MW01196848

COMMENTARY ON THE
NEW TESTAMENT

COMMENTARY ON THE
NEW TESTAMENT

Verse-by-Verse Explanations
with a Literal Translation

ROBERT H. GUNDRY

HENDRICKSON
PUBLISHERS

Commentary on the New Testament
© 2010 by Hendrickson Publishers Marketing, LLC
P. O. Box 3473
Peabody, Massachusetts 01961-3473

ISBN 978-1-56563-933-1

Printed in the United States of America

First Printing — July 2010

Library of Congress Cataloging-in-Publication Data

Gundry, Robert Horton.
     Commentary on the New Testament / Robert H. Gundry.
        p. cm.
     ISBN 978-1-56563-933-1 (alk. paper)
     1. Bible. N.T.—Commentaries. I. Title.
     BS2341.52.G86 2010
     225.7′7—dc22
                                        2009044843

CONTENTS

ACKNOWLEDGMENTS

My sincere thanks to Shirley Decker-Lucke, Editorial Director at Hendrickson Publishers, for accepting this exposition of the New Testament for publication, and to Mark House, Phil Frank, and others for their work there on the publication. My brother Stan Gundry, whose contributions to Christian publishing are deservedly well-known, encouraged me to write the exposition. Connie Gundry Tappy copyedited the manuscript. Her copyediting included not only the correction of errors and the refinement of style, but also a host of interpretive improvements and scriptural cross-references arising out of her comprehensive knowledge of the Bible. To her, my daughter as well as my copyeditor, I affectionately dedicate this volume.

Robert H. Gundry
Westmont College
Santa Barbara, California

INTRODUCTION

Above all, this volume aims to serve Christian ministers, Bible study leaders, and serious-minded lay students who are either too busy or otherwise unable to plow through technical commentaries on individual books of the New Testament. I've therefore omitted scholarly documentation and discussions of authorship, date, sources, historicity, harmonization, and similar topics and concentrated instead on what is likely to prove useful for expository preaching, teaching, group discussion, and private edification. As a result, my comments plunge into the text of each New Testament book with only minimal introductions. Nevertheless, even scholars and seminarians may discover in the comments many particulars not to be found elsewhere yet worthy of consideration.

To suit the orality of preaching, teaching, and group discussion, I've avoided almost all abbreviations and freely used contractions (for example, "we'll," "you're," "they've") and italics (the italics mostly for vocal emphasis), plus occasional colloquialisms. In the same vein, I've portrayed the New Testament authors as speaking rather than writing and their original addressees as hearing rather than reading. For first-century authors would normally have dictated their words to a writing secretary; and given the low rate of literacy and the scarcity of private copies, first-century addressees would normally have heard the text read to them.

Present-day readers will have to make their own practical and devotional applications of the scriptural text. But such applications shouldn't disregard or violate the meanings intended by the Scripture's divinely inspired authors and *should* draw on the richness of those meanings. So I've interpreted them in detail. Bold print indicates the text being interpreted. Translations of the original Greek are my own. Because of the interpretations' close attention to detail, my translations usually though not always gravitate to the literal and sometimes produce run-on sentences and other nonstandard, convoluted, and even highly unnatural English. Square brackets enclose intervening clarifications, however; and seemingly odd word-choices in a translation get justified in the following comments. It needs to be said, moreover, that the very awkwardness of a literal translation often highlights features of the scriptural text obscured, eclipsed, or even contradicted by loose translations and paraphrases.[1]

Literal translation also produces some politically incorrect English. Though "brothers" often includes sisters, for example, "sisters" doesn't include brothers (see Matthew 12:48–50). Similarly, masculine pronouns may include females as well as males, but not vice versa. These pronouns, "brothers," and other masculine expressions that on occasion are gender-inclusive correspond to the original, however, and help give a linguistic feel for the male-dominated culture in which the New Testament originated and which its language reflects. Preachers, Bible study leaders, and others should make whatever adjustments they deem necessary for contemporary audiences, but not adjustments that obscure or change the text's intended meaning.

Because of context and tradition, a Greek word often has to be translated differently from one passage to another. Take *hagios*: it's usually translated "holy" or, in the plural, "saints." For most English readers these translations connote moral superiority. But the Greek word's basic meaning has to do with consecration and consequent sacredness regardless of such superiority. So I've often translated with "consecrated" and "sacred." Yet "Holy Spirit" and "saints" have become so traditional that at other times I've retained these translations, occasionally with an explanation of the basic meaning. Despite sounding stilted, the traditional exclamation "behold!" has likewise been retained for lack of a sufficiently good synonym in contemporary English, at least for lack of one that suits a variety of passages with reasonable consistency. Other English versions of the New Testament often ignore the *men . . . de* construction

---

[1] See the article by Raymond C. Van Leeuwen at http://www.christianitytoday.com/ct/2001/october22/5.28.html.

in Greek, and do so because the only adequate English translation, "on the one hand . . . on the other hand," is ponderous in English as it is not in Greek. Nevertheless, I've refused to sacrifice meaning for lightness of touch.

The translation "scribes" is both traditional and literal. It originally referred to copyists of Scripture. But copying produced expertise, so that the term came to connote scholarship without regard to the work of copying. Hence my use of the translation "scholars" instead of "scribes." To highlight the identification of "the Lord" with "Jesus Christ," a comma usually appears between the two ("the Lord, Jesus Christ"). Similarly, a comma usually appears between "God" and "the Father." In both instances the comma substitutes for an implied "namely."

Square brackets enclose not only clarifications of awkward English resulting from literal translation, but also interior cross-references and words in English that don't correspond to words in the Greek text but do need supplying to make good sense. (As a language, Greek has a much greater tendency than English does to omit words meant to be supplied mentally.) Where a Greek verb occurs in the present tense for a past condition or event, I've used a present tense also in English whether or not such a translation looks and sounds awkward; and in my comments I've noted this usage as vivid or otherwise emphatic. Similarly, "is" or "are" plus the -ing form of a verb brings out the frequently progressive meaning of Greek verbs in the present tense.

In English, verbs of command carry an implied "you," which may be either singular or plural. By contrast, Greek verbs of command express the "you" outright, distinguish between the singular and the plural, and also occur in the third person ("he/she/it/they"). Traditionally, this latter construction is translated with an introductory "let," as in the nonbiblical "let them eat cake" (often but wrongly attributed to Marie Antoinette). But that sort of translation can sound like a permission rather than a command. So I've used "is/are to . . . ," as in "the person who is thirsting *is to come* . . . to take the water of life as a gift" (Revelation 22:17). In a few passages, however, "must . . ." or "had better . . ." gives a translation superior to "is/are to . . . ."

Readers who know New Testament Greek may note that my translations of Greek words don't always correspond to translations given in standard Greek lexicons, but do often fit better both the substance of the Greek and the New Testament context. For instance, "nitwits" corresponds to the Greek *aphrones* more exactly than does the usual translation, "fools"; and though humorously cumbersome, "a multitudinous multitude" corresponds to the highly emphatic Greek *poly plēthos* more exactly than does the usual translation, "a large [or 'great'] multitude." I've consistently translated *hostis* in its various forms with "who as such" or "who, to be sure" rather than with a simple "who"; for its contexts regularly support the notion of character, function, or the like which "as such" or "to be sure" adds to "who." Where ancient texts of the New Testament differ from each other in their wording, I've made my own judgments about what wording is mostly likely to have been original; but these judgments seldom stray from Nestle-Aland, *Novum Testamentum Graece* (27th edition; Stuttgart: Deutsche Bibelgesellschaft, 1993).

Out of respect for the abilities of my readers so far as English is concerned, I've not dumbed down the vocabulary used in translations and interpretations. Like the translations, interpretations are my own. Rather than reading straight through, most readers will consult this volume for the interpretation of individual passages in the New Testament. So a certain amount of repetition has had to supplement cross-references. To offset the repetition and thus keep the volume in bounds, I rarely discuss other interpretations. But I've not neglected to canvass them in my research.

On the theological front, careful readers will notice that lest one side or the other seem to lose its gravity I don't try to square New Testament affirmations of divine sovereignty, as in the doctrine of election to salvation (though I prefer to call it selection), with indications of human responsibility, as in the commands to repent of sins and believe the gospel. For the same reason I don't try to square New Testament affirmations of security in salvation for true Christians with warnings to professing Christians that they not apostatize. If squaring is needed, though, let it be that since God already knows who is true and who is false, apostates lose *out* on salvation rather than *losing* it; and since human beings can't tell ahead of time whether they'll apostatize, the warnings against apostasy are to be taken just as seriously as the affirmations of security.

In support of all who strive for faithfulness to the New Testament, my prayers accompany this volume.

MATTHEW

Very early church tradition attributes the writing of this Gospel to the apostle Matthew, also called Levi (compare Matthew 9:9 with Mark 2:14; Luke 5:27). The Gospel has in view persecution that exposes a rift between Christians who remain faithful to their Christian profession despite the persecution and those who because of it are proving themselves unfaithful. Matthew encourages faithfulness by highlighting Jesus' messiahship and divine sonship, defines faithfulness in terms of Christian behavior and verbal testimony, and warns against unfaithfulness by accenting its eternally dreadful consequence.

THE GENEALOGY OF JESUS CHRIST
Matthew 1:1-17

This passage divides into a heading for Jesus' genealogy (1:1), the genealogy proper (1:2–16), and a numerical summary of the genealogy (1:17). The genealogy proper subdivides into generations from Abraham to David (1:2–6a), from David to Jeconiah and his brothers (1:6b–11), and from Jeconiah to Jesus (1:12–16).

1:1: The record of the genesis of Jesus Christ, the son [= descendant] of David the son [= descendant] of Abraham. "The genesis of Jesus Christ" will consist in his genealogy. In Genesis 5:1, whose phraseology Matthew echoes in part, a genealogy takes its name after the first on the following list ("Adam"). But Matthew titles this genealogy after the last on the following list ("Jesus"). This reversal and the borrowing of Old Testament phraseology make the genealogy portray Jesus as the goal and fulfillment of the Old Testament. Matthew designs the portrayal to confirm in their Christian faith his audience of Jewish Christians, who are suffering persecution and tempted to save their necks by recanting. Strengthening this portrayal of Jesus are Matthew's additions of (1) "Christ," the Greek equivalent of the Hebrew "Messiah," which refers to the one God has "anointed" to bring salvation to his people; (2) "the son of David," David being the prototype of the messianic king; and (3) "the son of Abraham," father of the Jewish nation. This last phrase probably refers to David rather than Jesus as Abraham's descendant, though of course Jesus too descended from Abraham. The omission of all ancestors prior to Abraham suits the coming identification of Jesus as "the king of the Jews" (2:2; contrast the tracing of Jesus' genealogy as far back as Adam, father of the whole human race, in Luke 3:38). In the following genealogical list "fathered" has to do solely with impregnating the mother of the next male or males on the list.

1:2–6a: Abraham fathered Isaac, and Isaac fathered Jacob, and Jacob fathered Judah and his brothers, [3]and Judah fathered Perez and Zerah by Tamar, and Perez fathered Hezron, and Hezron fathered Aram, [4]and Aram fathered Amminadab, and Amminadab fathered Nahshon, and Nahshon fathered Salmon, [5]and Salmon fathered Boaz by Rahab, and Boaz fathered Obed by Ruth, and Obed fathered Jesse, [6a]and Jesse fathered David the king [compare 1 Chronicles 1:34; 2:1–2, 4–5, 9–12, 15; Ruth 4:18–22]. Since Davidic kings came from the tribe of Judah, Jesus' descent from Judah prepares for the presentation of Jesus as the messianic king in David's line. Mention of Judah's brothers, unnecessary in a purely genealogical list, portrays the old people of God as a brotherhood in anticipation of Matthew's portrayal of the church, God's new people, as also a brotherhood (5:22–24, 47; 7:3–5; 18:15, 21, 35; 23:8; 25:40). The mention of Tamar, emphasized by the inclusion of her son Zerah despite his falling outside Jesus' lineage, brings a Gentile into the genealogy. For she was probably a Gentile (see Genesis 38) and was certainly thought to be so by many Jews in the New Testament era. Thus she becomes for Matthew a prototype of Gentiles who convert to Jesus the Messiah and whose conversion Jesus will promote in 28:18–20. Two other women, Rahab and Ruth (both of them Gentiles without question and celebrated by Jewish rabbis as converts to Judaism), join Tamar as further prototypes of Gentile converts to the church (see Joshua 2, 6; Ruth 1–4). The introduction of Rahab is especially striking in that the Old Testament contains no indication of Salmon's fathering Boaz by her. The designation of David as "the king" adopts a designation of him that's frequent in the Old Testament and prepares for Matthew's portrayal of Jesus as the messianic king after the likeness of David and in fulfillment of God's promise to David (2 Samuel 7:1–17).

1:6b–11: And David fathered Solomon by the [wife] of Uriah, [7]and Solomon fathered Rehoboam, and Rehoboam fathered Abijah, and Abijah fathered Asaph, [8]and Asaph fathered Jehoshaphat, and Jehoshaphat fathered Joram, and Joram fathered Uzziah, [9]and Uzziah fathered Jotham, and Jotham fathered Ahaz, and Ahaz fathered Hezekiah, [10]and Hezekiah fathered Manasseh, and Manasseh fathered Amos, and Amos fathered Josiah, [11]and Josiah fathered Jeconiah and his brothers during the period of the deportation to

Babylon [compare 1 Chronicles 3:5, 10–16]. Here we have a list of Jewish kings in David's line, so that the list foreshadows Jesus as the Davidic king of the Jews. Again, however, a woman comes into the list. Unlike the previously mentioned women, however, she isn't named, though in fact she was named Bathsheba (2 Samuel 11:3; 12:24). Matthew omits her name and leaves "wife" to be inferred so as to center attention on her husband Uriah. Though she was a Jewess so far as we can tell from her father's name (2 Samuel 11:3; compare 2 Samuel 23:34), she was—so to speak—a Gentile by marriage. For Uriah was well known to be a Gentile, as indicated by his repeatedly being called "the Hittite" in 2 Samuel 11–12. Thus "the [wife] of Uriah" joins the previously mentioned women as vanguards of the Gentiles who'll convert to Christ and whose conversion he will promote (see 28:18–20 again). The Old Testament speaks of a king named Asa. Despite English translations to the contrary, Matthew adds "-ph" to "Asa-" for a reference to the psalmist Asaph, part of whose Psalm 78 he'll quote as fulfilled prophecy and whom he'll call "the prophet" (13:35). With this massaging of the name, then, the king himself becomes a kind of prophecy concerning Jesus the king of the Jews. Similarly, the Old Testament speaks of a king named Amon. And again despite English translations to the contrary, Matthew replaces "-n" with "-s" to get a reference to the prophet Amos, to whose prophecy in Amos 3:5 Matthew's quotation of Jesus' saying in 10:29 will conform. With the massaging of his name, this king too becomes a kind of prophecy concerning Jesus the king of the Jews. Just as Matthew mentioned Judah's brothers as well as Judah himself, he mentions the brothers of Jeconiah. But the Old Testament, which also calls him Jehoiachin, registers only one brother of Jeconiah (1 Chronicles 3:16; 2 Chronicles 36:10). So Matthew's ascribing to him brothers, perhaps in the sense of his fellow Jews deported with him to Babylon (2 Kings 24:10–16), puts renewed, extra emphasis on the old people of God as a brotherhood in anticipation of the church, God's new people, as also a brotherhood (compare the comments on 1:2).

Matthew omits the three successive kings Ahaziah, Joash, and Amaziah (for whom see 1 Chronicles 3:11–12), all of them belonging to the line of Athaliah, daughter of the infamous King Ahab in the northern kingdom of Israel and each of them suffering a violent death because of their wickedness (2 Chronicles 22:1–9; 24:20–27; 25:14–28). So even though the three omitted kings descended on their father's side from David, Matthew's omitting them conforms to the Lord's visiting the iniquity of Ahab up through the third and fourth generations of his children, here through his daughter's line (Exodus 20:5; Numbers 14:18 [compare 1 Kings 21:21; 2 Kings 10:30]). But a more important reason for these omissions will come out in 1:17; and to make that reason viable, Matthew now omits a fourth king, Jehoiakim (for whom see 1 Chronicles 3:15). As the addition of "the king" to "David" brought the first subdivision of the genealogy to a close, so the addition of "during the

period of the deportation to Babylon" brings the second subdivision to a close. This deportation also spelled the end of rule by David and his descendants and therefore paves the way for its revival in Jesus.

1:12–16: **And after the deportation to Babylon Jeconiah fathered Shealtiel, and Shealtiel fathered Zerubbabel, [13]and Zerubbabel fathered Abiud, and Abiud fathered Eliakim, and Eliakim fathered Azor, [14]and Azor fathered Zadok, and Zadok fathered Achim, and Achim fathered Eliud, [15]and Eliud fathered Eleazar, and Eleazar fathered Matthan, and Matthan fathered Jacob, [16]and Jacob fathered Joseph the husband of Mary, by whom** [referring to Mary] **Jesus who is called Christ was born** [compare 1 Chronicles 3:17–19a]. The Lord disqualified Jeconiah's sons (Jeremiah 22:24–30) but restored to favor Jeconiah's grandson Zerubbabel (Haggai 2:23). So Luke's saying that Neri fathered Shealtiel has to do with biological lineage, whereas Matthew's saying—with an eye on the Lord's disqualification of Jeconiah's sons—that Jeconiah fathered Shealtiel has to do with legal lineage, Shealtiel belonging to another branch of David's family (so also 1 Chronicles 3:17). In Zerubbabel the biological and legal lines reunite (compare Ezra 3:2). By taking "Abiud" as meaning "my father [is] Judah," Matthew points again to Jesus' belonging to the tribe from which the Davidic Messiah was to come. "Eliakim" likewise points to Jesus' Davidic messiahship in that according to Isaiah 22:20–24, a passage Matthew will echo in 16:19, this name belongs to a man who'll receive "the key of the house of David." "Azor" is a shortened form of "Azariah," an alternate name of the Davidic king Uzziah, already listed in 1:8–9, and therefore another pointer to Jesus' Davidic ancestry. There was an earlier Zadok who ministered as high priest during David's reign, so that "Zadok" here in Jesus' genealogy points yet again to Davidic royalty. As a shortened form of Ahimaaz, "Achim" does the same since Ahimaaz was a son of David's high priest Zadok. Matthew presents "Eliud" as meaning "God of Judah" to connote the royal tribe to which Jesus belongs as the king of the Jews. So these names, differing from those we find in reverse order in Luke 3:24b–27b, symbolize Jesus' qualification as a descendant of David to inherit David's throne.

Except for a slight difference in spelling, Matthew agrees with Luke 3:24 in "Matthan." But instead of "Heli" (Luke 3:23) he writes "Jacob," so that this Jacob fathered Jesus' foster father Joseph just as the Old Testament Jacob fathered as one of his twelve sons the Joseph who was sold into Egypt (compare Matthew's writing "Joseph" in 13:55 instead of the "Joses" of Mark 6:3 and often conforming the wording of this Gospel elsewhere to that of the Old Testament). The addition of "the husband of Mary" to "Joseph" shows that Jesus, though not fathered biologically by Joseph, belonged legally to David's line. For legal rights came through the father even though he was only a foster father, and Joseph took Mary to wife before Jesus' birth (1:20–25). "By whom [referring to Mary] Jesus . . . was born" prepares for divine action in the conception and birth of Jesus, for Matthew has carefully avoided saying that Joseph fathered Jesus. "Who is called Christ" draws the conclusion that so far as legal ancestry is concerned, Jesus is qualified to be the messianic king.

1:17: **Therefore** [drawing a conclusion from the foregoing list] **all the generations from Abraham to David** [are] **fourteen generations, and from David to the deportation to Babylon** [are] **fourteen generations, and from the deportation to Babylon to the Christ** [are] **fourteen generations.** 1 Chronicles 1:34; 2:1–15 provided fourteen generations from Abraham through David. But why does Matthew divide the rest of the genealogy into two more sets of fourteen generations each, and do so at the cost of omitting four Davidic kings in the second set and listing eight fewer generations than Luke does in the third set? He wants to say numerically what the listed names have already said genealogically, which is that in Jesus the Davidic Messiah has come. For the numerical values of the Hebrew consonants in David's name add up to fourteen: D (4) + V (6) + D (4) = 14. (Before the introduction of Arabic numerals, letters of the alphabet stood for numbers; and Hebrew was written without vowels.) The omissions mean that for the second and third sets "all the generations" refers to the generations listed by Matthew, not to all the generations found in the Old Testament. That Matthew constructs three sets of fourteen also corresponds to the spelling of David's name in Hebrew with three consonants and puts a triple emphasis on Jesus' Davidic ancestry. So the first set ended with royal power ("David the king"), the second with loss of royal power ("the deportation to Babylon"), and the third with a revival of royal power ("the Christ"). But to get his third set of fourteen Matthew counts Mary as well as Joseph. In other words, the one chronological generation represented by them carries within it two other kinds of generation, a legal (Joseph's) and a physical (Mary's). Otherwise we have only thirteen, since Jeconiah belonged to the second set of fourteen just as David belonged to the first. The counting of Mary harmonizes with Matthew's distinguishing between Jesus' royal lineage through Joseph (compare Joseph's being addressed with "son of David" in 1:20) and Jesus' divine generation through Mary. Since Jesus fulfills the Jews' messianic hope, Matthew's audience of persecuted Jewish Christians mustn't give up their faith to avoid further persecution.

THE BIRTH OF JESUS CHRIST AS DAVID'S SON AND "GOD WITH US"
Matthew 1:18–25

On the one hand, this passage explains how Jesus came to have the legal status of a descendant of David even though Joseph didn't father him: Joseph, himself a "son [= descendant] of David," brought Jesus into David's line by taking Mary to wife prior to Jesus' birth and by naming him at his birth. Without this explanation the preceding genealogy of Jesus through Joseph is pointless (see especially 1:16). On the other hand, this passage highlights Jesus' deity by noting that Mary became pregnant after her betrothal to Joseph but before her marriage to him and sexual intercourse with him. So she bore a divine child as the result of generation by the Holy Spirit.

1:18–19: **And the genesis of Jesus Christ was thus** [= happened in this way]. Here "the genesis of Jesus Christ" has to do with his *birth* as a followup to "genesis" as his *genealogy* in 1:1. **When his mother Mary had been engaged to Joseph, before they came together** [in marriage] **she was found to have** [a child] **in** [her] **womb by the Holy Spirit.** "By the Holy Spirit" parallels "by Tamar," "by Rahab," "by Ruth," "by the [wife] of Uriah," and "by whom [Mary]" in 1:3, 5–6, 16—all in reference to women—so that Matthew carefully avoids portraying the Holy Spirit as performing a male function through carnal intercourse in impregnating Mary. Thus she will still be virginal when she gives birth to Jesus (contrast pagan myths in which a god impregnates a human female carnally). Joseph found Mary to be pregnant, but he didn't yet know she was pregnant by the Holy Spirit. Matthew mentions the Holy Spirit's role as advance information which emphasizes that role. [19]**But Joseph her husband, being righteous and not wanting to disgrace her, planned to divorce her privately.** In Jewish society full betrothal was so binding that breaking it required a certificate of divorce, and the death of one party during the period of betrothal made the other party a widow or widower. So before his marriage to Mary, Joseph was her husband in the sense of a husband designate (compare Deuteronomy 22:23–24). Joseph's "being righteous" refers to his planning to divorce Mary on the ground she'd fornicated with another man, so that it would have been wrong for Joseph to marry her (compare Deuteronomy 22:23–24, which stipulates the stoning to death of an engaged girl and a man not her fiancé who'd impregnated her without her yelling out in protest; also Numbers 5:11–31; Matthew 5:32; 19:9). Joseph's "being righteous" also makes him a prototype of Jesus' disciples, whose righteousness Matthew will repeatedly stress after the pattern of Jesus himself (see, for example, 3:15; 5:10, 20; 25:37, 46; 27:19). Likewise, Joseph's "not wanting to disgrace [Mary]" characterizes him with the mercy that will mark Jesus' disciples (5:7; 18:33). Planning to divorce Mary "privately" means planning to divorce her in the absence of two or three witnesses. The Mosaic law didn't require them (see Deuteronomy 24:1–4), but they'd become customary to protect the husband against a denial of the divorce by his ex-wife's father. To spare Mary disgrace before witnesses, Joseph planned to waive this precaution.

1:20–21: **But when he'd mulled over these things, behold, an angel of the Lord appeared to him in a dream, saying, "Joseph, son** [= descendant] **of David, don't be afraid to take along Mary as your wife. For the** [infant] **conceived** [literally, 'fathered'] **in her is by the Holy Spirit."** "Behold" emphasizes the appearance of "an angel of the Lord," and together they emphasize the following message of Jesus' virginal conception and birth and of his saviorhood. Joseph's Davidic sonship will insure Jesus' Davidic sonship if Joseph carries out the angel's instructions. The Holy Spirit replaces what Joseph thought to be the role of another man. Ordinarily, of course, "fathered" has to do with the sexual role of a male. But as in 1:18, "by the Holy Spirit" maintains the virginity of Mary by negating carnal intercourse—therefore the foregoing translation "conceived." "Don't be afraid to take along Mary as your wife" shows, as did "before they came together" in 1:18, that "her husband" in 1:19 meant her husband designate. [21]**"And she'll birth a son; and you shall call his name Jesus, for he himself will save his people from their sins."** "A son," because the Christ is to be a king like David, not a queen. "She'll birth" is predictive. "You shall call" is prescriptive. And "he himself will save" is predictive again. By naming Jesus, Joseph is to adopt him as his legal though not biological offspring. He must bring Jesus into David's line for Jesus to become the messianic king. Naming by Mary wouldn't avail. But to *be* a king one must *act* like a king by saving his people from oppression (compare 1 Samuel 10:25–27, especially 27a, with 1 Samuel 11:1–11), just as David did (2 Samuel 5:1–3). Jesus' Davidic kingship therefore implies that "he himself will save his people," as indicated in the personal name to be given him. For according to popular etymology "Jesus," Greek for the Hebrew name "Joshua," means "the Lord [is] salvation." To draw out this meaning, the angel quotes Psalm 130:8 but replaces the psalmist's "will redeem" with "will save" for a closer link with the meaning of "Jesus." Also, "his people" replaces the psalmist's "Israel" because Jesus' people will turn out to be the ethnically inclusive church rather than Israel (see 16:18, where he says "my church"; 3:12, where John the baptizer refers to "his [Jesus'] wheat" [compare 21:43]). And "from their sins" replaces the psalmist's "from all his [Israel's] iniquities" to anticipate Jesus' forgiveness of sins (9:1–8; 26:28) and therefore deliverance from their oppressively judgmental consequences. The intensive "he *himself*" accents Jesus as the Savior; and this accent will lead to an affirmation of his deity, since only deity can save from sins by forgiving them.

1:22-23: And this whole thing has happened in order that what was spoken by the Lord through the prophet would be fulfilled, saying, [23]"Behold, the virgin will have [an infant] in [her] womb and birth a son; and they'll call his name Immanuel," which is translated, "God [is] with us [Isaiah 7:14]." In Psalm 130:7–8 it's "the Lord" who'll redeem Israel from all his iniquities. So here in Matthew it's Jesus as "God with us" who'll save his people from their sins. He's "with us" as God, not in static presence, but in saving activity. "Has happened" indicates a past event that has a continuing effect. "In order that" indicates divine purpose. "This whole thing" encompasses within that divine purpose all the preceding and following items that make up this episode. Nothing happened by chance. Instead of mentioning Isaiah's name, Matthew writes "by the Lord through the prophet" to draw a parallel with the convey-

ance of a message by "an angel of the Lord" (1:20; see also 2:15 with 2:13). "Would be fulfilled" cites fulfilled prophecy as a reason Matthew's audience of Christians shouldn't recant under the pressure of persecution. He's so eager to impress this reason on them that he cites the prophecy before narrating its fulfillment (as also in 2:15; 21:4–5). "Behold" calls special attention to Mary's virginal conception and birthing of Jesus. But Matthew replaces Isaiah's "And *she* will call his name Immanuel" with "And *they* will call his name Immanuel." "They" are Jesus' church, the people just mentioned whom he'll save from their sins. And he'll save them from their sins because they, unlike Israel as a whole, will confess that he is "God with us." The transliteration of the Hebrew "Immanuel" enables Matthew to draw out its meaning, "God [is] with us." Jesus is with his people to save them from their sins, not merely on behalf of God, but *as* God (compare the sandwiching of Jesus as "the Son" between "the Father" and "the Holy Spirit" in 28:19).

1:24-25: And on getting up from sleep [the angel had appeared to him "in a dream"], **Joseph did as the angel of the Lord had ordered him and took along his wife [25]and didn't know her** [sexually] **till she'd birthed a son. And he called his** [the son's] **name Jesus.** Joseph's obedience is immediate and as such presents an example to be emulated. By itself, his not having sex with Mary till she'd birthed Jesus doesn't necessarily imply that he did have sex with her afterwards. But later references to Jesus' brothers (12:46–47; 13:55) and sisters (13:56) heavily favor this implication. The delay in sexual union then preserves the virginity of Jesus' birth in addition to that of his conception (for loss of virginity comes by sexual penetration from outside, not by extrusion of a baby from inside). Matthew's emphasis falls on the maintenance of Mary's virginity up through Jesus' birth, not on the birth as such. Joseph's naming Jesus amounts to a formal acknowledgment of him as his legal son and clinches Jesus' place in the Davidic line.

THE WORSHIP OF JESUS BY A
VANGUARD OF GENTILES
Matthew 2:1–12

2:1-2: And after Jesus was born in Bethlehem of Judea during the days of Herod the king, behold, astrologers from the East arrived in Jerusalem, saying, [2]"Where is the one who has been birthed [as] **king of the Jews? For we saw his star at** [its] **rising and have come to worship him."** "In Bethlehem" stresses yet again Jesus' correspondence to King David, for David grew up in Bethlehem (five miles south of Jerusalem). "Of Judea" joins a recurrence of this phrase in 2:5 and the similar phrase "land of Judah" in 2:6 to heighten Jesus' royal status: he came from the tribe and territory that produced the Davidic kings (compare 1:2; Genesis 49:10). And the designation of Herod as "the king" joins recurrences of this designation in 2:3, 9 for a contrast with Jesus as "king of the Jews." (This Herod, known as "the Great," was born in 73 B.C., became governor of Galilee in 47 B.C., was named "King of Judea" by the Roman Senate in 40 B.C., gained control of Judea in 37 B.C., and died in 4 B.C.) The astrologers were Gentiles (compare Daniel 2:2, 10). So just as the four women (besides Mary) in Jesus' genealogy pointed forward to the influx of Gentiles into the church (compare 1:3, 5–6 with comments and 8:10–12; 28:18–20), so too the coming of these astrologers points forward to the same. "Behold" accents the point. As astrologers they saw the star of the king of the Jews "at [its] rising" (not "in the East," despite traditional translations). The star's *rising* indicated the *birth* of the Jews' king. Like Balaam, a Gentile prophet in Old Testament times, the astrologers arrived "from the East" (Numbers 23:7). Balaam too saw a rising royal star, one that represented David just as the present rising star represents Jesus as a king in David's lineage and likeness (Numbers 24:17–19). The astrologers' arrival "in Jerusalem" introduces that city as the center of antagonism toward Jesus already at his birth (compare 23:36). The astrologers' adding "of the Jews" to "king" contrasts with Herod's bare title, "the king," and hints at the legitimacy of Jesus' kingship over against the illegitimacy of Herod's. He wasn't a descendant of David, or even a full-blooded Jew, but a half-Idumean. (The Idumeans descended from Jacob's brother, Esau.) And the astrologers' having come "to worship [the newly born king of the Jews]" agrees with his deity, highlighted in 1:23 ("God [is] with us").

2:3: And on hearing [the astrologers' question and the reason for it], **King Herod was disconcerted, and all Jerusalem with him.** Herod was well known for harboring psychopathic suspicions that others were trying to seize his throne. The disconcerting of "all Jerusalem *with* him" allies Jerusalem with Herod against the prospect of another king. "*All* Jerusalem" intensifies the shared antagonism toward the infant Jesus. This antagonism will reach its zenith in his later trials and crucifixion. It also forecasts the persecution of his followers, such as Matthew's audience. They should therefore regard their persecution as patterned after that of Jesus and, therefore again, as a badge of honor (compare 5:10–12). The blame for this persecution rests most heavily on Jewish authorities, whom Herod now assembles for their cooperation in his attempt to destroy Jesus.

2:4–6: And on assembling all the chief priests and scholars of the people, he was inquiring of them where the Christ is born [= where the Messiah was to be born]. **⁵And they told him, "In Bethlehem of Judea, for it's written through the prophet in this way: ⁶And you, Bethlehem, land of Judah, are by no means least among the governors of Judah; for out of you will come a governing one who as such will shepherd my people Israel** [Micah 5:2; 2 Samuel 5:2; 1 Chronicles 11:2]." "Assembling" is a verbal form of the noun "assembly" or, as it's usually translated, "synagogue." So Herod's assembling the chief priests and scholars makes a kind of synagogue opposed to Jesus (compare Matthew's writing about "*their/your* synagogues" in 4:23; 9:35; 12:9; 13:54

and especially 10:17; 23:34). "*All* the chief priests and scholars" underlines the breadth of opposition to Jesus among the Jewish authorities. High-ranking priests, including the current high priest and past high priests, made up "the chief priests." The scholars (called "scribes" in traditional translations) had expertise in the Old Testament. "Of the people" alludes to the scholars' leading the Jewish people astray and contrasts their people, duped as they are, with Jesus' people, saved from their sins in recognition of him as "God with us" (1:21–23). Matthew mentions the chief priests because their position entailed working with King Herod, and the scholars because their expertise enabled them to answer his question. Herod wants to know where the Christ is to be born in order that he might find and destroy him. His expression "the Christ" replaces the astrologers' expression "king of the Jews," because he wouldn't refer to anyone but himself as the Jews' king. But for Matthew's audience, Herod expresses—in spite of himself—the truth about Jesus' messiahship.

The answer to Herod's question comes out of Micah 5:2. "In Bethlehem of Judea" echoes 2:1 and stresses the hometown and territory of David, prototype of the messianic king. "It's written *through* the prophet" implies that the prophet wrote as the Lord's penman (compare the comments on 1:22). Matthew edits the following quotation to bring out Jesus' Davidic messiahship: it's as though he subpoenas the chief priests and scholars to testify on his behalf about Jesus as the fulfillment of Micah's prophecy. "Land of Judah" replaces Micah's "Ephrathah" for an allusion to the man Judah, progenitor of David's royal tribe (1:2–3). Then Matthew inserts "by no means" to deny emphatically the leastness of Bethlehem in Micah's text. For Matthew, in other words, Jesus' birth has transformed Bethlehem from the unimportant village it was during Micah's time into the supremely important birthplace of the messianic king from David's line. Matthew reads "governors" instead of Micah's "thousands" or "clans" to ally Jesus as "the governing one" with Judah's previous Davidic governors (= kings) just as the genealogy, especially its second set of fourteen, has already done (1:1–17). Jesus' governorship undermines that of Pontius Pilate, who'll repeatedly be called "the governor" in chapters 27–28. "Who as such [that is, as one who governs] will shepherd my people Israel" replaces Micah's "one who is to be ruler in Israel" and comes from the Lord's promise in 2 Samuel 5:2; 1 Chronicles 11:2 to make David, who'd been a shepherd boy, the shepherd-king over Israel. These multiple emphases on Jesus' taking after David are designed to reinforce faith in Jesus as the promised Christ. So don't deny him to save your neck (compare 10:32–33).

2:7–8: Then Herod, on privately calling the astrologers, ascertained from them the time of the appearing star [that is, the time of its appearance]. **⁸And sending them to Bethlehem, he said, "On going** [there], **check out accurately concerning the little child. And whenever you've found** [him], **report to me** [where he is] **so that on going** [there] **I may worship him."** Since in 2:9

the astrologers will set out for Bethlehem under starlight after getting instructions from Herod, their private meeting with him is likely to have taken place at night. His malevolence, evident in the private meeting, contrasts with the righteousness and mercy of Jesus' father Joseph in planning to spare Mary disgrace by divorcing her "privately" (1:19). The contrast highlights Joseph's virtue as well as Herod's malevolence. Adding to that malevolence is the care with which Matthew says Herod went about plotting Jesus' destruction. For "ascertained" and "accurately" make a wordplay in Matthew's original Greek. By representing the same root, they emphasize Herod's care. The plot also foreshadows the Jewish authorities' plotting against Jesus' life just prior to his crucifixion (26:3–5). They'll have learned from Herod. His plotting with their help foreshadows their persecution of Jesus' disciples too (10:28; 23:34–37a; 24:9). To deceive the astrologers Herod says, "so that I may worship him." They'll need to be disabused of this deception.

2:9–10: And they, on hearing the king, traveled; and behold, the star that they'd seen at [its] rising led them forward until, on coming, it stood still over where the little child was. The redesignation of Herod as "the king" and the reappearance of the star set the legitimacy of Jesus' kingship and the illegitimacy of Herod's in opposition to each other again. "Behold" spotlights the star as symbolic of Jesus the Davidic king of the Jews. According to 2:8 the astrologers know to go to Bethlehem. But what road should they take to get there? The star, which they'd seen only at its rising so far as Matthew has written, reappears, this time to lead them to Bethlehem and pinpoint the location of baby Jesus. Efforts to explain the star and its movement astronomically have failed. But the ancient belief in stars as beings of a heavenly order may explain this star's movements in a nonastronomical way, and the star itself as personal. [10]**And on seeing the star, they rejoiced a great joy exceedingly** [or as we'd say, rejoiced with exceedingly great joy]. The combination of "rejoiced," intensified by "exceedingly," and "joy," magnified by "great," puts enormous emphasis on the astrologers' joy, which anticipates the joy of Christian disciples in the gaining of God's kingdom (13:44), in the discovery of Jesus' resurrection (28:8–9), in their eternal reward (25:21, 23), and even in their present persecution (5:10–12).

2:11–12: And on coming into the house [which defines "where the little child was" in 2:9]**, they saw the little child with Mary his mother.** Joseph drops out of sight for the time being now that he has brought Jesus into David's royal line. For prominence, "the little child" comes forward in the order of mention. And "his mother" is attached to "Mary" as a reminder of Jesus' virginal conception and birth and therefore of his deity (compare 1:18–23). The reminder of his deity prepares for the next statement: **And falling down they worshiped him.** Worship consisted in kneeling and bowing one's head to the ground in front of the object of worship, in this case Jesus as "God with us" (1:23). "Fall-

ing down" sharpens the point, for in 4:9 falling down will accompany worship in the alternatives of worshiping God and worshiping Satan, also in some disciples' worshiping Jesus at his transfiguration (17:6). **And on opening their treasure chests they offered him gifts: gold and frankincense** [an aromatic resinous gum] **and myrrh** [another aromatic resinous gum]. Elsewhere in Matthew "gift(s)" is used exclusively and often for offerings to God (5:23–24; 8:4; 15:5; 23:18–19), and the verb "offered" has to do with such offerings in 8:4 and throughout the Old Testament. So the astrologers' offering of these expensive gifts adds further emphasis on Jesus' deity and kingship; and the astrologers stand as prototypes of his disciples, who give up earthly treasures for heavenly treasures (6:19–21; 19:21). Like the Gentile kings in Psalm 72:10–11, 15, the astrologers bring gifts of gold to a superior king in Israel. Like the Gentile kings in Isaiah 60:2–3, 6, they bring gold and frankincense. And as Solomon the immediate son of David is perfumed with myrrh and frankincense in the Song of Solomon 3:6; 4:6, Jesus the later son of David is given frankincense and myrrh. These offerings confirm that in 2:2 we should understand "birthed [as] king of the Jews" rather than "birthed [to be] king of the Jews." [12]**And on being warned in a dream not to return to Herod, they withdrew to their country by another way.** The dream informs the astrologers of Herod's malevolence, and their withdrawal offers an example for persecuted Christians of fleeing from persecution (see 10:23 for Jesus' commanding such flight).

THE PRESERVATION OF JESUS AS A SIGN OF HIS DIVINE SONSHIP
Matthew 2:13–15

2:13: And after they [the astrologers] **had withdrawn, behold, an angel of the Lord appears to Joseph in a dream, saying, "On getting up, take along the little child and his mother and flee to Egypt. And be there till I tell you** [to leave]. **For Herod is going to seek the little child to destroy him."** Just as the astrologers' withdrawal feeds Matthew's theme of fleeing persecution (see the comments on 2:12), so the flight of the holy family does the same (see 10:23 again). "Behold" grabs attention for the angel's appearance and together with the vividness of the present tense in "appears" heightens emphasis on the divine intervention that signifies Jesus' status as God's Son. "The little child and his mother" (not "your child" in the sense of Joseph's biological offspring) recalls 2:11 and, as there, echoes 1:18 in a further reminiscence of Jesus' virginal conception and birth and therefore of his deity. The Egyptian sojourn of this Joseph and his family will correspond to the Egyptian sojourn of the Old Testament Joseph and his family (Genesis 37, 39–50; compare Matthew's listing "Jacob" as the father of the present Joseph just as the Old Testament Joseph had Jacob for his father [1:16]). The story of Moses follows that of Joseph and his family in the Old Testament. It's natural, then, that Herod's seeking to destroy Jesus echoes Pharaoh's seeking to slay Moses in Exodus 2:15. Matthew is making Jesus the greater Moses just as he has already made him the greater David (see also the comments on 2:20–21). These correspondences are supposed to fortify the faith of persecuted Christians, especially Jewish ones, by showing Jesus to be the fulfillment of Old Testament patterns as well as of Old Testament prophecies.

2:14–15: And he [Joseph], **on getting up, he took along the little child and his mother** [for which phrase see the comments on 2:11] **at night and withdrew to Egypt** [15]**and was there till Herod's end** [= decease]**, in order that what was spoken by the Lord through the prophet might be fulfilled, saying, "Out of Egypt I called my son** [Hosea 11:1].**"** The phraseology of 2:14–15a resembles that of 2:13b–d (see earlier comments). The resemblance points up the exactitude of Joseph's obedience as a model for Christian discipleship (compare 1:24). The addition "at night" displays immediacy of obedience, another exemplary point, and recalls "from sleep" in 1:24. Nighttime fits flight from persecution better than sleep would. "Withdrew" revives the allusion to Exodus 2:15 and echoes Matthew 2:12–13a. With Herod's "end" compare Pharaoh's decease in Exodus 4:19. See the comments on 1:22b for the formula of fulfillment that introduces the quotation of Hosea 11:1. In Hosea 11:1 the nation of Israel is addressed as the Lord's youthful son. The many parallels drawn between Israel's history and Jesus' life show that Israel's history is both recapitulated and anticipated in Jesus, "the king of the Jews": (1) like Israel in the messianic age, he receives homage from Gentiles (2:11); (2) as a youthful son, he like Israel as a youthful nation receives both fatherly protection in Egypt—then from death by famine, now from death by slaughter—and a calling out from Egypt (2:15); (3) his oppression brings sorrow just as Israel's oppression brought sorrow (2:17–18); and (4) like Israel, he's tempted in the wilderness (4:1–10). The quotation of Hosea 11:1 comes before the holy family's return from Egypt to the land of Israel. So as in 1:22–23; 21:4–5 Matthew is so eager to impress on his audience the fulfillment of prophecy that he cites the prophecy before finishing the narrative of its fulfillment. And again as in 1:22–23, "by the Lord through the prophet" draws a parallel with the conveyance of a message by "an angel of the Lord" (here in 2:13).

A PREVIEW OF JEWISH CALAMITIES RESULTING FROM THE REJECTION OF JESUS
Matthew 2:16–18

2:16: **Then Herod, on seeing that he'd been made fun of by the astrologers, was very angered. And on sending** [soldiers] **he did away with** [= had them kill] **all the male children in Bethlehem and in all its borders** [= in its entire vicinity] **from two years** [old] **and under, in accord with the time that he'd ascertained from the astrologers** [compare 2:7]. Here we have another correspondence with the story of Moses, for Pharaoh had

the male babies of Israelites slaughtered at the time of Moses' birth and preservation (Exodus 1:15–22 [compare the foregoing comments on Matthew 2:13–14, 20–21]). Since the present slaughter, traditionally called the Slaughter of the Innocents, came about through the chief priests' and scholars' cooperation with Herod (2:4–6), this episode previews the calamities to befall the Jewish nation for their, and especially their leaders', rejection of Jesus (compare 23:33–39; 27:20–25). The verb "had been made fun of" will reappear in 27:29, 31, 41 (also in 20:19 under the translation "mocking"). There, Jesus the true king of the Jews will be made fun of. Here, Herod their illegitimate king, with whom their leaders have cooperated, has been made fun of. The verb also makes a wordplay with "children," for the Greek behind "had been made fun of" literally means "had been treated like a child." Herod had been treated like a child though he was an adult, a king no less! "Exceedingly" magnifies his anger and warns of similar calamities to come. "Did away with" echoes Exodus 2:15 and compensates for its displacement in an otherwise similar echo at Matthew 2:13. "*All* the male children" and "in *all* its borders" echo Exodus 1:22 and enlarge the slaughter so as to escalate the warning that calamities will befall the entire Jewish nation for their rejection, by and large, of Christ. An infant would have been considered two years old immediately on entering his second year, so that Matthew's "two years [old] and under" means in our way of speaking "under one year old."

2:17–18: **Then was fulfilled what was spoken through Jeremiah the prophet, saying,** [18]**"A voice was heard in Ramah** [a city about six miles north of Jerusalem], [that is,] **weeping and much** [= loud] **lamentation, Rachel weeping for her children** [here in the sense of offspring rather than, as earlier, youngsters]. **And she wasn't wanting to be comforted** [that is, she refused comfort], **because they don't exist** [any more] [Jeremiah 31:15].**"** As later in 27:9–10, "Then was fulfilled" replaces "in order that [it] might be fulfilled" (1:22; 2:15, plus later passages) for a limitation of the fulfillment to God's *permissive* will. He didn't want this tragedy to happen. But he allowed it to happen. It happened primarily because of the Jewish authorities' cooperation with Herod (2:4–6). The dropping of "by the Lord," which occurred in 1:22–23; 2:15, and the insertion of "Jeremiah" (contrast the anonymity of the prophets in 1:22–23; 2:15) also distance God from the Slaughter of the Innocents. Rachel, Jacob's favorite wife, bore him Benjamin, whom she called Ben-oni, which means "the son of my sorrow" (Genesis 35:18). So in the quotation she figures as Israel's representative mother, particularly in her sorrow, as she lies—poetically speaking—weeping in her sepulcher at Ramah over the fate of the nation, portrayed as her offspring. In Jeremiah that fate is the deportation of northern Israelites as captives into Assyria. Matthew applies the fate to the Slaughter of the Innocents, so that "they don't exist [any more]" has to do with death rather than deportation—in other words, a very literal fulfillment. The huge emphasis on sorrow in the quotation relates to

27:25, where "all the people said, 'His [Jesus'] blood [be] on us and on our children [in the sense of offspring, as here in 2:18]!'" By taking Herod's side here and forcing Pilate's hand there in rejection of Jesus, the Jewish authorities have brought and will yet bring sorrowful consequences on the innocent children of the people they influence. To prepare for the correspondence between 2:17–18 and 27:25, Matthew replaces "sons," which occurs in Jeremiah 31:15 (despite English translations that have "children"), with "children," which will occur again in 27:25. (Sadly, it needs emphasis that Matthew doesn't write out of anti-Semitism; for as a Jew himself, he wants to save Jews from calamity, not contribute to it.)

THE RETURN OF THE GREATER MOSES TO BECOME DAVID'S BRANCH
Matthew 2:19–23

2:19–21: **And after Herod had come to an end** [= died], **behold, an angel of the Lord appears in a dream to Joseph in Egypt** [compare 1:20; 2:13 with comments], **saying,** [20]**"On getting up, take along the little child and his mother and travel to the land of Israel** [compare 2:13 with comments]. **For those who were seeking the little child's life have died."** Because the persecution has passed, the command to "travel" replaces the command to "flee" of 2:13. We read "the land of Israel" instead of "land of Judah" (2:6), because Matthew needs a term broad enough to cover Galilee, the unplanned but eventual destination, as well as Judea, the planned destination. The angel's instruction, emphasized by the present tense of "appears," echoes the wording of Exodus 4:19–20, where the Lord told Moses, "'Go return to Egypt, for all those who were seeking your life have died.' And Moses took his wife and his sons . . . and returned to the land of Egypt." Likewise here in Matthew: [21]**And he** [Joseph], **on getting up, took along the little child and his mother and went into the land of Israel.** So further parallels with the story of Moses come into play, though place-names and directions of travel differ and Moses is now an adult whereas the earlier parallels in 2:13, 16 had to do with his infancy. Matthew substitutes "went" for "returned," however, because Joseph won't return to Jesus' birthplace, whereas Moses did return to his birthplace. Matthew mentioned the death of Herod alone in 2:15, 19. Yet he wants so much to conform the story of Jesus to that of Moses that he quotes the angel as referencing the death of "those [plural] who were seeking the little child's life" in parallel with the death of "all those who were seeking [Moses'] life." The "all" of Moses' enemies drops out because Matthew's angel is speaking only of Herod, though in the plural to include the soldiers to whom he gave orders. The reference to Mary as Jesus' mother rather than as Joseph's wife and the mention of the little child ahead of her, both in contrast with Exodus 4:19–20, do not let us forget that the virgin-conceived, virgin-born Immanuel surpasses Moses. Once again, Joseph's obedience to the divine command makes a good example (as in 1:24–25; 2:14–15).

2:22–23: **And on hearing, "Archelaus is ruling Judea** [southern Israel] **in place of his father Herod,"** **he** [Joseph] **feared to go there from** [Egypt]. **And having been warned in a dream, he withdrew to the parts of Galilee** [northern Israel]. [23]**And on coming** [to Galilee], **he settled down in a city called Nazareth so that what was spoken through the prophets would be fulfilled, that he** [Jesus] **will be called a Nazarene.** In Matthew's original Greek, "is ruling" is a verbal form of the noun "king." So despite Archelaus's never getting the title "king," Matthew's use of the corresponding verb implies that Archelaus, like his father, is another illegitimate rival with whom the Jewish authorities would cooperate in plotting the death of Jesus, the legitimate king of the Jews. Adding to this implication are the phrase "in place of his father Herod" and the specification "Judea," the place of Jesus' former rejection (2:1, 5). Archelaus ruled so badly that the Romans banished him after a couple of years or so. Apparently the ruthlessness of his rule made Joseph afraid to go back to Bethlehem, Jesus' birthplace. A dream confirmed his fear, so that "he withdrew to the parts of Galilee," that is, to the parcels of land that made up the Galilean region (compare the astrologers' having been warned in a dream not to return to Herod [2:12]). Like the astrologers' withdrawal, Joseph's withdrawal sets an example of avoiding persecution geographically rather than recantingly (10:23). "Go . . . from" echoes Exodus 4:19–20 yet again (though the echo isn't so evident in English translations) for another parallel with the story of Moses. Joseph "withdrew" to the parts of Galilee rather than returning there, because Matthew's account has nothing about having originated in Galilee, Nazareth in particular. "Settled down" means to establish a home. The plural in "through the prophets" points to a theme found in more than one prophetical book rather than a direct quotation from a single prophetical book. "That" introduces an indirect summary of that theme, as indicated also by the absence of "saying" (contrast 1:22–23; 2:15, 17–18 and so on, but compare 26:54, which also refers in the plural to "prophets"). "He will be called a Nazarene" occurs nowhere in the Old Testament. But Isaiah 11:1 predicts the springing up of "a branch" from the roots of Jesse, David's father. The Hebrew word for branch (*netzer*) sounds a lot like the place-name "Nazareth," which underlies "Nazarene" (= somebody from Nazareth; compare 21:11; 26:71). And other prophets chime in with prophecies of such a branch that will revive David's dynasty (Jeremiah 23:5; 33:15; Zechariah 3:8; 6:12). They use a Hebrew word different from the one Isaiah uses for "branch." But in 1:21 Matthew played with different Hebrew words in connection with the name "Jesus." So his relating Jesus as a Nazarene, a man from Nazareth, to a similar sounding Hebrew word for the branch that represents a Davidic king who is yet to spring up provides a fitting capstone to Matthew's version of Jesus' nativity, which began with a reference to "Jesus Christ, the son of David" (1:1). Thus Matthew marries phonetics with Christology.

JESUS' BAPTISM BY JOHN AS A
MODEL OF RIGHTEOUSNESS
Matthew 3:1–17

This passage breaks down into an introduction of John the baptizer (3:1–6), his upbraiding of Pharisees and Sadducees (3:7–10), his prediction concerning Jesus (3:11–12), and his baptism of Jesus (3:13–17).

3:1–3: And in those days [the time of residence in Nazareth (2:23)] **John the baptizer arrives** [on the scene], **preaching in the wilderness of Judea and saying,** ²**"Repent, for the reign of heaven has drawn near."** ³**For this** [John] **is the one spoken about through Isaiah the prophet, saying, "The voice of one crying out in the wilderness, 'Prepare the way of the Lord. Make his paths straight** [Isaiah 40:3].'"** Though John is called "the baptizer" to distinguish him from others named John (for example, the apostle John), the initial emphasis falls on his preaching. Matthew uses the present tense in "John the baptizer *arrives*" and "this [John] *is* the one spoken about" to stress that John's preaching starts the proclamation of the good news concerning "the reign of heaven," a proclamation that will continue to the end (4:23; 9:35; 11:12; 24:14; 26:13). Indeed, just as Matthew made Joseph prototypical of Jesus' disciples in the practice of righteousness (1:19), so he makes John prototypical of disciples in preaching—they too are to preach that "the reign of heaven has drawn near" (10:7)—and even prototypical of Jesus himself. For John "arrives" just as Jesus "arrives" later on (3:13); and what John preaches furthers the parallel with Jesus, because in 4:17 Jesus preaches the very same message: "Repent, for the reign of heaven has drawn near." The word for "reign" can also mean "kingdom," the sphere in which reigning takes place. But a kingdom hardly *draws* near, whereas the activity of reigning can be on the verge of happening, so that "reign" is a better translation here. As in 26:46–47, "has drawn near" means nearness as a result of arrival; and the nearness is spatial in addition to temporal because God is about to reign in the person, presence, and activity of Jesus (compare 26:46–47 again, where the spatial nearness of Judas Iscariot marks the temporal nearness of his giving Jesus over to his enemies). "Of heaven" substitutes for "of God" (compare the prodigal son's saying to his father, "I've sinned against *heaven* and in your sight" [Luke 15:18, 21]) and connotes the majesty and universality of God's reign inasmuch as heaven overarches the entire earth (compare Daniel 4). Furthermore, "of heaven" allows for Jesus as well as God the Father to reign (see 13:41; 16:28; 20:21; 25:31 for Jesus' reign/kingdom).

John's "preaching in the wilderness" matches "crying out in the wilderness" in the quotation of Isaiah 40:3. "Of Judea" shows that he's preparing the Davidic territory of 2:1, 5–6, 22 for the Davidic Messiah. The passage in Isaiah predicts the return of Jewish exiles from Babylonia. Here the passage applies to the beginnings of a greater deliverance, but with emphasis on the straightness of the paths that constitute the way of the Lord, that is, the way of righteousness, on which he'll save his people from their sins (1:21; 21:32). Whereas "the Lord" is *God* in Isaiah, then, here "the Lord" is *Jesus*, who is about to arrive on the scene. But according to 1:23 Jesus is "God with us," so that the difference is inconsequential. At the end of the quotation "his" replaces Isaiah's reference to God, because that reference could cause Matthew's audience to think mistakenly of God in contradistinction to Jesus. "*For* the reign of heaven has drawn near" makes its nearness the reason for *John's* audience to repent. "*For* this is the one spoken about" makes John's identification with the one crying out in the wilderness a reason for *Matthew's* audience to maintain their Christian belief that the events beginning with John's preaching corresponded to ancient prophecy. "*Through* Isaiah" implies God as the source of the prophecy, and Isaiah as his mouthpiece. Making straight paths defines preparing the way of the Lord. Together they symbolize repenting. The dignity of Jesus as Lord calls for a road and paths that are straight and easily traveled, not like the twisting roads and paths in hilly, mountainous Israel.

3:4–6: And John himself [as distinguished from "the Lord"] **had his clothing from camel's hair and a leather belt** [just a strip of hide] **around his waist; and his nourishment was locusts and wild honey.** John was no city-slicker in his clothing and diet. For they carry forward the preceding theme of a wilderness and characterize him as a prophet in the mold of Elijah, whose return was predicted in Malachi 4:5 (see 2 Kings 1:8 for a similar description of the Old Testament Elijah, and compare Matthew 17:11–12). Locusts and wild honey not only indicate a sparse diet appropriate to the wilderness, but also a specially holy one devoid of flesh from which blood has had to be drained (hence locusts) and devoid of wine (hence honey, which like wine is sugary but unlike wine is nonalcoholic). ⁵**Then Jerusalem and all Judea** [southern Israel, where Jerusalem was located] **and all the region around the Jordan** [River] **were traveling out to him** [in the wilderness] ⁶**and were getting baptized by him in the Jordan River while confessing their sins.** A wilderness was by and large devoid of human population—hence the need to "cry out" if anyone was to hear—but not necessarily devoid of vegetation. In fact, plenty of vegetation grew along the banks of the Jordan River. The sparsity of human population highlights by contrast the traveling of "Jerusalem and all Judea and all the region around the Jordan" (in the sense of their inhabitants) out to John. The large number indicated by these phrases anticipates the even larger numbers of people whom Jesus will attract to himself. The references to Jerusalem, Judea, and the region around the Jordan River imply that John was preaching and baptizing toward the southern end of the river, close to where it empties into the Dead Sea. Repentance led to baptism; and confession of sins accompanied baptism to verbalize repentance, which means a change of mind that results in a change of behavior. For baptism, see further the comments on Mark 1:4–5.

3:7–10: **And on seeing many of the Pharisees and Sadducees coming to his baptism, he said to them, "Offsprings of vipers, who warned you to flee from the wrath that's going to come?** [8]**Therefore** [because of the necessity to repent if you want to avoid this wrath] **produce fruit in keeping with repentance.** [9]**And you shouldn't think to say among yourselves, 'We have Abraham as** [our] **father.' For I tell you that God can raise up children** [in the sense of offspring] **for Abraham out of these stones** [lying around here in the wilderness]. [10]**And the axe is already lying at the root of the trees. Therefore every tree that's not producing good fruit is being cut down and thrown into fire."** Pharisees and Sadducees composed the two leading factions in the Judaism of that period, though most Jews didn't belong to any faction at all. In 16:1–4 Jesus will upbraid both groups just as John does here—a further parallel between John and Jesus that will tell Matthew's audience to hang tough under persecution because Jesus really was the true heir of the prophet John and the fulfillment of his prophecy. "Many" helps explain why John responds to the Pharisees' and Sadducees' coming to his baptism. "*To* his baptism" carries a note of antagonism (compare, for example, 24:7, where the same preposition has the sense of "against") and intimates that John refused to baptize them. "To *his* baptism" indicates that he baptized people rather than their baptizing themselves. His addressing the Pharisees and Sadducees with "offsprings of vipers" restrikes the note of antagonism and implies they hadn't repented. Jesus will use the same epithet in 12:34; 23:33, so that the parallel between John's and Jesus' ministries will be extended yet again. "Who warned you . . . ?" isn't the kind of question that calls for an answer. It means, "Since you haven't repented, why are you coming to me for baptism?" The Pharisees and Sadducees want to avoid the wrath without repenting. This wrath consists in an outburst of divine anger that will purify the world of the ungodly in preparation for what Jesus later calls "the regeneration" (19:28; compare 13:36–43). "*Going* to come" indicates that the outburst is soon and sure. (For John's audience, one thinks of the Jewish War against Rome that started in A.D. 66 and came to a climax with the destruction of Jerusalem and its temple in A.D. 70—a preview of the "great affliction" preceding Jesus' second coming [24:15–41].)

To flee the coming wrath successfully requires repentance, a feeling sorry for one's sins that shows itself in getting baptized while confessing those sins. "Fruit in keeping with repentance" means conduct that verifies repentance. Absence of right conduct falsifies repentance and makes baptism meaningless. The command to produce such fruit implies that the Pharisees and Sadducees haven't produced it; and Abrahamic ancestry doesn't substitute for it. As to their bloodline, they're offsprings of Abraham. But as to their moral ancestry, they're still offsprings of vipers. So they shouldn't even "*think*" to encourage one another that they have a bloodline that'll exempt them from the coming wrath. Much less should they *actually* encourage one another in this way. God doesn't need them to fulfill his promise to Abraham that Abraham would have innumerable posterity (Genesis 13:16; 16:10). "For I tell you" and the proverbial deadness of stones magnify God's ability to "raise up children for Abraham out of these stones." "The axe" represents the coming wrath. "The trees" represent people. The axe's "already lying at the root of the trees" means that God is taking aim with his wrath right now, so that there's no time to lose in producing fruit in keeping with repentance. "At the *root* of the trees" means this is your last chance; for once the roots of a tree are cut, it can't revive (as it could if a stump were left). Like the plural of "offsprings" and "trees," "*every* tree" points both to individual judgment and to judgment that will spare no one who hasn't demonstrated repentance in his conduct. "*Not* producing good fruit" means failure to behave in keeping with repentance. The wrath is so soon and sure to come that it might as well be bursting forth at the present time—hence, "*is being* cut down and thrown into fire." The fire is the fire of hell (5:22; 18:8–9; 23:33; 25:41). And Jesus' saying the same thing in 7:19 will extend the parallel with John still yet again.

John continues to speak in *3:11–12*: **"I, on the one hand, am baptizing you** [plural] **in water with reference to repentance** [= as a sign and consequence of your repentance]. **On the other hand, he who's coming behind me is stronger than I** [am], **whose sandals I'm not qualified to carry away** [= remove]. **He** [as distinguished from me] **will baptize you in the Holy Spirit and fire,** [12]**whose winnowing shovel** [is] **in his hand. And he'll clean his threshing floor thoroughly and gather his wheat into the granary, but he'll burn the chaff with inextinguishable fire."** John *refused* to baptize the Pharisees and Sadducees (3:7–10). Here he addresses people whom he *is* baptizing. So "you" no longer refers to the Pharisees and Sadducees. Emphasis falls on the coming one, who'll turn out to be Jesus, as stronger than John in that the coming one will be able to do what John can't, that is, baptize people in the Holy Spirit and fire. He's coming "behind [John]" in both a spatial sense and a temporal sense. The temporal sense has to do with arriving on the public stage later than John. The lack of qualification to carry the coming one's sandals arises out of John's falling far short of the coming one's ability to baptize people in the Holy Spirit and fire. On this baptism, the winnowing fork, the threshing floor, and so forth, see the comments on Luke 3:16–17. Matthew's version has "*his* wheat," which corresponds to "*his* [Jesus'] people" (1:21) and "*my* [Jesus'] church" (16:18; compare Jesus' kingdom in 13:41; 16:28; 20:21, to which "*his* threshing floor may correspond).

3:13–15: **Then Jesus arrives from Galilee at the Jordan,** [coming] **to John to be baptized by him.** "Then" spotlights that John has hardly spoken of the coming one before that one arrives. The present tense of "arrives" accents the arrival itself and advances the parallel between Jesus and John in that Jesus "arrives" here just as John "arrives" in 3:1. "To be baptized by him" makes baptism by John the very purpose of Jesus' coming. Thus Jesus sets an example to be followed by those who become his disciples (compare 28:19: "disciple all nations by baptizing them . . ."). [14]**But John was trying to prevent him** [from being baptized] **by saying, "I have a need to be baptized by you** [in the Holy Spirit]. **And are you coming to me** [to be baptized in mere water]**?"** (Or rather than translating with an astonished question, we could translate with an astonished exclamation: "And you're coming to me!") [15]**But answering, Jesus told him, "Permit** [me to be baptized in water] **right now, for to fulfill all righteousness in this way is proper for us."** Jesus' insistence and "right now" emphasize the significance of this baptism as a model for Christian baptism: converts aren't to delay this first step on "the way of righteousness" (21:32). "Is proper" denies any impropriety such as John feared. "To fulfill all righteousness" means that as an example to be followed, this baptism is the entirely right thing to do. It fulfills all the righteousness that the present occasion calls for, though not all the righteousness that other occasions as well as this one call for. "For *us*" brings the baptizer together with the baptizee in doing the entirely right thing (compare Jesus' commanding the disciples to baptize converts [28:19]). **Then he** [John] **permits him** [Jesus]. We might have expected Matthew to write, "Then John baptized him" or "Then he [Jesus] got baptized." But Matthew's way of putting the matter accents John's yielding to Jesus, the one stronger than he, so that John becomes an example to be followed in the doing with Jesus of what Jesus says is right and proper. The present tense of "permits" underscores John's example alongside that of Jesus. It's good to baptize as well as to get baptized.

3:16–17: **And on getting baptized, Jesus immediately came up away from the water.** That is, Jesus clambered up onto the river bank without confessing sins, as other baptizees did while they were still in the water (see 3:6). He had no sins to confess. **And behold, heaven was opened; and he saw God's Spirit descending, as if** [the Spirit were] **a dove, and coming on him.** [17]**And behold, a voice out of heaven, saying, "This is my beloved Son, in whom I took delight."** The first "behold" underscores Jesus' enduement with the Spirit, so that he can baptize others with the Spirit (for which see the comments on Mark 1:6–8). The second "behold" highlights the statement of the voice out of heaven. "Heaven was opened" echoes Ezekiel 1:1. "This is my beloved Son" echoes Psalm 2:7 in regard to a Davidic king. And "in whom I took delight" echoes Isaiah 42:1 in regard to the Servant of the Lord. Such echoes of Old Testament phraseology, scattered as they are throughout Matthew's Gospel, serve to assure its audience that Jesus' life and ministry conformed *to* the Old Testament and is thus confirmed *by* the Old Testament. He *saw* God's Spirit descending . . . and coming on him" makes Jesus aware of his enduement. Usually Matthew writes about the "*Holy* Spirit" (1:18, 20; 3:11; 12:32; 28:19). But here he writes about "*God's* Spirit" for a trinitarian allusion: God, Jesus

his beloved Son, and the Spirit of God (so too in 12:28). This allusion makes for continuity between Jesus' baptism and Christian baptism in trinitarian terms (28:19) and in this way gives Jesus' baptism stronger exemplary force. The Spirit's "descending" complements Jesus' "coming up away from the water." "As if [the Spirit were] a dove" compares the descent to a dove's fluttering down from the sky. "*Coming* on him," creates a correspondence between the Spirit and Jesus as "the coming one" of 3:11. "Coming *on him*" anticipates the quotation in 12:18 of Isaiah 42:1 for another echo of the Old Testament. "A voice out of *heaven*" that says, "This is my beloved *Son*," implies the voice of Jesus' heavenly Father (compare 7:21; 10:32–33 and so forth). "*This* is . . . in *whom*" makes what Jesus' heavenly Father says about him a declaration of Jesus' divine sonship to Matthew's audience (not to John, for he has already shown awareness of Jesus' identity [compare 17:5]). So just as Joseph owned Jesus as his legal son (1:25), God owns Jesus as his divine Son. "In whom I took delight" means that God took delight in Jesus' getting baptized despite John's attempt to deter him, and therefore that God will take delight in those who without delay follow Jesus in baptism, and do so despite the persecution that will ensue.

JESUS AS A MODEL OF OBEDIENCE TO DIVINE COMMANDS
Matthew 4:1–11

This passage divides into an introduction to the temptation of Jesus (4:1), the first temptation (4:2–4), the second temptation (4:5–7), the third temptation (4:8–10), and the aftermath (4:11).

4:1: **Then Jesus was led up** [from the valley of the Jordan River] **by the Spirit into the wilderness to be tempted by the Devil.** But Jesus was already in the wilderness; for 3:1–6 placed John, who baptized him, "in the wilderness." So "into the [surrounding upland] wilderness" draws a parallel with the temptation of the nation of Israel in the wilderness of Sinai. "To be tempted" also means "to be tested," because every temptation tests your resistance to sin, and every test tempts you to sin. Matthew drew earlier parallels between the history of Israel and Jesus' life (see 2:15, 18 with comments). Here, the parallel has to do only with temptations in a wilderness, not with their outcomes. For where Israel failed her test by yielding to temptation, Jesus will pass his test by resisting temptation. This parallel and the earlier ones serve to assure Matthew's audience that the life of Jesus follows Old Testament patterns as well as fulfilling Old Testament prophecies and that therefore they (the audience) should pass their own tests by resisting the temptation to recant under the pressure of persecution. "The Devil" means "the accuser." If Jesus were to yield to temptation, the Devil would accuse Jesus to Jesus' heavenly Father of being a disobedient Son. "By the Spirit . . . to be tempted by the Devil" makes the temptation the very purpose of the Spirit's leading Jesus up into the wilderness, just as the Lord led Israel in the wilderness to test them. So far as the Lord and his Spirit are concerned, both Israel and Jesus are tested with temptations to see whether they'll obey divine commands (see Deuteronomy 8:1–3, the last verse of which Jesus is about to quote). In parrying the Devil's temptations, which in the first two instances will consist of commands (though conditional ones), Jesus will quote the divine commands that he is obeying; and all the quotations come from parts of Deuteronomy that have to do with the Lord's testing Israel in the wilderness. As Jesus' insistence on being baptized made an example for believers in him to follow, so his obedience to divine commands becomes for those believers an example of post-baptismal obedience, only in their case to his own commands as "God with us" (1:23; 28:19–20: "baptizing them . . . teaching them to keep all things, as many as they are, that I've commanded you").

4:2–4: And on fasting forty days and forty nights, afterward he hungered. ³And on approaching [him], the tempter said to him, "If you're God's Son, say that these stones become loaves of bread." ⁴But he, answering, said, "It's written, 'A human being shall not live on the basis of bread alone, but on the basis of every word proceeding out through God's mouth [Deuteronomy 8:3].'" Matthew doesn't say why Jesus fasted. So the accent falls on another parallel, this time between Moses and Jesus (as already in 2:13, 16, 20–21). As Moses fasted forty days and forty nights in the wilderness (Exodus 34:28; Deuteronomy 9:9), Jesus does too. Later he'll instruct his disciples how to fast (6:16–18), so that his fasting becomes another example for them to follow. Matthew doesn't say whether Jesus hungered during the forty days and forty nights as well as afterward. So the sole mention of hungering afterward simply prepares for the first temptation. Matthew switches from "the Devil" (4:1) to "the tempter," so that the Pharisees, their disciples, the Sadducees, and the Herodians will all be playing a devilish role when they, too, "tempt" Jesus in 16:1; 19:3; 22:18, 35.

"If you're God's Son" flashes back to "This is my beloved Son" (3:17). The Devil isn't tempting Jesus to doubt his divine sonship—rather, to use it for his own advantage, which would amount to disobeying his commission to "serve [others], even to give his life as a ransom in substitution for many [people]" (20:28). Since John the baptizer spoke of God's raising up children for Abraham "out of these stones" (3:9), "say that these stones become loaves of bread" probably means that as God's Son Jesus should ask his heavenly Father to turn the stones into loaves of bread. A loaf of bread in that culture was like what we call pita bread, and therefore resembled a stone. As a lone individual, Jesus needed only one loaf; but the tempter is quoted as using the plural, "these stones . . . loaves of bread," which echoes John the baptizer's reference to "these stones" when upbraiding the Pharisees and Sadducees (3:9). And in 16:11–12, where Jesus will warn against "the leaven of the Pharisees and Sadducees," which is "the teaching of the Pharisees

and Sadducees," we read again about "loaves of bread" (plural). So here the tempter appears again as a type of the Pharisees and Sadducees. By quoting Deuteronomy 8:3, Jesus obeys God's command that a human being subordinate living on the basis of bread to living on the basis of God's every word. That is to say, Jesus pursues his role as "a human being" rather than capitalizing on being "God's Son." Living on the basis of bread alone means eating for physical survival. Living on the basis of God's every word means obeying it for divine blessing and, ultimately, eternal life (compare 19:17). "*Every* word" calls for complete obedience (compare 28:20 again). So Jesus sets an example of complete obedience over against the disobedience of falsely professing Christians who'll repeatedly be said in this Gospel to suffer eternal damnation with those who make no profession of belief in Jesus at all (see, for example, 24:45–51).

4:5–7: Then the Devil takes him along into the holy city and had him stand on the winglet of the temple ⁶and says to him, "If you're God's Son, throw yourself down; for it's written, 'He'll command his angels concerning you; and on [their] hands they'll lift you up lest you strike your foot against a stone [Psalm 91:11–12].'" ⁷Jesus said to him, "Again it's written, 'You shall not test out the Lord your God [Deuteronomy 6:16].'" The present tense in "takes him along" and "says to him" dramatizes this temptation, as though it's taking place right in front of our eyes. Matthew calls Jerusalem "the holy city" because the temple was located there. That he'll call Jerusalem "the holy city" again in 27:51b–53 suggests that the resurrection of "holy [= consecrated] people" who then appear to many people in that city after Jesus' own resurrection will provide the demonstration of his divine sonship that the Devil tempts him to give here. "The winglet of the temple" probably refers to the southeast corner of its outer court, which drops off precipitously into the Kidron Valley. But there are other possibilities. In any case, Jesus' throwing himself down would prove suicidal if God's angels weren't to catch him in midair. The Devil backs up his (conditional) command with a quotation of Psalm 91:11–12, which references a command of God to his angels. But the Devil omits the psalmist's phrase "in all your paths," because the deliberate throwing of yourself from a high perch wouldn't correspond to accidental stumbling over a stone in your path (as in the psalm). (In 26:53–54 Jesus will say that if it weren't for scriptural necessity that he suffer and die he could call successfully for angelic help to save him from a danger *not* of his own making.) Matthew introduces Jesus' reply abruptly ("Jesus said to him"), as though to say Jesus has grown indignant with the Devil's tempting him—a righteous kind of indignation. "*Again* it's written" echoes this indignation and counters the Devil's misquotation of the Old Testament with another, correct quotation that contains a divine command opposed to the Devil's command. It's that we shouldn't test out God. He's our examiner, not we his. The addition of "out" to "test" intensifies the prohibition.

For a second time Jesus proves himself to be an example of postbaptismal obedience to divine commands.

4:8–10: Again the Devil takes him along [as he did in 4:5] **to a very high mountain and shows him all the kingdoms of the world and their glory.** [9]**And he said to him, "I'll give you all these things if on falling down you'd worship me."** [10]**Then Jesus says to him, "Go away, Satan! For it's written, 'You shall worship the Lord your God, and you shall do religious service for him alone** [Deuteronomy 6:13].'"** The present tense of "takes along" and "shows" makes vivid this climactic temptation. The mountain is *"very"* high to give Jesus an unimpeded view. "All" leaves none of the world's kingdoms out of sight, and "their glory" adds high quality to high quantity. This time the Devil doesn't issue a conditional *command* contrary to a divine command; rather, he makes a conditional *offer*. And it's the condition, not the offer, that goes against a divine command. (The earlier condition, "If you're God's Son," agreed with a divine declaration.) What a generous offer, too: *"all* these things"! But since they're "of the world," they stand in opposition to "the kingdom of heaven." To get all the kingdoms of the world and their glory would be to get what the Devil presently rules, and therefore can give, as opposed to the world that God will regenerate and give as a single kingdom to his Son if his Son proves obedient (see especially 19:28; 25:31–46). As to the Devil's condition, it's that Jesus fall down and worship him just as the astrologers fell down and worshiped Jesus (2:11). Whereas an unemphatic past tense introduced this temptation ("And he [the Devil] said to him"), an emphatic present tense introduces Jesus' retort ("Then Jesus *says* to him"). And whereas the Devil issued (conditional) commands in the first two temptations, now it's Jesus who imperiously issues a command ("Go away, Satan!"). *"For* it's written" makes the quotation of Deuteronomy 6:13 the reason for Jesus' command. Just as he has put himself under the authority of Scripture, he now puts Satan under that same authority. In the quotation itself Jesus adds "alone" (not in the Old Testament text) to exclude Satan from sharing worship with God. As God's Son, Jesus shares worship with him. Satan has no share in it, though. And Jesus addresses him with "Satan," the Hebrew equivalent of "Devil," perhaps to suit the following quotation from the Old Testament, originally written in Hebrew.

4:11: Then the Devil leaves him; and behold, angels approached and began serving him. So Satan obeys Jesus' command, supported by Scripture, to go away. The obedience arises out of defeat, though, not out of devotion. The present tense of "leaves" highlights the departure. "Behold" then highlights the approach of angels and their starting to serve him. They serve him *food* (the usual meaning of "serve") because he didn't capitalize on his divine sonship to get bread for his hunger. As *angels* they serve him thus because he didn't capitalize on his divine sonship by throwing himself down from the temple's winglet so as to require their catching him in midair. And they serve *him* because he *did* capitalize on his divine sonship to make Satan go away. So Jesus stands as an example of the postbaptismal obedience that his disciples should emulate and as the issuer of new commands that they should obey just as even the Devil did (28:20). And the angels' serving Jesus becomes an example for his disciples' serving him through their kindnesses to the least of his brothers (25:31–46). Finally, this episode encourages Matthew's audience to resist temptations to benefit themselves in persecution, to test God's faithfulness to them in their persecutions, and to avoid persecution by giving up the exclusive worship of the God who is with us in Christ (1:23).

GOING INTO GENTILE TERRITORY BECAUSE OF PERSECUTION
Matthew 4:12–16

4:12–16: And on hearing that John had been given over [into prison], **he** [Jesus] **withdrew into Galilee.** For the time being, to avoid John's fate Jesus withdrew from the wilderness of the Jordan, where John had been ministering and was imprisoned, to Jesus' home territory of Galilee. Thus Jesus himself becomes an example of fleeing from persecution (10:23 [see 2:12–14, 22 for earlier uses of "withdrew" in the sense of avoiding persecution]). Matthew's audience of persecuted Christians should follow suit. "Given over" stands for imprisonment but is used very often later in Matthew for Jesus' being given over to his enemies (particularly by Judas Iscariot) and for the giving over of Jesus' disciples to their enemies. So John's fate prefigures the fates of Jesus and his disciples. [13]**And on leaving Nazareth, coming he settled in Capernaum, the seaside** [city] **in the borders of Zebulun and Naphtali** [tribal territories], [14]**in order that what was spoken through Isaiah the prophet might be fulfilled, saying,** [15]**"Land of Zebulun and land of Naphtali,** [located] **along the road of the sea** [= toward the sea], **across the Jordan, Galilee of the nations—** [16]**the people sitting in darkness have seen a great** [= bright] **light; and for the ones sitting in the region and shadow of death** [= the region of death's shadow, where death threatens]**—for them light has risen** [= dawned] [Isaiah 9:1–2]**."** See the comments on 1:22–23 for Matthew's introduction to the quotation. He describes Capernaum as a seaside city in the borders of Zebulun and Naphtali to match the quotation. In Isaiah "the sea" refers to the Mediterranean Sea. Matthew transfers its reference to the Sea of Galilee (really a lake, but now called a sea by tradition). "Across the Jordan" is probably meant from the standpoint of John's ministry on the east side of the Jordan River, so that "across the Jordan" would describe Galilee as west (as well as north) of the river. Though many Jews lived in Galilee and though Jesus will minister to them, the description of Galilee as "of the nations" makes Jesus' ministry there prefigure his disciples' making further disciples of "all nations" (28:19 [compare 8:11 and the four Gentile women in Jesus' genealogy and the astrologers from the east in chapters 1–2]). He moves from Nazareth to Capernaum for the express purpose of conforming his ministry to Isaiah's prophecy. And the rising of the light reminds us of Jesus' star, which the astrologers saw "at its rising" (2:2, 9). The great and risen light is Jesus as the light of salvation for those otherwise headed for damnation in "the darkness farther outside" (8:12; 22:13; 25:30). Isaiah prophesied that northern tribes would see this messianic light first because they'd gone into exile first (some 135 years before the Judahites did). Matthew cites Jesus' fulfillment of this prophecy to fortify Christians suffering persecution.

JESUS AS A MODEL DISCIPLER
Matthew 4:17–25

Here Matthew gives a programmatic introduction to Jesus' Galilean ministry. Jesus appears as a model discipler for those he'll send to disciple all nations (28:19).

4:17–20: From then on Jesus began preaching and saying, "Repent, for the reign of heaven has drawn near." See the comments on 3:2. [18]**And as he was walking around to the side of the Sea of Galilee, he saw two brothers—Simon, the one called Peter, and Andrew, his brother—casting a net into the sea. For they were fishermen.** "Walking around" indicates the itinerant character of Jesus' ministry and makes an example for his disciples to follow when he tells them to go disciple all nations (see 28:19 again). "Two brothers" isn't necessary in view of the following identification of Andrew as "his [Simon Peter's] brother." But this redundancy helps make the biological brotherhood of Simon and Andrew represent the discipular brotherhood of all believers in Jesus (compare the comments on 1:2, 11). The word for "net" means a net with weights attached to its perimeter. When cast into the sea it would enclose fish as it sank to the bottom. Then the fishermen drew the weighted perimeter together to prevent the fish from escaping and raised the net containing the fish. [19]**And he says to them, "Here—behind me! And I'll make you fishers of human beings."** [20]**And they, immediately leaving the nets, followed him.** The present tense of "says" stresses Jesus' command and prediction. Disciples of a teacher followed behind him instead of walking beside him, much less ahead of him. "Fishers of human beings" is a figure of speech for disciples of Jesus who make other disciples for him, as they should. The immediacy of Simon's and Andrew's leaving the nets and following him makes them an example of obeying Jesus without delay. Matthew's Gospel puts great emphasis on obedience to Jesus' commands, as opposed to what theologians call antinomianism—that is, the sort of disobedience that professing Christians often practice to keep themselves undistinguished from non-Christians and thus avoid persecution (among other reasons). Leaving the nets indicates the forsaking of an occupation for a vocation. The word for "nets" isn't so specific as the word for "net"; and its plural number indicates that though Simon and Andrew had been casting one net into the water, they

had others too. But they left them all, including the one still in the water.

4:21–22: And on going forward from there, he saw two other brothers, James the [son] of Zebedee and John his brother, preparing their nets in a boat with Zebedee their father. And he called them [James and John, not Zebedee as well]. "Two other brothers" reinforces the earlier representation of Christian brotherhood, this for the sake of mutual encouragement under the stress of persecution. "And he called them" summarizes the command and prediction addressed to the former pair of brothers. In other words, Jesus said the same thing to James and John as he'd said to Simon and Andrew. [22]**And they, immediately leaving the boat and their father, followed him.** "Leaving the boat and their father" corresponds to Simon's and Andrew's having left their nets, and the immediacy of leaving stresses again the need to obey Jesus without delay (compare the comments on Mark 1:16–20).

4:23: And he was going around in the whole of Galilee, teaching in their synagogues and proclaiming the good news of the kingdom [called "the reign of heaven" in 3:2; 4:17; see the comments] **and healing every kind of disease and every kind of ailment among the people.** "Going around" prefigures again the itinerant evangelism that Jesus will send his disciples to do. "In the *whole* of Galilee" prefigures the worldwide extent of their itineration, especially since 4:15 described Galilee as being "of the nations," and tells us that Jesus fulfilled Isaiah's prophecy completely (4:14–16). Matthew has already drawn parallels between Jesus and Moses. "Teaching" starts another parallel in that Jesus instructs his listeners in synagogues, where the law of Moses was read every Sabbath. This parallel will come to full flower in the Sermon on the Mount (chapters 5–7). As often, "*their* synagogues" reflects the lamentable separation of church from synagogue by the time Matthew wrote. "Healing every kind of disease and every kind of ailment" rounds out the summary of Jesus' activities in a way that makes them—the teaching, preaching, and healing—a pattern for Christians to follow. "Among the people" indicates a symbolic fulfillment of the prediction in 1:21 that Jesus will save his people from their sins. For salvation from physical diseases and ailments symbolizes salvation from sins (see Matthew's use in 8:17 of Isaiah 53:4). "*Every kind* of disease and *every kind* of ailment" magnifies the symbolism.

4:24: And the news about him went off into the whole of Syria. And people brought to him all who were sick with various diseases and racked with pangs and demon-possessed and subject to seizures [epilepsy, for example] **and disabled** [in particular, unable to walk]. **And he healed them.** Matthew mentions Syria in anticipation of Jesus' ministry to a Gentile woman who lived in the Phoenician part of Syria (15:21–28) and for the purpose of giving Jesus' ministry among Galilean Jews (indicated by "their synagogues") overtones of later evangelization of Gentiles. The mention of Syria also implies that those who on hearing about Jesus brought the afflicted to him must at least include Syrians. So Jesus' Galilean ministry not only *anticipates* later evangelization of Gentiles. It also expands that ministry to *include* Gentiles, so that Jesus' own ministry sets an example for his disciples' ministry to Gentiles throughout the world (see 24:14 as well as 28:19). The length of the list of afflictions healed by Jesus adds emphasis to these ministries in both their literal and symbolic senses. The demon-possessed are "healed" in the sense that exorcism relieves them of the physical symptoms of such possession.

4:25: And many crowds followed him from Galilee and Decapolis and Jerusalem and Judea and Transjordan [east of Jerusalem and the Jordan River]. "*Many* crowds" not only points up the success of Jesus' ministry. In combination with the geographical designations that cover all parts of Israel except Samaria—the northwest (Galilee), the northeast (Decapolis, largely Gentile by the way), the southwest (Jerusalem and Judea), and the southeast (Transjordan)—"*many* crowds" also augurs well for the success of the disciples' worldwide ministry and encourages them to engage in that "fishing expedition" despite persecution. The crowds' "*following* Jesus" makes them his disciples, at least symbolically; for following Jesus characterized his first disciples, Simon and Andrew, James and John (4:20, 22). But as will come out later and repeatedly, Jesus' disciples in Matthew are a mixture of the true and the false, of the genuine and the merely professing (for two examples, see 24:45–25:13), so that the many crowds anticipate the large, mixed church at Matthew's time of writing.

THE SERMON ON THE MOUNT
Matthew 5–7

The law of Moses is contained in the Pentateuch, the first five books of the Old Testament. To further the parallel begun in earlier chapters between Jesus and Moses, chapter 5 starts the first of correspondingly five great discourses of Jesus in this Gospel (see chapters 10, 13, 18, and 23–25 for the remaining discourses). He has just appeared as teacher, preacher, and healer (4:23); and Matthew has already indicated the content of Jesus' preaching (4:17). Now he will detail Jesus' teaching (chapters 5–7) and healing (chapters 8–9) in the order of their mention in the preceding summary (4:23).

THE ENCOURAGING WORD OF GOD
AS TAUGHT BY THE GREATER MOSES
TO HIS PERSECUTED DISCIPLES
Matthew 5:1–10

5:1–2: And on seeing the crowds, he went up onto a mountain [as Moses went up onto Mount Sinai to receive and then promulgate the Law]; **and when he'd sat down** [that is, taken the posture that rabbis took to teach the Mosaic law], **his disciples approached him.** [2]**And**

opening his mouth he started teaching them, saying . . . . Since Jesus speaks to his disciples (by definition "learners"), we should take the Sermon on the Mount as instruction for discipleship, not as the good news of salvation or as a program for the social betterment of the world at large (though the world at large might well adopt such a program). And since at the conclusion of the Sermon on the Mount it'll be said that "the *crowds* were awestruck at his teaching" (7:28), the disciples who approach him and whom he starts teaching here in 5:1 are the same crowds that were portrayed in 4:25 as disciples (a mixture again of the true and the false), not a smaller group that separated themselves from the crowds by following Jesus up the mountain. This portrayal exhibits Matthew's desire to make Jesus' teaching the Law to the crowds anticipate and symbolize the mission described in 28:19–20, where Jesus will order his original disciples to teach newly made disciples from all nations to obey "all things" that he has commanded them. And since he's "God with us" (1:23) and human beings are to live "on the basis of every word proceeding out through God's mouth" (4:4), what now proceeds out through Jesus' mouth when he opens it are the very words of God, like the law of God promulgated through Moses on Mount Sinai. Thus Jesus as God incarnate and Jesus as the new and greater Moses merge.

5:3: "Fortunate [are] **the poor in spirit, because** *theirs* **is the reign of heaven."** (Here and following, italics indicate points of emphasis and implication: "*theirs* rather than others," "*they* rather than others," and so on.) The traditional translation, "Blessed," is sometimes updated to "Happy." But "Happy" wouldn't fit those who in 5:4 "mourn"; and Jesus is stating a matter of fact, not a matter of what should be, as though the poor in spirit should be happy whether or not they are. So "Fortunate" is a better update to "Blessed." "Poor in spirit" echoes the word of the Lord in Isaiah 66:2 and thus furthers the identification of Jesus' words with the words of God, as in 5:2 with 4:4. Poverty in spirit means inward dependence on God by disciples who because of persecution have no outward means of support. The use of the third person (not "you" and "yours" but "they" and "theirs") both here and in the following verses makes these beatitudes (as they are traditionally called) into statements that teach the characteristics and effects of true discipleship. "The reign of heaven" belongs to "the poor in spirit" in that though they're persecuted now, someday they'll share in reigning over the regenerated earth (compare 19:28; 25:21, 23, 28).

5:4: "Fortunate [are] **those who are mourning** [that is, grieving over their persecutions], **because** *they* **will be comforted** [when Jesus comes back and the reign of heaven fully takes over]." This beatitude echoes Isaiah 61:1–2.

5:5: "Fortunate [are] **the meek, because** *they* **will inherit the earth** [again, when Jesus comes back and the reign of heaven fully takes over]." "The meek" are those who suffer persecution without retaliating. This beatitude echoes Psalm 37:11.

5:6: "Fortunate [are] **those who hunger and thirst for righteousness, because *they* will be sated.**" But since they're being persecuted "on account of righteousness [their own, that is (5:10)]," they're already righteous; and Jesus will soon speak of "your righteousness" in addressing his disciples (5:20 [compare 1:19; 5:45; 10:41 and so on]). So the righteousness they hunger and thirst for is the righteousness of God in the sense of his vindication of them. They want him to do the right thing by way of rewarding them and punishing their persecutors. "They will be sated" alludes to being filled to satisfaction with divine vindication at the messianic banquet, which will take place when the reign of heaven fully takes over (compare 8:11–12; 22:1–10; 26:29). This beatitude echoes Isaiah 49:10; 61:1.

5:7: "Fortunate [are] **the merciful, because *they* will be treated mercifully.**" Now their persecutors treat them mercilessly, and in return they show only mercy toward their persecutors. So when the reign of heaven fully takes over, God will treat the merciful with mercy (and their persecutors without mercy, we might add from passages such as 23:29–36). This beatitude echoes Psalm 18:25.

5:8: "Fortunate [are] **the pure in heart, because *they* will see God.**" Great stress falls in Matthew's Gospel on inward purity as opposed to a merely outward show of purity, piety, and the like (see, for example, 6:1–6, 16–18). For it's only inward purity that can fortify a professing Christian against temptations to recant in times of persecution. "*They* will see God" when the reign of heaven fully takes over. To see him is to be brought into his glorious presence, as opposed to being thrown into outer darkness (for which see the comments on 4:16). This beatitude echoes Psalm 24:3–6.

5:9: "Fortunate [are] **the peacemakers, because *they* will be called sons of God.**" "The peacemakers" have their counterparts in those who persecute them ("people" who "hate you," as Luke 6:22 puts it). They make peace with their persecutors. "*They* will be called sons of God" means that when the reign of heaven fully takes over, God will acknowledge them as his sons. ("Sons" functions generically here and thus includes females as well as males.) This beatitude echoes Psalm 34:14; Hosea 1:10.

5:10: "Fortunate [are] **those who've been persecuted on account of righteousness, because *theirs* is the reign of heaven.**" As noted in connection with 5:6, here it's not God's righteousness but the disciples' righteousness for which they've been persecuted. Literally, to be persecuted means to be pursued, to be hounded—hence the withdrawals that we've noted in earlier chapters and the later command to flee (10:23). This beatitude echoes Psalm 15:1–2; Isaiah 51:7. So every one of these beatitudes displays unity between the teaching of Jesus, who is "God with us" (1:23), and the words of God in the

Old Testament. Repetition from the first beatitude of the promise, "*theirs* is the reign of heaven," brings the series to a close (see further the comments on 5:3). The first four beatitudes emphasized the persecuted condition of Jesus' disciples. The last four have emphasized the ethical qualities that characterize the persecuted. Accordingly, the first four end on the note of righteousness as divine justice, the last four on the note of righteousness as the disciples' good conduct. So in these beatitudes we don't have a gospel for the unevangelized, but words of encouragement for a suffering church.

THE DISCIPLES' PERSECUTION AND
MISSION IN THE WORLD
Matthew 5:11–16

Though this passage begins with "Fortunate," it doesn't belong with the preceding series of beatitudes which begin the same way. For no longer do we read a "because"-clause right after the "Fortunate"-clause, and the person changes from third ("they," "theirs," and "those") to second ("you" and "yours" in the plural). At this point, therefore, the term "Fortunate" simply forms a link between the beatitudes proper (5:3–10) and the following description of the persecutions to be endured by Jesus' disciples because of their mission in the world (5:11–12). There follow two descriptions of that mission, the first under the figure of salt (5:13), the second under the related figures of a light, a city, and a lamp (5:15–16). These three subdivisions of the passage close, respectively, with an encouragement to rejoice, a warning, and an exhortation.

5:11–12: "**Fortunate are you whenever people vilify you and persecute [you] and on account of me say every kind of evil thing against you, lying** [when they do]. [12]**Rejoice and be glad, because your reward in heaven [is] much. For in this way they persecuted the prophets before you.**" Here persecution takes the form of verbal abuse in addition to physical pursuit. The redundancy of "vilify" and "say every kind of evil thing against you" magnifies the verbal abuse. So too does "every kind of." "Lying" qualifies the verbal abuse to ensure that it's undeserved. "On account of me" has the same purpose but qualifies physical pursuit as well as verbal abuse, corresponds to "on account of [disciples'] righteousness" in 5:10, and thus points to Jesus as the one whose teaching produces righteousness in those who obey it. The redundancy of "Rejoice and be glad" underlines the coming good fortune of those who suffer such abuses undeservedly. "Your reward" defines the good fortune as deserved, in contrast with the abuses. Since the meek "will inherit the *earth*" (5:5), "in heaven" doesn't mean you'll get your reward when you go to heaven. It means, rather, that your reward is already packaged in heaven, so to speak, and only awaits delivery when the reign of heaven fully takes hold on earth. "Much" describes the reward as quite sufficient to compensate even for the saying of "*every* kind of evil thing against you." The similarity between the way people persecuted the Old Testament prophets and the way Jesus' disciples are persecuted supplies the reason "your reward in heaven [is] much." You're being persecuted no less than and no differently from those ancient prophets, and you don't doubt that their reward is much. In fact, some of you are prophets just as they were (10:41; 23:34). All in all, compare Genesis 15:1; Isaiah 51:7; 66:5.

5:13: "You are the salt of the earth. But if the salt is made foolish [in the sense of losing its saltiness], **with what will it be made salty?"** Implication: nothing can resalt the salt. **"It's no longer strong for anything** [that is, capable of doing its job], **except on being thrown out to be trampled by people."** "Earth" means "soil" and stands for the world of human beings (compare 5:14, 16). Behind this figure lies the ancient agricultural practice of using a light sprinkling of salt as fertilizer. So disciples in the world are like fertilizer in the soil. They're capable of producing "fruit in keeping with repentance" (3:8), that is, "righteousness" (5:10) consisting in "good deeds" that contribute to others' conversion (5:16). But salt can lose its saltiness through adulteration or leaching. As in the foregoing translation, the verb for losing saltiness literally means "to be made foolish." Elsewhere in Matthew a foolish person is a falsely professing disciple (5:22 [with comments]; 7:26; 25:2–3, 8 [compare 23:17 for hypocrisy]). Here, then, for salt to be made foolish is for a disciple to be proved false in his profession. Persecution has a way of bringing out such falsity. "With what will it be made salty?" means that the falsity is irreversible. "It's no longer strong for anything" means that because of its falsity the discipleship has lost its usefulness for converting others. "Except on being thrown out to be trampled by people" stands for being thrown out of the kingdom of heaven into eternal punishment (8:12; 22:13; 25:30, 46). (People threw refuse, like useless salt, into the street, where people walked.) So the last part of this verse warns against allowing persecution to cause apostasy from discipleship, for such apostasy puts one under an irrevocable sentence of judgment.

5:14–16: "You are the light of the world." In other words, you disciples are like the sun, which illuminates the whole world. **"A city situated on a mountaintop can't be hidden."** For easier defense, many ancient cities were built on mountaintops or, by modern standards, hilltops. [15]**"Neither do people light a lamp and place it under a basket** [used for measuring and equivalent to almost ¼ bushel or eight quarts], **but on a lampstand; and it gives lamplight to all those in the house.** [16]**In this way your light is to give lamplight in people's presence, so that they may see your good deeds and glorify your Father in heaven."** The light of the sun is visible to all throughout the world. A city situated on a mountaintop is visible to all in the vicinity. And the light of a lamp placed on a lampstand is visible to all in the house. Despite the threat and actuality of persecution, Jesus says, you must behave as a disciple out in the open, where your discipleship is visible. No hiding it to

save your neck. Your discipleship consists in doing good deeds as defined by Jesus' teachings. Given the emphasis on mercy and neighborly love in 9:13; 12:7; 19:19; 22:39 and elsewhere, "good deeds" means especially works of charity. So the doing of good deeds is to back up the proclaiming of good news. "And glorify your Father in heaven" requires that the motive for the doing of such deeds be not for your own glory (6:1–18; 23:5) but for the glory of God the heavenly Father, whose "sons" are "the peacemakers" (5:9). But how do nondisciples who see your good deeds glorify him? By becoming disciples themselves as a result of the good deeds that back up the proclamation of good news. There comes about, then, a chain reaction of disciples' making disciples who make even further disciples, and so on. "Of the *world*," "on a *mountaintop*," "to *all* those in the house," and "in *this* way" point forward to Jesus' telling the disciples to go disciple "*all* nations" (28:19).

THE AFFIRMATION OF THE OLD TESTAMENT IN JESUS' TEACHING OF THE LAW AND FULFILLMENT OF THE PROPHETS
Matthew 5:17–20

5:17–18: "You shouldn't think that I've come to tear down the Law or the Prophets. I haven't come to tear down [the Law]—**rather, to fulfill** [the Prophets]. [18]**For amen I tell you, till heaven and earth pass away, by no means will a single iota or a single horn pass away from the Law till all things have happened."** "The Law and the Prophets" comprise the first two sections of the Hebrew Old Testament from which passages were read every Sabbath. But the use of "the prophet" in 13:35 to introduce a citation from the third and final section (the Writings, read during festivals) suggests that "the Law and the Prophets" may include also that third section by implication. In 5:17 and 7:12 references to the Law and the Prophets bracket Jesus' teaching of the Law, which makes up the main body of the Sermon on the Mount. Here the portrayal of Jesus as the new and greater Moses attains its greatest clarity. To tear down is, literally, to "loosen down," as in the loosening of stones from each other so as to bring down a building or a wall. To tear down the Law would be to teach against it by word and example. To tear down the Prophets would be not to fulfill their prophecies (in the sense of their predictions). The second reference to not tearing down relates in particular to the Law, and the following reference to fulfillment relates in particular to the Prophets. The redundancy of "I haven't come to tear down" after "You shouldn't think that I've come to tear down" puts enormous emphasis on the necessity that disciples of Jesus obey the Law as taught by him, and that they do so despite the temptation to disregard and disobey it for the sake of avoiding persecution.

"Amen" is a term of strong affirmation. "For amen I tell you" therefore gives strong affirmation of the continuing validity of the Law as taught by Jesus and of the continuing validity of the Prophets as fulfilled by him.

Their continuing validity forms the basis of his teaching and actions. "By no means" intensifies the denial of having come for a dismantling operation. "Pass away from the Law" relates in particular to Jesus' teaching. It will interpret the Law correctly. "Till all things have happened" relates in particular to Jesus' deeds. They'll fulfill the Prophets truly. So the phrases swing back and forth between Jesus' teaching of the Law and his fulfilling of the Prophets. "Iota" refers to the smallest letter in the Greek alphabet (and by Jesus' time the Hebrew Old Testament had been translated into Greek). We don't know for sure what a "horn" represents. It could represent the smallest letter in the Hebrew alphabet, shaped like a horn, or a little hook or extension of a stroke that distinguishes some letters from similar ones. In any case, "a single iota or a single horn" stresses the validity of the Law down to its finest details—but, again, as taught and fulfilled by Jesus. "Till heaven and earth pass away" doesn't mean that heaven and earth will pass away and that the Law and the Prophets will then lose their validity. It means instead that so long as anything exists, the Law and the Prophets will retain their validity.

5:19–20: "**Therefore** [because of the continuing validity of the Law as taught by Jesus] **whoever tears** [down] **a single one of these least commandments and teaches people in this way** [= by way of words and example that teach against it] **will be called least in the kingdom of heaven. But whoever does and teaches** [these least commandments]—**this person will be called great in the kingdom of heaven.** [20]**For I tell you that unless your righteousness abounds more than** [that] **of the scholars and Pharisees** [abounds]**, by no means will you enter the kingdom of heaven."** Since Jesus is talking to his professing disciples, "whoever" means anybody within their circle. Thus his having come *not* to tear down the Law provides for Christian teachers a positive example of what *not* to do. Here the verb for dismantling lacks the element of "down" (contrast the comments on "loosen down" in 5:17), because Jesus is dealing with only one commandment rather than with the many commandments whose loosening would result in a teardown of the building- or wall-like Law. "A single *one* of these *least* commandments" stresses the importance of every commandment in detail. "*These* least commandments" heightens the stress by referring back to "a single iota or a single horn [of the Law]" (5:18). No resting easily in the so-called spirit of the Law, or even in the pervasive principle of love alone (compare especially 23:1–3; 28:20). "*Will* be called least in the kingdom of heaven" and "*will* be called great in the kingdom of heaven" look forward to a time when heaven's reign takes full control of the world (compare 6:10). "Will be *called* least" and "will be *called* great" mean to *be* least and to *be* great and recognized as such. "Will be called *least*" and "will be called *great*" imply varying ranks in the kingdom, variations depending on the degree of adherence in word and deed to the Law as taught by Jesus. With poetic justice those guilty of some nonadherence will be

called least in the kingdom. At a certain undefined and therefore scary point, however, nonadherence reaches a degree that causes exclusion from the kingdom (see 7:15–23 as well as later passages). "Will be called great" may also play on the literal meaning of "rabbi," that is, "my great one" (see 23:7–8; 26:25 for "rabbi").

"For I tell you" makes the following statement an emphatic reason to keep from tearing down any part of the Law and, on the contrary, to practice and teach it in detail. "Your righteousness" arises out of and consists in your adherence to the Law as taught by Jesus. Such adherence will produce a righteousness that surpasses that of the scholars and Pharisees, and entrance into the kingdom even at the lowest rank (because of some nonadherence) requires a righteousness superior to theirs. If mere entrance requires so much, greatness requires even more—that is, adherence to all the least commandments too. Not all scholars belonged to the Pharisaical faction in Judaism, and not all Pharisees took the scholars' role of teaching the Law. But the associating of the scholars with the Pharisees arises out of the dominance of the Pharisees among the scholars, out of the Pharisaical scholars' providing the main source of opposition to Jesus, especially on questions of the Law, and out of Matthew's desire to distinguish the disciples of Jesus as scholars who teach Jesus' interpretation of the Law from the Pharisaical scholars (see 8:19; 13:52; 23:34 for the disciples as scholars).

THE RIGHTEOUSNESS WHICH SURPASSES THAT OF THE SCHOLARS AND PHARISEES
Matthew 5:21–48

This passage contains six sayings starting with "You have heard that it was said" and, after a quotation of the Law, continuing with Jesus' interpretation, starting with "But I tell you." The sayings are traditionally called "the Antitheses." But this designation seems to imply that after stoutly affirming the Law in 5:17–20, Jesus contradicts it. We'll see on the contrary that he escalates it. He takes the Law up to the goal toward which it was already headed, so that we should stop calling these sayings "the Antitheses" and perhaps start calling them "the Culminations."

5:21–22: "**You have heard that it was said to the ancients, 'You shall not murder** [Exodus 20:13; Deuteronomy 5:17],' **and whoever murders shall be subject to the judgment.** [22]**But I tell you that everyone who's angry with his brother shall be subject to the judgment. And whoever says to his brother, 'Raca,' shall be subject to the Sanhedrin** [the Jewish Supreme Court]**. And whoever says** [to his brother]**, 'You fool,' shall be subject to the gehenna of fire."** "You have *heard*" refers to the reading of the Law in synagogues Sabbath by Sabbath. "That it was *said*" refers to God's speaking the Law (see Deuteronomy 5:4, 17, 22). "To the *ancients*" references the Israelites to whom God addressed the Law at Mount Sinai. "His brother," which occurs twice and is implied a third time, carries forward the theme of Christian brotherhood begun as early as 1:2, 11 (see the comments on those verses) and limits Jesus' interpretation to interpersonal relations among his disciples. "Angry" denotes an inward feeling. He portrays this feeling as issuing in the addressing of a fellow disciple with "Raca" (an Aramaic epithet meaning "empty person," rather like our epithets "empty suit" and "airhead") and with the epithet "fool." Elsewhere in this Gospel "fool" refers to someone who professes discipleship falsely (7:26; 23:17; 25:2–3, 8; compare the comments on 5:13). "Raca" appears to be a variation on "fool" and therefore to carry the same meaning. Though it's sometimes necessary for a church to make the judgment that one of their members should be treated as a false disciple (18:15–17), Jesus here prohibits the private expression of such a judgment (compare 7:1–5; 13:24–30, 36–43, 47–50). "The judgment" prescribed in the Old Testament for a murderer consisted in capital punishment imposed by a court of fellow Israelites (Numbers 35:9–21, 29–31 [compare Deuteronomy 17:8–13]). "The judgment" predicted by Jesus for a professing disciple who angrily declares a fellow disciple false—that judgment consists in eternal punishment ("the gehenna of fire" or, as we'd say, "hellfire") imposed by God's high court (symbolically called "the Sanhedrin"). So such disrupters of fellowship among Christian brothers will find themselves eternally doomed as the very kind of false disciples they'd accused others of being. Consequently, we don't have here a principle of legal justice for the whole body politic. Jesus isn't proscribing anger because it might lead to murder in society at large; rather, he's making anger and its offspring within the brotherhood of disciples to be offenses just as grave as murder outside the brotherhood. "Everyone" and the two occurrences of "whoever" disallow any exceptions. "Gehenna" referred at first to the Valley of Hinnom, a ravine on the south side of Jerusalem where fire-worship of the god Moloch and child-sacrifice took place and where refuse was burned. Out of that use developed a metaphorical use for hell, the place of fiery punishment for the wicked in an afterlife.

5:23–24: "**Therefore** [because of the foregoing warnings] **if you** [singular] **were to be offering your gift at the altar** [of the temple in Jerusalem] **and there remembered that your brother** [= fellow disciple] **has something against you,** [24]**leave your gift there in front of the altar and go. First get reconciled to your brother; and then, on coming** [to the altar], **proceed to offer your gift.**" A command to brotherly reconciliation naturally follows the warnings against anger and verbal abuse. Thus Jesus escalates the prohibition of murder (5:21) not only to avoidance of anger and verbal abuse (5:22) but also to appeasement of a fellow disciple's anger. Without reconciliation a gift offered at the altar lacks acceptability to God. This principle holds right through the shift from offerings at the temple in Jesus' day to other forms of worship in the time of the church.

To illustrate the necessity of reconciliation between disciples at odds with each other, Jesus now portrays an insolvent debtor whose only hope lies in coming to an agreement with his creditor before landing in a debtors' prison. **5:25–26:** "**Reach good terms with your opponent** [in a lawsuit] **quickly,** [that is,] **while you're with him on the way** [to court], **lest the opponent give you over to the judge, and the judge** [give you over] **to the bailiff, and you be thrown into prison.**" In other words, settle out of court. "Quickly" and its specification, "while you're with him on the way," emphasize the need for a disciple who has committed a fault against another disciple to achieve reconciliation with the other disciple immediately. [26]"**Amen I tell you** [still singular], **by no means will you come out of there till you've given back the last quadrans** [a Roman coin worth about ¼ cent, or ¹⁄₆₄ of a manual laborer's daily wage]." But in prison you can't earn money to pay back your debt! So like anger (5:21–22), failure to make things right with a brother in the church falsifies your profession of discipleship and lands you in hell, the prison of eternally hopeless debtors, that is, of sinners (compare the calling of sins "debts [of a moral sort]" in the Lord's Prayer [6:12], and note the wordplay between "give . . . over" and "give back"). Since you can't earn *any* money in prison, "the *last* quadrans" joins the minimal value of a quadrans to accent the eternality of punishment in hell. "Amen I tell you" and "by no means" add a double accent on this much-to-be-avoided punishment. Jews didn't throw debtors into prison, though. So Jesus uses this cruel practice of Gentiles to shock his Jewish disciples concerning eternal punishment for false discipleship. Persecution brings out the falsity of some disciples' profession just as it brings out the truth of other disciples' profession.

5:27–30: "**You** [plural] **have heard that it was said, 'You** [singular] **shall not commit adultery** [Exodus 20:14; Deuteronomy 5:18].' **[28]But I tell you** [plural] **that every** [man] **who looks at a woman so as to lust after her has already committed adultery with her in his heart.**" "*Every* [man]" leaves no room for exceptions— even, or especially, of professing disciples. On the one hand, Jesus isn't condemning the natural desire of a man for a woman (see 19:5–6). On the other hand, Jesus does escalate the Mosaic prohibition by condemning the leering look. In the Bible, adultery means having sex with somebody else's spouse, here with another man's wife. Like irreconciliation with your fellow disciple and like adultery in the flesh, adultery in the heart (we'd say, in the mind) will land you in hell: [29]"**And if your right eye causes you to stumble** [into the inward adultery of lustful looking], **gouge it out and throw** [it] **away from you** [singular]. **For it's advantageous to you that one of your** [body] **parts perish and not your whole body be thrown into gehenna** [for which see the comments on 5:22]. [30]**And if your right hand causes you to stumble** [into self-gratification of your lust for another man's wife], **cut it off and throw** [it] **away from you. For it's advantageous to you that one of your** [body] **parts perish and not your whole body go away into gehenna.**" What irony! Eyesight is supposed to keep you from stumbling. But though it does keep you from physical stumbling, it can cause you to stumble morally. And your hand is supposed to steady you (with the use of a walking stick, for example) so as not to stumble physically. But it can cause you to stumble morally. Since most people are right-handed, Jesus chooses the right hand as the one most liable to cause moral stumbling. And on the supposition that the right eye is stronger than the left one just as the right hand is stronger than the left, Jesus also chooses the right eye as the most liable to cause moral stumbling. (We could replace "stumble" with "fall into a trap," for Jesus' verb carries both meanings.) Alongside a death penalty, the loss of just one eye or hand—even the right one—seems preferable. How much more preferable alongside a whole-bodied eternity in hell. (Assumed is resurrection of the body for those who've died in the meantime.) True discipleship, then, will show itself through sexual self-discipline in the heart as well as in act. Gouging out and cutting off suffice for riddance of the offending eye and hand, so that the two additional occurrences of "and throw [it] away" underscore the absolute necessity of self-discipline.

The topic of adultery leads naturally to that of divorce. **5:31–32: "And it was said, 'Whoever would divorce his wife is to give her a** [written] **dismissal** [Deuteronomy 24:1].' ³²But I tell you that everyone who except for the reason of sexual immorality** [in her case (again see Deuteronomy 24:1)] **divorces his wife makes her to be adulterated** [by another man's marrying her when she really belongs to her first husband, sexually speaking, its being assumed that another man will marry her]. **And whoever marries a divorced** [woman] **adulterates himself** [by having sex with a woman who, again sexually speaking, still belongs to her first husband]." The Mosaic law didn't prohibit divorce, but according to Jesus it did require a husband who divorced his wife to give her a written dismissal so that he couldn't later accuse her of desertion. (Jewish women didn't have the right to divorce their husbands.) Jesus escalates this discouragement of divorce to a nearly exceptionless prohibition of divorce in that apart from the exception, divorce entails adultery through remarriage. "Except for the reason of sexual immorality" means that it won't be the wife's first husband who makes her to be adulterated by divorcing her. She has already been adulterated. But emphasis falls on the responsibility of husbands not to put their *un*-adulterated wives in a position that pretty much dooms them to adulteration by remarriage out of economic necessity. The passive voice in "be adulterated" reflects male dominance in Jewish marital culture. Strikingly, on the other hand, the man who marries a divorcée adulterates himself whether or not he himself is divorced.

5:33–37: "Again you [plural] **have heard that is was said to the ancients** [see the comments on 5:21], **'You** [singular] **shall not break an oath** [Leviticus 19:12],' **'and you shall give back to the Lord your oaths** [by carrying them out, for they are verbal debts owed to him] [Psalm 50:14].' ³⁴But I tell you** [plural] **not to swear** [an

oath] **at all—neither by heaven, because it's 'the throne' of God** [Isaiah 66:1], ³⁵nor by the earth, because it's 'the footstool of his feet' [Isaiah 66:1 again],' neither by Jerusalem, because it's 'the city of the great king** [= God, whose temple is located in Jerusalem though his reign originates in heaven (Psalm 48:2)].' ³⁶Neither should you** [singular] **swear** [an oath] **by your head, because you can't make a single hair white or black. ³⁷But** [in contrast with swearing oaths] **your word is to be 'Yes, yes; no, no.' What's in excess of these** [words by way of oaths] **is from the evil one** [= the Devil]." Here Jesus escalates the Mosaic requirement that oaths be carried out up to the requirement of such absolute truth-telling that oaths become wrong, not just unnecessary. Jesus doesn't base his prohibition on the need for credibility apart from oath-taking. He bases it on the detraction from God's majesty in oath-taking. Note, for example, the designation of God as "the *great* king." Never mind the vulgarizing of his name by an oath taken in it. Substitutions for his name also detract from his majesty in that they stand in association with him because of his universal authority. Over your head he has an authority that even you yourself don't have. Jesus' borrowing expressions from the Old Testament shows him conforming his words as Immanuel, "God with us" (1:23), to the ancient, written word of God. The doublings of "yes" and "no" either emphasize truth-telling without oaths or require truth-telling without oaths on successive occasions, or do both. The attribution to the Devil as "the evil one" of "what's in excess of these [words, 'Yes, yes; no, no']" makes oath-taking itself evil and therefore off-limits for Jesus' true disciples. Thus he brings the old strictures against careless oaths to culmination in a prohibition of oaths as such. "At all" makes the prohibition absolute.

5:38–42: "You [plural] **have heard that it was said, 'An eye for an eye' and 'a tooth for a tooth** [Exodus 21:24; Leviticus 24:20; Deuteronomy 19:21].' ³⁹But I tell you not to resist** [that is, fight back against] **the evil one** [= the Devil, as in 5:37, but as represented in your persecutors]. **Rather, whoever slaps you** [singular] **on your right cheek—turn to him also the other** [cheek]. ⁴⁰And to the one wanting to sue you and take your tunic** [= inner robe]—**let him** [have your] **cloak** [= outer robe] **too. ⁴¹And whoever requisitions you for one mile—go with him two** [miles]. ⁴²Give to the one asking you** [for something of your own, as poverty-stricken beggars do (6:1–4)], **and you shouldn't turn away from the one wanting to borrow from you."** Not only did the so-called law of retaliation, quoted by Jesus from the Mosaic law, have the purpose of working for justice by demanding that wrongdoers be punished (see especially Deuteronomy 19:15–21). It also had the purpose of working against cruelty by demanding that punishments match crimes rather than exceed them. For punishments often did exceed crimes in ancient cultures. Jesus escalates this latter purpose to the height of what can be summarized as the very meekness before the cruel and generosity toward the needy that he himself exemplified (11:28–30 [compare 5:5]). "Your *right* cheek" implies that a disciple should take meekly a backhanded slap by a right-handed person despite the specially insulting character of that kind of slap, which drew double the fine for a slap with the open palm. "Turn to him also the other [cheek]" indicates that even the worst insult doesn't exhaust Jesus' demand for meekness. An opponent in court couldn't sue you for your cloak, because the Mosaic law prohibited the keeping of someone else's cloak beyond sunset. For at nighttime a cloak provided the warmth of a blanket (Exodus 22:26–27; Deuteronomy 24:12–13). But Jesus demands of his disciples that they go so far as to let go even what is legally their inalienable right to retain. Requisitioning for one mile reflects the practice of soldiers' forcing nonsoldiers to carry gear for them (compare 27:32). Some of Jesus' phraseology echoes Isaiah 50:6, 8, especially in its Greek version (compare the comments on 5:33–37). Unlike a beggar, the borrower has an obligation to pay back what he borrowed. So Jesus commands generosity both in giving to people so needy that they can't pay back and in lending to those who can.

5:43–48: "You [plural] have heard that it was said, 'You [singular] shall love your neighbor [Leviticus 19:18]**,' and you shall hate your enemy** [a paraphrase of Psalm 139:21–22 that takes the psalmist's statements, 'Do I not hate those who hate you, O Lord? . . . I hate them with perfect hatred; I count them my enemies,' as a scriptural example meant to be emulated (compare Deuteronomy 30:7; Psalm 26:5)]. **⁴⁴But I tell you [plural], love your enemies and pray for the ones persecuting you, ⁴⁵so that you may become sons of your Father in heaven, because he makes his sun rise on evil [people] and good [people] and makes it rain on righteous [people] and unrighteous [people].** The growth of crops requires both sunshine and rain. **⁴⁶For if you love those who love you, what reward do you have** [awaiting you]**?"** Answer: none, for mere entrance into the kingdom requires abounding in righteousness even more than the scholars and Pharisees do (5:20). **"Even the tax collectors do the same, don't they? ⁴⁷And if you greet only your brothers** [= fellow disciples]**, what extra are you doing? Even the Gentiles do the same, don't they? ⁴⁸Therefore** [since disciples have to do a lot more than the tax collectors and Gentiles do] **you shall be perfect as your heavenly Father is perfect** [compare Deuteronomy 18:13: 'You shall be perfect before the Lord your God']**."** The parallel between "your enemies" and "the ones persecuting you" shows that your enemies are those who persecute you because of your discipleship (compare Deuteronomy 30:7 again: "on your enemies and on those who hate you, who persecuted you"). So "your neighbor" means by contrast your fellow among God's persecuted people (Israel in the Old Testament, the church in the New Testament). But Jesus escalates the law of loving your fellow among God's persecuted people to a law of loving your hostile persecutors. Thus even *perfect* hate fades into oblivion along with those other features of the Old Testament law that let anger and lust go unpunished and allowed merciless divorce, oaths, and standing up for your rights. Such features didn't have their origin in

God's will so much as they accommodated people's hard-heartedness (compare 19:8). The Old Testament center of gravity lay in counteractive tendencies that Jesus carries out fully for the new time of the kingdom.

"Love" means "*do* good to," not merely "*feel* good toward." "So that you may *become* sons of your Father in heaven" means "so that you may *prove* yourselves to be his sons." Like father, like son. So the heavenly Father's blessing with sunshine and rain evil, unrighteous people, whose Father he is *not*, as well as good, righteous people, whose Father he *is*, provides the reason why behavior similar to his is required to prove your sonship to him. Tax collectors were notorious for their dishonesty and Gentiles for their idolatry and immorality, so that to do no more than they do by way of loving and greeting people doesn't meet the requirement for entrance into the kingdom. (Greetings didn't consist in a bare "Hello," but included expressions of desire for the welfare of the person greeted.) The perfection that Jesus commands is a perfection of love in that he escalates both the Old Testament command to love a neighbor and the Old Testament's prescriptive example of hating enemies perfectly—he escalates them to the requirement of loving even your enemies, the ones persecuting you.

THE TEACHING OF JESUS THE SAGE
Matthew 6:1–7:27

Just as the expression "your righteousness" stands at the head of the legislative part of the Sermon on the Mount (see 5:20 with 5:21–48), that same expression here in 6:1 marks a fresh start for the sermon's final section, 6:1–7:27. In it we read no quotations from the Old Testament with Jesus' teaching attached. Their absence contrasts sharply with the many such quotations in 5:21–48. So Jesus now appears as the supreme sage, who after expounding the Law now teaches the wisdom of righteousness (see especially 7:24–27). The subsection 6:1–7:12 consists of prohibitions. They start with a general prohibition of ostentation in religious practices (6:1). Following are particular prohibitions of ostentation in almsgiving (6:2–4), in praying (6:5–15), and in fasting (6:16–18). Each of these prohibitions mentions the ironic results of ostentation and concludes with the proper way to practice righteousness. Next we read a prohibition of hoarding earthly wealth (6:19–21), with related references to greed (6:22–23) and anxiety (6:24–34), and a prohibition of judging (7:1–12). The sermon ends with a command to practice righteousness despite the fewness of righteous people (7:13–14), in contrast with false prophets (7:15–23), and like a wise man (7:24–27).

Against Ostentation
Matthew 6:1–18

6:1: "But take precaution not to perform your righteousness before human beings for the purpose of being observed by them. Otherwise you don't have a reward [awaiting you] **alongside your Father in heaven."**

This criticism of religious ostentation doesn't contradict the command in 5:14–16 to do good deeds before other people. For there Jesus was concerned with the temptation to hide your discipleship in order to escape persecution (compare 5:10–12), and he took care to command the doing of good deeds for the glory of your Father in heaven. Here he prohibits the doing of good deeds for your own glory. For "a reward [awaiting you] alongside your Father in heaven," see the comments on 5:11–12.

Prayer, fasting, and almsgiving formed the three main pillars of Jewish piety. Jesus first takes up almsgiving (sharing your wealth with the poor) and then steps back for prayer and fasting. **6:2–4: "Therefore** [since religious ostentation will keep your heavenly Father from rewarding you] **when you're performing almsgiving, you shouldn't have a trumpet sounded before you, as indeed the hypocrites do in the synagogues and in the lanes so that they may be glorified** [= honored/admired] **by human beings** [as distinguished from God, alongside whom they otherwise might have a reward awaiting them]. **Amen I tell you, they have their reward in full** [in the form of glorification by the human beings who see them performing almsgiving ostentatiously]." Jesus doesn't forbid almsgiving as such; rather, he prohibits publicizing it with the fanfare of a trumpet. We have no evidence that any Jews had a trumpet blown ahead of them as they went to dispense charity, though. So the prohibition probably carries a bitingly sarcastic hyperbole: it's *as though* the hypocrites had trumpets blown ahead of them. Since the synagogues were houses where people were supposed to glorify God, "in the synagogues" sharpens the sarcasm of trumpeting almsgiving there so that attenders would glorify the almsgiver. "In the lanes" sharpens the sarcasm further in that the hypocrites look for their own glorification even in narrow streets. They're not satisfied to have the crowds attending synagogues glorify them. They milk glory also from the few to be found in what we might call the back alleys of town. "Hypocrites" means "actors" and here refers to acting in pretense of concern for the needy when the real concern is for admiration from other human beings. The hypocrites receive their reward in full when they get that admiration, which is what they wanted in the first place. But they'll get no reward from God, for "have in full" appears in commercial language and on receipts of the New Testament period with the meaning "Paid in full." "Amen I tell you," which means something like "Mark my words!" underlines the point. ³**"And when you're performing almsgiving, your left** [hand] **is not to know what your right** [hand] **is performing,** ⁴**so that your almsgiving may be in secret."** That is to say, the charitable gift should be slipped unobtrusively to a beggar with the right hand alone (most people being right-handed), not offered with both hands so as to attract the attention of people nearby. Thus the almsgiving can take place secretly even in public places haunted by beggars and populated by others. **"And your Father, the one who** [unlike your earthly father] **sees in secret, will give back**

to you [what you doled out in charity, and he'll do so by way of rewarding you in the hereafter]."

6:5–6: "And when you're praying, you shall not be like the hypocrites, because they love to pray standing [the normal posture for prayer] **in the synagogues and at the corners of broad** [streets] **so that they may appear to human beings** [as praying]. **Amen I tell you, they have their reward in full."** "You shall not be" issues a prohibition, not a prediction. But Jesus doesn't prohibit standing and praying in public as such. Instead, he prohibits doing so for the purpose of being heard by other human beings rather than by God. "Love" highlights this hypocritical purpose. Along with the synagogues, the intersections of wide streets provide a maximum number of admiring human auditors. ⁶**"But you—when you're praying, go into your storeroom and, on locking your door** [compare 2 Kings 4:33; Isaiah 26:20], **pray to your Father in secret. And your Father, the one who sees in secret** [see the comments on 6:4], **will give back to you** [what glory you lost by praying in secret]." Ordinarily, your storeroom had the only lockable door in the house. Thus privacy demanded the use of that room. Private prayer ought to be secret so as to avoid being corrupted by the desire for public admiration.

Ostentation in prayer also takes the form of wordiness. So Jesus speaks against wordiness by comparing it to pagan babbling. **6:7–8: "And when praying you shouldn't babble ineffectually as indeed the Gentiles** [do], **for they suppose that they'll be heeded in their much speaking."** Gentiles larded their prayers with long lists of divine names and hoped that at least one of the names might prove effective for an answer to their prayer. (Knowing the name of a god and pronouncing it correctly was supposed to give a certain power to manipulate the god.) Jesus describes the practice as ineffectual. ⁸**"Therefore** [because of the false supposition] **you shouldn't be like them** [in your praying]. **For your Father knows the things you have need of before you ask him** [for them]." Since he already knows your needs, in other words, "much speaking" will only bore him.

6:9–10: "You [in contrast with the Gentiles] **therefore** [because of your Father's foreknowledge]—**pray in this way: 'Our Father, the one in heaven** [as distinguished from earthly fathers to highlight his majesty], **your name be treated as sacred.** ¹⁰**Your reign come. Your will come to pass on earth as also** [it comes to pass] **in heaven.'"** "In this way" points forward to the Lord's Prayer, characterized by an economy of words rather than pagan-like wordiness. "Our," "us," and "we" make the prayer communal, but in view of the petition for daily bread (6:11) probably communal for families in their daily prayers more than for praying with other Christians less frequently in church meetings. In accord with the emphasis on God's being the Father of Jesus' disciples (5:16, 45, 48; 6:1, 4, 6, 8 and so on), "Father" is the name of God that's to be treated as sacred, that is, as inviolable, not to be profaned or maligned but to be held in deepest reverence. "Father" goes back to the Aramaic "Abba" (Mark 14:36; Romans 8:15; Galatians 4:6), which means something like "Dadda" or "Daddy" *except that it remained in use during adulthood for addressing one's father, so that after childhood it didn't continue having the sound of baby talk.* "The one in heaven" not only distinguishes God "our Father" from our earthly fathers. It also points to his high majesty as a counterbalance to the familiarity of his fatherhood. No "daddy-o" he! The request that the heavenly Father's reign come may sound like a request that his reign soon take full control of the earth, as at Jesus' second coming. But according to 12:28 the Father's reign has already arrived in the activities of Jesus. Moreover, "Your will come to pass on earth" looks synonymous with "Your reign come"; for 7:21; 12:50; 21:31–32; 26:42 all portray the Father's will as something to be done during the present age, as by way of example Jesus himself does (26:42). Moreover again, throughout this sermon and elsewhere in the Gospel of Matthew, Jesus lashes out against false disciples, whose disobedience to the Law as taught by him stems from failures to treat the Father's name as sacred and to recognize his high majesty (see 7:15–27, for example). These considerations favor that requesting his reign to come and his will to come to pass on earth means asking that more people become Jesus' disciples by taking on themselves the yoke of discipleship and so do the will of God on earth as it's done in heaven (11:28–30). That is, we're to ask for success in discipling all nations (28:19–20).

Jesus has made the coming to pass of the Father's will in the present age an anticipation of the consummated reign of heaven in the coming age. Now he turns attention to the daily needs of his disciples for food and forgiveness. **6:11–13: "'Give us today our bread for the coming** [day]. [12]**And forgive our debts** [= our moral debts to God] **for us as we also have forgiven our debtors** [those morally indebted to us by having sinned against us (compare Deuteronomy 15:1–11, which has to do with financial debts, however)].'"** "*As we also have forgiven our debtors*" draws a comparison. Our forgiveness of others presents God with an example of the forgiveness sought from him and demonstrates the sincerity of our asking him to forgive us. The comparison will shortly turn into a condition. If we don't forgive others, God won't forgive us. But a condition isn't a cause, so that his forgiveness of our debts will still arise out of mercy and grace, not out of any merit in our having forgiven others (compare 18:21–35). "Bread" stands for what's needed in a basic diet. Receiving bread "today" for "the coming day" suits a morning prayer that the next day's bread be supplied during the day that has just begun; so there'll be no need to "worry about tomorrow" (6:34). [13]**"'And you shouldn't** [in the sense, "please don't"] **lead us into temptation.'"** This request doesn't ask that the Father should keep us from confronting temptation. It means instead that he should keep us from succumbing to temptation (see 26:41, where Jesus tells Peter, James, and John, "Stay

awake and pray lest you enter into temptation," even though temptation had already confronted them and they'd fallen asleep). As usual, "temptation" also means "test," because every temptation tests our resistance to sin, and every test of our resistance tempts us to sin (see 5:27–30 for the drastic consequence of succumbing). The mention of temptation naturally leads to a mention of that archtempter, the Devil, who has already tested Jesus (4:1–11): **"'Rather, rescue us from the evil one.'"** This evil one has recently appeared in connection with present temptations/tests (5:37, 39), so that rescue from him would consist in coming through such temptations/tests victorious over the persecutions and enticements that tested our resistance to sin (13:18–22).

Now Jesus explains why we should ask God to forgive us in accordance with our having forgiven others. (The familiar doxology, "For thine is the kingdom . . . ," is a later liturgical addition that's unoriginal to the New Testament.) **6:14–15: "For if you forgive human beings their trespasses, your heavenly Father will forgive you too** [your trespasses]. [15]**But if you don't forgive human beings** [their trespasses]**, neither will your Father forgive your trespasses."** "Their *trespasses*" shows that in 6:12 "our debtors" didn't refer to those who owe us money, but referred to those morally indebted to us by having trespassed against us, as when they persecuted us. "*If* you forgive" and "*if* you don't forgive" leave the question open whether as true disciples we've forgiven others or as false disciples we haven't. By contrast, there's no question as to what God will do in either case—hence "*will* also forgive" and "neither *will* . . . forgive." As our "Father," God will graciously forgive us or sternly not forgive us. Twice Jesus speaks of "human beings" where he might have spoken of "brothers," that is, of fellow disciples. So "human beings" indicates that his disciples should forgive others their trespasses whether or not the trespassers are fellow disciples.

Jesus' last criticism of religious ostentation deals with fasting; for fasting often accompanied prayer, which he has just discussed, as an indication of the sorrow that prompted prayer and of the seriousness that accompanied it (see 2 Chronicles 20:1–12, for example). He himself provided an example of fasting (4:2), and he'll teach that his disciples should fast after he's been taken away (9:14–15). **6:16–18: "And whenever you're fasting, don't become somber-looking like the hypocrites. For they make their faces disappear** [by pouring ashes on their heads, with the result that the ashes settle on their foreheads, cheeks, noses, and chins and make the hypocrites unrecognizable] **so that they may appear to human beings** [as opposed to God] [to be] **fasting."** Ironically, the hypocrites make themselves unrecognizable in order to be recognized. Far from expressing the genuine sorrow that prompts fasting for the purpose of prayer, their ashen look is designed to earn human admiration for fasting. "Amen I tell you, they have their reward in full [see the comments on 6:4]. [17]**But you—when fasting anoint your head** [with olive oil] **and wash your** face [18]so that you don't appear to human beings [as] fasting but [appear as fasting only] to your Father, the one [who sees] in secret [compare 6:4]." Putting olive oil on the head and washing the face are to replace putting ashes on the head and adopting a pale, somber look. The resultant glistening of the hair and brightness of countenance keep other human beings from knowing about the fasting and thus protect its Godward address. The Jews observed a national fast on the Day of Atonement. But Jesus is referring to fasts by hypocrites who want admiration from the nonfasting public. Regular such fasting took place on Mondays and Thursdays. "And your Father, the one who sees in secret, will give back to you [see the comments on 6:4, 6]."

Against Hoarding Earthly Wealth
Matthew 6:19–34

The mention of reward in 6:16–18 leads to a prohibition of hoarding earthly wealth out of greed (6:19–24) and anxiety (6:25–34). Positively, Jesus' disciples are to exchange earthly treasures for heavenly treasures by avoiding such greed and anxiety. 6:19–21: "Don't be treasuring up for yourselves treasures on the earth, where moth and eating make [clothes] disappear and where thieves dig through and thieve." The word translated "eating" is often translated "rust" but elsewhere means eating rather than rust. So initially the treasures don't refer to coins, subject to rust—rather, to clothes such as fill the wardrobes of the wealthy (compare the theme of ostentation in 6:1–16 and see especially 13:52: "who as such [that is, as a 'houseowner'] thrusts forth new [garments] and old [garments] out of his treasure [wardrobe]"). By eating clothes, moths make them disappear. Well, not entirely; but Jesus is using hyperbole for a wordplay: as hypocrites make their faces disappear (to an extent) under a coating of ashes when they fast (6:16), eating by moths makes clothes disappear (to an extent). Thieves don't steal moth-eaten clothes, but they do steal money and valuables other than clothes. So eating by moths and thieving by thieves clear a house of all its owner's treasures just as all earthly treasures will finally be obliterated (compare James 5:2–3). "Dig through" refers to thieves' digging through the mudbrick wall of a house, though the expression may have come to have the general meaning of breaking and entering. [20]"But be treasuring up for yourselves treasures in heaven, where neither moth nor eating make [clothes] disappear and where thieves don't dig through and don't thieve. [21]For where your treasure is, there will be your heart too." Your affection resides in your heart, and the location of your treasures determines the location of your heart and therefore the objects of your affection. Jesus isn't saying that building up earthly wealth is wrong only if it captures your affection. He's saying that building it up is wrong precisely because it will capture your affection. By contrast, building up heavenly wealth will draw your heart to heaven, where your eternal reward is banked indestructibly and securely.

The mention of "your heart" in 6:21 leads to sayings about the body and the eye. 6:22–23: "The lamp of the body is the eye. So if your eye is clear [that is, unclouded by disease], your whole body will be light [in the sense of illuminated by the healthy eye, which sparkles like a lighted lamp]." Jesus is playing on the ancient view that the eye emits light. According to this view a healthy eye not only emits light outward, away from the body. It also emits light inward, into the body. [23]"But if your eye is evil [that is, dull and clouded by disease], your whole body will be dark [because the cloudiness will block the rays of light]. So if the light in you is darkness, how utter the darkness!" "But if your eye is evil" and "So if the light in you is darkness" set forth unsure conditions. The two occurrences of "will be" set forth sure results given the turning of the conditions into actualities. The two occurrences of "your whole body" stress the all-or-nothing of inward light versus inward darkness. So much for the ancient biophysical background. Metaphorically, clarity stood for generosity (see Romans 12:8; 2 Corinthians 8:2; 9:11, 13; James 1:5, in all of which passages the expressions for generosity rest on words whose literal meaning has to do with clarity). So a clear eye is an eye that sees clearly the needs of people, gives generously to meet their needs, and thus treasures up treasures in heaven (6:20). Metaphorically again, an evil, clouded eye is an eye that doesn't see clearly the needs of people and doesn't give generously to meet their needs but stingily, greedily treasures up treasures on earth (6:19 [compare 20:15]). Thus the physical and moral meanings of "evil" merge. The filling of the body with light points forward to the enjoyment of heavenly treasures. The filling of the body with darkness points forward to the loss of earthly treasures. "So if the light in you is darkness" presents an oxymoron that emphasizes how utter is the darkness of eternal loss.

6:24: "No one can slave for two masters. For either he'll hate the one and love the other, or he'll be devoted to one and despise the other. You can't slave for God and for Mammon." "Mammon" means "wealth," whether much or little, and comes from the Aramaic language most often used by Jesus. Since Matthew brings the word into his Greek text without translating it, we too should keep it in its Aramaic form. In that form it's being personified as a deity opposed to God. Hence its capitalization. We do know of slaves that served more than one master (see, for example, Acts 16:16). So Jesus means either that no one can at the same time slave for these two masters, "God and Mammon" (their demands being contrary to each other), in which case "you can't slave for God and for Mammon" defines the statement that "no one can slave for two masters." Or Jesus means that no one can slave well for any two masters at the same time (its being psychologically impossible to do so), in which case "you can't slave for God and for Mammon" applies the general principle that "no one can slave for two masters." In either case, the reason for the impossibility lies in the resistance of human nature to divided loyalties. "He'll hate" matches "he'll . . . despise," and these two expressions refer to disaffection as shown in slackness of labor. Conversely, "he'll . . . love" matches "he'll be devoted to," and these two expressions refer to affection as shown in faithful labor. For the comparative use of love and hate, see especially Genesis 29:30, 33, where hating one wife means not loving her as much as another wife. All in all, slaving for God means treasuring up treasures in heaven by generously giving away your wealth to the needy, whereas slaving for Mammon means treasuring up treasures on earth by stingily hoarding away your wealth in unconcern for the needy. And Mammon will enslave you if you don't give it away in charity.

6:25–30: "**On account of this** [the impossibility of serving both God and Mammon] **I tell you, don't be worrying about your soul** [= yourself, with particular reference to the part of you that animates your body and therefore represents physical life], **as to what you should eat or what you should drink** ['should' not in the sense of obligation but in the sense of availability, given the spare diets of most people then], **nor about your body, what you should clothe yourself with** [given the financial inability of most people to afford very much clothing]." "I tell you" emphasizes the command not to worry. "**The soul is more than food, isn't it, and the body than clothing, isn't it?**" That is to say, food has only the lowly task of serving the soul, or self, by sustaining physical life; and clothing has only the lowly task of serving the body by providing it warmth and protection. ²⁶"**Gaze at the birds of the sky** [and note] **that they don't sow** [seed] **and don't reap** [crops] **and don't gather** [wheat] **into granaries, and your heavenly Father provides them with food.**" "Your heavenly Father" distributes emphasis between divine sovereignty ("heavenly") and divine care ("Father"). "**You're much more valuable than they, aren't you?** ²⁷**And who of you by worrying can add one bit to his lifespan?**" Implied answer: None of you can. ²⁸"**And why do you worry about clothing? Learn well** [as disciples should do, since 'disciple' means 'learner'] **the lilies of the field** [though some other kind of wildflower, or wildflowers in general, may be in view] [by noting] **how they grow. They don't toil** [as men do in the fields], **and they don't spin** [flax into thread or yarn, as women do at home]. ²⁹**Yet I tell you** [again emphatic] **that not even Solomon in all his glory was arrayed like one of these.**" The splendor of Solomon's royal robes didn't match that of even one lily! ³⁰"**And if God decks out the grass of the field in this way** [with lilies of greater glory than Solomon's raiment], **though it** [the grass] **exists today and is thrown into an oven tomorrow** [for burning], **much more** [will he dress] **you, people of little faith, won't he** [since despite the short life of wild grass, in contrast with Solomon's and your much longer lives, God decks out that grass with lilies of glory greater even than that of Solomon's raiment]?**" Disciples who worry about food, drink, and clothing betray little faith in God.

6:31–34: "**Therefore don't worry, saying, 'What should we eat** ["should" again in the sense of availability,

not obligation]?' or '**What should we drink?' or 'What should we wear?'** ³²**For the Gentiles** [in the sense of pagans] **seek after all these things. For your heavenly Father knows that you have need of all these things.**" So Jesus cites two reasons not to worry: (1) its being pagan-like to seek after food, drink, and clothing out of worry; for as pagans the Gentiles don't believe in God or have him as their providential heavenly Father; and (2) your heavenly Father knows of your needs without your having to inform him (an encouraging thought especially in times of persecution). ³³"**But seek first God's reign and his righteousness, and all these things will be added to you.**" "First" doesn't imply permission to seek earthly security after seeking God's reign. Since God will add "all these things," disciples should never seek them. So "first" *emphasizes* seeking God's reign and righteousness rather than *permitting* the seeking of other things. "His righteousness" doesn't mean the right conduct that God requires on *our* part, with which "seek" wouldn't fit since our right conduct stems from doing, not from seeking (6:1). Instead, "his righteousness" means right conduct on *God's* part by way of vindicating the persecuted disciples of Jesus (see 5:6 with comments). To seek his vindication is to strive for it by persevering under persecution, which brings economic deprivation that might easily lead to anxiety over food, drink, and clothing. Since vindication won't come till the final judgment, so too the addition of "all these things" won't come till then. But that addition is the form which the vindication will take (compare 19:27–29). In the meantime, disciples are to accept the hardship of economic deprivation due to persecution. ³⁴"**Therefore** [since plenty of food, drink, and clothing will be added to you in the end] **don't worry about tomorrow** [since worrying won't eliminate the economic deprivation you're presently suffering through persecution], **for tomorrow will worry about itself** [so that *you* needn't worry about tomorrow]. **Sufficient for the day** [is] **its hardship.**" In other words, each day has enough hardship of its own, so that it's excessive as well as needless and fruitless to worry about the next day's hardship. The sufficiency of the hardship is emphasized by the neuter gender of the Greek word for "sufficient," thus highlighting the quality of sufficiency, whereas the Greek noun for "hardship," which "sufficient" describes, is feminine. The hardship comes from persecution. So acquiesce to persecution today in confidence of vindication and reward at the end.

Against Judging
Matthew 7:1–12

This passage opens with commands not to judge your fellow disciple (7:1–2) but to correct yourself (7:3–5). The prohibition of judgment is then balanced by a precautionary note that nondisciples ought to be barred from church fellowship (7:6). The passage then closes on the positive note of doing good as God does (7:7–12).

It may be that the command in 6:33 to seek vindication from God, which will feature his judging the disciples' persecutors, shifts here to a discussion of the disciples' judging one another. Whatever the case, Jesus now discusses such judging. *7:1–2:* **"Don't ever judge, lest you be judged. ²For with the judgment by which you judge** [that is, by the standard that you use in judging others] **you will be judged, and with the measure by which you measure** [judgment symbolized by a measure, such as a bushel basket in the measuring out of grain (compare the 'bowls' of God's wrath in Revelation 16)] **it will be measured to you."** References in the next two verses to "your brother" show that Jesus prohibits the judging of a fellow disciple. But what sort of judgment is Jesus talking about? Well, we've seen that he warned of hellfire for any disciple who individually arrogates to himself the divine prerogative of pronouncing a fellow disciple false in his profession of discipleship (see the comments on 5:22). So Jesus is prohibiting that kind of judgment (compare James 2:12–13; 4:12), and "lest you be judged" cites as a deterrent to it God's judging *you* to be the false disciple that you individually judge someone else to be ("individually," because 18:15–17 commands corporate judgments of this kind in certain cases). And since hellfire awaits a false disciple, God's judging you to be a false disciple refers to God's consigning you to hell at the last day. Measuring and being measured carry the same thought in figurative language.

7:3–5: **"And why is it that you** [singular] **see a chip** [a little fault] **in your brother's eye but don't notice the plank** [the big fault] **in your eye? ⁴Or how is it that you'll say to your brother, 'Let me thrust out the chip from your eye,' and behold, a plank** [is] **in your eye? ⁵Hypocrite, first thrust out the plank from your eye; and then you'll see** [with your eye] **wide open** [rather than squinting because of a plank in it] **so as to thrust the chip out of your brother's eye."** In other words, instead of judging a fellow disciple to be false because of some little fault, get rid of your own big fault so that you can effectively help him get rid of his little fault. Disciples should correct each other to improve each other's quality of discipleship (see 18:15–17 again), but they shouldn't take it on themselves as individuals to judge each other's eternal fates. Without self-correction, though, correcting a fellow disciple makes you a hypocrite in that you're pretending to be a better disciple than he is though in fact you're worse. "Behold" and the hyperbole of having a plank in your eye, as if that were possible, emphasize such hypocrisy; and "*thrust* out" instead of the expected "*take* out" emphasizes both the hypocrisy and the necessity of self-correction.

7:6: **"Don't give what's sacred** [the meat of a sacrificial offering] **to dogs and don't throw your pearls in front of pigs, lest they** [the pigs] **trample them** [the pearls] **with their feet** [because pearls are inedible] **and** [lest] **on turning** [from tasting the meat that has whetted their appetites] **they** [the dogs] **tear you to pieces** [the dogs being ferocious street scavengers, not household pets]." Avoiding judgments of fellow disciples and awaiting God's final separation of false disciples from true ones

might lead to letting into the church people who show no behavioral evidence of repentance (compare 3:8). So this prohibition warns against lax conditions of entrance into the church. Such conditions would result in the influx of those who not only contaminate the church but who also turn against true disciples by informing on them in times of persecution (see 24:10, 49). That is what the "trampling" and "turning tear you to pieces" refer to figuratively. And the dogs and pigs refer figuratively to those false disciples who do the trampling and tearing to pieces (compare Psalm 22:16). Jews detested street-scavenging dogs and unclean pigs and therefore used "dogs" and "pigs" as epithets for Gentiles. So just as among Jesus' disciples "Gentiles" can refer to nondisciples instead of non-Jews (as in 5:47; 6:7, 32; 18:17), so too "dogs" and "pigs" can refer to *false* disciples as in reality *non*disciples. And just as it would be ridiculous to toss a piece of sacred meat to dogs and throw valuable but inedible pearls in front of pigs, so too it would be ridiculous to let obviously undiscipled people into the church.

7:7–12 opens with the beggar's wisdom that persistence pays off, and closes with the Golden Rule: **"Keep asking, and it** [whatever you're begging for] **will be given to you. Keep seeking, and you'll find** [whatever you're looking for]. **Keep knocking, and it** [the door] **will be opened for you. ⁸For everyone who keeps asking receives, and** [everyone] **who keeps seeking finds, and for** [everyone] **who keeps knocking it** [the door] **will be opened. ⁹Or who from among you is a man whom his son will ask for a loaf of bread—he** [the father] **won't give him an** [inedible] **stone** [which looks something like a round 'loaf' of pita bread (compare 4:3)], **will he? ¹⁰Or** [whom his son] **will also ask for a fish, he won't give him a** [poisonous] **snake** [which because of its scales looks something like a fish], **will he? ¹¹If therefore you** [plural], **though you're evil, know to give good gifts to your children** [not 'know *how* to give good gifts,' as though it were a matter of method, but 'know *to* give good gifts,' since it's a matter of course—and this despite the depravity of human fathers], **how much more your Father in heaven** [who has no depravity at all] **will give good things to those who keep asking him. ¹²Therefore all things, however many they are, that you're wanting human beings** [as distinguished from your heavenly Father] **to be doing for you—thus too you yourselves be doing for them** [whatever they want you to be doing for them]. **For this is the Law and the Prophets** [about which see the comments on 5:17 (compare 22:40)]."

At first this passage looks like an instruction on praying with persistence. But Jesus has already given instruction on praying (6:5–15), and the "Therefore" that introduces the Golden Rule makes God's *giving* good things in answer to persistent prayer the example that Jesus' disciples should follow in treating one another. That is to say, instead of judging each other and turning on each other when persecuted (see the comments on 7:1–6), they should "give good things" to each other—by way of supporting their persecuted fellows, for example (see 25:31–46; also 8:27; 9:8; 13:44–45, 52; 27:57 for other instances of "human being[s]" in reference to Jesus' disciples rather than to people in general). "All things, however many they are" emphasizes the lengths to which such mutual help should go. The wordplay between "*thus* [literally, 'in *this* way'] too you yourselves be doing for them" and "*this* is the Law and the Prophets" implies that the Father's giving good things sets an example of doing what's written in the Law and the Prophets. For in Matthew's original Greek "this" isn't neuter, as we'd expect it to be in referring to the doing of good; rather, it's masculine, referring to the Father himself as personifying by example the Law and the Prophets. Notably, the Golden Rule demands doing *good* for other disciples, not merely avoidance of doing them evil. Furthermore (and despite modern misunderstanding), your treatment *of* them as you'd like to be treated *by* them doesn't rest on egoism. It rests on readiness to disown yourself in order to serve them in a way you'd like to be served. So in its context the Golden Rule doesn't tell people in general how they should treat others. It doesn't even tell Jesus' disciples how they should treat people in general (though they might well treat them accordingly). It tells them how they should treat one another in the Christian brotherhood.

Exhortations to Obey Jesus' Teaching of the Law
and to Avoid the Influence of False Prophets
Matthew 7:13–27

The Sermon on the Mount concludes with a series of exhortations set in the framework of a contrast between the two ways—that is, roads—of righteousness and lawlessness and a warning against false prophets who divert professing disciples from the way of righteousness onto the way of lawlessness. The narrow gate and constricted road contrast with the wide gate and broad road (7:13–14). Hearing and doing Jesus' words contrast with hearing and not doing them and define entering the narrow gate as hearing and doing those words, the broad road as hearing and not doing them (7:24–27). In between lies a warning not to heed the siren call to lawlessness of those false prophets, whose use of "Lord" for Jesus contrasts with their disobedience to his teaching concerning the heavenly Father's will (7:15–23). And the contrast between entrance into life and consignment to destruction at the Last Judgment overarches the whole passage.

7:13–14: "**Enter** [the city of salvation; compare Isaiah 4:3; Revelation 3:12; 21:1–22:5] **through the narrow gate** [for two reasons]: [1] **because the gate** [is] **wide and the road** [is] **broad that leads away** [from the city of salvation] **to destruction** [so that you could easily miss the narrow gate, go through the wide one, and set off to the city of destruction] **and the ones entering through it** [the easily recognized wide gate] **are many** [so that you could be swept along with the crowd]; [2] [14]**because the gate** [is] **narrow and the road** [is] **constricted that leads away** [from the city of destruction] **to life** [in the city of salvation], **and the ones finding it** [the easily missed narrow gate] **are few** [so that you might not notice and join them]." "The narrow gate" refers to a small, door-like gate set in a city wall at a location hard to find, so that only knowledgeable citizens enter the otherwise closed city at night and in times of danger. The big gate is shut! Hurry into the city of salvation by the one available way. The narrowness of the small gate prevents the entrance of more than one person at a time and represents the strict righteousness that Jesus has just taught as a requirement for entering the kingdom of heaven and the fewness of those who satisfy this requirement. Such righteousness has to surpass even the righteousness of the scholars and Pharisees (5:20). The constrictedness of the road leading to life (which is eternal) in the city of salvation implies a city situated impregnably atop a mountain, so that the mountainside constricts the width of the road; and this constrictedness represents the persecution of Jesus' true disciples, characterized as they are by conduct that satisfies the requirements he has laid down. For "constricted" is a verbal form of the noun "affliction/tribulation," which refers to persecution (13:21; 24:9, 21, 29 [compare persecution on account of righteousness in 5:10–12]). The broad road leading to the city of destruction signifies a city situated defenselessly on an open plain that unlike a mountainside is suitable to a broad road, and the road's breadth represents the lawless course of least resistance, that is, false disciples' escaping persecution through disobedience to Jesus' teaching of the Law. The wideness of the big gate leading into the city of destruction allows many people to enter at the same time but by the same token beckons invaders and represents the lax behavior of false disciples in violation of the Law as taught by Jesus. So "enter through the narrow gate" means "accept the strictures of Jesus' teaching."

The next subsection opens with a leading statement that offers the key for explaining the following figure as a reference to false prophets, who teach laxity to others as well as practicing it themselves (7:15). The figure itself has to do with fruits (7:16–20). Finally, the Lord's rejection of the false prophets at the Last Judgment comes into view as a pattern to be followed by true disciples at the present time. *7:15*: "**Take precaution against the false prophets, who as such** [that is, as 'false'] **are coming to you** [my disciples] **in sheep's clothes but from within are ravenous wolves.**" Jesus is referring to false prophets *in the church*, so that the present tense of "are coming" makes their future coming so vivid it's as though they were already arriving in Jesus' day. This vividness highlights the danger posed by them to the church. The donning of sheep's clothing stands for the false prophets' claim to Christian discipleship (compare Zechariah 13:4). The wolf-like ravenousness of these prophets exposes their falsity and represents the luxuriousness of their lifestyle, bought at the expense of their duped followers, and their heavy-handedness in exercising authority over them (compare 24:45–51; Ezekiel 22:27; Zephaniah 3:3–4; John 10:12; Acts 20:28–30). "*From* within" indicates that such behavior originates in their nature, comparable to that of ravenous wolves.

Jesus isn't telling his disciples *why* to take precaution—rather, *how* to do so, which is by recognizing the false prophets according to their behavior.

7:16–20: "**By their fruits** [= their behavior] **you'll recognize them** [to be false prophets]." Recognition of them is supposed to result in rejecting them now, just as according to 7:21–23 Jesus will reject them at the Last Judgment. "You'll recognize them" expresses both a command ("You *shall* recognize them") and a prediction ("You *will* recognize them"). To emphasize good deeds as a sign of true discipleship (especially in the case of prophets) and evil deeds as a sign of falsity, Jesus now utters both a negative statement and a positive statement about bearing good fruits and evil. "People don't gather grape clusters from thornbushes or figs from thistles, do they?" Of course not! So in the same way you're not going to get anything good from the false prophets, because they're like thornbushes and thistles as well as like wolves. [17]"**Thus** [according to the law of nature that thornbushes don't produce grape clusters and that thistles don't produce figs] **every good tree produces good fruits, and the rotten tree produces evil fruits.**" A good tree is a healthy one that produces edible fruits and stands for a prophet who teaches and practices the Law as interpreted by Jesus. "*Every* good tree" stresses that no true prophet will fail to do so. A rotten tree is a diseased one that produces inedible fruits and stands for a prophet who teaches and practices lawlessness, that is, disobedience to the Law as interpreted by Jesus. ("*Evil* fruits" connotes inedible fruits in a literal sense and moral evils in a figurative sense.) The plural of "fruits" points to a variety of good and evil behaviors. [18]"**A good tree isn't able to produce evil fruits, nor** [is] **a rotten tree** [able] **to produce good fruits** [compare James 3:12]." So strong is the link between inward condition and outward behavior, in other words, that a true prophet doesn't even have the capacity to pervert and disobey Jesus' teachings; nor does a false prophet have the capacity to uphold and obey them. So you can be sure in your distinguishing of false prophets from true. [19]"**Every tree that's not producing good fruit is being cut down and thrown into fire** [= John the baptizer's statement in 3:10 (compare the comments on 4:17)]." The switch from "fruits" to "fruit" collectivizes good behaviors. The present tense of "is being cut down and thrown into fire" portrays the condemnation and consignment of false prophets to hellfire at the Last Judgment as so certain that it might as well be happening already. Another "every" allows no exceptions. [20]"**Indeed, then, you shall recognize them by their fruits** [note the return to the plural of evil behaviors]." This repetition reinforces both the *command* to recognize false prophets for what they are and the *prediction* that they'll be recognized as such (see 7:16 with comments). "Indeed" strengthens the reinforcement, and "then" draws an inference from the intervening explanation.

7:21–23: "**Not everyone who says to me, 'Lord, Lord,' will enter into the kingdom of heaven; rather, the one who does the will of my Father in heaven** [will enter into the kingdom of heaven]. [22]**Many will say to me in that day** [the day of the Last Judgment], '**Lord, Lord, we prophesied in your name** [compare "Thus says the Lord" in the introduction of Old Testament prophetic messages] **and in your name cast out demons and in your name performed many miracles, didn't we** [compare Jeremiah 14:14; 27:15]?'" This protest implies Jesus' having refused to let them enter the kingdom. [23]"**And then I'll declare to them, 'I never knew you** [despite your having used my name]. **Depart from me, you workers of lawlessness** [= you false prophets who taught and practiced disobedience to my interpretation of the Law].'" Past disobedience will falsify a future confession of Jesus as Lord; for "Lord" means "Master," and a true slave will have obeyed his master. Not even a doubling of the confession ("Lord, Lord") will suffice to erase such disobedience, though for Matthew and his audience the two doublings of "Lord" highlight Jesus' deity (see 23:3 for another contrast between saying and doing). "Will enter into the kingdom of heaven" takes us back to "enter[ing] through the narrow gate" into the city of salvation, identified here with that kingdom (7:13–14). By saying, "the will of my Father in heaven," Jesus equates his interpretation of the Law in 5:17–7:12 with his heavenly Father's will. "*My* Father in heaven" relates back to 2:15; 3:17; 4:3, 6, contrasts with "*your* Father in heaven" and "*your* heavenly Father" over a dozen times earlier in the Sermon on the Mount (5:16, 45, 48 and so on), and prepares for Jesus' acting as his Father's authorized representative at the Last Judgment. In reference to the false prophets on that future occasion, "many" shows the seriousness of their threat to the present well-being of the church and ties in with the "many" who'll enter the city of destruction through the wide gate (7:13). Past prophecies, exorcisms, and miracles—even "*many* miracles"—won't erase former disobedience any more than a double confession of Jesus as Lord in the future will erase it. The past tense in "I never knew you" accents falsity of prophetic ministry in the past in addition to nonrecognition by Jesus at the Last Judgment. Furthermore, to know can mean not only to recognize but also to select, as in the Lord's statement to Israel, "Among all the families of the earth, you alone have I known" (Amos 3:2; also Genesis 18:19, translated literally). So the past tense in "I never knew you" also means that Jesus never selected the false prophets for salvation (compare 22:14: "For many are invited, but few [are] selected"). "Depart from *me*" implies that Jesus is the locus of the kingdom of heaven, and therefore of salvation, and that he'll determine who'll enter and not enter that kingdom. "Depart from me, you workers of lawlessness" echoes Psalm 6:8a and thus contributes to the equation of the words proceeding out through Jesus' mouth (5:2) with "every word that proceeds out through God's mouth" in the Old Testament (4:4), for Jesus is "God with us" (1:23).

7:24–27: "**Therefore everyone who as such hears these words of mine and does them** ['as such' meaning 'as a hearer and doer of them'] **will be like a prudent man who as such** [= as prudent] **built his house on bedrock.**

[25]**And the rain descended and the streams came and the winds blew and they** [the rain, streams, and winds] **fell against that house; and it didn't fall, for it had been founded on bedrock.** [26]**And everyone who hears these words of mine and doesn't do them will be like a foolish man, who as such** [in reference to his being foolish] **built his house on sand.** [27]**And the rain descended and the streams came and the winds blew and they** [the rain, streams, and winds] **beat against that house. And it fell, and its falling was great** [in the sense of a total collapse]**."** "Therefore" makes the story of the prudent and foolish builders illustrate both the final doom of false prophets and their followers, whose lawless conduct exempts them from persecution now, and the ultimate security of true disciples, though they're presently persecuted because of their obedience to the Law as interpreted by Jesus. The two occurrences of "everyone" stress the inescapability of eternal doom on the one hand and the certainty of eternal life on the other hand. The two occurrences of "these words of mine" point to Jesus' interpretation of the Law in 5:17–7:12. Building a house represents behaving in one way or another. The "bedrock" represents Jesus' words. Building a house on bedrock represents hearing and obeying them. Since according to 16:18 Jesus will build his church "on this bedrock"—that is, on the bedrock of his words—a disciple's building on this bedrock is to be done within the framework of the visible, institutional church. Note: the bedrock of Jesus' words doesn't *support* the foundation; it *is* the foundation. A person is prudent to hear and do these words, foolish not to. As usual throughout Matthew, "foolish" describes a false disciple and "prudent" describes a true one (see the comments on 5:13; compare 25:1–13).

The rain, streams, and winds represent the Last Judgment—hence the two occurrences of "*will* be like." Their "*falling* against" the house founded on the bedrock highlights that because of its rock-foundation that house "didn't *fall*." Thus the disciple who obeys Jesus' words will be as impregnable on the Day of Judgment as the whole church will be to "the gates of Hades" (see 16:18 again). The plural of "streams" alludes to the flooding of normally dry ravines during rainstorms, accompanied as those rainstorms are by battering winds. The sand on which the foolish man builds his house doesn't deserve to be called a foundation, nor is it; and it consists of the alluvial soil washed down into a concourse of steep ravines. With the "beat[ing] against that house" by rain, streams, and winds compare the "beat[ing of] themselves" by "all the tribes of the earth" at Jesus' second coming (24:30). "Its falling was great" gives a pictorial equivalent of "Depart from me, you workers of lawlessness" (7:23).

A TRANSITIONAL FORMULA CONCLUDING THE FIRST "BOOK" OF JESUS' LAW
Matthew 7:28–29

7:28–29: And it happened that when Jesus had finished [saying] **these words, the crowds were awestruck at his teaching.** [29]**For he was teaching them as** [one] **having authority and not as their scholars** [taught].

This comment forms a bridge from this first of Jesus' five, Pentateuch-like sermons in Matthew to the following narrative (compare 11:1; 13:53; 19:1; 26:1). "The crowds" identifies Jesus' "disciples" who went up the mountain to him and heard his teaching there (5:1b–2) with "the crowds" mentioned previously (4:25–5:1b). Since "the ones finding [the narrow gate into the city of salvation] are few" (7:14), these crowds represent the church as a mixed body containing many false disciples (the "many" who "enter through [the wide gate]" into the city of destruction [7:13]). "*Their* scholars" contrasts non-Christian Jewish scholars with Christian scholars (probably mostly Jewish in Matthew's setting; compare 8:19 [with 8:21]; 13:52; 23:34). These non-Christian Jewish scholars appealed constantly to past scholars of their kind. By contrast, Jesus has been teaching on his own authority, as in "but *I* say to you" throughout 5:21–48. So a final accent falls on the authority of his interpretation of the Law, an authority binding on his disciples.

THE AUTHORITY OF JESUS' WORDS IN THE PERFORMANCE OF DEEDS
Matthew 8:1–9:34

Now begins a long section of narrative in which Matthew gathers together stories of Jesus' deeds, mainly miracles and exorcisms. These stories contain fewer details than the parallel stories in Mark and Luke. As a result, emphasis falls on the authority of Jesus' words in performing miracles and exorcisms as well as in teaching. First come three miracle stories concerning a leper (8:1–4), the disabled servant of a centurion (8:5–13), and Peter's mother-in-law (8:14–15). Then comes an interlude consisting of a summary with an Old Testament quotation attached (8:16–17) and two dialogues on discipleship (8:18–20, 21–22). A second trio of miracle stories follows: the stilling of a storm (8:23–27), the deliverance of two demoniacs (8:28–34), and the healing of a disabled man carried by four others (9:1–8). Another interlude tells of Matthew's becoming a disciple (9:9–13) and Jesus' giving instructions on fasting (9:14–17). A third trio of miracle stories rounds off the section: healing a woman with a flow of blood and raising Jairus's daughter (the two miracles being intertwined; 9:18–26), giving sight to two blind men (9:27–31), and making a dumb man speak (9:32–34).

JESUS' AUTHORITY IN FULFILLING THE LAW CONCERNING LEPROSY
Matthew 8:1–4

The Sermon on the Mount has carried the theme of fulfilling the Law (see especially 5:17–20). So to show fulfillment of the Mosaic law concerning leprosy in particular (Leviticus 13–14), Matthew puts first in this section the story of Jesus' cleansing a leper.

8:1–2: And when he'd come down from the mountain, many crowds followed him. [2]**And behold, a leper, having approached, was worshiping him,**

saying, "Lord, if you're willing, you are able to cleanse me [of my leprosy]." The story opens with a reminiscence of Moses' coming down Mount Sinai (compare Exodus 19:14; 32:1, 15; 34:29) and thus furthers Matthew's portrayal of Jesus as the new and greater Moses (see 5:1, 21–48, for example). The statement that "many crowds followed him" echoes 4:25, so that those earlier crowds equate with the ones that heard the Sermon on the Mount and now follow him down the mountain. Naturally they follow him, for Matthew has called them Jesus' "disciples" (5:1 [see 4:20, 22 for following as a sign of discipleship]). This repeated and deliberately unrealistic portrayal of the crowds as disciples shows that Matthew sees in them a foregleam of the disciples who'll come en masse from all nations (28:19) and include many false disciples as well as true ones (7:13–23). See the comments on Mark 1:40–42 for "leper" and "leprosy." "Was worshiping him" means that the leper was kneeling before Jesus and repeatedly bowing his head to the ground. "Behold" highlights his worship of Jesus. Though "Lord" may have meant little more than "Sir" in the mind of the leper, for Matthew the leper's body language joins the addressing of Jesus with "Lord" to underline Jesus' identity as "God with us" (1:23). "If you're willing" sets out an unsure possibility. "You *are* able" sets out a sure fact. Thus the leper expresses uncertainty about Jesus' willingness but certainty about Jesus' ability. The ability to cleanse has to do with curing the leper of his *disease*, not with declaring him *ritually* clean, for only a priest could do that.

8:3–4: And on stretching out [his] hand, he [Jesus] touched him while saying, "I'm willing. Be cleansed." And immediately the leprosy was cleansed. ⁴And Jesus says to him, "See [that] you tell nobody; rather, go show yourself to the priest [at the temple] **and for a testimony to them offer the gift that Moses prescribed."** As Jesus taught by his own authority, "not as their scholars" (7:29), so he doesn't attribute the miracle to God his Father but performs it by his own authority: "*I'm* willing. Be cleansed." The unsure possibility of his willingness has turned into a definite affirmation of it, so that his *ability* to cleanse issues in the *actuality* of a cleansing. For Jesus' stretching out his hand and touching the leper and for the immediacy of the cleansing, see again the comments on Mark 1:40–42. The leper had spoken of *his* being cleansed, and Jesus had commanded that the *leper* be cleansed. But now we're told that "the *leprosy* was cleansed." This shift stresses the departure of the leprosy, and its departure stresses a cure by Jesus over a priest's declaration of ritual cleanness. The present tense in "Jesus *says* to him" emphasizes Jesus' command not to tell anybody but to go for examination by a priest and offer the Mosaically prescribed sacrificial gift. A simple "Tell nobody" and "show yourself" would have sufficed, but the prefixing of "See" to "tell nobody" and of "go" to "show yourself" reinforces the command. "See [that] you tell nobody" has the purpose of getting the Mosaic law fulfilled as quickly as possible, and the

story ends without our being told what the ex-leper did. So a final, heavy emphasis falls on Jesus' commanding immediate fulfillment of the Law and on his wanting to become known as commanding it (compare 5:17–20).

At 5:21–48 we saw that Jesus' fulfilling the Law through teaching doesn't mean mere repetition of the Law. It consists, rather, in carrying forward the tendencies of the Law to their divinely appointed ends. But Jesus' touching the leper and cleansing his leprosy seem at first to contradict Mosaic stipulations against contact between lepers and nonlepers (see Leviticus 5:3; 13:1–46; Numbers 5:2–3). In fact, though, the healing touch carries forward the tendency of the Law to provide cleansing for lepers. The offering of a gift testifies to Jesus' miracle as a fulfillment of that tendency. Since "priest" is singular, "them" to whom testimony is borne are people in general.

JESUS' AUTHORITY IN PRONOUNCING BELIEVING GENTILES ACCEPTED AND UNBELIEVING ISRAELITES REJECTED
Matthew 8:5–13

8:5–6: And when he'd entered into Capernaum [see 4:13], **a centurion approached him, imploring him ⁶and saying, "Lord, my servant has been thrown** [on a bed] **at home disabled, being tormented terribly."** A centurion in the Roman army commanded one hundred soldiers. Quite possibly, though, "centurion" here means a military official from nearby Syria in the service of Herod Antipas, ruler of Galilee, where Capernaum is located. As in 8:2, the addressing of Jesus with "Lord" (whatever the centurion had in mind) highlights Jesus' deity as "God with us" (1:23). Disablement of some sort has rendered the centurion's servant bedridden. The servant's having been "thrown" on a bed and "being tormented terribly" portray the disablement as a malevolent force that Jesus will have to overcome with his lordly authority. Success will confirm and exhibit such authority. Though Jesus set up house in Capernaum (4:13), "at home" refers to the centurion's house, presumably also in Capernaum but at some distance from Jesus' house.

8:7–9: And he [Jesus] tells him, "On coming [to your house], **I'll heal him."** The present tense of "tells" puts emphasis on Jesus' words, and the words themselves display his readiness to heal the servant even though the centurion hasn't asked him to. He has only described his servant's plight. This readiness of Jesus to heal the servant of a Gentile, such as the centurion is, forecasts Jesus' commissioning his Jewish disciples to go make disciples of all nations (28:19). **⁸And answering, the centurion said, "Lord** [which gives this story a second emphasis on Jesus' deity], **I'm not worthy that you should enter under my roof."** Centurionship pales before Jesus' lordship, and a recognition of this fact gives the centurion his sense of unworthiness. **"Rather** [than entering under my roof], **only speak with a word** [of command] **and my servant will be healed. ⁹For even I am a human being**

under authority, though having under myself soldiers. And I say to this one, 'Go,' and he goes, and to another, 'Come,' and he comes, and to my slave, 'Do this,' and he does [it]." "*Only* speak with a word" magnifies the authority of Jesus' speaking as "Lord." So too does the centurion's confidence that even at a distance and despite the malevolent force of the servant's disablement, a lordly command by Jesus will effect healing. Though having soldiers and a slave under him, the centurion describes himself as "a human being *under* authority." But under *whose* authority? Caesar's, it's usually said, or perhaps Herod Antipas's authority. But nothing in this passage favors either of these answers. The centurion's having addressed Jesus twice with "Lord," confessed his unworthiness that Jesus should enter under his roof, and expressed confidence in Jesus' mere word of command—these factors favor that at least for Matthew the centurion describes himself as under the authority *of Jesus* (compare Jesus' statement in 28:18: "*All* authority in heaven and on earth has been given to me").

8:10–12: And on hearing [the centurion's statement], **Jesus marveled and said to the following** [crowds (see 8:1)], **"Amen I tell you, with nobody in Israel have I found such great faith.** [11]**And I tell you that many will come from the east and the west** [compare Psalm 107:3] **and recline with Abraham and Isaac and Jacob in the kingdom of heaven,** [12]**but the sons of the kingdom will be thrown out into the darkness farther outside. Weeping and gritting of teeth will be there."** The believing centurion stands for the Gentiles who were later to believe and become disciples of Jesus (28:18–20). Jesus' lauding the centurion's faith is underlined (1) by Jesus' "marvel[ing]" at his statement; (2) by Jesus' speaking about the centurion's faith "to the following [crowds]"; (3) by introducing his own statement with "I tell you"; (4) by prefixing this introduction with an emphatic "Amen"; and (5) by describing the centurion's faith as greater than any he'd found not only in Israel as a whole, but with *anybody* in Israel. "*Such* great faith" heightens the faith yet more by implying that Jesus has found great faith in Israel, but not so great as that of the centurion. "Amen I tell you" and another "I tell you" in the immediately following statement also underline the authority of Jesus' words. "Many" stresses the large number of Gentiles who'll become, and have become by the time Matthew writes, disciples through the worldwide mission of the church. "Will come . . . and recline . . . in the kingdom of heaven" refers to the banquet of salvation when Jesus comes back; for in that culture banqueters reclined on cushions with feet extended away from a low table, weight concentrated on the left elbow, and the right hand left free for bringing food to the mouth. "With Abraham and Isaac and Jacob" indicates continuity with the patriarchs of Israel and borrows from the Old Testament an oft-repeated expression, so that as often in Matthew the current words of Jesus as "God with us" conform to God's ancient words (compare 22:32). That believing Gentiles will recline on cushions to eat with the

sainted patriarchs at the banquet of salvation, commonly called "the messianic banquet," strikes an astoundingly happy note for the Gentiles and a dreadfully ominous note for unbelieving Jews, called "the sons of the kingdom" in the sense that but for disinheriting themselves through unbelief, as God's chosen people they should inherit the kingdom. Their destiny to be "thrown out into the darkness farther outside" refers to darkness outside the brightly lit hall where the festivities of the banquet will take place. "*Farther* outside" stresses the distance of that darkness from the banqueting hall. Such a distance will preclude any hope of late entry. Sorrow over exclusion from the kingdom will lead to weeping and gritting of teeth. Subsequent references to weeping and gritting of teeth have to do with the fate of false disciples (13:42, 50; 22:13; 24:51; 25:30 [compare Psalm 112:10]). So the fate of faithless Israel in the present passage stands as a warning to the church in those later passages.

8:13: And Jesus told the centurion, "Go. It's to happen for you as you've believed." "It's to happen" is what grammarians call a third person imperative—in other words, a command spoken indirectly rather than directly. Jesus commands the *event* to take place though he's addressing the *centurion*. (English grammar has nothing comparable.) **And the servant was healed in that hour** [compare 9:22, 29; 15:28; 17:18]. The centurion believed that Jesus' mere but authoritative word of command would effect the servant's healing (8:8–9). To justify and reward that faith, Jesus does effect the healing with a mere word exhibiting his authority. And the healing of the servant "in that hour" magnifies this authority; for Jesus' word takes effect at the very time he utters it, an hour being the smallest unit of time employed in that culture. (People then didn't deal in minutes, much less in seconds and fractions thereof.) We're not told that the centurion went home in accordance with Jesus' telling him, "Go." So the story closes on the note of a healing effected by the authority of Jesus' mere but authoritative word.

JESUS' AUTHORITY IN HEALING PETER'S
MOTHER-IN-LAW, CASTING OUT
DEMONS, AND HEALING ALL THE SICK
IN FULFILLMENT OF PROPHECY
Matthew 8:14–17

8:14–15: And on coming into Peter's house, Jesus saw his [Peter's] **mother-in-law thrown** [on a bed] **and burning with fever.** [15]**And he touched her hand, and the fever left her. And she got up and started serving him** [food (see the comments on 4:11)]. Jesus dominates the stage. With lordly authority he takes the initiative by entering Peter's house uninvited so far as we can tell from Matthew's narrative, by seeing Peter's mother-in-law bedridden with a fever without having her pointed out to him so far as Matthew says, and above all by healing her without a request that he do so. And her starting to serve him food pays tribute to his exercise of that authority. That she was "thrown" on a bed portrays the fever as a malevolent force, just as in 8:6 a servant's having been "thrown" on a bed by some disablement portrayed the disablement as a malevolent force. In both cases, Jesus' conquest of the force exhibits lordly authority. Highlighting the exhibition here is the fever's departure at Jesus' merely touching the woman's hand, much as a mere word of Jesus got rid of the servant's disablement (8:8, 13). The woman's getting up on her own (Matthew doesn't say that Jesus raised her) gives physical evidence that the fever, which had "thrown" her on a bed, has left.

8:16–17: And after evening came, people brought to him many who were demon-possessed. And he cast out the spirits [that possessed them] **with a word** [of command]**; and he healed all who were sick,** [17]**so that what had been spoken through Isaiah the prophet would be fulfilled, saying, "He himself has taken our weaknesses and carried away our diseases** [Isaiah 53:4]**."** It looks as though the serving of food to Jesus by Peter's mother-in-law occupied the late afternoon, so that people didn't bring their demoniacs and sick till evening. "He cast out the spirits with a [mere] word" displays Jesus' authority (compare 8:8, 13), and his casting them out even though their victims were "many" enhances the display. So too does his healing "*all* who were sick." "So that" indicates that he *purposed* to fulfill prophecy, just as he said he came to do (5:17); and "what was spoken *through* Isaiah the prophet" indicates that God used Isaiah as his (God's) mouthpiece. As often, Matthew cites the fulfillment of prophecy to encourage perseverance on the part of persecuted Christians. In the quotation, "he *himself*" accents Jesus' role. "Has taken our weaknesses [in the sense of 'illnesses'] and carried away our diseases" doesn't mean that Jesus suffered our illnesses and diseases in his own body; rather, he took them and removed them from those he healed.

JESUS' AUTHORITY IN THE DEMANDS OF DISCIPLESHIP
Matthew 8:18–22

Matthew has established Jesus' authority in word and deed. Now Matthew shows his mixed audience of true and false disciples that Jesus' authority demands total commitment—hence the insertion of teaching on discipleship.

8:18–20: And on seeing many crowds around him, Jesus commanded [them] **to come away** [with him (see 8:23)] **to the other side** [of the Sea of Galilee]. [19]**And on approaching** [Jesus], **one scholar told him, "Teacher, I'll follow you wherever you go away to."** [20]**And Jesus tells him, "The foxes have holes, and the birds of the sky** [have] **nests; but the Son of Man doesn't have anywhere to incline** [his] **head."** "Many crowds" recalls the "many crowds" of 4:25–5:1, identified there as "his disciples," who "followed him" as Peter, Andrew, James, and

John had just done (see the comments on that passage, and compare Mark 3:31–35; 4:10, where Jesus identifies "a crowd . . . around him" as his true family, those "who do the will of God"). But as usual in Matthew, the crowds are made up of false disciples as well as true, just as the church is. Jesus takes the initiative, not by commanding the twelve apostles to accompany him on a getaway from the crowds. The Twelve won't appear in Matthew till 10:1. Jesus takes the initiative by commanding *the crowds* to come away with him to the other (east) side of the Sea of Galilee. Those who obey his command will prove themselves true disciples. Those who don't obey will prove themselves false disciples. "One scholar" represents true disciples, just as Jesus' disciples are called "scholars(s)" in 13:52; 23:34 because of their having learned his teaching and put it into practice ("disciple" = "learner"; see 11:28–30). In contrast with 7:29, this scholar isn't called "one of *their* [the non-Christian Jews'] scholars." "*One* scholar" (not "*a* scholar," as in some translations) contrasts with the "*many* crowds" and spotlights this true disciple as an example to be emulated (compare especially 23:8–10 for the emphatic use of "one"). His addressing Jesus with "Teacher" suits the scholarship of a disciple/learner and corresponds to Jesus as the disciples' "*one . . . teacher*" (23:8). And his responding obediently to Jesus' command with "I'll follow you wherever you go away to" gives evidence of true discipleship. He'll follow to learn from Jesus' teaching and example. The present tense in "Jesus *tells* him" underlines Jesus' immediately following statement, as though in speaking to the scholar he's also speaking to the contemporary church. The statement about "foxes," "birds of the sky" (= wild birds as distinguished from domesticated fowl), and "the Son of Man" looks forward to Jesus' having to sleep in a boat (8:24) despite his exalted status as the Son of Man who in a vision at Daniel 7:13–14 comes with the clouds of heaven, as God himself does, and is given everlasting dominion over all peoples and nations. Earthbound foxes have holes and sky-flying birds have nests, but a boat isn't suitable for a human being to sleep in, much less for the glorious Son of Man to do so. In following Jesus the Son of Man, true disciples will suffer similar deprivations.

8:21–22: And another of the disciples said to him, "Lord, allow me first to go away and bury my father [compare Genesis 50:5–6]**."** [22]**But Jesus tells him, "Follow me, and let the dead bury their own dead."** "*Another* of the disciples" confirms that the preceding "scholar" was also a disciple. "Another *of the disciples*" confirms that the "many crowds around him" in 8:18 consisted of professing disciples. But is this disciple true or false? The addressing of Jesus with "Lord, Lord" by those whom Jesus will condemn at the Last Judgment (7:21–23) raises the possibility—perhaps a probability, because few will find the narrow gate that leads to life (7:13–14)—that this disciple's addressing Jesus with "Lord" bespeaks falsity. "Allow *me* first to go away and bury my father" confirms falsity (contrast the scholar's "I'll follow you wherever *you* go away to" and the immediacy with which Peter, Andrew, James, and John followed Jesus [4:20, 22]). False disciples find supposedly legitimate reasons not to meet the rigorous demands that Jesus makes. Again the present tense in "Jesus *says* to him" underlines Jesus' command to follow him and to let the dead bury their own dead, which probably refers to secondary burial, the custom of boxing up the bones of dead people after the decomposition of their flesh. The custom made room for further corpses on burial shelves in tombs. In the present passage, if the father had just died his son would have been already engaged in the initial burial of his father rather than talking to Jesus. But if the father was already buried, his son might want to delay following Jesus till the father's remains were ready for secondary burial, a filial duty just as the initial burial was. "The dead" who should "bury their own dead" then refers to family members already dead and secondarily buried in the same tomb with the father: they should take care of his secondary burial since he's already in their midst. As though they could! But Jesus is speaking ironically. His point is that an immediate following of him takes precedence over all else, even over the duty of a son to take care of his father's bones (compare 1 Kings 19:19–21). The respective truth and falsity of two representative disciples having been established, this episode ends on the note of Jesus' imperious demand.

THE AUTHORITY OF JESUS AS SEEN IN A STORM
Matthew 8:23–27

8:23–24: And when he got into the boat, his disciples followed him. That is, his true disciples from among the "many crowds" of professing disciples followed him. For following Jesus "*wherever*" he goes, as the "one [representative] scholar" of 8:19–20 said he would, indicates genuine discipleship. [24]**And behold, a great quaking took place in the sea, so that the boat was being covered by the waves. But he was sleeping.** "Quaking" usually refers to an earthquake. So "in the sea" clarifies its present use for the quaking of sea water because of a storm, and "great" adds severity to this effect of the storm. Though earthquakes are mentioned in 24:7; 27:54, in 28:2 we'll read again, "And behold, a great quaking took place," and this in connection with the announcement of Jesus' resurrection (compare 21:10). Literally, then, and despite the disciples' subsequent misunderstanding, the present great quaking previews the majesty of Jesus in resurrection rather than posing a threat to the disciples' lives (compare the risen Jesus' claiming "all authority in heaven and on earth" [28:18], plus Jonah 1:4 with Matthew 12:40 [see Exodus 19:16–25; Psalms 29:1–11; 107:23–32; Isaiah 64:1–3; Ezekiel 1:4–28 for examples of storms as a sign of divine majesty]). Since there's a great quaking in the sea, the boat is being covered, not in the sense of being swamped, but in the sense that the upheaval of the waters veils the boat from view as it descends into troughs between the waves. Jesus' sleeping shows him unperturbed; for the great quaking signals his divine majesty, not a mortal threat.

8:25–27: And on approaching, they aroused him [from his sleep], **saying, "Lord, save** [us]**! We're perishing!"** Compare the fright of the women and guards at Jesus' empty tomb because of the great quaking there (28:2–4). [26]**And he says to them, "Why are you craven, people of little faith?** [compare 6:30; 14:31; 16:8; 17:20]**." Then, on getting up, he reprimanded the winds and the sea, and there came about a great calm.** [27]**And the human beings marveled saying, "How marvelous is this** [man] **in that even the winds and the sea obey him!"** For Matthew and his audience the address, "Lord," highlights Jesus' divine majesty. But for the disciples, who misunderstand the great quaking in the sea as a threat to their lives rather than as a sign of that majesty, the address issues in a plea for salvation from perishing at sea. We're reminded that Joseph was instructed to name his adopted son "Jesus," which means "the Lord [is] salvation," because Jesus was to "save his people from their sins" (1:21)—a more important kind of salvation than salvation from winds and waves. The present tense in "he *says* to them" underlines yet again Jesus' following question. "*Why* are you craven . . . ?" implies that because of his miracles, exorcisms, and didactic authority, the disciples should have recognized in the great quaking a sign of his divine majesty rather than a threat. "Why are you *craven* . . . ?" implies they should have reacted with worship of him because of that majesty as signified by the great quaking. "People of little faith" doesn't imply total absence of faith. They'd asked him to save them, after all. But they didn't have enough faith to recognize in the great quaking a sign of his divine majesty. The reprimand of the winds and sea produces "a great calm" that replaces "a great quaking," disabuses the disciples of their timidity, and transforms it into spoken admiration of him for his having exercised authority over the winds and sea. Matthew calls the disciples "the human beings" to point up by contrast the deity of Jesus in addition to his humanity. The deity underlies his authority. For other instances of a contrast between human beings and deity see 6:1–18; 7:9–11; 9:8; 10:32–33; 16:23; 19:26; 21:25–26. There follows another story involving the sea.

JESUS' AUTHORITY IN CAUSING
THE DEATH OF DEMONS
Matthew 8:28–34

8:28–29: And when he'd come to the other side [the east side of the Sea of Galilee], **to the region of the Gergasenes, coming out of the tombs there met him two demon-possessed** [men], **very violent, so that nobody was strong enough** [by way of subduing them] **to pass by** [the demoniacs] **through that road** [which traversed the region]. [29]**And behold, they yelled saying, "What do we and you have to do with each other, Son of God? Have you come here to torture us ahead of time?"** See the comments on Mark 5:1 for "Gergasenes" versus "Gerasenes" and "Gadarenes" in different ancient manuscripts. That *two* demoniacs address Jesus with "Son of God" satisfies the law that "every matter shall be established on the basis of the mouth [= testimony] of two or three witnesses" (18:16). The description of the demoniacs not only as "violent" but also as "*very* violent" combines with their twoness to make the coming exorcism a heightened display of Jesus' divine authority. The tombs were cave-like rooms naturally or artificially formed in rock, or small room-like structures. The inability of anybody to pass by "through that road" may have some significance. For in 7:14; 21:32; 22:16 "road" is used for the "way" of righteousness and therefore could indicate here a symbolic reference to discipleship, for which Jesus authoritatively clears away demonic roadblocks (compare 8:23–27, which likewise started on the note of discipleship and climaxed with Jesus' majestic authority). "Behold" highlights the demoniacs' identification of Jesus as God's Son. Since knowing and pronouncing correctly the name of a deity was thought to gain a certain power over the deity, the identification of Jesus as God's Son joins the question, "What do we and you have to do with each other . . . ?" for an attempt to get rid of Jesus. The attempt arises out of the demoniacs' fear that he has come to their region to torment them ahead of time—that is, prior to the Last Judgment (see 13:30 for "time" as a reference to the Last Judgment, and 18:34 for "torturers" in connection with eternal punishment).

8:30–32: And at a distance from them a herd of many pigs was feeding. [31]**And the demons** [not the demoniacs!] **were imploring him, saying, "If you cast us out, send us into the herd of pigs."** [32]**And he told them, "Go." And they, on coming out, went off into the pigs. And behold, all the herd rushed down the slope into the sea. And they died in the waters.** "At a distance" implies that the pig herders (yet to be introduced) were keeping themselves and their pigs far enough away from the demoniacs to avoid being attacked by them. The description of the pigs as "many" makes impressive the rushing of "*all* the herd down the slope into the sea." The demons' "imploring" Jesus and saying "*send* us" show that the attempt to get rid of him has quickly morphed into a recognition of his authority over them despite their ability to prevent anybody else from passing by their way. They even seem resigned to his exorcising them, so that they can only plead for new, substandard housing in the herd of pigs. Talk about downward mobility! It takes only a single word of command, "Go," to effect both an exit of the demons and their going off into the pigs. "Behold" dramatizes all the herd's "rush[ing] down the slope into the sea" and "dy[ing] in the waters [plural for a large body of water]." Deprived of their porcine hosts, the demons began suffering ahead of time—that is, before the Last Judgment—the eternal torture they feared Jesus had come to inflict on them (8:29). Their torture previews what will happen to false disciples.

8:33–34: And those who'd been herding [the pigs] **fled and, on going off into the city, reported all things and** [in particular] **the things concerning the demon-possessed** [men]. [34]**And behold, all the city came out for a meeting with Jesus; and on seeing him, they implored that he move away from their borders.** "All things" includes what happened to the pigs and the demons. "The things concerning the demon-possessed men" calls special attention to the men's deliverance. In 8:29 "behold" underlined Jesus' divine sonship. In 8:32 it stressed the effect of Jesus' command. Here it spotlights the city's meeting and seeing Jesus, so that his majestic figure entirely crowds out the former demoniacs. Furthermore, it's "*all* the city" that comes out "for a meeting with Jesus." Such a meeting often connoted citizens' meeting a visiting dignitary outside their city to escort him into the city. These citizens feel such awe on seeing Jesus, though, that they "implored" him to leave their region much as in recognition of his divine authority the demons had been "imploring" him (8:31; compare the centurion's feeling unworthy to have Jesus enter under his roof [8:8]).

JESUS' AUTHORITY TO FORGIVE
SINS AS A MODEL OF THE DISCIPLES'
AUTHORITY TO FORGIVE SINS
Matthew 9:1–8

Matthew has shown Jesus' authority over the Law (chapters 5–7), over diseases and demons (8:1–4, 14–17, 28–34), over other human beings (8:18–22), and over winds and waves (8:23–27). Now he shows Jesus' authority to forgive sins (9:1–8) but will go back to Jesus' authority over other human beings (9:9–13, 14–17), over diseases (9:18–26, 27–31), and over demons (9:32–34). Matthew designs his stress on Jesus' authority to steel the audience of this Gospel against their persecutors, whose merely human authority can't match Jesus' divine authority.

9:1–2: And on getting into a boat, he crossed [the Sea of Galilee] **and came to his own city** [Capernaum, on the northwest shore (4:13)]. [2]**And behold, people were bringing to him a paralytic, thrown on a bed.** "Paralytic" doesn't necessarily imply the effect of a stroke, but it does indicate some sort of neuromuscular inability to walk. Much as in 8:6, "thrown on a bed" portrays the man's paralysis as a malevolent force that Jesus will have to overcome (see also 8:14). "Behold" dramatizes Jesus' confrontation with that force. **And on seeing their faith** [that is, the faith of those who were bringing the paralytic], **Jesus said, "Take courage, child! Your sins are being forgiven."** "Take courage, child!" carries a note of endearment and creates the expectation of a healing. But Jesus springs a surprise. Instead of healing the paralytic he tells him his sins are being forgiven right then and there. (It isn't stated that the paralysis was directly caused by these sins.) The Jews of that day expected forgiveness of their sins in the messianic age, but they didn't expect the Messiah to do the forgiving. Jesus' pronouncing forgiveness of the paralytic's sins amounts to a fulfillment of the angel of the Lord's prediction that Jesus would "save his people from their sins" in accord with the meaning of "Jesus," namely, "The Lord [is] salvation" (1:21).

9:3–6: And behold, some of the scholars said within themselves, "This [guy] is blaspheming." [4]And on seeing their imaginations, he said, "Why are you imagining evil things in your hearts? [5]For what's easier, to say, 'Your sins are being forgiven,' or to say, 'Get up and walk'? [6]But in order that you may know that the Son of Man on earth has authority to forgive sins"—then he says to the paralytic, "On getting up, pick up your mat [which was used as a stretcher by those who brought him] **and go to your house."** "Behold" dramatizes Jesus' confrontation with the scholars just as the earlier "behold" dramatized his confrontation with the malevolent force of paralysis. In 2:4 the scholars cooperated with Herod the Great in his attempt to kill Jesus. Here, on their own, they imagine that Jesus is blaspheming. It's evident that they're equating his pronouncement of forgiveness with blasphemy. But to blaspheme is to slander someone. Matthew doesn't tell whom they imagined Jesus was blaspheming. For the moment, then, attention focuses solely on the imagining as such. "On seeing their *imaginations*" portrays Jesus as a mind reader and contrasts with "on seeing their *faith*" in 9:2. In other words, the scholars' imagining that Jesus is blaspheming contrasts with the faith of those who brought the paralytic to him. "Evil things" describes the imagining of blasphemy. So it's the scholars' imaginations rather than Jesus' pronouncement that merits the description "evil." "*For* what's easier . . . ?" makes Jesus' question substantiate this description. He asks the question from the standpoint of a skeptic who wants visible confirmation of an unobservable and therefore questionable forgiveness. It's easier to pronounce forgiveness of sins than to command a paralytic to get up and walk. For nobody can falsify the pronouncement, but inability to obey the command would unmask the pronouncer of forgiveness as a pretender. "But in order that you may *know* that the Son of Man . . . has authority" contrasts with their "*imagining* evil things." See the comments on Mark 2:10–11 for "the Son of Man." "Authority to forgiven sins" indicates that as "the Son of Man on earth," Jesus himself forgave sins rather than that he merely announced sins as forgiven by God in heaven. That is, the heavenly man-like figure of Daniel 7:13–14 exercised such authority on earth in the person of Jesus, for Jesus is that figure. Dramatizing this authority are (1) Jesus' breaking off the statement, "But in order that you may know . . ." (he doesn't complete the sentence); (2) the sudden shift from the plural "you" that addresses the scholars to the singular "you" embedded in the command addressed to the paralytic; and (3) the vivid present tense in "he *says* to the paralytic."

9:7–8: And on getting up he went off to his house. [8]And on seeing [him do so], the crowds feared and glorified God, who'd given such authority to the human beings. "He went off to his house" corresponds to Jesus' telling the paralytic to go home and suggests obedient discipleship on his part, just as in 8:18–22 going off to the other side of the Sea of Galilee represented obedient discipleship. As in 4:25–5:1; 7:28; 8:1, 18, "the crowds" stand for Jesus' disciples, who in contrast with the skepti-

cal scholars fear God and glorify him (compare 10:28; 15:31; 17:6). Since Jesus forgave the paralytic's sins, we expect God to be described as the one "who'd given such authority *to the Son of Man*," that is, to Jesus. Instead, God is described as the one "who'd given such authority *to the human beings*" (note the plural). Who are these human beings? They can hardly differ from Jesus' disciples, whom Matthew strikingly called "the human beings" when Jesus calmed the storm (8:27). There, he called them such to make them a foil to his deity. So too here. In other words, Jesus is the "God with us" (1:23) who gives his disciples as human beings the authority to forgive sins. The disciples share his divine authority to forgive sins on earth (compare 16:19; 18:18; John 20:23). And just as his healing of the paralytic demonstrated his authority to forgive sins on earth, so the authority he'll give his disciples to exorcise demons and heal the sick (10:1) will demonstrate the disciples' authority to forgive sins on earth. For Matthew, then, Jesus is the God whom the crowds of professing disciples fear and glorify; and Jesus' forgiving and healing the paralytic provides a model for their own forgiving of sins on Jesus' behalf and performing miraculous cures to substantiate the forgiveness. (But we shouldn't substitute the disciples' authority to forgive sins committed against God for their obligation to forgive those who've sinned against them.)

JESUS' AUTHORITY TO EXERCISE MERCY ON TAX COLLECTORS AND SINNERS IN ACCORD WITH THE OLD TESTAMENT
Matthew 9:9–13

9:9: And as he was going along from there [from the spot where he'd healed the paralytic] **he saw a human being called Matthew sitting at** [his] **tax booth. And he** [Jesus] **tells him, "Follow me." And on standing up, he followed him.** The description of Matthew as "a human being" makes him another foil to Jesus as "God with us" (1:23; compare the comments on 9:7). The tax collector Matthew represents other tax collectors and sinners in the following part of this episode. Appropriately, Jesus' calling a sinner, such as this tax collector was, follows Jesus' forgiving the paralytic's sins (9:1–8). Matthew was collecting taxes from fishermen and/or collecting taxes in the form of tolls from merchants who were transporting their goods. The present tense in "he [Jesus] *tells* him" stresses the authority of Jesus in commanding Matthew to follow him and suggests that Jesus is still commanding people to follow him. So strong is his authority that despite the lack of prior contact with Jesus, Matthew's standing up and following him replace sitting at a tax booth. As did Peter, Andrew, James, and John, Matthew forsakes his occupation right in the middle of pursuing it (compare 4:18–22).

9:10: And it happened while he was reclining at home that, behold, many tax collectors and sinners, having come, were reclining [at table] **with Jesus and his disciples.** At special meals the diners reclined on cushions laid on the floor. "At home" links up with

Jesus' having set up house in Capernaum (4:13) and thus makes him the host at a banquet in his own house (compare 9:28; 13:1, 36; 17:25). "Behold" highlights the reclining of tax collectors and sinners with him and his disciples. The role of host enhances his authority in the coming exercise of mercy on sinners. Tax collectors were despised for collaboration with Gentile overlords, for handling currency with pagan inscriptions and iconography, and for dishonesty. The tax collectors in the Gospels seem to be Jewish customs officials (working under Herod Antipas in Galilee) rather than Roman tax collectors. In Jewish vocabulary "sinners" referred to pagan Gentiles and to notably wicked Jews, including tax collectors. That such people had "come" to Jesus at his home implies their having come for discipleship at his invitation (compare 8:18–19), and that they were "many" adumbrates the worldwide discipling of "all nations" by those who were already disciples, like the disciples here (24:14; 28:19–20).

9:11–13: **And on seeing** [this state of affairs], **the Pharisees were saying to his disciples, "Why is your teacher** [compare 17:24] **eating with the tax collectors and sinners?"** It was customary in the Near East for outsiders to stand around observing banqueters, as the Pharisees do here. Pharisees stressed avoidance of moral and ritual contamination—hence their asking why Jesus is hobnobbing with degenerates. Apparently his putdown of scholars in 9:1–8 leads the Pharisees to address his disciples rather than him. "Your teacher" echoes especially 5:1–2, recalls for Matthew's audience the didactic authority of Jesus in contrast with "their scholars" (7:28–29), prepares for "learn" here in 9:13, and previews Jesus' identifying himself as "your teacher" in 23:8. He hears the Pharisees' question and authoritatively takes the initiative by performing another putdown, this time a purely verbal one: [12]**But he, on hearing** [the question], **said, "Those who are strong** [= healthy] **have no need of a physician; rather, those who are sick** [have need of a physician]. [13]**But go learn what it is** [= means], **'I want mercy and not sacrifice** [Hosea 6:6 (compare Matthew 12:7)].' For I didn't come to call righteous** [people]—**rather, sinful** [people]." In the proverb that Jesus cites, righteous people correspond to the strong, the healthy. Sinners correspond to the sick. Jesus corresponds to the physician. The figurative use of illness for sin comes from the causal relation between sin and illness (whatever the directness or indirectness of that causal relation) and makes appropriate the presence of this passage among stories of healing. But Jesus is speaking at a special meal. So his calling sinful people carries the connotation of inviting them to the banquet of salvation, for which he's the host (compare 8:11; 22:1–14). "Go" implies that the Pharisees have no part in this banquet, at least not until and unless they learn what Hosea 6:6 means. "Learn" produces a wordplay with "disciples," which means "learners," and also with "Matthew" in that "Matthew," "learn," and "disciple" all begin with *math-* in the original Greek (though the meaning of "Matthew"

differs). "Mercy" characterizes disciples (5:7). In Hosea 6:6 it's the Lord who wants mercy and not sacrifice. Here it's Jesus as Lord who wants the Pharisees to learn mercy, because he himself came to show mercy to sinners by inviting them to the messianic banquet of salvation, anticipated in his having invited them to enjoy table fellowship with him at his home (compare his having come to fulfill the Prophets, like Hosea [5:17]). "*For* I didn't come . . ." makes Jesus' coming to call sinful people the reason for learning mercy. Righteous people have appeared in 1:19; 5:45 and will reappear throughout this Gospel. They don't need to be invited, because they've already accepted Jesus' invitation.

JESUS' AUTHORITY IN THE
PRESERVATION OF FASTING
Matthew 9:14–17

Appropriately, a question about fasting follows a question about eating (9:10–13). **9:14–15: Then the disciples of John** [the baptizer] **approach him** [Jesus], **saying, "Why are we and the Pharisees fasting but your disciples aren't fasting?"** The present tense of "approach" grabs attention for a question about fasting. The question arises out of the importance Jews attached to fasting as a religious practice. The occasion for the fasting of John's disciples and the Pharisees isn't identified, or the question may refer to fasting in general ("Why do we and the Pharisees fast but your disciples don't fast?"). In either case, the accent rests on fasting versus nonfasting as such, not on an occasion or occasions for fasting. [15]**And Jesus told them, "The sons of the bridal chamber** [= the bridegroom's attendants] **can't mourn so long as the bridegroom is with them, can they?"** Of course not! Wedding feasts lasted for days. It isn't just inappropriate for the attendants to mourn during such a feast. They *can't* mourn during it, for otherwise the feast wouldn't be a feast. It would be a funeral. But why do we read about mourning where we expect to read about fasting? The answer lies in Jesus' next statement: "But days will come whenever the bridegroom is taken away from them, and then they'll fast." The taking away of the bridegroom will cause mourning such as can't characterize his attendants so long as the bridegroom is with them, and the mourning will be indicated by fasting. "The sons of the bridal chamber" represent Jesus' disciples. "The bridegroom" represents him. "*So long as* the bridegroom is with them" represents the period of Jesus' earthly ministry. His being *"with them"* represents his being "God with us" (1:23). Their inability to "mourn" so long as he's with them represents the disciples' inability to mourn at banquets such as they've just enjoyed at his home in Capernaum. His being "taken away from them" represents the violent death he'll suffer (compare Isaiah 53:8). The "days" that will then come represent the following age of the church. "When*ever*" (where we expect a simple "When") stresses the resumption of fasting by Jesus' disciples once he's taken away from them. "Then they'll fast" contains a prediction of their fasting and links with Jesus' instructions on fasting in 6:16–18. Thus he closes the door against false disciples' enjoying a luxurious life in which fasting never plays a part (see 24:48–51 for a description of such a life by false disciples).

9:16–17: "And no one throws [in the sense of 'sews'] **a throw-on** [in the sense of 'a patch'] **of unshrunk cloth on an old garment."** The wordplay between "throw . . . on" and "a throw-on" is obvious. **"For its fullness** [the part of the patch that overlaps the old garment and is sewn onto it] **takes away from the garment** [when at its first washing the patch but not the previously washed garment shrinks] **and the rip** [that was supposed to be remedied by the patch] **becomes worse.** [17]**Nor do people throw** [in the sense of 'pour'] **new wine into old wineskins. Otherwise, indeed, the wineskins burst** [because the new wine swells as it ages whereas the old wineskins have already been stretched to their limit through prior use]**; and the wine is spilled out and the wineskins are ruined. Rather, people throw** [= pour] **new wine into new wineskins; and both are preserved together."** These saying support the taking up and continuance of the old practice of fasting once Jesus is taken away. "Indeed" strengthens this support. We should avoid individual identifications of the patch of unshrunk cloth, the old garment, the new wine, the old wineskins, and the new wineskins. For such identifications spoil simple metaphors concerning the need to preserve a good religious practice, that of fasting. Its hiatus during Jesus' earthly ministry offers no excuse for failure to practice it during his absence.

JESUS' AUTHORITY OVER DEATH AND
IN THE SALVATION OF A WOMAN
WITH A FLOW OF BLOOD
Matthew 9:18–26

Here we have intertwined stories of two miracles. **9:18–19: And while he** [Jesus] **was saying these things to them** [the disciples of John the baptizer (9:14–17)], **behold, one ruler, having approached, was worshiping him while saying, "My daughter has just ended** [= died]. **But come lay your hand on her, and she'll live."** "Behold" and the "one" that singles out the ruler highlight his worshiping Jesus. As elsewhere, worshiping means kneeling before the object of worship and touching one's head to the ground. This body language doesn't have to imply that the ruler thought Jesus to be divine; but for Matthew and his audience it certainly does. And being a ruler makes the worship of Jesus more noteworthy than if the ruler were an ordinary fellow. That Matthew doesn't tell what the ruler ruled centers attention solely on his worshiping Jesus despite his own status as a ruler. "And she'll live" states a confident prediction that displays the ruler's faith and implies Jesus' authority over death. The mere laying of Jesus' hand on the dead daughter will convert her death into life. So the ruler believes, and so Matthew wants us to believe. [19]**And on getting**

up [from reclining at meal at home, where the ruler approached him (9:10)]**, Jesus started following him; and his disciples** [did too].

9:20–21: And behold, a woman who'd been flowing with blood for twelve years, on approaching [Jesus] **from behind, touched the tassel of his garment.** [21]**For she was saying within herself, "If I were only to touch his garment, I will be saved."** As "behold" highlighted the ruler's worshiping Jesus (9:18), so another "behold" highlights this woman's touching Jesus' garment. Because her flow of blood made her ritually unclean and defiling to others (Leviticus 15:19–33), she approached from behind to sneak a touch. The tassel she touched was a Mosaically commanded attachment to the garments of Jews (Numbers 15:38–40; Deuteronomy 22:12 [compare Matthew 14:36; 23:5]). So Matthew's mentioning the tassel portrays Jesus as conforming to the Mosaic law (compare 5:17–20), all the more so in that the tassel had the purpose of reminding Jews of "all the Lord's commandments so as to do them." "If I were . . . to touch his garment" sets out an unsure possibility. "I will be saved" sets out a sure result. "If I were *only* to touch his garment" (compare 14:36) parallels the centurion's saying, "*Only* speak with a word" (8:8). Only a word, only a touch—such emphases portray Jesus' authority as so great that for miraculous cures it needs but little exercise. In the woman's mind, "I will be saved" has to do with deliverance from the chronic flow of blood that has afflicted her for twelve years. ("Hemorrhage" is too strong a term, for she couldn't have survived twelve years of suffering the amount of blood loss usually connoted by that term.)

9:22: And on turning and seeing her, Jesus said, "Take courage, daughter! Your faith has saved you." And the woman was saved from that hour. Matthew doesn't say what prompted Jesus to turn and see the woman. (Did he feel a tug on his garment, or healing power go out from him, for example?) So the accent falls on what he said. "Take courage!" echoes 9:2 and prepares for the gift of salvation by faith. "Your *faith* has saved you" shows that it wasn't her touch as such that saved her—rather, her faith that *led* her to touch Jesus' garment. This salvation by faith from a physical ailment symbolizes the salvation by faith that Jesus provides from sins (1:21). To stress the immediacy and permanence of both kinds of salvation, Matthew says "the woman was saved *from that hour*" (see the comments on 8:13 for "that hour"). Jesus' addressing her with "daughter" links her story with that of the ruler's daughter and portrays the woman as a member of Jesus' true family, that is, as a daughter of God the heavenly Father and therefore as a true sister of Jesus (12:46–50).

9:23–24: And on coming into the ruler's house and seeing the flutists and the crowd making an uproar, [24]**Jesus was saying, "Back off! For the little girl hasn't died; rather, she's sleeping." And they started laughing him to scorn.** For a funeral, Jewish rabbinical literature

directs even the poorest families to hire at least two flutists and one female wailer. The present crowd makes
an uproar of wailing while the flutists play their instruments. The presence of a crowd reflects the father's status
as a ruler. The crowd hasn't been following Jesus and
therefore doesn't stand here for his professing disciples.
But he puts his authority over them on exhibit with the
terse command, "Back off!" and then explains why they
should back off and thus cease bewailing the little girl's
death. The explanation that she hasn't died but sleeps,
at which the listeners start laughing, presupposes his
raising her shortly. Her death will amount to no more
than a nap (compare Daniel 12:2; John 11:11–13). The
crowd's laughing substantiates that they don't stand for
Jesus' professing disciples. He'll have the last laugh.

**9:25–26: And when the crowd had been thrown
out, on entering he grasped her hand; and the little girl
got up.** [26]**And this report** [= the news of Jesus' raising
her] **went out into that whole land.** "Had been thrown
out" underlines the effectiveness of Jesus' command to
back off. Since he'd already come into the ruler's house
(9:23), "on entering" refers to further entrance into the
room where the girl lay. Then the revival took place as a
result of his merely grasping her hand. Because she was
nappingly dead, she couldn't touch Jesus. So his grasping
her hand complements the touching of his garment by
the woman with a flow of blood. Mere contact brought
health in the one case and life in the other. "Into that
whole land"—what land? "Land of Zebulun and land of
Naphtali . . . Galilee of the nations," where Capernaum
was located (4:13–15)? Perhaps the best guess. But the
anonymity of the land into which went the report of
Jesus' raising the girl foreshadows the proclamation of
the gospel in "the whole inhabited [earth]" (24:14).

JESUS' LORDLY AUTHORITY IN THE
HEALING OF TWO BLIND MEN
Matthew 9:27–31; compare 20:29–34

9:27–28: And as Jesus was going along from there
[= from the ruler's house (9:23–26)], **two blind** [men]
**followed him, shouting and saying, "Have mercy on
us, Son** [= descendant] **of David!"** [28]**And when he'd
gone home** [= into his house in Capernaum (see 4:13
and 9:10 with comments)], **the blind** [men] **approached
him. And Jesus says to them, "Do you believe that I
can do this** [that is, have mercy on you by giving you
sight]**?" They say to him, "Yes, Lord."** The following of
Jesus by the blind men casts them in the role of disciples
from the very beginning of this story. But how could
they see to follow? Perhaps by using their ears instead
of their eyes. But Matthew's leaving the *physical* question unanswered supports their following as *theologically* indicative of discipleship. "Shouting" implies that
they were lagging behind, as well they might because
of their blindness. The addressing of Jesus with "Son of
David" suits Matthew's emphasis on Jesus as the Davidic
Messiah (see the comments on chapters 1–2); and their
"approach[ing]" him evinces a respect for him that suits

his followers. The present tense in "Jesus *says* to them"
and "They *say* to him" enlivens the dialogue, as though it
were going on right now. The question of belief in Jesus'
ability echoes 8:2, 10, 13; 9:2, 22; and the answer, "Yes,
Lord," evinces a truly discipular belief and confession of
Jesus' lordship. Thus both his Davidic ancestry (a necessary qualification for messiahship) and his deity receive
a double witness in line with the Mosaic requirement
that every matter be established by the testimony of two
or three witnesses (18:16, quoting Deuteronomy 19:15).

**9:29–31: Then he touched their eyes, saying, "It's to
happen for you in accordance with your faith** [compare
9:22; 13:58]**." ** [30]**And their eyes were opened** [in the sense
that they could now see; compare 2 Kings 6:20; Isaiah
35:5a; 42:7a]**. And Jesus growled at them, saying, "See
[that] no one knows** [that I've healed your blindness]**."**
[31]**But they, on going out, publicized him in that whole
land.** "Then" makes Jesus' touching the eyes of the blind
men consequent, as he himself says, on their confessing
faith in his ability as the Lord to give them sight. As in
8:3, 15; 9:20–21, 25, mere contact with Jesus effects healing. His growling doesn't display anger. It displays the
forcefulness of his command. Adding further forcefulness is its starting with "See [that]," where a simple "Let
no one know" would have sufficed. The ex-blind men
couldn't hide that they now had sight. But they could
keep secret that it was Jesus who had healed their blindness in the privacy of his home. The command to secrecy
starts an emphasis on Jesus' humility (see further and
especially 11:29; 12:16, 17–21; 21:5), and the forcefulness of this command adds to the emphasis. Despite that
forcefulness, the ex-blind men publicize Jesus, not just
their healing, the forcefulness of his command making
a foil against which their publicizing him stands out in
bold relief. Does their disobedience pay tribute to Jesus'
lordly ability to heal blindness in that they couldn't contain themselves, or does Matthew cite their disobedience
disapprovingly? Or should we think of both possibilities
at once? It's hard to be sure. But at least the publicizing
of Jesus makes his humility, seen in the command not to
publicize him, also stand out in bold relief. For "in that
whole land" see the comments on 9:26.

JESUS' MARVELOUS AUTHORITY IN
EXORCISING A DEMON FROM A DEAF-MUTE
Matthew 9:32–34; compare 12:22–24

9:32–33a: And as they [the two ex-blind men of
9:27–31] **were going out** [from Jesus' house in Capernaum; see 9:28 with comments], **behold, people
brought to him a demon-possessed deaf-mute.** [33a]**And
after the demon had been cast out, the deaf-mute
spoke.** As often elsewhere, "behold" adds drama to this
episode. The bringing of a deaf-mute "*as* [the ex-blind
men] were going out" has Jesus exercising his lordly authority without interruption. Muteness, a result of deafness, gets emphasis in the story because its reversal in the
gift of speech is more quickly obvious than the implied
reversal of deafness. Nevertheless, deafness is implied by

Jesus' not speaking to the demon in performing the exorcism, whereas apart from an exorcism at long distance (15:21–28) he speaks when exorcising demons (8:32; 17:18; cf. 11:5; 12:22).

9:33b–34: And the crowds marveled, saying, "Never has it appeared like this in Israel!" That is to say, the giving of speech and hearing to a deaf-mute has never been observed before in the whole history of Israel (but see the prophecy in Isaiah 35:5b). "Like this" adds the note of manner—by means of exorcizing a demon—to the fact of the gift. The presence of "the crowds" with Jesus at his home (see 9:28, 32 with comments) continues Matthew's portrayal of them as professing disciples. Their marveling suits discipleship. **34But the Pharisees were saying, "He's casting out demons by the ruler of the demons."** The Pharisees are running true to form (see 3:7–10; 5:20; 9:11). They attribute not only this exorcism but also Jesus' other exorcisms (note the plural of "demons" here versus the singular of "demon" in 9:33a) to the authority of the demons' ruler (identified in 12:24, 26–27 as "Beelzebul," a name for Satan) rather than to Jesus' authority as the lordly Son of Man. As critics of him, the Pharisees foreshadow those who oppose the church at the time Matthew writes his Gospel.

THE WORK AND COMPASSION OF THE LORD OF THE HARVEST
Matthew 9:35–38

As in 4:23–25, a summary of Jesus' activities rounds out the largely narrative chapters 8–9 and helps make a bridge to Jesus' second long discourse in chapter 10 (see chapters 5–7 for the first one).

9:35–36: And Jesus was going around all the cities and towns, teaching in their synagogues and proclaiming the good news of the kingdom [for which see the comments on 3:2] **and healing every kind of disease and every kind of ailment.** See the comments on 4:23. **36And on seeing the crowds he felt sorry for them, because they were harried and huddled, "as if** [they were] **sheep not having a shepherd** [compare Numbers 27:17; 1 Kings 22:17; 2 Chronicles 18:16; Ezekiel 34:5]." The description of the crowds as "harried and huddled, as if [they were] like sheep not having a shepherd" portends persecution of the disciples in Matthew's day, the period when Jesus as "the bridegroom" will have been "taken away from them" (9:15 [compare 2:6 for Jesus as a shepherd, like David]). (In 28:20 Jesus will promise to be with them always, but he'll have made clear in 18:20 that such presence will differ in kind from his current physical presence with them on earth.) Matthew has repeatedly made the crowds that follow Jesus stand for professing disciples of his (see the comments on 4:25–5:1; 7:28; 8:1, 18; 9:8, 33) and stressed the persecution of those disciples (most explicitly in 5:10–12, 44). For Matthew's audience, then, the compassion of Jesus for his harried and huddled sheep is designed to comfort and encourage them in their persecution.

9:37–38: Then he tells his disciples, "The harvest [is] **plentiful, but the workers** [are] **few. 38So you should ask the Lord of the harvest** [the one who hires workers and sends them to his field] **that he thrust out workers into his harvest."** The present tense in "he *tells*" has the effect of making Jesus address his following words to the contemporary church as well as to his original disciples. But who are these disciples? Since in 4:25–5:1 Matthew identified the crowds with professing disciples of Jesus (as confirmed by 7:28–29), we're to see the same progression here: Matthew identifies the harried and huddled crowds with Jesus' disciples, so that Jesus tells the crowds of disciples that because the evangelistic harvest is plentiful yet few of them are engaged in the work of evangelism, they should pray the Lord of the harvest to thrust workers from their own midst out into his harvest. Then he does exactly that in chapter 10 by summoning the Twelve from their midst and sending them on an evangelistic tour. This sending will preview his later sending them, minus Judas Iscariot, to make further disciples of all nations (28:16–20). So he himself is "the Lord of the harvest" to whom the disciples are to pray for the thrusting out of workers. The workers he thrusts out originate among the very disciples who are to pray that he thrust out workers. And the harvest is "his" in that it will consist of converts to him.

THE WORKERS OF THE LORD OF THE HARVEST AND THEIR AUTHORITY
Matthew 10:1–4

10:1: And on summoning his twelve disciples [from among "the crowds" of "his disciples" in 9:36–37], **he gave them authority over unclean spirits so as to cast them out and** [authority] **to heal every kind of disease and every kind of ailment.** Matthew mentions the Twelve without explanation, because his Jewish Christian audience already know about them. Jesus has authority (7:29; 9:6) and now shares it with the Twelve (compare 9:8). "Unclean spirits" is a Jewish way of referring to demons. The authority to cast them out matches Jesus' own authority to do so (4:24; 8:16, 31–32; 9:34), and the authority "to heal every kind of disease and every kind of ailment" likewise matches his own authority to heal them (4:23; 9:35).

10:2–4: And the names of the twelve apostles are these: first Simon (the one called Peter) and Andrew (his brother) and James (the [son] **of Zebedee) and John (his brother); 3Philip and Bartholomew; Thomas and Matthew (the tax collector** [see 9:9]**); James (the** [son] **of Alphaeus) and Thaddaeus; 4Simon (the Cananean) and Judas (the Iscariot, who also gave him** [Jesus] **over** [to his enemies]**).** In 10:1 Matthew called the Twelve "disciples." Now he calls them "apostles," because Jesus has given them his own authority, because he's about to send them to reap an evangelistic harvest, and because "apostles" means "those sent with their sender's own authority." "*First* Simon" puts this Simon forward as the leading and representative apostle. "The one called

Peter" distinguishes him from a later "Simon," called "the Cananean." The linking of Simon, Andrew, James, and John with three intervening occurrences of "and" keeps them a foursome in line with their call to discipleship in 4:18–22. The two occurrences of "his brother" (one each with Andrew and John) point to the larger brotherhood of the church (compare the comments on 1:2, 11; 4:18, 21; 5:22–24, 47; 7:3–5 and so on). "The [son] of Zebedee" distinguishes James in the foursome from a later James, called "the [son] of Alphaeus." The remaining names are paired in conformity with the law of two or three witnesses (18:16; Numbers 35:30; Deuteronomy 17:6; 19:15), because the Twelve will testify as witnesses (10:18 [compare 24:14]). "The Cananean" doesn't mean "the Canaanite"—rather, "the zealot" ("Cananean" being an Aramaic word). But Matthew makes nothing of that meaning; so for him it merely helps distinguish the two Simons. "The Iscariot" has an uncertain meaning but distinguishes Judas the betrayer of Jesus from Judas the brother of Jesus (13:55).

JESUS' COMMISSIONING THE TWELVE TO HARVEST ISRAEL
Matthew 10:5–15

10:5–8: These twelve Jesus sent after ordering them, saying, "You shouldn't go off into a road of Gentiles [that is, into Gentile territory] and you shouldn't go into a city of Samaritans. ⁶But journey, rather, to the lost sheep [consisting] of the house of Israel [compare Jeremiah 50:6]. ⁷And as you journey preach, saying, 'The reign of heaven has drawn near.' ⁸Heal sick people. Raise dead people. Cleanse lepers. Cast out demons. You've received freely [the authority to perform these deeds]. Give freely [by performing them without remuneration]." Gentile territories bounded Galilee on all sides except the southern. There, Samaria bounded Galilee. Consequently, the prohibitions against taking a road into any Gentile territory and against entering any Samaritan city limit the twelve apostles initially to Galilee; and "to the lost sheep of the house of Israel" limits them to Jews living there. Thus the apostles' ministry follows the pattern of Jesus' ministry, which began in Galilee (4:12–17). This correlation will be strengthened later by the stated limitation of his ministry "to the lost sheep of the house of Israel" (15:24). Exceptionally, some Gentiles do believe in him during his ministry (8:5–13, 28–34; 15:21–28); but a planned mission to Gentiles doesn't start till after the Jewish authorities have engineered his crucifixion and he has risen from the dead—that is, not till the kingdom ("the reign of heaven") has been transferred to the church (see especially 21:43 with 28:18–20). The present limitation belongs to an initial stage alone, then, and rests on the correlation between the ministries of Jesus and the Twelve. Like teacher, like disciples. This correlation gets further strength from Jesus' ordering the apostles to proclaim the very same message he has been proclaiming (see 4:17), to perform the very same

deeds he has been performing, and to do so without financial charge just as he hasn't charged the beneficiaries of his ministry and just as the apostles haven't had to pay for the authority he has given them. The gospel is good news partly because it offers salvation without cost to the recipients, who have only to exercise repentance and faith.

10:9–10: "You shouldn't acquire gold or silver or copper [coins] for your belts [of cloth, in whose twisted folds the coins would be kept], ¹⁰nor a bag for the road [to carry food for sustenance along the way] nor two tunics [robes worn under an outer robe and next to the skin] nor sandals nor a staff. For the worker is worthy [= deserving] of his maintenance." Since Jesus has just told the Twelve to give their services freely, "You shouldn't acquire" means they shouldn't seek or accept payment in the form of money or items for travel—not even copper coins of little value, much less gold coins of great value and silver ones of middling value. "Nor a bag for the road" implies depending for sufficient food on the hospitality of those in the cities and towns visited during the itineration. Don't worry, for your heavenly Father will see to it that you've had enough to eat before leaving and that you'll have enough to eat on arriving in the next city or town (compare 6:25–34). To acquire from beneficiaries of your services two tunics in addition to the tunic you're already wearing would give what we'd call two changes of underwear for the mission. To acquire from such beneficiaries a pair of sandals would give you a change of footgear once your present pair wears thin from journeying. And to acquire from beneficiaries a staff in addition to the one you're already using would provide extra support on steep terrain and extra protection against wild beasts. So we have an ascending order of desirability: the lunchbag for a mid-trip snack to be desired least, two tunics for changes of underwear to be desired somewhat, an extra pair of sandals for protecting the feet to be desired much, and an extra staff for warding off wild animals and steadying yourself on dangerously steep and slippery mountain paths to be desired most of all. "For the worker is worthy of his maintenance" identifies the Twelve as "the workers" whom Jesus, "the Lord of the harvest," is thrusting out "into his harvest" and gives the reason why they shouldn't acquire the foregoing items from beneficiaries along the way. It's that their hosts' provision of hospitality ("maintenance" of room and board) is what these workers deserve. But for them to acquire the forbidden items from beneficiaries of their services would amount to self-aggrandizement and thereby disobey the command to "give freely" as they've "received freely" (10:8).

But who will provide the Twelve hospitality? **10:11–13:** "And into whatever city or town you go, check out who in it is worthy and stay there till you go out [of that city or town]. ¹²And as you enter into the house [that is, whatever house you enter for possible hospitality], greet it [that is, the household]. ¹³And if on the one hand the household is worthy, your peace is to come on it [or 'on them,' since the household will consist of the people living in the house]. **But if on the other hand it isn't worthy, your peace is to return to you."** What constitutes worthiness here? Answer: readiness to provide the Twelve, or pairs of them, with the hospitality that consists in room and board. And who will provide them with such hospitality? Answer: other disciples of Jesus who'll demonstrate the genuineness of their discipleship by so doing, as opposed to still other disciples who'll demonstrate the falsity of their discipleship by refusing such hospitality (see 25:31–46, where Jesus says that his true disciples gave him room and board when they gave others of his disciples room and board, and the reverse for false disciples). In view of these alternatives, "peace" represents messianic salvation in addition to a simple Semitic "hello" (*shalōm* in modern Hebrew). So the Twelve are to check out who in a city or town is worthy by going into a house and greeting its inhabitants ("the household") to see whether they offer them hospitality. If they do, the Twelve's "peace" sticks and they themselves are to stay there till they exit the city or town. If the household refuses them hospitality, the Twelve are to retract their "peace" and find hospitality elsewhere, because there'll be no messianic salvation for those people. The Twelve have Jesus' own authority in the granting and retracting of such peace, and their staying in a worthy household cements that household's salvation. Jesus has already made disciples throughout Galilee. The Twelve, then, aren't to stay just anywhere. They're to stay in homes where the proclamation of the reign of heaven has already found a true and favorable reception (compare Matthew's emphasis on Christian brotherhood and 25:31–46).

10:14–15: **"And whoever doesn't welcome you and doesn't heed your words—as you go outside that house or city, shake out the dust of your feet. ¹⁵Amen I tell you, it will be more endurable for the land of Sodom and Gomorrah in the day of judgment than for that city."** "Your words" harks back to the Twelve's proclaiming, "The reign of heaven has drawn near" (10:7), the very words Jesus proclaimed (4:17), so that "your words" equate with his own words ("these my words," as he said in 7:24, 26). Here, exit is consequent on rejection rather than on completion of ministry (as in 10:11). "Shake *out* the dust of your feet" means to shake out of your clothing the dust kicked up by your feet in the course of walking on unpaved paths. So the Twelve have Jesus' authority to pronounce judgment with this gesture on those who refuse them and their words. And because it's his authority they exercise as apostles, judgment is certain to strike. "I tell you," reinforced by an initial "Amen," underlines the severity as well as certainty of the judgment. Since Sodom and Gomorrah had become proverbial for their wickedness, "It [the judgment] will be more endurable for the land of Sodom and Gomorrah" raises that severity to new heights (compare Genesis 18–19). And "in the day of judgment" tells when the judgment will strike, that is, at the Last Day. "*More* endurable" implies different degrees of eternal punishment.

JESUS' WARNING OF PERSECUTION IN A MISSION THAT WILL EVOLVE INTO THE INCLUSION OF GENTILES
Matthew 10:16–42

This long passage divides into a description of persecution with instructions to beware of informers, not to worry about preparing statements for trial ahead of time, and to flee from one city to another rather than staying suicidally in a city that poses a threat to life and limb (10:16–23). Reasons not to fear persecution follow (10:24–42). They include the solidarity in suffering of the disciples and their master (10:24–25), the impossibility of hiding the truth (10:26–27), the inconsequentiality of physical martyrdom as compared with eternal punishment of the whole person (10:28), the value God the Father places on Jesus' disciples (10:29–31), the necessity of confessing Jesus before other human beings if you're to be confessed by him before God (10:32–33), the unworthiness of anyone who draws back through fear of personal abuse (10:34–39), and the conveyance of eternal life in Christ through such costly ministry (10:40–42).

10:16: **"Behold, I'm sending you off like sheep in the midst of wolves. So become shrewd, as serpents** [are], **and guileless, as doves** [are]." In Matthew's Greek, "I'm sending" is a verbal form of the noun "apostle" (10:2). Just as sheep in the midst of wolves are exposed to attack, so the Twelve will be exposed to persecution, martyrdom in particular. Therefore they need to develop shrewdness for avoidance of martyrdom, so far and so long as is possible without miscarrying their mission; for martyrdom would cut short their ministry (see 10:23 for flight as a shrewd way of avoiding martyrdom). The comparison to serpents' shrewdness reflects Genesis 3:1–13. But shrewdness needs the balance of guilelessness; for without guilelessness shrewdness degenerates into deception, the mainspring of hypocrisy such as characterizes false prophets ("wolves in sheep's clothing" according to 7:15 [compare Romans 16:19; Philippians 2:15]). Ever since Noah sent out a dove that returned with "a freshly picked olive leaf" as the sign of a world cleansed of evil by the flood (Genesis 8:8–12), the dove has symbolized the purity of guilelessness.

10:17–18: **"And take precaution against the human beings** [as distinguished from the serpents and the doves just mentioned in 10:16]. **For they'll give you over to sanhedrins** [Jewish local courts], **and in their synagogues they'll flog you** [compare Deuteronomy 25:1–3; Acts 22:19; 2 Corinthians 11:24]. **¹⁸And you'll be led before both governors and kings on account of me for a testimony to them and the nations."** "For a testimony to them ['governors and kings'] and the nations" signals that Jesus' instructions for the Twelve's immediate Galilean mission to Jews alone have now evolved into instructions for a later mission to all the world's nations, not just to the Jews (24:14; 28:18–20). "Before governors and kings" will give the disciples a megaphone to reach those nations. "On account of me" puts Jesus at the center of the disciples' coming testimony. "You'll be led" indicates duress. Being given over "to sanhedrins" and flogged "in their synagogues" indicates a start of persecution in Jewish quarters before the expansion of persecution among Gentiles. The disciples will be flogged as Jesus was flogged (see 20:19 with 10:24–25). But who are "the human beings" against whom disciples are to take precaution? Unbelievers in general? Perhaps. But in view of the use of "the human beings" for disciples in 8:27 (with 8:23); 9:8 and in view of Jesus' prediction that "many . . . will betray *one another*" (24:10), the present warning may have in view especially false disciples who'll hand over true disciples to authorities to save their own necks in times of persecution.

10:19–20: **"And whenever they give you over, you shouldn't worry about how or what you should say. For what you should say will be given to you in that hour** [= the hour of your trial]. [20]**For you're not the ones speaking; rather, the Spirit of your Father** [is] **the one speaking in you."** The prohibition of worry over how or what to say parallels the prohibition in 6:31, 34 of worry over what to eat, drink, and wear. The omission of "how" with the second "what you should say" shows that "how" with the first one has to do with the content of speech, not with its style (see 10:7 for the content). And this content comes from the Spirit speaking in the disciples, so that when speaking themselves they use his words. Not to worry, then, as reinforced by the assuring designation of the Spirit as "of your Father."

10:21–22: **"And a brother will give** [his] **brother over to death, and a father** [will give his] **child over** [to death]. **And children will rise up against** [their] **parents and have them put to death** [as a result of accusations before the authorities (compare Micah 7:6)]. [22]**And you'll be hated by all** [kinds of people as well as your family members] **because of my name. But the one enduring to an end—this one will be saved** [compare Micah 7:7; Daniel 12:12–13]." "Because of my name" refers to the use of Jesus' name in prophesying, exorcising demons, and performing miracles (compare 7:22). The treachery of nondisciples and false disciples toward true disciples in their own families expands into a general hatred of true disciples on the part of all. But Jesus promises salvation to those who hold out "to an end." Since he has just spoken of being "put to death," "the one enduring to an end" is the disciple who endures persecution to the point of martyrdom. "This one" gives special recognition to such a disciple. Jesus' promise has the purpose of steeling disciples against treachery, hatred, and martyrdom. Sticking true will demonstrate a genuineness of discipleship that ensures eternal salvation (see further the comments on Mark 13:9–13).

10:23: **"But whenever they persecute** [literally, 'pursue'] **you in this city** [where you've gone], **flee into another** [city]. **For amen I tell you, you'll by no means have ended** [= finished visiting] **the cities of Israel till the Son of Man comes."** There's a fine contrast between pursuit and fleeing. Flight is the only legitimate way to avoid persecution, which could issue in martyrdom; and flight has the added benefit that disciples minister the gospel in the farther cities into which they flee. Hence the *command* to flee (compare examples of withdrawal from danger in 2:12–14, 22; 4:12; 12:15; 14:13; 15:21). But just as the warning of persecution ended in an assurance of salvation for the tried and true (10:16–22), so the command to flee from one city to another ends in an assurance of the Son of Man's coming before the disciples have run out of cities to flee to. "I tell you," reinforced with a prefixed "Amen," strengthens the assurance. Since Matthew wrote long after the Twelve's mission in Galilee and the Son of Man hadn't yet returned, by implication the mission to Israel has remained open at the same time it has expanded to include all nations (see 24:14; 28:18–20 again).

As an antidote to fear, Jesus now draws a parallel between the persecution of his disciples and his own persecution. *10:24–25*: **"A disciple isn't above** [his] **teacher, nor a slave above his master** ['above' in the sense of rank and consequent authority]. [25][It's] **enough for the disciple that he become like his teacher and the slave like his master."** "Disciple" means "learner" and therefore complements "teacher." The word translated "master" also means "Lord," and Jesus has often appeared as the Lord (3:3; 7:21–22; 8:2, 6, 8, 21, 25; 9:28, 38 and later). So as applied to Jesus' disciples, "slaves" stresses subordination to Jesus as their Lord even more than "disciples" stresses subordination to him as their teacher. "Like his teacher" and "like his master" have to do with similarity in the suffering of persecution, and "[It's] enough" means that Jesus' disciples shouldn't try to outdo him by avoiding martyrdom at all costs, as he did not. Following statements will explain that they could avoid martyrdom, though at eternal cost, by failing to proclaim the gospel and by disowning Jesus before others (10:26–33). **"If people have nicknamed the houseowner 'Beelzebul,' how much more** [will they stigmatize] **the members of his household."** "The houseowner" stands for Jesus. People's having nicknamed him "Beelzebul" anticipates the charge that he casts out demons by Beelzebul, the demons' ruler (12:24, 27; compare 9:32–34); only here people have nicknamed Jesus *himself* Beelzebul. There's a connection between "Beelzebul" and "houseowner" in that "Beel-" can be related to a Hebrew word for "owner," and "-zebul" to a Hebrew word for "house." "The members of his household" stand for Jesus' disciples. And it's easier to stigmatize them than him, because they're his subordinates (compare 5:11).

We come now to three prohibitions of fear. First, Jesus tells his disciples not to fear those who stigmatize him and them, because the truth will out (10:26). Second, he tells them not to fear those who can kill the body, because they can't kill the soul (10:28a). Third, he tells them not to fear, because they're more valuable than many sparrows, not one of which falls unless the

Father wills it to (10:29–31). The first two prohibitions lead to commands to proclaim Jesus' teachings publicly (10:27) and to fear God, who can destroy both soul and body in gehenna (10:28b). The third prohibition leads to a declaration that Jesus will confess those who confess him in public but disown those who disown him in public (10:32–33). **10:26–27: "Therefore** [because of your solidarity with me in being stigmatized] **you shouldn't fear them** [the stigmatizers]. **For nothing is covered that won't be uncovered, and** [nothing is] **secret that won't be made known."** In other words, the lies told about Jesus and his disciples will be exposed for what they are. This exposé will happen at the Last Judgment. So be patient. [27]**"Speak in the light what I'm telling you in the dark, and proclaim on the housetops what you're hearing in the ear."** "In the dark" and "in the ear" point to Jesus' teaching the disciples in private. "In the light" and "on the housetops" point to the disciples' proclaiming in public what they've heard him say in private. (Ordinarily, housetops were flat and had an outside stairway leading up to them.) So despite stigmatization, Jesus says, go ahead and publicize the gospel. You have nothing to fear in the end.

10:28: "And don't shy away in fear from those who kill the body but can't kill the soul. But fear, rather, the one who can destroy both soul and body in gehenna [see the comments on 5:22 for 'gehenna' as hell]." To shy away in fear would be to fail to proclaim the gospel in public. "Those who kill the body" are those who might make martyrs out of you for such proclamation. "But can't kill the soul" implies that although the soul's departure leaves the body dead, the soul lives on in a disembodied state till the resurrection. The addition of "rather" to "But" accentuates the contrast between needless fear and needful fear. "The one who can destroy both soul and body in gehenna" isn't Satan (see James 4:12) and is usually thought to be God the Father. But in view of Jesus' consigning people to hell in 7:23; 25:31–32, 41–46, he's the one we need to fear. For he'll judge turncoats as false disciples. "Destroy" carries the sense of ruination rather than annihilation.

10:29–31: "Two sparrows are sold for an assarion, aren't they?" They were sold for food. An assarion was worth one-sixteenth of a denarius, and a denarius was a day's wage for a manual laborer (20:1–16). **"And not one of them** [the sparrows] **will fall on the ground** [dead] **apart from your Father** [compare Amos 3:5]. [30]**And even the hairs of your head are all numbered** [by God your Father]. [31]**So don't fear** [martyrdom]. **You're more valuable than many sparrows."** Two sparrows' costing only one assarion highlights by contrast Jesus' disciples' being "more valuable than many sparrows." "All" and "even" emphasize God's having numbered "the hairs of your head" as being more impressive than his presence with "one" sparrow that will fall on the ground dead. And "will fall on the ground apart from your Father" makes God's presence at that sparrow's death a guarantee of his fatherly presence with Jesus' disciple at the

disciple's martyrdom, for the disciple is much more valuable. The Father's presence evacuates martyrdom of its frightfulness. The future tense in "will fall" points forward to the martyrdom of Jesus' disciples and promises the Father's presence.

10:32–33: "Therefore [because of your great value to the Father] **everyone who as such will confess me before human beings—I'll also confess him before my Father in heaven.** [33]**But whoever disowns me before human beings—I'll also disown him before my Father in heaven** [compare 1 Samuel 2:30]." "As such" means "in his function as a confessor of me in public." "Everyone" gives assurance that Jesus will neglect no such confessor. To confess Jesus is to acknowledge him. "Before human beings," earthbound as they are, makes a nice contrast with "my Father in heaven." The conjunction of "*my* Father" with "*your* Father" (10:29) makes Jesus' confession an acknowledgment of shared parentage. "Who . . . will confess me" sets out a desirable possibility, "whoever disowns me" an undesirable one. And the grammatical breaks represented by dashes in the translation accent these possibilities.

10:34–36: "You shouldn't think that I've come to thrust peace onto the earth. I haven't come to thrust peace—rather, [to thrust] **a sword** [onto the earth (compare 5:17 for phraseology, Ezekiel 38:21 for content)]. [35]**For I've come to pit 'a man against his father, and a daughter against her mother, and a daughter-in-law against her mother-in-law';** [36]**and 'a man's enemies** [will be] **members of his household** [Micah 7:6].'" Here "peace" means neither messianic salvation nor absence of conflict between nations and in society at large. It means accord within a family. "A sword" represents discord within a family. "Onto the earth" implies the discord's origin in heaven. The discord has to do not only with the difference between one household member's confessing Jesus publicly and another household member's disowning him publicly (as in 10:32–33). It also has to do with a nondisciple's giving a disciple over to the authorities to be put to death even though the two belong to the same household (as in 10:21; 24:10). Because of the cultural expectation of religious unity in a family, these sayings of Jesus put enormous emphasis on the sovereignty of loyalty to him over loyalty to one's biological family.

10:37–39: "The one who loves [his] **father or mother above me isn't worthy of me, and the one who loves** [his] **son or daughter above me isn't worthy of me.** [38]**And the one who doesn't take his cross and follow behind me isn't worthy of me.** [39]**The one who has found his life will lose it, and the one who has lost his life on account of me will find it."** Jesus continues to play on the theme of his upsetting family loyalties in favor of loyalty to him. "Who loves . . . *above* me" links back to 10:24, which said that "a disciple isn't *above* [his] teacher, nor a slave *above* his master." A professing disciple's failure to risk betrayal by the members of his own family shows him to be false and therefore unworthy of Jesus as his teacher and Lord. Jesus won't start predicting his death till 16:21–23, and even then not death by crucifixion. That kind of death doesn't come into view till 20:19. So a person's not taking up his cross and following behind Jesus stands for a professing disciple's failure to expose himself through public discipleship to the possibility of martyrdom. Again the failure shows his falsity and unworthiness to have Jesus as his teacher and Lord. And this unworthiness translates into *not* having Jesus as such. (Those sentenced to be crucified had to carry the crossbar of a cross on public thoroughfares from the site of sentencing to the site of crucifixion.) "The one who has found his life" is the false disciple who has preserved his present life by drawing back from public discipleship. But he'll lose the eternal life that would otherwise be his. "The one who has lost his life" is the true disciple who has suffered martyrdom for public discipleship. But he'll find eternal life. Not that eternal life *requires* martyrdom; rather, Jesus is encouraging his disciples not to draw back from *risking* martyrdom. "On account of me" stresses him as the focus of discipleship.

10:40–42: "The one who welcomes you welcomes me, and the one who welcomes me welcomes the one who sent me. ⁴¹The one who welcomes a prophet in the name of a prophet will receive a prophet's reward, and the one who welcomes a righteous person in the name of a righteous person will receive a righteous person's reward. ⁴²And whoever in the name of a disciple gives one of these little ones just a cup of cold [water] to drink—amen I tell you—will by no means lose his reward." Welcoming means harboring those who are fleeing persecution in accordance with 10:23. "You" refers to the twelve apostles, whom Jesus is addressing (10:1–5). "A prophet" refers to a Christian prophet (compare 7:22; 23:34). "A righteous person" refers not simply to someone who *lives* righteously—rather, to someone who also *teaches* righteousness (compare 28:20: "teaching them to keep [= obey] all things, as many as they are, that I've commanded you"; also 5:19; Daniel 12:3). "These little ones" refers to disciples who don't occupy positions of leadership in the church (hence "in the name of a disciple" with reference to "these little ones" [compare 18:6, 10]). So we have a hierarchical list descending from apostles through Christian prophets and teachers of righteousness to ordinary church members. Because of their greater exposure to public view, church leaders—the apostles, prophets, and teachers of righteousness—are first to suffer persecution. But even obscure ("little") disciples need help in fleeing from their persecutors. Who will harbor such refugees? Only their fellow disciples, for who else would dare to? So these sayings of Jesus indicate that willingness to risk danger by harboring fleeing disciples characterizes true disciples. Only false disciples will refuse. "In the name of" means "with acceptance that the refugee is what his designation—whether apostle, prophet, righteous person, or little disciple—indicates." "Reward" refers to entrance

into the kingdom of heaven at the end (5:12; 6:1), not through merit but through demonstration of genuine discipleship. To receive a prophet's or a righteous person's reward will be to receive the same entrance into that kingdom that a prophet or a righteous person will receive. Because of their leadership it might be tempting to harbor an apostle, prophet, or teacher of righteousness but not a "little one." So Jesus underlines the necessity of harboring ordinary disciples by saying "*one* of these little ones," "*just* a cup of cold [and therefore refreshing water]," "*amen* I tell you," and "will *by no means* lose his reward." The interruption of this sentence by "amen I tell you" intensifies the emphasis. The welcoming of Jesus in the welcoming of an apostle reflects the Twelve's having been given Jesus' own authority (in accordance with the connotation of "apostle" [10:1–2a]); and the welcoming of God, who sent Jesus, in the welcoming of Jesus reflects Jesus' having been given God the Father's own authority (in accord with the connotation of "sent," a form of the Greek verb *apostellō*).

A CONCLUDING FORMULA FOR THE SECOND "BOOK" OF JESUS' LAW, PLUS AN INTRODUCTION TO THE FOLLOWING NARRATIVE
Matthew 11:1

For Matthew's Moses-like pentateuch of Jesus' discourses, see the introduction to the Sermon on the Mount (chapters 5–7). *11:1: **And it happened that when Jesus had finished** [compare 7:28a] **giving orders to his twelve disciples** [compare 10:1, 5a], **he moved away from there** [wherever he was when he gave them orders (compare 9:35–10:1)] **to teach and preach in their** [the Galilean Jews'] **cities** [compare 4:23; 9:35]. "*Their* cities" echoes "*their* synagogues" and "*their* scholars" in 4:23; 7:29; 9:35; 10:17 and therefore rules out a reference to the twelve disciples' hometowns and implies, as in those earlier passages, an estrangement from each other of Israel and the church. Though "had finished giving orders" explains the instructions in chapter 10 as a commissioning of the Twelve, Matthew writes nothing about any teaching and preaching by them. Jesus instructed them to preach (10:7); but now it's he, not they, who proceeds to do so—and in the very cities where the disciples were supposed to go. Remarkable! At the level of Matthew's text, then, the disciples' mission to Israel shades into their mission to all nations (24:14; 28:19–20) for fulfillment during the present age of the church (compare the comments on 10:23).

THE OPPOSITION AND PERSECUTION INCURRED BY JESUS AND HIS DISCIPLES
Matthew 11:2–12:50

A narrative section that goes through 12:50 starts at 11:2. As usual, though, Matthew puts emphasis on Jesus' words even in narrative. Just as chapters 8–9 carried out the theme of Jesus' authority prominent in the Sermon on the Mount (chapters 5–7), so too chapters 11–12 carry out the theme of opposition to and persecution of Jesus and his disciples, a theme prominent in the discourse on mission (chapter 10). The story about the messengers of John the baptizer (11:2–24) reaches a peak in the saying on suffering violence (11:12). The associated sayings about the rejection of John and Jesus by "this generation" (11:16–19) reiterate the theme of opposition; and those concerning the unrepentant cities of Chorazin, Bethsaida, and Capernaum (11:20–24) give assurance to Matthew's audience that their persecutors will be judged. Jesus' gentleness toward his disciples, called "infants," provides a foil to the heavy-handed scholars and Pharisees, the source of Jesus' and the disciples' trouble (11:25–30). The Pharisees' criticisms of the disciples for plucking grain on the Sabbath (12:1–8) and of Jesus for healing on the Sabbath a man with a withered hand (12:9–13) climax in a plot to destroy Jesus (12:14) and in his consequent withdrawal (12:15–21). The withdrawal provides another foil to the murderous initiative of his opponents (compare the comments on 10:23). The charge that he casts out demons by Beelzebul (12:22–37) harks back to the similar charge in 10:25 and includes further assurances of coming judgment on persecutors. Yet another such assurance appears in Jesus' response to the demand for a sign (12:38–45). This narrative section closes with a more positive assurance regarding the members of Jesus' true family (12:46–50).

THE SUFFERING OF VIOLENCE BY
THE KINGDOM OF HEAVEN
Matthew 11:2–24

11:2–3: And John, when he'd heard in prison about the deeds of the Christ, sending [word] **through his** [John's] **disciples** [3]**said to him** [the Christ], **"Are *you* the coming one, or should we wait expectantly for *someone different?*"** In 4:12 Matthew wrote that Jesus had heard about John the baptizer's being taken into custody. Now he writes that John hears in prison about the deeds of Jesus, whom Matthew from his own standpoint calls "the Christ." Literally, "prison" means "a place for keeping [someone] in bonds"; and 14:3 will mention the binding of John. The present allusion to his imprisonment puts the following in a framework of persecution and makes John a prototype of persecuted Christians (compare 25:36, 39, 43–44). "The deeds of the Christ" make Jesus a model of doing good deeds—a model for his disciples to replicate (compare 5:16). "Deeds" differ from "words" (see 23:3, for example), but the rest of this passage will feature Jesus' words. "The" with "Christ" makes a title, the Greek equivalent of "the Messiah" (Hebrew). "*You*" and "*someone different*" are emphatic for stress on the question whether Jesus was fulfilling John's prediction concerning the one who was to come after him (3:11 [see also 21:9; 23:39; Psalm 118:26]). The "we" in John's question refers to John and his disciples—to John because he'd made the prediction, to his disciples because along

with him they expected its fulfillment. He'd said that the coming one would baptize people in the Holy Spirit and fire, save the repentant, and judge the unrepentant. Apparently Jesus' failure thus far to have fulfilled these predictions, at least the judgmental ones, had raised a question in John's mind, a question particularly nettlesome because of John's imprisonment. But Matthew doesn't tease out the reason for John's question. So the question serves only to set the stage for Jesus' response.

11:4–6: And answering, Jesus told them, "Go report to John the things you're hearing and seeing: [5]**blind people are seeing again and lame people are walking about. Lepers are being cleansed and deaf-mutes are hearing and dead people are being raised and poor people are getting good news** [compare Isaiah 26:19; 29:18; 35:5–6; 61:1]. [6]**And whoever isn't tripped up in regard to me** [= doesn't fall into the sin of unbelief because I'm not meeting his expectations] **is fortunate** [because such a person will be saved by faith in me]." "The things you're hearing and seeing" implies that John's disciples were hearing Jesus proclaim good news to the poor (compare the comments on 5:3) and seeing him perform the listed miracles right then and there. Healing the blind and healing the lame are paired. But the remaining miracles and the proclamation of good news are listed pell-mell with one connective "and" after another, as though to overwhelm John (and us as Matthew's audience) with the cornucopia of Jesus' salvific activities. He hadn't conformed to popular Jewish messianism by bringing political, social, and economic deliverance or by coming in the wake of such deliverance by God. But his performing miracles was more than what the Jews expected the Messiah to do, and his doing miraculously what according to Isaiah only God was going to do more than counterbalanced his failure to conform to Jewish expectations. Political, social, and economic deliverance could wait till his coming "on the clouds of the sky with power and much glory" (24:30). That is the import of his answer to John. Doubtless Matthew also wants us to see an indication of deity in Jesus' doing what Isaiah predicted God would do (compare 1:23). The beatitude on whoever doesn't take offense at Jesus makes John's doubt an example to be disregarded by Christians who find themselves in straits similar to John's.

11:7–10: And as these [disciples of John the baptizer] **were traveling** [back to John], **Jesus started saying to the crowds concerning John, "What did you go out into the wilderness to look at? A reed being shaken by wind?"** Obviously not. [8]**"Rather, what did you go out to see? A man dressed in soft** [garments]**?"** Again no, because John "had his clothing from camel's hair and a leather belt [just a strip of hide] around his waist" (3:4). **"Behold, the ones wearing soft** [garments] [are] **in kings' houses** [not in the wilderness, where you went to check out John]! [9]**Rather, what did you go out to see? A prophet? Yes, I tell you, and more than a prophet!** [10]**This is the one about whom it's written, 'Behold I'm sending my messenger before your face, who'll pave your road ahead of you [Exodus 23:20; Malachi 3:1 (compare Matthew 3:3; Isaiah 40:3)].'" John's disciples go off not to be heard from again. Nor is he heard from again. Matthew shows no more interest in how John reacted to his disciples' report than he showed in the reason for John's question. Instead, he shines a spotlight on what Jesus had to say. Appropriately, "*started* saying" introduces a rather long reflection by Jesus on John. "To the crowds"—as usual in Matthew, they stand for Jesus' professing disciples, to be distinguished from "this generation" of peevish little children who've rejected both John and Jesus (11:16–19). These crowds had traveled out to the wilderness not only to see John but also to get baptized by him as they repentantly confessed their sins (3:1, 5–6). A wilderness was devoid of many human inhabitants, though not necessarily of very much vegetation. So Jesus refers to "a reed" such as grows along the banks of the Jordan River, where John was preaching and baptizing. We might think that Jesus is saying it's ridiculous to imagine the crowds went out to see vegetation blowing in the wind. But for that thought we'd expect the plural, "reeds," not the singular, "a reed." This singular and the addition of "being shaken in the wind" suggest a contrast with the moral sturdiness of John in preaching a baptism of repentance, in calling many of the Pharisees and Sadducees "offsprings of vipers," and in warning them of fiery judgment (3:7–10). His rough clothing suited this moral sturdiness and contrasted with the soft garments of those who live in kings' houses rather than in the wilderness, as John did. "Behold" stresses the contrast. John was no wimp!

A prophet is a spokesman for God. Such was John. Jesus affirms that the crowds went out to see John because they recognized him to be a prophet. Several features buttress the affirmation: (1) a second "Rather," which negates the preceding reasons for the crowds' venturing into the wilderness; (2) Jesus' answering his own question with "Yes"; and (3) his adding an emphatic "I tell you." "And more than a prophet" adds John's even higher function of fulfilling what's written in the quoted Old Testament texts. As applied to John and Jesus, the sender ("I") in the quotation is God, his "messenger" is John, Jesus is the "you" before whom John was sent and who paved Jesus' road ahead of him, and John's preaching and baptizing constituted the paving.

11:11–15: "Amen I tell you, a larger than John the baptizer didn't arise among those born from women. But the littler one in the kingdom of heaven is larger than he [John]. [12]**But from the days of John the baptizer till now the kingdom of heaven suffers violence, and violent** [men] **plunder it.** [13]**For all the Prophets and the Law prophesied till John.** [14]**And if you're willing to welcome** [him]**, he himself is Elijah, the one who is going to come.** [15]**The person who has ears had better hear!"** Twice Jesus adds "the baptizer" to "John" even though he as well as Matthew has just used "John" without that addition and shortly will do so again (11:2, 4, 7, 13, 18). These two additions set forth John as an

example for Jesus' disciples to follow when discipling all nations (28:19: "baptizing them . . ."). "Larger" and "littler" have to do with status and function. Another "I tell you," this time reinforced by "Amen," underlines John's superiority over his predecessors in that he prepared the way for Jesus. Now that the reign of heaven has arrived in what 11:2 called "the deeds of the Christ," though, the littler person in that kingdom—that is, the disciple of low status and function (10:42)—is larger than John in the sense of being greater than he is (compare 18:4: "whoever humbles [literally, 'lowers'] himself like this little child [that is, to a childlike status and function] is largest in the kingdom of heaven"). That the littler one is larger than the previously largest one is as much a challenge as it is a statement of fact—a challenge to humble Christian service that exposes a disciple to persecution (20:25–28; 23:11–12). "The kingdom of heaven suffers violence" in the persecution of its members, compared to a plundering in which they're seized and imprisoned. "*But . . .* the kingdom of heaven suffers violence" contrasts the suffering of persecution with greatness in that kingdom. Despite greatness, there's persecution. This persecution started with John's imprisonment (4:12). Once again, then, he's a prototype of persecuted Christians (compare the comments on 3:1–3 concerning John as a prototype of Christian preachers and indeed of Jesus himself; also 17:9–13 for John and Jesus as partners in suffering). But the present tense of "suffers" and "plunder" links up with "till *now*" to indicate persecution as current at the time of Matthew's writing. "*For all the Prophets and the Law prophesied till John*" makes the transition from the time of the Prophets and the Law the reason for including John in the present period of persecution. For "the Prophets and the Law" see the comments on 5:17–18. Here Jesus reverses the Old Testament order ("the Law and the Prophets") because it was a prophet—Malachi—who predicted the coming of Elijah (Malachi 4:5), and Jesus is about to equate John with Elijah. Malachi's prophecy of Elijah's coming is but one of many prophecies now being fulfilled, however. So Jesus adds "all" to "the Prophets." "And if you're willing" gently urges a welcoming of John as the Elijah who was to inaugurate the messianic time, and to welcome him as such despite the persecution of him, which contradicted Jewish expectation concerning a returned Elijah. Welcoming him as such would lead to the welcoming of Jesus' persecuted disciples (10:14, 40–42). This gentle urging evolves into a firm command to heed what Jesus has just said. For persecution is inevitable.

11:16–19: "But to what should I liken this generation? It's like little children sitting in the marketplaces who, calling to the others, [17]**say, 'We played the flute for you, and you didn't dance. We wailed, and you didn't beat your breasts.'** [18]**For John came neither eating** [regular food (see 3:4)] **nor drinking** [wine]**; and they** [the people of 'this generation'] **say, 'He has a demon.'** [19]**The Son of Man has come eating** [regular food] **and drinking** [wine]**; and they say, 'Behold, a gluttonous**

man and a wino, a friend of tax collectors and sinners.' And wisdom has been vindicated by her deeds." "*But* to what should I liken this generation?" draws a contrast between the willingness and heedfulness urged and commanded in 11:14–15 and the stubbornness of "this generation." Jesus' contemporaries—more particularly, those of them who've rejected John and him—make up "this generation" (see 12:38–42; 16:1–4; 17:17; 23:29–36 for "this generation" as scholars, Pharisees, Sadducees, and unbelievers in general). The plural of "marketplaces" matches the plural of "their cities" in 11:1. Each of those cities had a marketplace. In the comparison to little children, one group of them tried flute-playing to get another group of them to play mock wedding with them. But that group didn't respond with the dancing that typified weddings. So the first group tried wailing to get the second group to play mock funeral with them. But that group didn't respond with breast-beating, which typified funerals. They just couldn't, or wouldn't, be pleased. Likewise, the same people ("this generation") have failed to respond both to the ministry of John and to that of Jesus. Neither John's funeral-like abstentiousness nor Jesus' wedding-like partying has pleased them. Jesus is addressing "the crowds" (11:7). So if he were identifying "this generation" with them, we'd expect him to say "*you* say" rather than "*they* say" when introducing the charges that John has a demon and that Jesus is a glutton and a wino. So the crowds maintain their role as Jesus' professing disciples, whereas "this generation" refers to nondisciples, that is, people who've refused to believe no matter what they've seen, with the consequence that John's abstentiousness out in the wilderness has led them to charge him with demon-possession. And Jesus' partying in town with tax collectors and sinners has led the nondisciples to charge him with gluttony and drunkenness (compare Deuteronomy 21:20). As a self-designation derived from Daniel 7:13–14, "the Son of Man" connotes Jesus' authority to transgress the boundaries of ritual purity; and it's easy to think that his transgressing them led "this generation" to exaggerate his festive behavior just as they exaggerated John's abstentiousness into demon-possession. "The deeds" of "wisdom" match "the deeds of the Christ" in 11:2, so that Jesus as the Christ is equated with wisdom. Therefore the vindication of wisdom by her deeds means the vindication of Jesus by his deeds over against the charge that he's "a gluttonous man and a wino." "Behold" puts emphasis on this charge, which his deeds have refuted.

11:20–24: **Then he started denouncing the cities in which his very many miracles had taken place, because they** [the cities] **hadn't repented:** [21]**"Alas for you, Chorazin! Alas for you, Bethsaida! Because if the miracles that took place in you had taken place in Tyre and Sidon, they'd have repented long ago in sackcloth and ashes.** [22]**Nevertheless** [that is, despite the pride and prosperity for which these unrepentant cities were noted (see especially Ezekiel 26:1–28:24)] **I tell you, in the day of judgment it'll be more endurable for**

Tyre and Sidon than for you! [23]**And you, Capernaum, won't be lifted up as far as heaven, will you? You'll go down as far as Hades** [compare Isaiah 14:15]! **Because if the miracles that took place in you had taken place in Sodom, it would have remained till today** [instead of being obliterated]. [24]**Nevertheless** [that is, despite the notorious wickedness of unrepentant Sodom] **I tell you that in the Day of Judgment it'll be more endurable for the land of Sodom than for you!"** The named cities stand for their inhabitants. "Very many" stresses the miracles' large number, which heightens the guilt of the Galilean cities that have failed to repent; and the miracles as such heighten these cities' guilt by authenticating Jesus' call to repentance (4:17). "In sackcloth and ashes" heightens the degree of repentance that would have characterized the heathen cities of Tyre and Sidon if they'd seen Jesus perform miracles in them (for sackcloth and ashes as signs of repentance and mourning, see Esther 4:3; Isaiah 58:5; Jeremiah 6:26; Daniel 9:3; Jonah 3:5–6; and for Tyre and Sidon as typically heathen cities, see Isaiah 23; Jeremiah 25:22; 27:3; 47:4; Joel 3:4; Amos 1:9–10; Zechariah 9:2–4). The two occurrences of "I tell you" emphasize the greater severity of judgment on the Jewish cities in Galilee than on those heathen cities. Even Sodom would have repented and survived had its inhabitants seen Jesus' miracles. "The *land* of Sodom" adds the surrounding plain, with its other cities, to Sodom itself (see Genesis 19:23–28, for example). "In the *Day* of Judgment" specifies the Last Day as the time of judgment and implies a resurrection of the unrighteous. "Till today" complements "long ago" and puts further emphasis on the judgment-worthy guilt of Capernaum. Concerning "sackcloth and ashes" and the several Galilean cites, see the comments on Luke 10:13–15.

KNOWING GOD THROUGH
LEARNING FROM JESUS
Matthew 11:25–30

God's and Jesus' recognition of each other as Father and Son comes out in 11:25–27, and that recognition provides the basis for learning from Jesus (11:28–30).

11:25–26: **Answering, Jesus said during that time, "I acknowledge to you, Father, Lord of heaven and earth, that you've hidden these things from wise and intelligent people and revealed them to infants.** [26]**Yes, Father, because** [to do so] **became a pleasure before you."** "Answering"—but whom is Jesus answering? Nobody in the preceding context has asked him a question or done anything to which he could be responding. Ah, but what he says addresses God his Father in regard to the Father's hiding things from wise and intelligent people and revealing them to infants. So Jesus answers in the sense of responding to the Father's hiding and revealing. "During that time" connotes a suitable time in that Jesus' response is apropos to the Father's hiding and revealing. "Father" prepares for the reference to Jesus' disciples as "infants." "Lord of heaven and earth" balances that fatherhood with God's universal lordship, which makes remarkable in the extreme his hiding things from the wise and intelligent and revealing them to mere infants. "I acknowledge to you" shows that even Jesus, God's very Son, is struck by how remarkable the hiding and the revealing have been. Contextually, "these things" consist in "the deeds of the Christ" (11:2), that is, in "the deeds" of "wisdom" (11:19), the significance of which God has hidden from the wise and intelligent and revealed to infants. Since "the deeds of the Christ" equate with "the deeds" of "wisdom," the hiding of these things from the wise and intelligent reduces their supposed wisdom to folly, and their supposed intelligence to stupidity. The wise and intelligent foolishly depend on their native insight rather than on divine revelation. "Infants" describes the disciples figuratively as people who humbly accept divine revelation rather than depending on native insight. The hiding from wise and intelligent people and the revealing to infants highlight the sovereign grace of God as "Lord of heaven and earth." "Yes, Father" underlines that grace; and "because [to do so] became a pleasure before you" personifies the pleasure of God in doing such hiding and revealing and reemphasizes the sovereignty of his grace. This pleasure of his stands before him, so to speak, as a constant source of delight.

Now Jesus switches from talking *to* his Father to talking *about* him and their relationship to each other. **11:27: "All things have been given over to me by my Father; and except for the Father no one recognizes the Son, nor does anyone recognize the Father except for the Son and the person to whomever the Son decides to reveal** [the Father]." "All things" knows no limits (compare the Devil's offering Jesus "all the kingdoms of the world and their glory" [4:8–9]). God has given all things over to Jesus because Jesus is his Son and therefore his heir. "Except for the Father no one recognizes the Son" means that only God recognizes Jesus as his Son; for biologically speaking, Jesus has no human father (1:18–25; 2:15; 3:17). Hence, God has no heir except for Jesus. Correspondingly, "nor does anyone recognize the Father except for the Son" means that only Jesus recognizes God as his Father; for biologically speaking, no human being except for Jesus has God as his Father (see again the aforementioned passages). But to this exception of himself Jesus adds "the person to whomever the Son decides to reveal [the Father]," so that just as Jesus addressed God with "Father," he taught his disciples to do the same (6:9; see also his many references to "your Father" and 5:9, 45). "To whom the Son *decides* to reveal [the Father]" reemphasizes sovereign grace, only this time the Son's in addition to the Father's. Since 16:16–17 will make Jesus' identity as the Christ, the Son of the living God, the subject matter of God the Father's revelation to Simon Peter, the subject matter of the Son's revelation is the identity of God as the Father of believers in Jesus.

11:28–30: "[Come] **here to me, all you who are laboring** [like workers in a field] **and burdened** [like pack animals (compare Jeremiah 31:25)], **and I'll give you relief** [or 'rest' (compare Exodus 33:14)]. [29]**Take my yoke on you and learn from me, because I'm meek and humble in heart, and 'you'll find relief for your souls'** [Jeremiah 6:16]. [30]**For my yoke [is] comfortable and my burden is light."** Jesus' addressing "you" (plural) implies that in 11:27, too, he wasn't talking to himself any more than he was talking to God his Father (as he *had* been doing in 11:25–26). "[Come] here to me" shows that Jesus is now addressing nondisciples, for his disciples are already following him. In other words, he speaks in this text as an evangelist; and since the context provides no audience of nondisciples, he's addressing the nondisciples to whom Matthew's audience of disciples are to take the gospel. "All" casts a wide evangelistic net. "Laboring" connotes fatigue, and "burdened" connotes encumbrance. Since no ox could put a yoke on itself, "yoke" has to be taken as a figure of speech. And indeed it was a commonly understood figure of speech for obligations, such as obligations people could themselves take on (compare Acts 15:10; Galatians 5:1). Jesus' yoke and burden consist in the obligations he has commanded his disciples to take on themselves (as in chapters 5–7, for example). The comfortableness of his yoke and the lightness of his burden contrast with the heavy burdens the scholars and Pharisees have put on their followers according to chapter 23 (see especially verses 1–4). But in what do this comfortableness and lightness consist? In an interpretation of the Law less stringent than that of the scholars and Pharisees? Hardly! According to the Sermon on the Mount, Jesus interpreted the Law more stringently than they did (see especially 5:17–48). The heaviness of the burdens loaded by the scholars and Pharisees on their followers consisted in demands that those followers fawn on them in ways that fed their pride: "they do all their deeds to be observed by people. . . . And they love the prestigious couch at banquets and the prestigious seats in synagogues and greetings in the marketplaces and to be called 'Rabbi' [= 'my great one'] by people" (compare 6:1–6, 16–18). In contrast, the comfortableness of Jesus' yoke and the lightness of his burden consist in his meekness (= gentleness, considerateness) and humility of heart. These characteristics make his demands, more stringent though they are, easier to bear than the lesser demands of the scholars and Pharisees, whose overweening desire for recognition made them treat common folk like camels or donkeys to be overloaded rather than as yokefellows with whom to share in pulling. The relief Jesus promises doesn't wait for the consummation. It begins immediately on coming to him. "Learn from me" means to learn from Jesus' words and example, "learn" being the verbal form of "disciple" in Matthew's original Greek. God's and Jesus' recognition of each other as Father and Son makes learning from Jesus an education of the highest possible order. Since soul and body are distinguished from each other in 10:28 (compare 6:25), "your souls" probably means "your inner selves."

THE PHARISEES' PLOT TO DESTROY JESUS
Matthew 12:1–21

Since he has just written about the relief—that is, rest—that Jesus gives to those who labor (11:28–30), Matthew now brings in two stories about the issue of resting on the Sabbath. (The very word "Sabbath" means "rest.") The first story has to do with the disciples' plucking heads of wheat on the Sabbath (12:1–8), the second with Jesus' healing a man's withered hand on the Sabbath (12:9–14). These activities and Jesus' defending their legitimacy against Pharisaic criticism lead the Pharisees to plot against his life, so that he withdraws in accordance with Scripture (12:15–21). As a whole, then, this passage fits into the theme of persecution, a theme that pervades this part of Matthew's Gospel.

12:1–2: During that time Jesus traveled on the Sabbath through [fields] sown [with grain], and his disciples got hungry and started plucking heads of wheat and eating [them]. ²And the Pharisees, on seeing [them do so], said to him, "Behold, your disciples are doing what's unlawful to do on the Sabbath!" The word for "time" connotes seasonality, here a season of harvest. The Mosaic law allowed plucking grain on a journey through another man's field (Deuteronomy 23:25); but the Pharisees regarded the action as reaping and therefore as labor, prohibited on the Sabbath (compare Exodus 34:21). Hence their accusation of Jesus' disciples. "Behold" adds exclamation to accusation.

12:3–4: But he said to them, "You've read, haven't you, what David did when he got hungry, also the ones with him, ⁴how he entered into God's house and [how] they ate the loaves of presentation, which eating wasn't lawful for him [to do], nor for the ones with him [to do], except for the priests alone [to do] [1 Samuel 21:1–6]?" "You've read, haven't you . . . ?" implies an affirmative answer. *Of course* the Pharisees have read 1 Samuel 21:1–6, which tells what David did—and did without blame so far as that scriptural passage is concerned. So they know better than to accuse Jesus' disciples. Their doing so anyway makes the accusation sinister in its motivation. Jesus wasn't said to have gotten hungry, plucked heads of wheat, and eaten them. Only his disciples were said to have done so. David doesn't represent Jesus, then. Along with his companions, rather, David represents Jesus' disciples in hungering and eating. The comparison is apropos also because bread, such as David and his companions ate, comes from grain, such as Jesus' disciples were eating. Since Solomon hadn't yet built the first temple, "God's house" refers to the tabernacle (a tent, about which see Exodus 25:1–31:11; 35:4–40:33). "The loaves of presentation," one each for the twelve tribes of Israel, were kept there and replenished every Sabbath, the old loaves being eaten by priests in the tabernacle's outer room (Exodus 25:30; Leviticus 24:5–9). Often by inference, Jesus reads into 1 Samuel 21:1–6 a number of elements not mentioned there, at least not explicitly: (1) David's having companions with him; (2)

his and his companions' having gotten hungry; (3) God's house; (4) David's entering it rather than merely asking for bread to be brought out to him; and (5) the eating of the bread by David and his companions. According to Jesus, then, David and his companions broke the Law. By implication, Jesus' disciples have likewise broken the Law. So how can he, who said he didn't come to tear down the Law (5:17), defend them? Or will he?

12:5–8: "Or you've read in the Law, haven't you, that on the Sabbath the priests in the temple profane the Sabbath [by working there] and are innocent? ⁶And I tell you that something greater than the temple is here. ⁷And if you'd known what it is [= means], 'I want mercy and not [= more than] sacrifice [Hosea 6:6 (compare Matthew 9:13)],' you wouldn't have convicted the innocent [= my disciples]. ⁸For the Son of Man is Lord of the Sabbath." As in 12:3, "you've read . . . , haven't you?" implies an affirmative answer. This time Jesus adds "in the Law" for an allusion to the Old Testament legal requirement that priests do the work of offering burnt offerings, grain offerings, and drink offerings "every Sabbath" (Number 28:9–10). Jesus adds "in the temple" to this requirement in order to contemporize it with respect to the priests' working there every Sabbath in his and the Pharisees' own day. So the law of the temple, whose precincts render innocent—*legally* innocent—priests who profane the Sabbath by working there, overrides the law of the Sabbath, as the Pharisees would have to admit. To describe priestly service on the Sabbath as a *profanation* of it is a shocking way to say that the temple is more important than the Sabbath (presumably because the temple was made for God, but the Sabbath for human beings [Mark 2:27]). So it is, however. By the same token, though Jesus' disciples have profaned the Sabbath, they're innocent—*legally* innocent—because they're in the precincts, so to speak, of "something greater than the temple." With this phrase Jesus refers to himself. For just as God is greater than the temple in which his Spirit dwells, so too Jesus is greater than the temple in that he's "God with us" (1:23; see the comments on Mark 13:1–4 for the temple's greatness). We'd expect "greater" to be in the masculine gender because it refers to Jesus. But in Matthew's original Greek, "greater" is neuter to emphasize Jesus' quality of greatness instead of his personal identity. "I tell you" adds to this emphasis and thus helps make his argument *a fortiori*: if being in the temple precincts exempts priests legally from keeping the Sabbath, *how much more* does being in his presence exempt the disciples legally from keeping the Sabbath. "Is *here*" points up Jesus' presence as "God *with us.*" "And if you'd known what it is" introduces a quotation of Hosea 6:6 to the effect that if the Pharisees had known the Lord wants mercy and not sacrifice (such as the priests offer in the temple every Sabbath and thereby profane the Sabbath, yet innocently), they'd also have known not to convict the disciples for profaning the Sabbath innocently. "For the Son of Man is Lord of the Sabbath" tells *why* the Pharisees wouldn't have convicted Jesus' innocent disciples if they'd known the meaning of Hosea 6:6. The reason is that as "the Son of Man" who is "Lord of the Sabbath," Jesus himself is the "I" who wants mercy and not sacrifice, as already in 9:13 (see the comments on 9:11–13; and Daniel 7:13–14 for the authority of "one like a son of man"). And as "Lord of the Sabbath" he has mercifully allowed his disciples to pluck and eat heads of grain on the Sabbath.

12:9–12: And on moving from there [= from the grain fields of 12:1], **he went into their synagogue.** So Jesus moves from one place to another because of opposition, just as he told his disciples to do (10:23). As usual, "*their* synagogue" reflects the separation of church and synagogue from each other, only in this case "their" makes a particular reference to the antagonistic Pharisees' synagogue. [10]**And behold, a human being having a withered hand!** Thus the stage is set for a demonstration of what is meant by the Lord of the Sabbath's wanting mercy and not sacrifice. The exclamatory "behold" matches that in 12:2 and thus sets up a parallel between the story in 12:1–8 and the present one in 12:9–14. Both stories feature opposition from the Pharisees. A reason for the translation "a human being" rather than the usual "a man" will come out shortly. The presence of a human being with a withered hand raises a question concerning the legality of healing on the Sabbath: **And they** [the Pharisees] **asked him** [Jesus], **saying, "**[Tell us] **if it's lawful to heal** [a human being] **on the Sabbath**" [the Pharisees deliberately egging him on], **in order that they might accuse him** [if he gave them what they considered a heretical answer]. Rabbinic law allowed medical help on the Sabbath if life was immediately endangered, but the healing of a withered hand could wait a day. The Pharisees presuppose that Jesus can indeed perform a miraculous healing! [11]**And he said to them, "What human being will there be from among you who'll have one sheep—and if this** [sheep] **should fall into a pit on the Sabbath, he'll grab hold of it and raise** [it out of the pit], **won't he?"** Implied answer: Of course he will, even though it's the Sabbath. [12]**"Therefore how much more valuable is a human being than a sheep!"** "Therefore" implies that if a human being will rescue a sheep from a pit on the Sabbath, it makes sense that he'll rescue a disabled human being on the Sabbath by healing him. For a human being is much more valuable than a sheep. Now we see the reason for translating with "a human being" rather than with "a man": Jesus constructs an argument that compares the relation of human beings to each other with the relation of human beings to an animal. Having "*one* sheep" makes the human being's case physically as bad as the case of someone who has only one sheep is economically bad. **"And so, it's lawful to act well on the Sabbath."** "And so" introduces a legal conclusion drawn from the much greater value of a human being, and "act well" describes the healing of a human being on the Sabbath.

12:13–14: Then he says to the human being [with a withered hand], **"Stretch out your hand." And he**

stretched [it] **out; and it was restored, healthy like the other** [hand]. The present tense of "says" highlights Jesus' command. Obedience leads to a healing of the hand. "Healthy like the other [hand]" describes the healing as complete. So Jesus has thrown down the gauntlet not only by *saying* it's lawful to heal a human being on the Sabbath but also by *performing* a healing on the Sabbath. (The Pharisees had only asked for an opinion.) [14]**And on going out** [of the synagogue mentioned in 12:9], **the Pharisees took counsel** [= consulted with one another] **against him, as to how they might destroy him.** This murderous plot of the unmerciful Pharisees against the merciful Jesus intensifies the motif of persecution that Matthew is pursuing. His audience should consider it an honor to be persecuted as their Lord was persecuted (compare 10:24–25).

12:15–21: And Jesus, on coming to know [about the plot], **withdrew from there. And many crowds followed him, and he healed them all.** Jesus' withdrawal from the location of danger to his life and limb results in a continuation and extension of ministry and sets again an example for the disciples to follow (compare 10:23; 12:9). As in 4:25; 8:1, the "many crowds" that "followed" Jesus stand for his professing disciples. Here they follow him in his exemplary withdrawal from mortal danger. That he "healed them all" displays his mercy, also exemplary, especially against the backdrop of the Pharisees' lack of mercy. [16]**And he reprimanded them that they not make him manifest,** [17]**in order that what was spoken through Isaiah the prophet might be fulfilled, saying,** [18]**"Behold, my servant, whom I've chosen, my beloved, in whom my soul has taken delight! I'll put my Spirit on him, and he'll announce justice for the nations.** [19]**He won't wrangle. Neither will he shout. Neither will anyone hear his voice in the broad** [streets]. [20]**He'll not break off a crushed reed and he'll not extinguish a smoldering wick until he thrusts forth justice to victory** [that is, successfully]. [21]**And nations will hope in his name** [Isaiah 42:1–4; 44:2b]**."** "That they not make him manifest" means that Jesus didn't want his followers to publicize his whereabouts, lest the murderously plotting Pharisees track him down. His example of fleeing persecution comes to the fore yet again. "He *reprimanded* them" suggests that his followers verged on publicizing his whereabouts. The sternness of his command that they not do so carries a woeful implication for false disciples who give true disciples over to their persecutors (24:10). The reprimand has the purpose of fulfilling "what was spoken through Isaiah the prophet" (see the comments on 3:3). So Jesus goes about fulfilling Old Testament prophecy quite deliberately. As "God with us" (1:23), why shouldn't he?

"Behold" highlights the servant in Isaiah's prophecy. "My" and "I" refer there to the Lord God. His having "chosen" the servant alludes to Jesus' distinctive relation to God. But since the word for "servant" also means "boy, child," the prophecy proceeds to describe the servant as God's "beloved," in whom God's innermost being ("soul") has taken delight, just as at Jesus' baptism: "This is my beloved Son, in whom I took delight" (3:17 [compare 17:5]). Through Isaiah the Lord said he would put his Spirit on his chosen, beloved servant. And again at Jesus' baptism, God's descending Spirit came on Jesus (3:16). Jesus hasn't, and won't, announce justice *to* the nations; for apart from several nonprogrammatic exceptions, his ministry is limited to "the lost sheep of the house of Israel" (15:24). But he'll announce justice *for* the nations by sending them his disciples to proclaim the good news of God's reign (24:14; 28:18–20). "Justice" refers to the justice of God in soon opening his kingdom to believers from all nations, not from the Jewish nation alone. He'll announce such justice for the nations rather than wrangling to get justice for himself. Meanwhile, because of withdrawing to avoid mortal danger, he won't shout or preach on main streets. Otherwise, the Pharisees could track him down easily (see 12:14). "A crushed reed" and "a smoldering wick" represent the harried and huddled, tired and burdened Jews to whom he's presently ministering. His not breaking such a reed or extinguishing such a wick represents the mercy of his ministry to them, again in contrast to the mercilessness of the Pharisees in their disapproval of Jesus' healing a withered hand on the Sabbath. His ministry to the Jews will last till he successfully "thrusts forth justice." The thrusting forth will be verbal, as twice in 12:35 (with 12:34), 36–37, and will consist in Jesus' announcing the Great Commission, according to which all nations, not only the Jews, are to be discipled (28:18–20). The nations' hoping in the servant's name will mark the Great Commission as successful (see 1:21 for "Jesus" as the salvific name of the servant). Thus Jesus' withdrawing from persecution and pursuing unobtrusive itinerant evangelism along the way forecasts the disciples' flight from place to place in a persecuted ministry that carries the gospel to all nations.

THE PERSECUTORS' FALSE AND UNFORGIVABLE ACCUSATION
Matthew 12:22–37

Matthew has just quoted Isaiah to the effect that the Lord God has put his Spirit on Jesus (12:18). So now he narrates a story in which Jesus' healing of a demoniac draws the charge that he exorcises demons by Beelzebul rather than by God's Spirit. As usual in this Gospel, though, the words of Jesus preponderate.

12:22–24: Then a demon-possessed blind and deaf-mute [man] **was brought to him** [Jesus]**; and he healed him, so that the deaf-mute spoke and saw.** [23]**And all the crowds were amazed and were saying, "Is this** [Jesus] **perhaps the Son of David?"** [24]**But the Pharisees, on hearing** [what the crowds were saying]**, said, "This** [guy] **isn't casting out demons except by Beelzebul, ruler of the demons** [or, as it could be translated, 'by the Beelzebulian ruler of the demons' (compare 9:32–34)]**."** "So that the deaf-mute spoke and saw" emphasizes Jesus'

having *healed* the man. The Pharisees, who've caught up with Jesus so as to pursue their plot (12:14), shift the emphasis to Jesus' having *exorcised* the man's demon. Meanwhile "all the crowds," representing as usual the large, mixed church of Matthew's day, raise the possibility that Jesus is "the son of David," as in fact Matthew's audience know he is (see 1:1–17 with comments; compare 9:27). Some translations have the crowds asking, "This [Jesus] isn't the Son of David, is he?" That would be a preferable translation if it weren't for the crowds' amazement, which turns a question that would imply a negative answer (as in those translations) into a question raising the possibility of an affirmative answer ("Is this [Jesus] perhaps the Son of David?"). The mere possibility of an affirmative answer sparks the Pharisees' charge that Jesus is casting out demons "by Beelzebul" (see the comments on 10:25). Implied is that as the demons' ruler, Beelzebul has given Jesus authority to cast them out, as though Jesus is acting as Beelzebul's hatchet man.

12:25–28: And knowing their imaginations, he said to them [the Pharisees], **"Every kingdom divided against itself is devastated, and every city or household divided against itself won't stand.** [26]**And if Satan is casting out Satan, he was divided against himself. So how will his kingdom stand?"** Implied answer: it won't, because it'll self-destruct. [27]**"And if I'm casting out demons by Beelzebul, by whom are your sons casting** [them] **out? On account of this** [the hypocrisy of your accusing me but not your sons of casting out demons by Beelzebul]**, *they* will be your judges** [in that none other than your own offspring will condemn you for implying that if I'm casting out demons by Beelzebul, they must be doing the same]**.** [28]**But if I'm casting out demons by God's Spirit, then God's reign has come upon you."** "Knowing their imaginations" echoes "seeing their imaginations" in 9:4, where the phrase refers to what the scholars said "within themselves," and therefore implies here Jesus' clairsentience. Thus he pierces through the hypocrisy of the Pharisees' pious appearance. "Imaginations" implies the falsity of the Pharisees' thinking. "*Every* kingdom" and "*every* city or household" indicate the inevitability of collapse in cases of internal division. Civil war in a kingdom results in the kingdom's devastation. Civic strife leads to the subjugation of a city by a besieging army. And contention within a royal household, as when princes vie with each other for the throne, makes that household easy prey for usurpers. "If Satan is casting out Satan" implies both that he's Beelzebul and that the demons are so much his agents that for him to oppose them by enabling Jesus to exorcise them would be for Satan to oppose himself and ensure the downfall of his kingdom. But he isn't that stupid! The switch from present tense in "if Satan *is* casting out Satan" to a past tense in "he *was* divided against himself" makes the hypothetical division against himself a precondition for Satan's supposedly casting out Satan. "Your sons" implies a generational distinction between the Pharisees, who are charging Jesus, and their sons, who are practicing exorcism. His argument doesn't necessarily imply the actuality of their sons' exorcisms. It need only point to the hypocrisy of stigmatizing Jesus' exorcisms but not purported exorcisms by their sons. Jesus then presses home the alternative that his exorcism of demons signals the recent arrival of God's reign, which is defeating the reign of Satan over human victims through his demons. "By God's Spirit" provides an exact antithesis to "by Beelzebul," displays fulfillment of the recently quoted prophecy of Isaiah that the Lord God would put his Spirit on Jesus his servant (12:18), anticipates blasphemy of the Holy Spirit in 12:31–32, and supplies a trinitarian allusion to the Spirit, God, and Jesus (as in 3:16–17; 28:19). Instead of Matthew's usual "reign *of heaven*" we have here "*God's* reign" for a sharper contrast with foregoing references to *Satan's* kingdom/reign.

12:29–30: "Or how can anyone enter into the house of the strong [man] **and plunder his** [household] **effects unless he first ties up the strong** [man] [compare Isaiah 49:24–25]**?"** Implied answer: no one can. **"And then** [if he ties up the strong man] **he'll plunder his house.** [30]**The person who isn't with me is against me, and the person who isn't gathering with me is scattering."** Jesus is addressing his opponents, the Pharisees, and therefore equates them with someone who doesn't accompany him as his disciples do accompany him, and with someone who isn't gathering with him but instead is scattering what he (Jesus) has gathered. So scattering represents opposition to Jesus. But what has been gathered that's now being scattered? And in what do the gathering and scattering consist? The gathering consists in Jesus' gathering "his wheat into the granary," that is, in Jesus' bringing people into God's kingdom (3:12); and the scattering consists in persecution by opponents of Jesus, so that his people flee (10:23; compare 26:31, where scattering has to do with persecution, and 9:36, which occurs as here in connection with harvesting [9:37–38]). So we have the language of persecution such as dominates chapters 10–12. Who then is the strong man? Answer: Jesus, whose plundered household effects are his disciples (compare Jesus as a householder in 4:13; 9:10, and 10:25 for his disciples as members of his household). "Strong" has described him before (3:11), and "plunder" has referred to persecution in 11:12 and will describe satanic activity in 13:19 (there translated "snatches away"). The introductory "Or" makes the plundering—that is, the persecution—an alternative opposed to the arrival of God's reign in Jesus' Spirit-empowered exorcisms. But just as the questions beginning with "How?" in 12:26, 34 implied an impossibility, so too here the question, "Or how can anyone enter . . . and plunder . . . unless he first ties up the strong [man]?" implies an impossibility. Satan can't tie up Jesus. In the end, therefore, persecution won't prevail (see 10:26–33 and 16:18: "the gates of Hades won't overpower it [Jesus' church]"). "And then he'll plunder his [the strong man's] house" is therefore reduced to a nonevent.

12:31–32: "On account of this I tell you, every sin and blasphemy will be forgiven for human beings [=

for their benefit]**, but the blasphemy of the Spirit** [in the sense of 'slander against the Spirit'] **won't be forgiven.** [32]**And whoever speaks a word** [= a statement] **against the Son of Man—it** [that slanderous statement] **will be forgiven for him, but whoever speaks** [a word/statement] **against the Holy Spirit—it won't be forgiven for him either in this age** [present time] **or in the coming** [age]**."** "On account of this" means on account of opposition to Jesus, accompanied by the charge that he casts out demons by Beelzebul/Satan rather than by God's Spirit. Jesus has shown the Pharisees the *absurdity* of their charge. Now he shows them its *gravity*. "I tell you" stresses this gravity. In view of Jesus' call to repentance (4:17), "every sin and blasphemy will be forgiven for human beings" means they'll be forgiven on condition of repentance. "*Every*" underlines comprehensiveness of forgiveness. "Blasphemy of the Spirit" consists here in attributing Jesus' exorcisms to Beelzebul/Satan rather than to God's Spirit. "Speaks a word against" equates with "blasphemy." "Whoever" eliminates any exceptions on either side of the ledger, whether for forgiveness in the case of repentance for every sin and blasphemy, even blasphemy against Jesus the Son of Man, or for unforgiveness in the case of blasphemy against the Holy Spirit. "Either in this age or in the coming [age]" underscores the eternality of unforgiveness. And the repetition of these truths by means of synonymously parallel statements ("every sin and blasphemy . . ." and "whoever speaks a word . . .") adds a final emphasis. The possibility of forgiveness for someone who speaks against the Son of Man seems at first to contradict Jesus' denying the person who denies him according to 10:33. In Matthew, however, the forgivable sin of blaspheming the Son of Man is committed by someone who has never professed to follow Jesus, whereas he'll unforgivingly disown a professing disciple who has disowned him (see the comments on 10:33).

Jesus' knowing the Pharisees' "imaginations" (12:25) now leads him to talk about the relation between thinking and doing. **12:33: "Either make a tree good and its fruit good, or make a tree rotten and its fruit rotten. For a tree is known by** [its] **fruit."** The earlier axiom that a good tree *produces* good fruits and a rotten tree rotten fruits (7:17) here turns into a command either to *make* the tree and its fruit good or to *make* the tree rotten and its fruit rotten. Why this shift? It's to avoid disparity between inward condition and outward appearance—that is, to avoid hypocrisy, such as characterizes the Pharisees whom Jesus is addressing (15:7; 22:18; 23:13, 15, 23, 25, 27–29). To avoid hypocrisy you shouldn't only make the tree and its fruit good. You should also make the tree and its fruit *rotten*! Jesus doesn't say to make the fruit of a *good* tree good, and that of a *rotten* tree rotten. Rather, make the tree and its fruit *correspond* to each other. The tree represents a person's thinking. Its fruit represents the person's doing. "*For* a tree is known by [its] fruit" makes Jesus' ability to *recognize* hypocrisy (see again 12:25 with 6:2, 5, 16; 7:5 and the aforementioned passages) a reason for avoiding it.

12:34–35: "**Offspring of vipers** [describing Jesus' addressees, the Pharisees], **how can you, being evil, speak good things?**" Implied answer: you can't. "**For the mouth speaks out of the surplus of the heart** [as though your thoughts overflow in spoken words]. [35]**A good person thrusts good things** [= legal tender, representing truthful words] **out of** [his] **good treasure** [= his fund of truthful thoughts], **and an evil person thrusts evil things** [= counterfeit coins, representing deceptive words] **out of his evil treasure** [= his fund of deceptive thoughts]." So the character of your thoughts determines the character of your words. For example, speaking against the Holy Spirit is determined by a thought (in this case an "imagination" according to 12:25) so wrongly evil that the speaking will never be forgiven (12:31–32).

12:36–37: "**And I tell you** [plural, as earlier] **that every deedless word that people speak—they'll render an account concerning it in the Day of Judgment. [37]For by your words you'll be justified, and by your words you'll be convicted** ['your' and 'you' being singular in this statement]." The traditional translation, "every *idle* word," leaves the misimpression that Jesus is talking about random remarks. A truer translation is "every *deedless* word." It goes without saying, at least for the moment, that in the Day of Judgment people will give an account of all their deeds (see 7:22–23, for example). Jesus is saying here that in the Day of Judgment people will give an account of their words as well as, and even apart from, their deeds—that is, whether or not their words had issued in deeds. "Every" individualizes the words and takes in all that's spoken, whether good or evil. Whether or not followed up by a corresponding deed, speaking against the Holy Spirit examples an evil word that will lead to conviction. But a word of repentance, as in the confession of sins (see 3:6 with 3:2), that produces good deeds ("fruit in keeping with repentance" according to 3:8)—now there's a basis for justification in the Day of Judgment! The striking shift from a string of plurals in "you" to the singular of "your" and "you" brings the issue of conviction versus justification down to the individual level. Since the Pharisees have "convicted" Jesus' innocent disciples (12:7), the coming conviction of the Pharisees for their having spoken against the Holy Spirit makes for poetic justice.

THE WICKEDNESS OF JESUS' PERSECUTORS AND THEIR COMING JUDGMENT
Matthew 12:38–45

12:38: Then some of the scholars and Pharisees answered, saying, "Teacher, we want to see a sign from you." The Pharisees continue to hound Jesus (compare 12:24). Because Jesus' response will deal with the Old Testament, the field of the scholars' expertise, Matthew mentions them too. The Pharisees included scholars in their number, anyway. In fact, Matthew's phraseology could well be interpreted to mean "some of the scholars who were Pharisees." "Answered" makes their request

for a sign a retort to Jesus' foregoing pronouncement of eternal condemnation on them for their having blasphemed the Holy Spirit (12:24–37). Addressing him with "Teacher" suits the ambience of scholarship due to the introduction of scholars. Since the Pharisees have charged that Jesus was casting out demons by Beelzebul/Satan (12:24), now they're asking for a sign not subject to interpretation as satanically aided. In effect they're saying, "You deny you're casting out demons by Beelzebul. Show us that you're not. We want evidence, not assertion."

12:39–40: And he, answering, told them, "An evil and adulterous generation seeks after a sign, and a sign won't be given to it except for the sign of Jonah the prophet. [40]For just as 'Jonah was in the belly of the sea-monster for three days and three nights [Jonah 1:17],' **thus the Son of Man will be in the heart of the earth for three days and three nights.**" Jesus' counter reply first takes the form of an accusation: it's "an evil and adulterous generation" that "seeks after a sign," as "some of the scholars and Pharisees" have done. He doesn't say, "*You* are an evil and adulterous generation," though. So the generalizing phrase, "*An* evil and adulterous generation," while including those scholars and Pharisees, can refer also to unbelievers in other times and places. The addition of "adulterous" to "evil" echoes Old Testament phraseology for religious infidelity (Isaiah 57:3; Jeremiah 3:1–4:2; 13:27; Ezekiel 23; Hosea 1–3; 5:3–4 [see also Mark 8:38; James 4:4]). Since Jesus' deeds have counted as "the deeds of the Christ" and "the deeds of wisdom" (11:2, 19), seeking for a sign different from those deeds counts as a rejection of them and justifies a description of the seekers as "evil and adulterous." Jesus adds "the prophet" to "Jonah" to stress his own coming fulfillment of the prophetic typology apparent in what happened to Jonah. "In the heart of the earth" corresponds to "in the belly of the sea-monster," picks up the term "heart" from "in the heart of the seas" in Jonah 2:3, refers to the realm of the dead (not simply to a grave), and points forward to Jesus' time in that realm. The limitation to three days and three nights alludes to his resurrection (compare the explicit references to resurrection in the very next verses [12:41–42]). Jesus stayed in the realm of the dead only parts of three twenty-four hour periods (part of Good Friday, all Saturday, and part of Easter Sunday), not three whole days and nights. But the reference to three days and three nights comes out of Jonah 1:17 and causes no problem, because the Jews reckoned part of a twenty-four hour period for the whole (see Genesis 42:17–18; 1 Samuel 30:1, 12–13; 2 Chronicles 10:5, 12; Esther 4:16–5:1 [compare the comments on Matthew 27:63]). So the sign of Jonah, the only sign these scholars and Pharisees are going to get, will consist in the limitation of Jesus' sojourn in the realm of the dead to three days and three nights. Prospective martyrs in the church may then take heart from this allusion to his resurrection, for it guarantees their own resurrection to eternal life.

12:41–42: "The Ninevite men will be resurrected at the judgment with this generation; and they'll condemn it, because they repented at Jonah's preaching [see Jonah 3]; and behold, something more than Jonah [is] here! 42The queen of the South will be raised at the judgment with this generation; and she'll condemn it, because she came from the extremities of the earth [= a very long way] to hear Solomon's wisdom [for which see 1 Kings 10:4, 6, 8]; and behold, something more than Solomon [is] here!" "The sign of Jonah" in 12:39–40 leads naturally to Jonah's "preaching" to "the Ninevite men." "This generation" narrows "A . . . generation" of 12:39 down to Jesus' contemporaries, in particular the scholars and Pharisees who've just asked him for a sign. Since "the sign of Jonah the prophet" alluded to Jesus' coming death and resurrection, the "something" that's "more than Jonah" is Jesus in that his death-and-resurrection exceeds Jonah's being preserved in the belly of the sea-monster for three days and three nights. And since the deeds of Jesus as the Christ (11:2) equate with the deeds of wisdom (11:19), the "something" that's more than Solomon is Jesus in that his deeds exceed even those of that wise king, the one who built the first temple in Jerusalem. For Nineveh, "the South," "condemn," the two instances of "behold," and the neuter gender in two instances of "something," see the comments on Luke 11:29–32; but note that "something more than" carries different references in these two Gospels. The condemnation of Jesus' persecutors at the Last Judgment stands as an encouragement to his persecuted disciples, who can expect like vindication.

12:43–45: "And whenever an unclean spirit comes out from a human being, it goes through waterless places seeking rest and doesn't find [it] [contrast the "rest/relief" that those who come to Jesus do find (11:28–29)]." Waterless places are devoid of houses, whose inhabitants would require a supply of water nearby. 44"Then it says, 'I'll return to my house [the human being in whom I dwelt earlier], from where I came out.' And on coming [back], it finds [the house] empty, swept, and put in order. 45Then it goes and takes along with itself seven other spirits more evil than itself and, on entering [the house], settles down there. And the last [circumstances] of that human being become worse than the first [circumstances]. It'll be this way also for this evil generation." "This evil generation" relates the present material to the condemnation of "this generation" at the judgment (12:39–42), and the metaphor of a house inhabited by evil spirits recalls the possible relation of "Beelzebul" to "houseowner" (10:25). The human being that houses the unclean spirit stands for the generation consisting of scholars and Pharisees. The unclean spirit itself stands for the evil of this generation. The unclean spirit's absence stands for this generation's lack of enough righteousness to fill the void (compare 5:20). The return of the unclean spirit with seven others worse than itself stands for an outburst of fully multiplied evil on the scholars' and Pharisees' part,

an outburst that will belie their righteousness. They'll help engineer Jesus' crucifixion; and they'll bribe the guards at Jesus' tomb to suppress, if possible, the truth of Jesus' resurrection (26:57; 27:41, 62; 28:11–15). The unclean spirit's having found the house empty, swept, and orderly stands for this generation's readiness to be taken over by multiplied evil, and it's this multiplied evil that the Ninevite men and the queen of the South will condemn at the judgment (12:41–42).

THE PERSECUTED AS THE FAMILY
OF THE HEAVENLY FATHER
Matthew 12:46–50

Matthew now finishes out chapters 11–12 with a contrast between Jesus' true family and those who persecute him and them.

12:46–47: While he was still speaking to the crowds, behold, his mother and siblings were standing outside, seeking to speak to him. 47And someone told him, "Behold, your mother and your siblings are standing outside seeking to speak to you." "While he was still speaking to the crowds" implies that in 12:43–45 Jesus had switched from addressing some of the scholars and Pharisees in 12:24–42 to addressing the accompanying crowds, whom he'd addressed earlier in 12:15–16. The first "behold" calls attention to the surprising appearance on the scene of his mother and siblings. (Since Jewish men usually married women a number of years younger than they, presumably Joseph the husband of Mary and foster father of Jesus is dead by now; and because of Jesus' virginal conception and birth, his siblings are half siblings [compare the comments on 1:24–25].) They were "standing outside," but outside what? "The house" according to 13:1. So when Jesus withdrew in 12:15, he apparently went to his house in Capernaum (compare 4:13), and everything that Matthew has narrated since then has taken place there. The standing of Jesus' mother and siblings outside therefore symbolizes that they—unlike the crowds, whom Matthew is about to call Jesus' "disciples" (compare the comments on 4:25–5:1; 7:28–29) and whom Jesus is about to call his true family (12:48–50)—don't belong to his household, his true family. The fact that someone has to tell him, with a second "Behold," about his mother's and siblings' seeking to speak to him emphasizes their not belonging. And Matthew's omitting to say why Jesus' mother and siblings were seeking to speak to him leaves the emphasis solely on their not belonging (but see 27:56, 61; 28:1; Acts 1:14; 1 Corinthians 9:5; Galatians 1:19 for a later change in this respect).

12:48–50: And he, answering, said to the one who'd told him [about his mother and siblings], "Who is my mother, and who are my siblings?" 49And stretching out his hand toward his disciples [that is, pointing at them], he said, "Behold, my mother and my siblings! 50For whoever does the will of my Father in heaven—

he/she is my brother and sister and mother." Jesus doesn't address his words concerning those who do the heavenly Father's will *to* the crowds *about* his disciples. To do so would distinguish the crowds *from* his disciples. Instead, he addresses these words to his informant *about* the crowds *as* his disciples (see again the comments on 4:25–5:1; 7:28–29). The unrealism of more than one crowd's presence in Jesus' house adds support to Matthew's making the crowds who follow Jesus represent the large number of professing disciples from all nations in the later church. "Behold" makes this representation exclamatory, and "For" makes doing the will of Jesus' heavenly Father explanatory of the representation. Doing his will activates the petition, "Your will come to pass on earth as also [it comes to pass] in heaven" (6:10), and presupposes learning the Father's will from Jesus, who as the Son knows God as his Father (11:25–30). The picking up of "whoever does the will of my Father in heaven" with "he/she" underscores Jesus' identification of his true family. His biological half sisters haven't yet come into view, but they will in 13:55–56. So the mention of his true "sister" alongside his true "brother" (both in the singular) justifies the foregoing translation "siblings" (plural) rather than the usual translation "brothers." Jesus has taken notice of young women as well as young men and older women in the crowds of his disciples. But "father" is missing in his family of disciples, not only because his foster father Joseph hasn't come with his mother and half brothers and sisters, but also because God is the sole Father in this new kind of family. So in the midst of persecution Jesus' disciples may comfort and encourage themselves that they belong to the family to which he belongs, the family of his caring heavenly Father.

FALSE DISCIPLES AS THOSE WHO LACK UNDERSTANDING, TRUE DISCIPLES AS THOSE WHO HAVE IT AND GAIN FURTHER UNDERSTANDING
Matthew 13:1–52

In 13:1–52 Matthew brings together eight parables for Jesus' third long discourse in this Gospel (see chapters 5–7 and 10 for the first two). After the introductory gathering of many crowds (13:1–2), the parable of the sower portrays the reason for Jesus' speaking in parables (13:3–9). When disciples from among the crowds approach him with a question concerning that reason, his answer includes an explanation of the parable (13:10–23). As it turns out, he speaks in parables because those who don't have understanding—that is, false disciples—fall under the judgment of hearing only parabolic riddles and because those who do have understanding—that is, true disciples—come into the good fortune of gaining further understanding through Jesus' explanation of these riddles (compare 11:25–27; 16:17).

After that parable about parables and its interpretation, Matthew puts six more parables. In contrast with the introductory parable of the sower, they all begin with a reference to the kingdom of heaven. The first deals with wheat and tares and emphasizes their separation at the end (13:24–30). The second and third constitute a pair dealing with a mustard tree (13:31–32) and a leavened lump of dough (13:33) and emphasizing large size. At the close of these first three of the six there's a citation of fulfilled prophecy concerning Jesus' parabolic speech to the crowds (13:34–35). At the start of the second three Jesus leaves the crowds, enters "the house," entertains the approach of disciples, and explains to them the tares and wheat in order to portray them as true disciples who gain understanding because of their already having some (13:36–43). Further understanding comes through a second pair of parables, those of the treasure (13:44) and pearl (13:45–46), both of which emphasize the value of understanding for entrance into the kingdom. The last of the six parables deals with good and foul fish and makes a bookend with the first of the six by reemphasizing separation at the end (13:47–50). Matthew's breaking up the pair of parables concerning the wheat and tares and the good and foul fish in order to use them as bookends for the other two pairs causes the main stress to fall on the separation of true and false disciples at the Last Judgment (compare 5:19–20; 7:13–27; 22:11–14; 24:45–25:13).

This stress explains in turn the distinction between the crowds and the disciples. The crowds represent the whole mixed body of professing disciples, the false as well as the true—therefore the addressing of parables that emphasize large size (the mustard tree and the huge lump of dough) to the crowds. The disciples who approach Jesus out of the crowds and receive further understanding because of prior understanding represent the true among the false (see especially 13:2, 10–17, 24, 31, 33–34, 36)—therefore the addressing of the parables of value (the treasure and the pearl) to the true disciples alone. The concluding eighth parable of a disciple as a scholar who speaks what he has recently learned ("new things") as well as what he'd already understood ("old things" [13:51–52]) underscores the difference between the true and the false among the crowds who follow Jesus. The true had understanding prior to the parables and gain more of it through those parables, whereas the false lacked it prior to the parables and lose it in the parables.

OLD UNDERSTANDING AS A HUMAN RESPONSIBILITY
Matthew 13:1–23

***13:1–2*: On that day, after going out of the house Jesus was sitting alongside the Sea [of Galilee]. ²And many crowds were gathered together to him, so that on getting into a boat he was sitting down; and all the crowd were standing on the shore.** "On that day" refers to the day when the episodes of 12:15–50 took place. See the comments on 4:13; 9:10; 12:15, 46 for "the house" as Jesus' house in Capernaum. "Going out" anticipates the going out of the sower in the upcoming parable about a sower and thus preliminarily identifies Jesus with that sower (13:3). By sitting, Jesus takes the authoritative posture of a teacher (compare 5:1; 23:2). A doubling of the reference to sitting emphasizes his didactic authority. The gathering together of "many crowds" to him previews the masses who later came into the church as professing disciples. Once clustered together, the many crowds become a single "crowd." The crowd's "standing on the shore" contrasts with Jesus' sitting and thus lays further emphasis on his didactic authority. "All" keeps the entirety of this crowd onshore so as to protect the uniqueness of his authoritative position and posture.

13:3–6: And he spoke many things to them in parables, saying, "Behold, a sower went out to sow [seeds]. ⁴And in his sowing, some [seeds] fell on the edge of a path; and on coming, birds devoured them." A parable contains a comparison and may refer to a proverb, riddle, fable, or allegory. "Behold" calls special attention to the sower who went out to sow seeds; and after Jesus' "going out," we can hardly miss the identification of the sower with Jesus (compare 13:37: "the one sowing the good seed is the Son of Man"). In the sowing near a path, some seeds fell on the edge of the path accidentally. There, hardness of soil packed down by human traffic left those seeds exposed to voracious birds, which took advantage of the exposure. **⁵"But other [seeds] fell on rocky [ground], where they didn't have much soil; and immediately they rose up out of [the ground] because of not having depth of soil. ⁶But when the sun had risen up, they [the seed sprouts] were scorched, and because of not having root, they were dried out [by the sun]."** For explanation, see the comments on Mark 4:5–6.

13:7–9: "But other seeds fell on thorns, and the thorns came up and choked them." We can't tell whether some seeds fell where the sower couldn't detect seeds of thorns hidden in the soil, or whether some seeds fell accidentally among dried up thorns from the previous year (compare Jeremiah 4:3). But so much emphasis falls on the thorns' coming up and choking the sower's seeds that the seeds' sprouting doesn't even get mentioned. **⁸"But other [seeds] fell on good soil and were giving fruit, one [seed] a hundredfold, but another [seed] sixtyfold, but another [seed] thirtyfold."** The good soil is receptive rather than hard like that of the pathway, deep rather than thin like that overlying some rock, and free of competition rather than infested like that containing thorns. The seeds falling on this good soil turn out to be three in number. "A hundredfold" comes first as the best example (see Genesis 26:12 for a hundredfold yield as excellent). Two instances of "but" introduce the less desirable examples of sixtyfold and thirtyfold. As elsewhere in Matthew, "fruit" stands for deeds, here for good deeds (3:8, 10; 7:16–20; 12:33 and so on). **⁹"The [person] who has ears [to hear with] had better hear!"** This indirect command ("The [person] who has" rather than "You") includes anyone outside as well as inside Jesus' immedi-

ate audience, so that everyone in the audience of Matthew's Gospel, for instance, is included. Such a person is supposed to put his ears to good use by listening to the parable, which in 13:18–23 Jesus will interpret as a parable about listening, about hearing. Having ears to hear with doesn't imply there are people without ears. It emphasizes that having ears obligates their owner to use them for hearing.

13:10–12: And on approaching [Jesus], the disciples said to him, "Why are you speaking to them in parables?" ¹¹And answering, he said to them, "Because to you it has been given to know the secrets of the kingdom of heaven, but to those [= 'them' in the disciples' question] it hasn't been given [to know those secrets]. ¹²For whoever has [knowledge]—it'll be given to him [to know the secrets]; and it [his knowledge] will be made to flourish [compare Proverbs 1:5]. But whoever doesn't have [knowledge], even what he has will be taken away from him." The secrets will be given to these disciples in Jesus' upcoming explanations of parables. His giving them the secrets indicates the genuineness of their discipleship, so that "them" and "those" refer to the rest of the crowd. Because the rest haven't understood Jesus' plain—that is, unparabolic—speech (as in 4:17, for example), they haven't borne the fruit of good deeds and have thereby belied their profession of discipleship. So Jesus uses parables to hide the secrets from them—but not from his true disciples, because for them he'll add explanations. He'll add them because true disciples *have* understood his plain speech and consequently borne the fruit of discipleship. The saying on the haves and have-nots rests on the economic truism that the rich increase in wealth by investing their capital while the poor sink deeper into poverty for lack of capital to invest. Thus Jesus takes away his plain speech from a false disciple by confusing him with parables, but furthers the knowledge of a true disciple (13:51–52) by explaining the parables to him (13:18–23, 36–43, 49–50). The switch from the plural "you" in 13:11 to the singular "whoever," "him," and "he" in 13:12 puts an individualizing stamp on the economically based saying. "And it [the true disciple's knowledge] will be made to flourish" emphasizes the gift of further knowledge. He'll have more than enough of it. At the level of Matthew's text, the plural of "parables" in the true disciples' question anticipates the parables to follow. But since these disciples are said to have approached Jesus, he must no longer be sitting in the boat. So it looks as though Matthew has advanced what in historical terms happened later—that is, these disciples' question and Jesus' answer, which will include an explanation of the parable of the sower—so as to make this parable the key to understanding the purpose of the following parables. For Jesus will go back to telling the crowds parables, seemingly from the boat, and won't leave the crowds till 13:36.

13:13–15: "On account of this I'm speaking to them in parables, because though seeing they don't see, and though hearing they don't hear, nor do they under-

stand. ¹⁴**And in them is being completely fulfilled Isaiah's prophecy that says, 'By hearing you'll hear and never understand** [what you hear], **and though seeing you'll see and never perceive** [what you see]. ¹⁵**For the heart of this people has become impenetrable, and with** [their] **ears they've heard ponderously** [that is, they've heard hardly at all], **and they've closed their eyes lest they perceive with** [their] **eyes and hear with** [their] **ears and understand with** [their] **heart and convert and I heal them** [Isaiah 6:9–10 (compare Mark 4:12; Luke 8:10; John 12:40; Acts 28:26–27; Romans 11:8)].'" So far as false disciples are concerned, then, Jesus isn't telling parables because those disciples haven't been *able* to understand his plain-spoken teaching and the parables will help them understand; rather, he's telling parables because as false disciples they've *refused* to understand his plain-spoken teaching and the parables will confuse them judgmentally for that refusal. "On account of this" points forward to "*because* though seeing they don't see [and so forth]." Thus the emphasis falls on the culpability of false disciples. They have eyes and ears but haven't used them well. Prior to the direct quotation of Isaiah 6:9–10, the references to seeing and hearing come out of that Old Testament text, but in reverse order. The false disciples don't even *see* what they see! They don't even *hear* what they hear! Such is the extent of their refusal to perceive, to understand. Forget the seeming self-contradiction in seeing but not seeing and in hearing but not hearing. This is a way of highlighting the deliberateness with which false disciples don't translate Jesus' plain-spoken teaching into behavior consistent with discipleship. "Is being *completely* fulfilled" highlights this deliberateness even further. Unusually, Jesus rather than Matthew quotes the Old Testament as fulfilled; and the usual "what was spoken [by the Lord] *through* [Isaiah] the prophet" (1:22; 2:15, 17, 23; 3:3; 4:14; 8:17; 12:17; 13:35; 21:4; 27:9) is replaced by "*Isaiah's* prophecy is being completely fulfilled . . . that says" to avoid even the slightest implication of divine causation that might be mistaken as a lessening of human responsibility. "For" makes the false disciples' obtuseness rather than the Lord's speaking through Isaiah the reason for failure to understand and perceive. "*Never* understand" and "*never* see" pronounce, in effect, eternal damnation. "They've closed their eyes *lest* they perceive . . . and understand . . . and convert and I heal them" puts a final accent on the deliberateness of false disciples' refusal to translate Jesus' plain-spoken teaching into behavior consistent with discipleship. They don't want to be healed of their hardheartedness, mental blindness, and willful deafness.

For a renewed and contrastive portrayal of true disciples Jesus now says in *13:16–17*: "**But fortunate** [are] **your eyes, because they see, and your ears, because they hear. ¹⁷For amen I tell you that many prophets and righteous** [people] **longed to see the things that you're seeing and didn't see** [them], **and to hear the things that you're hearing and didn't hear** [them]." "*Because* they see" and "*because* they hear" accentuate

human responsibility once again, but this time happily by attributing the good fortune of seeing the deeds of Jesus and hearing his words to true disciples' deciding to see and hear instead of refusing as false disciples do. Providing the basis for this pronouncement of good fortune is the unfulfilled longing of past prophets and teachers of righteousness—many of them, no less—to see the deeds of the Christ and to hear his words (compare 11:2–6, 19; and see the comments on 10:41 for righteous people as teachers of righteousness). "I tell you," reinforced by "amen," underlines the pronouncement.

13:18–22: "**You therefore** [since your eyes and ears are fortunate (13:16–17)]—**hear the parable of the sower. ¹⁹When anyone hears the word about the kingdom and doesn't understand** [it], **the evil one** [Satan] **comes and snatches away what was sown in his** [the hearer's] **heart. This is the person sown on the edge of a path. ²⁰But the person sown on rocky ground—this is the person who hears the word and receives it immediately with joy. ²¹But he doesn't have a root in himself, but is temporary. And when affliction or persecution comes about because of the word, he's immediately tripped up. ²²But the person sown in the thorns—this is the person who hears the word. And concern for this age** [as opposed to concern for his eternal fate] **and the seductiveness of wealth choke the word, and it becomes unfruitful.**" As a title, "the parable of the sower" centers attention on the sower, that is on Jesus, since the sower represents him (see the comments on 13:3–4, 37). So the title means "the parable told *by* Jesus the sower" as well as "the parable told *concerning* Jesus the sower." But why the command to hear this parable? These disciples have already heard it. Ah, but they don't yet understand it, though they've understood Jesus' earlier plain speech, as shown by their having borne fruit in keeping with discipleship. So he tells them to hear the parable in explanatory form. Thus their understanding of Jesus' earlier, plain speech will be augmented with an understanding of his parabolic speech (see 13:11–12a). "The word about the kingdom" harks back to Jesus' proclaiming, "Repent, for the kingdom of heaven has drawn near" (4:17 [compare 3:2]). He has attributed lack of understanding to people's having deliberately "closed their eyes lest they perceive with [their] eyes and hear with [their] ears and understand with [their] heart" (13:15). The resultant lack of understanding enables Satan to come and snatch away the word that was sown in their heart. Such people had their chance. They botched it. Since Jesus has just distinguished between what's sown and the person in whose heart it's sown, "the person sown" means a person who has received the seed of the word as though he were seeded soil. This turn of phrase lays emphasis on the individual person and his or her responsibility to hear and understand (compare 13:23). As for "the person sown on the rocky ground," "with joy" reflects the goodness of the news concerning the arrival of the reign of heaven and tells why this person "receives it [the word of good news] immediately." But "he doesn't have a root in himself" because he himself is the thin soil onto which the seeds fell. The thinness stands for superficiality in the reception given to the word, a superficiality that translates into temporariness. "Tripped up" translates into apostasy so as to avoid persecution. Sadly, the immediacy of this apostasy cancels the immediacy of having received the word with joy. This-worldly concern defines the thorns of "the person sown in the thorns." The persons sown on rocky ground and in the thorns are identified; but then the sentences regarding them are broken off, and "this" picks up the identified persons (see the dashes in the translation). This broken grammatical construction highlights their on-again, off-again characteristics.

13:23: "But the person sown on the good soil—this is the person who hears the word and understands [it]**, who indeed bears fruit and produces a hundredfold in one instance, sixtyfold in another instance, and thirtyfold in another."** Hearing and understanding contrast with the hearing and not hearing in the sense of not understanding (13:13). And fruit-bearing—that is, producing good deeds in keeping with discipleship (7:17–19; 21:43 [compare 3:8, 10])—gives evidence of hearing and understanding. "Indeed" highlights such fruit-bearing. See the comments on 13:8 for the gradations of yield. It's up to those who hear the word about the kingdom to let that word become fruitful.

NEW UNDERSTANDING AS A GIFT FROM JESUS
Matthew 13:24–52

This section contains six parables about the kingdom of heaven.

The Future Judgment of False Disciples in the Kingdom
Matthew 13:24–30; see 13:36–43 for an explanation

13:24–26: He presented another parable to them, saying, "The kingdom of heaven was like a man who'd sowed good seed in his field. 25But while the men were sleeping, his enemy came and oversowed tares in the midst of the wheat and went away. 26But when the grass sprouted and produced fruit [that is, when the grass-like blades shot up and developed ears of grain]**, then the tares also became apparent."** "Presented" echoes a verb used in the Old Testament for Moses' presenting the words of the Lord to the people of Israel and their elders (Exodus 19:7; 21:1; Deuteronomy 4:44). This echo supports Matthew's continuing portrayal of Jesus as a new and greater Moses. Though Jesus has most recently been speaking to his true disciples, segregated from among the crowds that also contained false disciples (13:10–23), the statement in 13:36 that "on leaving the crowds, he went into the house; and his disciples approached him" will imply that Jesus now speaks again to the crowds before explaining the present parable to his true disciples. This implication will be confirmed by 13:34: "Jesus spoke all these things in parables to the crowds." "Was like" points

to the whole of the following parable, not just to the immediately following phrase ("a man"). The past tense in "was like" calls attention to the mixture of wheat and tares in the kingdom as already having come about (see also 18:23; 22:2). Given Jesus as the sower in the parable of the sower, "a man who'd sowed good seed in his field" suggests a reference to Jesus, which will be confirmed in 13:37. That this "man" (singular), not his "men" (plural), himself sows the good seed suggests Jesus' establishment on earth of the kingdom of heaven. But who are "the men" who "were sleeping" while the man's "enemy" came and sowed the tares? The use of "the men" in 8:27; 9:8 (or "the human beings," a preferable translation in those passages) for Jesus' disciples suggests the same usage here. And just as the sleeping of "the men" in the parable allows tares to be sown among the wheat ("the man" isn't said to have slept!), so too the sleeping of Jesus' disciples allows the kingdom of heaven to be corrupted with the influx of false disciples (compare the comments on 7:6 and the sleeping of Jesus' disciples in Gethsemane while he stays awake to pray [26:36–45]). But to say so is to anticipate Jesus' upcoming explanation; so let's delay identifying "his enemy." Combined with the implied nighttime of sleeping, "came" and "went away" allude to the enemy's stealth. "*Over*sowed" alludes to the enemy's sowing the seeds of tares on top of the already sown seeds of wheat. "In the midst of the wheat" stresses the mixture of tares with wheat. Tares are a poisonous plant, also called darnels, that looks like wheat until the wheat develops ears of grain easily distinguished from the black seeds produced by tares.

13:27–28: "And on approaching, the slaves of the houseowner said to him, 'Master, you sowed good seed in your field, didn't you?'" Implied answer: Yes. **"'From where then does it have tares?'"** "The men" are now called "the slaves" because "the man" is now called "the houseowner," a designation Jesus used for himself in 10:25. The slaves are members of the man's household, but he owns a field ("his field" [13:24]) as well as a house. The slaves address him with "Master" because he owns them too. But the word translated "Master" means not only "owner," but also "Lord," and thus—like "houseowner"—suits the man's representation of the Lord Jesus. The appearance of some tares wouldn't have surprised the slaves. So their surprise implies a large number due to deliberate sowing, and their question confirms the enemy's stealth and reflects their having slept during the sowing of the tares. 28**And he told them, "A hostile man has done this."** In Matthew's original Greek, "hostile" is the adjective form of "enemy," the noun that appeared in 13:25. But "a hostile *man*" makes a sharp antithesis to "a *man* who'd sowed good seed in his field" (13:24). **"But the slaves say to him, 'Then do you want us, on going away** [from your house into your field]**, to collect them** [the tares]**?'"** The present tense of "say" reflects the eagerness of the slaves to weed out the tares and represents the eagerness of some in the church to weed out fellow disciples against whom they've made individual judgments (compare 7:1–5).

13:29–30: "But he says, 'No, lest while gathering the tares you uproot the wheat together with them. ³⁰Allow both to grow together till the harvest; and in the time [= season] **of harvest I'll say to the reapers, "First collect the tares and bind them in bundles so as to burn them up, but gather the wheat into my granary."'"** The present tense of "says" emphasizes the master's negation of the slaves' suggestion. But you can understand the suggestion. For volunteer tares were usually weeded out when the formation of heads of wheat did away with the similarity between mere sprouts of wheat and tares. Here, though, deliberate sowing resulted in so many tares that their roots were intertwined with those of the wheat. Collecting the tares would therefore entail a massive uprooting of the immature wheat along with the tares. For burning as a symbol of judgment and for gathering into a granary as a symbol of salvation, see 3:10–12. The harvesters differ from the slaves. This difference anticipates a later identification of the harvesters as angels in distinction from the slaves (= "the men" of 13:25), who represent Jesus' disciples. Usually, harvesters cut the grain just below the heads on the stalks, left the shorter tares standing uncut, and burned off the tares and the remaining stalks of wheat in the open field. So the collecting of tares first and their being bound in bundles for burning, like wood, are further elements of unrealism designed to emphasize the final judgment of those represented by the tares.

The Magnitude of the Kingdom
Matthew 13:31–33

13:31–32: He presented another parable to them, saying, "The kingdom of heaven is like a grain of mustard which [grain] **a man, on taking** [it], **sowed in his field—³²which** [mustard] **is on the one hand smaller than all the seeds. Whenever it** [the mustard] **has grown, on the other hand, it's larger than the vegetable plants and becomes a tree, so that 'the birds of the sky come and nest in its branches** [Daniel 4:12, 21 (compare Ezekiel 17:23; 31:6)]**.'"** The present tense in "is like" calls attention to the magnitude of the kingdom as indicated by the parable, a magnitude current in Matthew's day because of the astounding growth of the church, so that it includes large numbers of false disciples in addition to the true (compare 7:13–14; 28:18–19, and contrast the past tense of "was like" in 13:24 with comments). On close inspection, the seemingly irrational and confusing shift from the *grain* of mustard to the *mustard* makes sense. For "which [grain]" suits its being sown, whereas "which [mustard]" suits its being smaller than all the seeds. (In Matthew's original Greek it's clear that the first "which" refers to "grain," and the second "which" to "mustard.") A mustard seed was the smallest of Palestinian seeds visible to the naked eye and had become proverbial for smallness. But the mustard plant attains a height of 8–12 feet, so that Jesus takes

the liberties of calling it a tree and of describing it as larger *than* the vegetable plants rather than the largest *of* them. It has graduated hyperbolically from the category of a vegetable plant to the category of a tree. Similarly, "smaller than all the seeds" has made the mustard grain so small that it doesn't even count as a seed. (To signal this demotion, Jesus called the unsown mustard "a grain" rather than "a seed.") "On the one hand . . . . on the other hand" and birds' nesting in the branches of the mustard tree clinch the metaphorical contrast between the kingdom's smallest of beginnings (with only four disciples [4:18–22]) and largest of endings (disciples from all nations [28:18–19]). As in the parables of the sower and of the wheat and tares, the man who sowed the grain of mustard is Jesus. His field will turn out to be the world (13:38), and the man's having sown the grain of mustard in the field represents Jesus' having already established the reign of heaven in the world (compare 12:28).

13:33: He told them another parable: "The kingdom of heaven is like leaven which a woman, on taking [it], **hid in three satons** [about a bushel, or almost fifty pounds] **of wheat flour until the whole was leavened."** Leaven consisted of a portion of fermenting dough that was mixed with a batch of fresh dough to make the batch rise, much as yeast is used nowadays. Usually, leaven symbolizes the pervasive power of evil (see, for example, 16:5–12; 1 Corinthians 5:6–8; Galatians 5:8–9). The exceptionality of Jesus' presently using leaven for something good emphasizes the pervasive growth of the kingdom of heaven. It seems odd that the woman "hid" the leaven in the flour. But this very oddity portrays the large amount of flour as engulfing the small amount of leaven. So just as it was hyperbolic for Jesus to call the mustard plant a tree, it's also hyperbolic for him to speak of a woman's leavening "the whole" of a bushel of wheat flour to make one enormously large lump of dough. Thus the pervasiveness of the leaven illustrates the magnitude of the kingdom, which has to do with the huge number of professing disciples, true and false, throughout the world.

The Fulfillment of Prophecy in the
Parabolic Conundrums
Matthew 13:34–35

13:34–35: Jesus spoke all these things in parables to the crowds; and apart from a parable he was saying nothing to them, ³⁵so that what was spoken through the prophet would be fulfilled, saying, "I'll open my mouth with parables, I'll belch [an attention-getting figure of speech for speaking] **things hidden since the founding of the world** [Psalm 78:2]**."** "All these things" are the contents of the preceding parables—but not Jesus' explanation of the parable of the sower; for he gave that explanation only to his true disciples, whereas "the crowds" includes false disciples as well as true. "Apart from a parable he was saying nothing to them" reemphasizes his having used parables judgmentally to obscure the secrets of the kingdom from false disciples, whom he doesn't privilege with explanations of the parables (13:10–15). As in his other activities, Jesus has deliberately set about to fulfill Old Testament prophecy ("so that what was spoken through the prophet would be fulfilled"); and, as usual, "*through* the prophet" casts the prophet as the Lord's mouthpiece. According to Jewish tradition, Asaph composed Psalm 78. He was a cymbalist, singer, and choir leader (1 Chronicles 15:19; 16:4–7, 37; 25:6–7; 2 Chronicles 5:12; Nehemiah 12:46); but 1 Chronicles 25:2 and 2 Chronicles 29:30 also call him a prophet and seer. Matthew pluralizes Asaph's "parable" (singular) to suit the plurality of parables that Jesus has told. "Things hidden since the founding of the world" describes those parables as containing the secrets of the kingdom that the parables have hidden from false disciples because they didn't do the good deeds that would have demonstrated true discipleship (compare 11:25). Especially prominent in the parables thus far told is the secret that the kingdom includes a large number of false disciples. In context, then, Matthew reverses the meaning of Psalm 78, which has the psalmist using parables to reveal hidden things rather than to keep them hidden (see verses 3–4 in the psalm). Fulfillments of Old Testament prophecy often take a surprisingly different turn.

The Future Judgment of False Disciples in the Kingdom
Matthew 13:36–43

Now comes an explanation of the parable of the wheat and tares. **13:36–38b: Then, on leaving the crowds** [which included false disciples, unworthy of an explanation], **he went into the house** [Jesus' house in Capernaum (see 4:13; 9:10; 12:15, 46 with comments)]. **And his disciples** [the true ones] **approached him, saying, "Clarify for us the parable of the tares of the field."** The omission of wheat from the parable's title puts emphasis on the current presence and future judgment of false disciples, represented by the tares. [37]**And answering, he said, "The one who was sowing the good seed is the Son of Man** [compare the designation of the sower as 'the man' in the parable proper (13:24)]. [38a–b]**And the field is the world."** "World" emphasizes the widespread extension of the kingdom through evangelism, started by Jesus in the land of Israel and continued far and wide through the agency of his disciples, with whom he'll promise to be present (5:14; 24:14; 26:13; 28:18–20). He doesn't mean that all the world's inhabitants will become disciples. He means, rather, that throughout the world large numbers will profess discipleship (compare the parables of the mustard tree and the leaven). We would err to interpret "the world" as the church, for Jesus is quite capable of using "church" in this Gospel (16:18; 18:17). And to equate "the world" with a universal kingdom of the Son of Man would go too far in the other direction by overlooking that the Devil sowed tares *later* and in the *midst* of the wheat. So the world is the sphere into which the Son of Man brings his kingdom through preaching the gospel. Worldwide extent—yes; but not total domination of the world, at least not till the second

coming. **"And the good seed—these are** [= stand for] **the sons of the kingdom."** The broken grammatical construction, indicated by a dash, calls special attention to the good seed as a counterbalance to the tares. The plural of "these" makes "the good seed" a collective singular. In 8:12 "the sons of the kingdom" referred to the Jews as God's chosen people, who as such would inherit the kingdom except for their failure to repent and believe (though, of course, some did repent and believe and thus retain their status). Here, though, "the sons of the kingdom" refers to Jesus' true disciples, the very ones he's privileging with an explanation of the parable in order to add further understanding to their prior understanding (13:12).

13:38c–43: "But the tares are [= stand for] **the sons of the evil one** [who'll now be identified as the Devil, "sons of" indicating that they take after the Devil's evil on the principle of like father, like son]. [39]**And the enemy who sowed them** [the tares] **is the Devil."** So the infiltration of false disciples into the church is the work of the Devil. **"And the harvest is the consummation of the age** [when everything is bundled together at the end of present history]. **And the harvesters are angels.** [40]**Therefore** [because of the consummation] **just as the tares are collected and burned up by fire, thus it'll be in the consummation of the age:** [41]**the Son of Man will send his angels, and they'll collect out of his kingdom all the snares and those who practice lawlessness** [that is, who disobey the Law as interpreted by Jesus (see, for example, 5:21–48)], [42]**and will 'throw them into the furnace of fire** [Daniel 3:6].' **Weeping and gritting of teeth will be there** [because of the fire (compare Psalm 112:10)]." "Into the furnace of fire" tells why the tares were bound in bundles, like pieces of wood, rather than burned while standing in the open field. According to 24:30–31 the Son of Man "will send his angels . . . and they'll gather his selected ones [true disciples]" to inherit the kingdom (25:34). He says here, on the other hand, that his angels will collect false disciples, who ensnare others into sinning by disobeying the Law as interpreted by Jesus and teaching others to do the same (compare 5:19; 18:6–7; Zephaniah 1:3). Notably, Jesus claims the angels and the kingdom as his own (compare 16:28; Daniel 7:13–14 and Jesus' phrase "*my* church" in Matthew 16:18). But given that he's "God with us" (1:23), what else should we expect? [43]**"Then the righteous will shine out like the sun in the kingdom of their Father** [compare Daniel 12:3]." "The righteous" are true disciples, who not only live righteously but also—unlike false disciples, who ensnare others with their lawless teaching and conduct—teach righteousness to others by word and example. The kingdom is the Father's as well as Jesus', and "*their* Father" recalls many, many instances of Jesus' calling God the disciples' Father (5:16, 45, 48 and so on). This designation of God and the promise of shining out like the sun in his kingdom give encouragement and assurance to disciples who, because of their fidelity as true disciples, suffer persecution. **"The** [person] **who has ears** [to hear with] **had better hear** [because of a fiery furnace for false disciples and Jesus' and the Father's kingdom for true disciples]!" See further the comments on 13:9.

The Surpassing Value of Understanding
for Entrance into the Kingdom
Matthew 13:44–46

Just as 13:31–33 contained a pair of parables dealing with the kingdom's magnitude, the present passage contains a pair dealing with the surpassing value of understanding for entrance into the kingdom.

13:44: "**The kingdom of heaven is like a treasure hidden in a field, on finding which** [treasure] **a man hid** [it] **and from joy over it goes and sells all things that he has, as many as** [they are]**, and buys that field** [so that he can legally possess the treasure he found and re-hid there] [compare Proverbs 2:1–11]." The frequency of invasions often led people to bury their treasures in the ground. We're probably meant to understand a day laborer plowing in another man's field, discovering an old treasure buried there before the present owner's lifetime or acquisition of the field (for the present owner wouldn't sell the field knowing the treasure to be intact), and not extracting the treasure but carefully covering it back up so as to purchase the field and forestall the present owner's claiming to have buried the treasure himself. The necessity of selling absolutely all to purchase the field reflects the day laborer's relative poverty. "A treasure" connotes high value and here, as in Proverbs 2:1–11, stands for understanding, the kind of understanding that gains entrance into the kingdom of heaven. The treasure's hiddenness echoes the woman's hiding leaven in a bushel of wheat flour (13:33) and alludes to Jesus' explaining to true disciples the secrets of the kingdom that he hid in parables from false disciples. "In a field" echoes the same phrase in the parables of the tares and the mustard tree (13:24, 27, 31), where it represented "the world" (13:38), throughout which the reign of heaven extends in the discipling of all nations (28:18–20). So too here. Several features of the parable highlight the man's joy over finding the treasure: (1) his hiding it again; (2) the present tense in "goes and sells . . . and buys that field"; (3) his selling "all" his possessions; and (4) the reinforcement of "all" with "as many as [they are]." So this man's joy proves genuine, as opposed to the superficial joy of a "temporary" disciple represented by the rocky ground in the parable of the sower (13:20). In 19:21–22 Jesus will tell a young man to go sell all his possessions, give the proceeds to the poor for the gaining of treasure in heaven, and come follow him. But because of having "many acquisitions," the young man will go off sorrowing. Contrast the present man's joy in selling all he has to buy the field in which the treasure is hidden. So the accent falls on the surpassing value of the treasure, a value that devalues all else by comparison and makes the understanding required for entrance into the kingdom joyfully worth any cost.

13:45–46: "**Again, the kingdom of heaven is like a businessman seeking beautiful pearls. ⁴⁶And on finding one very valuable pearl, going off he sold all things that he had, as many as** [they were]**, and bought it.**" "Again" links this parable with the preceding one about the treasure. As did the treasure in that one, the pearl stands for the understanding that gains entrance into the kingdom. The selling of all possessions without exception gives evidence of true discipleship (compare the pearls at 7:6 in a context likewise dealing with true and false discipleship) and illustrates the surpassing value of understanding. "*One* very valuable pearl" underlines the value in that the pearl is worth any cost *even though* it's only one. Pearls were fished in the Red Sea, Persian Gulf, and Indian Ocean. The businessman's "*seeking* beautiful pearls" marks him as a wholesale dealer who travels to such places, not a small-time, shop-keeping retailer.

The Future Judgment of False Disciples
Matthew 13:47–50

The following parable pairs up with the parable about the tares, and with that parable bookends the intervening two pairs of parables (see the introduction to 13:1–52).

13:47–48: "**Again, the kingdom of heaven is like a dragnet that was cast into the sea and gathered** [fish] **of every kind, which** [dragnet], **⁴⁸when it had been filled, on drawing which** [dragnet] **up onto the beach and sitting down, they** [fishermen] **collected the good** [ritually pure and edible fish] **into containers; but they threw out the foul** [ritually impure and inedible fish, such as those without scales or fins (Leviticus 11:9–12)]." "Again" links this parable with the one about the pearl (13:45–46), so that these two parables join the one about the treasure (13:44) to form a triplet matching the earlier triplet of those that each started with "another parable" (13:24, 31, 33). The dragnet, weighted at the bottom, was either dragged to shore between two boats or laid out by a single boat in a circuit from the shore and back again and then drawn to shore by hand. "Into the sea" parallels "in his field" in the companion parable of the tares (13:24) and, as there, symbolizes the worldwide extent of Christian evangelism (13:38 [compare the frequent Old Testament portrayal of the nations of the world as a sea]). Like fishing as a figure for evangelism in 4:18–19, the gathering of every kind of fish stands for the coming into the church of both true and false disciples (compare 13:2: "And many crowds *gathered* together to him"; also the mixture of wheat and tares in 13:24–30, 36–43). The filling of the dragnet stands for the large number (by Matthew's time) of professing disciples. The "containers" into which the good fish are collected correspond to the "granary" into which the wheat was gathered in the parable of the tares (13:30). Strikingly, Matthew uses the neuter gender of "the good" and "the foul," though the implied word for "fish" is masculine. The neuter gender points beyond the fish as physical objects to their qualities of goodness or foulness, and—since "foul" and "rotten" translate the same Greek word—the neuter of these two words recalls the similar images of "a good tree" and "a rotten tree" (both neuter) in 7:17–18; 12:33. Jesus is still speaking in private to his true disciples, to whom alone he explains the parables (13:36). So an explanation now follows.

13:49–50: **"Thus it'll be in the consummation of the age: the angels will come forth and separate the evil** [false disciples] **from the midst of the righteous** [true disciples] [50]**and 'throw them** [the false disciples] **into the furnace of fire** [Daniel 3:6]**? Weeping and grinding of teeth will be there** [because of the fire (compare 13:41–42; Psalm 112:10)]**."** The coming forth of the angels corresponds to the sending of the angels by the Son of Man (13:41 [compare 16:27; 25:31]). But the angels' coming forth doesn't correspond to the fishermen's sitting down after beaching the dragnet. This incongruity shows that Jesus is deliberately relating the parable of the good and foul fish to the one about the wheat and tares. "Separate" will occur twice in 25:32 for the separation of true and false disciples at the Last Judgment. "The evil [false disciples]" correspond to "the sons of the evil one" in 13:38. "*From* the midst" forms an antithetic parallel to "*in* the midst" at 13:25. Like the phrase to which it corresponds, this phrase also shows that the evil are to be understood as false disciples within the kingdom rather than as evil people in general. Otherwise, "the righteous" would have been located in *their* midst and separated from them rather than vice versa (for "the righteous" see the comments on 13:43). The figure of a fiery furnace is inappropriate to fish, referred originally to the fate of bundles of tares (13:42), and thus ties the two parables together again for a double emphasis on the fearsome doom of false disciples, though the present parable makes this emphasis *exclusively* (contrast 13:43a).

The True Disciple as a Knowledgeable Scholar
Matthew 13:51–52

An appendant parable now stresses that understanding distinguishes true disciples from false as Jesus continues without interruption. **13:51–52**: **"Have you understood all these things?" They tell him, "Yes."** The introduction of "They tell him" without a preceding "And" and the present tense of "tell" underline the affirmative answer, which confirms these disciples as true (compare 13:23, where the good soil represents the disciple "who hears and *understands* the word"). "These things" refers to the contents of the parables; and "all" indicates a comprehensive understanding on the disciples' part, thanks to Jesus' explanations. (He didn't explain every parable to them; but the explanations he did give them included elements, like that of sowing seed in a field, which carried over to the parables otherwise unexplained.) [52]**And he said to them, "Because of this** [your understanding all these things]**, every scholar who has been discipled to the kingdom of heaven is like a houseowning man, who as such** [= in his capacity as a houseowner] **thrusts forth new things and old things out of his treasure."** A disciple's understanding qualifies him to be called a scholar. Since to be discipled means to be made to learn (for "disciple" means "learner"), to be discipled to the kingdom means to have been made to learn about it, as in the parables and their explanations. "*Every* scholar" indicates that thrusting forth new things and old things necessarily characterizes a true disciple. Jesus isn't talking about a special class among true disciples. He called himself a houseowner in 10:25. Like teacher, like disciple. "His treasure" refers to the contents of what we'd call a clothes closet. "New things and old things" refers to new clothes and old clothes. (Such an abundance of clothes signaled wealth.) The new clothes represent new understanding that a true disciple has gained from the parables and their explanations. The old clothes represent earlier understanding of Jesus' plain speech. He rewarded that earlier understanding with the new (13:12). And as usual, understanding includes conduct as well as cognition. In 12:33–37 "thrusts forth" had to do with speaking words out of one's "treasure." So too here, the houseowner's thrusting forth new things and old things out of his treasure means that a true disciple will draw on his new and old understandings when speaking as well as acting. For as Jesus himself did, "the righteous" teach by both word and example (compare 5:19).

DIFFERENT PEOPLE'S UNDERSTANDING
AND LACK OF UNDERSTANDING
Matthew 13:53–17:27

Matthew continues his practice of putting a block of narrative after each major discourse of Jesus. This block encompasses 13:53–17:27. As usual, the narrative illustrates the theme of the foregoing discourse, here the contrast between understanding and lack of understanding.

LACK OF UNDERSTANDING
IN UNBELIEVING JEWS
Matthew 13:53–58

13:53–57a: **And it happened that when Jesus had finished** [speaking] **these parables, he moved away from there** [his house in Capernaum (4:13; 13:36; see 7:28 for this concluding formula)]. [54]**And on coming into his hometown, he started teaching them** [his fellow townspeople] **in their synagogue, so that they were awestruck and were saying, "From where does this** [guy] **have this wisdom and** [these] **miracles?** [55]**This** [guy] **is the carpenter's son, isn't he? His mother is called Mary, isn't she, and his brothers** [are called] **James and Joseph and Simon and Judas**[, aren't they]? [56]**And his sisters are all with us, aren't they? So from where does this** [guy] **have all these things?"** [57a]**And they were taking offense at him.** Though Jesus had set up house in Capernaum (4:13), Nazareth remained the town of his upbringing (2:23). So "his hometown" refers to Nazareth. "*Their* synagogue" makes the synagogue there typify the synagogues of unbelieving Jews at the time of Matthew's writing. Jesus' fellow townspeople are awestruck not only at his teaching in their synagogue but also at his miracles; but instead of believing in him, they question the source of his wisdom and miracles. ("Wisdom" explains why they were awestruck at his teaching; it contained a stunning degree of wisdom.) As for the question of source, Matthew's audience will recollect the alternative answers, Satan and God's Spirit (12:22–32). And for Matthew's audience (but not for the townspeople), Jesus' being said to "*have* this wisdom and [these] miracles" makes the wisdom and miracles belong to him in his own right. For he's "God with us" (1:23), not just God's purely human agent. The townspeople betray their lack of understanding by misidentifying Jesus as "the carpenter's son" (biologically speaking, in their view), whereas Matthew's audience know him to be the Son of God (2:15; 3:17 and so on). Later, his disciples will confess him as such (14:33; 16:16). The naming of Jesus' mother and brothers but not of Joseph the foster father suggests strongly that Joseph had died and that his son Joseph, named after him, had replaced him, so to speak (compare the nonmention of the elder Joseph in 12:46). Naturally, the townspeople didn't think of Jesus' brothers as only his half brothers. Again for Matthew's audience, the mention of Jesus' mother, brothers, and sisters recalls the identification of his true family as those who do the will of God the Father rather than these his blood relatives (12:46–50). Though Jesus' biological half sisters aren't named, the question, "And his sisters are *all* with us, aren't they?" strikes a note of irony in that his true sisters are other and elsewhere (see 12:46–50 again). The townspeople's taking offense at Jesus displays their lack of understanding: they understand neither the source of Jesus' wisdom and miracles nor the identity of his true family. Since to take offense means to fall into a trap, lack of understanding has trapped the townspeople in unbelief.

13:57b–58: But Jesus said to them, "A prophet isn't dishonored except in [his] **hometown and in his household** [so that because of joining the other townspeople in dishonoring Jesus, his listed blood relatives don't count as his true family, at least not yet]**." 58And because of their unbelief, he didn't do many miracles there.** So lack of understanding has led to unbelief. Jesus wasn't *unable* to do many miracles in Nazareth. Because of the townspeople's unbelief in response to the few he did do, he *refused* to do many miracles. Even so, those few had left the townspeople awestruck.

LACK OF UNDERSTANDING IN
HEROD THE TETRARCH
Matthew 14:1–12

14:1–2: During that time Herod the tetrarch [a small-change ruler of Galilee (west of the Sea of Galilee) and Perea (east of the Jordan River)] **heard the news about Jesus 2and said to his servants, "This** [guy] **is John the baptizer. He** [John] **has been raised from the**

dead; and on account of this [his having been raised], **miracles are at work in him."** Here we have Herod Antipas, not his father Herod the Great of chapter 2. As in 11:25; 12:1, "During that time" connotes a suitable time. Herod's misidentification of Jesus as John the baptizer risen from the dead suits the preceding misidentification of Jesus by his fellow townspeople (13:53–58). "The news about Jesus" had to do with Jesus' miracles. But to say that "the miracles are at work in him," though it grants their actuality, is to deny that he himself works them. It's to say he's only their instrument. So Herod lacks understanding in three respects: (1) in his wrong identification of Jesus as John; (2) in his wrong deduction that John has been raised from the dead; and (3) in his wrong assignment of Jesus to his miracles rather than of the miracles to him (contrast his "hav[ing]" miracles in 13:54).

Herod's lack of understanding triggers a flashback to John's death. **14:3–5: For Herod, having seized** [= arrested] **John, had bound** [him, presumably with chains] **and put** [him] **away in a prison on account of Herodias, his brother Philip's wife. 4For John had been telling him, "It's unlawful for you to have her." 5And though wanting to kill him, he feared the crowd, because they held him as** [= to be] **a prophet** [compare 21:46]. Naturally it was unlawful for Herod to have somebody else's wife. (Matthew doesn't say that Herod had married Herodias, only that she was Philip's wife.) Herod wanted to kill John just as his father had wanted to kill the infant Jesus (2:1–18), and his arresting and binding of John anticipates the arresting and binding of Jesus in 26:4, 48, 50, 55, 57; 27:2. So two more parallels develop between John and Jesus (see the comments on 3:1–3). Herod's fear of the crowd was due to their holding John to be a prophet (compare Jesus' calling John a prophet in 11:9).

14:6–12: But when Herod's birthday took place, the daughter of Herodias danced in the midst [of the partyers] **and pleased Herod, 7with the result that he declared with an oath** [that he'd] **give her whatever she asked for. 8But she, having been prompted by her mother, said, "Give me here on a platter the head of John the baptizer."** So it looks as though Herodias as well as Herod had it in for John, though she isn't so concerned as Herod to avoid a popular uprising over an execution of John. **9And though grieved** [not for John but for himself because of not wanting to risk a popular uprising], **the king commanded** [John's head] **to be given** [to Herodias's daughter (14:5)] **because of** [his] **oaths and those reclining** [at banquet] **with** [him]**.** On the designation of Herod the tetrarch as "the king," see the comments on Mark 6:14. Here the switch from "the tetrarch" to "the king" suits the verb "commanded." The plural of "oaths" refers to the words of the "oath" (singular) mentioned earlier. Herod didn't want to lose face before his guests by reneging on his oath. "Those reclining with [him]" implies a formal dinner party, at which the partyers reclined on cushions around a low table. **10And on sending** [an executioner], **he had John beheaded in**

the prison. [11]**And his** [John's] **head was brought on a platter and given to the little girl, and she brought** [it] **to her mother.** Execution by beheading went against Jewish law but agreed with Greek and Roman custom. The littleness of the girl exposes Herod's weakness in that he has foolishly fallen prey to a youngster, a then undervalued female one at that. This early foolishness adds to his present lack of understanding in regard to Jesus. [12]**And on approaching, his** [John's] **disciples took away the corpse** [literally, "a fallen (body)"] **and buried him. And on coming, they reported** [John's beheading] **to Jesus.** The delivery of John's head on a platter and the taking away of his headless corpse provided the unmistakable evidence of John's death that has led to Herod's misidentifying Jesus as John risen from the dead. The taking of John's corpse by his disciples anticipates the taking of Jesus' corpse by one of his disciples (27:57–60) and thus contributes again to the parallel between John and Jesus that runs throughout Matthew. The reporting of John's death to Jesus sets up for Jesus' withdrawal in the next episode.

THE TWELVE DISCIPLES' OBEDIENT UNDERSTANDING AND A FORESHADOWING OF THE LORD'S SUPPER
Matthew 14:13–21

14:13a: And on hearing [the report of John's death], **Jesus withdrew from there in a boat to a deserted place by himself.** John's execution signaled danger to Jesus' life and limb in that John had announced the coming of Jesus as someone stronger than he and therefore more threatening to Herod (3:11–12) and in that Jesus had called John a prophet, more than a prophet, and greater than any of his predecessors (11:7–11a). So in line with Jesus' having told his disciples to flee persecution (10:23), he himself withdrew "from there." The last we heard of his whereabouts, he was in his hometown of Nazareth (13:53–58). But we're still in a flashback to the earlier incident of John's execution and its immediate aftermath. "From there" doesn't mean "from Nazareth," then. That meaning wouldn't have made sense of Jesus' withdrawing "in a boat," anyway; for Nazareth is landlocked. "From there" means, therefore, that he withdrew from his house in the seaside city of Capernaum, just as in 13:53 (with 13:36) on an earlier occasion. The "deserted place" to which he withdrew to be "by himself" will make it difficult for Herod's arm to reach him (compare Jesus' withdrawal to Galilee from the wilderness of Jordan, where John had been ministering and was arrested, when he heard of John's imprisonment [4:12; see also 12:15; 15:21]). "By himself" indicates that not even his disciples accompanied him in the boat.

14:13b–14: And on hearing [about Jesus' departure]**, the crowds followed him on foot from** [their] **cities.** [14]**And on coming out** [of his seclusion]**, he saw a large crowd and felt sorry for them and healed their sick.** The crowds' following of Jesus makes them stand, as they usually do in Matthew, for the large numbers of true and false disciples that have flocked into the church by the time this Gospel was written (compare most recently 13:24–33, 36–43, 47–50). Given Herod's fear of "the crowd" (14:5), these crowds gave Jesus protection in addition to that provided by the out-of-the-way place devoid of a settled population. Now that "the crowds" (plural) from various cities have congregated in one spot, Matthew calls them "a large crowd" (singular). Jesus feels sorry for them because of their sick. His healing their sick displays the sort of mercy he both exemplifies and calls on his disciples to exercise (compare 5:7; 9:10–13; 12:1–8).

14:15: And when evening had come, his disciples [the Twelve] **approached him, saying, "The place is deserted** [= void of a settled population] **and the hour has already passed away. Dismiss the crowds in order that on going away into the villages they may buy foods."** Normally, people took their main meal late in the afternoon. But that hour had "already passed away." So the upcoming feeding of five thousand families will be an evening meal—like the Lord's Supper, introduced in 26:20, as here, with the clause, "And when evening had come" (compare Jesus' praying in 26:39 that the cup of his sacrificial blood, represented in the Lord's Supper, might "pass away," if possible). So the feeding of five thousand families will foreshadow the Lord's Supper as it's celebrated in the large, mixed church of Matthew's (and our) day, by which time "the hour" of Jesus' shedding his blood will have "passed away." The failure of the twelve disciples to address Jesus respectfully with "Lord" (or the like) betrays as inappropriate their telling him what to do. On the other hand, "Dismiss the crowds" indicates that his hold over the crowds is so strong that, past normal mealtime or not, they wouldn't leave unless he told them to. After all, they stand for the church at large. The disciples speak of "the crowds" (plural), because if Jesus dismisses them to go away "into the villages" (plural), they'll break up into more than one crowd again (compare 14:13–14). "Going *away* into the villages" indicates that the villages are at some distance from the "deserted place," but near enough to be reached before nightfall. And the plural of "foods" probably anticipates the two kinds of food, bread and fish, that the twelve disciples have in short supply.

14:16–19: But he told them, "They have no need to go away. You give them [something] **to eat."** Eating something separately in somewhat distant villages wouldn't qualify to foreshadow the Lord's Supper. In a certain sense, "You give them [something] to eat" becomes a command to distribute its elements. The disciples understand Jesus' command but respond in a way that betrays little faith: [17]**And they tell him, "We don't have** [any foods] **here except for five loaves of bread and two fish."** Good understanding doesn't guarantee great faith (compare 6:30; 8:26; 14:31; 16:8), and the present tense of "tell" accents the disciples' statement exemplifying little faith. Bread and fish made up the basic diet of poor people in Galilee (compare 7:9–10). [18]**And**

he said, "Bring them here to me." "Here" underlines that where Jesus is, the bread is; for in the Lord's Supper, foreshadowed by the imminent feeding, bread stands for his body (26:26). ¹⁹**And on commanding the crowds to recline on the grass, on taking the five loaves and the two fish, on looking up into heaven** [where God dwells] **he blessed** [= praised God in thanksgiving for the bread and fish] **and, on breaking** [the loaves into pieces], **he gave the loaves** [in broken form] **to the disciples, and the disciples** [gave them] **to the crowds.** Reclining was for formal meals such as provided plenty of food. So the command to recline was an auspicious omen (compare the reclining at the Last Supper [26:20]). The grass made a suitable cushion on which to recline. Twice Matthew echoes his own and the disciples' earlier references to "the crowds" (plural [14:13, 15]) to underline the crowds' symbolizing the large, mixed church of his (and our own) day. Jesus himself commands the crowds to recline and thus acts as their host and Lord, because they foreshadow his church at the Lord's Table. The staccato-like effect of commanding, taking, and looking up enhances his lordly hosting. The taking of bread and fish, blessing God for them (not blessing the bread and fish themselves), breaking the loaves into pieces, and giving the pieces to the disciples foreshadow the institution of the Lord's Supper in 26:26–28. Breaking the loaves into pieces enables each of the disciples, who number more than five, to distribute the bread. Throughout the New Testament breaking has bread, not fish, as its object (see especially Mark 8:6–7). At this point, then, fish drop out of sight so as to turn the feeding into a preview of the Lord's Supper, in which fish don't figure. The disciples obey Jesus' command to give the loaves to the crowds just as he'd given the loaves to the disciples. Like Jesus, like his disciples.

14:20–21: **And all ate and were sated** [= filled to satisfaction]. "All" includes the Twelve as well as the crowds so as to foreshadow the institution of the Lord's Supper, which all Twelve—including the false disciple, Judas Iscariot—partook of (26:26–29). Similarly, the whole church, consisting of professing disciples—some true, some false—is to eat the Lord's Supper. And as the Lord's Supper will look forward to the messianic banquet in the coming kingdom (26:29), so too does this feeding—hence the being filled to satisfaction. **And they picked up a surplus of the broken pieces** [of bread], **twelve full hampers** [compare 2 Kings 4:38–44]. To continue a foreshadowing of the Lord's Supper, Matthew again omits the fish in describing the picking up of a surplus. "A surplus" and "full hampers" (hampers being large baskets) emphasize an inexhaustibility of supply. The bread of the Lord's Supper will never run out. There'll be more than enough for everyone, so that all discipled nations may come and eat. The number of hampers corresponds to the twelve tribes of Israel and the twelve apostles. Thus the new people of God, represented by the Twelve, have a full supply of bread. In view of 16:9 the Twelve, exclusive of "the crowds," picked up the surplus. ²¹**And the**

husbands who were eating were about five thousand, besides wives and children.** We expect "who'd eaten," as in Mark 6:44, rather than "who were eating" (compare 15:38: "the ones eating"). The latter suggests the church's ongoing eating of the Lord's Supper because of the inexhaustible supply. To stress the current magnitude of the church as a gathering of Christian families on the model of the holy family in chapters 1–2, Matthew adds "besides wives and children." That is, these five thousand families symbolize the later church at the Lord's Table. Of course, you wouldn't think that so many would leave a surplus so large out of only five loaves. But such is the overabundance of salvation as represented in this preview of the Lord's Supper and, ultimately, of the messianic banquet.

UNDERSTANDING JESUS AS SAVING
LORD AND GOD'S SON
Matthew 14:22–36

Matthew presents the story of Jesus' walking on the sea in a way that emphasizes the disciples' understanding of Jesus as the saving Lord and God's Son. The story includes a summary of his healings subsequent to walking on the sea.

14:22–23: **And immediately he compelled the disciples** [the Twelve] **to get into the boat** [that he'd used to go to the deserted place by himself (14:13)] **and go ahead of him to the other side** [of the Sea of Galilee] **until he'd dismissed the crowds** [implying that the disciples' going ahead of him has its limit: he'll rejoin them shortly]. Since Jesus went across the Sea of Galilee from Capernaum on the west side (see the comments on 14:13), the disciples are to go back there from the east side. "Compelled" implies that he exercised his authority on them against their will. Disciples want to stay with their master. "Immediately" stresses Jesus' exercise of authority. ²³**And after dismissing the crowds he went up onto a mountain by himself to pray.** As in 5:1, Jesus' going up onto a mountain makes a parallel with Moses' going up onto Mount Sinai. Since Moses acted as a lone intercessor on Mount Sinai (Exodus 32:31–32; 33:12–23; 34:8–9), "by himself to pray" adds to the portrayal of Jesus as the new and greater Moses. **And when evening came, he was there alone.** Thus Matthew reinforces the parallel between Jesus and Moses.

14:24–25: **And the boat was already many stades distant from the land** [one stade = just over 200 yards (192 meters)], **being buffeted** [literally, "tortured," as though the boat were a person] **by the waves. For the wind was contrary** [to the boat's direction]. ²⁵**And in the fourth watch of the night** [about 3:00 A.M.–6:00 A.M.] **he** [Jesus] **came to them walking across the sea.** The indefinitely long distance of the boat from land heightens the wonder of Jesus' walking across the billowing sea. It might be thought that the contrary wind and the waves symbolize persecution of the church. But elsewhere in Matthew "buffeted/tortured" never occurs for persecution, it's the boat rather than the disciples who are buffeted/tortured, and they aren't said to be in any danger nor do they express any feeling of danger (contrast 8:25). So the point of this episode has to do with the disciples' soon-to-be-expressed understanding of Jesus' deity. For only deity can walk across the sea (Job 9:8; 38:16; Psalm 77:19), and Jesus is both "God with us" and God's "beloved Son" (1:23; 2:15; 3:17 and so on).

14:26–27: And the disciples, on seeing him walking on the sea, were disconcerted, saying, "It's an apparition [= ghost]," and screamed from fear. [27]**But Jesus immediately spoke to them, saying, "Take courage! I am! Stop being afraid."** The disciples' disconcertedness and fear stem from nonrecognition of Jesus, not from failure to understand that as deity he could walk on the sea. So between his commands to take courage and stop being afraid, he identifies himself with "I am," where we'd say, "It's me" (compare John 9:9, for example). For Matthew's Jewish Christian audience, though, "I am" also equates with the divine title, "I AM," by which God identified himself to Moses in Exodus 3:14. The equation contributes to walking on the sea as a demonstration of deity. The immediacy with which Jesus speaks this encouraging self-identification underscores his deity, which makes him greater than Moses.

14:28–29: And answering him, Peter said, "Lord, if you're [the one we see walking on the sea]**, command me to come to you across the waters** [plural for a large body of water]**."** The address "Lord" shows Peter's understanding of Jesus' deity. "If" shows that Peter only wants to make sure it's Jesus whom he and the other disciples see walking on the sea. And "command me to come to you on the waters" shows that Peter understands not only that Jesus, if it is Jesus, can walk on the sea but also that the waters will hold Peter up if Jesus commands him to come to him. [29]**And he** [Jesus] **said, "Come." And on getting down from the boat** [onto the waters]**, he walked across the waters and came toward Jesus.** Peter is portrayed, then, as a typical disciple, one who seeks Jesus' command and then obeys it. Here the obedience consists in walking across the waters as Jesus walks on the sea. Like master, like disciple. But whereas Matthew uses "on the sea" for Jesus' walking, he uses "on the waters" for Peter's walking, because the multiple "waters" connote a turbulent threat to Peter, a mere human being, whereas the single "sea" connotes a stable pavement for Jesus, the divine human being.

14:30–31: But on seeing the wind, he [Peter] **got scared and, on beginning to sink down** [into the waters]**, he screamed, saying, "Lord, save me!"** Peter mistakenly turns his gaze from Jesus to the wind. Earlier, Matthew described the wind as "contrary" in relation to the boat's direction. Now he mentions it in connection with Peter's walking across the waters. Peter is threatened with being blown over, then, not with sinking. But he does start sinking out of fear of the wind and screams for Jesus to save him from drowning. And what he screams includes an understanding of Jesus' deity in

a second addressing of Jesus with "Lord." [31]**And immediately on stretching out** [his] **hand, Jesus took hold of him** [so that Peter stopped sinking] **and says, "You of little faith, to what purpose did you doubt?"** "Immediately" highlights that Jesus saved Peter in the nick of time. The present tense of "says" underlines Jesus' addressing Peter as someone of little faith and asking him what purpose he had in doubting. The question is ironic in that Peter's doubting had no purpose. At the same time Jesus defines as doubt Peter's getting scared by looking at the strong wind. So little faith leaves room for doubt; and again it comes out that good understanding doesn't guarantee great faith, and that great faith needs to supplement good understanding.

14:32–33: And when they'd gotten up into the boat, the wind died down. [33]**But the ones in the boat worshiped him, saying, "Truly you're God's Son."** The waves stirred up by the wind had buffeted the boat but not impeded Jesus, so that once he gets up into the boat with Peter the wind dies down. It can't affect the boat any longer. "The ones in the boat" exclude Jesus and Peter. Twice Peter has addressed Jesus with "Lord." So it remains only for the remaining eleven disciples to worship Jesus and confess him as God's Son. "Truly" highlights both the disciples' understanding of Jesus' true identity and the truth of their confession, which belies the designation of Roman emperors as God's sons. Worshiping Jesus—that is, bowing low before him—adds bodily confession to verbal confession so as to highlight even further the disciples' true understanding.

14:34–36: And on crossing over [the Sea of Galilee]**, they came upon land, [that is,] to Gennesaret** [a plain on the west side of the Sea of Galilee and south of Capernaum]. [35]**And on recognizing him, the men of that place sent** [word] **into the whole of that surrounding** [region]**; and people brought to him all who were sick.** [36]**And they** [the sick] **were imploring him that they might only touch a tassel of his outer garment. And as many as did touch** [it] **were brought safely through** [their sickness to health]. Displaying understanding are the recognition of Jesus, the sending of word about his arrival in the vicinity, the bringing of sick people, and their imploring to touch a tassel of his outer garment. As in 9:20, the tassel portrays Jesus as conforming to the Mosaic law (see the comments on 9:20–21). "*Only* touch" deepens the understanding of Jesus' miraculous power and displays great faith in it. Being brought safely through sickness to health shows the salvific effect of true understanding combined with great faith. "As many as" shows that, given the combination, this effect is a sure thing.

A GRANT OF UNDERSTANDING TO THE DISCIPLES CONCERNING TRUE DEFILEMENT
Matthew 15:1–20

15:1–2: Then Pharisees and scholars come to Jesus from Jerusalem, saying, [2]**"Why are your disciples**

transgressing the tradition of the elders? For they don't wash [their] hands whenever they eat bread." Compare the comments on 12:38 for the combination of "Pharisees and scholars." Their coming all the way from Jerusalem to Galilee (about ninety miles) shows a high degree of opposition to Jesus, implies a claim to authority on their part (especially given the centrality of Jerusalem to Judaism), and magnifies Jesus' upcoming exposé of their ignorance. They don't address Jesus respectfully (as with "Teacher," for example), but brusquely ask a question that contains an accusation of his disciples, for whose behavior they hold him responsible. Matthew leaves it to be inferred that they observe Jesus' disciples eating with unwashed hands, or at least that they'd heard of the disciples' doing so. The omission of an observation or report intensifies the element of brusqueness. "The tradition of the elders," rejected by Sadducees but highly esteemed by Pharisees, consisted in legal comments and case decisions made by past teachers of the Old Testament law. The hand-washing prescribed by the elders didn't have to do with physical hygiene so much as with ritual purity (compare Exodus 30:17–21; Deuteronomy 21:6–7, which the elders extended to hand-washing before eating). The mention of bread links this episode with Jesus' having recently fed five thousand families with five loaves of bread and may imply that the disciples have been eating with unwashed hands the leftovers of bread they'd picked up after that feeding (14:15–21).

15:3–6: And he, answering, said to them, "Why do even you transgress the commandment of God on account of your tradition? ⁴**For** *God* **said, 'Honor** [your] **father and mother** [Exodus 20:12; Deuteronomy 5:16]**,' and, 'The one who badmouths** [his] **father or mother is to be terminated by death** [Exodus 21:17; Leviticus 20:9]**.'** ⁵**But** *you* **say, 'Whoever says to** [his] **father or mother, "Whatever of mine by which you'd be benefited** [is] **a gift** [dedicated to God]," ⁶**shall by no means honor his father.' And you've nullified the word of God on account of your tradition."** Jesus answers with a counter question. In it, *"even* you transgress the commandment of God" shines an accusatory spotlight on the Pharisees and scholars as opposed to Jesus' disciples. What he proceeds to say indicates that though his disciples do transgress the tradition of the elders, they don't transgress the commandment of God. For the elders' tradition and God's commandment don't equate with each other; rather, they're opposed to each other. Jesus' "Why?" and "transgress" echo the Pharisees' and scholars' "Why?" and "transgress." "For" introduces a reason why the elders' tradition opposes God's commandment. The singular of "commandment" points to "Honor [your] father and mother," combined with the prescribed capital penalty for verbally dishonoring either one of them. Though Moses relayed this commandment, Jesus cites God as its author to sharpen the opposition of the elders' tradition to a scriptural command: "For *God* said" versus "But *you* say." By using *"you"* instead of "the

elders," which we might have expected in an echo of the Pharisees' and scholars' question, Jesus brings out their adherence to the elders' tradition rather than to God's word. The elders said that if you declare something of yours is going to be offered as a gift to God—say, as a sacrifice at the temple in the case of your ox—nobody else can have it or use it in the meantime, not even your needy parents. And this tradition applies whether or not you ever make good on your declaration, or even intend to. According to Jesus, then, the declaration counts as badmouthing your parents. And whereas God said that a badmouther of his parents is to be executed, the Pharisees and scholars say the badmouther "shall *by no means* honor his father," and thus with their own commandment "nullify the word of God on account of [their] tradition." "The tradition *of the elders"* (15:2) becomes *"your* tradition" because the Pharisees have accepted the elders' tradition as their own despite its nullification of God's word. "Whoe*ver*" and "what*ever*" stress the comprehensiveness of this acceptance.

Jesus continues in *15:7–9:* **"Hypocrites, beautifully did Isaiah prophesy about you, saying,** ⁸**'This people** ["the Pharisees and scholars" of 15:1] **honors me** [the Lord is speaking through Isaiah] **with lips, but their heart is far away from me.** ⁹**And they worship me faultily by teaching commandments of human beings** [as though they were] **teachings** [of God] [Isaiah 29:13].'" "Beautifully" makes the introduction to a quotation from Isaiah drip with sarcasm. "Hypocrites" interprets the quotation in terms pretense, the difference between religious talk and irreligious affections. This difference then transmutes into a substitution of humanly originated commandments (the elders' tradition, which qualifies as honoring God with the lips) for divinely originated teachings (the Old Testament, inspired by God himself). As a result, worship based on the substitution is faulty.

15:10–11: And on summoning the crowd, he said to them, "Hear and understand [what you hear]. ¹¹**What goes into the mouth doesn't defile a human being. Rather, what comes out of the mouth—this defiles the human being."** The Pharisees and scholars got only a scathing rebuke (15:3–9). The crowd get a lesson in the understanding of defilement, because throughout Matthew the crowds—in particular the ones that follow Jesus around—stand for professing disciples (= learners). So Jesus teaches them. The command to hear recalls similar commands in 11:15; 13:9, 18, 43. Addition of the command to understand amounts to a command to be like the person sown on good soil in the parable of the sower, who "hears the word and understands [it]" (13:23 [contrast 13:13–15, 19])—in other words, a command to be a true rather than false disciple. "What goes into the mouth doesn't defile a human being" shifts the topic from *how* to eat (whether or not with unwashed hands) to *what* to eat, but still deals with defilement and sounds at first like a downright abrogation of Old Testament dietary laws (Leviticus 11). But Jesus said he didn't come to tear down the Law (5:17). So his added statement that "what comes out of the mouth—this defiles the human being" shows that rather than abrogating the dietary laws he's escalating them into prohibitions of evil speech just as in 5:21–48 the series of statements, "You've heard that it was said to the ancients [+ a quotation or a paraphrase of the Old Testament] . . . but I tell you [+ Jesus' interpretation]," didn't abrogate the Law but escalated it to a new level. By pointing back to "what comes out of the mouth," "this" puts emphasis on evil speech as what "defiles the human being."

15:12–14: Then the disciples, on approaching [Jesus], say to him, "Do you know that the Pharisees, on hearing the word, were tripped up [= offended rather than informed by your statements]**?" ¹³And he, answering, said, "Every plant that my heavenly Father didn't plant will be uprooted. ¹⁴Leave them [the Pharisees]! They're blind guides. And if a blind person is leading a blind person, both will fall into a pit."** The present tense of "says" accents the disciples' asking whether Jesus knows the Pharisees took offense, that is, refused to accept Jesus' teaching on defilement. The Pharisees "hear[d] the word" but didn't understand it as the disciples did understand as well as hear it. The disciples' question seems to show some fear of the Pharisees, though. So Jesus' reply implies that it's the Pharisees who ought to be afraid—of the Last Judgment. He doesn't say he knows about the Pharisees' having taken offense, but his answer implies he does. He compares the Pharisees to plants that his heavenly Father didn't plant—rather like the tares that will be uprooted at the Last Judgment (13:24–30, 36–43), only the tares stood for false disciples whereas the plant-like Pharisees have never made a profession of discipleship. Their fates will be the same, though. Like the false disciples represented by satanically sowed tares, the Pharisees represented by plants not sowed by Jesus' heavenly Father are to be abandoned. They'll be judged not only for their own willful blindness to the truth but also for leading others, likewise blinded by the elders' tradition, with themselves into the pit of eternal destruction (compare the willful blindness of false disciples in 13:13–15). "Leave them" to God's judgment. Implied: you have better things to do, in particular, the discipling of all nations (28:18–20). "If a blind person is leading a blind person"—but of course that wouldn't happen in real life. If it were to happen, though, it's a certainty that "both will fall into a pit." Such is the certainty of the Pharisees' judgment. It would appear from Romans 2:19 that they or their elders claimed "leader of the blind" as an honorific title for themselves; and falling into a pit represents disaster also in Psalm 7:15; Proverbs 26:27; Isaiah 24:18; Jeremiah 48:44.

15:15–20: And answering, Peter said to him, "Interpret this parable for us" [compare 13:36]. **¹⁶But he said, "Are you too without understanding still? ¹⁷You do comprehend, don't you, that everything which goes into the mouth makes its way into the stomach and is thrust out into a toilet?"** Implied answer: Of course you

know that it does. **¹⁸"But the things that come out of the mouth issue from the heart** [in the figurative sense of a person's thinking as well as feeling, for 'as a man thinks in his heart, so is he'], **and those things defile the human being."** "*Those* things" puts them at a morally desirable distance. **¹⁹"For from the heart issue evil contrivances: [namely,] murders, adulteries, sexual immoralities, thefts, false testimonies, slanders. ²⁰These are the things that defile a human being** [all of them moral rather than ritual], **but eating with unwashed hands doesn't defile a human being."** "This parable" refers to Jesus' puzzling statement about defilement (15:11). "You" is plural, referring to "the disciples" (mentioned in 15:12). In response to Peter's request for an explanation, Jesus asks whether as true disciples Peter and the others are still without understanding as are false disciples, who made up the rest of "the crowd" (15:10). Then Jesus answers his first question with another question that implies these disciples do have some understanding of his statement on defilement. "What goes into the mouth doesn't defile a human being" (15:11a) is plain speech by Jesus, which he now rewords as something true disciples understand: "everything which goes into the mouth makes its way into the stomach and is thrust out into a toilet." Since true disciples get further understanding of parables on top of their understanding of Jesus' plain speech (13:12), he adds an explanation of the rest of his parable on defilement: "But the things that come out of the mouth . . . defile the human being," as emphasized by the broken grammatical construction in which "those things" resume "the things that come out of the mouth." They issue from the heart and consist in various evil contrivances. In 15:4 Jesus cited "Honor [your] father and mother" from the Ten Commandments; so he now proceeds in order down those commandments to murders, adulteries (to which he adds sexual immoralities in general), thefts, and false testimonies (to which he adds the related slanders). Because coveting stays within the heart, he stops short of listing it. The evil contrivances from murders through thefts issue from the heart but don't come out of the mouth. False testimonies and slanders do come out of the mouth, though, so that the list circles back to defilement consisting in evil speech. The lack of "and" before the last-listed evil ("slanders") suggests, however, that the list is open-ended. Further evils could be added; but they too would issue from the heart, and perhaps come out of the mouth as well. "But eating with unwashed hands doesn't defile a human being" returns to the original issue (15:2) with a denial that keeps all the emphasis on moral defilement and erases the elders' tradition.

A GENTILE'S UNDERSTANDING OF JESUS AS LORD AND SON OF DAVID
Matthew 15:21–28

15:21–22: And on going out from there [Gennesaret (14:34)]**, Jesus withdrew into the districts of Tyre and Sidon** [heathen cities on the Mediterranean coast north of Galilee]. The antagonism of the Pharisees and scholars from Jerusalem (15:1–2) prompts Jesus to withdraw, much as he told his disciples to flee persecution (10:23). But it's also appropriate for him to withdraw into Gentile districts after transmuting Jewish dietary taboos, foreign to Gentiles, into moral taboos, applicable to them as well as to Jews. And just as the flight of disciples leads to further evangelization, so too does Jesus' withdrawal lead to evangelization—and of a Gentile at that (compare 28:18–20). **²²And behold, a Canaanite woman from those borders** [bounding "the districts of Tyre and Sidon"], **having come out** [presumably from her home], **started yelling, saying, "Have mercy on me, Lord, Son** [= descendant] **of David! My daughter is severely demon-possessed!"** "Behold" stresses that the woman was a Gentile, called a "Canaanite" to conform to Old Testament terminology. At least for Matthew and his audience the woman's plea for mercy amounts to a confession of Jesus as divine "Lord" and messianic "Son of David." The addressing of Jesus with "Son of David" anticipates the limitation of his ministry to Israel (15:24, 26) and indicates the woman's understanding of that limitation. That is, she shows her recognition that he came to Israel as the Davidic Messiah. But her prefixing of "Lord" shows that she also hopes to win from Jesus an exceptional benefit in view of his universal dominion. She seeks mercy for herself ("Have mercy *on me*"), because her daughter's demon-possession pains her motherly heart. "*Severely* demon-possessed" emphasizes the Gentiles' need of salvation in that the daughter's case represents the case of all heathen. And "started yelling" implies a repetition that prepares for the disciples' annoyance.

15:23–24: But he answered her not a word. And on approaching, his disciples were requesting him, saying, "Dismiss her, because she's yelling behind us." Jesus' refusal to say even a single word in answer to the woman will play up her faith, which is about to be featured. So too will the disciples' request that he dismiss her (without granting her plea [compare 14:15]). "Approaching [Jesus]" implies that his disciples were following him at a little distance, as disciples should do, and had to catch up for the making of their request. "Because she's yelling behind us" implies that the woman, yelling all the while, is coming up from behind the disciples. To make Jesus hear her from a longer distance, then, she has had to yell. **²⁴And he, answering** [the disciples, not the woman, for they've just spoken to Jesus and she hasn't yet come close to him], **said, "I've not been sent except** [= 'I've been sent *only* . . .'] **to the lost sheep of Israel's household** [compare Jeremiah 50:6]." Jesus' answer harmonizes with the disciples' request that he dismiss the woman unsatisfied. So her faith faces the obstacles of his silence, the disciples' annoyance, and the limitation of his mission to the masses of needy Jews (compare 10:5–6 with comments). But recollection of the exception made for a Gentile centurion in 8:5–13 gives Matthew's audience an inkling that a turnaround is presently in the offing.

15:25–26: And she, on coming, started worshiping him [= bowing to the ground repeatedly before him], **saying, "Lord, help me!"** The woman has caught up to Jesus. Whatever she meant historically speaking, for Matthew's audience she's portrayed as a worshiper of Jesus as her divine Lord. The repetition of her obeisance underscores the portrayal. Now that Jesus has agreed with his disciples that as a Gentile she shouldn't be granted her request, she drops the earlier, Jewishly limited address, "Son of David," and uses only the universally oriented address, "Lord." Lordship implies ability. So absent "Son of David," "help me!" replaces the earlier "have mercy on me!" **²⁶But he, answering, said, "It isn't good** [in the sense of fitting] **to take the children's bread and throw** [it] **to the little dogs."** "The children" stand for Jews, called in 15:24 "the lost sheep of Israel's household." The "bread" stands for the benefits of Jesus' messianic ministry. "The little dogs" stand for Gentiles. And the inappropriateness of taking the children's bread and throwing it to the little dogs stands for the inappropriateness of Jesus' extending his mission to Gentiles. Though Jews commonly used "dogs" as an epithet for Gentiles, here we have puppies ("little dogs") as opposed to the street-roaming scavengers referred to in the epithet. (Except for tethered watchdogs, full-grown dogs weren't kept in ancient Middle Eastern homes.) The inappropriate throwing of bread to the puppies implies a setting around the dinner table, an implication the woman is about to pick up. Jesus isn't snubbing the Gentile woman, then, so much as he's reflecting the divinely ordained limitation of his mission to Jews. But the woman could well take his answer as a snub.

15:27–28: But she said, "Yes, Lord [her third recognition of Jesus' lordship!], **for even the little dogs eat from the crumbs falling from their masters' table."** "Yes" states her agreement with the limitation of Jesus' mission to Jews. "For" introduces a basis for him to heal her daughter despite that limitation, though. It's that such a healing would count as only a crumb that accidentally falls from the table rather than as a loaf of bread deliberately thrown to the puppies. A falling crumb doesn't upset the task of feeding the children. Behind "their masters'" is the same word otherwise translated "Lord," so that the woman portrays Jesus as the Lord/Master of Gentiles, like her, and as the Lord of the Lord's Table (compare 1 Corinthians 10:21 and Matthew's eucharistic interpretation of Jesus' feeding of five thousand families [14:13–21]). **²⁸Then answering, Jesus told her, "O woman, great** [is] **your faith! It's to happen for you as you wish!" And her daughter was healed from that hour.** "*Then* answering" indicates a quick response due to the woman's expression of great faith. "O woman" turns Jesus' observation of her great faith into an exclamation; and by recalling Matthew's phrase, "a *Canaanite* woman," "O woman" notes the presence of such faith in a Gentile (compare 8:10, 13). Her "*great . . .* faith" contrasts with Peter's and the disciples' "*little* faith" (14:31; 16:8) and with the "*un*faith" of Jesus' fellow townspeople in Nazareth (13:58). In a tribute to the greatness of her faith, the healing of her daughter took place without Jesus' having to go and speak a word of exorcism. "From that hour" makes a similar tribute. And the healing means relief from the physical effects of demon-possession. All this because of faith based on a Gentile's understanding of Jesus as both Lord and Son of David. With 8:5–13, it's looking better and better for the salvation of Gentiles as well as Jews (compare 24:14; 28:18–20).

UNDERSTANDING JESUS' WILL TO HEAL AND FEED THE GENTILES
Matthew 15:29–38

This passage expands the theme of Jesus' ministry to the Gentiles, a theme begun in 8:5–13 and revived in 15:21–28. And Matthew portrays the disciples—at least the true ones—as understanding Jesus' will to minister to Gentiles as well as Jews.

15:29–31: **And on moving away from there** [the districts of Tyre and Sidon (15:21)], **Jesus went to the side of the Sea of Galilee. And on going up onto a mountain, he was sitting there.** [30]**And many crowds approached him, having with themselves lame people, blind people, crippled people, deaf-mutes, and many others. And they threw them at his feet; and he healed them,** [31]**so that the crowd marveled as they saw deaf-mutes speaking, crippled people healthy, and lame people walking around and blind people seeing** [compare Isaiah 29:18–19; 35:5–6]. **And they glorified the God of Israel.** Jesus' going up onto a mountain and taking the seated posture of a teacher revives the portrayal of him as a new and greater Moses (see 5:1 with comments). The revival is remarkable in that Jesus doesn't proceed to teach the Law, as would be expected, but heals many people with a variety of maladies. Who are the crowds that throw them at his feet? "Many crowds" have stood for professing disciples before (4:25–5:1; 8:1; 13:2). As buttressed by their glorifying God, they do so here too—with a particularly strong indication that they're Gentiles and therefore point forward to the masses of Gentiles who've flocked into the church by the time of Matthew's writing. "And they glorified the God of Israel"—by itself this phraseology could mean that Jews glorified their own God (Psalm 41:13; 106:48; Luke 1:68; Acts 13:17). But in the preceding passage at 15:24 as well as earlier in 10:5–6, the related phrase "the household of Israel" stands in opposition to Gentiles, so that in Matthew's context it's Gentiles who "glorified the God of Israel" (and compare Matthew's present reference to "the Sea of Galilee" with his use in 4:12–16 of Isaiah 9:1–2 to describe Galilee as "of the Gentiles [or 'nations']" in connection with "the road of the sea"). Once the "many crowds" (plural) have clustered in one place, where Jesus is, they become "the crowd" (singular), as in 13:2. Their throwing the afflicted "at his feet" indicates a vigorous recognition of Jesus' lordship (see 5:35; 22:44; 28:9 for a position at the feet as implying someone's lordship). The

many and various healings Jesus performed exhibit his marvelous mercy extended toward Gentiles.

15:32–33: **And on summoning his disciples, Jesus said, "I feel sorry for the crowd, because they're staying with me—already three days!—and don't have anything to eat. And I don't want to dismiss them hungry, lest they faint on the way** [to their homes]." Now Jesus expresses mercy for the crowd in addition to having mercifully healed their afflicted. Along with mercy, though, his authority comes out in a summoning of the disciples and in an implication that even though the crowd has stayed with him three days already and have no food, they can't leave unless he dismisses them. [33]**And the disciples say to him, "From where in the wilderness do we have** [= get] **so many loaves of bread as to sate** [= fill to satisfaction] **such a large crowd?"** The disciples ask where to get a supply of food, but they do understand their responsibility to get it so that the crowd can eat to the full. Jesus doesn't even have to tell them. They've learned from 14:16, 19. The present tense in "the disciples *say*" stresses that their understanding of the responsibility indicates true discipleship (13:10–12, 19, 23, 51–52). This responsibility symbolizes their responsibility to disciple all nations (28:18–20). "Such a large crowd" points forward again to the masses of Gentiles who were to come into the church.

15:34–38: **And Jesus says to them, "How many loaves do you have?" And they said, "Seven, and a few small fish."** The present tense in "Jesus *says*" corresponds to the present tense in the disciples' question and accordingly stresses his recognition of their understanding the responsibility they have to feed the crowd. For the rest, see the comments on Mark 8:4–5. [35]**And on directing the crowd to recline on the ground,** [36]**he took the seven loaves and the fish and, on giving thanks, he broke** [them in pieces] **and started giving** [them] **to the disciples, and the disciples to the crowds.** [37]**And all ate and were sated** [filled to satisfaction]. **And they picked up a surplus of the broken pieces, seven baskets full.** [38]**And the ones eating were four thousand husbands besides wives and children.** Jesus' authority comes out again in his directing the crowd to recline. "Giving thanks" presages the same at the institution of the Lord's Supper (26:27). Matthew reverts to the plural, "crowds" (see 15:36 with 15:30), after several occurrences of the singular, "crowd" (15:31–33, 35), to reemphasize the large number of people. For the reclining, the breaking in pieces, the disciples' giving to the people, the sating of all, the surplus of broken pieces, and the families of husbands, wives, and children, see the comments on 14:19–21. These repetitions have the point of bringing Gentiles as well as Jews into a preview of the Lord's Supper. Differences in numbers and hampers versus baskets distinguish the two events from each other. Since the number seven often denotes completion (as in the six days of creation and a seventh of rest, for example), "seven baskets full" symbolizes a full complement; and the number "four" in "four thousand" symbolizes the coming conversion of multitudes, including Gentiles, "from the four winds" from which the angels of the Son of Man will gather his elect (better, "his selected ones") at the second coming (24:31 [compare Revelation 7:1]).

FAILURE TO UNDERSTAND THE
SIGNS OF THE TIMES
Matthew 15:39–16:4

15:39–16:1: And on dismissing the crowds, he [Jesus] **got into a boat and went into the borders of Magadan** [location uncertain]. The plural of "the crowds" accents their standing for the large, mixed body of the church in Matthew's time. Jesus goes by boat alone again (compare 14:13a and the comments on 16:5 for the disciples' catching up with him). [1]**And on approaching** [him], **the Pharisees and Sadducees, testing** [him], **asked him to show them a sign from heaven.** Thus Jesus has the same opponents that John the baptizer had (3:7), so that the parallel between these two is extended. By testing Jesus, the Pharisees and Sadducees play a devilish role; for "testing" equates with "tempting." They go back to the same Greek word that Matthew used for the Devil's tempting Jesus (4:1, 3). And the Greek verb underlying "asked" connotes insistence. That is, the Pharisees and Sadducees insist on Jesus' showing them "a sign from heaven," which means some heavenly display not subject to interpretation as satanically aided (see the comments on Mark 8:11).

16:2–4: And he, answering, told them, "When evening has come, you say, 'Fair weather, for the sky is fiery [= red]'; [3]**and in the morning** [you say,] **'Today a storm, for the sky is fiery** [= red], **glowering** [and therefore ominous].' **On the one hand you know** [how] **to discern the face of the sky** [that is, to distinguish between what a red sky portends in the evening and what it portends in the morning]. **On the other hand you can't** [discern] **the signs of the times.** [4]**An evil and adulterous generation seeks after a sign, and a sign won't be given to it except for the sign of Jonah." And abandoning them, he went away.** Jesus starts with evening because Jews counted a day as starting at sunset, and he excoriates the Pharisees and Sadducees for being adept at meteorology but clueless at eschatology. They're so ignorant of the end times that they don't recognize the coming of God's reign in the words and deeds of Jesus (= "the signs of the times" [compare 11:2–6; 12:28]). We expect the plural "signs," but not the plural "times." The latter matches the different kinds of weather in the preceding analogy, however; and the word for "times" connotes suitability. So the times are suitable to Jesus' messianic words and deeds. "The *signs* of the times" refers to those already provided by Jesus in his words and deeds but attributed to satanic power by his enemies, whereas the only sign of the irrefutable sort demanded by them is yet to come. It'll be his staying in the realm of the dead for only three days and three nights (see 12:40 with comments). "*Abandoning* them" connotes giving up on the Pharisees and Sadducees. As "an evil and adulter-

ous generation" (for which see the comments on 12:39), they're doomed to damnation.

THE DISCIPLES' GAINING UNDERSTANDING
CONCERNING THE EVIL TEACHING OF
THE PHARISEES AND SADDUCEES
Matthew 16:5–12

16:5–12: And the disciples, on coming to the other side, had forgotten to take loaves of bread. After feeding four thousand families, Jesus alone got in a boat and went into the borders of Magadan (15:39). Now the disciples catch up with him, apparently on foot overland. "To the other side" means the west side of the Sea of Galilee, opposite the east side, where Jesus fed the four thousand families. The loaves of bread that the disciples had forgotten to take probably consisted of leftovers from the feeding (15:37 [see 14:19 for "loaves" in the form of broken fragments]). [6]**And Jesus said to them, "Look out for and take precaution against the leaven of the Pharisees and Sadducees."** Jesus' exhortation to wariness contrasts with the disciples' forgetfulness. See the comments on 13:33 for leaven as a symbol of pervasive evil. [7]**But they** [the disciples] **were reasoning among themselves, saying, "We didn't take loaves of bread."** Whereas Jesus is concerned to warn the disciples against the Pharisees' and Sadducees' leaven, the disciples are concerned over their having forgotten to take bread with them and reason that his mention of leaven pointed to their forgetfulness. It's as though they missed the note of warning in his statement. So he addresses their concern over lack of bread: [8]**And on coming to know** [what they were reasoning among themselves], **Jesus said, "Why are you reasoning among yourselves,** [men] **of little faith, that you don't have loaves of bread? [9]Don't you yet comprehend or remember the five loaves of the five thousand and how many hampers** [of leftovers] **you took? [10]Nor the seven loaves of the four thousand and how many baskets** [of leftovers] **you took? [11]How is it that you don't comprehend that I didn't speak to you about loaves of bread? But take precaution against the leaven of the Pharisees and Sadducees."** Jesus attributes the disciples' incomprehension and forgetfulness to "little faith," which he corrects by reminding them of how many were fed with how little, yet with leftovers far exceeding the original amounts—and this on two occasions. The "not yet" of his question implies that the deficiency in their comprehension will be eliminated. And it is, for despite the absence of an explanation of what he meant by "the leaven," Jesus' denial that "leaven" had to do with "loaves of bread" and the repetition of his warning enlighten them: [12]**Then they understood that he hadn't said to take precaution against the leaven of loaves of bread—rather, against the Pharisees' and Sadducees' teaching.** So they'd thought that he warned them against literal leaven in the bread they'd forgotten to take. Now it strikes them that "of the Pharisees and Sadducees" made "leaven" a figure of speech for the Pharisees' and Sadducees' pernicious teaching (for which see 15:1–11; 22:23–33 and large parts of chapter 23). As true disciples, they understand.

UNDERSTANDING THE SON OF MAN
TO BE THE CHRIST AND GOD'S SON
Matthew 16:13–20

16:13–16: **And on coming into the districts of Philip's Caesarea** [a city located about twenty-five miles north of the Sea of Galilee, enlarged and renamed by the tetrarch Herod Philip, a son of Herod the Great, in honor of Caesar Augustus and himself, and distinguished from Caesarea on the Mediterranean coast and to the south], **Jesus was asking his disciples, saying, "Who do men say the Son of Man is?"** There's a wordplay between "men" and "the Son of Man." [14]**And they said, "On the one hand, some** [say,] **'John the baptizer.' On the other hand, others** [say,] **'Elijah.' But different ones** [say,] **'Jeremiah' or 'one of the prophets.'"** As usual, Jesus uses "the Son of Man" in reference to himself. By using it here he prepares for an equation of himself as the Son of Man with "the Christ, the Son of the living God" (16:16) and for his suffering, getting killed, and being raised in all three of these capacities. That is to say, by divine necessity as indicated in the Old Testament he'll suffer, get killed, and be raised as the Son of Man, as the Christ, and as God's Son. [15]**He says to them, "But who do you** [plural] **say I am?"** The present tense of "says" heightens tension over the disciples' understanding or misunderstanding of Jesus' identity, and "I" identifies Jesus as "the Son of Man" in his earlier question. [16]**And answering, Simon Peter said, "You're the Christ, the Son of the living God** [compare 26:63]**."** Matthew prefixes "Simon" to "Peter" in preparation for Jesus' upcoming use of "Simon." The addition of "the Son of the living God" to "the Christ" echoes the worshipful confession of the disciples (on whose behalf Peter is presently speaking) in 14:33, "Truly you're God's Son," and anticipates Jesus' upcoming statement that his Father in heaven has revealed Jesus' christhood and divine sonship to Simon (compare 11:25–27). Though "son of God" might connote no more than a purely human messiah adopted by God as his vicegerent, the title "Immanuel . . . God [is] with us" (1:23), the whole account of Jesus' virginal conception and birth (1:18–25), and the sandwiching of Jesus as "the Son" between "the Father" and "the Holy Spirit" in a baptismal formula (28:19) demand the stronger connotation of deity. The description of God as "living" echoes Old Testament language (see Hosea 1:10, for example), prepares for Jesus' assurance that the gates of Hades—that is, death—won't overpower the church (16:18), and distinguishes God from the false gods worshiped by Gentiles, whose conversion Jesus will commission his original disciples to seek (28:19).

Since Peter has told Jesus who Jesus is, Jesus now tells Peter who, or what, Peter is. ***16:17–18:*** **And answering, Jesus told him, "You're fortunate, Simon Barjona, in that flesh and blood didn't reveal** [my identity] **to you; rather, my Father in heaven** [revealed it to you]. [18]**And I tell you that you're Peter** [which means 'a loose stone'], **and on this bedrock I'll build my church, and the gates of Hades won't overpower it** ['my church']**."** "Bar-" is Aramaic for "son." So "Simon Barjona" means "Simon son of Jonah." But according to John 1:42; 21:15–17, Simon was "the son of John"; and though they're similar to each other, "Jonah" differs from "John." Here, then, Jesus is calling Simon "the son of Jonah" in the way the Old Testament spoke about "the sons of the prophets," that is, those apprenticed to prophets and destined to become prophets themselves (see 2 Kings 2, for example). Jesus associates Simon with the prophet Jonah, whom Jesus recently referenced in "the sign of Jonah the prophet" (12:39–40; 16:4). That sign had to do with Jesus' spending only three days and three nights in the realm of the dead—hence, by implication, with his death and resurrection. To call Simon "the son of Jonah" is therefore to predict his death by martyrdom and a following resurrection to eternal life. Thus we're led from "the sign of Jonah" through "the son of Jonah" to the inability of "the gates of Hades"—death, especially death by martyrdom—to overpower the church, and finally in 16:21–28 to the necessities that Jesus suffer, get killed, and be raised and that his disciples take up their crosses and lose their lives in order to gain them.

"Flesh and blood" connotes human frailty and inadequacy (compare 1 Corinthians 15:50; Galatians 1:16; Ephesians 6:12; Hebrews 2:14) and contrasts in these respects with Jesus' "Father in heaven." "I tell you" lends certainty to the further part of Jesus' statement. Actually, "you're Peter" could equally well be translated with "you're a [loose] stone" (*petros* in Greek). Obviously, a loose stone is unsuitable for the foundation of a building; but "bedrock" (*petra* in Greek) *is* suitable for such a foundation. "Cephas," the Aramaic word corresponding to "Peter" that appears elsewhere in the New Testament (John 1:42, for example), doesn't make the distinction between a loose stone and bedrock. But Matthew is writing in Greek. So the distinction between Peter as a loose stone, on the one hand, and bedrock, on the other hand, means that he isn't the bedrock on which Jesus will build his church. Besides, for Peter/*petros* or Cephas as the bedrock that forms the church's foundation, we'd expect "on *you* I'll build my church." What then is "this bedrock" as distinguished from Peter, the loose stone? It's the words of Jesus, his teaching. For in 7:24 he said, "Therefore everyone who hears these words of mine and does them will be like a wise man who built his house on bedrock." The image of building is the same as here. "These words of mine" define the "bedrock" on which building takes place, and "*this* bedrock" on which Jesus will build his church corresponds to "*these* words of mine" in 7:24. Furthermore, the identification of "this bedrock" with Jesus' words suits Matthew's overall portrayal of Jesus as a teacher (see especially 23:8). Peter isn't the church's *foundation*, then. To the extent he's an obedient disciple, along with all other such disciples he's part of the *superstructure* of the church, no longer a loose stone but one stone among many others fitted together to make a building that Jesus calls his church. It might be objected that 16:18 is too distant from 7:24 for "this bedrock" to recall the "bedrock" of "these my words" in 7:24. But a book like Matthew's Gospel was meant to be read orally long stretches at a time, even as a whole; and it takes only forty minutes or less to read aloud from 7:24 to 16:18. So an audience might easily be expected to understand 16:18 in the light of 7:24.

"*My* church" corresponds to "*his* selected ones," "*his* [the Son of Man's] kingdom," "*his* throne," "*his* glory," and "*his* angels" (13:41; 16:27–28; 24:31; 25:31; contrast "*their* synagogues" in 4:23; 9:35; 10:17; 12:9; 13:54 and "*your* synagogues" in 23:34). "Church" refers to the new people of God, Jesus' disciples; and the metaphor of building a people occurs also in Jeremiah 18:9; 24:6; 31:4; 42:10; 1 Corinthians 3:9; Ephesians 2:19–22; 1 Peter 2:5. "The gates of Hades" echoes Isaiah 38:10, where the expression stands for death (compare "the gates of death" in Job 38:17; Psalms 9:13; 107:18). The figure of a foundation resistant to flood and storm from the underworld appears in Isaiah 28:15–18. Persecution to the death won't threaten the bedrock of Jesus' words, but it will threaten the church he'll build on them. Nevertheless, such persecution won't overpower his church; and a resurrection like that of Jesus awaits the martyrs as well as all other true disciples.

The alluding of "this bedrock" to "these words of mine" leads to a portrayal of Peter as a Christian scholar (for which see 13:52) who uses keys—that is, Jesus' words—to bind and loosen things—that is, to prohibit and promote various kinds of behavior on the part of those who make up Jesus' church (compare the association of binding and loosing with church discipline in 18:15–18, and see 5:19 for loosening as a figure of speech for allowing [though in that case for allowing a commandment to be broken]). *16:19*: **"I'll give you the keys of the kingdom of heaven** [compare Isaiah 22:22]; **and whatever you bind on earth will have been bound in heaven, and whatever you loosen on earth will have been loosened in heaven."** Keys are used for locking and unlocking, and in 23:13 Jesus will excoriate the scholars and Pharisees for locking the kingdom of heaven with their teaching so as neither to enter it themselves nor to allow others to enter it. As a Christian scholar, Peter is to use the keys of Jesus' words to prohibit the kind of behavior that falsifies discipleship and blocks entrance into the kingdom, and to promote the kind of behavior that verifies discipleship and gains entrance into the kingdom. "Will have been bound in heaven" and "will have been loosened in heaven" indicate that Peter's binding and loosening will have already been determined in heaven. In other words, Peter will have already received direction for this activity. It will consist in Jesus' words, already spoken and derived from heaven. But other disciples too have heard them. Every true disciple is a scholar according to 13:51–52 (see also the comments on 8:19). And in 18:18 Jesus will give all disciples the authority to bind and loosen in accordance with what

has been bound and loosened in heaven. So Peter is only representative. He shares this authority with all other true disciples (compare the prohibition in 23:8–11 of calling any fellow disciple "Rabbi," "Father," or "Tutor"). All in all, then, Peter represents every disciple in confessing Jesus as the Christ and Son of the living God, in having received the revelation of Jesus' identity from the Father in heaven, in making up the church built on the bedrock of Jesus' words, in facing the threat of martyrdom with an assurance of resurrection, and in having been commissioned by Jesus as a scholar who teaches the discipled nations "to keep all the things, as many as they are, that [Jesus] has commanded [them]" (28:19–20a). The final accent in this passage now falls on the disciples' understanding Jesus to be the Christ and on the need to keep this information from everybody else, including false disciples who—because they haven't yielded fruit in keeping with true discipleship—don't deserve to know the secrets of the kingdom of heaven (13:10–15). *16:20*: **Then he ordered the disciples that they tell no one, "He's the Christ."**

UNDERSTANDING JESUS' LORDSHIP FOR THE SUFFERING OF PERSECUTION
Matthew 16:21–28

16:21: **From then on Jesus began showing his disciples that he must go away** [from Galilee] **into Jerusalem and suffer severely from the elders and chief priests and scholars and be killed and raised on the third day.** Just as in 4:17 "From then on Jesus began . . ." introduced Jesus' public proclamations of the kingdom in Galilee, here the same phraseology introduces private predictions of his passion and resurrection in Jerusalem. "Must" points to God-willed necessity as foretold in the Old Testament, so that Matthew will pepper his account of Jesus' passion and resurrection with quotations of fulfilled Old Testament passages. "Go away [from Galilee]" strikes a contrast with Jesus' having withdrawn "into Galilee" (4:12). "Into Jerusalem" pinpoints the location of Jesus' passion and resurrection and anticipates 20:17–19. "Suffer *severely*" prepares for "be killed." "From the elders and chief priest and scholars" identifies Jesus' persecutors as those who make up the three factions of the Sanhedrin, the Jewish Supreme Court (see the comments on 2:4–6; 15:2). Against Jesus they'll present a united front. "On the third day" refers to Easter and counts Good Friday and the intervening Saturday as the first and second days. So Jesus adds his own prediction to those in the Old Testament. Almost certainly the Jews of Jesus' time didn't think that the Christ would have to suffer (compare 16:22–23; 17:23; Mark 9:31–32).

16:22–23: **And on taking him aside, Peter started reprimanding him, saying,** "[God will be] **merciful to you, Lord! By no means will you have this** [as your fate]!**" "On taking him aside" means that Peter came up beside Jesus to take him apart for a private conversation. He doesn't want to shame Jesus before the other disciples. Peter's reprimand takes the form of a prediction that contradicts Jesus' foregoing prediction. But it contains an addressing of Jesus as "Lord" and arises, though incorrectly, out of Peter's correct understanding of him as "the Christ, the Son of the living God" (16:16). In particular and because of an assumption that God's Son (in the strict sense meant throughout Matthew) would share with his Father uninterruptably eternal life, "the Son of the *living* God" seems to exclude Jesus' being killed. Or so Peter thinks. [23]**But he** [Jesus]**, on turning, said to Peter, "Go behind me, Satan. You're a snare to me, because you're not thinking the things of God; rather,** [you're thinking] **the things of human beings."** Jesus turns to address Peter, who is standing beside him, and tells him to go back behind him, where disciples are supposed to be, following their teacher. Calling Peter "Satan" means that Satan is using him in an attempt to snare Jesus into refusing to fulfill God's scripturally revealed will that he suffer, get killed, and be raised. Hovering in the background is the danger that false disciples in the church will snare fellow disciples into refusing to take the path of possible martyrdom. "The things of God" are the items of his scripturally revealed will. "The things of human beings" are the items of mistaken human expectation concerning the Christ (compare the comments on Mark 8:33).

16:24–26: Then Jesus said to his disciples, "If anyone wants to come behind me, he has to disown himself and pick up his cross and follow me." Jesus is describing the nature of true discipleship, not its preconditions such as repentance and faith. So the sayings in these verses augment the disciples' understanding (compare 13:11–12) and thereby counteract Peter's failure to think the things of God (16:23). "Then" establishes a connection between these sayings and Peter's failure. For coming behind Jesus, self-disowning, picking up one's cross, and following Jesus, see the comments on Mark 8:34. [25]**"For whoever wants to save his life will lose it. But whoever loses his life on account of me will find it** [compare 10:38–39]. [26]**For in what way will a person be profited if he gains the whole world but forfeits his life? Or what will a person give as an exchange for his life?"** The string of future verbs—"*will* lose," "*will* find," "*will* be profited," and "*will* . . . give"—points ahead to the Last Judgment. For the rest, see the comments on Mark 8:35–37.

Now Jesus connects the Last Judgment, just alluded to in 16:25–26, with his second coming as the Son of Man. **16:27: "For the Son of Man is going to come in the glory of his Father with his** [the Son of Man's] **angels, and then 'he'll give back to each** [person] **in accordance with his** [that person's] **behavior** [Psalm 62:12; Proverbs 24:12]*.'"* This is the third successive time a saying of Jesus has begun with "For." The first saying (16:25) gave a reason for cross-bearing. The reason was that you lose eternal life by saving your present life, but find eternal life by losing your present life for Jesus' sake. The second saying (16:26) explained why the paradox in the first saying holds true: even gaining the whole world won't save your eternal life at the Last Judgment. And now the third

saying (16:27) provides the reason for the second saying. It's that the Son of Man will come and repay each person according to his behavior, not according to his possessions (for Jesus the Son of Man as the final judge, see also 7:21–23; 13:41–43; 25:31–46). The conjunction of "the Son of Man" with "his Father" implies that the Son of Man is also the Son of God. His glory will be no less than that of God his Father because it'll *be* his Father's glory. As in 13:41, he claims the angels as his own. "*Each* [person]" indicates he'll judge all humankind individual by individual, and "in accordance with his [that individual's] behavior" points to behavior consistent or inconsistent with true discipleship as the criterion of judgment. Salvation occurs by grace through faith, but the truth or falsity of faith comes out in behavior.

16:28: "Amen I tell you that there are some of those standing here who as such [that is, as standing here] **will by no means taste death** [a figure of speech for dying] **until they see the Son of Man coming in his kingdom** [compare 10:23; 19:28; 24:30; 25:31]**."** "Amen I tell you" stresses the truth of this prediction. As Jesus has just claimed the angels as his own, so he now claims the kingdom as his own. "Coming in his kingdom" corresponds to "com[ing] in the glory of his Father" in 16:27 and indicates that his "giv[ing] back to each [person] in accordance with his behavior," also in 16:27, has to do with entrance or nonentrance into his kingdom. "*Some* [people] standing here" implies that others standing there won't see the Son of Man coming in his kingdom. But the emphasis falls on the some who will.

UNDERSTANDING JESUS AS THE
NEW AND GREATER MOSES
Matthew 17:1–8

17:1–3: And after six days Jesus takes along Peter and James and John his brother [that is, the brother of James]**, and he takes them up onto a high mountain by themselves.** [2]**And he was transfigured in their presence, and his face shone as the sun** [shines]**, and his clothes became white as the light.** [3]**And behold, there appeared to them** [that is, to Peter, James, and John] **Moses and Elijah, speaking with him** [Jesus]. "After six days" ties this transfiguration of Jesus to the prediction in 16:28 that some standing there wouldn't taste death till they saw the Son of Man coming in his kingdom, so that the transfiguration fulfills the prediction; and Peter, James, and John qualify as the predicted "some." "By themselves" and the present tense in "takes along" and "takes . . . up" underscore their qualifying. The shining of Jesus' face as the sun shines and his clothes' becoming white as the light correspond to his prediction in 16:27 that he'd come in his Father's glory. But the prediction in 16:28 included "coming in his kingdom" and connected with his predicting in 16:27 that he'd come not only in his Father's glory but also "with his angels" and with the outcome of judging everybody—features absent from the transfiguration. So the transfiguration marks only a preview and partial fulfillment of the second coming.

But more is at work in this account. Matthew's repeated paralleling of Jesus with Moses justifies that he presents the "high mountain" as a new Sinai, and that he presents Jesus' going up onto it after six days as a parallel to Moses' going up onto Sinai after six days, that is, on the seventh (Exodus 24:16). Both times a cloud of divine glory (yet to be mentioned here) covered the mountain. In Moses' immediately preceding ascent up Sinai, he took Aaron, Nadab, and Abihu, plus seventy elders of Israel, who saw God there (Exodus 24:9-11). The seventy elders don't interest Matthew; but the three men Aaron, Nadab, and Abihu probably reminded him of the trio Peter, James, and John. And Joshua, whose name is the Hebrew form of "Jesus" and who succeeded Moses in leadership later on, accompanied Moses up Mount Sinai (Exodus 24:13). The addition of "his brother" to "John" both distinguishes this John from John the baptizer and reminds us that Jesus' disciples form a brotherhood (see the comments on 1:2, 11; 4:18, 21; 5:21-24 and so on). The shining of Jesus' face like the sun echoes the shining forth of the righteous like the sun (13:43), but the addition of "face" to Jesus' shining makes an allusion to the shining of Moses' face as a result of his meeting with God on Mount Sinai (Exodus 34:29-35; compare 2 Corinthians 3:7-18). With "white as the light" in regard to Jesus' clothes, compare the shining light of the disciples' good deeds (5:14-16). "Behold" highlights the appearance of Moses and Elijah. Matthew mentions Moses first to further the parallel between Jesus and Moses (contrast Mark 9:4). Both Moses and Elijah conversed with God on Sinai (also called Horeb [see Exodus 19:18-24; 32:7-14; 33:17-34:28; 1 Kings 19:9-18]). And Jesus is "God with us" (1:23) as well as the new and greater Moses.

17:4-5: And answering [in the sense of responding, since no question has been asked], **Peter told Jesus, "Lord, it's good we're here. If you want** [me to], **I'll make here three tents, one for you and one for Moses and one for Elijah." ⁵While he was still speaking, behold, a luminous cloud overshadowed them; and, behold, a voice** [came] **out of the cloud, saying, "This is my beloved Son, in whom I took delight. Hear him!"** For the fourth time in this Gospel Peter addresses Jesus with "Lord" (see also 14:28, 30; 16:22). "It's good we're here" implies that Peter, James, and John are like the good soil sown with "the word of the kingdom" and bearing the fruit of good deeds (13:8, 23). "If you want [me to]" underlines Peter's recognition of Jesus' lordship and submission to it. "*I'll* make here three tents" indicates Peter's desire to fulfill, by himself, Jesus' wish. "Three *tents*" recalls the tent, traditionally called the tabernacle, that Moses made for the Lord. But "*three* tents," including tents for Moses and Elijah as well as for Jesus, disagrees with the sole lordship of Jesus as "God with us" (1:23) and therefore as greater than both Moses and Elijah. To check this disagreement, "a luminous cloud overshadowed them [probably referring to Jesus, Moses, and Elijah]." But since a luminous cloud *shines*, it can't cast a shadow of *darkness*. So "overshadowed" has the sense of envelopment rather than that of darkening.

This envelopment forestalls the making of tents (compare Moses' inability to enter the tent of meeting because "the cloud had settled on it and the glory of the Lord filled the tabernacle" [Exodus 40:34-35]). "Behold" calls special attention to the cloud, and another "behold" calls equal attention to the voice coming out of the cloud and to what it says to the three disciples. The luminosity of the cloud and "*my* beloved Son" and "*I* took delight" indicate God the Father's presence and voice in reminiscence of his presence in a cloud and his speaking out of it on Mount Sinai (Exodus 24:16). "Hear him!" calls on the disciples to listen to Jesus, for he has replaced Moses and Elijah as God's spokesman for the new age of the kingdom (see Deuteronomy 18:15, where Moses himself says, "The Lord your God will raise up for you a prophet like me from among you, from your brothers. You shall hear him" [compare Matthew 11:15; 13:9, 18, 43; 15:10]). For the first part of the Father's statement, see the comments on 3:17.

17:6-8: And on hearing [the voice out of the cloud], **the disciples fell on their face and became exceedingly afraid. ⁷And Jesus approached and, on touching them, said, "Get up and stop being afraid." ⁸And on lifting their eyes, they saw no one except Jesus himself, alone** [so that from now on the disciples are to hear Jesus in monologue, not in conversation with Moses and Elijah]. "Face" is a collective singular. "Fell on their face" indicates deep disturbance (compare 26:38-39; Ezekiel 1:28; Daniel 8:17-18; 10:7-9, 15-17). The disciples "became exceedingly afraid" because they've heard God the Father, just as the Israelites feared when he spoke to them at Sinai (Exodus 20:1, 18-21; Deuteronomy 5:22-27; 18:16). Jesus' touch gives the disciples assurance, and the cessation of God the Father's speaking gives Jesus reason to tell them to stop being afraid. Since they've fallen on their face, they have to lift their eyes to see Jesus by himself. "Himself, alone" underscores his solitary presence and the need to listen only to him.

UNDERSTANDING JOHN THE
BAPTIZER AS ELIJAH
Matthew 17:9-13

17:9-10: And as they were coming down from the mountain, Jesus commanded them, saying, "Tell the vision to no one till the Son of Man has been raised from among the dead." Publicizing the vision would counteract Jesus' teaching that as the Son of Man he must suffer severely and be killed before being raised (16:21). "The vision" emphasizes the transfiguration's revelatory character. ¹⁰**And the disciples asked him, saying, "Why then do the scholars say, 'Elijah must come first'?"** "Then" establishes a logical connection between this question and the foregoing mention of the Son of Man's resurrection: since his resurrection implies his death, why do the scholars say Elijah must come first? Won't Elijah's restoration of all things forestall the Son of Man's being killed? This latter question implies that Peter, James, and John have understood Jesus' passion prediction. See Malachi 4:5–6 for Elijah's coming prior to the Day of the Lord, and the comments on Mark 9:11.

17:11–13: And he, answering, said, "On the one hand, Elijah is coming, and he'll restore all things. [12]On the other hand, I tell you that Elijah has come already, and people didn't recognize him [to be Elijah]**; rather, they did in him** [we'd say 'to him,' but 'in him' means something like 'in his case'] **as many things as they wanted** [to do]**."** Jesus is referring to the failure of Herod Antipas and Herodias to recognize John the baptizer as the prophesied Elijah and to their consequent arrest, binding, imprisonment, and beheading of John (14:1–12). Yet the statements that "Elijah *is coming*" and that "he *will* restore all things" indicate that although Elijah has already come in the person of John, he didn't restore all things. Otherwise he'd have been recognized and would have avoided imprisonment and execution. So he has to come again for the restoration of all things. In the meantime, absent that restoration the Son of Man will have to suffer severely and be killed after the pattern of John himself. "I tell you" underscores Elijah's fate in the person of John. Jesus' answering the disciples' question adds further understanding to the understanding they already have of Jesus' coming passion, an understanding that prompted their question. **"In this way also the Son of Man is going to suffer by them** [= by the agency of the elders, chief priests, and scholars (16:21)]**."** So the parallel between John and Jesus develops further. "Is *going* to suffer" connotes the certainty that grows out of divine necessity (see 16:21 again). [13]**Then the disciples understood that he'd spoken to them about John the baptizer.** Their added understanding contrasts with the failure of Herod Antipas and Herodias to recognize Elijah in John. Overall, then, Matthew uses this episode to stress both prior understanding and added understanding as distinguishing marks of true disciples (compare 13:11–12).

THE THREAT OF LITTLE FAITH
Matthew 17:14–20

The disciples' increased understanding (17:9–13) needs to be supplemented with larger faith. Hence the present passage exposes the danger of their little faith.

17:14–16: And when [they'd] **come to the crowd, a man approached him** [Jesus]**, kneeling before him and saying, [15]"Lord, have mercy on my son, because he's subject to seizures and suffers badly. For he often falls into a fire and often into water. [16]And I brought him to your disciples, and they couldn't heal him."** The crowd of professing disciples produces a man whose kneeling before Jesus and addressing him with "Lord" suit discipleship in addition to desperation. As usual, "Lord" connotes Jesus' deity for Matthew and his audience. The two instances of "often" tell how badly the man's son suffers. The seizures result in falling, and "into a fire" and "into water" identify the elements that inflict the suffering.

17:17–18: And Jesus, answering, said, "O unbelieving and perverted generation [compare Deuteronomy 32:5]**, how long shall I be with you? How long shall I put up with you? Bring him** [the son] **here to me."** The verb "Bring" has a plural "you" hidden in it. So the disciples whom Jesus didn't take up the mountain and to whom the father brought his son—these disciples are the ones whom Jesus tells to bring the man's son. Therefore also, these disciples are the ones whom Jesus addresses as an "unbelieving and perverted generation." The unbelief and perversion have to do with the present case in particular. (It's not a blanket description.) Unbelief amounts to a perversion of discipleship. "O" lends gravity to Jesus' exasperated questions. "How long shall I be *with* you?" alludes to Jesus as "God *with* us" (1:23). In 28:20 he'll answer his own question of how long: "And behold, I am with you *all the days till the consummation of the age.*" The command to bring the son to Jesus shows Jesus' determination to expose the baselessness of unbelief. [18]**And Jesus reprimanded him, and the demon came out from him, and the boy was healed from that hour** [onward]. Matthew leaves it to be assumed that the boy had been brought to Jesus and now indicates that demon-possession lay behind the boy's seizures. At first it's ambiguous whether Jesus reprimanded the boy or reprimanded the demon. But the demon's coming out from the boy makes clear that Jesus reprimanded the demon. The boy's healing consisted in deliverance from the physical effects of demon-possession. For "healed from that hour," see the comments on 8:13 and 9:22.

17:19–20: Then the disciples [the Twelve, minus Peter, James, and John]**, on approaching, said to Jesus in private, "Because of what weren't we able to cast it** [the demon] **out?" [20]And he says to them, "Because of the littleness of your faith. For amen I tell you, if you have faith like a grain of mustard, you'll say to this mountain, 'Move away from here to there,' and it will move away; and nothing will be impossible for you** [compare 1 Corinthians 13:2]**."** Privacy enables Jesus to instruct his true disciples on matters deliberately hidden from false disciples. The present tense in "he *says* to them" underlines this instruction. If even faith as small as a grain of mustard could move a mountain but the faith of the disciples couldn't so much as cast out a demon, their faith must have been even smaller than a grain of a mustard (for which see the comments on 13:31–32). "*This* mountain" refers to the Mount of Transfiguration (17:1). Ancient people often thought of mountains as pillars that support a solid sky and hold in position the disc of the earth over subterranean waters. The great depth of the bases of the mountains made the mountains a natural symbol of stability. In this conceptual framework you could hardly think of a more hyperbolic figure of power than that of moving a mountain. "*If* you have faith like a grain of mustard" indicates what *could* be. "It will move away; and nothing will be impossible for you" indicates what *would* be if the "could" turned into an actuality. "Amen I tell you" adds assurance. And the introductory "For" makes the whole statement an explanation of "Because of the littleness of your faith." The earliest and best manuscripts don't have 17:21.

UNDERSTANDING JESUS' DEATH
AND RESURRECTION
Matthew 17:22–23

17:22–23: **And as they** [the disciples] **were assembling in Galilee, Jesus said to them, "The Son of Man is going to be given over into the hands of men,** [23]**and they'll kill him, and on the third day he'll be raised." And they were exceedingly saddened.** The disciples are assembling in Galilee for a pilgrimage to Jerusalem, where they'll celebrate the Passover festival. The pilgrimage will start soon (see 19:1). To prepare the disciples for what will happen to him in Jerusalem, Jesus predicts again his passion and resurrection there. This second such prediction fulfills the implication in 16:21: "From then on Jesus *began* showing his disciples . . . ." "Is *going* to be given over" connotes certainty. "To be *given over*" predicts for the first time Judas Iscariot's giving Jesus over to the Jewish authorities (20:18; 26:15–16) and their giving him over to Pilate and the Gentiles (20:19; 27:2, 18 [compare 26:45]). "Into the *hands* of men" connotes an exercise of power over Jesus (compare Genesis 31:29: "It's in the power of my hand"; see also 2 Samuel 24:14 for the connotation of violent treatment). And just as in 16:21–23 Peter's protest, though misconceived, displayed an understanding of Jesus' prediction, so here the disciples' being "exceedingly saddened" displays that same understanding. As often, Matthew stresses understanding as a mark of true discipleship; for by definition, discipleship means "learning."

AVOIDANCE OF CAUSING UNBELIEVING
JEWS TO REJECT THE GOSPEL
Matthew 17:24–27

This unique story of what is popularly called "Peter's Penny" forms a transition from the foregoing narrative to the following discourse (chapter 18). In the story, Jesus teaches against leading others to sin.

17:24–26: **And when they** [Jesus and his disciples (17:19, 22)] **had come into Capernaum, those who were taking the double drachmas approached Peter and said, "Your teacher pays the double drachmas, doesn't he?"** "The double drachmas" refers to a tax levied on male Jews over twenty years old, including those living outside Israel, for upkeep of the temple (see Exodus 30:11–16; Nehemiah 10:32–33). Priests were exempt because of their service at the temple. A double drachma was a Greek silver coin worth about two denariuses, that is, approximately two days' wages for a manual laborer. The plural in "the double drachmas" reflects the collection of this tax year after year. [25]**He** [Peter] **says, "Yes."** So Peter knows that as a Law-observant Jew, Jesus customarily pays the tax. The abruptness of "He says" and the present tense of "says" emphasize Jesus' yearly payments. **And when he'd come into the house** [Jesus' house, we'd judge from 4:13], **Jesus anticipated him by saying, "How does it seem to you, Simon? From whom do the kings of the earth take custom duties and a poll-tax? From their sons or from** [sons] **belonging to others?"** [26]**And after** [Simon had] **said, "From** [sons] **belonging to others," Jesus told him, "Then the sons** [of kings] **are free indeed** [since freedom from taxation means freedom from subservience].**"** Presumably Peter entered Jesus' house to tell him the tax collectors had come to take his double drachma. But Matthew doesn't say so. Therefore the accent falls on Jesus' anticipating Peter—perhaps an indication of divine prescience. Jesus distinguishes between kings' sons (members of royal families) and sons belonging to others (members of nonroyal families). So the contrast between kings' sons and sons belonging to others isn't a contrast between citizens and noncitizens. Citizens pay taxes too. It's a contrast between members of a royal household and all others in the kingdom and implies that Jesus' disciples belong to God's royal household, whereas unbelieving Jews don't (see 5:35 for God as king in addition to references to God's kingdom). This implication fits well Matthew's emphasizing the transfer of the kingdom from Israel to the church (see especially 21:43).

Jesus continues in **17:27**: **"But lest we trip them up** [that is, trap unbelieving Jews into the sin of rejecting the gospel of the kingdom], **on going to the Sea** [of Galilee, beside which Capernaum is located], **throw a fishhook** [into the lake] **and take up the first fish that comes up. And on opening its mouth, you'll find a stater** [a silver coin worth four drachmas and therefore sufficient to pay the tax for Peter as well as for Jesus]. **On taking that** [coin], **give** [it] **to them** [the tax collectors] **in place of me and you."** "In place of" reflects the redemptive nature of the tax; the tax substitutes for those who pay it (Exodus 30:11–16). The tax collectors asked only about Jesus' payment. But he tells Peter to pay for himself as well as for Jesus. Why? To make Peter a model imitator of Jesus in paying the temple tax despite his and Jesus' nonobligation to do so because of their membership in God's royal family (compare 12:46–50) but for the purpose of not putting a stumblingblock in the way of Jews who might convert to the Christian gospel. There's no provision for the tax to be paid by disciples other than Peter. But that lack comes from the portrayal of him as a *representative* disciple. Matthew doesn't relate Peter's catching the fish, extracting the stater, and paying the tax. So the emphasis rests on Jesus' adding to Peter's understanding that Jesus pays the tax the further understanding that because Peter too has membership in God's royal family, he's tax-exempt but should pay the tax to avoid offending others.

MAINTAINING BROTHERHOOD
IN THE CHURCH
Matthew 18:1–35

Chapter 18 contains the fourth great discourse in this Gospel (after chapters 5–7, 10, and 13:1–52). The topic of maintaining churchly brotherhood overarches the chapter. As to subtopics, the discourse begins with the requirement of childlikeness for entrance into the kingdom of heaven (18:1–3). Humility defines childlikeness (18:4). The welcoming of disciples, childlike as they are, constitutes a welcoming of Jesus himself (18:5). But your causing one of them to sin (in the sense of apostatizing) brings judgment on you (18:6–7). And you need self-discipline to keep from sinning yourself (18:8–9). The heavenly Father wants those who are headed toward apostasy not to be despised, but to be rescued through personal reproof, church discipline, and prayer (18:10–20). And a wronged brother must forgive an offending fellow disciple, repeatedly if necessary (18:21–35).

18:1: In that hour the disciples approached Jesus, saying, "Who then is greater in the kingdom of heaven?" "In that hour" relates the disciples' question *chronologically* to the preceding discussion of taxation and freedom (17:24–27). "Then" relates the question *logically* to that discussion. (It's implied that the other disciples overheard or otherwise knew about Jesus' preceding conversation with Peter; and though the Twelve are in view, as elsewhere in this part of Matthew, they represent all Jesus' disciples, the church.) If Jesus' disciples are the tax-exempt sons of God the king, who of them is greater than the others? Might it be Peter? As we'd expect from Matthew's emphasis on understanding as a mark of true discipleship, the disciples' question presupposes that they understand their status as God's sons. Since there's no indication of a prior dispute among them as to which of them is greater than the others, the question is innocent as well as knowing. And since a kingdom entails hierarchy, a question of rank arises naturally. But rank in the kingdom as it presently manifests itself in the church, or in its future imposition on the entire world? "Who then *is* greater . . . ?" and Jesus' following instructions on behavior within the church favor the kingdom in its present manifestation. And Jesus is about to make humility in the present kingdom a condition (though not a cause) of entry into the coming kingdom.

18:2–5: And summoning a little child, he [Jesus] **had him stand in the midst of them** [the disciples]. **³And he said, "Amen I tell you, if you don't turn around and become like little children, by no means will you enter into the kingdom of heaven. ⁴Therefore whoever will lower himself** [= 'humble himself'] **[to be] like this little child—this** [person] **is larger** [= greater] **in the kingdom of heaven. ⁵And whoever welcomes one such little child on the basis of my name welcomes me."** Jesus starts by ignoring the question of greatness in the kingdom and addressing the unspoken issue of entrance into the kingdom. You can forget about greatness in it if you aren't there. What's necessary for entry is turning around, a figure of speech for conversion, and becoming like little children, represented by the little child whom Jesus makes an object lesson. (His "summoning" the little child excludes the child's being an infant.) "Amen I tell you" and "by no means" underscore this necessity. "In the midst of them" makes the object lesson of the little child unmistakable

to the disciples and even associates the child with them, especially since Jesus has summoned the child as he summoned the disciples (10:1; 15:32; also 20:25). But why the object lesson of a *little* child? In contrast with little children's high rank in contemporary western society, little children ranked low in ancient society. So references to childlike trustfulness or innocence are misplaced when applied to the present passage; and Jesus isn't referring to little children as such. "*Like* little children" and "*like* this little child" present them as objects of comparison, so that "one such little child" is a figure of speech for a disciple of Jesus. He means that entry into the kingdom requires humbling yourself to his lordship (compare 23:12). Bowing down before him is like lowering yourself to the stature of a statusless little child.

Having brought up and taken care of the issue of entrance, Jesus then addresses the disciples' question of greatness. "Therefore" indicates that since entry requires self-humbling for entry into the kingdom, greatness within the kingdom requires continued self-humbling. Now the self-humbling has to do with treatment of fellow disciples, represented by the little child. Which is to say that Jesus shifts from portraying the little child as a model of what *you* should be like by way of self-humbling to portraying the little child as a model of your *fellow disciple*, whom you should treat inside the kingdom with the same humility that characterized your entrance into the kingdom. Jesus' name constitutes the basis of such treatment; for your fellow disciple belongs to the people of Jesus who "call his name Immanuel, which is translated 'God [is] with us'" (1:21–23). And the welcoming of Jesus in the welcoming of your fellow disciple shows recognition that Jesus is "with" your fellow disciple as he promised to be with all his disciples (18:20; 28:20)—a solid basis for continuing humility in relation to them. In particular, welcoming your fellow disciple means showing him hospitality, especially when he's fleeing persecution (see 10:40–42 with 10:23; also 25:31–46, where taking in one of the littlest of Jesus' brothers equates with taking Jesus in).

18:6: "But whoever trips up [that is, causes to stumble into apostasy] **one of these little ones who believe in me—it's advantageous to him that an upper millstone be hung around his neck and he be drowned in the depth of the sea."** "Who believe in me" describes "these little ones" as believers in Jesus, not little children as such. A nonwelcome could cause apostasy in that the pressure of persecution would seem too much to bear given the refusal of help by a fellow disciple. A millstone is large, flat, round, and used of course for grinding grain. Literally, "upper" means "having to do with a donkey" and therefore describes the millstone as so heavy it has to be turned by donkey-power. Such a stone, hung by rope around the neck, would not only ensure drowning but also kill all hope of the drowned body's rising to the surface and floating ashore for burial, especially since "the *depth* of the sea" refers to the open sea far from shore. People of the Bible looked with horror on any kind of death that precluded burial. The un-Jewishness of execution by drowning intensifies the horror. But if such a fate is advantageous as compared with causing a fellow disciple's apostasy, how much more horrible must be the judgment of the disciple who causes the apostasy! The broken grammatical construction ("But whoever . . .—it's advantageous to him") lays stress on this greater horror. "Be drowned" echoes Peter's "beginning to drown" in 14:30 and suggests that his brush with drowning symbolized the danger of eternal damnation for disciples who don't live up to their profession.

18:7: **"Alas for the world because of snares** [= stumbling blocks that trip up disciples, so that they fall into apostasy]**! For** [it's] **a foregone conclusion that snares come. Nevertheless, alas for the person through whom the snare comes!"** In other words, the inevitability of snares doesn't release the snare-setter from culpability for having caused the apostasy of a persecuted fellow disciple by failing to welcome him hospitably. "*For* [it's] a foregone conclusion that snares come" explains why Jesus pronounced the first woe ("Alas"). Those who set snares endanger others in the world according to the first woe, whereas a snare-setter also endangers himself according to the second woe.

18:8–9: **"But if your hand or your foot is causing you to stumble** [= is tripping you up, ensnaring you into apostasy]**, cut it off and throw** [it] **away from you. It's** *good* **for you to enter into life** [eternal] **maimed or lame rather than that having two hands or two feet you be thrown into eternal fire.** ⁹**And if your eye is causing you to stumble, gouge it out and throw** [it] **away from you. It's** *good* **for you to enter into life** [eternal] **one-eyed rather than that having two eyes you be thrown into the gehenna of fire** [about which see the comments on 5:22]**."** Again sinning is in view, but now sinning caused by a member of your own body, not by someone else. And again eternal damnation for apostasy is in view, but this time for self-made sinners, not for those who cause others to sin. For further interpretation see the comments on 5:29–30, except that the present passage adds "your foot" but lacks the specifications of sexual misconduct and of a *right* eye and a *right* hand. Repetitiousness in these two sayings adds emphasis to the requirement of moral self-discipline.

18:10: **"See** [that] **you not despise one of these little ones."** Not even *one* of them! To despise them is yet again to refuse them hospitality when they're fleeing persecution (10:23, 40–42; 25:31–46). **"For I tell you that their angels in heaven are continually seeing the face of my Father in heaven."** As usual, "I tell you" adds emphasis to the following. And just as the Son of Man and even the Devil have angels (13:41; 16:27; 24:31; 25:31, 41; 26:53), so too do Jesus' disciples, "these little ones" fleeing persecution. Angels aid those they belong to. To see the face of someone connotes access to that person and can carry the special connotation of access to a sovereign (see 2 Samuel 14:24; 2 Kings 25:19 [where advisors to a king are called "those who see the king's face"]; Esther

1:14). It's unusual to have access to any sovereign. So it's all the more striking to have access to God, and continual access at that. How greatly the heavenly Father must value Jesus' little ones, then, to allow their angels an unrestricted access into his presence that other angels don't enjoy! All the more reason not to despise those little ones, but to welcome them hospitably. There's no 18:11 in the earliest and best manuscripts.

18:12–14: **"How does it seem to you** [plural, referring to the disciples (18:1)]**? If it happens that a certain man has a hundred sheep and one of them is led astray** [by someone in the church who despises 'a little one' by not welcoming him]**, he'll leave the ninety-nine on the mountains, won't he, and go seek the one being led astray** [compare Ezekiel 34:10–11, 13, 16]**?"** The first question implies that the disciples will understand Jesus' following parable. The second question implies an affirmative answer. Jesus doesn't state that the man would leave the ninety-nine under someone else's care. So all the emphasis falls on seeking the stray even though it's only one out of a hundred. To make sure no sheep were missing, shepherds counted their flocks before putting them in a pen for the night. "On the mountains" reflects the mountainous character of much of Israel and links with the danger of getting lost in such terrain. Jesus stops short of saying the stray is already lost, because the stray is going to represent a professing disciple rather than a nondisciple. But there remains a danger of lostness—that is, of apostasy and consequent eternal doom. ¹³**"And if it happens that** [he] **finds it, amen I tell you that he rejoices over it more than over the ninety-nine that haven't been led astray.** ¹⁴**Thus it isn't the wish before my Father in heaven that one of these little ones be lost."** "*If* it happens that [he] finds it" leaves open the possibility of eventual lostness, eternal doom because of apostasy. But "amen I tell you" accents the happier possibility of rejoicing over the found stray, that is, over a disciple rescued from his or her backsliding. In view of 10:11, 23, 40–42; 25:34–45, backsliding toward apostasy under the pressure of persecution is particularly in view. "More than over the ninety-nine that haven't been led astray" strengthens the accent on this possibility of rescue. "Thus it isn't the wish before my Father in heaven . . ." personifies the Father's not wanting even one persecuted disciple of Jesus to be lost forever. The Father's not wanting that to happen stands before him, so to speak, as a topic of his constant concern. It's always there and consequently always on his mind. By the same token, Jesus' disciples should be ever concerned to rescue endangered fellow disciples from eternal lostness.

18:15–17: **"And if your brother sins, go reprove him between you and him alone** [compare Leviticus 19:17]**. If he hears** [= heeds your reproof]**, you've gained your brother."** "Your brother" refers to your fellow disciple and portrays Jesus' church as a brotherhood. Jesus makes a disciple responsible to correct his fellow disciple who sins. The command to "go" to your fellow disciple highlights this responsibility (compare 7:1–5, especially

7:5b). "You've *gained* your brother" contrasts with the possibility of his becoming "*lost*" (18:14) and therefore means winning back a professing disciple who stands in danger of forfeiting salvation through sin, which tends toward apostasy. [16]"**But if he doesn't hear** [= doesn't heed you], **take along with you one or two more** [brothers] **in order that 'on the mouth of two or three witnesses** [= on the basis of their testimonies] **every matter may be established'** [Numbers 35:30; Deuteronomy 17:6; 19:15]." Jesus is in the process of emphasizing the need to exhaust every possibility in the effort to correct a disciple. "Take along with you one or two more" anticipates the law of two or three witnesses, which Jesus then quotes. He leaves no indication that the one or two additional brothers shall have witnessed the sin that has been committed. So their being taken along doesn't have the purpose of establishing the sin (the actuality of which is taken for granted) or at this point of enabling them to act as witnesses before the church in case of a second refusal to be corrected—rather, of strengthening the reproof. The purpose of strengthening the reproof is now confirmed: [17]"**But if he refuses to hear them** [= heed them], **tell the church** [that is, a local manifestation of the church]. **But if he also refuses to hear** [= heed] **the church, he's to be for you** [singular] **even as a Gentile and a tax collector.**" Presupposed is that the one or two others and now the church will join you in reproving the sinning brother. Here we have the ultimate application of pressure to receive correction. "A Gentile" has the sense of a pagan, and "a tax collector" has the sense of an especially sinful Jew (see the comments on 9:10). In Jewish society Gentiles and tax collectors were shunned. So to treat a fellow disciple like one of them was to ostracize him from Christian fellowship in the hope he would miss it, heed the correction, and come back into fellowship. The singular of "you" in "he's to be for *you* as a Gentile and a tax collector" pinpoints you as the initial reprover. But the cooperation of one or two others, and then of the whole church, plus the immediate switch to the plural of "you" in the next verses favors a church-wide shunning as well.

18:18–20: "**Amen I tell you** [plural], **however many things you bind on earth will have been bound in heaven, and however many things you loosen on earth will have been loosened in heaven.**" Essentially, this saying repeats the one in 16:19. But "Amen I tell you" adds emphasis. So too does the replacement of "whatever" (twice) with "however *many* things." The verbs of binding and loosening have changed from the earlier singular (in reference to Peter) to plural for an indication that all disciples are to share with Peter in the binding and loosening. As binding and loosening had to do with prohibiting behaviors inconsistent with discipleship and with promoting behaviors consistent with it, so here the binding and loosening have to do with applying these behavioral standards by way of disciplinary action. [19]"**Again amen I tell you that if two of you on earth agree concerning any matter that they may ask for, they'll have** [it] **from my Father in heaven.**

[20]**For where two or three are gathered in my name, I'm there in the midst of them.**" Here the binding and loosening of "however *many* things . . ." broadens out to praying for "*any* matter," and the prior binding and loosening *in* heaven becomes the future granting of the prayer request *from* heaven. "Again" signals this shift, and another "amen I tell you" adds as much assurance to the promise of future answers to prayer as was attached to the promise of prior validation of church discipline. "If two of you . . . agree" harks back to the law of two or three witnesses (18:16), only this time by way of strengthening the prayer to God rather than by way of strengthening the reproof of a brother. "Where two or three have gathered" harks back yet again to the law of two or three witnesses, only this time by way of strengthening the character of their having gathered together "in my name," that is, by way of joining together in "call[ing] his name Immanuel, which is translated 'God [is] with us'" (1:23). Gathering together in this way establishes a basis for God the Father's granting the disciples' requests and corresponds to the fact that Jesus is "in the midst of them" (compare 28:20). How could the Father refuse those who pray gathered in the name of his Son and blessed with the presence of his Son? Since in 18:2 Jesus had a little child stand "in the midst of them," by promising to be in their midst Jesus himself takes the role of a little child, a model of humility (compare 11:29; 21:5). He says "two or three" rather than "the church" to assure the two or three that they don't need the rest of the church to pray successfully as they did need the rest for disciplinary action against the sinning brother.

18:21–22: Then on approaching [Jesus], **Peter said to him, "Lord, how many times shall my brother sin against me and I forgive him? Up to seven times?"** [22]**Jesus says to him, "I don't tell you, up to seven times—rather, up to seventy times seven times!"** With "Lord" Peter acknowledges Jesus' lordship. Peter's question introduces an emphasis on the need for a brother sinned against to forgive the brother who sinned against him. Presupposed is repentance on the part of the brother who sinned (see 18:23–35). Because the number seven connotes completeness (there are seven days in a full week, for example), "Up to seven times?" seems to project a wholly sufficient number of forgivenesses. But out of Lamech's formula of seventy-sevenfold revenge in Genesis 4:24 Jesus constructs a formula of four hundred and ninetyfold forgiveness: "up to seventy times seven times!" (compare the requirement that you forgive others their trespasses to have God forgive you your own trespasses [6:14–15]). Several features put great emphasis on this formula of what amounts to *limitless* forgiveness: (1) abruptness due to the lack of a conjunction such as "And" or "But" preceding "Jesus says to him"; (2) the present tense in "Jesus *says* to him"; (3) "I *don't* tell you up to seven times"; (4) the introduction of "up to seventy times seven times" with "rather"; (5) the connotation of completeness in the number "seven"; and (6) the enhancement of that connotation with the multiple, "seventy."

Jesus has answered Peter's question concerning how many *times* a disciple ought to forgive his fellow disciple. Now the slate is clean for Jesus to talk about how *much* a disciple ought to forgive. **18:23–27: "Because of this** [the demand for limitless forgiveness] **the kingdom of heaven was like a man, a king, who wanted to settle accounts with his slaves.** ²⁴**And when he'd begun to settle accounts, there was brought to him one debtor of ten thousand talents** [= who owed that many talents, each talent worth the wages for around six thousand days of work by a manual laborer]. ²⁵**And because he didn't have** [the money] **to pay off** [his debt], **the master commanded him to be sold, also** [his] **wife and children and all things that he has, as many as they are, and** [his debt] **to be paid off.** ²⁶**So the slave, on falling down, was doing obeisance to him, saying, 'Be patient with me, and I'll repay you all** [those talents].' ²⁷**And feeling sorry** [for him], **the master of that slave dismissed him and forgave him the loan."** Jesus' remarks take the form of a parable. In it, a man is said to be a king for correspondence with the kingdom of heaven. Since elsewhere in Matthew the king of this kingdom is Jesus as well as God his heavenly Father (13:41; 16:28; 20:21), "a man [= a human being]," such as Jesus is, appropriately precedes "a king." In 18:35 he'll bring in his "heavenly Father" as an additional identification of "a king." The settling of accounts starts with forgiveness and unforgiveness in the present age and ends with the same at the Last Judgment. So "the kingdom of heaven *was* like . . ." reflects a temporal standpoint that looks back on the present age and the Last Judgment. The king's slaves stand for Jesus' disciples (see also 10:24–25; 13:27–28; 24:45–51; 25:14–30). "One" focuses attention on the debtor who owed ten thousand talents. A talent was the largest of monetary units; and "ten thousand," the largest numeral, was often used for an indefinitely and incalculably large number, like "zillions." A king wouldn't have loaned so much money to a slave. So the hyperbole emphasizes the enormity of our moral debt to God (see 6:12 for sin as a moral debt).

The talk about slaves shifts the vocabulary from "a man, a king" to "the master." But "master" translates the word elsewhere translated "Lord" and used for both God and Jesus, so that the king's standing for both of them is confirmed. Though people were sold to pay their debts (2 Kings 4:1; Nehemiah 5:1–13; Isaiah 50:1; Amos 2:6; 8:6), Jewish practice didn't allow the sale of a wife; and children constituted a man's dearest possession. Here, even the debtor's wife and children—plus his other possessions—are commanded to be sold. "As *many* as they are [note the present tense]" underlines the completeness of the sale. But such a sale wouldn't even come close to bringing in enough money to pay off the huge debt. So the absurdity of commanding the sale for paying it off represents the impossibility that we sinners could pay off our moral debt to God, and also plays up the master's ensuing compassionate act of forgiveness by emphasizing the hard justice of his prior sentence. The slave's falling down and doing obeisance to his master suits the mas-

ter's standing for the Lord Jesus and his heavenly Father, especially since "doing obeisance" translates the word that's elsewhere translated with "worship." The impossibility of paying off our moral debt to God achieves fine irony in the slave's plea for patience and his promise to repay all the talents, as though a slave could pay off an incalculable debt if given time. Compassionately, however, the master does better than his slave asked for. Instead of having him, his family, and all his possessions sold, he dismisses him. And instead of granting him time to pay off the debt, he—like God and Jesus, both of whom he represents—forgives the entire debt (see 6:12, 14 for the Father's forgiveness and 9:2–7 for Jesus' forgiveness).

18:28–30: "But on going out, that slave found one of his fellow slaves who was owing him a hundred denariuses [each denarius worth the wage for one day of work by a manual laborer]. **And on seizing him, he started choking** [him], **saying, 'Pay** [me] **back if you owe anything.'** ²⁹**So his fellow slave, on falling down, was imploring him, saying, 'Be patient with me, and I'll repay you.'** ³⁰**But he wasn't willing. Going off, rather, he threw him into prison till he would pay back what was owed."** "*That* slave" puts him at arm's distance, morally speaking. "*Found* one of his fellow slaves" indicates a purpose to do the opposite of what his master had done for him. "*One* of his fellow slaves" focuses attention on the fellow slave just as "*one* debtor" focused attention on the first slave (18:24). Over against the first slave's debt, incalculably huge and impossible to pay off, stands the debt of only a hundred denariuses, easy to pay off. Over against the first slave's having been "brought" stands his "seizing" the fellow slave and starting to choke him. And in the demand for repayment, "*if* you owe" and "*any*thing" make the fellow slave's debt so negligible as to be doubtful and unworthy of the preceding specification. The second slave falls down and implores the first slave but doesn't do obeisance to him, for the obvious reason that the first slave doesn't represent God and Jesus as the master does. The second slave isn't willing to grant more time for paying off the debt, much less to forgive it as the master forgave his debt. "Rather" stresses the contrast between his unwillingness and the master's compassion. Whereas the master "dismissed" the first slave, the first slave, "going off" with his fellow slave in tow, "threw him into prison till he should pay back what was owed." Imprisonment prevented escape and prompted dependents to raise money, if possible, for paying off the debt and ransoming the debtor. To underscore how paltry is the second slave's debt in comparison with the first slave's debt—hence, how insignificant are the sins committed by others in the church against us as compared with our own sins committed against God—there's no "all" with "what was owed" (contrast 18:25–26, 32). And underscoring the first slave's cruelty is the unrealism of a slave's having the right to imprison a fellow slave of his master.

18:31–35: "So his fellow slaves, on seeing the things that had happened, were exceedingly saddened and, on coming, related to their own master all the things

that had happened. ³²Then on summoning him, his master says to him, 'Evil slave, I forgave you all that debt, since you implored me. ³³It was necessary, wasn't it, that you too have mercy on your fellow slave as I too had mercy on you?'" Implied answer: Yes, it *was* necessary. ³⁴"And angered, his master gave him over to the torturers till he would pay back all that was owed. ³⁵In this way will my heavenly Father, too, treat you if you each don't forgive from your hearts his brother." The exceeding sadness of the other fellow slaves represents the extreme sorrow that ought to characterize churches over unforgiveness in their midst. At the Last Judgment the law of two or three witnesses will still be in effect (compare 12:41–42). So these other fellow slaves report what has happened. "*All* the things" points to a thorough airing at the Last Judgment. Nothing will remain hidden (10:26). The present tense of "says" highlights the master's response. Calling the unforgiving slave "evil" exposes him as a false disciple, for being forgiven by Jesus demands forgiving others as a sign that you've truly repented of your own sins. "All that debt" emphasizes both the enormity of the debt of sin owed to God and the infinitude of his grace. He cancelled the debt in response to a mere plea ("since you *impl*ored me").

The necessity of exercising the mercy of forgiveness toward a fellow disciple harks back to 6:14–15 ("For if you forgive human beings their trespasses, your heavenly Father will also forgive you [your trespasses]. But if you don't forgive human beings [their trespasses], neither will your Father forgive your trespasses") and 9:13; 12:7 ("I want mercy and not sacrifice" [compare 5:7]). The smallness of the fellow slave's debt implies that disciples ought to forgive their fellow disciples all the more because God's forgiveness is expansive, and that they ought to do so "from [their] hearts," that is, sincerely, not merely with their lips (compare 15:8; Isaiah 29:13). The warning against unforgiveness reaches its height in the master's anger, reversal of forgiveness, and instead of putting the unforgiving slave, his family, and all his possessions up for sale, as previously commanded, giving him "over to the torturers till he would pay back all that was owed"—a dreadfully ironic impossibility. Normally, torture of a debtor would give his family and friends incentive to raise the money necessary to pay off the debt. Here, though, the hopelessly large size of the debt makes the torture unending. So consignment to the torturers stands for consignment to eternal punishment. "If you *each* don't forgive" disallows any exceptions. Though Jesus began by addressing Peter (18:21–22), the plural of "you" and "your" in the closing explanation (18:35) shows that the parable applies to all disciples.

WELCOMING UNMARRIED PEOPLE IN THE CHURCH
Matthew 19:1–12

As usual, Matthew carries the theme of the preceding discourse into the following narrative. So the theme of churchly brotherhood in chapter 18 spills over into chapters 19–22. In particular, we read about the church's obligation to welcome unmarried people (19:1–12); young people (19:13–26); Gentiles (19:27–20:16); the blind, the lame, and (again) young people (20:17–21:16); and tax collectors, prostitutes, and (again) Gentiles, the welcoming of whom has God's rejection of the Jewish leaders as its counterpoint (21:17–22:46).

First, Matthew writes his formula concluding the foregoing discourse and introducing the following narrative. *19:1–2:* **And it happened that when Jesus had finished** [saying] **these words, he moved away from Galilee and came into the borders of Judea across the Jordan. ²And many crowds followed him, and he healed them there.** "Had finished [saying] these words" reminds us that Jesus' words form the bedrock on which he'll build his church (see the comments on 16:18 in relation to 7:24–27). His moving "away from Galilee" and coming "into the borders of Judea" prepare for the fulfillment of his prediction of going away to Jerusalem for suffering, death, and resurrection (16:21). As in 4:15, "across the Jordan" means the west side of the Jordan River and implies that Jesus had traveled down the east side of the river and crossed over into Judea toward Jerusalem, farther to the west. The crowds follow him as disciples follow their teacher, so that Matthew continues to make them stand for professing disciples (see the comments on 4:25–5:1; 7:28). And his describing them as "many" looks forward to the discipling of all nations (28:19). Jesus' healing them symbolizes saving them from their sins and authenticates "these words" of Jesus in chapter 18.

19:3–6: **And Pharisees approached him, testing him and saying,** "[Tell us] **if it's lawful for** [a man] **to divorce his wife for any cause** [at all]." The Pharisees play a devilish role, since "testing" represents the same word translated with "tempted" in the account of Jesus' temptation by the Devil (4:1–11 [see also 16:1]). "For any cause [at all]" prepares for "not on the basis of sexual immorality" (19:9) and puts the issue in the framework of a debate between the rabbinic schools dominated by Hillel and Shammai, respectively. The Shammaites interpreted Deuteronomy 24:1 strictly as allowing divorce mainly on the basis of a wife's unchastity. The Hillelites interpreted Deuteronomy 24:1 loosely as allowing divorce for almost any reason whatever. So the Pharisees are testing Jesus on a debated point of Old Testament law. Presumed throughout is the limitation of the right of divorce to husbands in Jewish society. ⁴**And he, answering, said, "You've read, haven't you, that from the beginning the one who created** [man and woman] **'made them male and female** [Genesis 1:27]'**?"** ⁵**And he** [Jesus] **said, "'On account of this a man shall leave** [his] **father and mother and cleave to his wife, and the two shall be one flesh** [Genesis 2:24]**.'** ⁶**And so they're no longer two; rather,** [they're] **one flesh. Therefore what God has yoked together** [by commanding male and female to be one flesh in marital coitus, the leaving of father and mother and cleaving to the wife implying marriage rather than a casual liaison] **a man is not to separate** [compare Malachi 2:15–16]." Jesus immediately steps forward with quotations of the Law, for he didn't come to tear it down but to perfect it by taking it further in the direction it was already headed (5:17–48). Since the Pharisees have indeed read the Old Testament passages that he quotes, they have no excuse for asking their malevolent question. To underscore his portrayal of Jesus as upholder and perfecter of the Law, Matthew introduces Jesus' second quotation of the Law with "And he said." For the rest, see the comments on Mark 10:6–9.

19:7–9: **They say to him, "Why then did Moses command** [a man] **to give** [his wife] **'a certificate of dismissal** [Deuteronomy 24:1]' **and divorce** [her]**?"** [8]**He says to them, "**[With a view] **toward your hardheartedness Moses permitted you to divorce your wives. But from the beginning it didn't happen this way.** [9]**But I tell you that whoever divorces his wife not on the basis of sexual immorality** [committed by her] **and marries another** [woman] **commits adultery."** The present tense in "They *say*" and "He *says*" enlivens the exchange. The Pharisees quote Deuteronomy 24:1 to qualify Genesis 1:27; 2:24, which Jesus has just quoted. In response he corrects the Pharisees' wrong interpretation of Moses as *commanding* divorce in Deuteronomy 24:1 with a right interpretation: Moses only *permitted* divorce. And Jesus attributes the permission to a consideration of hardheartedness, which he assigns to the Pharisees ("*your* hardheartedness"), not just to Moses' contemporaries. The requirement that if a man divorces his wife he must give her a certificate of dismissal—this requirement had the purposes of protecting her from a false accusation of desertion and of authenticating her right to remarry. Furthermore, the permission of divorce in Deuteronomy 24:1–4 arose as a sidelight to the main point of the passage, which was to prohibit a man's remarrying a woman whom he had divorced and whom another man had then married only to divorce her or die and leave her a widow. In fact, the second marriage of a woman is said to "defile" her. So Deuteronomy 24:1–4 limits divorce; and in escalating the limitation Jesus appeals to God's intent from the beginning, as indicated in the commands that a man "*leave* [his] father and mother" and "*cleave* to his wife" and that the two of them be "*one* flesh." In Genesis 1:27 and 2:24 we have true, fundamental *commands*, not mere permissions. Furthermore, Jesus extends the defilement of the woman by a second marriage to include a second marriage by the man, so that he commits adultery by marrying another woman. "But I tell you" underscores his committing adultery in this way (compare the repeated "But I tell you" in 5:21–48, where Jesus escalated the Law in other respects too). For the rest, including the exception for sexual immorality, see the comments on 5:31–32.

19:10–12: **The disciples say to him, "If the case of a man with a wife is this way, it's not advantageous to marry."** The disciples understand Jesus to mean not merely that divorce with remarriage is permitted only in cases of a wife's sexual infidelity, but that remarriage isn't permitted after divorce even in the case of such infidelity by the wife. Hence the disciples' comment that it's not advantageous for a man to marry in the first place. The present tense of "say" highlights this understanding. Now Jesus confirms the correctness of his disciples' understanding (throughout this Gospel they're portrayed as understanding his teaching) by admitting the seeming intolerability of what he has just said and reinforcing the disciples' understanding. After all, he has already said that entry into the kingdom requires a righteousness surpassing that of the scholars and Pharisees, who included Shammaites as well as Hillelites (5:20). [11]**And he told them, "Not all** [men] **make room for this word** [in the sense of tolerating Jesus' statement]. **Nevertheless,** [those] **to whom it has been given** [do make room for it]. [12]**For there are eunuchs who as such were born this way from** [their] **mother's womb; and there are eunuchs who as such were eunuchized** [castrated] **by human beings; and there are eunuchs who as such eunuchized themselves** [figuratively, by not remarrying] **on account of the kingdom of heaven. The** [man] **who can make room for** [eunuchry] **had better make room for** [it]**!"** That is to say, a disciple of Jesus can and *should* accept his stricture against remarriage even after divorcing his wife for sexual infidelity. "On account of the kingdom of heaven" means that because this kingdom is governed by Jesus' words, the disciple can and *will* live as a eunuch though not born as such or made such by anyone else. "Those to whom it has been given" echoes 13:11: "to you [true disciples] it has been given to know the secrets of the kingdom of heaven, but to those [false disciples] it hasn't been given [to know those secrets]." The echo favors that "this word" points back to Jesus' statement in 19:9 rather than to the disciples' statement in 19:10. And "the [man] who can make room for [eunuchry] had better make room for [it]!" echoes 11:15; 13:9, 43: "The person who has ears had better hear [= take heed]!" Genuineness of discipleship and therefore entrance into the kingdom are at stake. "Who as such eunuchized themselves" could be taken literally in terms of self-castration, but the contextual equation of remarriage with adultery favors denying oneself sexual intercourse through a new marriage, which self-denial is a kind of eunuchry. Despite the near insistence on marriage in Jewish society, then, Jesus portrays the single life of Christian men who haven't remarried after having had to divorce their immoral wives as obedience to his teaching, and therefore these men as worthy of welcome in the churchly brotherhood (contrast Deuteronomy 23:1, but compare Isaiah 56:3–5; and see Matthew 1:19 for divorcing an immoral wife as what a "righteous" husband ought to do).

WELCOMING YOUNG PEOPLE IN THE CHURCH
Matthew 19:13–26

Jesus' fortification of marriage leads him to bless little children, the offspring of marriages. Jewish parents took children to elders, or scholars, for blessing and prayer right after the Day of Atonement (compare Genesis 48:8–20). **19:13–15: Then little children were brought to him in order that he might lay** [his] **hands on them and pray** [for them]. **But the disciples reprimanded them.** [14]**But Jesus said, "Let the little children** [be brought to me], **and stop forbidding them to come to me. For the kingdom of heaven belongs to** [little children] **such as these."** [15]**And on laying** [his] **hands on them, he traveled on from there.** Presumably it was parents who were bringing their little children, but Matthew doesn't say so. Presumably the imposition of Jesus' hands that was being sought was for blessing, but again Matthew doesn't say so. And presumably the disciples reprimanded the parents, not the children; but yet again Matthew doesn't say so. He doesn't even say why the disciples engaged in reprimand. The interest centers solely on Jesus' response. In 18:1–6 Jesus made a little child the model of a humble station such as everyone is required to take, regardless of age, for entrance into the kingdom of heaven. Here, on the other hand, Jesus responds by declaring little children as such, when they "come to [him]," to be possessors of the kingdom (in the sense that they'll inherit it [compare 5:3, 5, 10]). The declaration, reinforced by the imposition of Jesus' hands, provides the reason for his commanding the disciples to let the little children come to him and to stop trying to keep them from doing so. Who are the disciples to presume they can keep heirs of the kingdom from coming to the king? Though the little children "were *brought*," they also "*come*," so that they count as youth, not as infants. But "such as these" limits the youth to be welcomed in the church to those who come to Jesus for his blessing and prayer (compare 18:6: "one of these little ones *who believe in me*"). After writing that Jesus laid his hands on such youth, Matthew writes that Jesus "traveled on from there." Matthew is more interested in getting Jesus closer to Jerusalem, where the passion-and-resurrection predictions will reach fulfillment, than in noting that Jesus prayed for the little children as well as laying his hands on them. He leaves the praying to be inferred.

19:16–17: And behold, on approaching him [Jesus], **one said, "Teacher, what good thing should I do in order that I may have eternal life?"** [17]**But he** [Jesus] **said to him, "Why do you ask me about the good? One is the good person. If you want to enter into life, keep the commandments."** "Behold" stresses the following "one" to highlight a parallel between the "one" who approaches Jesus with a question and the "one" who is "good." The address "Teacher" suits the content of the first one's question and agrees with a future self-designation by Jesus, again with the use of "one": "For one is your teacher" (23:8). Leviticus 18:5 says "a person may live" if he keeps the Lord's statutes and judgments. But there, "live" has to do with a prosperous and long *present* life. Here, Jesus' interlocutor specifies "*eternal* life." In Jesus' counter question "the good" is ambiguous. It can refer either to the "good *thing*" that the interlocutor asked about. Or it can refer to a good *person*. In his

immediately following comment, Jesus takes advantage of this ambiguity by shifting from the "good thing" of the interlocutor's question to a good person: "One is the good person ['good' being masculine rather than neuter, as it was earlier]." And who is this good person? Well, in a soon-to-be-told parable "the owner of the vineyard," also called "the householder," says outright, "I am good" (20:1, 8, 11, 15). Now "owner" goes back to the same word elsewhere translated "Lord" and used repeatedly for Jesus. Moreover, he has also used "householder" for himself (10:25; 13:27). In shifting from the one good thing to the one good person, then, Jesus is nudging his interlocutor to recognize him—that is, Jesus—as the answer to Jesus' counter question, "Why do you ask me about the good?" The reason is that because Jesus is the one good person, he's the right one to be asked about the good thing one has to do for eternal life. As the one good person, Jesus is also the one to follow, as he'll tell his interlocutor to do in 19:21. And in his answer to the interlocutor he shows himself to be an upholder of the Law: "keep the commandments" (compare 5:17–20).

19:18–19: He [the interlocutor] **says to him, "What** [commandments]**?"** "What?" connotes "what *sort* of?" or "which ones *in particular*?" The present tense of "says" and the lack of an introductory "And" or "But" before "He says" imply eagerness to know which commandments to keep. **And Jesus said, "The** [following]: **'You shall not murder, you shall not commit adultery, you shall not steal, you shall not give false testimony,** [19]**honor** [your] **father and mother,' and 'you shall love your neighbor as** [you love] **yourself** [Exodus 20:12–16; Deuteronomy 5:16–20; Leviticus 19:18]**."** Jesus starts reciting commandments from the second table of the Decalogue but skips the tenth commandment ("you shall not covet"), doubles back to the fifth commandment ("you shall honor [your] father and mother"), and adds from outside the Decalogue the commandment to love your neighbor (see the comments on Mark 12:29–31 for the meaning of "as [you love] yourself"). All these commandments have to do with interpersonal relations and are easier to keep than the skipped commandment not to covet, which deals with an inward desire. In view of the interlocutor's "having many acquisitions" (19:22), Jesus selects these commandments partly because he wants to leave the door open for the interlocutor's claim to have "guarded all these things" (19:20), partly because the acquiring of wealth can come at the expense of interpersonal relations, and partly because he plans to tell the interlocutor to sell all his possessions, give the proceeds to the poor, and come follow him (19:21). Though Matthew hasn't yet written about those possessions, Jesus omnisciently knows about them, so that the prohibition of coveting looks conspicuous by its absence. In the end, the interlocutor's reaction will show him guilty of covetousness.

19:20–21: The young man says to him, "I've guarded all these things. In what respect am I still lacking?" Again the lack of an introductory "And" or

"But" and the present tense imply eagerness (compare 19:18), and for the first time we learn that the interlocutor is young. He refers to "all these *things*" rather than to "all these *commandments*." "Things" calls attention to not murdering, not committing adultery, and so on. The young man claims to have guarded these things in the sense of being careful to avoid such wrong *activities* and to engage in the good *activities* of honoring his parents and loving his neighbor as he loves himself. You can almost hear him breathe a sigh of relief when saying he has guarded "*all* these things." Whatever the young man means, "In what respect am I still lacking?" stresses for Matthew and his audience the young man's lacking the superior righteousness required for entrance into the kingdom of heaven (5:20). [21]**Jesus told him, "If you want to be perfect, go sell your possessions and give** [the proceeds] **to the poor, and you'll have treasure in heaven. And here! Follow me!"** The lack of "And" or "But" before "Jesus said" lends a certain abruptness to his reply. "If you want to be perfect" echoes 5:48: "Therefore you shall be perfect as your heavenly Father is perfect." There it referred to the perfection of love (see the comments on that verse). But since the word behind "perfect" connotes maturity as a concomitant of perfection, Jesus also achieves a contrast between the youthfulness of his interlocutor and the perfection of maturity demanded by Jesus in 5:48. In other words, lack of perfection—that is, of maturity—means lack of discipleship. Not a high level of discipleship, but discipleship pure and simple. For the question has to do with attaining eternal life, and elsewhere Matthew doesn't distinguish between levels of true discipleship. Perfection doesn't imply complete sinlessness and full virtue as matters of fact. But it does imply observable dedication to those qualities of conduct. That Jesus didn't command each and every one of his followers to sell all their possessions gives comfort only to the kind of people to whom he *would* issue that command. For treasure in heaven, see 6:19 (compare 13:44). Such treasure is a figure of speech for eternal life, not for any reward above and beyond eternal life.

19:22: But on hearing the word [= Jesus' statement], **the young man went away sorrowing. For he had many acquisitions.** "The word" is reminiscent of the parable of the sower (13:19–23 [see also 7:24, 26, 28; 15:12; 19:1, 11]). Unfortunately, this word hasn't fallen into good soil. "Went away" contrasts with Jesus' "And here! Follow me!" (19:21). "Sorrowing" contrasts with the "joy" of the man who, on finding a treasure hidden in a field, "goes and sells all things that he has, as many as [they are], and buys that field" (13:44). In telling why the young man went away sorrowing, the explanation "for he had many acquisitions" illustrates Jesus' having said that "where your treasure is, there will be your heart too" (6:21 [see also 6:24; 19:23–24]). "He had many acquisitions" contrasts both with the selling he'd told the young man to do and with Jesus' having told the Twelve, "You shouldn't acquire gold or silver or copper [coins] [and so on]" (10:9–10a). "Acquisitions" defines the young man's possessions as things he'd gotten as a result of coveting

in violation of the commandment left conspicuously unquoted. This youth's *going away* from Jesus therefore presents a sad contrast with the little children who *came to* Jesus in 19:13–15. But just as that earlier passage threw open the church to youth, the present passage calls on youth to renounce affluence in order to become true disciples of Jesus.

19:23–26: **And Jesus said to his disciples, "Amen I tell you that a rich person will hardly enter into the kingdom of heaven.** [24]**And again I tell you, it's easier for a camel to go through a needle's eye than for a rich person to enter into God's kingdom."** "Amen I tell you," "again I tell you," and the repetitiveness of the following statements put enormous stress on the difficulty of a rich person's entering into the kingdom. Entering into it equates with entering into eternal life in 19:16–17. For the rest, see the comments on Mark 10:24b–25. [25]**And on hearing** [these statements], **the disciples were exceedingly awestruck, saying, "Who then can be saved?"** "Be saved" equates with entering into the kingdom and entering into eternal life (19:16–17, 23). The inferential "then" shows that the disciples have understood Jesus well enough to see an apparent contradiction between wealth as a hindrance to entering God's kingdom and wealth, when combined with piety, as a sign of God's favor. For according to Deuteronomy 28:1–14; Job 1:10; 42:10; Proverbs 10:22, wealth combined with piety signals God's favor. So if a pious rich person can't be saved, what hope of salvation is there for someone who doesn't have wealth as a sign of God's favor? No wonder it floors Jesus' disciples to hear him say that "it's easier for a camel to go through a needle's eye than for a rich person to enter into God's kingdom." [26]**But gazing intently** [at them], **Jesus told them, "For human beings this is impossible, but for God all things** [are] **possible** [compare Genesis 18:14]**."** The disciples' question elicits Jesus' saying something that augments their understanding (see 13:11–12). The intensity of his gaze adds visual impact to the verbal impact of his affirming the power of God to do the humanly impossible, not only to save a rich person but also to do *anything* God wishes to do. Thus Jesus doesn't answer the question who can *be* saved, but points the disciples to the only one who can *do* the saving because he's all-powerful.

WELCOMING GENTILES IN THE CHURCH
Matthew 19:27–20:16

19:27–28: **Then answering, Peter said to him, "Behold, *we*'ve left all and followed you. What then will we have?"** Matthew's "Then" is temporal and indicates a new beginning. Peter's "then" is logical and points to a hoped-for consequence. He speaks on behalf of the Twelve. His emphatic "*we*" contrasts their having left all and followed Jesus with the rich young man's sad departure upon Jesus' telling him to sell all, give to the poor, and follow him. "Behold" emphasizes the contrast. [28]**And Jesus said to them, "Amen I tell you that you who've followed me—in the regeneration *even you*** will sit on twelve thrones judging the twelve tribes of Israel whenever the Son of Man sits on the throne of his glory [= his glorious throne]." Since Peter spoke on behalf of the Twelve, Jesus addresses "them," not just Peter. Jesus' emphatic *"even you"* matches Peter's emphatic *"we,"* and "Amen I tell you" adds further force to Jesus' promise of compensation. In the promise, sitting on twelve thrones and judging the twelve tribes of Israel compensate for following Jesus and suit the nature of a kingdom. In 5:18; 24:35 he speaks of the passing away of heaven and earth. So "the regeneration" refers to their renewal or, to use the terminology of Isaiah 65:17; 66:22; 2 Peter 3:13; Revelation 21:1, "a new heaven and a new earth" (compare Hebrews 12:25–29). Just as "the Son of Man . . . will sit on the throne of his glory," with all nations gathered before him, to separate the righteous and the unrighteous from each other and assign them their respective fates (25:31–46), here Jesus promises the Twelve that they'll sit on twelve thrones judging the twelve tribes of Israel similarly. But "of his glory" exalts the Son of Man's throne above the thrones of the Twelve, so that the Twelve are promised to *assist* him in judging those tribes.

19:29–30: **"And everyone who as such has left houses or brothers or sisters or father or mother or children or fields for my name's sake will receive a hundred times as much and inherit eternal life. 30But many first ones will be last, and [many] last ones first."** "As such" stresses the feature of having left houses, brothers, and so forth. "Everyone" stresses that no person who has done so will be left uncompensated. The list of things left defines the "all" in Peter's statement, "Behold, we've left all" (19:27). For the order of those things listed, see the comments on Mark 10:29. "For my name's sake" alludes to the calling of Jesus "'Immanuel,' which is translated 'God [is] with us,'" by "his people" (1:21–23). "Will receive a hundred times as much" is reminiscent of the hundredfold yield in the good soil of 13:8, 23 but looks forward here to corresponding compensation in the coming kingdom. "And will *inherit* eternal life" puts the compensation in familial terms (compare 12:46–50). The coming parable will define the "many first ones" who'll be "last" as Jews, and the "[many] last ones" who'll be "first" as Gentiles (20:1–16; compare 8:11–12 and the expansion in chapter 10 of a Jewish mission to include Gentiles as well; also 28:18–20 for the discipling of all nations after Jesus' resurrection).

20:1–2: **"For the kingdom of heaven is like a man, a houseowner** [in the sense of a landowner], **who as such** [= in his capacity as a landowner] **went out together with the early morning to hire workers for his vineyard."** The chapter break is unfortunate, because Jesus continues without interruption. In fact, *"For the kingdom of heaven is like . . ."* makes the following parable substantiate and explain the saying in 19:30: "But many first ones will be last, and [many] last ones first." As already in 10:25; 13:27, "a houseowner" stands for Jesus. The houseowner's hiring of "workers" harks back to Jesus' sending the Twelve as "workers" to gather a harvest of converts (9:36–10:5a) and suits Matthew's emphasis on good works (see, for example, 5:16; 21:28–32). "Together with the early morning" is a striking way of saying "early in the morning" that stresses the earliness of this hiring. The stress will contribute to a contrast with a very late hiring yet to come. The metaphor of a vineyard comes from the Old Testament (see especially Isaiah 5:1–7; Jeremiah 12:10). 2**"And on agreeing with the workers on a denarius for the day** [the normal wage for one day of work by a manual laborer], **he sent them into his vineyard."** This agreement will later leave these early comers, "first ones," without grounds for grumbling.

20:3–7: **"And on going out about the third hour, he saw others standing in the marketplace without work.** 4**And he said to those, 'You too go into the vineyard, and I'll give you** [as a wage] **whatever is right.' And they went off** [into the vineyard]." The twelve hours of day were counted from sunrise, when work began. So "about the third hour" means "about 9:00 A.M." This time the houseowner doesn't go out to hire workers. But on seeing some unemployed men he hires them anyway. "You *too* go" either assumes they'd seen him hire the first batch of workers or, more probably, represents the vantage point of the houseowner. As to a wage, the present batch trust his justice. 5**"And again, on going out about the sixth** [hour] **and ninth hour** [= about noon and 3:00 P.M.], **he did likewise.** 6**And on going out about the eleventh** [hour (= about 5:00 P.M.)], **he found others standing** [in the marketplace]. **And he says to them, 'Why are you standing here the whole day without work?'** 7**They say to him, 'Because no one has hired us.' He says to them, 'You too go into the vineyard.'"** Because the workers hired at the eleventh hour will become a focus of this parable, the dialogue of the employer with them comes alive with the present tense in "he *says*," "They *say*," and "He *says*." The lack of an introductory "And" or "But" in the last two of these phrases adds to the liveliness. Jesus leaves it to be inferred that those hired later than the morning went off into the vineyard just as did the first- and second-hired workers. So some worked twelve hours, some nine, some six, some three, and some only one.

20:8–12: **"And when evening came, the owner of the vineyard tells his foreman, 'Call the workers and give back** [in return for the work] **the hire** [= wage], **beginning from the last ones** [hired and proceeding] **to the first ones** [hired].'" Since "owner" translates the word elsewhere translated "Lord," the landowner appears again to stand for Jesus, "the Lord of the harvest" (9:38). The present tense of "tells" emphasizes the upcoming payment and what it represents. The practice of paying workers every day comes from the Old Testament (see Leviticus 19:13; Deuteronomy 24:14–15). The singular of "the wage" derives from the single denarius each worker is going to receive. Ordinarily, the early comers would receive their wage first and leave without seeing how much the later comers receive. But Jesus reverses the expected order of payment to illustrate the firstness of the last and the lastness of the first in accordance with 19:30 and to make possible the grumbling of the early comers (20:11–12). ⁹**"And on coming** [to receive their wage], **the ones** [who'd been hired] **about the eleventh hour received a denarius each.** ¹⁰**And on coming, the first ones** [hired] **supposed that they will receive more. And they—they too received the denarius each."** "They *will* receive more" makes for a stronger supposition than the expected "they *would* receive more." Skipping over the ones hired at intermediate hours lays a heavy weight of emphasis on the reception of only a denarius by those who'd worked a full twelve hours. Adding to this weight is the construction, "And they—they *too*," which could also be translated, "And they—*even* they." ¹¹**"And on receiving** [a denarius each], **they started grumbling against the houseowner,** ¹²**saying, 'These last ones made one hour, and you've made them equal to us who've borne the burden of the day and the scorching east wind.'"** The repetition of "the houseowner" (compare 20:1) reemphasizes the sovereignty of Jesus, whom he represents. In the first comers' grumbling there's a wordplay: "*made* one hour" means "*worked* one hour," whereas "you've *made* them equal" means "you've *treated* them as equal." The first comers charge their employer with two injustices: (1) failure to take account of the difference between twelve hours of work and one hour of work and (2) failure to take account of the difference between the burdensome heat and scorching east wind of midday and the cool and calm of late afternoon. The absence of a polite address shows the first comers' indignation. In contrast, the employer will address one of them politely, even affectionately despite the affection's being undeserved (as also in 22:12; 26:50).

20:13–16: **"But he, answering one of them, said, 'Comrade, I'm not doing you an injustice. You agreed with me on a denarius, didn't you?** ¹⁴**Take your** [denarius] **and go. But I want to give** [a denarius] **to this last**[-hired worker] **as also** [I'm giving a denarius] **to you.** ¹⁵**It's lawful for me, isn't it, to do what I want with the things that belong to me? Or is your eye evil** [= covetous, greedy, stingy (compare 6:23)] **because I am good** [compare 19:17]**?'** ¹⁶**In this way the last ones will be first, and the first ones** [will be] **last."** What then does Jesus mean by this parabolic explanation of the saying about first and last? His promising that the Twelve will sit on twelve thrones judging the twelve tribes of Israel (19:28) shows that he took Peter's statement and question (19:27) as a reference to Jesus' original Jewish disciples—that is, in terms of the parable, first comers. So the latest comers in the parable stand for Gentiles who enter the church later in consequence of a carrying out of the Great Commission: "disciple all nations" (or, as it could also be translated, "disciple all the Gentiles" [28:19–20]). Thus the parable invalidates anti-Gentile bias among Jewish disciples, and demands that believing Gentiles be welcomed into the church. It's wrong for Jewish believers (or any others) to grumble against

Jesus' generosity to others when they themselves (or any others) have received justice. Any less than a denarius would have fallen below a subsistence wage for a man supporting his family; and the denarius represents eternal life. So this payment will take place at the Last Judgment. Eternal life will come only to workers—that is, disciples—but as a gift based on generosity, not as a wage based on calculation. Those who worked all day and got exactly what they deserved are a foil to those who got far better than they deserved, as shown by the contrastive selection only of those who worked just one hour. Despite the element of work, then, the employer's generosity consists in grace. The eleventh-hourers didn't earn a denarius. Implicitly, this parable warns Peter not to take his statement and question in 19:27 further by way of comparing the Twelve's sacrifices with the performance of other disciples.

CHURCHLY WELCOME OF THE BLIND, THE LAME, AND YOUNG PEOPLE
Matthew 20:17–21:17

This passage begins with the ascent of Jesus to Jerusalem and ends with his arrival there. He predicts again his death and resurrection (20:17–19), answers a request for special honor by pointing to his service for others (20:20–28), and exemplifies such service by giving sight to two blind men (20:29–34) and entering Jerusalem and the temple to heal the blind and the lame and defend the young people who praise him there (21:1–16). In these ways he sets an example for the church to follow by way of welcoming and serving the disenfranchised.

20:17–19: **And as Jesus was about to go up to Jerusalem he took along the Twelve privately and on the road said to them,** ¹⁸**"Behold, we're going up to Jerusalem, and the Son of Man will be given over to the chief priests and scholars, and they'll condemn him to death** ¹⁹**and give him over to the Gentiles for mocking and flogging and crucifying. And on the third day he'll be raised** [compare 16:21; 17:22–23]**."** "As Jesus was about to go up to Jerusalem" and "we're going up to Jerusalem" point up Jesus' determination to meet his fate there, a fate that he'll interpret in 20:28 as a service performed for others. "Behold" dramatizes this determination and its soon and certain accomplishment. "Go up" reflects the steep ascent from the Jordan Valley to Jerusalem, and the privacy of Jesus' prediction reflects his practice of reserving the secrets of the kingdom for disciples (13:11–12). But to keep the rest of the Twelve from thwarting his betrayal by Judas Iscariot, Jesus doesn't name him as the betrayer. Despite deep theological and other differences between the chief priests and scholars, to whom Jesus will be given over, he speaks of them as a united front opposed to him (compare 16:21). They'll condemn him to death, but because their Roman overlords reserved to themselves the right of capital punishment, they won't be able to stone him to death (the usual Jewish method of capital punishment). So "they'll

. . . give him over to the Gentiles." The Romans practiced crucifixion as the most demeaning form of capital punishment. For the first time Jesus specifies it as his fate. But preliminarily, he says, the Gentiles will mock and flog him. "*For* mocking and flogging and crucifying" indicates the *results* of his being given over to the Gentiles, but it also indicates the chief priests' and scholars' *purpose* in giving him over to the Gentiles (see chapters 26–27). His being raised on the third day certainly won't conform to their purpose, though!

20:20–21: Then the mother of Zebedee's sons approached him with her sons, [the mother] doing obeisance and asking for something from him. ²¹And he said to her, "What do you want?" She tells him, "Say that these two sons of mine should sit, one on your right and one on your left, in your kingdom." "Then" correlates the mother's request that Jesus grant her sons special honors with his just having predicted his passion and resurrection. The present tense of "tells" introduces the request with verve, but the request overlooks the passion of Jesus and settles on his kingdom following the resurrection. He himself has claimed, and will yet claim, the kingdom for himself (13:41; 16:28; 25:31, 34, 40). So her attributing it to him combines with her doing obeisance, which at least for Matthew and his audience means "worshiping," to highlight the deity of Jesus. But in addition to the overlooking of his passion, her asking him at first for an indefinite "something" (so that he asks her to specify her request) and her failure to address him politely (with "Lord," for example) undermine her request. We know from 4:21; 10:2 that Zebedee's sons are James and John, but their remaining unnamed here protects them somewhat from blame for their mother's request. That she makes the request in behalf of them also gives them some cover. Her approaching "*with* them" prepares for her saying "*these* two sons of mine." "*Say* that [they] should sit" implies that Jesus' saying so would guarantee their occupying the positions of highest honor next to him. And sitting harks back to his promise that the Twelve will sit on twelve thrones judging the twelve tribes of Israel (19:28), only the mother wants to make sure her sons' thrones will be located *immediately* to the right and left of Jesus' glorious throne.

20:22–23: But answering, Jesus said, "You [plural] don't know what you're asking for! Can you drink the cup that I'm about to drink?" They tell him, "We can!" ²³He tells them, "On the one hand, you *will* drink my cup. On the other hand, to sit on my right and on my left—this isn't mine to give; rather, [it'll be given] to those for whom it has been prepared by my Father." The plural of "you" brings the sons into the picture and attributes to them the request made by their mother. In other words, she acted as their spokesperson. "The cup" stands for Jesus' suffering and anticipates the cup at the institution of the Lord's Supper (26:17–28 [see also 26:39]). "That I'm about to drink" correlates with "as Jesus was about to go up to Jerusalem" (20:17) and indicates the purpose of his going up there. "You don't know what

you're asking for!" implies that the kind of honor they're asking for would require them to drink first the bitter dregs of suffering. "*Can* you . . . ?" implies the danger of inability to endure such a prior fate. "That I'm about to drink" implies the ability of Jesus to endure it. The present tense in "They tell him" highlights the sons' "We *can*!" Jesus accepts their declaration of ability and shifts to the coming actuality of their drinking his cup. The present tense in "He *tells* them" highlights this actuality. "*My* cup" unites their suffering with his because they'll suffer for his sake and the gospel's just as he'll suffer for their sake so as to bring about the gospel. Despite the unity of their suffering with his, though, the prerogative of assigning honorary positions on his right and left doesn't belong to him. It belongs to his Father, who has already prepared those positions. Jesus doesn't identify the honorees. Nor does he quite say that his Father has already assigned the positions, only that the positions have already been prepared for some. Whether or not the Father has already assigned the positions, think what envy would be incited by an identification of the assignees. "My *Father*" makes a striking contrast with "the *mother* of Zebedee's sons," and making an equally striking contrast will be the crucifixion of two bandits with Jesus, one on his right, the other on his left (27:38). James died an early martyr (Acts 12:2); and though John died a natural death according to tradition, he first suffered exile on the island of Patmos (John 21:22; Revelation 1:9).

20:24–25: And on hearing [the foregoing dialogue], the ten got indignant over the two brothers. ²⁵But Jesus, on summoning them [the ten, since the two brothers were already with him], said, "You know that the rulers of the Gentiles wield lordship against them, and [that] the great ones wield authority against them." With "over the two brothers" Matthew reminds us that the church is a brotherhood, represented here by biological brothers. "You know," addressed to all the Twelve, contrasts with "You don't know," addressed earlier to the two brothers (20:22), and points to knowing something true in society at large that unbeknown to them does *not* hold true in their brotherhood. But Jesus will add further knowledge to what they already have (13:11–12). The Gentiles' "great ones" recalls the disciples' asking him who is greater in the kingdom of heaven (18:1), and the rulers' and great ones' wielding lordship and authority "against" the Gentiles connotes conquest by violence and government by oppression, as opposed to the beneficial service that Jesus will now talk about.

20:26–28: "It shall not be this way among you. Rather, whoever wants to become a great one among you shall be your servant, ²⁷and whoever wants to be a first one among you shall be your slave, ²⁸just as the Son of Man didn't come to be served—rather, to serve, even to give his life as a ransom in substitution for many." "Shall not be" and the two instances of "shall be" are commands just as much as predictions. For a contrast with the violence and oppressiveness of the Gentiles' overlords, we might have expected an introductory

"But" before "It shall not be this way among you." The lack of such an introduction lends the command an emphatic abruptness. "Who*ever*" (twice) poses the possibility that the ten might entertain a selfish ambition like that of Zebedee's sons in concert with their mother. For emphasis, "a great one" escalates to the superlative "a first one," and "your servant" de-escalates to "your slave," this latter pair also in opposition to the Gentiles' "rulers" and "great ones." "*Your* servant" and "*your* slave" mean service and slavery to the rest of you. Since Jesus is the disciples' only Lord/Master and since a slave can serve only one master (6:24), for them to serve one another is to serve fellow slaves on behalf of Jesus. And not only on his behalf, also in imitation of him: "*just as* the Son of Man . . . ." The shift from negative, "didn't come to be served," to positive, "rather, to serve," underscores the example Jesus sets. "*Even* to give his life [as a] ransom in substitution for many" specifies his service as the ultimate in self-sacrifice and interprets his death as substitutionary for many people. Not for many as *opposed* to all, but for many because the all *are* many. Jesus will die in their place to ransom them from slavery to Satan, sin, and death, so that they may have the eternal life which only the righteous will inherit (25:46). His slavery spells their liberation from slavery on condition of believing in him. And his death will constitute the ransom price. Jesus' example doesn't exclude kinds of service that fall short of giving one's life for others. But it does point up the extent to which serving them may need to go, and did go in Jesus' exemplary case.

20:29–31: And as they were going out from Jericho, a large crowd followed him. [30]And behold, two blind [men] sitting on the edge of the road, on hearing that Jesus is passing by, shouted saying, "Lord, have mercy on us. Son of David, [have mercy on us]." [31]But the crowd reprimanded them so that they'd be quiet. But they shouted louder, saying, "Lord, have mercy on us. Son of David, [have mercy on us]." "As they were going out from Jericho" puts the episodes in 19:1–20:28 between the west bank of the Jordan River and the city of Jericho. The following of Jesus by a large crowd stands as often in this Gospel for the future masses of professing disciples from all nations. "Behold" calls special attention to the two blind men. For Matthew and his audience, their shouting "Lord" two times puts a double emphasis on Jesus' divine lordship, and their shouting "Son of David" two times puts a double emphasis on Jesus' human kingship. Their double plea for mercy (the second one implied) asks him to exercise the mercy that he commanded others to exercise (9:13; 12:7 [compare 5:7]). The greater loudness of their shouting a second time and its coming despite the crowd's reprimand strengthen the plea.

20:32–34: And on standing still, Jesus called them and said, "What do you want [that] I should do for you?" [33]They say to him, "Lord, that our eyes be open." [34]And feeling sorry [for them], Jesus touched their eyes. And immediately they saw again and followed him. "Standing still" indicates that Jesus heard the blind

men's shouts. "Called them" indicates that because he'd been "passing by," he was already some distance from them. They'd asked for mercy; but they hadn't specified what form the mercy should take, and if Jesus had seen them he would've already known they were blind and wanted sight. But he hadn't seen them and didn't know, so that he asks them what they want him to do for them. Their answer contains a third addressing of Jesus as "Lord," which—whatever they meant—points up for Matthew's audience Jesus' deity yet again. "That our eyes be open" compares their blindness to having closed eyes. His "feeling sorry" for them shows merciful emotion. His "touch[ing] their eyes" shows merciful action. All in all, this merciful healing exemplifies service to the needy (compare 20:24–28). "They saw again" probably implies that the two men had gone blind at some earlier point. The immediacy of their seeing again highlights that the two of them have become a unique pair of *eye*witnesses in that their healing testifies sufficiently—just because they're two in number—to Jesus' merciful service to them (compare 18:16; Numbers 35:30; Deuteronomy 17:6; 19:15). Their following Jesus now that they see again turns them into disciples whom the large crowd, representing the later, large church of Matthew's day, should welcome into their midst though—or perhaps because—they come from a disadvantaged class.

21:1–3: And when they drew near to Jerusalem and came to Bethphage, [that is,] to the Mount of Olives [or "of Olive Trees"], then Jesus sent two disciples, [2]telling them, "Go into the village opposite you. And immediately you'll find a tethered donkey and a colt with her. On loosening [them], bring [them] to me. [3]And if anyone should say anything to you, you shall say, 'Their owner has need [of them].' And immediately he [= the 'anyone' who says 'anything'] will send them [with you here to me]." The Mount of Olives is located to the east of Jerusalem just across a ravine called the Kidron Valley. Arrival in Bethphage leaves the need for another village to which Jesus may send two of his disciples for animals. "Then" ties the arrival to the sending, but "the village opposite you" remains anonymous. The immediacy of finding the animals means that the disciples will find them at entry. They won't have to hunt around farther inside the village. "And if anyone should say anything to you" is indefinite and ambiguous both as to possibility and content, and the succeeding verses will say nothing about anyone's saying anything to the two disciples when they untie the animals. So the entire stress lies on Jesus' telling the disciples to call him the animals' "owner" in saying he needs them. "Owner" translates the word otherwise translated "Lord" and therefore alludes to Jesus' lordship. As Lord, his ownership of the animals obliterates anyone else's owning them and gives him the right to use them. Matthew includes nothing about Jesus' returning the animals. So the stress stays on his divine ownership of them (contrast Mark 11:3). And their being sent to Jesus by the possible "anyone," underlined with "immediately," caps the stress on his owning them.

21:4–5: And this has happened in order that what was spoken through the prophet might be fulfilled, saying, 5"Say to the daughter of Zion [that is, the inhabitants of Jerusalem, built on Mount Zion], **'Behold, your king is coming to you, meek and mounted on a donkey and on a colt, the foal of an** [animal] **under a yoke.'"** "This" refers back to Jesus' sending two of his disciples to fetch a female donkey and a colt with her. In other words, he acted deliberately so as to fulfill prophecy. "Has happened" indicates the completion of an event that has continuing significance. That is to say, this past fulfillment of Old Testament prophecy authenticates for today the messianic kingship of Jesus. "Through the prophet" implies the Lord's using a prophet as his mouthpiece. The main part of the quoted prophecy comes from Zechariah 9:9. But that text begins with the command, "Rejoice greatly, daughter of Zion!" and goes on to announce Israel's deliverance. But according to Matthew 21:43 God is going to transfer his kingdom to the church (compare 16:18); and in 21:10 the city of Jerusalem, located on Mount Zion, will be upset rather than joyful over Jesus' entry (compare 2:3). So Matthew switches to a similar but contextually more appropriate line in Isaiah 62:11, "Say to the daughter of Zion," before proceeding to Zechariah 9:9. The substitution of Isaiah's "Say to" for Zechariah's "Rejoice greatly" makes "Behold, your king is coming to you . . ." an evangelistic proclamation to unconverted Israel. By omitting Zechariah's description of the king as "righteous and saving," Matthew concentrates on Jesus the king's being meek and mounted on a donkey and her colt. His meekness adds appeal to the evangelistic proclamation, as shown by his own invitation in 11:28–30: "[Come] here to me . . . . Take my yoke on you and learn from me, *because I'm meek and humble in heart*." Since a conqueror would have mounted a warhorse, "mounted on a donkey and on a colt, the foal of an [animal] under a yoke [that is, a *working* mother donkey]" supports the description "meek." "Behold" highlights Jesus' coming as this kind of king, and "*your* king" and "coming to *you*" emphasize that the Jews need this kind of king, not a militaristic conqueror. Where Zechariah spoke in synonymous terms of only one male donkey ("the foal") as being mounted, Matthew's use of "donkey" for the mother in 21:2 makes "a donkey" in the present quotation the mother rather than the foal. So he has Jesus mounted both on the mother donkey in accord with 21:2 and on her foal in accord with Zechariah 9:9. Since Matthew will write that Jesus "*sat*," he doesn't mean us to think of Jesus as a trick rider *standing* with one foot on the mother and the other on the colt. Rather, the pairing of the two animals so closely that sitting on the one amounts to sitting on the other as well—this pairing is designed to stress the involvement of two animals, not just one, because Zechariah did mention the mother of the male foal that's being ridden. And again, the involvement of the mother, an animal that works "under a yoke," reinforces Jesus' coming as a meek and humble king whose "yoke [is] comfortable" and whose "burden is light" (see 11:28–30 again).

21:6–7: And on going and doing just as Jesus had ordered them [to do], 7**the disciples** [that is, the two to whom he'd given instructions in 21:1–3] **brought the donkey and the colt and placed on them** [their outer] **garments; and he sat upon them.** "Going and doing just as Jesus had ordered them [to do]" spotlights exact obedience, the kind that characterizes true disciples. These same two disciples also do Jesus the honor of placing their garments on the two animals to provide him with a kind of saddle. "*Upon* them" differs slightly from "*on* them" and therefore favors that Jesus sat upon the garments. So Matthew balances the meekness of Jesus with the majesty of Jesus by picturing the two beasts as a very wide throne draped together with the same garments. Thus Jesus rides sidesaddle, so it seems, royally as well as meekly into his domain (compare the bringing of King Amaziah's corpse to Jerusalem "on horses [plural]" [2 Kings 14:17–20]).

21:8–9: And a very large crowd spread their own garments in the road [we would say "*on* the road"], **and others were cutting branches off the trees and spreading** [them] **in the road.** Matthew's description of the crowd as "very large" makes them stand for the numerous converts that were going to come into the church (28:19). "Their *own* garments" distinguishes their garments from those of the two disciples who have already honored Jesus with a kind of saddle. The spreading of garments and branches on the road honors him further with a kind of pavement—indeed, a double pavement—suitable for a king to ride over while his subjects only walk (compare 2 Kings 9:13). "Off the trees" alludes to the olive trees after which was named the mountain where the procession was starting (21:1). 9**And the crowds going ahead of him and the** [crowds] **following** [him] **were shouting, saying, "'Hosanna' to the Son of David! 'Favored** [is] **he who's coming in the Lord's name!' 'Hosanna' in the highest** [places] [Psalm 118:25–26]**!"** The plurality of the crowds that both precede and follow Jesus strengthens their symbolizing the numerous converts who were going to come into the church. The crowds' preceding and following Jesus make up an honorary escort. The double "Hosanna!" heaps further honor on him. See the comments on Mark 11:9–10 for the meanings of "Hosanna," "Favored," "coming in the Lord's name," and "in the highest [places]." "To the Son of David" harks back to Jesus' Davidic ancestry, acknowledges his succeeding to the messianic throne after the pattern of Solomon, David's original and wise royal son, and echoes the shouts of the two men whose blindness Jesus has recently healed (compare 1:1–17; 9:27; 12:23; 15:22; 20:30–31 with 11:2, 19; 12:42).

21:10–11: And when he'd come into Jerusalem, all the city was quaked, saying, "Who is this?" "Was quaked" connotes Jesus' divine majesty (see the comments on 8:23–24). Here the quaking has to do with a psychological shaking up of Jerusalem's populace. "*All* the city" adds emphasis to the connotation of Jesus' divine majesty. "Who is this?" exposes the Jerusalemites' ignorance in contrast with the crowds' knowing and acknowledging Jesus as "the Son of David." This contrast is furthered in Matthew's next statement: **[11]But the crowds were saying, "This is the prophet Jesus from Nazareth of Galilee."** So standing for numerous future converts from all nations, the crowds accompanying Jesus exhibit their knowledge of him as a prophet as well as David's son. In 13:57 he portrayed himself as a prophet: "A prophet isn't dishonored except in [his] hometown and in his household."

21:12–13: And Jesus entered into the temple and threw out all those who were selling and buying in the temple; and he overturned the moneychangers' tables and the chairs of those who were selling doves. The crowds have just identified Jesus as a prophet. Now he proves the identification correct by acting as a prophet in cleansing the temple. His throwing out "*all*" the sellers and buyers magnifies the irresistibility of this prophet, whose divine majesty caused all Jerusalem to be psychologically quaked if not earthquaked (though earthquakes are coming in 27:51, 54; 28:2). See further the comments on Mark 11:15–16, though Matthew writes nothing about carrying vessels through the temple and doesn't mention that the temple-cleansing occurred a day later than the triumphal entry. [13]**And he says to them** [the sellers, buyers, and moneychangers], **"It's written, 'My house will be called a house of prayer** [Isaiah 56:7]**,' but you yourselves are making it 'a den of bandits** [Jeremiah 7:11]**.'"** The present tense in "he *says*" lays emphasis on Jesus' prophetic word, which follows up on his prophetic deed. "It's written" backs up the deed with scriptural authority, for Jesus didn't come "to tear down the Law or the Prophets. . . . rather to fulfill [the Prophets]" (5:17). Isaiah 56:7 *predicts* that the temple will be called "a house of prayer." This meaning would here imply that with their commerce the sellers, buyers, and moneychangers are thwarting the fulfillment of that prediction. In Matthew's context, however, "*will* be called" could equally well be translated "*shall* be called" and understood as also a command that they are disobeying with their commerce. "You *yourselves* are making it 'a den of bandits'" pinpoints the blame. "You yourselves *are* making it 'a den of bandits'" contemporizes the desecration of the temple that was taking place back in Jeremiah's day. Jesus doesn't identify God as the speaker in the quoted Old Testament passages; so "*my* house" could mean *Jesus*' house. If it does, he's claiming an ownership, like his ownership of the donkeys, which justifies his cleansing the temple of the bandit-like commercialism that has taken away its proper use for prayer.

21:14–17: And blind and lame people approached him in the temple, and he healed them [compare 11:5; 15:30–31]. [15]**And on seeing the marvelous things that he did and the children who were shouting in the temple** [courts] **and saying, "Hosanna to the Son of David!" the chief priests and the scholars got indignant and said to him, "Do you hear what these** [children] **are saying?"** [16]**But Jesus tells them, "Yes. Haven't you ever read, 'Out of the mouth of infants and sucklings you have restored praise** [Psalm 8:2]**'?"** [17]**And abandoning them, he went outside the city to Bethany and lodged there.** According to 2 Samuel 5:8 the saying, "The blind or the lame shall not come into [the Lord's] house," arose out of David's statement that he hates "the lame and the blind." But David was using "the lame and the blind" as a figurative epithet for the Jebusites, from whom he was about to seize control of Jerusalem, and was referring to the royal palace, for the temple had yet to be built. So by healing physically blind and lame people in the precincts of the temple, the Lord's house, Jesus corrects Jewish misinterpretation of David's statement, and does so as the very son of David that the crowds have just acclaimed him to be. Furthermore, the healing of the blind and the lame means that *no longer* are there any blind and lame in the Lord's house. Matthew describes the healings as "marvelous" and indicates that children now add to the crowds' acclamation their own identical acclamation (see the comments on 19:13–15, and compare 18:1–6). The indignation of the chief priests and scholars at Jesus' healing blind and lame people in the temple and at the children's acclamation of him as the son of David leads them to ask whether he hears the acclamation—as though he might be deaf to the children's shouting and as though he should put it to a stop. His "yes," emphasized by the present tense of "says," answers their question. But he counters with a question of his own that implies the chief priests and scholars have indeed read the Old Testament passages about to be quoted, so that their indignation will stand exposed as unscriptural. The infants and sucklings of Psalm 8:2 don't quite correspond to the children in Matthew, who are old enough to visit the temple and shout an acclamation. But if even infants and sucklings can restore praise, much more can children do so. And "you have *restored* praise" indicates that the Lord has replaced illegitimate commerce in the temple with the children's proper acclamation of Jesus. And this acclamation counts for praise of the Lord in the psalm, because Jesus is both Lord and "God with us" (1:23). Abandoning the chief priests and the scholars and lodging outside the city in Bethany symbolize judgment on both the city and the Jewish authorities there. Apart from this symbolism, the crowding of Jerusalem during festivals, especially during Passover, forced many pilgrims to find lodging outside the city.

CHURCHLY WELCOME OF TAX COLLECTORS, PROSTITUTES, AND GENTILES AS SUPPORTED BY GOD'S REJECTION OF THE JEWISH AUTHORITIES
Matthew 21:18–22:46

In this section Matthew justifies the church's welcoming tax collectors, prostitutes, and Gentiles—in general, those whom Jewish authorities despised—by stressing God's rejection of those authorities.

THE WITHERING OF THE FIG TREE
Matthew 21:18–22

21:18–19: And early in the morning, as he was returning into the city, he [Jesus] got hungry. ¹⁹And on seeing one fig tree by the road, he went to it and found nothing on it except leaves only; and he says to it, "No longer should fruit come from you—forever!" And the fig tree withered at once. "One" singles out a fig tree to represent the city of Jerusalem, into which Jesus is returning and in which his enemies, the Jewish authorities, reside. The road by which the fig tree is located has appeared several times recently as the road leading into Jerusalem (20:17, 30; 21:8) and therefore ties the fig tree symbolically to that city. Matthew avoids a horticultural explanation for Jesus' finding nothing on the tree to eat. So the tree has no excuse for its offering nothing with which Jesus could satisfy his hunger, just as the chief priests and scholars in Jerusalem, precisely because they *had* read Psalm 8:2, lacked an excuse for getting indignant at the children's acclamation of Jesus in the temple (21:14–16). The redundancy of "nothing" and "leaves only" intensifies the authorities' lack of an excuse and of the fruit consisting in faith and good deeds. The present tense in "he *says*" underscores the following pronouncement of judgment—a judgment that corresponds to the symbolism in Jesus' having abandoned the authorities and gone outside their city (21:17). In the pronouncement itself, inability to bear fruit represents punishment; and "no longer . . . forever" puts a double emphasis on the eternality of punishment for the morally fruitless Jerusalemites. The immediacy of the fig tree's withering dramatizes their coming judgment.

21:20–22: And on seeing [the withering], the disciples marveled, saying, "How is it that the fig tree withered at once?" ²¹And answering, Jesus said to them, "Amen I tell you, if you were to have faith and not doubt, not only will you do the thing of the fig tree [= its withering], but even if you were to say to this mountain, 'Be lifted up and thrown into the sea,' it'll happen. ²²And you'll receive all things, however many they are, that you, if believing, might ask for in prayer." The immediacy of the withering makes the disciples marvel, just as Jesus' healing blind and lame people in the temple made the evangelist Matthew describe the healings as marvels (21:14–15). This marvelous immediacy stresses the certainty of eternal punishment for the Jerusalemites. The fulfillment of Jesus' symbolic pronouncement is as good as already done. The disciples ask about the *fact* of immediate withering ("*How is it that . . . ?*"). Jesus answers in terms of the *method* by which they too could perform such a marvel, though they hadn't asked for such instruction ("*How* did the fig tree wither at once?" as the text could also be translated). As usually in Matthew, Jesus is augmenting their knowledge with further knowledge (13:11–12). "Amen I tell you" stresses the truth of his answer, and the answer sets forth praying with faith as the method. "And not doubt" defines "faith" negatively. "Believing" defines it positively (though in

Matthew's original Greek "believing" is the verb form of "faith" or, the other way around, "faith" is the noun form of "believing"). Mountains represented stability of the highest degree (see the comments on 17:20). So the success of merely telling with faith "this mountain" (the Mount of Olives according to 21:1) to be lifted up and thrown into the sea (probably the Dead Sea, visible from the Mount of Olives on a clear day) represents the peak of the power of undoubting faith. "*Even if*" underlines this mind-boggling power. But who does the lifting and throwing? Jesus' following reference to prayer points to God. The lack of an explicit mention of God leaves emphasis on the power of faith, however. And "all things, however many they are" multiplies beyond counting the possibilities of answers to prayer offered in faith.

JESUS' AUTHORITY AND THE PARABLE OF THE TWO SONS
Matthew 21:23–32

21:23: And after he'd gone into the temple [its courts and cloisters, not the sanctuary, which was off-limits to lay people like Jesus], as he was teaching [there] the chief priests and the elders of the people approached him, saying, "By what sort of authority are you doing these things? And who gave you this authority?" Jesus' cleansing of the temple and performance of healings there took place the preceding day, and Matthew writes that Jesus is now teaching. So "*these* things" that the chief priests and elders refer to must at least include the teaching. Perhaps they're limited to the things he's teaching, so that the chief priests and elders challenge "*this* authority" of his to teach in the temple. Matthew attaches "of the people" to "the elders" to link the general populace of Jerusalem with the elders in opposition to Jesus (see 27:25). By failing to address him respectfully—say, with "Teacher" or "Rabbi"—the chief priests and elders show their contempt for him. "What sort of . . . ?" centers attention on the nature of the authority they ask him to cite. "And who . . . ?" centers attention on its source, if he has any authority. They don't think he does, of course. Their questions aren't designed to elicit information—rather, to embarrass Jesus, to expose him as an imposter. So he'll play with them at their own game.

21:24–25a: And answering, Jesus said to them, "I'll also ask you one word [= one thing], which if you tell me I'll also tell you by what sort of authority I'm doing these things." Jesus will question them as they've questioned him. But it'll take only one question of his to embarrass them, whereas their two questions will have failed to embarrass him. Here's Jesus' question: ²⁵ᵃ**"John's baptism [that is, baptism as administered by John the baptizer]—where was it from? From heaven [and therefore from God, 'heaven' being a reverential substitute for God's name] or from human beings ['from' in the sense of derivation and consequent authority, or lack thereof]?"** The sort of authority asked about depends on the source of that authority. So Jesus focuses on two possible sources of John's authority to baptize.

21:25b–26: But they started reasoning among themselves, saying, "If we say, 'From heaven,' he'll say to us, 'Why then didn't you believe him?' ²⁶But if we say, 'From human beings'—we fear the crowd, for they all hold John as [= to be] a prophet." John predicted that the one coming after him—that is, Jesus—would be stronger than he was (3:11). So if the chief priests and elders attribute heavenly authority to John's baptism, Jesus will ask them why they didn't believe John's prediction that Jesus has fulfilled, as proved by the marvels they've seen him perform the previous day right in the temple. From the quotation of Scripture in 3:3, of course, Matthew's audience know that John's baptism had divine authority behind it. "The crowd" consists of those who submitted to John's baptism because they considered him a prophet and who now follow Jesus as the stronger one predicted by John. With "we fear the crowd" the chief priests and elders confess to one another their principle of expedience and thus expose their guilt to Matthew and his audience. This fear of the crowd is exacerbated by its breaking into the dialogue before the consequence of saying "From human beings" is drawn. The consequence is never drawn, in fact, so that the accent stays on the chief priests' and elders' fear of the crowd. "They *all*" points to the universality of this crowd's holding John to be a prophet (compare 14:5).

21:27: And answering Jesus, they said, "We don't know." So with a single question he has reduced them to the embarrassment that their two questions were designed to reduce him. **He told them—even he, "Neither am I telling you by what sort of authority I'm doing these things."** The abruptness of Jesus' answer (there's no "And" or "But" introducing "He said") signals victory: Game over! Jesus wins! And "*even* he" spotlights him as the winner. The chief priests and elders didn't really want to know the nature and source of his authority. They only wanted to embarrass him. So he doesn't tell them what they didn't want to know anyway, and embarrasses them instead.

The game of embarrassment has ended, but Jesus continues speaking to the chief priests and elders. *21:28–32:* **"But how does it seem to you? A man had two boys** [here in the sense of offspring rather than youngsters]. **And on approaching the first, he said, 'Boy, go work today in the vineyard.' ²⁹But answering, he said, 'I'm not willing.' But on suffering remorse later on, he went off** [into the vineyard]. **³⁰And on approaching the other** [offspring], **he** [the father] **spoke the same way as** [he'd spoken to the first one]. **And answering, he said, 'I** [am willing], **master,' and he didn't go off** [into the vineyard]. **³¹Which of the two did the father's will?"** They [the chief priests and elders] **say, "The first." Jesus says to them, "Amen I tell you that the tax collectors and the prostitutes are going ahead of you into the kingdom of God** [compare 9:10–11]. **³²For John came to you in the way** [= path, road] **of righteousness, and you didn't believe him. But the tax collectors and the prostitutes did believe him. But you, on seeing** [that

they did], **didn't even suffer remorse later on so as to believe him."**

This parable initiates a series of three parables, each having to do with the Jewish authorities' rejection of Jesus and John his predecessor (see also 21:33–46 and 22:1–14). The lack of an address such as "father" in the first boy's statement of unwillingness shows insolence, but the following remorse and going off to the vineyard show repentance. The second boy's address, "master," surpasses the expected address, "father." Moreover, his leaving "am willing" to be inferred after "I" makes it sound as though his willingness can be taken for granted. Yet his failure to go work in the vineyard belies his profession of respectful willingness (compare the Jewish authorities' hypocrisy). Since "master" translates the word elsewhere translated "Lord," the command to go work represents Jesus' commanding the good deeds of Christian discipleship (in 5:14–16, for example). The present tense in "They *say*" and "Jesus *says*" enlivens the exchange between Jesus and the Jewish authorities. "Amen I tell you" puts extra weight on Jesus' response to their answer, which answer unwittingly amounted to a self-condemnation. In Matthew we usually read about "the kingdom of *heaven*." Here, however, we read about the "kingdom of *God*," because the vineyard represents his kingdom. The tax collectors' and prostitutes' "going *ahead*" of the chief priests and elders doesn't imply that these Jewish authorities will enter the kingdom after the others do. For the authorities are unbelievers, as Jesus proceeds to say. They're standing still while by faith the tax collectors and prostitutes are going on in. John's coming "in the way of *righteousness*" implies that believing him entailed repentance in accord with the content of his message and with the character of his baptism. It also confirms that working in the vineyard represents doing the good deeds that are in keeping with repentance (see 3:1–10 [compare Psalm 1:6; Proverbs 8:20; 12:28; 16:31]). Not only did John preach righteousness as "the way of the Lord" (3:3). He himself trod the way of righteousness when he baptized Jesus (see 3:15). Believing and not believing John stem from Jesus' having raised the question of John's baptism in 21:23–27. The second boy isn't said to have seen his brother's conversion. But Jesus goes beyond the parable in saying that the chief priests and elders, represented by the second boy, did see the conversion of the tax collectors and prostitutes yet didn't follow suit. So the guilt of their unbelief looms even larger than that of the second boy, who had pretended his willingness to work in the vineyard but didn't.

THE TRANSFERAL OF GOD'S KINGDOM FROM THE JEWISH AUTHORITIES TO THE CHURCH
Matthew 21:33–46

Now Jesus tells another parable concerning a vineyard. The parable deals with tenant farmers, who stand for the chief priests and elders (21:23).

21:33: "Hear another parable: There was a man, a houseowner [= landowner] who as such planted a vineyard and put a fence around it and dug in it a winepress and built a tower [in it] and gave it out [= leased the vineyard] to [tenant] farmers and went on a journey [compare Isaiah 5:1–2]." The command to hear recollects similar commands in chapter 13 (especially) and reminds us that Jesus will build his church on the bedrock of his words (see 16:18 with 7:24–25). Since this parable will later feature the son, representing Jesus, the owner himself represents God the Father rather than Jesus. The fence protected the vineyard from wild beasts and other intruders. The tower served as a shelter and high vantage point for a watchman.

21:34–36: "And when the season of fruits [= harvest time] drew near, he sent his slaves to the farmers to take his fruits. ³⁵And on taking his slaves, the farmers beat one and killed one and stoned one [compare 2 Chronicles 24:20–22]." "Fruits" stand for good deeds in keeping with repentance (3:8). "The *season* of fruits" and its "draw[ing] near" stand for the kingdom's having drawn near so as to necessitate the doing of those good deeds. The drawing near also harks back to Jesus' drawing near to Jerusalem (21:1), where in God the Father's behalf he should receive from the Jewish authorities a like payment of good deeds in keeping with repentance. The farmers' "taking his slaves" reverses what should have happened—that is, reverses the slaves' "tak[ing] his fruits." Ordinarily, tenant farmers were bound to pay their lessor only a portion of the harvest, as in Mark 12:2: "*some* fruits of the vineyard" (similarly Luke 20:10). Here, "to take his fruits" overlooks such a limitation and implies that all the harvest belongs to the lessor, who had, after all, gone to a lot of trouble in establishing the vineyard. Thus the theological symbolism of God's demanding the totality of people's lives swallows up economic realism. In 23:37 Jesus will speak of Jerusalem's killing and stoning the prophets sent to them. So the slaves in this parable that are beaten, killed, and stoned stand for mistreated Old Testament prophets. Stoning carries the connotation of execution on grounds of religious apostasy and therefore implies disgrace as well as death (see especially Deuteronomy 13:1–11). For a long time, then, Jewish authorities in Jerusalem have treated God's true prophets as false prophets. ³⁶"**Again he sent other slaves, more than the first ones; and they** [the tenant farmers] **treated them the same way.**" These more numerous other slaves represent later prophets in the Old Testament period, more numerous than the earlier ones (compare Jeremiah 7:25–26). The maltreatment of them in addition to the maltreatment of the slaves sent earlier heaps more guilt on the farmers and, through them, on the current Jewish authorities and their predecessors. Their behavior is inexcusable. The unrealism of the owner's sending more slaves after the beating, killing, and stoning of the first three intensifies the guilt by highlighting the owner's forbearance in giving the farmers a further opportunity to pay him.

At this point we don't expect the owner to send anyone else, but to go himself. It therefore comes as a surprise to read in *21:37–39:* "**And later on he sent his son to them, saying, 'They'll respect my son.' ³⁸But on seeing the son, the farmers said among themselves, 'This is the heir. Here! Let's kill him and possess his inheritance!' ³⁹And on taking him, they threw** [him] **outside the vineyard and killed** [him]." The son represents Jesus. "Later on" reflects the delay of God's sending Jesus his Son after the sending of prophets in Old Testament times. In their culture it would be expected that peasants such as the tenant farmers would accede to someone of the son's status. After all, he's the son of the owner. But the owner's saying, "They'll respect my son," adds pathos to the killing of his son by the farmers. Their speaking "among themselves" recalls the chief priests' and elders' reasoning "among themselves" and thereby confirms that the farmers represent those Jewish authorities. "This is the heir" implies the farmers think the owner has died and that the son is coming to take over the vineyard as his inheritance. So by killing him they can possess the vineyard by squatters' rights. But before killing him they take him and throw him outside the vineyard, just as Jesus will be crucified outside Jerusalem (27:32; Hebrews 13:12–13). *Throwing* the son outside shows how utterly the farmers reject the son, and therefore how utterly the Jewish authorities in Jerusalem will reject Jesus.

The delusion that the owner has died makes for an ironic turn of events in *21:40–41,* which Jesus introduces with a question: "**Therefore, whenever the owner** [= 'Lord'] **of the vineyard comes, what will he do to those farmers?**" "*Those* farmers" puts them at a moral distance to stress their wickedness. ⁴¹**They** [the chief priests and elders, represented by the farmers] **tell him, "He'll destroy them horribly, horrible** [as they are]**, and lease the vineyard to other farmers, who as such** [= as different from the horrible first ones] **will give back to him the fruits in their seasons** [compare Psalm 1:3]." By answering Jesus' question in this way the Jewish authorities unwittingly pronounce judgment on themselves, with emphasis on their own evil and on the severity of the judgment that God, represented by the owner, will inflict on them—as in fact he did at the destruction of Jerusalem and the temple in A.D. 70. The abruptness and present tense in "They *say*" dramatize their unwitting pronouncement of judgment on themselves. But who are the "other farmers" to whom the owner will lease his vineyard? Jesus will answer this question shortly. In the meantime, though, the chief priests and elders are not only pronouncing horrible judgment on their horrible selves. They're also predicting their replacement by others, who'll give back to God the fruits consisting in good deeds that accord with repentance. The plural in the phrase "in their seasons" looks forward to the prolongation and regularity of such giving back to God.

Just as "They say to him" introduced the Jewish authorities' answer abruptly and emphatically, so too does

"Jesus says to them" now introduce his identification of the "other farmers" who'll replace them. **21:42–44: Jesus says to them** [note the present tense and the lack of an initial "And" or "But"], **"Haven't you ever read in the Scriptures, 'The stone that the builders rejected—this has turned into the head of an angle. This** [head of an angle] **has come on the scene from the Lord and is marvelous in our eyes** [Psalm 118:22–23]'**? ⁴³On account of this I tell you that God's kingdom will be taken away from you and given to a nation producing its fruits. ⁴⁴And the person who falls on this stone will be shattered, and on whomever it falls—it will pulverize him."** "Haven't you ever read in the Scriptures . . . ?" implies that they have indeed read the passage that Jesus quotes; therefore they should understand the meaning of his parable. For the rejected stone, which has become "the head of an angle," see the comments on Mark 12:9–11. "On account of this" refers to the exaltation of the rejected stone as the basis for Jesus' following pronouncement. "I tell you" underscores the pronouncement. It's that God's kingdom, represented by the vineyard, will be transferred from the chief priests' and elders' leadership to the church—to the church as a whole ("a nation"), not just to her leaders; for *not* as in the Jewish nation, church members are all brothers in service to each other, and none of them is to be called "Rabbi," "Father," or "Tutor" (23:8–12). The church is called "a nation" because it will replace the nation of Israel with disciples from all nations, blended together into a new people of God. Implied is a comparison of this nation to a building (compare 16:18; Isaiah 5:7) whose key- or capstone will be the resurrected Jesus. But that kind of stone turns into a judgmental stone that shatters and pulverizes (see the comments on Luke 20:18 for interpretation).

21:45–46: And on hearing his parables, the chief priests and the Pharisees knew that he is speaking about them. "The elders of the people" in 21:23 are now identified theologically as "the Pharisees." The present tense of "is speaking" underlines their and the chief priests' coming to the realization that Jesus' parables contained damaging representations of them. ⁴⁶**And though seeking to seize him, they feared the crowds, since they** [the crowds] **held him for a prophet.** The plural of "the crowds" previews the discipling of "all nations" (28:19). The crowds' holding Jesus to be a prophet recalls their correctly identifying him as such at the triumphal entry (21:11; compare their holding John the baptizer as a prophet in 21:26, so that the parallel between John and Jesus reappears).

THE SHARED CONDEMNATION OF THE JEWISH AUTHORITIES AND FALSELY PROFESSING DISCIPLES
Matthew 22:1–14

22:1–3: And answering, Jesus spoke to them again in parables, saying, ²"The kingdom of heaven was like a man, a king, who as such [= as a king] **made a wedding banquet for his son. ³And he sent his slaves to invite to the wedding banquet those who'd been invited. And they weren't willing to come."** Jesus is still speaking to the chief priests and Pharisees (21:45 [compare 21:23]). The plural of "parables" includes the two preceding parables (21:28–32, 33–44) as well as the following one. The first of these three centered on the ministry of John the baptizer. The second peaked in the mission of Jesus, God's Son. The third will now advance to the mission of the church. "Answering" makes this third parable a response to the chief priests' and Pharisees' understanding that in the previous parable Jesus spoke about them and to their seeking to seize him but fearing the crowd, who held him to be a prophet. "The kingdom of heaven was like a man, a king" echoes 18:23 and compares the kingdom not to the kingly man alone but also to what he proceeds to do and its consequences. Though in 25:31–46 Jesus the Son of Man will be called "the king," here the king represents God the Father (compare 21:31, 43). But the kingdom belongs to both Jesus and his Father. The past tense in "*was* like" looks on the Jewish authorities' rejection of Jesus, shortly to be portrayed, as already consummated. As in 21:37–39, but here only implicitly, the son represents Jesus. And as in 21:34–35, the first contingent of slaves represents early prophets in the Old Testament period. "To invite . . . those who'd been invited" means to call to the banquet those who had previously accepted an invitation. Their previous acceptance makes their present unwillingness to come an affront to the king and harks back to the issue of willingness versus unwillingness in the parable of the two boys (21:28–32). The wedding banquet stands for the messianic feast of salvation (compare 8:11; Revelation 19:7–9).

22:4–6: "Again he sent other slaves, saying, 'Tell those who've been invited [referring to the initial invitation that they accepted], **"Behold, I've readied my meal. My oxen and fatlings** [are] **butchered, and all things** [are] **ready. Here! To the wedding banquet!"'** ⁵**But they, paying no attention, went off—one to his own field, one to his business; ⁶and the rest, on seizing his** [the king's] **slaves, manhandled and killed** [them]**."** As in 21:36, the second contingent of slaves represents later prophets in the Old Testament period. Sending them exhibits forbearance on the king's part. He gives the invitees a second chance despite their previous unwillingness to come. "Behold" underlines the readiness of the meal, as does also the detail of butchering and the generalization that "*all* things [are] ready." Given the scarcity of meat in the diets of ordinary people at that time, the menu of oxen and fattened livestock makes the banquet specially inviting. "Here!" and "To the wedding banquet!" redouble the invitation. But "my meal" implies that the banquet was to take place in the morning, because the word for "meal" properly refers to a breakfast or a brunch. (Jesus' use of this word leaves room for the king's quick military attack during the balance of the day on those who refuse the invitation [22:7], so that the banquet will be delayed till darkness has fallen [22:13].)

The farmer and the businessman don't even bother to give excuses. Paying no attention to the redoubled invitation, they brusquely go off to their normal round of daily affairs. No explanation. No request to be excused. Brazen unwillingness. Refusal of a king's invitation amounted to rebellion; but the remaining invitees do even worse by seizing, manhandling, and killing the king's slaves, just as the Jewish authorities did to Old Testament prophets and will yet do to those who proclaim the gospel of the kingdom (23:29–36 [compare 21:33–39]).

22:7–10: "And the king was enraged and, on sending his armies, had them destroy those murderers and set their city on fire. ⁸Then he tells his slaves, 'On the one hand, the wedding banquet is ready. On the other hand, those who'd been invited weren't worthy. ⁹Therefore go to the outlets of the streets [that is, to the places where the city streets pierce through the walls and turn into country roads] and invite to the wedding banquet as many people as you find.' ¹⁰And on going out into the roads, those slaves gathered all whom they found, both evil people and good people. And the wedding hall was filled with recliners [on cushions placed around the tables]." The king's rage represents the wrath of God, directed as it is against those who ignore his invitation to the banquet of salvation, and especially against those who like the chief priests and Pharisees make pretense of willingness to come (compare 3:7 and the boy in 21:30). "Sending his armies" indicates a wholesale military expedition. "Destroyed those murderers" echoes the destruction of the murderous tenant farmers in 21:41 and points toward the eternal destruction of the ungodly (5:29–30; 10:28, in which passages destruction means ruination rather than annihilation). Just as Isaiah 5:1–2 provided background for the preceding parable of the vineyard (see especially 21:33), so too does Isaiah 5:24–25 provide background for the king's having his armies torch the city. For Isaiah's parable about the Lord's vineyard leads to a threat against Jerusalem that reaches a climax in "fire" and "flame [compare the king's having the city set on fire] . . . for they've rejected the law of the Lord of hosts [compare Jesus' preoccupation with the Law in Matthew's Gospel] . . . . Therefore the Lord's rage has burned against his people [compare the king's rage here]; and he has stretched out his hand against them and struck them down; . . . and their corpses were like garbage in the middle of the streets [compare the destruction of the murderers here, also the mention of streets]." The setting of the city on fire points forward to the eternal fire of gehenna (= hell [5:22; 18:8–9; 25:46; see also 3:10–12; 7:19; 13:40–42, 49–50]). "*Those* murderers" and "*their* city" put them at a moral distance and imply a separation between Jerusalem and God's kingdom (compare "*those* tenant farmers" in 21:40; "*their* scholars" in 7:29; "*their* cities" in 11:1; and "*their* [or '*your*'] synagogues" six times throughout Matthew).

The present tense in "Then he *tells* his slaves" accentuates the king's commissioning a third contingent of slaves. Since the earlier-mentioned slaves were killed, we have to think here of further slaves. If the first two contingents represented earlier and later Old Testament prophets, as they certainly did in 21:34–36, and if the destruction of the murderers and burning of their city symbolized God's rejecting the Jewish authorities based in Jerusalem, this third sending of slaves stands for the mission of the church to disciple all nations, beginning right after Jesus' resurrection. In fact, the command of the king to his slaves that they "go" will be echoed in the Great Commission (28:19). The unworthiness of the initial invitees, now destroyed in the parable but still representing the chief priests and Pharisees—their unworthiness consisted in a refusal to come by way of repenting and producing "fruit in keeping with [literally, 'worthy of'] repentance" (3:7–8 [compare 10:11–13, 37–38]). "Therefore" makes the initial invitees'—that is, the Jewish authorities'—unworthiness the reason for going out into country roads to invite others—that is, to invite all nations to the banquet of salvation. The city has gone up in smoke; so people will be found only in the countryside, representing the whole wide world. "*Those* slaves" puts them at a geographical (not moral) distance because of their far-flung mission (compare Acts 1:8). "As many people as you find" combines with "both evil people and good people" to portray the church, resulting from a carrying out of the Great Commission, as made up of false as well as true disciples or, to use one of Jesus' figures of speech, tares as well as wheat (13:24–30, 36–43 [compare 13:47–50; 25:1–13]). This portrayal sets the stage for 22:11–14. The filling of the wedding hall represents evangelistic success throughout the inhabited earth (compare 24:14), but Jesus' having mentioned the evil people before the good people reflects concern over a preponderance of false disciples (compare 7:13–14, 24–27).

22:11–14: "And on entering [the wedding hall] to view the recliners [at table], the king saw there a man not garbed with a wedding garment. ¹²And he says to him, 'Comrade, how is it that you came in here not having a wedding garment?' But he was muzzled [a figure of speech for being reduced to silence, here by the king's question]. ¹³Then the king said to the servants [who've been serving the food], 'After binding his feet and hands, throw him into the darkness farther outside. Weeping and gritting of teeth will be there. ¹⁴For many are invited, but few [are] selected.'" This appendage to the parable warns against false discipleship. In first-century middle eastern culture a host might have his guests eat by themselves but come in on them during their meal. The present host, a king, is affronted by a recliner at table who isn't wearing a wedding garment. A wedding garment probably means a newly washed garment (compare Zechariah 3:3–5; Revelation 3:4–5, 18; 19:8; 22:14). It stands for good deeds that give evidence of true discipleship. Jesus doesn't bother himself with the question how country folk could have washed and dried their garments in time for the banquet. After all, the slaves had gone out and gathered them, apparently in such a way as to allow no interval between their being invited and their coming. Are we to infer that the king made available a clean garment for each guest (compare 2 Kings 25:29; Esther 6:7–9; Revelation 19:7–9)? Probably not, since Jesus offers no hint to that effect. The present tense in "he *says* to him" underscores the unacceptability of coming to the banquet without a wedding garment, that is, the unacceptability of false discipleship. Despite the affront to him, the king addresses the man not wearing a wedding garment with a polite, even affectionate, "Comrade" (compare 20:13; 26:50). "How is it that?" introduces a question concerning the *right* to enter, not the *means* of entrance. "But he was muzzled" points up this guest's lack of an excuse (compare 22:34). Likewise, false disciples in the church have no excuse for their falsity and will be judged accordingly.

Earlier in this parable, a third contingent of slaves represented disciples carrying out the Great Commission (22:8–10; compare 28:18–19). Still earlier in Matthew, though, it was angels who gathered false disciples out of the kingdom and threw them into a fiery furnace (13:41–42). So Jesus switches now from "the slaves" to "the servants." As a result, the servants differ from the slaves and represent the same angels that did the judgmental work in the parables of the tares and foul fish. And just as in the parable of the tares angels bound the tares and threw them into the fiery furnace, so too the servants are told to bind the man without a wedding garment and throw him out—but here into the darkness outside the wedding hall. "*Farther* outside" stresses the distance of that darkness from the hall. Such a distance precludes any hope of re-entry later on, as does also the binding of feet and hands. No means of locomotion are left. "Weeping" indicates sorrow over exclusion from eternal salvation. "Gritting of teeth" comes from the pain of eternal punishment. And why this fate? Because "many are invited, but few [are] selected" (compare 7:13–14). "Many" describes as numerous "all whom they [the king's slaves] found, both evil people and good people" (22:10). That is, the "many" represent the massive mixture of false and true disciples in the church. By the same token, the "few" represent the minority in that mixture who manifest genuineness of discipleship with deeds of righteousness. Since only one wedding guest is thrown into the darkness of night, whereas the rest of the guests remain in the lighted wedding hall, the proportions seem topsy-turvy. But Jesus could hardly have emptied the wedding hall of most of the king's guests without ruining the festivities. So turning the proportions upside down with "few [are] selected" goes to show the pervasiveness of false profession in the church and the strength of Jesus' concern over that problem.

The parable has contained a large number of unrealistic features: (1) the unwillingness to come of those who'd previously accepted an invitation; (2) their pleading no excuse and not even asking to be excused; (3) the concert of their refusal to come; (4) the repetition of the invitation even after such a refusal; (5) the refusers' manhandling and murdering the slaves who brought a gracious re-invitation; (6) the king's *sending* his armies to his own city; (7) the king's sending them to *torch* his

own city; (8) the carrying out of this military expedition on the afternoon of the very day of the wedding banquet; (9) the delay of the banquet only till evening; (10) the holding of the banquet in the burned-out city; (11) the bringing in of guests formerly deemed unsuitable; (12) a man's getting in without a wedding garment; and (13) the others' having wedding garments without any indication of how they could have gotten them so quickly. But all these unrealisms highlight the points of the parable: (1) the Jewish authorities' damnable rejection of God's invitation to the banquet of salvation; (2) the judgment coming on them for that rejection; (3) the successful shifting of evangelistic effort to all nations; and (4) the frightful fate of false disciples who have come into the church as a result of that effort.

THE EVIL OF THE PHARISEES IN TESTING JESUS ON THE ISSUE OF PAYING TAXES TO CAESAR
Matthew 22:15–22

22:15–17: Then, after going, the Pharisees took counsel so that they might trap him in a word [= in a statement of his]. **¹⁶And they send to him their disciples with the Herodians, saying, "Teacher, we know that you're truthful** [contrast the chief priests' and elders' untruthful claim in 21:27 *not* to know the origin of John's baptism] **and teach God's way in truth** [= truthfully], **and** [that] **it doesn't matter to you about anyone, for you don't look into the face of human beings** [in other words, you don't care what anybody thinks about you, because you're not impressed by their appearance, superficial as it is]**."** Thus the attempt to trap Jesus begins with a respectful address ("Teacher") and fulsome flattery designed to mask from him the purpose of entrapment. For Matthew's audience, though, the present tense in "they *send*" stresses this purpose and, ironically, the actual truth of what they intend only as flattery. Sending their disciples rather than going back to Jesus themselves, and sending them with the Herodians, form part of the Pharisees' stratagem. After Jesus' directing three successive parables against them, they hope he won't perceive who is trying to trap him into making a self-damaging statement. It's possible that "saying" tells what the Pharisees are saying *through* their disciples rather than what their disciples are saying. If so, further emphasis falls on the Pharisees' subterfuge. Normally they and the Herodians opposed each other, but having a common enemy in Jesus now makes them co-conspirators. **¹⁷"Therefore tell us how it seems to you. Is it lawful to give** [= pay] **a poll tax to Caesar or not?"** "Therefore" sets this request on the foundation of Jesus' true and impartial teaching of God's way. Concerning the Herodians, the flattery, the poll tax, and the dilemma in which the Pharisees are trying to trap Jesus, see the comments on Mark 12:13–14.

22:18–22: And knowing their evil [especially that of the Pharisees, who'd sent their disciples with the Herodians], **Jesus said, "Why are you testing me, hypocrites? ¹⁹Show me the coin of** [= used for paying] **the poll tax."**

And they brought him a denarius. ²⁰And he says to them, "Whose image [on the denarius is] this, and [whose] inscription?" ²¹They say to him, "Caesar's." Then he says to them, "Therefore give Caesar's things back to Caesar, and God's things back to God." ²²And on hearing [this statement], they marveled; and leaving him, they went away. The present tense in "And he *says* to them," "They *say* to him," and "Then he *says* to them" makes for a vigorous exchange, and "Therefore" makes Jesus' answer depend on the stamp of Caesar's likeness and inscription on the denarius. See the comments on Mark 12:15–17 concerning the hypocrisy of Jesus' interlocutors, the denarius, its image and superscription, Jesus' argument, the identities of Caesar's things and God's things, the distinction between giving and giving back, and the marveling at Jesus' statement.

THE CULPABLE ERROR OF THE SADDUCEES IN DENYING THE RESURRECTION
Matthew 22:23–33

22:23–24: On that day Sadducees, saying there's no resurrection, approached him and questioned him, ²⁴saying, "Teacher, Moses said, 'If some [man] were to die not having children, as next of kin his brother shall marry his wife and raise up seed [= father an heir] **for his** [deceased] **brother** [Deuteronomy 25:5; Genesis 38:8 (compare Ruth 4:5, 10)].'" "On that day" refers to the very day Jesus has just confounded the Pharisees on the issue of paying a poll tax to Caesar (22:15–22). The Pharisees believe in resurrection. The Sadducees don't (Acts 23:8). So they're going to try embarrassing Jesus, who—they seem to know—believes in resurrection as do their theological rivals the Pharisees (12:41–42). "Saying there's no resurrection" interprets the Sadducees' coming question as a denial of resurrection. "Teacher" introduces a scriptural question suitably but masks antagonism toward Jesus. And "Moses" comes forward to set up a possible conflict between Jesus as a teacher and Moses as a legislator. Since the Sadducees accept Moses' law (which doesn't refer explicitly to resurrection) but not the rest of the Old Testament (which does refer explicitly to resurrection, most clearly in Daniel 12:2; but see also Isaiah 26:19; Ezekiel 37:12–14), the Sadducees quote what's known as the law of levirate marriage. By wordplay, "raise up" in the quotation relates also to the question of resurrection; for this verb is used for God's raising up the dead as well as for a man's raising up offspring (in the sexual sense, not in the sense of child-rearing). But for the Sadducees, raising up offspring was the only kind of raising up to be hoped for. "*Shall* marry his wife and raise up seed" issues a command, not a prediction.

22:25–28: "But there were seven brothers with us. And after marrying [a wife], **the first one came to an end** [= died]; **and because of not having seed** [= offspring], **he left his wife to his brother. ²⁶Similarly also the second and the third** [married her, died without having offspring, and left her to the next brother] **up to the seven** [all of whom did the same]. ²⁷**And later than** all [the seven], **the woman died. ²⁸In the resurrection, therefore, of the seven whose wife will she be? For they all had her** [as a wife]." The introductory "But" contrasts the just-quoted law with the following case, put forward by the Sadducees as inconsistent with the law if there's going to be a resurrection. "With us" implies that they're citing an actual case, though they may be pretending to do so. Such pretense would indicate deception on their part. "Seven" connotes completeness, as though the case will seal the argument against resurrection. Whereas getting married and not having seed are indicated only in participles (-ing forms of the verb), dying and leaving the wife are indicated in main verbs for a stronger contrast with resurrection. "Therefore" makes the Sadducees' question stem from the story of the woman. According to them, resurrection would make shambles of Moses' law by giving to the woman *at one and the same time* the seven husbands whom the law had required her to have *one after another* during her mortal life. A man might practice polygamy. Many did, including the patriarchs. But a woman? In the resurrection? Absurd! Therefore the law of levirate marriage rules out the doctrine of resurrection. How will Jesus tackle this conundrum without joining the Sadducees in a denial of resurrection, including his own as already predicted to the Twelve (16:21; 17:22–23; 20:18–19)?

22:29–30: But answering, Jesus told them, "You're deceived because of not knowing the Scriptures and not [knowing] **God's power. ³⁰For in the resurrection people neither marry** [as men do] **nor are they given in marriage** [as happens to women]. **Rather, they are like angels in heaven** [the existence of whom the Sadducees also denied according to Acts 23:8, but see the comments on that passage for these denied angels as disembodied human spirits awaiting the resurrection of their bodies]." The Sadducees' ignorance, declared flatly by Jesus, contrasts with the knowledge that characterizes true disciples, as he has constantly emphasized in this Gospel. In view of the Sadducees' rejecting all the Old Testament except for Moses' law and in view of their denying the existence of angels, Jesus' reference to angels and use of the plural in "the Scriptures" lend sarcasm to the answer he gives the Sadducees. Presupposed by Jesus is that angels don't marry. And the present tense in "*marry*," "*are . . . given in marriage*," and "*are* like angels in heaven" projects the future resurrection as so certain it might as well be taking place already. The Sadducees' ignorance of God's power has deceived them; and this ignorance consists in a failure to understand not only that he can raise the dead but also that he can change conditions of life—and that he *will* change them at the resurrection so as to discard the institution of marriage since immortality will make procreation and the rearing of children needless. Consequently, levirate marriage now will pose no difficulty then.

22:31–33: "And concerning the resurrection of the dead, you've read, haven't you, what was spoken to you by God, saying, ³²I am the God of Abraham and the

God of Isaac and the God of Jacob [Exodus 3:6]'? He's not the God of dead people—rather, of living people." ³³And on hearing [Jesus' answer to the Sadducees], the crowds were awestruck at his teaching. "You've read, haven't you?" implies that the Sadducees have indeed read what God spoke in the Scriptures, so that the Sadducees have no excuse for their ignorance of his power. They've read the Scriptures but haven't understood them. Jesus doesn't identify the scriptural passage where God spoke, and he substitutes "to you" for the original addressee, Moses. This substitution exacerbates the Sadducees' ignorance in that they don't even understand what God spoke *to them*. Their ignorance is inexcusable. The exacerbation of this culpable ignorance achieves yet greater intensity with the substitution of "what was spoken to you *by God*" where—on the analogy of "what was spoken by the Lord *through the prophet*" (compare 1:22; 2:15, 17, 23; 4:14; 8:17; 12:17; 13:35; 21:4; 27:9)— we would expect "what was spoken to you by the Lord *through Moses.*" The spokesman Moses drops out of sight altogether to let the spotlight shine solely on God as having spoken to the Sadducees—directly, it would seem. Differently from Mark 12:26–27, where "am" is left out to be only inferred in the quotation ("I [am] the God of Abraham . . . "), here Jesus deduces from the expressed verb in the present tense ("I *am* the God of Abraham . . .") that God would not and does not identify himself as *now* the God of those who have died without hope of resurrection. For him to do so would amount to a confession of powerlessness over death. In accord with biblical anthropology, Jesus assumes that the hope of life after death includes physical life to fulfill God's intent for human beings at creation (compare the meaning of "resurrection" as a "standing up" of bodies that have been lying supine in graves). The amazement of the crowds "at his teaching" harks back to the Sadducees' addressing Jesus with "Teacher" (22:24) and highlights his having confounded them with his teaching just as he'd confounded the Pharisees in the preceding episode that very day. Two down. One to go. As usual, the awestruck crowds represent the future masses who'll come into the church as professing disciples.

THE PHARISEES' GATHERING AGAINST JESUS IN A QUESTION ABOUT THE GREAT COMMANDMENT
Matthew 22:34–40

22:34–36: And the Pharisees, on hearing that he'd muzzled the Sadducees, gathered together to the same [place]. ³⁵**And testing him, one of them, a lawyer** [= an expert in Old Testament law], **questioned** [Jesus]: ³⁶**"Teacher, what sort of commandment in the Law** [is] **great?"** "He'd *muzzled* the Sadducees" underscores with a colorful figure of speech Jesus' having silenced the Sadducees in the preceding episode. The Pharisees' having heard about the muzzling shows that Jesus' refutation of the Sadducees was so convincing that word got around. By "gather[ing] together to the same [place]" the Phari-

sees cast themselves in the role of heathen rulers who in the Greek version of Psalm 2:2 "gather together to the same [place]" against the Lord and his anointed (= his Christ). This antagonistic reaction to Jesus' having muzzled the Sadducees contrasts with the crowd's awestruck reaction and puts the Pharisees in a bad light. Though the Pharisees and Sadducees opposed each other theologically, there's no indication here that the Pharisees took delight in the muzzling of the Sadducees. They simply want to succeed where the Sadducees failed. And by "testing" Jesus, the lawyer who represents this coalition of Pharisees casts himself in a devilish role. For it was the Devil who first tested (= tempted) Jesus (4:1, 3 [see also 16:1; 19:3; 22:18]). The address "Teacher" echoes 22:24 and, as there, introduces a scriptural question suitably but masks antagonism toward Jesus. "What *sort of*" suits a question of "great" in the sense of important.

22:37–40: And he told him, "'You shall love the Lord your God with your whole heart and with your whole soul and with your whole mind [Deuteronomy 6:5]'. ³⁸**This is the great and first commandment** [in importance]. ³⁹**The second** [commandment is] **like it: 'You shall love your neighbor as** [you love] **yourself** [Leviticus 19:18 (compare Matthew 5:43; 19:19b)]'. ⁴⁰**On these two commandments hangs** [= depends] **the whole Law, also the Prophets."** The lawyer had asked what sort of commandment was great. Jesus' pairing of "first" with "great" implies that for him "great" escalates to "greatest." But the lawyer's "what *sort of*" left room for more than one great commandment. So Jesus adds a second commandment, great like the first one but not foremost in greatness; for as the object of your love the Lord God outranks your neighbor. The whole Law, plus the Prophets, "hangs" on these two commandments in the sense that they derive from and depend on these two, so that love for God and neighbor must permeate obedience to all the other commandments. This permeation keeps careful obedience from turning into mechanical rule-keeping. To leave emphasis on the first and second commandments, Matthew breaks off this episode without telling the lawyer's reaction. It's enough to know that Jesus taught the Law and the Prophets, which he came not to tear down but to fulfill (5:17–18). For the meanings of loving the Lord God with your whole heart, soul, and mind and of loving your neighbor as you love yourself, see the comments on Mark 12:29–31 (though note that to conform to the trio of phrases in Deuteronomy 6:4, Matthew omits loving God "with your whole strength").

JESUS' BESTING THE ASSEMBLED PHARISEES
Matthew 22:41–46

22:41–44: But since the Pharisees had gathered together [as mentioned in 22:34], **Jesus questioned them** [as their lawyer had questioned him in 22:35 (see also 22:23)], ⁴²**saying, "How does it seem to you concerning the Christ? Whose son** [= descendant] **is he?" They say to him, "David's." ⁴³He says to them, "Therefore how is it that David in the Spirit calls him 'Lord,' saying,**

[44]"The Lord [= God] **said to my Lord** [the Christ], **"Sit at my right** [hand] **till I put your enemies under your feet** [Psalm 110:1]"'?" Now that Jesus' enemies have failed miserably in their interrogation of him, he turns interrogator. "But" introduces this reversal of roles. The remention of the Pharisees' having gathered together revives Matthew's portrayal of them as acting like the heathen rulers in Psalm 2:2 (see the comments on 22:34). With "How does it seem to you?" Jesus echoes a locution that the Pharisees' disciples used in questioning him (22:17). Turnabout is fair play. "The Christ" is Greek for "the Messiah" in Hebrew. The present tense and abruptness in "They *say* to him" and "He *says* to them" enliven the dialogue at its crucial points. As in 21:31, 40–41; 22:20–21, Jesus forces his enemies to answer him. At the start of his riposte "Therefore" implies the correctness of their answer: "David's." As a result, Jesus' next question is protected from being misunderstood as an unscriptural denial of the Christ's Davidic ancestry (see 1:1–17!). But the introduction of a quotation from Psalm 110:1 with "how is it that?" implies that Davidic ancestry isn't all that needs to be said about the Christ's pedigree. "In the Spirit" describes David as under divine inspiration when calling the Christ "Lord." If "in the Spirit" indicates a visionary state, as it does in Revelation 1:10; 4:2; 17:3; 21:10, David's statement gets a prophetic stamp. (The Pharisees would have agreed with Jesus on the traditional ascription of Psalm 110 to David.) "Till I put your enemies under your feet" spells out the Christ's lordship (compare the emphasis throughout Matthew on Jesus' deity as "God with us" and "God's Son" as well as "Lord").

Jesus draws a conclusion in **22:45–46: "Therefore if David calls him** [the Christ] **'Lord,' how is it that he** [the Christ] **is his** [David's] **son?"** Matthew's audience know the answer, of course. It's that Joseph, himself a descendant of David, brought Jesus into David's family line by adopting and naming Jesus, though Mary had conceived Jesus by the Holy Spirit, so that he was also David's Lord (chapter 1). [46]**And no one was able to answer him a word. Neither did anyone dare from that day** [forward] **to question him any more.** The Pharisees are flummoxed. They don't know what Matthew's audience know. Not even one of the Pharisees knows, and not even a word of answer comes from their lips. Nor did anyone, Pharisee or Sadducee or other, dare to question him any more. To do so would prove too embarrassing for the questioner. The redundancy of "from that day [forward]" and "any more" stresses the danger of such embarrassment.

JESUS' REJECTION OF FALSELY PROFESSING JEWISH-CHRISTIAN WOULD-BE LEADERS AS PORTRAYED IN JESUS' REJECTION OF ISRAEL'S LEADERS
Matthew 23:1–13, 15–25:46

Chapters 23–25 constitute Jesus' fifth great discourse in Matthew. It balances the first one, the Sermon on the Mount, in its length, in its association with a mountain (24:3), in Jesus' taking the seated position of a teacher (24:3; compare 23:2), in the contrast between woes (here) and beatitudes (in the Sermon on the Mount), and in the closing judgmental scenes, each of which includes the addressing of Jesus with "Lord" by the condemned (7:21–23; 25:44–46). In their immediate context chapters 23–25 carry on and sharpen the condemnatory portrayal of Israel's leaders already begun. Those leaders stand not only for Jewish officials who were persecuting the church at the time of Matthew's writing, but also, it appears, for ecclesiastics—"loophole lawyers" coming from the Pharisaical sect—who had entered the church and were encouraging behavior lax by Jesus' standards. His earlier rejection of the Jewish leaders serves as a warning to Pharisaical scholars in the church, about whose Christian profession Matthew entertains suspicion.

A PROHIBITION OF HONORIFIC TITLES IN THE CHURCH
Matthew 23:1–12

23:1–2: Then Jesus spoke to the crowds and his disciples, [2]**saying, "The scholars and the Pharisees sat on Moses' seat."** "Then" means "at that time," not "later on." Earlier on this occasion "the crowds" were awestruck at Jesus' teaching (22:33). As usual in Matthew, they stand for the mass of disciples, both false and true, who have come into the church by Matthew's time, whereas "the disciples" stand for the true among them (see especially the comments on 4:25–5:1; 7:28–29). Not all scholars were Pharisees, and not all Pharisees were scholars. But scholars were the most prominent Pharisees, and Pharisees were the most prominent faction in Judaism. So Jesus pairs the scholars and the Pharisees. Sitting in Moses' seat means passing on the authoritative words of Moses, as the scholars and Pharisees did in public readings of the Law. The past tense of "sat" looks back from the standpoint of Matthew and his audience on a time when they attended synagogue and heard the scholars and Pharisees reading the Mosaic law.

23:3–7: "Therefore do and keep [in the sense of 'obey'] **all things, as many as they are, that they've told you** [when they read the Law to you]. **But don't do according to their deeds** [that is, 'don't imitate their behavior,' though imitation of a teacher's behavior was expected in addition to obeying his words]. **For they speak** [the Mosaic commandments] **and don't do** [them]. [4]**And they tie up heavy burdens and lay** [them] **on people's shoulders, but they themselves aren't willing to remove them with their finger** [or, as we'd say, 'they aren't willing to lift a finger to remove the heavy burdens they've laid on people's shoulders']." "Therefore" makes hearing the Law in past attendance at synagogues the basis for Jesus' commanding obedience to all that the scholars and Pharisees said when they read the Law in synagogues. So he's commanding obedience to all the Law. But he isn't commanding obedience to their interpretations, the tradition of the elders, by which they nullify the Law and against which he has put his own interpretation (15:1–20 [compare 5:21–48]). ⁵"But [as opposed to removing the heavy burdens] **they do all their deeds for the purpose of being observed by people** [compare 6:1]. **For they broaden their phylacteries and lengthen** [their] **tassels** [about which see the comments on 9:20]." "*All* their deeds" exempts not a single deed from the condemnation of being done for public viewing. Phylacteries were copies of texts taken from Exodus and Deuteronomy and tied to the Jews' left hand and forehead (see, for example, Deuteronomy 6:8: "And you shall bind them [the commandments in the Law] as a sign on your hand, and they shall be as emblems on your forehead"). Broadening the phylacteries and lengthening the tassels gave the appearance of extraordinary piety. ⁶"**And they love the prestigious couch at banquets and the prestigious seats in synagogues** ⁷**and greetings in the marketplaces and to be called 'Rabbi' by people.**" They're not satisfied unless they occupy the one most honorable couch beside the host (compare Luke 14:7–11; John 13:23–25; James 2:2–3). The prestigious seats in synagogues were located up front and facing the congregation, so that occupants of those seats enjoyed much visibility. Greetings of the scholars and Pharisees were fawning, starting with the address "Rabbi," which means "my great one." Such greetings attracted attention in marketplaces. So the heavy burdens the scholars and Pharisees place on people's shoulders don't consist in interpretations of the Law that are too strict. Jesus demands righteousness stricter than that of the scholars and Pharisees (5:20–48). Those heavy burdens consist, rather, in the scholars' and Pharisees' overbearing attempts to win people's adulation (see further the comments on 11:28–30, especially for a contrast with the lightness of Jesus' burden).

23:8–12: "**But *you*** [the crowds and disciples Jesus is addressing according to 23:1]—**you shouldn't be called 'Rabbi.' For one is your teacher, and all you are brothers.** ⁹**And you shouldn't call** [anyone] **on the earth your father. For one is your Father, the heavenly** [one]. ¹⁰**Nor should you be called tutors, because your tutor is one, the Christ.**" Here Jesus starts applying his criticism of the scholars and Pharisees to church life. An emphatic "*you*" underscores the application. The following series of prohibitions strikes against any striving for prestige in the church. By Matthew's time, scholars converted from Phariseeism may have been guilty of such striving right within the church. "One," referring in each instance to Jesus or God, stands in stark contrast to "all," which allows no disciple to rise above the equality of Christian brotherhood and subjection to Jesus' didactic authority. After "one is your teacher" we expect "all you are *disciples*," so that the unexpected reference to "brothers" underscores that equality. There will be teachers in the church; indeed, Jesus will order his disciples to teach (28:20). But teachers shouldn't be addressed as such; nor should fathers, authority figures though they are, be addressed as fathers. To do either one would spoil the egalitarian character of the church.

¹¹"**But your greater person will be your servant.** ¹²**And whoever will lift himself up** [= exalt himself] **will be lowered** [= humbled], **and whoever will lower himself will be lifted up.**" "Will be lowered" and "will be lifted up" imply divine action, but the passive voice accents the humbling and the exalting as such. And the future tense in these expressions points forward to the Last Judgment as the time of humbling and exaltation (compare 18:4; 20:26–27).

WARNINGS AGAINST HYPOCRISY
Matthew 23:13, 15–39

In 23:1–2 Jesus started speaking to the crowds and his disciples *about* the scholars and Pharisees. Now he starts speaking *to* the scholars and Pharisees a series of seven woes, translated with "alas" to indicate the sorrowful fate of the scholars and Pharisees due to their hypocrisy. Yet since there's no introduction to indicate a shift of address (such as "And Jesus said to the scholars and the Pharisees"), the crowds and the disciples are themselves to take warning from the woes.

23:13: "**But alas for you, scholars and Pharisees, hypocrites, because you're locking the kingdom of heaven in front of people! For you yourselves aren't entering, nor are you allowing those who are in the process of entering to enter.**" Jesus portrays an open door that the scholars and Pharisees are shutting and locking in the face of others who have begun to enter the kingdom (contrast 16:19 with comments). He doesn't specify what shutting and locking consist in. So the stress falls solely on their preventing others from entering and on the calamitous misery that is coming on the scholars and Pharisees as a result. "Hypocrites" makes their action a show of false piety, as though preventing others from entering the kingdom is a good thing to do. The earliest and best manuscripts don't have 23:14.

23:15: "**Alas for you, scholars and Pharisees, hypocrites, because you go around sea and dry** [land] **to make one proselyte** [convert]; **and whenever he becomes** [a proselyte], **you make him more than twice as much a son of gehenna** [= somebody destined for hell] **as you!**" "Go around" occurred in 4:23 and 9:35 for itineration that had the purpose of making converts, and "sea and dry land" occurred in Jonah 1:9 in a context dealing as here with Gentiles to be converted. There's irony in that the enormity of effort to make a convert has more than doubly disastrous results—also in that the enormity of effort actually contributes to the hypocrisy because the effort is itself designed to make a show of piety.

23:16–22: "**Alas for you, blind guides, who say, 'Whoever swears** [an oath] **by the sanctuary—it's nothing** [= the oath doesn't have to be kept], **but whoever swears by the gold of the sanctuary is obligated** [to keep his oath]!' ¹⁷**Foolish and blind** [guides]! **For which is greater** [in sanctity], **the gold or the sanctuary that** sanctifies the gold?" The answer is so obvious that Jesus doesn't bother to provide it. It goes without saying that as God's house the sanctuary (which doesn't include the surrounding courts and cloisters) has the greater sanctity, one that makes sacred any gold given to decorate it. [18]"'**And whoever swears by the altar** [just outside the sanctuary]—**it's nothing. But whoever swears by the gift upon it is obligated.**'" "Blind guides" echoes 15:14, creates irony in that a blind person can't act as a guide in the first place, and intimates that what the scholars and Pharisees say presents an interpretive path just as erroneous as the path taken by a blind person. The addition of "foolish" to the second occurrence of "blind" points to a destiny of hellfire and exclusion from the kingdom, as indicated by the use of "foolish" in 5:22; 7:26–27; 25:1–13 (compare making a proselyte more than doubly destined for hell [23:15]). Jesus' calling the scholars and Pharisees "foolish" doesn't contradict the prohibition in 5:22. For here he's addressing the scholars and Pharisees. There he was prohibiting use of the epithet in addressing a "brother," that is, a fellow disciple. [19]**Blind** [guides]**! For which is greater** [in sanctity]**, the gift or the altar that sanctifies the gift?**" Again it goes without saying—hence a third occurrence of "blind"— that the altar has greater sanctity, and Exodus 29:37 says explicitly that "whatever touches the altar will be sacred." Behind the scholars' and Pharisees' interpretation of oaths lies the rationale that a creditor can't place a lien on the sanctuary or the altar. For they belong to God. So the sanctuary and the altar provide no surety and make oaths taken in their name meaningless. It's not in the creditor's power to seize the sanctuary or the altar if the debtor fails to pay. But a creditor might well seize the gold dedicated by his debtor for a future gift to the sanctuary, or the animal dedicated by his debtor for a future sacrifice upon the altar. By charging the scholars and Pharisees with hypocrisy in making these distinctions Jesus doesn't approve swearing by the sanctuary and by the altar. For in 5:33–37 he prohibited swearing by anything at all. At issue here is the teaching of invalid distinctions, the following of which enables people to break certain oaths without losing a reputation for godliness and even encourages them to take oaths they can break with supposed impunity. [20]"**Therefore** [since the sanctuary and the altar obviously have the greater sanctity] **the person swearing by the altar swears by it and by all the** [gifts] **upon it;** [21]**and the person swearing by the sanctuary swears by it and by the one inhabiting it** [that is, God]. [22]**And the person swearing by heaven takes an oath by God's throne and by the one who is sitting upon it** [compare 5:34]."

23:23–24: "**Alas for you, scholars and Pharisees, hypocrites, because you tithe** [give for religious service a tenth of] **mint and dill and cumin** [herbs you grow for flavoring, aroma, and medicine]**, and you've left** [= neglected] **the weightier matters of the Law: justice and mercy and faith! It was necessary to do these things** [that is, to tithe the herbs that grow in your gardens (compare Leviticus 27:30)] **and not to leave those**

things [that is, not to neglect those weightier matters of the Law]. [24]**Blind guides, who strain out a gnat but swallow a camel!**" Jesus affirms the necessity of obeying the Law even down to the detail of tithing lightweight garden herbs. But tithing them to make a show of piety without practicing the weightier obligations of justice, mercy, and faith constitutes hypocrisy. In 12:18 "justice" referred to God's justice in soon opening his kingdom to believers from all nations, not from the Jewish nation alone. Jesus has called earlier for the exercise of mercy toward repentant tax collectors and sinners and toward his disciples (9:13; 12:7 [see also 5:7]). And though most translations have "faithfulness" here, elsewhere in Matthew this noun always means "faith," especially faith in Jesus (8:10; 9:2, 22, 29; 15:28; 17:20; 21:21). So he's saying that the Old Testament law supports his teaching not only the justice of discipling all nations to himself and the exercise of mercy toward repentant tax collectors and sinners and toward his disciples, but also faith in him—naturally, for he came to fulfill the Law and the Prophets (5:17). Since in 11:28–30 Jesus described his burden as "light" in the sense of easier to bear because of his meekness and humility, here "weightier" means "more difficult to practice," not "more important to practice" as though it wouldn't matter a great deal if you didn't tithe the garden herbs. In other words, Jesus is saying that in tithing those herbs the scholars are doing what's easier to do than practicing justice, mercy, and faith, which they neglect doing. No credit there! Another "blind guides," emphasized as usual by its occurrence in an exclamation, rounds out this woe. The scholars and Pharisees strained out gnats (or their larvae) by pouring wine (and perhaps other drink) through a cloth or a fine wicker basket. A gnat and a camel, the smallest and largest animals seen in daily life, represented ritually unclean food that the Mosaic law commanded not to be eaten (see Leviticus 11:4, 41). Jesus' humor, which borders on sarcasm, makes the point that the scholars' and Pharisees' straining gnats out of their wine is like their tithing of garden herbs for a show of punctilious piety, and that their neglect of justice, mercy, and faith is like swallowing a ritually unclean camel—as though one *could* swallow a camel even if it *were* ritually clean! This wry humor is heightened in the Aramaic language that Jesus was almost certainly speaking. For in it there's a wordplay between *galma* ("a gnat") and *gamla* ("a camel").

23:25–26: "**Alas for you, scholars and Pharisees, hypocrites, because you cleanse the outside of a cup and of a dish** [we'd say the *under*side of a dish]**, but inwardly they are full of extortion and self-indulgence!** [26]**Blind Pharisee, first cleanse the inside of the cup in order that also its outside may become clean.**" Collectively, the cup and the dish represent the scholars and Pharisees. So "*they* are full of extortion and self-indulgence" means that the scholars and Pharisees *as represented by the cup and the dish* are full of extortion and self-indulgence. (A cup and a dish wouldn't literally be full of such evils.) The extortion robs other people of what rightfully belongs to them and enables the larcenous scholars and Pharisees to live self-indulgently. This inward corruption makes their show of righteousness hypocritical. Jesus abbreviates by omitting "scholars and" between "Blind" and "Pharisee" and by omitting "and of the dish" after "the inside of the cup." The omissions allow an individual address to the Pharisee, whose blindness has to do with overlooking his inward corruption, like overlooking residue in a dirty cup. The command to cleanse first the inside recalls Jesus' emphasis in chapters 5–6 on the priority of inner righteousness.

23:27–28: "Alas for you, scholars and Pharisees, hypocrites, because you're like plastered tombs, which as such [= as plastered] appear outwardly as beautiful, on the one hand. Inwardly, on the other hand, they're full of dead people's bones and of every impurity. **[28]In this way you too, on the one hand, appear outwardly to people as righteous. Inwardly, on the other hand, you're full of hypocrisy and lawlessness."** As tombs contain within themselves ritual corruption, so the scholars and Pharisees contain within themselves moral corruption. Since Jesus' point lies in the disguising of inward corruption, the plastering of tombs doesn't allude to whitewashing tombs to alert people against accidentally brushing against them and thereby contracting ritual impurity. The plastering alludes rather to beautifying them to divert attention from their inward corruption (see also 6:1; 23:25, 29). "*Full* of dead people's bones and of *every* impurity" puts a double emphasis on ritual corruption inside plastered tombs. Correspondingly, "*full* of hypocrisy and law*less*ness" puts a double emphasis on moral corruption inside the scholars and Pharisees. Though by definition "hypocrisy" has to do with outward pretense that masks inward reality, Jesus locates hypocrisy on the inside. For there is its origin. "Lawlessness" has to do with disobeying the Old Testament law, reaffirmed and perfected by Jesus (5:17–48; 7:23; 13:41; 24:12).

23:29–33: "Alas for you, scholars and Pharisees, hypocrites, because you build the tombs of the prophets and decorate the monuments of the righteous **[30]and say, 'If we'd existed in the days of our [fore]fathers, we wouldn't have been their partners in the blood of the prophets [= "we wouldn't have participated with them in shedding the prophets' blood"].' **[31]**And so you testify against yourselves that you're sons [= descendants] of those who murdered the prophets. **[32]**And you—fill up the measure of your [fore]fathers! **[33]**Snakes, offsprings of vipers, how would you flee from the judgment of gehenna?"** For the combination of prophets and righteous people, see also 10:41; 13:17. The prophets contrast with those in 23:28 who are full of hypocrisy in that the prophets spoke for God at cost to themselves, whereas the hypocrites advertise themselves to their own advantage. The righteous people contrast with those in 23:28 who are full of lawlessness. Jesus interprets the scholars' and Pharisees' building the prophets' tombs and decorating the monuments of righteous people as self-incriminating testimony (compare 21:31, 41; 22:21, 42). "That you're the *sons* of those who murdered the

prophets" means more than that the scholars and Pharisees descended from those murderers. For "sons of" connotes shared characteristics. Beyond shared characteristics, though, Jesus interprets the scholars' and Pharisees' building and decorating, not as a repudiation of the forefathers' murders, but as an admission of solidarity with those murderers. And such solidarity amounts to lawlessness, a breaking of the command not to murder (5:21; 19:18). Doubtless the scholars and Pharisees would have said they built the tombs and decorated the monuments to honor the prophets and righteous people. But because of the scholars' and Pharisees' inward hypocrisy and lawlessness, which will come out in their murderously engineering the crucifixion of Jesus, his interpretation exposes the hypocrisy in their saying they wouldn't have gone along with their forefathers in shedding the prophets' blood.

A "measure" is a unit of measurement—like a bushel basket, to take but one example. Here "the measure" stands for a basket, so to speak, of murderous deeds. But the forefathers' murderous deeds didn't fill up the basket. So Jesus issues to the scholars and Pharisees an ironic command: "And *you*—fill up the measure of your [fore]fathers!" The emphatic "*you*" highlights the irony. They'll fill up the measure, not by continuing to build tombs and decorate monuments, then, but by repeating their forefathers' deeds through the murder of Jesus and his disciples (compare 1 Thessalonians 2:14–16). In effect, Jesus is telling the scholars and Pharisees to fulfill his predictions that they'll engineer both his murder by crucifixion and the martyrdom of his disciples—and thus prove his predictions correct! The irony of Jesus' command consists in the Law's prohibition of murder. For other ironic commands, see Isaiah 8:9–10; Jeremiah 7:21–22; Amos 4:4–5; Nahum 3:14–15. The mention of murders leads Jesus to address the scholars and Pharisees as venomous snakes and offsprings of vipers. The latter expression echoes 3:7; 12:34. The prefixing of "Snakes" sharpens the invective. "How *would* you flee from the judgment of gehenna?" presents such flight as only a theoretical possibility. "*How?*" indicates that you couldn't flee successfully even if flight were an actual possibility. And "flee" portrays the judgment of gehenna as in pursuit of the scholars and Pharisees. "The judgment *of* gehenna" means "the judgment *consisting in* gehenna." For "gehenna," which echoes 23:15, see the comments on 5:22.

23:34–36: "On account of this [your 'fill(ing) up the measure of your (fore)fathers'] **I'm sending to you prophets and sages and scholars** [that is, disciples who'll preach as prophets, give wise counsel as sages, and teach the Law as scholars in accord with Jesus' correct interpretation of it (compare 10:16–31; 24:14; 28:18–20)]. [Some] **of them you'll kill and crucify** [= get crucified, since Jews didn't ordinarily practice crucifixion, but the Romans did (compare 10:21, 28)]. **And** [some] **of them you'll flog in your synagogues** [compare 10:17; Deuteronomy 25:2–3; 2 Corinthians 11:24] **and persecute** [= pursue with the purpose of killing] **from city to city** [compare 10:23], **[35]so that on you may come all the**

righteous blood that was being shed on the earth from the blood of Abel, the righteous one [murdered by his brother, Cain (Genesis 4:1–15)], up to the blood of Zechariah, Barachiah's son, whom you murdered between the sanctuary and the altar [in the immediately surrounding courtyard]. ³⁶Amen I tell you, all these things will come on this generation." "On account of this" indicates that Jesus is sending his disciples in order that the scholars and Pharisees may fill up the measure of their forefathers with murders even beyond his own. Their hypocrisy and lawlessness deserve a judgmental chance to express themselves! The present tense in "I'm sending" portrays the Great Commission of 28:18–20 as so soon and certain to be given that Jesus might as well be giving it right now (but see 10:16 for a preliminary sending). The disciples appear as prophets and scholars in 5:12; 8:19; 10:41; 13:52. The Christ was wisdom in 11:2, 19. Here his disciples are wise ones, sages. Like master, like disciples (10:24–25). Ironically, the scholars and Pharisees will carry out their murders "so that" all the righteous blood that's been shed may come on them. It's as though they want to suffer the coming wrath while at the same time fleeing from it (3:7). Nonsense—and therefore irony. Not quite nonsense, though; for in 27:25 all the people, incited by the chief priests and the elders, will say, "His [Jesus'] blood [be] on us and on our children." Here, "on you may come all the righteous blood" means condemnation for blood-guiltiness (compare Jeremiah 26:15, among other Old Testament passages). "All the righteous blood" magnifies the blood-guiltiness, and the shedding of "righteous blood" indicates martyrdom (compare Lamentations 4:13).

Abel counts as the first martyr in the Old Testament, Zechariah as the last (canonically though not temporally speaking [see Jeremiah 26:23]). Zechariah's martyrdom appears in 2 Chronicles 24:20–22. Originally one book, Chronicles stands last in the arrangement of books making up the Hebrew canon of the Old Testament. Chronicles calls this Zechariah "the son of Jehoiada"; but Jesus calls him "Barachiah's son," which agrees with Zechariah 1:1. The Chronicler's Zechariah lived and died before the Babylonian exile, however, whereas the career of Zechariah the minor prophet followed that exile. So what is Jesus doing by calling the preexilic Zechariah the son of a man who fathered the postexilic Zechariah? Well, in 27:3–10 Matthew will quote the postexilic Zechariah 11:12–13 in regard to "innocent blood," "the price of blood," and "the field of blood." But Matthew will ascribe the quotation to Jeremiah, from whose prophecy part of the quotation does indeed come. So the martyred preexilic Zechariah is here associated with the father of the postexilic Zechariah to make up in advance for the nonmention in 27:3–10 of the postexilic Zechariah in favor of Jeremiah and to correlate the betrayal of Jesus' innocent blood, which fulfilled the prophecy in the Minor Prophets by Zechariah the son of Barachiah, with the shedding of the righteous blood of Old Testament martyrs, which culminated in the murder of Zechariah the son of Jehoiada in Chronicles. Thus theology trumps

biology. (Incidentally, Jesus' stopping short of martyrs mentioned in the Old Testament apocrypha, written later, shows that he didn't consider those books a part of Scripture.) The coming of all the Old Testament martyrs' blood on the scholars and Pharisees means they'll be held responsible for shedding it all. The extent of their evil and their coming role in the murders of Jesus and his disciples make it right and just that they be held responsible for the totality and judged accordingly.

"On the earth" echoes the story of Abel, where emphasis falls on the earth that received his blood. The description of Abel as "the righteous one" anticipates the description of Jesus as "that righteous one" (27:19). Both of them, and the martyrs in between, were Law-abiding. In regard to the martyr Zechariah, "whom you murdered" indicates that the scholars and Pharisees participated with their forefathers in that bygone murder. The gap between generations has disappeared. The "sons of those who murdered the prophets" (23:31) have become murderers themselves. "All these things" anticipates the same phrase in 24:8, 33–34 for the events of the coming age of the church and the tribulation. Retribution for all the righteous blood of the Old Testament martyrs will take the form of those events yet to be predicted as fulfilling the forecast concerning "this generation." By context "this generation" means the scholars and Pharisees. The next verse will narrow the reference further to the scholars and Pharisees in Jerusalem. But Jesus' involving them in the murder of an Old Testament prophet shows that he doesn't take "this generation" in a sense chronologically limited to his contemporaries, but in a qualitative sense concerning the "unbelieving and perverted" in the whole of Israel's history (11:16; 12:39, 41–42, 45; 16:4; 17:17). Hence we read, "in order that on you may come . . . you murdered [regarding a centuries-old incident] . . . will come on this generation." In other words, if the "you" who constitute "this generation" includes those who murdered Zechariah in Old Testament times, "this generation" can hardly bear the chronological limitation usually imposed on it. "Amen I tell you" underscores that "all these things will come on this generation."

23:37–39: "Jerusalem, Jerusalem, the [city] that kills the prophets and stones those who've been sent to her, how often I've wanted to gather your children [= residents] together the way a hen gathers her chicks together under [her] wings! And you didn't want [to be gathered together]. ³⁸Behold, your house is being left to you—deserted. ³⁹For I tell you, by no means will you see me from now on till you say, 'Favored [is] he who's coming in the Lord's name [Psalm 118:26 (compare Matthew 21:9 and see the comments on Mark 11:9–10 for the meanings of 'Favored' and 'coming in the Lord's name')]!'" The doubling of "Jerusalem" introduces this lament with pathos. At first Jesus speaks about the city ("to her"), but since he's now there he quickly shifts to direct address ("your children," several occurrences of "you," and your house"). "That kills the prophets and stones those who've been sent to her" personifies the city, specifies stoning as the method of killing, and describes the prophets as sent (by God according to the Old Testament). But in view of Jesus' sending his disciples as prophets (23:34), such killing will continue. The desire of Jesus to gather the city's residents together the way a hen gathers her chicks together under her wings refers to his desire to bring those residents under protection from God's coming wrath (compare 3:7). "How often" intensifies Jesus' desire by multiplying it. The Jerusalemites' not wanting to be gathered together by him presages the killing of Jesus in their city. "Your house" is the temple. "Is being abandoned" refers to Jesus' soon and certain desertion of the temple, where he has been speaking since 21:23 and whence he'll exit in 24:1–2 with a prophecy of its destruction. "Behold" dramatizes this desertion. Absent Jesus, the temple will no longer be the *Lord's* house (as it still was in 21:13; Jeremiah 12:7), but "*your* house" (compare Jeremiah 22:5; Ezekiel 11:22–23). The reason for Jesus' deserting the temple consists in the Jerusalemites' failure to welcome him in the Lord's name. It was the *Galilean* crowds of his followers that welcomed him thus at the triumphal entry (21:9). "From now on" stresses the immediacy of Jesus' judgmental desertion of the temple and intimates a delay till the Jerusalemites welcome him at what we call his second coming (compare the regeneration in 19:28; also Romans 11:25–27).

A TRANSITIONAL UNIFICATION OF CHAPTERS 24–25 WITH CHAPTER 23
Matthew 24:1–2

Just as the transition in 13:34–36 united the two parts of Jesus' parabolic discourse on the kingdom of heaven, so too the transition in 24:1–2 unites Jesus' upbraiding of the scholars and Pharisees in chapter 23 with the rest of chapters 24–25 so as to produce a single discourse dealing with the history of the kingdom. This history stretches from the final phase of Jesus' conflict with the Jews' religious authorities, who have their counterparts in the church, through the second coming and on to the Last Judgment. The first two verses of chapter 24 relate to the end of chapter 23 by giving a further indication of the way "your house is being left to you—deserted" (23:38–39).

24:1–2: **And on coming out, Jesus was going away from the temple** [and thus leaving it deserted of his presence]. **And his disciples approached to point out to him** [in a backward look] **the buildings of the temple** [which consisted not only of the sanctuary proper but also of surrounding courts and cloisters]. ²**But he, answering, said to them, "You see all these things, don't you? Amen I tell you, by no means will a stone be left here on a stone that won't be torn down!"** Whereas the disciples point out the temple buildings to *Jesus*, he turns attention to *their* seeing those buildings. "*All* these things" prepares for his prediction of total destruction. "Here" pinpoints the location as close at hand, so that fulfillment of the prediction will be easily confirmable; and underlining the certainty of fulfillment are "Amen I

tell you" and "by no means." The singular in the two occurrences of "a stone" indicates how detailed the fulfillment will be. In A.D. 70 the Romans burned the temple as well as tearing it down. If someone had put these words in Jesus' mouth after the temple's destruction to make them look like a prediction, we'd expect a reference to burning as well as tearing down.

THE PERSECUTION OF JESUS' DISCIPLES, LAX BEHAVIOR AMONG THEM, AND WORLDWIDE PROCLAMATION OF THE KINGDOM AS NONSIGNS OF THE END
Matthew 24:3–14

A question from the disciples prompts Jesus now to spell out features of the church age that will *not* signal the end, that is, his return. *24:3:* **And as he was sitting on the Mount of Olives, the disciples approached him privately, saying, "Tell us, when will these things be, and what** [will be] **the sign of your coming and the consummation of the age?"** "As he was sitting" puts Jesus in the authoritative posture of a teacher (compare 5:1–2). "Privately" excludes nondisciples, so that the disciples will gain more knowledge than they already have (see 13:11–12). They've just learned about the coming destruction of the temple buildings. The plural in "these things" treats the tearing down of each stone and building as an event in and of itself. Since Jesus hasn't yet predicted the events to be described in 24:4–28, the disciples don't yet know about them and therefore can't be asking when those events will occur. From his earlier teaching in 10:23; 16:28; 20:21, however, they do know about his future coming, which they correctly associate with "the consummation of the age" (compare 13:39; Daniel 12:4, 13). They use a word for his "coming" that often connotes the public arrival of a dignitary (compare Jesus' own emphasis on publicness in 24:27–30). He won't tell them when the temple buildings will be torn down; and whereas they ask for a sign that will alert them that he's about to come, he will tell them that the publicness of his coming will itself be the sign (24:30).

24:4–8: **And answering, Jesus told them, "Watch out lest someone deceive you.** ⁵**For many will come on the basis of my name, saying, 'I am the Christ,' and deceive many.** ⁶**And you're going to hear battles and reports of battles** [compare Daniel 11:44]." "*Going* to hear" indicates nearness and certainty. **"See that you're not alarmed."** "See that" adds emphasis to the command not to be alarmed. **"For it's necessary that** [these things] **happen** [because they're part of God's plan (compare Daniel 2:28)]. **The end isn't yet, however.** ⁷**For nation will rise up** [in arms] **against nation, and kingdom against kingdom** [compare 2 Chronicles 15:6; Isaiah 19:2]**; and there'll be famines and earthquakes from place to place.** ⁸**But all these things** [are] **the beginning of birth pains** [and therefore not signs of my coming and of the consummation]." "*All* these things" rules out each of them from being such a sign. For the rest, see the comments on Mark 13:5–8.

24:9–14: "Then people will give you over to afflic-tion** [in the sense of persecution; compare Daniel 12:1] **and kill you** [compare 10:28; 21:35; 22:6; 23:34, 37], **and you'll be hated by all nations on account of my name.**" "By all nations" implies that worldwide evangelism has taken place (compare 10:18; 24:14; 28:19). For "on ac-count of my name," see the comments on 10:22. [10]**"And then many will be tripped up and give one another over** [to affliction] **and hate one another.**" In other words, persecution by outsiders will lead the many false disciples to avoid persecution by apostatizing and be-traying their true, fellow disciples to the persecutors. They'll even hate their true, fellow disciples for provok-ing persecution with evangelism and righteous conduct. Through failure to condemn the loss of brotherly love, easygoing false prophets will exacerbate this problem of treachery in the brotherhood: [11]**"And many false proph-ets will arise and deceive many** [into thinking it's okay to cover up their profession of Christian discipleship]. [12]**And because lawlessness** [in the church] **will be mul-tiplied** [compare Daniel 12:4], **the love of the many will grow cold** [compare 7:13–14, 21–23; 22:14, where false disciples are described as 'workers of lawlessness' and as 'many' in contrast to the 'few' who are 'selected' and find the narrow gateway into 'life']." Their lawlessness will make cold—that is, extinguish—their love of God and neighbor, especially of fellow disciples. [13]**"But the one enduring to an end—this one will be saved** [for which see the comments on 10:22 and Mark 13:13b]. [14]**And this gospel of the kingdom will be proclaimed in the whole inhabited** [earth] **for a testimony to all nations, and then the end will come** [compare Daniel 11:35]." "This" identifies "gospel" with the message in Matthew's book (though not with the book itself). "Of the kingdom" echoes 4:23; 9:35, gives the disciples assur-ance of divine sovereignty in the face of persecution and martyrdom, and reminds them of the authority under which they're to live. "In the whole inhabited [earth]" and "to all nations" put a double emphasis on worldwide evangelism (compare 28:18–20). This emphasis counter-acts the withdrawal from evangelistic enterprise by false prophets and those deceived by them. To avoid persecu-tion and martyrdom, not only will they have stopped liv-ing in open obedience to Jesus' interpretation of the Law (as commanded in 5:14–16). They'll also have stopped proclaiming the gospel of the kingdom. "*Then* the end will come" implies the necessity that the Great Com-mission be carried out for the end to come (28:18–20).

THE ABOMINATION OF DESOLATION AS
THE BEGINNING OF THE END, AND THE SON
OF MAN'S COMING AS A PUBLIC EVENT
Matthew 24:15–31

24:15–19: "Therefore whenever you see 'the abomi-nation of desolation,' the [abomination] **spoken about through Daniel the prophet** [Daniel 9:27; 11:31; and especially 12:11], **standing in the holy place** [compare Daniel 8:13]—**the reader had better understand!**— [16]**then the ones in Judea had better flee to the moun-tains,** [17]**and the** [man] **on the roof had better not come down to take things out of his house,** [18]**and the** [man] **in the field had better not turn back to take his cloak** [which he shed for fieldwork]. [19]**And alas for** [women] **who are pregnant and** [women] **who are nursing** [their babies] **in those days.**" "Therefore" indicates that because the preceding paragraph detailed events that will characterize the church age but *not* signal the near-ness of the end, the present paragraph is going to detail events that *will* signal its nearness. The first such event will be "'the abomination of desolation' . . . standing in the holy place," that is, a sacrilege such as the image of a pagan god or deified ruler set up in the sacred precincts of the temple (compare 2 Thessalonians 2:3–4; 1 John 2:18; 4:3; Revelation 13). "Of desolation" describes the sacrilege as causing worshipers of the one true God to desert the temple, to abandon it, because it has been profaned. "Desolation" can hardly refer to destruction; for then the abomination wouldn't be standing there, and it would be too late to flee. So Jesus is still ignor-ing the disciples' question about the time of the temple's destruction. "Spoken about *through* Daniel the prophet" portrays Daniel as God's mouthpiece in predicting the abomination. This reference to Daniel favors that the reader who'd better understand is a reader of Daniel's prophecy, or a reader of Matthew's Gospel since it medi-ates Daniel's prophecy (compare Daniel 12:9–10). The disciples in Judea are to flee into the nearby mountains of the Judean wilderness, a traditional hideout for refu-gees, so as to escape persecution for not worshiping the abomination. The disciple lounging on the flat roof of his house (compare Acts 10:9) would be tempted to come down an outside staircase, enter the house, and take household articles unnecessary but dear to a person of leisure and means. The disciple working in a field would be tempted to dash back to the edge of the field and fetch his cloak, a necessity for warmth at night. But no, says Jesus. As hasty a getaway as possible is needed, even if it means leaping from roof to roof to avoid clogged streets, even if it means leaving a supposed necessity such as a cloak. Too bad for women who are pregnant or nurs-ing, for pregnancy and nursing will hamper or prevent a speedy escape. Such women stand a high chance of getting caught.

24:20–22: "But be praying that your flight not occur during winter [when heavy rains in Judea would make flight into the mountains difficult or impossible because of flooded roads and ravines] **or on the Sabbath** [when services to travelers would be suspended and trav-eling when others aren't traveling would expose you to capture]." Jesus envisions a state of affairs in which only his disciples will be exposed to mortal danger. [21]**"For then** [= at that time] **there'll be great affliction** [in the sense of persecution (compare Revelation 7:14)] **such as hasn't occurred since the beginning of the world till now and will by no means occur** [later on, for the Son of Man's coming will put an end to persecution of the disciples (compare Daniel 12:1)]. **[22]And if those days** [of unprecedented and final affliction] **hadn't been cut short, no flesh would have been saved** [from martyrdom]." The context of instructions for Jesus' disciples living in Judea, mainly in Jerusalem, limits "no flesh" to those of them living there. For they're the ones exposed to persecution for refusal to worship the abomination in the temple. **"But because of the selected ones, those days will be cut short."** That is, to preserve from martyrdom at least some of Jesus' Judean disciples, the period of unprecedented persecution won't last as long as otherwise it would last. In effect, Jesus is saying that mercifully the 1,260 days of Revelation 11:3; 12:6 won't be allowed to run their full course (compare the cancellation of the seven thunders in Revelation 10:1–7). The future tense in "will be cut short" shows that the earlier past tenses ("hadn't been cut short" and "would have been saved") were used to emphasize the cutting short as so sure to be done that it might as well be done already. Most translations have "the elect" or "the chosen ones" rather than "the selected ones." But in contemporary English "elect" suggests democratic voting, and "chosen" doesn't quite connote selection out of a larger number. Jesus' term does carry that connotation and describes true disciples as selected for eternal salvation.

Now Jesus gives another warning against deception—deception that if successful would keep his disciples in Judea from fleeing to the mountains for safety. The last time, he warned against their being deceived by those who'll come claiming to be the Christ and against being alarmed by warfare and natural disasters (as we call them) so as to think the end has come (24:4–8). At this point, though, the abomination is standing in the temple; and unequaled affliction has set in. So the end *is* near, resulting in a heightened danger of deception. *24:23–24:* **"Then** [= 'during these days'] **if anyone should say to you, 'Behold, here** [is] **the Christ!' or 'Here** [he is in another location]**!' don't ever believe** [him]. **[24]For false christs and false prophets will arise and give great signs and wonders so as to deceive, if possible, even the selected ones."** The danger of deception comes now not so much from the false christs as from their false prophets, who proclaim that the Christ is "here . . . or here." (We might expect "here . . . or *there*"; but one false prophet will say "here" where *he* is, and another will say "here" where *he* is, each false prophet proclaiming his own "here" for the location of the Christ.) The backing up of their proclamations with the performance of great signs and wonders will heighten the danger of deception. Since in contrast with 24:5 the false christs are *being* proclaimed rather than proclaiming themselves, the performance of signs and wonders is probably limited to the false prophets (compare Revelation 13:1–18; 16:13; 19:20; 20:10). "If possible, *even* the selected ones" puts emphasis on the extremity of this danger of deception.

The warning against deception continues in *24:25–26:* **"Behold, I've told you beforehand."** To be fore-

warned of the danger is to be forearmed against it. "Behold" emphasizes the forewarning. **[26]"Therefore** [because of the forewarning] **if they** [the false prophets] **say to you, 'Behold, he** [the Christ] **is in the wilderness!' you shouldn't go out** [to see him there (compare 11:7–9)]. **'Behold,** [he's] **in the storerooms!' you shouldn't believe** [them]." For their own emphasis, false prophets will also use "Behold!" Jews often thought that messianic salvation would begin in the wilderness (compare Israel's exodus from Egypt into the wilderness as deliverance from slavery, and Israel's entrance into Canaan out of the wilderness as the gaining of a homeland). "Storerooms" contrasts hideouts in the city with the wilderness. False teaching in the church is seldom brazen. It's usually offered with theological justification, such as a claim to have had direct and recent contact with the Christ, so that attention supposedly needs to be paid to a new communication that outdates his traditional teaching. Jesus warns, then, against contacts said to have taken place in the isolation of the wilderness and in the secrecy of urban hideouts, where public authentication that the Christ has returned and communicated with these false prophets is lacking. But people in the church can be easily taken in by false prophets who enhance their proclamations with claims to private contacts with the Christ and new communications from him. So Jesus will now play up the publicness of his return.

24:27–28: **"For just as lightning comes out from the east and shines as far as the west, so will be the coming of the Son of Man."** "For" makes the wide visibility of the Son of Man's coming the reason not to go out into the wilderness or squeeze into urban storerooms to see him. **[28]"Wherever the corpse is, there will the vultures be gathered together."** In other words, people will see the Son of Man coming in the sky as easily as they see vultures circling in the sky over a corpse (compare Job 39:26–30). So begone with claims of clandestine meetings and private revelations!

24:29–31: **"And immediately after the affliction of those days 'the sun will be darkened, and the moon won't give its light, and the stars will fall' from heaven, 'and the powers of the heavens' will be shaken** [see Isaiah 13:10; 34:4]. **[30]And then will appear the sign of the Son of Man in heaven, and then all the tribes of the land will beat their breasts** [in mourning (compare Zechariah 12:10)] **and see 'the Son of Man coming on the clouds of heaven** [Daniel 7:13]**' with power and much glory** [compare 16:27; 25:31]. **[31]And he'll send his angels with a loud trumpet** [compare Isaiah 27:1]**, and they'll gather together his selected ones out of the four winds, from the extremities of heaven to its extremities."** "Immediately" denies a temporal gap between "the affliction of those days" and the celestial disasters that will accompany the Son of Man's publicly visible coming. The two occurrences of "and then" put those disasters and that coming in the same time frame. They'll take place concurrently. The celestial disasters provide a dark backdrop against which the glory of the Son of Man's coming will shine all the brighter. These disasters will feature a darkening of our primary luminaries, the sun and the moon. Jesus doesn't say what will darken them, so that the point lies solely in the contrast between their darkening and the glory of the Son of Man's coming, a glory emphasized with "much." "The powers of the heavens" equate with "the stars" and personalize the stars as heavenly beings whose power is so shaken by the Son of Man's coming "with power" that they'll totter and fall out of the sky, as in a shower of meteorites.

"The sign of the Son of Man in heaven" is his appearance itself, not some kind of standard or ensign waved ahead of him. Thus "the sign of [Jesus'] coming" (24:3) and "the sign of the Son of Man in heaven" (24:30) are one and the same. Throughout, the word for "heaven" doubles for "sky." "In heaven" anticipates the heaven, or sky, that provides the clouds on which the Son of Man will come. They're a divine mode of transport (17:5; 26:64; Exodus 34:5 and many other biblical passages). All in all, Jesus emphasizes unmistakable visibility in the sky as opposed to hiddenness in the wilderness or backrooms (26:64). We might translate with "all the tribes of the *earth*," but Jesus' reference in 19:28 to "the twelve tribes of Israel" combines with an allusion to Zechariah 12:10 and the reference to Judea here in 24:16 to favor "all the tribes of the *land* [of Israel]." "Will beat their breasts" (*kopsontai* in Greek) makes a fine wordplay with "will see" (*opsontai* in Greek). "Till you say, 'Favored [is] he who's coming in the Lord's name'" (23:39) favors that the tribes will mourn in repentance (compare Zechariah 12:10–13:1). But the main point lies in the wide extent of mourning over against supposed private manifestations in deserts and backrooms. According to 13:41 "the Son of Man will send his angels" at the consummation of the age to "collect out of his kingdom all the snares and those who practice lawlessness" and "throw them into the furnace of fire." Here he sends his angels to gather together his few selected ones, true disciples as opposed to the many false ones (22:11–14, especially 22:14). Since the angels belong to him, they do his work. "The four winds" represent what we'd call the four points of the compass. To double the emphasis on universality over against the earlier restriction to "Judea" and "the land" (24:16, 30), Jesus adds "from the extremities of heaven to its extremities," that is, from one horizon to its opposite, whichever direction you look (compare Deuteronomy 30:4). A trumpet will blast so loudly that wherever they are, the selected ones will be aroused for the gathering.

THE NEARNESS OF THE SON OF MAN
Matthew 24:32–35

24:32–33: "And learn a parable from the fig tree: Whenever its branch has already become tender and is putting out leaves, you know that summer [is] near. ³³So also you—whenever you see all these things, know that he [the Son of Man] is near, at the doors." The introductory command to *learn* the parable anticipates the closing command to *understand* ("know") the

point of the parable and reminds us that "disciple" means "learner." Being evergreen, most trees in Israel keep their leaves throughout winter. As an exception, the almond tree loses its leaves in winter, and buds and leafs early in spring (or *toward* winter's end, since Jesus and his contemporaries spoke of only two seasons, winter and summer, both of them including portions of what we call spring and autumn [see Psalm 74:17]). The fig tree also loses its leaves in winter, but it doesn't bud and leaf till late in spring (or, as they would say, *at* winter's end). So its budding and leafing announce the approach of summer. "These things" doesn't refer to the destruction of the temple, for Jesus has ignored that topic ever since the disciples asked him about its timing and a prior signal. Nor can "these things" mean the events he predicted in 24:4–14, because they *won't* indicate the nearness of the Son of Man's coming. So "these things" must mean the events Jesus predicted in 24:15–28, for they *will* indicate its nearness. And "*all* these things" indicates that disciples need to see the precursive events not at the start of their fulfillment but in its completion before concluding that the Son of Man "is near, at the doors." As in 24:4–5, 23–28, Jesus is counteracting premature announcements by false christs and their false prophets.

24:34–35: "Amen I tell you that by no means will this generation pass away till all these things happen. ³⁵Heaven and earth will pass away, but by no means will my words pass away [= fail to be fulfilled]**."** "All these things" continues to mean the events predicted in 24:15–28. But since the Son of Man will come "immediately" afterwards (24:29), his coming also has to fall in the lifetime of "this generation." Since in 23:34–36 "this generation" included in addition to Jesus' contemporaries those who murdered Zechariah in Old Testament times, and probably earlier martyrs all the way back to Abel, at least in Matthew "this generation" may carry a qualitative as well as temporal meaning (compare the description "evil and adulterous" in 12:39; 16:4) and therefore indicate that this murderous *kind* of people will continue on till the Son of Man's coming. But see also the comments on Mark 13:28–31, and 2 Peter 3:10; Revelation 20:10; 21:1 for the passing away of heaven and earth.

UNCERTAINTY CONCERNING THE EXACT TIME OF THE SON OF MAN'S COMING
Matthew 24:36–44

24:36–41: "But concerning that day and hour, no one knows—not even the angels of heaven or the Son—except the Father alone." "Alone" stresses the exclusivity of the Father's knowing the day and hour of the Son of Man's coming. For the meaning of "that day and hour" and for the Son's as well as others' ignorance of the exact time of the Son of Man's coming, see the comments on Mark 13:32. ³⁷**"For just as the days of Noah [were], so will be the Son of Man's coming. ³⁸For as in those days before the flood people were munching [food] and drinking [beer/wine/water], marrying [as men do] and giving [their daughters] in marriage [as**

fathers do], **till the day that Noah entered into the ark,** [39]**and they didn't know** [that these activities of theirs were about to cease] **till the flood came and took them** [the people] **all away, so too will be the coming of the Son of Man.** [40]**Then** [= at that time] **two** [men] **will be in a field; one is taken along and one is left.** [41]**Two** [women will be] **grinding** [grain] **with a** [hand] **mill; one is taken along and one is left.**" "For just as the days of Noah [were]" introduces an illustration of the kind of unknowability that characterizes the day and hour of the Son of Man's coming. "For as in those days before the flood . . ." explains how the days of Noah were. Jesus doesn't cite the activities of eating, drinking, marrying, being given in marriage, working in a field, and grinding with a hand mill because they're abnormal and wicked. He cites them because they're normal and innocent. The point has nothing to do with the wickedness of Noah's contemporaries prior to the flood, wicked though they were. It has to do, rather, with the unexpectedness of the flood for people engaged in their routines. "They didn't know" contrasts the ignorance of the antediluvians, who represent nondisciples and false disciples, with the understanding of true disciples. The latter will be watching for the Son of Man's coming. They'll have recognized its signals detailed in 24:15–28, and they also know that the cutting off of those days makes its exact time incalculable and their own alertness necessary. The two instances each of the present tense in "*is* taken along" and "*is* left" are preceded by the future tense in "*will* be in a field" and "*will* be grinding." So Jesus uses the present tense to emphasize the certainty of being taken along and being left. They're as good as happening right now. The taking away of people by the flood favors that being taken along has to do with judgment at the Son of Man's coming (compare the separation of the wicked out from among the righteous in the parables of the tares and foul fish [13:30, 40–42, 49–50]). Then being left means being spared from judgment. The accent doesn't rest on the separation of people in proximity so much as on the occurrence of this separation during the round of daily activities and therefore unexpectedly—unless you're watching.

24:42–44: **"Therefore stay awake, because you don't know at what particular day your Lord is coming.** [43]**And know this, that if the houseowner had known at what particular watch** [of the night] **the thief is coming, he'd have stayed awake and not let him dig through his house.** [44]**On account of this** [the certainty of being caught unprepared if you don't stay awake] **you too** [as well as the houseowner] **get ready, because the Son of Man is coming at an hour that you don't think** [he'll come]." To stay awake means to keep watching for the events that will signal the nearness of the Son of Man's coming. "Therefore" bases the command to stay awake on the already stated impossibility of knowing the day and hour of the Son of Man's coming. The consequent redundancy of "because you don't know at what particular day your Lord is coming" adds further emphasis on that impossibility. "Your Lord" attributes deity to Jesus the Son of Man. He's divine as well

as human. "*Is* coming" makes his future coming just as certain as an event currently in progress. "Know *this*" could be translated more literally with "Know *that*." But for two reasons such a translation would cause confusion in English: (1) "that" would sound like a conjunction introducing a clause telling what should be known; and (2) immediately following is another "that" which really does introduce a clause telling what should be known. Nevertheless, the first "that" in a literalistic translation means something over there as distinct from something right here. The something over there is the statement about the houseowner, which is then introduced by the second "that" ("that if the houseowner had known . . ."). Jesus puts his illustration of the houseowner at a distance ("that *over there*") to make it a negative example of the danger a disciple shouldn't fall into. A watch of the night was a period of several hours when somebody stood guard—hence, "stay awake." For "the thief *is* coming" and "*dig* through his house," see the comments on Luke 12:39–40.

MALTREATMENT OF FELLOW DISCIPLES AS CHARACTERISTIC OF FALSE DISCIPLESHIP, WHICH WILL DRAW JUDGMENT AT THE LORD'S COMING
Matthew 24:45–51

Jesus defines further what it means to stay awake for the Son of Man's coming. It means not only to look for the predicted indications of its nearness so as to be ready for it. It also means that the consequent readiness includes brotherly treatment of fellow disciples. Unpreparedness allows abusive treatment of fellow disciples, and such treatment marks the abuser as a false disciple destined for the same judgment that will fall on the hypocritical scholars and Pharisees (compare 18:23–35 and chapter 23).

24:45–47: **"Who then is the faithful and prudent slave, whom the master put in charge over his household to give them** [their] **food on schedule** [compare Psalm 104:27]? [46]**Fortunate** [is] **that slave whom his master, on coming, will find doing so.** [47]**Amen I tell you that he'll put him in charge over all his possessions.**" "Then" draws an inference from the preceding stress on the impossibility of knowing the exact time of the Son of Man's coming. The word for "master" is elsewhere translated "Lord," so that the present master represents the Lord Jesus; and the slave represents a disciple of his. "Faithful and prudent" describes the slave as a true disciple and indicates that it's wise to be faithful in carrying out the master's—that is, Jesus'—orders. The present order to give fellow domestic slaves their food on schedule teaches that disciples, particularly those in leadership, should treat their fellow disciples well. (In the Roman Empire of the first century, masters often put one of their slaves in charge of the household.) The "coming" of the master represents the second coming of the Lord Jesus as the Son of Man. The good fortune of the slave whom the master, on coming, finds doing his job faithfully—that good fortune consists in a promotion, that is, in being put in charge over all the master's possessions. In other words, Jesus will richly reward his disciple who treats other disciples well.

24:48–51: "But if that wicked slave says in his heart, 'My master is delaying,' [49]and starts beating his fellow slaves, and eats and drinks with drunkards, [50]the master of that slave will come on a day that he doesn't expect [him to come] **and at an hour that he's not cognizant of. [51]And he'll slice him in two and put his portion with the hypocrites. Weeping and gritting of teeth will be there."** "*That* wicked slave" puts him at a moral distance and thereby makes him an example not to be followed. "*If* that wicked slave says . . . ," "starts . . . ," and "eats and drinks . . ." set out possibilities that shouldn't turn into actualities (contrast "Who then *is* the faithful and wise slave . . ." and "whom his master . . . *will* find [him] doing so" [24:45–46]). "Starts" implies some length of time remaining till the master's coming. But "My master is *delaying*" may well mean that the wicked slave tells himself his master won't come *at all* (see Deuteronomy 23:21–23 for this sense of "delay"). In charge of the household, this slave could abuse his authority by beating his fellow slaves, who make up the rest of his master's domestic help, and also by carousing with drunkards, who represent other false disciples. Together, they waste their resources on partying instead of sharing them with fellow slaves, who represent true disciples proclaiming the gospel, living openly according to Jesus' teachings, and fleeing resultant persecution. The abuse and the carousing breed carelessness, so that the master's coming—though delayed, and precisely *because* delayed—takes the slave in charge by surprise. "On a day" and "at an hour" denote the next shortest and very shortest units of time used by people then and therefore stress again the impossibility of knowing beforehand the exact time of the Son of Man's coming. "Slice him in two" warns of horrible judgment for unbrotherly behavior, and "put his portion with the hypocrites" means that Jesus will judge as false those professing disciples who engage in such behavior. As false, their portion—that is, their inheritance—will be to spend eternity with the hypocrites, namely, the scholars and Pharisees of chapter 23, who are destined for "the judgment [consisting] of gehenna" (23:33). "Weeping" arises out of sorrow over this fate, and "gritting of teeth" arises out of the pain associated with it (compare the figures of being sliced in two and elsewhere of hellfire). "There" refers to gehenna, hell, as the place of punishment (see the comments on 5:22).

WATCHING AS DOING GOOD DEEDS IN OBEDIENCE TO JESUS' TEACHING
Matthew 25:1–13

25:1: "Then the kingdom of heaven will be like ten virgins, who as such, on taking their own lamps, went out to meet the bridegroom [compare 1 Thessalonians 4:16–17]**."** "Then" means at the time of the Son of Man's coming, portrayed in 24:45–51 as the coming of a master. "*Will* be like" looks toward this coming as an event in the future. "Who *as such*" refers to the ten virgins as participants in a wedding celebration. "Their *own* lamps" stresses personal responsibility for the lamps. Since "went out to meet the bridegroom" indicates a coming use of the lamps outdoors, "lamps" probably means torches, because a lamp for indoors wouldn't stay lighted in a breeze, wouldn't provide enough light for outdoors, and wouldn't need a supply of oil in addition to what the bowl already contained (as these lamps will need more oil [25:8–10]). A torch resists a breeze, gives a bright light, burns only about fifteen minutes, and then needs to have the rags that are wrapped around the end of the stick soaked in oil again. Here a bridegroom comes to his wedding with the expectation that some virgins will have torches ready for a procession to the wedding hall. "Went out to meet the bridegroom" anticipates the virgins' going out to meet him in 25:6. They hardly go out twice. So the waiting that's about to be mentioned in 25:2–5 precedes the going out mentioned here in 25:1. The bridegroom represents Jesus (compare 9:15; 22:2). The virgins represent Jesus' professing disciples. Note: no bride appears in the parable to confuse these representations.

25:2–4: "But five of them were foolish, and five [were] **prudent. [3]For the foolish, on taking their lamps, didn't take oil with themselves. [4]But the prudent did take oil in flasks along with their own lamps."** "For" introduces a reason for the designations "foolish" and "prudent." "Foolish" recalls the man who built his house on sand, and "prudent" recalls the man who built his house on bedrock (7:24–27). Like them, the foolish virgins represent false disciples and the prudent virgins represent true disciples (compare also 5:13; 8:18–22; 13:24–30, 36–43, 47–50; 22:1–14). Taking oil to fuel the torches represents preparedness for the Son of Man's coming. Failure to take oil represents unpreparedness. Since in 7:24–27 "prudent" described the man who "hears and does" Jesus' words and "foolish" the man who doesn't, these descriptions bear the same meaning here. And since hearing and doing Jesus' words meant doing good deeds (see especially 5:14–16, where lamplight equated with "good deeds"), the same applies here. Not to hear and do Jesus' words is to practice lawlessness (see 7:23 and the allusion to that verse below in 25:12). As in chapters 5–7, good deeds contrast with the scholars' and Pharisees' hypocrisy, decried in chapter 23. The taking of oil in flasks "along with their *own* lamps" by the prudent virgins highlights these virgins' taking responsibility for preparedness. The absence of "own" in the taking of "their lamps" by the foolish virgins combines with their not taking oil to emphasize irresponsible lack of preparedness. Since the foolish virgins will later say that their lamps "are going out" (25:8), their not taking oil means that they didn't take oil to replenish their lamps—that is, to resoak the rags—after the oil in which the rags were originally soaked was used up. Olive oil was used as fuel for lamps.

25:5–6: **"But while the bridegroom was delaying, they all got drowsy and started sleeping. ⁶But in the middle of the night a shout has happened: 'Behold, the bridegroom! Come out to meet** [him].'" The first "But" contrasts the going to sleep because of a delay with the implied expectation of an immediate arrival. The second "But" contrasts the arrival with the delay. "Has happened" dramatizes the shouted announcement of the bridegroom's arrival, and "Behold!" dramatizes the arrival itself. Jesus is concerned with unpreparedness for his coming, not with the delay in his coming. The foolish virgins aren't foolish because they don't take oil to keep their torches burning continuously during the delay, or because they fail to consider the possibility of a delay. The torches aren't yet burning and won't be set alight till the bridegroom's coming is announced (25:7). They'll burn about fifteen minutes (as noted above) and go out, not while the virgins are sleeping (for which there's no criticism; even the prudent ones fall asleep), but during the interval between the announcement and the arrival. Five of the virgins are foolish, then, in that they don't take oil for the procession, which will take place when the bridegroom arrives.

25:7–9: **"Then all those virgins got up and fitted out their own lamps** [that is, they checked the oil-soaked rags wrapped around the end of the stick and set them aflame]." "All" calls attention to the mixture of the foolish and the prudent, like the mixtures of tares and wheat and of good and foul fish in 13:24–30, 36–43, 47–50—that is, the mixture of false and true disciples in the church. "*Those* virgins" reflects the distance that has separated the virgins and the bridegroom from each other. "Their *own* lamps" emphasizes individual responsibility once again. ⁸**"But the foolish said to the prudent, 'Give us some of your oil, because our lamps are going out** [note the absence of "own" between "our" and "lamps"].' ⁹**But the prudent answered, saying, '[No,] lest by no means there be enough for us and for you. Go instead to the sellers and buy** [oil] **for yourselves.'"** The going out of torches represents conduct that's not righteous enough to demonstrate genuine discipleship (compare 5:20). The prudent virgins rightly refuse, for division of the oil would cause a breakdown in the festivities. No one would have enough oil to complete the procession, to say nothing of the theological impossibility ("by no means") of riding into the kingdom on the coattails of someone else's true discipleship.

25:10–13: **"But as they** [the foolish virgins] **were going off to buy** [oil], **the bridegroom came; and the prepared** [virgins] **entered with him into the wedding hall, and the door was shut. ¹¹But later on, the rest of the virgins come too, saying, 'Master, master, open** [the door] **for us.' ¹²But he, answering, said, 'Amen I tell you, I don't know you.' ¹³Therefore stay awake, because you don't know the day or the hour** [of the Son of Man's coming]." Since Jesus doesn't indicate whether the foolish virgins were able to buy oil in the middle of the night, the warning grows out of their deficient preparation

prior to the bridegroom's coming. The prudent virgins' entering the wedding hall "with him" forms a counterpart to Jesus' saying to his true disciples, "I am with you" (28:20 [compare 1:23]). The shutting of the door includes its being locked to prevent further entrance. There's no second chance once Jesus returns. "The *rest* of the virgins" sounds a doleful note of being left out. "But later on" underlines the futility of their coming, and the present tense in "come too" underlines their desperation to enter. The doubling of "Master" in their address deepens that desperation. And since "Master" goes back to the same word elsewhere translated with "Lord," we hear an echo of 7:21–23: "Not everyone who says to me, 'Lord, Lord, will enter into the kingdom of heaven—rather, the one who does the will of my Father in heaven. Many will say to me in that day, 'Lord, Lord . . . ' And then I'll declare to them, 'I never knew you [compare "I don't know you" here in 25:12, reinforced with "Amen I tell you"]. Depart from me, you workers of lawlessness.'" It would be wrong to think that the closing exhortation to stay awake criticizes the earlier sleeping of the prudent as well as foolish virgins. For by the time the bridegroom arrived, all had awakened. More to the point, Jesus wants to teach that staying awake means preparedness through doing good deeds. So the bridegroom's delay, the drowsiness and sleep of the virgins, and their being aroused in the middle of the night don't contradict the exhortation to stay awake. They illustrate ignorance concerning the exact time of the Son of Man's coming.

ONCE MORE, WATCHING AS DOING GOOD DEEDS
Matthew 25:14–30

25:14–15: **"For** [the kingdom will be] **just as a man, going on a journey, called his own slaves and gave his possessions over to them. ¹⁵And to one** [slave] **he gave five talents, and to one** [slave] **two** [talents], **and to one** [slave] **one** [talent]—**to each** [slave] **according to his own ability. And he went on** [his] **journey."** "For" makes the following parable a further basis for the exhortation to stay awake in 25:13. The man represents Jesus. His going on a journey represents the soon departure of Jesus from his disciples (compare 9:15). The man's slaves represent Jesus' disciples. "His *own* slaves" stresses Jesus' lordship over the disciples. The man's giving "his possessions" over to the slaves represents Jesus' putting the disciples under obligation to obey his teachings. The man's possessions are monetary, a talent being the largest denomination of money and, if of silver, being enough to pay twenty manual laborers for about a year of work. So the slaves are entrusted with considerable sums of money. That the sums are considerable magnifies the obligation under which Jesus puts his disciples to obey his teachings (compare 5:20, where he says that entrance into the kingdom requires righteousness surpassing that of the scholars and Pharisees). The talents represent opportunities to do good deeds in obedience to Jesus' teachings. So "to each [slave] according to his own ability" refers to differences in the number of such opportunities, not to differences in native aptitudes. "His *own* ability" stresses the responsibility to take advantage of opportunities to do good deeds.

25:16–23: "Immediately going, the one who'd received the five talents worked with them [= invested them] **and gained five other talents. ¹⁷Likewise the one** [who'd received] **the two** [talents] **gained two other** [talents]. ¹⁸**But on going away, the one who'd received the one** [talent] **dug a hole in the ground and hid the silver of his master."** So the talent was one of silver rather than gold or copper. (A talent was about twenty-six pounds of gold, silver, or copper, the value depending of course on which metal was being weighed.) The third slave's "going *away*" to bury a talent contrasts with the first two slaves' "*going*" to invest the talents entrusted to them. The immediacy of the first two slaves' going exhibits eagerness to do their master's bidding. ("Likewise" makes the second slave's action match that of the first slave.) The third slave's hiding the talent given over to him represents hiding your supposed discipleship to avoid persecution. ¹⁹**"But after much delay** [representing the long delay of Jesus' coming till after the church age] **the master of those slaves comes and settles accounts with them.** ²⁰**And on approaching** [him], **the one who received the five talents brought five other talents** [as well], **saying, 'Master, you gave five talents over to me. Look! I've gained five other talents.' ²¹His master said to him, 'Well** [done], **good and faithful slave! You've been faithful over a few** [talents]. **I'll put you in charge over many** [talents]. **Enter into the joy of your master.** ²²**And on approaching** [him], **the one** [who received] **the two talents also said, 'Master, you gave two talents over to me. Look! I've gained two other talents** [as well].' ²³**His master said to him, 'Well** [done], **good and faithful slave! You've been faithful over a few** [talents]. **I'll put you in charge over many** [talents]. **Enter into the joy of your master.'"** The use of "worked" for investing alludes to the necessity of doing good works as proof of the true discipleship that will constitute preparedness for the Son of Man's coming (compare 5:13–16; James 2:14–26). The multiple instances of "master," which also means "Lord," emphasize the lordship of Jesus, represented by this master. "But after much delay" pits the master's coming and settling accounts against the third slave's hiding the talent given over to him. "Of *those* slaves" echoes "*those* virgins" in 25:7 and, as there, reflects the distance that during the delay has separated the slaves and the master from each other.

The present tense in "comes and settles accounts" underlines the certainty of the Son of Man's future coming and judging between true and false disciples according to their deeds. "I've gained five other talents" and "I've gained two other talents" constitute the first two slaves' appeal to good deeds as proof of true discipleship. "Look!" and references to the original number of talents given over to these slaves intensify the appeal. "Well [done] . . . !" denotes acceptance of this appeal

and delight in this proof of true discipleship. No "And" introduces the two instances of "His master said," so that the abruptness of this introduction indicates that the master can hardly wait to commend his first two slaves. The twofold description of them, "good and faithful," highlights the need for faithfulness during persecution, which makes persistence in the good works of open discipleship risky and therefore all the more commendable. Though of great worth, the talents were "few"—five and two in number. But the reward of being put in charge of "many [talents]" is indefinitely large (compare 5:12: "Rejoice and be glad, because your reward in heaven [is] *much*"). "The joy of your master" means his joy in the good and faithful service of the first two slaves, and his now putting them in charge of many talents gives evidence of that joy. They enter into his joy, then, by taking charge of these many talents. Similarly, at the Last Judgment true disciples will enter Jesus' joy in their good and faithful service by engaging in expanded service to him throughout eternity.

25:24–25: "And on approaching, the one who had received the one talent also said, 'Master, I knew you, that you're a ruthless man, harvesting [= cutting grain] **where you didn't sow** [seed] **and gathering** [winnowed grain into a barn] **from where** [the threshing floor] **you didn't scatter** [grain in the process of winnowing, that is, in the process of shoveling trodden grain into the air to let wind blow away the chaff while the kernels fall scattered on the threshing floor (compare 3:12; 6:26; 13:30)]. ²⁵**And on getting scared, going away I hid your talent in the ground. Look! You have your** [original talent].'" Jesus described the first slave as the one "who *received* the five talents" and, in the case of the second slave, left "received" to be inferred. As comes out especially in the original Greek of Matthew, "the one who *had* received" presents a stronger verbal expression that highlights the responsibility which the third slave failed to work off. "Master" echoes the respectful address used by the first two slaves, but unlike them this third slave makes no reference to the master's having given a talent over to him. Instead, he attacks the character and activities of his master and then appeals to his own fear of the master. In effect, he says the master's ruthlessly robbing farmers of their grain made him scared he might lose the talent in a bad investment and suffer his master's wrath for the loss. "Look! You have your [original talent]" implies that the master should be happy the slave hadn't lost the talent through such an investment. The earlier slaves referred only to the additional talents made through investments and left the original talents unmentioned. Lacking an additional talent, this last slave can refer only to the original talent.

25:26–30: "And answering, his master said to him, 'Evil and hesitant slave, you knew that I harvest where I didn't sow and gather from where I didn't scatter. ²⁷Therefore it was necessary that you throw my silvers [= coins making up a talent in weight] **to the bankers. And on coming, I'd have gotten back my talent with**

interest. ²⁸**Therefore take the talent away from him and give** [it] **to the one who has the ten talents.** ²⁹**For** [further talents] **will be given to everyone who** [already] **has** [additional talents]**, and** [his talents] **will be made to abound** [and thus be more than enough]**. But the one who doesn't have** [an additional talent, representing the surplus of righteousness required for entering the kingdom (5:20)]—**even what he has** [the original talent, representing entrustment to do the good deeds of discipleship] **will be taken away from him** [so that the falsity of his discipleship is exposed]. ³⁰**And throw the useless slave into the darkness farther outside. Weeping and gritting of teeth will be there.'"** Jesus introduced the earlier responses with a mere "His master said to him." Here, though, to emphasize the following pronouncement of judgment on this representative of disciples who falsify their profession by failing to do good deeds, Jesus introduces the master's response more fully: "*And answering*, his master said to him." "Evil" describes the slave as unfit for the kingdom. "And hesitant" describes him as having feared to do in public the good works of discipleship indicated by the use of "worked" for investing. This twofold description transmutes the slave's self-descriptions as fearful into evil, and as protective of the original talent into hesitancy with it. The master also uses the slave's knowledge of the master's robbing farmers of their grain to say that he should have invested rather than hidden the talent.

Jesus' portraying himself as a ruthless master should bother us no more than his portraying himself as a thief who breaks and enters in the night (24:43). That earlier portrayal doesn't have to do with the ethics of thievery—rather, with unexpectedness. The present portrayal doesn't have to do with the ethics of robbery—rather, with the forcefulness of Jesus' demanding good deeds as proof of true discipleship. "It was necessary" encapsulates this demand. "*Throw* my silvers to the bankers" is a vigorous figure of speech for depositing money in a bank. As such, it adds emphasis to the necessity of doing good deeds. Because the master delayed his coming for a long time, a deposit of the talent would presumably have earned another talent, as in the cases of five talents' earning five more and two talents' earning two more. For reception of added reward the master—that is, Jesus— singles out the slave whose five talents earned five more (compare 13:12). "Therefore" makes the third slave's hesitancy the reason for commanding his one original talent to be taken from him and given to the first slave. Thus the first slave gets even more than he deserves. Similarly, at the Last Judgment true disciples will be rewarded even more than their good deeds deserve. The master's ruthlessness has morphed into generosity. And his saying that this surplus of reward "will be given *to everyone* who [already] has [additional talents]" indicates that those disciples represented by the slave who earned two talents will also be rewarded even more than their good deeds deserve. As a description of the third slave, "useless" implies that good deeds are useful in spreading the gospel of the kingdom, as already in 5:14–16. See the comments

on 22:13 for the throwing of the useless slave into the darkness farther outside and for the weeping and gritting of teeth. The reference to darkness implies that in accordance with 24:43 the master came unexpectedly during a watch of the night. In view of 13:41, 49; 25:31, those whom the master tells to throw the useless slave into the darkness represent the Son of Man's angels. Thus the parable closes with a threat that Jesus will mete out eternal punishment to disciples who belie their profession by failing to do good deeds.

THE CRITERION OF NEIGHBORLY LOVE AT THE LAST JUDGMENT WITH PARTICULAR REFERENCE TO DEMONSTRATING TRUE DISCIPLESHIP THROUGH DOING CHARITY TO THE PERSECUTED MESSENGERS OF JESUS
Matthew 25:31–46

25:31–33: "And whenever the Son of Man comes in his glory and all the angels [come] **with him** [compare Zechariah 14:5]**, then he'll sit on the throne of his glory** [= his glorious throne]**. ³²And all nations will be gathered together before him** [compare Isaiah 66:18; Joel 3:2]**, and he'll separate them from one another** [referring to the individuals making up all nations, not to the nations as such, as though he'll separate one nation from another]**, just as a shepherd separates sheep from goats. ³³And he'll have the sheep stand at his right, on the one hand, but the goats at his left, on the other hand."** In 16:27 Jesus spoke of his coming as the Son of Man "in the glory of his Father." Here he speaks of coming in his own glory. But since he's "God with us" (1:23), the glory of his Father belongs also to him. Again in 16:27 he spoke of coming "with his angels." Here he speaks of "all the angels" as coming "with him." Just as the turning of his Father's glory into his own glory enhances his self-portrayal as the Son of Man, then, so too the addition of "all" to "angels" and the change from his coming with the angels to their coming with him enhance that self-portrait. Enhancing it yet further is his "sit[ting] on the throne of his glory" (= 19:28). A throne indicates royalty, and sitting is the posture of authority. Subjects stand before their seated king, as do the sheep and the goats in this text. Nations of people are gathered before the seated, kingly Son of Man to be judged. "*All* nations" indicates a judgment of all humanity. He separates them individually from one another to distinguish between the righteous and the unrighteous, between the saved and the lost. Kings were often compared to shepherds, and their subjects to sheep. But to distinguish between the righteous and the unrighteous and include only the righteous as his sheep, Jesus compares the unrighteous to goats as well as the righteous to sheep and himself to a shepherd (compare 9:36; 26:31). Shepherds commonly herded mixed flocks of sheep and goats, but separated them in the evening because sheep prefer the open air at night while goats need the warmth of shelter. The greater value of sheep (because they provide wool in multiple shearings) and their usually white color (Isaiah

1:18) suit them to stand for the righteous. Because most people are right-handed, the right hand often symbolizes favor, as it does here. Though Jesus said in 13:49 that angels will separate the wicked from among the righteous, here he says the Son of Man will separate the sheep and the goats from each other. But in 13:49 he was talking about the separating of false disciples out from among true disciples. Here he's talking about separating the righteous and the unrighteous from each other in humanity at large.

25:34–36: "Then the king will say to those at his right, '[Come] here, you favored ones of my Father. Inherit the kingdom prepared for you since the founding of the world. **[35]For I hungered and you gave me** [something] **to eat, I thirsted and you gave me** [something] **to drink, I was a stranger and you gathered me** [into your home], **[36][I was] naked** [a hyperbole for emphasis on being in rags] **and you clothed me, I was sick and you looked after me, I was in prison and you came to me** [compare Isaiah 58:7].'" Prisoners depended on visitors to bring them food and other personal necessities. Since the kingdom of heaven is the Son of Man's (13:41; 16:28; 20:21), Jesus calls himself "the king." But the king's calling the sheep "you favored ones of my Father" implies that God favors them because they've believed the Son of Man to be the Son of God (compare 16:13–17). The Father not only favors them. He owns them. They belong to him. The inheritance of the sheep consists in the kingdom and equates with eternal life (see 25:46). Jesus portrays eternal life as an inheritance to assure his disciples they'll be compensated for the dispossessions they suffered under persecution (see 19:27–29), and he portrays eternal life as a kingdom to indicate they'll be compensated for their disenfranchisements, including martyrdoms, through persecution. The preparation of the kingdom ever since the founding of the world shows that despite all their persecutions, disciples needn't despair: their reward already exists, reserved for them. They suffer for a present, though as yet undelivered, reality, not for an uncertain hope (compare 5:3, 10; 19:14; 21:43).

25:37–40: "Then the righteous will answer him, saying, 'Lord, when did we see you hungering and feed [you], **or thirsting and give** [you something] **to drink?** **[38]And when did we see you a stranger and gather** [you into our homes], **or naked and clothe** [you]? **[39]And when did we see you sick or in prison and come to you?'"** "The righteous" tells whom "the sheep" represent. Their addressing the king with "Lord" calls to mind the lordship of Jesus as deity (compare 1:23). Their unconsciousness of having ministered to the king's needs shows them to be unhypocritical. They lack pretense. **[40]"And answering, the king will say to them, 'Amen I tell you, to the extent that you acted** [charitably] **toward one of these littlest brothers of mine, you acted** [charitably] **toward me.'"** Perhaps the best commentary on the king's answer appears back in 10:40–42, where in speaking to his disciples Jesus said, "The one who welcomes you welcomes me, and the one who welcomes me welcomes the one who sent me. The one who welcomes a prophet in the name of a prophet will receive a prophet's reward, and the one who welcomes a righteous person in the name of a righteous person will receive a righteous person's reward. And whoever in the name of a disciple gives one of these little ones just a cup of cold [water] to drink—amen I tell you—will by no means lose his reward" (see the comments on this passage). The "little ones" are believers in Jesus (18:6). Here in 25:40 he calls them his "brothers," identified in 12:48–50 as those who do the will of his Father in heaven, that is, his (true) disciples. Here, "little" escalates to "littlest" and combines with "one" in the phrase, "for one of these littlest brothers of mine," to emphasize that doing charity even for a single disciple of low profile counts as doing it for Jesus. "Amen I tell you" underscores his identifying himself with one of them, and "these" invites the righteous to recognize *one another* as his brothers. They hungered and thirsted, were homeless and naked, and sick and imprisoned because they were suffering persecution and fleeing from it in obedience to Jesus' command (10:23). So he isn't talking about general humanitarianism (for that, go to passages such as Luke 10:30–37). He's talking about disciples' risking persecution of themselves by helping fellow disciples already under persecution. Such charity demonstrates true discipleship.

25:41–43: "Then he'll also say to those at [his] **left, 'Go away from me, you accursed ones, into the eternal fire prepared for the Devil and his angels. **[42]**For I hungered and you didn't give me** [anything] **to eat, I thirsted and you didn't give me** [anything] **to drink, **[43]**I was a stranger and you didn't gather me** [into your homes], **naked and you didn't clothe me, sick and in prison and you didn't look after me.'"** Far from doing charity for Jesus' persecuted disciples, the so-called goats have neglected their needs. "Go away from me" strikes an ominous contrast with "[Come] here" (25:34) and recalls 7:23. "From me" also contrasts starkly with the king's having identified himself with his littlest brothers. "You accursed ones" strikes another ominous contrast, this time with "you favored ones of my Father" (25:34). "Into the eternal fire" echoes 18:8, another passage featuring Jesus' "little ones." Whereas the kingdom was prepared for the righteous and they inherit it, the eternal fire was prepared for the Devil and his angels; and nondisciples go into it—not because it was prepared for them as an inheritance, but because they're "the sons of the evil one ['the Devil' (13:38–39)]." His angels contrast with those of the Son of Man, and the past preparation of eternal fire means that the nondisciples' punishment already exists. It only awaits their entry. The kingdom was prepared for the righteous "since the founding of the world," but the eternal fire isn't said to have been prepared since then. Why? Because God's initial, primary purpose was for eternal life; but the evil of the Devil and his angels, and now of the unrighteous, has brought about the preparation of eternal fire for a later, secondary purpose of punishment.

25:44–46: "Then they themselves, too, will answer, saying, 'Lord, when did we see you hungering or thirsting or a stranger or naked or sick or in prison and not serve you [= minister to your needs]?' ⁴⁵Then he'll answer them, saying, 'Amen I tell you, insofar as you didn't act [charitably] toward one of these littlest [brothers of mine], neither did you act [charitably] toward me.' ⁴⁶And these [represented by the goats] will go away into eternal punishment, but the righteous [will enter] into eternal life [compare Daniel 12:2]." "Themselves" stresses the following attempt to deflect the charge of uncharity. The goats' addressing Jesus with "Lord" has nothing in their previous lifetime to back it up. The accursed don't claim evidence of discipleship, as the false prophets of the church did in 7:22, but only express ignorance that they've ever faced the king and failed to meet his needs. In Jesus' reply, "Amen I tell you" once again stresses his identifying himself with even one of his low profile disciples. "Eternal punishment" tells the purpose of "the eternal fire," and "eternal life" defines "inherit[ing] the kingdom." Fire wouldn't need to be eternal if the punishment weren't everlasting any more than life would need to be eternal if inheriting the kingdom weren't everlasting. So punishment needs to be understood as everlasting in its suffering just as life needs to be understood as everlasting in its enjoyment.

THE DISCIPLES' UNDERSTANDING THAT JESUS MUST BE CRUCIFIED
Matthew 26:1–5

26:1–2: And it happened that when Jesus had finished [speaking] all these words, he said to his disciples, ²"You know that after two days the Passover is taking place and the Son of Man is being given over to be crucified." "All these words" refers to the lengthy, just-finished discourse in chapters 23–25; and the whole clause, "when Jesus had finished [speaking] all these words," echoes Deuteronomy 32:45: "And Moses finished speaking all these words." So Matthew's portrayal of Jesus as the new and greater Moses crops up again. Jesus' present statement to the disciples isn't so much another prediction of his crucifixion (for which see 20:19) as it's an observation that the disciples know not only the approach of the Passover festival (a matter of course) but also the Son of Man's upcoming delivery to crucifixion, because they've understood his earlier predictions of the passion (16:21; 17:12, 22–23; 20:18–19). They know even the mode of his execution. As often in Matthew, then, the accent falls on understanding as a necessary element of discipleship (see 13:11, 23, 51; 16:12; 17:13). The present tense in "is taking place" and "is being given over" portrays the Passover and the Son of Man's delivery to crucifixion as so soon and sure to fulfill his earlier predictions that they're as good as happening right now. For the taking place of the Passover "after two days," see the comments on Mark 14:1.

26:3–5: Then the chief priests and the elders of the people gathered together in the courtyard of the high priest, called Caiaphas; ⁴and they plotted together in order that they might seize Jesus with cunning and kill [him (compare Exodus 21:14; Psalms 2:2; 31:13)]. ⁵But they were saying, "[Let's not seize him] in the festal assembly, lest there be a riot among the people." "Then" means that at the very time Jesus mentions his being given over to be crucified, Jewish authorities are setting in motion the events that will fulfill his passion predictions. As in 21:23, Matthew attaches "of the people" to "the elders" so as to link the general populace of Jerusalem with the elders in opposition to Jesus (see 27:25). The chief priests and elders were based in Jerusalem. "In order that" highlights their malevolent purpose. The contrast between this purpose and the resolve to use cunning for avoidance of a riot emphasizes their treachery and recalls their fear of the crowds in 21:46. They presume that Jesus will head back to Galilee after the Passover, to which was attached the weeklong Festival of Unleavened Bread, so that they plot to seize and kill Jesus while he's still in Jerusalem during the festival but apart from the crowds of people assembled during daytime in the temple courts. Judas Iscariot will give them their opportunity to seize Jesus in Gethsemane, just outside Jerusalem, in the middle of night (26:36–56).

THE CONTRAST BETWEEN A WOMAN'S LARGE EXPENDITURE FOR THE PERFUMING OF JESUS' BODY AND JUDAS ISCARIOT'S BARGAIN TO BETRAY JESUS FOR A PALTRY SUM
Matthew 26:6–16

26:6–9: But when Jesus came to be in Bethany [on the Mount of Olives (see the comments on Mark 11:1 for further details)] in Simon the leper's house, ⁷there approached him a woman having an alabaster flask of very expensive perfume. And she poured [it] on his head as he was reclining [at table]. ⁸But on seeing [what she'd done], the disciples got indignant, saying, "To what purpose [is] this waste? ⁹For this [perfume] could have been sold for much [money] and [the money] given to poor people." "But" introduces the following act of devotion to Jesus as a contrast with the foregoing plot against Jesus' life. Concerning Simon the leper, the woman, the perfume, and the act of devotion, see the comments on Mark 14:3. Matthew's description of the perfume as "very expensive" sets up for a contrast with the paltry price of thirty pieces of silver that the chief priests will pay Judas Iscariot for Jesus (26:14–16; 27:3–10).

The disciples have asked a question: "To what purpose [is] this waste?" Jesus now adds to their knowledge by answering the question in 26:10–13 (compare 13:10–12); but he begins with a question of his own: And on coming to know [what the disciples were saying], Jesus said to them, "Why are you causing the woman troubles [= bothering her, with the implication that the disciples have been either addressing her with indignation or voicing to one another their indignation in her hearing]? For she has worked on me [as distinct from 'poor people' in your statement] **a good work** [in contrast with 'this waste' that you've talked about; also in contrast with the dastardly plot of the chief priests and elders in 26:3–5]. [11]**For you always have the poor with yourselves** [compare Deuteronomy 15:11], **but me you don't always have** [a predictive allusion to his soon-coming death and therefore also a hint of his supernaturally knowing about the plot just now hatched against him]." The allusion to Jesus' soon-coming death now becomes more than an allusion: [12]**"For by throwing this perfume on my body, this** [woman] **did** [it] **to prepare me for burial.** [13]**Amen I tell you, wherever in the whole world this gospel** [= good news] **is proclaimed, also what this** [woman] **has done will be told, with the result of her being remembered."** Verses 10–12 present a series of three statements beginning with "For" and thus giving three reasons why the disciples shouldn't give the woman "troubles": (1) the goodness of her deed, emphasized by the wordplay in "*worked* a good *work*"; (2) the constancy of having the poor with them versus Jesus' impending physical absence; and (3) the nature of the anointing as a preparation of his body for burial. The word for "body" can also mean "corpse," though of course Jesus' body isn't a corpse quite yet. The constancy of having the poor implies that apart from having Jesus present, selling the perfume and giving the proceeds to poor people would be obligatory (compare 6:1–4). "*Throwing* this perfume on my body" portrays the woman's "pour[ing] it on his head" with a vigorous figure of speech that sets the stage for a contrast with Judas's "throwing" the thirty pieces of blood money into the sanctuary (27:5). Burial implies death. Jesus' interpretation of the woman's deed doesn't necessarily imply she had in mind the meaning he gives it. On the contrary, she perfumed only his head, whereas he speaks of his body; and for corpses Jews ordinarily used cheap olive oil, not expensive perfume. Nevertheless, anticipatory preparation for burial adds a detail that hasn't appeared in the earlier passion predictions—namely, that Jesus' corpse won't be prepared in the usual manner between death and burial. He adds further predictions: (1) that "this gospel," referring to "this gospel of the kingdom" mentioned in 24:14 and explicated in Matthew, will be proclaimed throughout the whole world and (2) that the woman's good deed will be told along with this gospel, so that she'll be remembered for her good deed rather than criticized (as here). Her anonymity and "the *whole* world" make a fulfillment of these predictions unlikely and therefore the fulfillment more impressive when it actually happens (as it has!). "Amen I tell you" gives Jesus' disciples assurance of the unlikely fulfillment.

26:14–16: **Then on going to the chief priests, one of the Twelve, called Judas Iscariot,** [15]**said, "What are you willing to give me, and I'll give him over to you?"** "One of the Twelve" harks back to 10:4, highlights the treachery he's about to exhibit, and makes him a negative example of those Christians who'll betray one another (24:10). "*Called* Judas Iscariot" puts him in parallel and

company with the high priest "*called* Caiaphas" (26:3). Imagine! One of Jesus' chosen twelve goes to the chief priests to help their plot succeed. Judas's treachery runs so deep that he asks for money, leaves the amount open, as though he'll accept whatever they're willing to give him, and promises to give Jesus over to the chief priests. The greed of Judas intensifies his guilt and casts a bad light on betrayers of one another in the church. "Then" associates Judas's going to the chief priests with the woman's pouring expensive perfume on Jesus' head to prepare his body for burial. Ironically, Judas's treacherous action contributes to the outworking of the woman's good deed. **And they weighed out to him thirty silver coins** [which he must have taken, since in 27:5 he'll throw them into the sanctuary (see Zechariah 11:12)]. [16]**And from then on he started seeking a favorable opportunity to give him over** [to the chief priests]. According to Exodus 21:32, thirty shekels of silver were the value of a slave. So to betray Jesus, the Lord who is "God with us" (1:23), Judas accepts the price of a slave. For shame! Just as in 4:17 "from then on" indicated the beginning of Jesus' Galilean ministry, and in 16:21 indicated the beginning of his teaching the disciples about his coming passion and resurrection, here the phrase indicates the beginning of the passion-and-resurrection itself. "A favorable opportunity" will have to conform to the chief priests' and elders' determination to avoid a riot in the festal assembly (26:5), and Judas's "seeking" such an opportunity shows determination to carry out his treacherous purpose of giving Jesus over to them.

THE PREPARATION OF THE PASSOVER AND THE OBSERVANCE OF THE LORD'S SUPPER AS OBEDIENCE TO JESUS' COMMANDS
Matthew 26:17–29

26:17–19: **And on the first** [day] **of** [the Festival of] **Unleavened** [Bread] **the disciples approached Jesus, saying, "Where** [in Jerusalem] **do you desire that we prepare for you, so as to eat the Passover** [meal]**?"** [18]**And he said, "Go into the city to so-and-so and tell him, 'The teacher says, "My time is near. [On coming] to you, I'm doing the Passover with my disciples."'"** For "the first [day] of [the Festival of] Unleavened [Bread]," see the comments on Mark 14:12. Jesus is such a Law-abiding Jew that he doesn't have to tell the Twelve he's going to eat the Passover. They know he will. Their only question is where he wants them to prepare the meal. "For you" goes with "prepare," not with "to eat the Passover." So the emphasis doesn't rest on preparation for eating—rather, on preparation for Jesus. "To so-and-so" reflects Old Testament terminology for referencing someone or something whose identity is unimportant (compare Ruth 4:1; 1 Samuel 21:2; 2 Kings 6:8, though English translations don't always bring out this usage). As a result, attention is riveted solely on Jesus, called "The teacher" in an echo of 23:8: "For one is your teacher." The word for Jesus' "time" connotes an appropriate time, here the time appropriate for the fulfillment of his passion-and-resurrection predictions. This time is "near" in that he's speaking on the Thursday before Good Friday. Near indeed! There's a wordplay between Jesus' "time" and the "favorable opportunity" Judas is seeking in that the Greek word for "opportunity" contains a variant form of the word for "time." The present tense in "I'm doing the Passover" portrays his celebrating it as so soon and certain that the celebration might as well be taking place already. "With my disciples" recalls Jesus' being called "'Immanuel,' which is translated 'God [is] with us'" (1:23). ¹⁹**And the disciples did as Jesus had ordered them** [compare 21:6], **and they prepared the Passover** [meal]. So this paragraph ends with emphasis on the disciples' exemplary obedience to his ordering them to prepare for his adherence to the law of Passover along with them.

26:20–22: And when evening had come, Jesus was reclining [at table] **with the Twelve.** Jews usually ate their late meal toward the end of the afternoon, but evening was the proper time for a Passover meal (Exodus 12:8). ²¹**And while they were eating he said, "Amen I tell you that one of you will give me over** [to those plotting to have me crucified (26:1–5)]**."** This prediction is shocking, because although Jesus has spoken before of being given over to his enemies (17:22–23; 20:18–19), up till now he hasn't identified the betrayer as one of his disciples, much less one of his intimates, the specially chosen twelve. The unlikelihood of betrayal from within the ranks of the Twelve, who are eating the Passover with him, will make the fulfillment of his present prediction just as impressive as his many fulfillments of Old Testament prophecy, detailed throughout Matthew. "Amen I tell you" underlines certainty of fulfillment despite this unlikelihood. ²²**And being exceedingly saddened, they—each one** [of them, including Judas Iscariot]— **began saying to him, "Surely I'm not** [the betrayer]**, am I, Lord?"** The disciples' exceeding sadness echoes their exceeding sadness after Jesus' second passion prediction (17:22–23) and puts them in a good light. For emphasis, "each one [of them]" individualizes their sadness. "*Began* to say to him" implies that they asked their question one after another. Their addressing him with "Lord" implies what they think is an incapability of betraying him, except that for Judas Iscariot the address disguises his "seeking a favorable opportunity" to do just that. As usual when addressed to Jesus, "Lord" points to his deity.

26:23–25: And he, answering, said, "The one who has dipped [his] **hand with me in the bowl—this one will give me over. **²⁴**On the one hand, the Son of Man is going away, just as it's written concerning him. On the other hand, alas for that man through whom the Son of Man is being given over! It would have been good for him if he—that man—hadn't been born."** "And answering" puts some emphasis on Jesus' response to the disciples' question. For the rest, see the comments on Mark 14:19–21; but note that Matthew lacks "himself" between "who" and "is dipping," and lacks "one" before "bowl." ²⁵**And answering, Judas, the one giving him

over, said, "Surely I'm not** [the betrayer]**, am I, Rabbi?" He tells him, "You yourself have spoken."** "Each one [of them]" in 26:22 must have included Judas. So he responds to Jesus' second pronouncement of betrayal with a second question, repetitive of his first question to Jesus except for a change of address from "Lord" to "Rabbi." In 23:8 Jesus implied that as the disciples' one teacher he was their rabbi. But Judas's addressing him presently with "Rabbi" anticipates his addressing Jesus with "Rabbi" in the very act of giving him over to the chief priests and elders (26:49). Judas's question exudes hypocrisy. He knows very well that he's the betrayer. He has been paid to betray Jesus. The thirty silver coins are jingling in Judas's pocket, and he's currently seeking a favorable opportunity for the betrayal (26:14–16). So his question, which like that of the other disciples is worded in a way that expects a negative answer, lacks sincerity. "And answering" adds emphasis to his pretending loyalty to Jesus with the question. "The one giving him over" echoes 10:4 and adds further emphasis on Judas's pretense. The abruptness and present tense in "He [Jesus] tells him" underscore Jesus' answer, "You yourself have spoken," which amounts to a refusal to answer, as if to say, "Your words, not mine." Jesus won't identify Judas as the betrayer, because if he were to do so the other disciples would stop Judas, and Jesus' prediction that one of the Twelve is going to betray him wouldn't come to pass.

26:26–29: And while they were eating, Jesus, on taking bread and saying a blessing [= praising God for the bread]**, broke** [it into pieces, as was especially appropriate for unleavened bread, its being cracker-like] **and, on giving** [it] **to the disciples, said, "Take** [these pieces of bread]**. Eat** [them]**. This is my corpse."** In the context of Jesus' being given over to death, the word for "body" is better translated "corpse" (compare the use of this same word in reference to Jesus' burial at 26:12; 27:58–59). ²⁷**And on taking a cup and giving thanks, he gave** [it] **to them, saying, "Drink from it, all of you.** ²⁸**For this is my covenant-blood** [compare Exodus 24:8] **that's being poured out in behalf of many** [people] **for forgiveness of sins. **²⁹**And I tell you, by no means will I from now on drink from this produce of the vine till that day whenever I drink it anew with you in my Father's kingdom."** Still alive and well, Jesus is reclining bodily with his disciples and, as just noted, "corpse" better suits the context of his coming death and burial than "body" does. So "This *represents* my corpse" correctly interprets "This *is* my corpse." Similarly, since Jesus' blood has yet to be poured out (though "is *being* poured out" makes the outpouring as good as happening already), "this [cup containing red wine] *represents* my covenant-blood" interprets "this *is* my covenant-blood" correctly (but see John 6:47–60 with comments on the offensiveness of what on the unintended literalistic level is cannibalistic language). The separate mention of outpoured blood indicates a violent death, as in our term "bloodshed." We have then a symbolic as well as verbal prediction of Jesus' passion. The covenantal character of the blood and its "being poured out *in behalf of many*" also indicate the sacrificial character of Jesus' approaching death, its atoning value for others, as brought out clearly in the added phrase, "for forgiveness of sins." Whereas the blood of animal sacrifices under the Mosaic covenant covered sins only provisionally and temporarily, Jesus' blood remits sins, that is, takes them clean away. Since the Old Testament uses a cup of wine figuratively for divine punishment (see Psalms 11:6; 75:8; Isaiah 51:17, 21–23), the cup of Jesus' covenant-blood suggests that he is to endure vicariously the punishment deserved by others for their sins.

The terse commands, "Take," "Eat," and "Drink . . ." make the taking, eating, and drinking matters of obedience. "All of you" commands drinking from the one cup that represents Jesus' covenant-blood. There's only one source of atonement, to which all must repair if their sins are to be forgiven. So the taking, eating, and drinking represent appropriation by faith of the benefits of Jesus' sacrificial death. "For many" enlarges the number of beneficiaries beyond the Twelve to include those to be discipled among all nations (28:18–20). Matthew never gets around to saying that the Twelve did take, eat, and drink. So the accent stays on Jesus' authoritative commands, which thereby become part of his updating the Old Testament law through escalating the Passover Supper into the Lord's Supper. "For" introduces the outpouring of his covenant-blood as the reason for drinking. Not to drink would represent failure to appropriate the benefits of that outpouring. Since the forgiveness of sins depends on the outpouring, obedience to Jesus' commands is evidential of true discipleship, not meritorious of forgiveness (compare Isaiah 53:12; Jeremiah 31:34).

The passage ends with Jesus' saying he'll abstain from wine till he drinks it in his Father's kingdom. "And I tell you," "by no means," and "from now on" stress the abstinence. "With you" implies that Jesus' physical absence from the disciples in the coming church age—a time of persecution for them, as he has repeatedly predicted—would make wine-drinking, a celebratory sort of drinking, inappropriate for him. He'll hardly be able to celebrate while his disciples are suffering. But a physical "with you" in the future kingdom will consummate his being physically "Immanuel . . . God [is] with us" (1:23) until his death, burial, resurrection, and implied departure to heaven, whence he'll come back. "Anew" implies that Jesus has drunk with his disciples in the past and perhaps on this occasion—though probably not the wine of the Eucharist, for he gave the cup to them for the drinking of that wine. And since drinking that wine represented appropriating forgiveness of sins by faith in his atoning blood, it would have spoiled the symbolism for him to drink it. His blood was shed for others' sins, not for any sin of his own. "In my Father's kingdom" means "when my Father fully establishes his reign on earth." The use of "my Father's kingdom" rather than "God's kingdom" or "the kingdom of heaven" calls attention to Jesus' divine sonship. One of the Twelve will betray him, but his heavenly Father will vindicate him.

JESUS AS AN EXAMPLE OF PRAYERFULNESS AND PETER AS AN EXAMPLE OF PRAYERLESSNESS THAT WILL LEAD TO DISOWNING JESUS IN TIME OF PERSECUTION
Matthew 26:30–46

In accordance with custom the Passover meal ends by the middle of the night, so that Jesus and the disciples now leave for the Mount of Olives. (Matthew doesn't tell at what point Judas parted from their company, so that the emphasis will fall solely on the coming betrayal as such.) **26:30–32: And after hymn-singing** [probably some of Psalms 114 (or 113)–118] **they went out to the Mount of Olives.** [31]**Then** [= during their going] **Jesus tells them, "You, all of you, will be tripped up in** [regard to] **me during this night** [compare 11:6; 13:57]**. For it's written, 'I'll strike the shepherd, and the sheep' of the flock 'will be scattered** [Zechariah 13:7]**.'** [32]**But after I've been raised, I'll go ahead of you into Galilee."** "You" and "*all* of you" are designed to keep the disciples from trying to deflect Jesus' dire prediction concerning them. "In [regard to] me" makes him the cause of their getting tripped up, and "during this night" tightens the time frame for fulfillment. Adding "of the flock" (not in Zechariah) to "the sheep" makes a figure of speech for "the church," which Jesus earlier compared to a building (16:18). Concerning the rest, see the comments on Mark 14:26–28.

26:33–35: But answering, Peter told him, "Though all will be tripped up in [regard to] **you, I myself will never be tripped up."** "Answering," "myself," and "never" add weight to Peter's denial. [34]**Jesus told him, "Amen I tell you that during this night, before a rooster crows, you'll disown me three times."** The abruptness of "Jesus told him" exhibits impatience with Peter's contradicting his prediction. "Amen I tell you" sets the certainty of this prediction's fulfillment opposite Peter's counterprediction. "During this night" matches the tightened time frame of Jesus' prediction concerning all the disciples, only now he predicts Peter's disowning him in addition to their being scattered. "Before a rooster crows" tightens the time frame further. "Three times" specifies the number of disownings. Astonishing detail! And Peter's disowning Jesus to save his own life will be the polar opposite of disowning himself to follow Jesus at the possible cost of his own life (16:24). [35]**Peter tells him, "Even if it's necessary that I die with you, by no means will I disown you." And all the disciples spoke likewise.** Peter matches Jesus' abruptness with his own. The present tense of "says" and "by no means" underline Peter's misplaced self-confidence. "*Even* if it's necessary that I die with you" underlines the extent to which he claims he's ready to go for proof of his loyalty. In 16:21–23 he predicted Jesus wouldn't undergo the passion. But after Jesus' rebuke, he must have come to recognize its necessity; for the disciples' extreme sadness after the second passion prediction (17:22–23) implied Peter's acceptance of the divine necessity that Jesus die. "Even if it's necessary that I die with you" therefore means that Peter will join Jesus in that necessity before disowning him. See further the comments on Mark 14:29–31, though Matthew lacks some of Mark's features just as Mark lacks some of Matthew's features.

26:36–38: Then Jesus comes with them to a parcel of land called Gethsemane; and he tells his disciples, "Sit here while, after going over there, I pray [compare Genesis 22:5]**."** [37]**And on taking along Peter and the two sons of Zebedee, he started being saddened and dismayed.** [38]**Then he tells them, "'My soul is very sad, to** [the point of] **death** [Psalms 42:5, 11; 43:5; Jonah 4:9]**.' Remain here and stay awake with me."** "Then" relates the arrival of Jesus at Gethsemane to his just having predicted that Peter will disown him three times before cockcrow this very night. Thus Matthew portrays Peter's upcoming prayerlessness as the reason Peter will fulfill Jesus' prediction. The present tense in "comes" and in two instances of "tells" adds drama to the episode. The coming of Jesus "with them" recalls again his being "God with us" (1:23). "While . . . I pray" means "as long as I pray." The anonymity of "the two sons of Zebedee" leaves "Peter" standing out as the representative disciple, whose prayerlessness and subsequent failure will wave a red flag of warning to all disciples. The addition of "with me" to "Stay awake" complements Jesus' having come "with them." They're to stay with him just as he has stayed with them. For the elements shared with Mark 14:32–34, see the comments on that passage.

26:39: And on going forward a little, he fell on his face, praying and saying, "My Father, if it's possible, this cup is to pass away from me. Nevertheless, not as I want—rather, as you [want]**."** Jesus' "going forward *a little*" allows Peter and Zebedee's sons to see before they fall asleep what he does and to hear what he prays. (In that culture even private prayer was usually spoken out loud.) "He fell on his face" represents body language for the sadness and dismay that Jesus has just expressed in words (compare 17:6; Genesis 17:3, 17; Numbers 14:5; 16:4 and so on). "My Father" echoes Jesus' recently spoken phrase, "my Father's kingdom" (26:29), and suits Matthew's emphasis on Jesus' divine sonship. "This cup" alludes to the literal cup representing Jesus' covenant-blood at the institution of the Lord's Supper (26:27–28) and here refers figuratively to Jesus' sacrificial death that the sins of many people may be forgiven. This figure of speech appeared in 20:22–23; but "the cup" and "my cup" in that passage have turned into "*this* cup," because his death is on the verge of taking place. The traditional translation, "let this cup pass away from me," sounds as though Jesus is asking God to act directly on his behalf. Not so. Grammatically, Jesus is using his Father as a sounding board for a command *issuing from Jesus* that the cup pass away from him (Jesus), if possible. Even in the midst of his extreme sadness and dismay, he's too reticent to ask the Father himself to make the cup pass away from him. This same reticence leads Jesus to add "Nevertheless, not as I want—rather, as you [want]."

Thus Jesus' prayer exemplifies the prayer he taught his disciples, in particular, "Your will come to pass on earth as also [it comes to pass] in heaven" (6:10).

26:40–41: And he comes to the disciples and finds them sleeping and tells Peter, "In this way [that is, by going to sleep] **you** [plural] **weren't strong enough to stay awake with me for one hour!"** As in 26:36–38, the present tense in verbs—here, "comes," "finds," and "tells"— adds drama to the episode. See the comments on Mark 14:37 for translating Jesus' words as an accusatory exclamation rather than as a question. Though Jesus speaks to Peter, the plural "you" includes Zebedee's sons along with Peter and thus makes him represent other disciples. "With me" echoes 26:38 and, as there, complements Jesus' having come "with them" as "Immanuel . . . 'God [is] with us'" (1:23). "For one hour" indicates the length of time Jesus' first prayer vigil occupied. [41]**"Stay awake and pray lest you enter into temptation. On the one hand, the spirit** [is] **eager. On the other hand, the flesh** [is] **weak."** Earlier, Jesus told them only to stay awake (26:38). Now he tells them also to pray. In that culture people prayed not only out loud but also with their eyes open, not with their eyes shut. Praying would help the disciples stay awake, then, so as not to enter into—that is, succumb to—the temptation to sleep. The command echoes the Lord's Prayer (compare 6:13: "And you shouldn't lead us into temptation"). The spirit of the disciples may be eager to help Jesus, but their flesh is weak in the sense of tired ("You weren't strong enough"). It's late at night, and they've had an unusually full meal. Only prayer can help their eager spirit win its tug-of-war with their weak flesh. As in Psalm 51:12, to which Jesus alludes, we should think of their human spirit, not of God's Spirit.

26:42–44: Again, on going away a second [time] **he prayed, saying, "My Father, if it isn't possible that this cup pass away unless I drink it, your will come to pass."** Again the address, "My Father," accents Jesus' divine sonship. Instead of Jesus' wanting the cup to pass away from him (as in the first prayer), we discover now an expectation that he must drink it. "Drink" echoes Jesus' usage in 20:22–23; 26:27, 29. "*Unless* I drink it" implies that the cup *will* pass away if Jesus does drink it. It will pass away in that by drinking it he'll have emptied it of its poison of death. In that sense it will have passed away, but not from him, because he'll have drunk that poison—hence his omitting the earlier "from me." And instead of a contrast between Jesus' will and the Father's will (as in the first prayer), we discover a reference only to the Father's will. "Your will come to pass" echoes the Lord's Prayer exactly: "Your will come to pass" (6:10). Again Jesus is using his Father as a sounding board for a command issuing from him (Jesus) that the Father's will come to pass. [43]**And on coming again, he found them sleeping; for their eyes were weighed** [down (= heavy with sleep)]. [44]**And on leaving them again, going away he prayed a third time, speaking the same statement again.** Jesus' staying awake and praying three times contrasts with the disciples', and especially Peter's, threefold going to sleep and failing to pray (see 26:45 for the third time). This failure will have its consequence in Peter's three disownings of Jesus, as predicted by Jesus—one disowning for each failure to stay awake and pray with him. So Peter, the representative disciple, stands as an example warning all other disciples that failure to pray beyond the limits of physical comfort will result in succumbing to temptation, that is, in yielding to the temptation to disown Jesus for the purpose of saving their necks in time of persecution. On the other hand, Jesus' staying awake and praying three times presents an example to be followed. He'll save his life by losing it, and that's a lot better than losing your life by saving it (compare 16:25). "Speaking the same statement" brings up for the third time Jesus' wanting the Father's will rather than his own. And the redundancy of a second "again" adds yet more weight to Jesus' example of staying awake and praying.

26:45–46: Then he comes to the disciples and says to them, "Are you sleeping for the remainder [of the time till the betrayer arrives] **and resting?"** Jesus' question arises out of disgust at the disciples' sleepy prayerlessness. Or we could translate with a disgusted exclamation: "You're sleeping for the remainder of the time and resting!" Under either translation, the present tense of "comes" and "says" highlights the disgust. **"Behold, the hour has drawn near; and the Son of Man is being given over into the hands of sinners. ⁴⁶Rouse yourselves! Let's go! Behold, the one who's giving me over has drawn near."** "The hour" is that of Jesus' betrayal and arrest, as indicated by the Son of Man's "being given over into the hands of sinners" and by the parallel between the drawing near of the hour and the drawing near of the betrayer, both emphasized by a "Behold" (see also 27:55). Jesus' hour of betrayal and arrest follows upon the hour of his praying (26:40). "Is being given over" makes the betrayal as good as taking place already. So the disciples have to rouse themselves. "Let's go" doesn't mean "Let's get out of here and escape." It means "Let's go meet the betrayer and the 'sinners' into whose 'hands' he's giving me over" (see the comments on Mark 9:31 for the connotation of violence in the phrase "into the hands of sinners"). "Sinners" highlights the injustice Jesus will suffer, but going to meet the betrayer and the sinners shows him carrying out his Father's will, not his own. Thanks to Judas, the sinners who make up the chief priests' and elders' posse can now arrest Jesus in the dead of night apart from the festal assembly, where in view of his popularity an arrest would have caused a riot (26:3–5).

JESUS' DEATH AS A FULFILLMENT OF OLD TESTAMENT PROPHECY
Matthew 26:47–56

26:47–48: And while he was still speaking, behold, Judas—one of the Twelve—came, and with him a large crowd with swords and clubs, [a crowd] **from the chief priests and elders of the people.** The arrival of Judas while Jesus was still speaking puts on display Jesus' knowing that he was in the process of being betrayed and that the betrayer had drawn near (26:45–46). The "behold" that highlights Judas's arrival echoes the "Behold" that highlighted Jesus' announcement of Judas's approach. "One of the Twelve" echoes 26:14 and, as there, highlights in turn the treachery in Jesus' betrayal by one of his inner circle (compare 10:4). This treachery foreshadows the treachery of false disciples who'll betray their fellow disciples in times of persecution (24:10). The large size of the crowd with Judas contrasts with the fewness of Jesus and his band and gives the crowd an unfair advantage. The chief priests and elders didn't want to seize Jesus in the crowds of the festal assembly (26:3–5). But now they've drummed up their own crowd and armed them with swords and clubs. Despite the arms and the large size of the crowd, though, the chief priests and elders don't risk themselves by coming with their crowd. Cowards! ⁴⁸**And the one giving him over gave them a signal, saying, "Whomever I kiss—it's he. Seize him."** Though the moon shone during Passover (except when clouds covered it, of course), the nighttime, the presence of the Eleven, and the possibility of a melee dictated the need for Judas to identify Jesus in an ostensibly peaceful way. Hence the signal of a kiss. A simple pronoun would have referred to Judas well enough ("And *he* gave them a signal"). But Matthew designates him with the phrase, "the one giving him over," to keep attention focused on the treachery of betrayal and on the fulfillment of Jesus' prediction that one of the Twelve would give him over (26:21–25). Kissing Jesus as a signal to seize him deepens the treachery with a show of affectionate homage. "Seize him" exposes the show as a charade. In view of Jesus' thrice-repeated submission to his Father's will (26:39, 42, 44) and going to meet Judas and the arresters (26:46), there's irony in Judas's instruction, "Seize him," as though Jesus might try to escape.

26:49–50: And immediately on approaching Jesus, he said, "Hail, Rabbi," and kissed him. ⁵⁰But Jesus told him, "Comrade, [do] what you're here for." Then, on approaching, they [the crowd] **laid hands on Jesus and seized him.** To forestall a getaway by Jesus, Judas acts immediately. Accompanying the signal of a kiss is Judas's greeting Jesus and addressing him with "Rabbi," which echoes 26:25, where he pretended not to know whether he was going to be the betrayer though he'd gotten advance payment and was seeking a favorable opportunity (26:14–16). "Hail" anticipates "Hail" in 27:29, where soldiers will mock Jesus with this greeting. Judas, then, stands on the side of those who'll mock Jesus. Indeed, his present words and deeds constitute a mockery of Jesus. Additionally, the cheerful greeting, the respectful address, and the affectionate kiss represent hypocrisy at its height. Irony too. The greeting is ironic in that it literally means "Rejoice" or, as we'd say, "Have a nice day," whereas Jesus is going to be killed. The address is likewise ironic in that "Rabbi" means "my great one," yet Judas has gotten only the price of a slave for betraying Jesus (26:14–16). And the kiss is ironic in that the verb for it either intensifies the connotation of affection or denotes kissing the hand or feet rather than the face. So Judas was feigning affection or humility. "Comrade" occurred for a false disciple in 22:12–13 (compare 20:13), so that Jesus' addressing Judas with this term, itself ironic in that Judas is proving himself a betrayer rather than a comrade—Jesus' addressing him as such designates him a false disciple. Nor does the irony stop even here. For Jesus goes on to issue Judas an ironic command to proceed with what he has come to do, as though to say, "You've called me 'Rabbi.' Well, obey my command to do what you've come for. It's my Father's will, and I've submitted to it." By laying their hands on Jesus and seizing him, the crowd of thugs both obey Judas's instruction and fulfill Jesus' statement in 26:45 (see the comments on that verse).

26:51: And behold, one of those with Jesus, on stretching out [his] **hand, drew out his sword and by striking the high priest's slave lopped off his ear.** "One of those with Jesus" identifies the swordsman as one of Jesus' disciples. The crowd are armed with swords. So this disciple, unnamed by Matthew, responds in kind. His swordplay doesn't *contrast* with Judas's betrayal as good to bad; rather, it *corresponds* with the betrayal as evil to evil. "Behold" highlights the evil of the swordplay just as "behold" highlighted the evil of the betrayal (26:47). In this way Matthew shows that a violent response to persecution is no better than betraying others to persecutors (compare 5:5, 38–48). The striking of the high priest's slave reminds us of the striking of Jesus the shepherd in 26:31, quoting Zechariah 13:7. But only God's striking of Jesus, in accordance with Scripture, is legitimate.

26:52–54: Then Jesus tells him, "Return your sword to its place. For all who've taken hold of a sword [to use it] **will perish by a sword. ⁵³Or do you suppose that I can't implore my Father and** [that as a result] **he'll right now put at my disposal more than twelve legions of angels? ⁵⁴How then** [if I were to get twelve legions of angels to defend me] **would the Scriptures be fulfilled that it** [my sacrificial death] **must take place in this way?"** The present tense of "tells" lends emphasis to Jesus' response. The response carries forward his teaching against retaliation and presents Jesus himself as an example of carrying out that teaching (5:38–48). "*All* who take a sword" allows no exception to the teaching against retaliation or, more particularly, to using violence in resistance to persecution. Six thousand made a single legion. Twelve legions would provide plenty of protection, one legion each for Jesus and the eleven disciples (compare 4:6 and the guardian angels in 18:10). Though Jesus can gain the assistance of so many angelic warriors, and even more, he won't go against God's will as revealed in the Scriptures; for he didn't come "to tear down the Law or the Prophets . . . rather, to fulfill" (5:17–18).

26:55–56: In that hour Jesus said to the crowds, "As against a bandit have you come out with swords and clubs to take me with [you]**?"** This question could be repunctuated as an indignant statement; but either way, Jesus' response foreshadows the crucifixion of two bandits with him (27:38) and exposes the injustice of

his arrest by indirectly and ironically calling to mind his beneficial healings and exorcisms instead of banditry. It's the chief priests and elders, who sent the crowds to arrest Jesus, that sponsored banditry—in the temple no less (21:13)! "The large crowd" of 26:47 has turned into "the crowds" (plural) to reemphasize both the contrast with the fewness of Jesus and his band and the chief priests' and elders' fear of causing a riot by arresting Jesus in the festal assembly. "In that hour" links with 26:45: "Behold, the hour has drawn near." Only now the hour is no longer near. It has arrived, and Jesus finds himself within it. **"Day by day I was sitting in the temple** [courts]**, teaching, and you didn't seize me."** This sarcastic observation refers to Jesus' teaching in the temple courts as exemplified in 21:23–23:39 and exposes the discrepancy between the Sanhedrin's launching against him a kind of military expedition, as though he were a bandit to capture whom they've had to arm crowds of thugs and send them out into the countryside—the discrepancy between that and Judas's having just greeted him, called him "Rabbi," and kissed him. "Day by day" and "in the temple [courts]" emphasize this discrepancy by indicating closeness, frequency, and therefore plenty of opportunity for them to have arrested Jesus earlier. The teaching recorded in 21:23–23:39 took place during a single day, so that that teaching exemplifies teaching which took place on other days too. Sitting was the authoritative posture taken by teachers. So by saying, "I was sitting . . . teaching," Jesus portrays himself as the one legitimate rabbi-teacher (see 23:8), whom they might have seized very easily. He wasn't hiding or fleeing. He was sitting in plain view and teaching within earshot! **⁵⁶"But this whole thing has happened in order that the Scriptures** [= writings] **of the prophets might be fulfilled** [compare 1:22; 2:23; 26:54]**."** "This whole thing" refers to Judas's having given Jesus over to his enemies. "Has happened" indicates a past event that has a continuing effect. The rest of the statement tells the purpose of this betrayal, the purpose of fulfilling prophetic scriptures concerning Jesus' sacrificial death. But little did Judas and those who seized Jesus know they were contributing toward that purpose. Those scriptures include at least Zechariah 13:7, quoted by Jesus in 26:31 (see the comments on Mark 14:48 for further such scriptures). **Then leaving him, all the disciples fled.** In addition to the fulfillment of prophetic scriptures, we now have the fulfillment of Jesus' own prediction in 26:31 that all the disciples would be tripped up because of him and scattered this very night, a prediction backed up by a prediction in Zechariah 13:7. The flight of "all the disciples" contrasts also with the earlier protestations of loyalty to Jesus by "all the disciples" (26:35).

JESUS' EXAMPLE OF NONRETALIATION AND REFUSAL TO TAKE AN OATH
Matthew 26:57–68

26:57–58: But the ones who'd seized Jesus led [him] **away to Caiaphas, the high priest, where the scholars**

and the elders had gathered together. "But" marks a contrast between the disciples' having left Jesus and the crowds' now leading him away. Matthew identifies the high priest by name or, rather, identifies Caiaphas as the high priest. "The scholars and the elders" refers to the Sanhedrin, a kind of supreme court for the Jews. Matthew mentions "the scholars" first because the upcoming session will feature theological issues regarding Jesus' messiahship and divine sonship (contrast 26:47, which mentioned "the chief priests" ahead of "the elders of the people"). The high priest chaired the Sanhedrin; so it was natural for Jesus to be taken to Caiaphas and for the Sanhedrin to convene at Caiaphas's residence, where Caiaphas would naturally have been in the middle of the night. Their convening begins to fulfill Jesus' prediction that he'd be rejected and condemned by them (16:21; 20:18–19). **58And Peter was following him at a distance as far as the high priest's courtyard; and on going inside** [the courtyard], **he was sitting with the servants to see the end.** The distance at which Peter follows avoids a contradiction with his having fled and thus preserves the fulfillment of Jesus' prediction that "all" the disciples would be scattered (26:31, 56). Though Peter's flight has put him at a distance, his following shows a determination to die with Jesus if necessary, as Peter predicted contrary to Jesus' prediction (26:35). The determination makes it look unlikely that Peter will disown Jesus three times this very night, before a rooster crows (26:34). Making it look even more unlikely is Peter's bravely following Jesus right inside the high priest's courtyard and sitting with the high priest's servants, who could (and will) identify Peter as one of Jesus' disciples. But the greater the unlikelihood of fulfillment, the greater the impressiveness of a fulfillment. "To see the end" correlates the outcome of Jesus' trial in his death and resurrection with "the end" of the church age at his second coming, preceded by unprecedented persecution of disciples (24:6, 14 [see 27:51–53 for preliminary signs of the end in connection with Jesus' death and resurrection]). Understanding characterizes disciles in this Gospel (see 13:11, 23, 51; 16:12; 17:13), and Peter's "sitting . . . to see the end" shows that from having heard Jesus' passion-and-resurrection predictions he understands the necessity that the mortal life of Jesus come to an end. From having heard Jesus' predictions of the second coming, furthermore, Peter appears also to understand that the end of Jesus' mortal life will foreshadow the end at which Jesus will come "with power and much glory" (24:30).

26:59–61: And the chief priests and the whole Sanhedrin were seeking false testimony against Jesus, so that they might put him to death. 60But they didn't find [it], **though many false witnesses did come forward. But later on, two, having come forward, 61said, "This** [Jesus] **said, 'I can tear down God's sanctuary and build** [it] **in three days.'"** "The *whole* Sanhedrin" stresses the completeness with which Jesus' predictions are coming to pass and heightens the Jewish authorities' guilt in that all of them are implicated in the purpose to put him to death. Worse yet, to attain their goal they are all seeking *false* testimony rather than true. They find false testimony, a lot of it in fact ("*many* false witnesses"), but none of it grave enough for passage of a capital sentence. Ironically, they're seeking testimony whose *content* would justify putting him to death at the same time they're seeking testimony whose *character* would violate the law against false testimony (15:19; 19:18; Exodus 20:16; Deuteronomy 5:20). Finally, though, witnesses come forward charging that Jesus said something which now sparks an interrogation of Jesus by the high priest. Despite the falsity of their testimony—or, rather, *because* of its falsity, since the Sanhedrists were *seeking* false testimony—it helps that the witnesses are two in number to accord with the law that every matter shall be established "on the mouth of two or three witnesses" (18:16; Numbers 35:30; Deuteronomy 17:6; 19:15). The falsity of this testimony is threefold: (1) Jesus predicted that the whole temple complex, not just the sanctuary proper, would be torn down—but didn't say *he* could or would tear it down (24:2); (2) he said he'd be raised on the third day after being killed—but he didn't say *he* could build the torn-down temple in three days (16:21; 17:23; 20:19); and (3) he predicted to his disciples *in private* the destruction of the temple and his being raised on the third day—but then the two nondisciples who reported highly distorted versions of these predictions couldn't have been the witnesses they pretended to be. Does Matthew mean us to infer that Judas had fed them such distorted versions? Or that they themselves distorted what Judas had told them?

26:62–64: And on standing up, the high priest said to him, "Are you making no answer at all in regard to what these [two witnesses] **are testifying against you?" 63But Jesus kept silent. And the high priest said to him, "I adjure you by the living God that you tell us if you're the Christ, the Son of God." 64Jesus tells him, "You yourself have spoken. Nevertheless I tell you** [plural], **from now on you'll see 'the Son of Man' sitting at the right** [hand] **of the Power and 'coming on the clouds of heaven** [Daniel 7:13 (compare Matthew 22:44; Psalm 110:1)].'"** By standing up, the high priest abandons his rightful role as a judge and wrongly takes up the role of a prosecutor. In his opinion, the charge that Jesus said he could tear down the temple and build it in three days demanded an answer from Jesus. Why? Because the high priest controlled the temple (compare 21:15, 23, where the chief priests and their cohorts challenged Jesus' authority to cleanse the temple and perform marvels and receive praise there). Jesus maintains his silence, though, just as he'd refused to say by what authority he cleansed the temple (21:24–27). Because he has submitted to his Father's will that he drink from his cup the poison of death (26:39, 42, 44), he'll not defend himself. So the high priest puts him under oath (the meaning of "I adjure you by the living God") to say whether he's "the Christ, the Son of God." Caiaphas's comment makes you think he'd heard Peter's telling Jesus in 16:16, "You're the Christ, the Son of the living God" (see the comments on that passage). Only the Christ, God's Son, could tear down the temple and build it in three days. So the high priest implies. "Jesus tells him" introduces Jesus' response tersely. But the response doesn't tell the high priest what he has asked to know. For he has put Jesus under oath, and Jesus won't violate his own prohibition of oath-taking (5:33–37). Instead of saying whether he's the Christ, the Son of the living God, then, he tells the high priest, "You yourself have spoken," which echoes what Jesus told Judas in 26:25 and, as there, amounts to a refusal to answer, as if to say, "Your words, not mine." The echo also weds Judas and Caiaphas in the conspiracy to destroy Jesus. Moreover, if according to 5:33–37 it would have been wrong for Jesus to *answer* under oath, it was wrong to *put* him under oath. So while Jesus exemplifies obedience to his prohibition of oaths, the high priest exemplifies disobedience to it.

Jesus does add a statement, but one that doesn't answer under oath the high priest's question. "Nevertheless" stresses the difference between this voluntary statement and answering a question under oath. Differently from "You've said [it] yourself," Jesus now speaks his own words with a magisterial authority that owes nothing to an oath. "I tell you" adds legitimate force in place of the illegitimate force of an oath. The switch from the singular "you" to the plural "you" underlines this difference and directs Jesus' following words to the whole Sanhedrin, not just to the high priest. "From now on" refers to the church age, which dates from Jesus' time onward to the second coming. But how is it that the Sanhedrists will "see" him sitting at God's right hand from that time all the way through the church age, and then see him coming on the clouds of heaven? Jesus is speaking ironically, as though to say, "On the basis of your own high priest's using 'the Christ, the Son of God' in reference to me, you should see me sitting at God's right hand and coming on the clouds of heaven." Of course they won't; but they should expect to, given Jesus' having said to the high priest, "You've said [it] yourself." Jesus' replacement of the high priest's "the Christ, the Son of God" with "the Son of Man" indicates a reversal of roles. For "the Son of Man" connotes judgmental authority (16:27; 25:31); and at his coming as the Son of Man, Jesus will judge the Sanhedrists legitimately, not be judged by them illegitimately (as now). "The Power" is a reverential substitute for "God" both in view of "God's power" by which he'll resurrect people (22:29) and in view of the "power" with which the Son of Man will come after sitting at God's right hand (22:44; 24:30). "At the *right* [hand]" indicates the side of God's favor (see the comments on 25:33). "Sitting" is the posture of authority, and "coming on the clouds of heaven" gives Jesus the Son of Man a divine mode of transport (see the comments on 24:30).

26:65–68: **Then the high priest tore his garments, saying, "He has blasphemed! Why do we still have a need of witnesses? Look! You've now heard blasphemy!** [66]**How does it seem to you?" And they, answer-**ing, said, **"He's liable to death** [that is, deserving of the death penalty]**."** By tearing his garments the high priest adds emphatic body language to his pronouncement that Jesus has uttered blasphemy. Strengthening the emphasis are (1) the question implying that no further witnesses are needed; (2) the exclamation "Look!"; and (3) the reiteration that Jesus has uttered blasphemy. "*You've* now heard blasphemy" prepares for the question how it seems to the rest of the Sanhedrin, and "You've *now* heard blasphemy" pinpoints the statement Jesus has just uttered. For the character of the supposed blasphemy, see the comments on Mark 14:63–64. The verdict, "He's liable to death," fulfills Jesus' prediction in 20:18 that the Sanhedrin would condemn him to death. [67]**Then they spat in his face and punched him; and some slapped** [him], [68]**saying, "Prophesy to us, Christ. Who's the one who hit you?"** The spitting in Jesus' face echoes and fulfills Isaiah 50:6, where the suffering Servant of the Lord says, "I didn't hide my face from shame and spitting." (Jesus has submitted to his Father's will in this regard.) The Sanhedrists' punching Jesus fulfills his prediction that he'd "suffer severely from the elders and chief priests and scholars" (16:21; also 17:12). And by allowing some of them to slap him he exemplifies obedience to his own law of nonretaliation (see especially 5:39). On the ground that a prophet has supernatural knowledge, they challenge Jesus to prophesy who hit him with an open palm, that is, to identify each assailant by name. They think that his not identifying them by name exposes him as a false prophet and a false christ. Ironically, their very mistreatment of him is fulfilling both Old Testament prophecy concerning the Christ and his own prophetic predictions of suffering at their hands. Again ironically, their addressing him with "Christ" gives him a true designation even though they mean it only as a mocking echo of their high priest's question to Jesus, "Are you the Christ . . . ?" (26:63). Perhaps Jesus' prophecy in 26:64 prompted the challenge that he prophesy again.

THE NEGATIVE EXAMPLE OF PETER'S DENIALS AS A CONTINUATION OF THE WARNING AGAINST PRAYERLESSNESS
Matthew 26:69–75

The debilitating effect of prayerlessness on discipleship shows up especially in the disowning of Jesus during persecution. So in this passage Matthew completes the warning started in 26:30–46.

26:69–70: **But Peter was sitting outside** [the room where the Sanhedrin was meeting] **in the courtyard. And one maid approached him, saying, "You too were with Jesus the Galilean."** [70]**But he disowned** [Jesus] **before all** [the high priest's servants, with whom Peter was sitting according to 26:58]**, saying, "I don't know what you're talking about."** Matthew is moving his narrative backward to pick up what Peter was doing during Jesus' trial before the Sanhedrin. "But" introduces Peter's disowning of Jesus to avoid persecution as a contrast with Jesus' concurrent endurance of persecution. The "maid" would be a slave girl. "One" stresses that because of Peter's prayerlessness it took only a lone slave girl to make him stumble into a disowning of Jesus. So beware of prayerlessness. It will make you as weak as that! The maid's "You *too*" means Peter as well as the rest of the Twelve. His disowning Jesus "before all" recalls Jesus' warning that he would disown before his Father in heaven whoever disowns him before human beings (10:33). In the context of this Gospel, then, Peter is forfeiting his salvation, so that his name will disappear from the story of Jesus' resurrection (contrast 28:7 with Mark 16:7), and by his own words Peter confirms that he isn't the bedrock on which Jesus will build his church (see the comments on 16:18). (Though Peter will be counted among the Eleven in 28:16, his present disowning of Jesus makes him a tare among wheat, so to speak [13:24-30, 36-43], and probably one of those who "doubted" Jesus' resurrection [28:17].) Whatever the biographical reality, Matthew makes the figure of Peter symbolize a wide range of possibilities in discipleship: (1) apostolic ministry (10:1-2); (2) little faith (14:28-31); (3) confession of Jesus as the Christ, God's Son (16:16); (4) reception of special revelation (16:17); (5) interpretive authority (16:19); (6) satanic agency (16:23); (7) prayerlessness (26:36-46); and (8) apostasy in a time of persecution with the consequent forefeiture of salvation (the present passage). Since knowledge characterizes true disciples in this Gospel (see 13:11, 23, 51; 16:12; 17:13), by saying, "I don't know what you're talking about," Peter portrays himself as a false disciple.

26:71-72: And after he'd gone out [of the courtyard] **into the gateway, another** [maid] **saw him and says to the ones there, "This** [guy] **was with Jesus the Nazarene."** [72]**And again he disowned** [Jesus]—[this time] **with an oath: "I don't know the guy."** Peter exits the courtyard to escape the pressure. But Jesus' prediction of three disownings is catching up with him. Three failures to pray in Gethsemane, three disownings of Jesus. Especially after the past tense of "saw," the present tense of "says" underlines this second maid's statement. She doesn't address Peter as the first maid did, but speaks about him to others. But he's so concerned to dissociate himself from Jesus that he responds despite not being addressed. "Again" marks his second disowning of Jesus. Two down. One to go. "With an oath" intensifies this disowning, violates Jesus' prohibition of oaths (5:33-37), and contrasts with Jesus' refusal to answer under oath a question asked him by the high priest (26:63-64). With "I don't know the guy" Peter portrays himself for a second time as an unknowledgeable false disciple. This maid's "Jesus the Nazarene" parallels the first maid's "Jesus the Galilean" and thus echoes the association of Galilee and Nazareth in 2:22-23. In fact, whereas in that passage Joseph "settled down in a city called Nazareth so that what was spoken through the prophets *would* be fulfilled, that he [Jesus] will be called a Nazarene," here he *is* called a Nazarene. Unwittingly, the maid has fulfilled the prophecy.

26:73-75: And after a little [while]**, the** [men] **standing** [there]**, on approaching, said to Peter, "Truly you too are** [one] **of them, for even your speech makes you obvious** [as a Galilean]**."** [74]**Then he started cursing and swearing** [in the sense of speaking again under a self-imposed oath]**: "I don't know the guy." And immediately a rooster crowed.** "After a little while" shows that the fulfillment of Jesus' prediction is hastening toward fulfillment before a rooster crows. "Truly" calls attention by way of contrast to Peter's having uttered falsehoods. As in 26:69, "too" means "in addition to the Twelve." Peter's Galilean accent supports the identification of him with one of Jesus' disciples, for Jesus was a Galilean (26:69) and most of his followers came from there. "*Started* cursing and swearing" indicates *extended* cursing and swearing. Furthermore, cursing is added to the swearing of an oath, such as Peter has already done. Again, then, he violates Jesus' prohibition of oaths in contrast with Jesus' refusing to answer under oath (5:33-37; 26:63-64). Worse yet, the verb for cursing elsewhere takes an object, so that Jesus is probably implied as the object of Peter's cursing. If so, Matthew omitted "Jesus" out of reverence for him. (There'd have been no reason for Matthew to omit "himself" for a self-cursing by Peter.) For a third time Peter falsely claims not to know Jesus and therefore describes himself as an unknowledgeable false disciple to whom at the Last Judgment Jesus will declare, "I never knew you. Depart from me . . ." (7:23 [see also 25:12]). The lack of knowledge is mutual. The immediacy of the rooster's crowing shows that Jesus' prediction of Peter's three disownings of him this very night before the rooster crowed has come to pass in the nick of time and that Peter's counter prediction has failed to come to pass (26:34-35). [75]**And Peter remembered the word that Jesus had spoken: "Before a rooster crows, you will disown me three times." And on going outside, he wept bitterly.** Peter's remembering Jesus' prediction gives Matthew an opportunity to requote it and provides a basis for Peter's emotional reaction. "During this night" drops out of the requotation (contrast 26:34) to let emphasis concentrate on the number of disownings predicted: three, one for each failure to pray in Gethsemane. Peter's weeping dramatizes with pathos the fulfillment of Jesus' prediction, and the bitterness with which Peter weeps comes not from his feeling bad about disowning Jesus three times but from his having forfeited salvation by disowning Jesus before human beings (see 26:70 with 10:33 again). In this Gospel, then, Peter has turned into the example par excellence of "the person sown on rocky ground [compare the meaning of 'Cephas,' that is, 'rock, stone'] . . . who hears the word and receives it immediately with joy. But he doesn't have root in himself, but is temporary. And when affliction or persecution comes about because of the word, he's immediately tripped up" (13:20-21). Peter's going "outside" recalls Jesus repeatedly describing the fate of the damned as being thrown outside, and into the darkness farther outside (5:13; 8:12; 13:48; 22:13; 25:30).

THE MALICE OF JEWISH OFFICIALDOM
Matthew 27:1–2

In this snippet Matthew emphasizes the malice of Jesus' persecutors. They're the Jewish authorities who are also persecuting the church in Matthew's day (10:17–20, 23).

27:1–2: And when it got to be early morning, all the chief priests and the elders of the people took counsel [= consulted with one another] **against Jesus so as to put him to death.** "And when it got to be early morning" marks a chronological advance from the night of Peter's disownings of Jesus. Stressing the malice of the Jewish officials are Matthew's adding "all" to "the chief priests and the elders," describing the consultation as "against Jesus," and assigning them the purpose of "put[ting] him to death." See the comments on 26:3 for Matthew's attaching "of the people" to "the elders." ²**And on binding him, they led him away and gave** [him] **over to Pilate, the governor.** In Gethsemane Jesus was only "seized" and "led away" (26:47–57). Here the binding of him before he's led away starts a parallel with the later-mentioned Barabbas in that the word for "prisoner," which will twice describe Barabbas, literally means "a *bound* person" (27:15–16). The binding of Jesus also prepares for a contrast with Barabbas's later release in that the verb for releasing means "to *loosen* [bonds]" (27:15–16). The giving of Jesus over to Pilate, a Gentile, begins to fulfill Jesus' prediction that the Jewish authorities were going to give him over to the Gentiles (20:18–19). See John 18:31 for the Sanhedrin's legal incompetence in capital cases. But for Matthew it's the necessity that Jesus' prediction be fulfilled, not the Sanhedrin's incompetence, which determined the giving of Jesus over to Pilate. Addition of "the governor" to Pilate's name makes Jesus a model for his disciples, who'll "be led before both governors and kings on account of [Jesus] for a testimony to them and the nations" (10:18). See the comments on 2:4–6 for a comparison between Pilate as a governor and Jesus as a governor.

THE DREADFUL END OF JUDAS: AN EXAMPLE THAT WARNS AGAINST TREACHERY IN THE CHURCH DURING PERSECUTION
Matthew 27:3–10

The story of Judas's end shows the fulfillment of Jesus' dire prophecy in 26:24. More especially, though, this story complements the warning example of Peter's disownings of Jesus (26:69–75) with that of Judas's death. Both stories have unhappy endings: bitter weeping in one, suicide in the other. Both relate to problems caused by persecution: professing disciples' disowning Jesus to avoid persecution and professing disciples' betraying fellow disciples to avoid persecution. Both stories carry the same point: Don't do it, or you'll be sorry!

27:3–5: Then on seeing that he [Jesus] **had been condemned** [by the Sanhedrin], **Judas, the one giving him over** [to the Sanhedrin]—**on suffering remorse—returned the thirty silver coins to the chief priests and elders,** ⁴**saying, "I've sinned by giving innocent blood over** [to you] [compare Deuteronomy 27:25; 1 Samuel 19:5]." **But they said, "What** [is that] **to us? You shall see** [to it] **yourself!"** In other words, "Salve your conscience by yourself; don't try to enlist our help." This curt reply shows that disciples won't win the good will of persecutors by betraying fellow disciples to them. ⁵**And on throwing the silver coins into the sanctuary, he withdrew and, on going away, hanged himself.** The delivery of Jesus to Pilate (27:2) makes it apparent to Judas that the Sanhedrin has sentenced Jesus to death, since only a Roman governor could legally have a capital sentence carried out. For emphasis, the description of Judas as "the one giving him over" (compare 26:25, 46, 48) makes it look as though Judas is still betraying Jesus (contrast 10:4: "who also *gave* him over") in that copycat disciples are now giving each other over to their persecutors (see 24:10 for Jesus' prediction to this effect). As demonstrated by the obedience of faith, the feeling of remorse portrayed in 21:29, 32 equated with repentance. But Judas's hanging himself portrays lack of faith rather than the obedience of faith, so that the remorse he feels doesn't equate with repentance. Thus his remorse, though accompanied by a confession of sin and a return of the blood money, is hopeless, just as Jesus said about him in 26:24: "It would be good for him if he—that man—hadn't been born." The return of the money warns that ultimately there'll be no reward for betraying your fellow disciples. "Innocent blood" echoes Old Testament language (see especially Jeremiah 19:4). By using this expression Judas himself emphasizes the dastardly character of his betrayal of Jesus. The reference to blood implies the imminent outpouring of Jesus' blood, and the description of the blood as innocent makes room for its being poured out "for forgiveness of [others'] sins" (26:28). Judas's throwing the silver coins into the sanctuary reflects Zechariah 11:13: "So I took the thirty silver coins and threw them to the potter in the house of the Lord." And Judas's hanging himself parallels Ahithophel's suicide by hanging (2 Samuel 17:23). Ahithophel was a friend of David, and Matthew has played up Jesus as the Davidic Messiah. As Ahithophel turned against David, Judas has turned against Jesus, David's greater son. For Matthew, then, Judas's remorseful return of the blood money and committing suicide make the point: "Don't betray your fellow disciple. You'll belie your profession of discipleship, regret the betrayal, and lose all hope of salvation."

27:6–8: But the chief priests, on taking the silver coins, said, "It isn't lawful to toss [them] **into the treasury** [of the temple], **since they're the price of blood** [compare 1 Chronicles 22:6–10]." ⁷**And on taking counsel** [= consulting with one another], **they bought with them the Potter's Field for the burial of aliens.** ⁸**Therefore that field has been called "The Field of Blood" till today.** Here the chief priests act alone, because they have charge of the temple. Their saying it's unlawful to toss the silver coins into the treasury reemphasizes the dastardliness of Judas's betraying Jesus, as does also the reference to the money as "the price of blood." The chief priests avoid Judas's description of Jesus' blood as "innocent," however. To them, Jesus is a blasphemer who deserves execution. There's irony in their consulting with one another for the purpose of avoiding the unlawfulness of putting blood money in the temple treasury right after consulting with one another against Jesus so as to put him to death, that is, to kill him (16:21; 17:23; 21:38-39; 26:4; contrast 19:18: "You shall not murder," quoted from the Mosaic law [Exodus 20:13; Deuteronomy 5:17]). "The Potter's Field" combines the potter mentioned in Zechariah 11:13; Jeremiah 19:1, 11 and the field mentioned in connection with Judas's death in Acts 1:18-19. "For the burial" comes from and alludes to Jeremiah 19:11. But where Jeremiah spoke of Judeans, particularly Jerusalemites, Matthew speaks of "aliens." Jeremiah 19:4 helped this switch, for there the Lord calls the valley outside the Potsherd Gate "an alien place" because of its profanation with heathen sacrifices. The switch has the purpose of highlighting again the dastardliness of Judas's betrayal: the field bought with the price of betrayal was fit only for a graveyard, and that only for aliens. "Of aliens" implies that Judas wasn't buried there, for he wasn't an alien. "Therefore that field has been called 'The Field of Blood'" echoes Jeremiah 19:6 in part and means that the name of the field derives from the blood of Jesus, the price of which provided the money for purchase of the field. "*That* field" puts it at a moral distance because of the purchase price. And "till today" makes the field a contemporary warning to would-be betrayers in the church.

27:9-10: **Then was fulfilled what was spoken through Jeremiah the prophet, saying, "And I took the thirty silver coins, the price of the priced one, whom some of the sons of Israel priced for themselves;** [10]**and I gave them** [the thirty silver coins] **for the potter's field, in accordance with the things that the Lord had ordered me** [to do].**" "*Then* was fulfilled" replaces the usual "*in order that* [it] might be fulfilled" (1:22; 2:15 and so on) for a limitation of the fulfillment to God's *permissive* will. He didn't want this tragedy to happen. But he allowed it to happen (compare the comments on 2:17). The absence of the occasional "by the Lord" (1:22; 2:15) also distances God from the tragedy. But "through Jeremiah the prophet" portrays Jeremiah as the mouthpiece of the unmentioned Lord. Most of the following quotation comes from Zechariah 11:13. But elements of Jeremiah 19:1-13 that have already appeared in Matthew 27:3-8 appear also in the quotation. So Matthew cites Jeremiah as the source more likely to be missed if not mentioned explicitly. In the quotation, "I" and "me" are collective for the Sanhedrists. (A number of ancient manuscripts have "*they* took" and "*they* gave"; but the unchallenged "me" at the end of the quotation favors "*I* took" and "*I* gave," "they" probably having arisen out of the plurality of the Sanhedrists who bought the potter's

field.) "The priced one" is Jesus, whose value was set at thirty silver coins (the price of a slave) by some of the Jews ("the sons of Israel") for their own advantage ("for themselves"). The triple wordplay in "the *price* of the *priced* one, whom [some] from the sons of Israel *priced* for themselves" stresses that the Sanhedrists bought Judas's betrayal of Jesus on the cheap. Though they were the purchasers, not the seller, they set the price and got a bargain (26:14-16 [compare Amos 2:6]). "In accordance with the things that the Lord had ordered me [to do]" echoes a number of Old Testament passages (see, for example, Exodus 9:12) and attributes the purchase of the potter's field to the Sanhedrists' unwitting obedience to the Lord's command, which brings the Lord back into the picture as controlling even an event like this that falls out of his direct will into his permissive will.

A DEMONSTRATION OF JESUS' SUBMISSION TO THE FATHER'S WILL
Matthew 27:11-14

27:11-14: **And Jesus stood before the governor; and the governor questioned him, saying, "Are you the king of the Jews?" But Jesus said, "You yourself are speaking."** See the comments on Mark 15:2-5 for the implied charge of insurrectionism in the governor's question. As in 26:25, 64, Jesus' answers amounts to a nonanswer, as if to say, "Your words, not mine." So Jesus doesn't deny he's the king of the Jews. Such a denial would contradict the truth that he is their king (see 2:2; 21:5). Nor does he affirm that he is, for then the blame for his crucifixion (compare 27:37) would be diverted from his enemies, who'll call for it, to himself for admitting to insurrectionism. Concerning this point, see again the comments on Mark 15:2-5. [12]**And while he** [Jesus] **was being accused by the chief priests and elders, he made no answer at all** [because he'd submitted to his Father's will that he drink the poison of death from "this cup" (26:39, 42, 44)]. [13]**Then Pilate says to him, "You're hearing how many things they're testifying against you, aren't you?"** Expected answer: Yes. [14]**And he didn't answer him in regard to even one word** [of antagonistic testimony], **so that the governor marveled exceedingly.** "Then" and the present tense of "says" add emphasis to Pilate's astonished question. The high number of accusations being hurled against Jesus adds to the astonishment. And the astonishment reaches its peak ("exceedingly") when Jesus refuses to answer even one of the many accusations. He won't say anything at all that might thwart his Father's will that he drink the cup of crucifixion.

THE ACKNOWLEDGMENT OF JESUS AS RIGHTEOUS BY THE GENTILES PILATE AND HIS WIFE
Matthew 27:15-26

27:15-18: **And at each festival** [of Passover] **the governor was accustomed to release to the crowd one prisoner whom they wanted** [to be released]. [16]**And at**

that time they had a notorious prisoner called Jesus Barabbas. [17]Therefore when they [the crowd] had gathered together [to ask for the annual release of a prisoner of their choosing], Pilate said to them, "Whom do you want me to release to you, Jesus the Barabbas or Jesus, the one called Christ?" [18]For he knew that they had given him [Jesus Christ] over because of envy. Who are the crowd that gather together? Not the Galilean crowd that followed Jesus to the festival (20:29; 21:8–9, 11), for it's his popularity with that crowd which has generated this crowd's envy. So this crowd is the crowd sent by the chief priests and elders to arrest Jesus in Gethsemane (26:47, 55). They seem not to have a particular prisoner in mind when they gather together to request the release of a prisoner. For though Matthew has introduced Barabbas, not till later will they ask for Barabbas—and then at the instigation of the chief priests and elders (27:20). The crowd certainly don't have in mind to ask for Jesus' release, for they've given him over to Pilate out of envy. Matthew describes Barabbas as "notorious"—that is, as infamous for his evil—to strike a contrast with the upcoming description of Jesus as "that righteous [man]" (27:19). To make the contrast more striking, Matthew mentions Barabbas's first name, so to speak, a name that's identical with that of Jesus. So we have two Jesuses: one notorious and the other righteous. Pilate takes the initiative by giving the crowd a choice between the two. He calls the first Jesus "the Barabbas," which makes "Barabbas" a kind of title comparable to "Christ" in "Jesus, the one called Christ." Hidden behind Matthew's Greek text is the meaning of "Barabbas," which is Aramaic for "the son of the father" (compare Jesus Christ's being the Son of God the Father and the use of "Abba" for addressing God as Father in prayer [Mark 14:36; Romans 8:15; Galatians 4:6]). "Jesus, the one called Christ" makes it sound as though the governor had read that very phrase in Matthew's genealogy of Jesus (1:16). Matthew doesn't tell how the governor came up with the designation "Christ" for Jesus. It's enough for Matthew that Pilate advertised Jesus' christhood.

27:19: And as he [the governor] **was sitting on the judgment platform, his wife sent** [a message] **to him, saying, "Have nothing to do with that righteous** [man], **for I've suffered severely today in a dream because of him."** "Sent" implies the wife's distance from the scene of judgment. "*That* righteous [man]" reflects this distance. There's no indication how at a distance she knew Jesus was standing trial before her husband. All we're told is that a dream about Jesus disturbed her deeply, and even then we're not told what it was in the dream that disturbed her so. For "Have nothing to do with that righteous [man]" isn't presented as a message conveyed in the dream (contrast 1:20; 2:12–13, 19, 22). It's presented as advice generated by the governor's wife herself because the dream had caused her anguish. As a result, the accent falls on her description of Jesus as "righteous"—not just innocent (guiltless), but righteous (positively good as well as guiltless [compare 23:35]).

So Jesus appears as the example par excellence of the righteousness which surpasses that of the scholars and Pharisees and without which no one will enter the kingdom of heaven (5:20).

27:20–23: But the chief priests and the elders persuaded the crowds that they should ask for Barabbas and [that] **they should destroy Jesus** [see 2:13; 12:14 for earlier designs to "destroy" him]. "The crowd" (singular) of 27:15 has become "the crowds" (plural) to stress the breadth of human guilt for Jesus' death. "That they should ask for Barabbas" is surprising enough, given his notoriety for evil. But that "*they* should destroy Jesus" is astonishing, for we'd have expected them to ask *Pilate* to destroy Jesus. Even with the understanding that they ask to have Jesus destroyed by Pilate, or by his soldiers, the destruction is to be done on the crowds' behalf, so that an enormous weight of guilt descends on their heads. And, of course, the chief priests and elders incur guilt for persuading the crowds to ask for Barabbas's release and Jesus' destruction. [21]**And answering, the governor said to them, "Which of the two do you want me to release to you?"** But the governor hasn't been asked a question. So he must be answering in the sense of responding to the chief priests' and elders' having persuaded the crowds to ask for Barabbas instead of Jesus. **And they said, "Barabbas."** [22]**Pilate says to them, "What then should I do with Jesus, the one called Christ?" They all say, "He's to be crucified!"** [23]**And he said, "Why? What bad thing has he done?"** That is, what crime has he committed? **But they were yelling vehemently, saying, "He's to be crucified!"** The abruptness and present tense in "Pilate says to them" underscore the following question and therefore within it the second designation of Jesus as "the one called Christ" (see the comments on 27:17 for the first such designation by the governor). In stark contrast, the abruptness and present tense in "They all say" underscore the following demand that the one called Christ be crucified. "All" adds further emphasis on the breadth of human guilt for Jesus' death. We might expect the crowds to say, "Crucify him!" But that would mean Pilate should crucify him, or have him crucified. And that meaning wouldn't correspond to the crowds' having been persuaded to ask that "*they* should destroy Jesus [or have him destroyed]." So "He's to be crucified" doesn't mean that the crowds are telling the *governor* what to do, or to have done. They're telling him what *they* want to do, or have done, even though crucifixion was a Roman rather than Jewish mode of execution. The governor is just a sounding board, so that the guilt for Jesus' crucifixion will fall on them, not on the governor. Indeed, the governor asks why they want to crucify Jesus, or have him crucified. Asking what crime Jesus had committed shows that the governor has accepted his wife's description of Jesus as "righteous." The crowds' repeating "He's to be crucified" rather than answering with the citation of a crime confirms that description. "Were yelling vehemently" substitutes decibels and repetition for evidence.

27:24–26: And on seeing that he was profiting in no way [= making no headway in his attempt to dissuade the crowds], **but rather that a riot is developing, on taking water Pilate washed off** [his] **hands over against the crowd, saying, "I'm innocent of the blood of this righteous** [man]. **You shall see** [to it] **yourselves!"** In other words, "You'll have to bear the guilt for Jesus' unjust crucifixion by yourselves, because I've tried getting you to ask for the release of Jesus rather than Barabbas. Yet you've demanded Jesus' crucifixion and Barabbas's release, and custom dictates that I accede to your demands despite my judging Jesus to be righteous." The crowd are willing to accept responsibility for Jesus' crucifixion—responsibility but not guilt, in their opinion, as evident by the omission of "innocent" in their following reference to Jesus' blood (contrast 27:4). Anti-Semites have taken this acceptance as legitimating the persecution of Jews, but such persecution goes against Jesus' prohibition of using a sword (26:52–54). **25And answering, all the people said, "His blood** [be] **on us and on our children** [compare 23:35]!" **26Then he released Barabbas to them; but after having Jesus flogged, he gave** [him] **over to be crucified.** The present tense of "is developing" highlights the danger that a fullscale riot will eventuate. Ironically, the Jewish authorities have started a riot against Jesus, whereas they had wanted to avoid a riot in his favor (26:3–5). "Over against the crowd" demarcates the governor from the crowd to emphasize his innocence over against their guilt (see the comments on 27:15–18 for the identity of this crowd). "Innocent" echoes 27:4. But there Judas was guilty of Jesus' innocent blood. Here Pilate is innocent of Jesus' blood; and according to many of the oldest and best ancient manuscripts and translations, which are probably to be followed, the governor echoes his wife's message by calling Jesus "this righteous [man]," not just "this [man]." By washing off his hands with water the governor follows a rite prescribed in Deuteronomy 21:1–9. The rite indicates real innocence. "Answering" and "all" emphasize the people's willingness, indeed desire, to take from Pilate the responsibility for Jesus' blood. Since they don't consider Jesus innocent, it doesn't seem to them dangerous to call down his blood on themselves and on their children. The switch from "crowd" to "people" reflects 26:5, where "a riot" was associated with "the people." Flogging was a usual preliminary to crucifixion. Though the governor's soldiers will take Jesus away in 27:27, their absence here implies that "he gave [Jesus] over to be crucified" means that the governor gave Jesus over to "all the people," whose demand the soldiers will carry out for them.

JESUS AS THE MODEL OF A PERSECUTED RIGHTEOUS PERSON
Matthew 27:27–50

27:27–31: Then the governor's soldiers, on taking Jesus along into the official residence [of the governor], **gathered together the whole cohort against him.**

"Against him" heightens the element of persecution. Throughout the rest of Matthew's account of the passion, he'll stress the persecution of Jesus to encourage Christians suffering persecution at the time of writing (see the comments on 27:45–50). That the soldiers who took Jesus gather together "the *whole* cohort" points forward to a large-scale fulfillment of Jesus' prediction that Gentiles would mock him (20:19). Normally, a cohort numbered about six hundred. **28And on disrobing him, they put a scarlet cloak around him; 29and on braiding a crown of thorns, they put** [it] **on his head; and** [they put] **a reed in his right** [hand]; **and on kneeling before him, they made fun of him, saying, "Hail, king of the Jews!"; 30and after spitting on him they took the reed and started beating** [him] **on the head; 31and when they'd made fun of him, they disrobed him of the cloak and put his clothes** [back] **on him and led him away to crucify** [him]. These details of the Gentiles' mockery of Jesus add thoroughness of fulfillment to its large scale. Here are the indignities done to him: (1) his being disrobed; (2) his being dressed up in a scarlet cloak, an ordinary soldier's mantle, as though it were a kingly robe; (3) his being crowned with braided thorns, as though they were a woven wreath like Caesar's; (4) his having a reed put in his right hand, as though the reed were a king's scepter; (5) his being knelt before and mockingly greeted as the king of the Jews; (6) his being spat on in mockery of his subroyal cloak; and (7) his having the reed taken from him and used to beat him on the head in mockery of his subroyal crown. Crowning Jesus with thorns had the purpose of mockery, not of inflicting pain, though presumably it did inflict pain. Ironically, what the soldiers intended as mockery in kneeling before him is exactly what they should have done seriously. For Jesus is "God with us" (1:23). See the comments on 26:49 for irony in the greeting, "Hail!" And there's even further irony in the soldiers' greeting Jesus as "the king of the Jews" (compare 27:11). For though they don't think so, Jesus really is the king of the Jews (2:2; 21:5). See the comments on 26:67 for his being spat on. A reed would be too flimsy to hurt him; so beating him on the head with it has to do again with mockery more than with inflicting pain. Putting his own clothes back on him prepares for the next episode, which will include soldiers' dividing the clothes among themselves.

27:32–37: And as they were going out, they found a Cyrenian man named Simon. This [man] **they requisitioned to take up his** [Jesus'] **cross** [= the beam to be affixed horizontally to a permanently planted upright stake or to a living tree]. Since the soldiers have already led Jesus away from the governor's official residence (27:31), "going out" means exiting from Jerusalem (see the comments on 21:39). Simon was from Cyrene, a city in North Africa. Matthew doesn't say whether Simon had emigrated from there or was only visiting Jerusalem as a Passover pilgrim. But several features of the text do suggest that Matthew puts Simon forward as a model of Jesus' cross-taking disciples in accordance with 16:24

and in contrast with that other Simon, Peter, who has disowned Jesus: (1) the abruptness with which the sentence, "This [man] they requisitioned . . . ," starts; (2) the placement of "This [man]" ahead of "they requisitioned"; and (3) the absence of any indication, such as weakness on Jesus' part because of having just been flogged, why the soldiers requisitioned Simon—or even of Jesus' having carried the cross to this point. ³³**And on coming to a place called Golgotha, which is called "Skull's Place,"** ³⁴**they gave him wine to drink mixed with gall** [a bitter, yellow-brown or greenish fluid, also called bile and secreted by the liver of an animal and stored in the gall bladder]. The mixture adds insult to injury. **And on tasting** [it], **he didn't want to drink** [it]. Nor did he, not just because it tasted bitter, but because he'd said he would no more "drink from this produce of the vine [that is, wine]" till he drank it "anew" with his disciples "in [his] Father's kingdom" (26:29). Saying that Jesus "didn't *want* to drink" rather than saying that he *didn't* drink stresses his determination to keep the vow of abstinence. "Wine . . . mixed with gall" alludes to Psalm 69:21a, fulfilled here, and adds to the indignities already done to Jesus. ³⁵**And on crucifying him, "they divided his clothes for themselves by casting a lot** [Psalm 22:18]." Matthew is so concerned to show correspondence with the Old Testament that he subordinates Jesus' crucifixion to the division of Jesus' clothing. So we have another match with ancient Scripture and another indignity done to Jesus in that he hangs on the cross naked. Suffering shame is as much a part of persecution as is the suffering of pain. ³⁶**And sitting down, they were keeping guard over him** [so that his followers couldn't take him down from his cross before he died]. ³⁷**And they put over his head the charge against him, written: "This is Jesus, the king of the Jews."** Soldiers had mockingly addressed him with "king of the Jews" (27:29). Pilate had asked him whether he was "the king of the Jews," and he'd refused to answer yes or no (27:11). Nor has Matthew said that the Sanhedrin accused him of claiming to be the Jews' king, or had heard any testimony to that effect (26:57-68). So in Matthew's text it remains a mystery where this charge came from. All the more remarkable it is, then, that "the charge" takes the form of a declaration: "This is Jesus, the king of the Jews" (compare "This is my beloved Son" [3:17; 17:5] and "This is the prophet Jesus" [21:11]; contrast what the chief priests wanted Pilate to write according to John 19:21: "That [man] *said*, 'I'm king of the Jews'"). To be sure, the declaration in Matthew takes the standpoint of Gentiles and means to poke fun at Jesus, just as the Gentile soldiers did when they hailed him as "king of the Jews" (27:29). But because of the Gentile astrologers' asking in 2:2, "Where is the one who has been birthed [as] king of the Jews?" Matthew's audience know that the inscription over Jesus' head expressed the truth, so that the last laugh is on the mockers.

27:38-44: Then they crucify with him two bandits, one on [his] right and one on [his] left. ³⁹**And the passers-by started blaspheming** [= slandering] **him by** shaking their heads ⁴⁰**and saying, "You who are tearing down the sanctuary** [the temple proper, exclusive of surrounding courts and cloisters] **and building** [it] **in three days, save yourself if you're the Son of God, and come down from the cross."** ⁴¹**Likewise also the chief priests along with the scholars and elders, making fun of** [Jesus], **were saying,** ⁴²**"Others he saved. Himself he can't save. He's king of Israel. Let him come down from the cross now, and we'll believe on him** [= base our faith on him (compare 12:38-40)]. ⁴³**He has trusted on God** [= based his trust on God and therefore trusts him presently]. **Let him** [God] **rescue** [him] **now if he likes him** [an echo of Psalm 22:8]. **For he** [Jesus] **said, 'I'm God's Son.'"** ⁴⁴**And in the same** [way] **the bandits who were crucified together with him were also jeering at him.** The crucifixion of two bandits with Jesus heaps a further indignity on him (compare 26:55), and the present tense of "crucify" underscores this indignity. But "one on [his] right an one on [his] left" echoes 20:21, where the expression was associated with Jesus' kingdom, so that the present echo may imply that despite appearances to the contrary, the crucifixion of two unnamed bandits on either side of Jesus previews the sitting of two unnamed disciples on either side of him when he comes in glory. The head-shaking by passers-by echoes Psalm 22:7; Lamentations 2:15 and implies crucifixion along a thoroughfare. Their blasphemy slanders Jesus in that he never said he'd tear down the sanctuary and build it in three days. This blasphemy stemmed from the false testimony of two witnesses who'd never heard him say anything of the sort. Furthermore, the blasphemy doesn't even echo correctly that earlier false testimony. For according to it, Jesus said only that he *could* tear down the sanctuary and build it in three days (26:61), whereas the blasphemers make it sound as though he said he *would* tear it down and build it in three days. And "who are tearing down . . . and building" adds ridicule to the blasphemy by making it sound as though Jesus is accomplishing these tasks as he hangs on a cross. So the one wrongly condemned for *speaking* blasphemy (26:65-66) has wrongly become the *object* of blasphemy. In the direct challenge that he save himself by coming down from the cross, "if you're the Son of God" echoes a gambit in the Devil's first two temptations of Jesus (4:3, 6) and therefore casts the blasphemers in a satanic role of tempters (compare also 26:63).

All three sectors of the Sanhedrin add mockery to the blasphemy of the passers-by. Matthew puts the chief priests at the head; for they controlled the sanctuary, just mentioned in the blasphemy. These mockers have to admit that Jesus saved others (though see 12:24 for the attribution of his salvific power to Satan). The statements come lickety-split, staccato-like. The passers-by *challenged* Jesus to save himself. The Sanhedrists *deny* that he can. As noted above, the inscription over Jesus' head reflected the standpoint of Gentiles: "the king *of the Jews*" (27:37). The Sanhedrists' mockery reflects the standpoint of Jews: "king *of Israel*." They mean their statement, "He's king of Israel," as mockery, of course. For Matthew, though, the statement is a serious declaration of Jesus' kingship, just as is the inscription, "This is the king of the Jews." The Sanhedrists issue an indirect challenge that Jesus come down from the cross. They don't address him with "you," but continue to speak *about* him. "*Let* him come down" and "*Let* him [God] rescue [him]" are to be understood as insistent, not as petitionary. The Sanhedrists' rationale is that Israel's king wouldn't be hanging on a cross. The twice-occurring "now" gives the challenge a temporal bite. If Jesus waits to come down, it'll be too late. He'll be dead. Ironically, of course, he saves others by *not* coming down from his cross; and but for his submission to the Father's will, he *could* save himself by imploring his Father to provide him with angelic rescuers (26:53). The Sanhedrists' followup, "And we'll believe on him," makes Jesus the proper object of faith so far as Matthew is concerned. "*If* he [God] likes him" has twice been corrected by the Father: "This is my beloved Son, in whom I took delight" (3:17; 17:5). The Sanhedrists' twofold mockery of Jesus' divine sonship stands in striking contrast to an upcoming confession of the same by the Gentile centurion and his fellow soldiers (27:54). "Likewise also" exposes the Sanhedrists' mockery as blasphemous, like the challenge of the passers-by; and "in the same way" makes the bandits' insults identical in content with the Sanhedrists' insults. Both have to do with Jesus' self-identification, "I'm God's Son," which they cite as the basis of their challenge that God rescue him, since in their opinion "he can't save himself." But nowhere in Matthew has Jesus said, "I'm God's Son." In fact, when asked by the high priest whether he was "the Christ, the Son of God," Jesus answered with a noncommittal, "You yourself have spoken." Once again, then, the mockery consists in a falsehood. Jesus' co-victims jeer at him despite their deserving crucifixion and his not deserving it. This jeering highlights the extent to which his prediction of mockery for himself (20:19), as well as Old Testament passages, has reached fulfillment.

27:45–50: And from the sixth hour [noon] **darkness came across all the land until the ninth hour** [about 3:00 P.M.]. The phraseology concerning the onset of darkness echoes Exodus 10:22 and Amos 8:9–10. In both of those passages supernatural darkness expresses God's displeasure, so that here too the darkness expresses God's displeasure at the killing of his Son. (Astronomically, a natural eclipse of the sun wouldn't have occurred during the Passover, a time of full moon, or lasted for three hours.) Emphasizing this displeasure are the onset of darkness at noon, when the sun is at its zenith, its covering "*all* the land," and its lasting till midafternoon. Since the passion of Jesus previews the persecution of his disciples, God's displeasure at Jesus' crucifixion carries over to their persecution and thus provides them encouragement. **46And around the ninth hour Jesus cried out with a loud voice, saying, "Eli, Eli, lema sabachthani?"** that is, **"My God, my God, why** [= 'for what purpose'] **have you abandoned me** [Psalm 22:1]**?"** The abandonment consisted in God's leaving Jesus to die rather than

stepping in to save him from death. So Jesus shares his persecuted disciples' sense of abandonment; or, rather, they share his. The loudness of his outcry heightens this sense. The Hebrew of Psalm 22:1, "*Eli, Eli*, lema sabachthani?" sets up for a mistaken impression that he's calling for *Elijah*. **47And on hearing** [Jesus' outcry]**, some of the ones standing there were saying, "This** [guy] **is calling for Elijah!" 48And immediately one of them, on running and taking a sponge and filling** [it] **with vinegary wine and putting** [it] **around a reed, tried to give him a drink. 49And the rest were saying, "Let's see whether Elijah is coming to save him." 50But on shouting again with a loud voice, Jesus dismissed** [his] **spirit.** Because Elijah went to heaven without dying (2 Kings 2:11), Jews believed he would come to save righteous sufferers. Since the soldiers were sitting (27:36) and others were passing by (27:39), "the ones standing there" appear to be the chief priests, scholars, and elders (27:41). They would have the said belief concerning Elijah. So one of them takes immediate action to give Jesus a drink of cheap, vinegary wine and thus slake his thirst. The effort fulfills Psalm 69:21b (compare Matthew 27:34 with Psalm 69:21a). The immediacy of this effort and the running are due to the danger that Jesus will die too soon. As the rest of the bystanders note, more time is needed to see whether Elijah is coming to save Jesus. They don't believe he will, of course. So the effort has the purpose of demonstrating his supposed unworthiness of a rescue by Elijah. (Vinegary wine doesn't prolong life in a medicinal fashion, but as simple refreshment it might keep Jesus going a little while longer.) By echoing the cynical use of "save" in 27:40, 42, the present use of "save" adds further ridicule. Jesus hasn't saved himself. He appears unable to do so even though he saved others. God hasn't rescued him. And time will tell that neither will Elijah save him. Too late, though. Instead of drinking the vinegary wine, Jesus shouts again with a loud voice, as he had earlier. Matthew doesn't tell what he shouted, so that the loudness combines with Jesus' "dismiss[ing] [his] spirit" to highlight his death as an act of will. He doesn't die with a last gasp, for his will has become one with that of God his Father (contrast 26:39; but see 26:42, 52–54 for a gradual assimilation of his will to the Father's will).

ENCOURAGEMENT TO THE PERSECUTED: THE CIRCUMSTANCES OF JESUS' DEATH AS ESCHATOLOGICAL PROOF THAT HE IS GOD'S SON
Matthew 27:51–54

27:51–53: And behold, the veil of the sanctuary was torn in two from top to bottom; and the earth was quaked; and the rocks were torn apart; 52and the tombs were opened; and many bodies of the sacred ones who'd fallen asleep [a euphemism for "died"] **were raised; 53and on coming out of the tombs after his** [Jesus'] **resurrection, they entered into the holy city** [Jerusalem (compare 4:5)] **and appeared to many.** "Behold" highlights the tearing of the veil. "In two" stresses the completeness of the tearing; and, given the great height of the veil, "from top to bottom" indicates a heaven-originated, divine action that shows God's displeasure with the temple establishment, who've engineered the persecution of Jesus, and that therefore vindicates Jesus. Since Matthew has been portraying Jesus' passion as a paradigm of Christians' persecution, this supernatural vindication encourages them to hold fast. Their vindication will come, too. The earthquake not only tears apart the rocks out of which tombs were hewn just as the veil was torn apart. It also anticipates the earthquake at Jesus' resurrection in 28:2 and echoes Ezekiel 37:7, 12–13; Zechariah 14:4–5, where an earthquake occurs, graves are opened, and the people of Israel come up out of their graves. The rocks that are torn apart anticipate the rock out of which was hewn the tomb where Jesus is to be buried (27:60). "The sacred ones" are the righteous of previous times. They're sacred to God just as "the holy city" is sacred to God ("holy" and "sacred" translating the same Greek word). The statement about bodies being raised echoes in part the language of Daniel 12:2 and stresses the physicality of resurrection, especially in connection with the spatial expressions, "coming out of the tombs" and "entered into the holy city." Since the "many" to whom they later appeared seem not to include all the Jerusalemites, the "many" whose bodies were raised seem not to include all the righteous of previous times (compare the topographical limitation to Jerusalem and, seemingly, to rocky tombs around that city). The many raised bodies correspond to the many to whom they appear. The verb "appeared" connotes a juridical appearance for the purpose of testimony (see Acts 23:15, 22; 24:1; 25:2, 15; Hebrews 9:24, for example), so that this appearance provides the miraculous demonstration of Jesus' divine sonship that he refused to give at the Devil's behest in the holy city (4:5–7). All in all, these events combine with Jesus' resurrection to preview the certainty of resurrection and vindication for all who are persecuted for the sake of righteousness (5:10–12).

27:54: And on seeing the [earth]quake and the things that had happened, the centurion and the ones with him who were keeping guard over Jesus became exceedingly afraid, saying, "Truly this was God's Son." "The things that had happened" summarizes the results of the earthquake: the rocks' being torn apart and the opening of tombs, plus the veil's being torn in two. The sanctuary had two veils, an outer one and an inner one. The centurion's and guards' seeing these events requires that the outer veil be in view here (and, incidentally, requires also the site of crucifixion to be at some height on the Mount of Olives facing toward the outer veil rather than at the sites now visited by pilgrims, which would have provided no view of the outer [or inner] veil). "Became exceedingly afraid" echoes 17:6, where it referred to several disciples at Jesus' transfiguration. Since such fear characterizes disciples, the echo suggests the centurion's and guards' conversion, or—if not a historical conversion—at least Matthew's using the fear to symbolize

conversion. Confirming this suggestion is the centurion's and guards' confessing Jesus to be God's Son just as the disciples have done (14:33; 16:16). "Truly" implies both the sincerity of the confession and the truth of its content. "Was" reflects the death of Jesus as ending his lifetime and implies that he had been God's Son all along. Whatever the historical centurion and guards meant ("a son of a god" or "a son of God," for example), Matthew wants us to understand "God's Son." At least symbolically, then, they become a vanguard of the Gentiles who'll flock into the church, just as the astrologers (magi) were in 2:1–12. And the confession of Jesus' divine sonship links with the supernatural phenomena prompting the confession to fortify those who suffer for his sake.

CHRISTIAN DEVOTION TO THE PERSECUTED
Matthew 27:55–61

27:55–56: And many women were there watching at a distance, [women] **who as such** [= as keeping vigil] **had followed Jesus from Galilee to serve him** [food (compare 4:11; 8:15; 25:44)], **⁵⁶among whom was Mary Magdalene** [Luke 8:1–3], **plus Mary the mother of James and Joseph, and the mother of Zebedee's sons** [compare 20:20]. These women helped Jesus on his journey from Galilee to the cross and thus furnish a positive example of Christian devotion to fellow believers who like Jesus are suffering persecution (see especially 25:44). The male disciples have fled (26:56); and after following Jesus at a distance (26:58), Peter has made an apostate's exit (26:75). So the women make up for those disciples' failures. That the women were "many" reminds us of the crowds Jesus drew in Galilee and therefore of the coming success of worldwide evangelism. "At a distance" keeps the women separate from their fellow Jews who'd been mocking Jesus. The naming of Mary Magdalene first (see also 28:1) makes her a leader among these women. "Mary the mother of James and Joseph" is none other than Jesus' mother (see 13:55!). Since Jesus has died, she now gets designated as the mother of two of his half brothers.

27:57–61: And when it became late, there came a rich man from Arimathea—Joseph by name—who also himself had been discipled to Jesus [= made a disciple of Jesus]. **⁵⁸On approaching Pilate, this** [man] **asked for Jesus' body.** Since Deuteronomy 21:22–23 required Jews to remove corpses of the hanged and crucified prior to sunset, "late" means just before sunset. **Then Pilate commanded** [the body] **to be given back** [to Joseph]. **⁵⁹And on taking the body, Joseph wrapped it in a clean linen cloth ⁶⁰and put it in his new tomb, which he'd hewn in the rock; and on rolling a large stone to the door of the tomb** [to block entrance], **he went away. ⁶¹But Mary Magdalene and the other Mary** [see 27:56] **were sitting there opposite the tomb.** Jesus' burial in the tomb of "a rich man" fulfills Isaiah 53:9, where we read concerning the suffering Servant of the Lord, "His grave was assigned [to be] . . . with a rich [man] in his death." "Also" makes Joseph "a disciple of Jesus" alongside the just-mentioned women. "Himself" underlines

Joseph's discipleship. The resumption of Joseph by "this [man]" puts him forward as a good example of devotion to Jesus. Pilate's commanding Jesus' body to be given Joseph, and doing so "then"—that is, on the spot, without investigation—agrees with Pilate's having declared Jesus righteous and himself innocent of Jesus' blood (27:24); and "to be given *back*" indicates a return of the body to someone to whom it rightfully belongs, that is, to a disciple who'll treat the body respectfully. The taking of Jesus' body avoids the indignity of its hanging on a cross overnight and throughout the Sabbath. So too do its being wrapped in a linen cloth and placed in a tomb. For Romans normally forbade a proper burial of those executed like Jesus under a charge of high treason (in his case as "king of the Jews" in opposition to Caesar). Matthew describes the linen cloth as "clean," and the tomb as "new." Thus the ritual purity of the shroud and tomb displays Joseph's respect for the body of Jesus. Adding devotion to respect is Matthew's saying that Joseph himself hewed the tomb in rock, or had it hewn in rock on his behalf. "*The* rock" associates the tomb with the tombs in the rocks where earlier righteous people had been buried (27:51b–53). This association helps the application of Joseph's burying Jesus to the devotion of Christians toward their fellows victimized by persecution (compare 14:12; 25:34–40) and also presages the resurrection of Jesus after the pattern of those earlier ones' resurrection. Tombs hewn in rock had shelves on which wrapped corpses were laid. Matthew's description of the entrance-blocking stone as "large" enhances Joseph's effort to make sure the tomb containing Jesus' body wouldn't be violated. Joseph's going away provides a foil for the vigil of the two Marys, who sit opposite the tomb. "There" emphasizes that they stay for a vigil, which like Joseph's treatment of Jesus' body exemplifies ministerial devotion to the persecuted, a devotion that true discipleship requires (compare 10:41–42; 25:41–46). The temptation is always to dissociate from the persecuted and martyred in order to avoid persecution yourself, as illustrated in Peter's disownings of Jesus (26:69–75).

A CONTRAST BETWEEN THE JEWISH AUTHORITIES' DECEITFULNESS AND JESUS' TRUTHFULNESS
Matthew 27:62–66

This passage, unique to Matthew, prepares for a complementary passage, likewise unique, in 28:11–15. Together, these passages draw a contrast between the deceitfulness of the Jewish authorities in trying to squelch a report of Jesus' resurrection and the truthfulness of Jesus in having predicted his resurrection after three days. Such truthfulness gives encouragement to his persecuted followers. They have reason to trust his word and have confidence for like vindication.

27:62–64: And the next day, which as such is after the Preparation [= Friday, so-called because preparation was made on Friday before sunset for cessation of work till sunset on Saturday, the Sabbath], **the chief priests and the Pharisees gathered together to Pilate,** [63]**saying, "Sir, we remembered that that deceiver said while he was still living, 'After three days I'm being raised.'** [64]**So command the tomb to be secured till the third day lest his disciples, on coming, steal him and tell the people, 'He has been raised from the dead,' and the last deception be worse than the first** [deception]**."** The chief priests and Pharisees make their request on Saturday. But instead of calling that day the Sabbath, Matthew writes "the *next* day, which *as such* is after the Preparation [Friday]" to highlight the succession of days that will eventuate in the resurrection of Jesus on Sunday, "the first [day] of the week" (28:1), and thus in the fulfillment of his predictions that he'd be resurrected "on the third day" after being killed (16:21, for example). But the chief priests and Pharisees quote Jesus as saying, "After three days I'm being raised." The request for security at Jesus' tomb "*till* the third day" shows, however, that "*after* three days" doesn't extend the period beyond the third day. Otherwise security would be requested for more than three days. So "after three days" is equivalent to "on the third day." On the other hand, "after three days" reflects 12:40, where Jesus told the scholars and Pharisees that "the Son of Man will be in the heart of the earth for three days and three nights" (see the comments on 12:40 that "for three days and three nights" doesn't contradict "on the third day"). Here in chapter 27 the chief priests and Pharisees say they remembered that statement (compare Peter's remembering Jesus' prediction concerning him [26:75]). The past tense of "remembered" looks back to their formulating the request for security shortly before submitting the request. They correctly interpret Jesus' statement, the only one of its kind spoken to others than the Twelve, in terms of resurrection. The present tense in "I'm being raised" emphasizes the imminence of Jesus' resurrection once the period of three days starts. In submitting their request, the chief priests and Pharisees address Pilate with "Sir." But "Sir" goes back to the same word otherwise translated "owner," "master," and "Lord." Because of its frequent use for Jesus in the sense "Lord," there's irony in the chief priests' and Pharisees' using this word for Pilate in one breath and in the next breath calling Jesus "that deceiver." When Jesus was still alive, they should have addressed *him* with "Lord" and *believed* what he said. "*That* deceiver" implies he's dead and gone. "The *last* deception" refers to a possible crowning deception of the general populace by Jesus' disciples, who but for a securing of the tomb might steal his body and say he'd been resurrected. The implied first deception probably has to do with the crowds' being convinced that Jesus was the messianic "son of David" (21:9). But nonspecification of the first deception leaves the accent solely on the danger of his disciples' deceiving the people that he was raised from the dead.

27:65–66: Pilate told them, "Have a guardsquad. Go. Secure [the tomb] **as** [well as] **you know** [how]**."**

Matthew introduces Pilate's response abruptly, as though Pilate knows that securing Jesus' tomb won't keep him from being raised. "As [well as] you know [how]" supports this inference by casting doubt on the success of securing it. The chief priests had temple guards at their disposal. But to use them the chief priests wouldn't have had to make a request to Pilate; nor would they later need to shield them from Pilate's anger for failure at guard duty, for their own guards weren't answerable to him (28:14). So "Have a guardsquad" means that Pilate is providing them with guards. **⁶⁶And they, on going with the guardsquad, secured the tomb by sealing the stone** [with which Joseph of Arimathea had blocked the entrance (27:60; compare Daniel 6:17)]. Since the chief priests and Pharisees secure Jesus' tomb by sealing it and setting the gaurdsquad, the upcoming opening of the tomb by an angel of the Lord (28:2) will utterly discredit those Jewish authorities.

THE RESURRECTION OF JESUS AS A DEMONSTRATION OF HIS DEITY AND TRUTHFULNESS
Matthew 28:1–10

28:1–2: And later than the Sabbath, as [night] **was twilighting into the first** [day] **of the week, Mary Magdalene and the other Mary** [see 27:56 with comments] **came to view the tomb** [that is, to renew the vigil they'd started late Good Friday afternoon (27:61)]. Why doesn't Matthew write simply, as we read in Mark 16:2, "And very early in the morning on the first [day] of the week"? Well, by mentioning the Sabbath even though it ended at sundown on Saturday, by using an unusual "later than the Sabbath" rather than the expected "after the Sabbath," and by expanding "very early in the morning on the first [day] of the week" into "as [night] was twilighting into the first [day] of the week," Matthew renews his emphasis on the succession of days that now eventuates in the resurrection of Jesus as a fulfillment of his predictions that he'd be resurrected "on the third day" (compare the comments on 27:62). **²And behold, a great quaking took place; for an angel of the Lord, on coming down out of heaven and approaching** [the tomb], **rolled away the stone and was sitting on it.** "Behold, a great quaking took place" matches a statement in 8:24. Only there the quaking took place "in the sea." Here we have an earthquake. Both quakings accompany manifestations of Jesus' majesty, though, earlier in the stilling of a storm at sea, now in resurrection. To highlight his majesty, "behold" punctuates the quakings and "great" intensifies them (compare Exodus 19:18; Judges 5:5; Psalm 68:7–8). The present quaking reprises the recent earthquake that split open the rocky tombs at the resurrection of sacred people from the past (27:51b–53). But this time not only is the quaking "great," but also an angel of the Lord opens the tomb where Jesus has been lying. The angel's rolling away the stone, previously described as "large" (27:60), causes the earthquake. As in 1:20, 24; 2:13, 19–20, the angel gives both an expla-

nation and instructions. "Out of heaven" points to their divine origin. "Rolled away the stone" exposes the tomb's emptiness. And "was sitting on it [the stone]" indicates there's nothing more for the angel to do except for giving the explanation and instructions.

28:3–7: And his appearance was like lightning [that is, flashing brightly (compare Daniel 10:6)], **and his clothing** [was] **white like snow** [compare Daniel 7:9]. **⁴And from fear of him** [compare Daniel 10:7] **the** [guards] **keeping watch** [over the tomb] **were quaked** [as the earth had been quaked!] **and became like dead** [men (compare 27:54)]. In an ironic reversal Jesus has sprung to life while the guards, shaken like the earth itself, drop to the ground as if dead. The several allusions to Daniel, a book heavy with astonishing revelations, suit the astonishing revelation of Jesus' resurrection. **⁵And answering** [= responding, since no question has been asked], **the angel told the women, "You—don't be afraid. For I know that you're seeking Jesus, the crucified one. ⁶He isn't here. For he has been raised, just as he said** [he'd be]. **Here! See the place where he was lying. ⁷And on going quickly, tell his disciples** [the Eleven according to 28:16], **'He has been raised from the dead. And behold, he's going ahead of you into Galilee. You'll see him there.' Behold, I've told you."** Since the women have already arrived by the time the angel descends, the angel responds to the guards' becoming like dead men. But dead-like men can't hear; so the angel speaks to the women in view of what has happened to those guards. Since fear has seized the guards, the angel tells the women not to fear. The emphatic "You—" distinguishes them sharply from the guards. The guards had reason to fear. The women don't. The reason they don't is that the angel knows they're seeking Jesus, not as the guards, who were securing the tomb to keep disciples from stealing Jesus' body. But chapter 28 opened with a statement that the women came "to view the tomb." The angel's adding that they're seeking Jesus therefore implies that their vigil has the purpose of awaiting his resurrection, as a result of which they would see him. But he's already on his way to Galilee. Pilate's skepticism has proved prescient (27:65).

The angel calls Jesus "the crucified one" for a foil against which the announcement that he has already been raised will stand out in bold relief. No theft was needed, for his predictions of resurrection on the third day after crucifixion have been fulfilled (16:21; 17:22–23; 20:18–19). Despite the Jewish authorities' having called him "that deceiver" (27:63), his word has proved true. The soldiers had been guarding the tomb; and the angel, frightful in appearance, has kept the women from approaching close enough to look inside. So the angel says, "Here! See the place where he was lying." "Where he was lying" provides another foil, this time for a contrast not only with the resurrection of Jesus (literally, his "standing up") but also with his "going ahead . . . into Galilee" in fulfillment of his prediction in 26:32. As emphasized by "behold," he's on the move, no longer lying motionless. And since he's presently on his way, the disciples need to get started on their own way to Galilee. Otherwise they'll miss seeing him there. Hence the angel's instruction that the women go "quickly" to inform the disciples. The statement, "He has been raised from the dead," matches 27:64 exactly. But there the statement occurred on the lips of the Jewish authorities for what they said would be spread as a *false* rumor *by* the disciples. Here the statement is to occur on the lips of the women in a *true* report *to* the disciples. Over against "the place *where* he was lying" stands the prediction, "You'll see him *there* [in Galilee]," which the angel adds to Jesus' prediction that he'd go ahead of the disciples into Galilee (26:32). "I've told you" refers to the angel's having told the women, and another "Behold" stresses the importance of his instructions to the women and of the message they're to pass on to the disciples.

28:8–10: And on quickly going away from the tomb with fear and great joy, they ran to report to his [Jesus'] disciples. ⁹And behold, Jesus met them, saying, "Hail!" And they, on approaching, seized his feet and worshiped him. ¹⁰Then Jesus tells them, "Don't be afraid. Go report to my brothers that they should go away into Galilee. And they'll see me there." "And *quickly* going away" shows the women's wasting no time to obey the angel's instructions. Despite his having told them not to fear, though, their fear lingers. But it's a godly fear mixed with joy. Given the news of Jesus' resurrection, Matthew describes the joy as "great" (compare the comments on 2:10). Not only do the women leave the tomb quickly. They proceed to run for the purpose of reporting to the disciples as soon as possible. But Jesus interrupts their running by meeting them on their way. They don't meet him. He meets them. For their vigil at his crucifixion and at the tomb, contrasting with the disciples' flight from Gethsemane, makes them deserve at his initiative the first sight of him as resurrected (contrast the disciples' having to go to Galilee for the sight of him). "Behold" highlights Jesus' initiative. The common greeting "Hail!" means "Rejoice!" But in 26:49 Judas hypocritically told Jesus to rejoice while giving Jesus over to be killed, and in 27:29 soldiers mockingly told Jesus to rejoice while preparing to crucify him. Now it's Jesus' turn to say "Rejoice!" but to do so without hypocrisy or mockery. The women already had "great joy." So Jesus' telling them to rejoice confirms that they have good reason for such joy. He was seized by his enemies to do away with him (21:46; 26:4, 48, 50, 55, 57). But these women seize his feet. Doing so requires them to bend down before him in the posture of worship, quite a different kind of seizing. "They . . . worshiped him" recalls his deity (compare especially 2:11; 14:33). "Then" relates his telling them not to fear to their worship of him. His worshipers have nothing to fear from him. Their great joy needs no admixture of fear. The present tense of "tells" underscores this assurance, and also the following instruction, both of which reiterate in part what the angel told them. The abruptness of "Go report" adds further emphasis to the instruction. Jesus' plaintive cry of abandonment on the cross (27:46) echoed the language of Psalm 22:1. But the

triumphant instruction that the women "report to [his] brothers" now echoes the language of Psalm 22:22. What a difference between these two echoes! The reference to the disciples as Jesus' brothers revives the portrayal of the church as a brotherhood of those who do the will of his heavenly Father (see especially 12:48–50, but also the comments on 1:2). "And they will see me there" looks like a statement made to the women. So it is. But since it's also part of what they should report to the disciples, Jesus shifts from a command to a prediction that echoes what the angel has already told the women. But whereas the angel told the women to report his statement that Jesus had been raised from the dead, Jesus doesn't have to tell them to do so. They've seen him for themselves.

A CONTRAST BETWEEN THE JEWISH AUTHORITIES' DECEITFULNESS AND JESUS' TRUTHFULNESS CONTINUED
Matthew 28:11–15

This passage completes the story begun in 27:62–66.

28:11–15: But as they [the women] were going [in obedience now to Jesus' as well as the angel's command (28:7, 10)], behold, some of the guardsquad, on going into the city, reported to the chief priests all the things that had happened. ¹²And on gathering together with the elders and taking counsel [= consulting with one another], they gave a considerable sum of silver coins to the soldiers, ¹³saying, "Say that his disciples, on coming during the night, stole him while we were sleeping. ¹⁴And if this [matter] should be aired before the governor, we'll persuade [him not to have you executed for failure at guard duty] and make you worry-free." ¹⁵And they [the soldiers], on taking the silver coins, did as they'd been taught [by the chief priests and elders]. And this word [= this false report that the disciples had stolen Jesus' body] has been publicized among Jews till today. "Behold" highlights the parallel between the women's going to tell the disciples about Jesus' resurrection and the going of guards to tell the chief priests and elders about it. The women were only two (28:1). So "*some* of the guardsquad" tightens the parallel by lessening any disparity between the number of the women and that of the soldiers. The chief priests and elders have no excuse for their unbelief. From unprejudiced eyewitnesses (some of the guardsquad) they now know that Jesus has indeed been raised from the dead, that the sign of Jonah, which he promised to give the scholars and Pharisees (12:38–40), has now been given. Furthermore, the soldiers' report included "*all* the things that had happened." So the chief priests' and elders' unbelief runs counter to full information as well as unprejudiced eyewitness. (The soldiers report to them because of Pilate's having put the guardsquad at the Jewish authorities' disposal.) And just as the chief priests and elders took counsel to kill Jesus in 27:1, here they take counsel to kill the news that he's alive again. The bribery of the soldiers exposes the Jewish authorities' lack of honesty, and the large size of the sum it took to silence the soldiers argues for the truth of Jesus' resurrection and the falsity of the rumor concocted by those authorities and about to be circulated by the soldiers. Moreover, "the considerable sum of silver coins" given the soldiers contrasts with the paltry sum of thirty silver coins given Judas Iscariot to betray Jesus (see the comment on 26:14–16). By paying more to the soldiers than they did to Judas, the Jewish authorities show greater concern to squelch the news of Jesus' resurrection than they did to get him killed. Well they might! How the governor is to be persuaded, if he hears, remains unstated. But the promise to persuade him and keep the soldiers worry-free brings to a climax Matthew's portrayal of the Jewish authorities as deceptive. Yet they had the gall to call Jesus "that deceiver" (27:63)! And they're the ones who are worried even as they promise to make the soldiers worry-free. The statement that the soldiers "did as they'd been *taught*" describes the chief priests' and elders' instruction as deceptive, false teaching over against Jesus' teaching, which they themselves had described as true (22:16). Matthew also calls the chief priests' and elders' teaching "this word" as opposed to Jesus' "word" about the kingdom of heaven (13:19–23).

THE MISSION TO ALL NATIONS AND RELATED MATTHEAN THEMES
Matthew 28:16–20

This paragraph contains a compendium of important Matthean themes: Jesus as the greater Moses, the deity of Jesus, the authority of his commands, the trinitarian associations of baptism, the danger of doubt among disciples, their ministry of teaching, discipleship as obeying Jesus' commands, the presence of Jesus with his disciples, and the directing of Christian hope to the consummation. Paramount among these themes, however, is the mission to all nations.

28:16–17: And the eleven disciples [Judas Iscariot having committed suicide] **went into Galilee to the mountain where Jesus had given them instructions.** The disciples' going implies the women's having completed the mission they started in 28:8. [17]**And on seeing him, they worshiped** [him]**; but some** [of them] **doubted** [that they were seeing a resurrected Jesus]. The mountain in Galilee where Jesus had given the disciples instructions is the mountain where Jesus gave his Sermon on the Mount, full as it was of instructions on how disciples should conduct themselves (chapters 5–7). He'll go on to mention those instructions as what the current disciples are to teach future disciples. So the present portrayal of Jesus as a legislator on the mountain revives the parallel between him and Moses, who also legislated from a mountain (Sinai). On the other hand, the disciples' worshiping Jesus—that is, kneeling and bowing their heads to the ground—points to his deity as well. But there are doubters even among the eleven worshipers. Alarmingly, doubt can coexist with worship. We

might be tempted to think this doubt exhibits a healthy absence of gullibility. But given the doubters' seeing Jesus for themselves after hearing the women's report, Matthew wants us to recognize in the doubt of some an unhealthy shortfall of faith. They have little faith (see 14:31 for the connection between doubt and little faith, there in Peter's case—here too? [compare the comments on 26:70, and see also 17:20 for little faith as smaller than that smallest of all seeds, the mustard seed]).

28:18–20: And on approaching [them], **Jesus spoke to them, saying, "All authority in heaven and on earth has been given to me.** [19]**On going, therefore, disciple all nations by baptizing them** [the people making up the nations] **in the name of the Father and of the Son and of the Holy Spirit** [20]**and by teaching them to keep** [= obey] **all things, as many as they are, that I've commanded you. And behold, I am with you all the days till the consummation of the age** [compare Daniel 12:13]**."** Usually others approach Jesus. But because the disciples are kneeling on the ground in worship, he approaches them. His claim to have been given all authority *in heaven* as well as on earth contrasts with the Devil's having offered to give him "all the kingdoms *of the world* and their glory" if only he'd fall down and worship the Devil (4:8–9 [compare Daniel 7:14]). "Therefore" makes this claim of universal authority the basis for the Great Commission. The passages 7:29; 9:8; 11:27; 21:23 show that Jesus has had such authority all along. But the present passage confirms that authority and lifts geographical restrictions on his exercise of it. "All nations" corresponds to "all authority." No nation lies outside the sphere of Jesus' authority, and therefore nobody is exempt from the obligations to follow his example of getting baptized (see 3:13–15 with comments) and to learn and keep his commands. To include Gentiles as well as Jews, the present commission expands the earlier commission to go only to "the lost sheep of the house of Israel" (10:5–6; but see previews of the expansion in 2:1–12; 4:24; 8:5–13; 10:22; 15:21–28; 20:1–16; 22:1–10 and Matthew's bringing Gentile women into the genealogy of Jesus, a descendant of Abraham, through whose seed God promised that all nations of the earth would be blessed [1:1–3, 5–6; Genesis 22:18; compare Genesis 12:3]). To disciple all nations requires going to them; and by definition, discipling means to make learners. Since learning includes doing as well as understanding, Jesus stresses obedience to his commands.

Baptism is the rite of initiation into Jesus' school. Baptism in the name of the Father, Son, and Holy Spirit puts a trinitarian cast on this baptism, especially in that all three are included in "the name," and thus highlights Jesus' deity by sandwiching "the Son" between "the Father" and "the Holy Spirit." "In the name of" indicates acceptance that God is both Jesus' and your Father, that Jesus is his Son in an unrivaled sense, and that the Holy Spirit (not Beelzebul [12:22–28]!) empowered Jesus. As a whole, the trinitarian formula distinguishes this baptism from John's baptism, which had to do only with repentance in view of the soon coming of the kingdom of heaven (3:1–12). "All things . . . that I've commanded you" links up with "as many as they are" to underline the obligation of complete obedience (compare Exodus 7:2; Deuteronomy 1:3; 30:8; Joshua 1:7; Jeremiah 1:7). "Behold" underscores Jesus' presence with the disciples wherever they go throughout the inhabited earth in fulfilling their commission (compare 24:14). He won't be physically present with them, as he has been heretofore, but he'll be with them in the way the Lord was with his people to help them in the past (compare 18:20; Genesis 26:24; 28:15; Exodus 3:12; Joshua 1:5, 9; Judges 6:12, 16 and so on) and in this sense will continue to be "Immanuel . . . God [is] with us" (1:23). (So as not to call such presence into question, Matthew omits an account of Jesus' ascension to heaven, though the return from heaven in 10:23; 16:28; 24:30; 26:64 implies an ascension.) In line with the deity of Jesus, his "I" in "I am with you" replaces "God" in the echo of "God [is] with us." "All the days" assures the disciples of Jesus' uninterrupted presence and implies an extended period of time such as a worldwide making of disciples will take. "Till the consummation of the age" assures the disciples of Jesus' untruncated presence. They'll need it especially throughout the time of unprecedented affliction just before the second coming (24:15–30).

Note: It is possible that we should translate with "all the Gentiles" rather than with "all nations." Even so, 10:23 indicated a mission to Israel that continues till the second coming. Given "all the Gentiles," 25:31–46 would describe a judgment of Gentiles (for the same phrase occurs there); and 19:28 would supplement their judgment by the Son of Man with the apostles' judgment of "the twelve tribes of Israel." Either way, everybody is included.

MARK

Reserved mainly for slaves and criminals being treated as slaves, crucifixion was considered the most shameful of deaths. This Gospel therefore counters the shame of Jesus' crucifixion by showcasing his power to perform miracles, cast out demons, teach authoritatively, best his opponents in debate, attract crowds, and predict the future (including his own death and resurrection). According to very early church tradition Mark, a sometime companion of the apostles Peter and Paul, wrote the Gospel and got his information about Jesus from Peter. Since Peter didn't associate with Jesus till their adulthoods, then, the Gospel starts not with Jesus' birth but with the beginning of his public ministry, introduced as it was by John the baptizer (not to be confused with the apostle John).

JOHN'S PREDICTING A MORE POWERFUL BAPTIZER THAN HE
Mark 1:1–8

1:1–3: The beginning of the gospel of Jesus Christ, God's Son, ²according as it's written in Isaiah the prophet, "Behold, I'm sending my messenger before your face [= ahead of you], **who'll pave your way** [= the road you'll travel], ³[the messenger who is] **the voice of one crying out in the wilderness, 'Prepare the way of the Lord. Make his paths straight.'"** "Gospel" means "good news." Jews would associate this good news with Isaiah 52:7: "How lovely on the mountains are the feet of him who brings good news, who announces peace and brings good news of happiness, who announces salvation, [and] says to Zion, 'Your God reigns.'" Non-Jews would think of the good news of an emperor's accession to power, birthday, visit to a city, military victory, or bringing of prosperity to the empire. But Mark's good news has to do with the salvation and victory brought by Jesus over evil in all its demonic and physical forms. "The gospel *of* Jesus Christ" therefore means "the gospel *about* Jesus Christ" and refers to a proclaimed message ("the *voice* of one *crying out*"), not a book (though because books like Mark's contain that proclaimed message, the term came to refer to those books in the capitalized form of "Gospels" to distinguish them from the message, kept uncapitalized as "gospel"). "Jesus" is a personal name, the Greek spelling of the Hebrew name "Joshua." "Christ" is a title, meaning "anointed one" in the sense of "someone divinely appointed for a task." It's the Greek equivalent of the Hebrew "Messiah," which has the same meaning. Somewhere along the line this title "Christ" evolved

into another personal name for Jesus. By itself, "God's Son" doesn't have to connote deity. The term occurs elsewhere for angels and ordinary kings, for example. But as this Gospel progresses, no doubt will remain that Mark means us to understand that as God's Son, Jesus is indeed divine.

"The *beginning* of the gospel . . ." takes place "*according as* it's written" in the following Old Testament quotation, which Mark applies to the introductory ministry of John. So this beginning covers John's ministry in 1:2–8 and no more. The agreement of his ministry with the quotation shows that God, who stands behind the writing of "the prophet," is working out his plan. Mark names Isaiah as the prophet, and indeed 1:3 contains the text of Isaiah 40:3. But in 1:2 "Behold, I'm sending my messenger before your face" comes from Exodus 23:20, and "who'll pave your way" comes from Malachi 3:1. Never mind, though. Isaiah deserved mention for providing the bulk of the quotation. God is the "I" who sends John as his "messenger" ahead of "you," who is Jesus Christ. In Exodus 23:20 the messenger is an angel, and "you" is the nation of Israel. In Malachi 3:1 God is the one whose way is paved. And in Isaiah 40:3 "the Lord" is God. So using acceptable literary license, Mark changes some of these referents to make his quotation apply variously to God, John, and Jesus. God sees to it that someone prepares for his Son's journey onto the public stage. As is fitting for so high a dignitary as the Christ, God's Son, the Lord, the road he travels onto that stage needs to be paved, clear, and straight—easily traveled, not like the twisting roads in hilly, mountainous Israel.

1:4–5: There came on the scene John, the one who was baptizing in the wilderness and preaching a baptism of repentance for the forgiveness of sins. ⁵And all the Judean region and all the Jerusalemites were going out to him and getting baptized by him in the Jordan River as they were confessing their sins. John's coming on the scene matches the sending of God's messenger in 1:2. Baptizing matches paving the way of the Lord, also in 1:2. The wilderness here matches the wilderness there. John's preaching matches the shouting of a voice in 1:3. And the baptism of repentance matches preparing the Lord's way and straightening his paths. A wilderness was by and large devoid of human population, but not necessarily of vegetation. There was, in fact, plenty of vegetation along the Jordan River. The sparsity of human population highlights by contrast the going of "all the Judean region and all the Jerusalemites" to John to have him baptize them. "The Judean region" stands for its inhabitants. The first "all" emphasizes the wide extent of this region and joins the second "all" to emphasize the large number who came to be baptized. This large number anticipates the even larger numbers of people whom Jesus will attract to himself. The references to Judea and Jerusalem, which was located in Judea (the southern part of Israel), imply that John was baptizing toward the southern end of the Jordan River, close to where it empties into the Dead Sea. Baptism represented the washing away of sins. Flowing water, such as that of the Jordan River, was especially suited to represent such a washing; and the very word "forgiveness" means a "sending away" that separates sin from the sinner. This separation indicates why Mark has called John's ministry "the beginning of the *good* news." In and of itself, baptism didn't result in the forgiveness of sins. It was repentance that did. Repentance led to baptism; and confession of sins accompanied baptism to verbalize the repentance, which means a change of mind that results in a change of behavior. The people didn't baptize themselves. To have done so would have symbolized self-cleansing and self-forgiveness (much as in some contemporary psychology). As a messenger of God, John baptized people to symbolize *God's* cleansing them and forgiving their sins.

1:6–8: And John was clothed with camel's hair and [had] a leather belt around his waist and was eating locusts and wild honey. ⁷And he was preaching, saying, "The one [who's] stronger than I is coming after me, the strap of whose sandals I'm not worthy, bending down, to loosen. ⁸I've baptized you with water, but he'll baptize you in the Holy Spirit." John was no city-slicker. His clothing and diet carry forward the preceding theme of a wilderness and characterize him as a prophet in the mold of Elijah, whose return was predicted in Malachi 4:5 (see 2 Kings 1:8 for a similar description of the Old Testament Elijah). The one who's coming after John is Jesus. "After" has a spatial meaning, "behind," and a temporal meaning, "subsequent to." Spatially, Jesus will follow as a disciple behind John to the extent of submitting to John's baptism. Temporally, Jesus will follow John by starting his ministry later than John's. John attracted all the Judean region and all the Jerusalemites and got them to submit to the baptism of repentance. So if Jesus will be stronger than John, he must be very, very strong. And John's unworthiness to perform even the extremely menial task of bending down and loosening Jesus' sandal strap adds yet more to the description of Jesus as stronger. Still further, Jesus' upcoming baptism of people in the Holy Spirit contrasts favorably with John's currently baptizing them with mere water. This contrast puts an exclamation mark on Jesus' greater strength, particularly because the Spirit connotes power (as in Acts 1:8, to take but one example: "you'll receive power when the Holy Spirit comes on you"). The Spirit will enter Jesus at his baptism in 1:9–11, so that he'll exercise power in preaching, teaching, casting out demons, healing the sick, raising the dead, and even (as we'll see) in dying as a ransom for people, not

to mention rising from the dead. In Mark's Gospel it's these very activities—not a later imparting of the Holy Spirit as in Luke-Acts, for example—that will constitute Jesus' baptizing people in the Holy Spirit (see especially Mark 3:20–30).

GOD'S EMPOWERMENT, ACKNOWLEDGMENT, AND APPROVAL OF JESUS
Mark 1:9–11

1:9–11: And it happened during those days that Jesus came from Nazareth of Galilee, and he was baptized by John into the Jordan. ¹⁰And immediately, while coming up out of the water, he saw heaven being split apart and the Spirit descending like a dove [and coming] **into him. ¹¹And a voice came from heaven: "You're my beloved Son; I've taken delight in you."** "Those days" refers to the beginning of the good news during John's ministry. The village of Nazareth contrasts with the allusion to the city of Jerusalem in 1:5, and Galilee (up north) contrasts with Judea (down south) also in 1:5. Mark doesn't say that anyone besides Jesus came from Galilee to be baptized. As the lone Galilean to do so, then, Jesus differs from "all the Judean region and all the Jerusalemites" that went out to John. Thus the spotlight now shines on Jesus. His coming to John for baptism fulfills the spatial meaning of "after me" in John's prediction of a coming stronger one (see the comments on 1:7, and 1:14 for the start of Jesus' ministry as the fulfillment of an additional, temporal meaning in "after me"). Jesus' doesn't confess any sins as he's being baptized (contrast the people in 1:5). His silence is eloquent; for replacing a confession are God's empowering him with the Spirit, acknowledging him as his beloved Son, and declaring his delight in him—all because Jesus has no sins to confess. The immediacy of God's acting thus and of Jesus' seeing heaven being split apart and the Spirit descending into him underscores the divine actions that replace a confession of sins. Heaven is split apart by the Spirit's descent (compare Isaiah 64:1). The descent is like the downward flight of a dove. This comparison suits a dove's being the only bird fit for sacrifice under the Jewish law (Leviticus 1:14). It also suits the dove's being considered a divine bird by pagans. The Spirit's splitting heaven apart signifies the power of the Spirit, and his entering into Jesus empowers Jesus for his ministry as John's coming stronger one (1:7–8). Jesus' *seeing* heaven being split apart and the Spirit descending into him makes him aware of his empowerment by the Spirit. To strengthen Jesus' awareness, audition is then added to sight. A voice comes. It comes from heaven because it's the voice of God the Father, who dwells there. "You're my Son" confirms the identification of Jesus Christ as "God's Son" in 1:1 and echoes Psalm 2:7, to which God adds "beloved" to blend affection with acknowledgment. "I've taken delight in you" echoes Isaiah 42:1 and adds approval to acknowledgment and affection. Whatever happens to Jesus from now on, then, we can be sure that God is on his side.

ACKNOWLEDGMENTS OF JESUS' STATUS AS GOD'S SON BY SATAN, WILD BEASTS, AND ANGELS
Mark 1:12–13

1:12–13: And immediately the Spirit thrusts him out into the wilderness. [13]And in the wilderness he was being tempted by Satan for forty days; and he was with wild beasts; and angels were serving him. The immediacy of the Spirit's thrusting Jesus out into the wilderness confirms and stresses Jesus' infusion with the Spirit. The present tense of "thrusts" adds to the emphasis. But since Jesus was baptized in the Jordan River, he was already in a wilderness. So "into the wilderness" means into the nearby wilderness of Judean mountains. Mark's repeating the theme of wilderness calls attention to Jesus' being alone there with Satan, wild beasts, and angels. That Satan, "the ruler of the demons" according to 3:22, tempts Jesus as long as forty days constitutes a backhanded acknowledgment of Jesus as God's beloved Son. Satan can't afford to ignore Jesus. The content of Satan's prolonged temptation gets no mention. Neither does Jesus' resisting temptation. So Satan's backhanded acknowledgment of Jesus makes up Mark's one and only point. Mark doesn't say that the wild beasts were with Jesus; rather, Jesus was with them—in their territory. Yet even there he suffered no harm from them, not even an attack. Their passivity gives eloquent witness to his being the stronger one who John predicted was coming. And for forty days angels serve Jesus. The verb for serving usually means to serve food. By such service the angels acknowledge Jesus' status as the beloved Son of God. Furthermore, by serving him food the angels show him to be superior to the Baptist, who had to forage for himself in the wilderness. All in all, then, Jesus receives a backhanded such acknowledgment from the demonic realm, a pacifistic such acknowledgment from the wild kingdom, and a ministerial such acknowledgment from the angelic world.

THE STRONGER ONE'S ARRIVING ON THE SCENE
Mark 1:14–15

1:14–15: And after John was given over, Jesus went into Galilee preaching the gospel of God [15]and saying, "The time has been fulfilled, and the reign of God has drawn near. Repent and believe in the gospel [of God]." "Was given over" refers to John's arrest, resulting in imprisonment and execution (6:17–29), and sets up a parallel with Jesus' being "given over" to arrest and execution (9:31; 10:33; 14:21, 41). That Jesus goes from the Judean wilderness into Galilee to preach only after John was given over fulfills the temporal meaning of "after me" in John's prediction that one stronger than he was coming (1:7). "The gospel *of* God" means the good news *about* him. Its content consists in the fulfillment of time and the drawing near of God's reign. In other words, the appropriate time has come for the arrival of God's reign. (Here "kingdom," the traditional transla-

tion, has to do with the activity of reigning, not with the sphere in which this activity takes place.) As in 14:42–43, "has drawn near" means nearness as a result of arrival. It's here! And the nearness is spatial as well as temporal because God is about to reign in the person, presence, and activity of Jesus, the Spirit-empowered stronger one (compare 14:42–43 again, where the spatial nearness of Judas Iscariot marks the temporal nearness of his giving Jesus over to his enemies). Jesus' call to repentance matches John's (1:4). But Jesus' additional call to believe in the good news about God replaces John's baptism with water, because Jesus will baptize people in the Holy Spirit instead of water (1:8; see the comments on that verse for the meaning of Spirit-baptism in Mark). We could paraphrase: "Repent *because* the time has been fulfilled" and "Believe in the good news *because* God's reign has drawn near." Again, "the time has been fulfilled *with the result that* God's reign has drawn near" and "Repent *with the result of* believing in the good news."

THE FIRST EXHIBITION OF JESUS' POWER OF ATTRACTION
Mark 1:16–20

1:16–20: And while going along to the side of the Sea of Galilee, he [Jesus] saw Simon and Andrew, Simon's brother, casting [nets] in the sea; for they were fishermen. [17]And Jesus said to them, "[Come] here—behind me! And I'll make you become fishers of human beings." [18]And immediately leaving the nets, they followed him. [19]And on going a little farther, he saw James the [son] of Zebedee and John his brother, and [he saw] them in a boat preparing nets. [20]And he called them immediately; and leaving their father Zebedee in the boat with [his] hired hands, they came away behind him [Jesus]. This paragraph exhibits Jesus' power of attraction despite the lack of prior contact or present rationale in his command and call. Several items highlight this power: (1) the immediacy of Simon's and Andrew's leaving their nets, which immediacy demonstrates the overpowering authority of Jesus' command (contrast 1 Kings 19:19–21); (2) the immediacy of Jesus' calling James and John, which immediacy exhibits the constant activity of Jesus' power; (3) James' and John's leaving their father Zebedee in his boat despite the patriarchalism in that culture; (4) the sons' leaving Zebedee despite the hired hands' staying with him; (5) both pairs of brothers' going after Jesus in the thick of practicing their trade, casting nets in the first case and preparing them in the second—indeed without even hauling in the nets in the first case and without finishing the preparing of nets and casting them in the second case; (6) the addition of following Jesus to the leaving of nets; (7) the addition of coming away behind Jesus to the leaving of Zebedee (compare 10:28–30); and (8) Jesus' promising to make Simon and Andrew fish for human beings, a task much more difficult than fishing for fish (see 3:13–19; 6:7–13, 30 for the fulfillment of this promise through the disciples' healing the sick, delivering the demon-possessed, and getting people to repent and believe in the gospel of God). Preparing nets complements casting them and included cleaning, mending, and folding them. Unlike regular rabbis, Jesus chose his disciples—not they him. So powerful was his choice that despite their not looking for a rabbi to whom they might attach themselves, they couldn't help but follow Jesus. Following behind him showed him due respect and had the purpose of their learning from everything they heard him say and saw him do. Regular rabbis and their disciples kept up a trade to earn a living and otherwise led a sedentary life of study. Without difficulty, Jesus attracts his disciples to an itinerant life devoid of earnings.

JESUS' EXERCISE OF AUTHORITY IN TEACHING AND EXORCISM
Mark 1:21–28

1:21–22: And they [Jesus and his newfound disciples] **go into Capernaum** [on the northwest shore of the Sea of Galilee]. **And having entered the** [local] **synagogue on the Sabbath** [Saturday], **he immediately started teaching.** [22]**And they** [the audience] **were awestruck at his teaching, for he was teaching them as** [one] **having authority and not as the scholars** [taught]. "Immediately" stresses the quickness with which Jesus takes didactic charge in the synagogue. His authority widens from calling several disciples in 1:16–20 to teaching a general audience. Mark gives no indication whatever of the content of Jesus' teaching. He features only its authoritative manner and percussive effect (see also 6:2; 7:37; 10:26; 11:18). "Were awestruck" translates a verb whose literal meaning is to be knocked out. Obviously it carries a figurative meaning here, but a very strong one that underlines the authority with which Jesus taught. His exercise of this authority fulfills again John's announcement of a coming one stronger than he, one who by stunning his audience with his didactic authority was baptizing them in the Holy Spirit that had entered him at his baptism. The word for "scholars" is usually translated "scribes"; but in contemporary English, "scribes" tends to be limited to copyists. Copying the text of the Old Testament made copyists expert in its contents, so that "scribes" developed the meaning of "scholars" even apart from the practice of copying. In 7:1–13 Jesus will contrast God's commandment with scholarly tradition. This contrast suggests that the scholars supported their teachings by citing the opinions of past scholars (as happens in rabbinic tradition). But here in chapter 1 Mark is content simply to pit Jesus' authoritative teaching against the unauthoritive teaching of scholars.

1:23–26: And immediately in their synagogue there was a man with an unclean spirit; and he yelled out, [24]**saying, "What do we and you have to do with each other, Jesus of Nazareth? You've come to destroy us. I know you,** [that is,] **who you are.** [You're] **God's Holy One."** [25]**And Jesus reprimanded him, saying, "Be muzzled and come out of him."** [26]**And convulsing him** [the man] **and screaming with a loud scream, the unclean spirit came out of him.** Just as in 1:21 "immedi-

ately" stressed the quickness with which Jesus exercised didactic authority, so here "immediately" stresses the quickness with which he exercises authority over an unclean spirit. Mark calls the spirit "unclean" to contrast him with the Holy Spirit that entered Jesus at his baptism, that constituted Jesus as "God's Holy One," and that empowered him to call disciples effectively, to teach in the synagogue authoritatively, and now to exorcise the unclean spirit. Since "spirit" connotes power, as evident in this spirit's control of a man, we have a contest shaping up. Who'll win? Who has the greater power? The unclean spirit is speaking through the man; but "we" and "us" refer not to the unclean spirit and the man—rather, to the unclean spirit and others like it. For Jesus came to *deliver* demoniacs, not to destroy them along with their demons. So a defeat of this unclean spirit would portend the defeat of other unclean spirits too, whereas a victory by this unclean spirit would portend a defeat of the Spirit-filled Jesus by the others as well (compare 1:27).

The present unclean spirit mounts a defense—even an attack, since thus far Jesus hasn't tried to exorcise the spirit—in a couple of ways: (1) by asking what unclean spirits and he have to do with each other; in other words, by asking why Jesus is interfering with them; and (2) by exhibiting a knowledge of Jesus' personal name ("Jesus"), hometown ("Nazareth"), purpose in coming ("to destroy us [unclean spirits]"), and title ("God's Holy One"). Knowledge is power, and by exhibiting such manifold knowledge of Jesus, the unclean spirit thought to overcome him. (As a declaration, "You've come to destroy us" fits the spirit's maneuver; but even translated as a question, "Have you come to destroy us?" implies knowledge as well as fear of Jesus' purpose.) The switch from "we" and "us" to "I" brings the narrative back to the case of this individual spirit. "Be muzzled" means "Shut up!" But the passive voice of "Be muzzled" shows the muzzling to be, not an act of voluntary obedience, but an act imposed on the spirit by his superior, Jesus. In other words, Jesus defends himself by putting a stop to the spirit's attempt to control him. Then he goes on offense by telling the spirit to come out. The convulsing of the man and the spirit's screaming give visible and audible evidence of the effectiveness of Jesus' double reprimand. The convulsion shows the agony of the spirit's defeat, and the loudness of the scream shows how utter is its defeat.

1:27–28: And all were astounded, so that they discussed [the matter] **with one another saying, "What's this? A new teaching** [in that it's done] **with authority! He commands even the unclean spirits, and they obey him."** [28]**And immediately the news about him went out everywhere into the whole surrounding region of Galilee.** Every detail of the text piles emphasis on Jesus' authority: (1) the astonishment of the onlookers; (2) the universality of their astonishment ("all"); (3) the prompting of discussion by their astonishment; (4) the puzzlement prompted by it ("What's this?"); (5) the recognition of novelty in Jesus' teaching; (6) the authority that defines its novelty; (7) the equation of this authoritatively new teaching with an exorcistic command;

(8) the inference that this one exorcisim shows Jesus to be in command of other unclean spirits too; (9) their inferred obedience to his command; (10) their inferred obedience to his command despite their power over other human beings ("*even* the unclean spirits"); (11) the implication that he has been exorcising them all along even though here is the only instance thus far; (12) the immediacy with which the news about him goes out; (13) its going into the surrounding region of Galilee; (14) its going into the "whole" of that region; and (15) its not missing any part of the region—rather, its going "everywhere" in it. Mark puts exorcism under the rubric of teaching, then, to authenticate Jesus' didactic authority with Jesus' exorcistic authority.

JESUS' EXERCISE OF POWER OVER SICKNESS, DISEASE, AND DEMONS
Mark 1:29–34

Jesus, the one stronger than John, has proved so powerful as to have compelled men to leave their occupation and father, so powerful as to have outdone the scholars, so powerful as to have defeated a demonic force, and so powerful as to have become the talk of a whole territory. Now he'll prove so powerful as to heal the sick and diseased and cast out many demons, not just one.

1:29–31: And immediately on coming out of the synagogue, they [Jesus and his first four disciples] **went into the house of Simon and Andrew with James and John.** [30] **And Simon's mother-in-law was lying down, burning with a fever. And immediately they speak to him about her.** [31] **And on approaching** [her], **he raised her by grasping her hand. And the fever left her, and she started serving them** [food (compare 1:13)]. The first "immediately" shows that Mark can hardly wait to report Jesus' further exercise of a power exceeding that of John. The remention of Simon and Andrew, James and John—and especially of the latter pair, since the house they enter isn't their own—calls attention back to the effectiveness of Jesus' having called them. They're still following him. The lying down of Simon's mother-in-law shows the severity of her condition (compare 2:4). According to the custom of the day, she should have been serving the men food. But before modern medicine a fever threatened death (see John 4:46–54). So the immediacy of the disciples' reporting her condition to Jesus combines with the present tense in "they *speak* to him about her" to underline how desperate is her plight. But they don't ask him to heal her, because he hasn't given them any prior examples of healing. He takes the initiative, then, by approaching her and, without even saying a word, by grasping her hand and raising her. Given the threat of death it's almost as though Jesus raises her from the dead. The action of raising her with a grasp of her hand exhibits his strength and conveys it to her through a physically therapeutic baptism in the Holy Spirit. Her serving the men gives evidence not only of the fever's departure but also of her restoration to full health and vitality.

1:32–34: And after evening came, when the sun had set, people started bringing to him all who were sick and demon-possessed. [33] **And the whole city was gathered together at the door** [of Simon's and Andrew's house]. [34] **And he healed many who were sick with various diseases; and he cast out many demons; and he wasn't allowing the demons to speak, because they knew** [= recognized] **him.** For Jews the Sabbath ended at sunset on Saturday. So Mark's narrowing down "evening" to after sunset explains that people could bring their sick and demon-possessed, often having to carry them, without violating the prohibition of work on the Sabbath. That they started bringing them in the evening rather than waiting till the next morning magnifies the power of Jesus' attraction. "*All* who were sick and demon-possessed" shows his power to be limitless. Apparently his healing Simon's mother-in-law prompted the bringing of sick people, and his exorcising an unclean spirit in the local synagogue prompted the bringing of demoniacs. Word got around. That "the *whole* of the city was gathered at the door" adds further lustre to Jesus' magnetism. His healing "many" doesn't mean that he healed many but not all the sick who were brought to him. It means, rather, that the "all who were sick" and whom he healed were "many"—a further tribute to his power. The variety of their diseases heightens the tribute. Likewise, the demons he cast out were "many." Their outnumbering him poses no problem to his exercise of authority over them. "They knew him," just as the unclean spirit in 1:24 said by way of an attempt to thwart him, "I know you." And just as Jesus muzzled that unclean spirit, so he doesn't allow these demons to speak. Even with their knowledge of Jesus, they're defenseless. It may also be that he doesn't want them to publicize his identity lest such publicity cause such a crush of crowds as to hamper his going elsewhere to minister (see 1:35–39, 45; 3:7–12, 20; 4:1; 7:24; 9:30 among other passages).

JESUS' EXHIBITING MAGNETIC POWER AGAIN
Mark 1:35–45

1:35–38: And on getting up early in the morning, while it was very dark, he [Jesus] **went out** [of Capernaum and Simon's and Andrew's house there]. **And he went away** [from the crowd of 1:32–34] **into a deserted place, and he was praying there.** [36] **And Simon and those with him pursued him** [Jesus]. [37] **And they found him and say to him, "All** [the people] **are seeking you."** [38] **And he says to them, "Let's be going elsewhere,** [that is,] **into the surrounding market-towns, in order that I may preach there as well. For I came out** [of Capernaum] **for this purpose."** Mark shifts from evening after sunset in 1:32 to the following morning before sunrise. The piling up of two temporal expressions, "early in the morning" and "while it was . . . dark," and the intensification of "dark" with "very" show Jesus' magnetism to be so great that he must take an extreme measure to avoid the crowd that had gathered where he was staying. Showing the same is his going under cover of darkness to pray in "a deserted place." His magnetism is such that in populated locations the press of crowds would forestall praying. His praying complements 1:11. There God spoke to him. Here he speaks to God. They're in communion with each other. Jesus is no charlatan, no magician. He does what he does as the Spirit-empowered, beloved, and God-delighting Son of God. Mark leaves the point at that by not disclosing the content of Jesus' praying. Simon's companions are his brother Andrew and the brothers James and John. Their hunting Jesus down shows the continuing effectiveness of his calling them to follow after him. Their statement that all are seeking him reemphasizes his magnetism and its extent in Capernaum, and presumes that by this time the sun has risen and the disciples and townspeople have gotten up only to discover Jesus' absence. He ignores the townspeople's seeking him and tells the disciples, "Let's be going elsewhere." The present tense in "he *says* to them" emphasizes this determination to extend the reach of his powerful activity, in particular his preaching. As with Jesus' praying, Mark doesn't disclose the content of the preaching Jesus is determined to do (contrast 1:14–15). So the accent lies solely on the extension of Jesus' preaching. Thus also in the activity of preaching he proves himself the one stronger than John (compare 1:7).

1:39: And he went into the whole of Galilee, preaching in their synagogues and casting out demons. Preaching in their synagogues recalls and complements teaching in a synagogue at 1:21–28. So also does the casting out of demons, for 1:21–28 featured the exorcism of an unclean spirit. In 1:38 Jesus stated only his purpose to preach elsewhere. Like the exorcism in 1:21–28, then, the present exorcisms support the authority of his verbal ministry. Only here, the plurality of synagogues and "the *whole* of Galilee" extend the authority of his preaching and exorcisms over a much wider compass (compare 1:14, which lacked the emphatic "whole" and exorcisms, however).

Now Mark adds a miraculous cure to Jesus' powerful preaching and awe-inspiring exorcisms. The absence of details concerning time and place focuses attention on the cure as such. **1:40–42: And there comes to him a leper, imploring him and falling on his knees and saying to him, "If you're willing, you can cleanse me** [of my leprosy]." **41And feeling sorry** [for him], **stretching out** [his] **hand he touched him and says to him, "I'm willing. Be cleansed." 42And immediately the leprosy left him, and he was cleansed.** The word for leprosy covered various skin diseases in addition to Hansen's disease, to which "leprosy" currently refers. But the desperation of the man in this story—a desperation highlighted by the present tense of "comes"—favors Hansen's disease over comparatively minor diseases of the skin (though one could think of skin cancer). So let's stick tentatively with "leper" and "leprosy." People compared this disease to death itself, so that curing a leper seemed like raising the dead (see Numbers 12:9–12; 2 Kings 5:7). Yet Jesus has such power. It takes two expressions, "imploring him" and "falling on his knees," to convey the full measure

of this leper's desperation. It's only Jesus' willingness that stands in question, for the leper doesn't question Jesus' ability. In fact, he affirms it. And he doesn't ask for cleansing in so many words. So all the emphasis falls on "you *can* cleanse me." The cure is put in terms of cleansing because leprosy made its victims ritually unclean, so that they had to keep their distance from other people and warn them by yelling, "Unclean! Unclean!" against the possibility of ritual contamination through physical contact (Leviticus 13:45–46). The failure of the present leper to obey this law demonstrates further his desperation. The ability of Jesus to cleanse the leper refers to his ability to *cure* the leprosy, not to an ability to *declare* the man ritually clean. For only priests could do that (see 1:44 with Leviticus 13–14).

The notation of Jesus' compassion points up the goodness of the news about him (compare 1:1). Your hand represents your strength, for you use it in putting that strength to work (see Genesis 31:29: "It's in the power of my hand"). Therefore Jesus' stretching out his hand signals his exercise of strength, *miraculous* strength. His touching the leper despite the leper's uncleanness (about which see Leviticus 5:3; 13:1–46; Numbers 5:2–3) confirms the prior notation of Jesus' compassion, as does also the statement of Jesus, "I'm willing [to cleanse you]." "Be cleansed" adds his powerful word to his powerful touch. This word, underscored by the present tense in "he . . . *says* to him," is a command. So the leprosy leaves. Its leaving "immediately" accentuates the authority with which Jesus issued his command. The leprosy can't stay even an instant longer. The immediacy of its departure rules out an effect of ordinary therapy and demands the recognition of a miracle. "And he was cleansed" shows that Jesus' power to cleanse exceeded the power of leprosy to contaminate him. It also corresponds to Jesus' powerful command, "Be cleansed," just as "the leprosy left him [the leper]" corresponded to Jesus' powerful touch. The doubling up of these statements reinforces the emphasis on Jesus as the one stronger than John.

1:43–44: And growling at him, he [Jesus] **immediately thrust him out 44and says to him, "See** [that] **you don't say anything to anyone. Rather, go show yourself to the priest and—for the purpose of a testimony to them—offer for your cleansing the things that Moses prescribed."** Jesus' growling doesn't display anger. It displays forcefulness—the forcefulness with which he thrusts out the ex-leper (compare 1:12, where the same verb occurred for the Spirit's thrusting Jesus out into the wilderness) and with which Jesus commands the ex-leper. "Immediately" and the present tense in "he . . . *says* to him" add to this forcefulness. So also do the two double expressions "See [that] you don't say . . ." and "go show . . . ." A simple "Don't say . . ." and "show" would have sufficed, but the additions of "See" and "go" reinforce Jesus' commands. Why so much emphasis on forcefulness? To anticipate the answer in 1:45, the greater the forcefulness of Jesus' commands, the greater the tribute to him in the ex-leper's giving an even more resounding testimony than Jesus told him to give. The command not to say anything to anyone has the purpose, not of keeping Jesus' miracle secret, but of getting the ex-leper to a priest as quickly as possible (compare Luke 17:14) in order that the priest might confirm the cure officially and in order that upon this confirmation the ex-leper might offer the sacrifices prescribed by Moses as a testimony to others besides the priest concerning Jesus' miracle. (The priest's allowing sacrifices for ritual cleansing would confirm that Jesus had performed a physical cleansing.)

1:45: But he [the ex-leper], **on going out, began to preach a great deal** [about Jesus' cleansing him] **and to publicize the word, so that he** [Jesus] **could no longer enter a city openly; rather, he was outside in deserted places. And** [even there!] **people kept coming to him from everywhere.** The ex-leper's going out to preach duplicates Jesus' having done so in 1:35–38. Since Jesus has been preaching in synagogues (1:39), it appears that the ex-leper exits a synagogue where Jesus cleansed him. The additions of "a great deal" and "to publicize the word" to the ex-leper's preaching punctuate the spontaneous effect of Jesus' healing power. Despite the forcefulness of Jesus' instructions, the ex-leper can't contain himself. For a testimony to Jesus, preaching and publicizing beat private sacrificing any day. Mark records no criticism of this happy disobedience. So we should think of super-obedience, obedience that surpassed Jesus' instructions. The publicized "word" may be a report concerning the miraculous cleansing or, more specifically, Jesus' powerful statement, "Be cleansed," or, more generally, the good news about God and Jesus (compare 1:1, 14; 2:2). The ex-leper's preaching and publicizing enhance Jesus' magnetism so much that for the time being he has to stay outside cities in deserted locations. And when he finally does venture into a city, he'll enter incognito (as implied in 2:1). Meanwhile, so powerful is his magnetism that because of his presence even those deserted locations become centers of population. People "*kept* coming to him," and did so "from everywhere." He's a magnet so powerful as to erase the limits of time and distance.

JESUS' EXERCISE OF AUTHORITY
TO FORGIVE SINS
Mark 2:1–12

This story of Jesus' exercising authority to forgive sins starts a string of similar stories. In 2:13–17 he'll exercise his authority to eat with tax collectors and sinners; in 2:18–22 to disallow fasting; in 2:23–28 to let his disciples pluck grain on the Sabbath; and in 3:1–6 to heal on the Sabbath.

2:1–2: And on [Jesus'] **entering again into Capernaum, it was heard after** [some] **days** [had passed], **"He's at home!"** [2] **And many** [people] **gathered together, so that not even the things toward the door** [= the open area outside the door but facing it] **had room any longer. And he started speaking the word to them.** In 1:45 Mark said that Jesus couldn't enter a city "openly." So apparently he entered Capernaum a second time (see 1:21

for the first) incognito and succeeded in staying that way for an unspecified number of days. But then news of his presence leaked out: "He's at home!" Since according to very early tradition Mark got his information from Peter, this statement probably reflects the standpoint of Simon Peter and therefore refers to his and his brother Andrew's home. Jesus' magnetism works again. It's stronger than ever. The crowd fills not only the house but also the area outside its door. Not having room "any longer" implies an overflow crowd, so that some people can't even get into the open area, restricted as it apparently is despite being outside. "The word" that Jesus starts to speak is "the good news" about "the reign of God" that Jesus himself is bringing in his Spirit-empowered preaching, healings, and exorcisms.

2:3–5: And they [= the four about to be mentioned] **come bringing to him a paralytic, being carried by four.** By writing "They *come*" rather than "they *came*" Mark dramatizes the bringing of the paralytic. "Paralytic" doesn't necessarily imply the effect of a stroke, but it does indicate some sort of neuromuscular inability to walk. [4] **And not being able to bring** [the paralytic] **to him** [Jesus] **on account of the crowd, they unroofed the roof where he was** [= over the spot where Jesus was speaking]. **And on digging out** [a big hole in the roof], **they lowered the mat where** [= on which] **the paralytic was lying.** [5] **And on seeing their faith, Jesus says to the paralytic, "Child, your sins are being forgiven."** That the paralytic has to be carried shows the severity of his paralysis. The severity will then magnify Jesus' power in healing him. The crush of the crowd forces the four to climb an outside staircase onto the roof, dig a big hole through it, and lower the paralytic. This crush, the extraordinary effort of the four, and the exhibition of their faith in that effort give further evidence of Jesus' magnetism. What vigorous faith it inspires! Digging out the hole implies a roof of mud plastered over a network of branches laid over rafters spaced far enough apart to allow passage of the paralytic once a big enough hole is dug. Lowering him to Jesus constitutes a nonverbal but visible request for healing. With the address "Child," Jesus puts himself in a position of authority over the paralytic. But Jesus doesn't grant the request for healing, at least not yet. Instead, he pronounces that the paralytic's sins are being forgiven—right then and there. (But there's no indication whether the paralysis came by way of divine punishment for the paralytic's sins, though people then would usually have assumed that it did.) The present tense in "Jesus *says*" underlines this surprising pronouncement of forgiveness. But who is forgiving those sins? Some Jewish scholars think they know who *isn't* forgiving them!

2:6–7: But some of the scholars were sitting there and reasoning in their hearts, [7]**"Why is this** [guy] **talking this way? He's blaspheming! Who's able to forgive sins except one,** [namely,] **God?"** In 1:22 the scholars appeared as merely unauthoritative by comparison with Jesus. Here they show themselves antagonistic toward him. Their sitting as antagonistic observers contrasts with the active faith of the four who've brought the paralytic. The heart was considered an organ of thought, not just of emotions. So "reasoning in their hearts" indicates thinking without speaking. "Blaspheming" means slandering and defines, in the scholars' opinion, the "way" Jesus "is . . . talking." Then the question according to which only God can forgive sins gives a basis for the charge of blasphemy. The scholars take Jesus' pronouncement as the slanderous pirating of an exclusively divine prerogative by a mere human being (for this divine prerogative see Exodus 34:6–7; 2 Samuel 12:13; Psalms 32:1–5; 51:1–2, 7–9; 130:4; Isaiah 43:25; 44:22; Daniel 9:9; Zechariah 3:4). In Mark 1:40–45 Jesus showed himself able to cleanse a leper, but the scholars deny his ability to forgive sins.

2:8–9: And immediately Jesus, knowing with his spirit that they were reasoning this way within themselves, says to them, "Why are you reasoning these things in your hearts? ⁹What's easier, to say to the paralytic, 'Your sins are being forgiven,' or to say, 'Rise and pick up your mat and walk'?" The scholars have said nothing out loud, but Jesus knows what they're thinking. So for the first time in this Gospel he displays his power of clairvoyance, which is like God's (1 Samuel 16:7; 1 Kings 8:39; 1 Chronicles 28:9; Psalms 7:9; 139:1–2, 6, 23; Jeremiah 11:20; 17:9–10). "Immediately" and the present tense in "*says* to them" stress this power of Jesus. He needs no time to figure things out. "With his spirit" refers to his human spirit, not to the Holy Spirit, and therefore contrasts with "in their/your [the scholars'] hearts" (2:6, 8) and with "in themselves" (2:8). Mark uses "spirit" instead of "heart" or "himself," and "with" instead of "in," because "spirit" connotes power (see Isaiah 31:3) and because "with" indicates the means by which Jesus exercises clairvoyance rather than its mere location. It's easier to pronounce forgiveness of sins than to command a paralytic to rise, pick up his mat, and walk. Nobody can falsify a pronouncement of forgiveness, but inability to obey the commands would unmask Jesus as a pretender. The piling up of three commands in "Rise and pick up your mat and walk" magnifies the difficulty of making obedience possible.

2:10–11: "But in order that you may know that the Son of Man has authority to be forgiving sins on the earth"—he says to the paralytic, ¹¹"I tell you, rise, pick up your mat, and go to your house." "Son of Man" is a Semitic way of saying "human being." "*The* Son of Man" alludes to a human-like figure that Daniel saw in a vision (Daniel 7:13–14). Contrasting with beasts that appeared earlier in the vision, this figure was coming with the clouds of heaven and receiving dominion and a worldwide kingdom. So Jesus changes a comparison ("one *like* a son of man" in Daniel) into a self-referential title ("the Son of Man") and transmutes dominion and a worldwide kingdom into authority to forgive sins. Or, better, God's reigning through him takes here the form of forgiving sins. "The Son of Man" forgives them in

God's stead, then; and "on the earth" as the place where the Son of Man is forgiving sins contrasts with heaven as the unspoken dwelling place of God, who alone can forgive sins according to the scholars. Jesus aims to prove them wrong. "In order that you may know" addresses the scholars' incredulous reasoning. Building anticipation of the following three commands are Jesus' leaving his statement to the scholars unfinished, the sudden shift from the plural "you" that addresses the scholars to the singular "you" that addresses the paralytic, the vivid present tense in "he *says* to the paralytic," and the "I tell you" that precedes the commands. The ability to obey these commands will confirm Jesus' authority to be forgiving sins—not just the paralytic's sins, but sins in general. Inability would disconfirm such authority. The third command, "go to your house," replaces "walk" in 2:9 and thus contrasts with the paralytic's having to be brought earlier, presumably from his house.

2:12: And he rose; and immediately, on picking up his mat, he went out in front of them all, so that all were amazed and were glorifying God saying, "We've never seen [anything happen] **this way!"** Jesus wins! His authority to forgive sins on earth is authenticated just as his exorcising an unclean spirit in 1:21–28 authenticated the authority of his teaching. The paralytic's getting up contrasts with his earlier lying down. Picking up his mat contrasts with his earlier being lowered on it. The immediacy of his picking up the mat underscores the contrast. We expect "he walked" to correspond to Jesus' question in 2:9, or "he went to his house" to correspond to Jesus' command in 2:11. Instead, we read "he went out in front of them all," so that the emphasis falls on the *observability* of Jesus' demonstrating his authority as the Son of Man to forgive sins on the earth. "All" strengthens this emphasis. A second "all" tells who are amazed. Even the scholars can't—and don't—miss the demonstration, a demonstration such as none of them have seen before. And so the false charge of blasphemy turns into a glorification of God.

THE MAGNETIC POWER OF JESUS OVER TAX COLLECTORS AND SINNERS AND HIS EXERCISE OF AUTHORITY TO EAT WITH THEM
Mark 2:13–17

2:13–14: And he [Jesus] went out again [from Capernaum, as in 1:35, 38] **to the seaside** [as in 1:16–20 to call Simon Peter, Andrew, James, and John]. **And all the crowd** [that saw him prove his authority to forgive sins by healing the paralytic in 2:1–12] **were coming to him.** His magnetism draws them "all." None of them can resist it. **And he was teaching them.** To teach is to exercise verbal authority. Jesus exercises such authority again, this time in the open air, where a larger crowd can gather than could gather in the synagogue where he taught earlier (1:21–22). Mark's omitting the content of this teaching leaves the emphasis entirely on Jesus' didactic authority. ¹⁴**And going along he saw Levi, the** [son] **of Alphaeus, sitting at** [his] **tax booth.** Levi was collecting taxes from fishermen and/or merchants in the form of tolls on the goods (fish in the case of fishermen) that they were transporting. **And he** [Jesus] **tells him, "Follow me** [compare 1:17–18, 20]**." And on standing up, he** [Levi] **followed him.** The present tense of "tells" highlights the forcefulness of Jesus' command. Levi's standing up and following him replace sitting at a tax booth. Such is Jesus' magnetism that even absent prior contact with him, Levi forsakes his occupation right in the middle of pursuing it (compare 1:16–20). And that tax collectors were despised sinners magnifies all the more the magnetic power of "God's Holy One" (1:24).

2:15: **And it happens that he** [Jesus] **was reclining** [at table] **in his** [Levi's] **house. And many tax collectors and sinners were reclining with Jesus and his disciples. For they were many and were following him.** At special meals diners reclined on cushions laid on the floor. By itself, reclining could signify this kind of meal; and it does so here, as the next verse will make clear. The house of Simon Peter and Andrew (1:29–31; 2:1–2) doesn't belong to Jesus; nor has either one of them appeared in the present story, and Mark hasn't said that Jesus had his own house in Capernaum. But Levi has been working there. So "his house" must be Levi's. "Were reclining *with Jesus*" implies, though, that "he" who "was reclining" is Jesus. That his and his disciples' fellow recliners were "many" calls attention to his power of attraction. Tax collectors were noted for their venality and graft, and "sinners" refers in general to the notably wicked. That even such people followed Jesus to Levi's house and reclined there with Jesus and his disciples magnifies his power of attraction all the more. Mark's repeating their description as "many" reinforces this point. He omits any indication that Levi invited these tax collectors and sinners, so that the sole emphasis, intensified by the present tense in "it *happens*," lies on Jesus' magnetism.

2:16–17: **And on seeing that he's eating with the sinners and tax collectors, the scholars of the Pharisees were saying to his disciples, "Why is he eating with the tax collectors and sinners?"** [17]**And on hearing** [the question]**, Jesus says to them, "Those who are strong** [= healthy] **have no need of a physician, but those who are sick** [do have need of a physician]**. I didn't come to call righteous** [people]**—rather, sinful people."** It was customary for outsiders to stand around observing banqueters, as the scholars do here. Pharisees stressed avoidance of moral and ritual contamination. Naturally, then, it's their scholars who ask accusatorily why Jesus, whom an unclean spirit called "God's Holy One" (1:24), is hobnobbing with degenerates. Apparently his putdown of the scholars in 2:1–12 leads the Pharisaical scholars here to address his disciples rather than him. They have no luck, though. Jesus hears their question and performs another powerful putdown, this time a purely verbal one, emphasized by the present tense in "*says* to them." In the putdown, righteous people correspond to the strong and healthy in the proverb Jesus cites. Sinners correspond to the sick. (Tax collectors drop out for a

cleaner contrast with sinners, who include tax collectors anyway.) And Jesus corresponds to the physician. Implied is a correspondence between Jesus' calling sinners and a physician's healing the sick. But Jesus is speaking at a meal. Mark hasn't said that Levi invited sinners to the meal, yet he has said that they were reclining at table not with Levi but with Jesus and the disciples, whom Jesus had called earlier, including Levi most recently. So Jesus' calling sinners carries the connotation of inviting them to the banquet of salvation, for which he's the host (see Matthew 8:11; 22:2–14; Luke 13:29; 14:16–24 for salvation as a banquet). Jesus' application of a medical proverb to the banqueting metaphor knocks out his critics in one blow. It's useless to ask who the righteous are, whether they're only self-righteous or really righteous or don't exist in any sense of the word. The point has to do with Jesus' calling sinners, against whom the righteous are only a foil that makes the sinners, and Jesus' authority to call them, stand out in bold relief.

JESUS' EXERCISE OF AUTHORITY IN REGARD TO FASTING
Mark 2:18–22

To Jesus' authority to eat with tax collectors and sinners Mark adds the authority of Jesus in regard to fasting. *2:18:* **And John's disciples and the Pharisees were fasting. And people come and say to him** [Jesus]**, "Why are John's disciples and the Pharisees' disciples fasting, but your disciples aren't fasting?"** This John is the baptizer, of course, not John the disciple of Jesus. A question about fasting follows naturally the preceding question about eating (2:16). Mark may even want us to understand that people came and asked their question about fasting *while* Jesus and his disciples were eating at Levi's house (2:13–17). We know that Jews considered fasting a very important part of their religious practice. Mark doesn't identify the occasion of this particular fasting by John's disciples and the Pharisees, however. So attention focuses on fasting and non-fasting as such and on Jesus' authority over the matter. The Pharisees' disciples are the disciples of Pharisaic scholars. These disciples are fasting along with their scholars just as John's disciples are fasting (though he's in prison by now [1:14]), all in contrast with Jesus' and his disciples' eating. But the accent, buttressed by the present tense in "people . . . *say* to him," falls on the practice of *disciples*, not on their teachers' practice. This accent lays groundwork for an emphasis on Jesus' authority over against that of the Pharisaic scholars and John.

2:19–20: **And Jesus told them, "The sons of the bridal chamber** [= the bridegroom's attendants] **can't fast while the bridegroom is with them, can they? For as long a time as they have the bridegroom with them they can't fast.** [20]**But days will come when the bridegroom is taken away from them, and then they'll fast on that day."** Jesus' saying implies that he's like a bridegroom, that his disciples are like the bridegroom's attendants at a wedding feast, and that his presence with them is like the presence of a bridegroom with his attendants at the feast. It's not just *inappropriate* for the attendants to fast during the feast. They *can't* fast during it, for otherwise the feast wouldn't be a feast. So Jesus' disciples can't fast while he's with them. It's not his teaching that keeps them from fasting. It's his mere presence that does. The double mention of his presence underlines this point. But the analogy breaks down. In real life a bridegroom isn't taken away from his attendants; rather, they leave at the end of the feast and he stays. So Jesus' nonanalogous talk of the bridegroom's being taken away hints at a violent end to the feast-like ministry of Jesus. On the day of his being taken away (Good Friday) the disciples will fast. (They'll have eaten a Passover meal the preceding evening.) And that day will be the start of Jesus' absence during following days. He doesn't say whether the disciples will fast during them too.

Now Jesus adds two more analogies. They fit the preceding analogy of a wedding feast, because you have to wear good clothes to such a feast and wine flows freely at wedding feasts. *2:21–22*: **"No one sews a patch of unshrunk cloth onto an old garment. Otherwise, the fulness** [the part of the patch that overlaps the old garment and is sewn onto it] **takes away from it** [the old garment]. **The new** [overlap of the unshrunk patch takes away from] **the old** [garment], **and the rip** [that was supposed to be remedied by the patch] **becomes worse** [because the patch, when washed, will shrink and pull away from the previously washed-and-shrunk rest of the garment]. [22]**And no one throws** [= pours] **new wine into old wineskins. Otherwise, the wine** [swelling with age] **will burst the wineskins** [already stretched to their limit through prior use], **and both the wine and the wineskins are lost** [the wine by spilling out when the wineskins burst]. **Rather,** [people pour] **new wine into new wineskins** [still expandable]. Just as the bridegroom's presence precludes fasting at a wedding feast, so the shrinkage of new cloth precludes using it to patch an old garment. And the expansion of new wine precludes putting it into old wineskins. The irresistible forces of shrinkage and expansion illustrate the absoluteness of Jesus' authority and its incompatibility with old Judaism. As in 2:17, his pronouncement ends the debate almost before it has begun. Such is Jesus' verbal power.

JESUS' EXERCISE OF AUTHORITY OVER THE SABBATH
Mark 2:23–28

Like fasting, observance of the Sabbath formed an important part of the Jews' religious practice. *2:23–24*: **And it happened that on a Sabbath he was going along through** [fields] **sown** [with grain], **and his disciples began to make** [their] **way, plucking heads of wheat.** Note: Jesus isn't plucking them. Only his disciples are. [24]**And the Pharisees were saying to him, "Look! Why are they doing on the Sabbath what's unlawful** [to do on a Sabbath]**?"** Plucking heads of wheat counted as har-

vesting, harvesting counted as working, and working on the Sabbath was prohibited (see Exodus 20:8–11; 34:21; Deuteronomy 5:12–15, plus Deuteronomy 23:25 for the Law's allowing passers-through to pluck heads of grain, so that the disciples aren't accused of stealing). As usual, the Pharisees speak as guardians of the Old Testament law; and they speak to Jesus because as a teacher he bears responsibility for his disciples' behavior.

2:25–26: **And he says to them, "Haven't you ever read what David did when he had need and got hungry, he himself and the ones with him,** [26]**how he entered into God's house** [= the tabernacle, because Solomon hadn't yet built the first temple]**—at** [the section of the Old Testament represented by] **Abiathar the high priest—and ate the loaves of presentation, which it's unlawful to eat, except for the priests, and gave** [the loaves] **also to the ones who were with him?** [see Exodus 25:30; Leviticus 24:5–9; Hebrews 9:2 on the loaves of presentation]**."** Of course the Pharisees have read 1 Samuel 21:1–6, which tells what David did without blame so far as that scriptural passage is concerned. So they should know better than to criticize the behavior of Jesus' disciples, and the present tense in "he *says* to them" emphasizes that they should know better.

Mostly by inference, Jesus reads into 1 Samuel 21:1–6 a number of elements not mentioned there, at least not explicitly: (1) David's having companions with him; (2) his and his companions' being needy and hungry; (3) God's house; (4) David's entering it rather than merely asking for bread; (5) Abiathar's being a "*high* priest," not just a "priest"; (6) David's eating the loaves; and (7) his giving some of the loaves to his companions. Jesus also omits David's deceiving the priest and mentions Abiathar the high priest rather than Ahimelech, who appears in 1 Samuel 21:1–6. But here Abiathar represents a section of the Old Testament, not the priest who gave David the sacred bread. Hence, the translation "at the *time* of Abiathar" is wrong (see Mark 12:26 for a similarly locative rather than temporal usage). Jesus mentions Abiathar instead of Ahimelech for a link with the added "house of God," which for Jesus and the Pharisees stood in Jerusalem, where Abiathar officiated (1 Samuel 22:20–23; 2 Samuel 15:24, 35; 17:15; 19:11), not in Nob, where Ahimelech gave bread to David.

According to Jesus, then, David and his companions broke the law by eating the loaves of bread presented to God in the tabernacle and reserved for the priests to eat. But Jesus himself isn't breaking the law by harvesting on the Sabbath. So David doesn't represent Jesus. David and to a lesser extent his companions represent Jesus' disciples instead. The disciples *are* breaking the law by harvesting on the Sabbath. Jesus doesn't deny that they are. But by mentioning the need and hunger of David and his companions, Jesus prepares for a statement that humanitarianism trumps Sabbath-keeping. Meanwhile, though, he doesn't exonerate the disciples by saying that they, like David and his companions, had need and hungered. And neither Mark nor Jesus even says that the disciples *ate* the wheat they harvested! *Harvesting* on the Sabbath and Jesus' authority to *allow* such harvesting—whatever the rationale he'll offer for the allowance—make up the only issue at stake.

Now Jesus states the humanitarian purpose of the Sabbath and claims authority to pronounce on that purpose. **2:27–28: And he was telling them, "The Sabbath came into being on account of** [= for the sake of] **humanity, and not humanity on account of** [= for the sake of] **the Sabbath.** [28]**And so the Son of Man is Lord also of the Sabbath."** A new introduction, "And he was telling them," lends gravity to Jesus' following statements. They wrap up the argument. Jesus infers from Genesis 1–2 that since God established the Sabbath after he created humanity, the Sabbath came into being for the sake of humanity rather than vice versa. But he subordinates the humanitarian purpose of the Sabbath to his own authority as the Son of Man (which *means* "the Human Being") to lord it over the Sabbath. Since 1:3 used "Lord" for Jesus, we should capitalize it as a divine title for Jesus here too. And it's this title rather than "the Son of Man" that gets emphasis. "And so" indicates Jesus' reasoning: since the Sabbath is subordinate to human needs and since he's no ordinary human being but "the Son of Man/ Human Being," he's Lord also of the Sabbath. "*Also* of the Sabbath" adds Jesus the Son of Man's lordship over the Sabbath to Jesus the Son of Man's God-like authority to forgive sins on the earth (2:10). So this passage advances from a question about the disciples' conduct to an affirmation of Jesus' authority as Lord.

JESUS' EXERCISING AUTHORITY
TO HEAL ON THE SABBATH
Mark 3:1–6

In the preceding story (2:23–28) Jesus was correctly held responsible for his disciples' harvesting on the Sabbath. Now he himself heals on the Sabbath. **3:1–2: And he entered again into the synagogue** [at Capernaum; see 1:21 for Jesus' first entry]. **And a man** [= "a human being"] **who had a withered hand was there.** [2]**And they** [the Pharisees who accused the disciples of Sabbath-breaking in 2:23–28] **were scrutinizing him** [Jesus] [to see] **whether he will heal him on the Sabbath.** [They did so] **in order that they might accuse him.** "A man who had a withered hand" not only recalls "a man with an unclean spirit" in 1:23. It also points to the sort of being (a member of "humanity") for whose sake Jesus said in 2:27 the Sabbath came into existence and therefore whose benefit would trump the prohibition of working on the Sabbath. In 2:24 the Pharisees had issued Jesus a warning about violating the Sabbath. A second violation would subject him to the possibility of capital punishment (compare Exodus 31:14). Performing a cure on the Sabbath was considered a violation unless the patient's life was in immediate danger. If it wasn't, the cure could wait a day. A withered hand didn't pose an immediate danger of death. So the Pharisees scrutinize Jesus for the purpose of taking legal action leading, they

hoped, to his judicial death should he violate the Sabbath a second time (see 3:6). His past violation leads them to look for another one, and his past healings lead them to look for another healing (hence the future tense in "whether he *will* heal").

3:3–4: And he says to the man who had the withered hand, "Get up [apparently he was sitting] **in the midst** [of the Pharisees]." [4]**And he says to them, "Is it lawful to do good on the Sabbath or to do harm, to save life** [on the Sabbath] **or to kill?" But they kept silent.** With his command to get up, Jesus exercises authority. Nor does the malevolent scrutiny of the Pharisees stop him from doing so. "In the midst" prepares for a public demonstration of his healing power that even they won't be able to deny. They'd denied legality in 2:24. Now he asks a question of legality. As the present tense in "he *says* to the man" highlights Jesus' command, so the present tense in "he *says* to them" highlights Jesus' silencing question. The Pharisees wouldn't deny the legality of doing good rather than harm on the Sabbath, of saving life on the Sabbath rather than killing. But they keep silent out of embarrassment over Jesus' implied argument: healing a withered hand would count as doing good, not healing it as doing harm; and healing it would count as saving life, not healing it as killing. But how could healing a withered hand count as saving life? Well, death is already invading the man by way of his hand. Its witheredness counts as the onset of death for the whole man. So its healing would count as saving life, which is doing good. Having the power to heal it but not doing so would count as killing, as doing harm by letting death continue its invasion of the man. Killing and doing harm are prohibited on every day of the week, most especially on the Sabbath, since it came into being for the benefit of humanity. Saving life and doing good are required on every day of the week, most especially on the Sabbath, again because it came into being for the benefit of humanity (2:27). With this implied argument Jesus once more shows himself Lord also of the Sabbath (2:28).

3:5: And on looking around at them [the Pharisees] **with anger, being deeply grieved because of the hardness of their heart he says to the man, "Stretch out the** [withered] **hand." And he stretched** [it] **out, and his hand was restored.** Jesus casts angry glances at the Pharisees because their murderous design against him blots out the sympathy they should have for the man with the withered hand. For them, this man is only a potentially handy tool with which to nail Jesus. And Jesus grieves deeply because of their lack of sympathy. Introduced with an emphatic "he *says* to the man," Jesus' powerful command that the man stretch out his hand effects the healing. The hand was stiff, immobile, limp. Stretching it out demonstrated its restoration to health and vitality, to goodness and life.

3:6: And on going out, the Pharisees immediately started plotting with the Herodians against him [Jesus] **as to how they might destroy him.** "The Pharisees" identifies "they," "their," and "them" in the earlier verses of this episode and links them with the Pharisees in the preceding episode, which deals with the same issue of the Sabbath. Because Jesus' argument for doing good by saving life on the Sabbath has dealt them a forensic defeat, they can't take legal action against him by charging him with the capital crime of breaking the Sabbath a second time. Instead, they plot to assassinate him. So far as we can tell, the Herodians with whom they plot are supporters of Herod Antipas, ruler of Galilee under Roman sponsorship. Herod Antipas wasn't a Jew. So ordinarily the Pharisees, who stressed Jewish purity, would be at loggerheads with the Herodians. But they need the Herodians' political "pull" in an effort to get Jesus killed. "Immediately" indicates that the conspiracy hatches on this very Sabbath. On the day that Jesus does good by saving life they conspire to do harm by assassinating him. That is, on the Sabbath they conspire to kill the "Lord of the Sabbath" (2:28 [compare 11:18; 12:12; 14:1]).

JESUS' EXERCISE OF MAGNETIC POWER YET AGAIN
Mark 3:7–12

3:7–8: And Jesus withdrew with his disciples to the sea, and a multitudinous multitude followed [him] **from Galilee. And hearing how many things he was doing, a multitudinous multitude came to him from Judea** [8]**and from Jerusalem** [south of Galilee] **and from Idumea** [even farther south] **and Transjordan** [east of the Jordan River] **and** [from] **around Tyre and Sidon** [north of Galilee]. The conspiracy against Jesus' life in 3:6 leads him to withdraw. But his admirers outnumber his enemies and refuse to let him out of their sight. There's safety in numbers; and these numbers are humongous, as the two occurrences of "multitudinous multitude" attest. (The phrase sounds humorously odd in English, but it's true to Mark's emphatic Greek.) One such multitude follows from the region where he's been ministering. Another such multitude comes to him from great distances though they've only heard of his many exploits. Such is his magnetism. Despite the distances they no sooner hear than they come. The Baptist drew only from Judea and, within it, especially from Jerusalem. Jesus is stronger (1:7).

3:9–10: And he told his disciples that a small boat should be ready for him on account of the crowd, lest they crush him. [10]**For he had healed many, so that as many as had afflictions were falling on him** [= were bearing down on him] **in order that they might touch him.** The multitudinous multitudes provide safety from the plotting Pharisees and Herodians—yes. But these multitudes themselves pose a danger, a too-friendly one, of crushing Jesus (compare 5:24, 31). This danger highlights his magnetism all the more. And the magnetism rests on the high number of those he has healed, so that without exception ("as many as") those who were afflicted bear down on him with the understanding that to heal them he won't even have to touch them. They'll only have to touch him, so radiant is his power (compare 5:27–34; 6:56).

3:11–12: And whenever they saw him, the unclean spirits were falling toward him [that is, prostrate before him] **and shouting out, saying, "You're the Son of God."** [12]**And he was insistently reprimanding them that they not make him manifest.** Repeatedly and invariably the unclean spirits declare Jesus' divine sonship. At his baptism God *delightedly* declared him to be his beloved Son (1:9–11). Here the unclean spirits *self-defensively* declare Jesus to be God's Son (compare Satan's backhanded acknowledgment in 1:13). As in 1:24, the unclean spirits hope that their knowledge of Jesus' identity will shield them from his power. And to their verbal declaration they add the body language of falling *toward* him (a wordplay on afflicted people's falling *on* him in 3:10). But at this point Mark isn't interested in exorcisms. He doesn't quote Jesus as issuing any commands that the unclean spirits come out. Much less does he say that any of them did come out—any more than he had said that Jesus healed sick people *on this occasion*. In fact, Mark doesn't even mention the people whom the unclean spirits possessed. His sole point consists in the magnetic power of Jesus that irresistibly draws vast multitudes, including the afflicted, and even obeisant unclean spirits. So powerful a crowd-drawer is he that he has to shut up the unclean spirits repeatedly and insistently. If he doesn't, their publicizing his divine sonship will heighten the danger of his being crushed by ever larger multitudes. He has to put a limit on his magnetism (compare 1:45; 9:30). The effort succeeds, since he doesn't have to use for an escape the small boat he told his disciples to get ready for him.

THE APPOINTMENT OF TWELVE APOSTLES AS EVIDENCE OF JESUS' OVERWHELMING MAGNETISM
Mark 3:13–19

Jesus has attracted so many people that he has to have helpers. **3:13–15: And he goes up a mountain and summons those whom he himself wanted. And they came away** [from the multitudes] **to him.** [14]**And he appointed twelve (whom he also named "sent ones"** [the meaning of the traditional translation "apostles"]) **in order that they might be with him and in order that he might send them to preach** [15]**and to have authority to cast out demons.** The mountain gives Jesus a position of authority as he surveys the multitudes below. Then he summons those he wants. The addition of "himself" to "he" emphasizes his will as the determining factor. Further emphasis accrues from the present tense in "he *goes* up a mountain and *summons* . . . ." The statement that those he wanted "came *away* [from the multitudes] to him" underscores the powerful effect of his summons. Since in 4:10 the Twelve will appear among a larger group of Jesus' insiders, it looks as though he here summons more than the Twelve he appointed (see also 6:7 with 6:1; 9:35 with 9:31; 10:32 and 11:11 with 11:1, 9; 14:17 with 14:12). Superiors name inferiors, as when Adam named the animals in Genesis 2:18–20 and when God gave Jacob a new name in Genesis 32:22–32.[1] So Jesus' naming the Twelve "apostles" exhibits his superiority. To leave the emphasis there, Mark doesn't say why Jesus settled on the number twelve. As noted, "sent ones" defines "apostles." But "apostles" connotes in addition the authority to speak and act on behalf of the sender, in this case Jesus, authority rather like our legal power of attorney and the authority of an ambassador plenipotentiary. Such authority therefore amounts to a multiplication of Jesus' authority via the apostles' preaching and exorcisms. The content of their preaching isn't important to Mark here. It's the multiplication of Jesus' authority in their preaching that Mark puts forward. The awkwardness of the expression "send them . . . *to have authority* to cast out demons" emphasizes the same point in regard to exorcisms. (We'd expect the simpler "send them . . . to cast out demons.") "*Also* named apostles" underlines this multiplication, necessitated as it is by the throngs attracted to him. And being "*with* him" will prepare the apostles to carry out their commission.

3:16–19: And he appointed the Twelve. And he put on Simon the name Peter. [17]**And [he appointed] James the [son] of Zebedee and John the brother of James, and he put on them the names Boanerges, which is** [= means] **"sons of thunder."** [18]**And [he appointed] Andrew and Philip and Bartholomew and Matthew and Thomas and James the [son] of Alphaeus and Thaddaeus and Simon the Cananaean** [19]**and Judas Iscariot, who also betrayed him.** To introduce a list of the Twelve, Mark repeats their appointment, first mentioned in 3:14. Strikingly, though, instead of saying that Jesus appointed Simon, he says that Jesus put on him the name "Peter." As explained in connection with Jesus' naming the Twelve "apostles," the act of naming exhibits the superiority of the namer over the named. So Mark is emphasizing Jesus' superiority. Mark's Greek-speaking audience would understand the meaning of "Peter," which is Greek for "stone" (less usually for "rock"). So Mark doesn't need to translate it. We'd expect Simon's brother Andrew to be mentioned next (see 1:16). But to reemphasize Jesus' superiority, Mark follows with James and John, because Jesus puts a name on them too. It's Boanerges, which Mark translates as "sons of thunder" because it's Aramaic. His Greek-speaking audience wouldn't understand it apart from a translation. It's one name, but Mark uses the plural "name*s*" because of its plural "son*s*" and because of Jesus' putting it on *two* apostles. Thus Mark doubles his emphasis on Jesus' authoritative act of giving James and John a new name. Mark doesn't say why Jesus gave new names to Simon, James, and John. The interest focuses solely on Jesus' exercise of authority as John the baptizer's "stronger one" (1:7). "Cananaean" is Aramaic for "zealot" (whether religious or political or both), but Mark doesn't translate it, because Jesus didn't give that name to this other Simon. Not representing Jesus' exercise of authority, then, it doesn't interest Mark except

for its helping distinguish this Simon from Simon Peter. Similarly, "the [son] of Alphaeus" distinguishes a James from James the son of Zebedee and brother of John; and "Iscariot" distinguishes Judas the betrayer of Jesus from Judas the brother of Jesus (6:3, where the name is traditionally brought into English as "Jude," though in Mark's Greek it's the same as "Judas"). "Who *also* betrayed him" doesn't imply that others, too, betrayed Jesus. It only sets the treachery of this Judas's coming betrayal of Jesus over against Jesus' trust in appointing him.

THE DERIVATION OF JESUS' POWER
FROM THE HOLY SPIRIT
Mark 3:20–35

Jesus has just appointed the twelve apostles to send them with his authority to preach and cast out demons. But where does this authority come from? **3:20–22: And he goes home** [that is, to Peter's home; see the comments on 1:29 and especially 2:1]. **And the crowd comes together again, so that they** [Jesus and the Twelve, whom he has just appointed to be "with him" (3:14)] **couldn't even eat bread** [= a meal]. [21]**And on hearing** [of Jesus' arrival at Peter's home in Capernaum], **his** [Jesus'] **kinfolk came out** [from Nazareth] **to seize him; for they** [the kinfolk] **were saying, "He's gone out of his mind."** [22]**And the scholars who'd come down from Jerusalem were saying, "He has Beelzebul" and "He's casting out demons by the ruler of the demons."** Mark can't let go of Jesus' magnetism. Nor does he want to, for it illustrates Jesus' power. So he highlights the magnetism with the present tense in "[Jesus] *goes* home" and "the crowd *comes* together again." The crowd here is the same as the one that gathered earlier at Peter's home in Capernaum (1:29–34; 2:1–4). Inability even to eat a meal because of the crowd heightens the effect of Jesus' magnetism. Mark doesn't tell just how the crowd kept Jesus and the Twelve from eating. It would be easy to speculate, but doing so would hazard our missing that the omission centers attention on the magnetism as such. In 3:31–32 the kinfolk will turn out to be members of his immediate family, his mother and brothers. But for now their attempt to seize him sets up a contest of power, theirs versus his. Again Mark omits to say just what it was that made them say Jesus had gone out of his mind. But the scholars from Jerusalem supplement the kinfolk's statement by saying that Jesus has Beelzebul. In other words, Jesus' having gone out of his mind according to his kinfolk left a void that according to the scholars Beelzebul now fills. And since Beelzebul rules the demons, the scholars go on to say that Jesus casts them out by exercising Beelzebul's authority over them. Despite the scholars' antagonism toward Jesus, their having come down from Jerusalem ("down" because Jerusalem was situated in the hill country of Judea and Jesus is presently located in Capernaum, well below sea level) pays tribute again to his magnetism.

3:23: And on summoning them [the scholars, but not the kinfolk (see 3:31) or the crowd, who are already gathered around Jesus (3:20, 32)], **he was telling them**

---

[1]Adam's calling Eve "bone *of my bones* and flesh *of my flesh*" makes his naming her an exception to this rule (Genesis 2:23).

in parables [= speech that deals in comparisons], **"How can Satan cast out Satan?"** So Jesus identifies Beelzebul, ruler of the demons, with Satan, and also identifies Satan with the demons that Jesus has been casting out. That is to say, Satan is bonded with the demons subject to him. Otherwise Jesus would have said, "How can Satan cast out the *demons* he rules over?" instead of "How can Satan cast out *Satan*?" It's as though the bond between Satan and the demons is something like the bond between God and members of his kingdom. So it's just as absurd that Satan would use Jesus to cast out Satan's own demons as it's absurd that God would use Jesus to cast out God's own subjects. Jesus therefore goes on to say in **3:24**: **"And if a kingdom be divided against itself, that kingdom can't stand."** Civil war makes a kingdom easy prey for invaders. And since kingdoms are ruled by royal households, Jesus continues in **3:25**: **"And if a [royal] household be divided against itself, that household can't stand."** Strife within a royal family makes it easy prey for usurpers.

Now Jesus applies the comparisons that constitute those parables. **3:26: And if Satan has** [in fact] **risen up against himself and been divided, he can't stand** [that is, he can't survive as the demons' ruler]; **but he has an end** [that is, his time as their ruler is finished]." So Jesus argues that Satan has *not* risen up against himself in Jesus' performance of exorcisms, nor does that performance give evidence of a self-defeating division within Satan's domain. He's suffering a downfall, though, one that portends his end. He's coming to an end, but not because of internal strife—rather, because of incursion from without. **3:27: "But no one is able on entering into the house of a strong man** [that is, the household and kingdom of Satan] **to plunder his property** [that is, demon-possessed people] **unless he ties up the strong man first** [as Jesus the stronger one has done]. **And then he'll plunder his house** [by rescuing demoniacs from their possessor]." The undeniable fact that Jesus has performed exorcisms therefore proves three things: (1) Satan's rule is coming to an end; (2) it's not coming to an end because Jesus is casting out demons by Satan; and (3) it's coming to an end because as Satan's antagonist Jesus is stronger than Satan just as he's stronger than the Baptist.

3:28–30: **"Amen I tell you that all will be forgiven for the sons of men,** [that is,] **the sins and the blasphemies (however many** [sins] **they may commit by uttering blasphemy** [= slander]); [29]**but whoever utters a blasphemy against the Holy Spirit has no forgiveness for eternity. Rather, he's guilty of an eternal sin."** [He said this] [30]**because they were saying, "He has an unclean spirit."** Jesus has shown the scribes the *absurdity* of their charge that he casts out demons by the ruler of the demons. Here he shows them the *seriousness* of their charge that he has Beelzebul. "Amen I say to you" stresses this seriousness. The charge itself attributes the power of the Holy Spirit at work in Jesus to the power of Beelzebul, whom he earlier called "Satan" but now calls "an unclean spirit" to contrast him with "the Holy Spirit."

Since the scholars should have been saying, "He has the Holy Spirit," such a scurrilous attribution constitutes slander against the Holy Spirit. And this slander will never, ever be forgiven. Jesus doesn't say why it won't. His authority is such that it's enough to know that he said so. "The sons of men" means human beings. "However many [sins] they may commit by uttering blasphemy" shows that "the sins and the blasphemies" means "the sins consisting in slanders apart from the one against the Holy Spirit." And in view of Jesus' call to repentance and belief in the gospel (1:15; 2:17), "all will be forgiven" means that all the blasphemous sins of those who repent and believe will be forgiven. "All" and "however many" highlight by contrast the one kind of blasphemy that will never be forgiven. Earlier scholars accused Jesus of blasphemy (2:6–7). On a far higher register and with unmatched authority he returns the compliment on the present scholars. Since forgiveness of sin means a sending away of sin from the sinner, "has no forgiveness for eternity" means that the sin of blaspheming the Holy Spirit sticks to the blasphemer forever and ever. By applying Jesus' declaration to the scholars' charge, Mark implies that Jesus has consigned these scholars to eternal *un*forgiveness much as he exercised the divine prerogative of *forgiving* sins in 2:1–12. The scholars have no answer. He has beat them at their own game. So the one unforgivable sin—that of interpreting in the worst possible way the Holy Spirit's working through Jesus—arises out of a determination not to repent and believe the gospel.

3:31–32: And his mother and his brothers come; and standing outside, they sent [word] to him, calling him. [32]**And a crowd was sitting around him; and they say to him, "Behold, your mother and your brothers outside are seeking you!"** "His mother," "his brothers," and "his sisters" now identify the kinfolk mentioned in 3:21 as Jesus' immediate family. (Since Jewish men usually married women a number of years younger than they, Joseph the husband of Mary and foster father of Jesus is presumably dead by now; for otherwise he'd probably be mentioned.) The present tense of "come" points up the surprise in their arrival. Literally, their standing "outside" means outside the house. Symbolically, it means outside the circle of Jesus' disciples, consisting of the Twelve plus the crowd sitting around him (see 4:10–12). By sending word to him and calling him, these kinfolk try to usurp his role; for he's the one who calls people to himself (1:16–20; 2:14, 17; 3:13). But because they lack his authority, their call will prove ineffective. At first those who inform Jesus of his family's seeking him seem to be the just-mentioned crowd sitting around him. But in 3:33–35 he seems to be speaking to others *about* the crowd. So the informers are probably the scholars from Jerusalem (3:22), whom he has been addressing since 3:23 and whose own words have been quoted as recently as 3:30 ("because they were saying, 'He has an unclean spirit'"). They and his family act in concert. Naturally, they don't tell him his family have come "to seize him" (3:21) and consequently leave the impression that the family are seeking him innocently. Unknowingly to the scholars, their echoing Mark's "outside" reemphasizes the family's not belonging to the circle of Jesus' followers.

3:33–35: And answering them [probably the scholars]**, he says, "Who is my mother, and** [who are] **my brothers?"** [34]**And looking around at those sitting in a circle around him** ["the crowd" of 3:32]**, he says, "Look! My mother and my brothers,** [35]**for whoever does the will of God—this person is my brother and sister and mother."** "In a circle" indicates a closed group which Jesus' mother and brothers have failed to penetrate and to which as nondisciples they don't belong. They're outsiders, and their calling him has proved ineffective, their seeking to seize him unsuccessful. He's stronger than they are. The strength of biological family ties in ancient Jewish culture highlights by contrast Jesus' authority to declare for himself a family of a different kind. He doesn't say what God's will is that these insiders are doing. So the accent stays on the authority of Jesus' pronouncement. Though some manuscripts mentioned his biological sisters in 3:32, he doesn't mention them in 3:33. So his mentioning a new kind of sister in 3:35 looks like an addition. His biological sisters hadn't come calling; but the insiders crowded around him did include younger women. So he includes them. But "father" is missing in Jesus' family of disciples, not only because his probably deceased foster father hadn't come with his biological mother and brothers, but also because God is the sole Father in this new kind of family. All in all, then, Jesus has the Holy Spirit, not the unclean spirit Beelzebul, and therefore has the authority to form a supernatural family rather than having to submit to search and seizure by his natural family.

JESUS' SPEAKING IN PARABLES TO ESTABLISH GOD'S REIGN AMONG THE DISCIPLES AND TO SHUT OUT NONDISCIPLES
Mark 4:1–34

Jesus' use of several parables in 3:23–27 now prompts Mark to introduce a large batch of parables. After an introduction in 4:1 we hear a parable about seeds and soils in 4:2–9, a statement about the meaning and purpose of parables in 4:10–12, an explanation of the parable about seeds and soils in 4:13–20, parables about a lamp in 4:21–23, about a measure in 4:24–25, about a growing seed in 4:26–29, about a mustard seed in 4:30–32, and an editorial conclusion in 4:33–34.

4:1: And again he began to teach beside the sea [see 2:13 for Jesus' first teaching at seaside]. **And a huge crowd gathers together to him, so that on getting into a boat he was sitting in the sea; and all the crowd were on the land** [facing] **toward the sea.** "*Began* to teach" forecasts extensive teaching and puts more emphasis on the teaching than a simple "was teaching" would have done. Jesus' taking the authoritative posture of a teacher in antiquity—that is, sitting—suits Mark's emphasis on

the didactic authority of Jesus (compare 1:22, 27). Mark's description of the crowd as "huge" joins the present tense of "gathers" to emphasize Jesus' magnetism and prepare for a distinction within the crowd between insiders (the Twelve plus others making up Jesus' true family according to 3:31–35) and outsiders (nondisciples [see 4:10–12 for the distinction]). That "*all* the crowd" turn their attention toward him adds to the emphasis on his magnetism. His sitting "*in* the sea" sounds odd, but it makes a nice contrast with the crowd's being "*on* the land," which in turn portrays the crowd as the soil of the upcoming parable and its explanation (4:5, 8, 20). That is to say, by teaching in parables Jesus will be sowing the seed of "the word" on "the land/soil" of the crowd.

4:2–7: And he was teaching them much in parables and saying to them in his teaching, [3]**"Hear! Behold, a sower went out to sow** [seeds]**."** Mark piles up two more references to teaching for further emphasis on Jesus' didactic authority. "Much" adds to this emphasis yet further and means "extensively" (till evening, as will become clear in 4:35). Appropriately for the didactic authority with which Jesus fills this day, he starts with a command: "Hear!" In other words, "Listen to the parable I'm about to tell you." "Behold" reinforces the command. [4]**"And it happened that in the sowing, a** [seed] **fell on the edge of a path; and birds came and devoured it."** The sower didn't deliberately sow any seed on the path; but in sowing as close to it as possible, a seed fell on its edge. There the hardness of the soil, packed down by human traffic, left the seed exposed to voracious birds. [5]**"And another** [seed] **fell on rocky** [ground]**, where it didn't have much soil; and immediately it rose up out of** [the ground] **because of not having depth of soil.** [6]**And when the sun rose up, it** [the sprout of the seed] **was scorched; and because of not having root, it was dried out** [by the sun]**."** Rocky soil doesn't mean soil strewn with stones. It means soil that thinly covers a substratum of rock. It's disputed whether thinness of soil leads to rapid growth because heat from the sun concentrates in the thin layer, whether nourishment concentrates in the upper part of the plant because of lack of space for a root, or whether dew saturates the thin layer of soil and causes rapid growth. Either the sower doesn't know that rock lies immediately below the surface, or the seed falls accidentally on the rocky ground. With depth of soil (and rainfall), sunshine would have made for healthy growth. [7]**"And another** [seed] **fell into thorns; and the thorns came up and choked it, and it didn't bear fruit."** Seed of last year's thorns may lie buried in this patch of soil, or the sower's seed accidentally falls among dried up thorns from the previous year. But the stress falls so much on the present *thorns*' coming up and choking the sprouted seed that the sprouting of the sower's *seed* doesn't even get mentioned. For the first time a failure to bear fruit does get mentioned, though; and its mention prepares for a contrastive result in the last stage of the parable. The first seed never got a chance to "grow." The second started growing but died. The third grew but didn't produce any grain.

4:8–9: "And other [seeds] **fell into good soil and were bearing fruit by coming up** [breaking through the soil] **and growing** [reaching maturity]**, and one** [seed] **was yielding thirtyfold and one sixtyfold and one a hundredfold.**" The other seeds turn out to be three in number ("one . . . one . . . one") for a contrast with the three seeds that fell on bad soil. The contrast defines good soil as receptive rather than hard like that of the path, as deep rather than thin like that overlying some rock, and free of competition rather than infested like that containing thorns. Jesus mentions the yielding of fruit before he mentions the seeds' breaking through the soil and reaching maturity. This reversal of chronological order underlines the happy circumstance of fruit-bearing. The thirtyfold yield is good, the sixtyfold yield better, and the hundredfold yield best of all—a crescendo of success. **⁹And he was saying, "**[The person] **who has ears to hear** [with] **had better hear!**" Jesus started with a direct command to his audience that they listen to this parable: "You [plural]—hear!" Now he both individualizes the command ("who *has*" [singular]) and makes it indirect ("*who* has" [rather than "You"]) to include anyone outside as well as inside his immediate audience, so that anyone in the audience of Mark's Gospel is included, for instance. Such a person is supposed to put his ears to good use by listening to the parable, which in 4:13–20 Jesus will interpret as a parable about different kinds of hearing. Having ears to hear with doesn't imply there are people without ears. It only emphasizes the usefulness of ears for hearing.

4:10–12: And when he [Jesus] **came to be alone** [as regards the crowd of outsiders, nondisciples]**, the ones around him with the Twelve were asking him about the parables. ¹¹And he was telling them, "To you has been given the secret of God's reign; but to those outside, all things are happening in parables ¹²in order that 'though seeing they may see and not perceive** [what they're seeing] **and though hearing they may hear and not understand** [what they're hearing]**, lest they turn back** [from their unbelief in the gospel of God (compare 1:15)] **and it** [their unbelief] **be forgiven them'** [see Isaiah 6:9–10 for the quoted phrases]**."** The description of Jesus as alone—despite the presence of the Twelve and other disciples surrounding him as his true family (3:33–35)—calls attention to his excluding the outsiders. "Those" stresses this exclusion by indicating the distance that separates them from Jesus and his insiders. It was the outsiders' as well as insiders' presence that made the earlier crowd "huge" (4:1). The insiders ask Jesus about the parables because as his true family they do God's will, because to do it they must know it, and because to know it they have to understand the parables Jesus tells about it. But he has told only one parable on this occasion and to this crowd. Why then do the insiders ask him about "the parables [plural]"? The plural anticipates some further parables in this chapter and implies that Mark advances the insiders' inquiry out of chronological order. He does so to emphasize Jesus' judgmental purpose—so far as outsiders are con-

cerned—in speaking these parables to them. Parables to be spoken by Jesus on future, dissimilar occasions, like the one in 12:1–12, will be understood even by outsiders. But they haven't repented and believed his plain speech about the gospel of God (see 1:15 again). So for the present, Jesus uses unexplained figurative language to keep the secret of God's reign hidden from them. Such is the penalty for not hearing the plain speech correctly. An equal emphasis falls on the giving of this secret to those who *have* heard correctly by doing God's will as expressed in Jesus' earlier plain preaching and teaching. This giving consists in Jesus' explaining the parables in private to the insiders. For them the secret turns into an *open* secret. There's no such "giv[ing]" to the outsiders, though. It's just that "all things *happen*" to them in parables—"*all* things" rather than "the secret" to stress the completeness of Jesus' judgment on outsiders. He won't give them even a shred of truth beyond what they've already rejected.

4:13–19: And he [Jesus] **says to them** [the insiders], **"You don't understand this parable, do you? And** [as a result] **how will you understand all the parables?"** The present tense of "says" stresses the point of these questions, which is that understanding the parable about different kinds of soil holds the key to understanding other parables spoken on this occasion. **¹⁴"The sower sows the word** [= 'the good news of God's reign' (1:14–15; compare 1:45)]**."** So if you don't understand the parable that tells you *how* to hear this word, and how *not* to hear it, how will you understand the parables that tell you *what* the word says? **¹⁵But these** [people represented by the first kind of soil] **are the ones on the edge of the path where the word is being sown; and whenever they hear** [it]**, Satan comes immediately and takes away the word that was sown in them."** So act on the word as soon as you hear it, for Satan will take advantage of even the slightest delay. **¹⁶"And these** [people represented by the second kind of soil] **are the ones being sown** [in the sense of receiving seed] **on the rocky** [places]**, who whenever they hear the word receive it immediately with joy."** Their immediate reception of the word contrasts with Satan's immediate removal of the word in the preceding case of people who don't receive the word immediately. "With joy" reflects the goodness of the news about the arrival of God's reign, gives the reason for immediate reception of this news, and suggests that the preceding folk didn't receive it immediately because they missed its goodness and therefore failed to see in it anything to be glad about. The switch from "rocky [ground]" (singular) to "rocky [places]" (plural) is due to the plurality of the people represented. **¹⁷"And they have no root in themselves; rather, they're temporary. Then, when affliction or persecution comes about because of the word, they're immediately tripped up."** They have no root in themselves because they themselves are the thin soil into which the seed falls. Their thinness represents the superficiality of the reception they give to the word, a superficiality that translates into temporariness. "Tripped up" translates into apostasy so as to escape the antagonism of unbelievers. Sadly, the immediacy of this apostasy cancels the immediacy of their joyful reception of the word. ¹⁸**"And others are the ones being sown among thorns. They're the ones who've heard the word;** ¹⁹**and the concerns of this age** [as opposed to concern for their eternal fate] **and the seductiveness of wealth and the cravings for the remaining things** [that characterize worldly success], **by entering into** [the lives of these people], **choke the word; and it becomes unfruitful."** So the thorns stand for this-worldly concerns.

4:20: **"And those are the ones sown on the good soil, who as such hear the word and welcome** [it] **and bear fruit, one** [seed bearing] **thirtyfold and one six-tyfold and one a hundredfold."** "Those" distances the people who not only hear the word but also welcome it and bear fruit from the people who upon hearing the word dilly-dally, wilt under pressure, or let other matters crowd in and don't bear fruit. The crescendo in the rate of fruit-bearing indicates abundant success when the word is heard well. But Jesus doesn't identify the fruit with anything, such as good works, evangelism, or eternal life. The emphasis lies solely on welcoming the word *immediately*, then, so that Satan doesn't get a chance to snatch it away; on welcoming it *deeply*, so that persecution because of it doesn't induce apostasy; and on welcoming it *exclusively*, so that other concerns don't stifle it. The secret consists, then, in the current establishment of God's reign, not by conquest, but by speaking the good news, so that a person gets on the right side of God's reign by hearing the word in right ways.

4:21–23: **And he was saying to them, "A lamp isn't brought to be put under a peck-measure** [a two-gallon basket or bowl used to measure dry goods] **or under a bed, is it?** [A lamp is brought] **to be put on a lampstand, isn't it?** ²²**For nothing is hidden** [in a parable] **except that it might be disclosed** [by way of explanation to the disciples]. **Neither does anything get concealed** [in a parable] **except that it might come into the open** [again by way of explanation to the disciples]. ²³**If anyone has ears to hear** [with], **he'd better hear!"** Mark jumped ahead both to Jesus' explanation of the purpose of the parables (4:10–12) and to his explanation of the meaning of the parable concerning seeds and soils (4:13–20). Jesus gave those explanations to his disciples in private. As will come out in 4:33–34, Mark now goes back to Jesus' addressing the huge crowd that included nondisciples in addition to disciples, just as when Jesus told the parable of the seeds and soils. The command to hear at the tail end of this parable about a lamp repeats the command at the tail end of the parable about seeds and soils and thus revives the theme of hearing. But this time the point is that you'd better hear Jesus' plain speech in the right ways (explained in 4:13–20) if you want to get an explanation of the parables. Jesus tells the parables in order to shed light on the secret of God's reign; but they shed such light only when Jesus explains them, and he explains them only in private to his disciples. So become

his disciple by repenting and believing his plain speech about the arrival of God's reign, that is, by hearing the plain speech in right ways. Otherwise you'll be left in the dark when it comes to the secret of that reign.

4:24–25: **And he was saying to them, "Watch out what way you hear! With the measure that you measure with, it'll be measured to you."** In other words, Jesus will treat you according to the way you treat—that is, hear—his plain speech about God's reign. **"And it'll be added to you."** In other words, Jesus will add an explanation of his parables to the parables themselves if you've heard his plain speech in right ways. ²⁵**"For** [the person] **who has** [enough]—**it'll be given to him."** Just as it takes some money to make more money (to use a modern analogy), it takes the right hearing of Jesus' plain speech to get an explanation of the parables in addition to the parables themselves. **"And** [the person] **who doesn't have** [enough], **even what he has will be taken away from him."** In other words, just as if you don't have enough money to invest you'll lose what little money you do have by spending it on necessities, you'll lose the meaning of the parables (by being excluded from the audience of their explanation) if you don't hear Jesus' plain speech in right ways.

4:26–29: **And he was saying, "God's reign is like this—as if a man were to throw seed on soil** ²⁷**and sleep and rise night and day, and** [as if] **the seed were to sprout and become long. How** [this happens] **he himself doesn't know.** ²⁸**By itself the soil yields fruit, first a stalk, then an ear, then full grain in the ear.** ²⁹**And whenever the fruit is ripe, immediately he** [the man] **sends the sickle, because the harvest has arrived."** Jesus doesn't need to explain this parable to the disciples any more than he needed to explain the parables of a lamp and a measure in 4:21–25. For the explanation of the parable of soils carries over well enough. As in that parable, throwing seed on soil represents preaching the word (4:3, 14). Since it produces fruitful growth, the soil in this parable matches the good soil in that parable and therefore implies hearing the word in right ways. But implication isn't emphasis. Here the emphasis falls on the mysterious power of the soil and seed—that is, of the well-heard word of the gospel—to produce a fruit-bearing plant. Jesus spells out its stages of growth, eventuating in a harvest, to highlight this power. Jews usually counted nighttime as the first part of a twenty-four hour day, daytime as its second part. So Jesus puts sleeping before rising and night before day. And to distance the man from any contribution to the growth of the seed into a harvestable plant, Jesus doesn't even call him a sower or say that he sows the seed. Jesus calls him only "a man," reduces sowing the seed to "throw[ing]" it, and has the man merely sleeping throughout the night and rising throughout the day rather than tending the crop during its growth. "By itself" locates the power of the soil and seed entirely outside the man's activity; and *sending* the sickle, where we'd expect the man to *wield* the sickle himself, distances him yet again. Nor does he determine the time of harvest. The ripeness of the fruit does, so that he sends the sickle "immediately." He's under compulsion. It's hard to imagine how Jesus could have laid more emphasis on the unaided power of God's reigning through the well-heard word of the gospel. The parable of the soils stressed different ways of hearing this word. The parable of the lamp stressed the purpose of revealing the hidden meaning behind the word to those who hear well. The parable of the measure stressed the means of revelation, that is, the adding of explanations to parables for those who have heard Jesus' plain speech well. And now the parable of the growing seed has stressed the marvelous process of fruition resulting from Jesus' well-heard word.

4:30–32: And he was saying, "How should we liken God's reign, or in what parable [= comparison] **should we put it?** [31][It's] **like a grain of mustard, which** [grain] **when it's sown on soil, though it** [the mustard] **is smaller than all the seeds on the earth—**[32]**and when it's sown it comes up and gets larger than all the vegetable plants and produces large branches, so that the birds of the sky can take shelter under its shade."** Again the interpretation of the parable of the soils (4:13–20) carries over well enough to eliminate any need for an interpretation of this parable. Just as in that interpretation, the sown seed stands for the heard word; and the large size of the mustard plant and its branches stands for the success of God's reign through its being preached just as the thirty-, sixty-, and hundredfold harvest stood for that same success. Only here the accent doesn't fall on hearing the word rightly as the ground of success. The accent falls, rather, on the current magnitude of this success in Jesus' preaching—and this by way of contrast with the small beginning of God's reign at the start of Jesus' preaching. In the land of Israel a mustard seed was the smallest seed that could be seen with the naked eye. But Jesus doesn't even call the mustard "a seed." He calls it "a grain" that's "smaller *than* all the seeds on the earth," not "the smallest *of* all the seeds on the earth." Similarly, "it . . . becomes larger *than* all the vegetable plants," not "the largest *of* all the vegetable plants." The hyperbole of making the mustard grain less than a seed and the grown mustard more than a vegetable plant highlights the contrast between a small beginning and the large outcome. The absence of a sower, and even of a thrower of seed (contrast 4:26–29), concentrates attention on this contrast. The double use of both "all" and "large(r)" and the added reference to birds' taking shelter from the sun under the mustard plant's shade top off the contrast (compare Daniel 4:12, 21; Ezekiel 17:23; 31:6).

4:33–34: And with many such parables he was speaking the word to them as they were able to hear. [34]**But apart from a parable he wasn't speaking to them, but privately he was explaining all things** [in the parables] **to his own disciples."** "Many" implies more parables than Mark records here, and "such" implies that they—like the ones he has recorded—also had to do with Jesus' bringing the reign of God through his pow-

erful preaching and teaching. Speaking the word about God's reign corresponds to the parabolic sowing of seed. The limitation of private explanations to the disciples (a larger group than the Twelve [4:10]) shows that "them" to whom Jesus spoke many such parables consisted of the huge crowd, which included nondisciples as well as disciples, and therefore revives the theme of Jesus' judging with obscure speech those who hadn't believed his plain speech. Since it took private explanation for even the disciples to understand these parables, the ability of the huge crowd to hear can't mean an ability to understand. It must refer to their ability to listen, that is, to their attention span or to the time they could afford for listening. The description of Jesus' disciples as "his *own*" reminds us that in contrast with unbelieving outsiders, they're insiders who as those who believed his plain speech got an explanation of his obscure, parabolic speech. That the explanation covered "all things" in the parables contrasts with Jesus' judgmentally hiding "all things" in parables from outsiders.

JESUS' EXERCISE OF AUTHORITY OVER THE WIND AND SEA
Mark 4:35–41

4:35–36: And he [Jesus] **says to them** ["his own disciples" of 4:34] **on that day, when evening had come, "Let's go through** [the Sea of Galilee] **to the other side** [the east side]." [36]**And on leaving the crowd they take him along, just as he was, in the boat** [from which he'd spoken to the huge crowd on shore (4:1–2)]**; and other boats were with him.** Since these other boats contain disciples in addition to the Twelve, who presumably have joined him in the boat from which he told parables, the phrase "with him" stresses the insider status of these additional disciples even though they're in boats other than the one in which Jesus and the Twelve are traversing the lake. The boatloads of disciples in addition to the Twelve testify again to his magnetism, as though they like the Twelve have left all to follow him. And the present tense in "they *take* him along" points up the obedience of all of them to his exhortation, "Let's go . . . ," just as the present tense in "he *says* to them" stresses the exhortation itself.

4:37–38: And a great gale of wind came about, and waves were breaking over into the boat, so that the boat was already being filled. [38]**And he** [Jesus] **himself was in the afterdeck sleeping on a headrest. And they arouse him and say to him, "Teacher, you care that we're perishing, don't you?"** Magnifying the threat of death by drowning are (1) the description of the windstorm as "a great [that is, powerful] gale"; (2) the breaking of waves over into the boat; and (3) the boat's being filled with water "already" (that is, quickly). So overwhelming are the elements that the Twelve appear unable to bail out the water and ride out the storm. But Jesus sleeps the sleep of utter calm, neither because he's tired (so far as Mark is concerned) nor because he trusts in God (for Jesus will still the storm *himself*). He sleeps because he knows his own ability. The afterdeck being elevated, Jesus could sleep there above the hold that was already being filled with water. The present tense in "they *arouse* him and *say* to him" highlights the disciples' alarm. "Teacher" reflects Jesus' having just taught in parables and explained them. The disciples assume that he does care that they, including him, are perishing; but their failure to ask him to do anything—even to pray God for deliverance—betrays their lack of faith in his divine power. They don't yet recognize his deity.

4:39–40: And on rising up [to his full height], **he reprimanded the wind and told the sea, "Be quiet! Be muzzled and stay that way** [so we can complete this voyage]**!"** See the comments on 1:25 for "Be muzzled!" **And the wind abated, and a great calm came about.** [40]**And he said to them, "Why are you craven? Don't you have faith yet?"** We'd expect Jesus to ask these questions *before* stilling the storm. So stilling the storm first puts emphasis on his reprimanding the wind and commanding the sea, on the stilling effect of the reprimand and commands, and on the disciples' not needing to have cowered through lack of faith. Adding to this emphasis are (1) Jesus' speaking to both the wind and the sea and commanding the sea twice; (2) Mark's doubling the effect by writing both about the wind's abatement and about the coming of calm; and (3) Mark's description of the calm as "great" for a counterpoint to his having described the gale as "great." Literally, the command that the sea shut up means, "Be muzzled and stay that way [so we can complete this voyage]!" (compare 1:25). Since the Old Testament portrays God as the one who reprimands and stills the stormy sea, which represents the power of chaos, Jesus' doing the same exhibits his deity (see Job 26:11–12; Psalms 65:7; 66:6; 106:9; 107:29–30; Nahum 1:4). No wonder the following reaction of the disciples!

4:41: And they feared a great fear and were saying to one another, "Who then is this, [seeing] **that both** [or 'even'] **the wind and the sea obey him?"** For lack of faith the Twelve had been scared of the *storm*. Now they react with a reverential fear of *Jesus*. The combination of a verb, "feared," and its noun-object, "fear," and the description of the fear as "great" highlight this reaction of theirs. The greatness of the fear matches the greatness of the calm that reversed the greatness of the gale of wind. The Twelve's speaking to one another rather than to Jesus gives further evidence of how great was their fear of him. "Then" draws a deduction from the wind's and the sea's obeying him and underscores the Twelve's recognition of his authority. They'll get an answer to their question, "Who . . . is this . . .?" in 5:7 ("Son of the Most High God"), though Mark's audience already know this answer from 1:1, 11 and though the Twelve should have known it from what was narrated in 3:11. At the moment, however, Jesus looms too large for their comprehension. To still the storm he didn't even need to pray or adjure it in God's name. He has successfully exercised his authority over demons, over diseases, and over what modern people call nature. He's the Godman.

JESUS' WINNING A DOUBLE VICTORY OVER LEGION
Mark 5:1–20

5:1: And they came to the other [east] **side of the sea,** [specifically,] **to the region of the Gergasenes.** Early manuscripts are divided between the readings "Gergasenes," "Gadarenes," and "Gerasenes." But the city of Gadara lies about five miles southeast of the Sea of Galilee, and Gerasa even farther—about thirty miles—southeast of the sea, whereas this story requires a location having a hillside sloping steeply into the sea (5:13). Gergasa meets this requirement. Moreover, the going "away" and preaching "in the Decapolis" (5:20) fits Gergasa because it isn't part of the Decapolis (a league of ten cities), whereas both Gadara and Gerasa are part of it and therefore wouldn't require a going away from the region. Furthermore, copyists would find it easy to substitute the better known cities of Gadara and Gerasa for the relatively obscure Gergasa.

5:2–5: And when he [Jesus] **had come out of the boat, immediately a man with an unclean spirit,** [coming] **out of the tombs, met him—**[3][a man] **who had his dwelling in the tombs. And no one could bind him any more, not even with a chain,** [4]**both because of his having been bound many times with shackles** [on his feet and legs] **and chains** [on his hands and arms] **and** [because of] **the chains' having been torn apart by him and the shackles' having been shattered** [by him]**. And no one was strong enough to subdue him.** [5]**And continuously, night and day, he was yelling and lacerating himself with stones in the tombs and in the mountains.** The immediacy of this demoniac's confronting Jesus signals the drama to follow. The description of the demon as an "*unclean* spirit" suits the demoniac's dwelling in tombs and coming out of them, for corpses and bones of the dead convey ritual uncleanness. (Tombs were cave-like rooms naturally or artificially formed in rock, or small room-like structures.) Tombs represent death; and ancient people regarded mountains as places of peril (not as places of refuge from the pressures of civilization as in much modern thinking). The demoniac's yelling evinces torment, and his lacerating himself evinces the life-destroying aim of the spirit that possesses him. The night-long and day-long continuity of the yelling and self-lacerating sharpens this aim. So the story is building up to a life-and-death struggle over the demoniac between Jesus and the unclean spirit. John the baptizer had proclaimed the Holy Spirit-empowered coming one—Jesus, as it turned out—to be stronger than he. But will Jesus prove himself stronger than this man possessed by an unclean spirit? Jesus has done so with previous demoniacs, but Mark takes multiple pains to stress the unusually great power of this demoniac by indicating (1) the inability of anyone to bind him; (2) the uselessness even of chains on the hands and feet and shackles on the feet and legs; (3) the failure of past efforts at binding him; (4) the large number of those failed efforts; (5) his having torn the chains apart and shattered the shackles; and (6) his having grown stronger in that nobody can now subdue him well enough to bind him again with shackles and chains. This confrontation will test Jesus' strength, then.

5:6–8: And on seeing Jesus from a distance, he ran and prostrated himself before him. Even at a distance he recognizes the threat to him that Jesus poses. The spirit inspires this recognition, of course, and prompts the demoniac's running to Jesus. The running indicates desperation to get rid of Jesus. Yet right off the bat the demoniac's bowing face down to the ground toward Jesus shows recognition of Jesus' superiority. The immediately preceding stress on the great power of this demoniac gives his prostration a sharp point. **7And yelling with a loud voice, he says, "What do I and you have to do with each other, Jesus, Son of the Most High God? I adjure you by God not to torture me."** The demon has been torturing the man but wants not to be tortured by Jesus. The loudness of outcry displays further desperation, and the present tense of "says" dramatizes it. Since knowledge is power, by indicating a knowledge of Jesus' name and status as the Son of the Most High God (that is, higher than all other supposed gods), the demoniac's question constitutes an attempt to disempower Jesus and thus disengage him. The unclean spirit's adjuring Jesus by God not to torment it consists in its trying to make Jesus swear in God's name that he won't torment the spirit by casting it out. (Though the spirit is personal, the use of "it" for the spirit avoids confusion with the possessed man.) Usually, adjuring occurs in formulas of exorcism, so that by using this verb the unclean spirit is trying to turn the tables on Jesus by exorcising him out of the region, and in the attempt is using the most potent name possible, "God," short for "the Most High God," which immediately precedes. The attempt will fail, though, because—as this unclean spirit itself knows— Jesus is God's Son. And not only God's Son but also, as Mark's audience know, God's *beloved* Son, in whom he's *delighted* (1:11). **8For he [Jesus] had been saying to him, "Come out of the man, you unclean spirit."** That the spirit hadn't yet come out despite Jesus' having commanded it to do so shows how difficult a case he's dealing with. The spirit isn't just resisting. It's counterattacking with an adjuration. But the greater the difficulty, the greater will be Jesus' victory.

5:9–10: And he [Jesus] was asking it [the unclean spirit], "What [is] your name?" And it says to him, "Legion [is] my name, because we're many." 10And it was imploring him urgently that he not send them outside the region. Now we find out the reason for the difficulty of this case and for the demoniac's unusually great strength: the unclean spirit is in fact "many." Many indeed, as stressed by the present tense of the introductory "says." For a legion in the Roman army normally consisted of about 6000 footmen, 120 horsemen, and a number of auxiliaries. Small wonder that nobody has been able to bind or subdue this demoniac successfully! The spirits hadn't come out, then, because Jesus had ad-

dressed them as though they were only one ("you unclean spirit" [5:8]). By irresistibly forcing them to reveal their name, and thereby their number, Jesus gains the advantage over them. Realizing he has gained it, they resign themselves to being cast out of the man and are reduced to begging that Jesus not send them outside the region. How different this groveling from their bold adjuration of Jesus earlier on!

5:11–13: And there on the mountain [in our terms, the hillside] a large herd of pigs was feeding. 12And they implored him, saying, "Send us into the pigs in order that we may enter them." Though the ritual uncleanness of the pigs fits the uncleanness of the spirits, Mark makes nothing of the fit; nor does he explain how it was that such unclean animals were feeding on the mountain. His only point is that their presence gives the spirits hope of gaining a new host, the herd of pigs, whose large number would accommodate the spirits' large number. As recognized even by them, Jesus has the authority not only to exorcise them but also to tell them where to go next. He grants their request, and by now they're so cowed that he doesn't even have to repeat his earlier command to come out. They just do. **13And he permitted them. And on coming out, the unclean spirits entered the pigs; and the herd rushed down the slope into the sea, about two thousand [of them], and were drowning in the sea.** The spirits almost succeeded in an effort to destroy the life of their human host. Now they succeed fully in an effort to destroy the lives of their porcine hosts. Though this success displays an exercise of great power over the pigs, it also highlights Jesus' exercise of even greater power over the spirits—this for the benefit of their former victim's life.

5:14–17: And those who'd been herding them [the pigs] fled and reported [the incident] in the city [of Gergasa] and in the [nearby] hamlets. And they [the people of Gergasa and hamlets] came to see what it was that had happened. 15And they come to Jesus and see the demoniac, the one who'd had Legion, sitting clothed and sane. And they feared [Jesus]. 16And those who'd seen [the incident] related to them how it had happened to the demoniac and about the pigs. 17And they [probably the herdsmen, plus the city- and countryfolk] started imploring him to go away from their borders. The herdsmen's flight and report and the city- and countryfolk's fear show them all awestruck at Jesus' exercise of power. The present tense in "they *come* . . . and *see*" dramatizes the effects of the report and of the coming. It's as though we're viewing those effects in real time. The ex-demoniac's sitting contrasts with his former breaking loose from chains and shackles. His being clothed contrasts with the nakedness implied by his lacerating himself formerly. And his sanity contrasts with his earlier incessant yelling as he dwelt among the tombs and roamed the mountains. The herdsmen have already reported to the city- and countryfolk the incident *as* such. Now they relate *how* it happened. We're tempted to think that the people of the region implore

Jesus to leave because they fear further loss in addition to that of the pigs if Jesus sticks around. But Mark doesn't say so. He states only the people's fear at seeing the man de-demonized by Jesus. The awesome power of Jesus leads them to implore him just as the unclean spirits had implored him, and imploring him *to leave* their borders recollects those spirits' trying to exorcise him out of their region. But such is his authority that he can't be ordered about. He can only be implored.

5:18–20: **And as he [Jesus] was getting into the boat, the ex-demoniac was imploring him that he** [the ex-demoniac] **might be with him** [compare Jesus' choosing the Twelve "in order that they might be with him" (3:14)]. [19]**And he didn't let him, but says to him, "Go home to your** [family] **and report to them how many things** [the details of deliverance from demon-possession and of restored tranquility, attire, and sanity] **the *Lord* has done for you and how much he had mercy on you."** [20]**And he** [the ex-demoniac] **went away and began proclaiming in the Decapolis how many things *Jesus* had done for him.** So the Lord who had done these things is none other than Jesus (see 1:2–3 for another equation of the Lord with Jesus). **And all marveled.** The ex-demoniac's imploring to be with Jesus contrasts with his earlier attempt to ward off Jesus and with the people's imploring Jesus to leave. The contrast exhibits how marvelously and mercifully Jesus has acted as the Lord by delivering him. Apparently the ex-demoniac's family haven't come with the others to see for themselves; so Jesus commands him to tell them. The present tense in "he . . . *says* to him" underlines Jesus' command to go tell them over against the ex-demoniac's plea to stay with Jesus. But he exceeds Jesus' command by going off and making proclamation throughout the ten cities called the Decapolis. Such is the effect on the man of Jesus' mercifully powerful deed. And its effect on those who heard it proclaimed was that they marveled—not just some of them, but *all* of them.

JESUS' EXERCISE OF POWER OVER DEATH
Mark 5:21–43

This section starts with an introduction to the story of Jairus's daughter, proceeds to the story of a woman with a continuous flow of blood, and ends with a conclusion to the story of Jairus's daughter.

5:21–24: **And when Jesus had crossed again in a boat to the other side** [the west side of the Sea of Galilee], **a large crowd gathered to him; and he was at seaside.** So strong is Jesus' magnetism that no sooner does he come ashore than a large crowd meets him. They make up for the Gergasenes' imploring him to quit their borders. [22]**And one of the synagogue rulers, Jairus by name, comes and, on seeing him, falls at his feet** [23]**and implores him urgently, saying, "My little daughter is at the point of death. Come so as to lay** [your] **hands on her in order that she may be saved** [from dying] **and live** [= get well and live a healthy life]." The present

tense of "comes," "falls," and "implores" highlights the urgency of Jairus's plea. His daughter will turn out to be twelve years old (5:42); so he uses "My *little* daughter" as a term of endearment. Death has come so close that saving her will count as saving her life. The combination of salvation and life may carry overtones of the salvation that consists in eternal life (see 9:43, 45; 10:17, 26, 30). [24]**And he [Jesus] went away with him [Jairus], and a large crowd was following him [Jesus] and crushing him.** Jesus' going away with Jairus shows an intention to save the daughter's life. Remention of the large crowd revives Mark's emphasis on Jesus' magnetism. Their following him and crushing him heighten the magnetism and prepare for the next episode, in which the woman with a continuous flow of blood won't stay incognito despite coming in the crowd behind Jesus.

By interrupting the story of Jairus's daughter this next episode intensifies the already existing suspense. Will Jesus arrive at Jairus's home too late to save the daughter's life? After all, she's at death's door. It was nip and tuck even without an interruption. *5:25–29*: **And a woman who'd had a flow of blood for twelve years** [26]**and suffered much at the hands of many physicians and spent all her resources and was benefited not one bit but rather went** [from bad] **to worse—**[27]**having heard about Jesus, on coming in the crowd from behind** [him], **she touched his clothing.** [28]**For she'd been saying** [to herself], **"If I but touch his clothes, I'll be saved."** As in 5:23, "be saved" may again carry overtones of eternal salvation. Mark piles detail on detail to present a worst case scenario: (1) twelve years of a blood-flow (but not of hemorrhaging, which connotes heavy bleeding such as the woman couldn't have survived for twelve years); (2) a high degree of suffering at the hands of physicians; (3) exhaustion of all the woman's resources in payment to the physicians; (4) the lack of any benefit whatever; and (5) her getting worse. The case seems hopeless, but hearing about Jesus gives her hope, and more than hope: faith so strong as to believe that merely touching his clothing will save her from her malady and, because of the crowd and her approaching him from behind, will save her without his even noticing either her or her touch. Such is Jesus' reputation for power. Sure enough, his power radiates right through his clothing: [29]**And immediately the fountain of her blood dried up, and she knew with her body that she is healed of her affliction** [literally, "of her whip" or "lash" as a figure of speech for the torment caused by her malady]. By contrast with the past twelve years of suffering at the hands of physicians yet going from bad to worse, the immediacy of the woman's cure underlines Jesus' power to save. So too does the hyperbolic magnification of her malady from a mere "flow" of blood to a "fountain" of blood and to torment comparable to a whipping—a pretty long one at that! Knowing with her body that she's healed means that she feels the flow of blood stop. At long last there can be no doubt of her cure. She's healed for good. The Greek verbal form behind "healed" indicates permanence. Jesus' power has eliminated any possibility of a relapse.

5:30–34: **And immediately knowing in himself the power that had gone out of him, Jesus—on turning around in the crowd—was saying, "Who touched my clothes?"** [31]**And his disciples were saying to him, "You see the crowd crushing you and you're saying, 'Who touched me?'"** [32]**And he was looking around to see the one** [feminine in the original Greek] **who'd done this.** [33]**And the woman, fearing and trembling, knowing what had happened to her, came and fell down toward him and told him the whole truth.** [34]**And he said to her, "Daughter, your faith has saved you. Go in peace and be well** [= free] **from your affliction."** The word behind "power" can also be translated with "miracle," for by definition a miracle is an act of power. In this case, then, we shouldn't think of the power as an attribute of Jesus that enabled him to work a miracle. "The power" *is* the miracle, an act of power. Jesus' knowing "in himself" the act of power that healed the woman is due to its originating in him. He's so charged with it that it goes out from him even when he doesn't will it to do so. But he knows *when* it goes out, and he knows it goes out through mere contact with his clothing if the contact is accompanied by faith. As indicated by his turning around to see who touched his clothing, he even knows in what direction the act of power went out from him and therefore knows that the woman approached him from behind. The immediacy of all this supernatural knowledge matches the immediacy of the woman's being supernaturally healed when she touched his clothing. The disciples' remark could be taken as an astonished exclamation ("and you're saying, 'Who touched me?'!") or as a sardonic question ("and are you saying, 'Who touched me?'?") or simply as an ironic observation ("and you're saying, 'Who touched me?' [Hmmm]"). In any case, their incomprehension puts Jesus' knowledge in bold relief. The woman's fear, trembling, and prostration before him bear witness to his supernatural knowledge. Her telling him "the whole truth" bears witness to his supernatural act of power. His addressing her with "Daughter" links her story with that of Jairus's daughter and portrays the woman as a member of Jesus' true family of disciples, that is, as a daughter of God the Father and therefore as Jesus' sister (see 3:31–35). "Your faith has saved you" confirms her healing and shows that it wasn't her touch as such that saved her—rather, her faith that *led* her to touch his clothing. "Has saved" indicates the permanence of her healing just as "is healed" did in 5:29. The "peace" of well-being replaces her earlier torment. And the commands to go and be well guarantee her future of well-being.

5:35–36: **While he** [Jesus] **was still speaking** [to the healed woman], **people come from the synagogue ruler's** [house], **saying** [to him], **"Your daughter has died. Why still bother the teacher?"** [36]**But Jesus, on overhearing the word being spoken** [the report and the question], **says to the synagogue ruler, "Don't fear. Just believe."** It looks hopeless, as emphasized by the present tense in "people *come*." For they come with news of the daughter's death The episode of the

woman with a blood-flow has delayed Jesus' arrival at the house of Jairus ever so slightly. (Jesus "is still speaking" to her.) In the meantime, though, Jairus's daughter has died. Too late to heal her now. The people who bring the news don't use the endearing expression "*little* daughter"—just "daughter." She isn't theirs. Jesus' overhearing the report and the question leads him to tell Jairus to ignore them. Jesus himself certainly does. Despite the daughter's death, Jairus has only to believe, as emphasized now by the present tense in "Jesus . . . *says*." Jesus doesn't tell Jairus what to believe. Jesus hasn't raised anybody from the dead before. So what he'll do will come as a surprise.

5:37–40a: **And except for Peter and James and John the brother of James, he** [Jesus] **didn't let anyone follow along with him.** [38]**And they come into the synagogue ruler's house, and he sees an uproar and** [people] **weeping and wailing loudly.** [39]**And having gone into** [the house], **he says to them, "Why are you making an uproar and weeping? The little child hasn't died; rather, she's sleeping** [and will wake up]." [40a]**And they started laughing him to scorn.** Mark doesn't say why Jesus allowed Peter, James, and John to enter the house with him. But if—as very early church tradition indicates—Mark got the information for his Gospel from Peter, the presence of Peter enabled Mark to include this story. In preparation for a command to secrecy in 5:43, Jesus doesn't allow the remaining nine of the twelve disciples or the huge crowd following him to enter. For the same reason he'll throw the weepers and wailers out of the house. Their weeping and loud wailing emphasize the seeming tragedy of a youthful death and also the seeming hopelessness caused by Jesus' late arrival. He's so sure of raising her from the dead, though, that he compares her condition to sleep rather than death. Calling her a "*little* child" picks up on the father's having called her his "*little* daughter" (5:23) and thus shows Jesus' sharing the father's affection for the girl. The mourners' scornful laughing indicates they think Jesus has made a ridiculously ignorant diagnosis. The joke will be on them.

5:40b–42b: **But on throwing them all out** [of the house], **he himself took along the little child's father and mother and those with him** [that is, Peter, James, and John] **and entered** [the room] **where the little child was.** "He himself" puts Jesus in opposition to those who were laughing him to scorn. Throwing them out exhibits his authority. Just as the father and Jesus endearingly called the child "little," now Mark does too. [41]**And on grasping the little child's hand, he says to her, "Talitha koum," which translated** [from the Aramaic] **means, "Little girl, I'm telling you, get up** [= 'rise']!" [42a–b]**And she stood up immediately and started walking around, for she was twelve years old.** Jairus had implored Jesus to come and lay *his* hands on the girl for her healing (5:23). But she's no longer sick. She's dead. So he grasps *her* hand. Mark doesn't say Jesus raises her, though. Mere contact is enough, as in the case of the woman with a flow of blood. The gesture of Jesus, plus his commanding the girl to get up, empowers her to do so. In talking *about* her, Jesus called her "the little *child*" (5:39). In talking *to* her he affectionately calls her "Little *girl*." Mark's quoting Jesus' original Aramaic, introducing it with the present tense in "he *says* to her," and inserting "I'm telling you" into the translation accentuate the empowering command. Even a dead person hears and obeys him! The immediacy of her standing up and walking around clamps together as closely as possible—and as cause and effect—Jesus' handgrasp and command and the girl's coming back to life. The handgrasp and command generate so much power that they need no time to take effect. "For she was twelve years old" not only links up with the twelve years the woman had suffered a blood-flow. It also rules out that her repeated description as "little" meant she was too young to have learned to walk.

5:42c–43: And they [the parents, Peter, James, and John] **were immediately astonished with great astonishment.** The immediacy of their astonishment matches the immediacy of the girl's standing up and walking around and thus enhances the miracle with its powerful effect on those who witnessed it. The greatness of their astonishment heightens this enhancement. [43]**And he strictly ordered them that no one should know this** [that had happened]**, and he said to give her** [something] **to eat.** In 5:19 Jesus commanded the ex-demoniac to go home and tell his family what had happened to him. Here the parents have seen with their own eyes. But they and Peter, James, and John are to keep the miracle secret. Naturally, the mourners whom Jesus had thrown out of the house and the large crowd that had come with him would sooner or later discover for themselves that the girl was alive. But given the absence of a report from inside and their having taken Jesus' comment to them literally rather than figuratively, they'd think he was right and they wrong: the girl had only been sleeping. But why doesn't Jesus want them to know the truth of the matter? Well, the large crowd that accompanied him had been pressing him to the point of crushing him (5:24, 31), whereas he has been wanting to get away for ministry elsewhere. Their knowing that he'd raised this girl from death to life would exacerbate the danger in being crushed and make it difficult if not impossible for him to leave for Nazareth, as the secrecy will allow him to do in chapter 6. Hence the strictness of the command to secrecy. Meanwhile, giving the girl something to eat will maintain in her the strength by which Jesus enabled her to rise from the dead and walk.

JESUS' INVALIDATION OF UNBELIEF BY MEANS OF ASTONISHING MIRACLES
Mark 6:1–6a

This next story pits the unbelief of Jesus' fellow townspeople against the faith of the woman with a blood-flow and of Jairus in the preceding story (5:21–43). In view of Jesus' miracles, Mark invalidates the unbelief.

6:1: And he [Jesus] **went out from there** [that is, from Jairus's house] **and comes into his hometown.** According to 1:9, 24, Jesus' hometown is Nazareth. But Mark writes "hometown" instead of "Nazareth" to make the point that the people there should have taken pride in their native son. **And his disciples follow him.** Because he'll summon the Twelve for a mission in 6:6b–13, here "his disciples" probably includes a larger group of disciples from among whom he later summons the Twelve (compare the "other boats" of disciples that were with him and the Twelve in a sea-crossing at 4:35–36). In preparation for the unbelief of Jesus' fellow townspeople, the present tense of "comes" headlines the arrival of Jesus there; and the present tense of "follow" foregrounds the discipleship of his followers for a contrast with the unbelief of the townspeople.

6:2: And when the Sabbath came, he started teaching in the synagogue [compare Jesus' "going out" to preach "in synagogues" in 1:38–39, 45]. **And while hearing** [him], **many were awestruck, saying, "From where does this** [guy] **have these things** [his wisdom and miracles, as the next two questions make clear]**? And what** [are] **the wisdom that has been given to this** [guy] **and the miracles such as are taking place through his hands?"** As in 1:21–22, 27, Mark highlights the stunning effect of Jesus' teaching rather than specifying its content. This effect confirms yet again John's description of Jesus as "stronger" than he (1:7). "Many" doesn't imply that others weren't awestruck. It implies, rather, that the awestruck hearers were many, not few, so that all the more emphasis falls on the authority of Jesus' teaching. Their raising questions about it even before he finishes—that is, while he's still teaching—heightens this authority by exhibiting the immediacy of its stunning effect. This effect derives in particular from the wisdom Jesus displays in his teaching and from his miracles that accompany it (compare the conjunction of authoritative teaching and exorcism, also with stunning effect, in 1:21–28). Again Mark doesn't detail Jesus' wisdom or miracles, but cares only about the power of their effect. But being awestruck doesn't necessarily equate with faith, or lead to it; and here does not. Each of the fellow townspeople's first two questions features a contemptuous "this [guy]." The first question implies an outside source ("From where . . . ?") for Jesus' wisdom and miracles. The townspeople won't give Jesus credit for them, so that in the second question they say that the wisdom has "been given" to him and that "his hands" are only an instrument used by the miracles, which "are taking place" by their own effort, not his. Yet "such as" stresses how remarkable these miracles are. And "what [are] the wisdom . . . and the miracles . . . ?" adds consternation over their nature to the earlier question of their source. Because of unbelief the townspeople, awestruck as they are, simply don't know what to think about the power of Jesus' wisdom and miracles. Unbelief leaves it unexplainable.

The townspeople's questions continue in **6:3: "This** [guy] **is the carpenter, isn't he, the son of Mary and** brother of James and Joses and Judas [traditionally translated 'Jude' to distinguish him from Judas the betrayer of Jesus, though the names are identical] **and Simon? And his sisters are here with us, aren't they?"** Familiarity breeds contempt. Surely a local carpenter couldn't teach authoritatively and work stupendous miracles on his own. We know not only Jesus, but also his mother, brothers, and sisters; and they're unexceptional. Why then should we attribute his wisdom and miracles to him and therefore believe in him? So his fellow townspeople think. Mark's audience know that identifying Jesus as a carpenter misses his identity as the one stronger than John (1:7); that identifying him as Mary's son misses his identity as God's beloved Son (1:1, 11; 3:11); and that identifying him as Mary's son (again) and brother of James, Joses, Judas, and Simon and of unnamed biological sisters misses his identity as the nonbiological son and brother of those who do God's will (3:31–35). Besides Jesus' brothers named James, Simon, and Judas, the New Testament mentions two other Jameses, two other Simons, and two other Judases (though one of the Judases will apostatize by betraying Jesus [see 3:31–35 with 3:16–19; Luke 6:16; John 14:22]). **And they were taking offense at him** spoils with unbelief their being "awestruck" at his wisdom and miracles (6:2). To take offense is to fall into a trap, figuratively speaking. Unbelief has trapped these people. By identifying Jesus as *himself* the source of his wisdom and miracles (1:21–22; 5:20), Mark tries to rescue people from falling into the trap of unbelief.

6:4–6a: And Jesus was saying to them, "A prophet isn't dishonored except in his home town and among his relatives and in his house." So Jesus considers himself a prophet, among other things, or at least compares himself to a prophet so far as being dishonored by his fellow townspeople, extended family, and immediate family is concerned (see 3:20–21, 31–35 for the unbelief of Jesus' immediate family). **⁵And he couldn't do there even one miracle, except that by laying** [his] **hands on a few sick people he healed** [them]. "Not even one miracle" sounds absolute. But just as the townspeople heard stunning wisdom in Jesus' teaching, they saw stunning miracles. So "not even one miracle *except that . . .*" implies that Jesus' healing power has elsewhere demonstrated itself so profusely that the present working of only a few miracles hardly counts (see 6:8; 10:18 for similar exceptions after seemingly universal negatives). Though only few, however, the miracles stunned the townspeople. **⁶ᵃAnd he was marveling on account of their unbelief.** Not lack of power on Jesus' part, then, but the townspeople's unbelief kept him from performing the multitude of miracles that he'd been performing elsewhere (see especially 1:32–34). He marvels that familiarity breeds unbelief despite the stunning effect of his wisdom and miracles, which the unbelievers can't deny and don't even try to deny. Mark's point: Jesus' acknowledged wisdom and miracles invalidate unbelief.

JESUS' EXTENDING HIS AUTHORITY THROUGH THE APOSTLES
Mark 6:6b–29

After summoning the Twelve and giving them instructions, Jesus sends them on a mission that extends his authority through their preaching, exorcisms, and miraculous healings (6:6b–13). The resultant enhancement of his reputation causes people and King Herod (Antipas, not his father Herod the Great of the nativity stories in Matthew and Luke) to come up with various identifications of Jesus (6:14–16). Herod's identification of Jesus as John the baptizer risen from the dead leads to a flashback concerning the arrest, imprisonment, and beheading of John by Herod (6:17–29).

6:6b–7: And he [Jesus] **was going about the towns in a circuit** [around his hometown of Nazareth], **teaching** [as he went]. **⁷And he summons the Twelve and started sending them two by two, and he was giving them authority over unclean spirits.** Again Mark doesn't specify what Jesus was teaching and thus showcases the authority with which he was teaching. As emphasized by the present tense of "summons," he exercises that same authority in summoning the Twelve and sending them. "Two by two" conforms to the law that two or three witnesses suffice to establish a matter (here, the necessity of repentance according to 6:12 [see Numbers 35:30; Deuteronomy 17:6; 19:15]). And giving the Twelve authority over unclean spirits shows that Jesus has so much of such authority that he can, and does, dole it out to others for use as his qualified representatives. They will preach and heal as well as exorcise demons (6:12–13), but for the moment Mark singles out the most dramatic extension of Jesus' authority, its extension through the Twelve over a wider geographical range than Jesus alone can reach.

6:8–9: And he ordered them that they should take nothing for the road [= journey] **except a staff only: no bread, no bag, no copper** [= small change consisting of copper coins, less valuable than gold and silver coins] **for the belt** [of cloth in whose twisted folds coins could be kept]. **⁹Rather,** [he ordered them that they should be] **shod with sandals. "And you shouldn't put on two tunics** [= robes worn under an outer robe and next to the skin]." These orders display Jesus' authority *over* the Twelve. In addition, though, giving his authority *to* them means that those to whom they minister will be obligated to give them board and room, so that the Twelve shouldn't take food, a knapsack for carrying it, even small change to buy food or rent a room, or an extra tunic for warmth in case of having to sleep outdoors. Jesus allows only a pair of sandals to protect their feet when walking from place to place, and a staff to steady themselves in mountainous terrain and perhaps also to fend off wild animals that might attack them between towns.

6:10–11: And he was telling them, "Wherever you enter into a home, stay there until you go out from there." In other words, don't move from one home to another in a locality. Stay in one home till you leave town. The authority I give you requires your host to keep you as long as you stay there. [11]**"And whatever locality** [meaning the people of the locality] **doesn't welcome you and doesn't listen to you—for a testimony against them shake out** [of your clothing] **the dust under your feet as you go out** [the dust under your feet that you kicked up with the result that it settled in your clothing]." So the Twelve have Jesus' authority to pronounce judgment with body language on those who refuse them and their message. And because it's *Jesus'* authority, the judgment is certain.

6:12–13: And on going out [from Jesus' presence], **they preached that people should repent** [of their sins (compare 1:4–5, 15)]; [13]**and they were casting out many demons** [for which function as well as preaching he chose the Twelve according 3:14–15] **and anointing with olive oil many sick people and healing** [them]. Armed with Jesus' authority, that is to say, the Twelve do exactly what he has been doing and thereby extend the scope and impact of that authority over human behavior, over demonic possession, and over disease. The "many" of both their exorcisms and their healings multiply by twelve the "many" of Jesus' exorcisms and healings (1:34; 3:10) and counterbalance the fewness of his healings in 6:5 because of people's unbelief. The Twelve's use of olive oil, then used not only for cooking and lamp fuel but also as a soothing medicament, makes them healers-once-removed. It's not by their personal touch that they heal, but only through Jesus' power, which miraculously speeds up the effect of the olive oil. This episode also shows a fulfillment of Jesus' prediction that he'd make the disciples—in particular, two pairs of brothers (compare "two by two" here in 6:7)—"fishers of human beings" (1:16–20). In addition to Jesus' powers of teaching, exorcism, and healing, his power of prediction will gain more and more prominence as Mark proceeds. Indeed, so great is his authority that his predictions *determine* the future.

6:14–16: And the king, [namely] **Herod** [Antipas], **heard.** Officially, this Herod wasn't a king; but Mark conforms to popular usage. Herod certainly ruled Galilee (west of the Sea of Galilee) and Perea (east of the Jordan River). Mark doesn't say *what* Herod heard. He's interested in *why* Herod heard. **For his** [Jesus'] **name** [including his reputation] **had become prominent; and people were saying, "John the baptizer has been raised from among the dead; and on account of this** [his having been raised], **miracles are at work in him."** [15]**But others were saying, "He's Elijah** [come back from heaven, to which he was translated without dying according to 2 Kings 2:1–12 and from which he was to return according to Malachi 4:5]." **And others were saying, "[He's] a prophet, like one of the prophets** [in the Old Testament]." So Herod hears because Jesus' name and reputation have become so publicly prominent that people are making religiously heroic identifications of him. The preaching, exorcising, and healing activities

of his representatives, the Twelve, have enhanced that reputation. The identification of Jesus with a raised John shows the great length to which some people have gone for an explanation of Jesus' miracles. Yet to say that "the miracles are at work in him" is not only to grant the actuality of Jesus' miracles. It's also to deny that he himself works them. It's to say he's only their instrument (compare 6:2). The identification of Jesus with Elijah is less remarkable, because Elijah was predicted to return and because he hadn't died. And the identification of Jesus as a prophet similar to earlier prophets is even less remarkable. Herod, though, opts for the first, most remarkable identification: [16]**But on hearing, Herod was saying, "[The man] whom I myself had beheaded, John—this** [one] **has been raised."** Herod didn't behead John, but he *had* him beheaded. Combined with the reference to beheading, the setting of "I myself" over against "this [John]" betrays alarm on Herod's part that the man he himself had had beheaded must be alive and well and gaining a reputation that sets abuzz the whole countryside over which Herod rules.

The flashback to John's beheading now forms a kind of footnote to Herod's thinking that John has come back to life. **6:17–20: For Herod himself, on sending** [some soldiers], **had seized** [= arrested] **John and bound him** [presumably with chains] **in a prison on account of Herodias, his brother Philip's wife, because he** [Herod] **had married her.** [18]**For John had been saying to Herod, "It's unlawful for you to have your brother's wife"** [see Leviticus 18:16; 20:21]. [19]**And Herodias had it in for him** [John] **and was wanting to kill him** [that is, have him killed], **and she couldn't.** [20]**For Herod feared John, knowing him** [to be] **a righteous and holy man; and he was protecting him** [from Herodias's murderous intent]. **And on hearing him a great deal, he was at a loss** [what to do with him]. **And he was listening to him gladly.** Herodias wasn't satisfied by John's imprisonment. She wanted him executed. So Herod was torn between not wanting to displease her and being convinced by hearing John that he should release him. Since Herod identifies Jesus with John, Herod's having found John to be righteous, holy, and well worth listening to implies—at least for Mark's audience—that Jesus too is righteous, holy, and well worth listening to.

6:21–25: And a day of opportunity having come, [that is,] **when Herod on his birthday put on a banquet for his court officials and military commanders and the foremost** [men] **of Galilee—**[22]**and when Herodias's daughter entered and danced, she pleased Herod and those reclining with** [him at table]. At formal meals the diners didn't sit on chairs; they reclined on cushions around a low table. Mark doesn't say what it was about the girl's dancing that pleased Herod and his fellow diners. It's only John's upcoming decapitation that interests Mark. **And the king said to the little girl** [probably a term of endearment, given the king's pleasure, as in 5:42], **"Ask me whatever you want and I'll give** [it] **to you."** Is he drunk? [23]**And he swore to her** [not *at* her!]

vehemently, "I'll give you whatever you ask me for, up to half of my kingdom." He must be drunk. ²⁴**And on going out** [from the dining room], **she said to her mother, "What should I ask for?" And she** [Herodias] **said, "The head of John the baptizer."** Since not even Herodias was dining with her husband Herod and his fellow diners, the birthday banquet was a stag party. Her absence works to her advantage, though; for now she can use her daughter to trap Herod in his oath for the sake of getting John executed. ²⁵**And on entering** [the dining room] **immediately with haste to the king, she** [the daughter] **asked** [him], **saying, "I want that you at once give me the head of John the baptizer on a platter."** Herodias hadn't told her daughter to say "at once" or "on a platter." But the daughter added "at once" to forestall a later change of mind on Herod's part, perhaps when he sobered up. And she added "on a platter" to suit the setting of a banquet (a gruesome touch to a grisly request!) and enable her to carry the head to her mother.

6:26–29: And though becoming very sorrowful [given his high regard for John], **the king—because of** [his] **oaths and those reclining** [at table with him]— didn't want to disregard her. He had even higher regard for his oaths to the girl and for his reputation with the guests than for John. ²⁷**And immediately sending an executioner, the king commanded** [him] **to bring his** [John's] **head.** The girl's "at once" translates into Herod's "immediately" and thus underlines his susceptibility to manipulation and fear of losing face. **And on going off, he** [the executioner] **beheaded him in the prison** ²⁸**and brought his head on a platter and gave it to the little girl. And the little girl gave it to her mother.** Now the littleness of the girl doesn't indicate endearment; rather, it exposes Herod's weakness in that he has fallen prey to a youngster, a female one at that. How foolish of him, given the patriarchalism and male chauvinism of their culture! ²⁹**And on hearing** [about the beheading of John], **his disciples came and took away his corpse and put it in a tomb.** The delivery of John's head on a platter and the burial of his headless corpse in a tomb provided unmistakable evidence of his death. What mighty powers Jesus must be exercising, then, to have pushed the king into identifying him with a man whose head the king himself had seen delivered on a platter to his own dining room, and then to his wife, and whose corpse had been interred in a different location!

JESUS' EXERCISE OF POWER IN THE FEEDING OF FIVE THOUSAND MEN WITH ONLY FIVE LOAVES OF BREAD AND TWO FISH
Mark 6:30–44

With the power delegated to them by Jesus, the Twelve have done what Jesus had been doing by way of teaching, casting out demons, and healing the sick. But in the following two so-called "nature miracles"— multiplying bread and fish and walking on water— Jesus displays his deity by topping anything the Twelve have done.

6:30: And the apostles gather together to Jesus and reported to him all things, [that is,] **as many things as they'd done and as many things as they'd taught.** "Apostles" is the noun related to the verb "send" in 6:7 and describes the Twelve as sent to speak and act with the authority of Jesus himself, the one who sent them. The flashback to John's beheading has ended. So too has the apostles' mission. Naturally, they report back to their sender. The present tense of "gather" accentuates the occasion for a report of success. "All things" and two occurrences of "as many things as" provide a triple emphasis on the extension of Jesus' power through the apostles' deeds and words. Their deeds consisted in exorcisms and healings according to 6:13. For their words, Mark shifts from preaching (6:13 again) to teaching for an accent on the extension of Jesus' didactic authority (1:21–22, 27).

6:31: And he says to them, "[Come] here—[I mean] *you*—to a deserted place [where we can be] **by ourselves, and rest a little." For the people coming and going were many, and they** [Jesus and the apostles] **weren't getting an opportunity even to eat.** Jesus' extremely forceful address, introduced with the emphatic present tense of "says," reminds us that the apostles' authority derived from him. They'd exercised it so much, though, that they were exhausted and needed a rest. But the traffic of people has created the need for privacy if the rest is to be gotten. The lack of opportunity even to eat shows how congested is this traffic and revives Mark's emphasis on Jesus' power of attraction.

6:32–33: And they went away by themselves in a boat to a deserted place. ³³**And many people saw them going and recognized** [them] **and ran together there** [to the deserted place] **on foot from all the cities and preceded them** [Jesus and the Twelve]. Apparently Jesus and the Twelve are sailing more or less parallel to the shoreline, so that people run along the shore and are already at the deserted place by the time Jesus and the Twelve put ashore. As a result, the place is no longer deserted. So much for "by themselves"! Jesus' magnetism gains increasing force. Those who see him and the Twelve leave by boat *run* so as not to lose him. They're not only "many." They're also from "*all* the cities" thereabouts. And their running "together" from all these cities shows that the many who saw Jesus and the Twelve leave are joined by others along the way. Such is the wide range of Jesus' magnetism, extended now to the apostles, so that people flock to them as well as Jesus.

6:34: And on coming out [of the boat] **he saw a large crowd and felt sorry for them, because they were "like sheep not having a shepherd"** [compare Numbers 27:17; 1 Kings 22:17, for instance]. **And he started teaching them much** [= extensively, as in 4:2]. The large size of the crowd continues Mark's emphasis on Jesus' magnetism. The compassion of Jesus imbues his power with sympathy. What excites his sympathy isn't any hunger for food on the crowd's part. Neither here nor later does Mark say they hungered for food. What excites Jesus' sympathy is their lack of a teacher. So he teaches them and in this way acts as their shepherd by leading them to pasture on the truth of God's good news (1:14–15). Both the image of a shepherd and the activity of teaching connote authority, and the extensiveness of Jesus' teaching intensifies this connotation.

6:35–36: And when the hour had already become late, on approaching him his disciples [the twelve apostles according to 3:14; 6:6b–7, 30] **were saying, "The place is deserted** [except for them and the large crowd, of course]**, and the hour is already late. ³⁶Dismiss them** [the crowd] **in order that on going away into the surrounding hamlets and villages they may buy for themselves something to eat."** The Jews' main mealtime at the end of the afternoon is fast approaching or has arrived. The lateness of the hour (mentioned twice) and the absence of any food markets on location make the disciples' suggestion reasonable. But this very reasonableness will make Jesus' power stand out in bold relief when he feeds the crowd in a way that defies reason. The disciples' failure to address Jesus respectfully with "Lord" (or the like) betrays as inappropriate their telling him what to do; but "dismiss them" indicates that his hold over the crowd is so strong that, mealtime or not, they'll not leave unless he tells them to. "Going away into the surrounding hamlets and villages" sets up for a contrast with reclining on green grass right where they are, and "buy for themselves something to eat" sets up for a contrast with Jesus' giving the crowd for free an overabundance of food.

6:37–38: But he, answering, told them, "*You* give them [something] **to eat."** This command sounds unreasonable and will therefore make Jesus' power stand out when it enables the disciples to carry out the command. They want the crowd to buy their own food, but he orders them—exercising his authority as usual—to give the crowd the food that they (the disciples) have on hand and hope to eat in privacy if he'll only dismiss the crowd. Remember, because of many comers and goers, the disciples and Jesus haven't had an opportunity to eat (compare 6:31 with 6:36). **And they say to him, "On going away, should we buy two hundred denarii worth of bread loaves? And shall we give to them** [the loaves] **to eat?"** Their loaves of bread were round and flat, like our pita bread, each loaf enough for one person for a day. The disciples know that the food in their lunchbox isn't enough to feed the crowd but assume that two hundred denarii worth of loaves would be enough. And so strong is Jesus' hold on the disciples that they stand ready to do Jesus' bidding even if it entails doing with their own money what they'd suggested that Jesus let the crowd do for themselves with *their* own money. Two hundred denarii amounted to about eight months' wages for a manual laborer. **³⁸But he says to them, "How many loaves do you have** [on hand, without having to leave for surrounding communities, buy bread, and bring it back; for it's already late]**? Go see." And on coming to know** [how many], **they say, "Five, plus two fish."** Not many!

The present tense in "they *say* to him," "he *says* to them," and (again) "they *say* to him" enlivens the dialogue in preparation for the following miracle.

6:39–40: And he ordered them [the disciples] **to make all** [in the crowd] **recline group by group** [the crowd is so large they have to be organized] **on the green grass.** Thus the disciples are to exercise on the crowd Jesus' authoritative will. The green grass reminds us of Psalm 23:1–2 ("The Lord is my shepherd . . . . He makes me lie down in green pastures") and of Jesus' acting as a shepherd in 6:34. The green grass also makes a suitable cushion on which to recline for the formal meal, complete with Jesus as host and the disciples as waiters, that he is about to provide. "All" means that despite the large size of the crowd and despite the small number of loaves and fish, nobody's going to be left out. **⁴⁰And they reclined in rows by hundreds and fifties** [that is, in one large rectangle filled with rows of men (6:44), longways each row containing one hundred and sideways each row containing fifty, so that 100 x 50 will equal 5,000]. Jesus has his work cut out for him!

6:41–44: And on taking the five loaves and the two fish, looking up into heaven he said a blessing [= praised God in thanksgiving for the bread and fish] **and broke the loaves and started giving** [the pieces] **to his disciples in order that they might present** [the pieces] **to them** [the crowd]**; and he divided the fish for all.** The crowd is so large that Jesus needs helpers, the disciples, to distribute the food. The large size of the crowd magnifies his miracle as well as his power of attraction. Even though the fish are only two in number, nobody in the crowd will lack fish to go with the bread. Breaking the loaves into pieces indicates multiplication of the bread. **⁴²And all ate and were sated** [= filled to satisfaction; compare Jesus' having taught them "much" (6:34)]. No exceptions. No empty stomachs, not even half empty ones. **⁴³And they** [the disciples] **picked up broken pieces, twelve baskets' fulnesses** [that is, twelve full baskets of leftovers, uneaten pieces that Jesus had broken]**, and** [some uneaten pieces] **from the fish.** Enough for each of the Twelve to have a basketful! They needn't have worried about donating their five loaves and two fish for the crowd to eat. As a good host, Jesus provided more than enough. Such is his power and generosity. **⁴⁴And those who'd eaten the loaves were five thousand men** [= adult males]. For a climax, Mark has saved the number of the crowd till last (contrast the less impressive numbers in 2 Kings 4:42–44).

JESUS' AMAZING FEAT OF
WALKING ON THE SEA
Mark 6:45–52

6:45–46: And immediately he compelled his disciples to get into the boat and go ahead to the other side [the east side of the Sea of Galilee]**, toward Bethsaida, while he himself dismisses the crowd. ⁴⁶And on taking leave of them** [the crowd or, possibly, the disciples]**, he**

went away onto a mountain to pray. The present tense of "dismisses" underlines Jesus' dismissal of the crowd as an exercise of authority over them. "Compelled" implies that he exercised his authority on the disciples against their will. "Immediately" stresses his desire to be left alone for prayer. As in 1:35, his praying shows him to be a godly man. Mark doesn't say what Jesus was praying for. Certainly he wasn't praying for power to work miracles, for such power has resided in him as a result of the Holy Spirit's entering him at his baptism (1:9–11). "*Toward* Bethsaida" hints that the disciples won't reach that city (see 6:53). But on the mountain that Jesus ascends he'll have a vantage point for seeing them at sea.

6:47–48: And when evening came, the boat was in the middle of the sea; and he himself [was] **alone on the land.** "He *himself*" underlines the contrast between his solitary location and that of the boat full of disciples. [48]**And on seeing them straining** [literally, "torturing themselves"] **in the rowing—for the wind was against them—about the fourth watch of the night** [3:00 A.M.–6:00 A.M.] **he comes to them walking on the sea. And he was wanting to pass by them.** The disciples had started before the onset of evening. By the evening they were already in the middle of the sea. But Jesus doesn't come to them till the last quarter of the night. So the disciples have been straining at the oars for a long time without making headway. The contrary wind hasn't endangered them (contrast 4:35–41). It has frustrated them by blowing opposite the direction they want to go, and without Jesus they're helpless. Though he has a vantage point on the mountain, the darkness of night probably implies supernatural sight when he sees the disciples out at sea. Without question, though, walking on the sea exhibits his deity. For only a divine being (and he's "God's Son" according to 1:1, 11; 5:7; 9:7; 14:61–62; 15:39) has such ability (Job 9:8; 38:16; Psalm 77:19). Dramatizing this exhibition of Jesus' deity is the present tense in "he *comes* to them walking on the sea"; and enhancing the exhibition is his "wanting to pass by them," for this phraseology is used for the parading of deity such as characterized appearances of God in the Old Testament (Exodus 33:19, 22; 34:5–6; 1 Kings 19:11; Job 9:8, 11; Amos 7:8; 8:2).

6:49–50: And they, on seeing him walking on the sea, thought, "It's an apparition [= a ghost]**!" and screamed.** [50]**For all** [the twelve disciples] **saw him and were terrified. But he immediately spoke with them and says to them, "Take courage! I AM! Stop being afraid."** To forestall any notion of an illusion, Mark mentions twice the disciples' seeing Jesus as he walked on the sea. To certify the point Mark takes pains to note that "all" of them saw Jesus walking on the sea. And the triple reaction of mistaking Jesus for an apparition, screaming, and terror highlights the parading of his deity. The immediacy of his speaking with them stresses both his following self-identification and his commands to take courage and stop being afraid. Speaking "*with* them" as well as "*to* them" adds a soft note of assurance. Ordinarily, "I AM!" is written "I am" and carries a simple self-

identification, "It's me," as in John 9:9. But Jesus' walking on the sea as only deity can do and thus parading his deity before the disciples favor the divine title, "I AM," by which God identified himself to Moses in Exodus 3:14.

6:51–52: And he went up to them into the boat, and the wind died down [compare 4:39]. **And they** [the disciples] **were more than exceedingly amazed within themselves,** [52]**for they hadn't understood** [Jesus' display of deity] **on the basis of the loaves** [the multiplication of which should have alerted them earlier to his deity]. **Rather, their heart had been hardened.** Getting into the boat ends the parade of Jesus' deity. The disciples' amazement emphasizes the divine presence of Jesus, evident now in the abatement of the wind as well as in his having walked on the sea. Just as the water provided him firm footing, now the wind's abatement will provide him, and them, easy boating. "More than exceedingly" heightens the disciples' amazement to the nth degree. They're so overawed that though they'd screamed in terror earlier, now they're speechless. Their amazement is bottled up "within themselves." Since the heart was considered an organ of understanding as well as emotion, hardness of heart equates here with the disciples' having failed to discern in the feeding of the five thousand a demonstration of Jesus' deity that would now have kept them from their more than extreme amazement.

AN OVERFLOWING OF JESUS' POWER TO HEAL
Mark 6:53–56

6:53–56: And on crossing over [the Sea of Galilee] **to the land, they came to Gennesaret and beached** [there]. But according to 6:45 they were headed toward Bethsaida, a city on the east side of the sea, whereas Gennesaret is a plain on the west side. Because the contrary wind had blown them off course, indeed backward, their landing site turns out to be different from the one originally intended; and "having crossed over" has to do with a reversal of direction from the midpoint the disciples had reached before being frustrated by the contrary wind. By the time the wind died down, continuance toward Bethsaida had become impracticable or undesirable. [54]**And when they'd gotten out of the boat, people—immediately recognizing him** [Jesus]—[55]**ran around that whole region and started bringing around the sick on mats** [to] **wherever they were hearing, "It's he!"** A number of items punctuate Jesus' magnetism and known power to heal: (1) the immediacy of the people's recognizing him; (2) their running; (3) the wide range of their running; (4) their bringing the sick; (5) the seriousness of the maladies that afflicted these sick (they have to be carried on mats, used as stretchers); and (5) the people's bringing their sick to "wherever" Jesus is reported to be. [56]**And wherever he enters into towns or into cities or into hamlets, they put those who were ill in the marketplaces; and they were imploring him that they might touch even the fringe of his** [outer] **robe. And as many as touched it were being saved** [from their illnesses]. The wide range of people's running around to bring their sick is now matched by the wide range of Jesus' itineration. It includes towns, cities, and mere hamlets, as emphasized by the present tense in "he *enters*." "In [their] marketplaces" suggests numerous healings in serial fashion. These healings occur without his performing a gesture or saying a word (compare the wind's abatement in 6:51 without his saying a word). So many are the sick and so many are the localities where they've been brought that they can only implore Jesus to come close enough for them to touch the fringe of his outer robe as he hurries through. "*Even* the fringe" will do (in some contrast with 5:27–28). And no matter how many they were, none who touched failed to be delivered from their maladies. For "as many as" rules out any power failures.

JESUS' DEMONSTRATION OF DOMINANCE OVER PHARISEES AND SCHOLARS AND OF AUTHORITY OVER THE OLD TESTAMENT LAW
Mark 7:1–23

In this passage Jesus powerfully puts down the Pharisees and some scholars (7:1–13) and authoritatively pronounces all foods lawful to eat despite Old Testament laws to the contrary (7:14–23).

7:1–3: And the Pharisees and some of the scholars, having come from Jerusalem, gather to him. So Jesus is still in Galilee, presumably in the plain of Gennesaret (6:53). **²And on seeing some of his disciples, that they're eating the loaves of bread** [left over in broken pieces from the feeding of the five thousand and, because of the crowds, uneaten during the itineration in Gennesaret (6:31, 53–56)] **with defiled (that is, unwashed) hands—³for the Pharisees and all the Jews, holding the tradition of the elders, don't eat unless they wash** [their] **hands with a fist ....** In other words, they cup the hand so as to form a fist, but with fingers held slightly apart to allow full coverage with the least possible amount of water. The washing amounts, then, to a light rinse for the purpose of ritual cleansing more than for hygiene. "The tradition of the elders" consists in legal comments and case decisions made by past teachers of the Old Testament law. Holding this tradition means carrying it out in practice. That "all the Jews" as well as the Pharisees among them carry it out will amplify Jesus' authority when he negates the tradition. Jews living in Galilee made pilgrimages to Jerusalem. But the coming of scholars all the way from Jerusalem to Galilee shows how far and into what important circles the report of Jesus' mighty acts has spread. The present tense of "gather" underscores the point.

Mark's explanation of the elders' tradition and its practice continues in **7:4: and** [when the Jews come] **from the marketplace, they don't eat unless they baptize themselves** [that is, immerse themselves in water]. **And there are many other** [practices] **that they've received** [as tradition] **to hold,** [such as] **baptisms** [immersions] **of cups and pitchers and copper kettles and**

dining couches—. The Jews might have picked up some ritual impurity in the marketplace—hence their practice of immersing themselves to get rid of the impurity before eating. Otherwise the impurity would contaminate the food. You wouldn't want to ingest ritually contaminated food, would you? You'd get contaminated on the inside just as you'd gotten contaminated on the outside. So they thought. Archaeologists have discovered in Israel many ritual bathtubs designed for self-immersions and immersions of cooking utensils and dining paraphernalia.

Mark's long explanation of Jewish ritual practices interrupted the sentence he began in 7:2. But he leaves that sentence incomplete and starts anew in **7:5–8: And the Pharisees and the scholars ask him, "Why aren't your disciples walking** [= conducting themselves] **in accordance with the tradition of the elders, but** [instead] **are eating bread with** [ritually] **defiled hands?"** The present tense of "ask" highlights the confrontational question of the Pharisees and scholars, but their question itself implies correctly that Jesus is responsible for the behavior of his disciples (compare 2:23–28). **⁶But he said to them, "Beautifully did Isaiah prophesy about you, the hypocrites** [described by Isaiah], **as it's written** [in Isaiah 29:13]: **'This people** ["the Pharisees and all the Jews" of 7:3] **honors me** [the Lord is speaking through Isaiah] **with** [their] **lips, but their heart is far away from me. ⁷And they worship me faultily by teaching commandments of human beings** [as though they were] **teachings** [of God].' ⁸**Having abandoned the commandment of God, you hold the tradition of human beings."** "Beautifully" makes the introduction to a quotation from Isaiah drip with sarcasm. "You, the hypocrites" interprets the quotation in terms of pretense, the difference between religious talk and irreligious affections. This difference then transmutes into a substitution of humanly originated commandments (the elders' tradition, which qualifies as honoring God with the lips) for divinely originated teachings (the Old Testament, inspired by God himself). As a result, worship based on the substitution is faulty.

Now Jesus substantiates the charge in 7:8 of abandoning God's commandment for the tradition of human beings, the elders. **7:9–13: And he was telling them, "Beautifully do you set aside the commandment of God in order that you may establish your tradition."** The correspondence between Isaiah's prophecy and the Pharisees' and scholars' hypocrisy made the prophecy beautiful in its accuracy. But the sarcastic accuracy of "Beautifully" in 7:6 now turns into sarcastic irony: setting aside God's commandment to establish human tradition makes the tradition beautiful in its piety, which in accordance with the nature of irony means just the opposite: *ugly* in its *im*piety. Next, Jesus cites an example of abandoning God's commandment to establish human tradition: ¹⁰**"For Moses said, 'Honor your father and your mother** [Exodus 20:12; Deuteronomy 5:16]' **and 'The person who badmouths** [his] **father or mother is to be terminated by death** [Exodus 21:17; Leviticus

20:9].' [11]**But you say, 'If a man says to** [his] **father or mother, "Corban (which means 'gift') with reference to whatever you** [my father or mother] **might benefit from me'"—**[12]**you** [Pharisees and scholars] **no longer allow him to do anything for** [his] **father or mother** [13][and by disallowing him in this way you're] **nullifying God's word by your tradition that you've traditioned."** Here is an example of badmouthing one's father or mother. What "*you*" say" nullifies what "*Moses* said." And since what "*Moses* said" counts as "the commandment *of God*," what "*you* say" also nullifies God's commandment and makes the beauty of legalistic piety ironic rather than admirable. But what is legalistic, and therefore nullifying of God's commandment to honor your father and mother, about the elders' traditional teaching of "Corban"? Mark translates the Hebrew or Aramaic "Corban" with the Greek for "gift." The elders had taught that if you declare something of yours is going to be offered as a gift to God—as a sacrifice at the temple in the case of an ox, for example—nobody else can have it or use it in the meantime, not even your needy parents. And this tradition applies whether or not you ever make good on your declaration, or even intend to. So much for honoring your parents by meeting their needs! Not only do the Pharisees and scholars abandon God's commandment to hold the tradition of past elders (7:8) and set aside the commandment of God to establish the tradition that has now become their own (7:9). They've also handed *on* this tradition (7:13). Jesus' final, sweeping statement, "And you're doing many such things," makes the foregoing example one of many that might be cited. The Pharisees and scholars don't retort. They can't. In debate Jesus is stronger than they are, just as he's stronger than demons, diseases, wind, and waves (chapters 5–6).

7:14–15: And on summoning back the crowd, he was saying to them, "All of you, hear me and understand [what you hear]. [15]**There's nothing outside a human being that can defile him by entering into him; rather, the things proceeding out of a human being are the things that defile the human being."** Mark hasn't mentioned a crowd of bystanders. But in 6:45–46 Jesus "dismiss[ed] the crowd" of five thousand that he'd miraculously fed. So having returned to the west side of the Sea of Galilee after the disciples encountered a contrary wind on an eastward voyage, and now having addressed the Pharisees and the scribes, Jesus summons "back" the crowd of five thousand that he'd dismissed after feeding them. Mark's emphasis lies on the summoning as an exercise of Jesus' authority. "Hear *me*" intensifies the emphasis. Despite the large number of people indicated by "the crowd," the address "*All* [five thousand] of you" forecloses anybody's exemption from obedience to Jesus' authoritative command. The command to understand as well as hear gives advance notice that what he's about to say is puzzling. It's puzzling because Old Testament food laws, which like the commandment to honor your father and mother count as the word of God—those food laws prohibit the ingestion of certain foods, because they'll defile the eater (Leviticus 11:1–47; Deuteronomy 14:3–20).

Yet Jesus denies such defilement. The change in audience from Pharisees and scholars to the crowd is accompanied by a shift in subject matter from *how* to eat (whether or not with washed hands in accordance with the elders' tradition) to *what* to eat (whether or not with restrictions in accordance with Old Testament law). Jesus' statement is puzzling also in that he doesn't identify the things which come out of a human being and defile him. And is this defilement ritual, moral, or both? Just as Jesus punished outsiders by explaining earlier parables only to disciples in private (4:10–12, 33–34), so he'll do here. The earliest and best manuscripts don't have 7:16.

7:17–19: And when he'd entered into a house away from the crowd, his disciples were asking him about the parable. [18]**And he says to them, "In this way** [= like the crowd] **are you also void of understanding? You perceive, don't you, that nothing entering into a human being from outside can defile him,** [19]**because it doesn't enter into his heart—rather, into the stomach and** [then] **proceeds out into the toilet?"** [He said so,] **declaring all foods clean** [that is, ritually pure and therefore okay to eat]. Here "the parable" isn't a comparison (as in chapter 4, for example) so much as a puzzle. Jesus solves the puzzle for his disciples by capitalizing on their knowledge of the alimentary process. The present tense of "says" underscores his appealing to what they already know. Then Mark breaks in with the notation that Jesus' statement rescinded Old Testament food laws—*all* of them. If as the Son of Man Jesus has authority to forgive sins on the earth (2:10), as God's beloved Son he likewise has authority to rescind an Old Testament law.

7:20–23: And he was saying, "What proceeds out of a human being—*that* **defiles the human being.** [21]**For from within,** [that is,] **out of the heart of human beings, proceed evil contrivances: sexual immoralities, thefts, murders, adulteries,** [22]**covetings, malicious acts, treachery, licentiousness, an evil eye** [= stinginess], **slander, insolence, folly."** "And he was saying" marks a shift from the editorial comment in 7:19 back to Jesus' words, and also a shift from what doesn't defile a person to what does. The twofold expression, "from within" and "out of the heart of human beings," stresses the inner source of various defilements (compare Jeremiah 17:9–10). "The evil contrivances" consist in the following list of defilements. The list eliminates the ambiguity intentionally left in 7:15. The defilements are moral rather than ritual. The nouns in the plural refer to evil deeds. The nouns in the singular, which complete the list, have to do with defects of character. "Sexual immoralities" and "adulteries" relate to each other. "Thefts" and "covetings" relate to each other. So also do "murders" and "malicious acts." "Treachery" relates to "slander," "licentiousness" (which means *open* debauchery) to "insolence," and "stinginess" to "folly." The lack of "and" before the final item, "folly," suggests that the list is open-ended. Further vices could be added, but they too would proceed from within. For "contrivances" are formed in the world of thought, and Jesus and his contemporaries considered the heart an organ of thought as well as of emotions. So he attributes evil acts and evil dispositions to the way a person thinks: "As a man thinks in his heart, so is he." A summarizing statement gives final emphasis to the inner origin and defiling effect of the vices featured in the new law of purity that Jesus has laid down: ²³**"All these evil things proceed from within and defile the human being."** "All" intensifies the emphasis. So Jesus has changed the laws of purity. The change doesn't count as human tradition, though. For Jesus is divine, and the elders behind that tradition are not.

JESUS' EXORCISING A DEMON AT A DISTANCE AND WITHOUT A COMMAND
Mark 7:24–30

7:24–26a: **And on standing up** [implied is a teacher's seated position of authority for Jesus' preceding instruction in 7:17–23], **he went away from there into the borders** [= region] **of Tyre** [a Syrian city on the Mediterranean coast north of Galilee]. **And having entered into a house, he wanted nobody to know** [that he'd come there]. **And he couldn't escape notice;** ²⁵**rather, a woman, having immediately heard about him**—[a woman] **whose little daughter had an unclean spirit—on coming** [to Jesus], **fell at his feet.** Again Jesus' magnetism is on display, and the immediacy of the woman's hearing about him and coming to him intensifies the magnetism. He has exercised his power so effectively and startlingly that even in this foreign region he's already known (3:8), and his arrival excites an instant report. The woman's falling at Jesus' feet suits not only her desperation but also his dignity. ²⁶ᵃ**But the woman was a Greek** [by culture], **a Syrophoenician by descent.** This description prepares for the following dialogue, which hinges on the difference between Jews and Gentiles.

7:26b–27: **And she was asking him to cast the demon out of her daughter.** ²⁷**And he was saying to her, "Let the children be sated** [filled to satisfaction with food] **first."** Neither Jesus nor Mark explicitly identifies "the children" or what their being fed means. But "first" implies that the time isn't ripe for the exorcism of a demon from the woman's little daughter, and the description of the woman in non-Jewish terms implies that her being non-Jewish would make untimely an immediate deliverance of her little daughter. By further implication, then, "the children" are Jews—but Jews in general or the Jewish disciples of Jesus? The later statement in 9:30–31 that Jesus "didn't want anyone to know" his whereabouts, "for he was teaching his disciples," suggests that here "the children" are his disciples, whom he wants to sate with his teaching and therefore doesn't want to take time out for an exorcism. The woman's little daughter can wait. (In the end, though, he performs the exorcism at a distance so as not to take time out.) **"For it isn't good** [in the sense of fitting] **to take the children's bread and throw** [it] **to the little dogs."** Jews called Gentiles "dogs"; but here Jesus uses the diminutive, "*little* dogs" (that is, puppies), to correspond to the woman's

"*little* daughter" (though "little" may be a term of endearment rather than an indication of size or age; see the comments on 5:21–23, 35–43). This second statement of Jesus is discouraging. It now seems not so much a question of priority ("first") as it does a question of Jesus' granting the woman's request at all ("it isn't good"). She refuses to be discouraged, though.

7:28–30: **But she answered and says to him, "Lord, even the little dogs under the table eat from the little children's little crumbs."** Whatever the woman meant by "Lord," whether merely "Sir" or "Lord" as deity, Mark intends us to understand the higher meaning. The double introduction, "She answered and says to him," and within it the present tense of "says" call special attention to Jesus' lordship. The woman exhibits wit along with determination. Capitalizing on Jesus' comparing her little daughter to a little dog, she compares Jesus' "children" to "*little* children" who eat so messily that "*little* crumbs" fall by accident under the table, where "*little* dogs" eat them. Jesus admires the woman's cleverness in conceiving that a little Gentile "dog" might enjoy a little crumb of his mighty power *at the same time* that some little Jewish "children" are enjoying a full portion. This admiration leads him to respond: ²⁹**And he told her, "On account of this statement** [of yours], **go. The demon has gone out of your daughter."** Strikingly, Jesus doesn't go with the woman to confront the demon and speak a word of exorcism. Instead, he tells her to go and announces the demon's exit as having happened. Such is Jesus' power of wordless exorcism at a distance! And such is his supernatural knowledge that without seeing the exorcism, he knows it to have taken place. ³⁰**And on going away into her house, she found the little child thrown on a bed and the demon gone out.** To underscore Jesus' power, "thrown on a bed" gives proof of the demon's exit (compare 1:26; 9:26). And to underscore his supernatural knowledge, "the demon gone out" echoes Jesus' announcement.

JESUS' STUPENDOUS HEALING OF A DEAF-MUTE
Mark 7:31–37

7:31–32: **And on going out again,** [this time] **from the borders** [= region] **of Tyre, he went through Sidon** [another Syrian coastal city twenty miles north of Tyre (compare the comments on 7:24)] **to the Sea of Galilee up the middle of the borders of Decapolis.** So Jesus goes north, then east and south to the east shore of the Sea of Galilee (see also 8:10, which tells of his getting in a boat to sail to the west shore). "Up the middle of the borders of Decapolis" references the area east of the sea, through which area Jesus travels to reach its eastern shore. ³²**And people bring to him a** [man] **deaf and mute and implore him to lay** [his] **hand on him.** The proclamation in Decapolis of the ex-demoniac out of whom Jesus cast Legion (5:20) has prepared for Jesus' excursion into this region, so that people bring the deaf-mute to him in confidence that the deaf-mute will be healed if only Jesus will lay his hand on him. He has used the gesture so often and effectively before that here it stands for the healing itself. The Greek word translated "mute" means "speaking with difficulty," that is, with inarticulate grunts; and, of course, deafness caused the muteness. Having never heard, he never learned to talk. The people's imploring Jesus stresses the helpless plight of the deaf-mute if Jesus refuses to heal him. The present tense of "bring" and of "implore" stresses the deaf-mute's plight. But the sorrier his plight, the more powerful the effect of a healing.

7:33–35: And after taking him aside—away from the crowd—by themselves, he stuck his fingers into his [the deaf-mute's] **ears and, after spitting** [on his own fingers], **he touched his** [the deaf-mute's] **tongue.** [34]**And on looking up into heaven, he groaned and says to him, "Ephphatha," which means, "Be completely opened."** [35]**And immediately his hearings opened, and the bond of his tongue** [= what tied down his tongue] **was loosened, and he started speaking correctly** [= plainly]. Apparently the people who brought the deaf-mute are the crowd. Their large number then testifies to Jesus' magnetism. His taking the deaf-mute away from the crowd for a private healing isn't designed to keep the healing secret from them. For in 7:36 he'll command *them* to keep it secret. It's the difficulty of performing a double healing—on ears and on tongue—that creates a need for privacy, which allows better concentration on the effort required (compare 5:40; 8:22–26 and the specially difficult exorcism in 5:1–13, though there not in private). This difficulty also prompts Jesus to use extraordinary means of healing. They consist in sticking two of his fingers in the man's ears (one finger per ear), then spitting on his own fingers, applying the saliva to the man's tongue, looking up into heaven, and groaning—all in addition to the usual word of healing and much more than the simple laying on of a hand that the people asked for. Sticking fingers into the ears mimics and thereby aids their being opened to hear. Spitting, as though getting rid of something in your mouth that keeps you from talking plainly, mimics and thereby—along with application of saliva from Jesus' well-functioning tongue to the man's bonded tongue—aids the loosening of the bond. Furthermore, physical contact transfers healing power, and saliva is curative (compare John 9:6 and the way human beings and animals lick their wounds).

Mark doesn't say that Jesus prayed. But his heavenward look indicates that the power to heal derives from the Holy Spirit, who descended into him at his baptism (1:9–11), and that this healing and the others constitute Jesus' baptizing people in the Holy Spirit, as John the baptizer prophesied "the stronger one" would do (1:7–8). Groaning requires the vigorous exhalation of breath, which has life-force (Genesis 2:7). Here, Jesus' groaning endues his command, "Be completely opened," with force enough to enliven the deaf-mute's "hearings," a term that refers to the ears but puts emphasis on their auditory function. "Completely" demands perfection of that function, not mere improvement. Without some

extra exertion on Jesus' part, the deaf-mute might not hear Jesus' command, the hearing of which constitutes the healing. Mark's retention of the Aramaic original, "Ephphatha," emphasized by the present tense in the introductory "says to him," ties in with Jesus' use of extraordinarily complex means to underscore the difficulty of this healing. Again, though, the greater the difficulty, the greater the exhibition of Jesus' healing power. "Immediately" emphasizes that despite the difficulty, his power is so overwhelming that it requires no delay to effect an opening of the man's ears and a loosening of the man's tongue. *What* the man said is of no interest. *How* he said it is what matters for the healing. "Correctly" tells how and thus certifies the other half of this twofold miracle.

7:36–37: And he ordered them [the crowd] **that they should tell no one. But however much he was ordering them** [to tell no one], **they were proclaiming** [the miracle] **all the more.** The crowd would right away pick up the man's speaking plainly. So it would have been of no use for Jesus to command *him* not to say anything. In fact, Jesus healed him so that he *could* speak. But the crowd might keep quiet about the healing, and Jesus orders them to do so. Mark doesn't say why Jesus wanted them to. For Mark's point lies in the stupendousness of the miracle. You just can't keep quiet about something so stupendous, and the crowd didn't. [37]**And they were awestruck beyond measure, saying, "He has done all things beautifully. He even makes deaf and dumb people hear and speak"** [compare Isaiah 35:5–6]. Though it was twofold, Jesus has performed only one miracle here. So "all things" that Jesus has done "beautifully" make this miracle exemplary of all his miracles in the beauty of their benevolence. Likewise, the plural number of "deaf and dumb people" makes the healing of this one deaf-mute an example of many such healings that Mark hasn't recorded. Since speaking with inarticulate grunts doesn't count as true speech, "speaking with difficulty" (7:32) changes here to "dumb," the literal meaning of which is "*unspeaking*." Because of Jesus' power, deaf-mutes' unspeaking has turned into "speak[ing]." Jesus spoke sarcastically in describing as beautiful Isaiah's prophecy concerning hypocrites (7:6–7), and spoke ironically in describing as beautiful the Pharisees' and scholars' setting aside God's commandment in favor of their tradition (7:9). Now the crowd speak sincerely in describing all Jesus' deeds as beautiful.

JESUS' EXERCISE OF POWER IN THE FEEDING OF FOUR THOUSAND PEOPLE WITH SEVEN LOAVES AND A FEW SMALL FISH
Mark 8:1–9

8:1–3: In those days, because there was a large crowd again and [because] **they didn't have anything to eat, on summoning the disciples he says to them,** [2]**"I feel sorry for the crowd, because they're staying with me—already three days!—and don't have anything to eat.** [3]**And if I dismiss them to their home hungry,**

they'll faint on the way. **And some of them have come from far off** [contrast the disciples' taking initiative in 6:35–36]." "In those days" refers to the period of time Jesus spent on the east shore of the Sea of Galilee (compare 7:31 with 8:10). "Again" compares this "large crowd" (of about four thousand according to 8:9) with the earlier "large crowd" (of five thousand) on the west shore (6:34, 44). Jesus' proceeding to feed the present crowd as he did the earlier one will make the comparison appropriate. As usual, the large size of the crowd calls attention to Jesus' magnetism; and his summoning the disciples calls attention to his authority. Intensifying his magnetism is the crowd's staying with him three days already without having anything to eat, plus the fact that some of them have come from afar. Intensifying his authority is the implication that they can't go home unless he dismisses them. Apparently they haven't had lodging for three days any more than they've had food, yet they've still stayed with him because of his powerful hold on them. But tempering Jesus' authority is his compassion for the crowd because of their need for food and the consequent danger of their fainting on the way home. The present tense of "says" introduces his statement of compassion emphatically.

8:4–5: And his disciples answered him, "From where will anyone be able to satisfy these people with loaves of bread here on a wilderness?" ⁵And he was asking them, "How many loaves do you have?" And they said, "Seven." Jesus doesn't rebuke the disciples for asking their question, nor does he criticize them for forgetting his feeding the five thousand. To the contrary, he'll ask a question in 8:18–19 that's based on their *remembering* that feeding. So here the point lies in a circumstance worse than the one in which the feeding of the five thousand occurred. Then, reasonably nearby hamlets and towns offered the possibility of buying enough bread (6:36–37). Now, the crowd aren't merely in "a deserted place" in otherwise populated territory (6:31–32, 35); they're "on a wilderness." No hamlets or towns are in easy reach, for the whole territory is unpopulated. And it isn't merely late afternoon after a partial day's teaching (6:35), for the crowd have been with Jesus three days without food. It's a good thing the disciples have seven loaves instead of only five!

8:6–9: And he directs the crowd to recline on the ground. And on taking the seven loaves [first], **giving thanks** [next], **he broke** [them in pieces] **and started giving** [them] **to his disciples in order that they might present** [them to the crowd]; **and they did present** [them] **to the crowd. ⁷And they** [the disciples] **had a few small fish. And on blessing them** [= praising God for the fish], **he said to present these too.** Jesus' authority over the crowd comes out in his directing them to recline. The present tense of "directs" accents the exercise of authority. The fewness and smallness of the fish will make their multiplication all the more remarkable. **⁸And they** [the crowd] **ate and were sated** [filled to satisfaction with food]. **And they** [the disciples according to

8:20] **took up leftovers, seven baskets of broken pieces. ⁹And there were about four thousand** [who ate]. **And he dismissed them.** Again no empty stomachs, not even half-empty ones. Again an abundance of leftovers. And again a multiple of thousands. Now the crowd can go home without fainting, and can go home because Jesus authoritatively dismisses them.

JESUS' EXERCISE OF AUTHORITY IN DENYING A REQUEST FOR A SIGN FROM HEAVEN
Mark 8:10–12

8:10: And immediately getting into a boat with his disciples, he went into the districts of Dalmanutha. After Jesus fed the five thousand, he immediately forced the disciples to get in a boat and leave while he stayed to dismiss the crowd, go up a mountain, and pray (6:45–46). Here, after feeding the four thousand, he immediately leaves by boat with the disciples. In both cases, though, his departure from the crowd frees him for ministry elsewhere. We don't know for certain exactly where Dalmanutha was located. But its first syllable, Dal-, may derive from the well-known Mag*dala*, just as in the parallel Matthew 15:39 the "Mag-" of "Magadan" may also derive from *Mag*dala. If so, both Dalmanutha and Magadan may be variants of Magdala, situated on the west shore of the Sea of Galilee and south of the Plain of Gennesaret.

8:11: And the Pharisees came out and began disputing with him by way of seeking from him a sign from heaven, thereby testing him. The Pharisees' testing of Jesus sets up a verbal skirmish between him and them. They think they can expose him as an imposter if he doesn't produce a sign from heaven. Nobody is present who needs a miracle; so the sign from heaven that the Pharisees seek is hardly another of the miracles such as Jesus has been performing over and over again. "From heaven" indicates that he should persuade God to produce some heavenly display—say, in the sun, moon, stars, or planets (compare 13:24–25)—to prove that Jesus' power doesn't come from an alliance with Beelzebul, Satan. Scholars from Jerusalem had, after all, accused Jesus of possession by Beelzebul and therefore of casting out demons by the ruler of the demons (3:22).

8:12: And on groaning forcefully with his spirit, he says, "Why is this generation seeking a sign? Amen I tell you, [I'll be damned] **if a sign will be given to this generation!"** Just as groaning intensified Jesus' word of healing in 7:34, so groaning intensifies the words of Jesus that follow here. "Forcefully" adds to this intensity, and the present tense of "says" adds force to his following words. The question "Why . . . ?" expresses judgmental exasperation. "This generation" doesn't simply mean Jesus' contemporaries. It means people of the sort that seek a sign from heaven (compare especially 8:38; 9:19). The present Pharisees are the generation Jesus is talking about. Perhaps, then, we should translate with "this *kind*" instead of "this *generation*." "Amen I say to you" strengthens the judgmental refusal of a heavenly sign,

"Amen" being a Hebrew word brought over into Greek (and English) and affirming the truth of something. Ordinarily, "Amen" followed what it referred to, as when Christians say "Amen" at the end of their prayers. But Jesus prefixed it to statements whose truth he wanted to emphasize right from the start. "If a sign will be given to this generation!" is likewise a Hebrew way of denying something very strongly. Implied is the speaker's calling down a curse on himself if the denial isn't true (see, for example, Numbers 5:19–22; 2 Kings 6:31; Psalm 7:3–5). So except for its sounding flippant and irreverent, "I'll be damned if . . ." gives a good English equivalent. All in all, then, Jesus authoritatively denies the Pharisees' request for a sign from heaven, so that instead of exposing him as an imposter they suffer exposure themselves as wickedly undeserving of receiving such a sign (compare the parabolic withholding of the secret of God's reign from outsiders [4:10–12]).

JESUS' PROVING HIS MIRACULOUS POWER TO BE MORE THAN ADEQUATE
Mark 8:13–21

8:13–15: And leaving them, again getting [into the boat], **he went off to the other side** [the east side of the Sea of Galilee]. **[14]And they** [the disciples] **had forgotten to take loaves of bread, and except for one loaf they didn't have** [any loaves] **with them in the boat. [15]And he was ordering them, saying, "Look! Watch out for the Pharisees' leaven and Herod's leaven."** By leaving the Pharisees without producing for them the heavenly sign they'd asked for, Jesus not only puts physical distance between himself and them. He also abandons them to their chosen status of unbelieving outsiders. They're beyond hope. In this life it's possible—in their case it was actual—to persist in unbelief beyond the point of redemption. As an old gospel song puts it, "There's a line that is crossed in rejecting our Lord, where the call of his Spirit is lost . . . . Have you counted the cost?" Getting into the boat "again" harks back to 8:10, where Jesus got into it for the voyage to the district of Dalmanutha. Since this new voyage "to the other side" will end up in Bethsaida, on the north*eastern* shore of the Sea of Galilee (8:22), he's starting from Dalmanutha on the west side. The repetition of the disciples' having no loaves of bread, except for one, underscores their need for more (contrast their having had five and seven loaves, plus fish, on previous occasions). One loaf isn't nearly enough for all of them. Their talk of bread leads naturally to Jesus' talk of leaven. Leaven consists of a portion of fermenting dough which, when mixed with a batch of fresh dough, makes the batch rise, much as yeast is used nowadays. But we expect Jesus to address the insufficiency of their one loaf, not switch to the topic of leaven. He has multiplied bread before, though; and it's more important for him to warn the disciples against the leaven of the Pharisees, whom he has just abandoned, and against the leaven of Herod Antipas, ruler of Galilee and beheader of the Baptist. Mark describes the warning as an order to stress the authority with which Jesus issues it. Strikingly, however, neither Jesus nor Mark defines these two kinds of leaven. The lack of definition leaves the emphasis entirely on Jesus' exercise of authority in issuing the order and on the following reference to his power.

8:16–21: And they were discussing with one another [the fact] **that they don't have** [enough] **loaves. [17]And knowing** [what they were saying to each other], **he says to them, "Why are you discussing** [the fact] **that you don't have** [enough] **loaves? Don't you yet understand or comprehend? Do you have your heart hardened** [compare Isaiah 6:10]? **[18]Having eyes, you see, don't you? And having ears, you hear, don't you?'** [Jeremiah 5:21; Ezekiel 12:2]. **And you remember, don't you, [19]when I broke** [in pieces] **the five loaves for the five thousand how many baskets full of broken pieces you picked up?" They say to him, "Twelve." [20]"**[And you remember, don't you,] **when** [I broke in pieces] **the seven** [loaves] **for the four thousand you picked up fullnesses of how many baskets of broken pieces?" And they say to him, "Seven." [21]And he was saying to them, "Don't you yet comprehend?"** The verb "were discussing" connotes *reasoned* conversation. The disciples seem to reason falsely that Jesus doesn't want them to buy additional loaves from the Pharisees or the supporters of Herod Antipas, just as Jewish rabbis might say to beware of the leaven or meat of the Samaritans, in case it be ritually contaminated. But Mark's point doesn't lie in a misunderstanding of Jesus' warning by the disciples. It lies rather in their misunderstanding of Jesus' feedings of the five thousand and four thousand. Those feedings should have kept the disciples from thinking Jesus was alluding to their not having enough bread. "Don't you *yet* understand or comprehend?" implies that the doubling of the miracle of feeding should by now have caused them to understand he wouldn't be concerned over their having only one loaf. "Do you have your heart hardened?" implies that only the dullest sensibilities could have failed to detect the miraculous element in those feedings. Yet incredible as it may seem, that's exactly what Jesus' questions indicate the disciples had failed to grasp! Hence their failure to apply to their present need the magnitude of Jesus' power to multiply bread. The collective singular of "heart" unites the disciples in hardheartedness. They do remember how many baskets full of leftovers they picked up, though, and they did indeed see and hear what Jesus did and said when he fed the two multitudes. But seeing, hearing, and remembering haven't added up to a comprehension of the miracles that should have eliminated a concern over failure to bring enough bread for the present boat trip. Emphasis falls not so much on the feedings of the five thousand and four thousand with only five and seven loaves, respectively, as on the huge surpluses. The baskets of leftovers were "full" as well as many in the case of the first feeding; and in the case of the second feeding the strikingly inverted phrase "*fullnesses* of baskets," where we expect an unexceptional "baskets full of . . . ," puts extra emphasis on the superadequacy of Jesus' miraculous power. Mark says nothing about a multiplication of the one loaf for the present voyage. So the emphasis stays on the superadequacy of Jesus' power in the prior feedings. Throughout, the present tense in "he *says* to them," "They *say* to him," "And they *say* to him," plus the absence of an introduction to Jesus' question concerning the seven loaves, adds to the dialogue a vigor that underlines its import. So too does the absence of "And" before the first "They say to him."

JESUS' EXERCISE OF HEALING POWER IN A PARTICULARLY DIFFICULT CASE OF BLINDNESS
Mark 8:22–26

8:22–24: **And they come into Bethsaida** [on the northeast shore of the Sea of Galilee]. **And people bring to him a blind man and implore him** [Jesus] **to touch him** [the blind man]. [23]**And on taking hold of the blind man's hand, he led him outside the town; and on spitting into his eyes, laying his hands on him he was asking him, "Do you see anything?"** [24]**And on seeing again, he was saying, "I see the people, in that I see** [them as looking] **like trees** [and I see them as] **walking about."** The present tense in "they *come* into Bethsaida" and in "people *bring* to him a blind man and *implore* [Jesus]" introduces this particularly difficult case with an element of drama (compare 7:32). The blind man can't see to touch Jesus; so *Jesus* is implored to give the blind man a healing touch. But just as in 7:31–37 Jesus took a deaf-mute aside from a crowd to perform a particularly difficult miracle with the use of extraordinary means, so here Jesus takes the blind man outside town for the same reason. Again Jesus uses saliva as a healing agent, but this time spits directly into the blind man's eyes, because they're exposed (contrast Jesus' spitting on his own fingers, sticking them into the deaf-mute's mouth, and touching his tongue). Jesus then lays his hands on the saliva-soaked eyes of the blind man. The combination of these two therapies, saliva and the laying on of hands, is designed to produce a miraculous result. And it does; but Jesus suspects that it hasn't, or at least that the result isn't good enough. Hence his question, "Do you see anything?" Well, the man does see people milling about in the town. But they look so indistinct to him that he compares them to a clump of trees whose many branches and leaves make them hard to distinguish from one another, especially when they're milling about like branches waving in the wind. He sees, in other words; but he's nearsighted. Things in the distance look blurry to him.

8:25: **Then he** [Jesus] **laid** [his] **hands on his** [the man's] **eyes again. And he** [the man] **opened** [his eyelids] **wide, and he was restored, and he was seeing all things distinctly at a distance.** "Then" forcefully identifies a second stage of healing. A second application of Jesus' hands, one hand for each eye, implies greater than usual difficulty in the effecting of a full cure and thereby magnifies such a cure once Jesus has effected it. The man's eyes are still moist from Jesus' having spit into them at first; so there's no need of further saliva. Mark sets out the effect in three distinct steps: (1) open-

ing the eyelids wide; (2) restoration (which implies he'd *gone* blind rather than having been *born* blind); and (3) seeing all things distinctly at a distance. The measured pace of the narrative prolongs attention to the fullness ("*all* things," not just the people in town) and long-range clarity ("distinctly *at a distance*") of vision that Jesus effected. Heroic deeds often require prolonged, strenuous effort to overcome special difficulties. So we shouldn't think that the prolongation of this miracle degrades Jesus' power. On the contrary, the special difficulty of this case makes the miracle especially impressive.

8:26: **And he** [Jesus] **sent him to his home, saying, "You shouldn't even go into the town."** Going home on his own rather than into town (presumably the public square or, as we'd say, "downtown") will demonstrate to the distant townspeople that, thanks to Jesus, the man can see again. He needs no one to lead him, as they'd led him to Jesus at the beginning of this episode. Nor does the ex-blind man need to go into town to beg anymore. (A blind man's having to beg went without saying [see John 9:1 with John 9:8].) "Not *even* into the town" stresses the man's not needing to take back his old occupation.

JESUS' DISPLAY OF POWER TO PREDICT HIS OWN FATE AND THAT OF OTHERS
Mark 8:27–9:1

Peter's confession of Jesus as the Christ takes up the first section of this passage (8:27–30). The next section shows Jesus responding to that confession with a prediction of his passion and resurrection (8:31–33). The third section deals with discipleship in view of Peter's confession and Jesus' response (8:34–9:1).

8:27–30: **And Jesus and his disciples went out** [of Bethsaida, mentioned in 8:22] **into the towns of Philip's Caesarea** [that is, towns in the vicinity of the Caesarea built by Herod Philip about twenty-five miles north of the Sea of Galilee, as distinguished from Caesarea on the Mediterranean coast and to the south]. **And on the road he was asking his disciples by saying to them, "Who do the people say I am?"** [28]**And they spoke to him, saying, "**[Some say you are] **John the baptizer, and others** [say you are] **Elijah. But others say, '**[He's] **one of the prophets'** [see 6:14–15 for these same three popular identifications of Jesus]." [29]**And he himself** [Jesus] **was asking them, "But who do *you* say I am?" Answering, Peter says to him, "You are the Christ."** [30]**And Jesus issued them an ultimatum that they should tell no one about him.** The emphatic "he himself" sets Jesus apart from the popular identifications of him. They're wrong. The emphatic "*you*" sets his disciples apart from the people who are making those wrong identifications. The present tense in "Peter *says* to him" and the prefixing of "Answering" add emphasis to Peter's confessing Jesus to be the Christ. "*The* Christ" emphasizes the use of "Christ" as a title, meaning "the Anointed One." God anointed Jesus with the Holy Spirit to establish God's reign among human beings (1:9–11, 14–15). The ultimatum not to tell anybody about him—that is, about his being the

Christ—has the purpose of gaining privacy for predicting to the disciples his coming passion and resurrection. He's about to make the first such prediction (8:31–33). More will follow (9:9, 12, 30–31; 10:32–34). By mobbing him, the crowds have been bothersome and dangerous enough even under their views that Jesus is John the baptizer, Elijah, or one of the prophets (1:35–37, 45; 2:1–2; 3:7–12, 20; 4:1; 6:31–33; 7:24). What would they do if they believed him to be no less a personage than the Christ? In the balance of Mark, as a matter of fact, the disciples *won't* tell anyone that Jesus is the Christ. The accent rests so heavily on Jesus' ultimatum, and therefore on his authority, that Mark doesn't even say whether Jesus accepts Peter's designation of him as the Christ. That he does accept it comes only by inference from his ultimatum not to tell. And he'll now refer to himself as "the Son of Man" rather than as "the Christ."

8:31–32a: And he began teaching them that the Son of Man must suffer severely, and be rejected by the elders and the chief priests and the scholars, and be killed, and after three days rise [literally, "stand up," as opposed to lying in the supine position of a corpse]. **³²ᵃAnd he was speaking this statement plainly.** Mark puts this prediction in terms of teaching to emphasize its authority and to distinguish it from the Jewish expectation that the Messiah, or Christ, would *not* suffer and die but only reign in great glory. The switch from "the Christ" in 8:29 to "the Son of Man" here in 8:31 helps the distinction; and sharpening it are the severity of the suffering, the rejection by none lower than the highest Jewish authorities, and the consequent killing of Jesus. The elders, chief priests, and scholars constitute the Sanhedrin, based in Jerusalem and amounting to the Jews' Supreme Court. Rising after being killed—and only three days afterwards—makes the most astonishing part of the prediction. ("After three days" doesn't mean "on the fourth day"; for Mark puts Jesus' resurrection on the third day, Sunday, after Good Friday, so that "after three days" equates with "on the third day.") And "must" puts every part of the prediction in the sphere of divine necessity as expressed in Scripture (see especially Psalm 118:22–23 in relation to Mark 12:10–11, and the use of "must" at Mark 9:11 in relation to Malachi 4:5). It's all part of God's plan. Mark's detailed narrative in chapters 14–16 will put on display both the carrying out of this plan and Jesus' power to have predicted accurately his own fate. This power and God's plan erase the shame that would otherwise be attached to Jesus' crucifixion. For ordinarily crucifixion was considered the most shameful way to die. Originally it was reserved for slaves convicted of a crime. Then it was used to execute rebels and others convicted of high crime. It had all the associations, and worse, of an electric chair or a gas chamber in our culture (compare 1 Corinthians 1:18). Mark's unusual comment that Jesus spoke this prediction of his passion and resurrection "plainly" (here is the only passage where Mark uses this expression) lays all possible stress on Jesus' power to predict his own fate. He really did, and there was no mistaking what he said or meant.

8:32b–33: And on taking him aside, Peter started reprimanding him. For the moment Peter stops being a disciple, for disciples respectfully follow behind their teacher at a little distance. Moreover, Peter compounds his error by reprimanding Jesus for predicting that he (Jesus) will have to undergo intense suffering, rejection, and an execution which will necessitate his resurrection. Jesus has the authority to reprimand his disciples, but not they him. Mark doesn't quote Peter's reprimand of Jesus. So the emphasis stays on the plainness with which Jesus made his prediction and which therefore evoked the reprimand by Peter. **³³But on turning around and seeing his disciples, he reprimanded Peter and says, "Go behind me, Satan, because you're not thinking the things of God; rather,** [you're thinking] **the things of human beings."** Jesus' turning around and seeing his disciples points up that they're following him as disciples should do whereas Peter is not, and Jesus' reprimanding him shows who really does have the authority to engage in reprimand. He tells Peter to go back to his position among the disciples, where he belongs, following behind Jesus rather than taking him aside as though he had the right to lead Jesus and reprimand him. The plainness with which Jesus made his prediction justifies his reprimanding Peter; and the divine necessity ("must" in 8:31) justifies the shocking epithet "Satan" with which Jesus addresses Peter. Since Peter is "thinking the things of *human beings*," Jesus doesn't mean that Peter *is* Satan. For then he'd have said that Peter is thinking "the things of *Satan*." Jesus means, then, that in reprimanding him Peter was acting *like* Satan. The comparison frighteningly highlights the seriousness of allowing yourself to be scandalized by Jesus' passion. "The things of God" consist in the divinely necessitated suffering, rejection, killing, and resurrection of Jesus as the Son of Man. To think these things is to accept them as divinely necessitated, so that they regulate your belief and conduct. This kind of thinking is attitudinal and behavioral as well as intellectual. "The things of human beings" consist in the repudiation of Jesus' suffering, rejection, killing, and resurrection. To *think* these things is to deny the divine necessity of Jesus' suffering, rejection, killing, and resurrection—as Peter has just done, with the attitudinal and behavioral result that he inexcusably left his position behind Jesus, took him aside, and reprimanded him.

8:34: And on summoning the crowd along with his disciples, he told them, "If anyone wants to come behind me, he has to disown himself and pick up his cross and follow me." The authority of Jesus comes out in his summoning the crowd along with his disciples. Mark hasn't mentioned a crowd since he noted Jesus' departure from Bethsaida (see 8:27 with 8:22). So the present introduction of a crowd without saying where they came from points again to Jesus' magnetism. "Along with his disciples" indicates that except for Peter they've been following Jesus at a distance which prevented them from hearing the conversation between Peter and him. But the disciples have already been following Jesus. So his saying that anyone who "wants" to come behind him has to "disown himself," "pick up his cross," and "follow [Jesus]" applies to would-be disciples in the crowd. "Come behind me" echoes Jesus' reprimand to Peter, "Go behind me" (8:33). Disowning yourself doesn't mean practicing asceticism. It means putting your very life at risk (see 8:35–37). "Pick up" has to do with the start of discipleship, that is, conversion. Literally, "his *cross*" means the horizontal beam of a cross, not the whole cross, which would be too heavy to carry. Besides, the vertical pole of a cross—or it could be a living tree—was a fixture at the place of crucifixion. It wasn't to be picked up. "*His cross*" isn't Jesus' cross. It's the disciple's cross and, figuratively, means allegiance to Jesus despite the hostility of others to him and his disciples. He has predicted that he'll be rejected and killed (8:31–32a). But he has said nothing about crucifixion as the method by which he'll be killed. Nor will he later. And in Mark (as well as in Matthew and Luke) he won't carry his cross. Simon of Cyrene will (15:21). So to pick up your cross and follow Jesus doesn't mean to follow his example, as though he picked up his cross and, carrying it, went to the place of his crucifixion. No, to pick up your cross and follow him means to expose yourself to shame, ridicule, persecution, and—in dire circumstances—martyrdom because of open discipleship to him. His suffering, rejection, and execution were divinely necessitated. A disciple's suffering, rejection, and execution are voluntarily risked.

8:35–37: "For whoever would want to save his life will lose it." Merely wanting to save your life by avoiding the risks of discipleship will make you lose it in the world to come, whether or not you succeed in saving it now. **"But whoever will** [in fact] **lose his life** [now] **on account of me and the gospel** [that is, the good news that God's reign has arrived in Jesus' activities (1:14–15)] **will save it** [for the world to come]." Jesus doesn't *command* his hearers to lose their lives on his and the gospel's account, or even to want to. But if they do lose them—not to worry! They'll have saved their lives for the coming world. Wanting to save your life now, and consequently refusing discipleship because of its risks, has the woefully opposite effect hereafter. [36]**"For in what way does gaining the whole world and forfeiting his life profit a man?"** In no way, of course. The answer is so obvious that Jesus doesn't have to state it. You can't enjoy the whole world you've gained if you're dead. [37]**"For what would a man give** [as] **an exchange for his life** [that is, to keep it rather than lose it]**?"** Implied answer: everything he could, even the whole world if he had it. But he can't— therefore "*would* give" rather than "*does* give." "Life" shifts in meaning between present life and eternal life. Saving your present life for this world results in losing the eternal life that you might have had. Losing your present life in this world on account of Jesus and the gospel results in saving eternal life for yourself. Gaining the whole world isn't worth losing your present life, much less worth losing your eternal life. And nothing will buy back even your present life, much less your eternal life, once you lose it. Because of "an exchange," "the whole world" means the world of wealth, not the world of human beings.

8:38: "For whoever would be ashamed of me and my words in this adulterous and sinful generation, also the Son of Man will be ashamed of him when he comes in the glory of his Father with the holy angels." "*Would* be ashamed" holds out a possibility but discourages it. Jesus' "words" are his prediction that he must suffer severely, be rejected by the elders, chief priests, and scholars, be killed, and rise again (8:31). To be ashamed of him and those words is to dismiss that he can be the Christ if he undergoes such a fate, because it would be humiliating to believe in such a Christ. "In this adulterous and sinful generation" identifies the circumstance in which a person has to decide whether to become a disciple of Jesus. It consists of people whose wickedness will lead them to abuse that person if he or she does become Jesus' disciple. As the ultimately judgmental Son of Man, Jesus will be ashamed of such a person. In other words, he'll dismiss that such a person could be his disciple. It would be humiliating for Jesus to accept the person as one of his own. "When he comes in the glory of his Father with the holy angels" adds the second coming of Jesus to the resurrection that he predicted for himself in 8:31. The glory in which he'll come will be no less than that of God his Father, for it will *be* his Father's glory. *He* isn't ashamed of his Son! And the accompaniment of the holy angels, an angelic escort that contrasts with this sinful and adulterous generation, helps the statement as a whole to compensate for Jesus' prior suffering, rejection, and execution. Nothing to be ashamed of here—but much to fear!

In summary of 8:34–38, why should you disown yourself, pick up your cross, and follow Jesus? (1) Because you'll save your life for eternity even if you lose it now. Here's a savings account better than you ever dreamed of. (2) Because your life, whether present or future, is much more valuable than even the whole world. So don't be duped into making a foolish deal. (3) Because once you've lost your life, there's no buying it back, no matter how much you offer. The opportunity to invest in futures is now. Don't let it slip by. (4) Because when the tables are turned on this wickedly hostile world, when the glorious Son of Man comes with the approval of God his Father and with the holy angels as his army, you'll want to be on his side, not the world's.

9:1: And he was saying to them, "Amen I tell you that there are some standing here who as such [that is, as standing here] **will by no means taste death** [a figure of speech for dying] **until they see God's reign** [as] **having come with power."** The prediction in 8:38 of the Son of Man's glorious coming leads to a prediction involving the powerful coming of God's reign. "Amen I tell you" emphasizes the truthfulness of this prediction (compare 8:12). Along with its fulfillment (for which see 9:2–8), the prediction will demonstrate Jesus' ability to forecast the future; and by taking place before the fulfillment of his earlier prediction of the passion and resurrection, the fulfillment of this present prediction will lend credibility to the earlier one. From now on, to counteract the scandal of the crucifixion Mark will capitalize on Jesus' predictive power whenever he can.

A SUPPLYING OF VISUAL AND AUDITORY
EVIDENCE THAT JESUS IS GOD'S SON
Mark 9:2–13

This passage divides into Jesus' transfiguration (9:2–8) and a conversation between him and three of his disciples on the way down the mountain where they'd seen him transfigured (Mark 9:9–13).

9:2–4: And after six days Jesus takes along Peter and James and John, and he takes them up onto a high mountain by themselves—alone. And he was transfigured in their presence, ³and his clothes became glistening, exceptionally white, such [clothing] **as a launderer on the earth can't whiten them thus. ⁴And there appeared to them** [Peter, James, and John] **Elijah with Moses, and they were speaking with Jesus.** "After six days" links the transfiguration of Jesus to his prediction in 9:1, so that the transfiguration fulfills the prediction and thereby displays his power to forecast the future. "By themselves—alone" stresses that Peter, James, and John are the "*some* . . . who'll by no means taste death till they've seen God's reign [as] having come with power" (9:1 again). Mountains symbolize power and dominion, as in Daniel 2:35, 44–45: "The stone that struck the statue became a great mountain and filled the whole earth. . . . The God of heaven will set up a kingdom that won't ever be destroyed . . . . It'll crush all these kingdoms and bring them to an end and stand forever, just as you saw that a stone was cut from the mountain not by hands . . . ." So the "high mountain" on which Peter, James, and John see Jesus transfigured symbolizes the power of God's reign; and the transfiguration itself shows these three disciples that in Jesus the reign of God has come with power. The glistening and unearthly, unmatchable whiteness of Jesus' clothing also shows the disciples that God's reign originated in heaven but has come to earth in Jesus' activities. It's not that God's reign came with power in the transfiguration. It's that the transfiguration enabled these disciples to *see* that Jesus' miracles (literally, "acts of power"), exorcisms, and authoritative teaching constituted the coming of God's powerful reign. "In their presence" underlines the disciples' seeing, yet again in fulfillment of 9:1 ("until they *see* . . ."). In accordance with Malachi 4:5–6, Elijah's appearance signals to the three disciples that God's reign has come with power also in fulfillment of the long-prophesied Day of the Lord, at which time human history reaches its divinely appointed end and God's will is done on earth as it is in heaven (see too 9:11–13). Despite Moses' coming before Elijah in the Old Testament, Mark mentions Elijah first to highlight this signal. Moses accompanies Elijah, because they're the only Old Testament figures to have heard God on a mountain (Exodus 19:1–25; 24:1–18; 32:1–20; 34:1–35; 1 Kings 19:11–18); and Peter, James, and John are about to hear God speak on this mountain. Elijah along with Moses *appears* to these disciples, but Elijah and Moses *converse* only with Jesus. They aren't transfigured as he is, though, because God's reign has come with power only in Jesus' activities. He's the center of attention. So some

of those who heard the prediction in 9:1 saw that God's reign had come with power even before the Son of Man's coming "in the glory of his Father with the holy angels" (8:38), a yet future event of which the transfiguration—along with his miracles, exorcisms, and authoritative teaching—is a preview and guarantee.

9:5–6: And answering [in the sense of responding, since no question has been asked], **Peter says to Jesus, "Rabbi, it's good we're here" and "Let's make three tents, one for you and one for Moses and one for Elijah." ⁶For he didn't know what** [or "how"] **he should answer** [= respond]. **For they'd become terrified.** This terror emphasizes the three disciples' seeing that God's reign has come *with power* before their very eyes, and thus emphasizes the fulfillment of Jesus' prediction and therefore his foreknowledge. Though the locations differ, "here" connects this fulfillment with that prediction ("it's good we're *here*" [9:5] and "some of the ones standing *here*" [9:1]). Apart from the prediction in 9:1, Peter's statement, "Rabbi, it's good we're here," would mean that the presence of Peter, James, and John is good for the making of three tents. But because of Jesus' prediction the statement means that their presence is good because they are seeing the fulfillment of his prediction. So "we" refers only to Peter, James, and John as "some of the ones standing here" in Jesus' prediction. The same goes for the "us" who Peter suggests should make tents for Jesus, Moses, and Elijah. Peter puts Moses before Elijah to conform to their chronological order in the Old Testament and to link his suggestion with Moses' having made a tent, traditionally called "the tabernacle," for God's dwelling in the wilderness (Exodus 26:1–37; 35:4–35; 39:32–40:38). The limitation to three tents—one each for Jesus, Moses, and Elijah and therefore none for the three disciples—shows that Peter has in mind places of honor, as though Moses and Elijah were transfigured along with Jesus. But they weren't. And though the present tense in "Peter *says* to Jesus" underlines Peter's enthusiasm, to keep his audience from overlooking Peter's error Mark explains that Peter didn't know how to respond. God himself will shortly correct the error. Meanwhile, the disciples' terror gives the reason for the error and underscores the overpowering glory of God's reign that they're seeing in fulfillment of Jesus' prediction.

9:7–8: And there came a cloud, overshadowing them; and a voice came out of the cloud: "This is my beloved Son. Hear him!" [compare Deuteronomy 18:15]. **⁸And suddenly, looking around, they no longer saw anyone; rather,** [they saw] **Jesus alone with themselves** [but not with Elijah and Moses]. The cloud signals God's presence, as in Exodus 16:10; 19:9; 24:15–16; 34:5; 40:34–35; Numbers 9:15–22; 1 Kings 8:10–11 and other passages. The overshadowing eliminates any need for tents and therefore corrects Peter's suggestion of making three of them. The location on a high mountain indicates complete envelopment rather than just shade overhead (compare Exodus 40:34–38). So everybody on the mountain is enveloped by the cloud. In it the disciples lose sight of Jesus, Elijah, and Moses. But they hear God's voice, which replaces Elijah's and Moses' speaking with Jesus. God tells the three disciples that Jesus is his beloved Son (compare God's similar statement in 1:11 to Jesus himself) and that they should listen to Jesus—not to Elijah and Moses, it's implied. Despite the evident pleasure the three disciples took in Elijah's and Moses' speaking with Jesus, whatever *they*'d been saying to him doesn't compare with what *he* says (see his own command in 7:14: "Hear *me*" and compare 4:3, 9, 13–20, 23–24, 33). "Looking around" implies that the cloud has lifted and that the disciples are looking to see Elijah and Moses with Jesus. But with the exception of Jesus they see no one, for Elijah and Moses have left under cover of the cloud. The suddenness of seeing Jesus alone underlines visually what they'd heard God say to them audibly. "With themselves" complements Jesus' choosing the apostles to be "with him" (3:14). The declaration that Jesus is God's beloved Son counteracts Peter's (and anybody else's) taking offense at Jesus' predicted passion and at his consequent command to take up your cross and follow him (8:31–38). Since the disciples have already heard that prediction and that command, though, the present command to hear him looks forward to Jesus' coming command not to relate what they've seen till after the resurrection.

9:9–10: And as they were coming down from the mountain, he ordered them not to relate to anyone the things they'd seen—except when the Son of Man had risen from among the dead. [10]**And they kept the saying** [in obedience to Jesus' order], **though discussing with one another what the rising from the dead** [that Jesus predicted for himself] **meant.** As in 5:43; 7:36; 8:30, Jesus orders silence to avoid the danger of being mobbed by his admirers. After the resurrection, which will issue in the ascension, that danger will have passed. Here, moreover, a premature publicizing of the transfiguration, glorious as it was, would undermine both the teaching that the Son of Man must suffer humiliatingly and the general summons to shameful cross-taking (8:31–38). And after his resurrection, these disciples' telling about the transfiguration would combine with a proclamation of the resurrection to counteract the scandal of his crucifixion. His having predicted both these events will lend weight to this counteraction. "The things they'd *seen*" reminds us again of the prediction in 9:1 that some of Jesus' audience at that time wouldn't die "until they'd *seen* God's reign [as] having come with power." It will now come out that Peter, James, and John were discussing the meaning of Jesus' predicted resurrection in relation to the expected return of Elijah—a natural topic of discussion in view of Elijah's appearance at the transfiguration.

9:11–12: And they were asking him, saying, "Why do the scholars say, 'Elijah must come first'?"—that is, before the Day of the Lord and therefore, in the disciples' view (since resurrection is associated with that day), before the Son of Man's resurrection. A combination of several factors gives rise to this question: (1) the scholars' teaching in accordance with Malachi 4:5–6 that God will send Elijah before the Day of the Lord; (2) Jesus' recent mention of the scholars in his first passion-and-resurrection prediction (8:31); (3) Elijah's appearance at the transfiguration; and (4) the immediately foregoing mention of the Son of Man's resurrection (9:9–10). [12]**And he told them, "Indeed on coming first, Elijah restores all things."** Jesus doesn't answer the disciples' question why the scholars say Elijah must come first by saying, "Because Malachi prophesied that he would." Instead, Jesus vaults over scholarly opinion, and even over Malachi's prophecy, not only by accepting that Elijah must come first but also by predicting that "Elijah restores all things." The futuristic present tense of "restores" stresses the certainty of the fulfillment. Malachi predicted only that Elijah was going to "turn the heart of fathers to children, and the heart of children to their fathers." "Restores *all* things" enlarges Elijah's coming ministry to include everything needed for the consummation, the Day of the Lord—but not before Jesus' passion, as now becomes clear in a rhetorical question of his own: **"And how** [is it that] **it's written against the Son of Man in order that he may suffer severely and be treated with contempt** [if indeed Elijah, having come beforehand, restores all things]**?"** In other words, an earlier restoration of all things would leave no room for Jesus' maltreatment. "It's written *against* the Son of Man" in the sense that the Old Testament says people will turn against him. And "it's written . . . *in order that* he may suffer severely [and so on]" in the sense that the Old Testament expresses God's purpose that the Son of Man should suffer, a purpose the writing of which in Holy Scripture ensures achievement. Jesus has asked a question: "And how [is it that] . . . ?" But he doesn't answer it. His nonanswer leaves it to be inferred that since the Son of Man's suffering hasn't yet occurred, neither has Elijah's restoration of all things. For the restoration has to follow the suffering.

9:13: "Nevertheless I tell you that even Elijah has come; and they did to him as many things as they wanted, just as it's written against him." "Nevertheless I tell you" calls attention to the authority of Jesus' teaching and sets his implication that Elijah is yet to restore all things over against Jesus' present affirmation that Elijah has already come and suffered maltreatment in accordance with God's purpose as expressed in the Old Testament. *Even* Elijah" shows that Jesus is referring to John the baptizer in terms of Elijah; that is, Elijah has already come in the person of John. The many things they did to him consisted in Herod Antipas's arresting, binding, and imprisoning him, Herodias's plotting his execution, her daughter's requesting his head, and Herod's having him beheaded (6:17–29). But neither Malachi nor any other Old Testament prophet predicted maltreatment of the *coming* Elijah. So "just as it's written against him" refers to the maltreatment of Elijah in Old Testament *history* (1 Kings 18–19). Like the old Elijah, so John the baptizer as the new Elijah (compare the old Elijah's persecutors, Ahab and Jezebel, with the new Elijah's persecutors,

Herod and Herodias). But the old Elijah's persecutors failed to kill him. The new Elijah's persecutors succeeded in doing "as many things as they wanted," including the taking of his life. But though he came as Elijah in fulfillment of Malachi's prediction (see the comments on 1:6 for John's Elijah-like appearance), John's maltreatment not only paralleled the coming maltreatment of Jesus but also prevented his restoring all things. Apparently Jesus looks forward to a yet further coming of Elijah for such a restoration (see Matthew 17:11). Mark's interest centers, however, on God's scripturally indicated plan that both the Johannine Elijah and the Son of Man Jesus suffer first. For that plan shows the crucifixion *not* to have been a tragic, shameful accident.

JESUS' DISPLAY OF SUPERPOWER IN A SPECIALLY DIFFICULT EXORCISM
Mark 9:14–29

9:14–15: And on coming to the disciples, they [Jesus, Peter, James, and John] **saw a large crowd around them** [that is, around the remaining nine of the Twelve] **and scholars arguing with them.** It'll turn out that the scholars are arguing over the nine disciples' inability to exorcise a spirit. [15]**And immediately on seeing him, all the crowd were utterly amazed and were hailing him as they ran toward** [him]. *Utter* amazement seems too strong for mere surprise at seeing Jesus turn up on the scene. Could it be that his garments are still glistening from the transfiguration? Perhaps not, since he told Peter, James, and John not to tell anyone what they saw on that occasion (9:9). On the other hand, the crowd didn't see the transfiguration in process and the three disciples don't tell them about it, so that an afterglow wouldn't have publicized it. In any case, Mark stresses the impact of Jesus' appearance. Heightening this impact are its immediacy, its affecting the whole of a large crowd, and their running toward him and hailing him. The running and the hailing add Jesus' magnetism to the impact of his appearance.

9:16–18: And he asked them [the scholars], **"Why are you arguing with them** [the nine disciples]**?"** [17]**And one of the crowd** [instead of one of the scholars] **answered him, "Teacher, I brought you my son, who has a mute spirit."** The spirit keeps him from speaking during seizures, so that the ability to speak between seizures will eliminate any need to mention a restoration of speech in 9:27 once the spirit is exorcised and no more seizures are in the offing (contrast 7:35). Furthermore, the coming descriptions of the seizures don't include the usual shrieking and adjurations (contrast 1:23–26; 3:11; 5:6–10). The spirit will let out a shriek in 9:26, but that shriek will signal Jesus' defeat of the spirit. The father's addressing Jesus with "Teacher" reminds us of Jesus' "new [kind of] teaching with authority" since "he even commands unclean spirits, and they obey him" (1:27). "I brought *you* my son" indicates that the father supposed Jesus would be where he found the nine disciples. Presumably the large crowd had gathered there under

the same supposition. The father continues, [18]**"And wherever it** [the spirit] **takes possession of him** [my son]**, it dashes** [him] **to the ground; and he foams** [at the mouth] **and grinds** [his] **teeth and stiffens up. And I told your disciples to cast it out, and they weren't strong enough** [to do so]**."** The spirit's dominion over the son goes beyond dumbness. The further details describing the seizures—and more are to come—will make Jesus' exorcism all the more impressive in its superior power. Despite their successful exorcisms earlier on (6:12–13), the disciples weren't strong enough to cast out this spirit (compare 5:4). Their powerlessness, too, will make Jesus' exorcism of the spirit all the more impressive. He is truly "the stronger one" of whom John the baptizer spoke (1:7).

9:19: But he, answering them, says, "O unbelieving generation, how long shall I be with you? How long shall I put up with you? Bring him to me." Though the father has just been speaking to Jesus, Jesus answers "them." So the father represents the crowd, including the scholars, in his unbelief (compare 9:24, where the father will say, "Help my unbelief"). The disciples aren't included in the unbelieving generation, though, because they stood opposite the crowd in the foregoing argument; and Jesus won't mention unbelief on their part when they ask him why they failed to exorcise the spirit (9:28–29). It looks as though he condemns the crowd for making the disciples' failure a reason to disbelieve in the power of Jesus himself. The present tense of "says," the prefixing of "answering," and "O unbelieving generation" lend gravity to Jesus' exasperated questions (compare 8:12). And the questions themselves, "How long shall I be with you? How long shall I put up with you?" hint at his being killed before long without actually predicting it in public (see 8:31–33 with comments). "Bring him to me" shows Jesus' determination to expose the baselessness of unbelief in him. (A plural "you" is hidden in "Bring" as its subject.}

9:20: And they brought him [the son] **to him** [Jesus]**. And on seeing him** [Jesus]**, the spirit immediately convulsed him** [the son]**. And falling on the ground he started rolling around, foaming** [at the mouth]**.** The spirit convulses the son to intimidate Jesus with a demonstration of its power, but the demonstration will serve only to heighten the superiority of Jesus' power. Sharpening this point are the immediacy of the convulsion and the details of falling on the ground, rolling around, and foaming at the mouth. Because the spirit causes muteness during seizures, there's no verbal attempt to ward off Jesus (contrast 1:24; 5:7).

Not content with the already vivid details concerning the spirit's power over the son, Mark incorporates a dialogue between Jesus and the father. The dialogue adds further details that will make a successful exorcism all the more impressive. **9:21–22: And he asked his** [the son's] **father, "How long a time is it since this has happened to him?" And he said, "From childhood.** [22]**And** many times it has thrown him both into fire and into water to destroy him. Nevertheless, if you're able [to do] anything, help us by having compassion on us." "From childhood" makes the possession nearly lifelong and therefore difficult to break (compare 5:25–26 in regard to a long illness). "Many times" adds frequency to duration—with the same effect of difficulty. The destructive purpose of the spirit comes out in its throwing the son sometimes into fire, for incineration, and sometimes into water, for drowning. The very variety of fire and water highlights this destructive purpose and by contrast will therefore highlight equally well the life-saving power of Jesus. The father's question whether Jesus can help arises out of the nine disciples' failure. If their ability derives from his, their failure casts doubt on his ability. "Nevertheless" puts emphasis on the father's appeal for help, however. He believes in Jesus' compassion more than he disbelieves in Jesus' ability. And whereas he asked the nine disciples for an *exorcism* (9:18), because of disbelief in Jesus' ability he now asks him to help only by way of "*anything*" he can do. Since the father has a stake in the welfare of his son, he includes himself ("help *us*") as a possible co-beneficiary of Jesus' help.

9:23–24: But Jesus told him, "As to the [phrase], **'If you're able,' all things** [are] **able** [to be done] **for the person who believes."** This answer neatly shifts the focus from Jesus' ability, about which there should be no question, to a petitioner's belief. The dropping of "[to do] anything" from the father's appeal, which Jesus here quotes in part, allows emphasis to fall now on "*all* things." They include the particularly difficult exorcism at hand. Even it can be performed for the believer in Jesus. **24Immediately shouting out, the father of the little child was saying, "I believe. Help my unbelief."** "From childhood" in 9:21 implied the son's adulthood, or at least his young manhood. As before, then, and in line with a common use of diminutives, "the *little* child" reflects the son's endearment to the father (compare 5:23, 39–42). Mark's description of the father's response as a shout, and an immediate one at that, portrays Jesus as worthy of belief. Apparently the father brought his son with belief in Jesus' ability to exorcise the spirit; but the failure of the disciples, who represent Jesus, crushed his belief in Jesus' ability—hence Jesus' outburst ("O unbelieving generation . . ."). And now the father's belief revives, but accompanied by some vestigial unbelief, for the overcoming of which he asks for Jesus' help. The present tense of the request for help (literally, "Be helping . . .") stresses the need for Jesus' help in getting rid of some unbelief that lingers because the disciples' recent failure has raised the spectre of failure on Jesus' part too.

9:25–27: And on seeing that a crowd is running together, Jesus reprimanded the unclean spirit by saying to it, "Mute and deaf spirit, I command you, come out of him and never again enter into him." It has been assumed that deafness underlies the muteness; but deafness is now mentioned explicitly. **26And on shrieking and convulsing** [the son] **severely, it** [the

spirit] **came out. And he became as if dead, so that the many were saying, "He died." 27But Jesus, on grasping his hand, raised him; and he stood up.** Back in 9:15 the crowd was running toward Jesus. To reemphasize his magnetism, Mark mentions their running again. Jesus wanted privacy to perform this very difficult *exorcism* of a spirit that causes muteness and deafness just as he'd wanted privacy to perform the very difficult *healing* of a deaf-mute (7:33–35). By now, though, the crowd running toward him is congealing around him. So seeing that they are, as stressed by "*is* running together," Jesus reprimands the spirit before things get too crowded for comfort. "Unclean" describes the spirit as deserving of exorcism, and Jesus' addressing it as "deaf" as well as "mute" heightens the difficulty of the exorcism and thus its success. The reprimand consists in the command to come out and never reenter. Jesus addresses the spirit as "mute and deaf" because it *causes* muteness and deafness. But the spirit itself can hear and speak. So it shrieks in despair and, though making a final attempt to destroy the son with a severe convulsion, comes out in obedience to Jesus' command. "And never again enter into him" contrasts with the frequency of the son's earlier seizures and raises Jesus' success to the level of permanence. Mark's saying that "the many" were saying the son was dead doesn't imply that others in the crowd drew a different conclusion. It means that the crowd consisted of many people, all of whom were inferring the son's death. They're still the "unbelieving generation" of 9:19. They believe the spirit has succeeded in killing the son rather than that Jesus has succeeded in exorcising the spirit. But no, he grabs the son's hand and raises him with the result that he stands up—alive. A marvelous victory for Jesus and defeat of the spirit after all! The raising of the son from seeming death and his standing up may look forward to the raising of Jesus from actual death and his resurrection, for "resurrection" means quite literally a "standing up" (compare 5:41–42; 8:31; 9:9).

9:28–29: And when he'd gone into a house, his disciples were asking him privately, "Why weren't we able to cast it out?" 29And he told them, "This kind [of spirit] **is able to come out by no means except by prayer."** The disciples' question recalls their failure as a foil against which Jesus' success stands out. But *he* didn't pray so as to exorcise the mute and deaf spirit (= "This kind"). So what does he mean by citing the necessity of prayer? He means that *they* must pray to be successful in so difficult a case. But he's John the baptizer's "stronger one" (1:7). He was able to exorcise the spirit without praying. The disciples' needing to pray in such a case therefore provides another foil for Jesus' superior strength.

JESUS' DISPLAY OF ABILITY TO PREDICT HIS OWN DEATH AND RESURRECTION
Mark 9:30–32

9:30–32: And on going out from there [that is, from the house mentioned in 9:28]**, they** [Jesus and the Twelve] **were traveling along through Galilee. And he didn't want anyone to know [hence the lack of ministry along the way]. ³¹**For he was teaching his disciples and saying to them, "The Son of Man is being given over into the hands of men, and they'll kill him. And on being killed, he'll rise** [literally, 'stand up'] **after three days." ³²But they didn't understand the pronouncement and were afraid to ask him** [what it meant]. Jesus' teaching the disciples about his death and resurrection gives the reason for their traveling incognito (compare the private setting of his first such teaching and the command to keep it secret [8:27–33]). Historically, he was redefining his messiahship in a way the disciples needed to accept but that the general Jewish populace were sure to reject. They were all looking forward to freedom from Roman dominance and to their own dominance, under the Messiah's leadership, over other nations. Jesus was taking the role of a suffering and then vindicated messiah. But Mark is writing for Gentiles, not Jews, as evident from his explanation of Jewish traditions in 7:3–4. So he doesn't mention Jewish nationalistic messianism as the backdrop against which Jesus sets his teaching. It's the teaching as *prediction* that interests Mark, for as such it carries great apologetic value in defanging Jesus' crucifixion. His ability to predict it and the resurrection to follow—this ability takes away the shame of his crucifixion by making the crucifixion an exhibition of his predictive power and God's plan. "Is being given over" refers to Judas Iscariot's coming betrayal of Jesus to the Jewish authorities (14:10–11, 18, 21 and so forth), to their giving Jesus over to Pontius Pilate (15:1, 10), and to Pilate's giving him over to the soldiers who crucified him (15:15). The use of the present tense for these future events shows the events to be certain of fulfillment. There's a wordplay between "the Son of Man" and "hands of men." This latter phrase connotes oppressive, violent treatment in contrast with God's mercy (see 2 Samuel 24:14 among many other passages; also Genesis 31:29 for the connotation of power). Despite the connotation of crucifixion as the execution of a criminal, then, Jesus will die not *as* a criminal but *at the hands* of criminals. "After three days" indicates the quickness of his vindication through resurrection. The disciples' failure to understand his prediction despite its clarity makes his foreknowledge stand out, and their fearing to ask him for an explanation shows him to be awesome. Just what it is about the prediction that they don't understand Mark doesn't say. So his emphasis falls on ignorance and fear as such, because they provide foils for Jesus' foreknowledge and awesomeness.

JESUS' TEACHING WITH EXPLOSIVE FORCE
Mark 9:33–50

This long passage, consisting mainly of Jesus' sayings, is set in Capernaum. Its first section grows out of a dispute over greatness (9:33–37). Its second section grows out of a rivalrous confrontation (9:38–50). Just as Jesus' power of prediction proved frightfully awesome in 9:30–32, here the power with which he shatters norms proves explosive.

9:33–34: And they entered Capernaum. And on coming to be in the house [Peter's (see the comments on 2:1)], **he was asking them, "What were you arguing about on the road?" ³⁴But they kept silent, for on the road they'd discussed with one another who** [of them was] **greater** [than the others]. "On the road" implies that Jesus had made his preceding passion-and-resurrection prediction on the road just as he'd made the first such prediction on the road (see 8:27 with 8:31; also 10:32–34). The disciples' failure to understand the preceding prediction shows up now in an argument over which of them is greater than the others. Had they understood the coming fate of their awe-inspiring teacher, such an argument would hardly have arisen. It's easy to think they keep silent out of sheepishness over discussing a self-centered issue, but Mark leaves the reason for their silence unidentified. For him, it's enough that their silence will enable Jesus to display his supernatural knowledge of the argument (compare 2:8) just as he displayed supernatural knowledge of his coming death and resurrection. He's equally aware of what *has* taken place and will *yet* take place. Such knowledge undercuts the notion that in his passion he'll be a victim. He'll be, rather, a victor.

9:35–37: And on sitting down, he called the Twelve and says to them, "If anyone wants to be first [in rank], **he shall be last of all and servant of all." ³⁶And on taking a little child, he had him stand in their midst. And on hugging him to himself, he told them, ³⁷"Whoever welcomes one of such children** [as I've hugged this one] **on the basis of my name** [for this child represents others likewise acceptable to me] **welcomes me** [in that I've welcomed the child]. **And whoever welcomes me doesn't welcome me; rather,** [he welcomes] **the one who sent me** [for I'm that one's messenger]." Jesus' sitting puts him in the authoritative posture of a teacher (see the comments on 4:1–2). "He *called* the Twelve" indicates the vigor with which he exercises his teacherly authority over them. "The Twelve" provides a numerical framework for the upcoming contrast between first and last, that is, between first and twelfth. Then Jesus says that "if anyone wants to be first, he shall be last of all"—"shall be" not as a prediction but as a command (compare 10:30, for example: "You shall love the Lord your God . . ."). The present tense in "he . . . *says* to them" lends force to the command, which shows Jesus' supernatural knowledge of their unconfessed argument (compare 10:41–44). "Of *all*" commands the wisher for firstness to demote himself to *utter* lastness, and "*servant* of all" defines this utter lastness in terms of subservience to the other disciples as well as to Jesus. Presumably the little child whom he takes, makes to stand in the midst of the Twelve, and hugs to himself lives in the house where they are. As before, then, "little" may connote endearment rather than toddlership. Since Jesus is sitting, he doesn't have to bend down to hug the child, whose standing posture enables Jesus to reach out and envelop the child in his embrace. Just as by sitting he took the authoritative posture of a teacher, so he has the child take the reverential posture of standing, as suits a representative of all children who according to 9:42 "believe in [him]." Hugging represents visually his welcoming such a child, and welcoming means acceptance into his new family of those who do God's will (3:31–35). The disciples' welcoming such a child entails welcoming Jesus himself, and welcoming Jesus entails welcoming God, who sent him. "Not me . . . rather, the one who sent me" is an emphatic way of saying "not me *so much as* the one who sent me." "*One* of such children" emphasizes the obligation to welcome even a single child who believes in Jesus. "On the basis of my name" specifies the ground of welcoming such a child. It's that *Jesus* has welcomed the child and thus associated his own name with that child. So adult believers shouldn't pursue greatness. For if they do pursue it, they'll shut out child-believers—hence Jesus himself and God. Thus Jesus turns the question of greatness inside out by shifting attention from greatness among the Twelve to their welcoming of children, which shows humility in contrast with the self-exalting pride that gave rise to their arguing who of *them* was greater than the others. The "all" whom the Twelve are to serve and with whom Jesus associates his name include children as well as the Twelve. Mark's point graduates from Jesus' supernatural knowledge of the Twelve's argument to the explosive force of Jesus' upsetting the societal norms of trying to be first and of denigrating children (as was done in that culture, contrary to current western culture). He even makes himself an example of welcoming children who believe in him.

9:38: John [the apostle] **told him, "Teacher, we saw someone casting out demons in your name and were telling him not to, because he wasn't following us."** "Teacher" calls to mind Jesus' didactic authority, represented in 9:35 by his seated position; and the unnamed exorcist's use of Jesus' name recalls the receiving of children on the basis of his name (9:37). That his name effects exorcisms even when used by an independent exorcist highlights Jesus' power. It's ironic that the Twelve had been telling this exorcist to stop doing successfully what they themselves recently tried and failed to do in 9:14–29. Their having told him to stop contrasts with the reception of children that Jesus has just told them to exercise and displays the same pretensions that had caused them to argue who of them was greater than the others. We expect John to say to Jesus, "because he wasn't following *you*." Instead he says, "because he wasn't following *us*." Since the "we" who were forbidding the exorcist didn't include Jesus, but only the Twelve, "us" probably excludes Jesus. In any case, the Twelve's pretension of greatness stands out: just as they follow Jesus, they too want to be followed. Highlighting this pretension is the abruptness of "John told him" (there's no preceding "And," "But," or "Then").

9:39–42: But Jesus said, "Don't tell him not to [cast out demons in my name]." Now Jesus backs up his prohibition with three reasons, the last of which is double-barreled: (1) **"For there's no one who'll perform a miracle on the basis of my name and be able to badmouth me quickly."** (2) [40]**"For the person who isn't against us is**

for us." (3) [41]**"For whoever gives you a cup of water to drink in name that you are Christ's** [= that you're in the category of belonging to Christ]—**amen I tell you that he'll by no means lose his reward;** [42]**and whoever trips up one of these little ones who believe in me—it's *good* for him, rather, if an upper millstone collars his neck and he's been thrown into the sea."** The expansive phrase, "there's no one who," makes for a stronger negation than the shorter, usual "no one." Jesus uses "miracle" to include acts of supernatural power in addition to exorcisms. He means that using his name to work a miracle and turning around right away to badmouth him can't go together, because a person who thinks so highly of Jesus' name as to use it in working a miracle won't badmouth Jesus, the owner of that name. "Quickly" leaves open the possibility of later apostasy, however. In giving his second reason, Jesus expands John's "us," if limited to the Twelve in 9:38, to include himself (Jesus) and changes John's reference to "following" to being for or against them all. As a result, Jesus remains the only one to be followed, though he associates the Twelve with himself in the battle against evil powers. He doesn't make the self-evident point that the person who's for them isn't against them—rather, the not-so-evident point that since the independent exorcist isn't against Jesus and the Twelve (after all, he uses Jesus' name), he's for them. So don't try to stop him. He's on our side.

Two "whoever"-statements make up Jesus' third reason. In the first of these statements he says that the extension of minimal hospitality to the Twelve (giving them a cup of water to drink) because they belong to Christ is enough to ensure the reward of entrance into God's kingdom. For such hospitality gives evidence of believing in the good news of that kingdom. General humanitarianism isn't in view. Jesus is speaking about treatment of the Twelve in their evangelistic travels. If giving them even minimal hospitality ensures eternal reward, then following the Twelve mustn't be required. So don't tell the independent exorcist to stop just because he's not following you. "You are Christ's" implies Jesus' acceptance of Peter's calling him "the Christ" (8:29) and casts the giving of a cup of water in the mold of an acted-out confession of Jesus as the Christ.

In the second "whoever"-statement, "one of these little ones who believe in me" alludes to the children represented by the child that Jesus had stand in the midst of the Twelve (9:36–37) and limits his reference to children who believe in him. He isn't talking about children in general. "Trips up" means "makes to sin" or, more probably, "makes to apostatize/lose faith," as the Twelve are liable to do if they strive for greatness rather than receiving and serving all, even children, in the circle of believers. Literally, "upper" means "having to do with a donkey" and therefore describes the millstone as so heavy that it has to be turned by donkey-power. (A millstone is large, flat, round, and used of course for grinding grain.) Such a stone, lying around the neck, not only ensures drowning but also kills all hope of the drowned body's rising to the surface and floating ashore for burial.

People of the Bible looked with horror on any kind of death that precluded burial. The unrealism of having your head shoved through the center hole of an upper millstone, worn like a collar, intensifies the horror. The un-Jewishness of execution by drowning also intensifies it. "He's *been* thrown into the sea" stresses permanence. The fate that Jesus thus describes contrasts sharply with the reward promised in 9:41. Yet he describes this fate as emphatically "good" in comparison with the fate of the adult who trips up a believing child. So this latter fate must be horrible beyond description. Well, not quite beyond description. For Jesus is about to describe it in terms of hellfire (9:43–49). He hasn't said that having an upper millstone laid around your neck and being thrown into the sea "*would* be" good by comparison. It "*is*" good by comparison. Jesus is speaking about a matter of fact.

In summary, the independent exorcist isn't to be hindered, (1) because suspecting fellow believers outside one's close circle underestimates the number of people on Jesus' side (9:39b); (2) because a sense of rivalry makes believers fail to recognize their friends (9:40); and (3) because welcoming a messenger of the gospel amounts to believing for salvation (9:41), whereas causing a mere child who believes to lose faith brings horrible judgment on the culprit (9:42).

Now comes a series of three sayings beginning "And if [a part of your body] is tripping you up," followed by a command, and ending with "it's good that you . . . ." **9:43, 45, 47–48** (9:44, 46 being absent from the earliest and best manuscripts and present as unoriginal additions in other manuscripts): **"And if your hand is tripping you up, cut it off. It's *good*** [again with emphasis] **that you go into** [eternal] **life maimed rather than that having two hands you go away into gehenna,** [that is,] **into the unquenchable fire."** Again sinning is in view, but now sinning caused by a member of your own body, not by someone else (as in 9:42). And again eternal judgment is in view, but this time for self-made sinners, not for those who cause others to sin. "Gehenna" refers to the Valley of Hinnom along the south side of Jerusalem. It was used as a garbage dump, where fire was constantly burning up combustible trash and maggots were constantly feeding on organic matter. But here "gehenna" stands as a figure of speech for the eternal torment of sinners. Jesus designs his warning not only to keep the Twelve (and us) from self-induced sinning, but also by deflating them to keep them from forbidding the independent exorcist and from rejecting children who believe in Jesus. Insiders and grownups like the Twelve have their own danger to avoid. **⁴⁵"And if your foot is tripping you up, cut it off. It's *good* that you go into** [eternal] **life lame rather than that having two feet you be thrown into gehenna. ⁴⁷And if your eye is tripping you up, throw it out** [= gouge it out]. **It's *good* that you go into God's kingdom** [here equivalent to eternal life in the future] **rather than that having two eyes you be thrown into gehenna, ⁴⁸where 'their worm doesn't come to an end and the fire isn't quenched'** [Isaiah 66:24]." "Their worm" is a collective singular for the maggots that, so to speak, will

endlessly feed on sinners; and the unquenching of the fire likewise stands for the eternality of their punishment. Thus Jesus raises the glories of God's kingdom and the miseries of hell to almost unimaginable degrees.

9:49–50: "For everyone will be salted with fire. ⁵⁰Salt [is] **good. But if the salt were to become saltless, with what will you season it? Have salt among yourselves, and be at peace with one another."** "For" (in the sense of "because") makes the *future* salting of everybody with fire the reason for obeying *now* the commands in 9:43–48. To be salted is to have salt thrown on you. To be salted "with fire" is to have fire thrown on you *as if* the fire were salt being thrown on you (compare the turning of Lot's wife into a pillar of salt when the Lord threw fire down on Sodom and Gomorrah [Genesis 19:24–26]). So having fire thrown *on* you complements your being thrown *into* the fire of gehenna—two ways of portraying the punishment of sinners. But Jesus says that "*everyone* will be salted with fire," whereas not everyone will be thrown into the fire of gehenna. Some will enter eternal life instead. So for them the fire with which they'll be salted will be a test, which they'll pass, rather than a punishment, such as sinners will suffer (compare 1 Corinthians 3:12–15). The figure of being "salted with fire" then leads to salt itself. Unlike the fire of eternal punishment, salt is "good," because it stands for peaceful relations between believers (contrast the Twelve's arguing with each other who of them was greater than the others, also their forbidding the independent exorcist [9:33–34, 38]; and compare the use of salt, because of its preservative power, for the perpetuity of a covenantal relationship [Exodus 30:35; Leviticus 2:13; Numbers 18:19; 2 Chronicles 13:5; Ezra 4:14; Ezekiel 43:24]). Salt can become saltless if sodium chloride dissolves away from impure salt, if unscrupulous dealers adulterate salt with cheaper ingredients, and if an admixture of gypsum masks the taste of salt. These possibilities stand for the breakdown of peace among disciples. There wasn't any substitute for salt as a seasoning, so that the impossibility of restoring saltiness to salt that has lost its saltiness underlines the need for disciples to keep peace with one another. For without such peace, hostility from unbelievers will lead believers to apostatize. Thus Jesus has crushed with overpowering authority the disciples' contentiousness.

JESUS' EXERCISE OF POWER IN
A PUTDOWN OF PHARISEES ON
THE QUESTION OF DIVORCE
Mark 10:1–12

10:1: And on standing up [from the seated position Jesus took in 9:35], **he goes from there** [the house in Capernaum (9:33)] **into the borders of Judea and Transjordan** [the east side of the river, so as to avoid going through Samaria, whose inhabitants could be antagonistic toward Jewish pilgrims passing through their territory]. **And again crowds travel together to him; and as he was accustomed** [to do], **he was teach-**

ing them again. The present tense in "he *goes*" stresses the determination of Jesus to meet his fate, for he now enters the region where his passion-and-resurrection predictions will come true (8:31; 9:31; 10:33–34). Even though Jesus goes through Transjordan before entering Judea, Mark mentions Judea first because it's there in particular that the fulfillments will take place. More particularly, in 11:1 he'll put Jerusalem first and work backward through Bethphage and Bethany, though Jesus will go through them in the reverse order. "Travel" suits what pilgrims do. But Mark won't mention the Festival of Passover till 14:1; and here in 10:1 he describes the crowds as traveling to Jesus rather than to Jerusalem, where they'll celebrate the festival. This surprising—we might even say odd—turn of phrase joins the present tense of "travel" to highlight Jesus' magnetism, which Mark never tires of emphasizing. "Together" suits the plural of "crowds." The plural adds to the emphasis on Jesus' magnetism. And "again" recalls his attracting crowds on prior occasions too (most recently in 9:25). Mark doesn't say what Jesus was teaching the crowds. So quite apart from subject matter, the accent reverts to Jesus' didactic authority that amazed people and drew them to him (1:21–22, 27–28, 35–39). His teaching "again" and "as he was accustomed [to do]" underlines this authority with frequency and sets the stage for some Pharisees' testing him. The *teacher* will get tested (compare 7:5; 8:11; 12:13–15)!

10:2–4: And on approaching [Jesus]**, by way of testing him** [some] **Pharisees were asking him if it's lawful** [according to the Old Testament] **for a husband to divorce** [his] **wife.** [3]**But answering, he said to them, "What did Moses command you?"** [4]**And they said, "Moses permitted writing a certificate of dismissal and divorcing** [the wife]**."** These Pharisees should know better than to test Jesus. But they do it anyway. Mark doesn't specify what was difficult or controversial about their question (contrast the qualification "for any cause" in Matthew 19:3). It's enough for him that Jesus will pass the test over the effort of the Pharisees to expose ignorance on his part. He starts outfoxing them by answering their question with one of his own: "What did Moses command you?" They'd asked indefinitely about "a husband." He could have asked in return, "What did Moses command?" But by adding "you," and by adding it rather than "him" (the husband) or "us," Jesus puts the onus on his interrogators. In effect, he's testing them rather than they him. "You" also distances Jesus from these Pharisees to prepare for his opposition to the Pharisaically held command of Moses. To emphasize divorce as a husband's privilege (which a Jewish wife lacked), they replace Jesus' verb of command with a verb of permission. They also avoid his pointed and distancing "you" by omission of a corresponding "us"; and they quote directly from Deuteronomy 24:1, which reads in part that a husband "writes for her [his wife] a certificate of dismissal and gives [it] into her hand and sends her out of his house." To emphasize further a husband's privilege, the Pharisees omit the Deuteronomic phrase "for her,"

omit the Deuteronomic clause "and gives [the certificate] into her hand," and summarize sending her out of her husband's house with a simple "divorcing."

10:5: But Jesus told them, "[With a view] **toward your hardheartedness he** [Moses] **wrote this command for you."** Jesus corrects the Pharisees' emphasis on husbandly *privilege* by describing Deuteronomy 24:1 as a *command*. In its Deuteronomic context, however, the quoted words are not a command—rather, a reference to what was customary. The custom of giving the wife a certificate of dismissal had the purposes of protecting her from a false accusation of desertion and of authenticating her right to remarry, which she would need to do for economic support. In his typically authoritative way, though, Jesus treats the custom as a command and by doing so elevates women's rights and protection above husbandly privilege. At the same time, he says Moses wrote the command with a view toward the Pharisees' hardheartedness, so that husbandly privilege not only yields to women's rights and protection. It will now drop into the sinkhole of a male chauvinistic failure to recognize God's purpose in creating male and female.

So Jesus continues in **10:6–9: "But from the beginning of creation** [compare Genesis 1:1] **'he** [God] **made them** [human beings] **male and female** [Genesis 1:27]*.'* [7]**For this reason a man shall leave his father and mother** [some manuscripts, though not the best, add "and cleave to his wife"]**,** [8]**and the two shall be one flesh** [Genesis 2:24]*.'* **And so they're no longer two; rather,** [they're] **one flesh.** [9]**Therefore what God has yoked together** [by commanding male and female to be one flesh in marital coitus, the leaving of father and mother implying marriage rather than a casual liaison] **a human being is not to separate** [compare Malachi 2:15–16]**."** The human being who isn't to break up the marriage is the husband, who alone had the right of divorce under Moses' law. According to Jesus, then, the husband, who's a mere human being in contrast to God, has no right of divorce—the Mosaic law's permitting it to the contrary notwithstanding. We'd expect Jesus to say "*those whom* God has yoked together." The surprising "*what* God has yoked together" stresses the oneness of fleshly union in marriage. Genesis 1:27, quoted by Jesus, doesn't deal with the question of divorce, but with fruitfulness—that is, with propagation of the human race so as to fill the earth, subdue it, and rule over other creatures in it (Genesis 1:28). And in Genesis 2:24, "For this reason" doesn't refer to God's making the first human beings "male and female," but to his making Eve out of Adam's side. So the reason for a man's leaving his father and mother to be one flesh with his wife has to do with Eve's origin in Adam: since woman came from man, he should unite himself with her to recapture their original unity. Jesus goes beyond Genesis, however, by inferring that marital coitus, commanded as it is by God himself, makes divorcing a wife fundamentally illegitimate despite the Mosaic command. Speechless in view of Jesus' authoritative pronouncement, the Pharisees fade from view.

10:10–12: And [when he'd gone] **into the house again, the disciples were asking him about this** [Jesus' pronouncement on divorce]. "*The* house" can't refer in particular to the house in Capernaum, Galilee, into which he last entered in 9:33; for Jesus has now come into the borders of Transjordan and Judea (10:1). So the house refers to a house that typifies the class of buildings in which he converses with his disciples. Their inquiry underlines the unexpectedness of his pronouncement on divorce. Mark doesn't specify the point of the inquiry, so that attention concentrates on unexpectedness as such. [11]**And he tells them, "Whoever divorces his wife and marries another** [woman] **commits adultery against her** [his earlier wife]. [12]**And if she, on divorcing her husband, marries another** [man], **she commits adultery."** Remarriage constitutes adultery because the one who remarries still belongs to the earlier spouse. So divorce *leads* to adultery through another marriage. It doesn't *free* from adultery in another marriage. Thus God's ordinance, evident since creation, makes divorce an *instrument* of sin rather than a way to *avoid* it. "Against her" heightens the explosive force of Jesus' pronouncement; for a man was thought to commit adultery only against the husband of the woman with whom he had sex, but not against his own wife. It's not so much that Jesus elevates women to equality with men (though his pronouncement tends toward such an effect) as that he elevates divine ordinance over husbandly privilege. The present tense in "he *tells* them" stresses this elevation.

The possibility of a wife's divorcing her husband reflects Gentile rather than Jewish culture. In a male-dominated culture it went without saying that if a *man* commits adultery against his wife by divorcing her and marrying another woman, then a *woman* certainly commits adultery against her husband by divorcing him and marrying another man (compare Romans 7:2–3). So there's no reason for Jesus to add "against him" for a match with "against her." But Gentiles didn't consider a woman who divorces her husband and marries another man an adulteress any more than Jews considered a man who divorces his wife and marries another woman an adulterer. Jesus' pronouncement is countercultural across the board, then. He has upset norms and expectations by saying that the Son of Man must be killed and rise after three days, that a person must lose life to save it, that Elijah has already come, that anyone who wants to be first must make himself last, that entering God's kingdom with a maimed body is better than going to hell with a whole body, and that the remarriage of a divorced man or woman is adulterous. Now he'll continue to upset one norm after another by blessing children, describing wealth as a disadvantage impossible for anyone but God to overcome, and advocating a life of voluntary servitude. Even on his way to crucifixion, *especially* on it, Mark's Jesus dumbfounds disciples and silences enemies with iconoclastic force.

JESUS' MAKING LITTLE CHIDLREN AN EXAMPLE OF MEMBERSHIP IN GOD'S KINGDOM
Mark 10:13–16

10:13: And people were bringing little children to him that he might touch them, but the disciples reprimanded them. Presumably it was parents who were bringing their little children, but Mark doesn't say so. Presumably the touch people were seeking for the children was a touch of blessing, but again Mark doesn't say so. And presumably the disciples reprimanded the parents, not the children; but yet again Mark doesn't say so. He doesn't even say why the disciples engaged in reprimand. His interest lies solely in Jesus' astonishing response.

10:14–15: And on seeing [what was happening], **Jesus got indignant and told them** [the disciples], **"Let the little children come to me. Stop forbidding them** [to do so]. **For God's kingdom belongs to** [little children] **such as these** [that is, to little children who like these ones come to Jesus]. [15]**Amen I say to you, whoever doesn't accept God's kingdom** [in the sense of submitting now to his reign] **as a little child** [accepts it] **will by no means enter into it** [in the sense of entering into the sphere where at the end God's reign will have defeated Satan, sin, and death and brought salvation and eternal life]." The disciples' taking it on themselves to engage in a wrongheaded reprimand angers Jesus. His command, "*Let* the little children come to me," shows that the disciples have been succeeding in their effort to keep the children from coming to him. Astonishingly, he not only accredits the possession of God's kingdom to children who come to him. In this respect he also makes them exemplars for adults. The kingdom is God's in that he reigns in it, and it belongs to such children in that they will own its benefits. "*Come* to me" signals a shift from the children's being brought by others to the children's approaching Jesus themselves, and this shift leads into his interpreting their coming as an acceptance of God's rule, evident in Jesus' activities. So the children belong to the class of "little ones" who "believe" in him (9:42) and therefore deserve reception on the basis of his name (9:37). Though the children are little, then, they're old enough to believe in Jesus. Parents loved their children then as now, but society at large disregarded them for the most part. So Jesus' making children's acceptance of God's reign an example for adults to follow—on pain of nonentrance into God's kingdom if their example isn't followed—needed extra emphasis. Hence the introduction, "Amen I say to you."

10:16: And on hugging them [the little children], **he was blessing** [them] **while laying** [his] **hands on them.** The hugging goes beyond the touching for which the children were brought and thereby heightens with body language Jesus' verbal approval of their coming to him. Subsequently, blessing them while laying hands on them combines spoken language with body language in a single act. It's as though the spoken words of blessing flow down through his hands onto the children. To bless (in Mark's original Greek) is to speak well of. Having addressed the disciples, then, Jesus addresses the children by way of speaking well of their coming to him.

JESUS' SHATTERING THE ACCEPTED ECONOMICS OF SALVATION
Mark 10:17–31

The first part of this passage consists in a dialogue between Jesus and a rich man (10:17–22), the second part in a dialogue between Jesus and his disciples (10:23–27), and the third part in a dialogue between Jesus and Peter (10:28–31).

10:17: And as he [Jesus] **was going out to a road** harks back to his having entered a house (10:10) and confirms that his blessing the children (10:13–16) took place in the house. **One** [man]**, on running to him and falling on his knees, was asking him, "Good teacher, what should I do to inherit eternal life?"** The man's running to Jesus and kneeling exhibits both Jesus' magnetism and the man's desperation (compare 1:40; 5:22). The kneeling surpasses the reverence shown to an ordinary teacher and thus reminds us of Jesus' divine sonship (1:1, 11; 5:7). "Good teacher" shows recognition not only of Jesus' didactic authority but also of his moral virtue (a point not to be lost on Mark's audience, who might draw an opposite inference from their knowledge that Jesus died by crucifixion, a method of execution used on criminals). The man's question what he should do to inherit eternal life therefore seeks an authoritative answer from a morally reliable source. Describing the man as "one" makes for a wordplay with "no one" and "except one" in Jesus' response.

10:18–19: But Jesus said to him, "Why do you call *me* **good? There** [is] **no one good except one,** [that is,] **God.** [19]**You know the commandments: 'You shouldn't murder. You shouldn't commit adultery. You shouldn't steal. You shouldn't give false testimony. You shouldn't defraud** [anybody]**. Honor your father and mother** [Exodus 20:12–16; Deuteronomy 5:16–20]**.'"** Nobody would be surprised to hear that God is good. But the Old Testament calls some human beings good (Proverbs 13:22; 14:14, 19), and neither the Jews nor the Gentiles of Jesus' day would say that God *alone* is good. Jesus says so, however. Here we have, then, another of his revolutionary pronouncements.[2] That God alone is good lays groundwork for the inadequacy of keeping commandments, even *his* commandments (see 10:19–21). "Except one, [that is,] God," echoes a phrase in the scribes' question at 2:7: "Who can forgive sins except one, [that is,] God?" There, Jesus proceeded to work a *miracle* for a demonstration of his divine prerogative

to forgive sins. The present echo makes his following *words* (which will display omniscience) a demonstration that he likewise possesses divine goodness. And this latter demonstration lays groundwork for following him, rather than keeping commandments, as the only way to inherit eternal life, have treasure in heaven, and enter God's kingdom (10:21). Jesus doesn't say, "*Keep* the commandments to inherit eternal life." He says, "You *know* the commandments," and goes on to recite some of them, starting with the second table of the Decalogue. But for the tenth commandment, "You shouldn't covet," Jesus substitutes a variant on the prohibition of stealing: "You shouldn't defraud [anybody]." It's easier to keep from defrauding others (an evil deed) than it is to keep from coveting their possessions (an evil desire). So Jesus leaves the door open for the man's coming claim to have "guarded all these things" (10:20). But before the man does make that claim, Jesus doubles back to the commandment to honor your father and mother, another commandment relatively easy to keep and, like the other ones quoted, dealing with interpersonal relations. He selects these commandments because of the damage wealth often does to such relations. Though Mark hasn't yet indicated that the man is wealthy, Jesus omnisciently knows of his wealth. In the meantime, the prohibition of coveting looks conspicuous by its absence; and in the end, the man's reaction will show him guilty of covetousness.

10:20–21: But he [the man] **said to him** [Jesus]**, "Teacher, I've guarded all these things since my youth."** [21]**But Jesus, gazing intently at him, loved him and told him, "One thing is lacking so far as you're concerned. Go, sell however many things you have, and give** [the proceeds] **to the poor; and you'll have treasure in heaven. And** [come] **here! Follow me!"** In addressing Jesus, the man no longer calls him "good." He has failed to catch the implication that Jesus' union with God as God's Son makes him share God's goodness just as he shares God's prerogative of forgiving sins. The man also refers to "all these *things*," the activities referenced in the commandments rather than the commandments as such, and thus calls attention to his not murdering, not committing adultery, and so on. The man claims to have guarded such activities in the sense of being careful to avoid the prohibited ones and to engage in the required one. You can almost hear him breathe a sigh of relief when saying he has guarded "*all* these things." "Since my youth" implies he's now an adult and probably takes its starting point from his having become fully obligated to keep the commandments at thirteen years of age.

The intensity of Jesus' gazing at the man and the recency of Jesus' having hugged children and laid hands on them in a physical demonstration of blessing them—these factors favor that loving the man includes another physical demonstration, such as putting his arm around him or patting him on the shoulder. The verb "love" can include a demonstration of that sort (see, for example, Luke 7:47 with Luke 7:38, 44–46). Jesus' loving the man exhibits divine goodness. "One thing is lacking so far as

---

[2]Elsewhere even Jesus calls some people good (Matthew 5:45; 12:35; 22:10; Luke 6:45; 8:15; 19:17), but only in comparisons with evil people, whereas in the present passage he limits absolute goodness—the kind that would merit eternal life—to God.

you're concerned" doesn't mean that the man's past obediences need the *addition* of one more thing, but that the man is lacking the one and *only* thing necessary for him to inherit eternal life. Jesus upsets the notion that keeping commandments brings eternal life. The "*one* thing" that the man lacks contrasts with "*all* these things" that he has guarded. "So far as you're concerned" pinpoints the lack as *his*. He mustn't ignore it. In Mark's original Greek text there's a wordplay between "is lacking" and "You shouldn't defraud." The wordplay doesn't come out in English translation; but it points up that the man's coming failure to go sell however many things he has and give the proceeds to poor people will amount to a covetousness that defrauds the poor by stealing from them what rightfully belongs to them. The prohibition of covetousness keeps lurking in the background despite its not being mentioned explicitly.

"However many things you have" underlines the stunning comprehensiveness of Jesus' command to go and sell. But "you'll have treasure in heaven" provides a motive for obedience which outweighs that comprehensiveness. Since the man asked about eternal life, "treasure in heaven" stands for eternal life, not for a reward above and beyond eternal life, and puts eternal life in terms of wealth far more abundant and desirable than this-worldly possessions (compare 8:35–37). "And [come] here! Follow me" implies that charity as such won't suffice to inherit eternal life any more than keeping some of the Ten Commandments will. The only charity that will count is what comes as the price of discipleship to Jesus. And it will count not as merit but as evidence of following him. But what charity! Some rabbis forbade selling all your property lest you be reduced to poverty and dependence on others. Jesus sovereignly reverses that prohibition.

10:22: But he [the rich man], **frowning at the statement** [of Jesus], **went away sorrowful. For he had many acquisitions.** The man reacts outwardly with a frown and inwardly with sorrow. As a net effect, he goes away without saying a word. In 10:21 the expression "however many things you have" didn't tell the amount of his possessions, whether few or many. Now Mark describes them as "many" and calls them "acquisitions." This word contrasts with the selling that Jesus had told him to do and alludes to the underlying theme of covetousness. For covetousness means the desire to have more, which leads to acquisitiveness. Thus the story sets the stage for Jesus' revolutionary teaching on wealth as a hindrance to entering God's kingdom.

10:23–24a: And on looking around, Jesus says to his disciples, "How hardly will those having means [= money gotten from the sale of prior acquisitions] **enter into God's kingdom!"** [24a]**And the disciples were astounded at his sayings** [what he'd said to the rich man and now to them]. According to Deuteronomy 28:1–14; Job 1:10; 42:10; Proverbs 10:22, wealth combined with piety signals God's favor. Jesus upsets that view by exclaiming that moneyed people will have a hard time entering God's kingdom. The present tense of "says"

intensifies this exclamation, which arises out of the rich man's having gone away gloomy and sorrowful. Even if he had sold all his acquisitions, he wouldn't have wanted to part with the proceeds by giving that money to the poor. To enter into God's kingdom means the same as inheriting eternal life (10:17), which is to have treasure in heaven (10:21), but the shift to entrance prepares for the impossibility of going through a needle's eye (10:25). The disciples' astonishment underlines Jesus' turning the economics of salvation upside down.

10:24b–25: And Jesus, answering, says to them again, "Children, how hard it is [for those having means] **to enter into God's kingdom!** [25]**It's easier for a camel to go through a needle's eye than for a rich person to enter into God's kingdom."** The disciples haven't asked a question. So Jesus' "answering" indicates a response to their astonishment. "Again" signals a repetition of his foregoing exclamation. But this time he introduces it with the address, "Children," which adds stress to the exclamation, shows affection, and puts Jesus in the role of a father explaining something that the disciples have naively failed to understand. And the present tense of "says" underlines Jesus' exclamation. "How!" echoes 10:23, but the shift from "*will* enter" in that verse to the present tense of "it *is*" transforms a prediction into an axiom. In the following amplification, "a needle's eye" comes into Jesus' answer as the smallest of openings, and "a camel" both as the largest beast of burden known in first-century Israel and as a figure of speech for a human being burdened with wealth. A burdenless camel couldn't go through a needle's eye. (There was no narrow gate in Jerusalem called "The Needle's Eye," nor do the best manuscripts have "a rope" instead of "a camel.") Much less could a camel saddled with burdens do so, and it goes without saying that it *would* be saddled with burdens. Since such a camel can't go through a needle's eye but it's "easier" for a camel to do so than for a rich person to enter God's kingdom, with humorously ironic hyperbole the entrance of a rich person into the kingdom turns out to be not *nearly* impossible or even *wholly* impossible, but *more than* impossible.

10:26–27: And they [the disciples] **were extremely dumbfounded, saying to themselves** [probably = "to one another"], **"And who can be saved** [= enter into God's kingdom as opposed to going to hell, on which see 9:43–48]**?"** "Extremely" escalates the disciples' dumbfoundedness to such a degree that they doubt anyone's possibility of salvation, and their doubt heightens the revolutionary force of Jesus' teaching. The introduction of their question with "And" implies that what they perceive to be the impossibility of anyone's salvation follows as a logical carry-over from Jesus' last statement: if a pious person, like the rich man, whose wealth is a sign of God's favor, won't be saved, what hope of salvation does someone without that sign have? Now starts a dialogue whose vigor, marked by the absence of an introductory "and" or "but" and in the first instance by a historical present tense in "Jesus *says*," highlights the hindrance of wealth and the rewards of discipleship: [27]**Gazing intently at them** [as he had at the rich man in 10:21], **Jesus says, "For human beings—impossible! But not for God, because all things are possible for God."** The intensity of Jesus' now gazing at the disciples (he'd already looked around to address them in 10:23) adds visual impact to the verbal impact of his affirming the power of God to do the humanly impossible, not only to save a rich person but also to do *anything* God wishes. Thus Jesus doesn't answer the disciples' question who can *be* saved, but points them to the only one who can *do* the saving because he's all-powerful.

10:28–31: Peter began saying to him, "Behold, *we*'ve left all and followed you." [29]**Jesus said, "Amen I tell you, there's no one who has left house or brothers or sisters or mother or father or children or fields on my account and on account of the gospel** [30]**but that he'll receive a hundred times as much now at this time—houses and brothers and sisters and mothers and children and fields, with persecutions—and in the coming age eternal life.** [31]**But many** [who are] **first will be last; and the last, first."** Peter speaks on behalf of all the Twelve. His emphatic "*we*" contrasts their having left all and followed Jesus with the rich man's sad departure upon Jesus' telling him to sell all, give to the poor, and follow him. Peter's statement also recalls Jesus' magnetism and carries factual truth, so that Jesus doesn't criticize Peter for a sense of self-sacrifice. Rather, he makes two predictions, first of present compensation and second of future compensation. "Amen I say to you" adds credibility to the predictions. The universal negative, "There's *no one* who has left . . . but that he'll receive . . ." makes the predictions more emphatic than the expected "you who have left . . . will receive . . ." would have been. The list of things the Twelve have left defines the "all" in Peter's statement. "House" leads to those with whom one has lived in it. Jesus lists them in an ascending order of closeness to the one who has left them: siblings, parents, and children. The omission of "wife" suits his having cited a man's becoming "one flesh" with his wife, so that they shouldn't be separated (10:6–9). At the end of the list "fields" complements "house" at the top of the list. The order in the list also reflects increasing value in a rural society. A house is of least value, because it offers no prospect for profit, provides no income, and costs to repair or—in cases of natural disaster—to rebuild. Brothers come next, but they compete for the family inheritance. Sisters are of more value, because they can be married off at a profit, though they drain family resources in the meantime. The mother is of even greater value because of her labors in the family's behalf; and the father of truly great value, because in addition to his labors the inheritance comes from him. Fields are of the greatest value, though, because they constitute the land that makes possible the family's existence from one generation to another. The connective "or" makes allowance for people whose "all" doesn't include everything on the list—like people with no brothers or sisters or children that they can leave, for example.

Jesus' switching from "or" to "and" in the following list of compensations means that those who didn't have a brother or a sister or children to leave will get such in the families of their fellow disciples. "On *my* account" harks back to his command to follow *him* (1:16–20; 2:14; 8:34; 10:21). "On account of the *gospel*" harks back to his command, "Repent and believe in the *gospel*" (1:15 [compare 8:35]) and implies that the disciples too will preach the gospel (as in 13:9–10). For the present time of persecutions, which discipleship and evangelism will incur, Jesus promises a hundredfold reward of houses, brothers, sisters, mothers, children, and fields. If they have to flee from their persecutors to as many as a hundred different places, they'll find a hundred different houses and families and fields through the hospitality of fellow disciples (compare 3:31–35). In this second list, "father" drops out, probably because Jesus' disciples have only one father in this new family. That father is God. Best of all, Jesus promises eternal life in the age to come. The many who are now first but will then be last are those who, like the rich man, don't heed Jesus' call to leave all and follow him. Those who are now last but will then be first are those who do. Final lastness means exclusion from God's kingdom, not leastness in it. Correspondingly, final firstness means entrance into that kingdom, not preeminence in it.

JESUS' DISPLAY OF ABILITY TO FORECAST HIS OWN DESTINY
Mark 10:32–34

10:32a–d: And people were on the road, going up to Jerusalem; and Jesus was proceeding on ahead of them. And they were astonished, but the ones following [him] **were afraid.** The "people . . . on the road" are pilgrims who, like Jesus, are going up to Jerusalem for the Passover Festival. But he's proceeding on ahead of them at some distance, and they're astonished at his pushing ahead like this. They don't know why he's doing so. Mark means us to infer Jesus' resolve to meet his self-predicted and divinely necessitated fate in Jerusalem (see 8:31 for its necessity). "The ones following" are pilgrims traveling close behind him. They're afraid, but not because they understand he's going to be killed in Jerusalem. They don't understand. Not even the Twelve do (see 9:32). These pilgrims' fear grows out of ignorance just as the distant pilgrims' astonishment grows out of ignorance. Why Jesus' onrush? It's unsettling as well as surprising—unsettling especially if you're trying to keep pace with him. Something's up. But what is it?

10:32e–34: And on taking along the Twelve again, he began to tell them the things that were going to happen to him: [33]**"Behold, we're going up to Jerusalem, and the Son of Man will be given over to the chief priests and the scholars, and they'll condemn him to death and give him over to the Gentiles.** [34]**And they** [the Gentiles] **will make fun of him and spit on him and flog him and kill** [him]. **And after three days he'll rise."** Jesus reserves his passion-and-resurrection predictions for the Twelve alone (compare upcoming references to "James and John" plus "the ten" in 10:35, 41, and see 8:31; 9:31 for earlier such predictions). "Taking along the Twelve" separates them from other followers. "Again" harks back to Jesus' other dealings with the Twelve (though he hasn't taken them along before). "*Going* to happen to him" stresses the certainty and nearness with which Jesus' prediction will be fulfilled. He has the ability to forecast his own destiny. "Going to *happen* to him" shows that he can forecast even events that aren't of his own making. "Behold" adds a note of drama suitable to nearness and certainty. "Will be given over to the chief priests and the scholars" looks toward betrayal by Judas Iscariot without naming him. The chief priests and the scholars had their base of power in Jerusalem. The rest of the prediction is loaded with details which, when they come to pass, will retroactively magnify Jesus' powers of prediction and thereby obliterate the shame of his crucifixion and the humiliations preceding it in that the chief priests and scholars as well as the Gentiles will make fun of him (15:20, 31), some members of the Sanhedrin as well as the Gentiles will spit on him (14:65; 15:19), and Pontius Pilate, a Gentile, will have him scourged as an extreme form of flogging (15:15). "After three days" calls attention to the quickness with which Jesus will rise after the Gentiles have killed him (compare 8:31).

JESUS' DISPLAY OF ABILITY TO PREDICT THE DESTINY OF HIS DISCIPLES
Mark 10:35–45

This passage falls into halves: a dialogue (10:35–40) and a monologue (10:41–45). The dialogue also subdivides into halves: a request by James and John (10:35–37) and Jesus' answer (10:38–40). In response to the other disciples' indignation at James and John, Jesus delivers the monologue on servanthood (10:41–45).

10:35–37: **And James and John, the sons of Zebedee, approach him, saying to him, "Teacher, we want you to do for us whatever we ask you** [to do for us]**."** ³⁶**And he said to them, "What do you want me to do for you?"** ³⁷**And they said to him, "Give us** [the following:] **that we may sit in your glory, one** [of us] **on your right and one** [of us] **on your left."** In its disregard of Jesus' immediately preceding passion-and-resurrection prediction, this request—highlighted by the historical present tense of "approach"—recalls Peter's protest after Jesus' first such prediction (8:31–33) and also the disciples' arguing after the second one which of them was greater than the others (9:30–37). So the present request doesn't arise out of the two brothers' looking beyond Jesus' passion to the resurrection. It arises instead out of their cluelessness concerning the passion, as explicitly noted in 9:32. Jesus' predictions of it haven't registered in the disciples' thinking, so that the brothers' cluelessness provides a foil against which Jesus' predictive power stands out and helps erase the scandal of the cross. The address, "Teacher," implies Jesus' authority. The follow-

ing request, though, is unintendedly humorous in its solicitation of a signed blank check. What James and John "want" recalls Jesus' prediction that whoever "wants" to be first will be last of all and servant of all (9:35). In view of that prediction, do James and John omit at first to say what they want? Whether or not they do, Jesus refuses to sign a blank check and asks what they want. Their reference to his glory stems from their having heard him speak of the Son of Man's coming "in the glory of his Father" (8:38), from their having transmuted the Father's glory into the Son of Man's glory and identified Jesus with the Son of Man, and from their having seen him transfigured (9:2–8).

10:38–40: **But Jesus told them, "You don't understand what you're asking for. *Can* you drink the cup that I'm drinking or be baptized with the baptism that I'm being baptized with?"** ³⁹**And they said to him, "We *can!*" And Jesus told them, "You *will* drink the cup that I'm drinking, and you *will* be baptized with the baptism that I'm being baptized with.** ⁴⁰**But to sit on my right or left isn't mine to give; rather,** [it'll be given] **to those for whom it has been prepared."** Jesus' explicit indication of their misunderstanding brings out yet again his foreknowledge by way of contrast. Contrary to their desire and expectation, they'll have to drink the bitter dregs of suffering and feel a flood of woe overwhelming them, just as Jesus has to do, if they're to share his later glory. Even then, though, the assigning of honorary positions on his right and left doesn't belong to him. Implied is the prerogative of God his Father to make those assignments. Jesus doesn't identify those for whom those positions have been prepared. Even if he knows, think what envy such an identification would have stirred up among the disciples. "*Can* you . . . ?" implies a fate for James and John that is foreboding and also a danger of inability to endure it. "Can you drink the cup *that I'm drinking* or be baptized with the baptism *that I'm being baptized with*" implies the ability of Jesus to endure his fate. The present tense of his drinking and being baptized is used for a future event to emphasize the certainty and nearness of fulfillment, as also in his response to the brothers' "We *can!*" Jesus doesn't criticize their "We *can!*" It simply provides him an opportunity to display foreknowledge of both their fate and their endurance in addition to his own.

Now Jesus stops predicting his death and interprets it as a model for disciples. The interpretation will contradict any notion that he died the death of a hapless criminal. *10:41–44*: **And on hearing** [the dialogue between the two brothers and Jesus]**, the ten began to get indignant over James and John.** "Over James and John" makes clear that the ten get indignant at them for what the two requested, not at Jesus for what he answered the two. ⁴²**And on summoning them** [the ten, for James and John have already been talking with Jesus]**, Jesus says to them, "You know that the ones recognized to be ruling the Gentiles wield lordship against them, and** [that] **their great ones wield authority against them."**

The summons and a use of the present tense in "Jesus *says* to them" reflect Jesus' own authority and knowledge of the ten's indignation. "You know" contrasts with "you don't know" in 10:38 and points to the disciples' knowing something true in society at large that unbeknown to them does *not* hold true among themselves. Ironically, then, even what they "know" highlights their ignorance, which in turn highlights the superior knowledge of Jesus. The Gentiles' "great ones" recalls the disciples' disputing which of them was "greater" (9:34). The rulers' and great ones' wielding of lordship and authority "against" the Gentiles connotes conquest by violence and government by oppression as opposed to the beneficial service that Jesus now talks about: ⁴³**"But it isn't this way among you"** states a principle. **"Rather, whoever is wanting to become great among you shall be your servant; ⁴⁴and whoever is wanting to be first among you shall be a slave of all."** This pair of statements forms not so much a prediction as a command, what grammarians call an *imperatival* future (like "You shall love the Lord your God . . ." [12:30]). "Whoever is wanting" poses the possibility that the ten might entertain a selfish ambition like that of James and John. For emphasis, "great" escalates to the superlative "first," and "servant" de-escalates to "slave," the latter pair also in opposition to the Gentiles' rulers and great ones. And "*your* servant"—that is, "a servant of the rest of you ten"—escalates to "a slave *of all*." Whether "all" means "all the rest of you ten" or "all disciples in general," the escalation from "your" to "all" intensifies and expands the notion of slavery; for ordinarily a slave serves only one master. Servanthood and slavery give a revolutionary new definition of greatness and provide a new way of attaining it.

10:45: **"For even the Son of Man didn't come to be served—rather, to serve, even to give his life** [as a] **ransom in substitution for many."** Jesus' service as the Son of Man provides a model, which because of his authority is also a reason, for this sort of behavior among the disciples. "*Even* the Son of Man" underlines his behavior as a service to many others despite his future coming as "the Son of Man . . . in the glory of his Father with the holy angels" (8:38). "*Even* to give his life [as a] ransom in substitution for many" specifies his service as the ultimate in self-sacrifice. Not for many as *opposed* to all, but many because the all *are* many. Jesus will die in their place to ransom them from slavery to Satan, sin, and death. His slavery spells their liberation from slavery if they'll believe in him. And his death will constitute the ransom price.

JESUS' SHOWING MERCY AS DAVID'S SON IN THE RESTORATION OF SIGHT TO BARTIMAEUS
Mark 10:46–52

10:46: **And they come into Jericho** sets the stage for a healing on the road leading out of Jericho and marks Jesus' progress toward Jerusalem, along the road to which lies Jericho. This progress, underscored by the present tense in "they *come*," heightens the sense that

a fulfillment of Jesus' passion-and-resurrection predictions is about to take place. Mark is playing up the power of Jesus to predict the destiny that awaits him in Jerusalem (see especially 10:33–34). Since Jesus took along the Twelve in 10:32, here "they" seems limited to him and them. On the way out from Jericho, though, a probably larger body of disciples and a crowd come into view: **And as he and his disciples and a considerable crowd were traveling out of Jericho, the son of Timaeus**—[namely,] **Bartimaeus** ["Bar-" meaning "son of" in the Aramaic language commonly used by Palestinian Jews in the first century], **a blind beggar** [What other than begging could blind people do in that culture?]—**was sitting on the edge of the road.** Many pilgrims flocked to Jerusalem for the Passover. But Mark describes this crowd of pilgrims as "considerable" in its size to revive his emphasis on Jesus' magnetism. "The son of Timaeus—[namely,] Bartimaeus" prepares for "Son of David, [namely,] Jesus" in 10:47. The blindness of Bartimaeus sets the stage for a miracle that will restore his sight. His begging sets the stage for a request that will procure the miracle. And his *sitting* on the edge of the road sets the stage for his *following* Jesus on the road.

10:47–48: **And on hearing, "It's Jesus the Nazarene," he started shouting and saying, "Son of David, [namely,] Jesus, have mercy on me." ⁴⁸And many were reprimanding him** [to the effect] **that he should be quiet. But he was shouting all the more, "Son of David, have mercy on me."** "Jesus the Nazarene" means "the Jesus from Nazareth" as distinguished from many other Jesuses (for "Jesus," Greek for the Hebrew "Joshua," was a popular name because Joshua, Moses' successor, led Israel into the promised land of Canaan and generaled its conquest). "Began shouting and saying" stresses the loudness and insistence of Bartimaeus's plea. His putting the honorific title "Son of David" (that is, descendant of David) ahead of the personal name "Jesus" shows respect for Jesus and suits a plea for mercy. "Many" reflects the considerable size of the crowd, indirectly renews attention to Jesus' magnetism, and both heightens the pressure of the reprimand that Bartimaeus should be quiet and highlights the loudness and insistence of his continued shouting. "All the more" intensifies the shouting of his plea.

10:49–50: **And on standing still, Jesus said, "Call him." And they call the blind** [beggar], **saying to him, "Take courage! Get up! He's calling you." ⁵⁰And he, flinging away his cloak, jumping up, went to Jesus.** Jesus' standing still and commanding the reprimanders to call Bartimaeus overturns their self-supposed authority in favor of Jesus' truly divine authority and implies that because of the considerable crowd, he hears but doesn't see Bartimaeus. Their calling Bartimaeus indicates capitulation to Jesus' authority. The present tense of "call" underscores the capitulation. "Take *courage!*" promises something good and issues in Bartimaeus's *flinging away his cloak.* "*Get up!*" issues in his *jumping up,* the doing of which his now discarded cloak would have impeded. And telling him that Jesus is *calling* him issues in his *going* to Jesus. In other words, Bartimaeus's actions exceed what the crowd tells him to do. His going to Jesus answers to Jesus' calling him. We might ask how he could go to Jesus since he was blind. Mark doesn't say. But his not saying highlights Bartimaeus's exceeding what the crowd tells him to do; and this excess of action adds body language to the verbal pleas, all of which provide a basis for Jesus' coming notation of Bartimaeus's faith. Jesus told *the crowd* to call Bartimaeus. But they tell him that *Jesus* is calling him. Ironically, then, they play the role of Jesus' agents to carry out his merciful will despite their earlier reprimand of Bartimaeus. How quickly Jesus' exercise of authority turns things about! The rat-a-tat-tat of the commands to Bartimaeus and of his flinging away his cloak and jumping up dramatizes this turnabout.

10:51–52: And answering him [= responding to Bartimaeus's plea and actions]**, Jesus said, "What do you want** [that] **I should do for you?" And the blind** [beggar] **said to him, "Rabbouni, that I should see again."** [52] **And Jesus told him, "Go. Your faith has saved you." And immediately he saw again and started following him on the road.** Jesus asks what Bartimaeus wants him to do for him. Give him some money? Bartimaeus has been begging. Or does he want Jesus to do something else for him? Mark's calling Bartimaeus "the blind [beggar]" rivets attention on the malady that Jesus will cure and prepares for a request that he cure it. "Rabbouni" introduces the request with a heightened form of "Rabbi" and thus emphasizes Jesus' authority. The command that Bartimaeus "go" implies that he doesn't have to sit on the edge of the road begging any more. His faith has saved him from blindness; but because Jesus has used "save" for eternal salvation in 8:35 and as recently as 10:26, Bartimaeus's salvation from blindness represents salvation from hell. "Immediately" emphasizes the effectiveness of Jesus' power. Bartimaeus's following him on the road contrasts with Jesus' command that he go. But the contrast doesn't damage Jesus' authority; rather, it enhances his magnetism and demonstrates his power to heal. For Bartimaeus couldn't be following Jesus unless he were seeing again.

JESUS PROVED TO BE AN UNERRING PREDICTOR AND ACCLAIMED TO BE THE COMING ONE
Mark 11:1–10

In this passage Mark narrates a triumphal procession outside Jerusalem, not a triumphal entry into Jerusalem. When Jesus enters Jerusalem in 11:11, the celebrating crowd of 11:1–10 go unmentioned. The present procession starts with a prediction that Jesus gives in his instructions on getting a colt (11:1–3), continues with the fulfillment of that prediction (11:4–6), and reaches its goal in Jesus' sitting on the colt to much acclaim (11:7–10).

11:1–3: And when they draw near to Jerusalem, to Bethphage and Bethany—[that is, when they come] **to the Mount of Olives** [or "of Olive Trees"]**—he** [Jesus] **sends two of his disciples** [2]**and says to them, "Go into the village opposite you. And as you enter into it you'll immediately find a tethered male colt** [compare Genesis 49:11] **that no one of human beings has yet sat on. Untie him and bring** [him]**.** [3]**And if anyone should say to you, "Why are you doing this?" say, "His owner has need** [of him, that is, of the male colt]**. And immediately he** [the owner] **sends him** [the colt] **back here** [to the entrance into the village]**."** A succession of verbs in the historical present tense—"draw near," "sends," and "says"—creates a sense of excitement for Jesus' coming triumphal procession. Mark mentions Jerusalem first, because Jesus' passion-and-resurrection predictions will be fulfilled there. Then Mark works backward through Bethphage, probably situated on the west slope of the Mount of Olives just across the Kidron Valley on the east side of Jerusalem, to Bethany, situated lower down on the south slope and farther east from the city. Pilgrims coming from Jericho would go past (but not through) Bethany and Bethphage in that order. "Opposite you" describes the village as off the road they're taking and probably points to Bethany, farther off the road than Bethphage and, as the first to be by-passed, farther from Jerusalem. So the triumphal procession will be very long, as befits Jesus God's Son.

The command to go fetch a colt contains a prediction, and the prediction contains a number of details whose fulfillments will contribute to Mark's emphasis on Jesus' predictive power. Here are the details: (1) The two sent disciples will find a colt. (2) The colt will be male. (3) They'll find him immediately while entering the village (not just right after entering it). (4) The colt will be tethered. (5) No one will ever have sat on it, much less ridden it, before. (6) Someone might ask why the two disciples are untying the colt. What Jesus tells them to say carries not only a promise that he'll return the colt right away but also a claim that as the colt's owner he needs to use the colt. So Jesus is exercising a lordly prerogative by requisitioning the colt as a means of transportation. As God's Son, his ownership trumps ownership by any merely human being. Mark won't narrate the colt's return, for narrating it would weaken the story's climax in the acclamation of Jesus. But by qualifying the promised return with "immediately" and putting the return in the present tense ("sends," as though the return were already taking place), Mark compensates in advance for not narrating the return. "Of human beings" qualifies "no one" so as to emphasize no one's having sat on the colt before and to imply that Jesus will sit on him as the more-than-human Son of God. In view of his having repeatedly done what others can't do, there may also be an implication that he'll sit on the unbroken male colt with such mastery as to eliminate the need of breaking him. In any case, no one's having sat on the colt before will bring great honor to Jesus as the first one to do so. This won't be a used, secondhand colt.

11:4–6: And they [the two disciples] **went off and found a male colt tethered at a gate** [into the village], outside on the street [leading into the village]. And they are untying him; [5]and some of the ones standing there were saying to them, "What are you doing by untying the colt?" [6]And they spoke to them just as Jesus had told [them to speak], and they [the bystanders] allowed them [to finish untying the colt and take him to Jesus]. The disciples obey Jesus' instructions. The present tense of "are untying" underlines the obedience, and Jesus' prediction comes to pass in detail. The fulfillment is magnified in its details, though. The chronologically general "immediately" in the prediction (11:2) transmutes into the locally specific "at a gate [into the village], outside on the street [leading into the village]" to emphasize just how soon it is that the disciples find the colt. The possibility of being asked what they're doing by untying the colt (11:3) escalates into the actuality of being asked. And the multiplication of a singular questioner ("someone" [11:3]) into the plural ("some of the ones standing there") casts the fulfillment in spades. The disciples' speaking to the questioners "just as Jesus had told [them to speak]" exhibits his lordship over the disciples as well as over the colt. And the questioners' allowing the disciples to proceed exhibits his lordship over the questioners, too; for the disciples have told them they're untying the colt because the colt's owner needs him. The fact that the Greek word behind "owner" also means "master" and "Lord" suits the lordship of Jesus as God's Son.

11:7–8: **And they bring the male colt to Jesus and throw their garments on him** [the colt]**, and he** [Jesus] **sat on him.** The disciples' continuing obedience, expressed again in the present tense ("bring"), underlines Jesus' lordship over them. They don't ride the colt, but save him for first use by Jesus; and they throw their garments on the colt to honor Jesus with a saddle. The present tense of "throw" likewise underlines their paying him honor in this way. By sitting on the colt he takes the posture of a dignitary. Ordinary pilgrims go on foot. Mark doesn't make clear that the colt is a humble young donkey (as in Matthew 21:4–5), but leaves the impression of a young male horse, a steed fitter for the sort of figure Jesus cuts in this Gospel. [8]**And many** [not just the two disciples] **spread their garments in the road** [to honor Jesus with a kind of pavement, like our rolling out a red carpet for some VIP (compare 2 Kings 9:13, though there on a much smaller scale)]**, and others** [spread] **straw** [in the road]**, having cut** [it] **from the fields.** The addition of "others" to the "many" makes for a very large number of people honoring Jesus, and the spreading of straw in addition to the garments heightens the honor paid to Jesus by doubling the pavement (like doubling the thickness of a red carpet, we might say). This double-paving of the road from a point farther away from Jerusalem than Bethphage and even Bethany makes for a "red carpet" whose astounding length (about two miles) magnifies the VIP that Jesus is. But red carpets are for pedestrians. Jesus doesn't need one. He doesn't need any pavement at all. He's sitting on a colt, not walking on foot. So the superfluity of spreading garments and straw adds to the astoundingness of length.

11:9–10: **And the people going ahead and the ones following were shouting, "Hosanna! Favored** [is] **he who's coming in the Lord's name!** [10]**Favored** [is] **the coming reign of our father** [= ancestor] **David! Hosanna in the highest** [places]**!"** Some of the crowd precede Jesus and others follow so as to form an honorary escort for him. Those who go ahead do so not to lead him but to lay the honorific double pavement. The acclamation of Jesus heaps further honor on him. The first and last parts of the acclamation come from Psalm 118:25–26. Originally "Hosanna" was a prayer for this-worldly deliverance ("Please save . . ."), so that "Favored [be] . . ." meant "*May* God show favor to . . . ." By the time of the New Testament, though, "Hosanna" had come to mean something like "Hurray!" (compare the evolution of "God, save the king" to "God save the king!"), so that "Favored [is] . . ." means "God *has* shown favor to . . . ." "In the Lord's name" describes Jesus as coming with authority to act on behalf of the Lord. This authority is to be displayed in a revival of King David's kingdom (though doubtless the crowd misconstrued that kingdom as immediately political [compare 2 Samuel 7:16], whereas Jesus delays it as such till his coming in the glory of his Father [8:38] and also universalizes it [13:24–27]). "The highest places" are heavenly places. So heaven rings with the angels' acclamation of Jesus just as earth rings with human beings' acclamation of Jesus.

JESUS' ISSUANCE OF A STRONG CURSE
Mark 11:11–14

11:11: **And he entered into Jerusalem, into the temple** [not the sanctuary proper, into which only priests could go, but the larger complex of courts and cloisters]**; and on looking around at all things** [in the temple], **because the hour was already late he went out to Bethany with the Twelve.** The crowd at Jesus' triumphal procession is now missing. Though Jesus will leave with the Twelve, Mark mentions only Jesus as entering Jerusalem and, within it, the temple. So we have an uneventful entry by a private pilgrim, not a triumphal entry by a crowd-accompanied celebrity. Jesus' entry into Jerusalem sets the stage for departure to Bethany. His entry into the temple and looking around at all things there sets the stage for his cleansing the temple the next day. "Looking around at all things" signals his irritation, for "all things" will turn out to be, or at least to include, commercial traffic going on in the temple and passing through it (11:15–16). Jesus told "the Twelve" that he'd be killed in Jerusalem (10:32–34). So his going out to Bethany "with the Twelve" reminds us of that prediction and thereby indicates that because of the threat posed by Jerusalem he doesn't stay there overnight. (Later, he'll even pray for release from the fate awaiting him there [14:35–36, 39].)

11:12–14: **And after they'd gone out from Bethany the next day, he got hungry.** [13]**And on seeing at a distance a fig tree that had leaves, he went** [to it]—**if then he will find something** [on it to eat]. **And on coming to**

it he found nothing except leaves. For it wasn't the season for figs. ¹⁴And answering [= responding to the tree's not having something for him to eat], he said to it, "May no one eat fruit from you any more—forever!" And his disciples were listening. "He got hungry" tells why the fig tree caught Jesus' eye. "At a distance" tells why he didn't yet notice the tree had nothing he could eat. "That had leaves" gives the reason why despite the distance, he went to the tree expecting he'd find something to eat. "Then" makes the leaves a basis for his expectation, and "if he . . . will find" (as opposed to "if he . . . might find") indicates a strong expectation. Mark does not say Jesus went expecting to find "figs" or "fruit," that is, ripe figs. Of course not. It wasn't the season for them. He could only hope to find "something" edible; and that would be buds which form just before and as the tree leafs, so that the leaves on this tree presented a realistic hope of finding such buds. They're not very good to eat, but they can be eaten—and sometimes people do eat them. Furthermore, Jesus' finding nothing but leaves fits the circumstance that these buds fall off before the real fruit appears. "For it wasn't the season for figs" doesn't explain why Jesus didn't find buds. It steps back to explain why he went to find "something" rather than "figs" or "fruit." Since Jesus hadn't expected to find mature fruit but only buds, "May no one eat fruit from you" makes for a strong curse. "Any more—forever!" adds further strength to the curse and implies that apart from Jesus' cursing it the tree would have produced figs later on. The expectation of buds was reasonable; so the curse is appropriate. No buds now in March–April (the time of Passover)? Well, then, no fruit in June—or ever afterwards. The leaves of the tree make a fulfillment of Jesus' curse (which comes close to a prediction) unlikely, especially in the immediate future. But the fulfillment will have taken place before twenty-four hours have elapsed (see 11:19–25). Such is the power of Jesus' words. The fact that the disciples were listening leaves no room for doubting a fulfillment once it has occurred. Their listening also prepares for Peter's remembering (11:21).

THE AWE-INSPIRING TEACHING OF JESUS AT HIS CLEANSING OF THE TEMPLE
Mark 11:15–18

11:15–16: And they [Jesus and the Twelve] **come into Jerusalem. And on entering into the temple, he started throwing out those who were selling and buying in the temple; and he overturned the moneychangers' tables and the chairs of those who were selling doves; ¹⁶and he wasn't allowing anyone to carry a vessel** [presumably containing something-or-other] **through the temple** [that is, through its courts and cloisters]. Mark doesn't say what the doves were for. (They were for sacrifice.) Nor does he say what else people were selling and buying. (They were selling and buying sacrificial animals.) Nor does he tell why money was being changed. (It was being changed into currency acceptable for payment of a temple tax.) Nor does Mark say what people were carrying through the temple in vessels. And not having mentioned sacrificial animals,

he doesn't say that Jesus drove them out (contrast John 2:15). Despite mentioning the doves, Mark says nothing about taking them away (contrast John 2:16). Instead, he concentrates attention on Jesus' ferocious exercise of authority over the human beings who were commercializing the temple, as apparently he'd seen them doing when he looked around its precincts late on the previous day.

11:17: And he was teaching and saying to them, "It's written, isn't it, 'My house will be called a house of prayer for all the nations [Isaiah 56:7],' but you've made it 'a den of bandits [Jeremiah 7:11].'"** By connecting "he was teaching" with "saying," Mark emphasizes Jesus' exercise of authority in what he says as well as in what he does. In fact, Mark casts this whole episode in the mold of a lesson taught by Jesus in deed and word. The authoritative condemnation here parallels the authoritative curse in the preceding episode. "It's written, isn't it?" implies that it is written. But Jesus doesn't identify God as the speaker in the quoted Old Testament passages. So "my house" appears to mean Jesus' house. If it does mean Jesus' house, he's claiming authority to cleanse it of the predatory commercialism that has taken away its proper use for prayer by all the nations.

11:18: And the chief priests and the scholars [who constituted the hierarchy] **heard** [what Jesus was saying to the traffickers in the temple]. **And they were seeking how they might destroy him** [and therefore unwittingly set going the fulfillment of his passion-and-resurrection predictions]. **For they were afraid of him.** And why were they afraid of him? **For all the crowd was awestruck at his teaching.** "His teaching" refers to what he taught in 11:17: "It's written, isn't it?" plus quotations of Isaiah 56:7 and Jeremiah 7:11. Just as people were awestruck at Jesus' teaching in 1:21–28 because he'd backed it up by casting out an unclean spirit, so here the crowd are awestruck at his teaching because he has backed it up by casting out the traffickers. By attaching "all" to the crowd Mark displays the effect of Jesus' didactic authority at its highest power. Nobody in the crowd escapes that effect. So the main point consists in the awe-inspiring power of Jesus' teaching, backed up as it is by his strong actions. He strikes fear even in the hearts of the hierarchy who are seeking to destroy him. In fact, they're trying to destroy him because they fear him; and they fear him because he has a powerful hold on the crowd—all of them. He'll be crucified, then, not because of any weakness in him. On the contrary, he'll be crucified because of his power. Furthermore, the power on account of which he'll be crucified is a power he exerts for the benefit of all the nations, Gentiles and Jews alike. For his crucifixion, then, Jesus deserves honor and worship, not scorn and ridicule.

THE STARTLING FULFILLMENT OF JESUS' CURSE AND HIS STARTLING ANSWERS
Mark 11:19–25

11:19–21: And whenever it got late they'd go outside the city. So the exit of Jesus and the Twelve from

Jerusalem late on the day of the triumphal procession (11:11) becomes habitual during Passion Week. As a result, the chief priests and scholars can't seize Jesus at night while his admiring crowd are sleeping. ²⁰**And as they were passing by in the morning** [on their way back into Jerusalem], **they saw the fig tree withered from** [its] **roots** [up]. Jesus had cursed the tree only one day earlier, and because of the sun's rays a tree or plant usually withers from the top down. His word is so powerful, though, that the withering started with the roots despite the soil's shielding them from the sun and surrounding them with moisture soaked in from the spring rains of Passover season. The withering has proceeded so fast that above ground the tree is already visibly dead, and withered roots means there's no chance of revival. So Jesus' curse, "May no one eat fruit from you any more—forever!" (11:14), is sure to be fulfilled. ²¹**And on remembering** [Jesus' curse], **Peter says to him, "Rabbi, look! The fig tree that you cursed is withered."** As emphasized by a vivid present tense in "says," Peter gives Jesus honor by addressing him with "Rabbi." "Look!" stresses how startling was the speedy and permanent withering of the fig tree. And "that you cursed" puts emphasis on the power of Jesus' word.

11:22–25: And answering, Jesus says to them [the Twelve], **"Have faith in God. ²³Amen I tell you that whoever says to this mountain** [the Mount of Olives, which they're traversing to Jerusalem], **'Be lifted up and thrown into the sea** [the Dead Sea, visible from the Mount of Olives on a clear day],**' and doesn't doubt in his heart but believes that what he's saying is happening, it will be** [= occur] **for him."** This promise of Jesus, highlighted by the present tense in the introductory "says," is more startling than the fulfillment of his curse, so startling that lest the disciples disbelieve his promise he introduces it with "Amen I say to you." Just as his curse against the fig tree came to pass, so a curse against the Mount of Olives will come to pass for anyone who believes without doubt that God is so sure to carry out the curse that it's as good as happening already. To tone down Jesus' promise, we're disposed to fasten on the condition of believing without doubt and thus to say, in effect, "Well, nobody believes without at least some doubt that God would do such a thing; so the promise is only academic." But Mark wants us to fasten on the startling character of Jesus' promise, not on its condition as an escape valve. The promise is doubly startling in that ancient people believed that mountains reach down to the very foundations of the earth, yet Jesus speaks of an uprooting and removal so complete that the mountain disappears in the depths of the sea. But he makes an even more startling promise: ²⁴**"On account of this I tell you, all things that you pray for and ask for—however many** [they are]—**believe that you have received** [them], **and they'll be yours."** "On account of this" implies that if believing in God without doubt guarantees the effectiveness of a *curse*, such as one addressed to the Mount of Olives, how much more will such faith guarantee the effective-

ness of *prayer* requests addressed to God. "All things" is more startling than a mountain's being taken up and thrown into the sea and would have been startling enough. Adding to the startlingness is "however many [things you pray and ask for]." And believing that what you say "*is* coming to pass" (11:23) escalates to believing that you "*have* received," as though the answer to your prayer preceded the prayer. Again we're disposed to treat the condition of such faith as a way of weakening Jesus' promise, but Mark wants us to be awestruck by Jesus' teaching (see 11:18). ²⁵**"And whenever you stand praying, if you have anything against anyone, forgive** [him] **in order that also your Father in heaven may forgive you your trespasses."** It was normal to stand when praying. Standing showed respect for God, seated on his heavenly throne. But finally—and this is the main point—what could be more startling than Jesus' telling disciples who have anything against anyone to exercise forgiveness as they pray rather than praying for vindication and retribution, and to exercise forgiveness in order that God may forgive them? His forgiving them requires their forgiving others *even though those others are in the wrong!* The earliest and best manuscripts don't contain 11:26, a later insertion by copyists of Mark.

A Special Note on the Cursing And Withering of the Fig Tree

Jesus curses the fig tree between his looking around the temple and cleansing it a day later, and another day later the fig tree is seen to have withered. Therefore many commentators treat the cursing as symbolic of God's displeasure with Israel because of Israel's failure to repent and believe the gospel as preached by Jesus. The Old Testament often portrays Israel under the figure of a fig tree. The withering of the fig tree is then treated as symbolic of the consequent destruction of Jerusalem and its temple that Jesus is going to predict (13:1–2) and that his cleansing of the temple is likewise supposed to symbolize. But in 7:3–4 Mark had to explain Jewish practices to his audience. So he'd hardly expect them to connect a fig tree with Israel no matter how much the Old Testament uses that tree as a figure of speech for Israel. Moreover, only a failure of Jesus to find *fruit*—that is, *figs*—could well symbolize a failure to repent and believe. But Mark carefully avoids saying that Jesus went to find fruit and failed to find any. He was seeking only *buds*, hardly a good figure of speech for repentance and belief. And Jesus equally carefully avoids saying that the curse of future inability to bear fruit corresponds to past failure to bear fruit. If this episode did symbolize Israel's failure to bear the fruit of repentance and belief, Mark's explanation that "it wasn't the season for figs" would absolve Israel of blame and thus take away any reason for a coming destruction! Finally, Jesus makes out of his cursing the fig tree and its withering a lesson of faith, not a symbol of coming destruction for Jerusalem and the temple.

JESUS' OUTWITTING ALL THREE
CLASSES OF THE SANHEDRIN
Mark 11:27–12:12

This passage divides into a dialogue between the Sanhedrin, the Jewish Supreme Court (11:27–33), and a parable spoken by him to and about them (12:1–12). This confrontation starts a series of verbal victories that he wins over these opponents of his (12:13–27). The last of them will turn into an admirer of Jesus (12:28–34). Then Jesus will expose to a large crowd his opponents' ignorance (12:35–37) and their dangerousness and doom (12:38–40). Having earned the crowd's admiration, then, he'll display to the disciples his insight (12:41–44) and foresight (13:1–37). With this preparation, Mark will portray the following passion of Jesus as a backlash against Jesus' defeat of opponents who were dangerous to society as well as to him. He wasn't crucified for any danger that he himself posed to society—rather, out of spite.

11:27–28: And they [Jesus and the Twelve] **come again into Jerusalem. And as he was walking around in the temple** [= its courts and cloisters], **the chief priests and the scholars and the elders** [= the three classes making up the Sanhedrin] **come to him** [28]**and were saying to him, "By what sort of authority are you doing these things** [putting a stop to selling, buying, moneychanging, and transport in the temple (11:15–17)]**? Or who gave you this authority to do these things?"** "Again" marks a third entry into Jerusalem (compare 11:11, 15). The present tense in "*come* to him" headlines the Sanhedrin's confronting Jesus upon his entry. They're worried about his having cleansed the temple. By failing to address him respectfully—say, with "Rabbi" or "Teacher"—they show their contempt for him. "What sort of . . . ?" centers attention on the nature of the authority they ask him to cite, "or who . . . ?" on its source—if he has any. The Sanhedrists don't think he does, of course. Their questions aren't designed to elicit information—rather, to embarrass Jesus, to expose him as an imposter. They also imply that he has usurped the Sanhedrin's authority over the temple; for they'd been controlling its traffic—indeed, sponsoring it. The combination of "*these* things" with "*are* doing" suggests, and perhaps implies outright, that he continues to have stopped commercial traffic in the temple.

11:29–33: But Jesus said to them, "I'll ask you one word [= one question, as opposed to the two questions they'd asked him]. **And answer me, and I'll tell you by what sort of authority I'm doing these things.** [30]**John's baptism** [that is, baptism as administered by John the baptizer]—**was it from heaven** [and therefore from God, 'heaven' being a reverential substitute for God's name, as when careful speakers say 'for heaven's sake' rather than 'for God's sake'] **or from human beings** ['from' in the sense of derivation and consequent authority, or lack thereof]**? Answer me."** Jesus' double demand for an answer shows that he's taking charge in the game of public embarrassment that the Sanhedrin started. They'll be

sorry they did. "By what sort of authority" alludes to the Sanhedrin's first question in 11:28 (using the very same phrase). The alternatives "from heaven or from human beings" in Jesus' counter question allude to the Sanhedrin's second question in 11:28 ("Or who gave you this authority . . . ?"). So pointed is the dilemma posed by these alternatives, so insistent is his demand for an answer, that the Sanhedrin fall into disarray: [31]**And they were reasoning to themselves** [= consulting with one another], **saying, "If we say, 'From heaven,' he'll say, 'Why then didn't you believe him** [John, who predicted that one stronger than he, as Jesus has proved to be, was coming (1:7–8)]**?'"** According to 1:5 "*all* the Jerusalemites" were getting baptized by John. The Sanhedrin is made up of leading Jerusalemites. To escape the dilemma into which Jesus' question has put them, then, by refusing to affirm the divine authority of baptism by John they'll silently crawfish out of their own submission to his baptism. From the quotation of Scripture in 1:2–3, of course, Mark's audience know that baptism by John had divine authority behind it. [32]**But** [if] **we say, 'From human beings'** [to the effect that John had no authority from God to baptize people]—**they feared the crowd. For all** [the crowd] **held John to have really been a prophet.** Because Jesus has fulfilled John's prediction that someone stronger than he was coming (1:7–8), the Sanhedrin didn't dare assign divine authority to baptism by John—and by implication to Jesus' actions—even though they might otherwise have regarded John as the fulfillment of Malachi 4:5 according to their own interpretation of that passage (see Mark 9:11–13). They omit "if" before "we say, 'From human beings,'" though we have to carry over "if" from the first alternative to make good sense. This striking omission and the Sanhedrin's leaving the second alternative incomplete show that they don't even want to contemplate it seriously. Mark tells why: they feared antagonizing the crowd by denying the crowd's universal conviction that John practiced baptism as a true prophet of God. [33]**And answering Jesus, they say, "We don't know."** So with a single question he has reduced *them* to the embarrassment their two questions were designed to bring *him*. **And Jesus says to them, "Neither am I telling you by what sort of authority I'm doing these things."** The present tense in "they *say*" and "Jesus *says*" enlivens this dialogue. The dialogue itself ends with Jesus' outwitting the Sanhedrin. Because they don't dare answer the one question he asked, he needn't answer their first question—much less their second question, to which he doesn't even allude. The shame to which he puts the very ones who'll get him crucified cancels out what would otherwise be the shame of his crucifixion.

Now Jesus follows up his refusal to answer the Sanhedrin's questions with parables concerning them and their predecessors' behavior as leaders of the Jewish people. **12:1: And he started speaking to them in parables.** But only one parable follows, so that it represents others that Mark doesn't record. Though not recording them, Mark mentions them to imply that Jesus overwhelms the Sanhedrin with parables like the one Mark does record. **"A man 'planted a vineyard and put a fence around** [it] **and dug a vat** [under the winepress] **and built a** [watch-]**tower' and gave it** [the vineyard] **out to farmers** [= leased it to them] **and went on a journey."** The phrases in single quotation marks come from Isaiah 5:1–2. As in Isaiah, the vineyard stands for the Jewish people; and the man who plants the vineyard stands for God. But Isaiah stressed that the vineyard failed to yield good grapes despite the planter's lavishing a capital investment on it—in other words, that the Jewish people failed to live righteously despite God's good treatment of them. Jesus shifts the emphasis, first by omitting the vine that according to Isaiah 5:2 was planted in the vineyard and expected to yield good grapes but yielded sour ones instead. Then Jesus brings in a new element, namely, tenant farmers (who don't figure in Isaiah). The planter-owner's leasing the vineyard to them stands for God's putting the Jewish people under leaders such as the Sanhedrin and their predecessors. So the large capital investment now tells why the planter-owner will repeatedly try to get something back from his investment. No longer does the quality of the vineyard's fruit stand in the center; rather, the behavior of those put in charge of the vineyard does.

12:2–5: **"And at the season** [of harvest] **he** [the owner] **sent a slave to the farmers in order that he** [the slave] **might take from the farmers some fruits of the vineyard** [that is, the portion of harvest owed to the owner]. [3]**And on taking him, they beat** [him] **and sent** [him] **away empty**[-handed, not because the vineyard hadn't yielded fruit, but because the farmers rejected the owner's right to be paid for their use of the vineyard]**."** So the intention of the owner that his slave "take" from the farmers some fruits of the vineyard turns into the actuality of the farmers' "taking" the slave, beating him, and sending him away empty-handed. The rental fee they were supposed to pay stands for justice and righteousness in Isaiah 5:7–12, so that the slave whom Jesus injects into the parable stands for prophets like Isaiah who tried to collect moral rent for God by calling his people to justice and righteousness. [4]**"And again, he sent another slave to them; and they hit that one on the head and insulted him.** [5]**And he sent another** [slave]**, and they killed that one. And** [he sent] **many other** [slaves]**, some** [of whom] **they beat, and others** [of whom] **they killed."** The fates of the slaves represent rejections suffered by the Old Testament prophets, and the fates of the individually mentioned slaves show increasing maltreatment—from a beating and empty-handed send-off to getting dangerously hit on the head and insulted, and finally to getting killed. The addition of "many others," with another progression from getting beaten to getting killed, heaps more guilt on the tenant farmers and, through them, on the Sanhedrin and their predecessors. Their behavior is inexcusable. The unrealism of the owner's sending many other slaves after the maltreatment and murder of the first three intensifies the guilt by highlighting the owner's giving the farmers further opportunity to pay him.

At this point we don't expect the owner to send anyone else, but to go himself. It therefore comes as a surprise to read in *12:6–8:* **"He still had one** [that he could send]**, a beloved son. He sent him to them last** [of all]**, saying, 'They'll respect my son.'"** We're surprised not only that the owner sends one more, but also that the one more is his beloved son. "Still one" implies he has run out of slaves to send, and "beloved" suits an only son. This beloved son stands for Jesus, whom God called his "beloved Son" at Jesus' baptism and transfiguration (1:11; 9:7). From our standpoint the owner is risking his beloved only son despite the farmers' maltreatment and murder of all his many slaves, and this risk adds pathos to our surprise. But the owner says the tenant farmers will respect his son, and in that culture it would be expected that peasants such as the tenant farmers would accede to someone of the son's status. After all, he's the son of the owner. But for us the owner's saying that the tenant farmers will respect his son heightens the pathos and sets the stage for their attempt to seize ownership of the vineyard by killing its heir (who therefore *has* to be an only son). [7]**"But those farmers said to themselves** [= to one another]**, 'This is the heir.** [Come] **here! Let's kill him, and the inheritance will be ours.'"** "Those" puts the farmers at a moral distance to stress the wickedness of their plot, which represents the Sanhedrin's plot to kill Jesus (11:18; 12:12; 14:1). The law allows the son to act on his father's behalf by evicting the tenant farmers, by taking legal action against them for their refusal to pay rent and for their crimes against the father's slaves, and by reclaiming the vineyard. On the other hand, the tenant farmers will be able to lay their own legal claim to the vineyard if the father has died and they kill the only heir. Not that killing him would legalize their claim, but it would make possible a legal claim by right of possession ("squatters' rights," so to speak). They wouldn't think that by killing the son the inheritance will be theirs unless they also think his father, the owner, has died. Their very words "heir" and "inheritance" arise out of a mistaken deduction that the son's coming signals the owner's death and the son's purpose to claim the vineyard for himself. This delusion imbues the parable with irony. [8]**"And on taking** [him]**, they killed him** [as Jesus has predicted he'll be killed at the instigation of the Sanhedrin (10:33–34)] **and threw him outside the vineyard."** "*Throwing* him outside the vineyard" shows how utterly the tenant farmers reject him: they don't even give his corpse a decent burial. "Throwing him *outside* the vineyard" shows their rejection of his authority over the vineyard and therefore of Jesus' having had authority to cleanse the temple (compare 11:28).

The tension that has been mounting with each increase in the tenant farmers' crimes has reached a breaking point. So in *12:9–11* Jesus switches first to a question: **"What then will the owner of the vineyard do?"** Jesus answers his own question by saying, **"He'll come and destroy the farmers and give the vineyard to others."** He won't destroy the vineyard, as God does in Isaiah 5:5–6. He'll destroy the tenant farmers, as God will see to it that the members of the Sanhedrin are destroyed in the destruction of Jerusalem and the temple in A.D. 70 (compare 13:1–2). The Greek word for "owner" doubles for "Lord" and implies the right to destroy those farmers. But whom do the "others" to whom the owner will give the vineyard represent? They represent Jesus and the Twelve, to whom God will give leadership over the new people of God, that is, whoever does his will (compare 3:31–35). But if the killing of the son represented the killing of Jesus, how can Jesus be given the vineyard as his inheritance? He's dead. [10]**"But you've read this Scripture, haven't you** [implied answer: Of course you have, especially the scholars among you]: 'The stone that the builders rejected—this has turned into the head of an angle. [11]This** [head of an angle] **has come on the scene from the Lord and is marvelous in our eyes** [Psalm 118:22–23]'**?"** Jesus is "the head of an angle," which means either a cornerstone or a key- or capstone, but probably a cornerstone in that it's laid as the first stone of a foundation, so that the rest of the foundation is laid out angularly from it (at a right angle, for example). Thus the rejected stone, representing Jesus as rejected by the Jewish leaders ("the builders"), has turned into the cornerstone. (The metaphor representing God's people has changed from a vineyard to a building, and the past tense of verbs treats future events as sure to happen.) Jesus turned into the cornerstone by rising from the dead, just as he predicted to the Twelve in 8:31; 9:31; 10:32–34. (The present metaphor veils his meaning from the Sanhedrin, though.) Once risen, Jesus can inherit the vineyard—that is, take charge of God's new people—despite his having been killed. The Sanhedrin's knowledge of the Scripture that Jesus quotes should have led them to expect the Lord would thwart their plot to destroy Jesus. (Incidentally, there's a wordplay in that the Hebrew for "stone" in Psalm 118:22–23 [*eben*] is very like the Hebrew for "son" [*ben*], so that Jesus is both "the son" and "the stone.") In the psalm, "this" that's "from the Lord" and "marvelous" refers to the rejected stone's having turned into the cornerstone. In Mark "this" refers to that stone itself—in other words, to Jesus himself. He's both "from the Lord" and, as resurrected, "marvelous."

12:12: And they [the Sanhedrin] **were seeking to seize him, and they feared the crowd. For they knew that he'd told the parable in reference to them. And leaving him, they went away.** The Sanhedrin's fearing the crowd contrasts with their seeking to seize Jesus, tells why they didn't seize him on the spot but skipped out (they feared his parable would turn the crowd against them), and recalls the strength of Jesus' hold on the crowd. He's John the baptizer's "stronger one" (1:7) even in the events leading immediately to his crucifixion.

JESUS' MARVELOUS ESCAPE FROM THE HORNS OF A DILEMMA
Mark 12:13–17

12:13–14: And they [the Sanhedrin] **send to him some of the Pharisees and** [some] **of the Herodians to trap him in regard to a word** [that is, in a statement that he might make]. Because people in general esteemed the Pharisees highly on account of their religiosity, the Pharisees could use a *theologically* self-damaging statement by Jesus—such as one that he's subverting the Jewish religion—to kill his popularity. Because the Romans sponsored the Herods as rulers, the local supporters of the Herods could use a *politically* self-damaging statement by Jesus to lodge an accusation against him—such as one that he's subverting Caesar's government—with the Roman governor of Judea, Pontius Pilate. The Pharisees and Herodians plotted together against Jesus in 3:6. So they make natural emissaries of the Sanhedrin here. The attempt to trap Jesus begins with a fulsome flattery designed to mask the purpose of entrapment and punctuated by Mark with the present tense of "say" to spotlight the flattery: [14]**And on coming, they say to him, "Teacher** [a respectful address], **we know that you're truthful** [contrast the Sanhedrin's untruthful claim in 11:33 not to know the origin of John's baptism] **and** [that] **it doesn't matter to you about anyone, for you don't look into a face of human beings** [in other words, you don't care what people think about you, because you're not impressed by their appearance, superficial as it is]; **rather, you teach God's way** [for us to conduct our lives] **on the basis of truth** [as opposed to currying human favor or showing favoritism]." Ironically, what the Sanhedrin's emissaries intend as flattery is *actually* true of Jesus. Since their society was highly stratified, not at all egalitarian, the proneness of ordinary people to fawn on eminent ones makes all the more remarkable Jesus' teaching God's way truthfully rather than massaging the teaching so as to curry favor or show favoritism. Now a theoretical question: **"Is it lawful to give** [= pay] **a poll tax** [levied by the Roman government on adult males] **to Caesar or not?"** Next a practical question: **"Should we give** [it]**, or should we not give** [it]**?"** The emissaries hope Jesus will advocate either paying the unpopular tax, so that the Pharisees can use his advocating its payment to kill his popularity, which has kept the Sanhedrin from arresting him, or will advocate not paying the tax, so that the Herodians can accuse him of sedition, which would lead the Romans to arrest him regardless of his popularity. Roman law required payment of the tax, but contrary to Exodus 20:4; Deuteronomy 5:8 it had to be paid in Roman coins stamped with an image of Caesar and an inscription proclaiming his supposedly divine ancestry.

12:15–17: But he, **recognizing their hypocrisy** [their pretense of wanting to know the true answer to serious questions but really wanting to entice Jesus into a self-damaging statement], **said to them, "Why are you testing me?"** This question exposes their flattery as hypocrisy. **"Bring me a denarius** [the kind of coin required for paying the tax] **in order that I may see** [it]**."** [16]**And they brought** [a denarius to him]. **And he says to them, "Whose image** [on the denarius is] **this, and** [whose] **inscription?" And they said to him, "Caesar's."** [17]**And Jesus said to them, "Give Caesar's things back to Cae-**

sar, and God's things back to God." It's usually thought that by producing a denarius the Sanhedrin's emissaries, including the Pharisees, acknowledge Caesar's ownership of the coin and right of taxation. But people use a coin for its value in exchange whether or not they acknowledge the sovereignty of the ruler whose image and inscription is stamped on the coin. And the coin belongs to the person who earned it or gained it in some other lawful way, not to the ruler whose image and inscription appear on its face. So Jesus' argument, introduced with a vivid present tense ("says"), isn't *logically* compelling. But in Jewish culture of the time, what counted as argumentatively persuasive didn't have to have logical validity. It was enough, or better, to display cleverness, wordplay, one-upmanship. So the shift from Caesar's image and inscription *on* the coin to Caesar's "things," that is, to the coin *itself* and others like it, entails a leap of imagination whose *artistry* convinces that paying the tax is giving back to Caesar what belongs to him. And giving him back his things leads to giving back to God the things that belong to him. Thus Jesus seizes both horns of the dilemma by satisfying both Roman law and divine law. The Sanhedrin's emissaries had asked whether to "*give*" the tax. Jesus answers with "give *back*," so that payment both to Caesar and to God is obligatory. Caesar and God own what's owed them. But what are "the things of God"? For Jesus they're the divine necessity of his suffering, rejection, and being killed (see 8:33 with 8:31). And right after mentioning them in chapter 8 he called on the crowd to disown themselves, take up their crosses, and follow him at the possible cost of their lives (8:34–38). So "the things of God" that people are obligated to give back to him in the present passage consist in following Jesus according to his earlier call. A tailpiece now highlights the ability he has to defeat his enemies in verbal combat: **And they were marveling at him.** Even those who came to trap him in his speech succumb to admiration of his person.

JESUS' EXPOSÉ OF THE SADDUCEES' IGNORANCE
Mark 12:18–27

In this passage Sadducees, aristocrats centered in Jerusalem, try to overpower Jesus in debate now that some Pharisees and Herodians have failed to trap him. In particular, the Sadducees try to get Jesus, a non-Sadducee, to admit that the doctrine of resurrection, which they deny, is absurdly unscriptural. He has predicted his own resurrection, but only to his disciples (8:31; 9:31; 10:32–34). As readers of Mark *we* know about those predictions, though. So for us the theological stakes surpass those of the Sadducees, who are interested only in embarrassing Jesus. His resurrection in chapter 16 will prove the Sadducees wrong, but in the meantime they try to outwit him in the way he outwitted the Pharisees and Herodians.

12:18–23: And Sadducees, who as such [that is, as Sadducees] **say there's no resurrection, come to him.**

They accept as authoritative only the law of Moses (Genesis–Deuteronomy) and don't find the resurrection taught there. So they deny the doctrine. **And they were questioning him by saying,** [19]**"Teacher, Moses wrote to us, 'If some** [man's] **brother were to die' and leave behind a wife 'and not leave a child'**—[he wrote] **that 'his brother should take** [= marry] **the wife and raise up seed for his brother** [that is, produce offspring to be his brother's heir]' [Deuteronomy 25:5; Genesis 38:8 (compare Ruth 4:5, 10)]." "Teacher" introduces a scriptural question suitably but feigns respect for Jesus. "Moses" comes forward to set up a possible conflict between Jesus as a teacher and Moses as a legislator. Since the Sadducees accept Moses' law (which doesn't refer explicitly to resurrection) but not the rest of the Old Testament (which does refer explicitly to resurrection, most clearly in Daniel 12:2; but see also Isaiah 26:19; Ezekiel 37:11–14), the Sadducees quote what's known as the law of levirate marriage. By wordplay, "raise up" in the quotation relates also to the question of resurrection; for this verb is used for God's raising up the dead as well as for a man's raising up offspring (in the sense of procreation, not in the sense of child-rearing). [20]**"There were seven brothers."** This statement sounds like an actual case but looks made up for the purpose of argument. "Seven" connotes completeness, as though this case will seal the conclusiveness of the Sadducees' argument against resurrection. **"And the first took a wife and left no seed** [offspring] **when he died.** [21]**And the second took her and died not leaving seed behind. And the third likewise.** [22]**And the seven didn't leave seed. Last of all, the woman died too.** [23]**In the resurrection** [if there is one], **when they rise** [literally, 'stand up'], **whose wife of them will she be? For the seven had her as a wife."** That is to say, resurrection would make shambles of Moses' law by giving to the woman *at one and the same time* the seven husbands whom the law had required her to have *one after another* during her mortal life. A man might practice polygamy. Many did, including the patriarchs. But a woman? In the resurrection? Absurd! So the law of levirate marriage rules out the doctrine of resurrection. How will Jesus resolve this conundrum without joining the Sadducees in a denial of resurrection—including his own, already predicted to the Twelve?

12:24–25: Jesus said to them, "Because of this you're deceived, aren't you, not knowing the Scriptures nor [knowing] **God's power."** "Because of this" makes the Sadducees' ignorance of the Scriptures and of God's power the reason for their being deceived. The plural of "Scriptures" contrasts with the singular of "Scripture" in 12:10, referring there to a single passage, and may therefore cast a slur on the Sadducees' rejecting all the Old Testament except for Moses' law. [25]**"For when people rise from among the dead they neither marry** [as men do] **nor are they given in marriage** [as happens to women]." "Nor are *they* given in marriage" puts women in the plural, so that "they neither marry nor are they given in marriage" can't be limited to the seven brothers and the one wife they all had in succession.

"**Rather, they are like angels in heaven** [the existence of whom the Sadducees also denied according to Acts 23:8, but see the comments on that passage for these denied angels as disembodied human spirits awaiting the resurrection of their bodies, not as 'God's angels' (Genesis 28:12)]." Rising "*from among* the dead" suggests a resurrection of the righteous, who'll be like heavenly angels, as distinct from resurrection of the unrighteousness, consigned to hell (compare Revelation 20).

12:26–27: "**But concerning the dead, that they're being raised** [as though God is so sure to raise them that he might as well be doing so right now], **you've read, haven't you, in the book of Moses** [the Pentateuch, which you as well as I accept as authoritative] **at** [the passage about] **the bush** [that was burning but wasn't burning up], **how God spoke to him, saying, 'I** [am] **the God of Abraham and the God of Isaac and the God of Jacob** [Exodus 3:6]: ²⁷**He's not God of dead people—rather, of living people. You're much deceived.**" The Sadducees' ignorance of God's power consists in a failure to understand not only that he can raise the dead but also that he can change conditions of life, and that he *will* change them at the resurrection so as to discard the institution of marriage since immortality will make procreation and the rearing of children needless. Consequently, levirate marriage now will pose no difficulty then. "You've read, haven't you?" implies that the Sadducees have indeed read Exodus 3:6 and therefore should know better than to deny the resurrection. But what kind of argument does Jesus draw out of Exodus 3:6? His inference, "He's not God of dead people—rather, of living people," doesn't follow as a *logical* deduction from God's statement to Moses, "I [am] the God of Abraham . . . ." For God was only stating that at the time of his speaking to Moses, God was the one whom the patriarchs had worshiped during their mortal lifetimes—no implication of an afterlife, much less of a bodily resurrection, favored or even hinted at. So just as in 12:15–17, Jesus' argument is *artistically* compelling. How so? By way of drawing a surprising inference never before thought of. "Concerning the dead" includes the patriarchs among those who are presently dead. God's being God not of dead people but of living people means then that presently dead people will have to come back to life by virtue of resurrection. In other words, Jesus transfers God's statement from its original timeframe, the past, to a new timeframe, the future. Just as that statement, when pointed backwards, demanded past physical life for Abraham, Isaac, and Jacob, so too when pointed forward the statement demands future physical life for them even though they're now dead. What counted argumentatively between Jesus and the Sadducees was ingenuity at playing with words by such means as transferring them to new frames of reference where they could be made to say new things— much as preachers still do! Notably, Jesus grounds the resurrection in the nature of God, not in that of human beings. "You're much deceived" gives an outright affirmative answer to the question, "You're deceived, aren't you?" "Much" makes this answer stronger than the ques-

tion, as though to say, "You're *dead* wrong!" Thus Jesus exposes the smart-alecky Sadducees' ignorance with a powerful putdown.

A SCHOLAR'S COMING TO RECOGNIZE THE TRUTH OF JESUS' TEACHING
Mark 12:28–34

Jesus' dialogue with a scholar is the first of a pair of passages dealing with scholars. The two passages go from good (Jesus commends a scholar here in 12:28–34) to bad (Jesus condemns the scholars in 12:35–40).

12:28: **And on approaching** [Jesus], **one of the scholars, having heard them** [Jesus and the Sadducees] **debating with** [each other], **having seen that he answered them well, asked him, "What sort of commandment is first of all** [= most important]**?"** Mark notes that even a scholar had to admit that Jesus had bested the Sadducees in debate. But we have no good reason to think this scholar approached Jesus less antagonistically than the Sanhedrin, Pharisees, Herodians, and Sadducees had just done (11:27–12:27). The scholar doesn't address Jesus respectfully at first. Even the antagonistic Pharisees, Herodians, and Sadducees addressed Jesus respectfully with "Teacher" (12:14, 19), but like the Sanhedrin in 11:28 this scholar doesn't. And the final statement in the present passage, "And no one was *daring* to question him [Jesus] any more" (12:34c), shows that with his question the scholar is daring to challenge Jesus antagonistically. Apparently he thinks he can succeed, where his predecessors haven't, in embarrassing Jesus by dragging him into a theological quagmire. "What *sort of*" suits a question of "first" in the sense of most important. The question then allows Jesus to display, not his cleverness in outwitting his opponents by posing them a dilemma (as in 11:27–12:12), or by overcoming a dilemma posed to him (as in 12:13–17), or by using a part of Scripture to defend a doctrine that doesn't seem to be taught there (as in 12:18–27). No, here the question allows Jesus to identify the most important element in God's law.

12:29–31: **Jesus answered, "The first** [commandment in importance] **is** [the following]: **'Listen, Israel. The Lord our God** [is] **one Lord** [not many lords]. ³⁰**And you shall love the Lord your God with your whole heart and with your whole soul' and with your whole mind 'and with your whole strength** [Deuteronomy 6:4–5].' ³¹**This** [next commandment] **is second** [in importance]: **'You shall love your neighbor as** [you love] **yourself** [Leviticus 19:18].' **No other commandment is greater** [in importance than these]." The lack of "And" before "Jesus answered" indicates a certain abruptness on Jesus' part because of the scholar's failure to address him respectfully. Adherence to many gods results in divided loyalty, but adherence to one God in exclusion of other gods entails a demand for undivided loyalty. Hence the command to love God with the "whole" of heart, soul, mind, and strength. "Heart" connotes both feelings and thoughts. "Soul" connotes physical and psychological energy and life itself, to the point of martyrdom if necessary. "Mind" connotes reasoning. And "strength" connotes physical and material capabilities, including property and other forms of wealth. "And with your whole mind" doesn't appear in Deuteronomy 6:4–5, but here it suits Jesus' replying to a scholar. To love God with the whole of all these includes a feeling of fondness for him but demands much more. It demands sacrificial service of every possible sort. But Jesus goes beyond the scholar's question by quoting what Jesus says is the second most important commandment. This addition makes the point that you mustn't stop at loving God, even that you can't love him without loving your neighbor as well, and that loving your neighbor grows out of loving God. Again, loving has to do with sacrificial service as well as feelings of fondness. "As [you love] yourself" neither commands, commends, nor condemns self-love. It only uses the love you naturally have for yourself as a standard for loving your neighbor. Love for God isn't the standard for loving your neighbor, for the command to love God outranks the command to love your neighbor. But loving yourself doesn't outrank loving your neighbor, for self-love isn't even commanded. So you should love your neighbor as much as you love yourself. You should meet his or her needs in the same way you meet your own needs. Thus the element of love unites the two commandments cited by Jesus and satisfies the demand to know "what *sort of* commandment is first of all."

12:32–33: **And the scholar told him, "Well** [said], **Teacher!"** The disrespectful abruptness of the scholar's question in 12:28 now gives way to a respectful address, preceded by an exclamation that lauds Jesus' theological discernment. **"You've spoken on the basis of truth"** echoes the Pharisees' and Herodians' phraseology in 12:14. But they were flattering Jesus to trip him up. By now he has so overpowered the bullying Sanhedrin, the tricky Pharisees and Herodians, the blundering Sadducees, and the enquiring scribe that the phraseology has lost every tinge of flattery and carries the tones of total assent and pure admiration—so total and pure that the scholar now paraphrases what Jesus has said: "**'He** [the Lord our God] **is one** [Deuteronomy 6:4 again]' **and 'there's no other** [God] **besides him** [Deuteronomy 4:35]'. [33]**And 'loving him with the whole heart and with the whole understanding and with the whole strength** [that one has (Deuteronomy 6:5 again)]' **and 'loving the neighbor as** [one loves] **himself** [Leviticus 19:18 again]' **is more** [important] **than all the whole burnt offerings** [sacrifices that the Law commanded to be burned on the altar in their entirety] **and sacrifices** [of other sorts]." By omitting "Listen, Israel" and adding "there's no other [God] besides him" the scholar brings out more clearly the connection between belief in one God and undivided love. The "soul" and "mind" in Jesus' quotation of Deuteronomy 6:5 collapse into "understanding" to chime in with the scholar's display of understanding. "More [important] than all the whole burnt offerings and sacrifices" displays the scholar's understanding what other commandments might wrongly vie with the two most

important ones, and also displays his understanding that Jesus has ruled out both the existence of commandments equally important as the first two and the existence of more important ones.

12:34: **And on seeing him, that he'd answered thoughtfully, Jesus told him, "You're not far from God's kingdom."** From the primacy of love the scholar has correctly deduced the inferiority of sacrifices in the temple. This deduction displayed thoughtfulness and showed that he's at least beginning to love God with his mind. Since the scholar started out antagonistic to Jesus, Jesus' saying the scholar isn't far from God's kingdom means he's not *now* far from it. He has come close to entering it during the course of his dialogue with Jesus. But Mark puts his final accent, not on the scholar's having come close to God's kingdom—rather, on the effect of Jesus' verbal conquests: **And no one was daring to question him any more.** From here on the initiative will shift to Jesus now that he has passed every test and won every contest. After all, one of his enemies' own experts—a scholar—has just confessed the truth of his teaching.

JESUS' EXPOSÉ OF THE SCHOLARS' IGNORANCE, PRETENTIOUSNESS, AND RAPACITY
Mark 12:35–40

Now that Jesus' enemies have failed miserably in their interrogations of him, he himself turns interrogator. *12:35*: **And answering, Jesus was saying while teaching in the temple, "How come the scholars say that the Christ is David's son?"** Jesus has already answered the scribe in 12:28–33, and according to 12:34 nobody is daring to question Jesus any more. So here, his "answering" means his responding to the lack of further questions by asking his own question about the scholars. "While teaching in the temple" revives the contrast between Jesus' teaching with authority and the scholars' teaching without authority (1:21–22, 27), for he's about to attack them. The redundancy of "teaching" after "saying" exhibits Mark's desire to revive this contrast. Since he hasn't mentioned a departure from the temple since Jesus' returning to it in 11:27, "in the temple" implies that he has stayed there since then. His question not only presupposes that the scholars call the Christ "David's son," that is, a descendant of David. "How come?" in the question also presupposes that the Old Testament never uses "David's son" as a designation of the Christ. So on the basis of this lack Jesus is challenging the scriptural accuracy of that designation by the scholars.

Jesus continues in *12:36–37*: **"In the Holy Spirit David himself said, 'The Lord** [= God] **said to my Lord** [the Christ], **"Sit at my right** [hand] **till I put your enemies under your feet** [Psalm 110:1]."' [37]**David himself says him** [to be] **'Lord.'"** "In the Holy Spirit" attributes divine inspiration to David's scriptural statement; and "David *himself*," which occurs twice for emphasis, sets his designation of the Christ as his "Lord" in sharp, damaging contrast with the scholars' uninspired, unscriptural designation of the Christ as "David's son." "Till I put your enemies under your feet" spells out the Christ's lordship. The heavily emphasized designation of the Christ as "Lord" now leads to Jesus' challenging question, "And from where is he his son?" In other words, from where in the Old Testament do the scholars get "David's son" as a designation of the Christ? Answer: from nowhere. So the scholars stand exposed. They pass for experts in Scripture, but their designation of the Christ doesn't even appear in it. Though not in connection with "the Christ," Bartimaeus had addressed Jesus with "Son of David" (10:47–48); and Jesus, though having referred to himself as "Christ" when speaking to the Twelve, didn't object to Bartimaeus's address. So here Jesus' point is not that he isn't a descendant of David, but that the scholars have no scriptural support for using "David's son" as a messianic title. **And the large crowd was hearing him gladly.** "Large" and "gladly" stress the extent and power of Jesus' grip on the crowd.

In 12:35–37 Mark laid out Jesus' exposé of what the scholars *say* ("How come the scholars say . . . ?"). Now in *12:38–40* Mark lays out Jesus' exposé of what they *do*: **And in his teaching he was saying, "Watch out for the scholars, who like walking around in long robes and greetings in the marketplaces** [39]**and prestigious seats in the synagogues and prestigious couches at banquets,** [40]**who devour widows' houses and for show pray a long time. These** [scholars] **will receive prodigious judgment."** "In his teaching" echoes Jesus' "teaching in the temple" (12:35) and reemphasizes Mark's contrast between Jesus as a teacher with authority and the scholars as teachers without authority (1:21–22, 27). Only now Jesus himself goes further by portraying them as pretentious and positively dangerous in that their pretensions bring them an influence that masks their evil activities—hence the warning to "watch out" for them. Their walking around in long robes and being greeted in marketplaces make a pair, because they're greeted as they walk around in the marketplaces. Since the crowd are those who fawningly greet the scholars, Jesus' denunciation must have shocked the crowd. Seats and couches make another pair, because both are "prestigious." Those seats in the synagogue were located up front and facing the congregation, so that the scholars occupying them enjoyed much visibility. Those couches, consisting of floor pillows on which diners reclined, were the ones closest to the host. The reference to "banquets" leads to "devour[ing]." But it's not food that the scholars devour. It's "widows' houses." That is, Jesus charges the scholars, who were not to accept wages for their teaching, with sponging off the hospitality of widows. (There were widows aplenty to take advantage of, for adolescent girls were often married off to men a number of years their senior.) As was customary, the scholars prayed aloud and in public (compare Matthew 6:5). But they extended their prayers to an unusual length to make themselves look good, all the while freeloading at the widows' expense. Jesus closes his warning to watch out for the scholars with a forceful prediction that in the end they'll receive a prodigious judgment.

JESUS' UPSETTING OF POPULAR OPINION ON THE SIZE OF GIFTS
Mark 12:41–44

The true piety of a widow now contrasts with the pretended piety of the scholars who "devour widows' houses" according to 12:40. *12:41–42:* **And on sitting down** [Jesus has been "walking around in the temple" since 11:27] **opposite the treasury** [which contained receptacles for cash offerings]**, he was observing how the crowd is throwing money** [in the form of coins] **into the treasury** [= into the receptacles located there]**.** "How" has to do with different amounts of money. **And many rich people were throwing** [in money] **voluminously.** The large number of rich people now contrasts with the singleness of a widow, and her poverty contrasts with their wealth: [42]**And on coming, one widow—a poor one—threw** [into the treasury] **two lepta, which are** [= amount to] **a quadrans.** Lepta were the smallest coins in circulation among the Jews. A quadrans was the smallest Roman coin. Two lepta were worth ¼ cent, or 1/144 of a manual laborer's daily wage at the time of Jesus. Mark emphasizes the widow's poverty. It's naturally taken as due to a scholar's having "devoured" her "house" in accord with 12:40.

12:43–44: **And on summoning his disciples, he said to them, "Amen I tell you that this poor widow has thrown** [money into the treasury] **more voluminously than all those who are throwing** [money] **into the treasury.** [44]**For they all threw** [money into the treasury] **out of their surplus, but this** [widow] **out of her lack threw** [in] **absolutely everything she had,** [that is,] **her whole livelihood."** "Summoning his disciples" shows Jesus exercising authority over them. "Amen I say to you" assures them of the accuracy of his following estimate, incredible though it may seem. "More voluminously" puts the poor widow's giving on a grand scale. "Than *all*" and "they *all*" emphasize that the volume of her giving surpasses not only the average giving of the crowd but also the heavy giving of the rich, even the heaviest of their giving. Thus the generosity of her giving for public benefit—that is, for support of worship in the temple—contrasts with the scholars' plundering for their private gain the assets of widows. Since the widow had two lepta, she could have given one and kept the other for her own needs. But she didn't. She gave not only out of her lack in contrast with those who gave out of their surplus. She gave "absolutely everything she had," as emphasized by the addition of "her whole livelihood"—as if "absolutely everything she had" weren't already emphatic enough! Jesus doesn't commend the widow or tell his disciples to follow her example. So Mark doesn't present him as teaching them, or us, how to give. As usual throughout this part of his Gospel, rather, Mark is putting on exhibit Jesus' power to revolutionize the usual view of things, to upset traditional norms, to establish superior criteria.

JESUS' DISPLAY OF ABILITY TO PREDICT THE FATES OF THE TEMPLE, THE WORLD, AND THE SELECTED ONES, AND TO PREDICT HIS COMING AS THE SON OF MAN
Mark 13:1–37

This chapter is generally known as the Olivet Discourse because of its setting on the Mount of Olives. The discourse starts with a dialogue (13:1–4) that shades into a long monologue (13:5–37). The dialogue breaks down into an exclamation by an unnamed disciple (13:1), a responsively menacing prediction by Jesus (13:2), and a consequent inquiry by Peter, James, John, and Andrew (13:3–4). After a narrative introduction (13:5a), the monologue breaks down into two main sections. The first centers on what precedes the coming of the Son of Man (13:5b–23). The second centers on his coming (13:24–37). Both as a whole and in detail this chapter lends great weight to Mark's stress on Jesus' power of prediction, a stress that has already been growing, that will keep on growing right to the end of this Gospel, and that insulates the coming story of Jesus' crucifixion against deductions damaging to him, such as that the sufferer of so shameful an execution can't possibly be the world's Savior or the stronger one of John the baptizer's prediction (1:8).

13:1–4: And as he's going out of the temple [see 11:27 for Jesus' last entrance into the temple], **one of his disciples says to him, "Teacher, look! What magnificent stones and what magnificent buildings!"** The present tense of "says" suits the disciple's admiring exclamation. "Stones" refers to Herodian masonry, admirable for its massive dimensions and handsome style. "Buildings" refers to surrounding structures along with the sanctuary proper, all of which make up the temple complex. Recent archaeological excavations favor the addition of this complex to the traditional "Seven Wonders of the Ancient World" so as to make eight of them. The magnificence of its stones and buildings now makes Jesus' menacing prediction both striking and unlikely of fulfillment. (But, of course, we know that it was indeed fulfilled in A.D. 70.) **²And Jesus said to him, "You're looking at these large buildings. By no means will a stone be left here on a stone that for sure won't be torn down."** Some translations have Jesus *ask* whether the unnamed disciple is looking at the buildings. But *of course* he's looking at them. Otherwise he wouldn't have broken out in an exclamation over them and told Jesus to look. So it's better to say that Jesus prepares him for a dire prediction by observing that this disciple *is* looking at the buildings. Jesus' description of them as "large" adds to the unlikelihood that they'll be torn down in fulfillment of his prediction. The utter destruction of not one stone's being left on another increases this unlikelihood yet further and therefore makes the fulfillment—and with it, Jesus' power of prediction—all the more impressive. "Here" pinpoints the prediction in a way that makes its meaning and fulfillment unmistakable. And "by no means . . . for sure" underlines the certainty

of fulfillment. **³And as he was sitting on the Mount of Olives across from the temple, Peter and James and John and Andrew** [compare 1:16–20; 3:16–19] **were asking him privately, ⁴"Tell us, when will these things be** [= occur] **and what** [will be] **the sign when all these things are about to be consummated?"** So these four disciples must have heard what Jesus predicted to the unnamed disciple in 13:1–2. "Privately" excludes the rest of the disciples. "When will these things be?" asks about the time of the temple's coming destruction. "And what [will] be the sign . . . ?" asks for a forewarning signal. The addition of "all" to "these things" suits the multiplicity of the magnificent stones and buildings. It's as though the tearing down of each stone and building will be an event in and of itself, the totality of which will bring Jesus' prediction to fulfillment. Caution: since he hasn't yet predicted the events to be described in 13:5b–27, the four disciples don't yet know about them and therefore can't be asking about their fulfillment. They're asking about the temple's destruction, which Jesus has predicted in 13:2 but won't mention again, not even in 13:14.

13:5–6: **But Jesus started telling them, "Watch out lest someone deceive you. ⁶Many will come on the basis of my name, saying, 'I am,' and deceive many."** We might expect that the greater the number of charlatans, the fewer the number of people taken in by their competing and therefore contradictory claims. But the deception will be so clever as to produce the opposite effect: an increase in the number of deceived people with each increase in the number of deceivers. "My name" refers to Jesus' name, of course. But to his personal name "Jesus" or to his titular name "Christ"? The expression "in *name* that you are *Christ's*" in 9:41 and Jesus' predicting shortly that false *christs* will arise (13:21–22) favor that here "my name" refers to Jesus' titular name "Christ" (see also 8:29; 14:61–62). So the deceivers' coming "on the basis of" Jesus' name and saying, "I am," means that they'll claim, "I am *Christ*," just as in answer to the question, "Are you the Christ . . . ?" Jesus will say "I am [the Christ]" (14:61–62). For a believer in Jesus to be deceived by some false christ would be to believe that the false christ is Jesus come back to earth.

13:7–8: **"And whenever you hear battles** [so near that you can hear their noise] **and reports of battles** [so distant that you only hear *about* them], **don't be alarmed. It's necessary that they take place. The end isn't yet, however. ⁸For nation will rise up** [in arms] **against nation, and kingdom against kingdom. There'll be earthquakes from place to place. There'll be famines. These** [are] **the beginning of birth pains."** All these disasters belong to God's plan. So don't think that history has gotten out of his control. And don't think that these disasters *signal* the end of the age any more than you should think that the appearance of this or that false christ *constitutes* the end of the age. The disasters and the appearance of false christs constitute only "the beginning of birth pains," that is, of the horrors whose intensity will subsequently increase until the coming of the Son of Man (13:14–27). So Jesus wants to keep his disciples from deception and alarm. Notably, he's not answering the disciples' question when the destruction of the temple will take place and what will signal that it's about to take place. In keeping with a theme that runs throughout his Gospel, on the other hand, Mark wants to exhibit Jesus' ability to predict coming disasters, including those that because of the Roman peace (Pax Romana) seemed at the time unlikely of fulfillment.

13:9–11: "But you—watch out for yourselves." Here Jesus turns the disciples' attention from the cosmic events just described to their own persons. The preceding warning had to do with the danger of deception. The present warning has to do with the danger of persecution—in particular, the danger that persecution will cause the disciples to disown Christ. Evangelism would then be thwarted. Yet in allowing them to be persecuted, God purposes that they bear witness to the good news before people and among nations that wouldn't otherwise hear it. **"People will give you over to sanhedrins** [scattered, lesser Jewish courts in addition to the Great Sanhedrin, or Supreme Court, in Jerusalem] **and to synagogues. You'll be beaten** [a Jewish form of disciplinary punishment (compare Deuteronomy 25:1–3; Acts 22:19; 2 Corinthians 11:24)], **and you'll be stood before governors and kings** [who'll be Gentiles, since at that time the Jews didn't have their own governors and kings] **for a testimony to them** [= in order that you may preach the gospel to them]**."** It seems unlikely that nobodies like the disciples will bear witness before the high and mighty. But Jesus predicts they will. And they did. The further prediction, [10]**"And it's necessary that the gospel first be preached to all nations,"** seems even more unlikely. But again in accordance with God's plan ("it's necessary"), the gospel was so preached (Romans 1:5, 8–17; 11:11–36; 15:14–21, 26; Ephesians 2:11–3:21; Colossians 1:6, 23, 27; 1 Timothy 3:16). "First" means "before the end" (compare 13:7). [11]**"And whenever people lead you** [to the aforementioned authorities] **by giving** [you] **over** [to them], **don't worry beforehand about what you should say; rather, whatever is given you** [to say] **in that hour—say this. For you're not the ones speaking; rather, the Holy Spirit** [is speaking through you]**."** So nobodies like the disciples needn't be overawed by the high and mighty, for Jesus has baptized his followers in the Holy Spirit (1:8).

13:12–13: "And brother will give over [his] **brother to death; and father** [will give over his] **child** [to death]; **and children will rise up against** [their] **parents and get them put to death;** [13]**and you'll be hated by all because of my name** [see the comments on 9:41: 'in my name that you're Christ's']. **But the** [disciple] **who perseveres to an end—this one will be saved"** [compare Micah 7:7; Daniel 12:12–13]. With the phrases that Jesus borrows, Micah 7:6 described a *general* breakdown in family life. But Jesus makes *discipleship* to him the reason for betrayals of his disciples by members of their own families. The specificity of this prediction, plus its eventual fulfillment, makes it remarkable in that the family

forms the most fundamental and stable unit of society. Betraying the members of one's own family to the point of getting them put to death shows the extreme either of desire to escape persecution oneself, or of hatred toward the gospel, or of both. Even persecution so severe as this won't signal the end, however. But persecution will come from "all," not just from within one's own family. "Because of my name" alludes to the disciples' confessing Jesus as the Christ and using his name in exorcism and miracle-working (compare 9:38–39). "*An* end" in 13:13 differs from "*the* end" in 13:7 and therefore refers to a disciple's own end in case of martyrdom, not to the end of the age (see also being "give[n] over . . . to death" and "put to death" in these very verses). Perseverance means loyalty to the point of martyrdom, if necessary, and proves genuineness of discipleship. To buttress his disciples against this possibility, Jesus assures martyrs of eternal salvation. "This one" gives special recognition to martyrs.

Jesus' earlier warning, "But you—watch out for yourselves" (13:9), now focuses on a severer danger than he has described so far, one that does start a series of events immediately preceding and signaling the end. **13:14: "But whenever you see 'the abomination of desolation'** [Daniel 9:27; 11:31; and especially 12:11, to whose phraseology Jesus' statement comes closest] **standing where he shouldn't** [stand] **(the one who's reading is to understand), then the ones in Judea are to flee into the mountains!"** "The mountains" are those of the Judean wilderness, a traditional hideout. But what, or who, is "the abomination"? Where is it, or he, "standing"? What does "desolation" mean? Who's the one "reading"? What's he reading? And what is he supposed to "understand"? "The abomination" is a sacrilege. "He" personalizes the sacrilege. "Standing where he shouldn't" identifies the sacrilege as the image of a pagan god or of a deified ruler set up in the sacred precincts of the temple, where the one true God alone ought to be worshiped (compare 2 Thessalonians 2:3–4; 1 John 2:18; 4:3; Revelation 13). "Of desolation" describes the abomination as causing worshipers of the one true God to desert the temple, to abandon it, because it has been profaned by the abomination. ("Desolation" can hardly refer to destruction; for then the abomination wouldn't be standing there, and it would be too late to flee.) The disciples in Judea are to flee into the nearby mountains so as to escape persecution for not worshiping the abomination. So Jesus is still ignoring the four disciples' questions about the temple's coming destruction. "The one who's reading" is the reader of Mark's Gospel, usually a public reader to an audience of listeners. For prior to the invention of the printing press, private copies for private reading were few and far between. And the public reader is to understand that "he" shouldn't be changed to "it" even though "the abomination" is neuter. "The abomination" is grammatically neuter but refers to a personal object—therefore "he." So Jesus makes the abomination of desolation a sign, not of a soon destruction of the temple, but of the Son of Man's soon coming (13:24–27).

13:15–17: "And the [man] **on the roof** [of his house in the city] **isn't to come down or enter** [his house] **to take anything out of his house;** ¹⁶**and the** [man] **in the field isn't to turn back to take up his cloak** [which he shed for fieldwork but needs for warmth at night]. ¹⁷**And woe to** [women] **who are pregnant and** [women] **who are nursing** [their babies] **in those days.**" The man lounging on the flat roof of his house is at leisure. The man out in the field is at work. Neither one is to spend time to retrieve anything, not even a supposed necessity. Get out and away as fast as you can, even jumping from roof to roof if you're on a housetop. Too bad for women who are pregnant or nursing, for pregnancy and nursing will hamper or preclude a speedy escape. Such women will suffer a higher risk of getting caught.

13:18–20: "**But be praying that it** [the abomination of desolation] **not occur during winter** [when heavy rains in Judea make flight into the mountains difficult or impossible because of flooded roads and ravines]. ¹⁹**For those days will be** [= consist in] **affliction** [in the sense of persecution] **such as hasn't occurred since the beginning of the creation that God created until now and will by no means occur** [afterwards, for the Son of Man's coming will put an end to persecution of the disciples]. ²⁰**And if the Lord hadn't cut short the days** [of unprecedented and final affliction], **no flesh would have been saved** [from martyrdom]." The context of instructions for Jesus' disciples living in Judea, mainly in Jerusalem, limits "no flesh" to those of them living there. For they're the ones exposed to persecution for refusal to worship the abomination in the temple. "**But because of the selected ones, whom he selected, he has cut short the days.**" That is, to preserve from martyrdom at least some of Jesus' Judean disciples, the Lord has cut the period of unprecedented persecution shorter than it otherwise would have lasted. (In effect, Jesus is saying that the Lord will mercifully not allow the 1,260 days of Revelation 11:3; 12:6 to run their full course [compare the cancellation of the seven thunders in Revelation 10:1–7].) The cutting short is future, but it's so sure to happen that like the Old Testament prophets, Jesus uses the past tense. Most translations have "the elect" or "the chosen ones." But in contemporary English "elect" suggests democratic voting, and "chosen" doesn't connote selection out of a larger number so strongly as the term used by Jesus does. This term describes the disciples as selected for eternal salvation.

Now Jesus gives another warning against deception, deception that if successful would keep his disciples in Judea from fleeing to the mountains for safety. The last time he warned against their being deceived by those who'll come claiming to be the Christ and against being alarmed by warfare and supposedly natural disasters so as to think the end has come (13:5–8). At this point, though, the abomination is standing in the temple, where he shouldn't; and unequaled affliction has set in. So the end *is* near, and its nearness results in a heightened danger of deception. *13:21–23*: "**And then, if anyone should say to you, 'Look, here** [is] **the Christ! Look, there** [is the Christ]!' **don't ever believe** [him]. ²²**For false christs and false prophets will arise and give signs and wonders to deceive, if possible, the selected ones.**" The danger of deception comes now not so much from the false christs as from their false prophets, who proclaim that the Christ is here or there. The backing up of their proclamations with the performance of signs and wonders will heighten the danger of deception. Since in contrast with 13:5–6 the false christs are *being* proclaimed rather than proclaiming themselves, the performance of signs and wonders is probably limited to the false prophets (compare Revelation 13:1–18; 16:13; 19:20; 20:10). "If possible, the selected ones" puts a final emphasis on the danger of deception. ²³"**But you—watch out!**" tells how they're to avoid deception. "**I've told you all things beforehand.**" In other words, the disciples now know ahead of time all they need to know for avoiding deception—if only they watch out for the events Jesus has foretold. For Mark, this statement fits nicely into his emphasis on Jesus' predictive power.

13:24–27: "**In those days, however, after that affliction** [persecution] **'the sun will be darkened, and the moon won't give its light,** ²⁵**and the stars will be falling' out of heaven, 'and the powers in the heavens' will be shaken** [see Isaiah 13:10; 34:4]. ²⁶**And then people will see 'the Son of Man coming in clouds' with much power and 'glory'** [Daniel 7:13]. ²⁷**And then he'll send the angels and have them gather his selected ones out of the four winds, from the extremity of earth to the extremity of heaven.**" The succession of phrases, "In those days . . . after that affliction . . . . And then . . . . And then . . . ," displays both Jesus' knowledge of God's timetable and, again, Jesus' predictive power. The celestial disasters add detail to that knowledge and power and provide a dark backdrop against which the glory of the Son of Man's coming shines out all the more. Those disasters feature a darkening of our primary luminaries, the sun and the moon. Jesus doesn't say what will darken them, so that the point lies solely in a contrast between their darkening and the glory of the Son of Man's coming. "The powers in the heavens" equate with "the stars" and personalize the stars as heavenly beings whose power is so shaken by the Son of Man's coming "with much power" (compare 9:1) that they'll totter and fall out of the sky, as in a shower of meteorites. Further details highlight the awesome manner of Jesus' coming again as the Son of Man: (1) the seeing of this event by people in general (compare 14:62; Revelation 1:7) or possibly by the fallen heavenly powers; (2) his coming in clouds, a divine mode of transport (9:7; 14:62; Exodus 34:5, and many other biblical passages); (3) his coming with glory (compare 8:38; 10:37); and (4) his sending angels to gather his selected ones, believers in him. As the Son of Man, Jesus will have angels at his disposal. The ones selected for salvation belong to him, and they'll number so many that the angels will have to go to the farthest horizons of earth and sky to gather them all. Since according to 13:20 "the Lord" selected them, their belonging to the Son of Man makes Jesus as the Son of Man also the Son of God and thus heir to the selected ones. His coming won't need any announcement from others, such as "Look, here's the Christ! Look, there's the Christ!" It will announce itself in the heavens and across the expanse of the earth. Only false christs will appear in a corner and need prophets to advertise their whereabouts. And the gathering of the selected ones from everywhere will further eliminate any need for invitations to come and see. "However" stresses the contrast between the deceptive, private way in which false christs will come and the overpowering, open way in which the Son of Man will come.

13:28–31: "And learn a parable from the fig tree: When its branch has already become tender and is putting out leaves, you know that summer is near. ²⁹So also you—when you see these things happening, know that he [the Son of Man] **is near, at the doors."** The introductory command to *learn* the parable anticipates the closing command to *understand* ("know") the point of the parable. "These things" doesn't refer to the destruction of the temple, for Jesus has ignored that topic ever since Peter, James, John, and Andrew asked him about its timing and a prior signal. Nor can "these things" mean the events Jesus predicted in 13:5–13, because they *won't* indicate the nearness of the Son of Man's coming. So "these things" must mean the events Jesus predicted in 13:14–23, for they *will* indicate its nearness. Concerning fig trees, see the comments on Matthew 24:32–33. ³⁰**"Amen I tell you that by no means will this generation pass away till all these things happen** [compare Daniel 12:7]. ³¹**Heaven and earth will pass away, but by no means will my words pass away** [= fail to be fulfilled]**."** With "Amen I tell you" and two occurrences of "by no means," Jesus gives the firmest possible assurance of fulfillment. At first glance "this generation" looks like a reference to his contemporaries. And well it might have turned out to mean them (hence "*this* generation" rather than "*that* generation"). But the preceding parable defines "this generation" as those living at the time of the unprecedented affliction leading up to the Son of Man's coming and, in the disciples' case, as those who recognize the events of that time as heralding the nearness of his coming. The addition of "all" to "these things" brings into view his coming itself alongside those preceding events. As soon as those events transpire, the Son of man will assuredly come.

13:32: "But concerning that day or hour, no one knows—not even the angels in heaven or the Son—except the Father." Jesus has predicted what will signal the nearness of his coming as the Son of Man and has stressed the certainty of fulfillment once the warning signs start taking place. Now he denies that anyone except God the Father knows the exact time of his coming, apparently because the Lord has cut off the foregoing days of unprecedented affliction and hasn't revealed how many of them he has cut off (13:20). "Day" represents the smallest unit of time on the calendar, "hour" the smallest unit of time in a day. (Ancients didn't deal in minutes

or seconds.) The pairing of "day" and "hour" therefore confirms the distinction between the nearness of the Son of Man's coming, known by the occurrence of premonitory events, and its exact time, unknown to all but God the Father. Since "the Father" complements "the Son" yet the preceding statements have referred to "the Son of Man," the Son of God the Father equates with the Son of Man. Theologically, we may say that just as Jesus didn't exercise his divine omnipotence except to further the kingdom (compare, for example, his refusal to make stones into bread for himself), so he didn't exercise his divine omniscience except to further the kingdom. To have known and made known the exact time of his coming would have damaged the work of the kingdom by encouraging carelessness during the interim. What Jesus *could* have done because he was divine didn't predetermine what he *did* do as also a human being. The incarnation didn't lessen his divine potencies, but it did lead him to limit the use of them.

13:33–37: "Watch out [because you don't know the exact time of the Son of Man's coming, and you don't want to be caught unawares]**! Keep alert** [so as to recognize the events that signal its nearness]**! For you don't know when the time** [of his coming] **is."** It has been set, but the Father has kept it secret. ³⁴**"[It's] like a man away on a journey, having left his house and given authority to his slaves, to each his task. And he commanded the doorkeeper to stay awake. ³⁵Therefore** [in view of this parable] **stay awake; for you don't know when the owner of the house** [a figure of speech for Jesus] **is coming, whether during evening or midnight or cockcrowing or early morning** [the four watches into which Romans divided the night (though they didn't name them as such), each watch lasting three hours, more or less, so that "midnight" doesn't refer to our 12:00 midnight, or "cockcrowing" to the particular moment of a rooster's crowing, or "early morning" to the hour(s) right after dawn], ³⁶**lest coming suddenly he find you sleeping** [a figure of speech for carelessness in one's professed discipleship]. ³⁷**And what I'm saying to you** [Peter, James, John, and Andrew, to whom Jesus has been speaking according to 13:3–5] **I'm saying to all** [my disciples]: **Stay awake!"** The parable pinpoints the doorkeeper to echo Jesus' reference to the Son of Man's being "at the doors" once the unprecedented affliction starts (13:29). But the parable doesn't mention the doorkeeper's task of opening the housedoor when his master returns at an unknown day and hour. So the accent falls on *readiness*, not on the unmentioned task. And this readiness requires staying awake, a figure of speech for alertful recognition of the events that will indicate the nearness of the Son of Man's coming, the events that will begin with the abomination of desolation ("But when you *see* the abomination of desolation . . ." [13:14]). The difficulty of staying awake at night matches the danger that even the Lord's selected ones might be deceived (13:22). Jesus stops the parable with the master's command that the doorkeeper stay awake and jumps immediately to his own command that the disciples stay awake. When did the slavemaster/houseowner return? Was the doorkeeper awake at the time? What reward or punishment did he receive? Jesus doesn't say and thus leaves exclusive stress on watchfulness. Incidentally, the word for "owner" (of the house) also means "master" (of the slaves) and "Lord" (in a figurative reference to Jesus). That Jesus speaks of *night* watches even though he has mentioned the "day" of his coming emphasizes the incalculability of its exact time. Since travelers don't usually arrive home at night, the comparison to arrival during one of the night watches adds further emphasis on incalculability. A final addition to this emphasis comes in Jesus' reference to suddenness: if you're sleeping you'll have no time to get ready.

JESUS' MAKING OF FURTHER PREDICTIONS AND THE STARTING OF FULFILLMENTS
Mark 14:1–11

This passage puts on exhibit Jesus' power of prediction in that the details of his passion predictions now start to be fulfilled. The passage also shows that he didn't suffer the disgrace of burial without the customary anointing beforehand, though such a disgrace was to be expected for someone crucified as a heinous criminal. And Jesus gets better than an anointing. He gets a perfuming.

14:1a: And the Passover and [Festival of] Unleavened Bread were [going to occur] **after two days.** The Passover commemorated the exodus of Israel from Egypt at the time of Moses. This festival started with the slaying of sacrifices in the afternoon and ended with the eating of a meal in the evening. The weeklong Festival of Unleavened Bread followed immediately. Since unleavened bread was to be eaten at the Passover meal, though, Passover was often referred to as "the first day of [the Festival of] Unleavened Bread" (see 14:12). But what does Mark mean by saying that these festivals were going to occur "after two days"? Well, Jesus predicted he'd rise from the dead "after *three* days" (8:31; 9:31; 10:34). He died on Good Friday and rose on Easter Sunday. So if we count fractions of a day as a whole day, as Jews commonly did, "*after* three days" comes out to mean "*on* the third day" (see Matthew 16:21; 17:23; 20:19; Luke 9:22; 18:33; 24:7, 21, 46; 1 Corinthians 15:4). In our present passage, then, "after *two* days" means "on the *second* day," that is, "the *next* day" rather than "the day after the next day" (as in the case of Good Friday and Easter Sunday). Here's the resultant chronology of Passion Week: Palm Sunday—the triumphal procession at the end of a day's walk from Jericho; Monday—the cursing of the fig tree and the cleansing of the temple; Tuesday—discovery of the fig tree withered, debates in Jerusalem, and the Olivet Discourse; Wednesday—the plot against Jesus, his being perfumed, and Judas Iscariot's offering to betray him (= our present passage, 14:1–11); Thursday—Passover; Good Friday—Jesus' arrest, trials, crucifixion, and burial; Saturday—Jesus' lying in a tomb. Easter Sunday will begin a new week with Jesus' resurrection.

14:1b–2: And the chief priests and the scholars were seeking how, by seizing him with cunning, they might kill him [compare 11:18; 12:12]. Thus Jesus' predictions in 8:31; 9:31; 10:32–34 are starting to come true. "With cunning" underlines the chief priests' and scholars' murderous intent and prepares for Jesus' nighttime arrest, made possible by Judas Iscariot's betrayal of him. **²For they were saying, "[Let's not seize him] in the festal assembly, lest there'll be a riot of the people"** [see 12:12 again for their not arresting Jesus earlier because "they feared the crowd"]. Their certainty of the people's rioting in Jesus' behalf if he's arrested in their midst plays into Mark's emphasis on Jesus' hold over the masses.

14:3–5: And while he was in Bethany [see the comments on 11:1] **in the house of Simon the leper, while he was reclining** [at table], **a woman came having an alabaster flask of perfume,** [which was] **very expensive, unadulterated nard** [the best of perfumes]. **On breaking the alabaster flask, she poured it** [the perfume] **on his head. ⁴But some were indignantly saying to themselves** [= to one another], **"For what purpose has this waste of perfume taken place? ⁵For this perfume could have been sold for over three hundred denarii** [that is, for more than a whole year's wages for a fully employed manual laborer (see Matthew 20:1–16)] **and** [the denarii] **given to the poor." And they were growling at her.** "The leper" distinguishes this Simon from Simon Peter (3:16), Simon the Cananaean (3:18), Simon the brother of Jesus (6:3), and Simon of Cyrene (15:21). We don't know anything more about this Simon (for example, whether Jesus had healed him of his leprosy), because Mark turns immediately to the actions of a woman in relation to Jesus. Nor does Mark name the woman or say anything else about her. All his attention focuses on her pouring perfume on Jesus' head, and doing so as he was eating a meal! (Ordinarily, people would have anointed themselves before going out [Matthew 6:17]; or a host might anoint them on their entry as guests into his house [Luke 7:46].) Details concerning the perfume—its being contained in an alabaster flask, consisting of unadulterated nard, and costing a lot—enhance the honor paid to Jesus and give apparent justification to the criticism that this woman wasted the perfume when it might have been sold for a high price and the proceeds given to the poor. Pouring out the perfume exceeds smearing on a bit of it; and the woman's breaking the flask punctuates the unexpected lavishness of the outpouring, makes the flask unusable in the future, and therefore dramatizes the completeness of the outpouring. Not a drop is held back. This seeming excess of honor counteracts the shame of Jesus' coming crucifixion. Mark doesn't say who growled at the woman after becoming indignant, for he wants to focus next on Jesus' reaction and interpretation of her act.

14:6–9: But Jesus said, "Leave her [alone]. **Why are you causing her troubles** [= bothering her by growling at her]? **She has worked a *good* work** [in contrast with "this waste" that you've talked about; also in contrast with the dastardly plot that Mark mentioned in 14:1–2 and with Judas Iscariot's upcoming offer of betrayal in 14:10–11] **in me** [in my very body, as distinct from "the poor" that you referred to]. **⁷For you always have the poor with yourselves; and whenever you want, you can do well for them. But me you don't always have** [= a predictive allusion to his soon-coming death and therefore also a hint of his supernaturally knowing about the plot just now hatched against him (14:1–2)]." The allusion to his soon-coming death now becomes more than an allusion: **⁸"She has done what she could."** In other words, what she had she used. **"She has anticipated perfuming my body in preparation for burial."** Burial implies death. Jesus' interpretation of the woman's deed doesn't necessarily imply she had in mind the meaning he gives it. On the contrary, she perfumed only his head, whereas he speaks of his body; and Jews ordinarily used cheap olive oil, not expensive perfume, for corpses. But Jesus' interpreting the pouring out of costly perfume on his head as an anticipatory preparation of his body (the word for "body" can also mean "corpse") for burial gives him a dignity in burial that will erase the shame of what turns out to be crucifixion. Anticipatory preparation adds a detail that hasn't appeared in earlier passion predictions—namely, that Jesus' corpse won't be prepared in the usual manner between death and burial. **⁹"And amen I tell you, wherever in the whole world the gospel is proclaimed, also what this** [woman] **has done will be told with the result of her being remembered."** Here Jesus adds two further predictions: (1) that the gospel will be proclaimed throughout the whole world and (2) that the woman's good deed will be told along with the gospel, so that she'll be remembered. Her anonymity and "the *whole* world" make a fulfillment of these predictions unlikely and therefore the fulfillment more impressive when it actually happens (as it has!). "Amen I tell you" gives Jesus' disciples assurance of the unlikely fulfillment.

14:10–11: And Judas Iscariot, one of the Twelve, went away to the chief priests to give him [Jesus] **over to them. ¹¹And on hearing** [Judas's purpose], **they rejoiced and promised to give him money. And he started seeking how he might give him** [Jesus] **over** [to the chief priests] **conveniently** [that is, apart from the crowded festal assembly, where a riot in Jesus' behalf would be sure to break out]. "One of the Twelve" harks back to 3:19. This addition to Judas's name highlights the treachery he's about to exhibit. Imagine! One of Jesus' chosen twelve purposes to give him over to those who are plotting his execution. Judas's going away *from* Jesus reverses his former discipleship, which entailed going away *to* Jesus in order to be *with* him (see 3:13–14). "To give him over" to the chief priests starts the fulfillment of Jesus' predictions that he'll be given over to his enemies (9:31; 10:33). They joyfully promise to give Judas money; but he doesn't get it yet, and—in contrast with prior mention of the more than three hundred denarii worth of perfume used to prepare Jesus' body for burial—Mark doesn't mention the amount of money they promised

Judas. The Sanhedrin's seeking how to seize Jesus with cunning now yields to Judas's seeking how to give him over to them "conveniently." But Mark doesn't attribute to Judas any reason or motive, whether disgruntlement with the seemingly wasteful perfuming of Jesus' body, with Jesus' defense of it, or with a desire for money. (The chief priests promised him money without his asking for it.) So the accent falls entirely on this beginning of the fulfillment of Jesus' predictions and on the treachery of Judas's offer and effort.

JESUS' MAKING OF PREDICTIONS CONCERNING A PREPARATION FOR THE PASSOVER, AND THEIR FULFILLMENTS
Mark 14:12–16

14:12: And on the first day of [the Festival] **of Unleavened Bread,** [that is, on the day] **when they** [the Jews] **sacrificed the Passover** [lamb], **his disciples say to him, "Where** [in Jerusalem] **do you want us, on going away** [presumably from Bethany (see 11:11, 12; 14:3)], **to prepare for you to eat the Passover** [a meal featuring above all a roasted lamb]**?"** This "first day" is the Thursday before Good Friday and the beginning of the Passover Festival, which lasts into the evening and thus equates with the beginning of the Festival of Unleavened Bread (see the comments on 14:1). The disciples' asking Jesus where he wants them to prepare the Passover meal underlines his authority. We expect them to say "for *us* [the Twelve plus Jesus] to eat." Instead they say "for *you* to eat," though in fact they'll all eat the meal (14:17–25). The concentration on preparing for Jesus to eat, plus the present tense of "say" in the introduction to the disciples' questions, puts further emphasis on his authority.

Now Jesus exercises both his authority and his predictive ability. **14:13–16: And he sends two of his disciples and says to them, "Go into the city, and there'll meet you a man carrying a jar of water. Follow him; ¹⁴and wherever he enters, say to the houseowner, 'The teacher says, "Where's my guest room where I may eat the Passover** [meal] **with my disciples?"' ¹⁵And he'll show you an upstairs room—large, furnished, prepared** [for our use]. **And there prepare** [the Passover meal] **for us."** Again, the vivid present tense of "sends" and "says" headlines this first prediction by Jesus. He fills it with details, so that its fulfillment will be astonishing. A man will meet the two disciples Jesus sends. The fact that he'll meet them rather than they him makes fulfillment extremely unlikely, for it would be remarkable enough if Jesus knew the two were going to meet a man by virtue of their approaching *him* at Jesus' instructions. But Jesus' knowing that a man is going to meet them by virtue of his approaching *them*—what a testimony to Jesus' foreknowledge! Not only that, but also the man will be carrying a jar of water—what a woman would usually do in those days, for a man would normally carry water in a skin. It's a mistake to think that Mark wants us to imagine prearrangements on Jesus' part, for (1) prearrangements would have required a time of meeting set by Jesus beforehand, whereas the disciples happen at the moment to have taken the initiative with their question; (2) Jerusalem is big and thronged with tens of thousands of Passover pilgrims as well as with tens of thousands of permanent residents, so that Jesus would have had to prearrange a particular place of meeting—but his instructions mention no such place; and (3) prearrangements would probably have eliminated any need for the question, "Where's my guest room where I may *eat* the Passover [meal] with my disciples?" and led instead to a different question: "Where's the guest room where my disciples may *prepare* the Passover [meal]?" We have a prediction, then, not prearrangements. It stays unknown whether the houseowner is expected to recognize "the teacher" as Jesus, or whether he's expected to provide out of respect for teachers in general a room without knowing that Jesus is the teacher. The lack of information on this point leaves the stress on Jesus' predictive power and on his authority. "*My* guest room" implies that as the teacher he has authority to commandeer the room. "My *disciples*" highlights his authority further. The second prediction is as remarkably detailed as the first. The room will be upstairs, large, furnished, and ready for use. That the houseowner will neither refuse nor hesitate to show the room makes the prediction and Jesus' authority yet more impressive. [16]**And the** [two] **disciples went out and came into the city and found** [things] **just as he'd told them. And they prepared the Passover** [meal]. The disciples' discovery exhibits the accuracy of Jesus' predictions, details and all. And since every matter is to be legally established by the testimony of at least two witnesses (Numbers 35:30; Deuteronomy 17:6; 19:15), the twoness of the disciples who made the discovery provides sufficient testimony to the fulfillment of these unlikely predictions by Jesus. Obedient preparation of the Passover meal calls attention back to his authority and sets the stage for the meal itself.

JESUS' EXHIBITING FOREKNOWLEDGE OF HIS BETRAYAL, VIOLENT DEATH, AND ULTIMATE VICTORY
Mark 14:17–25

Mark's account of the Last Supper divides into Jesus' prediction that one of the Twelve will give him over (14:17–21) and predictions of his violent death and ultimate victory (14:22–25).

14:17–18: **And when evening came, he comes with the Twelve** [to the upstairs room]. The present tense of "comes" introduces vigorously this account of Jesus' further predictions. Jews usually ate their late meal toward the end of the afternoon, but evening was the proper time for a Passover meal (Exodus 12:8). [18]**And while they were reclining** [at table, as was customary at formal meals, whereas sitting was customary at ordinary meals] **and eating, Jesus said, "Amen I tell you that one of you 'who's eating with me'** [Psalm 41:9] **will give me over** [to those plotting to kill me (14:1)]." This prediction is shocking, because although Jesus has spoken before of

being given over to his enemies (9:31; 10:33–34), up till now he hasn't identified the betrayer as one of his disciples, much less as one of his intimates, the specially chosen Twelve. Adding to this pathos is the expression "who's eating with me," for in that culture eating with someone connoted an almost sacred bond of friendship. The unlikelihood of betrayal from within the ranks of the Twelve, who are eating the Passover with Jesus, will make the fulfillment of his present prediction all the more impressive. "Amen I tell you" underlines certainty of fulfillment despite this unlikelihood.

14:19–21: **And they began to be saddened and to say to him one by one, "Surely I** [am] **not** [the betrayer], [am] **I?"** [20]**But he said to them, "[The betrayer is] one of the Twelve who himself is dipping with me into the one bowl** [which we all share], [21]**because on the one hand the Son of Man is going away** [to his enemies as a result of being given over to them], **just as it's written concerning him** [see Psalm 41:9 again]. **On the other hand, alas for that man through whom the Son of Man is being given over!** [It would be] **good for him if he— that man—hadn't been born."** The disciples' sadness heightens the pathos. All of them are dipping with Jesus into the one bowl. So his answer to their question doesn't identify which one of them will betray him. Instead, it deepens the betrayer's treachery by adding "who himself is dipping with me into the one bowl" to the earlier "who's eating with me." "Who *himself* is dipping with me ..." deepens the betrayer's treachery yet more by describing the dipping as intentionally false-friendly. The lack of information concerning what was being dipped, what was contained in the bowl, and therefore what was being eaten—this lack directs attention solely to the treacherous intimacy of dipping with Jesus into one and the same bowl. The ignorance of eleven of the Twelve as to who will betray Jesus lets Jesus' foreknowledge stand out by contrast. He cites Scripture as the reason for being given over, so that his fate carries out God's plan. "Through whom" describes the betrayer as God's unwitting agent in the carrying out of that plan as revealed in Scripture. A pronouncement of woe on the betrayer ("alas for that man . . . !") categorizes him as the true criminal and exonerates Jesus of any guilt that people might attach to him because of his crucifixion. "*That* man" puts the betrayer at a moral distance from "the Son of Man," and repetition of "that man" magnifies the distance. Its being "good for him if he . . . hadn't been born" exposes the enormity of treachery by headlining the horror of his fate, worse than that of the Son of Man, who'll be resurrected to come again in glory. "Is going away . . . is being given over": so sure is Jesus to be going away as a result of being given over that the fulfillment of his prediction is in process right now (14:10–11).

14:22–25: **And while they were eating, on taking bread, on saying a blessing** [= praising God for the bread], **he broke** [it into pieces, as was especially appropriate for unleavened bread, its being cracker-like] **and gave** [the pieces] **to them and said, "Take** [these pieces of bread]. **This** [bread] **is my corpse.**" In the context of Jesus' being given over to death, the word for "body" is better translated "corpse" (compare the use of this same word in references to Jesus' burial in 14:8; 15:43). ²³**And on taking a cup, after giving thanks he gave** [it] **to them; and they all drank out of it.** ²⁴**And he said to them, "This is my covenant-blood** [compare Exodus 24:8] **that's being poured out for many** [people]. ²⁵**Amen I tell you that by no means will I any more drink from the produce of the vine till that day when I drink it anew in God's kingdom.**" Still alive and well, Jesus is reclining bodily with his disciples and, as just noted, "corpse" better suits the context of his coming death and burial than "body" does. So "This *represents* my corpse" correctly interprets "This *is* my corpse." Similarly, since Jesus' blood has yet to be poured out (though "is *being* poured out" makes the outpouring as good as happening already), "This *represents* my covenant-blood . . ." correctly interprets "This *is* my covenant-blood . . . ." The separate mention of blood indicates a violent death, as in our term "bloodshed." So we have a symbolic as well as verbal prediction of Jesus' passion. The covenantal character of the blood and its "being poured out for many" indicate the sacrificial character of Jesus' approaching death, not only its violence but also its atoning value for others—an indication of divine approval in opposition to human condemnation and otherwise shameful crucifixion. That "all" drank out of the cup exacerbates the treachery of Judas Iscariot. The passage ends with another prediction by Jesus, that of abstaining from wine till he drinks it in God's kingdom. "Amen I tell you" and "by no means" stress the abstinence. But drinking afterward strikes a final, happy note. Jesus speaks of *drinking* in the kingdom rather than of the kingdom's *coming* and thus highlights his vindication in a celebration of final victory. He doesn't say he'll drink *with his disciples*, only that *he* will drink, so that attention centers on that vindication. "Anew" implies he has drunk in the past and perhaps on this occasion (though probably not the wine of the Eucharist; for he gave the cup to the Twelve for drinking that wine, nor would it do for him to drink wine that symbolized the outpouring of his blood for others). The betrayed one will celebrate victory in God's kingdom—a happy prediction sure to be fulfilled in view of Jesus' many predictions already fulfilled.

A CONTEST OF PREDICTIVE ABILITY: JESUS VERSUS PETER AND THE OTHER DISCIPLES
Mark 14:26–31

The Passover meal had to end by the middle of the night; so Jesus and his disciples now leave the guest room for the Mount of Olives. Mark doesn't tell at what point Judas Iscariot leaves the rest for the betrayal. *14:26–28*: **And after hymn-singing** [probably some of Psalms 114(or 113)–18], **they went out to the Mount of Olives.** ²⁷**And Jesus tells them** [apparently as they're going along], **"You'll all be tripped up, because it's written, 'I'll strike the shepherd, and the sheep will**

be scattered [Zechariah 13:7].' ²⁸**Nevertheless, after I've been raised, I'll go ahead of you into Galilee.**" The present tense of "tells" emphasizes Jesus' predicting that the disciples will be "tripped up." To be tripped up is to stumble into sinning because of some baneful influence. The Old Testament quotation defines the sinning that Jesus predicts his disciples will stumble into. It'll consist in allowing fear to scatter them when he's arrested. To save their necks they'll leave him in the lurch. It seems unlikely that those closest to Jesus will forsake him. But Scripture must be fulfilled (the scattering will happen "*because* it's written"), so that the passion and its effect on the disciples will happen according to God's plan as well as according to Jesus' prediction. It seems even more unlikely that "all" these disciples will forsake him. But the fulfillment of this element in his prediction (an element that he adds to the Old Testament prediction) will enhance the impressiveness of his predictive ability. The original text of Zechariah 13:7 reads a *command*: "Strike the shepherd." Jesus tweaks the wording so as to create a *prediction*, "I'll strike the shepherd," that supports his own prediction. But he doesn't identify the "I" whom he imports into Zechariah's text. As a result, the emphasis falls entirely on prediction as such, and therefore on the agreement between Jesus' and Zechariah's predictions. "The shepherd" stands for Jesus, his being struck for his Passion (in the first instance, his being arrested), "the sheep" for his disciples, and the sheep's being scattered for the disciples' fleeing (14:50). "Nevertheless" sets Jesus' going ahead of the disciples to Galilee after his resurrection in strong contrast with his being "struck" in Jerusalem, and also sets the disciples' regrouping in Galilee in strong contrast with their being scattered at Jerusalem. The regrouping in Galilee is only implied by Jesus' preceding them there, though. So the emphasis rests on his predicting his earlier arrival as the resurrected one. The disciples won't leave him in a tomb when they go back to Galilee. He'll arrive before they do (see 16:7).

Peter has shown loyalty to Jesus by confessing him to be the Christ (8:29), by reprimanding him for predicting the Passion (8:32), and by joining the rest of the Twelve in asking, "Surely I [am] not [the betrayer], [am] I?" (14:19). His loyalty rises to the present occasion with a prediction counter to Jesus' prediction. *14:29–31*: **But Peter told him, "Even if they'll all be tripped up, yet** *I* **won't** [be tripped up]." That is to say, "Your 'all' won't include me." Because of his demonstrated loyalty to Jesus, the prediction by Peter seems likely to falsify Jesus' prediction. But this very likelihood will elevate Jesus' predictive ability if he turns out to be right and Peter wrong. The contest intensifies with another prediction by Jesus: ³⁰**And Jesus says to him, "Amen I tell you that today, this night, before a rooster crows twice,** *you* [Peter] **will disown me three times.**" The present tense of "says" and "Amen I tell you" set the certainty of this prediction's fulfillment emphatically opposite Peter's counterprediction. The emphatic "*you*" underlines that the apostle most likely to falsify Jesus' first prediction will in fact fulfill Jesus' second prediction as well.

"Today" (in the sense of a twenty-four hour day) dramatizes this fulfillment by bringing it close at hand and thus displays the acuteness of Jesus' predictive ability. The successive expressions "this night," "before a rooster crows twice," and "three times" sharpen this acuteness with the addition of increasingly specific and therefore astonishing detail, the fulfillment of which will immeasurably heighten the impressiveness of Jesus' predictive power. Furthermore, the apostle most unlikely to forsake Jesus will also do worse. He'll even disown Jesus—three times for good measure! Similar but larger increases in the unlikelihood and therefore greater impressiveness of fulfillment accrue from Peter's adding a second counter prediction and from all the other disciples' chiming in: **³¹But he** [Peter] **was saying vehemently, "If it should be necessary for me to die with you, by no means will I disown you." And also they were all speaking similarly.** Strengthening this second counter prediction by Peter are his speaking "vehemently," adding *dying* with Jesus if necessary, escalating his (Peter's) earlier "not" to the emphatic "by no means," and getting the support of all his fellow disciples. The "all" that identifies those who counterpredict their loyalty equate with the "all" who Jesus initially predicted will be tripped up. Who'll win this contest of predictive ability? The question is silly, because Mark has already laid out so much evidence of Jesus' abilities, including this kind, that we know the answer in advance. No contest!

THE FLOWERING OF FULFILLMENT
FOR JESUS' PREDICTIONS
Mark 14:32–52

This passage contains an unusually high concentration of verbs that appear in the present tense for events that occurred in the past: "come" (14:32), "tells" (14:32), "takes along" (14:33), "tells" (14:34), "comes" (14:37), "finds" (14:37), "says" (14:37), "comes" (14:41), "tells" (14:41), "arrives" (14:43), "says" (14:45), and "seize" (14:51). The vividness of these verbs displays the excitement of Mark over Jesus' entrance into the passion, for with that entrance the fulfillment of the passion-and-resurrection predictions starts coming to full flower. On the other hand, verbs that introduce Jesus' praying in Gethsemane don't appear in the present tense, because Mark isn't very interested in the praying as such. He's interested, rather, in Jesus' being given over to the Jewish authorities and in the disciples' failure of loyalty, both in fulfillment of Jesus' predictions.

14:32–34: And they come into a parcel of land whose name [was] **Gethsemane; and he tells his disciples, "Sit here while I pray." ³³And he takes along Peter and James and John with him and began to be alarmed and dismayed. ³⁴And he tells them, "'My soul is very sad, to** [the point of] **death** [Psalms 42:5, 11; 43:5; Jonah 4:9]**.' Remain here and stay awake."** Jesus' taking along his three closest disciples shows him to be seeking their help and thus builds up to the initial breakdown of even *their* loyalty. They'll not stay awake. Ultimately,

they'll abandon him altogether by fleeing with the rest (14:50). Mark's description of Jesus as "alarmed and dismayed," plus Jesus' describing himself as "very sad, to [the point of] death," is designed to excite sympathy for Jesus. In 13:33–37 staying awake had to do with watching for his glorious coming as the Son of Man. Here it has to do with watching for the coming of Judas the betrayer; for when in 14:41 he discovers for the third time that they're sleeping rather than staying awake, he tells them to sleep on. Why? Because it won't be long before the betrayer arrives; so they might as well get as much rest as they can. Jesus had wanted the three to stay awake watching for Judas's coming in order that he (Jesus) might give himself entirely to praying through his emotional distress.

14:35–36: **And on going forward a little, he was falling on the ground and praying that if it were actually possible the hour might pass away from him. ³⁶And he was saying, "Abba, Father, all things** [are] **possible for you. Take this cup away from me** [as though Jesus is at table with God the Father as host]. **Nevertheless,** [I request] **not what I want—rather, what you** [want]**."** Jesus' "going forward a *little*" allows Peter, James, and John to see before they fall asleep what he does and to hear what he prays. (In that culture even private prayer was usually spoken out loud.) "Was falling on the ground and praying" probably includes Jesus' second and third prayers in addition to this first prayer. "The hour" will turn out to be "the hour" of his being given over "into the hands of sinners" (14:41). His asking to be spared from this hour exhibits foreknowledge of the betrayal. "This cup" stands for the poison of death (compare 10:38–39). "This" describes the cup as near (this *here* as opposed to that *over there*). No wonder, then, that Jesus falls on the ground. Standing was the normal posture for prayer (11:25). Kneeling was abnormal. But "falling on the ground"—that goes beyond kneeling and displays alarm (compare Hebrews 5:7). It's the nearness of the cup that causes alarm, which excites further sympathy for Jesus and dramatizes his foreknowing that betrayal and death are soon to happen. "Nevertheless, [I request] not what I want—rather, what you [want]" shows Jesus' betrayal and death to be God's will. That God *can* take away the cup ("all things [are] possible for you," Jesus says to him) but *won't* do so shows all the more that Jesus' betrayal and death will carry out God's will. In other words, Jesus' crucifixion is not to be mocked. It's to be admired, not least because in it he subordinates his will to that of God his Father. "Nevertheless" emphasizes this subordination. So also does the use of both "Abba" (Aramaic) and its translation "Father," for a son is supposed to carry out his father's will.

14:37: **And he comes and finds them sleeping** recalls Jesus' seeking the help of his three closest disciples (see the comments on 14:33–34). He interrupts his praying to see whether according to his instruction they've remained nearby and stayed awake. His finding them asleep highlights the breakdown of loyalty that he predicted, that starts here, and that he goes on to speak of: **And he says to Peter, "Simon, you're sleeping! You weren't strong enough to stay awake for one hour!"** Many translations have it that Jesus asks questions: "Simon, are you sleeping? Weren't you strong enough to stay awake for one hour?" But if these are questions, the second one should really be translated, "You were strong enough to stay awake for one hour, weren't you?" with the implied answer, "Yes." Jesus' upcoming statement that "the flesh is weak" (14:38) implies, though, that Simon Peter was *not* strong enough, whereas Jesus *was*. So it's better to take Jesus' words as accusatory exclamations that call attention to the start of a breakdown in loyalty, the breakdown that will fulfill Jesus' predictions and falsify Peter's. Though James and John, too, were sleeping, Jesus singles out Peter because more than all the rest, Peter made predictions counter to those of Jesus.

Now Jesus addresses all three disciples in *14:38*: "Stay awake and pray lest you enter into temptation. On the one hand, the spirit [is] eager. On the other hand, the flesh [is] weak." Earlier, Jesus told them only to stay awake (14:34). Now he tells them also to pray. In that culture people prayed with their eyes open, not with their eyes closed. Praying would help the disciples stay awake, then, so as not to enter into—that is, succumb to—the temptation of sleep. This temptation is a test of their strength. The spirit of the disciples may be eager to help Jesus, but their flesh is weak in the sense of tired. (The hour is very late, and they've had an unusually full meal.) Only prayer can help their eager spirit win its tug-of-war with their weak flesh. As in Psalm 51:12, to which Jesus alludes, we should think of their human spirit, not God's Spirit.

14:39–42: **And on going away again, he prayed speaking the same statement** [as in 14:35–36]. [40]**And on coming again, he found them sleeping; for their eyes were weighed down. And they didn't know what they should answer him.** [41]**And he comes a third time and tells them, "Sleep for the remainder** [of the time till the betrayer has drawn near] **and rest. He's distant** [so you might as well sleep on and rest while you can]. **The hour has come. Behold, the Son of Man is being given over into the hands of sinners.** [42]**Rouse yourselves! Let's go. Behold, the one who's giving me over has drawn near!"** Mark refers to Jesus' second prayer but doesn't quote it, and he doesn't even refer to Jesus' third prayer but only leaves it to be inferred from Jesus' coming "a third time." So Mark shows comparatively little interest in Jesus' prayers and instead goes directly to Jesus' finding the disciples asleep again. Mark also stresses the fleshly weakness of the disciples by noting that "their eyes were weighed down," so that "they didn't know what they should answer him [Jesus]." Their weakness furthers Mark's emphasis on the breakdown in loyalty that's beginning to fulfill Jesus' predictions and falsify the disciples' predictions, especially Peter's. For Peter, falling asleep three times forecasts his three disownings of Jesus, again in fulfillment of Jesus' prediction. The disciples' weakness also makes Jesus look strong by

contrast. He has stayed awake. To counteract the scandal of Jesus' coming crucifixion, Mark wants a strong Son of God, strong in flesh as well as eager in spirit—"the stronger one" of John the baptizer's prediction (1:7), so physically strong that he'll die with a loud shout (emphasized twice by Mark in 15:34, 37) rather than lapsing into unconsciousness. Jesus shows exasperation in telling the disciples to sleep on and rest while "he" (identified almost immediately as "the one betraying me") is still distant. But the remaining time to do so doesn't last long, because the hour of betrayal has struck, the betrayal is already in progress, and then the betrayer comes so close it's time to get up and meet him. So the disciples have to rouse themselves. "Let's go" doesn't mean "Let's get away from here and escape." It means "Let's go to meet the betrayer and the 'sinners' into whose 'hands' he's giving me over" (see 9:31 and the comments on it for the connotation of violence in "hands"). "Sinners" highlights the injustice Jesus will suffer, but going to meet the betrayer and the sinners shows him carrying out his Father's will, not his own. Now the "sinners" who make up the Sanhedrin's posse can arrest Jesus in the dead of night apart from the festal assembly, where in view of his popularity an arrest would have caused a riot.

14:43: **And immediately, while he was still speaking, there arrives Judas, one of the Twelve, and with him a crowd with swords and clubs,** [a crowd coming] **from the chief priests and the scholars and the elders.** "Immediately" stresses the speed with which Jesus' prediction is proceeding toward final fulfillment. "While he was still speaking" reinforces this speed by indicating that Judas comes right as Jesus is saying, "Behold, the one who's giving me over has drawn near" (14:42). As already in 14:10, 20, the identification of Judas as "one of the Twelve" helps Mark portray Jesus' coming crucifixion as stemming from an act of treachery rather than from a pursuit of justice. Stressing this treachery is the addition that with Judas, who as an apostle should have been with Jesus (3:14), arrives "a crowd with swords and clubs" who have come from the Sanhedrin. The reference to weapons and the listing of all three classes that compose the Sanhedrin, who have been plotting to kill Jesus (14:1–2), present the crucifixion as stemming from hellbent animosity.

14:44–47: **And the one giving him over had given them** [the crowd with swords and clubs] **a signal, saying, "Whomever I kiss—it's he. Seize him and lead** [him] **away securely."** The signal intensifies Judas's treachery by exposing how carefully planned it was. A simple pronoun would have identified Judas well enough ("And *he* had given them a signal"). But Mark designates him with the phrase, "the one giving him over," to highlight yet more both the fulfillment of Jesus' prediction and Judas's treachery. Kissing Jesus as a signal to seize him and lead him away deepens the treachery with a show of affectionate homage. "Seize him and lead him away" exposes the show as a charade. In view of Jesus' submission to God the Father's will (14:36) and going out to meet the betrayer (14:42), there's irony in Judas's instruction to lead Jesus away "securely." He would go with them willingly. **⁴⁵And on coming** [to Gethsemane], **immediately approaching him** [Jesus], **he** [Judas] **says, "Rabbi," and kissed him.** "Immediately" calls attention again to the speed with which Jesus' prediction is reaching fulfillment (see also 14:43). Judas's addressing Jesus respectfully with "Rabbi" deepens the treachery yet further. And Mark uses a strengthened form of the verb "kiss," which means either that Judas kissed Jesus affectionately or kissed his hand or feet rather than his face. So Judas was feigning affection or humility. His treachery has reached its nadir, so that he now disappears from Mark's account. Mark isn't interested in Judas's fate (for which see Matthew 27:3–10; Acts 1:15–20). He's interested only in the fulfillment of Jesus' prediction of betrayal by one of the Twelve. Judas has played his part in that fulfillment and from Mark's standpoint deserves no more notice. **⁴⁶And they** [the crowd] **laid hands on him** [in fulfillment of Jesus' predictions that he'd be given over "into the hands of men" (9:31) and "into the hands of sinners" (14:41)] **and seized him** [in fulfillment of the Sanhedrin's desire (12:12; 14:1) and Judas's instruction (14:44)]. **⁴⁷But a certain one of the bystanders, on drawing** [his] **sword, struck the high priest's slave and lopped off his ear.** Mark has said the crowd came "with swords" (14:43). Jesus will respond to the present incident by pointing to their having come "with swords" (14:48). Several further references to "bystanders" never include his disciples (14:69; 70; 15:35, 39). In Mark, *Jesus* says nothing about the swordplay; nor does he restore the victim's ear. It seems, then, that in this account the lopping off of an ear isn't a disciple's act of defending Jesus, but an accident in which one member of the crowd injures another member of the crowd with a misdirected swing of his sword (compare Psalm 37:14–15: "The wicked have drawn the sword . . . to slay those who are upright in conduct. Their sword will enter their own heart"). This bit of grim humor then leads into Jesus' response, which highlights the weapons of those who have seized him.

14:48–49: **And answering** [= responding], **Jesus said to them, "As against a bandit have you come out with swords and clubs to take me with** [you]**?"** This question could be repunctuated as an indignant statement: "you have come out." But either way, Jesus' response foreshadows the crucifixion of two bandits with him (15:27) and exposes the injustice of his arrest by indirectly and ironically calling to mind his beneficial healings and exorcisms instead of banditry. It's the Sanhedrin, who sent the crowd to arrest Jesus, that sponsored banditry—in the temple no less (11:17). **⁴⁹"Day by day** [as opposed to a bandit's nighttime raids and to your arresting me at night] **I was with you in the temple** [courts], **teaching, and you didn't seize me."** This sarcastic observation refers to the preceding week of Jesus' public ministry, beginning at 11:15, and exposes the discrepancy between the Sanhedrin's launching against him a kind of military expedition, as though he were a bandit to catch whom they've had to arm themselves and come out into the

countryside—the discrepancy between that and Judas's having just called him "Rabbi" and kissed him. "Day by day," "with you," and "in the temple [courts], teaching" emphasize this discrepancy by indicating face-to-face closeness, frequency, and therefore plenty of opportunity for them to have arrested Jesus earlier. "But [this has happened] **in order that the Scriptures might be fulfilled.**" "The Scriptures" include at least Zechariah 13:7, quoted by Jesus in 14:27 (but see also Exodus 24:8; Psalms 22:1, 7–8, 18; 37:14; 41:9; 69:21; 71:11; 109:25; Isaiah 53:12; Lamentations 2:15 with Mark 14:18, 24, 41, 44, 46; 15:14, 29, 34, 36). Despite the injustice, then—and even through it—God is achieving his purpose of salvation for humankind

14:50–52: **And leaving him, all** [the disciples] **fled.** Thus the fulfillment of Jesus' prediction that the disciples would "all be tripped up" and "scattered" (14:27). "All" in this fulfillment not only matches "all" in the prediction. It also contrasts the fleeing of these "all" with the protestations of loyalty and the drinking from the eucharistic cup by the very same "all" in 14:23, 31. Mark doesn't say what motivated the disciples to flee. His omission of their motive leaves only Jesus' earlier prediction as an explanation for their fleeing. **⁵¹And a certain young man, clothed with a linen cloth on** [his] **naked** [body]**, was following with him** [that is, close behind Jesus as opposed to Peter's later following "at a distance" (14:54)]. **And they seize him;** **⁵²but leaving the linen cloth behind, he fled naked.** Who is this young man? What's his name? Why is he wearing only a linen cloth? How come he's following with Jesus when the disciples have fled? Why do the crowd seize him prior to his slipping out of the linen cloth? Mark leaves all these questions unanswered; so the young man's significance lies elsewhere. The crowd's seizing the young man parallels their having seized Jesus (14:46). The young man's wearing a linen cloth anticipates the linen cloth in which Jesus will be buried (15:46, where "*the* linen cloth" recalls the mention here of "*a* linen cloth"). The young man's leaving behind the linen cloth anticipates Jesus' resurrection, portrayed as a leaving behind of his linen burial cloth. And Mark will call the angel who in Jesus' empty tomb announces Jesus' resurrection—Mark will call that angel "a young man" (16:5–7) to recollectively associate the present young man with Jesus' resurrection. The closeness of the young man's following ("*with* Jesus") supports this association. All in all, then, this episode symbolically anticipates a reversal of Jesus' crucifixion and burial by virtue of the resurrection. Mark's mentioning the young man's following with Jesus *before* mentioning that the crowd led Jesus away shows how eager Mark is to anticipate this reversal.

THE FULFILLING OF JESUS' PREDICTIONS OF HIS REJECTION BY THE SANHEDRIN AND OF PETER'S DISOWNINGS OF HIM
Mark 14:53–72

In this passage Mark narrates both Jesus' trial before the Sanhedrin (14:53–65) and Peter's denials of him

(14:66-72). A brief introduction sets the stage for both events, which take place simultaneously (14:53-54). By putting Jesus' trial alongside Peter's denials and giving the trial and the denials a common introduction, Mark produces a double appeal to Jesus' power of prediction. For what happens in each case corresponds exactly to what Jesus foretold.

14:53-54: And they led Jesus away to the high priest, and all the chief priests and the elders and the scholars come together. The high priest chaired the Sanhedrin; so it was natural for Jesus to be taken to him and for the Sanhedrin to convene at the high priest's residence, especially in the middle of the night. The coming together of the three classes that made up the Sanhedrin begins to fulfill Jesus' prediction that he'd be rejected and condemned by them (8:31; 10:33). "All" stresses completeness of fulfillment. **⁵⁴And Peter followed him** [Jesus] **at a distance, as far as inside,** [that is,] **into the high priest's courtyard; and he** [Peter] **was sitting with the servants and warming himself,** [facing] **toward the light** [of a fire]. Peter's following Jesus at a distance contrasts with the young man's following "with" Jesus—that is, close behind him—in 14:51. The distance at which Peter follows avoids a contradiction with his having fled and thus preserves the fulfillment of Jesus' prediction that "all" the disciples would be scattered (14:27, 50). Though Peter's flight has put him at a distance, his following shows a determination to die with Jesus if necessary, as Peter predicted contrary to Jesus' prediction (14:30-31). This determination makes it look unlikely that Peter will disown Jesus three times this very night, before a rooster crows twice, in fulfillment of Jesus' prediction (14:30). Making it look even more unlikely is Peter's following Jesus right inside the high priest's courtyard, sitting with the high priest's servants, and disclosing himself in the light of a fire that enables them to identify him as one of Jesus' disciples. Such courage! Such loyalty to Jesus! The chances for a fulfillment of Jesus' prediction look dim. But the greater the unlikelihood that Jesus will win the contest of predictive ability, the greater the victory if he does win.

14:55-59: And the chief priests and the whole Sanhedrin were seeking testimony against Jesus for the purpose of putting him to death, and they weren't finding [any testimony to support a capital verdict]. **⁵⁶For many were testifying falsely against him, and the testimonies weren't equivalent** [that is, didn't agree with each other]. **⁵⁷And on standing up, some were testifying falsely against him by saying, ⁵⁸"We ourselves heard him saying, 'I myself will tear down this handmade** [= manmade] **sanctuary** [= the temple proper, excluding the surrounding courts and cloisters], **and in three days build another** [sanctuary], **not handmade.'** **⁵⁹And not even in this respect was their testimony equivalent** [self-consistent]. "The *whole* Sanhedrin" stresses once again the completeness with which Jesus' predictions are coming to pass. Their seeking testimony "for the purpose of putting him to death" is also begin-

ning to fulfill those passion predictions. At the same time, their "seeking" such testimony creates sympathy for Jesus in that they show themselves so bent on his death that they've hauled him to trial before finding testimony against him. Their finding no testimony because false witnesses are contradicting each other implies that the Sanhedrin are seeking true testimony. Their failure to find true testimony serves Mark's defense of Jesus by showing that Jesus doesn't deserve condemnation, much less crucifixion. The large number of false witnesses ("many") and the plurality of their "testimonies" underscore the Sanhedrin's failure to find true testimony, for the agreement of only two witnesses would have been enough to establish the truth of an accusation (Numbers 35:30; Deuteronomy 17:6; 19:15). The false testimony of "some" merits particular attention. We know from 13:1-4 that only some of Jesus' disciples heard him predict a destruction of the temple and that though he predicted destruction of its whole complex, he didn't at all say *he* was going to tear down the sanctuary. Nor did he disparage it as "manmade," or say he was going to build another sanctuary in three days, or say this other sanctuary wouldn't be manmade, or imply that since it wouldn't be manmade yet he himself was going to build it he must be divine. On the contrary, we know from 11:15-17 that Jesus called the whole temple complex "my house" and cleansed it of commercial traffic so as to make it "a house of prayer for all nations." The false witnesses don't agree with each other even when restricted in number ("some" as opposed to "many") and even when testifying on the same topic (what Jesus purportedly said about the sanctuary).

14:60-62: And on standing up in the midst [of the whole Sanhedrin], **the high priest questioned Jesus by saying, "You're making no answer at all, are you? What** [is it that] **these** [witnesses] **are testifying against you?" ⁶¹But he kept silent and gave no answer at all. Again the high priest was questioning him and says to him, "Are you the Christ, the Son of the Blessed One?" ⁶²And Jesus said, "I am** [the Christ, the Son of the Blessed One], **and you** [plural] **will see the Son of Man sitting at the right** [hand] **of the Power and coming with the clouds of heaven"** [Psalm 110:1; Daniel 7:13]. The high priest's standing up parallels the false witnesses' standing up (14:57) and thus puts him, like them, in a prosecutorial role as opposed to his rightful role as a judge. As a judge he should have pronounced Jesus "not guilty" because of the admittedly false testimonies brought against him. Mark doubles Jesus' refusal of the high priest's demand for an answer—"but he [Jesus] kept silent and gave no answer at all"—to emphasize Jesus' strength in withstanding the attempt to browbeat him into an admission of guilt. He does answer the high priest's next question, however; for though he's no criminal, he *is* the Christ and God's Son. (In the question, "the Blessed One," which means "the One who is to be praised," is a reverential substitute for "God.") Mark emphasizes the question of Jesus' christhood and divine sonship by introducing it doubly with

(1) "the high priest *was questioning* him" and (2) "[the high priest] *says* to him." Jesus' affirmative answer feeds into Mark's writing this Gospel to argue for Jesus as the Christ and God's Son (1:1) despite the scandal of his crucifixion. And true to Mark's emphasis on the predictive ability of Jesus, especially the ability to predict his own fate, Jesus proceeds to predict that the whole Sanhedrin will see him, the Son of Man, sitting at the right hand of "the Power" (another reverential substitute for a divine name) and coming with the clouds of heaven. Naturally, this will happen by way of vindicating him after his death and resurrection. The current fulfillment of his passion predictions ensures the future fulfillment of this prediction of vindication. Notwithstanding the apparent shame of crucifixion, Jesus will sit (the posture of authority) at the right hand (the position of highest favor) of none less than God himself, who is "the Power." Sharing God's power (compare 13:26) will erase any supposed weakness in the crucifixion. And Jesus' coming "with the clouds of heaven" clothes him with God's own regalia (see the comments on 13:26). The prediction refers to a seeing of Jesus the Son of Man at the last day. At his coming he'll be seated at God's right hand in the chariot that Ezekiel saw carrying God's throne in a great cloud (Ezekiel 1). Jesus will come again, no longer subject to the Sanhedrin's judgment.

14:63–65: And the high priest, tearing his undergarments [as a sign of horror], **says, "Why do we still have a need of witnesses? ⁶⁴You've heard the blasphemy. How does it appear to you?" And they all condemned him** [as] **being liable to death** [that is, Jesus as deserving the death penalty]. The present tense of "says" underlines the charge against Jesus. We expect the high priest to tear only his outer garments. Tearing his undergarments down to the bare skin and the Sanhedrin's unanimity in condemning Jesus to death stress the high degree of fulfillment reached by the prediction of Jesus that the Sanhedrin would reject him and condemn him to death (8:31; 10:33). Blasphemy is slander, in this case Jesus' supposedly slandering God by predicting that he, a mere human being, will sit at God's right hand and come again in God's own regalia, the clouds. So they condemn Jesus out of his own mouth. But we know that his prediction contains no blasphemy, for God himself twice declared Jesus his own beloved Son, the second time in a followup to Jesus' predicting he'd come "in the glory of his Father with the holy angels" (1:11; 9:7). Leviticus 24:10–16 prescribes stoning as the method of execution for blasphemy. But the Sanhedrin have pronounced Jesus as only "liable" to the death penalty, and he has predicted that they'll give him over to the Gentiles for execution (10:33–34). For the fulfillment of this prediction, then, to the Gentiles he must go. But first some indignity perpetrated on Jesus: ⁶⁵**And certain** [members of the Sanhedrin] **started spitting on him and covering his face all around and punching him and saying to him, "Prophesy." And the servants treated him to blows.** These indignities put the Sanhedrin and the servants in a bad light and excite sympathy for Jesus as a victim of gross injustice. Mark doesn't say why some cover Jesus' face or what they challenge him to prophesy. It's their actions as such that interest Mark, because those actions fulfill Jesus' predictions that the Sanhedrin would reject him. In particular, the challenge to prophesy—this challenge itself ironically fulfills what Jesus has already prophesied about his fate, namely, rejection by his challengers. Mark's reference to "the servants" leads nicely into the account of Peter's denials—that is, disownings of Jesus—because at the servants' previous mention Peter was sitting with them at fireside (14:54). By framing the challenge to prophesy between fulfillments of Jesus' predictions of condemnation by the Sanhedrin and of Peter's denials, Mark shows Jesus to be the prophet that the Sanhedrin think he isn't.

14:66–68a: And while Peter was below in the courtyard [so Mark is moving his narrative backward to pick up what Peter was doing during Jesus' trial before the Sanhedrin], **one of the high priest's maids comes ⁶⁷and, on seeing Peter warming himself** [in "the light" of a fire (14:54)], **gazing intently at him, says, "You too were with the Nazarene, Jesus." ⁶⁸ᵃBut he denied** [that he'd been with Jesus], **saying, "I neither know nor understand what you're saying."** The present tense of "comes" and "sends" headlines the start of the fulfillment of Jesus' prediction that Peter would disown him three times this very night. The maid would be a slave girl, and a lone one at that. Her comment—and it's only a comment—prompts the first denial by Peter, so that his babbling weakness strikes a contrast with the quiet strength of Jesus, who resisted pressure from a personage no less imposing than the high priest. The contrast makes more impressive the fulfillment of Jesus' prediction, for it didn't seem as though Peter was liable to disown him under pressure from a mere slave girl. Mark's mentioning that she belonged to the high priest supports a contrast between Peter's behavior toward her and Jesus' behavior toward her master. Peter's second denial will feature this same slave girl and therefore double the contrast between Peter's and Jesus' behaviors—all to the damage of Peter's predictive ability and to the demonstration of Jesus' predictive ability (see 14:27–31, 69–70a). Her observation and statement were correct, of course. Jesus was from Nazareth and, more importantly, Peter had been with him. Indeed, Jesus had chosen Peter and the rest of the Twelve to be "with him" (3:14). Mark doesn't say how it was that the slave girl recognized Peter as one of Jesus' disciples. It's enough for Mark that Peter's denial, and two more denials to follow, are demonstrating the accuracy of Jesus' predictions. This first denial takes the form of feigned ignorance, emphatic in its doubling: "I *neither* know *nor* understand . . . ."

14:68b–70a: And he [Peter] **went outside into the forecourt** [= an outer courtyard as distinct from the inner courtyard], **and a rooster crowed. ⁶⁹And on seeing him, the maid started again to say to the bystanders, "This one** [Peter] **is** [one] **of them** [Jesus' disciples]." ⁷⁰ᵃ**But again he denied** [that he was]. Peter exits from the courtyard into the forecourt to escape the pressure. But Jesus' prediction will catch up with him. Before it does, though, Mark notes the first crowing of a rooster as a reminder of Jesus' prediction that a rooster wouldn't crow twice before Peter disowned Jesus three times (14:30). You get the feeling that events are going to transpire exactly as Jesus foretold. And so sure is his prediction to be fulfilled in detail that the first rooster crow fails to warn Peter off from his second and third denials. Nor does his exit rid him of the maid. Instead of addressing him, this time she addresses bystanders; and instead of observing his having been with Jesus she pronounces him one of a *number* of Jesus' disciples. Peter overhears what she says, and the "again" of this denial both matches the "again" of her second observation and marks this denial as his second. Two down, one to go. Mark is counting.

14:70b–72: And again, after a little [while], **the bystanders were saying to Peter, "Truly you are** [one] **of them, for you too** [like the other disciples] **are a Galilean."** [71]**But he began cursing and swearing** [in the sense of speaking under oath]: **"I don't know this guy that you're talking about."** "After a little [while]" shows that the fulfillment of Jesus' prediction is hastening toward completion. "Again" marks the third and final test of his predictive accuracy and refers to this third test as such, not to the bystanders' speaking to Peter (for they haven't spoken to him before). "Truly" reinforces the test and puts Peter's false denials in a contrastively bad light. "For you too are a Galilean" reinforces the test by giving a reason for the identification of Peter as one of the disciples (and probably alludes to a difference in accent [so Matthew 26:73], though Mark is interested only in the test as such and Peter's fulfillment of Jesus' prediction). Peter's starting to curse and swear corresponds to this reinforcement of the third test and leaves no doubt that Jesus' prediction of Peter's denials has reached fulfillment, all the more so in that "cursing" seems to imply Jesus as the object of Peter's cursing. Speaking under oath strengthens the denial yet further. The first denial was private and evasive, the second one still evasive but public. This third denial is direct, public, and immeasurably stronger. At first Peter only denied knowing *what* the maid was talking about. Now—in a far cry from his earlier confession of Jesus as the Christ (8:29) and from Jesus' confessing himself at this very time to be the Christ, God's Son—Peter denies knowing *whom* the bystanders are talking about. "This guy" is disparaging, as fits a cursing of Jesus. But the bystanders haven't said anything about Jesus! They've spoken only about the disciples as Galileans. So the incongruity between their statement and Peter's response goes to show that he is indeed fulfilling Jesus' prediction by disowning him even when—and though—the interlocuters haven't mentioned Jesus. [72]**And immediately, for the second time, a rooster crowed. And Peter remembered the word, how Jesus had told him, "Before a rooster crows twice, you will disown me three times." And he proceeded to weep.** "And immediately" dramatizes the fulfillment of the sole remaining detail in Jesus' prediction: the second

crow of a rooster. "For the second time" notes the exactitude of fulfillment. The unusualness of "the word" for a saying of Jesus and the combination with "how Jesus had told him" emphasize Mark's requotation of Jesus' prediction. Peter's remembering the prediction gives Mark an opportunity to requote it and provides a basis for Peter's emotional reaction. "Today" and "this night" drop out of the requotation (contrast 14:30) to let emphasis concentrate on the numerical exactitude of the prediction and its fulfillment. Peter's weeping dramatizes the fulfillment with pathos and amounts to lamenting to Jesus, "You win." In adding the agony of defeat to this contest of predictive ability that Peter has lost to Jesus, the weeping replaces the bravado that characterized Peter's counter predictions and unbelief in Jesus' prediction. The absence of information on Peter's purpose in going to the high priest's courtyard, on the reason for the maid's presence, on the way she knew Peter had been with Jesus and the other disciples, on what the bystanders did when Peter was unmasked, and on his departure, plus the absence of any condemnation and restoration of Peter—all these absences leave the emphasis solely on the fulfillment of Jesus' prediction.

THE FULFILLING OF JESUS' PREDICTION THAT HE WOULD BE GIVEN OVER TO THE GENTILES AND FLOGGED
Mark 15:1–15

15:1: And immediately, early in the morning, after holding a consultation the chief priests along with the elders and scholars—even the whole Sanhedrin—on binding Jesus [= tying him up], **carried** [him] **off and gave** [him] **over to Pilate.** "And immediately" hurries Mark's story line to the next point of emphasis, namely, the fulfillment of Jesus' prediction that "the chief priests and the scholars . . . will give him over to the Gentiles" (10:33). "Holding a consultation" pinpoints the activity which will bring that prediction to fulfillment. Mark's emphasis on the completeness of fulfillment is so strong that he not only echoes Jesus' references to the chief priests and the scholars. He also adds the elders for good measure and, backing up, refers to them all as "the whole Sanhedrin." Mark doesn't tell the ins and outs of their consultation. Only its outcome interests him, for that's what fulfills Jesus' prediction. The consultation issues first in a binding of Jesus. This binding starts a parallel with the later-mentioned Barabbas, who was also bound (15:7; compare 15:6, where the word for "prisoner" literally means "a *bound* person"). The binding of Jesus also prepares for a contrast with Barabbas's later release (literally, an "*unbinding*" or "*loosening* of bonds" [15:6–15]). In Gethsemane Jesus was only "seized" and "led away" (14:43–53). Here, binding (not just seizing) causes Mark to use the stronger verb "carried off" (not just "led away"). Not necessarily that they carried Jesus off on their shoulders or on a stretcher, but Jesus' being bound required at least that they give him assistance on his way to Pilate. Mark assumes we know that Pilate is a Gentile with Gentiles under his command, but he doesn't bother to mention Pilate's position as the Roman governor of Judea. This omission and Mark's total silence on the Sanhedrin's reason for giving Jesus over to Pilate rather than stoning Jesus themselves focus all possible attention on the fulfillment of Jesus' prediction in 10:33. For Mark, it's the necessity that that prediction be fulfilled, not any jurisdictional incompetence of the Sanhedrin, that determines Jesus' being given over to the Gentiles (see John 18:31 for the Sanhedrin's jurisdictional incompetence in capital cases).

15:2: And Pilate questioned him, "Are you the king of the Jews?" This question implies that to portray Jesus as an insurrectionist the Sanhedrin have converted what they judged to be his blasphemous claim to be the Christ, God's Son, who was going to sit at God's right hand and come with the clouds of heaven (14:61–64)—that they've converted that claim into a treasonous claim to be the Jews' king. Pilate would care nothing about blasphemy, of course; but he *would* care a lot about any threat to Caesar's authority. So taken up is Mark with the fulfillment of Jesus' prediction that he'd be given over to the Gentiles, however, that Mark omits the charge of insurrectionism implied by Pilate's question. **And he, answering him, said, "You yourself are speaking."** Jesus' answer simultaneously admits "the king of the Jews" as a *given* designation (compare Pilate's later statement to the crowd, "whom *you* call the king of the Jews" [15:12]), and rejects the phrase as a self-designation, as if to say, "That's not what *I've* called myself" (therefore Pilate's coming effort to release Jesus rather than execute him as an insurrectionist).

15:3–5: And the chief priests were accusing him much. Mark highlights the vigor of their accusation, because its vigor goes to show just how thoroughly Jesus' predictions that the chief priests would reject him are being fulfilled (9:31; 10:33). The vigor of their accusation leads to the following: [4]**And Pilate was questioning him again, saying, "You're making no answer at all, are you? Look, how many things they're accusing you of!"** So Pilate joins Mark in noting the vigor of the chief priests' accusation, the content of which remains only implied. It's as though Mark subpoenas Pilate to testify to the thoroughness with which Jesus' predictions regarding the chief priests' rejection of him are being fulfilled. The chief priests continue pressing their charge, because Jesus has refused to tell Pilate he's the king of the Jews. [5]**But Jesus no longer answered in respect to anything at all** [as he *had* answered Pilate's opening question], **so that Pilate marveled.** The reason Jesus now refuses to answer is that the chief priests are pressing a charge to which he has already responded. Pilate's marveling at Jesus' silence testifies to the strength of Jesus in withstanding efforts to elicit from him an admission of guilt (compare the comments on 14:60–61a). Furthermore, his silence will make Pilate's upcoming questions to the crowd all the more impressive; for if Pilate sees no crime in Jesus despite Jesus' refusal to defend himself further, how flimsy must be the case against him (15:9, 12, 14a).

A short explanation now introduces the next episode. **15:6–7: And at each festival** [of Passover] **he** [Pilate] **used to release to them** ["the crowd" of 15:8–15] **one prisoner whom they were asking for.** [7]**And the** [man] **called Barabbas was bound with insurrectionists who as such had committed murder in an insurrection.** The annual release of "one" prepares for the release of Jesus or Barabbas, but not of both. And "*called* Barabbas" sets up for Pilate's referring to Jesus as the one whom the crowd "*call* the king of the Jews" (15:12). Barabbas's being bound "with insurrectionists who as such had committed murder in an insurrection" makes him an insurrectionist and a murderer. "As such" stresses his insurrectionism. Against this foil Jesus' innocence stands out in bold relief: Barabbas deserves to be bound and crucified, Jesus does not. Mark avoids obscuring this contrast with details concerning the insurrection, about which we know nothing from other sources, either.

15:8–10: And on going up [to Pilate], **the crowd started asking** [him to do] **as he used to do for them** [by way of releasing a prisoner of their choice every Passover]. [9]**And Pilate asked them, saying, "Do you want me to release to you the king of the Jews?"** [10]**For he knew that the chief priests had given him over because of envy.** Who are "the crowd" that go up to Pilate? Not the crowd that came to arrest Jesus in Gethsemane (14:43), because they wouldn't need stirring up shortly to ask for Barabbas's release and Jesus' crucifixion (15:11–14). Nor would the chief priests be envious of Jesus' popularity with those who arrested him. He was *not* popular with them, and they arrested him as the chief priests' own agents. This crowd, then, is the one with which Jesus *is* popular, much to the envy of the chief priests and much to their fear of arresting him in the festal assembly, where an uprising in his behalf would have occurred if they had arrested him there (14:1–2). The crowd seem not to have a particular prisoner in mind when they request the customary release of a prisoner. For even though Mark has introduced Barabbas, he avoids mentioning him as the object of the crowd's request. Nor do they appear to have in mind the release of Jesus. For Mark gives no indication that they even know as yet of Jesus' standing trial before Pilate or of the Sanhedrin's having condemned Jesus as liable to the death penalty. And Mark avoids making Jesus the object of the crowd's request just as he avoids making Barabbas such an object. It's *Pilate* who insinuates Jesus into their request; and he doesn't give them a choice between Jesus and Barabbas, or even mention Barabbas. The chief priests will be the ones to insinuate Barabbas into the crowd's request.

Pilate asks whether they want him to release to them the king of the Jews. It's a test question which implies not only the Sanhedrin's charge that Jesus claims to be the king of the Jews. It also implies the Sanhedrin's warning to Pilate that a large number of Jews, represented now by the very crowd that asks Pilate to release a prisoner, regard Jesus as their king. Pilate might have said "*your* king," but that would have prejudged their attitude toward Jesus' putative claim of kingship over them.

"Of the Jews" better preserves the testing character of Pilate's question. He asks it because he knows that the chief priests have given Jesus over to him on account of envy, that is, envy of Jesus' hold on the crowd. Now that the chief priests have given him over to Pilate in consequence of a secret arrest and trial, it becomes appropriate to speak of their envy instead of their fear. "On account of envy" revives Mark's emphasis on Jesus' magnetism. If the crowd do ask Pilate to release Jesus to them, Pilate will conclude that in agreement with the chief priests' implied charge against Jesus, a large number of Jews consider Jesus their king because he really does claim to be such.

15:11–12: And the chief priests stirred up the crowd that he should release to them Barabbas instead. ¹²But Pilate, answering again, was saying to them, "What then do you want me to do with the one whom you call the king of the Jews?" The chief priests are unaware of Pilate's knowledge of their envy. So they mistakenly fear he'll grant a request by the crowd for Jesus' release rather than regarding such a request as evidence validating the chief priests' implied charge that Jesus claims to be the Jews' king, has a large following, and therefore should be crucified. So the chief priests stir up the crowd to combat the popularity that Jesus has had with them. By asking Pilate to follow the festive custom of releasing one prisoner of their choice, this very crowd have given the chief priests an opportunity to manipulate them in this way. Thus the preceding identification of Barabbas comes into play and accomplishes Mark's purpose of making a foil against which the injustice of Jesus' crucifixion stands out. Emphasizing this foil is "rather." At the chief priests' incitement, we may infer, the crowd lodge a request for Barabbas's release. But to emphasize the fulfillment of Jesus' predictions that the chief priests would reject him, Mark omits the crowd's request and leaves only the purpose of the chief priests' incitement of them. "Whom you call the king of the Jews" confirms the implication that the chief priests have warned Pilate of a large following ready to rebel against Caesar and make Jesus their king. But Pilate is also puzzled over what the crowd want him to do with Jesus if they consider him their king yet want to release Barabbas instead of Jesus—especially since the custom is to release only one prisoner.

15:13–14: But they yelled again, [this time saying,] "Crucify him!" ¹⁴But Pilate was saying to them, "Why? What bad thing has he done?" [= What crime has he committed?] But they yelled vehemently, "Crucify him!" "Again" implies that the crowd's previous request for Pilate to release Barabbas took the form of yelling. Pilate is in the right to follow a custom of releasing to the crowd a prisoner of their choice, and the crowd are in the right to make their choice known by acclamation. Yet Mark's having mentioned the chief priests' envy of Jesus and incitement of the crowd turns the yelling into a feature of Jesus' trial that smacks of a "kangaroo court" and contrasts both with the crowd's mild-mannered initial request in 15:8 and with their yelling "Hosanna! Favored

[is] he who's coming in the Lord's name" at the triumphal procession less than a week earlier (11:9). "Crucify him!" brings into view the horrid method of Jesus' execution that causes Mark to write his Gospel as an apology for the cross. And it adds to the look of a kangaroo court that a crowd of Jews should yell for imposition of a *Roman* method of execution on a fellow Jew. By yelling for his crucifixion, the crowd now give the lie to the chief priests' implication that the crowd call Jesus their king. Pilate is disabused of suspicion both that Jesus wants to lead an insurrection and that the crowd want him to lead one. So Pilate asks what crime Jesus has committed. In contrast with the committing of murder by Barabbas and his fellow insurrectionists, Jesus has done nothing bad to which the crowd can point. So they only repeat their demand for his crucifixion instead of answering Pilate's question. Thus is exposed a miscarriage of justice. The addition of "vehemently" to the final yelling strengthens this exposé.

15:15: And Pilate, wanting to do the thing satisfactory to the crowd, released Barabbas to them and, after having Jesus flogged, gave him over to be crucified. The miscarriage of justice shows up again in Pilate's wanting to satisfy the crowd despite knowing that the chief priests have incited them out of envy. The miscarriage of justice shows up yet again in Pilate's releasing Barabbas, the very one who deserves crucifixion for insurrection and murder. The giving of Jesus over (to soldiers according to 15:16–27) to be crucified after a flogging completes this miscarriage of justice. Jesus goes to his execution without even the formality of a verdict, false though a verdict of guilty would have been. Being given over to Roman soldiers completes the fulfillment of Jesus' prediction that he'd be given over to the Gentiles (10:33). And the flogging of Jesus fulfills the detail of his prediction that the Gentiles would whip him.

THE FULFILLING OF JESUS' PREDICTION THAT THE GENTILES WOULD MOCK HIM
Mark 15:16–20c

15:16: And the soldiers led him away [from Pilate] into the courtyard, which is [part of Pilate's] official residence; and they called together the whole cohort. The soldiers are Gentiles. Their *leading* Jesus away (as in 14:44, 53) rather than *carrying* him off (as in 15:1) implies that after his flogging, Jesus was untied in preparation for mocking him. Because it was surrounded by buildings of the official residence, the courtyard was part of that residence. That the soldiers call together "the *whole* cohort" points forward to a large-scale fulfillment of Jesus' prediction that Gentiles would mock him (10:33–34). Normally, a cohort of soldiers numbered about six hundred.

15:17–20c: And they dress him up with purple [probably a soldier's cloak in mock imitation of a royal robe] **and on braiding a thorny crown** [in mock imitation of Caesar's woven wreath], **they put** [it] **around him**

[that is, around Jesus' head]. **¹⁸And they started saluting him: "Hail** [literally 'Rejoice' or, as we'd say, 'Have a nice day'], **king of the Jews!" ¹⁹And they were hitting his head with a reed and spitting on him and, kneeling, they were prostrating themselves before him** [in mock homage]. **²⁰ᵃ⁻ᶜAnd when they'd mocked him** [that is, made fun of him], **they disrobed him of the purple and put his clothes** [back] **on him.** The present tense in "*dress* him up" and "*put* [the thorny crown] around [his head]" introduces the Gentiles' mocking of Jesus on a note of emphasis. The details add thoroughness of fulfillment to large scale. The salute, "Hail, king of the Jews!" adds verbal mockery on top of sartorial mockery and heaps insult on his falsely reported claim to kingship. A reed is too flimsy to inflict pain, so that the soldiers' repeatedly hitting Jesus on the head with a reed simply heaps insult on Jesus' thorny crown. Furthermore, the reed is a mock sceptre. But instead of having Jesus hold it to mock his supposed kingship, the soldiers double the mockery by using the reed to hit him on the head. The repeated spitting on him heaps insult on his pseudoroyal robe, itself another instrument of mockery. The spitting also fulfills a particular detail to this effect in Jesus' prediction (10:34; compare 14:65). Putting his own clothes back on him prepares for the next episode, which will include their dividing up his clothes among themselves.

JESUS' EXPIRING IN A WAY THAT DEMONSTRATES HIS DIVINE SONSHIP
Mark 15:20d–27, 29–41

Much as in 14:32–52, a concentration of verbs in the present tense for past events will dramatize the fulfillment of Jesus' predictions that he'd be killed: "leads," (15:20), "requisition" (15:21), "bring" (15:22), and "crucify" (15:24, 27). **15:20d–21: And they** [the soldiers] **lead him out to crucify him.** This statement headlines the fulfillment of Jesus' prediction that the Gentiles would kill him (10:33–34). **²¹And they requisition a certain passer-by coming from a field** [outside Jerusalem], [namely,] **Simon—a Cyrenian, the father of Alexander and Rufus—to take up his cross** [= the beam to be affixed horizontally to a permanently planted upright stake or to a living tree]. Cyrene was a city in North Africa. Mark doesn't say whether this Simon was visiting Jerusalem as a Passover pilgrim or had emigrated from Cyrene. But identifying Simon as "a Cyrenian" distinguishes him from Simon Peter, among others (see the comments on 14:3); and identifying him also as "the father of Alexander and Rufus" seems to imply that Mark's originally intended audience knew personally the two sons but not their father. Mark has put Jesus in contrast with the fleshly weakness of Peter, James, and John in Gethsemane (14:32–42) and will yet emphasize twice the loudness of Jesus' last outcry (15:34, 37). It seems doubtful, then, that Mark wants us to think that Simon was requisitioned to take up Jesus' cross because Jesus was too weak to carry it. Rather, it's to dignify Jesus that Mark notes the taking up of Jesus' cross by Simon of Cyrene. Mark's Jesus

doesn't even *take up* his cross, much less carry it and then relinquish it. Omission of a reason for the requisition of Simon focuses attention on this dignifying of Jesus rather than on whatever weakness or suffering of his might have prompted the soldiers to requisition Simon.

15:22–23: **And they bring him to the Golgotha place, which is translated "Skull's Place."** "Bring" (present tense) and the topographical detail portend the imminent fulfillment of Jesus' predictions that he'd be killed (8:31; 9:31; 10:34). We don't know why the place was associated with a skull, whether because of its shape, nearby graves, use as a polling place (that is, for counting heads), or some other reason; but "Golgotha" probably doesn't mean the dried-out skull of a skeleton. **²³And they were trying to give him myrrhed wine, but he didn't take** [it]. Wine spiced with myrrh is a delicacy. So whatever the motive of the soldiers, their attempt to give him such wine amounts in Mark's presentation to a dignifying of Jesus just as requisitioning somebody else to take up his cross did the same. His refusal to take the wine may indicate a rejection of continued mockery, but more likely it indicates a determination not to sleep on the cross. (The wine would have had a soporific effect on him.) He will die awake and strong in flesh just as in Gethsemane he prayed awake and strong in flesh (contrast the sleeping of Peter, James, and John through weakness of the flesh). We might also think of Jesus' saying he wouldn't drink "from the product of the vine" till his drinking it "anew in God's kingdom" (14:25).

15:24: **And they crucify him and "divided his clothes for themselves by casting a lot for them** [Psalm 22:18]," **who should take up what.** The soldiers' crucifying Jesus fulfills his prediction that Gentiles would kill him. Mark borrows phraseology from the Old Testament to narrate the divvying up of Jesus' clothes by lot-casting (similar to our throwing dice or drawing straws). Despite having to explain all things Jewish elsewhere (see especially 7:3–4), Mark doesn't explain here that he's quoting. So he must not be expecting his audience to detect a fulfillment of the Old Testament. Highlighted, instead, is the desirability of Jesus' clothing, which the woman with a flow of blood wanted to touch, and did touch, for her healing (5:27–28, 30) and which the sick in general sought to touch, even just the fringe of his garment ("and as many as touched it were being saved" [6:56]). Mark adds "who should take up what" after mentioning the soldiers' "casting a lot for them." The addition is unnecessary, but it emphasizes the desirability of Jesus' clothes and produces a parallel with Simon of Cyrene's "tak[ing] up" Jesus' cross (15:21). Both instances of "take up" dignify Jesus. Though the divvying up of Jesus' clothes implies his being crucified naked, Mark doesn't mention the nakedness explicitly lest it undermine his dignifying the crucifixion of Jesus.

15:25–27: **And it was the third hour** [about 9:00 A.M.], **and they crucified him.** To reduce the shame of crucifixion as much as possible, Mark is starting a chronology that will show how little time Jesus spent on the cross (see 15:44–45 with comments). The reference to crucifixion follows up a similar reference in 15:24 so as to tie Jesus' crucifixion tightly to this apologetic chronology. Mark doesn't want us to imagine that Jesus hung on a cross any longer than he actually did. ²⁶**And the inscription of his charge** [that is, the accusation brought against him] **had been inscribed** [as follows]: **"The king of the Jews."** ²⁷**And they crucify two bandits with him, one on** [his] **right and one on his left.** The chief priests don't believe in Jesus' kingship. The crowd have refused to acknowledge him as their king (15:9–14). And as for Mark himself, nowhere in his Gospel does he present Jesus as the king of the Jews or as claiming to be their king. So the inscription and the crucifixion of two bandits with Jesus simply prepare for the following mockery. According to 14:48–49 he has already been mistreated as a bandit though he isn't one. The crucifixion of two bandits on either side of him creates a foil for his innocence, then, and dignifies him with a central position. The mistreatment of him as though he were a bandit gains further emphasis from his having called traffickers in the temple "bandits" (11:17). Thus Jesus the temple-cleanser is crucified with bandits as though he were a temple-desecrator. (The earliest and best manuscripts don't have 15:28.)

15:29–32: And the passers-by were blaspheming [= slandering] **him by shaking their heads and saying, "Ha! You who are tearing down the sanctuary** [the temple proper, exclusive of surrounding courts and cloisters] **and building** [it] **in three days, ³⁰save yourself by coming down from the cross." ³¹Likewise also the chief priests, mocking** [Jesus] **to one another along with the scholars, were saying, "Others he saved. Himself he can't save. ³²Let the Christ, the king of Israel, come down from the cross now, so that we may see and believe." And the** [bandits] **who'd been crucified together with him were jeering at him.** This mockery continues the fulfillment of Jesus' prediction in 10:33–34. Two elements make up the slander of blasphemy by the passers-by: (1) the falsity of implying Jesus had said he'd tear down the sanctuary and build it in three days (see 14:57–59 for this falsity); (2) the implication that Jesus was powerless to save himself by coming down from his cross. A scornful "Ha!" introduces and underlines these elements. The one wrongly condemned for blasphemy (14:63–64) has wrongly become the object of blasphemy. In mocking Jesus among themselves (as opposed to addressing him as the passers-by were doing) the chief priests with the scholars don't use the false charge brought up by the passers-by. For on account of its falsity, the chief priests and the whole Sanhedrin threw that charge out of court and condemned Jesus instead for claiming to be the Christ, God's Son, whom they'd see sitting at God's right hand and coming as the Son of Man with the clouds of heaven (14:61–64). By implication, they'd converted this religious charge into a political charge with regard to kingship (15:1–20a). So they bring into their mockery both "the Christ" from the religious charge and "the king of Israel" from the

political charge (with a shift from the Roman way of putting it, "the king of *the Jews*," to the Jewish way of putting it, "the king of *Israel*"). They also bring in Jesus' having saved others for a contrast with his supposed inability to save himself. The passers-by *challenged* him to save himself. Along with the scholars, the chief priests *deny* that he can. Then they issue an indirect challenge that Jesus come down from the cross in order that they may see and believe. Their rationale is that a messianic king wouldn't be hanging there. "Now" gives the challenge a temporal bite. If Jesus waits to come down, it'll be too late. He'll be dead. Ironically, of course, he saves others by *not* coming down from the cross. "Likewise also" exposes the chief priests' and scholars' mockery as blasphemous like the challenge of the passers-by. Even Jesus' co-victims jeer at him despite their deserving crucifixion and his not deserving it. This jeering highlights the extent to which his prediction of mockery for himself has reached fulfillment.

***15:33–39: And when the sixth hour** [noon] **struck, darkness came across the whole earth till the ninth hour** [about 3:00 P.M.]. The delay of darkness till noon provided daylight for the writing of the inscription, the crucifixion of two bandits with Jesus, and the mockery. Darkness now shrouds the whole earth from noon till Jesus' death in midafternoon. The supernatural character of the darkness—it starts when the sun is at its highest and brightest and extends earth-wide—magnifies Mark's apologetic point: now that Jesus' prediction of mockery has reached complete fulfillment, God hides his Son from the blasphemers' leering and jeering. ³⁴**And at the ninth hour Jesus cried out with a loud voice, *"Eloi, Eloi, lema sabachthani?"* which is translated, "My God, my God, why** [= 'to what purpose'] **have you abandoned me** [Psalm 22:1]**?" ³⁵And on hearing** [Jesus' outcry], **some of the bystanders were saying, "Look, he's calling for Elijah!" ³⁶And on running and filling a sponge with vinegary wine, putting it around a reed somebody tried to give him a drink, saying, "Let's see if Elijah comes to take him down." ³⁷But Jesus, in letting loose a loud voice** [as he did in the outcry of divine abandonment], **had breathed out** [= expired]. ³⁸**And the veil of the sanctuary was torn in two from top to bottom. ³⁹And on seeing that he'd breathed out in this way, the centurion who was standing by opposite it** [that is, standing by the cross but with a full view of the temple across the way] **said, "Truly this human being was God's Son."** On the one hand, Mark wants to excite our sympathy for Jesus' being abandoned by God. The abandonment consists in God's leaving him to die rather than stepping in to save him from death. The possibilities of coming down from the cross, destroying the sanctuary, and rebuilding it in three days have now yielded to the actuality of abandonment by God.

On the other hand, Mark also wants to excite our admiration of the *way* Jesus died. Ordinarily, victims of crucifixion weaken bit by bit and lapse into unconsciousness before dying without even a whimper. But to portray

Jesus as strong right up to and at the moment of his death or, better, *in* his death—strong in flesh, superhumanly so—Mark stresses the loudness of Jesus' outcry. He mentions it twice for emphasis. Twice before, he noted "a loud voice"; and each time it represented superhuman strength (1:26; 5:7). So it does here as well. How else should the very Son of God die but in a burst of strength? The cross puts on exhibit his strength, not weakness. Furthermore, the verb "cried out" introduces the shout with a certain formality that dignifies the loudness of Jesus' voice. And Mark retains the original Aramaic of the outcry before translating it, because the mystique of an oriental language carries the connotation of power. Here, the power turns out so superhuman that the breath which Jesus exhales in his dying loud shout—this breath makes a wind so strong that it tears in two the veil of the sanctuary from top to bottom (compare the Lord's powerfully destructive breath in Exodus 15:8, 10; Job 4:9; Isaiah 11:4; 2 Thessalonians 2:8). And this strong breath of wind is nothing, or none, less than the Holy Spirit that descended into Jesus at his baptism to make him the "stronger one" of John the baptizer's prophecy (1:7–11). For our words "breath," "wind," and "Spirit" all go back to the same word in Mark's Greek (and also in Aramaic and Hebrew, for that matter [compare Ezekiel 37:5–14]).

Because Elijah went to heaven without dying (2 Kings 2:11), Jews believed he would return to save righteous sufferers. Here, therefore, some bystanders say Jesus is calling Elijah to save him. (Note the similarity between "*Eloi*" and "*Elijah*.") And somebody tries to give Jesus a drink of cheap, vinegary wine to slake his thirst (compare Psalm 69:21b). The hope is to prolong Jesus' life a little longer and see whether Elijah will indeed come to take him down. The use of a reed with a sponge attached to its tip may dignify Jesus by portraying him at a height otherwise impossible to reach, for no such reed with a sponge was needed in the attempt to give him myrrhed wine prior to the crucifixion (15:23). Jesus doesn't take the vinegary wine—not because he refuses it, but because he has already expired (compare 14:25). His shout of superhuman strength, mentioned twice, was his last breath. No wonder the one who filled the sponge was "running." But it was too late to revive Jesus. Dead men don't drink.

Jesus' breathing "out" the wind of the Spirit contrasts with the Spirit's coming down "into" him at his baptism (1:10) just as the "voice" of Jesus asking God why he has abandoned him contrasts with the "voice" of God telling Jesus at his baptism, "You're my beloved Son; I've taken delight in you" (1:11). And just as the force of the Spirit's coming "down" caused the heavens to be "torn apart" at Jesus' baptism (1:10), so the force of Jesus' exhalation of the Spirit causes the veil of the temple to be "torn in two" from the top "down." "In two" stresses the completeness of the tearing apart. And "from top to bottom" indicates divine action, for Jesus' Spirit is the Spirit of God that came down from heaven into Jesus because Jesus was God's Son, as now recognized by the centurion. Just as the voice of God declared Jesus' divine sonship

(1:11), the centurion, *seeing* that Jesus expired with such loud force that his last breath, the wind of the Spirit, completely tore apart the veil of the sanctuary, declares Jesus to be God's Son. "Truly" emphasizes the reliability of the centurion's testimony—in contrast with the false testimonies lodged against Jesus during his trial before the Sanhedrin (14:55–59) and in opposition to the high priest's judging Jesus' confession of divine sonship to be blasphemous (14:61b–64).

The sanctuary had two veils, an outer one and an inner one. The centurion's standing opposite the temple and seeing the veil-rending requires the outer one to be in view here (and, incidentally, requires also the site of crucifixion to be at some height on the Mount of Olives facing toward the outer veil rather than at the sites now visited by pilgrims, which would have provided no view whatever of the outer [or inner] veil). But Mark ignores the distinction between veils to concentrate attention solely on the item of supernatural force, which points to Jesus' divine sonship. Nor is Mark content to describe the centurion only as a bystander. He also describes the centurion as standing opposite the sanctuary. Some translations have "standing . . . opposite *him* [Jesus]," rather than "standing . . . opposite *it* [the sanctuary]." But Mark has mentioned the sanctuary last. Standing *opposite* Jesus would contradict standing *by* him. And the centurion's "seeing" connects better with the *visible* effect on the sanctuary of the way Jesus died—that is, with the veil-rending—than with the *audible* effect of the way he died—that is, with a loud outcry. So the centurion's standing opposite the sanctuary underscores that he enjoyed a full view of the veil-rending. This full view lends great weight, then, to his declaration, "Truly this human being was God's Son." In conjunction with the lasting of darkness "till the ninth hour" (15:33), "seeing" implies that the darkness has lifted and complements the "hearing" in 15:35. Whereas "hearing" pointed to the words that Jesus cried out, "seeing" points to the effect of his outcry on the veil of the sanctuary.

"In this way" refers to the way in which the wind of the Spirit, exhaled when in his last breath Jesus let loose a loud shout, tore that veil in two from top to bottom. It's "this way" that evokes the centurion's declaration. In it, "this human being" makes a foil of Jesus' humanity against which his deity as "God's Son" stands out. The similarity between "*thus*" (as "in this way" might also be translated) and "*this* human being" adds to the emphasis. Whatever the historical centurion meant ("a son of a god" or "a son of God," for example), Mark wants us to understand "God's Son" (see 1:1). "Was" reflects the death of Jesus as ending his lifetime and implies that he has been God's Son all along. The centurion remains only a military bystander, anonymous and otherwise unknown in the Christian community (contrast "Alexander and Rufus" in 15:21). But this fact makes his declaration of Jesus' divine sonship all the more remarkable.

15:40–41: And there were also women watching at a distance, among whom [were] both Mary Magdalene, and Mary the mother of James the little [= the younger

in relation to his brother Jesus] **and of Joses** [see 6:3 for Mary the mother of Jesus and his brothers James and Joses]**, and Salome, ⁴¹who when he was in Galilee were following him and serving him** [food (compare 1:13, 31)]**, and many other** [women] **who'd come up with him to Jerusalem.** The male disciples have fled (14:50), and Peter is nursing his regret (14:72). So to guarantee further that Jesus died in a way that evoked the centurion's declaration of Jesus' divine sonship despite crucifixion, Mark indicates that women were watching. He even lists the names of several of them. He doesn't explain why they were watching from a distance, but he does explain how it came about that they were watching and indicates that the named women were far from alone. "Many others" were watching with them. As a result, all of them make a large number that both compensates for the distance from which they were watching, revives Mark's emphasis on Jesus' power to attract large numbers of people, and thus enlists the present large number of women as fellow witnesses with the centurion to what he saw of the superhuman way Jesus expired. The centurion doesn't stand alone in seeing that Jesus died with a burst of divine strength.

THE DIGNIFYING OF JESUS' BODY IN BURIAL
Mark 15:42–47

15:42–43: And because it had already become late, since it was Preparation, which is Pre-Sabbath [= Friday]**, ⁴³Joseph from Arimathea, a distinguished councilor who also himself was waiting for God's kingdom—coming, taking a risk,** [Joseph] **went in to Pilate and asked for Jesus' body.** It's Friday, the day before Sabbath, and Jews counted a twenty-four hour day from sundown to sundown. So "already late" refers to late afternoon. And if Jesus' body isn't to hang disgracefully on the cross and throughout the next day, his body has to be buried before sundown, when the Sabbath starts and no work—such as burying a corpse—can be done till the next sundown. To erase the shame of the cross, Mark dignifies Jesus in burial as well as in death. He notes that the one who comes to ask for Jesus' body, Joseph from Arimathea, is "a distinguished councilor," and not only a man of political prominence but also one of religious devotion ("who also himself was waiting for God's kingdom") and of derring-do ("taking a risk . . ."). "Also" adds Joseph's religious devotion to his political prominence, and "himself" emphasizes the devotion as personal. Mark doesn't specify why it was risky for Joseph to ask for Jesus' body; so the point has to do with Joseph's bravery as such, not with why his request required bravery. It speaks well of Jesus that despite the disgraceful manner of his death such a man as Joseph should dangerously seek to bury his body. The compliment is especially powerful in that though Mark portrays Joseph as waiting for God's kingdom, he doesn't portray him as a disciple of Jesus; rather, he identifies Joseph as a member of the very Sanhedrin that *unanimously* condemned Jesus (see 14:64 with 14:55). As a "councilor,"

Joseph belongs to that court, the whole of which held a "consultation" issuing in the delivery of Jesus to Pilate (15:1). Thus Joseph's political prominence, religious devotion, and personal bravery are all the more exceptional in comparison with the rest of the Sanhedrin and hence all the more complimentary of Jesus in relation to the crucifixion.

15:44–45: And Pilate marveled if he [Jesus] **had already died; and on summoning the centurion** [who'd seen "the way" Jesus died]**, he asked him if he** [Jesus] **had died a long while earlier. ⁴⁵And on coming to know from the centurion** [that Jesus *had* died a long while earlier]**, he donated the corpse to Joseph.** Ordinarily, victims of crucifixion take a long time to die, even several whole days. No wonder, then, that Pilate marvels if Jesus has died "already," that is, after hanging on his cross a mere six hours. Since Jesus died about 3:00 P.M. and had to be buried before sundown about three hours later, "a *long* while earlier" is hyperbolic—an exaggeration designed to emphasize the shortness of time that Jesus hung on the cross. The centurion was an eyewitness. So his testimony convinces even Pilate, and should therefore convince us, that the shame of Jesus' crucifixion was chronologically minimal. Pilate's initial doubt—a doubt accented by a double "if," one for his marveling and another for his inquiry—sharpens the point once the doubt is overcome. Confirmation from the centurion leads Pilate to "donate" Jesus' corpse to Joseph. In contrast with Jesus' having been "given over" to his enemies, the verb of donation ennobles Jesus for the burial of his corpse. Though "body" can have the sense of "corpse," Mark's switching from "body" (15:43) to "corpse" puts a final accent on Jesus' having died too soon to have spent very much time on a cross.

15:46–47: And having bought a linen cloth, on taking him [Jesus] **down** [from the cross]**, he** [Joseph] **wrapped** [him] **in the linen cloth and placed him in a tomb that had been hewn out of rock. And he rolled a stone over the tomb's entrance. ⁴⁷And Mary Magdalene and Mary the** [mother] **of Joses were watching where he'd been placed.** The purchase of a linen cloth dignifies Jesus with a brand new shroud. His being taken down avoids the indignity of hanging on a cross overnight and throughout the Sabbath. So too does his being placed in a tomb. For Romans normally forbade a proper burial of those executed like Jesus under a charge of high treason (in his case as "king of the Jews" in supposed opposition to Caesar). That the tomb was "hewn out of rock" adds to the dignity of Jesus' burial—especially because this description is best understood, not of a cave hollowed out of rock, but of a freestanding monolith carved out of rock inside and out. Mark's omitting to say who owned the tomb rivets attention on its high grade. Conspicuous by its absence is the usual Roman practice of leaving victims of crucifixion on crosses for days while their corpses started decomposing in plain view and predatory animals and birds of carrion picked off their flesh. No such shame in Jesus' case! Furthermore, the rolling of a stone over the tomb's entrance shielded his corpse from shameful predation and public exposure and prepares for the question in 16:3: "Who will roll away the stone . . . ?" Observation of the location by the two Marys not only prepares for their and Salome's coming to the tomb in 16:1–2. It also provides eyewitness evidence of Jesus' honorable burial.

THE RESURRECTION OF JESUS AS A
FULFILLMENT OF HIS PREDICTIONS
Mark 16:1–7

16:1–2: And when the Sabbath had passed, Mary Magdalene and Mary the [mother] of the James, plus Salome, bought aromatic spices to anoint him [Jesus] on going [to the tomb]. ²And very early in the morning on the first [day] of the week, when the sun had risen, they come to the tomb. The Sabbath ended at sundown on Saturday. The women could hardly have bought aromatic spices Sunday morning earlier than sunrise. Therefore they must have bought them Saturday evening. Ordinarily, no one would think to give a victim of crucifixion the dignity of an anointing; and the anointing of those who'd died without shame was usually done with olive oil. Only kings and other high dignitaries got their corpses anointed with aromatic spices (see 2 Chronicles 16:14, for example). So along with the prior anointing in 14:3, the honorable burial, and Mark's many other devices, the three women's buying such spices to anoint Jesus helps remove the disgrace of his crucifixion. As the one whom a Roman centurion declared to have been God's Son (15:39), Jesus deserves no less than a king does. In 15:40 Mark called the second Mary mentioned above "the mother of James the little and of Joses." In 15:47 he shortened the designation to "the [mother] of Joses." To make up for the omission of James the little in 15:47, then, Mark now calls her the mother of "*the* James," that is, of the aforementioned James. Salome wasn't mentioned in 15:47 as watching where Jesus was buried, but here she comes to the tomb with those who'd been watching. It seems unnecessary for Mark to have written "on the first day of the week." *Of course* it's the first day of the week if the Sabbath has recently passed. The wording therefore highlights this day as that of Jesus' resurrection. "When the sun had risen" keeps "very early in the morning" from being misunderstood as the last part of the night instead of a time right after sunrise. Thus the women can see to come to the tomb and can see once they arrive. The present tense in "they *come* to the tomb" creates a sense of excitement about to be duplicated in the present tense of "they *see.*"

16:3–4: And they were saying to each other, "Who'll roll away the stone for us from the tomb's entrance?" ⁴And on looking up they see that the stone *is* rolled away. For it was extremely large. Who rolled away the stone? God? An angel? The resurrected Jesus? Graverobbers? Even at the risk of letting us think of graverobbers, Mark doesn't say who rolled away the stone. He's interested only in its having been rolled

away so as to allow the women's entrance into the tomb. "For it was extremely large" looks as though it tells why the women found the stone already rolled away. But it doesn't. The extremely large size would explain instead why the women should *not* have found the stone already rolled away. The notation of its extremely large size gives, rather, the reason why they were asking each other who would roll away the stone for them. But Mark is so excited he can't wait to mention the stone's being rolled away already. So he puts it before his explanation of the women's question.

16:5–7: And on entering into the tomb they saw a young man sitting on the right, wearing a long white robe. And they were astounded. ⁶But he tells them, "Stop being astounded. You're seeking Jesus the Nazarene [= man from Nazareth], the crucified one. He has been raised! He isn't here. Look, the place where they put him! ⁷But go tell his disciples and Peter, 'He's going ahead of you into Galilee. You'll see him there, just as he told you.'" Other ancient literature, both Jewish and Christian, uses "young man" for an angel. So also here in Mark's Gospel (compare Matthew 28:2). But he calls this angel a young man to recall the young man of 14:51–52 (see the comments on that passage). "Sitting on the right" (1) indicates this young man's authority; (2) contrasts with the women's expectation of seeing Jesus' corpse lying prone; and (3) makes the young man represent Jesus, who at the time of Mark's writing is sitting at God's right hand in accordance with 12:36; 14:62. "On the right" also augurs well, for the right side is the side of favor. "Wearing a long white robe" contrasts with the linen cloth used to wrap Jesus' corpse (15:46). The robe's whiteness associates the young man with Jesus, whose garment at the transfiguration turned an unearthly white (9:3), and begins to identify the young man as a heavenly figure, an angel, a messenger of Jesus. The young man's proceeding to interpret the meaning of the empty tomb and to instruct the women what they should do completes his identification as an angel, for interpretation and instruction are standard functions of angels. The very meaning of "angel" is "messenger." And suiting the appearance of an angel are also the women's being astounded, the young man's telling them not to be astounded, his knowing information that an angel but not a human being would typically know, and the authority with which he commands the women (see, for example, Daniel 8:15–27; 9:20–27; Luke 1:11–17, 26–36). "Stop being astounded" implies that what has astounded the women pales into insignificance by comparison with the announcement the young man is about to make.

"You're seeking Jesus the Nazarene" shifts attention to him whose power and glory the young man represents, astounding though that representation has been. "The crucified one" makes all the more remarkable the following announcement of Jesus' resurrection, consequent absence, and going ahead into Galilee. "He has been raised!" echoes "after I've been raised" in Jesus' prediction at 14:28 and negates the scandal of his crucifixion by noting its undoing in fulfillment of that prediction.

"Look, the place where they put him!" underscores the fulfillment. He's absent from the tomb because he's already on his way to Galilee. "They" implies that Joseph of Arimathea had help placing Jesus in the tomb. "*But go*" draws a contrast between what the women were intending to do by way of anointing Jesus' corpse and what the young man now tells them to do. "His disciples" refers to the Twelve minus Judas Iscariot, because of his having betrayed Jesus, and minus Peter, because of his separation from the rest of the Twelve by following Jesus at a distance into the high priest's courtyard (compare 14:50 with 14:54, 66, 68). So Judas deserves no report, and Peter requires a separate report (hence "and Peter" [compare Luke 24:34; 1 Corinthians 15:5]). Jesus' going ahead of the disciples into Galilee completes the fulfillment of his prediction in 14:28. "You'll see him there" adds a coming visible proof to the announcement and indicates that Jesus is preceding the disciples to Galilee, not leading them there; for otherwise they'd see him along the way, not just on arrival. Jesus' prediction in 14:28 didn't include the disciples' *seeing* him in Galilee. So "just as he told you" refers to the prediction there of his *going ahead* of the disciples into Galilee as a followup to his resurrection—and emphasizes the coming fulfillment of that prediction.

THE OVERAWING OF THOSE WHO HEARD THE NEWS THAT JESUS HAD BEEN RAISED
Mark 16:8

16:8: And on coming out [of the tomb] **they fled from the tomb, for trembling and astonishment was gripping them. And they said nothing to anyone, for they were afraid.** The women's fleeing contrasts with the mere going that the young man had commanded. The contrast requires the explanation that they were in the grip of trembling and astonishment; that is, they were shaking with astonishment. The contrast of flight with mere going also emphasizes the overawing effect of what the women have seen and heard (the tomb's emptiness and the young man's announcement of Jesus' resurrection). Their fearful dumbfoundedness—they were too scared to speak—reemphasizes the awesomeness of Jesus' resurrection as Mark's climactic apology for the cross. This dumbfoundedness and their flight don't characterize them as disobedient to the young man's command, "Go tell . . . ," so much as they characterize

the news of Jesus' resurrection itself as overawing. We wouldn't know this episode if the women hadn't told about it in the end.

A Special Note on Mark's Ending

The earliest and best manuscripts don't contain Mark 16:9–20 or another, much shorter ending without numbered verses. So we shouldn't think of either one of these endings as canonical and authoritative any more than we should think of the myriad other inauthentic and often conflicting changes in later, inferior manuscripts as authoritative and canonical. It's disputed, though, whether Mark's Gospel originally ended at 16:8 or had an ending that for some reason has been lost. The treatment here of 16:8 *not* as the completion of a paragraph that started at 16:1 reflects an opinion that 16:8 starts a new paragraph the rest of which has been lost. Among considerations favoring this opinion are the following: (1) Mark has regularly used notations of topographical movement, preceded by "and," to start new paragraphs, just as here: "And on coming out [of the tomb] they fled . . . ." (2) Mark has repeatedly and in detail narrated the fulfillments of Jesus' other predictions insofar as those fulfillments occurred during Jesus' time on earth; so it seems highly unlikely that Mark would have omitted to narrate the climactic fulfillment of Jesus' prediction that upon resurrection he'd go ahead of the disciples into Galilee. (3) The young man's enhancement of that prediction with the statement, "You'll see him there, just as he told you," makes it seem doubly unlikely that Mark would have omitted such a narrative. (4) For the most part Matthew and Luke seem to have been following Mark up through 16:8, yet both of them go on to write about the women's carrying out their commission to tell the disciples—as though they had an earlier text of Mark that contained such a narrative. (5) Appearances of the resurrected Jesus are mentioned so often in the New Testament (see especially 1 Corinthians 15:5–8 as well as the other three Gospels) that it seems unlikely Mark wouldn't have included such an appearance. (6) In the original Greek text, 16:8 ends with the conjunction "For," a highly unlikely ending for a book. (7) The manuscript tradition displays massive dissatisfaction with an ending at 16:8, a dissatisfaction best explained by knowledge that Mark didn't end there. Nevertheless, we must make do with 16:8 as the last *known* verse in Mark's Gospel.

LUKE

Very early church tradition attributes the writing of this Gospel to Luke, a physician who accompanied the Apostle Paul on at least some of his travels (Colossians 4:14; 2 Timothy 4:11; Philemon 24). In accord with eyewitness reports and earlier writings, the Gospel portrays Jesus preeminently as a model of religious piety, moral purity, and political innocence—and thus as an attractive, sympathetic, and beneficent Savior of others.

A PROLOGUE INDICATING LUKE'S PRECEDENTS, METHOD, AND PURPOSE
Luke 1:1–4

The prologue consists of one long sentence, here divided in half for purposes of comment. **1:1–2: Inasmuch as many have put [their] hand to drawing up a narrative about the matters that have been brought to fulfillment among us, ²just as those who from the beginning became eyewitnesses and assistants of the word gave [those matters] over to us [by way of testifying to them] . . . .** "Inasmuch as" is a fancy way of saying "Since" and therefore starts this prologue on a note of formality. The formality, which Luke carries throughout the prologue, lends credence to Luke's precedents, method, and purpose. In connection with the rest of the prologue, "Inasmuch as" also indicates that earlier narratives—that is, his precedents—prompted Luke to add his own narrative. His description of the earlier narratives as "many" points to an abundance of testimonial evidence. Luke's narrative will therefore result in a *super*abundance of such evidence. "Have put [their] hand to" indicates the successful production of many earlier narratives, not mere attempts at drawing them up. "Drawing up a narrative" means putting its events in a meaningful order. "The things that have been brought to fulfillment among us" consist in the events of Jesus' life and ministry. Their having been brought to fulfillment describes them as the result of God's activity in the fulfillment of his plan and promises dating back to the Old Testament (compare, for example, 24:44–47). "Among us" describes the fulfillment as having taken place in plain view and therefore as verifiable. "Just as" indicates an agreement between the earlier narratives and the fulfilling events themselves. Those narratives are reliable. (Luke doesn't identify the earlier narratives, but modern students hypothesize that he's referring to Mark's Gospel and possibly to Matthew's, among other, presently unknown narratives, whether written or oral.) That the things "brought to fulfillment among us" derive from eyewitnesses adds to the element of reliability. That the eyewitnesses saw these things "from the beginning" adds chronological comprehensiveness to the reliability. "Assistants of the word" describes the eyewitnesses as helping the word—that is, the message concerning the fulfilling events—get circulated. And "gave [those things] over to us" describes the circulation as a handing on of information to those who weren't themselves eyewitnesses.

The sentence continues in **1:3–4: it has seemed good also for me, having followed [= investigated] all things carefully from the start, to write for you in an orderly way, most excellent Theophilus, ⁴so that you may know [= recognize] the certainty of the words about which you were instructed.** Though not an eyewitness himself, Luke's investigation of the eyewitness tradition has made it seem good for him to add his narrative to the earlier narratives. The care and comprehensiveness ("all things . . . from the start") of his investigation lend credibility to the coming narrative. So also does the "orderly way" in which Luke will now write. (By the way, the order may be variously chronological, topical, and logical.) His organization of materials will reflect the carefulness of his investigation, make for clarity of presentation, and thus enhance its persuasiveness. This Theophilus can hardly be the Jewish high priest who occupied his office A.D. 37–41. So we know nothing more about the Theophilus whom Luke addresses except that Luke will also address to him the book of Acts (Acts 1:1). This address carries on the formality of tone that helps undergird Luke's credibility. "The words" about which Theophilus was "instructed" equate with "the matters that have been brought to fulfillment among us" (1:1) since the matters were conveyed in testimonial words. Recognition of their "certainty" marks Luke's purpose in writing. He wants to provide Theophilus, and us, a convincing historical basis for Christian belief. Historical writing doesn't consist in a bare chronicle of events, though. So Luke will present events in the framework of an interpretation. The interpretation will contribute persuasive power to his narrative.

THE PROMISE AND ONSET OF ELIZABETH'S PREGNANCY
Luke 1:5–25

1:5–6: In the days of Herod, king of Judea [that is, during his reign, 37–4 B.C.], **there was a certain priest— Zechariah by name—of the division of Abijah; and he had a wife from the daughters of Aaron** [that is, a wife descended from Aaron, the elder brother of Moses and the first high priest of Israel]; **and her name** [was] **Elizabeth. ⁶And both** [of them] **were righteous in God's sight by way of traveling** [a figure of speech for living their lives]—**blameless—in all the Lord's commandments and righteous requirements** [as recorded in the Old Testament]. Luke starts laying a solid historical basis for Christian belief by rooting the initial episode of his narrative in the historical period of Herod, king of Judea ("Judea" here referring to the whole land of Israel, as also in 4:44; 6:17; 7:17; 23:5; Acts 1:8; 10:37). Added to the details of Herod's name and title is a cavalcade of other names and details. Luke knows about a Zechariah, that this Zechariah was a priest; that he belonged to the priestly division of Abijah (which along with twenty-three other divisions served in the temple for two one-week periods each year, excluding festivals); that Zechariah had a wife; that his wife was descended from Aaron even though it wasn't required that the wives of priests, as well as the priests themselves, should have such a pedigree; that her name was Elizabeth; that both she and he were righteous; that even God considered them righteous; that their righteousness consisted in ongoing obedience to "the Lord's commandments and righteous requirements" (the twoness of this expression emphasizing the couple's obedience); that this obedience wasn't marred by any exceptions; and that as a result they were "blameless." These details exhibit the thoroughness of Luke's research and thus enhance the credibility of his narrative. But some of the details do more: they recommend "the word" that Luke narrates by calling attention to the moral attractiveness of those who played positive roles in the good news about Jesus. According to Luke's account, this same moral attractiveness will characterize Jesus too. Throughout, Luke will appeal to our highest ideals, to what some people call "the better angels" of our human nature. The certainty that calls for belief in 1:4 has an admirable moral basis as well as a credible historical one.

But here are further details, ones that evoke our sympathy, especially in view of Zechariah's and Elizabeth's distinguished statuses (priestly and, in her case, unnecessarily Aaronic) and exemplary conduct: *1:7:* **And they had no child, because Elizabeth was barren; and they were both advanced in their days** [that is, very old and therefore past child-producing age]. Their advanced age prepares for the coming miracle of Elizabeth's getting pregnant by her husband. Luke delights in miracles, for they contribute to the certainty of Christian belief.

1:8–12: **And it happened that while he was doing priestly service before God in the order of his division** [that is, when his division was on duty in the temple], **⁹according to the custom of priestly service he was chosen by lot to offer incense upon entering into the Lord's sanctuary** [more specifically, the first room of the temple building, called the Holy Place, where the altar of incense was located]. To offer incense was to put it on the altar and burn it. **¹⁰And all the multitude of people were praying outside at the hour of incense** [which could be either early morning or late afternoon, though the presence of a multitude favors late afternoon]. **¹¹And an angel of the Lord, standing at the right of the altar of incense, appeared to him. ¹²And on seeing** [the angel], **Zechariah was unnerved; and fear fell on him.** To Zechariah's priestly *status* (1:5) is now added ordinary priestly *function*. "Before God" enhances this function and connects the Christian story to Judaism. Because ancient people, unlike most moderns, distrusted novelty, Luke will keep playing on this theme of continuity, that is, Christianity as fulfilled Judaism—Judaism come of age. The custom of choosing by lot had the purpose of leaving the choice entirely to God (not to chance, for in his world nothing happens by chance [compare Acts 1:24–26]). And entering into the Lord's sanctuary to offer incense piles extraordinary priestly privilege on top of ordinary priestly service; for not every priest got this privilege, and once a priest got it, to give other priests a better chance he was removed from the pool of lot-casting. Adding to this extraordinary privilege, Luke then bathes what's about to happen in an aura of special sanctity—special because of its time ("the hour of incense"), because of what the people outside were doing at the time ("praying"), because of their large number ("the multitude"), and because of the inclusion of everyone in the praying of the multitude ("all"). The appearance of a divinely sent messenger, an angel of the Lord no less, heightens the sanctity immeasurably. The angel's standing at the right of the altar of incense augurs well, for—given the righthandedness of most people—the right side is the side of favor. Nevertheless, Zechariah is unnerved and frightened—appropriately, though; for such a reaction shows an absence of temerity and thus carries forward Luke's emphasis on the moral and religious attractiveness of those who contributed to "the word" about Jesus. And Zechariah's "seeing" the angel contributes to the theme of reliability based on eyewitness.

1:13–17: **And the angel said to him, "Stop being afraid, Zechariah, because your prayer request has been heeded** [that is, heard so as to be answered positively]. **And your wife Elizabeth will bear a son for you** [so Zechariah must have prayed for offspring]. **And you shall call his name John. ¹⁴And you'll have joy and gladness, and many will rejoice because of his birth; ¹⁵for he'll be great in the Lord's sight. And by no means shall he drink wine and strong drink** [that is, wine and other alcoholic beverages, like beer]. **And he'll be filled with the Holy Spirit while he's still in his mother's womb, and onward. ¹⁶And he'll turn many of the sons of Israel to the Lord their God. ¹⁷And he himself will proceed before him** [before the Lord their God] **in Elijah's Spirit and power to turn fathers' hearts to children, and disobedient people into the good sense of righteous people,** [that is,] **to prepare for the Lord a people that have been readied** [for the Lord's coming]." Showing God's favor toward Zechariah are the angel's quieting his fear and promising him, despite his and his wife's old age, a son in answer to a request he'd made in prayer and, as a result of the answer to that prayer, joy and gladness. "A son *for you*" underscores the favorable estimate of Zechariah and its result. Because he's associated positively with the story of Jesus, then, the Lord's favor toward Zechariah on account of Zechariah's godliness brushes Jesus with virtue by association (the opposite of *guilt* by association). But Zechariah's joy will spill over to "many." The son's birth will constitute the immediate basis of his and their joy. But its ultimate basis consists in the son's high status and coming activity.

The high status comes into view with the Lord's determining that Zechariah should name his son "John." Ordinarily, a father has freedom to choose his son's name. But the Lord has special plans for this son and therefore has the angel tell Zechariah what he must name his son. Moreover, the son will be great in the Lord's estimation, not just in that of mere mortals (compare 7:28). His abstinence from wine and other alcoholic beverages will set him apart as specially consecrated to the service of God (compare Leviticus 10:9; Numbers 6:1–4, 20; Judges 13:4–5). The Lord's filling him with the Holy Spirit while he's still in his mother's womb (compare 1:44) and onward will empower him for that service. The service will consist in turning many Israelites to the Lord. More than this, he *himself* will proceed ahead of the Lord. By implication, the Lord is coming—in the person of Jesus, but Luke has yet to reveal that wrinkle. And John will proceed in the power of God's Spirit that characterized the ministry of the Old Testament prophet Elijah (compare Malachi 3:1; 4:5). The purpose and result of this Spirit-empowered ministry will be the uniting of old and young in the obedience to God that alone makes good sense and characterizes the righteous. The further purpose and result will be the preparation of a people, consisting of "many of the sons of Israel," who are morally ready for the Lord when he arrives. Thus Jesus, on his arrival as the Lord's emissary, will have people prepared so as to have the good moral sense to believe on him. Again, Luke is using his material to make a moral as well as historical case for Christianity. Allusions to the Old Testament put Christianity in the flow of divinely guided history, and Christianity's orientation to genuine piety and righteous behavior recommends it to the human conscience. Of course, Christianity hasn't yet come into being in Luke's narrative. But when it does, it will appeal to the pious and righteous.

1:18–20: And Zechariah said to the angel, "How shall I know this? For I'm an old man and my wife is advanced in her days." So how can she bear a son for Zechariah? [19]**And answering, the angel told him, "I'm Gabriel, the one standing in God's presence."** That's his usual location. **"And I've been sent to speak to you and tell you these things as good news."** Gabriel changes Zechariah's singular "this," referring to the seemingly impossible birth of a son to such an aged couple, to the plural "these things," referring to the son's coming activities as well as birth. [20]**"And behold, you'll be silent and unable to speak until the day that these things have taken place** [which would seem to be the day of

the son's birth; but Zechariah won't recover his ability to speak till the eighth day after birth, the day of circumcision and name-giving (1:57–64), so that the birth doesn't count technically till circumcision and acknowledgment by name-giving], **because you didn't believe my words, which as such** [that is, as divinely commissioned] **will be fulfilled in their due time."** Here's a fly in the ointment: Zechariah doesn't believe the angel's words and therefore asks how he can be sure that what the angel told him will really happen. He defends his question by noting his and his wife's old age. He'll get an indication how he can be sure, but first the angel notes what Zechariah should have noted to forestall any unbelief. He should have taken into consideration that an angel of the Lord wouldn't deliver a happy message only to tease him with an impossibility. But since Zechariah didn't consider the obvious, the angel gets more specific. He's no less an angel than Gabriel, who stands in God's presence when he's not on a mission for God. And at the moment he's on just such a mission. It's to tell Zechariah the good news of the items recounted earlier. So Zechariah's unbelief lacks justification and, as emphasized by "behold," the tongue that expressed unbelief won't be able to speak until the unbelief is conquered by fulfillment. Through the narration of this story Luke is telling us not to disbelieve as Zechariah did. The news really is good, and God's promises do come to pass at their proper time. Not only is righteousness sensible. Belief in the gospel is, too.

1:21–23: And the people were waiting expectantly for Zechariah and marveling at his spending so much time in the sanctuary. It was Gabriel's appearance and dialogue with Zechariah that took up the time, of course. [22]**And on coming out, he couldn't speak to them.** This fulfillment of Gabriel's punitive prediction foreshadows and guarantees the later fulfillment of Gabriel's happy prediction. **And they recognized that he'd seen a vision** [an actual appearance, not a dream] **in the sanctuary.** Luke records the people's recognition to convince us of the vision. After all, they were there and saw its effect on Zechariah. To emphasize its demonstrative effect, Luke rementions it in a twofold expression: **And he himself** [as distinct from the people] **was gesticulating to them and remaining mute.** The gesticulations dramatize Zechariah's muteness and thus emphasize the fulfillment of Gabriel's prediction that ability to speak won't return till the happier predictions start happening. [23]**And it came to pass that when the days of his religious service** [at the temple] **were fulfilled, he went away to his home.** Luke doesn't tell the whereabouts of Zechariah's home. It's important only that before going home, Zechariah did his religious duty despite being mute. And, naturally, going home enables him by God's power to impregnate Elizabeth.

1:24–25: And after these days [the week that Zechariah spent serving at the temple] **Elizabeth his wife conceived.** So the fulfillment of Gabriel's happy predictions gets started. **And she hid herself for five months . . . .** Luke isn't interested in her motive for hiding herself the first five months of her pregnancy. He's interested only in the outcome, namely, that the news of her pregnancy comes in the sixth month as a divine revelation and encouragement, delivered again by Gabriel, to Mary the mother of Jesus (1:26–38). Meanwhile, though, Elizabeth gives all credit to God: **saying, 25"Thus has the Lord done for me during the days in which he looked** [on me] **to take away my disgrace among human beings."** The contrast between "the Lord" and "human beings" corresponds to the contrast between favor and disgrace. In that culture childlessness was considered disgraceful. The Lord's looking on Elizabeth so as to take away this disgrace exhibits the Lord's approval of *her* piety just as his promising a son for Zechariah exhibited the Lord's approval of *his* piety. Luke wants us to know that those who lie at the base of Jesus' story are good people, as are Jesus himself and his later followers. Join up. You'll like the company.

THE PROMISE OF MARY'S PREGNANCY
Luke 1:26–38

1:26–29: And in the sixth month [of Elizabeth's pregnancy] **the angel Gabriel was sent from God** [and therefore *by* God] **into a city of Galilee that had the name Nazareth, 27to a virgin engaged to a man named Joseph from the household of David** [that is, descended from King David]; **and the virgin's name** [was] **Mary. 28And on coming in to her, he said, "Rejoice, favored one; the Lord** [is] **with you!" 29But she was very perplexed at this saying and pondered what sort of greeting this might be.** The details of chronology, geography, and personal and place names breathe the air of factuality that suits Luke's purpose of providing a solid historical basis for Christian faith. God's sending Gabriel, as he'd sent him to promise John's supernatural birth, leads us to expect another startling promise. The designation of Mary as a virgin marks her as chaste, in line with Luke's theme of Jesus' people as admirably moral, and prepares for a child-bearing that will surpass even the birth of John to parents too old to have had a child naturally. And the designation of her as engaged to a descendent of David prepares for the birth of a son who'll occupy the Davidic throne, for legal rights—like throne rights—passed through the father's ancestral line even though he was only a foster father. Ordinarily, the greeting "Rejoice" meant no more than "Hello." But the following address, "favored one," and declaration, "the Lord [is] with you," suggest the stronger, literal translation, "Rejoice," because the Lord's favor and personal presence are matters to get happy about. There is, in fact, something of a wordplay in Luke's original text; for both "Rejoice" and "favored one" go back to the same root and therefore share some letters (*chaire* and *kecharitōmenē*), almost as if to say, "Rejoice, you who've been made [by the Lord] to rejoice."

Mary doesn't understand just how or why it is she's favored with the Lord's presence. So Gabriel explains in **1:30–33: And the angel said to her, "Don't fear, Mary,**

for you've found favor with God. 31And behold, you'll conceive and give birth to a son. And you shall call his name Jesus. 32This** [son] **will be great, and he'll be called the Son of the Highest. And the Lord God will give him the throne of David his** [fore]**father, 33and he'll reign forever over the household of Jacob** [= the nation of Israel, compared to a household, "Israel" being the other name of Jacob, whose twelve sons fathered the twelve tribes of Israel]. **And there'll be no end of his reign."** "Don't fear," plus Gabriel's addressing Mary by name, adds assurance to the initial greeting. "You've found favor with God" portrays her as yet another good person, like Zechariah and Elizabeth. But it also indicates that God is *treating* her with a favor, which Gabriel goes on to explain, introducing it with an exclamatory "behold." It's the promise that she'll conceive and give birth to a son. As in the case of John, God's stepping in to determine the son's name indicates that God has special plans for Mary's son. Since it was a father who normally named his son (as Zechariah will name John), the command that *Mary* should name her son "Jesus" implies that he won't have a human father, at least not a biological one. Indeed, he'll be great not just in the Lord's sight, as John will be (1:15), but great as the Son of the Highest, that is, of God as the highest of all beings and so-called gods. No higher sonship than this! He'll be *called* such because he'll *be* such. Because he'll be the Son of the Highest, the Lord God—who is the Highest—will give him the throne of his ancestor David. As a result, he'll reign over Israel forever, without end. The Davidic character of his reign establishes continuity between the gospel of Jesus and Israel's history and religion. Luke stresses tradition, not novelty.

1:34–38: But Mary said to the angel, "How will this be, since I don't know a man [that is, haven't had sexual intercourse with a male]**?"** Mary doesn't ask how she can *know* that this child-bearing will happen, as Zechariah did in unbelief (1:18–20). She accepts that it *will* happen and asks only *how* it will, given her virginity and the assumption that she'll conceive before having sex with Joseph. The command that she should name her son had implied that he wouldn't have Joseph or any other human being as a biological father. That implication, buttressed by the son's being called "the Son of the Highest," wasn't lost on her. So she gets an explanation. 35**And answering, the angel told her, "The Holy Spirit will come on you, and the power of the Highest will overshadow you. Therefore also the** [infant] **being generated** [as] **holy will be called God's Son."** *Generated* as holy because, like the Holy Spirit, he'll be holy—that is, not born of illegitimate parentage, but consecrated for the sacred task of reigning over the household of Jacob forever. *Called* God's Son because he'll *be* God's Son. So the power of the Highest, working through his Holy Spirit, will be the means by which Mary will conceive in a state of virginity and give birth to a son. To this explanation Gabriel adds some encouragement: 36**"And behold, your relative Elizabeth—even she has conceived a son in her old age, and this is the sixth**

month [of pregnancy] **for her who's called barren** [because she *is* barren till she bears a child]! [37]**For nothing will be impossible with God."** The encouragement consists in news of another pregnancy. "Behold" makes this news, too, exclamatory. "Your relative Elizabeth" makes it near and dear and readily available for checking. "This is the sixth month" also makes it readily *observable* for checking. "For her who's called barren," "even she," and "in her old age"—these three expressions put a triple emphasis on Elizabeth's pregnancy as supernatural, as Mary's will be. Luke uses the supernatural to undergird Christian faith. And, as Gabriel says, the basis of this supernatural pregnancy is that nothing is impossible with God in the picture. [38]**And Mary said** [referring to herself], **"Behold, the Lord's slave! May it happen to me according to your word." And the angel went away from her.** She *willingly* submits to the role of service that God has favored her with. There's a wordplay in the very word "word," because in Luke's original text this word is the same as what's translated "thing" in "no*thing* will be impossible with God." The wordplay suggests that no *word* of God, such as the word about her conceiving as a virgin and giving birth to a son, will prove impossible of fulfillment. His mission accomplished, Gabriel leaves. Unlike Zechariah, Mary needs no punitive guarantee; for she has believed and submitted. Luke wants us to note her piety, which recommends the gospel about her son.

MARY'S VISIT WITH ELIZABETH
Luke 1:39–56

This passage is framed by Mary's going to visit her relative Elizabeth (1:39–40) and leaving for home after the visit (1:56). The visit itself features Elizabeth's and fetal John's responses of recognition and blessing (1:41–45) and Mary's paean of praise to God (1:46–55).

1:39–40: **And on getting up** [presumably from a seated position in which she'd received Gabriel's message], **Mary traveled with haste during these days into the mountainous** [region, specifically]**, into a city of Judah** [= of Judea, territory allotted in the Old Testament to the tribe of Judah]. [40]**And she entered into the house of Zechariah and greeted Elizabeth.** People in Luke's world were fascinated with travel and did a lot of it. So the reference to Mary's traveling to visit Elizabeth appeals to this fascination. (The same goes for Luke's many further references to travel.) "During these days" refers to the time of Gabriel's appearance to Mary and puts her journey right afterward. "With haste" describes the journey itself. Why the hurry? Good news can't wait to be shared, and the story of Jesus is good news. Added to these chronological details are geographical and topographical details ("into the mountainous [region]," "into a city of Judah," and "into the house of Zechariah"). Such details provide Luke's narrative with data aimed at our recognizing its historical "certainty" (1:4).

1:41–45: **And it happened that when Elizabeth heard Mary's greeting, the infant** [whom Zechariah

was to name John] **jumped around in her womb. And Elizabeth was filled with the Holy Spirit** [42]**and cried out with a loud shout and said, "Favored** [are] **you among women, and favored** [is] **the fruit of your womb** [the infant you're going to bear]**.** [43]**And from where** [is] **this to me, that the mother of my Lord should come to me?** [Where does this privilege come from? I can hardly believe it!] [44]**For behold, when the sound of your greeting came into my ears, the infant in my womb jumped around with gladness!** [45]**And fortunate** [is] **she who believed that there'll be a completion for the things spoken to her from the Lord."** "When Elizabeth heard Mary's greeting" indicates immediate recognition of the unborn Jesus by the unborn John. So the virgin Mary has already conceived. Did she conceive as soon as she said to Gabriel, "Behold, the Lord's slave! May it happen to me according to your word" (1:38)? John's immediate recognition of Jesus takes the form of body language (jumping around in Elizabeth's womb), comes about through John's being filled with the Holy Spirit in fulfillment of Gabriel's saying in 1:15 that he'd be filled with the Holy Spirit "while still in his mother's womb," and provides divine substantiation for the good news about Jesus.

To add verbal language to the body language and provide further substantiation, Elizabeth too is filled with the Holy Spirit. The loudness of her resultant speech gives evidence of being filled and adds force to her Spirit-inspired outburst. Elizabeth pronounces favor on both Mary and Jesus ("the fruit of your womb" confirming that Mary is already pregnant). Because of Gabriel's announcement, it's evident that this favor comes from God. It also fits Luke's program of recommending the gospel by portraying Jesus and those associated with him as worthy of favor. For if they're worthy of God's favor, they're certainly worthy of favor from Luke's audience. The worthiness of Elizabeth herself comes out in the self-deprecation of her wondering how come she gets the privilege of a visit "from the mother of [her] Lord." Mary's being much her junior highlights the humility in Elizabeth's self-deprecation. And calling the fetal Jesus her "Lord" likewise displays humility. John's recognition of Jesus and its immediacy come in for a second and therefore emphatic—indeed, exclamatory—mention, this time by Elizabeth herself. And she adds that her infant jumped around "with gladness." Gabriel said there'd be gladness *at* John's birth (1:14). But John jumps with gladness even *before* Jesus' birth. That's better yet. The traditional translation, "blessed [is]," doesn't mean "happy [is]." It means "fortunate [is]" or "congratulations to." Elizabeth congratulates Mary because of her belief. So unlike Zechariah, who disbelieved (1:20), Mary becomes a model of belief in "the word" of the gospel, the belief that Luke wants to generate in us his audience. Which is to say that Mary's belief in the "completion"— that is, the carrying out—of the things Gabriel told her gives us a model for believing what remains to be carried out in the further part of Luke-Acts. Since Elizabeth is speaking to Mary, we might have expected "fortunate

[are] *you* who believed" and "the things spoken to *you*." Instead we read "fortunate [is] *she* who believed" and "the things spoken to *her*," as though Elizabeth is talking to *us* about Mary. The switch from Elizabeth's earlier "you" and "your" to "she" and "her" helps Luke present Mary as a model of believing.

1:46–49: And Mary said, "My soul magnifies the Lord, ⁴⁷and my spirit was glad because of God my Savior, ⁴⁸because he looked on the low status of his [female] slave. For behold, from now on all generations will call me fortunate, ⁴⁹because the Able One has done great things for me, and his name is holy." These and following verses draw heavily on the Old Testament, especially on 1 Samuel 2:1–10. In the present statements, Mary centers on what God has done for her. To magnify the Lord is to call attention to his greatness. Her present magnification of the Lord derives from the gladness she had when Gabriel, sent from God, announced to her that she'd conceive and give birth to God's Son. Mary's "soul" and "spirit" synonymously represent the inward, emotional source of her magnification and gladness. Her calling God "my Savior" starts the theme of salvation that will attain much prominence throughout Luke-Acts and include both the deliverance of Israel from her enemies, exorcisms and physical healings, and forgiveness of sin. Luke doesn't say exactly what Mary had in mind, but the highly personal "*my* Savior" suggests something akin to Acts 16:30–31: "'What must I do to be saved?' . . . 'Believe on the Lord Jesus, and you'll be saved—also your household.'" In any case, Mary models belief in God as Savior. God's looking on her low status equates with his doing great things for her, that is, enabling her as a virgin to conceive his Son. In one way or another, then, God's being her Savior has to do with Jesus as God's Son, whom she is carrying. What way that is will come out later. Mary's calling herself God's slave echoes what she said to Gabriel in 1:38 and reminds us of her humble submission to the task God assigned her. She calls God "the Able One" in recollection of Gabriel's statement that "nothing will be impossible with God" (1:37, translated more literally, "With God nothing will be *unable* [to be done]"). "Powerful One" is another good translation in that God is powerful enough to do anything he wants (compare 1:35: "the power of the Highest"). Mary declares God's *name* to be "holy" because *he* is holy, and the holiness of his name as "the Able/Powerful One" consists in the uniqueness of his power. He has done the seemingly impossible in Mary's virginal conception of Jesus. Whereas Mary believed *that* God would make her conceive supernaturally, we're called to believe because he *did* act supernaturally in that way.

Mary continues in *1:50–55*, but switches to what God has done in her conception of Jesus for all his people: **"And his mercy [extends] to generations and generations [= to one generation after another] for those who fear him. ⁵¹He has performed a powerful deed with his arm [a figure of speech for power in action]. He has scattered those who are arrogant in the thinking** of their heart. **⁵²He has brought down mighty [rulers] from [their] thrones and lifted up lowly people. ⁵³He has filled hungry people with good things, and people who are wealthy he has sent away empty. ⁵⁴He has helped Israel his servant by remembering mercy, ⁵⁵just as he spoke to our [fore]fathers, to Abraham and his seed [= descendants], forever."** The extension of God's mercy to one generation after another highlights the continuity of Jesus' story with Israel's divinely managed past history. "For those who fear him" concentrates God's mercy on the righteous, like Zechariah and Elizabeth (1:6) and—later—Gentiles who fear God and therefore affiliate themselves with Judaism. Luke persists in laying a traditional and moral basis for the gospel. The "powerful deed" that God has performed is his Spirit's causing Mary to conceive Jesus despite her virginity. The gospel's moral basis reappears in the justice of God's scattering those who have an arrogant attitude, dethroning rulers who misuse their might, lifting up their beaten-down victims, filling with delicious food ("good things") those who've gone hungry because of those abusive, arrogant rulers, and dismissing the wealthy so that they can't eat at table. It's understood that they've gotten their wealth at the expense of the poor. The past tense in "has performed," "has scattered," "has brought down," "has lifted up," "has filled," and "has sent away"—this past tense points to a future justice which God is so sure to establish that it can be spoken of as already done. Likewise in regard to God's helping the nation of Israel: their deliverance from foreign oppression is so sure to come that it might as well have come already. And it'll come because God mercifully remembers forever his covenantal promise made for the benefit of Abraham and his descendants. Again, then, the story of Jesus and—in Luke's second volume, the book of Acts—the story of the church carry forward the story of Israel. Continuity, not disruption. Tradition, not novelty. God is working out his plan from ages past into the present and throughout eternity. And all is going to happen because of God's acting in and through his Son Jesus, whom Mary has conceived and is carrying in her womb.

1:56: And Mary stayed with her [Elizabeth] about three months and returned to her home. John's birth has yet to occur; so Mary stays with Elizabeth for most of Elizabeth's last trimester but leaves just before the birth of John. Since then it was already the sixth month of Elizabeth's pregnancy when Gabriel appeared to Mary (1:36), Mary's staying with Elizabeth about three months prior to John's birth implies that Mary went to visit Elizabeth right after Gabriel appeared to Mary. She returns to "*her* home," not Joseph's, because they're still unmarried (see also 2:5).

FROM THE BIRTH OF JOHN
THROUGH HIS BOYHOOD
Luke 1:57–80

In this passage, 1:57–58 takes up the birth of John. His naming comes in 1:59–66. In 1:67–79 Zechariah prophesies concerning him and, indirectly, concerning Jesus. And 1:80 deals with John's maturation.

1:57–58: And for Elizabeth the time for her to give birth was fulfilled, and she bore a son. 58 And her neighbors and relatives heard that the Lord had magnified his mercy with her, and they were rejoicing with her. God is a promise-keeper. His promise to Zechariah that Elizabeth his wife would bear a son for him (1:13) has now reached fulfillment. The rejoicing together of her and her neighbors and relatives also fulfills the promise in 1:14 that "many will rejoice because of [John's] birth." These fulfillments exemplify the many fulfilling events that make for "the certainty" of "the words" constituting "the word" of the gospel (1:1–4). "The Lord had magnified his mercy with her" means in Elizabeth's case that he'd displayed his mercy in a big way. After all, she'd passed the age of child-bearing.

1:59–63: And it happened that on the eighth day they [the neighbors and relatives] **came to circumcise the little child.** God had instituted circumcision as the physical sign of his covenant with Israel, and it was to take place on the eighth day after birth (Genesis 17:9–14; 21:4; Leviticus 12:3; Philippians 3:5). So Luke is pointing out the obedience of John's parents, the neighbors, and the relatives. And John himself becomes a properly circumcised Jewish male. Luke's point: Christianity didn't originate in religious apostasy. It arose out of religious piety. **And they** [the neighbors and relatives] **were trying to call him after the name of his father, Zechariah.** 60 **And answering** [= responding to their attempt], **his mother said, "No! Rather, he'll be called John."** Either Elizabeth had overheard Gabriel's message to Zechariah that the son should be called John or, being mute, Zechariah had previously written out this name for her to see. 61 **And they said to her, "There's no one from your kinfolk who's called by this name."** 62 **And they were gesticulating to his father as to what he might want him to be called.** So Zechariah is deaf as well as mute. Otherwise they'd merely speak to him. Deafness and muteness often go together, of course. 63 **And on requesting a little tablet** [made of wood covered with wax (he must have made the request by gesticulating in return)], **he wrote, saying** [in his writing, not with his mouth and tongue, for he was still mute], **"John is his name."** So Zechariah obeys the Lord's injunction through Gabriel, "And you shall call his name John" (1:13). The contrary pressure of neighbors and relatives makes this obedience particularly admirable. **And they all marveled.** Their surprise underlines Zechariah's obedience yet again. That "they *all* marveled" magnifies the earlier social pressure to name the son "Zechariah" and thereby makes Zechariah's obedience all the more admirable. Luke doesn't tire of drumming up admiration for those who advance the story of Jesus, as he will for Jesus himself.

1:64–66: And his mouth was opened immediately, and his tongue [was loosened], **and he was speaking by way of praising God.** Here's the fulfillment of God's word through Gabriel that Zechariah wouldn't be able to talk "*until* the day that these things have taken place" (1:20). And to the piety of obedience to God's command that Zechariah name his son John is added the piety of Zechariah's speaking well of God (the literal meaning of "praising" him). 65 **And fear came on all their neighbors, and all these things** [= events] **were being discussed in the whole of the mountainous** [region] **of Judea,** 66 **and all who'd heard put** [these events] **in their heart** [that is, reflected on them], **saying, "What then will this little child be?"** What's in store for him when he grows up? What role will he play? **For also the hand of the Lord was with him.** This last statement explains the just-mentioned fear, discussion, and reflection. Fear is the appropriate response of pious people to God's powerful actions. "*All* their neighbors," "in the *whole* of the mountainous [region] of Judea," and "*all* who heard" magnify the impact of "*all* these things." They consist in Elizabeth's miraculous conception and birthing of a son, in the unusual naming of him, and in the removal of muteness from Zechariah as soon as he named his son John. The events didn't happen in a corner. They were open to public observation, confirmation, discussion, and reflection—and thus contribute to Luke's gospel of "certainty" (1:4). That the Lord's hand was with John means that the Lord was powerfully active in his birth.

In 1:67–79 Zechariah speaks under the Holy Spirit's influence. Strikingly, the first part of his speech alludes not to what God will do through Zechariah's son John but to what God will do through his own Son Jesus (1:68–75). Only then does Zechariah speak about his son John (1:76–79). **1:67–75: And Zechariah his father was filled with the Holy Spirit and prophesied, saying,** 68 **"Praised** [be] **the Lord God of Israel, because he has visited** [his people, that is, come to their aid] **and accomplished redemption for his people** [= their liberation from slavery] 69 **and raised up for us a horn of salvation in the household of David his servant** 70 **just as he spoke through the mouth of his holy prophets since long ago—** 71 **salvation from our enemies and from the hand** [= power] **of all who hate us,** 72 **so as to accomplish mercy with** [respect to] **our** [fore]**fathers and remember his holy covenant,** 73 [that is,] **the oath that he swore to Abraham our** [fore]**father** 74 **to give us** [that we,] **having been rescued from the hand of** [our] **enemies, might serve him in his sight fearlessly** 75 **with devoutness and righteousness all our days."** The Holy Spirit's filling Zechariah enables him to prophesy. As in the case of Elizabeth at 1:41–45, his prophecy adds verbal language to body language. Throughout Luke-Acts, being filled with the Holy Spirit gives observable and therefore credible evidence of God's powerful activity. Zechariah's prophecy starts with praise to God, as befits Zechariah's piety, but immediately proceeds to the reason for such praise, namely, God's salvation. The salvation is yet to come but is so sure to come that it's put in a past tense ("has visited . . . and accomplished . . . and raised up"). The salvation consists in the deliverance of Israel from foreign oppression in merciful fulfillment of past prophecies and of God's covenantal promises to

Israel's patriarchs, beginning with Abraham (Genesis 12:1–3; 15:1–20; 17:1–21; 22:15–18; 26:2–5, 24). (Note the designation of the Lord as *Israel's* God, and the synonymity of "Israel," "his people," and "us.") In this way Luke portrays the Christian gospel as a carrying forward of God's long-established plan for Israel. It'll turn out that the unbelief of most Jews will delay God's political deliverance of Israel, but eventually it will come (13:31–35; 19:44; 22:30; Acts 3:21 [compare Acts 1:6–8]). Meanwhile, Luke is content to stress, as often, the continuity of Jesus' story with the Old Testament. "To *accomplish* mercy" is to *do* something merciful, and "to *remember* his holy covenant" is not to forget the promise contained in the covenantal oath, but to keep it. "With [respect to] our [fore]fathers" means in consideration of the promise given to the patriarchs.

Jesus comes into the picture as "the horn of salvation." Like "hand" and "arm," "horn" is a figure of speech for active power, because an animal with horns uses them in combat to overcome foes. We know that "the horn of salvation" refers figuratively to Jesus, not to John, for God has raised up the horn "in the household of David." Jesus was a legal descendant of King David, who belonged to the tribe of Judah (1:32), whereas John belonged to the tribe of Levi since his father was a priest (and, to boot, his mother a descendant of Aaron [1:5]). The purpose of Israel's rescue from foreign domination is that the Jews might serve God emotionally without fear of persecution from their oppressors, religiously with devoutness in their attitude toward God, morally with righteousness in their conduct, and chronologically for as long as they live.

Zechariah now addresses his infant son in **1:76–79**: **"And also you, child** [in addition to 'the holy prophets' of 'long ago'], **will be called a prophet of the Highest; for you will go before the Lord to prepare his ways,** [77]**to give his people knowledge of salvation in the forgiveness of their sins** [78]**because of the entrails of our God's mercy, with which** [entrails] **the [sun]rise from the height** [of heaven] **will look on us** [79]**so as to shine on those sitting in darkness and death's shadow, so as to direct our feet in the way of peace."** "The Highest" is God, also called "the Lord." John will be *called* a prophet of the Highest because he'll *be* a prophet of God. His being such will entail preparing the Lord's ways ahead of the Lord's traveling them. The plural of "ways" probably refers to the variety of things the Lord will do as outlined in 1:68–75 (looking on his people, accomplishing redemption for them, raising up a horn of salvation for them, and so forth). The Lord will act in these ways through his Son Jesus, so that John's going before the Lord *amounts to* going before Jesus even though "the Lord" refers here to God, not to Jesus, and prepares for Jesus' being called "Christ, the Lord" in 2:11.

"His people" are Israel. Giving them "the *knowledge* of salvation" means giving them the *experience* of salvation. This experience will consist in God's forgiving their sins. Luke will narrate the fulfillment of this prophecy, and Gabriel's similar one at 1:17, in his account of John's

ministry (see especially 3:1–6). "Entrails" is a figure of speech for deep emotions, here God's emotion of pity for his oppressed people. This pity ("mercy") will characterize "the [sun]rise from the height [of heaven]" that will look on them. The sun doesn't literally rise from the *height* of heaven, though. So saying that it will is a figurative way of emphasizing the divine origin of the light of salvation that will mercifully shine on those sitting in the darkness of impending death at the hands of their enemies. And the Lord's purpose of directing the feet of those presently benighted people "in the way of peace" means getting them into a situation where they'll enjoy both freedom from oppressors and what politicians sometimes call "peacetime prosperity." The light of sunshine will make it possible for them to walk the path to this peace.

1:80: **And the little child was growing and getting strong in spirit, and he was in the deserted places** [probably the Judean wilderness] **until the day of his public appearance to Israel.** Physical growth and spiritual strengthening complement each other. Luke is pointing up the well-roundedness of John's maturation. Staying in deserted places probably implies the death of his aged parents; but Luke's point has to do with the contrast between John's dramatic appearance on the public stage, which Luke will introduce with great fanfare (3:1–6), and the seclusion of John's intervening years.

JESUS' BIRTH AND ASSOCIATED EVENTS
Luke 2:1–21

This passage takes up the birth of Jesus (2:1–7), the visit of the shepherds (2:8–20), and the circumcision and naming of Jesus (2:21).

For Jesus' birth Luke again provides a historical frame of reference (as in 1:5), though this time in greater detail and thus with greater fanfare (as also in 3:1–2). The greater fanfare suits the occasion of Jesus' birth, and the historical frame of reference suits Luke's intention to display "the certainty" of Christian faith (1:4). **2:1–3: And it happened in those days that a decree went out from Caesar Augustus** [ruler of the Roman Empire] **for all the inhabited** [earth] **to get registered.** [2]**This registration happened as the first** [one] **while Quirinius was governor of Syria.** [3]**And all were traveling to get registered, each to his own city.** Mary had just gotten pregnant when she visited Elizabeth in the sixth month of Elizabeth's pregnancy, and Mary left just before Elizabeth gave birth to John. So Mary was about three months pregnant when John was born. Since she's now going to give birth to Jesus, "in those days" refers to the last of her remaining six months of pregnancy. It's commonly assumed that the registration decreed by Caesar Augustus had to do with taxation. Luke doesn't say so, though. His point has to do, rather, with the registration as a means of getting Jesus, to whom "the Lord God will give the throne of David his [fore]father" (1:32), born "in the city of David," namely, David's hometown of Bethlehem (2:4, 11 [compare Micah 5:2]). In other words, the empire-wide registration plays into God's plan for Jesus' birth. ("All the inhabited [earth]" is a way of referring to the Roman Empire.) "As the first [registration]" seems to imply more than one registration, and "while Quirinius was governor of Syria" narrows Luke's purview down from the empire to a portion of it in which Galilee and Judea, about to be mentioned, are located. It's the traveling of each to get registered in his own city that in particular gets Jesus born in David's city; for "his own city" means the city of his ancestors, and Joseph was descended from David (1:27).

2:4–5: And Joseph, too, went up from Galilee out of the city of Nazareth into Judea, into David's city, which is called Bethlehem, because he was from David's household and family [line], ⁵in order to get registered—along with Mary, being pregnant, who'd been engaged to him. Luke doesn't tell whether Joseph and Mary were yet married; but even if they were, the reference to engagement implies that the marriage hadn't been consummated, so that Jesus' birth as well as conception will be virginal (compare the comments on Matthew 1:18–25). In line with his usual portrayal of those associated with Jesus as good people, Luke portrays Joseph as an obedient subject of Caesar. The accompaniment of Mary despite her pregnancy (late term as it was) ensures Jesus' birth in David's city. The journey from Nazareth to Bethlehem was about ninety miles, and we have no way of knowing whether Mary rode an animal or walked. But it's the location of Jesus' birth, not hardship on Mary, that concerns Luke.

2:6–7: And it happened that when they were there, the days were fulfilled for her to give birth. ⁷And she gave birth to her firstborn son and wrapped him in strips of cloth and laid him in a feed trough, because there wasn't space for them in the lodging place. So God fulfills his promise to Mary through Gabriel. "Her *firstborn* son" prepares for her and Joseph's obeying in 2:22–24 God's law concerning firstborn males and also points toward Jesus' being "called holy [= set apart] for the Lord" (2:23), particularly (in this context) set apart for kingship. By wrapping her baby in strips of cloth, Mary shows herself a dutiful mother; for such was the custom to keep baby's limbs straight. "A feed trough" implies a stable and thus prepares for the visit of shepherds—suitably in view of David's having been a shepherd and Jesus' destiny as a Davidic king. The lack of space in the lodging place serves this suitability rather than casting aspersions of inhospitality on an innkeeper, who in any case makes no appearance whatever. "A feed trough" suggests that the Holy Family took refuge in an animal shelter.

2:8–14: And shepherds were in the same region living outdoors and keeping guard over their flock during the night [more literally, "guard-watching the guard-watches of the night over their flock"]. *⁹And an angel of the Lord came and stood over them, and the glory of the Lord shone around them, and they feared a great fear* [that is, they were terrified]. The

shepherds remind us again of David, the shepherd-king whose throne Jesus will occupy. The nighttime makes all the more dramatic and terrifying the appearance of an angel of the Lord and the shining of the Lord's own glory "*around* them"—as though they *could* mistake it or escape it! They know for certain what they see and now hear: *¹⁰And the angel told them, "Stop being afraid. For behold, I'm announcing to you as good news a great joy, which will be for all the people* [of Israel (see 1:33, 54–55, 68–79)], *¹¹because today there has been born for you in the city of David a Savior, who is Christ, the Lord. ¹²And the sign for you* [is] *this: you'll find a baby wrapped in strips of cloth and lying in a feed trough."* "In the city of David" recaptures Jesus' destiny to occupy David's throne in fulfillment of both Old Testament prophecy and Gabriel's prediction in 1:32–33. As "Christ," meaning "anointed" for God's special service, Jesus will exercise his kingship as "Savior" of Israel from foreign oppression. As "Lord," he'll have the ability to succeed. His birth "today" brings him close at hand. Good news worthy of great joy indeed! "The sign" will guarantee this good news—for us as well as for the shepherds. But they'll be the eyewitnesses who'll then relay the sign to Luke, who's now relaying it to us ("that you may know the certainty of the words about which you were instructed" [1:4]). *¹³And suddenly there came on the scene, along with the angel, a multitude of the heavenly army* [of angels], *praising God and saying, ¹⁴"Glory* [= honor] [is] *in the highest* [places (that is, in heaven)] *to God, and peace* [= all the blessings of salvation] [is] *on earth among human beings of* [God's] *good pleasure* [that is, among those in whom he has taken delight]." So to the *earthly* sign of finding a baby wrapped in strips of cloth and lying in a feed trough is added this *heavenly* sign of an angelic army praising God for the birth of the Savior, who is Christ the Lord. A double guarantee of certainty! Heaven itself rings with praise to God for his bringing to earth the peace of salvation for people like Zechariah, Elizabeth, and Mary who pleasure him with their piety. This "good news" of "great joy" is "for *all* the people," like the shepherds (2:10), but it'll be *realized* only among those who have mended, or will mend, their ways.

2:15–16: And it happened that when the angels went away from them into heaven, the shepherds were saying to one another, "By all means, let's go as far as Bethlehem and see this thing that has taken place, which the Lord [through his angel] *has made known to us." ¹⁶And hurrying, they went and found both Mary and Joseph and the baby, lying in the feed trough.* The angels' departure "away from [the shepherds] into heaven" shows they'd been so close to the shepherds that the shepherds couldn't have mistaken what they saw and heard. Their knowledge was God-given and so certain that they emphasize with "By all means" their determination to go to Bethlehem. Luke doesn't say how far away they were from Bethlehem, but "as far as Bethlehem" implies some distance. The news is so good and joyful and guaranteed by the angels, though, that no distance can deter the shepherds from going to see "this thing" which was made known in "this word" of the Lord. (The word for "thing" also means "word.") And not just *going* as far as Bethlehem. Also *hurrying* there. Sure enough, they find baby Jesus lying in the aforementioned feed trough. But for "wrapped in strips of cloth" (as spoken by an angel of the Lord in 2:12) Luke substitutes "Mary and Joseph" to remind us of Jesus' legal descent from David through his foster father. Because of the virgin birth, though, Luke mentions Mary before Joseph. The shepherds' finding what the angel promised they'd find makes the gospel credible.

2:17-20: And on seeing [this thing]**, they made known** [the information] **concerning the word that had been spoken to them concerning this little child.** [18]**And all who heard marveled at the things that were told them by the shepherds.** By making known to others what the Lord had made known to them and they had found to be true, the shepherds act as "assistants of the word" (1:2), the certainty of which Luke is writing to set forth. Those who hear the shepherds' report marvel because the news is good and joyful. That "all" who heard it marvel underscores how good and joyful it is. [19]**But Mary was preserving all these things** [= words and events] **by throwing** [them] **together in her heart** [= organizing them in her thoughts and memory]. Here Luke hints broadly that the information about Jesus' birth derives from Mary herself and therefore merits belief. [20]**And the shepherds returned** [to their flocks]**, glorifying and praising God because of all the things they'd heard and seen, just as they** [those things] **had been told to them.** Added to Mary's long-term memory and to the shepherds' already mentioned report to *others* is the shepherds' glorifying and praising *God*. True religion, Luke wants us to know, has a vertical as well as horizontal axis. And the gospel represents true religion admirably (for Luke's continuation of this theme, see also 5:25-26; 7:16; 13:13; 17:15, 18; 18:43; 23:47; Acts 4:21; 11:18; 13:48; 21:20 and compare Luke 2:14; 19:38; Acts 12:23). "*All* the things they'd heard and seen"—not one of those things fell short of redounding to God's glory and praise, for none of them had failed to correspond to what the shepherds had been told. And "*heard* and *seen*" makes them both earwitnesses and eyewitnesses to gospel truth.

2:21: And when eight days were fulfilled for circumcising him [compare the comments on 1:59]**, his name was also called Jesus,** [that is,] **the** [name] **called** [= specified] **by the angel before he was conceived in the womb** [1:31]. Keeping the law of circumcision on exactly the right day shows Joseph and Mary to be good Jews—obedient to the law of Moses as well as to the decree of Caesar Augustus—and Jesus to be a valid Jewish male. Luke mentions the circumcision in passing so as to maintain continuity between Judaism and Christianity. But obeying the angel's command to name the baby "Jesus" looms even more important than obeying the Mosaic law. So Luke puts the naming in a main

clause (the circumcision being a sidelight), reminds us of the angel's command, and even reminds us that the command came prior to Jesus' conception. Mary didn't forget.

EVENTS IN JERUSALEM
Luke 2:22-39

This passage divides into four parts: (1) the Holy Family's going to Jerusalem to keep the law of Moses (2:22-24); (2) Simeon's praise and prophecy in the temple (2:25-35); (3) Anna's thanksgiving and broadcast in the temple (2:36-38); and (4) the holy family's return to Nazareth after keeping the Mosaic law (2:39).

2:22-24: And when the days of their purification were fulfilled according to the law of Moses, they [Joseph and Mary] **brought him** [Jesus] **up to Jerusalem** [from Bethlehem] **to present** [him] **to the Lord,** [23]**just as it's written in the law of the Lord, "Every male that opens a womb shall be called holy** [set apart, consecrated] **for the Lord** [Exodus 13:2, 11-15; 22:29; 34:19-20; Numbers 3:13]**,"** [24]**and to give a sacrifice in accordance with what's written in the law of the Lord, "a pair of turtledoves or two young pigeons** [literally, 'two young ones of pigeons'] **[Leviticus 5:11; 12:8]."** "*Their* purification" refers to the purification of Joseph and Mary. The Mosaic law required for poor people the sacrifice of two turtledoves or pigeons for the ritual purification of a mother forty days after she gave birth to her first son (Leviticus 12:1-4, 6). But Luke includes Joseph with Mary in the purification to enhance his portrayal of them as Law-abiding Jews. And to Jesus' circumcision on the eighth day is now added his presentation as a firstborn son to the Lord. Notably, Joseph and Mary present him *to* the Lord rather than redeeming him *from* the Lord with a payment of five silver shekels, as provided for in the Mosaic law (Numbers 18:15-16). Consequently, at the age of twelve Jesus will expect his parents to know that he must be in the house of God his Father (2:49). Gabriel's designation of Jesus as "the Son of the Highest" (1:32) deters Mary and Joseph from taking advantage of the provision for redeeming a firstborn son. For Jesus everything is now in good religious order. There's no reason to fault his Jewish qualifications. All in all, then, Joseph's and Mary's obedience is chronological ("when the days of their purification were fulfilled"), topographical ("up to Jerusalem"), dedicatory ("to present [Jesus] to the Lord"), sacrificial ("to give a sacrifice"), and—above all—legal ("according to the law of Moses . . . just as it's written in the law of the Lord . . . in accordance with what's written in the law of the Lord").

2:25-26: And behold, there was a man in Jerusalem who had the name Simeon; and this man [was] **righteous and devout, waiting expectantly for the consolation of Israel. And the Holy Spirit was on him.** [26]**And it was disclosed to him by the Holy Spirit that** [he] **wouldn't see death before he'd seen the Lord's Christ.** Luke delights in highlighting the moral and religious excellence of those making positive contributions to Jesus' story. And the Lord showed his delight in Simeon as one such person by putting his Spirit on him and promising him that he'd see the Christ before dying. The promise came in response to Simeon's expectant waiting for Israel's "consolation," which means God's comforting Israel by delivering them from foreign oppression. "The *Lord's* Christ" refers to Jesus as anointed by the Lord to bring this consolation. *Seeing* the Lord's Christ will make Simeon one of the eyewitnesses whose testimony produces the gospel's "certainty" (1:1–4). The Holy Spirit's disclosure provides him with a divine interpretation of what he'll see. And the mention of Simeon's name, location, and description testify to Luke's careful investigation of tradition to prepare for writing this Gospel (see 1:1–4 again). So the investigation, Simeon's eyewitness, and the Spirit's interpretation combine to triple the gospel's certainty. As Ecclesiastes 4:12 says, "A threefold cord is not quickly broken."

2:27–33: And he came in the Spirit into the temple [courts and cloisters, not into the sanctuary proper, where only priests and other members of the tribe of Levi could go]. **And when the parents brought in the little child Jesus in order that they might act according to what was required by the Law concerning him** [see the comments on 2:23], **²⁸even he himself** [Simeon] **received him** [Jesus] **into** [his] **arms and praised God and said, ²⁹"Now, Master, you are dismissing your slave in peace according to your word, ³⁰because my eyes have seen your salvation, ³¹which you've prepared before the face of all the peoples, ³²**[the salvation that's] **a light for revelation to Gentiles and** [for] **your people Israel's glory." ³³And his** [Jesus'] **father and mother were marveling at the things being spoken about him.** On top of the Spirit's disclosure to Simeon, Luke adds the Spirit's arranging Simeon's meeting up with the holy family in the temple. This meeting has the purpose of fulfilling the promise disclosed to Simeon ("your word," as Simeon calls it in addressing God). We can trust God's word. Luke reemphasizes Joseph's and Mary's obedience to God's law. Simeon's receiving Jesus carries the connotation of welcoming something offered. As implied in the disclosed promise and Simeon's upcoming praise, the offerer is God; and Simeon's welcoming reception of the offered child grows out of his expectant waiting for Israel's consolation. "Into his arms" strikes an attractive note of tenderness: Simeon cradles the baby Jesus as he (Simeon) praises God, that is, speaks well of him. In his praise of God (itself an evidence of piety), Simeon calls God "Master" (with emphasis on sovereignty) and himself God's "slave." This high privilege hasn't gone to his head.

Most translations have Simeon saying, "Now [that I've seen your Christ, O Master], *dismiss* your slave . . . [or '*let* your slave depart . . .']." That translation is possible, but it would be unusual. So it's better to translate, "Now, Master, you *are* dismissing . . . ," to indicate that the Lord is in the process of dismissing Simeon from this mortal coil now that he has seen the Lord's Christ.

In other words, Simeon knows he's going to die now. But he's dying "in peace," which probably doesn't refer to psychological well-being in the face of death. Rather, Simeon is dying in the peace of the salvation personified in the infant Christ whom he's cradling—hence, his immediate reference to "your salvation," that is, the salvation provided by God in and through the infant Christ. God is dismissing Simeon "because" his eyes have seen this salvation. Simeon is an eyewitness to whom the Holy Spirit has identified the infant Jesus with salvation. "Prepared" describes the salvation as ready and available in the person of Jesus. "Before the *face* of all the peoples" describes the preparation as open to public scrutiny and acceptance. "*All* the peoples" makes the salvation available to Gentiles as well as Jews. This salvation is a light that has the purpose of taking away the veil of pagan darkness which blinds the Gentiles. And it's a light that also has the purpose of bringing "glory" (= honor) to Israel, presently humiliated by pagan overlords. Joseph and Mary can only marvel at what God will do with and through their little baby.

2:34–35: And Simeon blessed them and said to Mary his [Jesus'] **mother, "Behold, this one** [the child] **is destined for the falling and rising of many in Israel and for a sign that'll be spoken against ³⁵(and also** [because of that speaking against the sign of your son] **a sword will go through your soul), so that the reasonings of many hearts may be revealed."** To bless is to say a good word about something or someone. So Simeon praises Joseph and Mary for their obedience to God's law. But then he prophesies (for the Holy Spirit is "on him" and he entered the temple "in the Spirit" [2:25, 27]) to Mary, not to Joseph, because as Jesus' birth mother she has a greater emotional investment in him than Joseph, only a foster father, does. Jesus is destined to become the occasion of many Jews' falling into judgment through unbelief in him and, on the other hand, of the rising of many of them to eternal life (Is there a hint of resurrection here?) through belief in him. Emphasis falls on the negative side, though, so that Simeon adds Jesus' destiny to be a sign that unbelievers will speak against. But why "a *sign*"? Because as a baby wrapped in strips of cloth and lying in a feed trough he has already been a sign to the shepherds (2:12). Because as an adult he'll be a sign, like "the sign of Jonah," in that his preaching of repentance will signal God's judgment on the unrepentant (5:32; 10:13–15; 11:29–32; 13:1–5 and so on). Because by forcing on people the decision whether or not to repent, this preaching will expose the inner thinking of many people; for by definition repentance is a change of mind that issues in a reformation of conduct. As a parenthetical aside, Simeon prophesies that "a sword will go through [Mary's] soul"—not just a dagger, but a full-sized sword piercing into the seat of her emotions. This piercing may start when Jesus is only twelve years of age (see 2:41–51), but it will certainly happen during his public ministry and at his death (see 8:19–20 and perhaps 23:49; Acts 1:14). Simeon's emphasis on the negative reaction to Jesus' coming ministry, a reaction that will pain Mary deeply, is due to the crucifixion that Jesus will suffer. But the prophecy that carries this emphasis shows that God has already taken account of the coming, predominantly negative reaction among the Israelites, the Jews.

2:36–37: And Anna, a prophetess, Phanuel's daughter, from the tribe of Asher—this [woman] **was advanced in many days** [= very old], **having lived with a husband for seven years from her virginity.** [37]**And this** [woman had been] **a widow for eighty-four years, who didn't leave the temple as she did religious exercises by way of fastings and prayers night and day.** Supporting the historical certainty of Luke's narrative (1:4) is an abundance of detail concerning this woman. He cites her name, her prophetic office, her father's name, her tribal identity, her advanced age, the length of her married life, the length of her widowhood, and her religious devotion. This devotion was outstanding in her constant presence in the temple, her fastings, her prayers, and the incessancy of those fastings and prayers. More particularly, her remaining a widow so as to give herself wholly to these religious exercises, plus the sheer length of time that she'd done so, distinguishes her as a supergodly prophetess. With credentials like these, she's to be believed.

2:38: And stepping up at that very hour [when Joseph and Mary brought the baby Jesus into the temple and Simeon received Jesus], **she was giving thanks back to God** [that is, in response to his sending Jesus as a Savior]. **And she was speaking about him** [Jesus] **to all who were waiting expectantly for the redemption of Jerusalem.** As in the case of Simeon (2:27), Anna's stepping up "at that very hour" indicates a divinely ordered synchronization of the Holy Family's entrance into the temple and Anna's movements. Her giving God thanks not only displays piety. It also recommends the news about Jesus as *good* news—thankworthy. And her speaking with prophetic authority to others about him recommends the news about him as worthy of propagation—too good to be kept to oneself. She was speaking to "all who were waiting expectantly for the redemption of Jerusalem" (compare 2:25), because they're the ones whose expectant waiting God has now rewarded. Both the prophetess and her audience are admirable in their godliness and therefore commendatory of the gospel. "All" indicates that the gospel is for every expectant person. "The redemption of Jerusalem" refers to the city's liberation from foreign oppression (compare 1:68). As the capital of Israel, Jerusalem represents the whole of the nation (compare, for example, Isaiah 52:9). But confined as Anna is to the temple, located in Jerusalem, Luke singles out that city. He singles it out also because Jesus' ministry will aim for Jerusalem as the place where redemption will be accomplished (see especially 9:31, 51) and because the apostles will fan out from Jerusalem to preach the good news of redemption far and wide (Acts 1:8).

2:39: And when they'd completed all things in accordance with the law of the Lord, they [the holy family] **returned to Galilee, to their own city of Nazareth** [as distinguished from the just-mentioned Jerusalem]. Again Luke stresses the piety of Joseph and Mary. Christianity didn't start in a rebellion against Old Testament regulations. It started with obedience to them, *thorough* obedience ("*all* things . . ."). Only after such obedience did the Holy Family return to their hometown.

JESUS' MATURATION
Luke 2:40–52

The initial maturation of Jesus is summarized in 2:40. An example of his maturation by the age of twelve occupies 2:41–51. And 2:52 summarizes his further maturation.

2:40: And the little boy grew and got strong, being filled with wisdom. And God's favor was on him [compare 1 Samuel 2:26]. Jesus grew in stature. With such growth came an increase in physical strength. These were accompanied by intellectual development. And God's favor added divine superintendance to Jesus' maturation (compare 1:28, 30). All these features of the maturation portray him as an ideal human being in the making.

2:41: And his parents used to travel to Jerusalem year by year for the festival of Passover. For the purpose of recommending the gospel of their son, Luke highlights the piety of Joseph and Mary yet again. Jews celebrated the Passover in what we call springtime (March–April). It commemorated the exodus of Israel from Egypt, where they'd been enslaved. Men within striking distance of Jerusalem were supposed to go there every year for the celebration, but women didn't have to go (see Exodus 12:1–20; 23:14–17; 34:18–24; Deuteronomy 16:16, in which passages Passover is combined with the immediately following week of Unleavened Bread). The eighty-some miles from Nazareth to Jerusalem took three or four days to walk. So Mary's unnecessary but regular accompaniment of Joseph exhibits special piety.

2:42–43a: And when he [Jesus] **got to be twelve years old, as they were going up** [to Jerusalem] **in accordance with the custom of the festival** [43a]**and when they'd completed the days** [of the Festival, including Unleavened Bread, for Passover occupied only one day], **Jesus the boy was staying in Jerusalem while they** [Joseph and Mary] **were returning** [toward Nazareth]. It's often thought that Jesus' parents took him to this festival for the first time to prepare him for the religious responsibilities of an adult that fell on Jewish males at the age of thirteen. But Luke makes nothing of such a purpose, and his wording doesn't require that this be the first time Jesus' parents took him to a festival in Jerusalem. Luke is interested only in what happened on this occasion, when Jesus was only twelve, still a minor. He's no longer the "*little* boy" of 2:40, but he's still a "boy." But what a boy! His staying in Jerusalem after the festival had ended may strike us as disrespectful of his parents. But Luke wants us to interpret his staying as indicative of extraordinary devotion to the city whose redemption he'll accomplish (2:38).

2:43b–47: And his parents didn't know [that he was staying in Jerusalem]. **⁴⁴And on supposing that he was in the caravan** [of pilgrims returning to Galilee]**, they went a day's journey. And they were looking for him among** [their] **relatives and acquaintances. ⁴⁵And on not finding** [him]**, they returned to Jerusalem, looking for him. ⁴⁶And it happened that after three days they found him in the temple, sitting in the midst of the teachers and listening to them and asking them questions. ⁴⁷And all who heard him were astonished at his understanding and answers.** Luke presents us with a child prodigy. Now we know the extent of Jesus' "being filled with wisdom" as he grew up (2:40). What he hears the teachers say prompts him to ask them questions. Apparently they can't answer his questions, though, because he answers his own questions—there's nothing about the teachers' asking *him* any questions—with an understanding that astonishes everybody, including the teachers themselves, who heard him. This student excels his teachers in a foreshadowing of his own later teaching, especially in the temple (19:45–21:38). Suitably, then, he sits in their midst as the center of attention and object of admiration. Luke doesn't specify what the teachers were teaching, what Jesus was asking them, or what he was answering. The point has to do solely with his exhibition of intellectual prowess at the tender age of twelve. In their search for Jesus, Joseph and Mary show natural parental concern. Their finding him "after three days" probably counts the day of traveling from Jerusalem as the first day, a day of traveling back to the city as the second day, and a day of searching for Jesus in the city as a third day. Alternatively, Joseph and Mary searched for three days after returning to Jerusalem.

2:48–50: And on seeing him, they [his parents] **were awestruck. And his mother said to him, "Child, why have you treated us this way? Behold, your father and I, being pained** [by your truancy]**, were looking for you." ⁴⁹And he said to them, "Why** [is it] **that you** [plural, for Joseph as well as Mary] **were looking for me? You knew, didn't you, that it's necessary for me to be in my Father's house?" ⁵⁰And they didn't understand the statement that he'd spoken to them.** What strikes with awe the parents of Jesus is his sitting in the midst of the teachers, asking them questions, and answering his own questions with understanding. He's their boy, but even they are awestruck. This reaction gives way to a motherly complaint, however. The pain about which she complains may start the fulfillment of Simeon's prophecy that a sword would "go through her soul" (2:35). Mary complains because she's the biological mother of Jesus (hence her addressing him with "Child"), whereas Joseph is not his biological father. Yet in her complaint she refers to Joseph as Jesus' "father." This reference sets up for a corrective reference in Jesus' counter question. The corrective reference shows an awareness that *God* is his Father (compare 1:32, 35) and that his first obligation is therefore to God: "it's *necessary*." This necessity arises out of his parents' having presented him to the Lord instead of redeeming him into

their own possession (see the comments on 2:22–23). Because he belongs to God, then, and belongs to him moreover as his Son, he belongs in the temple, God's house.[1] He's at home there, as his spending several days in the temple symbolizes. Jesus has gotten wise enough to know his divine sonship, his filial obligation, and his true home. "You knew, didn't you . . . ?" would ordinarily imply that Joseph and Mary did know. But "they didn't understand . . ." indicates that they didn't know what they *should* have known because of their having presented him to the Lord rather than redeeming him. Their lack of understanding highlights by contrast the marvelous understanding that this twelve year old boy has displayed.

2:51: And he went down with them and came to Nazareth, and he was subjecting himself to them. And his mother was keeping all the things [= words and events] **in her heart.** Staying in the temple wasn't disobedience to his parents. It was obedience to God his Father. But lest anyone think wrongly that Jesus rebelled against Joseph and Mary, Luke notes Jesus' returning to Nazareth with them and subjecting himself to them. Mary's keeping these things in her heart gives another broad hint that Luke's information derives from her memory and thus from an eyewitness whose testimony helps make for the certainty of the gospel (1:4; 2:19). "*All* the things" underlines the comprehensiveness of her memory in addition to its accuracy.

2:52: And Jesus kept advancing in wisdom and stature and favor with God and human beings. So Jesus attains even more wisdom than the astonishing wisdom he has already displayed at the age of twelve. And he attains greater physical stature, greater divine favor, and greater social favor—altogether a perfectly rounded intellectual, physical, spiritual, and social maturation. The Son of the Highest is also an attractive human being.

In these first two chapters, then, Luke has portrayed John the baptizer in glowing colors, but Jesus as John's superior. John is "great before the Lord" (1:15). But Jesus is not only "great." He's also "the Son of the Highest" and "God's Son" (1:32, 35). The narrative of John's birth gets one verse (1:57). That of Jesus' birth gets a whole paragraph (2:1–7). Neighbors and relatives rejoice with Elizabeth at John's birth (1:58), but a whole multitude of angels celebrate Jesus' birth in conjunction with the shepherds' praise (2:13–20). At John's birth Zechariah prophesies more about Jesus than about his own son John (1:67–79). Simeon prophesies exclusively about Jesus (2:28–35). John grows up in the wilderness away from other people (1:80). Jesus grows up in Nazareth, advances in wisdom and divine and social favor, and astonishes people in the temple at the age of twelve (2:39–52).

---

[1] In view of earlier references to David as Jesus' forefather (1:32, 69) we might think of "my father's house" as David's house. But David didn't build the temple. His son Solomon did. The Lord built for David a house in the sense of a household, however, a family line of royalty.

THE PREACHING OF JOHN
Luke 3:1–20

This passage breaks down into the appearance of John as a preacher (3:1–6), his call to repentance (3:7–9), his definition of repentance (3:10–14), his prediction concerning Jesus (3:15–17), and the imprisonment of John because of his having rebuked Herod (3:18–20). In the comments on this passage "John" will refer to the son of Zechariah and Elizabeth, not to John the apostle or John Mark, sometime companion of Peter and Paul.

3:1–2: And in the fifteenth year of Tiberius Caesar's rule, while Pontius Pilate was governor of Judea [southern Israel] **and Herod** [Antipas] **was tetrarch** [small-change ruler] **of Galilee** [northern Israel] **and his brother Philip was tetrarch of the Iturean-and-Trachonitian region** [north and west of Galilee] **and Lysanias was tetrarch of Abilene** [northwest of Galilee], **²at the time of the Annas-and-Caiaphas high priest, God's word came on John the son of Zechariah in the wilderness.** To forecast the universal address of the gospel, which John will introduce, Luke sets John's appearance on the canvas of world history and then narrows it down to local history. Such fanfare marks the importance of this background information; and the details of chronology, government, geography, and high priesthood point to its reliability. Luke knows what he's writing about and relates it to the whole wide world for which he's writing his Gospel and to which its message, the gospel, is addressed (for its universal reach see, for example, 3:6 and Acts 1:8). "God's word," which "came on John" like a burden he had to unload by preaching it—this word equates with the gospel in the Gospel (though it will get further elaboration, of course). Or is God's word not the *message* John is to preach but God's *calling* him to preach, as in Jeremiah 1:1–10? Luke doesn't detail a divine call to preach; and in Jeremiah 1:11, 13; 2:1 and later, the coming of the word of the Lord to Jeremiah has to do with Jeremiah's message rather than his call. So the coming of God's word on John probably relates to the message, the gospel itself. Strikingly, Luke uses the singular of "high priest" for Annas and his son-in-law Caiaphas, the two of whom occupied the high priestly office not concurrently but in A.D. 6–15 and 18–36, respectively. But though Annas wasn't officially the high priest during Caiaphas's tenure in that office, unofficially he exerted high priestly authority with and through his son-in-law, so that Luke merges them into a single high priest, so to speak (compare John 18:13–14, 24; Acts 4:6 and the fact that between their high priesthoods five biological sons of Annas occupied the office!). The description of John as "the son of Zechariah" reminds us of John's miraculous birth to aged parents and of Zechariah's prophecy that John would be "a prophet of the Most High" in that he would "proceed before the Lord to prepare his paths [and so forth]" (1:76–79). "In the wilderness" reminds us also of where John grew up (1:80) and prepares for his dramatic entrance onto the public stage. Luke omits a description of John as a wild man of the desert who wore a coat of camel's hair and a leather girdle and ate locusts and wild honey (Mark 1:6; Matthew 3:4). Such a description wouldn't serve Luke's purpose of appealing to a genteel cosmopolitan audience, represented by the "most excellent Theophilus," to whom he dedicated this Gospel (1:1–4).

3:3–6: And he went into all the region around the Jordan [River] **preaching a baptism of repentance for the forgiveness of sins, ⁴as it's written in the book of the words of Isaiah the prophet: "The voice of one crying out in the wilderness, 'Prepare the way of the Lord. Make his paths straight. ⁵Every ravine shall be filled, and every mountain and hill shall be lowered, and the crooked shall be** [made] **straight, and the rough** [shall be made] **smooth. ⁶And all flesh will see God's salvation** [Isaiah 40:3–5].'"** John's going "into *all* the region around the Jordan" makes his preaching adumbrate both Jesus' even wider preaching throughout Israel and the worldwide preaching of the gospel in Luke's book of Acts. "The baptism of repentance" that John preaches foreshadows baptism in the name of Jesus, also in the book of Acts. John preaches a baptism of repentance in the sense that he calls on people to submit to this baptism. It has to do with repentance in the sense that it represents outwardly the inward change of mind that the word "repentance" means. A person repents by turning negative toward his or her sinful conduct. Such a turning brings forgiveness of sins, that is, a sending away of sins from the sinner. They're no longer attached to the sinner, who therefore faces no punishment for them. John's preaching of this baptism agrees with "the words of Isaiah the prophet" and therefore carries out God's plan as revealed in those words (compare "the words" whose "certainty" Luke writes that we might "know" [1:4]). That Isaiah's words are written "in a book" makes them checkable and therefore contributory to certainty. For his voice to be heard in the wilderness, John has to "cry out." Otherwise people won't hear him. Preparing the way of the Lord by straightening, leveling (a combination of filling ravines and lowering mountains and hills), and smoothing out his paths is a figure of speech for repentance. The filling of "*every* ravine" and the lowering of "*every* mountain and hill" means that people should repent of every sin of theirs. No exceptions! The future tense of the "shall be"-verbs carries forward the commanding tone of "*Make* his paths straight" (compare other commands in the future tense, such as "Thou shalt not kill"). These commands lead then to a happily predictive future tense in "all flesh will see God's salvation." "All *flesh*" means all humanity in their frailty, mortality, and need of salvation; for at death their flesh returns to dust (Genesis 3:19) and only their bones remain. "*All* flesh" means that God makes salvation available for everybody who repents, Jew and Gentile alike. To "*see* God's salvation" is to *experience* it. That it's "*God's* salvation" means that "the Lord" whose way is prepared by repentance is God, not Jesus. But it will turn out that God is coming to bring salvation in the person of his Son and agent, Jesus.

3:7–9: Therefore he was saying to the crowds that were traveling out [into the wilderness] **to be baptized by him, "Offsprings of vipers, who warned you to flee from the wrath that's going to come? ⁸Therefore produce fruits in keeping with repentance; and don't start saying among yourselves, 'We have Abraham as a** [fore]**father.' For I tell you that God can raise up children** [= descendants] **for Abraham out of these stones. ⁹And also, the axe is already lying at the root of the trees. Therefore every tree that's not producing good fruit is being cut down and thrown into fire."** "Therefore" makes John's preaching a fulfillment of the passage Luke has just quoted from Isaiah. So there's continuity with the Old Testament yet again. "The crowds" travel out of their cities and towns of residence as John itinerates throughout the region. The combination of their traveling and John's itineration appeals, as often in this Gospel and Acts, to interest in travel on the part of Luke's audience. And throughout this Gospel and Acts, Luke delights in the numerical success of the gospel. This success argues for the gospel's divine origin. Good Jews often immersed *themselves* for the sake of ritual purification. But to be immersed *by John* marked an innovation which—because he was acting as God's prophet—symbolized the washing away of sins by God himself. "Offsprings of vipers" implies that though the crowds had come to be baptized for the forgiveness of their sins, they hadn't yet repented of those sins. They wanted forgiveness without repentance, as though baptism as such would effect the forgiveness. So John asked them who'd warned them to flee from the wrath that was going to come, that is, from God's judgment on the unrepentant. The question implies they were motivated by fear of that judgment without an accompanying sorrow for their sins. The question also implies that John hadn't warned them to come for baptism apart from repentance. The next "Therefore" means that since the crowds are fleeing the coming wrath, they need to demonstrate repentance in their behavior. The plural "fruits" points forward to particular good works that John will detail in 3:10–14. For the moment, though, he tells the crowds that they shouldn't even start substituting in conversation their Abrahamic ancestry for the good works that in their conduct would demonstrate repentance (see John 8:33 for just such a substitution, though). Then John says in effect that Abraham doesn't need the crowd for his posterity. Nor does God need them for the keeping of his promise to Abraham that Abraham's posterity would exceed in number the sand on the seashore and the stars in the sky (Genesis 15:5; 22:17; 26:4). Stones are proverbial for being lifeless. But if you don't repent, John says, to keep his promise to Abraham God can raise up descendants for him out of the very stones lying hereabout. And in addition to this possibility (note the "also") is the actuality of judgment on the unrepentant, for which the axing down and throwing of a tree into fire is the image. "The axe lies *already* at the root of the trees," so that judgment is imminent. "*At* the root" means that the cutting edge of the axe is aimed *toward* the root of trees, so that

the judgment is dangerous. Since "the *root*" supplies the nourishment without which trees die, a cutting of the root implies a judgment that'll be permanent. "*Every* tree that's not producing good fruit" means that nobody at all who's unrepentant will escape judgment. "Is *being* cut down and thrown into fire" describes future judgment as so soon and certain that it might as well be occurring right now. But people still have a chance to repent and escape. Read on.

3:10–11: And the crowds were asking him, saying, "So what should we do?" ¹¹And answering, he was saying to them, "The person who has two tunics is to give [the extra one] **to the person who doesn't have** [even one tunic], **and the person who has items of food is to do likewise** [that is, give the extra items to the person who doesn't have any food]. By referring again to the crowds Luke reminds us of the numerical success of John's Spirit-filled preaching (compare 1:15; 3:7). The crowds' question indicates their desire to "produce fruits in keeping with repentance" (compare 3:8). In Luke's original Greek text, in fact, the verb in "So what should we *do*?" is the same as the verb in "*produce* fruits in keeping with repentance." To capture the wordplay, we could translate 3:10, "So what should we produce [by way of fruits in keeping with repentance]?" "So" relates this question to John's having just upbraided the crowds for coming to be baptized without repentance and to his having warned them of imminent judgment—as though to say, "In view of your upbraiding and warning, John, what should we do to get you to baptize us?" John's preaching achieves moral as well as numerical success, then. And John defines morality so far as the crowds are concerned in terms of giving their extra clothing and food to those who lack clothing and food. (A tunic was a short robe worn next to the skin and under a long outer robe.)

3:12–13: And even tax collectors came to be baptized and said to him, "Teacher, what should we do [see the comments on 3:10–11 for the verb 'do']**?" ¹³And he said to them, "Collect not one** [coin] **more than what has been commanded you** [to collect]." How great the success of John's preaching—"*even* tax collectors came to be baptized"! They were known for their graft, which consisted in collecting more taxes than they were commissioned to collect and pocketing the excess. Yet they, of all people, come to learn what repentance requires of them so that they can be baptized. The introduction of their question with the address "Teacher" shows a respect that indicates willingness to carry out John's instruction, which adds financial honesty to the charity he'd commanded the crowds to exercise.

3:14: And even soldiers were asking him, saying, "What should we do—we too [or 'even we']**?" And he told them, "You shouldn't 'shake down' anyone or use extortion, and be satisfied with your wages."** The soldiers' question furthers the success of John's preaching ("*even* soldiers"). They themselves seem astonished at their willingness to produce fruits in keeping with repentance ("we *too*" or "*even* we"). Soldiers didn't make much money, so they regularly used their soldierly authority to shake down people and extort money from them to supplement their wages. John's instruction therefore adds nonviolence to the charity and the financial honesty of previous instructions.

3:15: And as the people were waiting expectantly and all wondering in their hearts about John, whether *he* might be the Christ . . . . What were the people expecting? Apparently the coming wrath that John had warned them about. And apparently they were wondering whether he might be God's anointed agent to bring judgmental wrath on the unrepentant. The people's expectation and wonderment testify yet again to the success of John's preaching. "Were . . . *all* wondering" heightens the success. That they were "wondering *in their hearts*"—that is, privately—makes it surprising that they were all wondering the same thing, and therefore heightens John's success yet further. But this success only previews the even greater success of Jesus.

3:16–17: John answered them all by saying, "On the one hand, I'm baptizing you with water. On the other hand, one who's stronger than I is coming, the strap of whose sandals I'm not qualified to loosen. He [as distinguished from me] **will baptize** [= immerse] **you in the Holy Spirit and fire,** [17]**whose winnowing shovel** [is] **in his hand to clean his threshing floor thoroughly and gather the wheat into his granary. But he'll burn the chaff with inextinguishable fire."** John responds to "them *all*," so that none of them can retain the thought that he, John, might be the Christ. According to John, the one who's coming is superior to him in several ways: (1) He's stronger. (2) He's so august that John, despite his own eminence, isn't qualified to do for the coming one even what only a slave was expected to do for his owner, that is, to untie his owner's sandals. (3) The coming one will immerse people in the Holy Spirit and fire, whereas John uses mere water to immerse people. It's immersing people in the Holy Spirit and fire that'll show the coming one to be stronger than John and august beyond comparison. For such an immersion will demonstrate that he has the Holy Spirit at his disposal and the authority to consign unrepentant people ("the chaff") to the inextinguishable fire of hell after he has cleaned his threshing floor by gathering into safe-keeping ("his granary") repentant people ("the wheat"). The thoroughness of his cleaning the threshing floor means that no one will be left in limbo. Everybody will be either saved or lost. The winnowing shovel was used to toss threshed—that is, trampled—grain into the air so that wind would blow the loosened husks ("chaff") to one side while the heavier kernels of grain fell back on the threshing floor, and then (as here) to clean the threshing floor by tossing the wheat into a granary and the chaff into a fire. Most important for Luke, though, is that John's preaching and description of the coming stronger one both fulfill Gabriel's prophecy that John would "turn many of the sons of Israel to the Lord their God [and so forth (see 1:16–17)]" and also fulfill Zechariah's Spirit-inspired

prophecy that John would "go before the Lord to prepare his ways, to give his people knowledge of salvation in the forgiveness of their sins [and so forth (see 1:76–79)]." For these fulfillments establish continuity between the coming one (Jesus) and John, so that John links the coming one to a moral reformation in Judaism. The gospel is good for morals.

3:18–20: On the one hand, therefore, he [John] **was preaching many and different things as good news to the people by way of encouraging** [them]. [19]**On the other hand, Herod the tetrarch** [about which title see 3:1], **on being rebuked by him** [John] **concerning Herodias, the wife of his brother, and concerning all the evil things that Herod had done,** [20]**added this too on top of all** [those evil things]: **he also locked John up in prison.** Luke sets John's preaching of good news to the people and rebuking of Herod in contrast to each other. The "many and different things" John tells the people as good news contrast with "all the evil things," including the taking of his brother's wife and climaxing in the imprisonment of John, that Herod has done. John preaches the many and different things as "*good news*" because the crowd have repented and been baptized, as "therefore" indicates. The good news they hear is "encouraging" in that because they've repented and been baptized they no longer have to fear the fire of coming wrath. Luke doesn't specify "the many and different things" that John preached. It's enough for Luke that in general they encouraged the people with good news— good news that will link up with the good news Jesus will preach to establish continuity between himself and John. Nor does Luke specify what it was about Herodias, the wife of Herod's brother, that prompted John to rebuke Herod. Luke leaves us to infer that Herod had illegitimately taken his brother's wife to become his own wife (in violation of Leviticus 18:16; 20:21). Thus Herod, a perpetrator of evil, stands as a foil to make the moral reform effected by John stand out. Luke wants us to know that the gospel is morally attractive.

DEMONSTRATIONS OF JESUS' DIVINE SONSHIP
Luke 3:21–38

In this passage God pronounces Jesus his Son (3:21–22), and Luke uses Jesus' genealogy to highlight the divine sonship of Jesus (3:23–38).

3:21–22: And it happened that when all the people had been baptized and Jesus had been baptized and was praying, heaven was opened [22]**and the Holy Spirit came down on him in bodily form, like a dove, and a voice came from heaven, "You're my beloved Son; I've taken delight in you."** "*When* all the people had been baptized" takes us back to a time prior to John's imprisonment, and the baptism of "*all* the people" testifies to the numerical and moral success of John's preaching. For he wouldn't have baptized them if they hadn't heeded his demand that they produce fruits in keeping with repentance. According to earlier statements, Jesus was to be born as the holy Son of God, God's favor was on him, and he advanced in favor with God (1:35; 2:40, 52). These statements rule out that Jesus was baptized as a sign of repentance from sins that he'd committed. But Luke shows no interest in the question why then Jesus *was* baptized. For Luke, Jesus' baptism holds interest only, but importantly, as an occasion on which Jesus exhibited piety (he was praying), on which the Holy Spirit came down on him to anoint him for his ensuing activities (compare 4:16–19), and on which God himself called Jesus his beloved, delightful Son in fulfillment of Gabriel's predictions to Mary (1:32, 35 [compare Psalm 2:7; Isaiah 42:1]). To rivet attention on these matters alone, Luke doesn't even mention John as performing the baptism. The Spirit's having assumed "bodily form" made the Spirit visible, as indicated not only by "bodily" but also by the meaning of "form" as "outward appearance." (The noun for "form" is related in Luke's Greek to the verb "see.") It's a question whether "like a dove" describes the bodily form that the Spirit assumed or the manner of the Spirit's descent (like the downward fluttering of a dove). "Came down" favors the manner of descent, but "bodily form" favors the Spirit's outward appearance (compare the appearance of the Holy Spirit like tongues of fire in Acts 2:3). So it's best to combine dove-like descent with dove-like appearance. The Spirit's descent onto Jesus was something that could be seen, then, and confirmed by eyewitnesses (compare 1:1–4).

3:23–38: And when beginning [his activities], Jesus himself was about thirty years [old], being the son— as it was being supposed—of Joseph, the [son] of Eli, [24]the [son] of Mathat, the [son] of Levi, the [son] of Melchi, the [son] of Jannai, the [son] of Joseph, [25]the [son] of Mattathias, the [son] of Amos, the [son] of Nahum, the [son] of Hesli, the [son] of Naggai, [26]the [son] of Maath, the [son] of Mattathias, the [son] of Semein, the [son] of Josech, the [son] of Joda, [27]the [son] of Joanan, the [son] of Rhesa, the [son] of Zerubbabel, the [son] of Salathiel [= Shealtiel], the [son] of Neri, [28]the [son] of Melchi, the [son] of Addi, the [son] of Cosam, the [son] of Elmadam, the [son] of Er, [29]the [son] of Jesus [= Joshua], the [son] of Eliezer, the [son] of Jorim, the [son] of Matthat, the [son] of Levi, [30]the [son] of Simeon, the [son] of Judah, the [son] of Joseph, the [son] of Jonam, the [son] of Eliakim, [31]the [son] of Melea, the [son] of Menna, the [son] of Mattatha, the [son] of Nathan, the [son] of David, [32]the [son] of Jesse, the [son] of Obed, the [son] of Boaz, the [son] of Sala, the [son] of Naasson, [33]the [son] of Amminadab, the [son] of Admin, the [son] of Arni, the [son] of Hezron, the [son] of Perez, the [son] of Judah, [34]the [son] of Jacob, the [son] of Isaac, the [son] of Abraham, the [son] of Terah, the [son] of Nahor, [35]the [son] of Serug, the [son] of Ragau, the [son] of Peleg, the [son] of Eber, the [son] of Shelah, [36]the [son] of Cainan, the [son] of Arphaxad, the [son] of Shem, the [son] of Noah, the [son] of Lamech, [37]the [son] of Methuselah, the [son] of Enoch, the [son] of Jared, the [son] of Mahalaleel, the [son] of Cainan, [38]the [son] of

Enosh, the [son] of Seth, the [son] of Adam, the [son] of God. Luke carefully dated Gabriel's announcements of the coming births of John (1:5) and of Jesus (1:26, 36), the length of Mary's stay with Elizabeth (1:56), the birth of Jesus (2:1–2), the circumcision and naming of Jesus (2:21), his visit to the temple (2:42), and the start of John's ministry (3:1–2). Now Luke dates the start of Jesus' ministry at a time when Jesus was about thirty years old. This cavalcade of dates lays a historical foundation supporting "the certainty" of the gospel (1:1–4). Moreover, a man was considered to have reached the height of his powers at the age of thirty. Therefore Luke is portraying Jesus as starting his ministry at just the right age (compare David's becoming king of Israel at thirty years of age [2 Samuel 5:4] and the Lord God's giving Jesus "the throne of his father David" [Luke 1:32; see also 1:69; 2:11]). By adding "himself" to "Jesus," Luke highlights a shift from John's ministry to that of Jesus. Because of Jesus' virginal conception and birth, the popular supposition that he was Joseph's biological son was false. "As it was being supposed" therefore calls attention to Jesus' divine sonship via a virginal conception and birth. Nevertheless, Luke traces Jesus' genealogy through Joseph because legal rights, such as the right to David's throne, passed through the father even though he was only a foster father (see 1:27, 32–33, 69; 2:4, 11). The tracing of Jesus' genealogy all the way back to Adam implies both that Luke has done his homework and that Jesus will be a Savior for the whole human race, as in 2:29–32. But the genealogy doesn't stop with Adam. It stops with God, behind whom it can't go. So the genealogy comes to its climax with a designation of Adam as the son of God. Luke, then, is drawing a parallel between God's generating Adam out of the dust of the ground and God's generating Jesus in the womb of Mary. Thus this genealogy helps demonstrate the divine sonship of Jesus.

JESUS' MORAL VICTORY OVER THE DEVIL
Luke 4:1–13

To further his presentation of the gospel as morally attractive, Luke narrates Jesus' moral victory over the Devil. The occurrence of this victory at the very start of Jesus' ministry sets a tone of morality that will run throughout that ministry—and beyond in what he'll continue to do and teach through his Spirit-filled apostles as recorded in Luke's book of Acts. For the present, Luke provides a topographical and chronological setting in 4:1–2a, details three temptations of Jesus by the Devil in 4:2b–12, and punctuates the Devil's defeat in 4:13.

4:1–2a: And Jesus, full of the Holy Spirit, turned away from the Jordan [River, in which he'd been baptized,] and was being led in the Spirit in the wilderness [2a]for forty days as he was being tempted by the Devil. At Jesus' baptism the Holy Spirit descended "in bodily form . . . *on* him" (3:22). But though having assumed a bodily form, the Spirit isn't essentially physical. So now the Spirit *fills* him and *leads* him. "*In* the Spirit" means "*by* the Spirit" in the sense that Jesus is so immersed in the Spirit that the Spirit determines his movements, here by leading him in the wilderness—not *to* the wilderness, but *within* the wilderness by way of itineration. (Luke likes travel, which was popular in the Roman Empire, and so appeals to this liking among his audience.) Notably, Jesus' location "in the Spirit" takes precedence over his location "in the wilderness." And it's remarkable that the Holy Spirit rests on Jesus, inhabits him, envelops him, and takes the lead ahead of him. To be *tempted* is to have one's moral fibre *tested*, so that we should use these verbs interchangeably. The Devil's testing Jesus and the Spirit's leading him take place concurrently, and for forty days. This length of time magnifies both the extent of the Spirit's leading Jesus and the extent of Jesus' temptation, so that in conclusion Luke will refer to the completion of "*every* temptation" (4:13).

4:2b–4: And he [Jesus] **ate nothing during those days; and when they were completed, he hungered.** [3]**And the Devil said to him, "If** [in fact] **you're God's Son, tell this stone to become a loaf of bread."** [4]**And Jesus answered him, "It's written, 'Not by bread alone shall a human being live** [Deuteronomy 8:3].'"** "*Son*" is emphatic; but the Devil doesn't tempt Jesus to doubt his divine sonship, of which God gave him assurance at his baptism (3:22)—rather, to capitalize on that sonship by drawing on his divine power to make a stone, lying close by, into a loaf of bread (not a big, puffy loaf such as is common nowadays, but a loaf something like pita bread). If "God can raise up children for Abraham out of these stones" (3:8), surely God's Son can turn a stone into bread. Along with Jesus' hunger because of going without any food for forty days, the rough similarity in appearance between a stone and a loaf of bread provides a further basis for this temptation by the Devil. Surely it would be a small thing to make a single loaf for so large a need of nourishment. But since Jesus is being led by the Spirit in the wilderness, where there's no bread, to make bread out of a stone would go against the Spirit's leading and betray distrust in God's sustenance of human life even apart from the eating of bread—hence Jesus' quotation of Deuteronomy 8:3, which has to do with *God's* testing Israel in the Sinai wilderness by letting them go hungry and then feeding them with manna so that they might understand that human beings don't live by *bread* alone. Neither Jesus nor Luke gives this background, though; and "*shall* a human being live" gives the quotation the character of a command. So Jesus behaves in accordance with Old Testament Scripture. He's both a good Jew and an obedient Son.

4:5–8: And on leading him up, he [the Devil] **showed him all the kingdoms of the inhabited** [earth] **in a moment of time.** [6]**And the Devil said to him, "To you I'll give all this authority** [represented by the kingdoms] **and their glory, because it has been given over to me and I'm giving it to whomever I want** [to give it]. [7]**You therefore—if you'd worship** [by prostrating yourself] **before me, all** [the authority, the glory] **will be yours."** [8]**And answering, Jesus said, "It's writ-** ten, '**You shall worship the Lord your God and serve him alone** [Deuteronomy 6:13; 10:20; 1 Samuel 7:3].'" The Devil leads Jesus up to where? Luke doesn't say. So the accent falls solely on the Devil's showing Jesus all the kingdoms of the inhabited earth, which in Luke's setting meant the Roman Empire. "All" stresses the magnitude of the empire. The showcasing takes place "in a *moment* of time" in order that "all *this* authority" may be present to Jesus at the same instant. He sees it all at once. "*All* this authority" tempts Jesus with absolute power and the glory that goes along with it. "Because it has been given over to me and I'm giving it to whomever I want" is the Devil's preemptive strike against the possibility that Jesus will say the authority and glory aren't the Devil's to give. ("It," which occurs twice, treats "authority" and "glory" as essentially one and the same.) "Therefore" means, "Since I can give it to whomever I want." Luke doesn't say whether the Devil really could give all this authority and glory to Jesus. So the entire emphasis lies on the temptation as such. In this temptation, the forward position of "To you" and the emphatic "*You* therefore" appeal to Jesus' self-interest. "*All* will be yours" reemphasizes the magnitude of the Devil's appeal to Jesus' self-interest. But the condition, "*if* you'd worship [by prostrating yourself] before me," exposes the Devil's own self-interest. Again, though, Jesus behaves in accordance with Scripture by parrying the temptation with another quotation from the Old Testament, one that represents Jewish monotheism. So neither hunger for food nor hunger for power has led him into sin. He sets a high moral and religious example.

4:9–12: And he [the Devil] **led him into Jerusalem and stood** [him] **on the tip of the temple and said to him, "If** [in fact] **you're God's Son, throw yourself down from here.** [10]**For it's written, 'He'll give his angels orders concerning you, to protect you** [Psalm 91:11],' [11]**and, 'On** [their] **hands they'll lift you up lest you strike your foot against a stone** [Psalm 91:12].'" [12]**And answering, Jesus said to him, "It's said** [in Deuteronomy 6:16], 'You shall not test out the Lord your God.'"** See the comments on 4:3 concerning "If [in fact] you're God's *Son*." The present testing of Jesus comes to a climax in Jerusalem, where the final test of his passion will also take place (see especially 22:28). "From here" implies that if God can be trusted to keep his Son safe anywhere, he can be trusted to do so especially at his temple in Jerusalem. "The tip of the temple" is a high point, but we don't know whether it's the pinnacle of the sanctuary proper, the lintel of the gateway into the temple, or the Royal Porch on the southeast corner of the precincts, which dropped off over four hundred feet into the Kidron Valley. In any case, since Jesus has appealed to the Old Testament, the Devil does too. He tries using Jesus' own weapon against him. In quoting Psalm 91:11, however, the Devil omits the phrase "in all your ways," because the *deliberate* throwing of oneself down from a high perch doesn't correspond to *accidentally* stumbling over a stone on one's path, as in the psalm. This telltale omission by the Devil leads Jesus to counter with a quotation not to test out the Lord

God. For deliberately throwing himself down from a high perch wouldn't count as the falling by stumbling from which the psalm promises protection. It would count, instead, as the testing out of God that Deuteronomy 6:16 prohibits and that betrays, not trust in God, but just the opposite—lack of trust in him. So for a third time Jesus behaves in accordance with the Old Testament. Again, he's both a good Jew and an obedient Son.

4:13: **And on completing every temptation, the Devil withdrew from him until an opportune time** [that is, until another opportunity presented itself]. "*Every* temptation" suggests that the three temptations represented a totality of possible temptations, so that Jesus has passed a comprehensive exam. In the face of Jesus' moral victory the Devil withdraws in defeat, but only for the time being. Nevertheless, this victory of Jesus augurs well for the future. Matthew 4:11 has angels feeding Jesus at this point. Not so, Luke. He omits the feeding in order to concentrate attention on the obedience of Jesus to the will of God his Father as recorded in Scripture.

A SUMMARY OF JESUS' TEACHING IN GALILEE AND THEREABOUTS
Luke 4:14–15

4:14–15: **And Jesus returned in the power of the Spirit to Galilee. And news about him went throughout the whole surrounding region.** [15]**And he was teaching in their synagogues, being glorified** [= honored with praise] **by all.** The Spirit that came on Jesus at his baptism (3:22), filled him in his turning away from the Jordan River (4:1a), and was leading him in the wilderness for forty days (4:1b–2) now empowers him in his return to Galilee for the activity of teaching. Luke portrays Jesus as doing nothing without the Holy Spirit. Jesus is the example *par excellence* of a Spirit-filled, Spirit-led, Spirit-empowered human being—a religious phenom. And a celebrity, to boot. But a celebrity for a good rather than glitzy reason, namely, his empowerment by the Spirit as evident in his teaching (compare Acts 1:8; 2:1–4). His fame spreads even throughout the whole region surrounding Galilee (see 3:3; 4:37; 7:17; 8:37; Acts 14:6 for Luke's using "the surrounding region" for territory wider than what's immediately at hand). "In their synagogues" shows Jesus to be conforming to Jewish religious practice. He's no renegade. "Being glorified *by all*" indicates universal admiration of him because of his teaching. Nobody failed to be impressed favorably, and none failed to *express* their favorable impression (compare the boy Jesus' progressing "in favor . . . with human beings" [2:52]). This summary covers Jesus' activity in and around Galilee that will occupy Luke through 9:50 of his Gospel.

JESUS' FULFILLMENT OF SCRIPTURE IN THE SYNAGOGUE AT NAZARETH
Luke 4:16–30

4:16–19: **And he went into Nazareth, where he'd been brought up. And according to what was custom-** **ary for him** [to do] **on the Sabbath day, he entered into the synagogue. And he stood up to read.** [17]**And a scroll of the prophet Isaiah was given to him. And unrolling the scroll, he found the place where it had been written,** [18]**"The Spirit of the Lord** [is] **on me, on account of which** [Spirit] **he has anointed me to preach good news to poor people. He has sent me to proclaim release to captives and recovery of sight to blind people, to send away oppressed people** [from their oppressors] **by way of release** [from those oppressors], [19]**to proclaim the welcome year of the Lord** [Isaiah 61:1–2a; 58:6]." The customariness of Jesus' attendance at synagogue on Sabbath days shows him to be a pious Jew. His standing up to read shows deference to Scripture. And his finding a certain passage in Isaiah indicates the deliberate choice of a text, one that he will apply to himself. The Holy Spirit's having come down on Jesus at his baptism (3:22) has shown in advance that the statement, "The Spirit of the Lord [is] on me," applies to Jesus. Hence, the Spirit's resting on Jesus constitutes the Lord's anointing of Jesus for the task that the passage goes on to detail. Ordinarily kings, prophets, and priests were anointed by having olive oil poured on their heads. Here, the Holy Spirit himself, whom the olive oil symbolized, is the ointment that empowers Jesus to preach good news to poor people (that is, to announce the coming of economic justice in the messianic age) and to carry out the Lord's commission that he proclaim release to captives (that is, to announce the coming of legal justice in the messianic age, a kind of Emancipation Proclamation), to proclaim recovery of sight to blind people (that is, to announce the coming of what we might call therapeutic justice, so that in the messianic age the blind won't have to beg any more), to release the oppressed (legal justice again), and to proclaim the welcome year of the Lord (economic justice again, for that year is the Year of Jubilee, when all debts are canceled and slaves freed—a welcome year indeed! [Leviticus 25:8–17]). It's tempting to spiritualize these activities of Jesus, to make them symbolic of heavenly salvation. But like Isaiah, Gabriel, Mary, Zechariah, the angel of the Lord outside Bethlehem, and Simeon, Jesus is speaking about good things that will happen to Jews in the messianic age (1:32–33, 54–55, 68–79; 2:10, 25–32). The proclamation of release to captives might relate to those possessed by demons. But nowhere else does Luke use the language of captivity for demon possession; and in 21:24 he uses such language for coming exile, so that the release of captives probably has to do with the restoration of Jewish exiles back to the land of Israel, as in Isaiah's original meaning.

By and large, the Jews will reject Jesus, so that the Christian church will fill a resultant gap for the time being. The church's makeup of Gentiles as well as Jews living in different homelands will necessitate some revision of Jesus' present proclamation; but we must think of a delay in its fulfillment, not of a cancellation (13:31–35; 19:44; 22:30; Acts 3:21). Notably, Jesus stops short of quoting Isaiah 61:2b: "[To proclaim . . .] the day of our God's vengeance." That day awaits Jesus' second coming and refers to God's taking vengeance on Israel's oppressors. It's as though Jesus anticipates rejection by most of his fellow Jews and the resultant delay of God's taking vengeance on Israel's oppressors and instituting the messianic kingdom for Israel. Meanwhile, though, Jesus gives his fellow Jews their chance.

4:20–21: And on rolling up the scroll, giving [it] **back to the attendant, he sat down. And the eyes of all in the synagogue were gazing at him.** [21]**And he started saying to them, "Today this Scripture has been fulfilled in your ears."** Sitting was the usual posture for teaching. It connoted authority (compare 5:3; Mark 4:1; Matthew 5:1; 23:2; 26:55). The eyes of all Jesus' audience were fixated on him. None of them could avert their gaze, so mesmerizing was the effect he had on them. Luke wants us to see Jesus as a superhuman power player and his audience as attentive and therefore credible eyewitnesses. "*Started* saying," coupled with "words [plural] of grace" in 4:22, implies more speech than Luke records here. Jesus' declaration that Isaiah's words have been fulfilled supports Luke's emphasis on the continuity of the gospel with Judaism. "Today" marks the fulfillment as having taken place on this very occasion. "In your ears" makes the fulfillment take place in Jesus' teaching. It also makes the fulfillment unmistakable; the audience are earwitnesses to the fulfillment (compare Luke's appeal to eyewitness testimony in 1:1–4).

4:22: And all were bearing him witness and marveling at the words of grace that were proceeding out of his mouth. And they were saying, "This [man] **is Joseph's son, isn't he?"** They thought he was—in a biological sense. But Luke has told us better. Jesus is the virginally conceived, virginally born Son of God by the miraculous action of the Holy Spirit. Jesus' fellow townspeople can't figure out how such marvelous words can be coming out of the mouth of someone they think is the biological son of a local acquaintance. Yet not a single one of them can deny what their own ears hear. *All* of them not only witness his words with their ears. They also *bear* him witness with their tongues. They tell how marvelous are his words of grace. "The words of grace" means "the gracious words," but not gracious merely in the sense of kindly—or gracious merely in the sense of displaying rhetorical skill, though such skill was highly admired by the likes of "most excellent Theophilus," a man of sophistication. Much more, the words are gracious in the sense of conveying the good news of God's grace, his favor toward the poor, captive, blind, and oppressed.

The people's question, "This [man] is Joseph's son, isn't he?" wasn't directed to Jesus, and he pays no attention to it. Instead, by way of exposing a latent skepticism that underlay their question, he puts words in their mouth. So we read in **4:23: And he said to them, "Surely you'll tell me this proverb, 'Physician, heal yourself.'** [And you'll say,] **'Do here in your hometown, too, as great things as we've heard took place** [at your doing] **in Capernaum.'"** The proverb contains a comparison of Jesus to a physician. The comparison makes the proverb a "parable," which is in fact the Greek word underlying the translation, "proverb." The combination of "Physician" and "heal" with the "great things" that took place in Capernaum means that those things reportedly consisted in miraculous healings, and that Jesus' fellow townspeople doubt what they've heard and therefore challenge him to perform miraculous healings such as they've heard about but don't believe he performed in Capernaum, a town on the shore of the Sea of Galilee. "Heal *yourself*" means heal your *reputation* among us by healing other people's *bodies*. Luke leaves it to be inferred that Jesus has already performed healings in Capernaum. Historically, the healings that according to 4:31–41 took place in Capernaum did so prior to Jesus' teaching in Nazareth. But Luke has reversed the chronological order in favor of a topical order that puts the teaching in Nazareth first as Jesus' programmatic statement concerning his ministry—as though to say, "Here's what I'm going to do: proclaim good news to poor people, release to captives [and so on]."

Jesus makes a new start in **4:24–27: And he said, "Amen I tell you that no prophet is welcome in his hometown.** [25]**And I'm speaking to you on the basis of truth** [that is, I'm telling you the truth]. **There were many widows in Israel in the days of Elijah, when the sky was shut for three years and six months** [so that it didn't rain], **when there was a great famine over all the land** [because of the drought]. [26]**And Elijah was sent to none of them, except to a widow woman in Sarepta** [= the town of Zarephath] **of the Sidonian** [region]. [27]**And there were many lepers in Israel at the time of Elisha the prophet; and none of them was cleansed, except Naaman the Syrian** [was cleansed]." "Amen" and "on the basis of truth" carry a double emphasis on the reliability of what Jesus says here, hard though it was for his audience to accept. Jesus' first statement counters the townspeople's proverb with another proverb, in which Jesus' portraying himself as a prophet replaces the townspeople's portraying him as a physician. In the words of Isaiah, he proclaimed the "welcome year of the Lord" (the Year of Jubilee). But though he proclaimed such a year, he himself isn't welcome in his hometown. Why? Because familiarity breeds contempt. That's Jesus' point. But Luke's point is that the rejection of Jesus by his fellow townspeople wasn't due to any fault in him. They should have welcomed him to the same high degree that they welcomed his message as marvelous. By going on to cite incidents in the ministries of the prophets Elijah and Elisha, Jesus furthers his self-portrayal as a prophet. Since the Old Testament records these incidents, Jesus cites them "on the basis of truth," as even his fellow townspeople would have to admit since they accept the Old Testament (1 Kings 17:1–24; 2 Kings 5:1–14). Jesus cites the incidents to warn that rejecting him will exclude them from his "words of grace," which they've admired, and that God will extend his grace to outsiders, Gentiles, like the widow and Naaman. The two occurrences of "none of them" stress the danger of exclusion.

4:28–30: And on hearing these things, all in the synagogue were filled with rage. [29]**And on standing up** [they'd been sitting in the synagogue], **they thrust him outside the city and led him to the brow of a mountain on which the city had been built, so as to throw him down the cliff** [compare 4:9–10]. [30]**But he, passing through their midst, was traveling on.** The townspeople's rage exposes their refusal to accept the scriptural examples cited by Jesus and thus highlights by contrast his fulfillment of Scripture and behaving in accordance with it. The "all" who are filled with rage correspond to the "all" who "were bearing him witness and marveling at the words of grace proceeding out of his mouth" (4:22). This correspondence portrays their rage as inexcusable. It's all the more inexcusable because of its murderous intent. They make a move to kill Jesus. So their rejection of him is due to a moral fault in them, not to any in him. And their rejection of him fulfills Simeon's prophecy in 2:34–35. Jesus' passing through their midst and traveling on illustrate Jesus' moving "in the power of the Spirit" (4:14) and show that God's plan for Jesus can't be thwarted. "Through their midst" makes his passing subject to eyewitness (he didn't just disappear) in accordance with 1:1–4. And Luke's note that Jesus "was traveling on" appeals again to the great interest in travel that characterized people in the Roman Empire (see the comments on 4:1–2a). As a whole, 4:16–30 adumbrates what will happen repeatedly: admiration followed by rejection and then by escape, ultimately escape through resurrection and ascension.

TEACHING, EXORCISMS, AND HEALINGS IN CAPERNAUM
Luke 4:31–41

This passage subdivides into Jesus' teaching in Capernaum on the Sabbath (4:31–32), exorcising a demon from a man in the synagogue there (4:33–37), healing Simon's mother-in-law (4:38–39), and performing a variety of healings and exorcisms right after the Sabbath ended (4:40–41).

4:31–32: And he went down [from "the mountain on which (Nazareth) had been built" (4:29)] **to Capernaum, a city of Galilee** [about 680 feet below sea level beside the Sea of Galilee]. **And he was teaching them** [the people of Capernaum] **on the Sabbath.** [32]**And they were awestruck at his teaching, because his word was with authority.** In 4:16 Luke emphasized that as a pious Jew, Jesus habitually *attended synagogue* on Sabbath days. Here Luke emphasizes Jesus' *teaching* on a particular Sabbath. The teaching strikes its audience with awe, not because of its content (for Luke doesn't specify its content), but because of the authority that characterizes Jesus' speech. Powerful oratory was highly prized in the culture of that day. The public treated as celebrities speakers who spellbound their audiences. So Luke portrays Jesus as just such a public speaker, a master of communication. Joseph and Mary were awestruck by the twelve-year-old Jesus' learned dialogue with teachers in

the temple (2:46–48). Now a whole town is awestruck by the authoritative teaching of Jesus himself.

4:33–34: And in the synagogue [where apparently Jesus was teaching] **was a man having a spirit of an unclean demon** [that is, who had a spirit *consisting* in an unclean demon—unclean in the sense of moral and/or ritual defilement]. **And he yelled out in a loud voice,** [34]**"Leave [us] alone! What do we and you have to do with each other, Jesus of Nazareth? You've come to destroy us. I know you, [that is,] who you are. [You're] God's Holy One."** The man and his demon speak as a twosome—hence "we" and "us." The loudness of the yell is designed to help the words of the yell ward Jesus off. On the principle that the best defense is a good offense, the demon and his victim go on the attack by brandishing their knowledge of Jesus' name, hometown, intention to destroy them, and identity as "God's Holy One," which—by the way—contrasts with the uncleanness of the demonic spirit but dovetails with Jesus' having been endued and filled with the Holy Spirit (3:22; 4:1 [see also 1:35; 2:23]). Knowledge is power, and such knowledge was thought to give power over a person.

4:35–37: And Jesus reprimanded him [the unclean spirit] **by saying, "Shut up and come out of him." And throwing him down in the midst** [of the synagogue attenders], **the demon came out of him without hurting him at all.** [36]**And astonishment came on all, and they were speaking to one another, saying, "What [is] this word? For he commands the unclean spirits with authority and power, and they come out!"** [37]**And news about him was traveling out into every locality of the surrounding** [region]. Here's part of an ancient pagan text on how to perform an exorcism: "Take oil made from unripe olives, together with the plant mastigia and lotus pith, and boil it with marjoram (very colorless), saying, 'Joel, Ossarthiomi, Emori, Theochipsoith, Sithemeoch [plus additional nonsensical tongue-twisters] . . . . Come out of so-and-so.' But write this phylactery on a little sheet of tin, 'Jaeo, Abraothioch, Phtha . . . ,' and hang it around the sufferer. . . . But when you're adjuring [the demon to come out], blow by sending your breath from above [down to your feet] and [bouncing it back] from the feet to the face; and he [the demon] will be drawn into captivity." Jesus doesn't need to perform any such shenanigans. His simple word of command does the job. Shutting up the demon closes down the defensive maneuver in "I know you . . . ." And the demon's throwing down the man "in the midst" of the onlookers gives them visible evidence of a successful exorcism. "Without hurting him at all" showcases the beneficial effect of the exorcism. Even the demon's last paroxysm has no ill effect whatever. Jesus is completely victorious. All the onlookers are so astonished that they set their synagogue abuzz by asking what is the meaning of Jesus' authoritative, powerful "word" that unclean spirits obey. He has proved himself to be the one "stronger" than John (3:16). That the news about Jesus spreads "to *every* locality in the surrounding [region]" testifies to his overpowering presence and activity. As the Apostle Peter will later say, "God anointed him with the Holy Spirit and power," so that "he went throughout [the whole of Judea/Israel] doing good and healing all who were being dominated by the Devil, because God was with him" (Acts 10:38). For further details, see the comments on Mark 1:23–28.

4:38–39: And on standing up [and going away] **from the synagogue, he entered into the home of Simon. And Simon's mother-in-law was being racked with a high fever. And they made a request to him concerning her. ³⁹And on coming and standing over her, he reprimanded the fever; and it left her. And at once standing up, she started serving them** [food]. "Standing up" implies Jesus had been sitting to teach (see 4:20 with comments). "From the synagogue" is a condensed way of saying he left there. Simon is better known to us as Peter, but Luke won't mention Jesus' giving him that nickname till 6:14. Simon has his home in Capernaum, and it looks as though his mother-in-law lives in the home. Luke doesn't specify who "they" are in Simon's home who ask Jesus to do something about the fever of Simon's mother-in-law. So attention goes exclusively to what Jesus does. The description of the fever as "high" (literally, "great") makes his task seemingly difficult. Jesus' "standing over her," plus her later "standing up," implies she's bedridden with the fever. Jesus reprimands the fever just as he reprimanded the demon (4:35). Not that the fever *is* a demon. Rather, Luke personifies the fever to set up a parallel between this healing and the preceding exorcism. Notably, just as he exorcised the demon by merely speaking, so he makes the fever leave by merely speaking. Visible evidence of the exorcism consisted in the demon's throwing down the possessed man into the midst of attenders at the synagogue without doing him any harm. Likewise, visible evidence of the fever's departure consists in the mother-in-law's standing up and starting to serve food to the unspecified "them." The immediacy of her doing so highlights the completeness of the healing. No need for convalescence in her case. Jesus is the Great Physician.

4:40–41: And as the sun was setting, all—as many as had those who were sick with various diseases—brought them to him. And by placing [his] **hands on each one of them, he was healing them. ⁴¹And demons, too, were coming out from many as they** [the demons] **were shouting and saying, "You're the Son of God." And reprimanding** [them], **he wasn't permitting them to speak, because they knew the Christ to be him.** The Sabbath ended at sunset on Saturday; so people could then do the work of bringing their sick to Jesus without violating the prohibition of work on Sabbath days. Stressing the large number of people whom Jesus healed are "all," "as many as," and "each one of them." His physicianly *charity* knows no bounds. The variety of diseases he heals shows that neither does his physicianly *power* know any bounds. He healed Simon's mother-in-law by merely speaking. Now he heals by merely touching. Whether by way of verbal language or body language,

the healing works. The "many" demoniacs whom Jesus delivers correspond to the many sick he heals. The demons try to defend themselves by brandishing their knowledge that Jesus is God's Son (see the comments on 4:33–35). But to no effect. Jesus succeeds in exorcising them right as they're making their defensive maneuver. The battle is over as soon as it starts. Jesus' reprimand consists in putting a stop to this self-defensive shouting. "Because they knew the Christ to be him" implies that if he hadn't silenced the demons, the brandishing of their knowledge would've worked to prevent his exorcising them (see the comments on 4:33–34). Luke interprets the demons' phrase, "the Son of God," as meaning "the Christ" (compare 9:20; 22:67 with 22:70; 23:35).

AN INTRODUCTION TO JESUS' WIDER MINISTRY
Luke 4:42–44

4:42–44: And when it got to be day [after the healings and exorcisms during Saturday evening, and after the following night], **on going out** [from Capernaum] **he traveled to a deserted place. And the crowds were seeking him. And they came to him and were trying to hold him back so that he wouldn't travel away from them. ⁴³But he said to them, "I must preach the good news of God's reign also to other cities, because I was sent for this purpose." ⁴⁴And he was preaching in the synagogues of Judea.** Again Luke uses Jesus' itineration to appeal to people's interest in travel. That crowds, not just one crowd but a plurality of them, were seeking Jesus and coming to him even in a deserted spot testifies to his popularity, based as it was on his powerful preaching, healing, and exorcisms. The effort to hold him back, unsuccessful though it was, underscores further his popularity. He then shows obedience to the commission laid on him, that is, the commission to spread elsewhere the good news of God's reign—a commission that he'll pass on to his disciples in Acts 1:8 (compare Jesus' being sent to preach good news in 4:18). His preaching now extends to "the synagogues of Judea." As in 1:5; 6:17; 7:17; 23:5; Acts 1:8; 10:37, Luke is using "Judea" not just for the southern region of Israel but for the whole land of Israel. Thus Jesus becomes the example *par excellence* of a traveling evangelist.

FOLLOWER-MAKING WISDOM DISPLAYED BY JESUS
Luke 5:1–11

Luke 2:40 said that as the little boy Jesus was growing up he was being filled with wisdom, and 2:52 that from the age of twelve onward he was advancing in wisdom. The present passage displays his wisdom as a full-grown adult at the height of his powers (compare the comments on 3:23). Appropriately to the theme of wisdom, the passage begins with his teaching (5:1–3). Then comes the display of wisdom in some practical advice he gives on fishing (5:4–7). The passage ends with a double reaction of astonishment and leaving all to follow him (5:8–11).

5:1–3: And it happened that while the crowd was pressing on him and hearing the word of God, he himself was standing alongside the Lake of Gennesaret [= the Sea of Galilee, but called by the name of a plain south of Capernaum and immediately west of the lake]. [2]**And he saw two boats standing alongside the lake; but the fishermen, having gotten out of them, were washing the nets** [that they'd used for fishing the whole preceding night according to 5:5]. [3]**And on getting into one of the boats, which was Simon's, he** [Jesus] **asked him to put out from the land a little. And on sitting down, he was teaching the crowds from the boat.** Jesus has been preaching in synagogues (4:44). Now he's speaking outdoors. The crowd have flocked to hear him even in the open air. And what they hear him say is nothing less than "the word of God," for God's Spirit is on him (4:18). Since he draws a crowd wherever he goes, Luke can write about "*the* crowd" as a fixed feature of Jesus' ministry. Their "*pressing* on him" magnifies his popularity. He'd taken a stand alongside the lake to speak God's word to the crowd. Having been beached, the two boats that Jesus saw were likewise standing alongside the lake. The twoness of the boats prepares for a mention of the brothers James and John, who'd apparently been using the boat other than Simon's (whom 4:38 mentioned in passing). Jesus commandeers Simon's boat and Simon himself (compare the authority of his word in 4:33–41). It goes without saying that Simon obeyed Jesus' request "to put out from the land a little." The *little* distance keeps the crowd within earshot of Jesus' teaching, which he delivers in the authoritative posture of sitting (compare 4:20). But "the crowd" (singular) now becomes "the crowds" (plural) to further the emphasis on his popularity.

5:4–7: And when he'd stopped speaking, he said to Simon, "Put out into the deep and lower your nets for a catch." [5]**And answering, Simon said, "Master, laboring through a whole night we took nothing. But on the basis of your word, I'll lower the nets."** [6]**And on doing this, they** [the nets] **enclosed a multitudinous multitude of fish. And their nets started to tear.** [7]**And they** [Simon and whoever was with him] **motioned to** [their] **partners in the other boat to come help them. And they** [the partners] **did come; and they** [all of them] **filled both boats, so that they** [the boats] **started sinking.** Because Simon owns the boat where Jesus is sitting, Jesus tells him to put out from near the shore into deep water. But Simon has anonymous helpers ("all those with him" in 5:9, who don't include James and John in the other boat [5:10]). So Jesus addresses his command to the helpers as well as to Simon: "[You, plural] lower your nets." Simon's addressing Jesus with "Master" displays a suitable recognition of Jesus' superiority. (A "master" is someone who figuratively "stands over" someone else.) Simon's noting his and his helpers' failure to catch anything despite a whole, wearisome night of fishing makes all the more admirable his compliance with Jesus' command and also sets up for an astonishingly different outcome. The fisherman in charge of his boat (Simon) is taking orders from a nonfisherman (Jesus) who nev-

ertheless knows more about fishing than Simon does. Several features of the subsequent catch highlight its magnitude: (1) the designation of it both as "a . . . *multitude*" and also as "a *multitudinous* multitude" (an admittedly awkward, even humorous translation, but one that corresponds exactly to Luke's Greek); (2) the nets' starting to tear as a result of the weight of such a catch; (3) the nets' being so heavy with fish that Simon and his helpers can't lift them by themselves and so need help from their partners in the other boat; (4) the filling of *both* boats with the fish; and (5) the boats' starting to sink under the weight of fish despite a division of the catch between them.

5:8–11: And on seeing [what had happened]**, Simon Peter fell on his knees toward Jesus, saying, "Go away from me, because I'm a sinful man, Lord."** [9]**For astonishment had engulfed him and all those with him because of the catch of fish that they'd taken;** [10]**and likewise also** [astonishment had engulfed] **James and John, Zebedee's sons, who were partners with Simon. And Jesus told Simon, "Don't fear. From now on you'll be catching human beings alive."** [11]**And on bringing the boats to the land, leaving all they followed him.** The addition of "Peter" to "Simon" calls attention to his reaction to the catch. Earlier, he stated compliance with Jesus' command and called him "Master." Now he does obeisance before Jesus and calls him "Lord." By itself, "Lord" could mean no more than "Sir" and no higher than "Master." But combined with obeisance it does carry a higher meaning, that of deity so far as Luke is concerned, whatever Simon Peter may have meant (compare 1:43; 2:11). His asking Jesus to go away from him because he, Simon, is a sinful man not only displays a proper sense of unworthiness on Simon's part. It also implies the holiness of Jesus, his moral distinctiveness (compare 1:35; 2:23; 4:34). Testifying to Jesus' practical wisdom is the astonishment not only of Simon but also of his helpers ("*all* of them," no exceptions) and his partners James and John. Even these seasoned fishermen could hardly believe their eyes. Jesus has shown himself the Compleat Angler. His telling Simon not to fear implies that Simon's astonishment led to fear and indicates that Simon needn't think his sinfulness requires Jesus to go away from him. On the contrary, from this point on Simon will be catching human beings instead of fish; and he'll be catching them "alive" in that unlike fish, which die as a result of being caught, these human beings will gain life, *eternal* life. Jesus doesn't explain his figurative language. He doesn't need to, because on bringing their boats to the land Simon and the others leave "all" and follow Jesus. Simon understands implicitly that Jesus will turn him into a fisher of human beings (for an outstanding example, see Acts 2:14–41). The others—they follow Jesus out of sheer astonishment at his wise counsel on fishing. The "all" that they and Simon leave behind includes their boats, their nets, and the haul of fish. But because of Luke's lack of specification, "all" has to include *whatever* might have kept these men there. Jesus hasn't told them to leave all and follow him. They just do. Such is their newfound devotion to Jesus, and such is his magnetism.

JESUS' PHILANTHROPY, FIDELITY, POPULARITY, AND PIETY
Luke 5:12–16

5:12: And it happened that while he was in one of the cities, behold, a man full of leprosy! And on seeing Jesus, falling on [his] **face he begged him, saying, "Lord, if you want** [to do so], **you can cleanse me."** "Behold" and "*full* of leprosy" make the man's malady a topic of exclamation. He's in a bad way (see 17:11–13; Leviticus 13:45–46; 2 Kings 7:3–10 for the ostracism of lepers). (In those days "leprosy" wasn't limited to Hansen's disease, as it is nowadays, but covered other skin diseases too: psoriasis and ringworm for example.) No wonder, then, that he falls on his face and begs Jesus. "Falling on his face" makes "Lord" carry the high connotation of deity—if not quite in the leper's intention, at least in Luke's (see 5:8 with comments). The leper shows admirable faith in Jesus' ability to cleanse him, and equally admirable acquiescence to Jesus' desire, of which he's uncertain. "Cleanse" applies to leprosy because of its rendering victims ritually unclean (hence their ostracism, mentioned above). Otherwise we'd expect the verb "heal."

5:13: And stretching out [his] **hand, he** [Jesus] **touched him, saying, "I want to** [cleanse you]. **Be cleansed." And immediately the leprosy went away from him** [the leper]. Ordinarily, touching a leper makes the person who touches him ritually unclean (compare Leviticus 14:46–47 and the repeated instructions in Leviticus 13 that priests who inspect for leprosy should only "look" for it). Here, though, leprosy leaves the leper rather than drawing Jesus into a zone of defilement. For the leprosy's departure marks a *cleansing* of the leper. Its immediacy dramatizes the power of Jesus to cleanse the leper, and his wanting to do so highlights his humanitarianism (compare Acts 10:38: "Jesus, the [man] from Nazareth—how God anointed him with the Holy Spirit and power—who went throughout [the land] doing good [to people] and healing all who were being dominated by the Devil"). The body language of stretching out the hand to touch the leper and the verbal language in "Be cleansed" combine to produce this happy result.

5:14: And he [Jesus] **ordered him to tell no one** [about his being cleansed]: **"Rather, on going away, show yourself to the priest and make an offering in regard to your cleansing, just as Moses prescribed, for a testimony to them."** The command that the cleansed leper not tell anyone has the purpose of making the subsequent report come from none other than the priest who'll officially confirm the cleansing that Jesus has effected (see 5:15). The command not to tell anyone also provides a foil against which the subsequent spread of the report will stand out (see 5:15 again). "*Show* yourself to the priest" will make the priest's report that of an eyewitness and therefore credible (compare 1:1–4). This showing to the priest and the making of an offering in regard to the cleansing conform to Mosaic law (see Leviticus 14:1–32). As usual, Luke delights to portray Jesus in conformity with the ancient traditions of Judaism. Note: neither the priest nor the making of an offering effects the cleansing; Jesus has already done that. Who are "them" to whom the self-showing and offering will be a testimony? We could guess they'll be the priest and all those who'll hear his report directly and indirectly. But the lack of specification suggests that Luke has in mind also the audience of his Gospel. In any case, it's the commanded obedience to Jewish law, not the cleansing, that constitutes the testimony in favor of Jesus' fidelity to Judaism. He's no renegade.

5:15–16: But the word [= the report] **about it went throughout** [the land], **instead, and many crowds were coming together to hear** [Jesus] **and be healed from their illnesses. [16]But he was withdrawing in deserted** [places] **and praying.** This "word" about Jesus' having cleansed the leper contributes to the overall "word" of the gospel, whose certainty Luke writes to demonstrate (1:1–4). "Instead" indicates that in place of a report by the ex-leper such as Jesus prohibited, a report by the priest came out of his visual confirmation of Jesus' having cleansed the man. The man himself didn't have to say anything, and the priest unwittingly became an "assistant of the word" of the gospel (1:2). In turn, a circulation of the priest's report led to an increase in Jesus' popularity. Emphasizing the increase is "crowds" (plural), "*many*" of them, and their "coming *together*." "To *hear* [Jesus] and be *healed* from their illnesses" puts his word and his humanitarianism together in a twofold accolade. Jesus' habit of withdrawing shows him not to be promoting himself for the sake of the popularity that he nevertheless receives. And his habit of praying in deserted places shows him to be pious.

THE BRINGING OF GLORY TO GOD THROUGH A MIRACLE OF JESUS
Luke 5:17–26

This episode starts with a general statement. **5:17: And it happened during one of the days** [of Jesus' activities]**—and he was teaching** [we'd say "*that* he was teaching"]. **And sitting** [there] **were Pharisees and teachers of the Law who'd come from every town of Galilee and Judea and Jerusalem. And the power of the Lord was for him to heal** [as will be shown in the following story]. The Pharisees were a Jewish sect who practiced punctiliously the Mosaic law and their teachers' interpretations of it. That they, including their teachers, had come "from *every* town" not only of Jesus' home territory of Galilee in the north but also of Judea down south and the capital city of Jerusalem, located there, shows how widely the report of Jesus' cleansing the leper had spread. (After all, the cleansed leper had to be certified as clean and offer a sacrifice at the temple in Jerusalem.) The sitting of the

Pharisees and teachers of the Law, who'll criticize Jesus, contrasts with both the vigorous faith of those who'll carry a paralytic to Jesus and the paralytic's standing up, picking up his bed, and walking home when Jesus heals him. In advance, Luke attributes the healing to the Lord's power that Jesus wields. The word for "power" is the singular of the word translated "miracles" in the plural. To highlight the humanitarianism with which Jesus wields this power, Luke writes that it had the purpose and result of healing.

5:18–19: And behold, men carrying on a mat a man who was paralyzed! And they were trying to bring him in and put him under the eyes of him [Jesus]. **¹⁹And on account of the crowd, not finding such** [a way] **that they might bring him in, going up on the roof they let him down with the little mat through the tiles into the midst** [of the crowd] **in front of Jesus.** The exclamatory "behold . . . !" calls attention to the sorry and seemingly hopeless plight of a man so severely paralyzed that others have to carry him on a mat, used as a stretcher. Their trying to bring him in and put him under Jesus' eyes indicates that the sympathy of Jesus for disabled people had come to be recognized. ("Paralytic" doesn't necessarily imply the effect of a stroke, but it does indicate some sort of neuromuscular inability to walk.) The men believed that the mere sight of the paralytic would excite Jesus' sympathy. The obstacle of the crowd surrounding Jesus (they were in addition to the Pharisees and teachers of the Law) revives emphasis on his popularity. As in 5:1, "*the* crowd" has become a fixture because of that popularity. The men's going up on the roof to let down the paralytic on his mat through the roof tiles (some of which they had to remove, of course)—their doing so exhibits a determination to get the paralytic healed. So to Jesus' humanitarianism is added theirs. Such people are drawn to him. Because of the tightness of the hole in the roof, Luke adds "little" to "mat." Only a little mat could be squeezed through. "Into the *midst*" will make the whole crowd eyewitnesses of Jesus' healing (compare 1:1–4). And "in front of Jesus" puts the paralytic in Jesus' full view.

5:20–21: And on seeing their faith [that is, the faith of the men who brought the paralytic, though the paralytic himself might be included]**, he said, "Man, your sins have been** [and therefore are] **forgiven for you."** **²¹And the scholars** [= "teachers of the Law" in 5:17] **and the Pharisees began to reason, saying, "Who is this who is speaking blasphemies? Who can forgive sins except God *alone*?"** Jesus *sees* the men's faith in the great effort they made in putting the paralytic "under his *eyes*." (The preposition usually translated "before" in 5:18 means "within the eyesight of.") "Man" isn't an unfriendly address, but neither is it friendly (despite the use of "Friend" in some translations). Jesus addresses the paralytic with "Man" for a wordplay with "the Son of Man," which he'll use for himself shortly (5:24). The point of the wordplay will be that as a human being Jesus has forgiven the sins of a fellow human being. Jesus' hu-

manitarianism shines out again. "For you," which occupies a prominent position in Luke's original text, stresses the benefit to the paralytic of having had his sins forgiven and highlights Jesus' humanitarianism yet further. He doesn't attribute the man's paralysis to any sins the man has committed, much less to one particular sin of his. So the emphasis falls entirely on gracious forgiveness, a better gift than even the healing expected by the men who'd brought the paralytic (compare 7:47–49). Who has forgiven his sins, though? Jesus hasn't said. But the scholars and Pharisees take him to mean that he himself has forgiven the paralytic's sins and therefore consider his statement blasphemous, since in their view God alone can forgive sins. Jesus has made only one statement, so that we expect the scholars and Pharisees to accuse him of "blasphemy" (singular). But they're so outraged that they accuse him of "blasphemies" (plural), as though every word of his statement constituted a discrete blasphemy. Supposedly, these blasphemies consisted in Jesus' arrogating to himself an exclusively divine prerogative, that of forgiving sins. Such an arrogation slanders God, they reason, by verbally robbing him of an authority he alone possesses. ("Blasphemy" means "slander.")

5:22–24: And on recognizing their reasonings [plural, because each of the scholars and Pharisees was reasoning privately and therefore individually] **Jesus, answering, said to them, "Why are you reasoning in your hearts? ²³Which is easier, to say, 'Your sins have been forgiven for you,' or to say, 'Rise and walk around'? ²⁴But in order that you may know that the Son of Man has authority on the earth to forgive sins"**—he said to the paralyzed [man], **"I say to you, rise and, on picking up your little mat, go into your home."** Since the scholars and Pharisees were reasoning "in their hearts" rather than out loud in discussion with one another, Jesus' recognition of their reasonings exhibits its supernatural clairvoyance. He answers in the sense of responding to their unvoiced reasonings. His question *why* they're reasoning in their hearts implies that what he's about to do will make their reasonings unreasonable. The followup question has an obvious answer: it's easier to *pronounce* forgiveness than to *prove* it with a miracle. So Jesus sets about to prove that as the Son of Man (about which self-designation see the comments on Mark 2:10–11) he has authority on the earth to forgive sins just as God has such authority in heaven. In other words, Jesus agrees with the scholars and Pharisees that his saying, "Man, your sins have been forgiven for you," meant that *he*, Jesus, had claimed to forgive them. In his command to the paralytic, he expands the earlier "walk around" to "on picking up your little mat, go into your home." Provided the command works, this expansion emphasizes the dramatic shifts from being *carried* on the mat to *carrying* it and from being brought *from* home to going *into* the home.

5:25–26: And at once standing up within their eyesight [see the parenthetical comment on 5:20–21]**, on picking up what he'd been lying on, he went away**

into his home, glorifying God. ²⁶And awe took hold of them all, and they were glorifying God, and they were filled with fear, saying, "We've seen unimaginable things today." The immediacy of the man's standing up shows Jesus' power to heal so great that it requires no time to take effect. "Within their eyesight" makes even the scholars and Pharisees eyewitnesses to this miraculous proof of Jesus' earthly authority to forgive sins. "What he'd been lying on" replaces "the little mat" of Jesus' command to highlight the shift from lying flat to standing up and going home. The man's glorifying God exhibits a good religious effect of Jesus' miracle in addition to its good physical effect (see the comments on 2:20). The word for "awe" connotes an amazement so overpowering it takes your breath away. That such amazement took hold of "all" heightens the effect of Jesus' healing power on the scholars, the Pharisees, and the crowd. And to this psychological effect is added the religious effect of their glorifying God just as the healed paralytic does. Even the scholars and the Pharisees join in! The gospel produces good religion, Luke wants us to know. And such religion includes "fear" of the kind that Psalm 111:10 says is "the beginning of wisdom." Awe took hold of all from the outside. Fear filled them on the inside. No wonder they say they've seen unimaginable things. Just as "blasphemies" portrayed Jesus' statement of forgiveness in the plural for emphasis, so also "unimaginable things" portrays his demonstrative healing in the plural for emphasis. What he's done bursts the bounds of human thought and grammatical accuracy. "We've *seen*" makes it credible, though, and brings us back again to the eyewitnesses whose testimony undergirds the gospel (1:1–4). "Today" locates what they've seen on this very occasion and therefore makes it unmistakable (compare 4:21). No time for memory loss!

JESUS AS A MORAL REFORMER
Luke 5:27–32

This passage starts with Jesus' calling a tax collector (5:27–28) and concludes with a banquet and dialogue (5:29–32).

5:27–28: And after these things he went out [from the tile-roofed house where he'd forgiven and healed the paralytic (5:17–26)] **and observed a tax collector (Levi by name) sitting at the tax booth and said to him, "Follow me."** ²⁸**And on leaving all, standing up he set out following him.** See the comments on 3:12 for the crooked practices of tax collectors. By going out, observing the tax collector Levi, and telling Levi to follow him, Jesus takes compassionate initiative to reform a sinner. Levi's "sitting at the tax booth" implies that he was collecting taxes from fishermen or from merchants in the form of tolls on commercial goods passing through. Jesus' "Follow me" sounds imperious. Indeed it was. After all, though, he's "Christ *the Lord*" (2:11). Levi's "leaving all" means the abandonment of his occupation in favor of devotion to Jesus. In this respect Levi does more than what John the baptizer required of tax

collectors, which was to collect no more than what they were required to collect (3:12–13). Levi's "standing up" reverses his "sitting at the tax booth," and his "following" Jesus displays obedience to Christ as his Lord. The standing up and the following circumscribe the leaving and thus confine the "all" that Levi leaves to the entirety of his tax-collecting business. (He still has a house in which to host a banquet.)

5:29–30: And Levi put on a great banquet for him [Jesus] **in his** [Levi's] **house; and there was a large crowd of tax collectors, plus others who were reclining** [at table] **with them** [the tax collectors]. ³⁰**And the Pharisees and their scholars were complaining to his** [Jesus'] **disciples by saying, "Why are you eating and drinking with the tax collectors and sinful people?"** The putting on of a banquet *for Jesus* pays him suitable honor and thus manifests Levi's religious devotion to his Lord. Luke's description of the banquet as "great" magnifies both the honor and the devotion. In that culture, banqueters reclined on cushions around a low table. The large crowd of tax collectors and the others who were reclining with them, making an even larger crowd, testify to Jesus' magnetism even over ne'er-do-wells. The Pharisees and their scholars reappear (compare 5:17, 21). Are these the same ones as before, though? Probably not, since the earlier ones were among the "all" who were glorifying God for the Lord's power with which Jesus healed the paralytic (5:17, 26). But as the earlier ones criticized Jesus at first, these ones criticize the disciples for eating with the tax collectors and sinful people. "Disciples" means "learners." The disciples of Jesus have learned to eat with tax collectors and sinful people from his doing so; but since Jesus is the guest of honor, the Pharisees and their scholars don't pick on him. Luke describes their criticism as complaining, that is, grumbling or muttering. The complaining takes the form of a question ("Why . . . ?") rather than an accusation ("You're . . . !"). Underlying the question is a presumption that holy people should maintain a social distance from tax collectors and sinful people, whereas eating and drinking with them establishes a close bond. "Sinful people" defines the "others" who were reclining with the tax collectors according to 5:29.

5:31–32: And answering, Jesus told them, "People who are healthy don't have need of a physician; rather, people who are sick [do]. ³²**I haven't come to call righteous people; rather,** [I've come to call] **sinful people to repentance."** Jesus answers the Pharisees' and scholars' question even though they didn't direct it against him or to him. But as his disciples' teacher, he's responsible for their behavior, especially since it mirrors his own behavior. In the answer he compares righteous people to healthy people, who don't need a physician, sinful people to sick people, who do need one, and himself to a physician. And his calling sinful people to repentance—he compares this to the healing work of a physician (though "call" also sounds like an invitation to the banquet of salvation such as the present banquet might represent).

Jesus' omission of "tax collectors" makes "sinful people" include tax collectors along with other sorts of sinners. It's often said that the righteous don't really exist, that they're only a fictional foil against which sinners stand out, or similarly but more specifically that the righteous are the Pharisees and scholars who are righteous in their own and others' eyes but not before God. Just such a Pharisee appears in 18:9–14 (see also 16:14–15; 20:20). So far in Luke, though, truly righteous people have appeared (see 1:6, 17; 2:25). As such, they're drawn to the gospel through a preexisting affinity. But Jesus has to "call" sinful people, as he did Levi. And this call is "to repentance" (see the comments on 3:3 for repentance). Jesus acts as a moral reformer, then, not as a religious or political insurgent.

JESUS' DEFENSE OF A TRADITIONAL RELIGIOUS PRACTICE
Luke 5:33–39

5:33: And they said to him, "The disciples of John [the baptizer] **fast often and make requests** [in prayer to God]—**likewise also the** [disciples] **of the Pharisees. But yours eat and drink."** The topic of fasting versus eating and drinking follows naturally upon the eating and drinking at a banquet in 5:27–32. At first "they" who speak to Jesus about this topic seem to be "the Pharisees and their scholars" of 5:30. But the speakers refer to "the [disciples] *of the Pharisees*" rather than to "*our* disciples." So "they" probably means "some people," otherwise unidentified. Fasting and making requests in prayer go together because fasting has the purpose of devoting yourself wholly to prayer, especially to the kind of prayer in which you're so desperate to have God grant your requests that you fast to demonstrate the desperation (compare 2:37). The present statement amounts to an accusation that Jesus' disciples aren't so religious as John's disciples and those of the Pharisees. (In 18:12 a Pharisee will mention his fasting twice a week.)

In his answer Jesus uses figurative language to explain that his presence constitutes a special occasion, one that makes it impossible for the accusers to force fasting on his disciples (though his omission of prayer implies that the practice of prayer continues). In other words, Jesus' presence trumps others' attempts to shame the disciples into a show of piety by fasting. **5:34: And Jesus said to them, "You can't make the sons of the bridal chamber** [= attendants of the bridegroom] **fast while the bridegroom is with them."** Jesus is the bridegroom. His disciples are the bridegroom's attendants. His presence with them is a wedding celebration. But such a celebration doesn't last forever. It's temporary. So Jesus continues in **5:35: "But days will come—and when the bridegroom is taken away from them, then they'll fast during those days."** The coming days are the time of the church. The bridegroom's being taken away is Jesus' being taken up from the disciples at the ascension (24:51; Acts 1:9–11). The wedding celebration of his presence will be over. As a result, the disciples

will go back to the traditional practice of fasting (see Acts 9:9; 13:2–3; 14:23). Luke writes his Gospel during "those days" of revived fasting. So nobody can now say that Jesus' disciples are less pious than those of John the baptizer and of the Pharisees.

5:36–39 backs up this return to fasting with a two-pronged parable (= a comparison) that defends old practices, such as fasting for the purpose of praying. Luke's Jesus won't be seen as an iconoclast when it comes to traditional piety. **And he was also telling them a parable: "No one, having torn a patch from a new garment, throws** [= sews] [it] **onto an old garment. Otherwise, indeed, he'll both tear the new** [garment] **and the patch from the new** [garment] **won't match the old** [garment]. **³⁷And no one throws** [= pours] **new wine into old wineskins. Otherwise, indeed, the new wine will burst the wineskins and it'll be spilled out; and the wineskins will be destroyed. ³⁸Rather, new wine must be thrown** [= poured] **into new wineskins. ³⁹And on drinking old** [wine], **no one wants new** [wine]. **For he says, 'The old is excellent.'"** Nobody spoils both a new garment and an old one by tearing a patch from the new and mismatching the old with such a patch. And nobody wastes new wine and destroys old wineskins by pouring the new, which expands through fermentation, into old wineskins already stretched to their limit through prior use. Two occurrences of "indeed" emphasize these points. Jesus doesn't deny he has brought something new. In 22:20 he'll refer to "the new covenant in [his] blood." But his concern is for the preservation of both the old and the new. In the end, though, emphasis falls here on the excellence of the old. Though the new wine of the gospel has to be put in the new wineskins of celebratory eating and drinking in Jesus' presence, the excellence of aged wine—that is, of the tried and true practice of fasting to pray—makes undesirable the new wine of celebratory eating and drinking once he has been taken away.

JESUS AS LORD OVER THE SABBATH
Luke 6:1–5

6:1–2: And it happened on a Sabbath that he was going through [fields that had been] **sown** [with grain], **and his disciples were plucking and eating the heads of grain as they were rubbing** [the heads] **in** [their] **hands. ²But some of the Pharisees said, "Why are you** [disciples of Jesus] **doing what's not lawful** [to do] **on the Sabbath?"** There was no law against going through grain fields, not even on the Sabbath. And Deuteronomy 23:25 explicitly allows the plucking of heads of grain by people who are going through somebody else's grain field. What wasn't allowed was working on the Sabbath (Exodus 20:8–11; 34:21; Deuteronomy 5:12–15); and the disciples' plucking heads of grain and rubbing them in their hands to separate the wheat from the chaff counted as work, specifically as reaping, threshing, and winnowing—that is, preparing food. (Meals to be eaten on the Sabbath were prepared prior to the Sabbath.) So the Pharisees' question is accusatory.

6:3–5: And answering, Jesus said to them, "But you've read this, haven't you, what David did when he got hungry—he and those who were with him—⁴how he entered into God's house [at that time the tabernacle, for the temple hadn't yet been built] and, on taking the loaves of presentation, ate [them] and gave [them] to those [who were] with him, which [loaves] aren't lawful to eat—except for the priests alone [to eat]?" ⁵And he was telling them, "The Son of Man is Lord of the Sabbath." Though the Pharisees directed their question to the disciples, Jesus answers their question with one of his own, since as the teacher of his disciples he's responsible for their behavior (so too in 5:30–31). His question, "But you've read this, haven't you . . . ?" implies the answer, "Of course you have, because as Pharisees you know the Old Testament!" Jesus is referring to the story of David in 1 Samuel 21:1–6 and to the instructions in Leviticus 24:5–9 that only priests should eat the sacred bread presented weekly to the Lord in the tabernacle and later in the temple. By drawing a parallel between the unlawful actions of David and his companions and that of his own disciples, Jesus implies that his disciples' actions do indeed break the Law. His portrayal of David as "taking" the sacred bread and "giv[ing]" it to others strengthens the parallel, because Luke will portray Jesus too—and him alone—as "taking" bread and "giv[ing]" it to others (9:16; 22:19; 24:30). The portrayal is all the more striking in that 1 Samuel 21:1–6 doesn't portray David as "taking" the sacred bread and "giv[ing]" it to his companions (or, for that matter, as hungering along with his companions, as entering God's house [contrast the priest Ahimelech's "com[ing]" with trembling to meet David"], as having companions with him [though he seems to be *pretending* he did], or as eating the bread). The giving and taking may be legitimate inferences, but Jesus' making the inferences links up with Luke's portrayal of Jesus himself. On the other hand, Luke doesn't portray Jesus as David-like in hungering along with his disciples, in entering God's house, or in eating grain after plucking it and rubbing it in his hands. The emphasis falls, then, on Jesus' lordship over the Sabbath. (In Luke's original text, "Lord" occupies an emphatic forward position.) As "the Son of Man" who "has authority on the earth to forgive sins" (5:24 [compare 5:34]), Jesus also has authority to let his disciples break the Law, given their hunger. Thus his humanitarianism feeds into his lordship (compare 2:10–11: "And the angel said, 'Stop being afraid. For behold, I'm announcing to you as good news a great joy, which will be for all the people, because today there has been born for you in the city of David a Savior, who is Christ, *the Lord.*'"

JESUS AS A BENEFACTOR
Luke 6:6–11

6:6–7: And it happened on another Sabbath [besides the one on which Jesus has just defended his disciples (6:1–5)] that he entered into the synagogue and was teaching. And a man was there, and his right hand was withered. ⁷And the scholars and the Pharisees were scrutinizing him [to see] whether he heals on the Sabbath. [They were doing so] in order that they might find [a basis] for accusing him. Jesus' entry into the synagogue revives emphasis on his piety (see especially 4:16, "And *according to what was customary for him* [to do] *on the Sabbath day*, he entered into the synagogue," but also 4:44). So much was this a practice of Jesus that "*the* synagogue" has become a fixture of his ministry just as "*the* crowd" has become such a fixture (compare the comments on 5:1–3). His teaching in the synagogue adds honorific authority to habitual piety (see especially 4:15, "And he was teaching in their synagogues, *being glorified* by all," and 4:32, "And they were awestruck at his teaching, because his word was *with authority*"). Luke notes that it was the man's *right* hand that was withered. Since most people are right-handed, Luke implies that the man had lost use of his most useful hand (see Psalm 137:5), so that Jesus' healing it will prove especially beneficial. As in 5:17–6:5, the scholars and the Pharisees appear on the scene, this time not merely to criticize Jesus or accuse his disciples but to bring a formal charge against him should he violate the prohibition of work on the Sabbath. For this purpose they watch him closely, out of the corner of their eyes, as though spying on him. The desire to find a basis for accusing him pits their malevolence against his benevolence.

6:8–9: But he knew their reasonings and said to the man who had the withered hand, "Get up, and stand in the midst [of these scholars and Pharisees]." And standing up, he stood [in their midst]. ⁹And Jesus said to them, "I ask you whether it's lawful to do good on the Sabbath or to do harm, to save life or to destroy [it]?" "Their reasonings" internalize the scholars' and Pharisees' purpose to accuse Jesus, if possible, of breaking the Sabbath. (In 6:1–5 they'd accused only his disciples of breaking it.) "[To see] whether he *heals* [present tense] on the Sabbath" (6:7) makes the issue one of principle, and perhaps of Jesus' habit as well. His knowing their reasonings exhibits clairvoyance, as already in 5:21–22 (see also 2:34–35); and his telling the man to get up and stand in the midst of the scholars and Pharisees prepares for their eyewitnessing the benevolent healing that Jesus is about to perform. Luke subpoenas, so to speak, Jesus' enemies to bear eyewitness on his behalf (compare 1:1–4). The man's standing up and standing in their midst displays obedience but mainly, so far as Luke is concerned, doubles an emphasis on the visibility of the coming miracle of healing. Here Luke uses a word for "man" that normally and specifically connotes a male adult, and "withered" has an emphatic position to stress Jesus' benevolence in restoring the man's right hand to usefulness. Jesus' question whether it's lawful to do good on the Sabbath or to do harm, to save life or to destroy it, puts the issue in terms of benevolence versus malevolence. Notably, not to do good and save life on the Sabbath isn't just neglectful. It's malevolent. But the scholars and Pharisees would have agreed that saving life on the Sabbath is lawful. So Jesus' question implies that if they can make an exception for saving life on the Sabbath, he can make an exception for doing good on the Sabbath. And restoring a withered hand would count as doing good (see the comments on Mark 3:1–6, especially verses 3–4, for a slightly different take in that Gospel).

6:10–11: And on looking around at them all, he told him, "Stretch out your hand." And he did, and his hand was restored. ¹¹But they were filled with blankmindedness and were discussing with one another what they might do to Jesus. The addition of "all" to "them" leaves none of the scholars and Pharisees out of the circle of eyewitnesses to Jesus' doing of good. One wonders whether they'd count his mere speaking as a violation of the Sabbath, or whether they'd think the curative effect *made* the speaking such a violation. In either case, stretching out the hand is opposed to the curling up of a withered hand. So stretching it out demonstrates its restoration for all to see, and therefore demonstrates Jesus' authority as well as ability to do good on the Sabbath. The scholars and Pharisees have had "their reasonings" reduced to "blankmindedness." To drive home the point, Luke writes with wry humor that "they were *filled* with blankmindedness," as if the *lack* of something could *fill* anyone. At their wits' end, the scholars and Pharisees can only discuss with one another what "they *might* do" to Jesus. At this point, then, all bets are off.

JESUS' PRAYING IN ADVANCE OF CHOOSING THE TWELVE AND NAMING THEM APOSTLES
Luke 6:12–16

6:12: And it happened during these days [of the events that Luke has just recorded] **that he** [Jesus] **went out** [from the synagogue in which he'd restored a man's withered hand (6:6–11)] **onto the mountain to pray, and he was spending the whole night in prayer to God.** Going out "to the mountain" brings Jesus closer to heaven for the purpose of prayer "to God." "The" calls attention to the special suitability of a mountain for such praying. So to the piety of Jesus' attending synagogue in 6:6 and earlier, Luke adds the piety of Jesus' praying (as also at his baptism in 3:21 [see too 5:16; 9:18, 28–29; 22:39–46]). "Spending the whole night in prayer" heightens the accent on this sort of piety. Though many commentators deduce that Jesus was praying for divine guidance in selecting and naming the twelve apostles (6:13–16), Luke doesn't relate the content of Jesus' praying. So the accent falls on praying as such. Consistently, Luke portrays Jesus as a paragon of piety.

6:13–16: And when day came, he summoned his disciples; and on selecting from them twelve, whom he also named apostles: ¹⁴Simon (whom he also named Peter) and Andrew (his brother) and James [= the Old Testament name "Jacob"] **and John and Philip and Bartholomew ¹⁵and Matthew and Thomas and James ([the son] of Alphaeus) and Simon (the one called Zealot) ¹⁶and Judas** [= the Old Testament name "Judah"] **([the son] of James** [other than the two previously mentioned, apostolic Jameses]**) and Judas Iscariot (who became a traitor)—** [Luke leaves his sentence incomplete]. Jesus' summoning his disciples not only displays his authority over them. It also implies his solitude during the whole night of prayer, so that his piety stands out all the more. His "*selecting* from them twelve" implies a number of disciples larger than twelve, an indication of evangelistic success. Why a selection of *twelve*, no more and no fewer? The answer will come in 22:29–30, where Jesus predicts that the Twelve will "sit on thrones judging the twelve tribes of Israel" (see Acts 1:6–7; 15:16 for a restoration of the kingdom to Israel and similar implications already in Luke 1:32–33, 54–55, 68–79; 2:25, 32b). Since superiors name inferiors, Jesus' naming these twelve "apostles" as well as selecting them displays again his authority (see the comments on Mark 3:13–15). So the Twelve are not only "learners" (the meaning of "disciples"). They're also "sent ones" (the meaning of "apostles"). Jesus will send them out as certified eyewitnesses of his ministry, which extended from John's baptism of him through his ascension (see especially Acts 1:1–26). Luke makes nothing out of the meaning of "Peter" as "stone" (not "rock," as usually said). So the emphasis stays on the naming as such, which displays Jesus' superiority again. "[The son] of Alphaeus" distinguishes one James both from a previously mentioned James and from a following James who fathered a Judas. But "Iscariot (who became a traitor)" distinguishes a later Judas from this earlier Judas. Likewise, "the one called Zealot" distinguishes a second Simon from the one Jesus named "Peter." "Zealot" may describe this second Simon as zealous in his practice and defense of Judaism (compare Paul's self-descriptions in Acts 22:3; Galatians 1:14; Philippians 3:6; but also John 2:17; Acts 21:20; Romans 10:2) or, possibly, zealous in his opposition to Roman rule. But Luke doesn't say; so the description serves only to distinguish this Simon from Simon Peter.

JESUS AS A HUMANITARIAN TEACHER
Luke 6:17–49

This long passage divides into a setting for Jesus' so-called Sermon on the Plain (6:17–19), his pronouncing beatitudes (6:20–23) and woes (6:24–26), and his teaching on love (6:27–36), judgment (6:37–45), and obedience (6:46–49).

6:17–19: And on coming down [from the mountain (6:12)] **with them** [the Twelve, plus other disciples, all of whom Jesus had summoned (6:13)]**, he stood on a level place.** [Also standing there were] **a multitudinous crowd of his disciples and a multitudinous multitude of the people from all Judea** [= the whole land of Israel (see the comments on 1:5)] **and Jerusalem** [the capital city] **and the coastal** [region] **of Tyre and Sidon** [just north of Israel]**, ¹⁸who'd come to hear him and be healed of their diseases. And those who were being oppressed by unclean spirits were being treated** [by way of exorcism]**. ¹⁹And all the crowd was seeking to touch him, because power was coming from him and healing all** [who touched him]. Jesus stood on a level place to accommodate the throng who could also stand there, and did. Jesus' standing puts him more in the role of an orator than in that of a teacher, whose normal posture was one of sitting. Luke describes the throng not only as "a *crowd*" of disciples but also as "a *multitudinous* crowd" of them, plus not only "a *multitude* of the people from *all* Judea and Jerusalem," its most populous city, and from the foreign coastal region to the north but also "a *multitudinous multitude*" of them (see the comments on 23:27 for this wordplay). This fulsome description raises Jesus' popularity to the nth degree. The throng had come to hear him. Luke is appealing to his own audience's admiration of skill in oratory (compare 4:22: "and all were . . . marveling at the words of grace that were proceeding out of his mouth"). Also, public knowledge of Jesus' combining in himself the power and goodwill to heal the diseased and deliver the demon-possessed attracted them to him. Luke describes the demon-possessed as "oppressed." (There's no difference between demonic possession and demonic oppression.) And he describes exorcism as being treated, or cured, in the sense of being healed from the oppressive effects of demonic possession (compare Acts 10:38 and Luke's being a physician according to Colossians 4:14). That "*all* the crowd was seeking to touch him" adds yet further to his magnetism. Despite its size the crowd acts as a single unit, so great is Jesus' power of attraction. But his power also goes out *from* him (compare 5:17) with the effect of healing *all* who touched him. He suffers no power failures. And the crowd had only to touch him to gain the effect (compare 8:43–47). It's no surprise that he became a celebrity for his humanitarianism.

6:20–23: And he, on lifting his eyes to his disciples, was saying, "Fortunate [are you] **the poor, because yours is the kingdom of God. **[21]**Fortunate** [are you] **who are hungering now, because you'll be sated** [= satisfied with food aplenty]. **Fortunate** [are you] **who are weeping now, because you'll laugh. **[22]**Fortunate are you when people hate you and when they ostracize you and vilify** [you] **and cast out your name as evil on account of the Son of Man. **[23]**Rejoice in that day and jump** [for joy]. **For behold, your reward** [is] **great in heaven. For their** [fore]**fathers were doing the same things to the prophets."** Because the people were touching him, Jesus had to lift his eyes—that is, look over those people—to see and address his disciples. He designates them as "the poor," which means the poverty-stricken, economically speaking. These aren't the poor in general, but Jesus' disciples, whom he's addressing. Why they're poverty-stricken has yet to come out. But despite their poverty, they're fortunate. Such is the meaning of the traditional translation, "Blessed are . . . ." Jesus congratulates them on the ground that God's kingdom belongs to them. In Jesus, God has come to take over the world as his property, so that as Jesus' disciples they have the world deeded to them. They have yet to possess it, but they already own it. By pronouncing this beatitude, Jesus is fulfilling his commission "to preach good news to poor people" (4:18 in quotation of Isaiah 61:1).

Hunger follows naturally from poverty. But the future of satisfaction with plenty of food will expunge the "now"

of the disciples' hunger. "Weeping now" follows naturally from "hungering now." (The first three beatitudes deal in cause-and-effect.) But on possession of God's kingdom, laughing with a stomach full of food will replace the present weeping for lack of sufficient food. The fourth beatitude addresses the disciples as hated, ostracized, vilified, and defamed by others. Through loss of jobs, business, social acceptance, and such like, these treatments had caused the poverty that had caused the hunger that had caused the weeping, so that the fourth beatitude circles back to the first one in the matter of cause-and-effect. "Your name" is you in that you're known by your name, and therefore carries the connotation of your reputation. To have your name cast out as evil amounts, then, to your being treated as a nonperson because of calumny. "On account of the Son of Man" makes Jesus, not his disciples, the reason for such treatment. His enemies have been treating him as evil, so that because of a relationship to him his disciples will receive the same treatment. But it should be an occasion of jumping for joy (compare 1:41, 44). The rejoicing should take place on the very day ("in that day") when the disciples suffer mistreatment for Jesus' sake, that is, *while* they're suffering it. The emotion of joy is to be matched by the body language of jumping, skipping. Why? Jesus gives two reasons, emphasized by an exclamatory "behold!" (1) "Your reward [is] great in heaven," so great that it will far outweigh your present poverty, hunger, sorrow, and mistreatment. "In heaven" doesn't mean you'll get your reward in heaven. It means your reward is already in heaven waiting for you to get it when Jesus comes back to earth (Acts 1:9–11). The reward is signed and sealed but not yet delivered. So there's a futuristic reason to rejoice. There's also a historical reason. (2) The ancestors of those who mistreat you mistreated likewise the prophets of old. In other words, you belong to a long and good tradition. Luke likes nothing if not that kind of tradition. Jesus concurs.

6:24–26: "However, alas for you the rich, because you're receiving in full your consolation. **[25]Alas for you who have now been filled** [with food]**, because you'll hunger. Alas for you who are laughing now, because you'll mourn and weep. **[26]**Alas** [for you] **whenever all people speak well of you. For their** [fore]**fathers were doing the same things to the false prophets."** Obviously, these woes reverse for nondisciples the beatitudes Jesus pronounced on his disciples. "*Alas* for you" means "You're unfortunate whether or not you realize it at present." "Alas *for you*" implies Jesus is no longer addressing his disciples—rather, the well-heeled, well-fed, jaunty, idolized persecutors of the disciples. Their destiny is dim, because the only good they're going to get is what they're getting right now. To their detriment, emphasized by the double expression "mourn and weep," God will balance the scales of justice.

6:27–31: "But I tell you who are hearing [= listening]**: Love your enemies; treat well those who hate you. **[28]**Bless those who curse you; pray for those who threaten you. **[29]**To the person who strikes you on**

the cheek, offer also the other [cheek]; and from the person who takes your outer garment you shouldn't withhold even [your] inner garment. ³⁰Give to everyone who asks you [for your possessions], and from the person who takes your things don't demand [them] back. ³¹And just as you wish that people would do for you [that is, for your benefit], do likewise for them [that is, for their benefit]." "Your enemies," "those who hate you," "those who curse you," and "those who threaten you" hark back to the persecutors of Jesus' disciples in 6:22–23. So he's telling the disciples how to behave toward their persecutors. Yet he addresses "you who are hearing," and according to 6:17–18 they include not only a crowd of his disciples but also a multitude of other people. So addressing behavioral instructions for disciples to nondisciples as well as disciples makes Jesus a teacher to be admired for his teaching in society at large. Luke's portrayal of him as such has the purpose of attracting converts, especially converts out of people with moral sensibilities. "Love" equates with "treat well" just as "your enemies" equates with "those who hate you," so that loving involves good deeds, not just good feelings, in this case for the ill-deserving. To bless people is to speak well of them, probably to God as in 23:34 (where Jesus says concerning his crucifiers, "Father, forgive them, for they don't know what they're doing") and Acts 7:60 (where the martyr Stephen says concerning those who are stoning him to death, "Lord, you shouldn't hold this sin against them"). Blessing people, then, is the opposite of cursing them, which means invoking God to punish them. Similarly, praying for people is the opposite of threatening them. So Jesus' disciples are to act toward their persecutors oppositely of the malicious ways their persecutors act toward them.

Next, Jesus switches from the plural "you" and "your" that he has been using to the singular "you" and "your." This switch marks an emphasis on individual responsibility to behave as a disciple should. Offering your other cheek after having the first one struck is the opposite of striking your striker's cheek in retaliation. Not withholding your undergarment after being deprived of your outer garment is the opposite of resisting somebody's taking the undergarment from you. (Some allowance should be made for hyperbole here and about, because otherwise Jesus would absurdly be teaching nudity; but no refuge should be taken in the hyperbole.) And *giving* your possessions to "everyone" (!) who asks you for them is the opposite of loaning them with a demand for their return. So Jesus' disciples are to exercise extraordinary magnanimity toward those who abuse them and take advantage of them. In the so-called Golden Rule Jesus switches back to the plural of "you," for the rule has general applicability. Treating others the way you want them to treat you is—in the case of persecuted disciples—the opposite of the way your persecutors treat you. But such is Jesus' teaching on love. How admirable an ethic! It recommends its teacher and his gospel.

6:32–36: "And if [as a matter of fact] you love those who love you, what sort of favor do you have [from God for doing so]? [Not the sort that counts as a recognition of righteousness,] for even the sinners love those who love them. ³³And if [as a matter of possibility] you were to do good to those who do you good, what sort of favor do you have [from God for doing so]?" Again, not the sort that counts as a recognition of righteousness. "Even the sinners do the same thing. ³⁴And if you were to lend [to those] from whom you expect to receive [a loan], what sort of favor do you have [from God for lending]?" Yet again, not the sort that counts as a recognition of righteousness. "Even sinful people lend to sinners in order that they may receive back equally [in the form of a reciprocal loan]. ³⁵Rather, love your enemies and do [them] good and lend, expecting nothing back [by way of a reciprocal loan]; and your reward will be great [in God's kingdom (compare 6:20, 23 with comments)]. And you'll be sons of the Most High [= God], because he's magnanimous to the ungrateful and evil. ³⁶Become merciful just as your Father is merciful." As in 6:27, loving consists in good deeds. You loan money to get back the principle plus interest. Yet Jesus speaks of getting back "equally," which rules out interest. So he's saying not to loan money only to people who could reciprocate by loaning you an equal amount if you were to need such a loan. In contrast with nondisciples, his disciples are to show the kind of magnanimity toward their persecutors and debtors that God himself shows to those who because of their evil are morally indebted to him yet ungrateful for his mercy. Such magnanimity will bring great reward—the kind of favor from God that is denied to self-serving sinners— and will demonstrate your morally divine parentage. Like father, like son. Jesus calls God "the Most High" to elevate the disciples to the noblest of pedigrees. Mercy is one aspect of the just-mentioned "magnanimity." To fit magnanimity, Jesus called God "the Most High." (A person of low station doesn't have the wherewithal to exercise magnanimity.) Now Jesus calls God "your Father" to fit "mercy." (Fathers show mercy toward their sons.) And if you disciples live up to my ethical standards, Jesus says, you're "sons of the Most High," so that he's "your Father." (Luke continues using these standards to recommend the gospel to people of moral sensibilities.)

The passage 6:27–36 had to do with the behavior of Jesus' disciples toward their enemies, their persecutors. A new passage has to do now with their behavior toward one another. This limitation to their own circle doesn't come out immediately; but the brotherly language in 6:41–42, which details what not-judging and not-condemning in 6:37 mean, indicates the limitation. *6:37–42:* "And don't judge, and by no means will you be judged. And don't condemn, and by no means will you be condemned. Pardon, and you'll be pardoned. ³⁸Give, and it'll be given to you; [that is,] they'll give into your lap a good measure, [one that's] pressed down, shaken, overflowing. For with the measure that you measure with, it'll be measured back to you." ³⁹And he also told them a parable: "A blind person can't lead a blind person, can he?" Implied answer:

No. "Both will fall into a pit, won't they?" Implied answer: Yes. [40]"A disciple isn't superior to the teacher; but having been fully trained, every [disciple] will be like his teacher. [41]And why do you [singular] see the chip in your brother's eye but don't notice the plank in your own eye? [42]How can you say to your brother, 'Brother, let me thrust out the chip in your eye,' when you yourself don't see the plank in your own eye? Hypocrite, first thrust the plank out of your eye, and then you'll see clearly to thrust out the chip in your brother's eye." "Don't judge" doesn't prohibit the making of moral distinctions. As the later statements indicate, to judge is to see a little fault ("chip") in your fellow disciple ("brother") without noticing your own, greater fault ("plank"). Likewise, to condemn is to try correcting a little fault in your fellow disciple without first correcting your own, greater fault. ("*Thrust* out" makes a stronger figure of speech for such correction than the expected "*take* out.") This kind of judging and condemning turns you into a hypocrite, somebody who pretends to have more piety than he actually has; and this kind of judging and condemning counts as moral blindness. The hyperbole of having a plank in your eye, as though that were possible, underlines the hypocrisy and blindness. A morally blind person can't lead, can't correct, another morally blind person. They'll both fall into a moral pit. To correct someone else, you have to take moral education from Jesus, the superior Teacher. His teaching gives you a graduate education, so that you're "fully trained," that is, fully equipped, to give corrective moral teaching to your fellow disciple after you've corrected yourself: "and *then* you'll see clearly to thrust out the chip in your brother's eye."

But in addition to the unhypocritical passing on of Jesus' moral teaching to a fellow disciple, disciples are to pardon one another in regard to their faults. (The verb of pardoning means to release from judgment.) And not only to pardon, but also to give, just as the early Christians in Jerusalem gave into a common treasury—a practice that commended them to prospective believers (Acts 2:44–47; 4:32–37). Jesus says you'll receive back "a good measure" for giving your own resources into that treasury. A good measure refers figuratively to the bounty that disciples will receive from the pooling of their resources. In its literal sense the good measure refers to pouring into your lap (the fold of your garment) grain that its seller has pressed down into a measuring container, shaken to fill up any empty space in the container, and topped off so as to be spilling over. Such is the superabundant generosity characteristic of Christian community. "They" who'll give you a good measure can't be God, for he's not a "they." They're your fellow disciples. Because of parallelism and the overall theme of interpersonal relations among disciples, then, not being judged and not being condemned, but being forgiven instead, mean not being judged or condemned but being forgiven *by your fellow disciples* rather than by God (as usually thought). Thus Luke's Jesus lays the basis for an admirable and attractive harmony among believers.

6:43–45: "For a good tree doesn't produce rotten fruit, nor again does a rotten tree produce good fruit. [44]For each tree is known by its own fruit. For people don't gather figs from thornbushes, nor do they pick a cluster of grapes from a briarbush. [45]The good person brings forth what's good out of the good treasury of [his] **heart, and the evil** [person] **brings forth what's evil out of the evil** [treasury of his heart]. **For his mouth speaks out of** [the] **heart's surplus."** This passage lays a basis for the preceding command to "thrust the plank out of your eye" (6:42). Three successive statements begin with "For" in the sense of "because." Why thrust the plank out of your eye, that is, get rid of your faults? Because you prove yourself to be a disciple by obeying Jesus' words, and because disobedience demonstrates nondiscipleship, whatever your profession (see 6:46–49). What you do externally, whether good or evil, reveals what you are internally, good or evil. And vice versa, what you are internally, whether good or evil, determines what you do externally, good or evil. Jesus expresses these truisms first in horticultural figures of speech. A good person is like a good tree, such as a healthy fig tree, or like a good, healthy grapevine. And an evil person is like a rotten (that is, diseased) tree, thornbush, or briarbush. Good fruit, figs, and a cluster of grapes represent obedience to Jesus' commands. Rotten fruit represents disobedience to them. Then Jesus switches to the anatomical figure of a heart, which he compares to a treasury. This figure stresses the interior state that produces observable actions. The production is a kind of surplus that the treasury-like heart, which has a limited capacity, doesn't have room for, so that the interior state, whether good or evil, necessarily expresses itself in good or evil actions. "For his mouth *speaks* out of [the] heart's surplus" harks back on the one hand to *saying* to your fellow disciple, "Brother, let me thrust out the chip in your eye," when you have a plank in your own eye, and on the other hand to saying the same thing only after you've thrust out that plank (6:41–42 [see also 6:28–29 for blessing, praying, and not withholding]). Throughout, Jesus' demanding that his disciples *be* good and *do* what's good advances Luke's portrayal of him as a teacher of high moral standards that make the Christian community a showpiece attractive to people of good conscience.

6:46–49: "And why do you call me 'Lord, Lord' and don't do the things I say? [47]Everyone coming to me and hearing my words and doing them—I'll show you whom he's like. [48]He's like a man building a house, who dug and went deep and laid a foundation on bedrock. And when a flood happened, the river burst against that house. And it [the flood] **wasn't strong enough to shake it, because it had been built well. [49]But the person who has heard and not done** [my words] **is like a man who built a house on soil without a foundation, against which** [house] **the river burst. And it** [the house] **collapsed, and the breakup of that house was disastrous."** In Jesus' audience are those who confess him as their Lord but don't obey his commands. This disobedience contradicts their confession. The doubling of "Lord" highlights the contradiction. And the question "Why . . . ?" doesn't expect an answer, because it makes nonsense to call Jesus "Lord, Lord" but disobey his words. "Everyone *coming* to me and *hearing* my words" harks back to 6:17–18: "and a multitudinous crowd of his disciples and a multitudinous multitude of the people from all Judea and Jerusalem and the coastal [region] of Tyre and Sidon, who'd *come* to *hear* him" (see also 6:27: "you who *are hearing*"). Building a house well represents obedience to Jesus' words, of course; and building a house without a foundation represents disobedience to them. The unshakeability of the well-built house illustrates the good sense of obedience. The collapse of the foundationless house illustrates the senselessness of disobedience. Jesus might have ended with a statement of the collapse. But to underline the senselessness of disobedience he adds a description of the collapse as a "breakup" that was "disastrous." In many other passages he'll explain this disastrous breakup in terms of eternal loss (see 13:22–30 for one example, but also 6:24–26 already). Nevertheless, no such explanation appears in the present passage. So the emphasis falls on the senselessness of disobedience as such. It really doesn't make sense to come and hear Jesus' words but fail to obey them.

A BENEFICENT CENTURION'S FAITH IN JESUS
Luke 7:1–10

7:1–2: After he'd completed all his words in the hearings [= ears] **of the people, he went into Capernaum.** **²And a certain centurion's slave, being sick, was about to terminate** [= die], [a slave] **who was esteemed by him** [the centurion]. "In the *hearings* of the people" and the coming request for a *healing* echo 6:17–18: "a multitudinous multitude of the people . . . who'd come to *hear* him and *be healed* from their diseases." The centurion's esteem for a sick slave of his provides the reason for an extraordinary effort to enlist Jesus' help.

7:3–5: And on hearing about Jesus, he [the centurion] **sent to him elders of the Jews, requesting him** [through the elders] **that on coming, he bring his slave safely through** [the illness]. **⁴And on reaching Jesus, they were imploring him earnestly, saying, "He's worthy for whom you'd grant this** [request]. **⁵For he loves our nation, and he himself had the synagogue** [here in Capernaum] **built for us."** The centurion's hearing about Jesus testifies to Jesus' celebrity as a healer. Why the centurion sent Jewish elders (elders being respected for their age) rather than coming in person will receive explanation a little later. Meanwhile, the elders act as his agents. The earnestness of their imploring Jesus emphasizes both the desperate straits into which the slave's illness has plunged him, the centurion's esteem for him, and the elders' indebtedness to the centurion for his benefaction. Detailing the benefaction is his love of the Jewish nation as shown in his having had a synagogue built for the Jews of Capernaum despite his being a Gentile and a centurion of the Jews' overlords. Such benefaction makes him worthy of Jesus' granting his request.

7:6–8: And Jesus started going with them [the elders]. **But when he was already not far from the** [centurion's] **house, the centurion sent friends, saying to him** [through his friends], **"Lord, stop bothering yourself** [to come here], **for I'm not worthy that you should enter under my roof. ⁷On this account I didn't even consider myself worthy to come to you. But speak with a word, and my servant is to be healed** [that is, his illness will leave at your command]. **⁸For I too am a man placed under authority, having soldiers under myself. And I say to this one, 'Go,' and he goes, and to another one, 'Come,' and he comes, and to my slave, 'Do this,' and he does** [it]." Here Jesus' traveling not only appeals to the interest of Luke's audience in itineration. It also shows Jesus' humanitarian rejection of racial and political barriers. He actually gets close to the centurion's house before the centurion stops him. The centurion does stop him, though, by sending some of his own friends, who act as further agents for him. His commendable sense of unworthiness (compare 5:8) implies Jesus' worthiness and makes the addressing of Jesus with "Lord" a contrast with the hypocritical addressing of Jesus with "Lord, Lord" in 6:46. As usual, Luke wants us to read divinity into the address, whatever the level of meaning intended by the centurion. He considered himself unworthy not only to have Jesus enter his house but also—and even—unworthy to go in person to Jesus. Hence the use of two successive delegations. And to this sense of unworthiness is added faith in Jesus' authority to command a healing successfully. Luke and the centurion, speaking through the elders, used "slave" for the object of concern (7:2–3). In speaking through his friends the centurion now uses "servant," a softer designation that reflects his esteem for him. ("Servant" can also mean "boy," not necessarily in a youthful sense but possibly in an affectionate sense.) "For" introduces a reason why the centurion believes that at Jesus' command the illness would leave. A centurion commanded one hundred soldiers. So this centurion reasons that just as he is himself under a ruler's authority and as a commissioned officer exercises that same authority over his soldiers, so also Jesus is under God's authority and as divinely commissioned can exercise that authority over the servant's illness. "I *too*" indicates this parallel.

7:9–10: And on hearing these things [that the centurion had said], **Jesus marveled at him; and on turning to the crowd that was following him, he said, "I tell you, not even in Israel have I found such great faith." ¹⁰And on returning into the** [centurion's] **house, the** [friends] **who'd been sent found the slave in good health.** Jesus' lauding the centurion's faith is underlined by Jesus' marveling at him, turning to the crowd that was following him, introducing his comment to them with an emphatic "I tell you," and describing the centurion's faith as greater than any he'd found "*even* in Israel." "*Such* great faith" heightens the faith yet more by implying that Jesus has found great faith in Israel, but not so great as that of the centurion. Luke wants to encourage his Gentile audience to exercise similar faith even though, like the centurion, they're neither face-to-face with Jesus nor Jewish. The gospel isn't just for Jews (see especially 24:47–48; Acts 10–11, 13–28). Unlike the Jewish elders, who wouldn't enter a Gentile's house (compare Peter's initial refusal in Acts 10:1–11:18), the presumably Gentile friends of the centurion enter his house on their return and find the slave in good health. (Luke returns to his own designation "slave.") There was no need for Jesus to finish his journey. Luke doesn't even say that Jesus spoke a word of healing at a distance, though that's what the centurion had urged him to do. It's as if the centurion's remarkable faith in Jesus' authority under God was all it took to effect the shift from sickness to health. Notably, Luke turns from the vocabulary of healing, a momentary event (so in 7:7), to that of ongoing health. This new vocabulary makes an impressive contrast with the slave's having been "about *to terminate*" (7:2) and an equally impressive fulfillment of the centurion's request that Jesus "bring [the] slave *safely* through" (7:3).

TAKING PITY ON A BEREAVED WIDOW
Luke 7:11–17

7:11–12: And it happened that after a while he [Jesus] traveled to a city called Nain, and his disciples and a large crowd were traveling with him. ¹²And when he drew near the gate of the city, also—behold—the only son of his mother was being carried out dead. And she was a widow, and a considerable crowd of [= from] the city was with her. As often, Luke appeals to his audience's interest in travel. The traveling with Jesus of both his disciples and a crowd testifies, again as often, to his well-earned popularity. Luke's describing the crowd as "large" (literally, "multitudinous") and their traveling with Jesus despite not being his disciples heighten the emphasis on his popularity. A funeral procession was coming out of the city when he got near. The corpse was to be buried, as customarily, outside the city wall. The straits of the bereaved widow are desperate. Not only is her husband dead. So also is her son, who's not just nearly dead like the centurion's slave in 7:2. He's completely dead. In fact, he's about to be buried. He was her only son, moreover. So she'll have no means of support and sink into destitution, for Jewish women lacked earning power. "Behold" calls special attention to her plight. When added to Jesus' disciples, plus the large crowd traveling with him, the considerable crowd from the city that's with the widow will make for a huge number of firsthand witnesses to Jesus' following words and deed (compare 1:1–4).

7:13–15: And on seeing her, the Lord felt pity for her and said to her, "Stop weeping." ¹⁴And on approaching, he touched the burial plank; and those who were carrying [it] stood still. And he said, "Young man, I say to you, be raised!" ¹⁵And the dead [young man] sat up and started speaking. And he [Jesus] gave him to his mother. Luke calls Jesus "the Lord" to intimate Jesus' mastery over the widow's tearful plight. To the mastery is added his pitying her. The combination

of mastery and pity gives reason for her to stop weeping. Luke portrays a Jesus who's both sympathetic and powerful. Corpses were carried to the cemetery on an open plank, not in a closed coffin. So everybody present will be able to see what happens. Jesus touches the plank rather than grasping the hand of the young man, because the corpse, being carried aloft, is out of reach (contrast 8:54, where Jesus grasps the hand of a corpse *not* being carried aloft). His touching the plank causes the pallbearers to stop, so that now he can at least speak to the corpse. And his addressing the corpse with "Young man" indicates that the widow's son is of an age that will enable him, if alive, to support his widowed mother by working, and to do so for as long as she's likely to live. "I say to you" underscores Jesus' following command, "Be raised!" (compare 7:9 with comments). The passive voice of "Be raised!" suggests that God is acting through Jesus for the young man's resurrection, for elsewhere in Luke-Acts God is often portrayed as the one who raises people, not least Jesus himself, from the dead. Here the dead young man "sat up" because he was being carried on a burial plank; so he could hardly *stand* up. His starting to talk adds audible evidence to the visible evidence of being raised from the dead. So the large number of eyewitnesses become earwitnesses as well. Jesus' giving the raised young man to his widowed mother fills out the exercise of compassion on her (compare 1 Kings 17:23). In her son she'll have a renewed means of livelihood.

7:16–17: And fear took hold of all [who were watching and listening]; **and they were glorifying God by saying, "A great prophet has arisen among us" and "God has visited his people." ¹⁷And this word about him** [Jesus as a great prophet] **went out in the whole of Judea** [= the whole land of Israel (see the comments on 1:5)] **and all the surrounding** [region]. The stupendousness of Jesus' miracle (you might even say it was eery) caused fear. Exacerbating the fear is Luke's saying it "took hold" of the bystanders. It grabbed them. They were helpless to resist. "All" indicates that *none* of them could resist, for no one could deny what they'd all seen with their own eyes and heard with their own ears. But in addition to this psychological effect, Jesus' miracle also has a good religious effect: "they were glorifying God" (see the comments on 2:20). The glorification of God takes the form of giving him credit for raising up a prophet, a *great* one, right among them, so that in Jesus, who is that great prophet, God has visited his people. They're probably thinking of Jesus as a prophet on the order of Elijah, who also raised from the dead the son of a widow (1 Kings 17:8–24 [compare 2 Kings 4:1–37]). In view of 4:25–26, Luke too may have in mind a parallel with Elijah, though he doesn't make it explicit. So Jesus' raising the young man for the sake of his widowed mother represents God's coming to the aid of his people Israel as a whole (compare 1:68, 78; 19:44). The broadcasting of a report about Jesus throughout "the *whole* of Judea and *all* the surrounding [region]" foreshadows the spread of the gospel throughout the world to both Jews and Gentiles (24:45–48; Acts 1:8). The gospel knows no boundaries.

ON JESUS, JOHN THE BAPTIZER,
THE MEN OF THIS GENERATION,
AND WISDOM'S CHILDREN
Luke 7:18–35

This passage divides into a question of John the baptizer to Jesus (7:18–20), Jesus' answer (7:21–23), Jesus' tribute to John (7:24–28), and Luke's and Jesus' drawing a contrast between the people and the tax collectors, on the one hand, and the Pharisees and the lawyers, on the other hand (7:29–35).

7:18–20: And his [John's] **disciples reported to John about all these things.** [19] **And on summoning a certain two of his disciples, John sent** [them] **to the Lord, saying, "Are _you_ the coming one or should we wait expectantly for _someone else_?"** [20] **And on reaching him** [Jesus]**, the men said, "John the baptizer sent us to you, saying, 'Are you the coming one, or should we wait expectantly for someone else?'"** By now John is in prison (3:19–20). His disciples' reporting to him while he's in prison implies they can visit him there. So through them "this word about [Jesus]" that "went out in the whole of Judea and all the surrounding [region]" (7:17) penetrated even the walls of John's prison. Such was the powerful effect of Jesus' raising the son of the widow of Nain ("_this_ word" [7:17]). But the report of John's disciples wasn't limited to that miracle. It included "_all_ these things." The totality of Jesus' deeds and words, electrifying as they were, generated the report. John's sending "a certain _two_ of his disciples" provides sufficient testimony to authenticate the question he relays to Jesus through them (Numbers 35:30; Deuteronomy 17:6; 19:15). By writing that John sent them "to _the Lord_," Luke underscores Jesus' superiority to John. "Are _you_ the coming one . . . ?" asks whether Jesus is fulfilling John's own prediction in 3:16: "but the one who's stronger than I _is coming_." The "we" in "should we wait expectantly for someone else" refers to John and his disciples—to John because he'd made the prediction, and to his disciples, particularly the two he'd sent with the question, because along with him they expected a fulfillment of his prediction. Luke doesn't say why John posed his question to Jesus. So it serves only to set the stage for Jesus' response.

7:21–23: In that hour he healed many people of diseases and afflictions and evil spirits, and to many blind people he graciously gave seeing [that is, sight, the ability to see]**.** [22] **And answering, he told them** [John's two disciples]**, "Go report to John the things you've seen and heard: blind people are seeing again, lame people are walking around, lepers are being cleansed, and deaf-mutes are hearing. Dead people are being raised. Poor people are getting good news.** [23] **And whoever isn't tripped up in regard to me is fortunate."** The abruptness with which this subsection starts highlights the miracles that Jesus performs even before he answers the question posed to him. To people in first-century Israel an hour was the shortest unit of time. They knew nothing of minutes or seconds, much less of nanoseconds. So "in that hour" pinpoints Jesus' present performance of miracles precisely at the time John's two disciples relayed his question to Jesus. Thus they become eyewitnesses to these miracles; and just as their twoness authenticated John's question to Jesus, so it will now authenticate their reporting Jesus' miracles to John upon their traveling back to him (compare 1:1–4). Moreover, Jesus' healing in their presence "many" and giving sight to "many" make the miracles convincing in their sheer number. There's an escalation in the initial list of healings: from "diseases" through "afflictions" to "evil spirits." The meaning of "diseases" is self-evident. "Afflictions" rests on a Greek word that means "whips, lashes" but that is used here in a way which compares ongoing physical maladies, such as lameness and deafness, to the traumas of being whipped. And "evil spirits" refers to demon-possession, worst of all. By exorcising the evil spirits Jesus heals their victims of the ruinous physical effects of such possession. So the wide range of healings joins their large number to make them doubly convincing. The giving of sight to many blind people is so impressive that it merits a sentence all by itself. Luke's describing the giving as gracious foregrounds the philanthropy of Jesus (compare the graciousness of his words according to 4:22).

Earlier, John's disciples "reported to John all these things" (7:18), but apparently by hearsay because of "this word concerning him [Jesus]" that had "gone out in the whole of Judea and all the surrounding [region]" (7:17). Now Jesus tells John's two disciples to "report to John the things" they've "seen and heard" for themselves. They've become earwitnesses as well as eyewitnesses. And Jesus lists what they've seen and heard. His list (7:22) is more specific than Luke's (7:21). When added to the large number of healings and their wide range, this specificity makes them triply convincing. The list draws on Isaiah 26:19; 29:18; 35:5–6; 42:18; 61:1, though Luke doesn't call attention to that fact. John's two disciples have _seen_ blind people receive their sight, lame people walking around, lepers being cleansed, deaf people hearing, and dead people being raised. They've _heard_ good news being preached to poor people (compare 4:18; 6:20). Jesus' raising of dead people and preaching of good news to poor people are so remarkable that each gets expressed in its own sentence. And the plurality of every item in the list makes the miracles and preaching numerous in each category as well as overall. Jesus has given an impressive display of his power exercised to the benefit of human beings and made all the more impressive by the Jews' not expecting the Messiah to perform miracles of healing. Then Jesus' pronounces a blessing of good fortune on whoever isn't tripped up in regard to him. To be tripped up in regard to him is to fall into the sin of unbelief and thus to incur eternal punishment. Not to be tripped up is to believe in him and thus to receive eternal life (compare 10:25; 18:18, 30; Acts 13:46, 48). Good fortune indeed! Jesus may be implying that John's question puts him in danger of being tripped up, though Jesus' following accolade to John and Luke's having failed to give a reason for John's question temper that possibility. In any case, "whoever" invites anybody and everybody to come under the umbrella of Jesus' blessing.

7:24–28: And when John's messengers had gone away, he [Jesus] **started saying to the crowds concerning John, "What did you go out into the wilderness to look at? A reed being shaken by wind?"** Obviously not. [25]**"Rather, what did you go out to see? A man dressed in soft garments** [= comfy clothes]**?"** Again no. **"Behold, those who have their existence in fancy clothing and luxury are in palaces** [not in the wilderness, where John was preaching]. [26]**Rather, what did you go out to see? A prophet? Yes, I tell you, and more than a prophet!** [27]**This is the one about whom it's written, 'Behold, I'm sending my messenger before your face, who'll prepare your way ahead of you.'** [28]**I tell you, among those born from women no one is larger than John. But the smaller one in God's kingdom is larger than he** [John]**."** John's messengers go off not to be heard from again. Nor is he heard from again. Luke shows no more interest in how John reacted to his messengers' report than he showed in the reason for John's question. Instead, Luke shines the spotlight on what Jesus has to say. Appropriately, "*started* saying" introduces a rather long reflection by Jesus on John. "To the crowds"—there's more than one crowd, so popular is Jesus for his humanitarianism as shown in the "many . . . many" healings and the preaching of good news to the poor (7:21–22). But since these crowds had gone out into the wilderness "to *see*" John, they're also "the crowds that were traveling out to be *baptized* by him" (3:7). A wilderness was devoid of many human inhabitants, not necessarily devoid of much vegetation. So Jesus refers to "a reed" such as grows along the banks of the Jordan River, where John had preached and baptized. We might think that Jesus is saying it's ridiculous to imagine the crowds went out to see vegetation blowing in the wind. But for that thought we'd expect the plural, "reeds," not the singular, "a reed." This singular and the addition of "being shaken in the wind" suggest a contrast with the moral sturdiness of John in preaching a baptism of repentance, in calling the crowds "offsprings of vipers," in warning them of fiery judgment, and—above all—in rebuking Herod the tetrarch (3:3–20). Soft garments don't contrast with rough garments, for Luke hasn't described John's clothing as consisting of camel's hair and a leather belt (for which see Mark 1:6; Matthew 3:4). So the contrast pits John's spartan living *in the wilderness* against the sumptuous lifestyle of those who live *in palaces*. "Behold" stresses this contrast.

A prophet is a spokesman for God. Such was John. Jesus' "Yes" affirms that the crowds went out to see John because they recognized him to be a prophet. "I tell you" emphasizes "and more than a prophet," which indicates Jesus' own recognition of John to be a prophet and adds the even higher function of John's having fulfilled what's written in Exodus 23:20; Malachi 3:1 (compare Luke 3:4–6; Isaiah 40:3–5). Thus we come back to Luke's now familiar theme of the gospel as in continuity with and

fulfillment of the Jewish scriptures. As applied to John and Jesus, the scriptural sender ("I") is God, his "messenger" is John, Jesus is the "you" before whom John is sent and who prepares Jesus' way ahead of him, and John's preaching and baptizing constitute the preparation. Another "I tell you" emphasizes that because of this preparatory function, John is larger—that is, greater in status—than all other human beings ever born. But there's an exception: "the smaller one in God's kingdom." Who's that? We might think Jesus means that an unimportant member of God's kingdom enjoys greater status than John because John lived up to the advent of God's kingdom but not long enough to enter it (compare Luke 16:16). There's a chronological as well as hierarchical element, though, in the contrast between "larger" and "smaller." A larger child is generally older than a smaller one, and the smaller one is generally younger than the larger one. So "larger" and "smaller" can be used for "older" and "younger" (compare Mark 15:40). Now Luke is the only evangelist to recount the nativities of both John and Jesus, and in doing so he carefully noted that John was born before Jesus (Luke 1:5–2:20). In the present text of Luke's Gospel, then, Jesus is "the smaller one" in the sense of "the younger one" who is "in God's kingdom" as John is not (see 16:16 again). But despite being John's junior in age ("smaller"), Jesus is John's superior in status ("larger").

7:29–30: And all the people, on hearing [John's preaching of repentance], **and the tax collectors admitted God to be right** [in his condemnation of their sins through that preaching] **by being baptized with the baptism of John.** That is, John baptized them upon their repentance; they didn't baptize themselves. [30]**But the Pharisees and the lawyers disregarded for themselves God's will by not being baptized by him** [John]. Here Luke breaks into Jesus' speech with an editorial flashback to the success of John's preaching as evidenced in the submission of "*all* the people" and even "tax collectors" to his baptism of repentance. This flashback supports Jesus' having called John greater in status than all other human beings thus far born. But just as there was an exception to John's superiority, there were exceptions to his success: the Pharisees and the lawyers. In recounting John's ministry Luke didn't mention their disregarding "God's will for themselves." But their already evident opposition to Jesus (5:17, 21, 30; 6:2, 7) shows that in their case John didn't succeed in preparing the way for Jesus. God's will was that they flee from the coming wrath by producing evidence of repentance and submitting to John's baptism (3:7–9). "For themselves" implies an exercise of their own will in opposition to God's. Not smart!

Having finished his editorial insertion, Luke returns to Jesus' speech in **7:31–35: "Therefore to what should I liken the men of this generation, and to what are they like?** [32]**They're like little children sitting in a marketplace and calling to one another, who say, 'We played the flute for you, and you didn't dance.' 'We wailed, and you didn't weep.' **[33]**For John the baptizer has come** not eating bread and not drinking wine; and you say, 'He has a demon.' [34]The Son of Man has come eating [bread] and drinking [wine]; and you say, 'Behold, a gluttonous man and a wino, a friend of tax collectors and sinners!' [35]And wisdom has been admitted to be right by all her children." "Therefore" provides a second reason for Luke's editorial flashback to John's ministry. It not only supported Jesus' high estimate of John; it also prepared for Jesus' damaging comparison of "the men of this generation" to peevish kids. And who are these men? They can't be "all the people" and "tax collectors," because on hearing John they admitted God to be right by submitting to John's baptism and because they now flock to Jesus in "crowds" (7:24, 29). "The men of this generation" must be "the Pharisees and the lawyers" who "rejected for themselves God's will by not being baptized by [John]," who now oppose Jesus, and whom Luke has just included in his editorial flashback to provide an identification of this generation's men. They're like kids who can't be persuaded by one another to play either mock wedding, represented by flute-playing and dancing, or mock funeral, represented by wailing and weeping. More particularly, men did a round dance at weddings; but the little boys can't be persuaded by flute-playing little girls to dance in a game of wedding. And women wailed at funerals; but the little boys can't be persuaded by wailing little girls to weep in a game of funeral. "For" introduces the reason underlying this comparison. It's that neither the abstinent John nor the commensal Jesus has persuaded them to accept for themselves God's will. It's their childish stubbornness, not the lifestyles of John and Jesus, that drives their rejection of God's will. In chapter 3 Luke didn't spell out the unusual diet of John (the locusts and wild honey mentioned in Mark 1:6; Matthew 3:4). So the only point here in chapter 7 is John's abstinence from regular food and drink, as in funeral-like mourning.

"And *you* say, 'He has a demon.'" Whether or not they're in absentia, Jesus is addressing the Pharisees and the lawyers. But why has John's abstinence from ordinary food and drink led them to deduce that he's demon-possessed? The deduction makes no sense. But that's the point! In the same fashion the deduction that Jesus' partaking of regular food and drink and partying, as at a wedding, in the company of tax collectors and sinners makes him a glutton, a drunk, and a friend of tax collectors and sinners—this deduction is likewise nonsensical, though even more serious than the deduction that John is demon-possessed; for according to the Mosaic law gluttony and drunkenness make a son subject to being stoned to death (Deuteronomy 21:18–21). Ah, but isn't it true that Jesus *is* a friend of tax collectors and sinners? No, because as John did, he calls them to repentance (see especially 13:1–5; 15:7, 10). Only then, when they become his disciples, does he call them "friends" (12:4). "Wisdom" represents a willingness to accept God's will and therefore stands opposite the Pharisees' and lawyers' stubborn rejection of it. "Her children" are those who do accept it and by doing so admit the rightness of such

wisdom (compare 7:29). "*All* her children" recalls attention to the wide success of John's and Jesus' ministries. It's foolish to mess with success.

JESUS' GRACIOUS GIFT OF FORGIVENESS
Luke 7:36–50

This episode starts with a sinful woman's gestures of appreciative love toward Jesus at a meal (7:36–38), proceeds to a dialogue between him and his Pharisaic host concerning those gestures (7:39–47), and ends with Jesus' addressing the woman while ignoring a question of his fellow diners (7:48–50).

7:36–38: And a certain one of the Pharisees was asking him [Jesus] **to eat with him; and on entering into the Pharisee's house, he reclined.** It was customary to recline on low couches at formal meals. [37]**And behold, a woman who was sinful in the city! And on coming to know that he's lounging in the Pharisee's house, bringing an alabaster flask of perfume** [38]**and standing behind** [Jesus] **at his feet** [which were stretched out away from the table as he was reclining on his couch], **she started raining his feet with tears as she wept. And she wiped off** [the tears] **with the hair of her head and was kissing his feet and anointing** [them] **with the perfume.** This Pharisee is one of "the men of this generation" who "rejected for themselves God's will" and whom Jesus has just compared to peevish "little children" (7:30–35). But Luke's Jesus wants to extend them forgiveness, too, if only they'll believe in him. So he accepts the Pharisee's invitation. Was it a friendly invitation or one designed to put Jesus on the spot, if possible, or perhaps to enhance his own reputation by hosting a renowned teacher? Luke doesn't say. The accent falls then on Jesus' liberality. "Behold" calls special attention to the mentioned woman, and more especially to her being "sinful *in the city*." Luke doesn't identify the city, so his point has to do with her reputation there. What naturally comes to mind is her being well-known as a town prostitute, maybe *the* town prostitute. Luke doesn't specify her sin, however, so that she becomes an example of every kind of sinner whom Jesus befriends on the condition of repentance and faith in him. The woman's bringing an alabaster flask of perfume shows her intention to anoint Jesus with the perfume. Her shedding of tears shows deep disappointment over her inability to perfume Jesus. His unsandaled feet, the only part of his body available to her, hadn't had dirt from the road washed off them; and you don't put perfume on dirty feet. Unexpectedly, though, the copious amount of her tears washed his feet. Her standing at his feet made her tears fall on them like rain. Luke himself makes the comparison. Later, Jesus will too. But you don't put perfume on wet feet, either. So the woman dries them by using her hair as a towel. She hadn't brought one, because she'd thought that in accordance with the code of hospitality Jesus' feet would have been already washed and wiped dry. Her kissing Jesus' feet, now clean and dry, shows worshipful affection. And her anointing them with perfume shows loving gratitude.

7:39–40: **And on seeing** [what the woman was doing], **the Pharisee who'd invited him spoke within himself, saying, "If this** [guy] **were a prophet, he'd have known who and what kind of woman** [this is] **who as such is touching him;** [he'd have known] **that she's sinful."** [40]**And answering, Jesus said to him, "Simon, I have something to say to you." And he said, "Teacher, say** [it]**."** Luke describes the Pharisee as the one "who'd invited him [Jesus]." This description prepares for Jesus' noting that the Pharisee had failed to perform the honorific courtesies that a cordial host might well have performed for a celebrated teacher and healer. At most, the Pharisee could conceive of the possibility that Jesus was a prophet and hence, for Luke's audience and for those who'd heard Jesus call John the baptizer "*more* than a prophet," inferior to John. But the Pharisee rejects even this possibility. His rejection rests on the mistaken assumption that Jesus doesn't know the woman who's touching him to be a sinner. "As such" underscores her sinfulness. Since "the Pharisees and the lawyers" have just called Jesus "a *friend* of tax collectors and sinners" (7:29–35), this Pharisee shouldn't have been surprised if he *had* thought that Jesus knew the woman to be sinful. The Pharisee's musing implies, though, that a prophetic knowledge of the woman's sinfulness would have kept Jesus from allowing the woman to touch him and thus defile him ritually. So his musing disagrees with his own Pharisaical characterization of Jesus as a friend of sinful people. (It's hard for those who reject Jesus to be consistent.) In his answer, Jesus hints that he isn't so ignorant as the Pharisee thinks he is. His addressing him by name with "Simon" shows courtesy in the face of the Pharisee's failures at courtesy, and also gives evidence of Luke's historical research (1:1–4). "I have something to say to you" sounds an ominous note. Simon's addressing Jesus with "Teacher" shows respect, though perhaps a feigned or grudging respect, and along with his failure to perform honorific courtesies for Jesus may suggest he invited Jesus to boost his own reputation by entertaining a celebrated teacher. Simon's telling Jesus to "say [it]" springs the trap in which he'll find himself caught. Since the trap is sprung, Luke doesn't even have to indicate a change in speakers, but goes directly into what Jesus says.

7:41–43: **"A certain lender had two debtors. The one was owing** [him] **five hundred denarii** [just over a year and seven months of wages for a fully employed manual laborer at six days a week]**, and the other** [was owing him] **fifty** [a tenth as much, that is, eight weeks and two days of wages]. [42]**When they didn't have** [the wherewithal] **to pay back** [the money]**, he exercised grace** [by canceling their debts]. **Therefore, which of them will love him more?"** [43]**Answering, Simon said, "I suppose that he for whom he exercised grace the more** [will love him more]**." He** [Jesus] **said to him, "You've judged correctly."** The lender represents Jesus. The two debtors represent sinners of different degrees. (Yes, there are degrees of sinning.) The debts represent sins, which are moral debts (compare the Lord's Prayer: "Forgive us our debts" [Matthew 6:12]). The large debt represents the many sins of the woman who anointed Jesus. The small debt represents the few sins of Simon. The gracious cancellation of the large debt represents Jesus' forgiveness of the woman's many sins. The gracious cancellation of the small debt *would* represent Jesus' forgiveness of Simon's few sins if only he would repent and believe in Jesus. By way of introducing the question which debtor will love the lender more, "Therefore" means "In view of the disparity between the amounts forgiven." The question presents love as the proper, even inevitable, response to forgiveness. By starting his answer with "I suppose," Simon clamps Jesus' trap tightly on himself; and Jesus' response, "You've *judged* correctly," characterizes Simon's answer as a self-judgment. Simon is judged out of his own mouth.

7:44–47: **And on turning to the woman, he said to Simon, "You're looking at this woman. I entered into your house. You didn't give me water for** [my] **feet; but this** [woman] **has rained my feet with tears and wiped off** [the tears] **with her hair.** [45]**You didn't give me a kiss; but since** [the hour] **that I entered, this** [woman] **hasn't left off kissing my feet.** [46]**You didn't anoint my head with olive oil; but this** [woman] **has anointed my feet with perfume,** [47]**on account of which** [anointing with perfume] **I tell you, her many sins have been forgiven.** [I tell you so,] **because she loved much. But the person for whom little is forgiven loves little."** The Greek language Luke is using doesn't have a question mark, so that the difference between a declaration and a question is a matter of interpretation according to context. Here, Luke has already written that Simon was looking at the woman (7:39). So it's better to translate Jesus' words as a declaration, "You're looking at this woman," than as a question, "Do you see this woman?" (as in many translations). By turning to the woman, Jesus uses body language to keep Simon's gaze riveted on her as he speaks to Simon. And by using "this" in reference to the woman no fewer than four times, Jesus keeps Simon's gaze riveted on her with verbal language as well.

Giving "bite" to the application of Jesus' foregoing story so far as Simon is concerned is the staccato-like succession of "You didn't . . . . You didn't . . . . You didn't . . . ." The objects of "You didn't . . ."—"water," "kiss," and "olive oil"—occupy forward positions in Luke's original text to emphasize Simon's inhospitality. Walking in open sandals on dusty paths made the giving of water for foot-washing an expected gesture of hospitality (see, for example, Genesis 18:4; 19:2). A kiss of greeting would also have qualified as such (see 1 Peter 5:14 for one of many examples). Anointing a guest's head with olive oil to make it shine prefigured a good time to be had by all (see Psalm 23:5). Simon's hospitality lacked all these gestures, as signaled immediately in 7:36 by Jesus' reclining at table as soon as he entered. The woman more than made up for Simon's omissions: with her own tears instead of water, with her own hair instead of a towel, with repeated kissing of Jesus' feet instead of a single kiss on his face, with perfume on his feet instead of ordinary olive oil on his head. And the quickness of the woman's gestures ("since [the hour] that I entered") and their pro-longation ("she hasn't left off") add to the exhibition of her love for Jesus. "She loved *much*" because "her *many* sins [had] been forgiven" ("much" and "many" being the singular and plural of the same word). "But the person for whom little is forgiven loves little" shows that the woman's loving gestures constituted *evidence* of forgive-ness, not a *basis* of forgiveness. So "she loved much," as shown by what she has done, spells out the reason why Jesus *tells* Simon "her many sins have been forgiven," not the reason *why* they've been forgiven. In other words, "on account of which" goes with "I tell you," not with "her many sins have been forgiven."

7:48–50: And he [Jesus] told her, "Your sins have been forgiven." ⁴⁹And those who were reclining with [him] started saying within themselves, "Who is this who even forgives sins?" ⁵⁰But he told the woman, "Your faith has saved you. Go in peace." Her extraor-dinarily loving gestures grew out of much love. Her much love grew in turn out of the forgiveness of her many sins. So Jesus' telling her that her sins have been forgiven assures her of a forgiveness that took place earlier and sparked her love and the resultant gestures thereof. (We might think, though, that he speaks almost as much for Simon's benefit as for hers.) Jesus doesn't mean that her sins are being forgiven right now (as in Mark 2:5, 7, 9–10), for otherwise her gestures couldn't be said to have grown out of a love based on forgive-ness. Neither Jesus nor Luke relates the circumstances of her prior forgiveness, so that attention focuses solely on the contrast between her gestures on this occasion and Simon's omission of even lesser gestures. "*Within* themselves" could be translated "*among* themselves." But the parallel with Simon's speaking "*within* himself" (7:39) favors the interior meaning here too (compare 12:17). The question of Jesus' fellow diners implies that he has arrogated to himself the divine prerogative of forgiving sins. He ignores their question, though, be-cause—with Pharisees present—he answered it already back in 5:17–26 (see especially 5:24: "But in order that you may know that the Son of Man has authority on the earth to forgive sins . . ."). Here he refuses to be diverted from speaking "words of grace" (4:22) to the woman. "Your faith has saved you" means that the forgiveness of her many sins has delivered her from God's judging her because of them (compare 5:20; Acts 16:31, for example). The statement also confirms that it wasn't her gestures of love for Jesus that led him to forgive her sins. Faith in him, not love for him, did that. "Go in peace" echoes the Old Testament (see 1 Samuel 1:17; 2 Samuel 15:9; Judges 18:6) and sends the woman traveling on her way with a personalization of the angels' promise of "peace on earth among human beings of [God's] good pleasure" (2:14).

JESUS' ITINERATION
Luke 8:1–3

8:1–3: And it happened in the following [time frame] that he was taking a road through one city and town after another, preaching and heralding God's reign as good news. And the Twelve [were] **with him.** ²**Also [with him were] certain women who'd been healed of evil spirits and illnesses: Mary (called Mag-dalene, from whom seven demons had gone out)** ³**and Joanna (wife of Chuza, Herod's manager) and Susanna and many others, who as such** [= in their womanly role] **were serving them** [Jesus and the Twelve] **out of their** [own] **resources.** Jesus' itineration appeals as often to the interest of Luke's audience in travel. Emphasizing the itin-eration is "taking a road *through one city and town after another*." Even towns, despite their being smaller than cities, don't fall between the cracks. The combination of "preaching" and "heralding" highlights Jesus' verbal ministry, and the "news" is "good" because "God's reign" brings salvation through Christ the Lord (2:10–11). The presence of the Twelve with Jesus will provide eyewitness testimony substantiating the good news (1:1–4; 6:13–16; Acts 1:21–22). The additional presence of many women expands the number of eyewitnesses. So Luke is portray-ing Jesus as a compassionate Savior who not only forgave the many sins of the woman in 7:36–50 but also healed many women. The recording of some of their names, plus other descriptions of them, testifies to the detailedness of Luke's historical research (1:1–4). Mary was called "Mag-dalene" because of her hailing from Magdala, a town along the west shore of the Sea of Galilee. She was one of the women out of whom Jesus had cast out evil spirits, but her case merits particular mention because of the severity of her possession—by no fewer than seven demons! Her traveling with Jesus, plus that of the other women he'd healed of the physical effects of demon-possession and of regular illnesses, expresses gratitude and devotion to him for his philanthropy (compare 7:36–50). With Jo-anna, wife of Herod's manager Chuza, Jesus' magnetism has effectively reached into governmental circles (for this Herod, see 3:1). Luke doesn't specify the nature of Chuza's managership, so that the accent remains solely on Jesus' drawing Joanna from the court. Not only were these women traveling with Jesus and the Twelve. They were also "serving them out of their [own] resources." Normally, "serving" has to do with food (see, for example, Acts 6:2). It appears, then, that with their own money the women bought, prepared, and served food to Jesus and the Twelve as they all itinerated from city to city and town to town. Such was the women's thankfulness for his having healed them.

THE GIFT OF KNOWING THE SECRETS OF GOD'S REIGN
Luke 8:4–15

This passage divides into a parable (8:4–8), the pur-pose of parables (8:9–10), and the meaning of the pres-ent parable (8:11–15). Jesus has been heralding God's reign as good news (8:1). Now he reveals the secrets of that reign to people of good and beautiful hearts.

8:4–8: And as a large crowd and travelers from city after city were coming together to him [Jesus],

he spoke [to them] **through a parable: 5"A sower went out to sow his seed** [a collective singular]. **And in his sowing, some** [seed] **fell on the edge of a path and was trampled, and the birds of the sky** [as opposed to domestic fowl] **devoured it. 6And other** [seed] **fell on bedrock; and on growing, it dried up because of not having moisture. 7And other** [seed] **fell in the midst of thorns; and the thorns, growing with** [it], **choked it off. 8And other** [seed] **fell into good soil and, on growing, produced fruit one hundredfold." While saying these things, he called out, "**[The person] **who has ears to hear** [with] **had better hear!"** The double reference to "a large crowd" and "travelers from city after city" carries forward Luke's emphasis on Jesus' magnetism. "From city after city" recalls his having itinerated "through one city and town after another, preaching and heralding God's reign as good news" (8:1). Here he wastes no time in speaking to the large crowd and travelers, for he speaks to them "*as* [they] were coming together to him." What he has to say needs to be heard without delay. And it takes the form of a parable, that is, a comparison.

This comparison consists in the story of a farmer's sowing seed. To take advantage of as much of his field as possible, he sowed seed close to a path. But some of that seed accidentally fell on the edge of the path rather than on tillable soil. To indicate that it fell *on* the edge rather than *alongside* the edge, Luke notes that it's trampled and only then devoured by wild birds. Other seed fell accidentally on a patch of bedrock. Obviously, bedrock consists of neither soil nor moisture enabling the seed to grow. But since this seed did grow before drying up for lack of moisture, there must have been a thin layer of soil covering the bedrock and just enough moisture in the layer to allow a bit of short-lived growth. The hyperboles of falling "on bedrock" and of "not having moisture" stress the insufficiency of soil and moisture, however. Since the thorns *grew* with the third batch of seeds, the thorns were themselves still in seed form and therefore invisible to the farmer when he sowed his seeds among them. By growing more vigorously than the grain, the thorns "choked off" the seedlings of grain in the sense of crowding them out. The soil into which fruitbearing seed fell was good in that it wasn't hardened by human traffic, as in the case of the path, or dislodged by an outcropping of bedrock, or infested with thorns. The yield of a hundredfold counted as very, very good (Genesis 26:12). "[The person] who has ears to hear [with] had better hear!" doesn't imply that some people don't have ears to hear with. Rather, it warns that people had better put their ears to good use by heeding the word of God that Jesus speaks (5:1; 8:11).

8:9–10: And his disciples were asking him, "What might this parable be [= mean]**?" 10And he said, "To you** [as my disciples] **it has been given to know** [= understand] **the secrets of God's reign. But to the rest** [nondisciples] [I speak those secrets] **in parables in order that 'though they see they may not see, and though they hear they may not perceive** [Isaiah 6:9]**.'"** The disciples' question shows they don't understand the meaning of the parable. So Jesus' statement that it has

been given them to understand will require his explaining the parable to them (see 8:11–15). "To know *the secrets of God's reign*" gives an advance indication, though, of the subject that the parable deals with. Once Jesus explains these secrets to his disciples, the secrets will be secrets only to nondisciples. But using words from Isaiah, Jesus says he speaks in parables in order that nondisciples may *not* see or perceive the secrets of God's reign hidden in parables. They see the parabolic picture but don't see its meaning. They hear the parabolic words but don't perceive their meaning. And Jesus doesn't want them to, because they haven't become his disciples. The plural of "parables" implies the same judgmental purpose in other parables of his. Why then did he close off this parable with a command to hear? The command must mean that people should become disciples by hearing and believing the word of God that Jesus speaks in plain language (see again 5:1; 8:11 plus 8:21; 11:28 and many passages in Luke's book of Acts). Then they'll receive the gift of knowing the secrets of God's reign through Jesus' explanation of the parables. That is to say, we must believe to understand as well as understand to believe. In the following explanation, those secrets have to do with the present coming of God's reign through persuasive speech rather than through brute force.

8:11–15: "And the parable is [= means] **this: The seed is God's word** [the gospel that Jesus speaks in plain language]. **12And the** [people] **on the edge of the path are the ones who've heard** [God's word]. **Then the Devil comes and takes away the word from their heart lest they be saved by believing** [that word]. **13And the** [people] **on the bedrock** [are] **the ones who receive the word with joy when they hear** [it]. **And these** [people] **have no root.** [They're people] **who believe for a time and in a time of testing apostatize. 14And as for what fell into the thorns, these** [people] **are the ones who've heard** [the word] **and, going on, they're choked by life's anxieties and wealth and pleasures and don't bear** [fruit] **to maturity. 15And as for** [what fell] **in beautiful soil, these** [people] **are the ones who as such** [that is, as beautiful soil]**, on hearing the word in** [or 'with'] **a beautiful and good heart, hold** [it] **fast and bear fruit with perseverance."** Jesus has spoken about ears with which to hear God's word (8:8). Now he speaks about a heart with which to believe the heard word and be saved (compare Romans 10:9–10). But in the case of some people, Jesus explains, the Devil takes away the word that's heard, so that it's no longer in the heart to be believed. The parable talked about the *bedrock's* lacking *moisture*. The explanation switches to *people's* lacking *root*. That is, just as bedrock contains no moisture, seeds that fall on bedrock have no soil into which they can sink a root, so that the drying up that ensues represents apostasy—departure from initial belief—an apostasy occasioned by trials that test their faith and find it wanting (compare 1 Timothy 4:1; Hebrews 3:12). The thorns represent anxieties, wealth, and pleasures which, as people go on in life after hearing the word, keep them from bearing fruit to maturity. They're not said to have believed, but "not to maturity" implies some growth, only incomplete growth. So the Devil, trials, and diversions lie behind these failures, all three of which represent failure to be saved. To his description of the soil that produces the fruit of salvation as "good," Jesus adds "beautiful" for emphasis. (Farmers can appreciate the description of this soil as beautiful.) The beautiful and good soil represents "a beautiful and good heart." That is to say (and this fits Luke's emphasis elsewhere too), people of inward moral excellence are predisposed to hold fast the heard word against the Devil's attempts to take it away, and to persevere in belief despite being tested by trials and tempted by anxieties, wealth, and pleasures. We might conjecture that the hundredfoldness of these people's fruitbearing represents the eternality of the life they'll receive. But Jesus doesn't explain the large yield, so that the emphasis rests on a virtuous heart.

A POSTSCRIPT ON HEARING
THE WORD OF GOD
Luke 8:16–18

The parable and its explanation in 8:4–15 dealt with hearing God's word. The present passage adds to that subject.

8:16–17: "And no one, after lighting a lamp, covers it with a jar or puts [it] underneath a bed; rather, he puts [it] on a lampstand in order that people who come in may see the light. [17]For nothing is hidden [in a parable] that won't become manifest [in an explanation of the parable], nor is anything concealed [in a parable] that won't be known and come into manifestation [through an explanation of the parable]." Jesus compares his parabolic speaking to lighting a lamp in order that people who enter the room may see light—in other words, that people may understand the secrets of God's reign. But parabolic speech hides those secrets unless it's explained. Without explanation it's like a lamp covered by a jar or put under a bed. Explaining the parable is like putting the lit lamp on a lampstand for people's enlightenment. Then the purpose of lighting the lamp is attained. But who are those people who enter and receive enlightenment in Jesus' explanations of the parables? They are those, indeed exclusively those, who hear well the *non*parabolic word of God that Jesus has preached and taught, the very people represented by the beautiful and good soil in the preceding parable. **8:18:** "**Therefore** [in view of the fact that only good hearers of the gospel will get an explanation of the secrets of God's reign embedded in parabolic speech] **watch out *how* you hear** [the gospel]." Hear it with persevering faith (8:15), not carelessly (8:12), temporarily (8:13), or distractedly (8:14). "**For whoever has** [persevering faith in God's word, the gospel]—**it** [the explanation of parables] **will be given to him. And whoever doesn't have** [such faith]—**even what he thinks he has** [God's word, the gospel] **will be taken from him** [just as in the preceding parable the Devil took away the word, trials undermined it, and worldly concerns suppressed it]."

THE ALLEGIANCE TO JESUS OF
HIS NATURAL FAMILY
Luke 8:19–21

This snippet of a passage links up with the preceding theme of God's word (8:11–21 and, earlier, 5:1). **8:19–21: And his** [Jesus'] **mother and brothers came to him and couldn't meet with him because of the crowd.** [20]**And it was announced to him, "Your mother and your brothers are standing outside, wanting to see you."** [21]**And he, answering, told them, "My mother and my brothers—these are the ones who are hearing God's word and doing** [it]." So great is the popularity of Jesus that even his biological family can't get close enough to meet with him. The crowd is pressing around him too thickly. The family's wanting to see him, though, shows allegiance to him, their son and brother. He, in turn, describes them as those who hear God's word and do it (compare 6:46–49, where Jesus' words are in view, but he speaks the word of God). Jesus' speaking to the crowd about "these" (his mother and brothers) favors that here in Luke's Gospel he's describing his biological family as *examples* of those who "hear the word with a beautiful and good heart" (8:15) rather than referring to whoever hears God's word and does it. Moreover, a description of his natural family fits Luke's favorable portrayals of Jesus' mother Mary in Luke 1–2; Acts 1:14, of Jesus' half brothers in Acts 1:14, and of his half brother James in Acts 12:17; 15:13; 21:18. So those who knew him best, his immediate family, heard his words as God's word and put that word into practice. A convincing recommendation of Jesus!

THE IRRATIONALITY OF UNBELIEF IN JESUS
Luke 8:22–25

8:22–23: And it happened on one of the days that he got in a boat—also his disciples [got into it]—**and told them, "Let's go through** [the Sea of Galilee] **to the other side of the lake." And they set out.** [23]**And as they were sailing, he fell asleep. And a gale of wind came down into the lake** ["down" because the lake is about seven hundred feet below sea level], **and they were being filled up and endangered** [for their lives]. At the moment, the reason for Jesus' going to the other side of the lake doesn't matter. It's what happens during the voyage that matters. Nor does the reason for Jesus' falling asleep matter. But his sleeping does prepare for a striking contrast with the disciples' coming panic. The boat was being filled up with water because waves, stirred up by the violent wind, were washing over the sides of the boat. Since danger to the boaters counted as more important than danger to the boat, however, Luke writes that "*they* were being filled up."

8:24–25: And on approaching [Jesus], **they roused him** [= woke him up], **saying, "Master, Master, we're perishing!" And having been roused, he reprimanded the wind and the surge of water. And they stopped, and there came a calm.** [25]**And he said to them, "Where**

[is] **your faith?" And having become frightened, they marveled, saying to one another, "Who then is this, in that he commands even the winds and the water and they obey him?"** Boats in those days were so rickety that a severe storm posed great danger. No wonder, then, that the disciples panic. Their doubling of "Master" betrays a high degree of panic. They rouse Jesus with the announcement that they're perishing, but his noting later their lack of faith shows that they don't expect him to save them from perishing. Nor do they ask him to. It doesn't cross their minds that he can. Yet he does, with a mere reprimand of the wind and surge of water. The disciples correctly interpret the reprimand as a command. The resultant calm exhibits both Jesus' supreme authority and the gale's obedience, an obedience such as human beings ought to emulate. Jesus' display of power over wind and waves has *frightened* the disciples, so that they don't answer his question, "Where [is] your faith?" The display also *amazes* them, so that instead of answering his question they ask one another a question about Jesus' identity. But this question too goes unanswered, because so far as Luke's audience are concerned, if not the disciples, the question has already been answered. Jesus is God's Son (1:32, 35; 3:22; 4:3, 9, 41), King of Israel (1:32–33, 69), the Lord (1:43; 2:11), Savior (2:11), Christ (2:11, 26; 4:41), and the Holy One of God (4:34)—quite enough to be the master of wind and waves as well as of the disciples. So it doesn't make sense not to have faith in him.

EYEWITNESSING AND TESTIFYING IN REGARD TO JESUS' EXORCISM OF LEGION
Luke 8:26–39

The first half of this passage deals with the exorcism of demons called "Legion" (8:26–33). The second half deals with a report of the exorcism by eyewitnesses, others' coming to see the results of the exorcism, and the ex-demoniac's own proclamation (8:34–39).

8:26–27: And they [Jesus and his disciples] **sailed across** [the Sea of Galilee] **to the region of the Gergasenes, which as such is opposite Galilee. ²⁷And when he'd come out** [of the boat] **onto the land, there met him a certain man from the city** [of Gergasa] **who had demons and for a considerable time hadn't worn clothing and wasn't staying** [= living] **in a house, but in the tombs** [just outside the city]. Ancient manuscripts differ on whether to read "Gergasenes," "Gerasenes," or "Gadarenes." Only the city of Gergasa fits the geography and topography of this episode, however; and the greater prominence of Gerasa and Gadara, combined with similarities of spelling and pronunciation, made it easy for these other cities to crowd out an original Gergasa in the scribal tradition (see further the comments on Mark 5:1). "From the *city*" shows that the name of "the *region*" corresponds to the city just outside of which the exorcism will take place. "Opposite Galilee" indicates the east side of the lake, for Galilee lies on the west side. The geographical notations give evidence of Luke's histori-

cal research (1:1–4). Underscoring the sorry state of the demoniac who meets Jesus are (1) the plurality of the demons possessing their victim; (2) the considerable time he'd suffered possession; (3) his resultant nakedness; and (4) his living in tombs instead of a house. "*In* the tombs" implies caves used as tombs, though the phrase could be translated "*among* the tombs" without regard to caves. But the contrastive parallel with "*in* a house" favors "in the tombs." Either way, the severity of this demoniac's possession will make for a difficult exorcism and therefore greater success in the end.

8:28–29: And on seeing Jesus, he fell down screaming before him and said with a loud voice, "What do I and you have to do with each other, Jesus, Son of the Most High God? I beg you not to torture me." ²⁹For he'd commanded the unclean spirit to come out from the man. For many times it had seized him violently; and he was repeatedly bound with chains [on his hands and arms] **and shackles** [on his feet and legs], **being guarded; and tearing the bonds apart, he was repeatedly being driven by the demon into uninhabited places.** "And on seeing Jesus, he fell down . . . before him" adds detail to the demoniac's meeting Jesus in 8:27. The falling down before Jesus and begging him show recognition of his superiority. But the screaming and loudness of voice denote a desperate attempt to ward him off ("What do I and you have to do with each other . . . ?"). The attempt is supplemented by an exhibition of the knowledge of Jesus' personal name and status as "Son of the Most High God." (It was thought that knowledge of a person's name and status gives a certain power over that person.) Luke identifies the reason for this attempt as Jesus' having commanded the unclean spirit to come out. Strikingly, the man speaks as though an exorcism would torture *him*. But of course the spirit is speaking through the man about its own possible torture. Luke's description of the spirit as "unclean" suits the demoniac's living in tombs, for corpses and bones of the dead make tombs ritually unclean. The command to come out leads Luke to elaborate further the man's sorry condition and makes this condition the reason for Jesus' command: (1) numerous and violent seizures by the spirit; (2) others' repeatedly putting him in chains and shackles and under guard; and (3) his breaking loose only to be repeatedly driven by the demon into uninhabited places. So in addition to living in tombs he wanders in the wilderness. If Jesus succeeds in exorcising so strong and oppressive a demon, then, the exorcism will have displayed extraordinary power and compassion.

8:30–31: And Jesus asked him, "What's your name?" And he said, "Legion," because many demons had entered into him. ³¹And they were imploring him not to order them to go off into the abyss [the underworld]. Despite Jesus' earlier command, the demon hadn't come out. Why? Because Jesus thought of only one demon (as indicated by the singular form of "your" in Luke's original Greek), whereas readers of this Gospel have known since 8:27 that a number of demons possessed the man. (Theologically speaking, Jesus didn't always exercise his divine omniscience; he wasn't play-acting when he asked questions, for example.) Disclosure of the name "Legion," a Roman military term indicating here "*many* demons," gives Jesus the information he needs to pursue this exorcism to success. His superiority has forced them to disclose their name, and the disclosure makes them recognize the certainty and imminence of their exorcism. Resigned to it, they shift from their earlier vociferous attempt to ward off Jesus to imploring him not to order them into the underworld, a place of confinement. They'd rather wander topside.

8:32–33: And there on the mountain[side] **was grazing a herd of a considerable number of pigs. And they** [the correspondingly many demons] **implored him to let them enter into those** [pigs]. **And he let them.** [33]**And on coming out from the man, they entered into the pigs; and the herd rushed down the slope into the lake and drowned.** The negative entreaty that Jesus not order the demons into the underworld turns into a positive entreaty that he let them enter the pigs. This entreaty for permission shows once again the demons' recognition of his authority over them. One could almost say that in granting the permission, he shows compassion on them. There's no indication that he called on his foreknowledge to know how the pigs would react. So the demons play a humorously disastrous trick on themselves.

8:34–36: And on seeing what had happened, the herdsmen fled and reported in the city and in the hamlets [what had happened]. [35]**And they** [residents of the city and the hamlets] **came out to see what had happened, and they came to Jesus and found the man from whom the demons had come out, sitting at Jesus' feet, clothed and sane. And they were afraid.** [36]**And** [the herdsmen] **who'd seen** [what had happened] **reported to them how the demon-possessed** [man] **had been saved** [from his possession]. In agreement with his prologue (1:1–4), Luke emphasizes both the herdsmen's eyewitnessing of the difficult but successful exorcism and their widespread testifying both to *what* they'd seen and to *how* it had happened. In the same vein he also emphasizes the coming of their audience to see for themselves the results of this exorcism. That they come not only from the city but also from the hamlets of the region augments mightily the number of eyewitnesses. The evidence of exorcism that they see consists in contrasts with the man's former state: sitting at Jesus' feet rather than living in tombs and being driven into the wilderness, clothed rather than naked, sane rather than tearing apart the chains and shackles with which he'd been put under guard. The sight of this transformation strikes fear in the eyewitnesses.

8:37–39: And all the multitude of the surrounding [region] **of the Gergasenes asked him to go away from them, because they were gripped by great fear. And he, on getting into a boat, returned** [to Galilee on the west side of the lake]. [38]**And the man from whom the demons** **had come out was begging him to be with him. But he** [Jesus] **dismissed him, saying,** [39]**"Return to your house and relate** [to your family] **how many things God has done for you." And he went off, proclaiming throughout the whole city how many things Jesus had done for him.** "And *all* the *multitude* of the *surrounding* [region]" heightens Luke's emphasis on the large number of eyewitnesses. Their fear comes in for a second mention, this time intensified by its description as "great" and as having "gripped" them. Luke's intensification of their fear heightens also the awesomeness of the exorcism and explains the request that Jesus leave. It's often said that they don't want to lose any more pigs or whatever else they had that his actions might dispossess them of. But Luke doesn't make such a point, so that the accent falls on the fear-inspiring character of the exorcism as such. Just as Jesus consented to the demons' entreaty to enter the pigs, gracious as ever he consents to the multitude's request that he leave. The ex-demoniac's begging to be with him doesn't just show gratitude for deliverance from demon-possession. It gives further evidence of that deliverance by contrasting with his earlier, vociferous attempt to ward Jesus off. But gracious though he is, Jesus doesn't grant this request. He has something more important for the ex-demoniac to do. It's to return to his house, which he hasn't lived in for a considerable time, and relate to his family, from whom he has been estranged, how many things God has done for him. "How *many* things" calls attention to the details of deliverance: from tombs and wilderness to home, from nakedness to wearing clothes, from berserk behavior to sound-mindedness. The man does more than Jesus told him to do; he proclaims these many things throughout the whole city. So his preaching supplements both the eyewitness report of the herdsmen and the eyewitnessing by those who came to check out that report. These things didn't take place in a corner (Acts 26:26). They were open to public view, and the general public did view them. Hence the certainty of the gospel (1:1–4). With "how many things *God* has done for you" Jesus piously gives God the credit. With "how many things *Jesus* had done for him" the ex-demoniac piously gives Jesus the credit. Piety on both sides—without disagreement, for God is working through his Son Jesus. Luke stresses that Jesus and believers in him represent the best in true religion. And "*for him*," which occurs in both statements, highlights the beneficence of Jesus as God's Son and agent.

FAITH IN JESUS TO HEAL AND TO RAISE THE DEAD
Luke 8:40–56

This passage starts with a request for Jesus to save someone from imminent death (8:40–42), continues with an interruptive story of an unintended healing (8:43–48), and comes to a climax with Jesus' raising the one whose death had turned in the meantime from imminent to actual (8:49–56).

8:40: And as Jesus was returning [from the region of the Gergasenes, on the east side of the Sea of Galilee, to Galilee, on the west side], **the crowd welcomed him; for they were all waiting expectantly for him.** Several features of this statement highlight Jesus' popularity: (1) the crowd as a large number of people; (2) their welcoming him; (3) their doing so contemporaneously with his return ("*as* Jesus was returning"); (4) their welcoming him without delay because they were "waiting expectantly for him" in the sense of looking *forward* to seeing him; and (5) the inclusion of everybody in the crowd ("they were *all* waiting expectantly for him"). This grand welcome stands in contrast to the fear-filled request of residents on the other side of the lake that Jesus leave them (compare Acts 2:41; 18:27; 21:17).

8:41–42b: And behold, a man came who had the name Jairus. And this [man] **was a ruler of the synagogue. And on falling at Jesus' feet, he was imploring him to come to his house,** ⁴²ᵃ⁻ᵇ**because he had an only daughter, about twelve years old; and she was dying.** "Behold" calls attention to the coming of Jairus. Mention of his name supports historical trustworthiness. His "falling at Jesus' feet" points both to the desperation of Jairus and to his recognition of Jesus' superiority despite being himself "a ruler of the synagogue" (that is, chief elder in charge of organizing services there). The entreaty that Jesus come to Jairus's house isn't followed by an additional entreaty that Jesus heal Jairus's daughter of whatever had made her death imminent, for her coming death will make such an entreaty irrelevant. She's not merely ill. She's already in the throes of dying. Moreover, she's Jairus's only offspring and dying at the young age of twelve, the very age of the boy Jesus when with his understanding and answers he astonished all who heard his dialogue with the teachers at the temple (2:41–51). Sadly from the standpoint of Jairus, his daughter is dying without having been married off so as to bear children. We can appreciate his desperation.

8:42c–44: And as he [Jesus] **was going, the crowds were squeezing him.** ⁴³**And a woman who'd had a flow of blood for twelve years, who as such couldn't be healed by anyone,** ⁴⁴**on approaching from behind, touched the fringe of his** [Jesus'] [outer] **garment. And immediately her flow of blood stanched.** Jesus' going toward Jairus's house shows compassion for him. "The crowd" (singular) of 8:40 has turned into "the crowds" (plural) to magnify Jesus' celebrity, and their pressing around him so closely as to squeeze him adds to the magnification and also prepares for the woman's extraordinary effort to come close enough for a touch. She has suffered a flow of blood for as long as Jairus's daughter has been alive—only in the case of the daughter the accent falls on the shortness of her life thus far, whereas in the woman's case the accent falls on her medical problem as longstanding. Some early manuscripts add that the woman had spent in vain her whole livelihood on physicians (so Mark 5:26). But the early manuscripts followed here say simply that she couldn't be healed by anyone. If Jesus heals her, then, he'll have done what no one else could do. On the other hand, he doesn't intend to heal

her; for she has approached him from behind, hasn't made herself known to him, and therefore hasn't asked for healing. She believes that merely touching his garment, and only the fringe of it at that, will bring her healing. And Jesus is so radiant with power that the touch works (compare 6:19). The immediacy with which the blood-flow stanches underscores his power.

8:45–46: And Jesus said, "Who [is the person] **that touched me?" And as all were denying** [that they'd touched him]**, Peter said, "Master, the crowds** [plural, as in 8:42b] **are thronging you and pressing** [against you]**."** ⁴⁶**But Jesus said, "Someone touched me, for I recognized power as having gone out from me."** Jesus didn't know who touched him (there was no need for him to call on his omniscience here, or on prophetic clairvoyance), but he did know that power had gone out from him because somebody had touched him with faith for a healing. The crowds' pressing against him doesn't count as that effective kind of touching; and because of faith, touching only the fringe of his outer garment counts as touching Jesus himself. Peter's use of two expressions, "are thronging you" and "are pressing [against you]," maintains Luke's stress on Jesus' popularity. Peter's statement doesn't criticize Jesus' question so much as it answers the question—in effect, "You're so popular, and rightly so, that everybody is touching you!" Peter's statement also gains force from its contradicting the denial of "all" that they'd touched Jesus.

8:47–48: And the woman, on seeing that she hadn't escaped notice, came trembling; and on falling down before him, she reported in the sight of all the people the reason on account of which she'd touched him and how she'd been healed at once. ⁴⁸**And he told her, "Daughter, your faith has saved you. Go in peace."** Jesus' stating his knowledge that power had emanated from him made the woman see that she hadn't escaped notice. But why doesn't she deduce from Jesus' question, "Who touched me?" that she *had* escaped notice? If she hadn't escaped it, why does Jesus have to ask who touched him? And why didn't she deduce from his question that he knew *only* that power had gone out from him, not additionally that it had gone out *to her?* Here's the answer to these questions: Like the speech of Jesus in general, his mere question carried an authority that forced the woman to reveal herself as the one who'd touched him, much as his question, "What's your name?" forced the demons to answer, "Legion" (8:30). That the woman "came" to Jesus suggests either that she'd shrunk back into the crowds or—more likely, since she'd approached him "from behind" and now falls before him—that she came around to face him. In either case, trembling, falling before him, and reporting the reason why she'd touched him and how she'd been immediately healed show her recognition of the authority with which he'd asked his question. "At once" defines the "how" of her healing and for a second time magnifies Jesus' power (see 8:44 for the first time). Her reporting "in the *sight* of all the people" makes her a proclaimer of Jesus' beneficent power and makes the crowds a mass of eye- as well as earwitnesses to that power (compare 1:1–4 on eyewitnesses). "*All* the people" leaves no one present outside the circle of eye- and earwitnesses. Confirmation aplenty!

Jesus' addressing the woman with "Daughter" helps intertwine this story with that of Jairus's "daughter" (8:42). For the rest of Jesus' statement, see the comments on 7:50. But there, salvation by faith meant deliverance from eternal judgment for a woman's sins. Here, salvation by faith means deliverance from a temporally physical malady. But the two deliverances aren't unrelated, for the present physical deliverance anticipates a resurrection of the body for the peaceful—that is, healthful—enjoyment of eternal life. And to an even brighter such anticipation Luke now proceeds.

8:49–50: While he was still speaking, someone comes from the synagogue ruler's [house], saying, "Your daughter has died. Don't bother the teacher any more." 50But Jesus, on hearing [what Jairus had been told], answered [= responded], "Don't fear. Just believe, and she'll be saved [that is, saved from the death that she has already died]." "While he was still speaking" puts the bad news of the daughter's death in immediate conjunction with Jesus' words of salvation and peace to the healed woman and therefore raises the possibility that the death of Jairus's daughter will offset the healing of the woman. And the daughter's death makes for a more difficult case than that of the woman with twelve years of a blood-flow. The daughter was already dying when Jairus came to Jesus, so that she died during the delay caused by the interruptive healing of the woman. Luke's writing about "the synagogue ruler's [house]" suits the reference to Jesus as "the teacher," since teaching was regularly done in synagogues. "Don't bother the teacher any more" betrays unbelief that Jesus can raise the dead. But Luke's audience know that he can from his having raised the widow of Nain's son during the son's funeral procession (7:11–17). And Jesus, sympathetic as he is, *wants* to be bothered for the benefit of human beings. He's the great philanthropist in Luke's Gospel. Jesus responds to Jairus that by itself faith will gain his daughter's salvation from death. On the conjunction of faith and salvation, see not only 7:50 but also 8:12; 17:19; 18:42; Acts 14:9; 15:11; 16:31.

8:51–53: And entering the house, he didn't let anyone enter with him except for Peter and John and James and the child's father and mother. 52And all were weeping and beating themselves [that is, beating their breasts] over her. But he said, "Stop weeping. For she didn't die; rather, she's sleeping." 53And knowing that she'd died, they started laughing at him. Presumably, the house is too small for the mourners and the crowds that have accompanied Jesus. Soon he'll take Peter, John, and James to see his transfiguration too (9:28–36). They supply two or three witnesses from within the band of apostles. The father and mother, also allowed in, supply sufficient witnesses from outside that band (see Num-

bers 35:30; Deuteronomy 17:6; 19:15 for the sufficiency of two or three witnesses). Since Jesus, the three apostles, and the parents entered the house in 8:51 and Jesus didn't let anyone else inside (notice how he takes charge even in someone else's house), 8:52 steps back to describe the weeping and breast-beating that was being done outside the house before the entry of Jesus and the five others. "Stop weeping" shows his confidence of raising the dead daughter. He knows his power and determines to use it in nullifying the bad news and establishing the good news, the gospel. As a euphemism, sleeping usually refers to long-term death (as in 1 Thessalonians 4:15–16, for example). Here, not-dead-but-sleeping portrays the daughter's death as a short nap, since Jesus is about to awake her. "Knowing that she'd died" shows that Luke as well as the mourners knows she's dead. The mourners' laughing at Jesus provides a foil against which his raising her will stand out. He'll have the last laugh.

8:54–56: But he, on grasping her hand, called out, saying, "Child, arise." 55And her spirit returned, and she stood up at once. And he ordered that she be given [something] to eat. 56And her parents were amazed, but he commanded them to tell no one what had happened. Being dead, she couldn't touch Jesus as the woman with the blood-flow did. So Jesus grasps her hand. "Called" connotes an authoritative summons away from the realm of death. Jesus addresses her with "Child" to indicate that he's raising her for the benefit of her otherwise childless parents. "Arise" calls for a kind of resurrection (though not the final one) aided by Jesus' having grasped her hand to help her up (compare 7:14, where the passive "Be raised" implied God's raising the widow of Nain's son, since Jesus hadn't grasped his hand but was only touching his burial plank, held aloft so that the corpse was out of reach). First "her spirit returned" to her body (contrast Jesus' committing his spirit to God at the crucifixion [23:46]). Then "she *stood up*" (= the verbal form of "resurrection," which means a "standing up" of formerly supine corpses), and did so "at once" (compare the two occurrences of "at once" in reference to the healing of the woman with a blood-flow [8:44, 47]). Again, Jesus' power requires no time to take effect. The command that she be given something to eat proves her resurrection to be physical, just as Jesus will eat some fish to demonstrate to the disciples the physicality of his resurrection (24:36–43). The parents are amazed, but Luke mentions no amazement on the part of Peter, John, and James. They've seen him raise the son of the widow of Nain. Apparently Jairus and his wife haven't. Jesus doesn't need any more publicity. The crowds have been pressing him. So he says not to tell anybody what has happened.

AN EXPANSION OF JESUS' MINISTRY THROUGH THE TWELVE APOSTLES
Luke 9:1–6

9:1–2: And on calling the Twelve together, he gave them power and authority over all demons and

[power and authority] **to cure diseases.** **²And he sent them to preach God's reign and to heal the sick.** Jesus convenes the Twelve to segregate them for a commission. The giving of his own power and authority to them ensures continuity between his ministry and theirs, so that the apostolic church in Luke's book of Acts won't represent a break from Jesus any more than he represents a break from God's dealings in the Old Testament. Luke promotes continuity, because his audience is likely to trust it. "Power" indicates ability, and "authority" indicates freedom to use that ability. Luke's using both terms underlines the comprehensiveness of the continuity between Jesus' ministry and that of the Twelve, as does also the phrase "over *all* demons." Furthermore, this phrase indicates that the ministry of the Twelve will be just as unstoppable as that of Jesus. And their exercise of his power and authority is to work for the benefit of people possessed by demons and suffering from diseases. Luke uses the verb for "sent" that's cognate to the noun "apostle," which in turn connotes being sent with authority to act on behalf of the sender (rather like our legal power of attorney [compare 6:13]). By sending the Twelve to heal the sick, Jesus expands his program of philanthropy. "The sick" include, but aren't limited to, those suffering from the physical effects of demonic possession; for elsewhere Luke associates healing with exorcism as well as with the curing of diseases (6:18; 7:21; 8:2; 9:42; 13:10–14; Acts 5:16; 10:38 and perhaps Luke 4:40–41). Added to physical therapy is the preaching of God's reign, which makes the therapy part of God's beginning to impose his reign on earth by driving out the deleterious effects of sin as well as sin itself.

9:3–5: And he told them, "Take nothing for the road [= for your itineration]: **neither a staff nor a bag nor bread nor money nor two tunics each** [that is, only one per person]. **⁴And into whatever house you enter—stay there; and don't be going out from there** [to look for better quarters in another house in that locality]. **⁵And however many** [people] **don't welcome you—as you go out from that city** [where they live], **shake the dust** [of that city] **off your feet for a testimony against them."** A staff would have been for steadying themselves on difficult paths and defending themselves against wild animals. A bag would have been for carrying foodstuffs and money. Bread would have been the food itself, taken for nourishment during a journey from here to there. Money would have been for the purchase of bread. Tunics were robes worn next to the skin as undergarments. No need for more than one. So the Twelve are to travel light and depend on divine protection and local hospitality (for the latter of which the Middle East is still famous). They're not to aggrandize themselves even to the tune of a sack lunch, much less money offered them or gained by begging. They're to be satisfied with whatever lodging is given them. They're to minister for others, not for themselves. People's refusal of hospitality to them will bring a symbolic testimony against those people, however. God will see the testimony (the Twelve's shaking the city's dust off their feet as they exit) and remember

it at the Last Day. So there's an edge to the preaching of God's reign. Refusal to hear it ensures judgment; the good news turns into bad news (see 3:7–9; 13:1–5 for two examples from among many).

9:6: And on going out, they went throughout [Galilee (see 8:40 with comments)], **town by town, proclaiming the good news** [of God's reign (see 9:2)] **and healing** [people] **everywhere.** "Everywhere" relates to both the proclaiming and the healing. "Throughout," "town by town," and "everywhere" prefigure the spread of the gospel by the Twelve and others that Luke's book of Acts will detail. For the present, though, we see an initial fulfillment of 5:10: "From now on you'll be catching human beings alive" (see also 6:12–16). What starts here won't end till Jesus comes back (24:46–48; Acts 1:8–11). In 9:5 he spoke of whatever "city" might reject them. Here Luke writes "town by town." Towns are smaller than cities (though by our standards most of their cities were small). Because of Jesus' instructions, the evangelization of cities goes without saying. Luke adds towns to stress the thoroughness with which the Twelve carried out their mission.

THE GOSPEL'S REACHING AS FAR AS THE COURT OF HEROD ANTIPAS
Luke 9:7–9

9:7–9: And Herod the tetrarch [concerning whom see 3:1] **heard about all the things that were happening; and he was bewildered because of its being said by some, "John** [the baptizer] **has been raised from the dead,"** **⁸and by some, "Elijah has appeared"** [as prophesied in Malachi 4:5], **and** [by] **others, "A certain prophet of the ancient ones has resurrected** [literally, 'stood up']." **⁹But Herod said, "John I had beheaded. But who is this about whom I'm hearing such things** [compare 7:19–20, 49; 8:25]**?" And he was seeking to see him** [as he *will* see Jesus in 23:6–12]. "All the things that were happening" refers to what Jesus was doing both on his own and through the Twelve. That even this tetrarch, sitting on his high perch, hears about these things puts emphasis on the far reach and unstoppable progress of God's reign. That Herod hears "*all* the things that were happening" also puts emphasis on the openness of the gospel to public scrutiny. Neither Jesus nor the Twelve have anything to hide (compare Acts 26:26: "this hasn't been done in a corner"). Herod's perplexity is caused by others' conflicting, false identifications of Jesus and by Herod's own apparent doubt that the man he had had beheaded (John the baptizer) could be the man who was doing "such things" as Jesus was doing but John never did. Herod's seeking to see Jesus testifies to Jesus' celebrity.

JESUS' FEEDING ABOUT FIVE THOUSAND MEN
Luke 9:10–17

This account starts with an unsuccessful attempt at privacy (9:10–11) and proceeds to the feeding (9:12–17).

9:10–11: **And on returning** [from their mission], **the apostles related to him how many things they'd done. And taking them along, he withdrew privately into a city called Bethsaida.** [11]**But on knowing** [that he'd withdrawn], **the crowds followed him. And on welcoming them, he was talking to them about God's reign and healing those who had need of a cure.** "How *many* things they'd done" points to the success of the Twelve's mission. It could hardly be otherwise, given Jesus' having shared his own power and authority with them (9:1; compare the success of the later mission in Acts). Bethsaida lay at the northeast corner of the Sea of Galilee. But Jesus is so magnetic that the crowds from Galilee, on the west side, follow him there. He can't escape them even when trying to (compare 4:42). His welcoming them despite having tried to escape them displays bigheartedness (compare 4:43). Luke paints Jesus in attractive colors. Jesus combines speaking about God's reign with healing those in need of a cure, just as he'd sent the Twelve to do (9:2). Both he and they speak good words and back up those words with good deeds.

9:12–14a: **But day began to wane; and on approaching** [Jesus], **the Twelve said to him, "Dismiss the crowd in order that by traveling into the surrounding towns and hamlets they may get lodging and find something to eat, because here we're in an uninhabited place."** [13]**But he told them, "You give them** [something] **to eat." But they said, "We have no more than five loaves of bread and two fish—unless indeed we go buy items of food for all this people."** [14a]**For they** [the people] **were about five thousand men.** The waning of the day signals it's getting time to eat. The Twelve show a commendable concern for the crowd's well-being; but by failing to address Jesus with "Master" or the like, the Twelve betray as inappropriate their telling Jesus their Master what to do. "Dismiss the crowd" indicates that his hold over the crowd is so strong that, mealtime or not, they'll not leave unless he tells them to. "The crowds" (plural) of 9:11 have turned into "the crowd" (singular) to suit the upcoming number of "about five thousand men." (You wouldn't call five thousand men "the crowds.") And it's evident that this crowd is the same as the crowds that followed Jesus all the way from Galilee to Bethsaida (see the comments on 9:10–11), for a crowd of locals wouldn't have to "*get* lodging and *find* something to eat" in the surrounding towns and hamlets. Their homes would be there. So "the surrounding towns and hamlets" and "here we're in an uninhabited place" imply that the crowd has followed Jesus not only to Bethsaida, but also beyond that city into a wilderness. So many of them, too! How's that for Jesus' magnetism?

The Twelve have brought up the predicament of the crowd, and Jesus has given the Twelve power and authority (9:1)."You give them [something] to eat" therefore implies that he expects the Twelve to feed the crowd miraculously. But the Twelve take him to be thinking they have food enough to feed the crowd. After noting the insufficiency of their food supply—only five loaves of bread and two fish—they insinuate that Jesus means

them, rather than the crowd, to "go buy items of food" (probably a further supply of both bread and fish). Luke attributes the Twelve's reference to "all this people" to the number of "about five thousand men," as though it would be unreasonable for Jesus to expect them to buy enough food for so many. The word for "men" means adult males.

9:14b–17: **But he told his disciples, "Have them** [the five thousand males] **recline in groups of about fifty each."** [15]**And they** [the disciples] **did so, and all** [the five thousand] **reclined** [on the ground]. [16]**And on taking the five loaves of bread and the two fish, looking up into heaven he blessed them and broke** [them] **in pieces and was giving** [the pieces] **to the disciples to set before the crowd.** [17]**And they all ate and were sated** [= filled to satisfaction]**; and the surplus, twelve baskets of broken pieces, was taken up for them.** Jesus ignores the Twelve's insinuation that he means them to go buy food, and tells them instead to have the five thousand recline in groups of about fifty each. He has something in mind that they don't imagine, something that will enable them to obey his original command, "You give them [something] to eat," without having to go buy food in the surrounding towns and hamlets. Reclining was for formal meals such as provided plenty of food. So reclining is an auspicious omen. Jesus' "looking up into heaven," where God dwells, and "bless[ing]" the bread and fish display piety. Blessing them means praising God in thanksgiving for the food, so that in effect Jesus is giving God the credit for the multiplication of bread and fish that's about to take place. Since there are only five loaves and two fish, Jesus has to break them in pieces for each of the Twelve to have some that they can present to the crowd. Testifying to the abundance of Jesus' beneficence are the satiation of the crowd, of all five thousand of them, and the surplus of broken pieces that far exceed the original supply. The baskets are large. They aren't little lunch bags, and there are twelve of them. But who are the "them" for whom the baskets of surplus are taken up? Since Luke introduced Jesus' disciples as "the Twelve" in this very account (9:12), it looks as though the surplus of twelve baskets is for them in answer to their dismay at having to feed so many with so little. Jesus is generous. Luke doesn't say that the Twelve took up the surplus—rather, that it was taken up for them. So who took it up? Jesus? The five thousand? In either case, the point is that those who serve others get served.

THE PIETY, IDENTITY, AND FATE OF JESUS
Luke 9:18–22

9:18–19: **And it happened while he was praying by himself that his disciples were with him. And he asked them, saying, "Who do the crowds say I am?"** [19]**And they, answering, said, "'John the baptizer.' But others** [say], **'Elijah.' And others** [say], **'A certain prophet of the ancient** [prophets] **has resurrected.'"** The notation of Jesus' praying portrays him as pious. His praying "by himself" enhances the piety in that though "his disciples were with him," he's the only one praying. Their being with him allows him to ask them a question. By asking, "Who do the crowds [plural] say I am?" Jesus himself—like Luke—takes note of his popularity. The disciples' answer matches the popular identifications of Jesus that came to the ears of Herod Antipas in 9:7–9.

9:20–22: And he said to them, "But who do *you* say I am?" And Peter, answering, said, "God's Christ [compare 23:35; 2 Samuel 23:1]." **²¹And issuing an ultimatum, he** [Jesus] **ordered them to tell this** [that he's God's Christ] **to no one, ²²saying, "It's necessary that the Son of Man suffer severely and be rejected by the elders and chief priests and scholars and be killed and on the third day be raised."** Luke's audience know that Jesus' ultimatum not to tell anybody doesn't imply that Jesus isn't God's Christ; for Jesus' identity as God's Christ has been established long since (see 2:11, 26; 4:41). "Christ" means "anointed one," of course. Jesus is "*God's* Christ" in the sense that God anointed him to do the work of salvation ("a *savior*, who is Christ the Lord" [2:11]). He didn't anoint Jesus with any liquid, such as olive oil, but with the Holy Spirit (3:21–22; 4:16–21). Several times in Luke's account people, including the Twelve, have asked who Jesus is (7:49; 8:25; 9:9). Peter has now answered that question correctly, and done so on behalf of all the Twelve. But if he answered correctly, why does Jesus issue an ultimatum not to tell others? Well, the ultimatum includes an explanation that the Son of Man must suffer by being rejected and killed and afterwards raised. This explanation goes against Jewish expectations for the Messiah (Hebrew for "Christ" [see 24:18–21a]). So to tell others at this point that Jesus is God's Christ would steer people away from accepting his suffering, rejection, and execution as part of his fate as the Christ. Not till he's been raised from the dead will they be willing to accept his fate—precisely because of his resurrection (see, for example, Acts 2:22–36, 41). By referring to himself as "the Son of Man" rather than as "God's Christ" Jesus exemplifies what he has ordered the disciples to do, that is, to avoid telling people he's God's Christ. "It's necessary" puts Jesus' coming suffering, rejection, execution, and resurrection squarely in God's plan (see also 24:26; Acts 17:3). So there's no good reason to take offense. And once these events have taken place, Jesus' having predicted them as the outworking of God's plan will provide a positive reason not to take offense.

REQUIREMENTS FOR FOLLOWING JESUS
Luke 9:23–36

This passage divides into Jesus' stating what's required to follow him (9:23–26), and then God the Father's seconding Jesus' statement (9:27–36).

9:23–26: And he was saying to all [not just the twelve disciples, with whom he's been conversing in 9:18–22], **"If anyone wants to come behind me** [as students of rabbis did rather than walking with their teachers (the rabbis) side by side], **he's to disown himself** [= give up self-interest for the present] **and take up his cross day by day and follow me. ²⁴For whoever wants to save his life will lose it; but whoever loses his life because of me—this person will save it. ²⁵For in what respect is a man benefited by gaining the whole world but losing or forfeiting himself? ²⁶For whoever is ashamed of me and my words—the Son of Man will be ashamed of this person whenever he comes in his and the Father's and the holy messengers' glory."** Since Jesus' disciples are already following him, the phrase "wants to come behind me" targets most especially those present who aren't yet following him. Nevertheless, "day by day" includes in the address those, too, who are already following him. Discipleship requires ongoing, daily commitment, which starts with picking up your cross every morning and following Jesus with it. *Your* cross. Not Jesus' cross. He has predicted he'll be killed but has said nothing about death by crucifixion. So what does it mean to pick up your own cross and follow him? The cross was a horizontal crossbeam, not including a vertical stake. A combination of the two would have been too heavy to pick up; and anyway, the vertical stake was probably a permanent fixture. A person sentenced to crucifixion had to pick up the crossbeam at the place of sentencing and carry it to the place of crucifixion. People lining the route hurled insults, taunts, and ridicule at the condemned person. So picking up your cross and following Jesus is a figure of speech for willingness to endure social persecution because of open discipleship to him. This willingness defines the self-denial he demands.

Three statements beginning with "For" give reasons to meet the demand. The first is that self-interest for the present leads to self-loss in the end, whereas self-loss for the present, if it's for Jesus' sake, leads to self-interest in the end. Self-interest for the present means avoiding discipleship because of unwillingness to endure persecution. Self-loss for the present means willingness to endure it. Self-interest in the end means eternal life. Self-loss in the end means eternal ruin. So what do you want? Immediate gratification at the cost of hell later on, or delayed gratification at the cost of present persecution? Jesus' second reason for picking up your cross and following him makes losing or forfeiting yourself in hell the price of gaining the whole world, as if gaining it were possible. To gain the whole world you'd have to avoid persecution by pleasing the world. But in hell you wouldn't be able to enjoy what you'd gained. And "*forfeiting* himself" defines "*losing* yourself" as punishment for unwillingness to pay the price of persecution. Jesus' third reason for picking up your cross and following him attributes that unwillingness to your being ashamed of him and his words, and contains the warning that as the Son of Man he'll reciprocate by being ashamed of you at his second coming. To be ashamed of Jesus and his words is to reject them so as not to suffer insults, taunts, and ridicule. Likewise, his being ashamed means rejecting whoever out of shame has rejected him and his words. And contrasting with such shame is his coming glory, a glory not only that belongs to him but also that is accompanied by the glory of God his Father and the messengers' glory. This triple glory makes being ashamed of Jesus and his words ridiculously foolish, and makes the suffering of persecution on account of him a triflingly small price to pay. And his describing the messengers as "holy" makes being ashamed of him and his words *unholy*. But who are these messengers? Most translations have "angels" at this point. Later, though, we'll have reason to understand them as a couple of departed human beings (see the comments on 9:30–31).

9:27–29: **"And I tell you truly, there are some of** [those] **standing here who'll by no means taste death till they've seen God's reign."** [28]**And about eight days after these words, it happened that taking along Peter and John and James, he went up onto a mountain to pray.** [29]**And while he was praying the appearance of his face became different, and his clothing** [became] **white, flashing out** [like lightning]. "Truly" puts special emphasis on this prediction by Jesus. Death is like a fatal poison. So to "taste death" is a figure of speech for dying, not for having a mere brush with death. Seeing God's reign suits Luke's emphasis on eyewitnesses (1:1–4). "About eight days after these words" probably includes the day Jesus spoke the preceding words and the day of the following event, traditionally called "the transfiguration," so that six days intervened (compare Mark 9:2; Matthew 17:1). The addition of "after these words" to "about eight days" links the following event ("it happened") to the immediately preceding prediction that some standing there wouldn't die till they'd seen God's reign. In other words, the transfiguration is going to fulfill the prediction. Peter, John, and James will constitute the "some" in Jesus' prediction. As elsewhere, Luke notes Jesus' praying to portray him as worthy of admiration for his piety. Luke's omitting to identify the mountain keeps attention on the praying. The mountain provides a place close to God, the addressee of prayer (compare 6:12). For more emphasis on Jesus' piety Luke mentions the praying a second time. By occurring while Jesus is praying, the transfiguration confirms his piety. "The appearance of his face became different," but in what way? For now, Luke doesn't say, so that the accent falls on "the *appearance* of his face." In Luke's original text, "appearance" is the noun form of the verb of seeing in Jesus' prediction ("till they've *seen* God's reign"). So again in agreement with 1:1–4, Luke is stressing the element of eyewitness that helps give the gospel its "certainty." That Jesus' clothing became "white, flashing out [like lightning]" begins to look like a preview of Jesus' glory when he comes again according to 9:26.

9:30–31: **And behold, talking with him were two men, who as such** [= as fellow conversationalists] **were Moses and Elijah,** [31]**who on being seen** [that is, on appearing] **in glory, were telling about his exodus** [= departure], **which he was going to fulfill in Jerusalem.** "Behold" calls special attention to Moses' and Elijah's talking with Jesus. Their "being seen" emphasizes yet again the element of eyewitness. "In glory" echoes "the glory" of

"the holy messengers" with which according to 9:26 Jesus will come again, and therefore identifies those messengers as "two *men*" rather than as angels (so also the "two men" of 24:4; Acts 1:9–11 [compare the use of "messenger" in 7:27 for John the baptizer rather than for an angel; also 9:52 for human messengers who travel ahead of Jesus]). Thus the appearance of Moses and Elijah in glory helps make the transfiguration a preview of Jesus' glorious second coming. The use of "exodus" for Jesus' departure helps Luke establish continuity between the Old Testament, which in the book of Exodus features the exodus of Israel from Egypt, and the story of Jesus. That he'll "fulfill" his exodus puts this continuity in terms of a fulfillment of that Old Testament pattern. Moses' and Elijah's "*telling* about his exodus" adds prediction to the pattern. "*Going* to fulfill" makes the fulfillment certain and soon. "In Jerusalem" specifies the location of Jesus' exodus (compare 9:51; 13:22; 17:11; 18:31; 19:11, 28). And since in 24:26 he'll speak of "entering into his glory" after suffering, the exodus must refer to his ascension. He'll exit the earth to enter his glory in heaven (24:50–51; Acts 1:9–11).

9:32–33: **And Peter and those with him were weighed down with sleep. But on waking up, they saw his** [Jesus'] **glory and the two men standing with him.** [33]**And it happened that while they** [Moses and Elijah] **were being withdrawn from him, Peter said to Jesus, "Master, it's good we're here," and "Let us** [Peter, John, and James] **make three tents, one for you and one for Moses and one for Elijah," not knowing what he's saying.** So Jesus was praying while the three disciples were sleeping, much as all the Twelve, except for Judas Iscariot, will be sleeping while Jesus prays on the eve of his crucifixion (22:39–46). But Moses' and Elijah's "*standing* with him" indicates that instead of kneeling to pray, as on the eve of his crucifixion (22:41), Jesus had been standing to pray as Jews normally did (18:11, 13) and still do (at the Western Wall in Jerusalem, for instance). That "they [Peter, John, and James] *saw* his glory" (1) echoes still again Luke's appeal to eyewitnesses (1:1–4); (2) defines as glorious the difference in the appearance of Jesus' face and the flashing whiteness of his clothing; (3) interprets the seeing of God's reign in 9:27 as the seeing of Jesus' glory; (4) fulfills Jesus' prediction that some wouldn't die before seeing God's reign; and (5) makes the transfiguration a preview of both the Christ's entry "into his glory" (24:26) and "the Son of Man['s] . . . coming in his glory" (9:26), that is, "in a cloud with power and much glory" (21:27). Suitably to Moses' and Elijah's being withdrawn, the mention of Jesus' glory replaces the earlier mention of Moses' and Elijah's appearance "in glory" (9:31). Seeing Jesus' glory makes Peter's addressing him with "Master" particularly appropriate. The address itself implies the necessity of Jesus' approval if Peter's suggestion is to be carried out. It's good for Peter, John, and James to be there, Peter thinks, for the purpose of making three tents, one each for Jesus, Moses, and Elijah—recalling the tents the Israelites lived in on their way from Egypt to Canaan after the exodus that was alluded to in 9:31. We might think that Peter makes his suggestion to halt the withdrawal of Moses and Elijah. But Luke attributes the suggestion to Peter's ignorance, which is to say that he should have deduced that their being withdrawn signified God's wanting them *not* to stay.

9:34–36: And as he [Peter] was saying these things, a cloud came on the scene and was overshadowing them. And they got scared when they entered into the cloud. ³⁵And a voice came out of the cloud, saying, "This is my selected Son. Hear him." ³⁶And when the voice came, Jesus was found alone. And they kept quiet and announced to no one during those days any of the things they'd seen. "These things" that Peter was saying consisted in his two statements beginning, "Master, it's good . . . ," and "Let us make . . . ." The cloud's coming and overshadowing the three disciples and Jesus confirms that Peter had spoken out of ignorance. You don't construct tents on a mountain shrouded in a cloud. Moses and Elijah appeared in glory. The three disciples saw Jesus' glory. As often in the Bible, the cloud represents the glory of God (see, for example, Exodus 19:11, 16–18; Ezekiel 1:4–28), so that the glory of the Son of Man, of the Father, and of the holy messengers— the glory of all of them at the second coming (9:26) has been previewed in the transfiguration. The disciples' fear as they enter the cloud and the voice that comes out of the cloud confirm the presence of God the Father in this cloud. At Jesus' baptism, he'd said *to* Jesus, "*You* are my beloved Son . . ." (3:22). Here he says to the disciples *about* Jesus, "*This* is my selected Son." "Selected" replaces "beloved" to elevate Jesus above even Moses and Elijah, their appearance in glory notwithstanding (compare 23:35; Isaiah 42:1). And the followup, "Hear him," replaces "I've taken delight in you" (3:22 again) to tell the disciples they should heed Jesus rather than Moses and Elijah (compare Moses' own prediction in Deuteronomy 18:15; also Acts 3:18–24; 7:35–37). In particular, they should heed Jesus' comments on the requirements for discipleship (9:23–26). His being "*found* alone" when the Father's voice came implies that he was momentarily lost from view in the overshadowing cloud, but that on coming into view again he became the only one the Father could be referring to. The disciples kept quiet because of Jesus' command in 9:21 not to tell anyone he's God's Christ. For in a big way the transfiguration confirmed that he is. "The things they'd seen" puts yet another accent on eyewitnessing and marks again the transfiguration's fulfillment of Jesus' prediction in 9:27 that some standing there wouldn't die until they'd seen God's reign. But "during those days" makes their silence temporary; it lasts only till Jesus has been raised from the dead (see the comments on 9:21–22). Otherwise Luke couldn't be writing about the transfiguration.

GLORY TO GOD FOR JESUS' PHILANTHROPY
Luke 9:37–43a

This passage divides into a man's plea in regard to his only child (9:37–40) and Jesus' response to that plea (9:41–43a).

9:37–40: And the next day it happened that after they'd come down from the mountain, a large crowd met him. ³⁸And behold, a man from the crowd cried out, saying, "Teacher, I beg you to look on my son, because he's my one-and-only [offspring]. ³⁹And behold, a spirit takes him and suddenly shrieks and convulses him with foam and, crushing him, scarcely departs from him. ⁴⁰And I begged your disciples [the nine who hadn't gone up the mountain with Jesus] **to cast it out, and they couldn't."** The transfiguration had interrupted the sleeping of Peter, John, and James (9:32), so that afterward they spent the night, or the rest of the night if the transfiguration took place at night, finishing their sleep on the mountain. Hence their descent from the mountain "the next day." They came down with Jesus, of course. "*They*'d come down," but a "large crowd met *him*." As often, then, Luke stresses the popularity of Jesus due to his humanitarian ministry. The first "behold" calls attention to a man's crying out to Jesus. Sometimes "cried out" connotes crying out for help (see 18:7, 38). It does so here. The man's addressing Jesus with "Teacher" shows *respect*. The man's "beg[ging]" him shows *desperation*. He's desperate to *get* help, and "to look on" connotes looking so as to *give* help (see 1:48). That the son is the man's "one-and-only [offspring]" helps explain the desperation. A second "behold" (spoken by the man rather than interjected by Luke) shifts attention to a possessing spirit's baleful effects on the man's only offspring. The details: (1) "takes" indicates seizures; (2) "shrieks" implies pain (since the spirit shrieks *through* the son, the son is *experiencing* the pain); (3) "suddenly" describes the shrieking as compulsive; (4) "convulses him with foam" means that foaming at the mouth accompanies the convulsion; (5) "crushing him" means bruising him as a result of convulsion; and (6) "scarcely departs from him" means that the spirit rarely leaves him alone. Luke has referred to the father's begging Jesus for help. Now the father himself refers to his own earlier begging the nine disciples for an exorcism. This second reference to begging recalls attention to his desperation. Despite Jesus' having given the Twelve "authority over all the demons" (9:1), the nine of the Twelve whom he hadn't taken up the mount of transfiguration couldn't cast out this spirit. So if Jesus can do what they couldn't, his authority will stand out as unique.

9:41–43a: And answering, Jesus said, "O unbelieving and perverted generation, how long shall I be with you [plural] and put up with you [plural]? [You (singular),] bring your son here." ⁴²And as he [the son] was approaching, the demon threw him down and convulsed [him] violently. But Jesus reprimanded the unclean spirit and healed the boy and gave him back to his father. ⁴³ªAnd they were all awestruck at God's greatness. Jesus responds to the father's plea first by addressing the unsuccessful disciples. He explains their failure as due to their lack of faith. They *had* authority over all the demons (9:1 again); but having it didn't help, because they didn't *believe* their authority sufficient to cast out this spirit. By adding "perverted" to "unbelieving," Jesus interprets lack of faith as a kind of perversion, a distortion (compare Deuteronomy 32:5, 20). Since discipleship requires faith, lack of faith perverts discipleship. And Jesus is addressing his disciples because they, or nine of them, are the ones who failed to exorcise the spirit. "O" adds poignancy to his description of them as an unbelieving and perverted generation; and "generation" resonates with the spirit's victim as the man's one-and-only offspring, for "one-and-only" literally means "only generated." "How long shall I be with you and put up with you?" adds disgust on top of poignancy. "Bring your son here" indicates a shift from Jesus' addressing his failed disciples to his addressing the son's father. The demon's convulsing the son as the son was approaching Jesus makes the case and its outcome visible for all to see. Eyewitnesses again! Luke adds that "the demon threw [the son] down" and intensifies "convulsed him" with "violently." These additions highlight the demon's power, so that a successful exorcism by Jesus will highlight even more the superiority of *his* power. For the first time Luke describes this demonic spirit as "unclean." The description makes it a pollutant such as causes disease. So Jesus' reprimand "*healed* the boy" of its physical effects. To underscore Jesus' philanthropy, Luke writes nothing about the spirit's exit from the boy, only about the healing effect of its exit, plus Jesus' giving the father's one-and-only offspring back to him—"back" because the spirit had taken possession of the son away from the father. And "back to his father" indicates that Jesus exorcised the demon for the sake of the father rather than for the son's sake. It would have been tragic for the father not to have a son to care for him in his old age and carry on the family line (compare 7:15). That "they were *all* awestruck" despite their being "a large crowd" (9:37) magnifies the impressiveness of what had happened. But we might have expected a reference to their being awestruck at Jesus' overpowering authority. Instead, though, Luke writes about their being awestruck "at *God's* greatness." As elsewhere, then, Luke plays up the good religious effect of Jesus' philanthropy. It brought glory to God.

JESUS' PRESCIENCE VERSUS THE DISCIPLES' IGNORANCE
Luke 9:43b–45

9:43b–44: But while all were marveling at all the things that he was doing, he told his disciples, ⁴⁴"You—put these words in your ears. For the Son of Man is going to be given over into men's hands." The marveling of "all"—and there was "a large crowd" of them according to 9:37—at "*all* the things" Jesus was doing magnifies again his philanthropic activities. Nobody failed to be impressed, and none of his activities failed to excite appreciative amazement. But "*while* all were marveling" implies that this marveling might lead the disciples to mistake it as an indication that he wouldn't have to suffer rejection and persecution despite his prediction of such suffering in 9:22. With some revision, then, he reiterates that prediction and commands them to "put these words [of the following reiteration] in their ears"—a figurative

way of saying to heed the words (compare 8:8, 18; 9:35; 14:35; Exodus 17:14). "For" introduces the content of the prediction as a reason for giving heed. The prediction itself summarizes the suffering, rejection, and execution in 9:22 with a new element, namely, being "given over into men's hands." Judas Iscariot's betrayal of Jesus to the Jewish authorities will fulfill this element. "Into men's *hands*" connotes violent treatment, as in "manhandling" (compare 2 Samuel 24:14, for example), and "into *men's* hands" makes a wordplay with "the Son *of Man*." Human beings will manhandle a fellow human being. "*Going* to be given over" makes the betrayal and violent treatment soon and certain. Not as in 9:22, Jesus doesn't mention his subsequent resurrection, so that the emphasis rests entirely on what contravenes the misimpression that his good deeds will prevent his suffering, rejection, and execution.

9:45: But they [Jesus' disciples] **didn't understand this statement** [about his betrayal]**, and it was hidden from them lest they sense it** [= lest they sense its meaning]**. And they were afraid to ask him about this statement.** It's not that the disciples didn't understand *why* God's Christ would be given over into men's hands. Despite the clarity of Jesus' statement, it's that they didn't understand *that* he'd be given over. In 18:34 they'll still be ignorant of Jesus' meaning. Here, though, Luke excuses their ignorance on the ground that the meaning "was hidden from them lest they sense it." He doesn't say *who* hid the meaning from them, only *why* it was hidden from them. Thus the accent falls on their being faultless in the matter. And their being afraid to ask Jesus for his meaning excuses them further on the ground of their veneration of him. As much as possible, Luke is portraying Jesus' disciples in the best possible light so as to recommend the Christian community to prospective converts. On the other hand, the disciples' present ignorance provides a foil against which Jesus' prescience stands out.

THE ATTRACTION OF COMMUNITY
Luke 9:46–50

This passage divides into a question of greatness (9:46–48) and a question of competition (9:49–50). Jesus responds to both questions in a way that emphasizes a community of welcome and cooperation. For Luke, the church—as in his book of Acts—offers just such a community and therefore one that attracts people to the gospel.

9:46–48: And a thought came in among them [the disciples] **as to who of them might be greater** [than the others]**. ⁴⁷And Jesus, knowing the thought of their heart, taking hold of a little child, stood him beside himself ⁴⁸and said to them, "Whoever welcomes this little child on the basis of my name welcomes me. And whoever welcomes me welcomes the one who sent me. For the one among you who is smaller/younger** [than the others]**—this one is great."** Luke's turn of phrase, "And a thought *came in* among them," lessens blame on the disciples by making the thought an intruder into their company. "Who of them *might* be greater" is softer than "who *is* [or '*was*'] greater" would have been. And Jesus' "knowing the thought *of their heart*" shows that for Luke the disciples weren't arguing with each other. They were entertaining the question of relative greatness only in the privacy of their own thinking. In three ways, then, Luke is again putting the disciples in the best possible light so as to recommend the Christian community to prospective converts (see also 9:45).

Jesus' "*knowing* the thought of their heart" exhibits clairvoyance. By taking hold of a little child and making him stand "beside himself [Jesus]," he uses body language to associate the child closely with him. To welcome "this little child *on the basis of my name*" is to welcome the child as a fellow disciple. (Implied: little children, too, can believe in Jesus.) To do so is to welcome Jesus, he says, in that the child bears Jesus' name as a believer in him. By the same token, the person who welcomes Jesus welcomes Jesus' sender (God the Father) in that Jesus represents him. And why should you welcome Jesus' sender by welcoming Jesus, and Jesus by welcoming a little child on the basis of Jesus' name? Because as a bearer of Jesus' name the little child is "great." As noted in connection with 7:28, "smaller" can refer to being younger as well as littler. Here, the child is both younger and littler than the adult disciples, who are "greater" in both age and size. And to these temporal and spatial meanings Jesus adds the figurative meaning of importance. The child-disciple is great in importance even though younger and smaller than adult disciples.

9:49–50: And answering, John said, "Master, we saw someone casting out demons in your name; and we were trying to stop him, because he isn't following with us." [50]But Jesus told him, "Don't stop [him], for he who's not against you is for you." Jesus' mention of his name in 9:49 ("on the basis of my name") seems to have reminded John of someone who was using Jesus' name to cast out demons and whom John and the other disciples had been trying to stop, apparently unsuccessfully, because the exorcist wasn't following with Jesus' immediate disciples (presumably the twelve apostles). "With us" implies they thought that just as they were following Jesus, the exorcist should be following Jesus along with them. So John and the other disciples were looking out for Jesus, not for themselves. Jesus, on the other hand, is looking out for the community of his disciples, not for himself. So he turns attention to relations among them: "Don't stop [him]." Why not? Because "he who's not against *you* is for *you*." Cooperate. You're coworkers, not competitors, because—like that little child—you share my name.

JESUS' FORBEARANCE
Luke 9:51–56

9:51: And it happened as the days of his being taken up were being completely fulfilled that he fixed [his] **face to travel to Jerusalem** [= took resolute aim for that city as his destination]. "His being taken up" refers

to Jesus' ascension to heaven (24:50–51; Acts 1:9–11). But the plural "day*s*" includes events leading up to the ascension, too. Since the days of Jesus' being taken up are being fulfilled already at the time he takes resolute aim for Jerusalem, his being taken up includes not only his future passion and resurrection in addition to the ascension. It includes also his preceding ministry, the whole of which constitutes an upward movement from earth to heaven. (Technically, "assumption" would be better than "ascension," but "ascension" has become traditional.) "Being completely *fulfilled*" aligns this ministry with God's plan. "Being *completely* fulfilled" will leave nothing of God's plan unfulfilled. Jesus' resolve in carrying out the plan highlights his piety. "To *travel* to Jerusalem" appeals, as often, to the interest of Luke's audience in travel and makes Jesus a model for Christians who'll spread the gospel in their travels (though *from* Jerusalem rather than *to* Jerusalem [24:46–49; Acts 1:8]). Jesus' traveling to Jerusalem puts the completion of God's plan in continuity with the Old Testament and Judaism, for God had centered his presence in that city.

9:52–56: And he sent messengers before his face [= ahead of him]; **and traveling** [ahead], **they entered into a town of Samaritans to prepare for him. [53]And they** [the Samaritans of the town] **didn't welcome him, because his face was traveling to Jerusalem. [54]And on seeing** [this nonwelcome], **the disciples James and John said, "Lord, do you want us to tell fire to come down from heaven and consume them?" [55]And on turning** [because they were following behind him, as disciples should do], **he reprimanded them. [56]And they traveled to another town.** Luke writes "before his face" and "his face was traveling to Jerusalem" to underline the piety of Jesus' having "fixed [his] face to travel to Jerusalem" in complete fulfillment of God's plan. The sending of messengers and their going to prepare for Jesus recalls God's having sent John the baptizer as a messenger "before [Jesus'] face" to prepare Jesus' way ahead of him (7:27 [see also 1:17, 76; 3:4; Acts 13:24]). Here, Luke doesn't specify the nature of the preparation, whether for board and room or repentance, so that the point has to do with the extension of Jesus' and his disciples' missionary travels beyond Jewish boundaries (see again Acts 1:8: "You'll be my witnesses both in Jerusalem and in all Judea *and Samaria* and as far as the extremity of the earth"). The region of Samaria lay between Galilee in the north and Judea in the south, where Jerusalem was located (see further the comments on John 4:4, 7–9, 17–18 for the antipathy that caused the present Samaritans not to welcome Jesus). Reacting to the nonwelcome by one town of Samaritans, James and John ask Jesus whether they should tell fire to come down from heaven and consume them (compare 2 Kings 1:9–15). The question carries a suggestion. Jesus' reprimanding James and John for their suggestion points up his gracious forbearance. The accent falls, then, more on forbearance by him than on James' and John's vengefulness (compare 4:22). Jesus' and the disciples' traveling to another town carries forward the motif of missionary travel (compare 4:43).

THE GREAT COMMISSION IN ADVANCE
Luke 9:57–62

In this passage Jesus stresses that discipleship entails Christian witness.

9:57–58: And as they were traveling on the road, someone told him, "I'll follow you wherever you go away [to]." ⁵⁸And Jesus told him, "The foxes have holes, and the birds of the sky will nest [in tree branches after they've flown around]; but the Son of Man doesn't have anywhere to lay his head." "Traveling on the road" carries forward the motif of missionary travel yet again and casts the whole of the present passage in that mode. Someone's volunteering to follow Jesus wherever Jesus might "go *away* [to]" accentuates the motif. But the volunteer fails to address Jesus with a respectful "Teacher," "Lord," "Master," or the like. Correspondingly, Jesus doesn't address the volunteer's statement, but only describes his own situation of homelessness due to missionary travel. Thus he makes himself a model of such travel.

9:59–60: And he told another [man], "Follow me [compare 5:27; 9:23; 18:22]." And he said, "Lord, permit me, on going away, to bury my father first." ⁶⁰But he told him, "Leave the dead to bury their own dead. But you—on going away, announce throughout [this region] the reign of God [compare 4:43]." This episode starts with Jesus' commanding a man to follow him and ends with his commanding the man to go away and proclaim far and wide God's reign *rather than* following him! It's as though Jesus says to him, "Before following me you want to go away and bury your father. Okay, you can go away—but not to bury him; instead, to travel around preaching the gospel." In other words, this man is to become a precursor of all Jesus' disciples, whom he'll commission to be his witnesses throughout the world after he's gone (24:46–49; Acts 1:8) and who'll proceed to carry out that commission (the book of Acts as a whole). The man responds to Jesus with a respectful address: "Lord." From that standpoint, then, he's a good missionary candidate. To get rid of the impediment of the man's wanting to bury his father first, though, Jesus tells him to "leave the dead to bury their own dead." In 15:24, 32 "dead" describes someone physically alive but dead in the sense of alienated from his father. Here, similarly, "the dead" who are to be left to "bury their own dead" are people physically alive but dead in the sense of alienated from God and his reign. They can take care of burying the man's dead father and whoever else dies physically. The business of announcing far and wide the reign of God takes precedence even over the sacred duty of burying your father (on which duty see, for example, Genesis 50:5–6 and the command to honor your father and mother in Exodus 20:12; Deuteronomy 5:16).

9:61–62: And also another [man] said, "I'll follow you, Lord. But permit me first to say goodbye to those in my house." ⁶²But Jesus told him, "No one who has thrust [his] hand onto a plow and is looking backwards is useful for God's reign." As did the first man, this one volunteers to follow Jesus; and as did the second man, this one addresses Jesus with a respectful "Lord." Again there's an impediment, the request for permission to say goodbye to his household before following Jesus. In 1 Kings 19:19–21 Elisha made a similar request of Elijah; but whereas Elijah granted it, Jesus uses figurative language to declare the request out-of-line. Volunteering to follow Jesus is like thrusting your hand onto a plow. Asking to say goodbye to your household first is like looking backwards. But if you're looking backwards while plowing, you can't plow a straight line. So you're useless as a farmer. And unwillingness to make following Jesus your very first priority renders you useless for God's reign. But useless in what sense? Useless in the sense of unfit to proclaim God's reign.

CARRYING OUT THE GREAT COMMISSION IN ADVANCE
Luke 10:1–24

Jesus gave a preliminary form of the Great Commission in 9:57–62. Here he instructs seventy-two disciples on how to carry out that commission (10:1–12). (For its carrying out after his ascension, 22:35–38 will contain some revisions of the present instructions.) Then Jesus pronounces judgment on cities that haven't accepted his ministry (10:13–15) and assures the seventy-two that they represent him just as he represents God (10:16). There follow a report of the seventy-two on the success of their mission (10:17) and Jesus' response to their report (10:18–20), thanks to God (10:21), a soliloquy on the exclusivity of his relation to God (10:22), and a pronouncement of blessing on the disciples (10:23–24).

10:1: And after these things [the episodes in 9:57–62] **the Lord appointed seventy-two others** [besides the Twelve] **and sent them by twos before his face into every city and locality where he was going to go.** Luke refers to Jesus as "the Lord" to identify him as "the Lord of the harvest" in 10:2. The appointment of seventy-two in addition to the already chosen Twelve (6:12–16) points forward to a worldwide mission in the book of Acts. The Twelve have already gone on a mission (9:1–6). The mission of the seventy-two therefore marks an expansion. Jesus' sending them "by twos" prefigures the pairing of his witnesses in Acts 3–4 (Peter and John), 13–14 (Paul and Barnabas), 15:40–18:22 (Paul and Silas [compare Numbers 35:30; Deuteronomy 17:6; 19:15 on the sufficiency of testimony by two or three witnesses]). "Before his face" echoes 9:52 and recalls the piety of Jesus in fixing his face to travel to Jerusalem for the complete fulfillment of God's plan (9:51). "Into every city and locality" enroute points toward universal and thorough evangelism in time to come. "Where he was going to come" makes sure and soon his journey to Jerusalem for the complete fulfillment of God's plan.

10:2: And he was saying to them, "The harvest [is] plentiful, but the workers [are] few. So you should ask

the Lord of the harvest to thrust out workers into his harvest." The workers are proclaimers of God's reign, the gospel. The harvest consists in their converts. Its being plentiful indicates a large number of converts in the offing, which number will become even larger after Jesus' ascension and sending of the Holy Spirit (see, for example, Acts 2:41, 47; 4:4). Thus Jesus' attraction of crowds, which has gotten the spotlight till now, starts mutating into the conversion of large numbers through his followers' evangelistic labors. Luke's point: the Christian movement is unstoppable because it arises out of, and consists in, God's reign. So get on the winning side, the community of Jesus' disciples: "If you can't lick 'em, join 'em" (compare Acts 5:34–39). Though Jesus has added seventy-two to the Twelve, the workers remain few in comparison with the number of converts to be made. So the present workers should ask the Lord of the harvest to thrust out into the field of the world workers in addition to themselves. Help is needed! Since Jesus is thrusting out the seventy-two and has already thrust out the Twelve, he's the Lord of the harvest to whom the prayer request should be made (compare the comments on 10:1). And the harvest is "his" not only because he's its "Lord," the one who thrusts out workers, but also because the harvest will consist in converts to him.

Jesus continues speaking in *10:3–6*: "Go! Behold, I'm sending you as lambs in the midst of wolves. ⁴Carry neither a money-bag, nor a knapsack, nor sandals; and greet no one along the road. ⁵And into whatever house you enter, first say, 'Peace for this house!' ⁶And if a son of peace should be there, your 'Peace' will come to rest on him. Otherwise, indeed, it will come back on you." The command to go sends these workers away to make converts. "Behold" calls attention to the danger of persecution, compared to wolves' attacks on defenseless lambs. This danger will turn into actuality for Jesus' witnesses in Luke's book of Acts. The following instructions look similar to those given the Twelve in 9:3–5. The prohibitions of carrying a money-bag, a knapsack (comparable to a backpack nowadays), or sandals and of giving greetings while traveling on the road from here to there (compare 2 Kings 4:29)—these prohibitions have the purpose of speeding up the spread of God's good news. Just as there should be no delay in following Jesus (9:59–62), there should be no leisureliness in getting the gospel out. The seeming oddity of Jesus' saying not to *carry* sandals suggests to some that he prohibits carrying a pair in addition to those being worn. Not so, however, for you carry sandals on your feet just as you carry a money-bag and a knapsack on other parts of your body. The seventy-two are to go barefoot, then. Not even the weight of sandals, much less that of a money-bag and a knapsack, is to slow down the progress of evangelism.

The house that a pair of the seventy-two will enter is a building. The house for which they pronounce peace is a household, the family living in the building. So there's a play on two meanings of the word "house." There's also a play on the word "peace." It's the everyday greeting, like "Shalom" in Israel and "Hello" in America. But in view

of 2:14 ("on earth peace [be] among human beings of [God's] good pleasure"), the pronouncement of peace brings the message of salvation to the household (see also 1:79; 2:29; 7:50; 8:48; 19:42; 24:36; Acts 10:36). The coming of "your peace" to rest on "a son of peace" means salvation for the person who accepts your message. The peace is yours because you proclaim it. But your proclamation of peace will rebound off the person who doesn't accept it and back on you. Salvation rejected means salvation withdrawn. "Indeed" cements this danger.

10:7–9: "And in the very house [where there's 'a son of peace'] **stay, eating and drinking the things from them** [that is, the food and drink members of the household provide you]. **For the worker is worthy of his pay. Don't move from house to house. ⁸And into whatever city you enter and they welcome you, eat the things set before you; ⁹and heal the sick in it and say to them, 'God's reign has come near to you.'"** Jesus' witnesses are to waste no time moving from house to house in a locality or foraging for food and drink. They're to accept whatever hospitality of room and board is offered them, for in view of their evangelistic work they deserve such hospitality; and they should get to the all-important business of healing the sick and proclaiming the nearness of God's reign. Thus philanthropic deeds are to be accompanied by philanthropic words, for God's reign comes near in both deeds and words. But how near is that reign? In 15:1, 25; 18:40 nearness will mean within earshot. Since the present passage has to do with proclamation, God's reign has come near enough to be heard in the "Peace" spoken by Jesus' messengers. "To you" emphasizes the availability of God's peaceful reign as heard in the gospel.

10:10–12: "**But into whatever city you enter and they don't welcome you—on going out** [from the houses that refuse you hospitality] **into its broad** [streets], say, ¹¹**'Even the dust of your city that clings to our feet we're wiping off** [as a testimony] **against you. Nevertheless, know this, that God's reign has come near.' ¹²I tell you that it'll be more endurable on that day for Sodom than for that city."** Cities that don't provide hospitality won't hear the message of God's reign. Though in the persons of the messengers the reign has come near enough to be heard, then, it hasn't actually been heard—hence, the omission of "to you" after "God's reign has come near" (contrast 10:9, regarding cities that do welcome the messengers: "God's reign has come near *to you*"). The nonwelcoming city gets bad news instead of good news: at the Last Day even a city so evil as Sodom, on which God rained down fire and brimstone, will get less severe punishment than a city that rejects Jesus' messengers of peace. Among other passages, see Genesis 13:13; 18:16–19:29 on the wickedness and destruction of Sodom. So wicked is the city that doesn't provide hospitality for those messengers that even the dust of its streets isn't worthy to cling to the messengers' feet, which according to 10:3–6 are to be bare. Supplementing verbal language with body language, the messengers aren't to wait till they arrive at their next destination and wash their feet there.

They're to wipe off the dust even before exiting the city, and do so in plain view, on its main thoroughfares, where everybody can see as well as hear.

In *10:13–15* Jesus addresses cities where he has already ministered as though they were in his present audience: "**Alas for you, Chorazin! Alas for you, Bethsaida! Because if the miracles that have taken place in you had taken place in Tyre and Sidon, they'd have repented long ago, sitting in sackcloth and ashes.** [14]**Nevertheless** [that is, despite the pride and prosperity for which Tyre and Sidon were noted (see especially Ezekiel 26:1–28:24)], **at the judgment it'll be more endurable for Tyre and Sidon than for you!** [15]**And you, Capernaum, won't be lifted up as far as heaven, will you? You'll go down as far as Hades!**" Jesus' having mentioned cities that won't welcome his messengers reminds him of cities that by and large have rejected him despite the miracles he performed in them. And his having mentioned the pagan city of Sodom reminds him of the pagan cities of Tyre and Sidon. The mention of repentance recalls Luke's emphasis on moral reform (3:3, 8; 5:32, plus later passages). The addition of "sackcloth [a rough, hairy garment] and ashes [thrown on themselves in mourning for their sins]" intensifies the repentance in which Tyre and Sidon would have engaged had they witnessed Jesus' miracles (compare especially Daniel 9:3–19). "Long ago" intensifies Jesus' point yet more. Bethsaida, located at the northeast curve of the Sea of Galilee, appeared in 9:10. Capernaum, located on the northwest curve, appeared in 4:23, 31; 7:1, with stories of Jesus' miracles attached. Chorazin, located several miles northwest of Capernaum, hasn't appeared before in Luke's text. Since Jesus addresses these cities even though their residents aren't in his present audience, his pronouncing on them woeful judgment and hellish descent is designed to impress on his seventy-two messengers the gravity of their mission. It's no less important than his, as shown by the correlation between the fates of those cities that have rejected his ministry and the fates of those cities that will reject theirs.

Jesus secures this correlation with his statement in *10:16*: "**The person who hears you hears me, and the person who rejects you rejects me. And the person who rejects me rejects the one who sent me.**" The correlation rests not only between the message of the seventy-two and that of Jesus. It rests also between their persons and his person. They represent him in the truest sense, so that hearing them isn't just *like* hearing him. It *is* hearing him. Similarly in regard to rejecting them. The contrast between hearing and rejecting indicates that hearing entails accepting their message. To reject Jesus by rejecting his messengers means also to reject God, who sent Jesus with the message of salvation. Since Jesus doesn't go on to say that the person who hears him by hearing his messengers hears God, too, the final accent falls on the danger of rejection. For their own sake, Luke wants his audience to know that good news can turn into bad news all too easily.

10:17–18: **And the seventy-two returned** [from having been sent ahead in 10:1], **saying with joy, "Lord, even the demons submit to us in your name!"** [18]**And he told them, "I was watching Satan falling like lightning from heaven** [compare Isaiah 14:12; Revelation 12:7–9]." We know the results of the mission of the seventy-two through their own report to Jesus. To intimate the mission's success in advance of the report itself, though, Luke describes it as given "with joy," in line with an angel's having said in 2:10, "Behold, I am announcing to you as good news a great joy." Successful evangelism brings joy (see also Acts 8:4–8). The seventy-two's addressing Jesus with "Lord" not only shows reverence for him. It also highlights his authority so as to link up with the demons' submitting to the seventy-two "in [Jesus'] name." They submit in that name when the seventy-two use it to exorcise them (compare 9:49). "*Even* the demons" stresses the seventy-two's authority when using the name to exorcise superhumanly powerful spirits (compare 4:36; 8:29). Where the seventy-two were seeing demons being exorcised, Jesus was seeing in those exorcisms the fall of Satan out of heaven. Lightning appears to strike the earth from the sky, and it's visible to all (17:24). Likewise, Satan's fall out of heaven ("heaven" going back to the same word that means "sky") indicates his loss of authority over the demoniacs whom because of the exorcisms he no longer rules through his agents, the demons. And like lightning, these exorcisms have been visible for all to see (compare 1:1–4 for Luke's emphasis on eyewitnessing, and 4:33–37; 8:26–39; 9:37–43 for that emphasis in Luke's accounts of exorcisms performed by Jesus).

10:19–20: "**Behold, I've given you the authority to tread upon snakes and scorpions and on all the power of the enemy; and by no means will anything harm you.** [20]**Nevertheless, don't be rejoicing in this, that the spirits** [= demons] **submit to you; but rejoice that your names are inscribed in heaven.**" "Behold" calls attention to Jesus' having given the seventy-two authority not only to cast out demons but also to tread upon snakes and scorpions—barefoot, in view of the prohibition of their wearing sandals (10:4)!—and on all the power of Satan ("the enemy"). In other words, this additional authority defangs snakes, detoxifies scorpions, and disempowers Satan (compare Genesis 3:15; Deuteronomy 8:15; Psalm 91:13; Acts 28:3–6; Romans 16:20). This promise of invulnerability has to do with travel for evangelism, snakes and scorpions along the way, not with contrived demonstrations of supernatural power. "Don't be rejoicing in this, that the spirits submit to you" shows that back in 10:17 "with joy" described "saying," not "returned." Instead of rejoicing in their accomplishments, which could produce arrogance, Jesus' messengers should rejoice in their salvation. He portrays their salvation in terms of their names (representing them individually) as inscribed (therefore as officially recorded) in heaven (out of which Satan has fallen, so that he can't contest, steal, or destroy the record [compare Exodus 32:32; Daniel 12:1; Malachi 3:16; Hebrews 12:23]). We read about "the book of life" in Psalm 69:28; Isaiah 4:3; Philippians 4:3; Revelation 3:5; 20:12, 15; 21:27. But the absence of that phrase here in Luke 10:20 puts the emphasis solely on the joyful contrast between having names inscribed *in* heaven and Satan's having fallen *out* of heaven.

Next, Jesus addresses God and then slides into a soliloquy. **10:21–22: In that very hour he exulted in the Holy Spirit and said, "I acknowledge to you, Father, Lord of heaven and earth, that you've hidden these things from wise and intelligent [people] and revealed them to infants. Yes, Father, because [to do] so became a pleasure before you. ²²All things have been given over to me by my Father; and no one knows who the Son is except the Father, and [no one knows] who the Father is except the Son and the person to whomever the Son wants to reveal [him]."** "In that very hour" ties Jesus' exultation to his command in 10:20 that the seventy-two rejoice over their names' having been inscribed in heaven. Though different in wording, the content of his exultation matches theirs; for they're the "infants" who have received revelation from the Father through Jesus that their names are inscribed in heaven. His exultation in that revelation therefore provides a model for their rejoicing in it. Because Jesus "exulted," his saying "I acknowledge" carries a note of rejoicing. "In the Holy Spirit" describes his joyful exultation in a way that highlights the closeness of his relation to God's Spirit and, together with the address to God as his "Father" and the following declaration of the exclusivity of his relation to God as God's Son, lays a foundation for God as trinity: Father, Son, and Holy Spirit. Jesus' addressing his Father also as "Lord of heaven and earth" balances Jesus as "the Lord of the harvest" (10:2) and exhibits his piety in acknowledging God the Father's universal lordship. "These things" that Jesus' Father has hidden from wise and intelligent people and revealed to infants are the things Jesus has spoken to the seventy-two in 10:18–20. The contrast between "wise and intelligent [people]" and "infants" indicates that Jesus means "infants" in the sense of humanly unwise and unintelligent people (compare 18:17). The Father's having hidden these things from the wise and intelligent represents a judgment on their human wisdom and intelligence. And his having revealed these things to the infants represents a gracious gift to those "infants." "Yes" emphasizes the contrast between such hiddenness and revelation; and in preparation for 10:22, Jesus' addressing God a second time with "Father" reemphasizes his relation to God as God's Son. "[To do] so" refers to the aforementioned hiding and revealing. "Became a pleasure before you" is an indirect way of saying that God was pleased to have hidden these things from the wise and intelligent and revealed them to infants. But though it sounds odd to us, the very indirectness of this way of expressing the thought displays Jesus' great reverence for God his Father and therefore his piety, which Luke likes to put on display.

God has given all things to Jesus because Jesus is his sole Son and therefore his sole heir. And the inheritance consists of "all things" because God is "Lord [that is,

owner] of heaven and earth." No one knows the identity of God's Son except God the Father himself; and he has twice pronounced Jesus his Son (3:22; 9:35), the second time in an announcement to Peter, John, and James. According to 10:21, furthermore, the Father has revealed these things to infants. So the context indicates that the exclusivity of the Father's knowing who is his Son has the exception of those to whom the Father wants to reveal the identity of his Son, and does reveal it. A similar but explicitly stated exception appears in regard to the Son's knowing the identity of the Father: "and to the person to whom the Son wants to reveal him." Jesus states this exception explicitly to emphasize that a saving knowledge of God comes only through him. Such knowledge isn't attained by intellectual pursuit. It comes alone by way of Jesus' revelation of God. At the end of 10:21 the Father's pleasure determines who receives revelation. At the end of 10:22 Jesus' wish determines who receives revelation. This double emphasis on what we might call the doctrine of election—or, better, *se*lection—is designed not to discourage belief but to encourage dependence on divine revelation rather than on human wisdom and intelligence, and not to discourage evangelism but to encourage it with the assurance that God and Jesus are pleased to reveal themselves to the humanly unwise and unintelligent.

10:23–24: And on turning toward the disciples, he said in private, "Fortunate [are] the eyes that are seeing the things which you're seeing. ²⁴For I tell you that many prophets and kings [in the Old Testament] wanted to see the things that you're seeing and didn't see [them], and to hear the things that you're hearing and didn't hear [them]." Jesus has been addressing God (10:21) and soliloquizing (10:22), and his disciples are following him on the way to Jerusalem (9:51, 57, 59, 61). So he has to turn toward them to speak to them. "In private" limits to them the beatitude he pronounces. Only their eyes and ears are blessed, because unlike nondisciples they see and hear with an understanding born of faith (8:10). Naturally, the references to seeing Jesus' deeds and to hearing his words suits Luke's stated emphasis on eye- and earwitnesses of Jesus' ministry (1:1–4). The contrast with nonseeing and nonhearing by Old Testament prophets and kings—and this despite their desire to see and hear—forms a foil against which the disciples' eye- and earwitnessing stands out all the more.

JESUS' TESTING HIS TESTER ON DOING AS WELL AS KNOWING
Luke 10:25–37

This passage contains a dialogue, the middle part of which consists in the parable of the good Samaritan.

10:25–28: And behold, a certain lawyer [= an expert in the Old Testament law of Moses] **stood up, testing him by saying, "Teacher, by doing what shall I inherit eternal life"** ²⁶**And he said to him, "What's written in the Law? How do you read [it]?"** ²⁷**And answering, he said, "You shall love the Lord your God out of your whole heart, and with your whole soul, and**

with your whole strength, and with your whole mind [Deuteronomy 6:5]; and [you shall love] your neighbor as [you love] yourself [Leviticus 19:18]." [28]And he told him, "You've answered correctly. Do this, and you'll live [eternally]." "Behold" calls attention to the lawyer's standing up to test Jesus. "Stood up" implies a new setting in which others are sitting. The lawyer addresses Jesus with "Teacher," but "testing him" raises the question whether as a teacher Jesus knows his stuff. The raising of this question by an expert in the Law exacerbates the possible difficulty of the test, but the academic performance of Jesus as a lad only twelve years old (2:46–47) forecasted another sterling performance here. By asking a counter question Jesus tests his tester, as though to say, "You've called me 'Teacher.' So as a teacher I'll test you by asking you to answer your own question out of the Law, in which you're expert." By referring the lawyer to the Old Testament, Jesus shows—to Luke's delight—that he himself is no religious revolutionary. Rather, he's a traditionalist in continuity with God's ancient, scriptural revelation. Since reading was ordinarily done aloud in that culture, "How do you read [it]?" amounts to an injunction that the lawyer recite the Old Testament commandment obedience to which he thinks will guarantee him eternal life. Obedience to "what's *written* in the Law" will indicate that his "name" is "*inscribed* in heaven" (10:20). By reciting both Deuteronomy 6:5 and Leviticus 19:18, the lawyer combines two commandments into one in that they both deal with loving. To love God out of your heart is to love him out of your inmost thoughts and feelings. To love him with your soul is to love him with the capabilities of your physical and psychological life, even to the point of martyrdom if necessary. To love him with your strength is to love him with your physical and material assets, including property and other forms of wealth. To love him with your mind is to put your intellect in the service of God. The attachment of "whole" to each of these instruments for loving God leaves not even a smidgen of yourself undevoted to him. See the comments on Mark 12:31 for loving your neighbor as yourself. Jesus gives the lawyer a good grade on his knowledge of the Old Testament, but commands him also to obey it if he wants to live eternally. In line with Luke's stress on ethical behavior, Jesus teaches the practice of godliness in addition to a knowledge of its content. Not that such practice makes belief in him deserving of eternal life; rather, it proves this belief to be genuine (compare Acts 11:24; 26:18).

10:29: But he, wanting to justify himself, said to Jesus, "And who is my neighbor?" How does this question indicate a desire by the lawyer to justify himself? In this way: he designs the question to extend an academic dialogue at the expense of obeying the commandment he himself has correctly recited. Talk is cheap. Deeds aren't. So he'd rather keep talking in the vein for which Jesus has commended him. He can justify himself in discussion better than he can justify himself in practice. In agreement with his desire to justify himself, the "And" that introduces "who is my neighbor?" makes his question supercilious.

10:30–35: And taking up [the lawyer's question], **Jesus said, "A certain man was going down from Jerusalem to Jericho and fell among bandits who, on both** stripping him [of his clothes] **and laying blows on** [him (that is, beating him)], **went away, leaving** [him] **half dead.** [31]**And by coincidence a certain priest was going down that road and, on seeing him, passed by** [him] **on the opposite side** [of the road]. [32]**And likewise also a Levite, on having come down to the spot and seen** [the man], **passed by** [him] **on the opposite side** [of the road]. [33]**But a certain Samaritan, going along the road, came down to him and, on seeing** [him], **felt sorry** [for him]. [34]**And on approaching** [rather than passing by on the other side], **he bandaged his wounds, pouring olive oil and wine on** [them]. **And after mounting him on his own animal, he brought him to an inn and took care of him.** [35]**And on the next day, he gave two denarii to the innkeeper, thrusting** [them] **out, and said, "Take care of him, and whatever more you spend** [in taking care of him], **I'll repay you when I return."** "A certain man," "a certain priest," and "a certain Samaritan" recollect "a certain lawyer" in 10:25 and at the level of Luke's text raise a question whether the lawyer will someday be a victim in need of help, or a priest-like and Levite-like by-passer of those in need of help, or a Samaritan-like helper of those in need. The road from Jerusalem to Jericho went "down" about 3,400 feet in only seventeen or so miles and passed through gorges and ravines infested with bandits. It isn't surprising, then, that bandits waylaid the initial man. It is surprising, though, or at least disgusting that the priest and the Levite by-passed him after he'd been wounded, especially since you'd expect those who work in the temple of God to obey his command to love your neighbor as you love yourself. (Priests officiated in the temple, and Levites helped them by doing menial tasks.) Since "neighbor" means "someone near," passing by "on the opposite side [of the road]" shows that the priest and the Levite didn't want to make the wounded man their neighbor by coming near him or, as Jesus would put it, didn't want to make *themselves* a neighbor to the wounded man by coming near him. They kept their distance to avoid having to obey God's command. Jesus doesn't say why they wanted to avoid loving the man. So the point has to do with avoidance as such, whatever its motivation.

In view of the antipathy that existed between Jews and Samaritans and in view of a Samaritan town's refusal to welcome Jesus (9:51–53), it was shocking for him to portray the good neighbor as a Samaritan in contrast with the disgusting priest and Levite, both Jews. A Jew such as the lawyer would have expected Jesus at most to have made the Samaritan a person in need of help, so that the lesson would run: a Jew should help even a Samaritan in need. Instead it runs: even a Samaritan helps a Jew in need. End of ethnic pride in Jesus' ideal society!

As to the details of what the Samaritan did, "came down *to him*" and "*approaching*" rather than passing by on the other side of the road show the Samaritan to be making himself a neighbor by coming near the wounded man, who can't make himself a neighbor to the Samaritan—he's "half-dead"! The Samaritan's loving this man starts with pity and evolves quickly into concrete deeds: pouring oil on the wounds to soothe them and wine on them to disinfect them while bandaging them, mounting the man on the Samaritan's own beast of burden, bringing him to an inn, caring for him there overnight, paying the innkeeper two days' wages to take care of the man during two or three weeks of convalescence, and pledging to come back and pay the innkeeper any further costs incurred in caring for the man.

10:36–37: **"Who of these three seems to you to have become a neighbor of the** [man] **who fell among the bandits?"** [37]**And he** [the lawyer] **said, "The one who did mercy with him." And Jesus told him, "Go—you too** [as well as the Samaritan]**—and do likewise."** This question of Jesus reverses that of the lawyer in 10:29 ("And who is my neighbor?"). Instead of asking for an identification of the neighbor who was to *be* loved in the parable, Jesus asks for an identification of the one who by loving *became* a neighbor. Thus love defines neighborliness rather than asking for a definition of "neighbor." And neighborliness, which consists in loving, isn't a matter of your being close to those in need so much as it's a matter of *locating* yourself close to them so as to help them.

The lawyer can't bring himself to answer Jesus' question by saying, "The Samaritan." But in the answer that he does give, "the one who *did* mercy" shows that mercy, and therefore love, is something to be done, not just felt. The added phrase "with him" doesn't mean that the wounded man cooperated with the Samaritan in the doing of mercy. Rather, in doing mercy "with him" the Samaritan came into *association* with the wounded man. Merciful action brought him *near*, made him a *neighbor* to the man. Again the lawyer's answer is correct; but this time Jesus doesn't say so, presumably because he senses the lawyer's wanting to justify himself (10:28–29). So just as Jesus said earlier, "Do this and you'll live" (10:28), he now tells the lawyer to do as the Samaritan did. The time for discussion is over. The time for action is past due. "You too" emphasizes Jesus' command. But he introduces his command to "do likewise" with another command: "Go." This is the very verb that Luke often uses for evangelistic itineration (though not only for that). Is it possible that the command to go and do mercy with people in need intimates Jesus' commission to travel throughout the world spreading the gospel in good deeds as well as in good words?

JESUS' RELIGIOUS EMANCIPATION OF WOMEN
Luke 10:38–42

The travelogue continues with an episode that opens to women a privilege of discipleship heretofore reserved for males. *10:38–39*: **And as they** [Jesus and his disciples] **were traveling** [toward Jerusalem (9:51)], **he entered into a certain town. And a certain woman—by name, Martha—welcomed him** [contrast the nonwelcome in 9:53]. So far so good. [39]**And this** [woman] **had a sister called Mary who also** [in addition to Martha's having welcomed Jesus], **on seating herself at the Lord's feet, was listening to his word.** So far so good again. Martha's welcome of Jesus includes an offer of board and room. Hence the upcoming references to serving, that is, preparing food and setting table with it. Mary's having seated herself at Jesus' feet and listening to his word constitutes a deliberate choice *not* to do such serving. Luke calls Jesus "the Lord" to bring out the authority of "the word" Mary was listening to.

10:40–42: **But Martha was preoccupied with much serving** ["much" because of the many disciples accompanying Jesus—at least the Twelve, perhaps also the seventy-two]; **and on approaching and standing** [before Jesus, who according to custom was sitting to teach], **she said, "Lord, you care, don't you, that my sister has left me to do the serving alone? Therefore** [since you do care], **tell her that she should assist me."** Martha addresses Jesus with "Lord" to point up his authority to command Mary. [41]**And answering, the Lord told her, "Martha, Martha, you're fussing and fretting about *many* things. [42]But there's need of *one* thing. For Mary has selected the good portion, which as such** [= as good] **won't be taken away from her."** Now it's Luke who calls Jesus "the Lord," and he does so to imply Jesus' authority to emancipate Mary from a duty to help her sister Martha. The doubling of Martha's name in Jesus' address to her stresses that he wants her to take note of what he's about to say (compare 6:46; 8:24; 13:34; 22:31). In contrast with the many things Martha is doing to prepare and serve a meal, the one thing needed is to listen to Jesus' word; and this is "the good portion" that Mary "has selected" by "seating herself at the Lord's feet" and "listening to his word" (10:39). What then is the implied other portion? It's to prepare and serve a meal, as Martha is doing, which isn't bad to do. In fact, hospitality calls for it. But neither is it good to do by comparison with listening to Jesus' word. He may be using "portion" for a menu item, and this as a figure of speech for Mary's selecting to hear his word. More likely, though, "portion" refers to the part of an estate that a person inherits. If so, it's striking that Mary "has *selected* the good portion," for ordinarily it's the testator who apportions out an inheritance. And what Mary has selected as her portion—that is, listening to Jesus' word—won't be taken away from her, because she has made a good choice. Jesus would rather speak "the word" than be served food; and so long as he's speaking it, a woman who has chosen to listen is under no obligation to stop listening. The kitchen can wait. "For" makes Mary's having selected the good portion a reason why Martha should do the same by ceasing to fret and fuss about many things and by doing the one thing she needs to do.

THE PIETY OF PRAYING
Luke 11:1–13

To make the gospel religiously attractive to prospective converts, Luke regularly features the piety of

Jesus and his disciples. And so he does in this passage, which divides into the piety of praying for the right things (11:1–4) and the piety of praying with audacity (11:5–13).

11:1: **And it happened that while he was praying in a certain place, when he stopped, a certain one of his disciples said to him, "Lord, teach us to pray, just as also John taught his disciples** [to pray]." The piety of Jesus appears in his praying (as also in 3:21; 5:16; 6:12; 9:18, 28–29; 22:41, 44). The piety of one of his disciples appears in the disciple's waiting till Jesus stopped praying (he didn't interrupt Jesus' prayer) and in asking that Jesus teach him and his fellow disciples to pray. Addressing Jesus with "Lord" underlines his authority to teach praying. "Just as John too taught his disciples" brings into view the piety of Jesus' harbinger, the Baptist, and his disciples. Prayerful piety from the very start of Jesus' story.

11:2–4: **And he told them, "Whenever you pray, say: 'Father, your name be treated as sacred. Your reign come. ³Give us day by day our bread for the coming** [day]. **⁴And forgive our sins for us, for also we ourselves are forgiving everyone indebted to us. And you shouldn't** [in the sense, "please don't"] **lead us into temptation.'"** The piety of Jesus appears again in his teaching the disciples to pray. Since in Luke's book of Acts they pray with words other than those that Jesus teaches them here (Acts 1:24–25; 4:24–30 and so on), "*Whenever* you pray" doesn't mean they're limited to these words when praying. Rather, from time to time they should repeat this prayer—a communal one, as indicated by "us," "our," and "we." Twice in 10:21 Jesus addressed God with "Father" and went on to speak about his intimate relation to God. By instructing the disciples to address God with "Father," Jesus introduces them into a like intimacy with God. Though his intimacy with God remains unique, he has been pleased to reveal the Father to them (10:22), so that they can legitimately address him the way Jesus did.

As the first order of business in prayer, the disciples are to ask for the Father to be glorified as regards his reputation ("your *name* be treated as sacred," that is, as inviolable, not to be profaned or maligned but to be held in deepest reverence) and as regards his reign ("Your reign come"). God's reign has already come in part and will yet come in its fullness, so that the treatment of his name as sacred is ensured; and Jesus' disciples are to pray for this double-sided eventuality. As the second order of business in prayer, they're to ask for themselves food for the body, forgiveness of their sins, and protection from moral failure. "Bread" stands for what's needed in a basic diet. "For the coming [day]" means "for the next day" and translates a Greek word whose meaning is obscure, but the expectation in 11:5 that a friend would have three loaves in his house at midnight favors this translation. (Other possible translations are "daily" and "necessary.") "Day by day" looks forward to ongoing provision. "For us" indicates that God's forgiving our sins works

to our advantage. Obviously! "For also we ourselves are forgiving everyone indebted to us" portrays our sins as a moral debt owed to God and makes our forgiveness of others a model of the forgiveness for which we ask God. Hence, "*everyone* indebted to us" implies that we're asking God to forgive every one of our sins. We might consider the possibility that those indebted to us owe us money, and that we forgive them by canceling their financial debts in accordance with the Mosaic law concerning the Year of Jubilee (Leviticus 25:8–17 [compare Luke 4:19 with comments]). But Luke can hardly expect his Gentile audience to read that law into this request, and the parallel with God's forgiving our sins favors our forgiving those indebted to us by having sinned against us (see 7:41–43 for debts as a figure of speech for sins, and compare 13:4). From Luke's standpoint—whatever the kind of debt in view—the disciples' forgiving their debtors brings out a moral excellence that makes the disciples' company attractive to prospective converts.

The plea not to be led into temptation has something of a parallel in 22:40, where Jesus will tell his disciples, "Pray so as not to enter into temptation." In that context, entering into temptation means succumbing to moral failure, such as forsaking and disowning Jesus, because of sleeping instead of praying. So Jesus tells the disciples, "Pray *standing up*, lest you enter into temptation" (22:46). If they stand up to pray, they'll not succumb again to sleep and therefore won't succumb to moral failure. Praying that we not be led into temptation doesn't mean praying not to confront temptation, then. It means praying not to succumb to temptation by being sucked into it. But what kind of temptation is in view here? The word for "temptation" could also be translated "test." These two translations aren't so different as they might seem, though. For every temptation tests our mettle, and every test poses the possibility of failure. And following as it does on the heels of a request that God forgive our sins, the plea not to be led into temptation means naturally that we're asking him to keep us from succumbing to moral failure (compare 4:1–13).

11:5–8: **And he said to them, "Who of you will have a friend and go to him at midnight and would say to him, 'Friend, lend me three loaves of bread, ⁶because a friend of mine has come to me from the road and I don't have anything** [= food] **to set before him.' ⁷And answering from inside, that one** [your friend] **would say, 'Stop bothering me. The door is already shut and my little children are with me in bed. I can't get up and give you** [anything].' **⁸I tell you** [Jesus is speaking], **even though he** [the friend inside] **won't get up and give** [anything] **to him** [the friend with the request] **on account of being his friend, for sure on account of his** [the requester's] **audacity he'll get up and give him as many** [loaves] **as he needs."** Audacity consists in shameless boldness. The audacity to which Jesus here refers shows itself in asking a friend in the middle of the night to loan him three loaves of bread, this at the cost of rousing the friend from bed, waking up his little children, and opening the door. The awkward switch from "Who of you *will* have a friend and go to him" to "*would* say to him" implies the unlikelihood of making such an audacious request. Several items in the request put on display the requester's attempt to counterbalance its audacity: (1) the address "Friend," which appeals to friendship; (2) "lend me three loaves," which implies a promise of repayment; (3) "because a friend of mine has come to me from the road," which appeals to the middle eastern law of hospitality to travelers, in this case a law fortified by another friendship; and (4) "I don't have anything to set before him," which appeals to the requester's lack of provisions and suffering of shame if he doesn't feed his guest. Three loaves would be more than enough to feed him, but hospitality requires an excess of provisions.

"And answering from inside" implies that the requester has spoken from outside his friend's house. Another "*would* say" carries forward the unlikelihood of such a dialogue. The underlying audacity is outrageous. The answer of the friend inside contains no polite address and grumpily details why he thinks the request outrageous, so outrageous that he concludes, "I *can't* get up and give you [anything]." But Jesus contradicts the friend's "I can't" and turns an *unlikelihood* of giving because of *friendship* into the *certainty* of giving because of *audacity*. "I tell you," "for sure," and "he *will* get up and give" underline this certainty; and "as many [loaves] as he needs" enlarges it. Friendship won't bring the desired result. Audacity will. So pray with an audacity born of confidence that God will answer your prayers. For such audacity is a virtue. It pleases God. He's not like the sleeping friend. He never sleeps.

11:9–10: "And I tell you: keep on asking, and it [what you're asking for] will be given to you; keep on seeking [what you're looking for], and you'll find [it]; keep on knocking, and it [the door] will be opened for you. [10]For everyone who keeps on asking receives, and [everyone] who keeps on seeking finds, and it [the door] will be opened for [everyone] who keeps on knocking." So persistence marks audacity in prayer, and answers to audacious prayer will confirm the piety of praying audaciously. Another "I tell you" emphasizes the point. You ask for something in prayer. You seek for it in prayer. And you knock for it in prayer. Receiving, finding, and having the door opened for you represent the getting of positive answers to prayer. "Everyone" shows that God the Father plays no favorites when it comes to answering the prayers of his Son's disciples.

11:11–12: "And [your] son will ask what father from among you for a fish, and will he [the father] give him a snake instead of a fish? [12]Or also he'll ask for an egg. Will he give him a scorpion?" The father-son relationship about which Jesus speaks harks back to his teaching the disciples to address God in prayer with "Father" (11:2). Fish and eggs are nutritious, snakes and scorpions poisonous. Jesus' point is that as the disciples' Father, God will give them things good for them, not harmful to them, in answer to their prayers for such things. Jesus pairs a fish and a snake because both are

long and scaly, and pairs an egg and a scorpion because when curled up a scorpion looks something like an egg. Despite many English translations to the contrary, there's no "if" in Luke's text, as in "if your son asks" and "if he asks." What we have instead is affirmations ("the son *will* ask . . . . he *will* ask"), so that Jesus makes asking in prayer a characteristic of discipleship. There's no discipleship without prayer.

11:13: "If then you, though you're evil, know to give good gifts to your children, how much more will the Father from heaven give the Holy Spirit to those who keep asking him [for the Holy Spirit]**!"** Not "know *how* to give good gifts," as though it were a matter of method, but "know *to* give good gifts," since it's a matter of course—and this despite the depravity of all human fathers. Because God the Father is good rather than evil, he's even more likely than human fathers to give good gifts. Indeed, he will give them, most especially the gift of the Holy Spirit, to those who keep asking him. He's called "the Father *from* heaven" because he'll come on the disciples from heaven in the person of his Holy Spirit (Acts 2:2), and they'll have been praying (Acts 1:14).

ON JESUS' EXORCISMS
Luke 11:14–26

This passage discusses the source of Jesus' ability to perform exorcisms (11:14–20), describes them as victories over Satan (11:21–23), and warns against the danger of a vacuum following exorcism (11:24–26).

11:14–16: And he was casting out a demon, and it was mute. And it happened that after the demon had gone out, the mute [that is, the man who'd been mute] **spoke. And the crowds marveled. [15]But some of them said, "He's casting out demons by Beelzebul, the ruler of the demons." [16]And others, testing** [him]**, were seeking from him a sign out of heaven.** Since the demoniac spoke after the exorcism, Luke's description of the demon as mute probably means that it caused muteness in the man instead of, or at least in addition to, being mute itself. "The mute spoke" then gives audible evidence of a successful exorcism. Mention of "the crowds" (plural) revives Luke's emphasis on the popularity of Jesus because of his good deeds and gracious words. The crowds' "marvel[ing]" at this exorcism casts them as admiring eye- and earwitnesses (compare 1:1–4). "Some of them" and "others" pose exceptions to the admiration, though; yet even they can't deny what they've seen and heard. These "some" can only attribute Jesus' success to the power of Beelzebul, the demons' ruler, as though he would want to undo the very work he'd commanded them to do, that is, the work of possessing human beings. (Apart from identifying him with the demons' ruler, neither Luke nor those who make this accusation show any interest in the derivation or meaning of "Beelzebul," though 11:18 will identify Beelzebul as "Satan.") The "others" seek from Jesus a sign from heaven to rule out the possibility that he's casting out demons by means of Beelzebul. "A sign from heaven" means a heavenly display of some kind, as in the sun, moon, stars, and planets (21:26 [compare 2 Kings 20:8–11]). The setting back to back of the accusation that Jesus exorcises demons by Beelzebul and the demand that Jesus produce a sign from heaven exposes a disbelief unreasonable in its refusal to be satisfied by what should already have counted as adequate evidence. "Testing [him]" sets up a contest between Jesus and the "others" on this point.

11:17–20: **But he, knowing their thoughts, told them, "Every kingdom divided against itself is devastated, and** [every] **household** [divided] **against a household falls.** [18]**And if Satan too** [like 'every kingdom' and 'household'] **has been divided against himself, how will his kingdom stand?** [I ask you] **because you're saying that I cast out demons by Beelzebul.** [19]**But if I'm casting out demons by Beelzebul, by whom are your sons casting** [them] **out? On account of this** [their casting out demons but your not accusing them of doing so by Beelzebul as you do accuse me], *they* **will be your judges** [in the sense of exposing your double standard in accusing me but not them]. [20]**But if I'm casting out demons by God's finger, then God's reign has come upon you."** *"Knowing* their thoughts" displays Jesus' clairvoyance. And "knowing their *thoughts*" implies that he knew their seeking from him a sign from heaven to be motivated by a purpose to humiliate him (*"testing* [him]"). Dissension in a kingdom leads to its collapse. "Every" indicates the inevitability of collapse. Because of the parallel with "every kingdom," "household" refers to a royal family. Contention within such a family—for instance, princes' vying with each other for the throne—leads to the family's fall from power. "And if Satan too has been divided against himself" implies both that he's Beelzebul and that the demons are so much his agents that to oppose them by enabling Jesus to exorcise them would be to oppose himself. And to oppose himself would be to ensure the downfall of his kingdom. But he isn't that stupid!

As in Acts 19:13–16, "your sons" are Jewish exorcists accepted as *not* in league with Satan. Jesus' argument doesn't depend on the actuality of their exorcisms. The argument simply has to do with the inconsistency of stigmatizing Jesus' exorcisms but not those of the sons. Since fingers are used for close work (see Exodus 8:19; Deuteronomy 9:10; Psalm 8:3), "by God's finger" brings God into direct involvement with Jesus' exorcisms. And this involvement constitutes the arrival of God's reign, which is defeating the reign of Satan over human victims through his demons.

11:21–23: **"Whenever a completely armed strong** [man] **guards his own mansion** [a dwelling large and elaborate enough to enclose a courtyard], **his possessions are in peace** [that is, in safekeeping]. [22]**But as soon as a stronger** [man] **than he, coming upon** [him], **defeats him, he takes away his** [the first man's] **full armor, on which he'd relied, and distributes his spoils** [the first man's possessions, now plundered so as to become those of the stronger man]. [23]**The person who's not with me is**

against me, and the person who's not gathering with me is scattering." Jesus compares Satan to a strong man. "Completely armed" describes Satan as having plenty of resources to guard his possessions. Those possessions are made up of the human beings he has possessed through his demons. His mansion is "his kingdom" (11:18), in which demoniacs are subject to him. The stronger man is Jesus, as John the baptizer also described him (3:16). The stronger man's coming upon the strong man refers to Jesus' attacking Satan by ordering Satan's demons to come out of human beings (compare the sudden arrival of God's reign in 11:20). Jesus "defeats" Satan when the demons do come out. Taking away the full armor on which Satan has relied means making him defenseless before Jesus' superior power. The stronger man's distributing as spoils the former possessions of the strong-but-now-defenseless man refers to Jesus' giving the victims of demonic possession back to their families and friends— a humanitarian touch that suits Luke's emphasis on Jesus' philanthropy. "The person who's not with me is against me" refers to those who oppose Jesus by accusing him of casting out demons by means of Beelzebul and by seeking from him a sign from heaven (11:15–16). Referring to the same people is the statement, "and the person who's not gathering with me is scattering," only with figurative language that opposes the pernicious scattering of wheat at harvest time to the beneficial gathering of wheat into a granary (compare 3:17). The comparison of evangelism to a harvest in 10:2 suggests that here in 11:23 the person who scatters represents those who oppose evangelism, just as the person who gathers with Jesus represents those who join him in evangelism.

11:24–26: **"Whenever an unclean spirit comes out from a human being, it goes through waterless places seeking rest and not finding** [any]. **Then it says, 'I'll go back into my house** [the human being in whom I dwelt earlier], **from where I came out.'** [25]**And on coming, it finds** [the house] **swept and put in order.** [26]**Then it goes and takes along seven other spirits more evil than itself and, on entering** [the house], **settles down there. And the last** [circumstances] **of that human being become worse than the first** [circumstances]."** Because the context deals with exorcisms, the unclean spirit comes out as a result of exorcism. In 8:26–33 a herd of pigs hurtled down into a lake bearing with them demons that Jesus had cast out of a man and allowed to enter the pigs. So here the exorcised unclean spirit seeks rest (presumably in another human being) away from water. Not finding such rest, the spirit goes back to its former "house" and finds it swept and put in order, ready for reinhabiting (since the Holy Spirit isn't living there) and so attractive that the spirit gets seven other spirits more evil than itself and repossesses, along with the others, the human being. Now the human being, portrayed as a house, is much worse off than before. Such is the fate of those who are brushed by God's grace but don't keep asking him for the Holy Spirit (as they should in accordance with 11:13). Human nature abhors a vacuum just as the rest of nature does.

JESUS' REDIRECTING HONOR
FROM HIMSELF TO GOD
Luke 11:27–28

11:27–28: And it happened that while he was saying these things a certain woman, lifting up [her] **voice out of the crowd, said to him, "Fortunate** [is] **the womb that carried you and the breasts that you sucked."** [28]**But he said, "On the contrary, fortunate** [are] **those who are hearing God's word and keeping** [it in the sense of obeying it]**."** "The crowd" keeps attention on Jesus' popularity. By describing as "fortunate" the womb that carried Jesus and the breasts that he sucked, a woman expressed admiration for Jesus himself. Even as an embryo, a fetus, and an infant he brought high privilege to his mother. Naturally, it's appropriate for a woman to have expressed her admiration for him in this way. That she does while he's uttering his foregoing statements makes her outburst an interruption. "Lifting up her voice" heightens the interruption by indicating that she made herself heard over the voice of Jesus. The highly interruptive nature of this outburst intensifies her expression of admiration: she can't wait till Jesus stops talking to express it.

Piously, however, Jesus turns attention from himself as the supposed privileger of his mother to God, whose word it's a privilege to hear and obey. "On the contrary" denies that Jesus' mother Mary was fortunate to have carried and nursed him. But the angel Gabriel told her she'd "found favor with God" (1:26–33); and, "filled with the Holy Spirit," Elizabeth pronounced Mary "favored . . . among women" and "fortunate" (1:39–45 [compare 1:48]). In the overall picture, then, Luke must intend us to take Jesus' statement as comparative: it's a much higher privilege to hear and obey the word of God that Jesus preaches as an adult than it was for Mary to have carried him in her womb and nursed him at her breasts.

JESUS AS A PREACHER OF REPENTANCE
Luke 11:29–13:9

Throughout this section of his Gospel, Luke portrays Jesus as a preacher who condemns evil and teaches repentance from it. The portrayal suits Luke's appeal to prospective converts who in reaction against the moral degradation surrounding them are looking for, and attracted to, high moral standards. As intimated by the statement in 11:29 that Jesus "*started* saying," the section is so long that for purposes of commentary it'll be subdivided.

JESUS AS A GREATER PREACHER OF
REPENTANCE THAN JONAH WAS
Luke 11:29–32

11:29–30: And as the crowds were increasing, he started saying, "This generation is an evil generation. It's seeking a sign, and no sign will be given it except for the sign of Jonah. [30]**For just as Jonah became a sign to the Ninevites, so too will the Son of Man be** [a sign] **to this generation."** To heighten Jesus' popularity yet more, Luke pluralizes "the crowd" of 11:27 into "the crowd*s*" and says they "were *increasing*." As a preacher of repentance Jesus takes advantage of their presence to condemn them for their evil. "*This* generation" refers to them as his contemporaries in that they're seeking a sign—from him, it's to be inferred from 11:16. "This *generation*" refers to them as people of the same kind in that they're seeking a sign. And their seeking a sign after all that Jesus has said and done makes them an "*evil* generation." Because of their evil, they'll get no sign except for that of Jonah, who became a sign to the people of Nineveh, capital city of Assyria on the east bank of the Tigris River (northern Iraq in modern terms). For Jesus' contemporaries he himself ("the Son of Man") will be the sign of Jonah because of a similarity between him and Jonah. But what's that similarity?

11:31–32: "The queen of the South [of Sheba according to 1 Kings 10:1–10; 2 Chronicles 9:1–12] **will be raised at the judgment with the men of this generation; and she'll condemn them, because she came from the extremities of the earth** [= a very long way] **to hear Solomon's wisdom; and behold, something more than Solomon** [is] **here!** [32]**The Ninevite men will be resurrected at the judgment with this generation; and they'll condemn it, because they repented at Jonah's preaching** [see Jonah 3]**; and behold, something more than Jonah** [is] **here!"** Sheba was probably located in southwest Arabia. Because of parallelism with "will be resurrected," "will be raised" refers likewise to the resurrection of people for the Last Judgment. The queen of the South and the men of Nineveh will condemn the men of Jesus' generation, not in the sense that they'll act as judges, but in the sense that the coming to hear Solomon's wisdom in the one case and the repenting at Jonah's preaching in the other case contrast with this generation's seeking a sign. The contrast will testify against them, especially since the queen of the South had to travel far to hear Solomon's wisdom whereas "this generation" have only to stay where they are to hear Jesus, and also since the queen and the Ninevites were Gentiles whereas "this generation" and Jesus alike are Jews. Jesus is shaming his fellow Jews by citing favorably some Gentiles. Two instances of "behold" highlight the presence of "something more than Solomon" and of "something more than Jonah." We might have expected a personal "some*one*" (Jesus) rather than the neuter "some*thing*." But the neuter gender can be used for a person to stress a particular aspect of that person. So the "something more than Solomon" is Jesus in that his wisdom exceeds even that of Solomon, and the "something more than Jonah" is Jesus in that his preaching of repentance exceeds even that of Jonah. It's Jesus' preaching of repentance, full as it is of unrivaled moral wisdom, that constitutes him as the sign of Jonah to his generation.

JESUS' PREACHING OF REPENTANCE
AS MORAL LIGHT
Luke 11:33–36

11:33-34: "No one after lighting a lamp puts it in hiding [in a cellar, for example] **or under a basket** [used for measuring and equivalent to almost ¼ bushel or eight quarts], **but on a lampstand in order that those who enter** [the room] **may see the light** [compare 8:16]. [34]**The lamp of the body is your eye. Whenever your eye is clear** [that is, unclouded by disease and therefore healthy], **your whole body too** [as well as your eye] **is light** [in the sense of illuminated by the lamp-like eye]. **But as soon as** [your eye] **is evil** [that is, diseased and therefore clouded], **your body too is dark.**" First, Jesus compares his preaching of repentance to the lighting and shining of a lamp. The putting of a lit lamp on a lampstand for enterers to see the light represents the publicity of Jesus' preaching. Everybody could hear it just as everybody who enters a room can see the light of a burning lamp placed on a lampstand. Then Jesus compares your eye to a lamp. Your eye illuminates your body as a burning lamp illuminates a room, but only if the eye is healthy. If diseased ("evil," like "this generation" in 11:29), it won't shine and your room-like body will be dark. Which is to say that you should make the lamplight of Jesus' preaching of repentance your own moral lamp. Then you'll be fully illumined on how to behave. Otherwise moral darkness will characterize you. See the comments on Matthew 6:22–23 for the ancient biophysical view of eyes as emitters of light.

11:35-36: "**Therefore see to it that the light that's in you isn't darkness.** [36]**If therefore your whole body** [is] **light** [illuminated by the lamp that's your eye], **not having any part** [of it] **dark, it'll be wholly light, as whenever a lamp enlightens you with lightning**[-like rays]." The first "therefore" makes the possibility of moral darkness a reason for seeing to it that the light that's in you isn't darkness. You "see to it" by repenting at Jesus' preaching. If the light that's in you *is* darkness, it isn't light, of course. But that's the very point: if even that light is darkness, what moral hope do you have? All the more reason to repent! The second "therefore" makes repentance the engine of moral illumination. Emphasizing to the nth degree the moral light that comes from repenting at Jesus' preaching are (1) the illumination of "your *whole* body"; (2) its "not having *any part* dark"; (3) its being "*wholly* light"; and (4) the comparison of its lamplight to "*lightning*," which illuminates even the darkest sky.

JESUS' UPBRAIDING OF PHARISEES
FOR THEIR MORAL TURPITUDE
Luke 11:37–44

11:37-41: **And at** [the time of Jesus'] **speaking** [the foregoing statements], **a Pharisee asked him to dine with him. And on entering** [the Pharisee's house], **he reclined** [on a cushion around a low table, as was customary at formal meals]. [38]**And the Pharisee, on observ-**ing [Jesus], **marveled that he hadn't first gotten washed before the meal.** [39]**And the Lord said to him, "As it is, you Pharisees—you cleanse the outside of a cup and of a plate, but the inside of you is full of extortion and evil** [compare the evil spirits, the evil generation, and the evil eye of 11:26, 29, 34]. [40]**Nitwits, the one who made the outside made the inside too, didn't he?** [41]**Nevertheless** [that is, despite your being full of extortion and evil], **give as charity the things that are in** [you]; **and behold, all things are clean for you.**" Out of his Pharisaic concern for ritual purity this Pharisee marveled at Jesus' not first getting washed before the meal. "Washed" means "immersed," but Luke doesn't spell out an underlying reason for the expected immersion, so that the marveling simply provides an occasion for Jesus' responding to it. Since the Pharisee hasn't expressed his surprise, Jesus appears to have clairvoyance concerning it. By calling Jesus "the Lord" in his introduction to Jesus' response, Luke underlines its authority. With "as it is," Jesus cites a state of affairs that doesn't bear contradiction. Along with 11:45, 53–54, "you Pharisees" implies the presence of Pharisees besides the host and calls them emphatically to account. Their cleansing the outside of a cup and of a plate (we'd say the *under*side of the plate) doesn't describe a concern over the ritual purity of tableware, for then we'd read about outer cleansing *in addition to* cleansing the inside of cups and plates. So this cleansing only of the outside represents the Pharisees' keeping *themselves* externally, ritually pure to make a show of piety; for they are, so to speak, the cup and the plate. By contrast, Jesus says, their inside is full of extortion and evil, of a rapacity that wickedly impoverishes other people of what rightfully belongs to them. "Nitwits" makes the immorality of their rapacity foolish. Judgment is coming (11:31–32). God is the one who made the inside of people as well as their outside, so that he demands inward moral purity, not just outward ritual purity (though he hasn't demanded getting immersed before a meal even as a matter of ritual purity). And the only way for people full of evil extortion to get inwardly pure is to give away as charity the things they've gained thereby. Then, no longer in the possession of those people but to their advantage, all these things are clean—morally clean.

11:42-44: "**But alas for you Pharisees, because you tithe** [= give for religious service a tenth of] **the mint and rue and every** [other] **herb** [that you grow]; **and you bypass justice and love for God** [compare the by-passing of a wounded man by a priest and a Levite in the parable of the good Samaritan (10:31–32)]. **But it was obligatory to do these things** [justice and love for God] **and not to neglect those things** [the tithing of herbs]." Jesus continues to preach morality by pronouncing woe—that is, calamitous misery—on the Pharisees for their failures at justice (compare their evil extortion in 11:39) and at love for God, which would have been expressed with charity in place of extortion (11:41 [see also 10:25–37]). Not that tithing is unnecessary, but it doesn't save you from God's judgment if you don't do the necessaries of justice and love for him. Jesus unites social justice and religious devotion. ⁴³"**Alas for you Pharisees, because you love prestigious seating in synagogues and greetings in marketplaces** [compare 14:7–11; 16:14–15]. ⁴⁴**Alas for you, because you're like unmarked graves; and the people who are walking over them don't know** [that they are]." Jesus upbraids the Pharisees for their love of public recognition both in synagogues, where religious services are held, and in marketplaces, where commerce is carried on. "Prestigious seating" may refer to a row of seats up front and facing the rest of the congregation, so that the Pharisees are in full view. Because of their reputation for piety, "greetings" directed to them are fawning and flattering. Graves are full of ritual impurity, so that people come into contact with such impurity when inadvertently walking over graves that aren't marked as such. Jesus uses this inadvertent contact with *ritual* impurity to represent people's inadvertently coming into contact with the Pharisees' *moral* impurity when they greet them in marketplaces and sit below them in synagogues. The Pharisees' concern to avoid ritual purity themselves lends this woe some sarcasm.

JESUS' UPBRAIDING OF LAWYERS FOR THEIR MALEVOLENCE
Luke 11:45–52

After pronouncing three woes on Pharisees in 11:37–44, Jesus now pronounces three woes on lawyers. The lawyers were expert in the Mosaic law. So far as we can tell, most of them belonged to the Pharisaic sect, so that the woes already pronounced against the Pharisees in general applied to most of the lawyers in particular.

11:45–46: And answering, a certain one of the lawyers says to him, "Teacher, by saying these things [against the Pharisees] **you're insulting us too."** ⁴⁶**And he** [Jesus] **said, "Alas also for you lawyers, because you burden people with burdens hard to carry, and you yourselves don't touch the burdens with one of your fingers."** The present tense of "says" gives emotional intensity to the lawyer's complaint; and to lend it acceptability the lawyer addresses Jesus with a respectful "Teacher." But Jesus doesn't back down. He renews his attack, this time aiming specifically at lawyers. The hard-to-carry burdens with which they burden people consist in interpretations of the Mosaic law that go beyond it, so that keeping them in addition to the Law itself becomes difficult to do (compare Acts 15:10). On top of overburdening people in this way, the lawyers don't make any effort whatever to offer interpretations that would make Law-keeping easier to do. You help somebody carry a burden by grabbing it so as to share its weight. But Jesus says the lawyers don't even *touch* the burdens with even *one* of their fingers. In other words, they make not even the slightest effort to ease the burden of Law-keeping.

11:47–48: "Alas for you [lawyers], **because you build the tombs of the prophets, but your** [fore]**fathers killed them.** ⁴⁸**You're witnesses, then; and you agree with the deeds of your** [fore]**fathers, because on the one hand they killed them** [the prophets] **and on the other hand you build** [the prophets' tombs]." Doubtless the lawyers would have said they built the tombs of the prophets to honor the prophets. But because of the lawyers' wickedness Jesus interprets their building of those tombs as a completion of their ancestors' murderous deeds. The ancestors killed the prophets; the lawyers follow up by building tombs in which to bury the prophets. By building those tombs the lawyers bear witness to their agreement with the killing. Again, the lawyers would have strenuously objected to Jesus' interpretation of their building the tombs. But he bases his interpretation on a wickedness of theirs that's like their ancestors' wickedness. After all, they're among those who'll engineer the killing of him just as their ancestors killed the prophets (see especially 9:22; 11:53–54; 19:47; 20:19; 22:2, 66–23:12, in many of which passages the lawyers are called scholars, as also right here in 11:53).

11:49–51: "On account of this [your agreement with the killing of the prophets], **the wisdom of God too** [in addition to me] **said, 'I'll send them prophets and apostles; and they'll kill and persecute some of them** ⁵⁰**in order that from this generation** [recently described by Jesus as "evil" (11:29)] **may be exacted the blood of all the prophets that has been shed from the founding of the world,** ⁵¹[that is,] **from the blood of Abel** [murdered by his brother Cain (Genesis 4:1–15)] **to the blood of Zechariah, who was dispatched between the altar** [in the temple's courtyard] **and the house** [the temple building itself (2 Chronicles 24:20–22)]. **Yes, I tell you, it** [all the prophets' blood] **will be exacted from this generation.'"** Jesus quotes "the wisdom of God" to add a second testimony to his own against "this generation" (see Numbers 35:30; Deuteronomy 17:6; 19:15 on the sufficiency of two witnesses). We don't know the source from which Jesus gleaned this quotation; but by saying, "*I'll* send . . . ," God's wisdom personifies itself. And since God sent the prophets and, through his Son Jesus, sent the apostles, God's wisdom stands for God himself, because he's the fount and quintessence of wisdom (contrast Jesus' characterization of the Pharisees as "nitwits" in 11:40, and compare the association of wisdom with the Holy Spirit in Acts 6:3, 5, 10). Since the line of killed prophets started with Abel, the future tense of "I'll send" and "they'll kill" implies that God's wisdom spoke the quoted words even before the martyrdom of Abel.

"They" who'll kill some of the prophets and apostles and persecute others whom they don't succeed in killing—these "they" started with Cain but expanded into Israel, God's people. (In this context, "persecute" means to pursue with the purpose of killing.) The addition of apostles to prophets ties church martyrs together with ancient martyrs in agreement with Luke's stress on the continuity of Christianity with Judaism to allay ancient people's fear of novelty (compare 5:37–39). But since apostles are yet to be martyred, the blood of only the Old Testament prophets will be exacted from Jesus' contemporaries ("*this* generation"). He includes Abel among "all the prophets," perhaps because Abel's sacrifice of an animal testified to God's way of atonement (so Hebrews 9:22; 11:4). But Jesus doesn't say why. So his point has to do mainly if not solely with the shedding of Abel's (rather than the animal's) blood in the first martyrdom recorded by the Old Testament. Since Chronicles (originally one book), not Malachi, stands last in the arrangement of books making up the Hebrew Old Testament, the blood of Zechariah counts as the last martyrdom in the Old Testament used by Jesus. (This Zechariah isn't to be confused with Zechariah the minor prophet; and, incidentally, Jesus' not citing any later martyrs, such as those that appear in the already-written Old Testament apocrypha, shows that he didn't regard the Scripture as including those books.) The exacting of all this blood from Jesus' contemporaries means that they'll be held responsible for shedding it all. Their evil (see 11:29 again) and their coming role in the killing of Jesus, the acme of the prophetic line and fulfiller of its message (24:44–47), make it right and just that they be held responsible for the totality and judged accordingly. "Yes" and "I tell you" put a double emphasis on this judgment.

11:52: "Alas for you lawyers, because you've taken away the key of knowledge. You yourselves haven't entered, and you've forbidden those entering [to do so]." We might have expected "haven't entered" and "entering" to have the object, "God's kingdom," as elsewhere. But they don't, and throughout Luke-Acts entry and nonentry into that kingdom come at the end of present history even though acceptance and rejection of God's reign take place now. "*Have*n't entered" and "enter*ing*" would disagree with the futurity of nonentry and entry into God's kingdom if Jesus were here implying God's kingdom as the object. So the lack of an object preserves that futurity, and entry and nonentry have to do only with having and not having the key of knowledge. It's because of the lawyers' expertise in the Mosaic law that Jesus refers to knowledge. But he doesn't refer to their knowledge of the Law—rather, to a knowledge of the secrets of God's reign, as in 8:10. Knowing these secrets is the key to entering. But the door is locked, so that only those possessing this knowledge can use it as a key to unlock the door and enter. But just as "the Devil comes and takes away the word [concerning those secrets] from the heart [of those who hear it] lest by believing they be saved" (8:12), so too the lawyers—playing the Devil's part—"have taken away the key of knowledge" and "forbidden those entering [from doing so]." Their forbidding others in addition to not entering themselves draws Jesus' ire and prompts the pronouncement of a woe against them.

JESUS' WARNING AGAINST THE
PHARISEES IN THE FACE OF THEIR
TRYING TO TRAP HIM INTO SAYING
SOMETHING SELF-INCRIMINATING
Luke 11:53–12:12

11:53–54: And when he'd gone out from there, the scholars [= lawyers] and the Pharisees started to have it in for him bitterly and to interrogate him about very many things, ⁵⁴plotting against him so as to catch him in regard to something [coming] out of his mouth [that is, in regard to something he might say that they could use to bring a charge against him]. Jesus was engaged in table-talk at the house of a Pharisee (11:37). He has now gone out from there, but the Pharisees and the scholars—presumably Pharisees and lawyers who'd dined with him in that house—started having bitter feelings toward Jesus because of the woes he'd pronounced against them there. Out of these feelings came an interrogation of him. It had the purpose of trapping him into saying something self-incriminating. That the interrogation covered "very many things" shows a high degree of bitterness.

12:1–3: Meanwhile, when myriads of [people making up] the crowd had converged, and so were trampling one another, he began speaking first to his disciples: "Take precaution for yourselves against the Pharisees' leaven, which as such is hypocrisy. ²But nothing is completely covered [concealed] that won't be uncovered [revealed], and [nothing is] secret that won't be made known, ³because as many things as you've said in the dark will be heard in the light, and what you've spoken to the ear [whispered into somebody's ear] in inner sanctums will be proclaimed on rooftops." As usual, Luke headlines Jesus' popularity, this time by adding "myriads" to "the crowd" and saying they were so eager to see and hear him that they were trampling over one another as they converged. Leaven consisted of a portion of fermenting dough that was mixed with a batch of fresh dough to make the batch rise, much as yeast is used nowadays. Jesus makes leaven stand for the Pharisees' hypocrisy. Defining this hypocrisy is his recent upbraiding of them for their concern with outward, ritual purity while inside they're full of extortion and evil, for their care to tithe herbs while by-passing justice and love for God, for their love of prominent seating in synagogues and greetings in marketplaces, and for their similarity to unmarked graves (11:39–44). In other words, their hypocrisy consists in an outward show of piety that masks moral corruption within. But leaven permeates, as pointed up by "which *as such*." So Jesus commands his disciples to take precaution—for their own sakes—against permeation from the Pharisees' leaven of hypocrisy. To motivate such precaution, he then warns that what hypocrisy masks for the present will be unmasked in the future—at the Last Judgment, as intimated by an upcoming reference to being thrown into hell (12:5 [compare also 12:8–9; Acts 17:30–31; 24:15]). Even what's *completely* covered now will be uncovered then. Everybody will know your secrets. Even what you've whispered in the darkness of inner sanctums will be proclaimed, so to speak, on rooftops in the full light of day that all may hear what you said. And nothing will be exempted from such exposure. So it's hypocrisy in speech, saying things in secret that you wouldn't want known to the public, that Jesus highlights in his warning. Don't think you can get away with duplicitous talk.

12:4–5: "And I tell you, my friends, you shouldn't fear those who kill the body and afterward don't have anything more to do [to you]. ⁵But I'll point out to you whom you *should* fear. You should fear him who after the killing has authority to throw [you] into gehenna [a ravine south of Jerusalem where fire was constantly burning combustible trash, and therefore a figure of speech for fiery hell]. Yes, I tell you, you should fear *this one!*" Jesus' addressing the disciples with "my friends" projects a social ideal and indicates that he issues the following warning, like the preceding one, for the disciples' benefit. The first "I tell you" underlines the warning; and another "I tell you," buttressed by "Yes," underlines it a second time. Despite the possibility of martyrdom, Jesus' disciples shouldn't fear their persecutors, who can do no more than kill their bodies. But because of the possibility of being thrown into hell after being killed, the disciples should fear him who has authority to throw them there. That fear will keep them from denying Jesus so as to avoid being killed/martyred. Jesus doesn't say here who has such authority, but a reference to God in his immediately following statement points toward God (see also 12:20–21; 18:4, 7; 23:40).

12:6–7: "Five sparrows are sold for two assarions, aren't they? And not one of them [the sparrows] is forgotten in God's sight. ⁷But all the hairs of your head are numbered as well [= in addition to not a single sparrow's being forgotten]. Don't fear. You're worth more than many sparrows." After telling his disciples to fear God because of God's authority to throw them into hell (12:5), Jesus tells them not to fear that God will forget them after their persecutors kill their bodies. For not even cheaply sold sparrows—not even *one* of them—is forgotten, but remains in God's sight. And the disciples are worth more than many sparrows. (An assarion had a value of about one cent and amounted to ¹⁄₁₆ of a day's wage for manual laborers, so that one sparrow was worth less than ½ cent.) If God has counted up the hairs on the disciples' heads, he has shown so much interest in them that they shouldn't fear they'll be thrown into hell after being killed for Jesus' sake.

12:8–9: "And I tell you, everyone who confesses me before men—the Son of Man will also confess him before the angels of God. ⁹But the one who disowns me before men will be utterly disowned before the angels of God." Another "I tell you" stresses the following assurance and warning. To confess Jesus before men is to state in public that you believe in him—and this despite the danger of persecution and even martyrdom. To disown him before men is to state in public—for the purpose of avoiding persecution and martyrdom—that you don't believe in him. Jesus switches from "me" to "the Son Man" to make a wordplay on "men . . . Son of Man" and allude to his coming role at the Last Judgment (see especially 9:26; 21:36). Angels will attend that judgment as observers. For Jesus as the Son of Man to confess someone is for him to acknowledge that person as his disciple. His confessing "*everyone* who confesses

[him] before men" gives assurance. For someone to "be disowned"—particularly someone who at the judgment claims to be a disciple of Jesus but has disowned him before men—is for that person to be disowned as not a disciple. "*Utterly* disowned" implies eternal damnation. Whereas the statement that "the Son of Man will also confess him" divides attention between the Son of Man as the confessor and his confessing of someone, the phrase "will be utterly disowned" concentrates attention solely on the disowning. (There's no mention of Jesus as the disowner.) The final accent rests, then, on the judgment incurred by disowning Jesus.

12:10: "And everyone who'll speak a word against the Son of Man—it [that word] will be forgiven for him [= for his benefit]. But for the one who blasphemes [that is, slanders] the Holy Spirit there'll be no forgiveness." "Will speak a word against the Son of Man" is the same as a disciple's disowning Jesus before men in 12:9. The statement there warned that such a disowning will lead to Jesus' disowning the disowner before the angels of God. But now Jesus holds out to the disowner a possibility of forgiveness. "Will be forgiven" carries the sense, "can be forgiven." By the same token, "there'll be no forgiveness" carries the sense, "there can't be any forgiveness." This possibility encourages repentance by way of reversing a public disowning of Jesus with a public confession of him in accordance with 12:8. "Everyone" maximizes the encouragement. On the other hand, the impossibility of forgiveness for slandering the Holy Spirit, with whom God anointed Jesus (3:22; 4:18), warns against unbelievers' attributing to Beelzebul rather than the Holy Spirit Jesus' ability to exorcise demons and do other mighty works of salvation (11:15, 18–19). It is such a false attribution that constitutes slandering the Holy Spirit. Jesus doesn't explain why there can be forgiveness in the one case but not in the other. So the emphasis falls on the encouragement as such and on the warning as such.

12:11–12: "And whenever they bring you before synagogues and rulers and authorities, you shouldn't worry about how you should defend yourselves or what [you should offer in self-defense] or what you should say. ¹²For the Holy Spirit will teach you in that very hour the things that are necessary to say [compare 21:15]." Here Jesus addresses his disciples. "They" who "bring you before synagogues . . .?" are the disciples' persecutors who, like Jesus' opponents, slander the Holy Spirit by attributing to Beelzebul the disciples' mighty works of salvation and as a result of this false attribution haul the disciples before synagogal and other courts (compare "fighting against God" on the part of those who persecute the disciples, to whom "God has given the Holy Spirit" [Acts 5:32, 39], and Stephen's persecutors as "always resisting the Holy Spirit," who had filled him with "grace and power" to perform "great wonders and signs" [Acts 6:5, 8, 10; 7:51, 55]). The disciples shouldn't worry ahead of time about their self-defense, because the Spirit whom Jesus' and their persecutors slander will teach them "the things that are necessary to say." "Necessary" describes those things as fitting God's will and plan, of which the Holy Spirit is cognizant. "In that very hour" describes the Spirit's teaching as right on time (among other examples of the fulfillment of this promise, see Acts 4:8). So Jesus has proceeded from words of confession and disowning (12:8–9) through words of opposition and slander (12:10) to words of self-defense (12:11–12).

JESUS' TEACHING AGAINST GREED
Luke 12:13–21

In 12:1–12 Jesus taught morality in speech. Now he teaches economic morality. To attract people of moral sensibility, Luke is continuing to feature the high moral standards in Jesus' teaching.

12:13–15: And someone from the crowd said to him, "Teacher, tell my brother to divide [= share] the inheritance with me." ¹⁴But he said to him, "Man, who appointed me a judge or a divider over you [two brothers]?" ¹⁵And he told them [the crowd], "Look out and guard yourselves against every [kind of] greed, because the life of no one consists in the abounding of his possessions." The Old Testament contains laws of inheritance (see Numbers 27:1–11; 36:1–12; Deuteronomy 21:15–17), and teachers are supposed to know the Law. So Jesus is addressed with "Teacher" in the hope that he'll apply the Law to a dispute over inheritance. "Tell my brother to divide the inheritance with me" implies that the brother was resisting such a division and that by himself the petitioner of Jesus couldn't force his brother to divide the inheritance. Jesus' addressing the petitioner with "Man" doesn't show any disrespect—rather, that Jesus doesn't know the petitioner's name (compare 5:20; 22:58, 60). Jesus' question, "Who appointed me . . . ?" implies the answer, "Nobody," and amounts to a refusal to act as a judge by dividing the brothers' inheritance between them. He came to teach, but not to judge in that way. So he addresses the crowd with some teaching against greed such as that which motivated both his petitioner and the petitioner's brother. Literally, "greed" means the desire "to have more," with the understanding that the "more" is more than enough for basic needs. "*Every* [kind of greed]" enlarges the warning against greed beyond the bounds of disputes over inheritance. The doubling of the warning with both "look out" and "guard yourselves" underlines the danger of succumbing to greed (compare 8:14; 16:19–31; 18:18–30). And giving the reason why greed is dangerous is Jesus' statement that no one's life consists in the abounding—that is, the ever-increasing amount—of his possessions. Jesus doesn't use the word "livelihood." He uses the word "life," which means something more than those material things that make living possible and pleasurable (food, clothing, shelter, and so on). In this case, "life" may carry overtones of eternal life as well as of good relations with brothers and others (compare the inheriting of eternal life in 10:25; 18:18).

12:16–21: And he spoke a parable to them, saying, "The land of a certain rich man bore well [= yielded

abundantly]. ¹⁷**And he was reasoning in himself, saying, 'What should I do, because I don't have anywhere to store my crops?' ¹⁸And he said, 'I'll do this: I'll tear down my barns and build bigger ones, and I'll store there all my grain and goods. ¹⁹And I'll say to myself** [literally, "my soul," but "soul" is often used for "self"], **"Self, you have many goods laid up for many years. Take it easy. Eat. Drink. Have a good time."' ²⁰But God said to him, 'Nitwit! This night they're demanding back your self** [literally, "soul," here in the sense of physical "life"]. **And to whom will the things you've gotten ready belong?' ²¹Thus will be the person who amasses treasure for himself and isn't rich in relation to God."** The rich man's bumper crop exceeded his storage facilities. Even though they were multiple ("barns")—after all, he was already rich—their capacity fell short. His greed (the desire to have more) made him purpose to tear down his current barns and build bigger ones, there to store "*all* [his] grain." He had no thought of doing anything else with even a part of it. "And goods" may refer to other possessions, too, but probably describes the grain itself as "goods" in that the rich man falsely thinks of this excess of grain as good for him. That is to say, he falsely thinks that his "life consists in the abounding of his possessions" (12:15). Talking to himself about his goods as so "many" that they'll give him an easy life of eating and drinking (food and wine, of course) in constant revelry "for *many* years"—this talking betrays self-indulgence. By replacing the phrase "all my grain and goods," the phrase "many goods laid up for many years" adds emphasis on a false sense of security. And the staccato-like succession of "Take it easy," "Eat," "Drink," and "Have a good time" implies that the rich man can hardly wait to do these things. God's addressing him with "Nitwit" exposes the foolishness of his intention to amass more wealth for a long and supposedly good life. He'll die "*this* night," the very night that he's talking to himself in that vein. But who are the "they" who'll demand back his life? Jesus doesn't say. So it's only the losing of life that gets accented. Nor does Jesus indicate who'll get the rich man's amassed wealth. So another accent falls solely on the losing of it. "Amasses treasure *for himself*" is opposed to being "rich *in relation to God*." But what does it mean to be rich in relation to God? And what should the rich man have done with his increasing wealth? Again Jesus doesn't say, at least not here in this passage. So again the emphasis falls solely on the insecurity of wealth, the foolishness of amassing it, and the mistake in thinking that your life consists in material possessions. These are the moral lessons that Jesus teaches on the topic of personal economics.

SEEKING GOD'S KINGDOM RATHER THAN PHYSICAL PROVISIONS
Luke 12:22–34

12:22–23: And he said to his disciples [after addressing the crowd in 12:13–21], **"On account of this** [that is, because life doesn't consist of possessions, as illustrated in the parable of the nitwitted rich man (12:15–21)] **I tell you, don't worry about the soul** [= yourself, with particular reference to the part of you that animates your body and therefore represents physical life], **what you should eat** ['should' not in the sense of obligation but in the sense of possibility, given the spare diets of most people then], **nor about the body, what you should clothe yourselves with** [given the financial inability of most people to afford much clothing]. ²³**For the soul is more than food, and the body** [is more] **than clothing** [in that food only sustains the soul, or self, as physical life and in that clothing only protects the body]." Jesus doesn't say in what respect the soul and the body are more than food and clothing, so that his point is only, but importantly, that the disciples shouldn't be worried about having enough food and clothing. His address has shifted to them because only they come under the care of God the Father. Nondisciples aren't God's children.

12:24–31: "**Consider the ravens** [by noting] **that they neither sow** [seed] **nor reap** [crops (contrast the rich man in 12:16–21)]. **They don't have a storeroom or a barn** [not even one, yet the rich man had multiple barns (12:18)]. **And God provides them with food. How much more valuable are you than birds** [especially than ravens, a variety of crows despised by human beings]! ²⁵**And who of you by worrying can add a bit to his lifespan?**" Implied answer: None of you can. ²⁶"**So if you can't** [do] **even an extremely little thing** [like adding a bit to your lifespan], **why do you worry about the remaining things** [like getting food and clothing]? ²⁷**Consider the lilies** [though some other kind of wild-flower, or wildflowers in general, may be in view] [by noting] **how they grow. They neither toil** [as men did in the fields for food] **nor spin** [fibers into thread or yarn, as women did at home for clothing]." The lilies grow without working. "**Yet I tell you, not even Solomon in all his glory was arrayed like one of these.**" The splendor of Solomon's royal robes didn't match that of even one lily! ²⁸"**And if God dresses the grass in this way** [with lilies of greater glory than Solomon's raiment], **though it** [the grass] **is in the field today and thrown into an oven tomorrow** [for burning; that is, despite the short life of wild grass in contrast with Solomon's and your much longer lives], **how much more** [will he dress] **you, people of little faith.**" Disciples who worry about food and clothing betray little faith in God. ²⁹"**And you** [my disciples]—**don't seek what you should eat and what you should drink, and don't fret** [about such things]. ³⁰**For all the nations of the world seek after these things, and your Father knows that you need these things.**" Two reasons, then, neither to seek them nor to fret over whether you'll get them: (1) you're different from nondisciples in that God is your heavenly Father but not theirs; and (2) like a good father he'll provide you with food, drink, and clothing. ³¹"**Rather, seek his reign; and these things will be added to you.**" In addition to what? Read on.

12:32: "**Don't fear, little flock; for your Father was pleased to give you the kingdom.**" So disciples will receive provisions of food, drink, and clothing in addition to the kingdom—that is, the benefits of God's reign, the "peace" of salvation and eventually rulership (22:29–30). For "kingdom," "reign," and "rulership" all translate the same Greek word. And it brought God pleasure to give his kingdom to Jesus' disciples. The past tense of "was pleased" indicates that although full enjoyment of all the kingdom's benefits awaits the future, God has *already* given his kingdom to Jesus' disciples. As a result, they needn't fear they'll lack the provisions of food, drink, and clothing any more than a flock of sheep need to fear their shepherd won't lead them to green pastures and still waters (Psalm 23:1–2). Jesus' description of the flock as "little" draws a contrast with "all the nations of the world." God's pleasure in giving the kingdom to Jesus' disciples shows that they shouldn't think he cares little for them because they're only a little flock.

The disciples are to seek God's reign rather than physical provisions. But how are they to seek it even though he has already given it to them? *12:33–34:* "**Sell your possessions, and give** [the proceeds as] **alms** [to the poor]." As traveling evangelists given board and room by receptive hosts, you won't need those possessions (see 10:1–12); but the poor do need your charity, which will add good deeds to the good words of the gospel. So seeking God's rule starts with divestiture of possessions, proceeds to charitable giving, and eventuates in evangelistic travel. "**Make for yourselves money-bags that don't get old** [= wear out], **an inexhaustible treasure in heaven, where no thief comes near, nor does a moth cause ruin** [as moths ruin clothing on earth]. ³⁴**For where your treasure is, there will be your heart too.**" You're not to take a money-bag (singular) on your evangelistic travels (10:4), but you'll be manufacturing for yourselves everlasting money-bags (plural) filled with treasure that can never be depleted by spending—and this in the safe called heaven. Nor can any thief steal the treasure, or even come close to heaven so as to steal the treasure. Nor can a moth ruin the treasure (compared here to expensive clothing, more glorious than even Solomon's [12:27]), for the flight to the clothes closet called heaven is too far for earthbound moths. And you'll make such treasure in heaven "for *yourselves*" because "your *heart*" will be in heaven with your treasure. Your heart—that is, your inmost concerns—inevitably follows your treasure. It isn't that your treasure will be where your heart is, so that you'll have treasure in heaven if your heart is there. (Meanwhile, you could have treasure on earth so long as your heart was in heaven.) No, it's the other way around: the location of your treasure determines the location of your heart.

READINESS FOR THE SECOND COMING
Luke 12:35–48

12:35–38: "'**Your loins are to be girded**' [that is, in preparation for the work of evangelism, compared to harvesting in 10:2, the lower part of your outer robe is to be lifted up and tucked inside a belt cinched around your waist, so that you can have freedom of movement (Exodus 12:11)] **and your lamps burning** [in anticipation of what now follows]. ³⁶**And you—[be] like men waiting to welcome their own master at the time he gets back from a wedding celebration, in order that when he comes and knocks** [on the door], **they may open** [it] **for him immediately.**" "Their own master" implies that the "men" are slaves. It wouldn't do for slaves to keep their master waiting outside his own locked door while they groggily wake up and shuffle to the door to unlock and open it. Jesus doesn't say whether the wedding celebration is the master's or someone else's. So the stress falls solely on readiness to open the door immediately. ³⁷**"Fortunate [are] those slaves whom the master, on coming** [back from the wedding celebration], **will find awake** [and therefore ready to open the door immediately]. **Amen I tell you that he'll gird himself** [as I told you *your* loins should be girded (12:35)] **and have them recline** [at table for a formal meal] **and, on coming alongside** [them], **will serve them** [a meal]." Those alert slaves will enjoy the good fortune of having their master serve them as they've served him. What a reversal of roles! Yet that is what Jesus promises and now repeats for emphasis even after previously emphasizing the promise with "Amen I say to you": ³⁸**"And if during the second—and if during the third—watch** [that is, during the last two thirds of the night] **he should come and find them so** [that is, find them awake], **fortunate are those** [slaves]." The wedding celebration will probably have occupied the first third of the night, so that by the last two thirds of the night it would take considerable effort for the slaves to stay awake. So the master will show his appreciation of their staying awake. Thus their good fortune.

12:39-40: **"But know this, that if the houseowner had known at what particular hour the thief is coming, he wouldn't have let the thief dig through his house."** We'd say "break into" rather than "dig through"; but their houses often had windowless mudbrick walls, so that thieves might literally dig through the walls. ⁴⁰**You too** [as well as the houseowner]**—get ready, because the Son of Man is coming at an hour that you don't think probable."** Jesus shifts from the master of slaves to the owner of a house. The slavemaster represented the Lord Jesus, a representation made easy by the fact that "master" and "Lord" go back to the same Greek word. The slaves represented his disciples; his coming home to them represented his second coming; and his serving them a meal represented the messianic banquet (see 13:29; 22:29-30). Now the houseowner represents a disciple, and the coming of a thief represents the second coming of Jesus ("the Son of Man"). The oddity of "at what particular hour the thief *is coming*," where we'd expect "at what particular hour the thief *might come*"—this oddity sets up for a parallel with "the Son of Man *is coming*" and stresses the certainty of his coming (as though he were already on his way). Since an hour was the shortest unit of time used by people then, "at what particular *hour*" describes as unknowable the exact time of his coming. "At an hour that you don't think probable" intensifies this unknowability. The thief's digging through the owner's house represents the Son of Man's surprising the unprepared

with his coming (and has nothing to do with thievery). "But know this" means you should understand that the unknowability demands constant preparedness. Not to "let the thief dig through his house" is not to be caught unprepared by the Son of Man's coming. And "get ready" means to be prepared by girding one's loins and doing the work of harvesting converts to God's rule.

12:41-44: **And Peter said, "Lord, are you telling this parable for us or also for all** [people]." ⁴²**And the Lord said, "Who then is the faithful, wise manager, whom the master will put in charge of his domestic help to give** [them their] **food allowance on schedule** [compare Psalm 104:27]**?** ⁴³**Fortunate** [is] **that slave whom his master, on coming, will find doing so.** ⁴⁴**I tell you truly that he'll put him in charge of all his possessions."** "Then" draws an inference from the preceding stress on unknowability. Since "Lord" and "master" translate the very same Greek word, Peter's addressing Jesus with "Lord" and Luke's calling Jesus "Lord" confirm that "the master" in the preceding parable of 12:35-38 represented the Lord Jesus, and also that "the master" in the parable just starting likewise represents the Lord Jesus. Peter asks Jesus about that parable and the one in 12:39-40 concerning "the houseowner" as though they're a single parable in two parts. Peter's question whether Jesus is telling the composite parable only for the disciples or for a general audience ("all [people]") sounds as though Jesus isn't finished telling it. So instead of answering the question, Jesus picks up on Peter's use of the present tense ("*are* you telling") so as to continue telling "this parable" in a third constituent part. As in the earlier parts, the coming of the master represents again the second coming of the Lord Jesus as the Son of Man. "The manager" turns out to be a "slave." (In the Roman Empire of the first century, masters often made one of their slaves a manager.) The combination of "master/Lord" and "slave" makes clear enough the answer to Peter's question: Jesus is addressing "this parable" only to his disciples, at least those professing to be such. "The faithful, wise manager" is a true disciple. The combination of "faithful" and "wise" indicates that it's wise to be faithful in carrying out the master's—that is, Jesus'—orders. The present order to give fellow domestic slaves their food rations on time teaches that a disciple, particularly one in a high position, should treat his fellow disciples well. The good fortune of the manager whom the master finds doing so when he comes back—that good fortune consists in a promotion to managership over all the master's possessions. In other words, Jesus will richly reward his disciple who treats other disciples well.

12:45-46: **"But if that slave says in his heart, 'My master is delaying to come,' and starts beating the male servants and the female servants and both eating and drinking and getting drunk,** ⁴⁶**the master of that slave will come on a day that he doesn't expect** [him to come] **and at an hour that he's not cognizant of. And he'll slice him in two and put his portion with the unfaithful."** "But *if* that slave says . . ." sets out a possibility that shouldn't turn into an actuality (contrast "Who then *is* the faithful, wise manager . . . ?" and "whom his master . . . *will* find doing so" [12:42–43]). "But if that slave . . . *starts*" implies some length of time remaining till his master's coming. As a manager, the slave could abuse his authority by beating the subordinate servants who make up the rest of his master's domestic help, and also by indulging himself with excessive eating and drinking—so long as the master is absent. But such abusiveness and self-indulgence breed carelessness, so that the master's coming—though delayed, and precisely *because* delayed—takes the manager by surprise. "On a day . . . and at an hour" denotes the next shortest and very shortest units of time used by people then and therefore stresses again (as in 12:39) the impossibility of knowing beforehand the exact time of Jesus' return. "Slice him in two" warns of horrible judgment for unethical behavior, and "put his portion with the unfaithful" means that Jesus will judge as false those professing disciples who engage in such behavior. As false, their portion—that is, their inheritance—will be in hell, where they'll spend eternity with unbelievers, those who are "unfaithful" in the sense of not being full of faith.

12:47–48: "And that slave who knew his master's will and didn't get ready or act in accordance with his will will be beaten with many [blows]. **48But the** [slave] **who didn't know** [his master's will] **and did things deserving of blows will be beaten with few** [of them]. **And as to everyone to whom much has been given—much will be required from him. And as to the one with whom much has been deposited—they'll ask him** [for] **more."** Now the figure of speech for punishment in the hereafter changes from being sliced in two and given an inheritance with unbelievers to suffering a beating. The slaves in view are still those who profess to be disciples of the Lord Jesus. Here he teaches degrees of punishment according to knowledge and ignorance of what their master (representing Jesus) wants them to do. Hell won't be the same for everybody who's there. It'll be bad for all but worse for some than for others. But even the slave who's ignorant of his master's will gets punished, for such a slave will still have done things deserving of punishment. The giving and depositing of "much" relates back to the managership delegated to a slave in 12:42, but this time in terms of financial responsibility rather than the distribution of food rations. Who are "they" who'll "ask him [for] more [that is, for the return on an investment]"? Jesus doesn't say. So the accent falls alone on the principle that the larger the task, the larger the responsibility. Thus go the moral demands of Jesus as regards his disciples, a teaching Luke puts forward to attract people of high moral standards.

DISTRESS AND DIVISION
Luke 12:49–53

12:49–50: "I've come to throw fire onto the earth, and do I ever wish it was already kindled! 50And I have a baptism to be baptized with, and how I'm distressed till it has been finished [= accomplished]**!"** "I've come to throw fire" indicates a purpose of Jesus' present ministry. "Onto the earth" implies a throwing of fire from above—as from heaven, for example (compare 9:54: "Lord, do you want us to tell fire to come down from heaven"; but note the difference between *telling* it to come down from heaven and *throwing* it down from heaven). "And do I ever wish it was already kindled!" requires the throwing of fire onto the earth to be a future event as opposed to anything Jesus is already doing or has done. In Acts 2:1–4 Luke will describe the disciples' being "filled with the Holy Spirit" on the Day of Pentecost as originating "from heaven" and as appearing in the form of "tongues . . . as if of fire" coming "onto each one of them." In Acts 2:33 Peter then interprets this phenomenon as the exalted Jesus' having "poured out" the Holy Spirit. So just as Jesus will portray the pouring out of the Holy Spirit from heaven at Pentecost as a baptism in the Holy Spirit (Acts 1:5), here in Luke 12:49 he portrays the pouring out of the Holy Spirit from heaven as a casting of fire onto the earth. He wishes that this fire of the Holy Spirit which will sit on the disciples was already kindled, because between now and then (the Day of Pentecost) lies his suffering and death, which he portrays as a baptism that distresses him till it's accomplished. According to 22:43–44 Jesus was "in an [emotional] struggle" as he "prayed more earnestly" in Gethsemane on the eve of his crucifixion, and "his sweat became as if [it was] drops of blood going down onto the ground/earth [but compare his casting of fire 'onto the earth/ground' here in 12:49]." Blood flows freely; so the comparison of Jesus' sweat with falling drops of blood means that he was so drenched with sweat that it was as though he was baptized in it. Hence the portrayal of his coming passion in terms of a baptism. Thus his baptism in suffering and death while he's on earth will enable him upon his ascension to heaven to baptize his disciples in the Holy Spirit, that is, to fill them with the Holy Spirit, to pour out on them the Holy Spirit, or—in terms of the present passage—to cast fire ("tongues as if of fire") onto the earth. And Jesus' longing to get the job done despite the cost to himself exhibits a benevolent regard for those who belong to him.

12:51–53: "Do you suppose that I've come on the scene to give peace in the earth? No, I tell you! But rather, [to give] **division. 52For from now on, five in one household will be divided three against two and two against three. 53They'll be divided father against son and son against father, mother against daughter and daughter against mother, mother-in-law against her daughter-in-law and daughter-in-law against mother-in-law** [compare Micah 7:6]**."** Jesus has been addressing his disciples ever since 12:22. Here, after mentioning his own distress at having to undergo a baptism into suffering and death for their benefit, he tells them of family divisions they'll have to endure for his sake. Some in their families will oppose their discipleship, with the result of discord instead of peace. Jesus came to bring peace in the form of salvation (see 2:14; Acts 10:36, for example). But he didn't come to bring peace in the form of family unity as such or for its own sake. The peace of salvation takes precedence over domestic peace. Therefore if the gospel of peace causes divisions due to belief versus unbelief, so be it. "Do you suppose . . . ?" warns against the possibility of thinking otherwise, as would be easy to do because of family loyalty. "No, I tell you! But rather . . ." emphasizes the warning. And "from now on" warns the disciples to expect domestic divisions to begin immediately and to last for the duration, that is, till Jesus comes back (compare 9:26). We might have expected "father-in-law against son-in-law" (and vice versa) to complement "father against son" (and vice versa) the way "mother-in-law against daughter-in-law" (and vice versa) complements "mother against daughter" (and vice versa). But marriage didn't make a man belong to his wife's family as it did make her belong to his family. Hence the lack of "father-in-law against son-in-law".

NOW OR NEVER
Luke 12:54–13:9

12:54–56: And he was saying also to the crowds, "Whenever you see a cloud rising in the west, immediately you say, 'A downpour of rain is coming,' and so it happens. ⁵⁵And whenever [you see] **a southwest wind blowing, you say, 'It'll be scorching,' and** [so] **it happens. ⁵⁶Hypocrites, you have knowledge to appraise the face of the earth** [where wind blows] **and of the sky** [where clouds appear]. **But how is it you don't have knowledge to appraise the present time?"** The plural in "the crowds" revives Luke's emphasis on Jesus' magnetism. "A cloud rising in the west" brought rain from moisture that had evaporated out of the Mediterranean Sea. "A southwest wind" brought heat from the desert that we call the Sinai Peninsula. "When*ever* you see" (twice) and "*immediately* you say" stress the facility with which the crowds read these weather signs. "And so it happens!" (twice) stresses the accuracy of the crowds' readings. "Hypocrites" highlights the difference between knowing weather signs and not knowing the signs in Jesus' ministry that the time of salvation has arrived. The question beginning, "But how is it that . . . ?" expresses astonishment, if not disgust, at such ignorance. The signs are so visible in Jesus' deeds and words that it should be just as easy to recognize in "the present time" the time of salvation as it is to recognize the coming of a rainstorm or a scorcher.

12:57–59: "And why too don't you judge for yourselves [what's] **the right thing** [to do]**? ⁵⁸For while you** [singular, as for the rest of this paragraph] **are going with your accuser to a ruler, on the way give effort to be released from him** [your accuser, by settling with him out of court], **lest he drag you down to the judge** [for rulers acted as judges]**; and the judge will give you over to the bailiff** [an officer of the court], **and the bailiff will throw you into prison. ⁵⁹I tell you, by no means will you come out of there till you've given back** [to your accuser] **also the last lepton** [the smallest of coins]**."** So you owe your accuser money, and he's hauling you to court for nonpayment of your debt. Better to settle out of court than to land in debtors' prison, for there you'll have no way of earning money to pay off the debt. "*Also* the last lepton" implies that your accuser might have settled for less on the way to court, or at least that he won't settle for even the smallest coin less once you're in prison. (A lepton was worth only a tiny fraction of a denarius, the daily wage of a manual laborer, and thus worth only a few minutes of work.) "I tell you" and "by no means" accent the calamity of your being thrown into prison. And the change from "*lest* he drag you down to the judge" to "the judge *will* give you over to the bailiff, and the bailiff *will* cast you into prison"—this change accents the certainty of calamity by failure to do what's right to do while there's still time to do it. "For yourselves" indicates that the crowds are perfectly capable of coming up with a correct judgment if only they will. The phrase, "And why too," in the question, "And why too don't you judge for yourselves [what's] the right thing [to do]?" correlates this question with the question in 12:56, "But how is it you don't have knowledge to appraise the present time?" Together with 12:54–56, then, 12:57–59 warns the crowds that they'd better do the right thing by taking advantage of the present time of salvation, and do so before it's too late—that is, before Judgment Day.

13:1: And at that very time there arrived some who were reporting to him about the Galileans whose blood Pilate had mixed with their sacrifices. "That very time" refers to the time at which Jesus has just been speaking in chapter 12. Since the Galileans had to have been offering their sacrifices at the temple down south in Jerusalem, not in Galilee up north, and since Pilate was the Roman governor of Judea, where Jerusalem was located, but not of Galilee, he must have slain the Galileans in Jerusalem, so that their blood was mixed, so to speak, with the blood of their animal sacrifices. We know nothing more about this incident, such as why Pilate had these Galileans slain.

13:2–5: And answering, Jesus told them, "Do you suppose that because they suffered these things, these Galileans had become worse sinners than all [other] **Galileans? ³No, I tell you! Rather, unless you repent, you'll all perish likewise. ⁴Or those eighteen on whom the tower in Siloam fell and killed them— do you suppose they'd become greater debtors than all** [other] **Jerusalem-dwellers? ⁵No, I tell you! Rather, unless you repent, you'll all perish in the same way."** We don't know anything more about this latter incident, either; but by introducing it on his own, Jesus balances the death of Galileans with the death of Jerusalemites and thus doubles the force of his accompanying warning. Since sins count as moral debts owed to God, "debtors" here means the same as "sinners" (compare 7:41–43, 48 with comments). Jesus denies that those who perished were "greater sinners/debtors" than other Galileans and other Jerusalemites. But this denial accepts that those who perished were in fact sinners and perished for their sins. A tower's falling on eighteen Jerusalemites can have happened only for sins against God. And Pilate wouldn't have cared that certain Galileans had sinned against God, so that God must have used Pilate as his instrument to punish them (not *for* offering sacrifices but *while* offering sacrifices). At first blush, the perishing seems limited to physical death. But the statements of Jesus that unless his hearers ("the crowds" of 12:54) repent of their sins, they'll "all perish likewise/in the same way" can hardly mean that they'll all die physically—of course they will, for everybody does—or that they'll all die violently (as the Galileans did) or accidentally (as the Jerusalemites did)—of course they won't, for many will die of natural causes. So perishing has the added meaning of eternal lostness, as in 9:24–25; 17:33. The repeated "No, I tell you!" and "Rather" underline the necessity of repentance from sins if you're to avoid the loss of eternal life. "You *all*" allows for no exceptions. Jesus doesn't hesitate to use a scare tactic in the service of his call for moral reform. But it's more than a tactic. It's the truth (compare 10:13–15).

13:6–9: And he was telling this parable: "A certain [man] **had a fig tree, planted in his vineyard. And he came seeking fruit in it and didn't find** [any]. **⁷And he said to the vineyard worker, 'Behold, for three years now I'm coming** [= have been coming] **seeking fruit in this fig tree and am not finding** [any]. **Therefore, cut it down. Why should it also deplete the soil** [as well as fail to bear fruit]**?' ⁸And answering, he** [the vineyard worker] **says to him, 'Sir, let it be for this year too, until I dig around it and throw manure** [on it as fertilizer]. **⁹And should it produce fruit in the coming** [year]**—but if** [it does] **not in fact** [produce fruit]**, you shall** [have] **it cut down.'"** It's often said that the fig tree represents the nation of Israel; but there's no indication in Luke's text that it does, and the preceding context, dealing with individual repentance (see especially the singular "you" in 12:58–59), favors the same here. The figure of fruit recalls John the baptizer's calling for "fruits in keeping with repentance" (3:8) and in this way ties the present parable to the immediately preceding theme of repentance (13:1–5). "Behold" and the vivid present tense in "now I'm coming" highlight the lack of such fruit three years running. (Fig trees are supposed to bear annually.) "Cut it down" symbolizes the eternal punishment that perishing alluded to in 13:3, 5. Since the fig tree had been planted in a vineyard, the depletion of the soil refers to the tree's robbing the soil of nutrients that otherwise would nourish the grapevines. The word translated with "Sir" is the same as the one translated elsewhere with "owner," "master," "lord," and "Lord." Thus the "Sir" who's owner of the vineyard and possibly slavemaster of the vineyard worker represents Jesus the Lord. The vineyard worker requests an additional year for digging around the tree and fertilizing the resultant fallow ground in hope that this extra effort will lead to fruit-bearing the next year. That is to say, only a short time may be left for producing fruits in keeping with repentance. "*Should* it produce fruit" leaves the likelihood of repentance in

suspense, though. Worse yet, there's nothing about sparing the tree should it produce fruit in the coming year. It's as though fruit-bearing is so *un*likely that sparing the tree on that account isn't worth mentioning. On the other hand, "but if [it does] not in fact [bear fruit], you shall [have] it cut down" stresses the certainty of eternal loss for failure to bring forth the fruits of repentance. The owner gives no response to the request for another year's opportunity. This lack means that people can't count on even a short time remaining for repentance. So repent now!

THE GLORIOUS GROWTH OF GOD'S RULE IN JESUS' GOOD DEEDS
Luke 13:10–21

13:10–13: And he was teaching in one of the synagogues on the Sabbath. ¹¹And behold, a woman who had a spirit of infirmity [and had had it] **for eighteen years and was bent double and couldn't unbend at all! ¹²And on seeing her, Jesus summoned** [her] **and said to her, "Woman, you're released from your infirmity," ¹³and he placed** [his] **hands on her. And instantly she was straightened up, and she began glorifying God.** Another of Jesus' miracles shows happily that—despite prior warnings—it's still the time of salvation. "Teaching in one of the synagogues on the Sabbath" exhibits Jesus' piety and loyalty to the Jewish religion and its traditions. Luke wants his audience to know that Jesus was no renegade. "Behold . . . !" makes a woman's condition the object of an exclamation because of its severity. The severity will, in turn, heighten Jesus' success. The woman is too weak to stand up straight. "At all" raises her inability to the highest degree: she can't unbend herself even partially. The eighteen years of her suffering this weakness exacerbates the difficulty of her case. And the causing of her weakness by a spirit puts her case in terms of a contest between God's reign, carried out by Jesus, and Satan's reign, carried out by the spirit of infirmity. Jesus' addressing the woman with "Woman" shows respect, not disrespect, and simply implies that he doesn't know her name. "You're released from your infirmity" states a matter of fact and implies that the woman's weakness has kept her in a state of bondage, an appropriate way of describing her condition given its having been caused by a spirit. By placing his hands on her, Jesus transfers his power to her, so that it replaces her weakness. "She *was* straightened up" (rather than "she straightened up") testifies to the effect of his power. And her glorifying of God points out the good religious effect of Jesus' having delivered her from the spirit of infirmity. "*Began* glorifying God" makes this an ongoing effect (see the comments on 2:20).

13:14–17: And answering [= responding], **the ruler of the synagogue, angry because Jesus had healed on the Sabbath, was saying to the crowd, "There are six days on which it's necessary to work** [compare Exodus 20:9 = Deuteronomy 5:13: 'Six days you shall labor and do all your work']. **So coming on them** [those workdays], **be healed, and not on the day of the Sabbath** [which means 'rest'].**"** The ruler of the synagogue had responsibility for the order of worship and regarded Jesus' healing as working on the Sabbath and therefore as violating it. [15]**And the Lord answered him and said, "Hypocrites, each of you unties his ox or donkey from** [its] **stall on the Sabbath, doesn't he, and on leading** [it] **away has it drink?** [16]**And it was necessary, wasn't it, for this** [woman], **being a daughter of Abraham whom Satan had bound—behold, eighteen years!—to be untied from this bond on the day of the Sabbath?"** [17]**And as he was saying these things, all those who were opposed to him were being put to shame; and all the crowd were rejoicing at all the glorious things being brought about by him.** Despite his anger at Jesus for healing on the Sabbath, the synagogue ruler addresses the crowd rather than Jesus. The ruler is trying to exercise authority over the crowd. Is he also afraid to tangle with Jesus? The ruler's telling the crowd to come for healing on days of the week other than the Sabbath implies that the healed woman had come to the synagogue for Jesus to heal her, and indirectly blames her for doing so. By saying that "*the Lord* answered him," Luke underlines the overpowering authority of Jesus' answer. Though answering the synagogue ruler, Jesus uses the address "Hypocrites." The plural implies that the other elders of the synagogue supported their chairman in his anger at Jesus and indirect rebuke of the woman. "Hypocrites" intimates the discrepancy which Jesus is about to note. It's that the synagogue elders treat their animals better on the Sabbath than they want him to treat human beings on the Sabbath. "*Each* of you" keeps all the elders on the hook. Untying their animals on the Sabbath contrasts with their having wanted to keep the bent woman "bound" on the Sabbath. Adding to this contrast is her being not just another human being in contrast with animals, but also her being "a daughter [= descendant] of Abraham," a full-fledged member of God's chosen people, equal in this respect to a male. And just as it's horribly inappropriate that none other than Satan should have bound through one of his spirits a member of God's chosen people, it's wonderfully appropriate that she should be untied from this bond on the very day that God set aside for his people to rest—especially after eighteen years of bondage. Jesus' rhetorical questions are so argumentatively persuasive that his opponents are embarrassed ("put to shame") before the very members of the synagogue over whom they have charge. Their embarrassment takes place while Jesus is still speaking and covers *all* of them. None of them is able to slink into the shadows and out of view. Just as they "*all* were being put to shame," "*all* the crowd were rejoicing at *all* the glorious things being brought about by him." Besides the elders, none in the crowd failed to be caught up in the joy of the woman's release (compare 2:10: "For behold, I'm announcing to you as good news a great joy"). "All the glorious things" implies many other such joyful deliverances and the crowd's knowing about them. The description of them as "glorious"

draws a stark contrast with Jesus' putting the synagogue elders "to shame." And having rightly given glory to God (13:13), the crowd now give credit to Jesus as God's instrument ("being brought about by him").

13:18–19: Therefore he was saying, "What is God's reign like, and to what should I liken it? [19]**It's like a grain of mustard which a man, on taking** [it], **threw into his own garden. And it grew and turned into a tree, and the birds of the sky nested in its branches."** "Therefore" means that Jesus spoke this parable because "all the crowd were rejoicing at all the glorious things being brought about by him" (13:17). All these glorious things are represented, then, by the growth of a grain of mustard into "a tree" used by birds for nesting (see the comments on Matthew 13:31–32 for the use of "a grain" rather than "a seed" and for the hyperbole of "a tree"). The other way around, God's reign is growing large, despite its small beginning, in all the glorious deeds of Jesus. Similarly in **13:20–21: And again he said, "To what should I liken God's reign.** [21]**It's like leaven which a woman, on taking** [it], **hid in three satons** [about a bushel] **of wheat flour until the whole was leavened."** For leaven, see the comments on 12:1. Just as it was hyperbolic for Jesus to call the mustard plant a tree, it's also hyperbolic for him to speak of a woman's leavening a bushel of wheat flour to make one super-large lump of dough. And again, the leavening of "the whole" represents God's reign as growing very large in all the glorious deeds of Jesus. (Though the reign of God will take over the whole world at the end of time, here Jesus doesn't refer to that event.)

THE LOSTNESS AND LASTNESS OF MANY
Luke 13:22–30

13:22–27: And he was traveling through [the region] **city by city and town by town, teaching and doing his travel to Jerusalem.** The theme of travel, which appeals to the interest of Luke's audience, surfaces again in an emphatic double expression ("traveling through . . . and doing his travel"). Moreover, Jesus' traveling to Jerusalem city by city and town by town (see 9:51 for the start of this travelogue) forecasts the traveling of his witnesses from Jerusalem city by city and town by town (see Acts 1:8 and the whole book of Acts); and teaching is both what he does and what they will do. [23]**And someone said to him, "Lord, are the ones being saved few?" And he** [Jesus] **said to them,** [24]**"Strive to enter through the narrow door, because many, I tell you, will seek to enter and won't have the strength** [to do so]. [25]**Once the houseowner has gotten up and locked the door and you begin to stand outside and knock on the door, saying, 'Lord, open up for us,' and answering, he'll say, 'I don't know you, where you're from,'** [26]**then you'll begin to say, 'We ate and drank in your sight, and you taught in our broad** [streets].' [27]**And speaking to you, he'll say, 'I don't know you, where** [you're] **from. Go away from me, all you workers of unrighteousness.'"** As "Lord," the houseowner represents the Lord Jesus (contrast 12:39, where the houseowner portrays a disciple).

By addressing Jesus with "Lord," the questioner acknowledges Jesus' authority. But Jesus doesn't answer the question whether those who are being saved are few. Instead, he issues a warning, heightened by "I tell you," that the *unsaved* will be many, and therefore urges his audience to strive to enter through the narrow door. Striving to enter through the narrow door means taking pains to become Jesus' disciple right now so as to enter the door of salvation at the Last Judgment before that door is shut. Nondisciples will seek to enter after disciples have gotten in but won't have the strength to enter. For the door will be locked as well as shut, no amount of pounding on it will force it open, and congestion at the door will be too great. The narrowness of the door symbolizes that only disciples will be able to squeeze through. Not even a plea introduced with "Lord" and an appeal to having eaten and drunk in Jesus' sight and to his having taught in their main streets will succeed for the nondisciples. It'll draw only a terse command, repeated for emphasis, to depart (and departure from Jesus the Savior means departure from salvation itself) and the verdict, "Guilty of working unrighteousness," which particularly in Luke's Gospel includes injustice. In that culture, to know someone you had to know where the person was from. Not to know his or her place of origin was not to know the person him- or herself. So by itself neither proximity to Jesus nor his proximity to people makes them his acquaintances. Only the acceptance and practice of his teaching does. For his high moral standards exclude "workers of unrighteousness" from the circle of his acquaintances. As in 12:54–13:9, then, take advantage of your present opportunity; for dilly-dallying can only lead to eternal exclusion.

13:28–30: "Weeping and gritting of teeth will be there [outside the kingdom of God], **when you see Abraham and Isaac and Jacob and all the prophets in God's kingdom** [the realm of his reign] **but you being thrown outside."** The figure of being *shut* out in 13:25 has turned into the figure of being *thrown* out. 29**"And people will come from east and west, and from north and south, and recline** [at the celebratory messianic banquet] **in God's kingdom.** 30**And behold, there are last people who'll be first, and there are first people who'll be last."** The pain of exclusion from salvation in God's kingdom will cause weeping and gritting of teeth. Intensifying this pain will be the seeing of the patriarchs and all the prophets inside that kingdom at the very moment you as the unsaved are being thrown out. And in contrast with you who ate and drank in Jesus' presence and heard him teach on your main streets, people from the four directions of the compass who never had direct contact with him but heard about him later, repented, and believed in him—they'll come and enjoy the banquet of salvation. They're "last" because they'll have heard about him later, but they'll be "first" because they'll make it into God's kingdom before the door is locked shut. You who have direct contact with Jesus are "first" because he came to you in person, but you'll be "last" because by failing to repent and believe in him you'll be thrown out and the

door locked shut behind you. "Behold" focuses a spotlight on this pair of reversals; and quoting these words of judgment against those who heard Jesus in person, Luke makes an evangelistic appeal to us who haven't heard Jesus in person. We can be first!

JERUSALEM AS JESUS' DESTINATION AND DISAPPOINTMENT
Luke 13:31–35

13:31–33: In that very hour some Pharisees approached, saying to him, "Get out and go away from here, because Herod wants to kill you." 32**And he told them, "When you've gone, tell this vixen, 'Behold, I'm casting out demons and accomplishing cures today and tomorrow; and on the third day I am myself completing** [these activities].' 33**Nevertheless, it's necessary that I be traveling today and tomorrow and the following** [day], **because it's inconceivable that a prophet perish outside Jerusalem."** Luke gives no indication whether the Pharisees are genuinely concerned for Jesus' life, simply want him to leave their territory, or have some other motive. Luke likewise gives no indication whether Herod really wants to kill Jesus. He'd killed John the baptizer, Jesus' predecessor (9:9); but he'll refrain from killing Jesus when he has the chance (23:6–12). (This is Herod Antipas, a son of Herod the Great who was ruling at the time of Jesus' birth.) So the accent falls on what Jesus says to tell Herod, namely, that Jesus' philanthropic ministry of exorcisms and healings is ongoing—a point of emphasis in Luke's Gospel and highlighted here by "Behold." "Go" in the Pharisees' saying to Jesus, "go from here," is the verb elsewhere translated "travel." The same is true for "gone" in his saying to the Pharisees, "When you've *gone*, tell this vixen . . . ." And the same verb appears in his statement, "Nevertheless, it's necessary that I *be traveling*." In effect, then, Jesus is telling the Pharisees that they ought to take a trip (to Herod) since he (Jesus) is already taking a trip (to Jerusalem) and doesn't have to be told by them to do so. A vixen is a female fox and therefore not to be feared. By calling Herod a vixen, Jesus is saying he has nothing to fear from Herod. God's plan is that Jesus suffer the death of a prophet in Jerusalem, not in Galilee or Perea, where Herod rules. "And on the third day I am myself completing [the activities of exorcism and healing]" shouldn't be taken to mean that Jesus has only three days left of such activities. The same goes for his traveling "today and tomorrow and the following [day]." The point has to do with ongoing exorcisms and cures however many days it takes to reach Jerusalem. The three days are an open-ended sample. "I am *myself* completing [them]" underscores Jesus' role as a benefactor. "Nevertheless" means that despite his ongoing exorcisms and cures, God's plan necessitates that Jesus keep traveling to Jerusalem in order to perish there as a prophet. "Because it's inconceivable that a prophet should perish outside Jerusalem" strikes a sardonic note. Too many prophets have perished there for Jesus not to do so as well.

13:34–35: "Jerusalem, Jerusalem, the [city] that kills the prophets and stones those who've been sent to her, how often I've wanted to gather your children [= residents] together the way a hen [gathers] her own brood under [her] wings! And you didn't want [to be gathered together]! ³⁵Behold, your house [the temple] is being left to you [that is, abandoned by God's Spirit, who otherwise lives there—note: God's *Spirit* as opposed to an *image*, such as pagan temples were built to house]. And I tell you, by no means will you see me until it [the time] will have come when you say, 'Favored [is] he who's coming in the Lord's name [Psalm 118:26]!'" In anticipation of his arrival there, Jesus speaks about Jerusalem ("to *her*") as though he were already in that city, so that "*your* children," several occurrences of "*you*," and "*your* house" mark a shift to direct address. The doubling of "Jerusalem" deepens pathos in the following lament, in which the city is personified as a killer of the prophets. Stoning the ones sent to Jerusalem specifies the means of killing the prophets, whom the Old Testament often portrays as sent by God. The desire of Jesus to gather together the city's residents the way a hen gathers together her brood under her wings refers to his desire to bring those residents under protection from God's coming wrath (compare 3:7). "How often" intensifies Jesus' desire by multiplying it, and "her *own* brood" adds tenderness to it. The Jerusalemites' not wanting to be thus gathered together portends the killing of Jesus in the city. God's Spirit will abandon the temple there because of the killing. Though the abandonment is future, it's so sure to take place that Jesus uses the present tense: "is being abandoned." "Behold" dramatizes the abandonment. Though the temple is God's house in the sense of his dwelling-place, it's "your [the Jerusalemites'] house" in the sense of its being located in their city (compare 11:51; 19:46; Acts 7:47, 49). "I tell you" emphasizes their not seeing Jesus till he returns as the Son of Man. At that time, happily, they'll give him a warm reception, one that will issue in his "restor[ing] the kingdom to Israel" (Acts 1:6 [compare Luke 1:26–33, 54–55, 67–79; Acts 3:19–21]). (In 19:37–38 only his disciples, accompanying him from Galilee, will hail him with words taken from Psalm 118:26.) "Until it [the time] will have come" makes his return certain.

JESUS AT TABLE WITH HIGH-RANKING PHARISEES
Luke 14:1–24

In this passage Jesus overpowers some high-ranking Pharisees with both deed and word (14:1–6), advises them in regard to their present life (14:7–11), advises them in regard to their future fate (14:12–14), and warns them of exclusion (14:15–24).

14:1–4a: And it happened when on a Sabbath he went into the house of a certain one of the rulers of the Pharisees to eat bread [= to have a meal] that they were scrutinizing him. ²And behold, a certain [man] with dropsy [= edema, an excess of body fluids that results in swelling] was right in front of him. ³And answering [= responding to the Pharisaical rulers' scrutiny and the dropsical man's presence], Jesus spoke to the lawyers and Pharisees, saying, "Is it lawful to heal on the Sabbath or not?" ⁴ᵃBut they kept quiet. "The rulers of the Pharisees" doesn't mean those who ruled the Pharisees—rather, synagogue rulers who were Pharisees. The question Jesus asks them shows they were scrutinizing him to see whether in their opinion he would break the Sabbath by healing the dropsical man then and there. They considered healing to be work. "Behold" shines a spotlight on the case in point. Given the company of Pharisees, "the lawyers" probably belonged to the Pharisaical sect. Luke calls them "lawyers" to prepare for Jesus' question whether it's lawful to heal on the Sabbath. But Luke doesn't say why they don't answer the question. So the impression is left that Jesus simply overpowers them with it (see 14:6).

14:4b–6: And taking hold [of the man with dropsy], he healed him and dismissed [him]. ⁵And he said to them, "A son or an ox of which of you will fall into a well—? And you'll pull him up [out of the well] immediately on the Sabbath day, won't you?" ⁶And they weren't able [literally, "weren't strong enough"] to answer in turn with regard to these things [the extractions of a son and an ox]. By taking hold of the man, Jesus transfers to him his healing power. Dismissing the man indicates that he has no more need of that power. He's healed for good. "A son or an ox of which of you will fall into a well—?" sets out a supposition. "And you'll pull him up . . . , won't you?" sets out a certainty. The asking of this question before the preceding one is finished intensifies the certainty of an extraction even on a Sabbath. "Immediately" also intensifies it. The rhetorical question exposes the inconsistency of denying the legality of healing on the Sabbath at the leisure of a meal yet allowing the immediate pulling of a son or an ox up out of a well likewise on the Sabbath. Jesus' healing and dismissing the man before he (Jesus) asks the rhetorical question presents the Pharisaical lawyers with a concrete fact that would weaken any abstract argument they might put forward to make healing on the Sabbath illegal but extracting a son or an ox on the Sabbath legal. Hence, they're "not strong enough" in argument to take their turn. Jesus wins. His philanthropy wins (compare 13:10–17).

14:7–9: And on noticing how they were selecting the prestigious cushions [for reclining around a low table at a formal meal], he was telling a parable to those who'd been invited, saying to them, ⁸"Whenever you're invited by someone to a wedding [which would include a banquet], you shouldn't recline in a prestigious cushion, lest a more esteemed [man] than you had been invited by him [the host], ⁹and on coming [to the table] the one who invited you and him [the more esteemed man] will say to you, 'Give place to this [more esteemed man].' And then with shame [= embarrassment] you'll begin to occupy the last place [that is, the least prestigious couch]." The prestigious cushions were located close to the host. Jesus' "parable" takes the form of two illustrations concerning what happens to invitees at banquets. "Lest a more esteemed [man] than you had been invited" sets out a *possibility*. Should the possibility materialize, the host "will say to you . . . ." Then there's a *certainty* of your being demoted. Moreover, the host's words of demotion ("Give place . . .") will bring you public disgrace by not beginning with a respectful address, such as "Friend." Added to this disgrace will be the shame of your having to occupy the least prestigious cushion at table. "You'll *begin* to occupy the last place with shame" portrays the whole movement from first place to last, and then the occupation of last place throughout the whole banquet, as a loss of face.

The second illustration making up this parable comes in **14:10–11: "But when you're invited, on going** [to the wedding banquet] **lie down** [= recline at table] **in the last place, so that when the one who'd invited you comes, he'll say to you, 'Friend, go up higher** [that is, to a more prestigious cushion]**.' Then you'll have honor** [instead of shame] **in the sight of all those reclining with you, [11]because everyone who lifts himself up** [= exalts himself] **will be lowered** [= humbled], **and the one who lowers himself will be lifted up."** As before, "he'll say to you" sets out a certainty. You can count on being elevated if you humble yourself. And this self-humbling entails taking "the *last* place," the least honorable cushion, not just a cushion in the middle range of prestige. Your elevation will start with the host's addressing you respectfully, even endearingly, with "Friend," and will continue as all your fellow guests see you move higher and occupy your prestigious place throughout the banquet. On the other hand, "everyone who lifts himself up will be lowered" calls attention back to the shameful outcome of self-exaltation, with "everyone" allowing no exceptions. As a piece of practical wisdom, then, Jesus' prohibiting competition for honor lays a basis for harmony in the Christian community, a harmony attractive to prospective converts.

14:12–14: And he was also saying to the [Pharisaical ruler] **who'd invited him, "When you put on a dinner or a banquet, don't summon your friends or your brothers or your relatives or rich neighbors, lest they also invite you in return and you get a repayment. [13]Rather, when you put on a feast, invite poor people, maimed people, lame people, blind people; [14]and you'll be fortunate, because they don't have** [the wherewithal] **to repay you. For it** [your putting on a feast for them] **will be repaid to you at the resurrection of the righteous."** Apparently the use of "Friend" in Jesus' practical advice concerning the present life (14:10) triggers his giving advice about not inviting friends and others, advice with implications for the afterlife: give up present reciprocity for future reciprocity, and give up human reciprocity for divine reciprocity. Jesus doesn't attack the *motive* or *purpose* for inviting friends, brothers, other relatives, and rich neighbors, as though he said, "*in order that* you be

invited by them in return." Instead, he attacks the *outcome* of inviting them: "*lest* they also invite you in return and you get a repayment." That is to say, they'll reciprocate you in this life but you won't be reciprocated "at the resurrection of the righteous." Why not? Because you'll not participate in that resurrection. For the righteous are those who invite "poor people, maimed people, lame people, blind people." These are the destitute, economically reduced to beggary and religiously reduced to inferiority (see Leviticus 21:16–24; 2 Samuel 5:8 in contrast with Matthew 21:14). The lack of "and" before the last entry on this list of such people—that is, before "blind people"—suggests an open-ended list to which other sorts of disadvantaged people could be added. And the lack of "the" before each entry—we don't read about "*the* poor," "*the* maimed," and so on—stresses their abject state as such rather than the classes of people to which they belong. Thus charity toward the unfortunate marks "the righteous" and ensures for them the good fortune of participation in "the resurrection of the righteous."

14:15: And on hearing these things [that Jesus had just said], **a certain one of his fellow-recliners** [at table] **said to him, "Whoever will eat bread in God's kingdom** [is] **fortunate."** The present banquet and Jesus' talk of "the resurrection of the righteous" (14:14) makes another diner think of the messianic banquet to take place on that occasion. "In God's kingdom" associates that banquet with the full imposition of his reign on earth. "Will eat bread" doesn't describe the menu. It's an expression for eating a meal, whatever its menu. But who will be those fortunate enough to eat at the messianic banquet? The following parable answers this question.

14:16–20: But he [Jesus] **told him, "A certain man put on a big banquet and invited many** [guests]. **[17]And he sent his slave at the hour of the banquet to say to those who'd been invited, 'Come, because things are now ready.'"** The bigness of the banquet and the large number of invitees represent the generosity of God in his offer of salvation. As an old hymn says, "There's a wideness in God's mercy." The sending of a slave to tell the invitees to come indicates they had accepted a prior invitation. Otherwise, the host wouldn't have sent his slave to tell them the food was ready to be served. **[18]"And one after another they all began to excuse themselves."** "Began" starts a series of excuses. Though the series will include only three, the inviting of "many" and the phrase "they *all*" make the three representative of others. **"The first said to him, 'I've bought a field and have a necessity, on going out, to see it** [= I have to go out and see it]. **I ask you, have me excused.'"** As though he hadn't looked at the field before buying it! Or as if he needed to look at it again if he'd looked at it before! Or as if he couldn't wait till after the banquet to look at it if he'd bought the field sight unseen! In any case, a lame excuse. **[19]"And another said, 'I've bought five yoke** [= pairs] **of oxen and I'm going to examine them. I ask you, have me excused.'"** As if he hadn't examined them before buying them! Or as if he couldn't wait till after the banquet to examine them if in fact he hadn't examined them before the purchase! Another lame excuse. [20]**"And another said, 'I've married a wife and therefore can't come.'"** At last a good excuse? No, for in that male chauvinistic culture no self-respecting male would have missed a stag party (which was what such banquets were) just because he'd recently gotten married. So this man, like the others, refuses to come just because he doesn't want to. All three dishonor the banquet-giver both by their refusals and by the lame excuses they give for not coming. Though the third man gives an excuse, he adds an insult by not even *asking* to be excused and saying instead that he "*can't* come," though of course he could.

14:21–24: "And on arriving [back at the banquet-giver's house], **the slave reported these things to his master. Then enraged, the houseowner said to his slave, 'Go out quickly into the broad and narrow** [streets] **of the city and bring in here the poor and maimed and blind and lame.'"** Since "master" goes back to the word that's also translated "Lord," this master represents the Lord Jesus, who is extending God's offer of salvation. But the houseowner's rage portends judgment on those who reject the salvation offered through Jesus. The slave is to go out "quickly" and bring others into the banquet house because the food is ready to be served and eaten "now." The time of salvation is now. Later will be *too* late. The poor, maimed, blind, and lame are begging on the main and side streets of the city. Because they're *begging* there, they needn't be told to come. They'll come without being told to. The slave has only to bring them to the location where food is being served. By telling him to bring in the poor, maimed, blind, and lame, the master—representing Jesus—is doing exactly what Jesus told his host to do in 14:13: "when you put on a feast, invite poor people, maimed people, lame people, blind people." [22]**"And the slave said, 'Master, what you ordered** [to be done] **has taken place, and there's still room** [for more guests in the banquet hall].' [23]**And the master said to the slave, 'Go out into the roads and hedges** [that is, the roads that run along hedges enclosing fields in the open country] **and compel** [people] **to come in so that my house may be filled** [with diners]. [24]**For I tell you** [plural!] **that not one of those men who were invited will taste my banquet.'"** Subtly, Jesus has implied that those who refused to come and made excuses represent his critics, the Pharisaical rulers of 14:1. They may be reclining at table with him, but they've refused his message of salvation. As a result, disadvantaged Jews, represented by the poor, maimed, blind, and lame, are partaking of the banquet of salvation. But they're not numerous enough to fill the house. So the wideness of God's mercy extends outside the streets of Jewdom into the countryside of Gentiledom. And since Gentiles are "alienated from the citizenship of Israel and foreigners to the covenants of promise" (Ephesians 2:12), they have to be "compel[led]"—that is, strongly persuaded—to come in where by rights they don't belong. The filling of the house with banqueters thus represents the numerical success of the gospel, a success beginning among the down-and-outs of Jewish society and spreading out to Gentiles from all over the world. Luke will detail this success in his book of Acts and use it as an argument for the truth of the gospel and as an attraction for prospective converts, because a crowd draws a crowd. Here, however, the final accent falls on a warning that the original invitees won't taste the food of salvation. "I tell you" underscores the warning. "Not one" intensifies it, and "*those* men" sets the invitees at a telltale distance. The master has been addressing his slave alone, but suddenly a plural "you" appears. Thus Jesus has the master step out of the parable into the present banquet to pronounce judgment on Jesus' fellow diners, the Pharisaical rulers. Thus also he puts himself in the role of the master who sets the table of salvation and decides who's in and who's out.

THE NEED TO COUNT THE COST OF DISCIPLESHIP
Luke 14:25–35

14:25–27: And many crowds were traveling with him. And on turning [toward them], **he told them,** [26]**"If someone is coming to me and isn't hating his own father and mother and wife and children and brothers and sisters and, still, even his own self, he can't be my disciple.** [27]**Whoever isn't carrying his own cross and coming behind me can't be my disciple."** Luke's mention of "crowds" that were traveling with Jesus revives the theme of Jesus' popularity, which Luke uses to recommend the gospel in that Jesus was popular because of his humanitarian work. The plurality of the crowds and the addition of "many" accentuate this popularity. "Were traveling with Jesus" revives the theme of travelogue, interesting to Luke's audience and prospective of Christian missionaries' traveling in the book of Acts. Jesus' "turning" toward the many crowds implies their following him, which prompts him to explain what's entailed in *really* following him—that is, following him in a more than merely spatial sense. "If someone is coming to me" has to do with coming to Jesus for discipleship. "And isn't hating" is followed by a list of objects, twice paired. Because males dominated females in that culture, "father" precedes "mother" in one pair and "brothers" precedes "sisters" in the other pair. "Wife" stands opposite the male "someone" being referred to, and "children" covers both males and females. Because of their age, the pair "father and mother" outranks almost all others on the list and therefore comes first. Because of marriage, "wife" comes next. As the outcome of marriage, "children" follows. Lowest ranking goes to the pair "brothers and sisters." But saved till last is the highest ranking "his . . . self." "Self" translates the word that also refers to one's physical life, the "soul" that animates the body. Stressing the man's personal interest in his physical life/soul/self is "his *own*," which earlier stressed also the personal interest he has in his immediate family. As if hating his own immediate family weren't enough, "still" adds that *while* hating them a man must also hate himself. "Even" targets the hating of himself as the height of hatred. And "can't" makes hatred up and down the scale a requirement for discipleship. "My disciple" means a pupil of Jesus, someone who learns from him.

"Whoever isn't carrying his own cross" begins abruptly after the business of hating. This abruptness combines with a third "his own" and a second "can't be my disciple" to effect a close connection between hating, cross-carrying, and coming behind Jesus. "His *own* cross" distinguishes the disciple's cross from that of Jesus, which hasn't even been mentioned yet in Luke's Gospel. A disciple's cross-*carrying* doesn't refer to crucifixion. It refers to running the gauntlet of verbal, physical, and other abuse for the sake of Jesus and his gospel the way those sentenced to crucifixion had to run a similar gauntlet as they carried a cross-bar on their way from court to stake (compare the comments on 9:23). And whereas "coming *to* me" referred to approaching Jesus *for* discipleship, "coming *behind* me" refers to following Jesus *as* discipleship. And just as discipleship required hating, it also requires cross-carrying and going behind Jesus in allegiance to him. Because of the parallel between hating on the one hand and, on the other hand, cross-carrying and going behind Jesus, hating means putting allegiance to him so far ahead of all other interpersonal ties, and even ahead of self-preservation, that "hate" becomes an appropriate standard of comparison. (Note: the self-hate that Jesus refers to shouldn't be understood in terms of psychological self-loathing.) In its historical setting, the kind of discipleship Jesus was talking about had to do with forsaking all to take sides with him on his way to Jerusalem. Later, as in the book of Acts, that kind of physical following morphed of necessity into a following of Jesus' example rather than Jesus himself. He isn't here any more.

14:28–30: "For who of you, wanting to build a tower [such as a watchtower for the guarding of a vineyard (Mark 12:1; Matthew 21:33)]**, doesn't—on sitting down—first count the cost** [of building the tower]**, whether he has** [enough] **for** [its] **completion** [implied answer: Of course he'd first count the cost], **²⁹lest when he has laid a foundation and** [for lack of funds] **isn't able to finish** [building the tower]**, all those who are observing begin to poke fun at him, ³⁰saying, "This man began to build** [a tower] **and couldn't finish** [it]**."** "For" introduces an explanation of hating and cross-carrying in terms of cost-counting. Just as it costs a lot of money to build a tower, it costs a lot of personal and interpersonal loss to go after Jesus as his disciple. So the person who comes to him for discipleship had better, before starting out, count that cost to see whether he has enough allegiance to Jesus to run the entire gauntlet of nondisciples' abuse. For dropping out of discipleship in midcourse will incur a ridicule worse than that abuse (not to mention eternal damnation). "Sitting down" portrays the cost-counting as deliberate, and "*begin* to poke fun at him" portrays the fun-poking as ongoing. Every time the observers see the foundation lacking a tower they'll ridicule the would-be tower-builder. In the same fashion, observers of lapsed disciples will go on ridiculing them for their lapse from discipleship. In-

ability to finish the tower represents a shameful inability to run the entire gauntlet. Jesus is asking, Do you have the right stuff?

14:31–32: "Or what king, going to meet another king for battle, won't—on sitting down—first plan whether he's able with ten thousand [soldiers] **to confront the one coming against him with twenty thousand** [soldiers]**?"** Implied answer: No king would fail to do so. ³²**"And if not, indeed** [= And if he figures that in fact his ten thousand can't win a victory over the other king's twenty thousand], **while he** [the other king] **is a long way off, sending an embassy he** [the first king] **requests the** [terms] **for peace."** Here, counting soldiers replaces the counting of money in 14:28–30; but both countings have to do with calculating what it takes to follow Jesus as his disciple. Again, "sitting" portrays as deliberate the calculation necessary for long-term success. Better not to start discipleship at all than to start and fail at it because of opposition from nondisciples (like being defeated by the king with twice as many soldiers). Better to make peace with those nondisciples long before they engage you in a war of abuse. If you don't have what it takes to carry discipleship through to final success over the world's opposition, forget discipleship altogether. Go ahead and give up the peace of salvation for peace with the world. An unhappy trade, but better than having neither peace with the world nor the peace of salvation.

14:33: "In this way, therefore, everyone of you who doesn't take leave of all your own possessions can't be my disciple." Along with a third "can't be my disciple" (see 14:26–27 for the first two), "in this way" makes the divestment of one's goods comparable to cost- and soldier-counting. "Therefore" makes the divestment a necessary run-up to discipleship, a run-up apart from which you can't carry your own cross and go behind Jesus. "Everyone of you" allows no exceptions. "Your *own* possessions" underlines the break between discipleship and holding onto private possessions. "*All* your own possessions" demands complete relinquishment. (See the comments on 14:25–27 for the historical occasion of these statements as different from the situation of disciples after Jesus' death, resurrection, and ascension; but this difference shouldn't be used to neuter the demands of discipleship.)

14:34–35: "Therefore salt [is] **good. But if even salt is rendered saltless, with what will it be fixed? ³⁵It's useful neither for soil nor for a manure patty. People throw it out. The person having ears to hear** [with] **had better hear!"** "Therefore" draws a conclusion from the foregoing. The conclusion is that well-considered discipleship—the kind that lasts because its cost was calculated beforehand—is good. For the "salt" that Jesus declares to be good represents discipleship. Literally, the kind of salt that would be good for soil if it hadn't lost its saltiness isn't table salt, but the kind of salt we call potash, phosphate, and ammonia compounds. It's good for fertilizing the soil. And the salt that is good for the manure pile is what was used in making patties out of camel and donkey dung that were dried and then burned as fuel. This salt acted as a catalyst that made possible the burning. Mixed with gypsum and other substances, however, salt was often impure, so that when rain leached out the salt, the remaining substances lacked saltiness though still looking like salt. Therefore it was useless, and there was no substitute. So once impure salt lost its saltiness, there was nothing that could fix it for use as fertilizer or as a catalyst in manure patties. Hence, "with what will it be fixed?" Salt that has become useless by being rendered saltless characterizes a person who has become Jesus' disciple without counting the cost beforehand and as a result has lapsed along the way. "But if *even* salt is rendered saltless" denotes that even a presently professing disciple can in time lapse. Literally, "rendered saltless" means "rendered foolish" and thus implies the folly of falling from discipleship through failure to have counted its cost. And people's throwing out useless salt stands for the throwing of lapsed disciples outside the kingdom of God (13:28 [compare 3:9]). Punctuating this fate is the abruptness with which Jesus introduces it. No "therefore" or "so that" connects it with the preceding statement of uselessness. Because the many crowds traveling with Jesus to Jerusalem hadn't counted the cost of discipleship, he tells them they'd better heed what he has just now said.

JESUS' SAVING THE LOST
Luke 15:1–32

After a stage-setting that features some grumbling Pharisees and scholars (15:1–2), this chapter divides into three parables: the first about finding a lost sheep (15:3–7); the second about finding a lost coin (15:8–10); and the third about finding a lost son, plus the grumbling of his brother (15:11–32). All three of the lost represent sinners, lost as they are from God and his kingdom.

15:1–2: And all the tax collectors and sinners were drawing near to hear him [Jesus]. **²And both the Pharisees and the scholars were grumbling, saying, "This** [guy] **is welcoming sinners and eating with them."** Tax collectors were notorious for their dishonesty, and "sinners" refers also to people notorious for other sins. Because of Jesus' demand for repentance from sin, we might have expected such people to keep their distance from Jesus. But no, they "were drawing near" to him. How strong his magnetism! And that they were "all" drawing near maximizes it. Their purpose in drawing near? "To hear" Jesus. They of all people are heeding his immediately preceding admonition, "The person having ears to hear [with] had better hear!" (14:35). The Pharisees and the scholars grumble about Jesus' welcoming such people and eating with them (see 5:30 and 7:39 with comments). This off-putting self-righteousness of theirs makes a dark foil against which his magnetic congeniality shines out brightly.

15:3–7: And he told them [the Pharisees and the scholars] **this parable, saying, ⁴"What man from among you, if he has a hundred sheep and loses one of them, doesn't leave the ninety-nine in the wilderness** [an unpopulated area where pasture is found] **and go after the lost** [sheep] **till he finds it?"** Implied answer: Not one of you would fail to do so. **⁵"And on finding** [it], **he puts** [it] **on his shoulders, rejoicing. ⁶And on coming into** [his] **house, he calls together** [his] **friends and neighbors, saying to them, 'Rejoice with me, because I've found my sheep that was lost.' ⁷I tell you** [Jesus isn't quoting the shepherd any more but speaking himself] **that in this way there'll be joy in heaven over one repenting sinner rather than over ninety-nine righteous people who as such don't have need of repentance."** The lost sheep represents a sinner, but the ninety-nine don't represent the self-righteous Pharisees and scholars. They represent truly righteous people who, as Jesus plainly says, "don't have need of repentance" (see the comments on 5:31–32). That the shepherd leaves the ninety-nine untended in the wilderness, and does so for only one sheep at the expense of so many more, illustrates the depth of Jesus' concern to save sinners (compare 19:10). The shepherd doesn't stop searching till he finds the lost sheep. Nor will Jesus stop welcoming sinners and eating with them till he has brought them to repentance. But there's something of a mismatch between the parable and the circumstance in and for which he tells it. For unlike the shepherd, Jesus doesn't have to go searching for a sinner. The sinners are drawing near to him—all of them, not just one. He has only to welcome them and eat with them. So given both their drawing near and their large number in contrast with the one sheep that strayed away, how much more reason to rejoice over these sinners when they repent! In addition to rejoicing over finding his lost sheep, the shepherd puts it on his shoulder as a sign of affection. And his rejoicing over the salvation of the lost sheep complements the rejoicing of the saved themselves over their salvation (for which see 2:10; Acts 16:34). So great is the shepherd's joy that he goes home instead of returning to the ninety-nine, still untended in the wilderness, and calls on his friends and neighbors to rejoice with him. Such is the joy in heaven over even one repentant sinner. Think of the joy over the *many* repentant sinners coming out of Jesus' ministry!

"I tell you" emphasizes the joy in heaven. But who is rejoicing there? Jesus waits till 15:10 to answer the question, and then answers it indirectly. Meanwhile, he emphasizes the heavenly joy even further by contrasting it with *non*joy over the much larger number of righteous people who don't need repentance. Most translations supply "more" with "than" to produce rejoicing over one repenting sinner "*more* than over ninety-nine righteous [people]." But elsewhere in his Gospel, Luke uses "than" only five times for comparisons, and then always with an accompanying comparative adjective, such as "more" with "than" in 9:13: "We have no *more* than five loaves and two fish." There, *not* as here in 15:7, "more" is expressed and therefore doesn't need to be supplied (similarly in 10:12, 14; 16:17; 18:25). On the other hand, the word translated "than" occurs in Luke thirty-seven times for alternatives (hence its other translation, "or") instead of comparisons. Given the absence of a comparative adjective here, then, it's better to supply "rather" with "than" instead of "more" with "than" (see 17:2 for the closest parallel: "It's advantageous for him if an upper millstone collars his neck and he's been hurled into the sea *rather than* that he snare one of these little ones"). Thus the striking lack of joy in heaven over ninety-nine righteous people highlights the heavenly joy over one repenting sinner.

15:8–10: "Or what woman, having ten drachmas— if she should lose one drachma—doesn't light a lamp and sweep the house and search carefully [for the one lost drachma] till she finds [it]?" Implied answer: No woman would fail to do so. "And on finding [it], she calls together [her] female friends and neighbors, saying, 'Rejoice with me, because I've found the drachma that I lost.' [10]In this way, I tell you [again, Jesus isn't quoting the woman any more but is speaking himself], joy happens in the sight of God's angels over one repenting sinner." There's no "from among you" after "Or what woman," because Jesus is addressing an all-male audience of Pharisees and scholars (contrast 15:3: "What man from among you . . . ?"). A drachma was a coin that had the same value as a denarius, the daily wage for a manual laborer. It's possible but not certain that the woman is to be understood as wearing a headdress adorned with ten drachmas given to her as a dowry at her marriage and that one of them had come loose and fallen to the floor. She lit a lamp, not because it was nighttime, but because her house—a typical one for a peasant—had no windows, only a low door that let in little light. She swept her house to make the lost coin tinkle on the floor so that she could more easily determine its whereabouts, perhaps made harder to determine by its being hidden under straw spread over the floor because of domestic animals. "Carefully" describes her search so as to illustrate Jesus' care to bring lost sinners to repentance. Again, the mismatch between the woman's having to search for her *one* lost coin and *all* the sinners' drawing near to Jesus without his having to search them out—this mismatch gives more reason for rejoicing over the success of his ministry with sinners. Yet again, the woman's joy is too much not to share and be shared. "In this way" draws a comparison once more with the heavenly joy. "I tell you" emphasizes that joy still yet again. And "joy happens in the sight of God's angels" doesn't mean that the angels rejoice. It means that *God* rejoices in their sight. What a sight! So Jesus welcomes tax collectors and sinners and eats with them, not just out of sociability, but for the sake of their salvation through repentance from their sins. This theme suits Luke's appeal to prospective converts having moral sensibility, people looking for a religion of morality that contrasts with the immorality surrounding them.

15:11–12: And he said, "A certain man had two sons. [12]And the younger of them said to the father,

'Father, give me the portion of the estate devolving [on me].' And he [the father] distributed to them [the two sons] the assets [literally, 'the livelihood' made possible by the assets of the estate]." The request of the younger son to inherit his part of the father's estate before the father dies makes the respectful address, "Father," look like a ruse designed to mask the insolence of his request. Though asked to fork over only the younger son's part, the father distributes to the older son, too, his part. This excess of generosity forms a backdrop that will incriminate the older son's attitude later on. Jesus doesn't indicate the proportions in which the estate was divided for distribution to the two sons, so that speculation on the proportions is pointless.

15:13–16: "And after not many days [= 'After a few days'], having gathered together all [his assets], the younger son journeyed off into a distant region and there dissipated his [part of] the estate by living profligately. [14]And when he'd spent all [his assets], a severe famine came about throughout that region; and he began to be destitute. [15]And he went and attached himself to one of that region's citizens [to work for a living, since he had no more assets off which to live leisurely]. And he [the citizen] sent him into his fields to feed pigs. [16]And he was craving to eat his fill of the carob pods that the pigs were eating. And no one was giving him [anything to eat]." Gathering together all his assets for a long journey entailed selling them for cash, which can be carried. The distance of the region to which the younger son journeys represents sinners' alienation from God and plays into the appearance of pigs on the scene. For pigs wouldn't be raised in Jewish territory. The Mosaic law declared them unclean and not to be eaten (Leviticus 11:7; Deuteronomy 14:8). The son's lavish lifestyle has left him cashless. The arrival of a famine *"throughout* that region" makes it impossible to buy enough food even if he had leftovers of cash. The severity of the famine has driven the price of food out of reach anyway. "*Began* to be destitute" describes the son's condition as hopeless when looking down the road—until he goes to work feeding pigs for a local citizen, obviously a Gentile, since a Jew wouldn't be raising pigs. But what a comedown—working instead of spending freely, working as a Jew for a Gentile, and feeding animals forbidden to be eaten by a Jew! And even this work doesn't provide enough income for the purchase of food sufficient to alleviate his hunger pangs. They're so bad that he craves even the barely edible carob pods he has to give the pigs. The pigs' lives are more important to his employer than his own life is. So he doesn't even get pig feed. Nobody gives him anything to eat. The famine has destroyed human sympathy and fellow feeling. It's every man for himself and the Devil take the hindmost.

15:17–19: "But on coming to himself, he said, 'How many employees of my father are getting more than enough loaves of bread [representing food in general], yet here I'm perishing because of hunger! [18]On standing up, I'll travel to my father and tell him, "Father,

I've sinned against heaven and in your sight. ¹⁹I'm no longer worthy to be called your son. Make me like one of your employees.""" "Coming to himself" means "coming to his senses" and implies that he has strayed from himself, from his own best interests. His father's employees were neither members of the family nor household slaves, sure of daily provisions, but laborers hired a day at a time and only as needed. Yet even they have more than enough food to stay alive while in his famine-struck region the younger son is perishing (= dying) for lack of food. The word for "perishing" is the same as the word for "lost" in connection with the coin and the sheep in 15:3–10. Like that coin and that sheep, then, the son is lost from his father and has up till now been lost also from himself. But no longer, because he has come to himself. "On standing up" implies that he's sitting down as he plans what to do. A determination to confess his sin gives the plan to use the address "Father" a ring of genuine respect (contrast 15:12). "Heaven" is a reverential substitute for "God" (as when someone says, "For heaven's sake!" rather than "For God's sake!"), so that "I've sinned against heaven" means "I've sinned against God." Since *God* commanded children to honor their parents (Exodus 20:12; Deuteronomy 5:16), the son recognizes that dishonoring his father counted as a sin against God. "And in your sight" doesn't mean that the son has sinned against his father, however. It means his father has seen the son's sin against God and therefore can't be expected to treat the son *as* a son. Hence, "I'm no longer worthy ['in your sight'] to be *called* your son." "Make me *like* one of your employees" implies that though he's a son he should, because of his sin, be treated as an employee, a day laborer, not even a household slave.

15:20–24: **"And on standing up, he went to his own father. But while he was still a long way off from** [home], **his father saw him and felt sorry** [for him] **and, running, fell on his neck** [= wrapped his arms around the son's neck] **and kissed him. ²¹And the son said to him, 'Father, I've sinned against heaven and in your sight. I'm no longer worthy to be called your son.' ²²But the father told his slaves, 'Quickly bring out the first** [= the best, most prestigious] **robe and clothe him** [with it]. **And give** [him] **a ring for his hand** [we'd say "finger"] **and sandals for** [his] **feet. ²³And bring the fattened calf. Slaughter** [it]; **and eating** [it], **let's celebrate, ²⁴because this my son was dead and has come back to life. He was lost, and has been found.' And they began celebrating."** The son makes good on his resolve. That he went "to his *own* father" rather than simply "to *his* father" foreshadows a restoration of fellowship between father and son. We should resist the temptation to think that the father's seeing the son while the son "was still a long way off" implies a constant lookout for the son on the part of his father. The point is, rather, that when the father happened to see his son in the distance, he went to him despite the distance. "Felt sorry [for him]" implies that the father saw his son to be in tatters, unadorned, barefoot, and—unlike the coming fattened calf—emaci-

ated. And not only did he go the distance to his son. He *ran* the distance, a long one. Running is unusual for an elderly oriental man, but this father's compassion overpowers his sense of decorum, as though to say that even God forgets his dignity with a burst of joy when a sinner turns to him in repentance. Wrapping arms around the son's neck and kissing him display overwhelming affection.

As planned, the son blurts out his confession. Jesus doesn't say why "make me like one of your employees" drops off the end of the confession, whether because of the father's interruption, the son's deciding the request would insult his father after such an affectionate welcome home, or some other reason. In any case, the story line races to the father's instructions, addressed to his slaves. As the eldest in the family, the father still wields authority even though he distributed his estate to the two sons. Dramatically, his instructions imply forgiveness of the son, so that the father doesn't have to pronounce the forgiveness in so many words. "Quickly" implies his eagerness to demonstrate forgiveness. The best robe was long and flowing. The son won't even have to dress himself in it. The slaves will put it on him. Clothing the son with this most prestigious robe compares with "joy in heaven over one repenting sinner *rather than* over ninety-nine righteous [people] who as such don't have need of repentance" (15:7). The ring will adorn his finger. His bare feet will get sandaled. Eating the fattened calf, far better food than the carob pods he'd craved but had to give the pigs instead, will fatten him up; and—since meat seldom appeared on the menu; it wasn't part of a daily diet—the shared meal of meat will be an occasion of celebration all around, with one possible exception coming up. "Let's celebrate" includes even the slaves whom the father is instructing.

With "this my son" the father publicly owns the prodigal as his own offspring despite the son's earlier insolence and recent dissipation. But the father exaggerates when saying that his son "was dead and has come back to life." Nor is it entirely true that the son "was lost, and has been found." You could say that he'd been lost in that he'd strayed from his father and home the way the lost sheep had strayed from its shepherd and flock, and also from his own best interests (15:4, 17). But he hadn't been found, for the father hadn't gone looking for him as the shepherd did search for his lost sheep and the woman for her lost coin (15:4–5, 8–9). The son had come home of his own accord. But the exaggeration (which is deliberate) of being dead and coming back to life, and the half-truth of being lost and found, testify to the exuberance of the father's joy over his son's repentance, an exuberance that represents the exuberant joy of God over one repenting sinner. The festivities "began." In heaven they'll never end; for in the larger sense, "com[ing] back to life" represents resurrection to eternal life. Jesus can't wait to mention the festivities, so that he skips saying that the slaves carried out the instructions of their master, the father.

This parable ends with a tailpiece unparalleled in the parables of the lost sheep and the lost coin. **15:25–30:**

"And his [the father's] older son was in a field [doubtless working, in contrast with his younger brother's leisurely squandering in a far country]. And while he, coming [from the field], drew near the house, he heard music [of instruments being played together] and dancing [to the music (compare 15:10)]. ²⁶And on summoning one of the servants [another word for 'slaves'], he enquired what these things [the music and the dancing] might be [= mean]. ²⁷And he said to him, 'Your brother has come, and your father has had the fattened calf slaughtered because he's gotten him [your brother] back safe and sound [or as we might say, "all in one piece"].' ²⁸But he [the older son] got angry and didn't want to go into [the house to join in the celebration that was taking place there]. But on coming out [of the house], his father was urging him [to go in]. ²⁹But he, answering, told his father, 'Behold, I've slaved for you ever so many years and have never neglected [to obey] a command of yours! And you've never given me a goat [much less a fattened calf], so that I might celebrate with my friends. ³⁰But when this son of yours came, who has devoured your assets with prostitutes [by paying them for sex], you've had the fattened calf slaughtered for him.'"

The older son rudely fails to use the respectful address, "Father." He avoids calling the prodigal his brother and refers to him instead, and disdainfully, as "this son of yours." "Behold" calls attention to the many years he has worked like a slave for his father. "Ever so many years" underscores the length of his service; and "slaved for you" indicates that though the father had distributed to him a portion of the estate because he was a son and even though, unlike his brother, he hadn't asked for it (15:12), he'd worked for his father like a slave, and like a slave hadn't failed to obey a command of his father. Such voluntary supererogation! Whether rightly or wrongly, he attributes his brother's destitution to the cost of visiting prostitutes; and the "devour[ing]" of the assets given the brother by their father surely invalidates the celebratory devouring of a fattened calf. Or so the older brother thinks.

But what do those details mean? The older son represents "the Pharisees and the scholars" of 15:2. His anger and not wanting to join in the festivities represent the Pharisees' and the scholars' grumbling at Jesus for his welcoming sinners and eating with them (15:2). The father's urging his older son to go in represents God's wanting also the Pharisees and the scholars to join in celebrating the repentance and restoration of tax collectors and sinners. Like the older son, the Pharisees and the scholars serve God solely out of a sense of duty, pride themselves on their own merits, and therefore resent the gracious forgiveness of repentant sinners.

15:31–32: "But he [the father] said to him, 'Child [a more affectionate address than "Son" would have been], you're always with me [in contrast with your younger brother's having been absent for as many years as you, according to your own statement, have slaved for me]. And all my things are yours [because without exception I distributed to you all the estate left to me after your brother got his portion (which distribution may partly explain why the older son got angry at the father's having had the fattened calf slaughtered, for at bottom the calf belonged to the older son)]. ³²But it was necessary to celebrate and rejoice, because this brother of yours was dead and has come back to life, and [was] lost and has been found.'" The father's affectionate address, "Child," contrasts with this son's having rudely failed to use the respectful address, "Father." And over against that failure, the father points to his older son's privileges of having been "always" with him and possessing "all" the father's belongings. "Always" contradicts the son's "never" and along with "all" provides a twofold emphasis. Possessing all his father's belongings exposes the pretense of the son in saying the father hadn't "given" him even a goat. The son *owned* all the farm animals. He didn't need to be given any of them. Notably, the father doesn't acknowledge his son's self-righteous appeal to working as a slave for him. By replacing the older son's disdainful reference to "this son of yours," the father's reference to "this brother of yours" appeals to an affection that the older brother should feel for his younger brother. The exuberance of the father's joy comes out again in a second exaggerated statement about coming out of death back to life and in a second partial mismatch of lost and found (see the comments on 15:24). It's these happy reversals that make a celebration necessary. Not just appropriate, but necessary—because it's in the very nature of a father to rejoice over the return of his repentant son just as it's in the very nature of God to rejoice over a repentant sinner. Of necessity, nature will out.

What is the older brother's response? Jesus doesn't say, but leaves the parable open-ended because the Pharisees and the scholars and all others who trust in their own merits finish the parable themselves, either by renouncing their self-righteousness to join in the messianic feast of salvation or by shutting themselves out through maintaining their self-righteousness (18:9–14). Finally, the older brother shows that a person doesn't have to feel lost to be lost. You can be estranged from God right on home territory. But he invites everybody—flagrant sinner and decent older brother alike—on the same terms: forgiving grace.

HOW DISCIPLES OUGHT TO
DEAL WITH WEALTH
Luke 16:1–13

In this passage Jesus shifts his address from the Pharisees and the scholars (chapter 15) to his disciples (16:1a), tells them a parable about wealth (16:1b–8a), applies the parable (16:8b–9), and elaborates with comments on wealth (16:10–13).

16:1–8a: And he was also speaking to the disciples: "There was a certain rich man who had a manager. And this [manager] was accused to him of dissipating his possessions [that is, of mismanaging them for a loss]. ²And on calling him [the manager], he said to him, 'What [is] this I'm hearing about you? Render an account of your managership, for you can't manage [my possessions] any more.' The rich man believes the accusation and in connection with firing the manager demands an account so as to determine his losses. ³"And the manager said in himself [we'd say, 'to himself'], 'What should I do, because my boss is taking the managership away from me? I don't have the strength to dig. I'm ashamed to beg. ⁴I know what I should do in order that when I'm removed out of the managership people will welcome me into their homes [where I can live off their hospitality].' ⁵And on summoning each one of his own boss's debtors ['his *own*' stressing the obligation he had toward the boss, an obligation he's about to violate], he was saying to the first [debtor], 'How much do you owe my boss?' ⁶And he said, 'A hundred baths of olive oil [about 875 gallons].' And he told him [the debtor], 'Welcome your bill and, on sitting down, quickly write fifty [baths of olive oil].'" Most translations have "*Take* your bill" instead of "*Welcome* your bill," but elsewhere the verb regularly means to receive welcomely. Here, the debtor is to welcome his bill because of the manager's instruction to write down a radically reduced amount of debt. Welcoming the bill for the benefit of a discount will then translate into "welcom[ing the manager] into their homes" (16:4) once he's removed out of the managership. "Welcome your bill" also implies the manager had it in hand and therefore didn't need to ask for the amount of debt. But he does ask the debtor for the amount to impress on the debtor's mind the coming discount of 50 percent and thus ingratiate himself so as to gain future hospitality from the debtor. It was a practice for the debtor himself to write a promissory note. Naturally, writing required him to sit down. He's to write "quickly" lest the rich man appear on the scene before the note is written and stop the discounting. ⁷"Then he [the manager] said to another [debtor], 'And you—how much do you owe?' And he said, 'A hundred cors of wheat [about 1,100 bushels].' He tells him, 'Welcome your bill and write eighty [a 20 percent discount].' ⁸ªAnd the boss commended the manager of unrighteousness [= the unrighteous manager], because he'd acted shrewdly . . . ."

Elsewhere the word for "boss" is translated "master" and "Lord." We could therefore think that the manager was a high-ranking slave, and the rich man his master. But then the manager's being fired and leaving to find hospitable quarters in the homes of debtors grateful for the discounts wouldn't make good sense. Nor would a slave contemplate begging or hiring himself out as a ditch-digger. Hence the translation "boss [of an employee]" rather than "master [of a slave]." There's no ready explanation for the drop in discount from 50 percent to 20 percent. But is the manager getting worried about the reaction of his boss and so reducing the rate of discount? The past tense in "he [the manager] *told* him [the first debtor]" changes to the present tense in the second debtor's case: "he *tells* him." This change enlivens the dialogue and, along with the drop in discount, suggests

the manager's concern lest the boss show up too soon. Various suggestions have been offered to acquit the manager of dishonesty in reducing the debts—for example, that he reduces them by the amount of his commission. (Then why the wide divergence in the rates of commission?) Such suggestions have no basis in the parable itself, however; and they require that "unrighteousness" in the last sentence refer all the way back to the mismanagement mentioned in the first sentence without any indication there of dishonesty rather than incompetence. It's more natural to understand the "unrighteousness" as referring to the immediately foregoing reduction of debts before the boss can stop it. Why then does he commend the manager? Not for his dishonesty as such, for by it the boss suffered severe loss. Rather, the boss commends his manager for shrewdness in looking out for his own future as a member of the unemployed. Against taking offense at Jesus' making the dishonest manager a positive example of forward thinking, we should consider that Jesus has compared his second coming to the break-in of a thief with respect to unexpectedness rather than to break-in as such (12:39–40).

In *16:8b* Jesus begins to apply the preceding parable by completing a sentence begun in 16:8a: "because the sons of this age [= unrighteous people] are shrewder than the sons of light [righteous people] in their own generation." "Because" introduces a reason for the boss's commendation of his dishonest manager. The manager represents unrighteous people, called "the sons of this age" because they use wealth to advantage so far as their *temporal* future is concerned. "In their own generation" implies that righteous people, called "the sons of light," belong to a different time-frame, the age to come, even though for the moment they're living in the present age. So they should use wealth to advantage so far as their *eternal* future is concerned (in contrast with the rich man in 12:16–21). Sadly, though, the unrighteous use wealth more shrewdly for this age than the righteous use it for the coming age.

16:9–13: "And I tell you, make friends for yourselves with the mammon of unrighteousness in order that whenever it runs out people may welcome you into eternal tents. ¹⁰The person who's faithful [= trustworthy] in a very small matter is faithful also in much, and the person who's unrighteous [= dishonest] in a very small matter is unrighteous also in much. ¹¹So if you haven't proved faithful in respect to the unrighteous mammon, who'll entrust to you the true [mammon]?" Implied answer: No one. ¹²"And if you haven't proved faithful in respect to somebody else's [mammon], who'll give you your own [mammon]? ¹³No household slave can slave for two masters. For either he'll hate the one and love the other, or he'll be devoted to one and despise the other. You can't slave for God and for Mammon." "I tell you" underscores the importance of the following command. "For yourselves" indicates the advantage of making friends. Here the advantage is eternal. "Mammon" means "wealth" and comes from the

Aramaic language most often used by Jesus. Since Luke brings the word into his Greek text without translating it, we too should keep it in its Aramaic form. In that form and because of the parallel between "the mammon of unrighteousness" and "the manager of unrighteousness" in 16:8, mammon is being personified. "The mammon of unrighteousness" and "the unrighteous mammon" mean wealth in its devilish capacity of leading people who have it to *act* unrighteously, not wealth *gained* unrighteously; for one could hardly be "faithful" with regard to ill-gotten wealth. So just as the manager used mammon charitably to gain friends in this life, so Jesus' disciples should use mammon charitably to gain friends in the life to come. They should give it away (compare 11:4b: "For also we're forgiving everyone indebted to us"). The making of friends by charitable giving points up a social ideal such as Luke uses to appeal to his audience and illustrates in his account of the early church (Acts 2:44–45; 4:34–37; 11:27–30; 24:17). But in this age mammon runs out, and in the coming age there won't be any "mammon of unrighteousness" to use charitably for the making of friends. So use it charitably now, while you can. Then in the eternal state you'll get a hospitable welcome by the people you helped financially in your present life. They'll "welcome you into eternal tents" means they'll gratefully open their heavenly dwellings to you.

In the "faithful"-sayings there's synonymous parallelism between "a very small matter," "the unrighteous mammon," and "somebody else's mammon." That is to say, in and of itself worldly wealth has very little importance and, because it's only under your managership (as in the preceding parable), it really belongs to someone else. Jesus doesn't say to whom; so the point is simply that you shouldn't regard the wealth as your private possession. In the "faithful"-sayings there's also synonymous parallelism between "much," "the true [mammon]," and "your own [mammon]." That is to say, eternal wealth—what in connection with charitable giving Jesus elsewhere called "an inexhaustible treasure in heaven" (12:33)—such wealth has great importance, possesses everlasting value, and really does belong to you. Naturally, "much" contrasts with "very small," "true" contrasts with "unrighteous," and "your own" contrasts with "somebody else's." The manager in the preceding parable has now turned into a negative example, not of dishonesty (as in his discounting of debts owed to his boss), but of unfaithfulness (as in his mismanagement that led to the boss's firing him). If like the manager you mismanage the very small wealth of this world, you'll not be entrusted with very great wealth hereafter. But if you manage this-worldly wealth well by giving it away to the needy, you will be entrusted with great wealth hereafter. But watch out, because this-worldly wealth will enslave you if you don't give it away in charity; and then—because it's psychologically impossible to serve two masters—you won't be serving God. You'll be serving "Mammon" (capitalized as a personified deity opposed to God). But giving away this-worldly wealth enslaves you to God. Love and devotion to Mammon,

or love and devotion to God—one or the other but not both. It's your choice.

THE PHARISEES AS DETESTABLE LOVERS OF MONEY
Luke 16:14–31

A description of the Pharisees as lovers of money links this section to the preceding one on wealth. Their sneering at Jesus leads him to expose them as detested by God, though everyone—including them—is being urged to enter God's kingdom. The Pharisees' implied practice of divorce and remarriage and of marrying divorcees offers examples of their detestable violations of the Law through committing adultery despite their self-justification and despite the validity of the Law and the Prophets. Then Jesus tells a parable about a rich man resembling the Pharisees.

16:14–15: And the Pharisees, being lovers of money, were hearing all these things [that Jesus was saying about wealth]; **and they were sneering at him.** [15]**And he told them, "You're the ones who justify yourselves** [= make yourselves look good] **in the sight of human beings. But God knows your hearts** [where your love of money resides], **because what's high among human beings** [is] **an abomination in God's sight."** The Pharisees' love of money made them sneer at Jesus for his downgrading of this-worldly wealth and his portrayal of Mammon as their slavemaster to whom they give their love and devotion (16:10–13). Jesus doesn't specify just how the Pharisees justify themselves in the sight of other human beings. So his point lies in the contrast between those other human beings' regarding them as something high, and therefore admirable, and God's knowing their hearts to be an abomination, and therefore putrid. ("Abomination" means something that stinks—here used figuratively, of course.) "What's high" refers to the Pharisees, but the neuter gender of "What" matches the neuter gender of "abomination" and stresses the Pharisees' quality of highness in the mistaken opinion of others.

16:16–18: "The Law and the Prophets [were] **until John** [the baptizer]. **From then on** [= Since then] **God's reign is being preached as good news, and everyone is being insistently urged into it.** [17]**But it's easier for the heaven and the earth to pass away than for a single little stroke** [in its letters] **to fall from the Law.** [18]**Every** [man] **who divorces his wife and marries another** [woman] **commits adultery, and** [every man] **who marries** [a woman] **divorced from** [her] **husband commits adultery."** "The Law and the Prophets" refers to the Old Testament, especially its first two divisions according to the arrangement of books in the original Hebrew. Jesus doesn't say the Law and the Prophets were in force until John, or that they were preaching or being preached until John. Jesus merely mentions their existence as a backdrop against which a new phenomenon stands out. That's the preaching of God's reign as good news and the insistent urging of everyone to enter it (compare 14:23 with this insistent urging). Lest anyone think he's denigrating the Law and the Prophets, though, Jesus denies that even "a single little stroke" will "fall from the Law." (Here he concentrates on the Law alone, Genesis–Deuteronomy, in preparation for an allusion to its regulation concerning divorce and remarriage.) In other words, the Law in all its details stands forever. God's reign completes it but doesn't destroy it. Thus Jesus supports Luke's emphasis on the continuity of Christianity with Judaism, particularly with its Old Testament base. The gospel may be new in its flowering, but it has ancient, traditional roots.

According to the Law, a man who divorced his wife wrote her a certificate of divorce; and if another man married her and then divorced her or died, her former husband couldn't remarry her, "since she has been defiled" by the second marriage (Deuteronomy 24:1–4). Jesus doesn't abrogate this law. He has just said that the Law will stand forever. But he extends the Old Testament law of divorce and remarriage by inferring from a woman's defilement in a second marriage that it's adulterous for a man, whether or not *he* has been married before, to marry a divorced woman. Despite her divorce, she'll always belong sexually to her former husband. And adultery defiles. Strikingly, Jesus also infers that a man who divorces his wife and marries another woman, whether or not *she* has been divorced, commits adultery. For he'll always belong sexually to his former wife. Thus Jesus dots the i's and crosses the t's of the Law. Such is his adherence to and affirmation of the Old Testament, and such is his high standard of morality—a standard that Luke repeatedly holds up as an attraction to prospective converts of moral sensibility.

In *16:19–21* Jesus circles back to warn against the love of money that characterizes the Pharisees and breeds a lack of generosity (compare 16:14): **"And there was a certain rich man, and he was wearing purple and fine linen, enjoying himself splendidly day by day. **[20]**But a certain poor** [man]—**Lazarus by name—had been cast at his** [the rich man's] **gate.** [Lazarus was] **covered with sores **[21]**and craving to eat his fill of the** [items] **falling from the rich man's table. But coming** [to Lazarus]**, even the dogs were licking his sores."** The personalizing of the poor man with a notation of his name, "Lazarus," evokes sympathy for his poverty-stricken condition. By contrast, the anonymity of the rich man robs him of sympathy from Jesus' and Luke's audiences. Though Luke makes nothing of the fact, "Lazarus" is Greek for the Hebrew "Eleazar," which means "God is [his] help." Nobody else helps this Lazarus. Certainly the rich man doesn't, for the dogs' coming and licking Lazarus's sores to soothe them shows the dogs more sympathetically helpful than the rich man is. "But" introduces the contrast emphatically; and the fact that these are street scavengers, not household pets, makes the contrast even starker. Lazarus's exposed sores also contrast with the rich man's wearing of purple and fine linen. This contrast underlines Lazarus's sorry state and consequent need of help. The expensiveness of purple-dyed outer garments and linen undergarments contributes to this contrast, and underlining it

even more are Lazarus's having been "cast" at the rich man's gate (he's so weak or crippled that he can't move on his own and therefore is tossed there like a discarded piece of junk) and the further contrast between the rich man's "enjoying himself splendidly day by day" and Lazarus's "craving to eat his fill of the [items] falling from the rich man's table." "At [the rich man's] gate" makes Lazarus and his need for help evident to the rich man every time he passes in and out of the gate, and makes it easy for the rich man to help Lazarus if only he would. He wouldn't have to travel far, or at all, to help him.

16:22–24: **"And it happened that the poor** [man] **died and was carried away by angels into the bosom of Abraham. And the rich** [man] **also died and was buried. **[23]**And in hell, being in torments, on lifting his eyes he sees Abraham from far away and Lazarus in his bosoms. **[24]**And he, calling out, said, 'Father Abraham, have mercy on me and send Lazarus to dip the tip of his finger in water and cool down my tongue, because I'm suffering pain in this flame.'"** After mentioning the deaths of Lazarus and the rich man, Jesus begins to tell the story as though bodily resurrection has already taken place; for Abraham has a bosom, Lazarus a finger, and the rich man eyes and a tongue. On the other hand, later statements—"if someone from the dead were to go to them" and "if someone were to rise from the dead" (16:30–31)—presume that resurrection hasn't yet taken place. So we have to conclude that the parable doesn't teach a chronology of resurrection and reversal of fates, but only a reversal of fates. "Into the bosom of Abraham" implies that at the messianic banquet (on which see especially 14:15–24) Lazarus is reclining at table on his left side and leaning back onto Abraham's chest as the beloved disciple did on Jesus' chest at the Last Supper (John 13:23, 25). This position, plus being carried there by angels, accords Lazarus high honor.

By way of contrast, the rich man merely gets buried—by whom, Jesus doesn't say. Nor does he say who took him to hell. The plural of "torments" accentuates the "pain" the rich man is suffering in punishment for his failure to show Lazarus charity during their earthly lifetimes. In this respect the rich man is the reverse image of the manager who shrewdly prepared for his future by discounting debts (16:1–9). For correspondence with the plural of "torments," the singular of Abraham's "bosom" graduates to the plural of his "bosoms." This plural highlights the contrast between the rich man's suffering and Lazarus's pleasure. ("Bosoms" refers to the two sides, or breasts, of Abraham's chest.) The rich man's "lifting his eyes" stresses the distance he is from Abraham and Lazarus. Seeing them "from far away" adds more stress on this distance. Note: the stress doesn't fall on Abraham's and Lazarus's distance from the rich man; rather, on *his* distance from *them*, because he's the one disadvantaged by the distance. Despite the great distance, though, the rich man "sees" them. The present tense of this verb combines with the great distance to dramatize the difference between Lazarus's happy fate and the horrid one of the rich man. Because of the great distance, the rich man has to "call out" to be heard by Abraham. In an effort to gain his request, he uses the respectful address, "Father Abraham." Here, "Father" has the sense of "my ancestor." The rich man is appealing to his Abrahamic ancestry (compare 3:8). The request that Abraham "send Lazarus" shows that during his lifetime the rich man knew Lazarus by name yet did nothing to help him, and also shows that in his afterlife the rich man thinks Lazarus should serve his (the rich man's) needs as he hadn't served Lazarus's needs. Not even now does the rich man deign to talk to Lazarus. The tip of a finger and the tongue are only small parts of the human anatomy. But the torments of the rich man are so severe that he craves even the slightest relief just as Lazarus had craved even the items falling from the rich man's table. Lazarus had craved scraps of food for some nourishment. The rich man is in such pain from hell's flame that he'd be happy to get a drop or two of water to cool down his tongue.

16:25–26: "But Abraham said, 'Child, remember that during your life you received in full your good things, and likewise Lazarus [received in full] **bad things. But now he's being comforted, and you're suffering pain. ²⁶And among all these things** [= in addition to your torments and his comforts]**, a big chasm has been fixed between us and you** [plural]**, so that those wanting to pass through from here to you** [plural] **can't** [do so]**, nor can people cross over from there** [hell] **to us.'"** Since the rich man has called Abraham his ancestor ("Father Abraham"), Abraham calls him "Child" in the sense of his descendant. The only consolation Abraham can give the rich man is a memory of the good life he enjoyed on earth. "You received *in full* your good things" indicates, however, that because of his failure to be charitable he'll not receive any good things in his afterlife, certainly not in hell. By the same token, Lazarus's having received in full bad things indicates that he'll not receive any bad things in his afterlife. The reverse is also true: Lazarus is now enjoying a comfortable afterlife whereas the rich man is suffering pain. Then Abraham adds that "a chasm" separates him and Lazarus from the rich man. It's "big" (hence the rich man's having seen Abraham and Lazarus "from far away" [16:23]) and "fixed" (therefore uncloseable). Instead of using the singular of "you" in the phrase "between us and you," Abraham uses the plural, because the rich man represents the Pharisees in their love of money (16:14). In other words, Abraham steps out of the parable to address Jesus' audience of Pharisees. The same is true in the phrase "from here to you," and the "people" who "can't cross over from there to us" are these same money-loving Pharisees represented by the rich man. Once dead, then, their hellish fate is just as fixed as is the big chasm. There's no second chance. But who are "those wanting to pass through [the chasm] from here to you"? Who'd want to go from heaven to hell? Answer: the righteous, who'd like to show charity to the damned in hell. But alas, they can't. So all hope is lost for the uncharitable damned.

16:27–31: "And he [the rich man] **said, 'Therefore** [since the chasm is impassable] **I request of you, father, that you send him** [Lazarus] **into my father's house—** ²⁸**for I have five brothers—so that he may bear solemn testimony to them** [of my hellish condition]**, lest they also come into this place of torment.' ²⁹But Abraham says, 'They have Moses and the prophets. Let them** [your five brothers] **hear them** [not "let" in the sense of a permission, but in the sense of a command].' ³⁰**But he said, 'No, father Abraham, but if someone were to go to them from the dead** [a hypothesis]**, they'll repent** [a certainty, or so the rich man thinks].' ³¹**And he** [Abraham] **told him, 'If they don't heed Moses and the prophets, neither will they be persuaded if someone were to rise from the dead.'"** The rich man persists in thinking of Lazarus as someone who should now be sent to serve his needs though he hadn't served Lazarus's needs during their earthly lifetimes. In a continued appeal to his Abrahamic ancestry, he calls Abraham "father" a second and a third time, though he also makes a sidelong mention of his immediate father. The direct mention of his five brothers suggests an allusion to the five books of Moses (Genesis–Deuteronomy), in which the addressed Pharisees lay much store. The present concern of this rich man for his brothers, apparently rich as he'd been (for otherwise he needn't fear their joining him in hell for lack of charity), stands in contrast with his earlier lack of concern for poor Lazarus. The present tense in "Abraham says" and an omission of the earlier address, "Child"—despite the rich man's addressing Abraham again as his father—combine to show some judgmental impatience in Abraham's second reply (16:29). In 16:16 Jesus spoke of "the Law and the Prophets" as two sections of the Hebrew Old Testament. Here he has Abraham speak of "*Moses* and the prophets," not as writings so much as personal witnesses—in place of Lazarus—in and through their writings. "Let them *hear* them" refers to hearing the writings of Moses and the prophets read aloud in synagogues on the Sabbath (for their teaching on charity, see Deuteronomy 14:28–29; 15:4, 7–11; 24:14–15; Isaiah 3:13–15; 10:1–3; 32:6–7; 58:6–7, 10, and so on). Abraham's reference to Moses and the prophets advances Luke's presentation of Christianity as an ancient religion brought to maturity, not an unreliable upstart.

The rich man thinks mistakenly that his brothers will repent of their lack of charity if someone like Lazarus were to go to them from the dead with a testimony of the rich man's torments. Going from the dead doesn't equate with rising from the dead. It means going as a dead person to those still living. Abraham responds not just that a dead person's going to the living won't persuade the living to repent. If they don't heed Moses and the prophets on the necessity of charity, not even someone's resurrection will persuade them. Improbable as it might seem, then, the love of money will rob Jesus' resurrection of its persuasive effect. Because of its ability to attract such overpowering love and devotion, money is dangerous. In the story, the rich man's brothers never get the fearsome report of his torments in hell. But Jesus' and Luke's audiences do get it. So take heed!

ON OFFENSES, FORGIVENESS, FAITH, AND OBEDIENCE AMONG JESUS' DISCIPLES
Luke 17:1–10

In this passage Jesus remarks on various topics having to do with discipleship, first as regards the interactions of disciples with one another (17:1–4) and then as regards their exercising faith in God (17:5–6) and their obeying Jesus the Lord (17:7–10).

17:1–3a: And he told his disciples, "It's inevitable for snares to come. Nevertheless, alas [for the person] **through whom they come! ²It's advantageous for him if an upper millstone collars his neck and he's been cast into the sea** [rather] **than that he snare one of these little ones. ³ᵃTake precaution for yourselves."** Here Jesus shifts his address from the Pharisees (16:14) to his disciples. "Snares" are stumbling-blocks, tripping over which makes a person fall into sin or, more probably and particularly, into apostasy from discipleship to Jesus. He realistically recognizes the inevitability that into circles of his disciples will come such snares, set by some. We expect him to say the snare-*setters* come. But instead he personifies the snares and says *they* come. This personification portrays the snares as active agents waiting to trap the unwary. Despite the inevitability of their coming, though, the person who sets them faces lamentable doom. Jesus doesn't identify what kind of snare he has in mind, whether false teaching, a bad example, or something else. But coming as it does after a description of the doom, "Take precaution for yourselves" implies that his disciples should beware lest they set snares and suffer judgment for doing so. (The present concern isn't that they beware of being snared themselves by others.) For an explanation of being cast into the sea with an upper millstone laid around the neck like a collar, see the comments on Mark 9:42. If such a fate is advantageous as compared with the judgment of a snare-setter, how horrible that judgment! It must entail eternal hopelessness, just as there's no hope of giving even a decent burial to a person cast into the sea collared with an upper millstone. So instead of "he's cast into the sea," we read "he's *been* cast into the sea" for emphasis on permanence. But who are "these little ones" that the disciples will snare if they're not careful to avoid doing so? The context doesn't identify the little ones specifically. But an upcoming reference to "the apostles" (17:5) favors that the little ones are disciples below the apostolic level. Naturally, Jesus' warning applies to all subsequent church leaders, too. They're not above causing serious damage and thus incurring judgment of the worst sort.

17:3b–4: "If your brother [= fellow disciple] **sins, reprimand him. And if he repents, forgive him. ⁴And if he sins against you seven times during a day and seven times turns to you, saying, 'I repent,' you shall forgive him** [compare 11:4]**."** The switch from "forgive him" to the imperatival (*not* predictive) future, "you *shall* forgive him," highlights the obligation to forgive a sinner; and forgiveness is to take place even though the

sinning is "against you," not just sinning in general (as in the earlier "If your brother sins") and even though the sinning against you occurs seven times in a single day. Notably, though, sinning should draw a brotherly reprimand; for disciples bear responsibility for one another's conduct, not just for their own. Furthermore, forgiveness is conditioned on repentance. Thus Jesus establishes a community characterized by moral purity (in the reprimanding for sin and the repenting from it) and interpersonal harmony (through the mutual forgiveness of sins). A community of such characteristics attracts converts.

17:5–6: And the apostles said to the Lord, "Add faith to us [= Increase our faith]**." ⁶But the Lord said, "If you have faith like a mustard seed, you'd have been saying to this sycamine tree** [probably a black mulberry tree]**, 'Be uprooted and planted in the sea'** [compare the snare-setter's better but unrealized fate of being cast into the sea (17:2)]**, and it would have obeyed you."** No reason is given for the disciples' asking Jesus to increase their faith; so the point lies in his response. In effect, he responds that they don't need more faith. Just a little will do wonders. A mustard seed was the smallest seed visible to the naked eye in first-century Israel, and the sycamine tree was noted for its extensive root system, which enabled it to endure for centuries. Yet a command backed up by faith even so small as to be comparable to a mustard seed would have uprooted such a tree and planted it in the sea. The personification of the tree, as though it "would have *obeyed*" such a command, dramatizes the power of faith as tiny as a mustard seed. "The apostles" delimits to the Twelve "the disciples" who ask Jesus to increase their faith; and because Jesus' statement itself seems unbelievable, Luke twice calls him "the Lord" to stress the authority of his word about belief.

The followup in **17:7–10** implies that the apostles shouldn't think that because the sycamine tree would have obeyed them, they needn't obey Jesus their Lord: **"But which of you, having a slave plowing or shepherding, who when he has come in from the field will say to him, 'Coming alongside** [me]**, recline** [at table] **immediately'?"** Implied answer: None of you would say that. **⁸"Rather, he'll say to him, won't he, 'Prepare something for me to dine on; and on girding yourself** [with an apron, towel, or the like]**, serve me** [the food] **while I eat and drink; and after these things** [the preparation and serving of food] **you yourself shall eat and drink'?"** Implied answer: That's exactly what the slave would be told. **⁹"He doesn't have gratitude for the slave, does he, because he** [the slave] **did the things ordered** [for him to do]**?"** Implied answer: The slave doesn't get gratitude for following orders. **¹⁰"In this way you too, when you've done all the things ordered for you** [to do]**, say, 'We're useless slaves; we've done what we were obligated to do.'"** Jesus isn't approving the institution of slavery among human beings. But he is using it as a point of comparison for the apostles' relation to him as their Lord, that is, as a point of comparison for the apostles' relation to him as their owner and master (compare Luke's calling Jesus "the Lord" twice in 17:5–6). In other words, just as they wouldn't be grateful for a slave of theirs who had merely followed orders, they shouldn't expect the Lord Jesus to be grateful for their following his orders. It's their duty to follow them, and it's enough that after they've followed his orders here and now, he'll tell them at the messianic banquet, "*You yourself* shall eat and drink" (the future tense as a command). Compensation aplenty! In the meantime, though, even the doing of "*all* the things ordered" by Jesus should be belittled with a confession of uselessness. A slave is useful to his master when he carries out the master's orders, of course. But *saying*, "We're useless slaves; we've done what we were obligated to do," exhibits an appropriate sense of unworthiness.

THE GLORIFICATION OF GOD
BY A SAVED SAMARITAN
Luke 17:11–19

This passage starts with renewed attention to Jesus' traveling toward Jerusalem (17:11), proceeds to his cleansing of ten lepers (17:12–14), the gratitude of one of them (17:15–16), and Jesus' comment on the ungrateful nine (17:17–18) and assurance to the grateful one (17:19).

17:11: And it happened during the traveling to Jerusalem that he was going between Samaria and Galilee. Luke picks up again his recurrent theme of travel—here, in particular, Jesus' traveling to Jerusalem (for the start of which see 9:51). But "between Samaria and Galilee" seems puzzling at first, because in 9:52–54 he has already gone into Samaria on his way south from Galilee toward Jerusalem. Furthermore, traveling between Samaria and Galilee entails an east-west route rather than a southward route. (Luke doesn't locate the story of Mary and Martha [10:38–42] in Bethany near Jerusalem [though see John 11:17–19].) Luke probably means us to infer that because of the nonwelcome given Jesus by the first Samaritan village that he approached (9:52–54 again), he turned back toward Galilee (note that the town in 9:56 isn't identified as Samaritan, as the one in 9:52 was), took an easterly route between Samaria and Galilee to the Jordan River, and—skirting Samaria—turned south toward Jerusalem. In any case, the roundabout traveling of Jesus on his way to Jerusalem prefigures the roundabout traveling of the Apostle Paul (Acts 13–28). And the mention of Samaria prepares for the mention of a Samaritan among ten lepers in the immediately following episode.

17:12–14: And as he was entering a certain town, there met him ten leprous men, who stood far away. ¹³**And they raised** [their] **voice, saying, "Jesus, Master, have mercy on us."** ¹⁴**And on seeing** [them], **he told them, "Go show yourselves to the priests." And it happened that while they were departing, they were cleansed.** See the comments on 5:12, 14 for leprosy as various skin diseases, for the ritual uncleanness and os-

tracism of lepers, and for showing themselves to priests for confirmation of their cleansing/healing. Here, the ten leprous men "stood far away" to avoid defiling Jesus and those with him. More literally, they "stood *from* a distance." To their disadvantage, they were distant from Jesus and others rather than vice versa (compare the comments on 16:23). Because of the distance, to be heard they had to "raise their voice." The singular of voice indicates that they cried out for mercy in unison. And they respectfully addressed Jesus by his personal name and title. The title, "Master," doesn't translate the term that also means "Lord," "lord," "owner," and "master (of a slave)." It refers, rather, to somebody who's in charge. So this title indicates that in crying out for mercy, the ten lepers consider Jesus to be in charge of their fate. Indeed he is! The outcry catches Jesus' attention, so that he sees them, marks their leprous condition, and instead of healing them with a touch (they were distant, after all) tests their obedience and faith by telling them to go show themselves to the priests (plural, since the lepers, being plural, will require multiple priests when and if examined simultaneously). The instruction to show themselves to the priests exhibits Jesus' adherence to the Mosaic law. The lepers are cleansed—that is, rid of their uncleanness through the healing of their leprosy—as they depart in obedient faith to show themselves to the priests. They don't wait to depart till they've been cleansed.

17:15–16: But one of them, on seeing that he'd been healed, turned back, glorifying God with a loud voice. ¹⁶**And he fell on** [his] **face at his** [Jesus'] **feet, thanking him. And *he* was a Samaritan!** Now free of uncleanness that would defile others, this ex-leper doesn't have to stand "from a distance" any more, but falls prostrate, his face to the ground, at Jesus' feet and thanks him for having healed him. The gesture enhances Luke's portrayal of Jesus as the merciful and masterly physician. In 17:7–10, a slave isn't deserving of thanks for merely obeying orders. Here, though, Jesus *is* deserving of thanks; for he's in charge, as a slave isn't; and he has healed the lepers out of sheer grace, not out of duty. But even more importantly, as can be told from Luke's mentioning it before the leper's thanking Jesus, the leper glorifies God. For the glorifying of God shows the good religious effect of Jesus' ministry. It fostered piety rather than vitiating it (see the comments on 2:20). "With a *loud* voice" magnifies this good religious effect. And the notation that the ex-leper was a Samaritan adds further magnification in that Jews considered Samaritans to be apostates. Yet even an apostate glorifies God because of Jesus' having healed him.

17:17–18: And answering [= responding], **Jesus said, "The ten were cleansed, weren't they?"** Implied answer: Yes. **"But the nine—where** [are they]**?** ¹⁸**Except for this person of another race, they** [the nine] **haven't been found turning back to give glory to God, have they?"** Implied answer: They're nowhere to be found doing so. Emphasis falls once again on the Samaritan's giving God glory, and this despite belonging to a race other than the Jewish race (compare the role of the good

Samaritan in 10:30–37 and the coming conversions of many non-Jews throughout Luke's book of Acts [see Acts 8:4–25 for Samaritans in particular]). The implication that the unthankful nine were Jews strengthens indirectly both the inefficacy of the rich man's reliance on Abrahamic ancestry (16:19–31) and John the baptizer's denial of its efficacy (3:8).

17:19: And he told him, "Standing up, go [show yourself to a priest]. **Your faith has saved you."** To go, the Samaritan ex-leper will have to stand up, because he's presently prostrate on his face at Jesus' feet. The command to go repeats Jesus' original command to all ten that they go show themselves to the priests, and it renews the theme of Jesus' adherence to the Mosaic law, so that Christianity represents an outgrowth of the venerable religion of Judaism rather than a reaction against it. Since Jesus has healed all ten lepers, his telling this one worshipful and thankful Samaritan that his faith has saved him appears to include not only physical deliverance from leprosy but also eternal salvation, as in Acts 16:31: "Believe on the Lord Jesus, and you'll be saved—also your household" (compare Luke 7:50; 8:12, 48, 50; 18:42). The remaining nine lost out on eternal salvation (compare Acts 28:25–28).

GOD'S REIGN AS ALREADY PRESENT IN JESUS' PREACHING OF REPENTANCE
Luke 17:20–21

17:20–21: And on being asked by the Pharisees when God's reign is coming, he answered them and said, "God's reign isn't coming with observation. **[21]Neither will people say, 'Behold, here** [it is]!' **or 'There** [it is]!' **For behold, God's reign is in your midst!"** In 11:29 Jesus characterized "this generation" as "evil" because "it seeks a sign." So his present statement that "God's reign isn't coming with observation" means that it isn't coming accompanied by signs that people like the Pharisees can observe so as to be able to exclaim it's here or there. Then Jesus matches people's *false* "Behold" with his own *true* "behold" to underline that God's reign is in the midst of the Pharisees, though their question and Jesus' answer indicate they haven't recognized its presence because they haven't observed the signs they seek. Ah, but there was one sign according to 11:29–32. It wasn't a sign to be seen, though. It was a sign to be heard. That was the sign of Jesus' preaching repentance as the prophet Jonah had done. And this preaching in the Pharisees' midst constitutes God's reign. He's reigning through Jesus' preaching. So in an audible way his reign has already come. Its present whereabouts ("in your midst") makes the chronological question ("when?") irrelevant.

THE REVELATION OF THE SON OF MAN AS FUTURE
Luke 17:22–35, 37

Here Jesus shifts his address from the Pharisees to his disciples, and the topic from the coming of God's reign to the revelation of the Son of Man. Whereas God's reign has already come unobserved in Jesus' preaching of repentance, the Son of Man's revelation is yet to take place in a way impossible to miss.

17:22–25: And he told the disciples, "Days will come when you'll long to see one of the days of the Son of Man, and you'll not see [it]. **[23]And people will tell you, 'Behold, there** [he is]!' **or 'Behold, here** [he is]!' **Don't go off** [with them], **and don't chase** [after them to see the Son of Man where they'll tell you he is]. **[24]For just as the lightning shines, flashing from a** [region] **under the sky to a** [region] **under the sky** [= from one region under the sky to another region under the sky], **thus will be the Son of Man in his day. [25]But first it's necessary that he suffer severely and be rejected by this generation."** In 17:20–21 God's reign was to be heard right now rather than seen in the future. Here the Son of Man's day is to be seen in the future, for it will be a day of revelation (17:30). But that day will bring to a climax other days of the Son of Man (about which see the comments on 17:26–28). The disciples won't long to see any of those preceding days. They'll long to see "his day," the "one" day of his revelation. Meanwhile, because of his coming absence, they won't see it and shouldn't be deceived into thinking he has come covertly here or there. They won't have to go anywhere to see him on the day for which they long, because he'll be visible to everybody, like lightning that illuminates the earth and sky as far as the eye can see. So stay put, and be informed of the divine necessity (it's part of God's plan) that first the Son of Man suffer severely and be rejected by this generation (compare 9:22, 44; 13:33; 18:31–33).

Despite the necessity of the Son of Man's suffering and rejection, though, he'll win out in the end. **17:26–30: "And just as it happened in the days of Noah, so also it will be in the days of the Son of Man. [27]People were eating, drinking, marrying** [as men do], **being given in marriage** [as daughters are] **till the day that Noah entered into the ark. And the flood came and destroyed them all** [see Genesis 6–7]. **[28]Likewise, just as it happened in the days of Lot, people were eating, drinking, buying, selling, planting, building. [29]But on the day that Lot went out from Sodom, fire and sulfur rained from heaven and destroyed** [them] **all** [see Genesis 18–19]. **[30]It will be the same on the day that the Son of Man is revealed."** "Is revealed" rather than "comes" links up with Jesus' foregoing stress on wide, lightning-like visibility. The Old Testament stresses the evildoings of Noah's generation and the people of Sodom. Jesus' emphasis differs. The ancient destructions that he mentions only imply those evildoings. His explicit emphasis falls instead on what the Old Testament doesn't even mention—that is, the perfectly innocent and normal activities in which people were engaged at those times, so that their destruction came on them unexpectedly. And with the obvious exceptions of Noah, Lot, and their families, none of them escaped. The lack of "and" before the last-listed activities in the two lists of innocent, normal activities implies open-ended lists to which other such activities could be added. "Eating" and "drinking" occur in both lists. But in place of the "marrying" and "being given in marriage" in the days of Noah (compare Genesis 6:2: "they took wives for themselves"), Jesus mentions activities appropriate to a city like Sodom and its fertile surroundings: "buying, selling, planting, building" (compare Genesis 13:10: "And Lot lifted his eyes and saw all the circle of the Jordan [where Sodom was located], that it was well watered everywhere . . . like the garden of the Lord"). So as in the cases of Noah's generation and the citizens of Sodom, the revelation of the Son of Man and the accompanying destruction of all evildoers will come unexpectedly as they go about their daily business. That's what they'll be doing "in the days [plural] of the Son of Man" right up to "the day [singular] of the Son of Man." Because "the day" is that of his revelation (at the second coming), and because people have been engaged in ordinary activities ever since Jesus' time, "the days of the Son of Man" must have started then and must be continuing throughout the church age (compare Luke's church-historical book of Acts).

17:31–33: **"On that day** [of the Son of Man's revelation], **the** [man] **who'll be on the roof—and his goods in the house—mustn't come down to take them."** Their houses had flat roofs accessed by outside stairs and used for various purposes. For example, Acts 10:9 has the apostle Peter praying on a roof. **"And likewise the** [man] **in a field mustn't return** [to his house]. [32]**Remember Lot's wife.** [33]**Whoever seeks to preserve his life will lose it, but whoever loses** [it] **will keep it alive."** While fleeing from Sodom (just mentioned in 17:29), Lot's wife turned into a pillar of salt because of disobeying the Lord's command not to look back (Genesis 19:17, 26 [compare Luke 9:62]). But here in Luke there's no command to flee, for there's nothing to flee from (contrast Mark 13:14–17; Matthew 24:15–21). So Jesus' commands not to come down from a roof and not to return home from a field imply staying on the roof and in the field, from which places—it'll turn out in 17:34–35—the disciples will be taken. A man who seeks to preserve his life does so by coming down into his house, or by returning to it, to take his goods, which would make life possible except for the destruction that will come. A man who loses his life does so by not coming down into his house, or returning to it, to take his supposedly life-sustaining goods. His treasure, after all, is laid up in heaven. This man simply waits where he is for salvation from the coming destruction. Thus the losing of life and the keeping of life will both take place on the day of the Son of Man's revelation.

17:34–35, 37: **"I tell you, on that night two will be on one bed. One will be taken along, and the other will be left.** [35]**Two** [women] **will be grinding** [grain] **at the same** [place]. **One will be taken along, but the other will be left."** [37]**And answering, they** [the disciples] **say to him, "Where, Lord?" And he told them, "Where the carcass** [is], **there also will the vultures be gathered**

together." Taken along in judgment and left for judgment, or taken along in salvation and left for judgment— which? Well, in 9:10, 28; 18:31 "taken along" carries a friendly connotation. Vultures are attracted to a carcass that has been left. And in the stories of Noah and Lot, recently alluded to in 17:26–29, 32, those who were left suffered God's judgment. So Jesus is saying that on the day of his revelation, there'll be a separation in which disciples will be taken so as to be spared judgment, as were Noah and Lot; and nondisciples will be left as carrion that attracts the vultures, representing divine judgment. "I tell you" emphasizes the separation. "On one bed" represents the possibility that such a separation will happen at night, but "grinding [grain]" represents the possibility of its happening in the daytime. "On one bed" and "at the same [place]" stress that the separation will cut a fine line between the saved and the lost, that interpersonal associations won't obscure the difference between them. To the disciples' question where the lost will be left, Jesus answers in effect that they'll be left where the vultures of God's judgment will be gathered by the sight of their carcasses. The saved, on the other hand, merely have to wait, wherever they happen to be (as on a roof or in a field), for the Son of Man to take them from the region of judgment (compare 1 Thessalonians 5:3–11; 2 Thessalonians 1:5–2:2; Revelation 14:14–20). By introducing the disciples' question with a vivid present tense in "they *say*" and prefixing "answering," Luke ascribes to the disciples a commendable concern to understand Jesus' warning. There's no 17:36 in the earliest and best manuscripts.

PRAYING WHILE LONGING
Luke 18:1–8

In this passage Jesus continues addressing his disciples. He has just told them they'll long for the day of his revelation at the end of an indeterminate period of days (17:22–37). Now he tells them to pray during this period. Throughout Luke-Acts prayer is featured as part of the true piety fostered by Jesus and his gospel. In this way Luke appeals to people serious about religion.

18:1–5: **And he was telling them a parable to the effect that it's necessary to keep praying always and not give up,** [2]**saying, "In a certain city there was a certain judge who didn't fear God and had no consideration for a human being.** [3]**And there was a widow in that city; and she kept coming to him, saying, 'Give me justice against my adversary.'** [4]**And for a time he didn't want to. But after these things** [her repeated comings and pleas for justice] **he said in himself** [we'd say 'to himself'], **'Even if I don't fear God and don't have consideration for a human being,** [5]**because this widow is pestering me I'll indeed give her justice, lest by coming she wear me down completely** [literally, "give me a totally black eye," but here used figuratively].'" It's necessary for the disciples to pray because of their suffering the injustice of persecution during the days prior to the day of Jesus' revelation. He emphasizes this necessity by telling them both to keep on praying "always" and "not give up" doing so. Only by praying thus will they safeguard themselves from discouragement and apostasy.

For lack of a husband, widows occupied a weak and vulnerable position in that male chauvinistic society. So God had commanded that they be treated justly (Exodus 22:22–24; Deuteronomy 24:17–18). The judge in this parable shows his lack of a fear of God by not giving a widow justice at first despite her repeated comings and pleas. He also shows thereby his lack of consideration for a fellow human being. Not only does Jesus describe him in this way. The judge, too, describes himself thus. This double description emphasizes his not wanting to give the widow justice. The emphasis, in turn, underlines both her persistence, which the judge regards as pestering, and its success in gaining the result she desired. In the judge's own statement, "indeed" adds an accent to the success. Her not addressing him with a term of respect leaves the focus entirely on persistence. "I'll indeed give her justice" shows that he recognizes the widow's cause to be just; but the followup, "lest by coming she wear me down completely," shows that his decision to give her justice arises out of self-interest. To the very end he remains unfearful of God and inconsiderate of a fellow human being.

18:6–8: And the Lord [Jesus] **said, "Hear what the unrighteous judge is saying. ⁷And won't God by all means do justice for his selected ones, who cry out to him day and night, and be indulgent toward them** [as they cry out day and night for justice]**? ⁸I tell you that he'll do justice for them speedily. Nevertheless** [= despite this promise]**, will the Son of Man perchance find faith on the earth?"** Luke calls Jesus "the Lord" to underline his authority in issuing the following command. Though "unrighteous" summarizes the judge's lacking the fear of God and human sympathy, the command to "hear what the unrighteous judge is saying" centers on his decision to do justice for the widow against her adversary. But why the command to hear what an *unrighteous* judge is saying? Answer: because he's saying that he'll do justice for her *despite* his lacking both the fear of God and human sympathy, and because his saying so means that God will do the same for Jesus' disciples—not despite anything but because they're the ones God "*selected*" for salvation. If you hear what the judge is saying, then, you'll be encouraged "to keep praying always and not give up," that is, to "cry out to [God] day and night." He's far readier to do justice for his selected ones than is the unrighteous judge to do justice for a widow for whom he has no regard. "By all means" and the following up of a rhetorical question with the declaration, "[God] will do justice for them"—buttressed with a preceding "I tell you"—put enormous emphasis on God's readiness.

But what does "speedily" mean? It could mean "soon." But that meaning wouldn't fit very well Jesus' reference to the days during which the disciples will long for the Son of Man's revelation. Neither would it fit very well Jesus' commanding the disciples to keep praying always

and not give up, or comparing such praying to a widow's persistence over some period of time, or his saying that God will be indulgent to the disciples' crying out to him day and night rather than being exasperated by it (as in the judge's case). So "speedily" is better taken to mean that when God finally does justice for his selected ones after the extended interval that we call the church age, he'll do it fast. It won't take long. At the Son of Man's revelation one will be taken in salvation, another will be left for judgment. There won't even be time to grab your suitcase (see 17:22–37 again). Justice delayed can be regarded unbelievingly as justice denied, though. So Jesus closes with a pensive question whether on coming from heaven as the Son of Man he'll find on earth the kind of faith that will have kept his disciples praying. He leaves the question unanswered. We who are his disciples answer it by whether we keep on praying.

PRIDEFUL PRAYING VERSUS PENITENTIAL PRAYING
Luke 18:9–14

Now Jesus shifts his address from the disciples but continues to speak about praying. Instead of a focus on persistence in praying for God to do justice, as in 18:1–8, though, we have a contrast between prideful praying in self-justification and penitential praying for divine justification.

18:9–12: And he also spoke this parable to some who were trusting in themselves, that they're righteous, and were treating the rest [of humankind] **with contempt: ¹⁰"Two men went up to the temple to pray, one a Pharisee and the other a tax collector. ¹¹Standing, the Pharisee was praying these things in reference to himself: 'God, I thank you that I'm not like the rest of human beings,** [that is,] **predators, unrighteous people, adulterers, or even like this tax collector. ¹²I fast twice a week. I donate a tenth of all the things that I acquire, as many as** [they are].'" Because the temple was located on Mount Zion in Jerusalem, the two men "went up" to it quite literally (except for their doing so only in a parable, of course). As laymen they couldn't go into the temple building, but only into the surrounding courtyards. Since God dwelt as Spirit in the temple, it provided an especially appropriate place to pray. Jesus' identifying one of the men as a Pharisee implies a Pharisaic identification of the addressees who trusted in themselves, "that they're righteous," and despised everybody else. The present tense in "they're righteous" stresses their self-reliance. Despite his addressing God respectfully and thanking him, the Pharisee exhibits self-justification and contempt for the remainder of human beings, as though he were the only righteous one. His listing them as predators, unrighteous people, and adulterers amplifies his contempt; and "even like this tax collector" personalizes it. Pharisees fasted twice a week, on Mondays and Thursdays, and according to 11:42 tithed even the smallest of items. Here, though, the Pharisee stresses the large amounts of his tithing ("all the things that I acquire, as many as [they are]" [compare the money-loving, self-justifying Pharisees of 16:14–15]). Such fasting and tithing, plus not being rapacious, unrighteous, adulterous, or dishonest like a tax collector, constituted the Pharisee's righteousness in which he trusted, for which he thanked God, and by which he compared himself favorably with the rest of humanity. It was this self-exalting, others-disdaining comparison that subverted his thanks to God, especially since praying was done aloud, so that he was promoting himself in the hearing of others who were at the temple and shaming them, in particular the tax collector, by saying nasty things about them.

18:13–14: "But standing at a distance, the tax collector wasn't even willing to lift [his] eyes to heaven, but was beating his breast, saying, 'God, be propitiated [= appeased] for me, a sinner.' ¹⁴I tell you, this [man] went down [from the temple] to his house justified [= regarded as righteous by God] **rather than that** [man (the Pharisee)], **because everyone who lifts himself up** [= exalts himself] **will be lowered** [= humbled], **but the one who lowers himself will be lifted up** [compare 14:11]." Standing was the normal posture for prayer, so that the tax collector stands just as the Pharisee did. But the tax collector stands "at a distance" or, more literally, "from far away," indicating that he deliberately puts himself out of earshot. He has nothing to boast about in the hearing of others. His sense of unworthiness doesn't even let him lift his eyes heavenward (as was the usual practice, just opposite the modern practice of bowing one's head and closing one's eyes). The beating of his breast was body language for extreme sorrow, in this case of penitential sorrow for sins. He asks that God be appeased for him—in other words, that God withdraw the anger he rightfully entertains against the tax collector because of his sins—and that God do so for the tax collector's benefit. "I tell you" emphasizes that God regarded the tax collector as righteous rather than the Pharisee, whom bystanders as well as the tax collector probably regarded as righteous. And why? Because the lowering of yourself in penitential sorrow enables God to withdraw his wrath graciously, whereas the lifting of yourself in pride draws his wrath, pride being the quintessential, original sin (Genesis 3:5–6). And God's wrath brings low the self-exalted, but his grace lifts high the self-humbled (compare 14:7–11).

TODDLERS AS EXAMPLES OF HUMILITY
Luke 18:15–17

The preceding paragraph ended with a call to humility (18:14). Now Jesus makes some toddlers an example of the humility required for entrance into God's kingdom.

18:15: And people were bringing even infants to him that he might touch them [one after another]. **And on seeing** [what was happening], **the disciples were reprimanding them.** Presumably it was parents who were bringing their infants, but Luke doesn't say so. Presumably the touch people were seeking for the infants was a touch of blessing, but again Luke doesn't say so. And presumably the disciples were reprimanding the people, not the infants, but yet again Luke doesn't say so. Nor does he say why the disciples were reprimanding them. His interest focuses solely on the abnormality of infants' being brought to Jesus ("*even* infants"). This abnormality lays the groundwork for an astonishing response by him.

18:16–17: But Jesus summoned them [here definitely the infants in Luke's original text], **saying, "Let the little children come to me, and stop forbidding them** [to do so]; **for God's kingdom belongs to** [little children] **such as these** [that is, to little children who like these ones come to Jesus]. **¹⁷Amen I tell you, whoever doesn't welcome God's kingdom** [in the sense of submitting now to his reign] **as a little child** [welcomes it] **will by no means enter into it** [in the sense of entering into the sphere where at the end God's reign will finally have defeated Satan, sin, and death and brought eternal life (compare 13:22–30)]." Luke has used the term "infants" even though Jesus speaks of them as *coming* to him instead of being *brought* to him. Furthermore, Jesus speaks of them as "little children" who are "welcom[ing]" God's kingdom," whereas infants could hardly understand his "summon[ing] them" or the disciples' "forbidding them." So why Luke's exaggeration in calling the little children "infants" when they must have been at least toddlers? The answer lies first in the low position that little children occupied in that culture. (Theirs wasn't a youth culture like ours.) Next, the answer lies in the preceding statement of Jesus that the person who lowers himself, as the repentant tax collector did, will be lifted high (18:14). Luke uses "infants," then, to stress with hyperbole God's and Jesus' showing of favor to the lowliest of the low, to the smallest of the small. The point of comparison is one of humility, not of childlike trust, much less of childish innocence (compare 9:46–48). Oddly, Jesus summons the *infants* by speaking to the *disciples*. This oddity implies that the disciples should act as his agents in summoning the "infants" rather than as opponents to their coming. "*Let* the little children come to me" shows that the disciples had been succeeding in their opposition. "*Come* to me" signals a shift from the infants' being brought by others to the little children's approaching Jesus themselves, and this shift leads into his interpreting their coming as a welcoming of God's kingdom, evident in Jesus' activities. Though the children are little, then, they're old enough to welcome it. Jesus' making little children's welcoming of God's kingdom an example for adults to follow—on pain of nonentrance into the kingdom if their example isn't followed—needed extra emphasis on the authority of Jesus. Hence the introduction "Amen I say to you."

DIVESTMENT FOR GOD'S KINGDOM
Luke 18:18–30

The first part of this passage contains a dialogue between a ruler and Jesus (18:18–23), a dialogue between

Jesus and the audience of the first dialogue (18:24–27), and a dialogue between Peter and Jesus (18:28–30).

18:18–20: And a certain ruler asked him, saying, "Good teacher, by doing what will I inherit eternal life [compare 10:25]**?" ¹⁹And Jesus said to him, "Why do you call *me* good? There** [is] **no one good except one,** [that is,] **God. ²⁰You know the commandments: 'You shouldn't commit adultery. You shouldn't murder. You shouldn't steal. You shouldn't give false testimony. Honor your father and mother** [Exodus 20:12–16; Deuteronomy 5:16–20]**.'"** Luke doesn't identify what the ruler ruled (a synagogue? a court of law?). So calling the man a ruler has only the function, but an important one, of making more impressive his addressing Jesus with "Good teacher" and asking him what he should do to inherit eternal life. Even a ruler recognizes Jesus' didactic authority and moral virtue. Inheriting eternal life interprets what entering God's kingdom meant in 18:17 (see also 18:24–25). In and of itself Jesus' question, "Why do you call *me* good?" doesn't deny he's good. But the followup, "There [is] no one good except one, [that is,] God," does seem at first to deny Jesus' goodness. In 5:17–26, on the other hand, he took to himself the exclusively divine prerogative of forgiving sins, and demonstrated with a miracle his right to take it. Here, then, Jesus is implying with his question and followup that just as he possesses the exclusively divine prerogative of forgiving sins, he also has the exclusively divine attribute of goodness.[2] Just as "Why do you call *me* good?" takes up the ruler's addressing Jesus with "Good teacher," "You know the commandments" takes up the ruler's asking what he must do to inherit eternal life, and points him to commandments that he already knows and that Jesus proceeds to quote. For Luke, the quotations exhibit Jesus' fidelity to the Jewish Scriptures. Jesus quotes only those commandments out of the Ten Commandments which deal with the treatment of fellow human beings. A ruler such as this one, who'll also turn out to be rich, might be tempted to break such commandments by taking advantage of other people. The tenth commandment ("You shouldn't covet") also deals with one's relations to other people. But Jesus doesn't quote it. Instead, he circles back to the fifth and earliest such commandment ("Honor your father and mother"). His omission of the tenth looks as though he wants to make possible the ruler's following claim that he has obeyed all the quoted commandments. For the ruler's wealth may well have come through covetousness, or he may desire more wealth. In either case, enabling him to claim obedience paves the way for Jesus to tell him what he's lacking.

18:21–23: And he [the ruler] **said, "I've guarded all these things** [= guarded against the prohibited activities] **since** [my] **youth."** So he's now an adult looking back on his youth. **²²And on hearing** [this response]**, Jesus told him, "One thing still remains in your case. Sell all things that you have, as many as** [they are]**, and distribute** [the proceeds] **to poor people, and you'll have treasure in heaven. And** [come] **here! Follow me." ²³But he, on hearing these things, became very sad. For he was exceedingly wealthy.** This time the ruler doesn't address Jesus respectfully, but immediately claims to have obeyed all the quoted commandments. Jesus doesn't deny the claim. Only the doing of "*one*" remaining thing, in contrast to "*all* these things," will bring the ruler eternal life, though. "In your case" implies that others' cases may differ but that he'd better pay attention to his own case. (Zacchaeus, for example, won't be told to sell all his possessions to gain salvation [19:1–10].) Yet the attachment of this ruler to his wealth does require him to divest himself entirely and give to poor people if he truly wants to inherit the heavenly treasure of eternal life (compare 12:33–34). Charity as such doesn't bring eternal life, however. It's following Jesus that does. Charity counts as the precondition and evidence of following him. And good as it is to do, the keeping of Old Testament commandments doesn't make one an heir to eternal life. The great sadness of the ruler on hearing these things illustrates the truth of Jesus' saying in 12:34 that "where your treasure is, there will be your heart, too." The ruler's extreme wealth keeps his heart earthbound. He'll not have heavenly treasure. He'll not inherit eternal life (compare the comments on Mark 10:17–22).

18:24–27: And on seeing that he'd become very sad, Jesus said, "How hardly do those having means go into God's kingdom! ²⁵For it's easier for a camel to enter through a needle's eye than for a rich person to enter into God's kingdom." ²⁶And those who heard [these statements] **said, "And who can be saved?" ²⁷But he said, "The things impossible for human beings** [to do] **are possible for God** [to do]**."** The question of Jesus' audience arises out of passages such as Deuteronomy 28:1–14; Job 1:10; 42:10; Proverbs 10:22, which say that wealth combined with piety signals God's favor. Jesus upsets this view by exclaiming that people of means will have a hard time entering God's kingdom, for attachment to their wealth all too easily keeps them from giving charitably to poor people. And such charity is a concomitant of the one and only thing—discipleship to Jesus—that gains a person entry into God's kingdom. (The present tense in "do . . . go into God's kingdom" is axiomatic with reference to what will happen at the end [18:17], not descriptive of what's happening right now.) Just as entering God's kingdom equates with inheriting eternal life, so being "saved" equates with that entry and that inheritance. Jesus says "*enter* through a needle's eye" instead of "*go* through a needle's eye" to prepare for "*enter* into God's kingdom" (which replaces an earlier "*go* into God's kingdom"). A camel was the largest beast of burden known in first-century Israel. Here it represents a human being burdened with wealth. A burdenless camel couldn't go through a needle's eye,

---

[2]When Jesus describes some human beings as good in 6:45; 8:15; 19:17, he's comparing them with other human beings. Here he's dealing with absolute goodness.

the smallest opening in a hand tool. (Contrary to some modern interpretations, there was no narrow gate in Jerusalem called "The Needle's Eye"; nor do the best manuscripts have "a rope" instead of "a camel.") Much less could a camel carrying burdens do so, and it goes without saying that it *would* be carrying burdens. Since a camel can't go through a needle's eye but it's "easier" for a camel to do so than for a rich person to enter God's kingdom, with humorously ironic hyperbole the entrance of a rich person into the kingdom turns out to be not *almost* impossible or even *entirely* impossible, but *more than* impossible. "*And* who can be saved?" implies that the perceived impossibility of anyone's salvation follows logically from Jesus' statement. He doesn't answer the question who can be *be* saved, though, but points to the only one who can *do* the saving because he's all-powerful. That's God.

18:28–30: **And Peter said, "Behold, having left our own things we've followed you!"** [29]**And he said to them, "Amen I tell you that there's no one who has left a house or a wife or brothers or parents or children on account of God's kingdom** [30]**who'll by no means receive back much more in this time and eternal life in the coming age** [eternity]**."** Jesus' speaking "to *them*" shows that Peter was speaking about himself and the rest of the Twelve. He designs his "Behold" to galvanize Jesus' attention. Peter doesn't say they've *sold* all their possessions, as Jesus has just commanded the rich ruler to do. Not being rich, the Twelve presumably had nothing saleable. But they did have things *leaveable*, such as a house and its furniture. (These couldn't have been sold, for the families of the Twelve needed them.) Peter's calling the things they'd left to follow Jesus "our own" points up the sacrifice of having left them. Jesus adds the families of the Twelve to the "things" left behind. Itineration with him necessitated leaving their families too. The list of family members starts with those of generational equality, "wife" coming before "brothers" because a marital bond trumps a sibling one. ("Brothers" may be gender neutral so as to include "sisters" as well—hence "siblings" in some translations—but more likely "sisters" are omitted as having been married off or as soon to be married off.) "Parents" come next out of filial respect for their age, and "children" last on the list out of societal disdain for their youth. Jesus punctuates his promise of manifold compensation with "Amen I say to you," which is to say, "You can count on this." The compensation omits no one who has left all to follow Jesus for the sake of God's kingdom. "There's *no* one . . . who'll by *no* means" is an emphatically negative equivalent of "*every*one . . . by *all* means will." And the compensation will turn out to be an *over*compensation ("much more") that will cover both present time and the coming age. Jesus leaves the present compensation undefined to stress eternal life instead, for that future compensation will make present compensation negligible by comparison even though the present one is manifold. The promise of eternal life brings us back to the question of eternal life with which

this section started (18:18 [compare the comments on Mark 10:17–31]).

THE PASSION AND RESURRECTION OF JESUS AS AN ACCOMPLISHMENT OF PROPHETIC SCRIPTURE
Luke 18:31–34

18:31–33: **And taking along the Twelve, he said to them, "Behold, we're going up to Jerusalem; and all the things written through the prophets about the Son of Man will be finished** [= accomplished]. [32]**For he'll be given over to the Gentiles** [see 23:1, 6–7, 11 and compare 20:20] **and made fun of** [see 22:63; 23:11, 36] **and pooh-poohed** [see 22:63–65; 23:11] **and spat on** [see Mark 14:65; 15:19; Matthew 26:67; 27:30]. [33]**And after whipping** [him] [see Mark 15:15; Matthew 27:26; John 19:1]**, they'll kill him** [see 23:32–33, 46]. **And on the third day he'll resurrect** [see 24:5–8, 21]**."** Here Jesus makes the Twelve his private audience. "Behold" calls their special attention both to the journey to Jerusalem (on which see also 9:51, 53; 13:22; 17:11; 19:28) and to the accomplishment of prophetic Scripture in what will happen to him there (see also 9:22, 44–45; 12:49–50; 13:32–33; 17:25 for Jesus' prescience of his fate). The accomplishment of prophetic Scripture in Jerusalem, the headquarters of Judaism, will advance Luke's program of presenting Christianity as the flowering of a venerable religion rather than as a questionable novelty (see especially 24:25–27, 44–49). That "*all* the things written . . . about the Son of Man will be finished" underlines this presentation of Christianity, and "*through* the prophets" presents them as agents of God's Spirit in their writing about the Son of Man. Thus the very Spirit of God stands behind the evolution of Judaism into Christianity. "For" introduces an explanation of what will happen in Jerusalem to Jesus the Son of Man. Details in the explanation enhance both the theme of scriptural accomplishment and Jesus' prescience.

18:34: **And they** [the Twelve] **understood none of these things, and this saying was hidden from them, and they weren't comprehending the things being spoken** [by Jesus]. Despite the clarity of Jesus' passion-and-resurrection prediction, Luke presents the ignorance of the Twelve concerning its meaning as total ("*none* of these things"). By contrast, such ignorance enhances again Jesus' prescience and the coming accomplishment of the prophets' writings. Luke's mentioning the ignorance twice ("they understood none of these things" and "they weren't comprehending the things being spoken") adds to this enhancement. At the same time, however, and as he did in 9:45, Luke excuses the ignorance of the Twelve on the ground that "this saying [of Jesus] was *hidden* from them." He doesn't say *who* hid it, or even *why* it was hidden (though see 9:45). So the accent falls on the Twelve's being faultless in the matter. For the purpose of evangelism Luke exonerates them and thus portrays the Christian community, here its founding fathers, in the most attractive way possible.

THE GLORIFICATION AND PRAISE OF GOD BECAUSE OF JESUS' PERFORMING A MIRACLE
Luke 18:35–43

18:35–39: And it happened while he was drawing near to Jericho that a certain blind man was sitting on the edge of the road, begging. A blind person could do little or nothing else. **³⁶And on hearing a crowd traveling through, he was inquiring what this** [noise] **might be** [= mean]. **³⁷And they announced to him, "Jesus the Nazarene is passing by." ³⁸And he cried out, saying, "Jesus, son** [= descendant] **of David, have mercy on me." ³⁹And those who were proceeding forward were reprimanding him to the effect that he should be quiet. But he began shouting much louder, "Son of David, have mercy on me."** Jericho lay about seventeen miles northeast of Jerusalem. So in getting near to Jericho, Jesus is also getting near enough to Jerusalem to make it there in another day's walk. The crowd makes Jesus' passing by the reason for the hullabaloo that excites the blind beggar's curiosity. This hullabaloo and the crowd that caused it testify to the popularity of Jesus for his good deeds. "Nazarene" means "from Nazareth." "Jesus" is the Greek form of the Hebrew name "Joshua." Since Joshua figured heroically in the history of Israel, many Jewish parents named their baby boys after him. To distinguish this Jesus from other Jesuses, then, the crowd add "the Nazarene" to "Jesus." But the blind beggar adds "son of David" to "Jesus" and addresses Jesus a second time with "son of David" alone. For Luke, this repeated designation helps cement the relation of Christianity to Judaism and the fulfillment of God's ancient promises to David (compare 1:27, 32, 69; 2:4, 11; 3:31; Acts 15:16). The blind beggar's shouting "much louder" on being told to be quiet displays the faith that Jesus will shortly commend. Since those who told the blind beggar to keep quiet were "proceeding forward" ahead of Jesus, they didn't want Jesus to stop for him—hence their "be quiet."

18:40–43: And on standing still, Jesus commanded that he [the blind beggar] **be brought to him.** Ironically, those who told the blind beggar to be quiet are told to become Jesus' agents of bringing him to Jesus. **And when he** [the blind beggar] **had drawn near, he** [Jesus] **asked him, ⁴¹"What do you want me to do for you?" And he said, "Lord, that I should see again." ⁴²And Jesus told him, "See again! Your faith has saved you." ⁴³And at once he saw again and started following him, glorifying God. And on seeing** [the miracle Jesus had performed], **all the people gave praise to God.** With Jesus' standing still, commanding that the blind beggar be brought to him, asking what he wanted Jesus to do for him, and restoring his sight, Luke advances his portrayal of Jesus as a merciful and miraculously effective physician. The blind beggar's shifting his address from "son of David" to "Lord" evinces his belief that Jesus has the authority to effect a restoration of his sight. (Apparently he'd *gone* blind, since otherwise he'd have been described as *born* blind, as in another case recorded in John 9.) Jesus' mere command, "See again!" effects the restoration. Its immediacy accentuates the effectiveness of his merciful command. The command is salvific as well as merciful, and Jesus attributes his issuing it to the blind beggar's faith. As elsewhere, "Your faith has saved you" not only refers to a physical healing. It also alludes to eternal salvation (see 7:50; 8:48; 17:19 with Acts 16:31). Evidence of such salvation comes in the ex-blind man's starting to follow Jesus, a sign of discipleship. Naturally, the following also gives evidence of his seeing again. No longer does he have to be brought by others, as initially. His "glorifying God" exhibits the good religious effect of Jesus' miracle. The people's giving "praise to God" widens this effect. That "*all* the people" gave praise to God universalizes the effect so far as the crowd are concerned. As usual, Luke is recommending the gospel to prospective converts looking for a good, old-time religion (see also 2:20; 5:25–26; 7:16; 13:13; 17:15, 18; 19:37; 23:47; Acts 2:47; 3:8–9). And the crowd's "seeing" Jesus' miracle suits Luke's emphasis on eyewitnessing (1:1–4).

JESUS' SEEKING AND SAVING A LOST BUT REPENTANT TAX COLLECTOR
Luke 19:1–10

A blind beggar has just exercised faith (18:35–43). Now a rich tax collector will exercise repentance.

19:1–4: And on entering, he was going through Jericho. ²And behold, a man called Zacchaeus (as to [his] **name)—and he was a chief tax collector, and he** [was] **rich. ³And he was seeking to see Jesus, who he is, and couldn't on account of the crowd, because he** [Zacchaeus] **was small (as to** [his] **stature). ⁴And on running ahead to the front** [of the procession], **he climbed up on a sycamore tree in order to see him, because he** [Jesus] **was going to go through that** [way]. Jesus was getting near Jericho in 18:35. Now he has entered and is going through. "Behold" calls attention to the tax collector called Zacchaeus. Luke's knowledge of his name testifies to the historical character of this story (compare 1:1–4). More literally translated, "a *chief* tax collector" comes out as "a *ruler* tax collector." Add to this designation the description "rich" and you get a parallel with the "ruler" who was "rich" in 18:18–23. But Zacchaeus's response to Jesus will happily run counter to that of the earlier rich ruler. As a ruling tax collector Zacchaeus had other tax collectors working under him. Testifying to Jesus' well-deserved popularity are (1) Zacchaeus's seeking to see Jesus and (2) the crowd that Zacchaeus can't see over. The reference to Zacchaeus's diminutive stature marks another historical detail. It also prepares for Jesus' exercise of grace toward him, an outcast not only because he's a tax collector but also because ancient people generally despised anybody with a physical abnormality—and, shamefully from our standpoint, they considered unusual smallness just such an abnormality. "To see Jesus, who he is" implies that Zacchaeus has heard about Jesus but hasn't seen him before. He's curious to discover what Jesus looks like, but he'll unexpectedly discover much more about Jesus. He'll discover in him a shepherd who has come to seek and save him, a lost sheep (compare 19:10 with 15:3–7). The strength of Zacchaeus's desire to see who Jesus is comes out in his running (unusual for a person of consequence, who ordinarily walks with slow dignity) and climbing up a sycamore tree (which was rather like an oak with easily reached branches on which to climb). Again the details arise from historical reminiscence.

19:5–6: And when he [Jesus] **came to the place** [where Zacchaeus had climbed up the tree]**, looking up, Jesus said to him, "Zacchaeus, come down in a hurry; for it's necessary that I stay in your house today." ⁶And hurrying, he came down and, rejoicing, welcomed him.** As a tax collector, Zacchaeus was classified a sinner (5:27–32; 7:34; 15:1–2; 18:9–14; 19:7). But Jesus came to call sinners to repentance (5:32). So he takes the initiative with Zacchaeus. Luke doesn't say how Jesus knew Zacchaeus's name; so the point has to do with a respectful address. Since Zacchaeus is a sinful tax collector—a chief one at that—addressing him by name shows grace as well as respect and prepares for Jesus' inviting himself to stay at Zacchaeus's house for the day. The "hurry" in Jesus' command to come down implies that he doesn't want to delay his forging ahead to Jerusalem any longer than necessary. But the necessity of his staying at Zacchaeus's house arises out of God's plan just as does the necessity of his going to Jerusalem (13:33). Not only does Zacchaeus's "hurrying . . . down" display obedience to Jesus' command. It also accentuates the welcome he gives Jesus. Despite being a ruler, he obeys Jesus; and despite Jesus' having invited himself, Zacchaeus welcomes him joyfully. His "rejoicing" emanates from the good news of salvation represented by Jesus' wanting to stay at his house. Not only does the shepherd who finds his lost sheep rejoice (15:5–7). So too does this sinner, who was symbolized by the lost-and-found sheep of 15:3–7. Luke wants to attract prospective converts with the joy of salvation (see 2:10).

19:7–8: And on seeing [Jesus' entry into Zacchaeus's house]**, all** [the crowd] **were grumbling, saying, "He has entered to become the guest of a sinful man." ⁸But on standing still** [after entering the house with Jesus]**, Zacchaeus said to the Lord, "Behold, Lord, half of my possessions I'm giving to the poor; and if I've extorted anything belonging to anyone, I'm paying back four times as much."** "Seeing" recalls Luke's emphasis on eyewitnessing (1:1–4). The grumbling of the crowd recalls the Pharisees' and scholars' grumbling in 5:29–30; 15:1–2 and highlights by contrast Jesus' gracious initiative. "*All* [the crowd]" sharpens the contrast, for only he exhibits grace. Luke's "to the Lord" stresses Jesus' authority to exercise grace toward sinners; and Zacchaeus's addressing him with "Lord" amounts to a confession of Jesus' authority over him though he's a ruler as well as a tax collector. Salvation doesn't take place apart from repentance, including restitution; so Zacchaeus knows what he has to do. (Had he heard John the baptizer's instructions to tax collectors [3:12–13]?) His use of the

present tense in "I'm giving" and "I'm paying back" for what he has yet to do emphasizes that these actions are so sure and soon to be done that they're as good as in process right now. "Behold" adds stress to this evidence of repentance. Giving half his possessions to the poor shows charity to them such as the rich men in 16:19–31 and 18:18–23 didn't show. Zacchaeus needs the other half of his possessions to pay back fourfold the people from whom he has extorted more than they owed in taxes (compare Exodus 22:1; 2 Samuel 12:6, in contrast with only one-fifth restitution in Leviticus 5:16; Numbers 5:7). In Luke's original Greek there may be a wordplay between "I've extorted" (*esykophantēsa*) and "sycamore tree" (*sykomorean*), as though before God his extortions "put him up a tree" from which he has now come down in repentance. His charity and restitution exhibit the social benefits of Christianity, which Luke likes to feature.

19:9–10: And Jesus said to him, "Today salvation has taken place in this house [compare Acts 10:2; 11:14; 16:15, 31; 18:8]**, because he too is a son of Abraham. ¹⁰For the Son of Man has come to seek and to save what's been lost."** The "today" of Jesus' staying in Zacchaeus's house (19:5) has turned into a day of salvation for this rich but repentant tax collector. The salvation "has taken place," because it's an event. And it's an event in that Jesus' coming has effected it, almost as though his coming into the house *is* the event of salvation. Entrance into God's kingdom awaits the future (19:11–27), but the salvation that guarantees that entrance takes place "today." "A son of Abraham" means "a member of God's chosen people" and therefore someone eligible for salvation. Failure to repent would have disbarred him from such eligibility no matter his physical descent from Abraham (see 3:8–9). But repentance has saved his eligibility. Jesus' seeking what's lost interprets his inviting himself to stay in Zacchaeus's house and complements Zacchaeus's having sought to see who Jesus is. Curiosity motivated Zacchaeus's seeking. Salvation motivated Jesus' seeking. In Luke 15 he spoke of seeking and *finding* what's lost. Here he speaks of seeking and *saving* it. Saving interprets the figure of finding and links up with the "salvation" that has taken place in Zacchaeus's house. Jesus has come to Jericho and entered into Zacchaeus's house to effect this event. Moreover, saving what's lost keeps it from perishing. In fact, "been lost" and "perish" go back to the very same verb in Luke's Greek text. "*What's* been lost" is neuter for Zacchaeus and other persons like him. The neuter gender stresses the quality of lostness, the destiny to perish, of people apart from the salvation that Jesus provides for the repentant.

THE DELAY OF GOD'S REIGN AND WHAT TO DO IN THE MEANTIME
Luke 19:11–27

19:11–14: And as they [the crowd of 18:36] **were listening to these things, he** [Jesus]—**adding** [to what he'd said to Zacchaeus]—**told a parable, because he was**

near Jerusalem and they were supposing that God's reign was going to appear right away. ¹²Therefore he said, "A certain nobleman traveled into a distant region to receive for himself rulership and return [with the rulership in hand]. ¹³And having called ten slaves of his own [before he left for the distant region], he gave them ten minas [monetary units, each one worth three or four months' wages for a manual laborer working six days per week] and told them, 'Engage in business while I'm going and coming.' ¹⁴But his citizens [that is, the citizens of the region over which he was to receive rulership] were hating him; and they sent a delegation after him, saying, 'We don't want this [guy] to rule over us.'" Jerusalem was the center of Judaism. The crowd expected God to bring his reign there and impose it on earth from there. Jesus' preaching about God's reign and performing miracles and exorcisms had excited the messianic hopes of the crowd for the coming of God's reign. Now Jesus has come near Jerusalem. Naturally, then, the crowd suppose that God's reign is going to appear as soon as Jesus arrives in Jerusalem, that is, "right away." He tells the following parable to expose the mistake in the crowd's thinking, to tell them God's reign won't appear right away, and to indicate what his disciples should be doing in the meantime. The addition of "Therefore" after the "because"-clause doubles the emphasis on Jesus' corrective purpose in telling the parable.

In the parable, the nobleman represents Jesus. "Nobleman" literally means "a well-born [man]" and thus recalls Jesus' recently being called "son of David" (18:38–39), not to mention his having earlier been called the son of God (1:32, 35; 3:22; 4:3, 9, 41; 8:28; 9:35; 10:22 [compare 3:23]). Jesus' talk of the nobleman's traveling to a distant region to receive rulership over his own region seems to reflect some Jewish history of the period. For Herod the Great, who was ruling the land of Israel at the time of John the baptizer's and Jesus' births (1:5), had traveled to Rome in 40 B.C. to receive the right to rule over the land and on his return had to impose his rule by force. Similarly, after the death of Herod in 4 B.C. his son Archelaus traveled to Rome to receive kingship over Judea, Samaria, and Idumea (see the map) but had incurred the Jews' hatred, so that they sent a delegation to protest his coming rule. (Though he ruled for a while as an ethnarch, he never did gain the *formal* title "king.") Theologically, the nobleman's traveling to a distant region to receive rulership represents Jesus' coming ascension to heaven to receive rulership for the imposition of God's reign on earth (see 22:29–30 for God the Father's having decreed future rulership for Jesus; also Acts 2:32–36). God's reign is present in Jesus' ministry (see, for example, 11:20; 17:21), but its imposition over all the earth awaits the end. The "distant region" of heaven contrasts with Jesus' current proximity to Jerusalem. The nobleman's ten slaves represent professing disciples of Jesus. "His own" emphasizes Jesus' ownership of them and therefore lordship over them. Calling the slaves and giving them money with which to do business represent Jesus' giving the disciples tasks to perform for him while

he's "going and coming." For this phrase there's only one verb in Luke's original text, but the verb carries both meanings and refers to Jesus' going to heaven and coming back. The hatred of the nobleman by the citizens of his region represents the hatred of Jesus by his enemies. They didn't send a delegation to heaven to protest Jesus' receiving rulership over them. But they did protest it to Pontius Pilate (23:1–7, 13–25; Acts 3:13).

19:15–19: "And it happened when he came back after receiving the rulership that he said for these slaves to be summoned to him, [the slaves] to whom he'd given the money, in order that he might know what they'd gained through engaging in business. ¹⁶And the first [slave] came on the scene, saying, 'Master [which also means "Lord" in reference to Jesus], your mina has made ten minas more.'" So the nobleman had given one mina each to his ten slaves, not ten minas to each of them. ¹⁷"And he [the nobleman now made king] said to him, 'Well [done] indeed, good slave! Because you've become faithful in a very small matter, be having authority over ten cities [one for each of the minas made].' ¹⁸And the second [slave] came, saying, 'Your mina, Master, has made five minas.' ¹⁹And he said also to this one, 'And you—become over five cities [again one each for the minas made].'" The nobleman's coming back as king represents the return of Jesus at the end of the church age. The calling of the slaves to account represents the judgment of Jesus' disciples as to their doing the tasks of discipleship during his absence. In view of Luke's enormous emphasis on evangelism, especially between the first and second comings of Jesus (see 9:1–6, 52; 10:1–12; 24:47–49; Acts 1:6–8 and the entire book of Acts), the slaves' multiplication of minas probably represents the multiplication of converts through the disciples' evangelistic labors (as in Acts 2:41, 47; 4:4; 5:14 and, above all, 6:1, 7; 9:31; 12:24). The first two slaves' addressing the king with "Master" represents disciples' acknowledgment of Jesus' authority over them. The master's description of the first slave as "good" feeds into Luke's portrayal of Christians as good people. The commendation of the first slave for having become, through engagement in his master's business, "faithful in a very small matter" implies that in comparison with its future reward, Christian service—as in evangelism—counts for very little by way of self-sacrifice. The exercise of authority over ten cities, representing reward in Jesus' coming kingdom, far outweighs the effort put forth in a marketplace. Just as Jesus the servant will gain rulership for his service to God the Father, the disciples will gain authority for their work as Jesus' slaves (22:24–30).

The second slave in the parable gets authority over five cities for having made five minas with the one mina given him to work with. This difference from the first slave in work and reward teaches different levels of reward in Jesus' kingdom according to different levels of work done during earthly lifetimes. There'll be pure enjoyment in heaven but not equal enjoyment, just as there'll be different degrees of punishment in hell (12:47–48). The master's commendation of the second slave doesn't repeat from the first commendation "Well [done] indeed, good slave" and "Because you've become faithful in a very small matter." But the fact that the second slave's reward corresponds proportionately to the first slave's reward means that we're dealing with an abbreviation, not a slighting of the second slave.

19:20–23: "And the other came, saying, 'Master, behold, your mina, which I kept laid away in a cloth! ²¹For I feared you, because you're a demanding man. You take what you didn't deposit, and you reap what you didn't sow.' ²²He [the master] **says to him, 'I'll judge you out of your mouth, evil slave! You knew that I'm a demanding man, taking what I didn't deposit and reaping what I didn't sow. ²³And** [as a logical deduction from this knowledge] **for what reason didn't you give my money to the bank? And on coming I'd have claimed** [it] **with interest.'"** "The *other*" refers to a third slave; but because of his failure to do the master's bidding, for the moment he doesn't deserve to be called even a slave. "*The* other" dismisses the remaining seven slaves from individual mention later on. "Master" representatively implies a profession of discipleship, as in the first two cases, where the profession was backed up by obedience to the master's command. "Behold" reflects a hope, perhaps even an expectation, that the master will be glad to get back his mina safe and sound. At least "the other" hasn't lost it in a bad investment, and he even appeals to what seems to him an understandable fear of his master. But the explanation for this fear sounds like character assassination at the master's expense: he's demanding, and he robs other people of their money and crops. Surprisingly, though, the master admits to this characterization. So how can he represent Jesus? Well, Jesus robs Satan of Satan's subjects (see 11:20–22, where "take," used here, has already appeared in a similar connection) and expects his disciples through evangelism to do the same (see 10:1–2, 17–18, where evangelism is compared to reaping a harvest at the expense of Satan). In this respect Jesus *is* demanding (compare 12:49–53). "I'll judge you out of your mouth" means "I'll use your own words against you." The address, "evil slave," finally identifies "the other" as a slave but describes him as "evil" to make him represent a false disciple, one who doesn't do his master's bidding and therefore will get eternal judgment. Without investing the money, this slave could at least have had it draw interest in a bank. But despite the knowledge of his master's will and character, which knowledge represents false disciples' knowledge of Jesus' will and character, the evil slave didn't do even that much. The lesson: discipleship entails the work of evangelism. "For what reason . . . ?" makes failure to evangelize unthinkable for a true disciple. Luke introduces the master's words abruptly: there's no "And" or "But" before "he says to him." And the present tense of "says" energizes the following condemnatory quotation.

19:24–27: "And to the bystanders he said, 'Take from him the mina and give [it] **to the one who has ten minas.' ²⁵And they said to him, 'Master** [so the bystanders must be the seven other slaves], **he has ten minas.' ²⁶I tell you** [Jesus has the master break in preemptorily without an introductory change of speakers] **that to everyone who has,** [more] **will be given; but from the one who doesn't have** [= who hasn't made a profit for me], **even what he has** [such as the original mina which the evil slave was given to work with] **will be taken away. ²⁷Regardless** [of the slaves representing Jesus' disciples, both true and false], **bring here these enemies of mine** [representing Jesus' opponents], **the ones who didn't want me to rule over them, and slaughter them in front of me."** The command to take the evil slave's original mina from him stands for Jesus' exposé of a false disciple as in fact a nondisciple, one with no authority whatever in Jesus' kingdom, not even over a single city. For the grantings of authority over ten cities and five cities had to do with tenfold and fivefold profit exclusive of the original mina in each case. No profit, then, no position in Jesus' kingdom. But there'll be a surplus of reward for those who as true disciples do well for Jesus during his absence. They'll get even more reward than they deserve. The complaint of the other slaves emphasizes this generosity of the master, formerly described as "demanding." Because the evil slave had only the one mina he'd originally received, the master commands that it be given to the good slave with ten. But the master's saying that "to *everyone* who has, [more] will be given" indicates that those disciples represented by the slave who gained five more minas will also gain a surplus of reward, again more than they deserve. "I tell you" underlines both this surplus for true disciples and the loss of salvation for false ones (compare 8:18; 12:46). The parable ends with a fearsome representation of judgment on Jesus' outright enemies. "Slaughter them *in front of me*" indicates that he'll make sure of their perishing.

JESUS' RIDING TOWARD JERUSALEM TO THE GLORY OF GOD
Luke 19:28–40

19:28–31: And on saying these things [in the house of Zacchaeus according to 19:11–27], **he was traveling in front as he was going up to Jerusalem.** For the start of this trip to Jerusalem and for its theological significance, see the comments on 9:51, 53. As Jesus came near to Jericho in 18:35, others were preceding him (18:39). Now, however, he travels "in front." Doing so displays a determination to reach his goal. **²⁹And it happened that when he drew near to Bethphage and Bethany,** [that is,] **toward the mountain called "Of Olives Trees," he sent two of the disciples, ³⁰saying, "Go to the town opposite** [us], **in which as you're entering you'll find a tethered male colt that no one of human beings** [= no human being] **has ever sat on. And after untying him, bring** [him here]. **³¹And if anyone should ask you, 'For what reason are you untying** [him]**?' you shall speak in this way: 'Its owner has need** [of him].'" See the comments on Mark 11:1 for the locations of Bethphage and Bethany. Jesus' instructions to two of his disciples contain a half dozen predictions: (1) they'll find a colt; (2)

the colt will be male; (3) they'll find him *as* they enter the town, not *after* entering it; (4) he'll be tied; (5) he'll never have been sat on; and (6) someone might ask why they're untying him. The answer they're to give portrays Jesus as the colt's owner and as needing to use him. "Of human beings" qualifies "no one" both to stress the colt's never having been sat on and to imply that Jesus as the more-than-human Son of God will sit on him —and do so with such mastery as to eliminate the need of breaking the colt. (The word for "owner" also means "master" and "Lord.") Being the first to sit on the colt will bring honor to Jesus. As God's Son, he deserves not only a vehicle, but a brand new one.

19:32–34: And on going off, the [two disciples] **who'd been sent found** [things] **just as he'd told them.** So Jesus' predictions are fulfilled in detail. What he says is reliable. [33]**And as they were untying the colt, his owners said to them, "Why are you untying the colt?"** [34]**And they said, "His owner has need** [of it]**."** "His owners [plural]"? Jesus has just portrayed himself as the owner (singular [19:31]). So why does Luke speak of the colt's owners in the town and then quote the disciples to the effect that Jesus is the owner? This striking juxtaposition of "owners" and "owner" highlights the point that because he's the Lord, Jesus' ownership of the colt takes precedence over every other ownership. He out-owns what we own, so that he can requisition any of our possessions for whatever use he needs to put them.

19:35–38: And they led him [the colt] **to Jesus. And after throwing their outer garments on the colt, they mounted Jesus on** [the colt]. [36]**And as he was proceeding, they were spreading their outer garments in the road under** [Jesus and the colt]. [37]**And as he was by this time drawing near to the descent of the Mount of Olives** [that is, the descent on its west side just across the Kidron Valley from Jerusalem], **all the multitude of disciples, rejoicing, started to praise God with a loud voice concerning all the miracles they'd seen,** [38]**saying, "'Favored** [is] **the one coming'—**[that is,] **the king— 'in the Lord's name.' Peace** [is] **in heaven, and glory** [is] **in the highest** [places]**."** Obviously, the two disciples led the colt to Jesus. But who are the "they" who threw their outer garments on the colt, mounted Jesus on him, and spread their outer garments in the road? The two disciples are to be included, but they hardly comprise the totality of those who performed these actions. Luke's later reference to "all the multitude of disciples" probably identifies the two preceding instances of "they." A number of items give Jesus prestige: (1) the sacrifice of outer garments for a makeshift saddle; (2) the mounting of Jesus on the colt (not that *he* mounted the colt; rather, *they* mounted him on the colt); (3) the sacrifice of more outer garments to make a pavement over which he rides (compare our rolling out a red carpet for a VIP); (4) the acclamation of Jesus as "Favored," that is, as well spoken of by the Lord in accordance with Psalm 118:26; (5) the further acclamation of Jesus as "the one coming . . . in the Lord's name" (that is in this context, with authority delegated to him by God; for "name" connotes authority), again in accordance with Psalm 118:26; (6) the proclamation of Jesus as "the king" by way of an insertion into the quotation of Psalm 118:26; and (7) the participation of "all the multitude of disciples."[3]

"All" and "multitude" also carry forward Luke's stress on the popularity of Jesus; and the fact that "all the multitude" consist of "his disciples," quite apart from curiosity-seekers, testifies to the success of his ministry. This success prefigures the unstoppable progress and numerical success of the gospel in Luke's book of Acts. And the multitude's "rejoicing" advances Luke's theme of the gospel as joyful tidings (see 2:10). "*All* the miracles they'd seen" spotlights Jesus' miracles as large in number just as the multitude is large in number. "All the miracles they'd *seen*" supports Luke's emphasis on eyewitnessing as a basis for the gospel's certainty (1:1–4). But the multitude don't praise *Jesus* for performing many miracles in their sight. They praise *God*. As often pointed out by Luke, Jesus' ministry makes for good religion, God-glorifying religion, true piety. "With a *loud* voice" underlines this good religious effect. And elaborating it is the borrowing of phraseology from the angels' praise of God in 2:14. But there they say, "Peace [is] *on earth*" (that is, the birth of the Christ child has brought the blessings of salvation to earth), whereas here in 19:38 the multitude say, "Peace [is] *in heaven*"; for Jesus, in whom the blessings of salvation are wrapped up, is on his way to heaven (see 9:51 with comments for his journey to Jerusalem as the start of his ascension to heaven). "Glory [is] in the highest [places]" also echoes the angels' words in 2:14, where "to God" followed. But here Luke has said the multitude was praising God; so "to God" is unneeded. "Glory" means "honor." "In the highest [places]" refers to heaven and therefore implies the multitude's recognition that the angels are honoring God in heaven while the multitude are praising him on earth. In 2:14 the angels start with their glorification of God and proceed to the peace of salvation for human beings. Here in 19:38 the multitude start with the peace of salvation and proceed to glorification. This reversal of order lets the last accent fall on the glorification of God.

19:39–40: And some of the Pharisees from the crowd said to him, "Teacher, reprimand your disciples." [40]**And answering, he said, "I tell you, if these were in fact to fall silent, the stones will shout."** So great was Jesus' magnetism that despite their large number, "all the multitude of his disciples" in 19:37 didn't take in the whole of the crowd. For Pharisees from the crowd address him respectfully with "Teacher" but ask him to reprimand his disciples. But the disciples are praising God. So the Pharisees are opposing the praise of God! Their opposition thus highlights by contrast the good religious effect of Jesus' ministry, especially of his many miracles. "If these *were* in fact to fall silent" implies

---

[3]Since it isn't Jerusalemites but Jesus' disciples traveling with him toward Jerusalem who proclaim, "Favored [is] the one coming in the Lord's name," this event doesn't fulfill 13:34–35.

that in fact the disciples *won't* keep quiet. For it's characteristic of Jesus' disciples to praise God. They're truly religious. But if they weren't to do so, the stones *will* (in fact) shout the praises of God. Because stones are ordinarily dead silent, this statement of Jesus exhibits with maximal force his insistence on the praise of God. Again, good religion! All in all, then, Jesus' kingship is heavenly and peaceful, not earthly and seditious; and it features beneficial miracles, not acts of rebellion, and issues in the joyful praise of God.

JESUS' SADNESS OVER THE COMING DESTRUCTION OF JERUSALEM
Luke 19:41–44

19:41–42a: And when he'd drawn near [Jerusalem], on seeing the city he wept over it, ⁴²ᵃsaying, "If you, even you, had known on this day the things that make for peace—." Jesus might have completed this sentence with something like "God's reign would be coming immediately" (compare 19:11; also 11:2). But he leaves the sentence incomplete to put entire attention on Jerusalem's failure to understand the events of his ministry as bringing "on earth peace [that is, all the benefits of salvation] among human beings of [God's] good pleasure" (2:14). "On this day" pinpoints the present day of Jesus' approach and entry into the city. Of all days, this one should be the day when Jerusalem, especially its ruling elites, should hail him as the "Savior who is Christ the Lord" (2:11). But they don't, and won't. Instead, they'll challenge his authority, put him on trial, and have him killed. "Even you" underscores also that of all cities, Jerusalem—and again its ruling elites in particular—should know better than to act thus against him. For they stand at the center of the Jewish religion, which he has come to perfect and complete. And the Roman overlords have nothing to fear, for he doesn't approach with an army of rebels to take over the city and declare independence from Rome. No, he weeps over the city for its coming fate at the hands of Romans.

19:42b–44: "But they ['the things that make for peace'] have now been hidden from your eyes, ⁴³because days will have come upon you and [during them] your enemies will throw up an embankment against you and encircle you and hem you in from every [side] ⁴⁴and smash to the ground you [the personified city] and your children within you [your citizens] and not leave in you a stone on a stone, because you didn't know the time of your visitation [from God in the person of me, his Son]." Jesus is here predicting the siege and destruction of Jerusalem. The destruction, preceded by a siege, took place in A.D. 70. "Your enemies" are the Romans, against whom the Jews in Jerusalem started a rebellion in A.D. 66. An embankment consisted of earth thrown up against a city wall to give invading soldiers a slope up which to access the top of the wall. The things that make for peace "have now been hidden" from Jerusalem's eyes. Why? "Because" days of siege and destruction will have come in the future. But wouldn't we expect

the reverse—in other words, that the days of siege and destruction will have come because the things that make for peace have now been hidden from Jerusalem's eyes? As it is, though, the coming days of siege and destruction are the *cause*, not the *effect*, of present hiddenness. But the things that make for peace have now *been* hidden from Jerusalem's eyes. Why? Because for Jerusalem not to reject Jesus and the salvation he brings would be to thwart God's predetermined plan, as set out in Scripture, that Jesus suffer, die, and rise again for our salvation (24:7, 26, 44, 46; Acts 2:23; 3:18; 4:27–28; compare Acts 3:17 for his killers' having acted "in ignorance"). So divine sovereignty stands alongside human culpability in the matter of Jerusalem's rejection of Jesus.

JESUS' RECAPTURING OF SPACE FOR PRAYER
Luke 19:45–46

19:45–46: And on entering into the temple, he began to throw out the sellers, ⁴⁶saying to them, "It's written, 'And my house [the Lord is speaking] shall be a house of prayer [Isaiah 56:7],' but you've made it 'a den of bandits [Jeremiah 7:11].'" Jesus didn't enter the sanctuary itself. Only members of the tribe of Levi could, and he belonged to the tribe of Judah. So here "the temple" means the courtyards surrounding the sanctuary. "*Began* to throw out the sellers" implies that the action took some time. Luke doesn't say what the sellers were selling there. His concern has to do solely with an economically predatory use of space that the Lord wanted to be used for prayer. Though the Lord is making a prediction in Isaiah 56:7, "And my house *will* be a house of prayer," Jesus quotes it as a command, "And my house *shall* be a house of prayer," which the sellers as bandits have made into their den. But what are they robbing from people? Jesus doesn't mention exorbitant rates of exchange or exorbitantly high prices for sacrificial animals and birds. So here the robbery consists in the commandeering of space that should be used for prayer. Thus Luke portrays Jesus as throwing out the seller-bandits by way of a religious reformation pure and simple. Throughout Luke-Acts, Luke stresses the piety of Jesus and his followers, not least their piety in regard to prayer. Here too.

JESUS' STUMPING HIS WOULD-BE KILLERS
Luke 19:47–20:8

19:47–48: And he was teaching day by day in [the courts of] the temple; but the chief priests and the scholars were seeking to destroy him, and the aristocrats of the people [were doing the same]. ⁴⁸And they weren't finding the what-they-should-do [that is, a way they could destroy him]; for hearing him, all the people were hanging on [what they were hearing]. The aristocrats are usually called "the elders" (9:22; 20:1; 22:52). Here Luke calls them (in a more literal translation) "the first people" in an allusion to Jesus' having said "there are first people who'll be last" in that they'll be "thrown outside [God's kingdom]" (13:28–30). They, the chief priests, and the scholars made up the Sanhedrin, a kind of supreme court that under the Romans wielded considerable power, especially in Jerusalem. Naturally, Jesus' taking charge of the temple challenged their authority, so that they seek a way to get rid of him for good. But cowardly as they are, the popularity of his daily teaching in the temple keeps them from risking the people's wrath by destroying him. That "*all* the people" were mesmerized by his teaching testifies to the popularity that frustrates the Sanhedrin and that Luke has consistently used to present Jesus in attractive colors. The Sanhedrin seek to destroy him because he piously restored the temple to its divinely commanded use for prayer. Seeking to destroy him for this reason forms a particularly impious backdrop against which his piety stands out in sharp relief. Yet again, Luke presents Jesus as a paragon of true religion.

20:1–2: And it happened on one of the days when he was teaching the people in [the courts of] **the temple and proclaiming the good news** [= the gospel] **that the chief priests and the scholars along with the elders** [= "the aristocrats" of 19:47] **came up** **²and spoke, saying to him, "Tell us, by what sort of authority are you doing these things** [reforming the temple and teaching in it]**? Or who's the one that gave you this authority?"** No wonder all the people were hanging on what Jesus was teaching. He was telling them *good* news. The shift from "the aristocrats" in 19:47 to "the elders"—though the two terms refer to the same subgroup in the Sanhedrin—calls attention away from their eminence in society to their gravitas because of age. Societal eminence suited their helping seek for Jesus' destruction, and elderly gravitas suits their helping challenge Jesus' authority to reform the temple and teach there. The challenge has two prongs, the first one dealing with the nature of that authority ("what *sort* of authority?") and the second with its source ("who's the one that *gave* you this authority?"). Of course, they don't think he really has the kind of authority that would qualify him to reform the temple and teach there; nor do they think that anyone has given him such authority. So their challenge has the purpose of shaming him in front of his admiring public. He would then lose the popularity that has so far kept the Sanhedrin from destroying him.

20:3–4: But answering, he said to them, "I'll also ask you a question; and tell me, **⁴was John's baptism** [the one he administered] **from heaven or from human beings?"** So Jesus answers the Sanhedrists' questions with one of his own. In it the contrast with "human beings" makes "heaven" a reverential substitute for "God." The question, then, has to do only with the source of John's baptism. Did God authorize him to baptize people? Or did the idea of baptizing them spring from human imagination, whether John's or that of somebody else who influenced him? If this question of source is answered, the question of kind ("what sort of?") will take care of itself. "And tell me" demands an answer with an authority that did *not* characterize the Sanhedrists' two questions but *has* characterized Jesus' teaching and his reforming of the temple.

20:5–8: But they deliberated together, speaking to one another, "If we say, 'From heaven,' he'll say, 'For what reason didn't you believe him?' **⁶But if we say, 'From human beings,' all the people will stone us down** [= 'stone us to death'], **for they're convinced that John was a prophet."** **⁷And they answered that they didn't know where** [John's baptism] **came from.** **⁸And Jesus said to them, "Neither am I telling you by what sort of authority I'm doing these things."** Jesus' question catches the Sanhedrists between their having disbelieved John the baptizer in the past and their present fear of the people. Their fear of the people has kept them from destroying Jesus (19:48). Now it's keeping them from denying the heavenly origin of John's baptism. They want to avoid Jesus' shaming them to death (figuratively speaking) for their having disbelieved John; and they want to avoid being stoned to death (literally) by all the people for disagreeing with their conviction that John was a prophet. "*All* the people" makes this second possibility the more frightful in that the Sanhedrists would have no part of the populace to rely on for defense. (After all, the populace had submitted to John's baptism.) And to be shamed by Jesus, the very one they're seeking to shame and destroy—unthinkable! So they feign ignorance concerning the origin of John's baptism. This nonanswer to Jesus' question gives him a precedent not to answer their questions. But he mentions only their first question, the one about the sort of authority he has, and ignores their second question, the one about his source of such authority. For if he needn't answer even their first question, it goes without saying that he doesn't need to answer their second question. That is to say, the question concerning the source of Jesus' authority is irrelevant unless the question concerning the sort of authority he has (whether it qualifies him to reform the temple and teach there) deserves an answer. He has stumped his would-be killers.

A PARABLE OF JUDGMENT ON JESUS' ENEMIES
Luke 20:9–19

20:9–15a: And he began telling this parable to the people: "A certain man planted a vineyard [compare Isaiah 5:1–2] **and leased it out to farmers and went on a journey that took a long time.** **¹⁰And at the season** [of harvest] **he sent a slave to the farmers in order that they might give him** [the slave] **some fruit of the vineyard** [= the owner's share of the grape harvest]. **But after beating** [him] **the farmers sent him away empty**[-handed]. **¹¹And he** [the owner] **proceeded to send another slave. But they, after beating and insulting that one, sent** [him] **away empty**[-handed] **too.** **¹²And he proceeded to send a third** [slave]. **But they, after wounding** [him], **thrust out this one too.** **¹³And the owner of the vineyard said, 'What should I do? I'll send my beloved son. They'll probably respect this one.'** **¹⁴But on seeing him, the farmers were deliberating with one another, saying, 'This is the heir. Let's kill him in order that the inheritance may become ours.'** **¹⁵ªAnd on throwing him outside the vineyard, they killed** [him]**."** "*Began* telling" reflects the length of this parable. (It will continue further.) The planter-owner of the vineyard stands for God. (The word for "owner" also means "Lord.") The vineyard stands for Israel as God's chosen nation. The long time of the planter-owner's journey stands for the long history of Israel with God. The farmers stand for the nation's leaders. The sending of three slaves in succession stands for God's having sent a succession of prophets to Israel. The portion of fruit that the farmers were to give the slaves stands for Israel's obedience to God and his laws under the leaders of the nation. (To mention that the portion of fruit would have to be sold for carriable cash would have spoiled the figure of fruit for such obedience [compare 3:8–9; 6:43–45; 8:8; 13:6–9]). The farmers' mistreatment of the slaves, which advances from beating through beating-plus-insulting to wounding, stands for the leaders' persecution of the prophets. The sending away of the first two slaves empty-handed stands for the leaders' failure—indeed, refusal—to guide Israel into obedience to God and his laws; and the throwing out of the third slave stands for the leaders' utter rejection of God's prophets. The planter-owner's "beloved son," whom he sent last of all, stands for Jesus as God's "beloved Son" (3:22). The planter-owner's expectation that the farmers would respect his son stands for God's expectation that the current Jewish leaders would respect Jesus. The farmers' "deliberating with one another" on killing the son stands for the current Jewish leaders' seeking to destroy Jesus (19:47 [compare their "deliberating together" in 20:5 on how to answer his question]). The farmers' calling the son "the heir" and reasoning that the inheritance will be theirs by squatters' rights if they kill him implies that they think the planter-owner has died, that his son is an only son, and that he has come to claim the vineyard as his inheritance. Their thinking so portrays the Jewish leaders acting as though God is dead. Throwing the son out of the vineyard and killing him stand for the leaders' present rejection of Jesus and killing him shortly.

The parable, with a reaction to it, continues in **20:15b–18: "What then will the owner of the vineyard do to them** [the farmers]**? ¹⁶He'll come** [he isn't dead!] **and destroy these farmers and give the vineyard to others." And on hearing** [this]**, they said, "May it not happen!" ¹⁷And gazing intently at them, he said, "What then is** [the meaning of] **this that's written** [in Psalm 118:22]**, 'The stone that the builders rejected—this** [stone] **has become the head of an angle** [compare Acts 4:11]'**? ¹⁸Everyone who falls on that stone will be shattered; and on whomever it falls—it will pulverize him."** By referring to "*these* farmers" rather than "*those* farmers" Jesus fingers the Sanhedrists right there in his audience. The owner's coming and destroying the farmers represents God's coming through the agency of the Romans and destroying the Sanhedrists in A.D. 70. Poetic justice: those who are seeking to destroy Jesus (19:47) will themselves be destroyed. "He'll . . . give the vineyard to others" represents God's putting Jesus and the twelve apostles in charge of Israel (compare 22:29–30). "May it not happen!" refers to the farmers' destruction and the vineyard's

being given to others. But who are "they" who react with such dismay? Since the Sanhedrists will be said to understand the parable as directed against them, and since it teaches their destruction and loss of leadership, they are those who react with dismay. Jesus' "gazing intently at them" confirms their applying the parable to themselves and intensifies his following negation of their wish, "May it not happen!" In the negation he asks what else Psalm 118:22 can mean except that he, the stone which they, the builders, have rejected, has become "the head of an angle." Though Luke's Greek-speaking audience wouldn't pick it up, there's a wordplay between the Hebrew for "stone" (*eben*) and the Hebrew for "son" (*ben*), so that the "stone" here connects with the "son" in the preceding parable. And both terms refer to Jesus. "The head of an angle" refers either to a cornerstone or to a key- or capstone, but probably to a key- or capstone, since a cornerstone is the first to be laid whereas this stone was rejected at first. Installed last, a key- or capstone occupies the topmost position that suits the coming exaltation of Jesus (Acts 2:32–33; 5:31). But this figure of exaltation mutates suddenly into two figures of judgment: (1) that of a stone on which a person falls from a height and has his bones shattered (compare 2:34; Isaiah 8:14–15) and (2) that of a stone falling from a height (a tall cliff or wall, for example) and pulverizing him (compare Daniel 2:44–45). "*Every*one" and "whom*ever*" ensure the coming of this judgment on all the current leaders for their rejection of Jesus. None will escape.

20:19: And the scholars and the chief priests sought to lay hands on him [= arrest him] **in that very hour, and they feared the people** [compare 19:47–48; 20:6]**. For they** ["the scholars and the chief priests"] **knew that he'd spoken this parable in reference to them** [as the farmers]. The scholars were expert concerning the Old Testament. So Luke mentions them first because of Jesus' preceding quotation of Psalm 118:22 (contrast 19:47; 20:1). Next, Luke retains the chief priests, whom because of their political dominance he listed first in 19:47; 20:1. But for brevity he drops "the aristocrats of the people" and "the elders," who appeared as afterthoughts in 19:47 and 20:1, respectively. The seeking to arrest Jesus "in that very hour," that is, the hour of his telling the parable, arises out of their recognition that he directed the parable against them and shows them cut to the quick by the parable. They can't wait to arrest him—but they do wait, again because of their fear of the people, who were mesmerized by Jesus' teaching (19:48) and who would have stoned them to death if they had denied the heavenly origin of John's baptism, to which the people had earlier submitted (20:6).

THE FAILURE OF JESUS' ENEMIES TO TRAP HIM IN HIS SPEECH
Luke 20:20–26

20:20–22: And scrutinizing [him]**, they sent spies feigning that they themselves were righteous** [in the sense of "sincere"]**, in order that they might seize on his**

word [that is, get him to say something self-incriminating], **so as to give him over to the governor's rule and authority.** [21]**And they asked him, saying, "Teacher** [a feignedly respectful address], **we know that you speak and teach correctly and don't receive a face** [= play favorites]; **rather, you teach God's way** [for us to conduct our lives] **on the basis of truth** [as opposed to falsification so as to please people]. [22]**Is it lawful for us to give** [= pay] **tax to Caesar or not?"** The scholars and chief priests of 20:19 scrutinize Jesus by sending spies to seize on a statement of his that they could use against him before the Roman governor. The spies' feigning to be righteous points up by contrast that Jesus is genuinely righteous (23:47; Acts 3:14; 7:52; 22:14), and they design their flattery of him to mask the malevolent purpose that underlies their coming. Ironically, what the spies intend as flattery is *actually* true of Jesus. They hope that to save his popularity, he'll say it's against God's law to pay the unpopular tax required of adult males under Roman law, for then they could accuse him of seditious teaching. The tax had to be paid in Roman coins stamped with a Mosaically prohibited image of Caesar and with a blasphemous inscription proclaiming his supposedly divine ancestry. So the spies and their senders could easily have imagined that Jesus would teach against paying the tax.

20:23–26: And taking notice of their trickery, he said to them, [24]**"Show me a denarius. Whose image and inscription does it have?" And they said, "Caesar's."** [25]**And he told them, "Well, then, give Caesar's things back to Caesar, and God's things back to God."** [26]**And they were unable in the people's presence to seize on his saying; and marveling at his answer, they fell silent.** They don't fool Jesus. He asks the spies to show him a denarius, the kind of coin required for paying the tax; but Luke skips over their showing one and moves directly to Jesus' questioning them about the coin. It goes without saying that they have to do what he demands, and do it. For the character of his argument, see the comments on Mark 12:15–17. Luke's interest falls not so much on that argument as on the inability of the spies to seize on Jesus' saying for the purpose of accusing him of sedition. As a good subject of the Roman government, Jesus taught payment of the tribute tax. And the spies' inability was exposed "in the people's presence," so that there were eye- and earwitnesses to Jesus' fidelity to Caesar as well as to God (compare 1:1–4). Unable to accuse Jesus, the spies can only marvel at his answer and shut up.

JESUS' GETTING KUDOS FROM SOME SCHOLARS
Luke 20:27–40

20:27–33: And on approaching [Jesus], **some of the Sadducees, who contend there's no resurrection** [compare Acts 23:8], [28]**asked him, saying, "Teacher, Moses wrote for us, 'If the brother of some** [man] **dies having a wife and this** [brother] **was childless** [at his death], **that 'his** [surviving] **brother should take the wife** [of his deceased brother] **and raise up seed** [= progeny] **for his**

brother [Deuteronomy 25:5; Genesis 38:8].' [29]**So there were seven brothers. And after taking a wife, the first one died childless.** [30]**And the second** [31]**and the third** [each] **took her, and in the same way also the seven left no children and died."** The placement of "left no children" before "died," rather than in the more natural reverse order, puts emphasis on the childlessness. [32]**"Finally the woman died too.** [33]**So at the resurrection the woman becomes the wife of which of them? For the seven had her as** [their] **wife."** The Sadducees constituted a religious sect that disbelieved in resurrection because it's not taught explicitly in the Pentateuch (Genesis–Deuteronomy), the only part of the Old Testament they considered to be authoritative Scripture. Their addressing Jesus with "Teacher" suits their asking him a doctrinal question related to a particular law laid down by Moses in the Pentateuch. They quote that law, known as "the law of levirate marriage," and then cite a case they think makes belief in the resurrection of human beings look absurd. For although a man's having more than one wife at the same time was conceivable to them (the Pentateuch is replete with stories of polygyny), a woman' having more than one husband at the same time was not (the Pentateuch contains no stories of polyandry). If therefore the woman can't have seven husbands at the resurrection, there must be no resurrection. Thus the Sadducees argued.

20:34–38: And Jesus told them, "The children of this age marry [as sons] **and are given in marriage** [as daughters], [35]**but those who've been considered worthy to attain that age and the resurrection from among the dead neither marry nor are given in marriage.** [36]**For they can no longer die. For they're equivalent to angels and, being sons of the resurrection, they're sons of God.** [37]**But at the bush**[-passage in Exodus 3:6] **even Moses** [whose Scripture you accept as authoritative] **divulged that the dead are raised, when he calls the Lord 'the God of Abraham and the God of Isaac and the God of Jacob.'** [38]**And he isn't the God of dead people—rather, of living people. For all live in relation to him."** "The children of this age" are human beings characterized by living at the present time. "That age" is the coming age of eternal bliss for "those who've been considered worthy to attain [it] and the resurrection from among the dead [with which it starts]." Though Luke will include a reference to the resurrection of unrighteous people in Acts 24:15, Jesus here limits his remarks to the resurrection of righteous people. He calls them "sons of God" in that they're "sons of the resurrection," that is, "those who've been considered worthy to attain that age and the resurrection from among the dead." For Luke, their worthiness contributes to his portrayal of Jesus' followers as good people both morally, socially, and religiously—a portrayal designed to attract prospective converts. Just as "sons of God" are related favorably to God, so "sons of the resurrection" are related favorably to the resurrection of the worthy. Jesus gives a reason why their marriages won't be renewed at the resurrection: "they can no longer die," so that there's no more need of the procreation for which marriage was instituted. Then he gives a reason why they can no longer die: "they're equivalent to angels," who don't die. And how is it that they're forever deathless like the angels? By virtue of their resurrection "they're sons of God," just as angels are called "the sons of God" in the Pentateuch (Genesis 6:2, 4, as often understood in first-century Judaism [see also Job 1:6; 2:1; 38:7]). The Sadducees must have believed in "the angels of God," because such angels are mentioned in the Pentateuch at Genesis 28:12; but see the comments on Acts 23:8 that the Sadducees didn't believe in angels as disembodied human spirits awaiting the resurrection of their bodies.

Finally Jesus appeals to what Moses divulged, and uses the present tense to introduce the quotation vividly and therefore emphatically ("he *calls* the Lord . . ."). The use of the present tense also in Moses' divulging "that the dead *are* raised" pronounces their resurrection as so certain that it might as well be taking place right now (compare earlier instances of the present tense in "neither marry nor are given in marriage," "they can no longer die," "they're equivalent to angels," and "being sons of the resurrection, they're sons of God"). Similarly, "he isn't the God of dead people—rather, of *living* people" portrays the patriarchs as so certain to be resurrected that they might as well be living again already. Finally, Jesus supplies a reason for this portrayal. It's that "all live in relation to him [God]." That is to say, since God lives eternally, as not even the Sadducees doubt, those related to him will live eternally by virtue of resurrection. He'll not allow death to bereave him of those he has "considered worthy to attain that age and the resurrection from the dead."

20:39-40: And answering [= responding], some of the scholars said, "Teacher, you've spoken well [or, 'beautifully']." 40For they weren't daring any more to ask him anything. Along with the chief priests, the scholars had sought to arrest Jesus and, failing that, had sent spies to trick him into saying something seditious (20:19-20). Now that Jesus has vanquished the Sadducees in scriptural-doctrinal debate, some scholars give Jesus kudos for his interpretive brilliance. Most Jewish scriptural scholars were Pharisees; and because they believed in resurrection, some of them apparently enjoyed Jesus' putdown of the Sadducees on this point so much that they complimented Jesus and for fear of being put down themselves didn't pose him any more questions. "Some" implies that other scholars were so opposed to Jesus that they didn't join their colleagues in complimenting Jesus. For obvious reasons, Luke dwells on the kudos.

JESUS' QUESTION FOR THE SCHOLARS, WHO HAVE NO ANSWER
Luke 20:41-44

20:41-44: And he said to them [the scholars who'd complimented him but didn't dare question him any more (20:39-40)], **"How is it that people say that the Christ** [= the Messiah] **is David's son** [= descendant]? **42For David himself says in the book of Psalms, 'The Lord said to my Lord, "Sit at my right** [hand] **43until I place your enemies as a footstool for your feet** [Psalm 110:1]."' **44So David calls him 'Lord,' and how is it that he's his son?"** The questions how it is that the Christ is David's son and how it is that people say so—these questions don't deny the Davidic descent of the Christ. For from his birth onward Jesus has been identified as the Christ and given a Davidic descent (1:27, 32, 69; 2:4, 11, 26; 3:31 and so on). The questions are therefore designed to highlight that the Christ—that is, Jesus—is not only a descendant of David but also the Lord, as Jesus has repeatedly been called in Luke's Gospel, again from his birth onward (1:43; 2:11 and so on). The addition of "himself" to "David" emphasizes that no less a personage than this great king and psalmist—progenitor of Jesus though he was—called him "my Lord." "*For* David himself says" gives the reason for Jesus' leading question, and the present tense of "says" turns David's statement into a testimony contemporary in its significance. In Christian terms, the first Lord in Psalm 110:1 is God the Father; and the second Lord is Jesus his Son. Jesus assumes the scholars he's addressing agree with him that David wrote Psalm 110 and that the second Lord, the one David calls "my Lord," is the Christ (though of course he doesn't assume they identify the Christ with him). The paragraph closes with a repetition of Jesus' question, because the scholars have no answer. Either they're stumped, or they don't want to admit the lordship of the Christ.

JESUS' WARNING AGAINST PRETENTIOUS, PREDACIOUS SCHOLARS
Luke 20:45-47

20:45-47: And while all the people were listening, he told his disciples, 46"Take precaution against the scholars, who like to walk around in long robes and love greetings in the marketplaces and prestigious seats in the synagogues [compare 11:43] **and prestigious couches at banquets** [compare 14:7], **47who devour widows' houses and for show pray a long time. These** [scholars] **will receive a very harsh punishment."** Since Jesus addresses only his disciples, Luke's saying that "all the people were listening" adds to the emphasis on Jesus' popularity that pervades this Gospel. The humanitarianism of Jesus attracted people, all of them, to him. In his earlier use of "take precaution," Jesus added "for yourselves" to make warnings against falling into different vices (12:1; 17:3). Here, however, "for yourselves" is missing, so that the warning is to take precaution against the scholars themselves. Jesus portrays them as pretentious and positively dangerous in that their pretensions bring them an influence that masks their predacious behavior—hence the warning to take precaution against them. Their liking to walk around in long robes and loving to be greeted in marketplaces make a pair, because they're greeted as they walk around in the marketplaces. Since the listening people are those who fawningly greet the scholars, Jesus' denunciation must have shocked the people. Seats and couches make another pair, because both are "prestigious." Those seats in the synagogue were located up front and facing the congregation, so that the scholars occupying them enjoyed much visibility. Those couches, consisting of floor pillows on which diners reclined, were the ones closest to the host. The reference to "banquets" leads to "devour[ing]." But it's not food that the scholars devour. It's "widows' houses." That is, Jesus charges the scholars, who were not to accept wages for their teaching, with sponging off the hospitality of widows and thus dwindling the widows' already meager means. (There were widows aplenty to take advantage of, for adolescent girls were often married off to men a number of years their senior.) As was customary, the scholars prayed aloud and in public (compare Matthew 6:5). But they extended their prayers to an unusual length to make themselves look pious, all the while freeloading at the widows' expense. Jesus closes out his warning with a forceful prediction that the scholars will receive a very harsh punishment. The warning contributes to Luke's portrayal of Jesus as a teacher of true piety and high ethical standards.

JESUS' ESTIMATE OF GIFTS TO THE TEMPLE
Luke 21:1–4

21:1–4: And looking up, he saw the rich throwing their gifts [of money] *in the treasury* [= into the receptacles located there]. [2]*And he saw a certain widow, a poor one, throwing there two lepta* [the smallest coins in circulation among the Jews, two of them worth ¼ cent, or 1/144 of a manual laborer's daily wage]. [3]*And he said, "I tell you truly* [Jesus is still speaking to his disciples (see 20:45)] *that this poor widow has thrown* [money into the treasury] *more voluminously than all* [the others have done]. [4]*For all these threw* [their money] *into the gifts* [already deposited] *out of their surplus, but this* [widow] *out of her lack threw* [in] *all the livelihood that she had."* "I tell you truly" assures the disciples of the accuracy of his following estimate, incredible though it may seem. "More voluminously" puts the poor widow's giving on a grand scale. "Than *all*" emphasizes that the volume of her giving surpasses not only the heavy giving of the rich, but also even the heaviest of their giving. Thus the generosity of her giving for public benefit—that is, for support of worship in the temple—contrasts with the scholars' plundering for their private gain the assets of widows (20:45–47). Since the widow had two lepta, she could have given one and kept the other for her own needs. But she didn't. She gave not only out of her lack in contrast with those who gave out of their surplus. She gave "*all* the livelihood that she had." What counts, in other words, is the proportion of giving, not a raw amount. Again, Luke's Jesus shines as a teacher of true piety.

WHAT TO EXPECT AND DO PRIOR TO THE SON OF MAN'S COMING
Luke 21:5–24

21:5–6: And as some [of the disciples (see 20:45)] *were talking about the temple in that it was adorned with beautiful stones and dedicatory gifts, he said,* [6]*"As*

for these things that you're viewing, days are coming during which a stone won't be left on a stone that won't be torn down." Jesus is predicting the destruction of the temple complex that occurred in A.D. 70. The beautiful stones were Herodian masonry, noted for its massive dimensions and handsome style—stones of white marble up to nearly seventy feet long, eighteen feet wide, and twelve feet high. The dedicatory gifts included gold- and silver-plated gates, gold-plated doors, and multicolored tapestries of fine linen. Recent archaeological excavations favor the addition of this complex to the traditional "Seven Wonders of the Ancient World" so as to make eight of them. In Jesus' prediction of a future destruction, the plural in "days are coming during which a stone won't be left on a stone" implies a period of some length following that destruction and, as is about to become apparent, prior to the Son of Man's coming (compare the indications of delay in 17:22; 19:11; 20:9).

21:7–9: And they asked him, saying, "Teacher, so when will these things be and what [will be] *the sign when these things are about to happen?"* The respectful address, "Teacher," indicates that the disciples expect an informative answer. They ask for both the time of fulfillment and a forewarning signal that these things are about to happen. Since Jesus has so far predicted only the destruction of the temple complex, the plural in the disciples' use of "these things" treats the tearing down of each stone as an event in and of itself, as in the slow motion playback of a modern movie or televised event. [8]*And he said, "Watch out that you're not deceived. For many will come on the basis of my name, saying, 'I am* [Jesus],' *and, 'The time has drawn near.' You shouldn't go after them. [9]And when you hear battles and revolutions* [so near that you can hear their noise, as in the battles of the Jewish rebellion against Rome leading up to the destruction in A.D. 70], *you shouldn't panic. For it's necessary that these things happen first. Nevertheless, the end* [won't come] *immediately* [even after 'these things,' which now in Jesus' mouth include battles, outbreaks of revolution, and destruction, first take place]." The danger of deception is magnified by the large number of charlatans ("many"), by their claiming to have Jesus' name and therefore to be Jesus, and by their announcing that "the time [of destruction] has drawn near." The time *won't* be near, because it's necessary that battles and rebellious outbreaks happen beforehand (as in fact they did before the destruction of the temple complex). The necessity arises out of God's plan; for he controls even the history for which human beings are responsible because of their actions, evil as well as virtuous. And since the necessity arises out of God's plan, there's no need for the disciples of Jesus to panic. The delay of the end, when he'll come back as the Son of Man, till some time after the warfare and destruction of A.D. 66–70 gives a further reason not to panic.

21:10–19: Then he was telling them, "Nation will rise up [in arms] *against nation, and kingdom against kingdom;* [11]*and there'll be great earthquakes and,* from place to place, famines and plagues; and there'll be terrors and great signs from heaven. ¹²But before all these things [which according to 21:25–28 will immediately precede the Son of Man's coming], people will throw their hands on you [disciples of mine] and persecute [you], giving you over to the synagogues and prisons, [you] being led off to kings and governors on account of my name. ¹³It will turn out for you to result in a testimony. ¹⁴So settle it in your hearts not to rehearse beforehand what to say in self-defense. ¹⁵For I'll give you a mouth [= what to say] and wisdom that none of your foes will be able to withstand or contradict [= refute]. ¹⁶But you'll be given over [to them] even by parents and brothers and relatives and friends, and they'll get some of you killed. ¹⁷And you'll be hated by all because of my name. ¹⁸And by no means will a hair of your head perish [compare 12:6–7]. ¹⁹Gain your lives by your perseverance."

After racing ahead to the international conflicts, so-called natural disasters, and terrifying heavenly signs that will portend the end (21:10–11), Jesus steps back to predict the persecution of his disciples that will take place throughout what we call the church age, the start of which Luke will write about in the book of Acts. The persecution will come, not because of any rebellious or other misbehavior on the disciples' part, but "on account of [Jesus'] name" and "because of [Jesus'] name" in that his name represents him as the only Savior and in that the disciples will proclaim him as such (Acts 4:12). This proclamation will draw the ire of unbelievers. Furthermore, the persecution will lead to the disciples' testifying about Jesus even to the highest authorities, to whom their persecutors will have brought them for trial. So the persecutors' attempt to quash the spread of the gospel will actually amplify its spread—and its effectiveness, too, because Jesus himself will inspire with irresistible wisdom the self-defense of his disciples. Not to worry, then. But expect betrayal even by those closest to you, sometimes with a fatal outcome; and expect hatred of you by everybody else as well. To be forewarned is to be forearmed. Despite hatred and occasional martyrdom, though, "by no means will a hair of your head perish." But how can that be if you're killed? It can be only if Jesus is looking forward to the resurrection and eternal life. His looking forward to them is confirmed by the command, "Gain your lives by your perseverance," which puts into the imperative Jesus' earlier declaration, "Whoever seeks to preserve his life will lose it, but whoever loses [it] will keep it alive" (17:33 [see also 9:24]). "Perseverance" means enduring persecution without recanting.

21:20–24: "And whenever you see Jerusalem encircled by military encampments, then know [= understand] that her desolation has drawn near. ²¹Then the [disciples] in Judea [the region in which Jerusalem is located] are to flee into the mountains [those of the Judean wilderness, a traditional hideout], and the [disciples] in her midst [that is, inside Jerusalem] are to depart, and the [disciples] in the fields aren't to enter into her [compare 17:31], ²²because these are days of retribution** [for the city's rejection of Jesus (13:34–35; 19:41–44)] in order that all the things written** [in Scripture, what Christians call the Old Testament] **may be fulfilled. ²³Alas for** [women] **who are pregnant and** [women] **who are nursing in those days! For there'll be great adversity on the land and wrath against this people** [of Jerusalem]. **²⁴And they'll fall by the mouth of the sword** [as though the sword devours its victims] **and be led away as captives into all the nations, and Jerusalem will be trampled by Gentiles until the times of the Gentiles are fulfilled."**

Finally Jesus comes around to answering, if not the question when the stones of the temple will be torn down, at least the question about "the sign" that they're about to be torn down (compare 21:7). The sign turns out to be Jerusalem's encirclement by military encampments (compare 19:43–44). And the tearing down of the temple expands into the desolation of the whole city in which the temple is located. "Desolation" doesn't mean destruction so much as the abandonment of Jerusalem because of its destruction. "These *are* days of retribution" (where we expect "These *will be* . . .") stresses the certainty of this retribution. It's as good as taking place right now. Jesus' disciples are to escape, because they don't deserve retribution. They've accepted him, not rejected him as the Jerusalemites have done. The retribution has the purpose of fulfilling "all the things written." Jesus doesn't specify the Scripture where these events are written about, so that the accent falls solely on fulfillment as such and as entire ("*all* the things written"). One thinks, though, of Daniel 9:24–27; 11:1–12:13 and various other ancient prophecies of Jerusalem's destruction and the temple's desolation. To be sure, these prophecies came to pass within the Old Testament period and between the Old and New Testaments; but Jesus treats them as yet to reach a complete fulfillment—hence again, "*all* the things written." For women, pregnancy and the nursing of infants will hamper a speedy escape. So alas for them. The word behind "land" could be translated "earth." But the concentration on Jerusalem and Judea and the people living there favors a narrow reference to the land of Israel rather than a broad reference to the earth at large. The adversity and wrath will derive from divine retribution by way of the Roman sword and exile among all the nations, as indeed happened in A.D. 70. From then on, Gentiles will trample Jerusalem until their times of trampling it are fulfilled. The plural of "times" indicates a period of some length, and "are fulfilled" indicates a God-ordained limit to that period.

ENCOURAGEMENT, EXHORTATION, AND ADMIRATION
Luke 21:25–38

This passage divides into Jesus' encouraging the disciples by portraying his coming as their redemption (21:25–33), his exhorting them to be alert for its arrival (21:34–36), and the people's listening to him eagerly (21:37–38).

21:25–28: "And there'll be signs in the sun and moon and stars, and on earth [there'll be] **distress of nations in perplexity over the roar of the sea and of surging waves** [26]**as human beings faint from fear and anticipation of the things coming on the inhabited [earth]. For 'the powers of the heavens** [Isaiah 34:4]**' will be shaken.** [27]**And then they** [the human beings] **will see 'the Son of Man coming in a cloud** [Daniel 7:13]**' with power and much glory.** [28]**And when these things start happening, stand up straight and lift up your heads, because your redemption is drawing near."** Ancient people thought of "the sun and moon and stars" as superhuman beings and therefore as "the *powers* of the heavens." They'll be "shaken" by being thrown off course, and their being shaken will constitute individual "signs" of their loss of power in favor of the Son of Man's coming "with power"—and with "much glory," that is, glory exceeding that of the sun, moon, and stars. Corresponding to this shakeup in the heavens will be "distress" on earth. The distress will characterize "nations," but it's not to characterize Jesus' disciples. For they're to stand up straight, not cower in perplexity and foreboding over the events portended by ominous tsunamis. The "human beings" that make up the "nations" contrast with "the [personal] powers of the heavens." The fainting of human beings (whether taken literally, or figuratively for loss of composure) contrasts with the disciples' standing up straight and lifting up their heads (again whether taken literally, or figuratively for confident expectation of redemption at the Son of Man's coming). "These things" that will "start happening" are the heavenly signs and earthly distress. "*Start* happening" implies a period of time during which they'll happen. Emphasis falls on the encouragement of Jesus' disciples that when they see these things starting to happen they can be sure he'll soon redeem them—that is, liberate them—from their persecutors (compare 21:12–17). The "drawing near" of this redemption indicates that the period of heavenly signs and earthly distress won't be long. And just as people eyewitnessed Jesus' ministry in the past (a point of emphasis in Luke 1:1–4 and throughout), they'll eyewitness his coming as the Son of Man in the future. "In a cloud" indicates that he'll come in a divine means of transport (see Exodus 34:5 and many other biblical passages). After all, he's "the Lord," as Luke often calls him.

21:29–33: And he told them a parable: "Look at the fig tree and all the trees. [30]**Whenever they've already sprouted** [that is, as soon as they've put forth leaves]**, by seeing for yourselves** [that they've done so] **you know that the summer is already near.** [31]**In this way also you, whenever you see these things** [the heavenly signs and earthly distress of 21:25–28] **happening, know that God's reign is near.** [32]**Amen I say to you that by no means will this generation pass away till all things** [the Son of Man's coming as well as the preceding heavenly signs and earthly distress] **have happened.** [33]**Heaven and earth will pass away, but by no means will my words pass away** [= fail to be fulfilled]**."** Jesus features the fig tree among all the other trees because

its fruit is desirable just as for the disciples his coming to redeem them from their persecutors is desirable. Ancient Jews spoke of only two seasons, winter and summer (Psalm 74:17). So the sprouting of leaves on trees indicated that the early part of summer, what we call late spring, was near. The addition of "already" both to "sprouted" and to "near" advances the nearness: *very* near. "God's reign is near" substitutes for "your redemption is drawing near" (21:28) and thereby indicates that the coming of the Son of Man to redeem his disciples will mark the coming of God's reign on earth, for which reign Jesus taught them to pray (11:2). God's reign was present in the ministry of Jesus (17:21), but the complete takeover of the world by that reign awaits the second coming. Jesus gives the firmest possible assurance of nearness. At first glance "this generation" looks like a reference to his contemporaries. And well it might have turned out to mean them (hence "*this* generation" rather than "*that* generation"). But the parable of the fig tree and other trees defines "this generation" as those living during the period of heavenly signs and earthly distress. This period brings to a close "the times of the Gentiles," which are the indeterminately lengthy age of the church (represented in its initial stage by Luke's book of Acts); and seeing the start of the heavenly signs and earthly distress characterizing this period will enable Jesus' disciples to "stand up straight and lift up [their] heads, because [their] redemption is drawing near" (21:28). So *their* generation, not necessarily Jesus' contemporaries, are the generation "that by no means will pass away till all things have happened." The present heaven and earth will pass away (2 Peter 3:10–12; Revelation 20:11; 21:1), but these prophetic words of Jesus stand firm. Hence, "*Amen* I say to you."

21:34–36: "But take precaution for yourselves lest your hearts be weighed down with dizziness and drunkenness and anxieties about your livelihood** [compare 8:14; 10:41–42; 12:22–32, 45; 18:24–25]**, and [lest] that day** [when God's reign comes] **arrive on you as a sudden** [event]**, like a trap** [that springs on you unexpectedly (compare 12:39, 46)]**.** [35]**For it will come on all who dwell on the face of all the earth.** [36]**But stay alert at every time, praying that you be strong enough to escape all these things that are going to happen, and** [strong enough] **to stand before the Son of Man."** Weighed down hearts would contrast with the uplifted heads of 21:28. Through the wasting of your resources, dizziness and the drunkenness that causes it lead to anxieties about your livelihood; and the combination of the three weighs down your heart in such a way that you don't look up for the redemption that's drawing near. The day of the arrival of God's reign will come on everybody all over the earth, but it'll spring like a trap of judgment only on nondisciples. So make sure you're a true disciple by staying constantly alert and praying rather than carousing and worrying. "To escape all these things that are going to happen" doesn't mean to avoid confronting them, for Jesus has just talked about the disciples' seeing these things happen and anticipating redemption when they do (21:28, 30). To escape all these things means, then, to come out of them with eternal salvation intact because of avoiding dizziness, drunkenness, and anxiety through prayerful alertness (compare escape from within prison rather than avoidance of imprisonment in Acts 16:27, and an escape from within a house in Acts 19:16, the only other two instances of "escape" in Luke-Acts). The strength to escape in this sense and to stand before the Son of Man comes from such avoidance and such alertness. Standing before the Son of Man means maintaining your position in his presence as opposed to being "thrown out" (as in 13:28). And Jesus' railing against drunkenness and the dizziness and anxiety it causes, and his urging prayerfulness, contribute to Luke's portrayal of him as a teacher of virtue and piety.

21:37–38: And for days he was teaching in [the courts of] **the temple; but for nights, on going out** [of Jerusalem] **to the mountain called "Of Olive** [Trees]," **he was lodging** [there]. **³⁸And all the people were getting up early** [to go] **to him to hear him in** [the courts of] **the temple.** Jesus' teaching keeps him popular; and he teaches all day long, day after day. His popularity is so great that the people—*all* of them—get up early and go to the temple to hear him. Since he has just been teaching virtue and piety, how good an effect he's having in society! Therefore the gospel concerning him deserves belief.

THE SATANIC AND COWARDLY BARGAIN FOR THE BETRAYAL OF JESUS TO HIS ENEMIES
Luke 22:1–6

22:1–2: And the Festival of Unleavened [Bread], **the one said** [to be] **Passover, was drawing near. ²And the chief priests and the scholars were seeking how they might do away with him, for they were afraid of the people.** The Passover commemorated the exodus of Israel from Egypt at the time of Moses. This festival started with the slaying of sacrifices in the afternoon and ended with the eating of a meal in the evening. Since the weeklong Festival of Unleavened Bread followed immediately, however, and since only unleavened bread was to be eaten at the preceding Passover meal, Luke combines the two festivals with each other. The chief priests' and the scholars' "seeking how they might do away with [Jesus]" recalls 19:47, where with "the aristocrats of the people" they "were seeking to destroy him"; 20:1–2, where they challenged his authority; and 20:19, where they "sought to throw their hands on him [= arrest him]." Frustrated on those earlier occasions, their effort now concentrates on "*how* they might do away with him"; and just as in 19:47; 20:19 Jesus' popularity among the people made the chief priests and the scholars afraid to carry out their design, here their fear of the people—that is, their fear of a popular uprising against them and in Jesus' favor—makes them seek an undercover way of doing away with him (compare 20:1–8, where they fear being stoned to death by all the people if they deny the heavenly origin of John's baptism). Through the agency

of Judas Iscariot, Satan will show them the way. Meanwhile, their fear of the people adds to Luke's emphasis on the well-deserved popularity of Jesus and portrays the chief priests and scholars as looking out for their own skin rather than for the good of the people by way of preventing a Jesus-centered messianic rebellion that the Romans would crush.

22:3–6: And Satan entered into Judas, the one called Iscariot [as distinguished from other Judases, such as "Judas (the son) of James," also among the Twelve (6:16)], **being from** [= belonging to] **the number of the Twelve. ⁴And on going away** [from Jesus and the rest of the Twelve], **he spoke with the chief priests and officers** [of the temple guard] **as to how he might give him** [Jesus] **over to them. ⁵And they rejoiced and contracted to give him money. ⁶And he agreed** [to the contract, presumably a verbal one] **and started seeking a favorable opportunity to give him over to them apart from a crowd.** Satan's entering Judas makes the coming arrest and crucifixion of Jesus a result of the ultimate in demonic possession (Satan being the ruler of the demons according to 11:15, 18), not the result of any misbehavior on Jesus' part. As usual, Luke is stressing that Jesus was a good man, a paragon of probity. Satan's entering Judas also explains how such a dastardly deed as Judas's betrayal of Jesus could have been done by one of the twelve apostles. Otherwise, the deed would spoil Luke's picture of Jesus and the disciples as an ideal community worthy of converts. The identification of Judas as one of the Twelve lends treachery to his offer as well as pathos to his falling victim to satanic possession. Luke doesn't say that Judas asked for money, only that the chief priests and officers were so overjoyed by his offer that they contracted to give him money. If then he didn't ask for money, how deep his treachery and how strong Satan's hold on him! Luke replaces "the scholars" of 22:2 with "officers [of the temple guard]," because these officers will participate with the chief priests and Judas in Jesus' arrest (22:47–54a). Furthermore, their participation will put the military opposite Jesus' pacifism (22:49–51). Though a reformer, he's no insurrectionist such as governmental authorities should get rid of. The chief priests' and officers' rejoicing over Judas's offer contrasts ironically with the joy of salvation that Luke has highlighted from the start (1:14, 28; 2:10 and so on) and just as ironically contributes to that salvation by triggering the passion of Jesus that makes it possible. The chief priests rejoice because Jesus' cleansing of the temple had threatened their making money out of the commerce that was taking place at the temple. The officers of the temple guard rejoice because his cleansing of the temple had disrupted the order that they were responsible to maintain there. It's unclear in Luke's text whether Judas got his money on the spot or after giving Jesus over. Whether now or later, he got it according to Acts 1:18. His "seeking a favorable opportunity to give [Jesus] over to them apart from a crowd" shows that in speaking with them "as to *how* he might give him over to them" they stipulated their fear of the people (22:2). Cowards!

THE SO-CALLED LAST SUPPER
Luke 22:7–38

The risen Jesus will eat an evening meal with his disciples again in 24:30, 41–43, but this passage relates his last supper with them prior to the crucifixion. The passage divides into preparation for a Passover meal (22:7–13), the institution of the Lord's Supper during the Passover meal (22:14–20), Jesus' announcement of his betrayer's presence at the table (22:21–23), and Jesus' dealing with the disciples' dispute over which of them was greater than the others (22:24–27), assigning them rulership in his kingdom (22:28–30), praying for Simon Peter and predicting his denials of Jesus (22:31–34), and—for the disciples' future mission—revising the instructions he gave for their earlier mission (22:35–38).

22:7–13: And the Day of Unleavened [Bread] came, during which it was necessary that the Passover [lamb] be sacrificed. ⁸And he sent Peter and John, saying, "Go prepare for us the Passover [meal] in order that we may eat [it]." ⁹And they said to him, "Where do you want us to prepare [it]?" ¹⁰And he told them, "Behold, when you've entered into the city [Jerusalem, outside which Jesus and the Twelve have been lodging at night on the Mount of Olives (21:37)], there'll meet you a man carrying a jug of water. Follow him into the house that he goes into. ¹¹And you shall say to the owner of the house, 'The teacher says to you, "Where's the guest room where I may eat the Passover [meal] with my disciples?"' ¹²And that [houseowner] will show you an upstairs room—large, furnished. There prepare [the Passover meal]." ¹³And on going off, they found [things] just as he'd told them; and they prepared the Passover [meal]. "It was necessary" because of a scriptural requirement (Exodus 12:1–20; Deuteronomy 16:1–8). So Jesus' considering it a necessity that the Passover lamb be sacrificed shows him to have been a Law-abiding Jew, not an upstart renegade from the time-honored religion of Moses and the prophets. His taking the initiative by sending Peter and John to prepare the Passover meal underlines his adherence to the Mosaic law (compare 2:21–24, 39, 41–52). The mention of Peter and John by name prepares for their acting together in Acts 3:1–4:23; 8:14–25. "We" and "us" include the rest of the apostles along with Jesus, Peter, and John (see 22:14). "For *us* . . . in order that *we* may eat" brings all the apostles into the piety of celebrating the Passover. But to complement Jesus' designation as "the teacher," here they're called "disciples," which means "learners," rather than "the Twelve" or "the apostles."

"Behold" punctuates Jesus' ability to predict what Peter and John will find on entering Jerusalem to prepare the meal. Jesus fills the first part of his prediction with details whose unlikelihood will make fulfillment astonishing. A man will meet Peter and John. The fact he'll meet them rather than they him makes fulfillment extremely unlikely, for it would be remarkable enough if Jesus knew the two were going to meet a man by virtue of their approaching *him* at Jesus' instructions. But Jesus'

knowing that a man is going to meet them by virtue of his approaching *them*—what a testimony to Jesus' power of prediction! Not only that, but also the man will be carrying a jug of water—what a woman would usually do in those days, for a man would normally carry water in a skin. It stays unknown whether the houseowner is expected to recognize "the teacher" as Jesus, or whether he's expected to provide a room for Jesus without knowing Jesus' identity as he would provide one out of respect for any teacher. The lack of information concerning this point leaves the stress on Jesus' predictive ability. "Where I may eat the Passover [meal] with my disciples" recalls attention to the adherence of Jesus and the apostles to the law of Passover.

The second part of Jesus' prediction is as remarkably detailed as the first. The room will be upstairs, large and ready for use. Translated literally, the original behind "the owner of the house" comes out as "the houseowner of the house," which may imply that he'd had members of his household furnish the large guest room, so that it was ready for use. That the houseowner will neither refuse nor hesitate to show the room makes the prediction yet more impressive (see the comments on Mark 14:19–21 against Jesus' having made prearrangments). Peter's and John's going off and finding things "just as he'd told them" points up the accuracy of Jesus' prediction, details and all. And since every matter is to be legally established by the testimony of at least two witnesses (Numbers 35:30; Deuteronomy 17:6; 19:15), the twoness of Peter and John provides sufficient testimony to the fulfillment of Jesus' unlikely predictions. The actual preparation of the Passover meal carries forward the theme of adherence to the Mosaic law and sets the stage for the meal itself.

22:14–16: And when the hour [of the Passover meal] came, he reclined [at table], and the apostles [reclined] with him. ¹⁵And he said to them, "With longing I've longed to eat this Passover [meal] with you before I suffer. ¹⁶For I tell you that by no means will I eat it till it has been fulfilled in the kingdom of God." Luke's specification of "the hour" makes Jesus' adherence to the Passover law exact. The reclining of "the apostles with him" brings them also into such adherence. And Jesus' "longing" to eat the Passover meal with them makes his adherence one of genuinely felt piety, not of mere formality. Longing to eat the Passover meal "with them" makes for familial feeling on his part since the meal is to be eaten family by family (see Exodus 12:1–28, 43–46) and especially since the apostles represent his family of those "who hear God's word and do [it]" (8:19–21)—a family typified by table fellowship and the attraction of new members (Acts 2:46–47). The double expression, "With *longing* I've *longed*" adds depth to Jesus' piety and feeling of family. Luke doesn't tire of presenting Jesus and his followers as exemplars of true religion and good company. "Before I suffer" recalls the ability of Jesus to predict his own fate (see especially 9:22; 17:25, where he earlier used "suffer"); and since in Luke's original Greek the basic form of the word for suffering (*paschō*) looks much like the word for Passover (*pascha*), there may be a bit of wordplay here. If so, the point of it is that Jesus will suffer as the true Passover sacrifice, a theme that runs throughout John's Gospel (see also and explicitly 1 Corinthians 5:7). Jesus gives a reason for his longing to eat the Passover meal with the apostles. (Luke designates them with the title, "the apostles," to prepare for a coming dispute among them as to who of them was greater than the others [22:24–27].) The reason for Jesus' longing is that it's the last Passover meal he'll eat "till it has been fulfilled in the kingdom of God." "I tell you" and "by no means" put a twofold emphasis on the lastness of this Passover meal prior to its fulfillment in God's kingdom. "Till" implies that he'll eat it again in that kingdom, which as in 21:31 and elsewhere refers to the imposition of God's reign over the whole earth. But what does the Passover's fulfillment refer to? It can't refer to Jesus' death as a Passover sacrifice, because his death will occur almost momentarily, whereas the fulfillment awaits the more-or-less far future coming of God's kingdom (see also 22:18). The fulfillment therefore refers to the messianic banquet that will take place at that kingdom's coming with the coming of the Son of Man himself (13:29). So Jesus portrays the present Passover meal not only as looking back to Israel's exodus from Egypt but also as looking forward to the meal that will celebrate his coming and that of God's kingdom, the meal which will bring to fulfillment another exodus of God's people—that is, Jesus' disciples—from their persecution like that of Israel's bondage in Egypt (compare the exodus of Jesus himself which he's "about to fulfill in Jerusalem" according to 9:31).

22:17–18: And on welcoming a cup, after giving thanks he said, "Take this [cup] **and divide** [its contents] **among yourselves.** [18]**For I tell you that from now on I'll by no means take a drink from the produce of the vine** [that is, wine] **till God's reign comes."** In 22:42 Jesus will pray, "Father, if you're willing, take this cup [of suffering and death] away from me. *Nevertheless, not my will but yours come about.*" By writing that Jesus "welcom[ed]" a cup of wine, which he'll later make symbolic of a new covenant in his blood, Luke anticipates Jesus' welcoming God the Father's will that he suffer and die and thus highlights Jesus' piety. "Giving thanks" marks the piety of Jesus yet again. And his vow of abstinence from wine till the coming of God's kingdom complements the preceding vow of abstinence from eating the Passover meal till its fulfillment in God's kingdom (22:16). As there, "I tell you" and "by no means" underline the vow. Jesus will miss his disciples on earth too much to enjoy such eating and drinking. But they'll continue table fellowship among themselves when he's gone. So join in!

22:19–20: And on taking bread, after giving thanks he broke [it] **and gave** [the pieces] **to them, saying, "This is my corpse being given for you."** In the context of Jesus' being given over to death, the word for "body" is better translated "corpse" (as obviously in 23:52, 55; 24:3, 23). **"Be doing this for a reminder of me."** [20]**And**

[he gave them] **the cup likewise after the dining, saying, "This cup that's being poured out for you** [is] **the new covenant in my blood."** A second "giving thanks" marks Jesus' piety again. Unleavened bread is cracker-like. Jesus broke it so that each of the apostles could have a piece. So each apostle gets a representation of Jesus' corpse just as each apostle gets a portion of the wine representing Jesus' blood (compare the description of "wine" as "the blood of grapes" in Genesis 49:11). The separation of body and blood in his interpretation of the bread and wine points to a violent death (compare our term "bloodshed"), such as is required for a death to be sacrificial. (A natural death, such as by disease or simple old age, doesn't count as sacrificial.) Not all sacrifices inaugurated a covenant, but all covenants had to be inaugurated with a sacrifice; and Jesus interprets the shedding of his blood, which is about to take place, as inaugurating a new covenant which works to the benefit of the apostles and, it goes without saying, to all other believers in him ("for you"). The covenant is "new" in that it's based on the sacrificial death of Jesus rather than on that of an animal, the basis of the old covenant. But in this respect the new doesn't oppose the old; rather, it fulfills symbolism in the old (compare 16:16–17). The pouring out of the cup represents the shedding of his blood. The giving of the bread represents the giving of his corpse, and the giving of his corpse portrays salvation as a gift attributable to Jesus' sacrificial death and receivable by faith. "*Being* given" and "*being* poured out" make the sacrificial death of Jesus as good as in progress already. "Be doing this" commands repetition of the Lord's Supper in Jesus' absence (compare the command to repeat the Passover meal every year as a reminder of the Lord's having delivered Israel from slavery in Egypt [Exodus 12:42]). "For a reminder of me" gives the purpose of this supper, which is to remind us repeatedly of Jesus' sacrificial death for our salvation. Because Luke has written of Jesus' "*welcoming* a cup" rather than of *taking* it (see the comments on 22:17 for the reason why), here he refuses to write that Jesus "took" the cup and lets the earlier "welcoming" carry over as understood. (So "likewise" has to do only with the Words of Institution.) "*The* cup" refers to "*a* cup" mentioned before. Only now, after they've dined, does Jesus explain its significance. Luke doesn't narrate the actual eating of the bread or drinking of the wine, so that symbolism predominates in his account (see the comments on Mark 14:22–25 that "This *is* . . ." means "This *represents* [or '*symbolizes*'] . . .").

22:21–23: "Behold, however, the hand of the one giving me over [is] **with me on the table,** [22]**because the Son of Man is going in accordance with what has been determined. Alas, however, for that man through whom he is being given over!"** [23]**And they began discussing among themselves which of them might be the one who was going to do this** [the giving of Jesus over to his enemies]. Post-meal dialogue such as is taking place here appeals to Luke's audience (their own meals featuring this sort of dialogue) and adds to Luke's portrayal of a family at table. "However" draws a contrast between

Jesus' giving his corpse and shedding his blood for our salvation and the betrayer's imminent giving of Jesus over to his enemies. "Behold" headlines the contrast. The presence of the betrayer's hand with Jesus on the table—which represents fellowship at a meal, and this one a covenantal meal at that—makes the coming betrayal treacherous. Jesus uses the word "hand" not only because diners use their hands to reach for food set on a table but also because "hand" often stands for a means of taking action, as Judas Iscariot is about to do (see, for example, 1:66, 71, 74; 9:44; 20:19; 21:12; 22:53; 24:7; Acts 2:23). The "going" of the Son of Man refers to his ongoing journey, which started in 9:51, 53 and will carry him through crucifixion and resurrection right up to his "exodus" at ascension into heaven (9:31; Acts 1:9–11). (The word behind "going" is the same as that behind "travel" in 9:51, 53 and subsequent passages.) "What's been determined" alludes to God's predetermined plan, as also in Acts 2:23, and clears Jesus of any blame for the choice of Judas to become one of the Twelve. In Acts 1:15–20 the apostle Peter will cite Psalms 69:25; 109:8 as scriptural evidence of God's plan so far as Judas's part in it is concerned. Despite the predetermination of betrayal (thus the second "however"), the betrayer faces a woeful end that draws Jesus' "Alas" (which combines an announcement of doom and a lament for its victim) and categorizes Judas as a treacherous criminal over against the good and pious Jesus; and "that man" puts Judas at a critical distance from "the Son of Man." Yet alongside the treachery of Judas is Satan's using him to give Jesus over. For "*through* whom" rather than "*by* whom" combines with Satan's having entered Judas (22:3) to make Judas the agent of Satan. One could almost say, Satan's tool. Jesus has told the apostles before of being given over to his enemies (9:44; 18:32 [compare 24:6–7]), but this is the first time he has identified the betrayer as one of them. They're so shocked that they discuss among themselves which of them might be the betrayer. In their favor, the discussion indicates both an acceptance of Jesus' statement and a concern over its content. And the ignorance of all but Judas as to the betrayer's identity lets Jesus' foreknowledge stand out by contrast. This foreknowledge is so sure and certain that he uses the present tense in "is going" and "is being given over," as though the events are taking place right now.

22:24–27: **But also** [in addition to their commendable discussion concerning which of them might betray Jesus] **there took place a dispute among them as to which of them seems to be greater** [than the others]. [25]**And he told them, "The kings of the Gentiles wield lordship over them, and those who wield authority over them are called benefactors.** [26]**But you** [are] **not thus. Rather, the one among you** [who's] **greater** [than the others] **is to become like a youngster, and the one who leads like one who serves.** [27]**For who** [is] **greater, the one reclining** [at table] **or the one who's serving** [food to the recliner at table]**?** [It's] **the one reclining** [at table]**, isn't it? But I'm in the midst of you like one who's serving."** "*Seems* to be greater" casts doubt on the

apostles' opinions, and the present tense of "seems" enlivens their dispute. Despite Luke's putting the Christian community in the best possible light to attract converts, he's honest enough to mention this dispute over greatness. By way of compensation for the unflattering picture, though, the dispute provides a platform for Luke's presenting some of Jesus' admirable teaching. Jesus doesn't condemn the kings and authorities who rule the Gentiles, so that governmental authorities shouldn't suspect him or his followers of subversion. He notes on the contrary that those kings and authorities are called "benefactors." Nor does he contradict this designation. He only, but emphatically, rejects benefaction of the weak by the powerful among his disciples. The rejection starts with a description of the actual state of affairs: "But you [are] not thus." The following command is then designed to keep that state of affairs from morphing into a Gentile-like benefaction of the weak by the powerful: "the one among you [who is] greater [than the others] is to become like a youngster [who because of his youth has no lordship or authority], and the one who leads like one who serves." Since "greater" can mean larger in size as well as superior in authority, there's a wordplaying contrast with "a youngster" who hasn't grown to full size. Jesus' comments neither deny greatness and leadership nor redefine them as slave-like service. Instead, he tells great leaders that they ought to serve. And to impress on his disciples the importance of leading by serving from below rather than by ruling from above, he puts himself forward—great Lord and leader though he is—as the parade example of such service. "In the midst of you" makes his example impossible to miss, and therefore his command impossible to misunderstand. So we have no excuse for disobedience.

22:28–30: **"But *you*—you are the ones who throughout have stayed with me during my trials.** [29]**And just as my Father covenanted rulership to me, I'm covenanting** [rulership] **to you** [30]**in order that you may eat and drink at my table in my kingdom; and you'll sit on thrones judging the twelve tribes of Israel."** The initial "*you*" is emphatic (as indicated by the italics) and contrasts the faithfulness of the eleven apostles with the treachery of Judas Iscariot (22:21–23). By commending the Eleven's staying with Jesus during his trials, Jesus contributes to Luke's portrayal of the disciples as morally virtuous and attractively communal. "Throughout" enhances this portrayal by bringing the Eleven's loyalty up to the moment. Since trials pose tests that could end in yielding to temptation, "my trials" could come out equally well as "my tests" and "my temptations" (see 11:16 for Jesus' being tested with a demand that he provide "a sign from heaven," not to detail many other houndings by his enemies). As a reward for the Eleven's loyalty to him, Jesus covenants to them the rulership his Father covenanted to him. Covenanting has the sense of promising by way of a treaty. Here, then, just as God the Father will rule through his Son Jesus, so Jesus will rule through his apostles (compare 12:32 and 20:16 with comments). Jesus' present promise will attain its purpose in the future through their renewed eating and drinking during the messianic banquet at Jesus' own table (the one of highest prestige) in his kingdom (compare 13:29; 14:15–24). ("Kingdom" and "rulership" go back to the same original word because ruling takes place in a kingdom and a kingdom entails ruling.) Because of the Father's promise of rulership to his Son, Jesus can say "*my* table" and "*my* kingdom." And his present promise of rulership to the apostles has a future result: "you'll sit on thrones [as is appropriate for rulership] judging [as rulers do] the twelve tribes of Israel [as intimated by the angel Gabriel (1:32–33; compare 1:67–79; Acts 1:6–8; 3:18–21)]."

22:31–34: "Simon, Simon, behold! Satan has asked for you [plural, referring to the rest of the apostles as well] **with the purpose of sifting** [you] **like wheat.** [32]**But I've begged concerning you** [singular] **that your faith/faithfulness not run out. And** *you* [singular again]— **once you've turned back, reinforce your brothers."** [33]**But he** [Simon] **said to him, "Lord, I'm prepared to go with you both to prison and to death."** [34]**And he** [Jesus] **said, "I tell you, Peter, a rooster won't crow today until you've denied three times that you know me."** Sifting as wheat is sifted by being shaken in a sieve stands for an attempt by Satan to shake the apostles loose from their faith in Jesus and faithfulness to him. (The original word carries both of the meanings "faith" [= belief] and "faithfulness" [= loyalty based on belief].) That Satan has asked to sift them in this way indicates that as in the story of Job, Satan has to get permission from God. A number of features in Jesus' statements stress the danger of the Eleven's apostasy as approximated in the three denials he predicts Peter will make: (1) the old name "Simon" rather than the new apostolic name "Peter" that Jesus gave him (see 6:14); (2) the doubling of this old name (compare 8:24; 10:41; 13:34); (3) Jesus' singling out Simon despite the plural of the initial "you"; (4) "behold!"; (5) the request to sift by none less than the archdemon Satan (compare his having entered Judas Iscariot [22:3]); (6) Jesus' having "begged" in prayer that Simon's faith/faithfulness not run out; (7) the need for Simon to reinforce his "brothers" (= his fellow apostles) against apostasy once he himself has turned back from the verge of apostasy; and (8) the emphatic "*you*" that introduces Jesus' statement of this need. "Once you've turned back" implies the effectiveness of Jesus' begging that Simon's faith/faithfulness not run out. For Luke, then, the praying of Jesus is notable for its power as well as for its piety. "Have turned back" implies both a coming close to apostasy by Simon and his retreat from it. Jesus' calling Simon's fellow apostles "your brothers" portrays them as members of a family characterized by such mutual reinforcement that prospective converts should like to join up. Much as in Judas Iscariot's case (22:3–6), Satan's activity explains how Simon, the leading apostle, could be so disloyal as to verge on apostasy and how the rest of the Eleven could be in such danger of apostasy as to require Simon's reinforcement. Once again, Jesus isn't to be blamed for having chosen them. Even their responsibility is tempered by Satan's sifting them.

Simon's response to Jesus begins with the reverential address "Lord." For the moment his faith in Jesus is still intact and his faithfulness to Jesus pledged even to the extent of going with him "both to prison and to death." Simon's "to go" picks up the theme of Jesus' having traveled to Jerusalem (9:51, 53 and so on) and now traveling onward through crucifixion, resurrection, and ascension to heaven. (The verb is the same as the one elsewhere translated "travel.") Jesus has spoken of his and the apostles' being killed (9:22; 11:49; 12:4–5; 18:33; 20:14–15) and of their being imprisoned (21:12), but not of being imprisoned himself. Nevertheless, Simon thinks of imprisonment prior to death and declares his preparedness to accompany Jesus in both. This little mistake, plus the big one that he's *un*prepared, brings out by contrast the detailed accuracy of Jesus' predictions. Notably, Simon pledges his faithfulness without any self-exalting comparison with the other apostles. In predicting the three denials, then, Jesus shifts from the old name "Simon" to the new, apostolic name "Peter" in anticipation of Peter's just-mentioned turning back and reinforcement of his brothers. Yet "I tell you" puts Jesus' prediction of the three intermediate denials in emphatic opposition to Peter's affirmation of loyalty. Emphasis was needed because of the seeming unlikelihood that—of all the apostles—Peter, the confessor of Jesus as "God's Christ" (9:20), would deny three times that he knows Jesus, and would do so "today." (Though it was after dark, for Jews a new day had started at sundown.)

22:35–38: And he said to them, "When I sent you without a money-bag and a knapsack and sandals, you didn't lack anything, did you?" And they said, "Nothing." [36]**And he told them, "But now the one who has a money-bag is to take** [it], **likewise also a knapsack. And the one who doesn't have** [a sword] **is to sell his outer garment and buy a sword.** [37]**For I tell you that it's necessary that this that's written be brought to its goal in me: 'And he was counted with lawless** [ones] [Isaiah 53:12].' **For also the** [Scripture] **concerning me is having** [its] **goal** [= is reaching its goal of fulfillment]." [38]**And they said, "Behold, Lord, here** [are] **two swords." And he told them, "It's enough."** During their earlier missions in Galilee and on the way to Jerusalem, the Twelve and the seventy-two were to depend entirely on local hospitality from fellow Jews—hence no money-bag, knapsack, or sandals (9:2–3; 10:3–4). And that hospitality represented God's caring for their physical needs (compare 12:22–34). Looking forward to his disciples' mission throughout the largely Gentile world (24:47; Acts 1:8), in which they'll often have to pay for board and room (compare Paul's having to earn money in Corinth by making tents [Acts 18:1–3]), Jesus revises his instructions for evangelistic travel. The disciples will need to carry money and food for such travel. Jesus doesn't say they should henceforth wear sandals instead of going barefoot. Is it to be assumed that the much longer distances to be traveled outside Israel will require the wearing of sandals? Instead of answering the question, Jesus skips to the more important need for a sword to be used in defense against attackers, human and animal, that will lie in wait for them along the remote stretches of roads. So necessary is a sword that a disciple lacking one should even sell his outer garment to get money for the purchase of a sword.

Jesus then states the reason for this revision of his instructions. It's that he's going to die, so that his and the disciples' prior mission in Israel will expand into the disciples' world-wide mission. But he puts his imminent death in terms of its bringing Scripture to its goal of fulfillment. Stressing the attainment of this goal are (1) "I tell you"; (2) "it's necessary" (as part of God's plan revealed in Scripture); (3) the direct quotation of Isaiah 53:12; (4) the addition of actual attainment ("For also the [Scripture] . . . is having [its] goal") to necessary attainment; and (5) the vivid present tense in "is having [its] goal." The quotation, "And he was *counted* with lawless ones," implies that Jesus will die with criminals but isn't a criminal himself (see 23:32–33). In the apostles' response, "Lord" implies their future compliance with Jesus' instructions; and "Behold" calls his attention to their already having two swords. "It's enough" means that for the moment, having two swords suffices. Two won't be enough to prevent the imminent arrest of Jesus. So it remains to be seen what having two swords is enough for (see the comments on 22:49–51).

JESUS' ANGUISHED BUT ANGELICALLY STRENGTHENED PRAYING AND THE DISCIPLES' DANGEROUS THOUGH UNDERSTANDABLE SLEEPING
Luke 22:39–46

22:39–40: **And on going out** [from the guest room in Jerusalem], **he traveled in accordance with** [his] **custom to the Mount of Olives; and they followed him— that is, the disciples** [did]. [40]**And after coming upon the place** [the Mount of Olives], **he said to them, "Pray so as not to enter into temptation."** Luke's description of Jesus' traveling to the Mount of Olives as customary reflects 21:37, which says that he was regularly lodging there at night. "He traveled" keeps up the theme of travelogue: Jesus' journey from Galilee to Jerusalem and eventually to heaven. The disciples followed Jesus, as disciples are supposed to do according to 5:27; 9:23, 59; 18:22. Luke mentions their following Jesus to put them in a good light. And to portray Jesus as a teacher of moral piety, Luke mentions Jesus' telling the disciples to pray so as not to enter temptation—in other words, not to succumb to temptation (see the comments on 11:4). So Jesus teaches prayer as an antidote to moral failure.

22:41–44: **And he pulled himself away from them about a stone's throw and, on kneeling, was praying,** [42]**saying, "Father, if you're willing, take this cup away from me. Nevertheless, not my will but yours come about."** [43]**And there appeared to him an angel from heaven, strengthening him.** [44]**And on getting into a struggle, he was praying more earnestly; and his sweat became as if** [it was] **drops of blood going down onto the**

ground. Jesus immediately sets an example of the praying he has just told his disciples to do. "About a stone's throw" presents a detail arising out of Luke's historical research (1:1–4). Since Jews normally stood to pray (as in 18:11, 13, for example), Jesus' kneeling portrays him as specially pious. An angel's coming from heaven to strengthen him indicates God's approval of his prayer. The strengthening prepares him physically for the coming struggle in which he prays "more earnestly" (compare another physical strengthening in Acts 9:19). This increase in the earnestness of his praying magnifies his piety. He sweats so profusely that the beads of his sweat are comparable in their steady dripping to drops of blood falling to the ground. (Luke does *not* say that Jesus sweat blood, only that "his sweat became *as if* [it was] drops of blood going down on the ground.") The intensity of Jesus' struggling in prayer creates sympathy for him since he has done nothing but good for his fellow human beings. He has addressed God with "Father" just as he instructed his disciples to do in 11:2 (but see 10:21–22 for the uniqueness of the relation between God the Father and Jesus his Son). "This cup" that he asked his Father to take away from him is "the cup that's being poured out for [the disciples]" and represents "the new covenant in [Jesus'] blood" (22:20)—that is to say, the cup of his sacrificial death. Showing extraordinary piety, however, are the qualifications, "if you're willing" and "not my will but yours come about," this latter punctuated with "Nevertheless."

22:45–46: **And on standing up from the prayer, coming to the disciples he found them sleeping from** [= because of] **grief.** [46]**And he said to them, "Why are you slumbering? Standing up, pray lest you enter into temptation."** The angel's having strengthened Jesus enables him to stand up from his kneeling position. He finds the disciples sleeping instead of praying as he'd told them to do. But at least their sleeping because of grief shows that they feel sorry for Jesus. There's a lot of human sympathy in the family of Jesus' disciples (compare 8:21; Acts 8:2; 9:39). Though understandable, the disciples' sleeping instead of praying exposes them to the danger of succumbing to temptation, in particular to the moral failure of apostasy (see the comments on 22:31–34). So Jesus tells them again to pray lest they succumb, but this time to stand up while praying. In that posture they won't succumb again to sleep. Besides, as noted above, standing was the Jews' normal posture for praying. This paragraph started with Jesus' telling the disciples to pray so as not to succumb to temptation. Now it ends the same way. Luke wants us to see Jesus as both a teacher and an example of prayer for the avoidance of moral failure. True religion indeed!

THE FULFILLMENT OF JESUS' PREDICTION THAT ONE OF THE TWELVE WOULD BETRAY HIM
Luke 22:47–53

22:47–48: **While he was still speaking, behold, a crowd! And the** [man] **said** [to be] **Judas, one of the**

Twelve, was coming ahead of them. And he drew near Jesus to kiss him. [48]But Jesus said to him, "Judas, are you giving the Son of Man over [to this crowd] with a kiss?" The lack of an "and" before "While he was still speaking" accentuates the abruptness of the crowd's appearance on the scene. Doing the same are "behold . . . !" and the lack of a verb to tell what the crowd was doing. "Behold, a crowd!" also highlights that it will take a crowd to arrest Jesus even at night (compare "the authority of the *darkness*" in 22:53) and "apart from a [counter] crowd" of his supporters (22:6). The designation of Judas as "one of the Twelve" strikes the sour note of his treachery again and by the same token sets Jesus in a good and sympathetic light. In 6:16 we read a straightforward "Judas Iscariot," in 22:3 an oblique "Judas *called* Iscariot," and now in 22:47 a remote "said [to be] Judas" (compare 22:1: "said [to be] Passover"). This progressive distancing of Judas ballasts his pernicious membership in the Twelve. His coming "ahead" of the crowd puts him "near Jesus" so as to kiss him before the crowd can lay hands on him. There's nothing in Luke about the kiss as a means of identifying Jesus. In fact, Luke doesn't even say that Judas kissed Jesus, only that Judas intended to kiss him and that Jesus questioned him about this intention. Perhaps Luke doesn't want a man possessed by Satan according to 22:3 to plant a kiss on "the holy Son of God" (1:35). Or Luke may be diminishing the blame on Judas to protect as much as he can the reputation of the Twelve. Jesus shows that he knows what Judas is up to but has the good grace to address Judas by name. And instead of asking "are you giving *me* over?" he asks "are you giving *the Son of Man* over?" By using "the Son of Man," Jesus recalls to Judas's (and our) memory his predictions that as the Son of Man he would be given over, suffer, die, and rise again (9:22, 44; 17:24–25; 18:31–33; and especially 22:22 [see also 24:6–7]). "*Are* you giving the Son of Man over" indicates that the fulfillment of his predictions is underway.

22:49–51: And on seeing what will be [= what will happen]**, the ones around him** [that is, the disciples] **said, "Lord, shall we strike with a sword?"** According to 22:38 they have two swords and Jesus said that having them suffices. So should they use one of them? Addressing Jesus with "Lord" implies that the disciples want an authoritative answer. [50]**And a certain one of them struck the high priest's slave and lopped off his right ear.** So bent on defending Jesus is one of the disciples that he doesn't wait for Jesus' answer but defends him instantly. That the disciple's victim is "the *high priest's* slave" and has "his *right* ear" cut off testifies to Luke's searching out the reports of eyewitnesses (1:1–4 [compare "*seeing*" what will happen right here in 22:49]). [51]**And answering** [= responding to the swordplay, not answering the disciple's prior question]**, Jesus said, "Permit** [me] **up to this point." And touching the little ear** [that is the ear diminished by the swordstroke]**, he healed him** [the high priest's slave]. The verb translated "Permit" is often translated "Stop!" or "Enough of this!" or the like, as though Jesus were addressing the swordsman. But the verb contains a *plural* "you" (unexpressed in English translation), as opposed to "a certain one of them," and occurs a number of times elsewhere in Luke-Acts always in the sense of permission. So here Jesus is addressing the crowd and asking them for permission up to "this point," which turns out to be the healing of the ear. In other words, he buys time to perform the healing before they take him away. He's a physician, not a fighter. He isn't rebuking an overzealous disciple or saying the disciples shouldn't use a sword. For Luke, their concern for Jesus' well-being is commendable and indicative of an attractive mutuality in the Christian community just as Jesus' healing the ear makes an attractive example of "lov[ing] your enemies" and "treat[ing] well those who hate you" (6:27).

22:52–53: And Jesus said to the chief priests and officers of the temple and elders who'd sallied forth against him, "Have you come out with swords and clubs as [you'd come out] **against a bandit?** [53]**When I was with you day by day in** [the courts of] **the temple you didn't stretch out** [your] **hands against me. But this is your hour and the authority of the darkness."** Alongside the chief priests and officers of the temple, already mentioned together in 22:4, Luke brings in the elders to indicate a fulfillment of 9:22 (compare 20:1). The crowd ahead of which Judas was proceeding in 22:47 turns out to consist of these groups. They're not the Galilean crowds that acclaimed Jesus as he approached Jerusalem earlier in the week (19:37–40). His question draws a contrast between the present crowd's treating him as though he were a bandit to be captured by force, on the one hand, and on the other hand his having just healed the ear of one of their own. His comment about their not arresting him when he was teaching daily in the courts of the temple underscores their cowardice, as Luke has done more than once (20:1–8; 22:2, 6). "Your hour" of their arresting Jesus contrasts with—and will be reversed by—"the hour" of the Son of Man's coming in judgment (12:39–40, 46). Since in 4:6 Satan claimed to have all worldly authority, and since according to 22:3 Satan entered Judas, who has led the hostile crowd to Jesus' place of prayer, "the *authority* of darkness" looks satanic; and the darkness of this authority represents "the shadow of death" (1:79) and the darkness that will shroud the whole earth as Jesus is dying (23:44). Thus his arrest arises out of the most evil of influences, not out of any misbehavior on his part.

THE FULFILLMENT OF JESUS' PREDICTION THAT PETER WOULD DENY KNOWING HIM
Luke 22:54–62

22:54–57: And on seizing him, they led [him away] **and brought** [him] **into the high priest's house. And Peter was following at a distance** [literally, "from far away," emphasizing his distance from Jesus, not Jesus' distance from him]. [55]**And when** [they] **had kindled a fire in the middle of the courtyard and sat down together, Peter was sitting amidst them.** [56]**And on seeing**

him sitting [with his face] **toward the** [fire]**light and on gazing at him, a certain maid said, "This** [man] **too was with him** [Jesus]." [57]**But he disowned** [him], **saying, "I don't know him, woman." "**At a distance" draws a distinction between Peter's present following of Jesus and his earlier following so closely that they could carry on a conversation with each other. The distance bodes ill for Peter's having said he was prepared to go with Jesus both to prison and to death (22:33). He's starting to "enter into temptation" because he didn't pray (22:40, 45–46). "They" who kindled a fire and sat down together are unspecified, but Peter's sitting "amidst them" contrasts with his recent reclining at table with Jesus and again bodes ill for his declaration of loyalty to Jesus. (There's something of a parallel between the kindling of a fire "in the middle of the courtyard" and Peter's sitting "amidst them.") The maid would be a slave. Peter's facing toward the firelight enabled her, on close inspection of him, to recognize him as having accompanied Jesus. But Peter denied *knowing* Jesus, just as Jesus had predicted he'd do (22:34). At the same time that Peter falsely denies knowing *Jesus*, he addresses the maid with "woman" because he truly does *not* know her!

22:58–60: And after a short [while] **another one** [masculine], **on seeing him, said, "You too are from them** [Jesus' disciples]." **But Peter said, "Man, I'm not."** [59]**And after about one hour had passed, a certain other one** [masculine again] **was insisting, saying, "Truth** [be told], **this one too** [Peter] **was with him** [Jesus]; **for also he's a Galilean."** [60]**But Peter said, "Man, I don't know what you're talking about." And at once, while he was still speaking, a rooster crowed.** The temporal details, "after a short [while]" and "after about one hour," reflect Luke's historical research (1:1–4). In his second denial, Peter denies he's from the circle of Jesus' disciples, which is another way of saying he doesn't know Jesus. Again, then, Peter denies knowing the one he *does* know while using "Man" because he's addressing someone he does *not* know. Peter's third challenger "was insisting" on the "truth" while Peter was telling lies. The second challenger spoke *directly* to Peter, though without using a respectful address because in the challenger's opinion, belonging to the circle of Jesus' disciples was cause for *dis*respect. As did the maid, however, the third challenger talks to *others* about Jesus and renews the observation that Peter was with Jesus. Then he adds a reason for saying so ("for also"). It's that like Jesus and the other disciples, Peter is a Galilean. Luke doesn't say how the third challenger knew Peter was a Galilean. So the point is that Jesus was so popular in Galilee, where he'd ministered, that all Galileans—and therefore Peter—could be considered Jesus' companions. But Peter's "I don't know what you're talking about" makes it sound as though despite Jesus' popularity in Galilee Peter has never even heard about Jesus and therefore can't possibly know him or have been with him. The immediacy of the rooster's crowing after this third denial dramatizes the fulfillment of Jesus' prediction, unlikely though it seemed that "today" the leading apostle would three times deny knowing Jesus.

22:61–62: And on turning, the Lord looked intently at Peter [who was too far away to be spoken to; but looks can talk]; **and Peter was reminded** [by Jesus' look] **of the word of the Lord, when he'd said to him, "Before a rooster crows today, you'll disown me three times."** [62]**And on going outside, he wept bitterly.** Jesus' *turning* to look at Peter implies that Peter has denied him three times *behind his back*. Not a happy implication for Peter! The intensity of Jesus' look makes up for the distance that separated Peter from him. Luke's calling Jesus "the Lord" puts authority as well as intensity into that look, and Luke's calling the prediction of Peter's denials "the word of the Lord" gives to the prediction an authority that guaranteed fulfillment. Requotation of the prediction highlights its fulfillment in detail. And Peter's weeping bitterly after going outside represents the "turning back" that Jesus likewise predicted (22:32). Peter has come perilously close to apostasy by disowning Jesus (compare 12:9), but by weeping bitterly he hasn't entered into that temptation. "Outside," he's no longer sitting "amidst" Jesus' enemies, as he was in 22:55.

A MOCKERY OF JESUS
Luke 22:63–65

22:63–65: And the men who were holding Jesus in custody were making fun of him, beating [him]. [64]**And after blindfolding him they were asking** [him], **saying, "Prophesy! Who's the one hitting you?"** [65]**And slandering** [him], **they were saying many other things against him.** This mockery of Jesus fulfills his prediction of the same in 18:32 (see also 23:11, 36), so that by challenging him to prophesy who was hitting him the mockers themselves are ironically fulfilling an earlier prophecy of his. And to keep Jesus' reputation clean, as it deserves to be, Luke takes care to characterize the many other things they were saying against him as "slandering." Prospective converts need to know that.

JESUS' INTERROGATION BY THE SANHEDRIN
Luke 22:66–71

22:66–69: And when it became day, the people's council of elders gathered together, both chief priests and scholars, and led him off to their council chamber, saying, [67]**"If you're the Christ, tell us." But he told them, "If I tell you** [that I'm the Christ], **by no means will you believe** [that I am]. [68]**And if I ask** [you whether I'm the Christ], **by no means will you answer.** [69]**But from now on the Son of Man will be seated at the right** [hand] **of the Power of God** [= the Power which *is* God (compare Psalm 110:1)]." In 9:22 Jesus predicted his rejection by the elders, chief priests, and scholars. The prediction is now coming true. Chief priests and elders have already come to get Jesus on the Mount of Olives (22:52). Apparently they're now joined by others of their number and lead Jesus from the high priest's house (22:54) to their council chamber. They ask him to tell them if he's the Christ. Their purpose in doing so will come out in 23:2: they want to accuse him before

Pilate of claiming to be Caesar's rival in claiming to be the Christ. Perceiving their purpose, Jesus plays coy by shifting the ground of discussion from the question of his christhood to their refusal to believe and even to answer him lest by denying his christhood they antagonize the crowds that believe in him and risk being stoned to death by them (compare 20:3–8). Then he shifts again, this time to his heavenly exaltation as opposed to an earthly kingship that would rival Caesar's. "From now on" will begin at his ascension (24:50–51; Acts 1:9–11). And Jesus speaks of this exaltation in terms of himself as "the Son of Man," not in terms of himself as "the Christ." So the Sanhedrists have no grounds for an accusation of political subversion. Jesus is innocent.

22:70–71: And they all said, "Are you then the Son of God?" And he said to them, "You're saying that I am." 71And they said, "Why do we still have need of testimony? For we ourselves have heard from his mouth." Though Jesus has spoken of himself as "the Son of Man," his having also spoken of being "seated at the right [hand] of the Power of God" leads the Sanhedrists to ask whether he's God's Son. (They've failed to get him to say he's the Christ.) That "they *all*" asked him puts the utmost pressure on him. Again he doesn't buckle, though, but plays coy by saying, in effect, "'The Son of God' is your expression, not mine; for I referred to myself as 'the Son of Man.'" Since he hasn't told them anything accusation-worthy, why do they deny the need for testimony other than what they've now heard Jesus say? But that's Luke's point: Jesus' enemies are so perverse that they twist perfectly innocent statements into a basis for accusation.

ACCUSATION AND INTERROGATION
BEFORE PILATE
Luke 23:1–5

23:1: And on standing up, all the multitude of them led him to Pilate. "On standing up" implies that the Sanhedrists had been sitting down in their council chamber, and "all the multitude of them" looks ahead to a crowd of their fellow Jerusalemites. Luke has already identified Pilate as the governor of Judea (3:1). The Sanhedrists need his authority to get Jesus executed. Since Pilate is a Gentile, Jesus' prediction that he'd be given over to the Gentiles (18:31–32) starts being fulfilled right here.

23:2: And they began to accuse him, saying, "We found this [man] subverting our nation and forbidding [us] to give taxes to Caesar and saying [= claiming] himself to be Christ, a king." "*Began* to accuse him" intimates that they'll continue to accuse him, as in 23:5, 10. "We *found* this man" distorts the truth slightly, for they had *confronted* him (20:1). "Subverting our nation and forbidding [us] to give tax to Caesar" means subverting *by* forbidding and falsifies the truth flagrantly, for Jesus had said concerning taxes to "give Caesar's things back to Caesar" (20:25), quite the opposite of subversive instruction. At that time, "the scholars and the chief

priests" had sent "spies . . . in order that they might seize on his word" so as "to give him over to the governor's rule and authority," but upon Jesus' telling them to pay taxes to Caesar "they were unable in the people's presence to seize on his saying; and marveling at his answer, they fell silent" (20:20–26). Well, those people are no longer present; so the authorities lie to Pilate about Jesus' teaching. Since kings levy taxes, to support their lie the authorities say that Jesus has claimed "to be Christ, a king." But this too is a lie. Jews expected the Christ to be a king. And an angel of the Lord identified the infant Jesus as "Christ the Lord" to some shepherds (2:11). The Holy Spirit identified the infant Jesus as "the Lord's Christ" to the aged Simeon (2:26). Demons "knew him to be the Christ" (4:41). And in private conversation between Jesus and the Twelve, Peter confessed him to be "God's Christ" only to have him collar them with a gag order concerning this identification (9:20–21; compare 4:41). But neither in public nor in private has Jesus himself claimed to be Christ, and just a few minutes ago he refused before these very Sanhedrists to say he was the Christ (22:66–69). As to kingship, the angel Gabriel told Mary that Jesus would rule as king over the house of Jacob forever (1:33), and a crowd of Galilean pilgrims acclaimed him as such earlier in the week (19:38). Jesus did speak of his kingdom, but only during the preceding evening, only in connection with the coming of God's kingdom following the church age, and only in the privacy of the Last Supper (22:29–30 [compare 23:42]). So the Sanhedrists have fabricated this part of their accusation too, and in Jesus' favor Luke's audience can tell that they have.

23:3–5: And Pilate asked him, saying, "Are you the king of the Jews?" But he, answering him, said, "You're speaking." 4And Pilate told the chief priests and the crowds, "I find not even one thing culpable in this man." 5But they were adamant, saying, "He's inciting the people, teaching throughout the whole of Judea, even starting from Galilee [and coming] as far as here." As he did before the Sanhedrin, Jesus plays coy before Pilate. "You're speaking" means that the phrase "the king of the Jews" has come out of Pilate's mouth, not out of Jesus' mouth, as though to say, "Your words, not mine." Suddenly "the crowds" appear alongside "the chief priests"; and to all of them Pilate pronounces Jesus innocent of any subversion, as emphasized in "not even *one* thing culpable." But the chief priests and the crowds press their accusation relentlessly and elaborate it in terms of the effect of his teaching (incitation of the people) and its extent (throughout the land of Israel, "Judea" here standing for all of it, not just its southern part [see the comments on 1:5]). "As far as here" is designed to call up the specter of a messianic revolt centered in the capital city of Jerusalem. By "teaching," of course, the accusers mean that Jesus has been forbidding the payment of taxes to Caesar (nonpayment amounting to rebellion) and claiming to be Christ (a king in place of Caesar). Luke's audience know to the contrary that Jesus has been teaching morality and religious devotion.

But who are "the crowds" who join in these accusations, and why does Luke bring them in at this point? It's commonly thought that they consist in, or at least include, the Galilean pilgrims that acclaimed Jesus "the king" as he approached Jerusalem (19:38) and that, fickle as crowds can be, they've now turned on him. But with the exception of "some Pharisees," that "crowd" was made up of "the multitude of [his] disciples" (19:37, 39); and "all [Jesus'] acquaintances" and "women who together were following him from Galilee" will keep vigil and lament during the dark hours of Jesus' crucifixion (23:49). So it looks as though Luke isn't allying the crowds of Jesus' Galilean followers with the Sanhedrists, but instead is referring to the Sanhedrists' fellow Jerusalemites and portraying the lot of them as something like a lynch mob, except that they'll have to go through Pilate (compare 13:34; Acts 6:8–7:60).

ACCUSATION AND INTERROGATION BEFORE HEROD ANTIPAS
Luke 23:6-12

23:6-7: And on hearing [that Jesus had started from Galilee], **Pilate asked whether the man is a Galilean. ⁷And on coming to know that he's from Herod's jurisdiction, he sent him back to Herod, being also himself** [in addition to Pilate, who usually stayed in Caesarea on the coast] **in Jerusalem during these days** [of the Festival of Unleavened Bread]. Up north Herod (Antipas, not Herod the Great of 1:5) ruled Galilee under Roman sponsorship, whereas Pilate was governor only of Judea (strictly considered as southern Israel). Pilate's conviction that Jesus is innocent combines with the Sanhedrists' persistence in pressing charges against Jesus to make Pilate seize an opportunity to get Jesus' case off his hands. And Jesus' hailing from Herod's Galilean jurisdiction combines with Herod's presence in Jerusalem for the festival to give Pilate the opportunity he seizes by sending Jesus back to Herod. "*Back* to Herod" doesn't imply that Jesus had previously been before Herod. It means only that in Pilate's opinion Jesus belonged back under Herod's jurisdiction as he had been in Galilee. Since Herod like Pilate was a Gentile, Jesus' prediction that he'd be given over to the Gentiles (18:31–32) reaches complete fulfillment.

23:8-12: And on seeing Jesus, Herod rejoiced exceedingly; for he'd been wanting for considerable times to see him on account of hearing about him [compare 9:7–9]. **And he was hoping to see some sign being brought about by him. ⁹And he was questioning Jesus with a considerable number of words, but he** [Jesus] **gave him not a single answer. ¹⁰And standing** [there] **were the chief priests and the scholars, accusing him vehemently. ¹¹And even Herod, along with his soldiers, after treating him with contempt and making fun** [of him], **on throwing resplendent clothing around** [him] **sent him back to Pilate. ¹²And Herod and Pilate became friends with each other on that very day; for beforehand they were living in enmity,**

being against each other. "Herod rejoiced *exceedingly*" because "he'd been wanting *for considerable times*" to see [Jesus]." The plural of "considerable times" emphasizes how long Herod had had this desire. "Hearing about him" recalls Jesus' making news because of his miracles. But only out of curiosity, not out of a sense of need, was Herod hoping to see Jesus produce a miracle or, rather, "a sign" (compare 11:16, 29–30). The "*considerable* number of words" with which Herod questioned Jesus meets and contrasts with "not a *single* answer." Luke doesn't specify the content of the questions, so that the accent falls on Jesus' nobility in considering Herod and his curiosity unworthy of any answer (see 3:19–20; 9:7–9 for Herod's imprisonment and beheading of Jesus' predecessor, John the baptizer, and for "all the evil things he'd done" [compare 13:31–33; Acts 4:27]).

Apparently the chief priests and the scholars have gone with Jesus to Herod, for there they stand "accusing [Jesus] vehemently." Luke doesn't specify what they accuse him of before Herod. So here the accent falls on the vehemence of their accusations, as though vehemence made up for the lack of truth. "*Even Herod*" means that despite his long-held desire to see Jesus, he participated in treating him with contempt (literally, "as a nonentity"), making fun of him, throwing resplendent clothing around him to call attention by contrast to his seeming insignificance, and sending him back to Pilate as though Jesus wasn't worth Herod's time. But Pilate's gesture had made a friend out of Herod, and their enmity-replacing friendship makes a foil against which the hatred for Jesus of his enemies stands out in all its ugliness. At the same time, the Sanhedrists' rejection of Jesus and Herod's and the soldiers' making fun of him fulfill his predictions in 9:22; 17:24–25; 18:31–33.

PILATE'S GIVING JESUS OVER TO THE SANHEDRISTS' WILL TO HAVE HIM CRUCIFIED
Luke 23:13-16, 18-25

23:13-16: And on calling together the chief priests and the rulers and the people, ¹⁴Pilate said to them, "You brought me this man as one who is turning the people away [from giving taxes to Caesar (23:2)]. **And behold, on examining** [him] **in your sight, I've found in this man not even one culpability in regard to the accusations you brought against him. ¹⁵Be that as it may, not even Herod** [found in him a single culpability]; **for he sent him back to us. And behold, not even one thing deserving of death has been done by him. ¹⁶On disciplining him, therefore, I'll release him."** Together with the chief priests and the rulers, "the people" accused Jesus of turning "the people" away from paying taxes. Obviously, then, the people who accused him differ from the people purportedly misled by him. The latter are his Galilean followers. The former are Jerusalemites. A number of expressions underline Jesus' innocence of the accusations: (1) the "behold" that introduces Pilate's favorable judgment; (2) the reference to his having examined Jesus "in [their] sight," so that the examination was open and above board (compare Luke's emphasis on eyewitnessing [1:1–4]); (3) Pilate's finding in Jesus "not even *one* culpability"; (4) the failure also of Herod to find one, as shown by his sending Jesus back; (5) a second "behold" to introduce the repetition of Pilate's favorable judgment; (6) his declaring not just that he didn't *find* any culpability in Jesus but that "not even one thing deserving of death has been *done* by him"; and (7) the use of a passive verb in the foregoing expression to stress "not even one thing deserving of death" as the subject of the verb. Pilate leaves it unspecified what form of discipline he has in mind for Jesus; and Luke's audience have to wonder why Pilate, after declaring Jesus innocent three times (23:4, 14–15), plans to discipline him. Speculations about the form of discipline and Pilate's reason obscure the point that in Luke's Gospel the Sanhedrists' malevolence will deter Pilate from merely disciplining and then releasing Jesus. There's no 23:17 in the earliest and best manuscripts.

23:18–21: But as all the multitude they shouted out, saying, "Take this [man] away, and release for us Barabbas [19](who [Luke interjects] **had been thrown in prison because of a certain insurrection that took place in the city** [Jerusalem] **and** [because of] **murder)!"** [20]**But wanting to release Jesus, Pilate addressed them again.** [21]**But they counteraddressed [him], saying, "Crucify, crucify him!"** Behind the phrase "as all the multitude" is a word often translated "all together" or "in unison." But the word is a combination of "all" and "multitude" and therefore carries forward Luke's portrayal of the Sanhedrists and Jerusalemites as a kind of lynch mob (compare especially 23:1: "*all* the *multitude* of them" in reference to "the council of the elders of the people, both chief priests and scholars"). They demand that Jesus be taken away for execution and that Barabbas be released instead of Jesus. Luke interjects a thumbnail biography of Barabbas as an imprisoned rebel and murderer for a contrast with Jesus, a humanitarian who has taught payment of taxes and saved and restored people's lives. That the rebellion in which Barabbas actually participated took place in Jerusalem stands opposite the Sanhedrists' false accusation that Jesus had been "inciting the people . . . as far as here [in Jerusalem]" (23:5). And Barabbas's current imprisonment implies his having been convicted of rebellion and murder, whereas Pilate has declared Jesus innocent three times. He hadn't said, "I'll release [Jesus] *for you*," just "I'll *release* him." But the Sanhedrists demand, "Release *for us* Barabbas," so that they portray themselves as benefiting from the release of a rebel and murderer. So much for their feigned concern that Jesus not ignite a rebellion and that Caesar get paid their taxes! Wanting to release Jesus despite the contrary demands of the Sanhedrists testifies again to Pilate's judgment that Jesus is innocent of all charges. "Pilate addressed them again," but Luke doesn't quote what he said. It's as though the mob's counteraddress drowns him out. So Luke does quote their counteraddressing him with a demand that he have Jesus crucified, that is, be given the death of a criminal such as he is *not* but Barabbas *is*. In addition

to the horror and shame of crucifixion, the doubling of "Crucify" exposes the Sanhedrists' malevolence, which makes a dark backdrop against which Jesus' humanitarianism stands out.

23:22–23: And the third time he said to them, "Why, what bad thing has this [man] **done? I've found in him not even one thing deathly culpable. On disciplining him, therefore, I'll release** [him]**."** For the first two times Pilate addressed the Sanhedrists after Herod sent Jesus back, see 23:13–16, 20. [23]**But with loud voices they were insistent, asking that he be crucified; and their voices were overpowering** [Pilate's voice]. Pilate's persistence testifies to Jesus' innocence. He calls Jesus "*this* [man]" to distinguish him from Barabbas, who isn't present. And Pilate answers his own question concerning what bad thing Jesus has done. Yet again stressing Jesus' innocence is that answer: "not even one thing deathly culpable" (see also 23:4, 15). So too does Pilate's saying again that he'll release Jesus after disciplining him. The plurality and overpowering loudness of the Sanhedrists' and other Jerusalemites' voices and their insistence that Jesus be crucified reinforce Luke's portrayal of them as malevolent over against Jesus as innocent.

23:24–25: And Pilate decided that their request come to pass. [25]**And he released the one whom they were requesting, the one thrown into prison because of insurrection and murder; but he gave Jesus over to their will.** Not that "their request *should* come to pass" as a matter of *justice*, but that "their request *would* come to pass" as a matter of *injustice*. To highlight the injustice, Luke doesn't repeat Barabbas's name but does repeat the description of him as an imprisoned rebel and murderer. Though Pilate isn't guiltless of injustice (see Acts 4:27), his giving Jesus over "to *their* will" puts the onus of injustice on the Sanhedrists. Insistence has overcome justice. Loudness has substituted for evidence.

THE CRUCIFIXION OF JESUS
Luke 23:26–49

This passage divides into a procession to the place of crucifixion (23:26–31), the crucifixion itself (23:32–38), a repentant evildoer (23:39–43), Jesus' death (23:44–46), and the eyewitness of a centurion and many others (23:47–49).

23:26: And when they led him away, on taking hold of Simon, a certain Cyrenian [a man from Cyrene in North Africa who was] **coming from the countryside, they put on him the crossbeam to carry behind Jesus.** "A certain Cyrenian" distinguishes this Simon from Simon Peter and Simon the zealot, both members of the Twelve (6:14–15). The knowledge of the Cyrenian's name and place of origin testifies to Luke's historical research (1:1–4 [compare Acts 2:10; 6:9; 11:20; 13:1]). Simon the Cyrenian carries Jesus' crossbeam for him. "Behind Jesus" puts Jesus in the forefront of his journey to crucifixion just as "he was traveling in front as he was going up to Jerusalem" (19:28).

23:27–31: And there was following him a multitudinous multitude of the people, and of women who were beating [their breasts] **and wailing for him.** [28]**And on turning to them** [the women] **Jesus said, "Daughters** [= female citizens] **of Jerusalem, don't weep over me. On the contrary, weep over yourselves and over your children,** [29]**because—behold—days are coming during which people will say, 'Fortunate** [are] **the barren and the wombs that haven't given birth and breasts that haven't nursed.' **[30]**Then people will begin 'to say to the mountains, "Fall on us," and to the hills, "Cover us** [Hosea 10:8]," ' **[31]because if people do these things in the green tree, what's to happen in the dry** [tree]**?"** "A multitudinous multitude" makes awkward (even humorously awkward) English. But for emphasis Luke uses an adjective and a noun that go back to the same root. So something of the emphatic wordplay is lost in a relatively bland translation such as "a great multitude." The enormity of the multitude and the women's mourning (itself emphasized with the double expression, "beating [their breasts] and wailing for him") call attention to Jesus' popularity and the multitude's recognition of his truly good character over against the false accusations leveled against him by the Sanhedrin. Selflessly, on the other hand, he brushes aside the women's lamentation for him and tells them to weep over themselves and their children because of the coming siege and destruction of Jerusalem (compare 19:41–44; 21:5–6, 20–24). An interjected "behold" punctuates the calamity. It'll be so bad that despite the horror with which a woman's childlessness was viewed, the horror of the siege and destruction will make that horror look like a blessing. People will even call on the mountains and hills among which Jerusalem is situated to bury them. "*Begin* to say" implies a siege of some length (as indeed happened). The green tree, flowing with sap, stands for a favorable time of peace (see 19:42 again), the dry tree for an unfavorable time of war. So if an event so lamentable as Jesus' crucifixion takes place during a time of peace, how much worse the disaster to befall Jerusalem during the coming time of war. Jesus' sympathy for the women and their children matches their sympathy for him.

23:32–34: And also others—evildoers, two [of them]**—were being led to be executed with him.** [33]**And when they came to the place called "Skull," there they crucified him and the evildoers, one on the right** [of Jesus] **and one on the left.** [34]**But Jesus was saying, "Father, forgive them; for they don't know** [= understand] **what they're doing** [compare 6:28; Acts 7:60]**."** **"And they cast lots, dividing his garments for themselves** [Psalm 22:18]**."** The execution of two evildoers with Jesus fulfills his prediction in 22:37, which drew in turn on Isaiah 53:12. Luke's repeated designation, "evildoers [that is, criminals]," stresses by contrast all the good that Jesus has done and taught and the resultant injustice of his crucifixion (see especially 6:33–35; Acts 10:38). His goodness comes out now in the response he gives to his crucifixion. It's a prayer that God his Father forgive the crucifiers, whom he even excuses on the

ground of their ignorance. What boundless magnanimity! (It should be said, however, that some early and very good manuscripts omit this prayer, though it could be historical even if not an original part of Luke's Gospel.) Despite quoting Psalm 22:18 in regard to the lot-casting and dividing up of Jesus' garments, Luke doesn't say he's quoting. Consequently, the emphasis doesn't fall on a fulfillment of the Old Testament—rather, on the contrast between this injustice and Jesus' magnanimity. And starting from the leading away of Jesus in 23:26 up through the present verse (23:34), "they" has remained unspecified. For example, we might infer from other Gospels that it was soldiers who divided up Jesus' garments. But Luke doesn't say so. Consequently, "they" who led Jesus away, laid hold of Simon the Cyrenian, put the crossbeam on him, crucified Jesus and the two evildoers with him, became the objects of his prayer, cast lots for his garments, and divided them up—"they" appear to be the Sanhedrists and their fellow Jerusalemites, to whose will Pilate gave Jesus over (23:25). At least Luke holds them ultimately responsible for all these actions, and this responsibility enhances Jesus' piously prayerful magnanimity toward them all the more.

23:35–38: And the people were standing still, watching. But both the rulers were ridiculing [him]**, saying, "He saved others. Let him save himself if this** [man] **is God's Christ, the selected one** [compare 2:26; 9:35; Psalm 22:8]**,"** [36]**and also the soldiers, approaching, made fun of him by offering him vinegary wine** [37]**and saying, "If you're the king of the Jews, save yourself."** [38]**And there was also an inscription over him: "This** [is] **the king of the Jews** [compare 23:2–3]**."** The people's watching makes them eyewitnesses in accord with 1:1–4. Their standing still distinguishes them from both the rulers and the soldiers, who in their respective ways ridicule Jesus. Even on his cross, he's still popular with the people for all the good he has done for them (23:27). The rulers admit that he has saved others but reason that if he's God's Christ, the selected one, he should now use his power to save in his own behalf, that is, to save himself from dying on a cross. For in their view, the Christ should set up his kingdom, not die a criminal's death by crucifixion (compare Galatians 3:13; Deuteronomy 21:22–23). But Luke's audience know that Jesus is continuing to save others—this time for eternal life, not just for present life—*by* dying sacrificially on his cross (22:19–20). Luke's audience know as well that such dying by Jesus fulfills the plan of God for his Christ, the selected one, as recorded in Scripture (18:31–32; 20:17; 22:37 [see also especially 24:44, 46; Acts 8:26–35]). So the rulers' ridicule looks ignorant and foolish. "If you're the king of the Jews" implies that the soldiers, who speak these words to Jesus and fail to address him with a term of respect, aren't themselves Jews. Their challenge that he save himself therefore rests on a political ground rather than on the theological ground that underlay the rulers' comment. Luke doesn't say whether Jesus answered the soldiers and whether he drank the vinegary wine offered to him. So the accent falls solely on the fulfillment of

Jesus' prediction that Gentiles would make fun of him (18:32). The inscription adds to the mockery.

23:39–43: And one of the evildoers who'd been hung [on crosses] **was reviling him** [Jesus], **saying, "You're the Christ, aren't you? Save yourself and us."** **⁴⁰But answering, the other** [evildoer] **said, reprimanding him, "Since you're in the same condemnation** [as Jesus is, referring to crucifixion], **don't you fear God?"** Implied answer: Surely you do, so that you shouldn't be reviling Jesus. **⁴¹"And we indeed** [are in this condemnation] **justly, for we're getting things worthy of the things that we've done** [= what we deserve]. **But this** [Jesus] **has done nothing out of place** [= 'wrong']." **⁴²And he was saying, "Jesus, remember me whenever you come into your kingdom** [that is, into your rulership]." **⁴³And he** [Jesus] **said to him, "Amen I tell you, you'll be with me in paradise** *today***!"** Even on his cross Jesus fulfills the prophecy of Simeon that Jesus was "destined for the fall and rising of many in Israel and for a sign that'll be spoken against" (2:34). The evildoer who reviles Jesus fails to address him with a term of respect, speaks against him, and falls under God's judgment. The evildoer who defends Jesus rises into paradise. Like the rulers, the falling evildoer mistakenly supposes that Jesus should save himself and the two evildoers by setting up a messianic kingdom which would engulf all foreign powers, including Rome. Little does this evildoer know that by *not* saving himself, Jesus is proving to be the Christ of Scripture and making salvation available to others, including the two evildoers.

The other evildoer doesn't address his counterpart respectfully (he doesn't deserve respect) and confesses the justice of both their crucifixions and the injustice of Jesus' crucifixion because Jesus has done nothing wrong. So this evildoer adds his own verdict of "Not guilty" to that of Pilate and of Herod, and Luke's audience know not only that Jesus has done nothing wrong but also that he has done a lot that's right and good. Then, after addressing him respectfully with "Jesus," the evildoer who has confessed guilt asks Jesus to remember him (favorably, of course) whenever Jesus comes into his rulership, as though he won't come into it for some time, perhaps a long time—hence "remember," for the length of time might make Jesus forget him. Indeed, Jesus himself has intimated a long delay (see especially 19:11). You'd think that this evildoer had heard Jesus say so. But Jesus surprises him with a promise that he'll be with Jesus in paradise this very day, and guarantees the promise doubly with "Amen" and "I tell you." That is to say, they'll both die very soon rather than hanging on their crosses for several days (as usually happened to victims of crucifixion); and as disembodied spirits (for Jesus will commit his spirit to God and await his resurrection on Sunday [23:46; 24:1–8]) they'll go to heaven, portrayed as a pleasure-garden ("paradise"), like the garden of Eden in Genesis 2:8–9. Certainly a better locale than "Skull" (23:33)! Jesus has no need to remember this evildoer, then. They'll go to paradise together. Jesus saves *on* the cross and *from* the cross.

23:44–46: And it was already about the sixth hour [noon]**; and darkness settled on the whole land till the ninth hour** [about 3:00 P.M.]**, ⁴⁵because the sun failed** [to shine]**; and the curtain of the temple was torn in the middle; ⁴⁶and shouting with a loud shout, Jesus said, "Father, into your hands I commit my spirit"; and on saying this, he breathed out** [which means that in exhaling his last breath he committed his spirit to God, for "spirit" and "breath" go back to the same Greek word]. Though Luke explains the darkness of early afternoon as due to the sun's failing to shine, his audience can't help but recall that at his arrest Jesus said, "This is . . . the authority of darkness" (see 22:53 with comments). "The curtain of the temple" was a thick veil in the sanctuary proper (as distinct from its surrounding courtyards). In 21:5–6 Jesus predicted the destruction of the temple. But earlier, in 13:35, he'd said to Jerusalem, "Behold, your house [the temple] is being abandoned [by God's Spirit, who otherwise lives there]." The tearing of the curtain provides an exit for the Spirit. Henceforth the temple faces the destruction that will befall it in A.D. 70. The loudness of Jesus' final shout enables earwitnesses to hear it at a distance (compare 23:49 with 1:1–4). Suitably to Luke's emphasis on Jesus' piety as expressed in prayer, the last word from the cross consists in a prayer. It starts with the respectful but fond address, "Father," proceeds to a trustful committal of Jesus' spirit to the Father, and occurs at the ninth hour, the hour of prayer according to Acts 3:1. Thus Jesus remains to the end of his mortal life an admirable model of true religion, so that his spirit and God's Spirit—and the spirit of the repentant evildoer—fly up to paradise together. His body was given over into the hands of his enemies (9:44; 20:19; 22:53; 24:7; Acts 2:23), but they can't prevent the committal of his spirit into the Father's hands.

23:47–49: And on seeing what had happened, the centurion was glorifying God, saying, "Certainly this man was righteous." ⁴⁸And on seeing the things that had happened, all the crowds that had assembled for this sight were returning, beating [their] **breasts. ⁴⁹But standing at a distance were all his acquaintances, plus women who'd been following along with him from Galilee** [compare 8:2–3; 24:10]**, seeing these things.** Here Luke's emphasis on eyewitness testimony as supporting the certainty of the gospel comes out in full force: (1) The centurion *sees* what has happened and introduces his testimony with "Certainly." (2) The crowds, *all* of them, also *see* the things that have happened. (3) These crowds have assembled for the express purpose of seeing this "*sight*." And (4) "*seeing* these things" are also Jesus' acquaintances, again *all* of them, plus women who've been following along with him.

Luke has repeatedly noted the good religious effect of Jesus' birth and public ministry as shown in the glorifying of God (see 2:14, 20; 5:25–26; 7:16; 13:13; 17:15; 18:43; 19:38). Now even the death of Jesus produces this effect: "the centurion was glorifying God." You'd never think that this soldier, who along with those under his command had mocked Jesus (23:36), would turn into a

God-glorifier. But he did. Such is the effect on an eyewitness of the death of this righteous man. Indeed, he glorifies God *by* saying Jesus was certainly a righteous man. Thus the centurion joins Pilate, Herod, and the repentant evildoer in testifying to Jesus' good character. In the centurion's testimony Jesus is said to be not merely innocent of any wrongdoing, but also positively righteous, as opposed to the "evildoers" crucified on either side of him. Luke's reference to "all the crowds [plural!] that had assembled" indicates that even in his death Jesus remained popular because of his righteous and good deeds. The crowds' beating their breasts in lamentation as they were returning from "Skull" amplifies his popularity. They were sad to see him die. Instead of returning to the city, all Jesus' acquaintances and the female followers stay standing. Their exceptionless loyalty to him ("*all* his acquaintances and women who'd been following along with him") will keep them there till his corpse is taken down from the cross. Luke features such loyalty to attract converts. "At a distance" carries no negative connotation, but explains the reason Jesus had "shouted" his final prayer "with a loud shout" (see 23:46 with comments). He wanted his acquaintances and female followers to hear it. And, in fact, the first Christian martyr, Stephen, will imitate it (Acts 7:59–60).

JESUS' BURIAL
Luke 23:50–56

This passage divides into a request for Jesus' corpse (23:50–52), the burial proper (23:53–54), and the women's observing it, preparing for perfuming the corpse, and resting on the Sabbath (23:55–56).

23:50–52: And behold, a man by the name of Joseph, being a councillor [that is, a member of the Sanhedrin] **and a good and righteous man** [51]**(this one hadn't agreed with their plan and action) from Arimathea, a city of the Judeans, who was waiting expectantly for God's reign**—[52]**on approaching Pilate, this** [man] **requested Jesus' corpse** [compare Deuteronomy 21:22–23]. Luke's extensive description of Joseph carries a special emphasis. It's that even in his death by that most shameful mode of execution, crucifixion, Jesus is so good and righteous that he attracts Joseph, a good and righteous man like himself, as shown by Joseph's disagreement with the plan and action hatched and executed by the Sanhedrin. And he disagreed despite his own membership in the Sanhedrin and despite coming from a city in Judea rather than Galilee, where Jesus was popular. Like the "righteous and devout" Simeon back in 2:25, moreover, Joseph was "waiting expectantly for God's reign." Luke doesn't portray Joseph as a convert, but he does portray him as a prime candidate for conversion, given the correspondence between his admirable character and religious devotion and the same in Jesus. The request for Jesus' corpse, to be given a burial suitable to his goodness and righteousness rather than one suitable to an evildoer, supplies further testimony to Joseph's integrity.

23:53–54: And having taken down [Jesus' corpse], **he wrapped it in a linen cloth and placed him** [Jesus] **in a tomb carved** [out of rock so as to produce a cave-like room], **where no one had yet lain** [= had yet been buried]. [54]**And it was the day of preparation** [Friday], **and the Sabbath** [Saturday] **was breaking in on** [Joseph]. A linen cloth and a tomb so upscale as to have been carved out of rock suit Jesus' innocence and righteousness, accord him special and well-deserved honor, and enhance Luke's portrayal of Joseph as "a good and righteous man." Heightening these elements are the shift from "it" (the corpse that's taken down and wrapped in a linen cloth) to "him" (Jesus as the one placed in the tomb) and his being the first to be buried in the tomb. No secondhand tomb for him (compare his riding a previously unridden colt in 19:30, 35–36)! Friday was the day of preparation in that what was needed on Saturday, the Sabbath, had to be prepared beforehand so as to avoid working the next day. The Sabbath was breaking in on Joseph, but he succeeded—barely—in the work of burying Jesus before the Sabbath started at sunset. As a result, Jesus' burial didn't violate Sabbath law. Luke repeatedly points up the continuity of Jesus' story with the Old Testament and Judaism at its best.

23:55–56: And on following [Joseph], **the women who as such had come with Jesus out of Galilee** [compare 23:49] **saw the tomb and how his corpse was placed** [in it]. [56]**And on returning, they prepared aromatic spices and perfumed ointments. And throughout the Sabbath, on the one hand, they rested in accordance with the commandment.** "As such" highlights the women's having accompanied Jesus all the way from Galilee. Luke's emphasis on eyewitnessing comes out again in the statement that they now see the tomb and how Jesus' corpse was placed. There'll be no coming to the wrong tomb Sunday morning, then. ("*How* the corpse was placed" doesn't refer to the *manner* of its placement in the tomb; rather, to the *fact* of its placement there.) The preparation of spices and ointments with which to retard the decomposition of Jesus' corpse and mask its stench (24:1) marks the women's loyalty to him just as did their keeping in eyeshot of his crucifixion and burial (see the comments on 23:49). Their resting on the Sabbath implies that they had just enough time between the burial and sunset to make the preparation. "In accordance with the commandment" calls attention to their abiding by the Sabbath law. Jesus' followers weren't religious renegades, Luke wants us to know. They were good and decent and pious, the kind you might want to attach yourself to as a convert.

JESUS RESURRECTED
Luke 24:1–53

This passage divides into the announcement of Jesus' resurrection (24:1–8), Peter's confirming the emptiness of Jesus' tomb (24:9–12), Jesus' appearance to two disciples on the road to Emmaus (24:13–32), their report to the eleven apostles and the apostles' report to them about an appearance of Jesus to Simon (24:33–35), Jesus' appearance to all of them (24:36–49), and his ascension (24:50–53).

24:1–4: On the other hand [as opposed to resting on Saturday, the Sabbath, in 23:56]**, on the first** [day] **of the week** [Sunday] **at deep** [= early] **dawn they** [the women] **came carrying the aromatic spices that they'd prepared.** Magnifying the devotion of the women to Jesus are their coming not just at dawn but at *early* dawn and their carrying aromatic spices with which to anoint his corpse. They can hardly wait for the Sabbath and night to be over so that they can perform this act of devotion. And they'd prepared the spices late Friday afternoon to avoid any delay Sunday morning. [2]**But they found the stone rolled away from the tomb.** It had been used to close the opening. [3]**But on entering, they didn't find the corpse of the Lord Jesus.** Absence of the corpse prepares for a later demonstration of the physicality of Jesus' resurrection. Luke prefixes "Lord" to "Jesus" for a preindication of his risen authority. [4]**And it happened while they were dumbfounded at this** [the emptiness of the tomb] **that—behold—two men in flashing apparel came and stood over them.** "Behold" calls special attention to an encountering of the women by "two men in flashing apparel"—enough to scare them and make them bow their faces to the ground in subservience. The word for "men" connotes adult males, and these men recall 9:30–31: "And behold, talking with him [Jesus] were two men, who were Moses and Elijah, who on being seen [= appearing] in glory . . . ." The similarities not only in "two men" but also in "behold" and "in flashing apparel" vis-à-vis "in glory" strongly suggest that the two men encountering the women aren't angels that look like human beings, but the human beings Moses and Elijah (see also Acts 1:9–11 and the comments on 24:23). If so, the "flashing apparel" signifies their glorified state, which suits in turn the coming glorification of Jesus (see 24:26; Acts 3:13; 22:11 [compare Luke 9:26; 21:27]) and supports their imminent testimony to Jesus' resurrection as coming from a heavenly source. That there are two of them will provide testimony that's legally sufficient (Numbers 35:30; Deuteronomy 17:6; 19:15).

24:5–8: And when they [the women] **got scared and were bowing** [their] **faces to the ground, they** [the two men] **said to them, "Why are you seeking the living one** [Jesus] **with the dead** [that is, as though he were a dead person among other dead persons]**?** [6]**He isn't here; rather, he has been raised. You should remember how he spoke to you when he was still in Galilee,** [7]**saying, 'It's necessary that the Son of Man be given over into the hands of sinful men and crucified and on the third day resurrect** [a summary of Jesus' predictions in 9:22, 44; 17:24–25; 18:31–32; see the comments on those passages especially for 'It's necessary' and 'on the third day']**.'"** "*How* he spoke" refers to the fact of his speaking, not to its manner. Though Jesus spoke of being killed, he never spoke of being crucified, so that the two men interpret his predictions in the light of his crucifixion. [8]**And**

they remembered his words. Though women weren't explicitly mentioned as auditors of Jesus' passion-and-resurrection predictions, 8:2–3 indicated that certain women were serving him and the Twelve in Galilee; and 23:49, 55 recently identified the present women as those who followed him from Galilee to Jerusalem. Since the two men tell them, "You should remember how he spoke *to you* when he was still in Galilee," they must have heard Jesus predict his passion and resurrection. "And they remembered his words" confirms this conclusion; and remembering Jesus' words erases the women's dumbfoundedness, so that they will take a true and detailed report to the apostles and others (24:9–10). "He isn't here [in the tomb you've entered]," because it would be inappropriate for "the living one" to stay in a tomb such as is used for dead people. "He has been raised" implies that God has raised Jesus from the dead, as becomes repeatedly clear in Acts 3:15; 4:10; 5:30; 10:40; 13:30, 37.

24:9–12: And on returning from the tomb, they reported all these things to the Eleven and to all the rest [Jesus' "acquaintances" in addition to the Eleven (23:49)]**.** "All these *things*" refers to the stone's having been rolled away from the mouth of the tomb, the emptiness of the tomb, the encounter with two men in flashing apparel, and the announcement of Jesus' resurrection. "*All* these things" describes them as overwhelming in number, given their supernatural character. "The Eleven" excludes Judas Iscariot from the Twelve. "And to *all* the rest" (where Luke could have written "and to the rest") revives the theme of Jesus' popularity. He'd gained many disciples because of his good works. [10]**And they** [the women] **were Mary Magdalene and Joanna and Mary the** [mother] **of James** [Greek for the Hebrew "Jacob"] **and the rest** [of the women] **with them.** The names in this list give evidence of Luke's historical research (1:1–4). **And they were telling these things to the apostles,** [11]**and these words appeared in their** [the apostles'] **sight as if** [they were] **preposterous.** "As *if*" (where Luke could have written a simple "as") implies that the women's words were *not* preposterous despite the apostles' contrary impression of them. **And they** [the apostles] **weren't believing them** [the women]**.** [12]**But on standing up, Peter ran to the tomb and, bending down, sees the linen cloths alone** [that is, without Jesus' corpse wrapped inside them]**; and wondering what had happened, he went away** [from the tomb] **to his place of residence.** Apparently Peter had taken the report sitting down. His standing up and running to the tomb exhibit eagerness to confirm or disconfirm the women's report. His bending down implies a low opening into the tomb, a detail stemming from Luke's historical research. Peter's seeing the linen cloths alone—emphasized by the present tense of "sees"—fits Luke's interest in eyewitnessing and confirms the tomb's emptiness but not the resurrection of Jesus (for his corpse might have been stolen or otherwise removed). "The linen cloths" (plural) suggest that "a linen cloth" (singular [23:53]) had been torn into strips and wound around Jesus' corpse. Peter wondered what had happened, because—though he'd seen the tomb empty—the report of a resurrection still seemed to him preposterous. His eagerness for confirmation of the women's report and his ongoing wonderment display an unwillingness to believe in Jesus' resurrection on less than sure and certain evidence (compare 1:1–4). Since Peter was a Galilean, had a home in Capernaum, and will stay in Jerusalem till after Jesus' ascension and the Day of Pentecost (4:31, 38; 5:1, 3; 22:59; 24:49, 52; Acts 1:2–4, 12–13; 2:14 and so on), Peter's "place of residence" must mean a place of temporary residence in Jerusalem.

24:13–17: **And behold, two of them** [belonging to "all the rest," who were in addition to "the Eleven" (24:9)] **were traveling on that very day** [Sunday] **to a town that had the name Emmaus, being sixty stades** [= about seven miles] **distant from Jerusalem.** "Behold" introduces a lengthy narrative with a verbal exclamation. "Two," "on that very day," the town's name "Emmaus," and the precise notation of distance from Jerusalem give more evidence of Luke's historical research and provide circumstantial data supporting the reliability of the testimony by these two. In addition, "on that very day" allows no interval of time to blur the evidential value of the following story. [14]**And they were conversing with each other about all these things that had transpired.** As in 24:9, "*all* these things" describes the events as overwhelming in their number, given their supernatural character. [15]**And it happened during their conversation and discussion that Jesus himself, on drawing near, started traveling with them.** The addition of "discussion" to "conversation" implies different points of view. The addition of "himself" to "Jesus" highlights for Luke's audience, though not for the two discussants, the marvel of the resurrected Jesus' joining them. He's still "traveling," as he started doing in 9:51, 53, and won't stop doing till he has ascended to heaven (24:51; Acts 1:9–11). [16]**But their eyes were being restrained so as not to recognize him.** Luke doesn't say who or what kept the two discussants from recognizing Jesus, so that Luke is content to point out that they're not to be blamed for failure to recognize Jesus. Implied, however, is that apart from the restraining of their eyes, the two discussants would have recognized Jesus by sight; and he's about to blame them for something besides nonrecognition of him. [17]**And he said to them, "What** [are] **these words that you're exchanging with each other as you're walking along?" And gloomy-faced, they stood still.** "These words" refers to the verbal expression of "all these things" in their discussion. "Gloomy-faced" expresses in body language the disappointment they'll verbalize shortly. Their standing still expresses, likewise in body language, the surprise one of them will verbalize over Jesus' apparent ignorance of recent events. And their gloom and failure to recognize Jesus disfavor any fabrication by them out of an expectation that Jesus would rise from the dead.

2:18–20: **And answering, one by the name of Cleopas said to him, "Are you alone visiting Jerusalem and haven't come to know the things that have happened in it** [the city] **during these days?"** Luke's knowledge of Cleopas's name comes from historical research pursued by Luke to substantiate the truth of the gospel (1:1–4). Favoring reliability are the obscurity of Cleopas (he's otherwise unknown) and the anonymity of his companion (a fictionalizer would tend to provide names to both of them). [19]**And he said to them, "What sort of things?"** Many things have happened in Jerusalem during the Festival of Unleavened Bread, of course. But "what *sort* of things" have evoked the discussion taking place between Cleopas and his companion? **And they said to him** [now Cleopas's companion chimes in with him], **"The things concerning Jesus the Nazarene** [= the Jesus from Nazareth as distinguished from other Jesuses]**, who as a man became a prophet mighty in deed and word in the presence of God and all the people,** [20]**and how the chief priests and our rulers gave him over to a death-sentence and crucified him."** "As a man" marks Jesus as having been a male adult when he became a prophet (compare 4:16–21), and at the level of Luke's Gospel "as a man" alludes to Jesus' having grown up from the infancy and boyhood detailed in Luke 1–2. He had portrayed himself as a prophet and been regarded as such by others (4:24; 7:16; 9:8, 19; 13:33). Some Old Testament prophets, such as Elijah and Elisha, had been mighty in deed, that is, notable for their performance of miracles. Others had been mighty in word, that is, notable for their spoken messages. Isaiah comes to mind as an outstanding example. But Jesus was mighty in both deed and word. The addition of "word" to "deed" would have appealed to Luke's audience of Gentiles, who admired great oratory. "In the presence of God" implies God's approval of Jesus' deeds and words. "In the presence of . . . all the people" likewise implies their approval. "*All* the people" reflects the enormity of Jesus' popularity because of his good deeds and words of good news. "And *how* the chief priests and our rulers gave him over to a death-sentence and crucified him" doesn't have to do so much with the *manner* in which they did (though the injustice of that manner hovers in the background) as with the *fact* they did despite his good deeds, words of good news, divine approval, and—except for those authorities—popular approval.

Cleopas and his companion continue speaking in *24:21–24:* **"But we'd been hoping that he is the one who is going to redeem Israel."** "He *is* the one who *is* going to redeem Israel" tells how vivid their now disappointed hope was. "*Going* to redeem Israel" expresses how sure and soon they'd hoped for his redemption of Israel, and the redemption for which they hoped was liberation from domination by Rome (1:54–55, 68–75; 2:30–31). **"Nevertheless, indeed, also along with all these things** [the death-sentence and Jesus' crucifixion] **this is the third day since these things happened.** [22]**Nevertheless, also, certain women from among us astounded us by coming to be at the tomb early** [this morning]. [23]**And on not finding his corpse, they came saying they'd also seen a vision** [an actual appearance, not a dream] **of messengers, who say he's living.** [24]**And some of the ones with us went off to the tomb** and found [it] thus, [that is,] **just as the women had said. But they didn't see him."** "Nevertheless . . . also" and "Nevertheless, also" put a double emphasis on the contrast between the disappointment of hope because of Jesus' crucifixion and the glimmerings of renewed hope because of events earlier on this third day since the crucifixion. Tucked into the first occurrence of this phrase, "indeed" reinforces the emphasis. "The third day" echoes the words of the two men at the empty tomb (24:7), who quoted the words of Jesus himself (9:22; 18:33 [compare 24:46]). The women's "not finding his corpse" and "also see[ing] a vision of messengers, who say he's living" provide eyewitness evidence (1:1–4). The present tense of "say" lends a kind of immediacy to the messengers' statement. Most translations have "angels," but the underlying word can equally well mean "messengers" and refer to Moses and Elijah (see the comments on 9:30–31; 24:4). Confirmation of the tomb's emptiness by "some of the ones with us" implies that Peter wasn't the only one who checked out the women's report, and adds further evidence of an eyewitness sort (compare John 20:1–10). For the time being, however, not seeing Jesus alive leaves only the messengers' announcement of his resurrection. Unawares, the two travelers to Emmaus are themselves seeing the risen Jesus at the very moment they say visitors to the empty tomb have not seen him!

24:25–27: And he said to them, "O mindless and slow of heart to believe on the basis of all that the prophets spoke, [26]it was necessary, wasn't it, for the Christ to suffer these things and enter into his glory?" [27]And starting from Moses and from all the prophets, he interpreted to them the things about himself in all the Scriptures. Since the heart was considered a seat of intellect as well as of emotion, "slow *of heart*" means much the same as "mindless"—that is, mentally dull—and therefore doubles the reproach in Jesus' addressing them with "O mindless and slow of heart to believe." For Luke's audience, this reproach implies in reverse that, given what the Old Testament prophets said, it shows intelligence to believe right now that Jesus' suffering and glorification carried out God's plan for the Christ as revealed in the Scriptures. "*All* that the prophets spoke," "starting from Moses and from *all* the prophets," and "in *all* the Scriptures" stress the comprehensiveness with which this plan was revealed, and therefore the certainty on which belief in Jesus rests (1:1–4). His interpretation remedies mindlessness, speeds up belief, and shifts the focus from himself as "a prophet mighty in deed and word" (24:19) to himself as the Christ foretold by earlier prophets. "*Starting* from Moses" implies a lengthy interpretation, and "enter into his glory" anticipates his ascension as the culmination of the journey he began in 9:51, 53.

24:28–31: And they drew near to the town where [= to which] they were traveling, and he made as though he was traveling farther. [29]And they urged him, saying, "Stay with us, because it's toward evening and the day has already declined [to the point where it's almost

over]." **And he entered** [Emmaus] **to stay with them. [30]And it happened while he was reclining** [at table] **with them that taking a loaf of bread, he blessed** [it] **and, on breaking** [it into pieces]**, he gave** [the pieces] **to them. [31]And their eyes were opened and they recognized him. And he became invisible to them** [= vanished from their sight]. Urging Jesus to stay with them displays the virtue of hospitality, plus a concern that he not have to travel at night. His making as though he was traveling farther tested their hospitality and concern. By entering Emmaus to stay with them he gives them a passing grade. Though their guest, suitably to his lordship he acts as the host by taking a loaf of bread, blessing it, and giving the pieces to them. Since blessing the bread means praising God in thanksgiving for it, Jesus' piety comes into view again. *They* didn't open their eyes. "Their eyes *were* opened" in a reversal of 24:16: "But their eyes were *being* restrained so as not to recognize him." Whoever or whatever was restraining their eyes now opens them. They'd been seeing Jesus, of course; but perceptive seeing now enables them to recognize him for who he is. Thus they become eyewitnesses of Jesus as risen from the dead (compare 1:1–4). But no sooner do they become such eyewitnesses than he disappears to make others eyewitnesses like them.

24:32–35: And they said to each other, "Our heart was burning [within us], **wasn't it, as he was speaking to us on the road,** [that is,] **as he was opening** [= interpreting (see 24:27)] **the Scriptures to us?"** "Our heart" is a collective singular; the two speak as one. Figuratively, the burning of their heart may stand for excitement. Because of Jesus' addressing them with "O witless and slow of heart to believe on the basis of all that the prophets spoke" (24:25), however, the heartburn more probably stands for shame over their failure of wit and faith. [33]**And on standing up** [from reclining at table] **that very hour, they returned to Jerusalem.** So they travel at night as they'd urged Jesus not to do. But, of course, their news is too good to delay reporting for even the slightest amount of time—hence, "that very hour" (the shortest unit of time used by the ancients). **And they found the Eleven** [the Twelve minus Judas] **and the ones with them** [see 23:49; 24:9–10] **assembled, [34]saying** [to the two disciples from Emmaus], **"The Lord has been raised—really! And he has appeared to Simon** [compare 1 Corinthians 15:5]**." [35]And they** [the two from Emmaus] **started relating the things** [that had happened] **on the road and how he was made recognizable to them during the breaking of the bread.** "Assembled" prepares for large-scale eyewitnessing. Jesus' resurrection makes the reference to him as "the Lord" especially appropriate. "Really!" magnifies the actuality of his resurrection, and his appearance to Simon has made him an eyewitness in addition to the two from Emmaus. "By the mouth of two witnesses or by the mouth of three witnesses shall a matter be established" (Deuteronomy 19:15). Just as the two are told of Jesus' appearance to Simon, they relate Jesus' appearance to them, so that their testimonies confirm each other.

24:36–39: While they were saying these things, he [Jesus] **stood in the midst of them and says to them, "Peace** [be] **to you."** "Stood" shows that he's no longer lying supine as a corpse in a tomb. "In the midst of them" makes eyewitnesses out of them all, not just the two and Simon but also the rest of the Eleven and the ones assembled with them (24:33). The present tense of "says" contemporizes Jesus' pronouncement of peace. This peace makes not only a normal Semitic greeting (*shalōm* in Hebrew) but also the gift of salvation, guaranteed now by Jesus' resurrection (2:11, 14: "a *Savior*, who is Christ, the Lord. . . . and on earth *peace* [be] among human beings of [God's] good pleasure"). [37]**But panic-stricken and scared, they were supposing they were viewing a spirit** [= a ghost]. Ironically but understandably, Jesus' standing in the midst of them overpowers his pronouncement of peace with panic and fear. [38]**And he said to them, "Why are you troubled and for what reason are calculations coming up in your heart?** [39]**Look at my hands and my feet, that I am myself** [= 'that it's me']. **Feel me and see, because a spirit doesn't have flesh and bones as you view me having** [them]." "Troubled" refers to their panic and fear, "calculations" to the pros and cons arising in their "heart" (a collective singular for the mind as well as emotion) on the question whether they're seeing the resurrected Lord as Simon and the two from Emmaus have already done. Jesus helps their reasoning come to the right conclusion by appealing to what they see and inviting them to confirm their sense of sight with their sense of touch. He selects his hands and feet for seeing and feeling, not because of nail scars from crucifixion (which aren't mentioned), but because—apart from the head, which wouldn't be appropriate to feel—these are the exposed parts of his body featuring a combination of flesh and bones. "Look" and "see" put a double accent on eyewitness.

24:40–43: And on saying this, he showed them [his] **hands and** [his] **feet.** [41]**And while for joy they were still disbelieving and marveling, he said to them, "Do you have here anything edible?"** [42]**And they gave him a piece of broiled fish.** [43]**And on taking** [it], **he ate** [it] **in their sight.** "He *showed* them" and "in their sight" add further emphasis on eyewitnessing. "Hands and feet" and eating "a piece of broiled fish" demonstrate the physicality of Jesus' resurrection and thus destroy any thought of a ghostly apparition. (Because of his vow of abstinence from wine till God's rule comes [22:18], he eats but doesn't drink.) "For joy" excuses the disbelief and advances the theme of joyful salvation that started in Luke 1–2 (see especially 2:10–11: "For behold, I'm announcing to you as good news a great joy . . . a Savior"). "While . . . they were still disbelieving" means that what they were seeing seemed too good to be true, but "marveling" indicates that what they were seeing replaced that disbelief with amazement. Their initial disbelief does show again, though, that they didn't fabricate the story of Jesus' resurrection out of an expectation that he would rise from the dead.

24:44–49: And he told them, "These [are] **my words that I spoke to you when I was still with you: 'It's necessary that all things written about me in the Law of Moses and the Prophets and Psalms be fulfilled** [9:22; 17:24–25; 18:31–33 (compare 24:6–7)].'" [45]**Then he opened their mind** [a collective singular] **to understand the Scriptures** [46]**and told them, "Thus it's written that the Christ would suffer and rise from the dead on the third day** [47]**and that beginning from Jerusalem repentance for the forgiveness of sins would be proclaimed to all nations on the basis of his name.** [48]**You** [are] **witnesses of these things** [that is, of my suffering and resurrection as the Christ]. [49]**And behold, I'm sending on you the Father's promise. But you— sit** [tight] **in the city** [of Jerusalem] **till you're clothed with power from the height** [= heaven]." "These . . . my words" refers forward to the summarizing quotation of what Jesus told the disciples before his death and resurrection, and "thus" refers forward to what's written in the Scriptures concerning the Christ. So Jesus' words as well as the Scriptures have been fulfilled. "When I was still with you" implies that he's going to ascend to heaven so soon that he might as well be there already. "The Law of Moses and the Prophets and Psalms" constitute the three divisions of the Hebrew Old Testament, with the book of Psalms heading up and standing for the rest of the books in the third division. (Except for the Law of Moses [Genesis–Deuteronomy], the order of books in the Hebrew differs from the order in our English Bible; and since the third Hebrew division didn't include apocryphal books, written later, the Scriptures of Luke's Jesus exclude those books [see also the comments on Matthew 23:35].) "*All* things written about me" implies both a large amount of such material extending throughout the Old Testament and the completeness of its fulfillment. Rementioning the necessity of fulfillment emphasizes once again that Jesus' death and resurrection carry out God's plan rather than thwarting it and therefore bring the ancient religion of Judaism to fruition rather than running counter to it. "He opened their mind" implies that it was closed to understanding the Scriptures as predicting the Christ's suffering and rising from the dead. They thought only of his delivering them from Roman domination and reestablishing the Davidic kingdom. By opening the disciples' mind to understand the Scriptures, Jesus supplements what the disciples have eyewitnessed and about which they are to bear witness. Opening their mind also prepares them to give a scriptural proclamation on the basis of his name; for the Scriptures and his name agree with each other. "His name" connotes authority and refers back to "the Christ," so that "repentance for the forgiveness of sins . . . on the basis of his name" means that his suffering and rising from the dead on the third day *as the Christ* make forgiveness of sins possible for the repentant.

"Beginning from Jerusalem" and "to all nations" anticipate the Great Commission in Acts 1:8, which here in Luke 24:47 gets scriptural backing, so that the proclamation itself will join Jesus' suffering and resurrection in fulfilling the Scriptures and thus carrying out God's plan and bringing Judaism to fruition. "To all nations" enlarges the scope of the gospel to include Gentiles as well as Jews. "Behold" highlights the sending of God's promise on the disciples. Jesus' calling him "the Father" suits the comparison of God to a father who gives good gifts to his children—this in connection with God the Father's giving the Holy Spirit to those who ask him (11:11–13 [see Acts 1:8 for the combination of power, the Holy Spirit, and worldwide witness]). "The Father's promise" consists in "power from the height." But it's Jesus who'll send it. So he's the agent of empowerment for Christian witness as well as the agent of forgiveness. "*Clothed* with power" implies that the power won't be *inherent* in them but that it will *belong* to them. Not till the book of Acts will it become apparent that the promised power will come on them with the arrival of the Holy Spirit. Meanwhile, they're to "sit [tight] in the city [of Jerusalem]," because their proclamation to all nations would prove ineffective apart from empowerment originating in heaven.

24:50–53: **And he led them outside** [the city] **as far as Bethany** [on the Mount of Olives]; **and on lifting up his hands** [to God, not over the disciples]**, he blessed them** [= praised God for them, just as he'd blessed bread by thanking God for it (9:16; 24:30; compare 22:19) and just as the disciples praised God by pronouncing Jesus blessed on Palm Sunday (19:37–38), so that we're not to think here of Jesus' bestowing some sort of favor on them]. **⁵¹And it happened during his blessing them that he departed from them and was being carried up into heaven. ⁵²And on worshiping him** [as he was being carried up], **they returned to Jerusalem with great joy ⁵³and were continually in** [the courts of] **the temple blessing God** [again in the sense of praising him with thanksgiving, *not* in the sense of bestowing a favor on him]. Jesus blesses the disciples by thankfully praising God for them, because they'll be his (Jesus') witnesses proclaiming to all nations repentance for the forgiveness of sins in his name. His departure by being carried up into heaven marks both "his exodus," which on the Mount of Transfiguration Moses and Elijah were saying "he was going to fulfill in Jerusalem" (9:30–31), and also the "entering into his glory," about which he himself spoke (24:26 [compare 22:69]). The fulfillment comes as another indication that God's plan, predicted by two heroes of ancient Judaism and by Jesus, is being carried out. "Worshiping him" means kneeling with face to the ground as a bodily expression of submission to Jesus' lordship. The return to Jerusalem comes in obedience to his command that the disciples "sit [tight] in the city" until they're "clothed with power from the height." "With great joy" carries forward yet again the joyful effect of the gospel (see the comments on 24:41). And "were continually in [the courts of] the temple blessing God" carries forward yet again the good religious effects of the gospel. "In the temple" shows Jesus' disciples devoted to this institution of Judaism. "Continually" means "regularly," not "continuously," and underlines the devotion. And "blessing God" shows that belief in Jesus fosters piety rather than undermining it.

JOHN

In this Gospel Jesus appears as God's preexistent Son and agent of creation who therefore, on becoming a human being, carried out the will of God his Father completely, took full charge even of his own death and resurrection, and thus demands and deserves belief in him.

A PROLOGUE ON JESUS AS THE WORD
John 1:1–18

1:1: **In the beginning was the Word.** So starts the Fourth Gospel. Mark started his Gospel, the earliest one, with the phrase, "The *beginning* of the gospel of Jesus Christ" (Mark 1:1), and proceeded to the ministry of John the baptizer (from here on, "the Baptist" to distinguish him from John the evangelist, who wrote the Fourth Gospel, though the evangelist never calls him the Baptist). Matthew started with Jesus' genealogy and nativity; proceeded to the Baptist's ministry, Jesus' baptism, temptation, and move from Nazareth to Capernaum; and wrote, "From then on Jesus *began* preaching and saying, 'Repent, for the reign of heaven has drawn near'" (Matthew 4:17). In the prologue to his Gospel, Luke refers to "those who *from the beginning* became eyewitnesses and assistants of the word" (Luke 1:2). For Mark, then, the beginning consists in the *Baptist's* preaching and baptizing; for Matthew, in *Jesus'* preaching; and for Luke, in the ministry of *eyewitnesses* to Jesus' life on earth. Each of these beginnings came a little later in time: Jesus after the Baptist, and eyewitnesses after Jesus. John, who wrote last, breaks this pattern. His phrase, "*In the beginning*," echoes Genesis 1:1, "*In the beginning* God created the heavens and the earth," and so takes us all the way back to creation rather than marking another, still later beginning than those in the other Gospels.

But "created" is a verb of action in Genesis 1:1, just as Mark, Matthew, and Luke used verbs of action, such as the verbs of baptizing and preaching. In contrast, John uses the past tense of a verb of existence: "was." That is to say, in the beginning the Word already existed, because he himself had no beginning—or, as we read in Revelation 21:6; 22:13, "I *am* . . . the beginning." The Word preexisted. Because of the echo of Genesis 1:1 we expect the subject of John's first sentence to be God: "In the beginning was *God.*" As we've seen, though, Luke's prologue referred to "those who from the beginning became eyewitnesses and assistants of *the word* [that is, the *oral* gospel]." So John picks up this term, "the word," and—capitalizing it, so to speak—substitutes it for "God." But we don't yet know who this Word was, and if reading

John's prologue for the first time we won't know for quite a while. John keeps us in suspense. In the meantime he'll describe the Word without identifying the Word personally. On to that description, then.

And the Word was *with* God. Now the God of Genesis 1:1 comes into view. The Word and God preexisted together. In the beginning they were already there, both of them. "*With* God" distinguishes the Word *from* God and indicates a close, face-to-face relation with him. How close? **And the Word *was* God.** So close that the Word was identical with God at the same time as distinguishable from him. In other words, within himself—not just in relation to us, for neither human beings nor any other creatures existed already in the beginning—God was, is, and always will be a social being. (Add the Holy Spirit from later in John's Gospel [1:32–33 and following] and we get the Trinity.) But note the singular of "God." Despite the distinction between the Word and God we don't have "gods" (plural) even though God and the Word are both God. What we do have is plurality within singularity, and singularity pervading plurality.

In polytheistic religions the gods and goddesses engage one another in competition, jealousies, rivalries, battles, adulteries, murders, deceit, and so on. Since we seek to become like what we worship (as in the current "worship" of celebrities, called "stars" and "idols," in popular culture), the worship of those gods and goddesses encourages such behaviors instead of discouraging them. On the other hand, a god who alone is god and is only singular, who within himself is *non*social—that kind of god tends toward sheer power untempered by what we call social graces. He becomes, in short, a despot. So when his worshipers gain power, they tend toward despotism. By way of contrast the God of John's Gospel, being within himself social as well as singular, is both the God of love ("God loved the world" [3:16]) and the God of unity ("that they [the disciples] may be one just as we [the Word and God] are one" [17:22]).

1:2–4: **This one** [referring to the Word] **was in the beginning with God** repeats the thought of 1:1 to reecho Genesis 1:1 in preparation for introducing the creation, about which that Old Testament text goes on to speak. [3]**All things came into existence through him** [the Word], **and apart from him there came into existence not even one thing that did come into existence.** In Genesis God *spoke* things into existence. For example, "Then God *said*, 'Let there be light,' and there was light" (Genesis 1:3). So John turns God's *speaking* into God's

Word as the agent of creation. The "all things" that came into being through the Word include not only inanimate objects but also living creatures, human beings at their head according to Genesis 1:26–30. **⁴In him** [the Word] **was life.** But what kind of life is John writing about? The life that the Word conveyed to living creatures at the beginning? Probably not, because elsewhere in John "life" usually means *eternal* life for those who believe in the Word. This life is eternal because it's the very life of the eternal Word who was in the beginning with God. **And the life was the light of human beings.** God created light first (Genesis 1:3). But in John the light is the *un*created Word, God's agent in the creation of light along with everything else. The equation of life with light rests on some cultural background. Before the invention of matches, light bulbs, and the like, people had to keep a lamp burning if they wanted to avoid borrowing fire from a neighbor or laboriously rekindling fire by friction or percussion every time darkness fell. But when a living person wasn't present to keep the lamp burning, it went out, so that the going out of a lamp came to represent death, as in Job 18:5–6: "Indeed, the light of the wicked goes out and the flame of his fire gives no light. The light in his tent is darkened and his lamp goes out above him." On the other hand, life meant that the light of a lamp was kept burning.

John doesn't say that the *Word* was the light of human beings. Rather, "the *life* was the light of human beings." We get a hint that "the life" is not only life that was *in* the Word. More than that, the life is another way of referring to the Word himself. Later in John, as a matter of fact, the Word will say, "I *am* . . . the life" (11:25; 14:6; compare 1 John 1:1–2: "What was from the beginning, what we've heard, what we've seen with our eyes, what we've observed and our hands felt—[we're writing] about the Word of life, and the life was manifested, and we've seen [the life] and are testifying to [the life] and announcing to you the eternal life, who as such was with the Father and was manifested to us"). But *when* was the life the light of human beings? At the dawn of creation and ever since? Some have thought so. But 1:9 will talk about the light's *coming* into the world, and this coming is mentioned *subsequent* to the mention of the Baptist's testimony in 1:6–8. Furthermore, in 9:5 the Word says, "Whenever I'm in the world, I am the light of the world." In 12:46, "I've come into the world as light." And in 12:35, "the light is among you" for only "a little while yet." So 1:4 has skipped from creation "in the beginning" all the way to the Word's shining among human beings in the first century.

1:5: And the light is shining in the darkness . . . . Just as "the life" is a way of referring to the Word himself, so also "the light" is a way of referring to the Word himself (compare 8:12: "I am the light of the world"). But the light was going to be withdrawn with the Word's return to the Father after staying "a little while" in the world (see 12:35 again [compare 9:4–5]). So how should we take the present tense of "is shining"? It's what we call a "vivid historical present," the use of the present tense to

emphasize a past event as though it were happening right now. In other words, the light shone intensely, brightly.

In Genesis 1:4–5, "God separated the light *from* the darkness" and "called the light day and the darkness . . . night." But here in John "the light is shining *in* the darkness" to set up a confrontation between the two. And according to Genesis 1:4 "God saw that the light was good." Darkness didn't get the same description. So it's natural to associate light not only with life but also with goodness, and darkness not only with death but also with evil, as 3:19 will do: "the light has come into the world; and the human beings [who make up 'the world'] loved the darkness rather than the light, for their deeds were evil." We have then a confrontation between good and evil, but not in the abstract—rather, in concrete, personal terms. The good light is the Word who was with God and was God. Correspondingly, the darkness is the human beings whose works were evil. So John continues: **and the darkness** [that is, those human beings] **didn't apprehend it** [the light]. The verb "apprehend" carries two meanings: (1) take into custody, arrest, overpower and (2) take hold of mentally, perceive, understand, comprehend. Throughout the rest of John the human beings who make up the darkness constantly fail to understand. In fact they *mis*understand, as in 2:20–21: "Therefore the Jews said, 'For forty-six years this temple has been a-building, and *you*—will you raise it in three days?' But that one [the Word] was talking about the temple [consisting] of his body." Neither do they overpower the light. They don't even take the light into custody—not really. He will *volunteer* himself for arrest. Only then will they "take him along" (so a literal translation of 18:12 [contrast earlier, failed attempts to "seize" him in 7:30, 32, 44–46; 8:20; 10:39; 11:57]). How could the light be overpowered by the darkness if the light is none other than the Word who was God?

1:6–7: There came on the scene a human being sent from God. He had the name John [the Baptist]. **⁷This one came for the purpose of a testimony,** [that is,] **in order that he might testify concerning the light,** [and what was the purpose of his testifying?] **in order that all might believe through him.** In Mark the Baptist is primarily a baptizer. In Matthew he's equally a baptizer and a preacher of repentance. In Luke, primarily a preacher of repentance. In John, the Baptist is primarily a witness who bears testimony to the light. In the other Gospels he talks a little about "the coming one." But in this Gospel he actually points him out. He sees him coming toward him and says, "Look! The lamb of God that takes away the world's sin!" (1:29). His testimony has the purpose of getting people to believe in the light. So we can look at the whole of the Fourth Gospel as portraying a legal dispute in which various witnesses, like the Baptist, testify on behalf of the light while others accuse the light.

A negative statement balances a positive one in **1:8: That one** [the Baptist] **wasn't the light; rather,** [he came] **that he might testify concerning the light.** The negative suggests that some people at the time this Gospel was written still hadn't transferred their allegiance from the Baptist to the light. All the Gospels mention disciples of the Baptist who hadn't made the switch during the shining of the light in the world (Mark 2:18; Matthew 9:14; 11:2; Luke 5:33; 7:18–19, 24; John 3:25). Later, too, the Apostle Paul discovered twelve such disciples in Ephesus, far away in Asia Minor (Acts 19:1–7). He baptized them in the name of Jesus, so that they received the Holy Spirit (compare the early church tradition that the Fourth Gospel emanated from that city in the country now called Turkey). An ancient though probably unrelated sect of Baptist-followers, called Mandeans, still exists in Iraq.

There are several possible translations of **1:9**:

- **He** [the light who is the life who in turn is the Word] **was the true light that enlightens every human being who comes into the world.**

- **He was the true light that by coming into the world enlightens every human being.**

- **The true light that enlightens every human being was coming into the world.**

The main meaning is pretty clear, though. *First,* the description of the light as "true" not only keeps us from mistaking the Baptist for the light. It also associates the light with truth, which will become a major theme in this Gospel, as in 14:6, "I am . . . the truth," and 18:38, where the Roman governor Pontius Pilate asks, "What is truth?" when the truth is standing right in front of him. *Second,* although the people who make up the darkness don't come to the light because their deeds are evil (3:19–20), the light enlightens all human beings in the sense that he shines on all of them. Astronomically speaking, the sun is the light of the world; and it shines on the righteous and unrighteous alike (Matthew 5:45). So also this divine light is the light of the world in that he exposes human evil but brings the light of life to all who believe. *Third,* since elsewhere in John's Gospel coming into the world refers to the incarnation of the Word, here in 1:9 "coming into the world" probably relates not to "every human being" but to "the true light" and explains how that light shines. He shines by coming into the world. As the Word the light was with God in the beginning. But the Word became the light *for human beings* not till he left God and came into the world.

And what is this "world" he entered? *1:10*: **He was in the world, and the world came into existence through him.** So far, all we have to think of is the planet Earth. But the verse finishes with this statement: **and the world didn't know him.** So the world isn't planet Earth, or at least not exclusively or primarily this planet. It's the world of human beings who live here—in particular, unbelievers who make up the darkness that opposes the light and didn't recognize the Word for what he was: the way, the truth, and the life (14:6). "World" translates the Greek word *cosmos*, which contrasts with *chaos* and therefore means in John the society of human beings

organized around their unbelief, around their failure to recognize the true light.

1:11–13: **He came into his own things and his own ones didn't accept him.** "His own things" are the "all things" which came into existence through him and therefore belong to him as his proper home (1:3 [compare 16:32; 19:27]). That is, he entered his creation. "His own ones" are the Jews, who figure prominently later in John (compare 1:31; but avoid any anti-Semitic inference, for Jesus himself says in 4:22, "Salvation is from the Jews"). Not even they accepted him. And they didn't accept him because by and large they didn't recognize him. Happily, there were exceptions: [12]**But as many as did accept him—to them, the ones believing in his name, he gave authority to become God's children . . . .** To accept the light means to believe in his name. To believe in his name means to entrust our fate to him because of who his name indicates he is. But what name is in view? Not "Jesus" or "Christ" or "Lord" or "Son of God" or "Son of Man," because those names haven't yet appeared in John's text. The name could be "Word" except for the fact that later we'll read that the name belongs also to God the Father (17:11–12), yet John never calls the Father "Word." John has already mentioned a shared name, though. It's "God": "the Word was *with* God, and the Word *was* God" (1:1). To believe in the light's name, then, is to entrust our fate to him because of his being the Word who is God in communication with us human beings to give us the eternal life of God himself, a communication of light, the light of divine truth—a word of communication that stands in stark contrast with "Silence," which was a divine name in the Greco-Roman religions of John's era.

Since the light that is the Word shines on all human beings and since most of "his own ones" didn't accept him, those who did accept him became "God's children" as distinct from the children of Israel. But why does John say that the light gave them "authority" to become God's children instead of saying simply that as many as accepted him "became" God's children? Why does the word "authority" slip in? Probably because biological ancestry, even Israelite ancestry, gives nobody a claim on God. So John continues: [13]**who were born not out of bloods** [the bloodlines of biological parents] **nor out of the will of flesh** [sexual attraction of male and female] **nor out of the will of a husband** [who wants an heir to carry on his family line]**, but out of God.** That is to say, God himself is the source of this birth that carries the authority, the right, to become his children. Because it originates from God the birth will later be designated a birth "from above" (3:3, 7). It doesn't have its *source* in the flesh, but to make it possible the Word *became* flesh.

1:14: **And the Word became flesh and tented among us.** "Flesh"—not an apparition, but honest-to-goodness flesh, incarnation as a means toward communication. In the Word incarnate, God speaks the language of humanity, which we as human beings can understand. The Word's tenting "among us" indicates a communication at close range—open, immediate, and accessible. "Tented" indicates a temporary such communication, for tents don't have the permanence of buildings. We've already seen that the light shone for only a little while (see the comments on 1:4). But "tented" also alludes to the tent, traditionally called "the tabernacle," in which God dwelled for a while among his people Israel and where they met him (see Exodus 25 and following chapters). So believers met God when the incarnate Word, who was God, tented among them. John aims his statement, "And the Word became flesh," against certain heretics (called Gnostics) who out of a belief that everything physical is inherently evil denied the incarnation. According to them, the Word only *seemed* to be fleshly (hence "docetism," after a Greek verb that means "seem" [see further the introduction to 1 John]). **And we saw his glory, glory as of a one-and-only from the Father,** [glory] **full of grace and truth.** The traditional translation "only begotten" is misleading, because 1:13 has told us that believers were born—that is, begotten—from God, so that the Word can't be God's *only* begotten one. Furthermore, the Word's existing *already* in the beginning rules out being begotten then. Nor is there textual warrant for an eternally timeless begetting. And because the Fourth Gospel contains no account of a virginal conception and birth, that kind of begetting, though unique, is hardly in view. So "one-and-only" highlights the uniqueness of the incarnate Word as him who came from the Father bearing his own divine glory because he along with the Father was God. The term "Father" implies the Word is God's Son. This relationship doesn't imply that the Word had a beginning at a birth, though. It means only that the Word *relates* to God as a son relates to his father. The relationship is one of subordination by way of obedience alongside equally shared deity, as will come out explicitly and repeatedly later in John. Similarly, in human relationships a son is no less human than his father even though he obeys his father. And John's choice of "the Father" rather than "God" suggests that "a one-and-only" also implies God's fatherly love for the Word, for a one-and-only son naturally becomes the special object of his father's love (so also in the Old Testament, and see John 3:35; 5:20; 10:17; 15:9–10; 17:23–24, 26 for God the Father's loving Jesus his Son).

"The glory" isn't that of a cloud and pillar of fire such as hovered over the Old Testament tabernacle. It's a glory of "grace and truth" (compare Exodus 33:18–19; 34:5–7). Grace has an aesthetic dimension. It connotes beauty and attractiveness, but above all it means favor—here divine favor to an ill-deserving world of moral darklings. Truth is what is trustworthy as opposed to falsehood, but also what is real and genuine as opposed to imitation and superficiality. The Word's glory is *full* of such grace and truth. There's no lack. The supply is sufficient for all.

Who are the "we" who saw this glory? John seems to be referring to himself and his fellow disciples who with him saw in person the glory of the incarnate Word (compare 19:35; 21:24). And before those original disciples was John the Baptist. **1:15: John testifies** [note the emphasis in a vivid historical present tense again, as in 1:5] **concerning him and has shouted, saying, "This was he about whom I said, 'The one coming behind me** [in space and therefore as my follower, because disciples followed their teacher physically rather than walking side by side with him] **has come to be ahead of me** [in rank] **because he was prior to me** [in time, for he was "in the beginning" (1:1)] . . . .'"** So the Baptist testifies to the preexistence of the Word and therefore to the Word's superiority despite the Word's having followed the Baptist briefly.

The Baptist has given one reason why the Word outranks him: "because he was before me." In *1:16–17* he or, more probably, John the evangelist gives two more reasons: [1] **because from his** [the Word's] **fullness we've all received even grace in place of grace** [that is, one gift of grace after another—a never-ending succession of ill-deserved divine favors from the Word, whose supply of such grace is never diminished no matter how many favors he grants (compare the gracious signs and works that John narrates one after another in following chapters)], [2] [17]**because the Law was given through Moses; grace and truth came on the scene through Jesus Christ.** Finally, after seventeen and a half verses, after all the suspense stemming from nonidentification of the Word—finally we're told that the Word is none other than the historical figure of Jesus Christ, the Word-made-flesh. But because he was a *historical* figure it wouldn't have been appropriate to call him Jesus Christ in his preexistent, prehistorical, preincarnate state.

Some interpreters think that the first gift of grace back in 1:16 was the law of Moses. But here in 1:17 grace along with truth doesn't arrive on the scene till the Word's incarnation in Jesus Christ, so that law and grace seem to contrast with each other. We're reminded of Paul's contrasting the Law's command to *do* works of righteousness and the gospel's saying to *believe* because salvation comes by grace through faith, not by works (see, for example, Romans 10:5–10; Galatians 2:16; 3:10–14; Ephesians 2:8–9). As in 1:14, John adds "truth" to "grace," this time to imply that Jesus Christ embodied the divine *reality* to which Moses' law only *testified*. For this function of the Mosaic law in John see 1:45; 3:14; 5:45–46; 15:25 and, indirectly, 8:17; 10:34–37. The addition of "all" expands the meaning of "we" who have received grace to include every believer (contrast the limitation of "we" in 1:14).

John rounds off his prologue in *1:18*: **No one has seen God at any time.** The emphasis falls on "God" as distinguished from the Word-made-flesh, whose glory eyewitnesses saw. **A one-and-only** [who was] **God, the one existing in the bosom of the Father—that one has explained him.** Some manuscripts, followed by many English translations, have "a one-and-only *Son*" instead of "a one-and-only [who was] *God*." But those manuscripts are generally later and inferior. It seems that in order to suit the description of "a one-and-only" as having come "from the *Father*" in 1:14, here in 1:18 copyists would more likely have changed an original "God" to "Son" than vice versa. And since the Word wasn't only *with* God but also *was* God, the earlier manuscripts that have "God" instead of "Son" are probably correct. Here's the main, climactic point, though: Jesus Christ is called "the Word" in that he has *explained* God the Father. As a human being his words, his deeds, and his death and resurrection explain God in human terms that we can understand and believe. And this explanation is sufficient and reliable because it comes from the one who has a uniquely *intimate* relation to God: "in the *bosom* of the Father."

Note: It's popular to think that John borrows his description of the Word largely from Jewish descriptions of personified Wisdom (see Proverbs 8, for example) and that "Word" substitutes for "Wisdom," perhaps because in John's Greek language "Wisdom" is feminine, "Word" is masculine, and Jesus was a man, not a woman. But John uses a number of Greek feminine nouns for Jesus, such as those for "way," "truth," "resurrection," and "life." So John's universally acknowledged fondness for using synonyms (whatever their reference) makes it likely that he avoids using "Wisdom" in addition to "Word" because he wants *not* to portray Jesus as personified Wisdom. He may even be pitting Word-Christology *against* Wisdom-Christology. In either case, Genesis 1 plus the use of "word" for the oral gospel provides a more likely inspiration than Wisdom for John's portrayal of Jesus as the Word. The same holds true against the suggestion that John borrows from the ancient philosophical use of the Greek behind "Word," namely, *Logos* in the sense of "Reason." For where in this passage does John portray Jesus as divine Reason? The Word's "explaining" the Father points to communication, not reason (1:18).

MAKING THE FIRST DISCIPLES
John 1:19–51

Verses 19–28 constitute the first paragraph in this section. *1:19–20*: **And this is the testimony of John** [the Baptist] **when the Jews sent to him priests and Levites from Jerusalem so that they might ask him, "Who are you?"** The attention is so concentrated on the Baptist's testimony that we aren't told till much later where he was at the time or what he was doing, such as baptizing people. And his preaching of repentance never does get mentioned, nor his dress (a camel's hair shirt and a leather belt) or his diet (locusts and wild honey). We find those details in other Gospels (Mark 1:6; Matthew 3:4). Who'd want a wild man like that for a witness anyway? John the author of this Gospel doesn't. So he omits those details. [20]**And he** [the Baptist] **confessed and didn't deny—indeed, he confessed, "I'm not the Christ."** He didn't *deny* that he wasn't the Christ; rather, he *confessed* that he wasn't. So we have a triple emphasis: "he confessed . . . he didn't deny . . . he confessed." In Mark 1:5 and Matthew 3:6, too, there's confession. But it's the people who come to be baptized who do the confessing, and it's their sins that they confess. Here it's the Bap-

tist who does the confessing, and it's his nonidentification with the Christ that he confesses. In Luke 3:15 "the people" wonder whether the Baptist is the Christ. Here in John, then, do the emissaries of the Jews in Jerusalem ask him whether he's the Christ? No, they ask only who he is, *whoever* that might be—a completely open-ended question. And for the moment he doesn't answer the question by saying who he *is*. He says only who he *isn't*, and specifies that he's not the Christ. Saying that he isn't clears the ground for his later testimony concerning who *Jesus* is. It also goads the Baptist's questioners to ask who he is if he isn't the Christ, and even to suggest other possibilities since he doesn't seem to be very forthcoming.

1:21: **And they asked him, "What then? Are you Elijah?" and he says, "I'm not." "Are you the prophet?" and he answered, "No."** First-century Jews had various expectations of figures whom God would send in the end time. Not only was there the expectation of a coming Messiah, or even two Messiahs, a priestly one and a kingly one. ("Messiah" is Hebrew; "Christ" is Greek; and both terms mean "Anointed One," that is, someone specially chosen for a divinely commissioned task.) Also expected were a return to earth of Elijah (compare Malachi 4:5–6) and the appearance of a prophet like Moses (compare Deuteronomy 18:15–18). So the emissaries suggest these other possibilities. In the other Gospels such possible identifications are voiced concerning Jesus (Mark 6:15; 8:28; Matthew 16:14; Luke 9:8, 19), but John doesn't let in even a suggestion that Jesus is Elijah or "the prophet." The suggestion applies only to the Baptist, which he promptly denies in favor of his role as a witness for Jesus.

1:22–23: **So they said to him, "Who are you?** [Tell us,] **so that we may give an answer to the ones who sent us. What do you say about yourself?"** They insist on a positive identification; they're not satisfied with the Baptist's modesty. [23]**He said, "I'm the voice of one calling out in the wilderness, 'Straighten the way of the Lord,' just as Isaiah the prophet spoke** [see Isaiah 40:3]**."** In the earlier Gospels it's Mark, Matthew, and Luke—evangelists—who identify the Baptist with the voice prophesied by Isaiah. Here it's the Baptist himself who uses Isaiah's prophecy to identify his role, but he modestly shortens the quotation. It's longer in those earlier Gospels (see Mark 1:2–3; Matthew 3:3; and especially Luke 3:4–6). So the Baptist says he's a mere voice telling people to get ready for someone else. "Way" means "road." Making a crooked road straight makes it easier to travel, and you want a dignitary to have a pleasant trip to your place. So straightening a road is a figure of speech for getting ready for the visit of somebody important. Here that dignitary is the Lord, who turns out to be Jesus, the incarnate Word, who was in the beginning with God and was God. No higher dignitary than he!

1:24–25: **And they'd been sent by the Pharisees.** So the Jews of 1:19 turn out to be Pharisees, members of a leading Jewish sect (compare 3:1, where Nicodemus, who came to Jesus at night, is called not only a

Pharisee but also "a ruler of the Jews"). In Matthew 3:7 the Pharisees are among those who come to the Baptist, but here they just send as their emissaries some priests (who ministered at the temple in Jerusalem) and Levites (who helped the priests there). Apparently John saves the Pharisees themselves for a direct confrontation with Jesus, a confrontation between darkness and light. ²⁵**And they** [the priests and the Levites] **asked him and said to him** [the doubling of verbs emphasizes the emissaries' concern], **"Why then are you baptizing** [people] **if you're neither the Christ nor Elijah nor the prophet?"** Finally it comes out that the Baptist is a baptizer, but only as background for his testimony to Jesus. Baptism isn't the main point. In Matthew 3:7 the Baptist does the questioning; he asks the Pharisees and Sadducees (another leading Jewish sect), "Who warned you to flee from the wrath that is going to come?" In Luke 3:7 he asks the crowds the same question and in Luke 3:10 they ask, "So what should we do [to prepare the way of the Lord]?" John isn't interested in those questions. He wants only to highlight the Baptist's testimony to Jesus.

In *1:26–27*, then, **John** [the Baptist] **answered them** [the priests and the Levites], **saying, "I baptize in water. In your midst is standing one whom you don't know,** ²⁷[that is,] **the one coming behind me** [1:15], **the strap of whose sandal I'm not worthy to loosen."** In the other Gospels the Baptist says, "I am baptizing you in/with water" (Matthew 3:11; Mark 1:8; Luke 3:16). Here in John the pronoun "you" drops out because the Baptist is talking to the Pharisees' emissaries. He wasn't baptizing them, and they certainly hadn't come to be baptized— rather, to interrogate the Baptist the way a prosecutor interrogates a witness in court. Again in the other Gospels the Baptist goes on to say that the one coming after him is stronger than he is. But John omits that statement and substitutes the statement that in their midst is standing one whom they don't know. They don't recognize or acknowledge Jesus for who he is. We're reminded of 1:10, which said the light was in the world and the world came into existence through him but the world didn't know him. "Standing *in your midst*" recollects 1:14, "The Word became flesh and tented *among us*," and leaves the nonrecognition of Jesus without excuse. Has the Baptist answered the question why he baptizes people? No, he has ignored the question entirely and testified instead to the presence of someone the strap of whose sandal he's unworthy to loosen. Only a slave was obligated to perform this service for his master. But the Baptist exalts Jesus to such a high level, the level of preexistent deity, that even a slave's service for Jesus seems too honorable for the Baptist to perform.

1:28: **These things happened in Bethany, the other side of the Jordan, where John was baptizing.** From the standpoint of Jerusalem, "the other side" is east of the Jordan River. So John can't be referring to Bethany on the Mount of Olives just across the Kidron Valley (actually, only a ravine) from Jerusalem. Archaeologists may have discovered the remains of this other Bethany seven miles north of the Dead Sea and east of the Jordan River. There's also a possibility that Bethany beyond the Jordan is the same as Betharba, a village on the northeast side of the Jordan, or the same as Batanea, the northeastern territory of Transjordan. Whatever the exact location, Jesus will return to this Bethany (10:40) just before going to the Bethany near Jerusalem (chapter 11), where he will die as the lamb of God about to be announced by the Baptist here in the transjordanian Bethany (chapters 12–19).

Verses 29–34 constitute a second paragraph in this section. *1:29*: **The next day he** [the Baptist] **sees Jesus coming toward him and says, "Look! The lamb of God that takes away the world's sin!"** "The next day" implies a preceding day, reappears in 1:35, 43, and therefore sets up a succession of days that reaches a climax in 2:1: "On the third day" (after the last of the four days in chapter 1). The Baptist sees Jesus coming toward him, but there's no mention here or in the rest of this paragraph of Jesus' getting baptized by him. If we had only John's Gospel we'd never know that Jesus got baptized at all. A little later the Baptist will talk about the Holy Spirit's descending like a dove on Jesus, as happened at Jesus' baptism according to the other Gospels (Mark 1:9–11; Matthew 3:13–17; Luke 3:21–22). But John makes the Baptist a witness *for* Jesus, not a baptizer *of* Jesus. So he completely omits Jesus' baptism and thus forestalls any inference from such a baptism that Jesus was subordinate to the Baptist (to the contrary, see 3:22–4:2).

The testimony given by the Baptist is that Jesus is a lamb, that is, a sacrifice. According to 13:1 Jesus ate the Last Supper with his disciples "before the Festival of Passover," and according to 18:28 Jesus' accusers didn't enter the praetorium (official residence) of the pagan Roman governor Pilate lest by incurring ritual defilement they render themselves unable to eat the Passover meal that commemorated the exodus of Israel from Egypt. So in chapter 19 Jesus dies at the hour when Passover lambs were slaughtered, and his legs are left unbroken just as Passover lambs were not to have any of their bones broken—all because for John the true Passover sacrifice is the crucified Jesus (compare Exodus 12:46; Numbers 9:12; and 1 Corinthians 5:7: "For our Passover [lamb]—[namely,] Christ—has been sacrificed").

But Jesus is no run-of-the-mill lamb. He is *God's* lamb, the lamb provided by God himself. Ordinarily sinners offer their own lambs to God. Here we have the reverse: *God* offers a sacrificial lamb to take away the sin (a collective singular) of the world, the very world that according to 1:10 didn't know, recognize, or acknowledge the Word (compare Isaiah 53:3–12, where the rejected Servant of the Lord, bearing our sin, is led as a lamb to the slaughter, and Genesis 22:7–8, where Isaac asks his father Abraham, "Where's the lamb?" and Abraham answers, "God himself will provide a lamb"). What grace and truth—Jesus the true sacrificial lamb provided by a gracious God!

Echoing 1:15 is *1:30–31*: **"This is the one about whom I said** [the Baptist is speaking], **'Behind me is** coming a man who ranks ahead of me because he existed prior to me.' ³¹And I didn't know him, but in order that he might be manifested to Israel—for this purpose I came baptizing in water." "Behind me" suggests that Jesus started out as a disciple of the Baptist, but the Baptist testifies to Jesus' outranking him because Jesus preexisted as the Word (1:15). At first not even the Baptist recognized Jesus. Though Jesus is God's lamb to take away the sin of the *world*, he was manifested to *Israel*, a local and representative slice of the world. So now we know explicitly who the Word's "own ones" were back in 1:11 ("his own ones didn't accept him"). Note that in John the purpose of the Baptist's activity of baptizing people wasn't to straighten the way of the Lord by getting them to repent of their sins. There's nothing about repentance. Instead the purpose was to publicize Jesus as God's lamb that removes sin. Baptism simply drew an audience for the Baptist's testimony concerning Jesus.

That testimony starts in *1:32*: **And John** [the Baptist] **testified, saying, "I saw the Spirit descending like a dove out of heaven, and it abode on him."** In Mark and Matthew *Jesus* saw the Spirit descending (Mark 1:10; Matthew 3:16). (Luke 3:22 doesn't say anything about seeing.) Here, *the Baptist* sees the Spirit descending, and this sight supplies the content of his testimony. The word for "heaven" could also be translated "sky," but the Spirit's ultimate origin lies in heaven. That the Spirit "abode" on Jesus is matched in 14:10 by the Father's abiding in Jesus (hence the doctrine of the Trinity) and means that the Spirit stayed on him, didn't leave him—against the heresy of Cerinthus (a very early Gnostic), who distinguished between Jesus, a human being of flesh, and Christ, a divine spirit who came on Jesus at his baptism but left him before he died by crucifixion (see again the introduction to 1 John). Since to the contrary the Spirit stays on Jesus, John will be able to portray Jesus' *death* as a giving over of "the Spirit" with the result that on the first Easter Sunday evening Jesus breathes on his disciples and says to them, "Receive the Holy Spirit" (see the comments on 19:30; 20:22).

The Baptist's testimony continues in *1:33–34*: **"And I didn't know him, but the one who sent me to baptize in water—that one had said to me, 'On whomever you see the Spirit descending and abiding on him—this is the one who baptizes in the Holy Spirit.' ³⁴And I've seen and testified that this one is the Son of God."** Again we learn that the Baptist didn't recognize Jesus at first, but the Spirit's descending and abiding on Jesus made the Baptist recognize Jesus' true identity. Belatedly, baptism in the Holy Spirit comes into view. It appears earlier in the other Gospels, with the addition "and [in] fire" in Matthew 3:11–12; Luke 3:16–17. The fire burns up "the chaff" and therefore represents judgment on people who don't repent. Judgment will figure prominently later in John, but for now the attention focuses on the good news of Jesus as God's lamb that takes away the sin of the world. The removal connects with baptism in the Holy Spirit. In other words, having our sin taken away makes

this baptism possible. John's account of Jesus' crucifixion makes the connection. When a spear pierced Jesus' side, "immediately there came out blood and water" (19:34). The blood effected the removal of our sin by atoning for it. The water represents the resultant gift of the Holy Spirit, as indicated in 7:38–39: "The person who believes in me [Jesus]—just as the Scripture has said, 'Out of his belly will flow rivers of living water.' And he spoke this concerning the Spirit that those who'd believed in him were about to receive." *Living* water, because baptism in the Spirit brings eternal life: "The Spirit is the one who makes [people] live" (6:63).

Verse 12 called believers "God's *children*," but John's Gospel reserves "the *Son* of God" for Jesus alone. In Mark 1:11; Luke 3:22 it's God the Father who says to Jesus, "You're my beloved Son; I've taken delight in you," and in Matthew 3:17, "This is my beloved Son, in whom I took delight." But here in John it's the Baptist—ever the witness in Jesus' behalf—who identifies him as God's Son, so that "my" and "in whom I am well pleased" drop out. Jesus isn't *the Baptist's* well-pleasing Son! Not only does John omit Jesus' baptism (the occasion of God the Father's calling Jesus his beloved Son). He also omits the immediately following temptation of Jesus. Why? Because God can't be tempted (James 1:13), and the Word (Jesus) was God.

Verses 35–42 form the third paragraph in this section. *1:35–37*: **Again the next day John** [the Baptist] **was standing—also two of his disciples—³⁶and looking intently at Jesus walking around, he says, "Look! The lamb of God!" ³⁷And his two disciples heard him speaking and followed Jesus.** Once more the Baptist points out Jesus in their midst, this time with the effect that two of his own disciples start following Jesus. (No audience was designated for the Baptist's pointing out Jesus earlier in 1:29–34, so that the emphasis fell entirely on the testimony as such, regardless of its effect.) In Mark 1:16–20 and Matthew 4:18–22 Jesus calls his first disciples on a later occasion in Galilee, and they follow him (compare Luke 5:1–11). Here in John it's the Baptist, ever again the witness, whose testimony makes Jesus' first disciples. They learn from the Baptist who Jesus is, God's lamb. And though the Baptist doesn't tell them to follow Jesus they do so anyway, because like the Baptist but unlike the majority they accept Jesus for who he is.

1:38: **And turning and seeing them following, Jesus says to them, "What are you looking for?" And they said to him, "Rabbi (which translated means 'Teacher'), where are you staying?"** To speak to the two Jesus had to turn, because they were following behind him. The Jesus who had come behind the Baptist now has his own followers. He asks them what they're looking for rather than why they're following him. Then they ask where he's staying. "Staying" could just as well or even better be translated "abiding" (often a theologically loaded term in John). So the two were looking for an abode with Jesus. Later, abiding *with* Jesus turns into abiding *in* him (15:1–11). Jesus' "What?" has turned into the disciples' "where?" The question of where Jesus abides receives no earthly topographical answer. But it will receive a *theological* answer in 14:10–11: Jesus is in the Father just as the Father is in Jesus and abides in Jesus, so that to abide in Jesus—to stay where he stays—is to abide also in God the Father.

1:39: He says to them, "Come and you'll see." So they came and saw where he stays [= abides] **and stayed** [= abode] **with him that day. It was about the tenth hour.** The present tense and topographical ambiguity of Jesus' abiding open the door for his showing them God the Father as his abode. He can then say, "The person who has seen me has seen the Father" (14:9). The tenth hour from sunrise would be four o'clock in the afternoon. But then not much of the day would be left since Jewish days were commonly calculated to end (and begin) at sundown, and staying with Jesus "that day" wouldn't have very much point. On the other hand, 20:19 calls Easter Sunday evening the evening of the *first* day of the week. So John must calculate a day as ending not at sundown but at midnight. Otherwise Sunday evening would count as the first part of the *second* day of the week. "The tenth hour" from midnight, then, is ten o'clock in the morning; and staying with Jesus "that day," most of which remained, carries more meaning, a meaning that better symbolizes a permanent abiding in Christ.

1:40–42: Andrew, the brother of Simon Peter, was one of the two who heard from John [the Baptist] **and followed him** [Jesus]. **⁴¹This one** [Andrew] **first finds his own brother Simon and says to him, "We've found the Messiah" (which is translated 'Christ'** [= 'Anointed One']**).** These verses identify by name only one of the two former followers of the Baptist: Andrew. The anonymity of the other suggests that he's the author of the Fourth Gospel—that is, according to early church tradition, the Apostle John, unnamed in this Gospel just as the author never identifies himself by name. (The title, "The Gospel according to John," didn't belong to the original text but was later attached by way of tradition.) Andrew's announcement, "We've found the Messiah," reminds us of Jesus' question, "What are you looking for?" (1:38). Just as earlier the *what* turned into a *where*, so now the *what* turns into a *who*, namely, Jesus himself as the Messiah. So Andrew joins the Baptist as a witness in Jesus' behalf. **⁴²He** [Andrew] **brought him** [Simon] **to Jesus. Looking intently at him, Jesus said, "You're Simon the son of John** [*not* the Baptist]**."** Jesus knows Simon by name; for Simon is one of his sheep (a figure of speech for his disciples), and "he calls his own sheep name by name" (10:3). Though he doesn't call Simon's father, Jesus knows the father's name too and uses it to distinguish this Simon from other Simons. Better yet, he says to Simon, **"You'll be called Cephas," which is translated "Peter"** [= "Stone"]. Jesus knows not only Simon's present name. He knows also Simon's future name, which despite frequent translations to the contrary means a loose stone rather than bedrock. But the Fourth Gospel is pointing up Jesus' knowledge, not Peter's character or function (compare 1:43–51).

1:43: The next day he [Jesus] **wanted to go out** [from "Bethany beyond the Jordan" (1:28)] **into Galilee, and he finds Philip. And Jesus says to him, "Follow me."** Jesus hails from Galilee in northern Israel (7:53); so it's natural for him to return there. But John might have written simply that Jesus "went" into Galilee. Instead he writes the overloaded phrase, "*wanted* to go." The verb "wanted" often carries the stronger meaning "*willed*." So John may overload the phrase to imply that Jesus willed to go into Galilee for the express purpose of finding Philip, another of his "sheep," and of calling him to discipleship (compare 4:4; also 5:21: "the Son makes alive these whom he *wills* [to make alive]"). Andrew and his anonymous companion had found the Messiah down south. Now the Messiah himself, Jesus, has found Philip up north. Divine and human findings complement each other.

Human finding returns in **1:44–45: And Philip was from Bethsaida, from the city of Andrew and Peter. ⁴⁵Philip finds Nathaniel and says to him, "We've found the one that Moses wrote about in the Law and** [that] **the prophets** [wrote about]**, Jesus, Joseph's son from Nazareth."** Not only does Philip join the Baptist and Andrew in bearing witness about Jesus. He also enlists Moses and the prophets as fellow witnesses through their messianic prophecies recorded in Scripture. "*We've* found . . . ," says Philip, echoing Andrew's statement to Simon Peter in 1:41. But according to 1:43 it was the reverse: *Jesus* found Philip. Here, then, divine and human findings don't merely complement each other. They are fused in one and the same case, Philip's—a narrative example of the fusion of divine selection and human responsibility. "Joseph's son" provides a typical example of irony in John's Gospel, because 1:34 recorded the Baptist's divinely attested identification of Jesus as "the Son of God." And the erroneous "Joseph's son" sets up for another, corrective identification of Jesus as "God's Son" in 1:49. "From Nazareth" provides another irony. For although topographically correct, the phrase falls theologically short of Jesus as the Word who came into the world from the bosom of his Father in heaven (1:9, 18). At the same time, "from Nazareth" prepares for yet another irony in the next verse.

1:46: And Nathaniel said to him [Philip]**, "Can anything good be from Nazareth?" Philip says to him, "Come and see."** Nathaniel's question is ironic in that even some in the crowds at Jerusalem will say about Jesus, "He's good" (7:12); and Jesus himself will say, "I am the good shepherd" (10:11, 14). (Though the Greek word for "good" in 10:11, 14 differs from the one in 1:46; 7:12, John is fond of using synonyms with no distinction in meaning.) Philip's response to Nathaniel's question, "Come and see [whether anything good can be from Nazareth]," echoes what Jesus said to two of the Baptist's disciples back in 1:39: "Come and you'll see [where I am staying]." So eyewitness supplements verbal testimony.

1:47–49: Jesus saw Nathaniel coming toward him and says about him, "Look! [He's] truly an Israelite in whom there's no deceit [compare the phraseology of

1:29]." "Israelite" comes from "Israel," the name given to Jacob by "a man" identified as "God" in Genesis 32:24–32 (compare Jesus as the God-man here in 1:1–18). But Jacob was known for his deceit (Genesis 27:35). So Jesus highlights a contrast in the absence of deceit from Nathaniel. This absence agrees with the emphasis on truth in this very verse (note the opposition between "truly" and "deceit") and throughout John, as in 3:21: "But the one who is doing the *truth* comes to the light." Nathaniel is just such a person; so he comes to the light. ⁴⁸**Nathaniel says to him** [Jesus], **"From where do you know me?" Jesus answered and said to him, "Before Philip called you, while you were under the fig tree, I saw you."** Here we have another instance of what Jesus will say in 10:14: "I know my [sheep]." Just as they recognize him, he recognizes them. So Nathaniel asks about the *source* of Jesus' knowledge ("From where . . . ?"). But Jesus answers in terms of *time* ("Before . . ."), that is, in terms of *foreknowledge*, which on the larger theological canvas plays into John's theme of predestination, as in 6:37, 39: "Everything that the Father is giving me will come to me . . . . that I not lose anything that he has given me." ⁴⁹**Nathaniel answered him, "Rabbi, you're the Son of God; you're the king of Israel."** We've already been told in 1:38 that "Rabbi" means "Teacher," as is appropriate for the Word who has "explained" God (1:18). Nathaniel's recognition of Jesus as also "the Son of God" echoes the Baptist's testimony in 1:34. And as truly an Israelite, Nathaniel recognizes Jesus as "the king of Israel."

1:50–51: Jesus answered and said to him, "Because I said to you, 'I saw you under the fig tree,' do you believe? You'll see greater things than these." ⁵¹And he says to him, "Amen, amen I tell you, you'll see 'the heaven' opened and 'the angels of God ascending and descending' on the Son of Man." Nathaniel's believing marks him as one of those who accepted the Word by believing in his name (1:12). "Amen," a Hebrew word brought over into the Greek that John wrote, means "let it be" and ordinarily follows what it emphasizes, as at the close of a prayer. But Jesus advances "Amen" to the beginning to emphasize the truthfulness of what he's about to say. John doubles this "Amen" (it occurs only one at a time in the other Gospels) to put all possible weight on the truthfulness of the words of Jesus the Word, who is himself the truth. Adding to this weight is John's introducing the double "Amen" with "And he says to him" even though he has already written, "Jesus answered and said to him."

In John's original Greek text the "you" in "I say to you" and in "you'll see" is plural, so that the following statement includes Nathaniel's fellow believers along with him. (In English, of course, "you" may be either singular or plural.) The opened heaven and the angels' ascending and descending on the Son of Man constitute the things Nathaniel and his fellow believers will see that are greater than Jesus' preternaturally seeing and recognizing of Nathaniel seated under a fig tree. The seeing of these greater things will enlarge Nathaniel's and the others' eyewitness testimony. Some Jews understood the

name "Israel" to mean "he who sees" or "he who sees God," so that as truly an Israelite Nathaniel along with his fellow believers will see Jesus to be God.

"The Son of Man" recollects "one like a son of man"— that is, a human figure in contrast to preceding beasts— that Daniel saw coming "with the clouds of heaven" (Daniel 7:13). Clouds are emblems of deity, as when God descended in a cloud onto Mount Sinai (Exodus 19:9, 11, 16, 18). The ascending and descending of angels on the Son of Man borrows phraseology from Genesis 28:12, where in a dream Jacob, to whom John 1:47 has recently alluded, saw "a ladder . . . set on the earth with its top reaching to heaven; and behold, *the angels of God were ascending and descending on it.*" As the Son of Man, Jesus is a divine-human being who like Jacob's ladder connects heaven and earth. Since "angels" means "messengers," the ascending and descending angels portray Jesus as a ladder of *communication* between heaven and earth—suitably to his role as "the Word" (1:1–18). That they're *God's* angels ties in with Jesus as the Word who was both himself God and also God's one-and-only Son. The mention of ascending before the mention of descending reflects the *textual* order of ascending and descending in Genesis 28:12 and makes clear an allusion to that passage. But John 3:13, another text that refers both to the Son of Man and to ascending and descending, will make clear that *chronologically* speaking, Jesus' descent from heaven preceded his ascent back to heaven: "And no one has ascended into heaven except the one who has descended out of heaven, [namely,] the Son of Man." Since this later text has *the Son of Man* ascending and descending, it also makes clear that in 1:51 the ascending and descending *angels* are part of a complex representation of Jesus himself as a message-bearer. They don't refer here to heavenly beings different from him. They symbolize him in his revelatory function.

In the other Gospels heaven is opened at Jesus' baptism for the Spirit to descend on him. He sees the Spirit descending on him and hears the Father speak to him (Mark 1:10–11; Matthew 3:16–17; Luke 3:21–22, with the slight difference that in Matthew the Father speaks *about* him). Here in John, where his baptism goes unmentioned, Jesus himself speaks as the Word to the world throughout his earthly sojourn; and his disciples see in him the one who descended from a heaven opened for divine communication. In retrospect, the Word who was with God and was God became flesh to fill the roles of Messiah/Christ (1:20, 41), God's lamb (1:29, 36), baptizer in the Holy Spirit (1:33), Rabbi/Teacher (1:38, 49), God's one-and-only Son (1:34, 49), King of Israel (1:49), and ladder-like, message-bearing Son of Man (1:51).

THE SIGN OF WATER TO WINE
John 2:1–11

John used a great deal of symbolic *language* in chapter 1: "the Word," "light," "darkness," "tented," "lamb." Now he starts to narrate symbolic *actions* of Jesus. They're never called "miracles." By definition a miracle is an act of *power*. But John isn't interested in Jesus' actions for their display of power. He's interested in them for their theological *symbolism*. So he calls them "signs." They signify what happens when a person is "saved" (for which see 3:17; 5:34; 10:9; 12:47). They help make up Jesus' "works" of salvation ("works" being another one of John's favorite terms).

2:1–2: And on the third day a wedding took place in Cana of Galilee, and Jesus' mother was there. ²And Jesus and his disciples were also invited to the wedding. The third day from when? Chapter 1 has featured a succession of days. On day 1 the Baptist testified about Jesus (1:19–28). "On the next day" (day 2) the Baptist pointed Jesus out (1:29–34). "Again the next day" (day 3) the Baptist directed two of his disciples to Jesus (1:35–39). Since the two "stayed with him [Jesus] that day," Andrew's introducing his brother Simon Peter to Jesus (Andrew being one of the two who had stayed with Jesus for a day [1:40–42]) must have happened the next day (day 4). "On the next day" after that (day 5) Philip and Nathaniel started following Jesus (1:43–51). Fast forward to the death and resurrection of Jesus: his resurrection on a Sunday will mark the third day after his crucifixion on a Friday. So the third day will count both Good Friday as the first day and Easter Sunday as the third. By the same token, the third day after day 5 here in 2:1 is day 7 of the series begun in chapter 1. John says nothing about what happened on day 6, presumably because it was the Sabbath—that is, Saturday, a day of rest—just as he and the other evangelists say nothing about what happened on the Sabbath between Good Friday and Easter Sunday. "On the third day" therefore connects the following "sign" with the resurrection of Jesus. His resurrection will make possible the salvation symbolized by the turning of water to wine. Confirming this connection to Jesus' resurrection on the third day is his saying later in this very chapter that in three days he'll raise the disassembled temple, which John interprets in terms of the resurrection of Jesus (2:18–22).

Wedding celebrations could last a whole week, and the whole village plus friends and relatives from elsewhere joined in the festivities (Judges 14:12). Twice Jesus compared the kingdom of God to a wedding celebration (Matthew 22:1–14; 25:1–13), and Revelation 19:7–9 compares the union of Jesus and his saints at the second coming to a wedding celebration. So the wedding celebration here in John 2:1–11 anticipates that future event but portrays the present celebration as representing what happens in salvation here and now. Though Jesus and his disciples are invited guests, he will turn out to be more the true host than a guest. For he'll provide wine when the supply runs out.

2:3–4: And when the wine ran out, Jesus' mother says to him, "They have no wine." ⁴And Jesus says to her, "What do you and I have to do with each other, woman? My hour hasn't come yet." The present tense of "says" here and following makes for a lively dialogue, as though you can hear it in progress. As host, the bridegroom had a responsibility to supply enough wine for the entire celebration. Not to have enough would bring him serious shame in a culture that paid more attention to honor and shame than we do. And here, a lack of wine would spoil the symbolism of salvation—in particular, the symbolism of joy for one's salvation (compare the rabbinic saying, "There's no rejoicing except with wine," and the Jewish expectation that in the messianic age wine would flow freely). When Jesus' mother informs him of the lack, he addresses her with "woman" rather than with the expected "Mother." This address isn't disrespectful (compare 4:21; 20:15); but neither is it familial, or even familiar. And ancient Jewish, Greek, and Roman literature provides no example other than this one for a son's addressing his mother with "woman." John will keep Jesus' mother nameless also in 19:26–27, where Jesus addresses her again with "woman" and in addition tells her to regard the beloved disciple as her son and tells him to regard her as his mother. We could almost say that here in chapter 2 Jesus is already starting to treat his mother as belonging to the beloved disciple. Add John's keeping her nameless (in contrast with the other Gospels and Acts) to Jesus' addressing her with "woman" and you have John as well as Jesus disengaging Jesus from his mother. And Jesus' question, "What do you and I have to do with each other?" should dispel any further doubt about this disengagement. Attempts to soften Jesus' question and address, as with "*Dear* woman" or "Mother" and with "Why do you involve me?" or "What does this have to do with me?" violate what John actually wrote. Jesus' question uses the very same expression that demoniacs use when trying to disengage themselves from him, as in Mark 1:24; 5:7, for example; and the question has to do with Jesus and his mother, not with him and the lack of wine. In fact, he shifts the topic from lack of wine to the lack of a relation between his mother and him so far as the lack of wine is concerned. In other words, if he's to do anything about the lack, he won't do it because of her. As he'll say later and repeatedly, he carries out his heavenly Father's will, not any earthling's will, not even his mother's (5:19, 36; 8:28, 38; 10:25, 32, 37; 12:49–50; 14:10, 31; 15:10).

In accord with subsequent occurrences, Jesus' "hour" refers to the time of his death, burial, resurrection, and ascension. But what's the point of saying in this setting that it hasn't come yet? Jesus will proceed to turn water into wine; so saying that his hour hasn't come yet can't provide a reason for not making up for the lack of wine. Nor does John introduce Jesus' statement with "because" or "for." The introduction of Jesus' hour therefore links the wine he'll momentarily produce with the wine, so to speak, of his blood that will come out of his pierced side during the hour (19:34). Supporting his blood as a kind of wine to be drunk is Jesus' telling people after he feeds the five thousand that to have eternal life they must drink his blood, a figure of speech for believing in his blood as the cleansing agent for their sin (6:53–56; compare 1 John 1:7; Revelation 7:14 and the Word of Institution in Matthew 26:28: "For this is my covenant-blood that's being poured out in behalf of many [people] for forgiveness of sins"). No wonder, then, that John will omit the institution of the Lord's Supper during the Last Supper (13:1–11). The turning of water to wine and the exhortation to drink Jesus' blood will have taken care of that topic, and the outflow of blood from his pierced side (unique to John's Gospel) will bring closure to it.

2:5–6: His mother says to the servers, "Do whatever he *tells* you [to do]." John shows no interest in specifying what prompted the mother's instruction, but the instruction shifts the spotlight from her informing Jesus about a lack of wine to what he'll say. What he'll *say*, because he's the Word. It's almost as though his mother understood the purport of Jesus' disengaging himself from her. **⁶And six stone jars were situated there in accordance with the Jews' purification, each [jar] holding two or three metretes.** Ritual purification is in view, not hygienic purification. Being porous, earthenware jars contracted ritual impurity if something ritually unclean, like a mole or a mouse, fell into it. In that case the jar had to be broken and discarded (Leviticus 11:29–33). Not being porous, however, stone jars didn't contract impurity and were therefore used to hold the "holy water" with which the Jews purified themselves ritually. Thus this water symbolizes Judaism, which Jesus is going to change into something better, much better. Since in John's book of Revelation the number six is triply associated with the satanic "beast" (Revelation 13, especially verse 18), the sixness of the stone water jars may cast the Judaism symbolized by the water of purification in a light that falls short of a perfect seven, even in a satanic light (compare 8:44, where Jesus says to certain Jews, "You're from [your] father the Devil, and you want to do the desires of your father," and Revelation 2:9 and 3:9, both of which describe self-identified "Jews" as "Satan's synagogue," a religious appellation that in the meantime has been criminally misused to inspire and justify pogroms on the Jews). "Two or three metretes" puts the capacity of each of these stone jars at 20–30 gallons, so that the volume of wine produced by Jesus will be huge, more than enough for everybody, just as the blood of Jesus the lamb of God is more than enough for taking away "the sin of the *world*" (1:29).

2:7–10: Jesus says to them, "Fill the jars with water." And they filled them to the top. ⁸And he says to them, "Now draw [some] out and take it to the master of ceremonies." And they took [it to him]. ⁹And when the master of ceremonies tasted the water that had become wine and didn't know where it had come from (but the servers who'd drawn the water knew), the master of ceremonies calls the bridegroom ¹⁰and says to him, "Every man serves the good wine first; and when people have gotten drunk, [he] serves the inferior [wine]. You've kept the good wine till now!" "To the top" means to the brim and ensures a full supply and plenty to spare (compare 10:10: "I [Jesus] have come that they [the sheep, my disciples] might have life, and have [it] abundantly [which again means more than enough]"). John refers to "the water that had be-

come wine" without having told us that Jesus turned the water into wine. We're left to infer that it was the Word's word, "Now draw [some] out," that effected the transformation. To support the actuality of the change of water to wine, John mentions as a separate point that the servers knew the origin of the wine. But the master of ceremonies didn't know its origin and therefore called the bridegroom, mistakenly attributed this wine to the groom's generosity, and noted that hosts normally serve inferior wine after their guests have gotten drunk and can't tell its difference from good wine. He doesn't realize that the good wine, which symbolizes the cleansing blood of Jesus, has replaced the purificatory water that symbolizes Judaism (compare 1:17, "the Law was given through Moses; grace and truth came on the scene through Jesus Christ," and 10:32, "I [Jesus] have shown you many *good* works from the Father"). To abundant quantity is added superior quality, then. Such is the eternal life that Jesus brings. And as noted above, this wine makes it unnecessary for John to mention later the wine of the Lord's Supper.

2:11: Jesus did this beginning of the signs in Cana of Galilee and manifested his glory, and his disciples believed in him. "This beginning" forecasts further signs to be narrated later in John. The performance of this one in Cana of Galilee gives the answer to Nathaniel's question in 1:46: "Can anything good be from Nazareth?" For Nathaniel was from Cana (21:2). Good wine from the good man, Jesus of Nazareth! The interpretation of this sign as a manifestation of Jesus' glory undermines any interpretation that settles on his staying in the background and acting behind the scene—certainly not John's point (compare the publicity of Jesus' signs, works, and self-identifications right from the start of this Gospel and throughout). And 1:14 has answered in advance the question, What is the glory of Jesus that he manifested in this first of his signs? It's "glory . . . as of a one-and-only from the Father, [glory] full of grace and truth"—the ill-deserved favor of God's love and the truth of Jesus the Word's message concerning it. The disciples believed in Jesus. But in chapter 1 they'd already started following him and confessed him as the Christ, God's Son, the King of Israel, and the one about whom Moses and the prophets wrote. So what is meant by their believing in Jesus now? What's meant is that believing in Jesus for salvation requires ongoing belief, perseverance in faith, not apostatizing as many erstwhile believers will do later in this Gospel (6:60–71).

THE CLEANSING OF THE TEMPLE
John 2:12–22

For the cleansing of the temple John has to move Jesus from Cana in Galilee, the northern region of Israel, to Jerusalem in the southern region. **2:12–13: After this [the turning of water to wine in Cana] he, plus his mother and his brothers and his disciples, went down to Capernaum [because Cana was located in the hills,**

Capernaum on the northwest shore of the Sea of Galilee about sixteen miles away]; **and they stayed there not many days** [that is, a few days]. [13]**And the Passover of the Jews was near, and Jesus went up to Jerusalem** ["up" because Jerusalem was located on Mount Zion in the hill country of Judea]. The mother of Jesus reappears. His brothers make their first appearance. They won't play a part in the upcoming episode, but their present appearance prepares for a part they'll later play in connection with another pilgrimage to Jerusalem (7:2–13). It will turn out there that they don't believe in Jesus their brother. Here they and their mother accompany Jesus because the Passover, which was near, was an annual religious festival that brought many thousands of pilgrims to worship at the temple in Jerusalem. The festival celebrated the Israelites' exodus from Egypt and featured the slaughter and roasting of Passover lambs and the eating of a Passover supper (see Exodus 12 for further details). This festival will set the tone for John's ongoing portrayal of Jesus as the true Passover lamb. Jesus' disciples accompany him not only for the reason of a pilgrimage, but also because disciples (which means "learners") customarily followed behind their teacher wherever he went so as to learn from his words and exemplary deeds. John's statement that Jesus and these others didn't stay long in Capernaum, which lay on a road that led to Jerusalem, only *implies* that the others accompanied Jesus to Jerusalem (compare 2:17, 22). But because he alone will play a role there, John focuses on him: "and *Jesus* went up to Jerusalem." "Of the Jews" describes the Passover in a way that distances the festival from John and his audience at a later date. Now that Jesus has died as God's lamb that takes away the world's sin, there's no further need for the Passover and its sacrificial lambs.

2:14–17: And he found in the temple [not inside the building itself, but in an outer courtyard] **those who were selling oxen and sheep and doves, and moneychangers sitting** [at tables, according to a following statement]. [15]**And on making a whip out of ropes, he drove** [them] **all out of the temple, the sheep and the oxen too. And he poured out the coins of the moneychangers and overturned** [their] **tables** [16]**and said to those who were selling doves, "Take these things away from here. Stop making my Father's house a house of commerce."** [17]**His disciples remembered** [so they've come with him] **that it was written, "Zeal for your house will devour me** [Psalm 69:9]." The oxen, sheep, and doves—guaranteed to be ritually clean—were being sold for sacrificing at the temple. They're listed in descending order of expense. Pilgrims from other countries had to have their foreign currency exchanged for payment of the temple tax and purchase of the sacrificial animals and doves. All the other Gospels relate the story of Jesus' cleansing the temple, but only John mentions the sacrificial animals (oxen and sheep). And like Luke, he mentions only the sellers, not the buyers as well. Again, it is only John who mentions the whip. It's for driving out the animals along with their sellers. And John alone mentions the driving out of the animals in addition to their sellers. You can't

whip doves; so Jesus tells their sellers to take them away. Why John's concentration on the sellers and his distinctive attention to the expulsion of animals and doves to be sold for sacrifice? The answer lies back in 1:29, 36. There we have the Baptist's testimony—again distinctive of John's Gospel—that Jesus is God's sacrificial lamb that takes away the world's sin, a Passover lamb according to chapters 18–19 (see especially 19:36 with Exodus 12:46). Now that Jesus has arrived on the scene, oxen and sheep and doves aren't needed any more. So out with them! And as the Word who is himself God, he has the authority and therefore takes the initiative to drive them out. In effect, his symbolic action says, "I'm here. You go."

Mark 11:17 quotes Jesus as saying, "It's written, 'My house will be called a house of prayer for all the nations, but you've made it a den of bandits'" (see Isaiah 56:7; Jeremiah 7:11; similarly Matthew 21:13; Luke 19:46). That quotation has to do with the exorbitant prices and exchange rates being charged where Gentiles (as well as Jews) should have been able to come for prayer. But in John, Jesus makes a point of referring to God as his Father, so that by implication he is God's Son, and says to stop making his Father's house a shopping mall for sacrifices. Why? Not because of exorbitant prices and exchange rates or because of hijacking the Gentiles' place of prayer, as in the other Gospels. Rather (and again), because sacrificial oxen, sheep, and doves are outmoded now that the lamb of God has arrived (compare Zechariah 14:21: "And no longer will there be a merchant in the house of the Lord of hosts in that day").

John puts the cleansing of the temple here at the start of Jesus' ministry. The other Gospels put it in the last week. Did Jesus cleanse the temple twice? Or did the other Gospels delay the cleansing? Or did John advance it? Probably John advanced it to provide a quick followup to the Baptist's proclaiming Jesus the lamb of God. In any case, the comparisons still stand. Cleansing the temple recalls to the disciples' memory a statement in Psalm 69:9. But John changes the verb in that passage, "Zeal for your house *has* devoured me," from a past tense to the future tense: "Zeal for your house *will* devour me." In line with Jesus' stepping forward to replace sacrificial animals and birds, the future tense looks to his coming death as God's lamb. The zeal of Jesus will show itself in his taking the initiative to die as a sacrifice. He will say in 10:18, "No one is taking it [my life] away from me; rather, I'm laying it down on my own." He will even volunteer to be arrested and insist on drinking his cup of self-sacrifice (18:1–11). Such zeal will devour him in the sense of costing him his life. But what is his Father's "house" toward which that zeal is directed? Is it the temple building in Jerusalem?

2:18–22: Therefore the Jews [probably the Jewish authorities in particular, for they ran the temple] **answered and said to him, "What sign do you show us,** [seeing] **that you're doing these things?"** [19]**Jesus answered and said to them, "Disassemble this temple, and in three days I'll raise it."** [20]**Therefore the Jews said, "For forty-six years this temple has been a-building,**

and *you*—will you raise it in three days?" [21]But that one [Jesus] **was talking about the temple** [consisting] **of his body.** [22]**Therefore when he rose from among the dead, his disciples remembered that he'd said this; and they believed the Scripture and the word that Jesus had spoken.** The Jews answer in the sense of responding to the totality of Jesus' action ("these things" that "you're doing"). They demand that he show them a sign—apparently a display of miraculous power—to authenticate that God had commissioned him to cleanse the temple. His answer is both unbelievable and cryptic. Unbelievable because it has taken a crew of 18,000 full-time workmen forty-six years to renovate the temple—which was 300 feet wide, long, and high and covered on all sides with massive plates of gold—yet Jesus said that if they disassembled it he'd raise it in only three days. Cryptic because he was speaking about his body as the temple he'd raise in three days if they disassembled it, that is, killed him. No, not *if* they disassembled it. He *commands* them to disassemble it. In John, as a matter of fact, Pontius Pilate will deliver Jesus *to the Jews* for crucifixion (19:16), so that when they crucify him they will unwittingly be obeying his command to disassemble the temple. As an equal matter of fact, Jesus *will raise himself* from the dead. As the Word who is God he can do just that: "I have authority to lay down [my life], and I have authority to take it again" (10:18). The clue to the meaning of Jesus' cryptic saying lies in his using the verb "raise," which suits resurrection, rather than the Jews' verb "build," which suited the temple they mistakenly thought of.

Throughout this paragraph John uses a word for "temple" that doesn't include the surrounding courtyards (as the word in 2:14–17 did), but a word that means only the sanctuary proper, the building where God concentrated his spiritual presence. By definition a temple is a dwelling place for God or, in pagan religions, a god. Jesus is the Word that became flesh, and the Word is God. So his body is the dwelling place of God that outmodes the sanctuary in Jerusalem just as his being the lamb of God outmodes the animal sacrifices. He's both the new temple and the new sacrifice. The old is no longer relevant (compare Jesus' replacing the tabernacle, which preceded the temple [see 1:14 with earlier comments]). What then was "the house" of Jesus' Father back in 2:16–17? It turns out to have been Jesus' own body—itself to be sacrificed, itself to be devoured by his zeal to drink the cup the Father gave him.

Earlier, the disciples remembered an Old Testament text *at the time* of a remark by Jesus (see 2:16–17). Here they remember his remark not till *after* the resurrection. In 2:22 the verb is passive: "was raised." But the passive of this verb often means "rise"; and since Jesus has just said *he* will raise the temple consisting of his body, we should understand that the disciples remembered his saying "when he *rose* from the dead." This remembrance will issue in their believing the Scripture, presumably the passage quoted in 2:17 that has to do with Jesus' death, and in believing "the word" of Jesus the Word, which

has to do with his resurrection (2:19). Note that the resurrection will be of a body (complete with the scars of crucifixion according to 20:20, 27) and that another reference to the disciples' believing carries forward John's emphasis on saving faith as persevering faith (compare 2:11 with comments).

BELIEVING AND UNBELIEVING IN JERUSALEM
John 2:23–3:21

2:23–25: And when Jesus was in Jerusalem during the Passover in the festal assembly, many believed in his name because [they] **were seeing his signs that he was doing.** [24]**But Jesus himself wasn't entrusting himself to them, because of** [his] **knowing all** [human beings] [25]**and because he had no need that anyone should testify concerning a human being. For he himself knew what was in a human being.** John repeats his earlier reference to the Passover (see also 2:13). Coming as it does right after allusions to Jesus' death and resurrection (2:17–22), the repetition continues the portrayal of him as God's lamb who will sacrifice himself at a later Passover. He performs his signs in the festal assembly, the congregation of pilgrims, for all to see. We don't know what those signs were; but 20:30 will refer to many signs not written in this book, and 21:25 to so many deeds of Jesus that the world couldn't hold the books required to relate them one by one. To believe in his name is to trust in what his name means for eternal life. In 1:1, 18 John identified the name as "God," the one name that according to 17:11 Jesus and the Father share. So believing in his name means believing Jesus to be God in human flesh for our salvation (see the comments on 1:12). Flash-in-the pan belief doesn't count, however. Only believing for the long term does. So Jesus, calling on his omniscience as God, didn't entrust himself to those believers (contrast 1:10: "the world *didn't* know him"). Though for the time being they trusted in him, he didn't trust them. He knew they wouldn't keep on believing. And sure enough, 6:66 will say, "Many of his disciples went away as backsliders and were no longer walking with him" (see also the comments on 20:30–31).

3:1–2: And there was a man of the Pharisees, Nicodemus by name, a ruler of the Jews. [2]**This one came to him** [Jesus] **at night and told him, "Rabbi, we know that as a teacher you've come from God. For no one can do these signs that you're doing unless God is with him."** The word "man" is actually the same as "human being" in 2:25 (twice). So John brings Nicodemus forward as an example of the human beings whose inner contents Jesus knows. Jesus "knew what was in a human being" (2:25), and he knows what's in Nicodemus. "Pharisee" identifies Nicodemus by religious affiliation. John doesn't pay very much attention to the religious distinctives of the Pharisees. For him the Pharisees are simply prominent authorities in Jewish society. And so "a ruler of the Jews" identifies the Pharisee Nicodemus as a member of the Sanhedrin, the Jewish supreme court. In 19:39 John will remind us that Nicodemus came to

Jesus "at night," and will do so in connection with the secrecy of Joseph of Arimathea's discipleship "because of fear of the Jews" (19:38). It appears, then, that Nicodemus doesn't want to be seen coming to Jesus. But there's more. The Word, who became Jesus of Nazareth, has already been described as "the light of human beings," as "the light" that "is shining in the darkness," and as the light that "the darkness didn't apprehend" (1:4–5). Jesus will yet claim to be "the light of the world" and "the light of life" (8:12; 9:4–5 [see also 1:7–9; 11:9–10; 12:35–36, 46]) and right in the present chapter will associate darkness with evil and light with truth (3:19–21). In 11:9–10, furthermore, "light" and "night" stand opposed to each other; and in 13:30 "night" stands for the moral darkness into which Judas Iscariot enters when he exits from the presence of Jesus to betray the light of the world. So Nicodemus's coming to Jesus at night symbolizes an approach to the light of the world out of the darkness of sin and judgment.

"Rabbi" means "my great one" and therefore as an address pays honor to Jesus. "We *know*" uses the vocabulary of belief in Jesus, as for example in 6:69, "We've come to believe and *know* that you're the Holy One of God," and 17:3, "This is eternal life, that they *know* you, the only true God, and [that they know] Jesus Christ, whom you sent." Presumably the "we" who know include along with Nicodemus the believers in Jesus' name that John mentioned in 2:23–25. "Teacher" interprets "Rabbi," since John used "Teacher" as an equivalent of "Rabbi" in 1:38 (compare 20:16). "Come from God" agrees with a theme that runs throughout John. It's that God "sent" Jesus into the world. The theme will reappear shortly in Jesus' own teaching of Nicodemus (3:17). Nicodemus has said a lot of right things, and continues to do so in affirming that Jesus couldn't be performing the signs he does unless God were with him. Saying that God is with Jesus anticipates what Jesus himself will say in 16:32: "I'm not alone, because the Father is with me" (see 8:16 too). Nicodemus is looking good. But will he persevere? For a possible answer, see 7:50–52; 19:38–42.

3:3–7: Jesus answered and said to him, "Amen, amen I tell you, unless one has been born from above, he can't see the kingdom of God." [4]Nicodemus says to him, "How can a human being be born when he's old? He can't enter a second time into his mother's womb and be born, can he?" [5]Jesus answered, "Amen, amen I tell you, unless one has been born out of water, even the Spirit, he can't enter into the kingdom of God. [6]What has been born out of the flesh is flesh, and what has been born out of the Spirit is Spirit. [7]You shouldn't marvel that I told you [singular], 'It's necessary that you [plural] be born from above.'" For Jesus' front-loaded, double "Amen" see the comments on 1:51. The adverb translated "from above" can also mean "again," as indicated by Nicodemus's response. But Jesus follows up with talk of being born out of the Spirit. Most translations have "*by* (or a simple 'of') the Spirit" instead of "*out of* the Spirit," and similarly with regard to "the flesh"; but "out of" captures better the stated sense of origin as

distinct from means. Water symbolizes the Spirit according to 7:38–39—therefore the translation "water, *even* the Spirit" rather than "water *and* the Spirit." (Note that "water" drops out in the next references to the Spirit.) Although baptismal water hovers in the background, Jesus isn't talking about water baptism as such, much less about a mother's water breaking when she gives birth. He's talking about the Spirit, who comes out of heaven, as in 1:32: "I saw the Spirit descending like a dove out of heaven." So the talk of being born out of the Spirit shows that Jesus means "born *from above*" in a birth different from the physical. But Nicodemus's intervening questions about a "second time" show that he mistakenly thinks Jesus means "born *again*" in a physical sense. Jesus has to correct him. Of course, a human being *can* be born from above, out of the Spirit, when he's old.

It's obvious that what has been born *out of* the flesh *is* flesh. The flesh of a father and mother produces the flesh of their offspring (compare 1:13, where being born out of God—which here in 3:4–7 turns into being born out of God's Spirit—contrasts with being born out of parents' bloodlines, out of the fleshly attraction of a male and a female to each other, and out of a husband's will to have an heir). But what does it mean that what has been born out of the Spirit *is* Spirit? It can't mean that the Holy Spirit produces a human spirit (with a small "s," capitalization versus noncapitalization being a matter of interpretation since the ancient manuscripts don't make a distinction), because human beings have a human spirit quite apart from birth from above. What's meant is that birth from the Spirit produces people inhabited by the Holy Spirit (see 7:38–39 again, plus 14:16–17; 20:22). "The Word became flesh" (1:14), but also the Spirit descended and remained on him (1:32–33). Water, representing the Spirit, will come out of his pierced side (19:34); and he'll breathe the Holy Spirit into the disciples (20:22). So Jesus is both flesh and Spirit in the sense that he's in the flesh, and the Spirit is in him. Likewise in regard to believers, then: flesh as a result of natural birth, Spirit as a result of birth from above. But why shouldn't Nicodemus marvel at what Jesus has said? The answer will come in 3:10. *Seeing* the kingdom of God means *experiencing* God's reign by *entering* the sphere where he reigns. The shift from a singular "you" to a plural "you" makes Jesus tell all of us, not just Nicodemus, that we have to be born from above to enjoy the benefits of God's reign.

3:8: "The wind/Spirit blows where it/he wills [to blow], and you [singular again and following] hear its/his sound/voice. Nevertheless, you don't know where it/he is coming from and where it/he is going. Thus is everyone who has been born out of the Spirit." The word for "Spirit" also means "wind." So Jesus plays on these two meanings to draw an analogy with the Spirit's activity from the activity of wind. Until the last statement the accent falls on wind; but since the wind doesn't "will" anything, this verb implies the additional meaning "Spirit." For as personal, the Spirit *does* will. And "blows" is a verbal form of "wind/Spirit." So we could also translate as follows: "The Spirit spirits where he wills" (compare Genesis 1:2). This blowing, or spiriting, represents birthing people from above. "Where it/he wills" emphasizes divine sovereignty in the birthing from above: "the Son makes alive those whom he wills [to make alive]" (5:21), and "You didn't select me; rather, I selected you" (15:16 [for a balancing emphasis on human responsibility, see 7:17]). Hearing the sound of wind compares with hearing the voice of the Spirit so as to believe in Jesus. In fact, Jesus' voice is heard in the Spirit's voice (15:26 [compare Jesus' statements in 18:37, "Everyone who's from the truth hears my voice," and 10:27, "My sheep hear my voice . . . and they follow me"; see also 3:29; 5:25, 28; 10:3–5, 16; 11:43]).

Just as Nicodemus doesn't know where the wind comes from and where it goes, neither does he know where the Spirit comes from and goes. The Spirit's heavenly origin and destination are unknown to human beings because they've never been there. Contrast and compare Jesus' statements in 8:14, "I know where I came from and where I'm going. But you don't know where I'm coming from or where I'm going," and the statement about him in 13:3: "knowing . . . that he had come forth from God and is going to God." So there's a parallel between the Spirit and Jesus in the work of birthing from above, because he's the bearer of the windy Spirit. "Thus is everyone who has been born out of the Spirit" means that like the Spirit (and Jesus), those born out of the Spirit are from above in that the heaven-sent Spirit constitutes their true origin and guarantees their ultimate destination. Or as Jesus will put it, his disciples don't originate from the world though they're in the world (17:11, 14–16); and he'll ask that they may see him in his heavenly glory (17:24).

3:9–10: Nicodemus answered and said to him, "How can these things [being born from above, from water, even the Spirit] **happen?"** [10]**Jesus answered and said to him, "Are you the teacher of Israel and don't know these things?"** Nicodemus had described Jesus as a teacher (3:2). Ironically, perhaps even sarcastically, Jesus returns the compliment—and adds "the" and "of Israel" to heighten the irony of Nicodemus's teacherly ignorance. Nevertheless, the high rank of Nicodemus doesn't rise to the level of Jesus as a teacher who, according to Nicodemus himself, "has come from God" (3:2). Why *should* Nicodemus have understood these things? Because Ezekiel 36:25–27 quotes the Lord as saying, "Then I'll sprinkle clean water on you, and you'll be clean. . . . Moreover, I'll give you a new heart and put a Spirit in you . . . . And I'll put my Spirit in you . . . ." Now we know why Jesus told Nicodemus in 3:7 why he shouldn't marvel. As "the teacher of Israel" Nicodemus should have understood Jesus' words in terms of Ezekiel's prophecy.

3:11–12: "Amen, amen I tell you [singular] **that we speak about what we know and testify to what we've seen, and you** [plural here and following] **are not accepting our testimony.** [12]**If I told you earthly things and you don't believe, how will you believe if I tell you heavenly things?"** Who are the "we" who speak, know, and testify about what they've seen? Answer: Jesus the Word and teacher who has come from God, and the Spirit who has descended from heaven to birth believers from above. What they know and have seen is the truth about God the Father, to whom they alone have had direct access. For "no one has seen God at any time. A one-and-only [who was] God, the one existing in the bosom of the Father—that one has explained him" (1:18). "What he [Jesus] has seen and heard—this he testifies to" (3:32). "When the representative comes, whom I'll send to you from alongside the Father, the Spirit of the truth, who proceeds out from alongside the Father—that one will testify about me [that is, about Jesus the truth, whom to see is to see the Father according to 14:6–9]" (15:26). In switching from a singular "you" to a plural "you" Jesus addresses through Nicodemus those Jews who aren't accepting his and the Spirit's testimony (compare 1:11: "his own ones didn't accept him"). So unbelief consists in a refusal to accept testimonial evidence, the external, historical evidence of Jesus' testimony and the internal, existential evidence of the Spirit's testimony. Nobody asks you to believe without evidence. Nor is unbelief due to *lack* of evidence. It's due to *rejection* of evidence—testimonial evidence. The quality of this evidence will come up for discussion later in John (starting in chapter 5). What then are the earthly things that Jesus ("I") has told? Should we identify them with his language of birth and wind? But how can being born from the Spirit, who's *from above*, be described as *earthly*? And if it's something heavenly instead, what remains to be earthly? And why does Jesus imply that he hasn't yet spoken about heavenly things ("*if* I tell you heavenly things")? Perhaps the next verse will supply an answer.

3:13: "And no one has ascended into heaven except the one who has descended out of heaven, [namely,] **the Son of Man."**[1] In 20:17 the risen Jesus will put his ascension in the immediate future. So in referring here to the one who *has* ascended into heaven he is speaking from a standpoint *after* his coming death, resurrection, and ascension, as he often does in this Gospel (for example: "where I *am* you can't come" [7:34, 36], as though he's already back in heaven). The "earthly things" of 3:12, then, are the things Jesus spoke about while on earth. They're earthly not in their content but in the location at which they were spoken. It follows that the "heavenly things" of 3:12 are things that Jesus will speak after he ascends to heaven. They're heavenly in the location at which they'll be spoken, not in their content, as in 16:12–14: "I still have many things to say to you, but you aren't able to bear [them] now. But when that one, the Spirit of the truth, comes he'll guide you in all the truth. For he won't speak on his own; rather, he'll speak as many things as he'll hear and report to you the coming things. . . . he'll take ['the coming things'] from me

---

[1]According to 2 Kings 2:1–11 Elijah the prophet was taken up to heaven in a fiery chariot and whirlwind; but in John's Gospel Jesus ascends to heaven on his own (20:17), so that his ascension is one of a kind.

and report [them] to you [plus a repetition of this last statement in 16:15]." On his return to heaven, then, Jesus will speak through the Holy Spirit to the disciples. But what's the purpose for making the statement here in 3:13 anyway? Well, let's remember that "the Son of Man" is a Semitic way of saying "the human being," and also that according to the Gnostic heretic Cerinthus, the human being Jesus of Nazareth didn't ascend to heaven after resurrection—rather, the quite different divine Spirit Christ ascended to heaven just before the crucifixion of Jesus after descending on him at Jesus' baptism (see the introduction to 1 John). No, says John. You can't divide Jesus and Christ from each other. There was only *one* person, Jesus Christ, who as the Son of Man ascended to heaven *after* the crucifixion and resurrection just as he descended from heaven at the incarnation. The human and the divine aren't to be separated. The fleshly and the Spiritual aren't to be divorced. (Otherwise you fall either into mysticism or into materialism.)

3:14–17: "**And just as Moses lifted up the serpent in the wilderness** [see Numbers 21:5–9 for the story], **in this way it's necessary that the Son of Man be lifted up** [15]**in order that everyone believing might have eternal life in him;** [16]**for in this way God loved the world. And so he gave** [his] **one-and-only Son in order that everyone believing in him might not be lost, but might have eternal life;** [17]**for God didn't send** [his] **Son into the world in order that he might judge the world— rather, in order that the world might be saved through him.**" In 3:13 Jesus mentioned the ascension of the Son of Man. Here he speaks about the lifting up of the Son of Man. According to 12:32–33, that lifting up refers to the manner of his death, namely, death by being lifted up on a cross as opposed to two failed attempts to knock Jesus down by stoning him to death (8:59; 10:31). So the combination of ascension and being lifted up in 3:13–14 means that the crucifixion will mark the first stage of his ascension. Stated differently, John is starting to transform Jesus' shameful death (for crucifixion was considered the most shameful way to die) into the initial phase of his glorification. The verb "must" indicates divine necessity: the lifting up of the Son of Man on a cross won't happen by accident. It will happen in perfect accord with God's plan. "*Everyone* believing" occurs twice to emphasize the universality of the gospel: the invitation is open to all. Because of the statement, "In him was life" (1:4 [see also 11:25; 14:6; 1 John 1:1–2]), the phrase "in him" here in 3:15 probably describes the *location* where eternal life is to be found. In 3:16 a similar phrase (slightly different in John's original Greek though translated the same in English) indicates Jesus as the *object* of believing for eternal life. To believe in him (more literally, "*into* him") is to entrust yourself into his hand (compare 10:28, where Jesus says, "I give them [my sheep] eternal life, and by no means will they be lost . . . and no one will snatch them out of my hand").

"In this way" doesn't tell the degree of God's love, as though it were "so much." It *was* a love of high degree, but that's not the point here. Rather, "in this way" refers

back to the divine necessity of the Son of Man's being lifted up. That's the way God loved the world, by seeing to it that Jesus was lifted up on a cross. And it's "the world" that God loved in this way. What a vile world it is: a world that doesn't recognize the Word, the Spirit of truth, or believers in Jesus; a world that hates Jesus and his disciples, that persecutes his disciples; a world incapable of receiving the Spirit of truth; a world guilty of sin, full of lusts and pride, and located "in the evil one"; a world that loves darkness rather than light because its deeds are evil; a world whose ruler is Satan; a world that's the object of judgment (see 1:10, 29; 3:19; 7:7; 12:31; 14:17, 30; 15:18–19; 16:8, 11, 20, 33; 17:14; 1 John 2:16; 3:1, 13; 5:19). But vile as it is, God loved it. So his love consists in *giving* his one-and-only Son, and the giving doesn't allude to a divine Christmas gift. It alludes not to Jesus' birth but to his being lifted up on a cross—Good Friday, not Christmas Day (compare 6:51: "the bread that I'll give *for the world's life* is my flesh").

Unlike "in this way," the description of Jesus as God's "one-and-only Son" *does* indicate the high degree of love that led God to give his Son in death for the eternal life of a vile world. Traditional translations have "might not *perish*." But in English, perishing tends to connote passing out of existence, whereas the verb means rather to be lost (as in the parables of the lost sheep and the lost coin, which didn't pass out of existence [Luke 15:1–10]). Here it means to be lost to the possibility of having eternal life and instead to suffer the judgment of eternal punishment (Revelation 14:10; 20:11–15). God's sending his Son into the world had the purpose of averting this judgment in favor of saving everyone who believes.

3:18: "**The one believing in him isn't being judged. But the one not believing has been judged already, because he hasn't believed in the name of the one-and-only Son of God.**" As before, believing in Jesus doesn't mean only to believe what he says. It means also to rely on Jesus himself, his person and work. And believing in the *name* of the one-and-only Son of God is to believe in his name "God" (1:1, 18), the only name he shares with the Father (17:11–12 [see the comments on 1:12]); and to believe *in* his name "God" is to trust in his revelation of God for your eternal life in place of judgment. The verb "judge" is capable of more than one meaning. In 3:17 it stood opposite "save" and therefore meant to punish. Here in 3:18 it means to issue a verdict of guilty. A believer isn't being judged in the sense that he isn't being issued a verdict of guilty. The reverse for an unbeliever: he hasn't yet been punished, but he has already been issued a verdict of guilty; and the issuance of this verdict is due to unbelief. For if he'd believed, the lamb of God would have taken away his sin (1:29).

The verdict of guilty gets more detailed in **3:19–21**: "**And this is the judgment** [the verdict of guilty]: **that the light** [the Word who became Jesus according to 1:1–5, 14–18] **has come into the world; and the human beings** [who make up 'the world'] **loved the darkness** [which hides things] **rather than the light** [who makes things visible], **for their deeds were evil.** **²⁰For everyone who's doing evil things hates the light and doesn't come to the light** [who is Jesus, let it be repeated], **lest his** [the evildoer's] **deeds be exposed.** **²¹But the one who is doing the truth comes to the light in order that his deeds may be manifested** [to the effect] **that they were done in God."** Really to *believe* the truth is to *do* it. Doing it contrasts with "doing evil things." This contrast implies that truth has a moral quality about it, the quality of doing good deeds as opposed to evil deeds. So truth isn't just factuality that you believe in. It's also what you do in conformity with the way things really and truly are, the way God made them. The other way around, evil has the quality of falsehood. It's not just a lack of morality. To do evil isn't only to do what's bad. It's also to do what's false to the way God created us and the world we live in. Doing the truth isn't a human achievement about which the doer can boast, however, not something that merits God's favor. No, "the one who's doing the truth comes to the light in order that his deeds may be manifested [to the effect] *that they were done in God."* What does this last clause mean? Let's compare Jesus' statement, "Abide *in me* and I [will abide] in you. Just as the vine can't bear on its own, [that is, just as it can't bear fruit] unless it abides in the vineyard, so neither can you [bear fruit] if you don't abide *in me*" (15:4 [see the comments on chapter 15 for "vine" and "vineyard" rather than "branch" and "vine"]). The soil of the vineyard supplies nourishment for the vines to bear fruit. In the same way it's God who supplies through Jesus the wherewithal to do the deeds of truth. And those who do the truth come to the light for the express purpose of having their deeds shown to have had their genesis in God rather than in any natural human ability. To God alone be the glory!

THE BAPTIST'S FURTHER
TESTIMONY TO JESUS
John 3:22–36

The first three verses of this paragraph make a transition to the Baptist's testifying in favor of Jesus again. **3:22–24: After these things Jesus and his disciples went into the Judean countryside, and he was spending time there with them and baptizing** [people]. **²³And John too was baptizing** [people] **at Aenon close to Salim, because many waters were there; and people were arriving and getting baptized.** **²⁴For John** [the Baptist, as also above] **hadn't yet been thrown into prison.** Jesus and the disciples have been in Jerusalem for the Passover. Jerusalem is in Judea, but now they leave the city for the countryside. John 3:26 will put the Baptist—and therefore Aenon, where he was baptizing—*opposite* the other side of the Jordan River, where he'd been earlier. Since the other side is the east side, or Transjordan (compare 1:28; 10:40), Aenon opposite the east side must be located in territory west of the river—but probably not on its bank, because then John wouldn't have needed to say that "many waters were there." Apparently Aenon had many springs.

3:25–26: Therefore [because both Jesus and the Baptist were baptizing people] **a dispute concerning purification developed between some of John's disciples and a Jew.** **²⁶And they came to John and told him, "Rabbi, he who was with you the other side of the Jordan, about whom you've testified—look! This one** [Jesus] **is baptizing, and all are going to him."** The dispute had to do with ritual purification, such as baptism (compare 2:6). But the dispute is dropped before we find out about its particulars, and the Jew disappears. So the only purpose of 3:25 is to get the Baptist's disciples on stage. Some of them had already switched to Jesus—at the Baptist's own encouragement (1:29–42)—but some were still following the Baptist and disturbed that Jesus was attracting more people than their own rabbi/teacher. Nevertheless, they have to admit that the Baptist had testified to Jesus earlier. Maybe they wouldn't have minded if Jesus were drawing smaller crowds, or even equal crowds. But larger crowds? *"All* are going to him" exaggerates, because if the Baptist too is baptizing, *some* people are still coming to him. But the severity of his disciples' disturbance leads them to exaggerate. A similar exaggeration will come up in 12:19: "Look! The *world* has gone after him [Jesus]." Underlying these exaggerations is the world-wide success of the gospel by the time John writes the Fourth Gospel. The exaggerators said more than they realized. John's disciples don't ask a question, they express alarm. Their expression of alarm sets up for another testimony about Jesus by the Baptist and enhances the value of the Baptist's upcoming testimony, which will deny the need for alarm and go in the opposite direction.

3:27: John answered and said, "A human being can't take even one thing unless it has been given to him from heaven." The Baptist answers with a kind of proverb which means that human beings can't get any more from God than God wants them to have. As applied to the Baptist, the proverb means that God has given him a certain number of followers; and the Baptist couldn't get any more even if he wanted to. So if Jesus is getting more followers, that's the will of God.

The Baptist continues in **3:28–30: "You yourselves testify about me that I said, 'I'm not the Christ; rather, I've been sent ahead of that one** [the Christ]' [see 1:20–23, 29–30 for this earlier testimony]. **²⁹The one who has the bride is the bridegroom; and the bridegroom's friend, who stands and hears him, rejoices with joy because of the bridegroom's voice. Therefore this joy of mine has been fulfilled. ³⁰That one** [Jesus] **must increase** [so far as his following is concerned], **but I decrease** [so far as my following is concerned]." Jesus is the bridegroom. His followers are the bride (compare Revelation 19:7–9 with 21:2; 22:17). The Baptist is the friend of the bridegroom, a sort of best man (see the comments on 15:15 for the additional connotation that the "friend" of someone is an object of his love). That the Baptist hears the *voice* of Jesus the groom reminds us that Jesus is the *Word* (1:1–18). It also looks forward to the statements of

Jesus that his sheep hear his voice in the sense of recognizing it as the voice of their good shepherd (10:4, 16, 27). The Baptist isn't just *willing* to see more people flock to Jesus than to himself. He's *glad* to see them do so—glad to the max, for the awkward expression "rejoices with joy" means just that. His mission to testify about Jesus achieves success when people shift from him to Jesus. The success fulfills his joy. The glass is full—completely. More importantly, the shift arises out of a divine necessity: "That one *must* increase, but I decrease" (compare 1:30).

Now the Baptist elaborates his testimony. **3:31: "The one who comes from above is above all. The one who's out of the earth is out of the earth and speaks out of the earth. The one who comes out of heaven is over all."** There's a lot of redundancy in this verse. The first and last statements are exactly alike except for the explanatory substitution of "heaven" for "above." This repetitiveness puts all possible stress on Jesus' heavenly origin and consequent universal superiority (compare his description of birth out of the Spirit as a birth "from above" [3:3–8]). "The one who's out of the earth is out of the earth" is about as redundant a statement as you'll find anywhere. But it's this very redundancy that emphasizes the inferiority of the Baptist as compared with Jesus (contrast Jesus' playing up the greatness of the Baptist in Matthew 11:7–19; Luke 7:24–35, though with a qualification). The fact that the Baptist "speaks out of the earth" doesn't mean his message is untrue. It means that he speaks out of his own earthbound experience. Even a prophet of God, like the Baptist, gets his revelations on earth as an earthbound creature. But Jesus—he testifies to what he has seen and heard in heaven above (3:11–12), where as the Word he was with the Father in the beginning (1:1–2).

The Baptist continues speaking about Jesus in **3:32–34: "What he has seen and heard—this he testifies to, and no one is accepting his testimony. [33]The one who does accept his testimony has put his seal** [on the statement,] **'God is true.' [34]For he whom God sent speaks the words of God. For he doesn't give the Spirit measuredly."** "What he has seen and heard" portrays the preincarnate Son of God as an apprentice who learned a trade from his father's deeds and words. As the incarnate Son of God Jesus now testifies to his heavenly Father's deeds and words, so that what he speaks are the very words of God—naturally, since the Word who was *with* God *was* God (1:1). Jesus' voice brings the words of God from heaven above. In the other Gospels, at Jesus' baptism and transfiguration God the Father speaks from heaven. Here, according to the Baptist, Jesus speaks on earth the words of God that he has heard in heaven.

Take another look at the word behind "testify." It could just as well be translated "witness," which carries two meanings: (1) to see and hear, so that we speak of eyewitnesses and earwitnesses, and (2) to tell what has been seen and heard, that is, to bear witness, to testify. So just as the Baptist is a witness in that he testifies to what he has seen and heard about Jesus, now Jesus himself becomes an even more important witness in that

he testifies to what he has seen and heard in heavenly communion with God his Father. So the Baptist testifies to the superiority of Jesus' testimony over his own testimony. But "no one is accepting his [Jesus'] testimony." The statement sounds absolute, like what logicians call a universal negative. The statement is strong—certainly. But beware of universal negatives, and never say "never." There are exceptions. These exceptions put their seal on the statement that God is true. Wax seals, stamped with a signet ring, were used to certify ownership and authorship. So to put a seal on the statement that God is true isn't to certify that *Jesus* is true. (It's true that he's true, but that's not the point here.) Rather, people who accept Jesus' testimony to what he has seen and heard are certifying that *God* is true, because God is the subject of Jesus' words. He explains God (1:18).

"God is true" means that he's trustworthy (compare our expression, "He's for real," "She's for real"). In 3:34 we find two bases for people's certifying that God is true, that he's trustworthy. Each statement starts with the conjunction "For," which introduces a basis. The first is that Jesus speaks the words of God which he heard God speak in heaven and which God sent him to speak on earth. The second basis is Jesus' unlimited gift of the Spirit to those who believe in him. He doesn't measure out the Spirit cupful by cupful. No, he immerses them in the Spirit, drenches them with the Spirit (1:33). Once again, then, we have an external basis for believing, the testimony of the historical Jesus, and an internal basis as well, the experience of God's Spirit.

The words of God that Jesus speaks are more than sufficient. Hence **3:35–36: "The Father loves the Son and has given all things into his hand."** The hand stands for power, authority, ownership, control. God the Father hasn't held anything back from his beloved Son Jesus. So what Jesus says is all we need. **[36]"The one believing in the Son has eternal life."** Even though "eternal" has to do with the age to come, which we call eternity, believers in Jesus have eternal life now, ahead of time. Given the properly future meaning of eternal life, the present tense of "has" is blessedly astonishing. **"But the one who disobeys the Son** [through disbelieving him, as implied by the contrast with 'believing'] **won't see life** [in the sense of not experiencing eternal life with God and Jesus]**; rather, the wrath of God abides on him."** God is naturally angry with people who won't obey his Son through believing in him. God's wrath abides—that is, stays—on such people. It's already there, and it will stay there as long as they persist in the disobedience of unbelief (contrast the Spirit's abiding on Jesus in 1:32). We can appreciate the depth and breadth of God's love (about which see again the comments on 3:16) only against the background of his wrath.

JESUS AND THE SAMARITAN WOMAN
John 4:1–42

4:1–3: So when Jesus knew that the Pharisees had heard, "Jesus is making and baptizing more disciples

than John [the Baptist is making and baptizing]"—²**and yet indeed Jesus himself wasn't baptizing; rather, his disciples** [were baptizing]—³**he left Judea and went back into Galilee.** Jesus' making and baptizing more disciples than the Baptist made and baptized does two things: (1) it reemphasizes Jesus' superiority, and (2) it shows the fulfillment of the Baptist's statement, "That one must increase, but I decrease" (3:30). Jesus' knowing that the Pharisees heard doesn't have to imply his divine omniscience (somebody could have told him); but in view of such omniscience in 1:48; 2:24–25; 5:6, 42; 6:15; 16:19; 20:27; 21:17, it probably does here too. The Pharisees have already appeared as resident in Jerusalem and as antagonistic (1:19, 24, though see 3:1–2 for an exception in Nicodemus). So Jesus leaves Judea, the southern territory, where Jerusalem is located, and goes back to Galilee in the north, where Nazareth, Cana, and Capernaum are located. The qualification that Jesus deputized his disciples to baptize people for him heightens Jesus' superiority over John. Baptizing in water is for others to do. He will baptize people in a much superior element, the Spirit (1:33). Besides, so many people are coming to him that he has to use the disciples as his deputies.

4:4: And it was necessary for him to go through Samaria. It wasn't topographically necessary to go through Samaria on the way from Judea to Galilee. To go through Samaria was to take the direct route, in fact. Nor was it culturally necessary to go through Samaria. On the contrary, because of mutual antipathy between Jews and Samaritans strict Jews usually avoided Samaria by way of a detour. So the present necessity is divine, as always elsewhere in John too (ten times in toto). For example, "It's necessary that you be born from above": God requires it (3:7). "It's necessary that the Son of Man be lifted up": God requires it (3:14). The necessity that Jesus go through Samaria means, then, that Jesus is carrying out God's requirement. In terms of John 10:1–30, Jesus has other sheep, not of the Jewish pen but of the Samaritan pen: "I have other sheep that aren't of this [Jewish] pen. It's necessary that I bring those as well, and they'll hear my voice and become one flock" (10:16).

4:5–6: So he comes into a city [we'd call it a town] **of Samaria called Sychar near the plot of ground that Jacob had given to Joseph his son** [Genesis 33:18–19; 48:21–22; Joshua 24:32]. ⁶**And Jacob's well was there. So Jesus, tired out from the journey, was sitting thus** [that is, in a tired condition] **at the well. It was about the sixth hour.** The reference to Jacob prepares for a later reference to him (4:12). The term for "well" refers to the kind in which water bubbles up. Jesus' fatigue explains why he's sitting (probably on a low stone wall surrounding the well to keep people and animals from falling in) and prepares for his requesting a drink. Incidentally, the fatigue reinforces the Word's having become *flesh* (1:14). The reference to the sixth hour explains why Jesus was tired out and why a Samaritan woman is about to arrive. But what was the sixth hour? Counting from sunrise, it would be noon, in which case the woman comes then

because she's too ashamed of her sordid life to come with other women at dusk, when the heat has died down. But she'll give the impression of being shameless, and it's a real question whether she's a loose woman or a woman victimized by the men of Sychar. Counting from noon, the sixth hour would be 6:00 P.M., the normal hour for drawing water—and by that time Jesus would have been tired out from a *full* day's journey. Also, that hour suits the disciples' going into town to buy food for an evening meal (4:8), whereas Jews didn't eat a lunch. So 6:00 P.M. makes better sense than noon does (compare the comments on 1:39).

4:7–9: A woman of Samaria comes to draw water. Jesus says to her, "Give me [some water] **to drink."** ⁸**For his disciples had gone off into the city to buy food.** ⁹**So the Samaritan woman says to him, "How is it that you, though being a Jew, are asking** [for some water] **to drink from me, though being a Samaritan woman? For Jews don't co-use** [anything, such as a water bucket] **with Samaritans."** Jesus designs his question not to get a drink but to start a conversation that will issue in the woman's wanting to get a drink. The disciples' absence provides privacy for the conversation. A good Jew wouldn't defile himself by drinking water from the bucket of a Samaritan, for Jews regarded Samaritans and the things they used as ritually unclean. But at Cana in Galilee Jesus' changing the water of Jewish purification into wine symbolized that the old ritual taboos were now obsolete. The Holy Spirit, symbolized by baptismal water, was to be a new agent of cleansing.

4:10–12: Jesus answered and said to her, "If you'd known the gift of God and who's the one saying to you, 'Give me [some water] **to drink,' you'd have asked him and he'd have given you living water."** ¹¹**The woman says to him, "Lord, you have no bucket and the well is deep. So from where do you have the living water?** ¹²**You're not greater, are you, than our** [fore]**father Jacob, who gave us the well and himself drank from it, and his sons and his livestock** [also drank from it]**?"** In 4:5 John mentioned Jacob's gift of a nearby plot of ground to his son Joseph. Now Jesus refers to *God's* gift. What is it? The answer appeared in 3:16: "He [God] gave [his] one-and-only Son"—not a gift *to* his Son, as in Jacob's case, but the gift *of* his Son. So God's gift is Jesus himself. We could almost translate 4:10, "If you'd known the gift of God, *even* the one who's speaking to you." And note that Jesus calls himself a speaker ("the one saying to you"). He is, after all, the Word. But as the gift of God, Jesus is also a giver—of "living water," which is flowing water, spring water such as bubbles up in Jacob's well. So the Samaritan woman immediately thinks of that very water and asks how it is that Jesus has spring water out of Jacob's well since the well shaft is deep and he doesn't have a bucket with which to have gotten it. "From where . . .?" asks what source other than a bucket has provided him with a supply of living water from Jacob's well. And "you *have*" (not "you *get*," as in erroneous translations) shows her thinking that he claims to have *already* such water to give her. She addresses Jesus as "Lord" in the sense of "Sir," but of course John means us to understand "Lord" in the sense of deity. She spoke better than she intended or understood. So her question, "You're not greater, are you, than our [fore]father Jacob?" is deeply ironic. *Of course* Jesus is greater than Jacob. Jesus is the Word who was with God in the beginning and *was* God (1:1). He, the giver of living water, stands over against Jacob, the giver of the well according to a Jewish tradition not contained in the Old Testament. And the woman's statement that Jacob, his sons, and his livestock *drank* from the well tellingly omits any giving of the well's *water* by Jacob. He gave only the *well.* Jesus, by contrast, doesn't *drink* the living water that he has. He *gives* it. He is its source. "Our [fore]father Jacob" implies a claim to ancestry from Jacob on the part of Samaritans (compare "our [fore]fathers" in 4:20, where "our" can't include Jews along with Samaritans).

4:13–15: Jesus answered and said to her, "Everyone drinking some of this water will thirst again. ¹⁴But whoever drinks some of the water that I'll give him will never, ever thirst. Rather, the water that I'll give him will become in him a spring of water leaping up into [= with the result of] eternal life." ¹⁵The woman says to him, "Lord, give me this water so that I won't keep getting thirsty and [so that] I won't keep coming here to draw [water]." Again the woman means "Sir" but John means "Lord." Jesus now makes clear the distinction between the water he'll give and the water of Jacob's well. The woman catches the distinction but still thinks of Jesus' water as H2O, as though—if she drinks some of it—it will renew itself in her body and eliminate the daily chore of coming and drawing water. She misses the meaning of "eternal life" and thinks only that "will never, ever thirst" means "won't thirst for as long as present earthly life lasts." But Jesus means "will never thirst for all eternity." "Never, *ever*" stresses this point. By "living water," then, he means water in a figurative sense. Even in pre-scientific eras people knew about the connection between water and life, most especially in the largely arid Middle East. So living water isn't just the flowing water of a spring, as opposed to standing water in a cistern (of which there were many in ancient Israel). Living water is also water that *brings* life—life so vital that it leaps up to the level of eternal life. And being *in* you, this spring of life keeps you from ever thirsting again. In other words, you don't have to worry about your future. You have it secure in the form of eternal life within yourself, a part of your very being, as a gift from Jesus. Because it leaps up inside you, you don't even need a bucket to get it. The woman said, "so that I won't keep coming here to draw [water]." The verb for "come" actually means to come or go *through* some territory to arrive at your destination. For the woman it means to go through the countryside that separates her village from Jacob's well—a distance making her daily chore more onerous. But this is the same verb that John used in 4:4: "And it was necessary for him [Jesus] to *go through* Samaria." Because Jesus went through Samaria, then, this woman won't have to

go through anywhere to draw water. Oh sure, she'll have to for H2O, but not for the water of eternal life. And that's the water that she won't have to draw up with a bucket. It'll leap up within her. Later, John will interpret the water as the Holy Spirit that "makes [people] live" (see 6:63 with 7:37–39).

Suddenly Jesus turns the conversation away from water to the woman herself. **4:16–18:** He tells her, "Go call your husband and come [back] **here.**" "Here" echoes "here" in 4:15 to link Jesus' statement with the woman's statement even though Jesus has shifted the topic of conversation. There may already be a hint that Jesus knows she doesn't have a husband (as it will turn out) in the fact that the command to "come" is in the singular, not the plural that you might expect if the woman and her husband—if she had one—were both to come. ¹⁷The woman answered and told him, "I don't have a husband." Jesus tells her, "Well did you say, 'I don't have a husband.' ¹⁸For you've had five husbands, and him whom you now have isn't a husband of yours. You said this truthfully." Again Jesus exhibits his divine omniscience, and the woman shows that she's "from the truth" (18:37). There may be some underlying symbolism here too. Five husbands: in 2 Kings 17:24 we read that after taking most of the northern Israelites into exile, "the king of Syria brought people [1] from Babylon and [2] from Cuthah and [3] from Avva and [4] from Hamath and [5] from Sepharvaim, and settled them in place of the sons of Israel." Just maybe the woman's five husbands symbolize the fivefold heathen origin of the Samaritans. For by the time of Jesus these heathen had intermarried with Israelites left in the region, so that their religion had become a branch of Judaism considered heretical by the Jews. The Samaritans had once had a temple on Mount Gerizim, within sight of Jacob's well, though by now it lay in ruins. Furthermore, they had their own version of the Old Testament, limited to the law of Moses. How many books? Five! Genesis, Exodus, Leviticus, Numbers, and Deuteronomy—the Samaritan Pentateuch. John drew a contrast in 1:17 between the law of Moses and Jesus' grace and truth. Maybe we have something of the same contrast here, the woman's five husbands representing the Mosaic law, written down in five books. If so, the water of Jacob's well represents the Samaritan version of Judaism just as the purificatory water at Cana (2:6) represented the Jewish version, both to be superseded by the gospel of Christ.

4:19–20: The woman tells him, "Lord, I see that you're a prophet. ²⁰Our [fore]fathers worshiped on this mountain. And you [Jews] say, 'In Jerusalem is the place [that is, the temple] where it's necessary to worship.'" Yet again the woman means "Sir" but John means "Lord" in the sense of deity. The woman marvels at Jesus' supernatural knowledge but attributes it to a prophetic gift rather than to his deity, which she doesn't recognize, rather as Nicodemus attributed Jesus' signs to a divine gift of teaching rather than to deity itself (3:1–2). The Samaritans expected the Messiah to be, above all else, a prophet like Moses (Deuteronomy 18:15, 18 [compare their accepting only the Mosaic law]). Because of this expectation the woman is starting to think Jesus might be that prophetic Messiah, like Moses, despite Jesus' being a Jew rather than a Samaritan. So she asks him a question about the place where God requires people to worship. ("It's necessary" alludes to a divine requirement.) "Our [fore]fathers" refers to the patriarchs (Abraham, Isaac, Jacob, and others) as claimed by the Samaritans in that only they, not the Jews, regarded those patriarchs as having worshiped on Mount Gerizim. Despite the ruin of their temple there, the Samaritans still used this mountain as a place for sacrifice. Some interpreters think the woman is trying to steer the conversation away from a sordid life of her own making. But first-century Palestinian women didn't have very much say-so in their marriages, might suffer widowhood more than once, and lacked the right of divorce. So the woman here could well have been a victim. If so, her raising the issue of where it's necessary to worship appeals to Jesus' prophetic insight rather than constituting an attempt to avoid further embarrassment.

4:21–24: Jesus tells her, "Believe me, woman, that an hour is coming when you [plural] will worship the Father neither on this mountain nor in Jerusalem. ²²You [plural again, referring to Samaritans] worship what you don't know [= don't understand]. We [Jews] worship what we do know, because salvation is from the Jews. ²³Nevertheless, an hour is coming, and now is, when true worshipers will worship the Father in Spirit and truth. For the Father is seeking such [people to be] those who worship him. ²⁴God is Spirit, and it's necessary that those who worship him worship [him] in Spirit and truth." Since "Believe me, woman" is singular but "you will worship" plural, the woman represents a wider group made up of fellow Samaritans who along with her are shortly going to believe in Jesus. He says "neither on this mountain," where the Samaritan temple already lay in ruins, "nor in Jerusalem," where the Jewish temple was going to be destroyed in about forty years (A.D. 70). More importantly, he has already driven the sacrificial animals and their sellers out of the temple in Jerusalem, and he has cryptically declared his own body to be the new and true temple, the new and true dwelling place of God on earth (2:18–22). Theologically, then, the hour of a new kind of worship has already arrived in Jesus' arrival. But since the truth hasn't yet dawned even on his disciples, he also says that "an hour *is coming*"—it's yet future—when the Samaritan woman and others like her will actually worship neither on Mount Gerizim nor on Mount Zion (the site of the Jewish temple). Jesus doesn't mince any words when it comes to the Samaritans' heretical worship. But these words aren't any harsher than the whip with which he cleansed the Jewish temple, and no harsher than the words which accompanied that whip. And he's yet to say to Jews who'd believed him only superficially, "You're from [your] father the Devil" (8:44). But why does Jesus talk about worshiping "*what* you don't know" and "*what* we do know"? Since "the Father" is the object of worship,

in contrast with worship *by* the [fore]fathers, wouldn't we expect Jesus to say "whom" instead of "what"? The answer to this unexpected "what" lies in the following, "because salvation is from the Jews," which means that the Savior, the Messiah, comes from the Jewish people. So "what" does refer to God the Father, but shifts attention momentarily from his *person* to his *activity* of bringing salvation from the Jewish sphere into the world at large, including Samaritans. (By the way, Jesus' affirming that "salvation is from the Jews" undermines any interpretation of John's Gospel as anti-Semitic.)

What now does it mean to worship God the Father "in Spirit and truth"? Physically, to worship means to kneel down and bend one's head to the ground, as Muslims do today for example. So you might think that Jesus redefines worship as not prostrating your body but as prostrating your spirit. When "spirit" refers to a human spirit, though, it's normally made clear, as when the Apostle Paul says that God's Spirit bears witness "with *our* spirit" that we're the children of God (Romans 8:16). Jesus could have said, "The true worshipers will worship the Father in *their* spirits." But he didn't. Furthermore, we've already been told about the divine necessity of being born of water, even the Spirit—that is, the Holy Spirit, God's Spirit (see 3:5 with comments). So "Spirit" should be capitalized here as a reference to the Spirit of God. John has told us that Jesus the Word was full of grace and truth, and that grace and truth came on the scene through Jesus Christ (1:14, 17). John will yet quote Jesus as saying, "I am . . . the truth" (14:6). So "Spirit and truth" refers here, not to true worshipers' qualities of inwardness and sincerity, but to God's Spirit and to Jesus the truth. We have then the Trinity—God the Father, the Holy Spirit, and Jesus—wrapped together in Christian worship. There remains the preposition "in." What does it mean to worship God the Father *in* his Spirit and *in* his Son the truth. Well, just as we're to abide in Christ (that is, persevere in our Christian belief and conduct [15:1–10]), so also we're to abide in the Holy Spirit, whom Jesus sent as his replacement on earth (15:26). "Abide in" connotes permanence and closeness. It's only those who persevere in a close relation to Jesus and the Holy Spirit that the Father will accept as his true worshipers. And he's *seeking* such worshipers. Like the "Hound of Heaven" in Francis Thompson's famous poem, God is hunting us down—for our own sake as well as his—because he *loved* the world (3:16). "God is Spirit" confirms that the earlier reference to spirit is to the divine Spirit, not the human spirit: "Spirit" not just in a philosophical, metaphysical sense (spirit as opposed to dense matter), but also in a personal sense. And the *prediction* in 4:23 that true worshipers will worship the Father in Spirit and truth—this prediction turns in 4:24 into the divine *necessity* that those who worship him do so in Spirit and truth. Now, anything less than trinitarian worship on our part is unacceptable.

4:25–26: The woman tells him, "I know that Messiah is coming, the one called Christ. Whenever that one comes, he'll announce all things to us." ²⁶Jesus tells

her, "I am—the one speaking to you." The woman's statement reflects the Samaritan expectation that the Messiah would be a prophet. Jesus goes along with this expectation, as in his answer translated literalistically above. But there are several ways to take the answer: (1) "I'm the one speaking to you." But that's too obvious. *Of course* Jesus is the one speaking to her. (2) "I, the one speaking to you, am the Messiah, the one called Christ." Now that would fit nicely with the woman's preceding comment, "I know that Messiah is coming, the one called Christ." But why then does Jesus add the phrase, "the one speaking to you"? Why not just, "I'm the Messiah, the Christ," and forget about "the one speaking to you"? Well, by speaking to the woman, by telling her about her five husbands and her present, nonhusbandly man and answering her question about where to worship, Jesus was announcing all things to her, just as she expected of the prophetic Messiah. But his speaking also fulfills *our* expectations as readers of John's Gospel. We expect *the Word* to *speak*. And so he does. He speaks in this Gospel in a cascade of words, much more than in the other Gospels. There's more. Jesus doesn't say, "I am the Messiah, the one called Christ." He leaves "Messiah" and "Christ" to be supplied from the woman's preceding comment. It's what grammarians call an ellipsis: you leave out something to be supplied from the context. If you *don't* fill in the ellipsis here in 4:26, though, you get (3) "I am—the one speaking to you," which is a preview of Jesus' statement in 8:58, "Before Abraham came into existence, I am," and an echo of God's commanding Moses to tell the Israelites in Egypt that "I AM" had sent him (Exodus 3:14). So Jesus is not only Messiah, the Christ, not only the incarnate Word who speaks, but also the Word who because he was "in the beginning . . . with God" and "*was* God" (1:1) is the eternal I AM.

4:27–30: And at this point his disciples came and were marveling that he was talking with a woman. No one said to him, though, "What are you seeking?" or "Why are you talking with her?" 28So the woman left her bucket and went off into the city and tells the people, 29"Come see a man who told me all things, as many as they were, that I've done [compare 1:46]. Is this one perhaps the Christ?" 30They went out of the city and were coming to him. Even a married man wasn't supposed to talk with a woman, even his wife, in public space. For Jesus, a single man, to talk with a woman not his wife seemed scandalous. It still is in out-of-the-way Arab villages. The disciples' not daring to question Jesus gives an indirect testimony to his authority: he can talk with whomever he wants and ask for whatever he wants. The disciples' arrival and astonishment prompt the woman to go back into town. But she leaves her bucket. John makes a point of mentioning this detail. It's symbolic. She has discovered the source of living water, the water of eternal life; and in a theological but not physical sense she no longer needs the water of Jacob's well, the water of Samaritan religion. It's passé, just like the Jewish water of purification that Jesus turned into wine (2:1–11). That water represented Jewish religion just as

the water of Jacob's well represents Samaritan religion. Both are out-of-date, though Samaritan religion had also been spurious. The word translated "people" might refer only to the men of the town, but it can equally well include women. The woman's question whether Jesus is perhaps the Christ contains an element of uncertainty or even negativity, but urging her fellow townspeople to come and see Jesus favors that *she's* not uncertain. She's only accommodating her question to their not having had the experience with Jesus that she has just had. "All things, as many as they were, that I've done" is hyperbole, deliberate exaggeration for the sake of emphasis. From John's standpoint the expression points to Jesus' divine omniscience *without* exaggeration.

4:31–38: Meanwhile the disciples were asking him, saying, "Rabbi, eat." 32But he told them, "I have food to eat that you don't know about." 33So the disciples were saying to one another, "No one has brought him [anything] to eat, has he?" 34Jesus tells them, "My food is that I should do the will of the one who sent me and complete his work. 35You say, don't you, 'It's yet four months and the harvest comes'? Behold, I tell you, lift up your eyes and look at the fields in that they're already white for harvest. 36The one who reaps receives wages and gathers fruit [issuing] in eternal life with the result that the sower and the reaper rejoice together. 37For in this matter the saying is true, 'There's one who sows and another who reaps.' 38I've sent you to reap what you haven't labored on. Others have labored [on it] and you've entered into their labor." The disciples' questioning whether anyone has brought Jesus something to eat shows that they don't understand what he meant when he said he has food to eat that they don't know about. They take his words literally. He meant them figuratively, as with Nicodemus and the Samaritan woman. So he explains his figure of speech. Doing the will of God is like eating food—a necessity. Jesus calls God the one who *sent* him. The truth that God sent Jesus as a heavenly envoy to the world is going to get more and more prominent in John. Here it's based on Jesus as a prophet, because the Old Testament says repeatedly that God has sent the prophets, and the Samaritans expected the Messiah to be a prophet like Moses (as noted above). But in the larger context of John's Gospel, Jesus as the one whom God sent is also based on Jesus as the Word who preexisted with God in heaven, and on Jesus as God's Son, because a son was expected to take up his father's trade and carry on his father's work. In 4:34, then, Jesus talks about completing his Father's work. Here we have an anticipation of 19:28, where John says that on the cross Jesus knew that "all were now finished," and of 19:30, where Jesus says just before his death, "They're finished!" (see the comments on 19:30 for "*They're* finished!" instead of "*It* is finished"). And what is the Father's work that Jesus must complete? It's the work of accomplishing salvation for all who believe in Jesus as the one through whom God does the work of salvation (alternately "the works" [plural], as in 5:36; 6:28; 9:3–4; 10:32, 37; 14:10). You have only to believe.

It's usually thought that 4:35 contains a proverb: "You say, don't you [and here's the purported proverb], 'Yet four months and the harvest comes'?" as though it took four months from seedtime to harvest. But it takes considerably more than four months for grain to grow and ripen in Israel. So it's better to think Jesus is quoting what the disciples were saying about the grain at this particular point in the growing season. Harvest was still four months away. But Jesus refers to another kind of harvest that's right now—a harvest of converts: "Lift up your eyes." See, the Samaritans are coming! The woman that Jesus had been talking to was leading them out to see Jesus for themselves. They're within sight, their white garments compared by him to grain whitened and ripened for harvest. Jesus is the reaper. But who's the sower? Not the woman, because the sower is in the masculine gender, not the feminine. The sower must be John the Baptist since he started his ministry earlier than Jesus did, and 3:23–26 put the Baptist on the west side of the Jordan River, right next to Samaria, where the Samaritans likely heard him. In their culture, wages were paid at the close of every day and therefore indicated that a day's work was done. Here the wages consist of Jesus' joy, shared with the Baptist (compare the Baptist's statement in 3:29 that his joy is fulfilled in Jesus' ministry)—joy over the harvest of Samaritan converts that's about to take place.

Jesus hasn't yet sent the disciples to harvest converts, and he won't until 20:21 ("Just as the Father sent me, I too am sending you"). In the other Gospels Jesus sends the Twelve on a mission through Galilee (Mark 6:7–13; Matthew 9:35–10:42; Luke 9:1–6). But not in John's Gospel. Not till Jesus has completed his Father's work will Jesus send the disciples. So his statement in 4:38 that he sent them to reap what they hadn't labored on is spoken in anticipation, as is often done in this Gospel. Later, the disciples will continue the harvest of converts that Jesus has started here; and their harvesting will capitalize on the labor of Jesus throughout his ministry.

4:39–42: And many of the Samaritans from that city believed in him because of the word of the woman as she was testifying, "He told me all things that I've done." [40]So when the Samaritans came to him, they were asking him to abide [that is, stay] **with them. And he abode there two days; [41]and because of *his* word they believed in much greater measure [42]and were saying to the woman, "No longer do we believe because of your speaking, for we ourselves have heard [him] and know that this one is truly the Savior of the world."** John notes that many of the local Samaritans believed the report of a woman. How remarkable, in view of the male chauvinism in their culture! This remarkability enhances the value of the woman's testimony. Believing "because of the word" will occur also in 17:20 in reference to the disciples' testimony. So the woman here is acting as a disciple in getting others to believe. Jesus fulfilled the Samaritans' expectation that when the Messiah came he would announce to them all things (4:25). In a mundane sense abiding means staying, but for John it also carries

the theological meaning of a close and lasting relation between Jesus and believers in him. He stays here only two days, of course. But in the Jewish view two days with Samaritans is like forever! Jesus' word complements the woman's word—and surpasses it, for he is the Word. The word and words of the Word—they're what people get in John's Gospel. The greater measure in which the Samaritans believed may refer to numbers of believers (many more Samaritans believed) or to growth in belief (those who'd believed did so all the more [compare 2:11 with 1:35–51 and John's emphasis on perseverance]), or to both ideas. "The Savior of the world" harks back to 3:17: "For God didn't send [his] Son into the world in order that he might judge the world—rather, in order that the world might be *saved* through him." Saved from judgment. Saved for eternal life. And he's "truly" the world's Savior, because he is himself the truth (14:6). The Savior of the *world*—including even despised Samaritans!

JESUS' HEALING THE SON OF A ROYAL OFFICIAL BY MERELY SPEAKING AT A DISTANCE
John 4:43–54

4:43–45: And after the two days he went out from there into Galilee. [44]For Jesus himself testified, "A prophet doesn't have honor in his own fatherland." [45]So when he went into Galilee, the Galileans welcomed him because of having seen as many things as he'd done in Jerusalem in the festal assembly [during Passover]. **For they themselves had gone to the festival.** The two days refer of course to the two days Jesus stayed in Samaria according to 4:40, so that "from there" means from Samaria. Jesus' testimony reminds us that the whole of John's Gospel consists of a legal dispute, complete with witnesses, Jesus himself being a chief witness in his own behalf. In his testimony here, he accepts the title of "prophet" in agreement with the Samaritan woman's declaration back in 4:19. The Jews too expected an end-time prophet; for they asked the Baptist, "Are you the prophet?" (1:21). But a prophet doesn't have honor in his own country (the meaning of "fatherland"). Familiarity breeds contempt. Honor was—and still is—a big thing in Middle Eastern culture, as it used to be in ours. Just as we've lost much of our sense of shame, we've also lost much of our sense of honor. You can't have one without the other, not really. So for us, for whom shame has reduced to mere embarrassment, and honor to mere popularity, it's hard to appreciate the seriousness of Jesus' being without honor in his own country even though he's a prophet, a spokesman for God. And that's exactly what a prophet is, a spokesman for God (compare Exodus 7:1, where the Lord calls Aaron the "prophet" of Moses because he will speak for Moses). Beware, though. You don't dishonor a prophet of God, one of his spokesmen, and get away with it (see 2 Kings 2:23–24, where some young men ridicule the prophet Elisha for his baldness and two she-bears come out of the woods and tear some of them up).

But what is Jesus' "own fatherland," where he has no honor? In the other Gospels it's Galilee—particularly the city of Nazareth, where he grew up (Mark 6:1–6; Matthew 13:53–58; Luke 4:16–30). Here in John, though, he doesn't *leave* Galilee because he has no honor there. He goes *into* Galilee. Furthermore, the Galileans honor him by *welcoming* him; and the Samaritans have just *believed* in him. So his own fatherland must be Judea, where Jerusalem was located, not Galilee, where Nazareth was located. But Jesus wasn't a Judean. He was a Galilean. Nathaniel said about him, "Can anything good be from Nazareth?" (1:46). And in 7:52 the Sanhedrin will say that Jesus can't be a prophet, because "a prophet doesn't arise out of Galilee," whereas Jesus *has* arisen out of Galilee. So how can one say that Judea rather than Galilee is Jesus' "own fatherland," his home territory? Furthermore, 2:23 said that "when [Jesus] was in Jerusalem during the Passover . . . many believed in his name." And Nicodemus the Pharisee, who lived there, said to Jesus, "Rabbi, we know that as a teacher you've come from God. For no one can do these signs that you're doing unless God is with him" (3:2). Doesn't the belief of Nicodemus and others at the festival in Jerusalem count as honoring Jesus? If it does, then, Judea can't be Jesus' own fatherland that has failed to honor him.

On the other hand, however, the Jewish authorities in Judea challenged Jesus' authority to cleanse the temple: "What sign do you show us, [seeing] that you're doing these things?" (2:18). And Jesus left Judea for Galilee because he knew the Pharisees in Jerusalem had heard he was making and baptizing more disciples than the Baptist was—and they didn't like it (4:1). So Nicodemus seems to have been the exception, just as he will be when later he says to his fellow Sanhedrists, "Our law doesn't judge a man [in this case, Jesus], does it, unless it first hears from him and comes to know what he's doing?" (7:51).

Who then are those people who along with Nicodemus believed in Jesus' name when he was in Judea? Apparently Galileans who'd come to Jerusalem as pilgrims. As 2:23 says, they'd believed in his name because they'd seen the signs he was doing there. And here in 4:45 we read that now back in Galilee these Galileans welcomed Jesus because they'd seen as many things as he'd done in Jerusalem during the festival. Note that 4:45 doesn't say they'd seen "as many *signs*" as he'd done there (what the other Gospels call "miracles")—rather, "as many *things*," which include his cleansing the temple along with the signs. Unlike the Jewish authorities in Judea, then, the Galilean pilgrims accepted Jesus' right to cleanse the temple. "As many as" stresses the inclusion of temple-cleansing. In Jerusalem he didn't entrust himself to these Galilean pilgrims, though, because he knew their belief to be temporary (2:24–25); nor will he later, when after his feeding the five thousand in Galilee they'll try to take him by force and make him king (6:15). But here they honor him with a welcome.

Topographically, then, Galilee was Jesus' own fatherland, as in the other Gospels. But John is more concerned with theology than topography. So he presents Judea as Jesus' own fatherland, theologically speaking. The temple—his Father's house (2:16–17)—was there. The Pharisees and other Jewish authorities were there, the ones who should have led the nation to honor Jesus as king and Messiah. But they didn't. Instead, they challenged his authority. "He came into his own house [the temple, as 'his own things' can mean in 1:11], and his own ones [those in charge of his house the temple] didn't accept him." And why does John insert 4:43–45 anyway? Surely not just to tantalize us with a topographical problem that needs to be solved. John inserts these verses to explain how it happened that a royal official in Capernaum on the northwest shore of the Sea of Galilee came to hear about Jesus' presence in Galilee. Jesus had come back there because his theological fatherland of Judea hadn't honored him.

4:46–54: So he went again to Cana of Galilee, where he'd made the water wine. And in Capernaum there was a certain royal official whose son was ill. [47]On hearing, "Jesus has come out of Judea into Galilee," this [official] went from [Capernaum] to him and was asking that he should come down [to Capernaum] and heal his son. For he [the son] was about to die. [48]So Jesus said to him, "Unless you [plural] see signs and wonders, you [again plural] will never believe." [49]The royal official says to him, "Lord, come down before my child dies." [50]Jesus says to him, "Go, your son lives." The man believed the word that Jesus had spoken to him, and he started going. [51]And as he was already going down [to Capernaum] his slaves met him, saying that his child lives. [52]So he inquired from them the hour in which he [the son] got better. So they said to him, "The fever left him yesterday at the seventh hour." [53]So the father knew that [the fever left his son] in that hour in which Jesus had said to him, "Your son lives"; and he himself and his whole household believed. [54]And having come out of Judea into Galilee, Jesus again performed a sign, this [one as the] second [in Galilee]. Jesus isn't addressing the royal official alone when he says that "you" won't believe unless "you" see signs and wonders. He's addressing also the Galileans who've already believed because of the signs he performed in Jerusalem, and through them he's addressing all who read and hear this Gospel. Furthermore, he's implying that there's something wrong with belief that goes no deeper than admiration of the miraculous element. He adds "wonders" to "signs" to form a figure of speech that literary stylists call "hendiadys." You put two nouns together with "and," but one of them has the force of an adjective. So "signs and wonders" means "wonderful signs," "signs that cause wonder," with emphasis on the spectacular instead of the symbol in the sign, that is, the theological meaning of the sign. Saving faith requires an understanding of and belief in what God has done through his Son Jesus Christ, not just fascination, or even astonishment.

The royal official is so desperate, though, that he doesn't bother to say he believes without seeing signs and wonders. He addresses Jesus with "Lord" in the sense of "Sir," but again John wants us to understand "Lord" in the sense of deity (see 20:28). Cana, the location of Jesus at the moment, was situated in the Galilean hills; and Capernaum, where the official lived, was situated on the shore of the Sea of Galilee well over 600 feet below sea level. So he asks Jesus to come "down" before his child dies. The official uses the diminutive form of "child," so that it could be translated "little child," whereas his slaves use the normal form, simply "child." Whether the child really was little we don't know, because the diminutive form was also used for adults to express affection, as when John addresses his audience in 1 John with "[little] children" even though they're adults—and just as in popular love songs you call your sweetheart "baby" even though she's a grown woman: "Is you is or is you ain't my baby?" Even more, John is fond of using synonyms without distinguishing between their meanings (compare his use in 21:15–17 of a diminutive and a nondiminutive for sheep without any apparent distinction). So here the official's saying "little child" doesn't even have to express affection, though his desperation favors that it does.

Despite the official's desperate plea, Jesus doesn't go with him. Royal officialdom doesn't count with Jesus, who's king of his own kingdom, which isn't from this world (18:36). Instead, Jesus tells the official to go—without him—but with the announcement, "Your son lives." Well, my son may be alive still; but he might die if you don't come with me, the official could have thought or said. But he didn't. Rather, he hears—correctly—in Jesus' statement not just a description of the current state of the child, but also the promise of ongoing life. And note the shift from the verb of healing ("he was asking that [Jesus] come down and *heal* his son" [4:47]) to the verb of living ("Your son *lives*" [4:50, 53]). This shift signals a sign, a symbol. Healing morphs into living because the healing symbolizes a transfer from death (the child was about to die) to life—indeed, a transfer from *eternal* death to *eternal* life. "The *man* believed." He's not a high and mighty royal official any more, not in relation to Jesus. He's just an ordinary human being like the rest of us. He believes the spoken "*word*" that his son lives, the word spoken by Jesus, who is himself the Word spoken by God and who is "the Word *of life*" (1 John 1:1 [compare John 1:1–4]). He "believed . . . and started going." Here's true belief, belief that's acted out concretely—not just a mental event (though it is that in part) but, as the Apostle Paul puts it, "the obedience of faith" (Romans 1:5; 16:26).

The report of the man's slaves echoes the very verb that Jesus used, "lives," instead of the expected "is healed." So we have a second emphasis on the symbol of eternal life. But look at the adverb "already" in John's statement, "And as he was *already* going down his slaves met him saying that his child lives." John uses "already" (the underlying word can also be translated "now") a lot, as for example in 3:18: "The one not believing has been judged [= sentenced, condemned] already." But

here, since the child's living instead of dying symbolizes eternal life, "already" implies that believers get *eternal* life already in *this* life. They don't have to wait till eternity to get it. They have it *now, already*. The correspondence between the hour when Jesus said, "Your son lives," and the hour of the son's getting better proves the life-giving power of Jesus' word, that is, of Jesus *as* the Word. And for emphasis, that word is quoted a second time in 4:53. The seventh hour would be 1:00 P.M. if we count from sunrise, 7:00 P.M. if we count from noon. Since "yesterday" implies that the slaves stayed overnight in Cana after a day's walk from Capernaum (about twenty miles away), 7:00 P.M. seems the more likely time of Jesus' "word" (compare the comments on 1:39).

Now we learn that the boy's illness was a fever. The word for fever is a form of the word for fire. Is it too much to think that by specifying the illness as a kind of fire, John means the fire in the boy's body to symbolize the lake of fire into which John's book of Revelation says the wicked will be cast after the resurrection of their bodies and the Last Judgment (Revelation 20:11–14)? In any case, the fire of fever was dowsed by the water of life about which Jesus told the Samaritan woman. By leaving "the fever left his son" unwritten in verse 53 and to be supplied only mentally, John lets the emphasis fall on the healing word that Jesus the Word had spoken to the official: "Your son lives." The father believed when he heard his slaves' report. But he'd already believed when he heard *Jesus'* word, just as the disciples believed back in chapter 1 when they started following Jesus, and then believed again in chapter 2 when he turned the water to wine. They and this father believed again and again. They kept on believing. They persevered in their belief. That's true belief. And so remarkable is Jesus' life-giving word that the father's whole household believes along with him. In their culture the household included not only wife and children but also slaves. A household crisis has turned into household belief, and therefore into household salvation.

Finally, let's notice the redundancy in the last verse of chapter 4: "Jesus performed this *second* sign *again*." As reflected in the earlier translation, this statement doesn't mean that he repeated the second sign. It means that he performed a sign again, just as he had in Cana, so that this sign was the second one he performed in Galilee. John didn't need to use both expressions, "again" and "second." One of them would have been enough: "*Again* Jesus performed a sign" or "Jesus performed this *second* sign." But the redundancy of using both expressions puts all possible emphasis on this sign that represents life in place of death. No wonder Acts 3:15 calls Jesus the "Founder-Leader of life"!

THE HEALING OF A PARALYZED MAN
John 5:1–3a, 5–9a

5:1–3a, 5–9a: After these things there was a festival of the Jews, and Jesus went up to Jerusalem. ²And at the Sheep [Gate] in Jerusalem there's a pool called

Bethzatha in Aramaic, [a pool] **having five covered porches.** [3a]**In these were lying a multitude of invalid, blind, lame, paralyzed** [people]. [5]**And a certain man was there who'd been in his invalid state for thirty-eight years.** [6]**On seeing this** [man] **lying** [there] **and knowing that he'd already spent much time** [there], **Jesus says to him, "Do you want to get well?"** [7]**The invalid answered him, "Lord, I don't have a man to throw me** [probably in the weaker sense of helping put me] **into the pool when the water is stirred up. But while I'm coming, another person goes down** [into the pool] **ahead of me."** [8]**Jesus tells him, "Get up, pick up and carry your mat, and walk around."** [9a]**And immediately the man got well, and he picked up and carried his mat and walked around.** John doesn't tell the name of the festival, but describing it as "of the Jews" puts theological distance between Christians and Jews. Jesus went up as a pilgrim—"up" because of Jerusalem's location on Mount Zion in the hill country of Judea. Mention of the Sheep Gate suggests in anticipation of 10:1–16 that the man Jesus will heal is one of his sheep, and Jesus himself the good shepherd (compare the comments on 1:40–49). He'll certainly do something good for the invalid. Since John's text leaves "Gate" to be supplied mentally, his emphasis falls not on the identity of the gate but on the thought of sheep. For the pool, some manuscripts have "Bethsaida," "Belzetha," or "Bethesda" instead of "Bethzatha"; but "Bethzatha" is most likely original. These differences don't affect the theological meaning of the sign Jesus is about to perform, however.

Columns supported the roof of the porches that opened toward the pool. The number of porches, five, matches the number of the Samaritan woman's past husbands (5:16–18) and the number of books in the Mosaic law, claimed by both Jews and Samaritans. John's calling attention to this number suggests we should prepare for a symbolic allusion to what he stated outright in 1:17: "the Law was given through Moses; grace and truth came on the scene through Jesus Christ" (compare the portrayals of Jesus as the new Passover sacrifice and the new sanctuary, and his replacing the Jewish water of purification with the fine wine of his atoning blood [see 1:29–2:22 with 6:53–56]). In the fifth book of Moses the Israelites are said to have wandered in the wilderness for thirty-eight years because of their disobedience after receiving the Law (Deuteronomy 2:14). That number of years is the same as the number of years the man at the pool had been "in his invalid state." So just as the Jewish water of purification at the wedding feast in Cana represented the inadequacy of the Mosaic law, here the water of the five-porched pool represents the inadequacy of the Mosaic law. Mention of the Aramaic name of the pool just might add support for an allusion to the Mosaic law since that law was written in Hebrew, and the word translated "Aramaic," when translated literally, comes out as "Hebrew." (One and the same word does double duty for the two languages because of their close relation to each other.)

The earliest and best manuscripts don't contain 5:3b–4, concerning the invalid's waiting for the moving of the water, an angel's coming down and stirring up the water, and the healing of the first person to step into the water after it was stirred up. John's omitting an "and" before the last item in the list of disabled people suggests that the list is open to additions, as though the possibility of salvific healing is open to all. The word that describes the particular man in view—namely, "invalid"—doesn't have to do so much with a disease as with the effect of a disease or some other malady. "Paraplegic" and "quadraplegic" have been suggested here, but we can't be sure. Basically, this word means weakness; and it's the same word that in 4:46 described the effect of the nearly fatal fever on a royal official's son. So something of a parallel exists between these two stories. In both of them Jesus heals with a mere word, "Go, your son lives," and "Get up, pick up and carry your mat, and walk around." And just as the official's son got well in the very hour that Jesus spoke his word, here the invalid gets well "immediately." He was too weak to drag himself into the pool before someone else beat him to it; but now he's strong and healthy enough to get up, pick up his mat, carry it, and walk around. The official took Jesus' word not just as a statement about the current state of affairs but as a promise of ongoing life in place of death. The invalid takes Jesus' word not just as a command but as a promise of strength in place of weakness. And both men, the royal official and the invalid, exercise the obedience of faith. The official went home; the invalid gets up, picks up his mat, and walks around—even without knowing Jesus' identity, so strong is his belief in Jesus' word (see 5:12–13)! He has recognized the voice of his good shepherd (10:4).

But before the invalid does those things, Jesus *sees* this particular man (compare 1:48). Now 5:4 says that a multitude of variously incapacitated people were there. Jesus' singling out this one forecasts his statement in 15:16, "You didn't select me; rather, I selected you," and similar statements in 6:70; 13:18; 15:19. So we see divine initiative in the salvation represented by this healing, a divine initiative heightened by the invalid's not even knowing Jesus' identity. In the other Gospels people usually seek healing for themselves or their loved ones or friends. But here in John, Jesus takes the initiative, as he does in other respects too. For he is God incarnate. To use the language of 10:1–30 again, he also knows that this invalid is one of his "sheep." And he knows that this man has been an invalid for a long time ("much time"). Emphasis falls on the divine omniscience of Jesus rather than on his human compassion. (Not that he wasn't compassionate, of course; but we're looking for John's points of emphasis.) The age of the Mosaic law had been long. Now is the time of grace and truth (see 1:17 again). Jesus asks the invalid whether he *wants* to get well. So the selection of this one out of the multitude doesn't erase the element of human will (compare Revelation 22:17: "The person who wants [or 'wills' to do so] to is to take the water of life as a gift"). The two are complementary.

The invalid addresses Jesus with "Lord" in the sense of "Sir," but as usual John wants us to hear "Lord" in the sense of deity characterized by omniscience, selective grace, and the power to save. The invalid doesn't say he wants to get well, but he makes it obvious that he wants to by saying he doesn't have anybody to help him into the pool fast enough: "I don't have a *man* [that is, 'a human being']." Where merely human help is lacking, Jesus the divine as well as human Lord saves the day. And he doesn't have to wait till the water is stirred up. "Immediately" points to believers' possession of eternal life already in this age. They don't have to wait for the age to come.

A DISPUTE OVER THE SABBATH
BETWEEN THE JEWS AND JESUS
John 5:9b–47

5:9b–18: But it was Sabbath on that day. [10]**Therefore the Jews were saying to the healed** [man], **"It's Sabbath, and it's not permissible for you to carry your mat."** [11]**But he answered them, "The one who made me well—that one said to me, 'Pick up and carry your mat and walk around.'"** [12]**They asked him, "Who's the man that said to you, 'Pick** [it] **up and carry** [it] **and walk around'?"** [13]**But the one who'd been healed didn't know who it is, for Jesus had slipped out because a crowd was at the place.** [14]**After these things Jesus finds him in the temple** [courtyards] **and said to him, "Look, you've gotten well. Don't sin anymore, lest something worse happen to you."** [15]**The man went off and announced to the Jews that it's Jesus who made him well.** [16]**And on account of this** [the announcement] **the Jews started pursuing** [= persecuting] **Jesus, because he was doing these things on the Sabbath.** [17]**But Jesus answered them, "My Father is working till now, and I'm working."** [18]**So on account of this** [Jesus' answer] **the Jews were seeking all the more to kill** [him]**, because he was not only breaking the Sabbath, but also** [because] **he was calling God his own Father** [and thus] **making himself equal with God.** The very first verse in John's Gospel announced Jesus as the Word. The present story contains a triple reference to Jesus' performing this sign by speaking: (1) In 5:8 "Jesus *says* to him." (2) In 5:11 "the one who made me well—that one *said* to me." (3) In 5:12 "Who is the man that *said* to you . . . ?" In each of these instances, what Jesus said is quoted directly, "Get up, pick up and carry your mat, and walk around," except that in the third instance "Get up" is missing so as to draw attention to the question of working on the Sabbath (a piece of information John has withheld till now). It didn't break the Sabbath law for the invalid to get up. But it did break the Sabbath for him to pick up his mat and carry it as he walked around. That was work, and the very word "Sabbath" means "rest," the opposite of work. Exodus 31:14–15 prescribes the death penalty for Sabbath-breaking, and Numbers 15:32–36 records a carrying out of that penalty. Naturally, Jewish rabbis discussed what counted and didn't count as work. Otherwise, how would you know what you could and couldn't do on the Sabbath? And sometimes the rabbis

differed from each other on this question. But there's no question here of interpreting the Sabbath law. The ex-invalid doesn't argue that carrying his mat is allowable on the Sabbath. Nor does Jesus argue that carrying a mat doesn't break the Sabbath, or that the Jews have misinterpreted the Sabbath law. (Apparently "the Jews" are the Jewish authorities who try to enforce the prohibition of work on the Sabbath.) And in an editorial statement John, the author of the Fourth Gospel, says outright that Jesus was breaking the Sabbath (5:18: "because he was not only breaking the Sabbath"). We should note that *Jesus*, not just the healed man, was breaking it. Jesus wasn't carrying the mat, but he'd commanded the man to. So the fault lay with *him*, Jesus.

We have a contest of authority, then. It's not a contest between Jesus' authority and that of "the Jews." It's a contest between Jesus' authority and the authority of the Mosaic law prohibiting work on the Sabbath. According to 5:11 the ex-invalid considers his healing a sign of the healer's superior authority—whoever his healer is. He doesn't yet know the healer's identity. "He answered them," but his accusers hadn't asked him a question; so his answer is really a response to their accusation. The response, "The one who made me well—that one said to me, 'Pick up and carry your mat and walk around,'" amounts to what we might say: "Get lost! Resting every Sabbath, and every other day as well, for thirty-eight years didn't make me well. But the one who spoke to me did make me well, and he didn't just *permit* me to walk around carrying my mat. He *commanded* me to. So there!"

In 5:12 the Jews ask the healed man to identify his healer. It looks as though they expected him not just to name his healer but also to point him out then and there. And they call his healer "the man [the human being] that spoke to you." Jesus certainly was a human being, but he was more. He was God in human flesh: "the Word was God" (1:1). And this additional, divine identity of Jesus comes out clearly in 5:18: "[he was] making himself equal with God." According to 5:13 the reason the ex-invalid didn't know it was Jesus who'd healed him was that Jesus had withdrawn because a crowd was at that location. But did he want to get *away* from the crowd? Or did the crowd give him an opportunity to withdraw by melting *into* them? It's hard to say, but the latter is a good guess. And where's the location, "the place"? This could be a back-reference to the Pool of Bethzatha. If so, the crowd would presumably be the multitude of invalids mentioned in 5:3. The location would be somewhere else, unspecified, if the healed man had already walked away from the pool; and the crowd would consist of people other than the invalids at the pool. But in that case Jesus seems to have accompanied the man he'd healed, and the man's not yet knowing Jesus' identity becomes hard to understand. So again it's a good guess that they're both still at the pool, and that Jesus has melted into the crowd gathered there.

Later, and more importantly, Jesus *finds* the man—another instance of divine initiative. The physical healing won't truly represent the larger work of eternal salvation unless the man knows it's Jesus who healed him, for salvation requires knowing Jesus (10:14). And where does Jesus find the man? In the temple (a few hundred yards south of the pool). Now 2 Samuel 5:8 says that "the blind and the lame shall not come into the house ['of the Lord,' added by the Greek translation of the Old Testament]." And Jews understood this statement to mean that physically disabled people shouldn't enter the temple courts. That's what made the coming of blind and lame people to Jesus in the temple, and his healing them, so striking in Matthew 21:14. Here, though, the man is already healed; and his presence in the temple and his having *walked* there—he's no longer at the Pool of Bethzatha—demonstrate his healing. Jesus himself emphasizes the point: "Look! You've gotten well," as if to say, "You've walked all the way here, carrying your mat, and you're no longer lying on it at the pool. Hurrah!" But then Jesus adds, "Don't sin any more lest something worse happen to you." We know from 9:1–3 that physical ailments aren't necessarily punishments for particular sins. There, the disciples will ask Jesus, "Rabbi, who sinned, this [blind man] or his parents, with the result that he was born blind?" Jesus will answer, "Neither did this man sin nor did his parents." Here in chapter 5, though, the command not to sin *any more* implies that this man's disability *was* punishment for a particular sin. And that implication is supported by the allusion to the Israelites' wandering in the wilderness for thirty-eight years, because it was their refusal to enter the promised land immediately that led to their wandering as a punishment from God.

What might the command not to sin any more mean to the audience of John's Gospel back in the first century? John is writing to keep them believing in the true Christian gospel instead of apostatizing over to the heresy of Gnosticism. And one of the branches of Gnosticism taught that if you were one of the elite, one of the select—that is, if you were a Gnostic, somebody who had superior knowledge—you could ignore the moral and ethical rules that ordinary mortals think they have to live by. In fact, not only *can* you break those rules. You *should* break them, and by breaking them show your superiority. You're not sinning, because the sinning part of you—that's your body—isn't a real part of you. It's only your spirit that counts as your true self. This is the sort of teaching that John attacks in his first letter: "If we say, 'We don't have sin,' we're misleading ourselves and the truth isn't in us. . . . If we say, 'We haven't sinned,' we make him [God] a liar, and his Word isn't in us. My children, I'm writing to you in order that you not sin. . . . Everyone who is abiding in him [Christ] isn't sinning. Everyone who is sinning has neither seen him nor known him [despite the Gnostics' pretension to knowledge, the very term 'Gnostic' meaning 'knower']. . . . The person who is practicing sin is from the Devil . . . . Everyone who has been born from God isn't practicing sin" (1 John 1:8, 10–2:1; 3:6, 8–9 [see also the introduction to 1 John]). So John notes that Jesus says to the healed man, "Don't sin any more."

The healing represents salvation, and salvation means being saved from sin, not only from its penalty but also from its power over your life and conduct (compare Romans 8:3–4). "Lest something worse happen to you"—worse than the thirty-eight years of being an invalid. That sounds pretty bad. What is this worse something? Well, if the healing represents salvation, eternal life, the worse thing must be damnation, eternal death—an eternity of existence in separation from God, what John calls being lost; for human beings were made to live in communion with God, so that to exist apart from him is absolute ruination. And that will be the fate of those who don't stop the practice of sinning, including those who think they're above the rules.

According to 5:15 the healed man went away and reported to the Jews. Since Jesus had found him in the temple courts, the man's going away implies that the Jews weren't there. His report that it was Jesus who'd made him well doesn't answer their earlier question. They'd asked him, "Who's the man that said to you, 'Pick up and carry your mat and walk around'?" They hadn't paid any attention to the man's being healed. They were concerned only about his, and then his healer's, breaking the Sabbath. But the man answers in terms of Jesus' having healed him. That's all he cares about. And he gives all credit to Jesus, as he should. So we shouldn't think the man is informing on Jesus to save his own neck. After all, he omits Jesus' having told him to carry his mat when he reports back to the Jews. He mentions only Jesus' having made him well.

Starting 5:16 is the phrase, "On account of this." You might think "this" points backward to the man's report that Jesus had healed him. Read on, though. "On account of this the Jews pursued Jesus, because he was doing these things on the Sabbath." "This" refers forward to Jesus' doing these things on the Sabbath. But why the plural, "these things"? Hadn't Jesus done only one thing on the Sabbath? Actually, no. He'd done two things, both of which broke the Sabbath. First, he'd worked on the Sabbath by performing a sign, which John also calls a "work." "Signs" and "works" are largely synonymous in his vocabulary. The man had been lying at the pool for thirty-eight years. He wasn't a case for the emergency room. Jesus could have waited till the next day to heal him. But he didn't, and by not waiting he broke the Sabbath. Second, Jesus told the invalid to pick up his mat and walk around while carrying it. So Jesus broke the Sabbath by proxy, so to speak. He was responsible for the man's working on the Sabbath.

At this point most of our translations say the Jews were "persecuting" Jesus (5:16). That's not a wrong translation, and later—in 15:20—Jesus will use the same verb in telling his disciples, "If they've persecuted me, they'll persecute you too." But let's not forget that to persecute means to pursue quite literally, as in Matthew 10:23, for example: "But whenever they persecute you [that is, pursue you] in this city, flee into another [city]." So here the Jews pursue Jesus, physically, and catch up with him, as shown by his answering them in 5:17. Since they've not asked him any question, his answer is a response to their pursuit. And his response is astonishing. It doesn't interpret the Sabbath law in a way that allows humanitarian work. You'll find that defense in Mark 2:27: "The Sabbath came into being on account of [= for the sake of] humanity, and not humanity on account of the Sabbath." No, Jesus' present response is that when he heals, he's coworking with God his Father. Since he, Jesus, is breaking the Sabbath, then, so is God: "My Father is working till now, and I'm working." "Till *now*"—this very day, a Sabbath day at that! God hasn't stopped working for the sake of the Sabbath; so neither has Jesus, because as a dutiful Son he's an apprentice who does exactly what he sees his Father doing. And the "till" in "till now" implies that he and his Father started working long before now, as in 1:3: "All things came into existence through him [the Word, who became Jesus], and apart from him there came into existence not even one thing that did come into existence." As the preincarnate Word, Jesus was God's agent in creation. God rested on the seventh day, according to Genesis 2:2–3; but because of the fall of humanity into sin, he and Jesus have been working ever since for the healing of human beings from the sin that incapacitates them, that makes them moral invalids.

The Jews' expression, "*his own* Father," echoes Jesus' expression, "*my* Father." The Jews correctly understand that Jesus is claiming equality with God. So they seek "all the more" to kill him—for this claim of equality with God as well as for breaking the Sabbath. What began with a gracious healing turns into an ugly attempt to kill the healer. This is the first of repeated attempts in John (or we might say of a prolonged attempt) to kill Jesus. But Jesus' "hour" hasn't yet come (compare 2:4), and nobody takes his life from him. He'll lay it down on his own initiative. When his hour does come and he initiates his own death, Pilate will say to the Jews, "You take him and judge him according to your law." And, ironically, they'll have to admit, "It's not permitted for us to kill anyone" (18:31). To their shame, they'll have to get a special dispensation from Pilate, the Roman governor they hate. The most blessed irony, though, is that the killing of Jesus, which will take the form of Roman crucifixion, not the form of Jewish stoning—the killing of Jesus, once he allows or, better, determines it, will provide the very salvation from sin that the healing of the invalid symbolizes. You can't help but think of Isaiah 53:5: "He was pierced for our transgressions. He was crushed for our iniquities. The punishment that brought us peace came on him. And by his wounds we are healed."

5:19–23: Therefore Jesus answered and was saying to them, "Amen, amen I tell you, the Son can't do anything on his own, except [that he can do] **what he sees the Father doing. For whatever things that one does, these things also the Son does likewise.** [20]**For the Father loves the Son and shows him all things that he himself is doing, and he'll show him greater works than these in order that you may marvel.** [21]**For just as the Father raises the dead and makes** [them] **alive, in this way also the Son makes alive those whom he**

wills [to make alive]. [22]**For not even the Father judges anyone; rather, he has given all judgment to the Son,** [23]**in order that all may honor the Son just as they honor the Father. The person who doesn't honor the Son doesn't honor the Father who sent him."** Again Jesus' answer is a response, since the Jews haven't asked him a question. The reason for the response is their seeking to kill him. The subject matter of the response deals with their taking offense at his claim to equality with God as the basis for breaking the Sabbath. The front-loaded, double "Amen" emphasizes the truth of Jesus' response. What is that truth? It's that the relationship of the Son to the Father is so close that to say the Son doesn't *in fact* do anything except what he sees his Father doing is too *weak* a statement. The relationship is so close that the Son isn't even *able* to do anything other than what he sees the Father doing. Furthermore, the relationship is so close that *whatever* the Father does, Jesus the Son does too. And the Father shows his Son *everything* that he (the Father) is doing. No trade secrets here! Jesus, the apprentice Son, sees and imitates the workmanship of the master craftsman, God his own Father. Indeed, his work is *God's* work. God's work is *his* work. They work together on the same project: in this case, the healing of an invalid—something like two surgeons performing the same operation together.

The correspondence is complete, then. There's no slippage between Jesus' actions and those of God the Father. There's not even a difference. And the basis of this correspondence is the Father's love for the Son. It's what motivates him to show the Son everything he's doing. Theologians talk about the "hypostatic" union of the persons of the Trinity. "Hypostatic" means "having to do with the underlying divine essence, or nature, that all three persons of the Trinity have in common with each other." But the Trinity isn't only a matter of shared, static essence. It's also a matter of movement, interaction, social exchange—in our present passage, of love, divine love, God's love for Jesus his Son.

What the Father is doing and showing Jesus presently is works of salvation like the healing that Jesus and the Father have just performed in conjunction with each other. (Here "works" replaces "signs" because of the controversy over working on the Sabbath.) The greater works that they'll perform together in the future are resurrections, raisings of the dead. You can think ahead to chapter 11, where Jesus raises Lazarus from the dead, and to Jesus' raising himself from the dead (chapter 20 with 10:17–18). "In order that you may marvel" (5:20)—but marveling isn't believing, because believing entails personal commitment, the entrusting of your salvation to Jesus as God's Son. Even unbelievers such as Jesus' audience will marvel, though. The Son makes alive those whom he *wills* to make alive (5:21). Later, in 5:29, he'll distinguish between a resurrection of life and a resurrection of judgment, a resurrection that results in life and a resurrection that results in judgment. Since judgment contrasts with life, judgment must mean condemnation, lostness, "the second death" (Revelation 2:11; 20:6, 14;

21:8). So 5:21 must refer, not to a general resurrection of everybody, the righteous and the wicked alike, but only to the resurrection of the righteous. Only their resurrection results in life, eternal life. And this kind of resurrection includes only those whom Jesus wishes it to include. Here we have divine selection again: "You didn't select me; rather, I selected you" (15:16).

All this happens in cooperation with God the Father. But there's an exception to the cooperation between Father and Son. The Father doesn't judge anyone. He has given all judgment to the Son. Together, they raise the select to eternal life. But the resurrection to judgment—that's the business of the Son by himself, alone. Why has the Father delegated judgment to the Son alone? "In order that all may honor the Son just as they honor the Father" (5:23). So it isn't only that Jesus makes himself equal with God, as 5:18 says. God himself makes Jesus his equal! So important is Jesus' equality of honor with God that failure to give him such honor means failure to honor God. For God is the Father who sent his Son Jesus. It's therefore troubling to hear Christians talk a lot about God without talking very much about Jesus, as happens among Christians who try to be politically correct.

In summary of this paragraph (5:19–23), it begins with a leading statement to the effect that Jesus the Son can't do anything unless he sees God his Father doing it. After that comes a series of four explanations that unpack the leading statement. Each explanation starts with the conjunction "For": (1) For the Son imitates the Father's actions. (2) For the Father shows all his actions, present and future, to the Son. (3) For the Father and the Son cooperate in making certain people alive. (4) For the exception to their cooperation is the Father's having given all judgment to the Son.

5:24–30: "Amen, amen I tell you that the person who hears my word and believes the one who sent me has eternal life and isn't going into judgment; rather, he has transferred out of death into life. ²⁵Amen, amen I tell you that an hour is coming, and now is, when the dead will hear the voice of the Son of God; and those who hear will live. ²⁶For just as the Father has life in himself, in this way also he has given to the Son to have life in himself. ²⁷And he has given him authority to do [= execute] judgment, because he [the Son of God] is the Son of Man. ²⁸Don't marvel at this, because an hour is coming in which all those in the tombs will hear his voice. ²⁹And the ones who've done good things will come out into the resurrection of life [that is, with the purpose and the result of life], **but those who've done evil things** [will come out] **into the resurrection of judgment** [that is, with the purpose and result of judgment]. ³⁰**I can't do anything on my own. Just as I hear, I judge; and my judgment is right, because I don't seek my will—rather, the will of the one who sent me."** Jesus distinguishes between two different resurrections in 5:28–29, just as Revelation 20:4–6, 11–15 does. But 5:24 shows that his talk about making certain people alive refers not only to bodily resurrection in the future. It refers also to the possession of eternal life even before

bodily resurrection: "*has* eternal life" (present tense), "*has transferred* out of death into life." The body may die, but the eternal life remains, so that the resurrection will be a resurrection of life, not a resurrection of judgment: "isn't going into judgment" (5:24). To whom do these words apply? To the person who hears Jesus' word and believes the one who sent him. Here we have Jesus' own commentary on the healing of the royal official's son at the end of chapter 4 and on the healing of the invalid at the start of chapter 5. Jesus *said* to the official, "'Go, your son lives.' The man believed the word that Jesus had spoken to him" (4:50). Jesus *said* to the invalid, "Get up, pick up and carry your mat, and walk around" (5:8–9). Those healings symbolize hearing and believing Jesus' word for eternal life and eternal health. We can include eternal health because Revelation 22:2 says that the leaves of the tree of life in the New Jerusalem will be for the healing of the nations of the saved, so that not only death but also pain will be eliminated.

Where 4:50 talked about believing Jesus' word, though, 5:24 talks about hearing it and about believing the one who sent Jesus. Not that there's a contradiction here. Rather, 5:24 interprets believing Jesus' word to mean hearing it and believing God to be the sender of Jesus who speaks the word, because—as we learned in 5:19–23—Jesus and God are coworkers for our salvation and because—as we learned in 1:1–2—Jesus the speaker of the word is himself the Word who was with God and was God. And what is the subject matter of the word of this Word? It's Jesus himself. In John's Gospel Jesus is constantly talking about himself, presenting himself in his words. God sent me, he says. I'm his one-and-only Son. I'm the Son of Man, who came from heaven. I'm the bread of life, light of the world, good shepherd, the resurrection, the life, the way, the truth, and so on and on. In the other Gospels Jesus talks constantly about the kingdom of God; in this Gospel, about himself.

Another double "Amen" starts 5:25 just as it started 5:24. The *coming* hour is the future time of bodily resurrection. The hour which *now* is—that hour is the present time of receiving eternal life prior to bodily resurrection. Hearing the *voice* of the Son of God in 5:25 parallels hearing Jesus' *word* back in 5:24. You'd expect the Word to have a voice, wouldn't you? Sure enough, he does. Otherwise you'd never *hear* him. And 5:26 tells us *how* it is that the Son of God's voice gives life. That voice emanates from *within* him; and since *life* resides in him as God the Father's gift to him of the very same life that resides in the Father, that voice carries with it life, the shared life of the Father and Son—therefore *eternal* life.

In 5:27 Jesus shifts from life to judgment. Not only has the Father given the Son to have life in himself. He has also given the Son authority to execute judgment, that is, to impose the penalty of eternal death. And why? Because Jesus isn't only the Son of God. He's also the Son of Man. And in Daniel 7, Jesus' probable source for this expression, a figure like a son of man (that is, like a human being) is associated with a court that sits for judgment on the heathen. In 5:20 Jesus said that the

Father will show the Son the greater works of raising the dead and giving the select ones eternal life in order that the nonselect may marvel. (Elsewhere Jesus uses the language of human belief equally strongly, but here he uses the language of divine selection.) Now 5:27 tells the nonselect not to marvel at the Son of Man's executing judgment on them. They should *expect* it because of their evil doings.

We've already noted that 5:28–29 refers to two resurrections in the future. Jesus' voice comes into the picture again: it'll be so loud as to wake the dead from their slumber in the tombs. The ones who rise to enjoy the life of God the Father and his Son Jesus Christ—those people are described as the ones who did good things in their mortal lifetimes. The ones who rise to suffer judgment are described as those who practiced evil in their mortal lifetimes. It's not that doing good things makes you deserve eternal life. Throughout his Gospel John makes it clear and emphatic that you get eternal life as a pure gift, as a result of mere believing in Jesus as your Savior because of what he's done for you by dying for your sins and rising for your eternal life. But genuine belief shows itself in avoiding evil and doing good. Not *just* avoiding evil—there's no morally neutral zone—but *also* doing good. So the question for us Christians is: How much good are we doing? Enough to give evidence of genuine belief?

Wrapping up this paragraph is a reminder that Jesus can't do anything on his own (5:30). Even though the Father who sent him has given all judgment to him, he'll still judge according to what he hears is his Father's will. And that fact guarantees a right judgment. Whatever problems the doctrine of judgment throws up in our minds (and those problems were no less to the minds of ancient people than they are to us moderns)—whatever those problems, Jesus teaches that he'll make no mistakes in judgment. It'll be right. It'll be just. That thought is reassuring. It can also be frightening. "The fear of the Lord is the beginning of wisdom" (Psalm 111:10; Proverbs 9:10).

The theme of testimony, or witness, runs throughout John, so that the whole Gospel constitutes a legal dispute. The world puts Jesus on trial, a prolonged trial. But as 5:30 indicated, the reverse is true too. Jesus turns the tables and puts the world on trial: "Just as I hear, I judge; and my judgment is right." What we have, then, is a double trial. The paragraph 5:31–47 starts with Jesus on trial before the world and mutates into the world on trial before Jesus. He says in *5:31*: **"If I testify about myself, my testimony isn't true."** Jesus is speaking from the standpoint of the Jews, who considered self-testimony untrustworthy and therefore unacceptable. See, for example, 8:13: "Therefore the Pharisees said to him, 'You're testifying about yourself. Your testimony isn't true [= it's invalid].'" Jesus speaks from this standpoint, which isn't his own, to stress the Jews' unbelief. They won't believe his testimony no matter what.

Since Jesus' self-testimony is unacceptable to the Jews, he appeals to other testimony in his behalf. *5:32*:

"There's another who is testifying about me, and I know that true is the testimony he's testifying about me." "True is the testimony" is awkward English, but "true" comes first for emphasis—and for an emphatic contrast: "*not* true" in 5:31 versus "*true*" in 5:32. So here's testimony that according to the Jews' *own* standard is true. It's not self-testimony. Despite its conforming to their standard, though, they don't know this testimony to be true. Yet Jesus does. And the fact that he does—this fact calls attention to his divine omniscience and implies the Jews' ignorance. (And let's remember that they're a representative slice of "the world.")

But who is this other person that's giving true testimony about Jesus? We might think of John the Baptist, because the very next verse mentions him. *5:33*: **"You've sent** [priests and Levites] **to John, and he has testified to the truth."** But that possibility isn't likely, because Jesus goes on to say that he doesn't accept testimony from a human being, and the Baptist was a human being. *5:34*: **"But I don't accept testimony from a human being. Nevertheless, I'm saying these things that you might be saved."** So we might think that in 5:32 Jesus anticipated 5:36 by referring to the works that he does as testifying about him. But 5:32 spoke about a person, in the singular, not about works, in the plural. So the other person in 5:32 is probably God the Father, whom Jesus will get around to mentioning in 5:37. Meanwhile, in 5:33 Jesus summarizes the Baptist's testimony recorded in 1:19–27: "John [the Baptist] . . . has testified to the truth." What is this truth? It's the truth *about* Jesus and the truth that *is* Jesus (14:6).

Why doesn't Jesus accept the testimony, the witness, of a human being like the Baptist? Well, what is the other meaning of "witness"? If you witness something you're seeing it. And then you witness in the other sense: you *bear* witness, you testify, to what you've seen, to what you've witnessed. Let's keep these two meanings in mind and ask ourselves about Jesus' origin. According to John's Gospel, Jesus came from God the Father in heaven. Why then doesn't Jesus accept the witness of the Baptist, his testimony? Because in the very nature of the case, as a human being the Baptist didn't see, didn't witness, Jesus in Jesus' pre-existent state as the Word who was with God and was God "in the beginning" (1:1). So the Baptist's testimony is derived, secondary, mediated by divine revelation. Jesus wants and needs a primary witness. Nevertheless, he mentions the Baptist's testimony because it's just possible that the Jews who sent a delegation to the Baptist might get saved by believing his testimony, secondary though it is.

In *5:35* Jesus elaborates the possibility: **"That one** [the Baptist] **was the burning and shining lamp, and for an hour you were willing to bask in his light."** In 1:8–9 we were told that the Baptist wasn't the true light, but came to testify about the true light. Jesus is the light of the world, of course, the sun that sheds its rays everywhere (8:12). The Baptist's light was that of a mere lamp, such as you'd use in the darkness before dawn, before the sun comes up. The Baptist's lamplight represents his testimony concerning the true light. We read about his testimony in the middle of chapter 1 and at the end of chapter 3. And it was enough to lead some people to salvation. In chapter 1 it led Andrew and an unnamed person (probably John the apostle) to salvation, for they started following Jesus as a result of the Baptist's testimony (compare Revelation 1:9–3:22, where churches are portrayed as lampstands of Christian testimony to get people saved by leading them to the true light).

Sadly, though, the Jews in general were willing to enjoy the Baptist's lamplight for only a while, "an hour," but not an hour as sixty minutes. For them an hour was the shortest unit of time. So here an hour means a short while. In John's Gospel the Baptist had his hour, and Jesus will have one of his own. In what sense did the Jews enjoy the Baptist's testimony? Well, they came out in droves to hear his preaching and be baptized by him. The first-century Jewish historian Josephus attests to John's great popularity. But when in chapter 1 John denied being the Christ or Elijah or the expected prophet and testified about Jesus instead, the Jews' enjoyment of John petered out. It lasted just a little while. The lesson here is to beware of hitching your wagon to a lesser light, even one in the Christian world. There's only one true light, Jesus; and the lesser lights are duty-bound to testify about him, as the Baptist did, even at the cost of turning people away from themselves.

Jesus says in *5:36*: "**But I have a testimony greater than John's.**" This testimony turns out to be the works that God the Father has given him to complete: "**For the works that the Father has given me that I should complete them—the works themselves that I'm doing are testifying about me** [to the effect] **that the Father has sent me.**" Fast forward to 19:28, 30. There Jesus, knowing that "all were now finished," said as his last word from the cross, 'They're finished!'" (The verbs "complete" and "finish" have the same Greek stem.) That is, Jesus' works were finished, completed. These works are the signs that he does throughout the Gospel: turning water to wine, healing the royal official's son, healing the invalid, and doing more to come—all of them symbolizing the comprehensive work of salvation. When Jesus has finished these works, salvation will be complete for the taking. Nothing will need to be added. *Your* works aren't needed. Just believe. Believing is the only work God requires—if you can call it a work (though Jesus will in 6:29). Meanwhile, before Jesus finishes his works, they're already testifying about him to the effect that God has sent him. How do they do that? Note first that testimony isn't proof. It's evidence. Jesus' works testify that God sent him in that they provide evidence that he is working out God's plan of salvation—*God's* plan, as indicated by the fact that he *gave* Jesus these works. But precisely because he did, he's the ultimate witness to Jesus.

5:37: "**And the Father who sent me—that one has testified about me.**" The emphasis falls on "that one," referring to "the Father," in contrast with "that one" in 5:35, referring to the Baptist, a mere human being. When did the Father testify about Jesus? Not at Jesus' baptism, because Jesus says his audience have never heard the Father's voice: "**You've neither heard his voice at any time.**" Besides, John's Gospel doesn't quote what the Father said at Jesus' baptism: "This is my beloved Son, in whom I took delight" (Matthew 3:17; similarly Mark 1:11; Luke 3:22). John's Gospel doesn't even say that Jesus got baptized. "**Nor have you seen his form,**" Jesus adds. In 14:3–9 Jesus will tell Philip, "The person who has seen me has seen the Father." So the Father's "form" here in 5:37 must differ from Jesus, because the Jews have seen Jesus but they haven't seen the Father's form. Since 1:18 said that no one has ever seen God, maybe the Father's form is a projection of his glory, such as Old Testament prophets saw, an appearance different from God the Father himself. In any case, Jesus' audience haven't seen it. The Father's testimony about Jesus hasn't consisted in the Father's voice or form, then.

But now Jesus says in *5:38*: "**And you don't have his word abiding in you.**" The very next verse will refer to "the Scriptures." We would say, "the Old Testament." The psalmist says, "Your word have I hid in my heart" (Psalm 119:11). So Jesus seems to be saying that his audience haven't hid God's word, the Scriptures, in their hearts. Those Scriptures are the Father's testimony about Jesus. But there's probably a double meaning here. The first verse of chapter 1 identified Jesus as the Word who was with God and was God. And later, in 15:4, Jesus will talk about his abiding in believers as well as their abiding in him: "Abide in me, and I [will abide] in you." So when he says that his audience don't have God's word abiding in them, he also means that they don't have him, Jesus the Word, abiding in them. Why don't they? "**Because the one whom that one sent—this one you don't believe.**" They don't believe the one whom God sent, again Jesus, who is God's living Word alongside God's written word.

Some translations make the first part of *5:39* a command: "**Search the Scriptures.**" But that translation doesn't jibe very well with the followup, "because you think that in them you have eternal life." (The stress lies on "in them [the Scriptures].") For a command, you'd expect something like "Search the Scriptures, because in them you *have* eternal life" (not "you *think* . . ."). So the better translation is a statement rather than a command: "**You search the Scriptures because you think that in them you have eternal life.**" Do the Jews think so correctly? No. According to John, eternal life is to be found in Jesus the Word: "In him was life" (1:4). "I am the resurrection and the life" (11:25). "I am . . . the life" (14:6). Eternal life is to be found in Jesus, not in the Scriptures, contrary to what the famous first-century Jewish rabbi Hillel said: "The more study of the Law, the more life. . . . If a man has gained for himself words of the Law, he has gained for himself life in the world to come." But the Scriptures do *testify* to Jesus as the source of eternal life. So he adds "**and those are the ones testifying about me.**" Most English translations have "these" instead of "those." But the word is definitely "those" (over there) rather than "these" (right here). "Those" puts the Scriptures at some distance to stress that they aren't the source of eternal life—rather, witnesses to the source, which is Jesus.

Despite the Jews' searching the Scriptures, though, they don't accept the testimony of the Scriptures in Jesus' behalf. Why not? Jesus answers the question with his statement in *5:40*: **"And you're not willing to come to me that you might have life."** You were willing to enjoy the Baptist for a while, Jesus said, but you're not willing to come to me. It's a lack of willingness, then, not a lack of testimonial evidence, that keeps people from coming to Jesus for life. You'd think that for such a prize as eternal life people would be eager to come to Jesus with even less testimonial evidence than there actually is. But at bottom, the sin that corrupts our will contains a certain irrationality. Given the testimonial evidence, it doesn't make good sense not to come to Jesus for life. Not only nonsensical. Also dangerous. Is there any greater danger, any greater disaster, than to search the Scriptures and fail to arrive at their very goal?

We might wonder why Jesus' audience aren't willing to come to him for life. An answer comes in *5:41–44* and begins with Jesus' statement, **"Glory** [= honor] **from human beings I don't accept."** Emphasis falls on "glory from human beings," which comes first in the sentence. Why doesn't Jesus accept such glory? Because accepting glory from human beings would corrupt with self-love the love of God that's in him. By contrast, Jesus goes on to say, [42]**"But I know you, that the love of God you don't have in yourselves."** For emphasis "the love of God" moves ahead of the verb and its subject. Jesus' divine omniscience comes into prominence again. Jesus knows us from the inside out. It's a nice question whether "the love of God" means God's love for us (as in 3:16: "God loved the world") or the love of human beings for God (as in Deuteronomy 6:5: "You shall love the Lord your God . . ."). Perhaps both, since love from God and love for God are intertwined. It's God's love for us that prompts our love for him: "We love, because he first loved us" (1 John 4:19). "In yourselves" means that this love penetrates to the very core of our being and emanates from that core. There's nothing superficial about it.

Lacking the love of God equates with rejecting Jesus, because he's the expression of that love—and is himself God. So Jesus says, [43]**"I've come in my Father's name** [the name 'God,' which according to 17:11–12 Jesus shares with his Father, so that he represents God as also himself God in human flesh (see the comments on 1:1–18)], **and you aren't accepting me. If another person were to come in his own name** [and therefore not represent God], **that person you'll accept."** Jesus seems to be referring to false christs, or "antichrists," as they're called in 1 John 2:18, 22; 4:3; 2 John 7. He then asks, [44]**"How can you believe while accepting glory from one another, and you don't seek the glory** [that comes] **from the only God?"** "Glory" means "honor." Notice how be-

lieving lines up with having the love of God in yourself and with coming to Jesus for eternal life. Accepting glory from other human beings makes you incapable of seeking glory from God, because human standards of glory conflict with God's standards. The rabbis debated with each other over scriptural interpretation to parade their intellectual prowess. And in the Greco-Roman world, the rich and powerful gave banquets, sponsored sporting events, commissioned the production of art objects, decorated temples, and financed the construction of roads and public buildings—all for the express purpose of receiving praise for their generosity and good taste. Boasting of your magnanimity was considered normal and proper. Humility was despised. So human standards of glory, honor, and praise are corrupted by sin (pride, envy, lust, self-advantage, and so on). By contrast, God's standards are uncorrupted and incorruptible. So we have to make a choice. Do we want glory from one another, or glory from God? We can't have both. They contradict each other. The attaching of "only" to "God" is significant. The statement could do without that word: "You don't seek the glory that comes from God" instead of "the glory that comes from the *only* God." But the fact that "only" describes God implies that if you seek and accept glory from other human beings, you're treating them as though *they* were gods, whose approval you want; and you're *denying* your professed belief in one God alone.

In the Old Testament, Moses repeatedly and successfully interceded for Israel. But in *5:45–47* Jesus says, **"Don't ever think that I'll accuse you before the Father. The one who accuses you is Moses, in whom you've put your hope** [compare Deuteronomy 31:19, 21, 26; Romans 3:19]**."** Because Moses stands behind the first five books of the Old Testament, the reference to Moses echoes Jesus' earlier reference to "the Scriptures," where the Jews mistakenly thought life was to be found. Jesus concludes, [46]**"For if you'd been believing Moses, you'd have been believing me. For that one wrote about me.** [47]**But if you don't believe that one's writings, how will you believe my words?"** Note the distinction between the writings of Moses and the oral words of Jesus. They complement each other. Note also that the text doesn't talk about believing *in* Moses and believing *in* Jesus. Believing *in* has to do with personal commitment; and it's only Jesus, not Moses as well, in whom we're to believe. But before you can make a *personal* commitment to Jesus, you have to believe his *words* and what Moses *wrote* about him. Since such belief is impossible so long as you seek glory from your fellow human beings, forget that kind of glory. Go for glory from God. It's much better and longer-lasting.

JESUS' FEEDING THE FIVE THOUSAND
John 6:1–15

6:1–4: After these things Jesus went away across the Sea of Galilee, [that is] of Tiberias. [2]And a large crowd was following him, because they were seeing the signs that he was doing on those who were sick. [3]And Jesus went up onto a mountain and was sitting there with his disciples. [4]And the Passover was near, a festival of the Jews. Because of its size, we'd call the "sea" a lake. It was identified both by the region of its location, Galilee, and by a city located on its west shore, Tiberias. The city took its name after Tiberius Caesar, who was ruling the Roman Empire at the time the city was founded in the early A.D. 20s. The lake lies 650 feet below sea level and is thirteen by six miles at its longest and widest. Mountains 2,000 feet high bound it on the west and 4,000 feet high on the east. In the afternoon, cool winds blow in from the Mediterranean Sea through east-west valleys and collide with hot desert air from the east. The collision often produces storms on the lake, such as the one coming up in 6:16-21. Jesus' going across the lake and up a mountain means that he sailed with his disciples to the east side, where the higher mountains are located. Though he's sitting there temporarily, 6:15 will imply that he came back down to do what happens next before going up the mountain again. "With his disciples" prepares for a contrast with his going up again by himself. Elsewhere John mentions the Passover often (see 2:13; 11:55; 12:1; 13:1; 18:28, 39; 19:14), but always in connection with Jesus' going to Jerusalem, or with his presence there, for that festival—and also always in connection with his death as the true Passover lamb that takes away the sin of the world. But here Jesus isn't in Jerusalem, nor is he headed there. So John is going out of his way to mention that the Passover is near, and he does so to associate the feeding of the five thousand with Jesus' self-sacrifice for our salvation (see especially his own interpretation of the feeding in 6:25-58). "Of the Jews" describes the Passover festival in a way which indicates that for Christians the sacrifice of Jesus as the true Passover lamb has outmoded the Jewish festival with its sacrifices. Thus in coming to him instead of going to Jerusalem, the crowd in the next verse will be celebrating the true Passover.

6:5-6: Therefore, on lifting up [his] eyes and seeing that a large crowd is coming toward him, Jesus says to Philip, "From where should we buy loaves of bread in order that these [people] might eat?" [6]But he was saying this by way of testing him, for he himself knew what he was about to do. Jesus takes the initiative, as he regularly does in John's Gospel. In this case, taking the initiative to feed the five thousand with bread, which represents his sacrificial flesh, previews the initiative he will take when volunteering for his arrest—practically insisting on it, in fact—and subsequently laying down his life of his own accord (see chapters 18-19 with 10:17-18). "Therefore" relates back to the note in 6:4 that the Passover was near. In other words, Jesus takes initiative for the purpose of doing something that will symbolize his self-sacrifice as God's Passover lamb. The word for bread is plural, referring to multiple loaves, though not like our big, puffy ones—rather, like disc-shaped pita bread. By testing Philip, Jesus' question to him sets up for an answer by Philip that will provide a

contrast with Jesus' foreknowledge and magnify the sign Jesus is going to perform. John adds "himself" to "he" (Jesus) to emphasize the foreknowledge, which derives from Jesus' deity.

6:7-9: Philip answered him, "Two hundred denarii worth of bread isn't enough for them, that each [person] get a little bit." [8]One of the disciples, [namely,] Andrew the brother of Simon Peter, says to him [Jesus], [9]"Here's a boy who has five barley loaves and two fish. But what are these for so many [people]?" Implied answer: Not much, not by a long shot. Denarii were coins. Two hundred of them would be wages for two hundred days of manual labor by one man. But even the amount of bread that this much money could buy would fall far short of feeding a crowd as big as this one. So Jesus will have to do something very big indeed to match the size of the crowd. He had asked Philip from *where* bread might be bought. But the crowd is so big that Philip answers as though Jesus had asked him *how much* it would cost to buy enough bread. Too much! Jesus isn't concerned with whether there's enough, though. For him it's a question of source. Find the right source and there'll be volume enough. The description of Andrew as one of Jesus' disciples and as Simon Peter's brother is unnecessary in the light of 1:35-42. But John repeats the information to highlight Andrew's question. The question calls further attention to the seeming impossibility of feeding about five thousand people with only five loaves of barley bread and two fish. Barley bread was the bread of poor people. So the upcoming sign will show what Jesus can do with what's low in quality as well as small in quantity. And he will far outdo the prophet Elisha, who fed one hundred people with twenty loaves of barley bread (2 Kings 4:42-44). People used fish, usually dried or pickled, as a condiment on their bread.

6:10-11: Jesus said, "Make the men recline." And there was much grass at the place. Therefore [because the disciples made them do so] the men reclined—as to their number, about five thousand. [11]Therefore Jesus took the loaves and, on giving thanks, distributed [them] to the ones who were reclining—likewise also [he distributed to them] from the fish—as much as they wanted. Again Jesus takes the initiative. *Making* the men recline may correlate with, and symbolize, the effective call of God in salvation, as later in 6:44: "No one is able to come to me [Jesus says] unless the Father, who sent me, draws him." The second word for men ordinarily excludes women and children, but the first word for "men" differs from the second one and could include women and children. Just possibly, then, there were about five thousand adult men plus an unspecified number of women and children (compare Matthew 14:21). John is so fond of using synonyms without distinction, though, that it's doubtful he intended the inclusive sense. The notation of grass fits the Passover season, for that festival took place in springtime, when the grass was green. But the notation also reminds us of Psalm 23:1-2, "The Lord is my shepherd. . . . He makes me to lie down in green pastures," especially since the five thousand have just been made to recline on the grass. And the allusion to this shepherd psalm anticipates John 10:1–30, where Jesus speaks of himself as the good shepherd whose sheep find pasture, representing abundant life—that is, eternal life (see especially 10:9–10). That the grass here in 6:10 is "much" symbolizes this abundance. Similarly, the large size of the crowd ("about five thousand men") symbolizes the huge success of the gospel by the time John writes his Gospel (see the same symbolism in 12:12–20; 21:11).

In all the New Testament accounts of the institution of the Lord's Supper the night before Jesus was crucified, we read of his taking the elements and giving thanks, just as here. The parallel is especially close with reference to the bread in 1 Corinthians 11:23–26; Luke 22:15–20 (see also Mark 14:22–25; Matthew 26:26–29). The back-reference in 6:23 to Jesus' giving thanks for the bread accents this parallel. (We get "eucharist" from John's Greek verb for giving thanks.) So John makes the present feeding of the five thousand his substitute, in part, for the institution of the Lord's Supper—in part, because the turning of water to wine in 2:1–11 made up the rest of this substitute. The wine provided by Jesus there and the bread provided by him here—these will lead John to omit the institution of the Lord's Supper during the Last Supper in 13:1–11. (The two suppers aren't synonymous.) Taking the initiative yet again, Jesus himself distributes the bread and fish to symbolize that he will give himself, in particular his flesh, as a Passover sacrifice. No one will do it for him, and no one will make him do it. He will do it on his own (see 10:17–18 again and compare his giving the bread to the disciples at the institution of the Lord's Supper). The second mention of reclining suggests that those who receive salvation do so through no effort of their own. It comes solely as a gift from Jesus. "Distributed" implies that he gave the bread and fish individually to the five thousand (don't ask how long it took; we're dealing with symbolism built on top of a historical event) just as he gives salvation individually to each believer. John omits the breaking of the bread into pieces, partly to conform to the nonbreaking of the bones of a Passover lamb, such as Jesus is (19:33; Exodus 12:46; Numbers 9:12), and partly to indicate that each of the five thousand or so didn't get just the "little bit" that Philip talked about (6:7). They all got "as much as they wanted," just as believers get an abundance of life (see 10:10 again).

Abundance of life means *more* than enough life. So we read in **6:12–13: And when they were filled** [and therefore satisfied], **he tells his disciples, "Gather the excess fragments in order that nothing be lost** [compare 3:16]." [13]**Therefore they gathered** [the excess fragments] **and filled twelve baskets with fragments from the five barley loaves that were more than enough for those who'd eaten.** "Were filled" reemphasizes abundance in contrast with the subsistence diet of Galilean peasants. They had full stomachs very seldom, if ever. The mention of "excess fragments" reemphasizes the

abundance yet again. "That nothing be lost" symbolizes the eternal security of true, persevering believers (compare 6:27, "the food that *abides* with the result of eternal life," and 6:39, "that I not lose anything that he [the Father] has given me" [see also 10:28–29; 17:12; 18:9]). The filling of twelve baskets with excess fragments puts a final emphasis on abundance (compare the filling of water jars up to the brim in Jesus' making water into wine, the other part of John's anticipatory Lord's Supper, in 2:7). That there are twelve baskets full of excess fragments makes one for each of the twelve disciples (to be mentioned in 6:67 and following), more than enough for each one. They become the foundation for the new people of God, the church, on top of which foundation are built the rest of the church, represented by the five thousand (compare Ephesians 2:20; Revelation 12:17; 21:14). At the end, John omits the two fish and mentions only the five barley loaves. Since the number five has seemed to represent Judaism, enshrined in the five books of Moses (Genesis–Deuteronomy), the remention of the five loaves and the description of them as barley may symbolize Jesus' replacing Judaism, inferior like barley bread, with himself as the source of eternal life, just as he replaced the Jewish water of purification with the superior wine of his sacrificial blood (see 1:17; 2:1–11; 4:18; 5:2 with comments).

6:14–15: Therefore the men, having seen the sign that he'd done, were saying, "This is truly the prophet who was coming into the world." [15]Therefore Jesus, knowing that they're about to come and seize him in order to make him king, withdrew again onto the mountain himself alone. Jesus is more than a prophet. But he applied the term to himself in 4:44; so the crowd's present confession hits the mark. That is to say, John accepts their "truly" as itself true—doubly true, because "coming into the world" matches Jesus' portrayal of himself perfectly. On the other hand, though he's king, he'll tell Pontius Pilate that his (Jesus') kingdom isn't from this world (18:36–37; compare 1:49; 12:13, 15; 19:3, 14–15, 19–22). Nor has the "hour" of his exaltation yet come. So he withdraws when the crowd is about to surge toward him, seize him, and make him king. He's already a king, and his royal authority doesn't derive from them. It comes from his Father above. Jesus' knowing what the crowd is about to do displays divine omniscience again, and his going back up the mountain by himself prepares for the following episode.

JESUS' WALKING ON WATER
John 6:16–21

6:16–17: And when evening arrived, his disciples went down to the sea. They hadn't gone back up the mountain with Jesus; so their going down to the sea must refer to at least a slight descent to the shoreline. [17]**And on getting into a boat, they were going across the sea to Capernaum** [on the northwest shore]. **And darkness had now arrived.** In Jesus' absence it's theologically dark, as John means us to understand the symbolism of physical darkness; for Jesus is the light of the world, the sun that shines the light of eternal life on all who believe in him (1:4; 8:12; 11:9–10). **And Jesus hadn't yet come to them.** But "yet" implies that he *will* come to them, as he'll promise in 14:3; 21:22–23 and as he'll come to them several times after his resurrection (20:19, 24, 26; 21:13).

6:18–21: And because a strong wind was blowing, the sea was getting aroused [= getting rough with waves]. **¹⁹Therefore after rowing about twenty-five or thirty stades** [= about three or three and a half miles], **they see Jesus walking on the sea and getting near the boat. And they were frightened. ²⁰But he tells them, "I am. Don't be frightened." ²¹Therefore they wanted to take him into the boat; and immediately the boat arrived at the land to which they'd been going.** The surging sea represents the powers of chaos, evil, and death, as in John's book of Revelation 13:1, for example, so that the new heavens and earth, devoid of chaos, evil, and death, will have no sea (Revelation 21:1). Three or three and a half miles of rowing put the disciples in the middle of the sea, at their most vulnerable. Jesus' walking on the sea symbolizes divine omnipotence over the powers of chaos, evil, and death. The sight of him fills the disciples with fear. But they recognize his voice, the voice of the Word who is God, just as Jesus will say that his sheep recognize his voice as that of their good shepherd (10:4–5, 14, 16, 27). His "I am" means both a simple "It's me [Jesus]," just as the ex-blind man will say about himself (9:9), and also a divine "I AM," as in Exodus 3:14, where God tells Moses to say to the Israelites, "I AM has sent me to you," and as in John 8:58, where Jesus will say, "Before Abraham came into existence, I AM." So in agreement with his walking on water, he's proclaiming his deity. Hearing the proclamation and recognizing his voice change their fright, which he told them to get rid of, into wanting to take him into the boat. The verb "wanted" can escalate to the meaning "delighted," which would make an even stronger contrast with their former fright. In that case, Jesus did enter the boat (compare their wanting or delighting to "take" him into the boat with "accepting" Jesus by faith in 1:12 ["take" and "accept" translate the very same verb]; contrast 5:43: "I've come in my Father's name, and you aren't taking/accepting me"; and see Revelation 22:17 for the element of wanting, delighting, willing: "The person who *wants* to is to take the water of life as a gift"). The immediacy of their coming to land despite having been in the middle of the sea symbolizes the immediacy of getting eternal life once you accept Jesus. You don't have to wait till the hereafter to get it. The next verse will mention the next day, as though his arrival amounts to a sunrise, since he's the light of life (1:4–9 and following). Compare Psalm 107:23–30.

ON THE SACRIFICIAL FLESH
AND BLOOD OF JESUS
John 6:22–58

6:22–24: The next day the crowd [of five thousand] **that was standing on the other** [= east] **side of the sea saw that no other boat had been there except one** [the one used by Jesus and the Twelve to come to the east side] **and that Jesus hadn't gone into the boat with his disciples** [to go back to the west side the preceding evening]. **Rather, his disciples had gone away alone. ²³Other boats came from Tiberias** [on the west side] **near to the place where they** [the five thousand] **had eaten the bread after the Lord had given thanks. ²⁴So when the crowd saw that Jesus wasn't there, nor his disciples, they themselves got into the boats** [that had come from Tiberias] **and went to Capernaum seeking Jesus.** "After the Lord had given thanks" doesn't contribute to the movements to and fro, but John inserts this unnecessary detail to remind us that the feeding of the five thousand with bread symbolizes what the bread of the Lord's Supper symbolizes, that is, the self-sacrificed body—or flesh (the preferred term in John)—of Jesus, called "Lord" for the first time in John for an allusion to the Lord's Supper (compare 1 Corinthians 11:20). The five thousand know that he hadn't gone with his twelve disciples. They don't see him where they still are. And they know that he and the Twelve came in only one boat, so that there's no second one which he could have taken by himself. Where then could he be? The five thousand weren't privy to his walking on water to the Twelve, of course, or to the immediate arrival on the west side. So they go back to Capernaum and look for Jesus there.

They find Jesus—specifically in the synagogue at Capernaum according to a later reference in 6:59. **6:25–27: And on finding him on the other side of the sea, they said to him, "Rabbi, when did you get here?" ²⁶Jesus answered them and said, "Amen, amen I tell you, you're seeking me not because you saw signs— rather, because you ate from the loaves and were sated. ²⁷Don't be working for the food that perishes—rather, for the food that abides with the result of eternal life, which the Son of Man will give you. For this one** [the Son of Man] **God the Father has sealed."** The address "Rabbi" shows the crowd's belief in Jesus. Whether their belief will last hangs in the balance. Jesus doesn't answer their question, "*When* did you get here?" An answer would be irrelevant. The relevant question is *why* they're seeking Jesus. The answer to that question will expose the quality of their belief in Jesus. The quality won't be good. Jesus denies that they're seeking him because they've seen the signs he has been performing (most recently his feeding all five thousand or so of them). They *have* seen his signs, but seeing them isn't motivating their search for him. Instead, physical appetite is motivating it. So just as Jesus turned the Samaritan woman's attention away from water as H2O to water as a symbol of the life-giving Spirit of God (4:4–14), here he turns the crowd's attention away from food for the sustenance of mortal life to food for the sustenance of eternal life. Since water and food are necessary for mortal life, they make suitable figures of speech for the necessities of eternal life. Food for the sustenance of mortal life perishes, gets lost in the form of feces, so that working for *it* will bring you the same sort of fate—eternally. Food that doesn't perish, that doesn't get lost—it *abides*, and its abiding results in life that's eternal rather than mortal. But what kind of working is in view? Jesus has just mentioned their *seeking* him because he'd satisfied their physical appetite. So working equates with seeking. By the same token, then, to work for the food that abides is to seek Jesus as its source. And as the Son of Man he will give it to those who seek him for it rather than for physical satisfaction (compare Jesus' having distributed the bread and fish *himself* [6:11]). ("Which" could refer either to "the food that abides" or to the "eternal life" that it results in or even symbolizes—probably the food; but either way, the theology comes out the same.) Why does Jesus refer to himself as "the Son of Man" instead of using a simple "I"? The phrase is a Semitic way of saying "the human being." Jesus uses it here to set up for a speech about eating his flesh and drinking his blood, flesh and blood being characteristic of human beings capable of dying. (1 Corinthians 15:50 equates "flesh and blood" with "perishability.") And dying will make his sacrificial flesh and blood the food that abides with the result of eternal life for those who believe, and keep on believing, in him. The forward position of "this one," referring to the Son of Man, emphasizes that Jesus and no one else has God's seal of authority and approval to act in this capacity. The seal probably consists in God's putting the Holy Spirit on Jesus (1:29–34). The combination of "God" with "the Father" ensures that "the Son of Man" isn't misunderstood to mean that Jesus had a human rather than divine father (in opposition to the misunderstanding of Jesus as "the son of Joseph" in 1:45; 6:42).

6:28–29: Therefore they said to him, "What should we do to work the works of God [that is, to produce the works that God requires of us]**?"** **29Jesus answered and said to them, "This is the work of God, that you believe in him whom that one** [God] **has sent."** Jesus has just told the crowd not to work for perishable food, but to work for imperishable food. But they didn't catch the equation that he drew between working for imperishable food and seeking him as its source. So rather than thinking of the works that *Jesus* has been doing as signs of freely given salvation, they think of works that God requires *them* to do for eternal life. In his answer Jesus reduces the works of God to a single work, that of believing in Jesus as the one whom God sent for their salvation. But does Jesus pick up the crowd's use of "work" and, stretching its meaning, apply it to believing, so that God requires the "work" of believing in Jesus? Favoring a yes answer is Jesus' having just said to work for the food that abides (6:27). On the other hand, Jesus will soon say, "No one is able come to me *unless the Father, who sent me, draws him* . . . . It's written in the prophets, 'And they'll all be *taught by God.*' Everyone who has heard *from the Father* and learned [from him] comes to me" (6:44–45), and again, "No one is able to come to me *unless it has been given him* [to do so] *by my Father*" (6:65). The proximity of these statements to the one in 6:29, plus their sharing the portrayal of Jesus as God's sent one—these factors favor that Jesus means the work that

God *does* as well as the work that he *requires*. He does it by drawing people so as to enable their doing the work of believing in the one whom he has sent. This enablement keeps the work of believing from contradicting the character of eternal life as an unearned gift.

6:30–33: Therefore they said to him, "So what sign are you doing that we might see [it] **and believe you? What** [sign] **are you working?** 31**Our** [fore]**fathers ate manna in the wilderness, just as it's written, 'He gave them bread from heaven to eat** [Psalm 78:24 (compare Exodus 16:4, 15; Nehemiah 9:15; Psalm 105:40)]**.'"** 32**So Jesus said to them, "Amen, amen I tell you, Moses hasn't given you bread from heaven. Rather, my Father is giving you bread from heaven** [right now, because he's giving you *me*]**, the true** [bread from heaven]. 33**For the bread of God is he who comes down out of heaven and gives life to the world."** According to 6:2, 26 the crowd have already seen Jesus' signs. So here they're asking him for some further sign, as though he hasn't performed enough to satisfy them. After all, Jesus has said they were seeking for him to satisfy their physical appetite. It's the next day. They're hungry again. They've seen Jesus' past signs, but they haven't believed him. Which is to say they haven't believed what he has just told them about the work of God that by way of personal commitment they should believe *in* him as the one whom God sent. Then in response to Jesus' telling them that believing in him is the work God requires *them* to do, they sassily ask him what *he's* going to do by way of working. And the appeal to their ancestors' having eaten manna, a miraculous sort of bread from heaven, in the wilderness—this appeal implies that Jesus should fill their bellies with bread today just as he did yesterday. Then they'll believe him. Or so they say. But what about tomorrow, the day after tomorrow, and on and on? They want to turn Jesus into a daily bakery for as long as they live on earth. Never mind eternity. Solemnly, Jesus answers as though the Jews understand the unspecified "He" in "He gave them bread to eat from heaven" to mean Moses. Whether they do or not is another question. Certainly the Old Testament attributes to God, not to Moses, the giving of manna. In any case, though "the Law was given through Moses, grace and truth came on the scene through Jesus Christ" (1:17). He says "my Father" not only over against Moses but also over against "our [fore]fathers," the Jews' ancestors. Jesus is the true bread, given from heaven by God his Father. "True" not as opposed to what's false, but "true" as the ultimately real, toward which the manna only pointed. Manna was good for mortal life. God's bread is good for eternal life. Manna was only for the Jews' ancestors, Israelites. God's bread is for the whole world. And God's bread is "*from* heaven" as the abode of God rather than "*of* heaven" as the sky that dropped manna like dew (as in Exodus 16:13–14). To make this point John changes "*of* heaven," as Psalm 78:24 reads (despite English translations to the contrary), to "*from* heaven."

6:34–35: Therefore they said to him, "Lord, give us this bread always [in other words, day after day after day]." ³⁵Jesus told them, "I am the bread of life. The person who comes to me will never hunger, and the person who believes in me will never thirst—at any time!" "Therefore" harks back to 6:33, where "the bread of God is *he who* comes down out of heaven" could equally well mean "the bread of God is *that which* comes down out of heaven." Still thinking in terms of baked bread for their stomachs, Jesus' audience take the expression to mean "that which" and therefore ask him to give them such bread constantly as the further sign they seek according to 6:30. Otherwise they won't believe him (see also 6:36: "you don't believe"). So they mean "Lord" in the sense of "Sir," whereas John means us to understand "Lord" in the sense of deity. Finally Jesus identifies himself outright as the kind of bread he has been telling about, the bread of God from heaven. He's the bread "of life" in that he's *living* bread as opposed to baked bread (see 6:51) and also in that he's life-*giving* bread, for he gives to believers eternal life whereas baked bread sustains merely mortal life. Coming to him means believing in him. Hungering and thirsting stand for the human longing to keep on living, for which eating and drinking are necessary. Jesus converts these figures of speech from mortal life into figures of speech for eternal life. The two occurrences of "never" join "at any time" to emphasize the eternality of the life Jesus gives. Hungering leads to eating, and thirsting to drinking. But there was no thirsting and drinking in the feeding of the five thousand. So the present reference to thirsting echoes Jesus' conversation with the Samaritan woman concerning living water (chapter 4) and prepares for drinking another beverage besides water, namely, blood (6:52–58).

Jesus continues in *6:36–40*: "But I told you that you've both seen me and aren't believing. ³⁷Everything that the Father is giving me will come to me, and I'll never throw the person outside who comes to me, ³⁸because I've not descended from heaven to do my will but [to do] the will of him who sent me. ³⁹And this is the will of him who sent me, that I not lose anything that he has given me—rather, [that] I resurrect it on the last day. ⁴⁰For this is the will of my Father, that everyone who sees the Son and believes in him should have eternal life and [that] I should resurrect him on the Last Day." Since John hasn't recorded Jesus as having said earlier in so many words, "You've both seen me and aren't believing," the present statement of Jesus seems to interpret 6:26: "Amen, amen I tell you, you're seeking me not because you saw signs [though you did see them]—rather, because you ate from the loaves and were sated." According to the interpretation, seeing Jesus' signs amounts to seeing Jesus himself; and seeking Jesus as though he were a daily bakery amounts to disbelief in him. "Every*thing*," "any*thing*," and "*it*" turn out to be "the *person* who," "*everyone*," and "*him*." Why then doesn't Jesus use the personal expressions from the start and consistently? The reason is that the neuter expressions stress quality, in this case the quality of everyness. Absolutely no one of those the Father has given to Jesus will fail to come to him. Jesus will lose absolutely

none of them but will resurrect absolutely every one of them on the Last Day. So erstwhile believers who eventually apostatize weren't God's gift to Jesus in the first place. God's giving certain people to Jesus *effects* their coming to Jesus (compare 6:44, 65). Yet their coming to Jesus implies that this effectual giving doesn't cancel out responsible human willing (compare 7:17, "If anyone *wills* to do his [God's] will, he'll know about the teaching, whether it's from God or I speak on my own," and Revelation 22:17, "The person who *wants* to is to take the water of life as a gift"). To be thrown outside is to be thrown outside the vineyard of salvation into the fire of judgment and burned, as in the case of those who don't abide in Jesus (15:6), that is, to be thrown into the lake of fire and brimstone to suffer torment forever and ever (Revelation 14:10; 20:10, 14–15). And to "lose" is to allow ruination in that manner. But Jesus *won't* throw out or lose anyone who comes to him, because to do so would be to reject a gift from his Father and would violate the Father's will, the very will his Father sent him to carry out as a dutiful son. By claiming to have descended from heaven he equates himself with the Son of Man in 3:13. Standing as a counterpart to the impossibility of throwing out, losing, and allowing ruination is the certainty of resurrection to eternal life (compare 5:28–29). And Jesus himself will do the raising on the Last Day just as he raised himself on the first Easter Sunday according to 10:17–18. "The Last Day" refers to the day of what we call his second coming (compare 21:22–23 with Revelation 19:11–20:6). The paragraph ends with those who see the Son and *do* believe in him, in contrast with those at the beginning of the paragraph who see and *don't* believe. Thankfully in the case of the ones whom the Father has given to his Son, seeing *is* believing.

6:41–42: Therefore the Jews were murmuring about him because he'd said, "I am the bread that descended out of heaven." ⁴²And they were saying, "This is Jesus the son of Joseph, isn't he, whose father and mother we know? How is it that he's now saying, 'I've descended out of heaven?'" Jesus is teaching in the synagogue at Capernaum according to 6:59, and according to 6:60–65 his audience consists of disciples as well as unbelievers. So here "the Jews" probably means Jewish authorities, as often elsewhere in this Gospel. Descending out of heaven contradicts having a pair of human parents. At least it contradicts having a human father in view of Jesus' linking the descent from heaven with being sent by God as his Father. John knows that Jesus has a human mother, of course (2:1–5; 19:25–27). The Jews know her and her husband Joseph too, but mistakenly think he's the father of Jesus and therefore complain about Jesus' claim to be the bread that descended out of heaven.

6:43–46: Jesus answered and said to them, "Stop murmuring with one another. ⁴⁴No one is able to come to me unless the Father, who sent me, draws him; and I'll resurrect him on the last day. ⁴⁵It's written in the prophets, 'And they'll all be taught by God [Isaiah 54:13].' Everyone who has heard from the Father and learned [from him] **comes to me.** ⁴⁶**Not that anyone has seen the Father except the one who's from God. This one has seen the Father."** So the reason for the Jews' murmuring about Jesus' claim is that the Father who sent him hasn't drawn them. They haven't heard from the Father or learned from him. But without exception, all whom the Father does draw and teach have the ability to come to Jesus and do come. Though they hear and learn from the Father, they don't see him (compare 1:18). The privilege of seeing him belongs to Jesus alone, so that his explanation of God depends on sight as well as sound. Therefore to be taught by God and to hear and learn from the Father is to be taught by Jesus, who as the Word is himself God; and it's to hear and learn from Jesus, who is one with the Father (1:1; 10:30; compare the meaning of "disciple" as "learner").

6:47–51: "**Amen, amen I tell you, the person who believes has eternal life.** ⁴⁸**I am the bread of life.** ⁴⁹**Your [fore]fathers ate manna in the wilderness and died.** ⁵⁰**This one** [Jesus, who's speaking] **is the bread that descended out of heaven in order that anyone may eat from it/him and not die.** ⁵¹**I am the living bread that descended out of heaven. If anyone eats from this bread, he'll live forever. And also, the bread that I'll give for the world's life is my flesh."** A double "amen" gives firm assurance of eternal life for those who believe in Jesus. "Your [fore]fathers" contrasts with "the Father" of Jesus. "The wilderness" contrasts with the grassy place whose surrounding population provided the possibility of buying two hundred denarii worth of bread (6:10). And again Jesus builds a contrast within the parallel between manna and himself as bread. Here the contrast explicitly pits the mortality of ancient manna-eaters against the immortality of those who partake of the heavenly bread that is Jesus. Because of the previously mentioned resurrection, this immortality includes body as well as soul. The previous mention of resurrection also implies that "not die" means not suffering "the second death," which is eternal punishment (Revelation 2:11; 20:6, 14; 21:8). Again, but this time explicitly, the bread of life is living bread as well as life-giving bread. In fact, it is life-giving because it is the living Jesus who gives his own life *for* and, on the strength of his resurrection, *to* those who believe in such a way as to enter into him and abide in him. Eating him means believing in him not only so as to abide in him but also to ingest him, so that he abides in believers. "And also" underlines the identification of the living bread with Jesus' flesh, the flesh that the Word became (1:14). This identification may link with the fish that the five thousand ate as a condiment on the bread that Jesus distributed to them (compare Paul's reference to "flesh . . . of fish" in 1 Corinthians 15:39). And underlying the identification is an upcoming separation between Jesus' flesh and blood. The separation will make clear a violent death such that it's sacrificial. (Natural death can't be sacrificial.) For the time being, though, the reference to Jesus' flesh only hints at sacrifice—or *self*-sacrifice, since *he* will give it just as he himself distributed bread to the five thousand. According to 6:32 the Father gives

the bread, but Jesus and his Father "are one" (10:30), so that what the Father does Jesus does too. The future tense of "will give" points forward to the crucifixion as Jesus' self-giving, and we should remind ourselves that in John's Gospel Jesus volunteers for crucifixion (see, for example, 10:17–18 with 18:2–9). Implied is that the Word became flesh for the very purpose of crucifixion. "For the life *of the world*" means that the inability of people to come to Jesus except the Father draws them—this inability doesn't restrict either the value of Jesus' self-sacrifice or the breadth of the invitation to believe and be saved. "Eats *from* this bread" implies leftovers, an excess of bread that's enough and more than enough for the world, as already symbolized in the leftovers from the feeding of the five thousand (6:12–13).

6:52: Therefore the Jews were complaining to one another, saying, "How can this [man] give us his flesh to eat?" The question over which the Jews complain to one another doesn't arise out of disgust at the thought of eating Jesus' flesh. It arises out of puzzlement over a question of ability. Jesus has to be dead for his flesh to be eaten. Yet to give, to serve, his flesh the way he distributed bread to the five thousand, he has to be alive. So how can he be dead and alive at the same time? In answer, he disregards this question of his ability and shifts the focus to his audience.

6:53–56: Therefore Jesus said to them, "Amen, amen I tell you, unless you eat the flesh of the Son of Man and drink his blood, you don't have life in yourselves. ⁵⁴**The person who does eat my flesh and drink my blood has eternal life, and I'll resurrect him on the last day.** ⁵⁵**For my flesh is true food, and my blood is true drink.** ⁵⁶**The person who eats my flesh and drinks my blood abides in me, and I [abide] in him."** Whereas Jesus had earlier identified the bread of life with his flesh, here he drops the figure of bread, refers exclusively to flesh, and calls it the flesh of the Son of Man to emphasize the humanity of his flesh, "Son of Man" being a Semitic way of saying "human being." This emphasis strikes against the Gnostic heretical denigration and denial not only of the humanly fleshly incarnation of the Word but also of his humanly fleshly death and (as we'll see) resurrection. As noted before, along with the changing of water to wine, the feeding of the five thousand with bread and fish combines with Jesus' present explanation to replace the institution of the Lord's Supper at the Last Supper. At the institution of the Lord's Supper Jesus said, "This [bread] is my *body*" (1 Corinthians 11:24; Mark 14:22; Matthew 26:28; Luke 22:19). Here he uses "flesh" instead of "body" to stress tangibility over against the fleshless, bloodless spirituality on which Gnostics centered (see the introduction to 1 John). Jesus adds the drinking of his blood. In 6:35 he'd spoken of not thirsting any more, in an echo of drinking the water of life (4:14 [compare 7:37–39]). Here's another beverage—Jesus' blood, represented by wine at the institution of the Lord's Supper elsewhere in the New Testament and represented in John by the wine that Jesus made out of water at Cana (2:1–11).

The separation of blood from flesh indicates the violence of a sacrificial death in that "the life of the flesh is in the blood . . . for it is the blood by reason of the life that makes atonement" (Leviticus 17:11 [compare Hebrews 9:22]). For in the Old Testament, blood had to be drained out of an animal sacrifice (see Leviticus 1–7 and compare the outflow of blood from Jesus' pierced side in John 19:34). So the sacrifice of the Son of Man makes his life-blood the source of life for those who drink it. Such life becomes a very part of them just as food and drink become a very part of your constitution—hence "life *in yourselves*," just as 1:4 said that the preexistent Word has life "*in him*," 5:26 that "the Father has life *in himself*" and "has given to the Son to have life *in himself*," and 4:14 that the water that Jesus gives will become "*in him* [that is, in whoever drinks it] . . . a spring of water leaping up into eternal life." The resultant life is eternal as well as internal, for it's the life of the divine as well as human Word. And as such, it entails resurrection of the flesh both in the case of Jesus and in the case of those who eat his flesh and drink his blood—"the resurrection of life" rather than "the resurrection of judgment" (5:29).

Combined with John's pervasive symbolism, the description of Jesus' flesh and blood as "*true*" food" and "*true* drink" speaks against a literally cannibalistic meaning. This flesh and blood isn't ordinary food and drink any more than the life is ordinary. "True" has the sense, not of what's opposite to falsehood, but of what's ultimate and therefore brings life that's eternal. The eating and drinking equate with abiding. Now abiding means staying, remaining, and therefore persevering. But abiding "in" puts an accent on closeness and, indeed, union. Just as the body assimilates food and drink, so eaters and drinkers of the Son of Man's flesh and blood assimilate him. We'd therefore expect his abiding in eaters and drinkers to come first. But it doesn't. Coming first is their abiding in him, as though he ingested them. He didn't, of course; but abiding in him comes first to make the point that he won't abide in us unless we abide in him (compare 15:1–10).

6:57–58: **"Just as the living Father sent me and I live because of the Father, also the person who eats me—even that person will live because of me.** ⁵⁸**This one** [Jesus the Son of Man] **is the bread that descended out of heaven.** [It's] **not as the** [fore]**fathers ate and died. The person who eats this bread will live forever."** The Father shares his life with Jesus. So also Jesus shares his life with the person who eats him. Drinking his blood drops out here for a return to the theme of bread, a theme that arose out of Jesus' feeding the five thousand. And another contrast between the dying of ancient manna-eaters and the eternal life of Jesus-eaters caps this paragraph (compare 6:49–51). But what does it mean to eat his flesh and drink his blood?

APOSTASY VERSUS PERSEVERANCE
John 6:59–71

6:59–60: **He** [Jesus] **said these things while teaching in the synagogue in Capernaum.** ⁶⁰**On hearing** [these things]**, therefore, many of his disciples said, "This word is hard. Who is able to hear it?"** "Therefore" and "hard" refer back to the difficulty of understanding and accepting Jesus' foregoing remarks on eating his flesh and drinking his blood for eternal life. In particular, the seeming cannibalism of eating his flesh and, above all, the repeated Old Testament prohibition of ingesting blood contribute to this difficulty. But what was "this word" about? It was about Jesus, his flesh and blood. So this word is the Word who became flesh. So also the question of who's able to hear *it* (the word, the saying of Jesus) is also a question of who's able to hear *him* (Jesus the Word). Who then *is* able? The question is skeptical, but here's the answer: "everyone who has heard from the Father and learned" (6:45) or, according to later figurative language, Jesus' "sheep." Because the Father draws them by giving them the ability to hear (6:44, 65), they recognize his voice as that of their shepherd (10:3, 16, 27). Obviously, the hearing connotes recognition and acceptance, not mere listening. It's disconcerting that "*disciples*" of Jesus—indeed, "*many*" of them—don't hear in that favorable sense. We're being warned about the danger of temporary belief, of a lack of perseverance. Read on. The warning gets sharper.

6:61–64: **And Jesus, knowing in himself that his disciples are murmuring about this** [word/Word]**, told them, "This** [word/Word] **is making you stumble.** ⁶²[So will it make you stumble] **if you were to see the Son of Man ascending to where he was earlier** [that is, prior to the incarnation, 'In the beginning' (1:1)]**?** ⁶³**The Spirit is the one who makes** [people] **live. The flesh doesn't help one bit. The words that I've spoken to you are Spirit, and they are life.** ⁶⁴**But there are some of you who aren't believing."** **For from the beginning Jesus knew who were the ones that weren't believing and who is the one that was going to betray him.** Again Jesus' omniscience comes to the fore. Its location "in himself" parallels the "life" that's "in him" (1:4) and stresses that like life, omniscience is intrinsic to his deity as the Word who was God already in the beginning (1:1). In 6:41 "the Jews," nondisciples, were murmuring. Now Jesus' very disciples are murmuring. They're apostatizing. They don't have the perseverance in belief that characterizes those whom God has given to Jesus. And in murmuring about his word, what he has said, they're complaining about him himself. For he's the Word of his word, the subject of his message. (Note: perseverance has to do with *belief* that issues in corresponding behavior, not just with behavior.)

Jesus' response could be punctuated as a question: "Is this [word/Word] making you stumble?" But punctuating it as a declaration, "This [word/Word] is making you stumble," suits better the initial emphasis on Jesus' intrinsic omniscience. Stumbling is a figure of speech for taking offense so as to fall into unbelief, here from belief into the unbelief of apostasy. The Son of Man's ascending to where he was earlier recollects 3:13, which spoke of no one's having ascended into heaven except the one who descended out of heaven. But the question whether the disciples' seeing him ascending will make them stumble—this question is sarcastic. For at first blush, seeing him ascending should really *keep* them from stumbling, *keep* them from apostasy. Yet it won't. Why? The key to an answer lies in the *seeing* of his ascension. Nobody will see him ascending. Or so we might think. But in John's Gospel the Son of Man starts his ascent back to heaven by being lifted up on a cross. The very next verse after 3:13, cited above, said, "And just as Moses lifted up the serpent in the wilderness, in this way it's necessary that the Son of Man be lifted up" (3:14 [see Numbers 21:5–9 for the story]). Further, "Whenever you've lifted up the Son of Man, then you'll know that I AM" (8:28 [similarly 12:32, 34; compare the Son of Man's glorification in 12:23; 13:31]). The present audience will go as pilgrims to Jerusalem for the Passover at which Jesus will die (12:12). So they *will* see the Son of Man ascending. Yet they won't recognize it as an ascension. Yes, then, their seeing it *will* make them stumble. They'll mistake the crucifixion for a humiliation rather than taking it correctly as the start of an exaltation to preincarnate glory.

Suddenly Jesus switches from himself as the Son of Man to the Spirit, because it's the Son of Man's ascension, or glorification, that makes possible the giving of the Spirit: "And he spoke this concerning the Spirit that those who'd believed in him were going to receive. For the Spirit wasn't yet [received], because Jesus hadn't yet been glorified" (7:39). The Spirit's making people live (1) builds on being "born from above . . . from the Spirit" (3:3, 5, 7); (2) contrasts with stumbling (which eventuates in the second death; Revelation 2:11; 20:6, 14; 21:8); and (3) has to do with resurrection to eternal life at the Last Day, so that Father, Son, and Spirit all participate as one in making believers live (see 5:21 for the Father and the Son). "The flesh doesn't help one bit" builds on 3:6: "What has been born out of the flesh is flesh, and what has been born out of the Spirit is Spirit." But in 6:51 Jesus said "the bread that I'll give for the world's life is my flesh." *His* flesh is certainly helpful, then! So here in 6:63 he isn't referring to his own sacrificial flesh. He's referring to flesh in the sense of physical ancestry, Jewish ancestry in particular (compare "our/your/the [fore] fathers" in 6:31, 49, 58; also 7:22; 8:39, 56). Such ancestry doesn't guarantee eternal life. Only birth out of the Spirit does (compare birth out of God in 1:13). Jesus equates his words with Spirit and with life, because just as Jesus is the Word *of God* in that he speaks words that explain God (1:1, 18), so the Spirit is the words *of Jesus* in that he explains Jesus (see 16:12–15). And Jesus' words are life, because he himself is life (11:25, 14:6), is the subject matter of his words, and therefore is one with his words. Thus the Spirit uses them to communicate, even to generate, life—eternal life.

Since Jesus is speaking to his disciples at this point (6:60–61), the "some of you who aren't believing" are disciples whose belief has now lapsed and whose failure to persevere makes a warning to all professing disciples. (More disciples than the Twelve are in view.) Again, however, John's emphasis lies on Jesus' omniscience.

Jesus knew not only those who weren't believing at the time. He also knew ahead of time the one who was going to betray him. How far ahead of time? "From the beginning," which in line with 15:27 means from the time the disciples started to follow Jesus.

6:65: And he was saying, "On account of this I've told you that no one is able to come to me unless it has been given him [to do so] **by the Father."** The interruption of Jesus' speech with "And he was saying" adds emphasis to the following statement. "On account of this" means "because there are some of you who aren't believing." The statement itself is made to explain, and does explain, why "there are some of you who aren't believing" (6:64). The reason is that the Father hasn't given them the ability to come to Jesus, as Jesus said already in 6:44: "No one is able to come to me unless the Father, who sent me, draws him." Belief that perseveres is impossible apart from God's gift.

6:66–69: From this point on, many of his disciples went away as backsliders [literally, "to the things behind"] **and were no longer walking with him. ⁶⁷Therefore Jesus said to the Twelve, "You—you too don't want to go away, do you?" ⁶⁸Simon Peter answered him, "Lord, to whom shall we go? You have the words of eternal life. ⁶⁹And we've come to believe and know that you're the Holy One of God."** Peter's "Lord" means more than "Sir." Especially in John's intention it carries the connotation of deity. Peter's question implies that no one besides Jesus has the words of eternal life. The phrase "of eternal life" confirms that in 6:63 "the words" which "are life" bring life that's eternal. Peter's expression of belief and knowledge carries a note of permanence, of perseverance. The addition of knowing to believing makes a jab against Gnostics, whose very name (which means "knowers") carries their claim to a knowledge unshared with others. Elsewhere John describes as "holy" only the Father and the Spirit (1:33; 14:26; 17:11; 20:22). Here "holy" describes Jesus. Since "holy" means "set apart from others," these descriptions provide a scriptural basis for the doctrine of the Holy Trinity. As applied to Jesus, "holy" describes him as set apart for the salvific mission of bringing the words of eternal life into the world (10:36; 17:19).

6:70–71: Jesus answered them, "I've selected you, the Twelve, haven't I? And one of you is Devil." ⁷¹And he was speaking in reference to Judas, [the son] **of Simon Iscariot. For this one, one of the Twelve, was going to betray him.** Again the omniscience of Jesus is on display. His having chosen the Twelve links up with the Father's drawing certain people, but not others, and enabling them to come to Jesus (6:44, 65). Most translations have "*a* devil" rather than "Devil" (with a capital "D"). Other things being equal, it wouldn't be wrong to supply "a" so as to leave "devil" uncapitalized. But everywhere else in John, 1 John, and John's book of Revelation the word refers to the Devil. There are demons, but no devils. In 13:2 John will say that the Devil had already put it into Judas's heart to betray Jesus, and in 13:27 John will say that "Satan entered into that one" for the betrayal of Jesus. So here, without naming him, Jesus calls Judas "Devil." The absence of "the," which elsewhere precedes "Devil," emphasizes the quality of Judas's devilry. John, however, does name Judas as Jesus' referent. "[The son] of Simon Iscariot" distinguishes this Judas from another Judas to be mentioned in 14:22. John's explanation that Judas was going to betray Jesus defines what is meant by Jesus' calling Judas "Devil" (see 13:27 for Satan's entering into Judas at the start of the betrayal). "One of the Twelve" adds both pathos and a warning against apostasy, for you'd expect that *none* of the Twelve would betray Jesus. Yet one was going to.

HOW TO GO TO THE FESTIVAL
OF TABERNACLES
John 7:1–13

7:1: And after these things Jesus was walking around in Galilee; for he didn't want to walk around in Judea, because the Jews were seeking to kill him. They're the Jewish authorities based in the territory of Judea, specifically in the city of Jerusalem. Their seeking to kill Jesus echoes 5:18, which identified the reason for it as his making himself equal with God as well as breaking the Sabbath by healing on that day an invalid at the Pool of Bethzatha. Jesus wasn't unwilling to die; but as 7:6 will say, his time to do so wasn't yet ripe. Besides, as the Word who is God he'll die at his own initiative (10:17–18), not as a victim but as a victor.

7:2–5: But the Jews' Festival of Tabernacles was near. ³So his brothers told him, "Shift from here and go into Judea in order that your disciples too may see your works, which you're doing. ⁴For no one does anything in secret and himself seeks to be in public. If you're doing these things, manifest yourself to the world." That is, if you want to get noticed, don't hide in a closet. **⁵For not even his brothers were believing in him.** The Festival of Tabernacles lasted eight days, took place in late September–early October, and celebrated the harvest from fruit trees and vines. In the spring, Passover had celebrated the start of the grain harvest. Seven weeks later, Pentecost celebrated the end of the grain harvest. These were the three festivals for which pilgrims streamed up to Jerusalem in the hill country of Judea. As Passover recalled the Israelites' exodus from Egypt, Tabernacles recalled their living in tents during their wandering in the wilderness (the Sinai desert) on the way from Egypt to Canaan. For Tabernacles, then, the Jews built temporary booths to live in for the duration of the festival. Two further features bear mention: (1) Tabernacles came at the climax of a summer-long drought, so that by way of counterpoint, in 7:37–39 Jesus will proclaim himself the source of living water. (2) Tabernacles came at the autumnal equinox, after which darkness prevailed over light, so that in 8:12 Jesus will say, again by way of counterpoint, "I am the light of the world." Speaking of Jesus' biological half brothers,

John doesn't name them (though see Mark 6:3; Matthew 13:55), and he attributes their advice to unbelief in Jesus. Precisely because the advice stems from such unbelief, the advice that Jesus do his works in public doesn't make sense. Moreover, the disciples of Jesus have already seen his works both in Judea and in Galilee. He hasn't been doing them in secret—rather, in public. He has already manifested himself to the world. Such is the stupidity of not believing in Jesus: it misses the significance of what has happened in plain view. The redundant addition of "which you're doing" to "your works" emphasizes this stupidity by highlighting that the brothers themselves are acknowledging Jesus' works.

7:6–9: So Jesus tells them, "My time hasn't arrived yet, but your time is always opportune. ⁷The world can't hate you; but me it hates, because I testify about it that its works are evil. ⁸You—go up to the festival. I'm not going up to this festival, because my time isn't yet fulfilled." ⁹And on saying these things, he himself stayed in Galilee. Jesus' "time" is a synonym for his "hour," which has already appeared in 2:4. He has a schedule to keep, a work-schedule (compare the reference to his "works" in 7:3). His brothers don't. They're temporal vagabonds because, unlike Jesus, they aren't working the works of God. Unemployed by God, they don't even have a timecard to punch. Vagrant, they can do anything they want. But Jesus—he has a schedule for finishing his works. His time, his hour, hasn't yet come. There's more to do before he can shout, "It's finished," or—better—"They're finished" (see the comments on 19:28–30). Why can't the world hate Jesus' brothers? Because they *are* the world, at least a representative slice of it. As such, they don't testify about the evil of the world's works, which includes their own works. And as unbelievers in Jesus, they're the haters, not the hated. He's the hated, because he does testify about the world's evil works.

7:10–13: But when his brothers had gone up to the festival, then he himself also went up—not manifestly; rather, as it were, in secret. ¹¹So the Jews were seeking him at the festival and saying, "Where is that [fellow]?" ¹²And there was much murmuring about him among the crowds. On the one hand, some were saying, "He's good." But others were saying, "No! Rather, he's deceiving the crowd." ¹³Because of fear of the Jews, however, no one was speaking publicly about him. At first it sounds as though Jesus lied in telling his brothers, "I'm not going up to this festival" (7:8). We could think that on the principle, "All is fair in love and war," and in view of what amounted to warfare between the world and Jesus, he tricked his brothers into thinking he wouldn't go up to the festival. Or we could think that he changed his mind. But it's probably best to take a cue from "not manifestly; rather, as it were in secret" and think that whereas his brothers advised him to make a grand entrance into Jerusalem and "manifest [himself] to the world," as opposed to "in secret" (7:4), he meant he wouldn't go up *in that manner*, because the time for that kind of entrance wasn't to come till Palm Sunday (compare the Pharisees' exclamation on that later occasion, "Look! The *world* has gone after him!" [12:19]). So now, after some delay, he goes up in a way diametrically opposed to his brothers' advice—secretly rather than manifestly in a caravan of fellow pilgrims.

Again "the Jews" are Jewish authorities, especially those based in Jerusalem and associated with the temple. According to 5:18 and 7:1, they were seeking Jesus to kill him. Their question, "Where is that [fellow]?" asks people to inform them of his whereabouts. They assume he's in Jerusalem or, more particularly, in the festal assembly (for "festival" can refer to the assembly of pilgrims at the temple as well as to the time of their celebration). But he remains incognito for a while. The murmuring of some in the crowd, "He's good," supplies an affirmative answer to Nathaniel's skeptical question in 1:46, "Can anything good be from Nazareth?" and previews Jesus' portrayal of himself as the good shepherd and of his works as good (10:11, 14, 32). And his coming self-portrayal as the very embodiment of God's truth (14:6) will falsify the murmuring of others that Jesus is deceiving the crowd. Fear of the Jewish authorities kept anybody from speaking publicly about him. But why should those who portrayed him as a deceiver speak in hushed tones for fear of the authorities who wanted to kill him? Wouldn't those authorities agree with them and applaud a public proclamation of their view? Psychologically, the question defies an answer. Theologically, though, the hushed tones of negative as well as positive murmurings highlight by contrast the openness and boldness with which Jesus the Word speaks and on which John's Gospel repeatedly lays emphasis (7:26; 11:14; 16:25, 29; 18:20).

TEACHING AND DIALOGUE IN THE TEMPLE COURTS AT THE FESTIVAL OF TABERNACLES
John 7:14–52

7:14–15: And when it was now in the middle of the festival [which lasted eight days], **Jesus went up into the temple** [that is, into the courtyards surrounding the hilltop sanctuary itself] **and started teaching** [because he had a ready-made audience of pilgrims there]. **¹⁵So the Jews were marveling and saying, "How is it that this** [fellow] **knows letters without having learned** [them]**?"** The Jewish authorities have been seeking Jesus to kill him. So once he appears in public we expect them to seize him. But they can only marvel at his ability to teach. Such is the force of the words of the divine Word. "Letters" refers to letters of the alphabet used in written texts, in particular the text of the Old Testament, since that is what Jewish teachers taught. Modern scholars debate the degree of literacy among first-century Jews living in Israel, especially among men (since women were largely uneducated) and especially as to the ability to read (since the ability to write was probably less common). But the authorities' question doesn't deal with mere literacy so much as with the kind of expertise in the Old Testament

that enabled him to teach. They marvel that he has such expertise despite not having learned the letters of the Old Testament by way of a rabbinic education.

7:16: So Jesus answered them and said, "My teaching isn't mine; rather, [it] **belongs to the one who sent me** [God the Father]**."** The Jews hadn't accused Jesus of originating his teaching. They'd only asked how he got it. So his answer means that for him it's not a matter of having learned in school how to read or of having had a rabbinic education in the Old Testament. What he teaches consists in what the one who sent him told him to say. So even though his teaching relates to the Old Testament, what he says about it came to him from God the Father, the ultimate author of the Old Testament who therefore conveyed its true meaning to Jesus. But what it means has to do not only with information to be believed but also with demands to be obeyed. So Jesus follows up with **7:17: "If anyone wills to do his** [God's] **will, he'll know about the teaching, whether it's from God or I speak on my own** [literally, 'from myself']**."** Jesus doesn't say merely that willingness to do God's will is a necessary *condition* for knowing whether Jesus' teaching comes from God, though of course it *is* such a condition. The statement is stronger: it says that such willingness will *in fact* lead a person to such knowledge. Again John is making a jab against the Gnostics, whose misbehavior exposes an unwillingness to do God's will and therefore falsifies their claim to superior knowledge (for the Gnostics, see the introduction to 1 John).

Jesus continues in **7:18: "The person who speaks on his own is seeking his own glory** [= honor]**. But the person who is seeking the glory of the one who sent him** [and such a person is Jesus]—**this person is true** [that is, truthful in his teaching], **and there's no unrighteousness in him."** "The person who speaks on his own" is anyone who does so, though John may have his eye particularly on Gnostic heretics. Seeking your own glory corrupts truth by bending it to your own advantage. Seeking the Father's glory keeps Jesus' teaching from self-serving falsification. Notably, Jesus puts truth and unrighteousness in opposition to each other. You'd expect him to put falsehood opposite truth. But since unrighteousness means sinful behavior (1 John 1:7; 5:16–17), the point is that the sinful behavior which constitutes unrighteousness arises out of falsehood, a failure of truth. Misbelief and misbehavior are intimately linked with each other.

Jesus continues again in **7:19: "Moses has given you the Law, hasn't he?"** Implied answer: Yes. **"And none of you does the Law** [= keeps it, obeys it]**. Why are you seeking to kill me?"** According to 1:17 the Law was given through Moses. According to 1:45 Moses wrote about Christ. According to 5:45 Moses accuses the Jewish authorities. And according to 5:46 they'd be believing Jesus if they believed Moses, for he wrote about Jesus. So Jesus' present question sets a trap. The Jewish authorities, to whom he has been speaking since 7:15–16, are condemning themselves. In what way? By seeking to kill Jesus (see 5:18; 7:1, 11 again) in violation of the commandment, "You shall not kill" (Exodus 20:13; Deuteronomy 5:17). Killing in the sense of murder is implied.

7:20: The crowd [who've been listening in] **answered, "You have a demon. Who's seeking to kill you?"** The charge that Jesus is a demoniac sounds a bit like the charge that he has Beelzebul and casts out demons by this ruler of the demons (Mark 3:22; Matthew 12:24; Luke 11:15). But there's nothing here about exorcism of demons by Jesus. Why then do the crowd charge him with having a demon on the mere ground that he asked why the authorities were seeking to kill him? To us the question sounds more like paranoia than like demon-possession. According to 5:18; 7:1, 11 the Jewish authorities are out to get Jesus. According to 7:13 the crowd know the authorities dislike him so much that it would be dangerous to talk about him openly. But the crowd's present question implies they don't know of an actual plot to murder him. So back to the question, Why does Jesus' asking the authorities their reason for seeking to kill him lead the surrounding crowd to charge him with having a demon? Well, consider how demons reacted when he approached. Take Mark 1:24, for example: "You've come to destroy us." Apparently Jesus' question here in John ("Why do you seek to kill me?") sounded to the crowd like the premonition of a demoniac.

7:21–24: Jesus answered and said to them, "I did one work, and you're all marveling. [22]Because of this, Moses has given you circumcision (not that it's from Moses; rather, [it's] from the patriarchs [Abraham, Isaac, and Jacob]**); and on the Sabbath you circumcise a man. [23]If a man receives circumcision on the Sabbath lest the law of Moses be broken, are you angry with me because I made a whole man well on the Sabbath? [24]Stop judging according to outward appearance; rather, judge** [with] **right judgment."** Jesus' "one work" was the healing of an invalid on a Sabbath day at the Pool of Bethzatha, the healing that generated the Jewish authorities' seeking to kill Jesus (chapter 5). Despite the lapse of time and intervening events, the crowd are still marveling at this work of his. "Because of this" points forward in John's text but backward in history. It points to God's requiring circumcision as a Jewish covenantal sign not for the first time with Moses, but beginning with Abraham (Genesis 17:9–14). That's the reason Moses passed on this requirement in his law. Circumcision was to be done on the eighth day after a man's birth (Leviticus 12:3; Philippians 3:5). (Obviously, then, "man" refers to a baby boy in 7:22–23a or, as we might say of a baby boy, "a little man"). Circumcision counted as work, such as Sabbath law prohibited. But the requirement of circumcision superseded the prohibition of work on the Sabbath, so that if the eighth day after birth happened to fall on a Sabbath, the work of circumcision proceeded in violation of Sabbath law. Building on this practice, Jesus argues that if it's legally required to do that kind of work on the Sabbath, traumatizing a little man by cutting off a tiny piece of his flesh, it's not right to be angry with Jesus for making the whole of an adult man well on the Sabbath. His argument plays on contrasts between a baby and an adult, between a tiny piece of flesh and a whole body, and between injury and health. Just as Jews broke the Sabbath law to keep the law of circumcision, then, Jesus broke the Sabbath law to do one of the good works his Father sent him to do. A right judgment would recognize the legitimacy of Jesus' doing so. A contrary judgment is superficial. These references to judgment remind us that John's story of Jesus is the story of a prolonged trial.

7:25–27: So some of the Jerusalemites were saying, "This [fellow] **is the one that they're seeking to kill, isn't he?"** The crowd of Galilean pilgrims didn't know about the Jewish authorities' plot to kill Jesus (7:20). But some residents of Jerusalem, where those authorities also lived, knew about it. Word gets around. [26]**"And look! He's speaking in public, and they're saying nothing to him."** The Jerusalemites are astonished at two things: (1) Jesus' speaking in public despite the plot to kill him and (2) the authorities' saying nothing to him (much less seizing him, we might add). A quizzical question follows: **"The rulers haven't come to know truly, have they, that this** [fellow] **is the Christ?"** The form of the question suggests that maybe they *have* come to know. In fact, though, this may not be a question at all, but a declaration: **"Perhaps the rulers have come to know truly that this** [fellow] **is the Christ."** In either case, for John the word "truly" indicates the truth of knowing Jesus to be the Christ—against the Jerusalemites' intended meaning and against the Gnostic know-it-alls of John's day who falsely distinguished Jesus and the Christ and denigrated Jesus: [27]**"We know, however, where this** [fellow] **is from. But whenever the Christ comes, no one knows where he's from."** These statements exhibit unwarranted confidence in a knowledge of Jesus' origin as distinguished from ignorance of the Christ's origin. Yes, Jesus comes from Galilee (see especially 7:52). But his true origin, his ultimate one, is heaven, where as the preincarnate Word he dwelled with God his Father and from where the Father sent him into the world. Of that origin the Jerusalemites of Jesus' day and the Gnostics of John's day are ignorant. The Jews had a tradition that nobody would know the Christ's origin. On the ground of thinking they know that Jesus originated in Galilee they falsely deduce that he's not the Christ. But their ignorance of Jesus' heavenly origin makes ironically true their tradition that the Christ's origin will be unknown, and it ironically confirms—on their own terms—that Jesus *is* the Christ!

What I've just written seems to be contradicted in the first half of **7:28–29: So Jesus shouted while teaching in the temple and saying, "You both know me and you know where I'm from."** But Jesus' words can be translated equally well, or better, as a question: **"Do you both know me and know where I'm from?"** In other words, he calls in question their statements that they know who he is and where he's from. Then he informs them of his heavenly origin and contrasts their ignorance of the one who sent him with his own knowledge of that sender: **"And I've not come from myself** [that is, 'on my own,' just as according to 7:17 I don't 'speak from myself/on my own']; **rather, the one who sent me is true, whom you don't know. ²⁹I do know him, because I'm from him; and that one sent me."** The passage screams anti-Gnosticism: *Jesus* is the Christ. *Jesus* came from God. *Jesus* was sent by God. *Jesus* knows the true God. Despite their name, which means "knowers," the Gnostics are ignorant. So also are all those who claim knowledge superior to that of the human Jesus, the Word-made-flesh. And Jesus describes God his sender as "true" to indicate that what he (Jesus) speaks as a true messenger from God (7:18) is reliable, because God, the ultimate source of the message, is himself true (compare 3:33; 8:26; 17:3). In 7:28–29, then, Jesus has made five claims: (1) that he didn't come on his own; (2) that he has been sent; (3) that his sender is true; (4) that his audience don't know the sender; and (5) that he does know him because he's from him. Some in the audience are offended.

7:30–31: **So** [because of the claims just listed] **they were seeking to seize him; and no one laid a hand on him, because his hour hadn't yet come. ³¹But many of the crowd believed in him and were saying, "Whenever the Christ comes, he won't do more signs than those that this** [fellow] **has done, will he?"** The implied answer: "No, he won't; and that's the reason we're believing in Jesus as the Christ." Who are "they" who seek to seize Jesus? Probably "some of the Jerusalemites" mentioned in 7:25, and probably *not* the authorities; for they're about to make their own, later attempt in 7:32. Why does the this earlier attempt fail? Because until Jesus' "hour" strikes, all such attempts are useless. His timetable rules even in the hornets' nest. Who are the "many of the crowd" that believe in him because he has performed many signs? Probably pilgrims from Galilee, where he has recently fed five thousand of them (not to mention his other signs) and where they had tried to make him their king (6:1–15). They stopped following him (6:59–66), but in reconsideration of his performing many signs they swing back into believing in him—more specifically, into believing him to be the Christ (just maybe a new development). Their question implies that the Christ won't perform more signs than Jesus has done. So his signs suffice to substantiate that he's the Christ. For John, Christian faith isn't blind faith. It's not a leap in the dark. It's a leap, but a leap in the light of observable evidence, a leap in the evidential light of the light of the world, Jesus. The evidence doesn't force faith. Many who saw the signs disbelieved. But the evidence supports faith, and supports it sufficiently. (By the way, the Old Testament and other ancient Jewish literature show that the Jews didn't expect the Christ to perform the sorts of signs and works that Jesus did. So his signs and works made up for, or more than made up for, his disappointing their hope for a military-political Christ, which the New Testament delays till the second coming.)

7:32: **The Pharisees heard the crowd murmuring these things about him, and the chief priests and the Pharisees sent** [their] **officers to seize him.** Again the crowd consists of Galilean pilgrims. The things the Pharisees hear them murmuring are the just-quoted question favorable to Jesus. The Pharisees, a leading religious sect, appeared for the first time in 1:24. Here we meet the chief priests for the first time. They consisted of the current high priest, past high priests, and other high-ranking priests and members of priestly families. They had officers to carry out their wishes. Here the officers act rather like policemen. Most of the chief priests belonged to the sect called Sadducees. Pharisees and Sadducees opposed each other on many theological issues (compare Acts 23:1–11), but their common enemy Jesus made them strange bedfellows. They join in sending their officers to seize him, that is, to arrest him.

Now we expect John to tell whether the officers did arrest Jesus successfully. But he doesn't. We have to wait a dozen verses. Like a good storyteller, John keeps us in suspense, or at least in what little suspense might be left after telling us that Jesus' hour hadn't yet come. Instead, John tells us how Jesus reacted to the sending of the officers. *7:33:* **Therefore** [because the chief priests and Pharisees sent their officers to arrest him] **Jesus said, "Yet a little while I'm with you."** What's the implication? You can't arrest me quite yet. Well, we'll see whether they can or can't. We'll see whether Jesus' statement holds true. "And I'm going to the one who sent me." So when in chapter 18 they do take Jesus in the garden, it won't be the end of a journey so much as the beginning of a return trip, a journey back to his Father in heaven, the one who sent him, the completion of a roundtrip rather than the end of a one-way trip. The present tense, "I'm going," instead of the future tense, "I'll go," emphasizes the certainty of this return trip. It's as though Jesus has already started back home to the Father. *7:34:* **"You'll seek me and not find me."** Why not? Because he'll have gone to heaven. But won't they find him in the form of his corpse? No. The statement implies his bodily resurrection and ascension, which John will note later on. Why will they seek Jesus? He doesn't say. But ever since 7:1, 19–20, 25, 30 they've been seeking him to arrest and kill him. So apparently he means that as a result of his resurrection and ascension he'll be beyond their murderous grasp. "And where I am, you can't come." In 7:33 Jesus said, "Yet a little while I'm with you." But now he talks about being where his audience can't come to be with him, because he has said he's going to the one who sent him. So you expect him to say, "Where I'm *going* you can't come," not "Where I *am* you can't come." In fact, he'll say exactly that at 8:21: "Where I'm going you can't come." Why this unexpected, awkward, and seemingly illogical "I am" here in 7:34? Because throughout John's Gospel, Jesus portrays himself as the divine "I AM" who is eternally present, eternally existent, most astonishingly in 8:58: "Amen, amen I tell you, before Abraham came into existence, I AM" (compare Exodus 3:14). The fact that Jesus' listeners can't come to where he is with his Father in heaven shows that here he's addressing unbelievers, because in 17:24 he prays that his disciples may be with him, as he says, "where I am." A warning and fearful thought—that unbelief in Jesus shuts a person out of heaven.

7:35: So the Jews said to one another, "Where is this [fellow] **about to go that we won't find him? He isn't about to go to the Diaspora of the Greeks and teach the Greeks, is he?"** The Jews' question exposes their inability to understand Jesus' word. He has just told them that he's going to the one who sent him. They hardly think that the one who sent him lives in the Diaspora, because they know, or think they know, Jesus is from Galilee (7:41, 52). In view of what Jesus has told them, why do they even suggest the possibility of his going to the Diaspora? Their question doesn't make sense. In 7:17 Jesus said that the person who wills to do God's will—that person will understand Jesus' teaching. But these Jews in 7:35 aren't willing to do God's will; so they completely misunderstand what Jesus says.

"Diaspora" means "dispersion, scattering" and usually refers to Jews living outside the land of Israel, scattered among the Gentile nations. Here "the Diaspora of the Greeks" could mean Jews living among the Gentiles and called "Greeks" because of their adoption of the Greek language and culture. If so, Jesus' audience throw out the unlikelihood that Jesus would go to Jews in the Diaspora for the purpose of teaching them. But the followup, "and teach the Greeks," suggests that "Diaspora" just might refer not only to Jews living outside the land of Israel but also to Gentiles scattered across the Roman Empire. If so, the Jews' use of "Diaspora" links up with 10:16, where Jesus will say that in contrast with hired hands who flee from a wolf so that the sheep are scattered, he's the good shepherd who has other sheep, not of the Jewish pen; and he'll bring them, so that they'll all become one flock with one shepherd. We who believe in Jesus are even now that flock, once far from God, geographically scattered throughout the world, but theologically brought together as one flock by Jesus Christ, and in him, our good shepherd. Ironically but happily, later in John's Gospel some Greeks will come to see Jesus rather than his going to them: "And there were some Greeks from among those who were going up [to Jerusalem] to worship in the festal assembly [at Passover]. Therefore these approached Philip, the one from Bethsaida of Galilee [Philip being a Greek name, as in the case of Alexander the Great's father], and were asking him, saying, 'Sir, we want to see Jesus'" (12:21–22).

The Jews ask in **7:36, "What is this word that he has spoken, 'You'll seek me and not find me, and where I am you can't come?'"** He has just spoken about himself. In the other Gospels Jesus speaks predominantly about God's reign/kingdom. In John he speaks predominantly about himself, as he has done here. What's striking is that 7:36 could be translated not only with "*What* is this word that he has spoken?" but also with "*Who* is this Word that he has spoken?" Of course, this latter isn't what the Jews meant. But it could well be an additional meaning that

John saw in their question, because according to him Jesus is the Word who was with God and was God (1:1). He's the Word that's the subject matter of his own words. The Word speaks the Word that he himself is. The Jews said more than they themselves intended to say. And the fact that they ask a question which exposes their ignorance, "What/Who *is* this w/Word?" illustrates John's statement back in 1:5 that the darkness didn't *com*prehend the light of life that the Word was. A few verses later here in chapter 7 it will turn out that the darkness didn't *ap*prehend the Word, either. (The officers will fail to arrest him.)

But first take a look at **7:37: And on the last day, the great** [day] **of the festival, Jesus stood and shouted** [notice now how Jesus the Word not only speaks, but also speaks loudly and openly about himself, in contrast with the crowd's mere murmuring and not speaking openly about him for fear of the Jews (7:12–13, 32)], **"If anyone thirsts, let him come to me and drink."** "*Let* him" not in the sense of permission but in the sense of a command: he *should* come to me and drink. Thirst represents a longing for eternal life. Drinking represents the gaining of eternal life by believing in Jesus. He's the source of that life, just as he told the Samaritan woman at Jacob's well (4:14). The setting here is the Festival of Tabernacles in the fall, something like our Thanksgiving for an abundant harvest. As noted before, the festival lasted eight days. It also featured a daily ceremony of pouring water out of a golden flagon as a liquid sacrifice to God. The water recalled not only the rains that had made the harvests possible but also the water that God miraculously provided the Israelites in the wilderness on their way from Egypt to Canaan, when they were living in tents, that is, in tabernacles (Exodus 17:6; Numbers 20:2–11; Psalm 78:15–16).

7:38: "The person who believes in me—just as the Scripture has said, 'Out of his belly will flow rivers of living water.'" In 4:14 Jesus said to the Samaritan woman, "Whoever drinks some of the water that I'll give him will never, ever thirst. Rather, the water that I'll give him will become in him a spring of water leaping up into eternal life." But now the mere "fountain" of chapter 4 has turned into "rivers," not just one river, but multiple rivers to emphasize the abundance of eternal life. And not just leaping up *in* the believer, but flowing *out of* his belly, that is, *over*flowing—to emphasize an excess of eternal life, *more than enough*. Out of the *believer's* belly, not that of Jesus. (It's a mistake to draw a parallel with the outflow of water and blood from Jesus' side in 19:34 and deduce that here the rivers of living water flow out of Jesus' belly; for "side" refers to the rib cage rather than the belly, and the outflow of rivers of living water comes as a result of drinking the water that Jesus gives.) The water of these rivers is "living" not just because it's flowing instead of stagnant, though that much is true. It's "living" also because it brings life. In the world of nature, no water, no life. In the world of theology, the same. It's hard to know what Scripture Jesus has in view when he says, "as the Scripture has said." There's no Old Testament text that says exactly, "Out of his belly will flow rivers of living water." So we may have a paraphrase of a passage like Isaiah 58:11: "And the Lord will continually . . . satisfy your soul in scorched places . . . . And you will be . . . like a fountain of water whose waters do not fail." Additional help may have come from Isaiah 44:3–4, where the Lord says, "I will pour water on the thirsty [ground] and streams on the dry ground. I will pour my Spirit on your seed and my blessing on your offspring. And they will sprout up like a green tamarisk, like poplars beside channels of water."

John follows up with an editorial comment in *7:39:* **And he spoke this concerning the Spirit that those who'd believed in him were about to receive. For the Spirit wasn't yet** [received], **because Jesus hadn't yet been glorified.** In chapter 20 we'll read about Jesus' glorification and giving the Spirit to his disciples. For now we need only to note the echo of 3:5: "Unless one is born out of water, even the Spirit, he can't enter into the kingdom of God." Water symbolizes the Spirit of God as well as eternal life, because it's the Spirit who enlivens a believer with eternal life at the time of being born from above. The word for "Spirit" also means "breath." Life requires breathing just as life requires water. So water, Spirit, and life are all wrapped up with each other.

The next paragraph (7:40–44) gives us people's reaction to Jesus' statements. *7:40–41a:* **So on hearing these words, some of the crowd were saying, "This is truly the prophet."** Apparently they mean a great prophet that some Jews expected to appear in the end-time. Such a prophet was mentioned in 1:21 and distinguished there from a returned Elijah. Maybe these people expected a prophet like Moses, who'd brought water from a rock in the wilderness (Exodus 17:6; Numbers 20:11; Deuteronomy 18:15–18). *41a***Others were saying, "This is the Christ."** This designation is Greek for the Hebrew "Messiah," God's anointed king who was expected to rule over an Israel freed from foreign domination, and also over the nations. Both of the identifications, "the prophet" and "the Christ," are favorable; and though they don't tell the whole story about Jesus, John agrees with them (see 4:43–44; 20:31). But where these people distinguish between the prophet and the Christ, John unites them in the one person Jesus.

7:41b–42: **But some were saying, "Why, the Christ isn't coming out of Galilee, is he? ⁴²The Scripture said, didn't it, that the Christ is coming from the seed of David** [that is, will be a descendant of David] **and from Bethlehem, the town where David was?"** Apparently the "some" who talk about the Christ's "coming . . . from Bethlehem" differ from the "some" in 7:25–27 who said that "whenever the Christ comes, no one knows where he's from." Bethlehem was David's hometown, and Micah 5:2 predicted, "As for you, Bethlehem, . . . from you one will come forth to be ruler in Israel for me." The people don't know of Jesus' birth in Bethlehem as a descendant of David, and 1:45–46 portrays Jesus as coming from Nazareth. John doesn't deny Jesus' birth in Bethlehem as a descendant of David, for which see Matthew 1–2; Luke 1–2. But in the interests of what for him is the more important point of Jesus' origin in heaven as the Word who was with God as God's Son and was himself God, John never mentions Jesus' Davidic ancestry and birth in Bethlehem. Of Jesus' deity and heavenly origin the people are even more ignorant than they are of that human ancestry and birthplace.

7:43–46: **So because of him there developed a split in the crowd, ⁴⁴and some of them were wanting to seize him.** Presumably these were the officers sent to seize him back in 7:32, and perhaps they were joined by those who denied he was the Christ. **No one laid hands on him, however.** They wanted to, but they didn't. Why not? In 7:30 the Jewish authorities "were seeking to seize him; and no one laid a hand on him, because his hour [the divinely set time of his passion, resurrection, and ascension] hadn't yet come." But now we get an additional reason: ⁴⁵**Therefore** [since nobody had laid hands on Jesus] **the officers came to the chief priests and Pharisees** [who had sent them], **and those** [chief priests and Pharisees] **said to them** [the officers], **"For what reason haven't you brought him?" ⁴⁶The officers answered, "A human being has never spoken this way** [= the way Jesus has spoken]." Jesus is a human being, but he's also the Word who is *God.* Notice also, the *Word* who is God. So the words of this divine Word, who is Jesus, are so powerful, so eloquent, that they tie the hands of his would-be arresters. The ancient Greek orator Protagoras was nicknamed "Word" because of his eloquence with words; and Isocrates, a teacher of rhetoric, used the very word "words" as a synonym for eloquence. But according to John's text, Jesus out-orated them all—including Pericles, Demosthenes, Aeschines, Cicero—because he was superhuman to the degree of deity.

The Jewish authorities aren't pleased according to *7:47–49:* **So the Pharisees** [the main interpreters of the Old Testament law] **answered them** [the officers], **"You too haven't been misled, have you? ⁴⁸None of the rulers or of the Pharisees has believed in him, has he? ⁴⁹But this crowd that doesn't know the Law** [you can visualize the curl on their lips as they refer to the crowd disdainfully] **are accursed** [because if they don't know the Law they can't keep it and therefore fall under God's curse for unwittingly disobeying it (compare Deuteronomy 27:14–26)]." Surprisingly, Nicodemus the Pharisee, "a ruler of the Jews" and "the teacher of Israel" (as he was dubbed in 3:1, 10), pops up and speaks to his fellow rulers in *7:50–51:* **Nicodemus, the one who came to him** [Jesus] **earlier, being one of them, says to them** [the Pharisees, the present tense of "says" emphasizing the following statement], **⁵¹"Our law** [in which Nicodemus was expert as 'the teacher of Israel' (3:10)] **doesn't judge a man, does it, unless it first hears from him and comes to know what he's doing?"** See Deuteronomy 1:16–17: "I [Moses] charged your judges at that time, saying, 'Hear the cases between your brothers and judge righteously between a man and his brother or the alien who is with him. . . . You shall hear the small and the great alike."

Nicodemus is right, and his fellow Pharisees can't refute him. So they resort to ad hominem; they attack him instead of his argument in **7:52: They answered and said to him, "You too** [as well as Jesus] **aren't from Galilee, are you?"** They know he isn't; but they imply he might as well be, since he advocates giving Jesus a fair hearing. Then they think of a substantive argument: **"Search and see** [in the Old Testament] **that a prophet doesn't arise out of Galilee."** But the argument is plain wrong. The prophets Jonah and Nahum arose out of Galilee. The Old Testament says so (2 Kings 14:25; Nahum 1:1). Probably others as well, but the Old Testament is explicit about Jonah and Nahum. A very few ancient manuscripts of John have "*the* prophet" (of the end-time presumably) rather than "*a* prophet." If that's the correct text, the argument is still wrong, because the Old Testament doesn't say where the prophet of the end-time will come from. The Pharisees have said, "This *crowd* doesn't know the Law." It turns out that the *Pharisees* don't know it. Does John expect us to smile?

Note: The story of a woman taken in adultery occupies 7:53–8:11. But the earliest and best manuscripts of John don't have this story at all. They go straight from 7:52 to 8:12. The story was inserted in later, inferior manuscripts, usually here but sometimes after 7:36, or 7:44, or 8:12, or 21:25, or even after Luke 21:38 or Luke 24:53. The later manuscripts that do contain the story sometimes contain special markings to indicate its doubtfulness, and they contain an unusually high number of variations in wording. The reason the venerable King James Version (first published in 1611) included the story here is that the earliest and best manuscripts hadn't yet been discovered. Its translators had only the later, inferior manuscripts containing the story. And the King James Version exercised so much influence on the Christian public that more recent translators and publishers have sometimes included the story for fear of offending this public. The bottom line: John didn't write this story in his Gospel. It may be historically true, but it's not part of Scripture if you believe that Scripture consists only of what its Spirit-inspired authors originally wrote. After all, Jesus did and said many things in history that aren't recorded in Scripture (compare John 20:30–31; 21:25). And if we believe in addition that the later copyists who inserted this story at various points were inspired by the Holy Spirit, we should be consistent enough to think that the hundreds and hundreds of other copyists' insertions and revisions were equally inspired. But that's a hard pill to swallow. So we'll skip the story as noncanonical and go directly to 8:12–59, which in John's original text followed directly on 7:1–52.

DIALOGUE IN JERUSALEM AFTER THE FESTIVAL OF TABERNACLES
John 8:12–59

Jesus is still in Jerusalem following the last day of the Festival of Tabernacles. The whole of 8:12–59 consists of a dialogue between Jesus and the Jewish authorities.

8:12: Therefore Jesus spoke to them again, saying, "I am the light of the world. The person who follows me will by no means walk around in darkness; rather, he'll have the light of life." At the end of chapter 7 the Jewish supreme council asserted that "a/the prophet doesn't arise out of Galilee." Since the story of the woman taken in adultery doesn't belong in John's Gospel, "therefore" at the start of 8:12 makes Jesus' following statement a response to the council's using his Galilean origin to disqualify him from prophethood. He declares to them (apparently they're back in his audience) that he's much more than a prophet. He claims to be the light of the world. At the beginning of the festival that just ended the Jews lit four huge lamps in the area of the temple. The lamps were so large that it's said their light illuminated the whole of Jerusalem, and they were kept burning night and day for the whole week. But now the lamps have gone out. So Jesus takes advantage of the situation to say he's much more than a lamp. He's the light of the world, which—literally speaking—is the sun; for the sun illuminates not just the city of Jerusalem, but the whole world (see 11:9 for the light of the world as the sun, which rules out an allusion here to the pillar of fire that guided Israel at night in the wilderness). Predominantly in John, though, "the world" means the human race apart from God. And "light" represents eternal life. In the world of nature, life requires water—hence the water of life in chapters 4 and 7. In the world of nature, life also requires sunlight. As the light of the world, then, Jesus brings life, eternal life. Since he's the light that brings such life, those who follow him won't walk around in darkness. At first, following Jesus had to do with physical following, like that of the twelve apostles. But by the time John wrote his Gospel, following Jesus had come to mean believing in him, pledging allegiance to him, obeying him. Walking around in darkness leads to stumbling, to falling into God's eternal judgment, what the book of Revelation calls "the second death" (Revelation 2:11; 20:6, 14; 21:8). To "have" the light of life is to possess it, to own it as yours. This light is Jesus himself, because he is the life: "I am . . . the life" (11:25; 14:6).

The Pharisees, who among the Jewish authorities were experts on the Law, lodge a legal objection to Jesus' claim in **8:13–14: Therefore the Pharisees said to him, "You're testifying about yourself. Your testimony isn't true."** Jewish jurisprudence didn't allow a person to testify in his own behalf, because it was thought that self-interest would make him falsify the truth. So the Pharisees rule Jesus' self-testimony out of court, so to speak. It's neither valid nor true (compare 5:31 with comments). **[14]Jesus answered and said to them, "Even if I testify about myself, my testimony is true."** That is to say, Jesus' self-testimony is true even though the Jews' judicial rules don't allow it. And why is it true? Because in contrast to his audience, Jesus knows his origin and his destination, which are heavenly. Being earthbound, the Jews can't know them. Jesus continues: **"because I know where I came from and where I'm going. But you don't know where I'm coming from or where I'm going."** The shift from past tense, "where I came from," to present tense, "where I'm coming from," puts emphasis on Jesus' heavenly origin (just as using the present tense for a future event carries an emphasis). It's as though he's still coming. Jesus doesn't tell the Jewish authorities where he came/is coming from and where he's going. But readers of the Fourth Gospel know.

8:15–16: "You're judging according to the flesh. I'm judging no one. ¹⁶And if I judge, my judgment is true, because I'm not alone. Rather, I and the Father, who sent me [are together]." Judging according to the flesh stands opposite true judgment. So judging according to the flesh must indicate a false judgment—false because it's limited to Jesus' incarnate form, to his appearance in and as human flesh, in ignorance of his heavenly origin and destination. As in 7:24 ("Stop judging according to outward appearance [literally, 'face']; rather, judge [with] right judgment"), such judgment plays on the ancient practice of using the physical characteristics of a person (hair, facial features, complexion, posture, and so on) to assess his character. Jesus' judgment is true because, as 2:25 said, "he himself knew what was in a human being." But is there a contradiction between 8:15, where Jesus says he's judging "no one," and 8:16, where he says his judgment is true? No, because 8:16 implies that the kind of judgment Jesus denies he exercises is a false judgment. The kind of judgment he does exercise is a true judgment, and it's true because his Father is with him to guide his judgments, though the Father himself judges no one (5:22).

8:17–18: "And even in your law it's written that the testimony of two human beings is true. ¹⁸I'm the one testifying about myself, and the Father who sent me is testifying about me." Jesus is referring to the law of two or three witnesses in Numbers 35:30; Deuteronomy 17:6; 19:15. A literal translation is more forceful, though awkward in English: "even in the Law—yours." The emphatic "yours" shows that Jesus is using against the Jewish leaders what they themselves consider authoritative—a good debating maneuver. So the double testimony of Jesus and his Father satisfies the legal requirement, even surpasses it, because the Law required only the testimony of two *human* beings. Jesus is human, but he's also the Word who was God; and the one who sent him is God the Father. You can't get better witnesses than they. But the Pharisees don't believe that God is Jesus' Father (compare 5:18).

8:19: So they were saying to him, "Where is your father?" The Pharisees are thinking of a human father, whom "the Jews" in 6:41–42 said they knew as "Joseph," and ask Jesus to tell the whereabouts of his father so that they may go hear his testimony for themselves. **Jesus answered, "You know neither me nor my Father. If you'd known me, you'd have known my Father too."** Jesus refuses to answer where his Father is and stresses instead the Pharisees' ignorance of him and God his Father. Because the Pharisees don't follow him, they walk around in darkness, the darkness of ignorance. And whether or not they think they know Jesus, they don't—not really—any more than they know his Father. It takes believing in Jesus, following him, to know him; and it takes knowing him to know his Father.

8:20–21: He spoke these words in the area of the receptacles for offerings while teaching in the temple [courtyards]. And no one seized him, because his hour hadn't yet come. As usual, John's pointing up the "words" of Jesus recalls the identification of Jesus as "the Word." "In the area of the receptacles for offerings" locates Jesus' claim to be the light of the world near the huge lamps that had illuminated Jerusalem during the Festival of Tabernacles but whose light the light of Jesus replaces and far outshines. And John doesn't tire of noting that as the divine Word, Jesus determines the hour of his death, resurrection, and ascension, so that he can't be seized at others' initiative (compare 7:30, 44–46). **²¹Therefore he told them again, "I'm going, and you'll seek me** [a repetition of 7:33–34; but now instead of saying they won't find him, Jesus tells *why* they won't by referring to *their* death instead of his own], **and you'll die in your sin."** They'll die *in* their sin because they haven't believed in the lamb of God who takes *away* the sin of the world (1:29). And because they'll *die* in their sin, Jesus goes on to repeat what he said in 7:34b—with one difference: "Where I'm going you can't come." The difference is that in 7:34b he said, "where I *am* you can't come." Jesus is saving "I am" for a little later in this dialogue. In chapter 7 he didn't give the reason the Jews couldn't come. Here in chapter 8 he does give the reason. It's that they'll die in their sin; and we're meant to supply mentally that where he's going—to his Father in heaven—there's no sin.

The Jews react, but they avoid Jesus' reference to their dying in sin. It's human nature to avoid thinking and speaking about that possibility, but John would have us understand that on pain of eternal loss we'd better think and speak about it. **8:22: So the Jews were saying, "He won't kill himself, will he? [Surely not, but we ask whether he will] because he's saying, 'Where I'm going you can't come.'"** On the one hand, his saying they can't come where he's going prompts their question. On the other hand, they can't imagine that he'll kill himself. What they can't imagine will at a fundamental level actually take place, for he'll lay down his life at his own initiative (10:17–18) even though at a superficial level—and ironically—they, the Jews who ask this question, will kill him (19:16).

The dialogue switches back to Jesus in **8:23–24: And he was saying to them, "You're from the things below; I'm from the things above. You're from this world; I'm not from this world. ²⁴Therefore I told you, 'You'll die in your sins.' For if you don't believe that I am** [and it doesn't appear you will], **you'll die in your sins."** Obviously, "the things below" equate with "this world" ("earth" in 3:31). By implication and by contrast, "the things above" mean heaven, where the one who sent Jesus lives ("heaven" in 3:31). To be "from" means to have one's origin in. Jesus' origin is heavenly, not earthly. The

Jews' origin is earthly, not heavenly. If it weren't, they wouldn't die in their sins. Unbelief in Jesus is the sign of earthly origin and citizenship as opposed to being "born from above" (3:3, 7). (Since John often switches back and forth between the singular and the plural without any apparent difference in meaning, there's probably no difference between "sins" in 8:24 and "sin" in 8:21.) But what don't the Jews believe about Jesus? They don't believe "that I am." This expression doesn't make sense to the Jews, because they don't detect in it Jesus' claiming for himself the divine title "I AM" (Exodus 3:14).

The Jews think he should have completed his statement: "for if you don't believe that I am *so-and-so* . . . ." **8:25: Therefore they were saying to him, "Who are you?"** Fill in the blank, Jesus. Finish your sentence. In fact, though, Jesus' words have echoed the Greek translation of Isaiah 43:10–11. The Hebrew original reads: "You are my witnesses, says the Lord, . . . so that you may know that I am *he*. . . . I, I am the Lord, and besides me there is no savior." But the Greek translation reads, "so that you may know and believe that I *am*." There's no "he" after "I am," just as there's nothing after Jesus' "I am." The rest of 8:25 is hard to translate, so that English translations differ widely among themselves. I won't canvass them, but here's mine: **Jesus told them, "[I am] whatever I even speak to you,** [namely,] **the beginning.**" "The beginning" refers back to 1:1: "In the beginning was the Word." Jesus himself is what he speaks to the Jews, because he's the I AM in his preceding statement. It's as though he says, "I didn't need to finish my sentence, because it was already complete. I'm the Word who as I AM preexisted in the beginning and therefore am the beginning itself, as in Revelation 22:13, 'I [am] the alpha and the omega, the first and the last, *the beginning* and the end.'"

Jesus continues in **8:26: "I have many things to say and judge about you. But the one who sent me is true, and the things I've heard from him—these things I'm saying to the world."** Jesus draws a parallel between his saying and judging many things about "you" and saying things to "the world." "You're from this world" (8:23), because "world" means not only "the earth" but also *people*, especially unbelieving people. What guarantees the reliability of Jesus' words of judgment is the truth of God the Father, the source of Jesus' judgmental words. So Jesus brings a true message of judgment from God, and this message includes "*many* things." Thus the bounty of God's love is matched by the bounty of God's judgment. It's wrong, then, to stress the love of God at the expense of his judgment, which arises out of his wrath against human wickedness (3:19–20. 36). The Bible—including the Gospel of John, sometimes called "the Gospel of Love"— maintains a tensive balance between the two, because to the degree that judgment is diluted, love turns into sentimentality. And grace becomes less than amazing, just as to the degree love is diluted judgment turns into a mere temper tantrum, justice into personal animosity.

8:27: They didn't know [= understand] **that he was speaking to them in reference to the Father.** The phrase "in reference to" is supplied to make good English. If we omit it, the text reads, "They didn't know that he was speaking the Father to them," and thereby emphasizes that God the Father is the very essence of Jesus' speech (compare 1:18, which says that Jesus "explained" God). But how could the Jews fail to know, fail to understand? Twice in 8:16–19 Jesus referred to the Father who sent him, and in 5:16–30 the Jews seemed to have understood. Take 5:18, for example: "The Jews were seeking all the more to kill [him], because . . . he was calling God his own Father." Yet the ignorance of unbelief knows no limits. The truth may be as plain as possible, but unwillingness to do God's will not only prevents understanding. It also *deadens* understanding. Such unwillingness has now in chapter 8 killed the understanding that the Jews displayed in chapter 5.

8:28: So Jesus told them, "Whenever you've lifted up the Son of Man [a way of referring to himself obliquely], **then you'll know that I AM** [another claim by Jesus to this divine title] **and** [that] **I don't do even one thing on my own. Rather, just as the Father taught me—I speak these things."** In those days students learned by rote memory; so Jesus is saying that he speaks the words which before the Father sent him into the world he heard his Father speak and which he memorized at that time. But back to the Son of Man's being "lifted up": it refers to Jesus' being lifted up on a cross rather than knocked down by stoning; and because crucifixion is a lifting up rather than a knocking down, in John it marks the start of Jesus' exaltation back to heaven. "Son of Man" has particular connections with Jesus' descent and ascent, as in 3:13: "And no one has ascended into heaven except the one who has descended out of heaven, [namely,] the Son of Man." Who is going to lift up the Son of Man in this way? God? The Apostle Paul says so in Philippians 2:9: "Therefore [because 'Jesus humbled himself by becoming obedient to the point of death, even the death of a cross'] God lifted him above [everyone else]." But here in John it is the Jews ("you") who will lift Jesus up. What irony! Jesus' very enemies will be the agents of his exaltation, so that the cross becomes, not the depth of Jesus' humiliation at the hands of his enemies, but with their help his first upward step to glory (compare 19:16, where Pilate will give Jesus over to the Jews for crucifixion, though it should be stressed that as throughout the present passage, "the Jews" means the Jewish authorities at the time and therefore provides no scriptural basis whatever for anti-Semitism). We also see in 8:28–29 a parallel between the things Jesus does and the things he speaks. His deeds illustrate his words. His words interpret his deeds. His deeds imitate what he has seen the Father do. (The picture is that of a father showing his son how to practice a trade.) The words of Jesus repeat what he has heard the Father say. (The picture is that of a teacher and his pupil.) Jesus' deeds are visible words. Jesus' words are audible deeds. Thus it is that throughout his Gospel, John alternates the words and deeds of Jesus. They illustrate and interpret each other.

Jesus' speech continues in *8:29*: **"And the one who sent me is with me. He hasn't left me alone, because I always do the things pleasing to him."** Naturally Jesus always does the things that are pleasing to his Father. After all, he does and says *only* what he has seen his Father do and heard his Father say. Ordinarily, sending implies distance between the sender and the one sent. But not here, because as Jesus will later say, "I and the Father are one" (10:30). And just as Jesus the Word was with the Father in the beginning, prior to the incarnation, so now the Father is with Jesus during his earthly sojourn. It's no accident, then, that when John comes to the crucifixion, he won't quote Jesus' anguished outcry, "My God, my God, why have you abandoned me?" (Mark 15:34; Matthew 27:46). Rather, the triumphant but calm and confident "They're finished" (that is, his signs, works, and words [see the comments on 19:28–30]). Calm and confident, so that there'll be no shout, no loud voice, as in "The *Cry* of Dereliction." Only "Jesus said."

Some in Jesus' audience react positively. *8:30*: **While he was saying these things, many believed in him.** He responds to their belief in *8:31–32*: **Therefore Jesus was saying to the Jews who'd believed him, "If you abide in my word, you're truly my disciples; ³²and you'll know the truth, and the truth will set you free."** There's a subtle shift from believing *in* Jesus (8:30) to believing *Jesus* (8:31). Believing Jesus is believing what he says. Believing in Jesus is believing so as to commit yourself to his person. These two sorts of belief depend on each other. You can't commit yourself to his person unless you believe what he says; and given the content of what he says, which is about himself, you can't believe what he says without committing yourself to his person. "Disciples" means "learners"—here, those who learn Jesus' "word." But, of course, he *is* the Word, the subject matter of his own speech. So to abide in his word is to abide in Jesus himself, not just to learn *from* him but also to learn *him*. To abide is to stay, to remain. In other words, true learning requires perseverance till graduation day. It requires believing Jesus, and *in* him, till the Day of Judgment. Fleeting faith won't do. Dropouts won't make it. So when Jesus said back in 8:28 that the Jews would know that he's the I AM and that his words and deeds come from God the Father, he wasn't referring to all the Jews, but to those who after his crucifixion, resurrection, and ascension will believe him, and in him, and prove themselves true disciples by persevering in their belief. They're the ones who'll be in the know, who'll know his true identity and the true origin of his words and deeds. And as true disciples they'll know the truth, and the truth will set them free. According to 1:14, Jesus the Word was full of grace and truth. According to 1:17, grace and truth came on the scene through him. And he'll say in 14:6, "I am . . . the truth." So "you'll know the truth" means "you'll know *me*, Jesus, as the embodiment of God's truth; and as that truth *I'll* set you free." From what? We'll have to wait for an answer till 8:34. But for now Jesus establishes knowing the truth as the basis for liberation.

Jesus' audience don't think they need any liberation, though. *8:33*: **They answered back to him, "We're Abraham's seed** [= descendants] **and have never been enslaved to anyone. How come you're saying, 'You'll become free?'"** They're depending on Abrahamic descent rather than believing in Jesus. In 4:22 he said that "salvation is *from* the Jews," but he didn't say it's *being* a Jew. So they have a false faith—and a bad memory. For the Jews had fallen into slavery many times: to the Egyptians, Assyrians, Babylonians, Persians, and Greeks, for example. Jesus' audience don't even acknowledge their present plight. They're living under the heel of the Romans! They'll even say in 19:15 at Jesus' trial, "We have no king except Caesar." Oh how much these Jews need to learn! They've said, "We've never been enslaved to anyone."

But the word translated "any*one*" can also mean "any*thing*." Jesus picks up this second possible meaning in *8:34*: **Jesus answered them, "Amen, amen I tell you that everyone who's committing sin is a slave of *sin*."** So knowing the truth, that is, knowing Jesus, liberates you from slavery to sin. Not sin as guilt so much as sin as a dominating force in your life (compare Romans 7:14–15a, 19: "I'm fleshy, having been sold [as a slave so as to be] under sin [as my slavemaster]. For I don't know what I'm producing. . . . For I'm not doing the good that I want [to do]; rather, the bad that I don't want [to do]—this I'm doing"; and contrast Romans 6:17, 22: "Thanks to God that you *used to be* slaves of sin . . . . But now, having been freed from sin and enslaved to God, you have . . . the end result, eternal life."

8:35–36: **"A slave doesn't abide in the household forever."** Why? Because according to the Mosaic law of the sabbatical year, Hebrew slaves had to be released after six years (Exodus 21:2–4; Deuteronomy 15:12–13). And in pagan society they were often sold off or given away. They had no security in a family. **"A son does abide** [in the household] **forever."** He has a permanent place in the household. But *a* son represents *the* Son, Jesus as God's unique Son, because John uses the word "Son" for Jesus, but "children" for believers in Jesus. ³⁶**"Therefore if the Son frees you** [from sin, your slavemaster], **you'll be really free** [in the most important and fundamental way, because to die in your sins has eternally disastrous consequences or—perhaps better—because as God's Son, Jesus does a thorough job of liberation in that sin retains no hold whatever]." In 8:32 Jesus said "the *truth* will set you free." Here he talks about the *Son's* setting you free, because he the Son *is* the truth.

Harking back to the Jews' claim to be Abraham's seed is *8:37–38*: **"I know that you're Abraham's seed. Nevertheless** [despite that fact, which I acknowledge], **you're seeking to kill me, because my word has no space in you."** Jesus seems to be still speaking to the Jews who had believed in him (8:31). If so, he perceives that their believing is superficial and therefore temporary. In other words, Jesus' word doesn't find space to abide in them, which is another way of saying that Jesus himself, who is the Word, doesn't find space to abide in them, nor they in him or in his word (compare 14:20, 23; 15:4–5, where Jesus abides in believers; and 15:7, where his words abide in believers). What a turnaround, from believing in Jesus to seeking to kill him! ³⁸"I speak the things that I've seen alongside the Father [in my preincarnate state]. Therefore you too—do the things that you've heard from alongside the Father." We expect Jesus to *speak* what he has *heard*, and the Jews to *do* what they've *seen*. But here it's vice versa: he speaks what he has seen; they do what they've heard. This switcharoo shows the interchangeability in Jesus' vocabulary of seeing and hearing, of speaking and doing. Sight and sound complement each other. Words and deeds complement each other.

The things that Jesus' audience have heard from alongside the Father consist in what Jesus has told them from his having preexisted alongside God his Father. But the audience don't understand Jesus' reference to God. **8:39: They answered and said to him, "Our father is Abraham** [an echo of Jesus' acknowledging their Abrahamic ancestry in 8:37]**."** Jesus had told them to put in practice what they'd heard from the Father in the words of Jesus. But they distort Jesus' command into a declaration that they're doing the things they've heard from their ancestor Abraham. **Jesus says to them, "If you are Abraham's children, you'd be doing the works of Abraham."** The sentence is ungrammatical. Proper grammar would produce "If you *were* Abraham's children . . . ." The bad grammar deliberately underlines the contradiction between these Jews' acknowledged Abrahamic ancestry and their failure to follow Abraham's example. Ordinarily, children behave as their father has behaved. Jesus doesn't specify the works of Abraham; but Abraham was noted for his obedience to God, especially his obedience to the extent of offering his son Isaac except for God's intervention in the nick of time (Genesis 22).

8:40–41: "But now you're seeking to kill me, a human being who has told you the truth that I heard from alongside God. Abraham didn't do this [= didn't attempt murder]**."** The implication: Forget your biological ancestry. Morally speaking, Abraham is *not* your father. ⁴¹**"You're doing the works of *your* father."** Now "your" replaces the earlier, weak "the" before "father." But Jesus still doesn't identify the unbelieving Jews' father. We can detect an approach to the identification, nevertheless, in Jesus' mentioning their father's "works," which must be murderous since these Jews are seeking to kill Jesus. **So they told him, "We haven't been born as a result of fornication** [that is, 'We aren't bastards']**. We have one father, God."** Apparently the Jews now recognize that Jesus has shifted from biological ancestry to moral ancestry and therefore answer him in his own terms. And they describe God not simply as their father but as their "*one* father" because they worship the one and only God. They're not pagans, who worship many gods—gods who in mythology committed many fornications and the worship of whom included fornication in so-called cultic prostitution. No, these Jews are

*mono*theists. So to claim legitimacy they appeal to their monotheism in addition to their biological ancestry from Abraham.

8:42–44: Jesus told them, "If God were your Father, you'd love me [not be seeking to kill me so as to break one of the Ten Commandments, 'You shall not kill']**."** The claim of the Jews to have God as their Father is contradicted by their failure to love Jesus, God's Son. **"For I came forth from God, and I've arrived."** For emphasis Jesus distinguishes between his departure from heaven and his arrival on earth. **"For I've not come on my own; rather, that one** [God] **sent me. ⁴³Why don't you understand my speech?"** Jesus answers his own question: **"Because you aren't able to hear my word."** And why aren't they able to hear it? ⁴⁴**"You're from** [your] **father the Devil."** At last Jesus identifies their moral father. **"And you want to do the desires of your father."** At least in those days most children wanted to please their fathers. The word for the Devil's desires is often translated "lusts," desires that trespass the boundaries of legitimacy. **"That one** [the Devil] **was a murderer from the beginning."** He led Adam and Eve to eat the forbidden fruit, the eating of which caused them to die (compare 13:2, 27). **"And he doesn't stand in the truth, because truth isn't in him."** God had said, "In the day that you eat from it [the tree of the knowledge of good and evil] you'll surely die." The serpent, identified by Jesus as the Devil, said to Eve, "Surely you won't die" (Genesis 2:17; 3:4). **"Whenever he speaks a lie, he speaks out of his own things** [we'd probably say, 'he speaks in character']**, because he's a liar and the father of it** [= of lying]**."** Human sinning is based on the Devil's lying, so that sinning makes people children of the Devil. We're all the children of whom we believe.

8:45–47: "But because I'm telling the truth, you don't believe me." We might expect Jesus to have said, "*Although* I'm telling the truth, you don't believe me." But his "*because*" highlights that their being children of the father of lying causes them to rebel against the truth. For people to believe the truth, then, requires God's drawing them (6:44, 65). ⁴⁶**"Who of you convicts me of sin?"** This question assumes that Jesus has successfully defended himself against the charge in chapter 5 that he did wrong by healing an invalid on the Sabbath. The question also reminds us that John's Gospel presents the entirety of Jesus' ministry as a prolonged trial. The world puts him on trial. He produces witnesses in his behalf and then turns the tables by putting the world on trial, convicting and judging the world, as he does here. If they'd been able to convict him of sin, he couldn't have taken away the world's sin (compare 1:29). Nobody can convict him of sin, though. So he continues, **"If I'm telling the truth, why don't you believe me?"** Again Jesus answers his own question: ⁴⁷**"The person who is from God** [= has his origin in God] **hears the words of God** ['hears' in the sense of 'heeds,' hears with understanding and obedience; 'the words of God' as spoken by the Word of God, Jesus]**. For this reason you don't**

hear, [namely,] **because you aren't from God** [= don't have your origin in God, because you originated in your father the Devil]."

8:48: The Jews answered and said to him, "We say well, don't we, that you're a Samaritan and have a demon?" The preceding topic of ancestry leads them to insult Jesus with the epithet "Samaritan." The Jews considered Samaritans half-breeds and heretics. Having a demon means being demon-possessed. In the other Gospels Jesus exorcises demons from demoniacs, but here in John Jesus himself is accused of being a demoniac—for the second time (see also 7:20: "You have a demon"). In the earlier passage he was accused of having a demon because he'd accused the Jews of seeking to kill him, here because he accused them of not being of God but of the Devil. "Devil" makes them think of demons. By saying Jesus is demon-possessed they try to outdo him in this contest of accusations.

8:49–51: Jesus answered, "I don't have a demon." There's his answer to the charge of demon-possession. **"Rather, I'm honoring my Father."** There's his answer to the insult that he's a Samaritan: his ancestry is divine. And if we ask in what ways he honors his Father, the answer has to be that he does so by doing the works he has seen the Father do and by speaking the words he has heard and seen the Father speak (8:26, 32, 40). **"And you're dishonoring me."** Their accusations of mixed ancestry and demon-possession were designed to shame him. No matter, though: [50]**"But I'm not seeking my glory** [that is, 'glory for myself,' glory being what brings honor]. **He** [my Father] **is the one seeking** [my glory] **and judging** [me]." According to 5:22 the Father judges no one. But the context specifies the human race, whose individual judgments—for good or ill—he has given to his Son Jesus. Here the Father seeks Jesus' glory in the only judgment (a favorable one) that the Father exercises. [51]**"Amen, amen I tell you, if anyone keeps my word, by no means will he see death—forever."** Notice how Jesus the Word emphasizes his word. To keep it is to hear, believe, and obey it. To see death is to experience it. Not seeing death forever doesn't deny the possibility of an initial, physical death (see 11:25; 16:2; 21:19). It denies the possibility of experiencing what the book of Revelation calls "the second death," being "thrown into the lake of fire" (again see Revelation 2:11; 20:6, 14; 21:8).

8:52–53: So the Jews told him, "We've now come to know that you have a demon. Abraham died, also the prophets; and you say, 'If anyone keeps my word, by no means will he taste death [= 'see death' in 8:51]—**forever.'** [53]**You're not greater, are you, than our father Abraham, who died? And the prophets died. Whom are you making yourself?"** They don't ask, "Who *are* you?" They ask, "Whom are you *making* yourself?" The question implies that Jesus is making himself out to be someone he isn't. He doesn't say he won't die. He will in fact die; and the second death of those who keep his word will be encapsulated in his sacrificial death. He'll suffer it in their place, so that they won't have to suffer

it. But the Jews aren't thinking of the second death and therefore argue that by saying those who keep his word won't suffer death, Jesus is absurdly making himself greater than Abraham and the Old Testament prophets. A man so demon-possessed as to make such a claim can't be greater than them even though they're dead. But we who've read the prologue of this Gospel (1:1–18) recognize *truth*, not absurdity, in Jesus' statement. He *is* greater than Abraham and those prophets.

8:54–56: Jesus answered, "If I glorify myself, my glory is nil [= counts for nothing]. **The one glorifying me is my Father, in reference to whom you say, 'He's our God.'"** Culturally speaking, it's out of place for a son to glorify himself. To do so is to rob his father of the glory that belongs to him because of his status as the elder. And a father won't tolerate such theft. That's the reason a son's self-glorification counts for nothing. But a father's glorifying his son is another matter. To do that is the father's prerogative. You say that the one I call my Father is your God, Jesus tells the Jews. But he adds, [55]**"And you haven't come to know him** ['know' in the sense of personal acquaintance, which is the kind of knowledge that counts], **but I know him. And if I say, 'I don't know him,' I'll be a liar like you** [because your moral father is the Devil, the father of lying]. **Nevertheless, I do know him and keep his word** [as a good, obedient son keeps the word of his father]. [56]**Abraham your** [fore]**father** [so far as physical ancestry is concerned] **exulted that he would see my day. And he *has* seen it and rejoiced."**

There's a distinction between Abraham's exulting that he *would* see Jesus' day and *actually* seeing it and rejoicing at the sight of it. The Jews referred a few verses back to the Old Testament prophets. Those prophets prophesied a lot about the Day of the Lord, the time when the Lord will intervene to judge the wicked and save his people. Here Jesus claims to *be* the Lord of the Day of the Lord. As such he has intervened for judgment and salvation. And as a prophet, Abraham, forefather of the Jewish people, looked forward to this day and saw it. In Genesis 20:7 God himself called Abraham a prophet. Jesus doesn't identify when and where Abraham exulted that he would see Jesus' day, or when and where he did see it and rejoice. But Abraham laughed at the prospect of procreating a son in his and Sarah's old age (Genesis 17:17). Some Jewish tradition interpreted his laughter as joyful rather than doubtful. And much Jewish tradition had it that Abraham rejoiced at Isaac's birth. The very name "Isaac" means, "he [presumably Abraham] laughs." According to Genesis 21:6 "Sarah said, 'God has made laughter for me; everyone who hears will laugh for me.'" Furthermore, as Abraham and Isaac his son trudged up Mount Moriah, where Abraham almost sacrificed Isaac, he said to Isaac, "God himself will provide the lamb for the burnt offering." And John the Baptist announced in 1:29, "Look! The lamb of God that takes away the world's sin!" So maybe Jesus means that, symbolically speaking, Abraham saw the day of the Lord Jesus in his son Isaac, and in that promised lamb on Mount Moriah.

8:57–59: Therefore the Jews said to him, "You're not yet fifty years old, and have you seen Abraham?" Their question twists Jesus' words. He spoke about *Abraham's* seeing the far future day of Jesus. Their question makes it look as though Jesus had spoken about *Jesus'* seeing the long-deceased Abraham. So Jesus takes advantage of their twisting his words: **⁵⁸Jesus said to them, "Amen, amen I tell you, before Abraham came into existence, I AM."** Finally the Jews "get it": **⁵⁹So they picked up stones to throw at him. But Jesus was hidden and went out of the temple** [courtyards, where he has been since 7:14]. It's hard to know whether Jesus was hidden because he hid himself or because God hid him. But the main point is that the Jews don't succeed in stoning Jesus, because his death is going to be an upward movement back toward heaven, where he preexisted, not a falling down under a hail of stones. The cross will elevate him, not humiliate him—not in this Gospel. A comment of the early church father Augustine is apropos: "As a human being he [Jesus] flees from the stones. But woe to those from whose hearts of stone God flees."

THE SIGN OF JESUS' GIVING SIGHT TO A MAN BORN BLIND
John 9:1–41

Chapter 9 brings us to another of Jesus' signs, or works. Verses 1–7 tell what he did.

9:1–3: And as he [Jesus] was passing by, he saw a man blind from birth. In chapter 8 Jesus proclaimed himself the light of the world. But the man he sees here has never seen the light of the world that's the sun. He was *born* blind. Nor does he yet see the light of the world that is God's Son Jesus passing by. Just as the blind man has always dwelled in physical darkness, so every human being has dwelled in spiritual darkness since birth. But did this man's blindness come as a result of sin? Jesus' disciples think so. **²And his disciples asked him, saying, "Rabbi, who sinned, this [blind man] or his parents, with the result that he was born blind?"** The disciples suggest two possibilities: (1) The man had sinned in his mother's womb and had been suffering for his *own* prenatal sin ever since birth. (2) His parents had sinned and he'd been suffering since birth for *their* sin. Jesus rejects both possibilities. The man's blindness *represents* a state of sin but didn't *result* from sinning. **³Jesus answered, "Neither did this [man] sin nor [did] his parents. Rather, [he was born blind] in order that the works of God might be manifested in him."** It's true that all human beings sin and that all human suffering has its *ultimate* origin in sin. But it's equally true that not all human suffering has its *immediate* origin in a particular sin; and this is Jesus' minor point, a negative one, in regard to the present case. His main point is a positive one, that the man was born blind that the works of God might be manifested in him. What's about to happen to him will manifest those works. It's Jesus who'll perform the works; but since he's both the Son of God and himself God (1:1; 20:28), what *he* does counts as *God's* doing. Although Jesus will perform what

seems like a single work on the blind man, it will be so striking, so multiple in its symbolizing of salvation, that nothing less than the plural "works" suffices to describe it. The blind man will become an advertisement of a salvation that consists in God's working through Jesus rather than in our vain efforts. This symbolism overrides any questions we might raise about God's fairness in allowing the man to suffer blindness from birth for the purpose of manifesting in him the works of God.

Jesus continues in **9:4–5: "It's necessary that we work the works of him who sent me as long as it's day. Night is coming, when no one can work. ⁵Whenever I'm in the world, I am the light of the world."** By using "we" Jesus associates his disciples with himself in working the works of God. But he limits to himself God's *sending*, because as the preexistent Word he alone came as God's emissary from heaven. Despite Jesus' "we," the disciples won't help him bring sight to the blind man in the further part of this story. Yet because of Jesus' return to the Father the disciples will do even greater works than Jesus did (see the comments on 14:12), and he says here that works can be performed only so long as it's day (compare Psalm 104:23: "People go out to their work and to their labor until the evening"). Therefore the period after his return to the Father—what we call the church age—must count as an *extension* of the day that began with Jesus' earthly lifetime. Therefore also the night when no one can work must *follow* the church age. But Jesus is the light of the world only so long as he's in the world. Is he then in the world as its light also during the church age despite his return to the Father? Yes, for according to 14:23 he and his Father "will come to him [the believer] and make an abode alongside him" (compare 1 John 2:8: "the true light is *already* shining"). When will the night come, then, when no one—neither Jesus nor his disciples—can work? Answer: at "the Last Day" (6:39–40, 44, 54; 11:24; 12:48), when Jesus "comes" for the last time (21:23) and "the resurrection of life" and "the resurrection of judgment" occur (5:29). Then believers will "rest from their toils, for their works follow along with them" (Revelation 14:13).

9:6–7: After saying these things, he [Jesus] spat on the ground and made clay out of the spittle and smeared the clay on his [the blind man's] eyes ⁷and told him, "Go wash in the Pool of Siloam" (which is translated "Sent One"). So he went off and washed himself and came [back] seeing. Jesus takes the initiative. The blind man hasn't said a word, hasn't asked to receive sight. Salvation is *God's* work. At first the spitting and making of clay and smearing it on the blind man's eyes look like magic. In fact, though, these actions are merely a setup for the symbolism of salvation. The verb for smearing is the verb for anointing on which the title "Christ" is based. The Anointed One (Christ) anoints the man born blind. So salvation is *Christ's* work as well as God the Father's work.

Washing represents moral cleansing, as later when Jesus will wash the disciples' feet (13:1–11). The blind man's washing *himself* represents the exercise of faith. Throughout his Gospel, John lays just as much stress on human beings' believing in Jesus as he does on the works of God and Christ. But the effectiveness of this self-washing depends on the water in the pool whose Hebrew name means "Sent One." Jesus has just referred to himself as the one whom God sent (9:4). (The underlying Greek verbs for sending differ, but for variety John likes to use synonyms without any distinction in meaning.) So the water of the pool makes the self-washing effective because the name of the pool represents the Sent One, Jesus, whom God sent to perform the works of salvation. And of course the man's seeing represents salvation as seeing Jesus the light of the world. On the other hand, water represents the Holy Spirit (3:5; 7:37–39), whom Jesus will "send" according to 15:26; 16:7 just as the Father sent Jesus. So the Spirit and Jesus cooperate in this work of salvation. (By the way, archaeologists have discovered the Pool of Siloam.)

The next paragraph starts with the reaction of those who knew the ex-blind man. *9:8–12*: **So the neighbors and those who'd been observing him earlier—that he was a beggar—were saying, "Isn't this the one who was sitting and begging?"** [9]**Others were saying, "This is** [the one]**." Others were saying, "No, he's like him." That one** [the ex-blind man] **was saying, "I'm** [the one]**."** [10]**So they were saying to him, "How then were your eyes opened?"** Blindness often results in closed eyes. [11]**That one answered, "The man called Jesus made clay and smeared** [it] **on my eyes and told me, 'Go to Siloam and wash yourself.' So on going off and washing myself, I started seeing."** [12]**And they said to him, "Where is that** [man]**?" He says, "I don't know."** This paragraph provides confirmation of the works of God in the ex-blind man. The confirmation comes both from nondisciples of Jesus and from the man himself. In effect, they testify to Jesus' having performed the works of God even though John doesn't use the verb "testify" as he often does. And for the first time we learn that the ex-blind man had been a beggar. In that culture, before the welfare state, it was presumed that because a blind man couldn't work for a living he'd have to beg. But the explicit mention of begging sharpens the point that the salvation represented by this sign occurs as God's work through Jesus, not by virtue of our own efforts. It also comes out that the ex-blind man had learned Jesus' name. How he'd learned it we're not told. But the fact that he had suggests the start of a personal relationship with Jesus which will blossom as the story proceeds. The man's explanation of the way Jesus gave him sight revives all the theological symbolism we discovered in the first paragraph (9:1–7).

In 9:13–17 we read another dialogue. *9:13–15*: **They** [the neighbors and others who'd observed the man as a blind beggar] **bring him, the one who used to be blind, to the Pharisees.** The Pharisees were known for strict adherence to the Law. For example, the last time we met them in John they objected that Jesus' self-testimony was legally unacceptable (8:13). Here they enter the picture to pick up another point of legality, a point on which the ex-blind man's neighbors and others are unclear. [14]**But it was a Sabbath** [Saturday, when the Old Testament prohibited any work ("Sabbath" meaning "rest")] **on the day that Jesus made clay and opened his** [the blind beggar's] **eyes.** [15]**Again therefore they—that is, the Pharisees—were asking him how he'd started seeing.** "Again" may hark back to their legal objection in 8:13, but more likely to the legal objection in 5:10. The objection in 8:13 mentioned the Pharisees but didn't have to do with the Sabbath. The objection in 5:10 did have to do with the Sabbath, as here, but didn't mention the Pharisees, only "the Jews." Nevertheless, right here in chapter 9 John will later use "the Jews" synonymously with "the Pharisees." They're about to lodge another objection having to do with Sabbath law. "Therefore" makes Jesus' clay-making and healing of blindness the basis of this objection. The Pharisees' asking the man who'd been blind from birth how he'd started seeing gives him another chance to explain Jesus' method. **And he told them, "He put clay on my eyes and I washed myself and I'm seeing."** Some of the details are missing this time, but it's the third time we've learned how Jesus performed the works of God on this blind beggar. First there was John's own report, second the report of the ex-blind man to his neighbors and others, and now his report to the Pharisees—a triple emphasis on the symbolism of salvation in Jesus' method. The Pharisees asked how the man had *started* seeing, and in his earlier reports he did tell how he'd started to see (9:11, 15a with use of the past tense to indicate the start of an action). But in this report he uses the present tense, "I'm seeing," which stresses the ongoing effect of Jesus' work and also the incontestability of the evidence facing the Pharisees (compare 9:7: "he came [back] seeing").

9:16–17: **So some of the Pharisees were saying, "This man** [Jesus] **isn't from God, because he doesn't keep the Sabbath."** Making clay counted as work and therefore as violating the Sabbath, and because of the prohibition of working on the Sabbath they said cures couldn't be performed on a Sabbath unless life itself was in danger. This man had been blind from birth. Surely his cure could wait another day. **But others** [other Pharisees] **were saying, "How can a sinful man do such signs?" And there was a division** [in the sense of a disagreement] **among them."** So the Pharisees face a theological conundrum, and they can't agree on the solution. Ironically, then, these supposed know-it-alls when it comes to the Law ask the ex-blind beggar, who could never have even read the Law, *his* opinion. [17]**So they speak again to the blind man** [as though he were still blind]**: "Since he opened your eyes** [but he isn't blind any more after all]**, what do *you* say about him** [Jesus]**?"** Are the Pharisees so naïve as to think they'll get an unprejudiced answer from the man to whom Jesus gave sight for the first time in the man's life? Apparently so. They aren't so smart as they think they are, or as the man's neighbors and others who brought him for an expert opinion think the Pharisees are. The Pharisees turn out to be just as unclear on the legal point as the neighbors and others! **And he** [the ex-blind man] **said, "He** [Jesus] **is a prophet."** Jesus is more than a prophet; but the statement is correct, for in 4:44 he testified about himself that "a prophet doesn't have honor in his own fatherland" (compare 4:19; 6:14; 7:40, 52). Many Old Testament prophets performed miracles. We think especially of Moses, Elijah, and Elisha. So the healed blind man naturally deduces that Jesus is a prophet. But the interrogators can't imagine that a prophet would violate the Sabbath. So next they'll attempt to undermine the deduction that Jesus is a prophet.

9:18–19: **Therefore** [because of the ex-blind man's declaring Jesus to be a prophet] **the Jews didn't believe concerning him that he'd been blind and started to see, until they called the parents of the one who'd started to see.** [19]**And they asked them, saying, "Is this your son about whom you say, 'He was born blind'? How is it then that he now sees?"** Suddenly the Pharisees turn into "the Jews" because they represent all those Jews—but especially the Jewish authorities, whether Pharisees or not—who reject Jesus. Their two questions seem to conflict with each other. The first question raises the possibility that the ex-blind man *isn't* a son of these parents. The second question ("How is it then that he now sees?") assumes that he *is* their son. To eliminate this seeming conflict we have to insert something between the two questions: "Is this your son about whom you say, 'He was born blind'? [*If he is*,] how is it then that he now sees?" The question of *how* comes up a fourth time (compare 9:10, 15–16) and shortly will come up twice more. All this emphasis on Jesus' method calls attention again to its symbolizing the way salvation occurs, the symbolism of Christ as the anointed anointer, of washing as moral cleansing, and of the meaning of Siloam as "Sent One" in reference to Christ as the Savior whom God "sent" into the world (see the comments on 9:6–7).

9:20–23: **Therefore** [because of the Jews' two questions] **his parents answered and said, "We know that this is our son and that he was born blind,** [21]**but we don't know how it is that he now sees. Nor do we know who opened his eyes. Ask him. He's an adult. He'll speak for himself** [literally, 'about himself']**."** Of course the Pharisees had already asked the ex-blind man how he'd come to see. So the parents' "Ask him" implies they hadn't been around earlier. Maybe, then, they gave an honest answer. They really didn't know how their son had started seeing or who had opened his eyes. But John's editorializing falsifies their answer and implies that they'd at least heard about the how and the who: [22]**His parents said these things because they feared the Jews** [who were interrogating them]. **For the Jews had already agreed** [they've overcome the disagreement they had back in 9:16] **that if anyone confessed** [that is, declared] **him** [Jesus] **to be Christ, he** [the confessor] **would be de-synagogued** [that is, excommunicated]. [23]**For this reason** [not because of ignorance] **his parents said, "He's an adult. Ask him."** The implication

is that if they'd told how their son received sight and who gave it to him, they'd have been confessing Jesus to be *Christ*, not just a prophet as their son had said Jesus was. How then does "Christ" become a possibility for confession? Jews didn't expect the Messiah, the Christ, to do miracles when he came; and the Jews had objected earlier to the ex-blind man's declaring Jesus to be even so much as a prophet. He certainly hadn't declared Jesus to be Christ. Well, "Christ"—meaning "Anointed One"—becomes a possibility in the present passage because of *how* Jesus had healed the blind man. He had smeared—that is, anointed—the blind man's eyes with clay. And as already noted, that anointing pointed to Christ as the anointed anointer.

Fear of the Jews marks the parents for criticism. John mentions their fear twice. The parents feared ejection from the synagogue. John's message: Don't let fear of ostracism keep you from confessing Jesus as Christ. If you're one of God's selected ones, you're not from the world anyway—any more than Jesus himself was. Unfortunately the parents expose themselves as being from the world.

9:24–25: **Therefore** [because of the parents' evasiveness] **for a second time they** [the Jews] **called the man who'd been blind and said to him, "Give glory to God. We know that this man** [Jesus] **is sinful."** In Joshua 7:19 giving glory to God consists in confessing one's *own* sin. But here, giving glory to God would—in the Jews' opinion—consist in the ex-blind man's confessing *Jesus* to be sinful. And the Jews prompt the man to do so by appealing to their supposedly superior knowledge, based on legal expertise. [25]**Therefore** [because of the Jews' prompting] **that one** [the ex-blind man] **answered, "I don't know whether he's sinful** [that is to say, 'Unlike you I don't have legal expertise']. **I do know one thing, that though I used to be blind, now I'm seeing."** The experience of God's work through Christ in our lives always trumps the technicalities of others' supposedly superior knowledge.

9:26–29: **Therefore** [because the ex-blind man didn't obey the Jews' command that he give God glory by agreeing with them that Jesus was sinful] **they said to him, "What did he do to you? How did he open your eyes?"** This is the third time the ex-blind man has been asked the how-question, the second time by the Jews, or Pharisees. [27]**He answered them, "I've already told you and you didn't hear. Why do you want to hear again?"** He's exasperated. "Hear again" implies that they did hear the first time, but "You didn't hear" implies that they didn't hear what they heard. Two levels of hearing are in view: hearing but not paying attention to what's heard, like hearing background music while other things occupy the mind; and hearing with due attention, like listening to a symphony orchestra in a concert hall. The ex-blind man continues—sarcastically: **"You too don't want to become his disciples, do you?"** Since the disciples have faded into the background, "too" implies that the ex-blind man has himself become a disciple of Jesus.

The Jews pick up this implication: [28]**And they ridiculed him and said, "You're a disciple of that** [fellow], **but we're disciples of Moses** [the giver of the Sabbath law that Jesus violated]. [29]**We know that God has spoken to Moses; but as for this one** [Jesus], **we don't know where he's from."** In their culture you needed to know a man's place of origin before you could trust him, as in Nathaniel's question, "Can anything good be from Nazareth?" (1:46). So from the time of Jesus to our own day Christian discipleship has drawn ridicule. Persecution often takes that form; and given the importance of one's reputation and sense of self, this kind of persecution poses a serious danger of backsliding and apostasy. The ex-blind man doesn't succumb, though. He stands his ground. Indeed, he outargues the Jews on their own theological turf.

9:30–33: **The man answered and said to them, "Well now** [you can almost see his lips curl with increased sarcasm], **in this** [he's referring to what he's about to say] **is something marvelous, that you don't know where he** [Jesus] **is from and** [we would say 'yet'] **he opened my eyes** [the point being that their ignorance of Jesus' origin isn't compatible with his having opened the man's eyes]. [31]**We know that God doesn't listen to sinners; but if anyone is God-fearing and does his will, he** [God] **does listen to him.** [32]**Since the beginning of time it hasn't been heard that anyone opened the eyes of a person** *born* **blind.** [33]**If this one** [Jesus] **weren't from God, he couldn't do a single thing** [meaning a single thing of this sort, not anything in general; the ex-blind man is using a bit of hyperbole]**."** The ex-blind man can hardly believe the Jews' unbelief, which is "something marvelous" in the sense of surprising rather than admirable. They don't believe in Jesus because, as they themselves say, they *don't* know where he's from. But in 7:27 some Jerusalemites didn't believe in him because they *did* know where he's from: "We know, however, where this [fellow] is from [Galilee (see 7:52)]. But whenever the Christ comes, no one knows where he's from." The Jews are so deadset against Jesus that they contradict themselves in giving reasons to reject him. Even the powerful evidence staring them in the face—quite literally staring them in the face, because the ex-blind man *is* staring them in the face—even evidence so powerful as this doesn't convince them. They don't want to believe. They're determined not to.

The ex-blind man has outargued his intellectual superiors. So they resort to ad hominem: they attack *him* instead of his argument. *9:34:* **They answered and said to him, "You as a whole were born in sins. And are *you* teaching *us*?" And they threw him out.** Back in 9:18–23 his parents played coy because they feared ejection from the synagogue. Here their son suffers the fate they shamefully avoided, and suffers it because of his bold discipleship—chutzpah! "Are you teaching us?" implies that his interrogators, despite having solicited his opinion, don't think of themselves as having been born in sins, so that he should accept their teaching, not

they his. "Sins"—plural. At the start of this story Jesus' disciples asked about alternatives: Did the blind man or his parents sin prior to his birth, so that he was born blind? Here toward the end it's as though the Jews think of both/and rather than either/or: both of the man's own sin and that of his parents. And not only the plural "sins." Also "you *as a whole.*" No part of you escaped those sins, whatever they were. And your being born in them is what caused you to be blind from birth. Oh the irony! In this outburst the Jews unwittingly admit that the man whose identity they doubted in 9:18–19 and who now sees was born blind!

9:35: **Jesus heard that they'd thrown him out; and on finding him, he said, "Do you believe in the Son of Man?"** Jesus reappears on the scene. He doesn't ask, "Do you believe *in me*?" Nor does the ex-blind man know that Jesus uses "Son of Man" to refer to himself. Earlier in a conversation with Nicodemus Jesus portrayed himself as the Son of Man who descended from heaven and will ascend back to heaven (3:13). But the ex-blind man wasn't party to that conversation, and of course he hadn't read the Gospel of John. So *9:36* reads, **That one** [the ex-blind man] **answered and said, "And who is he, Lord, that I might believe in him?"** With his "And" in front of "who is he?" the ex-blind man insinuates that Jesus might have helped him out by continuing with an identification of the Son of Man. "Lord" could simply mean "Sir." The ex-blind man has confessed Jesus to be a prophet (9:17), and according to 9:30–33 he thinks that God hears Jesus because Jesus has reverence for God and does God's will and that Jesus comes from God. So maybe we're meant to think the ex-blind man views Jesus as no more than a prophet from God, like John the Baptist (1:6). But John the evangelist portrays Jesus as from God in the profounder sense of God's having sent Jesus from heaven into the world. So at least for us who read this Gospel the ex-blind man's addressing Jesus as "Lord" means more than "Sir." It carries the implication of deity just as later when the Apostle Thomas addresses the risen Jesus with the words, "My Lord and my God" (20:28).

9:37–38: **Jesus told him, "You've both *seen* him and the one speaking with you *is* that one** [the Son of Man]**."** "You've . . . seen him" calls attention to Jesus' having given him sight. And "the one *speaking* with you" recalls John's presentation of Jesus as the Word, who was with God in the beginning, was God, and explained God (1:1, 18). [38]**And he** [the ex-blind man] **said, "I believe, Lord." And he worshiped him** [that is, he knelt down with his face to the ground in front of Jesus]. Here, "Lord" has to mean more than "Sir" even for the ex-blind man.

9:39: **And Jesus said, "I've come into this world for the purpose of judgment, so that the ones who don't see** [like the blind man] **might see** [not just physically, but might see Jesus to be the Son of Man that he truly is (compare 1:51)] **and** [so that] **the ones who do see** [physically, as the Pharisees, or Jews, do] **might become** blind [not physically, but blind to Jesus' identity as the Son of Man]." According to 3:17 judgment in the sense of damnation (as indicated by a contrast with salvation) was *not* the purpose of God's sending his Son into the world. According to 5:27–29 and now 9:39 judgment in the sense of determining the respective fates of believers and unbelievers *was* the purpose of Jesus' coming into the world with authority given to him as the Son of Man. The blind man exemplifies believers. The Jews who threw him out of their synagogue exemplify unbelievers. The blind man's receiving physical sight symbolizes the positive judgment of salvation. And the Jews' loss of spiritual sight consigns them to the negative judgment of damnation.

9:40: **Some of the Pharisees who were with him** [Jesus] **heard these things** ["heard" in the sense of "overheard," since Jesus had been speaking to the ex-blind man] **and said to him** [Jesus again], **"We too aren't blind, are we?"** The question expects a negative answer. The Pharisees think only on the physical plane. They obviously have physical sight. Their failure to understand that Jesus spoke of mental, spiritual blindness shows just how blind in *that* sense they are. And the "too" in "We too aren't blind, are we?" seems to mean, "We aren't blind like the blind man, are we?"—as though the man were still blind, as though Jesus hadn't given him sight, and as though they hadn't recently admitted that the man had been blind from birth but now sees! Again they're thinking only on the physical plane.

9:41: **Jesus told them, "If you** *were* **blind, you wouldn't have sin. But now you're saying, 'We see.' Your sin abides."** John the Baptist proclaimed Jesus "the lamb of God that takes away the world's sin" (1:29). But the refusal of the Pharisees to admit their sin (instead they'd accused the ex-blind man of having been born as a whole in sins)—this refusal means that their sin won't be taken away. It abides, stays, remains (compare 3:36: "But the one who disobeys the Son . . . the wrath of God *abides* on him"). The Jews assume that their physical sight means they don't have sin. But if they were physically blind, Jesus says, they wouldn't have sin because—as in the case of the man born blind—Jesus would step in and give them mental sight as well as physical sight. This chapter began with the disciples' false assumption that sinning produced physical blindness (9:2). It ends with Jesus' saying that mental blindness produces sin.

JESUS AS THE GATE AND AS THE GOOD SHEPHERD
John 10:1–21

Chapter 10 proceeds from chapter 9 without a break. Jesus is still speaking to the Jews. So his continuing speech in chapter 10 will interpret his healing of the man born blind in chapter 9.

Jesus uses some figurative language in **10:1–6:** **"Amen, amen I tell you, the one not entering through the gate** ['door' carries a wrong connotation] **into the sheep pen but climbs** [over the wall] **from elsewhere—that one is a thief and a bandit.** [2]**But the one entering through the gate is the shepherd of the sheep.** [3]**To this one the gatekeeper opens, and the sheep hear his voice, and he calls his own sheep name by name and leads them out.** [4]**Whenever he thrusts out all his own** [sheep], **he proceeds ahead of them; and the sheep follow him, because they know** [= 'recognize'] **his voice.** [5]**But by no means will they follow a stranger; rather, they'll flee from him, because they don't know** [again = 'recognize'] **the voice of strangers."** [6]**Jesus spoke this figurative language to them, but those ones** [the Jews] **didn't know** [here in the sense of "understand"] **what the things were** [= "meant"] **that he was telling them.** The initial, double "Amen" emphasizes the truth of Jesus' figurative language. What this language stands for has to wait till the next paragraph, though. Meanwhile some explanation of the language itself:

Low stone walls (and there are plenty of stones in the land of Israel) enclosed sheep pens out in the hills where shepherds pastured their sheep. Apparently sheep-stealing was as common as cattle-rustling was in the American Wild West. So shepherds would leave their sheep overnight in a sheep pen under the guard of a gatekeeper—if a gatekeeper was available to give the shepherd some relief. Naturally, then, a thief or a bandit—because he wanted to avoid tangling with the gatekeeper, who was sleeping at the gate—would climb over the wall away from the gate to carry off some sheep.

More than one shepherd might bring their flocks to the sheep pen on a given night. So sheep belonging to different shepherds mingled with each other overnight. How then did a shepherd retrieve his own sheep the next morning? Well, he had given each of his sheep a name; and they'd grown to recognize his voice and their names. When the gatekeeper opened the gate, the shepherd entered the pen and one by one called out the names of his sheep. They'd come to him when he did. Sheep not belonging to him wouldn't come to him. (Of course the gatekeeper wouldn't open the gate to anyone who wasn't a shepherd of some sheep inside the pen.) The shepherd would then lead his own sheep out of the pen into pastureland, and they followed.

Shepherds didn't drive their sheep ahead of them. They led the sheep, because unlike the sheep they knew the location of good pasture. But "leads out" in 10:3 changes to "thrusts out" in 10:4. "Thrusts out" is unrealistic and at a literal level of meaning contradicts both "leads out," "proceeds ahead of them," and the sheep's "following" the shepherd. Why then does this verb appear here? Actually, "thrusts out" translates the same verb that we found back in 9:34–35, where the Jews "threw out" the ex-blind man from their synagogue. So this verb helps link together the story of Jesus and the blind man and the figurative language of the gate, the shepherd, and the sheep. But what a contrast between these thrustings out! The ex-blind man was thrust out to be abandoned. The shepherd thrusts out his sheep, so to speak, in order to go ahead of them as they follow. And he thrusts out *all* his own sheep. None are left behind. The shepherd won't lose a single one of his own (compare 6:39; 10:28–29; 17:12).

The shepherd's proceeding ahead of the sheep wouldn't necessarily guarantee they'd follow. But they do, 10:4 says, because they know his voice. So 10:4 adds *knowing* his voice as a complement to *hearing* his voice in 10:3. Later we'll learn that the shepherd knows his sheep—naturally, since he calls each one by name—so that there's mutual recognition between shepherd and sheep. In contrast with following their shepherd, the sheep not only won't *follow* a stranger. They'll *flee* from strangers, whether other shepherds or thieves and bandits, because they don't recognize the voice of a stranger. This behavior of the sheep stresses the exclusivity of the relation between sheep and their shepherd (compare Jesus' statement in 14:6: "No one comes to the Father except through me"). But the Jews don't know, don't understand, what Jesus has been saying. Apparently they don't know, don't recognize, his voice. They're not his sheep.

Now Jesus starts to explain his figurative language. **10:7–8: Therefore** [because the Jews didn't understand Jesus' figurative language] **Jesus spoke again, "Amen, amen I tell you** [the same emphasis on his truthfulness as in 10:1] **that I am the gate of the sheep.** ⁸**All—as many as they were—who came before me are thieves and bandits."** Jesus might be referring to false prophets and false christs; but in view of the way this chapter interprets chapter 9 he's probably referring to the Pharisees, the Jews, who had attained leadership and thrown the ex-blind man out of their synagogue. **"But the sheep didn't hear them."** The verb "hear" has the sense of hearing with recognition. The sheep didn't recognize the voice of the thieves and bandits and therefore didn't listen to them and, by implication, didn't follow them. So far the comparison isn't between a proper shepherd and the thieves and bandits. It's between the thieves and bandits and the gate, between those who climb over the wall and the gate, which they avoid and reject because of their evil intentions. The Pharisees, the Jews, have rejected Jesus the gate because their deeds are evil (3:19).

10:9–10a: "I am the gate." Jesus repeats what he said in 10:7. **"If anyone enters** [the sheep pen] **through me** [the gate], **he'll be saved and will enter and exit** [the sheep pen] **and find pasture."** So here the one who enters isn't the shepherd of 10:1–6. The one who enters is a sheep. Inside the pen the sheep gets security. Outside, the sheep gets food. Both security and food are necessary for life, and the sheep's physical life represents eternal life for human beings who believe in Jesus. Since the thieves and bandits don't enter through the gate, they won't be saved or get eternal security and sustenance. ¹⁰ᵃ**"The thief doesn't come except to steal and slaughter and destroy** [the sheep]." This statement describes in figurative language what the Jews did to the ex-blind man when they excommunicated him. The word for "slaughter" is commonly used for offering a sacrifice to God. In fact it's often translated "sacrifice." So we have here

a hint of what Jesus will say explicitly to his disciples in 16:2: "everyone who has killed you will think [himself] to be offering religious service to God." For background see Ezekiel 34.

10:10b: "I've come that they [the sheep] **might have life** [as opposed to being stolen, slaughtered, and destroyed], **and have** [it] **abundantly."** It's not the life that's abundant. It's the *having* of life that's abundant—therefore an adverb ("abundantly"), not an adjective ("abundant"). The difference is slight but meaningful. It means not so much that the sheep have a lot of life (though they will, because it's eternal). It means that they'll *have* it a lot. The accent falls on their experiencing of life, we might even say their enjoyment of it. And this enjoyment is more than enough, because "abundantly" indicates surplus—a surplus of enjoyment.

In the preceding paragraph Jesus claimed to be the gate and said that he has "come." But gates don't "come." They're stationary. So Jesus makes another claim, one that's appropriate to coming. **10:11–13: "I am the good shepherd. The good shepherd lays down his life** ['soul' in the sense of physical life] **for the sheep."** That's what his goodness consists in. What better thing could he do for his sheep? ¹²**"The one who's a hired hand and not a shepherd, whose own the sheep are not** [that is, to whom the sheep don't belong], **sees the wolf coming and abandons the sheep and flees—and the wolf snatches them and scatters** [them—that is, drags some sheep away to be eaten while the rest run in all directions to escape]—¹³**because he's a hired hand and isn't concerned about the sheep."** In this paragraph the shepherd takes the place of the gate. The hired hand takes the place of the gatekeeper. And the wolf takes the place of the thieves and bandits.

Jesus is the shepherd just as he was the gate. The hired hand doesn't stand for anybody in particular but acts as a foil to the shepherd just as the gatekeeper didn't stand for anybody in particular but acted as a foil to the gate. But the wolf stands for the Jewish authorities who mistreated the ex-blind man just as the thieves and bandits stood for them. Earlier the sheep fled from a stranger because of nonrecognition. Now the hired hand flees the wolf because of concern only for his own life. After all, he has no vested interest in the sheep. They aren't his. By contrast, Jesus' only concern is for the life of the sheep, as he showed when he healed the man born blind and led him to believe in the Son of Man for the removal of his sin. The sheep—that is, believers—belong to Jesus. He's concerned for their life, not for his own. The good shepherd saves his sheep from the wolf, then, by sacrificing his life in battling the wolf just as Jesus sacrificed his life in battling the Jewish authorities, to whom he'll yield himself at his arrest only on the condition that they let his disciples, his sheep, go—the very Jewish authorities who in John's Gospel will put him to death. (In 19:12, 16 Pilate will give Jesus over to them for crucifixion.) The wolf's snatching and scattering the sheep stands for what *won't* happen to them because of Jesus' self-sacrifice.

The next paragraph takes up Jesus' claim in the preceding paragraph to be the good shepherd and also circles back to 10:1–6 for a further interpretation of Jesus' figurative language in that paragraph. *10:14–16*: **"I am the good shepherd."** Jesus repeats what he said in 10:11. **"And I know my** [sheep], **and my** [sheep] **know me** [15]**just as the Father knows me and** [just as] **I know the Father. And I'm laying down my life for the sheep.** [16]**And I have other sheep that aren't of this pen. It's necessary that I bring those as well, and they'll hear my voice and become one flock. One shepherd!"** The mutual knowledge of the shepherd and his sheep echoes the theme in 10:1–6, but here the *shepherd's* knowing his sheep takes precedence over *their* knowing him. It was the reverse in the earlier verses. As before, knowing means recognizing. It's just as necessary that Jesus recognize those God has given him to shepherd as it is for those people to recognize Jesus as the shepherd God has given them. Again divine selection and human responsibility complement each other, balance each other.

Jesus even compares the mutual knowledge of shepherd and sheep to the mutual knowledge of God the Father and himself. The comparison supports the certainty and reliability of this mutual knowledge between Jesus and believers, the select. He won't fail to recognize his sheep and they won't fail to recognize him as their shepherd any more than God his Father and he would ever fail to recognize each other.

"I'm laying down my life for the sheep" restates 10:11 with the substitution of "I" for "the good shepherd" that Jesus is (and with the necessary change of the verb from third person to first person, of course). Since the "other sheep" that Jesus must bring "aren't of this pen" (the pen of the Jewish people), they represent Gentiles, who don't belong to his own people Israel (compare 1:11) but who'll come to Jesus just as "some Greeks" will do in 12:20 (compare 3:16, "God loved the *world* . . . in order that *everyone* believing in him might not be lost, but might have eternal life," and 12:32, "And I, if I'm lifted up from the earth—I'll draw *all* people to myself"). At present those other sheep aren't of this pen. They don't yet believe. But when Jesus brings them they'll form one flock along with present Jewish believers (perhaps with Samaritan believers too [see 4:39–42]). Jesus says "it's necessary" that he bring them just as "it was necessary" for him to go through Samaria and bring the woman at Jacob's well and her fellow townspeople (4:4). Their salvation is a divine necessity based on God's selective grace.

Just as the shepherd led his sheep *out* of the pen to pasture in 10:3, so now he leads them *in*. For the verb translated "bring" in 10:16 is the same as the one translated "leads" in 10:3. Numbers 27:15–23 provides background: "Then Moses spoke to the Lord saying, 'May the Lord, the God of the spirits of all flesh, appoint a man over the congregation who'll go out ahead of them and come in ahead of them and who'll lead them out and bring them in, so that the congregation of the Lord won't be like sheep that don't have a shepherd.' So the

Lord said to Moses, 'Take Joshua [a Hebrew name whose Greek form is 'Jesus'] . . . and commission him . . . . At his command [literally 'mouth'] they'll go out and at his command they'll come in . . . even all the congregation" (excerpts). As a shepherd Jesus leads his own *in* as well as *out*, into the security of the pen as well as out to the sustenance of pastureland (compare Psalm 23:1–2a). They'll hear his voice by way of recognizing that they belong to him.

That the sheep will be "one flock" rather than multiple flocks highlights the loving unity of all believers in Christ (compare 11:51–52: "Jesus was going to die for the nation, and not only for the nation, but that he might gather *into one* also the scattered children of God"). So Jesus will pray "that they may all be one just as you, Father, [are] in me and I [am] in you, that they too may be in us in order that the world may believe that you sent me . . . that they may be one just as we [are] one . . . that they may be completed in oneness" (17:21–23).

The text doesn't say "they'll be one flock *with* one shepherd," though some translations have it that way. "One shepherd" stands alone, grammatically unrelated to the preceding (or following) sentence. It's an exclamation: "One shepherd!" As before, this exclamation is a forceful way of saying what Jesus will spell out in 14:6: "No one comes to the Father except through me." As the *one* shepherd Jesus stands in contrast with "*all—as many* as they were—who came before me" (10:8). They were thieves and bandits. Jesus is the one shepherd, and his goodness contrasts sharply with thievery and banditry.

With an elaboration on his self-sacrifice Jesus continues speaking in *10:17–18*: **"Because of this** [because I'm laying down my life for the sheep, as I said earlier and am about to say again] **the Father loves me,** [that is,] **because I'm laying down my life . . . ."** But this time Jesus doesn't add "for the sheep." Instead he springs a surprise: **"in order that I might take it again."** He's obviously predicting his resurrection (compare 2:18–22), portraying his life as a piece of clothing that he takes off, lays down, picks up, and puts back on, and portraying his resurrection as a very purpose and result of his death. By itself the death of a shepherd would leave his sheep exposed to danger. Jesus doesn't die only to take away our sin, though. He dies to give us the life of his own resurrection, so that deceased believers too will rise from the dead to enjoy eternal life with him.

Then to make clear that he'll perform these feats at his own volition, Jesus denies that he'll die as a victim and affirms that he'll raise himself from the dead: [18]**"No one is taking it** [my life] **away from me; rather, I'm laying it down on my own. I have authority to lay it down, and I have authority to take it again. I've received this command from my Father."** So the authority consists in the Father's command. If the Father commands it, Jesus has authority to do it. Both the laying down of his life and the taking it again are acts of obedience, then. As God's Son, Jesus obeys his Father. What's striking, though, is that Jesus' taking his life again is as much an act of obedience as laying it down is an act of obedience.

But how can a dead man obey a command? How can a dead man raise himself from the dead? He's dead, isn't he? John portrays Jesus as the incarnate Word, though. As the Word he was God. As incarnate he was a human being. As a human being he was capable of dying and did die. As God he was capable of raising himself from the dead, and he did. Elsewhere in the New Testament Jesus is raised (passive voice) because God raised him (see for example Acts 4:10; 5:30; 10:40; 13:30, 37; Romans 4:24–25; 6:4, 9; 8:11). But since in this Gospel Jesus is God just as his Father is God, he raises himself at his Father's command. Already in 2:19 he said, "Disassemble this temple and in three days I'll raise it," and John editorializes in 2:21 that Jesus "was talking about the temple [consisting] of his body."

It isn't that a human part of Jesus died and a divine part of him raised the human part. He wasn't a half-breed, half human and half divine, part human and part divine. He was both fully and thoroughly human and fully and thoroughly divine. More than that we can't say because we bump up against the mystery of the incarnation. Mysteries aren't unbelievable if there's good evidence for them, as there is in this case. Given our current limitations, mysteries are just unexplainable, as in any number of matters—from the philosophical question why there's something rather than nothing to the physics of dark matter and the origin of the Big Bang to the psychology if not physiology of romantic love. But it's no mystery why Jesus' Father loves him for laying down his life and taking it again. His doing so constitutes an obedience that naturally draws such love. It should also draw us to love him who loved us to such an extent. "We love, because he first loved us" (1 John 4:19).

Looking back over 10:1–18 we can say that the lamb of God that John the Baptist proclaimed in 1:29, 36 has turned into a shepherd. But the shepherd sacrifices himself as though he were a lamb—or *because* he's also a lamb. And the lamb is a shepherd as in Revelation 14:4, where the redeemed are said to "*follow* the lamb."

10:19–21: On account of these words a division [in the sense of a disagreement] **developed among the Jews again. ²⁰And many of them were saying, "He has a demon and is raving. Why are you listening to him?" ²¹Others were saying, "These aren't the words of a demon-possessed person. A demon** [such as inhabits a demoniac] **can't open the eyes of blind people, can he?"** "A division . . . again" harks back to the division among the Pharisees over the ex-blind man (9:16) and connects Jesus' comments here with his giving sight to that blind man. The reference to "these words" of Jesus reminds us that he is the Word who explains God to us. The accusation of demon-possession comes up for a fourth time (see also 7:20; 8:48, 52). But this time the many Jews who make that accusation add that Jesus' words are the ravings of a madman. These Jews don't recognize Jesus' voice. They aren't his sheep. So they don't take his words for the voice of their shepherd. Instead, they mistake his words for the ravings of a man delirious because of demon-possession.

Others of the Jews—apparently a minority, because John doesn't describe them as "many" the way he described the accusers—these others doubt that Jesus has a demon. Instead they express a negative truth: Jesus' words don't come from demon-possession, because a demon can't give sight to blind people. All that's missing is the positive truth that Jesus' words do come from the Word who was with God and was God. Unfortunately, though, this omission is deadly. These Jews heard Jesus' words but they recognized his voice no more than those who accused him of demon-possession recognized it.

A DISPUTE OVER JESUS' DEITY
John 10:22–39

10:22–24: Hanukkah took place in Jerusalem at that time. ²³It was winter, and Jesus was walking around in the temple in Solomon's covered porch. ²⁴Therefore the Jews encircled him and were saying to him, "Until when are you keeping us in suspense? If you're the Christ, tell us outright." The Festival of Hanukkah started on the twenty-fifth of a Jewish month roughly equivalent to our December—hence John's reference to wintertime—and lasted eight days. "Hanukkah" means "renewal" and was so called because it celebrated the rededication of the temple by Judas Maccabeus in 165 B.C., that is, during the interval of four centuries between the end of Old Testament history and the beginning of New Testament history. The Syrian king Antiochus Epiphanes had desecrated the temple with pagan worship. Hanukkah was also named the Festival of Dedication and the Festival of Lights. This last name reflected the Jews' practice of lighting lamps and candles in their homes during the festival. Since the Old Testament didn't prescribe it (naturally, since it celebrated an event that followed Old Testament history), there was no requirement to make a pilgrimage to Jerusalem for the celebration. Nevertheless, we find Jesus there at the time. Since he'd made a pilgrimage to Jerusalem to celebrate the Festival of Tabernacles in what we call the fall, it looks as though he'd stayed there till winter. (We speak of four seasons, but ancient Jews spoke of only two, summer and winter [see, for example, Psalm 74:17].) Otherwise we have to suppose an unmentioned departure after Tabernacles and a return before Hanukkah.

As usual, "in the temple" doesn't mean in the sanctuary proper—rather, in its surrounding courts. The roof of Solomon's covered porch was supported by columns, as opposed to an open courtyard, so that it offered Jesus and his interlocutors some protection from the rain and cold of winter (compare 5:2). Though Jews thought differently, King Solomon couldn't have built the covered porch, because the temple he built was destroyed in 586 B.C. Here we have a second temple, the result of a rebuilding after the Jews' Babylonian exile and the subsequent return of some of them (Ezra–Nehemiah). Nonetheless, the covered porch went by the name of Solomon, builder of the first temple.

"Therefore" at the start of 10:24 means that "the Jews" (as normally, the authorities) take advantage of Jesus' walking around in the covered porch by encircling him. The encirclement has the purpose of trapping him so that he can't get away, as he did in 8:59 when they tried to stone him but he was hidden, or hid himself, and exited the temple courts (compare 12:36). We have to wait till 10:39 to see whether this encirclement works, but the encirclement shows that the Jews' question isn't open-minded. It's designed to get him to say something they can use for a capital accusation. They don't ask, "Until when *will* you keep us in suspense?" Instead, they use the present tense, "Until when *are* you keeping us in suspense?" to emphasize their present state of suspense, as though it has been going on for a while and is continuing without resolution.

Literally translated, "keeping us in suspense" comes out as "lifting up our soul." As in 10:11, 15, 17, "soul" has the sense of physical life. In those passages Jesus said that as the good shepherd he'll lay down his soul/physical life. So we have a contrast between a lifting *up* here and a laying *down* there, and the *Jews'* soul/life here and *Jesus'* soul/life there. They're distorting Jesus' sacrificing his present physical life for their eternal life into his interrupting their present physical life without regard to their eternal life. They hoped and expected the Christ to be a king in replacement of Caesar. If Jesus could be persuaded to declare himself the Christ plainly and publicly, the Jewish authorities would have a basis for accusing him of insurrection before the Roman governor. Then the governor would do away with him on their behalf.

10:25–26: Jesus answered them, "I've told you, and you don't believe. The works that I'm doing in the name of my Father—these [works] are testifying about me. ²⁶But you don't believe, because you're not from my sheep." In public Jesus hadn't told them plainly, "I'm the Christ." So what does he mean by saying, "I've told you"? As his next statement indicates, he means that his *works* have told them he's the Christ. Those works constitute the inaudible but visible public testimony to his messiahship. The "name" of his Father isn't a mere identification tag. It represents the character, status, power, and authority of God the Father of Jesus, so that doing the works in the name of his Father means that he's working for the Father and that the Father is working through him (compare 5:17, "My Father is working till now, and I'm working," and, more recently, 9:4, "It's necessary that we work the works of him who sent me"). And since as the Word, Jesus was God in the beginning (1:1), the works of God are Jesus' works as well as the Father's works. So the last part of 10:25 explains *how* Jesus had told the Jews he's the Christ (that is, by means of his works). Then 10:26 explains *why* they don't believe the works by which he'd told them he's the Christ: they're not from his sheep. They don't originate from the flock that belongs to him. The statement doesn't read that they're not from his sheep because they don't believe; rather, they don't believe because they're not from his sheep (compare again 6:44, 65; also 15:16, 19).

By way of contrast we read in *10:27–30*: "My sheep hear my voice, and I know them, and they follow me.

²⁸And I give them eternal life, and by no means will they be lost—forever; and no one will snatch them out of my hand. ²⁹My Father, which has given [them] to me, is greater than all; and no one can snatch them out of my Father's hand [compare 'the sheep of his (God's) hand' in Psalm 95:7]. ³⁰I and the Father are one." "My sheep" contrasts, of course, with "the Jews" of 10:24, who don't believe. Jesus' talking about his sheep presupposes the discourse on the good shepherd earlier in this chapter. Even though the occasion of Hanukkah is new, then, these Jews are the same as those at the Festival of Tabernacles in 7:14–10:21. Earlier, the hearing of Jesus' voice had to do with the good shepherd's calling his sheep by name. In the present passage it has to do with the testimony of Jesus' works (10:25). The sheep "hear" his voice in those works. The sheep's following Jesus out of allegiance to him puts in a bad light the Jews' encircling Jesus out of animosity toward him. It's Jesus, not God the Father, who gives his sheep eternal life, because it's Jesus who'll lay down his physical life and take it up again so as to give them eternal life.

Sheep have a proclivity toward getting lost, but Jesus' sheep will never get lost. "Forever" underlines their eternal security. Jesus will keep them in his hand. Because it's with your hand that you do things requiring strength, like twisting the lid off a vacuum-packed jar (not that they had such jars in Jesus' day, of course!), the hand had become a common figure of speech for strength. The hand of Jesus is so strong that no wolf, such as 10:12 talks about, can tear a sheep from its grip. Some ancient manuscripts have "my Father *who* has given [them] to me," but the probably better texts read "my Father *which* . . . ." Though it's awkward, "which" emphasizes the *quality* of fatherhood instead of the Father's personal *identity*. He's greater than all the wolves that try to snatch away Jesus' sheep. These sheep rest secure in the double, unbreakable grip of Jesus and his Father. But this double grip is really a single grip of doubled strength, because Jesus and his Father are one. "One" is neuter, not masculine. So Jesus and his Father are one in the *action* of gripping Jesus' sheep securely, and this oneness of action derives from their oneness in deity. They're not one person; for 1:1 made clear a personal distinction between the Word, who became Jesus, and God the Father of Jesus. On the other hand, 1:1 also made clear a oneness in deity by calling both of them "God." This oneness preserves monotheism (belief in one God alone [see Deuteronomy 6:4]).

10:31–32: Again the Jews picked up stones to stone him [just as they did in 8:59 after he'd said, "Amen, amen I tell you, before Abraham came into existence, I AM"]. ³²Jesus answered them [but they hadn't asked him a question; so his answer consists in a response to their picking up stones to stone him to death, their action being an inaudible but visible word just as his works have been inaudible but visible words], "I've shown you many good works from the Father ['good' because they symbolize Jesus' self-sacrifice as the 'good shepherd' for the benefit of his sheep (contrast 3:19: 'human beings loved the darkness rather than the light, for their deeds

[= works] were evil')]." "From the Father" describes the works because Jesus has performed them in his Father's name (10:25), because his Father has coworked with him (5:17; 9:3–4; 14:10), and above all because he has performed the works that the Father showed him and gave him to do (5:20, 36; 17:4). That they're "many" as well as "good" and "from the Father" indicates sufficiency for belief. **"Because of which work of them** [= out of the many good works that I've shown you] **are you trying to stone me?"** The question is ironic, even sarcastic. "Which . . . ?" carries the connotation "Which *kind* of . . . ?" and thereby challenges the Jews to identify any work of Jesus that doesn't match his description "good." Some translations have "you are stoning me," but 10:39 will show that the Jews are only making an unsuccessful attempt.

10:33: The Jews answered him [they're not amused], **"We're not trying to stone you for a good work, but for blasphemy, even because you, though you're a human being, are making yourself God."** They're correct on one count: Jesus *is* a human being. They're correct also in saying that he's making himself God in the sense of claiming deity for himself. But they're incorrect in the assumption that he's making himself out to be someone he isn't. So they mistake the mystery of the incarnation (the Word who was God became human flesh [1:1–18]) for blasphemy. Blasphemy means slander. The Jews charge Jesus with slandering God when he says that he's one with the Father in keeping believers from ever getting lost. But the human Jesus didn't make himself the God that he wasn't. Rather, without losing his deity the Word made himself the human Jesus that he, the divine Word, hadn't been but now forever is.

10:34–36: Jesus answered them, "It's written in your law, isn't it, 'I said, "You are gods."' [35]If it ['your law,' or 'he' in reference to God or the psalmist] **called those people gods to whom the Word of God has appeared on the scene (and the Scripture can't be broken!),** [36]**are you saying in reference to the one whom the Father consecrated and sent into the world, 'You're blaspheming,' because I said, 'I'm God's Son'?"** The sentence and its argument are complicated. The "law" is the Old Testament. "*Your* law" highlights what the Jews consider authoritative. Jesus is using their own weapon against them. He believes Scripture too, but "your" stresses his enemies' belief in it. The quotation comes from Psalm 82:6. Strikingly, other parts of this psalm speak of judgment, sin, and darkness, all of which link up with those very themes earlier in John (especially chapters 8–9); and the psalm uses "hand" as a figure of speech for strength just as Jesus has recently used it in the same way (10:28–29). (But "the hand of the *wicked*" in the psalm contrasts with the hands of Jesus the *good* shepherd and his Father.) More to the point, Jesus is addressing "the Jews," such as those who threw the ex-blind beggar out of their synagogue, just as Psalm 82:6 addresses those who afflict the poor and needy. It's hard to know whether "I" in the first "I said" above refers to the

psalmist, to personified Scripture, or to God speaking in the Scripture. But the point of the quotation doesn't lie in the identity of the speaker—rather, in the designation of those spoken to. In the psalm they're called "gods" because they act in God's stead, as the representatives of God, though they've done a bad job of it. The New Testament often applies Old Testament texts to new situations, though, and in the process changes the original meaning to something more up-to-date (the way modern-day preachers do with the New Testament as well as the Old Testament).

It's often thought that here in 10:35 "the Word of God" refers to Scripture, especially since the very term "Scripture" means "what is written" and because Jesus says, "It's written in your law" and "the Scripture can't be broken." Certainly "the Scripture" refers to "it's written . . . ," and in 5:38–39 "his [God the Father's] word" refers to "the Scriptures." But does "the Word of God" do the same in the present passage? Earlier, John called Jesus the Word who was with God, was God, and explained God (1:1–18)—pretty good evidence that in the vocabulary of John's Gospel, *Jesus* is also God's Word! In John, as a matter of fact, this portrayal of Jesus occupies far more attention than Scripture does. Furthermore, "appeared on the scene" in the present passage doesn't fit Scripture very easily; but it does fit Jesus' coming into the world (another constant theme in the Fourth Gospel), and this very expression occurred in 1:6–7, where it's synonymously parallel to "came," for another historical figure like Jesus, namely, John the Baptist. It also occurred in connection with Jesus at 1:17: "Grace and truth came on the scene through Jesus Christ" (compare 10:10, where he said, "I've come"). Furthermore again, the Scripture *can* be broken by disobedience to its commandments, and *is* broken thus (see 5:18; 7:23; also Matthew 5:17–19). But Scripture *can't* be broken so far as its prophecies are concerned. For God will see to their fulfillment.

So Jesus is referring to his own appearance on the scene as the Word of God and is treating Psalm 82:6 as a prophecy concerning the people to whom he has come as God's Word (see Revelation 19:13 for John's calling Jesus "the Word of God"; and for the Old Testament as prophecy see also John 5:39, 46; 12:34, 37–41; 13:18; 15:25; 19:24, 28, 36–37; 20:9). In other words, the "you" whom Psalm 82:6 calls "gods" are no longer the high and mighty of that psalm. They're Jesus' audience, called "gods" because of their exalted status in Jewish society—a status in which they should have acted in God's stead justly and fairly, but didn't, as in the case of the ex-blind man of chapter 9. And Jesus argues that since in Scripture his audience—that is, the audience of the Word of God that he himself is—are themselves called "gods," they shouldn't think it blasphemy for him to claim he's God's Son. After all, God his Father "consecrated" him, set him apart from them as his one-and-only Son, and sent him into the world from heaven, where he preexisted as the Word who was with God and was God (compare 17:19, where Jesus consecrates himself in order that his disciples may be consecrated in the truth). But has

Jesus ever said to the Jews, "I'm God's Son"? Not directly, not in so many words. But indirectly, yes—by calling God his "Father" time after time. (Incidentally, because John reserves "Son" for Jesus as God's Son in a unique sense, the second line of Psalm 82:6 is left unquoted: "and all you are sons of the Most High.")

10:37–39: "If I'm not doing the works of my Father [= the works that I saw my Father do and that he sent me to duplicate], **don't believe me** [= don't believe what I say]. **38But if I *am* doing them, even if you don't believe me, believe the works** [= believe what I *do* if you don't believe what I *say*; Jesus is capitalizing on the common observation that actions can speak louder than words] **in order that you may come to know, and continue to know, that the Father** [is] **in me and I** [am] **in the Father." 39Therefore they were seeking again to seize him, and he went out of their hand.** Coming to know refers to conversion, and continuing to know refers to perseverance. This double use of "know" undermines the falsely claimed knowledge of those self-proclaimed "knowers," the Gnostics, who denied that Jesus was the incarnation of God in human flesh (see the introduction to 1 John). True knowledge consists in recognition that the Father is *in* Jesus and Jesus *in* the Father, so that in addition to their relationship as Father and Son there's such a unity between them that Jesus could say they're "one" (10:30) and John could say that the Word who became Jesus *was* God as well as was *with* God (1:1).

Believing Jesus' works provides the basis for such knowledge. But what does it mean to believe them? Well, they're signs, symbols of what takes place in salvation: transformation from hunger to fullness, from blindness to sight, from death to life, and so forth—all on a plane that extends to eternity. So believing Jesus' works doesn't mean to believe simply that he performed miracles (a word that never appears in John). It means to believe the salvific symbolism of Jesus' works, with the result that the symbolized transformations take place in your own case. Their occurrence will let you know, and keep on knowing, that Jesus and the Father indwell each other. "Were seeking *again* to seize him" harks back to 7:30: "So they were seeking to seize him; and no one laid a hand on him, because his hour hadn't yet come." "He went out of their hand" means that he eluded them despite their having encircled him. Again, the hand represents strength. No one can snatch Jesus' sheep out of his and his Father's hands, but Jesus does escape from the Jews' hand. Theirs is too weak to grasp him. The hands of Jesus and his Father are too strong to be pried open.

THE RAISING OF LAZARUS
John 10:40–11:45

10:40–42: And again he went away, [this time] **across the Jordan** [to the east side, or Transjordan] **to the place where at the first John** [the Baptist] **was baptizing; and he abode** [= stayed] **there. 41And many came to him and were saying** [to each other, it turns out, not to Jesus], **"John didn't do a single sign. But all things—as many**

as they were—**that John said about this one** [Jesus] **were true." 42And many believed in him there.** In 6:1 Jesus went away to the other side of the Sea of Galilee. Here he goes away to the other side of the Jordan River. His abiding where the Baptist had been baptizing reminds us of 1:35–39 and its theme of symbolic abiding (for the location, see the comments on 1:28). In 10:40 we have a setup for the raising of Lazarus (chapter 11). In 10:41–42 people's believing because of Jesus' signs draws a contrast with the aforementioned Jews, who wouldn't believe either what he said or the works that he did. Those who now believe in him *come* to him; unlike the unbelievers in 10:24, they don't encircle him to trap and seize him. The Baptist's not having done even one sign contrasts with Jesus' having done many signs and works. The many things the Baptist said about Jesus are found in 1:19–36; 3:22–36. "*Many* came" and "*many* believed." The emphasis on "many" prepares for the triumphal procession in 12:12–19, where the large crowds will symbolize the many believers in Jesus scattered throughout the world by the time John writes his Gospel.

11:1: And a certain [man] **was sick, Lazarus from Bethany, from the town of Mary and Martha her sister.** In their culture people didn't have first and last names as we do. So to distinguish people of the same name, their places of origin or residence were often added, as in "Jesus of Nazareth" and "Saul of Tarsus." (There were many other Jesuses and Sauls.) Since the following story will feature Lazarus, he's the one identified as "from Bethany." According to 10:40–42 Jesus has been staying—and here in chapter 11 is still staying—where the Baptist used to baptize, that is, in Bethany east of the Jordan River (1:28). That Bethany probably wasn't a town but was a region, the northern part of Transjordan. The present Bethany *is* a town, not a region, considerably west of the Jordan River and, more specifically, on the east side of the Mount of Olives, which is just across a ravine from Jerusalem. Whereas Lazarus is identified by the name of this town, the town itself is identified by the names of Mary and Martha to distinguish it from the earlier Bethany. Mary is mentioned first because of what she'll do on a later occasion, as is mentioned in the next verse; and Martha is identified as her sister.

11:2: And it was Mary who anointed the Lord with perfume and wiped [it] **off with her hair, whose brother Lazarus was sick.** The story of that anointing doesn't come up till chapter 12; so this reference anticipates that story as well as distinguishing this Mary from other Marys. In particular, Mary's anointing Jesus and wiping off the ointment will symbolize his death, burial, and resurrection, so that John's mention of her actions here prepares for a preview of Jesus' death, burial, and resurrection also in the story of Lazarus. First-time readers of John's Gospel will notice this preview (and others like it) only in retrospect. For now, we may notice that John calls Jesus "Lord," which means "Master." Jesus will prove master of the seemingly impossible situation that's coming up. And for the first time John lets us know that Lazarus was Mary's brother, and therefore Martha's brother too. This sibling relation explains in advance the sisters' concern for Lazarus. After the statement in 11:1 that Lazarus was sick, the clause in 11:2, "whose brother Lazarus was sick," is redundant. But the very redundance highlights the crisis.

11:3: Therefore [because Lazarus was the sisters' brother and was sick] **the sisters sent** [a message] **to him** [Jesus], **saying, "Lord, look! He whom you love is sick."** Whatever the sisters may have meant by "Lord," John certainly intends us to think of Jesus as Lord in the sense of deity. Since Jesus is on the other side of the Jordan from Bethany, "look!" means "Pay attention! We have a crisis here. Come and see for yourself." For a third time Lazarus is described as "sick." But the sisters' message doesn't identify Lazarus by name. Instead, it identifies him as one whom Jesus loves. The sisters don't need to identify their brother by name. He's one of Jesus' sheep, and Jesus already knows his sheep by name. This is the first time in John that Jesus is said to love anyone, but it follows naturally after Jesus' portraying himself as the good shepherd who lays down his life for his sheep. He loves them, and Lazarus is one of them.

11:4: And on hearing [the message that Mary and Martha had sent], **Jesus said, "This sickness isn't for the purpose of death."** Though Lazarus's sickness will *result* in death, its *purpose* differs from death. **"Rather,** [the sickness is] **for the benefit of God's glory, in order that the Son of God may be glorified through it** [the sickness]." We're reminded of Jesus' saying that the blindness of the man born blind had the purpose of manifesting the works of God (9:3). But the glorification of God has the purpose and result of his Son's glorification too, because the Father and the Son are one (10:30).

11:5–6: And Jesus loved Martha and her sister and Lazarus. We've already learned that Jesus loved Lazarus. Here we learn that he loved Martha and Mary as well. This time John mentions Martha first and refers to Mary not by her name but only as Martha's sister, probably because later in the story Martha will take the lead and Mary will hang back. Perhaps Martha was older than Mary. The love of Jesus for the two sisters as well as for Lazarus heightens the tension created by Jesus' not responding immediately to the sisters' message. But what Jesus will finally do will demonstrate his love despite, and even because of, the delay. **⁶Therefore when he** [Jesus] **heard, "He** [Lazarus] **is sick,"** then he stayed two days in the place where he was. "Therefore" implies that Jesus stayed where he was *because* he loved Martha, Mary, and Lazarus. His waiting to arrive till Lazarus has been dead four days will demonstrate to them, when he raises Lazarus, that he is *their* resurrection and *their* life. It will be a demonstration that grows out of his love for them.

11:7–8: Then after this [that is, after the two days' delay] **he tells the disciples, "Let's go into Judea again."** Judea was the southern territory of the land of Israel, west of the Dead Sea, and the location of Jerusalem and

the nearby village of Bethany. Jesus and his disciples were there from 7:14 through 10:39. They've been away only since 10:40 ("He went away again across the Jordan"). **⁸The disciples say to him, "Rabbi** [which means 'Teacher' according to 1:38; 3:2], **the Jews were just now seeking to stone you** [10:31–33], **and are you going there again?"** The disciples can hardly believe their ears. And you can understand why. Not only had the Jewish authorities just tried for the second time to stone Jesus to death (see 8:59 for the first attempt). He'd also escaped and gone across the Jordan to get away from them. But Jesus' love for Lazarus, Martha, and Mary overpowers the threat to Jesus' life, just as the shepherd lays down his life for his sheep.

11:9–10: Jesus answered, "There are twelve hours of day, aren't there?" Of course! **"If anyone walks around during the day, he doesn't stumble, because he sees the light of this world. ¹⁰But if anyone walks around during the night, he does stumble, because the light isn't in him."** The light of this world is the sun, which shines during the day, so that people don't stumble over obstacles they can't see at night. But why does Jesus mention that the day lasts for twelve hours? Well, in 9:4–5 he portrayed himself as the light of the world, so that his earthly ministry constituted a day of salvation. But he also warned that night was coming, by implication because he would depart from the world. What would be the occasion of his departure? "His hour," the hour of his death, resurrection, and ascension back to heaven. So the mention of twelve hours here in 11:9 reminds us of that last hour of the daytime of Jesus' earthly ministry. Meanwhile, though, he has nothing to fear. He can elude his enemies so long as the day of his allotted lifetime lasts. But walking around in the light of day also represents discipleship to Jesus. And not stumbling because of the light of this world *that Jesus is* represents not falling into God's judgment, because believing in Jesus saves us from that fate. By contrast, walking during the night represents failure to have taken advantage of Jesus' earthly ministry, and the resultant stumbling represents falling into God's judgment. But what do we make of the last clause in 11:10: "because the light isn't *in him*"? You'd expect, "because he doesn't *see* the light of this world [the sun, representing Jesus]." The sun doesn't shine inside a person, does it? Well, *this* sun—Jesus—does! He indwells believers: "Abide in me, and I [will abide] *in you*" (15:4). So even when it's nighttime outside because Jesus is gone from the world, it's daytime inside. Not so for unbelievers, though. For them it's night inside as well as outside.

11:11: He [Jesus] **said these things, and after this he tells them** [the disciples], **"Lazarus our loved one has gone to sleep. But I'm going in order to wake him out of it."** The Greek noun behind "loved one" is usually translated "friend." But that translation obscures the use of the related Greek verb in 11:3: "He [Lazarus] whom you [Jesus] *love* is sick" (compare 11:5). Here, though, Jesus speaks of Lazarus as "*our* loved one"—in other words, "the one *we* love"—and thus includes his disciples with himself as those who love Lazarus. Hence a preview of the disciples' loving one another, so that, as Jesus said, "all people will know that you're my disciples" (13:34–35). Going to wake up Lazarus seems strange. After all, Jesus is a couple of days' journey or so away from Bethany—a long sleep for Lazarus if he won't wake up till Jesus arrives! The strangeness of Jesus' statement suggests a subtler meaning.

11:12–15: Therefore [because of Jesus' statement] **the disciples said to him, "Lord, if he** [Lazarus] **has gone to sleep, he'll be saved** ['saved' in the sense of getting well, because sleep has a healing effect]**."** But we'll find out that Lazarus's salvation will come about not by his sleeping, but by Jesus' waking him out of sleep. And this temporal salvation will symbolize eternal salvation—and something about Jesus too (for eternal salvation see 3:17; 5:34; 10:9; 12:47). **13But Jesus had been speaking about his** [Lazarus's] **death.** Because corpses are buried lying down, silent and motionless, death was often spoken of euphemistically as a kind of sleep. **But those ones** [the disciples] **thought, "He's speaking about the sleep of slumber."** They mistake the sleep of death for the sleep of slumber. **14So then Jesus said to them outright, "Lazarus has died; 15and I rejoice because of you, in order that you may believe, because I *wasn't* there. Nevertheless, let's go to him."** "Outright" means "plainly." Jesus doesn't say he rejoices because of Lazarus's death. Later, to the contrary, he'll shed tears over it. He rejoices because what he'll do for Lazarus will make the disciples believe. They've already believed; but in this Gospel believing in Jesus is an ongoing activity. Theologians call it the perseverance of the saints. "Because I wasn't there" means "because I wasn't there to keep Lazarus from dying by healing him." The implication? "You're going to see something better than a healing, something better that will advance your believing." "Nevertheless" means "despite the fact that it's too late to go heal Lazarus, let's go to him anyway." And Jesus' knowing at a considerable distance that Lazarus has died shows divine omniscience.

11:16: Therefore [since Jesus has said, "Let's go . . ."] **Thomas, the one called Didymus, said to** [his] **fellow disciples, "Let us go too in order that we may die with him."** The name "Thomas" is Aramaic, a Semitic language related to Hebrew. First-century Jews living in Israel spoke Aramaic more than either Hebrew or Greek (though Hebrew has "Thomas" in a form almost exactly like that in Aramaic). "Didymus" is the Greek equivalent of Thomas, and both of them mean "Twin." It looks as though the other disciples wouldn't go with Jesus apart from Thomas's urging—naturally, since they probably share Thomas's expectation of being stoned to death with Jesus. Ironically, though, the death of Jesus their shepherd will result, not in their deaths, but in eternal life for them—to be symbolized by his allowing himself to be arrested only on condition that they be let go (18:8–9).

11:17: On coming, therefore, Jesus found him [Lazarus] **entombed four days already.** "Already" em-

phasizes the length of time Lazarus had been entombed. "Four days" emphasizes that he seemed irreversibly dead, because Jews thought a dead person's soul hovered around its corpse for three days in hope of a resuscitation but then left. Too late then for a resuscitation, because putrefaction had become evident. So Lazarus's case looked hopeless. The next number of verses will tell what happened *before* Jesus entered Bethany and *before* he came to Lazarus's tomb. But here in 11:17 John has advanced Jesus' finding Lazarus entombed four days already to add even further emphasis on the apparent hopelessness of Lazarus's case.

11:18–19: And Bethany was near Jerusalem, about **fifteen stadia** [= about one and three-quarter miles] **away** [from Jerusalem]. This topographical note not only distinguishes the Bethany here from Bethany beyond the Jordan. It also associates the story of Lazarus with the story of what Jesus is going to do in Jerusalem. The parallels between these two stories will heap up as we go along. John's emphasis on the proximity of this Bethany to Jerusalem (notice not only the phrase "near Jerusalem" but also the specificity of the short distance) will support those parallels. **19And many of the Jews had come to Martha and Mary to console them about** [their] **brother.** Here's another reason for John's having mentioned how close Bethany was to Jerusalem. The Jews had come from Jerusalem because the journey was short, and some of them will take back to the authorities in Jerusalem a report of what happened in Bethany (11:46). This report combines with the topographical notations and the description of the Jews as "many" to differentiate them as Judeans in general from the Jewish authorities in particular who receive the report.

11:20–24: So when Martha heard, "Jesus is coming," she went to meet him. But Mary was sitting at home. **21So Martha said to Jesus, "Lord, if you'd been here, my brother wouldn't have died. 22Nevertheless, even now I know that God will give you as many things as you ask God** [to give you]**."** Jesus' approach leads Martha to go meet him outside Bethany. Meeting him leads her to make her statement. Her statement affirms the truth that God will give Jesus however many things Jesus asks of him. And this truth lays a basis for Jesus' prayer in chapter 17, and also for Jesus' saying later that God will answer whatever the disciples ask him in Jesus' name (15:16; 16:23–24). **23Jesus tells her, "Your brother will rise." 24Martha tells him, "I know that he'll rise in the resurrection at the Last Day."** The implication is that Martha wants Jesus to ask God to raise her brother from the dead right now, not on some future Last Day. Incidentally, "will rise" means "will stand up," and "the resurrection" means "the standing up." In other words, corpses lying supine in their tombs like sleepers will wake up and stand up alive. Resurrection has to do with renovated bodies, not with immortal souls.

11:25–27: Jesus told her, "I am the resurrection and the life. The one believing in me will live even though he dies. 26And everyone living and believing in me will by no means die—forever [that is as long as eternity lasts, and it has no end!]. **Do you believe this?"** [27]**She tells him, "Yes, Lord, I've come to believe that you are the Christ, the Son of God, the one coming into the world."** Jesus is the resurrection and the life in that he embodies them, so that he'll even raise himself from death to life (10:17–18). And because he has the power to do so, he's the source of bodily resurrection and eternal life both for Lazarus and for everyone who believes in him (5:21, 25–29; 6:39–40). Even though a believer dies, Jesus will raise the believer from death to live eternally.

Here's a problem, though. In 11:25 Jesus says the believer *may* die, but in 11:26 he says that the believer will *never* die. And here's the usual solution to the problem: 11:25 means that by virtue of resurrection the believer will live eternally even though he suffered *temporal* death (that is, the end of present life); and 11:26 means that by virtue of having eternal life the believer will never suffer *eternal* death ("the second death" in "the lake of fire" according to Revelation 2:11; 20:6, 14; 21:8). We can agree that the believer will never suffer eternal death, because in 8:51 Jesus said that the person who keeps his word "will by no means see death—forever." But there's something awkward in this solution. We'd expect Jesus to say in 11:26, "everyone believing in me and living," so that—as elsewhere throughout John—eternal life follows as a *result* of believing. As it is here, though, Jesus puts living *before* believing in him. Or we'd expect Jesus simply to omit the business of living: "everyone believing in me will never die." So why does he *mention* living and put it *ahead* of believing? Could it be that he uses "living" in a temporal as well as eternal sense just as he uses dying in a temporal as well as eternal sense (see 4:50–51, 53 for temporal living elsewhere in John)? Let's try that possibility: "And everyone living temporally and believing in me will never die even temporally, much less eternally." Living temporally when? At the Last Day, the day of resurrection, which Martha has just mentioned. Some people won't need resurrection, because they won't have died by then. They'll still be living. And if these people who are still living have believed in Jesus, they'll not only escape eternal death. They'll also escape temporal death. This solution makes sense of Jesus' placement of living before believing. Confirmation comes from 21:23, where Jesus will say to Peter about the beloved disciple, "If I should want him to remain till I come [that is, to stay alive till I come], what's [that] to you?" So those who'll never die are those who live up to the second coming, the Last Day, the day of resurrection, as Paul writes in 1 Thessalonians 4:16–18: "The Lord himself will come down from heaven with a summons, with the archangel's voice and with God's trumpet; and the dead in Christ will resurrect first. *Then we who are living and who are* [now] *being left behind* will be snatched up together with them in clouds to meet the Lord in the air. And in this way we'll always be with the Lord. Therefore comfort each other with these words."

If Martha hadn't introduced her answer to Jesus' question with "Yes," the answer would have implied that her belief in Jesus as the Christ, God's Son, and the one coming into the world *differed* from his claiming to be the resurrection and the life. As it is, her "Yes" implies an equivalence between his being the resurrection and the life, on the one hand, and his being the Christ, God's Son, and the one coming into the world, on the other hand. The two sets of identifications entail each other. If he weren't the one set, he wouldn't be the other. To put it another way, Martha tells Jesus she believes he's the resurrection and the life *because of* a prior belief that he's the Christ, God's Son, and the one coming into the world—therefore a belief in his preexistence (compare the Baptist's testifying to Jesus' preexistence in 1:30). Preexistence guarantees what we might call postexistence, that is, an eternality of life that carries with it the promise of resurrection for all deceased believers.

11:28–29: **And on saying this, she went off and called Mary her sister, saying** [to her] **in private, "The teacher is here and is calling you."** So Jesus is calling Mary through Martha. Martha calls Mary on Jesus' behalf, just as all believers need to call other people to Jesus on his behalf (compare 2 Corinthians 5:20). We might think privacy was necessary because of a hubbub of weeping and wailing in the middle eastern style. But John says nothing about such a hubbub. On the contrary, people have come to "console" the sisters (11:19, 31). The word for "console" means to cheer up with encouraging words—the opposite of weeping and wailing. So the privacy probably implies that Jesus is calling Mary because she's one of his sheep, but isn't calling the Jews from Jerusalem because they're not his sheep. Later, many of them will become his sheep by believing in him, but not yet. Earlier, Martha addressed Jesus with "Rabbi" (11:8). Here she refers to him as "the teacher," which "Rabbi" means. [29]**And when that one** [Mary] **heard, she got up quickly** [she'd been sitting according to 11:20] **and started going to him.** *What* did she hear? She heard Jesus' calling her through Martha. *Why* did she hear? She heard because she was one of Jesus' sheep; and when he calls his own sheep, they hear his voice (10:3–4, 16, 27). The quickness of Mary's response emphasizes her recognition of Jesus the good shepherd's voice and therefore her belonging to his flock.

11:30–31: **And Jesus hadn't yet come into the town, but was still in the place where Martha had met him.** [31]**Therefore the Jews who were with her in the house and were consoling her—seeing Mary, that she'd stood up quickly and gone out—followed her, thinking, "She's going to the tomb to weep and wail there** [as she will according to 11:33]**."** "Therefore" refers back to Mary's getting up and starting to go to Jesus. It doesn't refer to Jesus' still being outside the village. In the preceding verse, Mary "got up." Here she "stood up." Both verbs are used elsewhere for resurrection. Mary isn't resurrected, of course. But this twofold reference to getting/standing up hints at what Lazarus, who's not *sitting* down as Mary was but is *lying* down in the sleep of death—this twofold reference hints at what Lazarus will do, and after him Jesus too. This is the second time John mentions the quickness of Mary's response to Jesus' call. The double mention may not only emphasize her being one of the sheep that belong to him and recognize in him the voice of their shepherd. It may also imply that very shortly Lazarus will get up/stand up.

11:32–34: Therefore when Mary came where Jesus was, on seeing him she fell at his feet, saying to him, "Lord, if you'd been here, my brother wouldn't have died [exactly what Martha had said in 11:21 when she met Jesus, except for a slight difference of word order in John's original Greek]." ³³So when Jesus saw her weeping and wailing, and [saw] the Jews weeping and wailing who'd come with her, he growled with the Spirit and stirred himself up ³⁴and said, "Where have you laid him?" "Laid" is the same verb Jesus used in 10:17–18 when he said he would lay down his life on his own. They tell him, "Come and see." Philip used the same expression, "Come and see," when Nathaniel said to him, "Can anything good be from Nazareth?" (1:46).

The sight of Mary and the others weeping makes Jesus growl and stir himself up. In other words, he's working himself up to stop all this weeping by raising Lazarus from the dead. Other translations have it that Jesus "sighed" (or something like that) and "was troubled." But the first verb has a stronger meaning than sighing. It's used of horses snorting before they charge into battle, for example. In relation to human beings it means growling with indignation. Angry at death, in particular at the death of his beloved friend Lazarus, Jesus charges into battle like a snorting warhorse. The second verb isn't passive (as it will be in 13:21); it doesn't mean that Jesus *was* troubled, *was* stirred up. As the Word who was God, Jesus takes the initiative; he stirs *himself* up.

It's an open question whether "the spirit" refers to Jesus' human spirit or to the Holy Spirit. Favoring the human spirit is 11:38, which will say that Jesus growled again "in himself." But up to the present point in John, "the Spirit" has unmistakably referred to the Spirit of God no fewer than seven times and has never referred to Jesus' or anyone else's human spirit. So it's likely that here he growls with the Spirit of God that had come on him, and remained on him, back in 1:32. Since he's about to make Lazarus come to life, we should remind ourselves that in 6:63 Jesus said, "The Spirit is the one who makes [people] live." So the Spirit will work along with Jesus to make Lazarus live again. We'll see that the Father does too, so that the entire Trinity is involved (see 5:17, 19 for God the Father's coworking with Jesus).

At the same time, Jesus' humanity is evident. He *asks* where they've laid Lazarus. He doesn't call on his divine omniscience except when it's necessary to do so for the work of God's kingdom. Here it isn't necessary. And for Jesus' humanity look also at *11:35–38*: Jesus started crying. The verb means to shed tears. ³⁶Therefore the Jews were saying, "See how he loved him!" "How" has the sense of how *much*—enough to draw tears. ³⁷But some of them said, "This one [Jesus], who opened the eyes of the blind [man in chapter 9], could have done [something], couldn't he, so that also this one [Lazarus] wouldn't have died?" The implied answer is: Yes, he could have kept Lazarus from dying by healing him. The implied criticism is that he shouldn't have waited to come. ³⁸Therefore growling again in himself [where the Holy Spirit abides (see 11:33)], Jesus comes to the tomb. But it was a cave, and a stone lay on it [that is, over the mouth of the cave]. In Israel you can still see such ancient cave-tombs with a large stone disk that's rolled back and forth in a groove to open and close them.

11:39–40: Jesus says, "Take away the stone." Martha, the sister of him who had reached his end [= "died" for a bit of irony on John's part, for Jesus will soon show that Lazarus has *not* reached his end], says to him, "Lord, he already stinks; for he's on the fourth [day of being dead, so that putrefaction will be evident—too late now!]". ⁴⁰Jesus says to her, "I told you, didn't I, that if you believe, you'll see the glory of God?" But *did* Jesus previously tell Martha that she'd see God's glory if she believed? No, not in so many words. So seeing God's glory must be Jesus' interpretation of what he told her in 11:23–26, that her brother would rise again, that he was the resurrection and the life, and that a believer would live even though he died. Thus the raising of Lazarus will display God's glory, which 1:14 said is full of grace (God's ill-deserved favor) and truth (the reality and reliability of God's revelation of himself in the words and works of the Word incarnate).

11:41–42: So they took away the stone, and Jesus took away his eyes upward [there's a wordplay here between a horizontal taking away and an upward one] and said, "Father, I thank you that you've heard me." John hasn't recorded Jesus' prayer for the raising of Lazarus, but here it's implied; and Martha said earlier and correctly, "God will give you as many things as you ask God [to give you]" (11:22). Jesus continues: ⁴²"And I knew that you always hear me." When did Jesus know that God always hears him? He knew it when he prayed for Lazarus's raising. And this knowledge that God always hears him gave him confidence in that prayer. But why has Jesus thanked God *in public* for hearing him? Again he continues: "Nevertheless [that is, despite my knowing that you hear me *always*, not just occasionally], I've spoken on account of the crowd standing around, in order that they may believe that you sent me." What's about to happen will demonstrate to the crowd that God answers Jesus' prayer even for so difficult a task as raising a dead man. And this demonstration has the purpose of leading people to believe that God sent Jesus.

11:43–44b: And on saying these things [to God his Father], he shouted with a loud voice, "Lazarus, hither! Outside!" "Hither!" admittedly sounds old-fashioned. It means, "To here!" or, less literally, "Come here!" "Outside!" means to come outside the tomb, of course. ⁴⁴ᵃ⁻ᵇThe one who'd died came out, bound feet and hands with strips of cloth; and his face had been bound around with a napkin. Jesus called his sheep by name: "Lazarus." And Lazarus came out. Even though he was dead, he recognized the voice of his shepherd. Jesus' voice was loud so as to wake Lazarus out of the sleep of death. Jesus' words proved effective, because they were shouted by the Word who was with God in the beginning, who was God, who had life in himself, and who therefore was the resurrection and the life *for Lazarus*. Jesus' shouting brings life, but later the Jewish leaders' shouting several times will bring death to him (18:40; 19:6, 12, 15). And they will shout for his death because his shout brought life to Lazarus, for it's his raising of Lazarus that galvanizes their determination to kill Jesus (see 11:45–53; 12:9–11, 17–19). But out of Jesus' shouted death will spring the eternal life of shouted resurrection (see 12:24–25). That is to say, by killing him the Jewish leaders will unwittingly set the stage for his proving himself the resurrection and the life that he has just now claimed to be (11:25). What has happened in Lazarus's case dramatically illustrates what Jesus said in 5:25, 28–29: "Amen, amen I tell you that an hour is coming, and now is, when the dead will hear the voice of the Son of God; and those who hear will live. . . . an hour is coming in which all those in the tombs will hear his voice. And the ones who've done good things will come out into the resurrection of life, but those who've done evil things [will come out] into the resurrection of judgment."

To keep in place the long sheet (= a shroud) in which Lazarus's corpse was wrapped, and also to keep the feet together, thin strips of cloth had been tied over the sheet around the ankles. To keep the hands and arms against the torso, thin strips of cloth had been tied over the sheet around the torso at the wrists. And a napkin had been tied around the face, possibly to keep the mouth closed. The best Lazarus could do, then, was to shuffle or hop. **11:44c–45: Jesus tells them** [the crowd that should believe in him because he raised Lazarus], **"Loose him** [= untie those thin strips of cloth] **and let him go." 45Therefore many of the Jews who'd come to Mary and seen the things that he** [Jesus] **had done believed in him.** Why doesn't John mention Martha as well as Mary? Because it was Mary whose getting up and standing up hinted at Jesus' raising up Lazarus and raising up himself too (compare Mary's anointing Jesus' feet with perfume and wiping it off with her hair in 12:1–8, actions that will symbolize the death, burial, and resurrection of Jesus just as Lazarus's death, burial, and raising symbolize those events). The fact that John will mention the grave-wrappings of Jesus' corpse, and also the napkin over Jesus' face (19:40; 20:5–7), makes the story of Lazarus's raising symbolize and foreshadow the resurrection of Jesus down to its very details. Jesus will accomplish his own resurrection just as he accomplished the raising of Lazarus.

THE SANHEDRIN'S DECISION TO KILL JESUS
John 11:46–54

11:46–48: But some of them [the Jews] **went off to the Pharisees and told them the things that Jesus had done. 47So the chief priests and the Pharisees gathered**

a council [= a meeting of the Sanhedrin, the Jewish supreme court; apparently the Pharisees told the chief priests, who dominated the Sanhedrin] **and were saying, "What are we doing** [about the fact] **that this man** [a mere human being; they don't believe in his deity] **is doing many signs?"** Notice a contrast: the chief priests and the Pharisees are doing nothing; but Jesus is doing a lot, and even they have to admit as much. 48**"If we let him go on like this, *all* will believe in him."** *Some* already have. It could get worse. "All" is hyperbole, of course—an exaggeration for the sake of emphasis; for the chief priests and the Pharisees aren't about to believe in Jesus. **"And the Romans will come and take away both our place and** [our] **nation."** The Jews were already under the heel of Roman domination. But the Sanhedrin are afraid that since the Jews expect the Messiah to be a political savior, a messianic revolt will develop if more people believe Jesus to be the Messiah. And they're afraid that the Romans will then send an army to crush the revolt, as did happen about forty years later, but not because of anything having to do with Jesus.

"*Our* place" is the temple, which the chief priests controlled and which provided the base of the Sanhedrin's power (compare 4:20). "*Our . . .* nation" alludes to the large amount of control that the Romans allowed the Sanhedrin to exercise over the Jews living in Israel. The Roman overlords hold the Sanhedrin responsible for checking any revolutionary movements. So the Sanhedrin think they'd better put a stop to the Jesus movement while they can. The irony is that by the time John writes his Gospel, the Jesus movement will have spread all over the Roman Empire, and the Romans will have destroyed the temple and done away with the Jewish leadership. In fearing that the Romans will come and take away the Jewish leaders' place and *nation*, those leaders miss the point that Jesus came—according to John the Baptist—to take away the sin *of the world* (1:29).

11:49–50: But a certain one of them, Caiaphas, being high priest that year, told them, "You don't know anything [we'd say, 'You're stupid']. 50**Neither do you consider that it's to *your* advantage** [not the advantage of the nation, but the advantage of you its leaders] **that one man should die for the people and not the whole nation be lost** [= come to ruin]." The high priest presided over the council. But why does John add "that year" to Caiaphas's "being high priest"? (He'll add it again in 11:51 and 18:13.) The high priestly office wasn't passed around every year, and Caiaphas occupied it for nineteen years (A.D. 18–36). So why the singling out of "that year"? Well, we know that the "hour" of Jesus' passion has special significance in John. We also know from John's mentioning at least three different Passovers during Jesus' ministry that it must have lasted 2–3 years, since the Passover was an annual festival. And John will say in 11:51 that Jesus "was going to die." Apparently, then, John highlights the year of Jesus' death and associates it with Caiaphas's high priesthood to indict Caiaphas as the leader in the Jewish authorities' rejection of Jesus and to highlight the irony of Caiaphas's delivering an unwitting prophecy regarding Jesus' death despite being Jesus' main enemy.

Now John interprets Caiaphas's statement as just such a prophecy. **11:51–52: But he didn't say this on his own; rather, being high priest that year, he prophesied that Jesus was going to die for the nation, ⁵²and not only for the nation, but that he might gather into one also the scattered children of God.** They're Jesus' geographically scattered sheep that he'll gather into one theological flock, and he'll be their one shepherd (10:16; compare 6:12–13). His gathering the sheep to give them eternal life contrasts with the chief priests' and Pharisees' gathering a council to do away with Jesus. Ironically, though, their gathering to do away with him will make possible the gathering of the sheep for their eternal life. Where Caiaphas had in mind a sacrifice of Jesus to save the Sanhedrin's power over the temple and nation from the judgment of *Rome*, John sees a sacrifice of Jesus to save from *God's* judgment the whole nation, if only they'll believe in Jesus, and also God's children outside the nation. They will include Gentiles as well as Jews; for according to 1:12, "But *as many as* did accept him [Jesus the Word]—to them, the ones believing in his name, he gave authority to become God's children," and this without regard to physical ancestry (1:13). They've not yet been gathered, but they're called God's children by anticipation of their being gathered.

11:53–54: Therefore [because of Caiaphas's rebuke and advice] **from that day they planned to kill him** [Jesus]. So Caiaphas's supposed political realism triumphs over theological insight. The chief priests and Pharisees are blind. Their sin "abides/remains," just as Jesus said in 9:41. ⁵⁴**Therefore Jesus wasn't walking around publicly in Judea anymore; rather, he went away from there into a region near the wilderness, into a city called Ephraim, and he abode there with the disciples.** Just as Jesus previously eluded those who wanted to stone him to death, now he eludes the Sanhedrin, who plan to kill him. As far as we can tell, Ephraim was a town about twelve miles northeast of Jerusalem, within striking distance of Jerusalem but just far enough away and remote enough to provide cover.

THE ANOINTING OF JESUS
John 11:55–12:8

11:55–57: And the Jews' Passover was near, and many went up to Jerusalem from the countryside before the festival to purify themselves. Passover was one of the Jews' three annual pilgrim festivals. It took place in the spring; so several months have passed since the Festival of Hanukkah in late December (10:22). Pilgrims "went *up*" to Jerusalem because its elevated location in mountainous Judea required considerable climbing. The purification was ritual, and was required for participation in the ceremonies of Passover. ⁵⁶**So they** [the pilgrims] **were seeking Jesus and saying to one another while standing in the temple, "What do you think?**

That he won't come to the festival at all?" The pilgrims are standing in the courtyards of the temple complex, not inside the sanctuary proper, where only priests (descendants from Moses' elder brother Aaron within the tribe of Levi) and their helpers (Levites, that is, other members of the same tribe) could go. Jesus is still hiding out in the wilderness at Ephraim. The next verse tells why the pilgrims were wondering, even doubting, whether Jesus would come even though the Old Testament law required attendance by all able-bodied Jewish males within traveling distance. ⁵⁷**And the chief priests and the Pharisees had given orders that if anyone knew where he** [Jesus] **was, he** [that person] **should report** [the location of Jesus] **in order that they might seize him.** Apparently these orders came out of the chief priests' and Pharisees' planning to kill Jesus back in 11:53. They've enlisted popular support, as though Jesus were public enemy number one. This is the sixth time John has mentioned an effort to seize Jesus (see also 7:30, 32, 44; 8:20; 10:39). But until Jesus proceeds to Jerusalem with great fanfare and the Pharisees' full knowledge, the present effort won't work any better than previous efforts. Then it will work only because of the treachery of one of Jesus' disciples, not because of a report by someone in the general populace. And it'll work only halfway, because they won't be able to *seize* Jesus. He'll *allow* them to take him, almost *insist* on their taking him (18:1–14).

12:1–2: Six days before the Passover, therefore, Jesus came to Bethany, where Lazarus was, whom Jesus had raised from among the dead. ²Therefore they made a dinner for him [Jesus] **there, and Martha was serving. But Lazarus was one of those reclining with him.** "Therefore" implies that Jesus came *because* of his most-wanted status and so in *defiance* of it. No one will take his life from him. He'll lay it down on his own (10:17–18) and at his "hour," not earlier. Since in John the Passover will fall on the Saturday after Good Friday, "six days before the Passover" means the preceding Sunday. And since he counts days from midnight to midnight, not from sundown to sundown (see the comments on 1:39, for example), the dinner occurred late that Sunday. John identifies Bethany by Lazarus's presence, and the presence of Lazarus gives John a chance to remind us of Jesus' having raised Lazarus from among the dead—a preview of Jesus' raising himself from among the dead (as also in 12:9). The dinner was a formal meal prepared for Jesus as the honored guest. Martha is serving. Mary isn't. And Lazarus is reclining with Jesus along with others—including at least Jesus' disciples, since Judas Iscariot will show up shortly. For formal meals people didn't sit up in chairs. They reclined on mats placed on the floor around three sides of a very low table. The diners lay on their left side. Their left hand supported their head. They reached for the food with their right hand. And their legs stretched out away from the table.

12:3: Therefore [because Jesus' feet were accessible] **Mary, having taken a** [twelve-ounce] **pound of**

very expensive perfume [made] of pure spikenard oil, anointed Jesus' feet and wiped [the perfume] off his feet with her hair. And the house was filled with the fragrance of the perfume. Now we see why Mary wasn't serving. She had other business. Spikenard oil was extracted from the roots and spikes of nard plants, which grew in northern India. A Roman pound had twelve ounces instead of our sixteen. John emphasizes the purity and therefore expensiveness of the perfume. For having raised Lazarus from among the dead Jesus deserves only the best—and a lavish amount of it, one and a half cups, so much that Mary has to wipe his feet dry and so much that the fragrance fills the house. Ordinarily you anoint a guest's *head* with *oil*—cheap olive oil at that, not expensive perfume—and the feet only get washed with plain old water. Perfume for the feet? Almost unheard of! So Mary does the extraordinary for Jesus' having done the extraordinary on her brother.

12:4–6: **But Judas Iscariot, one of his disciples, the one who was about to give him over** [to the chief priests and Pharisees, who planned to kill Jesus], **says,** [5]**"Why wasn't this perfume sold for three hundred denarii and** [the three hundred denarii] **given to poor people?"** [6]**But he said this, not because he was concerned about the poor—rather, because he was a thief and was carrying the money-box that had the things** [= money] **being contributed** [to it]. "Three hundred denarii" indicates just how expensive the perfume was. It cost what amounted to a whole year's wages for a fully employed manual laborer. The description of Judas Iscariot as one of Jesus' disciples deepens the treachery of his upcoming betrayal of Jesus. The further description of Judas as a thief takes him out of the category of Jesus' sheep and puts him in the category of the thieves and bandits Jesus spoke about in 10:1–16. It also implies that Judas was stealing money from the box he carried as treasurer of the apostolic band. Elsewhere it's said that Judas got money from the Jewish authorities for giving Jesus over to them (Matthew 26:14–15; Mark 14:10–11; Luke 22:3–6; Acts 1:18). Bad enough. But even worse in John's Gospel, Judas steals money from his colleagues and Master and appears to betray Jesus gratis!

12:7–8: **Therefore** [because of Judas's statement] **Jesus said, "Let her alone in order that she may keep it** [the perfume] **for the day of my burial preparation.** [8]**For you always have the poor with yourselves** [compare Deuteronomy 15:11]**, but you don't always have me."** But how can Mary keep the perfume for the day of Jesus' burial preparation? She has already used it on Jesus' feet and wiped off the excess. So let's revise the translation by inserting an unexpressed but probably implied phrase: **"Let her alone. [It was intended] that she keep it** [the perfume] **for the day of my burial preparation."** And that day is *this* day, the day of Mary's anointing Jesus. She has prepared him for burial in advance of his death. Not that *she* intended to do so, but Jesus attributes to her anointing of him the *divine* intention of which she was unaware, just as Caiaphas

gave an unwitting prophecy concerning Jesus' death (11:49–52). By mentioning his burial, Jesus intimates his approaching death, which indicates in turn that they won't always have him available for acts of devotion like this anointing. In the same vein and with some superiority over Lazarus's case, Mary's wiping off the perfume symbolizes that Jesus will rise from the dead before the stink of putrefaction sets in, so that in the *final* analysis perfume is unneeded. The implied "you" in "Let her alone" is singular. Jesus is telling Judas to let Mary alone. The "you" in the statement about the poor is plural. So in that statement Jesus is addressing all his disciples and whoever else is present, such as Martha and Lazarus as well as Mary. The disciples know that Jesus, unlike Judas, is concerned for the poor. For according to 13:29, after Jesus sent Judas out to do quickly what he was going to do, "some [of the disciples] were supposing . . . that he [Judas] should give something to the poor." But here Jesus indicates that honoring him while there's still a chance to do so outranks for the moment the needs of poor people. Christology trumps humanitarianism, because Christology provides the basis of humanitarianism. Without Christology, humanitarianism lacks a sufficient basis. But the incarnation of God in Christ, God's becoming a human being and laying down his life for the eternal life of whoever will believe in him—now there's a solid basis for humanitarianism!

THE SANHEDRIN'S PLAN TO KILL LAZARUS
John 12:9–11

12:9: **Therefore** [because of the dinner for Jesus in Bethany] **a large crowd of Jews came to know that he's there; and they came, not on account of Jesus alone, but in order that they might see Lazarus too, whom he had raised from among the dead.** Back in 11:56 they were wondering whether Jesus would come to the Passover festival. Now that they learn he has come as close as Bethany, just on the other side of the Mount of Olives from Jerusalem, they go to see him for themselves. They also want to see Lazarus, apparently to confirm that Jesus really has raised him from among the dead. Since many Jews had come from Jerusalem to console Mary and Martha over the death of Lazarus, and then saw Jesus raise him, John probably means us to understand that the Jews here in 12:9 are others, who hadn't been present on that occasion. And John emphasizes that they were a *large* crowd to stress the huge, favorable impact of this sign that Jesus had performed.

12:10–11: **But the chief priests planned to kill Lazarus too** [in addition to Jesus, the only one they'd previously planned to kill according to 11:47–53], [11]**because on account of him** [Lazarus] **many of the Jews were going away** [apparently from Jerusalem to Bethany] **and believing in Jesus.** Many in the large crowd that came out of curiosity in 12:9 believe in Jesus, then, when they see that he has in fact raised Lazarus from among the dead. Seeing is believing—at least for them, though not for those determined not to believe. Again

John emphasizes the large number, "many," to stress the huge, favorable impact of this sign. The emphasis looms so large that John doesn't bother to say whether the Sanhedrin ever carried out their plan to kill Lazarus.

THE TRIUMPHAL PROCESSION OF JESUS
John 12:12–19

12:12–13: The next day a large crowd that had come to the festival, having heard, "Jesus is coming into Jerusalem," [13]**took branches of palm trees and went out to meet him; and they were shouting, "Hosanna! Favored [is] he who's coming in the Lord's name, even the king of Israel."** "The king of Israel" echoes part of Nathaniel's confession in 1:49: "Rabbi, you're the Son of God; you're the king of Israel" (compare Zephaniah 3:15). The king of Israel isn't the Lord. He's the one coming in the Lord's name, that is, with the Lord's authority. That's what the shouters mean. But of course readers of John's Gospel know that not only did Jesus come with the authority of the Lord, who is God his Father. Because of his oneness with the Father (10:30), Jesus is also himself the Lord. "The next day" means the day after the chief priests added their plan to kill Lazarus to their earlier plan to kill Jesus. (John doesn't specify what day of the week it was.) The fact that a large crowd acclaimed Jesus the very next day shows that from their own political standpoint the chief priests had good reason to kill Lazarus as well as Jesus if they could. Yet again John emphasizes the large size of the crowd to stress the favorable impact of Jesus' having raised Lazarus. Is this large crowd the same one that came from Jerusalem to Bethany to see Jesus and Lazarus in 12:9? Probably not, because John described the earlier crowd as "of the Jews," which tends to mean residents of Jerusalem and the surrounding territory of Judea. But John describes the large crowd at the triumphal procession as pilgrims who had come to the festival from elsewhere. If we have one large crowd in succession after another large crowd, a *double* emphasis falls on the impact of Jesus' having raised Lazarus.

Palm branches were a national symbol for the Jews. They appear on Jewish coins struck during rebellions against Rome, for example. Those rebellions occurred later, one in the first century and another in the second century. Here the national symbol of palm branches ties in with the acclamation of Jesus as Israel's king. "Hosanna! Favored [is] he who's coming in the Lord's name" comes from Psalm 118:25–26. Originally "Hosanna" was a prayer for quick salvation: "Save [us] now." But it had turned into an exclamation, something like "Hurray!" "Favored" (often translated "Blessed") doesn't mean that the crowd are pronouncing a blessing on Jesus the way he pronounced blessings on people in the beatitudes ("Blessed are the poor," for example, which means "Fortunate are the poor"). We have a different word here. It means "well spoken of, extolled." It pronounces praise—hence "Favored [with praise]." The crowd pronounce praise on Jesus, as well they might, because he has raised Lazarus from among the dead. And going out to meet Jesus as he approaches Jerusalem was a way of honoring him as the king of Israel. It was a regular practice when a king, emperor, or other dignitary visited a city for people to meet him outside and escort him the rest of his way into their city.

12:14–16: And on finding a little donkey, Jesus sat on it, just as it's written, [15]**"Don't be afraid, daughter of Zion. Behold, your king is coming, sitting on a donkey's colt."** So the donkey Jesus rides is little because it's young, the colt of an adult donkey. [16]**His disciples didn't understand these things at first. But when Jesus was glorified** [that is, lifted up on a cross, raised, and ascended], **then they remembered that these things had been written about him and** [that] **they had done these things for him** [in other words, that they had acclaimed him as he approached Jerusalem (for remembering, compare 2:17, 22; 14:26)]. The quotation comes partly from Isaiah 35:4; 40:9; 44:2; Zephaniah 3:16 ("Don't be afraid"), but mainly from Zechariah 9:9. Zion was the mountain that old Jerusalem was built on. Second Samuel 5:7 calls Zion "the city of David," who was the prototype of the messianic king that Jesus is. "Daughter of Zion" is a figure of speech for the people of Jerusalem, then. They shouldn't fear, because their king is coming to save them. Jesus brings salvation. But John omits Zechariah's "to you" after "your king is coming." The omission keeps Jesus' coming from being limited to Zion. He comes for the salvation of the *world*. Matthew 21:5 continues the quotation of Zechariah 9:9 to portray Jesus as "meek," because he's riding on a young donkey. But John doesn't portray Jesus as meek. He portrays a take-charge Jesus. After all, his Jesus is the Word who was God (1:1). It's Jesus, not two of his disciples, as in Mark 11:1–7; Matthew 21:1–7; Luke 19:29–35, who finds the young donkey. There's nothing in John about people's putting their garments on the colt and spreading garments and straw on the roadway. Luke even has them set Jesus on the colt. Not in John! Apart from the acclamation offered him, Jesus swallows up all the action. He's the one who sees to it that Scripture is fulfilled. The disciples don't even understand his action till a much later date. Much less to they contribute to it.

12:17–19: Therefore the crowd that was with him [Jesus] **when he called Lazarus out of the tomb and raised him from among the dead were testifying.** [18]**On account of this too** [their testimony as well as what Jesus had done] **the crowd met him, because they'd heard that he had performed this sign.** [19]**Therefore the Pharisees said to themselves** [= to one another], **"You see that you're not doing one bit of good. Look! The *world* has gone after him!"** Here we definitely have two different crowds: first, the one that bore testimony to their having seen Jesus raise Lazarus and, second, another crowd that went to meet Jesus because of the first crowd's testimony. So the "therefore" at the start of 12:17 refers back to the raising of Lazarus as the basis and content of that testimony. And the "therefore" at the start of 12:19 refers back to the second crowd's meeting Jesus. Their meeting him with acclamation throws the Pharisees into consternation. The Pharisees' plans to kill Jesus and Lazarus aren't working out. Instead of getting cooperation from the general populace (see 11:57 for their appeal to it), so large a portion of that general populace is going after Jesus that it seems to the Pharisees as though *the world* is acclaiming Jesus and believing in him (compare 4:42). As is typical of human beings, the Pharisees blame each other for the failure of their plans.

It's redundant of John to mention both Jesus' calling Lazarus out of a tomb and raising him from among the dead, but the redundancy accentuates the performance of a "sign" that Jesus truly is the resurrection and the life for those who, like Lazarus, belong to him (11:25). The Pharisees' statement that the world has gone after Jesus turned out to be less of an exaggeration than it was when they uttered the statement, because by the time John writes his Gospel belief in Jesus has spread throughout the Roman Empire and among many different peoples, not just the Jews. All in all, then, John's version of the triumphal procession stresses the large crowds whose acclamation of Jesus augured the worldwide success of the gospel (compare Acts 17:6; Colossians 1:6). And to make sure we don't miss this point, John immediately writes about some Greeks who wanted to see Jesus.

JESUS' RESPONSE TO SOME GREEKS' WANTING TO SEE HIM
John 12:20–26

John has written that a large crowd heard Jesus was coming to Jerusalem, and both the crowd and John have quoted Old Testament texts that speak about Jesus' coming. But John stops short of describing Jesus' entry into Jerusalem (therefore the use above of "triumphal *procession*" rather than the traditional "triumphal *entry*"). John is interested only in the honor that the crowd paid to Jesus by meeting him outside the city and acclaiming him to such an extent that the Pharisees say in consternation, "Look! The world has gone after him!" The world? Sure enough, certain representatives of the wider world—that is, wider than the Jewish world—suddenly show up.

12:20–21: And there were some Greeks from among those who were going up to worship in the festal assembly [on Mount Zion in Jerusalem]. [21]**Therefore** [because they were present] **these** [Greeks] **approached Philip, the one from Bethsaida of Galilee** [a back reference to 1:43–44], **and were asking him, saying, "Sir, we want to see Jesus."** "Greeks" doesn't necessarily mean people from Greece. It means Gentiles, probably because by and large they had adopted the Greek language and culture to a greater degree than the Jews had done (though the Jews weren't unaffected). "Going up to worship" implies that these Gentiles had converted at least halfway, perhaps fully, to Judaism. (According to the book of Acts the Apostle Paul had his best evangelistic success among such Gentiles.) The half-converts were called "God-fearers." They'd converted to monotheism

and the moral laws of the Old Testament. The full converts were called "proselytes." They'd converted to the ritual laws as well, starting for males with circumcision. "Philip" is a Greek name. For example, the father of Alexander the Great was Philip of Macedonia. And the Apostle Philip's hometown of Bethsaida was located in a region heavily influenced by the Greek language and culture. Not that Philip the apostle was a Gentile. He was a Jew, but the influence of the Greek culture even among Jews was such that many of them had Greek names. It's appropriate, then, for the Gentile Greeks in this episode to have approached a Jew who had a Greek name. Their expressed desire to see Jesus—that is, to meet with him—shows that they hadn't been part of the large crowd that went out to meet Jesus at the triumphal procession. And John doesn't say why they wanted to see Jesus. For two reasons John is content with their expression of a desire to see Jesus: (1) this expression illustrates the Pharisees' statement that the world has gone after Jesus, and (2) the Greeks' desire to see him previews the success of the gospel among Gentiles by the time John writes his Gospel.

12:22–26: Philip comes and tells Andrew [about both of whom see 1:35–51]. **Andrew comes—also Philip—and they tell Jesus.** Andrew's name, like Philip's, is Greek. [23]**And Jesus answers them, saying, "The hour has come for the Son of Man to be glorified. [24]Amen, amen I tell you, unless a grain of wheat dies by falling into the ground, it abides alone. But if it dies, it bears much fruit. [25]The person who loves his life loses it, and the person who hates his life in this world will protect it for life eternal. [26]If anyone serves me, he has to follow me; and my servant will also be where I am. If anyone serves me, the Father will honor him."** Because of their followups, the first "If anyone serves me" has the sense, "If anyone *is to serve* me, he has to . . ."; and the second has the sense, "If anyone *does in fact serve* me, the Father will . . . ." But who are the "them" whom Jesus "answers"? We might think of Philip and Andrew, who told him about the Greeks. But it was the Greeks who "were asking" (12:21). So Jesus' answering them might very well imply that the Greeks tagged along when Philip and Andrew went to Jesus. Verses 29 and 34 will indicate that a crowd, too, was standing around and listening.

"The hour" that "has come" is the time of Jesus' death, burial, resurrection, and ascension back to heaven. It hadn't yet come in earlier references. Now it has arrived. But Jesus doesn't describe it as an hour of suffering and shame, though crucifixion was considered the most shameful kind of death possible. It was called a slave's death, the kind of death fit for a slave guilty of some heinous crime. Whether or not you were a slave, you were being treated as one if they crucified you. And, of course, hanging stark naked on a cross in public view—as a warning to onlookers—wasn't exactly calculated to enhance your reputation. In a tour de force, though, Jesus backdates his glorification, so that it doesn't begin with his ascension back to heaven, or even with his resurrection. He makes it begin with his crucifixion. In what sense it does comes up later. Jesus calls himself "the Son of Man" in this connection, because that way of speaking about himself alludes to his descent from heaven, and also to his ascent back to heaven (see especially 3:13–14). So we have at least a hint that Jesus is treating his crucifixion as the start of his ascent.

A grain of wheat's abiding alone refers to its failure outside the soil to germinate and multiply itself in the reproduction of many grains. Its germination in the soil, on the other hand, involves disintegration, a kind of dying that produces a stalk containing many grains. In the first instance, Jesus appears to be talking about himself. He has just talked about his coming death as glorification, a benefit to him accomplished by God the Father. Now he's talking about his coming death as a benefit that he himself will accomplish for those who believe in him. His death will spell life through resurrection not only for himself but also for multiplied masses of believers throughout the world, represented by the Greeks who've come to see him. Their life as well as his constitutes the "much fruit" of his death as a grain of wheat. He has already spoken of "gather[ing] fruit [issuing] in eternal life" (4:36). In 15:5, 8 he'll speak of his disciples' bearing "much fruit," because as the Father sent him to bear the fruit of eternal life for many people, so he'll send his disciples to do the same through their evangelistic labors (20:21).

For the moment, though, the principle of life through death that applies to Jesus applies also to each individual. Loving your life means avoiding Christian discipleship out of fear of losing your life through persecution and martyrdom. But then you lose your life so far as eternity is concerned. The verb for "lose" (sometimes translated "destroy") is the same one that's translated "be lost" or "perish" in 3:16. Hating your life in this world means counting it as hateful insofar as loving it causes its loss in eternity. In other words, sacrifice it on the altar of martyrdom, if necessary for your Christian testimony. That's the only way to protect it for the life of eternity. That's the only way to serve Jesus—by following him in martyrdom, again if necessary, and certainly by living and testifying in a way that exposes you to this danger. Jesus promises people who serve him thus that they'll be where he is. He's speaking from a future standpoint. At the moment he's still on earth, but he's referring to his approaching presence with the Father in heaven. It's there, with God the Father, that those who serve Jesus by hating their lives in this world—it's in heaven where they'll be with him. And there's a plus for them. Not only will they be with Jesus in heaven. God the Father will honor them just as he glorified Jesus.

JESUS' DETERMINATION TO GO THROUGH HIS "HOUR"
John 12:27–36a

Jesus' response to the Greeks' wanting to see him shades into his stating a determination to go through his "hour." *12:27–29:* **"Now my soul is troubled, and what should I say? 'Father, save me from this hour'? But on account of this I came into this hour. 28"Father, glorify your name.'" Therefore a voice came out of heaven: "I've both glorified** [my name], **and I'll glorify** [it] **again." 29Therefore the crowd standing** [there] **and hearing** [the voice] **were saying, "It has thundered." Others were saying, "An angel has spoken to him."** "My soul is troubled" echoes Psalm 6:3. There's a wordplay here, because "soul" goes back to the same word that's translated "life" in the preceding statements about loving and hating your life, losing and protecting it. Here "soul" refers to the inward seat of Jesus' emotions. On his way to Lazarus's tomb, Jesus "troubled *himself*, stirred *himself* up, for the raising of Lazarus (11:33). Here Jesus "*is* troubled" (passive voice) by having entered his hour. So he asks himself whether he should pray that his Father save him out of it. He doesn't pray that his Father do so. He doesn't pray at all—not yet. He only asks himself *whether* he should pray in that vein. Then he answers his own question. The answer amounts to a no. The background of Jesus' troubled soul makes this no all the more emphatic of his determination to go through the hour. (To treat "Father, save me from this hour" as an actual prayer rather than a contemplated one makes little sense, probably nonsense, of Jesus' immediately following affirmation that he came for the purpose of entering the hour.) Not to go through the hour would defeat the very purpose of his coming, which was the giving of eternal life through his death. His works would go *unfinished*.

Now comes a prayer, quite a different prayer from the one Jesus contemplated only to reject it. Not a prayer to save him from his hour. Not even a prayer that God help him go through it. Not a prayer about himself at all. Instead, a prayer that his Father glorify his own name.

Jesus has already said the hour has come for himself as the Son of Man to be glorified (12:23). Here he prays that his own glorification entail the glorification of his Father. How different from Mark's portrayal of Jesus in the garden of Gethsemane! There Jesus prays "that if it were actually possible the hour might pass away from him. . . . 'Nevertheless, not what I want—rather, what you [want]'" (Mark 14:35–36). Because of Jesus' oneness with the Father, John replaces the submission of Jesus' wish to the Father's wish with Jesus' own determination to go through the hour. In John the will of Jesus and that of the Father are one and the same. And John replaces a prayer for exemption from the hour with a prayer for the Father's name to be glorified. "But on account of this I came . . . ," Jesus says. "This" refers to the troubling of his soul. (The grammar doesn't allow a reference to his hour.) So he came that his soul might be troubled by the hour. And because he came for *that* purpose, he'll be able to say to his disciples in 14:1: "*Your* heart isn't to be troubled." He bore our troubles so that we wouldn't have to bear them. And the adverb "now" at the beginning of 12:27 shows he has started to bear them right here, because his hour has arrived (12:23). Jesus doesn't pray for the Father to glorify himself—rather, to glorify his own "name." What name is that? Apparently "Father," which

Jesus has just used in addressing God. What then would it mean for God to glorify his name of "Father"? It would mean to display his glory by acting as a Father to Jesus, and acting as a Father also to believers in Jesus so as to accept them as his children (see 1:12: "God's children").

In the other Gospels, God spoke from heaven on the occasions of Jesus' baptism and transfiguration (Mark 1:11; Matthew 3:17; Luke 3:22). But John hasn't narrated those occasions. Here God speaks from heaven on the quite different occasion of Jesus' hour. His voice gives an immediate answer to Jesus' prayer. It says he answered the prayer in advance by glorifying his name in the past, presumably by acting as Jesus' Father in their coworking of signs and works (5:17: "My Father is working till now, and I'm working"). And the voice promises future such glorification too. That will consist in acting as Jesus' Father by restoring his Son to his former heavenly glory, and as the Father of believers in his Son by loving them as his children just as Jesus has loved them as his disciples (see chapter 17). The crowd heard the Father's voice but didn't understand it. They're an unbelieving crowd, it turns out in the following verses. So they don't recognize the voice of God the Father any more than they've recognized the voice of Jesus the good shepherd. They can think only of thunder or of an angel's speaking to Jesus.

12:30–33: Jesus answered and said, "This voice didn't come on my account—rather, on your account. [31]The judgment of this world is now. The ruler of this world will be cast out now. [32]And I, if I'm lifted up from the earth—I'll draw all people to myself." [33]And he was saying this to signify by what kind of death he was about to die. The crowd hadn't been talking to Jesus; so his answering means that he responded to what he'd overheard them saying. Because of his oneness with the Father, Jesus didn't need to hear his Father's voice. But because of their unbelief, the crowd needed to hear it as a sign of Jesus' authority even though they didn't recognize it to be God's voice or understand the words he addressed to Jesus. Jesus' telling the crowd this reason for their having heard the voice underscores the immediately following announcements that the world's judgment is now and that the casting out of the world's ruler will occur now. Jesus' unbelieving audience make up a representative slice of this world. The two announcements are more or less synonymously parallel. "This world" and "the ruler of this world" correspond to each other. "Judgment" and "will be cast out" also correspond to each other. And both announcements stress that "now" is the time of these corresponding events. "Now" is Jesus' "hour" that has finally arrived.

"This world" of unbelievers is ruled by their father the Devil, as Jesus put it in 8:44. And the Devil is called "the ruler of this world" to highlight the control he exercises over unbelievers (compare "slave of sin" in 8:34). In the other Gospels Jesus repeatedly casts demons out of individuals. Here the prince of demons, the Devil himself, is cast out of the world of unbelievers at large. So the Devil is robbed of his power over the world. But this omnibus exorcism does no good for the world. For the world suffers judgment just as the Devil suffers exorcism. And the death of Jesus in his hour signals this judgment and this exorcism. His death signals judgment on the world for their seeking his death. It signals exorcism of the Devil for his inspiring the world to seek Jesus' death. In Jesus' death, then, we see God's wrath as well as God's love. Apart from God's wrath, Jesus wouldn't have *had* to die. Apart from God's love, Jesus *wouldn't have* died. And just as believers enjoy the life of eternity by anticipation right now, so also the world suffers eternal judgment, and the Devil eternal exorcism, by anticipation right now.

There's the dark side. Here's the bright side: if Jesus is lifted up, he'll draw all people to himself (compare the Father's drawing people to Jesus in 6:44, 65, so that he and his Son cooperate in this effective attraction). Since Jesus has just spoken about the world's judgment and elsewhere has talked about a resurrection of judgment (5:29) and about God's wrath as abiding on unbelievers (3:36), Jesus can't mean that everybody will be saved. He means instead that he'll draw all *sorts* of people to himself, people from every tribe and tongue and nation, as Revelation 5:9; 7:9 put it. John interprets Jesus' statement as signifying the sort of death he was about to die, so that his being lifted up from the earth signifies elevation on a cross, in contrast with being knocked down to the ground by stones, as the Jews had tried doing to him more than once (8:59; 10:31–32). The addition of "from the earth" propels Jesus up toward heaven. And he sees in this elevation from earth toward heaven, not exposure to shame and ridicule by his human enemies, but the first step in God the Father's exalting him to his preincarnate glory, as he will pray in 17:5: "And now you, Father, glorify me alongside yourself with the glory that I had alongside you before the world existed" (compare Isaiah 52:13).

12:34: Therefore [because of what Jesus had just said] **the crowd answered him, "We've heard out of the Law that the Christ abides forever. And how is it that you say, 'It's necessary that the Son of Man be lifted up'? Who is this Son of Man?"** "The Law" is the Old Testament. They've heard it read to them in their synagogues. The crowd probably have in mind Ezekiel 37:25, where the Lord says, "David my servant will be [the Jews'] prince forever." Since David had died long before Ezekiel's prophecy, the Jews must have thought, probably correctly, that the Lord was calling the coming messianic prince by the name of his prototype, David. Earlier we noted Jesus' use of more or less *synonymous* parallelism (12:31). Here we note the Jews' use of *antithetical* parallelism. In their view "we've heard out of the Law" contrasts with "you say." "The Christ" contrasts with "the Son of Man." And "abides forever" contrasts with "must be lifted up." At least the last contrast is half right: being lifted up has to do with death—but they miss that it's death by an exaltation that eventuates in life, in abiding forever. And they totally miss that the Law testifies to Jesus rather than contradicting him, and that the Christ *is* the Son of Man, not that these two terms refer to different figures. As a matter of fact, Jesus hadn't told them, "It's *necessary* that the Son of Man be lifted up." He'd said to them, "*If* I'm lifted up from the earth." They've changed Jesus' "if" into a necessity, changed his "I" to "the Son of Man," and omitted "from the earth." But these changes aren't wrong, because Jesus told Nicodemus back in 3:14, "It's necessary that the Son of Man be lifted up," just what the crowd says here. It's as though Nicodemus had told them what Jesus said to him. Jesus ignores their questions. The crowd don't need explanation. They need exhortation.

12:35–36a: Therefore [because of their questions] Jesus told them, "The light is among you a little while yet. Walk around while you have the light, lest darkness apprehend you. And the one walking around in the darkness doesn't know where he's going. ³⁶ᵃWhile you have the light, believe in the light in order that you may become sons of light." Jesus is referring to himself as the light, of course, and to the fact that his luminous ministry will end soon. The exhortation to walk around while you have the light means to take advantage of Jesus' presence by becoming his disciple. The warning about darkness apprehending you is explained by the statement that the person who walks around in the darkness doesn't know where he's going. In other words, darkness equates with ignorance, a lack of the saving knowledge of God and Christ that Jesus will mention in his prayer to God the Father at 17:3: "And this is eternal life, that they know you, the only true God, and Jesus Christ, whom you sent." Most translations have "lest the darkness *overtake* you" instead of "*apprehend* you." That's okay, but it misses a contrast with 1:5, where the same verb occurs: "And the light is shining in the darkness, and the darkness didn't apprehend it," that is, didn't take it into custody, arrest it, overpower it. But like an evil force, the darkness of ignorance *does* overpower, *does* apprehend, those who don't walk in the light. Then their opportunity for salvation is lost. Too late. So believe in the light, Jesus says—that is, believe in me—while you have me as the light. Then you'll become sons of light. In biblical language, to be a son of this or that is to belong to it, to be characterized by it, to be destined for it. Judas Iscariot is called "the son of lostness," for example, because he's destined for eternal lostness (17:12). To be sons of light means then to belong to the realm of light, the light of eternal life in Christ, who is himself that light.

JOHN'S COMMENTARY
John 12:36b–43

12:36b–43: Jesus said these things and, on going away, he was hidden from them [the crowd]. ³⁷But though he'd done so many and great signs in their presence, they weren't believing in him, ³⁸in order that Isaiah the prophet's word might be fulfilled, [the word] that he spoke: "Lord, who has believed our report? And to whom has the arm of the Lord been revealed [Isaiah 53:1]?" ³⁹On account of this they *couldn't*

believe, because again Isaiah said, ⁴⁰"He has blinded their eyes and hardened their heart lest they see with [their] eyes and understand with [their] heart and be turned around and I heal them [Isaiah 6:10]." ⁴¹Isaiah said these things because he saw his [Jesus'] glory and spoke about him. ⁴²All the same, though, many even of the rulers believed in him. On account of the Pharisees, however, they weren't confessing [him], lest they become de-synagogued. ⁴³For they loved the glory of human beings rather than the glory of God. "Was hidden" could mean either that God hid Jesus or that Jesus hid himself, probably the latter since in this Gospel Jesus normally does things for himself. He was hidden in 8:59, too, when the Jews picked up stones to stone him to death. Here he's hidden again so as to be saved, or save himself, for death as the true Passover lamb on the afternoon several days from now when passover lambs are supposed to be slain (compare 1:29, 36). The signs he has performed are both many and great. Their performance in full view of the public makes the crowd's unbelief almost unbelievable. So John offers a reason for the unbelief. It's the necessity that Isaiah's prophecy be fulfilled. The prophecy consists in questions, and the questions imply that people haven't believed the word of the Lord which they've heard, meaning Jesus' words (for he is Lord).

"The arm of the Lord" is a figure of speech for his power to save, because you wield tools and weapons with the strength of your arm. Because of the people's unbelief, the Lord's arm, representing Jesus' powerful signs, hasn't been revealed to them. He hasn't shown himself strong to save them. That's John's use of Isaiah's text. Then in 12:39–40 John tightens the screw. He writes that the necessity that Isaiah's prophecy be fulfilled makes believing *impossible* for the crowd, and he quotes another passage from Isaiah to that effect. "Lord" carries over from the earlier quotation to become the subject in the later quotation: "He [the Lord, who is Jesus] has blinded their eyes [that is, the eyes of 'the crowd' mentioned in 12:29, 34]." Jesus gave sight to a man born blind in chapter 9. But that man believed in Jesus as a result of the sign Jesus had performed on him (9:35–38). Despite the many and great signs Jesus has performed in the crowd's presence, though, they *didn't* believe and they *couldn't* believe. Once again, as throughout John, human responsibility and divine determination dovetail. John doesn't explain *how* they do. They just *do*. Blinded eyes stand for mental blindness. A hardened heart likewise stands for mental ignorance, because the heart was considered an organ of thought. To be turned around would have been to be converted, set in the new direction of understanding and belief. To be healed would have been to be given mental sight and an understanding heart. Sadly, none of this is true of the present crowd.

Isaiah said these things because he saw the Lord's glory. The sight of it led him to say these things. When did he see the Lord's glory? When he received his prophetic call in the passage immediately preceding John's second quotation from the book of Isaiah: "In the year of King Uzziah's death, I [Isaiah is speaking] saw the Lord sitting on a throne, high and lifted up. [Jesus has recently talked of being lifted up (12:32, 34).] Seraphim . . . said, 'Holy, holy, holy is the Lord of hosts. The whole earth is full of his glory [there's the glory that Isaiah saw according to John].'" Then Isaiah gets his commission to prophesy because of having seen the Lord's glory: "Go and tell this people . . ." (Isaiah 6:1–9, excerpts). But who is the Lord whose glory Isaiah saw and about whom he spoke? Elsewhere John refers to the Lord with "he," "his," and "him." But in this passage he uses these same pronouns for Jesus—without making any distinction between Jesus and the Lord: "though *he* [Jesus] had done so many and great signs in their presence, they weren't believing in *him*" (12:37); "all the same, though, many even of the rulers believed in *him*" (12:42). So the Lord whose glory Isaiah saw and about whom he spoke was none other than the preincarnate Word, who became Jesus of Nazareth. And it's his arm that's mighty to save, while at the same time he's the one who exercises judgment by blinding eyes and hardening hearts. He's a lion as well as a lamb (compare Revelation 5:5–6).

But look! Even some rulers of the Jews, the higher-ups, believe in Jesus. No, not just "some"—rather, "many." Jesus' great and many signs did have their effect even in the upper echelons of Jewish society. But so did the love of high status, "glory" in the sense of honor bestowed by fellow human beings. Such love kept these believers from confessing Jesus. They didn't want to suffer the shame of the Pharisees' excommunicating them from the synagogue. You can't help but contrast the bold, brave, and even brash confession of Jesus by the healed blind man in chapter 9. There's irony in rulers' fearing what non-rulers like the Pharisees would do to them. And there's tragedy in the rulers' loving the cheap glory that comes from fellow human beings rather than the inestimably valuable glory that comes from God. Were these rulers true believers? It's hard to think so in view of Jesus' question in 5:44: "How *can* you believe [*truly* believe, we might add] while accepting glory from one another, and you don't seek the glory [that comes] from the only God?" Not all faith is saving faith; for "even the demons believe and quake" (James 2:19), but they're not saved.

JESUS' COMMENTARY
John 12:44–50

Jesus was hidden from the crowd in 12:36b. John inserted his own comments in 12:37–43. Now Jesus suddenly starts talking, indeed shouting, with no indication that he has come out of hiding and no indication that he has an audience. It's enough for John that Jesus the Word speaks loudly.

12:44–46: But Jesus shouted and said, "The person who believes in me isn't believing in *me*—rather, in him who *sent* me. [45]And the person who sees *me* is seeing him who *sent* me. [46]I've come into the world as light in order that everyone who believes in me may not abide [in the sense of 'remain'] in darkness." Shout-

ing puts emphasis on Jesus' words—Listen up!—and his shouting corresponds to the Father's thunderous voice in 12:28–29—naturally, since Jesus is the Word of God his Father (10:35–36). "Isn't believing in me—rather, in him who sent me" is a deliberately exaggerated way of stressing that the only way to believe in God truly is to believe in Jesus as the one whom God sent (compare 14:1). To see Jesus is to see God, who sent him, because Jesus is God in visible human flesh (compare 14:9: "The person who has seen me has seen the Father"). The sender and the sent merge at the same time they're distinguished from each other. As the light that God sent into the world (compare 1:9), Jesus makes it possible for believers not to abide in the darkness of sin, ignorance, death, and judgment. And they don't. Later the shift *from* abiding in the darkness will become a shift *to* abiding in Christ, who is the light (15:4–7).

12:47–50: "And if anyone hears my words and doesn't keep [them], I'm not judging him. For I haven't come to judge the world—rather, to save the world. [48]The person who rejects me and doesn't accept my words does have one who judges him. The word which I've spoken—that will judge him on the Last Day, [49]because I've not spoken on my own. Rather, the Father, who sent me—he himself has given me a command as to what I should say and what I should speak. [50]And I know that his command is life eternal. As to the things that I'm speaking, then—just as the Father has spoken to me, I'm speaking in this way." Not to *keep* Jesus' words is not to *obey* them. And obeying them begins with believing in Jesus and confessing him openly. Hearing his words without this kind of keeping makes the hearing inconsequential so far as salvation goes, but of great consequence otherwise, because hearing them without keeping them increases guilt and therefore builds up judgment (compare Romans 1:18–32). Jesus has repeatedly said that he judges, and came to judge: "The Father . . . has given all judgment to the Son" (5:22); "[The Father] has given [the Son] authority to do [= execute] judgment" (5:27); "Just as I hear [from the Father], I judge; and my judgment is right" (5:30); "I have many things to say and judge about you" (8:26); "I've come into this world for the purpose of judgment" (9:39). So how can Jesus now say that he's *not* judging the disobedient person, because he *didn't* come to judge the world but to save it—or rather *them*, since the world consists of human beings. This statement about not judging gets some support from 3:17: "for God didn't send [his] Son into the world in order that he might judge the world—rather, in order that the world might be saved through him." Actually, these two elements—Jesus' judgment and nonjudgment—appeared side by side in 8:15–16: "I'm judging no one. And if I judge, my judgment is true [not 'would be true,' but 'is true'], because I'm not alone. Rather, I and the Father, who sent me [are together]." So Jesus doesn't exercise judgment *apart from* what his Father tells him. But he does exercise judgment *in accordance with* what his Father tells him. And he exercises this kind of judgment only on those who disobey his words, the words of eternal life. He came as the divine Word to save the world with those words. But when they're disobeyed, those words become judgmental words instead of salvific words.

The purpose of the sun is to cast light. But when something stands in the way, the effect of the sun is to cast shadows. So it is with Jesus' words. Their purpose is to bring salvation. When the disobedience of unbelief stands in the way, their effect is to bring judgment, even to exacerbate it. Not to accept and keep Jesus' words is to reject *him*, because as the Word he is one with his words. So he himself—as well as his spoken word—is the Word that will exercise judgment on the Last Day, the Day of Judgment. And therefore the book of Revelation 19:11–16 calls him "the Word of God" when he comes back to "judge and make war." The fact that he hasn't spoken on his own, but only in accord with what the Father commanded him to say, shows again, as in 8:15–16, that it's judgment apart from his Father that he doesn't exercise, and won't exercise. But the Father's command spells eternal life for those who believe, because the Father's command translates into Jesus' words, which Peter described in 6:68 as "the words of eternal life" and which 1 John 1:1 transmutes into Jesus himself as "the Word of life."

JESUS' WASHING THE DISCIPLES' FEET AT THE LAST SUPPER
John 13:1–20

Chapter 13 carries us to the evening before Jesus' death the next afternoon and to his washing the disciples' feet during a meal that evening. The narrative includes a dialogue between him and Peter, and Jesus' explanation of the foot-washing (13:1–20). Since the explanation includes some references to Jesus' betrayal, the story of Judas Iscariot's exit comes next (13:21–30). Then starts a long discourse by Jesus that goes all the way through chapter 16 (13:31–16:33). Once in a while a disciple breaks in with a question or a request. The section closes with a chapter-long prayer of Jesus (17:1–26). Only then will the narrative of his arrest, trial, crucifixion, and resurrection appearances pick up (chapters 18–21).

13:1: And before the Festival of Passover Jesus, knowing that his hour had come for him to transfer out of this world to the Father, having loved his own [who were] **in the world, he loved them to the end.** "Before the Festival of Passover" pushes the Passover meal till the next evening, so that Jesus will die as the true Passover lamb the next afternoon, when the Jews were sacrificing the lambs that merely symbolized him as that true Passover lamb (compare 1:29, 36). "Knowing" highlights his divine omniscience as an indication that he's in control of his destiny. He's God in human flesh; and as such, he's in charge. The content of this knowledge, that he would transfer to the Father out of this world of unbelieving humanity, describes his hour not in terms of shame and suffering but in terms of what we might call a homegoing, a return to his Father in heaven. John's

calling God "the Father" contributes to this homey connotation. The thought of Jesus' going out of this world leads John to think of the disciples as destined to stay in the world after Jesus' departure. John's calling them "his [Jesus'] own" contrasts with "his own ones" who "didn't accept him" (1:11) but reminds us that Jesus himself called those who *have* accepted him "his own sheep" (10:3–4). He has already loved his own by coming into the world and calling them by name. By embracing his hour (12:27) he has now loved them to the end. "End" is simply the noun form of the verb "finish," so that in 19:30 Jesus will say, ". . . finished!" The statement won't indicate the end of his life so much as it will indicate that his love for those God has given him out of the world will have accomplished all things necessary for their salvation. That's the end, that's the goal.

13:2–5: And while the supper was going on, since the Devil had already thrown [it] **into the heart** [of Judas] **that Judas,** [son] **of Simon Iscariot, should give him** [Jesus] **over** [to the chief priests and Pharisees], [3]**he** [Jesus]**—knowing that the Father had given all things to him,** [in other words,] **into** [his] **hands, and that he had come forth from God and is going to God—** [4][Jesus] **rises from the supper and lays down his garments and, on taking a towel, tied** [it] **around himself.** [5]**Then he throws water into a wash basin and began to wash the disciples' feet and wipe off** [the water] **with the towel that he'd tied around himself.** Wash basins portrayed in ancient art and found by archaeologists are usually large enough to put your feet in and have water poured over them. The reference to supper shows that we're dealing with what is traditionally called the Last Supper. But there'll be no mention of Jesus' instituting the Lord's Supper during the Last Supper. Not in John's Gospel. Jesus' turning the water to wine back in 2:1–11 took care of the wine that in the other Gospels he made symbolic of his blood when instituting the Lord's Supper. And back in chapter 6 Jesus' having made the bread that he multiplied for the five thousand—his having made that bread symbolize his flesh took care of the bread symbolizing his body in the Lord's Supper. John doesn't need the Lord's Supper, then. So in the present section he replaces the brief Words of Institution ("This is my body. . . . This is my blood . . .") with a cavalcade of words from Jesus the Word. The words keep coming and coming all the way through chapter 17.

John's calling Judas "the son of Simon Iscariot" distinguishes this Judas from another Judas among the twelve disciples (see 14:22). The reference to this Judas's "giving" Jesus over to the chief priests and Pharisees seems unnecessary at this stage of the story—except that it sets up a contrast with the Father's having "given" all things into the hands of his Son Jesus. (Though used occasionally for convenience, the translation "betray" for Judas's action obscures this contrast.) "Into [Jesus'] *hands*" means into Jesus' *control*. The Father's having given all things into Jesus' control means that as the Son of God, Jesus has received his inheritance; and the inheritance consists of all that exists. No larger inheritance than that, because no larger inheritance is possible. And the giving of this universal inheritance to Jesus compensates—indeed, more than compensates—for Judas's giving Jesus over to his enemies. The Devil has "already" thrown it into Judas's heart to give Jesus over, but John uses the past tense for the Father's giving all things to Jesus, so that there's no interval even between Judas's *purpose* of giving Jesus over and the Father's giving, much less between Judas's *actual* giving and the Father's giving. The Father doesn't allow the slightest interval of noncompensation to his Son. On the other hand, the Devil's having already thrown it into Judas's heart to give Jesus over unmasks Judas. He's one of the Devil's children, like the unbelieving Jews in 8:44. Without naming him (because he calls his own sheep by name and Judas isn't one of them [10:3]), Jesus called Judas "Devil" in 6:70. Like father, like son. That the Devil had "thrown" it into Judas's heart is simply a vivid way of saying he had "put" it into Judas's heart, though the verb was used so often in this weak sense that in contexts like this one it had lost a lot of its vividness. Here, however, the verb sets up a contrast with Jesus' "throwing"—that is, "putting"—water into a wash basin. His action arose out of love for his disciples, as mentioned in 13:1. The Devil's action arose out of hatred toward Jesus (compare 3:20; 7:7; 15:18–19, 23–25; 17:14).

Jesus' divine omniscience comes up in 13:3 as well as in 13:1 to stress for a second time that he's in control. This time his omniscience is said to include his having come from God in addition to his going to God. The present tense of "is going" indicates either that he's already on his way (because his hour has arrived) or that his going is so sure and soon that it might as well be taking place already. His rising from supper ties in with the supper's being in progress (13:2) and implies a formal meal, at which the diners reclined on mats (see the comments on 12:2). Jesus' laying down his garments prepares for tying a towel around himself, but also symbolizes the laying down of his life for the eternal life of his sheep, as in 10:11, 15, 17–18. (The verb is the same.) The nudity (with the possible exception of a loincloth) of laying down his garments may even forecast the nudity in his crucifixion (compare 19:23: "the soldiers . . . took his garments"). Jesus himself will interpret the washing and wiping of his disciples' feet as a cleansing. So laying down his life has the purpose of washing away the sins of people who believe in him—another way of saying that by his death he "takes away" sin (1:29). You'd have expected the foot-washing to have occurred before the meal, though, not in the middle of it (see Luke 7:36, 44–46). So Jesus' interrupting the dinner to do what should have been done beforehand underscores the symbolism of cleansing from sin. It also prepares for, and puts emphasis on, his command to follow his example by washing one another's feet.

Now comes a dialogue between Jesus and Peter. *13:6:* **So he comes to Simon Peter** [as distinguished from "Simon Iscariot," the father of Judas in 13:2]. **He** [Simon Peter] **says to him** [Jesus], **"Lord, are *you* washing *my* feet?"** Peter's question is incredulous; he can hardly believe his eyes. It seems to him wholly inappropriate that the Lord, *his* Lord, should perform so lowly a task as washing the feet of a mere disciple, such as Peter. In all ancient non-Christian literature that has survived, there's no other instance of a person's washing the feet of someone lower in status than himself. In Jewish culture, disciples were to perform the tasks of slaves for their teacher—with the exception of washing their teacher's feet. Too lowly a task even for a disciple! And here it's not merely Jesus the *teacher* but Jesus the *Lord* who performs this lowliest of tasks. You can understand Peter's incredulity.

13:7–9: **Jesus answered and told him, "You don't know** [= understand] **now what I'm doing, but after these things you'll know."** Shortly Jesus will explain the foot-washing, but he'll say a little later yet that it will take the Holy Spirit to guide the disciples into all truth (14:26; 16:12–15). So "after these things" means after the events of Jesus' "hour" and the coming of the Holy Spirit. Only then will the foot-washing and Jesus' explanation of it make sense to Peter. [8]**Peter tells him, "By no means will you wash *my* feet—ever!"** Apparently, then, Peter's earlier question, "Lord, are you washing my feet?" (13:6), didn't imply that Jesus had already started washing them. Rather, Jesus had only approached Peter with the intention of doing so; and Peter was questioning that intention. Now he resists it. Literally translated, "ever!" comes out as "for eternity!"—a very strong expression. **Jesus answered him, "If I don't wash you, you have no part with me,"** meaning that Peter doesn't participate in the cleansing from sin that Jesus' washing represents if he (Peter) continues to resist. Jesus' warning leads Peter to overreact. [9]**Simon Peter says to him, "Lord, not only my feet, but also** [my] **hands and** [my] **head** [that is, the other exposed parts of my body]**."** We have to supply the verb "wash," of course: "Wash my hands and head as well. I can't get too much of a good thing, can I?" This time "Lord" shows Peter's submission to Jesus' foot-washing, just as the previous addressing of Jesus as Lord showed Peter's understandable but mistaken sense that foot-washing was below Jesus' dignity.

13:10–11: Jesus tells him, **"The person who has been bathed has no need** [to wash] **except to wash** [his] **feet. As a whole, rather, he's clean. And you** [plural] **are clean, but not all** [of you are clean]**."** [11]**For he** [Jesus] **knew the one giving him over** [Judas]. **On account of this** [knowledge] **he said, "Not all of you are clean."** Jesus distinguishes between being bathed and therefore clean as a whole, including hands and head, and needing only foot-washing because of getting the feet soiled by walking in open sandals over dusty paths and streets from the place of bathing to (in this case) the dining room. Being bathed may allude to baptism by immersion at conversion. But in 15:3 Jesus will tell his disciples, "You're already clean because of the *word* that I've spoken to you." So if being bathed alludes to baptism at all, the baptism only symbolizes a cleansing that took place because of belief in the word of the

John 13:12–15

gospel. Foot-washing, then, represents a maintainance of the original cleansing that took place at conversion. The original cleansing washed away all sin committed *prior* to conversion. Baptism represented that. Further cleansing is required for sin committed *after* conversion. Foot-washing represents this further cleansing, as in 1 John 1:8–9, written to Christians: "If we say, 'We don't have sin,' we're misleading ourselves and the truth isn't in us. If we confess our sins, he [God] is faithful and righteous, with the result that he forgives [our] sins for us and cleanses us from every [act of] unrighteousness." The fact that Judas isn't clean even though Jesus washes his feet shows that the foot-washing *as such* doesn't effect cleansing any more than baptism does. They don't work mechanically or magically. They're only representative of what took place if there was true faith and confession. For the third time in chapter 13 John mentions Jesus' divine omniscience, this time of Judas's giving him over, to keep stressing the control of Jesus over the events in his hour (compare 13:1, 3). As the Word who was God, how could Jesus *not* be in charge?

13:12–15: **Therefore when he'd washed their feet and taken his garments and reclined again** [at the supper table], **he said to them, "Do you know** [= understand] **what I've done for you?** ¹³**You call me 'the Teacher' and 'the Lord,' and well do you say** [so]. **For I am** [the Teacher and the Lord]. ¹⁴**Therefore if as the Lord and the Teacher I've washed your feet, you too ought to wash one another's feet.** ¹⁵**For I've given you an example, that just as I've done for you, you too should do** [for one another]." "Therefore" in 13:12 indicates that Jesus' washing the disciples' feet needs further explanation. If in 13:4 Jesus' laying down his garments represented laying down his life, taking his garments represents taking his life again, as in 10:17–18, where the same verb "take" is used for his resurrection. Peter has just called Jesus "Lord" twice (13:6, 9), as other disciples have done earlier. But Jesus adds here his designation as "the Teacher" to suit his teaching the disciples by example, the example of his washing their feet, as well as by his words of explanation. His commending them for calling him the Teacher and the Lord rests on the truth of these designations. Flattery they are not. And the truth of the designations provides the basis for a much-more kind of argument: if someone so exalted as the Lord and Teacher Jesus performed so lowly a task as washing the disciples' feet, much more should they wash each other's feet. The question arises whether Christians should still wash each other's feet literally. Christians did in the centuries immediately following the time of Jesus. So some Christians have continued the practice, and others are reviving it. But many Christians have discontinued it because it made sense only when people wore open sandals and walked on dirt, so that obedience to Jesus' command requires a cultural translation into other forms of lowly service even to your social inferiors. If you choose the route of cultural translation, it's also your responsibility to come up with particular equivalents to foot-washing. A lord is the owner and master of a slave.

Since Jesus as the Teacher and the Lord has just done a slave's service for his pupils and slaves (the disciples), he brings up the relation of masters and slaves in **13:16–17:** **"Amen, amen I tell you, a slave** [like the disciples] **isn't greater than his master** [= 'lord,' like the Lord Jesus], **neither a sent one** [Greek: *apostolos*, like the Twelve, whom Jesus will send as the Father sent him (20:21)] **greater than the one who sent him** [compare Matthew 10:24; Luke 6:40]. ¹⁷**If you know** [= understand] **these things, you're fortunate if you do them."** "These things" are Jesus' example and explanation of it. It's necessary but not enough to understand them. Congratulations ("you're fortunate") come only on those who follow his example by actually serving their fellow believers as he served them. He's speaking about service within the community of disciples, not about service to the world at large.

So he says in **13:18–20:** **"I'm not talking about all of you. I know** [= recognize, as the good shepherd knows his sheep] **certain ones that I've selected. But** [I've selected only certain ones] **in order that the Scripture might be fulfilled** [which says], **'The one eating my bread has lifted up his heel against me** [Psalm 41:9].' ¹⁹**From now on I'm telling you** [things] **before** [they] **happen in order that whenever they happen you may believe that I AM.** ²⁰**Amen, amen I tell you, the one receiving anybody I've happened to send is receiving me, and the one receiving me is receiving the one who sent me** [God the Father]." "Certain ones that I've selected" represents the doctrine of election or—more accurately, since Jesus explicitly denies he's speaking about everybody—the doctrine of *selection*. In Judas's case, the selection that left him out had the purpose of fulfilling Scripture. Eating bread with another person represented friendship with that person, but lifting up the heel against him represented rejection of him, as when walking away shows the walker's heel to the person being rejected. Put the two together, eating with Jesus as though his friend and showing a heel to him on the way out to give him over to his enemies—put these two actions together and you have the most dastardly deed imaginable, especially when the heel belongs to a foot that Jesus has just washed.

Jesus' divine omniscience comes up yet again. Now it includes what's going to happen in the future as well as what has happened in the past. Jesus' fore*knowing* leads to fore*telling*, and his foretelling has the purpose of getting the disciples to identify him, when what he has foretold happens, with the divine I AM (Exodus 3:14), for whom the distinctions between past, present, and future have no importance. His eternity makes him Lord of all time. He controls the future as easily as he controls the present and controlled the past. Jesus' foretelling starts here with a prediction of treachery within the ranks, so that the occurrence of that treachery will engender faith in him rather than destroying it. The treachery will eventuate in his departure from the world, and his departure will cause him to send others into the world as the Father sent him. So Jesus assures his disciples that

426

the reception of any of them counts as the reception of him, so closely does he identify himself as the sender with the one he sends. And receiving Jesus counts as receiving his sender, God the Father, so closely does the Father identify himself with Jesus his Son. Blest be the tie that binds together God, Jesus, and Jesus' disciples in the mission of world evangelism, a mission ironically helped along by Judas's treacherously untying himself from Jesus, and therefore from God.

THE EXIT OF JUDAS ISCARIOT
John 13:21–30

13:21: **After saying these things, Jesus was troubled by the Spirit and testified and said, "Amen, amen I tell you that one of you will give me over."** As in 11:33, it's an open question whether John is referring to Jesus' human spirit, which would be to say that Jesus was troubled inwardly, or is referring to the Holy Spirit, as later in chapters 14–16. In the latter case, the Holy Spirit troubles him to give a sad testimony (see the comments on 11:33). Jesus is troubled because one of his closest disciples is going to give him over to the chief priests and Pharisees. The addition of "testified" to "said" connotes a trial, with Jesus' prediction constituting a testimony against Judas for his coming betrayal of Jesus. "Amen, amen I tell you" stresses this second, more explicit form of Jesus' prediction so as to keep the disciples' faith from collapsing, and indeed to further their faith once the prediction reaches fulfillment. "One *of you*" adds pathos to the testimony.

13:22–26: **At a loss about whom he [Jesus] speaks** [this prediction]**, the disciples were looking at each other.** [23]**Reclining in Jesus' bosom was one of his disciples, whom Jesus loved.** [24]**Therefore Simon Peter nods to this one that he should inquire who might be the one about whom he [Jesus] is speaking.** [25]**On leaning back in this way onto Jesus' bosom, therefore, that one** [the beloved disciple] **says to him, "Lord, who is it?"** [26]**Jesus answers, "It's that one for whom I'll dip a morsel and give [it] to him." So after dipping the morsel, he takes [it] and gives [it] to Judas,** [the son of] **Simon Iscariot.** John's repeated use of the present tense, though awkward in English, lends great vividness to this passage. Dramatic intensity makes the episode in past history seem like a current event. The disciples are dumbfounded—literally: they don't speak to each other. They only look at each other. Their dumbfoundedness shows the innocence of all but one of them and sets up for the following inquiry. "One of his disciples . . . whom Jesus loved" (13:23) contrasts with and compensates for "one of you [who] will give me over" (13:21). Traditionally, the beloved disciple has been identified with the Apostle John, partly because the beloved disciple is associated closely with Peter here and elsewhere (see 20:2; 21:20) as John is in the other Gospels, where we read about the trio of disciples closest to Jesus—namely, Peter, James, and John. According to this identification, John was the very closest of the trio and, according to 21:24,

the author of the Fourth Gospel. He describes himself as the beloved disciple, then, to assure his audience that the contents of his Gospel come from a very reliable source. But remaining anonymous saves him from braggadocio and conforms to the anonymous authorship of the other Gospels. (Their titles are traditional rather than original to the books themselves.)

On the other hand, 11:3, 5, 36 named Lazarus as the disciple whom Jesus loved. According to 11:5, Jesus loved Martha and her sister Mary too; but here in 13:23 "one . . . whom" is masculine, so that the sisters are ruled out. Neither one of them can be the beloved disciple. Lazarus' residence in Bethany, next door to Jerusalem, tallies with this Gospel's emphasis on Jesus' ministry in Judea rather than Galilee. Yet whether or not Lazarus *was* a disciple, he's never *called* a disciple, as the beloved disciple *is* called one. And in John, "disciples" predominantly refers to the Twelve. In 6:70 Jesus said he'd selected "the Twelve," and at the present supper he has described his companions as selected (13:18). Chances are, then, that the beloved disciple was one of the Twelve and therefore not Lazarus. Furthermore, the fact that Jesus is said to have loved Martha and Mary as well as Lazarus shows that Jesus' special love wasn't limited to Lazarus. So it might have rested on the unnamed Apostle John too. This conclusion agrees with early church tradition.

In any case, whoever he was, the beloved disciple wrote this Gospel out of an intimate relationship with Jesus. Peter's nodding to the beloved disciple implies they were too far away from each other for Peter to whisper to him, and also that Peter was too far away from Jesus to ask him a question privately. Reclining on Jesus' bosom means that the beloved disciple was lying on his left side with his head tilted back toward the chest of Jesus, who was also lying on his left side. Contact wasn't made till the beloved disciple leaned back to ask for the identity of the betrayer. "In this way" refers to the leaning back against Jesus' chest and furthers the thought of the beloved disciple's intimate relation with Jesus (compare 1:18). The morsel was a piece of bread or other food. It was dipped into a sauce. By giving the dipped morsel to Judas, Jesus was acting as host at the meal. But he was changing what usually counted as a gesture of friendship and honor into one of identifying his betrayer.

13:27–29: **And after** [the giving of] **the morsel, then Satan entered into that one** [Judas]**. Therefore** [because of that entry] **Jesus tells him, "What you're doing, do very quickly."** [28]**But not one of the recliners** [at table] **knew** [= understood] **this,** [that is,] **for what** [purpose] **he** [Jesus] **had spoken to him** [Judas]**.** [29]**For some were supposing** [that] **since Judas had the money-box, Jesus tells him, "Buy the things we need for the festival," or that he** [Judas] **should give something to the poor.** "Satan" is the Semitic equivalent of the Greek term "Devil." The Devil has already put it into Judas's heart to give Jesus over to Jesus' enemies (13:2). Now called "Satan," the Devil himself enters Judas to activate Judas's betrayal of Jesus. But despite Satan's entry, Judas can do nothing apart from Jesus' permission or, rather, command. Jesus is in charge even in the face of this mother-of-all demonic possessions. He commands Judas to act "very quickly." Why very quickly? Because as the lamb of God, Jesus doesn't want to miss sacrificing himself at the proper moment for Passover sacrifices, that is, the next afternoon: "Get going, Judas. Time is limited." At least the beloved disciple must have known from Jesus' giving the morsel to Judas that Judas was the betrayer. But no one, not even the beloved disciple, understood Jesus' purpose in speaking to Judas. So they came up with mistaken possibilities. Their lack of knowledge lets the repeatedly mentioned divine omniscience of Jesus stand out in bold relief. Since they were all eating dinner, or had eaten it, the mistaken notion that Jesus had told Judas to buy provisions for the festival—that is, for the Passover—shows that the Passover hadn't yet arrived.

13:30: On taking the morsel, therefore, that one [Judas] **went out immediately. And it was night.** Judas's taking the morsel fulfills part of the Scripture quoted by Jesus in 13:18: "The one eating my bread." Judas's going out fulfills the rest of that Scripture quoted by Jesus: "[he] lifted up his heel against me" (see Psalm 41:9). By going out Judas shows Jesus the back of his foot, his heel. Together, these actions of Judas expose the treachery in his pretense of friendship during the course of betraying Jesus. The immediacy of Judas's going out shows again that Jesus is in charge, for Jesus has told him to act "very quickly." Judas does. It also intimates that Jesus will sacrifice himself at the proper time for Passover lambs to be sacrificed. John's mention of night wouldn't be necessary except for its symbolic import, namely, that it's too late for Judas to be saved. The night when no one can work the works of salvation has overtaken him. Not even Jesus can save him now (see 9:4; 11:9–10).

JESUS' DISCOURSE AT THE LAST SUPPER
John 13:31–16:33

13:31–33: Therefore when he [Judas] **had gone out, Jesus says, "Now the Son of Man has been glorified, and God has been glorified in him.** [32]**If God has been glorified in him, God will also in himself glorify him** [the Son of Man], **and he'll glorify him immediately.** [33]**Children, I'm still with you for a little while. You'll seek me; and just as I told the Jews, 'Where I'm going you can't come** [7:35–36; 8:21–22]**,' I'm now telling you as well."** "Now" and the three occurrences of "has been glorified" look as though the glorifications have already occurred. But "immediately" and the two occurrences of "will glorify" show that the preceding expressions hyperbolically emphasize the certainty and imminence of the yet-future glorifications. In other words, they are so sure and soon to happen that Jesus is speaking as though they've already happened. The glorifications will consist in the transformation of Jesus' crucifixion the very next day (hence "immediately") into an exaltation rather than a humiliation. Since this exaltation will propel his ascent to heaven, Jesus refers to himself as "the Son of Man," a des-

ignation that has to do with his descent and, as here, his ascent (3:13–14). The oneness of Jesus with God (10:30) means that God will be glorified in the glorification of Jesus and, vice versa, that Jesus will be glorified in the glorification of God. For either one to be glorified is for the other to be glorified too. But God's glorification is basic, the Son of Man's glorification derivative. "If God has been glorified in him, God will also in himself glorify him," because—as Jesus will say—"the Father is greater than I" (14:28 [see the comments on that statement for the sense in which the Father's greatness surpasses that of Jesus]). Later, Jesus will also say that while on earth he has glorified the Father (17:4); but here the emphasis falls on God's glorification of Jesus the Son of Man. "Children" is an endearing address that appears only here in John but often in 1 John (and compare John 21:5). The endearment suits the pathos of Jesus' departure and of the disciples' seeking him without success because they can't come to where he's going. The shortness of his remaining time with them adds to the pathos. But his telling them now forearms them against losing faith when he leaves them.

13:34–35: "I'm giving you a new commandment, that you love one another, just as I've loved you that *you* **also love one another.** [35]**By this will all people know that you're my disciples, if you have love among one another."** As the Word who is God, Jesus is in a position to give a commandment no less binding than, say, the Ten Commandments. This commandment is new in that, unlike the commandment to love your neighbor—that is, anyone in need who's near you—as you love yourself, it has to do only with loving fellow disciples. Yet it escalates the standard of loving from the natural self-love of human beings to the humanly unnatural but divine love of Christ for his disciples. "He loved them to the end" (13:1), and as the good shepherd he "[laid] down [his] life for the sheep" (10:15). A pretty high standard that! The repetition of "that you love one another," with emphasis on "you" the second time around in the original Greek, doubles the high standard. And in the eyes of all other people, meeting this standard will mark the disciples as having learned from Jesus' example ("disciples" means "learners"); for it will correspond to his love for them.

13:36: Simon Peter says to him, "Lord, where are you going?" Jesus answered him, "You can't follow me now [to] **where I'm going, but you'll follow** [me] **later."** Peter doesn't understand that Jesus is returning to his Father in heaven, and so wonders where *on earth* he might be going that the disciples too can't come. Instead of answering Peter's question "Where?" Jesus reiterates that Peter in particular can't follow him to where he (Jesus) is going, but adds the qualification "now" and the prediction that Peter will follow Jesus later—a vague prediction that will gain specificity in 21:18–19, where Jesus will further predict Peter's death in old age by crucifixion and, significantly, with the command, "Follow me" (21:22). There we have it: going to heaven, where Jesus is, by following him through death itself.

13:37–38: Peter says to him, "Lord, why can't I follow you now? I'll lay down my life for you." Finally Peter understands that Jesus has been speaking about dying and going to heaven. But he doesn't understand why he can't follow Jesus there presently by laying down his life for Jesus when Jesus lays down his life. It will happen, though, that Jesus will lay down his life for Peter while Peter is doing quite the opposite of laying down his life for Jesus, as the next verse now indicates. **38Jesus answers, "Will you lay down your life for me? Amen, amen I tell you, by no means will a rooster crow until you've disowned me three times."** Yet another prediction—a very specific and troubling one at that—whose sad fulfillment will shore up the disciples' faith despite Jesus' departure.

Jesus has been speaking to Peter. Now he speaks to all the disciples. **14:1a: "Your heart isn't to be troubled."** "Heart" is singular, but "your" is plural. So Jesus is talking about the individual heart of each disciple. The troubling of Jesus' soul in 12:27 made the troubling of his disciples' heart not only unnecessary but also forbidden. For Jesus is issuing a command. The reason why the disciples' heart *might* be troubled is his having told them that he was going where they couldn't come. But his departure is also the *reason* their heart shouldn't be troubled. What he's going to do upon his departure will make it wrong to have a troubled heart.

14:1b–c: "Believe in God, and believe in me." The original Greek could be translated several other ways—for example, as a statement followed by a command: "You believe in God. Believe also in me." But in view of the danger that Jesus' departure might shatter the disciples' faith in God because it was tied to their faith in Jesus, we probably do best to understand 14:1 as containing three commands: the first that your heart not be troubled, the second to believe in God, and the third to believe in Jesus. Your heart can't keep from being troubled unless you believe in God, and—whether or not you think so—now that the Word who was God became incarnate in Jesus, you can't truly believe in God without believing in his Son Jesus. Because of the contrast with being troubled, "believe" carries the connotation of trust (compare the comments on 3:14–17).

14:2: "In my Father's home are many abodes (and if not, I'd have told you), because I'm going to prepare a place for you." In other words, the reason there are many abodes in the Father's home is that Jesus is going to prepare a place for the disciples. The parenthetical comment that he'd have told them if it weren't so provides assurance that he's not withholding information which would add to the danger of their heart's being troubled. Again other translations are possible, but the foregoing produces the best logic. Most translations speak of the Father's "house" rather than "home." But "home" does a better job of connoting a house *that's lived in*. And most interpretations of Jesus' statement have it that he's referring to heaven. But in 2:16–17 he used "my Father's house/home" for the temple in Jerusalem and followed up by saying, "Disas-

semble this temple, and in three days I'll raise it" (2:19). Then John interpreted this claim as a reference to "the temple [consisting] of his body" (2:21). So the Father's home isn't heaven. It's the temple consisting of Jesus' disassembled and now resurrected body. We mustn't think of mansions in heaven, then, or even of rooms or apartments or dwelling places there. "Abodes" is simply the noun form of the verb "abide," which Jesus will use repeatedly in chapter 15 (for example, "Abide in me, and I [will abide] in you" [15:4]). To translate this noun with "mansions," "rooms," "apartments," "dwelling places," or the like rather than with "abodes" at least obscures, and probably misses completely, the relation between *Jesus* as the Father's home containing many abodes and the abiding of believers *in Jesus* as their home. Because the abodes are "many," each believer has "a place" in Jesus where he or she can abide, just as according to 14:23 Jesus and his Father "will come to him [each believer] and make an abode alongside him" (contrast the Jewish authorities' fearing in 11:48 that the Romans would come and take away their "place," that is, the temple which Jesus' body r*e*places as the Father's home). Jesus' going refers, of course, to his going immediately to the cross and ultimately to the Father, that is, to the crucifixion, resurrection, and ascension. And it is these events, not some architectural project after arrival in heaven, that constitute Jesus' preparation of a place in himself for each believer to abide. Without those accomplishments on his part (and in John's Gospel Jesus accomplishes his own death, resurrection, and ascension), believers wouldn't have abodes in him and therefore couldn't abide in him. Since his preparatory work lies in the future (though a very near future), the present tense in "*are* many abodes" underscores the certainty of their coming into being

14:3: "And if I go and prepare a place for you, I'm coming again; and I'll take you to myself in order that where I am, you also may be." Naturally believers will be where Jesus is if they're abiding in him, their abode. But when will he come again and take them "to himself" so as to abide in him? Aren't believers abiding in him now? Yes, of course. In this passage, then, his coming again can't refer to the second coming (as we usually call it), which is yet future, though he will refer to such a coming in 21:22–23. It must refer to his comings to the disciples immediately after his death, resurrection, and (as we'll see) ascension. And sure enough, John uses the verb "come" several times for the risen Jesus' meetings with the disciples (see 20:19, 24, 26; 21:13) *and is the only one of the Gospel writers to do so.* Furthermore, one of these meetings (20:26–29) will include an emphasis on the physicality of Jesus' self-raised body, "the Father's home" that's now the home of believers too, since they abide in Jesus. And counting as his taking them to himself will be his standing in their midst, greeting them with his "Peace," feeding them breakfast, and restoring Peter (20:19, 21, 26; 21:9, 12–13, 15–19).

14:4–6: "And you know the way to where I'm going." **5Thomas tells him, "Lord, we don't know *where* you're**

going. **How can we know the *way*?**" Thomas's point: you can't know the route if you don't know the destination. But he's wrong. Even though he and the other disciples don't yet know Jesus' destination, they do know the way there even though they don't *know* that they know it. They know the way there because they know Jesus; and he *is* the way, as he now says: [6]**Jesus tells him, "*I am the way and the truth and the life*."** Jesus doesn't satisfy Thomas's curiosity about Jesus' destination, though. Not yet. For now it's enough to identify himself as the way that Thomas mistakenly thought he and the others couldn't know without knowing Jesus' destination. But Jesus doesn't stop with his self-identification as "the way." He adds "the truth" and "the life" to prepare for the revelation of his destination as the destination of the disciples too. That destination will turn out to be the Father. Jesus is the way to the Father because he himself is the truth about the Father (see, for example, 1:18, according to which he "explained" the Father). And Jesus is the life because the truth about the Father brings eternal life to those who believe. Jesus continues, "No one comes to the Father except through me." So Jesus isn't just the way. He's the *only* way. And those who take this way will find themselves at the destination that is *his* destination. They'll go to the Father just as he will have gone to the Father.

14:7–11: "If you've come to know me [as you have], **you'll know my Father too. And from now on you do know him and have seen him."** The transition from "you *will* know" to "you *do* know" shows that the future is "now." *Seeing* the Father supplements *knowing* him. But one of the disciples isn't convinced that they've seen the Father as well as come to know him. [8]**Philip tells him, "Lord, show us the Father, and it's enough for us** [that is, 'we'll be satisfied']." [9]**Jesus tells him, "Am I with you** [plural, referring to all the disciples] **for such a long time and you, Philip, haven't come to know me? The person who has seen *me* has seen the Father. How is it that you say, '*Show* us the Father'?** [10]**You believe, don't you, that I** [am] **in the Father and** [that] **the Father is in me? I'm not speaking on my own the words that I'm speaking to you** [plural, as from here on, to include all the disciples]**. But by abiding in me, the Father is doing his works.** [11]**Believe me, that I am in the Father and** [that] **the Father** [is] **in me. But if** [you do] **not** [believe me, that is, my words]**, believe because of the works themselves."** The incarnation made God the Father visible in Jesus his Son. We'd expect Jesus to say, "Haven't I been with you . . . ?" But the present tense in "*Am* I with you . . . ?" takes account that he's with the disciples "for a little while still" (13:33). The equation of seeing Jesus with seeing the Father explains what Jesus meant in 14:7: "you've seen him ['the Father']." Jesus' oneness with the Father makes the equation possible or, rather, actual. The questions, "How is it that . . . ?" and "Don't you believe . . . ?" combine with the foregoing question to rebuke Philip's nonrecognition of that oneness, which Jesus affirmed as far back as 10:30. We'd also expect "But the Father abiding in me speaks the *words*." Instead, ". . .

does the *works*" draws a parallel between "words" and "works." They complement each other. They interpret each other. The abiding of Jesus and the Father in each other defines their oneness and provides the reason why Jesus' words don't originate with him, but with the Father, and also the reason why the works that elsewhere are said to be *Jesus'* works are here said to be the *Father's* works, which the Father does by abiding in Jesus. The words and works of Jesus originate in his Father. The affirmation of mutual indwelling then turns into a command to believe that affirmation. And if the disciples don't find believable the affirmation on its own merits, Jesus commands them to believe it because of the works. For they back up the affirmation.

Whether on the basis of the Father's words or works, believing will result in the *believers'* working. **14:12: "Amen, amen I tell you, the person who believes in me—that person too will do the works which I'm doing, and will do greater** [works] **than these** [which I'm doing]**, because I'm going to the Father** [compare 5:20]**."** Through evangelism believers will carry on Jesus' works of salvation. And because the disciples already outnumber Jesus and in the future will multiply many times over, believers' works will exceed those of Jesus in number and extent. This "greater" has its basis in his going to the Father. How will his going to the Father make possible the disciples' doing of Jesus' works and even greater ones? The answer awaits us in 20:21–23, where his glorification will have made possible a bestowal of the Holy Spirit, who enables the disciples to carry out the mission on which Jesus sends them (compare 7:37–39).

Now Jesus turns his going to the Father into a basis for the disciples' praying as well as working. The two activities supplement each other. Working without praying proves ineffective. Praying without working proves equally ineffective. **14:13–14: "And whatever you ask in my name—this I'll do in order that the Father may be glorified in the Son.** [14]**If you ask me anything in my name, I'll do** [it]**."** The first statement makes clear that Jesus will do whatever the disciples ask, but doesn't make clear to whom they'll direct their requests. The second statement makes clear that they'll direct them to Jesus. So his departure to heaven turns him into the addressee as well as the grantor of their requests. Strikingly, they'll make the requests "in [his] name" even though they'll be addressing him directly; and he'll be the one doing what they ask. As himself God, in other words, Jesus will play the roles usually associated with God the Father, the roles of addressee and answerer of prayers. But what does it mean to ask in Jesus' name? And what is that name? According to 17:11–12 Jesus' name is one that he shares with the Father, a name that 1:1 applied to both of them. The name is "God." To ask Jesus for something in his name, then, is to appeal to his status as God. Such an appeal therefore limits the requests to those that fall in line with his divine attributes of holiness, justice, mercy, love, and so on. Yet along that line the possibilities of requests and answers are limitless: "whatever" and "anything." Jesus' doing whatever the disciples ask in his name has the purpose of glorifying the Father. This glorification will take place "in the Son," because the Son does nothing apart from his Father, so that the Son's glorification counts as the Father's too.

Asking something in Jesus' name can't be done genuinely without loving him. So he continues in *14:15*: "If you love me, you'll keep my commands." Jesus uses the plural, "commands," but he has issued only one command *which has been designated as such*. That was to love one another. Yet he repeats this command several times (13:34–35; 15:12, 17; compare 14:21; 15:10, 14). For emphasis, the repetition of the command to love one another makes a multiplicity of commands out of one and the same command. And loving one another in obedience to Jesus' commands arises out of love for him, because he's "the Father's home," in whom believers abide. So you can't fail to love fellow believers if you love Jesus.

14:16–17: "And I'll ask the Father; and he'll give you another representative in order that he may be with you forever, [17][that is,] the Spirit of truth, whom the world can't accept, because it neither sees him nor knows [= recognizes] him. *You* know him, because he abides alongside you and will be in you." Jesus has just talked about the disciples' asking him to do things. Now he talks about himself as asking his Father to do something. But so sure is the Father to give him what he asks that Jesus doesn't even say what he'll ask. Instead, he skips right to the Father's granting the request, which is to give the disciples another representative. The Greek word behind "representative" is sometimes brought over in English characters as "paraclete." It's a hard word to translate adequately. Various translations such as "comforter," "helper," "counselor," "advocate," and "prosecutor" capture some but not all of its meaning. Perhaps we may settle for "representative" as broad enough to cover most of its meanings in John. "*Another* representative" implies that Jesus has spoken and acted as the Father's representative, and also implies that after Jesus' return to him the Father will send the Spirit to replace Jesus as his (the Father's) representative. Unlike Jesus, however, this new representative will never depart from believers. Yet like Jesus, who was "full . . . of truth" (1:14) and *was* "the truth" (14:6), this replacement for Jesus will be "the Spirit *of truth*," the truth about God and about his Son Jesus. If the world didn't accept Jesus the truth despite their seeing him, they certainly can't accept the Spirit of truth whom they don't see. Nor does the world recognize the Spirit any more than the world recognized Jesus the good shepherd of 10:14. Only his sheep recognized him as such. Likewise, Jesus says to his sheep, the disciples, that they recognize the Spirit of truth because the Spirit "abides alongside [them]." How so? Well, in 1:32–33 the Spirit descended out of heaven and abode on Jesus, so that as long as Jesus abode alongside the disciples (as

14:25 will say he did; but see also 1:38–39; 4:40; 7:9; 10:40; 11:6, 54) the Spirit who abode on *him* was also abiding alongside *them*. But upon Jesus' departure the Father will give them the Spirit to abide "in" them, not just "alongside" them (compare the Spirit as living water leaping up inside believers and flowing out of their bellies in 4:14; 7:37–39).

14:18–20: "I'll not leave you [to be] orphans. I'm coming to you. [19]Yet a little while and the world doesn't see me any more; but you see me. Because I live, you too will live. [20]In that day you'll know that I [am] in my Father and [that] you [are] in me and [that] I [am] in you." It's not enough that the Father will give the disciples the Spirit of truth as another representative. Jesus himself will come to them, but he uses the present tense, "am coming," for emphasis. He's so sure and soon to come to the disciples that he might as well be on his way. The same goes for the present tense of "you see me." Jesus isn't referring to their seeing him at the moment of his making this statement. He's referring to a future seeing as though it were happening already. But when will he come to them, so that they'll see him? A clue to the answer appears in his words, "because I live." Here's another use of the present tense not for his living at the moment but for his taking up his life in resurrection (10:17–18). It's *that* living of his which provides eternal life for believers—hence, "you too will live [eternally]." The world of unbelievers won't see Jesus very much longer, because after his death, burial, resurrection, and ascension he'll come only to the disciples, with the result of their seeing him (compare 14:3 with 20:19–20, 24–29; 21:1–14, and see the comments on 20:14–18, 21–23 for the disciples' seeing him again not till after his ascension). And in the day of their seeing him risen from the dead, they'll know for sure that he's in the Father, that they're in Jesus, and that he's in them. They won't be living in an orphanage. They'll be living in the Father's home, Jesus himself; and he'll be living in them as he lives in the Father. A blessed communion!

14:21: "The person who has my commands and keeps [= obeys] them—that person is the one who loves me. And the one who loves me will be loved by my Father, and I'll love him and make myself visible to him." Having Jesus' commands isn't enough. You also have to keep them. Again Jesus is referring to the commands to love one another in the Christian community. He has said earlier that if you love him you'll in fact keep his commands, so that the emphasis fell on keeping them as *a result* of loving him (14:15). Here the emphasis falls on keeping them as the *evidence* of loving him. And love for Jesus will be reciprocated by both the Father and Jesus. To that reciprocal love Jesus will add his self-manifestation. When will he make himself visible to the one who loves him? When he comes to the disciples in resurrected life, as in 14:19. Those who unlike the original disciples believe without seeing the risen Jesus will suffer no disadvantage, though; for he'll pronounce a special blessing on them (20:29).

14:22–24: Judas, not Iscariot, says to him, "And what has happened, Lord, that you're about to make yourself visible to us and not to the world?" ²³Jesus answered and said to him, "If anyone loves me, he'll keep my word. And my Father will love him, and we'll come to him and make an abode alongside him. ²⁴The person who doesn't love me doesn't keep my words, and the word that you hear isn't mine. Rather, [it's] the Father's who sent me." Jesus' answer is a nonanswer to Judas-not-Iscariot's question, for he doesn't identify such an event as Judas asks him to identify. But at least this Judas has caught on that Jesus has been talking about future rather than present visibility. For emphasis, Jesus repeats what he said in 14:15, 20–21, but replaces his "commands" with his "word" and "words." (The distinction between singular and plural is inconsequential, because John tends to use them without distinction.) The replacements offer variety of expression and highlight the word/words of Jesus. He also replaces his being in the Father and in the disciples with coming and making an abode alongside a disciple. Added, however, is the Father's joining Jesus in coming and making that abode alongside a disciple. Their abode alongside a disciple complements the disciple's abode in Jesus, the Father's home (14:2). The Father and the Son abide alongside as well as in a believer by virtue of the believer's having beside him other believers likewise indwelt by the Father and the Son (compare the Spirit's being alongside the disciples in the person of the Spirit-endowed Jesus as long as Jesus was physically present with them [14:16–17]). How then can a *physically absent* Jesus and his Father *in heaven* abide both in and alongside a believer *on earth*? The answer lies in the unity not only of the Father and the Son with each other but also in their unity with the Spirit. And Jesus has recently said that the Spirit will be "in" the disciples (14:17), so that the Spirit's indwelling entails the cohabitation of the Father and the Son too. To stress obedience to Jesus' words as the condition for this mutuality of indwelling, he declares that disobedience grows out of not loving him and warns that the heard word derives ultimately not from himself but from the Father who sent him with that word—indeed, *as* that Word.

14:25–26: "I've told you these things while abiding alongside you. ²⁶But the representative, the Holy Spirit, whom the Father will send in my name—that one will teach you all things and remind you of all the things that I've told you." So the Holy Spirit will represent the Father by teaching the disciples about the Father just as Jesus has taught them about him. "These things" that Jesus has told them consist of the preceding part of the present discourse. "Of truth" described the Spirit earlier (14:17). Now "Holy" describes him to jibe with his being sent by the Father, whom Jesus will likewise call "Holy" in 17:11. The Father's *sending* the Holy Spirit corresponds to his *giving* the Spirit of truth (14:16–17), just as the Father's *sending* Jesus corresponds to his *giving* Jesus (3:16; 6:32). Just as the disciples will make requests in Jesus' name, the Father will send the Holy Spirit in Jesus' name, that is, will send him to act in the capacity of Jesus as God (compare the comments on 14:14). And just as Jesus taught what the Father had taught him (8:28), the Holy Spirit will teach all the same things by reminding the disciples of them.

14:27: "I'm leaving you peace. I'm giving you *my* peace. I'm not giving [it] to you as the world gives [peace]. Your heart isn't to be troubled, nor is it to be cowardly." "Leaving" equates with "giving." Because of the command not to be inwardly troubled, we're tempted to think of the peace Jesus gives as psychological equilibrium. But "peace" (*shalōm*) was used not only as a Jewish "hello" and "goodbye." (Since Jesus is leaving the disciples, it's "goodbye" here.) It also carried connotations of security, prosperity, blessing, and even messianic salvation. So the peace Jesus gives isn't an untroubled heart. It's the salvation that gives rise to an untroubled heart. The world can't give that kind of peace. It can only say "hello" and "goodbye" (compare 16:33; 20:19, 21, 26). The prohibition of a troubled heart repeats 14:1a word-for-word; but in view of his coming arrest, interrogation, trial, and crucifixion—and also in view of the world's hating and killing the disciples afterwards (15:18–19; 16:2)—here Jesus adds a prohibition of cowardice. Sadly, the Apostle Peter will succumb to cowardice (18:15–18, 25–27). It will also show itself in the secrecy of Joseph of Arimathea's discipleship (19:38).

14:28: "You've heard that I told you, 'I'm going away, and I'm coming to you.' If you loved me you'd rejoice that I'm going to the Father, because the Father is greater than I." "You've heard that I told you" doesn't mean that somebody else reported to the disciples what Jesus had said, so that Jesus spoke to them only indirectly. It means that they themselves heard what he'd said. A simple "I told you" would have sufficed. But the prefixing of "You've heard that" puts more emphasis on the disciples' hearing than on Jesus' having spoken. This emphasis sharpens the criticism that they should have rejoiced when hearing that Jesus was going to the Father. The first part of 14:28 includes Jesus' coming to the disciples in addition to his going away. But since he has spoken repeatedly about coming to them (see 14:3, 18–19, 23 with comments), the last part of 14:28 drops the coming to them and substitutes "to the Father," as in 14:12, to provide the reason why they should have rejoiced. Love for Jesus would lead to joy over his homegoing to the Father. You rejoice in the good fortune of one you love. The Father isn't greater than Jesus in deity any more than a human father is greater than his son in humanity. For Jesus the I AM is the Word who wasn't only *with* God in the beginning. He also *was* God in the beginning (1:1; 8:58). The Father is greater than Jesus as a father is to a son in that Jesus carries out the will of God his Father, in that he says and does nothing but what he has heard and seen his Father say and do (5:19–23; 8:28, 38). The Father's functional superiority doesn't provide the reason Jesus is going to him. It provides the reason the disciples should have lovingly rejoiced at his going to the Father. For going to the greater one means sharing his greatness. Jesus will no longer have to carry out on earth the will of his Father (compare Jesus' prayer in 17:4–5: "I glorified you on the earth by completing the work that you've given me to do. And now you, Father, glorify me alongside yourself with the glory that I had alongside you before the world existed").

14:29–31a: "And now I've told you before it happens in order that whenever it does happen you may believe. ³⁰I won't speak with you much longer; for the world's ruler is coming, and he has nothing in me. ³¹ᵃNevertheless, in order that the world may know that I love the Father—even as the Father commanded me, thus I do [or, in easier English, 'I do exactly as he commanded me to do']." What's about to happen is Jesus' going to the Father. Jesus' foretelling it has the purpose, as before, of forging faith resistant to a disappointment that lapses into unbelief. It's not so much the soon departure of Jesus that will limit his further speech as it's the coming of the world's ruler. For it's that ruler's coming which will trigger the departure. The ruler is Satan. He'll come only to be cast out, as we can deduce from 12:31: "The ruler of this world will be cast out now." In the brief meantime, though, he has entered Judas Iscariot (13:27) and in the person of Judas is coming to the place where Jesus will get himself taken for interrogation. "He has nothing in me" means that Satan has no abode in Jesus, as believers and the Father do have, and therefore that Satan has no control over Jesus, as Satan does have control of Judas, whom he has entered. He may rule the world of unbelievers, but he doesn't rule Jesus. So whatever happens to Jesus will happen by the exercise of his own will, not Satan's. Yet Jesus will exercise his own will in exact accord with what the Father has commanded him to do. After all, the Father is greater than the Son in that a father has authority over his son. And Jesus' purpose in doing exactly what the Father has commanded is to show the world that he loves the Father. We might have expected a purpose to show the Father's love *for the world*, as in 3:16: "God loved the world." But here the Father's greatness overpowers all other considerations. It's a greatness that attracts the love of Jesus his Son, and his displaying love for the Father turns the world's attention to the Father. God's loving the world led him to give his Son that the world might be saved (3:16 again). Jesus' loving the Father led him to carry out the Father's command all the way to its finish on a cross (13:1; 19:28–30). So Jesus' love for the Father supplements Jesus' love for "his own," whom he has selected and whom the Father has given him "out of the world."

14:31b: "Get up, let's go from here." Having entered Judas (13:27), the world's ruler Satan is on his way toward the garden just outside of which Jesus will present himself for interrogation and crucifixion. Jesus won't be late. He'll keep to his Passover schedule so as to sacrifice himself as the lamb of God at the proper time for slaying a Passover sacrifice. Reclining at table must now yield to getting up, and eating must yield to leaving the dining room. But Jesus won't "go out" of the dining room till 18:1. He just keeps on talking to the disciples in chapters 15–16 and then talks to God his Father in chapter 17. We shouldn't be surprised. He's the Word, and as the Word he's loquacious. (We might compare the lengthy conversations that often ensue between "It's time to go home" after an evening's get-together and the actual leaving.)

15:1–4: "I am the true vineyard, and my Father is the vinegrower. ²Every vine in me that doesn't bear fruit—he takes it away. And every vine that does bear [fruit]—he cleans [= prunes] **it in order that it may bear more fruit. ³You're already clean because of the word that I've spoken to you. ⁴Abide in me, and I** [will abide] **in you. Just as the vine can't bear fruit on its own,** [that is, just as it can't bear fruit] **unless it abides in the vineyard, so neither can you** [bear fruit] **if you don't abide in me."** Traditionally, translations of this passage speak of a vine and its branches rather than of a vineyard and its vines. By the time John wrote, however, the words for a vine and its branches had come also and commonly to mean a vineyard and its vines. And since "cleans" means "prunes," it makes better viticultural sense to settle for a vineyard and its vines. For you prune a vine by cutting off its nonbearing branches. You don't prune branches by cutting off their twigs.

The Old Testament often portrays the land of Israel as a vineyard, and Israel herself as the Lord's vine planted in the land (see Isaiah 5:1–7, for example). So just as Jesus portrayed himself instead of the temple as "the Father's home" (see 14:2 with 2:19–22), now he portrays himself instead of the land as the true vineyard—"true" in the sense that he's the reality which the land symbolized. The land flowing with milk and honey, as the Old Testament often describes it (starting in Exodus 3:8, 17), provided rich nourishment for the vine of Israel. So also Jesus, who described his flesh and blood as true bread and drink (6:30–58), provides rich nourishment for every vine—that is, for every believer—planted in him.

As the vinegrower, God the Father takes away every vine that doesn't bear fruit, and removal from the soil of the vineyard brings death to the vine. In other words, false disciples face eternal damnation, the second death (Revelation 2:11; 20:6, 14; 21:8). But God prunes every vine that does bear fruit, that gives evidence of genuine discipleship. In the original Greek there's a wordplay between "takes away" (*airei*) and "cleans/prunes" (*kathairei*). Since the verb for pruning means to clean, the pruning has to do with cleansing true believers from occasional sins, just as Jesus' washing the sullied feet of already bathed disciples symbolized that kind of cleansing (13:1–11). "You're already clean" parallels being already bathed, so that only pruning—partial cleansing like washing only the feet—is needed (see also 1 John 1:7–2:2). Jesus' spoken word has brought cleansing, because he is himself the Word, the self-sacrifice of whose flesh and blood as God's lamb takes away sin (1:1, 14, 29).

Vines don't have to be told to abide in their vineyard. They're just there. So the analogy to Jesus and believers breaks down when he tells them to abide in him. But the surprise in this breakdown of the analogy highlights the importance of abiding in Jesus, of persevering in discipleship. The analogy breaks down even more surprisingly in his promise to abide in believers who abide in him. Vines abide in vineyards, but vineyards don't abide in vines. So a second breakdown in the analogy provides another point of emphasis: the reciprocal dwelling of Jesus in believers.

The fruit-bearing of a vine depends on its drawing physical nourishment from the soil of the vineyard in which it's planted. The fruit-bearing of a believer depends on his drawing spiritual nourishment from Jesus, in whom he's planted by faith. But what does fruit-bearing mean in a believer's case? If we were dealing with the Apostle Paul's letters, we might think of ethical behavior, as for example in Galatians 5:22–23 ("But the fruit of the Spirit is love, joy, peace, patience, magnanimity, goodness, faithfulness, gentleness, self-control"). But in John's Gospel fruit consists of converts, as in 4:36 ("gathers fruit [issuing] in eternal life," with a contextual reference to Samaritan converts) and 12:24 (the seed that falls into the ground and dies "bears much fruit," in contextual reference to Jesus' drawing all kinds of people to himself). So the kind of fruit-bearing that characterizes true disciples consists in their fulfilling the Great Commission, which Jesus will give them in 20:21, by way of getting other people to believe in him, as Andrew, Philip, and the Samaritan woman have already done in 1:40–51; 4:28–30, 39–42. The pruning away of disciples' occasional sins makes their Christian testimony more effective in gaining converts (hence, "*more* fruit").

Abiding in Jesus isn't the same as bearing fruit, then. It's the *condition* for bearing fruit. You can't bear fruit unless you abide in Jesus. So what does abiding in him mean more exactly? It means to keep on believing in Jesus as the Christ and Son of God (compare the comments on 2:11; 20:30–31, and in 6:59–71 contrast those who do and don't keep on believing). So at the base there's adherence to correct belief in Jesus. Then there's good behavior because of cleansing (pruning) from sin. Effective Christian witness (much fruit-bearing) follows naturally.

15:5–8: "I am the vineyard. You are the vines. The person who abides in me—and I [abide] in him—this person bears much fruit, because apart from me you can't do even one thing. ⁶If someone doesn't abide in me, he has been thrown outside as a vine [is thrown outside a vineyard]**; and it dries up, and people gather them and throw [them] into the fire and they're burned. ⁷If you abide in me and my words abide in you, ask for whatever you want; and it will happen for you. ⁸My Father has been glorified in this,** [which is] **that you bear much fruit and become my disciples."** "I am the vineyard" repeats 15:1a except for a dropping of "true" before "vineyard." Once given, that description is no longer needed. Where 15:1b identified Jesus' Father as the vinegrower, 15:5b identifies believers as the vines. Earlier statements only implied this identification. The inability to bear fruit without abiding in Jesus is intensi-

fied to the point of inability to do "even one thing" by way of successful evangelism, which fruit-bearing symbolizes (compare the inability of Jesus to do even one thing apart from his Father [5:19–20, 30]), so that success in evangelism comes ultimately as a result of Jesus' work, not human ingenuity, marketing techniques, or what-have-you.

We might expect a full stop after "this person bears much fruit" and a new, independent sentence to begin with "apart from me you can't do even one thing." Either that or "*and* apart from me you can't do even one thing." Instead of a full stop or "and," though, we have "because." Thus Jesus emphasizes that the inability to do any fruit-bearing at all apart from him is the *reason* why bearing much fruit depends on abiding in him. And "*much* fruit" contrasts with "not even one thing." To the inability to do even one thing apart from him is added the *certainty* of bearing much fruit if you do abide in Jesus. As abiding in Jesus is the condition that has to be met for fruit-bearing, "And I [abide] in him" is the cause of fruit-bearing. And to the taking away of fruitless vines, which is now expressed as their being "thrown outside," is added their drying up, being gathered, thrown into the fire, and burned. These additions punctuate with frightening detail the eternally deadly consequence of non-perseverance. We expect "*will* be thrown out," not "*has* been thrown outside." But the past tense dramatizes the certainty of future judgment. It's as though the judgment has already taken place. The plurals "them" and "they" show that "a vine," though singular, represents all who fail to persevere and thereby suffer damnation.

Jesus' abiding in believers becomes the abiding of Jesus' *words* in them, because as the Word he *is* his words. He's their subject matter; and he makes the granting of "whatever you want" in prayer conditional on abiding in him and on his words' abiding in the person who makes the request (see also 15:16; 16:24, 26 and compare 14:13–14). The person who abides in Jesus will want to please him, and the words of Jesus which abide in such a person will determine that person's desires. Nevertheless, the emphasis falls not on the conditions but on the promise of answered prayer provided the conditions are met. The bearing of much fruit, which is to say successful evangelism, brings glory to God, the vineyard-keeper and Father of Jesus. Again a past tense, "has been glorified," dramatizes the certainty of a future event. From the standpoint of John, writing late in the first century, the widespread success of the gospel has already redounded to God's glory; for multitudes now praise him as the Father of their Savior Jesus Christ. God is also glorified when those who bear much fruit through winning converts become *themselves* disciples of Jesus. But aren't those who convert others *already* his disciples? Well, yes—but discipleship isn't something you do and get it over with. It's a continuous process of becoming, or it's nothing at all. We're back to perseverance as a mark of true believers. And their perseverance brings glory to God.

15:9–10: "Just as the Father has loved me, I've also loved you. Abide in my love." God's love for Jesus his Son provides the standard of comparison for Jesus' loving us who believe in him. Abiding in Jesus himself morphs into abiding in his love for us. To abide in his love is to stay loved by him. [10]**"If you keep my commands, you'll abide in my love just as I've kept my Father's commands and abide in his love** [compare 10:17–18]." So abiding in Jesus' love depends on keeping his commands. He'll love us *as long as* we keep his commands. That's the implication of "If." To put it another way, if we don't obey him, he'll stop loving us. No unconditional love here! Again Jesus is pointing out the danger of apostasy and of consequently being taken away and thrown into the fire of eternal judgment (compare Ezekiel 19:10–12 and, for apostasy, 1 John 2:19). Jesus' keeping his Father's commands defines love in terms of obedience, not just feelings, and sets the example for our keeping Jesus' commands. And just as his obedience to the Father ensured that the Father would continue to love him, so our obedience to Jesus' commands ensures that he will continue to love us. God commanded him to love us, and Jesus commands us to love one another in the Christian community.

15:11: **"I've told you these things in order that my joy may be in you and** [that] **your joy may be fulfilled."** Jesus rejoices when we abide in him by actively loving one another in obedience to his command. And this obedience isn't onerous. It brings us joy just as it brings him joy. When Christians demonstrate love toward one another their joy is filled full, as a container is filled to its brim (compare Psalm 19:8: "The precepts of the Lord are right, *rejoicing* the heart"). The next verse (15:12) will now repeat the command Jesus gave in 13:34. Then 15:13 will define its extent; 15:14 will make obedience the condition of being loved by Jesus; and 15:15 will contrast being loved by him with slavery.

15:12–15: **"This is my command, that you love one another just as I've loved you.** [13]**No one has greater love than this, that someone lay down his life for his loved ones.** [14]**You're my loved ones if you do the things that I command you.** [15]**No longer do I call you slaves, because the slave doesn't know what his master is doing. But I've called you loved ones, because I've made known to you all the things that I heard from alongside my Father."** "Just as I've loved you" shows that Jesus is the "someone" who has laid down his life for his loved ones in the greatest possible act of love. He called believers his "disciples" in 15:8. Now he calls them his "loved ones." Most translations have "friends" instead of "loved ones." "Friends" isn't wrong, but it obscures the fact that the underlying Greek word is the noun form of one of the two verbs John uses for loving (including God's love for Jesus and for Jesus' disciples, Jesus' love for Lazarus and for the anonymous beloved disciple, and the disciples' love for Jesus [5:20; 11:3, 36; 16:27; 20:2; 21:15–17]). In the present context of the disciples' loving one another and especially of Jesus' loving them, therefore, "loved ones" brings out the overarching theme of love more clearly than "friends" does. Not loved ones in the sense of bio-

logical relatives, of course; but friends as the objects of love. As in 15:10, Jesus makes obedience to his commands the condition of being his beloved friends. His statement in 13:16, "A slave isn't greater than his master," implied that he was their master and they his slaves. Now he discards that comparison in favor of a loving relation between friends. Slavery entails blind obedience. A relation of love between friends entails obedience on the basis of full disclosure. And Jesus has disclosed to his beloved friends all that God the Father told him. That is to say, Christian believers are privy to the entire communication of God the Father to his Son Jesus Christ. They're not slaves. They're the ultimate insiders.

15:16: **"You didn't select me; rather, I selected you and appointed you that you should go and** [that] **you should bear fruit and** [that] **your fruit should abide in order that whatever you ask the Father in my name— he might give** [it] **to you."** Normally, Jewish disciples selected whatever rabbi they wanted to study under. Not so here. Jesus not only affirms his selecting of the disciples as his beloved friends. He also denies their having selected him, so that his loving them is the cause and their loving him is the effect (compare 1 John 4:19: "We love, because he first loved us"). His selecting them had a threefold purpose: (1) that they should "go" into the world of unbelievers; (2) that they should bear fruit by way of making converts; and (3) that they should keep on bearing such fruit (compare Matthew 28:19–20: "*On going*, therefore, *disciple* all nations . . . . And behold, I am with you *all the days till the consummation of the age*"). Perhaps "Get up, let's go from here" in 14:31 symbolically forecasts the Great Commission in 20:21: "Just as the Father has sent me, I too am sending you." The purpose and result of fulfilling this commission is answered prayer, for fulfilling the commission helps define what it means to ask for things in Jesus' name. To put it negatively, you aren't praying in Jesus' name if you aren't fulfilling the Great Commission by going, bearing the fruit of converts, and persisting in such evangelism (compare the comments on 14:13–14).

Yet again Jesus tells his disciples to love one another. **15:17–19**: **"I'm commanding you these things, that you love one another."** "These things" boil down to this single command, but by repetition this single command has become an emphatic plural. The repetition sets up a contrast with hatred: [18]**"If the world hates you, know that it has hated me before** [it hated] **you.** [19]**If you were from the world, the world would have been loving** [you as] **what belongs to them. But because you're not from the world (rather, I selected you** *out* **from the world), on account of this** [your not being from the world] **the world hates you."** Obviously, "the world" consists of unbelievers. Jesus' disciples aren't "from the world" because they've been born "out of *God*" and "from *above*" (1:12–13; 3:3, 7). They're a different breed from worldlings. So the worldlings hate them (compare 3:19–21). They hated Jesus first, because he too was from God and from above. God sent him into the world. As an antidote to discouragement, then, Jesus commands his disciples to understand both the world's prior hatred of him and the reason for the world's hating them. So he's the model of being hated by the world just as he's the model of being loved by his Father. And the flip side of Jesus' selecting the disciples to be his beloved friends is his selecting them out of the world's loving friendship into the world's hatred. Generally speaking, the world hates Christians for their claiming to have the absolute truth in Jesus over against the world's different beliefs and loose behavior.

15:20–21: "Remember the word that I spoke to you, 'A slave isn't greater than his master.' If they've persecuted me [as in fact they have], **they'll persecute you too. If they've kept my word** [as ironically they haven't], **they'll keep yours too** [as ironically they won't]." Though Jesus no longer *calls* his disciples slaves (15:15), he reminds them of the earlier such comparison (13:16) to draw a parallel between their persecution and his. Persecution shows that the aforementioned hatred has to do with actions, not just feelings, just as in the case of love. To be forewarned is to be forearmed, and Jesus forewarns his disciples not only of the world's persecution but also of the world's disobeying their word of command to believe in him. Only those whom God has given to him will obey their word (6:39, 65). [21]**"But they'll do all these things to you on account of my name, because they don't know the one who sent me."** The immediate cause of the world's persecuting believers in Jesus and disobeying their word—the immediate cause is their proclaiming Jesus' name as "God" (see 1:1 and especially the comments on 1:12; 17:11–12). The underlying cause is unacquaintance with God, who sent Jesus. For no one comes to God, and thereby knows him, except through believing that Jesus is God (14:6–11).

15:22–23: "If I hadn't come and spoken to them, they wouldn't have had sin." That is, they wouldn't have been guilty of the sin of disbelieving that Jesus is the Word who speaks as himself God. **"But now they don't have an excuse for their sin."** Jesus' having spoken to them as the Word who is God has robbed them of an excuse for their sin of unbelief. They do have sin, but they don't have an excuse for it. [23]**"The person who hates me** [see 15:18] **hates my Father too."** Why so? Because the Father abides in Jesus (14:10), so that Jesus and God his Father are one (10:30).

15:24–25: "If I hadn't done the works among them that no one else has done, they wouldn't have had sin." "Among them" stresses that Jesus did his works in full view of the world. The uniqueness of his works corresponds to the uniqueness of his divine sonship and underlines the world's lacking an excuse for their unbelief. So just as the *words* of the Word could have saved the world from the sin of unbelief (15:22), his *works* could have done the same. They didn't, though. **"But now they've both seen** [my works] **and hated both me and my Father."** Just as hearing the words of the Word robbed the world of an excuse for their unbelief, seeing his works has done the same. And despite the glory of grace and truth displayed in those works (1:17; 2:11), the world has not only disbelieved. The world has even hated Jesus and his coworker God the Father (compare 5:17). [25]**"[This happened,] however, in order that the word that's written in their law might be fulfilled, 'They hated me gratuitously** [= undeservedly, for no good reason]**.'"** The quotation comes from Psalm 35:19 or 69:4. So the world's hatred of Jesus happened for the fulfillment, not just of what's *written* in the Law, but of the *word* that's written there. That is to say, *Jesus* is the Word (with a capital W) that's written as the "me" in his quotation from their law. "*Their* law" refers to the *Jews'* law, the Old Testament. But from 15:18 onward, Jesus has been talking about "the *world*." In hating Jesus, therefore, the Jews—more particularly, their authorities—represent the world at large. Ironically, their law testifies against them by predicting their hatred of Jesus the Word (see especially 10:34–35 with comments, but also 1:45; 2:17; 5:46; 12:14–16, 37–41). Added irony comes from a literal translation of the word behind "gratuitously," that is, "as a gift." God loved the world by way of giving his one-and-only Son (3:16). The world reciprocated by giving the Son their hatred. Up to this point in chapter 15, then, we have three basic commands: (1) Abide in Jesus (15:1–8). (2) Love one another in the Christian community (15:9–17). (3) Understand the world's hatred of you (15:18–25).

15:26–27: "Whenever the representative comes, whom I'll send to you from alongside the Father, the Spirit of the truth, who proceeds out from alongside the Father—that one [again the Spirit] **will testify about me.** [27]**And you too are testifying** [about me], **because you're with me from the beginning."** Jesus' preceding talk about making converts in terms of fruit-bearing now leads him to talk about the means of making converts, namely, testifying about him. Pride of place in such testimony goes to the Holy Spirit. According to 14:16 God the Father will give the Spirit as his representative to be with the disciples in lieu of the absent Jesus. According to 14:26 God the Father will send the Spirit in Jesus' name to teach the disciples and remind them of Jesus' words. Now in 15:26–27, though the Spirit proceeds out from the Father (he has had a place "alongside the Father" just as the preincarnate Jesus had [see 17:5, for example)], it is *Jesus* who will send the Spirit. Since Jesus and the Father are one (10:30), they act as cosenders of the Spirit. Consequently, the Spirit will be sent not only in Jesus' name, as in 14:26. The Spirit will be sent also as Jesus' representative. Representing Jesus as well as the Father, the Spirit will add his testimony about Jesus to the disciples' testimony about him. This cotestimony satisfies the requirement of more than one witness to establish truth (8:17); and because of the Spirit's unity with Jesus the truth, "the Spirit of the truth" means not only that the Spirit will tell the truth when testifying but also that the Spirit is one with Jesus the truth, is also himself the truth as Jesus is, and will testify that Jesus is the truth.

Because this double testimony of both the Spirit and the disciples satisfies the law of two or more witnesses (Numbers 35:30; Deuteronomy 17:6; 19:15), their testimony will prove effective in bearing "much fruit," the making of many more converts. We could translate with a command: "And you too, testify." But favoring a statement, "And you too are testifying," is the parallel with the Spirit's testifying, which can't be taken as a command that the Spirit testify. "*Are* testifying" dramatizes the disciples' future testimony as though it were already occurring at the time of Jesus' speaking. He addresses these remarks specifically to the eleven original disciples, as can be told from the description of his addressees as with him from the beginning. Not from the precreational beginning of 1:1, of course, but from the beginning of his public ministry (see especially 6:64; 16:4). The present tense in "you're," where we expect "you've *been* with me from the beginning," reflects the disciples' continuing presence with Jesus at the time he speaks these words; and it alludes to these disciples' having persevered rather than apostatizing like those in 6:60–71. The testimony of these original disciples became the basis of later disciples' evangelism (1:14; 20:30–31; 21:24).

16:1–2: "I've told you these things lest you be caused to stumble." "These things" refers to the world's hatred and persecution of the disciples (15:18–21). Stumbling is a figure of speech for apostatizing through failure to persevere in belief that the Christ, God's Son, is none other than Jesus. It's the world's hatred and persecution that could cause the disciples to apostatize, but Jesus' foretelling them of the hatred and persecution will steel them against it. **²"They'll make you de-synagogued, but an hour is coming that everyone who has killed you will think** [himself] **to be offering religious service to God."** "They" refers to the Jewish authorities, who in their hatred and persecution of the disciples will represent the world at large. To be de-synagogued is to be excommunicated from a synagogue (see 9:22, 34–35). Just as Jesus had his "hour" to be killed for having testified about himself (5:31; 8:14, 18), the disciples will also have their "hour" to be killed for having testified about him. "But" contrasts the coming of their hour to be killed with their being merely de-synagogued. Though the latter will be bad enough, the contrast points up the extreme of martyrdom. We expect "the hour *when*." But the text reads "the hour *that*" to emphasize the *killing* which will take place during the *hour* rather than the hour during which the killing will take place. The killers will think of their killing as a kind of liturgy, such as takes place in the temple by way of worshiping God. How can they possibly think so?

The answer comes in **16:3–4c: "And they'll do these things because they've known neither the Father nor me** [compare 15:21]**."** Unacquaintance with God and Jesus will lead the world to mistake Jesus' disciples for enemies of God, so that killing the disciples will seem like worshiping God. And unacquaintance with Jesus carries with it unacquaintance with God, for no one

comes to God except through Jesus, or knows God except *in* Jesus (14:6–11). **⁴ᵃ⁻ᶜ"But I've told you these things in order that whenever their hour comes, you may remember them** [= 'these things'], **that I told** [them] **to you."** Though "their hour" could be the hour of the persecutors and killers, it's probably the hour of "these things," that is, the hour when the persecution and killing take place. Remembering them at the time, which means remembering that Jesus had predicted them, will confirm the disciples' belief in him so as not to apostatize.

16:4d–6: "But I haven't told you these things from the beginning, because I was with you. ⁵But now I'm going to him who sent me; and not a single one of you is asking me, 'Where are you going?' ⁶Rather, sadness has filled your heart because I've said these things to you." So long as Jesus was with his disciples he captured the world's murderous hatred all to himself. His physical presence and escapes from danger gave them assurance; and he protected them, as will come out especially in 18:7–9. With his imminent absence, however, they'll become objects of the world's murderous hatred. He didn't need to tell them so until the eve of his departure. But now he does need to in order that the memory of his forewarning may prolong their assurance throughout the hour of their persecution and martyrdoms, however long that hour may last. In 13:36 Simon Peter *did* ask Jesus, "Lord, where are you going?" (compare 14:5); and in 14:12 Jesus said outright, "I'm going to the Father." So what does Jesus mean by saying here that not a single one of the disciples is asking him, "Where are you going"? The answer lies in his immediately following statement that sadness has filled their hearts because he has forewarned them of their persecution and martyrdoms. Instead of sorrowing over their own future fates, at least one of the disciples should now be asking (notice the present tense) Peter's earlier question again. To have done so would have eclipsed their self-centered sadness with joy over Jesus' return to the Father.

Jesus tries next to erase the disciples' sadness, but not with his going to the Father—rather, with good news concerning them as disciples. **16:7–11: "But I'm telling you the truth** [in that as the Word Jesus is himself the truth that he *speaks*]**: it's better for you that I go away. For if I don't go away, the representative** [= the Holy Spirit] **won't come to you. But if I do go, I'll send him to you. ⁸And after coming, that one** [the representative, the Spirit] **will convict the world with regard to sin and with regard to vindication and with regard to judgment: ⁹with regard to sin, in that they** [the people who make up 'the world'] **don't believe in me; ¹⁰and with regard to vindication in that I'm going to the Father and you're no longer seeing me; ¹¹and with regard to judgment in that the ruler of this world has been judged."** Jesus has already mentioned advantages to the disciples in the Spirit's coming to replace him. Jesus' physical presence was localized, but the Spirit will be "in" them wherever they "go" to bear the "fruit" of converts (see 14:17 with 15:16). As they go, the Spirit will teach them and remind them of Jesus' words (14:26; 16:13–15). But here in 16:8–11 the Spirit's coming works to the disciples' advantage by convicting the very world that hates and kills them. "Will convict" connotes a legal verdict of guilty, not psychological persuasion such as "convince" would connote: (1) guilty of what in John is the quintessential sin of not believing in Jesus; (2) guilty as proved by God's vindication of Jesus, which is demonstrated by Jesus' going to the Father so as to be invisible to earthlings; and (3) guilty so as to be condemned to judgment in the judgment of their ruler, Satan. Most translations have "righteousness" instead of "vindication." But vindication means to be shown as right, and that is what Jesus' going to the Father shows him to be. He's in the right. The world is in the wrong. They murdered him. In other words, the Spirit reverses the world's verdict against Jesus and pronounces against the world a verdict of guilty. So in putting Jesus on trial, the world put themselves on trial.

It's "you," the disciples who aren't seeing Jesus any longer. They'll see him three times after his resurrection; but as often in chapters 13–17, he's speaking from the standpoint of the church age, as shown also by his saying "you *are* no longer seeing me" instead of "you *will* no longer see me." Strikingly, he doesn't say the *world* isn't seeing him any longer, though of course it isn't. He singles out the disciples instead; for if any could be expected to see him, they would be the ones. But not even they are seeing him, so complete is his vindication by returning to his preincarnate glory alongside the Father. That the world's ruler "has been judged" takes again a future standpoint. This time it depicts his judgment as so sure and soon that the judgment might as well have occurred already.

Now Jesus shifts back to the Spirit's ministry to believers. *16:12–15*: **"I still have many things to say to you, but you aren't able to bear [them] now. **[13]**But when that one, the Spirit of the truth, comes, he'll guide you in all the truth. For he won't speak on his own; rather, he'll speak as many things as he'll hear** [from Jesus, according to what follows] **and report to you the coming things.** [14]**That one will glorify me in that he'll take** ['the coming things'] **from me and report** [them] **to you.** [15]**All things, as many as they are, that the Father has are mine. For this reason I said that he** [the Spirit] **takes** ['the coming things'] **from me and will report** [them] **to you."** The disciples' sadness over their future persecution and martyrdoms makes further revelations by Jesus unbearable at the moment. On seeing him risen from the dead, however, their sadness will be turned to joy (16:19–22; 20:20), so that they can then bear further revelations by the Spirit, whom they'll receive on that occasion (20:22). Again Jesus calls him "the Spirit of the truth," because he'll represent Jesus the truth (14:6) and teach the truth about Jesus. It's a delicate question whether the Spirit will guide the disciples "in the truth" or "into the truth," but *in* the realm of truth hardly differs from *into* its realm. In either case, emphasis falls on "*all*

the truth" and on the Spirit's speaking "as *many* things as he'll hear." The revelation will be both complete and adequate. And just as Jesus spoke only what he'd heard from his Father (8:28, 38; 12:50; 15:15), neither will the Spirit speak on his own, but will speak only what he takes from Jesus. Since Jesus gets his words from the Father, then, following Jesus' departure we have a chain of communication from the Father to the Son, from the Son to the Spirit, and finally from the Spirit to the disciples—*these* disciples.

Here lies the main basis for treating the New Testament as canon, the authoritative guide—along with the Old Testament—for Christian belief and practice. According to early church tradition the New Testament consists of books written by Jesus' original disciples and their immediate associates who wrote down what those disciples had said. The Holy Spirit reminded those disciples of what Jesus had done and said and guided them in expounding it. The exposition included "the coming things" (particularized here) as well as Jesus' past ministry (particularized in 14:26). We think naturally of the book of Revelation, which Jesus got from God to give John "in the Spirit" and which contains "the things that must happen with speed" (Revelation 1:1, 10). During his absence, therefore, Jesus continued to be and act as the Word in that the Spirit mediated to the disciples further words of the exalted Jesus. And since the past and future words of Jesus have to do with him as the Word who was with God and was God and will come again as "the Word of God" (1:1; 10:35; Revelation 19:13), the Spirit's mediating them glorifies Jesus, honors him. All the many things that Jesus says belong to him as well as to his Father—these things are what the Spirit hears and passes on. By anticipation, the shift from "will take" to "takes" retrojects the future into the present, though "will report," immediately following "takes," puts the Spirit's reporting back into the future.

16:16–18: **"A little [while] and you'll see me no longer; and again a little [while] and you *will* see me."** [17]**Therefore some of his disciples said to one another, "What *is* this that he's telling us, 'A little [while] and you *won't* see me; and again a little [while] and you *will* see me,' and, 'I'm going to the Father' [16:10]?"** [18]**Therefore they kept saying, "What *is* this that he's saying, 'A little [while]'? We don't know [= understand] what he's saying."** Jesus' crucifixion and burial will occur the very next day, Good Friday. So it won't be long before he disappears from the disciples' sight. But he'll rise from the dead the following Sunday and appear to them that evening. So neither will it be long before they'll see him again. "What *is* this . . . ?" = "What does this *mean* . . . ?" Jews didn't expect their Messiah to die, rise, and reappear; and in John's Gospel Jesus makes no explicit predictions of his death and resurrection (contrast Mark 8:31; 9:31; 10:32–34 and parallels in Matthew and Luke). Jesus has only alluded to his death and resurrection in figurative, enigmatic language (2:19; 3:13–15; 6:53–58; 8:28; 12:32–34). Naturally, then, the disciples don't understand. They hardly do even in the other Gospels, where the predictions are explicit. The repetition of their question underlines their ignorance.

16:19–22: Jesus knew that they wanted to ask him [about these things] **and said to them, "You're seeking with one another** [the meaning] **concerning this, that I said, 'A little** [while] **and you *won't* see me, and again a little** [while] **and you *will* see me.'** [20]**Amen, amen I tell you that you'll weep and wail, but the world will rejoice. You'll be saddened, but your sadness will turn into joy.** [21]**When she gives birth, a woman has sadness** [in the sense of physical pain, for Jesus is playing on the double meaning of sadness as both emotional pain and physical pain], **because her hour** [of childbirth] **has come. But when she has given birth to a child, she no longer remembers the pressure** [of labor] **because of the joy that a human being has been born into the world.** [22]**On the one hand, then, you too have sadness now. On the other hand, I'll see you, and your heart will rejoice** [compare Isaiah 60:5; 66:14]**; and no one takes your joy away from you."** "Jesus knew . . ." brings out his divine omniscience, as often in John. "You're asking . . ." could be translated as a question, "Are you asking . . . ?" and often *is* translated as a question. But the reference to Jesus' omniscience favors a declaration that exhibits that omniscience. And again as usual, he takes the initiative by telling the disciples what they *want* to ask him but *don't* ask him, that is, the meaning of his earlier statements. But instead of answering the question they want to ask him, he elaborates the statements that gave rise to their question. Emphasizing the truthfulness of those statements is "Amen, amen I tell you." Weeping and wailing in the middle eastern style dramatizes the disciples' sadness upon his disappearance (because of death and burial, though he doesn't say so). The world's rejoicing will contrast with the disciples' weeping and wailing, and it will derive from the satisfaction of the world's murderous hatred of Jesus. The turning of the disciples' sadness into joy will derive from their seeing him again (because of his resurrection, though again he doesn't say so [compare 20:18, 20, 25, 29; 21:14]).

Jesus compares the disciples' coming transition from sadness to joy with the transition of a woman giving birth from labor pains to joy. Her "hour" of physical pain represents the disciples' little while of emotional pain, immediately follows Jesus' "hour" of death, and differs from the disciples' even later "hour" of being killed for preaching Jesus (16:2). It's surprising that he speaks of "a human being" rather than of "a child" (as at first) or perhaps "an infant" as born by the woman. "A human being" anticipates Pilate's saying when Jesus comes out wearing a thorny crown and a purple robe, "Behold, the man/the human being!" (19:5). Contrary to a Gnostic teaching, the King of kings and Lord of lords is none other than the human being Jesus (see the introduction to 1 John). "Has been born" would suffice, but Jesus adds "into the world" to portray his resurrection as a reentry into the world similar to his initial entry at the incarnation (compare 1:9; 6:14 and similar passages).

The disciples' joy at this reentry will erase from memory their short-lived sadness (20:20: "the disciples, on seeing the [risen] Lord, rejoiced"). Nor can their persecutors or killers or anyone else take away their joy, for it's as eternal as the eternal life that Jesus' resurrection gives them. Their heart, filled with sadness in 16:6, will then rejoice—when "I'll see you again," Jesus says. We expect him to say, "*You'll* see me," as in 16:16–17, 19 (compare again 20:18, 20, 25, 29; 21:14). But the shift to "*I'll* see you," plus the addition of "again," accents the initiative of Jesus and recalls his promise to "come again" and "receive" the disciples "to himself" (14:3). The mutuality of their seeing him and his seeing them corresponds to the mutuality of their abiding in him and his abiding in them (15:4). Behind this passage lies the Jewish expectation of "messianic birthpangs," a time of intense tribulation (that is, pressure) out of which would be born messianic salvation. In Matthew 24:8 Jesus himself echoed this expectation in reference to the end of the church age. Here in John those messianic birthpangs are advanced to the beginning of the church age and put in the microcosmic experience of the eleven disciples (compare Revelation 12 with comments).

16:23–24: "And in that day you'll not ask *me* for anything. Amen, amen I tell you, whatever you ask *the Father* in my name—he'll give [it] **to you.** [24]**Till now you haven't asked for anything in my name. Ask, and you'll receive** [it] **in order that your joy may filled."** "That day" is the day of Jesus' seeing the disciples again and of their rejoicing at the sight of him. In 14:13–14 he promised to give them whatever they asked *him* in his name. In 15:16 he said that he'd give them whatever they asked the *Father* in his (Jesus') name. Though he doesn't now prohibit their asking him (Jesus), he does predict that as a matter of fact they won't ask him for anything. They won't have to, because they can go all the way to the Father since Jesus is the way, the only way, to him (14:6). See the comments on 14:13–14; 15:16 on what it means to ask in Jesus' name. Receiving what they ask for will add the joy of answered prayer to the disciples' joy of seeing Jesus risen from the dead. This second joy will fill their cup of joy to its full capacity.

16:25–28: "I've told you these things in riddles [like that of a woman's giving birth]**. An hour is coming when I'll no longer speak to you in riddles; rather, I'll report to you plainly about the Father.** [26]**On that day** [= the aforementioned 'hour,' for John likes to use words synonymously] **you'll ask** [him] **in my name, and I'm not telling you that I'll ask the Father concerning you.** [27]**For the Father himself loves you, because you've loved me and believed that I came forth from alongside God** [so I won't need to ask him for you; you yourselves can go to him with your requests so long as you ask them in my name]. [28]**I did come forth from alongside the Father, and I've come into the world. Again** [I tell you], **I'm leaving the world and going to the Father."** For the first time Jesus has located his Father outside the world and equated him with God. So the disciples finally "get it."

16:29–30: His disciples say, "Look! Now you're speaking plainly and not saying anything by way of a riddle. ³⁰Now we know that you know all things and don't need anyone to ask you. In this [matter] we believe that you've come forth from God." The first "now" stresses Jesus' anticipatory shift from obscure to plain speech even ahead of the soon-coming "hour"/ "day." The second "now" stresses the correspondingly anticipatory shift of the disciples from ignorance to knowledge. But their knowledge is of his knowledge, indeed of his omniscience ("you know *all* things"). Believers can rest in the knowledge of Jesus' omniscience. Instead of saying, "*We* don't need to ask you," the disciples say, "*You* don't need anyone to ask you," because Jesus has carried out his Father's commission to tell them all that the Father told him to tell them. No further questions are necessary. Questions have given way to belief that Jesus came forth from God.

16:31–33: Jesus answered them, "Do you believe now? ³²Behold, an hour is coming, and has come, in order that you may be scattered each to his own home [compare 2 Kings 22:17]; and you'll leave me alone. And I'm *not* alone, because the Father is with me. ³³I've told you these things in order that in me you may have peace. In the world you have pressure. But take courage. I've conquered the world." Jesus' question, "Do you believe now?" could be translated equally well as a declaration: "Now you believe." Even as a question, though, Jesus doesn't deny the disciples' believing. (A denial would read, "You don't believe now, do you?") and under either translation Jesus is forewarning the disciples that they're about to be scattered, each to his own home (probably referring to temporary residences in Jerusalem [compare 19:27]). He designs this forewarning to give them peace *in him*, for by abiding in him despite their being scattered they'll retain the messianic salvation that "peace" connotes (see the comments on 14:27).

An hour has come "in order that" the disciples may be scattered. As it will turn out, the scattering will symbolize their preservation in salvation. For Jesus will insist that the disciples be let go before he lets his enemies arrest him (18:9: "in order that the word might be fulfilled which he'd spoken, 'The ones whom you [Father] have given me—I've not lost a single one of them [6:39; 17:12]'"). No blame attaches to the disciples for leaving Jesus alone, then. It's his *purpose* that they be scattered. He alone will accomplish their salvation. Alone so far as human companionship is concerned—yes. But God the Father is with him, so that John will omit Jesus' outcry on the cross, "My God, my God, why have you abandoned me?" (Mark 15:34; Matthew 27:46). How can the Word who is *one* with God (10:30) and *is* God (1:1) be forsaken *by* God? In this Gospel, to the contrary, God doesn't *abandon* Jesus to die on a cross. He *uses* Jesus' cross as an elevator taking him toward heaven and preincarnate glory.

The "pressure" that disciples have in the world—that is, among unbelievers—consists in the unbelievers' hating them by persecuting and killing them (compare

16:21). Such pressure "in the world" contrasts with the peace of eternal life that disciples have "in him [Jesus]." The present tense in "you have pressure" anticipates the world's hostility toward the disciples once Jesus leaves. His conquest of the world will take the shape of his resurrection, which is so sure and soon to happen that he speaks as though it has happened already. In his resurrection he conquers the world by reversing their murder of him. And this reversal gives the disciples reason to take courage, because his resurrection entails theirs too, a resurrection to eternal life—especially as a compensation for martyrdom. See Revelation 2:7; 20:4–6 and assorted intervening passages for believers' conquering the world as Jesus did.

JESUS' PRAYER
John 17:1–26

Jesus and eleven of the twelve disciples are still at the Last Supper. (Judas Iscariot left back in 13:21–30.) They won't leave till 18:1. So we shouldn't confuse the prayer that Jesus prays in chapter 17 with Jesus' later prayers in the garden of Gethsemane according the other Gospels. John will omit them in favor of this one. They're short, this one is long. They ask for exemption from death, if possible. This one accepts death. In Gethsemane Jesus falls on his face in a sweat of emotional turmoil—a perfectly natural human reaction to the prospect of dying the next day. Here Jesus is the picture of composure as he looks heavenward. How else would you expect God incarnate (as John portrays Jesus) to behave than with the composure of one who's in charge. In verses 1–5 Jesus asks God to glorify him. In verses 6–19 he asks him to keep the eleven disciples. In verses 20–23 he asks him to unite later believers with the Eleven. And in verses 24–26 he asks him to transport all believers to where he (Jesus) is.

17:1–2: Jesus said these things [that is, the things he had just told the disciples]; and on lifting up his eyes to heaven, he said, "Father, the hour has come. Glorify your Son in order that the Son may glorify you. ²Just as you gave him authority over all flesh in order that everything which you've given him—he might give them eternal life." Jews normally looked toward heaven, God's abode, when they prayed. Proving this rule is the exception of the tax collector so sorry for his sins that he wouldn't even "lift [his] eyes to heaven" (Luke 18:13). "Father" and "Son" complement each other by indicating the relationship between God and Jesus. "The hour" that has arrived is the occasion of Jesus' death by crucifixion, considered the most shameful of human deaths. To glorify his Son, then, the Father will have to make Jesus' crucifixion honorable rather than shameful, as indeed he'll do by making the uplifting of Jesus on a cross the first phase of his exaltation back to the Father's side in heaven. Honoring Jesus in this way has the purpose and result of Jesus' glorifying—that is, honoring—the Father, as a son ought to do according to one of the Ten Commandments (Exodus 20:12; Deuteronomy 5:16). And how might Jesus the Son honor God his Father in turn? By giving eternal life to everyone the Father has given him. Believers are God's gift to Jesus just as eternal life is Jesus' gift to believers; and Jesus honors God by giving them eternal life, a gift that indicates they're God's children (1:12–13). (In that culture, to have children was to have honor, childlessness being considered shameful.) "All flesh" refers to all human beings with special reference to their weakness and mortality, which contrast with the eternal life that Jesus gives to "everything" the Father has given him. "Everything" refers to "them" to whom Jesus gives eternal life. It sounds odd to us that "everything" turns out to be persons, but the use of "every*thing*" instead of "every*one*" accents the quality of every*ness*: not a single one of those the Father has given to Jesus will fail to receive eternal life. Just as Jesus' authority extends over all humanity, his gift of eternal life extends to all whom the Father has given him out of the mass of humanity. Since Jesus' authority extends over all humanity, not just over those whom the Father has given him, the door remains open to any who receive him by believing in his name (1:12). The Father's giving certain ones to the Son doesn't close the door to eternal life in the face of anyone who will believe.

17:3: "**And this is eternal life, that they** [those whom the Father has given to Jesus] **know you, the only true God, and** [that they know] **Jesus Christ, whom you sent** [into the world]." Knowing has to do with information, specifically with the truth that Jesus Christ embodied God and therefore provides the only way to God (14:6–11). But since this truth is personal, knowing includes acquaintance too—close acquaintance, very close (see 17:23). And the one person Jesus Christ, not a divine spirit Christ that came on a human Jesus at his baptism and left him before the crucifixion (as some Gnostics taught)—this one person made possible that kind of knowledge in his public ministry, a ministry commissioned by God. No secret revelations necessary! Compare the introduction to 1 John.

17:4–5: "**I glorified you on the earth by completing the work that you've given me to do. **⁵**And now you, Father, glorify me alongside yourself with the glory that I had alongside you before the world existed.**" Here Jesus anticipates the completion of his work at the cross (19:28–30). He prays as though it's already done. It's so sure and soon to be done that it's as good as done. The work consists in the revelation of his grace and truth (1:14). "On earth" sets up a contrast with heaven, described in terms of intimacy with the Father: "alongside yourself" and "alongside you." The glory that Jesus will enjoy alongside the Father rounds out the Father's glorification of Jesus by making the cross an instrument of honorable exaltation rather than shameful execution. "Before the world existed" reminds us of 1:1: "In the beginning was the Word" (the creation following in 1:3). But who gave honor to the preincarnate Word? God the Father did, and he did so by situating the Word right alongside himself.

17:6–8: "**I manifested your name to the human beings whom you gave me out of the world. They were yours, and you gave me to them, and they've kept your word. **⁷**They've come to know now that all things, as many as they are, that you've given me are from alongside you. **⁸[And those things are from alongside you] **in that I've given them the words which you gave me, and they accepted** [those words] **and came to know truly that I came from alongside you. And they believed that you sent me.**" "Your name" is "God." To manifest that name is to put in plain sight what it represents, the characteristics of the one who bears the name: holiness, righteousness, and love (to name several in the present context). "The human beings" means the eleven disciples (Jesus will broaden his prayer later) and sets them in contrast to "the only true God." "Out of the world" distances them from the society of unbelievers. The Father could give them to Jesus because they belonged to the Father. The giving to Jesus made them his, though they remain the Father's too (17:10); for the Father and Jesus are one and share the name "God" (1:1; 10:30; 17:11b). The Father's "word" is Jesus as God's Word, for Jesus made himself the subject of his speaking ("I am the bread of life/the light of the world/the good shepherd" and so on). The Eleven's having kept this Word means that they persisted in their belief. They didn't go away from Jesus, as many other disciples did in 6:66–69. "The words" that Jesus has given them make up all the many things that the Father has given him. Because Jesus as God's Word has given them these words, the disciples have come to know now that the words originated from God. Before, they were ignorant. No more! This knowledge came from acceptance. Accepting Jesus' words parallels accepting Jesus as the Word in 1:12. The disciples know "truly" because the object of their knowing is "the truth" (14:6), who came from alongside the Father. And accepting his words counts as believing that God sent him.

17:9–10: "**I'm asking in regard to them** [the Eleven]. **I'm not asking in regard to the world—rather, in regard to the ones you've given me, because they're yours.**" So Jesus disregards the world of unbelievers and appeals to God's ownership of the Eleven, as though to say, "You have a stake in them, Father. For your own sake, then, answer my prayer for them." Christians might well make the same sort of appeal when praying for their fellow Christians. ¹⁰"**And all my things are yours, and your things mine; and I've been glorified among them.**" This last statement shows that the "things" are people, the disciples in particular. But the neuter gender ("things") emphasizes that all eleven of them are co-owned by God and Jesus. And it's their perseverance in discipleship, in contrast with the apostasy of many other disciples, that has honored Jesus.

17:11a–c: "**And no longer am I in the world, and they are in the world, and I'm coming to you.**" For contrast, emphasis falls on "no longer," "they," and "in the world." Jesus' saying he's no longer in the world anticipates his soon departure, as though it has already occurred. "I'm coming to you" doesn't refer to his coming to the Father in prayer. It refers to Jesus' returning to the Father's side in heaven, so that his absence from the world of unbelievers and coming to the Father make up two sides of the same coin. Because of the contrast between being and not being in the world we want to say, "*but* they are in the world." John uses "and," however, so that "they are in the world" stands on its own two feet, not *just* as a contrast with Jesus' absence from the world. The disciples' continuing presence in the world creates the need for Jesus' prayer.

17:11d–f: "Holy Father, keep them in your name, which you've given me, in order that they may be one just as we [are one]." Here Jesus adds the description "holy" to "Father." Since holiness has to do with separation from the world, this description prepares for Jesus' description of the disciples and himself as not originating "from the world" and therefore of the disciples as needing protection in it (17:14–16). "Keep" refers to such protection and connotes a protection that is ongoing. The perseverance of believers rests, so to speak, on God's perseverance in protecting them. Not a bad foundation for their perseverance! But what does "in your name" add to the thought of keeping? And what is that name? Well, the name is one that the Father has ("*your* name") and that he has also given to his Son ("which you've given *me*"). So they share this name. What could it be, then? Not "Jesus," "Christ," "Son of God," "the Word," or any of the other names (or titles) that don't, and can't, refer to God the Father. Not "Father," which can't refer to Jesus. Not "I AM," because in John "I AM" never occurs for the Father, only for Jesus, and because Jesus never uses it as a name but only in statements (for example, "Before Abraham came into existence, I AM" [8:58] and "I am the way and the truth and the life" [14:6]). With the possible but unclear exception of 4:26, we never read anything like God's command to Moses, "Thus shall you say to the sons of Israel, 'I AM has sent me to you,'" in answer to Moses' asking what "name" of God he should use (Exodus 3:13–14). And though "Lord" applies to the Father twice and to Jesus many times in John, the two exceptions are determined by Old Testament quotations, which John can hardly change (12:13, 38). Otherwise, only Jesus gets the designation "Lord." But the very first verse in John's Gospel identifies the name that Jesus, the incarnate Word, and his Father share. It is "God": "In the beginning was the Word, and the Word was with God, and the Word was *God*" (1:1). Since names represent the characteristics of the named, to be kept in the name "God," which the Father and Son share, means to be kept by all those attributes which Scripture attaches to that name: love and grace, holiness and righteousness, mercy and faithfulness, omnipotence and omniscience, and so forth. That is to say, God is fully equipped to keep believers safe in their salvation. And since there's safety in numbers, especially when the numbers are accompanied by unity, Jesus prays that the disciples may be one in the kind of unity that characterizes him and his Father.

It's a unity of mutual love (13:34; 17:22–23). Such unity keeps disciples from apostatizing back into the world of unbelievers.

17:12: "When I was with them [again Jesus speaks from the standpoint of his upcoming absence], **I was keeping them in your name, which you'd given me, and I guarded** [them]." So Jesus' imminent absence is what has led him to ask for the Father's protection of the disciples. **"And not one of them** [the Twelve] **was lost except for the son of lostness, in order that the Scripture might be fulfilled."** "The son of . . ." is a Semitic way of expressing somebody's character or fate—here, obviously, fate. Jesus is referring to Judas Iscariot. Lostness doesn't mean annihilation. (The "lost" sheep in Jesus' parable at Luke 15:3–7 wasn't annihilated!) It means ruination—here, eternal damnation. "In order that" expresses purpose, but may also express result ("so that")—in other words, *attained* purpose. Neither the purpose nor the result of Scripture's fulfillment erases the responsibility of Judas for his actions. He embezzled the apostolic treasury entrusted to him (12:4–6), and he led Jesus' enemies to him under cover of night (18:2–3, 5). But the present passage stresses the sovereignty of God's will as expressed in Scripture. His will takes into account human evil and even uses human evil, as when in Old Testament times he used the evil empires of Assyria and Babylonia to punish apostate Israel and Judah.

17:13: "But now I'm coming to you [another reference to Jesus' return to the Father in heaven] **and saying these things in the world** [of unbelievers] **in order that they** [the Twelve except for Judas Iscariot] **might have my joy fulfilled in themselves."** "These things" are the contents of Jesus' prayer, which he's speaking while still in the world. The prayer has the purpose, and will have the result, of fulfilling his joy. In what does that joy consist? The context indicates that it consists in the preservation of his disciples in their Christian faith, and their being kept from apostasy. But not only does Jesus get joy out of their preservation. They do too: "have my joy fulfilled in themselves." The tacking of "-selves" onto "them-" stresses this sharing in Jesus' joy. Preserved and persevering believers are joyful believers.

17:14: "I've given them your word; and the world hated them, because they're not from the world just as I'm not from the world." "Your word" is the message the Father gave Jesus to teach those who belong to him and the Father. And since he proclaimed himself in this message, "your word" also means the Word who is Jesus (1:1–18). He has given himself to the disciples. "Not from the world" means not having their ultimate origin in the society of unbelievers. Though Jesus had a human birth (18:37), he had his origin in heaven. Likewise, believers in him are "born from above" (a more accurate translation than "born again," which was Nicodemus's largely mistaken understanding [3:3, 7]). This birth, also described as deriving from God's Spirit, supersedes biological birth and distances believers from the world.

17:15: **"I'm not asking that you take them out of the world** [which would exempt them from the world's hatred—but it's not their fortune to avoid that hatred, for removal would preclude their testifying to the world]— **rather, that you keep them from the evil one** [that is, Satan, but called evil in contrast with the 'holy Father' of 17:11 and because of Satan's efforts to subvert Jesus' disciples]." Thus, Jesus prays that in the very society where the evil one holds sway, the Father, who is holy, may keep the disciples from apostasy.

17:16–17: **"They're not from the world just as I'm not from the world."** This statement repeats what was said in 17:14. The repetition provides a platform for Jesus' following request: [17]**"Set them apart in the truth."** The request connects with Jesus' addressing his Father in 17:11 as "holy," which means "set apart, consecrated." As born from above, the disciples have a different origin from that of unbelievers and therefore need to maintain a religious though not physical distance from them. And it's "in the truth" where this essential distance is maintained. So Jesus goes on to say, **"Your word is truth."** Again, the word of God is the message about him as explained by Jesus, who is himself both the Word and God and the truth (1:1, 18; 14:6). Jesus refers to himself as well as to his message, for he's the content of it. In 14:6 Jesus identified himself as *the* truth," and in 17:17a he has just asked the Father to set the disciples apart "in *the* truth," which he (Jesus) is. But now in 17:17b the definite article drops off to emphasize the quality of truthfulness in the Father's word/Word. And since the disciples are to be set apart "*in* the truth/Truth," we have a parallel with their abiding *in* Jesus as a vine abides *in* a vineyard (15:1–8).

17:18: **"Just as you sent me into the world, I also sent them into the world."** Jesus' sending the disciples won't occur till after the resurrection (20:21). So here as elsewhere in his prayer he's taking a later standpoint. By implication from the preceding verse he sends the disciples with the word of the truth in which they're set apart (17:17). But though set apart religiously from the world of unbelievers, they're not only physically present "*in* the world" (17:11). They're positively sent "*into* the world." They're to penetrate human society with the very word of truth which sets them apart from that society.

17:19: **"And for them I'm consecrating myself so that they too may be consecrated in truth."** To consecrate is to set apart for a special purpose. The setting apart of the disciples depends on Jesus' setting himself apart. How is he doing that? By laying down his life and taking it up again for the disciples' sake—and doing so on his own. Just as according to 10:17–18 no one takes his life from him or gives it back to him, so also no one— not even the Father—is setting him apart. He's doing it to himself, by his own initiative. For he's not only God's Son; he's also himself God. And it's his self-accomplished death, resurrection, and exaltation that make possible the setting apart of his disciples for their mission to the world. "In truth" tells the location where they're set

apart. Again the dropping of "the" from "truth" emphasizes the quality of truthfulness in the word/Word that Jesus sends them to convey.

Now Jesus broadens his prayer beyond the eleven disciples. **17:20–21**: **"But not only in regard to these, but also in regard to the ones believing in me through their word, I ask** [21]**that they may all be one just as you, Father,** [are] **in me and I** [am] **in you, that they too may be in us in order that the world may believe that you sent me."** So the Father's word/Word (17:17) now becomes the word/Word of the Eleven too, that is, their message about Jesus with which Jesus sent them into the world (17:18). He prays for the oneness of the Eleven and their converts and defines that oneness in terms of being *in* one another—and in the Father and Jesus as well, just as they are in each other. As in 13:34; 17:11–12, 22–23, the oneness is a oneness of active love for one another; and this love is to unite them so closely that they are living inside the others' skin, so to speak. Such oneness has the purpose of engendering the world's belief, as indeed it does in the case of those whom the Father has given to Jesus out of the world. A society of love attracts people out of a society of hate. Believing that God sent Jesus arises out of, and corresponds to, Jesus' sending the disciples—and amounts to believing in Jesus.

Jesus elaborates in **17:22–23**: **"And I've given them the glory that you've given me in order that they may be one just as we** [are] **one—**[23]**I in them and you in me, in order that they may be completed in oneness, in order that the world may know that you sent me and loved them just as you loved me."** What glory has God given his Son? It's the glory of Jesus' cross transformed into the instrument that exalts him back toward his preincarnate position alongside his Father in heaven (17:1, 4–5). Being in Jesus by abiding in him therefore entails sharing his honorable position. The oneness of believers with one another and Jesus is both the purpose and the result of receiving Jesus' glory. Believers can't attain this oneness except by receiving that glory as a gift, for the gift of glory equates with the gift of eternal life. And their oneness reaches completion with Jesus' dwelling in them as the one in whom the Father dwells (compare, for example, 14:23). Without Jesus' indwelling, believers' oneness with each other would remain incomplete; and without the Father's dwelling in Jesus, the dwelling of Jesus in believers wouldn't bring them into oneness with the Father. The world's *knowing* that the Father sent Jesus parallels, and essentially means the same as, the world's *believing* that the Father sent him (17:21). But Jesus now adds the element of the world's knowing that the Father *loved* believers. And this love matches the Father's love for Jesus his Son, because believers are located *in* his Son Jesus. For the Father to love Jesus, then, entails loving believers too.

Now Jesus prays for both his eleven original disciples and those whom they will convert. **17:24**: **"Father, what you've given me—I want also those to be with me where I am in order that they may see my glory,** which you've given me because you loved me before the founding of the world." The simple address "Father" echoes the start of Jesus' prayer (17:1) and introduces a closing summary. "What" refers to believers in Jesus and collectivizes them as the Father's gift to his Son Jesus. "Where I am" anticipates Jesus' return to the Father's side. Since the Father has given believers to Jesus, it's only natural that Jesus wants them to be with him. But there's more: he wants them to be with him so as to see his glory, a glory that according to 17:22 he has given to them. *Seeing* his glory looks forward to the Last Day, the second coming, the general resurrection, and believers' enjoyment of eternal life forever after (compare 5:28–29; 11:23–26; 21:22–23). And seeing Jesus' glory inaugurates the fullness of that enjoyment, only a part of which believers have now. God's gift of glory to Jesus supplements God's gift of believers to him and stems from God's having loved his Son since forever past. (The Word was, after all, in the beginning with God, prior to all things coming into existence through the Word [1:1–3].)

17:25–26: "Righteous Father, even the world hasn't known you [though they should have]. **Yet I've known you, and these** [believers] **have known that you sent me.** [26]**And to them I've made known, and will make known, your name in order that the love with which you've loved me may be in them and I** [may be] **in them."** Just as Jesus added "holy" to "Father" in 17:11, here he adds "righteous" to "Father." He's implying that his Father will do the right thing by answering his prayer. The world's not knowing the Father means that they haven't come into personal acquaintance with him. Such an acquaintance comes only through believing in Jesus, for as God's Son he does have that acquaintance. The knowledge that believers have is informational ("that you sent me"). And their knowing this information leads to knowing God's name, which Jesus made known to them. Knowing this name means knowing all that the name represents, most especially the love of God (compare the comments on 17:11). At this point information about God shades into close personal acquaintance with him through experiencing his attributes in action, most especially his love that effects the salvation of believers (3:16). In this sense Jesus will continue to make God's name known to them through the coming Holy Spirit (16:13–14). The purpose-and-result of making God's name known is the placing of his love for Jesus in those who believe in Jesus. This placement doesn't mean that believers will love Jesus as God loves him. It means, rather, that God will love them as much as he loves Jesus because Jesus will be in them. Therefore the prayer ends with the request that Jesus may be in them so as to make possible God's loving them that much.

JESUS' GETTING HIMSELF ARRESTED
John 18:1–11

Finally Jesus leaves the site of the Last Supper (compare 14:31 and the comments on it). *18:1:* **After saying these things** [the prayer in chapter 17 and perhaps also the so-called Upper Room Discourse preceding that prayer in chapters 13–16], **Jesus went out with his disciples across the Kidron Ravine to where a garden was, into which he and his disciples entered.** Since Judas left in 13:30, the remaining eleven of the Twelve constitute "his disciples." Except during and just after rainstorms, the Kidron Ravine was a dry streambed dividing Jerusalem on Mount Zion to the west from the Mount of Olives to the east. The garden on the lower slope of the Mount of Olives contains a grove of olive trees. From Mark 14:32; Matthew 26:36 we know the garden as Gethsemane, and from Luke 22:39 its location on the Mount of Olives. But John omits both the name and the location (as also in 18:26) to associate the garden—even to equate it—with the garden where Jesus was crucified and buried and where he rose again (see 19:41, unique to John's Gospel). Does this garden then become a kind of new garden of Eden with the cross made into a tree of life by virtue of Jesus' resurrection? Maybe so.

For reasons explained in the introduction to chapter 17, John omits the prayers that Jesus prayed in Gethsemane according to the other Gospels and moves directly to Jesus' arrest. *18:2–3:* **But Judas too, the one betraying him, knew the place, because Jesus had gathered there with his disciples many times.** To betray means to give someone or something over to someone else. Only the context gives the action a good connotation or a bad one. Here, of course, the context gives Judas's action the bad connotation that "betray" has in English. [3]**So Judas, on taking a cohort—plus officers from the chief priests and from the Pharisees—comes there with lanterns and torches and weapons.** A cohort consisted of six hundred soldiers, though the number could vary; and this cohort was probably under Roman command, since John distinguishes between the cohort and the Jewish chief priests' and Pharisees' officers. Whatever the exact number of the cohort and the officers, emphasis falls on the large size of the band that Judas took to arrest Jesus. This large size will enhance the divine majesty of Jesus when they quail at his confronting them. And it's ironic that Judas takes so many to arrest one man. It's also ironic that the band take lanterns and torches, flickering as they do, to arrest the light of the world, comparable to the blazing sun (8:12). And the darkness that necessitated those lanterns and torches also reminds us of the night of sin and judgment into which Judas entered when he left Jesus to betray him (13:30). Yet again it's ironic that the band bear weapons which, in view of Jesus' laying down his life on his own initiative, they won't need and would prove useless if he did resist. Such ironies will abound throughout the narrative of Jesus' arrest, interrogation, trial, and crucifixion.

18:4–9: **Therefore** [because of Judas's coming with the large band of soldiers and officers] **Jesus, knowing all the things coming upon him** [as the Word who is God incarnate he's omniscient], **went out and says to them, "Whom are you seeking?"** The question drips with irony in view of Jesus' "knowing all the things coming upon him." [5]They answered him, "Jesus the Nazarene [= the Jesus who's from Nazareth]." He tells them, "I am [he]." (And even Judas, the one betraying him, was standing with them.) [6]When therefore he said to them, "I am [he]," they recoiled and fell to the ground. [7]Therefore he asked them again, "Whom are you seeking?" And they said, "Jesus the Nazarene." [8]Jesus answered, "I told you, 'I am [he].' Therefore if you're seeking me, let these [the eleven disciples] go." [9][He said this] in order that the word might be fulfilled which he'd spoken, "The ones whom you [Father] have given me—I've not lost a single one of them." Because of Judas's coming with the large band of soldiers and officers we might expect Jesus to flee. But no, seizing the initiative he exits the garden to offer himself to them. When on two earlier occasions his enemies picked up stones to stone him to death, he escaped (8:59; 10:31, 39; 11:8). Not here! His hour has come. We could almost say that Jesus insists on getting arrested—on condition, however, that his disciples be let go. John doesn't need to say they were let go. It's simply assumed that Jesus' sovereign word had its desired effect. And just as surely as the Old Testament word of God is fulfilled, the letting go not only fulfills a previous word of Jesus (17:12). It also symbolizes his keeping the disciples (the true ones) secure in their salvation. It symbolizes his preserving them from apostasy.

According to 17:12 Jesus did lose Judas in a fulfillment of Scripture. But the exception of Judas—a hardly believable exception ("*even* Judas")—doesn't need to be mentioned here since he's standing with the arresting band and has just been described as Jesus' betrayer. Evidence enough of the exception! But how pitifully timid Judas looks in contrast with the forceful Jesus. Judas doesn't approach Jesus, kiss him, and say, "Rabbi," as he does in the other Gospels. He just stands there with the arresting band. They recoil and fall to the ground when for the first time Jesus says, "I am [Jesus the Nazarene]." This phrase can be—and is—an ordinary self-identification, as when the man born blind but healed by Jesus said, "I am [he] [that is, the formerly blind beggar]" (9:9). But since "he" has to be mentally added for an ordinary self-identification, "I am" can also be taken without the addition. Then it turns into the divine title "I AM" of Exodus 3:14 (compare John 8:58). As such, Jesus' "I am" carries the meaning of deity as well as the meaning of a man from Nazareth. Since the arresting band are seeing a theophany, an appearance of God, and hearing the voice of God, they recoil, they go backwards, and fall to the ground—the involuntary reaction of human beings to a theophany. But instead of falling face down in worship, the arresting band fall backwards in defeat (compare Jesus' statement in 16:33: "I've conquered the world"). The repetition of "I am" underscores both the deity of Jesus and his will to lay down his life of his own accord (see again 10:17–18).

18:10–11: Therefore [because Jesus had offered himself for arrest] **Simon Peter, having a sword, drew it and struck a slave of the high priest and cut off his right ear. And the slave's name was Malchus.** [11]**Therefore Jesus told Peter, "Put the sword into [its] sheath. The cup that the Father has given me—by all means shouldn't I drink it?"** This question implies a resounding "Yes!" and thus reverses the first part of Jesus' preceding prayer in Gethsemane according to Luke 22:42, "Father, if you're willing, take this cup away from me," and changes the second part of that prayer, "Nevertheless, not my will but yours come about" (similarly Mark 14:36; Matthew 26:39), into a positive determination to drink the cup of death, so that his own will as a son accords with his Father's will. Peter's fighting, despite Jesus' later statement that his "officers" (the disciples) don't fight (18:36), forecasts Peter's verbal denials that he's a disciple of Jesus. That is to say, the swordplay shows Peter to be denying in *deed* what he will soon deny in *words*. Only John's Gospel mentions the name Malchus, perhaps because the unnamed disciple who'll get Peter admitted into the high priest's courtyard was acquainted with the high priest (18:16) and therefore knew the name of this slave of the high priest. John shares with Luke 22:50 the designation of the slave's severed ear as the right one, but John lacks Jesus' healing the ear according to Luke 22:51. John is more interested in Jesus' determination to die as the good shepherd for the salvation of his sheep.

JESUS' WITHSTANDING INTERROGATION BY CAIAPHAS IN CONTRAST WITH PETER'S DENIALS OF JESUS
John 18:12–27

18:12–13: Therefore [because of Jesus' determination to lay down his life despite Peter's effort to the contrary] **the cohort and the commander and the officers of the Jews** [in particular, of the chief priests and the Pharisees mentioned in 18:3] **took Jesus with** [them]. **And they tied him up** [13]**and led** [him] **first to Annas, for he was father-in-law to Caiaphas, who was high priest that year.** Since Jesus practically insisted on getting arrested, it's ironic that they tied him up. They wouldn't have had to, though you wonder why they didn't gag him to keep him from saying "I AM" again. John says nothing about the disciples' flight, because Jesus laid down as a condition of his arrest that they be let go. Dismissal doesn't count as flight. Annas had himself been the high priest. Five of his sons also became high priests at different times. And at the moment his son-in-law Caiaphas was the high priest. So Annas wielded considerable influence. Historically, his long-standing influence probably lay behind Jesus' being taken to him first. John shows no interest in such influence or in the earlier high priesthood of Annas, however. He shows interest only in Annas's relationship to Caiaphas, who was high priest that year. Why "that year" despite Caiaphas's holding the high priestly office nineteen years? Well, the other Gospels mention only the Passover at the close of Jesus' ministry. But by mentioning two earlier Passover festivals during the course of Jesus' ministry (2:13, 23; 6:4), John indicates that the ministry lasted about three years. For Jews celebrated the Passover once a year. So "that year" pinpoints the final one of those three years, the year of Jesus' "hour."

The mention of Caiaphas in 18:13 now leads John to write about him in relation to Jesus. *18:14–15: And Caiaphas was the one who'd advised the Jews* [that is, the Jewish supreme court, called the Sanhedrin] *that it was advantageous that one man die for the people* [11:47–53]. *¹⁵And Simon Peter and another disciple were following Jesus, and that* [other] *disciple was acquainted with the high priest, and he went with Jesus into the high priest's courtyard.* Concerning Caiaphas's advice, see the comments on 11:49–52. "Another disciple" will turn out to be the beloved disciple (see 20:2). His acquaintance with the high priest gains him entry into the high priest's courtyard. A courtyard is a walled enclosure, and John's word for it is the same one that's used in 10:1–18 for a sheep pen. Possibly, then, John wants us to think of Jesus' taking the role of the good shepherd, with whom Jesus identified himself in that passage. The matter hangs in doubt, though, because John doesn't make a point of Jesus' entering Caiaphas's courtyard through its gate, as Jesus did make a point of saying that the good shepherd enters a sheep pen through its gate. In fact, John will relate Peter rather than Jesus to the gate (18:16–17). And it's important to note that though Annas had been the high priest earlier, and even though ex-high priests continued to be called high priests, John hasn't called Annas a high priest. He has called only Caiaphas the high priest and stressed Caiaphas's being high priest "that year," almost as if to rule out a continuing designation of Annas as high priest or at least our thinking of him as such. So the courtyard is that of the high priest Caiaphas, not of Annas; and the high priest in the following verses continues to be Caiaphas.

18:16–18: And Peter was standing outside [facing] *toward the gate. Therefore the other disciple, the acquaintance of the high priest, went out and spoke to the gatekeeper and brought Peter in. ¹⁷Therefore the slave girl,* [that is,] *the gatekeeper* [for "the gatekeeper" is feminine in the original Greek], *says to Peter, "You too* [as well as 'the other disciple'] *aren't* [one] *of the disciples of this man* [Jesus], *are you?"* That one [Peter] *says, "I'm not* [one of his disciples]." *¹⁸And the slaves and the officers were standing, having made a charcoal fire because it was cold; and they were warming themselves* [around the fire]. *And Peter too was standing with them and warming himself.* The other Gospels don't explain how Peter gained entry into the high priest's courtyard. John does. The slave girl who kept the gate expects Peter to deny he's a disciple of Jesus. He meets her expectation. Ironically, the disciple who declared he'd lay down his life for Jesus (13:37) and who used his sword to prevent Jesus' arrest (18:10) is now cowed by a slave girl into denying he's a disciple of him. Appropriately, then, John refers to Peter in a way that cold-shoulders him: "That one." And, sadly, Peter is standing with the slaves

and the officers just as at Jesus' arrest Judas the betrayer was standing with the soldiers and the chief priests' and Pharisees' officers (18:5). Not good company!

18:19–21: Therefore [because Jesus had been brought into the high priest's courtyard] *the high priest asked Jesus about his disciples and about his teaching.* Earlier, concern was expressed that Jesus was leading people astray, deceiving them (7:12), and that the whole Jewish nation would believe in him so as to launch a revolt that the Romans would crush (6:14–15; 11:47–48; 12:19). Therefore the high priest's present questions. *²⁰Jesus answered him, "I've spoken publicly to the world. I've always taught in synagogue and in the temple* [that is, in its courtyards], *where all the Jews* [here not limited to the authorities] *gather together. And I've spoken nothing in secret. ²¹Why are you asking me? Ask the ones who've heard what I said to them. Look, these* [people who heard] *know the things that I've said."* At the insistence of Jesus his disciples were let go. So he doesn't answer the question about them. Nor does he describe the content of his teaching. But he doesn't remain silent. (After all, he's the Word; and as the Word he speaks—a lot.) Rather than describing the content of his teaching he emphasizes its publicity and extent. This emphasis contrasts Jesus' teaching with the covertness of his arrest in the dark of night. It also lays a basis for his challenging the high priest to procure witnesses. As usual in John, the Word who was God takes charge. Nobody was supposed to be forced into testifying against himself anyway.

18:22–23: And when he'd said these things, one of the officers standing by gave Jesus a slap, saying, "Is this the way you answer the high priest?" *²³Jesus answered him, "If I've spoken wrongly, testify concerning the wrong. But if* [I've spoken] *rightly, why do you strike me?"* Peter was cowed by a slave girl. Jesus isn't cowed by either the high priest or one of his officers. He's still in charge and answers the officer's question with a putdown that throws the onus back on the officer. What Jesus said to the high priest is right and true, and nobody could deny that fact. Just as it was wrong for the high priest to try getting Jesus to testify against himself, it was wrong for the high priest's officer to slap a prisoner, such as Jesus was. John has been describing a private, informal interrogation, not a trial. The Sanhedrin aren't present. No charges are laid. No witnesses testify. No verdict is delivered. For John, Jesus was on trial during the whole of his ministry, as exemplified by the Jews' twice trying to stone him after disputes with him (8:59; 10:31; 11:8). And for John this sustained trial reached a Sanhedric verdict back in 11:45–53, 57. From John's standpoint, then, and in contrast with the other Gospels, only the trial before the Roman governor, Pontius Pilate, remains. Thus we have had here a mere interrogation by the high priest, but an interrogation that highlights the verbal ministry of the Word.

18:24: Therefore Annas had sent him [Jesus], *tied up, to Caiaphas the high priest.* In 18:13–14 John identified Annas as the father-in-law of Caiaphas. That mention of Caiaphas then led John to fast forward to Caiaphas's interrogation of Jesus, during which Peter denied Jesus for the first time (18:15–23). Now John remembers that he didn't tell about Jesus' transfer from Annas to Caiaphas. So the present verse makes up for that omission; and "Therefore" means, "You readers can conclude from Caiaphas the high priest's interrogation of Jesus that Annas had sent him to Caiaphas." But why did John even mention the taking of Jesus to Annas first? We're told nothing about what happened there. An insignificant historical detail? Or perhaps John implies that Annas didn't know what to do with Jesus, had no authority over him, and therefore sent him to Caiaphas, who likewise—though he was the high priest that year—couldn't manage any better than an interrogation that backfired when Jesus took charge. Reappearing in 18:24 is the irony that Jesus is tied up despite his volunteering to be arrested and his determination to lay down his life at his own initiative (compare 18:12).

18:25–27: And Simon Peter was standing and warming himself. This reminder harks back to 18:18. **Therefore they** [the slaves and officers with whom he was standing and warming himself according to 18:18] **said to him, "You too** [in addition to the disciple acquainted with the high priest] **aren't** [one] **of his** [Jesus'] **disciples, are you?"** That one [John's second cold-shouldered reference to Peter (see 18:17 for the first one)] **denied** [that he was] **and said, "I'm not** [another of Jesus' disciples]." **²⁶One of the high priest's slaves, being a relative of him whose ear Peter had cut off, says, "I saw you in the garden with him** [Jesus], **didn't I?"** **²⁷Therefore Peter denied again** [that he was a disciple of Jesus]. **And immediately a rooster crowed.** John narrated Peter's first denial in 18:15–18. By switching back to Peter for Peter's second and third denials, John sandwiches the three denials around Jesus' challenges to the high priest and his officer. The contrast between timorous denials and forceful challenges ennobles Jesus at Peter's richly deserved expense. Peter's body may not have taken flight, but his former heroics certainly have. Notably, his saying twice, "I'm *not*" (18:17, 25), stands in stark contrast with Jesus' saying "I *am*" twice to those who came to arrest him (18:5–6, 8). And it's ironic that in his third denial Peter wilts before a relative of Malchus, whose ear he had cut off in a fleeting show of bravado. John's notation of a rooster's crowing suffices to point up the fulfillment of Jesus' prediction to Peter in 13:38: "Will you lay down your life for me? Amen, amen I tell you, by no means will a rooster crow until you've disowned me three times."

JESUS' WITHSTANDING INTERROGATION BY PILATE IN CONTRAST WITH PILATE'S YIELDING TO THE JEWISH AUTHORITIES
John 18:28–19:16a

18:28: Therefore [because of Caiaphas's inability to make Jesus testify against himself] **they lead Jesus from Caiaphas to the praetorium** [the Roman governor's of-ficial residence]. **And it was early in the morning. And they themselves didn't enter into the praetorium lest they be defiled** [that is, contract ritual impurity in the residence of a Gentile who didn't observe the law of Moses, which included rules for maintaining ritual purity]—**rather,** [that they] **might eat the Passover** [that is, celebrate the Passover Supper]. The Jews will slay their Passover sacrifices the afternoon of this very day, and eat the meat of those sacrifices in the evening. As an individual, Caiaphas fades out of the picture in favor of the Jewish authorities as a collective (the chief priests and the authorities of 18:3). Ironically, they maintain their ritual purity so as to eat sacrificial lambs that portray the lamb of God, Jesus, whom they'll unwittingly slay as the true sacrificial lamb, the one that takes away the world's sin (1:29, 36; 19:31–37; Exodus 12:46; Numbers 9:12).

18:29–30: Therefore Pilate went outside to them and says, "What accusation are you bringing against this man?" **³⁰They answered and said to him, "If this** [man] **hadn't been doing wrong** [the same word that Jesus used in 18:23 to deny that he'd spoken wrongly, but used here for some criminal misdeed], **we wouldn't have given him over to you** [the same verb that has been repeatedly used for Judas Iscariot's giving Jesus over to the Jewish authorities, so that their giving Jesus over to Pilate parallels Judas's betrayal of Jesus to them]. Though "praetorium" in the preceding verse refers to the governor's official residence, John doesn't identify Pilate as the governor. We'll find out why in 19:11–12. Ironically, the Jewish authorities have no accusation to bring against Jesus. Caiaphas's interrogation of him didn't produce one, and in 11:45–53 the decision of the Sanhedrin to kill Jesus didn't rest on any accusation. So this killing will count as a murder, not an execution.

18:31–32: Therefore Pilate said to them, "You take him and judge him according to your law." The Jews said to him, "It's not permitted for us to kill anyone." ³²[This exchange between Pilate and the Jewish authorities took place] **in order that Jesus' word might be fulfilled which he'd spoken by way of indicating what kind of death he was going to die.** The Jewish authorities could only tell Pilate that Jesus must have done something wrong, for otherwise they wouldn't have brought him to Pilate. Pilate is unimpressed. He'd wanted a specific, formal accusation; so he pushes Jesus' case back on them. But since they want it to be a capital case (they'd decided in 11:53 to kill him) they—ironically again—had to confess their incompetence. The Romans appear to have reserved to themselves the authority to impose capital punishment (see 19:10). (If so, the martyrdom of Stephen in Acts 6:8–8:3 counts as a lynching.) And in any case, the Jews' own law said, "You shall not kill," in the sense of prohibiting murder (Exodus 20:13; Deuteronomy 5:17). And absent a capital accusation and a capital verdict, their killing of Jesus will be exactly that—murder, a violation of God's law as well as Roman law. The Jewish authorities succeeded in avoiding ritual impurity, but they won't succeed in avoiding moral impurity by getting Pilate to let them kill Jesus. For he'll give Jesus over *to them* for the murder (19:16). Ironically yet again, despite their Jewishness they'll use a Roman method—crucifixion—to murder Jesus (19:16 again), just as Jesus indicated when he talked about the Jews' lifting him up (on a cross), as opposed to their trying to knock him down by stoning him to death (see 3:14; 8:28; 12:34 in contrast with 8:59; 10:31–33; 11:8). Their conversational exchange with Pilate will lead to the fulfillment of this word of Jesus. In fact, it's his word that *determines* not only the murder as such but also the way they'll murder him ("*in order that* the word of Jesus might be fulfilled"). By means of his word Jesus the Word is in charge—as usual. (Note: stoning would *draw* some blood but wouldn't *shed* blood, as Jesus' crucifixion will do [19:34], and therefore would negate his references in 6:52–58 to drinking his blood.)

18:33–34: Therefore Pilate went back into the praetorium and summoned Jesus and said to him, "Are *you* the king of the Jews?" ³⁴**Jesus answered, "Are *you* saying this on your own, or have *others* told you about me?"** The Jewish authorities haven't called Jesus their king, of course. They wouldn't have brought Jesus to Pilate if they'd regarded Jesus as their king. Nor have they accused Jesus before Pilate of claiming to be the king of the Jews. So the phrase is Pilate's alone, and John shows no interest in telling why Pilate thought to ask Jesus, "Are you the king of the Jews?" John cites its use here in private conversation with Jesus only (but importantly) to set the stage for Jesus' following explanation of his kingship, and also for Pilate's using the phrase to shame the Jewish authorities by repeatedly calling their king the man they're trying to get him to murder. This shaming of them highlights their guilt and provides a counterpoint that highlights in turn John's portrayal of the crucifixion as Jesus' glorification. "Of the Jews" may refer to the Jewish people in general, but in this context it points especially to their authorities, who've brought Jesus to Pilate. As he did with Caiaphas, Jesus ignores Pilate's question and fires back with a question of his own. Again he interrogates the interrogator. In a putdown, Jesus' emphatic "you" counters Pilate's emphatic "you," and Jesus' question suggests that Pilate doesn't know what he's talking about or that he's depending on the report of others whose reliability he hasn't confirmed.

18:35: Pilate answered, "I'm not a Jew, am I? Your nation and the chief priests gave you over to me. What have you done?" Thrown off balance by Jesus' having taken charge, Pilate asks, "I'm not a Jew, am I?" to imply that he himself wouldn't have come up with the possibility that Jesus was the Jews' king. But of course he had come up with that possibility—sarcastically, to be sure; yet he had. And the statement that Jesus' own nation and the chief priests had given him over to Pilate implies *they* had told him Jesus was their king, or claimed to be such. But of course they hadn't—not according to anything in John's text. Having tried his best to wriggle out of Jesus' question, Pilate abandons his own question

whether Jesus is the Jews' king and resorts to asking him what he has done to have caused his nation and the chief priests to give him over to Pilate. But of course the nation hasn't given Jesus over to Pilate. Only the chief priests have done so in an ill-considered and ill-fated attempt to save the nation from a messianic revolt that the Romans would crush mercilessly (11:47–53).

Again Jesus refuses to answer Pilate's question and shifts the topic back to kingship. **18:36: Jesus answered, "My kingdom isn't from this world. If my kingdom were from this world, my officers would have been fighting lest I be given over** [by Judas] **to the Jews. But now my kingdom isn't from here."** By saying "my kingdom" Jesus implies he's a king, though not necessarily "of the Jews"; and as one with God his Father, Jesus claims "the kingdom of God" (3:3, 5) as his own. Here "kingdom" means kingship, rulership. Jesus is denying that his kingly authority derives from human beings ("this world"). It doesn't derive from their support. Otherwise the Eleven would have been fighting to prevent his betrayal to the Jewish authorities. (He *stopped* Peter's brief swordplay, in fact.) Strikingly, Jesus calls the Eleven his "officers," that is, those who serve in an official capacity. The term suits the concept of kingship, so that just as the chief priests and the Pharisees have officers (7:32, 45–46; 18:3, 12, 18, 22; 19:6), so also does Jesus.

18:37–38a: Therefore Pilate said to him, "So then you're a king." Jesus answered, "*You* are saying that I'm a king. I was born for this purpose, and I came into the world for this purpose, that I should testify to the truth. Everyone who's from the truth hears my voice." ³⁸ᵃ**Pilate says to him, "What is truth?"** Pilate draws the correct conclusion that Jesus' phrases "my kingdom" and "my officers" imply that Jesus is a king. But missing is the earlier phrase, "of the Jews." Though Pilate will soon revive that phrase so as to mock the Jewish authorities, here in private conversation with Jesus his omission of the phrase shows at least a recognition that Jesus isn't the political threat to Rome which "the king *of the Jews*" connotes. Jesus then treats Pilate's statement as a testimony on his behalf: "*You* are saying that I'm a king." To Pilate's testimony Jesus adds his own: that he (Jesus) was born and came into the world to testify to the truth, which he said elsewhere he himself *is*, so that throughout this Gospel he has testified about himself as the truth of God incarnate. Since testimony relates to truth, Pilate's testimony leads Jesus to speak about his own testimony to the truth, a testimony for which he was born into the world and came into the world. The double occurrence of "into the world" emphasizes Jesus' heavenly origin. Since in his own person he is the truth of God (14:6), in testifying to the truth he has testified to himself throughout this Gospel. Since the truth is Jesus himself, to be *from* the truth is to have your *origin* in him (compare being born "from above" in 3:3, 7). Furthermore, origin determines nature: "What has been born out of the flesh is flesh, and what has been born out of the Spirit is Spirit" (3:6). So just as "it takes a thief to recognize a thief" (like understands like), it takes a person whose truthful nature has been determined by origin in the truth to recognize the truth. Such a person naturally hears Jesus' voice, just as the sheep that belong to him hear it, that is, recognize in it the voice of their good shepherd and follow him (10:3–5, 27). Sadly, Pilate's question, "What is truth?" shows that he hasn't recognized in Jesus' voice the voice of the truth. He's not one of Jesus' sheep. He's not from the truth.

18:38b–40: And on saying this, he [Pilate] went back outside to the Jews [again their authorities] and says to them, "I find in him [Jesus] no ground for an accusation [as implied already in 18:37 by Pilate's dropping 'of the Jews,' so that Jesus' kingship doesn't conflict with Caesar's ruling the Jews]. **³⁹But you have a custom that I release to you one** [prisoner] **during the Passover. Therefore do you want me to release to you the king of the Jews?"** Here Pilate reverts to the politically loaded phrase so as to ridicule the Jewish authorities by calling the man they want him to do away with their king. They react predictably: **⁴⁰Therefore they shouted back, saying, "Not this one** [Jesus], **but Barabbas." But Barabbas was a revolutionary.** Their shouting displays anger at Pilate's ridiculing them. The word translated "revolutionary" comes close to the meaning of "terrorist" and is the same as the word for "bandit" in 10:1, 8, where it stands opposite "shepherd." In calling for the release of a revolutionary bandit, then, the Jewish authorities show that they haven't recognized the voice of the good shepherd any more than Pilate did. They aren't Jesus' sheep either. Ironically, they choose a revolutionary of the kind they feared *Jesus* would be and therefore decided to have him killed (11:45–53). ("Barabbas" means "son of the father" in the Aramaic language, so that some have thought of a contrast between Barabbas as the merely human son of a merely human father and Jesus as the divine Son of God the Father. But John doesn't translate "Barabbas" as, by contrast, he does translate the Aramaic term "Gabbatha" in 19:13; and he could hardly expect his Greek-speaking audience to pick up a wordplay in a language unknown to all or most of them.)

19:1: Therefore Pilate then took Jesus and had him flogged. John doesn't mention the release of Barabbas, as the other Gospels do, because in the following verses Pilate will continue trying to persuade the Jews that he should release Jesus instead. And by the time those attempts fail, Barabbas is long forgotten. Combined with the preceding attempt, on the other hand, the further attempts will serve to exacerbate the Jews' guilt. But why does Pilate have Jesus flogged—that is, severely whipped—even though he found in Jesus no ground for an accusation? "Therefore" supplies the answer: the Jewish authorities' shouting for the release of Barabbas rather than Jesus provoked Pilate to add physical mockery to the verbal mockery of calling Jesus their king. He's using Jesus to mock *them*, not Jesus. John joins in the mockery by portraying them as unwittingly about to initiate Jesus' glorification by lifting him up on a cross. At the same time, blame accrues to the Jewish authorities for provoking Pilate into having Jesus flogged (compare 19:11).

19:2–3: And the soldiers, having braided a crown [made] **out of thorns, put** [it] **on his head and clothed him with a purple robe ³and were coming to him and saying, "Rejoice, king of the Jews!" and were giving him slaps.** Pilate has mocked the Jewish authorities by calling Jesus their king and having him flogged as such. Now the soldiers join in Pilate's mockery of those authorities by subjecting Jesus to a game of mock king. The game consisted in a mock coronation, a mock investiture, and a mock acclamation. The thorns probably pointed outward for the most part to imitate the radiate crown that emperors were often portrayed as wearing. The point lies in the shame of mockery more than in the pain caused by sharp thorns. The greeting, "Rejoice!" is roughly equivalent to "Good day" or "Have a nice day." Ironically and unbeknown to the soldiers, it *will* be a good and nice day for Jesus, because God his Father will shortly turn his crucifixion into a glorification, and thus a day of rejoicing indeed. The soldiers echo Pilate's "king of the Jews," and their slapping Jesus recollects the slapping of Jesus by an officer of Caiaphas (18:22).

19:4–5: And Pilate went back outside and says to them [the Jewish authorities], **"Look, I'm bringing him outside to you in order that you may know that I find in him no ground for an accusation." ⁵Therefore Jesus came outside wearing the thorny crown and the purple robe. And he** [Pilate] **says to them, "Behold, the man!"** Pilate says he's bringing Jesus outside (instead of having him led away for execution) to show the Jewish authorities that he (Pilate) finds no lawful reason to do away with Jesus. Pilate's finding him innocent a second time heaps further guilt on those authorities. But instead of writing that Jesus was *brought* outside, John writes that Jesus *"came"* outside. This shift in vocabulary may suggest—again—Jesus' voluntariness (10:17–18; 18:4–11). And the thorny crown and purple robe with which he appears further Pilate's derision of the Jewish authorities. He isn't trying to elicit their sympathy for Jesus. As before—and later in 19:20–22 too—he's using Jesus, whom he has called their king, to mock them. In effect he's saying, "I've declared him your king. The soldiers have crowned him, robed him, and hailed him as your king. Some king you have!" The thorny crown and purple robe were enough to portray Jesus as a mock king. So now Pilate refers to Jesus as "the man," an echo of Pilate's question in 18:29: "What accusation are you bringing against this man?" Why the switch from "king" back to "man"? Well, "man" means "human being" and therefore—at the level of John's text—prepares for a contrast with "God's Son" in 19:7. Jesus is a human being, of course; but readers of this Gospel have long since learned that he's much more: he's also the one-and-only Son of God, God in human flesh (1:14, 18). By calling Jesus "the man," Pilate was saying *less* than a mouthful.

19:6–7: When therefore the chief priests and the officers saw him, they shouted, saying, "Crucify [him]!

Crucify [him]!" **Pilate tells them, "*You* take him and crucify** [him], **for I find in him no basis for an accusation."** [7]**The Jews** [= the chief priests and their officers] **answered him, "We have a law; and according to the law he ought to die, because he made himself** [that is, claimed to be] **God's Son."** Pilate's derision of the Jewish authorities incites their anger again. So they shout for Jesus' crucifixion, a Roman rather than Jewish form of punishment and an advance on the generic verb "kill" in 5:18; 7:1, 19–20, 25; 8:37, 40; 11:53; 18:31. Since Jesus predicted his lifting up, as crucifixion will do for him, by shouting for his crucifixion the Jewish authorities are unwittingly helping fulfill his word and bringing about his glorificaiton. It determines the events that are unfolding. Their shouting not once but twice for Jesus' crucifixion adds yet again to their guilt, as does Pilate's telling them to take Jesus and crucify him. Is he giving them permission to crucify Jesus, or is he mockingly reminding them of their own admission that they're not permitted to kill anybody (18:31)? Probably this latter, though he will later let them crucify Jesus (19:16–18). The reason Pilate gives for this mockery of them—that he finds in Jesus no ground for an accusation—marks Pilate's third pronouncement of Jesus' innocence and once again exacerbates the Jewish authorities' guilt. Finally they appeal to a law, their law—probably Leviticus 24:16 in particular: "the person who blasphemes the name of the Lord shall surely be put to death." Jesus had claimed to be God's Son (5:18; 10:29–30), and the Jewish authorities considered his claim blasphemous and therefore him a blasphemer worthy of death. Being a pagan, of course, Pilate cared nothing about the Jews' religious law. According to pagan mythology, however, the gods sometimes masqueraded in human guise among human beings (compare the Lystrans' thinking Barnabas and Paul were the gods Zeus and Hermes, respectively, in Acts 14:8–18). So Pilate takes "God's Son" to mean, not God's one-and-only Son, but "a son of a god," some sort of a divine being who looks human, or is a combination of deity and humanity, and who'd be dangerous to mistreat, as Jesus has already been mistreated. The Jewish authorities' reference to Jesus' claim to be God's Son will make it unnecessary for John to cite the centurion's declaration, "Truly this human being was God's Son" (Mark 15:39), at the site of Jesus' crucifixion.

19:8–11: Therefore when Pilate heard this word he was frightened, rather. "Rather" indicates that up to this point he hadn't suffered any fear. [9]**And he entered into the praetorium again and says to Jesus** [we're left to infer that Jesus went back inside with Pilate], **"Where are you from?"** You said your *kingship* isn't from here, from this world. So where are *you* from? **But Jesus didn't give him an answer.** The nonanswer sets up for the following. [10]**Therefore Pilate says to him, "You're not speaking to me!"** Or it could be translated as a question: "You're not speaking to me, are you?" In either translation, "to me" gets the emphasis, for Pilate appeals to his authority. **"You know, don't you, that I have authority to release you and have authority to crucify you** [that is, have you

crucified]?" [11]**Jesus answered him, "You wouldn't have one bit of authority** [to exercise] **against me unless it was given to you from above. On this account the one who gave me over to you has a greater sin** [than you have]." Who has given Jesus over to Pilate? The singular, "the one who gave me over," might appear to point to Judas Iscariot. But he gave Jesus over to the Jewish authorities, not to Pilate. They're the ones who've given him over to Pilate. Apparently, then, the singular points in particular to Caiaphas, who acted on his own as the high priest that year. In John the Sanhedrin weren't with him when he interrogated Jesus. So he didn't act on their authority, much less on any authority given him by God above, as Jesus says Pilate is doing. Hence, the greater guilt of Caiaphas as compared with Pilate. "Not one bit of authority" contrasts with Pilate's twofold claim to authority: the authority to release Jesus and the authority to crucify him. The only authority Pilate has, to the extent he has any, derives from Jesus' Father in heaven, not from Caesar in Rome. Now we know why John didn't identify Pilate in 18:28–29 as a Roman governor. Roman authority doesn't count. Pilate's earlier question, "What is truth?" exposed him as not being from the truth and consequently as not recognizing it in Jesus, or Jesus *as* the Truth. So Jesus finds it useless to tell him where he, Jesus, is from. After all, he has already told him where his kingship is from; and for Pilate to have been told Jesus is from heaven would have only added to his fear of further mistreating a son of a god, whereas Jesus is determined to lay down his life.

19:12: For this reason Pilate was seeking to release him. But the Jews shouted, saying, "If you release this [man], **you're not a friend of the Caesar. Everyone making himself the king** [compare 12:12–15] **speaks against the Caesar."** "For this reason" makes better sense than the alternative translation, "From then on," because "For this reason" carries forward the emphasis on Pilate's fear that Jesus may be a divine being masquerading as a human being. Though now convinced of Jesus' innocence and bent on mocking the Jewish authorities, Pilate has been more or less content to let the Jewish authorities have their way. But now he positively seeks to release Jesus. The authorities' shouting yet again in reaction against Pilate's seeking to release Jesus adds to their guilt. Furthermore, they speak falsely. Jesus referred to his kingship in conversation with Pilate. But the Jewish authorities weren't privy to that conversation, and—more importantly—in it *Pilate* had called Jesus a king and Jesus had said his kingship was from above (18:33–37). So Jesus hadn't claimed it for himself. It had come to him, he said, from God his Father in heaven. Both ironically and unwittingly, then, the Jewish authorities turn Pilate's derisive designation of Jesus as their king into Jesus' making himself out to be such.

For Pilate it's only a possibility that Jesus is a son of a god. But it's a certainty what Caesar will do to Pilate if Pilate releases a reputedly rival king. Not a happy prospect for Pilate! Enter self-preservation and political realism. *19:13:* **Therefore Pilate, on hearing these words, brought Jesus outside to a place called "Stone Pavement," but in Aramaic "Gabbatha"; and he sat on a judgment platform.** Pilate hadn't recognized the truth in Jesus' words. Now he heeds the words of Jesus' enemies. A judgment platform was a platform on which a judge sat to hear judicial cases. But who sat on this one? Pilate, if we understand John to mean that "he [Pilate] sat"—but Jesus, if we understand John to mean that "he [Jesus] sat" or that "he [Pilate] seated [Jesus] on the judgment platform." Or John may want us to understand his text in both ways: superficially Pilate took the position of judge, but fundamentally and unwittingly he ceded judgment to Jesus in that God the Father "has given all judgment to the Son" (5:22). And if Pilate has Jesus sit on the judgment platform, Pilate continues using Jesus to ridicule the Jewish authorities even as he (Pilate) starts yielding to their shouts. In other words, Pilate's seating of Jesus amounts to telling them, "Your king (as I've designated him) is your judge." Ordinarily, of course, the accused stood below the platform.

19:14–16a: **And it was the preparation of the Passover** [that is, the day when they slaughtered and roasted the Passover lambs in preparation for eating the Passover Supper that evening]. **It was about the sixth hour** [that is, approximately 6:00 A.M. (see the comments on 1:39 against taking the sixth hour as noon)]. **And he** [Pilate] **says to the Jews, "Look, your king!"** [15]**Therefore those** [Jewish authorities] **shouted, "Take** [him] **away! Take** [him] **away! Crucify him!" Pilate says to them, "Shall I crucify your king?" The chief priests answered, "We have no king except Caesar."** [16]**Then, therefore, he** [Pilate] **gave him** [Jesus] **over to them** [the Jewish authorities, in particular the chief priests] **in order that he might be crucified.** John's noting the preparation of the Passover calls to attention that Jesus' crucifixion, for which the Jewish authorities are about to shout, will count as a slaying of God's lamb, Jesus, toward whose sacrifice to take away the world's sin the lambs to be sacrificed at the same time as Jesus' crucifixion pointed, and toward whose sacrifice the annually sacrificed lambs had pointed from time immemorial. "Look, your king!" shows that Pilate doesn't let up on ridiculing the Jewish authorities, and that John doesn't let up on magnifying the guilt of their murdering Jesus despite Pilate's seeking to release him. The doubling of their shout, "Take [him] away!" contributes to that magnification. The object of this taking away is left unexpressed. We have to supply it mentally from the context and from the parallel with "Crucify him!" where "him" *is* expressed. But the omission of "him" with "take away" (twice) may suggest that in the taking away of Jesus, *he* is taking away the sin of the world. That is, the Jewish authorities ironically and unwittingly shout for, and thereby contribute to, the sacrifice of the very lamb of God whom they oppose (compare Caiaphas's unwitting prophecy of Jesus' sacrificial death in 11:49–52). And "Crucify him!" defines the taking away of Jesus as an exaltation, a lifting up on the first rung of the ladder back to his heavenly glory.

(The verb "take away" ordinarily means to pick *up* and remove, as in "pick up and carry your mat" [5:8].)

For one last time Pilate seeks to release Jesus, but more weakly than before. He only asks a question, "Shall I crucify your king?" The question contains Pilate's usual barb of ridicule, "your king." The answer, "We have no king except Caesar," misquotes—or negates—a Jewish Passover hymn, which reads in part, "We have no king except you [O God]." And by declaring their allegiance to Caesar the chief priests rule themselves out from membership in God's kingdom. Pilate gives Jesus over to them for crucifixion without passing a verdict of guilty, without hearing a capital charge, and without taking testimony on such a charge. Nor in John have the Jewish authorities tried Jesus or passed a capital sentence on him. In having him crucified, then, they'll commit murder—despite their own admission in 18:31 that it's unlawful to do so.

JESUS' FINISHING HIS SIGNS, WORKS, AND WORDS AND THE START OF HIS GLORIFICATION
John 19:16b–30

19:16b–18: **Therefore they** [the Jewish authorities or, in accordance with 19:23, the soldiers who acted under their orders] **took Jesus along;** [17]**and carrying the cross by himself, he went out to the so-called "Skull's Place," which in Aramaic is called "Golgotha,"** [18]**where they crucified him, and with him two others,** [one] **on one side and** [the other] **on the other side, and Jesus in the middle.** "They *took* Jesus along" but "he *went* out." John keeps reminding us of Jesus' voluntariness. Carrying a cross means carrying the crossbar, not the vertical stake (a permanent fixture) as well. "By himself" dismisses Simon of Cyrene's carrying the cross for him (mentioned in the other Gospels), highlights again the nobility of Jesus in laying down his life on his own initiative, and probably rules out a developing heretical view that Simon of Cyrene not only carried Jesus' cross but also, instead of Jesus, died on it (compare the introduction to 1 John). Golgotha may mean Skull's Place not because of a skull-like shape or the finding of a skull there once upon a time, as often proposed, but because of its use as a place for counting heads, a polling place; for the Semitic word was used for living human heads, not for dried out skulls, and occurred often in connection with counting.

The crucifixion of Jesus finally fulfills his prediction that he would die by being lifted up. And in having him crucified, the Jewish authorities ironically and unwittingly obey his command to them in 2:19, "Disassemble this temple," which John interpreted in terms of "the temple [consisting] of his body" (2:21). Since the crucifixion of Jesus counts as disassembling the temple of his body, the rending of the veil in the temple building will go missing in John when Jesus dies. John doesn't call the two men crucified with Jesus "bandits/revolutionaries/terrorists," the word that Mark 15:27 and Matthew 27:38 use for them but that John 18:40 used for Barabbas, or "evildoers/criminals," the word that Luke 23:33 uses for the two men crucified with Jesus. For John to have used either one of these other two words would have spoiled his portrayal of Jesus' crucifixion as the start of Jesus' glorification. Instead, after writing that the two flanked Jesus (so also the other Gospels), John adds that Jesus was "in the middle." This emphasis on Jesus' central, prominent position enhances the portrayal of a glorification.

19:19–22: And Pilate also wrote a notice and put [it] **on the cross. And it was written, "Jesus the Nazarene, the king of the Jews."** Where the other Gospels have the two crucified with Jesus and the onlookers, including the Jewish authorities, mock Jesus, here in John Pilate just won't stop poking fun at the Jewish authorities. They suffer shame at the very moment Jesus' glorification is initiated by their lifting him up on a cross. [20]**Therefore many of the Jews read this notice, because the place where Jesus was crucified was near the city** [Jerusalem]. **And it** [the notice] **was written in Aramaic, Latin, Greek.** [21]**Therefore the chief priests of the Jews were saying to Pilate, "Don't write, 'The king of the Jews'—rather, 'That** [man] *said,* **"I'm king of the Jews."'"** [22]**Pilate answered, "What I've written I've written."** For the first (and only) time Pilate demonstrates knowledge that Jesus came from Nazareth. "The Nazarene" harks back to the account of Jesus' arrest (18:5, 7); and since he's sacrificing himself as the lamb of God that takes away the world's sin, "the Nazarene" shows that "something good" can indeed "be from Nazareth" (1:45–46). For some time John has been using "the Jews" to mean the Jewish authorities. But now *many* of the Jews" and "the chief priests *of* the Jews" expand the meaning of "the Jews" to include the general populace. Only John indicates that the notice was written in Aramaic (the Semitic language most spoken by the Jews), Latin (the language of their Roman overlords), and Greek (the language generally spoken by people in addition to their native language). This indication promotes the universal value of Jesus' death as "the lamb of God that takes away the *world's* sin" (1:29). "*Everyone* believing in him" will have eternal life (3:16). We'd expect "and" to introduce "Greek," the last in the list of languages. But it doesn't, as though to say that the list could go on and on, that the value of Jesus' death applies as well to each and every other linguistic group in the world (compare the comments on 5:1–3a, 5–9a). The chief priests feel the sting of Pilate's notice designating Jesus their king, but Pilate lets it stand. He refuses their request to change it into a self-claim by Jesus, whom they've contemptuously called "that one [over there]." In their request they ironically overlook that Jesus would be hanging right under such a revised notice, not at some distance. And of course John's Jesus never did claim to be the Jews' king. Though Pilate continues to mock the Jewish authorities, John omits the mocking of Jesus as he hangs on the cross. That too would spoil the portrayal of his crucifixion as a glorification. Nor does John mention the darkness that enveloped the scene according to the other Gospels. Here, the light of the world is shining from a cross. Many commentators see here a portrayal of Jesus as truly the king of the Jews, as enthroned on his cross, and as flanked by a royal retinue. But though John portrays him as "the king of Israel" (1:49; 12:13–15), he never portrays him as the king of the Jews, that is, of the Jewish authorities. This designation is only Pilate's jibe at them. They don't belong to Jesus' kingdom.

19:23–25a: Therefore the soldiers, when they crucified Jesus, took his garments and made [out of them] **four parts, a part for each soldier; and** [they took] **the tunic** [a robe worn next to the skin as distinct from an outer robe]. **But the tunic was seamless, woven from the top throughout the whole.** [24]**Therefore they said to each other, "Let's not divide it** [by tearing it into four pieces]; **rather, let's cast a lot** [like throwing dice or flipping a coin] **concerning it** [to see] **whose it will be."** [They did these things] **in order that the Scripture might be fulfilled that says, "They divided my garments among themselves and cast a lot for my clothing** [Psalm 22:18]." [25a]**On the one hand, therefore, the soldiers did these things.** Since Pilate had delivered Jesus to the Jewish authorities for crucifixion (19:16), the soldiers must be acting under the command of those Jews. Only John tells us that the soldiers, by implication four in number, divided Jesus' outer clothing into four parts, a share for each. Since the number four can indicate universality, as in "the four corners of the earth" (see John's book of Revelation 7:1; 20:8), this detail may symbolize the universal value of the lamb of God's self-sacrifice, just as the title's multiplicity of languages does. Since the soldiers decided not to tear Jesus' tunic into four parts, the division of his outer clothing must have entailed tearing. John is also the only one of the Gospel writers to mention the tunic, its seamlessness, the preservation of its wholeness, and the apparent limitation of the soldiers' lot-casting to the tunic. So just as the fourfold division of Jesus' outer clothing may symbolize the universality of the gospel (it's for all the world), the preservation of the seamless tunic's wholeness may symbolize the unity of all believers with one another, with Christ, and with God the Father (compare Jesus' prayer in 17:11, "Keep them . . . in order that they may be one just as we [are one]," and 17:21, "that they may all be one . . . that they too may be in us" [see also the comments on 21:11]). Without the soldiers' knowing so, what's written in the Scripture determined their actions. Everything is proceeding according to divine plan. No accidents are happening. God and his Son are in control. The division of Jesus' outer clothing has fulfilled the first line of Psalm 22:18 ("They divided . . ."). The lot-casting for Jesus' tunic has fulfilled the second line of Psalm 22:18 ("they cast a lot . . ."). The soldiers' having done "these things" because of the Scripture indicates not only that they carried out their decision not to divide the tunic. It also reemphasizes that Scripture determined their division of Jesus' outer clothing and their lot-casting for the tunic. They're acting under divine orders, not under the command of the Jewish authorities.

19:25b–27: Standing alongside Jesus' cross, on the other hand, were his mother and his mother's sis-

ter, Mary the [wife] of Clopas and Mary Magdalene. [26]Therefore on seeing [his] **mother and the disciple whom he loved standing alongside** [her], **he says to** [his] **mother, "Woman, look—your son!"** [27]**Then he says to the disciple, "Look—your mother!" And from that hour the disciple took her into his own home.** John locates the women and the beloved disciple close to Jesus' cross so that Jesus may address his mother and the beloved disciple. Conceivably, Mary the wife of Clopas could be the sister of Jesus' mother. But in that case the sisters would have the same name. It's likely, then, that John is listing two pairs of women, an unnamed pair ("his mother and his mother's sister") and a named pair ("Mary the [wife] of Clopas and Mary Magdalene"). He doesn't mention the name of Jesus' mother here any more than he did in 2:1–4. Her anonymity puts her in the shadows, and again as in 2:1–4 Jesus disengages himself from her with the address "Woman" to indicate that in his statement to her he's voluntarily carrying out the will of God his Father, not her will. "Woman" isn't disrespectful, but neither is it familial, or even familiar. The committal of her to the beloved disciple and his immediately taking her to his own home complete the disengagement and imply her husband Joseph's death. Jesus is heading home to his Father above.

19:28–30: **After this, Jesus, knowing that all were now finished, says in order that the Scripture might be completed, "I thirst."** [29]**A jug of vinegary wine was lying** [there]. **On wrapping a sponge full of the vinegary wine around hyssop, therefore, they brought** [it] **to his mouth.** [30]**Therefore when he'd taken the vinegary wine, Jesus said, "They're finished!" And bowing** [his] **head, he gave over the Spirit.** John highlights Jesus' omniscience. But what in particular were the "all" that Jesus knew were now finished? ("All" is plural as well as neuter, so that the singular translation "*everything* was now finished" is simply wrong.) Well, throughout this Gospel emphasis has fallen on Jesus' "signs," "works," and "words." It is these that he knows to be finished, although the fact that his death and resurrection are shortly to occur probably means that Jesus is anticipating the imminent accomplishment of those crowning signs and works (compare 20:30–31, which mentions "these signs" after the narration of Jesus' death and resurrection). He often speaks from a later standpoint (as repeatedly in chapter 17, for example).

Since clauses beginning with "in order that" usually depend on a preceding statement, "in order that the Scripture might be completed" could go with the preceding: "all were now finished in order that the Scripture might be completed." But since "I thirst" looks like a reference to Psalm 69:21 (compare Psalms 22:15; 63:1), "in order that the Scripture might be fulfilled" probably tells us Jesus' purpose in saying, "I thirst." Those exact words don't appear in any of those psalms, but Jesus' statement easily paraphrases their thought (compare 1:31 for another instance where "in order that . . ." goes with the following rather than the preceding). So the Scripture determines Jesus' knowledgeable action just

as the Scripture both has determined and will determine the soldiers' actions without their knowing it did (19:23–24, 31–37). Ironically but blessedly, Jesus thirsted so that believers in him might never thirst again (4:14; 7:37–38). "Finished" and "completed" are much closer in meaning than appears in English translation, perhaps even identical in meaning given John's fondness for synonyms. The variation may serve only to distinguish—while at the same time drawing a parallel between—the two accomplishments: of Jesus' signs, works, and words on the one hand and of the Scripture on the other hand. Vinegary wine slakes thirst better than fine wine does. Soldiers wouldn't have had fine wine available anyway. The wrapping of a sponge soaked with vinegary wine around a branch of hyssop points to the crucifixion as a sacrifice of God's Passover lamb, for it was with hyssop that at the exodus from Egypt the Israelites sprinkled the blood of their Passover lambs on the lintels and sideposts of their doors, so that the Lord passed over their homes without slaying their firstborn as he did slay those of the Egyptians (see Exodus 12:1–36, especially 12:22, and compare Psalm 51:7). Jesus' taking the vinegary wine fulfills Psalm 69:21: "And in my thirst they gave me vinegary wine to drink" (compare Jesus' determination to drink the cup that the Father had given him [18:11]).

By itself the final outcry of Jesus is ambiguous. But it should be translated "*They* are finished!" rather than "*It* is finished!" because it echoes the statement in 19:28 that Jesus knew "*all* were now finished." Again the reference is to all his signs, works, and words—done and said to take away the world's sin. The anguished outcry, "My God, my God, why have you abandoned me?" (that is, abandoned me to die [Mark 15:34; Matthew 27:46]), is missing from John. So far as John's portrayal of Jesus is concerned, how could the Word who *is* God be forsaken *by* God? Also missing is Jesus' committing his spirit to God the Father (Luke 23:46), breathing his last (that is, expiring [Mark 15:37; Luke 23:46]), and letting his spirit go (Matthew 27:50). In their stead John puts Jesus' bowing his head and giving over the Spirit. Jesus dies of his own accord, deliberately (10:17–18); and in doing so he gives over the Spirit. Since his glorification has started in his being lifted up on a cross, the giving of the Holy Spirit to the disciples has also started (see 7:39 for the giving of the Spirit upon Jesus' glorification, but not before, and 12:23, 28, 32–33; 13:31 for the crucifixion as glorification). Jesus will complete the giving of the Spirit to his disciples when his glorification has reached completion through his resurrection and return to the Father (see 20:22 with 20:17–18).

THE GLORIFICATION OF JESUS IN HIS BURIAL
John 19:31–42

19:31: **Since it was the preparation, therefore, the Jews—lest the bodies remain on the cross during the Sabbath, for the day** [consisting] **of that Sabbath was great—**[the Jews] **asked Pilate that they** [the soldiers] **might break their legs** [the legs of the crucified] **and**

[that their bodies, that is, corpses] **be taken away.** Since they deal with Pilate, "the Jews" are again the Jewish authorities. "The preparation" is again the day on whose afternoon they prepared the Passover supper, to be eaten in the evening. According to Deuteronomy 21:22–23 a corpse was not to hang on a tree overnight (compare Joshua 8:29). And since a Sabbath that coincided with the Passover was especially important (here the Saturday beginning at sundown on Good Friday), the Jewish authorities wanted all the more to avoid defiling it with hanging corpses "accursed by God" (Deuteronomy 21:23 again). As when they didn't enter the praetorium lest they be defiled and not be able to eat the Passover (18:28), the Jewish authorities ironically show greater fear of defilement (this time of their land [Deuteronomy 21:23 yet again]) than fear of having murdered Jesus. And they want the corpses of him and his companions in crucifixion taken away more than they want their sins taken away by the lamb of God. "The cross" is singular, perhaps a collective singular for the three crosses on which Jesus and his companions were hanging. It has been suggested, however, that all their crossbars were affixed to one and the same (living) tree. If so, is John implying that Jesus' companions (remember, John hasn't called them revolutionaries or criminals) stand for Christian believers who, being one with him, share in his exaltation on the cross, in his glorification by means of crucifixion?

19:32–34: On the one hand, therefore, the soldiers came and broke the legs both of the first one and of the other one who'd been crucified with him [Jesus]. [33]**And having come to Jesus, on the other hand, when they saw him already dead, they didn't break his legs.** [34]**Rather, one of the soldiers pierced the side of his rib cage with a spear; and immediately there came out blood and water.** Breaking the legs brought on death by shock for Jesus' two companions, already physically compromised as they were. The nonbreaking of Jesus' legs portrays him again as a Passover sacrifice, for the Mosaic law prohibited breaking any bones of such a sacrifice (Exodus 12:46; Numbers 9:12 [compare Psalm 34:19–20]). Most translations say that a soldier pierced Jesus' "side," but the word refers more specifically to the side of the rib cage as distinct from the abdomen. The blood that came out is the life-blood of God's Passover lamb that takes away the world's sin. It's blood separated from flesh by sacrifice, the blood that a person must drink, so to speak, by believing in Jesus (6:53–56) and the blood that "cleanses us from every sin" (1 John 1:7). The water that came out symbolizes the Holy Spirit, whom Jesus has just given over (19:30), by whom a believer is born from above (3:3–8), and who gives life eternal (6:63; 7:37–39 [see 1 John 5:6–8 for a conjunction of water, blood, and Spirit, though note the different order of mention]). The immediacy with which the blood and water came out ties the atonement and the gift of the Spirit as closely as possible to Jesus' death.

19:35: And the one who saw [the piercing and outflow of blood and water] **has testified** [to this event] **(and his testimony is true, and that one** [the testifier] **knows that he speaks truly) in order that you too may believe.** John uses "that one" instead of "this one," because the intervening clause, "and his testimony is true," has put some distance between "the one who saw" and the one who "knows that he speaks truly." In context only the beloved disciple, similarly spoken of in the third person and left anonymous, seems to qualify as the one who saw and testified about what he saw; and he testifies about it both by speaking and by writing this Gospel (compare 21:24). He emphasizes the truthfulness of his testimony to persuade the Gospel's audience to believe. Belief in the testimony concerning this particular event carries with itself belief in Jesus according to the entirety of John's Gospel.

19:36–37: For these things happened in order that the Scripture might be fulfilled: "Not a bone of him will be broken [Exodus 12:46 (compare Numbers 9:12; Psalm 34:20)]." [37]**And again another Scripture says, "They'll look at the one whom they pierced** [Zechariah 12:10]." The first Scripture relates the exemption of Jesus from leg-breaking to the exemption of Passover lambs from bone-breaking. In Zechariah 12:10, looking leads to repentant mourning and cleansing from sin. Revelation 1:7 cites Zechariah 12:10, as John 19:37 does, but there the looking leads to wailing in despair over coming judgment. Here in John the looking will reach fulfillment when the risen Jesus shows his disciples the scars left by his being pierced (20:20, 27). Naturally, then, "they" who look (the disciples) will differ from "they" who did the piercing (though in John's account only "one" of the soldiers did the actual piercing). For the moment, though, the accent doesn't fall on the looking. It falls on the piercing itself as a fulfillment of Scripture. Yet again the written word of God determines what happens to the Word-made-flesh.

19:38–40: And after these things Joseph from Arimathea, being a disciple of Jesus (but secretly because of fear of the Jews), asked Pilate that he might take away the body [= corpse] **of Jesus. And Pilate permitted** [him to do so]. **Therefore he went and took away his body.** Fear of the Jewish authorities inhibited people in 7:13; 9:22 and will lead the eleven disciples to meet behind locked doors in 20:19. Such fear doesn't rule out discipleship, but John's triple mention of it carries a note of criticism (compare 12:42–43). The solicitous taking of Jesus' body away from the cross balances—and compensates for—the Jewish authorities' angry shout, "Take [him] away! Take [him] away! Crucify him!" (19:15 [see the comments on that verse for the connotation of exaltation]). [39]**And Nicodemus also came, the one who'd originally come to him** [Jesus] **at night.** [He was] **carrying a mixture of myrrh and aloes** [that weighed] **about a hundred** [Roman] **pounds** [= about seventy-two English-American pounds]. [40]**Therefore they took the body of Jesus and bound it up with strips of linen cloth along with the scented powders, just as is the custom for the Jews to bury** [someone]. The reminder of Nicodemus's coming to Jesus "at night" links up with the preceding notation of secrecy in Joseph of Arimathea's discipleship. The partnership of Nicodemus with Joseph in the burial of Jesus implies that Nicodemus too is a disciple (compare Nicodemus's standing up for Jesus in 7:50–51). John has portrayed Jesus' crucifixion as a lifting up, a glorification. Now he portrays Jesus' burial as a further glorification. The glorification consists in the enormous amount of perfumery with which Jesus' body was wrapped. The Jews (here the Jewish people in general) customarily used a mixture of aromatic powders and linen cloth for burials, but a hundred Roman pounds of the powders? Lavish!

19:41–42: And a garden was at the place where he [Jesus] **was crucified, and in the garden a new tomb in which no one had yet been laid.** [42]**So because the tomb was nearby, on account of the Jews' preparation** [for the Passover meal that evening] **they laid Jesus there.** See the comments on 18:1 for the possibility, even likelihood, that John puts the crucifixion, burial, and resurrection of Jesus in the same garden where he volunteered to be arrested, and also that John portrays this garden as a new Eden where by virtue of Jesus' resurrection the cross turns into a tree of eternal life such as the one whose fruit Adam and Eve never ate because of their sin and expulsion from that garden (compare the comments on 19:31). In any case, the ambiance of a garden, the newness of the tomb, and the absence of any prior burial there all contribute yet further to John's portrayal of Jesus' burial as a continuing glorification. (Tombs were normally used for multiple burials, the bones of decayed corpses being collected in boxes so as to clear the shelf for a "fresh" corpse.) John makes the nearness of the tomb Joseph's reason for burying Jesus in it, whereas Matthew 27:60 identifies it as Joseph's and Mark and Luke don't tell why. For the third time John marks the day as the day during which lambs were slaughtered in preparation for the Passover meal to be eaten in the evening (see also 19:14, 31). This repeated synchronizing of Jesus' death with that slaughter puts huge emphasis on Jesus as the lamb of God who takes away the world's sin.

THE SELF-RAISING OF JESUS FROM HIS TOMB TO GOD THE FATHER IN HEAVEN
John 20:1–18

20:1–2: And early on the first [day] **of the week, while it was still dark, Mary Magdalene comes to the tomb and sees the stone taken away from the tomb.** [2]**Therefore she runs and comes to Simon Peter and to the other disciple, whom Jesus loved, and tells them, "They've taken away the Lord out of the tomb, and we don't know where they've laid him!"** Since darkness and light have assumed symbolic significance earlier in this Gospel, John's notation, "While it was dark," suggests that when Mary sees the risen Jesus a while later, he will appear to her as the risen sun, the just-risen light of the world who banishes the darkness of sin and judgment (compare 1:4–5, "In him ['the Word'] was life, and

the life was the light of human beings; and the light is shining in the darkness, and the darkness didn't apprehend it [in the sense of arresting and suppressing it]," and 8:12, "I am the light of the world. The person who follows me will by no means walk around in darkness; rather, he'll have the light of life"; also 12:35–36, 46, and 1 John 2:8, "The darkness is passing away, and the true light is already shining").

Just as the taking of Jesus' body away from the cross balanced and compensated for the Jewish authorities' shout, "Take [him] away! Take [him] away! Crucify him!" (19:15, 38), so also does the taking away of the stone from the tomb's mouth. Without looking into the tomb Mary concludes from the removal of the stone that the Jewish authorities (the probable reference of "they," since those authorities had shouted for Jesus to be taken away for crucifixion) have taken Jesus' body out of the tomb. But this time nobody has taken him away. He has himself taken up his life again (10:17–18, which uses a different verb that lacks the element of "away"). Mary calls Jesus "the Lord." This designation suits his mastery over his enemies and death without her knowing that it does. She also thinks that just as Joseph of Arimathea and Nicodemus had "laid" Jesus in a new, previously unused tomb (19:41–42), the Jewish authorities have "laid" Jesus somewhere unknown to her, Simon Peter, and the beloved disciple. (In John's text there's no indication that other women are present.) Her mistaken dismay, indicated by her running to Simon Peter and to the beloved disciple (apparently one after the other, since John repeats the preposition "to"), will soon turn into excitement (see 20:18). Meanwhile, though, the present tense in "comes," "sees," "runs," "comes," and "says" heightens her dismay. Throughout the rest of this passage, too, note should be taken of the present tense in that it creates an air of excitement as well as of concern.

20:3–9: Therefore Peter and the other disciple went out [from wherever they were] **and were coming to the tomb.** [4]**And the two were running together; and the other disciple ran ahead, faster than Peter, and came first to the tomb.** [5]**And on crouching down, he sees the strips of linen cloth lying** [there]. **He didn't go in, however.** [6]**So Simon Peter, following him, comes too and does go into the tomb and sees the strips of linen cloth lying** [there] [7]**and the face-cloth, which had been on his** [Jesus'] **head, not lying with the strips of linen cloth—rather, rolled up in one place by itself.** [8]**Therefore the other disciple, who'd come first, then went into the tomb too and saw** [the same things he'd seen before] **and believed.** [9]**For they didn't yet know** [in the sense of "understand"] **the Scripture that** [says] **it's necessary for him** [Jesus] **to rise from among the dead.** As in Mary's case, the running of Peter and the beloved disciple shows their dismay; and similarly to her case, their dismay will turn into joy (20:20). To peer into the tomb the beloved disciple had to crouch down, because the opening of such tombs was normally less than three feet high. Both of the disciples see the strips of linen cloth with which Jesus' body had been bound lying inside the tomb—Peter only after entering—and the face-cloth as well. So the legal requirement of at least two witnesses (8:17) has been met. The face-cloth wasn't scattered about like the strips of cloth, but was neatly rolled up and lying in one spot. The account of Jesus' burial didn't mention the face-cloth, but a face-cloth did appear in the account of Jesus' raising Lazarus from the dead (11:44). In fact, there are a number of parallels between the raising of Lazarus and Jesus' resurrection. In both there's a stone-closed tomb. In both the stone is taken away. In both the corpse is bound with strips of cloth. In both a napkin-like cloth covers the corpse's face. In both the risen body gets rid of its strips of cloth and face-cloth. So the raising of Lazarus anticipated Jesus' resurrection. But there are differences too. Because of being four days' old, Lazarus's corpse stank; but because of not being so old and because of an enormous quantity of perfumery, Jesus' corpse did not stink. Lazarus was raised, but Jesus raised himself. Lazarus came out bound up, but Jesus came out unbound. Lazarus was unbound outside his tomb; Jesus unbound himself inside his tomb. Others took away the stone from Lazarus's tomb. Jesus himself, it would appear, pushed aside the stone from his tomb. These differences highlight Jesus' omnipotence as the Word who was God. He didn't need any help.

What did the beloved disciple believe when he saw Jesus' grave wrappings lying in the empty tomb? Not that Jesus had risen from the dead, for John immediately says the beloved disciple and Peter didn't yet understand the Scripture that says Jesus had to rise from the dead. More than that, John says the beloved disciple believed *because* he and Peter didn't yet understand. So the beloved disciple can't have believed *that* Jesus had risen. Rather, he believed Mary Magdalene's report that the Jewish authorities had taken away Jesus' body. Since in that male chauvinistic culture a woman's report was often considered unreliable, John thinks it worth mentioning that the beloved disciple believed Mary's report because he himself saw the tomb empty of Jesus' body. (She'd only inferred its emptiness from seeing the stone taken away from the mouth of the tomb.) John doesn't identify or cite the Scripture that says it was necessary for Jesus to rise from among the dead. So the accent falls on scriptural necessity rather than on a particular passage in the Old Testament. Jesus raises himself of his own accord, but as the *living* Word of God he acts also in accord with the *written* word of God. Since he's one with God, how else could it be? "From among the dead" means "out from among those who've died." They remain dead. He has left their realm.

20:10–13: Therefore the disciples [Peter and the beloved disciple] **went back to themselves** [which means to their places of residence]. **¹¹But Mary was standing at the tomb—outside, weeping. Therefore as she was weeping she crouched down** [to peer] **into the tomb. ¹²And she sees two angels in white** [garments] **sitting where Jesus' body had been lying, one** [angel] **at the head and one at the feet. ¹³And those** [angels] **say to her, "Woman, why are you weeping?" She tells them,**

"They've taken away my Lord, and I don't know where they've laid him [compare 20:2]**."** Because 21:1 will shift the scene to Galilee, here the disciples' places of residence mean the places they were staying in or around Jerusalem during the Passover, not their homes in Galilee, where Peter and the beloved disciple had come from. They went back to their places of temporary residence because in ignorance of Scripture they still didn't believe Jesus had risen from among the dead (20:9). Mary's sorrow over the Jewish authorities' supposed removal of Jesus' body kept her at tombside, however, and issued in weeping, which would have included wailing in Middle Eastern fashion. Because she's standing there, also because she hadn't peered into the tomb before, now she crouches down, peers into it, and sees two angels. Just as the "two others" who were crucified with Jesus formed a kind of honor guard for him (19:18), so here the two angels do honor to the place where his body had lain. Their positions at the head and feet correspond to the positions of those two others on either side of Jesus. Apparently we're meant to infer that the two angels arrived in the tomb after Peter and the beloved disciple had left, for John didn't mention those disciples' seeing any angels. As often in John's book of Revelation, the whiteness of the angels' garments represents victory over sin and death, in this case Jesus' victory. And their seated posture represents the end of Jesus' victorious battle against sin and death. Despite the fact that "angels" means "messengers," these angels don't announce Jesus' resurrection to Mary. Instead, they ask Mary why she's weeping. Even when she tells them why, attaching an intensely personal "my" to "Lord," they don't announce the resurrection of Jesus. They leave that revelation to his initiative. Since they're unrelated to Mary and unacquainted with her, they address Mary with "Woman." This address leaves it for Jesus to address her by her name. As the good shepherd he knows it and will call her by it (10:3).

20:14–18: On saying these things she turned around [literally, "to the things behind"] **and sees Jesus standing, and she didn't know** [= recognize] **that it's Jesus. ¹⁵Jesus says to her, "Woman, why are you weeping? Whom are you seeking?" That one** [Mary], **supposing that he's the gardener, says to him, "Lord, if you've carried him** [somewhere], **tell me where you laid him and I'll take him away." ¹⁶Jesus says to her, "Mary." Having turned, that one** [Mary] **says to him in Aramaic, "Rabboni," which means "Teacher." ¹⁷Jesus tells her, "Don't hold me, for I've not yet ascended to the Father. But go to my brothers and tell them, 'I'm ascending to my Father and your Father, and** [to] **my God and your God.'" ¹⁸Mary Magdalene comes announcing to the disciples, "I've seen the Lord," and** [that] **he'd said these things to her.** "The things behind" are the area of the garden behind Mary when she was peering into the tomb. Jesus' standing shows him alive (compare 20:19, 26; 21:4 and the portrayal of him in Revelation 5:6 as a lamb that's standing even though he bears the scars of a sacrificial death). As one of his sheep Mary will recognize the voice of Jesus the good shepherd when he calls her by name (10:3–4, 16, 27), but for the moment she doesn't recognize him by sight. Since he doesn't call her by name at first but addresses her with "Woman," as the angels did, she still fails to recognize him. His second question, "Whom are you seeking?" shows that he already knows the answer to his first question why she's weeping (which repeated word for word the angels' question). Since she falsely supposes him to be the gardener, she intends the address "Lord" in the weak sense "Sir." But she spoke better than she intended, for the one she addresses is "Lord" in the larger, divine sense in which she used the word when she told Peter and the beloved disciple, "They've taken away the Lord" (20:2). In speaking to Jesus-mistaken-for-the-gardener, Mary doesn't refer again to Jesus as "my Lord." Referring only to "him," she apparently supposes that he has overheard what she said to the angels. And her mistaking him for the gardener makes her think he has carried Jesus' corpse somewhere and, as implied by her offer to take it away, laid it down temporarily to rid the tomb of it. For the second time, ironically, she uses the same verb "laid" that Jesus used for laying down his life of his own accord (10:17–18). So she unknowingly offers to take Jesus' corpse off the hands of Jesus himself!

Finally, Jesus calls Mary by name; and she turns. But according to the preceding verses she had already turned toward Jesus, seen him, and started conversing with him. To respond to his calling her by name, no further turning was necessary. Instead of saying that she turned on hearing her name, then, we should understand John to be *reminding* us that she had turned: "having turned [earlier]." This reminder has the purpose of emphasizing—with a kind of new start in the conversation—Mary's recognition of the good shepherd's voice when he called her by name. Her response, "Rabboni," is a heightened form of "Rabbi," which John translates with "Teacher." Literally, the term means "my great one" and was used as a title of honor for teachers. Here it contributes to John's transforming the account of Jesus' death, burial, and resurrection into the glorification of Jesus.

It's uncertain whether Jesus' command, "Don't hold me," implies that Mary shouldn't grab hold or that she'd already done so and should now let go. In either case, his imminent ascension requires her not to hold him but to go inform the eleven disciples of it. Notice—his *ascension*, not his resurrection. He leaves the resurrection for them to infer and centers on his ascension to indicate the completion of his exaltation, which started with being lifted up on a cross, continued with rising from the dead, and is now about to reach its pinnacle with a return to his preincarnate glory. He calls the disciples his brothers because they believe in him, whereas his blood brothers do not (7:3, 5, 10; compare 21:23 and Jesus' calling the disciples his "loved ones" in 15:14–15). Because believers are his brothers, he calls his Father theirs too, and his God theirs too. But in what sense is God "his"? Isn't he God's Son, and as the Word isn't he himself God? Why "*his* God," then? Because he's not only divine but also human, he speaks of his Father as his God. But

there's a difference: just as believers are "children" of God but Jesus is his one-and-only "Son" (1:12, 14; 3:16, 18; 11:52), so believers both *worship* God and *pray* to him but Jesus only *prays* to him. This distinction is preserved by Jesus' saying "my Father and your Father and my God and your God" instead of "*our* Father and *our* God." Jesus doesn't say he'll *be* taken up (passive voice), as in the descriptions of his ascension at Luke 24:50–51; Acts 1:9–11. Rather, he'll *go* up. Just as he raised himself from the dead (10:17–18), he'll ascend under his own divine power. In Mary's obedient announcement to the disciples of Jesus' ascension, "the Lord" reverts to its higher meaning even in her own intention.

THE FIRST COMING OF JESUS TO HIS DISCIPLES
John 20:19–25

20:19–20: Therefore when it was evening that day, the first of the week, and when for fear of the Jews the doors were locked where the disciples were, Jesus came and stood in the midst [of them] **and says to them, "Peace to you." [20]And on saying this, he showed them** [his] **hands and side** [= his rib cage]. **Therefore the disciples, on seeing the Lord, rejoiced.** By the Jewish reckoning of day as beginning at sundown, strictly speaking the evening of the first day of the week (Sunday) would be what we call Saturday evening, and what we call Sunday evening would be the evening that starts the second day of the week, Monday. But 20:1 introduced the morning of the *first* day of the week, that is, Sunday morning. So "evening that day" must mean Sunday evening, and John's calling it the evening of the first rather than second day of the week means that he's using the same reckoning of days that we do: from midnight to midnight rather than from sundown to sundown. As in the case of Joseph of Arimathea (19:38), the Eleven's fear of the Jewish authorities, though besmirching their discipleship, doesn't falsify it. Jesus' coming fulfills his promise to come again to them after going from them (14:2–3, 18, 28). John doesn't say that Jesus miraculously passed through the locked doors, but relates the locking of the doors to the disciples' fear of the Jewish authorities rather than to the manner of Jesus' entry. John simply doesn't say how Jesus came and stood in the midst of the disciples. His interest lies solely in Jesus' coming and standing as such. The standing indicates resurrection, because by definition "resurrection" means "a standing up" in contrast to the supine position of a buried corpse. "In the midst [of the disciples]" gives Jesus a central, prominent position such as he had "in the midst" between the two men crucified with him (19:18). "Peace" was the greeting normally used among Jews (*shalōm* in Hebrew). But Jesus had given the disciples a peace such as the world doesn't give (14:27; 16:33). His "peace to you" consists not only in peace of mind and peace with God but also in the abundance of eternal life. For "peace" carried the connotation of prosperity and blessing, in this case over against and in compensation for the tribulation that the disciples will have in the world (16:33). Jesus' showing them his hands (including the wrists) and side, bearing the scars of his crucifixion, guarantees for them that he's their crucified but now risen Lord and counteracts the Gnostic heresy that Jesus only appeared to be human (see the introduction to 1 John). Since a soldier had unusually pierced the side only of Jesus, the scar left there made the guarantee ironclad. The sight turns the disciples' fear of the Jews into the joy of the Lord in fulfillment of 16:22.

20:21–23: Therefore Jesus said to them again, "Peace to you. Just as the Father sent me, I too am sending you." [22]**And on saying this, he breathed into** [them] **and tells them, "Receive the Holy Spirit.** [23]**Whosoever sins you forgive, they're forgiven for them. Whosoever** [sins] **you retain, they're retained."** After repeating his greeting because of the disciples' joyful recognition of him, Jesus adds what we call the Great Commission, to which he prospectively referred in his prayer at 17:18. Unlike its other versions in the New Testament (Matthew 28:18–20; Acts 1:8 [compare Luke 24:47–48]), John's version draws a parallel between Jesus' sending the disciples and God the Father's having sent him. This parallel reflects John's portrayal of Jesus as God's Son sent from heaven and, to a certain extent, John's portrayal of the disciples as not *from* the world though they're *in* it (that is, in the world consisting of unbelievers [17:14–16]). To empower the disciples for the carrying out of this commission and to fulfill his promise of the Holy Spirit's coming (14:16–17, 26, 15:26; 16:7), Jesus completes the granting of the Holy Spirit to them that started at his crucifixion, which itself had started his glorification, when he "gave over the Spirit" (19:30). Believers couldn't receive the Holy Spirit till Jesus was glorified (7:39), and his glorification didn't reach completion till his ascension back to the Father (17:4–5). Just as he told Mary Magdalene not to hold him, because he was ascending, John means us to infer that Jesus did indeed ascend between his meeting with Mary Easter Sunday morning and the disciples' receiving the Holy Spirit from him Easter Sunday evening. His glorification complete, so too his granting of the Spirit is now complete (compare the Spirit's empowering the disciples to carry out the Great Commission also in Luke 24:46–49; Acts 1:8). This empowerment consists in the authority to forgive and retain people's sins, that is, to declare them forgiven if the people believe in Jesus, and to declare them unforgiven if the people don't believe in him. In the other Gospels Jesus forgives sins (Mark 2:1–12; Matthew 9:1–8; Luke 5:17–26). Here in John, so close is the union of disciples with Jesus and the Father (he and his Father dwell "in" them, and they abide "in" him [15:1–8; 17:21, 23]) that the disciples possess Jesus' and the Father's authority to forgive and retain sins. Some have compared Jesus' breathing the Holy Spirit into the disciples with the Lord God's breathing the breath of life into man at the creation (Genesis 2:7 [compare Ezekiel 37:9]), but there's nothing about the Spirit there and nothing about life here.

"Into" could be dropped from the verb John uses for "breathed," but because of Jesus' immediately saying to the disciples, "*Receive* the Holy Spirit," it's better here to retain "into" and supply "them."

20:24–25: But Thomas, one of the Twelve, the one called Didymus, wasn't with them when Jesus came. [25]**Therefore the other disciples were telling him, "We've seen the Lord." But he told them, "If I don't see in his hands the imprint** [that is, the scar] **of the nails and thrust my finger into the imprint of the nails and thrust my hand into his side** [that is, into the scar left on his rib cage by the soldier's spear]**, by no means will I believe** [that Jesus has risen from among the dead]**."** Because of Jesus' original choice of them, John refers to "the Twelve" even though Judas Iscariot has apostatized. "Thomas" means "twin" in the Aramaic language, which Jews spoke most often in their land. "Didymus" means "twin" in the Greek language, which most people in the Roman Empire used in addition to their native language (if it was different from Greek) and in which John wrote his Gospel. When despite the threat to Jesus' life and limb he decided to go into Judea to raise Lazarus from the dead, Thomas said to his fellow disciples, "Let's go too in order that we may die with him" (11:16). Once again, then, in the face of death Thomas shows lack of faith in Jesus as "the life" who has now raised himself just as he raised Lazarus (see 11:25; 14:6). Thomas wants tactile as well as visual evidence. And only the scars of crucifixion can convince him that his fellow disciples have seen the Jesus who died that kind of death.

THE SECOND COMING OF JESUS TO HIS DISCIPLES
John 20:26–29

20:26–29: And after eight days his disciples were inside again, and Thomas [was] **with them. Though the doors were locked, Jesus comes and stood in the midst** [of the disciples] **and said, "Peace to you."** [27]**Then he says to Thomas, "Reach out your finger here and see my hands, and reach out your hand and thrust** [it] **into my side, and stop being unbelieving. Rather,** [become] **believing."** [28]**Thomas answered and said to him, "My Lord and my God."** [29]**Jesus tells him, "You've believed because you've seen me. Fortunate** [are] **those who haven't seen** [me] **and** [nevertheless] **believed."** This time John does relate Jesus' coming to the locked doors, as though they posed no more of an impediment than the stone that blocked the mouth of his tomb. Are we to suppose that he unlocked the doors from the outside just as he rolled away the stone from the inside? For his coming, standing in the midst of the disciples, and greeting them, see the comments on 20:19–20. Showing divine knowledge of Thomas's insistence on *visual* evidence, Jesus has given it to him. And showing divine knowledge also of Thomas's insistence on *tactile* evidence, Jesus now offers that too. On his own initiative Jesus had shown himself, including his scarred hands and side, to the other disciples (20:20). So the implied criticism of Thomas in Jesus' telling him to shift from unbelief to belief doesn't aim at Thomas's insistence on visual and tactile evidence. It aims rather at the refusal of Thomas to believe the *testimony* of his fellow disciples. If he had believed their testimony he would have qualified for the congratulations that Jesus now pronounces on those who believe without seeing for themselves. The traditional translation, "Blessed are those . . . ," can be misleading, because "blessed" is often interpreted as meaning "happy." Wrong! To call people "blessed" isn't to describe them as happy, which would make nonsense, for example, of the beatitude, "Blessed are those who are *mourning*" (Matthew 5:4). To describe people as blessed is, rather, to congratulate them on the good fortune of being approved by God and therefore destined to be rewarded by him.

Ancient writers of Greek didn't use question marks. So the context determines whether to take a set of words as a declaration or a question. Jesus' declaration, "You've believed because you've seen me," could then be translated alternatively as a question: "Have you believed because you've seen me?" Since the question would imply a yes answer, though, the meaning would come out to much the same. But Thomas's having addressed Jesus with "My Lord and my God" favors that Jesus *declares* Thomas believed because he saw, rather than that Jesus is asking a *question* about Thomas's believing. Since Thomas doesn't take advantage of Jesus' invitation to touch the scars of crucifixion, Jesus attributes Thomas's belief only to seeing. And just as Jesus referred to "my Father and your Father, and my God and your God" (20:17, "your" referring to the disciples), here Thomas refers to *Jesus* as "my Lord and my God"—a double reference to Jesus' deity and, like Mary Magdalene's "*my* Lord" (20:13), an intimately personal one. The combination of "Lord" and "God" occurs in the Old Testament (see, for example, Psalm 35:23–24), and in paganism occasionally for the emperor. Some have argued that the lack of the definite article "the" before "God" in the original text of 1:1 means that we should translate it, "In the beginning was the Word, and the Word was with God, and the Word was *a god*." It's therefore important to note that a literal translation of 20:28 reads, "*The* Lord of me and *the* God of me." To avoid Thomas's recognition of Jesus' full deity would require, then, that Thomas be referring to God the Father rather than to Jesus. But John says he was *answering* Jesus and speaking to him!

THE PURPOSE OF JOHN'S GOSPEL
John 20:30–31

20:30–31: **So Jesus performed many other signs too in the presence of his disciples, [signs] that aren't written in this book [John's Gospel]. ³¹But these [signs] have been written in order that you might believe that the Christ, the Son of God, is Jesus and in order that by believing you might have life in his name.** The reference to many other, unwritten signs points to an excess of evidence. "In the presence of his disciples" implies their backing up John's claim that Jesus had performed those many other, unwritten signs. Like John, they saw Jesus perform those signs. (Literally, "in *the presence* of his disciples" means "in *the face* of his disciples," that is, right in front of their faces [compare our expression "in your face," but without its edginess].) John positions these verses after the account of Jesus' resurrection. He has portrayed Jesus as having raised himself from the dead. And the sign of Jesus' raising Lazarus from the dead previewed Jesus' raising himself. Therefore "these [signs]" that "are written" in this book include Jesus' resurrection. John addresses directly the audience of his Gospel in telling the purpose of his writing. Believing captures that purpose. But does John refer to believing initially, at conversion, or to persistence in believing as opposed to falling back into unbelief? On the one hand, the business of *receiving* the Word, being *born* from above, and thereby *becoming* God's children (1:12–13; 3:3, 7) combines with the stories of *coming* to faith, as in the cases of the woman of Samaria and the man born blind (chapters 4 and 9), to favor believing at conversion. On the other hand, 6:66–71 told of many disciples who left Jesus, of his asking the Twelve whether they too wanted to go away, of Peter's affirming their continuing belief, and of Jesus' pronouncing them the elect (that is, chosen or selected ones) except for Judas Iscariot the betrayer. Moreover, chapter 15 emphasized *abiding, remaining, staying* in Christ, and 10:28–29 and chapter 17 emphasized the *keeping* of disciples. Therefore it seems best to think that here in 20:30–31 John identifies his purpose as one of confirming believers in addition to converting unbelievers.

But why the need for confirmation as well as conversion? Well, it's likely that in John's day the heresy called Gnosticism had developed a teaching which distinguished between a human Jesus and a divine Christ and identified only the divine Christ with God's Son (see again the introduction to 1 John). John counters that Jesus is one and the same with the Christ God's Son (compare the comments on 19:16b–18). The translation, "The Christ, the Son of God, is Jesus," emphasizes this point somewhat better than the more usual translation, "Jesus is the Christ, the Son of God." It should also be noted that believing the truth *about* Jesus underlies believing *in* Jesus. You can't have a personal relation with Jesus apart from believing him to be the Christ, God's Son. The lack of "and" between "Christ" and "the Son of God" draws together the two designations as closely as possible. The Christ is divine as well as human. The Son of God is human as well as divine. And Jesus of Nazareth is both the Christ and God's Son. As described elsewhere, the life to be had by initial and persistent believing is eternal (so that some ancient manuscripts actually add "eternal" here). "In his name" points to the authority by which this life is granted to those who believe and persevere in believing. And the authority is of the highest possible order; it's divine, because Jesus' name is "God" (see the comments on 17:6).

THE THIRD COMING OF JESUS
TO HIS DISCIPLES
John 21:1–23

21:1–3: After these things Jesus manifested himself again to the disciples, [this time] at the Sea of Tiberias. And he manifested [himself] in this way: ²Simon Peter and Thomas (the one called Didymus) and Nathaniel (the one from Cana of Galilee) and the [sons] of Zebedee and two others of his disciples were together. ³Simon Peter tells them, "I'm going fishing." They tell him, "We too are coming with you." They went out and got into a boat and caught nothing during the night. Tiberias was a city located on the west shore of the Sea (really a lake) of Galilee (a region in the north of the land of Israel). Sometimes the Sea of Galilee was called, as here, after the city of Tiberias. Jesus fed the five thousand with bread and fish at the Sea of Tiberias (6:1, 23), as he will feed the disciples with bread and fish here in chapter 21. So the mention of the Sea of Tiberias begins to set up a parallel between the two incidents. "In this way" refers to Jesus' self-manifestation *to his disciples*. For Thomas see the comments on 20:24; and for Nathaniel see 1:45–51, which puts him in the region of Galilee but not specifically in Cana, as here (see 2:1–11; 4:46–54 for Jesus' performing two signs there). John doesn't name the sons of Zebedee, but from the other Gospels we know them as James and John. It's also the other Gospels that tell us James and John and another pair of brothers, Peter and Andrew, were fishers and that Jesus told them he would make them into fishers of human beings (see, for example, Mark 1:16–20). John conveys none of that information, but it seems to underlie Peter's going off to fish. It also favors that this fishing expedition will symbolize Christian evangelism in fulfillment of the Great Commission (20:21–23). Commentators regularly criticize Peter and the other disciples for going off to fish after the risen Jesus has appeared to them twice and given them the Great Commission. But neither here nor later in John's text do we find any such criticism. This lack of criticism favors again a symbol of Christian evangelism in fulfillment of the Great Commission, the very commission wrongly supposed to be negated, or at least neglected, by the disciples' fishing. The catching of nothing all night then symbolizes the futility of trying to fulfill this commission apart from the presence and instruction of the risen Jesus.

21:4–6: And when it now got to be early morning, Jesus stood on the beach. The disciples didn't know [= recognize] that it's Jesus, however. ⁵So Jesus says to them, "Boys, you don't have anything to eat, do you?" They answered him, "No." ⁶And he told them, "Throw the net on the right side of the boat, and you'll find [fish]." So they threw [the net on the right side of the boat] and couldn't any longer pull it in because of the multitude of fish [caught in the net]. Again Jesus' standing demonstrates his resurrection, which by definition means "a standing up" (see also 20:14, 19, 26), and the time of "early morning" suggests he has risen as the light of the world. He's the sunrise of salvation and eternal life. John doesn't say why the disciples don't recognize Jesus. Their nonrecognition simply provides the platform for Jesus' question. The question starts with the slightly ridiculing address, "Boys," and the implication in the question itself of a negative answer exhibits Jesus' divine omniscience that the disciples have caught nothing for their breakfast despite fishing all night. "Anything to eat" refers to the use of fish as a relish that they put on bread. Since most people are right-handed, the right side of anything—here of a boat—is the favorable side. And what a favorable side it proves to be! The almost unmanageable haul of fish symbolizes the huge success of Christian evangelism by the time John writes his Gospel, the success already symbolized by the throngs that acclaimed Jesus at the triumphal procession and that prompted the Pharisees to exclaim in hyperbolic dismay, "Look! The world has gone after him!" (12:12–19 [compare the immediately following arrival of "some Greeks" to "see Jesus"]).

21:7–8: Therefore that disciple whom Jesus loved tells Peter, "It's the Lord!" So on hearing, "It's the Lord!" Simon Peter wrapped [his] outer garment around himself (for he was naked) and threw himself into the sea. ⁸But the other disciples, dragging the net [full] of fish, came with the boat; for they weren't far from land—rather, about two hundred cubits [= about one hundred yards] away. The further demonstration of Jesus' omniscience (he knew not only that they hadn't caught any fish all night; he also knew where they *would* catch fish—a lot of them) causes the beloved disciple to recognize him. Since the word for Peter's outer garment means a robe worn over an undergarment, Peter's nakedness probably means that he was wearing only his tunic (a robe worn next to the skin). Throwing himself into the sea implies his swimming ashore, which sets up for his drawing the net ashore *from* the shore. Since you ordinarily *shed* as much clothing as possible to swim, Peter's *putting on* an outer garment despite swimming makes him presentable and thus shows deference to "the Lord."

21:9–11: Therefore when they [the disciples who stayed in the boat] disembarked onto the land, they see a charcoal fire situated [there] and a fish-for-relish situated over [the charcoal fire and therefore cooking] and bread [for which the fish was to be used as a relish]. ¹⁰Jesus tells them, "Bring some of the fish that you've now caught." ¹¹So Simon Peter went up [to the boat, to which the net was attached] and drew to land the net full of 153 large fish. And though there were so many, the net hadn't been torn. This charcoal fire is reminiscent of the charcoal fire around which Peter denied Jesus three times (18:15–18, 25–27) and therefore prepares for Jesus' eliciting from Peter three compensatory affirmations of love for Jesus (21:15–17). The already prepared bread and fish are likewise reminiscent of the bread and fish that Jesus multiplied to feed the five thousand (6:5–13). By supplying the bread and fish for these disciples in chapter 21, he acts as the bread of life for those who've persevered in belief as opposed to the many disciples who left him after the feeding of the five thousand and therefore won't get the benefit of eternal life.

Jesus' command to bring some of the fish that the disciples have just caught represents the success of Christian evangelism throughout the world among Gentiles as well as Jews (10:16; 12:20–24, 32). The large size of the fish and their large number add to this representation of such success. In drawing the net full of fish to shore, Peter acts as the evangelistic agent through whom, symbolically speaking, God draws people to Jesus (6:44) and through whom Jesus draws these same people to himself (12:32). Nothing is said about cooking and eating any of the 153 fish. To cook and eat them wouldn't agree with the symbol of successful evangelism. So the single fish that Jesus already has cooking and that the disciples then eat represents Jesus himself, given in sacrifice, just as the bread represents him in the same way (compare the five thousand's eating fish as well as bread [6:1–15], Jesus' reference to eating his flesh [6:52–59], and Paul's reference to the "flesh of fish" [1 Corinthians 15:39]). And in reminiscence of the soldiers' not tearing Jesus' tunic but preserving it whole (19:23), the preservation of the net from being torn represents again the unity, the oneness, of believers with one another, with Jesus, and with God the Father, a oneness that keeps them secure, so that with the sole exception of Judas Iscariot, scripturally destined to apostatize (13:18), not one is lost (6:12, 39; 10:16, 27–30; 17:11–12, 21; 18:9).

21:12–14: Jesus tells them, "[Come] here. Have breakfast." But none of the disciples, knowing that it's the Lord, was daring to ask him, "Who are you?" **¹³Jesus comes and takes the bread and gives [it] to them, and the fish likewise. ¹⁴This [was] now the third time Jesus was manifested to the disciples after rising from the dead.** As usual, Jesus takes the initiative with an invitation to the feast of salvation, portrayed here as the breakfast starting a new day (compare "early morning" at 21:4). The disciples' "knowing that it's the Lord" suits John's portrayal of eternal life as "knowing Jesus Christ" through a personal relationship with him (see especially 17:3). But why does John write that none of them "was *daring*" to ask Jesus who he was? Why not simply that they weren't *asking* him who he was because they knew he was the Lord? Answer: John writes at least partly against Gnostic heretics who didn't recognize the human Jesus as the divine Lord. They dared, in fact, to deny he was. So by way of contrast with those heretics John puts forward these disciples as true in that they *don't* dare to question the identity of the human Jesus as the divine Lord.

For the third time Jesus' coming fulfills his promise to come again and receive the disciples to himself (see also 20:19, 24, 26 with 14:3). The fact that he's already standing on the beach makes a reference to his coming superfluous except for emphasis on the fulfillment of that promise. His taking the bread and giving it to the disciples symbolizes the giving of his flesh in self-sacrifice for their eternal life (6:32–59). The added ref-

erence to fish makes clear the allusion to the feeding of the five thousand and its interpretation in chapter 6. The numbering of this manifestation of the risen Jesus as the third one indicates sufficiency and ties in with the threesome of Peter's past denials of Jesus and coming affirmations of love for him. The first verse of chapter 21 has said that Jesus manifested himself on this occasion. Therefore he's the implied subject of the passive verb "was manifested." Just as he raised himself from the dead (10:18), he has now manifested himself as risen.

21:15–17: So when they'd breakfasted, Jesus says to Simon Peter, "Simon, [son of] John, do you love me more than these [do]?" He tells him, "Yes, Lord. You know that I love you." He tells him, "Tend my sheep." **¹⁶He says to him again, a second time, "Simon, [son of] John, do you love me?" He tells him, "Yes, Lord. You know that I love you." He tells him, "Tend my sheep."** **¹⁷He says to him a third time, "Simon, [son of] John, do you love me?" Peter was grieved that he'd said to him a third time, "Do you love me?" and he tells him, "Lord, you know all things. You know that I love you." Jesus tells him, "Tend my sheep."** In this passage John uses different Greek verbs for loving, for knowing, and for tending (or shepherding), and different Greek nouns for sheep. Because he commonly uses synonyms without distinguishing their meanings in any way, however, the foregoing translation has stuck to one English equivalent in each case. (So far as John is concerned, then, forget the popular treatment of *agapē*-love as superior to *philē*-love.) Jesus' taking the initiative as usual in this Gospel and addressing Simon formally as a son of John (as in 1:42) lends gravity to the following question and distinguishes this Simon (Peter) from Simon Iscariot, father of Judas the betrayer of Jesus (13:2, 26). The question asks whether Simon loves Jesus more than the other disciples ("these") love Jesus. After all, Simon was the only one of the Twelve who'd said he would lay down his life for Jesus (13:37). Instead, however, he'd denied Jesus—hence Jesus' question.

To compensate for the denials Simon affirms not so much his love for Jesus as Jesus' *knowledge* of it. Since Jesus predicted Simon's denials (13:38), Jesus must surely know that despite the denials Simon loves Jesus—but not more than the other disciples love him. So Simon stops short of saying so. He has learned better. Simon's "Yes" would have implied he loves Jesus more than the other disciples do if it weren't for Simon's omission of "more than these." As it is, the "Yes" stresses Jesus' knowledge. Jesus responds by giving Simon the job of tending Jesus' sheep. To tend sheep is to feed them in the sense of shepherding them to pasture. They are, of course, people who because they've believed in Jesus belong to him (10:1–16, 26–29). Given his coming absence and Simon's chastened declaration, Jesus tells Simon to take care of future believers, represented earlier by the huge haul of fish the disciples caught but represented now under the figure of sheep.

Because the other disciples hadn't denied Jesus, Jesus doesn't have to recommission them. Simon's was a special case. The commission in 20:21-23 sufficed for the rest. Since pasturing the sheep in chapter 10 had to do with preserving them in eternal life, pasturing them here has to do likewise with preserving in eternal life those who like fish have been "caught" by evangelism. The addition of "a second time" to "again" (21:16) begins to clarify the compensation for Simon's three predicted denials of Jesus, and "a third time" (21:17a) completes the clarification as well as the compensation. The repetition of "a third time" (21:17c) stresses the correspondence to the three denials. In his second and third questions, Jesus drops "more than these [other disciples do]." The omission sharpens the question by casting doubt on Simon's loving Jesus *at all*. Simon doesn't grieve because he'd denied Jesus three times—rather, because Jesus asked him a third time and therefore seemed to cast a final doubt on his love for Jesus. In his third answer, then, Simon drops "Yes" in order to add "you know *all* things" after "Lord" and before "you know that I love you." The addition expands his earlier confession of Jesus' knowledge concerning him into a confession of Jesus' divine omniscience.

Jesus continues speaking to Peter in *21:18-19*: "**Amen, amen I tell you, when you were younger you used to clothe yourself and walk around wherever you were wanting** [to go]. **But when you get old, you'll stretch out your hands and somebody else will clothe you and bring you where you don't want** [to go]." [19]**And this he said signifying by what kind of death he'll glorify God. And on saying this, he tells him, "Follow me."** The double "Amen" emphasizes the truth of Jesus' following prediction, which Peter may not wish to believe. "When you get old" shows that "when you were younger" takes a later standpoint by way of anticipation. Peter is still young enough to clothe himself. Jesus predicts for him not only old age but also and, more ominously, his stretching out his hands and being brought to where he won't want to go. John interprets this prediction in terms of Peter's manner of death. Early church tradition says Peter died as a martyr by crucifixion sometime during A.D. 64-67. In 12:33; 18:32 Jesus used the same phraseology to reference crucifixion as the manner of his own death. (The earliest church tradition lacks the detail of crucifixion upside down for Peter, however.) So how does Jesus' phraseology relate to crucifixion? Peter would stretch out his hands to have them tied or nailed to the cross-bar of a cross. There's a wordplay on the verb "clothe." Peter was used to clothing himself with garments. But once he has stretched out his hands, someone else will clothe him. How so? The common practice was to *un*clothe victims of crucifixion, so that they hung on their crosses stark naked. The shame of crucifixion was deepened thereby. What we have, then, is a wordplay: whereas Peter used to clothe himself with garments, someone else will "clothe him," so to speak, with the cross-bar by tying or nailing it to his outstretched hands, and will then bring him, wearing the cross-bar, again so to speak, to the unwanted place of execution, where the vertical stake of the cross is situated. Though John points up the manner of Peter's

death, his main stress falls on Peter's glorifying God by such a death. As Jesus' death by crucifixion glorified God (13:31-32; 17:4), Peter's will too. But we should note a big difference: Peter won't want to go where he'll die; Jesus died voluntarily, insistently, with determination. And now, since Peter won't die till he's old, for the moment Jesus tells Peter to follow him—physically (compare Jesus' earlier statement to Peter in 13:36: "You can't follow me now [to] where I'm going, but you'll follow [me] later").

21:20-22: **On turning around, Peter sees the disciple whom Jesus loved following** [them], **[the disciple] who also reclined at the supper on his** [Jesus'] **bosom and said, "Lord, who's the one betraying you?"** [21]**On seeing that** [disciple], **therefore, Peter says to Jesus, "Lord, but what about this one?"** [22]**Jesus tells him, "If I should want him to remain till I come, what's** [that] **to you? You—follow me!"** In obedience, Peter has started following Jesus; but on turning around he sees the beloved disciple following both of them. John's describing the beloved disciple further as Jesus' closest confidant will support the truthfulness of this disciple's testimony in accordance with 21:24. Peter's asking about the beloved disciple's fate links up with Jesus' predicting that Peter won't want to be taken where he'll die. Will the beloved disciple die as a martyr too? Jesus answers that the manner of the beloved disciple's death should be of no concern to Peter. So what if Jesus wants the beloved disciple to remain till Jesus comes—a reference to the second coming (only so-called, for he has already come to the disciples three times since his resurrection)? Jesus reiterates that for the moment Peter's concern should be only to follow him.

21:23: **Therefore this word** [= saying] **went out to the brothers, "That disciple** [the beloved one] **isn't going to die** [but is going to remain—that is, keep living—till the second coming]." **But Jesus hadn't said to him** [Peter], **"He** [the beloved disciple] **isn't going to die"**—rather, "**If I should** *want* **him to remain till I come, what's** [that] **to you?"** "The brothers" is usually taken to mean believers in general, both men and women, including those living at the time of John's writing. But the last time "brothers" appeared in John's text, the term referred only to the eleven disciples: "Jesus tells her [Mary Magdalene], '. . . go to my brothers and tell them [plus words about Jesus' ascension]'" (20:17). So here "the brothers" more likely refers to the rest of the Eleven. The saying probably spread beyond their circle, but that wouldn't be John's point. His point is to deny that Jesus said the beloved disciple wouldn't die before the second coming.

THE RELIABILITY AND SELECTIVITY OF JOHN'S GOSPEL
John 21:24-25

21:24-25: **This** [the beloved disciple] **is the disciple who is testifying about these things and has written these things, and we know that his testimony is true.**

²⁵**And there are many other things too that Jesus did which if they were written one by one, I suppose not even the world itself has room for the books written.** So the beloved disciple declares himself the author of this Gospel and indicates his ongoing oral testimony about what he has written. (He's still alive, then.) The immediate shift from "we" to "I," after the author's referring to himself indirectly with "this one" and "his," implies inclusion of the author in the "we" who know his testimony to be true. And as in 1:14; 1 John 1:1–5; 3 John 12, the "we" enlists alongside the author the rest of the Eleven. For as eye- and earwitnesses of Jesus' ministry they were in a position to authenticate the truth of the author's testimony. His contemporaries at the time of writing were in no such position. So "we" could hardly include them. The present tense of "know"—despite the prior deaths of the Eleven—is then due to the author's being still alive as the primary witness. The whimsical supposition that the world couldn't hold all the books required to detail everything Jesus did—this supposition underlines the selectivity of John's account. And this selectivity underlines in turn the superabundance of Jesus' works, more than enough for our eternal life if we'll only believe in him.

ACTS

As a sequel to the Gospel of Luke, the book of Acts narrates Jesus' continuing, irresistible, and appealing work of salvation through the witness of his disciples (compare the introduction to Luke's Gospel).

AN INTRODUCTION BY WAY OF RECAPITULATION AND ELABORATION
Acts 1:1–26

This introduction to the book of Acts recapitulates subject matter in Luke's Gospel and elaborates the most recent parts of that subject matter. Luke alludes to his Gospel and its account of Jesus' activities (1:1–3), rementions Jesus' command that the apostles stay in Jerusalem till they're baptized in the Holy Spirit (1:4–5), records again the Great Commission (1:6–8), redescribes Jesus' ascension (1:9–11), and tells about the replacement of Judas Iscariot during the wait for baptism in the Holy Spirit (1:12–26).

Luke writes in *1:1–3*: **I produced the former word, Theophilus, concerning all the things which Jesus began both to do and to teach ²till the day that he was taken up** [to heaven] **after he'd given an order through the Holy Spirit to the apostles, whom he'd selected** [compare Luke 1:1–4; 6:13–16; 24:49–51], **³to whom also, after he'd suffered, he presented himself alive with many positive proofs, appearing to them throughout forty days and speaking the things about God's kingdom/reign.** "The first word" refers to Luke's Gospel, called a "word" because he put in writing the oral "word" of the gospel (see Luke 1:2; Acts 10:36 for two of many examples of "word" as the oral gospel). In fact, the expression Luke uses could legitimately be translated, "I *spoke* formerly." He dedicates Acts to Theophilus, as he did the Gospel. We know nothing more about Theophilus. "*All* the things which Jesus began both to do and to teach" recalls the overwhelming number of Jesus' good deeds and good words. Their sheer number recommends the gospel. "*Both* to do *and* to teach" stresses that the deeds backed up his teaching and that the teaching explained the significance of his deeds. The gospel isn't good news if either is missing. "*Began* both to do and to teach" implies that Jesus will continue doing good deeds and teaching good news through the agency of his apostles and other followers (compare 9:34: "And Peter said to him, 'Aeneas, *Jesus Christ* is healing you'"). "Till the day that he was taken up" marks the end of that beginning but notably includes

Jesus' death, resurrection, and postresurrection ministry in the doing and teaching. The "order" he'd given the apostles was that they should "sit [tight] in the city [of Jerusalem]" till they were "clothed with power from the height" (Luke 24:49). This clothing will consist in the Holy Spirit's coming on them from heaven (Acts 1:4–5, 8; 2:1–4). For now, though, Luke points out that Jesus gave the order "through the Holy Spirit." To the very end of Jesus' earthly lifetime, then, the Holy Spirit was inspiring the deeds and words of Jesus (see also Luke 4:18; Acts 10:38, for example).

Luke's remarking Jesus' selection of the apostles underlines their status as witnesses specially authorized by him. In particular, though disciples other than the apostles saw him risen from the dead, the apostles formed the solid core of that witness. For it was to them that "he presented himself alive"; and despite the fact "he'd suffered" crucifixion, that presentation included "proofs" which were "many" and "positive" and spread "throughout forty days" (compare "the certainty" of the gospel according to Luke 1:4; and contrast the Devil's testing Jesus forty days according to Luke 4:1–13, for which testing the forty days of proofs offer a kind of compensation). "Appearing to them" stresses the eyewitness character of the proofs (compare Luke 1:2 again), and the filling of the forty days with "speaking the things about God's kingdom/reign" establishes continuity between Jesus' ministry prior to passion-and-resurrection and his ministry afterwards. For that kingdom/reign had formed the main theme of his earlier deeds and words (Luke 4:43 and so on). Thus there's continuity not only between the Old Testament and Jesus' prior ministry. There's also continuity between that ministry and Jesus' post-resurrection ministry. And since those ministries are only the beginning of what he did and taught, there'll be continuity between them and what he's yet to do and teach through his apostles and other followers. In other words, apostolic Christianity is one with Jesus' deeds and words and, through them, with the Old Testament.

1:4–5: **And while eating with** [the apostles]**, he directed them not to withdraw from Jerusalem** [as they'd be tempted to do because of Jesus' crucifixion there and their Galilean origin] **but to await the Father's promise, "which you've heard from me, ⁵because John baptized with water, on the one hand, but you'll be baptized in the Holy Spirit *not* after these many days** [= in a few days]**."** "While eating with [the apostles]" refers back to

464

Luke 24:41–43, 49, where the risen Jesus ate with them to prove the physicality of his resurrection and directed them to "sit [tight] in the city [of Jerusalem]" because he was going to "send the promise of [his] Father on them." Baptism in the Holy Spirit interprets being "clothed with power from the height [= heaven]" in that promise. According to Luke 3:16, it was John the baptizer who said someone stronger than he would baptize people in the Holy Spirit. Here, Jesus adopts the statement as his own so as to establish continuity between his ministry and John's under the aegis of God the Father. Christianity has a good pedigree, then. That the fulfillment of the Father's promise will take place soon makes staying in Jerusalem tolerable. Putting the fulfillment's temporal proximity negatively ("*not* after these many days") stresses that the apostles won't have to wait long. The very awkwardness of this expression adds to the stress.

1:6–8: Therefore [since baptism in the Holy Spirit seemed to signal the messianic kingdom; see Ezekiel 36:22–38, especially verse 27] **they, on coming together, were asking him, saying, "Lord,** [we're wondering] **whether you're restoring the rulership to Israel at this time** [= the imminent time of baptism in the Holy Spirit that you've just talked about (compare Luke 24:21)]**." ⁷On the other hand, he told them, "It's not yours to know times or seasons that the Father has set by his own authority. ⁸Nevertheless, you'll receive power when the Holy Spirit has come on you, and you'll be my witnesses both in Jerusalem and in all Judea and Samaria and as far as the extremity of the earth."** As often in Luke's Gospel, "Lord"—here as a respectful address—suits Jesus' dignity as the Son of God. It's especially suitable in an address to Jesus as the *resurrected* Son of God. The angel Gabriel had promised to the Virgin Mary a restoration of rulership to Israel through Jesus (Luke 1:26–33). She exulted in that promise (Luke 1:54–55). Filled with the Holy Spirit, Zechariah prophesied such a restoration (Luke 1:67–79), and Jesus himself did too (Luke 22:29–30). So the apostles aren't to be blamed for asking whether the time for it has come. The use of the present tense in "you're restoring" for an event that isn't yet occurring shows the apostles hopeful of an affirmative answer. Jesus doesn't deny the restoration. How could he? As just noted, he'd recently predicted it. But he does deny the apostles' right to know the Father's timetable and interprets the imminent coming of the Holy Spirit on them as empowerment for witness rather than as a sign or concomitant of Jesus' restoring rulership to Israel. "Set by his own authority" implies that the apostles' hope for a quick restoration doesn't determine the Father's timetable. "Nevertheless" introduces the Holy Spirit's empowerment of the apostles as a compensation for their inability to know times or seasons. The empowerment has the purpose of enabling them to bear effective witness about Jesus and for him. Their witnessing will consist in testifying to what they've seen in his ministry and resurrection and in working miracles to back up their testimony (again see Luke 1:1–4). The starting of this testimony in Jerusalem implies and suits

continuity with Judaism, centered in that city. As ever, Luke wants his audience to know that Christianity is no upstart and therefore not a suspect religion. "And in all Judea and Samaria" probably refers to the whole land of Israel, including its central region of Samaria (see the comments on Luke 1:5), and thus adds to the theme of continuity with Judaism. "And Samaria" looks forward to the progress of the gospel into the region populated by religious cousins of the Jews (8:1, 4–25; 9:31; 15:3). (Samaritans used the Pentateuch, and still use it, as their Scripture.) "And as far as the extremity of the earth" projects the universal reach of apostolic witness (see especially Acts 13–28 and compare Luke 24:47–49).

1:9–11: And after he'd said these things, as they were watching he was lifted up; and a cloud hoisted him from their eyes [= out of their sight]. **¹⁰And as they were gazing into the sky while he was traveling** [up to heaven], **also—behold—two men in white clothes were standing alongside them. ¹¹And they said, "Galilean men, why do you stand looking into the sky? This Jesus, who has been taken up from you into heaven, will come in this way,** [that is,] **in the manner that you've viewed him traveling into heaven."** "As they were watching," "as they were gazing into the sky," "looking into the sky," and "you've viewed him" put a quadruple emphasis on eyewitness testimony concerning Jesus' ascension. In a backhanded way, "from their eyes" adds to this emphasis. Throughout, there's one original word underlying the translations "sky" and "heaven." The apostles were looking into the sky. Jesus was traveling up to heaven. He was lifted up by a cloud's taking him. Since God spoke out of a cloud at Jesus' transfiguration (Luke 9:34–35), here a cloud's taking him provides a divine mode of transport. According to Luke 21:27 it's this mode of transport that he'll have when he comes back—hence the two men's saying he'll come "in this way." The addition of "in the manner that you've viewed him traveling into heaven" ensures the parallel. The "two men in white clothes" recalls the "two men in flashing clothes" who announced Jesus' resurrection at the empty tomb (Luke 24:4–7) and, farther back, the "two men"—namely, Moses and Elijah—who "appeared in glory" and "were telling about his exodus, which he was going to fulfill in Jerusalem" (Luke 9:30–31). The ascension completes the final leg of that exodus. Here the men predict his second coming. "Also" and "behold" highlight the prediction, and their "standing alongside" the apostles makes the prediction unmistakably audible as well as the men's appearance to them unmistakably visible. "Galilean men" addresses the apostles in a way that stresses the difference between their place of origin and the city of Jerusalem, where Jesus has told them to await baptism in the Holy Spirit and where they're then to start bearing witness to what they've seen and heard (compare Luke 22:59). "Why do you stand looking into the sky?" indicates they should now expect a long interval before Jesus' return and fill that interval with worldwide testimony. He's not going to return while they're standing there.

Now Luke starts elaborating what went on after "they returned to Jerusalem with great joy" (Luke 24:52). *1:12:* **Then they returned to Jerusalem from the mountain called "Of an Olive Grove," which is near Jerusalem,** [the mountain] **situated a Sabbath day's journey** [from Jerusalem]. That would be only three-fifths of a mile distant. For a Jew, traveling any greater distance on a Sabbath was thought to violate the Sabbath by expending enough effort for it to count as work. But Luke offers no indication that the return to Jerusalem occurred on a Sabbath. Indeed, forty days from Easter Sunday rules out the Sabbath (compare 1:3). So the proximity to Jerusalem confirms instead the fulfillment of Jesus' "exodus" in Jerusalem (Luke 9:30–31). (Because pilgrims overflowed Jerusalem proper and bivouacked on the Mount of Olives, that mountain was considered part of greater Jerusalem.)

1:13–14: **And when they'd entered** [Jerusalem proper]**, they went up into an upstairs room where they were staying,** [that is,] **both Peter and John and James and Andrew, Philip and Thomas, Bartholomew and Matthew, James** [the son] **of Alphaeus and Simon the Zealot and Judas** [the son] **of James.** See the comments on Luke 3:14 for the apostolic list. As compared with that list, the present advancement of John to stand next to Peter prepares for their pairing in 3:1, 3–4, 11; 4:13, 19; 8:14. The resultant "Peter and John and James" echoes Luke 8:51; 9:28. "John and James" likewise echoes Luke 9:54. And though Andrew came second as Peter's brother in Luke 3:14, for lack of distinction elsewhere he comes last in the initial foursome here. For no reason expressed in Luke-Acts, Thomas advances ahead of Bartholomew and Matthew (but see John 11:16; 14:5–7; 20:24–29 for the increasing importance of Thomas). Judas Iscariot has been dropped from the list, of course. [14]**With mutual fervor all these were engrossed in the prayer together with women and Mary the mother of Jesus and his brothers.** Emphasizing the piety of the apostles and others are their engrossment in the prayer, the fervor of that engrossment, their sharing the fervor, and the unanimity of their fervent engrossment in the prayer. If "*the* prayer" alludes to prayer at an appointed time in Jewish practice, as in 3:1; 10:2–3, emphasis falls on the disciples' piety as a continuance of Jewish religious piety. "Women" harks back to the women who'd supported Jesus and the Twelve, followed along with him from Galilee, watched his crucifixion and burial, came to his tomb only to find it empty, and announced Jesus' resurrection to the apostles (Luke 8:2–3; 23:49, 55–56; 24:1–10, 22–23). The inclusion of Jesus' mother recalls her piety, displayed in Luke 1–2; and the inclusion of his brothers (half-brothers in view of his virgin birth) along with Mary recalls Jesus' describing their piety in Luke 8:19–21, particularly in verse 21: "My mother and my brothers—these are the ones who are hearing God's word and doing [it]" (see the comments on that passage for Jesus' talking about them, not about others as distinct from them; compare 1 Corinthians 9:5). As in his Gospel, then, Luke is highlighting the piety, comradery,

and inclusiveness—including gender inclusiveness—of Jesus' followers. All this to attract converts.

In 1:15–26 Luke continues to elaborate what went on between Jesus' ascension and the disciples' baptism in the Holy Spirit. *1:15–17:* **And during these days Peter, on standing up in the midst of the brothers and sisters, said (and a crowd of about one hundred and twenty names** [= persons] **was at the same** [place])**,** [16]**"Men, brothers, it was necessary for the Scripture to be fulfilled that the Holy Spirit foretold through David's mouth concerning Judas, the one who became a guide for those who took Jesus along** [= arrested him (Luke 22:54)]**,** [17]**because he** [Judas] **was numbered among us and obtained by lot** [that is, by God's will] **a portion of this service** [= apostolic ministry]**."** Peter's "standing up in the midst . . ." implies that the others were sitting down (compare 2:2). The previous mention of women (1:14) favors that "brothers" be supplemented with "sisters." The following notation of about one hundred and twenty persons indicates that "brothers and sisters" is being used in a religious sense (as in 6:3), not in a biological sense (as in 1:14). The use of "names" for persons allows for the presence of women as well as men. Luke puts the notation of how many persons were present between "said" and the quotation of Peter's words. The awkwardness of this placement calls special attention to what Luke considers a large number, especially given that "at the same place" refers apparently to the "upstairs room" of 1:13. Even after the ascension of Jesus to heaven, his popularity packs a room with people, even an upstairs room (compare Luke 5:18–19 and Luke's emphasis throughout the third Gospel on Jesus' well-deserved popularity). "At the same place" also points up the attractive unity of the disciples. But Peter addresses only his co-apostles, all male, whom he'll ask to participate in choosing a successor for Judas Iscariot. He interprets Judas's betrayal of Jesus as a guidance to Jesus of those who arrested him, and attributes the results of this betrayal to the divine necessity of fulfilling the Scripture. Thus even the betrayal's results carry out God's plan. He's ever in control. The Holy Spirit foretold the Scripture in the sense that the Scripture records the Spirit's foretelling. This foretelling passed through David's mouth onto a scroll of Scripture and dealt with Judas (see 1:20). Attributing the foretelling to the Holy Spirit and making David's mouth a mere channel puts enormous emphasis on the carrying out of God's plan. No accidents of history here! But the scripturally necessitated results of Judas's betrayal of Jesus have yet to be detailed in 1:18–26. Whatever they'll turn out to be, Peter says the Holy Spirit foretold them "because" Judas was numbered among the twelve apostles and had obtained a portion of apostolic ministry. "Numbered *among us*" confirms that Peter is addressing only his fellow apostles as originally twelve in number. It was Jesus who numbered Judas among the Twelve by selecting him along with the other apostles (Luke 6:13–16); and since Jesus spent all night in prayer right before selecting them, Judas obtained his portion by God's will (represented in the phrase "by lot"). But here Luke mentions neither God nor Jesus, so that the accent rests solely on Judas's membership and service in the Twelve as such. What's to happen now to that membership and service. What have been and will be the outcomes of Judas's betraying Jesus?

1:18–19: "**Therefore this** [Judas] **procured for himself a field with the reward of injustice; and on becoming prone** [= on falling headlong/facedown] **he burst open in the middle, and all his guts were spilled out.** [19] **And it** [this outcome] **became known to all who are inhabiting Jerusalem, so that in their own language that field was called** [= named] **'Hakeldama' (this is** [= means] **'Field of Blood').**" "Hakeldama" is Aramaic, the language of Peter and his audience. So "*their* own language" indicates that Luke is merging his own account of the past outcome into Peter's remarks so as to provide a basis for subsequent quotations of the Old Testament. According to Luke 22:4–5, the chief priests and officers of the temple guard covenanted to give Judas money for betraying Jesus. Now we learn that they kept their side of the covenant and that Judas used the money to purchase a field. Here Luke calls the money "the reward of injustice" to remind us that since Jesus was just—that is, righteous (see especially Luke 23:47)—his crucifixion was unjust. In view isn't the injustice of Judas's betrayal (Luke doesn't write "*his* injustice") so much as that of those who paid Judas for the betrayal. But he gets paid another way too by falling headlong, so that his abdomen bursts and his intestines gush out in a pool of blood. His blood then gives the field its name. Whereas Jesus' shed blood established a beneficial covenant (Luke 22:20), Judas's blood was shed as the result of a mercenary covenant that proved disastrous for him. The knowledge of this outcome throughout the populace of Jerusalem, plus their naming Judas's field after his blood, underlines the horror of his betraying Jesus even though the betrayal carried out God's plan. Divine determination and human responsibility coalesce.

Now Peter quotes the Scripture that he earlier said had to be fulfilled (1:16), and he introduces it as the reason for Judas's demise. **1:20**: "**For it's written in the book of Psalms, 'His homestead is to become deserted, and no one is to dwell in it** [Psalm 69:25],' **and, 'Another** [man] **is to take his supervisorship** [Psalm 109:8].'" "The Scripture" of 1:16 turns out to be two passages from the Psalms. The first one portrays the demise of a wicked person—in this case, Judas Iscariot—in terms of its result: the vacancy of his dwelling place. The second passage portrays the demise of a wicked person like Judas in terms of the need it creates to fill the supervisory role he has vacated. In this case, it's the supervisory role of an apostle.

1:21–22: **Therefore** [since Scripture demands that someone replace Judas in apostolic supervisorship] **it's necessary that of the men who came with us during all the time that the Lord Jesus came in and went out over us,** [22] **beginning from John's baptism till the day that he was taken up from us**—[it's necessary that] **one of these**

[men] **become a witness with us of his** [Jesus'] **resurrection.**" The Scripture is God's word, so that the necessity is divine because it's scriptural. "With us" refers to the apostles just as "among us" did in 1:17. "The men who came with us" refers to male disciples who accompanied the apostles. Peter defines "all the time" as spanning the period from John's baptism to Jesus' ascension. Apostleship among the Twelve required eyewitness of the entirety of Jesus' ministry, beginning with John's baptizing him (compare Luke 1:2: "the eyewitnesses from the beginning"). (Since the ascension had to do with Jesus alone, the baptism probably has to with John's baptizing Jesus in particular rather than people in general.) Between baptism and ascension Jesus entered and exited cities and towns "over us," Peter says. He means that Jesus was at their head, exercising leadership over them. As apostles they will supervise other disciples of Jesus, but he first supervised the apostles. Hence the placement of "Lord" before "Jesus." And to the apostles' supervisorship over other disciples is to be added witness-bearing to nondisciples concerning Jesus' resurrection. They're to tell nondisciples that they actually saw him resurrected from the dead. To make this testimony convincingly twelvefold, Judas needs to be replaced.

1:23–26: **And they** [the eleven apostles] **caused two to stand: Joseph** [a Hebrew name] **called Barsabbas** [an Aramaic name], **who was called Justus** [a Roman name in addition to the preceding Jewish names], **and Matthias.** [24] **And praying, they said, "You, Lord, knower of the hearts of all, out of these two point up the one whom you've selected** [25] **to take the place of this service and apostleship from which Judas deviated with the result that he went to his own place."** [26] **And they gave lots to them, and the lot** [that indicated apostleship] **fell on Matthias. And he was counted with the eleven apostles** [as the twelfth one]. Peter had stood up to speak according to 1:15. Now Joseph and Matthias are made to stand. Their standing is a matter of both posture and candidacy for Judas's former position among the Twelve. Luke's knowing all three names of the first candidate arises out of the historical research he mentioned in Luke 1:1–4. By causing these two qualified men to stand as candidates, by praying for divine direction, and by using lots to discern that direction, the Eleven leave the selection up to Jesus. (Giving lots was something like our drawing straws, but praying beforehand made the exercise a matter of Jesus' choice [compare Proverbs 16:33].) Since Peter has just called him "Lord" (1:21), the Eleven appear to be praying to Jesus with the address, "You, Lord"; and praying to Jesus that he might show whom he has selected to replace Judas harmonizes with his having selected the Twelve in the first place (Luke 6:13–16). The address, "Lord," acknowledges Jesus' authority to make the current selection. Only it's not current. Jesus has already made it. The Eleven merely need to have him point it out to them. The added address, "knower of the hearts of all," acknowledges the omniscience of Jesus. So his selection, though yet to be revealed, is recognized ahead of time not only as authoritative but also as wise. "To take the place of this service and apostleship" defines the supervisory role of apostles as a service for the benefit of others (see also 1:17) and shows that the Eleven have learned the lesson Jesus taught them in Luke 22:24–27: "the one among you [who's] greater [than the others] is to become like a youngster, and the one who leads like one who serves" (excerpt). Luke 22:4 described Judas's deviation: "And on *going away* [from Jesus and the rest of the Twelve], he spoke with the chief priests and officers [of the temple guard] as to how he might give him [Jesus] over to them." As a result, Peter says, Judas "went to his own place." What place was that? Answer: "Hakeldama," that is, the "Field of Blood." It was "his own," because he'd "procured [it] for himself with the reward of injustice"; and it was doubly his own in that he met a bloody demise there (1:18–19). We hear no more of Matthias, but the twelvefold apostolic witness has been restored.

BAPTISM IN THE HOLY SPIRIT
Acts 2:1–13

2:1–4: And when the day of Pentecost was being completely fulfilled, all were together at the same place. ²And suddenly there came from heaven a noise just as of a violent wind being carried along, and it [the noise] **filled the whole room where they were sitting. ³And there appeared to them tongues being divided as if of fire, and it** [the firelike appearance of the tongues] **sat on each one of them. ⁴And all were filled with the Holy Spirit and began to speak with other tongues** [= in other languages] **just as the Spirit was giving them** [ability] **to speak out plainly** [in those languages]. Pentecost was a one-day festival celebrating the end of the wheat harvest in early summer and falling on the fiftieth day after Passover. As at Passover, Jewish pilgrims and Gentiles who had converted to Judaism flocked to Jerusalem for the festival in accordance with Leviticus 23:15–21; Deuteronomy 16:9–12. "When the day of Pentecost was being completely fulfilled" means that the period from Passover to Pentecost was coming to an end with the day of Pentecost itself. It also alludes to the chronology in Jesus' prediction that the apostles would soon be baptized in the Holy Spirit (1:5). "All" includes the rest of the approximately one hundred and twenty besides the apostles (1:15). Their being "all . . . together at the same place" recollects their unity, which makes for a community attractive to potential converts (compare 1:15).

Making unmistakable the baptism in the Holy Spirit are (1) the suddenness of its occurrence; (2) the loudness of its noise ("just as of a violent wind"); (3) the comparison to wind (since "wind" and "Spirit" are cognate to each other in Luke's original Greek [compare John 3:8]); (4) the filling of the *whole* room with the noise; (5) the appearance of firelike tongues—that is, like tongues of flame—on the disciples; (6) their speaking in languages other than their own; and (7) the plainness with which they spoke out in those languages. The evidence was both unmistakably visible and unmistakably audible, rendering the disciples both eyewitnesses and earwitnesses.

"From heaven" denotes the origin of the Spirit. The violence of the wind with which the Spirit's coming is compared denotes the power that Jesus said the disciples would receive when the Holy Spirit came on them (1:8). The wind's "being carried along" implies that Jesus is carrying the Spirit to his disciples (compare 2:33). The division of the firelike tongues symbolizes the variety of the other tongues/languages that the Holy Spirit enables the disciples to speak. "The Spirit was giving them" makes this enablement a gift of the Spirit, undeserved but granted for use in evangelism, as in the rest of this chapter. The "other"-ness of the tongues/languages denotes the universality of the gospel. The tongues' sitting "on each one of them" and the filling of "all" with the Holy Spirit make baptism in the Holy Spirit universal as well as evident among believers, at least among true believers (compare 1 Corinthians 12:13). Jesus promised they'd "be *baptized* in the Holy Spirit" (1:5). Luke's present account of the fulfillment of that promise says they "were *filled* with the Holy Spirit." So the two expressions refer to the same experience. Since the wind of the Spirit "filled the whole room where [the disciples] were sitting," the room became a kind of baptistry in which they were immersed in the Spirit. But just as the Spirit filled the room, the Spirit also filled them just as the Spirit had filled Jesus upon his baptism in water (Luke 3:21–22; 4:1).

2:5: And residing in Jerusalem were Jews, devout men, from every nation of the [human beings] **under heaven.** Because of their Assyrian and Babylonian deportations during the Old Testament period, more Jews lived outside the land of Israel than inside. But some who lived outside had immigrated to the land and settled especially in Jerusalem. At the same time, those who continued living outside made pilgrimages to Jerusalem to join in celebrating festivals such as Pentecost. So Luke is referencing both permanent and temporary residents of Jerusalem (compare 2:9–10, which references residents of Macedonia, Cappadocia, Pontus, and other foreign regions, plus "*visiting* Romans," who therefore must be residing in Jerusalem only for the Festival of Pentecost, as well as residents of Judea, who must be living permanently in Israel [see the comments on 1:8 for "Judea" in the sense of the whole land]). The devoutness of these celebrants mirrors the religious sincerity of the audience of prospective converts toward which Luke pitches Luke-Acts; and though it has to do only with Jews and Gentile converts to Judaism, "from *every* nation of the [human beings] under heaven" prepares for the indiscriminate evangelization of Gentiles later in Acts.

2:6–8: And when this [aforementioned] **sound** ["of a violent wind" (2:2)] **came about, the multitude gathered together and were bewildered, because they were each one hearing them** [the apostles and other believers] **speaking in his own language.** The sound of the windy Spirit was so loud that it attracted the multitude residing in Jerusalem. Despite their large number, "each one" of them heard Jesus' disciples "speaking in his own language [referring to the language used by each auditor in the country of his origin or permanent residence]." Nobody's native language was left out. Here again we see a preview of multiethnic evangelism. No wonder the multitude's bewilderment at this Spirit-inspired miracle of speaking (*not* of hearing, for Luke doesn't write that each one was hearing them *as if* they were speaking in his own language). 7**And they** [the multitude] **were amazed and astounded, saying, "Behold, all these who are speaking** [in languages foreign to them but not to us] **are Galileans, aren't they?"** Implied answer: Yes. 8**"And how is it that we're each hearing** [them speak] **in our own language,** [the language] **in which we were born?"** Enhancing the miracle of this speaking in tongues is Luke's use of three terms for the listeners' wonderment: they were (1) "bewildered"; (2) "amazed"; and (3) "astounded." Also enhancing the miracle are (1) Luke's quoting the multitude directly in reference to their wonderment; (2) their use of "Behold" in the quotation; (3) their noting that none of the tongues-speakers originate from anywhere outside Galilee and therefore can't have learned the foreign languages in which they're speaking and which they the listeners recognize as their own native languages ("in which we were born" referring to the *language* of the country where they were born, not to the *country* of that language); and (4) the repetition of both "each" and "hearing them speak in his/our own language."

2:9–11: "We Parthians and Medes and Elamites and inhabitants of Mesopotamia, both Judea and Cappadocia, Pontus and Asia [a Roman province in western Asia Minor, not the continent of Asia], 10**both Phrygia and Pamphylia, Egypt and the parts of Lybia toward Cyrene, and visiting Romans, both Jews and proselytes,** 11**Cretans and Arabs—we hear them telling in our tongues** [= languages] **the magnificent** [deeds] **of God."** This list of nationalities and regions foreshadows the reach of the apostolic witness "to the extremity of the earth" (1:8) and the worldwide spread of God's kingdom in place of the Roman Empire. Since later in Acts "Roman" connotes Roman citizenship regardless of the region of residence, "visiting Romans" probably means Roman citizens visiting Jerusalem from various parts of the empire. Proselytes were Gentiles converted to Judaism. Their mention foreshadows the conversion of Gentiles to the Christian gospel. But the inclusion of "Judea" and "Jews" points to an ongoing mission to Jews. "Telling . . . the magnificent [deeds] of God" describes the good religious effect of the Spirit's outpouring. Since those deeds aren't specified, the accent rests on that effect as a recommendation of the gospel.

2:12–13: And they were all amazed and bewildered, saying one to the other, "What does this want to be?" That is, how does this speaking in tongues need to be understood? 13**But others, jeering, were saying,**

"**They** [the tongues-speakers] **are full of sweet wine** [= drunk on new, totally or largely unfermented wine, as though they're so susceptible that such wine *could* intoxicate them and *has* done so if they've drunk enough of it]." Enhancing again the miracle of tongues-speaking are (1) the repetition of the multitude's amazement; (2) the addition of yet another expression of wonderment, "bewildered"; (3) the indication that "all" were amazed and bewildered; and (4) another direct quotation of their wonderment. While all were amazed and bewildered, some of them were seeking to understand the meaning of the phenomenon but others were jeering. Presumably the jeerers were Judeans who hadn't resided in foreign countries and understood the disciples' Aramaic but didn't understand the other languages they were speaking and therefore accused them of drunken babbling. Luke savors, and expects us to savor, the stupidity of the accusation that the tongues-speakers were drunk on wine so unfermented as still to be sweet.

PETER'S SERMON AND ITS EFFECT
Acts 2:14–47

A sermon of Peter occupies the bulk of this passage (2:14–36). There follow a description of the sermon's effect in conversions (2:37–41) and the establishing of an ideal community (2:42–47).

***2:14–21*: And on standing with the Eleven** [so that the sermon will represent the twelvefold witness of the apostles as authorized by Jesus himself], **Peter lifted up his voice and spoke out plainly to them** [so that all the multitude could hear]: **"Men of Judea** [= permanent residents in Israel] **and all you who are residing in Jerusalem** [including visitors (compare 2:5 with comments)], **be this known to you and give ear to my words** [this double expression emphasizing the necessity of listening carefully]. 15**For these** [tongues-speakers] **aren't drunk, as you suppose** [them to be]." Here Peter aims his remark especially at the "others" who made the jeering accusation of drunkenness. **"For it's the third hour of the day** [about 9:00 A.M., too early to have gotten drunk]. 16**Rather, this** [tongues-speaking] **is what was spoken about through the prophet Joel** ['through' because Joel was God's mouthpiece]: 17**'And it shall be' in the last days, says God,** [that] **'I'll pour out some of my Spirit on all flesh; and your sons and your daughters will prophesy; and your young** [men] **will see visions; and your older** [men] **will dream dreams;** 18**and during those days, indeed, I'll pour out some of my Spirit on my male slaves and on my female slaves'; and they'll prophesy;** 19**'and I'll give wonders in the sky above and signs on the earth below: blood and fire and a haze of smoke.** 20**The sun will turn into darkness and the moon into blood before the great and obvious day of the Lord comes;** 21**and it shall be** [that] **everyone who calls on the name of the Lord will be saved'** [Joel 2:28–32a except for portions not enclosed in single quotation marks]."

"This is what was spoken about through the prophet Joel" advances Luke's overall emphasis on Christianity as the fruition of Old Testament religion rather than a questionable novelty. Into the first part of his quotation of Joel's prophecy Peter inserts two phrases: (1) "in the last days," which both interprets ahead of time Joel's phrase "during those days" and accents that the event of this Pentecost is helping bring Old Testament prophecy to fulfillment, so that "the last days" span the church age from beginning to end; and (2) "says God," which emphasizes that the fulfillment is carrying out God's preannounced plan. In the quotation itself the figures of being *clothed* with the Holy Spirit (Luke 24:49), being *baptized* in the Holy Spirit (Acts 1:5), and being *filled* with the Holy Spirit (Acts 2:4) have changed into being *suffused* with the Holy Spirit. All these figures of speech refer to the same experience; but their variety arises out of the difficulty of describing the experience adequately, so extraordinary it is.

"Some of my Spirit" implies that this outpouring won't void God of his Spirit. The supply never runs out. "On all flesh" means "on all *kinds* of human beings," as indicated by the following references to sons and daughters, young men and older men, male slaves and female slaves. The inclusion of young people and females stresses this diversity. Since "flesh" connotes frailty (because the flesh of a corpse decomposes though the bones don't) and "Spirit" connotes strength (see Isaiah 31:3), God's outpouring of the Spirit on all flesh empowers human beings to do things they're otherwise incapable of doing, such as prophesying (conveying messages from God) and seeing the visions and dreaming the dreams that provide the subject matter of prophecy. (Visions are seen in daytime while awake [see, for example, Luke 24:22-24]; dreams are dreamt at night while asleep [see, for example, Matthew 2:13-14].) The ability to speak in tongues—that is, in foreign languages never learned by the speaker—depends likewise on the outpouring of God's Spirit. "Indeed" highlights that God is pouring out his Spirit even on persons he counts his slaves, female as well as male. Again Luke makes an insertion into the quotation: "and they'll prophesy." This insertion probably indicates that he considers tongues-speaking—at least when it's understood, as here—equivalent to prophesying (compare 1 Corinthians 14:5, especially the "unless"-clause).

The wonders and signs that Joel proceeded to predict aren't taking place on this day of Pentecost; but since the preceding phenomena mark the beginning of the last days (the church age), Luke includes these wonders and signs to point forward to the end of the church age at Jesus' return ("the obvious day of the Lord"—obvious because of the visibility of his coming "in a cloud with power and much glory" [Luke 21:25-28]). Furthermore, Luke wants not to miss God's good news, spoken through Joel, that "everyone who calls on the name of the Lord will be saved." "Everyone" makes this good news universal in its address. "Calls on" has the sense of "appeals to." Just as the day of the Lord is the time of Jesus' return, "the name of the Lord" is the designation of Jesus *as* the Lord. Since the name "Lord" connotes authority,

divine authority indeed, appealing to him as the Lord brings salvation. He has the authority to save. But what does it mean to be saved? Neither Joel, Peter, nor Luke answers this question here. The question has already been answered in Luke 7:47-50, though, where Jesus himself interprets being saved as having sins forgiven by him (compare Luke 19:7 with 19:9-10 and Acts 2:38), and Luke 13:22-30, where he interprets being saved as having him open the door into God's kingdom (compare Luke 18:24-27). Not to be missed is also salvation from physical ills and demon possession in accordance with Jesus', the apostles', and others' miracles of healing and exorcism (Luke 8:36, 48, 50; 17:19; 18:42; 23:35; Acts 4:9, 12; 14:9).

2:22-28: "Men of Israel, hear these words: Jesus the Nazarene, a man accredited to you by God with miracles and wonders and signs that God performed in your midst through him, as you yourselves know— [23]**this [man], given over by God's ordained plan and foreknowledge, you did away with by nailing [him to a cross] through the hand [= agency] of lawless [men]—** [24]**[this man] whom God resurrected by loosening the birthpangs of death, because it wasn't possible for him to be held fast by it [death].** [25]**For David says regarding him, 'I was always seeing the Lord in front of my eyes, because he's at my right [hand], so that I'll not be shaken.** [26]**On account of this my heart was glad and my tongue exulted. Moreover, my flesh will pitch its tent on the ground of hope,** [27]**because you'll not leave my soul [= myself] in Hades, nor will you give your devout one [me] to see [= experience] putrefaction [such as corpses undergo].** [28]**You've made known to me the paths of life. You'll make me full of gladness with your face [= presence] [Psalm 16:8-11].'"** As in 2:14, Peter's addressing "men" probably implies that males alone constitute his audience. Otherwise his inclusion of females in the outpouring of God's Spirit (2:17-18) would most likely have led Peter to use a term mere amenable to the inclusion of women. "Of Israel" ties in with Luke's putting the onus of blame for Jesus' crucifixion most especially on the Jews' Jerusalem-based leaders. By citing his origin in Nazareth, "the Nazarene" distinguishes this Jesus from other Jesuses. "A man [= 'male']" designates him as a compatriot of the male Israelites whom Peter is addressing and who therefore should have accepted rather than rejected Jesus. Peter traces Jesus' "miracles and wonders and signs" back to God so as to make them a divine accreditation of Jesus. The wonders and signs also hark back to those that Joel prophesied would precede the obvious day of the Lord (2:19-20), so that those future wonders and signs have had a preview in Jesus' past ministry (compare Luke 2:12; 11:29-30). "In your midst" makes Peter's audience, particularly its Judeans (permanent residents in Israel), eyewitnesses of those wonders and signs. "As you yourselves know" underlines their having seen them. "Given over" refers to Jesus' betrayal; but whereas Luke 22:3-4 attributes it to Satan's having entered Judas, here it's attributed to "God's ordained plan and foreknowledge." God wasn't surprised, for he'd not only taken account of the betrayal. He'd also ordained it. Thus satanic, human, and divine responsibilities are intertwined. Peter's main point: everything has gone according to plan, *God's* plan. Eventually Peter will press the conclusion that his audience had therefore better fit into that plan by repenting and getting baptized (2:38–40).

"You did away with [Jesus] by nailing [him to a cross] through the hand of lawless [men]" puts the onus of blame for Jesus' crucifixion on the "men of Israel," represented by the Sanhedrin, and refers to the centurion and his underlings as their agents in the crucifixion. The centurion and his soldiers were "lawless" in that as Gentiles they weren't under the Mosaic law; but in a wider sense "lawless" also alludes to the murderous character of Jesus' crucifixion. God countered by resurrecting Jesus, says Peter. "By loosening the birthpangs of death" compares death to the suffering of birthpangs and then compares birthpangs to bonds that have to be loosened if one is to escape them. Because Scripture—divinely inspired as it is—must be fulfilled, it wasn't possible for Jesus to be held fast by those bonds; and Peter refers David's "I" to Jesus, as though David was impersonating Jesus. The quotation sets out the Lord's nearness to Jesus and Jesus' confidence, hope, and joy in expectation of deliverance from death. (Since David's "I" refers to Jesus, here "the Lord" about whom "I" speaks isn't Jesus, but is God the Father.) We're reminded that in Luke's Gospel Jesus predicted his resurrection several times (9:22; 18:33; 24:7) and maintained his composure while praying just prior to his arrest, getting arrested, standing trial, and dying (22:39–23:46). The hope of Jesus' "flesh" suits Luke's emphasis on the physicality of Jesus' resurrection (Luke 24:36–43). Not being left in Hades, the abode of the dead, implies being brought out of it by resurrection. The self-reference to Jesus as God's "devout one" likewise advances Luke's emphasis on Jesus' admirable piety. And God's not letting him experience putrefaction corresponds to Jesus' having been resurrected on the third day, that is, before putrefaction manifested itself. "You've made known to me the paths of life" indicates that Jesus' prediction of his resurrection came by way of communication from God his Father. And "you'll make me full of gladness with your face" expresses confidence of a happy reunion with God by way of ascension into the Father's presence (1:9–11; Luke 24:50–51).

2:29-32: "Men, brothers, [it's] **allowable to speak to you with boldness** [= I can speak to you confidently] **about the patriarch David, that he both came to an end and was buried. And his tomb is among us till this day** [with the implication that his bones are still there]. ³⁰**Being a prophet, therefore, and knowing that God 'had sworn to him with an oath to seat on his** [David's] **throne** [somebody] **from the fruit of his loin** [= his reproductive organ; that is, to seat a descendant of David on his throne (Psalm 132:11)]; ³¹**foreseeing** [that God would do so, David] **spoke about the resurrection of the Christ, that 'neither was he** [the Christ] **left in Hades' nor did his flesh 'see** [= experience] **putrefac-

tion** [Psalm 16:10]. ³²**God resurrected this Jesus, whose witnesses we all are** [that is, 'all twelve of us (see 2:14) testify to having seen him resurrected' (compare 1:8)]." For the third time Peter addresses his audience with "Men." Using a place-name, he first called them "Men *of Judea*" (2:14). Using a covenantally significant term, he then called them "Men *of Israel*" (2:22). Now he adds to "Men" the affectionately familial address, "*brothers*." This progression has the purpose of earning a favorable hearing, and the sheer multiplication of addresses has the same purpose. It's Jesus' having "presented himself alive with many positive proofs throughout forty days" after suffering crucifixion that allows Peter to speak with confidence on his own and his fellow apostles' behalf (1:3). A patriarch is a founding father. David was the founding father of a dynasty, a line of kings. On the basis of his foregoing quotation of a Psalm of David, Peter observes that David died and was buried, interprets the "flesh" of the "I" in David's psalm as enjoying life after death rather than suffering putrefaction, and concludes that David was prophesying the resurrection of Jesus as the Christ promised by God to descend from David's royal line (see Luke 1:27, 32, 69; 2:4, 11; 3:31; 18:38–39 for Jesus' Davidic descent). Peter doesn't spell out the premise that the corpse of David did suffer putrefaction because of God's leaving him in Hades rather than resurrecting him quickly. But Peter's audience would have agreed with that premise so readily that he didn't need to spell it out. The past tense in "neither was he left in Hades nor did his flesh see putrefaction" treats Jesus' resurrection, though future to David, as so certain as to have already happened; and the twelvefold apostolic witness to the resurrected Jesus contributes to the certainty of the gospel as undergirded by eyewitness testimony (Luke 1:1–4).

2:33-36: "**Therefore** [as a consequence of Jesus' resurrection] **having been exalted to God's right** [hand] **and having received from the Father the promise of the Holy Spirit, he** [Jesus] **has poured out this** [Spirit] **that you see and hear** [in the form of us whom you see and hear speaking in tongues]. ³⁴**For David didn't go up into heaven; but he does say, 'The Lord said to my Lord, "Sit at my right** [hand] ³⁵**till I place your enemies** [as] **a footstool for your feet** [Psalm 110:1].'" ³⁶**Therefore** [as a consequence of Jesus' exaltation] **let all the house of Israel know with certainty that God has made this Jesus, whom you crucified, both Lord and Christ.**" Peter draws the language of Jesus' "having been exalted" from his having seen Jesus "lifted up" and "hoisted" into heaven (1:9). "To God's right hand" puts Jesus in a position of shared deity and divine favor. "Having received from the Father the promise of the Holy Spirit" doesn't mean that Jesus received the promise in its *expression* to him by the Father. It means that he received the promise in its *fulfillment*. The Father fulfilled his promise by granting to Jesus his Son the Holy Spirit for the outpouring on Jesus' followers (see Luke 24:49; Acts 1:4 for the promise). By noting that his audience "see and hear," Peter underlines Luke's pervasive emphasis on eye- and earwitness as supportive of the gospel (Luke 1:1–4). David's not going up into heaven but saying the words of Psalm 110:1 provides the basis for Peter's interpreting the outpouring of the Holy Spirit as a result of Jesus' exaltation by God's right hand. As in Luke 20:42–43, "the Lord" in Psalm 110:1 refers to God the Father, and "my Lord" to Jesus as David's Lord. "Till I place your enemies [as] a footstool for your feet" looks forward to the subjugation of Jesus' enemies at the second coming (compare Luke 19:27; 21:25–27).

"Let all the house of Israel know" issues a command, not a permission, and portrays the nation of Israel as a household, a family (compare Peter's having addressed his audience of men as "brothers" [2:29]). With "all," Peter refuses to exempt any member of this national family; and "know with certainty" links with Luke's writing "that you may know the certainty of the things about which you were instructed" (Luke 1:4) but here refers specifically to God's having made Jesus "both Lord and Christ." Jesus was pronounced both Lord and Christ already at his birth (Luke 2:11, 26); but up till his exaltation by God's right hand he was, so to speak, Lord-elect and Christ-elect. He had yet to be installed into his office formally. His pouring out the Holy Spirit demonstrates that that installation has taken place. "*This* Jesus *whom you crucified*" not only distinguishes him from other Jesuses. It also stresses both the audience's guilt, which they need to repent of since soldiers crucified Jesus on their behalf (Luke 23:24–25, 36–37), and God's reversal of his fortunes, which should motivate repentance.

2:37–39: And on hearing [what Peter said]**, they were pricked at heart** [= conscience-stricken] **and said to Peter and the rest of the apostles, "What should we do, men, brothers?"** They recognize that Peter has testified on behalf of all twelve apostles and therefore address them all. "Men, brothers" reciprocates Peter's having addressed the audience the very same way (2:29) and betokens a favorable response to his sermon. [38]**And Peter tells them, "Repent—and each of you is to be baptized on the basis of the name of Jesus as Christ—for the forgiveness of your sins; and you'll receive the gift of the Holy Spirit.** [39]**For the promise is for you and your children and all** [who are] **far away, as many as the Lord our God may summon."** The present tense of "tells" highlights Peter's commands and promise. The command to repent has to do with their having had Jesus crucified and addresses them directly in the plural for a collective emphasis. The command to be baptized addresses them indirectly in the singular for an individual emphasis. "*Each* of you" rules out the exemption of anyone. Getting baptized symbolizes in outward fashion the inward change of mind that repentance consists in. "On the basis of the name of Jesus as Christ" makes this baptism a kind of body language (accompanied by verbal language according to 22:16) that confesses Jesus as the Christ and calls on him to exercise his christly authority by forgiving the sins repented of. The sign of this forgiveness will be reception of the Holy Spirit as Jesus' gift to the repentant. Such reception is promised,

and the promise is for Peter's Jewish audience, their children (compare "your sons and your daughters" in 2:17), and all Jews living outside the land of Israel ("all [who are] far away"). (Except for Gentile proselytes to Judaism [compare 2:11], Peter has yet to consider the evangelism of Gentiles, as shown in Acts 10.) But there's a condition besides repentance. It's God's summons ("as many as the Lord our God may summon"). As elsewhere, then, human responsibility and divine sovereignty are intertwined (compare 13:48b: "and as many as had been appointed to eternal life believed"). But the accent falls on God's summoning "many," so that evangelism will be numerically successful. Luke uses such success to argue for the gospel's divine origin and to persuade his audience to get on the winning side. "Our *God*" defines "the Lord" as God the Father, and "*our* God" appeals to the belief in God shared between Peter and his audience.

2:40–41: And with very many other words he [Peter] **was solemnly testifying and urging them, saying, "Get saved from this crooked** [= perverse, morally distorted] **generation** [compare Luke 9:41]**!"** [41]**On the one hand, therefore** [because of Peter's testimony and urging]**, those who welcomed his word** [= accepted his message] **got baptized. And on that day about three thousand souls** [= persons] **were added** [to the approximately one hundred and twenty disciples mentioned in 1:15]. Peter was testifying to Jesus' resurrection and exaltation as evidenced by the outpouring of the Holy Spirit, and he was urging his audience to get saved. "With very many words" and "solemnly" add weight to his testimony and heighten the urgency of getting saved. "From this crooked generation" alludes particularly to its perversity in having Jesus crucified unjustly and enhances Luke's presentation of the gospel as fostering moral reform in society. To "get *saved* from this crooked generation" is to escape from the judgment that will come on it (see Luke 11:29–32, 49–51). Baptism indicated acceptance of Peter's message. The addition of three thousand converts in one day exhibits the power for witness that Jesus promised his apostles would receive when the Holy Spirit came on them (1:8). Again Luke wants us to recognize and join the winning side. It's disastrous as well as useless to stick with losers, that is, with the crooked generation headed for eternal loss at the Last Judgment.

2:42–43: On the other hand [that is, in addition to the aforementioned mass conversion]**, they were engrossed with the apostles' teaching and with sharing, with the breaking of bread** [= eating with one another] **and with the prayers.** Their engrossment with the apostles' teaching advances a continuity of doctrine from Jesus through the apostles to their converts. Because it's tried and true, Luke likes tradition. Engrossment in sharing and eating together makes for an ideal social unit such as others would like to join. Engrossment in the prayers makes for an ideal religious unit and—if "*the* prayers" refers to appointed services of prayer in the practice of Judaism—portrays the converts as good Jews rather than apostates. And engrossment *as such* intensifies all these admirable practices. ⁴³**And fear was happening in every soul** [= person], **and many wonders and signs were happening through the apostles.** The fear seems related to the supernatural ("wonders and signs"), for displays of power that exceed human ability fill people with a certain dread even when that power works to their benefit. For it could work to their detriment too. Heightening the supernatural in the present instance are (1) the doubling of references to it with both "wonders" and "signs"; (2) the description of them as "many"; (3) their engendering fear "in *every* soul"; and (4) the portrayal of this fear and the wonders and signs as ongoing events ("was happening" and "were happening"). "Wonders" connotes awesomeness. "Signs" connotes significance in that the events point beyond themselves to a supernatural source and, in this case, to a salvific purpose. "Through the apostles" implies the Holy Spirit as the source of supernatural, saving power.

2:44–45: And all the believers were at the same [place] **and were holding all things** [their possessions] **in common;** ⁴⁵**and they were selling** [their] **pieces of property and goods and dividing them** [the proceeds of the sales] **among all** [the believers] **in accordance with anyone's having need.** Luke now elaborates his portrayal of believers as an ideal social unit by spelling out what he meant by their engrossment in sharing: they shared with each other both the same place (they stayed together) and their possessions. *All* of them shared *all* things with *all* other believers even to the point of selling both land holdings and what they otherwise possessed (though see 5:1–11 for an exception that will prove the rule). And the needs of other believers, not their status, determined the amount they received.

2:46–47: And being daily engrossed with mutual fervor in [the courts of] **the temple and breaking bread from house to house, they were taking nourishment** [= eating meals together] **with exultation and sincerity of heart,** ⁴⁷**praising God and having favor in relation to the whole people. And to the same** [place, where the believers spent time together] **the Lord was daily adding those who were getting saved.** Here Luke elaborates his portrayal of believers in Jesus as an ideal religious community. They share a religious fervor that engrosses them to the extent of going to the temple day after day, so that they prove themselves loyal to traditional Judaism. They open their places of residence to share meals with one another. With high spirits and heartfelt sincerity they praise God. This socioreligious behavior makes a favorable impression not just on some of the people outside but on "the whole people" (compare 5:13). (And Luke wants admiration to produce conversion.) Apparently the believers' behavior makes a favorable impression on the Lord, too; for he matches their daily admirable behavior with daily additions of those who are getting saved (compare 2:40: "Get saved from this crooked generation"). And these were additions "to the same [place]," so that unity wasn't compromised by growth.

THE HEALING OF A LAME MAN
Acts 3:1–10

3:1–3: And Peter and John were going up into [the courts of] **the temple at the hour of prayer,** [that is,] **the ninth** [hour (about 3:00 P.M.)]. ²**And a certain man who'd been lame since** [he'd come] **out of his mother's womb was being carried, whom people placed day after day at the gate of the temple called "Beautiful" for the purpose of** [his] **requesting alms** [charitable gifts] **from those proceeding into the temple** [courts], ³**who on seeing Peter and John about to go into the temple** [courts] **was asking to receive alms** [from them]. The going of Peter and John into the temple courts at the hour of prayer shows them to be piously observant Jews. The ninth hour is counted from sunrise. That the lame man has to be carried by others shows how debilitated he is: by himself he can't even limp along. And being so lame from birth, he never learned to walk. Such lameness makes him unable to work for a living. So others put him at the temple gate called "Beautiful" to ask for alms. For several reasons the gate makes a good place to ask for them: (1) a large number of worshipers enter and exit the gate; (2) its being a gate of the temple puts the comers and goers in a religious frame of mind; and (3) charitable giving formed an important part of Jewish piety. Will Peter and John fulfill this religious obligation?

3:4–8: And gazing at him, Peter along with John said, "Look at us." It appears that when Peter and John didn't give him anything, the lame man diverted his attention to other possible almsgivers. ⁵**And he, expecting to receive something from them** [from Peter and John because of their command to look at them], **started paying attention to them.** ⁶**But Peter said, "I don't have silver and gold, but what I do have—this I'm giving to you. In the name of Jesus Christ the Nazarene get up and walk around."** Of course Peter had no silver and gold, for with other believers he'd divested himself of his private possessions and donated the proceeds to a common treasury (2:44–45). So he gives what he can give, a gift better than money. He gives the gift of salvation from lameness. Peter doesn't issue his *command* in the name of Jesus Christ the Nazarene. Rather, the lame man is to *get up and walk around* in that name. To do so will require belief that Jesus of Nazareth is named Christ truly. Such belief will transfer to the lame man enough of Jesus' power to enable his getting up and walking around. ⁷**And seizing him by the right hand** [the hand of strength for most people], **he** [Peter] **raised him. And instantly his** [the lame man's] **feet and ankles were firmed up;** ⁸**and jumping up he stood and started walking around and entered with them** [Peter and John] **into the temple** [courts] **walking around and jumping and praising God.** "His feet and ankles" tells us the exact location of lameness. It's not enough that he got up and walked around in obedience to Peter's command. His *jumping up* exceeded the command and exhibits the abundance of power transferred from Jesus when a person believes him to be Christ, the one God anointed to bring us salvation (compare Isaiah 35:6). The repetition of his jumping and walking around accents the miracle of healing. Its happening "instantly" does too. The healed man's entering the temple courts with Peter and John—obviously for prayer, since it was the hour of prayer—and "praising God" demonstrate the good religious effect of the healing that came about through obedient faith in the name of Jesus Christ. Moreover, since ancient people regarded weakness in the ankles and feet as a sign of weak morals, and sure-footedness as a sign of strong moral character, the firming up of this man's ankles and feet symbolizes moral strength. So the gospel doesn't damage either morals or religion. The gospel enhances them.

3:9–10: And all the people saw him walking around and praising God; [10]and they were recognizing him, [that is, recognizing] **that he was the one who used to sit at the Beautiful Gate of the temple for the purpose of** [requesting] **alms; and they were filled with astonishment and dumbfoundment because of what had happened to him.** The people, *all* of them, become eyewitnesses to the truth and power of the gospel as demonstrated by the man's "walking around" (mentioned the third time for emphasis) and to the gospel's good religious effect as demonstrated by the man's "praising God" (mentioned the second time for emphasis). The people's recognizing in the healed man a former beggar, in particular the one who used to sit at the temple's Beautiful Gate, gives their eyewitness the element of certainty. This was no case of mistaken identity. Hence all the people's "astonishment," to which Luke adds "dumbfoundment" for yet more emphasis. And even more emphasis on the miracle accrues from their being "filled" with astonishment and dumbfoundment. No measured reaction here! "What had happened to him" was all too obvious and marvelous. It took their breath away (so, more or less, the meaning of Luke's Greek word behind "dumbfoundment").

ANOTHER SERMON BY PETER
Acts 3:11–26

3:11–15: And while he [the healed man] **was clinging to Peter and John, all the people, completely astonished, ran together to them at the portico** [a roofed and colonnaded walkway] **called Solomon's. [12]And on seeing** [them], **Peter answered** [= responded] **to the people, "Men of Israel, why are you amazed at this, or why do you gaze** [at us] **as though by our own power or piety we've made him** [the formerly lame man] **walk around? [13]'The God of Abraham and Isaac and Jacob—the God of our** [fore]**fathers** [Exodus 3:6, 15]'—**has glorified his servant Jesus** [compare Isaiah 52:13], **whom you on the one hand gave over** [to Pilate] **and denied in Pilate's face** [= presence] **after that one had decided to release** [him]. **[14]On the other hand, you disowned the Holy and Righteous One and requested that a man who's a murderer be granted to you; [15]and you**

killed the Founder-Leader of life [= had him killed], **whom God has raised from among the dead, whose witnesses we are."** The healed man's clinging to Peter and John is more than psychologically understandable. It also indicates his having joined the company of believers in Jesus. All the people's astonishment of 3:10 now escalates to "*complete* astonish[ment]." This escalation and their running together to Peter, John, and the healed man heap further emphasis on the miraculous character of what has happened and also indicate that through the apostles Jesus is continuing his salvific work; for during his earthly ministry it likewise astonished and attracted large numbers of people.

As he did in 2:22, Peter addresses the people with "Men of Israel" to remind them of their religious heritage; and he takes pains to divert their amazement and gaze from himself and John lest anyone mistakenly attribute the miracle to their own power or piety. Of course, this refusal to take credit is itself an evidence of piety, though still not an indication that the piety produced the miracle. Peter then extends his reminder of the people's religious heritage by referring to the God of Abraham, Isaac, and Jacob as the "the God of our [fore]fathers." By including Peter and John with the people, "our" portrays the apostles as observant members with them of God's chosen nation. Peter's calling Jesus God's "servant" implies that Jesus carried out God's bidding and contrasts sharply with the Jews' having given Jesus over to Pilate and disowning him before Pilate. According to Luke 23:18–25, this disowning took the form of demanding Jesus' crucifixion and, adding insult to injury, requesting that the imprisoned murderer Barabbas be released to them as a gift. Pilate's having decided to release Jesus (Luke 23:16) and Jesus' holiness and righteousness, acknowledged even by the centurion overseeing the crucifixion (Luke 23:47 [see also Luke 1:35; 4:34]), exacerbate by contrast these Jews' guilt (but not, it has to be said, that of Jews in all times and places). Peter's description of Jesus as holy and righteous paints him rather than Peter and John in glowing colors of virtue, though elsewhere it's appropriate for *Luke* to portray Peter and John as virtuous in a way it's inappropriate for *Peter* to do. God's glorification of Jesus started with his raising Jesus from among the dead. This raising made Jesus both the founder of the life that's eternal for believers in him and the leader of such believers into that life (contrast his enemies' getting him killed). Peter and John are Jesus' witnesses in that they saw him resurrected and are now testifying about him (see 1:8: "you'll be my witnesses").

3:16: "And on the basis of faith in his [Jesus'] **name, his name has firmed up this** [man], **whom you see and know; and the faith that's through him** [Jesus] **has given him** [the formerly lame man] **this total fitness fronting you all."** "On the basis of faith in his name" confirms that in 3:6 the lame man was to get up and walk around in the name of Jesus Christ rather than that Peter commanded him in that name. To obey the command it took faith in the name; and on the basis of this faith the name itself firmed up the man, in particular his feet and ankles (3:7), so that he jumped up, stood, and walked around (3:8). Perhaps we shouldn't say the name *itself* firmed him up, though; for the name represents who Jesus is as a *person*—that is, the Christ. Nevertheless, Luke attributes the miracle to this name to stress that it's Jesus' identity as the Christ that enabled him to firm up the lame man. "Whom you see and know" appeals to the audience's eyewitnessing the effect of the miracle and to their knowledge of his prior incapacity. Again, you can't disbelieve your eyes or hypothesize mistaken identity. "*Fronting* you all" makes for eyewitness and recognition at close range, and "fronting you *all*" confidently invites a challenge from anyone who saw what had happened. None is forthcoming or possible. Neither does the totality of the man's present physical fitness brook any challenge, and it enhances the miracle with completeness. The intertwining of divine sovereignty and human responsibility appears again in the firming up of the man by Jesus' name and the man's being given total fitness by his faith, and in the man's exercising faith and the coming of that faith "through" Jesus.

3:17–18: "**And now, brothers, I know that you acted in ignorance, just as also your rulers** [did]. [18]**But the things which God announced beforehand through the mouth of all the prophets—that his Christ would suffer—he has fulfilled in this way.**" "And now" looks beyond past guilt. "Brothers" appeals to co-citizenship in God's chosen nation. "I know that you acted in ignorance" lessens the blame for Jesus' crucifixion (compare his prayer in Luke 23:34, "Father, forgive them; for they don't know what they're doing," which comparison shows that Jesus is continuing to act and speak through Peter in accordance with the implication of Acts 1:1). "As also your rulers [did]" spreads the blame around but concentrates it on the rulers since they *are* rulers. The preannouncement of the Christ's sufferings demonstrates their fitting God's plan. That *God* announced them (the prophets acting only as his mouthpiece) emphasizes the point. "Through the mouth of *all* the prophets" makes the preannouncement so multiple that it can't be gainsaid. Since "Christ" means "anointed one," "*his* Christ" indicates that *God* anointed Jesus to fulfill the messianic role "in this way," that is, by suffering.

3:19–21: "**Therefore** [because you've sinned by having Jesus killed] **repent and turn around** [= be converted] **in order that your sins be wiped out, so that seasons of relief may come from the Lord's face** [= presence] [20]**and** [so that] **he may send the Christ, who was hand-picked for you beforehand,** [namely,] **Jesus,** [21]**whom it's necessary for heaven to welcome till times of the restoration of all things, which** [times] **God spoke about through the mouth of his holy prophets,** [who've prophesied] **since long ago.**" "Repent" has to do with a change of attitude toward your sins: you feel sorry for having committed them. "Turn around" has to do with a consequent change in behavior: you stop committing those sins. (*How* you stop is a question Peter and Luke don't take up, but see Romans 6:1–8:11.) The wip-

ing out of sins is a figure of speech for forgiveness: your sins aren't on the books any more. "Seasons of relief" equate with "times of the restoration of all things" but in this context have special reference to God's relieving the nation of Israel from foreign domination or, as the apostles put it in 1:6, to Jesus' "restoring the rulership to Israel" (see the comments on 1:6 with cross-references). In other words, "the restoration of all things" has as a special feature the restoration of rulership to Israel so as to give Israel its long-awaited relief. The plural of "seasons" and "times" suggests a lengthy period. But it will come only when Israel's sins are wiped out because of their repentance and conversion (compare Romans 11:25–27). It can come only "from the Lord's face," that is, by the Lord's doing. And it will come only when the Lord (here, God the Father) sends Jesus, prechosen to be the Christ "for you" (= "for your benefit"). "Hand-picked for you beforehand" alludes yet again to God's plan, this time for Jesus Christ in regard to Israel's future benefit. Meanwhile, his plan for the present is that heaven must welcome him till those future seasons of relief and restoration come up on God's calendar. Assuring that they will in fact come up are (1) God's speaking about them through the mouth of prophets; (2) the holiness of the prophets through whose mouth he spoke; and (3) their having prophesied those seasons "since long ago." The longer the tradition, the greater its reliability.

Peter proceeds to detail some of that ancient prophecy in **3:22–24:** "**On the one hand, Moses said, 'The Lord your God will raise up for you a prophet like me from among your brothers** [= fellow Israelites]. **Him you shall heed in accordance with all things he tells you, however many** [they are]. [23]**On the other hand, every soul** [= person], **whoever** [he is], **that doesn't heed that prophet will be obliterated from among the people** [of Israel] [Deuteronomy 18:15, 19 (compare Leviticus 23:29)].' [24]**And all the prophets from Samuel and the ones succeeding** [him], **as many as they** [were], **spoke about and announced these days.**" Peter identifies Jesus as the Moses-like prophet that Moses himself prophesied the Lord God would raise up in Israel for the Israelites' benefit. Does "raise up" allude somewhat to God's raising Jesus up from among the dead as well as to God's previously raising him up from within Israelite society? In view of those who don't heed Jesus as that prophet, "Him you shall heed" comes across as a command. But in view of the relief promised to result from repentance and conversion, "Him shall you heed" is also a prediction that some *will* heed Jesus as that prophet. "*All* the things he tells you, however *many* [they are]" demands and predicts total obedience. The warning of obliteration for not heeding the prophet Jesus is self-explanatory, and "*every* soul, who*ever* [he is]" underlines the warning by ruling out any exceptions. The addition to Moses of "all the prophets . . . as many as they [were]" from Samuel onward reinforces both the command, the promise, and the warning related to "these days" of fulfilled prophecy. The double expression, "spoke about and announced," adds further reinforcement.

3:25–26: "And you're the sons [= descendants] **of the prophets and** [sons = heirs] **of the covenant that God covenanted with your** [fore]**fathers, saying to Abraham, 'And in your seed** [= descendants] **all the people groups of the earth will be favored** [Genesis 12:3; 18:18; 22:18; 26:4].' **²⁶Raising up his servant** [Jesus], **God sent him first to you, favoring you by turning each** [of you] **away from your evils."** Calling the audience descendants of the prophets and heirs of the Abrahamic covenant strengthens Peter's appeal for repentance and conversion. Also strengthening this appeal are (1) the implication that repentance and conversion will make the audience themselves a fulfillment of the promise to Abraham that in his descendants "all the people groups of the earth will be favored"; (2) God's sending Jesus his servant to Israel "first"; and (3) Jesus' favoring them by turning each one away from their evils. (In Luke's grammar, "favoring" tells what God's servant does, not what God does.) For now, the favoring of individual Jews by turning them away from their evils won't eventuate in the conversion of them all, but it will eventuate in the favoring of all the people groups of the earth through worldwide evangelism by those Jews who do repent and convert, as later in Acts. God's sending Jesus to Israel "first" also implies a subsequent expansion of divine favor to include Gentiles.

THE TRIAL OF PETER AND JOHN
Acts 4:1–31

This passage divides into the arrest of Peter and John (4:1–4), Peter's defense at their trial (4:5–12), their release (4:13–22), and the effects of their release on other believers (4:23–31).

4:1–4: And while they were speaking to the people, the priests and the officer of the temple [guard] **and the Sadducees confronted them, ²being annoyed because they were teaching the people and announcing in Jesus the resurrection from among the dead. ³And they laid hands on them** [= arrested them] **and put them in a guardhouse till the next day, for it was already evening. ⁴But many of those who'd heard the word** [the gospel in Peter's sermon] **believed, and the number of the men came to be about five thousand.** Only Peter was speaking in 3:11–26. But just as he spoke on behalf of the Eleven as well as himself in 2:14–40, so in 3:11–26 he has been speaking on behalf of John as well as himself. So Luke writes, "And while *they* were speaking to the people" and "because *they* were teaching the people." In their teaching, Peter had announced that Jesus was resurrected from among the dead. But Luke's way of putting it—"in Jesus *the* resurrection from among the dead"—makes Jesus' resurrection a preview of others' resurrection. Since Sadducees didn't believe in resurrection (see 23:6–8 and Luke 20:27 with comments) and didn't want Peter to persuade the people of Jesus' resurrection and of that of others to come, they were annoyed. And since the leading priests were Sadducees and controlled the temple guard, they along with the officer

of the guard and lay Sadducees confronted, arrested, and put in a guardhouse Peter and John. They were so annoyed, in fact, that they couldn't wait for Peter to finish his sermon—hence its lack of an appeal to repent and get baptized (contrast 2:38–41). Because it was already evening, a trial was delayed till the next day. Despite the cutting short of Peter's sermon by the arrest, though, many who'd heard it believed, so that the number of men who believed swelled from about three thousand (2:41) to about five thousand (not counting women and children) in addition to the approximately one hundred and twenty (1:15). Because the disciples received power with the coming of the Holy Spirit on them (1:8), the progress of the gospel they preach is unstoppable.

4:5–7: And it happened on the next day that their [the Jews'] **rulers and elders and scholars—⁶including Annas the high priest and Caiaphas and John and Alexander and as many as were of high priestly stock—gathered together in Jerusalem. ⁷And on making them** [Peter and John] **stand in the midst** [of them], **they were inquiring, "By what sort of power or by what sort of name did you do this** [the healing of the lame man in 3:1–10]**?"** The rulers were the chief priests. The elders were the upper crust of lay society. Both of these groups were largely if not exclusively Sadducean. The scholars were experts in the Old Testament law. Most of them belonged to the party of Pharisees, who—unlike the Sadducees—believed in resurrection. Together, all three groups made up the Sanhedrin. Though Annas wasn't high priest at the time, he had been and still was the dominant figure in priestly circles. His son-in-law Caiaphas held the high priestly office currently (see the comments on Luke 3:2; John 18:13). The identity of this John is uncertain, and we know nothing more about this Alexander; but Luke's including them along with Annas and Caiaphas gives evidence of historical research supporting the claim in Luke 1:1–4. Though not all members of the Sanhedrin were of high priestly stock or belonged to the Sadducean party, Luke features those that were because of their opposition to the preaching of resurrection. "In Jerusalem" would seem unnecessary to say except for Luke's desire to remind us that the apostles were to start witnessing for Jesus in Jerusalem and have been hauled to court for doing so (1:8). The Sanhedrists' inquiry doesn't deny the performance of a miraculous healing. Eyewitness made the miracle undeniable. So the inquiry asks for the *sort* of power and the *sort* of name by which Peter and John performed it (compare Luke 20:1–2). (The plural of "you" in "did you do this" includes John as Peter's partner.) Was the power demonic or divine? Was the name demonic or divine? Because of their opposition to the teaching of resurrection, the Sadducees in the Sanhedrin are fishing for the demonic so as to condemn Peter and John (compare Luke 11:14–19).

4:8–10: Then Peter, filled with the Holy Spirit, said to them, "Rulers of the people and elders, ⁹if we're being interrogated today for a good deed [done] **on a weak man** [he was so lame he couldn't even limp]—

[as to] **by what** [power or name] **this** [man] **was saved** [from his weakness; but there are overtones of eternal salvation]— [10]**be it known to all you and to all the people of Israel that by the name of Jesus Christ the Nazarene, whom you crucified, whom God raised from among the dead—by this** [name] **this** [man] **stands in your sight healthy.**" For a second time Peter is filled with the Holy Spirit (compare Acts 2:4). Or is it that he's still filled because of what happened on the Day of Pentecost? Either way, the Spirit empowers him, a former fisherman, to speak boldly even to the Jewish supreme court. In addressing the Sanhedrin, Peter may leave out the scholars because they wouldn't object to resurrection as such, though Jesus' resurrection is another matter. Peter's describing the miracle as "a good deed" puts a bad face on the Sanhedrin's interrogation of him and John. For a good deed merits commendation, not judicial interrogation. Peter attributes the miracle to "the name of Jesus Christ the Nazarene" (see the comments on 3:6, 16). Because there's power in a name, "the name" answers the question, "By what sort of power . . . ?" "Of Jesus Christ the Nazarene" answers the question, "By what sort of name . . . ?" Though soldiers crucified Jesus (Luke 23:36–37), they did so on the Sanhedrin's behalf (Luke 23:24–25)—hence "whom *you* crucified." But both in Peter's speech and in Jesus' experience, "whom you crucified" is quickly reversed by "whom God raised from the dead." The reversal puts a bad face on the Sanhedrin once again and gives prospective converts a divine recommendation of Jesus. "Be it known to all you and to all the people of Israel" addresses the healing beyond immediate eyewitnesses to all the Sanhedrists and all Israelites whether or not they saw firsthand the healing and its effect. One thing all the Sanhedrists do see, though, is "this man" standing before their very eyes ("in your sight," Peter says) in a state of health. So the man is there with Peter and John, as to be expected from his clinging to them according to 3:11 (see also 4:14). "Stand[ing]," not sitting to beg for alms. "Healthy," not weak. "By this [name]" echoes "by the name of Jesus Christ the Nazarene" so as not to lose sight of that name and its power to save.

4:11–12: "**This** [Jesus] **is the stone, the one treated with contempt by you the builders, the one that has become the head of an angle** [compare Psalm 118:22 and the comments on Luke 20:17 for the meaning of 'the head of an angle']. [12]**And there's salvation in no one else, for under heaven there's no other name that's been given among human beings by which it's necessary for us to be saved.**" Peter echoes Jesus' own use of Psalm 118:22 when Jesus was answering, much as Peter is here, the chief priests', scholars', and elders' questions as to what sort of authority he had to act as he did and who gave him such authority (Luke 20:1–19). Presumably the present Sanhedrists are the same as those Jesus addressed and so are hearing this explanation of Psalm 118:22 for the second time. But whereas Jesus' explanation looked forward to his passion and resurrection as yet to be accomplished, Peter's looks back on those

events as already accomplished. He identifies Jesus with "the stone." But whereas the psalmist speaks of a "rejected" stone, Peter speaks in personal terms of the stone as "treated with contempt." "By you" identifies the Sanhedrists with "the builders" who treated Jesus the stone with contempt (compare Luke 23:11). The announcement of salvation in Jesus, in no one else, and in no other name—this announcement confirms that the salvation of the lame man from his lameness carried overtones of eternal salvation rather than being limited to physical healing. For not everybody needs physical healing, yet "it's necessary for *us* [whether physically incapacitated or not] to be saved." "There's salvation in no one else" and "there's no other name . . . by which it's necessary . . . to be saved" make the name of Jesus Christ the exclusive means of salvation (see the comments on 3:6, 16 for the exercise of faith in him as a necessary element in the saving effect of his name; also 2:21). "Under heaven" and "that's been given among human beings" further exclude salvation by any other means. But these expressions also make Jesus' name a means of salvation *open to all*—as a gift.

4:13–14: And seeing Peter's and John's boldness and on detecting that they're unlettered and unprofessional men, they were marveling and recognizing them, [that is, recognizing] **that they'd been with Jesus.** [14]**And seeing the man who'd been healed standing with them** [that is, with Peter and John], **they had nothing to say by way of contradiction.** "Unlettered" means either "uneducated (as to the Old Testament law)" or, more stringently, "illiterate." Either way, how could such laymen have used Psalm 118:22 in boldly accusing the Sanhedrists of miscarrying justice in Jesus' death when they themselves (Peter and John) were on trial before this very body? Ah, they've been with Jesus and heard him apply Psalm 118:22 to himself and the Sanhedrists in direct confrontation with them (Luke 20:17–19). The Sanhedrists see not only Peter's and John's boldness. They see also the healed man standing with them— again, "standing" rather than sitting and begging for alms. The Sanhedrists' own eyewitnessing robs them of anything they might say against Peter's and John's performance and explanation of the miracle. The inability to contradict Peter and John fulfills Jesus' promise in Luke 21:15: "I'll give you a mouth and wisdom that none of your foes will be able to withstand or contradict" (see also Acts 6:10).

4:15–17: And on commanding them to go outside the Sanhedrin [= outside the council meeting], **they were conferring with one another** [16]**saying, "What should we do with these men? For that a known sign has taken place through them is obvious to all who inhabit Jerusalem, and we can't deny** [it]. [17]**But lest it spread yet further among the people, let's warn them** [Peter and John] **not to speak any more on the basis of this name** [of Jesus Christ] **to even one human being.**" The Sanhedrists are so embarrassed and nonplussed that they don't want Peter and John to hear their deliberation.

The description of the miracle as "a sign" points to its theological significance. Though not for the Sanhedrists, for Luke the sign supports Peter's claim that there's salvation in Jesus' name and in no other. The description of the sign as "known" and of its having taken place through two of Jesus' apostles as "obvious" doubles the Sanhedrists' own emphasis on undeniability. "To *all* who inhabit Jerusalem" adds a third emphasis on undeniability. "Lest it spread further among the people" expresses fear that the sign will be reported to Jews living outside Jerusalem too. The decision to put a gag order on Peter and John carries a warning that threatens unspecified punishment for disobedience. "Not to speak any more on the basis of this name" reflects that they had spoken on the basis of Jesus' name. But according to 3:6-8, 16 the lame man *got up and walked around* in/on the basis of Jesus' name. Here the Sanhedrists transfer "on the basis of this name" to Peter's and John's *speaking*, since these apostles proclaimed the name as bringing salvation to believers in it. "To even one human being" betrays an extremity of fear that the gospel will be propagated. Subsequent events will prove the Sanhedrists' fear to be well-founded and their warning useless, for the gospel can't be stopped even by high authorities such as they are.

4:18-20: And on calling them, they ordered [them] **neither to speak nor to teach at all on the basis of Jesus' name** [as they had been doing]. [19]**But Peter and John, answering, told them, "You judge whether it's right in God's sight to heed you rather than God. [20]For we aren't able *not* to tell the things that we've seen and heard."** The double expression, "neither to speak nor to teach," plus "at all," reinforces the Sanhedrists' prohibition and therefore makes all the bolder the apostles' refusal to comply. "You judge" puts an onus on the Sanhedrists. After all, they were judges. But "whether it's right in God's sight" subordinates their judgment to a higher court. In effect, "to heed you rather than God" preannounces God's verdict. For he demands obedience to his commands, and it's implied that the apostles' telling what they've seen and heard has been commanded them by God. Indeed, he *has* commanded them to do so—through Jesus (see 1:8). And as Jesus' apostles, they're bound and determined to. "The things we've seen and heard" fits Luke's overarching emphasis on eye- and earwitness as certifying the gospel (Luke 1:1-4).

4:21-22: And they, on warning [them] **further, finding nothing as to how they might punish them, released them on account of the people, because all were glorifying God for what had taken place. [22]For the man on whom this sign of healing had taken place was more than forty years** [old]. The further warning responds to the apostles' statement of noncompliance. The Sanhedrists are so afraid of the people's opinion (as they were also in Jesus' case according to Luke 19:48; 20:6, 19, 26; 22:2) that instead of responding to Peter's and John's statement of noncompliance with further prosecution, they're reduced to giving them only a further warning. Even the statement of noncompliance doesn't count as

a ground for punishment. The people's glorifying God for the healing carries forward Luke's stress on the good religious effect of the gospel, in this case of what Jesus has continued to do and teach through the apostles (1:1). That "all" the people are glorifying God heightens the stress, and helping explain why all are glorifying God is the healed man's age of "more than forty years." To his natal lameness are added over four decades of never having walked or learned to walk. No wonder the people's universal praise of God for the healing! Luke borrows from the Sanhedrists the word "sign" to reemphasize the healing as a pointer to salvation through Jesus' name.

4:23-26: And on being released, they went to their own [people—that is, fellow believers] **and reported as many things as the chief priests and the elders had said to them.** "Their own" brings out the attractively close fellowship of Jesus' followers. "As many things as" indicates a full report, so that the reaction of Peter's and John's fellow believers won't be colored by any ignorance of the Sanhedrists' threats. "The chief priests and the elders" leaves out "the scholars" of 4:5 (see the comments on 4:8 for a possible explanation). [24]**And they, on hearing** [the report], **lifted** [their] **voice to God with mutual fervor and said, "Sovereign, you 'who made the heaven and the earth and the sea and all the things in them** [Psalm 146:6], [25]**who said through the Holy Spirit, the mouth of our** [fore]**father David your servant, 'Why do nations strut and peoples plot empty** [= futile] **things? [26]The kings of the earth took a stand and the rulers gathered together at the same place against the Lord** [God the Father] **and against his Christ** [Psalm 2:1-2].'"** Peter's and John's fellow believers react to the reported threat of the Sanhedrin with prayer. Such is their piety, which recommends the gospel. "*Lifted* their voice to God" suits his superiority in heaven above. The singular of "voice" suits the "*mutual* fervor" of their prayer. The address "Sovereign" exhibits both respect and confidence that God is in control of all that happens in the universe. If he made heaven, earth, sea, and all things in them, he surely has universal control and, more particularly, control over human events—as stated by God himself through the Holy Spirit. The collocation of "the Holy Spirit" and "the mouth of our [fore]father David your servant" without even an "and" connecting the two phrases, so that they stand cheek by jowl as joint objects of "through"—this collocation draws the closest possible equation between the quoted psalm of David and God's speaking through the Holy Spirit. And "your servant" makes David serve up God's word in the psalm just as the Holy Spirit does. "*Our* [fore]father David" calls attention to believers in Jesus as Jews loyal to their heritage. The strutting and plotting of nations and peoples have to do with both past opposition to Jesus and his followers and future such opposition. Its scripturally stated futility ensures the opponents' defeat. The prayer applies to Jesus and his opponents the kings' and rulers' gathering against him in Jerusalem. But their opposition to him is at the same time opposition to "the Lord." Hence its futility.

The prayer continues in *4:27–28*: "**For in truth both Herod and Pontius Pilate along with Gentiles and peoples of Israel gathered together in this city against your holy servant Jesus, whom you'd anointed, 28to do as many things as your hand and your plan had predetermined to take place.**" This sentence explains the meaning of Psalm 2:1–2, just quoted. "In truth" underlines the fulfillment of that Old Testament text by the opponents of Jesus and thus supports the affirmation that their actions carried out God's "plan." Since the hand stands for active power, "your hand" emphasizes that it's the power of God that has made his plan operative; and Herod Antipas and Pontius Pilate, along with their underlings (Gentiles all), joined with Israel to play their predetermined but at the same time guiltworthy roles (compare Luke 23:12). "The *peoples* [plural] of Israel" differs from "the people [singular] of Israel" in Luke 2:32; Acts 4:10; 13:17, 24. Peter uses the plural instead of the singular to draw a close connection with the "peoples" in Psalm 2:1–2. There, "peoples" paralleled "nations," and both referred to Gentiles. Here, by adding "of Israel" to "peoples" Peter casts Israel in the role of pagans so far as Israel's treatment of Jesus the Christ is concerned. "Gathered together in this city against your holy servant Jesus" harks back to the Sanhedrin's gathering together in Jerusalem against Jesus (Luke 22:66). The designation of him as God's "holy servant" highlights Jesus' virtue (contrast the criminality of Barabbas [Luke 23:18–25]). "Whom you'd anointed" brings out the meaning of "his Christ" in 4:26 (quoting Psalm 2:2; compare 10:38; Luke 4:18). "As many things as" makes the maltreatment of Jesus fulfill *all* God's plan for that episode.

The prayer closes with *4:29–30*: "**And as for the present, Lord, look on their threats** [4:17, 21] **and give your slaves** [= us] **to speak your word with all boldness 30as you stretch out your hand to bring about healing and signs and wonders through the name of your holy servant Jesus.**" The preceding has recollected how Jesus was maltreated. Now the prayer turns to the maltreatment, or threats thereof, of his followers. They'd addressed God with "Sovereign" in 4:24. To introduce their request they readdress God, this time with "Lord," which fits their self-characterization, "your slaves," since one meaning of "lord" is "slaveowner." This self-characterization puts them at God's disposal. "Look on their threats" means "pay attention to their threats." But to what end? Is it for protection, as we might expect? No. It's for speaking God's word, the gospel, with boldness—"*all* boldness," that is, without any thought of holding back to lessen danger. "As you stretch out your hand" expresses confidence that God will accompany their bold witness with healing, signs, and wonders certifying that witness. Luke's text could also be translated in such a way as to make these certifications the means by which God grants boldness ("*by* stretching out your hand"). Both accompaniment and means may be meant. For sure, the name of Jesus is the means of God's bringing about healing, signs, and wonders (see the comments on 3:6, 16). "Your holy servant Jesus" renews attention to Jesus' virtue (compare 4:27).

4:31: **And when they'd prayed** [in the sense of asking for something], **the place in which they'd gathered together was shaken, and they were all filled with the Holy Spirit and were speaking the word of God with boldness.** They'd prayed for boldness in speaking God's word. He answers their prayer. The boldness comes from being filled with the Holy Spirit, who empowers them (1:8). As on the Day of Pentecost (2:4), none of them failed to be filled. And the shaking of their place of assembly answers to their expectation of and/or request for signs and wonders certifying the word of God that they're speaking. Presumably an audience has gathered to hear them, as in 2:5–13, or they go forth to speak. But Luke doesn't say. Therefore the accent falls solely on God's answering their prayer (see Luke 11:9–13).

COMMUNAL LIVING
Acts 4:32–5:11

The first section of this passage describes an ideal community (4:32–35). The second section relates the contrasting cases of Barnabas and Ananias with his wife Sapphira (4:36–5:11).

4:32–35: **And the heart and soul of the multitude of those who'd believed was one.** "The multitude" recalls the unstoppable success of the gospel as an indication of its divine origin and as an inducement to conversion (see 2:41, 47; 4:4). "Heart" and "soul" hardly differ in meaning here, but Luke's using both of them magnifies the believers' unity, expressed with the help of "one." **And not even one** [of them] **was saying that any of his possessions was his own; rather, they possessed all things in common.** 33**And with great power the apostles were giving witness to the resurrection of the Lord Jesus.** The relinquishing of private ownership for communal ownership gives evidence of unity, included *every* believer, and excluded *none* of their possessions. As "the Lord," Jesus is the true owner of those possessions and is recognized to be such. Though elsewhere power is associated with the Holy Spirit's coming on the apostles (1:8), here power is associated with the favorable impression made on unbelievers by the believers' communal ownership and distribution that left no believer in need. That is to say, this favorable impression lent "power" to the apostles' eyewitness testimony concerning Jesus' resurrection. **And great favor was on them all,** 34**for there was no one needy among them. For as many as were owners of fields or houses, selling** [the fields or houses], **were bringing the prices** [= proceeds] **of the things being sold** 35**and were placing** [the money] **at the apostles' feet. And it was being distributed to each** [person] **according as anyone had need.** The power was "great" in that it attracted many converts. The "great power" derived from the "great favor." The selling of fields and houses, donating to a common treasury, and distributing to each person according to that person's need explains why this favor was "on them"; and it was "great" because "all" of them shared according to their ability ("as many as were owners"; compare the favor from unbelievers in 2:47). The result: no one of them suffered want (compare 2:44–45; Deuteronomy 15:4). You'd like to belong to a community like that, wouldn't you?

4:36–37: And Joseph—a Levite [= member of the tribe of Levi], **a Cypriot by birth** [= born on the island of Cyprus], **nicknamed by the apostles "Barnabas," which is translated "Son of Encouragement"** [= someone characterized by encouraging others with comfort and exhortation]—37**on selling a field that belonged to him, brought the cash and placed** [it] **at the apostles' feet.** Here's a particular example of the communal sharing that Luke has been describing in general terms (contrast Judas Iscariot's *buying* a field with the money he got for betraying Jesus ([1:18–19]). Barnabas's placing the cash at the apostles' feet shows the apostles to be in charge of the common purse. Next we'll get an insight into what happened when a fly of deception spoiled the ointment of communal sharing.

5:1–4: And a certain man by the name of Ananias, along with Sapphira his wife, sold a piece of property 2**and kept back for himself some of the price** [= proceeds of the sale], **the wife also colluding with** [him]. **And on bringing a certain part** [of the proceeds], **he placed** [it] **at the apostles' feet.** 3**But Peter said, "Ananias, for what reason has Satan filled your heart so as to beguile the Holy Spirit and keep back for yourself some of the price of the field** [that you sold]? 4**While staying** [unsold], **it was staying yours, wasn't it? And on being sold,** [the proceeds] **were in your authority** [= at your disposal], **weren't they? Why** [is it] **that you put this deed in your heart** [= conceived it]? **You haven't lied to human beings—rather, to God."** Peter's use of "beguile" and "lied" implies that Ananias pretended to bring all the proceeds of the sale but didn't, that he therefore pretended to be wholly dependent on the church for his livelihood though he'd kept some cash from the sale, and that with supernatural insight Peter detected the ruse. Since you can't beguile a stick or a stone but Ananias tried to beguile the Holy Spirit, the Holy Spirit is personal; and since trying to beguile the Holy Spirit equates with lying to God, the Holy Spirit is divine. Luke has spoken of the Holy Spirit's filling believers (2:4; 4:8, 31), but here is a quite different case. *Satan* has filled Ananias's heart, and done so with the result that Ananias has exercised guile in relation to the Holy Spirit and held back some of the proceeds (compare Luke 22:3, there also in relation to money). At the same time, though, Ananias *himself* has conceived in his heart the lying and holding back. So just as God's predetermination and human responsibility coalesce without either one's canceling out the other, so Satan's influence and human responsibility coalesce without either one's canceling out the other.

Normally, Peter's addressing Ananias by name would show respect; but here it may show sorrow or righteous indignation instead. The questions introduced with "for what reason?" and "Why?" don't expect an answer so much as they exhibit—again—sorrow or righteous indignation. In fact, there wasn't any reason why Ananias

should have lied. "While staying [unsold], [the field] was staying yours, wasn't it?" indicates that he was under no obligation to sell it. "And on being sold, [the proceeds] were in your authority, weren't they?" indicates that he was under no obligation to contribute even part of the proceeds, much less all of them. Contributions were entirely voluntary, which fact made those who did contribute everything they had all the more virtuous. "You haven't lied to human beings—rather, to God" implies God's presence in the community of believers.

5:5–6: And while hearing these words [of Peter], **Ananias, falling down, expired. And great fear came to be on all who were hearing** [Peter's words]. 6**And on standing up, the younger** [men], **wrapped him** [Ananias] [in a shroud] **and, on carrying** [him out], **buried him.** Both Ananias and others present are hearing Peter's words. But the effects differ radically. Ananias falls down and dies. Fear comes on the others. Not ordinary fear, either. "*Great* fear"—naturally, for they've just seen the sudden death of one of their number. And "on *all* who were hearing"—no exceptions—so stunning was the event. Peter hadn't told Ananias to drop dead or even threatened a punishment. So Ananias's sudden death was solely and recognizably an act of God that dramatized at the beginning of church history his concern for truth and purity in the community of believers (compare the sudden deaths of Nadab and Abihu at the beginning of Israel's history as a nation [Leviticus 10:1–7]). Because of their lower status and youthful strength, it's younger men who dispose of Ananias's corpse. Their "standing up" to do so presupposes a sit-down audience.

5:7–11: And an interval of about three hours elapsed, and his [Ananias's] **wife came in not knowing what had happened.** 8**And Peter answered** [= responded] **to her, "Tell me whether you** [plural, for Sapphira and her husband Ananias] **sold the field for such and such** [a price]." **And she said, "Yes, for such and such** [a price]." 9**And Peter** [said] **to her, "Why** [is it] **that it was agreed between you** [plural again] **to test the Spirit of the Lord? Behold, the feet of those who've buried your husband** [are] **at the door, and they'll carry you out!"** 10**And instantly she fell at his feet and expired. And on entering, the young men found her dead and, on carrying** [her] **out, buried** [her] **close to her husband.** 11**And great fear came to be on the whole church and on all who were hearing about these things.** The description of the interval as about three hours long gives evidence of historical research on Luke's part. Such an unnecessary detail isn't likely to have been manufactured out of thin air. And if Luke were in the business of fictionalizing such details, he'd likely have specified the price rather than leaving it an ambiguous "such and such." Of course, it was the price that Ananias had claimed he sold the land for and placed at the apostles' feet, not the higher price, part of which he and Sapphira had deceptively kept back. Peter addressed Ananias by name. He doesn't address Sapphira by name, though, but speeds right to "Tell me." This abruptness exhibits his disgust at the deception and his expectation that Sapphira, too, will die on the spot. She answers without addressing Peter respectfully. Her eagerness to deceive overpowers any sense of decorum, and her false "Yes" enables Peter to infer collusion between her and her husband. Again, Peter's "Why?" doesn't expect an answer so much as it exhibits sorrow or righteous indignation. The phraseology shifts now from trying to beguile the Holy Spirit (5:3) and lying to God (5:4) to "test[ing] the Spirit of the Lord." The Spirit is the Lord's in that the Lord is the ultimate owner of Ananias's and Sapphira's property and proceeds ("owner" being a meaning of "lord"), and is the Lord's also in that the Spirit is divine, that is, one with God. To try beguiling this Spirit—that is, lying to God—is to test the Lord's Spirit in the sense of tempting him to punish you for the lie.

On the ground of what happened to Ananias, Peter predicts Sapphira's sudden death. Beware tempting the Lord's Spirit to do justice by giving you a deserved punishment. He may justly yield to that temptation rather than showing you mercy. "Behold" punctuates the imminence of Sapphira's death. "Instantly" underlines its occurrence. Ananias placed the false price at the apostles' feet (5:2). With poetic justice his accomplice Sapphira now drops dead at Peter's feet, and the feet of the young men who've just buried her husband are at the door, ready to bury her as well. An ironic use of "feet" from beginning to end. Many English translations say the young men buried Sapphira "beside her husband." But that phrase reflects the modern practice of burying spouses side by side in cemeteries. Literally, Luke's Greek preposition means "toward" and in the present case points to a location close to her husband—as on a shelf in the same tomb, for example. This time great fear comes "on the *whole* church," not just on those believers who happened to be present, and "on *all* who were hearing about those things," not just those who happened to be listening at the time (see the comments on 5:5 concerning this fear).

WONDERFUL HEALINGS
Acts 5:12–16

5:12–13: And many signs and wonders were taking place among the people through the hands of the apostles. And with mutual fervor they were all in Solomon's portico [see 3:11 with comments]. **¹³And none of the rest was daring to join them. Nevertheless, the people were magnifying them** [in the sense of extolling them as great]. Luke uses the twofold expression "signs and wonders" to highlight the evidential value of the miracles. Their large number ("many") adds to that value. "Among the people" makes the people eyewitnesses of the miracles and therefore the miracles unmistakable. "Through the hands of the apostles" shows that the miracles took place for the purpose of bearing witness to Jesus, who selected these disciples to be apostles for this very purpose. That "they were *all* in Solomon's portico" at the temple made for a united

witness to the people who congregated there. That the apostles were there "with mutual fervor" exhibits their zeal as good Jews to worship God at the temple. "None of the rest"—that is, none of the unbelieving Jews who'd congregated there—was daring to join the apostles, because the apostles' supernatural power made them seem dangerous. Might they turn that power against unbelievers? Despite this possibility but because of the power, the unbelievers extolled the apostles as great.

5:14–16: And more than ever, those who were believing the Lord [compare 18:8]—**multitudes of both husbands and wives—were being added, ¹⁵so that** [they] **even carried the sick out into the broad** [streets] **and put** [them] **on cots and mats in order that as Peter was coming by, at least** [his] **shadow might overshadow someone of them. ¹⁶And also the multitude from the cities round about Jerusalem were coming together, carrying those who were sick and oppressed by unclean spirits, all of whom** [the sick and the oppressed] **were being healed.** On the one hand, the apostles' signs and wonders scared off unbelievers even when those signs and wonders drew unbelievers' admiration. On the other hand, the signs and wonders drew others beyond admiration into belief. "Were *believing* the Lord" means believing what the Lord Jesus was continuing to do and teach through his apostles according to the implication of 1:1 (about which see the comments). Yet Luke's original could just as well be translated, "And more than ever, believers—multitudes of both husbands and wives—were being *added* to the Lord" (compare 11:24), which would imply a union of believers with the Lord Jesus (compare his question to Saul of Tarsus, who was persecuting believers: "Saul, Saul, why are you persecuting *me*?" [9:4]). Perhaps Luke leaves the matter ambiguous to include both believing the Lord and being added to him. Either way, or both ways, stressing the growing success of the apostles' Spirit-powered witness are the addition of believers "more than ever," their being so many as to merit the plural "multitudes" (as recently as 4:32 there was only a single multitude of believers, large though it was), and the inclusion of both husbands and wives (or "both men and women," but see the comments on 8:12). Just as the signs and wonders led to the addition of multitudes, their addition led in turn to an increase in the bringing of sick people for healing. It isn't clear who carried the sick out into the main streets and put the sick there on cots and mats. So the focus rests solely on how remarkable the healings were, remarkable in that it took only contact with Peter's shadow to effect a healing. In addition to the multitudes of new believers in Jerusalem and regardless of distance, a multitude from cities surrounding Jerusalem came together carrying their sick and demon-oppressed. Word gets around. None failed to be healed. Luke distinguishes between sickness and demon-oppression (which doesn't differ from demon-possession) but uses "heal" for both since the symptoms of demon-possession often match those of sickness. Luke's stress on the supernatural and its beneficial use is designed to win converts.

MORE TROUBLE WITH THE SANHEDRIN
Acts 5:17–42

This passage divides into the arrest and escape of the apostles (5:17–21a), their teaching in the temple courts to the surprise of the Sanhedrin and being brought before that court (5:21b–26), the apostles' testimony during interrogation (5:27–31), and their being beaten, warned, and released but ignoring the warning (5:32–42).

5:17–21a: And when he stood up, the high priest and all those with him (the existing faction of the Sadducees) were filled with envy [because of the popularity of the apostles, comparable to that of Jesus in Luke's Gospel]. **¹⁸And they laid hands on the apostles** [= arrested them] **and put them in a guardhouse publicly. ¹⁹But during the night an angel of the Lord, on opening the doors of the jail and leading them out, said, ²⁰"Go and, on taking a standing position, speak in the temple** [courts] **to the people all the words of this life." ²¹ªAnd on hearing** [what the angel said], **they went into the temple** [courts] **at dawn and started teaching.** Luke expects us to recall that in 4:1–3 the Sadducees arrested Peter and John for announcing in Jesus the resurrection from the dead. (The Sadducees didn't believe in resurrection [23:8; Luke 20:27].) The high priest's standing up amounts to body language for taking action (see 4:5 on the high priest). "*All* those with him," that is "the existing faction of the Sadducees," paints the apostles' foes as formidable. Indeed they were, for they were the most politically powerful Jews in the land. And to have all of them against you—not good. But though Luke correctly portrays them as formidable, he also portrays them, again correctly, as very self-serving: "*filled* with envy." Their envy and consequent arrest and incarceration of the apostles (all of them now, not just Peter and John as in 4:1–3) make the apostles' previously mentioned humanitarian healings stand out contrastingly in a good light. In many English versions we read "put them in a *public* guardhouse" rather than "put them in a guardhouse *publicly*." Grammatically, the translations are equally possible. But "publicly" better suits Luke's emphasis on eyewitnessing and in this case makes the apostles' subsequent escape a matter of public knowledge embarrassing to the Sanhedrin as well as supportive of the apostles. An angel of the Lord's enabling the apostles to escape during the night shows whose side the Lord is on. Better not fight against him (see 5:39). The angel's command to go stand in the courts of the temple for the purpose of speaking there counters the high priest's standing to arrest the apostles and keep them from speaking. In the command to "speak all the words of this life," "*this* life" means the eternal life that Jesus' resurrection ensures for believers (2:28; 3:15; 13:46, 48; Luke 18:30); and "*all* the words of this life" means that the apostles are not in the least to trim their teaching out of fear of further persecution (compare 4:19–20). Their going into the temple at dawn and starting to teach shows them quickly obedient and admirably bold. They're the kind of people you'd do well to associate with.

5:21b–26: And when the high priest and those with him [all of them Sadducees (5:17)] **arrived** [at their meeting place], **they called together the Sanhedrin— that is, all the tribunal of the sons of Israel—and sent to the prison for them** [the apostles] **to be brought. ²²But on arriving, the servants** [temple guards] **didn't find them in the jail; and on returning they reported, ²³saying, "We found the prison locked altogether securely and the guards standing at the doors, but on opening** [them] **we found no one inside." ²⁴And when both the officer of the temple** [guard] **and the chief priests heard these words, they were bewildered about them as to how this** [state of affairs] **might turn out. ²⁵And on arriving** [from the temple], **someone reported to them, "Behold, the men whom you put in the jail are standing in the temple** [courts] **and teaching the people. ²⁶Then the officer** [of the temple guard], **on going away with the servants** [= guards], **was bringing them** [the apostles] **not with violence; for they were afraid of the people lest they be stoned** [by the people]. "All the tribunal" included the elders and the scholars as well as the ruling priests (see 4:5). So these priests want to array the entirety of the high court against the apostles. "Of the sons of Israel" describes the tribunal as national, not just local, and therefore as a kind of supreme court. How mortifying, then, for the ruling priests to have called together all the tribunal only for a no-show of the apostles. Worse than a no-show, the apostles are teaching the people in the temple courts, the very activity the Sanhedrin had commanded Peter and John not to engage in (4:1–22, especially 4:17–18, 21). "Behold" dramatizes the surprise caused by the report of the apostles' teaching in the temple courts despite their having been jailed. In view of their great escape, "altogether securely locked" and the guards' "standing at the doors" of the jail add some humorous irony. Since an angel of the Lord had opened these doors to let out the apostles, the angel must have shut and locked the doors behind them. Had he also cast a spell on the guards, or had they merely fallen asleep on duty? In either or any case, the emptiness of the jail bewildered both the officer of the temple guards, who was responsible for the apostles' detention, and the chief priests, who'd called together the whole tribunal. "Both . . . and" highlights their perplexity. They wondered what might happen next. Things looked out of their control.

So the officer and his guards brought the apostles without doing violence to them, but not out of fear that through his angel the Lord had enabled the apostles to escape—rather, out of fear that the people listening to the apostles would stone them if they took the apostles forcibly, much as in Jesus' case (Luke 20:19; 22:2). The popularity of Jesus is duplicated in the apostles' popularity, for they're his witnesses. And in both their case and his, the popularity is well-deserved because of their and his telling good news and doing good deeds. Their "standing in the temple [courts] and teaching the people" shows them obedient to the angel of the Lord's command to go stand in the temple and speak to the people (5:20).

It also matches Jesus' having done the same (Luke 19:47; 20:1) and shows him continuing to do so through the apostles (compare the implication in Acts 1:1 of Jesus' continuing activity). Their standing in the temple courts neutralizes both the high priest's standing in 5:17 and the guards' standing at the door of the jail in 5:23. But now the apostles go compliantly, so that nobody has to lay hands on them. They have nothing to fear.

5:27–28: And on bringing them, they [the officer and his guards] **had them stand in the Sanhedrin. And the high priest asked them,** [28]**saying, "With an order we ordered you not to teach on the basis of this name** [of the Lord Jesus]. **And behold, you've filled Jerusalem with your teaching; and you're planning to bring on us the blood of this man** [Jesus]." Luke keeps mentioning the standing position of the apostles to counteract the high priest's having stood up to take action against them (5:17) and the guards' standing at the prison doors to keep them (unsuccessfully) from escaping (5:23). Luke's writing that "the high priest *asked* them" leads us to expect a question, such as follows this verb everywhere else it appears in Luke-Acts. Instead, what follows is a declaration: "With an order we ordered you . . . ." The combining of "With an order" and "we ordered" makes the declaration strong, and the unexpectedness of a declaration after "asked" makes it even stronger (so strong, in fact, that some copyists of Greek manuscripts, but not of the earliest and most reliable ones, changed the declaration into a question implying an affirmative answer: "With an order we ordered you, *didn't we*, not to teach on the basis of this name?"). The super strength of the declaration puts all possible emphasis on the apostles' boldness in violating the previous gag order, that is, in obeying God rather than human beings. And how successful the violation! The high priest's charge is also an admission of the apostles' success: "you've *filled* Jerusalem with your teaching." An introductory "Behold" showcases the success, which gives evidence of the apostles' having received power with the coming of the Holy Spirit on them (1:8). The high priest's consternation then turns into paranoia with "you're planning to bring on us the blood of this man," as though the apostles were teaching the people that since the Sanhedrists had engineered Jesus' execution, the people should take justice into their own hands by inflicting capital punishment on them.

5:29–32: And answering, Peter and the apostles said, "It's necessary to mind God rather than human beings. [30]**The God of our** [fore]**fathers raised Jesus, whom you savaged by hanging him on a tree** [or 'on wood,' that is, on a cross (compare Deuteronomy 21:22–23)]. [31]**God has exalted this one to his right** [hand] **as Ruler-Leader and Savior for the purpose of giving repentance to Israel and forgiveness of sins** [compare 2:33–34; Luke 2:11]. [32]**And we** [apostles] **and the Holy Spirit, whom God has given to those who mind him, are witnesses of these things."** The individual mention of Peter, who does the answering, makes him spokes-

man for all the apostles, so that in effect they're saying what he says. But the main point is that they give a united testimony (compare 2:14; 3:12 with 4:1; and 4:8–9 with 4:13). The unanimity of their testimony lends it gravity. And its piety and boldness, expressed in "It's necessary to mind God rather than human beings [such as you Sanhedrists]," add further gravity. In 4:19 Peter and John told the Sanhedrists to "judge" whether it's right to heed them rather than God. Here the apostles don't ask the Sanhedrists to judge. They just *tell* them it's necessary to mind God rather than human beings. And this necessity isn't limited to the apostles. It's a general necessity and therefore applies to the Sanhedrists as well as the apostles and everybody else. The Sanhedrists are getting a Sunday School lesson. With "the God of *our* [fore]fathers" the apostles position themselves squarely in Jewish religious tradition and ethnic heritage. That this God raised Jesus makes Jesus' resurrection a fruition of that tradition and heritage. "Whom you savaged by hanging him on a tree" makes his resurrection God's negation of their criminal maltreatment of Jesus. That this whole sentence and the next one begin without a conjunction and both have God as their subject makes for a forceful, double-barreled affirmation of divine counteraction.

"God has exalted this one to his right [hand]" affirms the fulfillment of what Jesus predicted about himself in Luke 22:69. See the comments on 3:15 for Jesus as "Ruler-Leader." "For the purpose of giving repentance to Israel and forgiveness of sins" makes Jesus' resurrection and exaltation the basis for God's forgiving the sins of those who repent. Without Jesus' resurrection and exaltation, repentance would prove ineffectual and forgiveness wouldn't be forthcoming. As usual till Acts 10–11, Peter limits his focus to Israel and thus proves himself a traditional Jew. "And we [apostles] are witnesses of these things" refers to their seeing the resurrected Jesus and his ascension into heaven (see Luke 1:1–4 for eyewitnessing as certification of the gospel). Witnessing as seeing has issued in witnessing as testifying. Strikingly, Peter brings in the Holy Spirit as the apostles' co-witness. "Whom God has given to those who mind him" recalls the giving of the Spirit at Pentecost, the evidence of which gift was speaking in tongues. Such evidence, plus other signs and wonders produced by the Holy Spirit, makes him a witness too.

5:33–39: And they [the Sanhedrists], **on hearing** [what the apostles had said], **were being sawn through** [a figure of speech like our "cut to the quick," only referring to infuriation rather than to hurt feelings] **and were wanting to do away with them.** [34]**But on standing up in the Sanhedrin, a certain Pharisee by the name of Gamaliel, a teacher of the Law** [who was] **held in honor by all the people, commanded** [the guards] **to make the men** [go] **outside a little** [while] [compare 4:15]. "The men" are the apostles, but Gamaliel wouldn't have called them such. [35]**And he told them** [his fellow Sanhedrists], **"Men of Israel, take precaution for yourselves as to what you're about to do to**

these men. [36]**For before these** [current] **days Theudas stood up saying himself to be somebody** [= claiming to be a mover and shaker (compare 8:9; Galatians 2:6)], **whom a number of men (about four hundred) joined, who was done away with. And all**—[that is,] **as many as were being persuaded by him—were dispersed and came to nothing."** Theudas's falsely claiming to be somebody contrasts with Jesus' having been truly exalted to God's right hand as Ruler-Leader and Savior (5:31). [37]**"After this one** [Theudas], **Judas the Galilean stood up during the days of the registration** [compare Luke 2:1] **and incited people to follow him in an uprising."** "The Galilean" distinguishes the Judas here from other Judases, such as Judas Iscariot and Judas the son of James (see 1:13, 16; Luke 6:16, for example). **"That one** [Judas] **also perished, and all**—[that is,] **as many as were persuaded by him—were scattered.** [38]**And as for the present, I tell you: stand away from these men and leave them alone, because if this plan or this action be from human beings, it'll be demolished.** [39]**But if it's from God, you won't be able to demolish them** [the apostles]. [I say this] **lest you be found fighting even against God."** The wish to execute the apostles out of sheer rage puts the Sanhedrists in a bad light, especially because the apostles had stated the obvious necessity of minding God rather than human beings and had described what they'd actually seen (Jesus resurrected and ascending into heaven). Whereas the high priest had stood up to take action against the apostles (5:17), Gamaliel now stands up to urge inaction. As a Pharisee he believes in a future resurrection, but not in Jesus' past resurrection. By describing Gamaliel also as "a teacher of the Law [who was] held in honor by all the people [not just by some of them]," Luke preannounces his vote in favor of Gamaliel's upcoming advice.

The advice begins with the address, "Men of Israel," which makes Gamaliel sound like Peter, who has used this address twice (2:22; 3:12). Indeed, what Gamaliel is about to say could well have been said by an apostle like Peter. It's as though Gamaliel acts as Peter's mouthpiece. The precaution that Gamaliel advises is to stand away from the apostles and leave them alone rather than executing them (the meaning of "do away with them"). There's a wordplay between "stand away from" in the sense of "leave alone," on the one hand, and Judas the Galilean's "incit[ing] people . . . in an uprising," on the other hand. For this latter expression, if translated literally, comes out as "caus[ing] people to stand away from" by way of rebelling so as to gain freedom. Gamaliel's advice that they should free themselves of the apostles contrasts starkly with "what you're about to do to them," that is, impose on them a death penalty. Gamaliel knows that the Sanhedrin's "wanting to do away with them" won't be fulfilled unless it's God's wish, too; and he cites two cases, those of Theudas and Judas the Galilean, to prove the point. A double use of "all—[that is,] as many as" for the dispersed and scattered followers of Theudas and Judas stresses the futility of banding together to pursue an action unwanted by God. Gamaliel's "I tell you"

underlines the futility, and the escape of the apostles from prison should have taught the Sanhedrin as much. So far as Luke is concerned, the apostles' witness has already achieved so much success that the Sanhedrin has all along been fighting a losing battle against God.

Various kinds and purposes of standing have tied together the elements of this episode thus far. The high priest stood up to arrest and imprison the apostles (5:17–18). On freeing them from prison, an angel of the Lord told them to stand in the temple for the purpose of preaching (5:19–21). The guards are left standing at the prison doors (5:22–23). A report comes that the apostles are standing in the temple (5:24–25). They're brought to stand in the midst of the Sanhedrin (5:26–28). After Peter's speech (5:29–32), Gamaliel stands up to cite the two standings-up in rebellion of Theudas and Judas the Galilean and to advise standing away from Peter and John (5:33–38).

5:40–42: And they [the Sanhedrists] **were persuaded by him** [Gamaliel]. **And on summoning the apostles, after beating** [them] **they ordered** [them] **not to speak on the basis of Jesus' name** [compare 4:17–18]; **and they released them.** [41]**On the one hand, therefore, they were going from the face** [= presence] **of the Sanhedrin rejoicing in that they'd been deemed worthy to be dishonored for the name.** [42]**And every day in the temple** [courts] **and house by house they didn't cease teaching and preaching the good news of the Christ as Jesus.** Nothing like a good beating to emphasize the present gag order as well as to punish the apostles for violating the previous one. Gamaliel has persuaded the Sanhedrists only to the extent of releasing rather than executing the apostles. "On the one hand" expects "on the other hand," which won't come till 6:1, however. The apostles leave the Sanhedrin because of being released. But they don't rejoice in their release, as we might have expected them to do. They rejoice, rather, for the privilege of having been dishonored for the name of Jesus that they've used in preaching and performing miracles and that they've just now been prohibited from using any more. Their dishonor consisted in the Sanhedrin's arresting, imprisoning, and beating them. Their rejoicing grows out of having been "deemed worthy." But doesn't being dishonored contradict being deemed worthy? Not necessarily if the sources differ. And definitely not in this case; for the dishonor derived from a self-servingly enraged Sanhedrin, whereas it was God who deemed the apostles worthy for obeying him rather than mere human beings no matter how high and mighty those human beings seemed to be. And why is being dishonored for Jesus' name deemed a sign of worthiness? Because that's the only name by which we must be saved (4:12). As before and as emphasized by "they didn't cease," the apostles go right on obeying God rather than human beings through daily teaching and evangelizing. And these activities overflow from the temple courts into people's homes. "Preaching the good news of Jesus *as the Christ*" brings us right back to Jesus' saving name.

THE AMICABLE SETTLEMENT
OF A COMPLAINT
Acts 6:1–7

6:1: During these days, on the other hand [that is, over against the joy of 5:41–42], **as the disciples were multiplying** [in number] **there developed a complaint of the Hellenists** [= Jewish believers who habitually spoke Greek and had adopted some other elements of Greek culture] **against the Hebraists** [= Jewish believers who habitually spoke Aramaic, a language related to Hebrew, and who resisted Greek culture though they weren't entirely unaffected by it], **because their widows were being overlooked in the daily serving** [of food]. Luke keeps stressing the numerical success of the gospel as an indication that God's Spirit is empowering the evangelism, that merely human opposition to it can't succeed, and that therefore Luke's audience should cast in their lot with this movement. He doesn't say why Hellenistic widows were being neglected in the doling out of food rations. It's enough for him that a complaint which develops will get resolved.

6:2–4: And on summoning the multitude of the disciples [again Luke stresses numerical success], **the Twelve said, "It isn't feasible for us to serve at tables by abandoning the word of God** [= at the expense of neglecting to teach God's word, for there's not enough time and there are too many of you for us apostles both to wait on tables and to teach]. ³**But, brothers, look for seven recommended men from among you** [that is, seven that are receiving good testimonials from others], **full of the Spirit and of wisdom, whom we'll appoint over this need** [= put in charge of making sure the Hellenistic widows get their fair share of food]. ⁴**But we** [apostles] **will devote ourselves to the prayer and to the service of the word** [that is, to serving God's word through teaching rather than to serving food by waiting on tables]." The apostles' addressing with "brothers" the multitude of fellow disciples portrays the church in familial and therefore attractive terms. "Brothers" also presages an amicable settlement of the complaint that has been registered. Since throughout Luke-Acts "seven" seems regularly to carry a sense of sufficiency (see Luke 11:26, for example), the appointment of seven with high approval ratings seems to imply that that number of men will suffice for the job at hand. Besides having high approval ratings, though, they'll need to be full of the Spirit and of wisdom. Or perhaps we should say that their high approval ratings should depend on the recognizability of their being full of the Spirit and of wisdom. It takes being filled with the Spirit to imitate Jesus in serving at tables (see Luke 12:37; 22:26–27), and imitating him turns a menial task into an honorable one. The requirement of wisdom also recalls Jesus' growth in wisdom (Luke 2:40, 52; compare Luke 7:35) and suits the present need to mend a rupture of ecclesiastical concord. Given their authority, the apostles will appoint such men, but it's the multitude of disciples that will put forward the

men for appointment. For the multitude will know better than the apostles which of their own satisfy the stated requirements. Thus a combination of hierarchical and congregational government. As in 1:14; 2:42; 3:1, "*the prayer*" may refer to scheduled prayer in Jewish practice and therefore indicate again the disciples' carrying forward traditional piety rather than undermining it.

6:5–6: And the word [= the proposal of the apostles] **was feasible in the sight of all the multitude.** This time "all the multitude" not only recalls attention to the numerical success of the gospel (see 6:2). It also headlines the congeniality that brought about consensus. "*All* the multitude": there weren't any holdouts. Here's the unanimity of a community so ideal that you'd want to join it. **And they** [all the multitude] **selected Stephen, a man full of faith and of the Holy Spirit, and Philip and Prochorus and Nicanor and Timon and Parmenas and Nicolas, a proselyte from Antioch,** ⁶**whom** [referring to all seven] **they stood in the sight of the apostles. And praying, they** [the apostles] **placed** [their] **hands on them.** The congregation did the selecting. The apostles did the ordaining, which consisted in placing their hands on the selectees while praying. The hand-placing conferred authority to perform the appointed task. Luke doesn't say the apostles prayed for the seven that they might perform their task well (though we might conjecture that the apostles prayed thus). As often in Luke-Acts, then, the mention of prayer simply but emphatically highlights the admirable piety of Jesus and, here, of his apostles. Strikingly, the names of all seven selectees are Greek. So instead of selecting representatives from both sides, Hellenistic and Hebraist, the multitude selects only Hellenists, whose widows were being overlooked. What magnanimity—we might even say chivalry—on the part of the Hebraists! They weren't looking out for their own interests but trusted the fair-mindedness of the Hellenists they themselves helped select. They even helped select a Gentile, for "a proselyte" describes Nicolas as a Gentile who'd converted to Judaism and was now a believer that the Messiah was Jesus. And Nicolas was all the way from Antioch in Syria. Ethnic diversity or, better, ethnic universality is already making inroads into the church, and this even at high levels. Stephen stands out as a man "full of faith" as well as "of the Holy Spirit." He'll need fullness of faith, and of faithfulness, for his soon martyrdom.

6:7: And the word of God was growing, and the number of disciples in Jerusalem was multiplying enormously, and a large crowd of the priests were obeying the faith [compare Romans 1:5; 16:26]. To grow is to get big. The multiplication of disciples shows that the word of God is getting big, for people become disciples by believing his word, the good news about Jesus. "Enormously" magnifies the growth of this word. It's getting *very* big—right in Jerusalem, the center of Judaism, so that the gospel represents the fruition of that ancient, well-respected religion. Moreover priests, representing the very core of the Jewish religious establishment, are obeying the faith. And "a large crowd" of them at that. How big can the word of God get? But why "*obeying the faith*" instead of "*believing the word*"? Not that the two expressions contradict each other. Yet "obeying the faith" implies that believing is obeying the command to believe the gospel, and that the faith, which is the same as the belief (for these two English words go back to one and the same Greek word)—that the faith *is* the gospel because it's to be believed. The object and exercise of belief/faith are inseparable. Without an object there's no believing. Without believing, there's no object. So this episode doesn't end with the seven's serving food to Hellenistic widows. For Luke, that goes without saying. The episode ends, rather, with a stupendous enlargement of the church (believers, *not* a building) in Jerusalem (compare 1:8). The amicable settlement of an internal complaint makes the gospel attractive to outsiders.

THE MARTYRDOM OF STEPHEN
Acts 6:8–8:1a

This long passage divides into the ministry and arrest of Stephen (6:8–12), false accusations against him (6:13–15), his reply (7:1–53), and his being stoned to death (7:54–8:1a). His reply subdivides into a rehearsal of Israel's patriarchal history (7:2–16), the Mosaic period (7:17–43), the period from Joshua to King Solomon (7:44–50), and Stephen's accusing the Sanhedrin (7:51–53).

6:8–10: And Stephen, full of favor and power, was performing great wonders and signs among the people. [9]But some of the ones from the synagogue called "Freedmen's [Synagogue]"—both Cyrenians and Alexandrians and some from Cilicia and Asia—stood up, debating with Stephen. [10]And they weren't strong enough [in argument] **to withstand the wisdom and the Spirit with which he was speaking.** "Full of favor" means that Stephen was of such sterling reputation that he enjoyed a great deal of favor from people (compare 2:47; 4:33). "Full . . . of power" means that as a result of being "full of the Holy Spirit" (6:3, 5) he had great power to bear witness for Jesus through both words and miracles (which by definition are "acts of power")—thus his "performing great wonders and signs" and the inability of his opponents "to withstand the wisdom and the Spirit with which he was speaking." Their inability to withstand fulfills a promise of Jesus in Luke 21:15. Luke indicated in 6:3 that Stephen had to be "full of the Spirit and of wisdom" for selection as one of the seven to resolve a complaint in the serving of food (6:3). Here he puts his wisdom to work also in serving up God's word, and puts his Spirit-filledness to work also in the performing of miracles. The addition of "great" to "wonders and signs" heightens the degree of power with which he performs them. And Luke's addition of "among the people" makes them eyewitnesses to these great wonders and signs (compare Luke 1:1–4). Stephen's opponents arose out of a synagogue devoted to Jews who'd been freed from slavery, or whose fathers

had been freed from slavery, and who had immigrated to Jerusalem from Cyrene and Alexandria, both cities in North Africa (Egypt in particular for Alexandria), and from Cilicia and Asia, both regions in Asia Minor.

Unable to withstand Stephen in debate, his opponents resort to subterfuge, which for Luke's audience only betters Stephen's standing and recommends the gospel for which he argued. **6:11–12: Then they** [the freedmen] **induced men,** [who were] **saying, "We've heard him speaking blasphemous** [= slanderous] **words against Moses and God." [12]And they incited the people and the elders and the scholars; and on confronting** [Stephen], **they seized him violently and brought him into the Sanhedrin.** Luke doesn't tell whether the inducement involved a bribe. In any case, both the inducement and the falsity of what the induced men said make Stephen look good by contrast. In fact, irony runs thick in that the men slander Stephen by claiming to have heard *him* engage in slander! One way or another, Luke regularly showcases the virtues of Jesus' followers as a recommendation of their gospel. It's unclear whether the inciters are the falsifiers or those who induced their falsifying. This unclarity leaves the focus on the falsifying and its inducement as such. "The people" who are incited are unbelievers, of course; and "the elders and the scholars" represent two of the three sectors of the Sanhedrin (see 4:5). So "they . . . brought him into the Sanhedrin" means that they brought Stephen into a meeting of the whole Sanhedrin, which included the chief priests as well as the elders and the scholars. Those who seized and brought him are those who were incited.

6:13–15: And they stood false witnesses [before the assembled court], **who said, "This man didn't cease speaking words against this sacred place and the Law. [14]For we've heard him saying, 'This Jesus, the Nazarene, will tear down this place and change the standards that Moses gave over to us.'" [15]And gazing at him, all those sitting in the Sanhedrin saw his face as if** [it were] **an angel's face.** The falsity of the witnesses contrasts with the testimony of the apostles and others concerning what they've actually seen and heard. "This man" refers to Stephen, of course, and therefore sets up a parallel with "This Jesus," whose witness Stephen is. "Didn't cease speaking words against" echoes "speaking blasphemous words against" in 6:11, only "didn't cease" takes up the slack left by the omission of "blasphemous." "Against this sacred place" refers to the temple and therefore echoes "against God" in 6:11, for the temple is sacred as a house of God (but see 7:48–50 with comments). "Against . . . the Law" refers to the Pentateuch (Genesis–Deuteronomy) and therefore echoes "against Moses" in 6:11, since it's that part of the Old Testament which contains the Mosaic law. From earlier descriptions of Stephen as well spoken of and as full of the Holy Spirit, wisdom, faith, favor, and power, Luke's audience can hardly believe the false witnesses' accusation. And Luke's repeated emphasis on the congregating of Jesus' disciples in the temple courts and observing there Jewish times of prayer falsifies even further the testimony of Stephen's opponents. Jesus predicted the destruction of the temple but didn't say *he* would destroy it (Luke 21:5–6). And far from speaking against the Mosaic law, he repeatedly appealed to it (Luke 16:29, 31; 20:37; 24:27, 44) and even said to follow its prescriptions (as in Luke 5:14; compare Luke 2:22–24). So if Stephen were saying that Jesus was going to tear down the temple and change Mosaic standards, he'd be contradicting the very Jesus in whom he's urging people to believe. Not likely! Luke writes that Stephen's face looked angelic. We may presume that an angel's face looks somehow glorious (compare 9:29; Exodus 34:29–35), but as a matter of fact neither here nor elsewhere in Luke-Acts are we told what an angel's face looks like. Since "angel" means "messenger," therefore, the likening of Stephen's face to that of an angel connotes that he's the Lord's messenger to the Sanhedrin (compare the use of this word for human messengers in Luke 7:24, 27; 9:52 and the comments on 24:23). They—*all* of them—see him as such and therefore without exception become eyewitnesses to his role as the Lord's messenger. All the greater, then, their guilt in stoning him, as they're going to do.

7:1–3: And the high priest said, "[I ask you] whether these things are so?" In other words, "Is it true that you've been speaking words against this holy place and the Law?" **²And he said, "Listen, men, brothers, and fathers."** To gain a fair hearing, Stephen addresses the Sanhedrin genderwise as all males, familially as his fellow Jews, and respectfully as his seniors in age; and he tells them to hear what he has to say, much as Jesus did (Luke 8:8; 14:35). **"The God of glory appeared to our** [fore]**father Abraham while he was in Mesopotamia** [northern Syria], **before he dwelt in Haran** [a city in eastern Turkey], **³and said to him, 'Come out from your land** [Mesopotamia] **and from your relatives. And** [come] **here into whatever land I show you** [Genesis 12:1].'" "The God of glory" anticipates Stephen's seeing "the glory of God" in 7:55. Genesis 12:1 says only that the Lord spoke to Abraham. But Stephen adds that God "appeared" to him, which fits Luke's overall theme of eyewitness as well as earwitness (Luke 1:1–4). Abraham eyewitnessed an ancient revelation just as the apostles and others have eyewitnessed a recent revelation. Thus gospel history is knotted together with Jewish history. And Stephen's calling Abraham "*our* [fore]father" ties the knot tighter. Stephen also backdates God's appearance and instruction to Abraham, perhaps on the basis of God's bringing him out of his original home, Ur of the Chaldeans, according to Genesis 15:7; Nehemiah 9:7. For Genesis 12:1, which Stephen quotes, is set after the move from Ur to Haran, not before that move (compare Genesis 11:31). The backdating makes Abraham's pilgrimage the result of obedience to God's command from the very start, in Ur, rather than along the way, in Haran. The indefinite "*whatever* land I show you" heightens admiration for Abraham's obedience, which deepens reprobation of the Sanhedrists' disobedience to the plain and definite instructions spoken through Jesus and his disciples.

7:4–5: "Then, on coming out from the land of the Chaldeans [= Mesopotamia, where Ur was located], **he dwelt in Haran; and from there, after his father died** [Genesis 11:32], **he** [God] **removed him into this land** [Israel]**, in which you now dwell."** So God determined Abraham's migration from Haran to Israel as well as from Ur to Haran (compare Luke's emphasis on the fulfilling of God's plan in human history, as in Luke 3:1–6; 24:25–27, for example). "This land, in which *you* now dwell" pinpoints the Sanhedrists in the very land where God was working out his plan and prepares for Stephen's charge that, unlike Abraham, they're not following God's directions. **⁵"And he** [God] **didn't give him an inheritance in it, not even the stride of a foot** [about a yard in length]**; and he promised 'to give it to him for a possession, and to his seed** [= offspring/descendants] **after him** [Genesis 17:8]**,' though he didn't have a child."** Abraham didn't inherit from God any portion within the land, not even the length of a stride, much less the whole of the land. But he did receive from God a promise that God would give him the land for a possession, and this possession was to be realized in his descendants despite his not having a child. That is to say, the present possession of the land by Abraham's descendants demonstrates that God's plan always prevails no matter what the obstacles (compare Gamaliel's advice in 5:38–39).

7:6–7: "But God spoke in this way: 'His seed will be resident aliens in a foreign land, and they [the citizens of that land] **will enslave it** [his seed] **and maltreat** [his seed] **four hundred years. ⁷And I'll judge** [in the sense of "punish"] **whatever nation they serve as slaves,'** God said, **'and after these things** [events] **they'll come out** [Genesis 15:13–14; Exodus 2:22]**' and do me religious service in this place."** Stephen refers to the Israelites' moving to Egypt, where they lived as resident aliens till the Egyptians enslaved and maltreated them. The indefinite "*whatever* nation" is due to God's not identifying Egypt as the nation at the time he spoke to Abraham. The judging of that nation consisted in the ten plagues God sent on Egypt (Exodus 7:14–12:30). "They'll come out" refers to Israel's exodus from Egypt; "and do me religious service in this place" refers to the worship of God in the temple at Jerusalem (see 6:14 for "this place" as the temple). This last statement echoes Exodus 3:12 except that Stephen changes "at this mountain [Horeb/Sinai]" to "at this place" for an update, since the Jews had long since left Mount Sinai as a place of worship. Stephen cites these Old Testament passages to show again that nothing was happening apart from God's foreknowledge and plan. He foreknew and predetermined even the number of years that Israel would be enslaved and maltreated.

Now Stephen backtracks for more detail. **7:8: "And he** [God] **gave him** [Abraham] **a covenant of circumcision; and thus he fathered Isaac and circumcised him on the eighth day** [after birth in accordance with God's command (Genesis 17:9–14; 21:4)]**. And Isaac** [fathered and circumcised] **Jacob, and Jacob** [fathered and circumcised] **the twelve patriarchs** [ancestors of the twelve tribes of Israel].” The covenant included a promise of seed (descendants) and the requirement of male circumcision. “And *thus* he fathered Isaac” emphasizes that God kept his promise by giving Abraham offspring. “And *thus* he . . . circumcised him on the eighth day” emphasizes that Abraham met the requirement of circumcision even to the prescribed day. And so on down the line God kept his promise of offspring and the patriarchs obeyed the command to circumcise. As God long ago fulfilled his promise to Abraham, he has recently fulfilled his promise of salvation (2:38–40). But unlike their forefathers Abraham, Isaac, and Jacob—also unlike a large crowd of current priests—the Sanhedrists haven’t “obeyed the faith” (6:7).

7:9–10: **“And on getting envious of Joseph, the patriarchs sold** [him] **into Egypt. And God was with him** [10]**and took him out of all his afflictions and gave him favor and wisdom in the presence of Pharaoh, king of Egypt, and appointed him ruler over Egypt and over his** [Pharaoh’s] **whole household** [compare Genesis 39:2–3, 21, 23; 41:39–44; 45:8; Psalm 105:21]**.”** Not even the envy of the patriarchs and their selling Joseph into Egypt thwarted God’s plan. On the contrary, the envy and the selling carried it out in accordance with what God had said to Abraham (7:6–7). “All [Joseph’s] afflictions” alludes not only to his being sold into Egypt but also to his enslavement to Potiphar, the false charge leveled against him by Potiphar’s wife, and his resultant imprisonment, all of which look remarkably close to the current afflictions of Jesus’ disciples, the false charges leveled against them, and their imprisonment. But just as God was with Joseph, God has sent his Spirit on the disciples. Just as God took him out of all his afflictions, an angel of the Lord has taken the disciples out of prison. Just as God gave Joseph favor from Pharaoh, God has given the disciples such favor from the general populace that the Sanhedrin have feared to punish the disciples. Just as God gave Joseph wisdom, God has given wisdom to the disciples, most especially to Stephen, who is speaking (6:10). The appointment of Joseph as ruler over Egypt and Pharaoh’s whole household prepares for the next stage in the fulfillment of God’s plan as stated to Abraham. But we should note that in accordance with Genesis 45:8 it’s God, not Pharaoh, who appointed Joseph ruler over Egypt and over Pharaoh’s whole household. As God was in control then, he’s in control now (see Genesis 37, 39–50 for the whole story of Joseph).

7:11–16: **“And a famine came on the whole of Egypt and Canaan, and** [as a result] **great affliction** [came with it]**. And our** [fore]**fathers weren’t finding provisions** [to satisfy their hunger]**.** [12]**And on hearing there was food in Egypt** [in particular, food made from grain]**, Jacob sent our** [fore]**fathers out** [from Canaan to Egypt] **the first time.** [13]**And during the second** [visit] **Joseph was made known again to his brothers.”** “Again” indicates reacquaintance after an interval. The Old Testament says Joseph made *himself* known to his brothers. But Stephen uses the passive voice, “*was* made known,”

to imply that events are being guided by the unseen hand of God. **“And Joseph’s family became evident to Pharaoh. And sending** [a summons], [14]**Joseph called away to himself** [from Canaan] **Jacob his father and all** [his] **relatives, in** [number] **seventy-five persons.** [15]**And Jacob went down into Egypt and came to his end** [died]**, he and our** [fore]**fathers** [too]**.** [16]**And they were transferred to Shechem and put in the tomb that Abraham had purchased for a sum of money from the sons of Hamor in Shechem.”** Though these patriarchs died in Egypt, that is, their remains were carried back to the promised land of Canaan and interred there. Stephen has Jacob and his twelve sons buried in Shechem, whereas the Old Testament has him buried in Mamre (= Hebron) and only Joseph buried in Shechem (Genesis 49:28–33; 50:12–14, 25; Exodus 13:19; Joshua 24:32 [compare Hebrews 11:22]). Moreover, Stephen has Jacob and his twelve sons put in a tomb purchased by Abraham from the sons of Hamor, whereas according to the Old Testament that burial site was purchased from them by Jacob (Genesis 33:18–20), Abraham having purchased the burial site in Mamre/Hebron from Ephron the Hittite (Genesis 23:1–20). Since Joseph has dominated Stephen’s preceding remarks, then, Stephen has made Joseph’s burial in Shechem a template for the burial also of Jacob and Jacob’s other sons, so that the whole lot of them are buried unitedly in the same place. Thus the unity of believers in Jesus, which unity Luke has highlighted repeatedly even with respect to their physical location (1:14; 2:1, 44, 46; 4:31–32; 5:12), matches the topographical unity of the patriarchs and thereby exhibits continuity between believers in Jesus and the Jewish patriarchs.

7:17–20a: **“And as the time of the promise was drawing near that God had declared to Abraham, the people grew and multiplied in Egypt** [18]**till ‘there arose over Egypt another king, who didn’t know about Joseph** [Exodus 1:8]**.’** [19]**Manipulating our race, this** [king] **maltreated our** [fore]**fathers to the end of exposing their infants, so that they wouldn’t be kept alive,** [20a]**at which time Moses was born.”** “The time of the promise” was the time for it to be fulfilled. The promise itself was that through his descendants Abraham would possess the land of Canaan (7:3–7), as they did under the leadership of Joshua, Moses’ successor (see the book of Joshua). God “had *declared*” the promise in the sense of affirming it strongly. Abraham’s descendants (“the people”) “grew” in the sense that they “multiplied” in Egypt. Since the word of God has “grown” and the number of disciples “multiplied” (6:1, 7), Stephen’s mentioning the earlier growth and multiplication of Abraham’s descendants exhibits yet again a continuity between believers in Jesus and God’s ancient people (see the comments on 7:15–16). Luke is ever concerned to stress that the Jesus movement is rooted in the ancient, well-respected religion of Judaism. New is good only if it has a good pedigree.

Since Abraham’s descendants were to be enslaved in Egypt four hundred years, the Pharaoh (“king”) Stephen mentions here couldn't have known Joseph, who lived at the beginning of that period whereas this Pharaoh lived at its end. So he "didn't know *about* Joseph." His manipulating the Hebrew race took the form of maltreating them, and maltreating them took the form of getting them to expose their infants, as Moses' mother did by putting him out among reeds by the bank of the Nile River. Pharaoh expected such exposure to result in the deaths of those infants and therefore in the cessation of Israelite multiplication, which posed a threat to Egyptian dominance (Exodus 1:7–2:4). Stephen sees no need to mention the limitation of Pharaoh's stratagem to male infants. Or does he deliberately exaggerate by including female as well as male infants ("their infants") and thereby make the failure of Pharaoh's stratagem a stronger preview of the failure of the Sanhedrin to thwart the multiplication of believers in Jesus, female as well as male (5:14)?

7:20b–22: "**And he [Moses] was charming to God, [Moses] who was brought up three months in his father's house. ²¹But when he'd been exposed, Pharaoh's daughter took him up for herself and brought him up as her own son [Exodus 2:1–10]. ²²And Moses was tutored in all the Egyptians' wisdom and was powerful in his words and deeds.**" Exodus 2:2 says Moses was charming to his *mother* (compare Hebrews 11:23). To play up Moses as a religious figure, Stephen says Moses was charming to *God*. Exodus 2:1–10 says nothing about Moses' being "tutored in all the Egyptians' wisdom," but the addition of this historically likely element forms a parallel with the wisdom of Stephen himself and others of the seven (6:3, 10). As did the wisdom of Joseph (7:10), the parallel contributes yet again to the continuity of believers in Jesus with their Old Testament counterparts. "In *all* the Egyptians' wisdom" underlines the parallel. Moses' being "powerful in his words and deeds" sets up another parallel with Stephen; for Stephen was "full . . . of power" and "was performing great wonders and signs," and his opponents "weren't strong enough [in argument] to resist the wisdom and the Spirit with which he was speaking" (6:8, 10; see also the description of Jesus in Luke 24:19 as "powerful in deed and word"). This parallel, too, extends the theme of continuity with Judaism; and despite Moses' self-attested and divinely acknowledged lack of eloquence (Exodus 4:10–16), the desire to establish the parallel for the sake of continuity reaches such a high pitch that it leads to a description of Moses as "powerful in his words," like Jesus and Stephen.

7:23–25: "**But when a forty-year time period was being fulfilled for him** [= when he was approaching forty years of age], **it got on his heart to visit his brothers, the sons of Israel** [= his fellow Israelites]. ²⁴**And on seeing a certain one** [of them] **being injured, he defended** [him] **and by striking the Egyptian avenged the one being abused** [Exodus 2:11–12]. ²⁵**And he was supposing his brothers were understanding that through his hand God is giving them salvation** [that is, deliverance from the oppression of slavery, the present tense of

"is giving" representing the certainty of that deliverance, as though it were already happening]. **But they didn't understand.**" Obviously, the Israelite slave was being injured by an Egyptian taskmaster. Since Moses thought his fellow Israelites would understand that God would use him to save them from their slavery, his "visit" must have had a larger purpose than making a social call; and Moses must have understood his role as that of a savior. ("Through his hand" means by his agency, "hand" standing for active power, as in Genesis 31:29: "It is in the power of my hand.") But the Old Testament makes no mention of such a self-understanding on Moses' part at that time. So Stephen's adding it sets up a parallel with Jesus, who similarly understood his role as that of Savior (see especially Luke 19:10). Stephen's further addition, "But they didn't understand," extends the parallel in that according to 3:17 the Jews, and especially their rulers, acted in ignorance when rejecting Jesus (compare Luke 23:34: "But Jesus was saying, 'Father, forgive them, *for they don't know what they're* doing'").

7:26–29: "**And the next day he appeared to them** [two of his fellow Israelites] **as they were fighting each other, and he was trying to reconcile them for the purpose of peace** [between them], **saying, 'Men, you're brothers** [fellow Israelites]. **Why are you injuring each other?' ²⁷But the one who was injuring** [his] **neighbor pushed him** [Moses] **away, saying, 'Who appointed you a ruler and an adjudicator over us? ²⁸You don't want to do away with me the way you did away with the Egyptian yesterday, do you?'**" Now it comes out that Moses had struck the Egyptian *dead*. ²⁹"**And at this word** [= remark], **Moses fled and became a resident alien in the land of Midian, where he fathered two sons** [see Exodus 2:13–22; 4:20; 18:3–4 for the story and some of the foregoing phraseology]." The Old Testament text doesn't say Moses "appeared" to the Israelites who were fighting each other. Since "appeared" occurs often for Jesus (see 9:17; 13:31; 26:16; Luke 24:34), Stephen's injection of this verb suggests a further parallel between Moses and Jesus. Along the same line, Moses' trying to reconcile the two Israelites "for the purpose of peace" (phraseology that doesn't appear in Exodus 2:13–14) looks like Jesus' having come to bring the "peace" that consists in salvation (10:36; Luke 2:14; 7:50; 8:48; 19:41–42). Moses' saying to the fighters, "Men, you're brothers" (again without support in Exodus 2:13–14), stands comparison with Jesus' establishing a brotherhood of disciples (Luke 6:41–42; 17:3; 22:32; Acts 1:15–16). Stephen also adds to the verbal rejection of Moses that one of the fighters "pushed him away" (compare 7:39). This addition reminds us of Jesus' rejection by the Jews, most especially by the Sanhedrists, whom Stephen is addressing. And the open-ended question in Exodus 2:14, "Are you intending to kill me as you killed the Egyptian?" becomes in Stephen's mouth a question that implies a negative answer: "You don't want to do away with me the way you did away with the Egyptian yesterday, *do you*?" The implication of a negative answer keeps Moses from wanting to destroy life, just as Jesus came as "the Ruler-Leader *of life*" (3:15), not as a killer. Moses' fleeing at the word of a fellow Israelite, becoming a resident alien in Midian (the east coast of the Gulf of Aqaba), and fathering two sons there imply that except for his following commission from God, he wouldn't have returned to Egypt.

7:30–34: "And after forty years had been fulfilled [= had passed], **an angel appeared to him in a bush's flame of fire in the desert of Mount Sinai** [Exodus 3:2]. [31]**And Moses, on seeing** [this appearance], **was marveling at the sight; and as he was approaching to investigate, the Lord's voice came:** [32]**'I** [am] **the God of your** [fore]**fathers, the God of Abraham and Isaac and Jacob** [Exodus 3:6].'" So the "angel" turns out to be the alter ego of God himself. In other words, since "angel" means "messenger," Stephen calls God's alter ego "an angel" because God is conveying a message to Moses; and "God" and "Lord" interchange here just as they do in Exodus 3:1–10. **"And becoming tremulous** [that is, quivering with fear], **Moses wasn't daring to investigate.** [33]**And the Lord said to him, "Loosen the sandal of your feet** [= 'Take off your sandals'], **for the spot on which you're standing is sacred ground.** [34]**By looking, I've seen the maltreatment of my people in Egypt; and I've heard their groaning; and I've come down to take them out** [of Egypt]. **And** [come] **here now! I would send you into Egypt** [Exodus 3:5, 7–8, 10].'"" "The Lord's voice came" doesn't occur in Exodus 3, but we do read of "a voice com[ing]" in Luke 3:22; 9:35–36. It's the voice of God speaking to and about Jesus, so that its use for the Lord's speaking also to Moses advances further the parallel between him and Jesus. This parallel supports the continuity of God's dealings through Jesus in the recent past with God's dealings through Moses in ancient times. And Stephen's quoting the Lord's statement, "I [am] the God of your [fore]fathers, the God of Abraham and Isaac and Jacob," extends the continuity even further back than Moses so as to authorize Stephen's message with the most ancient tradition possible. In Exodus 3:2–6, Moses sees the bush burning but not burning up, so that he turns aside to see why. Then God tells him not to come near but to take off his sandals, and identifies himself as the God of the patriarchs. At this, Moses hides his face out of fear to look at God. Stephen omits that the bush wasn't burning up, also omits God's telling Moses not to come near, delays the instruction to take off his sandals, and substitutes Moses' trembling and not daring to investigate in place of Moses' hiding his face out of fear to look at God. In Stephen's account, then, Moses' pious reaction needs no prompting from God (compare Luke's having repeatedly stressed Jesus' piety). In the Lord's statement, the combination of "By looking" and "I've seen" accents the certainty of the Lord's observation. And the Lord's saying to Moses, "I would send you into Egypt," reminds us of the Lord's having "sent" Jesus (see 3:26; Luke 4:43; 9:48; and, especially because it parallels Moses' being sent as God's agent to deliver Israel from slavery, Luke 4:18, where Jesus says, "He [the Lord] has sent me to proclaim release to the captives, . . . to send away oppressed people [from their

oppressors] by way of release"). "I *will* send you" would make a prediction. But the text reads, "I *would* send you," which indicates God's intention and thus leaves room for Moses' obedience, similar to that of Jesus.

Now Stephen reminds the Sanhedrin of the initial disowning of Moses and goes on to rehearse additional disownings of him despite his performance of wonders and signs and his liberating Israel from slavery. Israel's disowning of Moses previews Israel's disowning of Jesus, as in 3:13, despite Jesus' performance of wonders and signs and fulfilling "his exodus" by which he, like Moses, "accomplished redemption [= liberation from slavery] for [God's] people" (Luke 1:68; see also Luke 2:38; 24:21).
7:35: "**This Moses, whom they'd disowned by saying, 'Who appointed you a ruler and an adjudicator?'** [so Stephen treats this question of *one* Israelite in 7:27; Exodus 2:14 as typifying the *whole* nation's disowning of Moses: 'whom *they'd* disowned']—**this** [Moses] **God sent** [to be] **both a ruler and a redeemer** [= liberator] **with the hand of the angel who appeared to him in the bush.**" "A ruler" despite "who appointed you a ruler . . . ?" "A redeemer" despite "Who appointed you . . . an adjudicator?" And "a redeemer" improves on "an adjudicator," for an adjudicator judges between disputants whereas a redeemer liberates from slavery. As in 7:25, "the hand" stands for active power; but there it was Moses' hand. Here it's the angel's hand. Moses' hand was strong in that the hand of the angel, God's alter ego, worked with him. See the comments on 7:34 for the parallel between God's sending Moses and God's sending Jesus.

7:36–40: "**Performing wonders and signs in the land of Egypt and in the Red Sea and in the desert for forty years** [compare Jesus' wonders and signs according to 2:22], **this** [Moses] **led them out.** [37]**This is the Moses who said to the sons of Israel, 'From among your brothers God will raise up for you a prophet like me** [Deuteronomy 18:15].'" According to 3:22, Jesus was that prophet like Moses (see the comments on 3:22). [38]"**This** [Moses] **is the one who came to be in the church in the desert along with the angel that was speaking to him in Mount Sinai and** [along with] **our** [fore]**fathers, who** [referring to Moses] **received living oracles to give you,** [39]**to whom our** [fore]**fathers weren't willing to become obedient. Rather, they pushed** [him] **away** [as the quarreling Israelite did earlier in 7:27] **and returned in their hearts to Egypt** [Numbers 14:3] [40]**by saying to Aaron, 'Make for us gods who'll proceed ahead of us** [into Egypt]; **for this Moses, who led us out of the land of Egypt—we don't know what has become of him** [Exodus 32:1, 23, where "the people saw that Moses delayed coming down from the mountain (Sinai)"].'" "The church" means "the congregation" of Israel assembled in the Sinai desert. Just as Moses had his "church," then, Jesus has his "church" (as already in 5:11, for example). The parallels between Moses and Jesus keep building up. And since Jesus will ask Saul of Tarsus, persecutor of the church (8:1; 9:1–2), "Why are you persecuting *me*?" and say, "I'm Jesus, whom you're persecuting" (9:4–5), Jesus must be "in" his church just as Moses was "in" his church.

"Along with the angel [God's alter ego] that was speaking to him in Mount Sinai" refers back to the angel that appeared to Moses at the bush and prepares for a reference to Moses' receiving the Law on Mount Sinai. By identifying Moses' "church in the desert" as "*our* [fore]fathers," Stephen allies himself, a member of Jesus' church, not only with his audience but also with Moses' church, so that Jesus' church is an outgrowth of Moses' church. Continuity reigns. The "oracles" are the Law Moses received on Mount Sinai. They're "living" in that if you "do" them (that is, obey their commandments), you'll "live" (that is, "inherit eternal life" [Luke 10:25–28]). Moses "received" them in the sense of welcoming them, whereas the forefathers responded quite oppositely. He gave the living oracles "to *you*," Stephen says, not "to *us*" (as relatively inferior manuscripts say). "To you" prepares for Stephen's charging the Sanhedrists with a disobedience similar to that of the forefathers. Stephen shares these forefathers with the Sanhedrists, but he doesn't share the guilt that the Sanhedrists have brought on themselves by disobeying Moses through their disowning of Jesus, the prophet like Moses whom Moses predicted God would raise up for them. The forefathers' unwillingness to obey Moses has been replicated in the Sanhedrists' unwillingness to obey Jesus (compare Luke 7:30; 15:28; 19:14, 27). The forefathers' pushing Moses away has been replicated in the Sanhedrists' shouting to Pilate, "Take this [Jesus] away!" (Luke 23:18). And the forefathers' returning to Egypt "in their hearts" reminds us at least somewhat of Jesus' criticizing his opponents for what was in their "hearts" (Luke 5:20–23; 16:14–15). Stephen's use of these expressions furthers the parallels between the forefathers' disowning of Moses and the Sanhedrists' disowning of Jesus and thus contributes to the continuity of Israelite history from ancient times right on into present church history. So much for the false charge that Stephen had been speaking against Moses (6:11, 14). As for the Israelites' asking Aaron, Moses' older brother, to make gods who'd proceed ahead of them into Egypt, there's irony in the request. For such gods, fashioned as idols, would have to be *carried*. They couldn't "proceed ahead."

7:41–43: "And during those days they made a calf and offered a sacrifice to the idol and were reveling in the works of their hands [Exodus 32:2–6]. **⁴²And God turned away** [from the Israelites] **and gave them over to do religious service for the host of heaven** [= the sun, moon, stars, and planets regarded as an army of heavenly deities], **just as it's written in a book of the prophets, 'House of Israel, it wasn't to me, was it, that you offered immolations and sacrifices forty years in the desert** [Israel being addressed as a household, a family]? **⁴³And you took up the tent of Moloch and the star of your god Raiphan, the images that you made' in order to worship them, 'and I'll remove you beyond Babylon** [Amos 5:25–27].'" The Jews of Stephen's time, including the Sanhedrists to whom he's speaking,

didn't practice idolatry but opposed it vociferously. So Stephen's calling to mind the idolatrous history of their forefathers—and this in immediate connection with Moses, whose story he has narrated in terms reminiscent of Jesus—is designed to cut the Sanhedrists to the quick. Their disowning of Jesus in favor of the insurrectionist and murderer Barabbas is like their forefathers' disowning of Moses *in favor of idolatry*! The forefathers' offering a sacrifice to the calf-idol and "reveling in the works of their hands" contain further irony in that lifeless idols don't merit sacrifice and celebration by their living makers. Though the mission to Jews will continue throughout Acts, God's turning away from the Israelites foreshadows a turning to the Gentiles (13:46; 18:5–6; 28:23–28). "And God . . . gave them over to do religious service *for the host of heaven*" in the desert after the exodus strikes a note of judgment (compare Romans 1:24, 26, 28) and makes a sorry contrast with God's saying, "They'll do *me* religious service in this place [the temple]" (7:7). Whereas in Amos 5:25–27, quoted by Stephen, the Lord portrays the Israelites who exodused from Egypt as worshiping God truly, Stephen's insertion of "was it . . . ?" into the Lord's question after "It wasn't to me" portrays them as idolaters right on from the incident of the idolatrous calf. They "took up the tent of [the false god] Moloch" instead of the Lord's tent, traditionally called "the tabernacle" (a portable sanctuary for the years of wandering in the desert [compare 7:44]). "The star of your god Raiphan" means "your star-god Saturn" (the planet being a wandering star worshiped as a deity). It drips with sarcasm to replace the Lord's tent with "the tent of Moloch" and to substitute "the star of your god Raiphan" for the Lord himself. "And you *took up* the tent . . . and the star [that is, the idol of the star-god]" means they took them up to carry them while wandering in the desert. "The images *that you made*" repeats the irony in "the works *of their hands*" (7:41, on which see the foregoing comments). Stephen also inserts into his quotation the phrase "in order to worship them," so that the worship of Moloch and Raiphan replaces worship of the Lord. And Stephen changes "I'll remove you beyond Damascus" to "I'll remove you beyond Babylon." From the standpoint of Israel, Babylon is beyond Damascus, so that "beyond Babylon" is even farther away from Israel. In fact, the removal "beyond Babylon" takes Israel back to Ur, from which Abraham started out, and therefore stands in stark contrast with his removal to the promised land (7:2). Thus Stephen modifies the text of Amos to heighten the degree of divine punishment for idolatry, with which Stephen is comparing the Sanhedrin's disowning of Jesus.

7:44–47: "Our [fore]**fathers had the tent of the testimony in the desert, just as the one who was speaking to Moses ordered** [him] **to make it according to the blueprint that he'd seen, ⁴⁵having received which** [tent] **in turn our** [fore]**fathers, along with Joshua, also brought in during the possessing of the Gentiles'** [land of Canaan], **whom God pushed out from the face** [= presence] **of our** [fore]**fathers, till the days of David, ⁴⁶who**

found favor in God's sight and asked for himself that [he might] **find a tenting place for the house of Jacob** [compare Psalm 132:5]. **⁴⁷But Solomon built a house for him** [Jacob]. "The tent of the testimony" was the Lord's tabernacle, or portable sanctuary, in which were kept the tablets inscribed with the Ten Commandments. The commandments are called "the testimony" because they testify to what the Lord requires of his people ("You shall have no other gods before me," and so forth). It was on Mount Sinai that the Lord gave Moses a blueprint for the tabernacle (Exodus 25–30, 35–40). Since the Israelites already had the tabernacle, the Lord's tent, it was reprehensible for them to take up the tent of Moloch (7:43). Making it doubly reprehensible was their idolatrous worship of other gods in violation of "the testimony" that was housed in the Lord's tent. The forefathers received the tent "in turn" from Moses, to whom initially the Lord had shown the blueprint. Joshua, the Greek spelling of whose name is that of "Jesus," appears as a mere tag-along to the forefathers because he was loyal to the Lord whereas Stephen is stressing the forefathers' apostasy. The mention of Joshua does mark a transition, however, from the time of Moses, who never entered Canaan, to that of Joshua, when God "pushed out" the Gentiles to fulfill his promise that Abraham's seed would possess the land (7:5). Despite the forefathers' apostasy, then, God's plan proceeded forward just as—despite the Sanhedrin's opposition—God's plan is continuing to proceed forward. "Until the days of David" tells how long the period of the tent/tabernacle lasted. Stephen's saying that David "found favor in God's sight" not only draws a contrast with the forefathers. It also sets up a parallel with Jesus, on whom God's favor rested (Luke 2:40) and who "kept advancing in . . . favor with God" (Luke 2:52). And Jesus has been given the throne of his forefather David (Luke 1:32 [compare Acts 15:16]). The description of both of them as enjoying God's favor puts in a bad light the Sanhedrin's disowning of Jesus. It's as though they would have disowned David too. He wanted to find a tenting place "for the house of Jacob," that is, for a temple as distinguished from the tent/tabernacle. "A *tenting* place" for the temple reflects that the temple, though a solid building, was patterned after the tent/tabernacle. We expect to read "for the house *of God*," and indeed some relatively inferior manuscripts contain that phrase because it seems more natural. But Stephen calls the temple "the house *of Jacob*," Jacob representing the whole nation of Israel, to prepare for a denial that the temple can encompass God. It's Jacob's house in that it's the central location of worship for the Jews, including Jewish believers in Jesus. Stephen leaves it as understood that God prohibited David from building the temple, so that the building of it shifted to Solomon, David's son.

7:48–50: "Yet the Most High doesn't reside in hand-made [houses], just as the prophet says, ⁴⁹Heaven [is] my throne, and earth [is] the footstool of my feet. What sort of house will you build for me, says the Lord, or what [is] my place of rest? ⁵⁰My hand made all these things,' didn't it?" The contrast with *God's*

hand shows that "handmade" means "made by *human* hands." Stephen's designation of God as "the Most High" suits the inability of houses made by human hands to encompass him. The plural of "handmade [houses]" implies that even multiple temples couldn't encompass him. And if heaven (= the sky with all its heavenly bodies) is his throne and earth is his footstool, neither can the whole universe encompass him. It consists only of pieces of furniture that he made for his own use. So human beings could never build the sort of house that would encompass him or provide him a place to rest. Stephen's quotation comes from Isaiah 66:1–2, but he turns the Lord's declaration, "My hand made all these things," into a question by adding "didn't it?" The question is designed to elicit from the Sanhedrin the answer "Yes" in preparation for the immediately following accusatory address to them.

7:51: "Stiff-necked and uncircumcised in hearts and ears, you're always resisting the Holy Spirit. As your [fore]fathers [resisted him], you too [are resisting him]." "Stiff-necked" means "stubborn," as shown in "resisting the Holy Spirit" (compare Isaiah 63:10). Circumcision of the penis was the sign of God's covenant with Abraham (7:8). That kind of circumcision the Sanhedrists had. But "uncircumcised in hearts and ears" (compare Leviticus 26:41; Deuteronomy 10:16; Jeremiah 4:4; 9:26; Ezekiel 44:7) means that the Sanhedrists lack the inward circumcision that would consist in an obedient hearing of the gospel. They're resisting the Holy Spirit in that the Holy Spirit is empowering those who preach the gospel which the Sanhedrists are refusing to hear obediently. ("Resisting" literally means "*falling* against" and therefore calls to mind what Simeon said to Mary about her son Jesus: "Behold, this one is destined for the *fall* . . . of many in Israel" [Luke 2:34].) The Sanhedrists' resistance, put in terms of uncircumcision, makes them deniers of the covenant. "*Always* resisting" amplifies their denial. And this continuous resistance leads Stephen to say "*your* [fore]fathers" rather than "*our* [fore]fathers," which he has used nine times earlier. By saying that their forefathers resisted the Holy Spirit as they themselves are doing, and vice versa, Stephen indicates that the present work of the Spirit continues the past work of the Spirit.

Stephen keeps speaking in **7:52–53: "Which of the prophets didn't your [fore]fathers persecute?"** Implied answer: None. And there it is again: "*your* [fore]fathers" rather than "*our* [fore]fathers." **"And they killed those who announced beforehand the coming of the Righteous One, whose betrayers and murderers you've now become, ⁵³[you] who as such received the Law by angels' orders and didn't keep it** [that is, disobeyed its commands]." Just as there's continuity in the history of salvation, there's continuity in the history of damnation. The Sanhedrists' betraying Jesus to Pontius Pilate and managing Jesus' murder follow the pattern set by their forefathers. Stephen's description of "the prophets" as "those who announced beforehand the coming of the Righteous One" calls us back to the point that Jesus came in fulfillment of God's preannounced plan, not as an interloper. Calling Jesus "the Righteous One" renews Luke's overarching theme of Jesus' virtue, echoes 3:14 ("the Holy and Righteous One"), and reminds us of the centurion's exclamation when Jesus expired: "Certainly this man was righteous!" (Luke 23:47). "As such" describes the Sanhedrists and their forefathers as traitorous and murderous despite having received the Law. "By angels' orders" makes the Law a set of orders delivered as a message from God, for "angels" means "messengers." This way of expressing the giving of the Law establishes a parallel with angels' having given the good news of Jesus' birth (Luke 1:26–38; 2:8–14 [compare 1:8–17]). "And didn't keep it [the Law]" scores the Sanhedrists for breaking the Law, in particular "You shall not murder" (Exodus 20:13; Deuteronomy 5:17), by murdering Jesus.

7:54–58: And as they were hearing these things, they were being sawn through [a figure of speech for "infuriated" (see the comments on 5:33)] **and were gritting** [their] **teeth at him.** ⁵⁵**But being full of the Holy Spirit, gazing into heaven he saw the glory of God and Jesus standing at God's right** [hand]. ⁵⁶**And he said, "Behold, I see the heavens opened and the Son of Man standing at God's right** [hand]**!"** ⁵⁷**And shouting with a loud voice, they muffled their ears** [so as to shut out what Stephen was saying] **and rushed at him with mutual fervor.** ⁵⁸**And on throwing him outside the city** [Jerusalem]**, they started stoning him. And the witnesses laid their outer garments at the feet of a young man called Saul.** The gritting of teeth shows the Sanhedrists to be "sawn through." Sometimes the truth hurts. In this case it did. On the other hand, Stephen's being full of the Holy Spirit enables him to become an eyewitness of the glory of God in heaven and of Jesus' standing at God's right hand, and empowers Stephen to testify about what he's seeing (see Luke 1:1–4 for Luke's emphasis on eyewitness testimony as certifying the gospel). Stephen highlights what he sees with "Behold." Earlier, Jesus has been said to be *seated* at God's right hand (2:33–34). Here, though, Stephen sees him *standing* there; and in an echo of Jesus' own statement at Luke 22:69, Stephen calls him "the Son of Man." In that passage, too, and in Luke 20:42 Jesus' posture is one of sitting. But now he stands as after his resurrection "he stood in the midst of [the disciples] and says to them, 'Peace [be] to you'" (Luke 24:36). He stands here, then, in opposition to the Sanhedrists' rushing at Stephen, throwing him outside the city, and stoning him. Jesus stands to welcome Stephen's spirit, about to be disembodied by the stoning, with the peace of salvation that includes a coming resurrection like Jesus' own. The Sanhedrists' fury issues in a loud shout and a muffling of their ears. They don't want to hear any more of what Stephen has to say, but they want him to hear their fury, inarticulate though it is. (Luke doesn't quote them as using words.) Along with the singular of "a loud voice," "with mutual fervor" shows them united in their misbegotten zeal to murder Stephen, just as he has told them they murdered Jesus

(contrast the godly fervor shared by believers in 1:14; 2:46; 4:24; 5:12; 15:25). Stephen's being thrown outside the city of Jerusalem recalls Jesus' being thrown outside the city of Nazareth (Luke 4:29) and the throwing of a son, representing Jesus in one of his parables, outside a vineyard (Luke 20:15 [see also Luke 6:22]). This action and that of stoning Stephen demonstrate rejection of his true testimony in favor of the false testimony borne by "the witnesses" who laid their outer garments at the feet of Saul (Jewish name of the Apostle Paul, but note that "Paul" was *not* a name given to him when he became a Christian [see the comments on 13:9]). Laying aside their outer garments gave them freedom of movement for throwing stones at Stephen.

7:59–8:1a: **And they kept stoning Stephen as he was calling** [on the Lord] **and saying, "Lord Jesus, welcome my spirit."** ⁶⁰**And on putting his knees** [to the ground]**, he shouted with a loud voice, "Lord, you shouldn't cause this sin to stand against them."** In other words, "You shouldn't hold this sin against them." **And on saying this, he fell asleep** [a euphemism for "died"]. ¹ᵃ**And along with** [the Sanhedrin]**, Saul was taking delight in** [their] **doing away with him** [= in their stoning Stephen to death]. Stephen addresses Jesus with "Lord" because he has seen Jesus standing at God's right hand. Not even the authority of the Sanhedrin can match that of Jesus. The standing of Jesus has preannounced a favorable response to the petition that he welcome Stephen's spirit. Whereas Jesus addresses *God* in his similar dying statement, "Father, into your hands I commit my spirit" (Luke 23:46), Stephen addresses *Jesus* as Lord. This shift puts on display the height to which God has exalted Jesus (compare 2:33; 5:31). But putting greater stress on Stephen's *second* petition are his kneeling, shouting with a loud voice, and repeating the address "Lord." His shouting articulately with a loud voice cancels out the Sanhedrists' shouting inarticulately with a loud voice (7:57) and recalls Jesus' shouting "with a loud voice" in his aforementioned dying statement. The petition that the Lord shouldn't hold against the Sanhedrists this sin of murdering Stephen headlines Stephen's piety and compares well with Jesus' piety in praying from the cross, "Father, forgive them, for they don't know what they're doing" (Luke 23:34). Like Jesus, like disciple. A forgiving community will be a community attractive of converts. Though falling asleep is a common euphemism for dying, you wonder whether in the case of a believer like Stephen there may be the suggestion of awaking to eternal life at the resurrection. Saul's taking delight with the Sanhedrin in the stoning of Stephen sets the stage for Saul's coming persecution of the church at large (9:1–2). This mutual delight exacerbates the reprehensibility of their murder. And it was a murder, not a judicial execution. For the Sanhedrin pronounced no verdict that Stephen had committed a capital crime; rather, they rushed at him like a lynch mob to do away with him. This criminal behavior makes Stephen's piety stand out in such bold relief as to draw converts to the gospel he proclaimed.

GENERAL PERSECUTION
Acts 8:1b–3

8:1b–c: And on that day there took place a great [= severe] persecution against the church in Jerusalem; and but for the apostles, all [the believers] were scattered down through the regions of Judea and Samaria. So the martyrdom of Stephen immediately triggered a general persecution of the church in Jerusalem (which at the time was the only church). The persecution was so severe that all the believers, thousands though they were (2:41; 4:4), fled town to save their necks. They went "*down* through the regions of Judea and Samaria" because of Jerusalem's higher elevation. Putting some distance between themselves and the Sanhedrin, who had lynched Stephen, gave the believers a measure of safety. The apostles' staying in Jerusalem reflects the inability of the Sanhedrin to rein them in successfully; for an angel of the Lord had delivered them from prison despite the Sanhedrin's best efforts, and the Sanhedrin had decided at Gamaliel's advice to leave them alone (5:17–42).

8:2–3: And devout men took care of Stephen's burial and made a great lamentation over him. ³But Saul was ravaging the church by going into house after house; and dragging away husbands and wives, he was giving them over into jail. All believers except the apostles have left Jerusalem, and Luke doesn't identify the devout men as apostles. So the devout men who took care of Stephen's burial appear to be pious though unconverted Jews like Joseph of Arimathea, who buried Jesus (Luke 23:50–54). That men of this calibre should take care of Stephen's burial and even make great—that is, loud—lamentation over him testifies to their admiration of Stephen. Such admiration recommends the gospel, for the preaching of which he was murdered. On the other hand, Saul's ravaging the church stands in stark contrast to the devout men's actions. This contrast will heighten the coming drama of Saul's conversion. The ravaging went to the extreme of house-to-house searching for believers, dragging husbands and wives away from their homes and children, and imprisoning them (see the comments on 8:12 for "husbands and wives"). Their imprisonment either implies that Saul pursued the scattered believers into Judea and Samaria or limits the "all" who were scattered to those he hadn't yet imprisoned and explains why all the rest fled. In either case, Saul turns out to be more than a bystanding coatkeeper at Stephen's stoning (7:58; 9:1–2).

THE EVANGELIZATION OF SAMARIA
Acts 8:4–25

8:4–8: On the one hand, therefore [= because of the aforementioned "great persecution" (8:1)], those who'd been scattered went throughout [the regions of Judea and Samaria (as follows from 8:1)] proclaiming the word as good news. ⁵On the other hand [that is, more specifically], Philip, having gone down [from the height of Jerusalem] to the city of Samaria, was proclaiming the Christ to them [the folks of that city]. ⁶And with mutual fervor the crowds were paying attention to the things being said by Philip as they were listening and seeing the signs that he was performing. ⁷For many of those having unclean spirits—shrieking with a loud voice [the spirits] were coming out [of them], and many paralyzed and lame people were healed. ⁸And great joy came about in that city. "The word" is the gospel, which means the good news of salvation in the name of Jesus Christ (4:12). Proclamation of the word throughout the regions of Judea and Samaria fulfills Jesus' commissioning the disciples to be his witnesses in those very regions (1:8), so that—ironically—the persecution contributes to that fulfillment. As in Jesus' commission, Judea stands for the whole land of Israel except for Samaria, which took a bite out of the middle (see the comments on 1:8; Luke 1:5). (The disciples have already borne witness in Jerusalem.) Since the apostles stayed in Jerusalem (8:1), the Philip who goes to Samaria must be the Philip chosen with Stephen and five others to serve at tables (6:5), not Philip the apostle (Luke 6:14). "To the city of Samaria" could mean "to the city whose name is Samaria" or "to the main city in the region of Samaria." Nothing theological rides on the choice between these alternatives, however.

"Proclaiming Christ" equates with "proclaiming the word as good news," because he *is* the good news of that word. Philip's drawing not just a crowd but "crowds" (plural) takes after Jesus' having done the same (Luke 4:42, to take but one example) and exhibits the Holy Spirit's empowerment of Philip to bear witness about Jesus (1:8). Adding to this popularity and power are the "mutual fervor" with which the crowds pay attention and "the signs" that Philip performs (contrast the "mutual fervor" of the Sanhedrists in their murder of Stephen [7:57]). The crowds pay attention not to Philip himself, but to "the things being said" by him. Those things are what counts, not Philip. Except in Jesus' case, the proclamation outranks the proclaimer. "*Seeing* the signs" makes the crowds eyewitnesses of the power of the Christ whom Philip is proclaiming. The signs are comprised of exorcisms and healings of paralyzed and lame people (for the meaning of "paralyzed," see the comments on Matthew 9:2). That both the exorcisms and the healings are "many" magnifies this exhibition of Christ's power. The loud shrieking of the unclean spirits as they were coming out gave audible evidence of their frantic exit. The broken grammar, represented in translation by the long dash between "unclean spirits" and "shrieking," dramatizes the exorcisms. Just as an angel of the Lord proclaimed "as good news a great joy" at the birth of "Christ the Lord" (Luke 2:10–11), so here the proclamation of Christ as the word of good news brings great joy. Luke wants us to join in that joy.

8:9–13: And a certain man by the name of Simon had previously been practicing magic in the city and astonishing the nation of Samaria, saying himself [= claiming] to be someone great, ¹⁰to whom all—from

small to great—were paying attention, saying, "This [Simon] is the power of God that's called great." [11]And they were paying attention to him because for a considerable time he'd astonished them with magic arts. [12]But when they believed Philip as he was proclaiming good news about God's reign and the name of Jesus Christ, they were getting baptized, both husbands and wives. [13]And Simon—even he—believed and, on being baptized, was adhering to Philip; and he was astonished as he observed signs and great miracles taking place. The Samaritans viewed Simon's practice of magic as evidence of supernatural power, not as clever tricks designed for entertainment; and he capitalized on their view by claiming to be someone great. So long-term and successful was his capitalization that the Samaritans—all of them, great as well as small, "the nation" as a whole—called him the great power of God, as though he were the personification and bearer of God's great power, and were paying attention to him. "Previously" indicates that Philip's performance of exorcisms and healings had outclassed Simon's magical arts, so that he (Simon) was no longer astonishing the Samaritans with them. Now the Samaritans were paying attention to Philip, not to Simon, and believing Philip, not Simon.

Whereas Simon had talked about himself, Philip proclaimed the "good news about God's reign" (in opposition to pagan rule, represented by Rome at the time) and "good news about . . . the name of Jesus Christ" (by which we're saved if we believe [4:12]). "Both husbands and wives" could come out in translation as "both men and women." But in view of Saul's entering homes to drag out husbands and wives (8:3) and in view of household baptisms later in Acts (10:47–48 with 11:14; 16:15, 31–33; 18:8) and the baptisms here in 8:12, we should probably think of husbands and wives in particular. "*Both* husbands *and* wives" elevates the status of women in that wives might otherwise go unmentioned (see 4:4; Luke 9:14, for example). The belief, baptism, and astonishment even of Simon are themselves astonishing since Philip has invaded his territory and won Simon's admirers over to Jesus. Along with the other Samaritans, Simon has become an eyewitness to the power of Christ. For Simon "observed" the "signs and great miracles [literally, 'acts of great power']" that were taking place. The addition of "great miracles," where earlier Luke wrote only about "the signs" (8:6), shows that the great power of God doesn't reside in Simon after all. It resides in Christ, and Simon himself—once the astonisher but now the astonished—confesses that it does by believing, getting baptized, and adhering to the evangelist Philip (compare 21:8).

8:14–17: And on hearing that Samaria had welcomed the word of God, the apostles, [who were] in Jerusalem, sent to them [the Samaritan believers] Peter and John, [15]who as such [that is, as apostles] on going down [in elevation from Jerusalem to Samaria] prayed for them so that they would receive the Holy Spirit. [16]For he hadn't yet fallen on any of them, and they'd only been baptized into the name of the Lord Jesus.

[17]Then they [Peter and John] laid [their] hands on them, and they [the Samaritan believers] were receiving the Holy Spirit [as the laying on of hands progressed from one believer to another]. "The word of God" equates with "the word" that's "good news" (8:4) and with the "proclaiming" of "the Christ" (8:5). The apostles' sending two of their number, Peter and John, down to the Samaritan believers runs counter to the traditional antipathy between Jews and Samaritans (for which see the comments on John 4:4, 7–9, 17–18) and puts on display the healing of social divisions through Christian community. Peter's and John's praying for the Samaritan believers to receive the Holy Spirit shows concern for them, Samaritans though they are, and likewise displays such healing. The gospel makes for mutuality and peace and therefore deserves to be welcomed with faith. In this passage, *receiving* the Holy Spirit equates with the Spirit's *falling* on believers, so that we have yet another way of expressing being *baptized* in the Holy Spirit (1:5), his *coming* on believers (1:8), their being *filled* with him (2:4; 4:8, 31; 6:3, 5; 7:55), and his being *poured* on them (2:17, 33) and *given* to them (2:38). "Baptized *into* the name of the Lord Jesus" indicates transference into the ownership and authority of Jesus as Lord. "They'd *only* been baptized into the name of the Lord Jesus" implies that ordinarily baptizees would have received the Spirit. Why not in the case of these Samaritan believers? Answer: to give Jewish believers in the persons of their two leading apostles firsthand evidence that God had accepted Samaritan believers on equal terms with Jewish believers. As shown by their praying and the laying of their hands on the Samaritan believers, Peter and John were more than willing to act as Jesus' agents in this respect. The laying on of hands gestured solidarity between Jewish and Samaritan believers. Reception of the Holy Spirit at this gesture evinces Jesus' approval of such solidarity (see 2:33 for Jesus as the one who pours out the Spirit).

Back to Simon in *8:18–23*: And on seeing that the Spirit is being given through the laying on of the apostles' hands, Simon offered them cash, [19]saying, "Give this authority also to me in order that on whomever I lay [my] hands—[that person] may receive the Holy Spirit." The present tense of "is being given" makes vivid the giving of the Spirit and thus makes understandable Simon's offer to purchase authority to bestow the Spirit by the laying on of hands. Magicians were paid for their services. So Simon figured that by charging a fee for transmitting the Holy Spirit to his customers he would be getting a handsome return on his investment, that is, on the cost of acquiring the authority of transmission. He mistakenly assumes the apostles can convey the authority and will do so for cash. And he doesn't know that cash laid at the apostles' feet goes for communal needs, not for special favors done to the donor (4:32–37). [20]But Peter said to him, "May your silver perish with you [literally, 'be for destruction with you'], because you thought to acquire God's gift with cash. [21]You have no part or portion [= assignment] in this matter, for your heart isn't straightforward before God. [22]Therefore repent from this evil of yours and beg the Lord, if then the intention of your heart will be forgiven for you. [23]For I see you [as] being in the gall of bitterness and [in] the bond of unrighteousness."

God's gift is the Holy Spirit (11:17; compare 2:38; 10:45; Luke 11:13). "To acquire God's gift" doesn't mean to receive the Spirit *oneself*. It means to purchase the authority to *transmit* the gift of the Spirit to others through a laying on of hands. Peter's sharp refusal of Simon's offer to purchase the authority exhibits pecuniary virtue. Peter can't be bought any more than the authority itself can be bought. This authority is "God's *gift*," not an item for sale. "May your silver perish with you" implies that Simon, despite his having believed and gotten baptized, is headed for destruction and that Peter wishes Simon's money to be destroyed with him. Peter doesn't wish *Simon's* destruction; he assumes it and wishes only the co-destruction of Simon's *money*. So strong is Peter's revulsion at Simon's offer. "You have no part or portion in this matter" rules Simon out of acquiring the authority to transmit the Holy Spirit. But "in this matter" could also be translated "in this word" and refer back also to "the word of God" that Samaria had received (8:14). That is to say, Simon's offer had either vitiated his belief in that word and his consequent baptism or shown them to be superficial, if not hypocritical, in the first place. God looks inside, at Simon's heart, and sees there crookedness rather than straightforwardness. Simon lacked straightforwardness in that he omitted mentioning his intention to make a profit at the expense of the Samaritan populace. Peter calls the omission "this evil" and makes it a reason for repentance. "Repent *from* this evil of yours" calls for a change of mind from wanting to make a profit. Such a change would issue in begging the Lord for forgiveness, and such begging would reverse his earlier attempt to buy influence. The Lord won't be bought any more than Peter could be bought. Simon must reduce his status to that of a beggar. And like any beggar, he can only hope for the desired result: "*if* then [as a result of your begging] the intention of your heart will be forgiven for you." Forgiveness is up to the Lord—he's under no obligation—and would come, if it comes at all, only by grace. Peter's command arises out of observing that Simon is "in the gall of bitterness"—immersed, so to speak, in bitter poison—and "[in] the bond of unrighteousness"—chained, so to speak, to the evil of his heart. The poison *is* the unrighteousness, and is bitter in that unrighteousness binds its victims. Repentance and forgiveness would neutralize the poison and loosen the chain.

8:24: And answering, Simon said, "You [plural]— beg the Lord on my behalf so that none of the things you've said come on me." Simon had wanted to equal Peter and John in their authority to transmit the Holy Spirit. Now he's so scared of perishing forever under the all-seeing eye of God that he doesn't even consider himself capable of begging successfully for forgiveness, but asks Peter and John to do it on his behalf. Surely the Lord will listen favorably to them. The story of Simon ends

here. Luke doesn't tell whether Peter and John begged the Lord on Simon's behalf or whether the Lord forgave Simon. Instead of resting on Simon's fate, then, the point of the story rests on the high standard of morality upheld by Peter and John in the matter of money. Luke features this high standard to win converts. They needn't fear defraudation or extortion if they join the church.

8:25: On the one hand, therefore, after solemnly testifying and speaking the word of the Lord, they [Peter and John] started returning to Jerusalem and [along the way] were proclaiming the good news [the gospel] to many towns of the Samaritans. To balance "On the one hand," "On the other hand" will come in 8:26. "Therefore" means that Peter and John started returning to Jerusalem because they'd successfully transmitted the Holy Spirit to the Samaritan believers. "After solemnly testifying and speaking the word of the Lord" refers to their preaching in "the city of Samaria" (8:5). "Solemnly" may describe the testifying in the light of Peter's heavy warning to Simon. Proclamation of the gospel "to many towns of the Samaritans" on the way back to Jerusalem expands the fulfillment of Jesus' commission in 1:8 and points to the unstoppable progress of evangelization.

AN ETHIOPIAN EUNUCH'S CONVERSION
Acts 8:26–36, 38–40

8:26–28: On the other hand [as distinct from Peter's and John's returning to Jerusalem], an angel of the Lord spoke to Philip [not the apostle, but Stephen's associate (6:5)], saying, "Stand up and travel south [or 'at midday'] on the road going down from Jerusalem to Gaza." (This is a desert [road].) [27]And on standing up, he traveled [south on that road]. And behold, a man, an Ethiopian, a eunuch, a powerful [functionary] of Candace, queen of the Ethiopians, who [referring to the man] was over all her treasury [= in charge of it], who had gone to Jerusalem to worship [28]and was returning and sitting on his chariot [perhaps little more than an ox-drawn wagon, since by running Philip will be able to catch up with it] and reading the prophet Isaiah! As in his Gospel, Luke appeals to his audience's interest in travelogues. His editorial description of the road is designed to highlight that Philip had divine guidance, for on his own he would hardly have taken a desert road going south (or at midday in high heat as the alternative translation puts it). Despite such a road, Philip follows orders. "And behold . . . !" (roughly equivalent to our colloquialism, "And get this!") dramatizes Philip's discovery of a fellow traveler on the road. And what a traveler! Luke lists his identifications one after another: (1) "a man"; (2) "an Ethiopian" (a black from far away); (3) "a eunuch"; (4) "a powerful [functionary]"; and (5) a worshiper of the one true God and consequent reader of Isaiah's prophecy. This amount of detail gives evidence of Luke's historical research (Luke 1:1–4). Just as "Pharaoh" was a title for the king of Egypt, "Candace" is probably a title for the queen of Ethiopia (which was what we now call the Sudan, not modern Ethiopia). The eunuch's having charge "over *all* her treasury" accents the power of his position. What a triumph for the gospel it will be if a man of such power and piety converts to belief in Christ!

8:29–31: And the Spirit told Philip, "Approach and join this chariot." [30]And on running to [the chariot], **Philip heard him** [the Ethiopian eunuch] **reading Isaiah the prophet** ["heard" because almost all reading, inclusive of private reading, was done aloud in those days]; **and he** [Philip] **said, "So do you really understand the things you're reading?"** The question contains a wordplay in that the original word for "reading" is built on the one for "understand." [31]**And he said, "Well, how might I be able** [to understand] **unless someone will guide me?" And he urged Philip to sit with him on coming up** [into the chariot]. Since Philip was "full of the Spirit" (6:3, 5), the Spirit takes over from an angel of the Lord and directs Philip to the Ethiopian. Philip frames his question in a way that casts doubt on the Ethiopian's understanding the prophet Isaiah; for such an understanding requires a knowledge of Christ, which the Ethiopian doesn't have (see Luke 24:25–27, 32, 44–47). Luke has called him "a *powerful* [functionary]." So there may be something of another wordplay when the Ethiopian asks in a more literal translation, "Well, how might I *have the power* [to understand] if no one will guide me?" This question could be paraphrased, "Why do you even ask? For *of course* I can't understand without a guide!" He follows up this confession of incompetence with an invitation that Philip join him in the chariot. But no, he doesn't just *invite* Philip. He *urges* him and thus exhibits a strong desire to understand. That the gospel is put in terms of understanding scriptural prophecy makes the gospel good news about old, reliable tradition rather than news about some specious novelty.

8:32–35: And the passage of Scripture that he was reading was this: "He was led as a sheep to slaughter; and as a lamb before the one who shears him [is] **voiceless, in this way he doesn't open his mouth. [33]In the humiliation** [of him], **his judgment was taken away** [in the sense that Jesus suffered the shameful death of crucifixion despite the thrice-repeated judicial verdict of 'not guilty' (Luke 23:4, 14–15, 22)]. **Who will recount his progeny? For his life is being taken away from the earth** [Isaiah 53:7–8]." In other words, he's being killed without having any offspring whom someone could later list in a genealogy. [34]**And answering** [= responding], **the eunuch said to Philip, "I beg you, about whom is the prophet saying this? About himself or about somebody else?" [35]And opening his mouth and starting from this scripture, Philip proclaimed to him Jesus as good news.** So Jesus' death was a slaughter, not an execution (in the judicial sense, of course). Though he told Pilate, "*You're* saying [I'm the king of the Jews]," he didn't utter a word of self-defense and was completely voiceless before Herod Antipas (Luke 23:3, 9). His silence contrasted with the loud shouts of those calling for his crucifixion (Luke

23:18, 21, 23). Thus he fulfilled Isaiah's ancient prophecy, which—though referring to the future—is put in a mixture of past and present tenses to indicate such certainty of fulfillment that it might already have happened or be happening back in Isaiah's time. What happened to Jesus has justified Isaiah's use of those tenses. The Ethiopian's use of the present tense ("about whom *is* the prophet saying this?") makes Isaiah's words come to life (compare the "living oracles" of 7:38). And "I beg you" registers the high intensity of the Ethiopian's desire to understand. He makes an outstanding example of a seeker after truth such as Luke wants to win over to the gospel. In effect, Luke is saying, "You should be like the Ethiopian." To provide salvation through his sacrificial death, Jesus didn't open his mouth (8:32). But Philip now opens his mouth to proclaim Jesus as good news. "Starting from this scripture" roots Philip's proclamation in the old, the tried and true; and the proclamation presents Jesus as good news in that he has fulfilled Scripture.

8:36, 38–40: And as they were traveling down the road, they came to some water. And the eunuch says, "Behold, water! What hinders me from being baptized?" Implied answer: Nothing, because the very desire for baptism gives evidence of belief in Jesus. [38]**And he ordered the chariot to stand still, and both went down into the water (both Philip and the eunuch), and he** [Philip] **baptized him.** Note: the earliest and best manuscripts lack 8:37, an insertion by later copyists. [39]**And when they came up out of the water, the Spirit of the Lord snatched Philip away; and the eunuch didn't see him any more, for he was traveling his road rejoicing.** Luke is so intent on highlighting the joy of salvation that he makes the Ethiopian's joyful continuance of travel the reason for not seeing Philip any more (see Luke 2:10 for the "great joy" that constitutes the "good news," plus many other passages in Luke-Acts). "Was traveling his road" strikes a contrast with Philip's having been "snatched away." [40]**But Philip was found in Azotus** [a city on the coast of southern Israel], **and going through** [the region] **he was proclaiming the good news to all the cities till he came to Caesarea** [a city on the north-central coast]. "The Spirit" spoke to Philip in 8:29. Here, Luke adds "of the Lord" to "the Spirit" to bring out the Spirit's exercise of authority in snatching Philip away to pursue evangelism elsewhere. His being "*found* in Azotus" as a result of the snatching away forms a contrast with the eunuch's not "*see[ing]* him any more." And, yet again, Philip's "proclaiming the good news to *all* the cities" as he goes through the region from Azotus to Caesarea displays the unstoppable progress of the gospel under the Spirit's power and direction.

THE CONVERSION OF THE PRIME PERSECUTOR
Acts 9:1–19a

This passage divides into what happened to Saul of Tarsus on the road to Damascus and its effect (9:1–9) and what happened to him in Damascus (9:10–19a).

9:1-2: And Saul, still breathing terrorism and murder against the Lord's disciples, on approaching the high priest [2]requested from him letters to the synagogues in Damascus so that if he were to find any people belonging to the Way, both husbands and wives [or "men and women" (see the comments on 8:12)], **he would bring them bound to Jerusalem.** Those who stoned Stephen had laid their outer garments at Saul's feet, and Saul was pleased with Stephen's being killed (7:58; 8:1a). So "*still* breathing terrorism and murder against the Lord's disciples" implies that as a young hothead, Saul was somehow behind the murder of Stephen (see 7:58 for Saul as a young man). "Terrorism" connotes the threat of murder like that of Stephen, and "breathing" doesn't connote breathing *out* threats so much as it connotes blowing threats *into* the disciples so as to frighten them. "The *Lord's* disciples" prepares for Saul's addressing Jesus with "Lord" (9:5). Jesus' lordship will overpower Saul despite Saul's getting from the high priest writs authorizing him to persecute the believers in Damascus. His going to Damascus in the next paragraph will imply that he got the writs he requested. That they consisted of "letters to the synagogues in Damascus" implies both that believers in Jesus were living in that city and that, as good Jews, they attended synagogues there. As usual, Luke is concerned to point out believers' loyalty to the ancient religion of Judaism. Obviously, Saul expects to find in Damascus people "belonging to the Way." But what does "the Way" mean? Well, "the way" means "the road"; and throughout Luke-Acts we read about the road trips of Jesus, his apostles, and other disciples. We read also about "the way/road of salvation," "the way/road of peace [= the blessings of salvation]," "the way/road of the Lord," and "the way/road of God" (Luke 1:79; 3:4 [compare 7:27; Isaiah 40:3]; 9:3, 57; 10:4; 19:36; 20:21; Acts 16:17; 18:25-26). The risen Jesus appeared to two of his disciples on the way/road to Emmaus (Luke 24:32, 35). The Ethiopian eunuch was converted on the way/road from Jerusalem to Gaza (8:26, 36, 39). And Jesus is about to appear to Saul as Saul journeys on the way/road to Damascus (9:17, 27; 26:13). "The Way," then, means the gospel as it is worked out, propagated, and received in the travels of Jesus, evangelists, and recipients. Saul's purpose of tying up believers and bringing them "bound" to Jerusalem implies that he wants them to stand trial before the Sanhedrin and suffer at their hands the fate of Stephen.

9:3-7: And as he was traveling, it happened that he was drawing near to Damascus; and suddenly a light from heaven flashed around him. [4]And after falling on the ground, he heard a voice saying to him, "Saul, Saul, why are you persecuting me?" [5]And he said, "Who are you, Lord?" And he [answered], **"I'm Jesus, whom you're persecuting. [6]Nevertheless, stand up and go into the city** [Damascus], **and it'll be told you whatever is necessary for you to do." [7]But the men who were journeying with him stood speechless, hearing the voice on the one hand but seeing no one on the other hand.** Saul's nearness to Damascus sets the stage for entrance into the city. The flashing of a light from heaven, its suddenness, and its flashing "around him" didn't *knock* him to the ground. Because of the light's flashing suddenly around him he voluntarily *fell* on the ground (compare the flashing of Jesus' clothing at the transfiguration [Luke 9:29] and see Acts 10:25; Luke 5:12; 8:41; 17:16 for falling as voluntary). Saul already recognizes the start of a heavenly revelation. But Luke doesn't say that Saul saw Jesus, only that he heard Jesus' voice, at first without knowing whose voice it was. The doubling of Saul's name in Jesus' address to him lends poignancy to Jesus' question why Saul is persecuting him. And whereas Saul was "still breathing terrorism and murder *against the Lord's disciples*" (9:1), Jesus asks, ". . . why are you persecuting *me*?" He associates himself so closely with his disciples that to persecute them is to persecute him. Saul is so overwhelmed that he doesn't answer why he's persecuting Jesus. For Luke, of course, the virtues of Jesus and his disciples mean that Saul doesn't have a good reason for persecuting them. Instead of saying why he does, then, Saul asks who is speaking to him. Whom *in heaven* could he be persecuting when he's headed for Damascus to persecute believers *there*? He's puzzled, but in view of the suddenly flashing light he has the good sense (or is it a gut reaction?) to address his interlocutor with "Lord." Then Jesus identifies himself both as the one Saul addressed with that title (compare 2:36) and once again as the one Saul is persecuting when he persecutes believers in Jesus as Lord. "Nevertheless" means "despite the fact that you're persecuting me" and therefore points to God's grace in the following conversion and commissioning of Saul. Since he has fallen on the ground, he has to stand up to proceed into nearby Damascus. Jesus has a surprise for him: "it'll be told you whatever is necessary for you to do." The phrase "whatever is necessary" is open-ended yet indicative that the "whatever" arises out of God's predetermined plan. Unlike Saul, his fellow travelers stood instead of falling on the ground and said nothing rather than engaging the heavenly voice. After all, it had addressed only Saul. But whereas he puzzled over the identity of the speaker, they puzzled over the speaker's invisibility.

9:8-9: And Saul got up from the ground; but though his eyes were open, he saw nothing. And leading [him] **by the hand, they** [his co-travelers] **led him into Damascus. [9]And for three days he wasn't seeing** [anything] **and neither ate nor drank** [anything]. The suddenly flashing light had blinded Saul, so that—ironically—the leading pursuer of believers (for by definition "to persecute" is "to pursue") has to be led. The prolongation of his blindness for three days prevents him from pursuing believers in the local synagogues, and his total fasting during that period is a mark of piety that goes together with his praying (to be mentioned in 9:11).

9:10-12: And there was a certain disciple in Damascus by the name of Ananias; and the Lord said to him in a vision, "Ananias." And he said, "Behold, [here am] **I, Lord** [compare 1 Samuel 3:4, 6, 8; Isaiah

6:8]." [11]**And the Lord** [said] **to him, "On standing up, go to the lane** [a *narrow* street] **called 'Straight' and seek in Judas's house a Tarsian** [= a man from Tarsus, a city in what we call Asia Minor] **by the name of Saul. For behold, he's praying!** [12]**And in a vision he has seen a man by the name of Ananias coming in and laying** [his] **hands on him so that he'd see again."** Luke's knowing the name of a relatively obscure figure like Ananias (different from the husband of Sapphira in 5:1–11, of course) and knowing the name of a mere lane in Damascus testify to the historical research mentioned in Luke 1:1–4. "Behold" emphasizes the readiness with which Ananias recognized the Lord in a vision. For though the Lord called Ananias by name, he didn't identify himself. The heart of Simon the magician wasn't "straight" before God (8:21). So there may be some symbolism in Saul's residing in a house on a lane called "Straight." Certainly his "praying" shows his heart to be straight before God. "Behold" calls special attention to his piety in praying, a piety that has been rewarded with a vision of Ananias's restoring his sight. Saul may be a persecutor, but he's a pious persecutor. So his conversion will be both another triumph of Jesus' saving power and a testimony to piety as a mark of those who come to believe in him.

9:13–14: **But Ananias answered, "Lord, I've heard from many people about this man as to how many harmful things he has done to your sacred people in Jerusalem.** [14]**And here** [in Damascus] **he has authority from the chief priests to bind all who call on your name."** Since elsewhere in Acts calling on the name of the Lord means to appeal to Jesus as the Lord (see especially 7:54–60, but also 2:21; 22:16), it's evident that Jesus is the one who has appeared to Ananias in a vision and is conversing with him. "Lord, I've heard from many people about this man" indicates that Saul has gained notoriety as a persecutor of believers in Jesus. "As to how *many* harmful things he has done to your sacred people in Jerusalem" indicates further that Saul not only had something to do with the murder of Stephen. He also spearheaded the "great persecution against the church in Jerusalem" that scattered all the local believers except the apostles (8:1–3; 22:20). (Traditional English translations have "your saints" instead of "your sacred people"; but whereas "saints" tends to connote outstanding moral purity, "sacred" more accurately connotes a consecrated status—here in relation to Jesus: "*your* sacred [people].") And Saul's having "authority from [no less a body than] the chief priests to bind *all* [in Damascus] who call on [Jesus'] name" makes him very dangerous in Ananias's estimation. Though Saul had requested writs from the high priest (9:1–2), it now appears that the chief priests joined the high priest in supplying the writs. Those writs gave Saul authority not only to bind believers in Jesus but also to bring them to Jerusalem (9:2), but Ananias mentions only what's liable to happen right in Damascus. All in all, Ananias's description of Saul and his mission will make Saul's conversion stellar evidence of the gospel's power.

9:15–16: **But the Lord told him, "Be going, because this** [man] **is a select instrument of mine to carry my name in the sight of both Gentiles and kings and Israel's sons.** [16]**For I'll show him how many things it's necessary that he suffer for my name."** Luke keeps calling Jesus "the Lord" to underline his authority. As the Lord, Jesus repeats his command that Ananias go to Saul (compare 9:11), adds emphasis to it by putting it in the present tense ("Be going"), and tells why he should go. The reason outweighs Ananias's fear-filled objection and consists in Saul's coming role in spreading the gospel to Gentiles and potentates as well as to Jews, called "Israel's sons" (that is, descendants of Jacob, whose nickname was "Israel"). "A *select* instrument of mine" points forward to the leadership of Saul in this coming role. "To carry my name" relates to Jesus' name as the only one by which it's necessary to be saved (see 4:12 with comments). "In the *sight* of both Gentiles and kings and to Israel's sons" will make them eyewitnesses of the gospel in its victorious march throughout the world. "For I'll show him" introduces an explanation of what will accompany Saul's evangelistic travels. It will be suffering for the sake of Jesus' name, the very name on which believers were calling when Saul came to Damascus to persecute them (9:14) but now the name that he'll carry to Gentiles, potentates, and Jews. Saul's suffering will be multiple ("many things") and divinely planned ("it's necessary"), but it will actually help spread the gospel (compare 8:4).

9:17–19a: **And Ananias went off and entered into the house** [of Judas on the lane called "Straight" (9:11)] **and, laying** [his] **hands on him** [Saul], **said, "Saul, brother, the Lord has sent me—**[that is,] **Jesus, the one who appeared to you on the road by which you were coming—so that you'd see again and be filled with the Holy Spirit."** [18]**And** [something] **like scabs immediately fell from his eyes, and he saw again and, on standing up, was baptized.** [19a]**And on taking nourishment, he gained strength** [for he'd neither eaten nor drunk anything for three days (9:9)]. Ananias relents and goes to Saul. Addressing him with "brother" as well "Saul" is designed to establish rapport (as in 2:29; 3:17; 7:2, for example). "The Lord has sent me" tells Saul the reason for this visit from a total stranger. Ananias's identification of the Lord as Jesus, who'd appeared to Saul on the road to Damascus, implies that somehow Ananias had learned of that appearance. For Luke it isn't important how Ananias learned about the appearance. It's important only that the language of appearance has made Saul into an eyewitness of the resurrected, exalted Christ (compare Luke 1:1–4). And this language has for the first time indicated that Saul saw Jesus in the flashing light of 9:3 (compare his own statements in 1 Corinthians 9:1; 15:8). As in 8:17–19, the laying on of hands constitutes a gesture of solidarity, here between Ananias and his formerly would-be persecutor, and transmits to Saul the fullness of the Holy Spirit, a concomitant of salvation (2:38). Because of his blindness, though, the laying on of hands also transmits the healing that restores Saul's sight (compare 28:8; Luke 4:40; 13:13). The immediacy of this restoration signals a miracle. Standing up and getting baptized amounts to a public confession of belief in Jesus by this ex-leader of persecution. And gaining strength from the taking of nourishment enables him to start preaching immediately.

SAUL'S PREACHING IN DAMASCUS
Acts 9:19b–22

9:19b–22: And he came to be with the disciples in Damascus for some days. Exactly how many, Luke doesn't say and probably doesn't know. But "*with* the disciples" contrasts with "*against* the Lord's disciples" in 9:1. A transformation has taken place. **20And in the synagogues he immediately started proclaiming Jesus,** [saying,] **"This is God's Son."** The immediacy of Saul's preaching matches the immediacy of his seeing again (9:18). He can't wait to proclaim Jesus instead of persecuting him. "In the synagogues" has him fulfilling the role of carrying Jesus' name "to Israel's sons" (9:15). By proclaiming Jesus to be God's Son, Saul echoes what the angel Gabriel and God the Father himself said about Jesus (13:33; Luke 1:32, 35; 3:22; 9:35). **21And all who were hearing** [him say this] **were astonished and saying, "This is the one, isn't he, who wreaked havoc in Jerusalem against those who call on this name** [Jesus] **and had come here for this** [purpose], **that he might bring them bound to the chief priests?"** Saul's notoriety as a persecutor was so great that *all* who heard him proclaiming Jesus were astonished. They knew both about the havoc Saul had wreaked in Jerusalem and what he'd intended to do in Damascus, and they can hardly believe the reversal. **22And Saul was becoming more and more powerful** [in his proclaiming of Jesus as God's Son] **and was confounding the Jews residing in Damascus by demonstrating that this** [Jesus] **is the Christ.** Because he was filled with the Holy Spirit (9:17), Saul's power as a witness for Jesus increases (see 1:8). The power frustrates local Jews who don't believe, because they can't refute Saul's demonstration that just as Jesus is God's Son, he's the Christ—or, better, that he's the Christ *because* he's God's Son. Luke doesn't say how Saul made his demonstration; so the point consists solely in the power with which the gospel proceeds in Saul's proclamation.

SAUL'S ESCAPES TO JERUSALEM
AND THEN TO TARSUS
Acts 9:23–30

This passage divides into Saul's escape to Jerusalem from Damascus, where the Jews had plotted to kill him (9:23–25), and his escape to Tarsus from Jerusalem, where he'd associated with the apostles, preached, and became the object of another plot to kill him (9:26–30).

9:23–25: And as a considerable number of days were being fulfilled [= were elapsing], **the Jews plotted together to do away with him;** **24but their plot was made known to Saul. And they** [the Jews] **were also guard-ing the gates** [of Damascus] **closely both day and night so that they** [the Jews] **might do away with him.** **25But on taking** [him] **at night, his disciples lowered him through** [an opening in] **the wall by letting** [him] **down in a basket** [compare 2 Corinthians 11:32–33]. The converted persecutor quickly becomes an object of persecution, obviously because of his overpowering in debate the unbelieving Jews who lived in Damascus (9:22). Unable to refute him, they plot to kill him. The ultimate ad hominem! Luke doesn't indicate who made known to Paul the plot against his life. So the insertion here of that leak of information, plus the close, round-the-clock guarding of the city gates, implies that the plotters discovered the leak and were trying to prevent an escape by Saul. Given the lowering of Saul through an opening in the wall, the failure of their effort merits a chuckle. The lowering by "*his* disciples" indicates that Saul had gained converts, for "disciples" means "learners." They'd learned from him that Jesus is the Christ (9:22). The gospel wins even in the face of deadly opposition.

9:26–27: And on arriving in Jerusalem, he was trying to attach himself to the disciples; and not believing that he's a disciple, they were all afraid of him. **27But on taking hold of** [him], **Barnabas brought him to the apostles and related to them how he** [Saul] **had seen the Lord on the road** [to Damascus] **and that he** [the Lord] **had spoken to him and how in Damascus he** [Saul] **had spoken boldly in the name of Jesus.** Saul's trying to attach himself to the disciples strikes a contrast with his earlier "breathing terrorism and murder against the Lord's disciples" (9:1) and reveals that he now identifies himself as one of them. Since persecution had scattered from Jerusalem all the disciples except for the apostles (8:1), we might think that here "the disciples" include only "the apostles." But Barnabas wasn't one of the Twelve, yet he's here in Jerusalem. To be sure, he'll be called an apostle in 14:4; but in the immediately following chapter 15 we read of "the church" in Jerusalem in addition to "the apostles and the elders" (15:4). So it appears that the twelve apostles, who stayed in Jerusalem, made further converts after the scattering of the first converts. Either that or at least some of the first ones, like Barnabas, drifted back into Jerusalem after the "great persecution" of 8:1. Perhaps we should think of both developments. But whoever these disciples were, Luke points out their ignorant and therefore understandable fear of Saul. Barnabas rides to the rescue, though, by bringing Saul to the apostles and relating to them the story of Saul's conversion and subsequent preaching in Damascus. The story highlights Saul's having become an eye- and earwitness of the risen Lord, and also his boldness in preaching—just as the apostles themselves had become such witnesses and preachers (1:1–3; 2:29; 4:13, 29, 31). "In the name of Jesus" makes Saul's bold speaking a presentation of Jesus' name as the only means of salvation (4:12). Luke doesn't say how Barnabas knew the story of Saul's encounter with Jesus and subsequent preaching and therefore lets the accent rest on Saul's transformation as such.

9:28–30: **And he was with them, going in and going out in Jerusalem** [= moving about in the city], **speaking boldly in the name of the Lord.** [29]**And he was also debating with the Hellenists** [Greek-speaking Jews who didn't believe], **but they were undertaking to do away with him.** [30]**And on coming to know** [of this plot], **the brothers brought him down to Caesarea** [on the Mediterranean coast] **and sent him off to Tarsus** [his home city]. "And he was with them" signals the success, thanks to Barnabas, of Saul's attempt to attach himself to the disciples. But he isn't content merely to associate with them. He moves about in Jerusalem, all the while "speaking boldly in the name of the Lord" just as in Damascus "he'd spoken boldly in the name of Jesus" (9:27) and drawn a plot against his life for doing so. Admirable boldness! Admirable bravery! Since Jesus is Lord, speaking boldly in the name of the Lord equates with speaking boldly in the name of Jesus. In addition to this bold speaking, Saul disputes with Greek-speaking Jews, as well he could since he wrote all his New Testament letters (Romans–Philemon) in Greek. For Luke it goes without saying that these Hellenists differed from those Hellenists who according to 6:1 had become disciples (but see 6:9 for others, probably Hellenists, who debated with Stephen). As in Damascus, the debate degenerates into a plot against Saul's life. His arguments are too powerful to refute. So to get rid of *them* the unbelieving Hellenists have to get rid of *him*. But fellow believers whisk him to the coast and send him off to Tarsus. Luke calls them Saul's "brothers" to underline that Saul is now an accepted member of Jesus' family of believers. The initial fear of him has evaporated.

THE PEACE AND GROWTH OF THE CHURCH, WITH A COUPLE OF EXAMPLES INVOLVING PETER
Acts 9:31–43

This passage divides into a general statement (9:31), Peter's healing of Aeneas (9:32–35), and Peter's raising of Dorcas (9:36–43).

9:31: **On the one hand, therefore** [because of Saul's departure], **the church throughout the whole of Judea and Galilee and Samaria was having peace, being built up. And traveling in the fear of the Lord and the urging of the Holy Spirit, it was being multiplied.** Judea in the south, Galilee in the north, and Samaria in between comprise the land of Israel. "The *whole*" of these three regions stresses the breadth of evangelistic success generated by the Holy Spirit. Luke told about the expansion of the church into Judea and Samaria (8:1–40). Here we learn of the church in Galilee, too—a natural (you could say inevitable) development in view of Jesus' having made many disciples there. Because of this geographical spread and the meaning of "church" as an assembly, a congregation, it might be expected that Luke would use a plural: "the churches." But he uses a singular, "the church," to indicate that the many local congregations, separated as they are on earth, make up a single congregation before God: the church universal. This picture of a widespread church contributes to Luke's emphasis on the relentless advance of God's reign through gospel-preaching. It's pointless to resist. It's advisable to participate. "Having peace" means enjoying a respite from persecution. (Saul wasn't persecuting them any more, nor was his preaching acting as a lightning rod to draw persecution.) "Being built up" is explained in terms of (1) "traveling in the fear of the Lord," that is, seeking not to displease him in one's conduct (the Christian life as a journey on the road of moral purity [compare Luke 1:6]), and (2) "traveling in . . . the urging of the Holy Spirit," that is, bearing witness at the Spirit's urging (the Christian life as a journey on the road of evangelistic outreach). The combination of moral purity and evangelistic outreach produced numerical multiplication of the church.

9:32–35: **On the other hand, it happened that as he was going through all** [those territories], **Peter came down** [from Jerusalem (see 8:1c)] **also** [= "and in particular"] **to the sacred ones residing in Lydda.** [33]**And he found there a certain man by the name of Aeneas, bedridden for eight years, who was paralyzed.** [34]**And Peter told him, "Aeneas, Jesus Christ is healing you. Stand up and spread out** [a couch] **for yourself."** The couch would be for reclining at meal, as was the custom (compare 9:19a; Luke 8:55 for taking nourishment after a healing and after a raising from the dead). **And he stood up immediately.** [35]**And all those residing in Lydda and Sharon saw him, who as such** [referring to the residents as eyewitnesses] **turned to the Lord.** "All [those territories]" refers to Judea, Galilee, and Samaria (9:31). Peter's "going through" all of them presents an individual example of "traveling in . . . the urging of the Holy Spirit" (9:31). Lydda was about two-thirds of the way toward the Mediterranean Sea northwest from Jerusalem. See the comments on 9:13 for believers in Jesus as "the sacred ones." Aeneas's having been bedridden with paralysis for eight years makes his healing so stupendously miraculous that all the residents of Lydda and of the surrounding coastal plain of Sharon who saw Aeneas up and about turned to the Lord. "To the *Lord*," not to Peter, because Peter had said to Aeneas, "*Jesus Christ* is healing you." There's no indication that Aeneas had believed in Jesus Christ before, so that Peter's command, "Stand up and spread out [a couch] for yourself," amounts to an injunction to believe in Jesus Christ then and there. The immediacy of Aeneas's standing up gives evidence of belief as well as of healing. Luke doesn't add that Aeneas spread out a couch for himself. It's enough for Luke that Aeneas stood up, because this is what proved the miracle that led to the conversion of *all* the eyewitnesses. Huge evangelistic success yet again.

9:36–37: **And in Joppa** [on the Mediterranean coast northwest of Jerusalem] **there was a certain woman disciple by the name of Tabitha, which** [name] **when translated** [from Aramaic into Greek] **means Dorcas** [= "gazelle" in both languages]. **This** [woman] **was full** of good deeds and acts of charity that she kept doing. [37]But it happened during those days that on getting sick, she died. And after washing [her corpse], people placed her in an upstairs room. As with Aeneas in the preceding paragraph, Luke's knowledge of place names and personal names shows evidence of the historical research he referred to in Luke 1:1–4. "Acts of charity" means gifts to the poor and specifies the good deeds of Dorcas. That she was *full* of good deeds and acts of charity" indicates extraordinary activity of this sort. Luke puts her forth as an example of the humanitarian impulse generated by Jesus and thus as a good and true advertisement for the gospel. It was customary to wash a corpse before anointing and then burying it. Presumably the washed corpse of Dorcas was placed in an upstairs room so as to be anointed. But Luke mentions only the placement, because something is going to happen that will forestall anointing and burial.

9:38–39: But because Lydda was close to Joppa [only about ten miles away, as a matter of fact], **on hearing, "Peter is in it** [= in Lydda]**," the disciples sent two men to him, urging** [him]**, "You shouldn't hesitate to come through as far as us** [because our Joppa is close by]**."** [39]**And on standing up, Peter went with them, whom** [referring to Peter]**, when he arrived, they led up into the upstairs room. And all the widows** [who may have been getting ready to anoint the corpse] **stood beside him weeping and displaying on themselves how many undergarments and outer garments Dorcas used to make while she was with them.** The sending of *two* men strengthens the request that Peter come to Joppa. "You shouldn't hesitate" doesn't mean "Come *quickly*" so much as it means, "Be *sure* to come." The two men cite the proximity of Joppa as a reason to come. Though they don't tell Peter about the death of Dorcas, he goes with them. Unexpectedly, Luke doesn't say Peter saw Dorcas's corpse on being led to the upstairs room where it lay. No, Luke is so concerned to attract people to the gospel by highlighting the good and charitable deeds of believers in Jesus that he (Luke) features the widows' displaying on themselves the many inner and outer garments Dorcas used to make for the poor and needy. They were wearing those garments. (Inner garments were short robes, called "tunics," and outer garments were long robes.) Since most widows were poor, these widows were almost certainly showing Peter the garments Dorcas had made *for them*. Hence they had a special reason to weep over her death.

9:40–43: And on ejecting all [the widows and the two men who had led him upstairs] **and kneeling, Peter prayed; and on turning to the corpse, he said, "Tabitha, stand up."** The ejection of all the widows keeps their weeping and displaying the garments from preventing his prayer. Luke doesn't say what Peter prayed, so that the accent rests on the piety of Peter in kneeling and praying. His piety combines with Dorcas's good deeds to recommend the gospel, which the two of them represent. "Turning toward the corpse" implies Peter's having looked toward God in heaven when he prayed. As an Aramaic-speaking Jew, Peter then addressed Dorcas with the Aramaic form of her name, "Tabitha." Compare Luke 8:54 with Peter's command that she stand up. **And she opened her eyes and, on seeing Peter, she sat up.** So she's alive again! [41]**And on giving her** [his] **hand** [so that she could grab hold]**, he helped her stand up.** So the miracle is complete. **And on calling the sacred ones** [see the comments on 9:13 for this designation of disciples in general] **and the widows** [in particular]**, he presented her alive.** So they become eyewitnesses of her having come back to life, and also witnesses in the sense of testifying to it. [42]**And it became known throughout the whole of Joppa, and many believed on the Lord.** So just as the miracle led to many conversions in Joppa, it joins Peter's piety and Dorcas's good deeds in recommending to Luke's audience that they put their faith in Jesus as Lord. [43]**And it happened that** [Peter] **stayed a considerable number of days in Joppa with a certain Simon, a tanner** [of animal skins]. This notation sets up for the next episode.

THE CONVERSION OF A
HOUSEFUL OF GENTILES
Acts 10:1–48

This passage divides into a vision seen by a centurion named Cornelius (10:1–8); a complementary vision seen by Peter (10:9–16); Cornelius's invitation to Peter (10:17–23a); their meeting each other (10:23b–26); Peter's explanation of why he came (10:27–33); his presentation of the gospel (10:34–43); and the conversion of his Gentile audience (10:44–48). The dovetailing of the two visions that make this episode possible displays God as inaugurating his plan to bring Gentiles en masse into his kingdom.

The passage begins with a long sentence in *10:1–3*: **And a certain man in Caesarea by the name of Cornelius—a centurion of the cohort called "Italian,"** [2]**pious and fearing God with all his household, doing many acts of charity for the** [Jewish] **people and praying to God constantly—**[3]**saw clearly in a vision at about the ninth hour of the day** [= about 3:00 P.M.] **an angel of God coming in toward him and saying to him, "Cornelius."** A centurion commanded one hundred soldiers or thereabouts, and a cohort numbered six hundred soldiers or thereabouts. The present centurion, Cornelius, recalls both the centurion whose faith Jesus found unequaled in Israel (Luke 7:2–10) and the centurion who at Jesus' death "was glorifying God, saying, 'Certainly this man was righteous'" (Luke 23:47). So we might expect some good in Cornelius too. Luke doesn't disappoint our expectation. Though a Gentile and an officer in an occupying army, Cornelius isn't only reverent toward God (the meaning of "pious"). He also fears God (in the sense of fearing to displease him). He has drawn all the members of his household into this God-reverencing, God-fearing piety. He performs acts of charity to benefit poverty-stricken people—indeed, *many* such acts. And he prays to God constantly, that is, regularly. If such a superlative specimen of virtue will be attracted to the gospel, what a good gospel it must be. Clearly, God is attracted to him; for in midafternoon he causes an angel to appear to Cornelius in a vision and greet him by name. Cornelius saw the angel "clearly." His eyewitnessing was mistake-proof. God saw to that.

10:4–6: And gazing at him [= at the angel] **and becoming terrified, he** [Cornelius] **said, "What is it, lord?"** An angel deserves to be addressed with "lord," but only with a small "l." Since the angel has spoken only Cornelius's name, Cornelius naturally wonders what's up; and he's terrified. Yet there's no need to be: **And he** [the angel] **said to him, "Your prayers and your acts of charity have come up as a memorial before God. ⁵And now send men to Joppa; and send for a certain Simon, who's nicknamed Peter. ⁶This** [Simon] **is lodging with a certain Simon, a tanner, who has a house alongside the** [Mediterranean] **sea."** Here we have proof that God is attracted to Cornelius. Prayers ascend to heaven naturally because they're directed upward. But Cornelius's acts of charity are directed outward to poor people on earth. Nevertheless, these acts haven't remained earthbound. They too have ascended to heaven, and neither they nor the prayers have been forgotten. They're a memorial before God in that he keeps them in the forefront of his memory. It's people such as Cornelius, then, that God goes out of his way to bring in contact with an evangelist; and it's to people such as Cornelius that the gospel of Jesus Christ should appeal, and does appeal. The angel's directions to Cornelius are clear and specific.

10:7–8: And when the angel that had been speaking to him went away, on calling two of [his] **household slaves and a pious soldier from** [the number of] **those who waited on him, ⁸and after relating to them all things** [in his vision], **he sent them to Joppa.** We've already been told that all Cornelius's household were pious (10:2). So now Luke has only to say that the soldier Cornelius sends along with two household slaves is pious. Apparently Cornelius has had a godly influence on at least one of his soldiers too.

10:9–14: And the next day as those [household slaves and the soldier] **were proceeding on the road** [to Joppa] **and were drawing near to the city, Peter went up on the housetop** [of Simon the tanner's home] **to pray at about the sixth hour** [= about noon]. Here Peter's piety comes out, as that of Cornelius has already done. The piety of a disciple and that of a prospective disciple make for a good match. **¹⁰And he** [Peter] **got hungry and was wanting to eat. But as they** [members of Simon the tanner's household] **were preparing** [food for Peter], **a trance came over him; ¹¹and** [in it] **he observes heaven opened and a container coming down, something like a large sheet being let down on the earth by** [its] **four corners . . . .** The present tense of "observes" makes vivid Peter's eyewitnessing. Luke compares the container to a sheet such as is used for a sail or an awning, because as a sail billows out when filled with wind or as an awning dips

in the middle no matter how tightly stretched, so this container billows downward or dips under the weight of the objects it supports. And it's "large" to accommodate the large number of those objects. Its coming down from an opened heaven indicates a *divine* revelation. Its being "let down on the earth" indicates a revelation *to Peter*. In view of the traditional expression, "the four corners of the earth" (as in Revelation 7:1; 20:8), "on the earth by [its] four corners" may forecast a revelation concerning the universality of the gospel, that it's for the whole earth (compare 1:8: "as far as the extremity of the earth"). Luke's sentence continues: **¹²in which** [container] **were all the four-footed** [animals] **and reptiles of the earth and birds of the sky. ¹³And there came a voice to him, "On standing up, Peter, slaughter** [these four-footed animals, reptiles, and birds] **and eat** [them]." After all, he was hungry (10:10). **¹⁴But Peter said, "By no means, Lord, because I've never eaten anything** [ritually] **impure and unclean."** "*All* the four-footed [animals] and reptiles . . . and birds" includes those that the Mosaic law prohibited the Jews from eating (see Leviticus 11:1–47). Peter recognizes the voice speaking to him as the Lord's and addresses the speaker with "Lord." "By no means" is at odds with this acknowledgment of authority, but Peter thinks that obedience to the dietary laws given by the Lord to Moses outweighs the present command to violate those laws. Perhaps he thinks the Lord is testing his obedience to the dietary laws. For Luke, in any case, Peter's lifelong adherence to those laws proves him to be a good Jew, faithful to the ancient Scriptures and therefore not a religious renegade.

10:15–16: And again, a second time, the voice [came] **to him, "The things that God has cleansed** [that is, declared ritually clean and therefore free to be eaten] ***you* aren't to go on considering** [ritually] **impure." ¹⁶And this happened three times over, and immediately** [after the three instances] **the container was taken up into heaven.** For the sake of universality, God's present declaration outdates a component of the Law given by him through angels (7:53). So Peter must accede. To underline the necessity that he accede, the command comes to him three times over. Ah, that number three! It reminds Peter of his disowning "the Lord," who is now addressing him, three times (Luke 22:34, 54–62). The reminder heaps further emphasis on the present necessity that he accede. The immediacy of the container's being taken up to heaven, where it originated, makes temporal room for the arrival of Cornelius's men and Peter's meeting them. The significance of the vision will then dawn on Peter.

10:17–20: And as Peter was puzzling in himself as to what the vision he'd seen might be [= might mean, or signify], **behold, the men who'd been sent by Cornelius, having successfully asked for** [directions to] **the house of Simon** [the tanner], **arrived at the gate. ¹⁸And calling out, they were inquiring if Simon, the one nicknamed Peter** [as distinct from Simon the tanner], **is lodging here.** "*Is* lodging *here*" echoes the actual wording of the inquiry. [19]**And while Peter was mulling over the vision, the Spirit told him, "Behold, three men seeking you!** [20]**Rather** [than continuing to mull over the vision], **on standing up, go down and, doubting in no respect, travel with them, because I myself have sent them."** The first "behold" introduces a clause that highlights for Luke's audience the arrival of Cornelius's men. The second "Behold" introduces an exclamation that highlights for Peter the men's looking for him. Since Cornelius had been told that the house of Simon the tanner was "alongside the sea" (10:6), Cornelius's men must have discovered more than one house alongside the sea and therefore had to ask which of them belonged to Simon the tanner. The angel had told Cornelius that Peter was lodging in that Simon's house. To make sure they're at the right house, then, Cornelius's men inquire if Peter is lodging there. Since they've arrived "at the gate," they have to "call out" their inquiry. Simultaneously, the Spirit tells Peter that "three men" are seeking him. There's that number three again, bedeviling Peter for his three disownings of Jesus. Because of them, what ordinarily would require only two men from Cornelius requires three (compare the comments on 10:16). That Peter is to *stand up*, go down from the housetop, and travel with them corresponds to the command in 10:13 that he *stand up*, slaughter, and eat. The meaning of the vision is already starting to take shape. "Doubting in no respect" corresponds to the three statements of that command over against Peter's refusal in 10:14 to stand up, slaughter, and eat. "Because I myself have sent them" indicates both that an "angel of God" acted as the Spirit's agent in telling Cornelius to send men (10:3–6) and that Cornelius acted in turn as the Spirit's agent in the actual sending (10:7–8).

10:21–23a: And on going down, Peter said to the men, "Behold, I'm the one you're seeking! What's the reason that you've come for?" [22]**And they said, "Cornelius—a centurion, a righteous and God-fearing man and attested by the whole nation of the Jews—was instructed by a holy angel to send for you** [to come] **into his house and to hear words from you."** [23a]**So on calling them in, he** [Peter] **gave them lodging.** "Behold . . . !" dramatizes the fulfillment of the angel's statement to Cornelius that his men would find Peter at the house of Simon the tanner. Peter knows no more than that he's to go with the men. So he asks them why they've come. Their answer features an identification of Cornelius by his name and occupation and a description of his character reminiscent of Luke's own description in 10:2 except that "righteous" replaces "pious," and "attested by the whole nation of the Jews" replaces and undergirds Cornelius's "doing many acts of charity for the [Jewish] people." "By the *whole* nation of the Jews" magnifies Cornelius's many acts of charity to the nth degree. "God-fearing" matches Luke's earlier description, though "with all his household" drops off because the three men themselves, or at least the two nonmilitary ones, are members of his household and would hardly describe themselves glowingly. Luke, of course, delights in showing that a

man of such sterling character and widespread repute as Cornelius is being attracted to the gospel because God is attracted to him. The earlier description of Cornelius as "praying *to God* constantly" also drops off in favor of an immediate introduction of the instruction *to Cornelius* that he send for Peter. The men attribute this instruction to "a holy angel." This phrase substitutes for "an angel of God" in 10:3, but of necessity an angel of God would be holy. As usual, "holy" doesn't mean morally pure so much as special and sacred. Luke's account of Cornelius's vision in 10:3–6 contains no instruction that he "hear words from [Peter]," but the three men add this instruction to their account. The addition sets the stage for a sermon that Peter will preach in Cornelius's house. By this time it was too late for a journey from Joppa to Caesarea; so Peter calls them in to stay overnight.

10:23b–26: And on standing up the next day, he went out [from Joppa] **with them; and certain of the brothers from Joppa went with him.** "The brothers" are Peter's fellow believers, doubtless Jewish like Peter himself. Their accompaniment of him, though not commanded by the Spirit, will provide multiple eyewitness attestation of what is going to happen in a houseful of Gentiles (see 10:45–46; 11:12–18). [24]**And on the next day** [after the previous "next day"] **he went into Caesarea. And Cornelius, having called together his relatives and close friends, was waiting expectantly for them** [his three men and Peter]. The angel told Cornelius that his prayers and charitable acts had gone up as a memorial before God (10:4–6) and that he was to hear words from Peter (10:22). The favorable memorial inclines Cornelius to expect good words from Peter. Hence the calling together of relatives and close friends in addition to the household (11:14). Good words deserve a large audience. [25]**And when it happened that Peter came into** [Cornelius's house], **on meeting him Cornelius worshiped** [him] **by falling on** [Peter's] **feet** [that is, kneeling down—or perhaps even lying prone—and putting his forehead down on Peter's feet in deep obeisance]. Thus Cornelius shows reverence toward Peter as the Lord's messenger. Now Peter shows piety toward God by refusing reverence: [26]**But Peter raised him, saying, "Stand up. I myself, too** [= as well as you], **am a human being."** Cornelius is to stand up now that Peter has arrived in Caesarea just as Peter stood up in Joppa to come to Caesarea (10:13, 20, 23). Both of them are human beings of equal standing. Again for the sake of the gospel, Luke takes delight in these complementary expressions of piety.

10:27–29: And as he [Peter] **was conversing with him, he** [Peter again] **went in and finds many people assembled.** The present tense of "finds" calls attention to Peter's discovery of so many. In accordance with learning that an angel had told Cornelius to hear words from Peter, Peter expected an audience of only one. For Luke's audience as well as for Peter, his companions, and all other Jewish believers, the "many" in Cornelius's house—relatives, close friends, and members of the household—represent a quantum leap in the propagation of the gospel to Gentiles. **²⁸And he said to them, "You yourselves understand how it's taboo for a Jewish man to be adhering or coming to a person of another tribe** [that is, to be associating himself intimately and having close converse with anyone outside the tribes of Israel]. **And God has shown me to say** [that] **not a single human being** [is] **impure or unclean** [ritually speaking]." "You yourselves understand" indicates that Gentiles were well aware of Jewish taboos. We expect Peter to say, "And God has *told* me." Instead, he says, "And God has *shown* me," with reference to the vision he'd seen. God *had* told him not to go on considering ritually impure what God has cleansed (10:15). But that statement seemed to, and perhaps did in part, deal with the four-footed animals, reptiles, and birds that Peter saw in his vision. Now it dawns on him that they stood for non-Jewish human beings, none of whom he should say is impure or unclean. Actually, he puts the point in a stronger, positive form: "to *say* [that] not a single human being [is] impure or unclean" (rather than "*not* to say [that] any human being [is] impure or unclean"). **²⁹On this account** [because of what God has shown me] **also** [in addition to it]**, I came without objection when sent for** [in contrast with my saying, 'By no means, Lord,' when he told me to slaughter and eat those animals, reptiles, and birds]. **So I'm inquiring for what reason you** [plural, to include the three men along with Cornelius] **sent for me."** In 10:22 Cornelius's men told Peter the reason, namely, that Cornelius sent for him so as "to hear words from [him]." Here, Peter asks to hear the reason from Cornelius's own mouth; and the question gives Cornelius opportunity to spell out in detail his vision, its circumstances, and his and the others' eagerness to hear the Lord's message from Peter.

10:30–33: And Cornelius said, "Four days ago, up to and including this hour I was in my house praying the ninth hour [in the sense of continuing to pray through the ninth hour (about 3:00–4:00 P.M.)]." "Four days ago" includes the day he was praying and the present day of his speaking, with two days intervening according to 10:9, 23. "Up to and including this hour" draws a happy parallel between the ninth hour of his praying and the present hour that has come as a result of his praying. But 10:3 didn't say that Cornelius was *praying* through the ninth hour, only that he received a *vision* "at about the ninth hour." So the addition here of praying makes the vision a divine response to the prayer. Nor did 10:3 indicate that Cornelius was in his house at the time. So the addition here of "in my house" draws another happy parallel, not this time a temporal one—rather, a topographical one in which the location of the prayer and the location of God's response to it match each other. "And behold, a man in resplendent apparel stood in my sight." Instead of "in my sight," most translations have "before me," "in my presence," or the like. But these translations miss Luke's emphasis on eyewitnessing, which is here contained in a phrase that connotes eyesight. The phrase corresponds to "Cornelius . . . saw

clearly" in 10:3. There, he saw "an angel [= messenger] of God." Cornelius now speaks of "a man in resplendent apparel." Such apparel suits an angel and enabled Luke to call him an angel. Cornelius's whole expression therefore implies that the angel projected himself as a man wearing heavenly garments. "Behold" marks the surprise caused by his appearance. **³¹"And he says** [the present tense enlivening Cornelius's quotation of the man's words], **'Cornelius, your prayer has been heeded and your acts of charity remembered in God's sight.'"** "Your prayer" refers specifically to what Cornelius was praying the ninth hour four days earlier. "Has been *heeded*" represents an advance on the going up of his prayers as a *memorial* before God (so 10:4). The remembering of Cornelius's acts of charity does correspond to the going up of those acts as a memorial, though (so 10:4 again). But replacing "before God" (10:4) is "in God's sight" for a parallel with the standing of a man wearing resplendent clothing "in [Cornelius's] sight." What *God* sees leads him to make *Cornelius* see by way of compensation. Cornelius continues quoting the man: **³²"Therefore** [because your prayer has been heeded and your acts of charity remembered] **send to Joppa and call for Simon who is nicknamed Peter. This** [Simon] **is lodging in the house of Simon, a tanner, alongside the** [Mediterranean] **sea.'"** "Call for" replaces "send for," perhaps—but only perhaps—as a counterpart to Peter's "calling [Cornelius's men] in" to stay overnight (10:23). **³³"Therefore** [because of the command] **I sent** [my men] **to you at once, and you've done well by coming. Now, therefore** [as a result of your arrival]**, we're all present in God's sight to hear all the things commanded you by the Lord."** "At once" highlights the immediacy of Cornelius's obedience. "You've done well" highlights Peter's obedience to the Spirit's instruction. "We're *all* present *in God's sight* to hear *all* the things commanded you by the Lord" highlights the readiness of Cornelius and his household, relatives, and close friends to hear the entirety of the Lord's message spoken by Peter. Virtue all around!

10:34–38: And opening [his] **mouth, Peter said, "In truth I apprehend that God doesn't play favorites** [as he would if he limited evangelism to the Jews]. **³⁵Rather, in every nation the person who fears him and works righteousness** [as Cornelius does according to 10:2, 4, 22] **is welcomed by him** [hence his arranging a meeting between Cornelius and Peter for the hearing of the gospel]. **³⁶The word** [in the sense of a message] **that he** [God] **sent to the sons of Israel by proclaiming as good news peace through Jesus Christ—this one is Lord of all. ³⁷You yourselves know the word** [in the sense of a reported event] **that took place throughout the whole of Judea** [the entirety of Israel (see the comments on Luke 1:5)], **beginning from Galilee after the baptism that John proclaimed, ³⁸**[the word] **in regard to Jesus, the** [man] **from Nazareth—how God anointed him with the Holy Spirit and power—who** [referring to Jesus] **went throughout** [the whole of Judea/Israel] **doing good** [to people] **and healing all who were being dominated by the Devil, because God was with him."** "In truth" stresses that Peter has caught on to the meaning of his vision. "In every nation" stresses God's welcoming God-fearing, righteous Gentiles as well as Jews by seeing to it that such people hear the gospel, as in Cornelius's case. Luke uses two different words for "word," one to indicate a message, the other an event. Though God welcomes God-fearing, righteous Gentiles, he sent the word as a proclamation of peace-filled good news through Jesus Christ originally to the descendants of Israel (Jacob); and this sending started with the angelic message at Jesus' birth: "For behold, I'm announcing to you as good news a great joy, which will be for all the people [of Israel], because today there has been born for you in the city of David a Savior, who is Christ, the Lord. . . . peace [= all the blessings of salvation] [is] on earth among human beings of [God's] good pleasure [that is, among those with whom he's well pleased—like Cornelius]" (Luke 2:10–11, 14). Through his angel, God himself was proclaiming as good news the peace of salvation through Jesus Christ. "To the sons of Israel" preserves the rootage of the gospel in old, respected Judaism.

On mentioning Jesus Christ, Peter breaks off his sentence for an independent declaration that this Jesus Christ is "Lord of all." The declaration affirms that though God sent the message originally to "the sons of Israel," Jesus' lordship isn't limited to them, but extends to all peoples and therefore to Cornelius and those with him in his house. "You yourselves know" points to the popular and therefore well-known success of Jesus' ministry. Peter denotes it as an event, word of which came even to the ears of Gentiles in Caesarea. "Throughout the whole of Judea, beginning from Galilee" stresses the breadth of Jesus' ministry, especially since "beginning" doesn't agree grammatically with "the word" and therefore has to agree with "Jesus Christ" in Peter's previous declaration. "After the baptism that John proclaimed" strengthens the ties of Jesus' ministry with the Old Testament and Judaism in that according to Luke 3:3–6, John's proclaiming a baptism of repentance fulfilled Isaiah 40:3–5. In effect (and perhaps grammatically as well), "in regard to Jesus" identifies him *as* the word/event that took place. God anointed him with the Holy Spirit at his baptism by John (Luke 3:21–22; 4:17–19)—hence another reason for the preceding notation of John's proclamation of baptism. And because the Holy Spirit brings power (1:8), the anointing with him was at one and the same time an anointing of Jesus with power (Luke 4:14). The Spirit is God's. So the anointing with the Holy Spirit means that "God was with him." Since God is good and all-powerful, then, Jesus went about "doing good and healing all those who were being dominated by the Devil [through demon-possession]" (see the comments on Luke 6:18 for the sense in which demoniacs are healed). "Throughout" and "healing *all*" reemphasize the breadth and success of Jesus' ministry. The greatest emphasis falls, though, on its humanitarianism. Jesus was—and is—good for people. That's a reason the news about him is good, and why you should believe in him.

10:39–41: "**And we are witnesses of all the things that he did both in the countryside of the Jews and in Jerusalem, whom also they did away with by hanging** [him] **on a tree** [= by crucifying him]. [40]**God raised this** [Jesus] **on the third day and granted that he become visible,** [41]**not to all the people, but to witnesses handpicked beforehand by God,** [that is,] **to us who as such** [= as previously handpicked] **ate and drank with him after he resurrected from among the dead.**" In its two occurrences, "witnesses" carries first and foremost the meaning of "eyewitnesses." The resurrected Jesus' becoming "visible" to the witnesses confirms this meaning. On the other hand, Peter's proclamation means that he's also bearing witness to what he and others have seen. Thus he contributes to Luke's program of certifying the gospel with eyewitness testimony (Luke 1:1–4). That Peter and others "are witnesses of *all* the things that he [Jesus] did both in the countryside of the Jews and in Jerusalem" defines the witnesses, whom Peter calls "us," as the twelve apostles. For they were those who accompanied Jesus continuously from the beginning of his ministry right up through his postresurrection appearances (1:21–22). "*Both* in the countryside of the Jews *and* in Jerusalem" underlines the comprehensiveness of the apostles' eyewitnessing and thus strengthens their certification of the good news about Jesus. "Whom *also* they did away with" implies the injustice of the Jews' adding a crucifixion of Jesus to his good deeds. God's raising Jesus on the third day counteracted their crucifixion of him and fulfilled Jesus' predictions of the same (Luke 9:22, 43–45; 17:25; 18:31–33; 24:6–7, 44–46). Emphasizing this counteraction is the abruptness with which Peter introduces his declaration that God raised Jesus. (There's no "and" or other connective word.) "*Granted* that he become visible" underlines the privilege of the apostles in seeing the resurrected Jesus. To be sure, others as well—for example, Cleopas and another disciple on the road to Emmaus—saw the resurrected Jesus (Luke 24:13–35). But Peter is centering on the apostles as previously handpicked and therefore as official eyewitnesses. They were handpicked back in Luke 6:13–16. There it's said that Jesus selected them. Here it's said they were handpicked by God. But Jesus had prayed before selecting them, and Judas Iscariot's replacement was chosen after prayer by a divinely determined casting of lots (1:24–26). So Peter can attribute the handpicking to God. Luke 24:41–43 says that after his resurrection *Jesus* ate a broiled fish in the apostles' sight (see also Acts 1:4). Here Peter adds drinking to eating and puts the matter the other way around: *he and the other apostles* ate and drank with Jesus. This way of putting it accents the apostles' role and privilege as handpicked by God. Since Jesus had asked whether the apostles had anything edible (Luke 24:41), it makes sense that they had provisions for a meal. As usual, "resurrected" means resurrection "from among the dead," who remain in their graves. The contrast with Jesus highlights the miracle of his resurrection.

10:42–43: "**And he directed us to preach to the people and testify solemnly, 'This** [Jesus] **is the one** designated by God as judge of living people and dead people.'" In Luke 24:47; Acts 1:8 Jesus directed the apostles to preach and testify. "To the people" means "to the Jews" (compare 13:31 with 13:16). In Luke 24:47, however, Jesus spoke of a proclamation "to all nations." That phrase includes Gentiles as well as Jews, of course; but here Peter speaks only about an order to preach to the Jewish people. This narrow focus links up with the solemnity of the testimony that God has designated Jesus, the very one the Jews crucified, as judge. Those Jews in particular have something to fear from him at the judgment (from *him*, according to Peter, not from his peaceable followers). "Designated by God as judge" attributes to Jesus a divine prerogative. "Of living people and dead people" makes Jesus' judgment universal, covering the whole human race, and implies a general resurrection of the dead for that judgment. ⁴³**"To this** [Jesus] **all the prophets bear witness that everyone who believes in him receives forgiveness of sins through his name** [compare especially 3:18, 24; Luke 24:25–27, 44]." The witness of the prophets roots the gospel again in the ancient Scriptures of Judaism. "*All* the prophets" multiplies their witness. And "*everyone* who believes" includes not only Jews, but also Gentiles such as Peter's audience. Believing *in* Jesus entails committal of one's fate to him. Reception of the forgiveness of a believer's sins defines the salvation that comes through his name, and only through his name (see 4:12 with comments).

10:44–46a: While Peter was still speaking these words, the Holy Spirit fell on all who were hearing the word. They're so ready to believe (see 10:33) that they believe before Peter has a chance to tell them to. In Peter's "words" (plural) they hear "the word" (singular) that constitutes the gospel. And for them, to hear is to believe. Otherwise the Holy Spirit wouldn't have fallen on them as they were hearing the word. The instantaneousness of the Spirit's falling on them gives powerful evidence of God's acceptance of believing Gentiles. In the case of Samaritan believers there was a delay so that the apostles Peter and John, both Jews, could go down to Samaria and see for themselves the Samaritan believers' reception of the Spirit (8:14–17). But Peter and Jewish believers from Joppa are already here at Cornelius's house in Caesarea. So no delay is necessary. ⁴⁵**And believers from the circumcision** [= Jewish believers], **as many as had come with Peter, were astonished that the gift of the Holy Spirit had been poured out on the Gentiles.** Apparently Peter wasn't astonished, because he'd seen the Samaritan believers receive the Spirit. The description of Jewish believers as "from the circumcision" underscores that these Gentiles have received the Spirit despite noninclusion in the "covenant of circumcision" (7:8). "As many as had come with Peter" emphasizes that there were no exceptions to the astonishment of Peter's Jewish companions. ⁴⁶ᵃ**For they were hearing them speaking with tongues and magnifying God.** "Speaking with tongues" (about which see the comments on 2:1–13) gave audible and therefore undeniable evidence of receiving the Holy Spirit. And "magnifying

God" describes the good religious effect of the Spirit's outpouring (compare 2:11: "we hear them telling in our tongues the magnificent [deeds] of God"; also the comments on 8:14–17 for figurative expressions, such as "fell on" and "had been poured out," in reference to reception of the Holy Spirit).

10:46b–48: Then Peter answered [= responded], ⁴⁷**"Surely no one is able to withhold the water, is he, for these to be baptized who as such** [= who as tongues-speakers] **have received the Holy Spirit as also we** [did]**?" ⁴⁸And he ordered that they be baptized in the name of Jesus Christ. Then they asked him to stay for some days.** "As also we [did]" sets forth the equality of Gentile believers with Jewish believers in God's sight. Peter seems not to have baptized these Gentile believers. Rather, "he ordered that they *be* baptized," presumably by his Jewish companions, who were duly astonished. If so, social healing is to occur between Jews and Gentiles in the believing community. The Gentiles' asking Peter to stay for an open-ended number of days gives further evidence of such healing, which lends attractiveness to the gospel. "In the name of Jesus Christ" describes the baptism as administered with the authority that his name represents. So no one should dare to deny the legitimacy of the baptism. Luke doesn't say whether the baptism was carried out or whether Peter stayed. We may assume an affirmative in each case, but the lack of explicitly stated affirmatives leaves the stress on Jewish believers' obligation to treat Gentile believers as their equals, and on Gentile believers' desire for fellowship with Jewish believers like Peter. Thus far in Acts, then, the gospel has won large numbers of converts among Jews, Samaritans, and Gentiles.

THE GLORIFICATION OF GOD BECAUSE OF THE GENTILES' CONVERSION
Acts 11:1–18

11:1–3: And the apostles [who except for Peter were still in Jerusalem (8:1)] **and the brothers** [= fellow believers] **who were throughout Judea heard that the Gentiles too had welcomed God's word. ²And when Peter went up** [from coastal Caesarea] **to Jerusalem** [in the Judean hill country]**, those of circumcision** [= Jewish believers] **were taking issue with him, ³saying, "You went in to men having uncircumcision** [= entered a house full of uncircumcised Gentile men] **and ate with them."** Chapter 10 said nothing about Peter's eating with uncircumcised Gentile men. But Peter won't deny the present accusation that he did, and his nondenial implies that he'd accepted the Gentiles' invitation to stay a while with them and had eaten with them during the stay (10:48). Eating with someone, especially in that someone's home, constituted the kind of intimate association and close friendship forbidden to Jews in relation to Gentiles (10:28). Therein lies the reason behind the Jewish believers' objection to Peter's behavior. Moreover, his having eaten with a Gentile and in the Gentile's home shows that Peter understood his vision of the sheet containing unclean as well as clean four-footed animals, reptiles, and birds to mean that God had abolished Old Testament food laws, so that he could legitimately eat whatever food his Gentile host served him. In other words, the vision had to do with foods as well as with human beings.

Now Peter rehearses his vision in some detail, though also with abbreviations, for his Jewish fellow believers, whereas he'd only alluded to the vision in his remarks to the Gentiles in Cornelius's house (10:28). **11:4–10: And starting [to speak], Peter was setting out to them [the particulars] in an orderly way, saying, ⁵"I was in the city of Joppa praying, and in a trance I saw a vision, a container coming down, something like a large sheet being let down by [its] four corners out of heaven. And it came as far as me, ⁶gazing into which [sheet] I was noticing and saw the four-footed [animals] of the earth and the wild beasts and the reptiles and the birds of the sky. ⁷And I also heard a voice saying to me, 'On standing up, Peter, slaughter and eat [them].' ⁸But I said, 'By no means, Lord, because a [ritually] impure or unclean [item] has never entered into my mouth.' ⁹And a voice answered from heaven a second time, 'The things that God has cleansed [that is, declared ritually clean and therefore free to be eaten] you aren't to go on considering [ritually] impure.' ¹⁰And this happened three times, and all [those] things were pulled up into heaven again."** Luke has Peter set out the particulars "in an orderly way" just as Luke says he himself set out the particulars of Jesus' ministry "in an orderly way" (Luke 1:1–4). "And *starting* [to speak]" appropriately introduces the first of these particulars. In 10:9–11 Luke said Peter went up to Simon the tanner's rooftop to pray, got hungry there, fell into a trance, and received a vision. Here, Peter ties his trance and vision directly to his praying: he was praying at the time. This direct connection establishes a cause-and-effect relation between his piety and God's communication to him.

By replacing the sheet-like container's being let down "on the earth" (10:11) with "it came as far as me," Peter indicates that the contents of the container were within his reach, so that he could easily have stood up and slaughtered them for food. And whereas 10:11–12 says that Peter observed heaven opened and the container coming down, here he uses "gazing into [the sheet]" and adds "I was noticing and saw," with the contents of the sheet rather than the sheet itself as objects of the noticing and seeing. Especially given the twofold verbal expression, this addition puts emphasis on the contents as a point of dispute between Peter and the Lord. Also emphasizing them as such is Peter's addition of "the wild beasts," which aren't listed separately from the four-footed animals, reptiles, and birds in 10:12 but which distinguish the four-footed animals as domesticated. "And the wild beasts" also makes up for the omission of "all" (describing the four-footed animals and so on in 10:12); and now that "*on* the earth" has disappeared, "*of* the earth" advances without competition to describe

the four-footed animals instead of the reptiles. Peter's substitution of "has never entered into my mouth" for "I've never eaten" (so 10:14) strengthens his revulsion so as to assure fellow Jewish Christians that he didn't violate dietary laws cavalierly. According to 10:15, "the voice [came] to him" a second time. Peter says here that "a voice answered from heaven" a second time. "Answered" and "from heaven" stress the authority with which the following declaration of divine cleansing was issued. And where 10:16 has "the container . . . taken up into heaven," Peter has "all [those] things were pulled up into heaven again." "*All* [those] things" puts emphasis on the contents of the sheet, including those considered taboo, as objects of God's cleansing. "*Pulled* up" implies some effort in lifting a sheet containing so many things. And "again" stresses the threefold repetition of the action. See the comments on 10:9–16 for remaining details, such as the comparison to a sheet, the possible significance of "four corners," and so forth.

11:11–14: "And behold, at once three men, sent from Caesarea to me, arrived at the house in which we were [Peter and his companions from Joppa]. ¹²And the Spirit told me to go with them, making no distinction. And these six brothers [= fellow Jewish believers, the companions from Joppa] also went with me, and we went into the house of the man [who'd sent the three men from Caesarea to me]. ¹³And he announced to us how he'd seen the angel standing in his house and saying, 'Send to Joppa and summon Simon, the one nicknamed Peter, ¹⁴who will speak to you words by which you'll be saved, also all your household.'" "Behold" highlights the immediacy of the three men's arrival. This immediacy substitutes for their arrival while Peter was mulling over his vision in 10:17 and dramatically quickens the pace of narrative. "Sent from Caesarea to me" substitutes for "sent by Cornelius" in 10:17 and thereby pushes Cornelius into the background, where he remains anonymous in chapter 11, in favor of Peter as the one with whom some Jewish Christians have taken issue. "Arrived at the *house* in which *we* were" substitutes for "arrived at the gate" in 10:17. This substitution brings in Peter's Jewish fellow believers alongside Peter himself to provide in advance multiple testimony to what happened in the house. "Also" and the specification of the fellow believers as six in number, which doesn't appear in chapter 10, accentuate the multiplicity of that testimony. The same is to be said about the substitution of "*we* went into the house" for *Peter's* entry in 10:25, and of "he announced to *us*" for Cornelius's answering Peter alone so far as can be told in 10:28–30. "Making no distinction" substitutes for "doubting in no respect" in 10:20. This substitution shifts the focus from doubting whether to go with Cornelius's men to ignoring the distinction between circumcised Jews and uncircumcised Gentiles. The latter focus corresponds to the criticism that Peter "went in to men having uncircumcision and ate with them" (11:3). "How he [Cornelius] had seen the angel" harks back to "an angel of God" in Luke's account at 10:3. "Standing in his house" substitutes for "he stood in my sight" in 10:30 and lays emphasis on the house of a Gentile as the objectionable place for Peter and his six companions to be, according to the opinion of other Jewish believers (see "you *entered*" in 11:3). In 10:22 Cornelius's three men reported to Peter, "Cornelius . . . was instructed by a holy angel . . . to hear words from you." Here, Peter picks up "words" from that report, turns the instruction into a prediction ("who *will* speak to you"), and adds a predictive description of those words: "by which you'll be saved, also your household." The addition intimates to the critics of Peter that God will put his stamp of approval on Peter's consorting with Gentiles by using the words he speaks as a means of salvation for all of them. The addition also equates "forgiveness of sins" (10:43) with salvation.

11:15–18: "And as I started speaking, the Holy Spirit fell on them just as also on us [Jewish believers] **at the start** [of what we now call the church age (2:1–4)]. [16]**And I remembered the word of the Lord** [Jesus], **how he was saying, 'On the one hand, John baptized with water; on the other hand, you will be baptized in the Holy Spirit.'** [17]**Therefore, if God gave them** [Gentile believers] **the same gift** [in the sense of an *equal* gift] **as** [he gave] **to us after** [they as well as we] **believed on the Lord Jesus Christ, who was I** [to be] **able to prevent God?"** [18]**And on hearing these things, they** [Peter's critics] **quieted down** [as to their objections] **and glorified God, saying, "Then God has granted also to the Gentiles** [as a class, not just to those in Cornelius's house] **the repentance resulting in life."** Actually, the Holy Spirit didn't fall on the Gentiles till Peter had been speaking for some time (10:34–44). But since the Spirit fell on them unexpectedly "*while* Peter was still speaking" (10:44), Peter uses hyperbole by saying, "And as I *started* speaking," to stress the Spirit's falling on them before he (Peter) finished and therefore as a dramatic indication of God's welcoming Gentile believers on an equal plane with Jewish believers. Peter says he then remembered Jesus' statement about baptism with water and baptism in the Holy Spirit. As in 1:5, which Peter quotes, "you" is missing as the object of baptism with water. Again as in 1:5, "and [in] fire" is missing after baptism "in the Holy Spirit" (contrast Luke 3:16 and see the comments on Acts 1:5 for the significance of these omissions). "The same/equal gift" is the Holy Spirit, who fell on the Gentile believers as a result of their believing on the Lord Jesus Christ. Where such belief was only implied by the gift in 10:44–48, here the belief is stated explicitly. To believe "*on* the Lord Jesus Christ" is to rest your eternal fate on him. And where Peter "answered" in 10:46–47 with a question, "Surely *no one* is able to withhold water, is he, for these to be baptized . . . ?" here he asks self-defensively in view of his critics' objections, "Who was *I* [to be] able to prevent God?" To prevent God from doing what? Not from baptizing them with water, as in 10:46–47; for God doesn't administer such baptism. The response of Peter's critics supplies the answer: he wasn't able to prevent God from granting "also to the Gentiles the *repentance* resulting in life [that is, eternal life]." So

repentance, which baptism represents, comes in alongside belief as a means of appropriating eternal life even before baptism and apart from circumcision. But like belief, repentance is a gift of God as well as an act of human will. And since the falling of the Holy Spirit on the Gentiles indicated that they'd already received the gift of repentance, Peter was chronologically as well as constitutionally unable to prevent God. The glorification of God even by Peter's former critics caps this episode with an expanded piety such as recommends the gospel to prospective converts.

MASS EVANGELISM OF GENTILES IN ANTIOCH, SYRIA
Acts 11:19–26

11:19–21: On the one hand, therefore, those who'd been scattered by the affliction [= persecution] **that took place over Stephen** [8:1, 4] **went as far as Phoenicia** [modern Lebanon] **and Cyprus and Antioch speaking the word** [= the gospel] **to no one except for Jews alone.** [20]**On the other hand, there were some of them—Cypriot and Cyrenian men—who as such** [that is, as non-natives of the land of Israel, though they'd immigrated there], **on coming to Antioch, were speaking also to the Greek**[-speakers; that is, because of the contrast with "Jews alone," to Greek-speaking *Gentiles*] **by way of proclaiming the Lord Jesus as good news.** "Therefore" implies that the conversion of a houseful of Gentiles in Caesarea (10:1–11:18) led to citywide conversions as far away as Antioch, Syria, the third largest city in the Roman Empire (after Rome, Italy, and Alexandria, Egypt). Cyprus is a nearby island, of course; and Cyrene was a city in North Africa. Having originally come from Cyprus and Cyrene, the Cypriot and Cyrenian men knew the Greek language well and therefore could use it easily in evangelizing Gentiles. The good news is that the Lord is Jesus, not Caesar or any one of the pagan gods (compare 1 Corinthians 8:5–6). [21]**And the Lord's hand was with them, and a large number that believed turned to the Lord.** "Hand" stands for active power, as in Genesis 31:29: "It's in the power of my hand." So "the *Lord's* hand" stands for omnipotence. Its being "with them [the Cypriot and Cyrenian evangelists]" resulted in "a large number" of conversions among the Gentiles. The progress of the gospel continues unabated so as to draw in Luke's audience too. The large number that believed are said to have "turned to the Lord [identified earlier as Jesus]." This way of putting their conversion implies that they stopped worshiping pagan gods (often called "lord[s]" and represented by idols) and started worshiping Jesus as the only true Lord.

11:22–24: And the word [in the sense of a report] **about them** [the many converts in Antioch] **was heard in the ears of the church that was in Jerusalem. And they** [= that church] **sent Barnabas as far as** [= all the way to] **Antioch,** [23]**who on arriving and seeing God's grace** [evident in the conversion of a large number of

Gentiles in this metropolis] **rejoiced and was encouraging all** [the converts] **to remain** [faithful] **to the Lord with determination of heart** [= inward resolve], [24]**because he was a good man and full of the Holy Spirit and of faith. And a considerable crowd were added to the Lord.** The conversions of Gentiles in Antioch were so numerous that word of them reached the church in Jerusalem. Despite distance, that church sent Barnabas, who was a Cypriot by birth (4:36) and therefore a fellow countryman of the Cypriots who helped evangelize Gentiles in Antioch. Luke doesn't specify the purpose behind the sending of Barnabas; so the accent falls on his seeing God's grace, rejoicing over the sight, and urging the converts to remain faithful to the Lord, to whom they'd turned. There's a wordplay between "grace" and "rejoiced" in that the two underlying Greek words used by Luke (*charin* and *echarē*, respectively) are cognate to each other. As throughout Luke-Acts, God's grace brings joy. "Was encouraging *all*" shows Barnabas living up to the meaning of his (nick)name, which is "son of encouragement" (that is, an encourager [4:36]), and renews emphasis on the divinely enabled success of evangelism. And "with determination of heart" stresses the importance of human will alongside that of divine grace. The description of Barnabas as "a good man and full of the Holy Spirit and of faith" suits Luke's constant highlighting of the moral and religious virtues of believers in Jesus and of many of those drawn to believe in him. Barnabas urged the converts to remain faithful "*because* he was a good man" (he had concern for them), "*because* he was . . . full of the Holy Spirit" (the Spirit inspired his encouragement), and "*because* he was . . . full of faith" (he believed that his Spirit-inspired encouragement would keep the converts faithful). But Luke immediately comes back to divinely powered evangelism with the addition of "a considerable crowd . . . to the Lord." "Were *added*" indicates many converts in addition to "the large number" mentioned in 11:21. So the number becomes even larger. "To the Lord" indicates that turning to Jesus as the Lord establishes the close connection that led Jesus to ask Saul of Tarsus, "Saul, Saul, why are you persecuting *me*?" and to say in a followup, "I'm Jesus, whom you're persecuting" (9:4–5).

11:25–26: And he [Barnabas] **went out** [of Antioch] **to Tarsus to look up Saul** [who'd gone there according to 9:30, Tarsus being his home city according to 9:11]. Earlier, Barnabas had introduced Saul to the apostles in Jerusalem (9:26–27). [26]**And on finding** [him]**, he brought** [him] **to Antioch** [to help teach the mass of newly converted Gentiles, it turns out]. **And it came about for them that throughout a whole year** [they] **gathered in the church** [this time the assembly of believers in Antioch, not Jerusalem] **and taught a considerable crowd.** That it takes a whole year for Barnabas and Saul to teach the "crowd" shows how "considerable" the crowd was. Here again, then, is Luke's stress on the divinely ordered success of the gospel. Get on board! "Church" is singular; but given the increasingly large number of believers, there must have been multiple as-

semblies meeting primarily in private homes. The believers' common confession of Jesus as Lord justifies the singular of "church," though. **And** [it happened] **that the disciples were first labeled Christians in Antioch.** Luke doesn't tell how this name was pinned on the disciples, whether by way of ridicule, for example. So he lets drop this bit of information either as a historical note or as an indication of popular recognition of the disciples' attachment to Jesus as the Christ (compare their turning to him as the Lord and being urged to remain faithful to him as the Lord [11:21, 23]).

CHRISTIANS' HELPING ONE ANOTHER
Acts 11:27–30

11:27–28: And during these days prophets came down from Jerusalem to Antioch. [28]**And on standing up, one of them by the name of Agabus indicated through the Spirit that a great** [= severe] **famine was about to be over the whole inhabited earth, which** [famine] **as such** [= as worldwide] **took place at** [the time] **of Claudius** [the emperor]. Luke has repeatedly referred to Jewish prophets dating from Old Testament times. Now he refers to Christian prophets. Their appearance confirms the continuity of Christianity with Judaism and indeed the outgrowth of the one from the other. Yet again, then, Luke undermines the suspicion of novelty and encourages confidence in a long tradition. Furthermore, the prediction of Agabus and its fulfillment show that God, the source of Agabus's prediction "through the Spirit," foreknows and thus controls history and that Christians have knowledge of God's plan. For first-century people living in the Roman Empire, "the whole inhabited earth" *was* the Roman Empire.

11:29–30: And according as anyone of the disciples was prospering [= to the extent of their financial capabilities]**, each of them decided to send** [something] **for relief to the brothers residing in Judea,** [30]**which** [sending of relief] **they also did by sending** [it] **to the elders** [of the church in Jerusalem] **through the hand** [= agency] **of Barnabas and Saul.** It's not said that the famine was less severe in Antioch than in Jerusalem. But famine inflates the price of food, and persecution had apparently impoverished Christians in Jerusalem (compare 8:1; 9:1, 13 with Romans 15:25–27; Galatians 2:10). Christians in Antioch hadn't been impoverished by persecution. So given the arrival of prophets from Jerusalem and the fulfillment of a prediction by one of them that a famine was coming, the Christians in Antioch decided to send relief to those in Jerusalem, and did send it. Though the financial capabilities of the ones in Antioch differed, "*each* of them" participated. Thus Luke features a unanimity of communal spirit that should attract prospective converts. His use of "brothers" for fellow believers underscores this spirit. And the use of "elders" for leaders of the church in Jerusalem marks again the outgrowth of the church from Judaism in that Judaism, too, had its elders both in synagogues and in the Sanhedrin. By taking financial aid to the church elders, Barnabas and Saul appear as traveling partners whose travels are shortly to expand.

PERSECUTION BY HEROD AND HIS DEATH
Acts 12:1–24

This passage divides into the martyrdom of the apostle James (12:1–2), the imprisonment and deliverance of Peter (12:3–17), Herod's frustration (12:18–20), and the death of Herod (12:21–24).

12:1–2: **And at that time Herod the king laid hands on some of the** [Christians] **from the church to harm them.** [2]**And by means of a sword he did away with James the brother of John.** Here we have Herod Agrippa I, a grandson of Herod called "the Great," who was ruling Israel at the time of Jesus' birth. Herod Agrippa I ruled the land A.D. 37–44, that is, some years after Jesus' death and resurrection, so that we shouldn't think of Herod Antipas—Herod the Great's son, ruler of Galilee during Jesus' public ministry, and beheader of John the baptizer—any more than we should think of Herod the Great. To pose as a champion of unbelieving Judaism, the present Herod has some Christians arrested for the purpose of harming them. Luke doesn't identify a particular church from which they come. Does he have in mind the church throughout the land of Israel or only the church in Jerusalem? Nor does he tell what kind of harm Herod intended to inflict on the Christians. So the emphases fall on persecution in general and on the martyrdom of the apostle James, brother of the apostle John (Luke 5:10), in particular. "By means of a sword" suggests a beheading.

Herod continues posing as a champion of unbelieving Judaism in *12:3–4*: **And on seeing that it** [the killing of James] **is pleasing to the Jews, he proceeded to arrest Peter too—and they were the days of Unleavened Bread** [that is, the weeklong Festival of Unleavened Bread was going on]—[4]**whom** [referring to Peter] **having seized he** [referring to Herod] **also put in prison, giving** [him] **over to four foursomes of soldiers** [making sixteen in toto] **to guard him, planning to bring him up to the people after the Passover** [the daylong celebration at the start of the Festival of Unleavened Bread, but standing here for the combined festivities]. The present tense in "*is* pleasing" takes us into Herod's mindset at the time. "He proceeded" carries the sense that Herod *added* the arrest of Peter to his doing away with James. The notation of the Festival of Unleavened Bread explains why Herod didn't immediately bring Peter up to the people for a showtrial. It would have been off-putting and perhaps counterproductive to interrupt their religious observances. After all, Herod was trying to please the people by doing away with leaders of what they considered a heretical movement. "Whom having seized" equates with "to arrest Peter," but may have a sharper edge. The detailing of sixteen soldiers to guard him will make what happens next quite remarkable.

12:5–7: **On the one hand, therefore** [because of Herod's delaying a showtrial], **Peter was being kept in the prison. On the other hand, prayer to God for him was earnestly being made by the church.** The piety of the Christians comes out in their praying; and the earnestness of their praying exhibits loving concern for a fellow believer, the apostle Peter. Luke never tires of mentioning the prayerfulness and communitarianism that attractively characterize the church. [6]**And on that** [very] **night when Herod was about to bring him forward** [in a public showtrial], **Peter, bound with two chains, was sleeping between two soldiers; and in front of the door, guards were guarding the prison** [more literally, to bring out the wordplay: "guards were keeping the guardhouse"]. So if Peter is to be delivered, it'll happen in the nick of time and therefore more dramatically than otherwise. And it'll happen despite his being double-chained and sandwiched between two soldiers, and despite the guarding of the prison door to prevent a jailbreak by Peter and to fend off any outside helpers he might have—the ancient form of a backup system for the sake of security. [7]**And behold** [a word Luke uses for dramatic effect], **an angel of the Lord came and stood over** [Peter], **and a light shone in the cell.** Peter will need the light to get dressed. **And striking Peter's side, he** [the angel] **roused him, saying, "Stand up in a hurry!"** "Striking" seems a bit strong for awaking Peter; but the getaway needs to be quick, and a contrastive parallel is coming up in 12:23. **And his chains fell from** [his] **wrists.** They weren't loosened. They *fell.* A miracle.

12:8–9: **And the angel said to him, "Gird yourself** [= 'Tighten the sash around your waist, the sash that you loosened for comfort during sleep'] **and bind on your sandals** [that you took off for sleeping]." **And he did thus. And he** [the angel] **says to him, "Don your outer garment and follow me."** The outer garment was used as a blanket for sleeping at night. So donning it and following the angel implies exiting the prison to go out into the cold night air. This implication is so startling that Luke uses the present tense ("says") to introduce the double command. [9]**And going out, he was following** [the angel] **and didn't know** [= understand] **that what was taking place through the angel is true. But he supposed he was seeing a vision.** "*Through* the angel" implies that the angel was acting as God's agent in what was taking place. The present tense in "*is* true" highlights the actuality of Peter's deliverance over against his mistaken supposition of a vision.

12:10: **And after passing through the first guard and the second** [guard], **they** [the angel and Peter] **came to the iron gate, the one leading into the city, which** [gate] **opened for them by itself** [in Greek, *automatē*, from which we get "automatically"]. **And on going out, they went forward down one lane** [= a narrow street]; **and immediately the angel departed from him.** Peter has already gotten up from his sleeping position between two soldiers. In addition, first and second guards were stationed at different points along the way leading to the prison gate. The opening of the gate by itself adds another miracle to the escape and shows God to be on Peter's side against Herod. The gate's being made of iron, strong and heavy, enhances the miracle and therefore its demonstration of divine favor toward Peter and disfavor toward Herod. "*They* went forward down one lane" gives befuddled Peter a start in the right direction, that is, into the city. The angel departs "immediately" because he's no longer needed.

12:11–12: And Peter, on coming to be in himself [as though he'd been out of his mind from befuddlement], **said, "Now I know truly that the Lord sent out his angel and took me out of Herod's hand** [= out of Herod's power] **and** [out of] **all the expectation of the people of the Jews** [= out of everything the unbelieving Jewish people expected Herod would do to me in view of his having done away with James by means of a sword (12:2; compare "release to the captives" in Luke 4:18)]." "Truly" accents Peter's shift from ignorance ("he . . . didn't know" [12:9]) to knowledge. Now his mind as well as his body is awake. [12]**And on seeing** [everything] **together** [that is, "connecting the dots," but with Luke's typical emphasis on eyewitnessing], **he went to the house of Mary the mother of John (the one also called Mark** [as distinguished most especially from John the baptizer and John the apostle]**), where a considerable** [number of believers] **were assembled and praying.** "The mother of John" distinguishes this Mary from Mary the mother of Jesus, Mary Magdalene, Mary the mother of James, and Mary the sister of Martha (for all of whom see 1:14; Luke 1–2; 8:2; 10:39, 42; 24:10). John Mark, traditional and likely author of the Gospel according to Mark, will shortly reappear (13:5). "A considerable [number of believers] were assembled and praying" reminds us (1) of the numerical success of the gospel; (2) of the believers' constantly meeting together in close and attractive community; and (3) of their equally attractive piety as evident in communal prayer. Verse 5 has made clear that the believers were praying to God for Peter, so that his deliverance marks God's answer to their prayers. Here, though, Luke mentions only the praying as such, so that the accent falls on their piety.

12:13–15: And when he knocked at the door of the gate [that is, the door *consisting* of the gate], **a slave girl by the name of Rhoda approached to obey** [the knock by opening the door]. [14]**And on recognizing Peter's voice, out of joy she didn't open the gate; but on running into** [the house], **she announced that Peter was standing in front of the gate.** [15]**But they said to her, "You're crazy!" But she kept insisting that** [he] **was thus** [= standing in front of the gate]. **But they were saying, "It's his angel."** The repeated use of "But" points to some vigorous thrust and counterthrust of a verbal sort. Luke's reporting the name of a slave girl presents remarkable evidence of his historical research (Luke 1:1–4). Her recognition of Peter's voice implies he'd spoken as well as knocked and merges with her joy at hearing his voice to show that she too, though a slave

girl, is a believer—indeed, a believer joyful over God's answer to her as well as the others' prayers for Peter. More than that, her very *failure* to open the gate and her *running* into the house to share the glad news of his arrival shows her to be *overjoyed*. The other believers' telling her she's crazy doesn't reflect badly on their faith (they've not heard Peter's voice as Rhoda has) so much as it magnifies the miracle of his deliverance. It seemed too good to be true (compare Luke 24:11). She's so sure of her having recognized Peter's voice, though, that she stands her ground despite being a slave girl. And her insistence achieves a partial victory in that her fellow believers drop their charge that she's crazy and shift to saying that Peter's angel has been knocking and speaking in the tones of Peter's voice. Presumably the angel is Peter's disembodied spirit (see the comments on 23:8); but since Luke doesn't say so, the point has to do only with the seemingly unbelievable fact of Peter's miraculous deliverance (compare Gamaliel's statement in 5:39 that if the apostles' activity is from God, "you won't be able to demolish them").

12:16–17: But Peter continued knocking. And on opening [the gate], **they saw him and were astonished.** They've become eyewitnesses of his deliverance, and their astonishment testifies to its miraculous character. [17]**And on motioning to them with** [his] **hand to quiet down, he related to them how the Lord had led him out of the prison. And he said, "Report these things to James and the brothers." And on going out, he traveled to another place.** "To quiet down" implies they were abuzz with astonishment. Since it was "an angel *of the Lord*" that led Peter out of prison (12:7), Peter attributes his deliverance to the Lord himself (compare the comments on 7:30–35 for an angel as the Lord's alter ego). James the apostle has been martyred (12:2). Another James is called "[the son] of Alphaeus," and yet another James is said to have fathered the apostle Judas *not* Iscariot (1:13; Luke 6:15). But James the half brother of Jesus will emerge as a leading figure in the church at Jerusalem (15:13; 21:18; compare Galatians 1:19; 2:9, 12; Mark 6:3; Matthew 13:55; Luke 24:10). So the present James looks to be Jesus' half brother, and "the brothers" look to be other half brothers of Jesus in accordance with 1:14 and, again, Mark 6:3; Matthew 13:55. None of them are at this prayer meeting, but the command of Peter that they be told implies their importance. Luke doesn't identify the "other place" to which Peter traveled. This nonidentification suits a location where Herod can't find him.

12:18–19: And when day came, there was not a little alarm [= there was a *lot* of it!] **among the soldiers over what then Peter had become.** Here, "then" doesn't mean "at that time." It means "because Peter's prison cell was empty." And "what . . . Peter had become" means "what had become of Peter." Had he turned into a ghost? [19]**And when Herod had searched for him and not found** [him], **on interrogating the guards he commanded** [them] **to be led away** [to execution for failure at guard duty; so they'd had good reason to be greatly alarmed over the absence of Peter from his prison cell]. **And on going down from Judea** [the hill country where Jerusalem was located, though that city hasn't been specified in the context] **to Caesarea** [on the coast, approximately at sea level], **he** [Herod] **was spending time** [there]. So Caesarea will now become the site of the following episode.

12:20–22: And he was quarreling fervently with the Tyrians and Sidonians [= people living in Tyre and Sidon on the coast of Phoenicia (modern Lebanon)]. **But with mutual fervor** [shared between themselves, not with Herod] **they came to him and after persuading Blastus, the king's valet,** [to get them a hearing with the king,] **they were asking for peace, because their country was supplied with food by the king's** [country]. Luke doesn't say what Herod's quarrel with the Tyrians and Sidonians was about. So Luke is interested only in the quarrel as a setup for what will happen in the aftermath of a meeting between the parties. There's a wordplay between the fervor of Herod's quarreling with the Tyrians and Sidonians and the fervor with which they unitedly sue for economic peace with Herod, whose country was agriculturally more productive than the more mountainous Phoenicia. [21]**And on a designated day Herod, having dressed himself in royal garb and having sat down on the rostrum** [an elevated platform used variously for speech-making, judicial pronouncements, and the like], **orated to them.** [22]**And the assemblage was calling out, "The voice of a god and not of a human being!"** For a king to dress himself in royal garb, take a seat on an elevated platform, and deliver an oration was to flaunt his authority. You suspect that his elocution didn't really sound so divine as the audience made it out to be, so that they were only buttering him up. In any case, he accepted the adulation.

12:23–24: But at once an angel of the Lord struck him because he hadn't given the glory to God [instead of taking it to himself]. **And on becoming worm-eaten, he expired.** So the Lord's angel struck him with a mortal disease, probably of some intestinal sort. The immediacy of the disease-dealing stroke underscores the cause-and-effect relation between Herod's acceptance of divine honors and the disease. So the divinely effected and gruesome death of Herod compensates for his putting the apostle James to death and stands in contrast with the divinely effected and thrilling deliverance of Peter from prison. Magnifying the contrast is the angel of the Lord's having struck Peter to deliver him *from* an execution like that of James and the angel of the Lord's striking Herod by *way* of execution. So much the better for the gospel: [24]**But the word of God went on growing and being multiplied.** The continuing growth of the gospel, God's word of salvation, has to do with its ongoing geographical spread à la 1:8. It's continuing multiplication has to do with its ongoing success in gaining large numbers of new converts. Such growth and multiplication give evidence of divine origin and activity, which—Luke wants us to know—help certify the gospel and show that the likes of Herod can't stop its progress (Luke 1:1–4).

AN EVANGELISTIC JOURNEY BY BARNABAS AND SAUL
Acts 12:25–14:26

This long passage divides into Barnabas's and Saul's return to Antioch, Syria (12:25); their being sent on an evangelistic journey (13:1–3); their proclamation of the gospel in Cyprus (13:4–12), Pisidian Antioch (13:13–50), Iconium, Lystra, and Derbe (13:51–14:20); and their return to Antioch, Syria (14:21–26). As a whole, the itinerary appeals to the interest of Luke's audience in travelogues.

12:25–13:1: And taking along John, the one also called Mark [see the comments on 12:12], **Barnabas and Saul returned** [to Antioch, Syria] **after fulfilling the service in Jerusalem** [that is, after delivering financial aid to the church there (11:27–30)]. [1]**And at the church that was in Antioch there were prophets and teachers: both Barnabas and Simeon (the one called Niger) and Lucius (the Cyrenian) and Manaen (a friend of Herod the tetrarch since childhood) and Saul.** Prophets spoke under divine inspiration. Teachers explained the gospel. Without distinguishing who was what, or whether they both prophesied and taught, Luke lists by name the prophets and teachers in the church at Antioch. It's enough for him to let us know that the Holy Spirit was inspiring prophetic messages and enabling teachers to explain God's word. "Simeon" is the Semitic form of Peter's original name ("Simon" in Greek), but "the one called Niger" distinguishes this Simeon from the apostle Simon Peter. The description of Lucius as "the Cyrenian" reminds us that Cyrenians were among those who first evangelized Gentiles in Antioch (11:20). Manaen had been reared with Herod the tetrarch and therefore was a convert of high social standing. Luke mentions him as such to show that because of its certainty, the gospel appeals as it should to the high as well as the low (compare Luke 1:3). This Herod is Antipas, who ruled Galilee and some nearby territories (Luke 3:1), had John the baptizer beheaded (Luke 3:19–20; 9:7–9), and mocked Jesus during Jesus' trial (Luke 23:6–12). Barnabas and Saul, respectively first and last on Luke's list, we've met before.

13:2–3: And as they were doing religious service for the Lord [by prophesying and teaching] **and fasting** [which shows the piety that Luke likes to highlight in his descriptions of Jesus and believers in him], **the Holy Spirit said, "All right, set apart for me Barnabas and Saul** [from the other prophets and teachers] **for the work that I've called them to."** "All right" adds a certain emphasis to the Holy Spirit's instruction, as though the church might be disinclined to let Barnabas and Saul go. "For me," as opposed to their keeping Barnabas and Saul for themselves, confirms such a disinclination. "The work" describes as laborious the far-flung evangelistic journey on which they're about to embark. That the Holy Spirit has "called them" to it implies his enablement of them, though (compare 9:15–16). [3]**Then, after fasting and praying and laying hands on them, they let go** [of them]. To the piety of fasting is now added the piety of praying. "Laying hands on them" indicates the church's adding their commission to the Holy Spirit's call. Barnabas and Saul will go as representatives of the church in Antioch. And "they let go [of them]" indicates the church's obedience to the Spirit's command that they set apart Barnabas and Saul.

13:4–5: On the one hand, therefore, having been sent out by the Holy Spirit they went down to Seleucia [a town about fifteen miles down river] **and from there sailed off to Cyprus.** The church in Antioch had let go of Barnabas and Saul, but it was the Holy Spirit that sent them out. He's in charge, then, so that God's plan is being worked out not only in the setting apart of Barnabas and Saul but also in the accomplishing of "the work [he has] called them to" (13:2). This is to be said despite the temptation to attribute their sailing to Cyprus to Barnabas's having hailed from there (4:36). ⁵**And on coming to be in Salamis** [toward the east end of Cyprus]**, they started proclaiming God's word** [the good news of what he has done through his Son, Jesus Christ] **in the synagogues of the Jews** [where Barnabas and Saul had ready-made audiences that included Gentile hangers-on as well as Jews]**. And they also had John** [Mark] **as an assistant.** This notation prepares for 13:13; 15:36–40.

13:6–7a: On the other hand, upon going through the whole island as far as Paphos [on the west end] **they found a certain man—a magician, a Jewish false prophet by the name of Bar-Jesus—**⁷ᵃ**who was with the proconsul Sergius Paulus, an intelligent man.** For a fee, magicians such as Bar-Jesus cast spells on behalf of others; and as a false prophet Bar-Jesus claimed to forecast their future, again for a fee. As a proconsul, Sergius Paulus was a Roman governmental official. Luke describes him also as "intelligent," but not because he had Bar-Jesus with him. After all, as a magician and false prophet who unlike Jesus and his followers had corrupted his Jewish heritage, Bar-Jesus traded on the ignorance of people like the proconsul. No, Luke describes Sergius Paulus as intelligent because this proconsul is about to hear and believe the word of God. That's the intelligent thing to do, Luke is telling prospective converts.

13:7b–8: On summoning Barnabas and Saul, this [proconsul] **sought to hear the word of God.** Here's evidence of the proconsul's intelligence. He made an effort to hear God's word. ⁸**But Elymas the magician (for that's the way his name** [Bar-Jesus] **is translated) was for his own sake opposing them by seeking to divert the proconsul from the faith.** "The faith" is God's word as the object of belief. Elymas doesn't want to lose influence and income, as he will if Sergius Paulus believes the word of God. There are difficulties in knowing just how "Elymas" relates as a translation to "Bar-Jesus." Suffice it to say that Luke's knowledge of personal names and place-names gives evidence of the historical research he referenced in Luke 1:1–4.

13:9–12: But Saul (the one also [known as] **Paul), on being filled with the Holy Spirit, glaring at him** ¹⁰**said, "O you** [who are] **full of every deceit and of every fraud, son of the Devil, enemy of all righteousness—you'll stop making crooked the straight paths of the Lord, won't you?** ¹¹**And now, behold, the Lord's hand** [is] **upon you** [for judgment, not for blessing] **and you'll be blind, not seeing the sun for a while." And at once dimness and darkness fell on him, and going around he was seeking people to lead him by the hand.** ¹²**Then the proconsul, on seeing what had happened, believed, being awestruck at the teaching about the Lord.** Saul was named after the first king of Israel, to whose tribe of Benjamin he too belonged (Philippians 3:5). "Paul" wasn't given to him as a new name for his becoming a Christian. Rather, it was a Roman name that as a Roman citizen he had borne since his birth (16:37; 22:25–29). "Paul" sounded similar to "Saul," his Semitic name. Luke introduces the name "Paul" here partly as a counterpart to Sergius Paulus (in Luke's original Greek there's no difference in spelling between "Paul" and "Paulus") and partly because the Roman character of "Paul" better suits Paul's primary focus on the evangelism of Gentiles like Sergius Paulus (compare Galatians 2:1–10). The Holy Spirit's filling Paul makes effective the pronouncement of temporary blindness on Elymas. The blindness itself is reminiscent of Paul's own temporary blindness (9:8–9). Even "seeking people to lead [Elymas] by the hand" parallels Paul's having been led by the hand. You wonder whether Paul drew on his own experience in the pronouncement. To begin with, though, he addresses Elymas with a series of condemnatory epithets punctuated with a glare and with "O," "full of," "the Devil," two occurrences of "every," an "all," and a rhetorical question: "*O you* [who are] *full* of *every* deceit and of *every* fraud, son of the *Devil*, enemy of *all* righteousness . . . ." These epithets decry magic as trickery at the financial expense of superstitious people who pay for it. The epithets also bring out by contrast the truth of the gospel, the scrupulous behavior of its propagators, the divine sonship of Jesus its subject, and its generation of righteousness in believers. More particularly, Elymas's being "full of every deceit and of every fraud" contrasts with Paul's being "full of the Holy Spirit."

Paul's rhetorical question contains an accusation that Elymas has been "making crooked the straight paths of the Lord"—in other words, that he has been diverting people from walking the straight and narrow way as required by the Lord in their conduct. In fact, the translations "making crooked" (13:10) and "divert" (13:8) go back to the very same verb in Luke's original text. Paul doesn't expect Elymas to answer "Yes" to his question, "you'll stop . . . won't you?" For by pronouncing blindness on Elymas, Paul gives his own "Yes" to the question. Since a hand stands for active power, "the Lord's hand" stands for omnipotence, so that Elymas can't resist the judgmental blindness pronounced against him. And he'll be so blind that he won't even be able to see the sun, bright though it is. Instead, dimness and—worse yet—

darkness. The immediacy of the dimness and darkness fulfills the "now" in Paul's prophetic pronouncement to demonstrate that the Lord's hand really is at work. And the falling of dimness and darkness on Elymas fulfills Paul's prophecy and makes a stark contrast with the falling of the Holy Spirit on believers (8:16; 10:44; 11:15). People used to seek the services of Elymas as a magician and (false) prophet. Now he seeks their services to lead him by the hand.

The proconsul's believing "on *seeing* what had happened" makes him an example of belief based on eyewitness evidence. He's awestruck—but by what? We want to say he's awestruck by the immediate fulfillment of Paul's pronouncement of instantaneous blindness. Surprisingly, though, Luke attributes the amazement to "the teaching about the Lord." So the judgmental miracle points away from itself as such to Jesus, the subject matter of Paul's and Barnabas's teaching, which is "God's word" (13:7). Thus Paul has acted as both a teacher and a prophet (compare 13:1). The episode ends with a reference to Jesus as "the Lord." The reference points up that the proconsul's governmental authority can't stand comparison with Jesus' authority, and that the proconsul himself acknowledges that fact by believing.

13:13–15: And on putting out to sea from Paphos, Paul's party came to Perga of Pamphylia [on the south coast of what we call Asia Minor]; **but on withdrawing from them, John** [Mark] **returned to Jerusalem** [where his mother had her home (12:12)]. Because Paul took the lead in the putdown of Elymas and conversion of Sergius Paulus, the "party" has become Paul's, so that Barnabas plays second fiddle. Luke doesn't say why John Mark withdrew and returned to Jerusalem. So mention of the return only prepares for a subsequent dispute between Paul and Barnabas over the taking of John Mark on another journey (15:36–40). ¹⁴**But they themselves** [Paul and the rest of his party], **on going from Perga through** [further territory] **arrived in Pisidian Antioch** [located in central Asia Minor and different from Antioch, Syria]. **And on entering into the** [local] **synagogue on the Sabbath day, they sat down.** As often, Luke points to a continuance of Jewish piety on the part of Christians. They represent an old religion come to flower, not a suspiciously new religion only now coming to bud. ¹⁵**And after the reading of the Law and the Prophets** [passages out of the first two divisions of the Hebrew Bible], **the synagogue rulers sent to them, saying, "Men, brothers, if among you there's any word of encouragement for the people, speak."** Readings from the Mosaic law and Old Testament prophetical books were regular parts of synagogue services. Synagogue rulers had charge of those services and would invite visitors to preach. "Men" limits the invitation to males. "Brothers" describes the visitors as fellow Jews. But the invitation is as much for a speech as for a speaker. Unwittingly, the synagogue rulers use a phrase, "any word of encouragement for the people," well suited to the good news that Paul is about to proclaim.

13:16–17: And on standing up and gesturing with [his] **hand, Paul said,** ¹⁷**"Men of Israel and you** [Gentiles] **who fear God, listen."** The hand gesture stresses the command to listen; and the address to Gentiles as well as Jews grows out of the evangelism of Gentiles in Antioch, Syria, where Paul had ministered (11:19–26 [compare 10:1–11:18]). It doesn't hurt that these Gentiles fear God, as evidenced by their attendance at synagogue (compare the attractiveness to God of Cornelius, a God-fearer [10:1–2, 4, 22, 34–35]). **"The God of this people Israel selected our** [fore]**fathers and uplifted the people during** [their] **sojourn in the land of Egypt and with an uplifted arm led them out of it."** To portray the gospel as Judaism come of age, Paul immediately connects his message to what God did for the patriarchs and Israel. God's uplifting the people during their sojourn in Egypt could be understood in terms of their numerical multiplication (7:17; Exodus 1:7–10). But the wordplay between uplifting them and "an uplifted arm" makes it more likely that his leading them out of Egypt defines his uplifting them. To lead them out, God lifted up his arm, so to speak, rather than letting it hang slack.

13:18–20: "And for about forty years' time he put up with them in the desert [compare 7:38–43]. ¹⁹**And after doing away with seven nations in the land of Canaan** [Deuteronomy 7:1], **he gave their** [the seven nations'] **land as an inheritance** [to the people of Israel (Joshua 14:1–5)]—**about four hundred and fifty years** [for the events from the time of the patriarchs to the inheriting of Canaan]. ²⁰**And after these things he gave** [the people] **judges till Samuel the prophet."** To enhance the fulfillment of God's promise to Abraham that Abraham's offspring would inherit Canaan (7:5), Paul mentions God's putting up with the Israelites. He kept his promise despite having to put up with them for a whole forty years or so, despite the necessity of destroying seven Canaanite nations, and despite the lapse of about four hundred and fifty years. Neither the trying of God's patience by a whole generation of the chosen nation nor the opposition of other nations nor the lapse of a long period of time kept him from fulfilling his promise. By making this point, Paul sets the stage for God's fulfilling another promise, that of a Savior from David's lineage. Samuel was one of the judges of Israel (1 Samuel 7:6, 15–17), but in accordance with 1 Samuel 3:20 Paul calls him what he also was: a prophet. This designation suits the theme of fulfilled prophecy that Paul is pursuing.

13:21–22: "And from there [in the temporal sense of 'afterwards'] **they requested a king; and God gave them Saul, Kish's son, a man from the tribe of Benjamin, for forty years** [of rulership]." Paul can't resist bringing in his fellow Benjamite Saul, after whom he himself was named (compare 13:9; Philippians 3:5). As did God's putting up with the people for about forty years in the desert, granting the people their request for a king displays God's patience. ²²**"And on removing him** [Saul], **he raised up David to be** [their] **king, in reference to**

whom he also spoke [= in addition to raising him up], **testifying, 'I've found David the** [son] **of Jesse** [to be] **a man in accord with my heart, who'll do all my wishes** [compare Psalm 89:20; 1 Samuel 13:14; Isaiah 44:28]**.'** "Testifying" lends weight to God's favorable appraisal of David's character, an appraisal that previews the character of Jesus as an offspring of David. "Who'll do all my wishes" means he'll carry them out and corresponds to "in accord with my heart," the heart being the inward seat of wishing. "*All* my wishes" looks forward to Jesus' carrying out God's will fully as David's greater counterpart. Paul doesn't give the reason why God removed Saul, so that the emphasis falls on God's raising up David and testifying favorably about him.

13:23–25: **"In accord with a promise, God brought to Israel from the seed** [= the progeny] **of this** [David] **a Savior,** [namely,] **Jesus,** [24]**after John had proclaimed to all the people of Israel beforehand—**[that is,] **before the face of his** [Jesus'] **entrance** [onto the public stage]— **a baptism of repentance** [on which see Luke 3:1–14 with comments]**."** "In accord with a promise" alludes to God's promise to David in 2 Samuel 7:8–16 that David would have progeny to rule over Israel forever, so that God has acted in accord with his promise to David just as David acted in accord with all God's wishes. But Paul defines God's promise to David not in terms of bringing Jesus to be a *king* but in terms of bringing him to be a *Savior.* The shift from king to Savior expands the scope of God's promise to include eternal life (see, for example, Luke 18:18–30). Yet "to Israel" maintains the connection of the gospel with that chosen nation. And the abruptness with which this sentence starts (unusually, there's no introductory conjunction) puts emphasis on God's having fulfilled the promise by bringing to them Jesus as the Savior. To give Jesus' entrance a moral dimension attractive to prospective converts of moral sensibility, Paul introduces John's prior proclamation of a baptism of repentance. "To *all* the people of Israel" reminds Paul's audience of the popularity with which John's proclamation was greeted. Will Paul's proclamation be greeted similarly? "Before the *face* of his entrance" means "before the *actuality* of Jesus' entrance." [25]**"And as John was fulfilling** [his] **race** [that is, completing his proclamation, as though it were a race to be run to the finish line], **he was saying, 'What do you conjecture I am** [the 'What?' of a God-ordained mission, not the 'Who?' of John's personal identity]**? I'm not** [what you conjecture]. **Behold, he the sandals of whose feet I'm not worthy to loosen is coming after me.'"** So Paul notes the transition from John's proclaiming the baptism of repentance to John's prediction of someone having infinitely more worth than he (compare Luke 3:15–16 with comments). "Behold" highlights the prediction.

13:26–29: **"Men, brothers** [= fellow Israelites], **sons belonging to Abraham's stock** [= descendants of Abraham], **and the** [Gentiles] **among you who fear God, the word about this salvation has been sent** *to us*! [27]**For because of not knowing this one and** [because of not knowing] **the prophets' voices when they're read every Sabbath by Sabbath, the ones residing in Jerusalem and their rulers fulfilled** [the prophets' voices] **by judging** [= condemning Jesus to death]. [28]**And despite finding not even one ground for death, they requested Pilate that he** [Jesus] **be done away with.** [29]**And when they'd completed all the things written about him, on taking him down from the tree** [= the cross] **they put** [him] **in a tomb."** To accent what he has to say about Jesus, Paul re-addresses his audience. "Men" comes over from his first address in 13:16, but for intimacy "brothers" replaces "of Israel" (more literally in 13:16: "Israelites"). Paul puts his audience and himself in the same ethnic family. "Sons belonging to Abraham's stock" harks back to "our [fore]fathers," whom God "selected" (13:17), and highlights the privilege of citizenship in God's chosen nation. And the God-fearing Gentiles come over from Paul's first address. The greater expansiveness of this second address as compared with the first one strengthens the accent on what Paul has to say about Jesus. Paul hasn't spoken about salvation before; but he has spoken about a Savior, Jesus (13:23). So Jesus is himself "*this* salvation." "The word about this salvation" is the good news about *him.* That it "has been sent *to us*" corresponds to the high privilege of being "sons belonging to Abraham's stock." But "to us" includes the God-fearing Gentiles, so that they enjoy no less a privilege. As in 10:1–4, 22, 31, 34–35; 13:16, the God-fearers' piety, like that of Luke's targeted audience, makes them attractive to God and amenable to the gospel. The Jerusalemites' and their rulers' "not knowing this one" means not *recognizing* Jesus to be "this salvation," and "[not knowing] the prophets' voices" means not *understanding* them. Paul's use of "voices" reflects the public reading of prophetical books during synagogue services every Sabbath. "Not knowing" leaves room for those guilty of engineering Jesus' death to repent, believe, and be saved (compare 3:17; Luke 23:34). Paul emphasizes Jesus' innocence of any capital offense to assure the audience that the crucifixion, ordinarily inflicted on heinous criminals, had no justification. Pilate appears as a pathetic tool in the hands of Jesus' enemies. "All the things written about him" refers to the prophetical texts written about Jesus and transmuted into the prophets' voices through weekly public readings. Unwittingly, Jesus' enemies "completed all the things written about him." Ironically, then, the enemies worked against their own intentions by providing the argument themselves from fulfilled prophecy, the argument that favors Jesus as the Savior. And by saying that "*they* put [him] in a tomb," Paul makes Joseph of Arimathea's interment of Jesus ironically represent their honoring Jesus with a respectable burial.

13:30–31: **"But God raised him from among the dead,** [31][that is, Jesus,] **who appeared for very many days to those who went up with him from Galilee to Jerusalem, who as such** [that is, as his fellow travelers at that time] **are now his witnesses to the people."** Paul is referring to the apostles, as Luke did in 1:1–8. The appearances of Jesus to them after his resurrection made them eyewitnesses of his risen state and therefore witnesses who presently testify about it to the Jewish people. This testimonial evidence certifies the gospel (Luke 1:1–4). "For very many days" describes the "forty days" of 1:3 as more than enough time for him to have proved himself risen from the dead. And "to those who went up with him from Galilee to Jerusalem" forestalls any theory of mistaken identity. The apostles knew him well.

13:32–33: "And we [as distinguished from the apostles] **proclaim to you as good news the promise that was made to** [our] [fore]**fathers** [as good news] **33in that God has fulfilled this** [promise] **for us, their children** [= the forefathers' descendants], **by resurrecting Jesus, as also it's written in the second Psalm: 'You're my Son; I've fathered you today.'"** So Paul uses Psalm 2:7 to compare God's resurrecting Jesus with the procreation of new life. And Psalm 2:7 becomes a prooftext for the plan of God and for his carrying it out in Jesus' resurrection.

13:34–35: "And that he resurrected him from among the dead, [him] **no more being about to turn into putrefaction** [as he was about to do just before his resurrection], **he** [God] **has spoken in this way: 'I'll give you David's devout, trustworthy things** [Isaiah 55:3].' **35Therefore he also says in another** [passage], **'You'll not give your devout one to see putrefaction** [= not allow his corpse to undergo decay] **[Psalm 16:10].'"** "You" is plural in "I'll give you David's devout, trustworthy things." So Paul interprets this quotation as meaning that God will give these things to the Jewish descendants of the patriarchs. What these things are remains to be identified in 13:38–39. But they're "David's" in that they're channeled through Jesus, to whom "the Lord God will give the throne of his [fore]father David" (Luke 1:32). They're "devout" in that just as David was a man "in accord with [God's] heart" (13:22), Jesus the channel is God's "devout one" (13:35; also 2:27). And David's things are "trustworthy" in that just as God testified concerning David, "[He] will do all my wishes" (13:22), Jesus submitted to God's will for him (Luke 22:42). "Therefore" means "because God promised to give Jesus David's things." But since Jesus was crucified, the fulfillment of God's promise required that he not allow his devout one to undergo putrefaction—in other words, that he raise Jesus from among the dead before putrefaction set in. The application of "devout one" to Jesus highlights, as usual in Luke-Acts, his piety as a magnet to prospective converts serious about religion.

13:36–37: "For on the one hand David, after doing service for God's plan in his own generation, fell asleep and was added to his [fore]**fathers and saw putrefaction** [= died and was buried with his ancestors, so that his corpse underwent decay]. **37On the other hand, he whom God raised** [that is, Jesus] **didn't see putrefaction** [because he was raised on the third day]." "After doing service for God's plan *in his own generation*" centers attention on David's service but implies that God's plan covers the whole history of salvation, not just its Davidic

phase, and that Jesus' resurrection marks a climactic moment in that plan. Paul argues that since David's corpse did undergo putrefaction, David couldn't be the one who according to God's promise would *not* undergo putrefaction. By virtue of speedy resurrection, only Jesus qualifies as the one in whom that promise reached fulfillment (contrast the case of Lazarus in John 11:17, 39).

13:38–39: "Therefore [since Jesus was resurrected] **be it known to you, men, brothers, that forgiveness through this** [one whom God raised]—[that is, forgiveness] **for you of** [your] **sins—is being proclaimed; 39and by this** [one] **everyone who believes is acquitted of all the things that you couldn't be acquitted of by the law of Moses."** The news of Jesus' resurrection is too good to be muffled. It calls for public proclamation. Paul adds "brothers" to "men" to highlight their sharing with him the Jewish tradition memorialized in the Scriptures he has just cited as fulfilled in Jesus. "Forgiveness" means the release of sins from the one who committed them. "Acquitted of" puts it the other way around: the release of the sinner from his/her sins. Together, forgiveness and acquittal define what was meant in 13:34 by "David's . . . things," given to "you [plural for the Jewish people]." Acquittal "*by* this [one]" parallels forgiveness "*through* this [one]." Combined, these expressions imply that Jesus acts as God's agent in forgiveness and acquittal. "*Everyone* who believes" enlarges the "for *you*" of forgiveness, and "everyone who *believes*" adds a condition—but a condition so easy to meet that the universality of "everyone" isn't compromised. "All the things that you couldn't be acquitted of by the law of Moses" defines the "sins" to be forgiven. His law had no power of acquittal. But the risen Jesus does have that power, and "all" leaves no sin outside it. So just believe.

13:40–41: "Therefore watch out lest what was said in the Prophets [= the prophetical section of the Old Testament] **come upon** [you]: **41"Look, you snobs, and marvel and vanish, because I'm working a work** [= performing a task/doing a job] **in your days, a work that by no means would you believe if someone were to relate it to you** [Habakkuk 1:5].'" "Therefore" means that in view of the audience's having been informed of forgiveness and acquittal to everyone who believes in Jesus, they should beware of the snobbery that would keep them from believing even if they were given eyewitness testimony. For if such snobbery takes effect, they'll be reduced to spectators who marvel at the forgiveness and acquittal but disappear from the scene without receiving the forgiveness and acquittal themselves. The staccato of the three commands—"Look," "marvel," "vanish"— produces a forceful effect. So too does the use of commands rather than a declaration, such as "they looked and marveled and vanished" would have been. Nobody likes to be called a snob, so that Paul quotes Habakkuk to motivate the audience not to put themselves in the category of snobs by disbelieving his proclamation. "In your days" makes forgiveness and acquittal a current possibility for them.

13:42–43: And as they [Paul and Barnabas] **were going out** [of the synagogue; see 13:14], **people were urging that these words be spoken to them the next Sabbath.** **⁴³And when the synagogue** [in the sense of "the congregation"] **had broken up, many of the Jews and of the devout proselytes** [Gentiles who attended synagogue and worshiped the one true God] **followed Paul and Barnabas, who in speaking to them aimed at persuading them to remain in God's grace.** "God's grace" defines the forgiveness and the acquittal that Paul had proclaimed, for they are ill-merited. "To *remain* in God's grace" implies that the Jews and proselytes who followed Paul and Barnabas had believed the gospel and therefore stood in that grace but needed to persevere. That these followers were "many" calls attention to the Spirit-empowered and therefore unstoppable success of evangelization; and Luke's description of the proselytes as "devout" calls attention, as often in Luke-Acts, to the attractiveness of the gospel to religiously serious people. The audience's "urging that these words be spoken to them the next Sabbath" sets up for the next episode.

13:44–47: And on the coming [= next] **Sabbath nearly all the city assembled to hear the word of the Lord.** An accent falls again on the numerical success of gospel-preaching ("nearly *all* the city"); and though it's Paul who proclaims the gospel, this message is nothing less than "the word of the Lord." **⁴⁵And on seeing the crowds, the Jews** [that is, those Jews who hadn't followed Paul and Barnabas the preceding Sabbath] **were filled with envy and, slandering** [Paul], **they were contradicting the things being spoken by Paul.** The envy implies that the earlier sermons of these Jews hadn't drawn "the crowds," the plural of which links up with "nearly all the city" to reemphasize the numerical success of gospel-preaching as evidence of divine empowerment (1:8). "*Filled* with envy" gives the reason behind the contradiction of Paul's words and the slandering of Paul himself that accompanied the contradiction: dialectic laced with personal attacks. **⁴⁶And speaking out boldly, Paul and Barnabas said, "It was mandatory to speak God's word first to you. Since you're pushing it away and not judging yourselves worthy of eternal life, behold, we're turning to the Gentiles. ⁴⁷For the Lord has ordered us in this** [following] **way: 'I've positioned you as a light for the Gentiles that you might be for salvation as far as the extremity of the earth** [Isaiah 49:6 (compare Acts 1:8)].'" Luke mentions the boldness of Paul's and Barnabas's speaking to build admiration for their courage. It was mandatory for them to speak first to Jews because of God's promise to their ancestors, the patriarchs (see Luke 1:54–55, 67–75 and so on [compare Romans 1:16]). "God's word" = "the things being spoken by Paul" (13:45) = "the word of the Lord" (13:44) = "these words" (13:42) = the "good news" of "the promise that was made to [our] [fore]fathers" (13:32). "Since you're pushing it away" starts a new sentence abruptly. The abruptness lends disgust to the observation that these Jews are rejecting God's word. Adding sarcasm to disgust is the statement that they aren't judg-

ing themselves worthy of eternal life. That is to say, Paul and Barnabas attribute to them a sense of unworthiness that they don't actually have but that they should have. For in fact they *are* unworthy of eternal life and therefore need to accept rather than reject God's word of "grace," that is, of ill-merited favor (14:3; 15:11; 20:24, 32; Luke 4:22). "Behold" headlines Paul's and Barnabas's turning to the Gentiles. The quotation of Isaiah 49:6 shows that this turning carries out God's foretold plan to save Gentiles wherever on earth they live. God is the "I" who has positioned "you [Paul and Barnabas, individually speaking] as a light [that is, placed each of them as a lamp on a lampstand to give the light of the gospel] for the Gentiles." "That *you* might be for salvation" implies that a gospel-preacher is just as necessary for people's salvation as is Jesus the Savior. For without hearing there's no believing, and without believing there's no being saved.

13:48–50: And hearing [what Paul and Barnabas were saying to the unbelieving Jews about turning to Gentiles for the Gentiles' salvation], **the Gentiles were rejoicing and glorifying the word of the Lord.** As usual, the good news of God's grace brings joy (see Luke 2:10 among many other passages in Luke-Acts). "Glorifying the word of the Lord" means acclaiming it because of its being directed as good news to Gentiles. **And as many as had been appointed to eternal life believed.** "Had been appointed to eternal life" states the biblical doctrine of election or, preferably, selection. Strictly speaking, though, believing isn't said to *depend* on such appointment. Rather, the appointment and the belief are coordinated. Each carries its own importance and validity. And Luke's point doesn't have to do with the limitation of God's selectivity. Quite the opposite! It has to do with God's having selected *many* Gentiles and with the believing of *all* of them ("as many as"). **⁴⁹And the Lord's word was being carried throughout the whole region.** Luke doesn't tell who carried it, so that the emphasis falls solely on the progress of the gospel, widespread as it was ("throughout the *whole* region"). **⁵⁰But the Jews** [who hadn't followed Paul and Barnabas] **incited the devout, eminent women and the foremost** [men] **of the city and stirred up a persecution against Paul and Barnabas and expelled them from their borders** [= from their territory]. On their own, apparently, the unbelieving Jews didn't have enough clout to drive out Paul and Barnabas—hence the incitement of Gentiles belonging to the upper class. We may deduce that the Jews even capitalized on the religious devotion of eminent Gentile women by persuading them that the message of Paul and Barnabas presented a theological hazard (take, for example, Paul's description of the Mosaic law as incapable of acquitting people of their sins [13:38]). Otherwise, why would Luke have mentioned the women's religious devotion? The foremost men may have been more concerned about the political and social unrest aroused by the introduction of new teaching. In any case, by using "incited" and "stirred up a persecution" Luke portrays the expulsion of Paul and Barnabas as unjustified.

13:51–52: **And on shaking out the dust of** [their] **feet against them, they** [Paul and Barnabas] **went to Iconium** [a city east of Pisidian Antioch]. Shaking out the dust symbolized both coming judgment on the unbelieving persecutors and Paul's and Barnabas's lack of liability for that judgment (for they had proclaimed to their persecutors the good news of salvation [compare 18:6]). Luke's wording doesn't mean that Paul and Barnabas shook dust off their feet; rather, they shook out of their clothing the dust kicked up by their feet. ⁵²**And the disciples were being filled with joy and the Holy Spirit.** Luke calls those in Antioch who'd believed "the disciples" because they'd "followed" Paul and Barnabas (13:43), following being a characteristic of disciples. The disciples' "being *filled* with joy and the Holy Spirit" indicates an abundance of joy (the joy of salvation [13:47]) and of the Holy Spirit (who'll now empower them in their own proclamation of the gospel [1:8]). This fullness of joy over forgiveness and acquittal of sins and over appointment to eternal life (13:38–39, 48) contrasts with the foregoing somber gesture that symbolized judgment to come on the unbelievers. And this fullness of the Holy Spirit for Christian witness compensates for the departure of Paul and Barnabas as evangelists.

THE EVANGELIZATION OF
ICONIUM AND LYCAONIA
Acts 14:1–7

14:1: **And the same thing happened in Iconium** [as had happened in Pisidian Antioch]: **they** [Paul and Barnabas] **went into the synagogue of the Jews and spoke in this way** [= in the way they'd spoken in the synagogue at Pisidian Antioch], **so that a multitudinous multitude of both Jews and Greeks believed.** "A multitudinous multitude" brings out Luke's emphasis on successful evangelism. "A multitude" would have sufficed for this emphasis. But "a *multitudinous* multitude" ratchets up the emphasis with a wordplaying use of an adjective and a noun stemming from the same root (see the comments on Luke 23:27). "Of *both* Jews *and* Greeks" heightens the emphasis yet another notch. Rather than stalling the engine of evangelism, then, the driving of Paul and Barnabas out of Pisidian Antioch revved it up. The Greeks were Greek-speaking Gentiles who attended synagogue services.

14:2–4: **But the Jews who'd disbelieved stirred up and damaged the souls of the Gentiles** [who didn't attend synagogue services and hadn't believed] **against the brothers** [that is, the fellow believers]. "Stirred up and damaged the souls of the Gentiles against the brothers" means incitement to think badly of the believers and mistreat them. Luke calls them "the brothers" to portray the Christian community as a close-knit family that a person should like to join. ³**On the one hand, therefore, they** [Paul and Barnabas] **spent considerable time** [in Iconium], **speaking out boldly** [in reliance] **on the Lord, who was testifying to the word of his grace by granting signs and wonders to take place through**

their hands. "Therefore" indicates that the prejudicing of unbelieving Gentiles against the Jewish and Gentile converts led Paul and Barnabas to stay longer than they might otherwise have stayed. Their converts needed support. "Speaking out boldly" draws admiration for courage in the face of concerted opposition. The opposition sparked such speaking rather than stifling it. And its boldness set an example for the converts not to wilt under the heat of prejudicial mistreatment. "[In reliance] on the Lord" describes the boldness as deriving from piety, not from self-generated bravado. The Lord added his stamp of approval "by granting signs and wonders to take place through their hands." "Signs" calls attention to the miracles' significance as supporting the truthfulness of the spoken message about the Lord's grace. "Wonders" calls attention to the miracles' stupendousness. "Through their hands" indicates that the Lord was using Paul and Barnabas as his agents. They weren't acting on their own or under their own power (compare 1:8). ⁴**On the other hand, the multitude of the city** [= its Gentile populace] **was divided; and some** [the unbelievers] **were with the** [unbelieving] **Jews** [that is, sided with them], **but some** [the believers] **with the apostles.** Ordinarily, "the apostles" refers to the Twelve, who according to 1:15–26 had to have accompanied Jesus from the time of John the baptizer up through Jesus' ascension. But "apostle," which means "sent one," came to refer also to other traveling evangelists (compare 22:21; 26:17 for Paul's case). This wider meaning of "apostle" applies here.

14:5–7: **And when both the Gentiles and the Jews along with their rulers** [unbelievers all] **made a move to assault and stone them** [Paul and Barnabas], ⁶**on becoming aware** [of it] **they fled to the cities of Lycaonia—**[namely,] **Lystra and Derbe—and the surrounding** [region]. ⁷**And they were proclaiming the good news there.** The opposition in Iconium looks more dangerous than that in Pisidian Antioch, so that Paul and Barnabas fled for their lives rather than being expelled (as they were from Antioch). Again, though, departure results in wider propagation of the gospel. It can't be muted.

MORE ON LYSTRA
Acts 14:8–20

14:8–10: **And in Lystra** [south-southeast of Iconium] **a certain man powerless in** [his] **feet was sitting, lame from his mother's womb** [that is, since his birth], **who'd never walked around.** ⁹**This** [man] **heard Paul speaking, who on gazing at him and seeing that he has faith to be saved** ¹⁰**said with a loud voice, "Stand up straight on your feet." And he jumped up and started walking around.** Presumably the lame man was sitting in public to beg. But Luke doesn't say so. As a result, the accent falls solely on the inability of the man's feet to support him well enough even to stand up straight, let alone well enough to walk around. "Lame from his mother's womb" worsens his plight in that he'd never learned to stand or

519

walk, so that the miracle will be more extraordinary than most miracles (which by definition are extraordinary). We're not told what Paul was saying that the man heard. So the accent here falls solely on the man's observable "faith to be saved," stressed by the present tense in "he *has* faith." "Saved" has the sense of being saved from his congenital lameness. But "saved" also carries the connotation of being saved for eternal life, which the physical healing symbolizes and presages. The loudness of Paul's command to stand up makes the bystanders ear- as well as eyewitnesses of the miracle. "Straight on your feet" stresses the power that will replace his feets' powerlessness. But the miracle exceeds Paul's command in that the man didn't just "*stand* up." He "*jumped* up." And instead of merely *standing* up straight, he "started *walking* around." No wonder the bystanders' following reaction.

14:11–13: And the crowds, on seeing what Paul had done, raised their voice, saying in Lycaonian [their native language], **"The gods, taking the likeness of human beings, have come down to us." ¹²And they were calling Barnabas Zeus** [the highest ranking of the pagan gods], **and Paul Hermes, since he was the leader of the word** [= the chief speaker]. Hermes was considered the messenger of the Greek gods, Zeus and Hermes being called Jupiter and Mercury in the Roman pantheon. The plural of "crowds" reflects the magnetism of Paul's and Barnabas's preaching, just as in the case of Jesus' preaching (see Luke 4:42; 5:3, 15 and so on). The singular in "their voice" indicates that the crowds, though multiple, were so awestruck by the miracle Paul had performed that they shouted as one. And the use of their native language indicates a spontaneity of reaction to the miracle. They couldn't help but shout in adulation. Pagan people had long thought that gods sometimes took the form of human beings, came down from heaven, and visited them incognito. And in the region where Lystra lay, Zeus and Hermes were associated with each other. We even know of a legend according to which an aged husband and wife entertained in their home Zeus and Hermes. Luke doesn't say why the crowds called Barnabas Zeus; so the emphasis falls on Paul, "the leader of the word." Luke uses this expression for Paul as the chief speaker to bring into view the word of the gospel that Paul proclaimed. **¹³And the priest of Zeus, whose** [temple] **was in front of the city** [that is, just before you enter the city], **on bringing oxen and garlands to the** [city] **gates, was wanting—along with the crowds—to sacrifice** [the oxen to Paul and Barnabas]. Sacrificial animals were often decked with garlands. Again the crowds enter the picture as a reminder of Paul's and Barnabas's Jesus-like magnetism. And the wish to offer them sacrifices testifies to the impact of their message and miracle.

14:14–18: And on hearing [what the priest and the crowds wanted to do], **the apostles Barnabas and Paul, tearing their clothes, sprang out into the crowd, shouting ¹⁵and saying, "Men, why are you doing these things? We too are human beings with sensitivities like** [yours] **as we proclaim good news to you in order**

that you turn from these ridiculous things to the living God, 'who made the heaven and the earth and the sea and all the things in them** [Exodus 20:11; Psalm 146:6],' **¹⁶who in bygone generations allowed all the Gentiles to go their** [own] **ways. ¹⁷And yet by doing good**—[that is,] **by giving you rains from the sky and fruitful seasons, by filling your hearts with food and cheer—he didn't leave himself without attestation."** Contrary to what you've thought, it wasn't Zeus who gave you these benefits. **¹⁸And despite saying these things, they** [Barnabas and Paul] **scarcely stopped the crowds from sacrificing** [the oxen] **to them.** Calling Barnabas and Paul "the apostles" distinguishes them from the gods Zeus and Hermes (see the comments on 14:4 for Paul and Barnabas as apostles outside the Twelve). Here Barnabas comes before Paul because the Lystrans had identified Barnabas with the chief god Zeus. Several actions of Barnabas and Paul highlight their horror at the prospect of having garlanded oxen sacrificed to them as though they (Barnabas and Paul) were gods: (1) their taking action as soon as they heard of the prospect; (2) the tearing of their clothes; (3) the vigor of their *springing* into action; (4) their springing "into the crowd" to identify themselves as fellow human beings with the crowd rather than standing apart as gods might do; and (5) their shouting. "The crowds" of 14:11, 13 become "the crowd," because Barnabas and Paul could hardly spring into more than one crowd at once (but see 14:18–19 for a reversion to "the crowds" to emphasize again the apostles' magnetism).

The verbal language of Barnabas and Paul matches their body language: "with sensitivities like [yours]" adds to "We too are human beings" the element of fellow feeling according to the axiom that like understands like ("It takes a thief to know a thief," for example). This addition underlines the humanity of Barnabas and Paul. Their affirmation of humanity carries with it a denial of divinity in that the gods weren't thought to have feelings such as human beings have. For Luke and his audience, this affirmation-plus-denial rules out any suspicion that Barnabas and Paul were charlatans. For charlatans would have taken advantage of being regarded as deities. "As we proclaim good news to you" shows it's out of fellow feeling that Barnabas and Paul preach the gospel. Human sympathy as well as divine commission impels their evangelistic labor. And the "news" they proclaim is intellectually "good" in that it entails "turn[ing] from these ridiculous things [= idols, such as that of Zeus in his temple nearby] to the living God." The idols are ridiculous because, unlike the living God, they're dead. The news is also economically "good" in that you can stop thinking you have to sacrifice to idols. And since the living God created all that exists, he doesn't need your garlanded oxen as sacrifices. He allowed all the Gentiles to take their wayward paths into idolatry. But "in bygone generations" implies that the time is ripe for you Gentiles to come back to him. It's not as though he abandoned you because of your idolatry. For he gave you a witness of himself in the form of what theologians call "common grace." It consists in God's having done you good by giving you rain that produced harvests, which in turn produced food that you enjoyed in the eating. "From heaven [or 'the sky']" stresses the divine origin of this common grace. We expect "filling your *stomachs* with food." But what we get is "filling your *hearts* with food" to emphasize the "cheer" brought about by eating the food. "Hearts" goes better with "cheer" than "stomachs" would. This attestation of God's general goodness points toward the specific goodness of the news of salvation through Jesus Christ. The difficulty of Barnabas and Paul in stopping the crowds from sacrificing to them highlights once again the stupendousness of Paul's having healed the man born lame.

14:19–20: But [unbelieving] **Jews arrived from** [Pisidian] **Antioch and Iconium and, on swaying the crowds and stoning Paul, they dragged** [him] **out of the city, supposing him to have died.** The Jews from Pisidian Antioch had expelled Paul and Barnabas from their city. Those from Iconium had moved to assault and stone them, so that they fled. Unsatisfied, the hatred of these Jews toward Paul and Barnabas drives them to Lystra for an attempt at killing them there. First, though, they have to turn the crowds against Paul and Barnabas, and they do so. Then they stone Paul, the miracle-worker and chief speaker. (For an unknown reason Barnabas temporarily drops out of sight, but see 2 Corinthians 11:25 for Paul's being stoned.) The stoning takes place without a prior trial or verdict of guilt for a capital crime. So Luke's audience will recognize both a gross injustice and a fulfillment of God's having said Paul would have to suffer many things according to plan (9:16). The dragging of Paul "out of the city" implies that the preceding events had taken place inside the city gates (compare 14:13) and compounds the injustice with an outrageous substitution of dragging what they thought to be a corpse instead of giving it a burial. It could rot there, away from their nostrils, for all they cared. "*Supposing* him to have died" suggests a mistaken opinion, though. **20But when the disciples had encircled him, on standing up he went into the city.** So not all in the crowds had turned against Paul. At least some had believed the good news and now dared to surround his body, probably to mourn and bury him. But Paul's standing up and going "into the city" reverses the opponents' having dragged him "out of the city." They hadn't gotten rid of him after all. God's plan for evangelism through Paul can't be thwarted even by a nearly mortal stoning. **And the next day he went out with Barnabas to Derbe** [east of Lystra]. "He *went* out" contrasts with his having been "*dragged* out." Lynching foiled!

THE RETURN TO ANTIOCH, SYRIA
Acts 14:21–26

14:21–22: And on proclaiming the good news in that city [Derbe] **and making a considerable number of disciples, they** [Paul and Barnabas] **returned to Lystra and to Iconium and to** [Pisidian] **Antioch,** **22stabilizing the disciples' souls, urging** [them] **to remain in the faith, and** [saying,] **"It's necessary that we enter God's kingdom through many afflictions."** So the stoning of Paul nearly to death aided the spread of the gospel rather than stopping it. And the gospelizing in Derbe proved so successful that "a considerable number" became disciples. On their return trip Paul and Barnabas seek to conserve their successes by "stabilizing" the disciples, with particular reference to their inward state ("souls"). "Urging [them] to remain in the faith" tells how Paul and Barnabas went about the stabilization and interprets the stabilization in terms of firming them up to endure afflictions. "It's necessary that we enter God's kingdom through many afflictions" quotes what was said by way of urging and implies that afflictions—that is, persecution—could shake their belief. Hence the urging to persevere. "It's necessary" assures them that the afflictions, even though they're "many," make up part of God's plan and will eventuate in entering his kingdom, where they'll suffer no more afflictions. The persecution of Paul and Barnabas in these cities gave them good reason to fortify their converts against what they themselves had undergone. "Enter God's kingdom" exhibits continuity with Jesus' teaching. This continuity inspires confidence in the words of Paul and Barnabas.

14:23: And on hand-picking elders for them church by church, praying along with fastings they [Paul and Barnabas] **committed them** [the disciples] **to the Lord, in whom they'd believed.** As synagogues had elders, so now churches gain elders. They're chosen to lead the churches with the wisdom of age now that Paul and Barnabas will leave the vicinity. The parallel with synagogue elders contributes to Luke's portrayal of Christianity as the legitimate outgrowth of Judaism. "Praying along with fastings" displays the piety of Paul and Barnabas. They're not self-serving charlatans; so their message is to be believed. The plural of "fastings" means they fasted for prayer at every church. Their departure means they could do little else but leave them in the Lord's care. And "in whom they'd believed" adds that the disciples had already entrusted themselves, including their eternal fate, to Jesus as their Lord.

14:24–26: And on going through Pisidia [an interior region, not a city], **they came to Pamphylia** [another region, but coastal]. **25And on speaking the word** [of the gospel] **in Perga** [a city close to the coast], **they went down to Attalia** [on the coast]. During their outgoing trip, apparently, Paul and Barnabas hadn't proclaimed the good news in Perga (see 13:13–14). Here they make up for that omission. **26And from there** [Attalia] **they sailed off to Antioch** [in Syria], **from where they'd been given over to God's grace for the work that they'd fulfilled.** This last statement ("given over . . .") explains in detail what was meant in 13:2–3 by the fasting, praying, laying of hands on Barnabas and Paul, and letting them go for the work to which they Holy Spirit had called them. As usual, "God's grace" means his favor, but here not the favor of salvation through Christ—rather, the favor required for doing evangelistic work. Without it, the work will fail. With it, the work will be fulfilled, that is, accomplished completely. And it was. Thus Luke stresses God's approval of evangelism. So believe the good news as proclaimed. It has divine backing.

THE DECREES OF THE JERUSALEM COUNCIL
Acts 14:27–15:33, 35

This passage divides into the start of a theological dispute within the church at Antioch, Syria (14:27–15:4), the settling of the dispute in Jerusalem (15:5–21), and the sending of resultant resolutions to the church in Syrian Antioch (15:22–33, 35). The settling of the dispute in Jerusalem subdivides into a speech by Peter to the other apostles and the church elders (15:6–11), a report to all of them by Barnabas and Paul (15:12), and a speech in reply by James the half brother of Jesus (15:13–21).

14:27: And on arriving [in Syrian Antioch] **and gathering the church together, they** [Paul and Barnabas] **were reporting the things, as many as they were, which God had done along with them; and** [they were reporting], **"He opened a door of faith for the Gentiles."** "*Gathering* the church together" shows the local church to be an assembly of people, not a building. "The things . . . God had done" refers to the miracles and conversions he'd effected. But "along with them" makes Paul and Barnabas coworkers with God and in this way re-emphasizes the grace of God, his favoring them with the work of evangelism (14:26). "As many as they were" describes the miracles and conversions as so numerous as to certify the gospel beyond doubt (Luke 1:1–4). Gentiles had been converted before, in Cornelius's house (10:1–48) and right here in Antioch (11:20–21). So why the statement at this late date, "He opened a door of faith for the Gentiles"? The answer lies in the word "faith," because the following account deals with the question whether faith alone suffices for the salvation of Gentiles, or whether observance of the Mosaic law, starting with circumcision for males, has to be added to faith. So "he opened a door *of faith* for the Gentiles" prepares for a dispute over this question and intimates the position of Paul and Barnabas that faith alone is enough.

14:28–15:2: And they [Paul and Barnabas] **were spending not a little time** [= a long time] **with the disciples** [in Syrian Antioch]. **¹And some** [Jewish believers], **on coming down from Judea** [where Jerusalem was located at a high elevation], **started teaching the brothers, "Unless you're circumcised in conformity with the standard of Moses** [that is, with the requirement laid out in the Mosaic law (for starters, see Genesis 17:10–14)], **you can't be saved."** Gentile converts to Judaism had to undergo circumcision (if they were males) and promise to keep the law of Moses. The Judeans taught the same requirement for Gentile converts to the Christian gospel. **²And when Paul and Barnabas had not a little dissension and debate** [= a lot of dissension and debate] **with them** [the men from Judea], **they** [the brothers, that is,

fellow believers in the church at Antioch] **appointed Paul and Barnabas and some others from among them to go up to the apostles and elders in Jerusalem with regard to this point of dispute.** The long time that Paul and Barnabas spent with the disciples in Syrian Antioch leaves room for the arrival of teachers from Judea and the development of a dispute over their teaching. Luke first calls the believers in Antioch "disciples," which means "learners," because of their having learned the Law-free gospel from the teaching of Barnabas, Paul, and others (13:1) and because of the Law-strapped doctrine they're now learning from the Judeans. Next, Luke calls these disciples "the brothers" as a reminder of the familial closeness to one another that believers enjoy and that prospective converts should find inviting. Paul and Barnabas disagreed and debated strongly with the Judean teachers, so that the brothers sent Paul and Barnabas and some of their own number to the apostles and church elders in Jerusalem for an opinion. Those of their own number will provide a check on whatever report Paul and Barnabas might bring back. Luke wants prospective converts to know that the church is concerned for truth. As in the appointment of elders for the churches in central Asia Minor (14:23), so the presence of elders in the church at Jerusalem exhibits continuity with Judaism, whose synagogues likewise had elders. Notably, none of the Judean teachers are said to have been appointed to go up to the apostles and elders in Jerusalem. So from the standpoint of the church in Antioch, it's the Law-strapped doctrine of the Judeans that's suspect, not the Law-free teaching of Paul and Barnabas. Otherwise the church would have sent Judeans to plead a case against Paul and Barnabas. Since Luke is writing in the main to convert Gentiles, it pleases him to note an already developing trend that will eventuate in a decree repudiating the Law-strapped teaching, which would inhibit the evangelism of Gentiles and lead many of those already converted to fall away from the church.

15:3–4: On the one hand, therefore [= because of the appointment to go to Jerusalem], **having been sent forward by the church they were going through both Phoenicia and Samaria, relating in detail the turning of the Gentiles to** [the living God from idols (see 14:15)] **and were producing great joy for all the brothers. ⁴On the other hand, after arriving in Jerusalem they were welcomed by the church and the apostles and the elders; and they reported the things, as many as they were, that God had done with them** [see the comments on 14:27]. Because of the parallel in 14:27, "they" refers to Paul and Barnabas alone. "In detail" underscores their self-reported success in the conversion of Gentiles. But the Gentiles' turning to the living God rather than to Paul and Barnabas, who had refused divine honors in Lystra (14:11–18), absolves Paul and Barnabas of any braggadocio. The "*great* joy" of "*all* the brothers" on hearing about the Gentiles' conversion portrays Christians as exceedingly and universally joyful over the salvation of others as well as themselves (compare the joy of God himself over even one sinner who repents [Luke

15:7, 10, 32]). And the welcome of Paul and Barnabas in Jerusalem corresponds to the joy with which their report of Gentiles' salvation was received along the way. The listing, "by the *church* and the *apostles* and the *elders*," magnifies the welcome. The church and its leaders are a welcoming community. So come on in.

15:5–6: But some of the ones from the faction of the Pharisees who'd believed stood up and out [from the rest], **saying, "It's necessary to circumcise them** [the Gentile converts] **and order** [them] **to keep the law of Moses."** ⁶**And the apostles and the elders gathered together to see about this word** [= to assess what these Pharisees were saying, as just quoted]. Luke's Gospel repeatedly casts the Pharisees in a bad light (5:17, 21, 30 and so on). So it comes as a pleasant surprise and testimony to the power of the gospel that some Pharisees have believed. At the same time, their insisting on the divine necessity of circumcision and other Law-keeping for Gentile converts is troubling—though understandable, given Pharisaic legalism. The apostles' and elders' gathering together to assess the matter corresponds to the Antiochian Christians' sending Paul, Barnabas, and others "to the apostles and elders in Jerusalem" (15:2). Cooperation makes for good community, and good community makes for evangelistic magnetism.

15:7–9: And after much debate had taken place, Peter, on standing up, said to them [the other apostles and the elders], **"Men, brothers, you understand that from olden days God made a selection among you** [to the effect that] **through my mouth the Gentiles would hear the word of the gospel and believe** [it]. ⁸**And the heart-knower, God, testified to them by giving** [them] **the Holy Spirit just as** [he did] **also to us** [Jewish believers]. ⁹**And in no way did he differentiate between both us and them when because of** [their] **belief he cleansed their hearts."** Luke's skipping the details of the debate lets the emphasis rest on Peter's speech, the report of Barnabas and Paul, and James's speech (the latter two yet to come)—all favorable to Gentile salvation by faith alone. But Luke describes the debate as "much" to assure his audience that the issue got a thorough airing, as it should have. Thus the decree to follow won't suffer from any inadequacy of deliberation. "Men, brothers" in Peter's address appeals to common interests between him and his fellow apostles and the elders (compare 1:16; 2:29 and so on). "You know" recalls Peter's reporting to Jewish believers in Jerusalem what had happened at Simon the tanner's house in Joppa and at Cornelius's house in Caesarea (11:1–18). That God's selection of Peter took place "among you" makes Peter's audience witnesses, like it or not, to the authority of what he now has to say. God's selection of Peter to evangelize the Gentiles in Cornelius's house lends further authority to Peter's present speech and alludes in particular to the vision Peter saw and, in it, to the instruction that he consider nothing ritually impure or unclean (10:15, 28; 11:9)—also to the synchronization of his vision with Cornelius's vision and sending men for Peter (10:1–23).

Perhaps with hyperbole, "from olden days" means "a long time ago." Whether or not hyperbolic, the expression emphasizes that God's acceptance of Gentile believers apart from circumcision and other Law-keeping already enjoys the status of tradition in the church. The Gentiles' "hear[ing] the word of the gospel and believ[ing] it]" satisfied God. And as a heart-knower, he perceived their inward belief without the outward evidence of submission to circumcision and other Law-keeping. Giving them the Holy Spirit just as he had to Jewish believers (2:1–4) constituted a testimony to his satisfaction with their faith alone. We expect Peter to say, "God testified to *us* [so that *we* could consider them saved apart from Law-keeping]." What Peter actually says, though, is that "God testified to *them*." So they haven't submitted to circumcision and the rest of Moses' law, not out of recalcitrance, but because of God's own testimony to them. They're not to be blamed or imposed upon. As to Law-keeping, "in no way" emphatically rules out any differentiation by God between circumcised Jewish believers and uncircumcised Gentile believers. Such a differentiation would have occurred at the Gentiles' conversion. But it didn't. The inward, moral cleansing of their hearts by the heart-knowing God made unnecessary any outward, ritual surgery on their bodies. And their "belief" sufficed for an inward, moral cleansing.

Peter continues in **15:10–11: "Now, therefore** [because of God's testimony to them], **why are you testing God by placing on the neck of the** [Gentile] **disciples a yoke that neither our** [fore]**fathers nor we** [Jewish offspring of theirs] **were strong enough to bear?"** Here, to test God is to try his patience by doubting his testimony that belief on the part of Gentiles sufficed for their salvation. Peter calls them "the disciples" to suit the issue of learning and keeping the Law. "A yoke" is a collar placed on the neck and attached to a plow, a wagon, or such like for the purpose of pulling it. Thus the weight of the object being pulled is transferred to the puller, usually an animal. Peter uses the yoke as a figure of speech for human beings' obligation to keep the Mosaic law. So to God's testimony to Gentile believers that their belief sufficed, Peter adds the history of Jewish disobedience to the Law, a history of repeated apostasies from the very beginning right up to the present time (see 7:35–53). The Jews haven't had the moral strength to bear the Law's weight by pulling it, that is, by obeying it. ¹¹**"But we** [Jewish disciples] **believe to be saved through the grace of the Lord Jesus in the same way that those** [Gentile disciples] **too** [believe to be saved]**."** Here Peter switches his emphasis from Law-free salvation for Gentile believers to Law-free salvation for Jewish believers. In other words, their circumcision and Law-keeping doesn't count toward salvation. Peter isn't saying he and his Jewish audience had all agreed *that* they're saved through the grace of the Lord Jesus. Some had insisted on Law-keeping for salvation (15:5). Otherwise there wouldn't have been "much debate" (15:7). Peter is saying, rather, that whatever some have thought and said to the contrary, as a matter of fact salvation comes to

Jews as well as Gentiles through grace in consequence of believing—period. And it's Jesus, the object of believing, who extends this grace, the ill-merited favor of salvation. Peter calls him "the Lord" to stress that Jesus has authority to confer such grace apart from our keeping the Law.

15:12: And all the multitude became silent and started listening to Barnabas and Paul as they related signs and wonders, as many as they were, that God had performed through them among the Gentiles. Now it comes out that in addition to "the apostles and the elders" mentioned in 15:6, many other believers were present, such as the Pharisees who insisted on Law-keeping (15:5). As usual, "the multitude" emphasizes evangelistic success as evidence of divine origin and approval. "*Became* silent" implies that Peter's speech had generated some hubbub. "Became *silent*" implies interest in what Barnabas and Paul have to say. Luke mentions Barnabas before Paul because of Barnabas's role in introducing Paul to the apostles (9:26–27, where Paul is called "Saul"). See the comments on 14:3 for "signs and wonders." "As many as they were" describes them as so numerous as to constitute unmistakable evidence of divine approval of the Law-free good news that Barnabas and Paul had proclaimed. *God*, not they, performed the signs and wonders. Hence *divine* approval. "*Through* them" portrays Barnabas and Paul as his instruments, whose Law-free proclamation therefore should now be approved by the Jerusalem council. "Among the Gentiles" makes the Gentiles eyewitnesses of God's approving with signs and wonders the Law-free good news and its proclaimers. The Gentile converts of Barnabas and Paul, then, are to be blamed for not keeping the Mosaic law no more than were Peter's Gentile converts in Cornelius's house to be blamed for not keeping it.

15:13–18: And after they [Barnabas and Paul] became silent [= stopped speaking], James answered [= responded], saying, "Men, brothers [about which address see the comments on 15:7], hear me. [14]Simeon has related how God first [in the incident concerning Cornelius and his household and friends] involved himself so as to take from among Gentiles a people for his name [compare Zechariah 2:11]. This James is the half brother of Jesus (see the comments on 12:17). The Semitic spelling "Simeon" replaces the Greek spelling "Simon" and thus reflects James's having spoken in the Semitic language, Aramaic, to a Jewish audience (compare 22:1–3). God's "involv[ing] himself to take from among Gentiles a people for his name" parallels God's having chosen Israel from among other nations (Deuteronomy 14:2) and thereby adds to Luke's portrayal of the church, Gentiles included, as the divinely planned enlargement of God's ancient people (compare 18:10). "For his name" means to become his property by having his name called over them or, as we would say, by having his name stamped on them (see 15:17 with comments). [15]**"And with this [salvation of Gentiles] the words of the prophets agree, just as it's written, [16]'After these things [the events of the Old Testament period]**

I [= God] **will return and rebuild the fallen tent of David** [a figure of speech for his royal dynasty] **and rebuild its ruins** [the result of Babylonian conquest (see 2 Kings 25:1–7, for example)] **and restore it** [through Jesus, David's descendant (Luke 1:26–33, 67–75; 2:4–14; 3:23–38, especially 3:31)], [17]**so that the rest of human beings** [besides Israel] **may seek out the Lord—even all the Gentiles over whom my name has been called,** [even] **over them,** [18]**says the Lord, making these things known since long ago** [Amos 9:11–12; Isaiah 45:21].'" To "seek *out* the Lord" is to find him. "Over whom my name has been called" refers to those Gentiles who've been branded, so to speak, with his name and therefore as his property. "*All* [such] Gentiles" indicates that none of them will fail to find the Lord. "Says the Lord" certifies his claim on them and promise of their finding him. "Making these things known" roots the Law-free salvation of Gentiles in divine revelation. And "since long ago"—that is, since Old Testament times—makes the revelation of their salvation a matter of ancient and therefore venerable tradition.

15:19–21: "Therefore [because God has involved himself so as to take from among the Gentiles a people for his name, just as prophesied] **I give judgment not to trouble those from the Gentiles who are turning** [from idols] **to God** [that is, not to trouble them with the requirement of circumcision and keeping the rest of Moses' law], [20]**but to write them a letter to the effect they should avoid the things polluted by idols** [which things will be specified in 15:29 as meat eaten in a pagan temple after the animal from which the meat comes has been sacrificed to the idol housed in the temple] **and** [to avoid] **sexual immorality** [practiced there in connection with feasting on the meat, for pagan temples and adjacent quarters featured prostitution and other sexual dalliance as well as dining] **and what's strangled** [as pagan sacrifices sometimes were] **and blood** [which was sometimes tasted or drunk at sacrificial ceremonies in pagan temples]." In other words, Gentile converts are to forgo their past participation in idolatrous and immoral activities at pagan temples (compare 1 Corinthians 8 and especially 10; also 1 John 5:21; Revelation 2:14, 20–21). [21]**"For ever since ancient generations Moses has city by city those who proclaim him by reading** [aloud his books, Genesis–Deuteronomy] **Sabbath by Sabbath in the synagogues."** It would scandalize weekly listeners to the Mosaic law, which condemns idolatry and the sexual immorality that accompanies it, if Gentiles were to keep attending pagan temples and participating in what goes on there. So Gentile converts should stay away, James says. Such participation is inherently wrong for Gentiles who according to 15:19 have turned to the living God from idolatry. Nor does James deny it's inherently wrong. But here he's concerned about its bad effect on his fellow Jews. He agrees with Peter that it would be wrong to trouble Gentile converts by placing the yoke of circumcision and other Law-keeping on their necks. Instead of making nonattendance and nonparticipation at an idol temple matters of Law-keeping, then, he makes them matters of deference to Jews. The emphasis falls on maintaining harmonious relations between Gentile converts and Jews. And in this book Luke puts such relations on exhibit to make the gospel and the Christian community inviting to prospective converts.

15:22–23a: Then it seemed good to the apostles and the elders, along with the whole church, to send to Antioch [in Syria] **men selected from among them** [= from their own number] **with Paul and Barnabas— Judas (the one called Barsabbas) and Silas, leading men among the brothers—**[23a]**having written through their hand** [which is to say that Judas Barsabbas and Silas hand-delivered the following letter, written by the apostles and elders along with the whole church]. Especially because of the "much debate" that preceded and the believing Pharisees' insistence on circumcision and further Law-keeping (15:5, 7), the unanimity of judgment achieved by the Jerusalem church and her leaders represents yet again the communitarianism that Luke highlights to attract prospective converts. Calling believers "the brothers" suits the same purpose.

Luke starts quoting the letter in **15:23b: "The apostles and the elders, brothers, to the brothers from among the Gentiles in Antioch and Syria and Cilicia: [We wish you] to rejoice."** It's unclear whether the first-mentioned "brothers" means that the apostles and the brothers are religious brothers to each other, whether only the elders are such, or whether they're all religious brothers to Christians in Antioch and Cilicia. It's also unclear whether the second-mentioned "brothers" are such in relation to each other or also to the brothers in Jerusalem. In any case, then, the emphasis falls again on attractive communitarianism among Christians. The present Antioch is located in Syria, so that mention of the country in addition to the city points to the evangelistically successful—and hence for Luke the evangelistically *useful*—spread of the gospel from city to country. The same is to be said about the mention of Cilicia; for Paul had spent time in the city of Tarsus, located in Cilicia, before going to Antioch, Syria (9:30). "[We wish you] to rejoice" is the Greek way of saying, "Greetings" or "Hello."

The letter continues in **15:24–26: "Since we've heard that some, on going out from among us, have stirred you up with words** [= their Law-strapped doctrine] **to the effect of upsetting your souls** [= your selves, with special reference to inner thoughts and feelings], **to which** [men] **we gave no orders,** [25]**it seemed good to us—after developing mutual fervor—on selecting men, to send** [them] **to you with our beloved Barnabas and Paul,** [26]**human beings who've given over their souls** [= devoted themselves and their lives, perhaps to the extent of risking them] **for the name of our Lord, Jesus Christ."** The party from the church in Antioch had informed the apostles and elders, authors of this letter, about the confusion and upset caused by the Judeans who without the apostles' and elders' authorization had

gone from the church in Jerusalem to the one in Antioch and taught the necessity of Law-keeping for salvation. The language of nonauthorization disavows any responsibility on the part of the apostles and elders for the confusion and upset. This language also combines with "it seemed good to us" to signal disagreement with the freelancers' teaching. "After developing mutual fervor" doesn't have to do so much with a common judgment as with a common zeal—here, to correct some false teaching. The selection of some believers from Jerusalem—namely, Judas Barsabbas and Silas—to accompany Barnabas and Saul will give the Christians in Antioch assurance of the letter's authenticity. Nobody will be able to accuse Barnabas and Paul of forging the letter. It mentions Barnabas before Paul because Barnabas was the one who introduced Paul both to the apostles in Jerusalem and to the church in Syrian Antioch (see 9:26–28; 11:22–26, where Paul is called "Saul"). "Our beloved Barnabas and Paul" puts the apostles and elders squarely on the side of those two and exudes the affection Christians typically feel toward one another—an affection the mention of which Luke includes to woo unbelievers caught in a societal web of love-destroying competition for honor and esteem. The designation of Barnabas and Paul as "human beings" sets off "Jesus Christ" as "our [divine] Lord." The citation of Barnabas's and Paul's having "given over their souls for the name of our Lord, Jesus Christ" commends them and thus indirectly recommends their Law-free teaching. "For the *name* . . ." means for the sake of Jesus Christ's reputation as "our Lord."

The letter comes to its conclusion in **15:27–29: "Therefore** [because 'it seemed good to us . . .' (15:25)] **we've sent Judas and Silas, even them, as announcers through word** [= through oral speech] **of the same things** [that are written in this letter]. [28]**For it seemed good to the Holy Spirit and to us to place on you not one more burden—but for these requisites:** [29]**to avoid** [meat] **sacrificed to an idol and blood and what's been strangled and sexual immorality, by keeping yourselves from which you'll do well** [see the comments on 15:19–21]. **Hang tough** [more literally, 'Be strengthened,' but used as a farewell like 'Goodbye']." Judas and Silas will provide oral confirmation of the letter's contents. In 15:25 the letter said "it seemed good to us . . . to send [selected men] to you with our beloved Barnabas and Paul." But to put extra weight on freedom from the Mosaic law, the letter says "it seemed good *to the Holy Spirit* and to us." Addition of "the Holy Spirit" (absent in 15:22) ahead of "us" gives him primacy, with the implication that he guided the apostles and elders in their judgment. His guidance undergirds the Law-free gospel with divine authority. "Not one more burden" alludes to Peter's question in 15:10 ("Now, therefore, why are you testing God by placing on the neck of the disciples a yoke that neither our [fore]fathers nor we were strong enough to bear?") and underlines freedom from Moses' law. Normally, "you'll do well" means "you'll prosper." But here it means "you'll do what's right" (by observing the requisites).

15:30–32: So on being let go, they [Judas Barsabbas and Silas along with Paul and Barnabas] **went down** [from Jerusalem] **to** [low-lying] **Antioch; and on gathering together the multitude** [of Christians there], **they delivered the letter.** [31]**And on having** [it] **read** [to them], **they** [the multitude] **rejoiced because of the encouragement.** "The multitude" calls attention back to the ongoing success of Christian evangelism, empowered as it is by the Holy Spirit (1:8). Join in, or be left behind. The reading of the letter consisted in someone's reading it to the assembled multitude, and the encouragement consisted in the letter's sparing them of any need to get circumcised and keep the rest of Moses' law for their salvation. As always, the good news of salvation by grace through faith brought joy. [32]**And Judas and Silas, also being prophets themselves, exhorted and stabilized the brothers through much speaking.** Prophets not only predicted future events, as Agabus did in 11:27–28. Under divine inspiration they also preached concerning the present. So Judas and Silas, called church leaders in 15:22 but now called prophets as well ("also"), preach by way of exhorting the Christians in Antioch to remain stable, that is, not to be shaken by false teaching such as they'd heard from unauthorized Judeans. In Luke's original Greek, "exhorted" in 15:32 is cognate to "encouragement" in 15:31. But there, association with joy favored the nuance of encouragement whereas here an association with stabilization favors the nuance of exhortation. "The brothers" portrays the believers, though multitudinous, as close-knit in their fellowship. "Through *much* speaking" displays *serious* concern on the part of Judas and Silas for the Christian fidelity of the brothers. These prophets weren't ministering for money.

15:33: And on spending time [in Syrian Antioch], **they** [Judas and Silas] **were let go with peace by the brothers** [Christians in Antioch] **to the ones who'd sent them** [those in Jerusalem]. "With peace" means "with a 'Shalom,'" the Semitic way of saying goodbye as well as hello—but here with overtones of peaceful relations among believers and of salvation through Christ, as in the angelic chorus at his nativity: "peace [is] on earth among human beings of [God's] good pleasure" (Luke 2:14). All in all, then, Luke paints a picture of Christian conciliation, a family of religious brothers who iron out their differences to the benefit of Gentile believers, but with reciprocal consideration on the Gentiles' part to avoid setting up barriers to social interchange with Jewish believers and to the evangelism of Jewish unbelievers. Joy and encouragement are spread all around. The ideal community stays intact. There's no 15:34 in the earliest and best manuscripts.

15:35: But Paul and Barnabas stayed on in Antioch, teaching and proclaiming—along with many others too—the word of the Lord as good news. Antioch has a big population, and a multitude of them have believed. Being so many, the believers need more teachers, and the unbelievers more evangelists. So the Lord supplies many of both in addition to Paul and Barnabas. Thus the work is shown to be the Lord's doing not only by the multiplication of converts but also by the multiplication of teachers and evangelists.

PAUL'S SECOND MISSIONARY JOURNEY
Acts 15:36–18:22

Travelogues appeal to Luke's audience. He uses this one to further his portrayal of the gospel as divinely irresistible in its advance across the Roman Empire. The travelogue proceeds from Syria through Cilicia (15:36–41), then through the cities of Derbe and Lystra (16:1–5), the Phrygian-Galatian region and northwest Asia Minor (16:6–10), the Macedonian cities of Philippi (16:11–40), Thessalonica (17:1–9), and Berea (17:10–15), and the Greek cities of Athens (17:16–34) and Corinth (18:1–17), and back to Syrian Antioch by way of Caesarea and Jerusalem in Israel (18:18–22).

FROM SYRIA THROUGH CILICIA
Acts 15:36–41

15:36: And after some days [spent in Antioch (see 15:35)] **Paul said to Barnabas, "All right, on returning let's check out the brothers each city by each city in which we proclaimed the word of the Lord.** [Let's see] **how they're doing."** "In which we proclaimed the word of the Lord" identifies the cities as those in Cyprus and Asia Minor (13:1–14:23). "All right" stresses Paul's concern for the welfare of converts in these cities. Calling the converts "brothers" points again to the winsomely familial spirit that characterizes Christian community. "Each city by each city" leaves none of the brothers outside Paul's concern.

15:37–41: But Barnabas was wanting to take along with [them] **John, too, the one called Mark,** [38]**whereas Paul was deeming it appropriate *not* to be taking along with them this one who'd deserted them** [by making off] **from Pamphylia and not going with them to the work** [of evangelizing the cities in central Asia Minor (see 13:13)]. [39]**And acrimony developed** [between Paul and Barnabas]**, so that they separated from each other; and Barnabas, taking along Mark, sailed out to Cyprus** [his homeland (4:36)]. [40]**But Paul, on picking Silas** [to be his traveling companion]**, went out** [from Syrian Antioch] **after being given over to the Lord's grace by the brothers** [in the church there]. [41]**And he went through Syria and Cilicia, stabilizing the churches.** If on their first journey John Mark refused to go with Paul and Barnabas to the cities in central Asia Minor, he shouldn't be taken on their second journey to those same cities. So thought Paul—and Luke too, since he describes John Mark as a deserter. Barnabas thought differently. (According to Colossians 4:10 John Mark was Barnabas's cousin.) Despite his concern to portray Christian communities as all sweetness and light, then, Luke can't—or doesn't—avoid mentioning the resultant acrimony that led to Paul's and Barnabas's splitting up. Not to have mentioned it would have left Luke's audience wondering why Barnabas doesn't accompany Paul from now on, and the wonderment would have cast doubt on Luke's authorial integrity. But he makes the best of the acrimonious splitup: Barnabas and John Mark sail out to Cyprus, which Paul and Barnabas evangelized on the first journey. Paul, on the other hand, will revisit the previously evangelized cities in central Asia Minor (16:1–6). Despite the splitup, then, Paul's proposal that the converts in each city evangelized on the first journey be revisited gets carried out. To replace Barnabas in the meantime, Paul picks Silas, who as a prophet and a leader of the church at Jerusalem had come to Antioch and returned to Jerusalem (15:22, 25–27, 30–32 [see Colossians 4:10; 2 Timothy 4:11; Philemon 24 for John Mark's subsequently restored companionship with Paul]). So Paul's picking Silas implies fetching him somehow from Jerusalem. In compensation for the acrimonious split between Paul and Barnabas, "after being given over to the Lord's grace by the brothers" renews emphasis on Christian community; and, much as in 14:26, "the Lord's grace" refers, not to the favor of salvation through Christ, but to the favor required for doing the work of evangelism (see further the comments on 14:26, which refers to "*God's* grace," so that if here in 15:40 "the *Lord's* grace" is the grace of Jesus as Lord, Luke comes close to equating Jesus with God). Since this Antioch lay in Syria, "he went through Syria and Cilicia" means that Paul traveled overland through northwest Syria and then through Cilicia, a region in southeastern Asia Minor where Paul's home city of Tarsus was located (22:3). "Stabilizing the churches" implies that the gospel has spread there too even though Luke hasn't provided any details (but see 9:30; 11:25 for Paul's having spent time in Tarsus after he'd been converted and started preaching).

THROUGH THE CITIES OF LYSTRA AND DERBE
Acts 16:1–5

16:1–2: **And he** [Paul] **arrived both at Derbe and at Lystra. And behold, a certain disciple was there by the name of Timothy—the son of a believing Jewish woman but of a Greek** [and therefore Gentile] **father— **[2]**who** [referring back to Timothy] **was being attested** [to Paul during his visit] **by the brothers in Lystra and Iconium.** "Behold" highlights the sterling reputation of Timothy, which advances Luke's program of advertising the virtues of Jesus and his disciples for Luke's evangelistic purpose in writing Acts. As usual, "the brothers" advertises their communitarianism as well, and for the same purpose. Son of a mixed marriage, Timothy was half Jewish and half Gentile. "Disciple" means "learner," and Luke notes the belief of Timothy's mother. So Luke's calling Timothy "a certain *disciple*" suggests that Timothy learned from his mother to believe in Jesus (compare 2 Timothy 1:5).

16:3: **Paul wanted this** [Timothy] **to go out with him** [as a helper replacing John Mark in the work of evangelism]; **and on taking** [him for this purpose], **he circumcised him on account of the Jews who were in those**

localities. **For they all knew that his father had been Greek.** "Had been" implies the father was now dead. Greeks considered the ideal of beauty to be the nude body of a male human being and therefore wouldn't hear of circumcision, the partial mutilation of their ideal. And in that male-dominated culture fathers had the say-so over their newborn sons. Despite the Jewish mother of Timothy, then, his Greek father hadn't circumcised him. So without the benefit of physical inspection the local Jews' knowledge that he had a Greek father gave all of them the further knowledge of Timothy's uncircumcision. Not to keep the law of circumcision, then, but to avoid putting a roadblock in the way of evangelizing the local Jews and stabilizing those who believed, Paul circumcised Timothy. As in the decrees of the Jerusalem Council, conciliation reigned supreme.

16:4–5: **And as they were traveling through the cities, they gave over to them** [particularly to the Christians in the cities of that region] **the decrees adjudicated by the apostles and elders in Jerusalem** [for them] **to keep.** "The decrees" consisted in commands to avoid ingesting meat sacrificed to an idol, sexual immorality, what's been strangled, and blood at festivities in pagan temples (see 15:20, 29 with comments). Originally, the decrees were addressed to Gentile converts in Antioch, Syria, and Cilicia (15:23). But since they applied to Gentile converts everywhere, Paul and Silas distribute the decrees also in this further region. [5]**So on the one hand the churches were being stabilized in their belief** [because the decrees also included a repudiation of the disturbing doctrine that Gentile believers had to get circumcised and keep the rest of Moses' law] **and were increasing in number day by day.** Evangelistic success keeps on growing. Become part of it! "On the other hand" awaits in the next episode.

THROUGH THE PHRYGIA-GALATIAN
REGION AND NORTHWEST ASIA MINOR
Acts 16:6–40

16:6–8: **On the other hand** [compare 16:5], **they** [Paul, Silas, and Timothy] **went through the Phrygia-and-Galatian region** [in central Asia Minor], **having been forbidden by the Holy Spirit to speak the word in Asia** [not the continent; rather, a province in western Asia Minor]. [7]**And on coming down to Mysia** [a province in northwest Asia Minor], **they were assaying to travel into Bithynia** [a province in northern Asia Minor]; **and the Spirit of Jesus didn't allow them** [to do so]. [8]**And on going along the edge of Mysia, they went down to Troas** [a seaport in the northwest corner of Asia Minor]. To speak the word of the gospel is good; but the Holy Spirit tells where to speak it, and when to speak it there. So his forbidding Paul and Paul's party to speak the word in Asia and not allowing them passage to Bithynia shows that evangelism proceeds under the control as well as power of the Holy Spirit. For this reason, too, it can't be thwarted, only surrendered to— if you're smart. Since "the Spirit of *Jesus*" controls the where-and-when of evangelism in just the same way "the *Holy* Spirit" does, the two equate with each other in the sense that the Holy Spirit *is* Jesus' Spirit, so that again Luke comes close to ascribing absolute deity to Jesus (compare the comments on 15:40).

16:9–10: And a vision appeared to Paul during the night: a man, a certain Macedonian, was standing and urging him and saying, "On coming through [that is, on crossing the Aegean Sea, which lies between Asia Minor and Macedonia-Greece], **help us." ¹⁰And when he'd seen the vision, immediately we sought to go out from** [Troas] **into Macedonia, concluding that God had summoned us to proclaim the good news to them** [the Macedonians]. "Concluding" means something like our colloquial expression, "connecting the dots." In other words, Paul and his companions, to whom he must have reported the vision, put the Spirit's forbidding them to speak the word in Asia and not allowing them passage to Bithynia together with the vision of a Macedonian's call for help. Just as 2 + 2 = 4, the conclusion followed that God had summoned them to help. And when we put together the Holy Spirit's forbidding, the disallowing by Jesus' Spirit, and God's summoning, something very like the doctrine of the Trinity emerges. The Macedonian's "standing" in Paul's vision suggests a note of desperation in the "urging" to come over and help. But through ignorance of the gospel the Macedonian doesn't know what kind of help is needed. So Paul and his companions have to interpret the need for help in evangelistic terms. The immediacy with which they sought to cross the Aegean Sea stresses their obedience to the divine summons and their eagerness to proclaim the good news to needy people. "We *sought* to go out from [Troas] into Macedonia" implies they needed to find a ship sailing there that would take them aboard. "*We* sought" and "summoned *us*" imply that the author of Acts is a member of Paul's party, probably (though not certainly) by having joined at this point.

16:11–13: And on setting sail from Troas, we ran a straight course to Samothrace [an island in the northern Aegean Sea], **and the next** [day] **to Neapolis** [a harbor city on the coast of Macedonia], **¹²and from there** [inland about ten miles] **to Philippi, which is a first city** [= a prominent one] **of a district of Macedonia, a** [Roman] **colony** [referring to Philippi, not to "a district" or to "Macedonia"]. "A straight course" and "the next day" indicate that Paul and his companions wasted no time answering God's summons that they proclaim the good news to Macedonians. The description of Philippi as prominent also hints that they aim to reach with the good news a city of some importance. The further description of Philippi as a Roman colony, settled by veterans of the Roman army as we know from other sources, prepares both for a charge that Paul and his companions advocate behavior illegal by Roman standards (16:20–21) and for the appeal of Paul to his and Silas's Roman citizenship (16:37–39). **And we were spending some days in this city.** This statement, along with others in the passage that use "we" and "us," makes the account derive from an eyewitness, the author (compare Luke 1:1–4). **¹³And on the Sabbath day we went outside the gate** [of the city] **to a riverside where we were thinking a place of prayer was. And on sitting down, we were speaking to the assembled women.** Apparently there *was* a place of prayer beside the river. Luke doesn't say whether it was a building, such as a synagogue; for his interest runs to the telling of good news to the assembled women. Apparently no men are present. Again Luke doesn't say why, but the upcoming description of one of the women as "worshiping God" (16:14) suggests a group of Gentile women who apart from their husbands had started worshiping and praying to the one true God. In any case, Luke focuses on the evangelizing of these women. This focus helps balance the emphasis elsewhere in Acts on men. The gospel is for women as well as men.

16:14–15: And a certain woman by the name of Lydia from the city of Thyatira, a seller of purple-dyed [fabric], **worshiping God, was listening, whose heart the Lord opened so as to attend to the things being spoken by Paul. ¹⁵And when she and her household had been baptized, she urged** [us], **saying, "If you** [plural] **have judged me to be believing the Lord** [as apparently you have by baptizing me], **on coming into my house, stay." And she prevailed on us.** The gospel's attracting a pious woman like Lydia shows it to be worthy of belief by other religiously sensitive people as well. Her baptism indicates that "attend[ing] to the things being spoken by Paul" entailed believing the gospel. "Worshiping God" and "was listening" are so closely connected that it seems her listening constituted worship of God. The opening of her heart by the Lord stresses that salvation is his work in the receiving of it just as in making it available. The baptism of Lydia's household broadens this evangelistic success; and her insistence on providing hospitality to Paul and his companions exhibits Christian hospitality, and therefore an attractive communitarianism, right from the start.

16:16–18: And it happened that as we were going to the place of prayer, there met us a certain slave girl, having a spirit of divination, who as such [referring to the slave girl] **was providing her masters** [= owners] **much profit by fortune-telling** [for a fee]. **¹⁷While following behind Paul and us, this** [slave girl] **kept shouting, saying, "These men are slaves of the Most High God** [compare Luke 8:28], **who as such are announcing to you** [the surrounding populace] **the way of salvation." ¹⁸And she kept doing this for many days. But on getting annoyed and turning around, Paul said to the spirit, "I order you in the name of Jesus Christ to come out of her." And it came out that very hour.** "As we were going to the place of prayer" calls attention to the piety of Paul and his companions. They didn't meet the slave girl. She met them. "Having a spirit of divination" indicates it was this spirit that prompted the girl to meet them, and then to follow them and shout repeatedly and persistently. "These men" reflects her proximity while following. "These *men*" sets off Paul and his companions as human beings over against "the Most High God," and "slaves" describes their "announcing the way of salvation" as a service to God, so that the spirit of divination is giving supernatural attestation to Paul, his companions, and their message, an attestation that Luke cites to impress prospective converts with the truth of the gospel. "To you" implies that those to whom Paul and his companions have been speaking are also hearing what the slave girl shouts. "While following behind Paul and us," "kept shouting," and "kept doing this for many days" underline that Paul exercised great patience before getting annoyed and that therefore the upcoming seizure, dragging, charging, disrobing, beating, and imprisonment of him and Silas will have no justification. At this point it would be easy to speculate that Paul finally got annoyed because he didn't like being advertised by a fortune-teller. But Luke doesn't say so. Therefore his emphasis falls on the success of Paul's exorcism. The annoyance merely sets up for the exorcism, and the exorcism proves successful because of Paul's using "the name of Jesus Christ." Thus the slave girl, who'd been shouting that Paul and his companions were announcing the way of salvation, is herself saved (compare 4:12). "The *way* of salvation" is the road that leads to salvation at the end (compare the comments on 9:2 and see Luke 13:23–24; Matthew 7:13–14).

16:19–21: But on seeing that their hope of profit had gone out [with the exit of the spirit that had enabled the slave girl to tell fortunes], **her masters—on taking hold of Paul and Silas—dragged** [them] **into the marketplace before the rulers.** ²⁰**And on bringing them to the officers, they said, "These men, being Jews, are throwing our city into confusion;** ²¹**and they're announcing standards that are unlawful for us, being Romans, to welcome or practice."** After calling the city authorities "the rulers," Luke calls them "the officers," probably by way of reflecting the military background of those who'd settled Philippi as a Roman colony (compare 16:12). Putting the slave girl's masters in a self-serving and otherwise bad light are (1) their valuing her profitability to them above her deliverance from the spirit that had possessed her; (2) their *dragging* Paul and Silas; (3) their pejorative citation of Paul's and Silas's Jewishness; (4) their blowing up the exorcism into city-wide confusion; (5) the covering up of their pecuniary motive with a false charge that Paul and Silas were announcing standards unlawful for Romans to welcome or practice; and (6) their failure to specify any such standards. The standards *supposedly* being announced by Paul and Silas contrast with "the way of salvation" *actually* being announced by them.

16:22–24: And the crowd rose up together against them; and the officers, on ripping off their [Paul's and Silas's] **clothes, were commanding** [policemen] **to beat** [them] **with rods** [compare 2 Corinthians 11:24–25]. ²³**And after laying many blows on them, they threw them into prison, ordering the jailer to guard them**

securely, ²⁴**who** [referring to the jailer] **on receiving such an order threw them into the inner prison** [for maximum security] **and secured their feet in the wood** [= in stocks for even further security]. The crowd acts as a mob, the officers like dupes of the slave girl's owners. Paul and Silas are given no chance to answer the charges brought against them. They're beaten with many blows of a rod and thrown into prison without so much as a verdict of guilty. But their suffering carries out God's preannounced plan, particularly for Paul (see 9:16). Luke's introduction of the jailer and the emphasis on keeping Paul and Silas securely prepare for the next episode, which will reverse the jailer's role and wreak havoc on the rulers' order and the means of security.

16:25–26: But toward midnight Paul and Silas, praying, were singing praise to God; and the prisoners [that is, the rest of them] **were listening to them.** ²⁶**And suddenly a great earthquake occurred, so that the foundations of the prison were shaken. And at once all the doors were opened and the fetters of all** [the prisoners] **came loose.** As often, Luke highlights the piety of Christians, this time by noting Paul's and Silas's praying and singing praise to God even in prison and even toward midnight. What good news it must be to produce such piety under such circumstances! The listening of other prisoners makes them earwitnesses to this piety. Suddenness dramatizes the earthquake as a divine response to the injustice perpetrated on Paul and Silas. The greatness of the earthquake magnifies this response and is certified by the shaking of the prison's foundations, the immediate opening of all the prison doors, and the loosening of all the prisoners' fetters. The double use of "all" leaves no door unopened, no prisoner still fettered.

16:27–29: And the jailer, on waking out of [his] **sleep and seeing the doors of the prison opened, drawing** [his] **sword he was about to do away with** [= kill] **himself, supposing the prisoners had escaped.** He was responsible for keeping them securely in prison. Better to kill himself than to suffer the indignity of public punishment, perhaps even execution. ²⁸**But with a loud voice Paul called, saying, "You shouldn't do yourself any harm, for we're all here."** Paul hasn't taken the opportunity to escape; and despite the jailer's having thrown him into the inner prison and secured his feet in stocks, Paul calls out to save the jailer—in more than one way, it'll turn out. The loudness of Paul's voice stresses the strength of his concern for the jailer's salvation. Luke doesn't tell how it happened that none of the other prisoners took the opportunity to escape. It's enough that their not doing so will make possible the jailer's salvation. ²⁹**And on asking for lights, he jumped in and fell down trembling before Paul and Silas.** The jailer wanted lights to see for himself whether all the prisoners were still there. "*Asking* for lights" implies his enlisting help, probably that of his household since they're to be mentioned shortly. His jumping in shows eagerness to check out the truth of Paul's statement. That he "fell down . . . before Paul and Silas" implies his discovery that all the prisoners are indeed still there. Together with the falling down, the trembling that accompanied it contrasts with the jailer's earlier rough treatment of Paul and Silas. God has turned the tables, for the gospel can't be stopped.

16:30–32: And on bringing them outside, he said, "Lords, what must I do to be saved?" ³¹And they said, "Believe on the Lord Jesus, and you'll be saved—also your household." ³²And they spoke the word of the Lord to him along with all those in his household. Most English translations have "Sirs" instead of "Lords." It's true that the underlying Greek word can carry either meaning, in addition to the meaning "master" or "owner," as for the slave girl's masters/owners (16:16, 19). But here it looks as though the jailer—because of the great earthquake, perhaps also because he thought Paul and Silas had supernaturally kept the other prisoners from escaping—is addressing Paul and Silas as though they're deities in human guise who can save him if he does what they tell him to do. His having fallen at their feet with trembling supports this impression. But they quickly point away from themselves to Jesus as "the Lord" who'll save him if he rests his faith on him (compare 4:12: "And there's salvation in no one else, for under heaven there's no other name that's been given among human beings by which we must be saved"). "Also your household" expands the evangelistic enterprise that Paul and Silas are making out of the earthquake. From his own standpoint, the jailer may have been asking what he must do to be saved from execution for failure to keep the prisoners secure, in which case Paul and Silas answer in the far more important terms of eternal salvation. At the level of Luke's text, though, it's a question of eternal salvation from the very start. "The word of the Lord" that Paul and Barnabas proceed to speak will have consisted in particulars of the gospel. Since this word is spoken not only to the jailer but also to "all those in his household," it appears that they're the ones on whom he'd called for lights (16:29).

16:33–34: And on taking them along at that hour of the night, he washed away [the blood] **from the blows** [they'd received]**; and he was baptized—also all his** [household members]—**at once.** ³⁴**And on bringing them up into** [his] **house, he set a table** [with food] **and, having believed God, exulted with all** [his] **household.** The jailer had thrown Paul and Silas into the inner prison, secured their feet in stocks, and then feared they and the other prisoners had escaped. In a dramatic turnaround, he now takes Paul and Silas alongside himself from the prison, cleanses their wounds, gets baptized, brings them to his home, and treats them to a celebratory meal. "At that hour of the night" (midnight according to 16:25) adds to the drama. The jailer can't wait to make amends. Nor can he wait to get baptized, as "at once" indicates; and his baptism indicates he has believed on the Lord Jesus to be saved. The baptism also of "all his [household members]" indicates they too have

believed. "*All* his household" stresses the power of "the word of the Lord" that they'd heard. "Having believed God" replaces "believ[ing] on the Lord Jesus" and thus comes close yet again to equating Jesus as Lord with God. At least the association is close enough to point toward Jesus' deity alongside that of God the Father. Exultation reflects the joy generated by believing the gospel, a theme prominent in Luke-Acts (see an early instance in Luke 2:10). "Exulted with all his household" portrays a family happy and united in their newfound faith, the kind of family prospective converts should want to make for themselves by believing God, which is to believe on the Lord Jesus.

16:35–36: And when day came, the officers [= the city rulers] **sent** [their] **policemen, saying** [to the jailer]**, "Let those men go." ³⁶And the jailer reported these words to Paul: "The officers have sent** [orders] **that you** [plural, for Silas as well as Paul] **be let go. On coming out** [of the jail]**, then, travel on now** [from the city] **in peace."** So Paul and Silas have returned to jail. We might speculate that the city rulers wanted Paul and Silas let go to forestall further earthquakes, or that they figured a night in jail had taught Paul and Silas a lesson. But Luke doesn't say so, because his interest focuses solely and appropriately on the *salvific* effect of the earthquake: it resulted in the salvation of the jailer and all his household. "Travel on now *in peace*" contrasts with the upset that Paul and Silas were falsely accused of causing and also with the beating, jailing, and stocks they'd suffered.

16:37: But Paul said to them, "Though we're Romans, they threw [us] **into prison after beating us in public without condemnation** [that is, without putting us on trial and reaching a verdict of guilty]**. And now they're throwing us out in secret? No way! Rather, on coming** [here] **they themselves are to bring us out!"** Though it was the jailer who'd reported to Paul the words of release, Paul replies "to *them*," who'll turn out to be the policemen sent by the city rulers. For the first time it appears that both he and Silas have Roman citizenship. This makes ironic the false charge that they'd been announcing standards unlawful for Roman citizens (16:20–21). What in fact had happened was that their rights as citizens had been grossly violated, whereas they'd shown good citizenship by passing up an opportunity to escape the jail and by returning there after the jailer had taken them to his home. The mistreatment of Roman citizens such as Paul and Silas—in violation of their rights—could backfire on the city rulers, so that Paul is now emboldened to demand they escort him and Silas out of prison rather than surreptitiously throwing them out. As the counterpart of "threw [us] *into* prison," "throwing us *out*" portrays the release as a self-serving attempt by the city rulers to keep Paul and Silas from pressing their own charges against them.

16:38–40: And the policemen reported these words to the officers [= city rulers]**. And they got scared on hearing, "They're Romans." ³⁹And on coming** [to the prison] **they implored them and, on bringing** [them]

out, they were asking [them] **to go away from the city.**
⁴⁰But on coming out from the prison they went into
Lydia's [house]**; and seeing the brothers, they encour-**
aged [them] **and went out** [of the city]. So the very
rulers who publicly humiliated Paul and Silas suffer
themselves the humiliation of acceding to Paul's demand
that they come and serve as a kind of honor guard by
escorting him and Silas out of the prison. Adding to the
rulers' public humiliation is their having to implore Paul
and Silas to come out of the prison, as though they had
to say, "*Please* come out, because you don't deserve to
be there despite our having thrown you in." The request
that Paul and Silas go out of town as well as come out
of the prison piles yet more humiliation on the rulers.
They can't handle the presence of these preachers. And
adding a final touch of humiliation is Paul's and Silas's
snubbing the rulers' request by going to Lydia's house,
seeing the brothers there, and encouraging them before
leaving town. "The brothers" calls to mind the attractively familial character of Christian communities.

IN THE MACEDONIAN CITY
OF THESSALONICA
Acts 17:1–9

17:1–3: And after taking a road through Amphi-
polis and Apollonia [cities in southeast Macedonia]**,**
they came to Thessalonica [a seaport also in southeast
Macedonia]**, where there was a synagogue of the Jews.**
²And in accordance with what was customary for Paul,
he went in [the synagogue] **to them** [the Jews congregated there] **and for three Sabbaths conversed with**
them from the Scriptures ³by opening [the Scriptures]
and adducing, "It was necessary for the Christ to suf-
fer and resurrect from among the dead," and, **"This**
Jesus whom I'm proclaiming to you [as distinguished
from other men named Jesus] **is the Christ."** To reemphasize the piety of Paul, Luke describes Paul's entering
the synagogue as customary for him (see 13:5, 14; 14:1
and compare 16:13, 16). "To them" seems unnecessary
for Luke to write. *Of course* Jews would be in attendance
at "a synagogue of the Jews." But Luke inserts "to them"
to accent Paul's ongoing concern for the Jews' salvation
despite his earlier (but only local) turning from Jews to
Gentiles (13:44–47). Thus the link with Judaism, an ancient and therefore venerable religion, is strengthened.
Paul's conversing with the Jews "from the Scriptures,"
their own Bible, strengthens this link yet more. "Opening" the Scriptures means interpreting them (see Luke
24:32 with 24:27). "Adducing, 'It was necessary for the
Christ to suffer and resurrect from among the dead,' and,
'This Jesus . . . is the Christ'" specifies Paul's interpretation (compare Luke 24:25–27, 46). More particularly, "it
was necessary" situates the suffering and resurrection of
Jesus as the Christ in God's plan, foretold in Scripture, so
that the suffering and resurrection carried out the plan
and fulfilled the Scripture. "For three Sabbaths" displays
the length to which Paul went in his attempt to bring the
Jews to salvation.

17:4: And some of them [the Jews] **were persuaded**
and allotted to Paul and Silas; and a multitudinous
multitude of devout Greeks and not a few of the fore-
most women [were allotted to Paul and Silas]. Paul's conversing from the Scriptures proved persuasive to some
of the Jews. But Luke emphasizes the larger numerical
success among Gentiles. "A multitude" would seem to
suffice for this emphasis. But to heighten it Luke writes
about "a *multitudinous* multitude" (see the comments
on Luke 23:27 for this wordplay). By negating "a few,"
"*not* a few" means "many." The devoutness of the Greek
converts and the eminence of the women converts add
religious and social distinction to the numerical success.
In effect, Luke is telling prospective converts, "Follow the
crowd and the elites. You'll be far from alone, and you'll
be in lofty company both religiously and socially. For the
good news attracts the best as well as the many." But what
does it mean that those who believed "were allotted" to
Paul and Silas? Most English translations have "joined"
or a similar verb, but the original really means to assign
by lot or, in the passive, to be allotted to (compare the
casting of lots to determine the Lord's choice for Judas
Iscariot's replacement [1:26; also 1:17; 8:21; 26:18; Luke
23:34]). So the allotting of converts to Paul and Silas refers to God's giving Paul and Silas the fruit of their evangelistic labor—in other words, evangelistic success again.

17:5–9: But the [unpersuaded] **Jews, on getting**
jealous and taking certain evil men of the shiftless
ones [hanging around the marketplace] **and forming a**
crowd, were setting the city in an uproar. And on ar-
riving at Jason's house they were seeking to bring them
[Paul and Silas] **forth to the populace. ⁶But on not find-**
ing them, they were dragging Jason and some brothers
before the city rulers, screaming, "These upsetters of
the inhabited [earth] **whom Jason has welcomed** [as
guests] **have come here too. ⁷And these** [men] **are all**
acting against Caesar's decrees by saying there's an-
other king, Jesus." ⁸And they stirred up the crowd and
the city rulers who were hearing these things. ⁹And
on receiving a considerable [sum] **from Jason and the**
rest [of the believers]**, they** [the city rulers] **let them**
go. The jealousy of the unpersuaded Jews arises out of
Paul's and Silas's having persuaded a very large number
of the Greeks who'd been attending the Jews' synagogue,
reemphasizes the huge success of the gospel, and tars
those unpersuaded Jews' subsequent actions with a base
motive. The recruiting of evil ne'er-do-wells from the
marketplace to help do their dirty work tars their actions further. The crowd they form with the ne'er-do-
wells' help turns into an uproarious mob that stands in
stark contrast with the harmoniously family-like communities of Christians that Luke portrays throughout
Acts and alludes to here in his reference to "Jason *and*
some brothers." Luke uses this contrast as an evangelistic
tool. "Seeking to bring [Paul and Silas] forth *to the popu-*
lace" betrays mob-lynching as their enemies' purpose.
"*Dragging* Jason and some brothers before the city rulers" displays both savagery and the attribution of guilt by
association with Paul and Silas. For the city rulers—but

not for Luke's audience—"screaming" masks falsity with high decibels. Paul and Silas haven't "upset the inhabited earth." They've been proclaiming "peace on earth" (Luke 2:14). And though Paul proclaims the kingdom *of God* (14:22; 19:8; 28:23, 31), he hasn't been presenting *Jesus* as a kingly rival to Caesar, that is, as a king who requires his subjects to act "against Caesar's decrees." On the contrary, Paul, Silas, and their converts stand as model subjects of Caesar (compare Luke 20:20–26 and see Luke 23:2–3 for Jesus' own refusal to say he was the king of the Jews). "These [men] are *all* acting against Caesar's decrees" alludes indirectly to the evangelistic success of Paul and Silas and raises the accusation to a height of falsity. Because of this false accusation the crowd and the city rulers were "stirred up." As a result, Jason and the rest of the believers had to purchase their own release for a considerable sum of money. Their having to do so counts as a final item of injustice. If Paul and Silas were guilty as charged, we'd call the purchase of their release a bribe. But since they weren't guilty, we could call it bail—of a permanent sort.

IN THE MACEDONIAN CITY OF BEREA
Acts 17:10–15

17:10: And immediately, during the night, the brothers sent both Paul and Silas out of [Thessalonica] **to Berea** [a city southwest of Thessalonica but still in Macedonia], **who as such** [referring to Paul and Silas], **on arriving, went right into the synagogue of the Jews.** Christian brotherly love led the Thessalonian believers to send Paul and Silas away immediately even though it was nighttime or, from another angle, *because* it was nighttime. The cover of darkness made escape easier, and the mob scene of the preceding day posed so great a danger to Paul and Silas that no precaution seemed too great. "Who *as such*," meaning "as fugitives," points up that despite their having to flee from unbelieving Jews in Thessalonica, on arrival in Berea they "went right into the synagogue of the Jews." Most English translations don't have "right" or any word corresponding to it. But to stress the admirable evangelistic courage of Paul and Silas, Luke uses a verbal form that merits the translation "went *right* into . . . ."

17:11–12: And these [Jews] **were better-bred than the ones in Thessalonica, who as such** [referring to the Berean Jews as better-bred] **welcomed the word** [of the gospel] **with all eagerness, examining the Scriptures day by day** [to see] **whether these things** [the contents of "the word"] **might be so.** "All" pitches up these Jews' "eagerness" to the nth degree. According to Luke, then, to "welcome the word with all eagerness" by way of "examining the Scriptures day by day [to see] whether these things might be so" signals good breeding. It's high class to give the gospel a fair investigation. [12]**On the one hand, therefore, many of them** [the Jews] **believed; also not a few of the eminent Greek women and men** [believed]. "Therefore" indicates that eager, daily, and open-minded examination of the Scriptures leads to

belief in Jesus because he fulfilled those Scriptures. The word of the gospel tallies with them. "*Many* of [the Jews] believed" highlights the persuasiveness of the correlation between the Jewish Scriptures (the Old Testament) and the good news concerning Jesus. This correlation proves persuasive even to not a few Gentiles ("*Greek* women and men"). As in 17:4, by negating "a few," "*not* a few" means "many." Luke mentions the eminence of the non-Jewish converts to show that believing the gospel isn't an unclassy thing to do. On the contrary! And the mention of women as well as and before men underlines that the good news is for women at least as much as for men.

17:13–15: On the other hand [as opposed to the classy behavior of the Berean Jews], **when the Jews from Thessalonica came to know that the word of God had been proclaimed by Paul also in Berea, they came there as well, shaking and stirring up the crowds.** So a mob scene, like the one in Thessalonica, threatens. Exacerbating the threat is the use of both "shaking" and "stirring up" for these Jews' whipping the Berean populace ("the crowds") into a frenzy. Thus the Thessalonian Jews brand themselves even further as hellbent opponents of God's word rather than as fair-minded students of the Scriptures. [14]**But immediately then** [= at that very time] **the brothers sent Paul out of** [Berea, which was inland] **to travel as far as to the** [Aegean] **sea, and both Silas and Timothy stayed there** [in Berea]. See the comments on 17:10 for "the brothers" and the immediacy of their sending Paul away. Here the adding of "then" to "immediately" increases the emphasis on immediacy. [15]**And the ones who were escorting Paul brought** [him] **as far as Athens.** The *sending* of Paul gives way to the *escorting* of Paul, and "as far as the *sea*" gives way to "as far as *Athens*." These shifts mark an escalation of brotherly concern for Paul's welfare. Luke wants prospective converts to know that Christians look out for each other. **And on receiving** [from Paul] **a command** [to be relayed] **to Silas and Timothy that they should come to him as quickly as possible, they** [the Berean brothers] **left.** We weren't told why Silas and Timothy had stayed in Berea, nor are we told here why Paul wanted them to rejoin him post haste in Athens. So it's his authority, represented by "a command" and representing the lordship of Jesus who sent him (9:15), that stands out.

IN THE GREEK CITY OF ATHENS
Acts 17:16–34

17:16–17: And while Paul was waiting for them [Silas and Timothy] **in Athens, his spirit was getting exasperated within him as he was observing that the city was teeming with idols.** [17]**On the one hand, therefore, he was conversing in the synagogue with the Jews and the devout** [Gentiles who attended there (compare 17:2 with comments)], **also in the marketplace every day with those who happened to be there.** By noting Paul's inner exasperation with Athenian idolatry, Luke appeals to prospective converts who have themselves become disaffected with idolatry and thus open to the gospel. "Therefore" means that the irritation motivated Paul to use both the local synagogue and the marketplace as venues for conversing with people for the purpose of getting them to believe in Jesus. So far as the synagogue is concerned, Paul was limited to Sabbath days. But the marketplace provided him a daily opportunity for evangelism, and he took advantage of it.

17:18: On the other hand [that is, as distinguished from Paul's evangelistic efforts], **some of both the Epicurean and Stoic philosophers were having a discussion with him. And some were saying, "What might this plagiarist want to say?"** That is, what's he getting at? The word for "plagiarist" literally means "a seed-picker," but here it's used figuratively for somebody who picks up scraps of knowledge from here and there and passes them off as his own. **And because he was proclaiming Jesus and resurrection as good news, some** [were saying], **"He seems to be a proclaimer of foreign deities."** Apparently they think Paul is proclaiming "Jesus" and "resurrection" as two deities unfamiliar to them— perhaps as male and female consorts, since the Greek word for resurrection (*anastasis*, from which we get the personal name Anastasia) is feminine. The Greek word underlying "deities" appeared numerous times in Luke's Gospel for demons. The philosophers wouldn't have in mind the bad connotation that "demons" conjures up. But Luke and his audience would think of that connotation and regard the philosophers as foolish for using such a word for "Jesus" and "resurrection." Luke pays no attention to the philosophies of the Epicureans and Stoics, though what he'll quote Paul as saying will both agree and disagree with their philosophies. Both he and the Epicureans criticize sacrificing to idols, but his emphasis on God's proximity to human beings goes against Epicurean philosophy. Both Paul and the Stoics trace the human race back to a single source, but his portrayal of God in personal terms disagrees with the impersonalism of Stoic pantheism.

17:19–21: And on taking hold of him they [the philosophers] **led** [Paul] **to the Areopagus** [the city council, perhaps meeting on the hill of that name but popularly called in English Mars' Hill], **saying, "Can we know what this new teaching** [is] **that's being spoken by you?** [20] **For you're bringing into our ears some** [deities] **that are foreign. So we want to know who these** [deities] **are."** [21] **(And all the Athenians and foreign visitors used to spend** [their] **time for nothing other than telling or hearing something novel.)** The philosophers take Paul to the city council for a judgment on the legality of his proclaiming what they thought to be foreign deities, but they address *him* in the presence of the city council instead of addressing the city council in reference to him. This address to him gives him opportunity to present his case. (The hearing will end in conflicting responses rather than in a judgment.) Since in 17:18 the philosophers were speaking of "foreign *deities*," here again it's foreign deities in particular that they ask about, not just "foreign (or 'strange') *things*," as in most English

translations. So the philosophers ask Paul *who* these foreign deities *are*, not *what* these strange things *mean*. And again the reference is to Jesus and resurrection as a supposed pair of deities. Luke attributes the question to a dilettantish but all-consuming thirst for novelty on the part of the Athenians—all of them, including visitors as well as permanent residents. Given Luke's predilection for the tried and true of old tradition, this attribution puts the Athenians in a very bad light. They weren't serious. They were only curious.

17:22–23b: And standing in the midst of the Areopagus [the city council], **Paul said, "Men, Athenians, I observe how very solicitous of** [your] **deities you** [are] **in all respects** [= in every possible way you try to please them and avoid offending them]. [23a–b]**For while going through** [town] **and observing closely your objects of worship, I found even an altar platform** [used for sacrificing] **on which had been inscribed, 'To an unknown god.'"** The Athenians are so concerned not to omit and thus antagonize an object of worship—that is, a deity— who hasn't come to their attention that they've tried to placate him with an altar platform despite his being anonymous to them. No wonder they want to know who the seemingly new deities Jesus and resurrection are! For to know who they are is to be better able to deal with them for one's own benefit.

Paul continues in **17:23c–25: "Therefore** [because of my finding the altar platform for an unknown god], [the object of worship] **that you reverence though not knowing** [who he is]—**I proclaim to you this** [object of worship/deity]." So Paul is proclaiming only one deity, not two; and that deity isn't foreign to the Athenians, for they have an altar platform dedicated to him right in their city. [24]**"The God who made the world and all things in it—this one, being Lord** [= master and owner] **of heaven and earth, doesn't inhabit handmade temples** [compare 7:47–50]. [25]**Nor is he cared for by human hands as though he needs anything, he himself giving life and breath and all things to all** [human beings (compare Isaiah 42:5)]." It's neither appropriate nor needed that the Creator of all should be confined, as idols are, to a temple made by his creatures' hands. And since he provides all human beings with life and all its necessities and benefits, he doesn't need human beings to care for him the way they care for their idols by giving them the shelter of a temple and offerings of food and drink that they supposedly consume overnight. (Actually, the pagan priests surreptitiously take the food and drink.) Human beings don't have to care for God. He cares for them.

17:26–28: "And from one [human being, Adam] **he made every nation of human beings to inhabit all the face** [= surface] **of the earth, having determined fixed seasons and the boundaries of their habitation** [27]**so that they would seek God, if then indeed they might grope for him and find** [him]—**his being not far, even indeed, from each one of us.** [28]**For in him we live and move** [= go here and there] **and exist, as even some of**

your own poets have said: 'For we too are this one's [that is, God's] **offspring**' [a quote taken from Aratus, though nearly the same statement occurs in Cleanthes' 'Hymn to Zeus']." To prepare for a universal call to repentance (17:30) Paul declares that God has given all humanity a common ancestor and a common place of habitation (as opposed to the Athenians' belief that they originated from the soil of their own part of Greece, Attica). God's predetermination of agricultural seasons specifies one way in which he has given "life and breath and all [things] to all people" (17:25 [compare 14:17]). "The boundaries of their habitation" refers to geographical boundaries within which he has also predetermined that each nation live—this too for the sake of human life and breath and all things (compare Deuteronomy 32:8). So "all the face of the *earth*" means all the surface of the *ground* (divided up among the nations) as distinct from the seas. God has granted all human beings this common grace, Paul says, so that they might seek God. "Then" introduces a possible consequence of seeking God, the consequence of finding him. "Indeed" stresses the need to grope for him. But "if," "might," and "grope for" reflect the difficulty of finding God through common grace alone even though he's "not far . . . from each one of us." This difficulty lays the foundation of need for a clarion proclamation of the gospel. Another "indeed," buttressed by "even," underlines God's proximity; and "from each one of us" makes the proximity both universal and individual. So Paul has proceeded from "every *nation*" to "each *one*" in further preparation for an upcoming call to individual repentance. With "of us" Paul includes himself among his audience as an indication of God's common—that is, universally shared—grace. "*In him* we live and move and exist" explains just how close God is to us: he's our very environment. And Paul backs up his point with a quotation from the pagan poet Aratus, whom Paul's and Luke's non-Jewish audiences held in high regard. The use of this quotation by other pagan poets justifies the plural in "even some of your own poets." With "we too are this one's [God's] offspring," compare Luke's having traced Jesus' genealogy back through Adam to God himself (Luke 3:23, 38).

17:29–31: "**Being God's offspring, therefore, we ought not suppose the deity to be like gold or silver or stone,** [that is,] **a sculpture of a human being's craftsmanship and imagination.**" Since we human beings aren't sculpted out of gold, silver, or stone yet are God's offspring, he shouldn't be thought to be like such images. If we take after him and live, move, and exist in him, he can't be like lifeless, stationary idols that have no existence apart from human artifice. [30]"**On the one hand, therefore** [since God isn't like an idol], **having overlooked the times of ignorance, God is now directing human beings everywhere that they should all repent,** [31]**because he has established a day on which he's going to judge the inhabited** [earth] **with righteousness** [compare Psalm 9:8] **by a man whom he has designated, having provided confirmation to all** [human beings] **by resurrecting him from among the dead.**"

The idolatry of pagans shows them to have been, and presently be, ignorant of God the Creator—this despite his previously mentioned common grace and proximity. Such ignorance on the part of the Athenians in particular is encapsulated in their inscription on an altar platform, "To an unknown God"; for in Luke's Greek, "ignorance" and "unknown" are noun and adjective forms of the same basic word. Sadly and ironically, "the times of ignorance" coincided with the "fixed seasons" of the agricultural cycle that were designed to dispel ignorance of God. He "overlooked the times of ignorance" by not bringing human beings to the final judgment. But his having recently resurrected "a man whom he has designated" to carry out such a judgment signals that God will no longer overlook idolatrous ignorance. He now demands repentance, here especially of idolatry. "Everywhere" and "all" make the demand universal in its application to people, called "human beings" to indicate their subservience to God. The man he has designated will act as his agent in judging the inhabited earth—that is—its inhabitants. God's having "*established* a day [= fixed it on his calendar] on which he's *going* to judge" underscores the certainty of that day of judgment. So too does his "having provided *confirmation*" by resurrecting the designated man. The addressing of this confirmation "to all" makes it sufficient for everybody whether or not they act on it. "With righteousness" puts the judgment on a moral basis.

At this point we expect Paul to identify Jesus as the man whom God designated to judge on his behalf and whom he resurrected from among the dead. But the Athenians interrupt Paul. *17:32:* **On the other hand** [as opposed to God's now directing all to repent (17:30)], **on hearing about a resurrection of dead people, some started sneering; but others said, "We'll hear you about this again too** [= in addition to the present occasion]." Strikingly, Luke completes *Paul's* "On the one hand" (17:30) with *his own* "On the other hand." The completion is designed to complement the demand for repentance with the audience's mixed response. The plural in "a resurrection of *dead people*" indicates that the audience took the judgment of all human beings by the agency of a resurrected man to entail the resurrection of other deceased human beings as well (compare 10:42; 23:6; 24:15). At best, most Greeks could contemplate the possibility of immortality for a disembodied soul. Most of them didn't consider even that a possibility, though. Bodily resurrection therefore seemed absurd. So it's no surprise that some started sneering at the talk about resurrection. Even in this climate of skepticism, however, Paul's proclamation—truncated though it is by the Athenians' interruption—proves its power. Others desire more of Paul's preaching. "Again too" is redundant. But the very redundancy emphasizes the others' desire to hear more.

17:33–34: **Thus Paul went out from their midst.** "Thus" describes Paul's exit as accompanied by a mixed response. [34]**And having joined him, some men believed, among whom** [were] **both Dionysius the Are-**

opagite [= a member of the city council], **plus a woman by the name of Damaris, and others with them.** Testifying to Luke's historical research (Luke 1:1–4) are the names "Dionysius the Areopagite" and "Damaris." These and other Athenians joined Paul to hear more about the gospel (17:32), and this hearing issued in their believing it. Dionysius, a member of the city council no less, believed. His belief demonstrates that the gospel appeals to the high and mighty, and rightly so, as well as to the down and out. So don't let your high social status, if that's what you have, make you think that Christian conversion is beneath you. And the mention of a woman by name broadens the appeal genderwise too. "And others with them" strikes as often the note of numerical success, which success confirms evangelism as God's program (compare 5:33–39).

IN THE GREEK CITY OF CORINTH
Acts 18:1–17

18:1–3: **On withdrawing from Athens after these things** [that had happened there], **he went to Corinth** [on the isthmus connecting central and southern Greece]. ²**And on finding a certain Jew by the name of Aquila (a Pontic by birth)** [in other words, he was a native of Pontus, a region in northeast Asia Minor], **having recently come from Italy—and Priscilla his wife—because Claudius** [emperor at this time] **had ordered all the Jews to withdraw from Rome,** [Paul] **approached them** ³**and because of being of the same trade was staying with them and working** [with them]. **For they were tentmakers by trade.** So the forced withdrawal of Aquila and Priscilla from Rome and their recent coming to Corinth coincided with Paul's voluntary withdrawal from Athens and present coming to Corinth. Claudius's having "ordered *all* the Jews to withdraw from Rome" may hint at divine providence for Paul, since Aquila and Priscilla might otherwise have stayed in Rome. Whatever the case, Paul has companions with whom to stay, Silas and Timothy being in Macedonia still (17:14), and also partners in tentmaking so as to support himself (compare 1 Corinthians 9:8–18; 2 Corinthians 11:9; 12:13–14, 16).

18:4–5: **And he was conversing in the synagogue every Sabbath and trying to persuade both Jews and Greeks** [who attended along with the Jews]. From 17:2 we know that Paul was conversing from the Scriptures (the Old Testament) to show it was necessary for the Christ to suffer and resurrect from among the dead and that the Christ is Jesus. "*Every* Sabbath" indicates a prolonged, persistent effort to persuade the audiences. "*Both* Jews *and* Greeks" stresses the universal address of the good news. ⁵**And when both Silas and Timothy came down from Macedonia** [a mountainous region, whereas Corinth lay barely above sea level (compare 17:15)], **Paul started being engrossed with the word by way of solemnly testifying to the Jews that the Christ is Jesus.** The arrival of Silas and Timothy released Paul from having to make tents for a living, so that he could (and did) proclaim the gospel fulltime. Had Silas and Timothy

brought an offering of money from Christians in Macedonia (compare 2 Corinthians 11:8–9; Philippians 1:5; 4:14–16)? "*Both* Silas *and* Timothy" may imply an earlier coming of Timothy alone from Macedonia (see 1 Thessalonians 3:1–6). The engrossment of Paul "with the word"—that is, in "testifying that the Christ is Jesus"—is itself a testimony to the gospel's power. It turned the chief persecutor into the chief evangelist! "To the Jews" shows that despite rejections of the gospel by Jews in other localities (but not by all of them), Paul keeps trying to persuade them from one locality to another. The link between Judaism and the gospel isn't to be broken except by unbelieving Jews themselves. And when they break it, they delink themselves from their own Scriptures. For the gospel stands foursquare on those ancient, inspired writings. The word order in "the Christ is Jesus" shows that Paul starts with the Jewish Scriptures and proceeds to their fulfillment in Jesus just as in Athens he started with an unknown god and proceeded to the one true God, who has revealed himself in Jesus (17:16–31).

18:6–8: **And because they were opposing and slandering** [Paul], **shaking** [the dust] **out of** [his] **clothes** [compare 13:51 with comments] **he told them, "Your blood** [is] **on your head."** In both instances, "your" is plural; so "head" is a collective singular. The shaking and the statement match up; they both indicate a coming judgment for which Paul isn't responsible, as follows: **"I'm clean** [= free of responsibility, because you've now heard the gospel from my lips]. **From now on I'll go to the Gentiles** [so far as Corinth is concerned (see 19:8–10; 28:17–24 for Paul's further gospelizing of Jews in other localities)]**."** The abruptness with which Paul introduces both "I'm clean" and "From now on I'll go to the Gentiles" lends force, even disgust, to his statements. ⁷**And on moving from there** [the synagogue] **he went into the house of a certain** [Greek] **worshiper of God by the name of Titius Justus, whose house was next door to the synagogue.** You'd think that Paul's moving right next door to the Jews' synagogue would have infuriated them, most especially the ruler of the synagogue. ⁸**But Crispus, the synagogue ruler, believed the Lord along with his whole household! And hearing** [that he and his household had believed], **many of the Corinthians were believing and getting baptized** [compare 1 Corinthians 1:14]. The conversion of no less a personage than a synagogue ruler, plus all the members of his household, exhibits the power of the gospel and triggers other conversions, whose abundance exhibits the gospel's power even further. This power originates from the Holy Spirit, who fills evangelists like Paul (1:8; 9:17). "Believed the Lord" means believing what the Lord was saying through his Spirit in Paul. "Getting baptized" gives outward evidence of inner belief. So if you believe, show it by getting baptized.

18:9–11: **And the Lord told Paul through a vision at night, "Don't be afraid** [compare 1 Corinthians 2:3]. **Rather, go on speaking. And you shouldn't hush up,** ¹⁰**because I'm with you and no one will lay** [hands] **on** you so as to harm you, because I have much people [= many people, but in a collective sense for the church as a new people of God, as in 15:14] in this city." [11]And he settled [there] a year and six months, teaching God's word among them. In view of the close shaves Paul had in Philippi, Thessalonica, and Berea, his settling in Corinth for a year and a half exhibits admirable courage. As a matter of fact, he's about to get accused before a provincial governor. In accordance with the Lord's promise, though, no harm will come to him. So he needn't be afraid. Alone, "go on speaking" or "you shouldn't hush up" would have sufficed. But the latter is added to the former to underline that the Lord has "much people" in Corinth, which underlines in turn the ongoing success of the gospel. "Teaching God's word" defines what Paul should "speak," and does speak in courageous obedience. In effect, "because I'm with you" and "because I have much people in this city" change Gamaliel's "*if* this plan or this action . . . is from God, you won't be able to demolish them [evangelists]" to "*since* this plan or this action . . . is from God . . . ." For to resist is to "be found fighting even against God" (5:39).

18:12–13: And while Gallio was proconsul [provincial governor] **of Achaia** [central and southern Greece], **with mutual fervor the Jews assaulted Paul and brought him to the judgment platform** [the same word as for an altar platform in 17:23, but here a platform used for hearing cases rather than for offering sacrifices], [13]**saying, "This** [guy] **is successfully persuading people to worship God in a fashion contrary to the Law."** The "mutual fervor" of these unbelieving Jews gives their assault against Paul threatening vehemence. By itself, "is persuading" in their accusation would indicate some success on Paul's part. But though Luke uses the simple verb many times throughout Luke-Acts, here he compounds it so as to stress the success (hence, "is *successfully* persuading") and thus make the unbelieving Jews themselves testify to the success of Christian evangelism. From their standpoint the successful persuasion amounted to seduction, but from Luke's standpoint it confirms the truth of the gospel. "To worship God in a fashion contrary to the Law" means either that "God's word," which Paul has been teaching, contradicts the law of Moses or that the Jews are lodging a false accusation against Paul. If a false accusation, he's being charged with the same offense said to have been committed by Stephen, over whose martyrdom Paul presided (6:13; 7:58 [compare 21:27–29, but see 24:14; 25:8; 28:23 for a positive attitude of Paul toward the law of Moses]).

18:14–17: But when Paul was about to open [his] **mouth** [to speak], **Gallio said to the Jews, "On the one hand, O Jews, if it were some crime or evil act of fraud, I'd put up with you in accord with reason** [= it would be reasonable for me to judge the case you've brought against Paul]. [15]**But if there are disputes about a word** [such as the word of God that Paul has been teaching] **and names** [such as the names 'Jesus,' 'Christ,' and 'Lord'] **and your own law** [the Mosaic law as distinguished from

Roman law], **you yourselves shall see** [to it; that is, you'll have to iron out your differences]. **I don't want to be a judge of these things."** [16]**And he** [Gallio] **had them driven away from the judgment platform.** [17]**And they all started beating Sosthenes, the synagogue ruler, in front of the judgment platform after taking hold of him. And none of these things** [that is, neither the beating nor the charge brought against Paul] **was of any concern to Gallio.** So in fulfillment of God's promise that no harm would come to Paul in Corinth (18:9–10), Gallio dismisses the case brought against Paul. And what happens further even exceeds that promise. Gallio has the accusers *driven* away from the judgment platform; and at a little distance but still within full view, the accusers—all of them, no less—beat the ruler of their own synagogue. We could speculate endlessly why they did so, but Luke gives us no clue. As a result, the emphasis falls on the contrast between what might or would have happened to Paul (barring God's promised protection) and what did happen to the leader of Paul's opposition at the hands of that leader's own brothers-in-arms. See 1 Corinthians 1:1 for a Sosthenes associated with Paul in writing that letter—the same Sosthenes as here, only now converted? Perhaps in part as a result of being beaten by his fellow Jews?

BACK TO SYRIAN ANTIOCH BY WAY OF CAESAREA AND JERUSALEM IN ISRAEL
Acts 18:18–22

18:18: And on staying a considerable number of days still, Paul sailed out to Syria after taking leave of the brothers [in Corinth]—**and Priscilla and Aquila** [were sailing] **with him—after getting his head** [of hair] **cut in Cenchrea** [a seaport of Corinth]; **for he had a vow.** Paul's staying a long time in Corinth "still"—that is, after and despite being opposed, defamed, and accused before Gallio—shows him obediently devoted to evangelizing the "much people" the Lord had there. "Paul sailed out to Syria"—but not directly to Syrian Antioch, as Luke will shortly indicate. "Taking leave of the brothers" connotes the familial closeness of Christian community that Luke repeatedly employs to attract converts. The advancing of "Priscilla" ahead of "Aquila" (contrast 18:2) and their accompanying Paul prepare for their teaching the orator Apollos in Ephesus, apparently with Priscilla taking the lead (18:24–26). Luke likes showing to whatever extent he can the prominent role played by women in the Christian movement. Doing so enhances the gospel's appeal to prospective converts among women. And by associating Paul's getting a haircut with a vow he'd taken, Luke underlines the piety of Paul. Luke doesn't explain the vow (though compare 21:23–24; Numbers 6:13–21), so that the accent falls on Paul's piety as such. He's truly religious, not a traveling charlatan. So believe the gospel he proclaims.

18:19–22: And they arrived in Ephesus [a major city in western Asia Minor], **and he** [Paul] **left those** [companions Priscilla and Aquila] **there** [in Ephesus].

But he himself, on going into the synagogue [as opposed to the city at large, where he'd left Priscilla and Aquila], **conversed with the Jews** [about which conversing see the comments on 17:2]. Upon the Jews' rejection of the gospel in Pisidian Antioch and Corinth, Paul turned from them to the Gentiles (13:44–47; 18:5–6). But Ephesus gives him a fresh opportunity to convert Jews. He takes it. [20]**But though they were requesting** [him] **to stay for a longer time, he didn't consent** [to do so]. [21]**Rather, on taking leave of them and saying, "I'll return to you, God willing," he set sail from Ephesus.** [22]**And after coming down to Caesarea** [from the high sea], **on going up** [to Jerusalem] **and greeting the church** [there], **he went down to Antioch** [in Syria]. The Jews' request that Paul stay longer in Ephesus displays the gospel's power of attraction. "God willing" exhibits again the piety of Paul and implies that God directs his evangelistic activities. So they can't be thwarted. And Paul's going up to Jerusalem in Judea and greeting the church there shows that Christian harmony has prevailed over the dispute caused by those from Judea who taught observance of the Mosaic law, beginning with circumcision, as necessary for salvation (15:1).

THE PREPARATORY MINISTRY OF APOLLOS DURING THE START OF PAUL'S THIRD JOURNEY
Acts 18:23–28

18:23–26a: And after spending some time [in Syrian Antioch], **he** [Paul] **went out, going successively through the Galatian region and Phrygia** [in central Asia Minor (compare 16:6)], **stabilizing all the disciples** [converted and also stabilized on Paul's first journey, though "all" may imply further conversions in the meantime (see 14:22 and compare 15:32, 41)]. [24]**And a certain Jew—Apollos by name, an Alexandrian by birth** [Alexandria, Egypt, being the second largest city in the Roman Empire], **an eloquent man—arrived in Ephesus,** [he] **being mighty in the Scriptures** [or, as we might say, knowing the Old Testament thoroughly and able to use it convincingly]. [25]**This** [man] **had been instructed as to the way of the Lord** [which John the baptizer had proclaimed in preparation for the coming of one stronger than he, that is, Jesus (Luke 3:1–17)]. **And being ardent in spirit, he started speaking and teaching accurately the** [facts] **about Jesus, though understanding only John's baptism** [= the baptism of repentance without further knowledge of baptism in Jesus' name and baptism in the Holy Spirit]. Apollos's ardor of spirit imbues his eloquence in public speaking with heartfelt passion. No mere crowd-pleaser he! And the accuracy of his teaching the facts about Jesus adds truth to eloquence and ardor. A happy, threefold combination! [26a]**And this** [man] **started speaking boldly in the synagogue.** So boldness is added to eloquence, ardor, and accuracy to make an even happier, fourfold combination that Luke uses to recommend the gospel to prospective converts. People admired boldness in orators, such as Apollos was.

18:26b–28: And on hearing him, Priscilla and Aquila took him aside and expounded to him the way of God more accurately. Not that what Apollos had been teaching was inaccurate. But it was incomplete. So the greater accuracy had to do with added information, not with the correction of mistakes. The mention of Priscilla before Aquila implies her leadership in explaining "the way of God," which refers then to an enlarged version of the earlier-cited "way of the Lord." [27]**And because he** [Apollos] **was wanting to go through to Achaia, encouraging** [him to do so] **the brothers wrote to the disciples** [in Achaia] **to welcome him, who on getting there contributed a great deal to those who'd believed through the grace** [of God]. [28]**For in public he was vigorously confuting the Jews by demonstrating through the Scriptures** [in which he was "mighty"] **that the Christ is Jesus.** Athens and Corinth, which Paul had evangelized, were located in Achaia. "Go *through* to Achaia" entailed either sailing across the Aegean Sea or taking a land route that looped north, west, and south. "The brothers" implies that conversions had taken place in Ephesus, where Paul had briefly preached and Apollos had now spoken boldly; and as usual "the brothers" calls attention to the familial community of believers. Their "encouraging" Apollos enhances the communitarianism, as does also the writing of a letter to the effect that the disciples in Achaia should welcome Apollos. Churches are communities of encouragement and welcome. Come join. Luke attributes the Achaian disciples' belief to God's grace—in other words, to God's ill-deserved favor. People must will to believe, but also—and apart from any merit of their own—God must will them to believe. His will and theirs work in concert, neither one canceling out the other. Apollos contributes a great deal to the Achaian believers by confuting the unbelieving Jews there. It's implied that the unbelievers were trying to disprove the gospel. Apparently the believers didn't have the eloquence or learning to confute them as Apollos did. His confutation was vigorous, public, and scriptural—a forensic victory of the first order. The gospel wins in open forum. See the comments on 18:5 for "demonstrating through the Scriptures that the Christ is Jesus."

PAUL AT EPHESUS
Acts 19:1–41

This passage subdivides into Paul's baptizing in Jesus' name some disciples of John the baptizer (19:1–7), speaking in the local synagogue and the school of Tyrannus (19:8–10), performing miracles and exorcisms to the effect of converts' giving up their magical practices (19:11–20), and on the eve of departure for Jerusalem becoming in absentia the object of a riot (19:21–41).

19:1–4: And it happened that while Apollos was in Corinth, on going through the upper districts [inland Asia Minor] **Paul came down to Ephesus** [almost on the west coast] **and found some disciples.** [2]**And he said to them, "**[I'd like to know] **whether you received the Holy Spirit on believing." And they** [said] **to him,**

"To the contrary, we haven't even heard whether there is a Holy Spirit." ³And he said, "Into what then were you baptized?" And they said, "Into John's baptism." ⁴And Paul said, "John baptized with a baptism of repentance, telling the people that they should believe in the one coming after him, that is, in Jesus." Paul's reference to these disciples' having believed agrees with Luke's use of "disciples" for believers and thus shows that despite a deficiency, we're to consider these disciples/believers "saved." Paul's question whether they'd received the Holy Spirit implies they showed no evidence thereof, such as speaking in tongues, performing of miracles and exorcisms, and boldness and effectiveness in proclaiming the gospel. "On believing" is ambiguous. It could refer to receiving the Holy Spirit sometime after believing, as in the case of Samaritan believers (8:14–17), or at the time of believing, as in the case of Cornelius and his household (10:44–46). So Paul's question centers on the whether, not on the when, of receiving the Holy Spirit. And it's of concern to him that there's no evidence of these disciples' having received the Spirit, the source of power for Christian witness (1:8).

The disciples answer that they "haven't even heard whether there *is* a Holy Spirit." Since Luke 3:16 indicated that John the baptizer predicted a coming baptism in the Holy Spirit, it's tempting to say that these Ephesian disciples hadn't heard about the fulfillment of John's prediction on the day of Pentecost (see 1:5 with 2:1–4). At face value, though, they deny ever having heard of the Holy Spirit's existence. Since the Holy Spirit is more a matter of experience than a topic of instruction, then, Paul shifts to the topic of baptism and asks what they were baptized into. The question expresses surprise that as baptized believers they haven't yet received the Holy Spirit. Was something wrong with their baptism? According to 8:16 Samaritan believers had been baptized "into the name of the Lord Jesus" but hadn't yet received the Holy Spirit (see the comments on 8:16 for baptism *into* the name of the Lord Jesus as indicating transference into the ownership and authority of Jesus as Lord). The Ephesian believers answer, however, that they were baptized "into John's baptism." But what would being baptized into a baptism mean? It would mean that being baptized signifies a transference of the baptizee into the demands of his/her baptism. So Paul answers that the Ephesian believers' having been baptized into John's baptism signified their transference into the demands of repentance, which his baptism signified. Then Paul adds to John's baptism of repentance John's telling people to believe in the one coming after him, and Paul identifies that one as Jesus. So the Ephesian believers have heard neither about the existence of the Holy Spirit nor about the coming of Jesus as the one whose coming John predicted. What they'd believed so as to become disciples consisted only in the baptism of repentance as preparation for the coming one, not yet identified to them at the time they were baptized. Up till now, in other words, they've been more deficient than Apollos, who knew about Jesus though at first he knew only John's baptism (18:25).

19:5–7: **And on hearing** [about Jesus], **they got baptized into the name of the Lord Jesus** [see again the comments on 8:16]. ⁶**And when Paul laid** [his] **hands on them, the Holy Spirit came on them; and they started speaking in tongues and prophesying.** ⁷**And all the men were about twelve** [in number]. We never read about a rebaptizing of people who'd undergone John's baptism of repentance during the lifetime of John. It seems, then, that Paul rebaptizes these people because they underwent John's baptism of repentance at a later date and in ignorance of Jesus' and the Holy Spirit's having come. That is to say, John's baptism counted for Christian baptism only if it took place prior to the comings of Jesus and the Spirit. And if the Ephesians' initial baptism took place later and therefore in John's absence, it's easy to think they hadn't heard that John spoke about the Holy Spirit as the element in which the coming one would baptize people. Here, getting baptized into the name of the Lord Jesus indicates believing now in him in addition to believing in John's message of repentance and a coming one, as they did earlier. And just as Peter and John laid their hands on Samaritan believers who'd been baptized into the name of the Lord Jesus (8:17), so too Paul lays his hands on the Ephesian believers who've now been baptized into the name of the Lord Jesus. The purpose of the gesture is the same, that is, to indicate solidarity between Spirit-baptized believers and believers not yet baptized in the Holy Spirit. The result is also the same, reception of the Holy Spirit, which equates with baptism in the Holy Spirit. And just as the original disciples spoke in tongues and prophesied on getting baptized in the Holy Spirit (2:4, 17–18), so too do these Ephesian believers. Speaking in tongues and prophesying give Paul the evidence, heretofore lacking, that they have the Holy Spirit. Nor will they themselves need ever again to plead ignorance even of the Spirit's existence.

19:8: **And on going into the synagogue, he was speaking boldly for three months, conversing** [with the Jews from the Scriptures (see 17:2; 18:19)] **and persuading** [the Jews] **in regard to the things concerning God's kingdom/reign.** Paul's going into the synagogue fulfills the promise he made to the Jews of the Ephesian synagogue, "I'll return to you, God willing" (18:21). They'd asked him to stay longer (18:20). Luke wants the boldness of Paul's speaking to draw admiration, and "persuading [the Jews]" indicates evangelistic success. As a matter of fact, boldness and persuasiveness in speech were highly admired in the culture of that time. "In regard to the things concerning God's kingdom/reign" brings out the continuity between Paul's ministry and Jesus' ministry. For that kingdom/reign constituted Jesus' main theme (compare 1:3; 8:12; 14:22 and see many passages in Luke's Gospel, starting with 4:43). So continuity with Jesus' ministry comes on top of continuity with the Old Testament Scriptures to show that the gospel has an unbroken pedigree stretching back through recent times to ancient times.

19:9–10: But when some were hardening themselves [= becoming obstinate] **and refusing to be persuaded, badmouthing the Way in the sight of the multitude, he** [Paul], **disengaging from them, separated the disciples off** [from the obstinate badmouthers], **conversing day by day in the lecture hall of Tyrannus.** [10]**And this went on for two years, so that all the residents of Asia** [a Roman province in western Asia Minor]—**both Jews and Greeks—heard the word of the Lord.** Since the gospel has the support of Scripture, Luke attributes unbelief to obstinacy and refusal to be persuaded. His use of two verbal expressions ("hardening themselves" and "refusing to be persuaded"), where one would have sufficed, highlights the unreasonable basis of disbelief. In effect, he's saying to prospective converts, "Don't let obstinacy keep you from believing, for believing is the reasonable thing to do." See 9:2 with comments on "the Way" as a designation of the gospel. "Badmouthing the Way" contrasts with Paul's persuasive speech. The contrast portrays the badmouthing as unjust and casts the badmouthers in a bad light. "In the sight of the multitude" probably means that the obstinate unbelievers were badmouthing the Way before the very same large congregation with whom Paul was conversing. So to avoid mere wrangling, he disengages from the badmouthers by leaving the synagogue, takes his converts with him, and continues conversing with people in Tyrannus's lecture hall. We know nothing more about Tyrannus, so that the mention of him by name gives evidence of Luke's historical research (compare Luke 1:1–4). "Day by day" multiplies Paul's evangelistic efforts far beyond once-a-week presentations during Sabbath services in the synagogue. And "for two years" extends those efforts over a long time. As a result, not only the residents of Ephesus but also the residents of the whole province in which the city was located "heard the word of the Lord." Implied is the coming of people who lived outside the city into the city and hearing Paul in Tyrannus's lecture hall. By including "*all* the residents of Asia—*both* Jews *and* Greeks," Luke emphasizes that the progress of the gospel can't be impeded even by people who badmouth it. Indeed, their badmouthing it leads to its wider distribution.

19:11–12: And God was performing extraordinary miracles [literally, "miracles that don't usually happen" (even by the standard of miracles)] **through the hands** [= agency] **of Paul,** [12]**so that wipes** [such as handkerchiefs used to mop sweat off a public speaker's brow] **and waistcloths** [worn in his tent-making] **were being carried away from his skin to those who were sick; and** [their] **diseases were being removed from them and evil spirits were going out** [of them]. Here Luke brings forward the humanitarian features of Paul's ministry, healings and exorcisms, much as he brought forward the same in Jesus' and Peter's ministries. The gospel is good for the body as well as for the soul, good for this life as well as for the next. The tracing of the miracles back to God shows him to be the power behind Paul's ministry. The extraordinariness of the miracles magnifies that power. So, as Gamaliel said, don't fight against

God (5:39). Yield to his reign and you'll enter his kingdom (compare 14:22). Contact with Paul's skin invested the wipes and waistcloths with curative and exorcistic properties much as physical contact with Jesus, and even with his clothing, had also done (see, for example, Luke 8:43–44; compare Acts 5:15). Only here the wipes and waistcloths are carried away, so that the healings and exorcisms occur at a distance from Paul (compare Jesus' healing at a distance with only a word—at John 4:46–54, for example). Paul's wipes and waistcloths don't have to be in contact with him at the moment. How extraordinary!

19:13–16: But also some of the Jewish exorcists who went about [plying exorcism as a trade-for-hire] **undertook to name the name of the Lord Jesus over those who had evil spirits, saying, "I adjure you** [to come out] **by the Jesus whom Paul proclaims."** Though many Jews had become Christians, "*Jewish* exorcists" implies *non*-Christian exorcists in contrast with the apparently *Christian* carriers of Paul's wipes and waistcloths. Will the use of Jesus' name by non-Christians work as well as the use of Paul's wipes and waistcloths has worked? If so, the power is magical. If not, it's divine. [14]**And seven sons of a certain Sceva, a Jewish chief priest, were doing this** [using Jesus' name in exorcisms with a side reference to Paul]. [15]**And answering** [in a particular case], **the evil spirit said to them, "On the one hand, I know about Jesus and am apprised concerning Paul. On the other hand, who are you?"** Mention of the Jewish chief priest's name, "Sceva," and of the number of his sons gives more evidence of Luke's historical research. It's often said that Sceva wasn't really a chief priest—that is, a leading priest who as such belonged to the Jewish supreme court, the Sanhedrin in Jerusalem—but only laid a false claim to being a chief priest. But Luke gives us no reason to think of a false claim, so that we're meant to think of Sceva as an actual chief priest whose sons had emigrated to the province of Asia and taken up the role of traveling, non-Christian exorcists. The evil spirit recognizes the names of Jesus and Paul and thus testifies to their eminence. But since he doesn't recognize Sceva's sons to be Christian, as he does recognize Paul to be, those names prove ineffective when spoken by Sceva's sons. Worse than ineffective: [16]**And jumping on them, the man the evil spirit was in—mastering one and all** [of Sceva's sons]—**prevailed against them, so that naked and wounded they fled out of that house** [previously unmentioned but implying here that the demoniac was in a house at the time]. A number of items stress the utter defeat of these imposters, who by using Jesus' name pretended to be Christian exorcists: (1) the demoniac's "jumping on them"; (2) the demoniac's "mastering" them; (3) the demoniac's mastering them "one and all" though the odds against him were seven to one; (4) the demoniac's "prevailing against them" (he proved stronger than they); (5) the sons' having to flee; (6) the sons' having been stripped naked, much to their shame in flight; and (7) their having been wounded. Preliminary outcome: divine power proved; magic disproved.

Luke records final outcomes in *19:17–20*: **And this** [episode] **became known to all, both Jews and Greeks, who were residing in Ephesus; and fear fell on them all; and the name of the Lord Jesus was being magnified.** Naturally, the sight of naked would-be exorcists streaking through town in full flight made such news that the Ephesians came to know about the episode. *"All"* and *"both* Jews *and* Greeks" emphasize the disproval of magic in favor of the divine power wielded by Paul (compare 19:10). And the falling of "fear on them all" strengthens the emphasis. But why fear? Answer: because if Paul is wielding a divine power that succeeds against evil spirits that can overpower exorcists such as Sceva's sons, who use magic, then the Ephesians' own use of magic endangers them rather than protecting them. "The name of the Lord Jesus was being magnified" because it was proving effective in healings and exorcisms when Paul, a Christian believer, used it. So you, too, believe in Jesus as the Lord. [18]**And many of those who** *had* **believed were coming, confessing and announcing their practices.** [19]**And** [more particularly,] **considerable numbers of those who'd practiced magical arts, on bringing** [their] **books** [of magical formulas and instructions], **burned** [them] **up in the sight of all.** Ephesus was noted for the publication there of such books, and as usual Luke features eyewitnessing. **And they counted up the prices of them** [= of the books] **and found** [the prices to add up to] **fifty thousands of silver** [coins]. [20]**In this way the Lord's word was growing mightily and prevailing.** The episode concerning Sceva's sons exposed the ineffectiveness and danger of practicing magic. So believers in Jesus burned their books of magic in a public bonfire. *"Confessing . . . their practices"* means stating their practice of magic as wrong. *"Announcing* their practices" means reciting the magical formulas and instructions in those books being burned. The effectiveness of those formulas and instructions was thought to depend on their being kept secret. So this public recitation made them useless even in the eyes of the unbelieving audience of onlookers, who consisted of "all" the Ephesians. What rascals, those Christians! The "considerable numbers" of book-burners and reciters and the huge value of their books show both what massive, growing, mighty, and prevalent effect the Lord's word had on Ephesian society—all to the good. So the final outcomes of the episode concerning Sceva's sons include its publication throughout Ephesus, universal fear of the power Paul wields in Jesus' name, the magnifying of that name, the exposure of magical formulas and instructions so as to make them useless, the burning of books containing them, and the growth in power of the Lord's word. Don't fight it. Surrender to it.

19:21–22: **And when these things had been fulfilled** [= come to completion], **Paul placed** [a plan] **in** [his] **spirit** [that is, he resolved] **to travel to Jerusalem after going through Macedonia and Achaia, saying, "After I've come to be there** [in Jerusalem], **it's necessary that I also see Rome."** "It's necessary" implies that God plans for Paul to see Rome. Paul himself plans to *travel* first to Jerusalem. But God's plan that he also *see* Rome

leaves room for his going there not as a traveler but as a prisoner (see chapters 27–28). [22]**And after sending into Macedonia two of those who were serving** [= assisting] **him,** [namely] **Timothy and Erastus, he himself stayed on for a while in Asia** [the province in western Asia Minor]. This is the first and only time Luke mentions Erastus (but see Romans 16:23; 2 Timothy 4:20). So the appearance of Erastus's name at this point gives further evidence of Luke's historical research.

19:23–26: **And at that time** [just when Paul had resolved to travel to Jerusalem] **there took place not a small disturbance concerning the Way** [= a big riot took place concerning Paul's proclamation of the gospel]. [24]**For a certain Demetrius (as to** [his] **name), a silversmith, by making** [miniature] **silver sanctuaries of Artemis** [in imitation of the local temple of this goddess] **was providing the craftsmen not a little business** [that is, a lot of profitable work] **. . . .** Apparently Demetrius employed the craftsmen or headed up their trade guild. Luke's sentence continues: [25]**on assembling whom** [= on Demetrius's bringing together the craftsmen], **plus the workers with regard to such things** [unskilled workmen in this industry], **he said, "Men, you understand that we have prosperity from this business.** [26]**And you're observing and hearing that this Paul has brainwashed a considerable crowd not only of Ephesus—rather, of nearly all Asia** [the province]—**by persuading** [them], **saying, "The** [gods] **that come into being through hands** [= idols fashioned by human hands, like images of Artemis] **are** *not* **gods."** The appeal to prosperity in business immediately exposes a self-aggrandizing motive. *"This Paul"* is derogatory. We expect "a considerable crowd . . . of *Ephesians* . . . of nearly all *Asians*." Instead, we get ". . . not only of *Ephesus* . . . of nearly all *Asia*." Demetrius has already referred to a large number of people with "a considerable *crowd*." So he switches to place-names for emphasis on geographical extent. Thus even Paul's opponent highlights both the numerical and the widespread success of the gospel and therefore (though unintentionally) its divine origin.

Demetrius continues in *19:27*: **"And not only is this trade of ours in danger of going into disrepute, but also the temple of the great goddess Artemis** [is in danger of] **being counted as nothing, and she whom the whole of Asia and the inhabited earth worship** [is in danger of] **even being about to be deprived of her greatness."** Demetrius adds to his base, mercenary motive the motive of avoiding public shame through having his and his colleagues' trade "going into disrepute." He also appeals to pride in the temple of Artemis, one of the Seven Wonders of the Ancient World. It rested on a platform over 400 feet long and almost 240 feet wide. The building itself was 360 feet long and 180 feet wide (that is, considerably larger than a football field) and had well over 100 columns more than 55 feet high (that is, as high as a six-story building), plus a peaked roof resting on the columns, all of which dimensions made it four times the size of the Parthenon in Athens. The ancient epigrammist Antipater wrote: "I've set eyes on the wall of lofty Babylon, on which is a road for chariots; and the statue of Zeus by the Alpheus; and the hanging gardens; and the colossus of the Sun; and the huge labor of the high pyramids; and the vast tomb of Mausolus. But when I saw the house of Artemis that mounted to the clouds, those other marvels lost their brilliance; and I said, 'Lo, apart from Olympus [the mountain on which the gods were believed to dwell], the Sun never looked on anything so grand.'" For Paul, Luke, and Luke's target audience, though, this magnificence of architecture was spoiled by the idolatry it represented. (Luke aims his work especially toward Gentiles disillusioned with idolatry and disgusted by the immorality that went with it.) Finally, Demetrius appeals to reverence for Artemis, whom he calls "the *great* goddess." Whereas he'd earlier said, "Paul has brainwashed . . . *nearly* all Asia," he now expresses fear that "the *whole* of Asia" and, indeed, "the inhabited *earth*" will no longer worship Artemis. Well, her temple no longer stands, and nobody worships her any more.

19:28–29: And on hearing [Demetrius's speech] **and becoming full of fury, they started yelling, saying, "Great** [is] **Artemis of the Ephesians!"** Civic pride in Artemis now takes over on the basis of "fury," even "full[ness]" of fury, as opposed to Paul's having "reasoned" in the synagogue and in Tyrannus's lecture hall. This contrast recommends the gospel over against opposition to it. [29] **And the city was filled with tumult, and with mutual fervor they rushed into the** [outdoor] **theater, having violently seized Gaius and Aristarchus— Macedonians, fellow travelers of Paul.** Full fury fills the city with tumult. The mutual fervor with which they rush into the theater is reminiscent of the mutual fervor with which Stephen's murderers rushed at him (7:57; compare also the mutual fervor with which Corinthian Jews assaulted Paul (18:12]) and contrasts with Christians' mutual fervor in prayer, praise, attendance at the temple, and reaching agreement over a disputed question (1:14; 2:46; 4:24; 5:12; 15:25; compare crowds' paying attention with mutual fervor to Philip's proclamation of the gospel in 8:6). The reminiscence and the contrast recommend the gospel again. Ruins of the theater still stand in fairly good shape. It seated about 25,000. The violence with which Gaius and Aristarchus were seized disrecommends opponents of the gospel. And Luke's identifying Gaius and Aristarchus by name, country, and association with Paul gives evidence yet again of historical research.

19:30–31: But when Paul was wanting to go into the assemblage, the disciples weren't letting him. [31] **And even some of the Asiarchs** [= rulers of the province of Asia], **being friendly to him, sending** [a message] **to him were urging** [him] **not to give himself into the theater** [= not to venture into it]. Luke draws admiration for Paul's courage, and hence for the gospel he proclaims, by noting Paul's desire to enter the riotous assemblage. So strong was his desire that only the disciples' not letting him enter kept him back. In addition, though, the Asiarchs' friendly urging of him not to venture into the theater gives him high level support of a provincially wide extent. The Asiarchs aren't portrayed as Christians, so that their concern for the safety of Paul makes his integrity stand out all the more.

19:32–34: On the one hand, therefore, some were yelling one thing, some another; for the assembly was tumultuous and the majority didn't know on whose account they'd come together. [33] **On the other hand,** [some] **of the crowd concluded** [it was] **Alexander** [on whose account they'd come together], **because the Jews had thrust him forward.** The switch from "the assembly" to "the crowd" indicates that what was supposed to be a proper meeting of citizens was really the congregating of a mob. **And shaking** [his] **hand downward** [a gesture designed to quiet down the crowd] **he was wanting to speak to the assemblage in self-defense** [by way of dissociating himself and his fellow Jews from Paul and the idolatry-destroying effect of the gospel among Gentiles]. [34] **But on recognizing that he is a Jew** [note the vividness of "he *is* a Jew"], **there came a voice from all for about two hours, yelling, "Great** [is] **Artemis of the Ephesians."** The Jews' trying through Alexander to dissociate themselves from Paul's anti-idolatry fails. The crowd's recognition that as a Jew Alexander too opposes idolatry triggers about two hours of acclamation for Artemis, whose idol stands in her famous local temple. The acclamation keeps Alexander from speaking; and the length and loudness of the acclamation bespeak irrationality, as opposed again to Paul's having "reasoned" in the synagogue and in Tyrannus's lecture hall. The singularity of the "voice" that comes "from *all*" confirms the irrationality of a mob.

19:35–40: But calming down the crowd, the scribe [= the clerk who wrote down and kept the city records] **says, "Men, Ephesians, now who of human beings is there that doesn't know the city of the Ephesians** [as] **being custodian of the great Artemis and of what fell from Zeus** [presumably a meteorite, perhaps in a shape thought to represent Artemis and therefore not to be a manmade image]?" Implied answer: No one doesn't know, so great is our fame. [36] **"Since these things are undeniable, therefore, it's necessary that you keep calm and do nothing impulsive.** [37] **For you've brought these men** [Gaius and Aristarchus, who are] **neither robbers of temples nor slanderers of our goddess.** [38] **On the one hand, therefore, if Demetrius and the craftsmen with him have a word** [= complaint] **against someone, assizes are being held** [= tribunals are open to the public from time to time] **and there are proconsuls** [governmental officials to hear your complaints]. **Let them accuse one another** [before the proconsuls during the assizes]. [39] **But if you're seeking anything further** [that is, more than in a private lawsuit], **it'll be resolved in the legal assembly** [as opposed to tribunals for private lawsuits and as opposed to this riotously illegal gathering]. [40] **For we're even in danger of being accused of an uprising in connection with today, since there's no cause we can give back [by way of answering the accusation] as a reason for this turbulence." The Romans could take away the city's privileges, such as the right to an assembly of its citizens to do business. And on saying these things, he dismissed the assembly. Luke likes this speech so much that he introduces it with a lively present tense in "the scribe *says*"; and he likes it because its scolding of Demetrius, the craftsmen, and the rest of the mob comes not from a Christian but from a believer in "the great Artemis," in the sacred meteorite as having fallen "from Zeus," and in Ephesus as "custodian" of both. Besides the scolding, the speech appeals to Luke in its exoneration of Paul's companions, Gaius and Aristarchus, and in its pronouncement of the uproar both as unjustifiable (so that loss of business by the makers of silver sanctuaries doesn't count as robbery) and as dangerously illegal (so that it is opponents of the gospel rather than evangelists who disturb the civic order). Dismissal of the mob amounts to dismissal of the case, if you can even call it a case. And for Luke and his audience there's humorous irony in the city clerk's statement that the greatness of Artemis, the falling of a meteorite from Zeus, and Ephesus' custodianship "are undeniable." They're not only deniable. They're downright false!

FROM EPHESUS TO MACEDONIA AND GREECE AND BACK THROUGH MACEDONIA TO TROAS
Acts 20:1-12

This passage divides into accounts of Paul's travels (20:1-6) and of his reviving Eutychus in Troas (20:7-12).

20:1-6: And after the uproar [in Ephesus] had ceased, on sending for the disciples and encouraging [them], saying farewell Paul went out [of Ephesus] to travel to Macedonia. Because of the antagonism that sparked the uproar, the disciples needed encouragement, which included exhortation to persevere despite opposition. ²And on going through those districts [of Macedonia] and encouraging them [the Christians living in those districts] with much speaking, he came into Greece. "Much speaking" arose out of Paul's deep concern that people continue in the faith after coming to faith. ³And after doing three months [in Greece], because there developed a plot against him by the Jews as he was about to set sail for Syria, he decided to return through Macedonia [where he'd just been]. It looks as though unbelieving Jews plotted to do away with Paul during his planned voyage to Syria. Again Luke points up the skullduggery and treachery of the gospel's opponents, whether Jewish or Gentile, and uses the contrast with Christians' probity to win converts to the gospel. ⁴And accompanying him were Sopater [the son] of Pyrrhus, a Berean [referring to Sopater], and Aristarchus and Secundus of the Thessalonians, and Gaius, a Derbean, and Timothy, and the Asians Tychicus and Trophimus. The camaraderie of these fellow travelers makes a good advertisement for their gospel. ⁵And on proceeding ahead, these [men] were awaiting us in Troas. Since they'd been accompanying Paul, they

must have proceeded ahead from some point on the way north, and then east, from Greece through Macedonia toward Troas. "Us" brings in the author of Acts (Luke) as an additional companion of Paul. ⁶And after the days of Unleavened Bread [beginning with the day of Passover and lasting for a week thereafter during springtime (Luke 22:1)] we sailed out from Philippi and within five days came to them [Sopater and the others] in Troas, where we spent seven days. The abundance of detail testifies to Luke's own involvement in addition to the historical research that he did according to Luke 1:1-4.

20:7-9: And on the first [day] of the week, when we'd gathered to break bread [that is, to eat a meal together], Paul started conversing with them since he was going to leave on the morrow. Luke writes "with them" rather than "with us" because he has been Paul's only traveling companion since Sopater and the others went ahead and waited for Paul and Luke in Troas. And he prolonged [his] speaking till midnight [compare the "much speaking" of Paul in Macedonia as a sign of his deep concern that people continue in the faith after coming to faith (20:2)]. ⁸And there was a considerable number of lamps in the upstairs room where we'd gathered. ⁹And sitting on the window sill, a certain young man— Eutychus by name—getting weighed down with deep sleep as Paul was conversing more and more, when [completely] weighed down from sleep, fell down from the third floor and was picked up dead. Luke mentions the lamps, which burned olive oil, to shift blame for this accident from the length of Paul's speaking to the soporific effect of lampsmoke. Don't blame Paul. His speech is golden, so the longer the better! Blame the lamps. Luke's highlighting their large number emphasizes the point. The presence of Eutychus suggests but doesn't require that "them" and "we" include believers living in Troas as well as Sopater and Paul's other traveling companions.

20:10-12: But on going down, Paul fell on him [in the sense of throwing himself on Eutychus's corpse]. And on wrapping [his arms] around him, he said, "Stop being upset, for his life is in him." Paul's "going down" indicates that "picked up dead" didn't entail bringing Eutychus's corpse back upstairs. Since Eutychus was dead, it was contact with Paul—through Paul's wrapping his arms around him—that restored Eutychus's life and enabled Paul to give the others assurance (compare the healings and exorcisms that took place through contact with wipes and waistcloths taken "from [Paul's] skin" [19:11]). ¹¹And on going [back] up [to the third floor room] and breaking bread and eating and talking for a considerable [time], [that is,] till dawn, he went out in this way [which is to say that his departure from Troas took place in the fashion of a Christian fellowship that prospective converts should love to enter and enjoy]. ¹²And they led the boy alive and were comforted not measuredly [= were comforted *im*measurably]. Luke doesn't say where they led the boy. So the last accent falls entirely on his being so alive that they didn't have to pick him up again and carry him. What a miracle!

FROM TROAS TO MILETUS
Acts 20:13–38

This passage divides into a journey to Miletus (20:13–16), Paul's farewell speech at Miletus to the elders of the church in Ephesus (20:17–35), and their bidding him a sad goodbye (20:36–38).

20:13–16: And we, on proceeding ahead to the ship, set sail for Assos [a seaport in northwest Asia Minor], [where] **we were going to take Paul aboard. For thus he'd directed, since he was going to foot it** [that is, walk the route from Troas to Assos]. Luke doesn't tell why Paul took the trip on foot, so that his directing the others, including Luke the author, captures the spotlight. Already taking shape is the determination of Paul to go to Jerusalem despite the danger awaiting him there and despite other Christians' reservations (to put it mildly). Luke wants to build up admiration for Paul's courage and devotion, and therefore confidence in Paul's gospel (compare Luke 9:51). [14]**And as he was meeting us in Assos, on taking him aboard we went to Mitylene** [the main city on the island of Lesbos, off the northwest coast of Asia Minor]. [15]**And on sailing off from there we arrived the following day opposite Chios** [another island off the coast of Asia Minor, but farther south than Lesbos]. **Another** [day] **and we crossed over to Samos** [yet another island off the coast of Asia Minor, but still farther south], **and the subsequent** [day] **we came to Miletus** [a seaport on the west coast of Asia Minor thirty-five miles south and a little west of Ephesus]. [16]**For Paul had decided to sail past Ephesus so that spending time in Asia might not happen to him** [in better English: so as not to spend time in Asia, where he'd already spent well over two years according to 19:8, 10]. **For he was hurrying to get to Jerusalem, if it were at all possible for him, by the day of Pentecost** [about which see the comments on 2:1]. People in Luke's world were interested in travelogues; so this portrayal of Paul as an inveterate traveler breeds admiration for him and his gospel—this in addition to the details that continue showing Luke's own participation in these travels. Paul's drive to get to Jerusalem for the Festival of Pentecost also shows him true to the ancient religion of Judaism and its Scriptures. No renegade he, no spouting of a newfangled religion lacking a solid basis in antiquity.

20:17–21: And sending from Miletus to Ephesus he called for the elders of the [Ephesian] **church.** We've not read about these particular elders before, but the mention of them links the church, like Paul himself, to Judaism since church elders duplicated synagogue elders (compare 11:30; 14:23 and so on). [18]**And when they'd come to him, he told them, "You yourselves know how I was with you for all the time from the first day I set** [foot] **in Asia . . . ."** Despite their already knowing, Paul reminds them just how he'd been with them from the start: [19]**"slaving for the Lord with an entirely lowly attitude** [toward the Lord, as befits a slave of his (compare Luke 17:7–10)] **and tears** [out of concern for you

and others in Asia] **and trials that had happened to me through the plots of the Jews** [the unbelieving ones, of course], [20]**how I didn't shrink from reporting to you a single one of the things beneficial** [to you] **and** [from] **teaching you publicly** [in the synagogue and Tyrannus's lecture hall (19:8–10)] **and from house to house,** [21]**testifying solemnly both to Jews and to Greeks about repentance toward God and faith in our Lord,** [namely,] **Jesus."** "For all the time from the first day" points to Paul's constancy and consistency. As a slave, he has labored for the Lord, not for the Ephesians, though they've benefited from such labors. "With an entirely lowly attitude [toward the Lord]" shines a light on the piety of Paul, "with . . . tears" on his sincerity, and "with . . . trials that happened to me" on his endurance. "Through the plots of the Jews" alludes to incidents in Pisidian Antioch, Iconium, Lystra, Thessalonica, Berea, and Corinth (chapters 13–14, 17–18). And we see patience as well as concern in Paul's not shrinking from telling the Ephesians, whatever the efforts required of him, *everything* they needed to know. His teaching in public took courage. His teaching from house to house took persistence. The solemnity of his testimony displayed seriousness. "Both to Jews and to Greeks" displayed cosmopolitanism. "About repentance . . . and faith" displayed the negative and positive sides of what it takes for conversion. "Toward God" tells to whom a person has to address his/her sorrow for sins. "In our Lord, [namely,] Jesus" identifies the one into whose lordship a person has to commit his/her fate.

20:22: "And now, behold, I'm traveling to Jerusalem, having been bound in the spirit, not knowing the things that will happen to me in her [= in the city of Jerusalem] **. . . ."** Many translations, perhaps most of them, have "bound by the Spirit," that is, by the Holy Spirit. But in his very next statement Paul will qualify "the Spirit" with "Holy"; and if he meant the Holy Spirit in the present statement, too, we'd expect him to say "the Holy Spirit" here and shorten the reference with "the Spirit" the second time around. Besides, Luke has been pointing out Paul's own intentions: "For thus he'd directed, since he was going to foot it. . . . For Paul had decided . . ." (20:13, 16). So it seems better to translate with "having been bound in the spirit" and treat the phrase as a reference to Paul's own human spirit, the source of his compulsion to travel to Jerusalem in pious Jewish fashion for Pentecost. "Not knowing the things that will happen to me in her" strikes a note of foreboding and thus draws admiration for the piety of Paul's courage in forging ahead despite the foreboding. "Behold" punctuates both the piety and the courage, and "*now . . .* I'm going" underlines the determination of Paul by describing his pilgrimage as already and irreversibly in progress.

Though the compulsion to travel to Jerusalem originated in Paul's human spirit at a time he didn't yet know what would happen to him there, his statement continues in **20:23–24** with more recent indications of what to expect: **"except that the Holy Spirit** is solemnly testifying to me in city after city, saying that bonds [such as prison chains] and afflictions await me." "Bonds and afflictions" do indeed add solemnity to the testimony, but the solemnity has more to do with the forcefulness of the testimony than with its content. The binding of Paul in his spirit will eventuate in the binding of his body; and his continued determination to go in spite of now being repeatedly told by the Holy Spirit (through Christian prophets according to 21:4) what will happen to him in Jerusalem—this determination elevates his courage and piety to a new height. And to personal courage and Jewish piety he adds Christian evangelistic fervor: 24"But on no account do I make my life valuable to myself so long as I finish my race, even the service that I received from the Lord Jesus, [which is] to testify solemnly concerning the good news of God's grace." So Paul's solemn testimony concerning God's grace balances the Holy Spirit's solemn testimony concerning what awaits Paul in Jerusalem. He won't allow the Spirit's testimony, solemn though it is, to deter him from pursuing his own testimony; for his own testimony consists in a service that he "received from the Lord Jesus." The lordship of Jesus over his slave Paul keeps Paul from falling out of his race (a figure of speech for his evangelistic service) before he reaches the finish line (compare 1 Corinthians 9:24–27). "God's grace" makes good news for the people to whom Paul gives solemn—that is, forceful—testimony. But his "service" is rendered to Jesus as his Lord. And so strong is his recognition of Jesus' lordship over him that he doesn't care if *worse* than "bonds and afflictions" await him in Jerusalem. He values the completion of his evangelistic service to Jesus more highly than his own life. How good must be the news of God's grace to inspire such obedient devotion! Believe it!

20:25-27: "And now, behold, I know that you all, among whom I went around proclaiming the kingdom [God's reign, according to 19:8]**, will never again see my face."** "And now, behold" punctuates Paul's *knowing* just as "And now, behold" in 20:22 punctuated Paul's *going*. Whether or not martyrdom in addition to imprisonment awaits him, he knows none of the Ephesian elders will ever see him again (the meaning of "you all . . . will never again see my face"). He might have said he'd never see *them* again. But "will never again see *my* face" accents what's going to happen to him. So whereas the Holy Spirit has been using others to prophesy what awaits Paul, here Paul himself prophesies. For Luke, "among whom I went around proclaiming God's kingdom/rule" displays continuity between Paul's proclamation and that of Jesus. And continuity breeds confidence in reliability. 26"Therefore [since none of you will ever see me again] I testify to you this very day that I'm clean from the blood of all [of you]." "This very day" (or, more literally, "the today day") calls special attention to Paul's last chance to affirm his innocence face to face. "Blood" stands for life (Genesis 9:4; Leviticus 17:11, 14; Deuteronomy 12:23). So Paul is saying that if any of the elders fail to attain eternal life because of apostasy, he'll not be responsible.

27"For I didn't shrink from reporting all God's plan to you." You learned it from me; so if you don't stick true to it, I'm not to blame, especially since I left out none of it. Luke uses Paul's self-portrayal as an evangelistic tool: the plan of God that Paul has proclaimed, as recorded in this book of Acts, is all you need to know for salvation. Note the emphatic use of "all" in "all [of you]," "all God's plan," and—in the upcoming statement—"all the flock."

20:28: "Take precaution for yourselves and for all the flock, within which the Holy Spirit has positioned you as supervisors for the purpose of shepherding the church of God, which he acquired with his own blood." So just as the Holy Spirit "sent out" Barnabas and Saul/Paul on an evangelistic journey (13:4), the Holy Spirit has also "positioned" the Ephesian elders "as supervisors" to care for the well-being of converts. Paul calls the converts in Ephesus "the flock," that is, "the church," and compares the elders' supervision to shepherding. But the church belongs to God, not to the elders (hence, "the church *of God*"). And it's his by acquisition "with his own blood," which most naturally means that the blood was the price of acquisition—just as Judas Iscariot "went to his own place," which was the "Field of Blood," because he'd "procured it for himself . . . with the reward of injustice [the money he'd gotten for betraying Jesus]" (1:15–19, 25; Luke 22:3–6). Some translations read "the blood of his Own," meaning the blood of God's own *Son*. Perhaps so, but the predominant use of "own" elsewhere in Luke-Acts, particularly in the singular, makes it a bit more natural to think here of God's blood. Luke 22:20 speaks of Jesus' blood, though. So the association between Jesus and God is so close that Jesus' blood counts as God's (compare 15:40 with comments). And as in 20:26, "blood" stands for life, but this time for God's life in Jesus sacrificed for our eternal life.

Next, Paul tells why the elders should take precaution for themselves and for all the flock, not leaving out anybody in the church. The reason has to do with the possibility of apostasy, and therefore of exclusion from eternal life, through the influence of false teachers. The abruptness with which Paul introduces this reason (there's no "because" or "for") gives it a jagged edge. *20:29-31*: "I know that after my departure dangerous wolves will come in among you, not sparing the flock; 30and from among you yourselves there'll stand up men speaking perversions so as to draw away the disciples after them [that is, to establish their own personal followings apart from the true church]." Just as Paul prophesied that the Ephesian elders would never again see his face, so now he prophesies an entrance into the church, and an arising within the church, of false teachers, whom he compares to wolves. And just as wolves kill sheep—hence "dangerous" and "not sparing the flock"—so will the false teachers kill their duped followers' chance of eternal life by perverting the gospel. 31"Therefore stay awake, remembering that night and day for three years I didn't stop putting each one [of you] on notice with tears [that mortally dangerous false teachers will achieve some success]." We'd say "day and night." But Paul puts "night" before "day" partly because for Jews like him a day started at sunset but mainly here because he has exhorted the elders to "stay awake" so as to spot and counteract the speakers of "perversions." Luke uses the exhortation to tell his own audience of prospective converts to beware of such speakers. Believe the authentic gospel that Paul proclaimed.

20:32–35: "And as for the present [prior to the coming of false teachers], I'm committing you to God [for safekeeping, since you won't see me anymore] and to the word of his grace [= the good news that salvation is by grace through faith], which [word] is able to build [you] up [as opposed to being torn down by perversions that end in apostasy] and give [you] an inheritance among all the sacred ones [that is, eternal life along with all other believers, whom God has segregated for himself from unbelievers]. ³³I've lusted after no one's silver or gold or clothing." Like silver and gold, extra clothing counted as wealth. ³⁴"You yourselves know that these hands [you can picture in your minds Paul's stretching them out to the elders] did service for my needs and for those who were with me." The manual labor of Paul provided financial support not only for him but also for his colleagues; so he can't be rightly accused of preaching for money. The gospel of God's grace has been matched with Paul's grace in preaching without remuneration, and therefore made more believable. ³⁵"In all things I've shown you that by laboring in this way it's necessary to help those who are sick and to remember the words of the Lord Jesus, in that he himself said, 'It's more fortunate to give than to receive.'" "In *all* things" leaves no room for exceptions to Paul's setting an example of earning money to help the sick, who because of their sickness can't work for their own living. Paul supported not only himself and his colleagues, then. He also helped sick people financially. His example shows it to be a divine requirement that the elders also should fulfill in remembrance of a saying of Jesus. Paul backs up his example with a quotation of that saying and calls Jesus "the Lord" to underline the authority of Jesus and his saying. Though good fortune does fall on the sick who are financially helped, the saying pronounces even better fortune on the helpers. (We have no other record of this saying in the New Testament.)

20:36–38: And after saying these things, putting his knees [on the ground] he started praying with them all. As often, Luke highlights Christians' piety. The kneeling and the inclusion of "all" add emphasis. ³⁷And a considerable weeping of all took place. And falling on Paul's neck they were kissing him, ³⁸being distressed especially because of the statement which he'd spoken [to the effect] that they weren't going to view his face ever again. Altogether an emotional parting that illustrates the heartfelt and attractive camaraderie of Christians. Again "all" adds emphasis. Luke invites others to come share in this camaraderie. But they were conducting

him to the ship [despite their sorrow at his leaving, for he was determined to travel to Jerusalem].

FROM MILETUS TO JERUSALEM
Acts 21:1–17

This passage divides into voyages of Paul and his party from Miletus to Tyre (21:1–6), from Tyre to Ptolemais (21:7), and from Ptolemais to Caesarea (21:8–14), plus an overland trip from Caesarea to Jerusalem (21:15–17). This travelogue caters to the interest of Luke's audience in travel and points up Luke's own involvement, indicated by "we" and "us."

21:1–3: And when it happened that we set sail, after being drawn away from them [that is, parted from the Ephesian elders], on running a straight course we came to Cos [an island in the Aegean Sea], and the next [day] to Rhodes [an island off the southwest corner of Asia Minor], and from there to Patara [a city on the southwest coast of Asia Minor]. Though normally "being drawn away from" indicates no more than being parted from, here the drawing away reflects the love of Christians for each other, as shown in the sorrow of their parting (20:37–38), and contrasts with the coming of false teachers who'll "draw away the disciples after them" (20:30). ²And on finding a ship crossing over to Phoenicia [roughly modern Lebanon, on the east coast of the Mediterranean Sea], after getting aboard we set sail. So they changed ships in Patara. ³And on sighting Cyprus and leaving it behind on the left, we kept sailing to Syria and came down to Tyre. So they sailed on the open sea south of the island of Cyprus and arrived at the port of Tyre in Phoenicia, which was considered part of the larger region of Syria (compare the "Syrophoenician" woman of Mark 7:26). For there [in Tyre] the ship was unloading [its] cargo.

21:4–6: And on finding the disciples [living in Tyre], we stayed there seven days—[the disciples] who as such were telling Paul through the Spirit not to set [foot] in Jerusalem. That is, in their capacity as disciples they were speaking through the Spirit. ⁵But when it happened that we'd concluded the [seven] days, on going out [from Tyre] we started traveling while all [the disciples] with [their] wives and children were conducting us as far as outside the city. And on putting [our] knees on the beach, after praying we said farewell to one another. ⁶And we went up into the ship, but those [disciples with their wives and children] returned to their own [homes]. Finding the disciples in Tyre entailed looking them up, a sign of Christian communitarianism. These disciples' telling Paul not to go up to Jerusalem exhibits concern for his well-being, yet another sign of communitarianism. And capping it is that the disciples—all of them, no less—take along their wives and children, conduct Paul and his party "as far as outside the city," kneel on the beach, pray, and join him and his party in reciprocal farewells. They escorted Paul and his party as far as they could without boarding the ship themselves. Who wouldn't want to belong to such a close-knit community as that? And praying together adds piety to the communitarian spirit. As for Paul, his determination to go to Jerusalem for the Festival of Pentecost comes to the fore again (compare 20:16) and gets emphasis from the contrast between the disciples' telling him "not to *go up* to Jerusalem" and "we [Paul and his companions] *went up* into the ship" that was headed toward Jerusalem. (The verb is the same in both statements.) The determination of Paul displays his allegiance to the ancient religion of Judaism (whose hopes he considers fulfilled in the gospel)—antiquity deserving respect—and displays also his courage in that he knows that "bonds and affliction," and perhaps death, await him in Jerusalem. "Through the Spirit" could mean that the Holy Spirit, using the disciples as his mouthpiece, forbade Paul to go to Jerusalem. But 20:23 indicated that the Holy Spirit had repeatedly told Paul what awaited him in Jerusalem, and did so without forbidding him to go. Moreover, 21:10–14 will contain yet another Spirit-inspired prophecy of what will happen to Paul in Jerusalem, nor will this prophecy contain a command that he not go. Instead, out of their own concern for Paul, his companions and the local disciples will urge him not to go. So it seems better to say that here in 21:4 Luke is using shorthand for the disciples' telling Paul not to go to Jerusalem because of what the Holy Spirit revealed to them would happen to Paul if he went, not that the Holy Spirit forbade him to go.

21:7–9: And we, completing the voyage from Tyre, arrived at Ptolemais [a seaport south of Tyre]; **and on greeting the brothers** [there], **we stayed one day with them.** Christian community is on display again. Paul and his companions take advantage of every opportunity to fellowship with other believers. Luke uses such fellowship as a magnet to attract prospective converts. **⁸And after going out** [of Ptolemais] **on the morrow, we went to Caesarea** [a seaport on the central coast of Israel and seat of the Roman governors]. **And on going into the house of Philip the evangelist** [= a proclaimer of the good news (see 8:5–40)], **who was one of the seven** [chosen to wait on tables in 6:1–6], **we stayed with him.** The emphasis doesn't lie on Philip's offering Christian hospitality so much as it lies on Christians' seeking hospitality from another believer for the sake of fellowship. **⁹And this** [Philip] **had four prophesying virgin daughters.** Luke's audience will immediately remember Peter's quotation in 2:17 of Joel 2:28, "'And it shall be' in the last days, says God, [that] 'I'll pour out [some] of my Spirit on all flesh; and your sons *and your daughters* will prophesy,'" and may recall as well that the aged widow Anna, who gave thanks over the baby Jesus, was a prophetess (Luke 2:36–38). And just as her lengthy widowhood had enabled her to devote herself fulltime to fasting and praying in the temple, the virginity of Philip's daughters enabled them to devote themselves fulltime to prophesying (compare 1 Corinthians 7:25–35). So Christian community is imbued with Spirit-inspired prophecy, as next becomes further evident.

21:10–11: And while we were staying more days [than "the morrow" of arrival in 21:8, or perhaps "quite a few days"], **a certain prophet from Judea—Agabus by name—came down** [to Caesarea]. **¹¹And on coming to us and appropriating Paul's belt** [a long strip of cloth unless stated to be leather, as in Mark 1:6], **binding his own feet and hands** [with the belt] **he said, "The Holy Spirit speaks as follows: 'In this way the Jews will bind in Jerusalem the man whose belt this is, and they'll give** [him] **over into the hands of Gentiles** [for them to do to him what they will or, rather, whatever God will allow them to do].'" The Holy Spirit has already and repeatedly given solemn testimony to Paul that he'll be bound in Jerusalem (20:22–23). The present confirmation adds two details: (1) the Jews (unbelieving ones) will do the binding, and (2) they'll give him over to Gentiles.

21:12–14: And when we heard these things, both we and the locals were urging that he not go up to Jerusalem. Yet another example of fellow Christians' concern for Paul's well-being. So join the fellowship of believers and you'll receive such concern yourself. **¹³Then Paul answered, "What are you doing by weeping and breaking my heart? For I'm prepared not only to be bound but even to die in Jerusalem for the name of the Lord Jesus."** Paul's heart is breaking because he hates to see his fellow disciples weeping. Their sorrow over him triggers his sorrowing over them. This mutuality of sorrow arises out of the communitarian spirit on which, as already noted, Luke trains a spotlight to attract prospective converts. "*For* I'm prepared . . ." gives Paul's fellow disciples a reason to stop weeping and breaking his heart. *His* preparedness to be bound, even to die, should prepare *them* for such an eventuality. "For the name of the Lord Jesus" adds evangelistic devotion to Paul's admirable courage; for in its proclamation this name brings salvation to everyone who believes (4:12). **¹⁴And because he wasn't being persuaded** [not to go up to Jerusalem], **we fell silent after saying, "The Lord's will come about."** "He wasn't being persuaded" puts a final accent on Paul's courageous devotion to Jesus and the gospel, and "The Lord's will come about" adds an accent on the piety of Paul's fellow believers, a piety like that of Jesus himself (see Luke 22:42).

21:15–17: And after these days, on getting ready [for the journey] **we started going up to Jerusalem.** So Paul's determination to go up to Jerusalem now turns into the actuality of going. **¹⁶And also** [some] **of the disciples from Caesarea went along with us, bringing** [us] **to Mnason—a certain Cypriot, a long-time disciple—with whom we were lodged.** And still yet again Luke brings out the communitarianism of Christians, here in the Caesarean disciples' accompanying Paul and his party and making sure they had a place to lodge on the way up to Jerusalem. Like Barnabas, Mnason had immigrated to Israel from the island of Cyprus (compare 4:36). **¹⁷And when we'd gotten to Jerusalem, the brothers welcomed us gladly.** Ah, Christian community again, punctuated with a familial term ("the brothers") and a welcome augmented with "gladly."

A DEMONSTRATION THAT PAUL WASN'T AN APOSTATE JEW
Acts 21:18–26

21:18–19: And on the morrow Paul was going in with us to James, and all the elders [of the Jerusalem church] **were present.** This James is Jesus' half brother (see the comments on 12:17). "All the elders" relates the church to the synagogue, which had elders, and thus implies that Christianity is Judaism brought to fruition. [19]**And after greeting them, he** [Paul] **was relating each one by each one the things that God had done among the Gentiles through his** [evangelistic] **service** [compare 20:24]. The credit goes to God. Evangelists such as Paul don't promote themselves. Nor does Luke promote Paul for Paul's sake—rather, for the glory of God in the success of the gospel. This is good religion. "Each one by each one" points to a multiplicity of God's deeds that Paul details. And "among the Gentiles" reveals a door of salvation wide open for the Gentile majority in Luke's audience, who of course differ from Paul's Jewish audience. Because he has taken the initiative by going in to James and the elders, he greets them rather than they him. His greeting exhibits amicability toward them (contrast the false charge in 21:28).

21:20: And they, on hearing [Paul's report]**, were glorifying God.** Those who heard included "all the elders" in addition to James (21:18), so that everybody in Paul's audience was giving God the credit for what he'd done through Paul. Here then we have an ideal religious community, for they all glorify God. **And they said to him, "You observe, brother, how many tens of thousands there are among the Jews of those who've believed; and they're all Law-zealots."** Though they've believed in Jesus for their salvation, in other words, they're zealous about keeping the Mosaic law. That "they're *all* Law-zealots" points up further that Christianity carries forward the ancient religion of Judaism rather than negating it. The address, "brother," shows affection for Paul. "How many tens of thousands" makes the success of the gospel among Jews match its success among Gentiles—this as evidence that God is at work in Christian evangelism (compare 5:38–39). "You observe" describes Paul as an eyewitness to this success among the Jews. He has already seen it among the Gentiles.

21:21–25: "And they [the Law-zealous believers] **have been instructed concerning you that you teach all the Jews among the Gentiles apostasy from Moses by saying they should neither circumcise** [their] **children nor walk** [= behave] **in line with** [Mosaic] **standards.** [22]**So what's** [to be done]**?"** This question indicates that Paul's auditors don't believe, or at least doubt, the rumor concerning what he teaches Jews living outside Israel. "*All* the Jews" suggests not just Jewish believers but also the unbelieving Jews whom Paul has been trying to con-

vert with his Law-free gospel. **"Surely they'll hear that you've come.** [23]**Therefore do this that we're telling you: We've got four men having a vow on themselves** [or, as we would say, they're under a vow]. [24]**Taking along these** [men], **be purified with them and pay expenses for them in order that they may have their head** [a collective singular where we'd use the plural 'heads'] **shaved. And all will know that there's nothing to the things they've been instructed concerning you—rather, that you yourself also toe the line by keeping the Law."** The overall effort here is to avoid a split and maintain Christian community. Luke says that head-shaving was entailed and that for it, ritual purification was required (compare Numbers 6:1–21). Otherwise he doesn't explain the nature of the vow, nor for his purpose does he need to. For purification, sacrifices had to be offered; and they cost money. So James and the elders tell Paul to join the four men in the ceremonies of purification and pay for the sacrifices. Then also the tens of thousands of Jewish believers in Jerusalem will recognize the falsity of the rumor told about Paul, and Luke's audience will recognize again the continuity of Christianity with age-old, venerable Judaism. [25]**"But concerning the Gentiles who've believed, we wrote** [them] **a letter after deciding they should keep themselves both from** [meat] **sacrificed to an idol and blood and what's been strangled and sexual immorality** [see the comments on 15:28–29]**."** Here, "sexual immorality" is saved till last so as to keep the three ritual matters together. James and the elders mention these decrees to draw a parallel between what they've told Paul to do and what they earlier told Gentile believers to do. In both instances, the purpose is to avoid offending Law-keeping Jews, not to add Law-keeping on top of belief as a further requirement for salvation.

21:26: Then Paul, on taking along the men the following day, after being purified with them started going into the temple [courts] **announcing throughout** [those courts] **the fulfilling of the days of purification** [that the four men accompanying him were undergoing] **until the offering for each one of them was offered** [to bring to an end the period of fulfillment, which 21:27 will specify as seven days in length]. For the sake of Christian community and continuity with Judaism, then, Paul accedes to James' and the elders' bidding. "The following day" shows that Paul wasted no time in doing so. He's eager to maintain Christian community. Though the totality of purification will take seven days, he and the four have to undergo purification every time they enter the temple courts. "*Until* the offering for each one of them was offered" implies that the week of purification hasn't yet reached a conclusion, so that "the fulfilling" is still in progress. "Announcing throughout [the temple courts]" doesn't refer to a private notification addressed to priests in the temple. It refers to public announcements by Paul—again every time he and the four enter the temple courts—so that the Law-zealous Jewish believers will hear about his participation in the rites of purification and his paying for the offerings at the end. Then they'll know that the rumor they've heard about him is false. The offering "for each one of them" stresses his bearing the expense of *all* the offerings. As in 15:1–29, salvation comes by faith without any necessary addition of Law-keeping. But a keeping of the Law by Paul, his paying others' expenses for doing the same, and his doing so to maintain fellowship with other Jewish believers who keep the Law out of custom—these are acts of magnanimity that recommend the gospel he proclaims.

THE SEIZING OF PAUL IN THE TEMPLE COURTS
Acts 21:27–30

21:27–29: **And when the seven days** [of purification] **were about to be consummated, the Jews from Asia** [the Roman province in western Asia Minor]**, on catching sight of him in the temple** [courts] **started agitating all the crowd and laid hands on him,** [28]**shouting, "Men of Israel, help! This is the man who's teaching all** [Gentiles] **all over** [= everywhere] **against** [our] **people and the Law and this place** [the temple]**; and still** [more]**, he has even brought Greeks into the temple** [courts; that is, beyond the barrier that Gentiles, on pain of death, weren't supposed to go] **and has** [ritually] **defiled this sacred place."** [29]**For they'd previously seen Trophimus the Ephesian in the city with him, whom** [referring to Trophimus] **they were supposing that Paul had brought into the temple** [courts]. Since Ephesus was located in the province of Asia and Trophimus was an Ephesian, the Jews from Asia recognized him and knew him to be a Greek, that is, a Gentile. But they mistakenly supposed that because they'd seen him accompanying Paul in the city, he must now be accompanying Paul in the temple courts too. Moreover, they extrapolate that if Paul has brought one Gentile into the Jews-only temple courts, he has brought more than one ("Greeks," plural). Whether deliberately false or innocently false, the extrapolation is designed to help agitate the crowd. "*All* the crowd" shows the extent of agitation, and "laid hands on him" starts the fulfillment of Agabus's prophecy, which tagged Jews as those who'd take the first action against Paul (21:10–11). The contrast with "[our] people" makes "all" refer to Gentiles. "All [Gentiles] all over" is an exaggeration as well as a wordplay. Paul hasn't gone everywhere, nor has he spoken to every Gentile. But like the extrapolation, the exaggeration is designed to help agitate the crowd that's jammed into the temple courts. Luke's audience will immediately recognize that Paul's preaching in synagogues wherever he could, circumcising Timothy (16:3), coming to Jerusalem in time for Pentecost if possible, getting a warm welcome from fellow Jewish believers there, greeting the leaders of the Jerusalem church, and undergoing purification and paying for the prescribed offerings at the temple *belie* the Asian Jews' shouting that he teaches against the Jewish people, against the Law, and against the temple. The Asian Jews might have shouted, "This man *is* teaching . . . ." Instead they shout, "This *is* the man who's teaching . . . ," as though they've known of such a man, have been on the hunt for him, and have finally found him. But if he has brought Greeks into the temple courts, as they say he has, those Greeks might spring to his defense. So addressing the "men of Israel" as distinguished from the Greeks, the Asian Jews yell for help. It comes.

21:30: **And the whole city was moved** [with anger]**, and a convergence of the people took place.** Those Jews in the city ran to join their compatriots already in the temple courts. **And on taking hold of Paul they were dragging him outside the temple** [courts]**. And the doors** [into the courts] **were immediately shut.** The mistaken supposition and false charges of the Asian Jews circulated quickly throughout Jerusalem so as to rally a vast lynch mob. The mob dragged Paul outside the temple courts to do their worst on him without defiling those courts as he'd been falsely charged with defiling them by bringing in Greeks. (To kill Paul in the courts would have defiled them.) The doors were immediately shut to keep any more supposed Greeks from entering and defiling the courts further with their presence.

PAUL'S RESCUE
Acts 21:31–40

21:31–32: **And as they were seeking to kill him** [now that they'd dragged Paul outside the temple courts]**, a report went up to the commander of the** [Roman] **cohort** [a company of six hundred soldiers stationed by the temple] **that the whole of Jerusalem was in tumult** [the cohort being stationed there to prevent such a tumult and to take care of one if it took place]**,** [32]**who** [referring to the commander] **at once taking along soldiers and centurions** [each one the commander of a hundred soldiers] **ran down upon them** [the tumultuous populace of Jerusalem]**. And they, on seeing the commander of the cohort and the soldiers, stopped beating Paul.** So the mob that ran together against Paul get run down themselves. "They were seeking to kill him" and "they . . . stopped beating Paul" add up to an attempt to beat him to death—this without a trial, much less a verdict of capital guilt. Presumably they'd bound Paul in order to beat him. But Luke's not saying so shows he doesn't create fulfillments of prophecy out of thin air; for otherwise Agabus's prophecy that the Jews in Jerusalem would bind Paul hands and feet (21:10–11) would have induced Luke to mention explicitly a binding of Paul at this point. The mob's cowering at the sight of the commander and his cohort makes a nice contrast with Paul's courage in having come to Jerusalem despite knowing this sort of thing would happen to him here.

21:33–36: **Then, on drawing near, the commander of the cohort took hold of him and commanded that he be bound with two chains.** Well, this doesn't quite correspond to Agabus's prediction, according to which the *Jews* would bind Paul hands and feet and give him over into the hands of Gentiles (21:10–11). For here it's *Gentiles* who bind Paul. Nor do the Jews *give him over* to Gentiles' hands. They try to *kill* him, and a Gentile yanks him to safety. Moreover, the word for "chains" has to do with binding the *hands*, not the feet, whereas Agabus predicted the binding of Paul's *feet* as well as hands. (You have to admire Luke's honesty in preserving these differences.) But the correspondences are close enough to be impressive: there's a transfer of Paul from Jews to Gentiles, and he's bound. **And he** [the commander] **was inquiring who he** [Paul] **might be and what he'd done** [worthy of a lynching]. ³⁴**But some in the crowd were calling out one thing, and others something else.** This very difference in the responses to the commander's inquiry betrays ignorant fury rather than knowledgeable zeal as the basis of the crowd's assault on Paul. **And since because of the uproar he couldn't come to know the certainty** [of who Paul might be and what he'd done], **he commanded him to be led into the barracks** [adjoining the temple courts]. ³⁵**But when he** [Paul] **got to the stairs** [leading up into the barracks], **it happened that because of the crowd's violence he was being carried by the soldiers.** This violence underscores both the ignorant fury of the crowd and, by contrast, the good news of "peace on earth among human beings of [God's] good pleasure" (Luke 2:14). ³⁶**For the multitude of the people were following, shouting, "Take him away."** Their following kept Paul in danger, and the shout of this multitude echoes the shout of "all the multitude" at Jesus' trial before another Roman, Pontius Pilate: "Take this [Jesus] away" (Luke 23:18). Since they led Jesus away to crucifixion, the present echo suggests that "Take [Paul] away" means, "Take him away to crucifixion [a Roman method of execution]," not just removal from the scene.

21:37–40: **And as he was about to be brought into the barracks, Paul says to the commander of the cohort, "[Tell me] if it's permissible for me to say something to you."** The circumspection of Paul's request contrasts with the rampageous demand of the multitude. The contrast puts him, and therefore his gospel, in a good light. The present tense in "Paul *says*" vivifies the contrast for emphasis. **And he** [the commander] **said, "You know** [how to speak] **in Greek!"** Apparently Paul had made his request in Greek. ³⁸**"Then** [since much more Greek is spoken in Egypt than in Israel] **you're the Egyptian, aren't you, who before these days** [= some time ago] **incited and led out into the desert four thousand men** [consisting] **of the Assassins** [men who carried concealed daggers with which to assassinate fellow Jews who collaborated with the Roman overlords]**?"** Implied answer: Yes, you're that Egyptian. ³⁹**But Paul said, "On the one hand, I'm a Jewish man, a Tarsian from Cilicia** [not Egypt], **a citizen of not an insignificant city** [= a positively significant city, as indeed Tarsus was]. **On the other hand, I beg you, permit me to speak to the people."** Paul takes pride in his home city and appeals to his citizenship there. He's no rebel. Again his circumspection ("I beg you, allow me") contrasts with the multitude's rampageous demand. ⁴⁰**And when he** [the commander] **had given permission, Paul, standing on the stairs, shook** [his] **hand downward at the people** [a gesture designed to quiet them down]. **And when much silence came about, he addressed them in**

the Aramaic language, saying . . . ." Aramaic, the predominant language of Jews living in first-century Israel, was considered a version of Hebrew; for these languages are very closely related.

PAUL'S DEFENSE BEFORE HIS FELLOW JEWS
Acts 22:1–21

22:1–5: **"Men, brothers, and fathers, listen to my defense** [that I] **now** [make] **to you."** ²**And on hearing that he was addressing them in the Aramaic language, they provided more quiet** [for him to speak]. "Men" addresses males. "Brothers" appeals to Paul's sharing the Jewish heritage of his peers and juniors in the audience. And "fathers" shows respect to his seniors. "*More* quiet" implies that the "much silence" in 21:40 wasn't total. **And he says, ³"I'm a Jewish man, born in Tarsus of Cilicia but brought up in this city, educated accurately at the feet of Gamaliel in accordance with** [our] **ancestral law, being God's zealot, just as you all are** [God's zealots] **today,** ⁴**who** [Paul is referring back to himself] **persecuted this Way** [see the comments on 9:2 concerning 'the Way' as a designation of Christianity] **to the death, binding and giving over into prisons both husbands and wives** [8:3], ⁵**as also the high priest testifies concerning me—all the council of elders** [= the whole Sanhedrin] **too—from whom** [plural, for both the high priest and the council] **on having also received letters to the** [non-Christian Jewish] **brothers, I started traveling to Damascus for the purpose of bringing even the** [Christians] **there to Jerusalem, after they'd been bound, to be punished."** Paul had told the commander of the Roman cohort that he was a Jewish man and citizen of Tarsus in Cilicia. But speaking now to an antagonistic Jewish audience leads Paul to replace the reference to his Tarsian citizenship with a reference to his being brought up in that audience's own city of Jerusalem despite having been born in Tarsus. And to his upbringing in Jerusalem he adds his education under the famous rabbi Gamaliel, so well respected (Luke expects us to remember) that the Sanhedrin earlier took his advice to release the apostles Peter and John rather than killing them (5:33–40). Paul also emphasizes the accuracy of his education as regards the Jews' ancestral law— that is, the law of God as passed down through the Jews' ancestors, beginning with Moses—and complements his education with action: "being God's zealot," which means persecuting Christians as violators of God's law much as Phinehas showed similar zeal for God's law in early Israelite history (Number 25:6–8) and just as all Paul's audience have been doing to him this very day of his speaking to them.

At first, "just as you all are [God's zealots] today" looks as though Paul is throwing his audience a bouquet. But then one realizes that he's referring to their persecution of him, against which he's defending himself. "To the death" indicates that his own persecution of Christians had resulted in martyrdom, as in Stephen's case (7:54–8:1), and parallels the present crowd's attempt to kill Paul (21:31). His persecution included binding and imprisoning "both husbands and wives." Though the underlying phrase is usually translated "both men and women," the pairing of these nouns favors "husbands and wives"; and the point seems to be that Paul was so zealous as to include in his persecution the wives of his male victims. And lest such family-destroying zeal seem unbelievable, he cites the high priest and the whole Sanhedrin both as witnesses to such zeal on his part and as backers of his persecution through their writing letters of reference to show Jews living in Damascus that he had authority to arrest, bind, and take back to Jerusalem for punishment any Christians he found in Damascus. "*Even* the [Christians] there" stresses the distance Paul's zeal would take him, and "for the purpose of bringing [them] . . . to Jerusalem . . . to be punished" draws a parallel with the crowd's attempt to punish him in Jerusalem. As to the letters of reference, "received" connotes a welcoming reception. Paul was glad to receive such letters so that he could pursue Christians all the way to Damascus. The detailing of this zeal has the purpose of making his conversion inexplicable apart from what happens next in his autobiographical account.

22:6–10: "But it happened that as I was traveling and drawing near to Damascus, around midday a brilliant light from heaven suddenly flashed around me; ⁷and I fell to the ground and heard a voice saying to me, 'Saul, Saul, why are you persecuting me?' ⁸And I answered, 'Who are you, Lord?' And he told me, 'I'm Jesus the Nazarene [= the Jesus from Nazareth], **whom you're persecuting.'" ⁹And those who were with me saw the light, on the one hand. On the other hand, they didn't hear the voice of the one speaking to me. ¹⁰And I said, 'What should I do, Lord?' And the Lord told me, 'On standing up, continue traveling to Damascus; and there it'll be told you all the things that are assigned for you to do.'"** As compared with Luke's account in 9:3–7, Paul adds the temporal note "around midday" and a description of the light as "brilliant." This description implies that the light outshone the sun even at its height. "Falling *to* the ground" may imply falling from a beast of burden as "falling *on* the ground" in 9:4 didn't necessarily do. (The Greek words for "ground" also differ in these two passages, the one used here suggesting a bottom to be reached by falling, as from a beast.) See the comments on 9:4–5 for Jesus' initial question and Saul's/Paul's counter question. To Jesus' answer, "I'm Jesus," Paul adds "the Nazarene" to distinguish this Jesus from other Jesuses known to the audience. There followed in 9:6–7 Jesus' command to stand up and go into Damascus, where it would be told Saul/Paul what he must do. Only then did the experience of his traveling companions come into play. But to stress the brilliance of the light, Paul now replaces their speechlessness (so 9:7) with their seeing of the light, which also replaces their having seen no one (that is, their not having seen who was speaking to Paul [so 9:7 again]). Here at 22:9, in fact, Paul says his companions didn't even hear Jesus' voice, much less see him. He replaces his companions' "*hearing* the voice" (9:7) with "they *didn't* hear the voice

of the one speaking to me." It's possible that 9:7 meant they heard the voice as noise and that 22:9 means they didn't hear the voice as articulate speech. But the point of emphasis remains that they saw the light, whereas 9:3–7 said nothing of the sort. In other words, Paul now cites his companions as eyewitnesses for certification of his account just as Luke cited some of his sources as eyewitnesses for certification of his own account (Luke 1:1–4). And however "hear" in 22:9 is to be understood, the conversation between Jesus and Paul remains private so as to highlight Paul's adding the question (missing in 9:6), "What should I do, Lord?" This question exhibits further that Paul was "God's zealot" even in his conversion.

Since Saul/Paul has asked what he should do, the Lord's "Nevertheless" in 9:6 isn't needed any more. That is to say, Jesus no longer issues the command to stand up and go into Damascus to be told what to do *despite* his having said, "I'm Jesus, whom you're persecuting." He issues the command *because* Paul has asked what he should do. And since he has asked for an assignment, Jesus speaks of "all the things that are *assigned* for you to do," whereas in 9:6 he spoke of "whatever is *necessary* for you to do." Necessity was to be *imposed* on a Saul/Paul who didn't ask what he should do. Now an assignment is to be *given* to a Saul/Paul who did ask what he should do. And "*all* the things that are assigned" replaces the earlier "*whatever* is necessary" for a veiled forecast of Paul's evangelistic success instead of a veiled forecast of what he'll have to suffer for the sake of Jesus' name (compare 9:6 with 9:16).

22:11: "And when I wasn't seeing because of the glory of that light, being hand-led by those who were with me I came to Damascus." Luke wrote in 9:8 that Saul/Paul saw nothing *despite* his eyes being opened. Here, Paul says he wasn't seeing *because of* "the glory of that light." Since Jesus was speaking to him, this glory gives evidence that Jesus had indeed "entere[d] into his glory," just as he said it was scripturally necessary for him to do after suffering (Luke 24:26 [compare Luke 9:26, 32; 21:27]). Paul doesn't say how it was that the glory of that light blinded him but not his companions, who also saw the light (22:9). Did they not see its glory, as Paul did? In any case, he's more concerned to point out Jesus' glory than to provide a lesson in ophthalmology.

22:12–13: "And a certain Ananias, a devout man in accordance with the Law, being recommended by all the Jews residing [in Damascus], **¹³on coming to me and standing over** [me] **told me, 'Saul, brother, look up!' And that very hour I looked up at him."** Ananias will turn out to be a Christian. So the description of Ananias as "a *devout* man," and this "in accordance with the *Law* [of Moses]," highlights both the piety of Christians and the continuity of Christianity with the age-old religion of Judaism. The favorable testimony concerning Ananias by the Jewish residents of Damascus, indeed by *all* of them, undergirds this piety and this continuity both for Paul's audience and for Luke's audience. Furthermore, Paul omits his neither seeing, eating, nor drinking "for three days," and omits Ananias's vision as well (9:9–16). These omissions let all the emphasis rest on Christian Law-faithful piety and continuity with Judaism. As in 9:17, Ananias is said to have addressed Saul both by name and with "brother" to establish rapport. But here the command "look up!" replaces Ananias's references to the visions he and Saul/Paul had seen. This command and Paul's saying that he "looked up" at Ananias, who was "standing over [him]," concentrate attention on the restoration of sight "at that very hour." Since an hour was their shortest unit of time, this phrase highlights the immediacy with which Paul's sight was miraculously restored.

22:14–16: "And he [Ananias] said, 'The God of our [fore]fathers hand-picked you beforehand to know his will and see the Righteous One and hear a voice [coming] out of his mouth, ¹⁵because you'll be a witness for him to all people of the things you've seen and heard. ¹⁶And now, what are you going [to do]? On standing up, get baptized and get your sins washed away by calling on his name [the name of Jesus the Righteous One].'" See the comments on 2:21 for "calling on his name." "The God of our [fore]fathers" appeals yet again to continuity between Christianity and Judaism. "Hand-picked you beforehand" alludes to God's plan, which is to be worked out through Paul (among others), so that Christianity isn't an aberration. "To know his will" implies that what Paul has since been proclaiming and doing corresponds to divine revelation. It hasn't popped out of his imagination. "To . . . see the Righteous One" alludes to Paul's vision on the road to Damascus. Earlier, Paul said he "was *not* seeing because of the *glory* of that light" (22:11). His present statement indicates that the glory of that light was the glory of the Righteous One, who identified himself as Jesus; that he *did* see the glorified Jesus; and that the brilliance of the light of Jesus' glory blinded him. The designation of Jesus as "the Righteous One" calls attention to his virtues (compare 3:14; 7:52; Luke 23:47). "To . . . hear a voice [coming] out of his mouth" makes Paul an ear- as well as eyewitness to Jesus as the risen, glorified Lord (compare Luke 1:1–4). It follows, then, that "you [Paul] will be a witness for him . . . of the things you've seen and heard." "To *all* people" prepares for Jesus' later sending Paul "far off [from Jerusalem] to Gentiles" (22:21). "And *now*" aims at what Paul is to waste no time doing. He says that Ananias answered his own question, "what are you going to do?" The answer was that on standing up, Paul should get baptized and get his sins washed away by calling on Jesus' name. So Ananias's question turned into a command. "On standing up" confirms that Paul had had to "look up" at Ananias, who was "standing over [him]" (22:13). To call on Jesus' name is to get one's sins washed away, as pictured in baptism. The picture of sins being washed *away* made immersion in *flowing* water preferable, though not necessary, in the early church. Paul leaves it to be assumed that he followed Ananias's orders, but Luke's account in 9:18 leaves no doubt for the audience of Acts. (Mainly

because of Paul's having omitted Ananias's vision, some details that appeared in 9:17–19a don't appear here.)

22:17–18: "And it happened to me upon returning to Jerusalem that as I was praying in the temple [courts] I came to be in a trance ¹⁸and saw him [Jesus the Righteous One] **saying to me, 'Hurry up and go out of Jerusalem quickly, because they won't welcome your witness concerning me** [compare 9:26–30].'"** Paul's returning to Jerusalem and praying at the temple display his piety and loyalty to Judaism. His seeing Jesus in a trance makes him for the second time an eyewitness of Jesus as the risen and glorified Lord (compare the comments on 22:11) and indicates Jesus' approval of Paul's praying in the temple courts. But the command to get out of Jerusalem indicates Jesus' disapproval of the Jerusalemites' nonwelcome of Paul's testimony concerning him. The testimony had as its subject matter Paul's *initial* eyewitnessing of Jesus as the risen, glorified Lord. Paul doesn't quote Jesus as mentioning the plot of "the Hellenists," Greek-speaking Jews, to do away with Paul (for which see 9:29), so that the accent falls here on the nonwelcome of Paul's testimony. Since that plot goes unmentioned here and since Paul's present audience of Jerusalemites in general will erupt against him, "they" who according to Jesus will reject Paul's testimony include more than those Hellenists—rather, the present audience themselves. "Hurry up" means get out as *soon* as possible. "Quickly" means get out as *fast* as possible.

22:19–21: "And I said, 'Lord, they themselves understand that synagogue by synagogue I used to imprison and bind [with chains in the prisons] those who believe on you [= who rest their eternal fates on you]. **²⁰And when the blood of Stephen your witness was being shed, even I myself was standing over** [the incident] **and taking delight** [in the bloodshed] **and guarding the garments of those who were doing away with him.' ²¹And he** [the Lord] **told me, 'Start traveling, because I'll send you far off to Gentiles.'"** Paul cited his past persecution of Christians as a reason not to get out of Jerusalem soon and fast. Surely the Jerusalemites' knowledge of him as a former persecutor would make them accept his testimony. Paul readdressed Jesus with "Lord" to make his argument respectful (compare 22:8, 10) and detailed the persecution to strengthen his argument: (1) "Synagogue by synagogue" describes the persecution as extensive and thorough. (2) "I used to imprison and bind . . ." describes it as ruthless. (3) Participation in Stephen's bloodshed describes the persecution as murderous. "Even I myself was standing over [the incident]" probably means that Paul had charge of Stephen's murder, so that he wasn't a mere bystander. That is, he guarded the clothes of those who were carrying out his bidding and took delight in its accomplishment (compare how 8:3 follows up on 7:58; 8:1). But Jesus wasn't convinced by Paul's argument. Jesus' order to leave because of the Jerusalemites' nonwelcome of Paul's witness now morphs into an order to start traveling because Jesus will send him on a far-flung mission to Gentiles. Luke's audience know, of course, that Jesus' prediction came true.

THE SEIZURE AND NEAR TORTURE OF PAUL
Acts 22:22–29

The mention in 22:21 of a far-flung mission to Gentiles is too much for Paul's audience. **22:22–24: But they** [the audience] **were listening to him up to this statement and raised their voice** [the singular indicating a united outcry], **saying, "Take away such** [a man] **from the earth** [that is, execute him], **for it isn't fitting that he live** [compare Luke 23:18]." In other words, he's too disgraceful to be left alive. Luke's largely Gentile audience will recognize in this outcry the prejudice, indeed hatred, of these Jews against them. He hopes their recognition will translate into a favorable reception of the gospel. [23]**And as they** [the crowd] **were shouting and throwing off** [their outer] **garments and tossing dust into the air** [all signs of violent displeasure with Paul], [24]**the commander of the cohort commanded him to be brought into the barracks, saying he should be interrogated with whips in order that he** [the commander] **might know the charge** [against Paul] **on account of which they were calling out to him in this way** [that is, calling out to the commander to take Paul away from the earth by executing him]. The obvious hatred of the crowd for Paul and the equally obvious injustice of the commander's order to torture him raise sympathy for Paul in Luke's audience and therefore make likely a sympathetic hearing of the gospel.

22:25–29: But when they'd stretched him out for the thongs [that were attached to a handle, making a whip to be used by the soldiers interrogating Paul], **he said to the centurion standing** [there], **"[I ask you] whether it's lawful for you to whip a man who is Roman and uncondemned?"** The answer is obvious: No, it isn't lawful to whip an uncondemned Roman citizen. (The thongs of the whip were often strung with knucklebones, lead pellets, or other sharp objects, sometimes to fatal effect.) It's also obvious that Paul hasn't been condemned. No trial has taken place. It's not so obvious that Paul is a Roman citizen, but his question implies that he is. [26]**And on hearing** [Paul's question], **the centurion, on approaching the commander of the cohort, reported by saying, "What are you about to do? For this man is a Roman."** [27]**And on approaching** [Paul], **the commander of the cohort said to him, "Tell me, are you a Roman?" And he said, "Yes."** [28]**And the commander of the cohort answered, "I acquired this citizenship with much capital** [= I bought it with a large sum of money]." **And Paul said, "But I was even** *born* [a Roman citizen]!" Citizenship by birth outranked citizenship by purchase, and citizenship by purchase meant bribery. [29]**Immediately, therefore, those who were about to interrogate him** [with the whips] **disengaged from him; and also the commander of the cohort got scared on recognizing that Paul is a Roman and that he'd bound**

him [with two chains (see 21:33)]. "Also" implies that the commander got scared for what he'd done by having Paul bound just as the interrogators were so scared that they disengaged from Paul without having whipped him. And the present tense in "Paul *is* a Roman" stresses his citizenship and therefore the illegality of what had already been done to him and what was planned to be done to him.

THE SELF-DEFENSE OF PAUL
BEFORE THE SANHEDRIN
Acts 22:30–23:11

22:30: And on the morrow, wanting to know the certainty [= the facts] **in regard to what he** [Paul] **is being accused of by the Jews, he** [the commander of the cohort] **had him loosened.** Earlier, he'd had Paul bound with two chains (21:33). "*Is* being accused of" represents the action as it was at the time. **And he commanded the chief priests and all the Sanhedrin** [that is, its other members as well] **to come together; and on bringing Paul down** [the stairs from the barracks (compare 21:34–35, 40; 22:24)], **he had** [him] **stand among them.** The day before, the commander had inquired of the uproarious crowd at the temple who Paul might be and what he'd done worthy of a lynching; but some called out one thing and others something else (21:33–34). So now the commander convenes the Sanhedrin for a formal session apart from the crowd.

23:1–3: And gazing at the Sanhedrin, Paul said, "Men, brothers, with an entirely good conscience I've lived as a citizen for God up to this day." Paul's gaze adds emphasis to his words, and the addition of "brothers" to "Men" appeals to the common ground of Jewish heritage. He knows that the Roman commander is listening as well as the Sanhedrin. For the commander, then, he says that he has lived as a citizen with an entirely good conscience. Since he and the commander conversed the preceding day about their respective Roman citizenships (22:25–28), the commander will understand Paul to be describing his life as a Roman citizen. At least for the audience of Acts, then, Paul's "entirely good conscience" may reflect badly on the commander's having bought citizenship by way of a bribe. But since Paul said in 22:3 that he'd been brought up in Jerusalem, the Sanhedrin will understand Paul to mean that he has lived for God as a citizen of Jerusalem with an entirely good conscience. "Up to this day" describes his Roman and Jewish conduct as blameless right through the uproar of yesterday. He had *not* brought any Gentiles into the temple courts forbidden them. [2]**But the high priest Ananias** [who of course differed from Ananias the Christian in Damascus] **commanded those standing beside him** [Paul] **to strike his mouth.** [3]**Then Paul told him, "God is going to strike you, you whitewashed wall! And you—you sit judging me in accordance with the Law, and violating the Law you command me to be struck!"** A divine stroke is more to be feared than any stroke inflicted by a human being. Nobody has asked Paul to speak. On the contrary, the commander has stood him among the Sanhedrists to find out *from them* what Paul was being accused of. Nevertheless, Paul takes the initiative by speaking. So the high priest commands that he be struck on the mouth to shut him up. He refuses to shut up, though. His further speaking combines with the absence of any indication that the high priest's command was carried out to show that in fact Paul never was struck on the mouth. Instead, he openly predicts God's judgment on the high priest and describes him with the figure of a decoratively plastered wall. This figure indicates turpitude masquerading as sanctity. The masquerade is exemplified, Paul notes, by the high priest's sitting in judgment on him according to the Law while violating the Law in commanding that Paul be struck (see Leviticus 19:15).

23:4–5: And the ones standing beside [Paul] said, "You're insulting God's high priest." ⁵And Paul said, "I didn't know that he's a high priest, brothers. For it's written, 'You shall not badmouth a ruler of your people [Exodus 22:28].'" With "brothers" Paul reaffirms his sharing a Jewish heritage with the Sanhedrists. We're to take his words, "I didn't know . . . ," at face value. He really didn't know. *"For* it's written" explains why he wouldn't have called the high priest a whitewashed wall if he *had* known he was speaking to the high priest. Ignorance of the Law is no excuse. But Paul knows the Law and quotes it. He was ignorant only of the high priest's identity. On the other hand, the high priest comes out as knowingly violating the very Law according to which he's supposed to judge Paul.

23:6–8: And on recognizing that the one part [of the Sanhedrin] consisted of Sadducees and the other [part] of Pharisees, he shouted out in the Sanhedrin, "Men, brothers [for which address see the comments on 23:1], I'm a Pharisee, a son of Pharisees. I'm being judged in regard to hope and resurrection of dead [people]." We don't read, "I'm a Pharisee *and* a son of Pharisees." The absence of an "and" gives independent force to "a son of Pharisees," as in "I'm a Pharisee. [I'm a] son of Pharisees." The consequent emphasis on Pharisaic heritage strengthens Paul's self-identification as a Pharisee. As comes out later, the Pharisees believed in resurrection. The Sadducees didn't. So Paul's identifying himself as a Pharisee and as a descendent of Pharisees not only allies him with the Sanhedrin's Pharisaic faction. It also leads naturally to his and their "hope and resurrection." "Hope" means expectation, not merely a wish. Paul doesn't say he's being judged in regard to the hope *of* resurrection. He says, rather, that he's being judged in regard to two topics: (1) "hope" and (2) "resurrection." True, resurrection is the object of hope; and Paul might have left out hope with the result: "I'm being judged in regard to a resurrection of dead [people]." But by making both hope and resurrection the topics of judgment, he weights equally his *belief* in resurrection (for which he's being judged) and resurrection *itself* (for it's a topic on which Sadducees and Pharisees disagree). **⁷When he'd said this, there developed a dispute on the part of the Pharisees and Sadducees [that is, they wrangled with each other]; and the multitude was divided.** The Sanhedrists, all of whom the Roman commander had convened (22:30), numbered over seventy, so that for a court of justice they were a "multitude." **⁸For on the one hand Sadducees say there's not a resurrection, nor an angel or spirit. On the other hand, Pharisees affirm both.** The Sadducees accepted as Scripture only the Pentateuch (Genesis–Deuteronomy), and no explicit teaching of resurrection appears there. Hence their disbelief in resurrection. God's Spirit, the angel of the Lord or of God, and "the angels of God" (Genesis 28:12) do appear in the Pentateuch. But importantly for Sadducean unbelief, no disembodied human spirits, such as in Paul's and the Pharisees' belief will reinhabit resurrected bodies, appear in the Pentateuch. Furthermore, in Luke 24:36–43 the disciples think at first that they're seeing the resurrected Jesus as a disembodied spirit. In Acts 12:15 Peter is mistaken for "his angel," apparently his disembodied spirit, since an angel is a spirit. In 23:9 "angel" and "spirit" will appear to be alternative designations. And right here in 23:8 "both" is best taken as a reference to "resurrection" on the one hand and to "an angel or spirit" as alternative designations of a disembodied soul awaiting resurrection on the other hand. If not, "both" would have to reference three rather than two items, which is possible (as in 19:16: "one and all") but unlikely (because of the usual reference to only two).

23:9–11: And there came about a great [= loud] clamor; and on standing up, some of the scholars of the part [of the Sanhedrin] consisting of the Pharisees were contending [against the Sadducees], saying, "We find nothing bad in this man. And if a spirit or angel has spoken to him, [so be it]." What stands out is the declaration of Paul's innocence by non-Christian Pharisees. They contemplate the possibility that in the visions Paul reported (22:6–10, 17–21) a spirit or angel, perhaps that of a disembodied Jesus, had spoken to him. The Pharisees aren't prepared to think of a resurrected—that is, reembodied—Jesus, though. **¹⁰And since a serious dispute was developing, the commander of the cohort—fearing lest Paul be torn to pieces by them—commanded the troops, on coming down [from their barracks], to snatch him out of their midst and bring him into the barracks.** For Luke the division between Pharisees and Sadducees argues that since non-Christian Jews disagree among themselves, their disagreement with Christians doesn't rule Christians out of Judaism. As a whole, the incident reflects badly on the Sanhedrin, especially on its leaders, the Sadducees, in their denying a resurrection, angels or spirits, and in their threatening to tear Paul limb from limb in an effort to wrest him from his Pharisaic defenders. He himself looks both admirably clever in causing an intramural dispute and theologically cheerful in affirming hope and resurrection of dead people (not just of Jews!). **¹¹And the following night [= the night following the day of standing amidst the Sanhedrin] the Lord, on standing over him, said, "Maintain courage;**

for as you've borne solemn witness in Jerusalem to the things concerning me, so it's necessary that you testify also in Rome." Presumably Paul was lying down as the Lord stood over him. Since Paul has been testifying about Jesus, "the Lord" who describes that witness as "concerning *me*" must be Jesus. "It's *necessary*" makes Paul's testifying "also in Rome" part of God's unthwartable plan. Hence the command to maintain courage despite current confinement. Indeed, this confinement will promote the testimony in Rome. Note: Paul is to maintain courage in the promotion of his testimony, not in his own well-being.

THE THWARTING OF A PLOT TO KILL PAUL
Acts 23:12–35

This passage divides into the forming of a plot to kill Paul (23:12–15), a discovery of the plot (23:16–21), preparations for a safe transfer of Paul (23:22–30), and the transfer itself (23:31–35). The thwarting of this plot shows the *un*thwartability of God's plan that Paul testify concerning the Lord Jesus also in Rome (compare 23:11). The gospel has divine momentum behind it; so you'd do well to join in.

23:12–15: And when it became day [compare the Lord's speaking to Paul during the night in 23:11], **forming a conspiracy the Jews put themselves under a curse, saying** [they] **would neither eat nor drink till they'd killed Paul.** Otherwise, the curse would take effect, or so they thought (and Luke too?). [13]**And those who formed this plot were more than forty,** [14]**who as such** [that is, as plotters and conspirators] **on approaching the chief priests and the elders said, "With a curse we've put ourselves under a curse to partake of nothing** [that is, neither food nor drink] **until we've killed Paul.** [15]**Now, therefore, you—along with the Sanhedrin** [which includes the scholars as well as you chief priests and elders]—**inform the commander of the cohort that he should bring him** [Paul] **down to you, as if you're going to determine the things** [= the facts] **concerning him more accurately** [than you've been able to do thus far]. **But we're ready to do away with him before he comes near** [to you, so that you'll bear no blame and suffer no retaliation]." So strong is the Jews' opposition to Paul and his gospel that they form their conspiracy the very next day after the Sanhedrin's failed session with him. Since the conspirators go to members of the Sanhedrin, they themselves don't belong to the Sanhedrin. And since the conspirators number more than forty, "the Jews" doesn't include all the Jews in Jerusalem. But more than forty of them makes a formidable force for the assassination of one man in their immediate locality. And they know both his whereabouts and the route on which he'll be taken if he's brought back to the Sanhedrin. Moreover, putting themselves under a curse not to eat or drink till they've killed Paul shows them fanatically determined—no, *terroristically* determined—to kill him. The redundancy of "with a curse . . . under a curse" stresses their determination. Other things being equal,

it doesn't look good for Paul. But the Lord's nighttime encouragement of him in 23:11 showed that other things aren't equal. "The chief priests and the elders" would have been Sadducees, ill-disposed toward Paul because of his having identified himself as a Pharisee and believer in the resurrection, which they denied. Naturally, then, the conspirators go to those segments of the Sanhedrin antagonistic toward Paul and tell them to schedule another meeting of the whole Sanhedrin, presumably to schedule it without revealing to the rest of the Sanhedrin (particularly the Pharisees, who had taken Paul's side) about the plan for assassination.

23:16–21: And having heard about the [planned] **ambush, the son of Paul's sister, on arriving and going into the barracks, reported** [it] **to Paul.** [17]**And on summoning one of the centurions, Paul said, "Lead this young man off to the commander of the cohort, for he has something to report to him."** Since Paul was brought up in Jerusalem though born in Tarsus (22:3), it seems likely that he not only has or had a sister but also that she too was brought up in Jerusalem and had a son who lives there currently. The main point, though, is that the plot against Paul's life is beginning to unravel in favor of God's plan for him. [18]**Taking him along on the one hand, therefore, he** [the centurion] **led** [the young man, Paul's nephew] **to the commander of the cohort and says, "On summoning me, the prisoner Paul requested** [me] **to lead to you this young man, who has something to tell you."** Unknowingly, the centurion cooperates with God's plan for Paul. The present tense in "says" highlights the centurion's carrying out Paul's request, which God will use to save Paul from assassination and thus get him to Rome for further witness. [19]**And on taking hold of his hand and withdrawing, he** [the commander] **was inquiring in private, "What is** [it] **that you have** [in the sense of possessing, not in the sense of necessity] **to report to me?"** Now the commander as well as the centurion is beginning to be drawn into the working out of God's plan for Paul. But the commander is aware of his function no more than the centurion was. The nearly friendly gesture of "taking hold of his hand" shows how unsuspectingly cooperative with God is the commander, as does also the withdrawing for a private inquiry that won't alert the conspirators to the discovery and thwarting of their plot. [20]**And he** [the young man] **said, "The Jews have agreed to make a request of you,** [which is] **that tomorrow you should bring down Paul into the Sanhedrin as if they're going to inquire somewhat more accurately about him.** [21]**Therefore** [= in view of the 'as if'] **you shouldn't be persuaded by them, for out of them more than forty men are waiting to ambush him,** [men] **who as such** [= as would-be ambushers] **have put themselves under a curse neither to eat nor to drink till they've done away with him. And they're ready now, expectantly awaiting your promise** [to bring Paul down into the Sanhedrin]." Though he doesn't know God's plan for Paul to testify in Rome, the young man has played his part in bringing it to fruition.

23:22–24: Therefore the commander of the cohort dismissed the young man, having directed [him] to speak out to no one "that you've informed me of these things." The commander continues to carry out God's plan both secretly and unknowingly. To do so, in a reversal of roles the commander even starts to follow the young man's telling him that he shouldn't bring Paul down into the Sanhedrin. The shift from indirect discourse ("having directed him to speak out to no one") to direct discourse ("that *you*'ve made these things clear to *me*") emphasizes the commander's concern for the secrecy that will ensure a successful transfer of Paul from the danger zone. **23And on summoning a certain two of the centurions, he said, "Get ready two hundred soldiers, plus seventy horsemen and two hundred spearmen, so that by the third hour of the night** [= by nine o'clock tonight] **they may travel to Caesarea"; 24and [he said] to provide mounts in order that after putting Paul on** [a mount] **they might save [him] through to Felix the governor** [in Caesarea on the Mediterranean coast] .... To the commander, Paul was a Roman citizen who stood in danger of assassination by fanatical Jews and whose protection would add a credit to the commander's military record. To Luke and his audience, Paul was also and more importantly a herald of the gospel, which God wanted him to proclaim as far away as Rome, capital of the empire. From both angles, then, the preparations for a quick and safe transfer from Jerusalem to Caesarea didn't seem excessive. The expression "*save* [him] through to Felix the governor," where we might have expected a simple "*bring/take* [him] to . . . ," accents the element of saving Paul for his divinely planned proclamation in Rome. What chance will forty-plus would-be assassins have against two hundred soldiers, seventy cavalry, and two hundred spearmen? They won't even know that Paul is being taken away under cover of darkness. They're waiting to ambush him next morning right in Jerusalem. By then he'll be gone. And though the foot soldiers and spearmen will have to walk, multiple mounts are supplied for Paul to ride on, one after another, all the way to the coast—or perhaps for him and his baggage and/or companions. Little does the commander understand the evangelistic significance of what he's doing under the guidance of God's hidden hand.

Luke's sentence continues in reference to the commander of the cohort. **23:25–30: having written a letter possessing this form: 26"Claudius Lysias to the most excellent governor Felix:** [I wish you] **to rejoice** [= the Greek way of saying, 'Greetings' or 'Hello']. **27This man, having been seized by the Jews and being about to be done away with** [= killed] **by them, I extricated** [from their clutches] **by coming on them with troops after learning that he's a Roman."** False! The commander, whose name we now know, didn't learn of Paul's citizenship till later. It was a tumult in the temple courts that brought the commander and his troops on the scene. And the so-called extrication consisted in clamping chains on him illegally (21:31–33). The commander is lying to make himself look good. But his lying makes the truth of the gospel look good by contrast. **28"And wanting to know the charge** [against Paul] **on account of which they** [the Jews] **were accusing him, I brought** [him] **down into their Sanhedrin, 29whom** [referring to Paul] **I found being accused in regard to moot points of their law, but having no charge** [against him] **deserving of death or bonds** [= imprisonment in chains]**."** Here the commander tells the truth. Paul is innocent. It's not the gospel as such that causes social unrest. It's opposition to the gospel that does. And a non-Christian military man says as much. **30"And when a forthcoming plot against the man was disclosed to me, I sent** [him] **to you at once, having ordered also those accusing** [him] **to say before you the things** [they have] **against him."** The governor outranks the commander, so that the commander refers Paul's case to the governor. But on discovering that Paul hadn't done anything deserving of death or bonds, why didn't the commander just release him? Ah, then Paul would have been completely exposed to assassination. The continuation of his case saves him from that fate and will eventually propel him to Rome for Christian witness there. The Romans, of all people, are unwittingly carrying out God's plan.

23:31–35: On the one hand, therefore, in accordance with what had been directed them [= their orders] **the soldiers, on taking up Paul** [probably to hoist him onto a mount (compare 1:9 with 1:11)]**, brought** [him] **by night to Antipatris** [a city in Judea]**. 32The next day, on the other hand, after letting the horsemen go off with him they** [the foot soldiers and spearmen] **returned to the barracks** [in Jerusalem]**, 33who as such** [referring now to the horsemen in their capacity as horsemen, since Paul too was riding a mount]**, on entering into Caesarea and delivering up the letter to the governor, presented also Paul to him** [that is, Paul in addition to Claudius Lysias's letter]. Mission accomplished! God's plan in progress! **34And on reading** [the letter] **and asking from what province he is** [the present tense reflecting the question at the time] **and being apprised that** [Paul is] **from Cilicia, 35he said, "I'll hear your case whenever your accusers also arrive," commanding him to be guarded in Herod's palace** [built by Herod the Great for himself, but that Herod was long dead by now]. The promise to hear Paul's case and the command that he be kept under guard in Herod's palace appear to be given in close conjunction with each other. The palace doesn't sound like a bad place to be kept. Is Luke playing up the Romans' well-disposed treatment of Paul as an indication of God's providential care over this evangelist?

PAUL UNDER THE JURISDICTION OF GOVERNOR FELIX
Acts 24:1–6b, 8b–27

This passage divides into accusations against Paul (24:1–6b, 8b–9), his defense (24:10–21), the extension of his case (24:22–23), and private meetings between him and Felix (24:24–27). The earliest and best manuscripts don't have 24:6c–8a.

24:1–3: And after five days the high priest Ananias came down [from Jerusalem to Caesarea] **with some elders and a certain orator** [by the name of] **Tertullus, who as such** [referring to them all in their function as Paul's accusers] **informed the governor** [of their charges] **against Paul.** Using his skill as a public speaker, Tertullus is going to act as a prosecuting attorney. Other things being equal, the high social status of Ananias and the elders could weigh heavily against Paul. **²And when he** [Paul] **had been called, Tertullus began to accuse** [him]**, saying, "Having attained much peace through you—and because reforms are happening for this nation through your forethought—³we welcome** [this peace and these reforms] **both every** [way] **and everywhere, most excellent Felix, with all thanksgiving."** To get on Felix's good side, Tertullus starts with an oratorical flourish of fawning compliments. Though largely untrue to the facts of Felix's governorship, they're geared to the accusations Tertullus is about to bring against Paul in that according to those accusations Paul has been disturbing the peace. And by mentioning Felix's supposed reforms, Tertullus is implying in advance that doing away with Paul will add another reform to Felix's resumé.

24:4–6b, 8b–9: "But in order that I not bore you further, I urge you to hear us briefly at your indulgence. ⁵For on finding this man [to be] **a pest** [in the sense of a troublemaker] **and a mobilizer of uprisings among all the Jews throughout the inhabited** [earth] **and a ringleader of the faction of the Nazarenes** [= Christians, designated this way because Jesus was from Nazareth], **⁶ᵃ⁻ᵇwho even tried to profane the temple** [by bringing a Gentile past the court of Gentiles into an inner court forbidden them (see 21:27–29)]**, whom also we seized, ⁸ᵇ⁻ᶜfrom whom you yourself by interrogating** [him] **will be able to ascertain all these things about which we're accusing him."** With "not to bore you further," "briefly," and "at your indulgence," Tertullian completes his initial attempt to ingratiate himself, the high priest, and the elders with Felix. "For" introduces the reason Felix should continue listening. We know, of course, the falsity of Tertullus's charges. It's unbelievers, not Paul, who've made trouble and mobilized uprisings. "Among all the Jews throughout the inhabited earth" would be a gross exaggeration even if it were true that Paul had made trouble and mobilized uprisings. The word translated "ringleader" refers to a man of front rank, a leader, and here occurs in relation to "uprisings." In fact, these two words have the same root, so that Tertullus falsely charges Paul with being a leader of uprisings—hence, "a ringleader." "Of the faction of the Nazarenes" casts a slur on Paul as a leader of believers in "this Jesus, the Nazarene," who according to a false report "will tear down this place [the temple] and change the standards that Moses gave over to us [the Jews]" (6:14). The charge that Paul had tried to profane the temple implies that the Jewish authorities should have jurisdiction over his case and that therefore Lysias was wrong to take Paul from them. (Tertullus studiously avoids mentioning the near lynching of Paul and speaks instead about a seemingly orderly arrest.) But we also know that Paul didn't try to profane the temple. On the contrary, he was undergoing rites of purification there and even paying for others' such rites (21:17–26). Tertullus's attributing to Felix the ability to confirm with his own interrogation all the charges against Paul adds a final touch to the inflated, fawning compliments showered on Felix. **⁹And the Jews, too, joined in laying** [these charges against Paul]**, alleging these things to be so.** "Too" either means the rest of the Jews (the high priest and the elders of 24:1) or, more naturally, implies that Tertullus is a Gentile (compare 24:5, where he speaks of "the Jews"). If he's a Gentile, "*we* welcome" and "*we're* accusing" in 24:3, 8 represent his speaking on behalf of the Jews though speaking as a Gentile to a Gentile governor; and there's irony in the Jews' using a Gentile as a hired gun in an intra-Jewish dispute concerning a purported profanation of the temple by a Gentile.

24:10–11: And when the governor had nodded for him to speak, Paul replied [to the charges brought against him]**, "Understanding you to have been a judge for this nation over many years, as to the things concerning myself I make my defense optimistically, ¹¹since you're able to ascertain that I've not had more than twelve days since I went up to Jerusalem for the purpose of worshiping."** Paul doesn't flatter Felix. He doesn't even address him by name and status (contrast Tertullus's "most excellent Felix" [24:3]). He only notes Felix's long experience in judging Jewish affairs as giving Paul optimism that Felix will judge fairly. And this optimism is supported further by Felix's ability to ascertain Paul's having gone up to Jerusalem for the purpose of worshiping God, not for the purpose of mobilizing an uprising, as Tertullus has charged him with doing (24:5). "You're able to ascertain" echoes Tertullus's "you yourself by interrogating [Paul] will be able to ascertain." But in line with his not flattering Felix, Paul omits the emphatic "yourself." He also omits "by interrogating," because Felix would need only to hear testimony from unaccused witnesses. "Not . . . more than twelve days" makes Paul's going up to Jerusalem for worship so recent as to render the memory of witnesses reliable and the actions of Paul directly contradictory to Tertullus's charge that he tried to profane the temple at the time. Paul ignores the charge that he has mobilized uprisings elsewhere throughout the inhabited earth. After all, the high priest and the elders haven't themselves witnessed such uprisings, nor do they have others on hand to testify concerning them.

24:12–15: "And neither in the temple [courts] **nor in the synagogues nor throughout the city did they find me conversing with anybody** [which could have resulted in an argumentative disturbance] **or causing the onset of a crowd** [such as could have resulted in a massive uprising]. **¹³Nor are they** [my accusers] **able to demonstrate** [the things] **about which they're now accusing me. ¹⁴But I declare this to you, that according to the Way, which they say** [is] **a faction—in this manner I do religious service for the God of** [our] [fore] fathers, believing all the things in accordance with the Law and [all] the things written in the Prophets [= two of the three main divisions of the Hebrew Old Testament], ¹⁵having a hope in God that also these [my accusers] themselves are expectantly awaiting, [that] there's going to be a resurrection of both righteous and unrighteous people." They've falsely accused Paul of trying to profane the temple. Not only does he truthfully deny that he did. He says he hasn't even engaged anyone in conversation or done anything else that would have drawn a crowd whether in the temple courts, the synagogues, or elsewhere in the city. See the comments on 9:2 for the designation of Christianity as "the Way." By noting that *his accusers* say the Way is "a faction," Paul implies that it's not one faction among others within Judaism, like the Pharisaic and Sadducean factions (5:17; 15:5; 26:5). No, it's the true, one and only culmination of Judaism. "In this manner I do religious service for the God of [our] [fore]fathers" describes the Way as having an ancient pedigree in its fidelity to the God of Abraham, Isaac, and Jacob, and describes Paul himself as serving God religiously in his Christian activities. His "believing *all* the things" that are "in *accordance* with the Law" makes him completely faithful to what's written in the Pentateuch without committing him to rabbinical add-ons (compare Luke 11:46). His "believing all the things . . . written in the Prophets" and "having a hope in God . . . [that] there's going to be a resurrection" ally him with the Pharisees, the most popular of the Jewish religious factions, and distinguish him from the Sadducees, who don't accept the Prophets as Holy Scripture and who disbelieve in resurrection (23:6–8). "A resurrection of *both* righteous *and* unrighteous people" reflects Daniel 12:2 (compare Luke 14:14; 20:35–36; John 5:28–29; Revelation 20:11–15) and therefore implies Paul's belief in the third main division of the Hebrew Old Testament, the Writings. But "having a hope *in God*" bases Paul's confidence of a general resurrection not on the Writings as such but on God, whose Spirit inspired them and who alone can raise the dead. "A hope that also these [my accusers] themselves are expectantly awaiting" implies either that none of his present accusers are Sadducees (an unlikely possibility, since surely the high priest and probably the elders were Sadducees) or that Paul refers to at least some of the elders as Pharisees (a better possibility, since in the midst of the Sanhedrin he declared his belief in resurrection on noting a mixture of Pharisees and Sadducees [23:6]). Or Paul is speaking ironically in that neither the high priest nor the elders believe in resurrection (the best possibility, since after the Pharisees defended Paul against the Sadducees in a meeting of the Sanhedrin [23:9], his would-be assassins colluded with the chief priest and the elders, apparently anti-Pauline Sadducees, but not with the rest of the Sanhedrin, apparently pro-Pauline Pharisees [23:12–15]). If speaking ironically, Paul is indirectly accusing his accusers of theological heresy.

24:16–18: "In this [= in view of the coming resurrection] I myself also [= in addition to having hope] try always to have an irreproachable conscience toward God and [toward] human beings [that is, to have no consciousness of anything in my conduct that would offend either God or my fellow human beings]." "Try" has the connotation of exercising. "Always" points to the practice of moral exercise without letting up. These self-descriptions of Paul contribute to Luke's overall emphasis on the moral and religious virtues of Jesus and his followers. Luke designs this emphasis to appeal to prospective converts who have moral and religious sensitivities. ¹⁷"And after very many years I arrived to do alms [= to bring charitable gifts] for my nation and [to do] offerings [= to pay for the purificatory sacrifices of the four men mentioned in 21:23–26], ¹⁸in which [= in the doing of which alms and offerings] they found me, having been [ritually] purified, in the temple [courts], not with a crowd and not with an uproar." Paul describes his doing of alms as for the Jewish nation, which he also owns as *his* (note the shift from "*this* nation" in 24:10 to "*my* nation" here). And he describes his doing of offerings as performed in the temple courts (to be distinguished from his taking an offering of money to the church in Jerusalem [Romans 15:25–28; 1 Corinthians 16:1–4; 2 Corinthians 8–9; Galatians 2:10]). So his Jewish accusers can't rightly consider him an enemy. And he arrived to do alms and offerings despite an absence from Jerusalem of "very many years." Those years, numerous though they were, didn't erase his concern for the poor and needy in the city of his upbringing. Charitable giving was highly valued as a moral and religious virtue, so that Paul's self-description contributes again to Luke's overall emphasis. "To do alms" expresses a *purpose* of coming to Jerusalem. Since elders of the church there didn't tell Paul to pay for purificatory sacrifices till after his arrival (21:18–26), "to do . . . offerings" expresses a *result* of his coming to Jerusalem, and also supports his earlier claim to believe "all the things in accordance with the Law" (24:14). The same goes for his having been ritually purified when the Jews found him in the temple doing these Mosaically prescribed activities. "Not with a crowd and not with an uproar" circles back to "neither in the temple [courts] . . . did they find me . . . causing the onset of a crowd [such as could have resulted in an uproar (24:12)]" to reemphasize that Paul bore no responsibility for the riot that centered on him in the temple courts.

24:19–21: "But some Jews from Asia [found me in the temple courts], whom it was necessary to be present before you and to accuse [me] if they were to have anything against me." By implication, Paul's present accusers—Tertullus, the high priest, and the elders—aren't eyewitnesses. So they can't be trusted. The eyewitnesses are missing. For lack of them, Felix needs to dismiss the case against Paul. And "if they *were* to have anything against me" implies that the Jews from Asia who found Paul purified in the temple wouldn't be able to substantiate a charge even if present. ²⁰"Or let these themselves [= the high priest and the elders present] tell what crime they found when I stood before the Sanhedrin, ²¹other than this one pronouncement, that I shouted out while standing among them, 'I'm being judged before you today in regard to the resurrection of dead people [compare 23:6].'" Paul knows that Felix won't consider Paul's pronouncement a crime and that given the Pharisees' belief in resurrection, Tertullus, the high priest, and the elders won't dare put forward the pronouncement as a crime. Moreover, because of earlier indications of the Pharisees' belief, Luke knows that his own audience won't consider the pronouncement a crime.

24:22–23: And because of knowing the things [= the facts] **concerning the Way quite accurately, Felix put them** [Paul's accusers] **off by saying, "Whenever Lysias, the commander of the cohort, comes down** [from Jerusalem to Caesarea, here on the coast], **I'll decide the things according to you** [plural, referring to Paul's crimes according to Tertullus, the high priest, and the elders],"** .... In other words, Felix knows Christianity better than to decide against Paul on the basis of the charges that have just been brought against him. Lysias, who sent Paul to Felix, won't come down, so that Felix never will sort through the charges to make a final judgment. Besides, he already knows Lysias's opinion, favorable toward Paul, from the letter Lysias sent him (23:25–30). Despite putting off Paul's accusers rather than releasing Paul, Felix's refusal to condemn Paul, and refusing because of quite accurate knowledge of the Way, recommends the gospel to Luke's audience of prospective converts. But there's more to Felix's inadvertent recommendation in the continuation of Luke's sentence: **23directing the centurion that he** [Paul] **be guarded** [for his safety more than to prevent his escape] **and have relief** [from the rigors of imprisonment] **and** [that the centurion] **prevent none of his own** [that is, Paul's relatives and/or friends] **from serving him** [= from meeting his needs, such as for food and clothing, which Romans didn't provide to prisoners]. In other words, the governor goes so far as to grant Paul protective custody with broad privileges. Romans used imprisonment to keep the accused available for trial and the condemned available for punishment, but not for punishment itself.

24:24–27: And after some days Felix, having arrived with Drusilla his own wife, who was a Jewess, sent for Paul and heard him concerning belief in Christ Jesus. Arrived where? Perhaps the audience hall in Herod's palace (compare 25:23), for presumably Paul was being kept elsewhere in the palace (see 23:35). But Luke doesn't say, so that the emphasis falls on Felix's being interested enough to hear Paul talk about belief in Christ Jesus and to bring along his wife to listen in. "His *own* wife" highlights that Drusilla belonged to Felix even though she was Jewish and he Gentile. Since she was Jewish, Luke attaches "Christ" (Greek for the Hebrew "Messiah") to "Jesus." **25And as he** [Paul] **was conversing about righteousness and self-control and the judgment that's going to come, on getting scared Felix answered, "For the time being, go; and on gaining an opportune time I'll call for you," 26at the same time also hoping that**

money would be given him by Paul. For this reason, too, on sending for him he was talking with him quite often. Here, "righteousness" means right conduct as scripturally defined, and "self-control" instances a virtue strongly emphasized by Greco-Roman philosophers, especially the Stoics. So Luke portrays Paul as a preacher of virtues both scriptural and philosophical and therefore Christianity as fostering desirable social reform. This portrayal contributes yet again to Luke's writing for an audience of morally sensitive people ripe for Christian conversion. More particularly, "righteousness" targets Felix's governing unjustly; and "self-control," which has the connotation of sexual chastity (see 1 Corinthians 7:9), targets Felix's having lusted for Drusilla, his present wife, while as a teenager she was the bride of King Azizus of Emesa, a city in Syria. It's the coming judgment according to standards of righteousness and self-control that scares Felix, though not to the effect of repentance (compare 17:30–31). His putting Paul off and the frequent recalls of Paul arose out of Felix's hoping Paul would offer a bribe for his freedom as well as out of Felix's fearful fascination with Paul's message of morality and judgment. No bribe is passed, so that Paul maintains his moral purity as a representative of the gospel. Just as importantly, his staying in custody for failure to bribe his way to freedom will eventuate in the fulfillment of God's plan that he bear witness in Rome (23:11). **27But when two years had been fulfilled, Felix received a successor** [= was succeeded by], **Porcius Festus; and wanting to lay down a favor for the Jews** [after all, Paul hadn't come through with a bribe], **Felix left Paul bound** [as a prisoner]. Not to worry, though. These are only Roman governors. God is in control.

PAUL UNDER THE JURISDICTION OF GOVERNOR FESTUS
Acts 25:1–26:32

This long passage divides into negotiations between Festus and Jewish leaders (25:1–5), Paul's appealing his case to Caesar (25:6–12), Festus's consultation with King Agrippa (25:13–22), and Paul's defense before King Agrippa, Festus, and others (25:23–26:32). This last section subdivides into Festus's opening the session with introductory remarks (25:23–27), Paul's defense proper (26:1–23), Festus's dialogue with Paul (26:24–29), and conversation between Festus and King Agrippa (26:30–32).

25:1–5: Therefore [because of appointment as Felix's successor] **Festus, on setting** [foot] **in the province, went up to Jerusalem from Caesarea after three days. 2And the chief priests and the foremost** [laymen] **of the Jews informed him** [of their charges] **against Paul and were urging him 3by way of requesting a favor against him** [Paul], **so that he** [Festus] **would send for him** [to come] **to Jerusalem, while they were arranging an ambush to do away with him along the road** [from Caesarea]. The combination of "were urging" and "requesting" underlines the strength of the Jews' determination to kill Paul. But the stronger their determination, the more impressive the undoing of their plot—should it be undone. The present plot revives the one described in 23:12–22, and the failure of that one leads us to believe that God's plan for Paul to bear witness in Rome will prevail again. Sure enough, **⁴Festus therefore answered on the one hand that Paul was being kept in Caesarea and, on the other hand, that he himself [Festus] was going to travel out** [from Jerusalem] **shortly. ⁵"Therefore," he says, "on going down** [to Caesarea] **with [me], the dominant ones among you are to accuse him if there is** [in fact] **anything deviant in the man."** Foiled again! There'll be no ambush. Ironically, Paul's enemies rather than he will have to travel for a second time the road between Jerusalem and Caesarea.

25:6–8: And after spending not more than eight or ten days among them [the Jews in Jerusalem], **on going down to Caesarea, taking a seat the next day on the judgment platform** [see 18:12 with comments] **he commanded Paul to be brought.** "Not more than eight or ten days" specifies Festus's "shortly" in 25:4. **⁷And when he** [Paul] **had arrived, the Jews who'd come down from Jerusalem stood around him bringing against [him] many and weighty** [= serious] **charges that they weren't able to demonstrate** [= prove], **⁸while Paul was saying in self-defense, "I've not done anything wrong either against the Jews' law or against the temple or against Caesar."** "Stood around him" suggests a verbal attack from all sides, or at least a verbal siege. The multitude and weight of the charges brought against Paul make the accusers' failure to prove them and the success of his self-defense all the more remarkable. "They weren't *able* to demonstrate" more literally reads, "they weren't *strong* [enough] to demonstrate," an ironic turn of phrase in that the accusers counted as "the *dominant* ones" or, more literally again, "the *powerful* ones." Paul's not having sinned against the Jews' law or against the temple shows him faithful to Judaism—in line with Luke's stress on Christianity as the true and legitimate fruition of Judaism; and Paul's not having sinned against Caesar shows him to be a good Roman citizen, not a dangerous revolutionary. Prospective converts needn't fear they'll be joining a subversive society if they convert.

25:9–12: But wanting to lay down a favor for the Jews, Festus said in answer to Paul, "Are you willing, on going up to Jerusalem, to be judged there before me concerning these [charges]?" The Jews had requested the favor of bringing Paul to Jerusalem when Festus first visited that city (25:3). To establish good relations with the Jewish leaders, Festus now proposes to Paul a trial in Jerusalem (compare Felix's having left Paul imprisoned to do the Jews a favor [24:27]). If Paul assents, the earlier foiled ambush could now come off. But why does Festus ask him whether he's willing instead of exercising authority as governor by setting a trial in Jerusalem *regardless* of Paul's willingness? Apparently he knows that as a Roman citizen Paul has the right to appeal his case to Caesar, so that to please the Jews Festus is trying to

prompt Paul to go to Jerusalem for trial instead of appealing to Caesar in Rome. The ruse doesn't work. **¹⁰But Paul said, "I'm standing before Caesar's judgment platform, where it's necessary that I be judged. In no way have I harmed Jews, as also you yourself very well recognize. ¹¹Therefore if on the one hand I'm harming [them] and have done anything deserving of death, I'm not asking to be excused from dying. If on the other hand there's nothing to the things these [Jews] are accusing me of, no one can grant me to them. I'm appealing to Caesar!"** Not that Paul is appealing a verdict already rendered. None has been rendered. Rather, Paul is appealing to Caesar for a verdict. "No one [not even you, Festus] can grant me *to them*" exhibits Paul's knowledge that because of an ambush, by going to Jerusalem he would fall into his enemies' hands along the way and suffer assassination (compare 23:16). And since in Luke's Greek the verb "grant" has the same root that "favor" has, "can *grant* me to them" exhibits Paul's knowledge that Festus wants to do the Jews "a *favor*." So too does Paul's saying that Festus "very well *recognize*[s]" his innocence. By saying "it's *necessary*" that he be judged before Caesar's judgment platform, Paul exhibits his knowledge that God's plan for him to bear witness in Rome, where Caesar is, must prevail—and in part will prevail by Paul's taking advantage of his right as a Roman citizen to appeal his case to Caesar (compare 23:11). The present tense in "I'm standing before Caesar's platform" portrays God's plan to be as good as already being carried out. And Paul's willingness to die if he so deserves underlines that his conscience is clear. **¹²Then, after speaking with [his advisory] council, Festus answered, "You've appealed to Caesar. To Caesar you'll go!"** Paul wins. The Jews won't be able to ambush him. God's plan is proceeding apace.

25:13–21: And after some days had elapsed, Agrippa the king and Bernice arrived in Caesarea, greeting Festus [that is, paying their respects to him as the new governor of Judea]. Agrippa was the son of the Herod in 12:1 (about whom see the comments there). The Romans had made Agrippa king of territories close to Judea, mainly to the north, and curator of the temple in Jerusalem. Bernice was his sister. **¹⁴And as they were spending very many days there, Festus laid Paul's case before the king, saying, "There's a certain man left as a prisoner by Felix, ¹⁵concerning whom** [referring to the prisoner, Paul], **when I'd come to be in Jerusalem, the chief priests and the Jews' elders informed [me], asking for a sentence of condemnation against him, ¹⁶to whom** [referring to the chief priests and elders] **I answered, 'Romans don't have a [legal] standard of granting any person** [to his accusers (compare 25:11 with comments)] **before the accused has had a chance to meet [his] accusers face to face and get a place [= an opportunity] for a defense in regard to the charge.'"** So the governor portrays the Jewish leaders as making an illegal request, and Roman trial procedure as eminently fair. **¹⁷"Therefore when they'd gathered here [in Caesarea], not delaying at all, taking a seat on the**

judgment platform the next [day], I commanded the man to be brought, [18]concerning whom the accusers, on standing [before me], were bringing not a single charge of the evil things I'd been suspecting [they'd bring against him]. [19]But they had some moot points of disagreement with him over their own religious tenets and over some dead Jesus, whom Paul was alleging to be living." Festus's "not delaying at all" and "taking a seat on the judgment platform the next [day]" contrast favorably with Felix's having kept Paul imprisoned two years while hoping to be bribed by Paul and wishing for a self-serving purpose to do the Jews a favor. The speed with which Festus acted on Paul's case indicates that the carrying out of God's plan for Paul to bear witness in Rome was on the move again. Luke described the charges brought against Paul as "many and weighty" but unable to be "demonstrate[d]" (25:7). Now Luke quotes Festus as describing these charges as having to do, not with any "evil things"—that is, crimes—such as he'd expected to hear about, but with "some moot points of disagreement . . . over their own religious tenets and over some dead Jesus, whom Paul was alleging to be living" (compare 23:29). This weakened description, emphasized by "not a single charge," reflects Festus's judgment that Paul has committed no crime and that the charges consist only in intra-Jewish theological disagreements. Thus Luke has cited a Roman governor as confirming that Christianity represents a form of the ancient religion of Judaism. Not for Luke and his audience but probably for the pagan Festus, "their *own* religious tenets" carries a connotation of superstition; and his phrase, "over *some* dead Jesus," reflects a lack of specific knowledge concerning Jesus. And "whom Paul was alleging to be living" makes Festus Paul's mouthpiece in testifying to Jesus' resurrection. [20]"And being at a loss as to the investigation of these things, I was saying [= asking] whether he might be willing to go to Jerusalem and there be judged concerning these things. [21]But when Paul appealed to be kept [in custody] for the decision of His Majesty [= Caesar], I commanded that he be kept [in custody] till I send him up to Caesar." According to 25:10–11, Paul appealed his case to Caesar. Here it's added that he appealed to be *kept in custody* till his being sent up to Caesar, and that Festus granted this appeal. These additions spotlight Paul's being kept safe from assassination, so that God's plan that he bear witness in Rome can reach fulfillment.

25:22–27: And Agrippa [said] to Festus, "I too would like to hear the man myself." "Tomorrow," he [Festus] says, "you'll hear him." The present tense of "says" stresses that the hearing will occur soon. **[23]So on the morrow, when Agrippa and Bernice had come with much pomp and entered into the audience room along with commanders of cohorts and also prominent men of the city, and when Festus had given the command, Paul was brought. [24]And Festus says, "King Agrippa and all you men who are present with us, look at this [man], about whom all the multitude of the Jews approached me both in Jerusalem and here, clamoring** that he mustn't live any longer. [25]But I apprehended that he'd done nothing deserving of death [compare 25:10]; and since this [man] himself appealed to His Majesty, I decided to send [him], [26]about whom I don't have anything certain to write to the lord [in the sense of 'the emperor']. Therefore I've brought him forward before you [plural] and especially before you, King Agrippa, so that after the [present] examination has taken place, I may have something that I may write. [27]For it seems absurd to me in sending a prisoner not also to indicate the charges against him."** The elevated social status of Paul's audience—royalty (King Agrippa and his sister), high-ranking military commanders, prominent urbanites, and the governor (Festus)—serves Luke's purpose of recommending the gospel as suitable to elites, and if to them, to others as well (compare 9:15; 17:34; Luke 21:12–13). "With much pomp" adds to this purpose, as does also "*all* you men who are present with us [that is, with King Agrippa, his sister, and me (Festus)]." Instead of the command to "look at this [man]," most translations have a declaration, "you're looking at this [man]." But for a declaration we might have expected "you're looking at *a* man about whom . . . ," so that "*this* [man]" slightly favors a command: "look at this [man], about whom . . . ." "Look" connotes a continuing gaze rather than a passing glance.

"The chief priests and the elite [men] of the Jews," that is "the dominant ones among [them]," constituted Paul's accusers in both Jerusalem and Caesarea according to 25:2, 5, 7. Here they're expanded into "*all* the multitude of the Jews both in Jerusalem and here." (Though "multitude" occurred for the Sanhedrin in 23:7; Luke 23:1, the Pharisaic faction in it defended Paul; and here in 25:24 "all the multitude of the Jews" appears to include far more than the whole Sanhedrin.) Furthermore, the request that Paul be brought to Jerusalem (25:3) and the leveling of "many and weighty charges" against him (25:7; compare 25:15) now escalates into all the multitude's "clamoring that he mustn't live any longer." The multiplication of accusers and the escalation of their accusations into a hue and cry for his execution magnify the opposition to Paul and to the gospel he proclaims. But the greater the opposition, the greater a victory over it and the more reason to repent and believe. "He *mustn't* live any longer" represents the opponents' plan. But the "must" of God's plan that Paul bear witness in Rome will prevail (see 23:11 again). "But I apprehended that he'd done nothing deserving of death" reaffirms Paul's innocence in Festus's judgment. "I *decided* to send him [to Caesar]." Oh? According to 25:11 Festus *had* to send Paul to Caesar: "no one *can* grant me to them [my accusers]," said Paul; "I'm appealing to Caesar!" And just previously, "I'm standing before Caesar's judgment platform, where it's *necessary* that I be judged" (25:10). Divine necessity uses Roman law to reduce Festus's decision to a mere expedient in the working out of God's plan. "Especially before you, King Agrippa" intimates that Agrippa has expertise in Jewish affairs (see 26:2–3) and therefore may be able to help Festus compose a letter explaining to Caesar the charges against Paul. No such letter will be written, though, because as Festus and Agrippa leave the audience room they'll agree that Paul "is doing nothing deserving of death or bonds [= imprisonment]" and therefore "could have been released if he hadn't appealed to Caesar" (26:30–32). Meanwhile, what starts as an examination and self-defense of Paul will turn into his trying to persuade the audience to become Christians (see especially 26:24–29).

26:1–3: And Agrippa said to Paul, "It's permissible for you to speak concerning yourself." Then Paul, stretching out [his] hand, started defending himself: ²"Concerning all the things that I'm being accused of by Jews, King Agrippa, I consider myself fortunate for being about to defend myself before you today, ³especially since you're an expert on both all the standards [= religious customs] of the Jews and moot points [of their law]. For this reason [= because you're expert in the Jewish subject matter of my speech] I beg you to hear me patiently." Since Festus has had Paul brought to be heard by Agrippa, it's Agrippa rather than Festus who gives Paul permission to speak autobiographically. The gesture of Paul in stretching out his hand typifies an orator. And an orator would be expected to address royalty like Agrippa by name and title and to compliment him, as Paul does (see also 26:7, 13, 19). (Agrippa was indeed very knowledgeable of Jewish law and customs.) By mentioning these features in the opening of Paul's speech, Luke portrays him as an orator. And since oratorical skill was highly esteemed in that culture (they even held oratorical contests), this portrayal of Paul has the purpose of recommending to Luke's audience the gospel that Paul proclaims.

26:4–5: "Therefore [= in view of my speaking of Jewish matters to an expert on them], all the Jews know my lifestyle from youth on up, which [referring to 'my lifestyle'] took place from the beginning in my nation and in Jerusalem, ⁵[they] knowing me from time past, [that is,] from the start, if they're willing to testify, that according to the most accurate faction of our religion I lived as a Pharisee." "All the Jews" includes Paul's accusers and claims that none of the Jews could truthfully deny the following description of his lifestyle. "If they're willing to testify" suggests unwillingness to testify but at the same time implies that were they willing and truthful, they'd confirm his self-description. Emphasizing that Paul's lifestyle has never been other than Jewish are four phrases: (1) "from youth on up"; (2) "from the beginning"; (3) "from time past"; and (4) "from the start." The very redundancy of these phrases adds to the emphasis. Two similarly redundant phrases emphasize the easy observability of Paul's Jewish lifestyle: (1) "in my nation" and (2) "in Jerusalem." With "*my* nation" Paul declares his personal allegiance to the Jewish nation. "In Jerusalem" harks back to his having been brought up in the Jewish capital (22:3) and implies that his Jewish lifestyle has long been observed in the very city where according to a false accusation he tried to profane the temple. With

"*our* religion" he declares *fellow* allegiance to Judaism. "According to the most accurate faction . . . I lived as a Pharisee" describes his lifestyle as not only Pharisaic but also, in being Pharisaic, as closer than all other Jewish factions to the requirements of their religion (see 22:3 again). For Luke, Paul's strictly Jewish conduct supports the theme of Christianity as Judaism brought to fruition.

26:6–8: "And now I stand being judged [referring to Paul's ongoing trial, not especially or in particular to the present hearing] for the hope of the promise made by God to our [fore]fathers, ⁷to which [promise] our twelve-tribed [nation] hopes to attain by earnestly doing religious service night and day, concerning which hope I'm being accused by the Jews, O King. ⁸Why is it judged unbelievable with you [plural] if God raises dead [people]?" This question makes clear that "the hope" is hope of resurrection and implies a deficient view of God's power on the part of Paul's audience. The plural "you" who judge resurrection to be unbelievable refers to Paul's audience of Agrippa, Bernice, Festus, commanders of cohorts, and urban elites (25:23). As non-Pharisees and, in most cases, as non-Jews, they don't believe in a resurrection. Here Paul speaks of a general resurrection. Jesus' resurrection will come into view later. Hope of resurrection means confident expectation of resurrection, not just a wish for it, and refers to the raising of dead bodies to live again, not just to an ethereal afterlife of disembodied souls. "*If* God raises dead [people]" doesn't imply any lack of confidence on Paul's part, but it does recognize disbelief on the part of his audience. He describes the hope of resurrection (1) as "the promise made by God to our [fore]fathers" (compare the comments on 24:14–15 and note that "our" renews Paul's declaration of allegiance to the Jewish nation, as in 26:4); (2) as the promised goal which "our twelve-tribed nation hopes to attain"; and (3) as the hope for the having of which the Jews have been accusing Paul. These last two descriptions may seem to contradict each other. For "our *twelve-tribed* [nation]" stresses the prevalence of this hope throughout the Jewish nation. It isn't limited to Pharisees. Why then has Paul been accused by the Jews of sharing their hope? Luke's audience know the answer: "the Jews" who have been accusing Paul are the Sadducees, who in denying resurrection make an exception to the prevalent national belief in resurrection (23:8; Luke 20:27–33 [compare Acts 24:9; 25:7, 9 with 25:2 for similarly restricted references of "the Jews"]). But it's still preposterous that the Sadducees have been pressing for Paul's execution because he holds a belief in resurrection that the vast majority of other Jews also hold. "By . . . doing religious service" compliments "our twelve-tribed [nation]." "Earnestly" and "night and day" heighten the compliment. ("Night" comes before "day" in that the Jewish day starts at sunset and Paul, a Jew, is speaking primarily to Agrippa, an expert on Jewish matters.) The compliment confirms loyalty to his nation and its religion and again plays into Luke's theme of Christianity as the fruition of Judaism. "O King" invites Agrippa to marvel at the incongruity of Paul's having been accused of holding a hope that the vast majority of Jews likewise hold. "And *now*" stresses the continuity of his holding this hope with his past life as a Pharisaic Jew.

26:9–10a: "**Therefore I thought to myself that doing many things contrary to the name of Jesus the Nazarene** [= the Jesus from Nazareth] **was necessary,** [10a]**which also** [in addition to thinking] **I** [actually] **did in Jerusalem.**" "Which" refers to the doing of those many things (= which *doing* I *did*). "In Jerusalem" recalls Paul's persecution of Christians as described in 7:58; 8:1–3. "*Many* things" underlines the severity of that persecution to emphasize in turn the religious zeal of Paul. "Contrary to the *name* of Jesus the Nazarene" alludes to the proclamation of Jesus' name as the only one by which it's necessary to be saved (4:12). We might have expected Paul to say "contrary to the *disciples* of Jesus the Nazarene." But in line with Jesus' asking him, "Saul, Saul, why are you persecuting *me*?" and adding, "I'm *Jesus*, whom you're persecuting" (9:4–5), Paul refers to Jesus' name as the name he was doing many things contrary to (see 26:11 below). "I thought to myself" indicates that the doing of these things arose out of Paul's own thinking, not out of Scripture, other divine revelation, or even Judaism as such. "Was necessary" means he supposed he was doing God's will, carrying out God's plan. "Therefore" harks back to 26:5 and means "because of my lifestyle as a Pharisee."

26:10b–13: "**And on receiving authority from the chief priests, I also locked up in prisons many of the sacred ones** [= Christians as sacred to God and therefore wrongly imprisoned by me]**; and when they were being done away with** [= killed]**, I cast a vote against** [them] [= for their execution]**.**" In 8:1–3 Luke mentioned Paul's imprisonment of believers and ravaging of the church in Jerusalem but not Paul's having received authority from the chief priests (though see 9:1–2, 13–14 in connection with a projected persecution in Damascus). Nor did 8:1–3 contain a reference to the killing of Christians in Jerusalem and Paul's voting for their execution. So these present additions implicate the chief priests with Paul and interpret the earlier-mentioned ravaging of the church in terms of killing as well as imprisonment. His ratcheting up of the persecution continues: [11]"**And throughout all the synagogues** [still in Jerusalem]**, by punishing them I was often trying to force** [them] **to blaspheme** [= to slander 'the name of Jesus the Nazarene']**. And being exceedingly enraged at them, I was pursuing** [them] **as far as even to the cities outside** [Jerusalem], [12]**in which** [activities], **while traveling to Damascus with authority and the chief priests' commission,** [13]**at midday along the road, O King, I saw a light above the brightness of the sun shining from heaven around me and the ones traveling with me.**" "Punishing them" probably refers to the thirty-nine lashes Paul himself later suffered no fewer than five times (2 Corinthians 11:24). It looks as though the failure of such punishment to make Christians blaspheme Jesus' name infuriated Paul so much that he pursued

Christians right into the cities throughout Judea and Samaria to which they'd fled from Jerusalem (see 8:1b). The enraged pursuit both certifies his zeal for Judaism and makes his transformation into a Christian Jewish evangelist all the more impressive. "In which [activities]" adds to this impressiveness by pointing out that the transformation occurred not during a lapse of such zeal but at its height. As in 9:2 and especially 22:5, "with authority and the chief priests' commission" enlists the Jewish authorities as witnesses to that zeal. Just as the "light" in 9:3 became the "brilliant light" of 22:6, the "brilliant light" of 22:6 now becomes "a light above the brightness of the sun"; and the light is now said to have shone around Paul's fellow travelers as well as around him. These escalations heighten the force of Jesus' self-revelation from heaven.

26:14–18: "**And when we'd all fallen to the ground, I heard a voice saying to me in the Aramaic language, 'Saul, Saul, why are you persecuting me? It's hard for you to kick against goads.'** [15]**And I said, 'Who are you, Lord?' And the Lord said, 'I'm Jesus, whom you're persecuting.** [16]**Nevertheless, stand up and stand on your feet. For to this** [purpose] **I've appeared to you, to handpick you beforehand as an assistant and a witness both of the things you've seen in regard to me and of the things** [in which] **I'll appear to you** [in the future], [17]**rescuing you from the** [Jewish] **people and from the Gentiles, to whom I'm sending you** [18]**to open their eyes, so that** [they] **may turn from darkness to light and** [from] **Satan's authority to God, so that they may receive forgiveness of sins and a portion among those who've been consecrated by faith in me** [see Isaiah 42:6–7, 16; 49:6; Jeremiah 1:7–8; Ezekiel 2:1–3 for some of the phraseology in this passage]**.**'" Escalations continue in that as compared with 9:4; 22:7, not only does Paul fall to the ground, all his fellow travelers do, too, so that the force of Jesus' self-revelation is heightened yet again. Since Paul is speaking to a largely Gentile audience, he specifies that Jesus spoke to him "in the Aramaic language." (Because Paul was speaking to a Jewish audience in chapter 22, he put his whole account in Aramaic [21:40; 22:2].) The originally Greek proverb, "It's hard for you to kick against goads," applies to Paul in two ways: (1) By persecuting Christians, he's resisting God's will the way an animal pulling a cart, a wagon, or a plow resists the will of its driver by kicking against a goad, the pointed stick used to prod it forward by pricking its hind quarters. (2) The futility of an animal's kicking against a goad represents the futility of Paul's resisting God's will, a futility demonstrated in Paul's falling to the ground under the force of Jesus' self-revelation.

As in 26:16, the accounts in 9:11 and 22:10 had Jesus telling Paul to stand up. But here Paul adds to "stand up" the further "and stand on your feet." Why a second "stand" plus "on your feet" instead of "up"? Well, in the earlier accounts Jesus tells Paul to stand up for the purpose of proceeding into Damascus, where he'll receive information—mediated by Ananias, as it turned out—concerning what he should do by way of bearing witness

(9:15–16; 22:12–16). Here, however, Jesus himself commissions Paul on the spot (as he does later in the temple at Jerusalem according to 22:17–21) and there's no command to go into Damascus (though Paul will go there), so that the addition, "and stand on your feet," has to do with Jesus' sending Paul to bear witness to Jews and Gentiles (compare Paul's own use of Isaiah 52:7 in Romans 10:15: "How beautiful the *feet* of those who are proclaiming good things"). "Nevertheless" means "despite the fact you're persecuting me" and thus highlights by contrast Jesus' now commissioning Paul to proclaim the good news about him (compare the comments on 9:3–9; 22:6–11 for this and other features of these parallel passages). For the first time, "I've *appeared* to you" interprets the light from heaven as illuminating Jesus himself—for Paul but not for his companions, since "you" is singular. This appearance counts as Jesus' "handpick[ing]" of Paul "beforehand as an assistant [compare 'assistants of the word' in Luke 1:2] and a witness." "Beforehand" means that the present handpicking precedes Paul's assisting Jesus by spreading the word of the gospel (compare 1:1: "all the things which Jesus *began* to do and to teach," implying that he continues doing and teaching through his assistants). As a witness Paul was to testify about his vision of Jesus on the road to Damascus ("the things you've seen in regard to me"), as Paul did in 22:6–11 and is doing right here in 26:12–18, and also about a further vision in Jerusalem ("the things [in which] I'll appear to you"), as Paul did in 22:17–21 (see also 18:9–10; 23:11). By now, Luke's audience know the fulfillment of Jesus' promise to rescue Paul from antagonistic Jews and Gentiles (13:50–51; 14:5–6, 19–20; 16:19–40; 17:5–10, 13–14; 18:12–17; 19:23–20:1 and chapters 21–25). But Paul will open, and by now *has* opened, the eyes of other Jews and of Gentiles. People whose eyes are shut live in darkness. People whose eyes are open live in the light. So the opening of eyes results in "turn[ing] from darkness to light." "Satan's authority" interprets "darkness" (compare Luke 22:53) and means domination by Satan. "God" interprets "light" in terms of God's forgiving the sins of believers in Jesus and giving them an inheritance ("portion") among those God has set apart as sacred to himself because of their belief in Jesus (compare 15:9).

26:19–20: "**Consequently, King Agrippa, I didn't prove disobedient to the heavenly vision** [an actual appearance, not a dream]; [20]**rather, both first to those in Damascus and Jerusalem and throughout all the region of Judea, and** [then] **to the Gentiles, I started proclaiming that they should repent and turn to God by doing deeds of repentance** [that is, deeds of righteousness instead of evil deeds and, in the case of Gentiles, forsaking idolatry for worship of the one true God (compare Luke 3:8)]." "Consequently" underscores the effect of Paul's "heavenly vision." "I didn't prove disobedient" represents the radical change from persecutor of the church to proclaimer of the gospel. His proclamation in Damascus and Jerusalem was reported in 9:26–30; but here is added his proclamation "throughout all the region of Judea," which magnifies the change from persecutor to proclaimer in that Paul had led "the great persecution against the church" not only "in Jerusalem" but also "throughout the regions of Judea and Samaria" (8:1). "And to the Gentiles" magnifies the change in Paul yet more by highlighting a shift from narrow-minded concern for Pharisaic purity to broad-minded concern for the salvation of Gentiles as well as Jews. And his preaching of repentance (sorrow for sins) and of corresponding behavior marks him as a religious-moral reformer whose message should appeal to Luke's audience of morally and religiously highminded people.

26:21–23: "**On account of these** [activities] **Jews, having seized me while I was in the temple** [courts], **were trying to kill me with their hands** [compare the beating of Paul in 21:31–32]." So some Jews tried to kill him barehandedly because he was preaching repentance and deeds of repentance! How absurd, Paul means Agrippa to understand, as Luke also means us to understand. [22]"**Therefore** [= because of the attempt on my life], **having obtained help from God right up to this day, I stand testifying to both a small** [person] **and a great** [one], **saying nothing except for the things that the prophets and Moses stated were going to happen,** [23]**whether the Christ** [is] **subject to suffering** [by dying], **whether as first by resurrection from dead** [people] [= as the first to rise from among the dead] **he's going to proclaim light both to the people** [of Israel] **and to the Gentiles** [compare 13:47; Luke 2:32; Isaiah 49:6]." God's helping Paul right up to the day of his speaking to Agrippa supports the truth of Paul's proclamation. So believe it! The singular of "a small [person]" and of "a great [one]" individualizes the addressees of his testimony in a way that puts King Agrippa in particular, whom Paul is addressing, on the same plane of need for repentance and belief as a seemingly unimportant person occupies. That Paul's message excludes anything not predicted by the prophets and Moses bases the entire gospel firmly on ancient Scripture. "*Whether* the Christ [is] subject to suffering, *whether* as first by resurrection from dead [people]" sounds initially as though uncertainty has weakened Paul's preaching. But no, the two instances of "whether" allude to questions *raised by Jews*: How could it be that the Messiah would suffer by dying and then be the first to rise from the dead for a proclamation of light to both Jews and Gentiles? Paul answers that it could be, and indeed *had* to be, because of predictions by the prophets and Moses. "First" implies that Jesus' resurrection as the Christ constitutes a guarantee of the general resurrection yet to come. "Light" harks back to the "light" of God's "forgiveness" and of "a portion among those who've been consecrated by faith" (26:18). This light was represented by the "light above the brightness of the sun" that shone "from heaven" around Paul and his fellow travelers (26:13).

26:24–29: And as he [Paul] **was saying these things in self-defense, Festus says in a loud voice, "You're insane, Paul! Many letters** [= much book-learning as represented by written letters of the alphabet] **is turning**

[you] **to insanity.**" [25]**But Paul says, "I'm not insane, most excellent Festus; rather, I'm uttering words of truth and sensibleness.** [26]**For the king** [Agrippa], **to whom I'm speaking freely, knows about these things; for I'm not persuaded that any of these things is escaping his notice. Not one thing** [is escaping it], **for this** [that I've related to him] **hasn't been done in a corner.** [27]**Do you believe the prophets, King Agrippa? I know that you believe** [them]." [28]**But Agrippa** [said] **to Paul, "Are you making me a Christian** [by saying I believe the prophets, who you say predicted the Christ's death and resurrection] **with little** [argument] [referring to the brevity of Paul's speech]**?"** [29]**And Paul** [said], **"I could pray to God that both with little** [argument] **and with great** [argument] **not only you but also all who are hearing me today would become even such as I am, except for these bonds** [= chains]." The vividness in the present tense in "Festus says" and the loudness of his voice suit the charge that Paul has gone crazy—crazy in the sense of propounding crazy ideas. Paul's great book-learning refers to his expertise in the Old Testament; and though Festus puts it forward as the cause of Paul's supposed insanity, for Luke and his audience Festus's recognition of this book-learning supports the scriptural truth of the gospel. The present tense in "Paul says" underscores Paul's denial of insanity and affirmation of the truth and sensibleness of his words, that is, the gospel. To the advantage of Paul, his courteous address, "most excellent Festus," contrasts with Festus's rude interruption. Paul proceeds to enlist King Agrippa as a witness to that truth and sensibleness in that because Agrippa is expert in Jewish matters (26:3) he surely knows about the things Paul has reported. For they happened in public view. The addition of "not one thing" to "any of these things" stresses the thoroughness of Agrippa's knowledge. It's this knowledge that emboldens Paul to speak freely. Agrippa won't contradict him. "Freely" connotes boldness, and boldness of speech was admired in orators. So Paul appears again as a superb public speaker. "To *whom* I'm speaking freely" amounts to a putdown of Festus because of his having interrupted Paul's address to Agrippa. Paul then turns from Festus back to Agrippa with the question whether Agrippa believes the prophets and with the affirmation that he does. Agrippa takes advantage of Paul's question with a question of his own, a wry and evasive one that implies Paul would need to offer more argument to convert Agrippa successfully. Agrippa can hardly say he agrees with Paul right after Agrippa's host, Festus, has called Paul insane. Neither can Agrippa say he doesn't believe in the prophets without damaging his reputation among the Jews. "*Both* with little [argument] *and* with great [argument]" stresses Paul's pious concern for the conversion of his whole audience and implies his willingness to spend whatever length of time it takes to convert them. "Become even such as I am" means, become a Christian. "Except for these bonds" implies that despite his Roman citizenship, Paul has been chained again (compare 21:33; 22:29–30), probably in connec-

tion with his request to be kept in custody (24:22–23, 27; 25:21).

26:30–32: And the king stood up, also the governor and Bernice and the ones sitting with them; [31]**and on withdrawing, they were speaking to one another, saying, "This man is doing nothing deserving of death or bonds** [= chains]." [32]**And Agrippa said to Festus, "This man could have been released if he hadn't appealed to Caesar."** The commander of a cohort, Claudius Lysias, declared Paul innocent (23:29). Festus, an expert on Roman matters, did too (25:25). Now Paul's whole audience—but most especially King Agrippa as the expert on Jewish matters—declare him innocent (compare Luke 23:13–15). So Paul's gospel isn't to be suspected of subversion, and prospective converts needn't fear they'd be joining either an anti-Jewish or an anti-Roman movement should they believe in Jesus.

SURVIVING A SHIPWRECK ON THE ISLAND OF MALTA
Acts 27:1–44

This passage divides into the start of a voyage across the Mediterranean Sea (27:1–8), a seastorm (27:9–26), and a consequent shipwreck on the island of Malta (27:27–44), though not till 28:1 will the island be identified as Malta. Luke appeals as usual to the interest of his audience in travelogues. Here, though, suspense heightens their interest. Earlier parts of Acts have assured the audience that Paul will reach Rome to bear witness for Jesus (see especially 23:11). Such assurance may be thought to eliminate the suspense. But the question of *how* the Lord will rescue Paul from drowning at sea keeps Luke's audience on pins and needles.

27:1–5: And when it was decided that we sail away [from Caesarea] **to Italy, they were giving both Paul and some other prisoners over to a centurion of the Augustan cohort by the name of Julius.** These details concerning the centurion, plus many more details to follow, support that the account of this voyage comes from an eyewitness (compare the multiple occurrences of "we" throughout chapter 27). [2]**And on boarding an Adramyttian ship** [= a ship from Adramyttium, a seaport in northwest Asia Minor] **that was about to sail to places along Asia** [= the coast of the province of Asia in southwest Asia Minor], **we put out to sea, Aristarchus, a Macedonian of Thessalonica, being with us** [see 19:29; 20:4 for earlier mentions of Aristarchus]. [3]**And the other** [= next] **day we were brought down** [by the wind from the high sea] **to Sidon** [on the coast of Phoenicia, modern Lebanon]. **And Julius, treating Paul humanely, allowed** [him], **on going to** [his] **friends, to get sustenance** [for the voyage]. So God is using the centurion as well as Paul's friends to facilitate the journey to Rome, and the friends' giving provisions to Paul for his journey displays the helpfulness of Christians to each other—a feature that Luke uses to attract converts—and also exhibits the spread of the gospel to an important city (Sidon) whose evangelization Luke hasn't recorded. ⁴**And on putting out to sea from there, we sailed under Cyprus, because the winds were contrary** [= on the east side of Cyprus so as to be protected by the island from those winds]. ⁵**And after sailing through the open sea along Cilicia** [= a province in southeast Asia Minor] **and Pamphylia** [a province just west of Cilicia], **we came down** [from the high sea] **to Myra** [a city] **of Lycia** [a projection on the south coast of Asia Minor]. So the ship has been hugging the coast northward from Caesarea and then westward between Cyprus and Asia Minor, and after Cyprus farther westward but distant from the coast till reaching Myra.

In those days no ships were devoted exclusively to passengers. So travelers by sea had to take ships whose main business was the hauling of cargo. **27:6-8: And on finding there** [at Myra] **an Alexandrian ship sailing to Italy, the centurion put us aboard it.** Apparently the Adramyttian ship was headed north to its home port, whereas Rome, Italy, lay to the west. Skeptics will think that the centurion simply chanced on one of the many ships that carried grain from Egypt to Italy by way of Myra. But Luke's audience know better. The Lord, who wants Paul to bear witness for him in Rome (23:11), has provided another ship for Paul's transportation westward. ⁷**And sailing slowly for a considerable number of days and barely coming to be along Cnidus** [a city on the tip of a peninsula having the same name on the southwest corner of Asia Minor], **because the wind wasn't allowing us to proceed we sailed under Crete** [on the protective east side of this island in the middle of the Mediterranean Sea] **along Salmone** [a promontory on the northeast corner of Crete]. In the absence of a keel, an ancient sailing ship like the one Paul was on couldn't tack and therefore could proceed only under a favorable wind. The present lack of very much favorable wind sets the stage for a ferocious wind later on, and the slowness of the present pace will turn the question of how long it will take Paul to reach Rome into a question whether he'll get there at all. ⁸**And barely sailing alongside it** [= off the south coast of Crete], **we came to a certain place called Good Harbors, near which was the city of Lasea.** More lack of favorable wind. More of slow pace before being driven pell-mell.

27:9-12: And since considerable time had elapsed and the voyage was now dangerous because even the fast [connected with the Day of Atonement in late September or early October] **had now passed by, Paul was advising,** ¹⁰**saying to them, "Men, I observe that the voyage is going to be with damage and much loss not only of the cargo and the ship but also of our lives."** ¹¹**But the centurion was being persuaded more by the helmsman and the shipowner than by the things being said by Paul.** It looks as though the centurion has at least veto power over the timing of the voyage. Almost all shipping on the open sea ceased during winter; and winter (which included late autumn, since people then spoke of only two seasons, summer and winter [compare

Psalm 74:17]) was verging on the voyagers. So navigation was already dangerous. ¹²**And since the harbor was unsuitable for wintering, the majority settled on a plan to put out to sea from there, if somehow on arriving at Phoenix, a harbor of Crete facing southwest and northwest** [winds], **we might be able to winter** [there]. So Good Harbors didn't offer a harbor good enough for wintering.

27:13-20: And when a south wind began to blow gently, supposing to have gotten the opportunity [to sail onward to Phoenix], **on weighing** [anchor] **they started sailing alongside Crete quite close** [to shore]. By occasionally using "they" rather than "we" here and later, Luke dissociates himself, Paul, and Aristarchus from the rest, who had rejected Paul's advice. ¹⁴**But after not much time** [= in a short while] **a cyclonic wind, called Euraquilo** [a nor'easter], **blasted down from it** [that is, from the island of Crete and, more particularly, from its Mount Ida, 8000 feet high]. Paul's untaken advice is beginning to look good in hindsight. ¹⁵**And when the ship was violently seized** [by the wind] **and couldn't head into the wind, on giving** [ourselves] **up** [to the wind], **we were being borne** [by it]. ¹⁶**And after running under** [the shelter] **of a certain little island called Cauda** [south of Crete], **we were barely able to get the skiff under control,** ¹⁷**on the taking up of which** [= on hoisting the skiff aboard] **they were using supports** [= cables or ropes] **in undergirding the ship.** The skiff was a small boat being towed for transportation to and from shore and for use in emergencies. The cables or ropes were passed underneath and around the ship's hull and tightened to keep its timbers from breaking apart under added leverage from the mast, to which was attached the windblown mainsail. **And fearing lest they fall off** [course] **onto the Syrtis** [shallows with sandbars along the coast of modern Libya in North Africa], **on lowering the mainsail** [or perhaps the draganchor] **they were being borne** [by the wind] **in this way** [without a mainsail or, alternatively, dragging an anchor so as to slow down]. "They" must refer to the sailors. By now, Paul's unheeded advice has been fully confirmed as wise. ¹⁸**And because we were being violently storm-tossed, the next** [day] **they started jettisoning** [cargo], ¹⁹**and the third** [day] **they threw** [overboard] **the ship's gear with their own hands.** Desperation grows. Human life exceeds in value a ship's nonhuman cargo and gear. "With their *own* hands" stresses that the sailors' livelihood, represented by the ship's gear, amounted to nothing in comparison with their lives. ²⁰**And when neither sun nor stars appeared for very many days and not a little tempest** [= a large tempest] **was lying on** [us], **from then on all hope of our being saved was being taken away** [by the tempest]. Ancient people didn't think of the heavenly bodies as inanimate objects. They thought of them as personal beings of a higher order than earthbound human beings and therefore as beings whose observable movements in the sky affected events on earth (hence, astrology). More particularly, the storm-sighting of the constellation Gemini, containing the patron gods of sailors (namely,

Castor and Pollux), was considered a favorable omen. So the stormclouds' blotting out of the sun and stars, especially of Gemini, not only left the sailors ignorant of their position and unable to fix their course. It also seemed to indicate that those heavenly beings didn't care about the fate of this ship's passengers and crew. The crew had done all they could humanly do to save themselves and the passengers. Now all of them had to depend on the sun and the stars. Or so the non-Christians thought. But the sun and the stars had withdrawn behind stormclouds.

27:21–26: And when there was much lack of appetite [presumably because of seasickness, among other possibilities]**, then Paul, standing in the midst of them, said, "O men, it was necessary that** [you,] **following my advice, not have put out to sea from Crete and gained this damage and loss** [= 'I told you so!' with an ejaculatory 'O' and an ironic if not sarcastic use of 'gained' with 'this damage and loss']. **²²And as for now, I'm advising you to cheer up. For there'll be no throwing away of life from among you** [= no loss of any of your lives]**. Nevertheless** [there'll be a throwing away/loss] **of the ship."** The ship's cargo has been jettisoned (literally, "thrown out" from the ship's hold into the sea), but there'll be no throwing of human lives off the ship's deck. Good reason to cheer up despite an impending loss of the ship that presently keeps them from drowning! Paul continues, **²³"For this night** [just past] **there stood beside me an angel of God, whose I am, for whom also I do religious service,** ²⁴[the angel] **saying, 'Don't be afraid, Paul. It's necessary that you stand beside Caesar. And behold, God has granted you all the ones sailing with you.'** ²⁵**So cheer up, men! For I believe God, that it will be this way,** [that is,] **exactly as it has been told me.** ²⁶**But it's necessary that we fall off** [course] **onto some island."** The earlier advice of Paul was to slow down by wintering in Crete. Despite the rejection of that advice and despite the loss of all hope of being saved (27:20), here he advises cheering up. "It was *necessary* that [you] . . . not have put out to sea from Crete" implies that the rejection of his earlier advice amounted to a rejection of God's plan. For throughout Luke-Acts necessity regularly connotes a plan of God. But the angel's saying to Paul, "It's necessary that you stand beside Caesar," indicates that God's overarching plan for Paul to do so trumps the men's rejection of God's initial, subordinate plan that they winter in Crete. That rejection cost damage to the ship and loss of its cargo and gear, and will yet cost a total loss of the ship. And God's present plan revises Paul's earlier "observ[ation]" that "the voyage is going to be with . . . much loss . . . also of our lives" (27:10) to the effect that there'll be no loss of life whatever. In the introduction to Paul's report of the angelic message, he identifies himself as God's possession and servant and characterizes his service to God as religious in nature ("whose I am, for whom also I do religious service"). For *Luke's* audience, this self-description displays the piety of Paul as an ornament of the gospel. For *Paul's* audience, the self-description explains why God communicated to him through an angel, underlines the need of Paul's

audience to heed his present advice, and along with their mistake in rejecting his earlier advice makes it likely that they'll heed this advice. He transmutes the angel's telling him not to be afraid into his own telling the shipmates to cheer up. For emphasis, the advice to cheer up occurs twice and gets the support of Paul's believing God "that it will be this way." If Paul believes so, the others ought to as well. And for extra emphasis, he supplements "that it will be this way" with "exactly as it has been told me." Because the angel was *God's* angel, Paul's believing the angel's report equates with believing God himself; and believing God displays Paul's piety again.

It may seem strange that just as Paul says, "For this night there stood *beside* me an angel of God," so the angel told him, "It's necessary that you stand *beside* Caesar." In fact, most translations have "*before* Caesar" or the like. But elsewhere in Luke-Acts the expression refers to *by*standers (see Luke 19:24; Acts 1:10; 23:2, 4), and other expressions have to do with standing *before* someone or something (see Luke 1:19; 21:36; Acts 4:10; 6:6; 10:30; 12:14; 24:20; and especially 25:10). So Paul's standing "beside Caesar" lowers Caesar to Paul's level, or perhaps we should say it elevates Paul to Caesar's level. In either case, there's no hierarchical difference between them so far as God is concerned. In 18:9–10 Paul was told not to fear, because the *Lord* had many people in Corinth. Here the command not to fear is connected with God's granting to *Paul* all those sailing with him. "Behold" accents the grant, and "all" makes the assurance exceptionless. The temporal salvation of Paul's shipmates symbolizes the eternal salvation of those "allotted to Paul" (17:4 [compare those who "joined him" in 17:34]). God's angel didn't tell Paul it was necessary to "fall off [course] onto some island." So Paul is here speaking as a prophet. As such, he knows that God has planned a shipwreck, but not "onto the Syrtis" on the coast of North Africa as feared in 27:17—rather, "onto some island." Will Paul's prediction come true?

27:27–32: And when the fourteenth night [of the storm] **had come, as we were being borne through** [the sea by the wind] **in the Adria** [a part of the Mediterranean Sea between the islands of Crete and Sicily, though it also extends northward between the east coast of Italy and west coast of Greece]**, about midnight the sailors began to suspect some territory** [in the sense of terra firma, solid ground] **was approaching them.** We'd say they suspected they were approaching land; but Luke's putting it the other way around makes the land a looming danger, as though it threatens to strike the ship and smash it to smithereens. "The fourteenth night" adds seemingly interminable length to the unmanageable severity of the storm. ²⁸**And on heaving the lead** [= taking a sounding with a lead weight attached to a long rope] **they found twenty fathoms** [= they found the water to be 120 feet deep]**. And after being borne a little farther and heaving the lead again, they found fifteen fathoms** [90 feet]**.** ²⁹**And fearing lest they fall off** [course] **somewhere against rugged places** [= run aground against rocks]**, on throwing four anchors out of the stern** [so as to keep the prow landward] **they started praying for day to come** [so they could see where to beach the ship]. [30]**But when the sailors were seeking to flee out of the ship and had lowered the skiff into the sea by pretense, as if they were going to stretch out** [= lay out] **anchors from the prow,** [31]**Paul told the centurion and the soldiers, "If these** [sailors] **don't stay in the ship, you can't be saved."** Again Paul speaks as a prophet to whom "God has granted . . . all the ones sailing with [him]" (27:24), and his words take effect: [32]**Then the soldiers severed the skiff's ropes and let it fall off** [course] [that is, let it drift just as the ship had been doing]. So in accordance with God's promise to Paul, all will be saved, not just the sailors.

27:33–38: **And till the day was about to come** [that is, dawn], **Paul was urging all to partake of food, saying, "Today** [is] **the fourteenth day you're continuing without food, taking nothing for yourselves, waiting** [in suspense]. [34]**So I urge you to partake of food, for this** [partaking] **is for your salvation** [= physical welfare], **for a hair from the head of none of you will perish."** Yet again Paul speaks as a prophet. In view of the two weeks of fasting, his urging the eating of food gives practical advice. His urging "all" reflects once more that God has granted him "all the ones sailing with [him]." That not a hair of any one of them will perish extends the prediction of escape down to minutiae (compare 1 Samuel 14:45; 2 Samuel 14:11; 1 Kings 1:52; Luke 21:18 for this proverbial expression). [35]**And on saying these things and taking bread, he gave thanks to God in the sight of all; and on breaking** [the bread into edible pieces] **he started eating.** By eating bread, Paul demonstrates his belief in the coming escape of his shipmates and him. For there'd be no point in eating if they were on the verge of drowning. By giving thanks to God, Paul attributes to God the salvation that makes the bread thankworthy in that it will provide sustenance for continued living. "In the sight of all" makes the thanksgiving a promissory testimony of God's coming salvation of all of them and produces the following effect: [36]**And getting cheered up, they all—even they themselves— partook of food.** [37](**And all of us souls in the ship were two hundred and seventy-six.**) "Souls" has the sense of persons but connotes especially their physical lives, endangered but destined to be saved. Paul's thanksgiving and eating finally induce his shipmates to obey his repeated command to cheer up (27:22, 25). Where we might say, "without exception they all," Luke writes, "they all—even they themselves," to stress the cheerful effect of Paul's testimony; and "*all* of us souls . . . were *two hundred and seventy-six*" stresses the inclusiveness of that effect. It's hard not to think of Luke's emphases on the joy of *eternal* salvation and on the inclusivity of the *gospel* (see Luke 2:10; Acts 10:34–35, 44–48, for example). (We know of one first-century ship that carried about six hundred passengers along with cargo, and of a ship 180 feet long, over 45 feet wide, and over 43 feet deep.) [38]**And on eating enough food to get full, they started lightening the ship by throwing the grain out**

into the sea. They'd jettisoned some cargo of grain back in 27:18 but saved some for ballast. Now they proceed to jettison the remainder, for a ship of light weight will run aground farther up the beach than a heavy one would.

27:39–44: **And when day came, they weren't recognizing the land; but they were noticing a certain cove that had a beach onto which they were planning to drive the ship if perchance they could.** [40]**And by slipping the anchors they were leaving** [them] **in the sea while at the same time unfastening the crossbar that linked the steering paddles** [normally two] **to each other. And on hoisting the foresail to the blowing** [wind], **they were heading for the beach.** The succession of verbs with "were -ing" produces the effect of a moving picture. Hoisting the foresail to the blowing wind was designed to give extra speed for landing as far up the beach as possible. [41]**But on falling into a place of two seas** [that is, where a sandbar separated the sea behind from the sea between the sandbar and the beach], **they ran the ship aground. And on the one hand the prow, getting stuck** [in the sandbar], **stayed unmoved; and on the other hand the stern was being split apart by the force of the waves** [crashing in from the open sea behind]. [42]**And the soldiers' plan was that they'd kill the prisoners lest any escape by swimming away.** [43]**But planning to save Paul through** [to Caesar], **the centurion prevented them from** [carrying out] **the plan and commanded those who could swim to go as first ones to the land by throwing** [themselves from the ship into the water between the sandbar and the beach], [44]**and the rest** [to go to the land] **some on planks and some on any things** [= other pieces] **from the ship.** The soldiers' plan to kill the prisoners (see 27:1 for prisoners besides Paul) runs into the centurion's plan to bring Paul safely through the storm and on to Caesar. The centurion's plan prevails because he's carrying out God's plan that Paul bear witness before Caesar. That the centurion is carrying out God's plan unwittingly makes the defeat of the sailors' plan all the more impressive. **And in this way it happened that all were saved through to the land** [= brought safely through the storm to the land]. So Paul's prophecy is fulfilled. The Lord has kept his promise. And just as the eternal salvation of Paul through his conversion entailed the eternal salvation of all whom the Lord had allotted to him (17:4), so the temporal salvation of Paul entails the temporal salvation of all his shipmates.

WINTERING ON MALTA
Acts 28:1–10

This passage divides into Paul's being unaffected by a poisonous snakebite (28:1–6) and his humanitarian service to the inhabitants of Malta, who'd treated him and his shipmates with humanitarianism (28:7–10).

28:1–6: **And after being saved through** [to land], **we then discovered that the island is called Malta** [south of Sicily]. [2]**And the barbarians were showing us unusual humanitarianism. For on kindling a fire they** received us all because of the rain that had set in and because of the cold. The Lord continues to provide for Paul so that his plan that Paul bear witness in Rome may prevail (23:11). "Barbarians" connotes inability to speak Greek, not uncouthness or savagery. ³But when Paul had gathered a bundle of sticks and put them on the fire, a viper coming out because of the heat fastened onto his hand. Here's another threat to God's plan that Paul bear witness in Rome. ⁴And when the barbarians saw the wild beast hanging from his hand, they were saying to one another, "Surely this human being is a murderer whom, though saved from the sea through [to land], Justice [the goddess] hasn't allowed to live." Luke calls the viper a "wild beast" to point up its danger to Paul's life. The viper was venomous. "Hanging from his hand" adds to "fastened onto his hand" an emphasis on the viper's not letting go. It's determined to kill Paul with a prolonged injection of poison—hence the barbarians' "Surely." They call Paul "this human being" for a contrast with the goddess Justice, who they deduce is using the viper, perhaps even making the snake venomous and its bite lasting, to execute Paul for murder despite the seemingly contrary sign of his having escaped the storm with his life. Do they think the gods' concern for his *shipmates* had enabled him to escape, whereas it was really God's concern for *Paul* that had enabled the shipmates to escape? ⁵On the one hand, therefore [= because the viper was hanging from his hand], on shaking the wild beast off into the fire he suffered no harm [compare Luke 10:19]. ⁶On the other hand, they were supposing that he was about to swell up and suddenly drop dead. But because they were waiting expectantly for a long time and observing nothing amiss happening to him, changing [their minds] they were saying he's a god. Paul is saved again. Apparently the language barrier prevents both his disclaiming deity, as he and Barnabas did in 14:8–18, and his proclaiming the gospel to these barbarians.

28:7–10: And in the [places] around that place [where Paul and his shipmates had come ashore and built a fire] there was an estate belonging to the foremost [man] of the island, by the name of Publius, who on welcoming us lodged [us] amiably for three days. ⁸And it happened that Publius's father was lying [in bed] being racked with fevers [plural for recurrent bouts of fever] and dysentery [intestinal disease characterized by abdominal pain and diarrhea], on going in to whom and praying [for him], Paul healed him by laying [his] hands on him. Paul reciprocates the hospitality of Publius by healing Publius's father. The combination of "fevers" and "dysentery" makes the healing doubly remarkable. Paul's praying shows him piously dependent on God for the power of healing, and the healing itself sparks an extensive ministry of humanitarianism: ⁹And after this happened, also the rest [of the people] on the island who had diseases were coming [to Paul] and getting cured, ¹⁰who [referring to the people] also honored us with many honors and put on [board] the things for [our] needs [= needed provisions] as we were

putting out to sea. Again it seems that Paul's inability to speak the barbarians' native language and their inability to speak Greek kept him from evangelizing them. So his healing their sick exhibits humanitarianism even apart from evangelism. Such humanitarianism should attract people who do hear the gospel. The honoring not only of Paul but also of his shipmates consisted at least in part of providing them with supplies, or perhaps monetary funds, for the continuation of their journey. (In 4:34; 5:2–3; 7:16; 19:19 the word translated "price" is the same as the word translated "honors" here.) From now on "we" and "us" may be limited to—or at least concentrated on—Paul, Aristarchus, and Luke.

ON TO ROME
Acts 28:11–15

28:11–15: And after three months we put out to sea in an Alexandrian ship [= one from Alexandria, Egypt], figureheaded Dioscuri [that is, having on its prow carved figures of Castor and Pollux, the patron deities of sailors and twin sons of Zeus and Leda], that had wintered at the island. ¹²And on having been brought down [by the wind from the high sea] to Syracuse [a city on the east coast of Sicily] we stayed [there] three days, ¹³from where after casting off we arrived at Rhegium [a city on the "toe" of Italy]. And when a south [wind] came up after one day, on the second [day] we came to Puteoli [a city on the Gulf of Naples], ¹⁴where on finding brothers [fellow Christians] we were invited to stay with them seven days. And in this way we came to Rome. ¹⁵And on hearing the things [= news] about us, the brothers [yet other fellow believers] came from there [prior to our arrival in Rome] as far as the Forum of Appius [a market town on the Appian Road about forty-three miles south of Rome] and Three Taverns [on the Appian Road thirty-three miles south of Rome] to meet us, on seeing whom [referring to "the brothers"] Paul, thanking God, took courage. So Paul is in Rome. For God's plan to reach completion, it remains only that he bear witness there (23:11). But on the way up through southern Italy he, Aristarchus, and Luke take initiative to find Christians in Puteoli. The presence of Christians in that city testifies to the divinely irresistible spread of the gospel even apart from Paul's evangelistic labors. Staying in Puteoli seven days allows news of the approach of Paul and his companions to travel to Christians in Rome. The gospel has already spread to Rome too. So Christians there travel south to meet Paul and his companions and escort them the rest of their way to Rome. The search for fellow believers in Puteoli, their week-long provision of hospitality, the coming of other believers from Rome to meet Paul, Aristarchus, and Luke—these actions feature the Christian camaraderie that Luke has regularly highlighted to attract prospective converts. Underlining this camaraderie in the present passage are (1) the long distances ("as far as") traveled by two welcoming parties; (2) Luke's calling the believers in Puteoli "brothers"; and (3) the description of arrival at Rome as "in this way," which refers forward to a welcoming party's escorting

Paul and his companions all the way from the Forum of Appius to Rome, and to an additional welcoming party's doing the same all the way from Three Taverns to Rome. Paul's thanking God and taking courage on seeing these welcoming parties adds yet more emphasis on Christians' evangelistically attractive camaraderie and personal piety.

PAUL'S BEARING WITNESS IN ROME
Acts 28:16–28, 30–31

This passage divides into an indication of Paul's living arrangement in Rome (28:16), his initial meeting with leading Jews there (28:17–22), a second meeting with them (28:23–28), and Paul's bearing witness in Rome also to Gentiles for two whole years (28:30–31). There's no 28:29 in the earliest and best manuscripts.

28:16: And when we entered Rome, it was allowed to Paul that [he] **stay by himself with the soldier guarding him.** This living arrangement now enables Paul to fulfill God's plan that he bear witness in Rome despite being a prisoner awaiting trial.

28:17–20: And it happened that after three days he called together those who were the foremost [men] **of the Jews. And when they'd come together, he was saying to them, "Men, brothers, though having done nothing against the** [Jewish] **people or** [contrary to our fore]**father's standards, I was given over as a prisoner from Jerusalem into the hands of the Romans** [in Caesarea], [18]**who as such** [= in their capacity as our overlords] **on interrogating me were planning to release** [me] **because there wasn't a single ground for death in me** [= in my case]." Paul had hardly gotten settled before he took a step toward fulfilling God's plan that he bear witness in Rome (23:11). By addressing the Jewish leaders in Rome as "brothers," associating himself with the Jewish people, implying that their forefathers are therefore his too, claiming to have done nothing against the people or contrary to the forefathers' standards of behavior, and citing Jerusalem as the place from which he has come—by all these means Paul presents himself as these leaders' compatriot. And a good one, as further evidenced by the Romans' planning to release him, because interrogation turned up no reason whatever to execute him. Delicately, he avoids mentioning that in Jerusalem a Jewish mob tried to beat him to death, so that he had to be rescued by Roman authority. Instead, and so as not to offend his addressees or excite their suspicions regarding the reason for his imprisonment, he speaks vaguely of being "given over as a prisoner . . . into the hands of the Romans." He does feel a need, however, to explain his presence in Rome as a prisoner: [19]**"But because the Jews were speaking against** [the Romans' plan to release me], **I was forced to appeal to Caesar, though not as having anything to accuse my nation of."** "*My* nation" reiterates Paul's loyalty to God's chosen people and their religion, which he'll present as fulfilled in Jesus (28:23). With regret, "I was *forced* to appeal to Caesar"

pins blame on antagonistic Jews in Jerusalem. But "not as having anything to accuse my nation of" avers that Paul has come to Rome as a defendant, not as a prosecutor. He bears no ill will. For Luke's audience as well as for Paul's, this attitude exemplifies the Christian charity that makes the gospel attractive and its adherents admirable. [20]**"For this reason, therefore, I've called** [you together (28:17)] **to see you and talk to** [you]. **For I'm wearing this chain for the sake of Israel's hope."** The redundancy of "For this reason" and "therefore" stresses Paul's innocence and lack of ill will as reasons for seeing the Jewish leaders in Rome and talking to them. Presumably he's chained to the soldier guarding him (28:16 [compare the comments on 26:29]). Luke's audience will know from 2:24–32; 23:6; 24:15; 26:6–8 that "Israel's hope" is the confident expectation of resurrection of the dead, guaranteed according to the gospel by the already accomplished resurrection of Jesus. For believers in him, this hope makes good news because they'll participate in the resurrection of the righteous rather than in that of the unrighteous. It's an honor, not a shame, to be chained for the sake of such a hope.

28:21–22: And they said to him, "Neither have we received letters from Judea concerning you, nor on coming here [from Judea] **has any of the brothers** [= fellow Jews] **reported or said anything evil about you."** Are they telling the truth? Luke gives us no reason to think they aren't. So it's best to think that he presents their statement as a testimony to the innocence and uprightness of Paul. Because Paul's accusers in Jerusalem, located in Judea, knew their accusations against him to be false, they hadn't even bothered to convey those accusations to Jews living in Rome. The Jewish leaders in Rome continue: [22]**But we consider it worthwhile to hear from you the things you think. For regarding this faction** [Christianity], **it's known to us that it's spoken against everywhere."** So the absence of information damaging to Paul makes his opinion concerning the faction in Judaism known as "the Way" worth listening to despite its universally bad reputation or, rather, because of it. For the moment at least, his innocence and uprightness trump that reputation.

28:23: And after setting a day with him [we'd speak of making an appointment with him], **more of them** [than before] **came to him at his lodging, to whom by way of solemnly testifying and trying to persuade them concerning Jesus from both the Law of Moses and the Prophets** [the first two of three divisions of the Hebrew Old Testament] **from morning till evening he was expounding God's reign.** "More of them" gives Paul a bigger audience than before. A bigger audience befits the gospel. The solemnity of Paul's testimony and its extending from morning till evening spotlight its importance and the fulfillment of God's plan that Paul bear witness in Rome (23:11). Testimony for the gospel can't be stopped, and this unstoppability argues for the certainty of its truth (compare Luke 1:1–4) and hence for your need to believe it. Paul's use of the Law and the Prophets to persuade the audience concerning Jesus highlights Jesus' fulfillment of those Jewish Scriptures and therefore points up the continuity of Christianity with Judaism. The gospel has ancient roots that have now borne fruit. That fruit is the arrival of God's reign in the person and work of Jesus. Good news indeed! Believe.

28:24–28: **And some were being persuaded by the things being said** [by Paul], **but others were disbelieving.** ²⁵**And being in disagreement with one another, they started leaving after Paul had said one word** [that is, had issued a final statement]: **"Beautifully did the Holy Spirit speak through Isaiah the prophet to your** [fore]**fathers,** ²⁶**saying, 'Go to this people and say, "By hearing you'll hear and never understand** [what you hear], **and though seeing you'll see and never perceive** [what you see]. ²⁷**For the heart of this people has become impenetrable, and with** [their] **ears they've heard ponderously** [that is, they've hardly heard], **and they've closed their eyes lest they perceive with** [their] **eyes and hear with** [their] **ears and understand with** [their] **heart and convert and I heal them** [Isaiah 6:9–10; compare Luke 8:10; Mark 4:12; Matthew 13:14–15; John 12:40; Romans 11:8].'"'"** Here, healing is a figure of speech for salvation. ²⁸**"Therefore** [since you're just like your ancestors] **be it known to you that this salvation from God has been sent to the Gentiles** [compare 13:46–47; 18:6; Luke 2:30–32; 3:6; 24:47; Psalm 67:2]. **They too will hear."** The disparate responses to Paul's exposition follow an established pattern: some believe, some don't. Since he's a prisoner, though, even those who do believe have to leave (contrast converts' following and joining Paul in 13:43; 17:34). Paul quotes Isaiah 6:9–10 and addresses the quotation to those Jews who haven't believed his exposition of the gospel. "Beautifully" makes the quotation's introduction sarcastic (as in Jesus' introduction to another quotation of Isaiah at Mark 7:6–7; Matthew 15:7–9). The quotation itself is beautiful in its accuracy but ugly in its description of the Jews' ancestors, whom Paul calls "*your* [fore]fathers" to dissociate himself and other Jewish believers from the Jews whose disbelief makes them the theological progeny of Isaiah's contemporaries. To give the quotation ultimate authority, Paul says that the Holy Spirit was speaking through the prophet Isaiah. The start of the quotation, "Go to this people," applies the Lord's sending Isaiah to minister to the Jews of *his* time to Jesus' having sent Paul to minister to the Jews of *his* time (9:15; 26:17). In essence, the quotation attributes disbelief to a deliberate refusal to understand, perceive, and accept the gospel rather than

to any inability to do so (see especially the charge that "they've closed their eyes *lest* they perceive . . ."). This refusal then explains why some people disbelieve the gospel despite its "certainty" (Luke 1:4), the evidence for which Luke has put on display throughout Luke-Acts. Paul's announcement that "this salvation from God has been sent to the Gentiles" needles the Jews who won't believe by indicating that God has turned his attention away from them (but not from Jews who haven't yet heard the gospel) to the Gentiles, whom they despise. That "they [the Gentiles] too will hear" doesn't mean the Gentiles will believe, though many of them will believe. It means, rather, that the Gentiles in Rome will get the same opportunity to believe that the Jews in Rome have gotten, as has already happened elsewhere.

28:30–31: **And Paul stayed two whole years in his own rented quarters and was welcoming all who came in to him,** ³¹**proclaiming God's reign and teaching the things concerning the Lord,** [namely,] **Jesus Christ, with all boldness unrestrainedly.** Paul was still chained to a soldier (28:16, 20), of course; but he made his rented quarters an auditorium for continued proclamation to visitors (see the comments on 28:23 for the contents of God's reign and Jesus). His "*welcoming* all who came in to him" exhibits the virtue of hospitality; and "welcoming *all* who came in to him" exhibits the liberality of his hospitality, a liberality suitable to the gospel's universality. Luke calls Jesus Christ "the Lord" to deny the lordship of Caesar even though Paul is awaiting trial in Caesar's court. Why doesn't Luke tell the outcome of that trial? The most natural answer is to say that the trial hadn't taken place by the time of Luke's writing. For if by that time Paul *had* stood trial in Caesar's court, Luke is likely to have reported the trial to show the fulfillment of God's plan as stated to Paul by the angel in 27:24: "It's necessary that you stand beside Caesar." In any case, Luke's final emphasis falls on the fulfillment of God's plan that Paul "bear witness also in Rome" (23:11). "Two whole years" highlights the length of this fulfillment. "Welcoming *all* who came to him" stresses its breadth. And "with all boldness unrestrainedly" enhances its quality. The fulfillment suffered no external restraint, and "with *all* boldness" portrays it as meeting the highest standards of public proclamation. "His own rented quarters" allowed such freedom. So the gospel proves unstoppable despite imprisonment even in Rome, capital of the Roman Empire (compare 1:8); and its unstoppability implies its divine origin. So it's to be believed as sure and certain (compare Luke 1:1–4 again).

ROMANS

Paul wrote this letter in Corinth, Greece, during his third missionary journey (15:25–26; 16:23; 1 Corinthians 1:14). There being no public postal service, the commendation of Phoebe, a woman who lived in Cenchrea right next door to Corinth, probably indicates that she carried the letter to Christians in Rome (16:1–2). They were predominantly Gentile (1:5–6; 13, 11:13, 22–31; 15:15–16). Paul hadn't founded a church in Rome, but he planned to visit the Christians there and gain their support for a mission to Spain farther west (15:24, 28). So the letter takes the form of a self-introduction in terms of the gospel he proclaims.

INTRODUCTION
Romans 1:1–17

The introduction to Romans divides into a greeting (1:1–7), Paul's plan to visit Rome (1:8–15), and a statement of the letter's theme (1:16–17).

1:1–7: Paul, a slave of Christ Jesus, called [to be] **an apostle, having been set apart for the gospel of God** **²that was promised beforehand through his prophets in the Holy Scriptures ³concerning his Son, who in accordance with flesh came on the scene out of David's seed, ⁴who in accordance with the Spirit of Holiness was designated God's Son with power by resurrection from the dead—**[namely,] **Jesus Christ, our Lord, ⁵through whom we've received grace and apostleship for the purpose of bringing about the obedience of faith among all the Gentiles for the sake of his name, ⁶among whom** [referring to "all the Gentiles"] **also are you** [as] **Jesus Christ's called ones—⁷to all God's beloved who are in Rome, called** [to be] **saints: Grace and peace to you from God, our Father, and the Lord, Jesus Christ.** Paul identifies himself by name, by a self-designation ("a slave of Christ Jesus"), and by a designation placed on him ("an apostle"). To be the slave of an important personage gave one prestige, and the placement of "Christ" as a title (the Greek equivalent of the Hebrew "Messiah") before "Jesus" highlights Jesus' importance. So Paul's self-designation sounds a note of derived authority. Since most of the Roman Christians didn't know him, he needed to establish his bona fides right from the start. The note of authority carries over into the designation placed on him, for an apostle was someone sent to speak and act with the full authority of the sender. The mention of Christ Jesus makes clear that he's the one who called Paul to be his apostle. As

elsewhere, Paul uses "called" for an effective initiative on the part of the caller (compare Isaiah 49:1–6; Jeremiah 1:4–5). "Having been set apart" distinguishes Paul from Christians who aren't apostles and thus underlines his authority yet again. "For the gospel" identifies proclamation of the gospel as the purpose of his call to apostleship. For the gospel as "promised," compare Galatians 3:13–29. "Beforehand" indicates that the gospel was promised prior to the coming of Christ, whose death and resurrection made the gospel possible. "Through his prophets" casts the prophets in the role of God's mouthpieces, so that the gospel originated from God—hence, "the gospel *of God*." "In the Holy Scriptures" points to the written records of the prophetic promise and therefore assures the Roman Christians that Paul doesn't proclaim a gospel disagreeable with the Old Testament. "Holy" describes those scriptures as sacred, that is, as different from other writings because of divine inspiration.

"Concerning his Son" tells who Christ Jesus is in relation to God and thus implies Jesus' deity. As to humanity, Paul references Jesus' physical descent from David, because the prophetic scriptures promised that the Messiah, the Christ, would stem from David's royal line (2 Samuel 7:12–17; Isaiah 11:1–5, 10; Jeremiah 23:5–6; 33:14–17; Ezekiel 34:23–24; 37:24–25; Acts 13:22–23, 32–34; 2 Timothy 2:8). Since Paul has paired Jesus' divine sonship and humanly physical descent, the designation of Jesus as "God's Son with power" puts emphasis on his investment with the power of his messianic office. "By resurrection from the dead" identifies the occasion of this investment (compare Acts 2:29–36). "In accordance with the Spirit of Holiness" attributes Jesus' resurrection to the action of God's Spirit and indicates that it's characteristic of the Spirit to give life through resurrection just as "in accordance with flesh" indicated that it's characteristic of flesh to give life through procreation (8:11; 1 Corinthians 15:45). And just as "Holy" described the Scriptures as belonging to a different category from other writings because of divine inspiration, "of Holiness" describes the Spirit as belonging to a different category from human, angelic, and demonic spirits because of divinity. ("The Spirit of Holiness" differs from Paul's usual phrase, "the Holy Spirit," and thereby supports a hypothesis that he's quoting an early Christian confession.)

"Jesus Christ" identifies "God's Son," and "our Lord" identifies "Jesus Christ" in terms of his designation as "God's Son with power." "Our" would seem at first to include the Roman Christians along with Paul. But he immediately uses "we" for the recipients of "grace and apostleship" in distinction from "you" who are "among all the Gentiles." So who are the "our" and "we"? Because Paul hasn't mentioned any cosenders of the letter (whereas in his other letters he usually does) and because his apostleship concentrates distinctively on the evangelizing of Gentiles (see, for example, Galatians 2:2, 7–9), most commentators think that Paul is using an editorial "our" and "we" that excludes any others. Nevertheless, he will send the Roman Christians greetings from Timothy as his "fellow worker" (16:21); and elsewhere he regularly uses "we," "our," and "us" in close connection with his fellow workers, his traveling companions, and then switches to "I," "my," and "me" for himself alone. It seems likely, then, that here Paul includes Timothy, anonymously for the time being, not as an apostle but as a sharer in Paul's apostolic ministry to Gentiles. "Grace and apostleship" describes Paul's apostleship as a gracious gift, ill-deserved because prior to his call he persecuted the church (see especially Galatians 1:13–16, 22–24). "Through whom" portrays Jesus Christ as the agent of this gracious apostleship and alludes to his calling and commissioning Paul on the road to Damascus (Acts 26:12–18).

"The *obedience* of faith" makes believing the gospel an act of obedience in that the word translated "faith" can equally well be translated "belief" (10:16; 15:18); and "the obedience *of faith*" puts this obedience in the category of belief/faith rather than of works (see 4:4–5 for Paul's distinguishing between these categories). "Among *all* the Gentiles" establishes Paul's apostolic prerogative to proclaim the gospel in Rome. "For the sake of his name" means to bring Jesus Christ honor by getting Gentiles to confess him as Lord and to call on him as such for their salvation (10:9–10, 13). As "called ones," the Roman Christians don't simply belong to Jesus Christ. He himself called them to salvation just as he called Paul to apostleship. As usual, the call proved effective. God loves the Roman Christians because his Son, Jesus Christ, called them. "To all God's beloved who are in Rome" finally locates the addressees and includes a minority of Jewish Christians (see, for example, 4:1; 16:3 [with Acts 18:3], 7) in addition to the majority of Gentile Christians ("all the Gentiles . . . among whom also are you"), though there may be an allusion to groups of Christians scattered around the big city of Rome, in which case Paul is indicating that this letter should be circulated among them all (compare 16:4–5, 14–15). "Called [to be] saints" doesn't mean that they're urged to become godly in their behavior (though of course they should)—rather, that their call has already consecrated them to God and in this respect made them unlike the other Gentiles, pagans, among whom they live. For the greeting "Grace . . . and peace," see the comments on 1 Peter 1:2; 2 John 3. "From God, our Father, and the Lord, Jesus Christ" transforms an expected greeting from Paul into a greeting from God and Jesus Christ the Lord, so that once more the authority of this letter is underscored. Yet balancing the element of authority is the designation of God as "our Father," for it establishes a familial framework for Paul's coming explanation of the gospel. Since Jesus Christ is the divine Lord as well as a human being, Paul pairs him with God, so that the two become objects of one and the same preposition, "from."

1:8–12: **First, on the one hand, I'm thanking my God through Jesus Christ for all of you, because your faith is being heralded in the whole world.** [9]**For God, for whom I'm doing religious service in my spirit in the gospel of his Son, is my witness** [as to] **how incessantly I mention you** [10]**when begging** [God] **always on** [the occasion of] **my prayers if somehow now I'll sometime have my way paved in God's will to come to you.** [11]**For I long to see you in order that I may share with you some Spiritual gift so that you may be stabilized—** [12]**that is, on the other hand, so that** [I] **may be mutually encouraged among you through the faith** [that we share] **among one another, both your** [faith] **and mine.** Letter-writers customarily followed the introductory address with a thanksgiving or prayer for the addressees. Here Paul follows the custom and includes both a thanksgiving and a prayer to establish rapport with the Roman Christians, because most of them are personally unacquainted with him. Such rapport will dispose them to accept his explanation of the gospel in the rest of his letter. Thanking God for them both compliments them and gives God the glory for their Christian faith, that is, their belief in Jesus Christ his Son. For "all of you" see the comments on "all God's beloved who are in Rome" (1:7). "I'm thanking *my* God" reflects Paul's feeling of closeness to God. "*Through* Jesus Christ" portrays him as the way to God for Paul's giving of thanks to God. Rome was a big city and capital of a far-flung empire. It was natural, then, for the faith of Christian residents of that city to be heralded abroad: The gospel has reached Rome and prospered there! Since Paul aspires to proclaim the gospel where Christ hasn't yet been named (15:20) and since he plans to go to Spain (15:23–24), "in the whole world" means either that the Roman Christians' faith but not the substance of the gospel has been heralded in the whole world, or that Paul is using hyperbole. In either case, "the whole world" probably means for him and his audience the civilized world consisting of the Roman Empire.

Paul calls his apostolic work a religious service for God. "In my spirit" describes this service as taking place within Paul himself, and therefore sincerely, rather than in a temple, where other religious service is normally done. "In the gospel of [= about] his Son" describes this service as taking place also outwardly through Paul's proclamation of this gospel (15:15–16). "God . . . is my witness" emphasizes the truth of what Paul is about to say. Given God's witnessing how well Paul's words agree or disagree with the truth, Paul wouldn't dare lie to the Romans. The truth is that as shown in his prayers, he wants to visit the Christians in Rome. "Begging" intensifies his praying that his way be paved for such a visit. "Incessantly" adds persistence to intensity. A redundant and therefore emphatic "always" fortifies the persistence. "Somehow" indicates that Paul wants to visit the Roman Christians by any means possible, and "sometime" indicates he wants to visit them at any time possible. But "now" indicates his preference for a visit in the very near future. Nonetheless, "in God's will" subordinates Paul's desire and preference to the will of him "for whom [he's] doing religious service." So how does Paul's thanking God for the Roman Christians show itself? Answer: by the incessant mention of them in Paul's prayers. Why does he mention them incessantly in his prayers? Answer: because of "long[ing]" to see them. And what is the purpose of the desired seeing of them? Answer: the sharing with them of "some Spiritual gift" for their stabilization.

A Spiritual gift is a gift given to Christians by the Holy Spirit—hence the capitalization in "Spiritual." There's a multiplicity of such gifts (for listings, see 1 Corinthians 12:8–11, 28–30), and Paul has more than one of them (including apostleship, teaching, miracle-working, and speaking in tongues [see, for example, 1 Corinthians 14:18; 2 Corinthians 12:12]). Depending on what he sees the Roman Christians need, he'll share one of those gifts with them in the sense that he'll exercise it to their benefit. "So that you may be stabilized [in your faith]" defines the benefit in view of the pressure on them to apostatize (16:17–19). "On the other hand" balances mutual encouragement in a future visit over against Paul's thanking God for them during present absence (1:8: "on the one hand"). By being among them Paul would both give and get encouragement. "Through the faith [that we share] among one another" would provide the means of mutual encouragement. "Both your [faith] and mine" underlines the sharing of faith in Jesus as that means.

1:13–15: And I don't want you to be ignorant, brothers, [of the fact] **that I've often planned to come to you (and heretofore have been curbed** [from doing so]**) in order that I may have some fruit also among you, just as also among the rest of the Gentiles.** ¹⁴**To both Greeks and barbarians, to both wise people and mindless people, I'm a debtor—**¹⁵**thus my eagerness to proclaim the gospel also to you, the ones in Rome.** In several ways Paul continues trying to build rapport with the Roman Christians so that they'll accept his explanation of the gospel, which includes lifestyle as well as belief: (1) his addressing them affectionately with "brothers"; (2) his expressing a desire that they not be ignorant of his past plans; (3) his having planned to visit them; (4) his describing the planning as frequent; (5) his describing the planning as having been frustrated each time, so that his failure to visit them heretofore hasn't been his fault; (6) his describing himself as a debtor to the Romans, as also to others; and (7) his describing himself as eager to pay off his debt to the Romans by proclaiming the gospel to them.

At first blush, Paul's purpose to "have some fruit also among [the Roman Christians], just as also among the rest of the Gentiles" looks like a figurative reference to gaining converts, so that they have the fruit of eternal life (compare 6:21–22). But it's he, not they, whom he wants to have some fruit. Maybe fruit stands for successful ministry on his part, then (as in Philippians 1:22). In 15:22–29, however, Paul clearly uses "fruit" as a figure

of speech for the material support he hopes to get from the Roman Christians for his projected mission to Spain, and he includes indebtedness in the discussion just as he does here. Fruit occurs as figure for material support also in 1 Corinthians 9:7; Philippians 4:14–18 and probably in an anticipatory but oblique way in Philippians 1:11. So it looks more likely that as probably in Philippians 1:11, here too Paul is expressing in an anticipatory but oblique way his hope to gain material support for his mission to Spain when he's among the Roman Christians. He has gotten such support for further missions when among other evangelized Gentiles (see 1 Corinthians 16:6; 2 Corinthians 1:16 with comments). Why not when he's in Rome too? (In the first part of Romans he introduces a number of topics that he later spells out.)

"Among the *rest* of the Gentiles" implies that the addressees, at least the majority of them, are Gentiles. Paul switches from "Gentiles" to "Greeks" because the Greek language and culture had conquered even Rome, as shown by Paul's writing in Greek to the Christians living there. "Barbarians" refers to people ignorant of the Greek language and culture. The Latin language prevailed in Spain, which Paul planned to evangelize, so that his call to apostleship indebted him to the barbarians there too (as well as elsewhere). He owes both them and "Greeks" a proclamation of the gospel. Since Greeks were known for philosophy, which means "the love of wisdom," "to . . . wise people" probably means the same as "to . . . Greeks." Correspondingly, "mindless people" would refer to "barbarians."

1:16–17: For I'm not ashamed of the gospel; for it's God's power resulting in salvation for everyone who believes, both for a Jew first and for a Greek. ¹⁷**For God's righteousness is being revealed in it from faith to faith, just as it's written, "The righteous person will live by faith** [Habakkuk 2:4]**."** Paul is eager to proclaim the gospel to the Romans (1:15), because he isn't ashamed of it (1:16a). He isn't ashamed of it, because it's God's power resulting in salvation for everyone who believes (1:16b). The gospel is such power because in it God's righteousness is being revealed from faith to faith, as indicated already in the Old Testament (1:17). The gospel features a crucified Christ, and crucifixion was considered the most shameful way to die (compare 1 Corinthians 1:17–18, 23; Hebrews 12:2). So Paul might well have been ashamed of the gospel, so ashamed of it that he wouldn't proclaim it. But when proclaimed, it turns into God's power, so that the proclaimer needn't be ashamed of it (compare 1 Corinthians 1:23–25). "Salvation" means deliverance. But deliverance from what? Deliverance from God's wrath, which is already being revealed against human sinfulness (1:18–32) and which will culminate against it at the Last Judgment (2:1–16). Given the firmness of sin's grip on human beings (for which see especially 7:7–25), it takes *God's* power to deliver them from that grip and its consequences, both present and future.

"Who believes" makes the reception of available salvation depend on faith. Later, Paul will categorically distinguish belief/faith from works (4:4–5). "*Everyone* who believes" stresses that nobody needs more than belief/faith, and "both for a Jew . . . and for a Greek" stresses the availability of salvation to believers regardless of ethnicity. Paul uses "a Greek" rather than "a Gentile" because apart from an Old Testament quotation in 10:19 (and there in the sense of "a nation"), he never uses the singular of the Greek word underlying "a Gentile," as would be required here on account of the parallel with "a Jew," whereas he often uses "a Greek" in the singular. Besides, to a considerable extent Rome was Greek in its culture. "For a Jew *first*" alludes to the gospel's having been proclaimed to Jews before it was proclaimed to Gentiles (see Acts 3:26; 13:46; 26:20 as well as numerous passages in the Gospels and Paul's practice of preaching first in synagogues, if possible [Acts 13–28]).

"God's righteousness" supplements "God's power" and refers to God's doing the right thing in saving believers. It will come out in 3:21–26 why that's the right thing for him to do (see the comments on that passage, also on 1 Corinthians 1:30). God's righteousness is being revealed in the gospel *as proclaimed* unashamedly. "From faith to faith" means that the revelation proceeds from faith on the proclaimer's part to faith on the part of hearers (compare 10:17). The righteous person "will live" in the sense of having eternal life, not in the sense of behaving by faith in daily life (see 2:7; 5:21; 6:22–23). Having eternal life "by faith" shows that righteous behavior doesn't bring such life. So the believer isn't a "righteous person" by virtue of his or her righteous behavior—rather, by virtue of God's righteous behavior in that he treats a believer as righteous despite the believer's sinfulness. See again the comments on 3:21–26 on how it's right for God to do so, and compare the comments on Galatians 3:10–12. As often, Paul mentions an item only to explicate it later. In 6:12–23; 8:1–11 he'll speak of believers' becoming "slaves of righteousness" in their behavior, but "by faith" rules out that thought here (compare 10:6).[1]

THE SINFULNESS OF ALL HUMAN BEINGS
Romans 1:18–3:20

This section of Romans divides into the sinfulness of pagans (1:18–32), the sinfulness of Jews (2:1–3:8), and the sinfulness of Jews and pagans alike (3:9–20).

THE SINFULNESS OF PAGANS
Romans 1:18–32

1:18–23: For God's wrath is being revealed from heaven against every kind of ungodliness and unrighteousness of human beings, who by [their] unrigh-

[1]It's possible to translate 1:17 as follows: "For God's righteousness is being revealed *in him* [that is, in the case of the aforementioned believer]," much as in Galatians 1:15–16 God "was pleased to reveal his Son in me [= in Paul's case]" and much as here in 1:18–32 "God's wrath is being revealed" in his giving human beings over to their depravity. The overall meaning of 1:16–17 wouldn't be affected by this translation, however.

teousness are holding down [= suppressing] the truth, [19]because what's known about God is obvious among them. For God has made it obvious to them. [20]For since the world's creation the invisible things about him, both his everlasting power and deity, have been clearly visible, being understood by means of [his] products, so that they [the human beings] are inexcusable, [21]because though they knew God they didn't glorify [him] as God or thank [him]. Rather, they became ridiculous in their reasonings; and their stupid heart was darkened. [22]Though claiming to be wise, they became foolish [23]and exchanged the glory of the imperishable God for the likeness [consisting] of an image of a perishable human being and [of] birds and four-footed [animals] and reptiles [compare Psalm 106:20; Jeremiah 2:11]. The wrath of God, which brings punishment, counterbalances his righteousness, which brings salvation; and the unrighteousness of human beings, which refers to their doing what's *not* right, contrasts with God's righteousness, which refers to his doing what *is* right. His righteousness is being revealed at present in the gospel (as proclaimed). His wrath is being revealed at present from heaven (as experienced by human beings, it will turn out, in God's having given them over to their ungodliness and unrighteousness). "The truth" is "what's known about God," that is, "his everlasting power and deity." The suppression of this truth by unrighteousness shows that behavior affects belief. Bad behavior makes for bad belief. The revealing of God's *wrath* tells why his *righteousness* is being revealed (1:17): Because of their ungodliness and unrighteousness, human beings need to be saved from God's wrath by being made right with him. "From heaven" describes the revealing of his wrath as due to direct action by God himself. "Against *every kind* of ungodliness and unrighteousness" anticipates the many kinds about to be spelled out and disallows any exceptions. "Ungodliness" means lack of reverence for God, and "unrighteousness" means wrong behavior growing out of that lack of reverence.

The obviousness of what's known about God provides the reason for the revealing of his wrath. "Among them" puts the known truth about God close at hand, close enough that it has to be held down if it's not to be accepted in behavior and belief. It's obvious to human beings because God himself has made it so. His power and deity are invisible. So *how* has he made his power and divinity obvious to human beings? Answer: in the products of his creation, visible as they are in the world (compare Psalm 19:1–6). Who but deity of unimaginable power could have created the world? So the things about him that are *in*visible to the physical eye are *clearly* visible to the mind's eye—hence, "understood"—because of the physically visible products of God's creation. And God's power and deity are "everlasting" in that he had to exist prior to the world's creation. His preexistence translates into everlasting power and deity. "*Since* the world's creation" doesn't leave human beings a chronological excuse for their ungodliness and unrighteousness any more than they have the excuse of unclarity. God's everlasting power and deity have been clearly visible and thus understood from the very start. Ignorance is no excuse, but human beings can't even *plead* ignorance as an excuse. Why? Because "they knew God" but "didn't glorify [him] as God." They exchanged him, the proper object of glorification because of his imperishability, not even for *his* perishable creatures—that is, "human beings and birds and four-footed [animals] and reptiles"—but for their *own* creations consisting of mere likenesses— that is, images—of God's creatures, proceeding down from the crown of his creation (human beings) to the lowest (reptiles). What an insult to him! And how ridiculous they became in their reasonings, which Paul ascribes to the darkening of a stupid heart, the heart being portrayed as the seat of reasoning and darkness being used as a figure of speech for stupidity! This stupidity made them foolish, and not the least element in their foolishness was their "claiming to be wise." Their failure to glorify God consisted in their failure to thank him. But for what? For his having created the world with themselves and other creatures in it. Such thanksgiving would have kept them from deifying themselves and those other creatures in the form of ridiculous images. ("The likeness" and "an image" are collective singulars.)

1:24–25: Therefore God gave them over in the lusts of their hearts to impurity, so that among themselves their bodies were dishonored, ²⁵**who as such** [that is, as lustful, impure, and dishonored] **exchanged God's truth** [= the everlasting power and deity of God] **for the lie** [of idolatry] **and revered and did religious service for the creature rather than the one who created** [them]**, who is to be praised** [literally, "spoken well of"] **forever. Amen!** "Therefore" means "because of the pagans' idolatry." God's "giv[ing] them over" instances the revealing of his wrath in that he punishes *deliberate* sinning with delivery to *impulsive* sinning. "In the lusts of their hearts" adds lusts to idolatry as indicative of stupidity. "Lusts" are desires so strong that they lead to "every kind of ungodliness and unrighteousness" (1:18). "*In* the lusts of their hearts" points to such inward desires, and "*to* impurity" points to the outworking of them. "So that among themselves [= with each other] their bodies were disgraced" defines the lusts and their outworking as sexual. The exchange of God's truth for the lie of idolatry let down the bar against sexual immorality (and still does in modern forms of idolatry, as for example in the worship of stars of stage, screen, and athletic venues). Sexual immorality disgraces the body just as dirt disgraces it—hence, "impurity." In Paul's day people revered their idols in temples, and priests "did religious service" there. "For the creature" is collective for "a perishable human being and birds and four-footed [animals] and reptiles" and contrasts with "the one [= God] who created [them]." Pagans revered and did religious service for the creature by means of idolatry. The doxology, "who is to be praised forever," refers to the creator and provides temporary relief from Paul's depressing description of idolatry and its effects. The doxology also compensates for the idolatry. "Forever" matches the praise of God to

his "everlasting power and deity," and "Amen!" caps the doxology with an exclamatory affirmation.

1:26–27: Because of this [the exchange of God's truth for idolatry] **God gave them over to dishonorable passions. For also their females exchanged their natural use** [by males as regards sex] **for the** [use that's] **against nature** [= same-sex intercourse in lesbian relations]; ²⁷**and likewise also the males, having abandoned the natural use of the female, were inflamed in their ardor for one another, males committing the indecency** [of same-sex intercourse] **and getting back in themselves the requital that was necessary for their error.** For the second time, "God gave them over" instances the revealing of his wrath. "To disgraceful passions" echoes the previously mentioned "lusts" and the "disgrace[ing]" of bodies. "For also" adds homosexual intercourse as a specific and obvious example of the sexual impurity fostered by the exchange of God's truth for idolatry. That exchange has fostered both females' "exchang[ing]" their natural use for the [use that's] against nature" and males' "abandon[ing] the natural use of the female." The description "natural" alludes to the complementarity of female and male sexual organs (compare the comments on 1 Thessalonians 4:3–6; 1 Peter 3:7). "Inflamed in their ardor for one another" pictures the males' homosexual passion as a raging fire. "The indecency" that they commit is what has made their passions "disgraceful." "Getting back in themselves the requital that was necessary" points again to the revealing of God's wrath, refers to disease resulting from homosexual intercourse, and describes the disease as punishment and the punishment as necessary because homosexual intercourse is unnatural. It disagrees with the way God created males and females. "Error" means a going astray and here describes homosexual intercourse as males' straying from females as their physically natural partners for intercourse.

1:28–32: And just as they didn't approve having God in [their] **recognition** [that is, recognizing and acknowledging him as God]**, God gave them over to a disapproved mind, so that they were doing improper things,** ²⁹**having been filled with every kind of unrighteousness, evil, greed, malice; full of envy, murder, strife, deceit, maliciousness; [they are] whisperers** [of gossip], ³⁰**vilifiers, God-loathers, insolent, arrogant, boastful, inventors of bad things, disobedient to** [their] **parents,** ³¹**stupid, contract-breakers, unaffectionate, unmerciful,** ³²**who as such, though recognizing God's righteous decree that those who practice such things are deserving of death, not only do them but even take delight in those who practice** [such things]**.** For the third time, "God gave them over" instances the revealing of his wrath. The recognition of God would have consisted in glorifying him as God and thanking him (1:21). That the pagans "didn't approve" of this recognition has resulted in his "giv[ing] them over to a disapproved mind." "Just as" calls attention to this correlation. So not only are idolaters' reasonings ridiculous and their heart stupid (1:21), but also their mind is disapproved by God because it concocts the doing of "improper things," which means things that ill suit the human flourishing desired by God for his creatures. "Having *been filled* with every kind of unrighteousness [and so on]" and "*full* of envy [and so on]" stress the deplorable degree of human degradation. Added to this degree is the brazenness of the degradation: they practice manifold evil despite recognizing that their evil deeds deserve death, and they even delight in their fellow evil-doers. If misery loves company, so does evil. Evil-doers should want to save their fellow human beings from the penalty of death, the death they know that evil-doing will bring; but they're so reprobate that they care no more for their fellows' fate than for their own. Their recognition that evil-doing deserves death in accordance with "God's . . . decree" and that the decree is "righteous" intensifies their brazenness and shows that they know God to be not only everlastingly powerful and divine but also moral in himself and in his demands. In other words, they have a conscience, yet sin against it.

THE SINFULNESS OF JEWS
Romans 2:1-3:8

2:1-2: Therefore you are indefensible, O every human being who are judging [another human being]. **For while you're judging the other** [human being] **you're passing judgment against yourself. For you who are judging** [the other human being] **are practicing the same things.** ²**And we know that God's judgmental sentence is in accord with truth against those who are practicing such things.** It will come out gradually—with a hint in 2:9-10 and then explicitly in 2:17 and following—that Paul is addressing a Jew who relies on his Jewishness and the Mosaic law (with particular reference to fleshly circumcision) to save him at the Last Judgment. The Jew is therefore non-Christian. But since this letter is addressed to Christian believers, Paul addresses such a Jew imaginatively for dramatic emphasis. He imagines that the Jew has heard the broadside leveled against pagans in 1:18-32 and shouted "Amen!" a number of times in agreement with that broadside. But by not making clear right from the start of chapter 2 that he's addressing such a Jew, Paul is drawing him into a rhetorical trap (compare Amos 1-2 in regard to Judah and Israel). "And we know" baits the trap by bringing the imaginatively addressed Jew alongside Paul in the knowledge of God's truthful judgment, and also correlates this knowledge on Paul's and the Jew's part with pagans' previously mentioned recognition of "God's righteous decree" (1:32). (Here "we" doesn't refer in general to Paul and the addressees of Romans, but refers specifically to him and the imaginatively addressed judge of others.)

"The same things" and "such things" refer back to the evils of pagans that have been listed in 1:28-32. "Therefore" implies that if pagans "recogniz[e] God's righteous decree that those who practice such things are deserving of death" (1:32), then surely a Jew does too (compare the Jews' having been "entrusted with the oracles of God" [3:2]); and because a Jew does, he's "indefensible" when judging another human being, such as a pagan, for doing the same evils that he himself is practicing. "O every human being" marks this warning with an exclamation. "O *every* human being" warns against anyone's thinking—even a Jew's thinking—he can escape God's judgmental sentence, which carries a condemnatory meaning here. And "O every *human being*" puts the merely human judge of his fellow in the dock before God, where the human judge will stand self-condemned, not for judging his fellow—rather, for practicing the same evils he'd condemned his fellow for doing. Thus God's judgmental sentence will have only to confirm that self-condemnation, though the sentence will include "those who are practicing such things" whether or not they've judged others. "In accord with truth" describes God's judgmental sentence as accurate and thereby suggests that before God there'll be no success in attempts to hide one's own misdeeds.

2:3-8: But are you counting on this, O human being who are judging the ones practicing such things and [who] **are doing them** [yourself]**, that you'll escape God's judgmental sentence?** Surely not, for "we [you as well as I] know" about "God's judgmental sentence" (2:2). ⁴**Or being ignorant that the magnanimous quality of God is meant to lead you to repentance, are you flouting the wealth of his magnanimity and tolerance and patience?** Surely not, for "*we* know" (2:2) shows that you aren't ignorant. ⁵**But in accord with your hardness and unrepentant heart you're treasuring up wrath for yourself on the day of wrath and of the revelation of God's righteous judgment,** ⁶**who** [referring to God] **"will give back to each** [human being] **in accord with his** [the human being's] **works** [Proverbs 24:12 (compare Psalm 62:12]**." ⁷**[He'll give back] **eternal life to those on the one hand who in accord with perseverance** [in the doing] **of good work are seeking glory and honor and imperishability;** ⁸[he'll give back] **wrath and rage to those on the other hand who are characterized by status-seeking and are unpersuaded by the truth but are persuaded by unrighteousness** [compare 1:18]. This passage makes clear that "God's judgmental sentence" in 2:1-2 had to do with the Last Judgment, yet to come. "O human being" makes for another exclamatory warning that puts a merely human being in the dock before God. The additions of "tolerance" to "magnanimity" and of "patience" to "tolerance" justify Paul's use of "wealth" in connection with God's attempt to lead the judgmental Jew to repentance of his misdeeds. Since neither a miscalculation on escaping God's judgmental sentence nor ignorance of the purpose of God's magnanimity accounts for the Jew's practicing the same evils that he judges another person for doing, what does account for it? Answer: "hardness" (a figure of speech for sheer stubbornness) and an "unrepentant heart" (which arises out of such stubbornness).

But Paul isn't concerned to explain why the Jew practices the same evils he (the Jew) judges another for doing so much as he (Paul) is concerned to warn him that, ironically, he's "treasuring up wrath for [him]self in the day of wrath and of the revelation of God's righteous judgment," which contrasts with the Jew's judgment of others, unrighteous as it is because of his own misdeeds. "The *revelation* of God's righteous judgment" will make obvious the judgment's "accord[ance] with truth" (2:2), and "*treasuring up* wrath for yourself in the day of wrath" warns that the present delay produces a buildup of divine wrath so long as repentance doesn't take place. The quotation of Proverbs 24:12 supports the accuracy and justice of God's judgment and its inescapable individuality and inclusiveness ("*each* [human being]"). "Will give back" points up the correlation between works and the judgmental sentence. This correlation triggers an unexpected reference to "eternal life" as God's give-back to those "seeking glory and honor and imperishability," which terms spell out three characteristics of eternal life. The life's eternality corresponds to perseverance in the doing of good work while seeking glory, honor, and imperishability. (In chapter 4 Paul will flatly deny that good work *earns* salvation; so here he's noting that good work *accompanies* seeking the characteristics of eternal life.) Just as he switched from the doxology in 1:25b back to pagan evils, Paul now switches from the giving back of eternal life to the giving back of "wrath," to which for good measure he adds "and rage." Therefore nobody should doubt God's anger, or its intensity, toward "those . . . who are characterized by status-seeking [which underlies the Jew's judging others] and are unpersuaded by the truth [that is, don't repent despite knowing the truth regarding 'God's judgmental sentence' (2:2)] but are persuaded by unrighteousness [that is, practice evil despite such knowledge]." "On the one hand . . . on the other hand" highlights the contrast between the perseverers in good work and the practitioners of unrighteousness. Nonpersuasion and persuasion personify "the truth" and "unrighteousness," as though they're orators; and "unrighteousness" highlights by contrast "God's righteous judgment."

2:9–11: [There'll be] **the pressure and pinch** [of divine judgment] **against every human person who is producing the bad, both the Jew first and the Greek;** ¹⁰**but** [there'll be] **glory and honor and peace for everyone who is producing the good, both the Jew first and the Greek.** ¹¹**For there's no partiality with God.** "The pressure and pinch [of divine judgment]" describes the effects of God's "wrath and rage" (2:8) as crushing and confining. "Against *every* human person who is producing the bad" reprises the inescapability of punishment for evil-doing. "Producing" has to do with works—that is, behavior—and "the bad" again with those evils that are listed in 1:28–32. "Both the Jew first and the Greek," which occurs twice, echoes 1:16. Paul's repetition of the phrase emphasizes Jewish priority and thus prepares for a full discussion of it in chapters 9–11. See the comments on 1:16 for Paul's use of "the Greek." "Glory and honor and peace" repeats "glory and honor and imperishability" as characteristics of "eternal life" in 2:7 except that in substitution for "imperishability," "peace" connotes all

the blessings of eternal life. "For *everyone* who is producing the good" ranges the inevitability of these blessings for producers of the good over against the inescapability of punishment for producers of the bad. "For there's no partiality with God" explains why—despite being chronologically first to hear the gospel (see the comments on 1:16)—the Jew won't get any special favors from God at the Last Judgment.

Now Paul elaborates the foregoing explanation. **2:12–16: For as many as sinned outside** [the jurisdiction of] **the Law will also perish outside** [the jurisdiction of] **the Law, and as many as sinned within** [the jurisdiction of] **the Law will be judged through** [the instrumentality of] **the Law.** ¹³**For the hearers of the Law** [are]**n't righteous before God; rather, the doers of the Law will be declared righteous.** ¹⁴**For when Gentiles, who don't have the Law, do by nature the things of the Law** [= the things required by the Law]—**these** [Gentiles] **are a law to themselves though not having the Law,** ¹⁵**who as such** [that is, as being a law to themselves] **exhibit the work of the Law** [= the good work required by the Law] **written in their hearts** [compare Jeremiah 31:33] **as their consciousness testifies along with** [the work itself] **and as between each other** [their] **considerations accuse or else defend** [them] ¹⁶**on the day when in accord with my gospel God will judge through Christ Jesus the hidden things of human beings.** "The Law" is the Mosaic law, given to the Jews (or Israelites, as they were called in Old Testament times), so that at the Last Judgment "as many as [will have] sinned outside [the jurisdiction of] the Law" refers to Greeks, that is, all non-Jews. Though not having been under the Law's jurisdiction, they'll have sinned in that they "recognize[ed] God's righteous decree" (1:32) but did evil despite that recognition and will perish accordingly. Their "perish[ing]" references the effect of "the pressure and pinch" of God's "wrath and rage" (2:8–9) and contrasts with "eternal life" (though perishing means ruination of existence, not cessation of existence [see the comments on Matthew 25:46; Revelation 14:10–11]). Because God had placed Jews under the Law's jurisdiction, they'll be judged in accordance with its demands. Why? Because "the hearers of the Law [= Jews in that they hear it read in their synagogues every Sabbath] [are]n't righteous before God [that is, in comparison with God, whose righteousness is absolute]; rather, the doers of the Law will be treated as righteous." This answer seems so obvious that it doesn't need to be stated. But Paul does state it, because the Jew whom he's imaginatively addressing rests in his Jewish privilege of having been entrusted with the Law—a privilege not shared by non-Jews—and rests in that privilege at the expense of keeping the Law up to God's standard of perfection.

For an explanatory contrast, Gentiles, who don't have the Law, enter the picture as "doers of the Law." (The switch from "the Greek" to "Gentiles" signals that the echo of 1:16 has died out.) "Do[ing] *by nature* the things of the Law" makes a striking contrast with the *un*natural homosex in 1:26–27 and prepares for a description of the Gentiles presently in view as "a law *to themselves*" because of having "the work of the Law written *in their hearts*." But who are these Gentile Law-keepers? Well, just as Paul has barely mentioned his future plans in 1:8–15 and will elaborate them in 15:14–33, and just as in 1:16–17 he has barely mentioned God's righteousness as revealed in the gospel and will elaborate it in 3:21–4:25, so here he barely mentions Gentiles' doing by nature the things of the Law and will elaborate this doing in 8:1–17 (see especially 8:4). It will turn out there that these Gentiles, like their Jewish fellows in the church, are Christians, justified by faith (to use the traditional phraseology), not by keeping the Law, but through fulfilling the righteous requirement of the Law giving evidence of having received God's Spirit as a concomitant of justification. So "the doers of the Law will be declared righteous" not *because* they do it—rather, because they've believed in Christ with the *result* of doing it by virtue having received the Holy Spirit (compare Galatians 5:22–23). To keep his imaginary Jewish addressee in tow, however, Paul saves this key point till later.

"Exhibit" showcases the visible evidence of "do[ing] . . . the things of the Law" that's written invisibly in these Gentile believers' "hearts." "Their consciousness" differs from the more usual translation, "their conscience"; but see the comments especially on 1 Corinthians 8:7; 10:25, though "conscience" fits better in Acts 23:1; 24:16; 1 Peter 2:19; 3:16, 21. Here the term refers to a consciousness of deeds done. It's not this consciousness that accuses or else defends. It's "considerations" of those deeds—that is, thoughtful ruminations on them—that accuse or else defend. So these considerations will join the exhibited work of the Law to bring favorable testimony at the Last Judgment. "Or *else* defend [them]" accents the favorable testimony. But since the "considerations" of their "consciousness" of what they've done may "accuse" as well as "defend" them, Paul has artfully brought the non-Christian Jewish Law-breaker back into the picture. God's judging "in accord with [Paul's] gospel" shows that belief versus unbelief in the gospel that Paul proclaims, not Law-keeping as such, will constitute the criterion of judgment; and "through Christ Jesus" projects him as God's agent of judgment in that he (Jesus) is the topic of Paul's gospel, which relates especially to Gentiles according to Galatians 1:15–16; 2:7–8, for example. See the comments on 1:1 for the placement of "Christ" before "Jesus," a placement that suits well his function as God's agent at the judgment. As objects of judgment, "the *hidden* things of human beings" recalls "their *hearts*" but also indicates that nothing, whether good or evil, will fail to be judged.

2:17–21a: **But if you name yourself a Jew and rely on the Law and boast in God** [18]**and know [his] will and approve the things that are superlative by being instructed out of the Law** [19]**and by having convinced yourself that you're a guide of blind people, a light of those in darkness,** [20]**a disciplinarian of nitwitted people, a teacher of infants because of having in the Law the formulation of knowledge and of the truth,**

[21a]**you therefore who are teaching another person— you're teaching yourself, aren't you?** The Jewishness of Paul's imaginary addressee now comes into clear view. "If you name yourself a Jew" implies dependence on Jewish ethnicity (compare Philippians 3:4–6). "And rely on the Law" implies dependence on having the Law more than on obeying it. "And boast in God" implies dependence on monotheistic belief as opposed to polytheism. "And approve the things that are superlative by being instructed out of the Law" implies dependence on knowing and accepting the Law-based distinction between good ("the things that are superlative") and evil. "And having convinced yourself that you're a guide of blind people, a light of those in darkness [and so on]" implies dependence on falsely supposed superiority to Gentiles, thought of in disdainful terms. "Therefore" introduces a question based on the preceding characterization of the Jew. The question asks pointedly whether this Jewish teacher of another person is teaching himself. The implied answer is yes. So any conduct of the teacher that violates the teaching of himself will be flagrant.

2:21b–24: **You who are preaching that [people] not steal, do you steal?** [22]**You who are telling [people] not to commit adultery, do you commit adultery? You who abominate idols, do you burglarize temples?** "Abominate" plays on its literal meaning, "regard as stinky." For people shy away from stink. So to paraphrase Paul, "If you regard idols as stinky, for the purpose of burglary do you go into temples that stink with idolatry rather than keeping your distance from the stink?" [23]**You who are boasting in the Law dishonor God through [your] transgression of the Law!** [24]**For just as it's written, "Because of you God's name is being slandered among the Gentiles** [Isaiah 52:5]**."** Paul leaves open the questions about stealing, committing adultery, and burglarizing temples. In and of themselves they don't imply either a positive answer or a negative one, so that the imaginary Jewish addressee thinks himself free to answer negatively. But before he can, Paul lowers the boom on him with the accusation that the Jew's "transgression of the Law," what*ever* it is, dishonors God. To support this accusation, Paul quotes Isaiah 52:5 out of the Jew's own Scripture. Paul isn't implying that all non-Christian Jews commit all these transgressions. Like the imaginatively addressed Jew, the transgressions are representative and chosen as egregious examples of transgression, especially in that all three relate to the Ten Commandments (Exodus 20:4, 14–15; Deuteronomy 5:8, 18–19).

2:25–29: **For on the one hand circumcision benefits if you're practicing the Law. If you're a transgressor of the Law, on the other hand, your circumcision has turned into uncircumcision.** [26]**Therefore, if the uncircumcision is keeping the righteous decrees of the Law, his uncircumcision will be credited as circumcision, won't it?** [27]**And by completing the Law** [= by obeying it]**, the uncircumcision by nature will judge you, the transgressor of the Law through [its] letter and circumcision.** [28]**For the overt Jew isn't [a Jew],** and overt circumcision in flesh [is]n't [circumcision]. **29Rather, the hidden Jew** [is a Jew], **and circumcision of the heart by the Spirit and not by** [the Law's] **letter** [is circumcision], **whose praise [is]n't from human beings—rather, from God** (compare Leviticus 26:41; Deuteronomy 10:16; 30:6; Jeremiah 4:4; 9:25–26). To the preceding scriptural explanation of the charge that the Law-boasting Jew dishonors God through transgression of the Law, Paul adds an explanation of the effect that transgressing the Law has on the Jewish transgressor himself: the transgressor turns his physical circumcision, representing membership in God's chosen people, into moral uncircumcision, representing nonmembership in them (Genesis 17:9–14). So the circumcision that carries the benefit of membership consists in "practicing the Law." "Therefore" introduces the inverted conclusion that "if the uncircumcision is keeping the righteous decrees of the Law, his [physical] uncircumcision will be credited [at the Last Judgment] as [moral] circumcision." Only Paul puts this conclusion in the form of a question implying the answer "Yes" to draw agreement from the Jewish addressee.

"*Is keeping* the righteous decrees of the Law" and "*his* uncircumcision" imply the personification of "the uncircumcision." This personification treats the Gentile Law-keeper as defined by his uncircumcision and thus highlights the unnecessariness of physical circumcision and the necessity of moral circumcision. "By nature" describes the retention of foreskin as natural in that the male was born with foreskin. The statement that "the uncircumcision by nature will judge you [the unnaturally circumcised Jewish addressee], the transgressor of the Law"—this statement continues the personification of "the uncircumcision" and astonishingly makes the uncircumcised Law-keeper a kind of coagent with Christ Jesus of God's judgment (compare 2:16). So much for the Jewish addressee's falsely supposed superiority and disdainful epithets for Gentiles (2:17–21a)! "By completing the Law" identifies the basis of coagency in the judgment and implies both that by itself hearing the Law leaves it incomplete and that obedience completes it by bringing it to its goal. "Through [the Law's] letter and circumcision" describes the transgressor as caring for the Law only as letters of the alphabet written on scrolls and therefore as a talisman, and circumcision likewise as a talisman.

Paul justifies the uncircumcision's coming judgment of the circumcised transgressor by denying that "the overt Jew," one with "overt circumcision in flesh," is a Jew, and by denying that "overt circumcision in flesh" is circumcision. Then he explains what he means by these denials: The praiseworthy Jew is "the hidden Jew" in that the Spirit has circumcised his heart by bringing the Law to completion through an obedience that in the case of Gentiles by-passes the cutting off of fleshy foreskin and cuts off instead the metaphorical foreskin of such transgressive behaviors as stealing, adultery, and burglary of temples (2:21b–22 [compare 2:15: "the work of the Law written in their hearts"]). Note: there's no

contrast between the so-called spirit of the Law (in the sense of its tenor) and the letter of the Law (in the sense of its diction), for the contrast lies between God's Spirit as the enabler of Law-keeping and the Law as a dead letter on scrolls that can't enable obedience to it (compare 7:6; 2 Corinthians 3:1–11). Though human beings—in particular, non-Christian Jews—withhold praise from such a Gentile because he hasn't gotten physically circumcised, God will praise him at the Last Judgment. It helps Paul's line of reasoning that the Hebrew word for "Jew" plays on the Hebrew word for "praise," as in Genesis 49:8 according to the original Hebrew text. The Mosaic law required circumcision for membership in God's people, Israel; but Paul declares circumcision unnecessary for membership in God's people, the church. For Christians, then, the Law that's necessary to be kept and is evidentially kept consists in the moral law exclusive of ritual law.

3:1–4: "**Therefore** [since fleshly Jewishness and circumcision as such don't substitute for Law-keeping] **what** [is] **the Jewish person's surplus** [over what a Gentile has]**, or what** [is] **the benefit of** [fleshly] **circumcision** [as to salvation]**?**" **2Much** [surplus and benefit] **in every respect! For first, on the one hand, they** [the Jews] **were entrusted with the oracles of God** [as recorded in the Old Testament]. **3For what** [is to be said] **if some** [of the Jews] **have proved untrustworthy? Their untrustworthiness won't render God's trustworthiness ineffective, will it?**" **4To the contrary! But** [in contrast to the suggestion that the untrustworthiness of some Jews might render God's trustworthiness ineffective] **God is to be turning out as true, and "every human being as a liar** [Psalm 116:11]**," just as it's written, "so that you** [God] **may be declared righteous in your words and conquer when you're being judged** [Psalm 50:6 according to a pre-Christian Greek translation]**."** Here Paul starts taking up objections that his imaginary Jewish addressee, from here on called the interlocutor, might lodge against what Paul has just argued in chapter 2. Hence quotation marks demarcate the interlocutor's objections. To the question of what more a Jew has than a Gentile has, Paul answers, "Much in every respect!" and grounds his answer ("For . . .") in the Jews' entrustment "with the oracles of God," which pronounced Jews God's chosen people, so that they're both first and last when it comes to the benefit of salvation (1:16; 11:11–32, especially 11:25–27). "First" and "on the one hand" introduce this grounding; but there's no "second" or "on the other hand," because Paul has the interlocutor break in with a pair of further counter questions.

Another "For" introduces the first of these counter questions, "what [is to be said] if some [of the Jews] have proved untrustworthy?" as an explanatory deduction from the salvific advantage Paul has claimed the Jews possess in having been entrusted with God's oracles. Won't this advantageous entrustment exacerbate the guilt of Jews who've proved untrustworthy, particularly through unbelief in the gospel (compare 15:31), and thereby render God's trustworthiness ineffective in that despite their membership in his chosen people he won't save them after all? ("Untrustworthiness" and "unbelief" are equally valid translations of Paul's Greek word, though the contrast with God's trustworthiness favors an accent on untrustworthiness; for God's "belief" wouldn't make good sense.) The second counter question implies that surely those Jews' untrustworthiness won't render God's trustworthiness ineffective. So why shouldn't ethnic Jewishness and fleshly circumcision as such still count toward salvation? Paul emphatically agrees that the untrustworthiness of some Jews won't render God's trustworthiness ineffective and adds scriptural support to this agreement.

"But God is to be turning out as true [to his word], and [by contrast] every human being as a liar" is Paul's command, softened by its indirectness, that God demonstrate his truthfulness and—for the sake of highlighting God's truthfulness by contrast—that every human being expose himself as the liar that he is. We might even call this indirect command a prayerful command on Paul's part. For he longs that God be demonstrating his (God's) truthfulness by bringing Jews to salvation in fulfillment of oracular promises recorded in the Old Testament scriptures (compare 9:1–5; 10:1). "So that you [God] may be declared righteous in your words [in the sense of being declared truthful and therefore trustworthy] and conquer when you're being judged [by human beings]"—these words conjure up the scene of a battle in court, with God accused by human beings of having spoken untrue and therefore unrighteous words yet prevailing over his accusers, such as Paul's interlocutor, according to whom a circumcision-free gospel renders God untrustworthy in that it seems to deny the Jews' advantage that was stated in divine oracles.

Paul puts another pair of counter questions in the mouth of his interlocutor and then answers them with a question of his own. *3:5–6*: "**But if our unrighteousness** [= the unrighteousness of us Jews] **commends God's righteousness** [by contrastively highlighting it], **what shall we say?**" "We" means "you, Paul, and I, your interlocutor." "**The God who brings wrath against** [the unrighteous] **isn't** [himself] **unrighteous, is he?**" Implied answer: No, he isn't unrighteous. "**I** [Paul's interlocutor] **am speaking humanistically** [that is, from a standpoint that I don't really hold but that regards human beings as having the prerogative to judge whether God is unrighteous in his wrathful judgments]." Paul has his interlocutor make this statement in a show of sanctimony. Then Paul answers, [6]**To the contrary!** That is, of course the God who brings wrath against the unrighteous isn't himself unrighteous; for it would be unrighteous of him *not* to. And Paul supports his answer with a question of his own: **Since how will God judge the world** [if he's unrighteous]**?** Paul's question correctly assumes that as a Jew his interlocutor would agree that God will judge the world righteously.

Paul's interlocutor follows up with another question in *3:7*: "**But if by my lie** [a functional equivalent of 'un-

trustworthiness' in 3:3–4a] **the truth of God** [a functional equivalent of his 'trustworthiness,' also in 3:3–4a] **has flourished with the result of his glorification** [a functional equivalent of God's 'turning out as true,' so that he 'may be declared righteous' in his words 'and conquer' when he's judged, in 4:4], **why am I too still being judged as a sinner?**" Jews regularly referred to Gentiles as sinners (compare Galatians 2:15). So "I *too*" means "I as well as those pagans, the Gentiles." "*Still* being judged as a sinner" means "being condemned as a sinner even after God's getting glorified by my lie." Unable to tolerate such specious reasoning, Paul now breaks in with another question of his own, which takes that reasoning to its logically absurd end in *3:8a*: **And** [why] **not** [say], **as we are being slandered** [as saying] **and as some are asserting that we're saying, "Let's do bad things in order that good things may come"?** By using an introductory "And," Paul connects his question with his interlocutor's foregoing question and thereby makes his own question a reduction to absurdity of the foregoing one. The reference of "we" has shifted from the interlocutor and Paul to Paul and his fellow evangelists, such as Timothy (compare 1:5; 16:21). Tucked within Paul's question is a twofold indication that they were being falsely accused of taking their teaching to a morally wildcat conclusion. So before delivering his scriptural broadside against that very conclusion, Paul does his part in "declar[ing God] righteous" (3:4). *3:8b*: **The judgmental sentence against whom** [referring to the slanderers] **is right!**

THE SINFULNESS OF JEWS AND PAGANS ALIKE
Romans 3:9–20

3:9–18: "**What then?**" the interlocutor asks in view of Paul's affirming that Jews have much advantage in every respect (3:1–2). "**Are we** [Jews] **superior** [to the Gentiles]**?**" **Not at all!** Paul answers. **For we've already charged that both Jews and Greeks are all under sin,** [10]**just as it's written, "There's not a righteous person, not even one.** [11]**There's not a person who understands. There's not a person who is seeking out God.** [12]**All have degenerated. Together they've become depraved. There's not a person who is practicing magnanimity. There's not even one.** [13]**Their throat** [is] **an opened tomb. They've been deceiving** [people] **with their tongues** [= with their speech]. **The venom of vipers** [is] **under their lips,** [14]**whose mouth is full of cursing and bitterness.** [15]**Their feet** [are] **keen to shed blood.** [16]**Demolition and distress** [are] **in their paths** [as a result of their destructive deeds], [17]**and they've not known the path of peace** [because they haven't traveled it in their conduct]. [18]**There's no fear of God before their eyes.**" Here the quotation marks have enclosed a string of quotations taken in succession from Psalms 14:1–3; 5:10; 139:4 (the latter two according to a pre-Christian Greek translation); 10:7; Isaiah 59:7–8; Psalm 36:1. As in 3:8, "we" in "we've already charged" refers to Paul and his fellow evangelists. Throughout his letters he often includes them to bolster his statements. The present extensive quotation of scriptural passages bolsters even more the charge in 1:18–2:29 that "both Jews and Greeks are under sin" (see the comments on 1:16 for "Greeks"). "*Under* sin" implies enslavement to sin as humanity's overlord (see especially 7:14). Paul chooses his quotations for their emphasis on the universality and variety of humans' sinning. They all sin in one way or another.

3:19–20: And we know that as many things as the Law says, it says [them] to those in the Law [= under its jurisdiction] **in order that every mouth may be shut and all the world subject to God's righteous** [judgment], **²⁰because by works of the Law** [= deeds done in obedience to the Mosaic law] **"will no flesh at all be declared righteous in his sight [Psalm 143:2]." For through the Law** [is] **the recognition of sin.** "We" probably refers to Paul and his interlocutor. "In order that *every* mouth may be shut and *all the world* subject to God's righteous [judgment]" indicates that the Jews' sinfulness, as exposed by the Law, has become Exhibit A-1 of human sinfulness in general (compare 2:9). For only the Jews have been under the Law's jurisdiction. "*As many things as* the Law says, it says [them] to those in the Law" stresses the jurisdiction of the Law over Jews, and over them alone, but for the purpose of shutting the mouth of everybody, whether Jew or Greek, so as to prevent any pleas of "Not guilty." The phrase translated "subject to God's righteous [judgment]" has to do with being arraigned in court for a crime or, to use Paul's terminology, for a sin. And if not even deeds done by Jews in *obedience* to their Mosaic law will result in a divinely pronounced judicial sentence of "Not guilty," then pagans, whose egregious *sins* were detailed in 1:18–32, don't stand a chance of being cleared. "No flesh at all" underscores this impossibility ("flesh" being an allusion to humanity in their mortality, since flesh decomposes upon death). "For through the Law [is] the recognition of sin" tells why a Jew's "works of the Law" won't lead to God's declaring him righteous. No matter how many are the works of the Law, it exposes infractions of it; and God is the one who takes knowledge of these infractions.

THE JUSTIFICATION OF SINNERS WHO BELIEVE IN JESUS CHRIST
Romans 3:21–5:21

Having established the universal sinfulness of human beings as a judicial problem, Paul now explains God's remedy.

THE BASIS OF JUSTIFICATION IN THE PROPITIATORY DEATH OF JESUS
Romans 3:21–26

This passage elaborates 1:16–17.

3:21–23: But apart from the Law [as a way of being declared righteous because of keeping it] **God's righteousness, being attested by the Law and the Prophets,**

has now been disclosed. ²²But [now has been disclosed] **God's righteousness through belief** [= faith] **in Jesus Christ for all who are believing** [in him]. **For there isn't a distinction** [between Gentiles and Jews]. **²³For all have sinned and** [as a result] **are lacking God's glory . . . .** "God's righteousness" contrasts with the just-highlighted unrighteousness of all human beings, but also with "God's righteous [judgment against their unrighteousness]" (3:19) in that Paul now puts on display the righteousness of God that *saves* sinners who believe in Jesus Christ. God's righteousness saves them by declaring them righteous despite their sinfulness. How he can do so *rightfully*, especially when 3:5–6 has suggested the opposite, Paul will explain in 3:24–26. "Being attested by the Law and the Prophets" gives this salvific righteousness of God scriptural support like that given to human sinfulness in 3:10–18. (God's salvific righteousness and human sinfulness don't conflict with each other, of course; for the one complements the other.) "The Law" refers to the five books of Moses (Genesis–Deuteronomy) as the first section of the Hebrew Bible. "The Prophets" refers to its second section, which contains both historical books written from a prophetic standpoint and what we ordinarily think of as prophetical books. Paul adds "the Prophets" to "the Law" for an allusion to Old Testament prophecies of messianic salvation, prophecies fulfilled in and by Jesus Christ—thus, "God's righteousness has *now* been disclosed." "Through belief in Jesus Christ" tells how God's salvific righteousness has been disclosed in individual cases (compare its revelation through evangelism [1:16–17]). Most English translations have "through *faith* in Jesus Christ." "Faith" translates a word that can equally well be translated "belief," but "faith" obscures somewhat the word's interconnection with the subsequent expression, "are *believing* [in him]" (see the comments on Galatians 2:15–16 against a reference to "the faithfulness of Jesus Christ"). "For *all* who are believing" adds the element of universality to "belief in Jesus Christ." Not that all *do* believe in him, but that by his righteousness God saves *everybody* who believes in Jesus Christ. Why this universality? Because the universality of human sin has created a universal need for salvation: "*For all have sinned.*" "And [as a result] are lacking God's glory" alludes to pagans' having "exchanged the glory of the imperishable God for the likeness [consisting] of an image of a perishable human being and [of] birds and four-footed [animals] and reptiles" (1:23), but "all" now includes the Jews' having exchanged God's glory for doing the same things they condemn pagans for doing (2:1, 17–24).

3:24–26: [all] **being freely declared righteous by his** [God's] **grace through the redemption that** [is] **in Christ Jesus, ²⁵whom God set forth as a propitiation, through belief, in his blood for a demonstration of his righteousness because of the letting go, in God's tolerance, of the sins that had previously taken place— ²⁶[that is,] for the demonstration of his righteousness in the present season so that he might be righteous and the one who declares righteous the person who is**

of belief in Jesus. "Being . . . declared righteous" brings out the meaning of the traditional translation, "being justified." "Freely" means "as a gift" in opposition to a justification supposedly earned by Law-keeping (4:4–5). "By his grace" refers to God's favor, ill-deserved because of sin. "Through the redemption that's in Christ Jesus" tells the means by which "being freely declared righteous" is made graciously possible. The placement of "Christ," properly a title, before "Jesus" strikes a note of messianic dignity suitable to his role in the making of redemption possible. Redemption connotes the purchase and liberation of a slave. Paul has recently described "both Jews and Greeks" as enslaved "under sin" (3:9). Their liberation from this enslavement lies "in Christ Jesus, whom God set forth as a propitiation." There, in the propitiatory Christ, believers experience liberation from enslavement to sin. The propitiation refers to a sacrificial atonement that appeases God. Because of his wrath and rage at human sin (1:18; 2:5, 8; 3:5), he needed to be appeased if he was to declare believing sinners righteous and thus redeem them from enslavement to sin. At this point the analogy to enslavement ceases, because no price of redemption was paid to the slavemaster, sin. As just said, we have instead an appeasement of God the judge (compare 3:19–20).

That "God set forth [Christ Jesus] as a propitiation [of God himself]" points up God's earlier-mentioned "grace." "Through belief" doesn't tell the means of propitiation—rather, the means of a human being's capitalizing on Christ's propitiation. "In his blood" doesn't tell the object of belief—rather, the means of propitiation. For the blood of Christ represents his sacrificial death as what appeased God, wrathful and outraged as God rightfully was because of human sin (compare the parallel in 5:9–10 between the death of Christ and his blood, and death as the consequence of sin in 5:12–21; 6:15–23). On the Day of Atonement in Jewish ritual, moreover, the blood of a sacrificial animal was sprinkled on the gold lid, called "the mercy seat," of the ark of the covenant in the Holy of Holies, the innermost room of the Jewish sanctuary; and the word translated "propitiation" was used also to designate that lid as the place where God was appeased with the atoning blood of a sacrifice (see Hebrews 9:1–10:18 with comments for the symbolic, inadequate, and temporary nature of that atoning appeasement). So Paul portrays Christ's sacrificial death as the location where real and permanent appeasement by atonement happened.

"A demonstration of his [God's] righteousness because of the letting go, in God's tolerance, of the sins that had previously taken place" was needed because there was no real and permanent appeasement of God prior to his setting forth Christ Jesus as a propitiation. Yet in his tolerance (an Old Testament foregleam of his present grace) he let go sins committed prior to Christ's propitiation. At least he did for human beings characterized by faith, such as Abraham and David (see chapter 4). This earlier "letting go" foreshadowed the present redemption. It wouldn't have been right of God to let those ear-

lier sins go if he hadn't demonstrated his righteousness "in the present season" by setting forth Christ Jesus as a propitiation. For sins call for the judgmental penalty of death. As it is, God has proved himself righteous by that setting forth and has made available his salvific righteousness without violating his judgmental righteousness. His judgmental righteousness fell on Christ Jesus. His salvific righteousness ("declar[ing] righteous") falls to "the [sinful] person who is of belief in Jesus." "Of belief in Jesus" describes a person who gets his or her identity by believing in Jesus for salvation rather than by Law-keeping.

FAITH AS THE MEANS OF OBTAINING JUSTIFICATION
Romans 3:27–4:25

This passage divides into faith's exclusion of boasting in one's works (3:27–31) and examples of such faith in Abraham and David (4:1–25). The translations and comments will revert to the traditional term "faith," but its synonym "belief" and the cognate verb "believe" should be kept in mind.

3:27–28: "Where then [is] boasting?" the interlocutor asks. It was excluded! Paul answers. "Through what sort of law? Of works?" the interlocutor asks; and Paul answers, No ["for through the Law (is) the recognition of sin," so that "by works of the Law 'will no flesh at all be declared righteous in his (God's) sight'" (3:20)]—rather, [boasting in one's works—that is, in Law-keeping—was excluded] through the law of faith. Though the word for the Mosaic law can also refer to a principle outside that law, Paul is about to support being "declared righteous by faith apart from works of the Law" with an appeal to the story of Abraham, which appears in Genesis, the first book of the Mosaic law (see Romans 4:1–25). So "the law of faith" refers to the Mosaic law in that it supported being declared righteous by faith and at the same time excluded boasting by exposing sin for what it is, namely, transgression. The past tense in "was excluded" also favors this understanding of "the law of faith," because the story of Abraham and its recording in Scripture lie far back in the past. [28]For we're reasoning that a human being is declared righteous by faith apart from works of the Law. "For we're reasoning . . ." stresses that justification by faith (as it's usually called) is a deduction from the Law itself and therefore to be accepted as scriptural truth.

3:29–31: "Or [is God] the Jews' God only? [He's the God] of the Gentiles too, [is]n't he?" Yes—of the Gentiles too, [30]if indeed God [is] one, who [as a result] will [at the Last Judgment] declare righteous a circumcision of faith and an uncircumcision through faith. Paul personifies "a circumcision" to represent a Jew "of faith [in Christ]," and similarly personifies "an uncircumcision" to represent a Gentile "who through faith [in Christ]" will be declared righteous along with the Jewish believer. As implied by its introductory "Or," the opening question, which is asked like earlier questions by Paul's interlocutor, arises out of Paul's having just deduced justification by faith without works of the Law from the Mosaic law itself. If that law does indeed support such justification and if, as Paul said in 3:19, the Law speaks only to those under its jurisdiction—that is, the Jews— is the God of justification by faith the Jews' God only? "He's the God of the Gentiles, too [is]n't he?" implies on the interlocutor's part an affirmative answer to his own question. After all, he's a Jewish monotheist (Deuteronomy 6:4). But Paul is too. So he answers, "Yes—of the Gentiles too," and supports his answer with an appeal to the monotheism with which he knows his interlocutor agrees. ("If indeed God [is] one" doesn't call in question the oneness of God, but uses it as a sure basis ["indeed"] for the answer "Yes.") But instead of using God's oneness over Gentiles as well as Jews to argue that keeping the Law, given by God through Moses, is required of Gentiles as well as Jews, Paul uses God's oneness over all human beings regardless of their ethnicity to argue in favor of justification for *everyone* who'll believe in Jesus. For Paul has already noted that works-righteousness was excluded by the very Law that spells out the works required by such righteousness (see the comments on 3:27–28). As a consequence, Paul and company are establishing rather than invalidating the Law in regard to its true salvific meaning: [31]**Therefore are we invalidating the Law through faith?** he asks, and answers, **To the contrary! Rather, we're establishing** [the Law].

Paul's interlocutor speaks up again in *4:1–3*: **"Therefore** [in view of your claiming, Paul, that boasting has been excluded by 'the law of faith' (3:27–31)] **what shall we** [you and I] **say Abraham, our forefather as to flesh** [= as to biological descent], **has found?** [2]**For if Abraham was declared righteous by works** [= in consequence of his deeds, such as his immigration to Canaan at God's command and above all his willingness to sacrifice his son Isaac (Genesis 12:1–5; 22:1–19)], **he has a basis for boasting."** This *is* what he has found, the interlocutor says—a basis for boasting. So Paul is wrong to claim that boasting has been excluded by "the law of faith." The interlocutor's "For if Abraham was declared righteous by works" doesn't call in question that he was. For the purpose of concluding that he has a basis of boasting it *assumes* that he was declared righteous by works. By citing the interlocutor's own Scripture as *his* own too, Paul now refutes the assumption and the conclusion drawn from it: **Not in relation to God, however!** [3]**For what does the Scripture say?** [It says,] **"Abraham believed God, and it** [his believing God] **was credited to him as righteousness** [Genesis 15:6]."** "Not in relation to God, however!" doesn't necessarily imply that Abraham has a basis for boasting in relation to his fellow human beings. For at issue is only what Abraham might say to God at the Last Judgment—and what God will declare concerning him on that occasion. Human interrelationships aren't in view. Paul's scriptural citation proves that Abraham's believing God, not Abraham's works, were credited to him as righteousness. Paul will now go on to put believ-

ing and working in sharply different categories; but note first that he isn't talking about faith as a vaguely religious temperament—rather, about faith as believing God, in Abraham's case about believing that God would fulfill his promise to give him a biological heir and in the case of Christians about their believing that God will declare them righteous through Jesus Christ his Son.

4:4–8: **But to the person who works, the wage isn't credited in accordance with grace** [that is, as an unearned favor]—**rather, in accordance with a debt** [owed by the employer to his worker]. [5]**But to the person who doesn't work but believes** [= rests his faith] **on the one who declares the ungodly person righteous, his faith is credited as righteousness,** [6]**just as indeed David too speaks about the good fortune of the human being to whom God credits righteousness apart from works:** [7]**"Fortunate** [are] **those whose lawlessnesses have been forgiven, and whose sins have been covered up.** [8]**Fortunate** [is] **the man whose sin the Lord will by no means count** [Psalm 32:1–2]." Here Paul adds that God not only credits faith as righteousness though it is *not* righteousness in the sense of a behaviorally good work. He also credits the *ungodly* person's faith as righteousness. It has to be so if anybody at all is to be declared righteous. "For all have sinned and [as a result] are lacking God's glory" (3:23). "But to the person who . . . believes *on the one who declares the ungodly person righteous*" implies that even Abraham was ungodly and that saving faith includes a believer's recognition of his or her own ungodliness and of God's grace. For otherwise Paul needed only to say, "But to the person who . . . believes on God."

To elaborate God's grace in declaring the ungodly person righteous because of that person's faith and apart from works, Paul cites a Davidic psalm in which the forgiveness of transgressions being declared righteous and in which sins' being covered up so that "the Lord will by no means count [them]" complements the counting of faith as righteousness. "Just as *indeed* David *too*" underscores these complements. In Paul's leadup to the psalm, "*apart from* works" reprises the earlier person "who *doesn't* work" and thus adds another emphasis on the fundamental distinction between working in self-reliance and believing in reliance on God. The added citation of a Davidic psalm reinforces Paul's argument in that unlike Abraham, David lived after the promulgation of the Law, so that his word "lawlessnesses" refers to transgressions of the Law as objects of forgiveness. In 3:25 Paul alluded to the mercy seat, on which sacrificial blood was sprinkled during the Day of Atonement. Inside the ark of the covenant, whose lid was the mercy seat, were the tablets of the Ten Commandments—but the second set of them, because Moses had smashed to pieces the first set when he saw the Israelites worshiping a golden calf (Exodus 32:1–19; 34:1–4, 28–29; Deuteronomy 10:1–5). So the second set recalled an egregious transgression of the Law. For Paul, then, did the "cover[ing] up of sins in David's psalm refer to Christ's blood as covering up sins in a way similar to the covering up of the broken Law by sacrificial blood on the mercy seat? "Will *by no means* count" ratchets up the Lord's grace in not counting a believer's sins.

4:9–12: [Is] **this good fortune then** [pronounced] **on the circumcision** [alone], **or also on the uncircumcision?** Here again Paul personifies "the circumcision" and "the uncircumcision," so that they represent Jews and Gentiles respectively. **For we're saying, "Faith was credited to Abraham as righteousness."** This Pauline statement gives the reason for the foregoing question and thereby shows that that question was Paul's, not the interlocutor's. The Pauline character of the statement also shows that "we" refers to Paul and his fellow evangelists, and the replacement of "the *Scripture* says" (4:3) with "*we're* saying" highlights the extent to which they've appropriated Genesis 15:6 as gospel, the good news of justification by faith. [10]**How then was it credited? While** [he] **was in circumcision** [= in a circumcised state] **or** [while he was] **in uncircumcision** [= in an uncircumcised state]**? Not in circumcision; rather, in uncircumcision.** [11]**And he received the sign of circumcision as a seal of the righteousness of the faith** [that was credited to him as righteousness] **in** [his state of] **uncircumcision**.... Paul notes that the crediting of Abraham's faith as righteousness (Genesis 15:6) occurred earlier than Abraham's circumcision (Genesis 17:9–14, 22–27), calls circumcision a "sign" in an allusion to God's calling it "the sign of the covenant" between God and Abraham (Genesis 17:11), and interprets this sign as "a seal," God's certification that he had indeed credited Abraham's faith to him as righteousness.

The continuation of Paul's sentence lays out the purpose of this crediting prior to circumcision: **so that he** [Abraham] **might be the father of all who believe during uncircumcision, so that righteousness might be credited to them too—**[12]**and** [so that he might be] **the father of circumcision** [= the ancestor characterized himself by subsequent circumcision] **to those** [who are] **not only of circumcision** [that is, Jewish believers] **but also to those** [Gentiles] **who are tracing the steps of our father Abraham's faith during** [his former state] **of uncircumcision.** As "we" in 4:9 referred to Paul and his fellow evangelists, "*our* father Abraham" also refers to them but now includes the Roman Christians as well. "The *father* of all who believe during uncircumcision" makes Abraham's fatherhood religiously though not biologically genetic in the case of Gentile believers. "Of *all* who believe during uncircumcision" accents this sort of fatherhood with a sideswipe at the Jewish interlocutor's biological exclusivism. Adding to the accent are Paul's mentioning Abraham's fathering uncircumcised believers before mentioning that of circumcised believers (contrast the Jews' priority in 1:16; 2:9–10) and the addition of "those [who are] *not only* of circumcision *but also* to those [Gentiles] who are tracing the steps ...." We expect "tracing the steps *of our father Abraham*." But Paul surprises us with "tracing the steps of our father Abraham's *faith*." For emphasis, this phraseology (1) personifies the faith of Abraham, as though it rather than he was walking; (2) alludes to walking from Mesopotamia to

Canaan and then living there nomadically as an exercise of faith that God would fulfill his promise of an inheritance; and (3) compares Christians' faith to Abraham's in that Christians too believe that God will fulfill his promise of an inheritance. But what is that inheritance?

4:13: **For the promise to Abraham or to his seed** [= descendents] **that he'd be the heir of the world** [was]**n't through the Law—rather,** [the promise was] **through the righteousness of faith.** Paul might have written "through *faith*." But to keep in view sinners' need to be declared righteous he writes, "through the *righteousness* of faith," by which is meant the righteousness that sinners' faith is credited as being. Because of his expansion of Abraham's fatherhood to include Gentile believers among the offspring of Abraham, Paul expands God's promise to Abraham of the land of Canaan (Genesis 12:6–7; 13:14–17; 15:7, 18–21; 17:8) to include "the world" (compare 1 Corinthians 6:2). This inclusion implies believers' future occupation in redeemed bodies of a world delivered from the bondage of corruption (see 8:18–25, where the world is called "the creation"). We might have expected "to Abraham *and* to his seed." Instead we read "*or* to his seed," which suggests that though he'll be "the heir of the world," he'll be such only because his seed now includes believers *not* biologically descended from him. Paul's argument presupposes a knowledge that the Mosaic law wasn't promulgated till long after Abraham, so that "the promise to Abraham or to his seed ... [was]n't through the Law" and therefore *had* to be through the scripturally stated crediting of his faith as righteousness. Thus the argument ("*For* the promise to Abraham ...") provides a reason why in 4:9–12 Paul made Abraham "the father ... also to those [Gentiles] who are tracing the steps of our father Abraham's faith."

To the chronological and scriptural argument Paul adds a theological argument in **4:14**: **For if those of the Law** [are] **heirs, faith has been voided** [in that obedience to the Law as behavioral righteousness replaces faith credited as righteousness] **and the promise has been incapacitated.** Why so? Paul answers in **4:15**: **For the Law produces wrath.** Transgressions of the Law, which God promulgated, make him wrathful; and his wrath would make him withdraw the promise were not faith credited as righteousness on the basis of Christ's atoning propitiation (3:24–26). **But where the Law isn't** [as it wasn't in Abraham's time and place], **neither** [is there] **transgression** [of the Law with a consequent production of divine wrath, so that the crediting of Abraham's faith as righteousness was unimpeded by any wrath of God against transgression of the Law]. Which isn't to say that apart from the Law there's no sin. On the contrary, see 5:12–14 as well as 1:18–32. Strictly speaking and by definition, rather, "transgression" presupposes a stated law and therefore heightens guilt (compare our expression "*high* crimes and misdemeanors").

4:16–17: **Because of this** [the absence of transgression where the Law is absent] [the promised inheritance of the world (4:13) is] **by faith** [= in consequence thereof] **in order that** [the promised inheritance might be] **in accordance with grace** [that is, by way of an unearned favor (4:4–5)], **so that the promise might be firm for all the seed** [descendants of Abraham], **not only for the** [seed who are] **of the Law, but also for the** [seed who are] **of the faith of Abraham, who is the father of us all**—[17]**just as it's written, "I've made you a father of many nations** [Genesis 17:5]"—**in the presence of God, whom he believed,** [the God] **who makes dead people live and calls the things that don't exist as existing** [= so that they come into existence]. God's wrath would incapacitate the promise. The Law produces wrath (4:14–15). But in accordance with grace the promise is firm for all Abraham's seed. Therefore "the [seed who are] of the Law" refers to Jews who were circumcised in accordance with the Law but who in the meantime have followed Abraham's example and had their faith credited as righteousness. But Paul's emphasis falls on the inclusion of believing Gentiles as well: "for *all* the seed," "not only . . . *but also*," "the father of us *all*," plus a scriptural quotation that makes Abraham "a father of *many* nations." Whereas the scriptural quotation made Abraham the *biological* father of many nations, Paul adds that by his example of faith Abraham became the *religious* father of many nations. "In the presence of God" alludes to the Lord's appearing to Abraham and talking with him in Genesis 17:1–21, from which Paul takes his quotation. "Whom he believed" reprises Abraham's believing God, but this time—along with the description of God as him "who makes dead people live and calls the things that don't exist as existing"—sets the stage for God's having brought life and existence out of the procreative deadness of Abraham and Sarah, and also for God's having raised Jesus out from among the dead.

4:18–25: Who [referring to Abraham] **against hope believed on the basis of hope with the result that he became the father of many nations in accord with what had been spoken: "Thus will be your seed** [Genesis 15:5]." [19]**And not getting weak in faith, he accurately discerned his own body to have been put to death** [by old age so far as procreation was concerned], **he being somewhere around a hundred years old; and** [he accurately discerned] **the deadness of Sarah's womb.** [20]**But in regard to God's promise he didn't doubt by way of disbelief; rather, he was empowered by way of faith, giving glory to God** [21]**and being fully assured that what he** [God] **had promised he's able also to do.** [22]**Therefore also "it** [Abraham's faith] **was credited to him as righteousness** [Genesis 15:6]." [23]**But "it was credited to him" wasn't written for the sake of him alone**—[24]**rather, for the sake also of us, to whom it** [faith] **is going to be credited** [as righteousness at the Last Judgment]—[that is, us] [25]**who believe on him** [God], **who raised Jesus, our Lord, from among the dead, who** [referring to Jesus] **was given over** [to death] **because of our trespasses** [which needed atonement (compare Isaiah 53:12)] **and was raised because of our being declared righteous** [which will be needed at the Last Judg-

ment]. As usual in Paul, "hope" connotes confidence, not the uncertainty of a mere wish; and so it does here in Abraham's believing "on the basis of hope." Abraham's hope consisted in confidence that he'd become the father of many nations. The Lord's statement to this effect gave him confidence, because he believed the Lord. But what does Abraham's believing "*against* hope" mean? Well, the Lord's statement, "Thus will be your seed," occurs in a passage where Abraham expressed confidence that his servant Eliezer of Damascus would be his heir (Genesis 15:1–3). In opposition to *that* confidence, which Paul calls "hope," Abraham shifted his hope, his confidence, to belief in the Lord's statement, "Thus [like the innumerable stars in heaven] will be *your* seed [that is, your *own* offspring]."

Abraham's accurate discernment that old age had killed his and Sarah's procreative powers didn't weaken him so far as his faith was concerned. The statement that "he didn't doubt by way of disbelief" underlines his "not getting weak in faith," as does also his "being fully assured that what he [God] had promised he's also able to do." The present tense in "he's able," where we might have expected "he *was* able," implies that God is still able. With his full assurance Abraham gave glory to God by acknowledging God's ability to do what he'd promised. Abraham's empowerment by way of faith means empowerment to impregnate Sarah. Paul then returns to the topic of faith credited as righteousness and applies God's raising Abraham's and Sarah's procreative powers from death to God's raising Jesus "from among the dead." "Who [referring to Jesus] was given over [to death] because of our trespasses" recalls God's setting him forth as a propitiation because all have sinned (3:23–26). As he hasn't done till now, though, Paul brings Jesus' resurrection into relation with "our being declared righteous." A failure of God to have resurrected Jesus would have indicated that Jesus' propitiation didn't appease God, that our faith in Jesus couldn't be credited as righteousness on the basis of his propitiation, and that believers therefore wouldn't have any hope, any confidence, of eternal life (compare 1 Corinthians 15:16–19).

THE BLESSINGS OF JUSTIFICATION
Romans 5:1–11

5:1–2: Therefore, since we've been declared righteous by faith, we have peace with God through our Lord, Jesus Christ, [2]**through whom we've also come to have access by faith into this grace in which we stand; and we're boasting on the basis of hope for God's glory.** "Therefore" introduces a conclusion based on Jesus' having been "given over [to death] because of our trespasses" and "raised because of our being declared righteous" (4:25). So confident is Paul that faith "is going to be credited" as righteousness at the Last Judgment (4:24) that he now puts the declaration in a past tense: "since we've been declared righteous by faith." The declaration is as good as made already (compare the comments on 4:18–21 for hope as confidence). As a result of being declared righteous, believers (to whom "we" and "our" refer) "have peace with God" in that he'll no longer direct his wrath against them. He'll no longer consider them his enemies, but will bestow on them all the benefits of salvation that the word "peace" connotes (see also the comments on 1 Peter 1:2; 2 John 3). "Through our Lord, Jesus Christ" specifies him as the agent of this peace because he's also the object of saving faith. As such he's also and likewise the agent of access "into this grace," which refers to "peace with God" as an ill-deserved gift (3:24; 4:4, 16). "In which we stand" refers to this grace as a standing place over against works of the Law as not a good place to try standing. For standing connotes stability, whereas the Law produces God's wrath (4:15), not peace with him. And nobody can withstand his wrath. Here "boasting" has the sense of exultation. "Boasting on the basis of hope [which means confidence and therefore equates with faith]" contrasts with boasting in the Law (2:23) and in works (4:2). "For God's glory" identifies the object of hope and has to do with sharing God's glory in the eternal state (see, for example, 2:7, 10; 3:23; 8:18, 21; 9:23).

5:3–5: And not only [that], but we're also boasting in [our] afflictions, because we know that affliction produces perseverance, ⁴and perseverance [produces] probity [= tried and true integrity], and probity [produces] hope. ⁵And hope doesn't put [us] to shame [by failing to be fulfilled], because God's love has been poured out in our hearts through the Holy Spirit, who was given to us. To "boasting on the basis of hope for God's glory," Paul adds "boasting in afflictions," that is, in present persecutions as opposed to future glory. Again, "boasting" has the sense of exultation. Note: not just boasting in the *midst* of afflictions; rather, boasting in *reference* to afflictions, so that they become the subject matter of boasting (see 2:17, 23; 5:11 among other Pauline passages for this meaning of "boasting in"). The knowledge that "affliction produces perseverance, and perseverance probity, and probity hope" provides the reason why those who "are boasting on the basis of hope for God's glory" (5:2) "are also boasting in [their] afflictions." Those afflictions set off a chain reaction ending in the very hope—the confidence of sharing God's glory eternally—which provides the basis for boasting. Nor will that boastful hope shame believers before the unbelieving world (at the Last Judgment) by failing to reach fulfillment. How do believers know they won't be shamed in this way? The outpouring of God's love for them has told them so. "In our hearts" locates this outpouring in their organ of thinking and feeling (as the heart is viewed in the Bible). "Through the Holy Spirit who was given to us" makes believers' experience of God's Spirit the vehicle by which they hope in confidence of sharing God's glory.

Now Paul explains what he meant in 5:5 by "God's love." **5:6–8: For while we were still weak, at still the right time Christ died for ungodly people.** The twofold use of "still" makes the time of our weakness the

right time for Christ to have died for ungodly people. "Ungodly" defines the meaning of "weak" as moral sickness (compare 8:3), and according to 1:18–3:19, 23 all human beings fall into the category of ungodly people. Next, Paul explains why the time of our weakness was the right time for Christ to die for us. **⁷For hardly will anyone die for a righteous person. For someone might possibly even dare to die for a good person. ⁸But God demonstrates his own love for us in that while we were still sinful, Christ died for us.** The doubling of this explanation ("For . . . . For . . .") brings out both the unlikelihood and the bare possibility that someone would die for a good and righteous person. By contrast, God demonstrates his love for us *as sinners* rather than as good and righteous people. "His *own* love" sets his love apart as special in this respect. The "demonstrat[ion]" of it makes it available for us to capitalize on by believing in Christ. "While we were still sinful" recalls "while we were still weak," joins "ungodly" in defining our weakness as moral sickness, and thus underlines our need for God's love and his love's graciousness as demonstrated in the death of Christ on our behalf (compare 3:23–26).

5:9–11: Because of having now been declared righteous by his blood, therefore, much more will we be saved through him from [God's] wrath [1:18; 2:5, 8; 3:5]. ¹⁰For if while being enemies we were reconciled to God through the death of his Son, much more will we be saved by his [the Son's] life after being reconciled—¹¹and not only [that], but also while boasting in God through our Lord, Jesus Christ, through whom we've now received reconciliation. "Because of having *now* been declared righteous . . . therefore" reprises 5:1: "Therefore, since we've been declared righteous." But the addition of "now" accents that the declaration has already taken place, though final certification awaits the Last Judgment. "By his blood" supplements the human element, "by faith" (5:1), with the divine element of God's having set forth Christ Jesus "as a propitiation in his blood" (3:25). Paul argues that if we've now been declared righteous, our future salvation from the wrath of God that's yet to come on unbelievers is "much more" certain than the already-issued declaration, which has been preliminarily certified by the outpouring of God's love in our hearts through the Holy Spirit, who was given to us (5:5). Then Paul supports this "much more" by adding to "the *death* of his [God's] Son" another "much more" that involves the *resurrection* of God's Son: "much more will we be saved by his life" (compare Jesus' having been "raised because of our being declared righteous" [4:25]).

"After being reconciled" shows that being "saved by his life" follows and depends on reconciliation. "We were reconciled to God" shows that "being enemies" means our sinfulness made us his moral enemies (compare 8:7) and therefore objects of his wrath. "While being enemies" describes our relation to God "while we were still weak" (5:6) and "while we were still sinful" (5:8), and along with those expressions exhibits the marvel that the death of God's Son reconciled believers to God while they were still morally hostile to him (compare God's graciously declaring righteous "the *ungodly* person" [4:5]). "After being reconciled" parallels "having now been declared righteous" and supplements justification with reconciliation. For since God is righteous himself, reconciliation to him requires our being declared righteous as a prerequisite to reconciliation; but by the same token reconciliation comes by way of being declared righteous. "While boasting in God" tells what believers will be doing at the Last Judgment, when they'll "be saved by his [Jesus'] life." There'll be no boasting before God in our own works (4:2), only boasting in God "through our Lord, Jesus Christ." "Through whom we've now received reconciliation" parallels "having now been declared righteous by his blood," replaces any future boasting in our own works with an acknowledgment of Jesus as the agent of past reconciliation because of his sacrificially atoning blood, and makes the reconciliation of believers to God his act rather than theirs.

A CONTRAST BETWEEN ADAM AND CHRIST
Romans 5:12–21

Paul will start drawing a contrast between Adam and Christ, but before completing it will break off the contrast in the middle of 5:12 to expound the association of sin and death with each other. Then in 5:18 he'll resume and complete the contrast between Adam and Christ.

5:12–14: **Because of this** [Jesus' being the agent of an already received reconciliation], **even as through one human being sin came into the world and death** [came into the world] **through sin—and in this way death came through** [sin] **to all human beings, because all have sinned** [compare 3:23]. [13]**For until the Law** [was promulgated through Moses], **sin was in the world. But sin is not charged** [to an account] **when there isn't a law.** [14]**Nevertheless, death reigned from Adam till Moses even over those who hadn't sinned in a manner similar to the transgression of Adam, who is** [in Scripture] **an imprint** [in the sense of a personal foreshadowing] **of him who was going to come** [that is, Jesus]. The portrayal of Jesus as the agent of reconciliation (5:11) now prompts a parallel but counter portrayal of Adam as the agent through whom sin entered the world. Since Jesus was one human being and will be called such in 5:15 (compare 5:17, 19), the calling of Adam "one human being" prepares for this parallel but counter portrayal. To reinforce the portrayal Paul delays identifying Adam by name, so that the emphasis falls on him as "one human being" like the upcoming Jesus. In 3:9 Paul personified sin as a slavemaster under whom are all, both Jews and Greeks. He'll elaborate that personification in chapter 6, but here—because of the preceding reference to being saved by Jesus' life (5:10)—Paul reintroduces the personification of sin ("sin came into the world") only to the extent of enabling a parallel personification of death as a result of sin ("and death [came into the world] through sin [as death's agent]") and as a contrast with the eternal life that Jesus' resurrected life actualizes for believers in

him. "*As indeed*" and "*in this way*" cement the parallel between sin's coming into the world and death's coming into the world through sin's agency. But though "in this way" *implies* that death came "into the world" as sin did, "to all human beings" replaces "into the world" to bring out the universality of human death. (If Paul were asked, he'd probably say that the cases of Enoch [Genesis 5:21–24] and Elijah [2 Kings 2:1–18] are exceptions that prove the rule.)

"Because all have sinned" tells why "death came through [sin] to all human beings." ("Because" is an efficient way of translating a Greek phrase that means "on the basis of the fact that" [see also 6:21; 2 Corinthians 5:4; Philippians 3:12 for the causal meaning in Paul's use of the phrase].) Since "all have sinned" in 3:23 referenced everybody's having sinned individually, for himself, as indicated in 1:18–3:18, the present repetition of that statement points to everybody's having sinned individually, for himself. It's not that God counted Adam's sin as everybody else's too. Paul isn't talking here about accounting. He's talking here about invasion: Adam's sin gave sin as a personified force entry into the world, a force so powerful that "all have sinned," with the result that "death came through [sin] to all human beings." Paul goes out of his way, in fact, to deny he's talking about accounting. He affirms that "sin is *not* charged [to an account] when there isn't a law. *Nevertheless*, death reigned [as a consequence of sin] from Adam till Moses [during which interim there was no law to enable an accounting of sin] even over those who hadn't sinned in a manner similar to the transgression of Adam [whose sinful eating of the forbidden fruit constituted a transgression of God's explicitly stated command (Genesis 2:16–17), like the commands divinely stated later in the Mosaic law]." So the reign of death over those who didn't sin against an explicitly stated law, and therefore whose sin wasn't counted as the transgression of a law, shows that Paul is talking here about sin as a personified force that has enslaved everybody, not about a transgression by Adam that was put on everybody's moral account. The statement that Adam is a scriptural imprint of "him who was going to come" prepares for a comparison of Jesus with Adam. But the comparison will include contrasts; and to build up for a climax, Paul saves till later his identifying the coming one by name. Meanwhile, "was *going* to come" stresses the certainty of Jesus' coming "at the right time" to die "for ungodly people" (5:6).

5:15: **Nevertheless,** *not* **as** [was] **the trespass, in this way** [is] **also the gracious gift. For if by the trespass of the one** [human being, Adam] **the many have died, God's grace and the gift by the grace of the one human being, Jesus Christ, has flourished for the many much more.** "Nevertheless" signals a contrast within the comparison between the one human being, Adam, and the one human being, Jesus Christ. This contrast begins with the difference between Adam's trespass and the gracious gift given by Jesus Christ. Paul explains that Adam's trespass gave sin entry into the world, so that "the many died." "The many" doesn't leave out anybody but emphasizes instead that the all who've sinned and consequently died are indeed many. Again saving up for a climax, Paul doesn't identify "the gracious gift," though to underline its as-yet-undefined difference with the many's death, he ascribes the gift to "God's grace" and calls it "the gift by the grace of the one human being, Jesus Christ," so that it's doubly gracious and involves both God and his Son (compare 3:24–25). The singular verb, "has flourished," unifies the compound subject, "God's grace and the gift." Furthermore, "has flourished for the many much more" makes the gracious gift already available in more than enough quantity for the many, all of whom need it. The gracious gift has flourished for the many much more than death has flourished by the trespass of Adam. In other words, the universality of death in consequence of sin's having entered the world through Adam's trespass, so that everybody has sinned—this universality of death has been outstripped by the flourishing of God's and Jesus Christ's gracious gift to believers. But a gift has to be received, in this case by faith, whereas death reigns by irresistible force. So what counts in this contest between death and gift isn't the number of those who die versus the number of those who receive the gift. What counts is the character of the gift as gracious versus the character of death as deserved.

5:16–17: And what was given [is]n't like [what came about] through the one [human being, Adam] who sinned. For on the one hand the judgmental sentence [originated] out of one [trespass] with the result of condemnation—the gracious gift, on the other hand, out of many trespasses with the result of a sentence of justification. [17]For if by the trespass of the one [human being, Adam] death reigned through the one [human being, Adam], much more will those who receive the surplus of grace and of the gift of righteousness reign in life through the one [human being], Jesus Christ. Here Paul adds to the contrast within the parallel between Adam and Jesus. The addition has to do with "the judgmental sentence" that originated "out of one [trespass]" resulting in "condemnation." Paul is alluding to God's pronouncing the sentence of death on Adam for Adam's trespassing the command not to eat from the tree of the knowledge of good and evil (Genesis 2:16–17). "A sentence of justification" identifies the previously mentioned "gracious gift" with God's crediting the faith of sinners as righteousness. Astonishingly, this gracious gift of justification didn't come about *despite* the trespasses that followed in the train of Adam's one trespass. No, it originated "*out of . . .* trespasses"—indeed, "out of *many* trespasses" (which parallel "the many" who "have died" [5:15]). Those trespasses triggered the grace of God and Jesus Christ at the same time those trespasses triggered God's wrath, which Paul said in 1:18–32 is already being revealed, though its culmination awaits the Last Judgment. So astonishingly (it bears repeating), the contrast between the judgmental sentence and the sentence of justification doesn't lie in a difference of origin between a trespass and *non*trespasses—rather, between *one* trespass and *many* trespasses (compare 5:20: "where sin became

more, grace flourished *beyond* [what was needed]"). Paul explains this astonishing contrast in terms of receiving "the surplus of grace"—that is, more than enough grace to take care of "many trespasses"—"and of the gift of righteousness"—that is, a larger-than-needed gift consisting in a declaration of believing sinners to be righteous—larger-than-needed in that it adds to "the gift *of righteousness*" a "reign[ing] *in life* through the one [human being], Jesus Christ." In 5:21; 6:23 Paul will describe this life as "eternal." Meanwhile, reigning in life stands over against death's reigning. But where we expect life's reigning for a contrast with death's reigning, we read about the reigning "*in* life" of those who receive the surplus of grace and of the gift of righteousness. This further surprise highlights the recipients as victorious over death.

5:18–21: Therefore, then, as through one trespass [a judgmental sentence came about] for all human beings with the result of condemnation [compare 5:12], in this way also [the gracious gift came about] through one act of righteousness for all human beings with the result of a being declared righteous that results in life.[2] [19]For even as the many were made sinners through the disobedience of the one human being [Adam], in this way also the many will be made righteous through the obedience of the one [human being, Jesus Christ]. [20]But the Law sneaked in so that the trespass might become more; but where sin became more, grace flourished beyond [what was needed] [21]in order that even as sin reigned by means of death, in this way also grace might reign through righteousness with the result of eternal life through Jesus Christ, our Lord. The combination of "Therefore" and "then" (the latter in the sense of "therefore," *not* in the sense of "at that time") puts a very heavy accent on the following conclusion, drawn as it is from 5:12–17. The first conclusion is that "the gracious gift" came about through "one act of righteousness" which contrasted with the one trespass of Adam as distinguished from the many trespasses that followed (5:16). This one act of righteousness consisted in Christ's having died for all of us, weak and ungodly sinners though we are (5:6, 8, 10). Paul describes the act as "righteous" because it has resulted for believers in their "being declared righteous." This declaration "results in life" because it frees believers from the reign of death as the consequence of their having sinned because of sin's having come into the world. "For even as the many

---

[2]The contrast in 5:16 with "out of many trespasses" favored the translation "out of one [trespass]" over the translation "out of [the trespass] of one [human being]" and therefore favors here the translation "through one trespass" over the translation "through the trespass of one [human being]." Likewise, then, the present parallel between Adam's disobedience, which consisted in the single act of eating the forbidden fruit, favors that Christ's "one act of righteousness" consisted in his self-sacrificial death for us, not including his prior life of obedience to God's law (as thought by many theologians), which obedience only (but importantly) qualified him to die on behalf of sinners (compare Philippians 2:8).

were made sinners through the disobedience of the one human being" defines Adam's aforementioned trespass as disobedience and emphasizes that it made the many to be sinners by allowing sin's entry into the world as a force so powerful that all succumbed to it. "In this way also the many will be made righteous through the obedience of the one" defines Jesus Christ's aforementioned one act of righteousness as obedience, sets his obedience over against the disobedience of Adam in his one trespass, and lays out the result in a making of the many who believe righteous in the sense of being declared righteous at the Last Judgment.

"But the Law sneaked in" personifies the Law just as sin and death have been personified. "Sneaked in" portrays the Law as a latecomer on the scene (compare 5:13–14) and prepares for a notation of its effect as detrimental. "So that the trespass might become more" tells the purpose and result of the personified Law in sneaking in. The Law's sneaking in enlarged Adam's original trespass, which was a single disobedience of one command, by adding to it the many trespasses in disobedience to God's multiple commands in the Mosaic law, promulgated after the interim (between Adam and Moses) during which there was no divinely stated command that could be disobeyed (5:12–14). The purpose and result of this increase shifts to the location ("where") of sin's becoming more. This shift locates the increase among the Jews, to whom alone the Law was given (2:12–14, 17–18, 23; 3:19), and suits the repersonifying of sin in its "reign[ing] by means of death [its result]." In 5:17 *death* was said to have reigned. Now *sin* is said to have reigned, for sin and death go together as cause and effect. "Even as" underlines the reign of sin by means of death to enhance the reign of grace, which flourished beyond what was needed. We expect Paul to put a reign of righteousness over against the reign of sin. But to emphasize that righteousness is an *ill-deserved* declaration that believing sinners are righteous, he personifies grace instead of righteousness as a ruler, personifies righteousness as the agent of grace, and makes the reign of grace through righteousness flourish beyond even what was needed to displace death with life. "Eternal" describes this life as never to be overthrown by death. "Through Jesus Christ, our Lord" reminds that it's his "one act of righteousness" that made possible the declaration of believing sinners to be righteous, so that they receive the gracious gift of eternal life. Grace flourished where sin became more. Sin became more where the Law sneaked in. The Law sneaked in among the Jews. Therefore grace flourished among the Jews—for it was among them that "God demonstrates his own love for us in that while we were still sinful, Christ died for us" (5:8).

THE BEHAVIOR OF THOSE JUSTIFIED BY FAITH
Romans 6:1–8:39

This section of Romans divides into behavior and baptism (6:1–14), behavior and slavery (6:15–23), behavior and the Law (7:1–25), behavior and the Spirit (8:1–27), and behavior and God (8:28–39).

BEHAVIOR AND BAPTISM
Romans 6:1–14

6:1–2: **Therefore** [since grace flourished beyond what was needed where sin "became more" (5:20)] **what shall we say?** The "we" who as Paul will go on to say received God's grace and died to sin, as dramatized in baptism, can hardly include the non-Christian Jewish interlocutor whom Paul conjured up in earlier chapters. So "we" refers here to Christian believers, such as Paul and his addressees in Rome. **Should we be staying in sin in order that grace may become more? ²To the contrary!** Paul first reacts in moral outrage at the specious reasoning that Christians should continue behaving sinfully, as they did before their conversions, to prompt the exercise of more and more forgiving grace on God's part, as though God *would* exercise more and more of such grace and *be pleased* to do so for the garnering of greater credit than ever because he did. Next, Paul supports his horrified reaction with a counter question: **How shall we, who as such died so far as sin is concerned, still live in it?** Since Paul's first and second questions were deliberative ("Therefore what *shall* [not 'will'] we say?" and "*Should* we stay in sin . . . ?"), we should take this third question, too, as deliberative ("How *shall* we . . . ?") rather than predictive ("How *will* we . . . ?"), so that "How . . . ?" doesn't mean "In what way . . . ?"—rather, "How is it that . . . ?" (indicating incredulity). "Who *as such*" underlines the character of Christians as people who've died so far as sin is concerned—that is, who've been disconnected from their life of sin prior to conversion. "Still live in it [sin]" explains the earlier phrase, "stay in sin," and highlights the behavioral as well as logical contradiction of *living* in something you've died to.

6:3–4: Or are you ignorant [of the fact] **that as many of us as were baptized into Christ Jesus were baptized into his death? ⁴Therefore we were buried with him through baptism into death in order that as indeed Christ was raised from among the dead through the Father's glory, in this way we too might walk around in newness of life.** "Or are you ignorant . . . ?" introduces a question alternative to the preceding one, puts Paul's addressees on the defensive by suggesting they understand the import neither of his preceding question nor of their (and his) baptisms, and may even imply his suspicion (or knowledge) of sinful behavior among the Roman Christians. He puts them on the defensive to prompt their agreement: Oh no, Paul, we agree with you that as Christians baptized into Jesus' death we shouldn't continue living in the sin that we died to.

"As many of us as were baptized into Christ Jesus" doesn't imply that some of "us" weren't baptized into him. The expression simply emphasizes baptism as the initiatory rite that all Christians undergo (or did in the first century). Since baptism means immersion in water, "baptized into Christ Jesus" explains baptism in water as a dramatization of believers' union with Christ, as though he's the water into which believers are immersed. But he died for us, his burial followed, and immersion is like being buried after dying. So "baptized in his [Jesus'] death" and "buried with him through baptism into death" explain baptism as not just a dramatization of union with Christ, but as a dramatization of union with Christ *in his death and burial*. That is to say, God looks on Christian baptizees as having died and been buried with Christ when he died and was buried. For they are "in Christ" (a favorite phrase of Paul) because of having believed in him and received the Holy Spirit, who indwells Christ (8:1–11).

"Through baptism" can mean either that baptism is the means of such union with Christ or that it's a dramatization of such union with him. But Paul's shying away from saying that Christians have already been raised with Christ through baptism, though they *have* already been *buried* with him through baptism into death, favors dramatization over means. For means would have encouraged Paul to add that Christians have been raised with Christ through baptism. But dramatization discourages such an addition, because analogies (and a dramatization is a kind of analogy) break down at some point or another. Otherwise we'd have identity rather than analogy. It's true that in Colossians 2:12 Paul speaks of having been raised with Christ in baptism; but the addition there of "through faith" makes faith the means, so that baptism remains a dramatization even in that passage (see further the comments on Galatians 3:25–27).

"Therefore" bases a conclusion on the equation of baptism into Christ Jesus with baptism into his death. From burial with him through baptism into death the conclusion proceeds to the purpose of baptism to foster "newness of life." "Walk around" is a figure of speech for behavior and therefore interprets "newness of life" as a new kind of behavior, one that differs from living in sin (6:1–2). Paul compares this newness of life to Christ's having been "raised from among the dead," which suggests that Christians' new kind of life distinguishes them from the non-Christian walking dead (compare Ephesians 2:1–3) and implies that the resurrection of Christ launched him into a new life devoid of the sin that he bore on our behalf "once for all" (6:10).

"Through the Father's glory" recalls "God's glory" in 3:23 (see also 1:23; 3:7); but Paul shifts from "God's" to "the Father's" because "God's" put God over against sinful humanity, whereas "Father's" puts him in rapport with Christ and those who by faith are in Christ (compare 8:1). But wouldn't we expect "through the Father's *power*" as the means of Christ's resurrection and as in 1:4; 1 Corinthians 6:14; 2 Corinthians 13:4; Philippians 3:10? Why "through the Father's *glory*"? Well, "glory" is associated with "power," "might," and "strength" in Colossians 1:11; 2 Thessalonians 1:9. There's no such association here; but since God's power is glorious according to those other passages, Paul substitutes glory for power to highlight that the newness of Christ's resurrected life freed him from the sins of humankind, who because of their sins lack God's glory according to 3:23 (compare John 11:40–44).

As noted above, Paul stops short of saying Christians were raised with Christ through baptism into resurrec-tion, which would be comparable to coming up out of the water; and Paul stops short even though saying so would have strengthened his identifying the purpose of baptism as a dramatization of newness of life. Why then the stopping short? Answer: Paul is reserving the resurrection of Christians for what will happen to their bodies at the Last Day (see 6:5 and especially 6:8), and reserving it as a forward-looking motive for Christians to "be *considering*" themselves "living in Christ Jesus in relation to God" (6:11). Such a consideration will affect their behavior.

Now Paul tells why baptism has the purpose of prompting newness of life. **6:5: For if we've become united with** [Christ] **by the likeness of his death, we'll nevertheless be also of** [his] **resurrection . . . .** "The likeness of [his] death" refers to baptism as a dramatization of believers' union with Christ in his death. On the other hand, "nevertheless" differentiates resurrection sharply from death. "We'll nevertheless be also of [his] resurrection" puts in the future whatever it is of Christ's resurrection that Paul is talking about. It would make a certain amount of sense to fill the gap in his wording as follows: "we'll nevertheless be also [united with Christ by the likeness] of [his] resurrection." Such a fill-in would help the parallel with "we've become united with [him] by the likeness of his death"—but wouldn't help enough, because the future tense in "we'll . . . be" doesn't fit the past tense in "we've become united," so that a sup-plied "likeness" of Christ's resurrection couldn't refer to baptisms already undergone by Christians. Apparently Paul sensed that filling out the parallel would produce this misfit, so that he left the awkward gap in order to preserve and even emphasize the difference of a future bodily resurrection from the past baptismal dramatiza-tion of union with Christ in his death. As said before, this difference provides motivation for good Christian behavior in anticipation of that resurrection.

6:6–7: [we] **knowing this, that our old human being** [= our preconversion self] **was crucified with** [Christ] **in order that the body of sin might be incapacitated so that we'd no longer be slaving for sin.** [7]**For the person who has died has been emancipated from sin.** "The body of sin" means the physical body as dominated by sin in its behavior. (Recall the portrayal of sin as an overpowering force in 5:12–14, 21.) Paul compares this domination to enslavement, with sin as the slavemaster. But death incapacitates a body (it can't work any more) and thereby emancipates a slave from his master. (At this point there's a wordplay in that the Greek verb underly-ing "has been emancipated" is a form of the verb Paul has been using in the sense of being justified, declared righteous.) So death's incapacitation and emancipation of a body formerly enslaved to sin has to do with Chris-tians' ceasing to sin because God regards them as having been crucified with Christ so far as sin is concerned. It's their "knowing this," dramatized in their baptism, that leads them to stop sinning.

6:8–11: But if we died with Christ [as we did so far as God is concerned], **we believe that we'll also live**

with him [by way of resurrection or staying alive right through the second coming into eternity], ⁹[we] **knowing that Christ, having been raised from among the dead, dies no more. Death wields lordship over him no more.** ¹⁰**For as to** [the death] **that he died, he died once for all in relation to sin; but as to** [the life] **that he's living, he's living in relation to God** [because it was God who raised him from the dead (6:4)]. ¹¹**In this way you too be considering yourselves dead, on the one hand,** [as in fact you are from God's point of view] **in relation to sin. On the other hand** [be considering yourselves] **living in Christ Jesus** [as in fact you are] **in relation to God.** "We believe that" introduces an article of Christian faith with which Paul's Roman addressees agree, and "knowing that . . . Christ dies no more" supplements "knowing . . . that our old human being was crucified with him [and so forth in 6:6]." Just as death emancipates from enslavement to sin (6:7), so resurrection overthrew the lordship of death over Christ (see 5:12–14, 21 again for the personification of death as an overlord). Paul stresses the finality of Christ's death: "Christ dies *no more*. Death wields lordship over him *no more*. For as to [the death] that he died, he died *once for all*." The addition, "in relation to sin" hints at the reason for this stress on finality: the stress is meant to encourage Christians to stop sinning once and for all in view of their having been crucified, and thus died, once and for all with Christ so far as God is concerned. This encouragement evolves into a command that Christians look at themselves the way God looks at them, that is, as having died with Christ once for all: "*In this way* you *too* be considering yourselves dead, on the one hand, in relation to sin." For thinking determines doing, so that if you're *considering* yourselves dead to sin you'll not be yielding your bodies to sinful behavior. Then Paul commands Christians to be considering themselves also as living, the way God considers them because he looks on them as being in Christ, the one living by virtue of resurrection. But in line with his refraining from drawing out a baptismal dramatization of past resurrection, Paul delays drawing out the behavioral effects of Christians' considering themselves living in Christ Jesus.

6:12: **Therefore** [since you should consider yourselves dead so far as sin is concerned] **sin isn't to be reigning in your mortal body, so that** [you] **obey its lusts.** The personification of sin as a reigning force makes another appearance, but only to be negated. Paul isn't commanding the Roman Christians not to let sin reign. He's commanding *sin* not to reign, but addressing the command to the Roman Christians so that *they* may command sin not to reign. (Unlike Greek, English doesn't have an easily recognizable form of an indirect— that is, third person—command; but "So-and-so *is* to do [or not to do] such-and-such" does a fair job of it.) Since reigning implies a domain, Paul specifies the domain of sin's possible reign: "in your mortal body." And since "your" is plural in the original Greek, the singular of "body" is collective to balance the plural in "your [body] parts." Paul describes the body as "mortal" in view of

surrounding references to death. The result of sin's reigning in the mortal body would be obedience to its lusts, so that lusts are personified as objects of obedience just as sin has been personified as a ruler. "Lusts" covers all desires, especially sexual ones, so strong that they lead to sinning.

Now Paul issues commands directly to the Roman Christians. *6:13–14:* **Neither be presenting your** [body] **parts to sin as tools of unrighteousness; rather, present yourselves to God as if you're living from among the dead, and** [present] **your** [body] **parts to God as tools of righteousness.** ¹⁴**For sin won't wield lordship over you. For you're not under the Law; rather,** [you're] **under grace.** The personification of sin continues. It could use your body parts—hands, feet, eyes, and sexual organs, for example—as tools for the doing of deeds that aren't right, as though sin instead of you is doing them (compare 7:16–20). But on the basis of considering themselves dead in relation to sin, Christians are not to present their body parts to sin—rather, to present themselves to God. "Your [body] parts" shifts to "yourselves" in the command to "present yourselves to God as if you're living," because it would sound odd to speak of body *parts* as living. "From among the dead" defines "living" in terms of resurrection. But "as *if* you're living from among the dead" contrasts with "as *indeed* Christ was raised from among the dead" (6:4) and thereby reserves Christians' bodily resurrection for the Last Day and defines the presentation of themselves to God as living in terms of thinking, as was said in 6:11: "Be *considering* yourselves . . . ." Paul shifts back to "your [body] parts" in the command to present them "to God as tools of righteousness." As personified sin would use those parts as tools for the doing of deeds that *aren't* right, God will use them for the doing of deeds that *are* right, as though he instead of you is doing them (through his indwelling Spirit according to 8:1–14).³

Paul predicts that sin won't wield lordship over Christians (compare 8:4–5). But instead of making his prediction the *result* of presenting body parts to God, he makes it the *reason* for presenting them to God: "*For* sin won't wield lordship over you." In other words, use your future to determine your present, your coming emancipation from sin's lordship to determine your present behavior. Then the future will merge into the present, and vice versa. Next, Paul adds a reason for the foregoing reason. It's that "you're not under the Law; rather, [you're] under grace." We saw in 3:9 that "under sin" indicates enslavement to sin as an overlord and owner. This indication will become even clearer in 7:14: "sold [as a slave] under sin." But if "under sin" indicates enslavement to sin, "under grace" indicates enslavement to grace. What a desirable enslavement—to God's unearned and ill-deserved favor! But how is it that not being under the

---

³Sometimes Paul uses the word translated "tools" in the sense of "weapons" (2 Corinthians 6:7; 10:4; compare John 18:3), but there the contexts favor that sense. Here the context of slavery favors "tools."

Law but under grace provides the reason sin won't wield lordship over you? Chapters 7–8 will answer this question. Meanwhile, back to a question of specious reasoning such as chapter 6 started with.

BEHAVIOR AND SLAVERY
Romans 6:15–23

6:15–18: Therefore what [shall we say (compare 6:1)]**? Should we sin because we're not under the Law—rather, under grace? To the contrary!** [16]**You know, don't you, that to whom you present yourselves as slaves for the purpose of obedience—you're slaves** [of the one] **whom you obey, either of sin with the result of death or of obedience with the result of righteousness?** [17]**But thanks** [be] **to God that you used to be slaves of sin but were obedient from the heart to the teaching's imprint to which you were given over;** [18]**and having been set free from sin, you were enslaved to righteousness.** "Therefore" harks back to the statement in 6:14 that Christians aren't under the Law (that is, the Mosaic law), but under grace. Yet to fill out his question, "Should we sin . . . ?" Paul repeats that statement to make it a specious reason for sinning. As in 6:2, "To the contrary!" adds moral outrage to a negative answer. "You know, don't you . . . ?" implies that the Roman Christians do know the following and will therefore agree with his deduction from it. Of course they know that slavery entails obedience to a slavemaster and, the other way around, that obedience betokens slavery to a master. Then Paul sets out two possible masters to whom obedience is rendered, and the results of obedience to them. The contrasts are stark. First the possible masters: sin and obedience. Obedience? Isn't it what's to be *rendered* to a master, not *itself* a master? Don't we expect "God" rather than "obedience" in view of the command in 6:13 to present yourselves to God rather than sin? Yes, we do. But Paul surprises us by making obedience itself a master. Though obedience might be rendered to sin, Paul is so confident that "sin won't wield lordship over you" (6:14) that he turns a blind eye to the possibility of Christians' obeying sin and co-opts obedience as their master. So certain are Christians to obey God, if they're true Christians, that this obedience is itself their master. The results: death and righteousness. Righteousness? Don't we expect "life" in contrast with "death"? Yes, we do. But Paul surprises us again with "righteousness" to emphasize good behavior instead of life, which will get enough emphasis shortly.

Paul's confidence in regard to the Roman Christians leads him to break out in thanksgiving to God. Paul puts their slavery to sin in the past, that is, prior to their conversions. He attributes their liberation from sin to their obedience "to the teaching's imprint," to which imprint they "were given over." "From the heart" describes their obedience as unforced and unfabricated. What Paul economically called "the gospel" in 1:16 (compare 1:1, 9; 2:16) he now calls expansively "the teaching's imprint, to which you were given over." This expansion alludes to

the effect, for which "imprint" is a figure of speech, that gospel-teaching has had on the Roman Christians' behavior. But we expect Paul to say that this effect, this imprint, was given over *to them.* Instead, he says they were given over *to it.* They belong to the behavioral imprint of gospel-teaching. It doesn't belong to them. So neither they nor anybody else should dare tamper with it (compare 16:17–18). Then Paul sets liberation from sin and enslavement to righteousness in tandem with each other, so that there's no interval of nonenslavement. Human beings are enslaved either to sin or to righteousness. To righteousness? Hasn't Paul just spoken of righteousness as the result of enslavement *to obedience*? Yes, but in the imprint of teaching to which Christians have been given over, obedience and righteousness are so tightly bonded with each other that righteousness substitutes for obedience to underscore the *kind* of behavior entailed by specifically Christian obedience.

6:19–20: I'm speaking humanly [that is, using the human institution of slavery as an analogy] **because of the weakness of your flesh** [that is, because you might not understand a theological exposition devoid of a human analogy]. Because flesh decomposes upon death, weakness is commonly ascribed to flesh—but not usually in regard to mental capacities. Here, though, surrounding references to the body and body parts lead to a use of "flesh" for weakness in regard to mental capacities. Now Paul elaborates his human analogy. **For even as** [prior to your conversion] **you presented your** [body] **parts to impurity and lawlessness as** [their] **slaves with the result of lawlessness, in this way you've now** [through conversion] **presented your** [body] **parts to righteousness as** [its] **slaves with the result of consecration.** "Impurity" refers to moral impurity, especially of a sexual sort and especially when in association with body parts (1:24–27; 7:5; 1 Corinthians 6:15; 2 Corinthians 12:21; Galatians 5:19 and so on), and "lawlessness" to behaviors that violated the Mosaic law whether or not the violators were under its jurisdiction. (Most of the Roman Christians were Gentiles, who therefore had never been under its jurisdiction, though some were Jews, who had been under it.) Paul has personified impurity and lawlessness as slavemasters the way he personified sin as a slavemaster. Since lawlessness might seem to imply the liberty of license, it's especially striking that Paul personifies lawlessness along with sin and impurity as a slavemaster rather than as a liberator. "With the result of lawlessness" means that as a slavemaster, lawlessness reproduces itself in the behavior of its slaves. "In this way" draws a parallel between the self-presentations, which retain the element of human responsibility. "With the result of consecration" identifies the result of enslavement to righteousness as consecration, which means devotion to God as opposed to impurity and the lawlessness reproduced by lawlessness. Devotion to God requires moral purity and obedience to his commands. Now Paul explains that enslavement to sin excluded enslavement to righteousness: [20]**For when you were slaves of sin, you were free so far as righteousness was concerned.** It's presupposed that there's no concurrent enslavement to two opposing masters (compare Matthew 6:24; Luke 16:13).

6:21–23: Therefore [since slavery to sin kept you free as regards righteousness], **what fruit were you having then because of** [impure and lawless behaviors] **that you're now ashamed of? For the end of those** [behaviors is] **death.** [22]**But now, having been set free from sin and enslaved to God, you're having your fruit resulting in consecration; and the end** [of consecration is] **eternal life.** [23]**For the wages of sin** [is] **death, but God's gracious gift** [is] **eternal life in Christ Jesus, our Lord.** "Fruit" is a figure of speech for the outcome of something. "What fruit were you having *then* . . . ?" dates the *outcome* of the Roman addressees' impure and lawless behaviors, not just the behaviors themselves, to the period before the addressees were converted and therefore makes the outcome ("fruit") of their behaviors God's having given them over to their "lusts," "dishonorable passions," and "a disapproved mind" (1:24–32). So the fruit was a *near* outcome, cut short—thankfully—by being "set free from sin." The fruit of this liberation is consecration to God, likewise a near outcome in that it already obtains. "The end," however, points forward to a final outcome. The contrast of "death" with "eternal life" implies that here, death doesn't mean physical death. For though Christians will enjoy eternal life because of having been set free from sin, they die physically. In the present case, then, "death" means eternal damnation as "the end," sin's final outcome, whereas eternal life is "the end," the final outcome, of consecration to God. Paul has talked of enslavement to grace, to obedience, to righteousness, and to the imprint of Christian teaching (6:14–19). Here he talks of enslavement to God, which includes all those other enslavements and prepares for eternal life as "God's gracious gift" to his slaves. The miserly slavemaster sin gives no gifts, only wages—and dismally poor wages at that. For the Greek word translated "wages" connotes a pittance, such as soldiers are paid; and death is a poor wage indeed, whereas God's gracious gift of life is lavish, because the life is eternal. "In Christ Jesus, our Lord" tells where this gift is to be found by faith.

BEHAVIOR AND THE LAW
Romans 7:1–25

7:1–3: Or don't you know, brothers—for I'm speaking to those who do know the Law—that the Law wields lordship over a human being for as long a time as he or she lives? [2]**For a married woman is bound by the Law to her living husband. But if the husband dies, she has been discharged from the Law as regards** [her] **husband.** [3]**Therefore, then, while** [her] **husband is living she'll be labeled an adulteress if she becomes** [a wife] **to another man. But if** [her] **husband dies, she's free from the Law, so that she's not an adulteress if becoming** [a wife] **to another man.** At first, "Or don't you know . . . ?" suggests that in Paul's view the Roman Christians don't know. So he softens his ques-

tion with the affectionate address, "brothers," and then says he's asking the question because they do know the Law. Thus the question turns out to be rhetorical rather than accusatory. Since Roman law allowed wives as well as husbands the right of divorce but the Mosaic law allowed only husbands that right (Deuteronomy 24:1–4), "the Law" refers to the Mosaic law. For Paul says "a married woman is bound by the Law to her living husband" and is "discharged from the Law" only "if [her] husband dies." No right of divorce for her according to this law! Even Gentiles would have known from observable Jewish practice and, if they'd attended Jewish synagogues prior to Christian conversion (as many Gentile Christians had done), would have known from hearing the Mosaic law read Sabbath by Sabbath (compare Mark 10:12). Paul uses the married woman's being bound by this law of marriage to illustrate the Law's lifelong lordship over everyone under its jurisdiction (that is, every Jew [see the comments on 3:19]). The labeling of a divorced and unwidowed but remarried woman as an adulteress—a labeling reinforced by the twofold expression "Therefore, then"—underscores the illegitimacy of divorce and remarriage for a woman under Moses' law so long as her husband is living. But Paul's emphasis falls even more heavily on the husband's death as breaking the woman's bondage to this law—*more* heavily as evident in the repetition of "But if the husband dies," in the pairing of "she's free from the Law" with "she has been discharged from the Law as regards [her] husband," and in the conclusion that "she's not [then] an adulteress if becoming [a wife] to another man."

7:4: And so, my brothers, as regards the Law you too were put to death through the corpse of the Christ with the result that you've become [a wife] **to another—**[namely,] **the one who was raised from among the dead—in order that you might bear fruit for God.** "And so" introduces an application of the foregoing, and "my brothers" warms up the addressees to get in line with God's purpose that they "bear fruit" for him. In 7:2–3 Paul spoke twice of dying as breaking the legal bond of marriage. Now he switches to being "*put* to death" as the means by which believers are freed from the Law. This expression recalls 6:1–7, which talked of believers' having been united with Christ in his death, as dramatized in baptism. In other words, Paul's switching from dying to being put to death has the purpose of excluding natural death in the future and speaking instead of believers' having been (so far as God is concerned) *crucified* with Christ when he was crucified—hence, "through the *corpse* of the Christ" (compare also 6:6–11). The word translated "corpse" is usually translated "body." But "the body of the Christ" wrongly recalls the use of that phrase as a figure of speech for the church (1 Corinthians 12:12–27; Ephesians 4:12). In agreement with the present context of death and with early and still current usage, the word refers here to the corpse of Jesus that resulted from his crucifixion. Paul calls him "the Christ" to intimate Jesus' messianic role in giving himself over to crucifixion for our sake (compare Galatians 2:20).

Surprisingly, believers play the roles of both the husband who dies and the wife who lives to marry another man in 7:1-3: "you too were put to death [as the first husband died] through the corpse of the Christ in order to become [a wife] to another [man, whom the widowed wife marries]." But the widowed and remarried wife in 7:1-3 did *not* die though in fact believers, represented by her in respect to being freed from the Law, *were* put to death through the Christ's corpse. Correspondingly, Christ plays both the role of the first husband, who died, and—by virtue of his resurrection—the role of the second husband, whom the widowed wife marries. That these roles jostle against each other testifies to the overpowering strength of Paul's teaching that believers were united with Christ in Christ's death and will be united with him in his resurrection. "In order that you might bear fruit for God" echoes the fruit associated with consecration to God in 6:22, identifies the purpose of marrying (so to speak) the resurrected Christ, and looks forward to the righteous behavior outlined in 8:1-17 and detailed in 12:1-15:13.

Now Paul explains why it used to be impossible for him and his addressees to "bear fruit for God" but is now possible to do so. **7:5-6: For when we were in the flesh, sinful passions, which** [came about] **through the Law's instrumentality, were at work in our** [body] **parts with the result of** [our] **bearing fruit for death.** [6]**But now we've been discharged from the Law by having died as regards that by which** [referring to the Law] **we were being held down, so that we're slaving in newness of the Spirit and not** [in] **oldness of the letter.** Paul and the Roman Christians are still living in their physical bodies, but "when we were in the flesh" implies they're no longer living in the flesh though they once did. Therefore "in the flesh" doesn't concern their physical bodies as such—rather, those bodies as dominated in their "[body] parts" by "sinful passions" prior to conversion (compare the comments on "the body of sin" in 6:6). That the sinful passions "were at work in our [body] parts" personifies those passions just as sin was personified as a dominating force in chapters 5-6. "Bearing fruit for death" also revives the personification of death in those same chapters, contrasts with "bear[ing] fruit for God" (7:4), and recalls death as the wages of sin (6:23). Paul will explain in 7:7-25 how it was that sinful passions came about "through the Law's instrumentality." Meanwhile he explains the foregoing analogy of a wife's being discharged from the Law as regards her husband (7:2) in terms of being discharged from the Mosaic law as a whole. But unlike the discharge of the wife through the death of her husband, Christians have been discharged by their own death through union with Christ in his death (see the comments on 7:4 and 6:1-7). That they "were being held down" by the Law portrays the Law—like sin, lusts, unrighteousness, impurity, and lawlessness in 6:12-23—as a slavemaster, indeed a repressive one.

"So that we're slaving in newness of the Spirit" picks up the theme of enslavement to God, obedience, and righteousness in 6:12-23 but adds the element of the Spirit, who according to 8:1-17 *enables* believers to slave for God, obedience, and righteousness. "Oldness of the letter" refers to the Mosaic law as both written in Scripture (the Old Testament) and outdated. "Newness of the Spirit" highlights the transition from inability to obey the Law up to God's standard over to ability to do so (see the comments on 2:29; 2 Corinthians 3:4-6 against a contrast between the spirit of the law and the letter of the law). Since only Jews were under the Law's jurisdiction, Paul uses the freeing of Jewish believers from the Law to keep Gentiles from thinking they can keep the Law successfully enough to earn salvation.

7:7-8: What then shall we say [in view of "sinful passions" that have come about "through the instrumentality of the Law" (7:5)]**?** [Is] **the Law sin? To the contrary! Rather, I wouldn't have known sin** [to be what it is: sin] **except through the Law. For also** [= in particular] **I wouldn't have known lust** [to be what it is: lust] **unless the Law was saying, "You shall not lust** [Exodus 20:17; Deuteronomy 5:21]." [8]**But seizing** [its] **opportunity, sin produced in me through the commandment** [not to lust] **every sort of lust. For apart from the Law, sin** [is] **dead.** Paul is exonerating the Law by saying that it identifies sin and prohibits sinning, whereas sin (still personified as a powerful force) used the identifications and prohibitions to incite sinning (compare Proverbs 9:17). So "know[ing] sin" means knowing it experientially in one's conduct as well as knowing it intellectually in one's mind. Since Christians aren't under the Law, though (6:14-15), Paul is describing a pre-Christian experience under the Law; and since he uses "I," "me," and (later) "my" and "I myself," he's describing his own experience of sin's using the Law to incite his sinning prior to being discharged from the Law through union with Christ in death and prior to receiving the Spirit. Most translations read, "You shall not *covet*," in accordance with Exodus 20:17; Deuteronomy 5:21 (though even there coveting your neighbor's wife counts as lust). But Paul uses the verb ordinarily translated "lust"; and though lusting refers to all sorts of inordinate desires, his use of the verb and its cognate noun stresses above all sexual lusts (see "sinful passions" close by in 7:5 and the association of lusts with bodies, body parts, flesh, fornication, homosex, impurity, and pleasures in 1:24-28; 6:12; 7:5; 13:14; 1 Corinthians 10:6-8; Galatians 5:16-19, 24; Ephesians 2:3; Colossians 3:5; 1 Thessalonians 4:3-5; Titus 3:3 and compare 2 Timothy 3:6 and "youthful lusts" in 2 Timothy 2:22). As in 1:24-28; 1 Timothy 6:9; 2 Timothy 3:6; Titus 3:3, then, "every sort of lust" probably refers to various kinds or occasions of sexual lust, the Law's prohibition of which incited them in Paul. "For apart from the Law, sin [is] dead" implies that the Law's jurisdiction over a person enlivens sin by making it possible for sin to incite unlawful lusts in that person. Before his death to the Law through union with Christ, however, was Paul ever outside the Law's jurisdiction?

7:9-10: I was living apart from the Law once upon a time; but when the commandment came, sin sprang to

life. But I died ¹⁰and the commandment, which [was]
for the purpose of life—this [commandment] was
found in my case to result in death. "Once upon a time"
puts Paul's "living apart from the Law" before his death
to the Law through union with Christ, and therefore in
Paul's youth prior to his becoming old enough to bear
the responsibility of an adult to keep the Law (compare
the ceremony of bar mitzvah, whatever the date of its
origin). Jewish lads came to that responsibility at the age
of puberty and therefore at the age when the Law's prohibition of lusting could incite every sort of sexual lust. So
it was in Paul's case, he confesses. "The commandment
[not to lust] came" in the sense of impinging on him as
a lad both newly pubescent and newly responsible to
keep the Law. "Sin sprang to life" in the sense of using
that commandment as an incitement to sexual lusts. "But
I died" contrasts Paul's death with sin's springing to life
and recollects the entry of death into the world in the
train of sin (5:12) and death as the wages of sin (6:23).
Only Paul's is a *moral* death. The commandment had
the purpose of producing life (through obedience to it);
but because of sin's co-opting the commandment so as
to incite disobedience, a moral death occurred in Paul's
case. (And his case is paradigmatic of everyone's except
Christ's, whatever the commandment in view.) In retrospect, then, the Law's sneaking in so that the trespass
might increase (5:20) indicated the purpose of the Law
insofar as sin had co-opted it—but not otherwise—as
Paul now explains.

7:11–12: **For sin, seizing** [its] **opportunity through
the commandment** [not to lust], **deceived me and
through it killed me.** ¹²**And so, indeed, the Law** [is]
holy; and the commandment [in it not to lust] [is]
holy and righteous and good. Sin's having deceived
Paul and through the commandment killed him relates
to his saying that "the serpent deceived Eve with his
trickery" (2 Corinthians 11:3; see also 1 Timothy 2:14),
which goes back to the crafty serpent's telling Eve she
wouldn't die if she ate the forbidden fruit, despite God's
having said she would (Genesis 3:1–6). In Paul's case, sin
took the serpent's place, and sexual lusts took the place
of forbidden fruit; but the deception still consisted in a
denial that disobedience would end in death. To exonerate the Law and blame sin, Paul portrays sin as his killer
and the commandment as its unwitting instrument of
death. In and of itself, the Law is "holy" in the sense of
differentiated from sin. The Law's commandment not
to lust is likewise "holy," but also "righteous" in that it
corresponds to the character of God, and "good" in that
it benefits human beings to avoid lust.

Paul's exoneration of the Law continues in *7:13*:
Therefore [in view of sin's having killed me through
the commandment] **has the good become death in my
case? To the contrary! Rather, sin—in order that it
might be exposed as sin—produced death in my case
through the good** [contained in the commandment]
**in order that through the commandment sin might
become outrageously sinful.** "The good" emphasizes

the beneficial quality of the Law and, in particular, of its
commandment not to lust (compare 7:12). A second "To
the contrary!" highlights Paul's continued exoneration of
the Law (see 7:7 for the first one), this time by denying
that goodness, which benefits human beings, turned into
death—that is, Paul's moral death. The culprit was sin,
not the goodness characteristic of the commandment.
Over against an evolution of "the good" into "death,"
Paul puts the exposé of sin as "outrageously sinful." More
than that, he portrays this exposé as *self*-exposure on the
part of sin. And more yet, he portrays the self-exposure
as purposeful on sin's part ("sin—*in order that* it might
be exposed as sin . . . *in order that* . . . sin might become
outrageously sinful"). Sin flaunts itself as sinful (compare 1:32).

Now Paul tells why he has emphatically denied any
equation between the Law and sin, and between the
goodness of the commandment not to lust and death.
7:14–16: **For we know that the Law is Spiritual. But
I'm fleshy, having been sold** [as a slave so as to be]
under sin [as my slavemaster (compare 3:9)]. ¹⁵**For I
don't know what I'm producing. For what I** *want* [to
do]—**this I'm** *not* **doing. Rather, what I** *hate*—**this I** *am*
doing. ¹⁶**But if I'm doing this,** [namely] **what I** *don't*
want [to do], **I'm agreeing with the Law to the effect
that it's good.** "*We* know" draws the Roman Christians
into Paul's circle of knowledge, so that they'll agree with
his exoneration of the Law. "Spiritual" describes the Law
as nonsinful because it was given by God's Spirit (hence
the capitalization of "Spiritual"), or by God *as* Spirit.
(Compare the prohibition of making a graven image
of God [Exodus 20:4; Deuteronomy 5:8]; and contrast
Paul's saying in Galatians 3:19, where to reject works-
righteousness he needs to depreciate the Law, that the
Law "was promulgated through angels.") Since flesh connotes weakness (see the comments on 6:19, for example),
"I'm fleshy" describes Paul as morally weak (compare
5:6, 8) and therefore enslaved to sin, which has bought
him and thus owns him. But like his addressees Paul has
died to sin and thus been set free from it (6:2, 7, 18, 22).
So his switching from the past tense used in 7:5–13 to the
present tense is designed to animate the description of
his enslavement to sin, not to characterize his Christian
life as one of enslavement to sin. Reread 7:5–6 and look
ahead to 8:2–10! As evidence of his past enslavement
to sin Paul says he didn't know what he was producing,
which is to say he didn't recognize his behavior as representative of his desire. He desired to obey the commandment not to lust, but found himself lusting. He hated
lusting, but lusted anyway. Despite this lusting, his not
wanting to lust showed agreement with the Law that it's
good not to lust.

7:17–20: **But now** *I*'**m no longer producing it** [what
I don't want to do]; **instead, the** *sin* **that's residing in me**
[is producing it]. ¹⁸**For I know that good isn't residing
in me, that is, in my flesh. For** *wanting* [to do the good]
lies beside me, but as to *producing* **the good—no.** ¹⁹**For
I'm not doing the good that I want** [to do]; **rather, the**

bad that I don't want [to do]—this I'm doing. [20]But if I'm doing this, [namely] what I don't want [to do], I'm no longer producing it. Instead, the sin that's residing in me [is producing what I don't want to do but am doing anyway]. So different were Paul's deeds from his desire that though he didn't recognize them as stemming from his desire, he did recognize them—correctly, in view of 5:12—as stemming from sin, the overpowering force that "came into the world" through Adam (5:12 again) and recently took up residence in Paul's flesh, weak as it was. "But *now*" heightens the animation produced by use of the present tense for past experience. The switch from "we know" in 7:14 to "I know" concentrates attention on Paul as an individual whose enslavement to sin was paradigmatic, and whose recognition that "good isn't residing in [him], that is, in [his] flesh," was exemplary (in the sense of worth imitating). The inability to do the good that he wanted to do frustrated him especially because the desire to do good lay close at hand ("beside me") but was thwarted by the sin residing in him.

7:21–23: I find then the law that the bad lies beside me—[that is,] me [as] the one who wants to be doing the good [by way of not lusting (compare 7:18)]. [22]**For I take pleasure in God's law so far as [my] inner human being is concerned.** [23]**But I see another law in my [body] parts waging war against the law of my mind and making me a captive in the law of sin, [the law] that's in my [body] parts.** "For I *take pleasure* in God's law so far as [my] inner human being is concerned" ratchets up Paul's "*want*[ing] to be doing the good." Similarly, "that the bad *lies beside me*" is ratcheted up by "another law['s] . . . *waging war* against the law of [Paul's] mind," the result of which war is the "making [of Paul] a *captive*" who is imprisoned "in the law of the sin that's in [his body] parts." The "inner human being" of Paul equates with his "mind," and "in my [body] parts" equates with "in my flesh," which occurred earlier (7:18). But how does "God's law" relate to "the law of [Paul's] mind"? How do "the law that the bad lies beside [Paul]," the "law in [his body] parts waging war against [his] mind," and "the law of sin that's in [his body] parts"—how do these laws relate to each other, and also to "God's law" and "the law of [Paul's] mind"? (Some English translations use "principle" instead of "law" in some of these phrases.) Though "*another* law" may seem to distinguish the law that wages war from "God's law," Paul has already spoken of the Mosaic law in terms of its different uses (see the comments on 3:27–28). So here it's probable that the law of Paul's mind is God's law as the law in which Paul takes pleasure so far as his "inner human being"— that is, his "mind"—is concerned. "The law that the bad lies beside [Paul]" equates with "the law in [his body] parts." That "wag[es] war against the law of his mind and mak[es him] captive in the law of the sin that's in [his body] parts." These to-be-equated laws refer then to God's law *as used by sin* to thwart Paul's desire to be doing the good commanded by the Law—and, as previously said, to thwart this desire by using the Law as an incitement to sin.

7:24–25a: Wretched human being [that] **I** [am]! **Who'll rescue me from the body of this death?** [25a]**But thanks to God** [for such a rescue] **through Jesus Christ, our Lord!** Paul's outcry and question punctuate the distress he felt over enslavement to sinful lusts despite a desire to be free of them. Being private, this distress wasn't contradicted by Paul's public blamelessness as regards the Law according to Philippians 3:5–6. A possible translation, "this body of death," would stress the *body* as the locus of moral death's outworking through body parts. The translation, "the body of this death," stresses *moral death* as what works itself out by using body parts as its tools (compare 6:12–23). But the difference is only one of emphasis, a slight one at that; and in either case, though Paul has yet to wrap up the description of his pre-Christian moral defeat, he can't wait to thank God for God's having answered his question by rescuing him "through Jesus Christ." The addition of "our Lord" intimates that it took Jesus Christ's lordship to rescue Paul from sin's lordship, and intimates as well that the Roman Christians have had a similar rescue. Paul's thanking God contrasts with and perhaps compensates in part for pagans' failure to thank God (1:21).

7:25b: Therefore, then, I myself am slaving for God's law with [my] mind, on the one hand; on the other hand, [I myself am slaving] **for the law of sin with [my] flesh.** The twofold expression, "Therefore, then," lays heavy emphasis on this wrapup. The addition of "myself" to "I" emphasizes how deeply felt was the tug of war between Paul's mental enslavement to God's law and sin's using the Law to incite Paul's sinning with his flesh. "On the one hand" and "on the other hand" add to this emphasis. So sin is to be faulted, but not the Law. Why then Paul's extended exoneration of the Law? Answer: To prepare for a further emphasis on fulfilling the righteous requirement of the Law as characteristic of Christian behavior in that Christians now have God's Spirit, who is also the Spirit of Christ (8:1–15).

BEHAVIOR AND THE SPIRIT
Romans 8:1–27

8:1: For those [who are] **in Christ Jesus, then,** [there is] **now no condemnation.** "Then" means "because of God's rescue of the wretched human being in 7:24–25a." The rescue that was longed for there has taken place. "Those [who are] *in* Christ Jesus" explains how it came about that they were rescued—or, as Paul will put it here, "liberated"—"*through* Jesus Christ, our Lord" (7:25a [compare Christians' having been baptized into Christ Jesus, buried with him through baptism, united with him by the likeness of his death, and died with him in 6:3–5, 8, plus the "eternal life" that's "in Christ Jesus, our Lord" according to 6:23]). "Now" distinguishes the present, rescued condition of those who are in Christ Jesus from the past, unrescued condition of the "I" in 7:7–25 and thus confirms that the present tense in 7:14–25 was used for dramatic effect, not to describe Christian experience. "No condemnation" reverses the condemnation pronounced in 5:16, 18 and anticipates no condemnation at the Last Judgment according to 8:34.

Paul proceeds to explain the reason for no present condemnation. **8:2: For the law of the Spirit of life in Christ Jesus has liberated you** [singular] **from the law of sin and of death.** "The law of sin and of death" is the Mosaic law as used by sin to incite transgressions that result in a moral death that would have ended in eternal death (see the comments on 6:21 for this death as eternal). "The law of the Spirit of life in Christ Jesus" is the Mosaic law as obeyed by those in Christ Jesus because of their having the Spirit, who imparts to them eternal life (see 6:22–23 for this life as eternal and as in Christ Jesus; 7:3, 6 for liberation from the Law; and 6:18, 22 for liberation from sin). "Has liberated you": the singular of "you" indicates that though Paul was speaking autobiographically in 7:7–25 ("I," "I myself," "my," and "me"), his addressees should see *themselves* as individuals represented in *his* individual experience of liberation from former enslavement. Since the enslavement consisted in domination by sin so far as behavior was concerned, liberation consists in freedom from such domination, as Paul will go on to say. But first we should note, perhaps with some surprise, that it's "the *law* of the Spirit of life in Christ Jesus" which has brought liberation. This law is the Mosaic law that in 7:14 Paul described as "Spiritual," though, and a quotation of which in 4:9 he introduced with "*we* [Paul and his fellow heralds of the gospel] are saying." Though sin co-opted the Law, Paul has, so to speak, rescued the Law for employment in service to the gospel and Christian behavior.

8:3–4: For as to the powerlessness of the Law in that it was weak through the flesh, by sending his own Son in the likeness of sinful flesh and as a sin offering God condemned sin in the flesh [4]**in order that the righteous requirement of the Law might be fulfilled in us who aren't walking around** [= behaving] **in accordance with the flesh—rather, in accordance with the Spirit.** Here Paul explains both *how* it was that God made up for the powerlessness of the Law in relation to sin, and *why* it was that God did so. Paul starts by noting that the moral weakness of human beings, which he calls "the flesh," made the Law itself weak. Presupposed is that the Law was powerless to keep sin from using it to incite transgressions (7:7–11). How then did God make up for the Law's powerlessness? First, he sent "his own Son." The use of "Son" (rather than, say, "Jesus" or "Christ") and of "his *own*" highlights God's "demonstrat[ing] his *own* love for us" (5:8). "In the likeness *of sinful flesh*" describes the Son's flesh as capable of dying because of sin, but "*in the likeness* of sinful flesh" differentiates his flesh from the flesh of others. For in its moral weakness their flesh is dominated by sin. "As a sin offering" describes the Son's death as a sacrifice for the atonement of others' sins. The statement that "God condemned sin" shifts his condemnation of "all human beings" because of their sinning (5:16, 18) to a condemnation of sin itself in the case of "those [who are] in Christ Jesus" (8:1). (The

condemnation of sin, as though it had been arraigned in God's court, shows that Paul's personification of sin as an evil and powerful force continues.) "In the flesh" refers to the flesh of Christ, which constituted "a sin offering," and thus locates God's condemnation of sin in that sin offering, so that for Christians sin itself died under God's condemnation so far as its being their slavemaster is concerned.

"The righteous requirement of the Law" is the Law's requirement of righteous behavior, which the Law defines (see 7:7). That this requirement is moral, as in the commandment not to lust (7:7 again), but not ritual is indicated by Paul's having denied the necessity of circumcision while affirming the necessity of avoiding theft, adultery, and idolatry (2:17–29) and by Paul's coming citations of Mosaic moral commandments (13:8–10) while denying the necessity of observing dietary taboos and holy days (chapter 14 [see also 1:32; 1 Corinthians 7:19]). So the why of God's having condemned sin is answered in his purpose that the Law's righteous requirement be fulfilled; and that his purpose itself has indeed been fulfilled is shown by Paul's calling Christians "us who aren't walking around in accordance with the flesh—rather, in accordance with the Spirit" (see Isaiah 31:3 for "spirit" as connoting power in opposition to "flesh" as connoting weakness). Not that Christians never sin, but their pre-Christian enslavement to sin has been broken; and righteousness characterizes their overall behavior. If it doesn't, their Christian profession stands in doubt (to say the least).

8:5–8: For those who are in accordance with the flesh are thinking the things of the flesh, but those [who are] **in accordance with the Spirit** [are thinking] **the things of the Spirit.** [6]**For the thought of the flesh** [is] **death; but the thought of the Spirit** [is] **life and peace,** [7]**because the thought of the flesh is hostile to God. For it doesn't subject itself to God's law. For neither is it able** [to subject itself to God's law], [8]**and those who are in the flesh aren't able to please God.** First, Paul cites differences in thinking as the reason for the difference between behavior according to the flesh and behavior according to the Spirit. Second, he explains the final outcomes of the differences in thinking. Third, he explains why one of the final outcomes is destructive. For emphasis, this explanation gets elaborated several ways.

As mentioned, Paul traces behavior back to thinking ("For as a man thinks in his heart, so is he" [Proverbs 23:7; compare Romans 6:11: "be *considering* yourselves dead . . . in relation to sin . . . living in Christ Jesus in relation to God"]). "The things of the flesh" are sinful behaviors, to which the flesh succumbs. Those who are thinking such things because they're "in accordance with the flesh," morally weak as the flesh is, are non-Christians. "The things of the Spirit" are righteous behaviors, the doing of which the Spirit enables. Those who are thinking such things because they're "in accordance with the Spirit," powerful as he is, are Christians. For only they have the Spirit. "The thought of the flesh [is] death" in the sense that eternal damnation, which "death" represents, is the final outcome of the flesh's thinking. (Paul personifies "the flesh" as a thinker who is morally weak.) "The thought of the Spirit [is] life and peace" in the sense that eternal life and peace with God are the final outcome of the Spirit's thinking, which controls Christians' behavior (5:1; 6:20–23). "The thought of the flesh is hostile to God" in that "it ['the thought'] doesn't subject itself to God's law." Worse yet, and because of sin's enslavement of the flesh, the thinking of the flesh *can't* subject itself to God's law, so that neither are "those who are in the flesh" able to please God by fulfilling his law's righteous requirement in their behavior. To be "in the flesh" doesn't mean to be in the body as living human beings. It means to be living in the moral weakness that "the flesh" represents. There's a better place to live, though.

8:9–11: But you're not in the flesh—rather, in the Spirit—if indeed the Spirit of God is residing in you. But if anyone doesn't have the Spirit of Christ, this person doesn't belong to him. ¹⁰But if Christ [is] in you—. The body [is] dead, on the one hand, because of sin; on the other hand, the Spirit [is] life because of righteousness. ¹¹And if the Spirit of him [God] who raised Jesus from among the dead is residing in you, he who raised Christ from among the dead will make alive also your mortal bodies through his Spirit, who is residing in you. Paul reverts here to the plural of "you" and tells the Roman Christians they're "not in the flesh." Since they're alive and kicking, it's obvious that "not in the flesh" has nothing to do with bodiless-ness and has to do instead with fulfilling the righteous requirement of the Law through the power of the Spirit rather than transgressing the Law because of the moral weakness represented by flesh. And for you to be "in the Spirit" is for God's Spirit to be "residing in you," so that the Spirit is both your biosphere and your vitality, both the space you inhabit and the air you breathe. "If indeed the Spirit of God is residing in you" doesn't call in question that God's Spirit resides in the Roman Christians. Vice versa, it stresses that he does ("indeed") *because* they are Christians. "But if anyone doesn't have the Spirit of Christ, this person doesn't belong to him" does raise the specter, however, of a person falsely professing belief in Christ, perhaps even deluded into thinking of himself as a Christian believer though in fact he isn't, as indicated by failure—through lack of the Spirit—to be fulfilling the righteous requirement of the Law. "The Spirit of Christ" equates with "the Spirit of God" and thus points to Christ as the divine Lord to whom, as his slaves, Christians "belong." Since the Spirit is Christ's, to be in the Spirit is to be in Christ (8:1); and, vice versa, to have the Spirit in you is to have Christ in you. For just as the Spirit of God is the Spirit of Christ because Christ and God are one with each other, to have the Spirit in you is to have Christ in you because the Spirit and Christ are one with each other.

"Your mortal bodies" interprets the earlier statement, "the body [is] dead," as a strong way of saying that (barring Christ's return beforehand) Christians will die physically. In that sense, their body (a collective singular) is as good as dead already (compare 8:36). "Because of sin" harks back to 5:12–14, where Paul ascribed the coming of death into the world to the coming of sin into the world. The promise that God "will make alive also your mortal bodies through his Spirit" interprets the earlier statement, "the Spirit [is] life," as a strong way of saying that (again barring Christ's return beforehand) the Spirit's present residence in them guarantees their future resurrection to eternal life. The contrast with "because of sin," which has to do with sinful behavior, means that "because of righteousness" has to do with righteous behavior, what 8:4 called Christians' fulfilling "the righteous requirement of the Law" and what constitutes a necessary evidence of having the Spirit and thus belonging to Christ.

Paul can hardly mean that the Christ's residence in Christians is the condition of the deadness of their bodies, as though their body wouldn't be dead (= mortal) if Christ weren't in them. Apparently, then, "But if Christ [is] in you" starts a sentence that Paul breaks off (as indicated by the immediately following dash and period) in order to talk about the body as dead and the Spirit as life. Afterwards the sentence that he broke off restarts with "And if the Spirit . . . is residing in you," which is equivalent to "But if Christ [is] in you," since Christ resides in Christians through his Spirit. So this residence is the condition that has to obtain if resurrection to eternal life is to be attained. But as shown by Paul's describing God's Spirit as him "who is residing in you," emphasis falls on the fulfillment of this condition so far as Paul can tell in his addressees' case, not on any doubts he might have.

8:12–15: Therefore then, brothers, we're not debtors to the flesh so as to be living in accordance with the flesh. ¹³For if you're living in accordance with the flesh, you're going to die. But if by the Spirit you're putting to death the body's practices, you'll live. ¹⁴For as many as are being led by God's Spirit—these are God's sons. ¹⁵For you haven't received a spirit of slavery resulting again in fear. Instead, you've received the Spirit of adoption, in whom we're shouting, "Abba! Father!" "Therefore, then" introduces a conclusion from "not [being] in the flesh—rather, in the Spirit" (8:9). Paul uses both "Therefore" and "then" to underscore the conclusion. The endearing address "brothers" and the temporary switch from "you" (plural) to "we" underscore the conclusion even further. Nonindebtedness to the flesh grows out of not being in the flesh (for the meaning of which see the comments on 8:9). Indebtedness to the flesh would mean obligation to indulge its moral weakness ("living in accordance with the flesh"). Christians die physically despite their not living in accordance with the flesh (8:10–11). So the death that you're going to die "if you're living in accordance with the flesh" is eternal (compare the comments on 6:21–23). Paul writes "you're *going* to die" rather than "you'll die" to stress the certainty of such death. And this certainty makes nonindebtedness to the flesh an explanatory warning not to indulge the flesh. "By the Spirit putting to death the body's practices" contrasts with "living in accordance with the flesh," so that "the body's practices" means deeds done out of moral weakness through the instrumentality of the physical body (7:24). The word-play between "going to die [eternally]" and "putting to death [morally]" enhances the promise, "you'll live," on condition of putting to death the body's sinful practices. Moreover, the eternality in "you'll live" contrasts with the temporariness of "living in accordance with the flesh," which living ends in eternal death. The contrast likewise enhances the promise, "you'll live." This promise is supported by being "God's sons"; and "being led by God's Spirit" characterizes God's sons, for they're in the Spirit and the Spirit is in them (8:9–11). To be "led by God's Spirit" equates with "by the Spirit putting to death the body's practices" that arise out of indulging the flesh.

"For as many as are being led by God's Spirit—these are God's sons" adds assurance to the promise "you'll live." And Paul supports this assurance by noting, in connection with his calling those being led by God's Spirit "God's sons," that the Spirit isn't "a spirit of slavery resulting again in fear." For fear would undermine assurance. "Resulting again in fear" implies that fear characterized the lives of Paul and his addressees prior to their conversions: fear of not obeying the Law well enough in the case of Jews, fear of antagonizing the gods in the case of pagans. The fear itself was a form of enslavement. Reception of the Spirit results from God's having adopted as sons those who've believed in his Son. So "the Spirit of adoption" means the Spirit as evidence of adoption." And this evidence is experiential in that being "in the Spirit" (8:9) enables God's adopted sons to shout fearlessly, "Abba! Father!" Slaves fear their masters, but sons don't fear their fathers. See further the comments on Galatians 4:6.

8:16–17: The Spirit himself is testifying along with our spirit that we're God's children. ¹⁷And if children, also heirs—God's heirs on the one hand, Christ's coheirs on the other hand—if indeed we suffer together in order that we may also be glorified together. Paul carries forward the theme of assurance. The twofold testimony of God's Spirit and Christians' human spirit satisfies the law that at least two witnesses are required to establish a matter (Numbers 35:30; Deuteronomy 17:6; 19:15). This testimony consists in shouting to God the address, "Abba! Father!" His Spirit and the Christians' own spirit cooperate in this shouting. But the addition of "himself" to "The Spirit" accents his vocal role as the Spirit of adoption. For alone, "our spirit" couldn't shout with conviction, "Abba! Father!" Since heirship comes along with childship, Paul adds "heirs" to "children." He doesn't tell what Christians will inherit (for which see 4:13). It's enough for assurance that heirship as such certifies their belonging to God as his children. But not quite enough, on second thought. For Paul adds "Christ's coheirs," which because of the parallel with "God's heirs" probably doesn't mean heirs together with Christ—rather, heirs who together with one another belong to Christ just as they belong to God. Similarly, "If indeed

we suffer together" probably doesn't mean suffering together with Christ—rather, suffering together with one another for Christ, especially since the rest of chapter 8 will feature persecution for Christ's sake (see 8:35–36). "If indeed we suffer together" emphasizes that Christians' sharing of persecution with one another characterizes them as true Christians (compare the comments on Matthew 25:31–46 and contrast Matthew 24:10), and that this sharing of persecution ensures their sharing with one another a coming glorification that will more than compensate for the shared suffering of persecution (compare 2 Corinthians 4:16–18). The mention of coming glory now leads Paul to develop further that theme.

8:18–21: For I consider that the sufferings of the present season [are]n't worthy [to be compared] to the glory that's going to be revealed to us. ¹⁹For the creation's eager expectation is eagerly expecting the revelation of God's sons. ²⁰For the creation was subjected to futility, not voluntarily—rather, because of him [God] who subjected [it]—on the basis of hope ²¹that the creation itself will be liberated from the slavery consisting in perishability into the liberty of the glory of God's children. Paul has probably endured more sufferings for the gospel than any of his addressees have. So his considering such sufferings not worth comparing with the coming glory should prove convincing. "Of the present season" implies that these sufferings are suitable only for the present. "That's going to be revealed" stresses the certainty of the glory's revelation. "Revealed to us" indicates that the revelation of glory will occur at the revelation of Jesus Christ, his second coming (compare 1 Corinthians 1:7; 2 Thessalonians 1:7). To support the considering of present sufferings unworthy of comparison to future glory, Paul notes the expectation of that glory in creation itself, which glory—in view of believers' adoption as God's sons/children/heirs (8:14–17)—he now calls "the revelation of God's sons," so that the revelation of glory to them has become a revelation of them in their glorious state. Paul underlines this expectation in several ways: (1) He personifies the creation to make it expectant. (2) He personifies the expectation itself to make it as well as the creation expectant. (3) He describes the expectation of both as "eager." The "subject[ion]" of creation to futility," about which see Ecclesiastes 1:5–11, gives the reason for this expectation. "Because of him who subjected [the creation to futility]" harks back to God's curse on the ground in Genesis 3:17–19, and "not voluntarily" alludes to Adam's sin rather than to any fault of the creation as the reason for that curse.

"On the basis of hope" ameliorates creation's involuntary subjection to futility with confidence that "the creation itself will be liberated." "From the slavery consisting in perishability" defines the previously mentioned "futility" in terms of death, which has enslaved creation along with the human race, as well as in terms of "the thorns and thistles" of the curse in Genesis 3:17–19. The creation's coming liberation contrasts with the perishability that constitutes her present enslavement, and this liberation matches the liberty consisting in the glory that's going to be revealed to and in God's children. So just as resurrection will give them imperishable bodies (1 Corinthians 15:40–43, 50–55; 2 Corinthians 4:17; Philippians 3:20–21), the creation in which their bodies will live will likewise be imperishable, as Paul now goes on to explain.

8:22–23: For we know that all the creation is groaning together and suffering birth pangs together until the present [season]. **²³And not only** [that], **but also we ourselves too, having the firstfruits consisting of the Spirit, are groaning within ourselves as we eagerly expect the adoption,** [that is,] **the redemption of our body.** Intensifying creation's subjection to futility and the slavery consisting of perishability are Paul's (1) adding "all" to "the creation"; (2) describing the effects of the subjection and slavery in terms of both "groaning" and "suffering birth pangs" (note the continued personification of creation); (3) twice adding "together" to these effects for emphasis on "*all* the creation" (compare 8:17); (4) tracing the effects of the fall right up to "the present [season]"; and (5) appealing to common knowledge of the effects ("For we know . . ."). Then Paul adds the groaning of Christians too, including himself. Highlighting this addition are the combination of "And," "not only," "but also," "too," and the tacking of "ourselves" onto "we" and of "within ourselves" onto "are groaning." "Having the firstfruits consisting of the Spirit" ameliorates the Christians' groaning just as "on the basis of hope" ameliorated creation's subjection to futility (8:20). For "firstfruits," which are the first of a harvest, describes the Spirit, whom Christians possess (8:9), as a guarantee of the coming harvest through resurrection, which Paul initially calls "the adoption" and then calls "the redemption [that is, liberation from perishability] of our body." So the already accomplished adoption of believers, so that they're God's "sons," "children," and "heirs" (8:14–17), will graduate to an adoption of their mortal bodies into a resurrected state of glory and imperishability.

Next, Paul tells why Christians are eagerly expecting the redemption of their body. **8:24–25: For we were saved by hope. But hope being seen isn't hope, for who hopes for what he sees? ²⁵But if we hope for what we don't see, we're eagerly expecting** [it] **with perseverance.** Salvation from God's wrath will occur in the future according to 5:9–10. So the past tense here in "we were saved" anticipates that salvation, so sure and certain is it "for everyone who believes" (1:16). Because "hope" connotes confidence of receiving such salvation at the Last Day, "by hope" substitutes for "by faith," which we might have expected. Yet Paul draws hope close to faith by saying that hoping excludes seeing its object, for seeing it makes hoping for it unnecessary (compare 2 Corinthians 5:7: "For we're walking around by faith, not by visible form"). Then he links hope with eager expectation and adds "with perseverance" because of "the sufferings of the present [season]" (8:18). It's the confidence connoted by "hope" that enables both perseverance and eagerness of expectation.

8:26–27: And in the same way [as hope enables us to persevere with eager expectation in our sufferings for the gospel] **also the Spirit is helping our weakness.** Because the present context speaks of suffering in the course of testifying to the gospel and because Paul often associates bodily weakness with such suffering (see especially 2 Corinthians 11:30–13:9), "our weakness" that "the Spirit is helping" is of that sort. Now Paul explains why the Spirit is helping it. **For we don't know what we should pray for in accordance with what is necessary** [to pray for]. What is necessary to pray for is what accords with God's will as regards our suffering bodily weakness in the course of testifying to the gospel (see, for example, Paul's praying for relief from "a thorn in the flesh" and being told by God that such relief wasn't God's will [2 Corinthians 12:7–9]). Now Paul tells how the Spirit helps our weakness. **The Spirit himself is interceding for** [us], **however, with ineffable groans.** "Is interceding for [us]" means that the Spirit is conversing with God on our behalf, since we don't know what is necessary to pray for. The Spirit's groans match our groaning (8:23) and indeed surpass it, for "*ineffable* groans" means groans too deep to be put into words. Such groans show the Spirit's intercession for us to be of utmost earnestness and therefore of utmost likelihood of success. But likelihood becomes certainty, because intercession in accordance with God's will is added to intercession of utmost earnestness: **²⁷And he** [God] **who examines the hearts** [of human beings] **knows what the Spirit's thought** [is], **because he** [the Spirit] **intercedes for the consecrated ones** [= Christians as consecrated to God] **in accordance with God** [= according to his will]. The God who examines human hearts surely knows the thought of his own Spirit, and his own Spirit surely intercedes for Christians in accordance with God's will. Knowing his own Spirit's thought contrasts with Christians' not knowing what they should pray for, just as the Spirit's interceding "in accordance with God" contrasts with Christians' not knowing "what is necessary [to pray for]." Thus the Spirit's help is complete. That Christians are "consecrated" to God helps ensure the success of the Spirit's intercession for them.

BEHAVIOR AND GOD
Romans 8:28–39

The mention in 8:27 of God as the one in accordance with whom the Spirit intercedes leads next to a discussion of Christian behavior in relation to God, and of the results of that behavior. As shown by "we know," the first statement grows out of the confidence, called "hope," by which "we were saved" (8:24). **8:28–30: And we know that all things are working together for good for the ones who love God, the ones who are called in accordance with** [his] **program, ²⁹because the ones whom he foreknew he also predestined** [to be] **conformed to the image of his Son, so that he** [the Son] **might be the firstborn among many brothers. ³⁰And the ones whom he predestined—these he also called. And the ones** whom he called—these he also declared righteous. And the ones whom he declared righteous—these he also glorified. "All things" includes the aforementioned "sufferings" for the gospel (8:18 [see also 8:36]). The "good" for which they "are working together" is "the glory that's going to be revealed to us" in "the redemption of our body" (8:18, 23). See 1 Corinthians 2:9 for another association of future glory with those who love God. It goes without saying that loving him entails obeying him (see Deuteronomy 6, especially verse 5), so that "the ones who love God" equate with those in whose behavior "the righteous requirement of the Law" is fulfilled and who "aren't walking around in accordance with the flesh—rather, in accordance with the Spirit" (8:4). But lest anyone credit them with works on the basis of which they could boast before God (compare 4:2), Paul hastens to add that they're "the ones called in accordance with [God's] program." The call of God has effected their loving him so as to carry out his program for their lives. Paul then supplies the basis of Christians' knowing that all things are working together for their good. It's that God "predestined [them to be] conformed to the image of his Son." This predestination had to do with "the ones whom he foreknew," that is, those whom he decided beforehand to bring into an intimate and loving relationship with himself (see further the comments on 1 Peter 1:2 concerning foreknowledge).

"[To be] conformed to the image of his Son" tells the purpose of predestination and means to be made like Jesus, so that he might have believers in him as his younger brothers. But made like him in what respect? The series of following statements comes to a climax in the glorification of Christian believers. So in line also with 8:11, 17–18, 21–25; 1 Corinthians 15:49; 2 Corinthians 3:18; 4:16–5:5; Philippians 3:20–21; Colossians 3:4, conformity to the image of God's Son looks forward to coglorification with him through a resurrection like his. And the purpose of this conformation is that the Son "might be the firstborn among many brothers." To be firstborn is to be first in time and first in rank. God's Son Jesus was the first to be resurrected to a life in which neither sin nor its consequence, death, would play any further part. The similar resurrection of the foreknown and predestined is yet to come. God's Son Jesus will also outrank them at the same time they share brotherhood with him; and, of course, their being God's sons, as shown by their having received God's Spirit (8:14–17), makes them brothers of God's Son. That they are "many" heightens his rank and helps subordinate their glorification to his glorification. Because God foreknew them, he predestined them. Because he predestined them, he called them (that is, effected their faith). Because he called them, he declared them righteous (by crediting their faith as righteousness [3:21–5:1]). Because he declared them righteous, he glorified them. The foreknowledge, predestination, and call have already occurred. The declaration as righteous and the glorification have yet to occur, at the Last Judgment and on the Day of Resurrection, respectively. But Paul puts the declaration and the

glorification in a past tense out of confidence (= "hope") that nothing will bring to a standstill God's program for those he has foreknown, predestined, and called. Their future is as secure as their past.

8:31–34: **Therefore what shall we say about these things?** Here's what: **If God [is] for us** [as he obviously is from his having foreknown, predestined, called, justified, and glorified us]**, who [is] against us?** Implied answer: nobody of any consequence, for God is unrivaled. [32]**He who indeed didn't spare his own Son but instead gave him over for us all** [Jews and Gentiles alike, and for our trespasses according to 4:25]**, how is it that also together with him** [his Son] **he won't graciously grant us all things?** Answer: it's unreasonable to think that he won't. "Indeed" stresses the irrationality of thinking otherwise; and being graciously granted all things in partnership with God's Son harks back to being "Christ's coheirs" (8:17) and to inheriting "the world" (4:13 [compare 1 Corinthians 3:21–23]). [33]**Who'll bring an accusation against God's selected ones? God [is] the one who declares [them] righteous.** Nobody will dare accuse God's selected ones at the Last Judgment, because he'll have declared them righteous on that occasion; and he'll have done so because he selected them for adoption as his Son's brothers and coheirs. [34]**Who [is] the one that condemns [them]? Christ [is] the one who died** [for them according to 5:6, 8] **and conversely was raised, who is also at God's right [hand], who [referring to Christ] is also interceding for us** [compare Isaiah 50:8–9]. Paul asks this question and answers it because Christ shares with God his Father the function of judging (see 14:9 with 14:10 and 2 Corinthians 5:10; 2 Timothy 4:1). Ruling out any condemnation by Christ are (1) his dying for God's selected ones; (2) his being raised as the firstfruits heralding their resurrection to eternal life (1 Corinthians 15:20, 23), for which resurrection the Spirit, whom they possess, is the firstfruits guaranteeing it (8:23); and (3) Christ's interceding for them already, prior to the Last Judgment, at God's right hand (compare the Holy Spirit's interceding for them [8:26]). Since the right hand is the hand of favor (see Matthew 25:31–46, for example), Christ's intercessory position at God's right hand as the one who died for the selected ones leaves no doubt that God will declare them righteous.

8:35–39: **Who will separate us from the love of the Christ?** [Will] **affliction or a tight predicament or persecution or hunger or nakedness or danger or a sword** [used for beheading a Roman citizen, such as Paul was]**?** [36]**Just as it's written, "For your sake we're being put to death the whole day long. We've been regarded as sheep for slaughter** [Psalm 44:22]**."** [37]**Rather** [than being separated from the love of the Christ]**, in all these circumstances we're winning big through him who loved us.** [38]**For I'm convinced that neither death nor life nor angels nor rulerships nor current circumstances nor circumstances that are going to come nor powers** [39]**nor height nor depth nor any other creature will be** able to separate us from God's love in Christ Jesus, our Lord. The mention in 8:34 of Christ's death leads Paul to exult in "the love of the Christ," which ends up as "God's love in Christ Jesus, our Lord" (compare 5:5–8). In fact, "*the* Christ" points back to "Christ" as mentioned in 8:34 and connotes his messianic role as Savior. The Greek translated "Who . . . ?" can equally well be translated "What . . . ?" But the parallel with "Who . . . ?" in 8:34 and 8:35 favors "Who . . . ?" here as well, in which case Paul is personifying "affliction," "a tight predicament," "persecution," "hunger," "nakedness," "danger," and "sword" as possible separators of Christians from Christ's love in the sense of forestalling the happy outcome of his love in being declared righteous and glorified on the Last Day. The quotation of Psalm 44:22 shows that these possible separators all have to do with elements of persecution for Christ's sake (compare 2 Corinthians 11:23–27). "Being put to death the whole day long" means being constantly exposed to the possibility of martyrdom, portrayed figuratively as the slaughtering of sheep. "Rather" introduces with vigor a negative answer of Paul to his own question; and the answer goes far beyond a simple "No," as shown immediately by the phrases "in *all* these circumstances" and "we're winning *big* [or less informally, 'overwhelmingly']." Implied is a battle between Christians and the circumstances of persecution. The Christians are winning big in that even their sufferings for Christ are working together for good—yes. But not by their own means; rather, through the agency of the Christ who loved them. It's not that they'll not let *him* go. It's that he'll not let *them* go.

Then Paul, who (as noted above) has almost certainly suffered more persecution than any of the Roman Christians have, testifies to his own conviction that no creature of God can separate Christians from God's love as manifested in Christ Jesus, their Lord. The list of these would-be separators expands the earlier list of circumstances associated with persecution and includes both demonic angelic powers and personified elements of space, time, and personal history. Paul aims to make this list all-encompassing; but lest he has inadvertently omitted something, he adds "nor any other creature." Though common, the addition of "our Lord" to "Christ Jesus" alludes to his supremacy over all God's creatures, both personal and personified, none of whom therefore can separate Christians from his and God's love.

ISRAEL'S UNBELIEF
Romans 9:1–11:36

Paul has just declared that nothing can separate Christians as the adopted sons of God from God's love in Christ Jesus (8:39). But how can Paul or his addressees be sure? Haven't the Jews, whom Paul calls "Israelites" to recollect their status as the chosen people of God, his earlier adopted sons (as spelled out in 9:4–5)—haven't they been separated from God's love? For Paul has argued at length that salvation will take place only by faith in Christ, not by works of the Jews' law; and most of

the Jews haven't believed in Christ. These questions bear on the relation between Gentile and Jewish Christians in the Roman churches, for 11:17–24 will warn Gentile Christians in Rome against treating Jewish Christians with arrogance.

PAUL'S CONCERN FOR ISRAEL
Romans 9:1–5

9:1–3: I'm telling the truth in Christ—I'm not lying, my conscience testifying with [me] **in the Holy Spirit—** [2]**that I have great sorrow and unceasing anguish in my heart.** [3]**For I myself could pray to be accursed,** [cut off] **from the Christ, on behalf of my brothers, my kinfolk so far as flesh** [= biological descent] **is concerned . . . .** The abruptness with which this section starts bespeaks the intensity of concern Paul feels for his fellow Jews who haven't believed the gospel. To convince the Jewish Christians in Rome of his concern for these Jews and to hold up this concern as an example to be followed by his Gentile Christian audience (see chapter 11), Paul (1) adds "I'm not lying" to "I'm telling the truth"; (2) adds "in Christ" to his truth-telling and "in the Holy Spirit" to his not-lying, with the implication that in view of his union with Christ and the Holy Spirit he doesn't dare to lie rather than telling the truth (compare being both "in Christ Jesus" and "in the Spirit" according to 8:1, 9); (3) pairs the testimony of his conscience with his own testimony to comply with the law that it takes at least two witnesses to establish a matter (Numbers 35:30; Deuteronomy 17:6; 19:15); (4) uses both "sorrow" and "anguish" to express his concern; (5) describes his sorrow quantitatively as "great," his anguish temporally as "unceasing," and both of them locally as "in [his] heart," that is, as deeply felt; and (6) explains that his concern goes so deep that if it would do any good (though it wouldn't, because his justification and glorification are ensured [8:30–39]), he'd pray "to be accursed"—that is, damned forever (compare 1 Corinthians 16:22; Galatians 1:8–9)—in place of these unbelieving Jews, whom he endearingly calls both his "brothers" and his "kinfolk" (compare 10:1). The addition of "myself" to "I" accents this last evidence of concern. "[Cut off] *from the Christ*" harks back contrastively to "telling the truth *in* Christ" (contrast also 8:38–39 with 8:35), carries an overtone of Jesus as the Jews' Messiah, and implies that Paul's being cut off from him on the Jews' behalf would put *them* in Christ.

Paul's sentence continues in **9:4–5: who as such** [= as my biological kinfolk] **are Israelites, to whom** [belong] **the adoption** [as God's sons] **and the glory and the covenants and the legislation and the religious service and the promises,** [5]**to whom** [belong] **the** [fore]**fathers, and from among whom** [referring to the Israelites] [came] **the Christ so far as flesh** [= biological descent] **is concerned, who as** [himself] **God is over all,** [who is to be] **praised forever. Amen!** This list of privileges gives evidence of the Jews' special status before God, warns Gentile Christians again to avoid a supercilious attitude toward Jews, and prepares for Paul's announcement of massive Jewish salvation at the second coming (11:25–27). Calling the Jews "Israelites" recollects their privileged status in the Old Testament, for "Jews" connotes the tribal territory of Judah whereas "Israelites" connotes the chosen nation of Israel, so named after the nickname God gave to the patriarch Jacob (Genesis 32:24–28). For adoption of the Israelites as God's sons, see Exodus 4:22; Deuteronomy 14:1; Hosea 11:1, which associate their sonship to God with the exodus from Egypt (compare Isaiah 63:16; 64:8; Jeremiah 31:9). "The glory" recalls the glory of the Lord that appeared on Mount Sinai to the Israelites just after their exodus (Exodus 16:7, 10; 24:16–17) and that filled the tabernacle and, later, the temple at their dedications (Exodus 40:34–35; 1 Kings 8:10–11; 2 Chronicles 7:1–2), not to mention other occasions. Paul doesn't identify "the covenants" he has in mind, but his extensive discussions of Abraham and the Law up to this point and his current allusions to the exodus suggest that he has in mind at least the Abrahamic and Mosaic covenants (for which see especially Genesis 15:12–21; Exodus 24:3–8). Recollection of the Mosaic covenant probably led Paul to mention "the legislation" as a privilege of the Israelites, since he has exonerated the Law of blame for sin (7:7–25). The legislation included regulations for religious service to be performed in the tabernacle at first, and then in the temple. So Paul mentions "the religious service" next. Then come "the promises," two of which (heirship of the world and innumerability) have been mentioned in 4:13–14, 16, 20–21 and which 15:8 will describe as given to the Israelites' forefathers. The privilege of the Israelites in having those promises entails the further privilege of having Abraham, Isaac, and Jacob—to whom the promises were originally addressed—in the Israelites' pedigree. A good biological pedigree was nothing to be sneezed at. As a matter of fact, though, Paul doesn't name the forefathers, specify the promises, detail the religious service, employ his usual term "the Law," identify the covenants, explain "the glory," or date the adoption. So leaving these privileges more or less vague lets the spotlight shine on the most outstanding privilege of all, which Paul denominates with all specificity. It's that "the Christ," the messianic scion of all Israel, came "out from among" the Israelites "so far as flesh [= biological descent] is concerned." Breaking the pattern of the preceding privileges, though, Paul doesn't say that the Christ belongs to the Israelites. He doesn't belong even to Christians; they belong to him (1 Corinthians 3:23).

Since ancient Greek manuscripts lacked punctuation almost entirely, punctuation in English translations is a matter of interpretation. It's possible here, then, to punctuate 9:5 so as to produce several translations different from the foregoing—for example, "who [referring to 'the Christ'] is over all. God [as distinct from 'the Christ'] [is to be] praised forever" (compare especially 1:25; 2 Corinthians 11:31). But a switch from the Christ as the climax of the Israelites' privileges to God the Father seems unlikely. So to Jesus' messiahship is added deity,

attended by lordship "over all" and everlasting praise. "Amen!" caps this greatest of all the Israelites' privilege enthusiastically.

ISRAEL'S UNBELIEF AS A MATTER OF GOD'S PREDETERMINED PLAN
Romans 9:6–33

9:6–9: [It's] **not as though God's word has flopped** [= failed to attain its goal in regard to the Israelites]. **For not all these who** [descended] **from Israel** [= Jacob according to his nickname] [are] **Israel** [God's chosen people]. [7]**And** [it's] **not that all** [Abraham's] **children** [biological descendents] **are the seed of Abraham; rather, "in Isaac will your seed be called** [Genesis 21:12]." [8]**That is, these children of the flesh** [= biological descendents again] **aren't God's children; rather, the children of the promise are being counted as seed** [= descendants]. [9]**For this** [is] **the word of promise** [= the statement containing a promise]: **"At this season** [a time suitable for conception, gestation, and birth to have taken place] **I** [the Lord is speaking] **will come, and Sarah** [Abraham's wife] **will have a son** [Genesis 18:10, 14]." "God's word" refers in particular to "the promise" and to "the word of promise" drawn from Genesis 18:10, 14, for it's this word that has flopped if it isn't fulfilled in Israel's case. As his first argument against a failure of God's word, Paul distinguishes between those who are Israelites only by way of biological ancestry and those who are Israelites in another way (through divine selection, it will turn out in the rest of chapter 9 [compare the distinction in 2:26–29 between outward Jews and inward Jews]). Paul similarly distinguishes between Abraham's "children" only by way of biological ancestry and those who are Abraham's "seed" in another way, which he identifies here as "the promise," which will turn out to be a promise based on divine selection and for which Paul makes Isaac, the son promised to Abraham, symbolic. (Compare Galatians 4:21–31, where Paul contrasts Isaac as the son promised to Abraham and Ishmael [though unnamed there and not specifically referenced here in Romans] as Abraham's *un*promised son.) It remains to be seen in the present passage whether "the children of the promise" include nonbiological as well as biological descendants of the forefathers Abraham and Israel, but 2:26–29 (again) and the whole of chapter 4 have preestablished an inclusion of nonbiological descendants. In Genesis 21:12 the calling of Abraham's seed means merely the delimiting of his seed to Isaac and Isaac's descendants. Here in 9:7 and in accord with Paul's normal usage, the calling of Abraham's seed carries the additional meaning of God's effectively drawing them to himself (compare 4:17; 8:28–30).

9:10–13: And not only [that (referring to God's promise of Isaac)], **but also Rebekah** [Isaac's wife], **having a marriage-bed** [so as to conceive] **by one** [man], [namely] **Isaac our** [fore]**father—**[11]**for** [the twins, Jacob and Esau], **since they'd not yet been born and not done anything good or evil, in order that God's program in accordance with** [his] **selection might**

remain [immutable], [a selection] **originating not out of** [human] **works; rather, out of him who calls**—¹²it was told her, "**The bigger one** [= the older boy] **will slave for the littler one** [= the younger boy] [Genesis 25:23]," ¹³**just as it's written, "I** [the Lord is speaking] **loved Jacob, but I hated Esau** [Malachi 1:2–3]." Since older boys are generally bigger than younger ones, "bigger" came to be used figuratively for "older"; and "littler" came to be used figuratively for "younger." Though Jacob and Esau were twins, Esau came out of Rebekah's womb before Jacob did (Genesis 25:24–26), so that "bigger" and "littler" have here the purely figurative meanings of "older" and "younger"; and "bigger" describes Esau though he was barely older than Jacob. Nevertheless, custom privileged the older regardless of how much older he was. So God's privileging of Jacob, the younger, reversed human custom and thereby illustrates the independence as well as sovereignty of God's selection of Jacob over Esau, which Scripture puts in terms of love versus hate to underscore the difference between selection and nonselection. Reinforcing this independence as well as sovereignty is Paul's pointing out that God's selection of Jacob and nonselection of Esau occurred before either one of them had "done anything good or evil," and even before they'd "been born."

Lest someone think that God based his selection and nonselection on anything good or evil that he foresaw Jacob and Esau would do, Paul describes the selection of Jacob as "originating *not* out of [human] works; *rather*, out of him who calls [that is, God, who effectively draws to himself those whom he has selected]." For a contrast with "not out of [human] works," we expect "out of faith." But "out of him who calls" lays the emphasis here on God's effectively drawing to himself those he selected beforehand (see 8:28–30 again). Moreover, the purpose "that God's program . . . might *remain*" shows that his "selection" is no more determined by a *re*view of human beings' good and evil works than by a *pre*view of them. Adding yet more reinforcement is the interruption of Paul's sentence. It started with a reference to Rebekah's conception but then branched off into a long excursion into God's selection and call as unconditioned by human works. Only then did Paul cite what was told to Rebekah. By calling Isaac "*our* [fore]father," Paul includes as Isaac-like "children of the promise" and "God's children" (9:8) his Gentile Christian addressees as well as his Jewish ones; and by referring to Isaac as the "one [man]" by whom Rebekah conceived her twins, Paul sharpens the distinction between God's selection of Jacob and nonselection of Esau. Strikingly, non-Christian Jews turn out to be Esau-like—not a happy comparison for them since Esau was the rival of their biological ancestor Jacob and since Esau's descendants, the Edomites, did violence to the Jews (see Obadiah).

9:14–18: **Therefore** [= in view of the independence and immutability of God's selections and nonselections] **what shall we say?** [There's] **no unrighteousness with God, is there?** In other words, God doesn't act unjustly, does he? **On the contrary!** ¹⁵**For he says to Moses, "I'll show mercy to whomever I show mercy, and I'll show pity to whomever I show pity** [Exodus 33:19]." ¹⁶**Therefore, then,** [the selection does]**n't belong to the** [human being] **who wants** [to be selected], **nor** [does it] **belong to the** [human being] **who is running** [= exerting himself to attain selection]; **rather,** [the selection] **belongs to the mercy-showing God.** ¹⁷**For the Scripture says to Pharaoh, "I've raised you up for this very purpose, that I may demonstrate my power in you** [= in my dealings with you] **and that my name** [with overtones of a reputation for power] **may be announced throughout all the earth** [Exodus 9:16 (compare Proverbs 16:4)]." ¹⁸**Therefore, then, he shows mercy to whom he wants** [to show mercy]; **and he hardens whom he wants** [to harden]. See 2:5; 11:7, 25; 2 Corinthians 3:14; Ephesians 4:18 for hardness as figurative of insensibility, ignorance, unrepentance, and unbelief. Paul reacts violently against the suggestion that God is unjust in his selections and nonselections (compare 3:5–6). But Paul doesn't defend the justice, the righteousness, of God with an appeal to what human beings deserve. For because all of them have sinned (3:23), they all deserve nonselection. So the selection of some for his mercy and pity and the nonselection and indeed hardening of others in their disobedience and unbelief (as in Pharaoh's case [Exodus 4:21; 7:3, 13, 22; 8:19; 9:7, 12, 35; 10:1, 20, 27; 11:10; 14:8]) don't depend on the good or evil that human beings do, or might do. Nor does even the *evil* that they do form a basis of nonselection, for God might have selected the evildoers that he didn't select just as he did select other evildoers. Sinning explains death, then (5:12–14; 6:21, 23); but it doesn't explain nonselection.

As in the aforementioned likeness to Esau, the nonselection of non-Christian Jews, who are merely Abraham's "children of the flesh" (9:8), makes them strikingly like Pharaoh, the ancient oppressor of Israel. God's "rais[ing] up" of Pharaoh for the express purpose of "demonstrate[ing God's] power" in dealing with him underscores the nonselection of Pharaoh-like Jewish non-Christians. Paul pays no attention to Pharaoh's hardening his own heart according to Exodus 8:15, 32; 9:34; but in those passages that hardening appears to be generated by God's hardening, not vice versa (see especially 9:34 with 9:35). So instead of trying to rationalize God's selection and nonselection in accord with fallible humanism ("Man is the measure of all things" [Protagoras, an ancient Greek philosopher]), Paul cites infallible Scriptures to the effect that God's wish and will alone are determinative. Selection shows the mercy of God, because nobody deserves it. Nonselection shows his power, because nobody can resist the disastrous results of his nonselection. And he wants his reputation for such power to "be announced throughout all the earth." Two instances of the twofold expression, "Therefore, then," highlight the sovereign independence of his will and wish over against the suggestion that they're subject to human judgment. His will and wish *determine* what's right and just rather than *being* determined by some humanly constructed standard outside him.

9:19–21: **You'll say to me, then, "Why then does he** [God] **still blame** [anybody]**? For who has withstood his will?"** 20**Quite the contrary** [to your asking these questions], **O human being** [in contrast with God]**! Who are you,** [you] **who are retorting to God? What's molded won't say to** [its] **molder, "Why have you made me like this** [Isaiah 29:16; 45:9]**?" will it?** 21**Or the potter has authority over the clay, doesn't he, to make out of the same lump a vessel for honor** [in the way it's used]**, on the one hand, and a vessel for dishonor** [in the way it's used]**, on the other hand?** Paul has already told why God blames human beings. God blames them for their sins. As has already come out, though, their sins don't explain the nonselection of some; for God *has* selected other sinners mercifully. So Paul by-passes the question of blame. As for the question of who has withstood God's will, Paul lets stand the implication that nobody has withstood it and rails instead against a human being's right to ask the question (compare Job 38–41). For in comparison with God, a human being is no more than a molded lump of clay (compare God's molding the first human being out of moistened dust of the ground, that is, clay [Genesis 2:6–7]). And in comparison with a human being, God has as much authority over the human being as a potter has over a lump of clay. (Modern humanistic protests to the contrary notwithstanding, it might be added.) Paul's outburst, "Quite the contrary, O human being!" underscores these ridiculously unequal comparisons. "A vessel for honor" represents human beings selected to receive God's mercy. We might think of a decorative vase. "A vessel for dishonor" represents human beings not selected to receive God's mercy and therefore destined for damnation. We might think of a chamber pot (a vessel used as a toilet). The putting of merciful selection and merciless nonselection in terms of honor and dishonor illustrates the strong sense of honor and dishonor that characterized Paul and his contemporaries and that is largely lost in contemporary Western culture (see 2:7, 10 for associations of "honor" with "glory," "imperishability," "peace," and "eternal life").

9:22–26: **But** [what] **if God, wanting to demonstrate** [his] **wrath and to make known his power** [compare 9:17]**, has borne with much patience the vessels of** [his] **wrath, prepared for ruination?** 23**And** [what if he has done so] **in order to make known the wealth of his glory on the vessels of** [his] **mercy, which** [vessels] **he prepared beforehand for glory,** 24[that is,] **us, whom he has called** [= effectively drawn to himself] **not only from among the Jews but also from among the Gentiles?** 25**As also he** [God] **says in Hosea: "The not-my-people I'll call 'My people' and the not-loved** [wife] [I'll call 'my] **beloved** [wife]'**;** 26**and it shall be in the place where it was said to them, 'You['re] not my people,' there they'll be called 'sons of the living God'** [Hosea 2:23]**."** The question, "And [what] if God . . . has borne with much patience the vessels of [his] wrath . . . ?" isn't meant to draw an answer. It's meant to draw admiration of God's patience. Similarly, the question, "And [what if he has

borne with much patience the vessels of his wrath] in order to make known the wealth of his glory on the vessels of [his] mercy . . . ?" isn't meant to draw an answer. It's meant to draw admiration of God's mercy, exercised on those he has selected, as the very purpose of his exercising patience toward those he hasn't selected. As a group, "the vessels of [God's] wrath" are the same as "a vessel for dishonor" (9:21) and, like that vessel, represent those whom God hasn't selected for his exercise of mercy. "His wrath" interprets "dishonor." "Ruination" (as in the shattering of a potter's vessel) identifies the eternal effect of that wrath (see the comments on Matthew 25:46; Revelation 14:10–11). And "*prepared* for ruination" stresses God's "*wanting* to demonstrate [his] wrath and make known his power" in his judgment on those he didn't select for mercy. Yet the fact that he "has borne [them] with much patience" implies their responsibility for sinning, for which he did *not* prepare them, and shows him giving them leeway till the Last Judgment.

"To make known the wealth of his glory" parallels "to make known his power"; and just as the power of God will be made known in his wrath, his glory will be made known in his mercy (again at the Last Judgment). "The *wealth* of his glory" matches his toleration of the nonselected "with *much* patience"; and just as his wrath will have the effect of eternal ruination, his glory will have the effect of eternal glorification (see 2:6–10; 5:2; 8:18, 21, 30). "*Prepared . . . for glory*" implies God's wanting to demonstrate his mercy just as much as he wanted to demonstrate his wrath; and "beforehand" stresses that as in the case of Jacob and Esau, his selection wasn't based on anything good that the selected ones had done. Paul identifies the vessels God prepared beforehand for glory with "us," who include Gentiles as well as Jews. By emphasizing God's calling Gentiles ("not *only* [Jews] . . . but *also* [Gentiles]"), Paul implies that Gentile Christians should think themselves more fortunate than Jewish Christians rather than snubbing them (see again 11:17–24). "*From among* the Jews" and "*from among* the Gentiles" distinguish the called ones sharply from the uncalled, and highlighting both this distinction and the especially good fortune of the called Gentiles is Paul's citation of what "[God] says in Hosea." The present tense of "says" makes God's statement during Hosea's time currently applicable. In Hosea, "The not-my-people" and "the not-loved [wife]" refer to Israel, a nation that used to be God's wife-like people but that he temporarily put aside because of their apostasy. But "I'll call [them] 'My people' and . . . '[my] beloved [wife]'" and "they'll be called 'sons of the living God'" refer to Israel's restoration into God's good graces. Jewish Christians could easily be considered to have been restored as God's people because of God's call. The Gentile Christians in Rome never had been God's people, though. Paul includes them in this restoration nevertheless because, as he will figuratively explain later on, they've been grafted into the stock of Israel (11:17–18). So the accent stays on the privileged status of Israel (compare 1:16), lest Gentile Christians get uppity in relation to their Jewish Christian fellows.

Now Paul cites Isaiah, too, in support of Israel's privileged status. *9:27–29:* **And Isaiah shouts concerning Israel, "Though the number of the sons of Israel were like the sand of the sea, the remnant** [those who remain after God's judgment on Israel] **will be saved.** [28]**For the Lord will execute** [his] **word on the earth by consummating** [it] **and concising** [it] **[Isaiah 10:22–23; 28:22]."** [29]**And just as Isaiah has foretold, "If the Lord Sabaoth hadn't left us seed** [= a remnant of descendants], **we'd have become like Sodom and been like Gomorrah [Isaiah 1:9]."** Isaiah doesn't cry out in despair, according to Paul. Isaiah shouts in exultation that "the remnant [of Israel] will be saved," for the remnant's salvation demonstrates the continuance of Israel's privileged status. (Paul interprets this salvation as eternal.) "Though the number of the sons of Israel were like the sand of the sea" makes the remnant's salvation stand out as a glorious exception to the nonselection of other Israelites. "For the Lord will execute [his] word" refers to his saving a remnant of Israel and adds a note of assurance that he will. "On the earth" tells where the salvation will take place. From Isaiah's standpoint, the salvation was going to take place in the future. But a remnant of Israel is being saved on the earth right during Paul's lifetime. The Jewish Christians in Rome are representative of them (see 11:1–5). The Lord's "consummating" his word means that he'll bring it to completion, and his "concising" it means that he'll cut off his word by completing it. (The translation "concising" represents a rare use of "concise," ordinarily an adjective, as a verb for the sake of a wordplay with "consummating," a wordplay that corresponds to a wordplay in Paul's Greek.) The "seed" that the Lord has "left" in Paul's second quotation from Isaiah is the present remnant of Jewish Christians. The Lord's having left them has kept Israel from a complete obliteration like that of Sodom and Gomorrah. "Sabaoth" is Hebrew for "of hosts," in reference to armies of angels. Paul doesn't write "the Lord *of hosts*," though, because he's following a pre-Christian Greek translation of Isaiah that leaves the Hebrew word untranslated.

Now Paul turns his attention away from Israel's remnant consisting of Jewish Christians to a contrast between their Gentile Christian fellows and non-Christian Jews. *9:30–33:* **Therefore** [since God is saving a remnant of Israel] **what shall we say?** Answer: **That Gentiles who weren't pursuing righteousness have laid hold of righteousness—but the righteousness** [that's] **by faith.** [31]**But Israel, pursuing the law of righteousness** [= the Law as a means of laying hold of righteousness in good works] **didn't arrive at the Law.** [32]**For what reason? Because** [they did]**n't** [pursue the righteousness that's] **by faith; rather,** [they pursued righteousness] **as though** [it's] **by works. They've stumbled over the stone of stumbling,** [33]**just as it's written, "Behold, I'm laying in Zion a stone of stumbling and a rock of tripping; and the person who believes on him won't be shamed** [by having his faith turn out to be unfounded] **[Isaiah 28:16; 8:14]!"** The Gentiles weren't pursuing righteousness in that they weren't trying to keep the Mosaic law, whereas Israel was

trying—but failing, as in Paul's case (7:7–25). So instead of saying that by contrast Israel was pursuing righteousness, Paul says that Israel was pursuing "the law." But instead of stopping with "the law," he adds "of righteousness" for a contrast between a righteousness consisting in "works of the Law" (3:20, 28) and "the righteousness [that's] by faith"—in other words, faith credited as righteousness (chapter 4). And whereas Paul says that Gentiles "have laid hold of righteousness," he says that Israel "didn't arrive at the Law." Why the switch from "laid hold of" to "arrive at"? Because "arrive at" connotes arrival before others (see 2 Corinthians 10:14; Philippians 3:16; 1 Thessalonians 2:16; 4:15). Israel enjoyed a head start (3:1–2 [compare 1:16; 9:4–5]), but later-starting Gentiles have by and large forged ahead of them (see 11:11–27, especially 11:25: "a callousing has happened to Israel in part until the fullness of the Gentiles has come in"). "The stone of stumbling" is a stone that lies on a path and causes a walker to stumble. "A rock of tripping" is a rock that juts up out of the ground into a path and likewise causes a walker to trip. The stone and the rock represent Christ Jesus. The stumbling and the tripping represent disbelief in him and the unsuccessful attempt to attain righteousness by keeping the Law instead (compare 1 Peter 2:7–8). In sum, Paul marvels that *any* Jews are getting saved, and that *so many* Gentiles are. Only God's merciful selections explain why; yet while explaining why, the selections themselves remain inscrutable.

THE UNBELIEF OF ISRAEL AS A MATTER OF THEIR OWN-RIGHTEOUSNESS
Romans 10:1–21

10:1–4: **Brothers, my heart's desire and plea to God in behalf of them** [the Israelites] [is] **for** [their] **salvation.** [2]**For I bear them witness that they have a zeal for God—not in accordance with knowledge, though.** [3]**For being ignorant of God's righteousness and seeking to establish a righteousness of their own, they haven't submitted to the righteousness of God.** [4]**For so far as everyone who believes is concerned, Christ** [is] **the end of the Law for the purpose of righteousness.** The affectionate address "Brothers," which refers to Paul's *Christian* brothers in Rome, suits and emphasizes the emotion that characterizes his desire and plea to God for the salvation of Paul's *biological* "brothers," the Israelites (9:3). "My *heart's* desire and plea," where he might have said only, "my desire and plea," deepens the emotion. Notably, God's independent and prior selection and nonselection of people for salvation (so chapter 9) doesn't deter Paul from pleading with him for the Israelites' salvation. The inscrutability of the selections and nonselections *may* even give Paul some reason to plead as he does. "For [the Israelites'] salvation" implies that most of them remain unsaved (9:30–33), the previously mentioned "remnant" being exceptions to the rule (9:27–29). The Israelites' "zeal for God" *certainly* gives Paul reason to plead as he does. He says so: "*For* I bear them witness . . . ." He knew himself what an ignorant zeal for God was, as evident in Galatians 1:13–14 and Philippians 3:6, where he speaks of his own such zeal in persecuting the church and maintaining Judaistic traditions prior to conversion (see also Acts 9:1–5; 22:3–5; 26:4–5).

"Not in accordance with knowledge" makes even zeal for God ineffective for salvation. This lack of knowledge equates with ignorance of God's righteousness, which Paul defined as God's declaring righteous those people, sinners all, who believe in Jesus Christ (see especially 1:16–17; 3:21–26 with further comments). The "righteousness of their own" that the Israelites are "seeking [unsuccessfully] to establish" would consist in keeping the Law perfectly well (compare Philippians 3:9). But since the Law is God's, their misplaced zeal is still "for God." "They haven't *submitted* to the righteousness of God" implies, however, that "seeking to establish a righteousness of their own" puts them in prideful rebellion against God's righteousness despite their zeal for him (compare 2:17–29). That zeal explains why Paul pleads for the Israelites, and their ignorance of God's faith-based righteousness and attempt to establish their own works-based righteousness explain why their zeal is misdirected. Christ as the end of the Law for the purpose of producing works-based righteousness—at least the end of it so far as believers in him are concerned—then explains why it's wrong to use the Law for that purpose; and Paul has already cited the Law itself as advocating the righteousness that originates out of faith (see 1:17; 4:3, 9, 20–24 with Genesis 15:6).

Now Paul tells why he said that so far as everyone who believes is concerned, Christ is the end of the Law for the purpose of establishing their own righteousness. **10:5–8: For Moses writes about the righteousness originating out of the Law: "The human being who does them** [the things that the Law commands] **will live by means of them** [Leviticus 18:5]." For Paul, eternal life is in view (see the comments on 1:17; 2:7; 5:21; 6:22–23). He has earlier said, however, that despite the purpose of the Law to produce such life, sin took advantage of the Law by using it to incite sinning—that is, Law-breaking—which produces death (7:7–25). For him, then, the statement that he quotes out of Leviticus 18:5 ("The human being who does them will live by means of them") is academic because of unfulfillability (see the comments on Galatians 3:12). The present tense in "Moses *writes*" points up the unbelieving Israelites' current use of Leviticus 18:5 as a justification for using the Law to establish their own righteousness. Next, Paul quotes and interprets Deuteronomy 9:4; 30:12–13 in terms of "the righteousness originating out of faith" in the Christ, who has now descended out of heaven and been raised from the dead. ⁶**But the righteousness originating out of faith speaks in this way: "You shouldn't say in your heart, 'Who'll ascend into heaven** [Deuteronomy 9:4; 30:12]**?'"—that is, to bring Christ down** [from heaven]—⁷**or "Who'll descend into the abyss** [Deuteronomy 30:13]**?"—that is, to bring Christ up from among the dead.** ⁸**What does it** [the righteous-

ness originating out of faith] **say, instead?** Here's what it says: **"The word is near you,** [as near as] **in your mouth and in your heart** [Deuteronomy 30:14]**." This is the word about faith,** [the word] **which we're proclaiming . . . .** Paul personifies "the righteousness originating out of faith," so that this righteousness "speaks" just as "Moses writes," and speaks both for the present time and also against what Moses writes if what he writes is taken nonacademically, that is, as making out Law-keeping to be a realistic way to attain eternal life.

Strikingly, the statements Paul quotes out of Deuteronomy are just as much what Moses writes as is the statement Paul quotes out of Leviticus. In their original context, moreover, the statements Paul quotes out of Deuteronomy have just as much to do with the Law's commandments as does the statement he quotes out of Leviticus. But since Israel's history and Paul's own suffering of moral death under the Law have demonstrated the Law's weakness "through the flesh" (8:3), he pirates these statements for "the word about faith" as opposed to works of the Law. The nearness of the Law's word according to Deuteronomy—it's so near as to be in the Israelites' mouth and heart—did them no good, and still doesn't. That fact and the Law's own testimony to the righteousness originating out of faith justify Paul's putting the statements in Deuteronomy on the lips of faith-righteousness and applying these statements to Christ. Because Christ has already come down from heaven, it's absurd to ask who'll ascend into heaven to bring him down (compare Philippians 2:5–8 for his heavenly preexistence and coming down to earth). And because he has already been raised from among the dead, it's equally absurd to ask who'll descend into the abyss to bring him up from among the dead, "the abyss" being the bottomless shaft that connects the netherworld of the dead to the surface of the earth (see Revelation 9:1–2). Paul has been quoting what he takes to be statements by the righteousness originating out of faith. So what does he mean by asking what it says "instead"? He means what it says *contrary* to asking who'll bring Christ down from heaven and bring him up from among the dead. What it says *positively* is that "the word," which Paul then identifies as "the word about faith" (= the message that God credits faith as righteousness), is as near as "in your mouth and in your heart." How so? It's so because this word, which Paul and company proclaim, was believed in the hearts of the Roman Christians and confessed with their mouths, just as stated in Deuteronomy by the righteousness originating out of faith.

Paul's sentence continues in the same vein with **10:9–10: because if you confess with your mouth Jesus as the Lord and believe in your heart that God raised him from among the dead, you'll be saved.** ¹⁰**For with the heart** [the word about faith] **is believed with the result of righteousness, and with the mouth** [the word about faith] **is confessed with the result of salvation.** At first Paul puts confessing with the mouth ahead of believing in the heart. This order corresponds to the textual order of "mouth" and "heart" in Deuteronomy

30:14. But temporally speaking, believing in the heart precedes confessing with the mouth. So the second time around, Paul switches to the temporal order. The parallelism of "salvation" with "righteousness" shows that "righteousness" means being declared righteous because of faith, not righteous conduct as in 2:12–16; 6:12–23; 8:4. Paul says the word about faith requires a confession that Jesus is the Lord, who has come down from heaven according to 10:6, and says it requires a belief that God raised him from among the dead, which raising shows God to have been propitiated by Jesus' sacrificial death on believing sinners' behalf (4:25). Given the possibility of persecution, confessing with the mouth so that other people hear is required to give them evidence that the confessor's belief is genuine. But given the possibility of hypocrisy, believing in the heart is required to give God, who examines the heart, evidence that the confession is genuine. Those two requirements met, salvation from God's wrath and a crediting of faith in Christ as righteousness at the Last Judgment are assured. A scriptural citation will now support the assurance.

10:11–13: For the Scripture says, "Everyone who believes on him [Jesus as the Lord] **won't be shamed** [by having his faith proved to be unfounded] [Isaiah 28:16]." **¹²For there isn't a distinction between Jew and Greek** [in this matter of how to be saved]. **For the same** [Lord is] **Lord of all, being rich** [in mercy] **to all who call on him.** "For there isn't a distinction between Jew and Greek" supports "Everyone" in the statement, "Everyone who believes on him won't be shamed." Just as there's no distinction between Jew and Greek in that "all have sinned" (3:22–23), there's no distinction between them in that they both have to believe on the Lord if they're to be saved. "For the same [Lord is] Lord of all" supports this lack of distinction between Jew and Greek. The addition of the Lord's "being *rich* [in mercy]," as he has to be if "*all* who call on him" are to be saved, centers attention on Jesus' lordship in salvation, which then gets supported with another scriptural citation: **¹³For "everyone who'll call on the name of the Lord will be saved** [Joel 2:32]." Here, "call[ing] on the name of the Lord" is a variation on "believ[ing] on him." Calling on his *name* ("Lord") means making a petition to him that he exercise his lordship by saving the petitioner because of the petitioner's faith and confession.

10:14–15: How then would they call on [him] **in whom they haven't believed? And how would they believe** [in him] **about whom they haven't heard? And how would they hear** [about him] **apart from** [someone] **proclaiming** [him to them]**? ¹⁵And how would they proclaim** [him] **unless** [proclaimers of him] **be sent** [to them]**? Just as it's written, "How beautiful the feet of those who are proclaiming good things** [Isaiah 52:7]**!"** With "they" Paul reverts to talking about the Israelites, most of whom haven't believed "the word about faith." A series of rhetorical questions establishes that calling on the Lord's name for salvation requires believing in him—that is, Jesus—as the Lord, that believing in him as

such requires hearing about him, that hearing about him requires a proclaiming of him, and that a proclaiming of him requires a sending of proclaimers. The buildup to the requirement of sending is designed to prepare the Roman Christians for Paul's statement in 15:24 that after visiting them for a while he may be sent forward by them to proclaim the gospel in Spain. Such sending implies financial and perhaps other support (see the comments on 1:13–15). The citation of Isaiah 52:7 ("How beautiful the feet . . . !") is then supposed to make attractive the Roman Christians' participation in the sending of Paul forward to Spain. "The *feet* of those who are proclaiming good things" implies travel for the sake of proclamation where the good things haven't yet been proclaimed, and "good things" refers to the good news of salvation and of the righteousness that originates out of faith rather than the Law.

10:16–18: Not all have obeyed the gospel, though. For Isaiah says, "Lord, who has believed our report [Isaiah 53:1]**?"** Since Paul has spoken of "the Lord" as "Christ," who came down from heaven (see 10:9 with 10:6), he must be interpreting Isaiah's address, "Lord," to mean that Isaiah was speaking to Christ before Christ's descent from heaven. **¹⁷Faith originates out of hearing** [our report]**, then. And the hearing** [comes] **through the word about Christ.** Paul plays on a Greek word that means both a report that's heard and the hearing of a report, and on this word plus two others that also have the same root and mean (respectively) "to hear" and "to obey." **¹⁸I say, however, they haven't "not heard," have they? To the contrary, indeed** [they *have* heard]**! "Their speech has gone out into all the earth, and their words to the extremities of the inhabited** [earth] [Psalm 19:4]**."** Paul's use of "obeyed" where we expect "believed" suits Jesus' lordship and implies that the gospel is to be obeyed through believing in Christ as the Lord, for the gospel commands such believing (see 1:5 with comments; also 16:26; 2 Thessalonians 1:8). A remnant of Israelites have become Christians (9:27–29). But it amazes Paul that not all Israelites have obeyed "the gospel," for by definition it means "good news." So he satisfies himself with a citation of Isaiah, which in effect tells Paul that he shouldn't be surprised at the Israelites' unbelief. For him, "*our* report" in Isaiah equates with "the word about faith" that Paul and company "are proclaiming" (10:8). So his statement that "faith originates out of hearing [our report]" alludes to his earlier question, "And how would they believe [in him] of whom they haven't heard?" The further statement that "the hearing [comes] through the word about Christ" limits the report—that is, the gospel—to the orally proclaimed message about Christ. Paul strongly affirms and supports with statements borrowed from Psalm 19:4 that the Israelites have heard this report, this message. So unbelieving Israelites have no excuse for their unbelief. Notably, their nonselection by God (as per chapter 9) doesn't negate their responsibility for disobedient unbelief. The statements borrowed from Psalm 19:4 have to do with the heavens' telling about God's glory and the sky-dome's declaring the work of his hands (Psalm 19:1). Paul applies these statements, however, to the Israelites' having heard the words of the gospel spoken to them. "Into all the earth" and "to the extremities of the inhabited [earth]" were meant absolutely in the psalm but are used hyperbolically by Paul to stress widespread hearing of the gospel by Israelites living throughout the Roman Empire.

10:19–21: I say, however, Israel hasn't "not known," has he? As the first [to answer this question], **Moses says** [in the Lord's voice (so too in the following quotations from Isaiah)], **"I'll provoke you to jealousy with a non-nation; with a stupid nation I'll provoke you to anger** [Deuteronomy 32:21]." [20]**And Isaiah is very daring and says, "I was found by those who weren't seeking me, and I became evident to those who weren't asking for me** [Isaiah 65:1]." [21]**But in reference to Israel he says, "The whole day long I've stretched out my hands to a disobedient and disagreeable people** [Isaiah 65:2]." "I say, however, Israel hasn't 'not known,' has he?" echoes 10:18: "I say, however, they haven't 'not heard,' have they?" As there, "however" puts the question, which implies a positive answer, in opposition to the possibility that Israel's disobeying the gospel has been due to not hearing it and therefore not knowing it. Israel can't plead ignorance as an excuse, then; but neither can Israel plead lack of motivation. For now Paul cites Moses himself, Israel's legislator, to the effect that the Lord was going to provoke Israel to jealousy and anger. In chapter 11 Paul will interpret these provocations as the Lord's saving large numbers of Gentiles who believe in him. "A non-nation" describes them as nonmembers of ethnic Israel, God's chosen nation (compare 9:25–26). "A stupid nation" describes them as ignorant of the Mosaic law (in contrast to Israelites as described in 2:17–20). Jealousy of the Gentiles' salvation and anger at God's favoring so many of them with salvation should motivate Israel to get in on the action. But so far it hasn't. "As the first" applies to Moses but also looks forward to Isaiah as another scriptural witness to the Lord's provocations of Israel.

Paul describes Isaiah as "very daring" in quoting the Lord to the same effect as Moses had quoted him. By implication, Paul is picking up Isaiah's mantle of derring-do in applying the Lord's words to the current salvation of many Gentiles but of few Israelites. The daring consists in quoting the Lord as saying that he has been "*found*" by those who "weren't *seeking*" him, and that he has become "*evident* [in the sense of available]" to those who "weren't *asking* for" him, both of which statements seem almost self-contradictory, at least very unlikely. For Paul, the nonseekers and the nonaskers are Gentile Christians, of course, who because of their not seeking and not asking for the Lord illustrate God's sovereign and independent selection of them for mercy in accordance with chapter 9. "But in reference to Israel" makes clear that the people in the second quotation from Isaiah are Israelites. This quotation illustrates their recalcitrance despite the Lord's appeals to them. "The whole day long" describes those appeals as continuous. "I've stretched out my hands" describes the appeals as earnest. Once again, the nonselection by God in chapter 9 doesn't eliminate the responsibility of Israel (the majority of Jews) for disobeying the gospel, which they've heard, and indeed for speaking against it, which is what "disagreeable" means here. Nor does their nonselection by God or their recalcitrance keep him from appealing to them any more than it keeps Paul from pleading with him in their behalf (10:1).

THE PRESENT REMNANT OF ISRAELITE BELIEVERS
Romans 11:1–10

11:1–4: I say, therefore [in view of numerous conversions of Gentiles], **God hasn't pushed away his people, has he? On the contrary! For I too am an Israelite, from Abraham's seed,** [a member] **of the tribe of Benjamin.** [2]**God hasn't pushed away his people, whom he foreknew** [compare 1 Samuel 12:22; Psalm 94:14]. **Or you know, don't you, what the Scripture says in Elijah** [that is, in the passage about him], **how he intercedes to God against Israel?** [3]**"Lord, they've killed your prophets, they've torn your altars down** [to the ground], **and I alone have been left remaining. And they're seeking my life** [1 Kings 19:10, 14]!" [4]**What does the divine oracle say to him, however?** Here's what it says: **"I've left behind for myself seven thousand men who as such** [= as leftovers from the killing] **haven't bent** [their] **knee to Baal** [in worship of this false god] [1 Kings 10:18]." "Pushed away" is a figure of speech for discarding, rejecting. "His people" means Israel as God's chosen nation. Paul cites himself as evidence that God hasn't discarded ethnic Israel. How so? First, as implied by "I *too*," Paul is just as much an Israelite as are non-Christian Israelites. Second, he descended biologically from Abraham, father of the Israelite nation. Third, Paul even knows his genealogy well enough to cite his tribal membership, that of Benjamin (compare Philippians 3:5 and the fact that Paul's other name, Saul, echoes the name of Israel's first king, who came from the tribe of Benjamin [1 Samuel 9–10]). As a *Christian* Israelite, then, Paul is evidence that God hasn't discarded Israel. God's foreknowledge of Israel counts as further such evidence, for such knowledge doesn't mean only that he knows ahead of time what's going to happen. It means that he knows what's going to happen because he has predetermined it to happen, and foreknowing carries the further meaning of determining to enter into an intimately loving relationship with the object of foreknowledge (see the comments on 8:29; 1 Peter 1:2). Such a *predetermined* relationship isn't subject to reversal.

"Or you know, don't you . . . ?" implies that the Roman Christians do know the following and that their knowledge may have made Paul's citation of God's foreknowledge superfluous. This compliment is designed to solicit their agreement with Paul's continuing argument against a rejection of Israel by God. In the first century the Old Testament didn't have chapter divisions or verse divisions, which weren't inserted till the thirteenth and sixteenth centuries, respectively. So a passage was often cited according to a topic or personage featured in the passage—hence, "what the Scripture says in Elijah." Ordinarily we think of intercession as *in behalf of* people (see 8:27, for example). But Elijah "intercedes to God *against* Israel," so that God's saving a remnant already in Elijah's time stands out by way of contrast with the antagonism of Elijah toward Israel. "However" underscores the opposition of "the divine oracle" to Elijah's antagonistic intercession. In that intercession the killing of the Lord's prophets and the tearing down of his altars foreshadow most Israelites' unbelief in the gospel and perhaps also their violent opposition to it in Paul's day (compare 2 Corinthians 11:24, 26; 1 Thessalonians 2:14–16 and the persecution of the church by Paul himself prior to his conversion). Just as the Lord hadn't left Elijah alone (though Elijah doesn't seem to have known so), the Lord hasn't left Paul alone; for Paul is by no means the only Israelite of his time to have been graciously selected by God for salvation. "For myself" describes the Lord's leaving behind "seven thousand men" in Elijah's time. This description stresses the Lord's sovereign will in the selection of a remnant, then as now (see chapter 9). "Who *as such*" refers to the remnant as left over *for God's self*, so that his selection of them didn't grow out of their not having worshiped Baal. Just the reverse: their not having worshiped Baal grew out of God's having selected them. And "who as such haven't bent [their] knee to Baal" may imply that unbelieving Israelites in Paul's day are no better than the Baal-worshipers were in Elijah's day.

11:5–6: Therefore [that is, because of the precedent set by God in the time of Elijah] **in this way also at the present season a remnant has come to be in accordance with a** [divine] **selection characterized by grace.** "In this way," "also," and "at the present season" put a triple emphasis on the correspondence between the nonidolatrous remnant of Israel in Elijah's time and the Christian remnant of Israel in Paul's time. Combined with that correspondence, the growing of the present remnant out of "a [divine] selection characterized by grace [= unearned favor]" confirms that God did *not* select the seven thousand in Elijah's time because of their refusal to worship Baal any more than God has selected the present remnant because of their works of the Law. Sealing this confirmation is Paul's next statement: **⁶And if** [the selection is] **by grace,** [it] **no longer** [originates] **out of works, since the grace wouldn't be grace any longer.** "No longer" and "not . . . any longer" mean no longer in argument (that is, logically), not no longer in history (that is, temporally); for according to 9:11–13 divine selections never did originate out of works. To incorporate works as a consideration in the exercise of grace is to evacuate grace of its very meaning.

11:7–10: What then [shall we say]? Answer: **What Israel is seeking after—**[Israel] **hasn't obtained this. But the selection** [the remnant of Israel graciously selected by God] **has** obtained [it]. **But the rest have been calloused,** **⁸just as it's written, "God gave them a spirit of slumber, eyes characterized by not seeing and ears characterized by not hearing, right up to the present day** [Deuteronomy 29:4; Isaiah 29:10]." **⁹And David says, "Their table is to turn into a trap and into a net** [for snaring] **and into a stumbling block and into a payback to them. ¹⁰Their eyes are to be darkened so as not to see, and bend their backs double continually** [Psalm 69:22–23]." Israel is seeking righteousness (compare 9:31–32; 10:2–3). But they haven't obtained it. We already know the reason why. It's that they're pursuing the law of righteousness and seeking to establish their own righteousness through works of the Law (see 9:31–32; 10:2–3 again). Here, though, Paul isn't interested in the reason why. He's interested only in Israel's failure to obtain righteousness, and to stress this failure he uses a strengthened form of the verb: "seeking *after*," not just "seeking." The stronger the seeking, the more dismal the failure to obtain its object. Over against this failure is the obtaining of righteousness—the righteousness of faith credited as righteousness—by "the selection." Israel's remnant is so dependent on God's gracious selection rather than on works that Paul personifies "the selection" and makes it refer to the remnant.

The callousing of the rest of Israel stands for their hearts' imperviousness to the gospel (contrast 10:8–10). Paul supports this callousing with a scriptural citation. In it the eyes of a sleeper don't see (they're closed) and his ears don't hear (they're tuned out), and it is God who made them sleepily blind and deaf (compare 9:18b: "he [God] hardens whom he wants [to harden]"). In Deuteronomy 29:4, "right up to the present day" meant right up to the end of Moses' lifetime. Here in Romans it means right up to the time of Paul's writing this letter, so that God's callousing most of Israel has yet to end, though his nonrejection of Israel holds out hope of an end (see 11:25–27). In the added scriptural quotation, "their table" stands for non-Christian Israelites' apparent well-being (religiously speaking) in that a table is set with food. David says, though, that the table is to turn into a trap, a net for snaring, a stumbling block, and a payback. The piling up of these figures of speech for judgment stresses the dreadfulness of God's coming judgment on the calloused majority of contemporary Israel. The further figurative language in the darkening of their eyes so that they don't see suggests they don't see that judgment awaits them. "And bend their backs double continually" has them doubled up under divine disapproval right up to the end, when God's final judgment will fall on them. Grammatically, David doesn't ask God, "Turn their table into a trap . . . . Darken their eyes . . . ." He issues commands to their table and their eyes *indirectly* through God. This indirectness makes David's *direct* petition that God "bend their backs double continually" stand out as terrifying. And the present tense in "David says" makes what he says applicable to the divinely unselected majority of contemporary Israelites.

THE FUTURE RESTORATION AND
SALVATION OF ISRAEL
Romans 11:11-32

11:11-12: Therefore [in view of God's making most of Israel unresponsive and in view of David's calling for judgment on them] **I say, they haven't stumbled in order to fall, have they?** "They" refers to Israel as an ethnic whole, regardless of the distinction between a believing remnant and the unbelieving majority. "Stumbl[ing] in order to fall" refers to the effect of God's discarding Israel as an ethnic entity. **On the contrary! Instead, because of their trespass** [that is, Israel's disobedience, by and large, to the gospel] **salvation** [has come] **to the Gentiles for the purpose of provoking them** [the Israelites] **to jealousy** [see the comments on 10:19-20]. [12]**And if their trespass** [is] **the world's wealth and their defeat** [is] **the Gentiles' wealth, how much more their fullness** [will be the world's, the Gentiles', wealth]! "Their defeat" is the nonselection of the majority of contemporary Israelites, which nonselection corresponds to "their trespass" in disobeying "the word about faith" (10:8). "The world's wealth" and "the Gentiles' wealth" are one and the same in referring to the wealth of God's grace made available to the world of Gentiles (compare 10:12). The twofoldness of these expressions accents Israel's present disadvantage and the Gentiles' present advantage. "Their fullness" refers to a largescale salvation of Israelites which is yet come and which will be accompanied by a wealth of divine grace for Gentiles even greater than what they've already experienced in conversion (see 11:15). The provocation of Israel by largescale salvation of Gentiles (10:19) will have succeeded, and "fullness" connotes the salvation of all whom God has selected for salvation.

11:13-16: And I'm speaking to you Gentiles. Therefore, inasmuch as I am indeed an apostle to the Gentiles I glorify my service [14]**if somehow I might provoke to jealousy my flesh** [= my biological kinfolk] **and save some of them.** [15]**For if the casting off of them** [by God] [is] **the reconciliation of the world, what** [will be] **the acceptance** [of them] **if not life from among the dead?** [16]**And if the firstfruits** [are] **consecrated** [to God], **also the lump of dough** [is] **consecrated** [to him]; **and if the root** [is] **consecrated, also the branches** [are consecrated]. Paul narrows his address to Gentile Christians in Rome to prepare them for a warning that will start in 11:17-18. To support this warning he first cites his qualification to address them authoritatively. It consists in his apostleship to the Gentiles. That is to say, Christ sent him into the world of Gentiles to speak and act with Christ's own authority (1:5; Galatians 1:16; 2:7; Ephesians 3:8; Acts 9:15; 22:21). Emphasizing this authority are the formality of "inasmuch as" and "indeed." Paul's "service" is his serving the gospel to Gentiles by proclaiming it. He glorifies this service by making a fine display of it to Israelites so that they may, he hopes, become jealous of the Gentiles who are enjoying the grace of God and because of this jealousy get converted to the gospel themselves

(see Acts 13:44-47; 18:5-6; 28:16-28, especially 28:28, for Paul's making a point to Jewish audiences of Gentile evangelism). "If somehow" reflects the earnestness of Paul in desiring to save some Israelites through the exercise of his apostleship to Gentiles. His purpose in this exercise is to work toward God's acceptance of Israel as an ethnic whole. Currently God has cast this Israel off in that he has selected from among them only a remnant for salvation; and the casting off has resulted in "the reconciliation of the world," which means the turning of large numbers of Gentiles from enemies of God into his children and heirs (5:10-11; 8:15-17). (Because chapters 9-10 have stressed the distinction between the saved and the unsaved on account of divine selection and nonselection, "the reconciliation of the world" can't mean the salvation of everybody.) The coming acceptance of Israel as an ethnic whole will entail "life from among the dead," that is, resurrection to eternal life. Since the resurrection will occur at Christ's second coming, so too will Israel's acceptance by God; and the resurrection to eternal life will constitute the Gentiles' greater "wealth" of which 11:12 spoke.

As the first of a harvest, firstfruits guarantee a full harvest yet to come. Here, "the firstfruits" are Israel's patriarchs: Abraham, Isaac, and Jacob, to whom God gave irrevocable promises (11:28-29). "The lump of dough," which eventuates from a harvest of grain, is the patriarchs' offspring, Israel as a nation, whose consecration to God is guaranteed by the consecration of its forefathers (see Numbers 15:17-21 for the consecration of firstfruits to God). Paul shifts to the figure of a root and branches in preparation for the warning in 11:17-24. Like the firstfruits, "the root" stands for Israel's patriarchs; and the branches stand for Israelites as their descendants. The consecration of the root guarantees again the consecration of the branches. And this manifold consecration guarantees in turn God's "acceptance" of ethnic Israel after the present period of his casting off the nation in favor of largescale salvation among Gentiles.

11:17-18: But if certain of the branches were broken off and you, being a wild olive [branch], **were grafted in among them** [the remaining natural branches] **and became a sharer with** [them] **of the root characterized by the fatness** [= sap] **of the olive tree,** [18]**don't boast against** [= don't vaunt yourself over] **the** [natural] **branches. But if you do boast against** [them]—**you're not supporting** [= nourishing] **the root; rather, the root** [is supporting] **you** [compare Jeremiah 11:16-19; Hosea 14:6]. "Certain of the branches" represents individual Israelites. Their having been "broken off" represents "the casting off of them" (11:15) because of their unbelief and God's nonselection of them (which correlate with each other). "You," being singular, refers to an individual. "Being a wild olive [branch]" describes the addressed individual figuratively as a Gentile Christian. "Were grafted in among them" refers, again figuratively, to the incorporation of a Gentile Christian in among Israelite Christians, who because of their belief in Christ haven't been "broken off." The result of becoming "a sharer with [the Israelite Christians] of the root" means becoming what Paul earlier called becoming "Abraham's seed" through following that patriarch's example of faith (chapter 4). "The fatness [= sap] of the olive tree" stands for the righteousness consisting in faith credited as such (so in Abraham's case). The warning not to boast against the natural branches suggests that because of God's having turned his main attention to saving Gentiles, those Gentiles in Rome who've believed are vaunting themselves over their fellow Christians of biological descent from Abraham, or at least are liable to do so. The break in thought between "But if you do boast against [them]" and "you're not supporting the root . . ."—this break implies that such boasting is ridiculous. Drop even the thought of boasting against Israelite believers, because the nourishment consisting in eternal life stems from the root of membership by faith in the seed of Abraham, the forefather of all Israel.

11:19–22: Therefore you'll say, "Branches were broken off in order that I might be grafted in." [20][You've spoken] **well. They were broken off because of** [their] **unbelief, but you stand by faith. Don't be thinking high things** [about yourself]. **Instead, fear** [for yourself] [compare 1 Corinthians 10:12]. [21]**For if God didn't spare the natural branches, neither will he spare you** [if you think high things about yourself]. [22]**Therefore look at God's magnanimity and truncation** [= severity portrayed as a cutting off]: **truncation for those who've fallen, on the one hand; God's magnanimity for you, on the other hand, if you stay in** [his] **magnanimity— since you too will be cut off** [if you don't]. Paul's initial "Therefore" alludes to what he has just said. So too does the immediately following quotation of what "you'll say." In this quotation, "Branches" refers to biological Israelites. Their having been "broken off" refers to God's rejection of them. "In order that I might be grafted in" has a Gentile Christian concluding that the rejection of biological Israelites had the purpose of making salvific room for the Gentile Christian and his like. "[You've spoken] well" indicates Paul's agreement, for he has said as much in 11:17. But to the purpose of the breaking off, he adds its cause: "They were broken off *because of [their] unbelief.*" In view of chapter 9 we might have expected him to ascribe the breaking off to God's nonselection rather than to the Israelites' unbelief. But the nonselection and the unbelief are correlative, and Paul chooses at this point to cite unbelief for a contrast with belief—that is, faith—as the means by which Gentile as well as Israelite Christians stand. This standing contrasts in turn with falling under God's judgment (compare 11:8–11). And since faith is a nonwork that can't be boasted about (see 4:4–5 for the categorical distinction between faith and works), the "high things" about yourself that betray lack of faith and that Paul says not to think consist in whatever makes you think you deserve salvation as a wage rather than recognizing salvation to be an ill-deserved gift. The command to fear for yourself, instead, arises from the possibility of self-deception, such as has characterized Jews according to chapter 2 (compare

2 Corinthians 13:5). Supporting this command is the reasoning that God is as least as liable not to spare wild olive branches whose thinking high things about themselves corrupts their profession of faith as he was not to spare natural olive branches because of their unbelief. In other words, Gentiles who profess Christian faith suffer just as much danger of losing out on salvation as the Israelites did who've already lost out on it.

Looking at "God's magnanimity and truncation" is to take the place of thinking high things about yourself. "Magnanimity" comes close in meaning to "grace," but puts an accent on the kindness of a gracious God even to a Gentile, a nonmember of Abraham's biological seed. "Truncation" refers to God's severity, portrayed as a cutting off similar to the previously mentioned casting off (11:15) and breaking off (11:17, 19–20). "On the one hand . . . on the other hand" sets out magnanimity and cutting off in stark antithesis to each other. In 11:11 falling symbolized God's discarding Israel as an ethnic whole, at least for the time being. Here "fallen" describes those many individual Israelites whom God has discarded (compare 14:4; 1 Corinthians 10:12). "If you stay in [his] magnanimity" assures you of his magnanimity in salvation if you fear for yourself instead of thinking high things about yourself. For this fear and such nonthinking define, or at least ensure, staying in God's magnanimity. But the last accent falls on the danger of being cut off from that magnanimity through failure to fear instead of thinking self-exaltedly.

11:23–24: And those [natural branches that have already been cut off], **too, will be grafted in if they don't stay in unbelief. For God is able to graft them in again.** [24]**For if you were cut off from a naturally wild olive tree and were grafted contrary to nature into a beautiful** [= cultivated] **olive tree, how much more will these natural** [branches] **be grafted into their own olive tree!** "Grafted in if they don't stay in unbelief" means incorporation into true Israel, into Abraham's true seed (9:6–7), by believing in Jesus (10:9–10). So the "fullness" of Israel (11:12) will be accompanied by such faith. Otherwise it wouldn't happen. "To graft them in *again*" doesn't mean that biological Israelites had been ingrafted earlier. It means that they'll be grafted into the Israel of Abraham's faith just as they've always belonged to the Israel of biological descent from Abraham. Supporting this ingrafting is God's ability (compare 1:16, where the "power" [Greek: *dynamis*] of God to save is the noun form of "able" [Greek: *dynatos*] here in 11:23). And to support God's ability at ingrafting, Paul adds that it will be easier ("how much more") for him to ingraft believing Israelites, given their biological descent from Abraham, than it has been to ingraft believing Gentiles, given their not belonging to biological Israel.

In 11:11–12 Paul said Israel hasn't stumbled "in order to fall," and he predicted Israel's "fullness." In 11:24 he predicted the grafting of "these natural [branches] into their own olive tree." Paul now supports these predictions with greater detail, and does so to keep the Gentile Christians in Rome from arrogance in their relations with Jewish fellow Christians. *11:25–27*: **For I don't want you to be ignorant of this secret, brothers—lest you be wiseacres—that a callousing has happened to Israel in part until the fullness of the Gentiles has come in. ²⁶And in this way all Israel will be saved, just as it's written: "The rescuer will come out of Zion, he will turn ungodliness away from Jacob, ²⁷and this [is] my covenant with them when I take away their sins** [Isaiah 59:20–21; Jeremiah 31:33–34; Isaiah 27:9]." There's some irony in Paul's telling Gentile Christians he doesn't want them to be *ignorant* lest they be *wise-acres*. But ignorance does often make people think of themselves as wise when they aren't, so that knowledge may correct their mistaken self-image. Whatever the level of irony, the affectionate address "brothers" lowers it to make Paul's addressees amenable to the warning against arrogance. He uses the term "secret" here and elsewhere for a truth that human beings would never have surmised but that God has revealed to his own. The present secret is that biological Israel's callousing, which is partial in that a remnant of Jews have believed the gospel, will last until all the Gentiles whom God has selected for salvation have converted (see chapter 9 for the selecting, and 11:7 for the callousing). "In this way" describes the salvation of all Israel as occurring not until these Gentiles are all converted.

"All Israel" means all biological Israelites. Most recently, 10:9–10 has made belief in Jesus Christ a key to salvation, and 11:23 has talked of Israel's not continuing in unbelief. Paul assumes, then, that his audience will understand all Israel to be saved by believing in Jesus. Paul's concern relates here to the time when this salvation will occur, not with its means. So after identifying the time as when "the fullness of the Gentiles has come in," he uses Old Testament scripture to pinpoint the time at the second coming of Jesus, to which the prophecy, "The rescuer will come out of Zion," refers in Paul's interpretation. "The rescuer" is Jesus, and his "com[ing] out of Zion" is his exiting heaven (the Zion above [compare Hebrews 12:22; Revelation 14:1–3]) for a descent to earth. It's on this occasion that all biological Israel will be saved by Jesus' turning ungodliness away from them ("Jacob") and by the Lord's fulfilling his covenant with Israel by taking away their sins (see Isaiah 59:20–21; Jeremiah 31:33–34 for "covenant"). That only a remnant of Israel are being saved during the present period of massive Gentile salvation means that all Israel who'll be saved at the second coming will consist only, but massively, of Israelites living at that time (compare Paul's having himself been saved by a revelation of Jesus from heaven [1 Corinthians 9:1; Galatians 1:15–16; Acts 9:3–5; 22:6–8; 26:13–15]).

11:28–32: **As regards the gospel, on the one hand, [they (the Israelites) are] enemies for your sakes. As regards selection, on the other hand, [they are] beloved for the [fore]fathers' sakes. ²⁹For God's gracious gifts and call [are] irrevocable. ³⁰For as you [Gentiles] indeed were disobedient to God once upon a time but have now been shown mercy** [by him] **in view of the disobedience of these** [Israelites], **³¹thus these too have now been disobedient so that in view of the mercy shown to you they themselves, too, may now be shown mercy. ³²For God has confined all** [both Israelites and Gentiles] **in disobedience in order that he might show mercy to all.** Except for a remnant of them, the Israelites are God's enemies in that he has calloused them and given them a spirit of slumber, unseeing eyes, and unhearing ears (11:7–10); and he has done so for the sake of Gentiles in extending the gospel to them. The reduction of salvation among Israelites enhances the exhibition of God's grace for Gentiles and thereby leads to an enlargement of salvation among them. Yet God loves the Israelites "for the [fore]fathers' sakes," that is, because of the promises he made to Abraham, Isaac, and Jacob concerning their descendants (9:4–5). "On the one hand . . . . on the other hand" spotlights the balance between ethnic Israel's ancient "selection" as promised to the forefathers and the nonselection of most contemporary Israelites so far as individual salvation is concerned. The irrevocability of God's gracious gifts and call constitutes the reason why ethnic Israel is still beloved by God for the forefathers' sakes. He won't go back on his words of promise. Paul doesn't identify "God's gracious gifts and call," so that the emphasis falls here on the irrevocability of whatever God graciously gives and of the call whereby he effectively works his will on whomever he has selected for salvation—in this case by keeping his promises to Israel's forefathers. The mercy presently being shown to Gentiles substantiates the irrevocability of God's promise to Abraham that he'd be the father of many nations (see 4:16–25 with Genesis 17:5). "As you *indeed* were disobedient to God once upon a time" highlights his grace in showing the Gentiles, pagan as they were, mercy.

"In view of the *disobedience* of these [Israelites]" balances God's nonselective hostility toward most of them (11:28) with the responsibility they bear for not heeding his appeals (10:21). In his program, the present disobedience of most Israelites has the purpose of showing them mercy such as Gentiles are now receiving. Here is another way of saying that by saving large numbers of Gentiles, God has the purpose of provoking Israel to jealousy and anger so as to generate faith in them as well (10:19–20). Two occurrences of "too" and the addition of "themselves" to "they" underscore this purpose, which illustrates the irrevocability of God's gracious gifts and call. That the Israelites "may *now* be shown mercy" reflects God's desire to show mercy to all Israel immediately, though the conversion of the full number of Gentiles he has selected for salvation must occur first. "Confined . . . in disobedience" refers to God's nonselection for salvation (compare especially chapter 9). Such confinement of Israelites is currently achieving God's purpose of showing mercy to Gentiles. Such confinement of Gentiles once their fullness has come in will achieve God's purpose of showing mercy to all Israel, not just to a remnant thereof (11:25–27). Thus the confinement of "all" excludes the doctrine of universal salvation, and the showing of mercy to "all" has to do with the salvation of both Israelites and Gentiles. By the end, in other words, things will have evened out between them despite, or because of, the differences in God's salvific dealings with them from one era to another.

A DOXOLOGY TO GOD FOR
HIS WAYS OF WISDOM
Romans 11:33–36

11:33: O the depth of the wealth of both God's wisdom and knowledge! How inscrutable [are] **his judgments and untrackable his paths!** In contemplation of God's successive dealings with Israelites and Gentiles, whether by way of salvation or by way of damnation, Paul marvels at the wisdom and knowledge evident in those dealings. Using one term isn't enough; so Paul adds "knowledge" to "wisdom." Using two terms isn't enough; so he speaks of their "wealth." Using "wealth" with the two terms isn't enough; so he attributes "depth" to the wealth (compare our expression "deep pockets"). Using depth as an attribute of the wealth of both God's wisdom and knowledge isn't enough; so Paul introduces them all with an exclamatory "O . . . !" Not even this exclamation is enough, though; so he follows up with another exclamation ("How . . . !") that elaborates the foregoing "depth" with the inscrutability of God's judgments and the untrackability of his paths. "His judgments" are his decrees, for which "his paths" are a figure of speech; and "untrackable" is a figurative equivalent of "inscrutable," an equivalent that suits "paths" just as "inscrutable" suits "judgments." The adding of a figurative phrase highlights the inscrutably wise and knowledgeable judgments of God.

Now Paul justifies the preceding exclamations. **11:34–36: For "who has known the mind of the Lord, or who has become his counselor** [Isaiah 40:13]?" ³⁵**Or "who has first given** [something] **to him and it will be given back to him in restitution** [Job 41:11]?" The implied answer to these rhetorical questions is: Nobody at all! Nobody has known the Lord's mind, because his knowledge exceeds human capabilities of understanding. Nobody has become his counselor, because his wisdom needs no supplementing. Paul himself spells out the reason why nobody has first given to the Lord with the result that the Lord repays him: it's ³⁶**because all things** [are] **from him,** so that nobody can give anything to him "first." **And through him,** so that he's the agent of all initial gifts. And **for him,** so that he's the donee, not the donor, of gifts given in restitution. Reason enough, then, for Paul's finale: **To him** [belongs] **the glory forever. Amen!**

PRACTICAL EXHORTATIONS
Romans 12:1–15:13

Paul wants theology to affect the daily conduct of Christians. So the next major section of his letter contains exhortations dealing with the outworking of theology in practical ways.

CONSECRATION TO GOD
Romans 12:1–2

12:1: Therefore [in view of all I've said up to this point, but especially in view of God as the one to whom belongs the glory forever (11:36)] **I exhort you through God's mercies, brothers, to present your bodies as a sacrifice—**[one that's] **living, consecrated, pleasing to God—**[which presentation is] **your reasonable religious service** [to him]. The affectionate address "brothers" should make the addressees amenable to Paul's exhortation. The mercies of God consist in his selection of both Gentiles and a remnant of Israelites for salvation (chapters 9–11; see in particular 9:15). It is these mercies that make a presentation of Christians' bodies to God "a *reasonable* religious service" (contrast the pagans' *un*reasonable doing of religious service "for the creature rather than for the one who created [them]" [1:25]). "Through God's mercies" makes them the motivating factor in Paul's exhortation. In 12:2 he'll speak of "your mind," but now he speaks of "your bodies" as the physical instruments that carry out the thoughts of the mind. "Your [body] parts" were the objects of presentation in 6:13, 19. But here "your bodies" makes a better complement to "your mind," coming up in 12:2, and also suits better "a sacrifice" (compare Hebrews 10:4–12). The sacrifice is to be (1) "living . . . to [in the sense of 'for'] God" (compare 6:13); (2) "consecrated . . . to God" rather than dominated by sin (contrast pagans' dishonoring their bodies through acting on lusts according to 1:24); and therefore (3) "pleasing to God" (compare the description of burning animal sacrifices as giving off "a pleasing odor to the Lord" [Leviticus 1:9, 13, 17 and so on], only here in Romans the sacrifices are living). Thus "your reasonable religious service" encompasses the totality of bodily conduct rather than being limited to occasional or even regular ceremonies, as in the offering of animal sacrifices under the Mosaic law.

12:2: And don't be conforming yourselves to this age; rather, be transforming yourselves by the renewing of your mind that you may be proving out [in your conduct] **what** [is] **the good and pleasing and complete will of God.** In 1:18–32 Paul set out in detail the evil characteristics of this age, which in Galatians 1:4 he calls "this present evil age." So nonconformity to it means not participating in its evil practices. And this nonconformity requires transformation because of Christians' having participated in those practices prior to conversion, as was true even of Jewish Christians according to chapter 2. Since mental impulses produce bodily actions, the transformation requires a renewing of the mind (contrast the "disapproved [= reprobate] mind" of pagans in 1:28). For this new way of thinking, see 6:11: "be *considering* yourselves dead, on the one hand, in relation to sin; on the other hand, living in Christ Jesus in relation to God" (also compare 6:4; 7:6; 2 Corinthians 4:16; 5:17;

Galatians 6:15; Ephesians 2:15; 4:24; Colossians 3:10). Such thinking has the purpose and result of "proving out [in your conduct] what [is] the . . . will of God." Paul describes God's will (1) as "good," in that it corresponds to the goodness of God himself (compare Mark 10:18; Luke 18:19); (2) as "pleasing," in that like the presentation of your bodies as a sacrifice, his will pleases him when he sees it done; and (3) as "complete," in that his will includes all that he requires of human beings.

MINISTRIES IN THE CHURCH
Romans 12:3-8

12:3-5: For through the grace that was given me I say to everyone who is among you not to be thinking more highly [of himself] **than what it's necessary to think—rather, to be thinking so as to be thinking temperately** [that is, sanely], **as God has distributed to each** [of you] **a measure of faith.** **⁴For just as indeed we have many** [body] **parts in one body and not all the** [body] **parts have the same function, ⁵in this way we, who** [are] **many, are one body in Christ and individually** [body] **parts belonging to one another.** Here Paul starts explaining in detail what it means to prove out in your conduct what God's good, pleasing, and complete will is. In the first place it means not to think more highly of yourself than necessary. A comparison with 11:25 and its context suggests that Paul puts this exhortation first because of Gentile Christians' vaunting themselves over Jewish Christians and, given "I say *to everyone* who is among you," probably also because of what he perceives to be a danger of Jewish Christians' returning the favor (so to speak) in view of his just having spoken about the coming salvation of all Israel (11:26-27). "Through the grace that was given me I say to everyone . . ." parallels "I exhort you . . . through God's mercies . . ." in 12:1, but with an autobiographical concentration that indicates the consciousness with which Paul issues the present exhortation. Of all people Paul, who had persecuted the church violently, knew that despite his apostleship he shouldn't think of himself more highly than was necessary. For it was solely by the grace of God that he was saved and even made an apostle (see especially 1 Timothy 1:12-16). So he issues this exhortation more in exemplary humility than with apostolic authority. "Than what it's necessary to think" implies that it *is* necessary for Christians to think of themselves up to the level of their being graciously gifted to perform various functions in the church (12:6-8). Otherwise they wouldn't perform those functions. But that level of thinking comports with "thinking temperately," which is the first step in "the renewing of your mind" (12:2).

"As God has distributed to each [of you] a measure of faith" leaves no room for pride in your faith, as though it were self-generated, and doesn't have to do with faith for salvation—rather, with faith to perform the functions for which Christians are graciously gifted. Since those functions and the gracious gifts suited to them differ from one another in the amount of faith required for performance,

the amounts of faith God has distributed differ accordingly (see 14:1-2, 22-23 for different amounts of faith, and compare 1 Corinthians 7:17; 2 Corinthians 10:13). But "to each [of you]" leaves no Christian insufficiently supplied with such faith, for no Christian lacks a gracious gift needing to be exercised—as illustrated in the analogy of the body and its parts, all of which parts have a necessary function but not the same function. Paul first cites the multiplicity of body parts in a single body and the variety of their functions, but then switches to the oneness of the body and the belonging of its parts to one another. This switch and "indeed" have the purpose of reinforcing the exhortation not to think too highly of yourself, for such thinking is bound to destroy unity in a local church and in the church at large. To underscore unity, Paul describes the one body as "in Christ," so that just as Christians are individually "in Christ" (8:1; 16:7, 9-10), they're corporately in him too and therefore need to think temperately about themselves lest the body, the church, break down because of malfunctioning parts.

Now Paul switches back to an emphasis on variety, this time on the variety of the gracious gifts that Christians have. **12:6-8: And because of having different gracious gifts in accordance with the grace given to us, whether** [the gracious gift is] **prophecy,** [let us prophesy] **in accordance with the proportion of the faith** [that God distributed by measure to us]. **⁷Whether** [the gracious gift is] **service,** [let us be engaged] **in service. Whether the one who teaches** [has the gracious gift of teaching], [he's to be engaged] **in teaching. ⁸Whether the one who exhorts** [has the gracious gift of exhortation], [he's to be engaged] **in exhortation. The one who gives** [because of having the gracious gift thereof] [is to give] **with generosity. The one who presides** [because of having the gracious gift thereof] [is to preside] **with diligence. The one who shows mercy** [because of having the gracious gift thereof] [is to show mercy] **with cheer.** "The grace given to us" refers to the ill-deserved favor of God in salvation, a grace shared in common by all Christian believers (compare 12:3). But that grace entailed the granting of "*different* gracious gifts" necessary for the functioning of a local church and of the universal church. The following list of such gifts is representative, not exhaustive (for other, somewhat differing lists see 1 Corinthians 12:8-10, 28-31a; Ephesians 4:11). Paul doesn't mention the highest gift, apostleship, apparently because he knows the Roman church has no apostles to whom he could be addressing his exhortation (see the above-mentioned passages for apostleship as the highest gift). But he does begin his list with the next highest gift, that of prophecy, which means conveying to others a divine revelation given to the prophet. "In accordance with the proportion of the faith [that God has distributed to us]" means that prophets should prophesy as much as they believe God has revealed to them. They shouldn't hold back, for to do so would be to think of themselves *less* highly than necessary (see 12:3 with comments). (To say that Paul is telling prophets not to prophesy *beyond* what they believe the Lord has revealed to them is to violate the tenor of this passage, which is one of encouragement to use the gracious gifts to their *full* extent.)

The remaining gifts follow haphazardly, but this very haphazardness and the tailoring of an exhortation to each gift highlight the variety that's necessary to a well-functioning church. "Service" has to do with meeting the practical needs of others; "teaching" with explaining Scripture (the Old Testament in Paul's time) and newly minted Christian oral tradition and writings; and "exhortation" with what is less formally dubbed "urging," the urging of Christians to live christianly. In regard to service, teaching, and exhortation, Paul is saying: Just *do* it! Then he tells others *how* to exercise their gracious gifts. Generosity is to characterize the giving of financial and other aid to those in need of such aid. Otherwise, the needs won't be fully met. Diligence is to characterize the presiding done by those in leadership. Otherwise, by basking in the bright light of leadership they'll not complete their tasks. And cheer is to characterize the showing of mercy. Otherwise, the showing of mercy won't help its recipients as much as it should. That all these gifts are "gracious"—that is, un- and even ill-deserved yet bestowed by God—excludes pride both in their possession and in their exercise.

LOVE IN THE CHURCH WITH
ATTENDANT VIRTUES
Romans 12:9–13

12:9–13: **Love** [is to be] **unhypocritical** [= sincere rather than pretended]. [Be] **loathing what** [is] **wicked.** [Be] **cleaving to what** [is] **good.** The verb for "loathing" includes staying away from the object of loathing and therefore makes a strong contrast with "cleaving," which in its literal sense means to be glued to, welded with, and inlaid. [10] **As to brotherly love,** [be] **tenderly affectionate to one another.** In first-century Mediterranean culture and despite contrary examples, love between brothers was considered especially strong (for an Old Testament example full of tender affection, see Genesis 43:29–30; 45:14–15). **As to honor,** [be] **giving preference to one another.** Since in "this [present evil] age" (12:2 with Galatians 1:4) people compete for honor against one another, giving preference to one another offers a particularly outstanding example of nonconformity and a renewed mind (12:1–2). [11] **As to diligence, don't** [be] **indolent.** For diligence and indolence are incompatible. **As to the Spirit,** [be] **ebullient.** Literally, "ebullient" means "boiling, seething." But in English those expressions, when used figuratively, connote anger. Not so here. Paul is speaking of the zestful enthusiasm produced by God's Spirit for Christian life and witness. **As to the Lord,** [be] **slaving** [for him]. But you won't do so grudgingly if you have the ebullience of the Spirit! [12] **As to the hope** [= the confidence of Christians in Christ's return], [be] **rejoicing** [in it]. **As for affliction** [= persecution], [be] **enduring** [it]. The hope of Christ's return will enable you to endure the affliction (compare 5:3–5). **As for prayer,** [be] **engrossed** [in it]. Affliction should drive you to much praying. [13] **As for the needs of the saints,**

[be] **sharing** [your resources with the saints to meet their needs]. For affliction creates needs, and by definition "the saints" refers to those who are consecrated to God and therefore entitled to your help. [Be] **pursuing hospitality.** Affliction means persecution. Persecution means being pursued. Being pursued requires flight (Matthew 10:23). And flight creates a need for hospitality to Christians in flight from persecution. Dramatically, though, Paul commands pursuit of hospitality to those under pursuit—and this despite the exposing of yourself to persecution by giving hospitality to the persecuted.

RELATIONS WITH NON-CHRISTIANS
AS WELL AS CHRISTIANS
Romans 12:14–21

12:14–21: **Be blessing those who are pursuing** [= persecuting] **you. Be blessing** [them] **and not cursing** [them]. To bless them is to speak well of them in prayer to God, as Jesus and Stephen did at their martyrdoms (Luke 23:34a; Acts 7:60; compare Matthew 5:44; Luke 6:27–28). To curse your persecutors would be to call down God's judgment on them (compare Luke 9:54). "Those who are pursuing you" makes a contrastive play on your needing to pursue hospitality in 12:13. [15] **Be rejoicing with those who are rejoicing. Be weeping with those who are weeping.** The "brotherly love" commanded in 12:10 is to show itself "tenderly affectionate" in the sharing of both joy and sorrow. No competition here. [16] [Be] **thinking the same toward one another.** In other words, rank others as your equals, not your inferiors. **Don't** [be] **thinking haughty things** [about yourselves (compare 11:18, 20; 12:3)]; **rather,** [be] **leading yourselves away** [from such haughty things] **with lowly things** [in thinking about yourselves]. That is, rank yourselves lower than others. **Don't be becoming wiseacres** [again in thinking about yourselves (compare 11:25)]. [17] **Don't** [be] **returning anyone evil in place of an evil** [done to you (compare 1 Peter 3:9)]. [Be] **giving forethought regarding good things in the eyes of all human beings.** In other words, be concerned about your public reputation. [18] **If possible (so far as the possibility** [arises] **out of you),** [be] **living at peace with all human beings.** Realistically, it's not always possible; but make every effort to get along with non-Christians as well as Christians. This effort and your reputation for doing good may lead non-Christians to conversion. [19] **Don't** [be] **avenging yourselves, beloved; rather, give place to the wrath** [of God]. **For it's written, "Vengeance** [is] **mine; I'll repay** [Deuteronomy 32:35]**," says the Lord.** The address "beloved" highlights the command not to be avenging yourselves, but to let God's wrath, particularly his wrath at the Last Judgment, take care of present injustices. Scripture promises he will, and the supplementing of "it's written" with "says the Lord" underlines the promise. [20] **Rather** [than avenging yourselves], **"if your enemy is hungry, feed him. If he's thirsty, give him a drink. For by doing this you'll heap coals of fire on his head** [Proverbs 25:21–22]**."** Which is to say (modern western sentiments to the contrary notwithstanding), doing good to your enemy will, if he doesn't repent and believe in Jesus, increase the vengeance with which God will repay him. Further reason, then, not to take vengeance into your own hands (compare 2 Thessalonians 1:4–10; and for coals of fire as standing for judgment and punishment, see 2 Samuel 22:9, 13; Psalm 18:8, 12; Job 41:20–21; Psalm 140:10; Proverbs 6:27–29; Ezekiel 24:11). [21]**Don't let yourself be conquered by evil; rather, be conquering evil by means of good.** To be conquered by the evil that persecutors do to you would be to avenge yourselves. To conquer the evil done to you by them is to leave vengeance to God at the Last Day (2:5, 8; 5:9; 9:22) and in the meantime to feed your enemy if he's hungry and give him a drink if he's thirsty.

OBEDIENCE TO THE GOVERNMENT
Romans 13:1–7

Paul has just talked about Christians' taking forethought to make their public reputation attractive, about their conquering the bad with the good, and about leaving to the Lord the taking of wrathful vengeance on their persecutors (12:17–21). Instructions on how they should behave in relation to the government, centered in the very city (Rome) where Paul's addressees were living, therefore comes as a natural followup. For such behavior is publicly observable, open to judgment as bad or good, and liable to draw the wrath of governmental vengeance if bad.

13:1–2: Every soul is to be subjecting himself to governing authorities. For there's no authority except [those put in position] **by God, and the existing** [authorities] **have been positioned by God.** [2]**And so, the person who opposes the authority opposes God's imposition** [of the authority]**; and those who oppose will incur judgment on themselves.** The use of "every *soul*," meaning "every *person*," instead of a simple "everyone" accents that there are no individual exceptions to the rule of subjection to governing authorities. Paul bases this rule on God's having put the authorities in their positions. Emphasizing God's having done so is Paul's wordplay between "*po*sitioned," "*op*poses," and "im*posi*tion" (a wordplay lost in other translations but corresponding to the original Greek). Two conclusions follow: (1) to oppose the authority is to oppose God's imposition of the authority; (2) opponents will incur judgment on themselves. That is to say, the governing authority will sentence them to punishment; and since opposition to that authority entailed opposition to God's imposition of the authority, the punishment incurred now will foreshadow divine punishment at the Last Judgment. But Paul's description of the authorities as "existing" suggests he's referring to contemporary governmental authorities because at the time and on the whole they were maintaining peace and justice (as indicated in sources outside the New Testament).

13:3–4: For the rulers aren't a terror to good behavior—rather, to bad [behavior]**. And do you want not to be terrified by the authority? Be doing good, and you'll have praise from him** [the authority]**;** [4]**for he is God's servant to you for the good. But if you're doing bad, be terrified; for he** [the authority] **isn't bearing the sword without effect. For he's God's servant as an avenger for the purpose of** [bringing] **wrath on the person who's practicing the bad.** That the rulers Paul refers to aren't a terror to good behavior—rather, to bad behavior—supports the preceding suggestion that they're the governmental authorities ruling when he wrote. To God's imposition of these authorities as a reason to obey them, Paul adds two more reasons: (1) they terrorize bad behavior; (2) they don't terrorize good behavior. And yet another reason: they'll praise you for good behavior, which praising links up with Paul's concern that the Roman Christians establish a praiseworthy public reputation (12:17). In a context of governmental authority, bad behavior means criminal behavior at least, and good behavior means noncriminal behavior at least. A discussion of tax-paying will expand Paul's purview, though. Meanwhile he describes the authority as serving the addressees on God's behalf and for the good of praising them for good behavior and of scaring them away from bad behavior. The addressees don't serve the government, then; the government serves them. No room for totalitarianism here! Moreover, by serving them through terror and praise as *God's* servant for their good, the governmental authority is unwittingly helping Christians behave in a way that will benefit them in relation to God at the Last Judgment as well as in relation to the governmental authority here and now. Paul commands the Roman Christians not only to be doing the good, but also to be terrified if they're doing the bad; and he supports this command to be terrified by declaring that the authority "isn't bearing the sword without effect." In other words, your very life is at stake. Then Paul adds further support by declaring that the authority isn't only God's servant for the good. The authority is also God's servant for vengeance on the evildoer. Since vengeance belongs to the Lord according to 12:19, as an avenger the governmental authority is carrying out God's wrath now in anticipation of the wrath to come (see 1:18–32 for another anticipation of God's coming wrath).

13:5–7: Therefore [it's] **a necessity to be subjecting yourselves, not only because of the wrath—rather, because of conscience too.** [6]**For because of this** [the matter of conscience]**, also be paying taxes. For they** [the authorities] **are God's deputies, engrossed in this very thing** [praising good behavior and punishing bad behavior]**.** [7]**Pay off** [your] **debts to all** [to whom you owe them]**: tax to whom tax** [is owed]**, revenue to whom revenue** [is owed]**, fear to whom fear** [is owed]**, honor to whom honor** [is owed]**.** Here Paul cites yet another reason to be subject to the governmental authority: your conscience tells you it's the right thing to do, and it's bad to violate your conscience (compare 14:23c: "and everything that doesn't [stem] from faith is sin"). "*Also* be paying taxes" comes in *addition* to subjecting yourselves to the governmental authority by good rather than criminal behavior, or as an *example* of such subjection. The engrossment of the authorities as God's deputies for a just government makes a good reason to pay taxes. (God doesn't want his deputies to go unpaid.) Taxes count as debts that should be paid off (compare Mark 12:13–17; Matthew 22:15–22; Luke 20:19–26). Debts other than taxes, which are direct (like a poll tax or a property tax), also need to be paid off: revenue (an indirect tax such as a sales tax or a toll), fear (of the governmental authority as God's avenger of criminal behavior), and honor (of the governmental authority as God's servant to you for the good). "To *all*" encompasses the sum total of those who qualify as a governmental authority.

LOVE
Romans 13:8–10

13:8–10: Owe no one anything, except to love one another; for the person who loves another person has fulfilled the Law. ⁹For as to the [matter of commandments], **"You shall not commit adultery, you shall not murder, you shall not steal, you shall not lust** [Exodus 20:13–15, 17; Deuteronomy 5:17–19, 21]**," and if** [there's] **any other commandment, it's headed up in this** [statement]: **"You shall love your neighbor as** [you love] **yourself** [Leviticus 19:18]**." ¹⁰Love doesn't do a bad deed to a neighbor. Therefore love** [is] **a fulfillment of the Law.** The command, "Owe (*opheilete* in Paul's Greek) no one anything," connects with the command, "Pay off [your] debts [*opheilas* in Paul's Greek] to all [to whom you owe them]," in 13:7 and therefore doesn't mean not to incur debts—rather, to pay them off, which will establish a good public reputation for Christians (12:17). Whereas in 13:5–7 it was governmental authorities to whom the debts of tax, revenue, fear, and honor are owed, here "no one" and "anything" expand Paul's command to include payment of all other debts to all other creditors too, with the one exception of love. For the obligation to love one another is a debt always owed and therefore always to be paid *on* but never to be paid *off*. Since Paul is addressing Roman Christians, "to love *one another*" probably limits "your neighbor" and "a neighbor" to your fellow Christian (for a broader perspective see Luke 10:25–37).

Paul then cites fulfillment of the Law by loving one another as a reason for such loving (compare 8:4), and supports this statement of fulfillment by relating love of one another to four of the five last commandments in the Decalogue: loving one another keeps you from adultery with your neighbor's spouse, keeps you from murdering your neighbor, keeps you from stealing your neighbor's goods, keeps you from lusting after your neighbor's property. "And if [there's] any other commandment" is a catchall for further commandments having to do with interactions between human beings. The command to love your neighbor as you love yourself heads up all such commandments in the sense of capsulizing them (see the comments on Mark 12:31 for loving your neighbor "as yourself"). "Love doesn't do a bad deed to a neighbor" relates the command to love your neighbor as yourself to the negative commandments quoted from

the Decalogue. Notably, though Paul denies any need for Christians to fulfill the Law's ritual commandments (such as circumcision [2:25–29; 4:9–25]), he carries over the Law's moral commandments as necessary for Christians to fulfill. To fulfill these commandments means to fill them up with obedience. Moreover, love is defined by moral norms.

WATCHING FOR THE END
Romans 13:11–14

13:11–12: And as to this [the fulfilling of the Law], [be] **taking cognizance of the season** [the critical time], **that** [it's] **already the hour for you to be aroused out of sleep. For now our salvation** [is] **nearer than when we believed. ¹²The night has advanced. The day has drawn near. Therefore let's put off the deeds of darkness, and let's put on the tools of light.** To be "taking cognizance of the season" is to get motivation for fulfilling the Law. The season is "the hour for you to be aroused from sleep." Paul is already awake and is arousing the Roman Christians with this letter. His reason for doing so is that "now our salvation [is] nearer than when we believed." This salvation refers to final salvation. Paul includes himself in it. Since "the night has advanced" and since "the day has drawn near," the hour is just before dawn. So "the night" represents "this age" (12:2), and "the day" represents what Paul elsewhere calls "the Day of the Lord," when Jesus returns (see, for example, 1 Thessalonians 4:16–5:11). Here, though, Paul omits "of the Lord," so that emphasis falls on "the day" as a time of "light" rather than on the event accompanying the day. This emphasis suits the contrast with "darkness," which describes "the night" as a time when non-Christians do things unsuitable to the light of day (compare John 3:19–20; Ephesians 5:3–14). To "put off the deeds of darkness" is like taking off dirty clothes, morally dirty in this case. To "put on the tools of light" is like dressing in clean clothes, morally clean in this case. Paul calls such clothes "the *tools* of light" rather than "the *deeds* of light" (which we'd expect to form an antithetic parallel with "the deeds of darkness") for a back-reference to Christians' body parts as "tools of righteousness" in 6:13 (see the footnote to 6:13–14 for the translation "tools" rather than "weapons"). But here the tools represent the righteous deeds to be performed by the body parts. (Means have evolved into outcomes.) So Christians are to dress for daylight even though it's still dark. It won't be dark for long.

13:13–14: Let's walk around respectably, as in daytime, not in carousals and bouts of drunkenness, not in instances of lewdness and instances of licentiousness, not in strife and jealousy. "Let's walk around" is a figurative way of saying, "Let's behave." "Respectably" describes good behavior as suitable to daytime in that daytime exposes bad behavior as shameful. The immediately following reference to "carousals and bouts of drunkenness" suggests a contrast between walking respectably and the staggering of drunks. Like "carousals and bouts of drunkenness," "instances of lewdness and instances of licentiousness" typify "the deeds of darkness." Those instances are bred by carousing and drunkenness. And "strife and jealousy" are likewise bred by instances of lewdness and licentiousness. ¹⁴**Rather, put on the Lord, Jesus Christ; and don't be thinking ahead for the flesh** [your moral weakness] **with a view to** [its] **lusts** [that is, for their gratification]. So now Jesus Christ is himself the clothing suitable to daytime. The command to put him on is a figurative way of saying to let his lordship govern your deeds—hence, "*the Lord*, Jesus Christ" (compare Galatians 3:27, which states a fact rather than issuing a command, however). The only way not to think ahead for the flesh, so as to gratify its lusts once nightfall comes, is to put on Jesus Christ as your Lord.

FREEDOM AND AVOIDANCE OF OFFENSE ON NONMORAL ISSUES
Romans 14:1–15:13

14:1–4: **Be accepting of the person who is weak as to faith** [contrast 4:19], **not for squabbles consisting in arguments.** ²**On the one hand,** [there's the person] **who believes so as to eat all** [foods]. **On the other hand, the person who is weak** [as to faith] **eats vegetables.** ³**The person who eats** [all foods] **isn't to be disdaining the person who doesn't eat** [all foods]**; and the person who doesn't eat** [all foods] **isn't to be judging the person who does eat** [them]**, for God has accepted him.** ⁴**Who are you, you who are judging another's household slave? He stands or falls in relation to his own master. And stand he will, for the Lord** [= the Master] **is able to make him stand.** In the preceding paragraph Paul told the Roman Christians to "love one another" (13:8–10) and to avoid "strife and jealousy" (13:13); and earlier he spoke about "a *measure* of faith" (12:3) and about "the *proportion* of the faith [that God distributed by measure]" (12:6). A discussion of weak faith and the avoidance of giving offense follows naturally, then. "Weak as to faith" describes the Christian whose faith isn't strong enough to let him eat all foods with assurance that he's doing nothing wrong in eating them (compare the dietary taboos in the Mosaic law [Leviticus 11; Deuteronomy 14:3–21]), and indeed whose faith is so weak as to make him a vegetarian. (Ritual contamination rather than health is at issue here.) "Who believes so as to eat all [foods]" describes the Christian whose faith is strong enough to ignore such taboos and in all good conscience eat meat as well as vegetables. "On the one hand .... On the other hand" underscores the distinction between these Christians and thereby implies Paul's knowledge of disagreement over diet among the Roman Christians. To what extent the issue corresponded to that in 1 Corinthians 8–10 is unknown; and guesswork as to who in Rome was holding what position and why, especially in view of the fact that the Mosaic law allows the eating of some meats, doesn't materially affect the meaning of Paul's exhortations.

The exhortation to accept the person with weak faith is obviously addressed to the person strong in faith. Ac-ceptance means taking the other to oneself as a fellow Christian and having table fellowship with him despite dietary differences. "Not for squabbles consisting in arguments" tells the nonvegetarian to avoid arguing back and forth about diet when having fellowship at table with the vegetarian. Additionally, the nonvegetarian is to avoid treating the vegetarian with disdain, as though the vegetarian were a nobody because of his vegetarianism. Conversely, the vegetarian isn't to be judging the nonvegetarian. Why not? Because "God has accepted him [the nonvegetarian]." The contrast between God's acceptance and the prohibited judging indicates that judging means not accepting the other as a true Christian. Paul addresses his question, "Who are you [singular], you who are judging another's household slave?" to the vegetarian and implies the answer, "*You* aren't his master." "Another's" and "his own master" refer to "the Lord," for "Lord" and "master" translate the same Greek word. "Another's household slave" compares the church to a household, the Lord to its head, and Christians to his domestic slaves. "His *own* master" may sound as though the nonvegetarian has a master different from the vegetarian's. But Paul's question, "Who are you, you who are judging *another's* household slave?" portrays the judgmental vegetarian as playing the role of the nonveg-etarian's master, though in fact he as well as the nonvege-tarian is the Lord's household slave. So "his own master" emphasizes that the nonvegetarian belongs to the Lord, not to the vegetarian, whose judgmentalism ill suits his having the same master. Standing represents final salva-tion; falling represents final damnation (compare 11:11, 20, 22) "In relation to his own master" implies that the vegetarian is in no position to judge the nonvegetarian as doomed to damnation because of eating all foods. "And stand he [the nonvegetarian] will" implies that all foods are in fact okay to eat (compare 1 Timothy 4:3–5). "For the Lord is able to make him stand" tells why the non-vegetarian will have salvation at the Last Judgment. It's not just that the Lord *will* make him stand. It's that the Lord "is *able*" to make him stand." This way of putting it pits the Lord's ability against the vegetarian's inability to pass sentence on the nonvegetarian.

14:5–6: **For** [there's the person], **on the one hand, who judges** [one] **day** [to be above another] **day** [in re-ligious importance]. **On the other hand,** [there's the per-son] **who judges every day** [to be alike]. Here, judging a person in regard to salvation or damnation changes to judging days in regard to observing them or not observ-ing them. "For" introduces an explanation. Paul's mak-ing the difference between observers and nonobservers of holy days an explanation of the foregoing exhorta-tion concerning diet links days with diets in a way that equates the vegetarian with the observer of holy days and, conversely, equates the nonvegetarian with the non-observer of holy days (see the Mosaic calendar in Leviti-cus 23 and compare Galatians 4:10; Colossians 2:16–23). As in the matter of diet, "On the one hand .... On the other hand" underscores the distinction between the ob-server and the nonobserver. **Each person is to be fully**

assured in his own mind. This statement commands that observance and nonobservance alike stem from full mental assurance, and *"each* person . . . in *his own* mind" implies nonimposition of anybody else's opinion (compare "not for squabbles consisting in arguments" in 14:1; also the statement in 14:23 that "everything that doesn't [stem] from faith is sin"). The indirectness of Paul's command—he doesn't say, "[You] be fully assured in your own minds"—puts the observers and nonobservers at a distance that suits the optionality of their practices. **⁶The person who minds the day is minding** [it] **for the Lord.** Hence the observance is legitimate. **And the person who eats** [all foods] **is eating** [them] **for the Lord, for he's giving thanks to God** [for all the foods he eats]. **And the person who doesn't eat** [all foods], **for the Lord he doesn't eat** [them] **and gives thanks to God** [for the vegetables he does eat]. The switch back to diet furthers the equation of nonvegetarians with nonobservers of holy days, and of vegetarians with observers of holy days. Eating all foods "for the Lord" parallels minding a holy day "for the Lord." That is to say, the practice of a nonvegetarian, who doesn't observe holy days, is just as much for the Lord as is the practice of an observer of holy days, who eats only vegetables. And thanksgiving to God makes both diets equally valid and reflects the practice of thanking God for food (see especially 1 Timothy 4:4–5, and contrast pagans' unthankfulness to God according to 1:21).

14:7–9: For none of us lives for himself and none [of us] **dies for himself.** This statement spells out a negative reason why Christians conduct themselves "for the Lord" and give "thanks to God" (14:6). They do so because none of them "lives for himself" and none of them "dies for himself." They live and die for the Lord. *"None* of us . . . *none* [of us]" stresses that if they don't, they're not true Christians. Another statement now spells out a positive reason why Christians conduct themselves "for the Lord" and give "thanks to God": **⁸For if we live, we live for the Lord; and if we die, we die for the Lord.** Living for the Lord means that as his household slaves (14:4), Christians obey him. But dying for the Lord? Well, that seems to echo 8:36, which speaks of constant exposure to the possibility of martyrdom: "For your sake we're being put to death the whole day long. We've been regarded as sheep for slaughter." Next, Paul draws a conclusion from living for the Lord and dying for him. It's that we belong to him. The switch to "we" and "us" lumps everyone together—vegetarians and nonvegetarians, observers of holy days and nonobservers—and joins them with Paul and company as all alike the Lord's household slaves. **Therefore both if we live and if we die, we're the Lord's.** A further statement tells why Christians belong to the Lord: **⁹For to this purpose Christ died and came to life, that he might wield lordship over the dead and the living.** "Christ" identifies who "the Lord" is, and Christians belong to Christ as their Lord/ Master/Owner because he died and came to life for the purpose of wielding a lordship over them which at his

second coming will entail a raising of "the dead" and a snatching up with them of "the living" to "meet the Lord in the air" and be with him forever after (1 Thessalonians 4:13–18). The switch from the order of living and then dying to the order of "the dead and the living" points in that direction. So too does the use of "came to life" rather than "was raised" for Christ's resurrection.

14:10–12: But you [who eat only vegetables], **why are you judging your brother** [= fellow Christian who eats all foods]? **Or you too** [who eat all foods], **why are you disdaining your brother** [who eats only vegetables]? There's no good reason to judge a nonvegetarian or to disdain a vegetarian. So Paul supplies a reason to do neither: **For we will all stand before God's judgment platform.** Paul wrote Romans from Corinth, Greece (see the introduction to Romans). So his having stood before the judgment platform of the Roman governor Gallio in Corinth (Acts 18:12–17) probably sparked the foregoing statement. "We . . . all" stresses that not even Paul will be exempt from God's judgment. Since God will judge all of us Christians, none of us should presume to judge another Christian on nonmoral issues such as diet and holy days. (That *moral* matters *require* judgment by Christians, though, see 1 Corinthians 5.) And since as Christians we'll all stand before God's judgment platform, none of us should dare disdain a fellow Christian because of disagreement on nonmoral issues. Paul now supports these points with an Old Testament quotation and draws a conclusion from it. **¹¹For it's written, "'[As] I live,' says the Lord, 'every knee will bow to me, and every tongue will confess to God** [Isaiah 49:18; 45:23].'" **¹²Therefore, then, each of us will give an account of himself** [to God]. "[As] I live" underscores what the Lord then says. "Every knee will bow to me" stresses bodily acknowledgment of God's lordship at the Last Judgment over against human beings' presuming to exercise judgmental lordship on nonmoral issues during present lifetimes. "Every tongue" corresponds to "we . . . all" in the immediately preceding run-up to this Old Testament quotation, and to "each of us" in the followup. Similarly, "will confess to God" tells what will happen when we "stand before God's judgment platform" according to that same run-up, and gets explained by "will give an account of himself" in the followup. Since Christ is the Lord (14:9), it's noteworthy that Paul speaks of "*God's* judgment platform" in connection with "*the Lord*" to whom "every knee will bow" (contrast "the judgment platform *of the Christ*" in 2 Corinthians 5:10). Christ the Lord will act as God's agent at the Last Judgment, but Paul's calling the judgment platform "God's" highlights the judicial incompetence of mere human beings when it comes to nonmoral issues.

14:13–15: Therefore [because "each of us will give an account of himself"] **let's not be judging** [= condemning] **one another any more. Instead, judge** [= determine] **this rather: not to put a stumbling block or a snare before a brother.** "Not . . . any more" confirms that Paul knew vegetarian Christians in Rome to be judging their nonvegetarian fellow Christians for eating all foods. Since it's the vegetarians who have been judging in the sense of condemning the nonvegetarians, whereas the nonvegetarians have been disdaining the vegetarians, the exhortation not to be judging one another any more, though it's general ("let's"), relates especially to the vegetarians. But the nonvegetarians' eating all foods threatens to drive the vegetarians into apostasy by tempting them to violate their conscience through eating meat. So Paul issues a command directed especially to the nonvegetarians that they "judge this: not to put a stumbling block or a snare before a brother" by eating meat—presumably when at table with a vegetarian, for otherwise the commands that the vegetarian not be judging the nonvegetarian and that the nonvegetarian not be disdaining the vegetarian (14:3) lack a setting (compare 1 Corinthians 10:27–30 with comments; also Galatians 2:12–13). Thus judging as condemning another person (on the part of the vegetarian) shifts to judging as determining for oneself (on the part of the nonvegetarian). "Instead" and "rather" spotlight this shift, and both the wordplay on judging and the doubling up in "a stumbling block or a snare" lend force to the command. The vegetarians' eternal destiny is at stake. Then Paul states his own position: [14]**I know and have been convinced in the Lord, Jesus, that nothing** [is] **impure** [ritually speaking] **in itself** . . . . "I know" advances a claim to knowledge. Paul isn't expressing a merely personal opinion. So the vegetarians shouldn't dismiss Paul's following declaration that "nothing [is] impure in itself." "In itself" adds a qualification that leaves room for an exception. "I . . . have been convinced" implies that someone convinced him. "In the Lord, Jesus" indicates that Jesus did. In fact, the translation, "*by* the Lord, Jesus" would work just as well as "*in* the Lord, Jesus." Not that he spoke directly to Paul; rather, that Paul knew of Jesus' declaring all foods ritually pure (Mark 7:18–19; Matthew 15:11). Paul calls him "the Lord" to call attention to Jesus' authority in this declaration.

Now for the exception: **except for the person who considers some** [food] **to be impure, for that person** [it's] **impure.** The impurity isn't channeled through the food to such a person. It's channeled through that person to the food. Next comes a reason for the nonvegetarian "not to put a stumbling block or a snare before a [vegetarian] brother": [15]**For if because of food your brother is being nettled** [which nettling could lead him to apostatize by violating his conscience]**, you're no longer walking around** [= behaving] **in accordance with love** [though you've been commanded to love one another (12:9–10; 13:8–10)]. What might be the consequence of this unloving behavior? Ruination, which in the next command has to do with eternal damnation (see, for example, 2:12–13; 1 Corinthians 1:18; 8:11; 2 Corinthians 2:15–16; 4:3; 2 Thessalonians 2:10; and for the association of stumbling blocks and snares with such damnation, see 9:32–33; 11:9; 16:17–18; Mark 9:42; Matthew 18:6–7; Luke 17:1–2): **Don't be ruining with your food that** [brother of yours]**, for whom Christ died.** "That

[brother of yours]" lends pathos to the command, and "for whom Christ died" pits Christ's loving self-sacrifice for the vegetarian (compare Galatians 2:20) against self-indulgence by an inconsiderate nonvegetarian.

14:16–18: Therefore [= in view of ruining your vegetarian brother forever by influencing him to eat foods he thinks are impure] **your good** [that same food, which you correctly consider to be good] **isn't to be slandered** [as bad, impure, by the vegetarian brother when he sees you eating it at table with him]. Since Paul can hardly command the good food itself to avoid being slandered, he issues a third person command that it not be slandered. The nonvegetarians themselves will have to see to it that the command is carried out. And why should all foods be shielded from slander? Paul supplies two reasons why. Here's the first one: [17]**For God's reign isn't eating and drinking—rather, righteousness and peace and joy in the Holy Spirit.** For Christians the reign of God, which here has to do with his ruling their conduct, doesn't consist in their "eating and drinking." (So far as his reign is concerned, those activities await Jesus' second coming according to Luke 22:29–30; Revelation 19:7–10.) In "this age" (12:2) God's reign consists in righteousness of conduct (as in 2:12–16; 6:12–20; 8:4). Paul has just spelled out what such righteousness requires in regard to table fellowship and a religious calendar; and such righteousness will produce peace among Christians, another feature of God's reign (compare the prohibition in 14:1 of "squabbles consisting in arguments" and Colossians 3:15). Peace, in turn, produces joy, a still further feature of God's reign (compare 15:18; and for examples of Christians' taking joy in one another, see 2 Corinthians 2:3; 7:4, 13; Philippians 4:1; 1 Thessalonians 2:19–20; Philemon 7). "In the Holy Spirit" tells where such righteousness, peace, and joy take place; for according to 8:9 Christians are themselves "in the Spirit." Here's the second reason why nonvegetarians should shield all foods from slander by vegetarians: [18]**For the person who in this** [matter] **is slaving for the Christ** [is] **pleasing to God and approved by human beings.** "The person who in this [matter] is slaving for the Christ" is the nonvegetarian who to avoid ruining his vegetarian brother doesn't eat all foods when sitting at table with him. "Slaving" implies that this avoidance equates with obedience to Jesus in recognition of his lordship (compare 14:4). But Paul calls Jesus "the Christ" to suit his role as the messianic king who is presently reigning on God's behalf (see 1 Corinthians 15:23–28). "The person . . . is pleasing to God" recollects 12:1, so that the aforementioned avoidance counts as part of presenting your body to God as a living and consecrated as well as pleasing sacrifice. "Approved by human beings" supplements God's pleasure and refers to the vegetarians' approving the nonvegetarians' considerateness of their (the vegetarians') scruples when eating together. This approval contrasts both with the vegetarians' "judging" the nonvegetarians (14:3–4) and with the vegetarians' "being nettled" if the nonvegetarians don't show love in this way (14:15).

14:19–20a: Therefore, then, let's be pursuing the things that promote peace and the things that promote the building up of one another. ²⁰ᵃDon't be dismantling God's work for the sake of food. The use of both "Therefore" and "then" emphasizes the following exhortation and makes it grow out of what God's reign does and doesn't consist in (14:17) and out of divine pleasure in and human approval of slaving for the Christ in respect to disagreements over nonmoral issues (14:8). Since the unloving behavior of nonvegetarians disturbs the peace, the exhortation, though it's general ("let's"), relates especially to them. "Be *pursuing*" connotes energetic effort. As noted above, the eternal destiny of those weak in faith is at stake. "The things that promote peace" are the behaviors that promote peaceful relations between Christians, to which things Paul adds as another object of pursuit "the things that promote the building up of one another." This addition makes for emphasis and for a contrast with dismantling the work of God for the sake of food, in which the reign of God doesn't presently consist. His "work" is the vegetarian Christian. A dismantling would amount to the ruination of which 14:15 spoke and which meant eternal damnation on account of an apostasy caused by unloving, self-indulgent behavior on the part of those strong enough in faith to eat all foods.

Now Paul restates his own conviction positively (see 14:14 for his stating it negatively), but tells how it's sometimes wrong to eat all foods. **14:20b–21: All** [foods are] **indeed clean** [in the ritual sense]. **Nevertheless,** [such food is] **wrong for the human being who's eating** [it] **by way of** [putting] **a stumbling block** [in a brother's path]. "Nevertheless" marks a sharp distinction between the theological truth, underlined by "indeed," that "all [foods are ritually] clean" (compare 14:14) and the wrongness of eating all foods "by way of [putting] a stumbling block [in a brother's path]," which means eating them in a circumstance of table fellowship with a vegetarian brother weak in faith and therefore liable to apostatize by violating his conscience through joining in the eating of meat. For emphasis Paul now supplements what's "wrong" with what's "good": ²¹[It's] **good not to eat meat and not to drink wine and not** [to do anything] **by which your brother stumbles.** This supplement specifies meat as a food regarded by vegetarians as possibly impure (and certainly so in the case of pork, popular among pagans but detestable to followers of the Mosaic law). The supplement also adds wine-drinking to the eating of such food. We might speculate why Paul throws in wine-drinking despite no prohibition of it in the Mosaic law and despite his medicinal prescription of it for Timothy (1 Timothy 5:23). But whatever his reason, if wine-drinking or any other morally neutral behavior done in the presence of a fellow Christian weak in faith might lead him to apostatize by participating against his conscience, it's good to refrain. "Your brother" appeals to the affectionate brotherly love commanded in 12:10.

14:22–23: The faith that you have, have it in accordance with yourself in God's sight. "The faith that you have" refers to the amount of faith you have in regard to eating foods, not observing holy days, and drinking wine. "Have it in accordance with yourself" means to exercise faith in these regards up to the amount of faith that you have to do such things but, by implication here and an outright statement next, no further. "In God's sight" warns that he is looking to see whether in your behavior you violate the limit of your faith. **Fortunate** [is] **the person who isn't judging** [= condemning] **himself by what he approves. ²³But the person who is doubting is condemned if he eats, because** [his eating] **doesn't** [stem] **from faith; and everything that doesn't** [stem] **from faith is sin.** So "what he approves" means whatever foods he allows himself to eat. Faith that he's eating nothing prohibited by God leaves the eater fortunately uncondemned by his eating. (We'd say that his conscience is clear.) But eating something he believes God has prohibited from eating leaves the eater sinfully self-condemned—sinfully because behaving in violation of what you believe destroys your integrity and thus, so far as the issue of food is concerned, makes you unable to thank God for it (contrast 14:6).

15:1–2: And we, the ones capable [of eating meat, drinking wine, and treating every day alike without transgressing the boundary of our faith] **ought to be bearing the weaknesses of the ones incapable** [of engaging in those activities with faith] **and not to be pleasing ourselves.** With "we" Paul includes himself among those who recognize the obsolescence of ritual laws (compare 14:14). But "we . . . *ought*" puts him and the others in debt to those weak in faith, for loving them is a debt always to be paid on but never to be paid off (13:8). In this case, loving them entails bearing their weaknesses by not eating meat and not drinking wine when at table with them. For their weaknesses consist in an inability to eat meat and drink wine with faith that they're not breaking God's law. To be "pleasing ourselves" rather than "bearing [their] weaknesses" would be failing to pay on the debt of love. **²Each of us is to be pleasing** [his] **neighbor for the good, with a view to building** [him] **up.** "Each of us" allows no exceptions among the strong in faith, not even an exception of Paul. "Is to be pleasing [his] neighbor" opposes "to be pleasing ourselves" and harks back to the command, "You shall love your neighbor as [you love] yourself," and to the statements that "love doesn't do a bad deed to a neighbor" and that "therefore love [is] a fulfillment of the Law" (13:8–10; see the comments on that passage for "your neighbor" as someone near you because of being a fellow Christian). "Building [the neighbor] up" defines "the good" for which pleasing him is to be done, and "building up" puts improvement of his Christian life and witness under the figure of constructing a house, just the opposite of "dismantling God's work" in 14:20.

But why please your neighbor rather than pleasing yourself? **15:3: For even the Christ didn't please himself—rather, just as it's written, "The vilifications of those who vilify you have fallen on me** [Psalm 69:9]."

As a title, "the Christ" joins "even" to stress that despite his status as the Messiah, Jesus "didn't please himself." Then "rather" introduces sharply a contrast with self-pleasing. "Just as it's written" and the following quotation give the contrast scriptural support. It's not pleasant to take on yourself the brunt of another's misfortune, which in the quoted psalm consists in vilifications. Weakness of faith is a kind of misfortune that the strong in faith need to bear on behalf of those suffering that misfortune. Paul correlates the scriptural quotation to the Christ's not pleasing himself. So in the context of Romans "the vilifications of those who vilify you have fallen on me" means that the vilifications of those who vilify God have fallen on Christ. And since this statement exemplifies pleasing your neighbor rather than yourself, pleasing your neighbor takes its cue from Christ's pleasing God. Would it then be too much to say that pleasing your neighbor pleases God too?

Now Paul explains why he quoted Scripture. **15:4: For as many things as were written formerly** [in Scripture] **were written for our instruction in order that through the perseverance and through the exhortation of the Scriptures we might have hope.** "As many things as were written formerly" covers the entirety of the Old Testament, not only the just-quoted passage, and therefore prepares for a slew of upcoming quotations (15:9–12). "For our instruction" tells the purpose behind the writing and extends that purpose beyond those living at the time of writing to us who are living long afterward. As the writing had the purpose of our instruction, so our instruction has a purpose, that of giving us hope, which as usual in Paul's letters means confidence in the second coming of Christ. Paul doesn't speak of having hope through the Scriptures—rather, "through the *perseverance* and the *exhortation* of the Scriptures." That is to say, the Scriptures contain examples of perseverance, like the example in the just-quoted psalm, and thereby instruct us to persevere in pleasing our neighbor for the good with a view to building him up at a cost to ourselves, again as in the quoted psalm. This example amounts to an exhortation to follow suit (see 12:8, where the word translated "exhortation" here has already appeared in the same sense; and compare 5:3–5 for perseverance and hope).

15:5–6: And may the God of perseverance and exhortation give you to be thinking the same thing among one another in accordance with Christ Jesus ⁶in order that with mutual fervor you may be glorifying with one mouth the God and Father of our Lord, Jesus Christ. These verses contain a wish and a statement of its purpose. The wish starts with "the God of perseverance and exhortation." Paul has just spoken about "the perseverance and the exhortation of the Scriptures." These Scriptures are God's word. So God himself is "the God of perseverance and exhortation" in that through the Scriptures he provides a hortatory example of perseverance in the Christ who spoke in Psalm 69:9. Paul wishes that God may give the Roman Christians "to be thinking

the same thing," that is, to be united in their thinking. Not that they have to agree on nonmoral issues, for Paul has argued otherwise since the start of chapter 14. Instead, he wishes them to think of each other as equals in the one body that's in Christ. For this meaning see 12:16 with 12:4–5. Such thinking makes for the peace and building up of one another that 14:19 exhorts us to pursue (see also Ephesians 4:11–16); and here, "among one another" underlines that such thinking should be shared. "In accordance with Christ Jesus" qualifies the thinking that Paul wishes we do and corresponds to Christ's unself-centered thinking as represented in the quoted psalm. That Paul wishes God to *give* the Roman Christians to think in this way harks back to the moral incapability of human beings apart from the operation of God's Spirit in them (7:7–8:11).

"In order that" starts a statement concerning the purpose of what Paul wishes for. In this statement, "with *mutual* fervor" parallels "the same thing among one another" in the wish and suits the theme of unity. "With mutual *fervor*" grows out of "the God of perseverance and exhortation," for it's the perseverance and exhortation provided by him in the Scriptures that generate fervor. "In order that . . . you may be glorifying *with one mouth*" is to grow out of "thinking *the same thing* among one another," for thinking issues in speech. Like "the *same* thing," "with *one* mouth" is a striking expression of unity. But presumably the "*one* body in Christ" (12:5) has only one mouth. Paul doesn't want church unity for its own sake, though. He wants it for the glorification of God in congregational thanksgiving to him, as when those strong in faith and those weak in faith join at table in thanking God for their food (14:6). A disunited congregation can't glorify him either "with *mutual* fervor" or "with mutual *fervor*." The addition, "and Father of our Lord, Jesus Christ," supplies a reason to glorify God. As the Father of none other than our Lord, who is Jesus Christ, God is entitled to be glorified by us. See the comments on 2 Corinthians 1:3 and 1 Peter 1:3 for the whole expression.

15:7–13: Therefore be accepting of one another, just as also the Christ accepted you for the glory of God. "Therefore" means "in view of my wish that God may give you to be thinking the same thing among one another [and so forth in 15:5–6]." "Just as also the Christ accepted you" makes his so doing an example to be followed: if he did, surely you ought to. "*The* Christ" implies that if his messianic status didn't keep him from accepting you, how much more should you, who have no such status, let nothing keep you from accepting one another. "For the glory of God" echoes for emphasis the stated purpose of thinking the same thing among one another in 15:5–6. Only here the Christ himself sets an example of doing something for God's glory. ⁸**For I'm saying that Christ became a servant of the circumcision** [the Jews] **in behalf of God's truth to confirm the promises to the** [fore]**fathers** [of the circumcision, of the Jews], ⁹**and** [Christ became a servant of the circumcision in behalf of God's truth] **for the Gentiles to glorify God for** [his] mercy, just as it's written, "Because of this I'll confess you among the Gentiles, and I'll sing in praise of your name [2 Samuel 22:50; Psalm 18:49]." ¹⁰And again it says, "Celebrate, you Gentiles, along with his [God's] people [Deuteronomy 32:43]." ¹¹And again, "Be praising the Lord, all you Gentiles; and all the peoples are to praise him [Psalm 117:1]." ¹²And again, Isaiah says, "There'll be the sprout of Jesse, even he who rises to rule the Gentiles. In him the Gentiles will hope [Isaiah 11:10]." ¹³And may the God of hope fill you with all joy and peace in believing, so that you may be flourishing in hope by the power of the Holy Spirit.

Paul cites his speaking as a reason for accepting one another: "*For* I'm saying . . . ." But though he speaks with the authority of an apostle (1:1), the reason doesn't consist *only* in his speaking. It consists also in *what* he's saying, which is that "Christ became a servant of the circumcision." If Christ became the Jews' servant, Gentile Christians should accept their Jewish Christian brothers. (As already implied in 11:17–24, the Gentile Christians in Rome were *not* accepting them.) "In behalf of God's truth" means that Christ served the Jews to show God true to the promises he'd made to their forefathers Abraham, Isaac, and Jacob (see earlier mentions of these promises in 4:13–14, 16, 20–21; 9:4, 8–9; also Galatians 3:19). "To confirm the promises" isn't to fulfill them, for their fulfillment awaits the second coming (see chapter 11, especially 11:25–27). But the first coming of Christ guaranteed that future fulfillment (compare 1:2–4; 9:4–5). Furthermore, he became the Jews' servant so that Gentiles might glorify God for his mercy to them (concerning which see 9:22–26), non-Jews though they are (see chapter 4, especially 4:16–18, for the inclusion of believing Gentiles in the promises made to the Jews' forefathers).

Paul accents God's mercy to the Gentiles to show Gentile Christians why they should accept the Jewish Christians. A series of no fewer than four Old Testament quotations strengthens several times over the accent on God's mercy to Gentiles. In the first quotation, "Because of this" means "because of God's mercy to Gentiles" according to the context here in Romans. "I'll sing in praise of your name" defines the meaning of "I'll confess you among the Gentiles." Telling them to celebrate "along with his [God's] people [the Jews]" calls on Gentile Christians to join the Jewish Christians in congregational singing of praise to God (compare "one mouth" in 15:6). "*All* you Gentiles" and "*all* the peoples" leave no Gentile Christian unobligated to obey the call to mutual celebration. Jesse was the father of King David. For "the sprout of Jesse" as a figure of speech for the Christ, see the comments on Revelation 5:5. Since the noun related to the verb "rises" referred to Christ's resurrection in 1:4; 6:5, the rising of Jesse's sprout to rule the Gentiles may allude to the resurrection of Christ.

This paragraph, and indeed the whole of 14:1–15:13, closes with another wish of Paul. In it "the God of hope" echoes the preceding statement, "In him [Jesse's sprout] the Gentiles will hope," but encompasses as the object

of hope God as the Father of our Lord, Jesus Christ, along with Jesus Christ as Jesse's sprout. "*Fill* you with *all* joy and peace" is emphatic and reminiscent of 14:17 (concerning which see the comments). "In believing" locates the means of all joy and peace in faith, whether the faith is strong or weak. "Flourishing in hope" means having more confidence in Christ's return than is actually needed for enduring the trials and tribulations that beset Christians. "By the power of the Holy Spirit" echoes the Spirit's empowering of Christians as detailed throughout chapter 8 (compare Galatians 5:22–23; and see Isaiah 31:3; Zechariah 4:6 for the association of spirit with power).

PAUL'S PLAN TO VISIT ROME
Romans 15:14–32

15:14–16: And I, even I myself, am convinced concerning you, my brothers, that you, even you yourselves, are full of goodness, having been filled with every [kind of] knowledge, able to be admonishing one another. ¹⁵But rather daringly I've written to you, partly as [one who is] reminding you because of the grace given to me by God ¹⁶that I might be a minister of Christ Jesus to the Gentiles by ministering as a priest the gospel of God in order that the offering of the Gentiles may become fully acceptable, consecrated by the Holy Spirit. "I, *even I myself*" and "you, *even you yourselves*" underline Paul's favorable conviction concerning the Roman Christians. "My brothers" adds affection to this conviction (compare 12:10). Their "goodness" consists in *doing* good things (2:7, 10; 7:18–19; 9:11; 12:2, 9, 21; 13:3–4). So "*full* of goodness" means doing *lots* of good things (compare Galatians 5:22). The addressees' "having been filled with every [kind of] knowledge" has made them "able to be admonishing one another" (compare 1 Corinthians 1:5: "having been enriched . . . in every [kind of] knowledge"). They're so knowledgeable that Paul has had to be "rather daring" to write them, and so knowledgeable as to make what he has written partly a reminder of what they already know (though not wholly a reminder, for 11:25–27 has informed them of a "secret"). These compliments have the purpose of helping Paul win the Romans' support for his projected mission to Spain, about which he'll speak shortly (compare the brief compliment in 1:8).

Paul justifies writing the Romans despite their knowledge by citing "the grace given" to him "by God." In 1:5 "grace and apostleship" referred to Paul's apostleship as ill-deserved because prior to God's call, Paul had persecuted the church (12:3; Galatians 1:13–16, 22–24; 1 Timothy 1:12–16). Here, though, he calls himself "a minister of Christ Jesus," a priestly rather than governmental minister (as in 13:6) to prepare for the upcoming reference to his doing the work of a priest. Though it looks back to Paul's past evangelistic labors, "to the Gentiles" looks forward more especially to the Spanish mission for which he's going to solicit the Romans' support. For "the gospel of God" see the comments on 1:1. This gospel originates from him. "Ministering [it] as a priest" makes God's gospel what Paul teaches the Gentiles. And those who believe it become a kind of sacrifice which as a kind of priest he offers to God (compare 12:1–2, though there the Romans rather than Paul are to do the sacrificing). Since those who believe the gospel receive the Holy Spirit (8:1–11), the offering of the Gentiles will indeed become "fully acceptable" as "consecrated [that is, set apart for God] by the Holy Spirit." So God, Christ Jesus, and the Holy Spirit—all three of them—figure in Paul's ministry to the Gentiles.

15:17–19: **In Christ Jesus, therefore, I have a boast regarding the things pertaining to God.** [18]**For I'll not dare to say anything about the things that Christ has** *not* **accomplished through me by word and by deed—** [19]**with the power of signs and wonders, with the power of God's Spirit—resulting in the Gentiles' obedience, so that from Jerusalem and round about as far as Illyricum I've fulfilled the gospel about the Christ** [by proclaiming it] . . . . The boasting of Paul occupies a much lengthier passage in 2 Corinthians 10:7–12:13. In the present passage, "therefore" draws a conclusion from his God-given ministry to Gentiles. "In Christ Jesus" tempers the boasting in which Paul engages. He'll take no credit, so that his boasting has the character of exultation. "The things pertaining to God," about which he boasts, refer to Paul's aforementioned priestly kind of work; for such work consists in making an offering to God (15:16). A reason for boasting follows. But Paul introduces it by saying, "I'll not dare to say anything about the things that Christ has *not* accomplished through me." In other words, Paul won't exaggerate. "In Christ," as he is, Paul wouldn't dare exaggerate. At the same time, his statement implies that he has acted as Christ's agent, but only as Christ's agent, so that Christ gets the credit for the accomplishments. "By word and by deed" identifies the means of accomplishment. "By word" refers obviously to proclamation of the gospel. Paul himself explains "by deed" as referring to the doing of "signs and wonders," an emphatically twofold designation of miracles (compare 2 Corinthians 12:12; Galatians 3:5). Because "with the power of God's Spirit" parallels "with the power of signs and wonders," Paul attributes his working of signs and wonders to the Holy Spirit; and the twofold use of "power" (which in its plural form usually means "miracles," that is, acts of supernatural power) implies a divine authentication of the "word." As a result, Gentiles have obeyed the gospel (see the comments on 1:5, and the final ones on 15:7–13). The book of Acts, starting at 9:28–29, narrates Paul's "fulfill[ing] the gospel about the Christ" from Jerusalem onward and outward, but doesn't include Illyricum (the Dalmatian coastal region of modern Croatia and Albania across the Adriatic Sea from Italy's east coast [compare 2 Timothy 4:10]). So the narrative in Acts has a gap, though "as far as Illyricum" might mean "as far as but not including Illyricum" (see Philippians 2:30, for example, where the same Greek preposition, though translated differently, is noninclusive). "I've fulfilled the gospel about the Christ" indicates proclamation of it in

the mentioned cities and regions, thereby disfavors a noninclusion of Illyricum, and implies unfulfillment of the gospel if it isn't proclaimed. For then it does no good for people's salvation (see 10:13–15).

15:20–21: **and in this way** [the way I proclaimed the gospel from Jerusalem round about as far as Illyricum] **aspiring to be proclaiming the gospel not where Christ has been named, lest I be building on somebody else's foundation—** [21]**rather, just as it's written, "[People] to whom nothing about him** [Christ] **was announced will see, and** [people] **who haven't heard** [about him] **will understand** [Isaiah 52:15]**."** "Not where Christ has been named" doesn't only mean "where Christ hasn't been heard of." It also means "where Christ hasn't been confessed to be who his name says he is" (compare 2 Timothy 2:19). Paul is referring to virgin territory for evangelism. As the first to be establishing churches in such territory, Paul conceives of himself as a foundation-layer, not as one who builds up a church established by somebody else (see 1 Corinthians 3:10; 2 Corinthians 10:12–16). The mention of this self-conception will feed into his appeal for the Romans' help in a mission to Spain, implied by the present passage to be unevangelized territory. Paul caps the description of himself as not building on somebody else's foundation with an Old Testament quotation, which he's fulfilling by portraying Christ before the eyes of people heretofore ignorant of him and by speaking his name into their ears.

15:22–24: **Therefore I was also being hindered many times from coming to you.** [23]**But now, no longer having a place in these districts and for many years having a longing to come to you** [24]**while I'm traveling to Spain—for I'm hoping that when traveling through** [Rome toward Spain] **to see you and by you to be sent there with your help if I may first be filled for a while** [with your company]**—.** "Therefore" means that Paul's evangelizing "from Jerusalem round about as far as Illyricum" has hindered him from coming to the Romans. "Also" makes that evangelism a hindrance *as well as* a fulfillment of the just-quoted Old Testament passage (15:21). "But now, no longer having a place in these districts [where the gospel hasn't already been proclaimed]" confirms that "being hindered" referred to Paul's God-ordained evangelistic activities to the east of Rome. The combination of this reason for not having visited the Romans heretofore and Paul's "longing" to visit them (compare 1:10–11) should pave Paul's way into the hearts of the Roman Christians. He wants them to long for his visit just as he longs to visit them. The "many years" of his longing adds length of time to the "many times" of being hindered and thus heightens the longing. "While I'm traveling to Spain" makes Rome only a stopover because of its having been evangelized already and Paul's determination to lay foundations, not build on them. But an *important* stopover, for he hopes not just to see the Roman Christians but also to be sent by them to Spain. This sending should include at least financial help and perhaps also food for the journey (compare especially

Titus 3:13) and a traveling companion or two, such as one who knows Latin, because Greek wasn't spoken in Spain and Paul isn't likely to have known Latin (see, for example, Acts 13:2, 13; 15:40; 16:1–3 and so on, including many references in Paul's letters to his traveling companions). He leaves this long sentence incomplete and hurries on to start a new one having to do with his immediate plan.

15:25–27: But now I'm traveling to Jerusalem, serving the saints [who live there]. **²⁶For Macedonia and Achaia were pleased to make a certain contribution for the poor consisting of the saints** [= Christians] **in Jerusalem. ²⁷For they** [Macedonia and Achaia] **were pleased** [to do so]**, and they are debtors to them** [the saints in Jerusalem]**. For if the Gentiles have shared in their** [the Jewish saints'] **Spiritual things, they're indebted also to minister to them in fleshly things.** Paul's traveling to Jerusalem "now" alerts the Romans that despite his longing to visit them, the visit will be delayed a while. So they shouldn't take the delay as a sign of insincerity or flattery in his statements of longing. "Serving the saints" tells what he'll do in Jerusalem. Two statements then explain why he'll be serving the Christians there. In the first statement Macedonia and Achaia (Greece) stand for the Christians living in those territories. "Were pleased to make a certain contribution" identifies the nature of Paul's "serving the saints" as delivering to them the contribution, which means a sharing of financial resources. Many translations read "for the poor *among* the saints in Jerusalem." But "serving the saints" referred to the saints in Jerusalem without making an economic distinction between them. So too in 1 Corinthians 16:1; 2 Corinthians 8:4; 9:1, 12, all of which have to do with this very same contribution. Therefore the translation "the poor *consisting of* the saints in Jerusalem" (equally true to Paul's Greek) is to be preferred (see 1 Corinthians 16:1–4; Galatians 2:10). The second statement explaining the reason for Paul's serving the saints there repeats what was already said in the first such statement, namely, that Macedonia and Achaia "were pleased" to contribute. The double mention of their pleasure sets an example for the Romans to emulate in contributing to Paul's Spanish mission. He then appends another reason for serving the saints in Jerusalem. It's that the Gentiles who make up most of the Christians in Macedonia and Achaia "are debtors" to those in Jerusalem, who are Jews, so that Paul *should* help those Gentiles pay their debt by delivering the contribution. In other words, duty is delaying his visit to Rome. The reason for the Gentiles' indebtedness is that they've shared in the Jewish saints' "Spiritual things," which means the Spirit-empowered evangelism that originated from the mother church in Jerusalem. Ministry in merely "fleshly things," which in this context means money, is neither onerous nor unreasonable, then.

15:28–29: Therefore [since I'm now traveling to Jerusalem] **after completing this** [service to the saints in Jerusalem] **and myself sealing for them this fruit, I'll come away** [from Jerusalem] **to Spain by way of you.**

²⁹And I know that when coming to you, I'll come in the fullness of Christ's blessing. "After completing this [service]" means "after delivering this contribution." Since sealing connotes a stamp of ownership (see the comments on 2 Corinthians 1:22), "and myself sealing for them this fruit" means that Paul in person will transfer the contribution into the ownership of the saints in Jerusalem. "Fruit" stands for an outcome, here for the contribution as a financial outcome of the sharing by Jewish saints in Jerusalem of "their Spiritual things" with Gentiles in Macedonia and Achaia (15:27 [compare 1:13; Galatians 5:22–23]). "Blessing" means praise in the sense of saying something commendatory. So Paul's knowing that he'll come to the Romans in the fullness of Christ's blessing means that he's sure Christ will commend him for having delivered and sealed the contribution for the saints in Jerusalem before coming to Rome. "In the *fullness* of Christ's blessing" (not simply "with Christ's blessing" or even "with Christ's full blessing") accents Christ's approval of Paul's travel plans. So the Romans shouldn't criticize him for going to Jerusalem before coming to Rome.

15:30–32: But I exhort you, brothers, through our Lord, Jesus Christ, and through the Spirit's love to strive with me in prayers to God in my behalf, ³¹that I may be rescued from those in Judea who are disobeying [the gospel] **and** [that] **my service in Jerusalem may turn out to be fully acceptable to the saints** [there]**, ³²in order that on coming to you with joy through God's will I may have respite** [while] **with you.** The danger to Paul's life and limb in Judea and the possibility that the contribution he's carrying to Jerusalem may not prove fully acceptable make a strong contrast with the previously mentioned "fullness of Christ's blessing" on Paul for his "serving the saints" there and thus. Hence the exhortation to pray for him, to which the address "brothers" attaches a note of urgency. "Through our Lord, Jesus Christ" makes him the agent through whom Paul channels his exhortation to the Romans, so that it carries the authority of Jesus Christ as Lord. "Through the Spirit's love" (1) refers to the love for one another that the Spirit engenders in Christians; (2) personifies this love; and (3) makes it a coagent with Christ of relaying to the Romans the exhortation to pray. (Note that it isn't the *Spirit* that Paul puts alongside Christ—rather, the *love* engendered by the Spirit.) But not merely to pray. "To *strive* . . . in prayers." Strenuous prayer. Multiple prayers. "With me" makes Paul himself an example of such praying. "To God," for only he has the power to answer the prayers.

Paul defines "in my behalf" first in terms of his being rescued from unbelieving Jewish enemies in Judea, where Jerusalem was located. How he *needed* rescue from them! And *was* rescued! See Acts 21:27–36; 23:1–35. Besides those non-Christian physical enemies, the saints in Jerusalem included Christian theological enemies of Paul (see, for example, Acts 15:5; 21:17–26; Galatians 2:11–14). In the second place, then, Paul pleads for prayer that his service in Jerusalem "may turn out to be fully acceptable," that is, accepted by all the saints there, including his theological enemies. By implication, he's hoping that the contribution from largely Gentile churches in Macedonia and Achaia, churches that he established, will win his theological enemies from their Law-bound theology over to the Law-free theology he espouses. His coming to the Romans will be "with joy" if that service proves "fully acceptable," and will be "through God's will" if Paul is "rescued from those in Judea who are disobeying [the gospel]." Such rescue and full acceptance will give him "respite" with the Romans from present danger and apprehension before he undergoes the rigors of a mission to Spain. As it turned out, he went to Rome all right, but as a prisoner after a delay of several years because of imprisonment (Acts 25–28). We don't know whether he ever made it to Spain.

A BENEDICTION
Romans 15:33

15:33: And the God of peace [be] **with all of you. Amen!** Hoping for his own respite leads Paul to wish, not that the Romans have peace, but that *the God* of peace might be with them. This is the God who Paul hopes will bring peaceful relations between Jewish and Gentile Christians in Rome (11:17–24) just as Paul is praying that through the contribution he's taking to the saints in Jerusalem God will bring peace between these blocs in the church at large. "*All* of you" implies both Jews and Gentiles, and "Amen!" underscores the wish.

A COMMENDATION OF PHOEBE
Romans 16:1–2

16:1–2: And I commend to you Phoebe, our sister who is also a deacon of the church in Cenchrea, ²**in order that you may welcome her in the Lord as befits the saints** [to be welcomed] **and** [in order that] **you may stand beside her** [to help her] **in whatever business she may need you. For also she herself has become a benefactress of many and of me myself.** The Roman Empire had no public postal system. So letters had to be carried by a letter-writer's own agent, or the writer had to take advantage of someone's traveling on other business to the letter's destination. Here, "in whatever business she may need you" favors that Phoebe was going to Rome on personal business and that Paul is taking advantage of her trip by having her deliver his letter. So that the Roman Christians may welcome her, Paul commends her as "our sister"—that is, as their as well as his fellow Christian in God's family—and as "also a deacon of the church in Cenchrea"—that is, as an assistant to the elders of the church in Cenchrea, a seaport immediately southeast of Corinth, where Paul was at the time of writing (compare Philippians 1:1; 1 Timothy 3:1–13; also Acts 6:1–6). "In the Lord [who is Christ]" describes the Spiritual location of the welcome the Romans are to give Phoebe and thereby confirms that "our sister" identifies her as a fellow Christian (see 8:1–11 for being in Christ because of being in the Spirit, who himself indwells Christ); and "as befits the saints" describes the welcome as fitting for those whom, like Phoebe, God has

consecrated to himself (which consecration is the very meaning of sainthood). If he has consecrated her, surely the Romans should welcome her. Such a welcome is to include standing beside her for help in whatever business she has to undertake in Rome. The help could consist in providing her board and room, for example. A wordplay between the verb "stand beside [Greek: *parastēte*]" and the related noun "benefactress [Greek *prostatis*, literally, 'someone who stands in front of']" highlights the commendation's purpose. Paul's citing her benefaction as a reason for helping her suggests she's going to Rome on financial business. In any case, calling her "a benefactress of many and of me myself" probably implies that she's a woman of some wealth and that she has used it for the benefit of Paul and others. Enormous emphasis on her deserving both a welcome and help accrues from "also she *herself*," "a benefactress of *many*," and "of me *myself.*"

GREETINGS
Romans 16:3–16

16:3–5a: Greet Prisca and Aquila, my coworkers in Christ Jesus, ⁴**who as such risked their own neck for my life, to whom not I alone but also all the churches of the Gentiles give thanks;** ⁵ᵃ**and** [greet] **the church** [that meets] **in their house.** Literally, to greet is to embrace, though when greetings are sent over a distance, as in 16:21–23, the physical aspect falls out and only its verbal counterpart remains. Not satisfied with a merely verbal greeting, Paul doesn't greet anybody in Rome, not even his acquaintances. Instead, he tells his nonacquaintances there to greet his acquaintances there. He hadn't evangelized Rome or yet visited the city (1:8–15; 15:22–24), but he had become acquainted with a number of his addressees in the eastern part of the empire before they moved to Rome. In the case of Prisca and Aquila, they'd left Rome under duress, been joined by Paul in Corinth, Greece, and accompanied him to Ephesus in western Asia Minor (Acts 18:1–3, 18–19, 24–26); but by now they'd returned to Rome because of the decease of Claudius, the emperor who earlier had expelled them and other Jews from Rome. Since Prisca and Aquila were Jewish Christians, the command that Paul's nonacquaintances greet them and, in following verses, others like them looks to be a command that Gentile Christians stop acting arrogantly toward Jewish Christians and embrace them instead (compare 11:17–24; 15:7). Only then will Paul get unified support from the Roman Christians for his Spanish mission.

"Prisca" is the nondiminutive equivalent "Priscilla," which is diminutive ("little Prisca"). The unusual placement of her name before that of her husband gives greater prominence to her than to him, but for what reason we don't know. In any case, Paul's mentioning her first shows Paul unprejudiced toward Prisca as a woman. "My coworkers in Christ Jesus" overlooks Paul's making tents with her and her husband according to Acts 18:3 and centers attention instead on their sharing with Paul the work of evangelism, a work that takes place primarily in the Spiritual location of Christ Jesus (see again 8:1–11), only secondarily in a geographical location. "In *Christ* Jesus" reflects Paul's, Prisca's, and Aquila's proclaiming Jesus as the Messiah. "Who as such" relates Prisca's and Aquila's risking their neck for Paul's life to working together with him in that proclamation. "Their *own* neck" accents the risk they took to save Paul from martyrdom. (The singular of "neck" is collective for their necks, and risking their neck may be more than metaphorical by posing the possibility of beheading.) We don't know any more details, but such risk-taking merits both Paul's mentioning Prisca and Aquila first and their getting an embrace from the Roman Christians unacquainted with Paul. "To whom not I alone but also all the churches of the Gentiles give thanks" supplies those nonacquaintances with another reason to embrace Prisca and Aquila: if they don't embrace them, they'll stand out like a lone sore thumb in comparison with all the other Gentile churches. (Presumably Paul refers to those churches that as Jesus' apostle to the Gentiles he himself founded.) The Roman Gentile Christians shouldn't let their good reputation, mentioned back in 1:8, slip away. Paul's point stands whether all the churches of the Gentiles give thanks to Prisca and Aquila for risking their necks to save him from martyrdom, or whether for Prisca's and Aquila's own work of evangelism both with and apart from Paul, or whether for both. Since there were no church buildings yet, the church that meets in Prisca's and Aquila's house refers to an assembly of Christian people. And since other Roman Christians are to greet that church, there must be other such assemblies meeting elsewhere in Rome.

16:5b–7: Greet Epenetus, my beloved [Christian brother], who is the firstfruits of Asia for Christ. ⁶Greet Mary, who, to be sure, has labored a lot for you. ⁷Greet Andronicus and Junia, my kinsmen and my fellow prisoners, who as such are renowned among the apostles, who [referring to Andronicus and Junia] also came to be in Christ before me. The description of Epenetus as "the firstfruits of Asia for Christ" means that he was the first convert in the Roman province of Asia in western Asia Minor. As such, he deserves to be embraced. Mary's having "labored *a lot*" and "*for you* [Paul's nonacquaintances, largely Gentile]" makes her likewise deserving, as emphasized by "to be sure." The pairing of Andronicus and Junia probably implies their being husband and wife. "My kinsmen" describes them as Paul's fellow Jews (see 9:3–5 for this meaning of "kinsmen"). "My fellow prisoners" means that they had shared an imprisonment with Paul (compare 2 Corinthians 11:23) or that apart from him but like him they were imprisoned because of proclaiming the gospel. The combination of their renown among the apostles and having come to be "in Christ" before Paul—this combination suggests not that they were among the original Twelve but that they were among a larger group who saw the risen Christ and were commissioned by him prior to his ascension and therefore prior to Paul's conversion (compare 1 Corinthians 15:5–9).

16:8–13: Greet Ampliatus, my beloved [brother] in the Lord. ⁹Greet Urbanus, our coworker in Christ, and Stachys, my beloved [Christian brother]. ¹⁰Greet Apelles, a tried and true [brother] in Christ. Greet the [brothers] from the household of Aristobulus. ¹¹Greet Herodion, my kinsman. Greet the [brothers] from the household of Narcissus who are in the Lord. ¹²Greet Tryphena and Tryphosa, who've labored in the Lord. Greet Persis, the beloved [sister] who as such has labored a lot in the Lord. ¹³Greet Rufus [compare Mark 15:21], selected in the Lord, and his mother and mine. The various descriptions of these acquaintances of Paul tell why his nonacquaintances should embrace them. If one or more of the acquaintances are beloved by him; if they're "in the Lord" (who is Jesus) and equivalently "in Christ"; if one or more are Paul and company's coworkers, "tried and true," and his kinsmen (that is, fellow Jews); if they've labored in the Lord, even "a lot"; if they've been selected by God for salvation (see chapter 9); and if one has mothered Paul—then his nonacquaintances should embrace them. It's not too much to say that God has. We don't know what trial or trials had tested Apelles and proved him a true Christian brother. "From the household of Aristobulus" and "from the household of Narcissus" imply that Aristobulus and Narcissus themselves are unbelievers or that they're dead. The pairing of Tryphena and Tryphosa probably implies their being biological sisters. Paul calls Persis "the beloved [sister in the sense of a fellow Christian]" but doesn't prefix "my" lest damaging suspicions be aroused concerning his relation to her, a woman (contrast his calling several men "*my* beloved [brother]"). In what respect Rufus's biological mother acted as Paul's metaphorical mother evades our knowledge. The high number of women and of slaves' names testifies to the concentration of God's grace on the weak and powerless (compare 1 Corinthians 1:26–31), though some of those bearing slaves' names may have obtained their freedom. Notably, it's only women whom Paul describes as having "labored a lot" (so Mary and Persis) or as having simply "labored" (so Tryphena and Tryphosa). The verb connotes working to the point of exhaustion. Maybe as women they had more leisure time than most men had to devote to church work and evangelism. But if so, they certainly didn't use the time for leisure.

16:14–16: Greet Asyncritus, Phlegon, Hermes, Patrobas, Hermas, and the brothers with them. ¹⁵Greet Philologus and Julia, Nereus and his sister, and Olympas and all the saints with them. ¹⁶Greet one another with a sacred kiss. All the churches of the Christ greet you. "And the brothers with them" suggests that Asyncritus, Phlegon, Hermes, Patrobas, and Hermas and those brothers formed a house-church besides the one meeting in the house of Prisca and Aquila (16:3–5a). "And all the saints with them" likewise suggests that Philologus and Julia, Nereus and his sister, and Olympas and those saints formed yet another house-church in Rome. Maybe, then, those listed by name in 16:5b–13 helped form the church that met in Prisca's and Aquila's house (though some have thought that those from the households of Aristobulus and Narcissus formed two other house-churches). The high number of those names could then be explained by Prisca's and Aquila's corresponding with Paul because of past prolonged and close association with him. "And *all* the saints with them" leaves no room for exceptions and prepares for "*All* the churches of the Christ greet you." That is to say, if all the churches greet you, you in turn should greet all the saints who are with Philologus and Julia and the others. The pairing of Philologus and Julia probably indicates that they're husband and wife. Since Rome is capital of the Roman Empire, it's appropriate that all the churches elsewhere in the empire greet the Christians living in Rome. "All the churches of *the* Christ" gives the greeting a formality suitable to residents of the capital city. Those churches elsewhere—that is, the people making them up—can't greet the Roman Christians with a sacred kiss, but by virtue of living in the same city the Roman Christians can greet one another with such a kiss. So Paul commands them to supplement the embrace that constitutes a greeting with a kiss that he describes as "sacred" not to indicate it shouldn't be sexual (though it shouldn't be) but to indicate its symbolizing the acceptance of one another as "saints," which by definition means "consecrated to God" and therefore sacred to him.

A WARNING AGAINST FALSE TEACHERS
Romans 16:17–20a

16:17–18: **But I'm exhorting you, brothers, to be on the lookout for those who are effecting dissensions and snares contrary to the teaching that you've learned; and be avoiding them.** [18]**For such [people] aren't slaving for our Lord, Christ—rather, for their own belly; and through sweet talk and flattery they're deceiving the hearts of the innocent** [in the sense of the naïve]. This exhortation, which has the character of a warning, marks a contrast with the preceding exhortations to greet one another. The address "brothers" lends the present exhortation a note of familial concern. Most likely, "those who are effecting dissensions and snares" are nonvegetarians who are eating all foods at table with vegetarians. If so, the vegetarians are being put off by the nonvegetarians' behavior in their presence—thus "dissensions," on the one hand—and are being pressured by that behavior to apostatize through eating all foods themselves despite not having the strength of faith to do so conscientiously—thus "snares," a figure of speech for what causes apostasy, on the other hand. "Contrary to the teaching that you've learned" refers to Paul's having just taught the strong in faith not to eat all foods or drink wine at table with the weak-faithed vegetarians and teetotalers (chapter 14). (It bears mention here that wine was ordinarily mixed with several parts water to one part wine, and that drinking undiluted wine was considered intemperate (compare the comments on Revelation 14:10; see also Proverbs 9:2, 5; 23:30–31; Augustine, *Confessions* VI. ii [2]). Those who refuse to obey this teaching are to be avoided, says Paul. In other words, don't eat at table with them lest—if you're weak in faith

when it comes to diet and wine-drinking—the example of the meat-eaters and wine-drinkers lead you to apostatize. As for them, they're slaving for their own belly with their meat-eating and wine-drinking at table with those weak in faith. The statement that "such [people] aren't slaving for our Lord, Christ" puts them outside the circle of true Christians. So "be avoiding them." Their deceptively "sweet talk and flattery" has the purpose of getting the weak in faith to transgress the boundary of their faith in matters of diet and drink.

16:19–20a: **For your obedience has reached** [the ears] **of all. Therefore I'm rejoicing over you, but I want you to be wise in** [what is] **good but guileless in** [what is] **evil.** [20a]**And the God of peace will crush Satan under your feet shortly.** Here Paul adds another reason to obey his command to avoid "those who are effecting dissensions and snares contrary to the teaching that you've learned": don't spoil your reputation for obedience, a reputation that has spread throughout the church at large (compare 1:8). (In that culture of honor and shame, reputation ranked very high in importance.) This reason for avoidance is also a compliment to the Roman Christians that should prompt them to obey the command to avoid slaves of their own bellies just as they've obeyed the command to believe the gospel (1:5; 6:17; 10:16; 15:18). Adding to the compliment is Paul's rejoicing over them because of their reputation for obedience. Yet this joy is tempered by a desire that naïveté give way to wisdom so as to do what's good (that is, what's in line with faith) and guilelessly so as not to do evil (that is, what's out of line with faith), in particular reference to the nonmoral issues discussed in 14:1–15:13. If the Romans behave wisely by doing what's good and guilelessly by not doing what's evil—that is, if they prove to be true Christians—"the God of peace [who sponsors the good of peaceful relations among his people that eventuate in the peaceful good of eternal salvation (1:7; 2:10; 5:1; 8:6; 14:17, 19; 15:13, 33)] will crush Satan [whose name means "Adversary" and who as such sponsors the evil of dissensions and apostasy-causing snares among them (16:17)] under your feet shortly [that is, at the second coming of Christ (compare Genesis 3:14–15)]." This promise encourages further obedience.

A BENEDICTION
Romans 16:20b

16:20b: **The grace of our Lord, Jesus,** [be] **with you.** The promise that God will crush Satan shortly under the Roman Christians' feet leads Paul to wish them the grace of their and his Lord—namely, Jesus—in the meantime. As usual, "grace" means undeserved favor.

FURTHER GREETINGS
Romans 16:21–23

16:21–23: **Timothy, my coworker, greets you; and Lucius and Jason and Sosipater, my kinsmen,** [greet you]. [22]**I, Tertius, the one who in the Lord has written the letter** [at Paul's dictation]**, greet you.** [23]**Gaius,** my host and [the host] **of the whole church** [here in Corinth], **greets you. Erastus, treasurer of the city, greets you; and Quartus, the brother,** [greets you]. The earliest and best manuscripts lack 16:24. Because Timothy was Paul's closest and longest-standing co-worker, he heads the list of those with Paul at the time of writing (compare Paul's writing 1 and 2 Timothy to him; also Acts 16:1–3). Timothy's and the others' sending greetings reinforces Paul's call for peaceful relations among the Christians in Rome. Because of the distance separating Paul's companions in Corinth, Greece, from those Christians in Rome, Italy, these greetings take on the character of an epistolary rather than physical embrace. Jason is probably to be equated with the Jason of Acts 17:5–9, and Sosipater probably with Sopater of Acts 20:4 (Sopater being a shortened form of Sosipater). Paul describes them and Lucius as his fellow Jews ("kinsmen" [see 9:3–5]). Jason hailed from Thessalonica and Sosipater from Berea, cities in Macedonia (next to Greece, where Corinth was located). The Lucius of Acts 13:1 hailed from Cyrene, far away in North Africa, though he did minister with Paul in Antioch, Syria. Because of geography, then, the present Lucius is less likely to be equated with the Lucius of Acts 13:1. But who knows?

"In the Lord" describes the greeting of the secretary who wrote at Paul's dictation and thus describes the secretary himself as a Christian. His name, Tertius, is Latin for "Third." Apparently his parents gave him this name because he was their third child or third son. The later-mentioned Quartus has a Latin name meaning "Fourth." Were Tertius and Quartus brothers, then, the third and fourth children or sons of their parents? Quartus is called "the brother," but Paul's use of this term for biologically unrelated Christians and the interjection of Gaius and Erastus between Tertius and Quartus reduce, though they don't obliterate, the chance that Teritus and Quartus were biological brothers. Gaius is probably to be equated with the Gaius of 1 Corinthians 1:14, whom Paul baptized in Corinth on his second missionary journey (contrast Gaius of Derbe in Asia Minor and Gaius of Macedonia in Acts 19:29; 20:4). The Corinthian Gaius was hosting Paul at the time of writing and regularly hosted the entirety of the Corinthian church. Since the church met in his house, he must have been the owner of a large house and therefore a man of some means. Erastus may have been the Erastus of Acts 19:22; 2 Timothy 4:20, but it's hard to be sure. Paul's citing Erastus's status as the treasurer of Corinth and calling the others, respectively, a coworker, kinsmen, a host, and a brother give weight to their greetings as an endorsement of the letter.

A DOXOLOGY
Romans 16:25–27

16:25–27: And to him who is able to stabilize you in accordance with my gospel and the proclamation concerning Jesus Christ, in accordance with the revelation of the secret that was kept quiet for long ages **²⁶but that has now been disclosed and made known through the prophetic Scriptures to all the nations in accordance with the command of the eternal God to elicit the obedience of faith, ²⁷to the only, wise God, through Jesus Christ, to whom** [belongs] **glory forever—. Amen!** By definition a doxology consists in giving glory to God. Giving rise to the present doxology is his ability to stabilize the Roman Christians, so that they—especially the weak in faith among them—don't apostatize. "In accordance with my gospel" means that stability entails adherence to the gospel that Paul proclaims (compare 2:16). This gospel consists in "the proclamation concerning Jesus Christ," and this proclamation accords "with the revelation of the secret that was kept quiet for long ages," which is the secret that massive salvation of Israel is to be preceded by massive salvation of Gentiles (11:25–27). The secret was revealed in the Old Testament (see the scriptural quotations scattered throughout chapters 9–11); but during the "long ages" of Old Testament history the secret was "kept quiet," so to speak, by its nonfulfillment. The callousing of Israel for the massive salvation of Gentiles has set the fulfillment in motion, however, so that the fulfillment has now disclosed the meaning of those "prophetic Scriptures" quoted in chapters 9–11 and so that they now become the means by which Paul and company make known the secret to all the nations, Jews and Gentiles alike, but especially to the Gentiles till their "fullness comes in" (11:25). ("All nations" means all ethnic groups, not nation states.) Paul and company's making known the secret accords with God's command, his having commissioned them to make it known. Paul describes God as "eternal" to suit the "long ages" during which the secret was "kept quiet" despite its "revelation." "To elicit the obedience of faith," concerning which see the comments on 1:5, tells the purpose of Paul and company's making known the secret.

Paul brings the doxology toward its close by adding to his description of God as "able" (at the start of 16:25) a description of him as "only" (over against polytheism, the pagan belief in many gods) and as "wise" (in view of his organizing the history of salvation as he has [compare 11:33–36]). "Through Jesus Christ" makes him the channel through whom glory is given to God. "To whom [be] glory forever" probably gives glory to God rather than to Jesus. For otherwise "to him who is able" and "to the only, wise God" lack a finishing touch. *What* would be to him? "To whom [be] glory *forever*" completes an emphatic wordplay in the Greek behind "ages" (*aiōniois*), "eternal" (*aiōniou*), and "forever" (*aiōnas*). "To *him*" would complete the doxology in good grammatical style. But Paul, overwhelmed by the ability, oneness, and wisdom of God, has forgotten that the doxology lacks a main clause and says "to whom" instead, thus leaving his sentence incomplete. Somehow, though, its incompleteness fits the foreverness of God's glory. "Amen!" caps the doxology with a "So be it!"

FIRST CORINTHIANS

After a greeting to the Corinthian church (1:1–3) and a thanksgiving for them (1:4–9), this letter of Paul divides into two main parts: (1) his responses to a report he has heard or read about the church (1:10–6:20) and (2) his replies to questions asked him in a letter sent to him by the church (7:1–16:4). (The church's letter hasn't survived.) A set of miscellanea concludes the letter (16:5–24). See Acts 18:1–18a for Paul's evangelization of Corinth, a city located in Greece on a narrow isthmus between the Aegean Sea to the east and the Ionian Sea to the west. He writes this letter from Ephesus, close to the west coast of Asia Minor, on his third missionary journey (Acts 18:22–23; 19:20).

ADDRESS AND GREETING
1 Corinthians 1:1–3

1:1–3: Paul, called through God's will [to be] **an apostle of Christ Jesus, and Sosthenes,** [our] **brother, ²to the church of God that's in Corinth,** [that is, to those who] **have been consecrated in Christ Jesus, called** [to be] **sacred** [in him] **along with all who in every place call on the name of our Lord, Jesus Christ, their** [Lord] **and ours: ³Grace and peace to you from God, our Father, and the Lord, Jesus Christ.** "An apostle of Christ Jesus" means someone sent by Jesus to speak and act with the very authority of Jesus himself. The prefixing of "Christ," properly a title meaning "Anointed One" ("Messiah" in Hebrew), lays a basis for that authority in Jesus' messianic office. And "called through God's will" adds further emphasis on Paul's apostolic authority in that Jesus carried out God's will when commissioning Paul (for the details of which see Acts 9:15–16; 22:11–15, 21; 26:12–18; Galatians 1:15–16). All this emphasis on Paul's authority is designed to undergird both his responses to the disturbing report he has heard about the Corinthian church and his replies to disputed questions they've asked him in their letter (compare 12:28; 2 Corinthians 10:8; 13:10). Sosthenes is probably a Corinthian who happens to be with Paul at the time of writing (Acts 18:17). If so, Paul's inclusion of him in the greeting and affectionately calling him a "brother" enlist one of the Corinthians' own number in support of what he, Paul, is going to write.

For "the church of God" see the comments on 1 Thessalonians 2:14. "Consecrated in Christ Jesus" means "set apart as sacred to God" by virtue of being "*in* Christ Jesus" and thus distinguishes Christians from the rest of humanity. People come *to be* in Christ Jesus by *believing* in him; and when they believe in him they receive the Spirit of God, who is also the Spirit of Christ, so that having the Spirit of God that indwells Christ entails being in Christ (see especially Romans 8:1–11, but also 1 Thessalonians 1:1 for the additional entailment of being "in God, the Father"). "*Called* [to be] sacred [in Christ Jesus]" refers to God's effective drawing of certain people into this field of consecration to himself and sets up a parallel with Paul's apostolic calling. The parallel implies that the Corinthian believers are just as obligated to live out their consecration to God as Paul is to live out his apostolic commission. "Along with all who in every place call on the name of our Lord, Jesus Christ" indicates that though Paul has addressed his letter only to the Corinthian church and will take up topics specific to that church, what he has to say to them about living as people consecrated to God applies to all Christians everywhere, so that the Corinthians shouldn't think Paul is "picking on them" when he proceeds to spell out the requirements of their consecration. And they should make this letter available to Christians from elsewhere. "All" and "in every place" underscore the general relevance of Paul's instructions. "Calling on the name of our Lord, Jesus Christ" means appealing to him for salvation because he's the Lord and therefore *can* save (Romans 10:13). "*Our* Lord" distinguishes him from the Caesars and pagan deities whom pagans designated their lords. "*Their* Lord and *ours*" means "the Lord of all other Christians as well as of us," reemphasizes the general relevance of this letter, and puts forward all Christians' confession of Jesus' lordship as a backdrop against which Paul will criticize splits in the Corinthian church (1:10–4:21; compare 7:17; 11:16; 14:33, 36; 16:1). For "grace and peace" see the comments on 1 Peter 1:2; 2 John 3. "From God, our Father, and the Lord, Jesus Christ" transforms an expected greeting from Paul into a greeting from God and Jesus Christ the Lord, so that once more the authority of this letter is underscored. Yet balancing the element of authority is the designation of God as "our Father," for it establishes a familial framework for Paul's coming instructions. Since Jesus Christ is the Lord as well as a human being, Paul pairs him with God, so that the two become objects of one and the same preposition, "from."

A THANKSGIVING
1 Corinthians 1:4–9

1:4–8: On the basis of God's grace that was given to you in Christ Jesus I'm always thanking my God for you ⁵in that you've been enriched in him in every

[respect]—[that is,] **in every** [kind of] **speech and every** [kind of] **knowledge,** [6]**just as the testimony about the Christ** [= Paul's testimony that Jesus is the Messiah] **has been confirmed among you,** [7]**so that you aren't falling short in any gracious gift while eagerly awaiting the revelation of our Lord, Jesus Christ,** [8]**who will also confirm you until the end** [so as to be] **unaccusable in the Day of our Lord, Jesus Christ.** Having struck an authoritative note in 1:1–3, Paul now strikes a complimentary note. The compliment consists in stating his recognition that the Corinthians have a wealth of gifts having to do with speech and knowledge; and this compliment gets added emphasis from his "always thanking [his] God for [the Corinthians]," from his description of their enrichment as having "confirmed" among them "the testimony about the Christ," from his statement that as a group they "aren't falling short in any gracious gift," and from his description of them as "eagerly awaiting the revelation of our Lord, Jesus Christ." The details concerning the gracious gifts will follow in chapters 12–14. Meanwhile the multifaceted compliment has the purpose of winning an acceptance of Paul's coming responses and replies. Yet to forestall the Corinthians' taking pride in the compliment, he bases his thanking God for them on "God's grace [= ill-deserved favor] that was given to [them] in Christ Jesus [not because of what they were or are in themselves]" and describes their enrichment in terms of "gracious gifts." By calling God *my* God Paul supports what he has to say with a back reference to his being an apostle of Christ Jesus "through God's will" (1:1). "The revelation of our Lord, Jesus Christ" will happen at "the end," which equates with "the Day of our Lord, Jesus Christ"—in other words, the day when he comes back in a full display and exercise of his lordship (compare 1 Thessalonians 4:13–5:10; 2 Thessalonians 2:1–12). "Who will also confirm you until the end [so as to be] unaccusable in the Day of our Lord, Jesus Christ" assures the Corinthians that their "eagerly awaiting" that revelation is well justified. They'll be confirmed—that is, well-established in Christian faith—just as "the testimony about the Christ has [already] been confirmed among [them]." As a result, no one will be able to accuse them of apostasy when the Lord returns. The four occurrences in 1:1–8 of "*our* Lord" imply a foundation of shared faith on which Paul will build his coming responses and replies.

1:9: God [is] **faithful, through whom you were called into the fellowship of his Son, Jesus Christ, our Lord.** "God [is] faithful" continues the assurance in 1:8. So he'll *faithfully* confirm the Corinthians "until the end." "*Through* whom you were called" makes God the agent of calling, which way of putting it involves him as closely as possible in the calling itself. As indicated by "Jesus Christ, our Lord," "the fellowship of [God's] Son" refers to Christians' sharing Jesus Christ as their Lord (versus, as before, other lords: Caesars and pagan deities) and therefore once again implies a foundation of shared faith on which Paul will build his coming responses and replies.

RESPONSES TO A REPORT ABOUT THE CORINTHIAN CHURCH
1 Corinthians 1:10–6:20

ON SPLITS IN THE CORINTHIAN CHURCH
1 Corinthians 1:10–4:21

1:10–12: But I urge you, brothers, through the name of our Lord, Jesus Christ, that you all say the same thing and [that] **there be no splits among you but** [that] **you be put back together in the same** [turn of] **mind and in the same purpose.** [11]**For concerning you, my brothers, it has been pointed out to me by Chloe's** [household members] **that there are contentions among you.** [12]**I'm saying this** [in other words]: **that each of you is saying, "I belong to Paul," but "I belong to Apollos," but "I belong to Cephas," but "I belong to Christ."** As often, "brothers" introduces an exhortation on an affectionate note; but in view of Paul's discussion of divisions among the Corinthians, the present such address implies they should restore family unity in their church. "Through the *name* of our Lord, Jesus Christ" adds to the exhortation the authority of Jesus Christ *as Lord*. "That you all say the same thing" exhorts the Corinthians to adopt the same slogan rather than different slogans ("I belong to Paul" [and so forth]). "That . . . there be no splits among you" alludes to the divisive effect of those slogans. The unifying slogan won't become wholly apparent till 3:21–23. Everybody's "say[ing] the same thing"—that is, adopting the same slogan— will "put [them] back together." This mending of their fractured fellowship will issue in a shared mindset ("the same [turn of] mind") and in a shared objective ("the same purpose").

A repetition of the address, "brothers," and the addition to it of "my" deepen Paul's expression of affectionate concern over the report of internal contentions by members of Chloe's household. (We know no more about Chloe, the members of her household, or how they communicated with Paul, whether by oral report in a visit to him or by way of a letter.) The contentions consist in divided personal loyalties. "I belong to Paul" comes first on the list of slogans representing those loyalties in order to emphasize Paul's rejection of loyalty even to him. For Apollos, see especially Acts 18:24–19:7. "Cephas" is the Aramaic form of Simon's Greek nickname, "Peter," about which see the comments on Matthew 16:16–18 (and see 1 Corinthians 9:5; Galatians 2:11; 1 Peter 5:13 for his itinerant ministry). Though an explanation of "I belong to Christ" will appear in 3:21–23, Paul doesn't explain how or why these divided loyalties arose; so speculation serves no good purpose. At the same time, "*each* of you is saying" stresses the extent of the divisions; and a grammatical construction in Paul's Greek text stresses the slogans' divisiveness. (A *somewhat* literal translation of the construction goes as follows: "On the one hand . . . on the other hand . . . on the other hand . . . on the other hand." But then we have too many hands.[1])

1:13–17: Has the Christ been divided? Paul wasn't crucified for you, was he? Or were you baptized in Paul's name? [14][In view of my misbegotten followers] **I'm thanking God that I baptized none of you except Crispus and Gaius,** [15]**lest anyone [of you] should say that you were baptized in my name.** [16](**But I also baptized the household of Stephanas; as for the rest, I don't know whether I baptized anyone else.)** [17]**For Christ didn't send me to baptize [people]—rather, to proclaim the gospel, not with wisdom of speech, lest the cross of the Christ be voided.** Here Paul counters the divisive slogans with a satirical question that both he and the Corinthians hardly need to answer: "Has the Christ been divided?" This question arises out of Paul's teaching that all believers are "in Christ," so that divisions among them falsely imply a division of Christ himself. "*The* Christ" calls attention to his being the corporate Christ. Paul counters also with a question that the Corinthians are expected to answer: "*Paul* wasn't crucified for you, was he?" Of course not, as they well know; for otherwise he wouldn't be writing this letter. Then he counters with a question that he himself answers: "Or were you baptized *in Paul's name?*" But instead of answering that he hadn't baptized *any* of the Corinthians in his own name—that is, to gain a following for himself—he proceeds to answer that he hadn't baptized *very many* of them *at all*. Yet the exceptions of Crispus and Gaius (on whom see Acts 18:8; Romans 16:23) do prove that he hadn't baptized anyone in his name, for baptizing to establish a following of his own would have led him to baptize as many as he could. He's reminded of further exceptions ("the household of Stephanas"), but the very facts that he didn't at first remember having baptized them and that he doesn't remember whether he baptized anyone else add further proof of his not having baptized people to gain a personal following. So too does his thanking God that he didn't. For if he'd baptized people for that purpose and gained so few followers by doing so, he'd have little reason to thank God—and he wouldn't have the present argument with which to denounce divisions in the Corinthian church.

But why did Paul baptize anybody at all if Christ didn't send him to baptize people? The question is wrongly framed. Baptism as such isn't at issue. Baptism in Paul's name is at issue. Christ didn't send him to gain a personal following by baptizing people; but he did send Paul to proclaim the gospel, which has to do with "the cross of the Christ," not with anything having to do with Paul. (Incidentally, "send" is the verbal counterpart of "apostle" in 1:1.) Both philosophy (which means "love of wisdom") and eloquence ("speech") were highly prized—indeed, celebrated—in Greece and throughout Greco-Roman culture. So if Paul had proclaimed the gospel with eloquently expressed wisdom ("wisdom of speech"), a Corinthian audience would have attributed their conversions to his abilities as a philosopher and orator and for that reason would have declared subservience to him en masse. As it was, only a fraction of believers had, against his intention, declared subservience to him. Crucifixion was considered the very most shameful way to die. By human standards, then, Paul's proclamation of "the cross of the Christ" was guaranteed to prove that Jesus couldn't have been the Christ, the Messiah, and that the proclamation brought bad news, not good news (as "gospel" means). Whether or not Paul could have wowed an audience with "wisdom of speech," he didn't; and the conversion of Corinthians proved that the Christ's cross wasn't void. Christ himself purposed that his cross not be voided with eloquent wisdom. For to him, not to any herald of his, belongs all the glory. But what's meant by "voided"?

1:18–19: For on the one hand the speech about the cross is foolishness to those who are being destroyed. On the other hand, it's God's power for us who are being saved. [19]**For it's written, "I'll destroy the wisdom of the wise, and I'll nullify the astuteness of the astute** [Isaiah 29:14].**"** Here Paul explains the meaning of "voided" at the tail end of the preceding sentence. "Emptied [of power]" is what it means. The speech about the Christ's cross seems foolish to unbelievers, so that its ability to draw any belief at all demonstrates the power of God. But to emphasize this power, Paul writes "for us *who are being saved*" rather than "for us *who believe*," and also writes "to those *who are being destroyed*" rather than "to those *who don't believe*," because the destruction of unbelievers demonstrates God's power just as the salvation of believers does. (And to bring out the contrast with "who are being saved," the translation "who are being destroyed" does a better job than the translation "who are perishing" does.) The quotation of Isaiah 29:14 supports directly the demonstration of God's power in the destruction of the worldly wise and astute, who regard "the speech about the cross" as "foolishness," and supports indirectly the demonstration of God's power in the salvation of those who recognize that same speech to be good news ("gospel"). There may be something of a wordplay between the Greek word for "I'll destroy," *apolō*, and the Greek form of Apollos's name back in 1:12, *apollō*, but not with any detectable criticism of Apollos on Paul's part.

1:20–22: Where [is] the wise [man]? Where the scholar? Where the debater belonging to this age? God

---

[1]Some have suggested that the Corinthians weren't actually giving voice to slogans but that Paul is caricaturing the Corinthians by saying that because of their divisions it's *as though* they're saying they belong as slaves to Paul or Apollos or Cephas or Christ. But this suggestion runs into trouble at 3:21–23, where Paul says that Paul, Apollos, and Cephas belong to the Corinthians rather than vice versa. If the Corinthians weren't using the present slogans, Paul's later reversal of the slogans, at least of the first three, would pack no punch. The Corinthians could retort that they'd never used these slogans in the first place. Besides, it was considered an honor and privilege to belong as a slave to a prominent and powerful figure, such as Paul, Apollos, and Cephas were in Christian circles.

has made foolish the world's wisdom, hasn't he? [21]For since in God's wisdom the world didn't know God through wisdom, God delighted to save through the foolishness of the proclamation [of the Christ's cross] those who are believing, [22]since also Jews ask for signs and Greeks seek for wisdom. "The wise [man]" is one who thinks a crucified Christ makes no logical sense. "The scholar" is one who thinks a crucified Christ makes no scriptural sense. "The debater" is one who thinks a crucified Christ makes no rhetorical sense. That is to say, such a Christ lacks appeal. "Belonging to this age" describes "the debater" as thinking in terms of the here and now rather than in terms of what's coming at "the revelation of our Lord, Jesus Christ"—in other words, as short-sighted. By implication, "belonging to this age" probably applies also to "the wise" and "the scholar." In effect, God's having "made foolish the world's wisdom" and having "delighted to save those who are believing" answer the three questions beginning with "Where?" The wise man, the scholar, and the debater fall into the category of the foolish and unsaved. "The world" consists of unbelieving human beings. "God has *made* foolish the world's wisdom" by providing salvation through a means that seems like foolishness to them but is in fact his wisdom. And he did so not just because "the world didn't know God through [their] wisdom," but because it was "in *God's* wisdom" that they didn't know him that way. In other words, he wisely determined that they wouldn't, lest they take to themselves credit for knowing God.

God's saving those who are believing contrasts with his having made foolish the world's wisdom. But Paul doesn't say simply that God saves those who are believing. He says that "God *delighted* to save those who are believing," which at one and the same time suggests he has *not* delighted in making foolish the world's wisdom (for he desires the salvation of all [1 Timothy 2:3–4]) and gives assurance to believers (for his delighting in their salvation ensures it). "Through the foolishness of the proclamation [of the Christ's cross]" states the form in which salvation comes. It comes in the form of a proclamation that seems foolish from the standpoint of worldly wisdom, worldly scholarship, and worldly rhetoric. "Since also Jews ask for signs and Greeks seek for wisdom" brings out why "the world didn't know God through wisdom." The world is made up of Jews and Gentiles, but because of the use of the Greek language throughout the world as Paul knew it and also in this case because the love of wisdom ("philosophy") was associated especially with Greece, where Corinth was located, he calls the Gentiles "Greeks." He has already taken care of "the debaters" by referring to "the foolishness of the proclamation" in opposition to skillful rhetoric. He takes care of the scriptural scholar by referring to Jews, who ask for signs in fulfillment of Scripture (see Matthew 12:38–42, for example). And he takes care of the wise man by referring to Greeks, who seek for wisdom. Together, these references expose the sentiments of those who make up the unbelieving "world." See the comments on 1 Thessalonians 4:5 on not knowing God.

1:23–25: But we—we're proclaiming Christ crucified, a snare to Jews, on the one hand, foolishness to Gentiles, on the other hand, [24]but to them [who are] called [by God (1:2)]—both Jews and Greeks—Christ [as] God's power and God's wisdom, [25]because God's foolish [proclamation] is wiser than human beings' [wisdom], and [because] God's weak [proclamation is] stronger than human beings' [power]. The emphasis on "we" makes for a strong contrast between proclaimers of Christ crucified and the foolishly unbelieving Jews and Gentiles. The crucified Christ is a snare—that is, a stumbling block that causes those not called by God to fall into his judgment—to Jews because for them crucifixion isn't a sign of messiahship. Quite the opposite, in fact; for, generally speaking, they expected the Messiah to save them powerfully from Roman domination or, if God saved them first, to rule the world subsequently with power (compare Galatians 3:13; Deuteronomy 21:23). Likewise, the crucified Christ is foolishness to Gentiles because for them crucifixion indicates that something has gone amiss. Victims of crucifixion were a laughingstock. To stress the snare and the foolishness, Paul ignores Jesus' resurrection for the time being and focuses on Christ as forever the one who once was crucified. Because of the snare and the foolishness, it takes God's call to believe in the crucified Christ. Happily, though, he has effectively called "both Jews and Greeks" to do so. For those sign-seeking Jews who've been called, then, the crucified Christ is "God's power" for their eternal salvation, rather than an in*sign*ificant weakling who only pretended to messiahship; and for those wisdom-seeking Greeks who've been called, the crucified Christ is "God's wisdom" for their knowledge of God, rather than a Jewish fool who thought he could resist Roman authority successfully. Paul accepts that to Gentiles the proclamation of the crucified Christ is foolish and that to Jews it's weak, but declares that in fact this supposedly foolish proclamation decreed by God surpasses the wisdom of human beings, represented by Paul's switching from "Gentiles" to "Greeks" because of the Greeks' love of worldly wisdom, and declares that this supposedly weak proclamation decreed by God surpasses the power of human beings.

1:26–29: For look at [God's] calling of you [to salvation], brothers, because not many [of you are] wise according to flesh [= by human standards], not many [are] powerful, not many [are] well-pedigreed [= blue-blooded, born into aristocracy]. [27]Rather, God has selected the world's foolish things in order to shame the wise, and God has selected the world's weak things in order to shame the strong things, [28]and God has selected the world's unpedigreed things, and the things that are treated as nothings, the things that don't exist [by the world's standards], in order to incapacitate the things that do exist [*some*things by the world's standards], [29]so that no flesh at all might boast in God's sight. Paul explains that the supposedly foolish and weak proclamation of the crucified Christ corresponds to the supposed foolishness and weakness of most believers in such a Christ, and that this correspondence stems from God's purpose that no human being should boast. Since flesh turns to dust at death (Genesis 3:19), Paul uses "no flesh at all" to stress the frailty of human beings as compared to Almighty God. "In his sight" locates the site where boasting might otherwise occur, that is, in God's immediate presence and therefore at the Last Judgment. The command, "look at [God's] calling of you," has the purpose of keeping Christians from boasting even prior to their standing there and then. As often, the address "brothers" introduces the command with affection. Lying behind God's call is his selection of the world's foolish, weak, and unpedigreed things (compare Romans 8:29–30). Not only will no flesh boast in God's sight. Also, again at the Last Judgment, God will shame the worldly wise and powerful and well-pedigreed by making apparent his having selected, not them, but the world's foolish and weak and unpedigreed, to which Paul adds for emphasis "the things that are treated as nothings," so that they "don't [even] exist" so far as the world is concerned. He even adds that God has selected them "to incapacitate the things that do exist," that do count in the world's estimation. "The things" refers to people, but the neuter gender represented by "things" stresses the *qualities* of peoples as wise or foolish, powerful or weak, well-pedigreed or unpedigreed, existent or nonexistent by human standards.

1:30–31: And out of him you are in Christ Jesus, who from God became for us wisdom—both righteousness and consecration and redemption—³¹in order that just as it's written, "The one who's boasting is to be boasting in the Lord [Jeremiah 9:24]." "*Out of* him" means "by God's doing," but the more literal translation produces a better complement to "*in* Christ Jesus." To be in Christ Jesus is for God to relate to you as he relates to him, because so far as God is concerned you've been incorporated into him. And since the crucified Christ is God's wisdom (1:23–24), to be in Christ Jesus is to have from God the wisdom of God. Paul lists the ingredients of this wisdom, all three of which are beneficial to God's selected ones. See the comments on 2 Corinthians 5:21 that it's God's saving righteousness, not Christ's moral righteousness, that believers have in Christ. Similarly, it's God's consecration of them to himself, not Christ's consecration of himself to God, that they have in Christ. Again, it's God's redemption of them, not any imaginary redemption of Christ, that they have in Christ (see Romans 3:21–25a with Ephesians 1:7; Colossians 1:14). Confirming that God is the source of this righteousness, consecration, and redemption is the foregoing description of wisdom as originating "from God." For if righteousness, consecration, and redemption make up the ingredients of this wisdom, then they too must originate from God because they're God's. In accordance with preceding statements concerning the cross, "Christ Jesus became for us wisdom" in and through his crucifixion. "*For* us" means "in our case and for our benefit." "Righteousness" describes God's saving us as the right thing for him to do because we're

in Christ Jesus. "Consecration" describes God's saving us as segregating us from the world to be sacred to him because we're in Christ Jesus his Son as others are not. And "redemption" describes God's saving us as liberating us because we're in Christ Jesus, liberating us according to this context from enslavement to the world's foolishness.

Again Paul quotes the Old Testament, this time not to give a *reason* for the point just made (as in 1:19) but to issue a *command* growing out of the point just made. As to boasting, 1:29 has already dealt with that topic. But there we had an expression of divine purpose. Here we have an expression of scriptural and apostolic command. There we had a blockage of boasting. Here we have a command to boast. There we had a denial of boasting "in God's sight" as to location. Here we have an affirmation of boasting "in the Lord" as to subject matter. There we had God in view because of his coming judgment. Here we have the Lord, Jesus Christ, in view because of what he has already become for us. And since the Lord in whom one is to boast is Christ, Paul hints at the meaning of "I belong to Christ" in 1:12 and anticipates what he'll say plainly in 3:21–23, so that we're brought back to what prompted his introducing the proclamation of Christ crucified—namely, divisions in the church that were based on boasts of belonging to Paul, Apollos, and Cephas. It's looking as though the slogan, "I belong to Christ," may not be a divisive one.

2:1–2: And when I came to you, brothers, I did not come in accordance with superiority of speech or of wisdom while announcing to you the testimony of God. ²For I'd made a judgment not to know anything among you except Jesus Christ, and this one [as] **crucified.** The address, "brothers," suits Paul's putting himself forward as one whose style of proclamation at Corinth ("not . . . in accordance with superiority of speech or of wisdom") matched the previously mentioned content of proclamation ("Christ crucified, a snare to Jews . . . foolishness to Gentiles" [1:23]). "Superiority of speech" means oratorical eloquence, and "superiority . . . of wisdom" means philosophical brilliance (compare the comments on 1:17). By equating his seemingly foolish and weak proclamation of Christ crucified with "the testimony of God," Paul enlists God himself as a witness for that proclamation—and legitimately, because it contains God's superior wisdom.² Since Paul "did not *come* [to the Corinthians] in accordance with superiority of speech or of wisdom," it looks as though his "judgment not to know anything among [them] except Jesus Christ" was made earlier than his arrival. In any case, his mentioning a deliberate decision strengthens his denial that he wanted to gain a personal following. We might have expected him to say, "to *proclaim* anything among you except Jesus Christ." Instead, he says "to *know* . . ."

---

²A number of early manuscripts have "the secret of God" instead of "the testimony of God"; but the difference in meaning isn't great, because "the secret of God" consists here in Christ crucified just as "the testimony of God" means his testimony to the crucified Christ.

for emphasis on the acknowledgment in his proclamation that there's no room for allegiances to the likes of Paul, Apollos, and Cephas (compare the comments on 1:31; 3:21–23). "And this one [as] crucified" harks back to 1:10–25, where Paul pitted the proclamation of the crucified Christ against all boasting in celebrities such as Paul, Apollos, and Cephas. It's looking again as though the slogan, "I belong to Christ," isn't a bad one.

2:3–5: And I came to be with you in weakness and in fear and in much trembling, ⁴and my speech and my proclamation [were] **not** [couched] **in persuasive words of wisdom; rather,** [they were accompanied] **by a demonstration of the Spirit and of power, ⁵in order that your faith might not be in the wisdom of human beings—rather, in God's power.** In 2:1–2 Paul described how he did *not* come to the Corinthians. Now he describes how he *did* come to them, though with an echo of how he didn't. The two descriptions dovetail in that the weakness, fear, and trembling that characterized his coming complement his not coming "with superiority of speech or of wisdom." "Weakness" often means "illness, sickness," so that Paul may mean he was sick when he came to Corinth (compare 2 Corinthians 10:10; 12:5–10 and especially Galatians 4:13). If so, sickness may have contributed to, or even underlain, his fear and trembling. "Much" exacerbates the trembling. Might a bout of malarial fever have caused the trembling and led Paul to fear for his life? In any case, his weakness corresponds to God's weakness, which is stronger than human strength (1:25); and Paul mentions his coming in a state of weakness, fear, and trembling to portray himself as unworthy of anyone's saying, "I belong to Paul." To the same end Paul denies that the addressees were converted because of admirably wise and persuasive rhetoric on his part. He didn't use such rhetoric. The credit goes instead to the Spirit's accompanying demonstration of God's power. Since the plural of "power" is regularly used in the sense of "miracles" (that is, deeds of supernatural power), "a demonstration of the Spirit and of power" refers to miracles performed by Paul in the power of the Holy Spirit so as to confirm that his proclamation of the crucified Christ derived from God and represents God's power despite the proclamation's lack of eloquence and philosophical brilliance (compare Romans 15:18–19; 2 Corinthians 6:7; 12:12; Galatians 3:5; 1 Thessalonians 1:5). "In order that your faith might not be in the wisdom of human beings" criticizes the lionizing of Paul, Apollos, and Cephas that's represented in the slogans quoted in 1:12. "Rather, in God's power" implies that the Spirit's demonstration of power in miracles matches or represents "God's power" in "the speech about the cross" (1:18).

2:6–8: But we do speak wisdom among the mature, but not the wisdom belonging to this age, nor of the rulers belonging to this age, who are being incapacitated. ⁷Rather, we're speaking God's wisdom in [the form of] **a secret, the hidden** [wisdom] **that God predetermined prior to the ages for our glory, ⁸which**

[wisdom] **none of the rulers of this age knew** [= understood]. **For if they'd known** [it], **they wouldn't have crucified the Lord of glory.** "But we do speak wisdom" qualifies "my speech and my proclamation [were] not [couched] in persuasive words of wisdom [as counted by human standards of rhetoric and philosophy]" (2:4). "Among the mature" refers to those whom Paul has previously described as "called" and "selected" by God in distinction from the rest of humanity (1:9, 27–28), describes them here as mature in that by virtue of God's having called and selected them they've understood the wisdom of God in the proclamation of Christ as crucified, and implies that the rest of humanity, including its vaunted rulers, are immature and childish in their considering that proclamation to be foolish. "The wisdom of this age" means the wisdom which thinks in terms of the here and now rather than in terms of what's coming at "the revelation of our Lord, Jesus Christ"—in other words, wisdom that's short-sighted and therefore inferior to God's foolishness (compare 1:20, 25). "The rulers belonging to this age" likewise means rulers who are ruling only temporarily. Paul mentions them here to make a contrast between their political power and "God's power" in "the speech about the cross" (1:18). "Who are being incapacitated" indicates their growing loss of power—despite their having crucified Christ—through the effective proclamation of God's wisdom, and also looks forward to their complete loss of power at "the revelation of our Lord, Jesus Christ . . . in the Day of our Lord, Jesus Christ" (1:7–8).

According to 1:21, 24–25, 30, "God's wisdom" consists in his determining that the uncalled, unselected world would *not* know him through their brand of wisdom but that the called and selected *would* know him through the seemingly foolish and weak proclamation of the crucified Christ. Paul says that God hid this wisdom of his in the form of "a secret." That is to say, the gospel of Christ as crucified was hidden from all in the past (though see the next verses for its recent revelation to believers) and remains hidden to unbelievers. "Predetermined prior to the ages" describes God's hidden wisdom in a way which denies that Christ's crucifixion occurred by accident. The gospel concerning it is not at all an ad hoc solution to some unforeseen problem. That God's wisdom was hidden for so long a time highlights the privilege of knowing it now by faith in the crucified Christ; and a sense of this privilege will undercut divisive boasting in one or another ecclesiastical celebrity, as though they merit adulation. "For our glory" adds that in his wisdom God predetermined to glorify believers in compensation for their belief in the shamefully crucified Christ, a belief that brought shame on them too. For the occurrence of this compensation at Jesus' return and their resurrection, see 15:43; Romans 5:2; 8:18–25; Colossians 1:27; 3:4; 1 Thessalonians 2:12; 2 Thessalonians 2:14; 2 Timothy 2:10. The coming glorification of believers in general makes the present glorification of supposed celebrities among them both unnecessary and inappropriate. The earlier-mentioned "wisdom . . .

of the rulers belonging to this age" is undone by their ignorance of God's wisdom; but their very ignorance led to the outworking of his wisdom in that had they known it they wouldn't have crucified the Christ, whose crucifixion constituted that wisdom. But Paul calls Christ "the Lord of glory" to point up that Christ's glory as the now exalted Lord has eclipsed the shame of his crucifixion and thus ensured the coming glorification of those who've been "consecrated [to God] in Christ Jesus" (1:2; compare 1:30). For if they're in him, what's true of him is bound to be true of them as well.

2:9–11: **Nevertheless** [that is, despite the crucifixion of "the Lord of glory"], **just as it's written, "Things that an eye hasn't seen and** [that] **an ear hasn't heard and** [that] **haven't come up onto the heart of a human being** [= haven't entered human reason or imagination]**, things that God has prepared for those who love him"** [Isaiah 64:4]—¹⁰**yet** [in contrast with their previous nonrevelation] **God has revealed** [those things] **to us through the Spirit. For the Spirit investigates all things, even the deep things of God.** The things that in Isaiah's time hadn't been seen, heard of, reasoned out, or imagined but that God, in accordance with his predetermination, had already prepared "for those who love him"—these things make up "our glory," which is yet to come (2:7). "Those who love him" do so in appropriate response to God's having selected, called, saved, redeemed, consecrated, and redeemed them. Though not yet realized, the things that make up "our glory" have been "revealed to us" by God "through the Spirit," so that those who love God by having believed the proclamation of the crucified Christ aren't saddled with "the [false] wisdom of this age," which equates with the ignorance of "the rulers of this age." With "through the Spirit" Paul lays claim for himself and other Christians to new revelation communicated by God's Spirit and supplementing the Old Testament Scriptures as represented by the quotation taken from Isaiah. The Spirit's investigation of "*all* things" implies that those Scriptures contained only *some* things which God wanted his own to know, and that new revelation in the gospel makes up for the old omissions. "*Investigates* all things, even the *deep* things of God" portrays the Spirit as a kind of detective, explorer, or researcher who just because he's the Spirit of God can plumb the depths of God's predetermined wisdom. This portrayal carries an assurance of the new revelation's authenticity. Paul then elaborates this assurance, the elaboration starting with an analogy: ¹¹**For who of human beings knows the things of a human being except the human being's spirit within him? So too no one has known the things of God except God's Spirit.** According to a Greek truism it takes like to understand like (compare our saying that "it takes one to know one"). The application of Paul's analogy to God and his Spirit indicates that apart from revelation through the Spirit those who love God wouldn't know the things he has prepared for them. So whatever Paul, Apollos, and Cephas may have proclaimed, they don't deserve any credit for it and therefore shouldn't be adulated.

2:12–13: **But we haven't received the world's spirit. Rather,** [we've received] **the Spirit** [that has come to us] **out of God, in order that we may know the things bestowed us by God,** ¹³**which things we're also speaking, not in words taught by human wisdom—rather, in** [words] **taught by the Spirit as we interlink Spiritual** [things] **with Spiritual** [people]. Because of the references to speaking and teaching, "we" appears to mean Paul, Apollos, and Cephas—perhaps also Paul's missionary companions. "The world's spirit" is the spirit of human beings, just referenced in 2:11. Collectively, their spirits make up the world's spirit. Paul, Apollos, and Cephas *have* a human spirit, as do human beings who make up "the world" (compare 1 Thessalonians 5:23). But Paul, Apollos, and Cephas "haven't *received* the world's spirit" as they *have* received the Spirit who has emanated to them from God. Which isn't to deny that all believers have received God's Spirit (to the contrary, see 12:13; Romans 8:9, for example), but Paul is here concerned to attribute his and his colleagues' knowledge of the things they speak about to the Spirit's revelation rather than to any human insight of their own that should be celebrated by the Corinthians. "The things bestowed us by God" describes the "things that God has prepared for those who love him" as given for free. Again, then, there's no room for boasting except in the Lord. "Not in words taught by human wisdom" reprises the denial of having used rhetorical eloquence and philosophical acumen to persuade the Corinthians. "In [words] taught by the Spirit" sharpens the revelation by way of contrasting the unadorned wording of the Spirit's instruction with the polished wording of orators and philosophers. Paul and others "interlink Spiritual [things] with Spiritual [people]" when they speak the words taught them by the Spirit to people who receive the Spirit because God selected and called them (1:2, 9, 26–30). The capitalization of "Spiritual" underscores the role of God's Spirit as the basis for interlinking the things spoken with the people spoken to.

2:14–16: **But the soulish human being doesn't welcome the things of God's Spirit. For they're foolishness to him; and he can't know** [= understand] [them]**, because they're Spiritually examined.** ¹⁵**But the Spiritual** [human being] **examines all things, but he himself is examined by no one.** ¹⁶**For "who has known** [= understood] **the Lord's mind** [so as to be someone] **who will advise him?"** [Isaiah 40:13]. **But we have Christ's mind.** "The soulish human being" is one animated solely by his natural life (the soul), in contrast with "the Spiritual [human being]," who has received the Spirit of God because of believing and being in Christ (see the comments on 1:1–3). It takes the *possession* of God's Spirit to "welcome" and "understand" "the *things* of God's Spirit," what have just been called the "Spiritual things" "taught by the Spirit" to Paul and others and being spoken by them (2:12–13). Otherwise, those things seem like "foolishness . . . because they're Spiritually examined," that is, can be judged properly only by a "Spiritual [human being]," one who has God's Spirit. Such a human being "examines all things," which things refer specifically to "all things, even the deep things of God," that "the Spirit investigates" (2:11). The Spiritual human being "is examined by no one" in the sense of not being judged properly by any "soulish human being." That is to say, non-Christians' judgment that Christians are foolish to have believed the gospel of Christ crucified—this judgment is wrong. The quotation of Isaiah 40:13 supports the assertion that the un-Spiritual person doesn't judge the Spiritual one properly, and supports it by denying with a rhetorical question which itself denies that anyone apart from the Spirit has understood "the Lord's mind" so as to "advise him." Because "the soulish human being" lacks the Spirit, his judgment of "the Spiritual [human being]" doesn't correspond to "the Lord's mind." But having the Spirit includes "hav[ing] Christ's mind," because for Paul the Lord of whom Isaiah spoke is Jesus Christ, and the Spirit of God is also the Spirit of his Son, Jesus Christ (see especially Romans 8:1–2, 9). To have the mind of Christ is to know his thoughts, and they are one and the same as the things that "God has revealed to us through the Spirit" (2:10).

3:1–3a: And I, brothers, wasn't able to speak to you [in chapters 1–2] **as to Spiritual** [people]**—rather, as to fleshy** [people]**, as to infants in Christ. ²I caused you to drink milk, not** [to eat] **solid food. For you weren't yet able** [to eat solid food]. **Not even now are you yet able** [to eat solid food, however]; **³ᵃfor you're still fleshly.** Again the affectionate address "brothers" softens a criticism of the Corinthian believers (compare 1:10); and as in 2:12–16, "Spiritual people" refers to people who've received the Holy Spirit because of their believing in the crucified Christ. But though the addressees have all *received* the Spirit and therefore *are* Spiritual (see especially 2:12; 12:13), Paul says he can't *speak* to them as to Spiritual people. Their behavior doesn't correspond to their possession of the Spirit—rather, to their being made of flesh ("fleshy"), which represents frailty (here, moral frailty in a broad sense). The thought of frailty leads to "infants," weak as they are, and contrasts with "the mature" in 2:6.³ "In Christ" describes these infant-like adults as Christians despite their fleshiness. The analogy to infants leads in turn to Paul's having given the addressees "milk" to drink, as though he were a lactating mother (compare 1 Thessalonians 2:7; Galatians 4:19, which seem to rule out a present comparison of himself to a male nurse who in the ancient world fed infants with goat's milk). The milk stands for Paul's earlier exposition of the gospel concerning the crucified Christ. The "solid food" that Paul didn't feed them because of their inability to eat it represents further teaching that would make no sense to Christians whose behavior doesn't correspond to their possession of the Spirit. "*Not even now* are you

---

³In 2:6 the Corinthian believers were "mature" in that unlike nonbelievers they accepted God's wisdom in the proclamation of Christ crucified. Here they're like "infants" in that their divisive behavior has made them incapable of tolerating the solid food of further teaching.

yet able, however; for you're *still* fleshly" brings the addressees' past inability contrastively and therefore emphatically into the present so as to highlight a problem that needs solving forthwith, the problem of ongoing splits in the Corinthian church. But this time "fleshly" (which differs from "fleshy") stresses the *influence* of moral frailty on behavior more than moral frailty as the *makeup* of people who are misbehaving.

Paul's reference to fleshly influence gets an explanation in *3:3b–4:* **For insofar as jealousy and strife** [are] **among you, you're fleshly and walking about in accordance with human being, aren't you?** Implied answer: Yes, the weakness of your humanity ("human being"), represented by perishable "flesh," is evident in the jealousy and strife that characterize your behavior (for which "walking about" is a figure of speech). **⁴For whenever someone says, "I belong to Paul," but another** [says], **"I belong to Apollos," you're human beings, aren't you** [in the sense of behaving out of the jealousy and strife typical of human beings apart from the Holy Spirit]**?** As compared with 1:12, "I belong to Cephas" and "I belong to Christ" drop out, though both Cephas and Christ will come back into the picture at 3:21–23. So perhaps Paul cites the first two slogans listed in 1:12 simply as examples, though it's possible he omits the Cephas-slogan here because Cephas had never visited Corinth whereas Apollos had (Acts 18:27–19:1), and omits the Christ-slogan for a reason that will become apparent in 3:21–23.

3:5–7: Therefore [since you're behaving like fleshly human beings with your slogans, I ask you] **what is Apollos? And what is Paul?** [They're] **servants** [not slavemasters to whom you belong as implied in your slogans] **through whom you believed, and to each as the Lord gave!** That is, Jesus the Lord gave to each one, Apollos and Paul, a service to perform in getting the Corinthians to believe the gospel. **⁶I planted** [by evangelizing Corinth (Acts 18:1–18a)]. **Apollos watered** [by following up with further evangelism]. **God, however, was causing growth** [in the formation of the Corinthian church]. **⁷And so, neither is the one who plants anything** [to say that you belong to]**, nor** [is] **the one who waters—rather, God, who causes growth,** [is the one you belong to (compare "the church *of God*" in 1:2)]. Apollos was mentioned last in 3:4. So Paul starts out with him here in 3:5, switches back to himself, and then mentions Apollos again. The two of them are "servants" in the sense of having served the gospel to the Corinthians, as indicated by the clause, "through whom you believed." Paul compares this service to the work of farmhands in planting and watering. The verb for watering means "cause to drink" and here has soil as its implied object, standing for the Corinthians. In 3:2 this verb had the Corinthians as infants for its object.

3:8–9: But the one who plants and the one who waters are one [thing]**, yet each will receive his own wage in accordance with his own labor. ⁹For we** [Apollos and I] **are coworkers belonging to God. You are God's cultivated field, God's building.** "One [thing]" unites Paul the planter and Apollos the waterer in a common evangelistic task. Yet they'll receive separate wages, because the amount and quality of their respective labors may differ. "Coworkers" negates the rivalry suggested by the Corinthians' slogans, "'I belong to Paul,' but 'I belong to Apollos'" (1:12). "Belonging to God" makes Apollos and Paul owned by God rather than owners of the Corinthians, again in opposition to those slogans. And just as Apollos and Paul belong to God, so too do the Corinthians. "God's cultivated field" completes the agricultural metaphor, and "God's building" starts an architectural metaphor that Paul will develop next.

3:10–11: In accordance with God's grace that was given to me, as a wise master builder I laid a foundation [by establishing "the church of God that's in Corinth" (1:2)]; **but another** [presumably Apollos (see 3:6)] **builds on** [the foundation with further evangelism]. **But each** [whether Apollos or I or anyone else] **is to watch out how he builds** [on the foundation]. ¹¹**For no one can lay another foundation besides the one lying** [there already], **which** [foundation] **is Jesus Christ.** The grace of God that was given to Paul consisted both in a salvation that Paul ill-deserved, because he had persecuted the church, and in his equally ill-deserved apostolic commission (see 15:9–10). This grace provides motivation and guidelines for his task of church-building (not of church *buildings*, but of *assemblies* of believers likened to buildings). Though often used for a head contractor, "a wise *master* builder" has to do with Paul's being the *initial* builder of the Corinthian assembly in that he was first to proclaim the gospel in Corinth (hence "planted" and "laid a foundation"); for he isn't claiming a supervisory role over Apollos. Paul describes himself as "a *wise* master builder" in that the gospel he proclaimed there consisted in God's wisdom, that is, in a proclamation of the crucified Christ. "But each is to watch out how he builds" warns against gathering a personal following. Paul has even rejected one (1:13–17). "Each" rules out any exceptions to this rule. For a builder to gather a personal following would be to contradict the foundation already laid—that is, Jesus Christ—with the superstructure of the builder's personal following. "For no one *can* lay another foundation" doesn't mean merely that no one *should*. It means that Jesus Christ is the only foundation *possible* for a church (compare the comments on Matthew 16:17–19).

3:12–15: And if someone builds on the foundation with gold, silver, costly stones, lumber, hay, straw, ¹³**each** [builder's] **work will become apparent. For the day** [referring back to "the Day of our Lord, Jesus Christ" in 1:8, when our works will be judged (compare 2 Corinthians 5:10)] **will make** [the work] **evident, because it is being revealed by fire.** So sure is this revelation to take place that Paul uses the present tense, as though the judgment were already in progress. **And the fire itself will test the work of each** [builder as to] **what sort it is.**

¹⁴**If someone's work which he built on** [the foundation] **remains** [that is, survives the test of fire as gold, silver, and costly stones survive a fire], **he'll receive a wage.** ¹⁵**If someone's work will be burned down** [as lumber, hay, and straw burn], **he'll incur a loss; but he himself will be saved—yet in this way: as through fire.** Being decorative, gold, silver, and costly stones indicate a comparison of the (local) church to a temple; for temples, such as the Jewish one in Jerusalem, were decorated with such materials, and Paul will shortly make the comparison explicit (3:16–17; see also 6:19; 2 Corinthians 6:16; Ephesians 2:21). We should probably think of the "costly stones" as inlaid gems, though possibly also as marble or even as well-tooled masonry such as the famous Herodian masonry still visible in Jerusalem (compare 1 Chronicles 29:2; 2 Chronicles 3:4–7; Isaiah 54:11–12). Gold, silver, and stones are inflammable, of course, whereas lumber, hay, and straw are highly flammable. But who would use lumber, hay, and straw to build the superstructure of a fire-resistant temple? Nobody. So with this comparison Paul ridicules anyone who would gather a personal following. Two occurrences of "each" stress the individual responsibilities of church-builders. "Will become *apparent*" and "is being *revealed* by fire" point to public honor and shame at the Last Judgment. "A wage" for work well done will consist in public honor. "A loss" (or, as it could be translated, "a fine") for work poorly done will consist in the loss of honor, that is, in public shame. Salvation isn't in jeopardy, yet public shaming is bad enough to be compared to passing through fire.

3:16–17: You know, don't you, that you're God's temple and [that] **God's Spirit dwells in you?** ¹⁷**If someone despoils God's temple** [by gathering a following for himself], **God will despoil this person** [by depriving him of his "wage," that is, of public honor at the Last Judgment (see 3:14–15)]. **For God's temple is sacred, who as such** [referring to the temple as personified in the Corinthian believers] **you are.** The word for "temple" refers to a sanctuary proper, exclusive of surrounding courtyards and auxiliary buildings, and by definition means the dwelling place of a god. Pagan temples housed a god's image. But the Mosaic law prohibited images (Exodus 20:4; Deuteronomy 5:8). So God as Spirit indwelt his temple in Jerusalem. But Paul had taught the Corinthians that God shifted the dwelling of his Spirit from the Jewish temple to them as his new sacred space. Hence Paul appeals to their knowledge that God's Spirit indwells them. At one and the same time this appeal compliments them on the knowledge and excoriates them for regarding themselves as belonging to Paul or Apollos or Cephas rather than to God, whose temple they are. Because Paul has thus far been concerned over splits in the Corinthian church, he portrays the Christians there as *collectively* God's temple. ("You" is plural throughout.) The temple is "sacred" in that it's made up of those who've been "consecrated in Christ Jesus, called [to be] sacred [to God as others are not]" (1:2).

3:18–20: **No one is to delude himself. If someone among you is supposing** [himself] **to be wise in this age, he's to become foolish in order that he may become wise.** [19]**For the wisdom of this world is foolishness alongside God. For it's written, "**[He's] **the one who catches the wise in their trickery** [Job 5:13]**";** [20]**and again** [it's written]**, "The Lord knows the contrivances of the wise, that they** [the contrivances] **are inconsequential** [Psalm 94:11]**."** In 3:12, 14, 15, 17 "someone" referred to itinerant church-builders like Paul and Apollos, who came into town from outside. Here, "no one" and the addition of "among you" to "someone" make for a warning lest any one of the Corinthians' own number delude himself into supposing he's "wise in this age." Such a person would probably think of himself as wise—period. Paul's addition of "in this age" subverts the wisdom from the get-go. See the comments on 2:6 for the meaning of "wise *in this age*." Perish even the thought of such wisdom! But if someone does think so, "he's to become foolish" by shifting his attention to the crucified Christ. Only then will he become wise in the ways of God. "The wisdom of this world [that is, of unbelievers, who consider the proclamation of Christ crucified to be foolishness] is [itself] foolishness *alongside God*" in the sense that God, the all-wise, considers it foolishness. The quotation of Psalm 94:11 then explains why he considers the world's wisdom to be foolishness. He does, because he recognizes it to be what it truly is: "trickery" and "contrivances" designed to win fame and fortune by means of philosophical eloquence. And he describes the contrivances as "inconsequential" because they bring no benefit in the long run, that is, for eternity (compare the "loss" of "a wage" in 3:14–15).

3:21–23: **And so, no one is to boast in human beings. For all things belong to you,** [22]**whether Paul or Apollos or Cephas or the world or life or death or things present or things to come. All things** [belong] **to you,** [23]**and you** [belong] **to Christ, and Christ** [belongs] **to God.** Paul has just warned against taking the role of a worldly-wise man to be boasted *about* by his admirers (a warning for the likes of himself). Now Paul warns against taking the role of an admirer of such a man (a warning for the admiration-tipsy Corinthians). The contrast with "God" and "the Lord" in 3:19–20 gives "human beings" here in 3:21 the sense of *mere* human beings. "All *things*" include Paul, Apollos, and Cephas to emphasize that these human beings are mere possessions of the Corinthian believers rather than vice versa in accordance with the Corinthians' slogans (1:12). As earlier, "the world" refers to human beings, non-Christians in particular. Even they belong to the Corinthian believers, who according to 6:2 "will judge the world." Then to stress further that the Corinthians shouldn't have split up into factions that boast of belonging to merely human celebrities, Paul makes the Corinthians possessors also of "life," "death," "things present," and "things to come." The connecting of all these items, both personal and impersonal, with multiple instances of "or" implies that outside God and Christ, whoever and whatever the Co-

rinthian believers might think of as their owners are in reality their possessions. A repetition of "all things [belong] to you" caps this implication with a corresponding assurance. With "you [belong] to Christ" Paul sides with those in Corinth who were saying, "I belong to Christ" (compare 1:31; 2 Corinthians 10:7). They couldn't properly be called a faction, for theirs was a unifying slogan, the only such one. The other slogans were divisive. "And Christ [belongs] to God" then relates Christians' unity in Christ to Christ's unity with God.

4:1–4: **A person is to regard us** [Paul, Apollos, and Cephas] **in this way: as Christ's assistants and** [as] **managers of God's secrets.** As assistants rather than masters, then, Paul, Apollos, and Cephas belong to Christ; and the Corinthian Christians don't belong to mere assistants (see 3:21–23 in contradiction to the slogans listed in 1:12). Paul, Apollos, and Cephas are managers, to be sure, but "managers of *God's* secrets," not of any secrets—that is, long-hidden truths—of their own for the revelation of which they should be adulated. Moreover, a manager was a slave who had charge of his master's household so as, for example, to give household members their food on schedule and then give an account to his master (Matthew 24:45–51). Likewise Paul, Apollos, and Cephas dole out God's secrets and will have to give him an account of their work (compare 3:10–15). In 2:7 Paul used the singular of "secret" for the proclamation of Christ as crucified. Meanwhile, though, he has referred in the plural to "the deep things of God" (2:10) and to "solid food" that goes beyond the "milk" of Christ crucified (3:1–4) and therefore uses the plural, "secrets." [2]**Here in** [the case of] **managers, moreover, it is sought that one be found faithful.** "Found" connotes an examination and judgment. The slogans quoted in 1:12 imply that some of the Corinthians have examined Paul, judged him more faithful than Apollos or Cephas, and therefore proclaimed Paul to be their master. Others have done the same with Apollos, and others with Cephas. [3]**But to me it's a very minor matter that I should be examined by you** [and then Paul thinks of his examination in Corinth before the Roman proconsul Gallio (Acts 18:12–17)] **or by a human day.** "Day" refers to a day in court. "*By* a human day" personifies the day, as though it were the examining judge. And "by a *human* day" stands in contrast with "the Day of *our Lord*, Jesus Christ" (1:8), when the Lord will act as the examining judge (3:13–15; 5:5). **On the contrary** [so far as examination is concerned], **I don't even examine myself,** [4]**for I'm conscious of nothing against myself** [by way of unfaithfulness (compare Job 27:6)]. In other words, since Paul isn't conscious of having done anything in relation to the Corinthians that would lead some of them to favor Apollos or Cephas over against him, he doesn't bother to examine himself in self-judgment. **Nevertheless, I'm not justified by this** [unconsciousness of unfaithfulness on my part]; **and the one who examines me is the Lord.** He'll examine Paul on the coming Day of the Lord, Jesus Christ, to determine whether Paul has proved faithful as a manager of God's secrets (compare 2 Corinthians 5:10).

So sure is this future examination to occur, though, that Paul uses the present tense in "examines." If this external examination discovers managerial faithfulness, he'll be justified—that is, vindicated—over against those who've pitted Apollos and Cephas against him.

4:5: And so [because examining is the Lord's prerogative], **don't be judging anything ahead of time,** [that is,] **until the Lord comes, who will both bring to light the hidden things of darkness and disclose the intentions of the hearts** [of human beings]. **And then each** [of us, in reference to Paul, Apollos, and Cephas] **will get praise from God** [so that we have no need for you to boast in us]. "Don't be judging any*thing*" means "don't be judging any *person*, such as me, Apollos, or Cephas, as to the *quality* of our managerial faithfulness" (compare the use of the neuter for persons in 1:27–28; 2:2; 3:5, 7, 21 for emphasis on personal qualities). Paul's statements in Romans 13:12–14; 2 Corinthians 4:2; Ephesians 5:11–12 suggest that here "the hidden things of darkness" and "the intentions of the heart" smack of evil. But "each will get praise from God" shows Paul confident that the Lord won't find hidden evil and selfish intentions in him, Apollos, or Cephas. That is to say, just as Paul was conscious of nothing against himself (4:4), so too he's conscious of nothing against Apollos and Cephas. And since the slogans of 1:12 conferred praise on them (in effect, "I belong to Paul because he's praiseworthy" [and so forth in regard to Apollos and Cephas]), praise from God on *each* of them at the Last Judgment invalidates the *divisive* use of praise with those slogans at the present time. "Praise from God" identifies the "wage" to be gotten for work well done according to 3:8, 14. Considering its source, a high wage indeed and well worth suffering shame for proclaiming Christ crucified (compare Romans 2:29)! Since "the Lord" who "comes" and "will bring to light the hidden things of darkness" is none other than Jesus Christ, the getting of "praise from God" implies that Jesus' judgment is one and the same as God's judgment (compare the parallel between "the judgment platform of the Christ" in 2 Corinthians 5:10 and "God's judgment platform" in Romans 14:10).

4:6–7: And I've applied these things figuratively to myself and Apollos because of you, brothers, in order that in us [= in our cases] **you may learn the** [saying], **"Don't** [go] **beyond the things that are written," lest one be puffed up over one,** [that is,] **against the other.** [7]**For who differentiates you** [as superior to someone else]? **And what do you have that you didn't receive? And if also you received** [it], **why are you boasting as though not having received** [it]? Since Cephas has dropped out, leaving Paul and Apollos as in 3:4–15, the figurative application of "these things" refers to the application there to Paul and Apollos of farmwork and temple-building as figures of speech for their evangelistic labors (see the comments on 3:3b–4 for the dropping of Cephas). "Because of you" means "because you've taken sides against one another with your slogans featuring Apollos and me." The affectionately unifying address,

"brothers," signals the Corinthians' need to "learn the [saying], 'Don't [go] beyond the things that are written.'" "Learn" connotes obedience to the negated verb of command ("Don't [go]"), which has to be supplied from the sense of "beyond . . . ." Since Paul regularly uses "written" for what's written in the Old Testament, "the things that are written" probably refers to the Old Testament quotations in 1:19, 31; 2:9; 3:19–20. They deal with the futility of worldly wisdom in contrast with the Lord's wisdom. So to go beyond the things that are written would be to put a high estimate on worldly wisdom, in contradiction of Scripture, and thus be "puffed up" (a figure of speech for pride and arrogance). As Paul himself explains, "one . . . over one" means that self-puffery sets individual against individual. With the implied answers to three questions he then explains why self-puffery goes beyond Scripture. It does (1) because God treats each believer equally rather than playing favorites; (2) because whatever "enrich[ment] . . . in every [kind of] speech and every [kind of] knowledge" anyone enjoys (1:5) has come to that person as a "gracious gift" (1:7) for which he or she can't take credit; and (3) because boasting about a gift that he or she ill-deserved (so the meaning of "gracious") falsely implies that he or she did deserve the gift. At this point it becomes apparent that boasting in belonging to Paul, Apollos, or Cephas has evolved into the Corinthians' boasting about themselves, too, because of their enrichment in speech and knowledge.

4:8: Already you're glutted [with food and drink]! **Already you've gotten wealthy! You've started reigning** [as kings] **apart from us! And O that you had indeed started reigning in order that we too might have started reigning with you!** This passage drips with sarcasm, augmented both with two occurrences of "Already . . . !" and with "O that . . . !" and with the fact that not many of the Corinthian converts belonged to the upper classes of society (1:26–29). In view of the coming reference to "God's reign" (4:20), "you've started reigning apart from us" portrays the puffed up Corinthians as having started to share in God's reign before its arrival on earth. Not that they *actually* thought themselves to be sharing it as a present phenomenon. It's *as though* they did, because they were picking up on the worldly notion that wise people are superior to others as kings are superior to their subjects (compare Plato's "philosopher king," for example). Like kings they were glutted with food and had gotten wealthy, figures of speech for "hav[ing] been enriched . . . in every [respect]—[that is,] in every [kind of] speech and every [kind of] knowledge" (1:5). Enrichment? Yes. Paul said so. But reigning as kings apart from Paul, Apollos, and Cephas? No, as emphasized by the wish, "And O that you had *indeed* started reigning in order that we too might have started reigning with you!" The wish prepares for a very unkingly description of Paul and his fellow apostles.

4:9–10: For, I suppose, God has exhibited us, the apostles, as last ones [in that we haven't started reigning with you], **as sentenced to death, because we've become**

a spectacle to the world, both to angels and to human beings! ¹⁰**We're fools because of Christ, but you're shrewd in Christ! We['re] weak, but you['re] strong! You['re] esteemed, but we['re] dishonored!** Here Paul supplies the reason behind his wish for present kingliness (4:8b). It's that he and his fellow apostles are suffering in a most unkingly manner, that is, like criminals sentenced to die "as the last ones" in an act forming the climax of a show in the arena (compare 15:32), as buffoons laughed at by spectators in the world-theater, as despised weaklings who suffer the shame of dishonor. Even angels look on with amusement, as though joining unregenerate human beings in watching a comedy. No wonder the wish for kingliness. "We're fools because of Christ" means that the apostles are considered fools because of "the foolishness" of their "proclaiming Christ crucified" (1:18, 21, 23, 25). By contrast, "you're shrewd" (another reference to the Corinthians' enrichment in every kind of knowledge [1:5]), but Paul slips in the qualifying phrase "in Christ" to remind them of what he has already said: "you've been enriched *in him* ['Christ Jesus']," and this "on the basis of God's grace," not on the basis of any merit of their own (1:4–5). As the proclamation of Christ crucified is philosophically foolish by the world's standards, it's rhetorically weak by the world's standards (see 1:25, 27; 2:3). So its proclaimers, like Paul, Apollos, and Cephas, seem themselves weak as well as foolish. But the Corinthians' using their shrewdness, strength, and esteem—all three of which they have in Christ—for puffing themselves up betrays short-sighted attention to the "already" of "this age" (1:20; 2:6, 8; 3:18) rather than to judgment on the coming Day of the Lord.

4:11–12: To the present hour we both hunger and thirst and go naked [a hyperbole for wearing tattered clothes or a partial garment] **and are pummeled and unsettled** [because of moving from one place to another, often forced to flee persecution (see Acts 13:50; 14:5–6, 19–20 and so on)] ¹²**and labor, working with our own hands.** "To the present hour" sharpens the contrast with the Corinthians' being glutted "already" and reigning "already" (4:8), especially since an hour was the shortest unit of time identified by the ancients. The apostles' "hunger[ing] and thirst[ing]" contrasts with the Corinthians' being glutted like kings, comparatively speaking, with food and drink. The apostles' "go[ing] naked" contrasts with the royal attire worn by the wealthy kings to whom Paul likens the well-dressed Corinthians. The apostles' being "pummeled" by persecution as slaves were pummeled by their masters (1 Peter 2:20) contrasts with the unpersecuted Corinthians' reigning like kings over others. The apostles' being "unsettled" contrasts with the Corinthians' king-like settledness in a palace, their palace consisting of the prosperous city of Corinth. And the apostles' exhausting manual labor, despised as it was by the elite, contrasts with the Corinthians' king-like uppitiness (whatever their actual occupations).

4:13: Being ridiculed [for proclaiming Christ crucified], **we wish** [our ridiculers] **well. Being persecuted** [that is, pursued with intent to harm], **we put up with** [our persecutors]. **Being defamed** [with false accusations], **we speak cordially** [to our defamers]. **We've become like the world's scum, the scrapings of all things, till now.** Defamatory accusations included disturbance of the peace, sedition against the Roman government, and angering the gods for refusal to offer sacrifices to them, so that they bring fires, floods, earthquakes, and other disasters on humanity (compare the comments on 1 Peter 2:9–12). "The world" means its human population, so that the parallel "all things" (which in the original Greek can be masculine ["all people"] as well as neuter) means the totality of human beings. "Like the world's scum" compares the apostles to filthy residue that has to be cleaned off, as by washing or wiping; and "the scrapings of all things" compares them to filth so caked that it has to be scraped off. Sometimes these comparisons were used for criminals and otherwise worthless persons who were sacrificed to the gods (compare 4:9). "Till now" bookends "To the present hour" in 4:11 and thereby sharpens once again the contrast with the Corinthians' being glutted "already" and reigning "already" (4:8), and also makes ridiculous their hero-worship of Paul, Apollos, and Cephas.

4:14–15: I'm not writing these things by way of shaming you—rather, by way of admonishing [you] **as my beloved children.** ¹⁵**For though you were to have ten thousand attendants in Christ,** [you] **nevertheless** [do] **not** [have] **many fathers. For I fathered you in Christ Jesus through the gospel.** Paul's preceding sarcasm and self-depreciation ("these things") lead him to assure the Corinthians that he's not trying to shame them. Instead, he's trying to correct them as a father corrects his child. "My beloved children" strikes an even more affectionate note than does the usual address, "brothers." "Attendants" were household slaves assigned to lead young sons in elite families to and from school and, in general, to keep the boys in line, so that on Greek vases such attendants were often pictured with a stick in their hand. It's useless to speculate who the Corinthians' attendants might have been; for Paul says, "though you *were* to have," not "though you *have*." "In Christ" shows that he's using "attendants" as a figure of speech for ecclesiastical disciplinarians. "Ten thousand," being the largest numerical unit then used, could mean "myriads." In either case, the image of a comparatively few Christians in Corinth being kept in line by so many attendants is nothing short of comical. But the comedy highlights the singularity of Paul's having "fathered" the Corinthians earlier and therefore of his now having "admonish[ed]" them in a fatherly way rather than in the harsh way typical of "attendants." "In Christ Jesus" shows that he's using "fathered" as a figure of speech for having converted them; and "through the gospel" both identifies the means of their conversion and describes the earlier-mentioned proclamation of the crucified Christ as good news (= the meaning of "gospel"), especially in view of the previously noted fact that not many of the Corinthian converts belonged to the upper class of society (1:26–29). Paul's comparison of himself to a father balances the comparison of himself to a mother in 3:2.

4:16–17: Therefore [= because I fathered you] **I urge you, become imitators of me.** [17]**Because of this** [your need to imitate me] **I've sent you Timothy, who is my beloved child and faithful in the Lord, who** [referring again to Timothy] **will remind you of my ways in Christ, just as I teach** [them] **in every church everywhere.** Fathers are to set for their sons an example of proper behavior. Here, Paul tells the Corinthians to follow his example of self-depreciation, "lest one [of them] be puffed up over [another] one [of them]" (4:6). "My ways" refers to the ways in which he depreciates himself to set a good example. "In Christ" describes these ways as also suiting and commending the gospel of Christ, who "lowered himself by becoming obedient to the point of death—[not just any sort of death,] but the death of a cross [= a humiliating death by crucifixion]" (Philippians 2:8). Timothy's being sent to "remind the Corinthians of Paul's ways in Christ implies that they saw Paul behave self-depreciatingly when he was among them, but that in view of their self-inflation they need reminding of those ways. "My beloved child" describes Timothy in an echo of Paul's describing the Corinthians as his "beloved children" (see the comments on 4:14). "Faithful in the Lord" describes Timothy further as trustworthy in his service to the Lord Jesus, which trustworthiness carries even more importance than trustworthiness in helping Paul. These descriptions join "just as I teach" to assure the Corinthians that Timothy's reminder will be accurate in its representation of Paul's ways. So they'd better pay heed. "In *every* church *everywhere*" then assures the Corinthians of the consistency of Paul's teaching self-depreciation by word and example, so that they shouldn't think he's calling them unfairly to a behavior incumbent on them but not on other Christians too.

4:18–21: But some [of you] **have become puffed up as though I weren't coming to you.** [19]**But I'll come to you quickly, if the Lord wants** [me to]; **and I'll get to know, not the speech of the puffed up** [people]— **rather,** [their] **power.** [20]**For God's reign doesn't** [consist] **in speech—rather, in power.** [21]**What do you want? Should I come to you with a stick, or in love and the Spirit of gentleness?** "*Some* [of you]" seems to leave out others. If so, these others are those who say, "I belong to Paul"; for in their view he wouldn't berate his own fan club even if he were to come again to Corinth. But the rest have become puffed up out of confidence that they won't have to face Paul. He threatens them with a personal visit. "Quickly" indicates a need to get rid of the self-puffery as soon as possible for the sake of re-unifying the church. "If the Lord [Jesus, as usual] wants [me to]" indicates that the quickness of Paul's coming depends on the Lord's pleasure, not on Paul's (compare 16:7, and see 16:8 for what Paul himself considers a necessary delay). A consciousness of apostolic authority to act on the Lord's behalf underlies Paul's peremptoriness in saying he'll "get to know," whenever he comes, "not the

speech of the puffed up [people]—rather, their power." He's implying that despite their arrogant talk in his absence, they won't be able to resist the apostolic authority with which he'll deflate them in person. And why not? Because he represents God's reign, and it doesn't take hold in cheap talk—rather, in powerful deeds (compare the confirmation of Paul's speech and proclamation "by a demonstration of the Spirit and of power" [2:4 with comments]). It's up to the Corinthians whether Paul will come "with a stick," like the attendants who discipline naughty boys (see the comments on 4:15), or "with love," like a father who admonishes his beloved children (4:14). Since "gentleness" is a "fruit of the Spirit" (Galatians 5:22–23), "the Spirit of gentleness" refers to the Holy Spirit as gentle, not to Paul's human spirit as gentle (compare Galatians 6:1). Just as he fathered the Corinthians "in Christ Jesus" (4:15), he will come to them, if they heed this letter, "in . . . the Spirit of gentleness." And since gentleness characterizes Christ (2 Corinthians 10:1), "the Spirit of gentleness" would be enabling Paul to act as Christ himself would act.

ON A CASE OF FORNICATION IN THE CORINTHIAN CHURCH
1 Corinthians 5:1–13

5:1–3: Fornication among you is actually heard of [because of being reported to Paul in particular], **even fornication of such a kind that** [is] **not** [heard of] **among the Gentiles** [= pagans], **so that someone has** [= is cohabiting with] **the wife of** [his] **father** [in other words, his stepmother]. [2]**And you're puffed up and haven't mourned instead, so as to have the one who perpetrated this deed removed out of your midst.** [3]**For I, being absent in body on the one hand yet present in spirit on the other hand, have already passed judgment, as being present** [in spirit], **on the** [man] **who has committed this** [deed] **in this way.** "Fornication" is used for all sorts of sexual immorality but here applies to incest, which included cohabiting with a stepmother as well as with a close biological relative and which Paul says even pagans condemned (see also Leviticus 18:8; 20:11; Deuteronomy 22:30; 27:20). The use of "Gentiles" for pagans as distinct from Christians implies that Christians are a new breed, neither Gentile nor Jewish though drawn from among Gentiles and Jews (10:32; 12:2; Galatians 3:28). Paul may have heard about the present case of incest from members of Chloe's household, as he did concerning splits in the Corinthian church (1:11; see 16:17 for another possibility). He doesn't address the incestuous man's stepmother. Perhaps she didn't profess Christian faith and therefore lay outside the church's jurisdiction, though a culture of male dominance may have simply pushed her into the background. Since young women were often married off to men quite a bit older than they, the incestuous man and his father' wife, with whom he was cohabiting, could well have been close to each other in age. Paul doesn't address even the man, but reproves the Corinthian church for keeping him in their midst.

Pagans winked at many sorts of sexual immorality. But not only does their intolerance of incest make Paul astonished at the Corinthian Christians' tolerance of it. So too does their self-puffery. Paul doesn't say they're puffed up over the tolerance, as though they mistakenly thought Christian freedom included sexual freedom. It's just that their tolerance should have kept them from *any* kind of self-puffery, such as what he mentioned in 4:6, 18, 19. Instead of getting puffed up *despite* having in their midst a fornicator such as even pagans wouldn't tolerate, they should have mourned *because of* having him in their midst. We don't know why they didn't mourn as they should have, though it's a good guess that the man was one whose wealth and influence people in the Corinthian church depended on. Maybe they met in his home. Whatever the case, mourning suggests sorrow over a death, and a moral death has indeed occurred. So the church should have buried the incestuous man, so to speak, by removing him out of their midst the way a corpse, decaying as it does, is removed through burial. Paul is speaking of a social burial: ostracism. His "judgment" underlies this comment, and his judgment anticipates ("already") the Lord's at the Last Judgment. Better to face Paul's judgment now than the Lord's judgment hereafter. But Paul will want the Corinthians to carry out his judgment. Meanwhile, the addition of "in this way" to "the [man] who has committed this [deed]" reemphasizes the moral horror of the incest and of the Corinthians' tolerating it. "Is *actually* heard of" carried the same emphasis at the start. See the final comments on 6:15–17 on the way Paul's spirit could be present with the Corinthians while his body was absent from them.

5:4–5: When you and my spirit have gathered together in the name of our Lord, Jesus, together with the power of our Lord, Jesus, [5][I order you] to give [a man] such as this over to Satan for the destruction of the flesh, so that the spirit will be saved in the Day of the Lord. "In the name of our Lord, Jesus," and "with the power of our Lord, Jesus" parallel each other, so that Jesus' twice-mentioned title, "Lord," points up his power. "*Our* Lord" underscores Paul's and the Corinthians' sharing access to Jesus' power. Especially if the incestuous man is rich and influential, they'll have to draw on that power when they expel him from the church; for its undistinguished members—and most of the members *are* undistinguished (1:26–29)—could be too weak-kneed to do so on their own. Paul doesn't refer simply to "this [man]," but to "[a man] *such as* this" to stress yet again the horror of his sexual immorality and of his continuing presence in the church. "To give . . . over to Satan" parallels "to have . . . removed from your midst" in 5:2 and therefore means that expulsion from the church will confine the man to worldly society, dominated as it is by Satan (compare Colossians 1:13). Since Satan tempts people to engage in sexual immorality (7:5), it's appropriate that this sexually immoral man be given over to his tempter, Satan.

Though Paul has used "fleshy" and "fleshly" figuratively for human weakness (3:1, 3), elsewhere in 1 Co-

rinthians "flesh" has to do with physicality (1:26, 29; 6:16; 7:28; 10:18; 15:39, 50; see also 10:10 for physical destruction); and the present contrast with "spirit" favors a reference to physicality here too. ("The spirit" can hardly refer to the Holy Spirit, for it would make theological nonsense to say he "will *be saved*.") So "the flesh" refers to the incestuous man's physical flesh, which will decay away, leaving only his bones; and "the spirit" refers to his human spirit, which will be saved "in the Day of the Lord"—that is, when Jesus returns as Lord (1 Thessalonians 4:15–5:2; 2 Thessalonians 2:1–2)—by being given a new body in resurrection (see especially 6:13–14; 15:35–57; 2 Corinthians 4:16–5:4). "For the *destruction* of the flesh" then refers to a premature death, much as Paul will later say that some have fallen ill and even died for having desecrated the Lord's Supper (11:29–30). In 1 Timothy 1:20 Paul has given two men over to Satan for a corrective purpose: "in order that they may be educated not to slander." No such purpose appears here, though. Perhaps the offense is too serious. Be that as it may, the moral health of the Corinthian church constitutes Paul's main concern.

5:6–8: Your boast [is] not good. You know, don't you, that a little leaven leavens the whole batch of dough [compare Galatians 5:9]? [7]**Clean out the old leaven in order that you may be a new batch of dough, just as you are unleavened. For our Passover [lamb]— [namely,] Christ—has been sacrificed. [8]And so, let us be celebrating the festival, not with old leaven—that is, not with the leaven of wickedness and evil—rather, with unleavened [pieces of bread] consisting of purity and truth.** The boast isn't good, because it stems from being puffed up, that is, arrogant. Paul doesn't define the boast, but see 4:8. Of course the Corinthians know that "a little leaven leavens the whole batch of dough." Everybody does, so that Paul's question ("You know, don't you . . . ?") is tinged with sarcasm. Leaven consists of a portion of fermenting dough which, when mixed with a batch of fresh dough, makes the batch rise, much as happens with yeast nowadays. Just a little goes a long way. But leaven can get old and sour. Then it ruins a batch of dough, so that a new batch has to be introduced. Paul likens the "wickedness and evil" of incest to old leaven. Its presence has corrupted the Corinthian church, morally speaking. As old leaven, then, the wickedness and evil have to be cleaned out by removing the incestuous man (5:2) and giving him over to Satan (5:5). Then the Corinthians will be, so to speak, a new batch of dough. But instead of saying that as a new batch they *will be* unleavened because of the incestuous man's removal, Paul springs a surprise by saying they *are* unleavened despite the incestuous man's presence. In effect Paul is saying, "*Become* what you *are*." *In Christ* they're clean; so as a church they'd better get clean *in themselves*, too.

Mourning would lead to removing the incestuous man (see the comments on 5:1–2). But removing him clears the way for celebration, just the opposite of mourning. In anticipation of the removal, then, Paul says, "let us be celebrating the festival." He has in view the Festival of Unleavened Bread, starting with the Passover Festival. All leaven was to be removed from Jewish homes as a condition for this celebration, and *un*leavened bread was to be eaten throughout the seven days of festivity (Exodus 12:15–20; 13:6–7; Deuteronomy 16:1–4). So Paul makes the removal symbolize a disciplinary ostracism of the incestuous man, whose fornication he tags as "wickedness and evil," though the word for "wickedness" also means "malice" in anticipation of the malice which according to chapter 6 is leading the Corinthian Christians to sue each other. Since the removal of leaven was to precede Passover and Unleavened Bread, Paul's commanding a removal of the incestuous man *because* Christ has been sacrificed as our Passover lamb means that it's past time, and therefore high time, to remove the incestuous man by ostracizing him. Lack of leaven stands for "purity and truth." In this context purity means sexual morality, and truth means correspondence in conduct to the way God looks at us in Christ, that is, as morally clean. The Corinthian church is a single batch of dough, which in 10:17 Paul will call "one loaf of bread." But just as a cracker-like loaf of unleavened bread is broken in order that each person at the table may have a piece, so the Christians in Corinth, though making up one loaf, are to be characterized individually by purity and truth, like "unleavened [pieces of bread]."

5:9–10: I wrote you in [my previous] **letter not to associate with fornicators,** ¹⁰**not at all** [meaning to dissociate yourselves from] **this world's fornicators** [that is, non-Christians who fornicate] **or the greedy and predatory or idolaters, since then you'd be obligated to go out of the world.** Paul's previous letter to the Corinthians hasn't survived. "Not *at all*" underscores the denial that he meant they should dissociate themselves from sexually immoral people who make no profession of belief in Jesus. He doesn't say so, but such dissociation would kill chances to bear Christian witness to unbelievers. "Fornicators" comes first because of the case of fornication Paul has been dealing with. But he adds "the greedy and predatory or idolaters." The first two of these are paired with "and" because greed leads people to seize what belongs to others (compare the Corinthians' suing each other in court according to 6:1–11). And for a Christian to practice idolatry is for him to deny that Jesus is the one and only Lord (8:5–6 [compare Paul's discussion in chapters 8–10 of eating food sacrificed to an idol]). "Since then you'd be obligated to go out of the world" implies that it would have been absurd of him to command dissociation from non-Christians as well as professedly Christian fornicators, greedy predators, and idolaters. Surely the Corinthians don't think he'd be so silly. At least they shouldn't, especially since the world is full of such people and going out of the world is either impossible or suicidal.

5:11–13: **But now I've written to you not to associate with anyone named "a brother"** [= a fellow Christian] **if he's a fornicator or a greedy person or an idolater or a ridiculer or a drunkard or a predator, and**

not to eat with such a person [the doing of which would seal a social bond]. ¹²**For what** [authority] **do I have to judge those outside** [the church]? To judge them would be to cut off social ties with them at the present time (but see 6:1–2 for Christians' participating with God in judging the world at the Last Day). **You judge those inside** [it], **don't you?** ¹³**But God will judge those outside** [it]. **"Remove the evil** [man] **from among yourselves** [Deuteronomy 13:5; 17:7; 19:19; 21:21; 24:7]." "But *now* I've written to you" refers to what Paul has just written by way of clarifying the meaning of what he wrote in his previous letter (5:9–10). "A fornicator or a greedy person" comes over from 5:10, with only a shift from the plural number to the singular (as also in the following). Then Paul skips predatory persons for the time being (5:10) and advances "or an idolater," perhaps to bring idolaters a little closer to fornicators because sexual immorality often accompanied idolatry, both in temple prostitution and at idolatrous feasts. "Or a ridiculer" introduces a new category as compared with 5:10, refers to someone who ridicules as foolish the proclamation of Christ crucified (1:18–25), and suggests that those Corinthian believers who say, "I belong to Paul," are similarly ridiculing those who say, "I belong to Apollos," and those who say, "I belong to Cephas," and likewise in regard to the other sloganeers. "Or a drunkard" introduces another new category, but one that contributes to fornication, accompanies idolatrous feasts (compare 10:7), and indicates in advance that those who are getting drunk at the Lord's Supper are behaving like unbelievers (see 11:20–21). Finally, "a predator" comes over from 5:10, but with a change of "and" to "or" because the term is no longer paired with "the greedy" (see the comments there). "You judge those inside [the church], don't you?" calls for the answer, "Yes." But the Corinthians' failure to remove their incestuous fellow church member shows that they do *not* judge insiders. At least they haven't judged that one, as they should have. So Paul's question carries another tinge of sarcasm designed to shame them into compliance. The quotation of a repeated command in Deuteronomy brings this discussion to a close with the third command to remove the incestuous man, the first one having been inferential ("so as to have . . . removed" [5:2]), the second figurative ("Clean out the old leaven" [5:7]), and this one scriptural. But Paul's authority as an apostle makes it unnecessary for him to indicate that he's quoting Scripture. So the final accent falls on the church's responsibility to join Paul in disciplining the miscreant.

ON LAWSUITS BETWEEN CHRISTIANS
1 Corinthians 6:1–11

Paul has criticized the Corinthian Christians for failure to discipline one of their members (5:1–13). Now he criticizes them for lodging lawsuits against each other. The former had to do with sexual morality. The present has to do with economic morality. But in both, Paul deflates the Corinthians' self-puffery and stresses the responsibility of the local church for the behavior of its individual members, and the responsibility of its individual members to uphold the divinely ordained moral standards of the church.

6:1–2: Who of you, when having a plaint against another person [in the church], **dares to be judged** [= go to court] **before the unrighteous and not before the saints?** ²**Or you know, don't you, that the saints will judge the world? And if the world is being judged by you, are you unworthy of the smallest lawsuits** [that is, unfit to set up your own Christian tribunals for judging trivial suits between church members]? Naturally, lawsuits between Christians exacerbated the disunity criticized in 1:10–4:21. The singulars in "*Who* of you . . . *dares*" might suggest only one case of litigation between Christians in Corinth. But the plurals in 6:7 ("*lawsuits* along with *yourselves*") favor multiplicity. Paul could have written a declaration: "Some of you . . . have dared . . . ." But by using a question, "Who of you . . . dares . . . ?" he highlights his horror. We might think it took daring to lodge a lawsuit "before the unrighteous" because the unrighteous don't judge justly. But in the first century Roman Empire, judges so favored the elite, especially when bribed by the elite, that the nonelite weren't likely even to lodge a lawsuit for the getting of justice; and the elite were likely to lodge a lawsuit precisely for the getting of *in*justice favorable to them but unfavorable to the one they were suing. So "who of you . . . dares . . . ?" doesn't allude to the danger of suffering *in*justice in a court of unrighteous human judges, but to the danger of suffering *justice* in God's court for having lodged a lawsuit against a fellow Christian. It takes a daredevil to dare God. "And not before the saints" suggests that lawsuits were brought "before the unrighteous" so as to avoid a just judgment by fellow Christians. For the lawsuit's very purpose was predatory (compare the references to predatory people in 5:10, 11; 6:10); and as consecrated to God, the saints would be expected to rule against predators just as he will at the Last Judgment (6:9–10).

"You know, don't you . . . ?" implies that the Corinthian Christians do know and therefore shouldn't be suing each other in pagan courts. "*Or* you know, don't you . . . ?" implies that if you don't want to answer the *preceding* question ("Who of you . . . dares . . . ?"), then at least answer the *following* question. If "the saints will judge the world"—that is, "the unrighteous," who constitute the world—it makes nonsense for the saints to subject themselves to the world's judges. Apparently Paul had taught the Corinthians that as saints they would judge the world. Otherwise he could hardly have expected them to know that they would. There's no explanation of what judging the world will entail, but God's coming judgment of outsiders according to 5:13 implies that the saints' judging the world will entail participation in God's judgment of the outsiders. So "the world *is being* judged by you" puts that future judgment in the present tense to underline its certainty. The saints' judging the world proves that they are *not* unworthy to judge lawsuits among their own number. "Smallest" describes the lawsuits as trivial in comparison with the eternal is-

sues that will occupy the saints' attention when judging the world.

6:3–6: You know, don't you, that we'll judge angels—let alone, indeed, mundane matters? ⁴**So if you have merely mundane lawsuits, are you seating** [as judges] **these** [people]**: the ones being treated as nobodies in the church?** ⁵**I say this to your shame!** [Is it] **the case that among you there's not a single wise person who will be able to differentiate between his brother** [who deserves to win the suit and another brother who doesn't—that is, between his fellow Christians]? ⁶**Instead, is a brother being judged along with a brother** [= being hauled to court by a fellow believer], **and this before unbelievers?** The switch to "unbelievers" from "the unrighteous" (6:1) shows that lack of righteousness correlates with lack of faith. For the question, "You know, don't' you . . . ?" see the comments on 6:2. There's no explanation of what judging angels will entail; but judging them marks a step up from judging the world, and judging angelic matters marks a step up from judging the "mundane matters" of everyday human life over which the Corinthian Christians were suing each other (compare the superiority of angels to human beings according to Hebrews 2:7, 9). "Let alone" and "indeed" underscore these differences.

Paul is about to recommend lodging no lawsuits at all (6:7). So he's not commanding the Corinthians to seat "nobodies" among them as judges of lawsuits (as some translations say he is). "Nobodies" echoes his description of most of them from the world's standpoint (1:28). They're taking lawsuits before unbelievers, so that the question whether the Corinthians are seating nobodies among them as judges requires a *negative* answer, implies for the sake of argument—but only for its sake—that they *should* seat such people if they were to sue each other at all, and carries a *sarcastic* edge. "I say this to your shame!" (contrast 4:14) makes sure the sarcasm isn't missed and takes direct aim at the Corinthians' self-puffery and boasting (4:6, 18–19; 5:2, 6). Paul has described the Corinthians as "enriched in . . . every [kind of] knowledge," as "not falling short in any gracious gift," as having heard "God's wisdom," and as presumably having among them "someone . . . supposing [himself] to be wise in this age" (1:5, 7; 2:7; 3:18). Therefore sarcasm reaches a peak in Paul's next question, "[Is it] the case that among you there's not a single wise person who will be able to differentiate between his brother [and another brother]?" But sarcasm changes to sadness in the final question, which implies an affirmative answer and contrasts what for the sake of argument *should* have happened (Christians' settling disputes among themselves) with what *has* happened (Christians' suing each other before non-Christians).

6:7–8: So [the mere fact] **that you have lawsuits along with yourselves is actually a defeat for you already. Why not rather let yourselves suffer injustice? Why not rather let yourselves be defrauded?** ⁸**Instead, you perpetrate injustice and defraud** [people]**—and**

[you do] **this to brothers** [fellow Christians]! "Lawsuits *along with* yourselves" may sound strange, but it echoes "a brother being judged *along with* a brother" in the preceding verse. Paul draws an unexpected conclusion. In effect, he takes off the table what we might have inferred from the foregoing, namely, that Christians should sue each other only "before the saints" (6:1). Here he says that suing each other shouldn't happen at all. Even in an ecclesiastical court, what by mundane standards would count as a victory for one of the litigants counts by heavenly standards as a defeat for the whole local church. ("You" is plural in the phrase, "a defeat for you.") "Actually" stresses the truth of this judgment, and "already" inverts the Corinthians' being "glutted already" and "gotten wealthy already" (4:8) and advances the judgment from the Last Day to the present for current contemplation. So the questions, "Why not rather let yourselves suffer injustice? Why not rather let yourselves be defrauded?" imply that at the Last Judgment the suffering of present injustice and of present defraudation without resort even to an ecclesiastical court will turn out to be a victory in God's court. Because of this implication, Paul expresses astonishment that fellow Christians are perpetrating injustice on each other in pagan courts by means of lawsuits that defraud the losers of their rightful property.

6:9–10: Or you know, don't you, that unrighteous people won't inherit God's kingdom? Don't be deceived. Neither fornicators nor idolaters nor adulterers [those who have sex with someone else's spouse or with someone not their own spouse] **nor softies** [males who play the effeminate role in homosex] **nor sodomites** [males who play the masculine role in homosex (see Leviticus 18:22; 20:13)] ¹⁰**nor thieves nor greedy people, not drunkards, not ridiculers, not predators will inherit God's kingdom.** "You know, don't you . . . ?" implies that the Corinthian Christians do know and therefore should take care not to fall into the category of "unrighteous people" such as those Paul proceeds to list. "*Or you know, don't you . . . ?*" introduces this implied knowledge of theirs as an unutilized deterrent to their defrauding of fellow Christians by suing them in pagan courts. "Unrighteous people" harks back to "the unrighteous" in 6:1, where they're distinguished from "the saints." "Won't *inherit* God's kingdom" makes for a contrast with suing someone to *defraud* him of his mundane property. Better to inherit God's kingdom.

"Don't be deceived" suggests that the Corinthians have been deceived, or are in danger of being deceived, into thinking that their conduct doesn't matter to their inheriting God's kingdom. So Paul lists various sorts of unrighteous people who won't inherit it. The Corinthians can then judge for themselves whether their conduct rules them in or out of the inheritance. As in similar lists at 5:10 and 5:11, this list starts with "fornicators," such as the man to be expelled from the church according to 5:1–13. As in the similar list at 5:11, this one ends with "predators," such as those who are using lawsuits to defraud others in the church. The fornicator and the

predators had better repent—or else! Apart from differences in order, the list of unrighteous people in 5:11 repeated the categories in the list at 5:10, but added "a ridiculer or a drunkard" to "greedy people" and "idolaters." Again apart from differences in order, the list here in 6:9–10 repeats the categories in 5:11, but adds "nor adulterers nor softies nor sodomites nor thieves." At the head of the list and in preparation for a discussion of idolatry in chapters 8–10, "idolaters" comes right after "fornicators," because sexual immorality was often practiced in connection with idolatrous feasts. The following expansion of sexual sins with "adulterers," "softies," and "sodomites" reflects the prevalence and variety of sexual immorality in the Roman Empire and, specifically, in Corinth, and also prepares for a discussion in 6:12–20 of the body's sanctity over against sexual immorality. At the end of the list, a repetition of not inheriting God's kingdom reinforces Paul's warning that the professing Christians in Corinth should take care not to fall into the listed categories.

6:11: And some of you were these things. You let yourselves be washed, however. You were consecrated, however. You were justified, however, in the name of the Lord, Jesus Christ, and in the Spirit of our God. By reminding the Corinthians, at least some of them, of their pre-Christian selves Paul continues his program of puncturing their pride. "Were these *things*" refers to *people* ("fornicators," "idolaters," and so on); but as often, the neuter gender brings to the forefront their sinful qualities. Three instances of "however" emphasize what has made them *not* these things any more. "Be washed" means having their behavior washed clean of fornication, idolatry, and the other vices. "You *let* yourselves be washed" refers to their submitting to baptism as a symbol of the cleansing (compare Acts 22:16). "You were consecrated" refers to God's setting them apart from the rest of humanity so as to please him in their conduct. "You were justified" refers to his no longer counting them to be the "unrighteous people" he once counted them (correctly) as being. "In the name of the Lord, Jesus Christ" means that naming Jesus Christ as their Lord led God to justify them (compare Acts 22:16 again and Romans 10:13). "In the Spirit" means that God gave them his Spirit in conjunction with their justification. "Of our God" distinguishes this Spirit from "the *human being's* spirit" and "the *world's* spirit" (2:11, 12), and "*our* God" distinguishes the "one God" from the many "*so-called* gods" (8:4–5). To the extent that the Corinthians don't fit Paul's picture of them as changed in their behavior, doubt falls on the washing, consecrating, and justifying of them.

ON THE SANCTITY OF CHRISTIANS' BODIES
1 Corinthians 6:12–20

6:12–14: "All things are permissible for me." Not all things are beneficial, however. "All things are permissible for me." I'll not be dominated by anything, however. ¹³**"Foods [are] for the belly, and the belly [is] for**

foods; but God will incapacitate both this [the belly] and those [the foods]." But the body [is] not for fornication—rather, for the Lord; and the Lord [is] for the body. ¹⁴But God has also raised the Lord, and will raise us through his power. Because of Paul's foregoing emphasis on sexual sins, he himself would hardly say, as will be said in 6:18, "Every sin . . . is outside the body." And because of his immediately preceding attack on idolatry, thievery, ridicule, and predation, he himself would hardly say, "All things are permissible for me," and then repeat the statement for emphasis. It therefore appears that he's quoting some immoralistic slogans of the Corinthians, and then qualifying those slogans, somewhat as he quoted and rebutted the Corinthians' fan-club slogans in 1:12, only here without explicit indications of quotation. (The Corinthians would recognize their own slogans, though.) The qualification, "Not all things are beneficial, however," builds on Paul's having noted that "unrighteous people won't inherit God's kingdom" (6:9–10). Absence of benefit indeed! The Greek words behind "are permissible" and "be dominated" have the same rootage. So with a wordplay Paul qualifies the claim of entire moral permissibility with an allusion to libertines' becoming dominated by the very immoralities they feel free to engage in (compare Romans 1:24–32; 6:12–23).

The slogan concerning foods, the belly, and God's making the belly incapable at death of taking in foods and making foods incapable of feeding the belly once death has occurred—this slogan implies that the body's coming death makes bodily behavior, as in fornication, morally indifferent. God doesn't care about the body. Paul counters first that a permission of fornication doesn't follow from the body's coming death. "The body [is] not for fornication—rather, for the Lord" as "the belly [is] for foods"; and "the Lord [is] for the body" as "Foods [are] for the belly." As a second counter to this slogan of the Corinthians ("But . . . *also*"), Paul proves God's care for the body, and therefore the moral significance of human behavior through its use, by citing God's past raising of Jesus ("the Lord") and future raising of Christians ("us"). For emphasis on our body's moral significance, Paul uses an intensive verbal form in "will raise us." "Through his [God's] power" gives assurance that God can raise us just as well as he can incapacitate the belly and foods. Paul uses "the Lord" for Jesus Christ as distinguished from "God" to remind the Corinthians that they themselves named Jesus Christ their "Lord" (6:11). By their own confession, then, they aren't free to behave as they like. In fact, "the body . . . [is] for the Lord" could well be read in an alternative translation, "the body . . . [belongs to] the Lord," in which case "the body [does] not [belong to] fornication" (as though sexual immorality were to own the body as a master owns a slave) and "the Lord [belongs to] the body" (as though the Lord has subjected himself to serve the body). Similarly, foods and the belly belong to each other in that they serve each other.

6:15–17: You know, don't you, that your bodies are Christ's [body] parts? So on taking away the Christ's

[body] parts [from him], should I make [them] a prostitute's [body] parts? May it not happen! ¹⁶Or you know, don't you, that the one who joins himself to a prostitute is one body [with her]? For it [Scripture] says [alternatively, "for he [God] says" (compare Matthew 19:4–5)], "The two will be one flesh" [Genesis 2:24]. ¹⁷But the one who joins himself to the Lord [Jesus] is one s/Spirit [with him]. "You know, don't you . . . ?" implies that Paul had indeed taught the Corinthian believers that their bodies were the Christ's body parts (in the metaphorical sense spelled out in 12:12–31a, though there in more detail, probably, than prior to the present letter). "The Christ's [body] parts" alludes to Jesus' messiahship, according to which he's the anointed king who incorporates in himself the people of God. With "I," Paul makes himself an example. But since he has only one body to help make up the Christ's metaphorical body, the self-referential plural in the question whether he should take away "the Christ's [body] parts" and make them "a prostitute's [body] parts" highlights by its very awkwardness the applicability of Paul's example to the Corinthians. Since the Greek words for "a prostitute" and "fornication" have the same root, "a prostitute" reprises the topic of fornication, for which foods and the belly were introduced as an analogy.

"May it not happen!" expresses a horrifiedly negative answer to the question of transferring body parts from the Christ to a prostitute. "Or you know, don't you . . . ?" both implies that the Corinthians do know the answer to the following question and that if they don't want to answer the preceding question, they should at least answer the following one (compare the comments on 6:2). "Who joins himself to a prostitute" refers to coitus, in which two bodies come together as one, the male penetrating the female and the female enfolding the male. Paul quotes Genesis 2:24 in support. "One flesh" in the quotation equates with "one body" in Paul's statement. A person "joins himself to the Lord" by calling on the name of the Lord so as to be saved (Romans 10:13). In an alternative translation, a person "is being joined to the Lord" by doing the same. In either case, the supplicant's human spirit and the Lord's Spirit come together as one—hence "s/Spirit"—in a fashion analogous to the coming together of two bodies of flesh as one. Here's the reason Paul could say in 5:3–5 that his spirit, joined to the Lord's Spirit as we now know from 6:17, is present in the Corinthian church "with the power of our Lord, Jesus Christ" to discipline the fornicator. Only because Paul's spirit was joined to the Lord's Spirit could Paul's spirit be there and do that.

6:18: Flee fornication. "Every sin—[that is,] whatever [sin] a human being commits—is outside the body." But the one who fornicates sins against his own body. Paul uses the strong verb "flee" because the sexual urge is so strong that it easily leads to fornication (compare 10:7–8, 14). The quoted Corinthian slogan claims that bodily functions, such as sexual intercourse, have no moral or immoral significance, because no sin has anything to do with the body. So bodily urges may be satisfied without restraint. Paul rebuts this slogan by declaring that a fornicator sins against his body (compare Romans 1:24–27 for a probable reference to sexually transmitted diseases). We might have expected him to say that a person sins *with* his own body. But "*against his own body*" stresses the physical damage caused by sexual immorality, and "against *his own* body" stresses the foolishness of such self-inflicted damage.

6:19–20: Or you know, don't you, that your body is a temple of the Holy Spirit, whom you have from God, and [that] you're not your own? ²⁰**For you were bought at a price. Glorify God with your body, then!** Again, "you know, don't you . . . ?" implies knowledge of the following. "*Or* you know, don't you . . . ?" implies that if you don't accept that the fornicator sins against his own body, you should at least act on your knowledge of the following. The individual believer's body is "a temple of the Holy Spirit" just as the local church, consisting of believers, is "God's temple" as a dwelling-place of "God's Spirit" (see 3:16–17 with comments on the meaning and use of temples). It's there, in the body-temple, that the divine Spirit and the human spirit come together as one (6:17). "Holy" describes the Spirit as sacred in opposition to the unsanctity of a prostitute, who sells her body as common property to all comers. "From God" indicates that God himself occupies through his Holy Spirit the temple consisting of a believer's body. "You're not your own" indicates that your body belongs to God for his occupation, not to yourself for self-damaging pleasure. "For you were bought at a price" supports God's ownership and consequent occupation of your body (compare 7:22–23). Paul doesn't identify the price here (though see Galatians 3:13; 4:4–5), so that the accent lies on the legitimacy of God's ownership and occupation. Particularly in this context, "glorify God with your body" means "flee fornication." Doing so brings honor to God by keeping sacred—that is, set apart from common use—his temple, which consists of your body.

REPLIES TO QUESTIONS ASKED IN A LETTER FROM THE CORINTHIAN CHURCH
1 Corinthians 7:1–16:4

ON MARRIAGE, SINGLENESS, AND DIVORCE
1 Corinthians 7:1–40

7:1: And concerning the things you wrote about: "[It's] **good for a man not to touch a woman** [a euphemism for having sexual intercourse with her]." Two reasons stand out for thinking that here Paul quotes a Corinthian slogan, as he did in 1:12; 6:12a, 13a–c, 18b: (1) he will *command* sexual intercourse within marriage (7:2–5), so that the statement, "[It's] good for a man not to touch a woman," hardly represents his own judgment. (2) Paul will carefully balance his statements between male and female in 7:2–5, 10–16, 33–34, so that the lack of such a balance in the foregoing statement ("[It's] good for a *man* . . .") points to a Corinthian slogan. It ap-

pears that just as sexual promiscuity characterized some Christians in Corinth, sexual abstinence characterized others. Where promiscuity abounds, reactive abstinence often follows. Abstinence in the Corinthian church precluded marriage for some and prevented sexual intercourse within marriage for others. So the Corinthians' letter to Paul brought up the topic of sexual abstinence.

7:2–3: But because of fornications [a term for all kinds of sexual immorality, often in the case of men's having sex with prostitutes] **each** [man] **is to have his own wife** [in the sense of possessing her so as to have sexual intercourse with her]**, and each** [woman] **is to have her own husband** [in the sense of possessing him so as to have sexual intercourse with him]. ³**The husband is to pay back** [his sexual] **debt to** [his] **wife, and likewise also the wife** [is to pay back her sexual debt] **to** [her] **husband.** In 6:12–20 Paul prohibited sexual intercourse outside marriage. Now he commands it within marriage and grounds his command on the danger that without marital sex the sexual urge will lead to sexual immorality. This grounding demeans marriage as the proper outlet for the sexual urge *only if the body and its urges are considered vulgar*. But for Paul the body of a Christian is sacred, a temple for God's Spirit (6:19–20), so that the body's urges, including the sexual one, are *not* vulgar. Within marital and nonabusive bounds, then, their satisfaction isn't at all dishonorable. "Each [man]" doesn't mean all men (which would contradict Paul's coming recommendation of the single life for some), but all married men (individually speaking), as indicated by the reference to having sex with one's wife. Similarly in regard to "each [woman]." The husband owes his wife sexual satisfaction, and the wife owes it to her husband. Paul mentions the husband's sexual debt first, and does so despite writing in a male-dominated culture which gave men free rein when it came to sex but restricted women in this respect. The first mention emphasizes that a husband owes his wife sexual satisfaction just as much as she owes it to him. "Likewise also" points up the equality of obligation.

7:4–6: The wife doesn't have charge of her own body [in the matter of sexual intercourse]**; rather, [her] husband** [does]**. And likewise also the husband doesn't have charge of his own body** [in this matter]**; rather, [his] wife** [does]**.** Here Paul shifts from the foregoing language of indirect commands ("[So-and-so] is to . . .") and of debt to the language of declarative statements and of authority. But the underlying message stays the same—indeed, gets emphasis by being repeated in a different form. Two instances of "rather" underscore the lack of sexual authority that a spouse has over her or his own body and the possession of such authority over the body of his or her spouse. As the language of indirect commands and of debt started with the husband, the language of declarative statements and of authority now ends with the husband. Thus the obligation to give his wife sexual satisfaction frames her similar obligation; and another "likewise also" points up the equality of obligation over against a culture of male-domination. **5Don't be defrauding each other** [by refusing to have sexual intercourse with your spouse], **unless perhaps by mutual agreement for a spell in order that you might have leisure for prayer—and you should reunite lest Satan be tempting you because of your unrestraint** [that is, lest Satan take advantage of your inability to control the sexual urge and thereby tempt you to have sex outside your marriage]. Here Paul shifts from the foregoing indirect commands and declarative statements to direct commands ("you"). Nonpayment of a sexual debt and assertion of sexual authority over one's own body now count as defrauding your spouse of what rightfully belongs to her or him. Abstention for married couples has to be mutually agreed upon, temporary, for the sake of prayer, and followed by sexual reunion. Not that they're to pray only during spells of abstention (see 1 Thessalonians 5:17); rather, those spells will allow *more* time for prayer on suitable occasions. **6But I'm saying this** [about abstention for the sake of prayer] **by way of allowance, not by way of command.** In other words, Paul allows but doesn't command some abstention for the sake of prayer.

7:7: But I wish all [Christian] **people to be as also I** [am]. That is, unmarried (7:8; 9:5). **Nevertheless** [= despite my wish], **each person has his/her own gracious gift from God—on the one hand this way** [with marriage], **on the other hand this way** [with singleness]. It will come out in 7:25–35 why Paul wishes all his fellow Christians to be unmarried, as he is. "Nevertheless," meanwhile, introduces a realistic recognition that regardless of Paul's wish, God has graced some people with marriage as a gift, and others with singleness as a gift. So who is Paul, or anyone in the Corinthian church, to insist on sexual abstinence, whether by way of celibacy or by way of abstinence within marriage? "On the one hand . . . on the other hand" highlights the divinely determined difference between the gifts of marriage and singleness and thus adds emphasis to Paul's rejection of any demand that unmarried Christians not get married (much less have sex outside marriage) and that married Christians abstain from sexual intercourse.

7:8–9: But as for the unmarried and the widows, I say it's good for them if they remain as I also am [that is, single]. **9But if they aren't controlling themselves, they're to get married. For it's better to get married than to be burning** [with sexual passion]. Paul narrows his focus down from married couples and Christians in general to "the unmarried and the widows." (There were widows aplenty, including young ones, because girls were regularly married off to men appreciably older than they.) Singleness is good for unmarrieds and widows—unless they can't suppress a sexual passion burning within them. For otherwise they'll fall into sexual misbehavior (compare 7:2).

7:10–11: But I'm commanding the married—not I, rather the Lord [is commanding] **a wife not to get uncoupled from** [her] **husband** [by divorcing him] **11(but even if she were to get uncoupled, she's to remain unmarried or be reconciled to** [her] **husband), and** [the Lord is commanding] **a husband not to get rid of** [his] **wife** [by divorcing her]. Now Paul shifts from issuing his own apostolically authoritative command ("they're to get married" [7:9]) to relaying a command of Jesus, whom he calls "the Lord" to underline the divine authority that stands behind Jesus' command. This command is recorded in Mark 10:11–12. Paul gives its substance instead of quoting it. Ordinarily, divorce carried—and still carries—the right to marry someone other than the previous spouse. But for wives Paul allows at most a truncated divorce: separation from her husband without the right of remarriage to another man. For the husband, though, he doesn't allow even a truncated divorce. In other words, marriage is more binding for the husband than for the wife, though the prohibition of a wife's remarriage to another man makes marriage for her binding enough (compare 7:39). Perhaps the allowance of a truncated divorce for the wife has the purpose of giving her an out in case of physical abuse, of which there was plenty on the part of husbands, whereas in a male-dominated culture the husband doesn't stand in danger of such abuse from his wife.

7:12–14: But to the rest I, not the Lord, am saying, if any brother [= fellow Christian of ours] **has an unbelieving wife and this** [wife] **is glad to cohabit with him, he's not to get rid of her. 13And if any** [believing] **wife has an unbelieving husband and this** [husband] **is glad to cohabit with her, she's not to get rid of** [her] **husband. 14For the unbelieving husband has been consecrated in** [his] **wife and the unbelieving wife has been consecrated in the brother, since then** [= if it isn't so] **your children are unclean** [in the ritual sense of unconsecrated]. **But now** [as it is, since you're a believer though your spouse isn't] **they're consecrated.** "The rest" turn out to be believers married to unbelievers. "I, not the Lord, am saying" doesn't mean that what Paul then says lacks authority. He's the Lord's apostle, after all. He means that the Lord, Jesus, didn't say anything about religiously mixed marriages. So Paul can't reference him on the matter, as he did in regard to Christian couples at 7:10–11, and therefore must issue his own applicable commands on the Lord's behalf. Paul's use of "any brother" instead of "any believer" or "a believing husband" (either of which would parallel "an unbelieving wife") makes the local church a religious family similar to a biological family. Presumably one spouse has become a believer and the other hasn't in the sort of case Paul addresses, for in 7:39 he prohibits a believer's marrying an unbeliever. The unbelieving spouse "has been consecrated" in the sense of set apart from unbelievers who have an unbelieving spouse. Having a believing spouse distinguishes the unbeliever. "*In* [his] wife" and "*in* the brother" stress the closeness of this marital association with a believer and its consecrating effect. The consecration establishes a basis for the believer's staying with his or her unbelieving spouse, should the unbeliever be glad to maintain the marriage. "Since then [if there's no consecration of the unbeliever] your children are unclean" implies that believers married to unbelievers thought that though their *children* were consecrated because of having a believing parent, their *spouse* wasn't, so that the believer could divorce the unbeliever legitimately. The upshot of Paul's counter argument is that if the unbelieving spouse is consecrated as the children are, it would be just as wrong to get rid of that spouse as to get rid of the children. In reverse, if the believer were to get rid of the unbelieving spouse, the believer might as well get rid of the children. It needn't be said that riddance of the children would be undesirable as well as wrong. (In the first century Roman Empire fathers normally kept the children in cases of divorce, so that Paul's argument applies and appeals as much to fathers as to mothers.)

7:15–16: But if the unbeliever gets uncoupled, he/she is to get uncoupled, [because the believer, can't prevent the divorce]. **The brother or the sister isn't enslaved** [by the marriage] **in such** [cases]. **But God has called you in peace.** [16]**For how do you know, wife, whether you'll save** [your unbelieving] **husband? Or how do you know, husband, whether you'll save** [your unbelieving] **wife?** Since this letter is addressed to believers, not to unbelievers, Paul's command that "the unbeliever . . . is to get uncoupled" is indirect and therefore breathes the air of private resignation on the part of a believing spouse being divorced by an unbelieving spouse. And in fact a spouse couldn't fight divorce. Among Gentiles at least—and most of the Corinthians were Gentiles, biologically speaking—anybody who wanted a divorce could effect it by simply walking out of the marriage. By the same token, "the brother or the sister isn't enslaved in such [cases]" states a simple matter of fact. The believer is free of the marriage.[4] "But God has called you in peace" returns to the situation of a believer married to an unbeliever who is glad to maintain the marriage. The two were in a state of peaceful relations with each other when God called one of them, that is, effectively summoned one of them into the faith (compare 7:18 for "in" as meaning "in a state of"). So instead of breaking up the marriage the believer should preserve it in view of the possibility of saving the unbelieving spouse from eternal doom through converting him or her. Now we know the character of the unbeliever's and the children's consecration back in 7:14: separated from fellow unbelievers outside the home, the unbelieving spouse and the children have within their home a close-range exposure to the gospel through the believing spouse and parent—and therefore a good possibility of salvation through conversion.

---

[4]Whether freedom from the marriage implies freedom to remarry is a matter of dispute. Paul's later statement, "A wife is bound so long as her husband lives," so that only after her husband's death is she "free" to remarry (7:39; compare Romans 7:2–3), disfavors freedom to remarry. And though the language of freedom to remarry appears in ancient certificates of divorce, Paul's excluding such freedom when discussing divorce in 7:10–11 likewise disfavors it.

7:17: If not [that is, apart from the possibility of saving your spouse]**, as the Lord distributed** [an assignment] **to each** [believer]**, as God has called each** [believer]**, he** [the believer] **is to be walking about in this way. And in this way I'm giving orders in all the churches.** This verse forms a bridge to another topic, that of believers' assignments, or callings. Jesus is the Lord who "has distributed [an assignment] to each [believer]." God the Father is the one who "has called each [believer]." The call equates with the distribution, and both of them occurred at conversion. The believer "is to be walking around [that is, conducting his or her life] in this way [that is, in accordance with his or her distribution/calling]." Which means, as Paul will go on to explain, that the believer is to be content with his or her state in life as it was when conversion occurred. Meanwhile, a second "in this way" points to consistency in what Paul says here. "I'm giving orders" points to the authority with which he says it (compare 1:1; 4:17). And "in all the churches" points to the equal applicability to all Christians of what he says.

7:18–19: Was someone called who'd been circumcised? He's not to be pulling [skin] **over** [the head (glans) of his penis, as was done with surgical stitching to reverse the circumcision]. **Has someone in a state of uncircumcision been called? He's not to be getting circumcised.** [19]**Circumcision is nothing** [= insignificant]**, and uncircumcision is nothing. Rather, the keeping of God's commandments** [is everything (= significant; compare Romans 2:25–29)]. Paul introduces the states of circumcision and uncircumcision and will next introduce the states of slavery and freedom primarily, though not exclusively, as analogous to the states of marriage and singleness. Circumcision embarrassed some Jewish men when their penises were exposed at public baths and at athletic events in which they participated. (Athletes competed in the nude.) Gentiles usually considered circumcision a barbaric mutilation of the human body, but Jews and Gentiles heavily influenced by Judaism considered it a sign of belonging to God's covenant people. Paul says to let neither the usual Gentile ridicule of circumcision nor the Judaistic insistence on it make a Christian man reverse his circumcision or get circumcised. Circumcision is commanded in Genesis 17:9–14 for Abraham and his descendants through Isaac and Jacob. But the two occurrences of "is nothing" here in 7:19 reduce circumcision (and by extension other Old Testament rites prescribed for Israelites) to insignificance so far as churches, being multiethnic, are concerned. That "the keeping of God's commandments [is everything]" therefore draws a distinction between moral commandments which come over from the Old Testament (see Romans 13:8–10; Galatians 5:14, for example) and ritual commandments, such as circumcision, which don't come over. (Take as another example Paul's omission of the ritual commandment to observe the Sabbath day and his explicit rejection of the necessity to do so [Romans 14:5–6; Galatians 4:9–11; Colossians 2:16–17].) Similarly, neither marriage nor singleness counts as morally good, whereas fornication counts as morally evil. So the keeping of God's commandments, such as the one to flee fornication (6:18), is morally necessary whereas neither marriage nor singleness is in and of itself morally necessary.

7:20–22: Each person is to remain in this, [namely,] in the calling [= the state] in which he was called. ²¹As a slave were you called? It's not to be of concern to you. Nevertheless, if you can also become free, use [the opportunity] rather [than staying enslaved]. ²²For the person in the Lord who was called as a slave is the Lord's free person. Likewise, the one called as a free person is Christ's slave. "The calling in which he was called" is the state—whether married or unmarried, circumcised or uncircumcised, slave or free—in which the believer was at the time of his conversion. A state of slavery isn't to concern a Christian slave, as though that state denigrates his status before God the way it does in society at large. It should be noted that slavery in the Roman Empire didn't have a racial basis and that slaves had no human or legal rights. But slaves often had opportunities to gain freedom—by saving up money given them by their masters and buying their freedom, for example, and by pleasing their masters (though masters often freed their slaves when upkeep for them cost more than the slaves profited the masters through work). Paul bases his command to use an opportunity to become free from an earthly slaveowner on the Christian slave's being already the heavenly Lord's freed person. A freed person differs from a free person. The free person has never been a slave. The freed person *has* been a slave. The slave who is "in the Lord" by virtue of having the very Spirit of God that's in Jesus the Lord—that slave "is the Lord's freed person" inasmuch as the Lord acts as his patron. For he treats the Christian slave, not as a slave, but as a person whom he has freed from slavery but for whose welfare he takes responsibility and who in return owes him lifelong respect and specified services. Such is the meaning of "the Lord's freed person." By looking at himself in this way a Christian slave needn't be demoralized by his enslavement to a merely human master and, despite the admonition to remain "in the calling in which he was called," needn't hesitate to capitalize on an opportunity to gain freedom. Just as the Lord pays no attention to a Christian's earthly status as a slave, so he pays no attention to a Christian's earthly status as "a free person," but regards him as his own slave. But since "lord" was used for a slave's owner and master, we'd have expected "the *Lord's* slave" and, earlier, "*Christ's* freed person." Instead, Paul writes "the Lord's freed person" and "Christ's slave" and thus implies that just as the divine Lord acts as a Christian slave's patron, so the human Christ acts as the Christian free person's owner and master. (The divine Lord and the human Christ are one and the same, of course.) The Christian free person mustn't look down on the Christian slave, then; nor need the Christian slave grovel before the Christian free person.

7:23–24: You were bought at a price [see the comments on 6:20]. Don't become slaves of human beings. ²⁴Brothers, each [believer] is to remain alongside God in this, [namely, in the state] in which he was called. Being bought at a price follows naturally after the immediately preceding reference to "a free person" as "Christ's slave." In 6:20 "you were bought at a price" was addressed to all the Christians in Corinth. Here in 7:23, though, it's addressed only to the free Christians living there. Then Paul tells them, "Don't become slaves of human beings," which means that because Christ has purchased them to be his slaves, they're prohibited from selling themselves into slavery, as people sometimes did in those days. (Since a master supported his slaves, a poverty-stricken free person could often improve his economic condition this way.) In combination with Paul's command to take an opportunity for freedom, this prohibition undermines the institution of slavery in society. "Brothers" introduces a summation of the commands that started in 7:17. "*Each* [believer]" expands the summation to include all Christians, not just the free ones most recently addressed. "Alongside God" indicates that God himself stands with a believer in whatever state the believer found himself at the time God called him to salvation. Not bad company! So with the exception of slaves, it's quite satisfactory, indeed required, to stay in that class. Though Christian slaves are to take an opportunity for freedom, they aren't to revolt; and though within a church the barriers of class are to be broken down by common consent (see Galatians 3:28), in the world at large a forcible tearing down of such barriers by Christians would discredit the gospel. Stay put, then.

7:25: But concerning virgins I don't have a commandment of the Lord [as I did about marriage and divorce in 7:10–11]. But I'm giving a dictum as one who has been treated mercifully by the Lord so as to be faithful. "Virgins" appears to mean chaste young women of marriageable age (see 7:26–29); and because of a misguided opinion in the Corinthian church that all sexual intercourse was to be avoided (see 7:1 with comments), it appears that some in the church said these virgins shouldn't marry. To support the reliability of his following dictum on this issue, Paul cites the Lord's having shown him mercy so that he might serve the Lord faithfully. "Mercifully" alludes to Paul's having persecuted Christians prior to his conversion (15:9–10; 2 Corinthians 4:1; 1 Timothy 1:12–16). The dictum will arise out of a sense of unworthiness and obligation to be faithful, then, not out of arrogance or self-interest.

7:26–28: Therefore [because of my sense of unworthiness and obligation] I think this to be good because of the present crisis, that for a man to be this way is good: ²⁷Are you bound to a woman? Don't be seeking a loosening [of the bond]. Are you loosened from a woman? Don't be seeking a wife. ²⁸But even if you were to marry, you haven't sinned; and if the virgin were to marry, she hasn't sinned. But such people [as those who get married] will have affliction as to the

flesh, and I'm sparing you [by discouraging you from getting married]. "I think this to be good" starts an echo of a Corinthian slogan that Paul quoted in 7:1: "[It's] good for a man not to touch [= have sexual intercourse with] a woman." But Paul's dictum will revise and replace the Corinthian slogan. We don't know for sure what in particular "the present crisis" was that he makes the basis of his dictum. But whatever it was, his references in 7:29 to "the time" that "has been shortened" and to "the remainder [of time]" imply a crisis that points to the oncoming Day of the Lord, when Jesus returns (compare 10:11; Romans 13:11–14; Philippians 4:5b; 1 Thessalonians 4:13–5:2). "That for a man to be this way is good" completes the echo of the Corinthian slogan and identifies what "this" is that Paul thinks to be "good." The interjection of "because of the present crisis" required a repetition of "good"; but "in this way" looks forward to the following rhetorical questions, commands, and commentary, which together define Paul's dictum. Since he has announced the topic of virgins, "Are you bound to a woman?" asks whether a man is engaged to get married. If so, Paul tells him not to seek a breaking ("loosening") of the engagement for the sake of maintaining sexual abstinence. "Are you loosened from a woman?" asks whether a man has broken an engagement to get married. If so, Paul tells him not to seek a wife by getting engaged again and then marrying. "But even if you were to marry, you haven't sinned; and if the virgin were to marry, she hasn't sinned"—these statements show that "good" didn't have to do with morality, which would brook no exceptions like this one. Rather, "good" had to do with practicality, which Paul proceeds to spell out. He addresses the man but not the woman, because she had little or nothing to say about her engagement and marriage. Her family made such arrangements with the man. Paul warns that those who do get married despite his discouragement "will have affliction as to the flesh," by which he means the material pressures incurred by marriage on both husband and wife. "I'm sparing you" exhibits concern for the practicalities of his addressees' lives.

7:29–31: But I say this, brothers: the time has been shortened. As for the remainder [of time], [I say] **that both those who have wives should be as though not having** [wives], [30]**and** [that] **those who are weeping** [should be] **as though not weeping, and** [that] **those who are rejoicing** [should be] **as though not rejoicing, and** [that] **those who are making purchases** [should be] **as though not holding tight** [their purchases], [31]**and that those who are using the world** [should be] **as though not using** [it] **at all. For the complexion of this world is passing away.** Another affectionate address, "brothers," adds weight to the shortened time and therefore to the need to live as free as possible from worldly cares in the time left till the Day of the Lord. "As though not having [wives]" means that married Christian men should put a higher priority on living out the gospel than on pleasing their wives, though the latter isn't ruled out entirely (see, for example 7:2–3; Ephesians 5:25–33;

Colossians 3:19). "As though not weeping" means that weeping, as for example in mourning the dead, should not curtail a telling of the good news concerning salvation in Christ. "As though not rejoicing" means that rejoicing, as for example at a birth or a wedding, shouldn't rule out warning unbelievers of God's coming wrath. "As though not holding tight [their purchases]" means that Christians shouldn't lay up treasures on earth. And "as though not using [the world] at all" means that in their dealings with unbelievers Christians shouldn't make moral compromises. "The complexion of this world" means the way human society is presently shaped so as to give it a certain appearance. Sadly, sin has distorted its divinely intended shape, so that it will pass away under God's judgment. "*Is* passing away" makes that judgment so sure that it might as well be taking place already. So there's every reason *not* to make moral compromises in worldly dealings.

7:32–35: **And I want you to be free of care. The unmarried** [man] **cares about the Lord's things, how he may please the Lord.** [33]**But the married** [man] **cares about the things of the world, how he may please** [his] **wife;** [34]**and he's divided** [between pleasing his wife and pleasing the Lord]. **And the unmarried and virginal woman cares about the Lord's things, in order that she may be holy both in body and in spirit. But the married** [woman] **cares about the things of the world, how she may please** [her] **husband.** [35]**And I say this for your own benefit, not to throw a noose on you** [that is, not to restrict you]—**rather, for propriety and devotion** [in pleasing] **the Lord undistractedly.** In the Greek that Paul wrote, "free of care," "cares," and "is divided" have the same root. So there's a wordplay that highlights the divisive contest between caring about the Lord's things and caring about the world's things. Paul's recommendation of the single life shows concern both for his addressees and for the gospel. He plays off the demands of married life and the demands of the gospel against each other. Caring for the Lord's things equates with pleasing the Lord, and pleasing the Lord consists in bearing witness to the gospel in deed and word. Despite Paul's having addressed only men, he not only describes "the unmarried and virginal woman" as "car[ing] about the Lord's things" in like fashion to the unmarried man. He also and strikingly adds what he didn't say in connection with the unmarried man: "in order that she may be holy both in body and in spirit." Since "holy" carries first and foremost the ritual meaning of "set apart from ordinary use," the woman's holiness in body and in spirit means that her unmarried state keeps her from having to serve a husband's sexual and emotional needs and thus enables her to devote all her energies to serving the Lord (7:1–6). "Your *own* benefit" stresses Paul's concern that the unmarried will lose their freedom from worldly care if they marry. "Not to throw a noose on you" denies that staying single is restrictive. It's marriage that restricts. "For propriety and devotion [in pleasing] the Lord undistractedly" implies that it wouldn't be proper for a married Christian to devote him- or herself to "the Lord's things" undistractedly. For marriage rightly demands distractions. The emphasis falls, nevertheless, on pleasing the Lord undistractedly unless an unsatisfied urge to marry makes one vulnerable to inappropriate behavior.

7:36–38: But if anyone thinks [he's] **acting inappropriately toward his virgin, if he's over the top and thus it** [marriage] **ought to happen, he's to do what he wishes** [to do]. **He isn't sinning. They're to marry.** **[37]But he who stands firm in his heart, not having a necessity, but has authority as regards his own wish and in his own heart has decided this,** [namely,] **to keep his own virgin, will do well.** **[38]And so, both he who marries his own virgin does well and he who doesn't marry** [his own virgin] **will do better.** "Anyone" is the man who wants to marry. "His virgin" is the young woman he wants to marry. "Acting inappropriately" means fondling in unacceptable ways. "Over the top" means overflowing with sexual passion. "He's to do what he wishes"—that is, get engaged and marry the young woman—because of that passion, which creates a moral necessity ("ought" [compare 7:9]). The man will be incurring worldly cares, but he won't be sinning. "They're to marry" goes against English translations that treat the passage as dealing with whether a father (who is never mentioned as such) should marry off his daughter (who is never mentioned as such or identified with the virginal woman). A man "stands firm in his heart" by committing himself to celibacy. He's to do so only if his sexual urge doesn't create the moral necessity of marriage and thus enables him to keep his wish for sexual intercourse under control. Then his decision to stay single will be valid. "His *own* wish" and "his *own* heart" stress how deeply felt is his decision and how fundamentally different it is from the societal convention of marriage. But Paul puts the man's staying single in terms of "keep[ing] his own virgin," that is, preserving her a virgin so that "she may be holy both in body and in spirit" for the sake of "car[ing] about the Lord's things"—like a single man—"undistractedly." "His *own* virgin" points up the radicality of deciding for singleness. Though the marrying man "does well" to fulfill his overflowing sexual urge in the God-ordained way, the nonmarrying man will do better by enabling himself to please the Lord undistractedly.

7:39–40: A wife is bound [in marriage] **for as long a time as her husband lives. But if the husband were to fall asleep** [= die], **she's free to be married to whom she wishes, only in the Lord.** **[40]But according to** [my] **dictum** [7:25], **she's more fortunate if she remains thus** [that is, an unmarried widow]. **And I daresay** [that] **I too have God's Spirit.** Since according to 7:10–11 uncoupling from a husband doesn't allow remarriage to another man but requires keeping open the possibility of reconciliation, the marital bond lasts as long as the husband lives. "But if her husband were to fall asleep" brings us back to the widows mentioned in 7:8–9. As a single man is free to marry his own virgin in accordance with his wish, so a widow "is free to be married to whom she wishes." But "only in the Lord" limits her marital possibilities to a fellow believer in Jesus as Lord. Paul will have none of a Christian's marrying a non-Christian for the purpose of evangelism. Only the conversion of one spouse but not the other allows for evangelism within a marriage (7:12–16). But the widow who doesn't remarry is more fortunate for not reincurring worldly concerns having to do with pleasing a husband. "And I daresay [that] I too have God's Spirit" suggests, probably with some sarcasm, that Paul knew of some in the Corinthian church who laid claim to a revelation by God's Spirit that differed from what he has had to say. See 1 Timothy 5:3–16 for a differentiation between young and old widows.

ON FOODS, ESPECIALLY MEAT, SACRIFICED TO IDOLS
1 Corinthians 8:1–11:1

Now Paul proceeds to another topic that came up in the Corinthians' letter to him (7:1). The topic has to do with the question whether Christians can eat foods that they know came from sacrifices to idols. Take meat especially. Parts of an animal sacrificed at a temple housing the idol of a god were burned in honor of the god. The priests of the temple got some of the meat for their own consumption. The offerer got some for himself, his family, and guests to eat in the temple (more exactly, in a dining room adjacent to the temple) or at home. Any remaining meat was put up for sale to the general public. You could be sure that meat eaten in the temple had come from an animal sacrificed to the god of that temple. But elsewhere, in private homes and public markets, you wouldn't know unless you were told, because not all meat came from sacrificed animals. It turns out that Paul prohibits Christians from eating any food they know to have been sacrificed to an idol, but they don't have to enquire whether food had such an origin.

8:1–3: And concerning [foods] **sacrificed to idols, we know that "we all have knowledge." Knowledge puffs up, but love builds up. [2]If someone supposes he has come to know something, he hasn't yet known** [it] **as it's necessary to know** [it]. **[3]But if someone loves God, this person has come to be known by him** [God]. In 8:4–6 Paul will define the knowledge in view as a knowledge that there's only one God, the Father, and only one Lord, Jesus Christ, so that idols don't represent real gods and real lords as pagans mistakenly think they do. According to 8:8–13 even some Christians, acclimated to idolatry because of their pagan past, make that same mistake though they *worship* only God, the Father, and the Lord, Jesus Christ. Because of the mistake, Paul will deny in 8:7 that everybody has knowledge. Here in 8:1, then, "We all have knowledge" appears to be a slogan of those Corinthian Christians who, unlike the others, recognized the falsity of polytheism (the belief in many deities). Since Paul immediately follows with the observation that "knowledge puffs up," "we know that" represents Paul's sardonic prefix to the Corinthians' slogan. Furthermore, his quoting the slogan in connection with "[foods] sacrificed to idols" implies that the slogan rationalized unlimited freedom to eat foods sacrificed to idols, this on the ground that nonexistent gods and lords such as are represented by idols can't taint sacrifices offered to them. For nothing comes of nothing. But along with Paul's sardonic prefix to the slogan and his postfixed warning that "knowledge puffs up" whereas "love builds up," the use of "[foods] sacrificed *to idols*" instead of the usual pagan expression, "*sacred* sacrificial [food]" (as in 10:28), signals that he disagrees with the way the slogan is being used (compare his command in 10:14 to be fleeing from idolatry).

"If someone *supposes* he has come to know something" refers to thinking mistakenly that information is all that's needed for the governance of Christian conduct. Paul counters that loving God has to accompany the learning of information if knowledge is to govern such conduct correctly. Why so? Because by itself knowledge puffs up the knower, whereas love builds up others (compare 3:10–15 for the analogy of building); and love for others, particularly for fellow Christians, grows out of love for God, because they're his building (3:9b). And though building up others out of love for God may seem to deprive ourselves in a zero sum game, the supposed deprivation is more than compensated for by God's having come to know the person who loves him. For God's having *come* to know him doesn't have to do solely with divine omniscience (a matter of information). It has to do also with God's entering into an intimately and mutually loving relation with that person (compare the euphemistic use of "know" for sexual intercourse, starting in Genesis 4:1). In other words, God's knowledge too is information imbued with love. Better to be known by him in this way than to know anything by way of information without love (compare 13:2).

8:4–6: Concerning the eating of [foods] **sacrificed to idols, therefore, we know that an idol in the world** [is] **a nothing and that** [there's] **not one god except one** [God]. **[5]For even if there are, indeed, *so-called* gods, whether in heaven or on earth—as indeed there are** *many* [so-called] **gods and** *many* [so-called] **lords— [6][there is] for us, nonetheless, *one* God, the Father, from whom all things** [have their existence]**—and we** [exist] **for him—and** [there is for us] *one* **Lord, Jesus Christ, through whom all things** [came into existence]**—and we** [exist] **through him.** Paul adds the element of eating to the initial phrase with which 8:1 opened. "Therefore" bases the following on the aforementioned difference between knowledge, which puffs up, and love, which builds up. Paul's "we know" omits the "all" that appeared in the slogan quoted in 8:1 ("We all have knowledge"), because even some Christians mistakenly think of idols as significant somethings rather than as insignificant nothings (see 8:7). So "we" is here limited to those who recognize with Paul "that an idol in the world [is] a nothing and that [there's] not one god except one [God]."[5] Paul's addition of "in the world" to

"an idol" limits the idol's location to this-worldly society. The idol isn't transcendent.

The wordplay (regularly missed in translations) in "not one god except one [God]" stresses the falsity of polytheism (compare Deuteronomy 6:4, which Paul appears to split by distinguishing between God, whom he calls "the Father," and "the Lord," whom he calls "Jesus Christ"). "For" introduces an explanation of what Paul means in view of the pervasiveness of polytheism in the Roman Empire. "Even if" and two occurrences of "indeed" highlight his recognition of that pervasiveness. "In heaven" as well as "on earth" recognizes that though idols are confined to "the world," polytheists located some of their gods in heaven, though representing them on earth with idols. But Paul's "so-called" denies the gods' true existence both in heaven and on earth, and "*many* gods" contrasts with "*one* [God]." Because of Jesus Christ's identity as the Lord, Paul adds "*many* [so-called] lords" for a contrast with Jesus Christ as the "*one* Lord" ("L/lord" being another designation of a deity, though it has other applications too). "For us," which occurs twice, means "for us Christians in accordance with our knowledge (not merely in accordance with our opinion)." "Nonetheless" underscores the contrast between the falsity of polytheism and the truth of "one God, the Father . . . and one Lord, Jesus Christ." "The Father" implies that the Lord, Jesus Christ, is God's Son and therefore shares deity with his Father. "From whom all things [have their existence]" describes God as the source of all that exists. "And we [exist] for him" means that human beings, especially Christians, not only owe their existence to God but also owe fealty and homage to him. "Through whom all things [came into existence]" describes Jesus Christ as God the Father's agent in the creation of all things. "And we [exist] through him" means that Jesus Christ sustains human beings, especially Christians, in their existence.

8:7: Nevertheless, the knowledge [of the one God and of the one Lord] **doesn't** [exist] **in all people. And by custom as regards the idol up till now, some are eating** [the food] **as** [food] **sacrificed to an idol; and their consciousness, being weak, is being defiled** [when they eat in this way]. "Nevertheless" introduces the qualification that not everybody has the knowledge of what we call monotheism. Because of following references to fellow Christians, those who don't have this knowledge and therefore eat food sacrificed to idols as though the idols represent real gods and real lords, not just so-called ones, include some Christians. Though as Christians they now worship only God, the Father, and the Lord, Jesus Christ, their idolatrous past makes them still think polytheistically. Most English translations have "their conscience." But "conscience" probably overinterprets the underlying Greek word to mean a moral compass. "Consciousness"

---

[5]Some scholars favor the translation, "we know that [there's] no idol in the world." But since Paul elsewhere refers to idols as existent in the world (8:7; 10:19; 12:2; Romans 2:22; 2 Corinthians 6:16; 1 Thessalonians 1:9), those scholars are forced to interpret their translation as meaning that though idols exist as images, no idol exists as a deity.

may capture Paul's meaning more accurately. In this case he means that people's consciousness is being polluted with a false belief in many gods and many lords, so that when they eat food known by them to have been sacrificed to an idol, they do so with a false consciousness of a so-called god's or a so-called lord's association with the food. Their consciousness is weak, then, in that it lacks the robust knowledge that there's only one God and only one Lord. Such knowledge was robust, and had to be robust, because polytheism prevailed in the Roman Empire.

8:8–11: But food won't make us stand before God [to be judged for what we ate]. Compare Romans 14:10; 2 Corinthians 4:14; 11:2; Ephesians 5:27; Colossians 1:22, 28; 2 Timothy 2:15 for being made to stand before God at the Last Judgment. Because Paul doesn't refer specifically to "[foods] sacrificed to idols," for the moment "food" means food *as such*, not necessarily food that's been sacrificed to an idol; and in and of itself—that is, apart from other considerations—food won't subject us to God's judgment one way or another. **We're neither lacking** [God's favor] **if we don't eat, nor are we flourishing** [in God's favor] **if we do eat.** [9]**But watch out lest this authority of yours** [over whether to eat] **somehow become for the weak** [in consciousness] **a stumbling** [block]. "A stumbling [block]" stands for something that trips a person into sinning, most especially into apostatizing from Christian faith. Paul then explains the way apostasy might happen ("somehow"). [10]**For if someone were to see you, the one who has knowledge** ["that an idol in the world (is) a nothing" (8:4)], **reclining** [at table] **in an idol's temple, his consciousness—because he's weak** [for lack of the knowledge that you have]—**will be built up, won't it, so that he'll eat the** [foods] **sacrificed to idols?** Implied answer: Yes. Diners at formal meals reclined around a low table. Regardless of the understanding of believers in only one God and one Lord, it would be understood by believers in many gods and many lords that a meal eaten in a pagan temple is eaten in honor of the god of that temple and thus violates the Christian worship of only one God and only one Lord. Whereas according to 8:1 "love builds up" fellow believers so as to stabilize them in their Christian worship, Paul sardonically says that seeing a fully monotheistic believer dining in the temple of an idol will "buil[d] up" the regrettably semimonotheistic believer's consciousness, so that he too "will eat the [foods] sacrificed to idols" and thus, according to his own belief in many gods and many lords, apostatize. [11]**For by your knowledge the one who is weak, the brother on account of whom Christ died, is being ruined** [because of your dining in an idol's temple, which setting makes obvious that the food has been sacrificed to an idol]. "Is being ruined" points to eternal lostness because of apostasy; and "the brother on account of whom Christ died" appeals to what Paul hopes is the knowledgeable Christian's love of his theologically undereducated fellow Christian.

8:12–13: And by sinning in this way against [your] **brothers—that is, by mauling their consciousness,**

weak though it is—you're sinning against Christ. [13]**Therefore, indeed, if food trips my brother** [into apostatizing], **by no means will I ever eat meat, lest I trip my brother.** Strikingly, Paul reserves the vocabulary of sinning for those who eat with knowledge but without love rather than for those who eat without knowledge and therefore with a polytheistic supposition. To sin against fellow Christians is to sin against Christ, because all Christian believers are "in Christ." "Mauling their consciousness" tells why the sin goes "*against* [your] brothers." "Weak though it [their consciousness] is" exacerbates the sin in that it's unfair—or, in this case, unloving—to beat up on the weak. "Therefore" builds on the equation of "sinning . . . against your brothers" and "sinning against Christ." The addition of "indeed" underscores the back reference to this equation. Then Paul makes himself an example to be followed, but deliberately exaggerates to heighten his example. He exaggerates by saying, "if food [that is, food as such, not just food sacrificed to an idol] trips my brother, by no means will I ever eat meat [meat as such, not just meat from an animal sacrificed to an idol], lest I trip my brother." As though he'd become a vegetarian or even stop eating altogether to keep from causing his fellow Christian to apostatize! And "*by no means* will I *ever* . . ." adds a temporal dimension to this strongest possible negative.

Now Paul makes his *actual* behavior an example of not tripping the weak; and to maximize the example, he cites features of his status that could well make him care more for pleasing himself than for self-sacrificing to keep from tripping the weak. **9:1–2: I'm free, am I not? I'm an apostle, am I not? I've seen Jesus, our Lord, haven't I? You're my work in the Lord, aren't you?** The implied answer to all four of these questions is affirmative. [2]**If I'm not an apostle to others, I'm nevertheless** [an apostle] **to you, indeed. For in the Lord you're the seal of my apostleship.** Paul is no earthly human being's slave. He's not even a former slave, now freed but bound by certain obligations to his ex-master. He's free and always has been (compare the comments on 7:21–22). And not only a free man, but also an apostle, so that he speaks and acts with the very authority of Jesus, who sent him with that authority. And an apostle in the strict sense of one who has seen Jesus (15:8; compare Acts 1:22; 2:32; 3:15; 4:33), not just in the loose sense of one sent from church to church on an itinerant ministry (see 2 Corinthians 8:23, for example). "Our *Lord*" underscores the authority of Jesus that Paul has as Jesus' apostle. "*Our* Lord" puts the Corinthian believers, too, under Jesus' authority, but not as authorized apostles like Paul. They're Paul's "work" because he evangelized them (compare 3:6a with 3:13–15). But addition of "in the Lord" gives Jesus the credit (see 1:30–31). There are some Christians to whom Paul isn't an apostle. He didn't evangelize them and hadn't been sent to do so. But since the Lord sent him to evangelize the Corinthians, Paul is certainly an apostle to them. "Nevertheless" and "indeed" stress the point in order that they may heed his instructions. And he stresses this point further by explaining that their conversions confirm the Lord's having sent him as their apostle. Paul compares them to a seal stamped with his name to indicate their belonging to him as his converts. But a second occurrence of "in the Lord" gives Jesus the credit once again and indicates that his ownership of them supersedes Paul's.

9:3–6: My defense to those who examine me is this: ⁴**[It's] not [that] we don't have authority to eat and drink, is it** [that is, the right to get board (and room, presumably) from you who owe your conversions to our evangelizing you]**?** ⁵**[It's] not [that] we don't have authority, is it, to lead about a sister-wife** [= a wife who's a fellow believer] **as also the rest of the apostles and the Lord's brothers and Cephas have authority to do** [and apparently do]**?** ⁶**Or do only I and Barnabas not have authority not to work** [for a living but to depend on our converts for it]**?** According to 2:14–15 "the Spiritual person examines all things, but he himself is examined by no one." Since Paul claimed in 7:40 to have God's Spirit, then, he's not subject to examination by other human beings. So his defense to those who examine him is spoken tongue-in-cheek. It's not that anybody in particular is actually examining him, much less has the right to. He's conjuring up an imaginary scene to make a point, as indicated further by his immediately switching from "I," "my," and "me" to "we," which includes his missionary teammates. Like him, they didn't take along a believing wife in their travels (compare 7:7a). Though the reference to their "authority to eat and drink" has to do with authority to demand material support from the beneficiaries of their evangelistic labor, the subtext has to do with the question of food sacrificed to idols. If idols represent nonexistent gods and food sacrificed to them is therefore unaffected by those so-called gods, Christians have authority to eat such food. But should they exercise that authority when it's known that the food has been sacrificed to an idol? For "the Lord's brothers" see the comments on Acts 1:14. Apparently they traveled about in evangelism—Cephas, too (compare the slogan, "I belong to Cephas" [1:12]). Barnabas didn't help Paul evangelize Corinth (see Acts 15:36–40 with 18:1–17), but it looks as though the Corinthians knew him at least by reputation. He had traveled with Paul on Paul's first missionary journey (Acts 13–14); and by the implication of Paul's present comment, he too supports himself.

9:7: Who ever does military service with his own rations? Who plants a vineyard and doesn't eat its fruit [compare Deuteronomy 20:6]**? Or who shepherds a flock and doesn't eat** [we'd say, "drink"] **some of the flock's milk?** The army provided food rations to soldiers. Wages are not at issue here—just sustenance. Paul piles analogy on top of analogy to make his point that work deserves at least sustenance, so that as an apostle he has the right to get material support from his Corinthian converts.

9:8–11: I'm not saying these things in accordance with a human being [= on the basis of human authority]**, am I? Or the Law, too, says these things, doesn't it?** ⁹**For it's written in the law of Moses, "You shall not muzzle an ox while it's threshing** [= treading the grain to separate the wheat from the chaff] [Deuteronomy 25:4]**." God isn't concerned for oxen, is he?** ¹⁰**Or he's speaking entirely on our account,** [isn't he]**? For on our account it was written, because the one ploughing ought to be ploughing in the hope—and the one reaping** [ought to be reaping] **in hope—of sharing** [the crop (compare 3:6–8; 16:15 for the agricultural analogy)]**.** ¹¹**If we've sown Spiritual things for you,** [is it] **a big thing if we'll reap your fleshly** [things (= material support)]**?** Here Paul ratchets up his argument by turning from the human customs of supplying soldiers with their food rations and allowing planters of a vineyard to eat its fruit and shepherds to draw nourishment from their flock— Paul turns from these human customs to the Mosaic law, which derives ultimately from God himself. The implied answer to Paul's question whether God is concerned for oxen is "No," as confirmed by Paul's saying that God "is speaking [in the Mosaic law] *entirely* on our account." (Despite some English translations to the contrary, there's no "only" between "concerned" and "for oxen" in Paul's text; and his use in 5:10; 9:22; 16:12; Romans 3:9 of the Greek word underlying "entirely" favors this translation over weaker translations.) In other words, if it weren't for the right of Christian evangelists to draw material support from their converts, God wouldn't have seen to it that the Mosaic law demands keeping unmuzzled an ox which is treading grain, so that the ox can eat some of the wheat being trodden out for others. The figure of threshing leads naturally to prior ploughing and reaping and to prior sowing and reaping. See the comments on 2:12–13 for "Spiritual things," especially in regard to the capitalization of "Spiritual." Since "Spiritual things" have eternal value whereas "fleshly things" have only temporary value, it wouldn't be "a big thing" if Paul and company were to get material support from their Corinthian converts, who've received from them Spiritual enrichment. But to strengthen his point, he puts the possibility in the future tense ("if we'll reap your fleshly [things]") rather than in a hypothetical past tense (such as "if we had reaped your fleshly [things]"). As a result, his coming denial that he'll ever accept their material support gains in dramatic effect.

9:12: If others share the authority over you [to receive material support]**, we** [share this authority] **more, don't we? Nevertheless, we haven't used this authority. Nevertheless, we endure all sorts of things** [such as having to work for our living despite your obligation to support us] **lest we give any hindrance to the gospel about the Christ.** We don't know the identity of "others" who because of their ministry in Corinth shared with Paul and company the authority to get material support from the Christians there, though because "Apollos watered" in Corinth as a followup to Paul's "plant[ing]" (3:5–6), Apollos must have been one of them. Since the verb "share" also means "partake of," it's likely they exercised this authority as well as sharing it. Not Paul, though. Without exercising it he and company shared the authority "more" in the sense of having a stronger right than the others did to expect material support from the Corinthians. This stronger right derived from having been the first to evangelize Corinth. Two instances of "Nevertheless" highlight this nonexercise of the authority and consequent endurance of all sorts of hardships (for which see 4:11–13 and compare 2 Corinthians 11:23–33; 1 Thessalonians 2:9). Again, this nonexercise of authority presents an example designed to keep the Corinthian believers from exercising authority to eat food known to have been sacrificed to an idol, because eating such food might trip a fellow Christian into apostasy (chapter 8). "Lest we give any hindrance to the gospel about the Christ" implies that if Paul and company had demanded material support, they'd have been suspected of preaching for material gain, as many itinerant religious teachers, philosophers, and orators were known to do (compare 2 Corinthians 2:17). Such a suspicion would have hindered the proclamation of the gospel from achieving its purpose of converting people to belief in Jesus as the Christ, the one whom God anointed with his Spirit to be our Savior. "Lest we give *any* hindrance" exhibits the limitless extent to which Paul and company went to ensure evangelistic success. Should the Corinthians do any less in regard to the eating of food known to have been sacrificed to an idol? Compare 8:9, 13 and the statement in 8:1 that "knowledge puffs up, but love builds up."

9:13–14: You know, don't you, that those who work the sacred things [= perform services at the temple] **eat the** [foods] **from the temple,** [that] **those who are occupied at the altar are given, along with** [it], **a distribution** [from the altar]. **¹⁴In this way also the Lord ordered those who are proclaiming the gospel to be living off the gospel.** Paul's citation of the Mosaic law concerning oxen leads him here to the Law's stipulation that for their sustenance Jewish priests (descendants of Moses' brother Aaron within the tribe of Levi) and Levites (the remaining members of that tribe) be given portions of the sacrificial offerings brought to the temple (and originally to the tabernacle), where they served (see Numbers 18:8–32; Deuteronomy 18:1–8). The same practice was observed at pagan temples. Then Paul makes this practice analogous to Jesus' "order[ing]" those who are proclaiming the gospel to be living off the gospel" (see Mark 6:7–10; Matthew 10:5–11; Luke 9:1–4; 10:1–8) and calls Jesus "the Lord" to underline the authority of Jesus' order.

9:15–18: But I've used none of these [rights]. **And I didn't write these things** [just now in this letter,] **in order that it** [material support from you] **might happen thus in my case. For** [it would be] **good for me, rather, to die than—. No one will void my boast! ¹⁶For if I'm proclaiming the gospel, I don't have a boast. For necessity is imposed on me. For woe to me if I weren't to proclaim the gospel! ¹⁷For if I'm doing this willingly, I have a reward. But if** [I'm doing this] **unwillingly, I've been entrusted with a managership. ¹⁸What then is my**

reward? That while proclaiming the gospel I present the gospel free of charge, so that I haven't at all used my authority in the gospel.** Despite the Lord's order that proclaimers of the gospel be living off their proclamation, Paul didn't use his authority to get material support from the Corinthians. This nonuse implies that he considered the Lord's order to have been addressed *through* the original disciples *to their hearers,* so that Paul could legitimately give up his right to material support. And he goes out of his way to deny he's now hinting that he'll henceforth accept such support from the Corinthians. He'd rather die than do so! And where we expect him to say "rather, to die than *for anyone to void my boast,*" he breaks off his sentence after "than" (of all places) and exclaims, "No one will void my boast!" This broken grammar dramatizes his refusal ever to take, much less demand, the Corinthians' material support. His boast consists in this refusal.

But beyond the dramatically broken grammar, the boast gets spelled out in five explanatory sentences, each one beginning with "For" and supporting what immediately precedes. Why hasn't Paul written to get material support? Because he's determined that no one void his boast by persuading him to accept such support. Why that determination? Because by itself, proclaiming the gospel is nothing to boast about, whereas proclaiming it without taking remuneration *is* something to boast about.[6] Why is only proclaiming the gospel nothing to boast about? Because Paul *has* to proclaim it. The "necessity" of proclaiming it has been "imposed" on him, so that he can take no credit for doing his job (see Galatians 1:15–16; Acts 9:15–16; 22:15, 21; 26:16–20). Why this necessity? Because failure to proclaim the gospel would bring him "woe." And why woe? Because he'd lose the reward he'll get if he proclaims the gospel willingly. "But if [I'm doing this] unwillingly, I've been entrusted with a managership" means that an unwilling proclamation of the gospel would reduce him to a slave who has been put in charge of household affairs but doesn't get rewarded for doing his duty (compare Luke 17:7–10). We expect Paul to answer his question, "What then is my reward?" in terms of something to be received at the Last Judgment. But no, he answers in terms of what he can boast about right now, that is, "proclaiming the gospel . . . free of charge," with the result that he hasn't "at all used" his "authority" to charge people for proclaiming "the gospel" to them. The ability to make this boast is reward enough, thank you.

9:19–23: For though being free from all [men], **I've enslaved myself to all in order that I may gain more** [of them as converts to the gospel]. **²⁰And I've become to the Jews** [as myself] **a Jew in order that I may gain Jews, to those under the Law as** [myself] **under the Law (though not** [in fact] **being myself under the**

---

[6]In first century Greco-Roman culture, boasting could be good as well as bad, whereas in our culture we tend to say we're proud of our accomplishments rather than saying we're boasting about them (compare the current touting of "a good self-image").

Law) in order that I may gain those under the Law, ²¹to those Law-less [that is, Gentiles, who aren't under the Mosaic law] as [myself] Law-less (though not being lawless in relation to God—rather, in-lawed in relation to Christ) in order that I may gain the Law-less. ²²I've become weak for the weak in order that I may gain the weak. I've become all things for all people in order that by all means I may save some. ²³I'm doing all things on account of the gospel in order that I may become a sharer of it with others. Here Paul explains how he hasn't at all used his authority in the gospel. The foregoing reference to managership by a household slave (9:17) turns his mind back to the claim in 9:1 that he's neither a slave nor a freed man—rather, a free man. In the present text he stresses his social freedom by adding "from all [men]." This stress makes all the more remarkable the evangelistic enslaving of himself "to all" (compare and contrast his prohibiting Christians from selling themselves into slavery [7:23]). "That I may gain more" blends the language of economic profit with the language of evangelistic success and produces a seeming paradox in that self-enslavement of an evangelistic sort makes profit for the slave. The profit consists, of course, in the winning of more converts.

Paul proceeds to define his self-enslavement in reference to Jews and others. He has become to the Jews as himself a Jew in the sense of subjecting himself to Jewish jurisprudence (as for example when he received thirty-nine lashes each of five times [2 Corinthians 11:24]), even though as a Christian he didn't have to. But he did to keep in touch with his fellow Jews, whom he wanted to convert. "As [myself] under the Law" has the sense of observing some features of the Mosaic law, as for example when he attended the Festival of Pentecost (16:8; Acts 20:16), even though as a Christian he didn't have to. But he did to keep in touch with those under the Law, whom he wanted to convert (see also Acts 21:20-26). "As [myself Law-less]" has the sense of giving up his dependence on Law-keeping for justification before God, so that he can present himself to Gentiles as an example of how they may be justified by faith apart from subjecting themselves to the Mosaic law (see, for example, Philippians 3:4-11). Paul carefully qualifies his freedom from the Mosaic law, though, as not implying that he lives lawlessly toward God; rather, he abides by the law of Christ, that is, what Christ instructed his followers to do (see, for example, Galatians 6:2, but also 1 Corinthians 7:10-11; Acts 20:35). Paul doesn't say he has become *as* himself weak in correspondence with his having become *as* himself a Jew *as* under the Law, and *as* Law-less. For by reducing his lifestyle to bare subsistence for the sake of evangelism he has become *actually* weak, like "the world's weak things" that "God has selected" in preference (for the most part) to "the world's . . . strong things" (1:26-29)—and this to "gain the weak" whom God has selected. "That by all means I may save some" summarizes the preceding and interprets the several occurrences of "may gain" as saving in the sense of converting people to salvation (compare 7:16).

9:24-25: On the one hand you know, don't you, that those who run in a stadium are *all* running? Of course you do, for it's obvious that they're all running. **On the other hand** [you know, don't you, that] *one* **receives the prize?** Of course you do. (Second and third place prizes weren't awarded.) **Run in this way: that you may win** [the prize]. ²⁵**And everyone who competes exercises self-control in all respects. Therefore, on the one hand, those** [competitors do it] **in order to receive a perishable wreath. On the other hand, we** [do it to receive] **an imperishable** [wreath]. Athletes who competed in contests such as the ancient Olympics and the Isthmian games near Corinth had to undergo a months-long discipline of rigorous exercise, a strict diet, and abstinence in matters of sex and alcohol or, as Paul puts it, "in all respects." For him, such discipline is analogous to Christians' needing to avoid food known to have been sacrificed to an idol. The victorious athletes' "perishable wreath" consisted of laurel, pine, or celery, all of which withered quickly. Christians victorious because of their analogous self-control will receive "an imperishable [wreath]" consisting in eternal life (compare Philippians 3:7-14). For professing Christians defeated because of their lack of self-control are no Christians at all and therefore won't receive that imperishable wreath (see the comments on 9:26-27).

9:26-27: So I'm running in this way: as not aimlessly [that is, not without the prize clearly in view]. **I'm boxing in this way: as not beating the air** [that is, not missing my target]. ²⁷**Instead, I'm punching my body and leading it into slavery lest after proclaiming** [the gospel] **to others I myself were somehow to become disqualified.** The target of Paul's punches turns out to be his own body in that by refusing to get material support from the Corinthians he subjects his body to manual labor so rigorous as to be comparable to the bruised and battered body of a boxer and to a lifestyle so penurious as to be comparable to slavery. (The verb for punching means to hit under the eye and thus cause a black eye but here carries the expanded meaning of bruising the body all over.) "Lest after proclaiming [the gospel] to others I myself were somehow to become disqualified" shows Paul determined to win the prize of an imperishable wreath representing eternal life. "After proclaiming [the gospel] to others" deepens the tragedy of failing to win that prize. "I *myself*" heightens the warning example that such a failure on Paul's part would be. "Somehow" puts forward the possibility of failure no matter how unexpected in his case. And "to become disqualified" confirms that failure to win the prize would mean losing out on eternal life, for in 2 Corinthians 13:5 disqualification runs counter to being "in the faith" and having "Jesus Christ in you," which are matters of salvation itself (see also Romans 1:28; 2 Timothy 3:8; Titus 1:16). So the underlying issue of eating food known to have been sacrificed to an idol is of no small import.

10:1-4: For I don't want you to be ignorant, brothers, [of the fact] **that our** [fore]**fathers were all under**

the cloud and [that] **all went through the sea** ²**and** [that] **all were baptized into Moses in the cloud and in the sea** ³**and** [that] **all ate the same Spiritual food** ⁴**and** [that] **all drank the same Spiritual drink. For they were all drinking from the Spiritual rock that was following them. And the rock was the Christ** [compare the Lord God's being called "the rock" in Deuteronomy 32:4, 13, 15, 18, 30–31]. "For" introduces an explanation of the reason why Paul has just issued his warning of possible disqualification (9:24–27). Lending gravity to this reason, and thus to the warning as well, are his statement that he doesn't want his addressees to be ignorant and his addressing them with "brothers." This familial address suits the familial reference to "our [fore]fathers," moreover. "Our [fore]fathers" sounds at first as though Paul is portraying Gentile as well as Jewish Christians as religious if not biological descendants of the ancient Israelites (compare Romans 4, 11). On the other hand, in 10:32 he'll distinguish "God's church," which consists of Gentile as well as Jewish Christians, from "Jews" (as well as from "Greeks"). So it's probably better to say that here Paul calls the ancient Israelites "our [fore]fathers" in a simply experiential sense: their experiences were something like our Christian experiences, and their experiences support Paul's warning to the Corinthian Christians.

"Under the cloud" describes those Israelites who'd come out of Egypt (Numbers 14:14; Psalm 105:39). "Through the sea" describes their passage through the Red Sea (more accurately, the Reed Sea) on the way out of Egypt into that wilderness (Exodus 14:21–22; Psalm 78:13). Then the phraseology changes to "*in* the cloud [waters above] and *in* the sea [waters below]" to compare those Israelites' experience to Christian baptism—that is, a going under water and through it. The comparison attains its sharpest focus in the phrase, "baptized into Moses," which parallels "baptized into Christ" (Romans 6:3; Galatians 3:27) and suggests a union of the ancient Israelites with Moses similar to Christians' union with Christ. But just as being under the cloud and going through the sea didn't entail getting wet, so that the experience was only similar to Christian baptism, so the baptism into Moses was only similar to baptism into Christ in that there was no Spiritual union with Moses as there is with Christ.

But the ancient Israelites did eat "Spiritual food," the manna that God supplied them in the wilderness (Exodus 16; Psalm 78:23–29), and drink "Spiritual drink," water from "the Spiritual rock" (Exodus 17:1–7; Numbers 20:2–13; Psalm 78:15–16; 105:40; 114:8). Paul identifies this rock as "the Christ." But since the Christ wasn't yet incarnate, Paul alludes to him as "the *Spiritual* rock" in that it was as divine Spirit that the Christ provided drink (compare the identification of "the Lord" with "the Spirit" in 2 Corinthians 3:17). Paul's description of the rock as "following" the Israelites draws on an ancient Jewish tradition that the rock from which flowed water to slake their thirst was actually a large stone that rolled along behind them wherever they wandered in the wil-

derness—an easy inference from the biblical text, since in it the two instances of water's coming from a rock are positioned at the beginning and the end of the wandering. It seemed natural, then, to think of only one rock that followed them to provide water during the intervening decades of wandering (compare the use of other extrabiblical Jewish traditions in Acts 7:53; 2 Timothy 3:8; Hebrews 2:2; Jude 9, 14–15). Paul describes the drink as "Spiritual" in that it represented the Spirit, whom the Christ was later to give as a drink to believers in him (12:13b; see the comments on 2:12–13 for capitalizing "Spiritual"). Paul likewise describes the food as "Spiritual" in that it represented the Christ's future offering of himself to God "through the eternal Spirit" (Hebrews 9:14; compare 1 Corinthians 15:45).

So just as the Israelites' baptism into Moses in the cloud and in the sea foreshadowed Christians' baptism into Christ, the Israelites' eating Spiritual food and drinking Spiritual drink foreshadowed Christians' eating and drinking the Lord's Supper, which will come up explicitly in 10:16–17, 21; 11:20–34. Herein lies the point of Paul's not wanting the Corinthians "to be ignorant." In reference to the Israelites' reception of God's benefactions, six occurrences of "all," supplemented by "the *same* Spiritual food" and "the *same* Spiritual drink," leave no excuse for the displeasing of God by any of those Israelites. Correspondingly, the facts that "we [Christians] *all* partake of the *one* loaf ['the Christ's body' (10:16–17)]" and that "we've *all* been baptized in *one* Spirit into *one* body [of Christ (10:16–17; 12:27)] and have *all* been made to drink *one* Spirit" (12:13) leave no excuse for the displeasing of God by any Christian.

10:5: God wasn't pleased with most of them, however; for [= as evidenced by the fact that] **they were strewn about** [as corpses] **in the wilderness.** Of the adults who came out of Egypt, only Caleb and Joshua survived the wandering in the wilderness (Numbers 14:26–35; 26:65). That the rest had their corpses "strewn about in the wilderness" delivers a stern warning to Christians that they shouldn't displease God by misbehaving in ways like those of the ancient Israelites. Christians who do misbehave in such ways won't enter the Promised Land of eternal life, but "will pay a penalty, [namely,] eternal destruction away from the Lord's face" (2 Thessalonians 1:9).

10:6–7: And these things happened [as] **symbols of us, in order that we not be lusters after evil things as those** [forefathers of ours] **also lusted** [after evil things]. ⁷**And don't become idolaters as some of them** [did], **as indeed it's written, "The people sat down to eat and drink and stood up to play** [Exodus 32:6]." By "symbols of us" Paul means that we Christians should see the ancient Israelites as symbolizing us Christians, God's benefactions on them as symbolizing his benefactions on us, and his displeasure with them and its judgmental consequence as symbolizing both his displeasure with us if we misbehave and its judgmental consequence. Since Exodus 32:6 has to do with what the Israelites did after sacrificing to the golden calf, Paul's quotation relates "lust[ing] after evil things" to eating food known to have been sacrificed to idols. "And don't become idolaters as some of them [did]" indicates that such eating counts as idolatry—even apart from offering the sacrifice, for Paul omits to mention that and focuses exclusively on the idolatry of eating and drinking such food. For the drinking, we should probably think of libations poured out to the god of the idol. "As those [forefathers] *also* lusted" implies that some of the Corinthians are lusting after these evil things. "As *indeed* it's written" highlights the quotation as a warning to the rest of the Corinthians that they shouldn't become idolaters by eating food and drinking wine known to have been sacrificed to an idol. Such eating and drinking stands in stark contrast with the aforementioned eating of "Spiritual food" and drinking of "Spiritual drink." "And stood up to play" doesn't necessarily imply sexual play in Exodus 32:6. But given Paul's immediately following reference to the Israelites' fornicating on another occasion (10:8), here in 1 Corinthians "to play" probably carries the connotation of afterdinner revelry that degenerates into a sexual orgy.

10:8–10: And let's not be fornicating, as some of them fornicated, and twenty-three thousand fell [dead] on a single day. ⁹And let's not be testing out the Christ, as some of them tested [him] and were being dispatched [= killed] by snakes. ¹⁰And let's not be grumbling, as indeed some of them grumbled and were dispatched by the destroyer. By including himself in the exhortation, "And let's not be fornicating," Paul reprises his exemplary self-discipline as described in 9:26–27. The story of the Israelites' fornicating appears in Numbers 25:1–9 and starts with the eating of food sacrificed to pagan gods just as in Paul's day fornication often followed upon idolatrous feasts. The death of so many as "twenty-three thousand" in so short a time as "a single day" dramatizes how serious is the sin of fornication. Numbers 25:9 says that 24,000 died by a plague. Therefore Paul mustn't be exaggerating by speaking of 23,000. He's rounding off 24,000 to 20,000 and then adding 3,000 for an allusion to those who according to Exodus 32:28 were killed for worshiping the golden calf. This allusion is confirmed by the fact that Numbers 25:9 says nothing about 24,000 "*fall*[ing dead] on *a single day*" (so Paul), whereas Exodus 32:28 says that about 3,000 "*fell* [dead] on *that day*" (compare the comments on Matthew 1:1–17; Revelation 13:18 for two examples of similar plays on numbers).

"And let's not be testing out the Christ" implies that our misbehavior would strongly tempt him to judge us. (The underlying Greek word carries the meanings of both "test" and "tempt," since every test includes a temptation and every temptation includes a test.) In the ancient Israelites' case the Christ yielded to that temptation—rightfully, because their misbehavior deserved judgment. That they tested him out prior to his incarnation substantiates the earlier identification of "the Spiritual rock that was following them" with "the Christ" (10:4). "Were being dispatched by snakes" identifies the

punishment for the Israelites' testing him out with a complaint about lack of food and water—except for the manna, which they disliked (Numbers 21:4–6; Psalm 78:18). Apparently they didn't know that the water-producing rock was following them. The use of snakes to dispatch them for their tempting the Christ suited a snake's having issued the first temptation (Genesis 3:1–7). The incident of their grumbling, so that "some of them . . . were dispatched by the destroyer," is recorded in Numbers 16:41–50. In Numbers the Lord dispatched the grumblers by means of a plague. So Paul's saying "some of them . . . were dispatched by the destroyer" identifies the preincarnate Christ with the Lord and portrays him as the destroyer on that occasion just as Exodus 12:1–29 portrayed "the destroyer" as the Lord's alter ego (see especially Exodus 12:23 with 12:29). The portrayal by Paul is designed to frighten with good reason any Corinthian Christians who might grumble that avoidance of food known to have been sacrificed to an idol would disrupt their social relations with non-Christians, relations supposedly essential to their economic and other interests. But "indeed" underscores the grumbling and consequent dispatchment of the Israelites as a prophylactic against such grumbling by the Corinthians. Overall, the piling up of three specific instances of judgment on the Israelites sends the Corinthians a danger signal.

10:11–13: These things happened to those [forefathers] as symbols and were inscripturated for the admonition of us, on whom the ends of the ages have come down. ¹²And so, the person who supposes he's standing [and thus invincible to God's judgment] **is to watch out lest he fall** [under that judgment, as our forefathers fell dead in the wilderness]. **¹³No temptation has [over]taken you except a human one** [that is, one typical of temptations faced by other human beings too]. **But God is faithful, who won't allow you to be tempted above what you can** [resist]. **Rather** [than allowing you to face an irresistible temptation], **he'll make along with the temptation also an escape route so that** [you] **can bear up under** [the temptation]. For the phrase "as symbols," see the comments on 10:6; and compare 9:9–11 for "they [the things that happened] were inscripturated for the admonition of us." "The ends of the ages" portrays the present time as ending the succession of ages that have constituted human history. "On whom the ends of the ages have come *down*" points up the possibility that "the person who supposes he's *standing* is to watch out lest he *fall*." This possibility has to do with losing out on eternal life at the Last Judgment, which ends the ends of the ages. Meanwhile, living in those ends means that there's little time left for shaping up so as to avoid falling under that judgment.

Just as the knowledgeable Christian must "watch out" to avoid putting a stumbling block in the path of "the weak" (8:2, 9), so that same knowledgeable Christian (here called "the person who supposes he's standing") must "watch out" lest he himself "fall." See the comments on 10:9 for "temptation" as including the meaning of "a test," and vice versa. Furthermore, Paul plays on the ancient Israelites' tempting the preincarnate Christ to judge them for their misbehavior (so 10:8–10) and the Corinthian Christians' being tempted to sin through idolatry and fornication (so here in 10:11–13). But "*no temptation . . . except a human one*" covers temptations of other sorts too and thus drains uniqueness out of the Corinthians' particular temptations. Recognition that other human beings face the same temptations that you face illegitimizes any excuse for succumbing to temptation by appeal to special circumstances. "Who won't allow you to be tempted above what you can [resist]" defines God's faithfulness (compare Deuteronomy 7:9; 32:4) and makes succumbing to temptation your fault rather than his. "He'll make along with the temptation also an escape route" doesn't imply that God makes the temptation as well as the escape route—rather, that he doesn't allow you to face a temptation out of which you can't escape. And "so that [you] can bear up under [the temptation, here with emphasis on its aspect as a test]" defines the escape as successful endurance. But the endurance requires flight.

10:14–17: Therefore indeed, my beloved [children (compare 4:14)], **flee away from idolatry.** [15]**I'm speaking as to sensible people. You** [as such people]—**judge what I'm saying.** [16]**The cup of blessing that we bless is a sharing of the Christ's blood, isn't it? The bread that we break is a sharing of the Christ's body, isn't it?** [17]**Because** [there's] **one loaf** [of bread], **we many are one body; for we all partake of the one loaf.** "Therefore" harks back to God's providing an escape route from temptation as a basis for the following command. "Indeed" stresses the availability of the escape route. "My beloved [children]" makes the command flow out of Paul's love for them, love that he said in 8:1 "builds up [others]." His command to "flee away from idolatry" recalls the command in 6:18 to "flee fornication," which often accompanied idolatry, and like that earlier command uses the hyperbolic verb "flee," as though because of the strong pull of temptation and the likely consequence of yielding to it you should *run* away from occasions and places of idolatry and fornication, not just avoid them. By telling his addressees to judge as "sensible people" what he's saying, Paul compliments them on their good sense and thus elicits their agreement with what follows.

"The cup of blessing that we bless" refers to the cup of wine for which Christians praise God at the Lord's Supper. "Is a sharing of the Christ's blood, isn't it?" describes the cup as containing a representation of the Christ's blood and therefore the drinking of that representation as a sharing of it with one another. The bread in the Lord's Supper is broken so that each participant may eat a piece. The breaking of the bread parallels the blessing of the cup in that both actions prepare for a partaking of the elements. "Is a sharing of the Christ's body, isn't it?" describes the bread as a representation of the Christ's body—a representation in both cases, because when Christ instituted the Lord's Supper his blood and flesh were still united in living form, so that when he

identified the bread with his body and the wine with his blood the language had to be metaphorical (11:24–25). Paul simply echoes that language and uses "the Christ" (a title) to elevate the sharing of messianic blood and body over the sharing of demons at idolatrous feasts (10:18–21). Separation of the Christ's blood from his body in the elements of the Lord's Supper stands for a violent and therefore sacrificial death. Emphasizing the unity of Christians as represented in the Lord's Supper are the two instances of "a *sharing*," the two instances of "*one* loaf," and the two statements that "we many are one body" and that "we all partake . . . " (compare again "the *same* Spiritual food" and "the *same* Spiritual drink" in 10:1–4). This emphasis on unity puts forward a reason not to put a stumbling block in the way of a fellow Christian by way of participation in an idolatrous feast. Your idolatry will trip him into perdition along with yourself. "We many are one *body*" makes a wordplay on the Christ's body as a *corpse* (because its life blood has been shed) and Christians' being one *living* body because of his death.

10:18–20: Look at Israel according to the flesh. Those who eat the sacrifices are the altar's sharers, aren't they? [19]**So what am I saying? That** [food] **sacrificed to an idol is anything** [significant in itself] **or that an idol is anything** [significant in itself]**?** [20]**Rather,** [I'm saying] **that** [the foods] **which they sacrifice, "they sacrifice to demons and not to God** [Deuteronomy 32:17]**." And I don't want you to become sharers of the demons.** The allusive quotation of Deuteronomy 32:17, which has to do with ancient Israel's apostasy in the wilderness, shows that in a reprise of 10:7–10 "Israel according to the flesh" doesn't refer simply to biological Israel. The phrase refers to those Israelites who with their idolatry and fornications *behaved* in the wilderness "according to the flesh," that is, in accordance with moral frailty (see the comments on 3:1–4 for this use of "flesh" and compare Romans 8:5, 12–13). The phrase also suits especially well the eating of sacrificial flesh and the one-flesh fornication at Israel's idolatrous feasts in the wilderness (compare 6:16). The present tense in "those who eat the sacrifices are the altar's sharers, aren't they?" contemporizes for present application what those ancient Israelites did. They shared with the altar the flesh of sacrifices offered to idols. The altar got some for burning, and the Israelites got some for eating.

But lest his addressees think this sharing implies the real existence of gods, Paul reminds the addressees that neither the sacrificial food nor the idol has significance in itself (8:4–6). So we expect him to say that those ancient Israelites sacrificed to "so-called gods" (8:5). Instead, he springs a surprise by quoting Deuteronomy 32:17 to the effect that "they sacrifice to *demons* and not to God," which sacrificing to real demons is even worse than sacrificing to unreal gods. As before, the change of a past tense in Deuteronomy ("they sacrificed") to a present tense ("they sacrifice") contemporizes the text for application to the question currently at issue in Corinth. "Rather" introduces the shocking reference to demons with emphasis. And whereas Deuteronomy 32:17 disidentifies *demons* with God ("They sacrificed to demons, [who are] *not God*"), Paul changes the wording just enough to disidentify *sacrifices* to demons with sacrifices to God ("they sacrifice to demons and *not to God*"). The sharpness of the antithesis between demonic and divine recipients of sacrifice leads naturally to Paul's saying he doesn't want the Corinthians "to become sharers of the demons," which would conflict with "a sharing of the Christ's blood" and "a sharing of the Christ's body" (10:16). So the opposition between recipients of sacrifice *at altars* shifts to an opposition between sharings *at table*. The shift suits the dominant issue of eating. And the sharing of demons means that the eating of food known to have been sacrificed to idols represents an acceptance of the demons' life-destroying activity in the world just as the drinking and eating of the Christ's blood and body represent an acceptance of the life-saving benefits of his sacrificial death.

10:21–22: You can't drink the Lord's cup and the cup of demons. You can't partake from the Lord's table and from the table of demons. ²²Or are we provoking the Lord to jealousy? We're not stronger than he, are we? "The cup of blessing that we bless" (10:16) has here turned into "the Lord's cup" to make possible an antithetic parallel with "the cup of demons" at an idolatrous meal. "The Lord's table" likewise opposes "the table of demons" at such a meal. "The Christ" of 10:16 changes to "the Lord" for emphasis on his authority, which makes provoking him to jealousy dangerous and his judging us irresistible. But jealousy implies love in addition to lordship. "You can't" connotes incompatibility. This incompatibility is so sharp as to provoke jealousy because the Christ as Lord bought us at a price (6:20; 7:23), therefore owns us as his slaves, and demands our turning from demonic idols to serve him alone (compare 1 Thessalonians 1:9–10). "*Or* are we provoking the Lord to jealousy?" puts forward an alternative to the two instances of "You can't . . . ." That is to say, though you can't *compatibly* participate in the Lord's Supper and a supper of demons, you can *actually* participate in both—but only at the expense of provoking the Lord to jealousy (compare Hebrews 3:7–11; Psalm 95:7–11; Deuteronomy 32:21a–b). With the switch from "you" to "we" Paul includes himself among those who would be provoking the Lord to jealousy and be unable to resist the Lord's consequent judgment (compare 9:26–27).

But Paul doesn't want to be misconstrued as meaning that the Corinthian Christians shouldn't have anything to do with non-Christians (see 5:9–13 for just such a misconstrual of his earlier letter, which hasn't survived). The rest of the chapter deals, then, with the implications of what he has said for relations to non-Christians just as the preceding has dealt with relations among fellow Christians.

10:23–24: "All [foods] **are permissible." Not all** [foods] **are beneficial, however. "All** [foods] **are permissible." Not all** [foods] **build** [others] **up, however.** **²⁴No one is to be seeking his own** [benefit]**; rather,** [he's to be seeking] **the other person's** [benefit]**.** Despite most English translations but because of the overriding theme of foods sacrificed to idols, we should supply "foods" rather than "things" after each occurrence of "all." Paul has made clear by now that foods known to have been sacrificed to idols are *not* permissible for eating. So with the repeated statement, "All [foods] are permissible," he's quoting another Corinthian slogan (compare especially 6:12–13). "Not all [foods] are beneficial, however" is Paul's comment on that slogan: foods known to have been sacrificed to idols are impermissible *because they aren't beneficial*. On the contrary, they're deadly (8:7–13; compare 9:27; 10:5–12). Paul's next comment, "Not all [foods] build [others] up, however," defines "beneficial" in terms of building others up (compare 8:1). Earlier, building others up was opposed to defiling the weak consciousness of fellow *Christians* (8:7) and causing them to stumble back into idolatry with the consequence of losing out on salvation (8:9–13). Now, however, building others up is opposed to putting a stumbling block in the way of *non*-Christians' path to salvation. "Seeking" the other person's benefit connotes constant effort, in opposition to the natural human tendency to be constantly expending effort for one's own benefit.

Now Paul starts showing that *given ignorance of food's religious origin*, if any, what's beneficial is for the Christian to exercise freedom in diet. **10:25–26: Eat every** [food] **being sold in the market, not examining even one** [item] **because of consciousness** [that is, not examining any item so as to become conscious of whether it has been sacrificed to an idol]. **²⁶For "the earth and its fullness** [are] **the Lord's** [Psalm 24:1; 50:12; 89:11]**."** Apart from being known to have been sacrificed to an idol, all foods aren't just *permissible* for eating. Paul *commands* that they be eaten, because like the earth from which they spring they belong to the Lord (compare 1 Timothy 4:1–5). By implication, then, if food is sacrificed to an idol, the Lord is being robbed; and to appropriate stolen goods knowingly is to be an accessory to the crime. Paul's emphasis lies elsewhere, though: "Eat *every* [food] being sold in the market, not examining even *one* [item] because of consciousness. For 'the earth and its *fullness* [are] the Lord's.'" But why not examine even one item to determine whether it has been robbed from the Lord? Because it's more important to be thankfully conscious of the Lord's owning the earth and its fullness than to be unthankfully conscious of an idolatrous robbery.

Next, Paul shifts from the public market to the private home—of an unbeliever, as it turns out. **10:27–30: If anyone of the unbelievers invites you** [to a meal—in his home, it's to be understood from Paul's having forbidden eating in an idol's temple] **and you want to go, eat everything that's being set before you, not examining even one** [item] **because of consciousness** [see the comment on 10:25]. **²⁸But if someone should tell you, "This is sacred sacrificial** [food (for which expression see the comments on 8:1)]," **on account of that one who informed** [you] **and** [on account of] **the consciousness** [that the food was sacrificed to an idol], **don't ever eat** [it]. [29]**But** [this time] **I don't mean your own consciousness—rather, the** [consciousness] **of the other person** [that the food was sacrificed to an idol]. **For why is my freedom** [to eat any food of unknown origin] **being judged** [= condemned] **by another person's consciousness** [that the food was sacrificed to an idol]? [30]**If with thankfulness I partake of** [food whose origin I don't know], **why am I being slandered for what I give thanks for?** With his switch from "your" to "my" and "I" Paul puts himself sympathetically in the position of a knowledgeable Corinthian Christian. Because of parallelism, "being slandered" means "being judged." Which is to say that by calling attention to a food's idolatrous origin, the unbelieving informant puts the believing guest under God's condemnation if the believing guest eats the food. Paul leaves unanswered his two questions containing "why?" Rather than needing answers, these questions explain why he has just centered on an unbeliever's consciousness rather than on the believer's consciousness.

10:31–11:1: **Therefore, whether you're eating or drinking or doing anything** [else], **be doing all things for God's glory.** [32]**Become** *non*stumbling **both for Jews and for Greeks and for God's church,** [33]**just as I too am trying to please all people in all respects by not seeking my own benefit—rather,** [by seeking] **the** [benefit] **of many in order that they may be saved.** [1]**Become imitators of me just as I too** [am an imitator] **of Christ.** "Therefore" draws a consequence from the preceding two questions rather than answering them. The consequence consists in a command. Since your freedom is being judged by another person's consciousness and since you're being slandered, "be doing all things"— whether eating or drinking or anything else—"for God's glory" rather than for your own benefit. For doing everything to benefit others brings glory to God by removing stumbling blocks that would otherwise keep them from saving faith. "Become *non*stumbling" (and therefore benign) escalates, then, to "trying to please" (so as to be beneficial). "*All* people in *all* respects" stresses the need to save as many as possible by all means. Paul distinguishes between Jews and Greeks because they differed in what counted for them as an obstacle to their conversion. And he distinguishes God's church from both Jews and Greeks because Christians, who make up the church, differed from the Jews and Greeks in what counted for them (the Christians) as occasions for apostasy. Again Paul cites his own conduct as an example to be followed. "Just as I too [am an imitator] of Christ" correlates Paul's conduct with Christ's. Since Paul is "trying to please all people in all respects" and thereby "seek ... the [benefit] of many" rather than "[his] own benefit," his imitation of Christ implies that Christ had tried to please all people in all respects. In both cases the benefit consists in salvation from God's coming wrath (1 Thessalonians 5:9).

ORDER IN MEETINGS OF THE CORINTHIAN CHURCH
1 Corinthians 11:2–14:40

This section of 1 Corinthians deals with headcovering for women who pray and prophesy in church services (11:2–16), desecration of the Lord's Supper through disunity and overindulgence (11:17–34), and Spiritual gifts (12:1–14:40).

On Headcovering for Women
1 Corinthians 11:2–16

11:2: **But I praise you because you've remembered me in regard to all things and are holding tight the traditions just as I gave** [them] **over to you.** Paul's praise provides a mild contrast with his preceding command to imitate him, and itself precedes an upcoming criticism so as to make the criticism palatable. "You ... are holding tight" defines what he meant by "you've remembered," and "the traditions" defines what he meant by "all things." So the Corinthians have remembered Paul in regard to all things *by* holding tight to the traditions. "Just as I gave [them] over to you" adds scrupulosity to conservation. The traditions were given over to Paul. He in turn gave them over to the Corinthians. Two of the traditions will make an appearance in 11:23–26 and 15:1–8.

11:3: **But I want you to know that the Christ is every man's head, and** [that] **the man** [is] **a woman's head, and** [that] **God** [is] **the Christ's head.** "But I want you to know" makes plain that the following does *not* count as one of the traditions that Paul had given over to the Corinthians and that they have held tight. So it's likely that their letter to Paul raised a question about the headcovering of women. His reply starts by affirming Christ's headship over a man, proceeds to the man's headship over a woman, and reaches a climax in God's headship over the Christ. The headship of God over the Christ ameliorates the man's headship over a woman. For if even the Christ stands under another's headship, a woman's standing under the headship of a man, who himself stands under the Christ's headship, doesn't demean her. Moreover, the nonrepetition of "every" for the man's headship over a woman provides further amelioration by putting less emphasis on his headship over a woman than on the Christ's headship over the man. Twice Paul says "*the* Christ," because this title connotes the authority of Jesus' messianic office. Thus headship connotes in turn the supremacy of Christ over a man, of the man over a woman, and of God over Christ. Not that the Christ is any less divine than God (see, for example, Philippians 2:5–6 and Paul's frequent use of "Lord," the equivalent of "Lord" in the Old Testament, for Christ). Rather, as God's Son the Christ carries out the will of his Father. So too in the relation of a woman to a man: she is no less human than he, but she's to carry out his will because he's her head (in the figurative sense that headship implies [see Ephesians 1:22; 5:22–24; Colossians 2:10 for headship as supremacy of will]). The Greek words for "man" and "woman" also mean "husband" and "wife," respectively; and Paul will shortly reference the creation of Adam and Eve, the first married couple. So the relation between a man and a woman that Paul puts in view should be understood as primarily a marital one.

11:4–6: Every man praying or prophesying having [a covering] down over [his] head is shaming his head [the Christ]. ⁵And every woman praying or prophesying with an uncovered head is shaming her head [the man]. For she's one and the same thing with a shaved [woman]. ⁶For if the woman isn't covering her [head], she's also to be shearing her [head (that is, cutting off her hair)]. But if shearing or shaving her [head is] shameful for a woman [as it obviously is], she's to be covering her [head]. "Every man" and "every woman" allow no exceptions for either sex. The inclusion of prophesying alongside praying implies a church meeting in which the man or the woman is leading others in prayer or is prophesying—that is, delivering a Spirit-inspired message—to others in the meeting. Since 11:15 will identify a woman's long hair as the substitute for "a throwaround [that is, a scarf]" on her head, "[a coming] down over the head [of a man]" would here consist of long hair. But for a man to pray or prophesy with such a covering shames his head, who has just been identified as the Christ, because to cover the man's anatomical head that represents Christ, the Spiritual head, is to shame the Christ by symbolically putting him out of sight. The same doesn't hold true for a woman, though, because if she prays or prophesies with an uncovered head she shames her head—that is, her husband as represented by *her* anatomical head—by flaunting him as "God's image and glory" (11:7) in competition with the Christ, who's supposed to have his headship over the man recognized. "For she [the woman praying or prophesying with an uncovered head] is one and the same thing with a shaved [woman]"—this statement supports Paul's preceding pronouncement with an example universally acknowledged as shameful, as in shaving the head of an adulteress. "The same *thing*" stresses the quality of shamefulness. To reinforce his example, Paul backs it up with a statement that adds head-shearing to head-shaving and actually commands head-shearing if the woman doesn't cover her head. The counter command to cover it takes precedence, however, because of the obvious shame of a woman's shaving her head or shearing off its hair.

11:7–9: For on the one hand a man, being God's image and glory, ought not to be covering [his] head. On the other hand, the woman is a man's glory. ⁸For man isn't from woman—rather, woman [is] from man. ⁹For, in addition, man wasn't created because of the woman; rather, woman [was created] because of the man. "On the one hand . . . . On the other hand" stresses this contrast between a man and a woman. In 11:3–4 a man's shaming Christ, his head, implied that Christ is the glory of the man *as* the man's head. Here that implication becomes explicit except for Paul's saying that the man is

"*God's* image and glory." He shifts from Christ to God for a reference to Genesis 1:26–27, where God is said to have created man in his own (God's) image, which Paul interprets as God's glory and makes the reason why a man "ought not to be covering [his anatomical] head" because of its representing the man's Spiritual head, the Christ, in whom God has manifested himself. But given God's taking Eve out of Adam according to Genesis 2:18–23, for the moment Paul passes over the creation of the woman as well as the man in God's image according to Genesis 1:26–27 and equates the woman with a man's glory. And to reinforce that equation, Paul adds that woman was created for the man's sake ("because of the man") rather than vice versa (Genesis 2:18–22). So origin and purpose unite to support the woman's being the man's glory.

11:10–12: Because of this [the woman's originating from the man and having been created for him] **the woman ought to have authority on [her] head because of the angels.** As in Mark 2:10; Luke 5:24, "to have authority on" locates the place of authority. Revelation 11:6; 14:18; 16:9; 20:6 speak of "hav[ing] authority over," which specifies the object of authority rather than its location. But a woman's exercising authority over her anatomical head would make obscure sense here; and because her anatomical head represents the authoritative headship of her husband over her, exercising authority over her head would symbolically contradict his headship. So "authority on [her] head" refers to her head-covering, which represents authority for her to pray or prophesy without shaming her husband, represented by her anatomical head. In view of 4:9 ("we've become a spectacle . . . to angels"), "because of the angels" implies that angels observe church meetings and would be scandalized if women were to violate decorum by praying or prophesying with uncovered heads. ¹¹**Nevertheless, in the Lord neither** [is] **a woman apart from a man nor a man apart from a woman.** ¹²**For as the woman** [is] **indeed from the man, so too** [is] **the man through the woman. And all things** [are] **from God.** "Nevertheless" introduces a counter balance. "In the Lord" implies that the preceding stricture on women has to do with a norm in society rather than with a norm in Christ, the Lord. With "in the Lord neither [is] a woman apart from a man nor a man apart from a woman" Paul harks back again to Genesis 1:26–27, which says that God created "male *and female*" in his own image." "For as the woman [is] indeed from the man" likewise harks back again to Genesis 2:18–23; but Paul's addition of "so too [is] the man through the woman" alludes to women's giving birth to men, starting in Genesis 4:1, as an indication that "in the Lord" men and women are interdependent. "And all things [are] from God" makes men and women equally dependent on God.

11:13–15: Judge for yourselves: Is it proper for a woman to be praying to God uncovered [as to her head]**?** ¹⁴**Even nature itself teaches you, doesn't it, that if a man wears his hair long, on the one hand, he has disgrace—**¹⁵[that] **if a woman wears her hair long on**

the other hand, she [has] **glory, because** [her] **hair has been given to her in place of a throwaround?**[7] "Judge for yourselves" assumes a well-recognized norm. Then Paul appeals to the teaching of nature itself and balances the disgrace of a man who wears his hair long with the glory of a woman who wears her hair long. Furthermore, her being her husband's glory in society is now counterbalanced by her having her own glory if she conforms to nature's teaching. "Nature" refers to something inborn—here an inborn preference—whether it be good (as in Romans 2:14), bad (as in Ephesians 2:3), or indifferent (as in Romans 2:27). Over against letting her tresses hang loose, which was considered immodest, "in place of a throwaround" means that the long hair of a woman is to cover her head by being wrapped around it, so that she doesn't need any further headcovering, such as a veil (the specific word for which doesn't occur anywhere in this passage).

11:16: But if anyone thinks it good to be contentious, we don't have such a custom [as he or she wants to substitute for our custom in regard to a woman's headcovering]. **Neither** [do] **the churches of God.** "We" includes Paul's missionary teammates with him. Their inclusion strengthens his appeal to the custom. That "the churches of God" follow this custom strengthens the appeal further. The prior grounding of Paul's instruction in the theology of headship and creation and in nature itself undermines any attempt to treat the custom as culturally relative rather than culturally absolute.

On the Lord's Supper
1 Corinthians 11:17–34

11:17–19: And in commanding this [that follows] **I'm not praising** [you], **because you're not coming together for the better—rather, for the worse.** [18]**For first, I hear splits exist among you when you come together in church** [that is, in an assembly, not in a church building, of which there were none yet]; **and I believe a certain part.** [19]**For it's also necessary that there be factions among you in order that also the qualified people may become obvious among you.** In 11:2 Paul prefaced a criticism with a word of praise, because he hadn't given over to the Corinthians a tradition on the matter at hand. Their ignorance softened his approach to the criticism. Here, though, he *had* given over to them a tradition on the matter at hand (see 11:23–25). So they don't have the excuse of ignorance, and he introduces his criticism bluntly. The outright statement that he's not praising them is the reverse of 11:2, and "because you're not coming together for the better—rather, for the worse" alarmingly describes the Corinthian believers' church meetings as detrimental rather than beneficial. The splits

Paul has heard about recall those in 1:11–12. But those revolved around personality cults. These arise out of a wrong way of celebrating the Lord's Supper. In 11:34 Paul will refer to "the remaining matters" on which he "will give orders" when he goes to Corinth. The reference will retrospectively indicate that here in 11:18 "a certain part," which he believes, consists in a partial *report* of the splits, not that his *belief* is only partial.

"For first, I hear splits exist among you" explains why the Corinthians' meetings are "for the worse." "For it's also necessary that there be factions among you" follows up with a second explanation. But what does this one mean? In 1:10–3:23 Paul sided with the faction in Corinth who were saying, "I belong to Christ" (see especially 3:23). So his urging in 1:10 that there be no splits amounted to an urging that those who were saying, "I belong to Paul," "I belong to Apollos," and "I belong to Cephas" give up their slogans and join those with the one and only legitimate slogan, "I belong to Christ." Likewise here in chapter 11, "the qualified people" make up a faction that celebrate the Lord's Supper worthily. Since disqualification comes from not being in the faith and not having Christ in you (see 9:24–27 with 2 Corinthians 13:5), the issue of qualification is of such great importance that "it's also *necessary*" for factionalism to make the qualified people obvious. Better for that to happen now, so that the presently disqualified may make amends, than at the Last Judgment, when it will be too late for making amends.

11:20–22: Therefore [because of the splits and resultant factions] **when you're coming together to the same** [place], **it's not to eat the Lord's Supper.** The Lord's Supper included a full-scale meal, not just the bread and wine mentioned in Jesus' later-quoted words ("This is my body . . . . This cup is the new covenant in my blood"), which bread and wine were consumed at the close of the meal. [21]**For in the eating, each is going ahead** [of others] **to take his own supper** [that is, to eat it]; **and one person is hungry** [because of not having enough food to satisfy his hunger], **and another person is drunk** [because of excessive drinking]. [22]**For you don't** *not* **have homes for eating and drinking, do you?** Of course not, for you *do* have homes in which to eat and drink. **Or are you despising God's church and shaming those who don't have** [enough food and drink]? **What should I say to you? Should I praise you? In this** [matter] **I'm** *not* **praising** [you]! "The same [place]" would ordinarily be a house—hence our expression, "a house church" (compare 16:19; Romans 16:5, 23; Colossians 4:15; Philemon 2). In declaring that when the Corinthians come together it isn't to eat the Lord's Supper, Paul implies that church meetings ordinarily do have the purpose of eating it. He then justifies his declaration in the Corinthians' case on the ground that eating the Lord's Supper requires Christian unity, because the eating of it symbolizes unity in Christ, as noted earlier in 10:16–17: "The cup of blessing that we bless is a sharing of the Christ's blood, isn't it? The bread that we break is a sharing of the Christ's body isn't it? Because [there's]

---

[7]A number of English translations have "for" rather than "in place of," but Paul's use elsewhere of the underlying Greek preposition favors substitution in one form or another (see Romans 12:17; Ephesians 5:31; 1 Thessalonians 5:15; 2 Thessalonians 2:10).

one loaf [of bread], we many are one body; for we all partake of the one loaf." The factional splits in the Corinthian church have made the supper theirs rather than the Lord's, however. He's no longer the host, so to speak.

The statement that "one person is hungry" limits "each" to the person who "is going ahead to take his own supper," has gotten "drunk," has a home "for eating and drinking," and is "despising God's church and shaming those who don't have [enough food and drink]." Furthermore, "going ahead to take his own supper" indicates an eating and drinking by "each" before others arrive at the place of meeting (compare "wait for one another" in 11:33). Implied: the early-comers are the well-off who bring plenty of food and wine and consume their fare before the poor (including slaves), who have long working hours, can arrive. Nor can these poor bring enough food to satisfy their hunger, while the well-off have wined as well as dined to the point of getting drunk instead of waiting to share their food and drink equally with the poor. The hunger of the poor combines with the satiation and drunkenness of the well-off to exhibit the factious insensitivity of the well-off. And since only the well-off have homes with ample facilities for cooking and dining whereas most of the poor live in tiny apartments and therefore have to eat much of their food outside at fast-food shops, Paul addresses the well-off when asking, "For you don't *not* have homes for eating and drinking, do you?" This question adds a second justification of his declaring that when the Corinthians come together it isn't to eat the Lord's Supper. The justification is that the well-off don't need church meetings to enjoy their gastronomical affluence. Putting the justification in the form of a question which has an all-too-obvious answer gives the question a sarcastic edge. As an alternative to that question Paul asks seriously whether the gourmands are daring to despise God's church by shaming poor Christians—as though to say, "Who do you think you are to despise *God's* church in this way?" By leaving the question without an implied answer of either yes or no, Paul challenges the well-off to test themselves on their behavior (compare 11:28). "What should I say to you?" evinces his consternation, and his consternation produces yet another question, "Should I praise you?" plus the firmly negative answer, "In this [matter] I'm *not* praising [you]!" which for emphasis echoes 11:17. Paul shows no concern here to erase economic disparities. He's concerned only that the flaunting of those disparities is causing a church-splitting factionalism which dismantles the Lord's Supper. But this very concern runs counter to pagans' not only accepting but also flaunting such disparities, including feasting while empty-mouthed others look on.

11:23–24: For I received from the Lord what I also gave over to you: that the Lord, Jesus, on the night in which he was being given over took a loaf of bread [24]**and after giving thanks broke** [it in pieces] **and said, "This is my body,** [which is] **for you. Be doing this for my remembrance."** Here Paul begins the third justification of his declaring that when the Corinthians come

together it isn't to eat the Lord's Supper. It's that their having received this tradition leaves the well-off no excuse for turning the Lord's Supper into their own supper. "From the Lord" means that the tradition originated with Jesus' words that instituted the Lord's Supper at the Last Supper. The prefixing of "the Lord" to "Jesus" calls attention to Jesus' exaltation to heavenly lordship in compensation for his sacrificial death. "On the night in which he was being given over" locates the tradition's origin temporally and makes a wordplay on "gave over" as Paul's *relaying* the tradition and on "was being given over" as Jesus' being *betrayed* that night by Judas Iscariot. "After giving thanks" explains what Paul meant by "blessing" in 10:16, for the address of a thanksgiving to God equates with blessing something in the sense of praising him for it. Jesus' thanking God for representations of his sacrificial death makes a remarkable demonstration of his desire to save us. But the nonmention of his disciples, such as the betrayer Judas Iscariot, concentrates attention on Jesus as the Lord, the ownership of whose supper Paul is defending. Since Jesus was still alive at its institution, the equating of bread with his body has to be understood figuratively—in other words as meaning, "This bread *symbolizes* my body." But the breaking of the bread has no symbolic significance, as though Jesus' body was broken on the cross. To the contrary see John 19:31–37; and "which was broken" does not appear as a description of Jesus' body in the best textual tradition of the present passage. The loaf of bread was broken in pieces simply so that each disciple could have a piece to eat. "Be doing this" commands an ongoing repetition of eating the bread of the Lord's Supper. "For my remembrance" means "to remember me by way of recalling my dying for your salvation." In the present context, repeated remembrances of Jesus' sacrificing his body for others (more specifically, "for you") as represented in *one* loaf of bread to be eaten by his disciples *in unison* should have forestalled factious eating in the Corinthian church.

11:25–26: In the same way he also [took] **the cup after the supper, saying, "This cup is the new covenant in my blood** [compare Jeremiah 31:31–34]. **Be doing this for my remembrance as often as you drink** [from the cup]." [26]**For as often as you eat this bread and drink** [from] **the cup you're relating the Lord's death until he comes.** "After the supper" alludes to the Passover Supper (= the Last Supper) at which Jesus instituted the Lord's Supper with some bread and wine. "This cup" corresponds to "the loaf of bread," preceding. As before, and for the same reason, "is" means "symbolizes." "The new covenant" contrasts with the Mosaic covenant, instituted as it was with the blood of animal sacrifices (Exodus 24:1–8). This covenant is new in kind by being instituted in the blood of a human being, Jesus. The cup symbolizes the new covenant in Jesus' blood in that the wine which the cup contains is liquid and red, like blood. Since "the life of the flesh is in the blood" (Leviticus 17:11; see also Genesis 9:4; Leviticus 17:14; Deuteronomy 12:23), the symbolic separation of Jesus' body and blood in the Lord's Supper points to a violent death such as a sacrifice necessitates. See the comments on 11:24 for the presently repeated command, "Be doing this for my remembrance." Its repetition makes for emphasis. The addition this time of "as often as you drink [from the cup]" adds to the emphasis on continuing remembrance and prompts Paul's addition of a rationale for ongoing celebrations of the Lord's Supper. It's that the eating and drinking are accompanied by a relating of the Lord's death. We might think solely of a nonverbal relating in the symbolism of bread and wine. But "are relating" normally carries a verbal meaning, and Paul's emphasizing in 1:18, 21, 23 and throughout chapter 2 "the speech about the cross" and the "proclaiming [of] Christ crucified" favors the verbal meaning here too, especially since "the *Lord's* death" (rather than "*my* death," as spoken by Jesus) signals an addition by Paul. Only when Jesus returns will the need for proclamation cease—hence, "until he comes." Till then, constant retelling is required.

11:27–30: And so, whoever is eating the bread or drinking the cup of the Lord unworthily will be guilty of the Lord's body and blood. [28]**But a human being is to be testing himself and is to be eating from the loaf of bread and drinking** [unworthily] **from the cup in this way** [= with self-testing]. [29]**For the one who's eating and drinking** [unworthily] **is eating and drinking a judgmental sentence against himself because of not differentiating the body** [of the Lord]. [30]**Because of this** [failure to differentiate], **many among you** [are] **weak and sick; and a considerable number are sleeping** [the sleep of death]. The Lord's bread and cup represent his body and blood. In this context, eating and drinking these representations "unworthily" means eating and drinking them in conjunction with despising God's church through shaming those without enough food and drink, and this by feasting before they arrive (11:20–22). (Note: Paul speaks of unworthy *eating and drinking*, not of unworthy *people*.) Since the separation of body and blood indicates death, "guilty of the Lord's body and blood" means guilty of the Lord's death, so that the eating and drinking, which should symbolize an assimilation of salvation because of his death, symbolize instead an assimilation of guilt for his death. In view of this latter symbolism, Paul commands self-testing and sets "a human being" over against "the Lord" to underscore the importance of self-testing, which defines the way eating and drinking the Lord's Supper is supposed to be done.

To test oneself is to make sure one isn't eating and drinking unworthily by "shaming those who don't have [enough food and drink]" (11:22). As a reason to test oneself, Paul says that eating and drinking without "differentiating the body" incurs "a judgmental sentence against [one]self." But does the Lord's body refer to Jesus' physical body or, as in 10:16–17; 12:12–30, to the church as Christ's body? Or to both? The immediate context of the Words of Institution favors a reference to Jesus' physical body alone. To differentiate the Lord's body, then, is to eat the bread symbolizing it with recognition that it differs from all other physical bodies by its having been sacrificed for the eternal salvation of others ("for you [plural]"). A recognition of its uniqueness in this all-important respect will preclude self-centered eating and drinking. Bodily weakness, sickness, and death among the Corinthians constitutes an execution of the judgmental sentence passed against them for failure to differentiate the Lord's body. "Many" and "a considerable number" point up the large extent of the failure in Corinth and warn of further such punishment for any further failure.

11:31–32: But if we'd been differentiating ourselves, we wouldn't have been being judged. [32]**But when being judged by the Lord we're being disciplined lest we be condemned along with the world** [consisting of unbelievers]. Here, differentiating the Lord's *body* as symbolized by the bread of the Lord's Supper turns into differentiating *ourselves* from the Lord as inferior to him and therefore subject to his judgment if we eat and drink his supper unworthily. Such self-differentiation would have kept us, Paul says, from turning the Lord's unifying supper into a factious supper. Three occurrences of "we" bring out Paul's recognition, or confession, that he too is subject to the Lord's judgment. And "lest we be condemned along with the world" interprets the temporal judgments of bodily weakness, sickness, and death as satisfying the Lord's displeasure though falling short of eternal damnation.

11:33–34: And so, my brothers, when coming together to eat, wait for one another. [34]**If someone is hungry, he's to eat at home lest you be coming together with the result of judgment. As for the remaining matters** [presumably having to do with details missing in the report Paul had heard about the Corinthians' celebration of the Lord's Supper (see 11:18 with comments)], **I'll give orders whenever I come.** "And so" occurred in 11:27. There it introduced a statement of guilt. Here the expression introduces a command, obedience to which will avoid guilt. "Brothers" introduces the command affectionately and therefore in line both with the immediately preceding occurrences of "we" and with the following command to wait for one another. The well-off, who've brought most of the food and drink and eaten and drunk most of it before the poor could arrive, are to wait till those poor arrive and then share the food and drink equally with them. To forestall further judgment for eating and drinking the Lord's Supper unworthily, Paul commands the well-off to satisfy their hunger at home rather than doing so at the place of meeting before the poor arrive and thus shaming them.

On Spiritual Gifts
1 Corinthians 12:1–14:40

This section divides into a discussion of the diversity of Spiritual gifts (12:1–31a), the supremacy of love over Spiritual gifts (12:31b–13:13), and the superiority of prophesying and the inferiority of speaking in tongues (14:1–40).

12:1–3: And concerning Spirituals, brothers, I don't want you to be ignorant [compare 10:1]. **²You know that when you were Gentiles** [= pagans] **you were being led to voiceless idols whenever you were being led away. ³Therefore I'm informing you that no one speaking by God's Spirit says, "Jesus** [is] **anathema," and no one can say, "Jesus** [is] **Lord," except by the Holy Spirit.** As already in 7:1, 25; 8:1, "And concerning . . ." introduces a topic addressed in the Corinthians' letter to Paul. But "Spirituals" is ambiguous. In 14:1b Paul will use it to describe gifts, especially the ability to prophesy, as given by the Holy Spirit. But in 14:37 he'll use the term for someone's self-description. So here in 12:1 he uses it in a twofold way: (1) to describe people endowed with the Holy Spirit (the meaning intended in the Corinthians' letter to Paul) and (2) to describe abilities graciously given by the Holy Spirit to Christian believers (the meaning intended by Paul). Paul will shift the Corinthians' attention from people endowed with Spiritual gifts to the Spiritual gifts with which the people are endowed. This shift will replace the Corinthians' focus on personal privilege in having Spiritual gifts so as to puff themselves up (compare 4:6, 18–19; 5:2, 8:1; 13:4) with a Pauline focus on personal responsibility so as to use Spiritual gifts for others' benefit.

The address "brothers" links up with Paul's coming emphasis on communal benefit as well as helping to introduce a new topic. "I don't want you to be ignorant" implies ignorance on the Corinthians' part, the ignorance of focusing on themselves as Spiritual rather than on their gifts as Spiritual. "You know" starts a correction of that ignorance with a reference to what the Corinthian Christians do know. They know that in their pagan past they were repeatedly "being led to voiceless idols." "*Whenever* you were being led away" stresses the repetitiousness. "Being led away" refers to being caught up in pagan processions that ended up at the temple of an idol. "Voiceless" describes the idols not so much in contrast with the living God as in contrast with the Holy Spirit's giving believers a voice to say, "Jesus [is] Lord." As a leadup to that Spirit-inspired confession, Paul denies that anyone speaking by God's Spirit says, "Jesus [is] anathema." "Anathema" means "accursed," and the statement as a whole represents what an unconverted Jew would say about Jesus because the Mosaic law pronounced a curse on anyone hanged on a tree, as Jesus was in crucifixion (see Deuteronomy 21:23; Galatians 3:13). So as idolatry characterized the pre-conversion past of Gentile Christians, an estimation of Jesus as accursed characterized the pre-conversion past of Jewish Christians. "Therefore" makes idols' voicelessness, which renders them unable to speak, the basis for Paul's mentioning both the speaking of a curse and the speaking of a confession. "I'm informing you" has here to do with imparting new knowledge. It's that just as God's Spirit never prompts a Jew to say, "Jesus [is] anathema," so no one can say, "Jesus [is] Lord," except by the Holy Spirit. Paul is referring of course to a true confession, not to a mere mouthing of words. Because of the contrast between God and idols, "*God's* Spirit" follows naturally on the heels of "voiceless *idols*." Then Paul switches to "the Holy Spirit" in connection with the Christian confession. The main point: since "no one *can* say, 'Jesus [is] Lord,' except by the Holy Spirit," everyone who makes this confession *has* the Holy Spirit, so that no Christian (by definition a confessor of Jesus as Lord) can rightly look down on another Christian as not having the Holy Spirit (compare 12:13). Chapter 14 will make it look as though some Christians in Corinth thought that if you don't speak in tongues you don't have the Holy Spirit.

12:4–6: And there are distributions of gracious gifts, but the same Spirit. ⁵And there are distributions of services, and the same Lord. ⁶And there are distributions of activities, but the same God, who is activating all in all. Though the Holy Spirit enables a single confession of Jesus as Lord, the same Spirit distributes to the confessors a plurality of gifts, services, and activities. "Gracious" describes the gifts as ill-deserved but given anyway, and these gifts refer to authorized abilities. "Services" connotes the uses to which the abilities are put and implies an obligation to use the gifts in service to others. "Activities" connotes the effort required to use the abilities in such service and implies an assurance of God's working in and through the use of gifts in serving others. Paul confirms this assurance by adding to "the same God" the description, "who is activating *all* [the gracious gifts, services, and activities] in *all* [who by his Spirit say, 'Jesus is Lord']." This description joins with "*gracious* gifts" and the meaning of "*services*" to puncture any self-puffery over one's own gift. Nobody is to despise any of the gifts, for they all represent God's activity; and no confession of Jesus as Lord is to be despised, because God activates all believers. The three combinations of "distributions" and "the same . . ." prepare for emphasis on the way variety in the gracious gifts, services, and activities contributes to church unity. In line with the mention of "God's Spirit" and Jesus as "Lord" in 12:3, Paul associates "gracious gifts" with "the same Spirit," "services" with "the same Lord," and "activities" with "the same God," so that we have here the makings of a doctrine of the Trinity.

12:7–10: And to each is being given the manifestation of the Spirit for what's beneficial. ⁸For on the one hand a word of wisdom is being given to one person through the Spirit. On the other hand a word of knowledge [is being given] **to another person according to the same Spirit, ⁹to another person faith by the same Spirit, and to another person gracious gifts of healings by the one Spirit, ¹⁰and to another person workings of miracles, and to another person prophecy, and to another person differentiations of spirits, to another person kinds of tongues, and to another person the translation of tongues.** So every confessor of Jesus as Lord is gifted ("to each is being given"). The gift makes obvious that the confessor has the Holy Spirit ("the manifestation of the Spirit"). And the gift has a beneficial purpose (compare 6:12; 10:23). "For" introduces examples of the beneficial manifestation of the Spirit. "On the one hand . . . . On the other hand" and "to one person" plus eight instances of "to another person" highlight variety within the manifestation of the Spirit. The following up of "through the Spirit" with "according to the *same* Spirit" and "by the *same* Spirit" stresses that no believer should boast of having a better spirit because of his or her particular gift. "By the *one* Spirit" then prepares for the oneness of the church as the corporate Christ, illustrated by the oneness of the physical body (12:12–27). There may be some slight difference in "through" as indicating the Spirit's agency, "according to" as indicating the Spirit's will, and "by" as indicating the Spirit's activity. More likely, however, is variation for the avoidance of monotony.

"A word," which occurs twice, connotes speaking to others, so that they as well as the speaker might benefit. "A word of wisdom" consists in counseling others what they should do and comes first because the topic of wisdom came up prominently in the first main section of 1 Corinthians (1:10–2:16). "A word of knowledge" consists in informing others what they should understand and comes next because knowledge relates to wisdom and came up prominently within the second main section of 1 Corinthians (chapter 8). "To *another* person" indicates that "faith" consists in more than saving faith, for every Christian has that kind of faith. The gracious gift of faith consists, then, in an ability to believe God for extraordinary things above and beyond salvation (13:2; Mark 11:22–24; Matthew 17:20; 21:22; Luke 17:6). Since such faith has a lot to do with miraculous healings and other sorts of miracles, Paul follows up with "gracious gifts of healings" and "workings of miracles." The plurals in these phrases point to the occasions on which healings and other sorts of miracles are performed. "Gracious gifts" distinguishes the healings from medical cures. Since prophets often worked miracles, "prophecy" comes next. It consists in the receipt and delivery of divine revelations. Because spirits other than the Holy Spirit inspire false prophets, Paul follows up with "differentiations of spirits," that is, the ability on occasion to differentiate false prophecy from true. Closing out this list are "kinds of tongues" and "translation of tongues," because in combination with each other they rank with the just-mentioned prophecy (14:5). "Kinds of tongues" means speaking languages that the speaker hasn't learned, and "translation of tongues" means translating languages without ever having learned them.

12:11–13: One and the same Spirit activates *all* these [gracious gifts] **by distributing** [them] **to *each* person *individually* just as he** [the Spirit] ***wills*** [to do]. The italicized words leave no possible basis for self-puffery over one's Spiritual gifts. **¹²For just as the body, indeed, is one and has many parts, and all the parts of the body, though being many, are one body, so too** [is] **the Christ. ¹³For also, whether** [as] **Jews or Greeks or slaves or free persons, we've all been baptized in one Spirit into one body and have all been made to drink one Spirit.** The first "For" introduces a christological

explanation of the reason for the Spirit's distribution of gracious gifts. The second "For" introduces an additional (hence "also") but Spiritual explanation of the same. "Indeed" stresses the analogy to a human body, which runs through both explanations and beyond. The body's oneness, which Paul mentions three times, emphasizes close, working unity. "Many parts" and "all the parts, though being many" emphasize complementary variety (compare the plural, "distributions" in 12:4–6). Paul compares "the Christ," not the church, to one body composed of various parts, and does so because he sees all believers as "in Christ" and therefore as making up what we might call the corporate Christ. The variety of body parts is matched by the variety of persons who make up the corporate Christ: from the standpoint of ethnicity and culture, Jews and Greeks; from the standpoint of class and rank, slaves and free persons (see the comments on 1:22 for "Greeks").

To stress the unity of this corporate Christ, Paul includes himself with "we" and twice adds "all." Some English translations have "baptized *by* one Spirit," but elsewhere in connection with baptism the underlying Greek preposition indicates the element within which immersion occurs: hence, "baptized *in* the Spirit." Immersion in the Spirit puts a believer into the one body, consisting of the corporate Christ. For the Spirit is Christ's (Romans 8:9b; 2 Corinthians 3:17), so that to be immersed in the Spirit is at one and the same time to be incorporated into Christ. And just as baptism in the Spirit equates with being filled with the Spirit (see Acts 1:5 with Acts 2:4), baptism in one Spirit equates with having the Spirit within by being made to drink the Spirit. The two mentions of "*one* Spirit" join the thrice-mentioned oneness of the body to reemphasize unity over against splits in the Corinthian church, for those splits render the body parts useless to one another (compare 1:10; 11:18; 12:24–25).

12:14–17: For also the body isn't one [body] **part— rather, many** [body parts]. **¹⁵If the foot says, "Because I'm not a hand I'm not** [a part] **of the body," it's not on account of this** [just saying so] **not** [a part] **of the body, is it? ¹⁶And if the ear says, "Because I'm not an eye I'm not** [a part] **of the body," it's not on account of this** [just saying so] **not** [a part] **of the body, is it? ¹⁷If the whole body** [were actually] **an eye, where** [would] **the** [organ of] **hearing** [actually be]**? If the whole** [body were actually an organ of] **hearing, where** [would the organ of] **smelling** [actually be]**?** Whereas "For" in 12:12 introduced a *christological* explanation of the reason for the Spirit's distribution of gracious gifts and "For also" in 12:13 introduced a *Spiritual* reason for the same, another "For also" here in 12:14 introduces a *theological* reason (see especially the references to "God" in 12:18, 24b). Shades of the Trinity again, as in 12:4–6. Paul's elaboration of this reason in terms of "one body" made up of "many parts" will extend through 12:30. The twice-occurring "If [such-and-such a body part] says, 'Because I'm not [a such-and-such different part] of the body,'" stands for the divisive individualism of puffed-up church members in Corinth. Paul ridicules them by likening them to body parts that speak though none of them is a tongue or a mouth, body parts that speak nonsense, moreover.

Because the Greek word for a body part refers most particularly to limbs, Paul mentions first the foot and the hand as extremities of the limbs. Then he mentions the ear and the eye because of their location in the topmost extremity of the body—and later adds the organ of smelling, also located there. For the moment, the point isn't the need these body parts have for each other. The point is the absurdity of one part's declaring itself a nonmember of the body because it isn't another part. Emphasizing this absurdity is the double negative in "it's *not* on account of this [just saying so] *not* [a part] of the body, is it?" Are the foot and the ear making their statements out of pride that they're not a hand and an eye, respectively, or out of disappointment, even envy? Supposed nonmembership in the body would seem to favor disappointment and envy. In either case, though, the absurdity remains. The final two "If"-questions reinforce the absurdity of supposed nonmembership in the body with the deficiency of a body consisting of only one organ, as though the ear, wanting to be an eye, didn't recognize the necessity of its function of hearing and thought the whole body should be an eye; and as though the organ of smelling, wanting to be an organ of hearing, didn't recognize the necessity of its function of smelling and thought the whole body should be an ear. Paul uses a grammatical construction that asks what would be the case if such-and-such which is unthinkable were really true. The construction underscores how utter would be the deficiency of a one-organed body.

12:18–24a: **But now** [as it is], **God has positioned the** [body] **parts—each one of them—in the body just as he wanted.** So God has willed the variety of Spiritual gifts, and "each one of them" stresses that no Spiritual gift is unwilled by him. [19]**But if all** [of them] **were actually one** [body] **part, where** [would] **the body** [actually be]**?** [20]**But now** [there are] **many** [body] **parts, yet one body.** Whereas 12:17 called attention to the *deficiency* of a body consisting of only one organ, 12:19 calls attention to the *absence* of a body in a conglomeration of the same organ. [21]**And the eye can't say to the hand, "I don't have need of you," or again the head to the feet, "I don't have need of you."** [22]**On the contrary, the parts of the body that seem to be much weaker by far** [than the others] **are essential.** [23]**And those** [parts] **of the body that we think to be less honorable—we clothe these with extraordinary honor; that is, our unpresentable** [private parts] **have extraordinary presentability** [when well-clothed], [24a]**whereas our presentable** [body parts] **don't have need** [of extraordinary presentability]. Here Paul puts forward humble interdependence as an antidote to prideful independence. Because of their prominence at the top of the body, the eye and the head stand for Christians with Spiritual gifts that thrust them into the limelight, whereas the hand and the feet stand for Christians with Spiritual gifts that keep them backstage.

But without the hand, the eye has no means of manipulation, and without the feet the head has no means of locomotion. Similarly, the limelighters need the stagehands. (Does Paul use the singular "hand" because nearly all people do their primary work with one hand, depending on right- or left-handedness, but the plural "feet" because normal locomotion requires the use of both feet?) Thus "*can't* say" means that it wouldn't be true for the one body part to deny its need for the other body part.

Since physical strength is exerted by the hand and the feet, "the parts of the body that seem to be much weaker by far" shifts attention to the organs of the torso. "Weak*er* by far" casts doubt on the strength of the hand and feet, however; and "*seem* to be . . ." casts doubt on the weakness of the torso's organs. But whatever their weakness or strength, Paul stresses their essentiality. So what if the heart and lungs, the stomach and intestines, the liver and kidneys and other innards don't put strength on exhibit as the hand and the feet do? They're no less essential to the body's functioning than are the hand and the feet. Since the torso's organs are hidden from view by skin and clothing, Paul shifts attention again, this time specifically to the sexual organs ("unpresentable [private parts]"), which out of modesty human beings (so long as they don't consider themselves mere animals, we might add) take extraordinary pains to keep clothed (compare Genesis 3:7, 10, 21). To expose those parts is to dishonor them as being public property. To clothe them is to honor them as being private property. Hence, those Christians who have the most inconspicuous and unprestigious Spiritual gifts should get the most honor.

12:24b–26: **God has integrated the body, however, by giving extraordinary honor to** [the body part otherwise] **lacking** [honor] [25]**in order that there may be no split in the body** [between its parts]**—rather, that the** [body] **parts may have identical concern for one another.** [26]**And if one part is suffering, all the parts are suffering with** [it]**; if** [one] **part is being glorified** [by getting extraordinarily clothed], **all the parts are rejoicing with** [it]. So Paul makes the modesty of human beings, when it comes to their private parts, symbolize God's integrating the body for the avoidance of splits in it. But the physical body isn't split if its private parts aren't clothed. At this point, then, Paul is talking about the church and its members in terms of a body and its parts. God's "giving extraordinary honor to [the body parts otherwise] lacking [honor]"—and doing so through what the apostle Paul is just now writing—has the purpose of avoiding splits in the church, such as those mentioned in 1:10–11; 11:18 but here more especially splits arising out of pride and envy in regard to prominent gifts. To honor by clothing shades into honoring by showing identical concern for one another despite the differences in gifts. The suffering of all body parts in the suffering of one part refers to what *actually* happens in the physical body as an analogy for what *should* happen in a church. The rejoicing of all parts with a glorified part refers to the whole body's *actually* feeling good when its unpresentable parts are well-clothed and stands for how church members with prominent gifts *should* feel when those with inconspicuous gifts get honored.

12:27–28: And you are Christ's body and individual parts [of it]. [28]**And God has positioned some in the church first as apostles, second as prophets, third as teachers, thereafter miracles, thereafter gracious gifts of healings, helps, administrations, kinds of tongues.** Whether in a local church or in the church at large, unity and variety balance each other. "Some" is to be understood throughout this list, not just with "apostles." The command in 12:31a to "aspire after the greater gracious gifts" means that "first" ranks "apostles" as having the greatest gift, that "second" ranks "prophets" as having the next greatest gift, and that "third" ranks "teachers" as having the third greatest. Since in 14:1 Paul will skip over apostleship and say to aspire after prophesying, "apostles" must carry the strict sense of those to whom the resurrected Christ appeared and whom he himself commissioned to represent him (compare 9:1; 15:4–8 and see 4:9–13 for the world's contrastive denigration of them). You can't aspire to apostleship in that sense. Prophets are conveyers of divine revelations, and teachers are explainers of those revelations. Paul then shifts from people according to their functions to functions as people. Miracles and healings appeared in reverse order in 12:9–10, but there Paul wasn't ranking the gifts. Here the broader "miracles" outranks "healings," a subcategory of miracles. Again to differentiate them from physicians' cures, Paul describes "healings" as "gracious gifts." If his command that's quoted in Acts 20:35 is any guide, "helps" refers to people gifted for helping the sick. "Administrations" refers to people gifted for guiding a church in its policies and programs. The term was used for the helmsman of a ship and therefore suited especially well the church in Corinth, a maritime community through which sea traffic passed. See the comments on 12:10 for "kinds of tongues," which comes last in rank order. Because the top-ranking apostles, prophets, and teachers all have gifts of speaking, we might have expected kinds of tongues, also a gift of speaking, to be ranked toward the top. But the addition of a miraculous element to speaking in kinds of tongues sends this gift to the bottom lest it give rise to pride, as chapter 14 will indicate happened in the Corinthian church. It should be noted at the same time, though, that "administrations" comes next to last lest guidance turn into self-assured tyranny.

12:29–31a: Not all [are] apostles, are they? Not all [are] prophets, are they? Not all [are] teachers, are they? Not all [are] miracles, [are they]? [30]**Not all have gracious gifts of healings, do they? Not all are speaking in tongues, are they? Not all are translating [the tongues], are they?** [31a]**But be aspiring after the greater gracious gifts.** The implied negative answer to all the rhetorical questions stresses the need for variety and therefore its legitimacy. The equation of people with their gift in the question, "Not all [are] miracles, [are they]?" shows how closely linked are Christians with

their Spirit-given functions in a church. As compared with 12:27–28, the omission of "helps" and "administrations" gets Paul quicker to "speak[ing] in tongues," which he does not omit, because it had become problematic in the church at Corinth. Despite the Spirit's distributing a variety of gracious gifts, believers should be aspiring after the greater ones. In 14:3–4 Paul will use prophecy to explain why the greater ones should be aspired after: they build up the church rather than the self alone. Paul doesn't yet identify the means by which Christians should aspire after the greater gracious gifts, and the Spirit distributes them "just as he wills [to do]" (12:11). But 14:13 will identify prayer as the means of aspiration. Meanwhile, the accent falls on the greater gracious gifts as deserving of aspiration.

12:31b–13:3: And I'm showing you a pathway of unparalleled excellence: [1]**If I speak with the tongues of human beings and of angels but don't have love, I've become clanking brass or a clanging cymbal.** [2]**And if I have prophecy [as a gracious gift] and understand all secrets and all knowledge and if I have all faith so as to remove mountains but don't have love, I'm nothing** [or as we'd say, I don't amount to anything]. [3]**And if I dole out all my possessions, and if I give over my body with the result of boasting** [about having done so], **but don't have love, I profit in no respect whatever.** Paul presents love as a pathway along which to walk (compare his frequent use of walking around as a figure of speech for behavior, as in 3:3; 7:17 for instance), and he presents himself as an example of the worthlessness of exercising Spiritual gifts without love (compare also his making himself an example in 9:19–27; 11:1 among other passages). "Of unparalleled excellence" describes love as a pathway of such excellence that not even exercising the greater gifts, after which Christians are to aspire (12:31a), matches the excellence of exercised love. But Paul mentions tongues first, though along with translation it ranks last (see 12:10 and especially 12:30), because tongues-speaking was overestimated in the Corinthian church (see chapter 14) and because despite his low estimate of tongues he speaks in them more than they do (14:18). With prophecy he goes back to the top of the list, except for apostleship, which can't be aspired after (see the comments on 12:28). People can aspire after prophecy (14:1, 39); but even this gift, second only to apostleship, makes its recipient count for nothing if he doesn't have love.

"If I have prophecy . . . but don't have love" doesn't imply that Paul lacks the prophetic gift (to the contrary see 14:6; Ephesians 2:20). At issue is prophecy without love, not prophecy by itself. "Secrets" refers to hidden truths such as were often made known to prophets, so that Paul pairs "secrets" and "knowledge" in connection with "prophecy" (among other passages, see 2:7; 4:1; 15:51 for his knowledge of secrets). He certainly has faith (see Galatians 2:20, for example), as evidenced by his performance of miracles (2:4–5; Romans 15:18–19; 2 Corinthians 6:7; 12:12; Galatians 3:5; 1 Thessalonians 1:5). Doling out possessions has to do especially with feeding the hungry (Romans 12:20) and may relate to the gift of "helps" (12:28). See Acts 20:33–35 on Paul's dispossessing himself for others' benefit. He even contemplates the possibility of giving over his very body in addition to his possessions (compare 1 Thessalonians 2:8–9). "With the result of boasting" means "so that at the Last Judgment I could express pride in my self-sacrifice for others." [8] See the footnote on 9:15–18 for good boasting, and for other examples of Paul's boasting "in Christ Jesus" about what he (Paul) has accomplished for the gospel, see 15:31; Romans 15:14–21; 2 Corinthians 1:12; 11:5–12; Philippians 2:16; 1 Thessalonians 2:19.

Paul doesn't tell here what giving over his body would entail or how it would help others, but see 2 Corinthians 4:7–12 for being constantly given over to death as a possibility in evangelistic service. He has doled out his possessions, perhaps all of them, but hasn't given over his very body to the point of actually dying. This part of his statement is a suppose-so. Similarly, he has some faith, but not all faith. He hasn't removed a mountain (compare Mark 11:23; Matthew 17:20; 21:21). He has a prophetic gift and therefore understands some secrets and some knowledge, but he isn't omniscient (see Romans 11:33–35). By the same token, he speaks with the tongues of human beings (14:18), but not with the tongues of angels, which falls into the suppose-so category along with omniscience, mountain-moving faith, and body-giving. But without love, even speaking in angelic as well as unlearned human languages would grate on the ears. Without love, even omniscience and mountain-moving faith would count for nothing. And without love, even investing in other people not only all one's possessions but also one's very own body would give grounds for boasting but not bring any profit at the final judgment bar. Love must imbue all these activities, and those associated with the remaining Spiritual gifts; for only love makes speaking in tongues musical, prophecy and understanding helpful, and self-sacrifice profitable.

13:4–7: Love practices patience, practices magnanimity. Love doesn't envy. Love doesn't brag, doesn't puff itself up, ⁵doesn't behave indecently, doesn't seek its own [interests], doesn't get irritated, doesn't keep a tally of abuses, ⁶doesn't rejoice over injustice but rejoices with the truth, ⁷tolerates all things, believes all things, hopes all things, endures all things. Here Paul personifies love, so that he has switched from love as a person's possession (13:1–3) to love as a person's possessor, acting out through the person. The personification takes the form of describing personal characteristics evident in behavior. The descriptive verbs are all active. They start with behaviors that do character-

ize love, move quickly to those that don't, and end with further behaviors that do. What Paul says love does and doesn't do looks largely aimed at unloving behavior in the Corinthian church, so that the description subtly and perhaps ironically holds up that church for criticism and correction. For example, "doesn't envy" looks aimed at those who envy others' Spiritual gifts (3:3; 12:15–16); "doesn't brag, doesn't puff itself up" at those who do because of their superior knowledge (4:6, 18–19; 5:2; 8:1); "doesn't behave indecently" at those men who behave indecently, or think they do, toward their virgins (7:36); "doesn't seek its own [interests]" at those who bring lawsuits against fellow believers in pagan courts (6:1–6); and "doesn't rejoice over injustice" at those who take pleasure in winning unjust lawsuits against fellow believers (6:7–8). On the other hand, "tolerates all things" and "endures all things" bring us back to practicing patience and magnanimity and to not getting irritated or keeping a tally of abuses and link up with Paul's admonitions, "let yourselves suffer injustice" and "let yourselves be defrauded" (6:7). Because of being flanked by tolerance and endurance, "believes all things, hopes all things" refers to believing with confident expectation that in the end all injustices will be righted. Love is ebullient with this truth ("rejoices with the truth"), so that in this respect truth is personified alongside love.

13:8–10: Love never founders. But whether [there are] prophecies [as indeed there are], they'll be discontinued; whether tongues, they'll cease; whether knowledge, it'll be discontinued. ⁹For we know piecemeal and prophesy piecemeal; ¹⁰but when the complete comes, the piecemeal will be discontinued. "Love never founders" in the sense that it will never be discontinued or cease but will characterize the interrelations of God's people throughout eternity. By contrast, Paul selects tongues for cessation, and knowledge for discontinuance, because the Corinthians overvalue them (8:1; chapter 14). Yet he also mentions prophecies to indicate that even the greatest gift (after apostleship) will be discontinued. (Apostleship in its narrow sense is already discontinued [see 15:8 with comments].) "Piecemeal" means "incomplete." "For we know . . ." explains why prophecies and knowledge will be discontinued. (At this point tongues drop out, because incompleteness doesn't quite apply to them.) The coming of "the complete" refers to the final state of perfection. Then prophecies, which have the purpose of building others up and exhorting and reassuring them (14:3), won't be needed. The building will be complete, the exhortations fully heeded, the reassurance fulfilled. Then tongues, which are speaking to God in prayer (14:2, 14), will cease, because prayers too will no longer be needed. Then knowledge, the special gift of informing others (12:8), will be discontinued, because they'll have the full knowledge that will make any further informing redundant (13:12).

13:11: When I was a child, I was talking as a child [talks]; I was thinking as a child [thinks]; I was reasoning as a child [reasons]. When I became an adult, I

---

[8]Other English translations have "with the result of being burned" (or similar wording) instead of "with the result of boasting." But the earliest and generally best manuscripts favor a reference to boasting; and it's hard to see why a copyist would change being burned (as a martyr [compare Daniel 3]) to boasting (at the Last Judgment), but easy to see why a copyist would change boasting to being burned as a martyr. For the latter is more admirable.

discontinued the things of the child [that is, my childish talking, thinking, and reasoning]. The Greek word behind "complete" in 13:10 has to do with maturity and adulthood when it comes to human beings—hence the present segue into the contrast between childish and mature talking, thinking, and reasoning. Paul uses the contrast to illustrate the present incompleteness and future completion of prophecies and knowledge, a contrast that leaves love unaffected.

13:12: **For at present we see with a mirror puzzlingly, but then** [we'll see] **face to face. At present I know piecemeal, but then I'll know fully just as also I've been known fully.** "For" introduces the reason for an eventual discontinuance of the gifts of prophecy and knowledge. Paul puts the reason first in the form of an analogy, that of seeing with a mirror. His followup with "face to face" shows that he means seeing someone else in a mirror, not ourselves. The someone else therefore has to be located behind us so as to be reflected in the mirror. Ancient mirrors consisted of polished metal and were valued for accuracy of reflection (against the modern misinterpretation that Paul uses the analogy of a metal mirror because of its giving a fuzzy image). But such mirrors were small and therefore didn't give a full reflection; a puzzle remained as to the rest of the other person reflected. So Paul applies the analogy with his statement, "Presently I know *piecemeal*," and draws a contrast with knowing "fully" because of seeing "face to face," which enables seeing the other's whole body. By using "I" in connection with knowing piecemeal, Paul decries self-puffery because of knowledge (8:1). Not even he knows enough to brag. Only in the coming state of perfection will his knowledge attain the fullness that already characterizes his being known. "Face to face" implies a direct vision of God at the end (compare Revelation 22:4), which all believers will share with Paul, and implies God as the one who knows Paul fully. But the nonmention of God keeps attention glued to the contrast between an incompleteness that leaves puzzles and the completeness that will solve them.

13:13: **But now** [as it is] **these three remain: faith, hope, love. But love** [is] **greater than these** [first two: faith and hope]. Though the Greek nouns for "faith, hope, love" are all feminine, Paul uses the neuter gender in "these three" to stress their qualities as cardinal virtues (compare especially 1 Thessalonians 1:3; 5:8). These virtues "remain" in that they'll not be discontinued or cease, as the three Spiritual gifts of prophecies, tongues, and knowledge will (13:8). The virtues will continue to characterize God's people throughout eternity. There'll always be faith in God because of his love, hope in him because of it, and love of one another as an outgrowth of his love. So love is greater than faith and hope because neither faith nor hope could continue without the love of God.

14:1–3: **Be pursuing love, and be aspiring after the Spiritual** [gifts], **but especially that you may be prophesying.** [2]**For the person who's speaking in a tongue isn't speaking to human beings—rather, to God. For no one hears** [him with understanding]; **but by the Spirit he's speaking secrets.** [3]**But the person who's prophesying is speaking edification and exhortation and reassurance to human beings.** Pursuit is stronger than aspiration. Because love is paramount, then, Paul makes love the object of pursuit, and Spiritual gifts the object of aspiration. And since prophesying outranks all other Spiritual gifts except apostleship, which can no longer be aspired after (see 15:8 and the comments on 12:27–28), he makes prophesying the special object of aspiration. The first "For" introduces his rationale for singling out prophesying. The rationale starts with a description of what happens in tongues-speaking as opposed to what happens in prophesying. The case of a person speaking in a tongue presupposes that nobody with the gift of translation is translating it and that the tongue is a language nobody in the assembly has learned before. Otherwise Paul couldn't say that the speaker is speaking to God, who understands all languages, but not to human beings. "For no one hears [the tongues-speaker]" confirms this presupposition, and "he's speaking secrets" shows that "no one hears" refers to not hearing with understanding. Nonetheless, "by the Spirit" preserves the status of tongues-speaking as a genuinely Spiritual gift, just as prophesying is. Because a prophet speaks in a language that his human audience has learned, what he says builds them up through the imparting of divine revelations ("edification"), urges them to act on the revelations ("exhortation"), and encourages them as to the outcome of such action ("reassurance").

14:4–5: **The person who's speaking in a tongue is edifying himself, but the person who's prophesying is edifying the church** [that is, the people making up the local assembly]. [5]**And I'm wishing you all to be speaking in tongues, but more that you be prophesying** [compare Numbers 11:29]. **The person who's prophesying** [is] **greater than the person who's speaking in tongues, unless he** [the tongues-speaker] **is translating in order that the church may receive edification.** The tongues-speaker doesn't understand what he's saying unless he has the additional gift of translation. Then he can translate what he's saying so that his audience, too, might understand what he's saying. But Paul is presenting the case of a tongues-speaker without the gift of translation. Since such a tongues-speaker doesn't understand what he's saying, his self-edification contains no mental element, only an emotional element (what Paul will call praying and praise-singing with the human spirit apart from the mind [14:13–17]). Since others in the assembly aren't speaking by the Spirit in a tongue, they don't get edified even in their spirits, let alone in their minds, when someone else is speaking in an untranslated tongue. So Paul again differentiates prophesying as edifying others. Only this time he doesn't call the others "human beings" in contrast with "God," as in 14:2, but "the church" for a contrast with the lone tongues-speaker. Not that Paul despises tongues-speaking, though. To emphasize his lack of prejudice against it he states his wish that all the

Corinthian Christians spoke in tongues, so much value does it have. "But more that you be prophesying" reprises the superiority of prophesying, however (14:1–3). And it's not just prophesying that's greater than tongues-speaking. Paul ranks "the *person* who's prophesying" as "greater than the *person* who's speaking in tongues." This personal ranking implies that in the church at Corinth tongues-speakers ranked themselves, and were ranked, above others with different Spiritual gifts, probably because of the miracle of speaking in unlearned languages. For Paul, though, edification of the whole local church through prophesying counts for more than self-edification through tongues-speaking no matter what the miracle involved. Yet he adds a qualification that he'll later amplify. It's that a tongues-speaker who also translates because of having the additional gift of translation is just as great as the prophet. For then the church gets edified.

14:6–9: But now, brothers, if I come to you speaking in tongues, how will I profit you unless I speak to you either by way of a revelation or by way of knowledge or by way of a prophecy or by way of a teaching? ⁷Likewise lifeless things, whether a flute or a harp, when giving a sound—how will what's being fluted or harped be understood if they don't give a distinction in the tones? ⁸For also [= in addition to a flute and a harp] if a trumpet gives an unclear sound, who'll get ready for battle? ⁹So also you, unless you give a well-signaled word [= an intelligible statement] through the tongue, how will what's being spoken be understood? For you'll be speaking into the air. "But now" means "But given the criterion of edification for the whole local church." The address "brothers" introduces Paul's "I" appropriately on a familial note. "If I come to you speaking in tongues" still presupposes no accompanying translation (see the comments on 14:1–3). Since Paul will say in 14:18 that he speaks in tongues more than all the Corinthians do, the present reference to his speaking in tongues combines with the absence of a reference to his translating them, and with references to his other forms of communication instead ("a revelation," "knowledge," "a prophecy," "a teaching"), to suggest that he didn't have the gift of translation. The point: by itself tongues-speaking even by the apostle Paul, whom the Corinthian Christians are supposed to imitate (4:16; 11:1), wouldn't do them any good. Their good—or as he calls it, their profit—would come only by way of his imparting to them a divine revelation, an item of knowledge, a prophecy, or some teaching, all in the language they naturally understand (compare 12:8, 10, 28–29; 13:2, 8). Then he compares tongues-speaking with "lifeless things" such as "a flute or a harp" or "a trumpet." If a flute or a harp is monotone, no understandable music, no melody, comes forth. If a trumpet merely blares, doesn't give a recognizable signal, soldiers won't get ready for battle. The description "lifeless" implies that if even inanimate instruments of sound need to produce clarity of meaning, much more does the tongue of a living human being. "Through the tongue" plays on the tongue as both an organ of speech and a spoken language. "You'll be speaking into the air" describes tongues-speaking without translation as missing a target audience that needs to be edified, exhorted, and reassured (14:3) just as in 9:26 "beating the air" referred to a boxer's missing the target of his punches.

14:10–12: In the world there are such exemplary kinds of sounds [as those of a flute, a harp, and a trumpet], and none [of them is] soundless. ¹¹If therefore I don't know the power of the sound, I'll be to the person who's speaking a barbarian; and the person who's speaking [will be] a barbarian in me [= in my case or estimation]. ¹²In this way you too, since you're aspirants after Spirits, be seeking that you may be flourishing for the edification of the church. To say that no kind of sound is soundless sounds superfluous. Most interpreters therefore understand "soundless" to mean "meaningless." But Paul has just said in 14:6–9 that lack of clarity and of a distinction in tones does render some sounds meaningless. So his redundancy simply emphasizes the large variety of sounds in the world. Because of this variety it's important to know "the power of the sound." Now the element of meaning comes into the picture. The power of a sound lies in its meaning, for its meaning has effects (such as "edification and exhortation and reassurance" [14:3 yet again]). So Paul makes himself an example of the person who doesn't understand an untranslated tongue and says both that he'll be to the tongues-speaker a barbarian and that the tongues-speaker will be a barbarian in his (Paul's) estimation. "Barbarian" is a word that means what it sounds like. To Greeks, those who spoke a language other than Greek sounded as though they were mouthing a meaningless succession of the same syllable: "bar, bar, bar [and so on]." Here, then, Paul portrays speaking in tongues without an accompanying translation as divisive, just as the speaking of foreign languages divided barbarians from Greeks; and divisions in the Corinthian church over other matters had already elicited his concern (1:10–17; 11:18; 12:25). "In this way" doesn't refer to the preceding, for considering each other barbarian is exactly what Paul wants his audience *not* to do. So "in this way" references the following exhortation to aim for the edification of the church. "You *too*" means "you in addition to me." Paul makes himself an example to be imitated in this respect. And he uses the Corinthians' aspiring "after Spirits" as a springboard for the exhortation. The plural of "Spirits" refers to the Holy Spirit as distributed individually to Christians in their Spiritual gifts (compare 12:11 and the comments on Revelation 1:4). In his or her Spiritual gift, that is to say, each Christian has the whole Holy Spirit. From the standpoint of individual human experience, then, there are divine "Spirits," though from the standpoint of God's being, the Spirit is "one" and "the same" (12:4, 8–9, 11, 13).

14:13–17: Therefore [because the church needs edification] the person who's speaking in a tongue is to be praying that he may be translating [the tongue]. ¹⁴If I pray in a tongue, my spirit is praying but my mind is

unfruitful. ¹⁵**What then is** [to be done]**? I'll pray with** [my] **spirit, but I'll pray with** [my] **mind too. I'll sing praise** [to God] **with** [my] **spirit, but I'll sing praise with** [my] **mind too.** ¹⁶**Since if you praise with** [your] **spirit, how will the person who's filling the place of the nonpractitioner** [of tongues and their translation] **say the "Amen" on your giving of thanks, since as a matter of fact he doesn't know what you're saying?** ¹⁷**For you, to be sure, are giving thanks beautifully; the other person, however, isn't being edified.** The command that a tongues-speaker be praying for the additional gift of translation retroactively defines in terms of *praying* for the gift of prophecy what was meant by the command to be aspiring to prophesy (14:1). Now Paul justifies his command to pray for the gift of translation by appealing to the distinction between irrational but emotional praying and singing praises to God in an untranslated tongue, on the one hand, and praying and singing praises rationally as well as emotionally in a commonly understood language, on the other hand. "My spirit" represents the emotional, "my mind" the rational. Paul values the emotional, but fruitlessness of the mind creates for him a problem. So he converses with himself on how to solve the problem. He solves it by determining to keep praying with his spirit, but to add praying with the mind. The same goes for singing praise to God. Insofar as Paul describes the content of tongues-speaking, then, it includes prayer and praise. (But the equation of tongues-speaking plus translation with prophesying for the church's edification [14:5] favors that tongues-speaking includes messages to the congregation as well.) "The person who's filling the place of the nonpractitioner" is one who's seated and listening without understanding the untranslated praise-song and therefore doesn't know when to join the tongues-speaker in saying "Amen" at the conclusion of what Paul calls "your giving of thanks" as a description of "singing praise" (compare 2 Corinthians 1:20). Then Paul describes the giving of thanks itself as done "beautifully," because it is, after all, sung. But in the meeting of a church, musical beauty needs supplementing with a verbal understanding that brings edification.

14:18–19: I thank God I speak in tongues more than all of you. ¹⁹**Nevertheless, in church I want to speak five words with my mind in order to instruct others too** [= as well as myself]**, than ten thousand words in a tongue.** Paul claims to speak in tongues more than all the Corinthians put together do. This claim has the purpose of convincing them that his depreciation of untranslated tongues doesn't arise out of an unfulfilled desire on his part to speak in tongues or, as we'd say, out of "sour grapes." At the same time, "I thank God" eliminates self-glorification for having the gift of tongues-speaking in such greater abundance—God be praised for it—and implies by example that the Corinthians shouldn't get puffed up, or be idolized, for also having this gift. "Nevertheless" introduces the weightier value of speaking an understood language for the instruction of others in an assembly. The huge difference between "five

words" and the largest numerical unit in the Greek language—namely, "myriad," which means either "ten thousand" or an indefinitely large number—underscores how much more valuable is understandable instruction than tongues-speaking apart from translation. Paul's preference for "speak[ing] . . . with [his] mind" in a church service suggests that in the absence of someone with the gift of translation, he limited his tongues-speaking to private devotions.

14:20: Brothers, don't become little children in [your] **mentality. Instead, be infantile as to malice; but become mature in your mentality.** The familial address "brothers" suits the exhortation not to become "little children." Paul implies (1) that fascination with the miracle of speaking in an unlearned language has led to the overvaluation of tongues-speaking; (2) that this overvaluation has led to tongues-speaking apart from translation; and (3) that reveling in tongues-speaking because of its miraculous nature without even wanting to know the meaning of what's being said—and this despite the availability of translation through an equally miraculous gift of translation—betrays a childish disinterest in substantive content. When it comes to malice, though, Paul wants the Corinthians to be, not merely childish, but even infantile. Whatever else infants are, they aren't malicious. Nor should Christians be malicious. But why the mention of malice in a discussion of tongues? Probably because Paul still has in mind the malice that led some Corinthians to sue their fellow Christians in pagan courts (6:1–11; compare the comments on 5:6–8). The command to become mature in mentality returns to tongues and means to value them less than speaking in an understood language. "Don't *become* little children" suggests the Corinthians are *not* childish in their mentality, but "*become* mature" suggests they *are* childish. This delicate balance between childishness and maturity leaves it up to the Corinthians which category they'll fall into.

14:21–22: In the Law it's written, "With other tongues and with others' lips I'll speak to this people. And not even [when I speak to them] **in this way will they heed me," says the Lord** [Isaiah 28:11–12; compare Isaiah's preceding reference to childish talk in 28:9–10 with Paul's preceding reference to childish mentality here in 14:20]. ²²**And so, tongues are for a sign, not concerning those who believe—rather, concerning unbelievers; and prophecy** [is for a sign]**, not concerning unbelievers—rather, concerning those who believe.** Most English translations have it that "tongues are for a sign, not *to* those who believe—rather, *to* unbelievers; and prophecy [is for a sign], not *to* unbelievers—rather, *to* those who believe." In that case, tongues-speaking would be—because of its miraculous nature—an *evidential* sign of the truth of the gospel. Believers already believe the gospel, so that they don't need such a sign. Unbelievers do need such a sign—and get it through Christians' speaking in tongues. But in 14:23 Paul will say that on hearing tongues-speaking (apart from translation, it is still assumed), an unbeliever will be put off and conclude that Christians are crazy. In other words, tongues-speaking (again apart from translation) undermines evangelism rather than helping it. Something is wrong, then, with the translation "*to* those who believe" and "*to* unbelievers." The Greek can just as well be translated "*concerning* [that is, 'in *reference* to'] those who believe" and "*concerning* unbelievers." Consonant with this translation is Paul's using "And so" to indicate that his statements interpret the preceding quotation of the Law. (That the quotation comes from Isaiah 28:11–12 shows that he uses "the Law" for the Old Testament as a whole, not just for the law of Moses, contained in Genesis–Deuteronomy, as was natural since the Old Testament prophets, Isaiah being one of them, called God's people back to the Mosaic law.) In the quotation the Lord says through Isaiah that he will speak to Isaiah's Jewish contemporaries by way of the foreign languages of invaders, but that the Jews won't heed even this method of communication from the Lord. So speaking in foreign languages turns out to be a judgmental sign that does not foster real hearing ("heed[ing]") and therefore signifies the status of unbelievers as under God's judgment, like the unbelieving Jews of old, and as devoid of any benefit from languages they don't understand. Quite the opposite, in fact. Only believers get any benefit from tongues, though it's minimal when unaccompanied by translation. On the other hand, prophecy signifies the status of unbelievers as those for whose conversion the Lord successfully uses understandable language. Though prophecy carries other benefits for believers, it doesn't benefit them evangelistically. They're already converted. From the evangelistic standpoint, then, it doesn't signify their status. Since Paul regularly uses "the Lord" for Jesus Christ, Paul's appending "says the Lord" to the quotation makes the preincarnate Christ the speaker through Isaiah (compare the comments on 10:1–4).

14:23–25: If therefore the whole church comes together to the same [place] and all speak in tongues and housefolks or unbelievers come in, they'll say, "You're crazy!" won't they? ²⁴But if all prophesy and some unbeliever or one of the housefolks comes in, he's being convicted by all. He's being examined by all. ²⁵The hidden things of his heart are becoming apparent. And in this way, [that is,] falling on [his] face, he'll worship God while declaring, "God is really among you [Isaiah 45:14]!" "Therefore" builds the following on what Paul has just said about tongues-speaking and prophecy in relation to believers and unbelievers. But alongside unbelievers he now brings in "housefolks" as distinct from unbelievers ("housefolks *or* unbelievers . . . . some unbeliever *or* one of the housefolks"). Yet like unbelievers the housefolks will say believers are crazy if they all speak in tongues when they come together; and like unbelievers the housefolks are subject to prophetic conviction, examination, exposure, and conversion. So apparently the housefolks are a subcategory of unbelievers. The word translated "housefolks" is usually translated "unlearned," "ungifted," "uninitiated," or the like. Certainly the Greek

word carries those meanings, but it's built on an adjective that means "belonging to one's own self." Since therefore the people referenced by the word appear to make up a subcategory of unbelievers yet all unbelievers are equally unlearned, ungifted, and uninitiated so far as speaking in tongues by the Holy Spirit is concerned, the translation "housefolks" refers to the subcategory as unbelievers belonging to the believers' own households—say, the unconverted spouse, offspring, or slave of a believer.

To heighten the contrast between the effects of speaking in untranslated tongues and of prophesying in an understood language, Paul imagines a church meeting in which *all* the believers are speaking in such tongues, and another church service in which *all* the believers are prophesying in an understood language. And to highlight the positive effect of prophesying over against the negative effect of tongues-speaking apart from translation, he describes the negative effect singularly with "they'll say, 'You're crazy!' won't they?" but the positive effect plurally with references to conviction, examination, exposure, and conversion (as represented by face-to-the-floor worship of God and a declaration of God's presence among the believers). Prophecy subjects an unbeliever to an examination which brings to light "the hidden things of his heart," so that he has to face them in the glare of public scrutiny. This exposure convicts him in the sense of convincing him of God's presence among the prophetic Christians, and the conviction leads to conversion. By notable contrast, pagan religions paid little attention to sin, much less to secret sins, and therefore no attention to conversion from one religion to another. Pagans just added religions to each other.

14:26–28: What then is [to be done], **brothers?** Answer: **Whenever you come together, each person has a praise-song, has a teaching, has a revelation, has a tongue, has a translation. All** [these activities] **are to take place for the purpose of edification** [that is, for building up the whole assembly, not just for building up the person who has these things]. ²⁷**And if someone speaks in a tongue,** [it's to take place] **by twos** [from meeting to meeting]—**or at the most by threes—and in turn; and one person is to be translating.** ²⁸**But if there's no translator, he** [the tongues-speaker] **is to keep quiet yet be speaking to himself and God.** The address "brothers" introduces the following instructions in a way that implies an eldest brother's telling his younger brothers what to do. The brotherly relationship is supposed to make the instructions palatable as well as mandatory. "Each person has . . ." doesn't mean that each one necessarily has all the listed items. It means that each one has one or another of them. "A praise-song" may refer to a song sung in a tongue (see 14:15)—but maybe not, since "a tongue" is listed separately. "A revelation" may imply prophecy, since prophecy isn't listed separately. And otherwise what would "a revelation" mean? In any case, the list is representative rather than comprehensive, because gifts such as "a word of wisdom," "a word of knowledge," and "differentiations of spirits" are missing (compare 12:8–10, 28–30). What the list does do, however, is to bring out again the variety of Spiritual gifts so that Paul can reemphasize their purpose of mutual edification. More particularly, the restrictions on tongues and their interpretation have the purpose not only of making them edify the whole assembly but also of preserving time for the exercise of similarly edifying gifts. To ensure the edificatory effect of tongues Paul requires both their translation and their speakers' taking turns. The speaking of two or more at the same time would thwart the audience's understanding of any translation that was taking place. And only one person is to translate the tongue being spoken, lest two or more translators speaking at the same time make the translation incomprehensible. If the tongues-speaker also has the gift of translation, he can translate his own tongues-speaking, of course. The prohibition of tongues-speaking in the absence of a translator implies that it was known who had the gift of translation, and this prohibition joins the requirement of speaking in turn to imply also that tongues-speakers do not lose control of themselves. They can wait their turn or keep quiet till they're able to speak to themselves and God in private.

14:29–33a: And two or three prophets are to be speaking, and the others are to be differentiating [the prophecies as to truth versus falsehood, for there are false as well as true prophecies]. [30]**And if** [a prophetic message] **is revealed to another** [prophet] **while he's sitting, the first** [prophet, the one speaking] **is to keep quiet.** [31]**For you can all prophesy one by one in order that all may be learning and** [in order that] **all may be exhorted** [to act on what they've learned (compare 14:3)]. [32]**And the prophets' Spirits are in subjection to the prophets,** [33a]**for God isn't** [a God] **of disorder—rather, of peace.** Since tongues plus translation equals prophecy in value (14:5), the restrictions to two or three prophecies in a meeting and to prophesying "one by one" match the restrictions on tongues plus translation. In regard to tongues, Paul said three "at most." The absence of this phrase in connection with prophecies doesn't imply the allowance of more than three prophecies per church meeting. Otherwise why even mention "two or three"—unless it be *to demand* two or three prophecies per church meeting? But prophecies depend on revelations from God, not on human determination. So the present absence of "at most" simply reflects a greater need for the control of tongues-speaking than for that of prophesying. Since tongues can't be translated miraculously except by the Holy Spirit, no differentiating between truth and falsehood is required for tongues plus translation. But false as well as true prophecy can be spoken in a language commonly understood by a speaker and his audience. So Paul requires an exercise in differentiation. After the mention of "two or three prophets," "the others" might seem to mean other prophets; but the others' commanded activity of "differentiating" points back to those who are gifted with "differentiations of spirits" (12:10). Of course, other prophets as well as nonprophets might have that gift.

Not only are prophets to speak "one by one." They're also to stop prophesying if another prophet receives a revelation. Reception of the revelation while the first prophet is speaking indicates that the Lord wants the first prophecy concluded. Presumably the second prophet signals the first one in the event of a revelation. "*For* you can all prophesy one by one" gives the reason behind the command that a prophet stop talking if another prophet receives a revelation. This restriction parallels the restriction to one translator for each tongue. Since not all have the prophetic gift according to 12:29, the "all" in "you can all prophesy one by one" refers to believers who do have that gift, whereas the "all" in "that all may be learning and [in order that] all may be urged" refers to all the assembled. The limitation to two or three prophecies per church meeting, and these "one by one," implies that some prophets may have to wait till a future meeting for the speaking of their prophecies. The implied self-control of tongues-speakers becomes explicit in the case of prophets, though in both cases we should perhaps speak of controlling the Spirit rather than self-control. For in 14:12 "aspirants after Spirits" portrayed the one Holy Spirit as distributed in his wholeness to each recipient of a Spiritual gift. By the same token, "the prophets' Spirits" are the one Holy Spirit distributed in his wholeness to each prophet. But how can it be that God's Spirit is "in subjection" to a human prophet? Paul anticipates the question by explaining that "God isn't [a God] of disorder—rather, of peace." In other words, God has put his Spirit in subjection to the prophets for the sake of peace. Because of the contrast with "disorder," "peace" connotes orderliness due to the absence of one upmanship in the exercise of Spiritual gifts.

14:33b–36: As in all the churches [= assemblies] **of the saints,** [34]**the women are to keep quiet in the churches; for it's not permitted for them to be speaking. Instead, they're to be in subjection, just as the Law too** [in addition to me] **says.** [35]**But if they're wanting to learn something, they're to ask their own husbands at home; for it's shameful for a woman to be speaking in church** [= in an assembly]. [36]**Or did God's word emanate from you, or reach you alone?** "As in all the churches of the saints" recollects Paul's appeal to "custom" in "God's churches" with regard to women's praying and prophesying in church meetings (see 11:16 with comments). Here too the subject is women's speaking in such meetings, though differently from their legitimate praying and prophesying. As Paul anticipated an objection in 11:16, he does so here in 14:36. But the present appeal to churchly custom is separated from the anticipation of an objection, for Paul advances his appeal to the beginning of the paragraph (contrast 11:16). Here it functions as a preemptive strike against the objection that's implied at the end of the paragraph. "As in *all* the churches" strengthens the preemptive strike (contrast the absence of "all" in 11:16); and the addition, "of the saints," describes the churches as made up of those whom God has consecrated to himself and therefore whose customs represent his own holiness.

The command that corresponds to all the churches' custom is that "the women are to keep quiet in the churches; for it's not permitted for them to speak." But in 11:2–16 Paul laid down a condition under which women could indeed speak in church meetings—by way of praying and prophesying.[9] So what kind of speaking is prohibited here? The contrast with being in subjection indicates speaking by way of contradicting the message of a prophet. There may have been, incidentally, something of a women's liberation movement in the first-century Roman Empire, a movement that would have encouraged the speaking prohibited here by Paul. He's still concerned to avoid "disorder" and maintain "peace" (14:33a). On the other hand, he respects the desire of women to learn, but says they should direct enquiring questions to their husbands at home. For asking such questions in church would not only interrupt the prophesying but also hinder the purpose of prophecy "that *all* may learn" (14:31). Church meetings have the purpose of corporate learning, which is a form of corporate edification such as Paul has been advocating all the way through chapters 12–14. Individual learning can take place "at home." Paul says that the Law commands women to be in subjection but doesn't cite any passage in particular. Apparently, then, his arguing in 11:7–12 from Genesis 1–2 ("the Law") for the subjection of women carries over to the present passage. He's also concerned that they not shame their husbands with contrarian comments and interruptive questions directed to men not their husbands. In a culture that traditionally frowned on public discourse between a married woman and a man other than her husband, such shaming would disrecommend the gospel—hence Paul's command that women ask "their *own* husbands" (compare 11:5). The question, "Or did God's word emanate from you, or reach you alone?" suggests, maybe even implies, some disagreement with Paul in Corinth and sounds sarcastic since the question has an obviously negative answer: God's word didn't emanate from the Corinthians, it *came* to them—through the instrumentality of the very Paul who has just issued the foregoing commands. Nor has God's word reached the Corinthians alone, as shown by the foregoing reference to "all the churches of the saints." "Or" introduces the question as a ridiculous alternative to what Paul and the Law say and all the churches of the saints practice.

14:37–38: If someone supposes [himself] **to be a prophet or Spiritual** [= endowed with the Holy Spirit], **he's to be acknowledging the things that I'm writing to you,** [in other words, he's to be acknowledging] **that they're the Lord's command.** [38]**But if someone ignores** [the Lord's command that I'm writing to you], **he's being ignored** [by the Lord]. Paul has ordered a differentiation of prophecies (14:29; compare 12:10). Here he lays

down a criterion by which a true prophecy can be differentiated from a false one. Constituting this criterion is acknowledgment that what Paul is writing equates with the Lord's command—in other words, that the exalted Jesus is speaking through Paul. Disagreement with the equation will discredit a self-proclaimed prophet as un-Spiritual, lacking the Holy Spirit. To ignore the Lord's command is to disobey it. To be ignored by the Lord is to be forever lost (compare Matthew 7:22–23). Since 14:37–38 is bounded by commands concerning prophecy and tongues (see 14:39–40 as well as 12:1–14:36), "the things that I'm writing to you" refers to the contents of chapters 12–14, not to the whole of 1 Corinthians—though if asked, Paul would doubtless say the same about the rest of his letter (compare 7:40b).

14:39–40: And so, brothers, be aspiring to prophesy; and don't ever ban speaking in tongues. [40]**But all** [these activities] **are to take place decorously and in accord with orderliness.** "And so" introduces a wrap-up of chapters 12–14. "Brothers" imbues the wrap-up with affection. "Be aspiring to prophesy" reprises 14:1b (on which see the comments). "And don't ever ban speaking in tongues" is designed to guard against taking Paul's strictures on tongues-speaking as a reason to rule it out altogether. The overall command to maintain decorum and order has the complementary purpose of ensuring that prophesying, tongues-speaking, and the exercise of other Spiritual gifts don't get out of hand so as to impair the edification of Christians and the conversion of non-Christians.

ON RESURRECTION
1 Corinthians 15:1–58

Some of the Corinthian Christians denied a future resurrection of the dead, though they did believe in the past resurrection of Christ. So in 15:1–34 Paul points out that Christ's resurrection ensured the resurrection of Christians, and in 15:35–58 he explains what happens to the body both in resurrection and in a transformation of bodies still living on the day of resurrection.

15:1–2: And I'm making known to you, brothers, the gospel that I gospelized to you [= the good news that I told you *as* good news], **that you also received, in which also you've taken a stand,** [2]**through which also you're being saved if you're holding tight the said word** [= message] **I gospelized you with—unless you believed casually.** Paul uses "the gospel" and "gospelized" (the latter twice) because the upcoming affirmation of Jesus' resurrection as ensuring the resurrection of believers in him is indeed good news. The Corinthians received the gospel when Paul evangelized their city. They've taken a stand in the gospel by believing it. They're being saved through it in the sense that their salvation is ongoing till it reaches a culmination at Christ's second coming and the Last Judgment. But that culmination is conditioned on their holding tight the gospel, which Paul calls "the said *word*" in allusion to his having *spoken* the gospel

---

[9]Arguments for regarding 14:34–35 as a copyist's insertion into Paul's letter get rid of what proponents consider a disagreement with 11:2–16; but no surviving Greek manuscripts lack 14:34–35, though a very few (not considered the earliest and best) and some Latin translations place these verses after 14:40.

in Corinth. He lays down the condition because of the possibility that the Corinthians believed "casually," that is, without the seriousness of purpose that would keep them holding tight to the word of the gospel. It's the possibility of their having believed casually and therefore losing out on salvation that leads Paul to make the gospel known to them in this letter even though they already know it from having received it and taken their stand in it. The affectionate address "brothers" shows his concern over this possibility and helps introduce the new topic to be discussed in chapter 15.

15:3–7: For to you I gave over among the foremost things what I too received: that Christ died for our sins in accordance with the Scriptures, ⁴and that he was buried, and that he was raised on the third day in accordance with the Scriptures, ⁵and that he appeared to Cephas, then to the Twelve. ⁶Thereafter he appeared to over five hundred brothers at one time, the majority of whom remain [alive] till now (but some have fallen asleep [that is, died]). ⁷Thereafter he appeared to James, then to all the apostles. Along with "you received" in 15:1, "I gave over" and "I too received" indicate a passing on of the tradition concerning Christ's death, burial, resurrection, and appearances as resurrected. Paul doesn't say who gave the tradition over to him, for that bit of information wouldn't have related to the Corinthians. The introductory "For" makes the tradition an explanation of "the gospel" that Paul mentioned in 15:1–2. "Among the foremost things" puts the tradition among the first and therefore most important things he spoke on arriving in Corinth. "What I *too* received" draws a parallel between him and the Corinthians. The parallel is designed to give Paul a sympathetic hearing on the Corinthians' part. "That Christ died" sets out a historical event. "For our sins" interprets its significance. The significance is that Christ's death had the purpose of erasing our sins and their deadly effects. "In accordance with the Scriptures" refers to the Old Testament as a repository of indications that God had all along planned Christ's atoning death. Paul doesn't identify any particular passages in the Old Testament referred to by the tradition, so that emphasis falls on the point that Christ's death for our sins wasn't a last resort, much less a makeshift. The use of "Christ" rather than "Jesus" implies that his death and what followed it formed the climax of his mission as the one anointed by God to effect our salvation, for "Christ" means "anointed" and therefore chosen for a special task.

"That he was buried" comes as a natural consequence of death but more especially prepares for "he *was raised*." Like "have taken a stand" in 15:1, "was raised" indicates an action that was completed in the past but has a continuing result. In other words, Christ still lives in a resurrected state. Coming on the heels of burial, moreover, "was raised" implies that his buried body was raised in renewed life. Indeed, the very word "body" will figure prominently in Paul's continuing discussion of resurrection. "On the third day" tells when Christ was raised and implies a counting of Good Friday as the first day and therefore Easter Sunday as the third. Foregoing comments apply also to the second occurrence of "in accordance with the Scriptures." Paul shows no concern to clarify where, or whether, "on the third day" is included in scriptural foregleams of Christ's resurrection. So the emphasis stays on the point of God's having preplanned the event.

The tradition cites Christ's various post-mortem appearances as evidence that he'd been raised. The appearance to Cephas is listed first because he was the leading apostle among the Twelve, who come next on the list (see the comments on 1:12 for "Cephas"). Though Judas Iscariot had dropped out of the Twelve and therefore can't have seen the raised Christ along with his former apostolic colleagues, "the Twelve" had become a stereotyped expression that simply overlooked the exception of Judas. His replacement with Matthias may have helped the overlooking (see Acts 1:15–26). The appearance "to over five hundred brothers" strengthens the evidence of Christ's resurrection with a high number of eyewitnesses. "At one time" adds further strength by implying their agreement with each other that together on a single occasion they'd seen Christ as raised. To strengthen the evidence yet further, Paul adds to the tradition that most of the five hundred have remained alive. They can still vouch for having seen the raised Christ at one and the same time and together. "But some have fallen asleep" makes explicit the implication in "the *majority* of whom remain [alive] till now," but also prepares for a discussion of all deceased believers' resurrection as an awakening out of the sleep of death. As Cephas was listed before the Twelve because of his leading role among them, so James is listed before "all the apostles" because of his leading role among them. In accordance with Galatians 1:18–19; 2:9, this James was Jesus' half brother, not James the brother of John and one of the Twelve. Since the twelve apostles have already been mentioned, "all the apostles" includes a larger number than the Twelve and adds even further numerical strength to the evidence of Christ's having been raised. Paul cites all this traditional evidence to keep his audience "holding tight" so that they'll continue "being saved" till the end. They haven't stopped believing in Christ's resurrection. But Paul wants them to keep believing in it, because he's going argue that if believers in Christ aren't going to be raised from the dead, neither was Christ—a dangerous argumentative maneuver if belief in Christ's resurrection isn't settled and sure.

Now Paul adds his own seeing of Christ as raised (compare 9:1). **15:8–11: And last of all he appeared also to me just as if to a miscarriage. ⁹For I'm the least of the apostles, who am not fit to be called an apostle, because I persecuted God's church. ¹⁰But by God's grace I am what I am** [that is, an apostle], **and his grace** [that he extended] **to me hasn't turned out empty** [of its desired effect]. **Rather** [as opposed to ineffectuality], **I've labored a lot more than all of them** [the other apostles]—yet not I; rather, God's grace [that's] **with me.** **¹¹Therefore whether I**['m proclaiming Christ] **or those** [apostles are proclaiming him], **we're proclaiming**

[him] **this way** [that is, in accordance with the afore-mentioned tradition]; **and you believed in this way.** Since a couple of decades or so have passed since Paul saw the resurrected Christ, "last of all" implies that no more appearances of Christ to prove his resurrection are to be expected. Otherwise Paul would have said to aspire after apostleship, which required having seen the resurrected Christ, as the greatest Spiritual gift rather than after prophecy as the second greatest (12:28, 31a, 14:1). "Just as to a miscarriage" doesn't connect with Christ's appearing to Paul "last of all"; for a miscarriage occurs early, not late. The following statement, introduced with "For," explains the meaning of "a miscarriage." Paul is just like a miscarriage in that miscarriages eject an embryo or fetus smaller than a baby born fully formed in his mother's womb, and Paul is "the least of the apostles" (compare Numbers 12:12, where miscarriages are said to produce a stillborn "whose flesh is half eaten away"; also the meaning of *paulus* in Latin: "small"). So small physical size symbolizes the smallest of apostleships, that of Paul. Then he explains why he describes himself as "the least [or 'smallest'] of the apostles." It's that his having persecuted God's church (for which see Acts 8:3; 9:1, 13, 21; 22:4, 19; 26:10–11; Galatians 1:13, 23; Philippians 3:6; 1 Timothy 1:13) made him unfit to be called an apostle.

"To be called an apostle" refers to Christ's calling him *to be* an apostle rather than to others' calling him one— as shown by the immediately following reference to "God's grace," by which Christ called Paul into apostleship. If grace was ever *ill-deserved*, it was so in the case of Paul; and that he was called not merely into salvation but into apostleship, the greatest of Spiritual gifts, heightens to the nth degree God's grace as *favor*. Paul's resting his apostleship on God's grace shows him not to be puffed up like the Corinthians, who have only lesser Spiritual gifts (4:18–19; 5:2). Even Paul's claim to have labored a lot more than all the other apostles (put together, it would seem) doesn't betray self-puffery, because he ascribes his labor to "God's grace [that's] with [him]" rather than to himself—as though he's watching the grace of God doing the work of evangelism not through him or even in cooperation with him—instead, with Paul as an admiring spectator: "yet *not* I; *rather*, God's grace [personified as a laborer]." "Therefore" draws a consequence from the labor of God's grace, namely, that both Paul and the other apostles are proclaiming the gospel tradition that the Corinthians came to believe.

15:12–15: **But if Christ is being proclaimed, that he was raised from among the dead, how is it that some among you are saying, "There's no resurrection of dead people"? ¹³But if there's not a resurrection of dead people, neither was Christ raised. ¹⁴And if Christ wasn't raised, then too our proclamation** [of him is] **empty** [in the sense of hollow, worthless]**; and your faith** [= belief] [is] **empty; ¹⁵and we're being found** [to be] **even false witnesses about God, because we've testified against God that he raised the Christ, whom he didn't raise if in fact, then, dead people aren't raised** [as some of you say they aren't]. We now know why Paul

has brought up the topic of resurrection: some in the Corinthian church were denying a resurrection of dead people. Since Paul has said that the Corinthians believed the gospel, which includes Christ's resurrection as an event that has already occurred, the denial must have to do with a future resurrection of others.

At this point it's important to note that "resurrection" means "a standing up," so that a standing up of dead people means that their corpses, lying supine in graves, stand up because of renewed life. Paul doesn't explain why some Corinthians denied a future resurrection, though we know from extrabiblical sources that in the first-century Roman Empire there was a lot of skepticism about any sort of afterlife, and at most a belief in the soul's immortality apart from the body (with the exception of a belief in bodily resurrection by some but not all Jews). Instead of exploring the reason for some Corinthians' denial of a resurrection of dead people, Paul pounces on the inconsistency of denying it yet believing in Christ's resurrection. The blatancy of this inconsistency leads Paul to introduce it in the form of an astonished question: "how is it that some among you are saying … ?" So confident is he of the evidence for Christ's resurrection and of the Corinthians' belief in it that in effect he challenges them to deny Christ's resurrection if they persist in denying others' coming resurrection. Then he tightens the argumentive screw by saying that if Christ wasn't raised, as consistency with their denial demands, they've worthlessly believed a worthless proclamation peddled by false witnesses, who did *not* see the raised Christ as they claimed to have seen him. Gone is Christ's resurrection. Gone is the truth of the gospel. Gone is the validity of the Corinthians' faith in Christ. Gone is the truthfulness of Cephas, of the Twelve, of the more than five hundred, of James, of all the apostles, and of Paul himself. Furthermore, the witnesses would not only have been testifying falsely "*about* God." They would also have been testifying falsely "*against* God," as though he were in the dock being falsely accused of wrongdoing. Paul designs the otherwise otiose phrase, "against God," to highlight the absurdity of concluding for the sake of consistency that the witnesses to appearances of Christ as raised are false. "*Even* false witnesses" adds to the absurdity, and "being *found*" false portrays the deniers of a future resurrection as judges who are ignorantly throwing out of court the testimonies by all those from Cephas through Paul concerning Christ's past resurrection. "Whom he ['God'] didn't raise if in fact, then, dead people aren't raised" brings into the open God as the doer of the action in "he [Christ] was raised."

15:16–19: **For if dead people aren't raised, neither was Christ raised. ¹⁷And if Christ wasn't raised, your faith** [is] **inconsequential. You're still in your sins. ¹⁸Then also those who've fallen asleep** [= died] **in Christ have perished. ¹⁹If in Christ we've hoped only during this life, we're more pathetic than all human beings** [besides us]. To justify his foregoing list of losses, given a nonresurrection of Christ, Paul asserts for the third time that denial of resurrection entails a denial of

Christ's resurrection, repeats that the Corinthians faith is worthless ("inconsequential" being a synonym for the earlier "empty"), and adds three further losses: (1) "You're still in your sins," which contrasts with being "in Christ" and belies that "Christ died for our sins" (15:3) with any good effect. Forgiveness of sins means that they're sent away from the sinner, so that he doesn't have to be punished for them. So to be "still *in* your sins" means not just that they're still attached to you, but that you're attached to them as the very environment in which you live and will die. (2) "Then also those who've fallen asleep in Christ have perished." They'll never wake up in resurrection, because to have died in a *dead* Christ, one who himself didn't wake up in resurrection, is to be lost forever. (3) Similarly, in regard to those still living but hoping in a dead, unresurrected Christ: "If in Christ we've hoped only during this life, we're more pathetic than all human beings [besides us]." "*Only* during this life," because this life is all we have if dead people aren't raised; and "*more* pathetic than . . . ," because a nonresurrection of dead people makes pathetic those who live now with a vain hope of resurrected life. For it's those who understand and face reality, no matter how grim it is, who alone deserve admiration.

15:20–22: **But now [as it is], Christ *was* raised from among the dead as the firstfruits** [= the first installment] **of those who've fallen asleep. ²¹For since in fact death [came] through a human being, resurrection of dead people, too, [came] through a human being. ²²For just as in the Adam** [whose very name means "human being"] **all die, in this way also all will be made alive in the Christ.** Here Paul switches from his long series of deductions from what some Christians in Corinth don't believe in—that is, resurrection as such (15:12–19)—to what they as well as the rest of the Corinthians and he do believe in, namely, Christ's resurrection (though those who deny resurrection as such believe in Christ's resurrection inconsistently). "From among the dead" repeats a phrase that occurred at the start of the preceding series and thus signals a refutation of the denial on which the deductions were based. "As the firstfruits" supplies an element missing in Paul's argument up till now. He uses "firstfruits" as a figure of speech for the first of what is yet to come, as when the first sheaf of harvested grain holds the sure and certain promise of the rest of the harvest. Applied to Christ, this figure of speech means that his resurrection wasn't a fluke, the exception that proves a rule that dead people aren't raised. No, his resurrection holds the sure and certain promise of believers' resurrection yet to come, so that there's no rule that dead people aren't raised. (Only some Corinthians' denial of deceased Christians' resurrection occupies Paul's attention; so he doesn't discuss the question of unbelievers' resurrection.)

The reason Christ's resurrection holds the promise of believers' resurrection is that they're in Christ; so in union with him what happened to him is bound to happen also to them. Paul supports this premise by appealing to all human beings' dying as a result of being "in

the Adam," that is, of sharing humanity with the original human being, who died for committing the original sin (Genesis 3:1–24; 5:3–5). "In *the* Adam" makes "Adam" into a title for Adam as incorporating in himself all human beings; and "in fact" stresses the actuality of everybody's death as a result of this incorporation. "In *the* Christ" likewise makes 'Christ" into a title for Christ as incorporating in himself all human beings who believe in him. Just as shared humanity with the Adam makes possible incorporation in him, so shared humanity with the Christ makes possible incorporation in him. But since unbelief and even casual belief in him result in eternal lostness (1:18; 3:17; 5:13; 6:9–10; 9:27; 15:2), shared humanity with the Christ doesn't suffice for resurrection to eternal life, so that the "all" who "will be made alive in the Christ" consist only, but thankfully, of all who died believing in him, whereas the "all" who die in the Adam consist of all human beings without distinction. "Will be made alive" links the resurrection in view, that of believers, with eternal life as opposed to eternal death.

15:23–26: **But each in his own order: Christ, the firstfruits** [= the first installment of the resurrection]; **thereafter at his coming, those who belong to the Christ; ²⁴then the end, when he gives the reign over to God, even the Father, [that is,] when he has incapacitated every rulership and every authority and power. ²⁵For it's necessary that he be reigning till "he has put all enemies under his feet [Psalm 110:1]." ²⁶Death is being incapacitated as the last enemy.** To be in Christ by faith is to belong to him, and "those who belong to the Christ" confirms that the "all" who "will be made alive in the Christ" consist only of believers in him—though Paul accents that *all* of them will be made alive, as opposed to any notion that only believers still living at the second coming will thereafter have a bodily existence like Christ's (compare 1 Thessalonians 4:13–18). To set out a chronology, this paragraph returns to the analogy of Christ as the firstfruits of resurrection, pinpoints the resurrection of believers as occurring at his second coming, proceeds to "the end," defines the end as the time "when he gives the reign over to God, even the Father," and pinpoints this transfer as occurring when Christ "has incapacitated every rulership and every authority and power." "When he gives the reign over to God" implies that Christ will have been reigning on God's behalf. "Even the Father" implies that Christ will have been reigning on behalf of God because he's God's Son. And the whole expression implies the subjection of Christ to God as a son is subject to his father.

Paul doesn't identify what he means by "every rulership and every authority and power"; but their incapacitation by him implies antagonism toward his reign, and the piling up of three synonyms and two occurrences of "every" stress the completeness of their ultimate incapacitation by Christ. Nor does Paul say whether "the end," when Christ gives the reign over to God because of having incapacitated every opponent, will occur right after Christ's coming or only after an interval (such as the millennium of Revelation 20:1–6). In view is only the resurrection of believers in him. Since those who've "fallen asleep" in him will be resurrected at his coming, then, the incapacitation of Death "as the *last* enemy" in their resurrection indicates at least that Paul doesn't have in mind a following interval. (Our capitalization of "Death" reflects Paul's personification of it.) The quotation of Psalm 110:1 shows that the necessity of Christ's reigning till he has put all enemies under his feet is a scriptural necessity. The Scriptures must be fulfilled, because they're God's word.

15:27–28: For "he has placed all things in subjection under his feet [Psalm 8:6]." But when it says, "All things have been placed in subjection," [it's] **clear that** [all things have been subjected under his feet] **except for the one** [God] **who subjected all things to him** [Christ]. **²⁸And when all things have been subjected to him, then also the Son himself will subject himself to him who subjected all things to him, in order that God may be all in all.** According to 15:23–26, by incapacitating every one of his opponents *Christ* will ultimately have put all enemies under his feet. According now to 15:27–28, *God* will ultimately have placed all things under Christ's feet. No problem, though; for since Christ is reigning on God's behalf, what Christ does, God does. In 15:23–26 Christ's coming transfer of reign to God the Father implied Christ's subjection to him. Now in 15:27–28 Paul makes that implication explicit. For the self-subjection of Christ the Son to God the Father is to be seen in Christ's transfer of reign from himself to God. The subjection of the Son to his Father gets emphasis from the addition of "himself" to "the Son." We could even put an exclamation mark after "the Son himself." "Also" (or "even," as the underlying Greek word could be translated) precedes "the Son himself" and thus furthers the emphasis on the Son's subjection. This subjection has the purpose of God's being "all in all," an expression that underscores the totality of his reign, which includes even his Son, Christ, as a subject.

15:29–34: Since [if what I've said isn't true] **what will those who are getting baptized for the dead do? If dead people aren't being raised at all, why are they even getting baptized for them? ³⁰Why too are we in danger every hour? ³¹As truly as I boast of you—a** [boasting] **that I have in Christ Jesus, our Lord—I'm dying day by day. ³²If I fought with wild beasts in Ephesus in accordance with a human being** [that is, without hope that a human being could survive a gladiatorial contest with wild beasts], **what profit** [do] **I have? If dead people aren't being raised, "Let's eat and drink, for tomorrow we die** [Isaiah 22:13; compare Isaiah 56:12]." **³³Don't be led astray: "Bad company corrupts good morals** [a proverb by the poet Menander, *Thais* 218]." **³⁴Sober up, as is right** [for you to do]; **and stop sinning, for some have no knowledge of God. I say** [so] **to reproach you.** To take 15:29 apart from what immediately follows is to make 15:29 seem as though Paul is talking about living people getting baptized for others who are already dead

and gone. But he goes right on to describe himself, a baptized Christian (Acts 9:18), as "dying day by day" in the sense that the enemy Death is already at work in his body and in the afflictions he faces as a Christian (compare 2 Corinthians 4:8–5:4, especially 4:10–12, 16, all in the context of bodily resurrection, as here; and Romans 8:10). So Paul presents himself as an example of people who in the grip of death are getting baptized for themselves. To portray them as in the grip of death he speaks of them as *though* they're dead already and therefore as *though* they're different from themselves when in fact they're themselves *as* the living dead. "What will [they] . . . do?" asks out of utter perplexity what reason for baptism there can possibly be if the baptizees, already in death's grip as they are, won't be raised. Deepening the perplexity are Paul's use of the present tense for a future event in "aren't being raised," his addition of "at all," and his prefixing "even" to "getting baptized for them."

"Why too are *we* in danger every hour" puts Paul and his fellow believers together in hourly *danger* of dying. Then he buttresses the affirmation of his *actually* dying day by day (for which see again 2 Corinthians 4:10–12, 16) with an avowal that such dying on his part is just as true as is the fact that he boasts of the Corinthians. "A [boasting] that I have in Christ Jesus, our Lord" protects the boast from self-exaltation and has the purpose of keeping the Corinthians from getting puffed up because of Paul's boasting about them. The basis for boasting lies in Christ Jesus, not in Paul or in the Corinthians. Since fighting with wild beasts in a gladiatorial show would almost certainly have ended Paul's life, he uses such fighting as a figure of speech for encountering deadly opposition, as he did in Ephesus according to Acts 19:23–31 (compare 1 Corinthians 16:9b). But absent a coming resurrection, what profit is there in exposing oneself as a Christian to mortal danger. Better to enjoy life while it lasts. As a knee-jerk reaction to that conclusion, though, Paul immediately warns against being led astray into sinful behavior on the false ground that death ends all. His quotation of the proverb that "bad *company* corrupts good morals" suggests that the Corinthian deniers of resurrection are getting their denial from unbelievers, whose company will lead the believers into bad behavior (compare 2 Corinthians 6:14–7:1). "Sober up" makes drunkenness an example of corrupt rather than good morals and harks back to some of the Corinthians' getting drunk at the Lord's Supper (11:21). "As is right" describes sobering up as right not only to avoid desecration of the Lord's Supper but also to avoid noninheritance of God's kingdom (6:9–10). "And stop sinning" unites with "I say [so] to reproach you" to imply that the Corinthians *are* sinning, partly as a result of denying resurrection. "For some have no knowledge of God" implies that the sinning of Christians in Corinth is keeping their fellow Corinthians from coming to a knowledge of God, and this despite the Christians' both having such knowledge and boasting of it (1:5; 8:1–2, 10–11).

15:35–38: Somebody, however, will say, "How are the dead being raised? And with what kind of body are

they coming?" ³⁶**Stupid! What you sow isn't made alive unless it dies. ³⁷And as to what you sow, you don't sow the body that's going to turn out. Instead, [you sow] a bare grain of wheat, for example, or one of the rest [of the grains]; ³⁸and God gives it a body just as he wanted, and to each of the seeds its own body.** As before, the present tense in "are . . . being raised" and "are they ['the dead'] coming" straddles the undisputed resurrection of Christ in the past and the disputed resurrection of Christians in the future. Paul imagines that a Corinthian denier of resurrection will raise questions. His harsh reaction with "Stupid!" shows up the questions as asked by way of objection, not innocently. The objection is practical, and the question concerning the *kind* of body at a resurrection specifies what's meant in the question concerning *how* the dead are raised—not how it happens, but how it ends up. In answer, Paul uses an analogy that even a stupid objector should understand. "What you sow isn't made alive unless it dies" appeals to the stupid objector's observation of what happens in the aftermath of his own action, and the following statements appeal to the action itself. The dissolution of a seed sown in the ground is like the dissolution of a dead human body— so alike, in fact, that the seed "isn't made alive *unless* it dies." And though being made alive, it comes forth as a different body from the grain that was sown: continuity with change, identity with difference. "A *bare* grain" underscores the difference between what's sown and the resultant plant, which Paul calls "a body" to maintain the analogy. The analogy works in part because corpses, like seeds, are buried in the ground. Paul draws attention also to the variety of grains, to the individuality of each seed within its family, and to the reflection of God's will in this variety and individuality. (Against a denial of resurrection, the will of God for resurrection *will* be done.) The variety will serve a forthcoming stress on differences between the human body that dies and its replacement in resurrection. The individuality will serve a forthcoming distinction between those who are still living on the day of resurrection and those who've died.

15:39–41: Not all flesh [is] the same flesh; rather, [there's] one [flesh] of human beings, and another flesh of animals, and another flesh of birds, and another of fish. ⁴⁰And [there are] heavenly bodies and earthly bodies. The glory of the heavenly [bodies is] one sort [of glory], however; and the [glory] of the earthly [bodies is] different. ⁴¹[There's] one glory of the sun, and another glory of the moon, and another glory of the stars. For star differs from star in glory. Here the stress on variety continues, only with a switch to different kinds of flesh as a closer analogy than grains to the upcoming stress on differences between the mortal body and the resurrected body. In other words, Paul switches for the moment from emphasizing *renewed* life to emphasizing *different* life. The bodies of earthly creatures—human beings, animals, birds, and fish—are made up of different sorts of flesh. Likewise heavenly bodies—the sun, moon, and stars—have glories differing from each other. The earthly kinds of flesh and the

heavenly kinds of bodies are listed in descending orders of glory, the glory of earthly bodies having to do with beauty, the glory of heavenly bodies having to do with brightness. The fact that many ancient people thought of the sun, moon, and stars as personal beings with shining bodies helped Paul's analogy at this point. And just as in 15:35–38 Paul supplemented a stress on variety with a stress on individuality for a forthcoming distinction between those who are still living on the day of resurrection and those who've died, so too here—and for the same purpose—he notes differences in glory from star to star, though all the stars fall into the same category over against the sun and the moon.

15:42–44: So too [is] the resurrection of the dead. [The body] is sown in perishability; it's raised in imperishability. ⁴³It's sown in dishonor; it's raised in glory. It's sown in weakness; it's raised in power. ⁴⁴It's sown a soulish body; it's raised a Spiritual body. Here Paul returns to the analogy of sown seed but also retains his more recent emphasis on difference in terms of glory. As before, "is sown" represents death and burial, "perishability" the dissolution of the body's flesh, "dishonor" the shame of being reduced to a bare skeleton, "weakness" inability to stand up from a supine posture in the grave, and "soulish" the body's heretofore animation merely by a soul. As to being "raised" in "the resurrection of the dead," "imperishability" represents the resurrected body's immortality, "glory" the honor of the skeleton's reclothing with flesh (compare Luke 24:39), "power" the ability to stand up from a supine posture in the grave, and "Spiritual" to the Spirit's reanimation of the body.

15:45–46: If there's a soulish body, there's also a Spiritual [body]. So too it's written, "The first human being, Adam, became a living soul [Genesis 2:7]." The last Adam [became] a life-producing Spirit. ⁴⁶The Spiritual [body] [was]n't first, however—rather, the soulish [body]; then the Spiritual [body]. As mentioned before, "a soulish body" is one that's animated by the soul with which a person was born, and a "Spiritual [body]" is one that's reanimated by the Spirit at the resurrection (compare Romans 8:11). Note: a Spiritual body isn't one that's made of some ethereal substance called "spirit," for Paul regularly uses "Spiritual" in reference to the Spirit, as when he describes "gracious gifts" as "Spiritual" because they're distributed by the Spirit (chapters 12 and 14), and describes Christians as Spiritual because they're taught by the Spirit (2:12–14). Because the merely soulish body undergoes the degradation described in 15:42–43 and because Christ's resurrection has ensured the resurrection of those who've been incorporated into him, Paul concludes that a Spiritual body must succeed the soulish one. Then he quotes Genesis 2:7 to support the soulish body's priority (in a purely temporal sense). The mention of Adam in the quotation then leads Paul to call Christ "the last Adam"; for "Adam" means "human being," and Christ is a human being just as Adam was (15:21–22). But whereas Adam became a merely "*living* soul," Christ as the last Adam became "a life-*producing* Spirit," again because his resurrection has ensured the resurrection of those incorporated into him. By his Spirit, in other words, Christ will make alive believers in him; and his doing so by his Spirit confirms that "a Spiritual body" didn't refer to a body made of an ethereal spiritual substance—rather, to a body reanimated by the Spirit (see Romans 8:9; 2 Corinthians 3:17 for Christ's Spirit and for Christ as Spirit). "The *last* Adam" implies that as "the first human being," Adam incorporated in himself his physical descendants as a race of living souls like him, and that Christ has similarly incorporated in himself his Spiritual descendants as a new race to be eternally embodied as he is. To bring the discussion back to bodies, Paul applies the temporal order of "the *first* human being, Adam" and "the *last* Adam" to the order of the soulish body as "first," and "*then*" the Spiritual body.

15:47–49: **The first human being** [was] **from the earth, made of dust. The second human being** [was] **from heaven.** [48]**As** [the first human being was] **made of dust, such also** [are] **those** [human beings] **made of dust; and as** [was] **the heavenly** [human being], **such also** [will be] **the heavenly** [human beings]. [49]**And just as we bore the image of the** [first human being] **made of dust, we'll also bear the image of the heavenly human being** [the second one]. "From the earth" indicates the origin of Adam (Genesis 2:7). "Made of dust" alludes to his bodily constitution and to the returning of his soulish body to dust after death (Genesis 3:19 [compare "perishability" here in 15:42]). "From heaven" indicates the origin of the last Adam and implies his deity alongside his humanity. But Paul calls him "the *second* human being." Many human beings came and went between Adam and Christ. So Christ is the second human being in the sense that only he incorporated in himself a race of human beings as Adam did. "Such also [are] those [human beings] made of dust" alludes to the bodily constitution of Adam's race and to the returning of their soulish bodies to dust after death, as in Adam's case. "Such also [will be] the heavenly [human beings]" promises that just as Christ, the second human being, came from heaven in the past, so God will bring with Jesus those who've "fallen asleep in Jesus" when he descends "from heaven" (1 Thessalonians 4:13–16). (For the time being, Paul is talking about the resurrection of the dead, not about believers still living at the second coming.) "We bore the image of the [first human being] made of dust" means that believers, like all other human beings, have had bodies made of dust and therefore perishable. But in anticipation of the resurrection, Paul puts the bearing of such bodies in the past: "we *bore* . . . ." "The image of the heavenly human being" refers to the imperishable, glorified, powerful, Spiritual bodies produced by the last Adam as the life-producing Spirit—that is, to bodies like his (compare Philippians 3:20–21).

15:50: **And I'm saying this, brothers, that flesh and blood can't inherit God's kingdom; nor does perishability inherit imperishability.** "And I'm saying this," plus the address "brothers," introduces a new element into the discussion. It begins with a denial that flesh and blood can inherit God's kingdom. This denial is often misunderstood as a denial of the physicality of resurrection. But in addition to recognizing the natural meaning of "body" in connection with resurrection and the very meaning of "resurrection" as "a standing up" of bodies out of their graves, it's important to note that the phrase "flesh and blood" doesn't have to do with physicality *as such*—rather, with *perishable* physicality. The flesh and blood of a corpse decompose, perish, leaving only the bones, so that "flesh and blood" came to represent perishability itself, as Paul immediately goes on to explain: "nor does *perishability* inherit imperishability." And he has already noted the *im*perishability of believers' resurrected bodies. Just as "perishability" explains "flesh and blood," "imperishability" explains "God's kingdom."

Now Paul expands his purview on this matter to include believers still living at the second coming. **15:51–53**: **Behold, I'm telling you a secret: we'll not all fall asleep** [= die]; **but we'll all be changed** [52]**in an instant, in the blink of an eye, at the last trumpet.** "The *last* trumpet" suits Paul's designation of Christ as "the *last* Adam," and "the last *trumpet*" suits an awakening through resurrection of those who've fallen asleep in Jesus. **For the trumpet will sound, and the dead will be raised imperishable, and we'll be changed.** [53]**For it's necessary that this perishable** [body] **put on imperishability and that this mortal** [body] **put on immortality.** "Behold" marks Paul's "secret" with a joyful, triumphant exclamation. The secret consists in a new revelation for believers. It's that believers still living at the second coming will undergo a change which will make their bodies like those of resurrected believers: imperishable and immortal. "In an instant, in the blink of an eye" stresses the suddenness of change. "At the last trumpet" stresses the concurrence of this change with the resurrection of deceased believers. In 1 Thessalonians 4:13–18 Paul is concerned to show that deceased believers will be at no disadvantage. Here he's concerned that living believers will be at no disadvantage. "We" who "will be changed" refers to living believers as distinct from "the dead [believers]" (who "will be raised imperishable"), so that "this perishable [body]," also called "this mortal [body]," refers to the body of believers still living. For the bodies of believers who've "fallen asleep" aren't mortal. They're dead. As the first "For" introduces the chronology of change, the second "For" introduces the necessity of change. This necessity harks back to the impossibility that perishability inherit imperishability. "Put on" makes imperishability and immortality a kind of cloak that will protect a living believers' body from its erstwhile perishability and mortality.

15:54–57: **But when this perishable** [body] **puts on imperishability and this mortal** [body] **puts on immortality, then will come to pass the inscripturated word** [= statement], **"Death has been gulped down into Victory** [Isaiah 25:8]**."** [55]**Where, Death, is *your* victory? Where, Death, is *your* stinger** [Hosea

13:14]?" ⁵⁶**And Death's stinger** [is] **sin, and Sin's power** [is] **the Law.** ⁵⁷**But thanks** [be] **to God, who's giving us the victory through our Lord, Jesus Christ.** The joyful, triumphant exclamation signaled by "Behold" in 15:51 comes here to full throat, and to the necessity that an imperishable body inherit an imperishable kingdom is added the actuality of Scripture's coming to pass in the gulping down of Death into victory, as though personified Death were being cannabilized whole as a defeated enemy. Death's "stinger" (a weapon) is sin in the sense that sinning leads to death (Romans 5:12–14; 6:23; Genesis 2:17; 3:3–4, 19; 5:1–31). Then Paul personifies Sin by portraying it as exercising power, that is, the power to kill. He identifies Sin's power as the (Old Testament) Law in that the Law powerfully provokes and exposes sinning (as Paul explains with some detail in Romans 5:20; 7:7–24). Triumph over Death turns into thanks to God for using Jesus Christ to give believers victory over Death. "Our Lord" suits Jesus Christ as the first victor over Death.

15:58: And so, my beloved brothers, become resolute, immovable, always flourishing in the Lord's work, knowing that in the Lord your labor isn't empty [of its desired effect (compare 15:14)]. "My beloved brothers" introduces this exhortation on an affectionate note. The certainty of believers' resurrection, should they die before the second coming, and of transformation, should they live till then, ought to breed a resolve that prevents being moved away from faith and that prompts activity in the work of evangelism.

ON THE COLLECTION FOR THE CHURCH IN JERUSALEM
1 Corinthians 16:1–4

16:1–4: And concerning the collection for the saints, as I indeed gave orders to the churches of Galatia [a province in central Asia Minor (modern Turkey)], **so you do too:** ²**Every first** [day] **of the week** [that is, Sunday by Sunday] **each of you is to be individually putting** [some money in a collection], **treasuring up whatever he's being prospered with** [= saving up for each collection whatever he can afford], **in order that when I come no collections take place then.** ³**And when I've arrived, whomever you approve—I'll send these** [men] **with letters to carry your charity off to Jerusalem.** ⁴**And if it's worthwhile for me as well to be traveling** [to Jerusalem], **they'll travel with me.** "And concerning" introduces another topic broached in the Corinthians' letter to Paul (see the introduction to 1 Corinthians and compare earlier occurrences of the phrase in 7:1, 25; 8:1[4]; 12:1) and therefore implies they already know about "the collection for the saints" but await orders on how to go about collecting it. For "the churches of Galatia," see Acts 13–14. Paul's telling the Corinthian church to do what he ordered the Galatian churches to do has the purpose of keeping the Corinthians from thinking he's discriminating against them with his instructions (compare 11:16; 14:33). "As I indeed

gave orders" underlines his nondiscrimination. "*Every* first [day] of the week" orders regularity in the putting of some money in a weekly collection. "Every *first* [day] of the week" alludes to Christians' meeting together on that day as the day of the week on which Christ was raised from among the dead (compare Acts 20:7). These meetings make possible the taking of collections. "*Each* of you . . . individually" places a financial responsibility on every church member, so that the charity will be corporate, not a benefaction on the part of a few wealthy Christians motivated by a desire to be praised for their generosity. But each one's saving up whatever he can afford makes the giving proportional to his financial prosperity (compare Deuteronomy 15:14; 16:10, 17). Thus Paul wants the collection ready to go as soon as he arrives again in Corinth.

The Corinthians may approve whomever they wish to carry the collection, so that Paul needn't be exposed to a charge of embezzlement or of choosing from among them lackeys for embezzlement. Letters of recommendation will accompany the carriers, apparently one such letter for each carrier. As the sender, Paul will write the letters, presumably. He calls the collection "your charity" in that the Greek word behind "charity" is the same as the word often translated "grace." As God has shown "grace" to the Corinthian "saints" (1:1–3), they're going to show "grace" to fellow "saints." "To Jerusalem" tells the locale of those fellow saints. Its long distance from Corinth will prevent them from lauding the Corinthians in the Corinthians' own city. Yet in pagan society, getting lauded in one's own city provided the motive for exercising generosity. No wonder, then, that for this collection Paul uses the word "charity/grace"—a *free* gift, one that won't be remunerated locally with praise from its recipients. After saying he'll send the carriers, he poses the possibility of traveling to Jerusalem himself—and if so, of their traveling with him. "If it's worthwhile" suggests that he might ask the Corinthians whether they and other contributors trust him to take along the carriers of the money. For more on the collection, see Romans 15:25–32; 2 Corinthians 8–9.

THE TRAVEL PLANS OF PAUL, TIMOTHY, AND APOLLOS
1 Corinthians 16:5–12

16:5–9: But I'll come to you when I've gone through Macedonia [northern Greece], **for I'm going through Macedonia** [not in the sense that he's doing so at the moment, but in the sense that he's planning to in the future]; ⁶**and perhaps I'll stay with you, or even spend the winter** [with you], **in order that you may send me forward wherever I may go.** ⁷**For I don't want to see you in passing just now, for I'm hoping to stay with you for some time, if the Lord permits.** ⁸**But I'll be staying in Ephesus till Pentecost.** ⁹**For a big and serviceable door stands open to me, and many** [are] **set against** [me]. So Paul is writing from Ephesus in western Asia Minor, will travel north and west to Macedonia, and then make his way south and west to Corinth (Acts 19:1, 21; 20:1–2). "Perhaps," "wherever," "I'm hoping," and "if the Lord permits" show the uncertainty of Paul as to his future travel beyond going to Corinth via Macedonia after "staying in Ephesus till Pentecost." He expects the Corinthians to know that Pentecost, a Jewish pilgrim festival, occurs in late May or early June, when travel by sea becomes feasible after a winter's lull. Staying in Corinth "for some time" may force him also to "spend the winter" there; for winter storms and overcast skies, making navigation difficult, pretty much halt travel by sea (compare Acts 27; 2 Timothy 4:21; Titus 3:12). (Winter included our late autumn.) Paul doesn't say why he hopes "not . . . to see [the Corinthians] in passing just now" but "to stay with [them] for some time." So the Corinthians are to gather (1) that he expects them to send him forward with provisions to do further evangelism; (2) that they shouldn't take his censures of them in this letter as indicating he doesn't want to have anything further to do with them; (3) that the Lord's permission overrides Paul's wishes and hopes; (4) that the opening of "a big and serviceable door" (representing a largescale evangelistic opportunity [see 2 Corinthians 2:12; Colossians 4:3]) indicates that the Lord wants him to stay in Ephesus till Pentecost; and (5), perhaps surprisingly, that the opposition of many indicates likewise a largescale evangelistic opportunity and therefore the Lord's will that he stay to take advantage of it. "Big" points to the possibility of numerous conversions, and "serviceable" points to a good chance of success.

16:10–11: And if Timothy comes, be observing that he's with you fearlessly. For he's working the Lord's work, as I [am] too. [11]Therefore no one should treat him as a nobody. But send him forward in peace in order that he may come to me. For I'm waiting for him along with the brothers. See 4:17 for Paul's having sent his protegé Timothy to Corinth. "And if Timothy comes" doesn't express doubt that he'll come; it refers to his coming as what will enable the Corinthians to "be observing that he's with [them] fearlessly." In 4:17–21, the very passage in which Paul mentioned that he'd sent Timothy to Corinth, Paul spoke fearlessly against arrogant members of the Corinthian church. Here he tells the Corinthians that they're to observe Timothy's similar fearlessness when he's with them, a fearlessness that's grounded in his "working the Lord's work" as Paul is. Doing the *Lord's* work breeds fearlessness, because he's in charge. On observing Timothy's fearlessness as a result of doing the Lord's work, the Corinthians shouldn't "treat him as a nobody"—not because he's Paul's emissary; rather, because he's the Lord's emissary. Then they should send Timothy forward with provisions just as Paul expects them to send him forward with provisions at a later date (16:6). The added phrase, "in peace," prescribes a sendoff with best wishes for a safe and prosperous journey to rejoin Paul. We don't know the identity of "the brothers" whom Paul expects to accompany Timothy, but their mention reflects the practice of teamwork in early Christian evangelism.

16:12: And concerning Apollos, the brother, I urged him much to come to you with the brothers; and there wasn't at all a will that he come now. But he'll come when he has an opportune time. "And concerning Apollos" indicates that the Corinthians' letter to Paul contained an enquiry concerning Apollos's travel plans (compare the comments on 16:1). Paul's calling Apollos "the brother" and having "urged him much" to visit the Corinthians show that he considers Apollos a fellow evangelist, not a rival, despite the Corinthians' splitting over them (1:10–12; 3:1–9). Again Paul doesn't identify "the brothers" who might have accompanied Apollos, but their mention reflects yet again the practice of teamwork in early Christian evangelism. Whose will is lacking for Apollos to go now to Corinth? God's? Apollos's? Certainly not Paul's, because he "urged [Apollos] much" to go. Since Paul wouldn't have done so if God had made apparent *his* lack of will, Apollos's lack of will must be in view. "But he'll come when he has an opportune time" may therefore imply that an opportunity for evangelism where he is now makes *in*opportune an immediate trip to Corinth by him.

CONCLUDING EXHORTATIONS AND REMARKS
1 Corinthians 16:13–24

16:13–14: Stay awake; stay standing in the faith. Be acting like grownups; be getting strong. [14]All your [actions] **are to take place in love** [that is, do everything with love toward God, one another, and others]. Paul uses wakefulness as a figure of speech for constant vigilance. His pairing it with standing in the faith indicates vigilance against the loss of faith. "*The* faith" may sound like a reference to *what* is believed. But in 15:1–2 Paul spoke of "stand[ing]" in the gospel, "through which also you're being saved . . . *unless you believed casually*." So "the faith" refers to believing, not to what is believed; and to stand in the believing means not to retreat from believing the gospel, lest you lose out on salvation (compare 10:12; 2 Corinthians 1:24; Romans 5:1–2; 11:20; Ephesians 6:10–16). "Be acting like grownups" commands the Corinthians to give up their childish, indeed babylike, behavior (see 3:1–3; 13:10–11; 14:20). "Be getting strong" is paired with acting like grownups because childish, babylike behavior betrays weakness whereas grownups display strength (compare Luke 1:80; 2:40). Weakness and strength of character are in view. The command to act in love recalls 2:9; 8:1, 3; and especially 13:1–14:1a, but stresses here for the first time that love is to permeate "*all* your [actions]."

16:15–16: And I'm exhorting you, brothers— you know the household of Stephanas, that it's the firstfruits of Achaia [= the first converts in southern Greece] **and** [that] **they put themselves to service for the saints—**[16][I'm exhorting you] **that you also be putting yourselves in subjection to such** [people] **and to everyone who's working and toiling with** [them]. "Brothers" introduces a new exhortation with emphasis, and appropriately in view of the immediate reference to "the *household* of Stephanas." Back in 1:16 Paul mentioned having baptized Stephanas' household as well as two other Corinthians, and in 16:17–18 he's going to mention the coming to him of Stephanas along with two others. The description of Stephanas' household as "the firstfruits of Achaia" causes a bit of a problem, because Acts 17:34 mentions an earlier conversion of some Athenians, whose city also lay in Achaia. But "the firstfruits" needn't mean more than the first Achaian converts, collectively speaking, whatever city they lived in. Paul appeals first to the Corinthians' knowledge of Stephanas' household as firstfruits and as having "put themselves to service for the saints." They will have known whether the service consisted in providing a home for meetings, giving financial help to poverty-stricken believers, or distributing food during a famine. Other services are also possible. In any case, this part of 1 Corinthians commends Stephanas' household for their service, and especially Stephanas himself as their head, and goes on to exhort subjection to them. "To *such* [people]" showcases their service, and "to everyone who's working and toiling with [them]" broadens the exhortation to include subjection to the associates of Stephanas' household in the performance of self-sacrificial service. "That you *also* be putting yourselves in subjection" implies that by serving the saints, Stephanas' household have subjected *themselves* to the saints. So reciprocal subjection through service to one another is what Paul exhorts. How antithetic to the Corinthians' self-puffery, against which he has repeatedly inveighed (4:6, 18–19; 5:2; 8:1; 13:4)!

16:17–18: And I'm rejoicing over the coming of Stephanas and Fortunatus and Achaicus, because these [men] **have filled up the lack of you** [that is, have made up for my lack of your company]. [18]**For they've refreshed my spirit and yours. So be giving such** [men] **recognition.** There's joy in Christian fellowship, and Paul's saying he's "rejoicing over the coming of Stephanas and Fortunatus and Achaicus" (who may have brought the Corinthians' letter to Paul) shows again that his censures don't indicate a desire not to have anything further to do with them. Much to the contrary, the three men's making up for Paul's lack of the rest of the Corinthians' company implies that he'd like to have the company of *all* the Corinthian believers. For his censures of them have grown out of love for them (4:14; 10:14; 15:58; 16:24). Refreshment of spirit has to do with emotional refreshment (compare the use of "spirit" for emotion in 14:2, 14–16). Just as the coming of Stephanas, Fortunatus, and Achaicus has refreshed Paul's spirit, their return to Corinth will have refreshed

their fellow Corinthians' collective spirit when this letter (which they may be carrying with them) has arrived in Corinth. So the three men's service of refreshment calls for churchwide recognition.

16:19–20: The churches of Asia greet you. "Asia" refers to the Roman province in western Asia Minor where Ephesus is located. **Aquila and Prisca** [the name whose diminutive form is "Priscilla"] **along with the church** [that meets] **in their house greet you much in the Lord.** [20]**All the brothers greet you. Greet one another with a sacred kiss.** Greetings from the Asian churches imply that churches in widely separated localities considered themselves a network of friends because of their shared faith. Aquila and Prisca once lived in Corinth but have since moved to Ephesus, where Paul is writing this letter (Acts 18:1–3, 18–21). Because Aquila and Prisca knew the Corinthians in person, "much in the Lord" attaches to their greeting. Yet again Paul doesn't identify "all the brothers." See the comments on 1 Thessalonians 5:26 for greeting "with a sacred kiss."

16:21–24: The greeting in my (Paul's) hand[writing]. [22]**If anyone doesn't love the Lord, he's to be anathema** [= accursed]. **Marana tha.** [23]**The grace of our Lord, Jesus,** [be] **with you.** [24]**My love** [be] **with all of you in Christ Jesus.** The greeting of Paul in his own handwriting guarantees the authenticity of this letter and implies that he dictated the rest of it, as was usual (compare Romans 16:22; Galatians 6:11; Colossians 4:18; 2 Thessalonians 3:17; Philemon 19). Also as usual, "the Lord" refers to "Jesus." The Greek noun for a "kiss" in 16:20 (*philēmati*) leads Paul to speak of "anyone" who "doesn't love [*philei*] the Lord" and then to pronounce a curse on such a person (contrast an unbeliever's pronouncing *Jesus* accursed in 12:3). "He's to be anathema" isn't a prediction. It's an indirect command that the Lord himself anathematize nonlovers of him. Indirectness softens the command into something like a prayer request. And this softening leads to an outright prayer request in "Marana tha," which means "Our Lord, come"—a prayer for the second coming (compare Revelation 22:20). The retention of this prayer in its original Aramaic (as opposed to Greek) points to an early recognition of Jesus' lordship (compare the retention of "Abba," Aramaic for addressing God as "Father" in Mark 14:36; Romans 8:15; Galatians 4:6). But the Lord's "grace"—that is, favor rather than anathema—is to be enjoyed by the Corinthians as those who love the Lord. And Paul extends his own love to all the Corinthian believers, even those he has censured; for "in Christ Jesus" love reigns supreme.

SECOND CORINTHIANS

A good understanding of 2 Corinthians requires the collating of some background information. After writing 1 Corinthians from Ephesus, Paul found it necessary to make a sorrowful visit to Corinth and back, sorrowful because of the strained relations between him and the Corinthian church at the time. Though Luke doesn't record this visit in Acts, it's to be inferred from 2 Corinthians 12:14; 13:1–2, where Paul describes his *coming* visit as the "third." Moreover, Paul's statement in 2:1, "For I decided . . . not to come to you *again* in sorrow," implies a past sorrowful visit that can hardly be identified with his first and very successful visit to proclaim the glad tidings of salvation through Jesus Christ; and apart from the inferred sorrowful visit in the past, Paul's coming visit would be only his second, not his third. The past sorrowful visit failed to ease relations with the church. So on his return to Ephesus he wrote a tearful letter to the Corinthians, which at first he regretted having sent (2:4; 7:8). This letter can hardly be identified with 1 Corinthians, for 1 Corinthians exudes censure but not tears. The tearful letter, coming between 1 and 2 Corinthians, hasn't survived, just as Paul's letter referred to in 1 Corinthians 5:9–11 and therefore written and sent earlier than 1 Corinthians hasn't survived. Apparently the now-lost tearful letter commanded the Corinthian church to discipline an obstreperous individual who was leading opposition to Paul (2:5–11). According to 2:12–13; 7:4–16 Titus was returning from Corinth, probably after carrying that letter to Corinth. Meanwhile, knowing Titus would return via Macedonia and Troas (on the northwest corner of Asia Minor) and being anxious to hear from Titus the Corinthians' reaction, Paul left Ephesus and waited in Troas. When Titus failed to arrive quickly, Paul proceeded to Macedonia, where Titus finally met him and reported the good news that most in the Corinthian church had repented of their rebellion against Paul and had followed his instruction to discipline the leader of opposition to him. So apart from introductory and concluding matter, Paul wrote 2 Corinthians from Macedonia on his third missionary journey (1) to express relief and joy at the favorable response of the majority of Corinthian Christians (chapters 1–7); (2) to stress the collection he wants to gather from them for the Christians in Jerusalem (chapters 8–9 [compare 1 Corinthians 16:1–4]); and (3) to defend his apostolic authority to a still-rebellious minority (chapters 10–13).

ADDRESS AND GREETING
2 Corinthians 1:1–2

1:1–2: **Paul, an apostle of Christ Jesus through God's will, and Timothy, the brother** [= the fellow Christian], **to God's church that's in Corinth along with all the saints that are in the whole of Achaia:** **²Grace and peace to you from God, our Father, and the Lord, Jesus Christ.** For Paul's self-designation see the comments on 1 Corinthians 1:1. Here he adds his helper Timothy, whom he'd sent to Corinth at the writing of 1 Corinthians (see 4:17; 16:10–11 of that letter) but who has since returned to Paul. The inclusion of Timothy lends support to what Paul will write, and Paul's calling him "the brother" appeals to the Corinthians' having recently had Timothy in their midst. But "*God's church*" makes plain that the Corinthians belong to God, not to Paul or Timothy, and that therefore God cares for them. Compared to being God's, the location of the church "in Corinth" is incidental. "Along with all the saints that are in the whole of Achaia" indicates that this letter is to be made available to all the Christians living throughout southern Greece. Though Paul will address topics specific to the church in Corinth, others too need to learn from what he has to say. For "grace and peace from God, our Father, and the Lord, Jesus Christ," see the comments on 1 Peter 1:2; 2 John 3; and 1 Corinthians 1:3.

A THANKSGIVING FOR GOD'S ENCOURAGEMENT AND PROTECTION
2 Corinthians 1:3–11

1:3–5: **Praised** [be] **the God and Father of our Lord, Jesus Christ, the Father characterized by mercies** [= acts of mercy], **even the God characterized by all encouragement, ⁴who is encouraging us on the occasion of our every affliction so that we can be encouraging those in every affliction** [of their own] **through the encouragement with which we ourselves are being encouraged by God, ⁵because just as the Christ's sufferings are flourishing in us, in this way also the encouragement of us is flourishing.** God as the Father of believers (1:2) now shifts to God as the God and Father of Jesus Christ, and "our" shifts from "Father" (1:2) to Jesus Christ as "our Lord." Since Jesus Christ is Lord, God as the Father of him differs from God as the Father of believers. For Jesus Christ's lordship puts him on the level of deity alongside his Father, whereas God as the

Father of believers does nothing of the kind. "Our Lord" designates Jesus Christ the owner and master of believers and therefore the one to whom they owe obedience and worship. God is his God in that he represents God. So the accent falls here on praise to God for his acts of mercy, which bring encouragement. The "we/us/our" who are getting encouragement from him include Timothy (1:1) and perhaps others of Paul's company along with Paul, but not the Corinthians, as the contrast with "you/your" in following verses makes clear.

"*All* encouragement" is defined by "encouraging us on the occasion of our *every* affliction," and "affliction" goes back to a Greek word that means—when not used figuratively, as it is here—"pressure" (compare the English word "op*pression*"). The pressure of persecution is particularly in view (compare 1 Corinthians 16:9). No occasion of affliction for the gospel goes unaccompanied by God's encouragement. So Paul can't help but praise him. But God's encouragement of Paul has a larger purpose than Paul's benefit. It's that he may be able to encourage similarly afflicted Christians by citing to them God's ongoing encouragement of him. And the reason Paul can do so is that the flourishing of Christ's sufferings in him is matched by the flourishing of God's encouragement of him ("just as . . . in this way also"). Despite the *flourishing* of those sufferings (they come in extraordinary profusion), there's no shortfall of encouragement. Paul names his own afflictions "the *Christ's* sufferings," because when Paul is being afflicted as a Christian, so close is the union between him and Christ that the Christ, who by the Spirit indwells him and whom by the Spirit he indwells, is suffering (compare Acts 9:4–5; 22:7–8; 26:14–15). That is to say, just as Christ suffered individually *for* Paul (and others, of course) to make salvation *possible*, so he now suffers unitedly *in* Paul (and other evangelists) to make salvation *available*. For without its proclamation and consequent affliction by way of persecution, salvation doesn't eventuate through hearing with faith (compare Romans 10:13–15; Philippians 3:8–10; Colossians 1:24–29). "*The* Christ" connotes the corporate Christ: him and those united to him by faith.

1:6–7: And whether we're being afflicted, [it's] **for your encouragement and salvation. And whether we're being encouraged,** [it's] **for your encouragement, which is effective in the endurance of the same sufferings that we too are suffering.** [^7] **And our hope for you** [is] **firm, knowing** [as we do] **that as you're sharers** [with us] **of the sufferings, so too** [you're sharers with us] **of the encouragement.** Here the Corinthians' sufferings come to the fore, and the afflictions of Paul as well as the encouragement of him are said to have the purpose and effect of encouraging the Corinthians in their own sufferings for Christ. But how are Paul's *afflictions* supposed to encourage them? It would be easy to understand that the apostolic ministry *for* which he is suffering afflictions brings encouragement to the Corinthians. But the afflictions themselves as a source of encouragement? In what sense? In the sense that they

show the Christ to be suffering in Paul's afflictions (1:5); and if Christ is suffering in *Paul's* afflictions, the Corinthians can be sure that the Christ is suffering also in *their* sufferings. The knowledge of his presence brings encouragement. To the encouragement of the Corinthians Paul adds their salvation, because their sufferings could lead them to apostatize, to lose faith. So this encouragement has the purpose of ensuring endurance—that is, perseverance as opposed to apostasy—for the attainment of final salvation. Paul describes the encouragement as "effective" in this respect. "The *same* sufferings that we *too* are suffering" identifies the Corinthians' sufferings as afflictions for the gospel's sake, not as the troubles into which all human beings are born ("as sparks fly upward" [Job 5:7]). The firmness of Paul's hope for the Corinthians' endurance right on to ultimate salvation rests on his knowing that they share his encouragement as well as his sufferings.

1:8–11: For we don't want you to be ignorant, brothers, regarding our affliction that took place in Asia [a Roman province in western Asia Minor], **in that we were burdened excessively,** [that is,] **above** [our] **ability** [to bear the affliction], **so that we despaired even of living.** [^9] **Instead** [of expecting to live] **we ourselves had within ourselves the death sentence, so that we didn't trust in ourselves—rather,** [we trusted] **in God, who raises the dead,** [^10] **who out of extremely perilous deaths has rescued us and will rescue** [us likewise in the future], **in whom we've set our hope that he'll rescue us even yet,** [^11] **as you also join in helping by means of praying in our behalf, so that the gracious gift to us** [of our rescue] **through many** [who pray] **in our behalf may be the object of thanksgiving by many faces** [= many persons in the sense of players in a drama, since such players wore face-masks]. In 1:7 Paul spoke of knowing about the *Corinthians'* sufferings and encouragement. Now he says he doesn't want them not to know about *his own* affliction and encouragement. The address "brothers" softens with affection his not wanting them "to be ignorant." So this paragraph explains what they need to know to make fully reciprocal their and his sharing of sufferings and encouragement. Apart from locating Paul's affliction "in Asia," the explanation deals with its intensity rather than its composition—hence, "burdened excessively, [that is,] above [our] ability [to bear the affliction], so that we despaired even of living [and so forth]." This stress on the intensity of affliction will undergird Paul's defending himself later in chapter 1 against the charge that he didn't mean what he said in regard to his travel plans.

"We ourselves had within ourselves the death sentence" means that Paul was resigned to, and expectant of, martyrdom. This resignation and expectation resulted rightly in lack of self-trust and in trusting God instead. Against the background of Paul's discussion of resurrection in 1 Corinthians 15, he describes God as the one "who raises the dead" in that God has already raised Christ and will yet raise those who've "fallen asleep" in Christ. This description supplies the platform for saying that God "rescued us out of extremely perilous deaths [such as the one we were facing in Asia] and will rescue [us likewise in the future]," so that these preliminary rescues from death by martyrdom anticipate the final rescue from death at the resurrection of believers, including those who like Paul died by martyrdom after close scrapes with it. "In whom we've set our hope that he'll rescue us even yet" re-expresses confidence of further rescues from martyrdom so as to introduce the picture of the Corinthians' helping bring about through prayer the occurrence of such rescuing. "Through *many* [who pray]" suggests that Christians other than the Corinthians will join them in praying for the further rescuing of Paul. He describes this rescuing as "the gracious gift" for which many people will thank God. (Note: a Greek wordplay exists between "gracious gift" [*charisma*] and the "thanksgiving" for it [*eucharistēthē*].) So thanksgiving to the God who answers prayer takes precedence over Paul's rescue in answer to prayer. To God be the glory!

PAUL'S RELIEF AND JOY AT THE FAVORABLE RESPONSE OF THE MAJORITY OF CHRISTIANS IN CORINTH
2 Corinthians 1:12–7:16

AN EXPLANATION OF PAUL'S FAILURE TO VISIT CORINTH AGAIN
2 Corinthians 1:12–2:4

1:12–14: **For our boasting is this, the testimony of our consciousness that with God's candor and sincerity—and not with fleshly wisdom; rather, with God's grace—we've behaved in the world, but extraordinarily** [so] **toward you.** [13]**For we're not writing to you things other than the things you either read or also understand. And I'm hoping that you'll understand completely—**[14]**just as you've partly understood us— that we are your basis for boasting just as indeed you too** [will be] **ours on the Day of the Lord, Jesus.** The first "For" introduces Paul's behavior as a reason he expects that many will help him by praying for him (1:11). The second "For" introduces a particular explanation of his behavior in regard to his letters. See the footnote to 1 Corinthians 9:15–16 for good as well as bad boasting, and the comments on 1 Corinthians 8:7 for the translation "consciousness" rather than "conscience." Paul is legitimately proud of having behaved with "candor and sincerity" in society at large ("in the world"), but "extraordinarily" so toward the Corinthians. Several additions keep this "boasting" from degenerating into self-puffery: (1) Paul's tracing his boasting to the testimony of his consciousness, as though his consciousness were a third party testifying to him and now through him to the Corinthians; (2) his attributing the candor and sincerity to God ("God's candor and sincerity" being no more godly or godlike, despite many English translations to the contrary, than "God's grace" is only godly or godlike); (3) the ruling out of "fleshly wisdom," which in this

context means the humanly rhetorical trick of feigning candor and sincerity; and (4) the equation of "God's candor and sincerity" with "God's grace," so that the candor and sincerity came to Paul as a free gift from God, not something Paul can take credit for. Because of discord with the Corinthians, he has taken care to behave toward them with *extraordinary* candor and sincerity.

Next comes an explanation to the effect that Paul means exactly what they read in his letters, as follows from candor and sincerity. ("You . . . read" has a collective sense, because one person would be reading to the assembled others.) "Or also understand" makes their understanding of what they read an alternative to their reading, as though they might not be understanding everything they read in his letters to them. Highlighting this possibility are (1) a Greek wordplay between *anaginōskete* ("you read") and *epiginōskete* ("you understand") and (2) the contrast between Paul's hoping that the Corinthians will "understand *completely*" and their having "understood *partly*." What he hopes they'll understand completely is that they already have Paul to be proud of for his having evangelized them ("your basis for boasting"), just as "on the Day of the Lord, Jesus" (when he comes back as Lord for the Last Judgment) Paul will have them to be proud of as his converts. "Indeed" accents his having them as a basis for boasting and thus continues his fence-mending with the Corinthians.

1:15–17: **And in this confidence I planned earlier to come to you in order that you might have a second grace** [= the favor of a second visit by me], [16]**that is, to go through you** [= through your midst] **into Macedonia and to come again from Macedonia to you and be sent forward** [with provisions (compare 1 Corinthians 16:6, 11)] **by you into Judea.** [17]**So then, when planning this** [itinerary] **I wasn't acting with levity** [= being lighthearted]**, was I? Or do I plan in accordance with the flesh the things that I plan, so that with me there's "Yes, yes" and "No, no"?** "This confidence" refers to Paul's hope that the Corinthians will completely understand that they can take pride in him. His earlier plan to visit them—once on his way to Macedonia and again on his way back—grew out of such confidence. "When planning this [itinerary] I wasn't acting with levity, was I?" implies both that he'd changed his plan and that at least some Corinthians had criticized him for doing so. This implication comes out forcefully in the following, open-ended question whether he plans "in accordance with the flesh." The rotting away of flesh after death led to the use of "flesh" as a figure of speech for weakness. So fleshly planning means weak planning, which means planning without sufficient gravity to carry out the plan. As a result, the planner's yes can really mean a repeated no even when he repeats the yes, and vice versa (compare Matthew 5:37; James 5:12). You can't count on what he says. Do Paul's plans display such a lack of gravity?

1:18–19: **But God** [is] **faithful in that our word to you isn't "Yes-and-no."** [19]**For God's Son, Jesus Christ, who was proclaimed among you through us—through**

me and Silvanus and Timothy—didn't turn out to be "Yes-and-no." In him, rather, there has come into being a "Yes!" Instead of taking credit to himself for not speaking out of both sides of his mouth, Paul gives the credit to God, so that it's the faithfulness of God, his trustworthiness, that's to be seen in the straightforwardness of Paul's communications. Then Paul explains God's faithfulness in terms of the proclamation of Jesus Christ, whom Paul calls "God's Son" to associate him as closely as possible with the faithful God. In conformity to the law requiring two or three witnesses (13:1; Numbers 35:30; Deuteronomy 17:6; 19:15), "through us" makes Paul, Silvanus, and Timothy testifiers to God's faithfulness as proclaimed in the good news concerning his Son, so that again the credit goes to God (see the comments on 1 Thessalonians 1:1 for Silvanus and Timothy). The proclamation doesn't take back a divine "yes" with a divine "no": the good news hasn't turned into bad news, nor will it. For God is faithful. His word is trustworthy. This fact is to be seen in Jesus Christ, the subject of proclamation. And from the beginning, Paul's communications to the Corinthians have reflected the very same reliability, the very same absence of equivocation.

1:20: For however many [are] God's promises, in him [Jesus Christ] [they are] [God's] "Yes!" Therefore also, through him [Jesus Christ] [is] the "Amen!" to God for [his] glory through us. In other words, God's promises, proclaimed as they are in the gospel, haven't outstripped their affirmation in Jesus Christ; for he fulfills them all, regardless of their number. His fulfillment of them puts God's "Yes!" after each one. "Therefore" introduces a consequence, and "also" adds to God's "Yes!" the "Amen!" of Paul and company. "Through him" makes Jesus Christ the agent whose fulfillment of God's promises makes possible the "Amen!" "Through us" makes Paul and company the agents of God's glorification in saying to him, "Amen!" And in accordance with 1:19, this "Amen!" consists in their proclamation of God's Son, Jesus Christ, as God's "Yes!" in the fulfillment of all God's promises. Note the parallel between the "through us" of proclamation in 1:19 and the "through us" of saying "Amen!" in 1:20.

1:21–22: And the one who's confirming us along with you for Christ and [who] anointed us [is] God, [22]who has also sealed us and given [us] in our hearts the downpayment [consisting] in the Spirit. "Along with you" shows that "us" refers to Paul and company. Though God is confirming the Corinthian believers, and has also anointed them, sealed them, and given them the downpayment that consists in God's Spirit, Paul is still defending himself against the charge that he speaks lightheartedly out of both sides of his mouth. So "along with you" simply means that his claiming for himself God's confirmation, anointing, sealing, and downpayment doesn't exclude the Corinthians from the same. They should recognize that he has from God what they have from God. "Who's confirming us . . . for Christ" means that God is continuously maintaining Paul and

company in their relationship to Christ. "Anointed us" points to God's co-opting them for evangelism, and "sealed us" points to his putting in them the stamp of his ownership. This stamp consists in the gift of the Spirit as "the downpayment" that guarantees their final salvation. Since the Spirit indwells them, Paul writes "*in* our hearts" rather than "*on* us." In his Greek text there's a wordplay between *christon* ("Christ/Anointed One") and *chrisas* ("anointed [us]").

1:23–24: And I call on God as a witness against my life that by way of sparing you I've not yet come to Corinth [as originally planned (1:15–16)]. **[24]Not that I'm wielding lordship over you in respect to [your] faith; rather, we're coworkers of your joy** [= we're working together to produce joy in you]. **For as to [your] faith** [as distinct from joy] **you've taken a stand.** Paul decided against going yet to Corinth, not because his plan to do so lacked sincere resolve, but because he wanted to spare the Corinthians the apostolic thrashing that his coming would have entailed. To stress that he acted out of this consideration for them, he calls God to witness against his life, as though he were being tried on a capital charge, if he's not telling the truth. So far as Paul is concerned, the Corinthians' faith isn't at issue; for in that respect "they've taken a stand" and thus are standing firm (compare 1 Corinthians 15:1). So he isn't "wielding lordship" over them in respect to their faith. He doesn't need to. He's concerned instead about their joy—that is, the joy they should have in a happy relation with him—and he has acted out of that concern. Indeed, by canceling his plan to visit them earlier, by writing to them, and by sending them his traveling companions he and those companions have been working together to restore the Corinthians' joy in Paul, who first brought them the gospel.

2:1–4: For I decided this for myself: not to come to you again in sorrow. [2]For if I'm making you [plural] sorrowful, who too [in addition to me] [is] the one cheering me up except the one who's being made sorrowful by me? [3]And I wrote this very thing lest on coming [to you] I'd have sorrow from those [over whom] it was incumbent on me to rejoice, confident as I was and continue to be over all of you that my joy is [the joy] of all of you. [4]For out of much affliction and distress of heart I wrote you through many tears, not that you should be made sorrowful—rather, that you should know the love that I have for you in extraordinary measure. The first "For" introduces an explanation of Paul's delaying a visit so as to spare the Corinthians (1:23). The second "For" introduces the reason he didn't "come . . . again in sorrow." "I decided this for myself" distinguishes Paul from his coworkers, most especially from Titus, whom he'd sent to Corinth instead of going himself (2:12–13 [see the introduction to 2 Corinthians]). "In sorrow" contrasts with the Corinthians' joy, for which Paul and company are working in cooperation with each other (1:24). His tearful letter made them sorrowful, however; and his having written it "through many tears" stresses his own sorrow in writing it as a counterbalance to their sorrow in receiving and hearing it read to them. "I'm making you sorrowful" dramatizes the Corinthians' sorrow, as though it were taking place in the present. Yet it took place right after Paul "wrote this very thing [his tearful letter]"; and "this very thing" indicates that in his now-lost tearful letter Paul had said his sorrow could be turned to cheer only by "the one" whom he (Paul) was making sorrowful by means of his tearful letter. So apparently that letter commanded the Corinthians to discipline someone whose opposition to Paul caused Paul sorrow, and the discipline of whom at Paul's command caused that opponent sorrow in turn—and caused the rest of the Corinthians sorrow too. (Church discipline is sorrowful to all concerned, and should be.) The tearful and therefore sorrowful letter substituted for a sorrowful visit ("lest on coming [to you] I have sorrow"). Paul preferred letter-writing sorrow over face-to-face sorrow.

"From those over whom it was incumbent on me to rejoice" raises the desirability of rejoicing over converts to the level of a necessity, so that Paul has taken, and is taking, all possible measures to meet this necessity. Confidence in the Corinthians has accompanied the taking of these measures, and Paul's expression of this confidence compliments the Corinthians so as to cap what he's about to mention, namely, their disciplining of Paul's opponent. "Over all of you" leaves out none of them. "That my joy is [the joy] of all of you" reemphasizes the inclusiveness of his confidence and defines the confidence as an expectation that the Corinthians find their own joy in Paul's joy and therefore will do what cheers him up (compare Romans 12:15). A third "For" in this paragraph introduces an explanation of his having written "this very thing" to avoid a sorrowful visit. "Out of much affliction and distress of heart" identifies the source of writing instead of visiting. "Through many tears" identifies the accompanying circumstance in which the writing took place. "Not that you should be made sorrowful" denies one purpose (though not the result); and "rather, that you should know the love I have for you" affirms another purpose. "In extraordinary measure" highlights the superabundance of Paul's love for the Corinthians. "That you should *know* the love" points to experiencing it through the letter, not just to being informed about it in the letter.

AN INSTRUCTION TO FORGIVE PAUL'S DISCIPLINED, PENITENT OPPONENT
2 Corinthians 2:5–11

2:5–7: But if someone has caused sorrow, he hasn't caused me sorrow; rather, in part [= to some extent]—**lest I burden** [you with an exaggeration]—[he has caused] **all of you** [sorrow]. **⁶Sufficient for such** [a person as the one who caused sorrow] [is] **this punishment which** [was inflicted] **by the majority** [of you], **⁷so that instead, rather, you should graciously forgive and comfort** [him] **lest somehow such a** [person] **be gulped down by excessive sorrow.** In a large number of ways Paul exhibits pastoral tact: (1) He says "*if* some-

one has caused sorrow" concerning an *actual* case of sorrow-causing. (2) He uses an indefinite "someone" instead of the sorrow-causer's name. (3) He omits identifying the cause of sorrow. (4) Though later affirming his forgiveness of the sorrow-causer (2:10), he downplays his own sorrow to the point of hyperbolically denying he'd been caused any sorrow and (5) speaks instead of all the Corinthians' having been caused sorrow. (6) He also downplays the Corinthians' sorrow, however, by describing it as partial in its extent and (7) by stating his purpose not to burden them with exaggeration. (8) He declares the punishment inflicted on the sorrow-causer to be "sufficient" and (9) uses the neuter gender of the Greek word underlying "sufficient" to highlight the quality of sufficiency, whereas the Greek noun for "punishment," which "sufficient" describes, is feminine. (10) He prescribes gracious forgiveness and (11) comfort of the sorrow-causer. (12) He emphasizes this twofold prescription with both "instead" and (13) "rather." (14) He expresses concern lest the sorrow-causer "be gulped down by excessive sorrow." (We'd say "be drowned in excessive sorrow.") Presumably punishment by the majority caused the sorrow-causer to suffer his own sorrow. Thus Paul's pastoral tact obscures not only the identity of the sorrow-causer and the nature of what he did to cause sorrow, but also the nature of the punishment inflicted by the majority and what would be the long-term effect of his being "gulped down" by excessive sorrow. Overall, it comes out that church discipline is to have the purpose of restoration as well as punishment.

The next paragraph proceeds in the now-established pastoral vein. **2:8–9: Therefore** [= because of the danger of being gulped down] **I'm urging you to certify** [your] **love for him.** The Corinthians are to certify their love for the sorrow-causer by graciously forgiving and comforting him. "Certify" connotes an official declaration of such forgiveness and comfort so as to eliminate any doubt either in his mind or in others' minds concerning his restoration into the church's good graces. Since biblical love has as much to do with deeds as with emotion, the officialness of certification doesn't stand in tension with love. **⁹For I also wrote** [my tearful letter] **for this purpose: that I might know your mettle,** [that is,] **whether you're obedient in all things.** "For I *also* wrote for this purpose" means that Paul wrote his tearful letter not only to avoid a second sorrowful visit and to make known to the Corinthians his extraordinary love for them (2:1–4), but also to know for himself their mettle, which he defines in terms of their obedience. In view is their obedience to the commands that Paul, an apostolic stand-in for Jesus Christ, issued to them. "In *all* things" stresses the necessity of comprehensive obedience.

2:10–11: And whom you graciously forgive something, I also [graciously forgive him]. **For also what I've graciously forgiven, if I've graciously forgiven** [him] **something,** [I've done so] **because of you in the face** [= person] **of Christ, ¹¹lest we be exploited by Satan. For we aren't ignorant of his thoughts** [here in the sense of stratagems]. Paul supports his command that the Corinthians graciously forgive the sorrow-causer with his own gracious forgiveness of him. The indefiniteness of "something," concerning which Paul forgives him, carries forward Paul's pastoral tact. "*If* I've graciously forgiven [him]" doesn't call in question the forgiveness. Rather, it introduces the circumstance in which the forgiveness has occurred. This circumstance is threefold: (1) the need to set for the Corinthians an example of gracious forgiveness; (2) the presence ("face") of Christ, whose part Paul the apostle plays as though he were a stage-actor wearing the face-mask of Christ (compare the comments on 1:11); and (3) the danger of exploitation by Satan. The exploitation would take the form of Satan's defrauding Paul and company of their convert in the sorrow-causer. Paul's setting an example of forgiveness arises out of his and his colleagues' knowledge of Satan's stratagems. Two occurrences of "also" stress the gracious forgiveness. The past tense in "what I've graciously forgiven" and "if I've graciously forgiven [him]" indicates a forgiveness already granted on Paul's part. But the implied present tense in "I also [graciously forgive him]" makes the forgiveness sound current so as to encourage a concurrent forgiveness on the Corinthians' part ("whom you graciously forgive something").

PAUL'S RESTLESSNESS OVER TITUS'S FAILURE TO COME TO TROAS
2 Corinthians 2:12–13

2:12–13: **And when I came to Troas for the gospel of the Christ** [that is, to proclaim it] **and a door** [= an opportunity] **lay open in the Lord for me** [to do so (contrast Acts 16:6)], [13]**I had no rest for my spirit** [= I couldn't relax], **because I didn't find Titus, my brother. Instead** [of staying in Troas and taking advantage of the opportunity to proclaim the gospel there]**, on bidding goodbye to them** [the people in Troas] **I went out from** [there] **into Macedonia.** "The gospel of the Christ" refers to the good news that the messianic Savior came in the person of Jesus. "In the Lord" makes Jesus as Lord the very sphere in whom exists the opened door. So far as evangelism is concerned, then, opportune location in the Lord overshadows geographical location. Paul expected to find Titus in Troas on Titus's return trip from Corinth, but he didn't find Titus there. "My brother" expresses Paul's affection for him and indirectly illustrates the erasure in Christ of the distinction between Jews and Greeks, for Paul was a Jew and Titus a Greek (Galatians 2:3; 3:28). Paul wanted to hear from Titus how the Corinthians had responded to Paul's tearful letter. So he left Troas for Macedonia, which journey implies (as did his journey from Ephesus to Troas) a knowledge of Titus's expected route. "On bidding goodbye *to them*" implies the presence of Christians in Troas and may also imply that Paul gained converts there before cutting short an evangelization of the city. His overpowering urge to hear Titus's report proves to the Corinthians the extraordinary love Paul has for them (2:4).

THANKSGIVING
2 Corinthians 2:14–17

2:14–16a: **But thanks to God, who is always leading us in a triumphal procession in the Christ and making perceptible through us in every locality** [where we go] **the odor** [consisting] **in the knowledge of him,** [15]**because we are the fragrance of Christ for God in those who are being saved and in those who are being destroyed—**[16a]**to some, on the one hand, an odor deriving from death, resulting in death; to some, on the other hand, an odor deriving from life, resulting in life.** Paul is so thankful to God for Titus's good report concerning the Corinthians' response to the tearful letter that before mentioning Titus's report upon meeting him finally in Macedonia (7:5–7), he breaks out in a thanksgiving (2:14–17), which will evolve into an extensive elaboration concerning his and his colleagues' evangelism (3:1–7:4). The thanksgiving makes a striking contrast with Paul's having "no rest for [his] spirit" in Troas (2:13). The language of being led in a triumphal procession reflects a custom in which victorious Roman emperors and generals paraded into Rome with both their soldiers and captured enemies. So the question is whether Paul is portraying himself and his missionary companions as soldiers sharing God's victory in Christ, or as former enemies now captured by God in Christ. On the one hand, being led in a triumphal procession normally meant to be led as captives. On the other hand, being led as such put the captives to public shame (see, for example, Colossians 2:15); yet it would seem passing strange for Paul to be thanking God that he (Paul) is always being put to public shame. He gladly endures such shame for proclaiming the gospel; but that shame comes from opponents of the gospel, not from God, whereas here it would be God who is putting Paul and company to shame by leading them as captives in a triumphal procession. Since the normal meaning of leading in triumph and the connotation of shame conflict with Paul's thanksgiving, then, it's better to say that he uses this figure of speech, not for its own sake, but as a setup for what he goes right on to mention: God's "making perceptible through us in every locality the odor [consisting] in the knowledge of him." In Roman triumphal entries incense was often burned along the way and perfume spread to counteract for the celebration of a victory the stench of the big, crowded city of Rome, a stench that led well-to-do Romans to build villas at some distance from the city. So Paul's point has to do neither with captivity nor with victory, but with odor as a figure of speech for spreading the knowledge of God through proclamation of the gospel concerning Christ (see 4:6; 10:5 for knowing God through Christ).

"In *the* Christ" locates Paul and company in the corporate Christ for the pursuit of evangelism. "In every locality [where they go]," whatever its geography, they remain in him by virtue of having his Spirit. "Always" stresses the constancy of their evangelistic labor. An odor may smell either good or bad. Since the gospel concerning Christ is good news, then, Paul switches from "the odor [consisting] in the knowledge of him [God]" to "the fragrance of Christ" and says that he and his fellow evangelists *are* that fragrance in that everywhere they go, they make the good news concerning Christ pervade the atmosphere. It's as though they've become the very gospel they proclaim. But "thanks to God" gives credit to him rather than to them. "The fragrance of Christ" is "for God" in the sense that the activity of evangelism diffuses upwardly to him like the sweet odor of sacrificial incense and perfume as well as diffusing outwardly to human beings, both "those who are being saved" because of believing the good news and "those who are being destroyed" because of disbelieving it (see the comments on 1 Corinthians 1:18 for the translation "who are being destroyed" rather than "who are perishing"). Paul's switching from "fragrance" back to "odor" takes account of the disbelief of those who are perishing. Through their disbelief they smell in the evangelists an offputting odor which derives from death—that is, from a decaying corpse (compare 1 Corinthians 1:22–23)—and which is resulting in their own eternal death ("perishing"). Through belief, those who are being saved smell in the evangelists an odor which derives from life—that is, from living human beings perfumed with the knowledge of God—and which is resulting for them in eternal life. Since a smell is an internal sensation, Paul says "*in* those who are being saved and *in* those who are perishing."

2:16b–17: **And who** [is] **competent for these matters** [of death and life]? [17]**For we're not like the many, huckstering God's word** [as they do]. **In front of God—** [that is,] **in Christ—we're speaking rather as** [persons] **of sincerity, rather as** [persons sent] **from God** [not as selfishly motivated hucksters]. "God's word" identifies "the fragrance of Christ" (2:15). "Huckstering God's word" means preaching it for financial profit and adulterating it to make it more appealing to potential customers. "The many" indicates that a large number were huckstering God's word. In chapters 10–13 Paul will take further, detailed aim at some of them. Here he mentions them in passing to imply that he and his colleagues, different from the many hucksters, are competent to spread the fragrance of Christ. Two occurrences of "rather" highlight the difference. Paul and company, like all true Christians, are "in Christ"; and Christ is now exalted in heaven. So being in Christ entails being "in front of God." Paul's mentioning this location exhibits a consciousness of proclaiming the word of God in God's full view. This consciousness keeps Paul and company from huckstering, imbues them with sincerity, authenticates God's having sent them, and thus makes them competent for genuine evangelism.

THE LIVING RECOMMENDATION OF PAUL'S MINISTRY IN THE CORINTHIAN CONVERTS
2 Corinthians 3:1–3

3:1: **Are we starting again to commend ourselves?** Some self-commendation is legitimate, because it ac-

cents conscientiousness (see 4:2; 6:4–10; 7:11). Other is not, because it accents the self (compare our phrase, "the self-made man," and see 5:12; 10:12, 18). Here, what Paul said about himself and his colleagues in 1:12–14 makes him realize that what he has just said in 2:14–17 could lead the Corinthians to charge that for the second time in this letter (hence "again") he's engaging in illegitimate self-commendation. His question is open. But the alternative question that now follows contains within itself a negative answer that implies a similarly negative answer to the present question. **Or we don't need letters of recommendation to you or from you, do we, as some** [need such letters]? Paul and company don't need letters of recommendation from others *to* the Corinthians so that the Corinthians could satisfy themselves regarding the credentials of Paul and company, or letters of recommendation *from* the Corinthians so that others could satisfy themselves regarding the credentials of Paul and company. "As some [need such letters]" alludes to itinerant preachers (the hucksters just mentioned in 2:17, also to be called "false apostles" in 11:13) previously unknown to the Corinthians and therefore needing letters of recommendation for acceptance by the Corinthians as well as needing such letters from them once they leave Corinth to visit other churches still unacquainted with them.

3:2–3: **You yourselves are our letter** [of recommendation], **inscribed in our hearts, being understood and read by all people,** [3]**being displayed** [to the effect of the recognition] **that you're Christ's letter, served by us, inscribed not with ink—rather, with the Spirit of the living God; not in stone tablets—rather, in tablets** [that are] **fleshy hearts** [compare Exodus 31:18; Deuteronomy 9:10; Proverbs 3:3; Jeremiah 31:33; Ezekiel 11:19; 36:26–27a]. So Paul says that the Corinthians themselves constitute a kind of letter which recommends him and his colleagues in that as their converts, the Corinthians attest to the credentials of Paul and company. "Inscribed in our hearts" means that wherever Paul and company go, people understand and read, so to speak, the obvious affection Paul and company have for their Corinthian converts. This affection disproves hucksterism and displays sincerity (2:17). "Being understood and read by *all* people" indicates that no one doubts the authenticating affection. Since understanding comes from reading, we expect reading to precede it. But Paul unnaturally puts understanding first to underscore further that all people recognize the affection which Paul and company have for the Corinthians and which authenticates their sincerity. Only a small minority of people in the first century Roman Empire could read a physically written text. Again, then, Paul's saying that all people read the figuratively written text in the hearts of the apostle and his colleagues underscores the recognition of this authenticating affection.

"Our letter" meant "a letter recommending us." "Christ's letter" means "a letter written by Christ." Paul and company couldn't have a better letter of recommendation than that! And the Corinthians are themselves the letter written by Christ. "Served by us" stands for Paul and company's having evangelized the Corinthians successfully on Christ's behalf, as though Christ was dictating the letter and Paul and company were taking down the dictation. Paul inserts the verb "served" between two occurrences of "inscribe" to prepare for the theme of service (traditionally, "ministry") that will occupy the rest of chapter 3. Since the writing material consisted of hearts rather than papyrus (an ancient equivalent of paper), the Spirit substitutes for ink. Paul has identified the hearts as his and his colleagues', and the letter as the Corinthians themselves. "Inscribed . . . with the Spirit" means, therefore, that the Corinthians are the letter of recommendation by virtue of having been "baptized in one Spirit" and "made to drink one Spirit" (1 Corinthians 12:13 [compare 2 Corinthians 1:22]). "Of the living God" describes the Spirit in a way that sets the stage for a contrast between "the [alphabetical] letter," which "kills [people (as explained in the comments on 3:4–8)]," and "the Spirit," who "makes [people] live" (3:6). (Eternal doom and eternal life are in view.) Similarly, the contrast between "stone tablets" and "tablets [that are] fleshy hearts" sets the stage for a contrast between "the serving of death," a serving that's "chiseled in stones" (in reference to the stone tablets containing the Ten Commandments and representing the old covenant), and "the new covenant," in which there's "the serving of the Spirit," who (it bears repeating) "makes [people] live" (3:6–8). Paul started with the Corinthians as a letter of recommendation inscribed in his and his colleagues' hearts. So for a final emphasis on heartfelt affection for the Corinthians, "fleshy" describes Paul and company's hearts. Their hearts are soft with affection rather than unaffectionately hard, like stones.

THE SUPERIORITY OF THE NEW
COVENANT OVER THE OLD
2 Corinthians 3:4–18

3:4–6: And through the Christ in relation to God we have such confidence [as the following]: **⁵not that we are competent in ourselves so as to count anything as** [originating] **from ourselves; rather, our competence** [originates] **from God, ⁶who also made us competent as servers of a new covenant characterized not by a letter** [of the alphabet]—**rather, by the Spirit. For the** [alphabetical] **letter kills** [people]**, but the Spirit makes** [them] **live.** This paragraph starts with a further indication that Paul hasn't been, and isn't, engaging in illegitimate self-commendation. For he and his coworkers don't consider themselves competent *in themselves*. They're competent—yes. But their competence comes from God, not from themselves, so that they don't count "anything," such as evangelistic success, as having derived from their own abilities. They're confident as well as competent, then; but they're not self-confident, and their confidence, like their competence, comes from God, who channels it through Christ his Son. "Through *the* Christ" calls attention to Jesus' messianic office, which fits the ensuing

discussion of a new covenant. "Servers of a new covenant" means that through competent evangelism Paul and company serve a new covenant *to* people the way waiters at table serve food to diners, not that Paul and company are working *for* a new covenant as though it were their employer or master. "Also" introduces the serving of a new covenant as an additional element in God-given competence.

In the mid-first century, when Paul wrote this letter, the new covenant hadn't been written down in books gathered together in what we call the New Testament. The gospel was oral. This circumstance leads Paul to draw a contrast between "the old covenant" (3:14), encapsulated in the Ten Commandments and represented by "a [written] letter [of the alphabet]," and "a new covenant," represented by "the Spirit." Why a new covenant? Because "the [alphabetical] letter kills [people]" in that sinning against it brought death, and animal sacrifices didn't suffice to take away sins as according to 5:21 the sin offering that Christ was made *did* suffice to take them away. Paul's using the singular twice in "a letter [of the alphabet]" and "the [alphabetical] letter" stresses that even an infraction of a single element in the old covenant brought death without recourse to sufficient atonement (compare 1 Corinthians 15:56; Galatians 3:10–13; Romans 7:5–8:6). "But the Spirit makes [people] live" builds on the previous description of the Spirit as "of the living God" and describes the new covenant as life-making through the Spirit rather than death-dealing through an inanimate "letter [of the alphabet]" inscribed on stone tablets. So the new covenant is new in kind as well as new in time. It's superior in kind, too.

3:7–8: But if the serving of death, [a serving] **chiseled in stones in letters** [of the alphabet]**, came on the scene in glory, so that the sons of Israel** [= the descendants of Jacob, nicknamed Israel] **couldn't gaze at Moses' face because of the glory** [= the brightness] **of his face,** [a glory] **that was being rescinded, ⁸the serving of the Spirit will be a lot more in glory, won't it?** For an antithetical parallel with the serving of a new covenant characterized by the life-making Spirit (3:6), Paul now calls the alphabetical letter that kills people (3:6 again) "the serving of death" and echoes the phrase, "in stone tablets" (3:3), with "in stones" but changes "inscribed" (3:3 again) to the more specific—indeed, harsher—"chiseled." The connection with "chiseled" leads Paul to shift from the singular in "a letter [of the alphabet]" and "the [alphabetical] letter" (3:6) to the plural, "in letters [of the alphabet]"; for death was served in many such letters making up the Ten Commandments that were chiseled in stones. At the giving of those commandments, indeed, three thousand were killed for their disobedience in worshiping the golden calf (Exodus 32:1–28); and the reflection of God's glory made Moses' face so bright that the Israelites were afraid to go near him (compare Exodus 34:29–30, 34–35). If glory so bright as what characterized "the serving of death," Paul reasons, "a serving of the Spirit will be a lot more in glory." Paul will get around to comparing the degrees of glory.

For the moment, though, his reasoning has to do with a greater certainty of glory; and he puts his reasoning in the form of a question designed to engage his audience by eliciting from them an affirmative answer. "The serving of the Spirit" contrasts with "the serving of death" and parallels the "serv[ing] of a new covenant" (3:6), so that just as death was dished out under "the [alphabetical] letter" that "kills," the Spirit is dished out under "a new covenant." Though Christians have already received the Spirit (1:22; 1 Corinthians 12:13), Paul delays the serving of the Spirit "in a lot more glory" till the future ("will be"). He has recently said that "the Spirit makes [people] live" (3:6), and he has spoken of the Spirit as "life-producing" in reference to the future resurrection of believers' bodies "in glory" (1 Corinthians 15:43, 45). So Paul's present statement looks forward to that event, the glory of which according to 3:10 will eclipse the glory, bright though it was, at the serving of death, which resurrection will reverse. The rescinding of that earlier glory (Paul infers that it faded from Moses' face) previewed its coming eclipse.

3:9–11: For if the serving of condemnation [had] **glory, how much more does the serving of righteousness flourish in glory!** [10]**For also what was glorified** [that is, the face of Moses] **was *not* glorified in this case on account of the surpassing glory** [of the serving of righteousness]. [11]**For if what was being rescinded** [came on the scene] **through glory, how much more** [does] **what lasts** [flourish] **in glory!** Since condemnation leads to death, "the serving of condemnation" (for which see Deuteronomy 27:26) underlies "the serving of death" (3:7); and together these two expressions elaborate "the [alphabetical] letter" that "kills [people]" (3:6). The glory that the serving of condemnation had is the same as the glory in which the serving of death came on the scene. "The serving of righteousness" parallels "the serving of the Spirit" (3:8) but doesn't mean here that the Spirit makes Christians live righteously. As often elsewhere in Paul's letters, "righteousness" refers to salvation as the right thing for God to give people who've believed in Jesus his Son (see the comments on 5:21 and 1 Corinthians 1:30–31). "The serving of the Spirit . . . in glory" looked forward to the Spirit's resurrecting the bodies of believers in glory at the last day (3:8: "will be . . . in glory"). But though that resurrection will cap the serving of righteousness as salvation, the present tense of "flourish" shows that the serving of righteousness as salvation is already occurring and outshining the old glory.

"How much *more* does the serving [the dishing out, so to speak] of righteousness flourish in glory!" adds a greater *degree* of glory (than what accompanied the serving of condemnation) to the greater *certainty* of glory in 3:8. The first "For" introduces this greater degree of glory as a *reason* for the greater certainty of glory. In other words, the greater glory necessitated the greater certainty, because a glory that's greater in degree can't be held back. It must break out. The second "For," followed by "also," introduces the eclipse of the old glory by the greater glory as an added explanation of how much

greater is the glory that characterizes the serving of righteousness. The Milky Way is glorious, but you can't see its glory when the sun is shining in all *its* glory. A third "For" introduces the explanation why "what lasts"—that is, "the serving of righteousness"—flourishes in glory "much more." If "what was being rescinded" comes on the scene "through glory" as an attendant circumstance *despite its destiny to be rescinded*, "how much more [does] what *lasts* [flourish] in glory!" The permanence of the serving of righteousness that's already flourishing looks forward to the imperishability and immortality of believers' bodies, resurrected in glory by "the last Adam" (Christ) as "the life-producing Spirit" (1 Corinthians 15:42–44, 53–54).

3:12–13: Therefore [because of the surpassing glory of the serving of righteousness] **having such a hope** [that is, having confidence in the permanence of this glory], **we're acting with much boldness of speech** [in proclaiming the gospel], [13]**and** [are] **not** [acting] **as indeed Moses** [acted]. **He used to put a veil over his face so that the sons of Israel wouldn't gaze at the end of what was being rescinded.** "Hope" has as its object the consummation of salvation at Jesus' second coming. So Paul's introduction of this term confirms that the glory which will characterize the serving of the Spirit (3:8) had to do with the glory of believers' Spirit-produced bodies at the resurrection, occurring as it will at the second coming (1 Corinthians 15:43). Meanwhile, the confidence connoted by hope breeds "much boldness of speech." In view of the glorious resurrection to come, no danger of persecution for proclaiming the gospel need hush its proclamation. To the contrary! Then Paul draws a contrast between his and his colleagues' great boldness and Moses' veiling his face. The veiling grew out of embarrassment, the opposite of boldness. Which is to say, Paul *infers* that the glory of the serving of death and condemnation faded from Moses' face, and *interprets* Moses' veiling his face as motivated by embarrassment about the fading. Moses didn't want the Israelites to see "the end of what was being rescinded," the final fadeout of the glory. The veil didn't serve to shield the Israelites from the glory reflected off Moses' face. Instead, the veil kept them from seeing "the end of what was being rescinded" *as represented* in the fading. But since the serving of righteousness lasts, so that its glory will never fade away, boldness is in and embarrassment is out.

3:14–16: Their [the Israelites'] **minds were hardened, however. For right up to the today-day** [= this very day] **the same veil, not being divested, remains at the reading of the old covenant** [that is, when the Old Testament, particularly the Mosaic law, is read to the Jews Sabbath by Sabbath in their synagogues], **because in Christ it's being rescinded.** [15]**Till today, however, whenever Moses is being read a veil is lying over their heart.** [16]**But whenever he turns to the Lord, the veil is taken from around** [from around the face in Moses' case, from around the heart in the case of a Christian convert] [Exodus 34:34]. The first "however" signals a dramatic shift in Paul's interpretation of the veil. It no longer refers to Moses' using a literal veil externally to hide from view the end of the old glory, representing the future rescinding of the old covenant, and doing so out of embarrassment as opposed to boldness. Now the veil functions as a figure of speech for the internal hardening of the ancient Israelites' minds. "For" then introduces an explanation of that hardening as a prefiguration of the same hardening in Paul's Jewish contemporaries, "right up to the today-day" (compare Deuteronomy 29:4). "The *same* veil" unites these contemporaries with their forebears in the hardening, but "the today-day" puts an accent on the contemporaries' hardened minds. Paul describes their and their forebears' minds as "hardened" in the sense that those minds are characterized by ignorance because of unbelief (see Romans 11:7, 25; Ephesians 4:18). They've made their minds impenetrable to the gospel. The hardness of their minds corresponds to the stones of the tablets containing "the serving of death" and contrasts with the "tablets [that are] fleshy hearts" in which Christ has written letters of recommendation for Paul and company (3:3, 7).

"Not being divested" charges the Jews—at least the majority of them, those who attend synagogue and hear "the reading of the old covenant"—with failure to throw off the veil of ignorance-causing hardness (compare Romans 10:16, 21). Paul implies that if they understood the old covenant when it's read to them, in particular if they understood the symbolism of Moses' veil as just explained by Paul, they would recognize that the old covenant is antiquated because of having been rescinded "in Christ," who inaugurated "a new covenant" (3:6; 1 Corinthians 11:25). "*Because* in Christ it's being rescinded" makes rescinding of the old covenant the reason why failure to remove the veil of hardness results in permanent ignorance. The permanence of the veil keeps unbelieving Jews from recognizing the surpassing glory of the permanent new covenant (3:11). "Because in Christ it's *being* rescinded" means that every time a Jew comes to be in Christ by faith, the old covenant is rescinded in the believer's now-knowledgeable mind. A second "however" sets the veil of permanent ignorance over against the fact that the old covenant has been rescinded in Christ. "Till today" and "whenever Moses is being read" reemphasize the permanence of this ignorance among most of Paul's Jewish contemporaries. Since thoughts were conceived to be located in the heart, he says that "a veil is lying over their [the unbelieving Jews'] heart," so that the significance of what Moses wrote doesn't penetrate their thinking. (The reference to thinking, which occurs in the heart, has led to a transfer of the symbolic veil from Moses' face [3:13] to the Jews' collective heart.) Then Paul paraphrases Exodus 34:34, which in its Old Testament context refers to Moses' removing the veil from his face whenever he entered the sanctuary (a tent) to speak with the Lord. Paul treats Moses' entry into the Lord's presence as symbolic of a person's turning to the Lord, who in Paul's vocabulary is almost always Jesus, through believing the gospel. And Paul treats Moses'

removing the veil from his face as symbolizing the removal of ignorance from around the heart of a convert, particularly a Jewish one.

3:17: And the Lord is the Spirit; and where the Spirit of the Lord [is], **freedom** [is there]! 1 Corinthians 15:45 said that as "the last Adam," Christ became "a life-producing Spirit." As "the Lord" he's now said to be "the Spirit." *Personally*, Paul distinguishes between the (Holy) Spirit, the Lord (Jesus), and God (the Father), as in 1 Corinthians 12:4–6. Hence "the Spirit *of* the Lord" here in 2 Corinthians 3:17b (compare Romans 8:9). In 3:17a, however, Paul equates the Lord *functionally* with the Spirit, since the Lord (Jesus) works in and through the (Holy) Spirit. "The Lord" refers back to the Lord to whom one turns, so that the veil of hardening is removed (3:16); and turning to him locates one where he is as the Spirit, for Christians have the Spirit that, functionally speaking, the Lord Jesus is. Freedom is there, exclaims Paul. See 1 Corinthians 7:21–22; Galatians 2:4; 3:28; 5:1 for his associating freedom with Christ. Like the present passage, the passages in Galatians deal with the old covenant, the Law. So as in those passages, freedom means freedom from the death-dealing law of Moses. Compare the extensive contrast earlier in this chapter between the Spirit in the new covenant that makes people live and the alphabetical letters of the Ten Commandments that kill people.

3:18: And we all, looking with an unveiled face at the Lord's glory as in a mirror, are being transformed into the same image from glory to glory, just as indeed [this transformation is] **from the Lord, the Spirit.** "We all" includes all Christians in contrast with Moses as the lone figure who under the old covenant looked at the Lord's glory as in a mirror. But as Moses removed his veil when he entered the sanctuary (a tent) and looked at the Lord's glory, so Christians look at it "with an unveiled face." By faith they see it as unbelievers do not. "As in a mirror" compares the Lord (Jesus) to a mirror in that his glory is a reflection of God's glory. The comparison implies that Moses likewise saw the glory of the Spiritually preincarnate Christ, mentioned as such in 1 Corinthians 10:4 (see the comments there), as a reflection of God's glory. Looking at this mirrored glory with an unveiled face transforms believers "into the same image," which 4:4 will identify as Christ in that he is "God's image," the very representation of God (compare Romans 8:29; Colossians 1:15). That is to say, as believers look at the Lord Jesus' glory they're being transformed into the image of God that the Lord Jesus himself is. "From glory to glory" indicates a progressive transformation that will culminate on the day of resurrection (compare 1 Corinthians 15:49). Because God's glory, reflected in the glory of the Lord Jesus, stands in contrast to human sinning (Romans 3:23), the glory of the Lord Jesus refers now not to dazzlingly bright light, as in the story of Moses, but to the sinless perfection of the Lord Jesus. Consequently, the transformation of believers refers to their being morally perfected by degrees till they ultimately reach that same sinless perfection (compare 1 John 3:2–3 and contrast the fading of luminous glory from Moses' face with the ever-increasing moral glory in Christian believers' lives). Not by their own doing, though! For this transformation has its origin in the Lord because functionally speaking, he's the Spirit who keeps believers from vices, called "the works of the flesh," and develops in them virtues, called "the fruit of the Spirit" (Galatians 5:16–24). "Indeed" underlines that this moral transformation is "from the Lord, the Spirit."

THE DETERMINATION OF PAUL TO CARRY OUT HIS MINISTRY
2 Corinthians 4:1–6:10

4:1–2: Because of this [our being "transformed from glory to glory" (3:18)], **having this service, just as we've been treated mercifully we're not giving up.** ²**For ourselves, rather, we've renounced the hidden [deeds] of shame** [= deeds that their doer hides because they'd bring shame on him if they were exposed], **not walking around** [= not behaving] **in trickery and not counterfeiting God's word; rather, by the disclosure of the truth commending ourselves in God's sight to every consciousness of human beings.** "This service" refers to the serving of "Christ's letter" (3:3), of "a new covenant" (3:6), of "the Spirit" (3:8), and of "righteousness" (3:9). The "having" of this service came as a consequence of being "treated mercifully." Paul is alluding in particular to Christ's "laying hold" of him for salvation and apostleship despite Paul's blasphemy and persecution of the church (compare 1 Corinthians 7:25; 15:9–10; Philippians 3:12; and especially 1 Timothy 1:12–16 as well as Acts 7:58; 9:1–19a; 22:3–16; 26:9–18). "We're not giving up" has as its background the extreme affliction and sufferings Paul and company have been enduring because of their proclamation of the gospel (1:3–11). On the one hand, "not giving up" corresponds and responds to "hav[ing] been treated mercifully." On the other hand, "not giving up" has entailed "renounc[ing] the hidden [deeds] of shame," which deeds would exempt them from persecution since such deeds would align them with their persecutors. "For ourselves" underlines the behavioral difference between Paul and company and their persecutors, and "rather" draws a contrast between the possibility of giving up and the actuality of renouncing the hidden deeds of shame. "Not walking around" interprets the renunciation as behavioral, not just verbal. "Trickery" and "counterfeiting God's word" recall "the many who are huckstering God's word" according to 2:17 and exemplify the hidden deeds of shame that Paul and company have renounced. "The disclosure of the truth" contrasts with trickery and counterfeiting, which hide the truth to please people (for financial profit at their expense, if 2:17 is any guide). But disclosing the truth of "Christ crucified," which Jews consider "a snare" and Greeks consider "foolishness" (1 Corinthians 1:23 [compare 2 Corinthians 2:16]), is commendatory in God's sight and also commends Paul and company "to

every consciousness of human beings"—that is, makes everybody conscious that Paul and company aren't trying to trick them with a counterfeit of God's word.

4:3–4: But even if our gospel is veiled, it's veiled in those who are being destroyed, ⁴**[that is,] in those whom the god of this age has blinded the minds of the unbelievers** [= "those who are being destroyed"] **so that [they] won't espy the illumination consisting in the gospel concerning the glory of the Christ, who is God's image.** "The disclosure of the truth" by Paul and company (4:2) means that it's not their fault if the gospel "is veiled." Nor is it the fault of the gospel itself, for the gospel is illuminative. Blame for the veiling of the gospel rests on "the god of this age," who for the time being—till "the Day of the Lord" commences "the coming age" of eternity—"has blinded the minds of the unbelievers." In other words, Satan has veiled unbelievers' minds, so that they can't see with their mind's eye the truth of the gospel even though that truth has been disclosed by Paul and company's serving it to them (compare 3:14–16, where a veil represents the hardening of Israelites' minds and hearts). "*Our* gospel" means the good news as proclaimed by Paul and company. "Veiled *in* those who are being destroyed" reflects the interiority of their minds, and "are being destroyed" points to ongoing ruination caused by the blindness of unbelief inflicted on them by Satan (compare 2:15; 1 Corinthians 1:18). (It's unbelief, not faith, that's blind.) This ruination will culminate in eternal punishment just as ongoing salvation will culminate in eternal reward. "The glory of the Christ" confirms that in 3:18 "the glory of the Lord" referred to the glory of the Christ, not (except by reflection) the glory of God the Father, and consequently that in 3:16–17 "the Lord" referred to the Christ. Because the gospel concerns the *glory* of Christ, it brings illumination—except in cases of blind unbelief. The description of the Christ as "God's image" makes the glory of the Christ a mirror-like reflection of God's glory (compare the comments on 3:18; also Paul's calling the Christ "the last Adam" in 1 Corinthians 15:45 and the first Adam's having been created "in [God's] image" according to Genesis 1:26–27). "*The* Christ" connotes a title such as suits one who is God's image.

4:5–6: For we aren't proclaiming ourselves—rather, Jesus Christ as Lord, and ourselves as your slaves on account of Jesus, ⁶**because God, who said, "Out of darkness light shall shine** [Genesis 1:3; Isaiah 9:2]," **[is] the one who has shined in our hearts with the result of an illumination consisting in the knowledge of God's glory in the face of Jesus Christ.** This sentence elaborates 3:12–4:4, with a sidelong glance at 2:17. "We aren't proclaiming ourselves—rather, Jesus Christ as Lord and ourselves as your slaves on account of Jesus" shows that Paul and company aren't "walking around [= behaving] in trickery" like self-promoting, audience-fleecing hucksters (4:2). After "Jesus Christ *as Lord*" we expect Paul to describe himself and his coworkers as slaves of Jesus Christ. But "*your* slaves on account of Jesus" emphasizes the proclamation of Jesus as Lord for the Corinthians' benefit, not for that of Paul and company. "On account of Jesus" should keep the Corinthians from thinking there's anything about them that deserves the service of slaves, however. "Because God, who said, 'Out of darkness light shall shine,' [is] the one who has shined in our hearts with the result of an illumination" explains why Paul and company proclaim Jesus Christ as Lord and themselves as the Corinthians' slaves, but also balances out "the god of this age has blinded the minds of the unbelievers so that they won't espy the illumination consisting in the gospel" (4:4 [note the parallel between "hearts" and "minds"]). At creation God spoke physical light into being out of physical darkness. At conversion God himself shines as the light of knowledge that dispels the darkness of ignorance (compare the accounts of Paul's conversion in Acts 9, 22, 26, where physical light results in the light of saving knowledge). "The knowledge of God's glory in the face of Jesus Christ" explains "the glory of the Christ, who is God's image" (4:4) as the glory of God reflected off the face of the Christ because of his being the mirror image of God and producing a better reflection than that on Moses' face, and a permanent rather than fading reflection like the one on Moses' face (3:7–13). "The *knowledge* of God's glory in the face of Jesus Christ" means the *experiencing* of that glory through "being transformed into the same image from glory to glory" as a result of "looking with an unveiled face at the Lord's glory as in a mirror" (3:18; see the final comments on that verse for God's glory as sinless perfection). That Paul locates God's glory "in the face of Jesus Christ" confirms again the identity of "the Lord" in 3:16–18 as Jesus Christ. As an unveiled viewer of the preincarnate Lord's glory, Moses prefigured Christians. As a mirror-like reflector of God the Father's glory, Moses prefigured Christ.

4:7–10: But we have this treasure [God's having "shined in our hearts" (4:6)] **in clay vessels, so that the superiority of the power is God's and not from us—** ⁸[we] **in every** [way] **being afflicted—not crushed, however; being stymied—not despairing, however;** ⁹**being persecuted—not being abandoned, however; being thrown down—not being destroyed, however;** ¹⁰**always carrying around in the body the dying of Jesus in order that also the life of Jesus may be displayed in our body.** Because they're easily broken, "clay vessels" turns out to be a figure of speech for physical bodies, subject to being "afflicted," "stymied," "persecuted," and "thrown down." The putting of treasure in containers so fragile as clay vessels highlights "the superiority of the power," which according to 1 Corinthians 1:18 consists in "the speech about the cross." As in that verse, here too the power is God's. The addition of "not from us" excludes Paul and company from any contribution of power. "In every [way]" multiplies their affliction and probably their being stymied, persecuted, and thrown down as well. On the one hand, the four antitheses, emphasized by the repeated "however" and a strong form of "not," imply divine deliverances from what we call near-death

experiences. But Paul presents the experiences as a process of dying that God hasn't allowed to reach completion (compare Romans 8:36; 1 Corinthians 15:31). As will come out clearly in 4:11–12, moreover, the dying Paul puts in view isn't dying as the common lot of humanity. It's dying as a result of proclaiming the gospel.

On the other hand, somewhat as in 1:8 Paul admitted to despairing whereas he now denies doing so (presumably as a result of the past deliverance [1:9–10]), a more literal translation of the antitheses exposes them as almost humorously self-contradictory: **being pressured—not being cramped, however** [as though pressure doesn't cramp]; **being without a passageway—not being without a passageway out, however** [as though having no passageway at all doesn't include the lack of a passageway out of a difficulty]; **being pursued—not being abandoned, however** [as though pursuit isn't the opposite of abandonment]; **being struck down—not being destroyed, however** [as though to be struck down doesn't often mean to be overthrown and slain, destroyed like a gladiator felled in the arena]. Paul saves the biggest seeming self-contradiction till last but substitutes "in order that" for "however" to add purpose to paradox: "always carrying around in the body the *dying* of Jesus in order that also the *life* of Jesus may be displayed in our body," as though dying displays life. Paul will now explain what he means.

4:11–12: For we the living are continually being given over to death on account of Jesus in order that also the life of Jesus may be displayed in our mortal flesh. ¹²**And so, death is at work in us, but life in you.** The addition of "the living" to "we" highlights by contrast that "we . . . are always being given over to death." As God gave Jesus over to death (Romans 8:32), "being given over to death" implies that God is giving Paul and company over to death by "exhibit[ing]" them "as sentenced to death" through their evangelistic labors (1 Corinthians 4:9). "On account of Jesus" should keep the Corinthians from thinking there's anything about them that deserved Paul and company's risking their lives to evangelize them, that is, letting death go to work in Paul and company so that life of an everlasting kind because of Jesus' resurrection can go to work in the Corinthians (compare the comments on 4:5). So "carrying around in the body the dying of Jesus" (4:10) referred to Paul and company's dying by degrees because of proclaiming the gospel (contrast their being transformed by degrees "from glory to glory" in 3:18). Being afflicted, stymied, persecuted, and thrown down (4:8–9) referred to such dying. The use of "always" in 4:10 and of "continually" in 4:11 stresses the constancy of this dying, which is due in turn to the constancy of proclamation. "Dying" differs from "death" and in view of the present statements suggests that because Christians are united to Christ and therefore "in Christ," he is dying (though not atoningly) with Christian evangelists as they are gradually dying for the gospel (compare Jesus' statement to Paul on the road to Damascus, "I'm Jesus, whom you're persecuting" [Acts 9:5; 22:8; 26:15]).

"*Carrying around . . .* the dying of Jesus" (4:10) sounded odd. But the oddity of this expression reflected the *itinerant* character of dying because of evangelism. "In the/our body" interpreted "in clay vessels" (4:7, 10), but now in 4:11 "in our mortal flesh" substitutes for "in the/our body" to stress the possibility of martyrdom (hence "mortal"), and also to punctuate the paradox of displaying Jesus' life in a body whose flesh disintegrates at death (hence "flesh"). "The life of Jesus" in both 4:10 and 4:11 refers to the life he has by virtue of his resurrection. It's "displayed" both by the use of fleshy bodies to go around proclaiming the gospel, which includes not only Jesus' death but also his having been raised to new life (1 Corinthians 15:3–4), and also by the deliverances from death that Paul and company have thus far experienced. For these deliverances preview final deliverance through a resurrection to eternal life that will replicate Jesus' resurrection. Because of the statement, "that also the life of Jesus may be displayed in *our* [Paul and company's] mortal flesh," we expect Paul to conclude that "life [as well as death is at work] in *us*." But he springs a surprise by saying, "life in *you*." So his and his coworkers' continual dying because of evangelism has produced, and is producing, the eternal life of resurrection through a display of Jesus' resurrected life.

4:13–15: But having the same Spirit of faith in accordance with what's written, "I believed; therefore I spoke [Psalm 116:10]," we also believe; therefore we speak, ¹⁴knowing that the one who raised Jesus will raise us too along with Jesus and will present [us] along with you [to himself]. ¹⁵For all things [are] because of you in order that the grace [of God], having increased through the majority, may make thanksgiving flourish for God's glory. "Having the same Spirit of faith" makes Paul and company believe despite the fact that "death is at work" in them (4:12); and their believing issues in their speaking, which as in 2:17 refers to their proclamation of the gospel. Since faith is a fruit of the Spirit (Galatians 5:22–23) and since the preceding context here has featured the Spirit (3:17–18), "the . . . Spirit of faith" is the Holy Spirit, whom Paul and company possess (compare 1 Corinthians 7:40) and who produces in them faith. "In accordance with what's written" shows that "the *same* Spirit of faith" means the same as the Spirit of faith that the author of Psalm 116:10 had—hence, "we *also* [in addition to the psalmist] believe." The Corinthians would understand from 1:9 and 1 Corinthians 15:15, of course, that God is "the one who raised Jesus"; but Paul now adds that he and his coworkers speak the gospel because of knowing that God will raise them too if they suffer martyrdom. "Along with Jesus" makes their resurrection consequent on that of Jesus since he was "the firstfruits [= the first installment] of those who've fallen asleep [in death]" (1 Corinthians 15:20). Union with him by faith entails a coming resurrection like his. So knowing supplements believing and rests on the historical fact of Jesus' resurrection. Paul isn't implying that Christians other than him and his colleagues won't be resurrected. He's only centering on his own and his colleagues' res-

urrection as a mainspring for their dangerous work of evangelism. In a followup to their resurrection he mentions God's "present[ing]" them, apparently to himself much as Ephesians 5:27 talks about Christ's presenting the church to himself.

"Along with you" shows that here and earlier "we," "us," "our," and "ourselves" do not include the Corinthians (with the exception of "we *all*" in 3:18). Paul connects "along with you" with the presentation but not with the resurrection, because at the time it seemed likely that he and his fellow evangelists would be martyred before the second coming and therefore need resurrection, whereas the Corinthians might well survive till the second coming and not need it (compare 1 Corinthians 15:51–52). "All things" that are "because of you" consist in Paul and company's evangelistic and pastoral work among the Corinthians. So concern for the Corinthians supplies yet another reason, in addition to having the Spirit of faith and knowing that God will raise martyred evangelists, for speaking as they do. But beyond the Corinthians' benefit is the purpose of glorifying God through thanksgiving that flourishes because of an increase in his grace. This grace will have increased "through the majority." In 2:6 "the majority" referred to the majority of already converted Corinthians, and in 9:2 will refer to the majority of already converted Macedonians. So "through the majority" means that God's grace will increase by way of further conversions resulting from the life and witness of the majority of Christians, particularly those in Corinth, who have obeyed Paul (2:6–9; 7:5–16).

4:16–18: Therefore [because of resurrection to come (4:14)] **we're not giving up. Rather, even though our external human being is wasting away, yet our internal [human being] is being renewed day in and day out. ¹⁷For the momentary lightness of our affliction is producing for us an eternal weight of glory in accordance with superiority, with the result of superiority, ¹⁸while we're fixing our gaze not on the things that are being seen—rather, on the things that aren't being seen. For the things that are being seen [are] temporary, but the things that aren't being seen [are] eternal.** "We're not giving up" echoes 4:1. "Our external human being" refers to the physical body, also called "clay vessels" (4:7); and its "wasting away" refers to its gradual "dying" because of debilitation and possible martyrdom due to evangelistic work (4:10–12). "Our internal [human being]" refers to the human spirit that indwells the physical body (compare "my spirit" in 2:13). As shown by the contrast with giving up, renewal of the internal human being refers to the renewal of its "confidence" so as not to give up (compare 3:4). The adding of "day in and day out" to renewal but not to wasting away signifies that the renewal overcomes the wasting away, that confidence trumps giving up.

"Affliction" versus "glory," "momentary" versus "eternal," "lightness" versus "weight"—these contrasts tell why it is that confidence trumps giving up. And "in accordance with superiority, with the result of superiority" makes the glory doubly and ineffably superior in weight to the lightness of affliction. (Paul may have in mind a single Hebrew word that means both "weight" and "glory"; but he can hardly have expected the Corinthians, few if any of whom knew Hebrew, to have recognized the wordplay.) Since the lightness of affliction has to do with the debilitating effects of persecution on the body, the eternal weight of glory has to do with the glorifying effects of resurrection on the body, as in 1 Corinthians 15:43; Philippians 3:21. But it's not a *comparison* of the lightness of affliction with the weight of glory that generates a renewal of confidence. It's the *production* of the weight of glory by the lightness of affliction that generates the renewal. In other words, the knowledge that affliction produces glory renews the internals of persecuted evangelists like Paul and his coworkers. As this production goes on, they "aren't fixing [their] gaze on the things that are being seen"; that is, they're overlooking their "external human being," wasting away as it is. Instead, they "are fixing [their] gaze . . . on the things that aren't being seen"; that is, they're training their mind's eye on their resurrected body, presently invisible because it's yet to come. But it will be visible, just as Christ's resurrected body was visible (1 Corinthians 9:1; 15:3–8). The reason for this not-gazing, on the one hand, and gazing, on the other hand, is that presently visible bodies are temporary—they'll vanish—whereas presently invisible bodies are eternal—they'll be visible forever.

5:1–3: For we know that if our earthly house consisting of the tent [a figure of speech for our temporary body] **is dismantled** [= if we die (compare 4:10–11)], **we have a building from God, a house not handmade, eternal, in the heavens.** [2]**For also in this** [tent] **we groan, longing to put on our dwelling from heaven over** [our earthly house], [3]**if indeed after putting** [it] **on we'll also not be found naked.** The first "For" in this passage introduces another reason why Paul and company aren't giving up (see 4:16 with earlier reasons introduced by "For" in 4:17, 18b–c). "We know" harks back to 4:14: "knowing that the one who raised the Lord, Jesus, will raise us too"). "Our earthly house" represents the present physical body as a dwelling place of the human spirit (compare 2:13 ["my spirit"]; also 1 Corinthians 6:19 for the physical body as a temple in which the Holy Spirit resides). "Earthly" means "located on earth" and therefore contrasts with "our dwelling from heaven." "Consisting of a tent" connotes easy dismantlement, as in death (compare Paul's calling present physical bodies "clay vessels," easily broken [4:7]). "A building," also called "a house" for the human spirit, stands for a resurrected body. As a building is substantial and a tent insubstantial, so the resurrected body will be immortal whereas the earthly body is mortal. The present tense in "we *have* a building" makes Christians' coming to have an immortal body on the day of resurrection so certain that they might as well have it already (see 1 Corinthians 15:12, 15–16, 29, 32, 35, 42–43 for similar uses of the present tense in reference to future resurrection). As a building, the resurrected body will be "from God" in that God is "the one who . . . will raise us" (4:14; com-

pare 1 Corinthians 15:38)—hence "not handmade" in the sense of not manmade. "Eternal" describes the building—that is, the resurrected body—as permanent, unlike the temporary lightness of affliction in 4:17 as well as unlike the perishability of the earthly house (compare 1 Corinthians 15:42, 52–55). Since Paul speaks of "our dwelling *from* heaven," "*in* the heavens" can hardly mean that believers will indwell their resurrected bodies forever in heaven. Heaven marks a place of origin, not of destination or continuance (compare 1 Corinthians 15:40, 48–49; Philippians 3:20–21). So "in the heavens" doesn't go with "eternal"; rather, it adds a third description of the building/house that represents a resurrected body: (1) "not handmade"; (2) "eternal"; and (3) "in the heavens" (from where it will originate by the action of God, who dwells there).

The second "For" in this paragraph introduces yet another reason (hence "also") why Paul and company aren't giving up (see the comments on 5:1). "Longing" underlies and accompanies "groaning," and the two of them arise out of the "wasting away" of "the external human being" (4:16). "To put on our dwelling from heaven *over* [our earthly house]" refers to a longing to live right up to the second coming. In this event, the immortal body is put on over the mortal body—we might think of a remodeling—so that there's no bodiless existence between death and resurrection: "we'll also [in addition to having a body from heaven] not be found naked [as a human spirit disembodied by death is 'naked']" (1 Corinthian 15:51–52; 1 Thessalonians 4:15–17). "If" contemplates the possibility of living right up to the second coming so as not to undergo a disembodied existence between death and resurrection. "Indeed" stresses the certainty of not undergoing it in that case.

5:4–5: For also we who are in the tent [our temporary body] **groan, being weighted down, because we don't want to be unclothed** [= disembodied through death]**; rather,** [we want] **to put on** [our dwelling from heaven] **over** [our still living earthly body at the second coming] **in order that the mortal** [body] **may be gulped down** [= swallowed up] **by life.** [5]**And the one who has conditioned us for this very** [dwelling from heaven] [is] **God, who gave us the downpayment consisting in the Spirit** [1:22]. "For also" introduces an elaboration of the reason in 5:2–3 for not giving up. "Being weighted down" substitutes for "longing" and plays on "an eternal weight consisting in glory" (4:17). That is to say, the weight of groaning out of a desire to avoid disembodiment makes a striking contrast with "an eternal weight consisting in glory" (4:17). The degree of contrast underscores a longing for glorification at the second coming (see 1 Corinthians 15:51–52 again). In 2:7 Paul spoke of being "gulped down by sorrow," and in 1 Corinthians 15:54 of death's being gulped down into victory, an unhappy fate for death. Here he speaks of the body's being "gulped down by life," a happy fate for the body because "life" refers here to eternal life, attained in its completeness at the second coming. But it isn't the *dead* body that's to be gulped down by life. It's "the *mortal* [body]," so that Paul is still talking about the putting of a glorified body over a still living earthly body at the second coming, not about the resurrection of a dead body. "The one who has conditioned us for this very [dwelling from heaven] [is] God" echoes 4:14. "The [God-given] downpayment consisting in the Spirit" guarantees the dwelling from heaven in that the Spirit wouldn't be indwelling the present mortal body, as he does according to 1 Corinthians 6:19, unless he were going to produce a better replacement, as he will according to 1 Corinthians 15:44–45.

5:6–8: Always being confident, therefore, and knowing that while being at home in the body we're absent from the Lord— [7] **for we're walking around** [= conducting our lives] **by faith, not by visible form.** [8] **And we're confident and delighted, rather, to become absent from the body and at home with the Lord.** "Therefore" means that having "the downpayment consisting in the Spirit" (5:5) breeds confidence, and "always" means that no affliction, such as those mentioned in 4:7–12, ever shatters this confidence. "Knowing that while being at home in the body we're absent from the Lord" suggests that absence from the Lord, who is in heaven, because of our bodily existence on earth might shatter confidence even though affliction by itself doesn't. Without finishing his sentence, Paul explains a consequence of being at home in the body and therefore absent from the Lord. The consequence is walking by faith in the Lord, who is invisible from our earthly vantage point (compare 4:13 for the element of faith). Starting a new sentence, Paul revives the element of confidence and adds the element of delight. He and his colleagues have confidence that becoming absent from the body as a result of death, particularly martyrdom, would result in being at home with the Lord; and they take delight in that result. "Absent from the body" implies a disembodiment of the human spirit at death. "At home with the Lord" implies presence in heaven with Jesus, the Lord, on the part of a Christian's disembodied spirit. This confidence and delight counterbalance the longing to live till the second coming and thus skip a disembodied heavenly existence between death and resurrection (compare Philippians 1:21–23). "Rather" stresses the counterbalance.

5:9–10: Whether being at home [in the body] **or being absent** [from it], **therefore also we're making it our ambition to be pleasing to him.** [10] **For it's necessary that we all be manifested** [= exposed to view] **before the judgment platform of the Christ in order that each** [of us] **may be requited for the things** [done] **through the body, consistent with the things he has done, whether a good thing or an evil thing.** "Therefore also" introduces another consequence (besides the confidence and delight mentioned in 5:6–8) of God's having given the Spirit as a downpayment on a glorious body at the resurrection (5:5). "Making it our ambition to be pleasing to him [the just-mentioned 'Lord,' who is Jesus]" implies earnest effort, and the effort proceeds without regard to the possibilities of staying alive (so as to be "at home in the body") and dying (so as to be "absent [from

the body]"). What does drive Paul and company's effort, though, is the necessity of being "manifested before the judgment platform of the Christ." The retention of "we" and the addition to it of "all" combine to include the Corinthians, and by extension all other believers (see Romans 2:6–10 for the judgment of all human beings, Christians and non-Christians alike). "The judgment platform" recalls the judgment platform in Corinth before which Paul stood trial (Acts 18:12–17). But that one was Gallio's, who was a Roman governor. This one will be Christ's. "Of *the* Christ" suits with a title his coming role as the messianic judge. "Each [of us]" points to individual judgment. There'll be no coattails (1 Corinthians 3:13; 4:5). The judgmental requital will be consistent with the character of deeds done through the instrument of the body. But the singulars in "whether a good thing or an evil thing" underline the judgment of individual deeds as well as of individual persons. In view of 1 Corinthians 3:10–15, this judgment means that the Christ will reward a Christian for a good deed and inflict loss on a Christian for an evil deed. On the one hand, salvation won't *necessarily* be lost (see in particular 1 Corinthians 3:15), but the enjoyment of it will be diminished just as a reward will consist in enhanced enjoyment of salvation. On the other hand, the behavior of a professing Christian may be sufficiently evil for him to be judged as having believed only "casually" (1 Corinthians 15:2) and thus to have received God's grace "ineffectually" (2 Corinthians 6:1).

5:11–12: Knowing the fear of the Lord, therefore, we're trying to persuade human beings; but we've been manifested to God. And I'm hoping to have been manifested also in your consciousnesses. [12] **We're not commending ourselves to you again—rather, giving you a basis,** [that is] **a ground of boasting about us, in order that you may have** [such a basis in speaking] **to those who are boasting in face** [= outward appearance] **and not in heart** [= inward reality]. "Therefore" means "because we'll all be requited for our deeds at the Last Judgment" (see 5:10). "Knowing the fear of the Lord" means "fearing that the Lord will find evil deeds to requite us for." In the statement "we're persuading human beings," "we" has reverted to Paul and company; and "human beings" refers to their audiences (including the Corinthians) and highlights by contrast the deity of Jesus as "the Lord." But persuading the human beings of what? Paul follows up with statements about his being in a state of manifestation to God and, he hopes, in the Corinthians' consciousnesses, and also about his and his coworkers' not recommending themselves to the Corinthians but giving them a basis to boast about him and his coworkers. So "trying to persuade human beings" doesn't mean trying to persuade them of the gospel. It means trying to persuade them that he and his coworkers aren't hucksters. They're sincere (1:12; 2:17). Others' persuasion of their sincerity will, of course, enhance evangelistic success. But God doesn't need to be persuaded of their sincerity, because he knows their hearts. Switching temporarily to "I" instead of "we" because of some continuing opposition to him among the Corinthians, Paul states his hope that in their consciousnesses they will recognize his sincerity as God does. See the comments on 1 Corinthians 8:7 for the translation "consciousnesses" rather than "consciences," which would be particularly bad here because this English word refers to a moral monitor for one's *own* behavior, whereas here the opinion of *others* than Paul is in question. Though self-commendation appears in 4:2; 6:4, Paul denies it here. He has merely expressed a hope that his trying to persuade the Corinthians and others of his and his coworkers' sincerity has proved successful. And the expression of this hope is giving the Corinthians a basis—that is, a ground—for them to boast about Paul and company's sincerity "to those who are boasting in face and not in heart." It will turn out in chapters 10–13 that they are Paul's opponents, a minority within the Corinthian church and interloping false apostles as well (for starters, see 10:2, 12–13; 11:13).

5:13: For if we've gone out of our minds, [it's] **for God; and if we're sensible,** [it's] **for you.** We don't know for sure the specific reference in "we've gone out of our minds," but the "snare to Jews" and the "foolishness to Gentiles" of "proclaiming Christ crucified" (1 Corinthians 1:23) offers an attractive possibility. To unbelievers, proclaimers of a crucified Christ seem deranged. But in view of believers' contrary opinion, "if" casts doubt on actual derangement; and whether or not they're deranged, Paul and company do what they do "for God." Nor do we know for sure the specific reference in "we're sensible," but the proclamation of Christ as "God's power and God's wisdom" so far as those who are "called" are concerned (1 Corinthians 1:24) provides an attractive possibility. In view of unbelievers' contrary opinion, "if" casts doubt again, this time on actual sensibility; and whether or not they're sensible, Paul and company do what they do for the Corinthians ("for you") as well as for God. However it's evaluated, then, Paul and company's behavior gives the Corinthians a basis for boasting in them (5:12).

Now Paul explains why they do what they do for God and the Corinthians. **5:14–15: For Christ's love constrains us since we've determined this, that one died for all. The all have died, then.** [15]**And he died for all in order that those who are living should no longer live for themselves—rather, for the one who for them died and was raised.** Here Paul adds Christ's love to "knowing the fear of the Lord" (5:11) as a motivation. "Since we've determined this" means that Paul and company have come to the conclusions that follow. According to 5:14 Christ died for the all who've died. According to 5:15 he died for those who are living. Most naturally, "those who are living" refers to those living at the time of Paul's writing, especially since it's only the living who can any longer live "for the one who for them died and was raised" rather than "for themselves." Correspondingly and contrastingly, "the all" who "have died" most naturally means those who've died by the time of Paul's writ-

ing. So Christ died for both the living and the dead. In view of Paul's reference to the living, though, what does he mean by saying, "The all [for whom Christ died] have died"? He must be reminding the Corinthians that "in Adam all die" (1 Corinthians 15:22; compare Romans 5:12–18). Paul's referring to Christ as "one" signals this reminder. The dead have already died in Adam. Barring the second coming beforehand, the living are yet to die in Adam. The switch from the present tense in 1 Corinthians 15:22 ("die") to the past tense here ("died") makes a parallel with the past tense of "died" in regard to Christ's death and stresses that because "in Adam *all* die," the living are as good as dead already (again barring the second coming beforehand). But what is it about Christ's having died for all which leads Paul to *reason* ("then" in the sense of "therefore") that all have died? It's that their dying in Adam led Christ to die for them—to give them eternal life, attained after death, we might say. True enough, but Paul expresses a more immediate purpose, namely, that he and his contemporaries ("those who are living") shouldn't live out the remainder of their lives "for themselves—rather, for the one who for them died and was raised." Because Christ died for all, this purpose includes living Christians and living non-Christians alike. But the purpose is attained only in the case of Christians. That Christ was raised for all as well as died for all implies, in accordance with 1 Corinthians 15, a consequent availability of resurrection and translation to eternal life for all who'll believe seriously, not just casually (see in particular 1 Corinthians 15:1–4).

5:16: And so, from now on we know no one according to flesh [that is, in a superficial way (compare 5:12)]. **Even though we did know Christ according to flesh, yet now we no longer know** [him that way]. "And so" introduces a consequence stemming from the constraint of Christ's love. It's that because he loved all human beings to the extent of dying for them all, Paul and his fellow evangelists don't take a superficial view of anybody, for everybody is a candidate for eternal life. "No longer" implies that prior to their conversions, they didn't regard people as candidates for eternal life. "Even though we did know Christ according to flesh" doesn't refer to knowing him during his earthly lifetime—rather, to a superficial view of him prior to believing in him (compare 1 Corinthians 1:23). "Yet now we no longer know [him that way]" implies a factual view of Christ through believing in him.

5:17–19: And so, if anyone [is] **in Christ,** [he's] a **new creation. The old things have passed away. Behold, new things have come into existence.** [18]**And all the** [new] **things** [are] **from God, who reconciled us to himself through Christ and gave us the serving of reconciliation,** [19]**to the effect that God was in Christ, reconciling the world to himself by not counting their trespasses against them** [compare Romans 4:8; Psalm 32:2] **and by placing in us the word** [= message] **of reconciliation.** "And so" in 5:16 introduced a consequence stemming from the *constraint* of Christ's love. "And so" now introduces a consequence stemming from Christ's love *itself*. It looks as though Paul's prior references to "the new covenant" (3:6; 1 Corinthians 11:25) have prompted him to speak here of "a new creation" in the case of "anyone" who is "in Christ." A believer is in Christ by having the Spirit that indwells Christ, so that the believer too indwells Christ (Romans 8:1–11). "Anyone" stems from regarding everybody as a candidate for eternal life (5:16) and defines the "new creation" in terms of an individual. "The old things" imply an old creation—that is, a pre-Christian self—characterized by sinful behaviors. But they've "passed away" (1 Corinthian 6:9–11; compare Ephesians 4:17–24). "Behold" calls special attention to the coming into existence of "new things," which consist in godly behaviors (Galatians 5:16–24; 6:15–16). But Paul's tracing all these new things back to God denies to anyone in Christ any credit for them. There's no room for self-righteousness, in other words.

"Who reconciled us [Paul and company] to himself through Christ" gives credit to God for reconciliation as well as for the change from sinful to godly behaviors, and also implies hostility toward God prior to the reconciliation, so that Paul now considers his past persecution of the church (Galatians 1:13; Philippians 3:6), which at the time seemed to represent zeal for God, hostility toward him. "Through Christ" alludes to Christ's dying "for all" (5:14–15)—more specifically, "for our sins" (1 Corinthians 15:3)—as making possible a righteous God's reconciling people to himself. "And gave us the serving of reconciliation" refers to God's having commissioned Paul and company to offer through the gospel reconciliation to God. "How that" introduces an elaboration of this reconciliation. "God was in Christ" plays on the earlier "if anyone [is] in Christ" and affirms God's presence in Christ (compare Colossians 1:19; 2:9) whereas any human being's presence in Christ is only a possibility (though, thankfully, a realized one in cases of conversion). The past tense of "was" looks back to God's presence in Christ during Christ's earthly sojourn for the purpose of effecting reconciliation "through Christ." "Reconciled *us* to himself" changes to "reconciling the *world* to himself." "The world" is the world of all human beings, no longer just Paul and company. But by no means do all human beings accept reconciliation to God (see 2:14–16, for example). So "reconciling the world to himself" has the sense of laying the groundwork for an attempt at reconciliation. "By not counting their [the world's] trespasses against them" is conditioned by acceptance of "the word of reconciliation," as implied in 5:20 by Paul and company's "begging" the Corinthians to be reconciled to God. Otherwise, there'd be no need for God to have "plac[ed] in [Paul and company] the word of reconciliation." And "not counting [the world's] trespasses against them" shows that God has graciously taken the initiative despite being the offended party, whereas normally the offending party has to seek reconciliation.

5:20-21: Therefore [because of God's having placed in us the message of reconciliation] **we're acting as am-**bassadors for Christ since God is making an entreaty through us. On Christ's behalf we're begging: Get reconciled to God! [21]He [God] made him who didn't know sin [Christ] a sin offering on our behalf in order that in him we might become God's righteousness. The distinction between "we" and "you" shows that preceding instances of "we," "us," and "our" have referred to Paul and company as distinct from the Corinthians, though much that he has said about himself and his colleagues can have a broader application. "Begging on Christ's behalf" defines "acting as ambassadors for Christ." Ultimately, though, God is the one who urges reconciliation, for he's the one who "was in Christ, reconciling the world to himself" and "placing in [Paul and company] the word of reconciliation" (5:19). Paul doesn't say whom he and his associates are begging, or to whom God is making an entreaty through them. "The world" as objects of reconciliation in 5:19 and "human beings" as objects of persuasion in 5:11 suggest a general audience for the begging and the entreaty. But a general audience includes the Corinthians; Paul is about to entreat the Corinthians "not to receive God's grace [from which originated reconciliation and saving righteousness] ineffectually" (6:1); and a minority in the Corinthian church still oppose Paul and company, as implied both by "the majority" in the Corinthian church who according to 2:6 have punished Paul's opponent and by Paul's self-defense throughout chapters 10–13 (see 6:12, too). So the objects of God's entreaty and of Paul and company's begging include these opponents along with outright unbelievers. Since by God's commission Paul and company are acting as Christ's ambassadors, opposition to them counts as failure to be reconciled to God (compare 6:11–13; 7:2). Not only for the outside world, then, but also for some in the Corinthian church the salvation that reconciliation ensures stands in jeopardy (compare 13:5; 1 Corinthians 15:1–2).

To know sin is to experience it as a force that corrupts your conduct (compare Romans 7:7–8). "Him who didn't know sin" therefore describes Christ as sinless in his conduct and, therefore again, capable of being sacrificed as a sin offering on behalf of sinners (such as Paul and company, but all others too). Many translations read "sin" rather than "sin offering"; but in a Greek translation of the Old Testament that Paul often quotes, "sin" means "sin offering" in Exodus 29:14; Leviticus 4:24; Numbers 18:9 (compare Isaiah 53:9–11), so that Paul is playing on two meanings of a single word: (1) a wrongdoing in "didn't know sin" and (2) an atoning sacrifice for wrongdoing in "made him . . . a sin offering" (compare the requirement that animals sacrificed as sin offerings be unblemished with Christ's not knowing sin as qualifying him to be made a sin offering). That is to say, the transfer of sin from a sinner to the sacrificial offering is so thorough that the offering is called sin itself. In Christ, then, a believer has already died sacrificially for his own sins.

"Becoming God's righteousness in Christ" doesn't mean becoming righteous in conduct (though that should follow, and does follow, in cases of true conversion). For Paul references *God's* righteousness, not ours.

And what is that? It's God's doing the right thing by reconciling to himself sinners who by faith have come to be in Christ, their sin offering (compare Romans 3:21–26 and the frequent Old Testament parallels between God's righteousness and salvation, for example in Psalms 51:14; 71:15–16; 98:1–3; Isaiah 45:8, 21–25; 46:13; 51:5–6, 8; 56:1 [and so on]). "*Become* God's righteousness" matches God's having "*made* [Christ] . . . a sin offering." But what does it mean to become God's righteousness? Well, just as in Galatians 3:13 Christ "became" a curse in the sense that he became the object of God's curse (see Deuteronomy 21:23, which Paul quotes), so "becom[ing] God's righteousness" means becoming the objects of his saving righteousness, of his declaring sinners righteous because Christ as a sin offering has enabled God not to count their trespasses against them yet remain righteous himself in not doing so. Just as being made sin indicates a thorough unification of sin with a sacrificial offering for sin, so becoming God's righteousness indicates a thorough unification of that righteousness with believing sinners and thus ensures the salvation entailed in their reconciliation. The abruptness with which Paul introduces the whole statement in 5:21 lays great emphasis on it as a description of the mode of reconciliation.

6:1–2: And while working together we're also entreating you not to receive God's grace ineffectually [literally: "with an empty result"]. **²For he's saying, "I heeded you at an acceptable time, and during a day of salvation I helped you** [Isaiah 49:8]." **Behold, now** [is] **a fully acceptable time! Behold, now** [is] **a day of salvation!** Since in 5:20 Paul said, "God is making an entreaty through us," the phrase "while working together" refers here to Paul and company's working together with God. "We're *also* entreating *you*" specifies the Corinthians as among the "human beings" (5:11)—that is, "the world" (5:19)—whom Paul and company are trying to persuade to be reconciled to God. "Not to receive God's grace ineffectually" points to the danger that the Corinthians will lose out on salvation unless they're reconciled to him (see the comments on 5:20–21). A quotation of Isaiah 49:8 and two following exclamations support the entreaty with an indication that it's not too late for reconciliation and salvation. The escalation of "an acceptable time" to "a *fully* acceptable time" highlights this opportunity. But the two occurrences of "now" imply that the opportunity won't last indefinitely. Moreover, an acceptable time and a day of salvation imply an unacceptable time and a day of damnation looming on the horizon.

6:3–10: [We're] **not giving** [anyone] **even a single reason to stumble in even a single thing** [that we do or say], **lest the serving** [of reconciliation (5:18)] **be faulted. ⁴Instead, in everything as God's servants** [we're] **commending ourselves in much endurance: in afflictions, in hardships, in tight predicaments, ⁵in beatings, in prisons, in riots, in toils, in sleepless** [nights], **in fastings, ⁶in purity, in knowledge, in patience, in magnanimity, in the Holy Spirit, in unhypocritical love, ⁷in the word of truth, in the power of God, through the weapons of righteousness for the right** [hand] **and the left, ⁸through glory and dishonor, through ill repute and good repute, as deceitful and truthful, ⁹as being unknown and being well known, as dying and—behold, we're living!—as being disciplined and not being put to death, ¹⁰as being saddened but always rejoicing, as poverty-stricken but enriching many, as having nothing and having all things securely.** This description of Paul and company's evangelistic and pastoral work is designed to elicit a favorable response to the preceding entreaty that the Corinthians "not . . . receive God's grace ineffectually." How could they do so, given the sterling character of Paul and company's working together with God in their behalf? Points of emphasis are evident in "not giving [anyone] *even a single reason* to stumble in *even a single thing* [that we do or say]" and "in *everything* . . . commending ourselves." But "as God's servants" and "lest the serving [of reconciliation] be faulted" show Paul and company to be acting out of concern for the gospel, not out of self-aggrandizing interests (compare 1 Corinthians 10:32–33). There follows a list of vicissitudes, all of which have required "much endurance." Next comes a list of personal virtues describing the manner in which Paul and company serve reconciliation to people. These virtues are mixed with the Holy Spirit, the source of virtues (Galatians 5:22–23), and with "the word of truth" (= the speaking of the gospel as truth) and "the power of God" (which accompanies speaking the word of truth [4:7; 1 Corinthians 1:18; 2:4]). Paul will take no credit either for the virtues or for the power; but he does take care to describe his and his colleagues' love as "unhypocritical," for they aren't "huckstering God's word," as many do (2:17).

The mention of God's power leads to a military metaphor: "through the weapons of righteousness." This metaphor implies fighting. Under the assumption that most soldiers are right-handed, "for the right [hand] and the left" describes the weapons as offensive, the right hand being used to wield a sword, and defensive, the left hand being used to hold a shield. Paul doesn't specify the weapons, though (contrast Ephesians 6:16–17), so that the accent falls on the generality of being well-equipped to fight. The weapons bear some relation to "righteousness." Paul has recently mentioned God's saving righteousness (see 5:21 with comments). Afflictions, beatings, imprisonments, and riots made for a conflict not of Paul's choosing, but a conflict necessitating a fight if this righteousness of God was to prevail. So the weapons are to be used evangelistically in fighting for his righteousness. "*Through* the weapons" indicates means of warfare (compare 10:3–6). "*Through* glory and dishonor" and "*through* ill repute and good repute" indicate circumstances in which the fighting takes place. Fundamentally, it doesn't matter to Paul and company whether people heap on them glory or dishonor, defame them or laud them. Nor does it fundamentally matter to them whether people accuse them of deceit or recognize their truthfulness, whether people ignore them or promote them, whether people persecute them to the verge of death. At this juncture Paul breaks his pattern by interjecting the triumphant exclamation, "Behold, we're living!" (compare 1:8–11; 4:8–11, 16; Psalm 118:17–18), and then returns to his pattern with "as being disciplined [which refers to punishments imposed by Jewish and Roman authorities (11:24–25a)] and not put to death." "As being saddened" alludes especially to the sadness caused Paul by opposition to him in the Corinthian church (2:1–4; but see also Romans 9:1–3). "But *always* rejoicing" describes him and his coworkers as rejoicing even when saddened intermittently (compare Philippians 3:1; 4:4; Colossians 1:24; 1 Thessalonians 5:16). "As poverty-stricken" refers to their economic distress because of devotion to evangelistic work. "But enriching many" refers to their enriching people through evangelism with "the grace of our Lord, Jesus Christ" (8:9). "As having nothing" makes the poverty complete in that even meager possessions in the present age don't have lasting value. "And having all things securely" refers to the permanent possession of all that really counts (see 1 Corinthians 3:21–23 and Romans 8:16–39, especially 8:16–17, 32). With this whole paragraph compare 11:23–28 and see examples scattered throughout Acts 13–28.

AN EXHORTATION TO MUTUAL AFFECTION
AND SEPARATION FROM UNBELIEVERS
2 Corinthians 6:11–7:1

6:11–13: Our mouth stands open to you, Corinthians. In other words, Paul and company have spoken freely and frankly to the Corinthians, and are prepared to continue speaking thus. The direct address "Corinthians" suits this frankness and appropriately introduces a statement of affection: **Our heart stands widened** [so as to contain you with affection]. **¹²You're not being narrowed down in us, but you *are* being narrowed down in your affections** [so as to exclude us]. **¹³But by way of the same requital** [that is, in an equal exchange]—**I'm speaking as to children—you too be widened** [in your affections toward us]. "You're not being narrowed down in us" means that Paul and company aren't excluding the Corinthians from a place in their hearts. "But you *are* being narrowed down in your affections" means that the Corinthians are constricting themselves through a failure to include Paul and company in their affections. He's referring to ongoing opposition to him on the part of a minority in the Corinthian church. The false apostles whom Paul will attack in chapter 10–13 are probably aiding and abetting the opposition. (He uses a word for "affections" that in its collective physical sense refers to the heart, lungs, kidneys, liver, and spleen—all located in the upper torso—as distinct from the bowels, which are lower down.) The exhortation that the Corinthians "be widened" in their affections toward Paul and company as the heart of Paul and company is already "widened" toward them—this exhortation gets emphasis from the interjection, "I'm speaking as to children." Is Paul calling them *his* children, figuratively speaking, because of having converted them? Perhaps so, but we might have

expected him to attach "my" for that meaning, as in 1 Corinthians 4:14, 17; Galatians 4:19; 2 Timothy 2:1; Philemon 10. Exceptions occur only in letters to his associates (1 Timothy 1:2, 18; 2 Timothy 1:2; Titus 1:4). So it's likely either that Paul is trying to shame the Corinthians by comparing them to children who need a good talking-to, or that he's leaving it ambiguous whether the comparison shows his disgust or his affection. Then the Corinthians' response will decide the meaning.

6:14–18: Stop becoming disparately yoked with unbelievers. For what partnership [do] righteousness and lawlessness [have with each other]? Or what fellowship [does] light [have] with darkness? ¹⁵And what concord [does] Christ [have] with Beliar? Or what stake [does] a believer [have] with an unbeliever? ¹⁶And what agreement [does] God's temple [have] with idols? For we are the temple of the living God, just as God said, "I'll dwell in them and walk around in [them] **and be their God, and they'll be my people** [Leviticus 26:11–12; Jeremiah 32:38; Ezekiel 37:27]." ¹⁷**Therefore "come out from their midst** [compare Ezekiel 20:34] **and be marked off from them," says the Lord, "and don't ever touch an unclean thing** [Isaiah 52:11]," **and I'll welcome you in ¹⁸and be a father to you, and you'll be to me sons and daughters, says the Lord Almighty** [compare Deuteronomy 32:19; 2 Samuel 7:14; Isaiah 43:6]. Paul has just scored the Corinthians for unnaturally breaking off from him and his colleagues, and told them to ally themselves again with him and his colleagues. Now he scores the Corinthians for allying themselves unnaturally with non-Christians and tells them to break these alliances. "Disparately yoked" represents the alliances under the figure of different species of animals—say, an ox and a donkey—yoked together to pull something, such as a plow—a practice prohibited in Deuteronomy 22:10. To support the disparity in a yoking of believers with unbelievers Paul asks five rhetorical questions, to each of which the unstated but obvious answer is "None at all." Since he has recently said that believers "become God's righteousness" in Christ (5:21), "righteousness" stands for believers in the question, "For what partnership [do] righteousness and lawlessness [have with each other]?" But "righteousness" has shifted in meaning from God's saving righteousness (so 5:21) to the righteous behavior of believers, as indicated by the contrast with "lawlessness," which stands for unbelievers. (You *are* how you *behave*.) "Lawlessness" refers to the breaking of God's laws.

"Light" stands for believers as "sons of light" (1 Thessalonians 5:5; compare 2 Corinthians 4:6), whereas "darkness" stands for unbelievers (compare Ephesians 5:8). "Christ" represents believers, since they are in Christ (as most recently according to 5:21), whereas "Beliar," a derogatory name for Satan,¹ represents unbelievers, since he's "the god of this age" (4:4). These representations become clear-cut with "a believer" and "an unbeliever"

---

¹"Beliar" probably combines an Old Testament word for "worthlessness" with "Baal," the name of a pagan god.

in the fourth rhetorical question. And "God's temple" stands for believers—as explained in the followup, "For we are the temple of the living God" and also as indicated earlier in 1 Corinthians 3:16–17; 6:19—so that "idols" stands for unbelievers. (You *unite* with what you *worship*.) But lying behind this fifth and last rhetorical question is the lack of an idol in God's temple in Jerusalem, whereas pagan temples were built for the purpose of housing an idol. Righteousness and lawlessness oppose each other. So too do light and darkness, Christ and Beliar, God's temple and idols. Therefore believers should oppose unbelievers when it comes to religious and moral issues in which unbelievers take the wrong side. "Partnership," "fellowship," "concord," "stake," and "agreement" express synonymously what believers and unbelievers do *not* have with each other. "Lawlessness" and "idols" imply that disparate yoking with unbelievers leads to moral and religious degradation, perhaps apostasy (compare 1 Corinthians 6:18; 10:14).

Paul doesn't define what counts as a disparate yoke. But his insistence that Christians not have sex with prostitutes (1 Corinthians 6:15–18), that a Christian widow remarry "only in the Lord" (1 Corinthians 7:39), and that Christians not participate in idolatrous feasts (1 Corinthians 8–10) gives us some idea of what he means by a disparate yoke. (At the same time, 1 Corinthians 5:9–13; 10:27 keep us from thinking he's prohibiting morally and religiously uncompromising social relations with non-Christians.) "Living" contrasts "God" with "idols." His dwelling in believers constitutes them his temple, which by definition is the dwelling place of a god. Because they're dead, idols don't walk around in their temples. But because he's "living," God does walk around in believers, regarded collectively, so that they have fellowship with him (see 1 Corinthians 3:16; 6:19 for his doing so through the Holy Spirit). Since he's "their God" and they "[his] people," they should have nothing to do with idols. "Come out from their midst" calls for a moral and religious separation from unbelievers (morality and religion being at least intertwined if not indistinguishable). "Be marked off from them" calls for moral and religious distinctiveness. "Don't ever touch an unclean thing" shifts an Old Testament requirement of ritual purity to a requirement of moral and religious purity (7:1; compare 1 Thessalonians 5:22). As a temple building requires ritual purity, so Christians as the temple of God's Spirit are to maintain moral and religious purity. The imagery of a temple then shifts to that of a family into which God welcomes believers as their Father and them as his sons and daughters. This welcome *into* God's family compensates for Christians' coming *out* from unbelievers' midst. (But 1 Corinthians 7:12–14 calls for Christians to maintain, if possible, marriages made to non-Christians prior to the Christians' conversion.)

7:1: **Therefore, since we have these promises, beloved, let us cleanse ourselves from every defilement of the flesh and spirit, bringing consecration to completion in the fear of God** [compare 5:11]. "Therefore" would have sufficed by itself to base the following exhortation on the preceding promises of a divine welcome into God's family. But to highlight them, Paul adds "since we have these promises"; and their familial nature leads him to insert the affectionate address, "beloved." After all, he has been stressing his and his coworkers' affection for the Corinthians (6:11–13) and is about to do so again (7:3). "Let *us* cleanse ourselves" prolongs the familial note by including Paul and company along with the Corinthians. The exhortation interprets the commands in 6:14–17 against disparate yoking with unbelievers and against "touch[ing] an unclean thing" in terms of a self-cleansing; and "from every defilement of the flesh and spirit" interprets "the unclean thing" as moral rather than ritual. "Of the flesh" defines the defilement especially in terms of sexual immorality (see 1 Corinthians 6:9). "And [of] the spirit" defines the defilement in terms of idolatry and covetousness and their effects (see 6:16; 1 Corinthians 6:9–10). But *every* defilement" embraces all sins as moral stains, any one of which would prevent "bringing consecration to completion" (compare 1 Corinthians 7:34; 1 Thessalonians 5:23). To consecrate is to set apart for sacred use or activity, so that "consecration" suits the commands in 6:14–17 to "stop becoming disparately yoked with unbelievers," to "come out from their midst and be marked off from them," and to "never touch an unclean thing" (compare "being transformed into the same image [as Christ] from glory to glory" [3:18]). Paul sets out "complete consecration" as Christians' goal, and "the fear of God" as motivating the effort to reach that goal. Professing Christians not engaged in this effort have something to fear from God.

JOY OVER TITUS'S REPORT
2 Corinthians 7:2–16

7:2–3: **Make room for us** [in your hearts (compare 6:11)]. **We've treated no one unjustly. We've corrupted no one. We've exploited no one. [3]I'm not saying** [so] **to condemn** [you]**, for I've told you before that you're in our hearts so as to die with** [you] **and to live with** [you]. In 6:12–13 Paul told the Corinthians that they were being "narrowed down in their affections" so as to exclude him and his colleagues, and therefore commanded them to "be widened." Now he harks back to that command but shifts from "be widened" to "Make room for us" (the opposite of being "narrowed down"). Three denials eliminate reasons that would keep the Corinthians from making room in their hearts for Paul and company. A staccato-style in the renewed command and three subsequent denials lends emphasis to the whole. "We've treated no one unjustly" may deny any injustice in Paul's command to ostracize the man cohabiting with his father's wife (1 Corinthians 5) and/or in the command to discipline Paul's opponent (2:5–11; 7:12). "We've corrupted no one" probably has to do with morals (compare 1 Corinthians 15:33), and "we've exploited no one" probably has to do with financial matters (compare 2:17; 8:20–21; 12:17–18). "I'm not saying [so] to condemn [you]" means that Paul's denials don't imply charges of injustice, corruption, or exploitation on the Corinthians' part. "For I told you before that you're in our hearts" supports that nonimplication with a reminder of Paul's telling them in 3:2, "You yourselves are our letter [of recommendation], inscribed in our hearts" (compare 6:11: "Our heart stands widened [so as to contain you with affection]"). Here he adds "so as to die with [you] and to live with [you]," which indicates love so strong as to make him and his colleagues ready to die with the Corinthians (in martyrdom, presumably) as well as to stay alive with them (in Christian witness, again presumably). For emphasis, "to die" precedes "to live," because sharing death requires greater love than sharing life does (compare 2 Samuel 15:21).

7:4a–b: I have much boldness of speech toward you. I have much boasting about you. "I have much boldness of speech" interprets "Our mouth stands open to you" back in 6:11 as a figure for free and frank speech, but the switch from "our" to "I" focuses attention on Paul's speech in this letter. See the footnote to 1 Corinthians 9:15–16 for good as well as bad boasting. The present boasting is good, and for emphasis Paul describes both his boldness and his boasting as "much." In other words, he speaks very freely and frankly *to* the Corinthians and very proudly to others *about* the Corinthians; and the complimentary speech addressed to others about them offsets the critical speech addressed directly to them.

7:4c–7: I'm filled with encouragement. I'm overjoyed in every affliction of ours. ⁵For also when we came into Macedonia, our flesh had no rest at all; rather, [we were] being afflicted in every [way]: conflicts [stemming] from outside, fears [stemming] from inside. ⁶**But the one who encourages the dejected—** [namely,] **God—encouraged us by Titus's coming; ⁷and not only by his coming, but also by the encouragement with which he was encouraged by you, as he an**nounced to us your longing [for us], your mourning [for having rebelled against me], **your zeal in my behalf** [by way of disciplining my opponent], **so that I rejoiced** [even] **more . . . .** The mention of encouragement and joy follows naturally from Paul's "much boasting" about the Corinthians, but "*filled* with encouragement" and "*over*joyed" reinforce that boasting. "In every affliction of ours" escalates the encouragement and joy even further in that without exception they topped the afflictions. "For also" introduces an explanation of this topping as an additional comment. See the introduction to 2 Corinthians for Paul and Timothy's "com[ing] into Macedonia." "Our flesh had no rest at all" refers to persecution so severe that it attenuated and endangered their physical lives, as immediately indicated by the phrase, "being afflicted in every [way]." (Paul "had no rest in [his] spirit [= no peace of mind]" according to 2:13, but that had to do with emotional distress over not finding Titus in Troas before proceeding to Macedonia.) "Conflicts [stemming] from outside" refers to "being afflicted." "Fears [stemming] from inside" refers to a re-

newal in Macedonia of the despair that was felt earlier in Asia (1:8–9). Together, the external conflicts and the internal fears made for "being afflicted *in every way*" and consequently "dejected."

Always concerned for the glory of God, Paul both describes him as the one "who encourages the dejected" (compare 1:3–4; Isaiah 49:13; 54:11), for emphasis puts this description ahead of "God," and cites God's twofold encouragement of him and Timothy (1) "by Titus's coming" and (2) "by the encouragement with which he [Titus] was encouraged by you [the Corinthians]." "And not only by his coming, but also by . . ." underscores the Corinthians' encouragement of Titus as evident in his reporting the Corinthians' longing for good relations with Paul and company, mourning for having spoiled such relations with him, and exercising zeal to restore them by disciplining his opponent (compare 2:5–11). "So that I rejoiced [even] more" means that Paul's joy over Titus's report exceeded the joy over Titus's coming. The infliction of punishment on Paul's opponent "by the majority" and therefore not by all the Corinthians (2:6), plus Paul's saying *in this letter* that the Corinthians "are being narrowed down in [their] affections [so as to exclude him and his colleagues]" (6:12), means that Titus reported the longing, mourning, and zeal of the majority and that for the moment Paul is ignoring the continuing recalcitrance of the minority, and is doing so for a conciliatory lead into his plea that the Corinthians contribute generously to a collection (chapters 8–9). He's saving till chapters 10–13 the ammunition he'll use against the minority.[2]

To spell out a reason for rejoicing even more over Titus's report than over the coming of Titus, Paul continues his sentence in **7:8–11: because even though I made you sorrowful by** [my] **letter, I don't regret** [having done so], **even though I did regret** [it]. **For I see that that letter made you sorrowful, though even for an hour** [that is, only briefly]. ⁹**Now I'm rejoicing, not because you were made sorrowful—rather, because you were made sorrowful to the point of repentance. For you were made sorrowful in accordance with God, so that you weren't incurred a loss by us in anything.** ¹⁰**For sorrow in accordance with God works an unregrettable repentance resulting in salvation, but the world's sorrow works out death.** ¹¹**For behold, what eagerness this very being-made-sorrowful in accordance with God has worked out for you—rather,** [what] **defense** [of yourselves]; **rather,** [what] **indignation; rather,** [what] **fear; rather,** [what] **longing; rather,** [what] **zeal; rather,** [what] **retribution! In everything you've commended yourselves to be pure in the matter** [of my opponent]. Paul's letter that made the Corinthians sorrowful was the now-lost letter that he wrote to them "through many tears" (2:4). Out of love for the

---

[2]The explanation that opposition to Paul revived during a break in dictation between chapters 8–9 and 10–13, so that during the dictation of 1–9 the entirety of the Corinthian church had reconciled with him—this explanation neglects 2:6; 6:12.

Corinthians (see 2:4 again), he at first regretted having saddened them with that letter. But no longer, because their sorrow lasted only briefly. Not only does he no longer need to harbor regret, then. He now rejoices, not merely because their sorrow has ceased but also because it prompted them to repent, that is, to reform their attitude toward Paul and obey his instructions.

Four successive sentences beginning with "For" explain the repentance-prompting sorrow: (1) It agrees with God's will that people repent of their wrongdoings. (2) In the Corinthians' case, they didn't suffer any loss by repenting at Paul's behest. (3) On the contrary and again as in the Corinthians' case, such sorrow works a repentance that won't be regretted, because the repentance results in salvation. So nothing less than salvation was at stake in the Corinthians' relation to Paul, an apostolic stand-in for the Lord Jesus. The sorrow of the world—that is, of unbelievers—works out death because it lacks the element of repentance (see 1 Thessalonians 4:13 for the world's sorrow). As opposed to "salvation," "death" refers to eternal punishment (2:15–16). "Works out" seems stronger than "works" and probably stresses such death to highlight salvation by contrast.

The fourth successive sentence beginning with "For" and explaining the sorrow that prompts repentance adds "this very" to "being-made-sorrowful" and gets the exclamation, "behold what . . . !" for a climactic emphasis. The exclamation lists seven outcomes of this sorrow: (1) "eagerness" to do God's will as represented in Paul's instructions; (2) "defense" in the sense of the Corinthians' clearing themselves of guilt by repenting of their wrongs; (3) "indignation" over the opposition to Paul that arose in their midst; (4) "fear" of God (7:1); (5) "longing" to restore good relations with Paul; (6) "zeal" in disciplining the leader of opposition to him; and (7) "retribution" consisting in the discipline itself. The introduction of the second and remaining outcomes with a repeated "rather" creates a cascade of outcomes, as though each preceding outcome didn't suffice to put a finishing touch on the list, so manifold are the commendatory outcomes. "In everything" pronounces the outcomes as complete, and "as pure in the matter" declares the Corinthians absolved.

7:12–13a: Even though I wrote to you, then, [I did so] **not on account of the one who'd treated** [me] **unjustly, nor on account of the one who'd been treated unjustly** [me]—**rather, on account of** [the need that] **your eagerness in our behalf might be displayed to you in God's sight.** [13a]**We've been encouraged because of this.** As a consequence of having pronounced the Corinthians now "pure" in the matter of his opponent, Paul denies that he wrote his tearful letter to avenge himself as "the one who'd been treated unjustly" on "the one who'd treated [him] unjustly" (that is, his opponent). He wrote instead to prompt a display of the Corinthians' eagerness to do God's will in Paul and company's behalf—a display *to the Corinthians themselves*, as though they were unaware of their own eagerness. This way of putting their eagerness compliments them despite the temporary hiddenness of the eagerness, a hiddenness resulting from

the influence of Paul's opponent in their midst. "In God's sight" assures them that he too has seen this display—approvingly, it needn't be said, in view of preceding references to being made repentantly sorrowful "in accordance with God" (7:9–11). "We've been encouraged because of this [display of 'eagerness in our behalf']" implies that the display hasn't gone unnoticed by Paul and company, but stresses again the encouragement of them to set the stage for his next statement.

7:13b–14: And on [top of] **the encouragement of us** [by your display of "eagerness in our behalf"], **we rejoiced extraordinarily more over the joy of Titus, because his spirit has been refreshed by all you,** [14]**because if I've boasted somewhat to him about you I've not been shamed** [by you]; **rather, as we've spoken all things to you in truth** [= truthfully], **so too our boasting** [about you] **before Titus has turned out to be the truth.** Encouragement breeds joy, and Titus's joy has made Paul and Timothy's joy flourish all the more. Joy is contagious, and mutuality of joy heightens the degree of joy. "*Extraordinarily* more" indicates a heightening to the nth degree. "Because his [Titus's] spirit has been refreshed" brings out the inwardly restorative power of joy. "By all of you" ignores again the still-recalcitrant minority in the Corinthian church (see the footnote to 7:4–7). Paul is addressing the repentant majority. An added element in his joy consists in most of the Corinthians' having proved truthful his boasting about them to Titus when sending him on a delicate mission to the Corinthian church. Had a majority not responded with sorrowful repentance, they'd have shamed Paul because of a false boast. Happily, that was not to be. "*If* I've boasted *somewhat* to him about you" indicates that the majority's repentance-producing sorrow more than matched Paul's hesitant, low-key boasting about them.

7:15–16: And his affections for you are extraordinary as he remembers the obedience of all you, [that is,] **how you welcomed him with fear and trembling.** [16]**I'm rejoicing because in every respect I have confidence in you.** Paul continues addressing the majority and ignoring the minority, so that "all you" encompasses all within this limited address. To prepare them for another mission of Titus to them—that is, for taking up a collection (chapters 8–9)—Paul mentions Titus's affections for them, describes the affections as extraordinary, and attributes the affections to Titus's recollecting these Corinthians' obedience to Paul's instruction, relayed by Titus during his earlier visit, that the opponent of Paul be disciplined. It was that obedience which constituted the way they "welcomed [Titus] with fear and trembling," and it was a recognition that their very salvation was at stake (7:10) which sparked the fear and trembling. Finally Paul rementions his own ongoing joy (compare 7:7, 9, 13) on the basis of having confidence in them. The prefixing of "in every respect" implies confidence that just as they obeyed the instruction to discipline his opponent, they will obey his upcoming instruction to contribute generously to a collection.

AN EXHORTATION TO COMPLETE THE COLLECTION FOR CHRISTIANS IN JERUSALEM
2 Corinthians 8:1–9:15

This exhortation divides into several subsections: the good example of Christians in Macedonia (8:1–6); Jesus' good example (8:7–9); the ideal of equality (8:10–15); the coming of Titus and others to receive the collection (8:16–9:5); and God's reward for generosity (9:6–15).

THE GOOD EXAMPLE OF CHRISTIANS IN MACEDONIA
2 Corinthians 8:1–6

8:1–2: And [in this letter] **we're making known to you, brothers, God's grace, given among the churches of Macedonia, ²that in an extreme ordeal of affliction** [= persecution] **the flourishing of their joy and their abysmal poverty have flourished so as to result in the wealth of their generosity . . . .** The affectionate address "brothers" smooths Paul's way toward an exhortation to give generously out of financial resources. He sets out the Macedonian churches' generosity as an example of such giving. ("The churches of Macedonia" include at least those in Philippi, Thessalonica, and Berea [Acts 16:11–17:14], located in what is now northern Greece, where Paul was at the time of writing 2 Corinthians [2:13; 7:5–7].) To give credit to God rather than to the Macedonian churches, however, Paul "make[s] known" to the Corinthians "God's grace," which he describes as "given" among those churches, so that they've given generously because God has given them the grace of giving thus. All glory to him! And since "grace" means "favor," the opportunity to give is a sign of God's favor (compare 9:14 and 1 Corinthians 16:3, where the word here translated "grace" is translated "charity"). This divinely given grace/favor of giving is magnified by the circumstance of the Macedonians' "extreme ordeal of affliction" (compare Philippians 1:29–30; 1 Thessalonians 2:14; 3:4; Acts 16:11–17:14). Paul doesn't content himself with "affliction" alone, but describes it as "an ordeal" that's "extreme," all to magnify "God's grace." A still higher magnification of that grace, and derivatively of the Macedonians' example of generosity, accrues from the joy *with* which they've given and the poverty *out of* which they've given. Paul escalates their joy by saying that "the *flourishing* of their joy" has "*flourished.*" This redundancy is strikingly emphatic. And Paul deepens the Macedonians' poverty by describing it as "abysmal" and saying that it too has "flourished." You'd think that joy, especially the joy of giving, would have diminished rather than flourished when poverty, especially "abysmal poverty," flourished. But God's grace actualized the seemingly impossible flourishing of joy alongside the flourishing of abysmal poverty. And the result consisted not simply in "their generosity," but in "*the wealth* of their generosity." Only God's grace could have brought such wealth out of abysmal poverty.

8:3–6: because [the Macedonian churches contributed to the collection] **in accordance with** [their] **ability—even beyond** [their ability], **I'm testifying—as volunteers ⁴begging us with much urging for the grace** [= favor], **that is, the sharing of the service for the saints. ⁵And** [they gave] **not as we'd hoped; rather, they gave themselves first to the Lord and to us through God's will, ⁶so that we urged Titus that just as he'd earlier begun, so too he should bring to completion among you this grace as well.** This continuation of the sentence begun in 8:1–2 defines the just-mentioned "wealth of their generosity" in terms of the Macedonians' having given (1) according to their financial ability; (2) even beyond their financial ability; (3) as volunteers rather than as draftees; (4) as going beyond volunteering to the extent of begging to contribute; (5) as begging "with much urging" (compare the axiom of beggars that persistence pays off); and (6) as describing "the sharing of the service of the saints" as "the grace," that is, as a favor *for them*, the Macedonian contributors. It's a favor for the sharers to share, whereas the sharing is a "service for the saints." The Macedonians' giving voluntarily and beggingly beyond their financial ability seems so unlikely, if not impossible, that Paul testifies to his having witnessed for himself such giving. He doesn't identify where "the saints" who are to receive the collection live, but the Corinthians will have known from 1 Corinthians 16:1–4 and even earlier communication that those saints were living in Jerusalem. In distinction from non-Christians, "saints" designates Christians as consecrated to God. "The service for the saints" means serving them money to alleviate their poverty (about which see Romans 15:25–27, 31; Galatians 2:10). "Sharing" this service alludes to the participation also of churches outside Macedonia, such as the church in Corinth. "Not as we'd hoped" means that the Macedonians exceeded Paul and company's hope, not that they'd disappointed it; and "hoped" carries the connotation of expectation. Then Paul defines this exceeding of expectation as the Macedonians' giving themselves to the Lord (Jesus) and to Paul and company before giving their money generously to the collection. So the giving of money grew out of devotion to the Lord and his representatives. It also took place "through God's will." Not simply *in accordance with* God's will, but *through* it in that by giving the Macedonians his grace (8:1) he successfully willed the Macedonians' giving themselves to the Lord and his representatives (Paul and company). In view of 8:10–11; 9:1–2 it appears that on an earlier occasion, otherwise unspecified, Titus had begun taking a collection in the Corinthian church. The more recent example of the Macedonians has now prompted Paul and company to urge on Titus a completion of that task. Implied is that Titus will have carried this letter to the church in Corinth.

JESUS' GOOD EXAMPLE
2 Corinthians 8:7–9

8:7–9: Nonetheless, as indeed you're flourishing in every respect—[in] **faith and speech and knowledge**

and all eagerness and the love that [comes] **from us** [and settles] **in you**—[see] **that you flourish also in this grace.** ⁸**I'm not saying** [this] **by way of a command; rather,** [I'm] **making sure also of the genuineness of your love through the eagerness of others** [the Macedonian Christians]. ⁹**For you know the grace of our Lord, Jesus Christ, that because of you he, though being rich, became poor in order that by means of the poverty of that one** [Jesus Christ] **you might become rich.** "Nonetheless" signals a shift from the example of the Macedonians to the Corinthians, who are "flourishing in every respect." Paul defines this flourishing in terms of "faith" (which refers to an ability to believe God for extraordinary things above and beyond salvation), "speech" (which refers to prophesying, teaching, speaking in tongues, etc.), "knowledge" (which refers in particular to theological insight), "all eagerness" (about which see below), and "the love" that goes out from Paul and company and settles in the Corinthians (see 1 Corinthians 1:5, 7; 12:7–10; 13:2 with comments). Next, however, Paul tells them to "flourish also in this grace." At the moment, then, and despite their flourishing in every just-listed respect, they aren't flourishing in the grace/favor of contributing to the collection. Much less does their flourishing in the just-listed respects match the flourishing of the Macedonians' joy and abysmal poverty (8:1–2). But "indeed" emphasizes the Corinthians' flourishing in the respects they do flourish in; and this emphasis compliments them so as to make the following exhortation palatable. Moreover, the attachment of "all" to "eagerness" implies their eagerness to flourish in the grace of charitable giving just as according to 7:11–12 they eagerly mended fences with Paul by disciplining his opponent. A recollection of that earlier eagerness leads Paul to mention his and his colleagues' love for the Corinthians as a force that ought to spur their flourishing in the grace of giving too (compare 2:4). "Also in this grace" implies that their flourishing in faith, speech, knowledge, eagerness, and love is due to God's grace, as will prove true of their flourishing in contributions to the collection, and has already proved true in the Macedonians' case. Because the word translated "command" tends to carry a military overtone, "*not . . . by way of a command*" softens the exhortation to flourish in the grace of giving into a "making sure also of the genuineness of [the Corinthians'] love." Paul uses the Macedonians' "eagerness" as a metric with which to make sure of the genuineness of the Corinthians' love. "Also" implies that the Macedonians' eagerness proved their love genuine.

Because of Paul and company's love for the Corinthians, "your love" means the Corinthians' reciprocal love for Paul and company, to be expressed by an eager completion of the collection. "The grace of our Lord, Jesus Christ" constitutes the reason for making sure of the genuineness of the Corinthians' love. So his grace complements "God's grace" in 8:1. The Corinthians "know" the grace of Jesus Christ, whom Paul calls "our Lord" to distinguish him as the Christians' Lord from the

so-called lords worshiped by pagans (1 Corinthians 8:5–6) and to suit the description of him as "rich." For "Lord" means "Owner" (among other meanings). Knowing the Lord's grace includes experiencing it. Because of knowing it, the Corinthians can't plead ignorance as an excuse not to follow his example through giving—a more powerful example even than that of the Macedonians. Since elsewhere we have no evidence of Jesus' having been rich early in his earthly lifetime, the grace of Jesus Christ as Lord consists in his having given up his preincarnate heavenly wealth and becoming poor in earthly goods so that by means of his poverty others might become rich in eternal life. (Is Paul alluding to Jesus' dying so poor that even his clothes had been confiscated [Mark 15:24; Matthew 27:35; Luke 23:34; John 19:23–24]?) The Macedonians were involuntarily and purposelessly poor. But Jesus Christ made himself poor voluntarily and for the purpose of making others rich. "By means of the poverty *of that one*" highlights his example. "Because *of you*" and "in order that . . . *you* might become rich" apply the example pointedly to the Corinthians.

THE IDEAL OF EQUALITY
2 Corinthians 8:10–15

8:10–12: **And I'm giving a dictum in this** [matter of the collection]**, for this** [dictum-giving] **is beneficial to you, who as such started earlier—**[that is,] **last year— not only to do** [the collection] **but also to want** [to do it]**.** ¹¹**But now, complete the doing as well so that just as indeed** [there was] **the readiness of wanting** [to do it]**, so too** [there may be] **the completing** [of the collection] **out of** [your] **possessing** [of means to contribute]**.** ¹²**For if the readiness lies at hand,** [the contribution is] **very acceptable in accordance with whatever** [a person] **possesses, not in accordance with what he doesn't possess.** "Who *as such*" casts the Corinthians in the role of those who had "started earlier—[that is,] last year" and who therefore should play out their role by completing the collection. Paul's dictum that they *should* complete it is "beneficial" to them because it will *prompt* them to complete it. He supports the dictum (1) by complimenting them on their earlier "want[ing]" to do the collection," which he stresses with "the readiness of wanting," preceded by "indeed," and (2) by noting their possessing the means to contribute. Then he explains that given the readiness to contribute, financial resources determine what amount of contribution will be acceptable (compare 1 Corinthians 16:2: "whatever he's being prospered with"). But since the Macedonians have been lauded for giving beyond their means (8:3), "*very* acceptable" stresses that Paul doesn't expect the Corinthians to meet that standard.

8:13–15: **For** [I'm not saying this] **in order that others** [may have] **relief, you affliction—rather,** [I'm saying this] **out of** [a concern for] **equality.** ¹⁴**At the present time your surplus** [has] **the purpose of** [making up] **the deficit of those** [saints in Jerusalem] **in order that also the surplus of those** [saints] **may make up for your def-**

icit, so that equality may come about, ¹⁵just as it's written, "The one who [had] **much didn't have more** [than
he needed]**, and the one who** [had] **little didn't have
less** [than he needed] [Exodus 16:18]." "For" introduces
an explanation that Paul isn't showing favoritism toward
"others," that is, toward Christians in Jerusalem, who'll
get financial relief from the collection taken for them
and then delivered to them. Nor does Paul want the Corinthians to suffer an "affliction" consisting in financial
distress because of their having contributed to the collection. The lack of a connective, such as "and," between
"that others [may have] relief" and "you affliction" emphasizes Paul's denial of favoritism toward others. The
equality for which he aims characterizes true friendship
and has to do with Christians' meeting the basic needs
of one another. A reference to "the present time" implies
a future time and introduces an observation that over
the course of time, shifting financial circumstances will
determine who should give and who should receive. For
the moment the Corinthians' financial surplus has the
purpose, according to Paul's perception of God's will, of
meeting the financial deficit of Christians in Jerusalem.
But the reverse could be true in time to come. Paul draws
this principle of equality out of God's seeing to it, as recorded in Scripture, that the Israelites who'd gathered a
lot of manna didn't have any excess when it was measured, and that those who'd gathered little didn't have
any deficit when it was measured (see Exodus 16 for the
whole story concerning manna).

THE COMING OF TITUS AND OTHERS
TO RECEIVE THE COLLECTION
2 Corinthians 8:16–9:5

**8:16–17: But thanks to God, who gave the same
eagerness** [that we have] **for you in the heart of Titus,**
¹⁷**because he accepted** [our] **urging** [him to visit you
(see 8:6)]**, on the one hand. Being more eager** [than
mere acceptance of our urging]**, on the other hand, he
went out as a volunteer** [from us] **to you.** The past tense
in "he went out . . . to you" takes the standpoint of the
Corinthians after Titus's arrival with this letter. In 8:8
"eagerness" referred to the Macedonians' eagerness in
contributing to the collection. Here, then, "eagerness"
refers to Titus's eagerness to facilitate a completion of the
collection among the Corinthians. "The *same* eagerness"
matches this eagerness on the part of Titus with that of
Paul and Timothy (see 1:1 for Timothy in addition to
Paul). "In the *heart* of Titus" portrays his eagerness as
heartfelt and therefore genuine. With "on the one hand
. . . on the other hand" Paul sets out two evidences of this
heartfelt eagerness: (1) Titus's acceptance of Paul's and
Timothy's urging him to return to Corinth for a completion of the collection and (2) Titus's acceptance of their
urging because of his own independent will to return
for that purpose. His own will to return showed more
eagerness than accepting others' urging alone would
have shown. Overall, this portrayal of Titus's eagerness
recommends him in order that the Corinthians may co-

operate with him when he arrives, the present letter in
hand, to complete the collection. Nonetheless, thanks
for his eagerness don't go to him or to Paul and Timothy—rather, to God, who "gave" it to Titus (compare the
comments on 8:1, where the word translated "grace" is
the same as the word translated "thanks" here in 8:16).

**8:18–21: And we sent with him the brother, whose
praise in the gospel** [has spread] **throughout all the
churches,** ¹⁹**and not only** [that] **but also** [who] **has
been hand-picked by the churches** [to be] **our fellow
traveler** [from Corinth to Jerusalem] **with this grace** [=
charity] **that's being served by us** [to poverty-stricken
Christians in Jerusalem] **for the glory of the Lord
himself** [through thanksgivings for the financial relief
(9:11–13)] **and** [for] **our readiness,** ²⁰[we] **taking this
precaution** [of being accompanied by the unimpeachable brother] **lest anyone discredit us in this generosity**
[of the Macedonians and you] **that's being served by
us.** ²¹**For we're taking forethought in regard to good
things** [financially speaking] **not only in the Lord's
sight, but also in the sight of human beings** [compare
Proverbs 3:4]. Paul continues to take the temporal standpoint of the Corinthians after the arrival of Titus and
their consequent receipt of this letter. "The brother," a
fellow Christian, remains anonymous; but the Corinthians will have known him from his having accompanied Titus to Corinth. "Whose praise" recommends
the brother as trustworthy; so the Corinthians needn't
fear that he'll embezzle any of their contributions to the
collection. "In the gospel" portrays him as an evangelist
(compare Romans 1:9; Philippians 4:3; 1 Thessalonians
3:2). "Throughout all the churches" indicates that as a
widely traveled evangelist he's recognized universally
among Christians as trustworthy. "And not only [that]
but also" introduces with great emphasis the churches'
having "hand-picked" him to travel with Paul and company when they carry the collection to Jerusalem. That
the churches rather than Paul hand-picked him for this
mission forestalls any charge of cronyism on Paul's part,
such as the sending of Titus alone could have fostered.
Like other churches, then, the Corinthian church can
satisfy themselves that all their contributed money will
reach the recipients intended by the contributors. But
their satisfaction, though important, pales before the
purpose of bringing "glory" to "the Lord," whose person
is accented by the addition of "himself," and before the
purpose of putting into effect Paul and company's own
readiness to deliver all the money to poverty-stricken
Christians in Jerusalem. In other words, Paul and company are just as concerned as the churches are that all the
money reach those Christians—hence "this precaution."
"For" then introduces an elaboration of the precaution
in terms of "taking forethought" against the possibility
of someone's discrediting Paul and company by accusing
them of embezzlement, as though the large amount of
money indicated by "this generosity" could allow some
embezzlement to go undetected. The Lord sees all, but
human beings, whether Christian or non-Christian,
see only the obvious. Conscious not just of the Lord's

all-seeing eye but also of people's distrust, then, Paul and company are taking measures to make their rectitude obvious.

8:22–24: And we've sent with them [Titus and the aforementioned "brother"] **our brother, whom we've made sure of many times in many** [circumstances], [our brother] **being eager but now much more eager by reason of** [his] **much confidence in you.** ²³**And if** [someone has a question] **concerning Titus,** [he's] **my partner and fellow worker for you; and if our brothers** [are in question], [they're] **apostles of churches;** [they're] **the glory of Christ.** ²⁴**Therefore** [be] **demonstrating to them in the face** [= presence] **of the churches the demonstration of your love** [for them] **and of our boasting about you.** This second anonymous Christian brother differs from the preceding one and appears to be a member of Paul's team ("*our* brother"), whereas the preceding one ("*the* brother") appears to have been an itinerant evangelist independent from Paul but widely known and trusted among the churches and therefore hand-picked by them. As they have praised that brother, Paul now praises this one by saying he and his colleagues have made sure of their brother both "many times" and "in many [circumstances]," describing him as "eager" in the past and as "now *much more* eager" (in respect to the collection [see the comments on 8:16–17]). "By reason of [his] much confidence" tells why he's presently much more eager, and tells it in a way that should endear him to the Corinthians and thus make them cooperate with him in completing the collection. Though they know Titus face-to-face from his recent visit, Paul inserts a recommendation of him, too, by calling him "my partner and fellow worker"—therefore someone Paul himself trusts—and adds "for you" to assure them that Titus, like Paul, is looking out for their interests, not for his own and Paul's interests. Then Paul returns to the anonymous brothers. "Our" now applies to the one hand-picked by the churches as well as to Paul's associate, and this application undergirds the initial recommendation. To satisfy any lingering question about the brothers, Paul calls them "apostles of churches," that is, delegates sent by other churches to the church in Corinth to act on behalf of those other churches. Even Paul's associate is acting on their behalf (compare 1 Corinthians 16:3). So because those churches have sent these brothers as their apostles, the Corinthians need to show them love by cooperating with them in a completion of the collection. Otherwise the Corinthians will have openly thumbed their nose at fellow churches and broken Christian unity. Paul also calls the brothers "the glory of Christ," that is, a credit to Christ, men who bring him honor. For this reason, too, the Corinthians need to show them love. "The demonstration . . . of our boasting about you" implies that surely the Corinthians wouldn't want to shame themselves by showing themselves unworthy of that boasting. Never mind the shaming of Paul and company for having boasted about them unjustifiably. The redundant wordplay in "demonstrating . . . the demonstration" underscores the need to avoid shame.

9:1–2: For on the one hand it's superfluous for me to be writing to you about the service [= the collection] **for the saints** [in Jerusalem (see 1 Corinthians 16:1–4)]. ²**For I know your readiness, which I'm boasting about to the Macedonians in your behalf,** [saying,] **"Achaia** [the southern part of Greece, where Corinth is located] **has been prepared** [for the collection] **since last year"; and your zeal has enthused the majority** [of the Macedonian Christians to contribute]. Paul's knowing the Corinthians' readiness "since last year" to contribute to the collection supplies the reason why it's superfluous for him to be writing them about the collection, and this superfluousness supplies the reason why he and his associates have been boasting about the Corinthians as noted in 8:24 and reiterated here in 9:2. He has been writing them about the collection nevertheless, somewhat as we say, "Not to mention such-and-such," but mentioning it by saying we won't mention it. "Achaia" represents the Corinthian Christians according to their geographical location. Their "readiness" escalates to their "zeal," which in turn "has enthused the majority" of Macedonian Christians. Why "the majority" rather than "all"? Probably because their "abysmal poverty" (8:2) left some of them without any money at all to contribute.

9:3–5: On the other hand I've sent the brothers in order that our boast concerning you might not be voided [of truthfulness] **in this instance, in order that you may be prepared** [with your contribution] **just as I was telling** [the brothers you're prepared], ⁴**lest somehow if Macedonians come with me and find you unprepared we (not to say, "you") would be shamed in this assurance** [of your preparedness]. Paul wants to make sure that his assurance of the Corinthians' aforementioned "readiness" won't prove ill-founded. In particular, he wants to make sure that by the time he arrives in Corinth after the arrival of Titus and the anonymous brothers, the Corinthians' long-standing readiness to contribute will have translated into a contribution ready to be carried off to Jerusalem (compare 1 Corinthians 16:2: "in order that when I come no collections take place then"). It's for this purpose that he has sent Titus and the other two brothers ahead of him with the present letter. And he has another, underlying purpose—namely, that his boasting to the Macedonians about the Corinthians' readiness and zeal won't prove to have been unjustified and thus bring shame on Paul and company. The parenthetical "not to say, 'you'" includes the Corinthians' shaming of themselves should they not have their contribution prepared for sending. But Paul includes this possibility only as a sidelight to imply that they surely wouldn't want to shame themselves—though, given some of their members' continuing opposition to Paul, they might not mind the bringing of shame on Paul. The further possibility that Macedonians, to whom he has boasted about the Corinthians' readiness and zeal, will accompany Paul exacerbates any shame that would result. "Lest *somehow*" reflects Paul's hope—or is it a subliminal suggestion to the Corinthians?—that their shaming him and themselves is unlikely. ⁵**Therefore** [because of even the slight possibility of shaming us and yourselves by not having your contribution ready to go when I arrive] **I've considered it essential to urge the brothers that they should go to you in advance** [of me] **and arrange in advance your blessing** [= your contribution as a bountiful gift], **promised** [by you] **in advance** [at least "since last year" according to 9:2], **that this** [blessing] **might be ready in this way,** [that is,] **as a blessing** [a bountiful gift] **and not as covetousness** [a paltry gift due to the desire to have more for oneself (compare those Israelites who according to 8:15; Exodus 16:18 gathered more than the prescribed amount of manna)].

GOD'S REWARD FOR GENEROSITY
2 Corinthians 9:6–15

9:6–7: And [I'm saying] **this: he who sows sparingly will also reap sparingly, and he who sows blessingly** [= bountifully] **will also reap blessingly** [= bountifully] [compare Proverbs 11:24]. **⁷Each** [of you is to give] **just as he has purposed in advance in** [his] **heart, not out of sorrow** [over the sacrifice of his money] **or out of necessity** [due to being shamed if he doesn't give]. **For God loves a cheerful giver** [compare Deuteronomy 15:10; Proverbs 11:28; 22:8–9]. Paul uses an agricultural analogy both to explain what he meant in 9:5 by the contrast between "a blessing" and "covetousness" and to draw out their consequences. Sowing sparingly stands for giving money sparingly because of covetousness. Reaping sparingly stands for getting little help when financial fortunes plummet, and getting little because of having given little. Sowing bountifully stands for giving money bountifully because of cheer, that is, happiness in the letting go of money for others' benefit. Reaping bountifully stands for getting plenty of financial help when financial fortunes plummet, and getting plenty because of having given plenty (compare 8:13–15). "Each [of you is to give]" calls for every Corinthian believer to give, and "just as he has purposed in advance" bars the door against reducing the amount of money originally planned to be given. "In his heart" appeals to the heartfelt zeal that characterized the original plan. And God's love for a cheerful giver supplies a good reason to give bountifully as a result of giving cheerfully.

9:8–9: And God is able to make every grace [= favor] **flourish for you, in order that by always having all self-sufficiency in every** [circumstance] **you may flourish in every good** [= charitable] **deed, ⁹just as it stands written, "He scattered** [his money] **widely, he gave to the poor. His righteousness remains forever** [Psalm 112:9]**."** So cheerful givers in the Corinthian church needn't worry about falling into financial ruin because of their bountiful charity, for God is able to keep them from such ruin. Better yet, God is able to make every kind of financial favor ("every grace") flourish in their case, so that under no circumstances would they ever be at all financially dependent on other human beings, but instead would flourish in charitable giving every time fellow Christians in addition to those in Jeru-

salem need financial help. Of course, Paul has projected the possibility of a financial downturn for the Corinthians in the future (8:14). So here he says that God is *able* to make them flourish financially, not that God necessarily *will* do so. Not to worry, though. For either he'll do so, or he'll give to other churches the grace of giving to meet their financial needs. But to substantiate the possibility of financial flourishing, Paul cites Scripture. "He scattered widely" means that a cheerful giver distributes his money to others rather than hoarding it for himself. "The poor," who by definition are destitute and therefore dependent on charity, constitute the beneficiaries of his distribution, and the distribution counts as "his righteousness" (compare Matthew 6:1–4, where almsgiving counts as an element in "your righteousness"). The remaining of the giver's righteousness "forever" means that because his giving is cheerful, he'll continue giving charitably as long as he lives. ("Forever" doesn't always mean "eternally." See, for example, John 8:35, where because of the Mosaic law requiring a release of slaves every sabbatical year it's said that a slave doesn't abide in a household forever, but that a son does abide in a household forever, that is, as long as he lives.)

9:10–12: And he [God] **who abundantly supplies "seed to the sower and bread for eating** [Isaiah 55:10]**" will supply and multiply your seed and cause the produce of your righteousness to grow** [compare Hosea 10:12], **¹¹**[you] **being made rich in every** [circumstance] **for the purpose of every generosity, which** [generosity] **as such is effecting through us** [in the present case] **thanksgiving to God, ¹²because the serving** [up] **of this religious duty is not only filling up the saints' deficits completely, but also** [is] **flourishing through many thanksgivings to God . . . .** Paul predicts for the Corinthians financial prosperity due to God's abundant supply. As God abundantly supplies agricultural seed for farmers to sow and the consequent bread for them and their families to eat, so he'll multiply the Corinthians financial seed, just as seed harvested exceeds in volume seed sown, and "will cause the produce of [the Corinthians'] righteousness to grow," that is, will prosper them financially because of their almsgiving. "Being made rich" then interprets the agricultural metaphors in terms of financial prosperity. "In every [circumstance]" echoes 9:8. "For the purpose of every generosity" means that God will prosper the Corinthians financially so that they may give generously of their means on later occasions of fellow Christians' needs. Prosperity for philanthropy, in other words. Not prosperity for pleasure.

"Which [generosity] *as such* is effecting . . . thanksgiving" indicates that it's in the very nature of generosity to generate thanksgiving to God for his putting charity into the hearts of cheerful givers. "Through us" alludes to the coming delivery of the collection by Paul and company, including the anonymous Christian "brothers," to the poverty-stricken saints in Jerusalem, who'll thank God for the financial relief. Paul and company are "serving [up] this religious duty" to those saints by delivering the collection (8:19–20), but so too are the

Macedonians and the Corinthians by contributing to the collection (8:4; 9:1–2). "This religious duty" describes the service as just such a duty. Paul expects that the size of the contribution will alleviate completely the plight of the needy saints in Jerusalem, and he says that "the serving . . . is *flourishing*" by virtue of "*many* thanksgivings to God." As intimated by "flourishing," it brings pleasure to Paul that not only are financial needs in the church at Jerusalem being met but that also many thanksgivings to God are resulting from "the serving [up] of this religious duty" (compare 8:19). The shift from a singular "thanksgiving" to the plural "thanksgivings," reinforced by "many," heightens Paul's pleasure. And since the collection has yet to be delivered, the use of the present tense ("is effecting," "is not only filling up but also [is] flourishing") indicates what's bound to happen.

Paul's sentence continues in *9:13–15*: [you] **glorifying God through the proof consisting in this service** [of the collection] **on the basis of your confessional submission to the gospel about the Christ and** [on the basis of] **the generosity of** [your] **imparting** [your resources] **to them and to all** [others as well], [14]**while with** [prayer-]**requesting in your behalf they also long for you because of God's surpassing grace on you.** [15]**Thanks to God for his indescribable gift!** "Glorifying" seems parallel to "being made rich" in 9:11, which clearly describes the Corinthians, not the saints in Jerusalem. If so, the Corinthians will be glorifying God through proving themselves true to their original zeal by completing the collection ("this service"). The proof will rest theologically on their submission "to the gospel about the Christ," which they've confessed, and behaviorally on their "generosity" in "imparting [their resources]" to needy saints in Jerusalem and, in the future, to other needy saints. "To all [others as well]" could include non-Christians along with Christians except for the addition that they'll pray for the Corinthians and long for them "because of God's surpassing grace" on the Corinthians. So Paul must mean all other Christians, and charity given to needy fellow Christians constitutes a necessary behavioral evidence of having submitted obediently to the gospel that was confessed verbally. "About *the* Christ" lends an official tone to this requirement. All the needy saints will pray for the Corinthians as well as thank God for financial relief received from them; and this relief will forge in them an emotional bond with the Corinthians, a bond that will make them long to see the Corinthians face-to-face. But lest the Corinthians get puffed up by this result, Paul ascribes their generosity to the surpassing grace of God that rests on them, and then breaks out in thanks for God's gift, which because of its graciousness surpasses anyone's ability to describe it fully. In view of that gift, even the most generous of human gifts doesn't justify pride. "Grace" and "thanks" translate the same Greek word. So the wordplay on its two meanings highlights God's indescribable gift. In view of 8:9, this gift consists in Jesus' becoming poor that others might become rich; but in view of 8:1 it also includes the Corinthians' and

Macedonians' financial gift, prompted as it was by God's gift in the Lord, Jesus Christ.

PAUL'S RELATION TO THE CORINTHIAN CHURCH WITH SPECIAL REFERENCE TO A STILL-RECALCITRANT MINORITY
2 Corinthians 10:1–13:10

This third major section of 2 Corinthians subdivides into Paul's defense of himself against charges of weakness and cowardice (10:1–11); rightful claim on the Corinthians as his converts (10:12–18); concern over the danger of false apostles in Corinth (11:1–6); refusal to take financial support from the Corinthians (11:7–15); pedigrees of Jewish ancestry and Christian service (11:16–29); weakness as a topic of his boasting (11:30–12:10); apostolic miracles (12:11–13); and coming visit to Corinth, with a threat of harshness and an appeal for repentance (12:14–13:10).

PAUL'S DEFENSE OF HIMSELF AGAINST CHARGES OF WEAKNESS AND COWARDICE
2 Corinthians 10:1–11

10:1–2: **And I myself, Paul, am exhorting you through the Christ's meekness and mildness—**[I] **who face-to-face on the one hand** [am] **lowly among you; on the other hand I'm courageous toward you when absent—**[2]**yet I'm begging** [you] **that when present I may not be courageous with the confidence which I'm considering to dare** [using] **against some who consider us** [to be] **as walking around according to flesh.** The additions to "I" of "myself" and "Paul" signal the start of Paul's lengthy self-defense against a still recalcitrant minority in the Corinthian church and against their cohorts, some traveling preachers who've infiltrated the church and whom Paul will call "false apostles" (11:13) and has already described as "huckstering God's word" (2:17). In view of these opponents' later-cited description of his bodily presence as "weak" and his speech as "of no account" (10:10), he appeals to "the Christ's meekness and mildness" as the characteristics he (Paul) emulates in issuing his exhortation. But emulation doesn't capture the full meaning of his phrase. Because he's an apostle he speaks as the Christ's stand-in, so that the meekness and mildness are Christ's own, not just an emulated version thereof. "*The* Christ's meekness and mildness" calls attention to the messianic office, and therefore the authority, that Paul represents because of his apostleship. He doesn't explain how the Christ displayed meekness and mildness, but for possibilities see 8:9; 1 Peter 2:23; Matthew 5:5; 11:29; Zechariah 9:9.

After appealing to the Christ's meekness and mildness as represented in Paul's written exhortation, Paul interprets what his opponents call the weakness of his bodily presence. He interprets it as lowliness—that is, humility—when face-to-face with the Corinthians. But in Greco-Roman culture humility wasn't considered a virtue. So in mentioning his humility as "lowliness" Paul is both associating it with the Christ's meekness and mildness and admitting to not measuring up to the standard expected of him by his opponents (compare 12:21). In effect, "I'm courageous toward you when absent" likewise admits to their slur that by contrast only his letters are "weighty and strong" (10:10 [compare 2:3–4; 7:8]). Then he escalates "I . . . am exhorting you" to "I'm begging [you]" (compare 5:20) and counteracts the foregoing admissions ("*yet* I'm begging [you]") with what could have been a threat to deal roughly with his opponents on his coming visit. Well, maybe it is a threat; but if so, it's a veiled threat. For by begging the Corinthians, particularly Paul's opponents, to drop their opposition to him so that he won't have to be "courageous with the confidence which [he's] considering to dare [using]," he's slyly threatening to reverse his weighty and strong manner in the letters he writes and his weak manner when personally present. If necessary, in other words, he'll be confidently courageous in person just as he has been in writing and thus disprove the contention of his opponents that he and his colleagues are "walking around [= behaving] according to flesh." "According to flesh" refers to some kind of weakness (see the comments on 1:17), occasionally to moral weakness (as in Romans 8:4–5, 12–13). Here it refers to behavior that's considered personally weak by a prevailing cultural standard.

Paul adds "with the confidence" to "courageous" to reinforce his exhortation, including the veiled threat. But "which I'm *considering*" leaves his opponents time to spare themselves an apostolic drubbing as well as making a contrast with their "consider[ing]" Paul and company to be behaving weakly. Simultaneously, "*to dare* [using] against some" points back to the possibility of Paul's using his confident courage despite preferring not to do so. He doesn't identify who the "some" are that consider him and his colleagues to be behaving weakly. Possibilities are the false apostles, the minority of church members opposed to Paul, and both groups. At least it's apparent that he has the majority on his side.

10:3–6: For though walking around in flesh we're not waging war according to flesh. ⁴For the weapons of our warfare [are]n't fleshly—rather, [they're] powerful for God with the result of tearing down strongholds ⁵as we're tearing down considerations and every high thing that's being lifted up against the knowledge of God, and [as we're] capturing every thought for obedience to the Christ ⁶and standing ready to punish every disobedience whenever your obedience has been fulfilled [compare Proverbs 21:22]. First, Paul explains why those are wrong who think he and his colleagues are behaving weakly. Then he explains how it is that he and his colleagues are not behaving weakly. His opponents consider them to be "walking around *according to* flesh," that is, behaving weakly (10:2). But he admits only to "walking around *in* flesh," that is, living bodily, so that conformity ("according to") changes to location ("in"), and flesh as a figure of speech for weakness changes to flesh as the material that clothes the human spirit (compare 5:1–6). Next, Paul echoes his opponents' "according to flesh," but in place of "walking around" he substitutes

"waging war" and adds "not." So "flesh" returns to its figurative meaning of weakness, but "waging war" denies weakness and figuratively denotes Paul's coming attack on his and his colleagues' opponents. "The weapons of our warfare" aren't specified. So the accent falls on the fact that they "aren't fleshly"—that is, not weak—"rather, [they're] powerful." The opponents should be scared!

"For God" indicates that Paul and company will use their weapons in service to God, for by opposing Paul and company the opponents are opposing God himself. "With the result of tearing down strongholds" predicts the weapons' effectiveness, a result of their power. "As we're tearing down considerations" identifies the strongholds as the reasonings, the arguments, of "some who consider [Paul and company to be] as walking around according to flesh" (10:2). "Some" refers to Paul and company's opponents, false apostles who've infiltrated the Corinthian church plus a minority of its members who've been taken in by the false apostles. The tearing down of their strongholds will consist in Paul's refutation of their reasonings, that is, their arguments that Paul and company are weaklings. The repetition of "tearing down" stresses the crushing power of his coming refutation. "And every *high* thing that's being lifted up" portrays the strongholds as rampart-like arguments against Paul that grow out of pride in those who make them (see 11:20). "Tearing down . . . *every* high thing" will leave no such argument unrefuted. Strikingly, "against the knowledge of God" implies that arguing against Paul amounts to arguing against the knowledge of God. For Paul's apostolic ministry enables people, and has enabled the Corinthians, to know God, which means both to understand the truth about him and to enter into a right and intimate relation with him.

The figure of besieging a towering stronghold and tearing it down with siege engines ("weapons") shifts to capturing all its inhabitants ("every thought"). That is to say, Paul is aiming to refute his opponents' arguments so thoroughly that no adverse thought about him will remain unrefuted—indeed, that every thought about him will be turned favorable. And just as arguments against him amount to arguments "against the knowledge of God," favorable thoughts about Paul will amount to "obedience to the Christ." Moreover, right thinking ("every thought") leads to right action ("obedience"). "To *the* Christ" highlights the authority vested in Jesus by virtue of his messianic office, an authority that calls for obedience to him through obedience to Paul, the Christ's apostolic stand-in. Because of having been captured, "every thought" is bound to such obedience. For captives become slaves to their captors. But despite Paul's coming refutation of every argument leveled against him, it may be that not every one of his opponents will cease opposing him. So he states his readiness, like a soldier at the ready, "to punish every disobedience," that is, every remaining opposition to him. This punishment will consist in an unspecified form of discipline (but see 1 Corinthians 5 for excommunication from the church). The contrast between "every disobedience" and "whenever your obedience has been fulfilled [= fully carried out]" implies that in "*your* obedience" Paul is addressing those who by the time of his visit will have obeyed, and is disregarding those he'll punish. Presumably the obedience he's talking about consists in their rejecting the false apostles who've infiltrated their camp and wreaked havoc.

10:7–11: **Be looking at the things** [with which you're] **face-to-face** [compare 10:1]. "The things [with which you're] face-to-face" means things that are obvious. Paul goes on to detail them: **If anyone is persuaded regarding himself that he belongs to Christ, on the basis of himself he's again to be considering this, that just as** [by his own lights] **he himself** [belongs] **to Christ, so too** [do] **we.** In other words, if he's persuaded that he has a basis in himself for considering himself as belonging to Christ, he's to follow up ("again") with the consideration that Paul and company have at least as much basis for considering themselves as belonging to Christ. Now Paul starts to tell why such a person is to reason thus: **⁸For even if I boast somewhat excessively about our authority, which the Lord** [Jesus] **gave** [us] **for building** [you] **up and not for tearing you down** [compare Jeremiah 24:6], **I'll not be shamed, ⁹lest I seem as though** [I'm] **terrorizing you through** [my] **letters.** **¹⁰"On the one hand the letters," says** [the aforementioned "anyone" who's "persuaded regarding himself that he belongs to Christ"], **"[are] weighty and strong** [in the pejorative sense of heavy-handed and despotic]. **On the other hand** [his] **bodily presence** [is] **weak and** [his] **speech of no account."** Paul is leading up to boasting self-defensively about his apostolic authority (see especially chapter 11). Because of his colleagues' partnership with him, he presents them as sharing, or at least as representing, this authority—hence "*our* authority." He's embarrassed about having to boast about it, though. The embarrassment comes out in "*even* if I boast *somewhat excessively*." But "which the Lord gave [us]" justifies the authority as worthy of boasting, if necessary; and "for building [you] up and not for tearing you down" ameliorates the boasting by pointing to its intended beneficial rather than destructive effect on the Corinthians. Paul wants to tear down the arguments of his opponents (10:4–5), but not the Corinthians themselves. He wants to build them up (12:19; 13:10 [compare 1 Corinthians 3:9–15]). "I'll not be shamed" means that exercising his apostolic authority on arrival in Corinth (if he has to) will refute those who presently shame him with the charge that he terrorizes the Corinthians with heavy-handed, despotic letters but cuts a singularly unimposing figure and speaks without rhetorical skill when physically present with them (compare 11:6). **¹¹Such a person** [as says so] **is to be considering this, that the sort of persons we are in speech through** [our] **letters when absent, this** [is] **the kind of persons** [we'll be] **also in deed when present.** "Is to be considering this" calls for a reversal of the "considerations" that consist in "every high thing that's being lifted up against the knowledge of God" (10:5). This new

consideration would result in "obedience to the Christ" (10:5) through a revival of loyalty to his apostle Paul, who first evangelized Corinth.

PAUL'S RIGHTFUL CLAIM ON THE CORINTHIANS AS HIS CONVERTS
2 Corinthians 10:12–18

Here Paul tells why his self-confident opponents should on second thought take account that on arrival in Corinth Paul and company will deal forcefully with them (10:11). *10:12–13*: **For we aren't daring to classify or compare ourselves with any of those who are recommending themselves. When they themselves are measuring themselves by themselves, however, and comparing themselves with themselves, they don't understand** [what they're doing]. **¹³But we ourselves won't boast in reference to unmeasured things** [that is, regarding evangelistic successes lying outside the zone of ministry that God measured out for us]; **rather,** [we'll boast] **in accordance with the measure consisting in the zone that God measured for us as a measure to reach as far as even you.** According to 10:2 Paul considers daring to use courageous confidence against his opponents when he arrives in Corinth. But here in 10:12 he says it would be prohibitively daring, in the sense of courting God's judgment, for him and his colleagues to classify or compare themselves with "some of those who're recommending themselves"; for then he and his colleagues would be arrogating to themselves a divine prerogative of judgment. Or is Paul engaging in mock humility so as to criticize prideful self-recommendation on the part of his opponents, the false apostles in particular? In either case, "some of those" doesn't mean a group *selected* out of a larger group—rather, a group *consisting of* those who are recommending themselves. Paul is referring to the false apostles who've infiltrated the Corinthian church. Their self-recommendations identify what Paul meant in 10:5 when speaking of "every high thing that's being lifted up against the knowledge of God." Naturally, it's easy for them to recommend themselves when they measure themselves by themselves and compare themselves with themselves rather than measuring themselves by external criteria and comparing themselves with the likes of Paul and company. Much more is it easy to recommend themselves when they don't recognize that God will judge them for good or ill. "However" draws attention to the folly of such self-recommendation: "they don't understand [what they're doing]." "But *we* won't boast in reference to unmeasured things" implies that the false apostles *are* boasting of their success in fueling opposition to Paul among the Corinthians, and of doing so in a zone of ministry that by divine boundary-drawing belongs to him and his colleagues. The false apostles are poachers. By contrast, Paul and company will boast only about their success within the zone divinely surveyed for their evangelistic activities. "To reach as far as even you" underscores that Corinth falls inside that zone.

Now Paul explains why he and his colleagues *will* boast in accordance with the zone measured out to them by God and including Corinth. **10:14–16: For we're not overextending ourselves, as though not reaching to you** [= as though our divinely measured zone of ministry doesn't include you]; **for we arrived** [before any others] **as far as even you in the gospel of the Christ** [= by way of being the first to preach to you the good news that Jesus is the Messiah], [15]**not boasting to the point of unmeasured things in others' labors** [that is, we don't at all boast about successes in zones which God measured out for others to evangelize], **but having hope to be magnified among you in accordance with our zone as your faith grows with the result of** [our] **flourishing,** [16][that is,] **with the result of** [our] **proclaiming the gospel in the** [regions] **beyond you, not to boast in reference to things ready-made in another's zone.** "As far as even you" stresses the inclusion of Corinth in Paul and company's zone of evangelism and therefore stresses the legitimacy of their boasting of success in that city. "To be magnified among you" means to be extolled by you (see Philippians 1:20; Luke 1:46; Acts 5:13; 10:46; 19:17 for this meaning of "magnify" when a person or persons are its object). "Having hope" means having a confident expectation that the Corinthians, especially the recalcitrants, will extol Paul and company instead of opposing them. The expectation compliments those Corinthians and thus makes more likely their switching from opposition to extolment. "In accordance with our zone" bases the expected extolment on their recognition that they reside in territory divinely assigned to Paul and company for evangelism. "As your faith grows" correlates growth in Christian faith with extolment of the evangelists, just as opposition to them correlates with a shrinkage of faith. For opposition to them entails opposition to their gospel, whereas extolment of them entails extolment of their gospel. If the opponents become supporters, Paul and company will be able to turn their attention and efforts away from problems in the Corinthian church to evangelism in regions unevangelized by anyone else. Thus they'll "flourish" as missionaries. "*Not* to boast in reference to things ready-made in another's zone" takes a sideswipe at the false apostles, who do exactly that.

10:17–18: But "the one who's boasting is to be boasting in the Lord [Jeremiah 9:24 (compare 1 Corinthians 1:31)]." [18]**For the person who's recommending himself—that person isn't qualified; rather,** [the person] **whom the Lord recommends** [is qualified]. The command to be "boasting in the Lord" contrasts with the false apostles' "boast[ing] in reference to things ready-made in another's zone" (10:16). Therefore "boast[ing] . . . in accordance with the measure consisting in the zone that God measured for us [Paul and company]" (10:13)—this boasting on their part equates with boasting in the Lord. Then Paul tells why a boaster should boast in the Lord. First, the person who boasts about what he has done in someone else's zone of ministry is described as "the person who's recommending himself" rather than boasting in the Lord. Then that person is said to be disqualified.

In 13:5 disqualification stands over against being "in the faith" and over against having "Jesus Christ in you." So Paul is denying salvation to the false apostles. They masquerade as Christians, but they aren't. Reason aplenty not to follow their lead! True Christians are those whom the Lord recommends, because they boast in him rather than recommending themselves.

PAUL'S CONCERN OVER FALSE APOSTLES IN CORINTH
2 Corinthians 11:1–6

11:1–2: O that you'd put up with me in a little bit of nonsense! Rather, do indeed put up with me! [2]**For I'm jealous for you with God's jealousy, for I've betrothed you to one husband, to present** [you] **as a pure virgin to the Christ.** This paragraph starts with a wish ("Would that . . . !"), proceeds with a command, "do . . . !"), adds a reason for the command ("For I'm jealous for you . . ."), and ends with a reason for the jealousy ("for I've betrothed you . . ."). "Rather" emphasizes the switch from a wish to a command, and "indeed" strengthens the command. "Put up with me" appears in both the wish and the command. "In a little bit of nonsense," which appears in the wish, is probably to be supplied mentally in the command as well. All in all, then, Paul is insisting that the Corinthians put up with him as he goes on to write some nonsense. But it's only "a little bit of nonsense." So they should be able to tolerate it. Paul leaves them in suspense as to what the nonsense is, though, and delays it in order to tell them the reason why they should put up with him when he finally does engage in the nonsense. His jealousy for them is that reason. False apostles have captured their affection, at least the affection of some of them, and others may be similarly seduced. So it's only natural that as the founder of the Corinthian church he should be jealous, and jealousy can make people act nonsensically. But Paul's jealousy isn't his alone. It's also God's jealousy (among other Old Testament passages, compare Exodus 34:14; Deuteronomy 4:24). For the Corinthian church is God's, not just Paul's (1:1; 1 Corinthians 1:2).

Paul feels God's jealousy because acting in God's stead he has "betrothed" the Corinthians "to one husband." Paul can betroth them in God's stead because they live in a zone of evangelism that God has measured out to Paul (10:13–16). "To the Christ" identifies the one husband to whom Paul has betrothed them and thus implies that the jealousy of God that Paul shares is a jealousy for Christ's sake, that the false apostles are stealing for themselves affection that properly belongs to Christ, and that this theft threatens Paul's purpose to present to him the Corinthians "as a pure virgin." "To *one* husband" stands over against the plurality of the "false apostles," who "are recommending themselves" (10:12; 11:13; see Deuteronomy 22:23–24; Matthew 1:18–19, 24 for the use of "husband" during the period of betrothal). "To *the* Christ" stresses his messiahship over against the emptiness of their self-recommendations. "As a *pure* virgin" suggests the danger of religious fornication on the part of Corinthians who continue their dalliance with the false apostles, but 12:21 may well include sexual fornication too. In view of 4:14, the presentation to the Christ should occur on the day of resurrection, when he comes back (compare Ephesians 5:25–27; Colossians 1:21–22, 28). In presenting the Corinthians as a pure virgin to the Christ, Paul is playing the part of a father who on protecting his daughter from sexual violation gives her away in marriage to the man to whom he has betrothed her (see 1 Corinthians 4:15 for Paul as having fathered the Corinthian church).

11:3–4: But I fear lest somehow, as the serpent deceived Eve with his trickery, your minds be corrupted [so that they veer] **from the integrity and the purity** [that they should have] **in relation to the Christ** [your "one husband"]. **⁴For indeed if a person who comes** [to you] **is proclaiming another Jesus whom we didn't proclaim** [as in fact is happening], **or you receive a different spirit that you didn't receive, or** [you accept] **a different gospel that you didn't accept, you put up with** [him] **beautifully!** Over against his purpose "to present [the Corinthians] as a pure virgin to the Christ" Paul puts his fear that they'll let the false apostles thwart that purpose "somehow." He doesn't leave the "somehow" undefined, but defines it with a comparison to the serpent's tricky deception of Eve (Genesis 3:1–13). So the false apostles are playing the serpent's part, and the Corinthians are playing the part of Eve. Behind the serpent lies the figure of Satan, already referred to in 2:11; 4:4. Hence the false apostles are acting as his agents when corrupting the Corinthians' minds (so the explicit statement in 11:13–15).

The false apostles have deceived some of the Corinthians in proclaiming to them a Jesus other than the one Paul and company proclaimed, so that these Corinthians received a spirit different from the Holy Spirit they received at their conversion (1 Corinthians 12:13) and accepted a gospel different from the one Paul and company proclaimed. The false apostles' self-recommendations have constituted the trickery that made the deception effective. The deception has "corrupted" some Corinthians' "minds," so that their minds have disintegrated, being split between the true Jesus and a false one, between the Holy Spirit and an unholy spirit, between the authentic gospel and an inauthentic one. This deception has also corrupted some Corinthians' minds so as to compromise the purity of their affection for "the Christ," to whom alone Paul betrothed the Corinthians and to whom alone they should direct their affections. "For" introduces a reason why Paul fears this corruption of their minds. He states the reason with sarcastic irony: the Corinthians, at least those he's here addressing, put up with a false apostle "beautifully," and do so despite the false apostle's proclamation of another Jesus and the Corinthians' consequent reception of a different spirit and acceptance of a different gospel (compare Jesus' sarcastically ironic use of "beautifully" in Mark 7:9). Well now, if the Corinthians put up with a *false* apostle beautifully, they should consent to put up with their *founding* apostle, Paul, whether beautifully or not. "*Lest* your

minds be corrupted" states an unwanted possibility. "You receive a different spirit," "[you accept] a different gospel," and "you put up with [a false apostle] beautifully" state distressing actualities. This competition between a possibility and actualities reflects the competition in the Corinthian church between those who've thus far resisted the false apostles' allurements but stand in danger of succumbing and those who have succumbed but might yet be retrieved.

11:5–6: For in not a single respect do I consider myself to have come short of the super-apostles. ⁶But even if [I'm] **an amateur as to speech,** [I'm] **nevertheless not** [an amateur] **as to knowledge—in every way, nevertheless, having made** [this fact] **obvious in all** [our relations] **to you.** Here Paul introduces another reason why he fears corruption of the Corinthians' minds. It's that some Corinthians have been hoodwinked by false apostles despite the obviousness of Paul's expertise in knowledge—that is, knowledge of the gospel. This obviousness, reinforced by the phrases "in every way" and "in all [our relations] to you," should have kept the Corinthians from deception. But before appealing to his obvious knowledge Paul states his conviction that "in not a single respect" has he "come short of the *super*-apostles." They're not the *false* apostles about to be mentioned as such in 11:13, because he'll claim superiority to them (11:23) whereas here claims mere equality with the super-apostles. So we can only make an educated guess concerning their identity and the reason they're called "super-apostles." They're probably the original Twelve plus James the half brother of Jesus or, more probably, that same James, Cephas (Peter), and John (Galatians 1:18–19; 2:6–9); and Paul calls them "super-apostles" probably because the false apostles were calling those apostles "super" to denigrate Paul by comparison (see Galatians 2:6, 9 for his calling James, Cephas, and John "those who seem to be something" and "those who seem to be pillars"). In any case, Paul sets his expert knowledge over against his lack of rhetorical skill, presumably from not having been schooled in rhetoric, so that it looks as though the false apostles did have such skill and were deriding his lack of it (compare 1 Corinthians 1:22; 2:1–5). But better solid knowledge than empty eloquence. "*Even if* [I'm] an amateur as to speech" emphasizes the superiority of knowledge to eloquence. The first instance of "nevertheless" makes the same emphasis. The second, somewhat parallel instance of "nevertheless" emphasizes the obviousness of Paul's knowledge to imply that none of the Corinthians should have fallen prey to the false apostles. To include his colleagues, he switches (according to the Greek text) from "I" to the plural in "having made [this fact] obvious in all [our] relations to you."

PAUL'S REFUSAL TO TAKE FINANCIAL SUPPORT FROM THE CORINTHIANS
2 Corinthians 11:7–15

11:7–9: Or did I commit a sin by lowering [= abasing] **myself in order that you might be elevated** [= exalted], **in that as a gift** [= without charging you for it] **I proclaimed to you as good news the good news about God?** [8]**I robbed other churches by receiving provisions** [from them to go to you] **for the purpose of serving you!** [9]**And when present with you and deficient** [of funds], **I didn't put pressure on anyone** [of you to support me financially]. **For on coming from Macedonia, the brothers** [whom you know from having met them] **filled up my deficit completely; and in every respect I kept myself, and will** [in the future] **keep** [myself], **unburdensome to you.** Why does Paul defend himself for not taking pay from the Corinthians for his evangelistic work among them? Answer: because his opponents are saying that his not taking pay amounted to an admission of incompetence so far as rhetoric is concerned. He has just admitted to such incompetence. With sarcastic irony, then, he asks whether nonreception of pay, either by refusing it or by not insisting on it, amounted to *committing a sin*. Part of the irony consists in his calling the non-taking of pay a self-lowering for the sake of elevating the very Corinthians some of whom have joined the false apostles in deriding his lack of rhetorical skill (see 1 Corinthians 1:26–31 for the Corinthians' elevation). He then references his having evangelized them "*as a gift*," so that the very manner of his evangelizing them not only differentiated him from money-grubbing itinerants but also correlated with God's "indescribable *gift*," for which Paul gave thanks in 9:15. So the Corinthians should have been thanking Paul for not charging them just as he has thanked God for not charging human beings for that gift (compare Romans 3:24: "being *freely* declared righteous by his [God's] grace through the redemption that [is] in Christ Jesus"). The redundancy in "I proclaimed as good news the good news about God" brings out this correlation, and the correlation intensifies the irony of Paul's question.

"The good news about God" means the good news of what he has done in giving us his indescribable gift and distinguishes this good news sharply from the false apostles' "different gospel" about "another Jesus" and involving "a different spirit" (11:4). But Paul isn't done with irony. He portrays his receiving provisions and financial support from other churches as robbery for the sake of serving the Corinthians. Does receiving equate with robbing? Of course not! Those other churches gave voluntarily, but Paul's portraying himself as robbing them to support his free-of-charge evangelization of Corinth makes the Corinthians who are denigrating him look abysmally thankless. Several further details underline how totally Paul avoided taking support from the Corinthians: (1) his not pressing any of them for support though needing it; (2) the completeness with which funds from Macedonia met his financial needs; (3) his having kept himself financially unburdensome to the Corinthians "in every respect"; and (4) his resolve to keep himself thus (compare 2:17; 4:2; 7:2; 12:17–18; 1 Corinthians 9:3–18; Philippians 4:15–16).

11:10–11: **Christ's truthfulness** [is] **in me: this boasting won't be barred to me in the districts of Achaia** [= southern Greece]. [11]**Why? Because I don't love you? God knows** [I do]! Here Paul reaffirms his resolve to keep himself financially unburdensome to the Corinthians in the future as he has in the past. He has pressed them for a generous contribution to the collection that will go to poverty-stricken Christians in Jerusalem (chapter 8–9). But no such pressure will come from him for his own needs, not so long as he's resident among them. (According to 1:16; 1 Corinthians 16:6, 11, however, he does expect them to supply provisions for an evangelistic journey onward from Corinth.) "Christ's truthfulness [is] in me" means that the Corinthians should believe Paul's reaffirmation just as assuredly as they would if Christ himself were speaking to them (compare 13:3). In 11:7 Paul referred ironically to his taking no support from the Corinthians as self-abasement. Here he refers nonironically to it as a practice to boast about (see the footnote to 1 Corinthians 9:15–16 on good versus bad boasting); and he includes the surrounding region of Achaia, for 2 Corinthians is addressed "to God's church that's in Corinth along with all the saints that are in the whole of Achaia" (1:1). "The districts of Achaia" means the districts comprising Achaia, not the districts surrounding Achaia. Paul anticipates that some may ask why he won't take support from them and may answer their own question by saying he doesn't love them. Either that or he has heard of such a question and answer. *We* might ask why anyone would think free-of-charge shows lack of love. Well, love for others can show itself in willingness to let them help you when you're in need, as well as in not imposing on them when you're in need. So Paul's policy was subject to a negative as well as positive interpretation. He affirms the positive one by appealing to God's omniscience: "God knows [I love you]!" So "Christ's truthfulness" and God's omniscience bracket Paul's "boasting."

11:12–15: **But what I'm doing** [by way of taking no pay from you] **I'll also do** [in the future] **so that I may cut off the basis of those who want a basis** [for boasting of superiority to me], **so that in what they're boasting about they may be found just as also we** [are]. By not taking pay Paul is exposing the false apostles as money-grubbers. The exposé will lead the Corinthians to stop paying the false apostles. At least Paul hopes so. Then those apostles will be payless just like him and his colleagues and won't be able to boast of superiority on the basis of the Corinthians' paying them but not paying him and his colleagues. [13]**For such people** [as those who want a basis for boasting of superiority to me] [are] **false apostles, deceitful workers, refashioning themselves into Christ's apostles.** [14]**And no wonder! For Satan himself refashions himself into an angel** [= messenger] **of light.** [15]**Therefore it**['s] **not a big thing if also his servants refashion themselves as servants of righteousness, whose end will be in accordance with their works.** The parallel between "false apostles" and "Christ's apostles" indicates that these self-styled apostles falsely claimed to have gotten a commission straight from the resurrected Christ. "Deceitful workers" describes their activity in churches like that of the Corinthians as consisting in deceit, the false claim to be Christ's apostles. "Refashioning themselves" then describes the deceit as a masquerade in which they make themselves appear to be what they are not. "And no wonder!" exclaims that nobody should be surprised at their refashioning themselves. Why not? Because "Satan himself refashions himself into an angel of light," which he is not (see the parallel in 6:14–15 between "darkness" and "Beliar," another name of Satan, and also in that passage the representation of "righteousness" by "light" and of "lawlessness" by "darkness"). But Satan's refashioning himself in this way—that is, as an angel/messenger of light/righteousness—could be taken as a mere analogy. So Paul adds that in reality the false apostles are servants of Satan. It's *because* they are that they refashion themselves as Satan does. Analogy graduates to causation, in other words; and the addition of "himself" to "Satan" caps the graduation. "It's not a big thing if . . ." matches "And no wonder!" to emphasize again that nobody should be surprised at the false apostles' refashioning themselves. Paul is implying that the Corinthians should have found it easy to detect the deceit. The antithetical parallel between "servants of righteousness" and "his [Satan's] servants" implies that the false apostles portray themselves as serving righteousness, personified as their master, when in reality they're serving Satan. Since they're "deceitful workers," "whose end will be in accordance with their works" means that the false apostles will get a sentence of eternal damnation at the Last Judgment.

PAUL'S PEDIGREE OF JEWISH ANCESTRY AND CHRISTIAN SERVICE
2 Corinthians 11:16–29

11:16–17: Again I say, nobody should suppose I'm nonsensical; but if not indeed [that is, if in fact you don't heed my command to avoid supposing I'm nonsensical], **at least accept me as nonsensical in order that I too may boast a little bit.** Paul is referring back to 11:1: "Would that you'd put up with me in a little bit of nonsense! Rather, do indeed put up with me!" "In order that I *too* may boast" implies that the false apostles are boasting. "A little bit" points up Paul's hesitancy to boast, though, and probably also claims a contrast with the false apostles' boasting *more than* a little bit. [17]**What I'm saying I'm not saying in accordance with the Lord—rather, as it were in nonsense, in this assurance of boasting.** "What I'm saying" looks forward to what Paul is about to say by way of boasting. It's "not . . . in accordance with the Lord" because it's nonsense, and it's nonsense because it's self-assured boasting—that is (to anticipate Paul's next statement), it's the nonsense of "boasting in accordance with the flesh"—such as the Lord wouldn't want him to do, other things being equal. But other things aren't equal, and "as it were" makes this boasting mere play-acting on Paul's part. The Lord won't be displeased, then.

11:18–21a: Since many are boasting in accordance with flesh, I too will boast [in accordance with flesh (compare 11:16)]. [19]**For you, being sensible, are gladly putting up with senseless** [people (compare 11:4)]. [20]**For you're putting up with** [it] **if someone is reducing you to slavery, if someone is devouring** [you], **if someone is taking** [you], **if someone is lifting himself over** [you], **if someone is hitting you in the face.** [21a]**I'm speaking by way of disparagement** [of ourselves], **to the effect that we've been weak** [by comparison with the false apostles, who've manhandled you]. To boast "in accordance with the flesh" means to use superficial human standards rather than substantive divine standards in boasting (compare 5:12; 1 Corinthians 1:26) and therefore equates with not speaking "in accordance with the Lord" (11:17). If the false apostles don't make up the entirety of the "many" who are boasting in accordance with flesh, they are at least included among them. Paul is probably classifying the false apostles with the many pagan philosophers, teachers, and orators who traveled around the Roman Empire vaunting their learning and eloquence, taking fees from their admirers, and competing with one another for others' adulation. He cites the high number of fleshly boasters as a reason to enter himself into the competition. Then he cites another reason to do so, a reason relating specifically to the Corinthians: they enjoy being entertained with fleshly boasting.

From his own standpoint, though, Paul describes their enjoyment as a "putting up with." The Corinthians do it "gladly," nevertheless, because they're "sensible." But doing so makes *no* sense; sensible people don't gladly put *up* with the nonsense of senseless boasters. They're disgustedly put *off* by it. So Paul's calling the Corinthians' "sensible" strikes a deliciously ironic note. In actuality, putting up with the senseless false prophets makes the Corinthians senseless, too (compare the irony in 1 Corinthians 4:10). Furthermore, it makes no sense for them to put up *at all* with someone's reducing them to slavery, devouring them, taking them captive, exalting himself over them, hitting them in the face. Yet not only are the Corinthians putting up with these abuses. They're doing so *gladly*. Masochistic pleasure indeed! And Paul mocks it with a series of interrelated figures of speech: (1) "reducing you to slavery," so that you're working for the false apostle, not for yourselves and your families; (2) "devouring [you]," so that he's gobbling up your hard-earned money by taking it as payment for his senseless boasting; (3) "taking [you]," so that he's making you like captured prisoners of war; (4) "lifting himself over [you]," so that he's domineering you as slaves-by-capture are domineered; and (5) "hitting you in the face," so that he's abusing you as masters often abuse their slaves. Finally Paul supplements his mocking of the Corinthians' masochistic pleasure with mockery of his own and his colleagues' weakness in dealing with the Corinthians heretofore. He and his colleagues haven't enslaved, devoured, taken captive, domineered, or abused the Corinthians. But, of course, this mockery, which he calls "disparagement," is done tongue-in-cheek whereas the mockery of the Corinthians' masochistic pleasure was done seriously.

11:21b–23: But in whatever anyone dares [to boast]—**I'm speaking nonsensically: I too dare** [to boast in it]. **²²Are they Hebrews? Me too! Are they Israelites? Me too! Are they Abraham's seed? Me too! ²³Are they Christ's servants? I'm speaking as someone insane; I**['m] **more** [a servant of Christ than they are]: **in ever so many more labors, in ever so many more imprisonments, in a surpassing number of blows** [of a rod or a lash], **in deaths** [that is, mortal dangers] **many times** [compare 1:8–10; 4:11; 6:5, 9; Romans 8:36; 1 Corinthians 15:31]. "Anyone" refers to any false prophet who has infiltrated the Corinthian church. "Dares" describes the false apostles' boasting as presumptuous and therefore as inviting refutation. "In whatever" implies that Paul will leave no false prophet's boast of superiority unrefuted. "I'm speaking nonsensically" looks forward to his boasting by way of refutation and describes this boasting as embarrassingly nonsensical. "I too dare" revives the description of boasting as presumptuous, but we can be sure that Paul thinks his boasting *ir*refutable. The three terms "Hebrews," "Israelites," and "Abraham's seed" represent a backward progression in time. For "Hebrews" refers to Jews currently differentiated from fellow Jews by their resistance to Greco-Roman culture (compare Philippians 3:5; Acts 6:1; 22:3). "Israelites" refers to Jews as belonging to God's long-standing covenant people, Israel, who took their name after the nickname of Jacob (Genesis 32:28, 32). And "Abraham's seed" describes Jews as all descended from Abraham, Jacob's grandfather. Paul's questions imply that the false apostles qualify as such Jews. But he matches them in these respects, as indicated by his repeated "Me too!"

The combining of "Are they Christ's servants?" with "I more" implies that the false apostles claim to be Christ's servants and that for the purpose of his deliberately nonsensical boasting, Paul accepts their claim (compare 10:7). But his ascribing to them the proclamation of "another Jesus" and the purveying of "a different spirit" and "a different gospel" (11:4) and calling them "servants" of "Satan" (11:14–15) show that when speaking good sense, Paul doesn't at all consider them Christ's servants. Before boasting of superiority to them, Paul says, "I'm speaking as someone insane," to put even greater emphasis than before on the embarrassment he feels in boasting about himself. But the likeness of his boasting to insane speech comes out dramatically in the listed points of superiority to the false apostles. What sane person would boast about "so many more labors," about "so many more imprisonments," about "a surpassing number of blows," about "deaths many times"? Complaining about them would be sane. But boasting about them rather than about evangelistic successes? Crazy! At least crazy by the standards of "boast[ing] in accordance with flesh" (11:18). A warrior might boast about scars of battle on his chest, but scars of punishment on the back brands their bearer a miscreant.

The crazy boasting continues with enumerated instances of being in mortal danger ("in deaths"). **11:24–25: Five times I received from Jews forty** [lashes] **less one. ²⁵Three times I was beaten with rods. Once I was stoned. Three times I was shipwrecked. A night and a day I've spent** [adrift] **in the deep.** Jewish synagogues could impose punishments up to a limit of forty lashes (Deuteronomy 25:2–3), but the number was reduced to thirty-nine, perhaps to avoid going over forty through miscounting (compare Matthew 10:17; 23:34). Notably, Paul received the maximal number of lashes no fewer than five times; and even one such set of lashes could kill. Prior to his conversion he himself had imposed lashings on Christians (Acts 22:19; 26:11). Being beaten with rods was a Roman governmental punishment (see Acts 16:16–23). The one stoning of Paul is recorded in Acts 14:19. Though thought to have been killed, he survived (Acts 14:20). Each of his three shipwrecks entailed the danger of drowning. One of them also entailed floating a night and a day in the deep blue sea, presumably on a piece of flotsam. But none of them equates with his shipwreck recorded in Acts 27; for that one followed by some years the writing of 2 Corinthians. So apart from the stoning and one instance of being beaten with rods, the book of Acts contains only a sparse selection of Paul's apostolic sufferings for the gospel.

Now Paul lists a large variety of dangers to which he was exposed during his travels as a missionary. **11:26: On walking trips many times** [I was exposed] **to dangers of rivers** [= of drowning when fording the rivers], **to dangers of bandits** [along the way], **to dangers from kinfolk** [mobs of unbelieving fellow Jews], **to dangers from Gentiles** [mobs of pagans], **to dangers in a city** [from its antagonistic human inhabitants when arriving there], **to dangers in a wilderness** [from wild beasts when traveling between cities], **to dangers at sea** [from shipwreck and drowning when crossing a sea to get from one road to another], **to dangers among false brothers** [from treacherous pseudo-Christians].

Next Paul lists hardships in which he did his evangelistic work. **11:27:** [I subjected myself] **to labor and toil** [to support myself and thus make my evangelism free-of-charge] **in wakefulnesses many times** [= frequent spells of sleeplessness due to long hours of working as well as evangelizing], **in hunger and thirst** [due to lack of sufficient funds to purchase needed food and drink], **in fastings many times** [= often going without food to devote myself to labor, evangelism, and prayer], **in cold and nakedness** [on account of not having enough money to purchase needed clothing].

11:28–29: Apart from the things beside [the ones just listed], **I have the daily pressure** [which consists in] **anxiety concerning all the churches. ²⁹Who's weak, and I'm not weak?** Implied answer: No one, because I take to heart his or her condition. **Who's being tripped** [into apostasy (compare 1 Corinthians 8, 10)], **and I'm not being set aflame** [with rage]? Implied answer: No one, because I care for the eternal destiny of the person being tripped. Paul supplements the preceding catalog of physical sufferings, dangers, and hardships with the pressure of his anxiety, so that the psychological supplements the physical. Some of the anxiety falls due, doubtless, to the baleful influence of false apostles. That the psychological pressure of this anxiety is "daily" points up its constancy; and "anxiety concerning *all* the churches" points up that once Paul leaves a church, whether or not it was founded by him, he doesn't forget the church, as false apostles do after infiltrating a church and leaving it. For it's out of sight out of mind once geographical distance severs them from that church's financial support. By contrast, neither time nor distance neutralizes Paul's anxiety.[3] He illustrates it with examples of sympathy for the weak and stumbling.

The combination of weakness and stumbling recalls 1 Corinthians 8:7–13, where weakness represented an uninformed consciousness regarding food sacrificed to an idol, and where stumbling represented eternal ruination because of apostasy. Add to the recollection of that combination Paul's present attack on heretically false apostles and you get a strong impression that he's expressing concern for professing Christians so theologically weak that they're falling into eternally ruinous apostasy because false apostles are tripping them with "another Jesus," "a different spirit," and "a different gospel" (11:4). He's so enraged by this effect that he compares his rage to a fire burning within him. But his sympathetic weakness can't mean that he's theologically weak like a theologically weak church member who's stumbling into apostasy, for Paul is "not [an amateur] as to knowledge" (11:6). So his weakness isn't theological. It's physical, as he'll go on to note in 12:5–10 and as he noted earlier in 10:10; 1 Corinthians 2:3 (compare especially Galatians 4:13). His weakness isn't the same as the other's weakness just as his being set aflame isn't the same as the others' being tripped. Nonetheless, the correlations are close enough to point up his anxiety.

INSTANCES OF PAUL'S WEAKNESS AS A TOPIC OF HIS BOASTING
2 Corinthians 11:30–12:10

11:30–31: **If it's necessary to be boasting** [as it is because of the false apostles' "boast(ing) according to flesh" and your "gladly putting up with (such) senseless people" (11:18–19)], **I'll boast in reference to the things related to my weakness. [31]The God and Father of the Lord Jesus,** [the God] **who's forever praised, knows that I'm not lying.** "If it's necessary to be boasting" both reflects again Paul's embarrassment over boasting about himself and defends it as an activity forced on him. Others' weakness (11:29) leads him to spell out now his own corresponding weakness (also mentioned in 11:29). "I'll boast in reference to the things related to my weakness" differentiates his boasting from the false apostles' "boast[ing] in accordance with flesh" (11:18), that is, with the use of superficial human standards. "The things

[3]Paul had anxiety for the churches, whereas both he and Jesus taught against having anxiety for oneself (see Matthew 6:25–34; Luke 12:22–34; Philippians 4:6–7). So there's no contradiction.

related to my weakness" points forward to the events recorded in 11:32–12:10. Since some of what he'll record there is hard to believe, Paul affirms his truthfulness by appealing to God's knowing that he isn't lying, as though to say that at the Last Judgment God will certify Paul's truth-telling. To play up God as the one who knows he isn't lying, Paul identifies him as "the God and Father of the Lord Jesus," whom (referring to Jesus) the Corinthians have themselves confessed as their Lord (1:3; 1 Corinthians 1:2; 12:3), and describes God as "forever praised," which description undergirds Paul's appeal to God as the highest authority he can cite to underwrite his truthfulness.

11:32–33: **In Damascus the ethnarch** [probably a kind of governor or the leader of an ethnic group living in the city] **under Aretas the king was guarding the city of the Damascenes** [more exactly, was having it guarded] **in order to seize me, [33]and through a window** [that looked out] **through the wall I was let down in a rope-basket and escaped his hands** [compare Acts 9:19b–25]. Here Paul offers an example of his weakness in having to be helped out of Damascus by others. He didn't, and couldn't, leave on his own two feet. Just as he "was let down," we'll see next that he was "snatched up," again apart from locomotion of his own making.

12:1–4: **It's necessary to keep boasting. On the one hand** [it's] **not beneficial** [to keep boasting]. **On the other hand I'll come to visions and revelations of the Lord** [because it's necessary to keep boasting]. "Visions" stresses Paul's seeing. "Revelations of the Lord" stresses what Jesus as the exalted Lord showed him. Since Paul will mention only one incident of this sort, the plural in "visions and revelations" may imply the selection of an example or, perhaps more likely, a plurality of sights and disclosures within the one incident described. A later reference to "utterances" will indicate that sounds accompanied the sights. **[2]I know a human being in Christ;** [I know] **such** [a human being] **as having been snatched up as far as the third heaven fourteen years ago— whether in the body, I don't know, or outside the body, I don't know. God knows. [3]And I know such a human being—whether in the body or apart from the body, I don't know; God knows—[4]that he was snatched up into paradise and heard unutterable utterances that aren't allowed for a human being to speak.** Paul feels caught between the necessity to keep boasting about himself if he's to wean the Corinthians away from the false apostles, and the unprofitability of such boasting in and of itself. Necessity wins out. So he proceeds to "visions and revelations of the Lord." But the victory of necessity is only partial, because though describing his own experience, Paul refers to himself obliquely as "a human being" in contrast to "the Lord" and locates himself "in Christ," so that it's only by virtue of this location, not by virtue of any accomplishment of his own, that as a mere human being he received visions and revelations. Then he confesses his ignorance twice ("I don't know . . . I don't know") in contrast with God's knowledge, also mentioned twice ("God knows. . . . God knows"), as to whether he (Paul) was snatched up as far as the third heaven in an embodied state or in a disembodied state (which pair of possibilities, by the way, implies that human beings are made up of a body and a spirit, that the two are naturally united, but that they're separable [compare 5:6–8]). "I know *such* a human being" repeats Paul's referring to himself obliquely as merely human in contrast to the divine Lord and as having received heavenly visions and revelations only by virtue of being "in Christ." Another "I don't know" versus "God knows" contrasts again Paul's ignorance with God's knowledge as to an embodied state versus a disembodied one. Paul knows himself to be a human being in Christ, but he doesn't even know whether he was in his own body! He's doing all he can to depreciate himself while submitting to the necessity of unprofitable boasting. "Fourteen years ago" points to a definite, memorable experience. More importantly, the occurrence of the event two heptads earlier shows how long Paul has been suffering his "thorn in the flesh," which he's about to mention as given to him for the prevention of pride over the visions and revelations. His self-depreciation shows that the thorn worked. "As far as the third heaven" probably means "right up to the highest heaven," the heaven of the Lord's abode as distinct from the starry heavens (the second heaven) and the earth's atmosphere (the first heaven [compare 1 Kings 8:27]). The switch to "paradise" compares the third heaven to a walled pleasure garden (see the comments on Luke 23:43; Revelation 2:7). Supplementing what Paul saw were the "utterances" that he heard. He describes them as "*un*utterable" in that a mere human being, such as he is, isn't allowed to repeat them. Again, then, he's depreciating himself to distance himself from a prideful kind of boasting.

12:5–7a: **Concerning such** [a human being] **I'll boast, but concerning myself I'll not boast—except in [my] weaknesses.** [6-7a]**For if I want to boast, I'll not be nonsensical; for I'll tell the truth.** "Concerning *such* [a human being]" refers to Paul yet again obliquely as a mere human being who only by virtue of his location in Christ received heavenly visions and revelations. Paul says he'll boast about himself as such a human being; but astonishingly, he then distinguishes himself from that human being, as though the Paul who's writing is a different person from the Paul who had those visions and revelations. They belong to a former Paul, so to speak. The present Paul—he'll boast about himself only in reference to his weaknesses. "For if I want to boast" implies his wanting to boast by way of a necessary refutation of the false apostles and starts a justification of the preceding statement, "Concerning such [a human being] I'll boast." "I'll not be nonsensical" corresponds to the preceding statement, "but concerning myself I'll not boast—except in [my] weaknesses," and therefore implies that boasting in one's strengths *would* be nonsensical. "For I'll tell the truth" recalls 11:10, 31 and explains why Paul won't be nonsensical. It would be nonsensical *not* to tell the truth! **And I'm refraining** [from nonsensi-

cal boasting], **lest anyone credit to me even in regard to the extraordinariness of the revelations** [just described as having occurred in paradise] [anything] **above what he sees me** [to be] **or anything** [above what] **he hears from me.** For Paul, then, telling the truth means not exaggerating the facts concerning himself. It's the false apostles who deal in self-inflating exaggerations. "Even in regard to the extraordinariness of the revelations" shows that Paul was indeed referring to himself when talking about the human being who was treated to visions and revelations.

12:7b–9c: **So** [because of "the extraordinariness of the revelations"] **in order that I not be lifting myself up** [in pride] **over** [other people], **a thorn in the flesh was given to me,** [that is,] **a messenger of Satan, in order that he** [Satan's messenger] **might be pummeling me in order that I not be lifting myself up** [in pride] **over** [other people]. [8]**Concerning this** [messenger of Satan] **I urged the Lord three times that he** [the messenger] **might go away from me.** [9a–c]**And he** [the Lord] **has told me, "My grace is enough for you, for** [my] **power is being completed in** [your] **weakness."** People are compared to "thorns" in the sides and eyes in Numbers 33:55; Joshua 23:13; but for such a comparison here, perhaps to the false apostles, we'd expect the plural, as in those passages, rather than Paul's singulars, "a thorn . . . a messenger." So the attachment of "in the flesh" to "a thorn" makes the thorn a figure of speech for some sort of physical malady. (It's useless to try identifying it more particularly.) "A messenger of Satan" personifies the malady and describes it as inflicted by Satan (compare Satan's transforming himself "into an angel [which means 'messenger'] of light" [11:14]). "In order that he might be pummeling me" changes the figure of a thorn stuck in some flesh to that of a fist knocking down the whole body. "In order that I not be lifting myself up [in pride] over [the people]" then states in prosaic language the purpose of being figuratively pummeled to the ground.

"Was given to me" indicates that it was a gift for Paul to have something keeping him from self-exaltation over other people because of "the extraordinariness of the revelations" he'd received in "the third heaven," "paradise." He leaves ambiguous the giver of the thorn in the flesh. On the one hand, the equation of the thorn with Satan's messenger suggests that Satan gave Paul the thorn. On the other hand, the Lord rather than Satan had the purpose of keeping Paul from self-exaltation; for self-exaltation was a hallmark of the false apostles as Satan's servants (11:13–15, 20). So it looks as though both Satan and the Lord gave the thorn to Paul: Satan for the purpose of curbing Paul's evangelism, the Lord for the purpose of curbing self-exaltation by Paul and thus of safeguarding his evangelism (compare 4:11). The Lord's purpose, mentioned twice for emphasis, won out. Paul's urging the Lord "three times" that Satan's messenger go away shows how painful was Paul's malady, the thorn in his flesh. "And he has told me" sets the Lord's single, enduring reply over against Paul's three urgings. "Grace" means "favor," so that "My grace is enough for you" matches the Lord's favor to Paul's pain. To bear the pain it's enough to know the Lord's favor; and his favor is manifested in his power, such as characterizes Paul's proclamation of Christ crucified to the accompaniment of "both signs and wonders and miracles" (12:12; compare 4:7; 6:7; 1 Corinthians 1:18, 23–25; 2:4–5; 4:20). The Lord's power "is being completed" in that Paul's "weakness," which can also be translated "illness," makes obvious that all the power comes from the Lord, none from Paul.

12:9d–10: Most gladly therefore [because the Lord's power is being completed in my weakness] **I'll boast in my weaknesses rather** [than in "the extraordinariness of the revelations"] **so that the Christ's power may tent over me.** [10]**So** [on account of the tenting of Christ's power over me when I'm boasting in my weaknesses] **I'm delighting in weaknesses, in insults, in hardships, in persecutions and tight predicaments** [endured] **on Christ's behalf. For when I'm weak, then I'm powerful.** "May tent over me" makes figuratively clear that the power is Christ's, not Paul's. "*The* Christ's" calls attention to the power as tied to Jesus' messianic office and shows that "the Lord," whom Paul urged to send away Satan's messenger, was none other than Christ. Paul would rather have the Christ's power tenting over him while a thorn is stuck in his flesh and he's being knocked flat than to be rid of the thorn and the messenger's fist and not have that power. "Most gladly" raises this preference to the highest possible degree. *Boasting* in weaknesses, of which the thorn in the flesh is an example, clears the way for the tenting of the Christ's power over Paul, because then the Christ will get all the credit, which he deserves. This self-deflationary boasting is directed outward to others. *Delighting* in weaknesses has to do with inward emotion. Paul adds to weaknesses both insults and hardships and persecutions and tight predicaments, because these additions expose his weaknesses so that he can delight as well as boast in them. That they're endured "on Christ's behalf" triggers "the Christ's power." "For when I'm weak, then I'm powerful" explains that insults, hardships, persecutions, and tight predicaments bring out Paul's weaknesses with the result that he's powerful, not with his own power, but with the Christ's power that tents over him.

PAUL'S APOSTOLIC MIRACLES
2 Corinthians 12:11–13

12:11: I've become nonsensical. In 12:6 Paul said, "I'll *not* be nonsensical . . . . And I'm *refraining* [from nonsensical boasting]." But just now he has said that when he's weak he's powerful. So it hits him that declaring himself powerful *is* nonsensical even though he has ascribed his power to the Christ (12:9). But he blames the Corinthians for catapulting him into the nonsense of boasting that he's powerful: **You forced me** [to become nonsensical], **for I ought to have been commended by you.** The Corinthians were indeed blameworthy. They should have commended Paul rather than lionizing the

false apostles. Their lionizing them forced him to compete in a contest of nonsensical boasting. Now Paul tells why the Corinthians should have commended him: **For in nothing have I come short of the super-apostles, even though I'm nothing** [compare 1 Corinthians 15:9]. For the super-apostles as the original Twelve plus James the half-brother of Jesus or, more probably, as that James, Cephas (Peter), and John see the comments on 11:5. "In *nothing* have I come short . . . even though I'm *nothing*" makes a wordplay that emphasizes both Paul's total lack of shortcoming in comparison with the super-apostles and the totality of his nothingness. He doesn't say, "I'm nobody" or "I'm a nobody"—rather, "I'm nothing" or, as it could also be translated, "I'm not a single thing." His use of the neuter gender, "no-*thing*," emphasizes the quality of nothingness; and this quality looks the more remarkable in view of his comparing himself favorably with the *super*-apostles.

Next, Paul balances what he didn't do (by way of not coming short) with what he did do—only he uses the passive voice to divert credit from himself to the Christ, whose power tents over him. **12:12–13: Indeed, the signs of an apostle were produced among you with all persistence by way of both signs and wonders and miracles** [which by definition are "acts of power" (compare Romans 15:18–19; Galatians 3:5)]. "Indeed" underlines the production of apostolic signs, which Paul defines by adding "wonders and miracles," that is, awe-inspiring miracles. Though not limited to apostles, the working of these signs characterized apostles, because Christ produced them first; and then as his stand-ins, the apostles produced them with the very power that he himself had exercised. "Were produced" leaves room for Christ to have been producing the signs through Paul's agency as well as for Paul to have been producing them on Christ's behalf. "Among you" appeals to the Corinthians' having witnessed the production of Paul's apostolic signs, so that none of the Corinthians should have shifted their loyalty from Paul, a true apostle, to the false apostles. "With all persistence" may refer to this endurance of vicissitudes, as in 6:4; but the present close association with the production of signs favors an appeal to the continuation of signs-production throughout the entirety of the year and a half he spent evangelizing Corinth (Acts 18:11). For this reason, too, none of the Corinthians should have shifted their loyalty from Paul to the false apostles. So now he justifies with a question his appeal to the apostolic signs: [13]**For what is** [the respect] **in which you were treated worse than the rest of the churches, except that I myself wasn't a burden to you?** As though the multiplicity and persistence of apostolic signs that were produced for their benefit might have constituted *mis*treatment of them, indeed worse mistreatment of them than that of the rest of the churches established by Paul with (tongue-in-cheek) mercifully fewer signs! This irony heightens to sarcasm in his reference to having been financially unburdensome to the Corinthians (11:7–9), as though this was an even *worse* mistreatment than that of producing apostolic signs among them! Then the sarcasm reaches its peak: **Pardon me this injustice!** As though proclaiming the gospel to them free-of-charge was an injustice requiring a plea for absolution! Paul's opponents in Corinth should be ashamed of themselves.

PAUL'S COMING VISIT TO CORINTH
2 Corinthians 12:14–13:10

12:14–15: **Behold, I'm ready to come to you for this third** [time]; **and I'll not burden you** [financially], **for I'm not seeking your** *things—rather*, *you*! **For children oughtn't to be treasuring up** [things] **for** [their] **parents—rather, parents for** [their] **children.** [15]**And I'll most gladly spend and be spent out for your lives.** "Behold" calls special attention to Paul's future visit. "I'm ready to come to you" implies it will occur soon; so they'd better hurry up and get ready themselves. "For this third time" implies the first visit for evangelism and the second, sorrowful visit mentioned in 2:1. Paul says he'll continue his practice of not asking them to support him financially during his visit, and explains his motive as one of restoring good relations with them rather than milking them of their resources for his upkeep. Then he repeats the explanation under the figure of parents' treasuring up things for their children rather than vice versa. The reference is to parents' supporting their children as the children are growing up, not to saving up to leave the children an inheritance; for then the analogy wouldn't work, Paul being still alive and active. His converting them made him a kind of parent to them, and them rather like children to him (1 Corinthians 4:15). The word for "lives" refers to physical life (1:23; 1 Corinthians 15:45); so Paul is stating that not only will he avoid taking money from them for *his* upkeep. He'll also spend his own money for *their* upkeep—indeed, spend it all ("I'll . . . be spent *out*")—and do so "most gladly," just as he said he'll boast in his weaknesses "most gladly" (12:9 [compare the comments on Acts 20:32–35]). Such is the love of parents for their children. So Paul asks, **If** [I'm] **loving you extraordinarily more** [than merely not burdening you financially], **should I be loved less?** Even the *recalcitrant* Corinthians should be able to answer, "No."

12:16–18: **And it's to be: I didn't burden you.** We'd say: As a matter *of fact* I didn't burden you by taking pay for my upkeep, and you can't change that past history of mine with you; for it just *is*, and is bound to stay that way. **Being tricky, nevertheless, I took you in with cunning.** After noting the unchangeable fact of his not having taken pay from the Corinthians, Paul describes himself as "tricky," so that he "took [them] in with cunning." In their thinking they had it over on him because of his not having taken pay for evangelizing them, as though by his own recognition it hadn't been worth getting paid for. But he foresaw that not taking pay from them would enable him to contrast himself with money-grubbers like the false apostles. So he now has it over on the Corinthians. "Nevertheless" contrasts the appearance of unworthiness to take pay with the cunning

trickery of not taking it. The jocularity of this contrast now gives way to some serious questions: [17]**In regard to anyone of those I've sent to you, I've not exploited you through him, have I?** Implied answer: No. [18]**I urged Titus** [to visit you (compare 2:13; 7:6, 13–14)] **and sent the brother with** [him]. "The brother" remains anonymous, but the Corinthians will have known him from his having accompanied Titus. **Titus didn't exploit you in any way, did he?** Implied answer: No. **We've walked around** [= behaved toward you] **by the same Spirit, haven't we?** Implied answer: Yes. **In the same steps, haven't we?** Implied answer: Yes. So the same Spirit that has directed Paul's irreproachable behavior toward the Corinthians has directed Titus's similarly irreproachable behavior toward them (compare 1 Corinthians 12:9–11, and see Galatians 5:16 for walking around by the Spirit and Romans 4:12; 1 Peter 2:21 for "steps" as representing an example to be followed).

12:19: **Have you been thinking all along that we're defending ourselves to you? We're speaking in front of God,** [that is,] **in Christ.** Paul did defend himself in 1 Corinthians 9:3 ("My defense to those who examine me is this . . ."), but "all along" refers now to what he has been saying from 10:1 onward. How can he deny self-defense here, though? Well, the Corinthians are in Corinth. Paul and company are still in Macedonia (2:13; 7:5). So although what Paul has been saying does count as self-defense, he hasn't been speaking in person to the Corinthians. They can't hear him in Corinth as he dictates the letter in Macedonia. They'll hear it read to them later on, but they're not hearing it now. So Paul uses this temporal-and-geographical circumstance to point out that though at the time of dictation the Corinthians aren't within earshot, he and his colleagues are speaking "in front of God" because of their being "in Christ," who is enthroned in heaven with God (compare 2:17). The consciousness that God is their present audience ensures the truthfulness of the self-defense more securely than the expectation of the Corinthians' later listening could ever ensure it. For God can't be fooled, whereas Corinthians have been fooled—by the false apostles. **And** [we're saying] **all things, beloved, for the sake of building you up.** The purpose of building up the Corinthians supplements the consciousness of dictating the letter in God's hearing. "Beloved" assures the Corinthians of Paul's parental affection for them (compare 12:14). "All things" excludes a destructive purpose in any action of Paul relating to the Corinthians.

Now Paul tells why he's doing all things for the sake of building up the Corinthians as his beloved children. *12:20–21*: **For I fear lest somehow, on coming** [to you], **I find you such as I don't want** [to find you] **and** [lest somehow] **I be found by you such as you don't want** [to find me], **lest somehow** [there be] **strife, jealousy, outbreaks of rage, rivalries, malicious remarks, gossipings,** [self-]**pufferings, tumults,** [21]**lest when I've come my God humble me again in relation to you and I mourn over many who'd sinned previously and didn't** repent of the impurity and fornication and licentiousness that they'd practiced [previously]. Paul doesn't want to find the Corinthians full of strife, jealousy, and so on; and the Corinthians wouldn't want to find him wielding his apostolic authority against them. "I fear lest . . ." poses the possibility that 2 Corinthians won't have succeeded in its aim to bring around the still-recalcitrant minority (compare 2:1); and "somehow," which occurs twice, suggests that the false apostles might thwart this aim. "Lest . . . my God humble me again in relation to you" indicates Paul's fear that God might use continued recalcitrance by the minority to humiliate Paul a second time. An apostle shouldn't have to suffer humiliation at God's hands in the presence of the very people the apostle has evangelized. "Lest . . . I mourn" indicates Paul's fear that continued sinning on the part of supposed converts will make him mourn because of their disqualification from salvation (compare 13:5; 1 Corinthians 15:1–2). "Who'd sinned previously" refers to sinning prior to professed conversion (1 Corinthians 6:9–10). "And didn't repent" points to a failure to follow up the profession with reformation of conduct. Perhaps the false apostles' teaching had something to do with the failure to repent. "Impurity" means moral impurity of a sexual sort. "Fornication" means sexual immorality of any sort. And "licentiousness" means unbridled sexual immorality.

13:1–3: This [is] the third [time] **I'm coming to you. "On the mouth of two witnesses and three** [= on the basis of at least two testimonies] **every matter shall be established** [Deuteronomy 19:15]." [2]**I said before, when I was present** [with you] **the second time, and now, though being absent** [from you], **I'm saying before** [my upcoming third visit to you]—[I'm saying] **to those who've sinned before and to all the rest that if I come again I'll not spare** [anyone], [3]**since you're seeking proof of the Christ speaking in me,** [the Christ] **who isn't weak** [in dealing] **with you—rather, is powerful among you.** In 12:20 Paul expressed fear that on his upcoming visit he might be found by the Corinthians "such as [they] don't want [to find him]." That fear turns here into a forewarning predicated on their persistence in the vices listed in the further part of 12:20. The upcoming visit will be his third to Corinth. On the first one he evangelized the city (Acts 18:1–18). The second visit saddened him because of a failure to quell the rebellion against his apostolic authority over them (2:1). In 12:14 he pronounced himself ready to come. Hence, "I'm coming to you" makes his coming so sure and soon that he might as well be already on his way. Since the coming is so sure and soon, the Corinthians had better hurry up and mend their ways.

"This [is] the *third* [time] I'm coming to you" makes Paul's citation of the Mosaic law requiring at least two witnesses personify his three visits, including the imminent one, as though they testify to the state of affairs in the Corinthian church and justify his dealings with that church. The citation's abruptness dramatizes it as a scriptural support of these dealings. Since neither Greek nor Roman law required more than one witness, Paul's citation of the more demanding scriptural requirement underlines the sufficiency of his three visits as witnesses, one more than even the scriptural minimum. Added to the three visits as personified witnesses are two forewarnings, one that Paul issued during his second visit and a second that he's issuing right here in the present letter (compare an unmentioned forewarning earlier than either of these in 1 Corinthians 4:21). "Those who've sinned earlier" refers to the unrepentant sinners mentioned in 12:21 (see the comments there). "All the rest" refers to the remainder of Christians in Corinth. They too need a forewarning lest they be lured into sinful behavior by the example of the unrepentant and perhaps also by the false apostles' influence. "If I come again" doesn't take back the certainty of Paul's coming as expressed in 13:1. The "if"-ness has to do, not with his coming as such—rather, with his coming so as not to spare anyone. If all the Corinthians needing to repent *do* repent, he'll *not* come with an unsparing purpose. If *not* all of them repent who need to do so, he *will* come with an unsparing purpose. Not to spare the unrepentant would be to excommunicate them from the church, as in 1 Corinthians 5, for which excommunication Paul would have support from the majority of Corinthian believers (2:6; compare 10:6).

"Since you're seeking proof of the Christ speaking in me" addresses in particular Paul's opponents (a minority), makes the threat of excommunication his response to their proof-seeking, and relates the proof-seeking to his claim that the Christ is speaking in him and therefore through him—not just because Christ indwells him as he indwells every true believer (so 13:5) but because as an apostle, Paul is being used by Christ as a mouthpiece. "*The* Christ" invests Christ's words, spoken through Paul, with the authority of Christ's messianic office, as brought out further by Paul's describing the Christ as "not weak"—rather, as "powerful"—in his dealings with the Corinthians through Paul's agency. Just as the present tense makes Paul's coming sure and soon, so the present tense makes the Christ's not being weak in dealing with the Corinthians but being powerful among them likewise sure and soon in its excommunicatory outworking. Paul doesn't say what kind of proof his opponents are seeking, but certainly they aren't seeking their own excommunication as proof! That's what they'll get, though, unless they quickly repent.

13:4: **For he** [the Christ] **was also crucified because of weakness, yet he lives because of God's power. For in him we also are weak, yet** [in dealing] **with you we will live with him because of God's power.** These two sentences explain why up till now Paul has been "weak" in his dealings with the Corinthians (10:10; 11:21). The weakness consisted in "meekness and mildness" (10:1). But that meekness and mildness was "the Christ's" (so 10:1 again). Now Paul interprets it as the weakness by which the Christ subjected himself to crucifixion, and therefore a weakness not to be despised. The first "also" makes his crucifixion because of weakness an object of consideration additional to his just-mentioned power. The pendulum swings back to power, but this time Paul refers to God's power as the cause of Christ's resurrected and ongoing life post-crucifixion (compare Romans 1:4). Then Paul locates his and his colleagues' meek and mild weakness "in" the Christ, correlates it with the Christ's crucifixion because of such weakness (the second "also"), and interprets any forthcoming excommunications—because of their power (see 1 Corinthians 5:1–5, especially 5:4)—as anticipations of his and his colleagues' future resurrected and ongoing life with the resurrected Christ "because of God's power" (compare Romans 8:10; 1 Corinthians 6:14; 15:43; Galatians 2:20; Philippians 3:10).

13:5–6: Be testing yourselves [to see] **if you're in the faith. Be proving yourselves.** Some Corinthians are seeking proof that the Christ is speaking in Paul (13:3). So Paul turns the tables on them by telling them to prove themselves. The proof will have to start with self-testing as to whether they're "in the faith," that is, as to whether their conduct proves or disproves the genuineness of their professed belief in Christ. If they fail this self-test, they'd better repent of their opposition to Paul and of their immorality (the latter listed in 12:21). Otherwise they face Paul's unsparing excommunication (13:2). The present tense of testing and proving puts a spotlight on Paul's commands (compare 2:9). **Or you recognize about yourselves, don't you, that Jesus Christ** [is] **in you unless indeed you're disproved** [= disqualified, proved not to be a true believer]**?** The affirmative answer implied by this question compliments the Corinthians on their knowledge but leaves them without excuse. They know better than to assume they don't have to prove by their conduct that Jesus Christ is in them, which is the flip side of their being in the faith (compare Romans 8:10; Galatians 2:20). "Or," which introduces Paul's question, makes it an alternative to the preceding command, as though to say, "If you're not inclined to be proving yourselves because of my command that you do so, then be proving yourselves because of your knowledge that Jesus Christ is in you unless you're disproved." "Indeed" stresses the possibility of being disproved and thus unsaved despite a profession of faith (see the comments on 1 Corinthians 9:27, where the word translated "disproved" here in 13:5 is translated "disqualified" in accordance with the context there of athletic competition). Because of the frequency with which Paul portrays believers as "in Christ" we might have expected him to say here, "that you're in Christ." But he says, "that Jesus Christ [is] in you," for a parallel with the Corinthians' seeking proof of the Christ speaking "in" Paul (13:3). So the reversal of "in Christ" underlines Paul's turning the tables on the Corinthians by commanding them to prove themselves rather than seeking proof concerning him. Whereas the Christ is powerful in his dealings "among" the Corinthians as a body of believers (13:3), here he's present "in" believers individually unless they're disproved. **6And I'm hoping that you'll recognize that we aren't disproved.** For Paul, hoping means expecting, not merely wishing for. Here, then, he states his expecta-

tion that either because of repenting of their opposition or because of his not sparing the unrepentant, the Corinthians will recognize that, unlike the false apostles, he and his colleagues "aren't disproved" or, positively stated, are "in the faith" and have "Jesus Christ in [them]."

13:7–9: And we're praying to God that you do nothing evil, not in order that we be displayed as proved—rather, in order that you may be doing the good but we may be, as it were, disproved. So praying to God supplements Paul's letter-writing. Paul includes his colleagues with himself in praying that the Corinthians "do nothing evil." The praying superimposes God's sovereignty on the Corinthians' avoiding evil in answer to prayer. Thus he'll get the credit, and no room will be left for self-righteousness on their part. By informing them of this prayer Paul seeks both to forestall self-righteousness and to impress on them the will of God that they do nothing evil. The preceding context indicates in particular the evils of opposing Paul, a true apostle, of favoring the false apostles, and of engaging in sexual immorality. He denies that behind this praying of him and his colleagues lies a purpose of merely saving face ("*not* in order that we might be displayed as proved [to have Jesus Christ in us]"). Their praying has the contrary purpose of getting God to work in the Corinthians his will that they do "the good" of submitting to Paul's apostolic authority, rejecting the false apostles, and discontinuing their sexual immorality. "But that we may be, *as it were*, disproved" strengthens "not in order that we might appear proved," but not to the extent of being *really* disproved. After all, Paul has just said, "And I'm hoping that you'll recognize that we *aren't* disproved."

Now Paul supplies two reasons why he and his colleagues are praying to God that the Corinthians do good and not evil. Here's the first reason: **8For we can't** [do] **anything against the truth; rather,** [we do everything] **for the truth.** "The truth" consists in the gospel (4:2; 6:7; 11:10). Merely to save face would be to do something against the gospel, which is good news about the Christ, not self-recommendation such as the false apostles engage in. Paul says, "We *can't* [do] anything against the truth," because the Christ is speaking in him (13:3); and the Christ speaks nothing but the truth. To do everything for the truth is to support the proclamation of the gospel with self-effacement, as Paul has done even while boasting nonsensically about himself (11:16–12:10). Here's the second reason he and his colleagues are praying to God that the Corinthians do good and not evil: **9For we're rejoicing whenever we're weak and you're powerful.** "Whenever we're weak and you're powerful" means whenever Paul and company can afford to act toward the Corinthians with "the Christ's meekness and mildness" (10:1) because the Corinthians are behaving as true Christians should behave and therefore are exhibiting in their conduct the gospel's power (among other passages see 4:7; 6:7; 12:9–10; 13:3–4; 1 Corinthians 1:18, 23–24). **We also pray this: your being put back together** [compare 1 Corinthians 1:10]. "Also" adds praying that the Corinthians be put back together to the prayer that they do good and not evil. Since evil causes disintegration and good causes integration, these prayers complement each other. "Your being put back together" has special reference to bringing the minority in Corinth, who oppose Paul, together with the majority, who support him, so that they present a united front in his favor and against the false apostles.

13:10: **While being absent I'm writing these things because of this, [namely,] in order that when being present I may not deal sharply [with you] in accordance with the authority that the Lord gave me for the purpose of building up and not for the purpose of tearing down.** "In order that . . . I may not deal sharply" defines the reason why Paul is writing. His and his colleagues' praying that the Corinthians be "put back together" has prompted him to supplement such praying to God with writing to them this letter, especially chapters 10–13. He'd rather that God answer the prayer through using the letter than that he (Paul) have to use his apostolic authority to tear some of them down through excommunication ("deal sharply"). "Tearing down" through excommunication would diminish the size of the church, but the Lord Jesus commissioned Paul to build up the church through the winning of ever more converts (compare 10:8).

CONCLUSION
2 Corinthians 13:11–13

Making up the conclusion are final exhortations supported by a promise (13:11), greetings both commanded and given (13:12), and a benediction (13:13).

13:11: **As to the rest [of this letter], brothers, be rejoicing. Be putting yourselves back together. Be being exhorted. Be thinking the same thing [= agreeing with one another and me]. Be at peace [with one another and me], and the God of love and peace will be with you.** "As to the rest [of this letter]," traditionally translated "Finally," signals a conclusion. "Brothers" strikes a note of affection to assure the Corinthians that even in his harshest statements Paul has had their best interests at heart. The Corinthians will be able to rejoice in obedience to his initial command to rejoice if they obey his second command to put themselves back together (on

which see 13:9). They'll be able to put themselves back together if they obey his third command to be exhorted. The result of obeying this command will be obedience to his fourth command that they think the same thing, which matches being put back together. The result of thinking the same thing will be obedience to the fifth command that they be at peace with one another and Paul. Then, but only then, will God be with them as the God who loves them and extends to them the peace which consists in all the blessings of salvation. So they shouldn't shrug off these commands.

13:12: **Greet one another with a sacred kiss. All the sacred ones** [traditionally translated "All the saints," which obscures the wordplay with "a sacred kiss"] **are greeting you** [through this letter]. See the comments on 1 Thessalonians 5:26 for greeting "with a sacred kiss," which in the present context has special relevance to the split in Corinth between the majority, who support Paul, and the minority, who oppose him. The description of the kiss as "sacred" also has special relevance to the problem of sexual immorality among the Corinthians. See the comments on 1 Corinthians 1:1–3 for the designation of Christians as "the sacred [= consecrated] ones." The sending of greetings from "*all* the sacred ones" puts friendly pressure on the Corinthians to be putting themselves back together.

13:13: **The grace of the Lord, Jesus Christ, and the love of God and the fellowship of the Holy Spirit** [be] **with all of you.** "Grace" means "favor" (see further the comments on 1 Peter 1:2; 2 John 3). When identifying the source of grace in letter-closing benedictions elsewhere, Paul always refers to the Lord, Jesus Christ, as he does now. But here he adds, as he doesn't do elsewhere, God's love for the Corinthians to echo "the God of love" in 13:11, and also adds "the fellowship of the Holy Spirit"—that is, Christians' sharing the Spirit with one another—to echo "the same Spirit" by whom Paul and company walk "in the same steps" (12:18). This sharing of the Spirit should produce much-needed unity through truly Christian behavior (compare 1 Corinthians 12:13). "[Be] with *all* of you" underlines Paul's hope for such unity. And the trinitarian cast of this benediction shouldn't go unnoticed (among other passages, compare 1 Corinthians 12:4–6).

GALATIANS

Some Jewish Christians advocated that for salvation, Gentile Christians had to keep the law of Moses (beginning with submission to circumcision if they were males) in addition to believing in Christ. Here Paul refutes that view by advocating to the contrary that Jews and Gentiles alike gain salvation by faith apart from keeping the Mosaic law, though not at the expense of virtuous conduct.

ADDRESS AND GREETING
Galatians 1:1–5

1:1–2: Paul, an apostle [sent] **not from** [mere] **human beings nor through** [the agency of] **a** [mere] **human being—rather,** [sent] **through** [the direct action of] **Jesus Christ and God the Father, who raised him from among the dead—**²**plus all the brothers** [= fellow Christians] [who are] **with me, to the churches of Galatia** [in central Asia Minor (modern Turkey)]: . . . . As was customary for first-century letter writers, Paul starts by identifying himself as the author. Then he calls himself "an apostle," which means somebody who has been sent. "Not from [mere] human beings" denies that he has been sent by a church such as the one in Antioch, Syria, for example (see Acts 13:3, especially the translation "they let go [of them]" as opposed to "they sent [them]"). "Nor through [the agency of] a [mere] human being" denies even the involvement of a human intermediary in the sending of Paul (contrast "the coming of some from James" [2:12]). He makes these denials to establish a foil against which his being sent "through [the direct action of] Jesus Christ and God the Father" stands out in full flower. Since "apostle" connotes a sending with authority to act on behalf of the sender, Paul stresses the direct derivation of his apostleship from Jesus Christ and God the Father to impress on the letter's addressees (from now on "the Galatians") that what he has to say in the balance of the letter should bring them to their knees in submission rather than putting them in high dudgeon. For the balance of the letter contains some stinging rebukes.

Paul puts "Jesus Christ" ahead of "God the Father" because he has in mind Jesus Christ's commissioning him to apostleship in connection with his appearance to Paul as Paul was traveling on the road to Damascus (see 1:12; 1 Corinthians 9:1; 15:8; Acts 9:1–6, 15; 21:40–22:15; and especially 26:12–20). "Who raised him [Jesus Christ] from among the dead" describes God in view of the circumstance that unlike the twelve apostles, Paul's apostolic commissioning occurred after rather than before Jesus' resurrection. Since "God . . . was pleased to reveal his Son in [Paul] in order that [Paul] might proclaim the gospel among the Gentiles" (1:16), Paul includes "God the Father" with "Jesus Christ" as the source of his apostleship and thus doubles his apostolic authority. Because of the collocation of God and his Son in 1:15–16, here in 1:1 "God the Father" probably refers to God as the Father of the just-mentioned "Jesus Christ," though Paul will shortly widen God's fatherhood to include Christian believers (1:4; 4:6). The pairing of Jesus Christ with God the Father, the designation of him as God's Son, and the further designation of him as "our Lord" in 1:3 imply the deity of Jesus Christ. Yet he's also human—hence the two explanatory insertions of "mere" to distinguish him from other human beings.

Paul includes "all the brothers" who are with him at the time of writing as co-senders (though not co-authors) of the letter to let the Galatians know that he has his companions' support in what he'll proceed to say. So the Galatians had better not dismiss the letter as the rantings of an eccentric. "Plus *all* the brothers" sharpens this point. The brothers remain anonymous, and their and Paul's whereabouts remain unidentified. For what counts above all in this context is the apostolic authority of Paul. "To the *churches* of Galatia" implies a circular letter, one that's meant to make the rounds of local assemblies of Christians and be read aloud to them in those assemblies. Paul's omitting to describe the Galatians as "saints," "God's beloved ones," "believers," or "faithful" portends coming expressions of disgust with them, or at least of puzzlement about them (1:6; 3:1, 3; 4:9–11; 5:7). Similar omissions occur in the addresses of 1 and 2 Thessalonians, but there Paul quickly follows up with compliments, as he does *not* do here.

1:3–5: Grace and peace to you from God, the Father, and the Lord, Jesus Christ, ⁴**who gave himself for our sins so that he might deliver us out of this present evil age in accordance with the will of God, even our Father,** ⁵**to whom** [belongs] **the glory forever and ever. Amen.** For the greetings "grace" and "peace" see the comments on 1 Peter 1:2; 2 John 3. The issue in the rest of Galatians concerning salvation by grace apart from salvation by Law-keeping (1:6; 2:9, 21; 5:4) and the warning in 5:15 against internal strife give special pertinence to these greetings. Since grace and peace connote salvation, the greetings stem from God and Jesus Christ, not from Paul. As an apostle he can relay divine greetings to the Galatians, and so he does. "The Father" probably still describes God in relation to Jesus Christ. "*The Lord*" describes Jesus Christ with a term that in association with "God" connotes deity and distinguishes Jesus Christ as the deity worshiped by Christians from the so-called deities worshiped by pagans (see 1 Corinthians 8:5–6). Paul's reversion to the normal order, God and then Jesus Christ (contrast 1:1), enables him to add more about Jesus Christ. "Who gave himself for our sins" defines his and God's grace, which means ill-deserved favor, in terms of Jesus Christ's voluntary self-sacrifice by way of suffering for our sins the punishment that we deserved (compare 2:20–21; 3:13; 1 Corinthians 15:3). "So that he might deliver us out of this present evil age" defines the peace of God and of Jesus Christ in terms of the flourishing that will characterize eternal life in the age to come, free as that age will be of the evil that besets mortal life in the present age. Since we're living in the present evil age, deliverance "out of" it looks to the future (but see 2:20 for a present anticipation of the deliverance in that the crucified and resurrected Christ now lives in the believer). "In accordance with the will of God" means that just as a son *should* do, Jesus Christ obeyed God his Father in giving himself for our sins to deliver us from this present evil age. God's willing him to do so leads Paul to designate God as "*our* Father," for a father looks out for the welfare of his children (compare 4:4–7). And this beneficent fatherhood of God leads Paul to declare that eternal glory, which means eternal honor, belongs to God. "Forever and ever" heightens eternality to the nth degree, and "Amen," meaning "So be it!" adds an emphatic affirmation of the whole greeting.

PAUL'S REASON FOR WRITING
Galatians 1:6–10

1:6–7: I'm astonished that you're defecting in this way—[that is,] **quickly**—**from the one who called you in the grace of Christ into a different gospel, ⁷which isn't another** [gospel]—**except there are some who are stirring you up** [to defect] **and wanting to distort the gospel about the Christ.** Shockingly, Paul replaces the usual thanksgiving for his readers (see an example in 1 Corinthians 1:4–9) with an expression of astonishment which carries a note of rebuke, explains his omitting to call the Galatians "saints," "God's beloved ones," "believers," or "faithful" back in 1:2, and tells why he's writing this letter and why he started it with a heavy stress on his apostleship as having come directly from Jesus Christ and God the Father. The Galatians' defection is the reason. "You're . . . defecting" indicates a defection in progress, which the letter is designed to halt. "In this way—[that is,] quickly" describes the defection, but we don't know whether this description means soon after conversion or soon after the proclamation of "a different gospel" to the Galatians. There may be other possibilities of meaning. In any case, "quickly" makes the defection especially astonishing to Paul. He assumes that the Galatians will understand "God, even our Father" (1:4) to be

"the one who called [them] in the grace of Christ" (see 1:15–16 for God as a caller). As used by Paul, the call of God refers to his summons, powerful and effective as it is—here to salvation "in the grace of Christ," which refers to his ill-deserved favor in having given himself for our sins "so that he might deliver us out of this present evil age" (1:4). "*In* the grace of Christ" makes his grace the sphere in which God's call took place, for Christ's giving himself for our sins made it possible for God to summon people to salvation without violating his right and just standard that sins must be punished.

"Into a different gospel" stands in opposition to "in the grace of Christ." That is to say, the different gospel subverts Christ's grace. Since this grace makes the gospel what it is—namely, "good news"—the subversion of Christ's grace produces "a different gospel," even a *non*gospel ("which isn't another [gospel]"). Given our sins, the subversion of his grace makes for bad news, not good news. "Except there are some who are stirring you up [to defect]" implies that the defection is a kind of rebellion, a transfer of allegiance from the one who called the Galatians to the different gospel that's not really a gospel at all (compare 5:4). Because of the preceding emphasis on his apostleship, we might have expected Paul to portray the defection as a defection from him. But because both his apostleship and the grace and peace of salvation stem ultimately from God, Paul portrays the defection as a defection from God. And the description of God as "the one who called [the Galatians] in the grace of Christ" makes the defection not only unwarranted but also ungrateful. By writing "except there are some who are stirring you up," however, Paul takes exception to his own expression of astonishment at the Galatians' ungrateful defection. For the blame shifts now from them to "some who are stirring you up and wanting to distort the gospel about the Christ." This shift softens Paul's tone so as to make the Galatians amenable to his upcoming defense of Christ's grace and his critique of the nongospel. "*Wanting* to distort the gospel about the Christ" attributes purpose to the distorters (see 4:17; 6:12–13 for their selfish motives). They know they're changing the gospel that Paul proclaimed to the Galatians. "To *distort* the gospel about the Christ" represents Paul's judgment against their changing it. They haven't corrected it. They've distorted it. "About *the* Christ" lends an official overtone to Paul's gospel. The grace in its content is the grace of no less a personage than the one anointed by God to give himself for our sins, for "the Christ" means "the Anointed One."

1:8–9: Even if we or an angel [coming] **out of heaven were to be proclaiming a gospel overreaching the gospel that we proclaimed to you, however, he's to be anathema** [= a curse, a strong way of saying "accursed"]. **⁹As we've said before** [in the immediately preceding statement], **I'm also saying again—right now: if anyone is proclaiming to you a gospel overreaching what you received, he's to be anathema.** Stressing the lack of any exceptions to the accursedness of anyone who distorts the gospel of Christ's grace are (1) "*Even* if"; (2) the inclusion of Paul and company ("we" [compare 1:2]); (3) the additional inclusion of "an angel [coming] out of heaven"; and (4) "however," which sets Paul's "we" and "an angel" over against the distorters of the gospel in that "we" and "an angel" proclaim a different gospel *only hypothetically* ("Even if we or an angel . . . *were* to be proclaiming . . .") whereas the distorters actually *are* proclaiming a different gospel. Paul describes the different gospel as "overreaching" what he has just called "the gospel of the Christ." "Overreaching" has the sense of going beyond the grace of Christ—by requiring more than belief in him, it will turn out. "He's to be anathema" is a command, not a wish, much less a permission, as the usual translation, "*let* him be accursed," might be understood. Paul gives the command with the apostolic authority he ascribed to himself in 1:1. The repetition of the command redoubles the foregoing emphasis, and the introduction of this repetition with "As we've said before, I'm also saying again—right now" shows that the redoubling is downright deliberate. Far from pointing back to a curse leveled prior to the writing of this letter, "right now" sets the repetition ("I'm also saying again") emphatically alongside the foregoing curse in the present text ("As we've said before"). The shift from "*we*'ve said before" to "*I*'m saying again" concentrates attention on the curse as uttered by Paul, an apostle no less. The shift from "the gospel that we did proclaim to you" to "what you received" designates the undistorted gospel of Christ's grace as a traditional message that goes back to the Christ himself, so that overreaching it constitutes a distortive novelty.

1:10: For am I right now trying to win human beings, or [am I trying to win] **God? Or am I seeking to please human beings? If I were trying to please human beings, moreover, I wouldn't be Christ's slave!** "Am I . . . trying to win human beings?" equates with "Am I trying to please human beings?" The two maledictory commands in 1:8–9 make clear a negative answer to these questions. Curses don't make friends. "Or [am I trying to win] God?" presents an alternative to trying to win human beings and equates with "be[ing] Christ's slave." For God wants slaves for his Son. A slave tries to please his master; so "moreover" adds that "trying to please human beings" would disqualify Paul from being Christ's slave. The initial "For" makes the whole of 1:10 an elucidation of what the maledictions in 1:8–9 imply regarding Paul's motive. He wants to be winsome to God and pleasing to Christ by defending the gospel from distortion even at the cost of displeasing human beings.

AN AUTOBIOGRAPHICAL ARGUMENT FOR THE GOSPEL OF SHEER GRACE
Galatians 1:11–2:21

This major section of Galatians subdivides into Jesus' direct revelation to Paul of the gospel of sheer grace (1:11–12); the impossibility of this gospel's having originated from Paul's very Judaistic past (1:13–14); the impossibility of his having learned it from merely human sources (1:15–24); the later acknowledgment of this gospel by the church leaders in Jerusalem (2:1–10);

and Paul's rebuke of Peter for his behavioral compromise of it in Antioch, Syria (2:11–21).

JESUS' DIRECT REVELATION TO PAUL OF THE GOSPEL OF GOD'S SHEER GRACE
Galatians 1:11–12

1:11–12: But I'm making known to you, brothers, the gospel which was proclaimed as gospel [= as good news] **by me, that it isn't in accordance with a human being.** [12]**For I did not at all receive it from a human being, nor was I taught** [it by a human being]**; rather,** [I received it] **through a revelation of Jesus Christ** [compare 1:1]. Paul's having taken exception to his own expression of astonishment (1:6–7) now shades into the affectionate address, "brothers," which expands the brotherhood of 1:2 and softens his tone yet further to make the Galatians amenable to his upcoming defense of God's sheer grace and critique of the nongospel. "*But* I'm making known to you" means, "Despite not trying to please human beings, such as you are (1:10), I'm making known to you . . . the gospel."[1] As to its content, Paul made known the gospel to the Galatians when he evangelized them. Now in this letter he's making it known to them as regards his own reception of it. "For I did not at all receive it from a human being, nor was I taught [it by a human being]" explains what he means by saying "it isn't in accordance with a human being." "Through a revelation of Jesus Christ" identifies the means by which Paul received the gospel he proclaimed to the Galatians. The contrast with receiving the gospel from a human being or being taught by one favors that "through a revelation of Jesus Christ" means that God revealed Jesus Christ to Paul. Verses 15–16 will confirm this meaning (compare 1 Corinthians 9:1; 15:8). Since the gospel that Paul proclaimed to the Galatians came to him by divine revelation, they ought to correct their defection by realigning themselves with this gospel.

THE IMPOSSIBILITY OF THE GOSPEL'S HAVING ORIGINATED FROM PAUL'S VERY JUDAISTIC PAST
Galatians 1:13–14

1:13–14: For you've heard about my conduct once upon a time in Judaism [the Jewish religion as practiced in the first century], **that I was persecuting God's church outrageously and wreaking havoc on it;** [14]**and I was beating my way forward in Judaism beyond many contemporaries** [as to age] **among my kinfolk** [the Jews], **being an extraordinary zealot for my ancestral traditions.** The passage 1:13–24 explains Paul's having received the gospel "through a revelation of Jesus Christ"

---

[1]A number of early manuscripts have "*For* I'm making known to you . . . the gospel," but that may be due to parallel influence on copyists from "For" in 1:10, 12, 13. If "For" is original, though, Paul's denying that the gospel is "in accordance with a human being" tells *why* he isn't trying to please human beings (1:10).

(1:12). The explanation starts with common knowledge regarding Paul's practice of Judaism prior to that revelation. "You've heard" appeals to what the Galatians already know about it and therefore to what should have deterred them from defection. Paul mentions first his persecution of the church (here in a collective sense), and calls the church "God's" to point up the horror of having persecuted it. To underscore this horror Paul describes the persecution as outrageous and adds to it the wreaking of havoc on the church. In other words, the persecution attained a measure of success in its ravaging of Christians. The literalistic translation, "I was beating my way forward in Judaism," may mean no more than "I was advancing in Judaism"; but a literalistic translation resonates so uncannily well with "persecuting the church outrageously and wreaking havoc on it" that one wonders whether Paul intended to portray his advancement as bought at the expense of ravaged Christians. "Beyond many contemporaries among my kinfolk" portrays the advancement at least in comparative terms, perhaps also in competitive terms. Even if only in the comparative, we smell self-righteousness in the pre-Christian Paul (compare Philippians 3:6–7a, 9). "Beyond many contemporaries" may mean "beyond my contemporaries, who were many," in which case he claims to have surpassed all his contemporaries in the practice of Judaism. "Being an extraordinary zealot" is reminiscent of the extraordinary zealot Phinehas in Numbers 25:1–13. "For my ancestral traditions" doesn't refer to the Old Testament as such—rather, to it as interpreted in the Pharisaic school of thought. For Paul had been a Pharisee (Philippians 3:5; Acts 22:3; 26:4–5). That a revelation of Jesus Christ tore Paul loose from those traditions despite his extraordinary zeal for them should draw the Galatians away from the nongospel and back to the gospel he proclaimed to them.

THE IMPOSSIBILITY OF PAUL'S HAVING LEARNED THE GOSPEL FROM MERELY HUMAN SOURCES
Galatians 1:15–24

1:15–17: But when he who set me apart ever since [I was in] **my mother's womb and called** [me] **through his grace was pleased** [16]**to reveal his Son in me** [= in my case] **in order that I might proclaim him** [the Son] **as good news among the Gentiles, I didn't consult with flesh and blood immediately.** [17]**Nor did I go up to Jerusalem to those** [who became] **apostles before me** [= before I did]. **Rather, I went away** [from Damascus] **to Arabia and returned again to Damascus.** "To reveal his Son" makes clear that "he who set me apart" is God the Father. "Set me apart" has to do, then, with God's setting Paul apart from his many contemporaries among Jewish kinfolk in Judaism (1:14; compare Isaiah 49:1–6; Jeremiah 1:4–5). That God set him apart while he (Paul) was still in his mother's womb and then "called [him]" while Paul was persecuting the church and wreaking havoc on it testifies dramatically to God's sheer and sovereign grace, so dramatically in fact that the Galatians

should retrace their steps back to the gospel that features this grace undistorted and unappended. (See the comments on 1:6 for the meaning of "called," which here has to do with both Christian conversion and an apostolic commission.) And that God was actually "pleased"—or "delighted," as Paul's Greek verb could equally well be translated—to reveal his Son in Paul, again while Paul was persecuting the church and wreaking havoc on it, testifies all the more to the marvel of God's sheer and sovereign grace. Nothing need be added to it, Paul wants the Galatians (and us) to know. "In me" doesn't define the revelation of God's Son as an interior revelation that took place only in his mind, though the revelation certainly did change his mind. For elsewhere he says that he actually saw the risen Jesus and that the risen Jesus actually appeared to him (1 Corinthians 9:1; 15:8). So "in me" means "in my case" (compare 1:24; 4:20; 2 Corinthians 13:3; Philippians 1:30; 1 Timothy 1:16).

God's purpose that Paul "might proclaim him [Jesus the Son of God] as good news among the Gentiles," such as most of the Galatian Christians were by background, testifies further to God's grace in turning a persecutor into a proclaimer. Gentiles are pagans, so that God's purposing Paul to convert the Gentiles testifies yet again and even further to God's grace. But to stress the impossibility of having learned the gospel of grace from merely human sources, the main accent falls on Paul's neither "consult[ing] with flesh and blood" nor "go[ing] up to Jerusalem to those [who became] apostles before [him]" immediately after he received a revelation of God's Son. "Flesh and blood" connotes human frailty and inadequacy (see the comments on Matthew 16:17; 1 Corinthians 15:50) and implies that consultation with mere human beings wouldn't have qualified Paul to be "an apostle . . . [sent] through Jesus Christ and God the Father" (1:1). "*Up* to Jerusalem" alludes to that city's high elevation in the mountains of Judea. The revelation of God's Son, bad as the run-up to it was in Paul's case, was quite enough to convince Paul of God's grace in Jesus Christ.

1:18–20: Then after three years I did go up to Jerusalem to get acquainted with Cephas, and I stayed with him fifteen days. [19]**But I didn't see a different one of the apostles** [in addition to Cephas], **except** [that I did see] **James, the Lord's brother.** [20]**The things that I'm writing to you—behold,** [I assure you] **in God's sight that I'm not lying.** "Cephas" is the original, Aramaic form of the Greek "Peter." Paul does *not* say that he spent three years meditating in the Arabian desert away from Damascus so as to figure out the gospel in view of God's having revealed his Son to him. According to Acts 9:19–22, in fact, Paul started proclaiming Jesus as God's Son immediately in Damascus; and it remains unclear here in Galatians 1:17–18 how much of the three years Paul spent in Damascus and how much in Arabia. Since he'd started proclaiming the gospel three years before going up to Jerusalem to get acquainted with Cephas, he couldn't have gotten the gospel from Cephas. Besides, he stayed with Cephas only fifteen days; and he didn't see any of the other apostles, so that they weren't the source of Paul's gospel any more than Cephas was. Paul did see James, but doesn't make clear whether James was an exception *among* the apostles or an exception *separate from* the apostles. Paul does call James "the Lord's brother," however, to emphasize that Jesus Christ's lordship trumps whatever authority James had in the church at Jerusalem (compare 2:9, 12; Acts 12:17; 15:13–21; 21:18). (This James, traditional author of the letter of James, differs from James the brother of John and James the son of Alphaeus, both of whom were numbered among the twelve apostles.) To underline how very delayed, short, and limited were his Christian contacts in Jerusalem and therefore how impossible it was for him to have learned the gospel of grace by any means other than divine revelation, Paul assures the Galatians that he's not lying. "Behold" punctuates this assurance, and "in God's sight" implies that the assurance is given in full awareness that God will punish him if he's not telling the truth.

1:21–24: Then I went into the districts of Syria and Cilicia. [22]But I was unknown by face to the churches of Judea, [which are] **in Christ; [23]and they were only hearing, "The one who once was persecuting us is now proclaiming as good news the faith on which he was once wreaking havoc." [24]And they were glorifying** [= honoring] **God in me** [= in my case]. Syria was north of Israel. Even farther away was Cilicia, a province in southeast Asia Minor. Paul's hometown of Tarsus was the capital of Cilicia. So distance separated him once again from the apostles in Jerusalem (compare Acts 9:30). "But I was unknown by face to the churches of Judea [the territory outlying Jerusalem]" means that the churches there hadn't seen Paul, much less spoken to him so as to teach him the gospel, even during his fifteen days in Jerusalem. He describes those churches as "in Christ" to point up that their theological location outclasses their geographical location by virtue of their having been called "in the grace of Christ" just as the Galatians were (1:6). Their only hearing about the conversion of their former persecutor into a proclaimer of the gospel reemphasizes Paul's independence from them so far as the origin of his gospel was concerned. He calls this gospel "the faith" to prepare for an upcoming contrast between faith and works of the Mosaic law in the matter of gaining salvation. Faith means belief both in the sense of believing and in the sense of what is believed. "The faith" is so part and parcel of those who have it that Paul's having wreaked havoc on God's church (1:13) now turns into his having wreaked havoc on the faith itself. "And they were glorifying God in me" shows that they, the early churches in Judea, recognized that Paul's case demonstrated the gospel to be one of sheer grace. The Galatians should come to the same recognition.

THE ACKNOWLEDGMENT OF PAUL'S GOSPEL BY THE CHURCH LEADERS IN JERUSALEM
Galatians 2:1–10

2:1–2: Then [after going] **through fourteen years I went up again to Jerusalem with Barnabas, taking also Titus along with** [me]. **[2]And I went up in accordance with a revelation and presented to them** [Christians in Jerusalem] **the gospel that I proclaim among the Gentiles, but privately to those who seemed** [to be leaders] **lest somehow I were running or had run ineffectually** [literally, "with an empty result" (compare Philippians 2:16)]. "Then [after going] through fourteen years" may mean fourteen years after Paul's departing Jerusalem for the districts of Syria and Cilicia (1:21) and therefore seventeen years after his conversion and call three years prior to that departure (1:18). On the other hand, the parallel with "Then after three years" (1:8), and also between going up to Jerusalem in both instances, may favor a counting of the fourteen as well as the three from Paul's conversion and call. In either case, he's continuing to point out temporal and geographical distances from the apostles in Jerusalem. For given his well-known proclamation of the gospel during all this time, these distances support his having received the gospel of grace by divine revelation rather than from or through any merely human source or agency. "With Barnabas" may imply the Galatians' knowledge of Barnabas in accordance with his having helped Paul evangelize south Galatia on Paul's first missionary journey (but not on the second one [Acts 13:1–14:28; 15:36–41]). The Galatians may have known Titus, too, though Paul's telling them in 2:3 that Titus was a Greek might indicate they didn't know him and therefore had to be told his ethnicity and culture. See the comments on 1:17 for going *up* to Jerusalem.

"In accordance with a revelation" has nothing to do with the revelation of God's Son to Paul on the road to Damascus (1:15–16) and refers instead to a divine revelation of some sort that he should go up to Jerusalem. Whether the revelation came to him directly or someone relayed it to him (compare Acts 11:27–30), his mentioning it has the purpose of reinforcing the result of his visit. God was at work in what happened, so that the Galatians should accept the result rather than defecting. By now in this letter Paul has established the gospel as one of sheer, unaugmented grace. His presenting it "privately" to reputed leaders in the Jerusalem church suggests fear of opposition to such a gospel. "That I proclaim among the Gentiles" suggests the opposition might have to do with Gentile converts, as though opponents think something is missing in the Gentiles' conversions, and this at Paul's fault. "Lest . . . I were running or had run ineffectually" compares his evangelization of the Gentiles to a race that he may have been losing or had already lost. "Ineffectually" means without the result of salvation for the Gentiles so far as the opinion of the reputed leaders in the Jerusalem church was concerned. For the moment, "somehow" leaves obscure the element that opponents may think is missing from Paul's proclamation but crucial to the salvation of Gentiles.

2:3–5: However, even Titus, who [was] **with me, wasn't forced to be circumcised, though he was a Greek. [4]**[The question of circumcising him came up] **because of false brothers smuggled into** [the church], **who as such sneaked in to spy on our freedom, which**

we have in Christ Jesus, in order that they might en-slave us, [5]**to whom** [referring to the false brothers] **we didn't yield by way of submission even for an hour, in order that the truth of the gospel might stay with you throughout** [that is, unendingly despite the false brothers' attempts to take it away]. "However" marks a turn from fear of failure in 2:2 to a declaration of victory. It now comes out that there was definitely a question at issue, that is, whether Gentile converts should be circumcised in accordance with the Mosaic law and what was required of Gentile converts to Judaism. Paul explains that Titus was a Greek. "Gentile" means non-Jewish. But Paul uses "Greek" for Titus because, though Greeks were Gentiles, their ideal of beauty was the nude male body. This ideal made them think of circumcision as an ugly mutilation. We don't know whether Titus was a Greek by ancestry as well as by culture, or only by culture. In either case, that the reputed church leaders in Jerusalem didn't force him to be circumcised marked a victory for the gospel of sheer grace, unaugmented by a Gentile convert's circumcision as a first step in keeping the law of Moses. "Titus . . . wasn't forced" and the otherwise unnecessary remention of his accompanying Paul ("who [was] with me" [compare 2:1]) underscore this victory for the gospel of sheer grace (compare 6:12).

The suggestion of opponents in 2:1–2 now becomes an explicit reference to them. "False brothers" describes them as falsely professing Christians, not true Christians at all. "Smuggled into [the church]" may suggest a satanic subterfuge. Or was it one devised by non-Christian Jewish authorities? In any case, "who *as such*" emphasizes the brothers' falsity. "Sneaked in" heightens the subterfuge. "To spy" portrays the false brothers as enemies under the pretense of allies. "On our freedom" has to do with the freedom of Christians from keeping the Mosaic law as such (though Paul will adopt its moral elements for Christian conduct as a necessary evidence of having received the Holy Spirit in consequence of salvation by grace through faith [see 5:13–24]). Paul locates this freedom "in Christ Jesus" by way of anticipating death to the Law through participation by faith in Christ's having died for our sins under the Law's curse for transgressing it (see 2:19–21; 3:10–13 with 1:3–4). "In order that they might enslave us" describes the false brothers as theological slave-raiders such as the Galatians should beware of. "To whom we didn't yield by way of submission" sets an example for the Galatians to follow. Since an hour was the shortest unit of time used in first-century Mediterranean culture, "even for an hour" makes Paul and company's unyieldingness temporally total so as to shame the Galatians for yielding to distorters of the gospel "so quickly" (1:6). "In order that the *truth* of the gospel might stay with you throughout" contrasts with *false* brothers' attempts at enslavement and should therefore make the Galatians appreciate Paul and company's defending the gospel of sheer grace for their sakes. "The truth of the *gospel*" consists in "our freedom, which we have in Christ Jesus" and therefore includes behavior allowed by this gospel.

2:6–10: **And from the ones who seemed to be some-thing** [that is, who were looked on as leaders of the church in Jerusalem]—**whatever they were once upon a time** [that is, when they accompanied Jesus during his earthly lifetime] **makes not one difference to me; God doesn't accept a human being's face** [= doesn't show partiality based on appearance]—**for the ones who seemed** [to be something] **added not one thing to me.** [7]**On the contrary, rather, having seen that I'd been en-trusted with the gospel of the uncircumcision** [that is, with the task of proclaiming the gospel to Gentiles without forcing circumcision on them] **just as Peter** [had been entrusted with the gospel] **of the circumcision** [that is, with the task of proclaiming the gospel to Jews, circumcised as they are]— [8]**for the one who activated Peter for apostleship to the circumcision** [Jews] **activated also me for the Gentiles** [= to proclaim the gospel to them]— [9]**and on recognizing the grace that had been given to me, James and Cephas and John, the ones who seemed to be pillars, gave a right** [hand] **of fellowship to me and Barnabas in order that we** [might go] **to the Gentiles and they to the circumcision,** [10]**only that we might keep remembering the poor, which very thing I'd been eager to do.** The abundantly gracious revelation of God's Son to Paul the persecutor made him so confident of the freedom believers have in Christ Jesus because of sheer, unaugmented grace that the celebrity of church leaders in Jerusalem didn't faze him at all. He even sets his indifference to their celebrity alongside a similar indifference on the part of God himself! And despite their celebrity they "added not one thing" to Paul by way of making him augment his gospel with the requirement of circumcision for converts, or with any other requirement that would distort sheer grace. "On the contrary, rather" puts a twofold emphasis on those leaders' acknowledgment of God's having entrusted Paul with the gospel he'd been proclaiming to Gentiles, an acknowledgment that put this entrustment on par with God's having entrusted Peter, the leader of the twelve original apostles, with the gospel he'd been proclaiming to Jews—this acknowledgment drawing no distinction between Peter's gospel and Paul's gospel of sheer grace. Paul ascribes the acknowledgment to God's having activated Paul's and Peter's respective apostleships. In other words, the success of Paul in converting Gentiles just as Peter had in converting Jews made Paul's apostleship so obviously God-ordained that not only Cephas himself but also James ("the Lord's brother" according to 1:19) and John the apostle recognized "the grace that had been given to [Paul]." This grace refers at one and the same time to the grace that God gave to Paul in his conversion, in his commission as an apostle to the Gentiles, and in the gospel he proclaims to them.

Paul lists James before Cephas and John because of this James' having risen to leadership in the Jerusalem church despite not belonging to the circle of Jesus' twelve apostles (Acts 12:17; 15:13–21; 21:18; 1 Corinthians 15:7). "The ones who seemed to be pillars" describes them according to their reputedly stalwart leadership—

but not by way of demeaning their reputation as such; rather, by way of impressing on the Galatians that none other than the acknowledged such leaders of the mother church in Jerusalem "gave a right [hand] of fellowship" to Paul and Barnabas (compare the figure of "pillars" with Paul's describing both a local church and the universal church as God's temple [1 Corinthians 3:16–17; 2 Corinthians 6:16; Ephesians 2:19–22]). Since most people are right-handed and since "fellowship" means participation, "a right [hand] of fellowship" signals with body language an agreement to work cooperatively, though in different spheres—Gentile and Jewish. "Only that we might keep remembering the poor" has to do with Gentile Christians' continuing the Jewish practice of almsgiving. "Only" brings out that this obligation doesn't count as circumcision-like enslavement to the Mosaic law. "Which very thing I'd been eager to do" makes the same point, for otherwise Paul would have resisted the obligation (compare Acts 11:27–30; Romans 15:25–28; 2 Corinthians 8–9).

PAUL'S REBUKE OF CEPHAS FOR HIS BEHAVIORAL COMPROMISE OF THE GOSPEL OF SHEER GRACE
Galatians 2:11–21

2:11–13: **But when Cephas came to Antioch, I stood against him face to face, because he had condemned himself** [not verbally, but by his behavior, as Paul now goes on to explain]. **¹²For prior to the coming of certain ones from** [Jesus' brother] **James he'd been eating with the** [Christian] **Gentiles. But when they** [the ones from James] **came, he started withdrawing** [from table fellowship] **and separating himself off** [from the Gentiles] **because of fearing those of the circumcision. ¹³And the rest of the Jewish** [Christians]**, too, played hypocrite along with him, so that even Barnabas was led astray with them by the hypocrisy** [of Cephas]. For the church in Antioch, Syria, see Acts 11:19–26; 13:1–3; 14:25–15:2, 30–33. Paul's facing down Cephas, the leading apostle among the original twelve, gives ample evidence that Cephas's celebrity made "not one difference" to Paul (2:6). The truth of the gospel mattered more to him than celebrity did (compare 1:10). In first-century culture, eating with someone connoted acceptance of each other, even a bond. So Cephas's eating with Gentile Christians, who were uncircumcised, connoted acceptance of them as fellow Christians, their uncircumcision notwithstanding. After all, he hadn't insisted on the circumcision of Titus when Paul took Titus up to Jerusalem (2:1–3). This behavior showed that Cephas truly did believe in the gospel of grace unaugmented by the Mosaic law. So subsequently withdrawing himself from table fellowship with Gentile Christians and separating himself off from them constituted hypocrisy, which means playing a part that doesn't represent your true self. "The coming [to Antioch] of certain ones from James" led Cephas to engage in such behavior out of fear, and the redundancy in "withdrawing and separating himself off" underscores

the hypocrisy involved (compare his three disownings of Jesus out of fear of nondisciples [see Mark 14:66–72, for example]).

We don't know whether "those of the circumcision," which refers to Jews, equates with "certain ones from James." Neither do we know whether Cephas bowed to a fear on the part of James that Jewish Christians' eating with Gentile Christians would make it difficult to convert other Jews, who as much as possible avoided close contact with Gentiles, or would lead to further persecution by Jews who considered a Jewish Christianity wide open to Gentiles a threat to Judaism. Nor do we know that the ones from James accurately represented his views (compare Acts 15:24), though Paul's describing them as "from James" seems to imply as much. And though he mentions Cephas's initial table fellowship with Gentile Christians, Paul says nothing about Mosaic dietary restrictions (for which see Leviticus 11). So we don't even know whether insistence by word and/or example on the part of the ones from James that those restrictions not be violated underlay Cephas's withdrawal from that table fellowship (compare Acts 11:2–3). In any case, by saying certain ones came from James, Paul seems to implicate James along with Cephas either in reneging on their earlier approval of Paul's Law-free evangelization of Gentiles (2:7–9) or at least in drawing back from its social implications favoring table fellowship with Gentile believers. Drawing back from such fellowship with them could, moreover, have a doctrinal effect disastrous to the gospel of sheer grace. For doctrine doesn't always *determine* practice. Sometimes it *follows* practice. "The *rest* of the Jewish [Christians]" refers to Jewish Christians resident in Antioch and therefore additional to Cephas and the ones from James, who were only visiting. It goes without saying that Paul excludes himself, though he too is a Jewish Christian. But the inclusion of Barnabas and exclusion of no Jewish Christian besides Paul highlight how serious was the threat to the gospel of sheer grace. "*Even* Barnabas," Paul's partner-in-arms on the trip to Jerusalem for the purpose of defending the Law-free gospel! Along with the other Jewish Christians, he too "was led astray" by Cephas's hypocritical example.

2:14: **When I saw that they** [Cephas, Barnabas, and the rest of the Jewish Christians in Antioch] **aren't walking straight in relation to the truth of the gospel, however, I said to Cephas before all** [of them]**, "If you, though being a Jewish** [Christian]**, are living in a Gentile fashion and not in a Jewish fashion, how is it that you're trying to force the** [converted] **Gentiles to Judaize** [= live like Jews]**?"** We'd say "they *weren't* walking straight," but to dramatize the seriousness of the others' defection Paul uses the present tense, "they *aren't* walking straight," as though the Galatians are watching in real time what happened in Antioch. "They aren't walking *straight* in relation to the truth of the gospel" means that they're deviating from it in their behavior, for "walking" is a figure of speech for behaving in one way or another. As in 2:5, "the truth of the gospel" describes the truth as good news and the good news as true. "However" contrasts Paul's speech to Cephas with Cephas's behavior. "Before all [of them]" not only reinforces that Cephas's celebrity made "not one difference" to Paul (2:6, 11). It also makes Paul's denunciation of Cephas a criticism of those in Antioch who were led astray by his example, and an indirect criticism of the distorters of the gospel who are leading astray the Galatians (1:6–7). Apparently it was well-known that though Cephas had been circumcised, as all Jewish male babies were, he wasn't living in accordance with the rest of the Mosaic law ("not in a Jewish fashion" [compare Acts 10:1–11:18]). So Paul's question, "how is it that you're trying to force the Gentiles to Judaize?" points up the hypocrisy of Cephas and portrays his withdrawing himself from Gentile Christians, uncircumcised as they were, as an attempt to force Judaism on them, starting with circumcision, even though Cephas himself wasn't practicing Judaism. Examples carry force, especially when they're set by prominent figures.

2:15–16: We ourselves [are] Jews by nature [because of our ancestry] and not sinners from among the Gentiles. ¹⁶Yet knowing that a human being isn't justified [= treated as righteous by God] because of [the human being's performing] works of the Law—[in other words, knowing that he isn't justified] except through faith in Jesus Christ—even we ourselves [as Jews] have believed in Christ Jesus in order to be justified because of faith in Christ and not because of works of the Law, because no flesh at all will be justified because of works of the Law. Throughout this passage "because of" translates a preposition that indicates the source of justification so far as human activity is concerned. "We ourselves" refers of course to Cephas and Paul. "Jews by nature" contrasts with "sinners," who are so by their behavior. "We *ourselves*" underlines the contrast. Jews called Gentiles "sinners" because Gentiles didn't keep God's laws. "We ourselves . . . [are] not sinners *from among* the Gentiles" means that Cephas and Paul have neither their ancestral nor their behavioral origin in paganism. Despite this advantage, though, they know that a human being, even a Jew, isn't justified by God because that human being keeps "the Law," by which Paul means the Old Testament law. He assumes Cephas's agreement on this point, and also on the point that a human being, even a Jew, isn't justified "except through faith in Jesus Christ" (compare Acts 10:43; 11:17; 15:1–11). If so, the argument goes, Gentiles shouldn't have to be circumcised and keep the rest of the Law for their justification.

Some commentators prefer the translation "through Jesus Christ's faithfulness," but Paul's going right on to speak of "hav[ing] believed in Christ Jesus in order to be justified" favors the traditional translation, "through faith in Jesus Christ." Besides, it's hard to find in this passage anything or anyone to which or to whom Paul could be portraying Jesus Christ as faithful. These same considerations favor the translation "because of faith in Christ" over "because of Christ's faithfulness" just following "we ourselves have believed in Christ Jesus in order to be justified." "Because of faith in Christ" is

emphatically repetitious of the earlier "through faith in Jesus Christ" just as "we ourselves [as Jews]" is emphatically repetitious of the earlier "we ourselves [as Jews]" and just as the several occurrences of "be[ing] justified" and of "not because of works of the Law" are emphatically repetitious. It's important to note that so far as human activity is concerned, Paul locates the origin of justification in believing rather than in doing what the Law demands, so that to be justified is to be *treated* as righteous despite disobedience to the Law, not to *be* righteous by virtue of obedience to it. Since "flesh" connotes human frailty—here, moral frailty in particular—the statement that "*no flesh at all* will be justified because of works of the Law" roundly rejects the Law as providing a way of justification. (It comes out in Romans 7:7–25 that the Law actually *incites* sinning.) The switch from "in Jesus Christ" to "in Christ Jesus" and then to "in Christ" provides variety of expression.

2:17–18: But if by seeking to be justified in Christ we ourselves too [in addition to the Gentiles] have been found [to be] sinners, [is] Christ then a server of sin? To the contrary! ¹⁸For if I'm building again these things that I tore down, I'm showing myself [to be] a transgressor [of the Law (compare 3:19 with comments)]. Yet again "we ourselves" refers to Cephas and Paul as examples of Jews who "are seeking to be justified in Christ." "Seeking" indicates a deliberate attempt. "In Christ" provides a location for the sought-after justification because from God's point of view, believing in Christ puts believers within Christ, the object of their belief. Believing in him brings the gift of his Spirit, so that through the Spirit that indwells him believers too indwell him (see 3:2 with 4:6; Romans 8:1–17). But does seeking justification by believing in Christ rather than by obeying the Law equate with sinning through disregard of the Law? If so, as the object of belief Christ serves sin in the sense of prompting people to sin by disregarding the Law. Paul denies this conclusion vehemently and then gives a reason for his denial, but couches the reason in terms of sinfully rebuilding "these things that [he] tore down." They're "works of the Law" that he tore down by ceasing to depend on them for justification and by believing in Christ instead. To rebuild them would be to depend again on works of the Law, and this would imply that believing in Christ for justification was itself a transgression of the Law. Does any Christian really want to say that he transgressed the Law by believing in Christ? Paul certainly doesn't—hence his switching from "we ourselves" to "I" and thereby setting an example that Cephas, Cephas's fellow hypocrites, and the Galatians should follow.

2:19–21: For through the Law I died in relation to the Law in order that I might live in relation to God. ²⁰I was crucified with Christ, and remain so; and I'm no longer living, but Christ is living in me. And as to the fact that I'm living in flesh, I'm living by faith in God's Son, who loved me and gave himself over [to crucifixion] on my behalf. ²¹I'm not setting aside the grace of

God. **For if righteousness** [comes] **through the Law, then Christ died gratuitously.** This paragraph explains why it's theologically impossible to think that believing in Christ constitutes a transgression of the Law. Paul puts the reason in highly autobiographical and therefore movingly personal terms. It's that from God's standpoint (and it's his standpoint that counts) Paul was crucified when Christ was crucified, because Paul's believing in Christ made Christ the Spiritual habitat of Paul. Christ's crucifixion is unrepeatable, so that Paul's having been crucified with Christ (again from God's standpoint) is equally unrepeatable. In the sense of unrepeatability Paul "remains" crucified with Christ. Since in his crucifixion Christ suffered vicariously the Law's penalty for Paul's and others' sins (1:4), crucifixion with Christ severed Paul's relation to the Law; for the Law exhausts itself on a person in the exacting of capital punishment. A dead person is under no obligation to the Law, because he *can't* obey it—hence Paul's statement that "through the Law [that is, through the Law's exacting the death penalty on me in my crucifixion with Christ] I died in relation to the Law . . . . and I'm no longer living [under its jurisdiction]." But just as Paul was crucified *with* Christ because by faith he came to be *in* Christ, so by virtue of resurrection (plus the gift of the Holy Spirit according to 3:2; 4:6) Christ is living in Paul. Though no longer living in relation to the Law, then, through the resurrected Christ's living in him Paul is living in relation to God while living in flesh, that is, in a body destined either to die and be resurrected or to stay alive till the second coming and be immortalized (as guaranteed by Christ's resurrection [1 Corinthians 15:50–54]). Thus "living in flesh" means "living by faith in God's Son" outside the Law's jurisdiction and therefore where transgressing the Law—that is, the Mosaic law *as such*—is impossible. The switch from "Christ" to "God's Son" makes the relationship to God of a person in Christ by faith, as Paul is, one of sonship too (see 4:6). "Who loved me and gave himself over [to crucifixion] on my behalf" injects into Paul's theological reasoning a soulful observation on the soulful reason for Christ's crucifixion. In view of the theological and soulful reasons that Paul has spelled out, he refuses to "set aside the grace of God" by—and for the sake of—rebuilding "works of the Law." Specifically why? Because if righteousness (in the sense of God's treating people as righteous) comes through the Law (in the sense of obeying its precepts), "then Christ died gratuitously" (in the sense of needlessly).

A THEOLOGICAL ARGUMENT FOR THE GOSPEL OF GOD'S SHEER GRACE
Galatians 3:1–5:12

This major section of Galatians subdivides into the sufficiency of faith (3:1–5); the example of Abraham (3:6–9); the curse of the Law (3:10–14); God's covenantal promise to Abraham and his offspring prior to laying down the law of works (3:15–18); the purpose of the Law to demonstrate the necessity of God's sheer grace and of its reception through faith in Christ (3:19–4:7); and

a plea to retain trust in God's grace alone for freedom from the Law as illustrated allegorically in the story of Abraham (4:8–5:12).

THE SUFFICIENCY OF FAITH
Galatians 3:1–5

***3:1–5:* O mindless Galatians, who bewitched you, before whose eyes Jesus Christ was publicly exhibited as crucified?** [2]**Only this do I want to learn from you: Did you receive the Spirit because of works of the Law or because of a hearing** [of the gospel] **characterized by faith** [in Jesus Christ]**?** [3]**Are you mindless in this way—** [that is,] **after starting** [the Christian life] **in the Spirit** [whom you received], **are you now trying to perfect yourselves on the basis of flesh?** [4]**Have you experienced so many things casually, if indeed** [it] **really** [was] **casually?** [5]**So does he who supplies to you the Spirit and works miracles among you** [do so] **because of works of the Law or because of a hearing characterized by faith?** In this paragraph Paul subjects the Galatians to an interrogation consisting in five consecutive questions. The questions don't contain answers within themselves. Paul leaves to the Galatians the answering, but he asks with confidence that honest answers will support his position. In the first question, "mindless Galatians," punctuated by an initial "O," lampoons the Galatians for their irrationality in defecting "into a different gospel" and away from God, who called them "in the grace of Christ" (1:6). "Who bewitched you . . . ?" furthers the lampoon by escalating their absence of mind to being under a spell. "Before whose eyes Jesus Christ was publicly exhibited as crucified" makes mindlessness and bewitchment inexcusable. The Galatians hadn't seen Jesus' crucifixion. So it's not the crucifixion itself which they'd seen. It's the public exhibition thereof which they'd seen in Paul's preaching (compare 1 Corinthians 1:17–25; 2:2). We might therefore expect him to have referenced the Galatians' hearing rather than seeing. But spells were often cast with a supposedly evil eye. So Paul makes the point that seeing the exhibition with their own eyes should have immunized the Galatians against bewitchment with someone else's evil eye. The answer to "who bewitched you . . . ?" doesn't really matter. Only the bewitchment itself does.

With some sarcasm Paul introduces his second question by playing the role of a student wanting to learn from the Galatians, as though they're his teachers. "*Only this do I want to learn from you*" strengthens the sarcasm by implying that they could complete Paul's education satisfactorily with an answer to a single question, the second one in his arsenal of questions. Unlike the answer to the first question, the answer to the second one does matter—and is obvious. The Galatians received the Spirit because of hearing the gospel with faith, not because of works of the Law; for they received the Spirit immediately upon believing the gospel and therefore prior to starting to do works of the Law (whatever the extent to which they may have started doing them [compare 1:6 with 4:9–11, 21; 5:4, 7–8]). The third question builds on the second by implying the irrationality of self-perfection "on the basis of flesh" after having started out "in the Spirit." Self-perfection has to do with performing works of the Law, most decisively with circumcision, which in turn has to do with flesh in a quite literal sense (compare Romans 2:28; Philippians 3:2–5 for the association of "flesh" with circumcision). But flesh is weak. It disintegrates upon death, for example. So using it in an attempt to do all the works of the Law will inevitably fail. On the contrary, the Spirit is strong (Romans 8:3–4; Mark 14:38; Matthew 26:41; Isaiah 31:3). It makes nonsense to regress from the Spirit to flesh, then.

The "many things" that the Galatians "have . . . experienced" according to the fourth question consist in the Galatians' already-mentioned reception of the Spirit and the next-to-be-mentioned miracles that have been worked among them. "Experienced" points to felt effects of the Spirit on the Galatians, therefore to effects they can't deny; and "so *many* things" stresses the abundance of these effects favoring faith and the Spirit over works of the Law and flesh. "Casually" suggests the possibility of not having taken this abundance of effects seriously (compare 1 Corinthians 15:1–2). "If indeed [it] really [was] casually" holds out a hope that the Galatians didn't take it casually and therefore can be won back with an appeal to the abundance of effects. "He who supplies . . . the Spirit" to the Galatians and "works miracles among [them]" is God (see 4:6). He started supplying the Spirit and working miracles through Paul during Paul's proclaiming of the gospel to the Galatians and their believing. "Works of the Law" played no part, as emphasized by the wordplay between "works miracles" and "works of the Law." "So" introduces this fifth and last question as a crowning consequence of the preceding questions.

THE EXAMPLE OF ABRAHAM
Galatians 3:6–9

3:6–9: Just as Abraham "believed God and it was credited to him as righteousness [Genesis 15:6]"—⁷know then that people of faith [= people characterized by belief]—**these are Abraham's sons. ⁸And the Scripture, having foreseen that God is justifying** [= treating as righteous] **the Gentiles because of [their] faith, proclaimed the gospel to Abraham ahead of time: "All the Gentiles will be favored in you [Genesis 12:3; 18:18]." ⁹And so people of faith are being favored along with the believing Abraham.** Paul starts drawing an analogy to Abraham's having believed God. The force of the analogy lies in Paul's couching the analogy in the wording of Scripture, the Scripture which contains the Law—indeed, that part of Scripture which *is* the Law. Instead of completing the analogy, though, Paul breaks up his sentence by interjecting the command, "know," to correct the Galatians' mindlessness and bewitchment (3:1). "Know *then*" commands a rational deduction to complete the analogy. It's that since Abraham's believing God was credited to him as righteousness, people characterized by belief are "Abraham's sons." "Credited . . . as righteousness" doesn't describe believing as an act

of righteousness, such as a work of the Law. It means, rather, that believing is counted *as though* it were an act of righteousness when in fact it is not. For believing and working belong to different categories (Romans 4:4–5). "People of faith" means people who believe in Jesus Christ (2:16, 20). But since Abraham believed God rather than believing in Jesus Christ, who hadn't yet come on the scene, Paul tightens the analogy to Abraham by omitting to add "in Jesus Christ" to "people of faith." To highlight such people, on the other hand, Paul breaks up his sentence again so as to refer back to them with an emphatic "these." "Abraham's sons" will include females according to 3:28, but Paul uses "sons" because the story of Abraham featured his fathering a divinely promised son (Isaac) despite very old age (Romans 4:18–22). Whereas the Old Testament spoke of a biological son and subsequent offspring (Genesis 15:1–5), though, Paul enlarges the concept of Abrahamic sonship to include also those nonbiological descendants who follow Abraham's example of believing. "Because of [their] faith" conspicuously leaves out any reference to additional works of the Law.

Having already used scriptural wording, Paul then cites "the Scripture" explicitly to argue his case from the very Law to which the distorters of the gospel must have been appealing. The recognition of Scripture as the word of God underlies the personification in Paul's phraseology, "And the Scripture, *having foreseen.*" "That God is justifying the Gentiles because of faith" describes what's going on at the time of writing as a fulfillment of what was said to Abraham: "All the Gentiles will be favored in you." Paul describes this prediction, moreover, as a proclamation of good news to Abraham "ahead of time," that is, long before current Gentiles heard it. "*All* the Gentiles" stresses universality in opposition to Jewish exclusivism, including the insistence that Gentiles make themselves Jews of a kind by getting circumcised and keeping the rest of the Law. "Will be favored" alludes to having faith credited as righteousness, as in Abraham's case. A second occurrence of "people of faith" reinvigorates the emphasis on faith. "*Are* being favored" points up the present fulfillment of "*will* be favored." "Along with Abraham" interprets the quoted scriptural phrase "in you" in terms of a community that Abraham fathered by example. "The believing Abraham" identifies his exercise of faith as the manner in which he set an example.

THE CURSE OF THE LAW
Galatians 3:10–14

3:10–12: For as many as are of works of the Law are under a curse. For it's written, "Accursed [is] everyone who isn't abiding in [= obeying] **all the things written in the book of the Law so as to do them [Deuteronomy 27:26]." ¹¹And it['s] clear that in the Law** [that is, by behaving in obedience to it] **no one is being justified before God, because "the righteous person will live by faith [Habakkuk 2:4]." ¹²But the Law isn't of faith** [that is, doesn't arise out of faith as its guiding principle]; **rather, "the person who has done them** ['all the things written in the book of the Law'] **will live in them** [as his habitat] [Leviticus 18:5]." The first "For" in this paragraph introduces the reason why Abraham-like faith is necessary for God's favor. It's that "as many as are of the works of the Law"—that is, who in any part depend for their justification on keeping the Law—"are under a curse." The second "For" introduces the reason why such people are under a curse. It's that Scripture pronounces a curse on "everyone [compare the preceding 'as many as,' the two of which expressions allow no individual exceptions] who isn't abiding in all the things [which expression allows no exception of any commandment] written in the book of the Law so as to do them." "Who isn't *abiding* in" stresses the necessity of obedience uninterrupted by any disobedience. Paul skips saying that no one obeys the Law perfectly, so that some interpreters argue that since the Law provides for atonement of sins, he doesn't imply that the Law demands perfect obedience and that elsewhere he claims for himself pre-Christian blamelessness before the Law (Philippians 3:6). But that claim has to do with outward appearances ("in flesh" [Philippians 3:4–6]), whereas he confesses to moral defeat in the matter of inward lust (Romans 7:7–25). And it's more of an inference to import atonement under the Law than it's an inference to import imperfect obedience to the Law. For though speaking elsewhere and at length of sinning under the Law (Romans 3:9–23), nowhere does Paul speak of atonement under the Law. The passing over of sins committed under the Law (Romans 3:25) counts as overlooking them for the time being but hardly as their having been atoned for. Paul's immediately following statement right here, "And it['s] clear that in the Law no one is being justified before God" shows that he rules out atonement under the Law. "No one" makes not even the outwardly "blameless" Paul an exception, and "before God" puts even him, prior to his conversion, under a curse in that God could see the inward lust to which Paul had fallen prey. Furthermore, the combination of "everyone" and "no one" shows that Paul is thinking of individuals, not of Israel as a collectivity.

The Lord's quoted statement to Habakkuk is what makes "clear" that "in the Law no one is being justified before God." Paul's appeal to clarity puts to shame the Galatians for their mindlessness and bewitchment (3:1). What the Lord said to Habakkuk denies justification in the Law by basing justification on faith instead. "The righteous person" corresponds to "is being justified [treated as righteous]." "By faith" opposes "in the Law," as Paul goes on to assert: "But the Law isn't of faith." To what does "will live" refer in his interpretation? Not to daily conduct, as in "*walking around* through faith, not through sight" (2 Corinthians 5:7)—rather, to having eternal life in God's kingdom (see 3:21 and especially 5:21 with 6:8, but also 2:20; Romans 8:13; 1 Thessalonians 5:10). "By faith" tells how it is from the human standpoint that a person will live. Being treated as righteous and having eternal life harmonize with each other in that the former (justification) results in the latter (life). See Romans 5:18! Paul caps his disentangling of faith

from the Law by citing Leviticus 18:5: "the person who has done them [the Law's commandments] will live in them." Justification has to do with faith. The Law has to do with deeds. And since "as many as are of works of the Law are under a curse," the promise, "will live [= will have eternal life, again according to Paul] in them," turns out to be unfulfillable.

3:13–14: Christ bought us out from under the Law's curse by becoming a curse on our behalf, because it's written, "Accursed [is] everyone who hangs on a tree [Deuteronomy 21:23]," [14]with the result that in Christ Jesus the favor of Abraham [= God's favoring him by crediting his faith as righteousness (3:6–9)] **has appeared on the scene for the Gentiles, with the result that through faith we've received the promise of the Spirit.** Since Gentiles weren't under the Law (Romans 2:14–15), it might seem that "us" whom "Christ bought . . . out from under the Law's curse" refers only to Jews. But since the Galatians, at least most of whom were Gentiles (4:8), received the Spirit (3:2), "we" who "have received the promise of the Spirit" includes Gentile as well as Jewish believers and therefore works backward to include Gentiles as well as Jews in the preceding "us." And this inclusion makes sense in that Gentiles in Galatia were starting to put themselves under the Law (see especially 4:21; 5:4, but also 1:6; 3:1, 3; 4:9–11; 5:7–8) and therefore unthinkingly under the Law's curse. Christ's having "bought us out from under the Law's curse" came at the cost of his "becoming a curse on our behalf," that is, by taking on himself the curse we deserved for not keeping the Law perfectly. So thoroughly did Christ take on himself the curse we deserved that Paul doesn't speak in conformity with 3:10 simply of Christ's becoming accursed. He speaks of Christ's becoming the curse itself (compare 2 Corinthians 5:21 with comments). The Greek word translated "on our behalf" could also be translated "*in* our behalf," which would mean "for our benefit" or simply "for us" whereas "*on* our behalf" means "as our representative or agent." But "*becoming* a curse" because "accursed [is] everyone who isn't abiding in all the things written in the book of the Law so as to do them" calls for vicariousness ("on our behalf"), not just beneficence ("in our behalf").

"*Bought* us out from under the Law's curse" suggests redemption from enslavement (compare 4:1–11, 21–5:1). "Because it's written" introduces a scriptural reason, but not for Christ's buying us by becoming a curse—rather, for Paul's *saying* that he did. Christ's doing so conforms to a scriptural statement in that his crucifixion counts as "hang[ing] on a tree" or, as it could equally well be translated, "hang[ing] on wood." Most translations read two occurrences of "*in order that*" and/ or "so that" to indicate the purposes of extending to Gentiles God's favor and of granting them the Spirit. But the Greek conjunction often indicates *attained* purpose, hence result, and Paul has made abundantly clear that God's favor has indeed been extended to Gentile believers and that the Spirit has indeed been granted them (3:2, 6–9)—hence the foregoing translation, "with the result that" (twice). Christ's having hung on a tree as a curse on our behalf has resulted in the appearance on the scene "for the Gentiles" of God's favor toward Abraham. "Has appeared on the scene" marks a dispensational change so far as God's dealing with Gentiles is concerned. "In Christ Jesus" limits God's favor to those Gentiles who've been incorporated into Christ Jesus because they've believed in him and received his Spirit, just as in the case of Jews. Thus the reception of the Spirit stands alongside the appearance of God's favoring the Gentiles as another result of Christ's having "bought us out from under the Law's curse." Naturally, reception of the Spirit, undeniable as it is in the experience of believers (3:2–4), confirms to them the favor of God in crediting their faith, like Abraham's faith, as righteousness. "The promise of the Spirit" doesn't refer to a promise that the Spirit gave. It refers rather to the Spirit as promised. Paul will shortly interpret the reception of the Spirit as a fulfillment of God's promise to Abraham of the land of Canaan.

GOD'S COVENANTAL PROMISE TO ABRAHAM AND HIS PROGENY PRIOR TO LAYING DOWN THE LAW OF WORKS
Galatians 3:15–18

3:15–16: Brothers, I'm speaking in accordance with a human being [= in human terms]: **No one sets aside a validated testament/covenant or adds a codicil** [a legal supplement] **on top** [of it] **notwithstanding** [its being the testament/covenant] **of a** [mere] **human being,** [16]**and the promises were spoken to Abraham and to his seed. It** [the Scripture] **doesn't say, "And to your seeds,"** as [referring] **to many—rather, as** [referring] **to one: "and to your seed** [Genesis 12:7; 13:15; 17:8; 24:7, the repetition of the promise producing the constellation of aforementioned "promises" (plural)]," **who is Christ.** With "Brothers" Paul addresses the Galatians as fellow Christians whom he wants to save from apostasy. Introducing the address at this point indicates a new turn in his discussion. He describes the turn as an analogy drawn from human law, an analogy that even the mindless, bewitched Galatians (3:1) should be able to understand, though the address "Brothers" has now softened his tone. The analogy plays on two meanings of a single Greek word: (1) last will and testament and (2) covenant. Paul compares God's covenant with Abraham to a human being's last will and testament. Both that covenant and a last will and testament have to do with inheritance. Hence the aptness of this comparison. The validation of a last will and testament occurs upon the testator's death. From that point onward, no one can legally set it aside or add to it a codicil, which by definition would change it. In this respect, God's covenant with Abraham, validated as it was (though not upon a death of God—rather, with the death of animal sacrifices [Genesis 15]), isn't subject to being set aside or changed. But Paul calls God's covenant with Abraham "the promises" to link it with the just-mentioned "promise of the Spirit." Paul also quotes "and to your seed" (repeated

as it is several times in Genesis), stresses the singular of "seed" as opposed to "seeds" (plural), and identifies Abraham's seed as Christ to suit the incorporation "in Christ Jesus" of Gentiles as well as Jews who believe in him and thereby receive his Spirit. Originally, "seed" referred to biological offspring that the aged Abraham was to have despite his apparent inability to ejaculate semen (which means "seed"). Again originally, "seed" was a collective singular referring to innumerable offspring of Abraham (innumerable like the stars in the sky, for example). But Paul has already indicated that Abraham's offspring include those of faith like his as well as those with genes like his (3:6–9), and Paul is about to collectivize Christ by including in him as Abraham's seed all who belong to him (Christ) by faith, regardless of their ethnicity, class, or sex (3:26–29).

3:17–18: I'm saying this: The Law, which came on the scene four hundred and thirty years later [than the promises were spoken to Abraham] **doesn't invalidate a testament/covenant previously validated by God with the result of incapacitating the promise** [contained in the testament/covenant]. [18]**For if the inheritance** [originates] **out of the Law, no longer** [does it originate] **out of the promise. But through the promise God graciously bestowed** [the inheritance] **to Abraham.** "I'm saying this" introduces an application of the analogy introduced in 3:15 with "Brothers, I'm speaking . . . ." The Law's arrival on the scene later than the promises spoken to Abraham doesn't invalidate God's previously validated covenant with Abraham any more than a testament can be set aside or changed after it has been validated upon the testator's death. "Four hundred and thirty years later" strengthens the argument from analogy by highlighting how much later the Law arrived on the scene. Paul couches the verbal expressions "came on the scene," "previously validated," and "graciously bestowed" in a form that indicates an action completed in the past and having a present result. The Law arrived in the time of Moses. The present result of its arrival consists in the salvific effect of Christ's death under the Law's curse. The promises to Abraham were validated four hundred and thirty years earlier than the Law's arrival. The present result of their validation consists in the enjoyment of God's favor by believing Gentiles as well as by believing Jews. At the same earlier time and in the form of those promises an inheritance was graciously bestowed to Abraham. The present result of that bestowal consists in believers' having eternal life now and forever. For the land of Canaan inherited by Jews has expanded into Gentile as well as Jewish believers' inheriting the whole world (Romans 4:13) in conjunction with eternal life in God's kingdom (see the comments on 3:11; compare Romans 8:18–25, 32). "For" introduces the rationale that since the Law and the promise belong to opposing categories, the promised inheritance has nothing to do with the Law. The Law demands obedience, whereas "through the promise God has *graciously* [that is, apart from any 'works of the Law'] bestowed [the inheritance] to Abraham." So the promise calls for a faith like Abraham's.

THE PURPOSE OF THE LAW TO DEMONSTRATE THE NECESSITY OF GOD'S SHEER GRACE AND OF ITS RECEPTION THROUGH FAITH IN CHRIST
Galatians 3:19–4:7

3:19–20: So why the Law [since the inheritance doesn't originate out of it]**? It was added on account of transgressions until the seed would come to whom it** [the inheritance] **had been promised,** [the Law] **having been promulgated through angels in the hand of an intermediary.** **²⁰But the intermediary isn't of one; but God is one.** The Law wasn't added *to* the promise. It was added *separately* from the promise. For Paul has just made clear that the Law and the promise belong to opposing categories. But why was the Law added in any case? It was added "on account of transgressions," that is, to make sins into transgressions of a stated law. "Until the seed would come" turns the Law into a stopgap. That is all. According to 3:16, 29 Abraham's seed, "to whom it [the inheritance] had been promised," is the corporate Christ, that is, Christ and all those who by faith are "in Christ." "Had been promised" connotes a promise made in the past and having a lasting effect, one not to be negated by the Law's addition. "Having been promulgated through angels" reflects, apparently, a Jewish tradition (compare Acts 7:53; Hebrews 2:2 with Deuteronomy 33:2). "In the hand of an intermediary" may at first seem to reference Moses. But since Moses acted as God's intermediary (see Exodus 32:15; 34:4, 29; Deuteronomy 10:3), that reference wouldn't agree with Paul's immediate denial that the intermediary belongs to "one," whom Paul then proceeds to identify as God in accordance with Deuteronomy 6:4; Romans 3:30; 1 Corinthians 8:6. So the intermediary seems to reference the angels' unidentified intermediary rather than God's (Acts 7:38). Notably, the promulgation of the Law "through angels in the hand of an intermediary" makes the Law inferior both to God's unmediated promise to Abraham and to the gospel of God's sheer grace in that God revealed this gospel to Paul without an intermediary (1:11–24). But does inferiority imply opposition?

3:21–22: [Is] **the Law therefore against the promises of God? To the contrary! For if a law had been given that could make** [people] **live, righteousness really would have originated out of the Law.** **²²The Scripture has impounded all things under sin, however, in order that the promise might be given because of faith in Jesus Christ to those who believe.** "Therefore" makes Paul's opening question grow out of the inferiority of the Law because angels and their intermediary promulgated it. "To the contrary!" roundly denies that that inferiority equates with opposition to God's promises to Abraham and his seed, however. Paul supports his denial by saying that only if the Law had had an ability to make people live would the Law have opposed God's promises by presenting a competitive way to live. "*If* a law had been given that *could* make [people] live" implies the Law's inability, however; and the fact that people have mortal life

regardless of their having or not having the Law shows that Paul has eternal life in view (see further the comments on 3:11). "Righteousness" means a right standing before God, equivalent to justification and practically equivalent to salvation (see the comments on 1 Corinthians 1:30 and especially those on 2 Corinthians 5:21). "Righteousness *really* would have originated out of the Law" emphasizes the contrary necessity of God's bestowing the inheritance to Abraham and his seed "graciously," that is, without their deserving it (3:18). It's probably the Scripture quoted in 3:10 that "has impounded all things under sin" (but see Romans 3:9–18 as well). "All *things*" refers to people, but with an accent on the universality of their impoundment under sin. In view of Romans 8:20–22, however, the whole creation may also be in view. "Impounded . . . under sin" portrays Scripture as a judge who sentences "all things" to imprisonment, and portrays sin as their jailer. But the very purpose of this impoundment is to show faith in Jesus Christ as the only way of attaining a right standing before God. "To those who believe" stipulates faith as belief in Jesus Christ rather than as Jesus Christ's faithfulness, of which Paul has nothing to say in those terms either here or elsewhere.

3:23–24: And before faith came we were being held in custody under the Law, being impounded until the coming faith would be revealed. **²⁴And so the Law became our childminder until Christ in order that we might be justified because of faith.** Abraham exercised faith long before Christ appeared on the scene. But because faith is now tied inextricably to Christ as its object, the coming and revelation of faith amount to the coming and revelation of him (compare 1:15–16), but with emphasis on the faith that his coming and revelation call for. See the comments on 3:13 concerning "we." "Being held in custody under the Law" and "being impounded" portray the Law itself rather than sin as our jailer (contrast 3:22). But this shift makes sense in that the Law was added to make sins into transgressions (3:19). A custodial holding would imply some kind of protection except for the impounding, which implies custodial confinement instead. So the portrayal of the Law as a jailer evolves into a portrayal of the Law as a childminder, that is, as a slave assigned to keep in check free-born children (boys in particular) who would otherwise use freedom for license. Childminders didn't always succeed at their task, of course; nor did the Law succeed in keeping those under it from transgressing it. "Until Christ" interprets the coming and revelation of faith, and "in order that we might be justified because of faith" tells the purpose of Christ's coming as faith's object in view of the Law's failure as our childminder, necessary though the Law was to point up our need for God's sheer grace.

3:25–27: But because faith has come, we're no longer under a childminder. **²⁶For in Christ Jesus you're all God's sons through faith.** **²⁷For as many of you as have been baptized into Christ have been clothed with Christ.** See the comments on 3:23 for the coming of faith. Its coming marks the end of an era, the era of the Law as our childminder. Why so? Because by virtue of having the Spirit, who indwells Christ (see 3:2–3 with 4:6; Romans 8:1–11; Philippians 1:19), believers in Christ likewise indwell him; and though he came to be under the Law at his birth (4:4), his becoming the Law's curse on our behalf at his crucifixion (3:13) severed him from the Law, so that in him believers too are severed from the Law. It's no longer their childminder. They're God's grownup sons—all of them—like Christ Jesus himself, because without exception they're in him. And how is it that they're in him? By baptism into Christ. But since "through faith" defines the mode of becoming God's sons in Christ Jesus, baptism dramatizes incorporation into him through faith rather than effecting the incorporation. Because baptism means immersion into water, "into him" fits the dramatization. "*As many of you as* have been baptized into Christ" leaves open the possibility that in the assemblies where this letter will be read there may be unbelievers, who've never been baptized into Christ. But being surrounded with water through baptism is something like being surrounded with clothing or, we might say, like being immersed in clothes. Given that similarity and the custom of putting a new robe on a young man to mark his graduation from supervised boyhood to free adulthood, "baptized into Christ" morphs into "clothed with Christ" (compare Romans 13:14, though there Paul issues a command, whereas here he states a fact). The shift from "we" to "you" (plural) aims to assure the Galatians directly that they mustn't gravitate to Law-keeping (compare the comments on 3:13 concerning "us"). In Christ they have all they need. To put themselves under the Law would be to deny the sufficiency of incorporation into Christ through faith as dramatized in their baptism and as compared with being clothed with a robe of adulthood. (We don't know whether the practice of reclothing a person after his or her baptism generated the figure of being clothed with Christ, or whether this figure generated that practice.)

3:28–29: [In Christ] **there's not a Jew and not a Greek. There's not a slave and not a free person. There's not "a male and a female** [Genesis 1:27]**." For you're all one in Christ Jesus.** [29]**And if you**['re] **Christ's** [as you are if you're in him]**, then you're Abraham's seed, heirs in accordance with the promise** [that God made to him and his seed]**.** So ethnicity (with which is associated culture—hence "not a Greek" rather than "not a Gentile"), social class, and sex make no difference when it comes to a right standing before God because of being "one in Christ Jesus." In Paul's Greek text "one" is masculine to agree with "Christ Jesus," where this oneness is to be found. Whether the oneness makes no difference in regard to functions in church order as well as in regard to a right standing before God depends on what Paul has to say elsewhere on matters of church order (see 1 Corinthians 11:2–16; 14:34–36; 1 Timothy 2:11–14; 3:11 with comments). "*You*'re Abraham's seed" if you belong to Christ by being in him, because *he* is Abraham's seed

(3:16). And being Abraham's seed entails heirship "in accordance with the promise." See the comments on 3:11, 17–18 for the promised inheritance.

4:1–5: But I'm saying [this (compare 3:17)]**: For as long a time as the heir is a minor, though being owner of all the things** [that he'll inherit] **he differs in no respect at all from a slave.** [2]**Contrariwise** [to his ownership]**, he's under guardians and managers till the** [day] **previously fixed by** [his] **father.** [3]**So too we, when we were minors, were enslaved under the elements of the world.** [4]**But when the fullness of time had come, God sent his Son out of** [heaven]**,** [his Son] **arriving on the scene out of a woman, arriving on the scene under the Law,** [5]**in order that he might buy those under the Law out from** [under it]**, in order that we might receive from** [God] **adoption as** [his] **sons.** "The heir" echoes "heirs" in 3:29, and "For as long a time as the heir is a minor" develops the implication of youth in the comparison at 3:24–25 to being "under a childminder." That comparison now evolves into a comparison of the minor's being "under guardians and managers" (presumably after the father's death, which for Paul is beside the point), so that despite owning the estate as its heir, the minor's guardians and managers dominate him the way a master dominates his slave. Guardians took care of the minor's person, managers of the minor's estate. "He differs *in no respect at all* from a slave" emphasizes the completeness of this domination as to its degree, and "*for as long a time as* the heir is a minor" emphasizes the same as to its chronology. And "though being owner of *all* the things [that he'll inherit]" emphasizes the contrast between this domination and heirship. These emphases stress in turn the slave-like restrictedness of being under the Law (compare 3:23). "Till the day previously fixed by [his] father" refers to the day designated by the father before his death as the day when his son should be graduated from minorhood to adulthood and thus freed from the domination of guardians and managers.

"So too we" starts Paul's theological application of the foregoing custom. "When we were minors" refers to the time prior to Christ's coming. But where we expect Paul to say we were "enslaved under the Law" as a parallel to our being "held in custody under the Law" (3:23), he says instead that we were "enslaved under the elements of the world." Ancients spoke of the world as being made up of four elements—earth, air, fire, and water—and deified these elements. Furthermore, since such deified elements were thought to govern the world, the elements were also identified with the rules and regulations under which human beings are bound to live. For Jews, the Law consists in those rules and regulations. But Paul wants to compare Jewish believers' having been held in custody under the Law prior to conversion with Gentile believers' having been subject to the rules and regulations in pagan religion prior to conversion. So he uses "the elements of the world" to include both the Law and pagan rules and regulations. Thus "we" refers to both Jewish and Gentile believers; and so far as enslavement is concerned, the shocking coordination of the Law with pagan rules and regulations should keep the Galatians from subjecting themselves to re-enslavement—this time to the Law rather than to pagan rules and regulations, yet enslavement to elements of the world nonetheless. "But when the fullness of time had come" compares with the day previously fixed by a father for his son's graduation from minorhood to adulthood, and also corresponds to faith's coming, which ended the era of being under a childminder, that is, of being under the Law (3:25). But now it's not the coming of faith that Paul puts on view—rather, the coming of "the fullness of time" that resulted in God's sending his Son as the *object* of faith, so that in the Son believers might experience adult sonship, free alike from the Law and from the rules and regulations of pagan religion.

Perhaps all other translations describe the Son as "*born* of [or 'from'] a woman, *born* under the Law." Certainly the phrase "of/from a woman" alludes to birth; but Paul's verb carries the broader meaning of arriving on a scene, whether by birth (as in this case) or travel or some other means. Here, then, we have arriving on the scene as a consequence of God's sending, and "out of a woman" as a complement to "out of [heaven]." (Paul had no need to attach "out of" to "sent" unless he meant us to supply "heaven," the dwelling place of God the sender.) "In order that he [God's Son] might buy those under the Law out from [under it]" portrays being under the Law as enslavement to it, and emancipation from that enslavement as coming at a cost, the cost according to 3:13 of Christ's becoming a curse by being hung on a tree on our behalf. To pay this cost he had to arrive on the scene as himself "under the Law." From the broad phraseology, "under the elements of the world," Paul reverts twice in a row to the narrow phrase, "under the Law," because the distorters of the gospel aren't telling the Galatians to submit to pagan rules and regulations—rather, to the Law (though for Paul submission to either amounts to enslavement). If Jews, who are "those under the Law," have been emancipated from the Law because of faith in Christ, surely Gentile believers such as the Galatians shouldn't be selling themselves into slavery under the Law. And as the sending of God's Son had the purpose of emancipating slaves, the emancipation of slaves has the purpose of their adoption as God's sons, so that the freedom of sonship to God replaces enslavement under the Law. As 4:6 will make clear, "we" who "receive adoption" includes Gentile believers like the Galatians, who'd been under pagan rules and regulations, as well as Jewish believers, who'd been under the Law.

4:6–7: And because you're [his] sons, God has sent the Spirit of his Son out of [heaven] into our hearts, [the Spirit] shouting, "Abba! Father!" ⁷And so you're no longer a slave—rather, a son. And if a son, also an heir through God. So the Galatians' experience of the Spirit confirms their adoption as sons of God apart from works of the Law. If the Galatians were still under the Law, God wouldn't have sent the Spirit out of heaven into their hearts at their conversion just as he sent his Son out of heaven at his Son's birth. See the comments

on 4:4 for the supplying of "heaven" after "sent . . . out of." To submit to the Law would be to deny the divinely given evidence of adoption. "Into our hearts" stresses the felt effect of receiving the Spirit as such evidence. "The Spirit *of his Son*" (rather than "*his* [God's] Spirit") underlines the basis of believers' sonship to God. It's their being in Christ, God's Son, by virtue of having within them the very Spirit that indwells Christ. His sonship to God has thus become theirs too. Paul doesn't say here that as believers *we* shout, "Abba! Father!" (for which see Romans 8:15). Rather, it's *the Spirit* in our hearts who shouts, "Abba! Father!" For the Spirit is Christ's, and Christ is God's Son. But since we have Christ's Spirit in our hearts, the Spirit's shouting, "Abba! Father!" confirms our sonship to God in addition to reflecting Christ's. "Shouting" strengthens the confirmation to the highest possible degree. "Abba" is Aramaic for "Father" and so typified Jesus' addressing God intimately (see Mark 14:36) that it came to be used also by Greek-speaking Christians. (Aramaic is a Semitic language related to Hebrew.) "And so you're no longer a slave" implies that you used to be a slave ("under the elements of the world" [4:3]). Whereas the switch from "you" to "our" reflected the *shared* experience of the Spirit, "rather, a son [of God, your Father as well as Christ's]" individualizes the conclusion to be drawn by each believer from the Spirit's shouting within him, "Abba! Father!" And sonship entails heirship, which means the inheriting of eternal life in God's kingdom (see the comments on 3:11, 17–18, 21 and 5:21 with 6:8). "Through God" ascribes the attainment of this heirship to his adopting believers as sons.

A PLEA TO RETAIN TRUST IN GOD'S SHEER GRACE FOR FREEDOM FROM THE LAW
Galatians 4:8–5:12

4:8–11: On the one hand, however, then—when not knowing God—you slaved for those who by nature aren't gods [though at the time you thought them to be gods (compare 1 Corinthians 8:5–6; 10:20)]. **⁹On the other hand, having now come to know God—but rather having come to be known by God—how is it that you're turning back again to the weak and bankrupt elements for which you want to slave all over again? ¹⁰You're scrupulously observing days and months and seasons and years** [compare Colossians 2:16; Genesis 1:14]. **¹¹I fear for you, lest somehow I've labored for you ineffectively.** Stressing theological and chronological contrasts are (1) "On the one hand . . . . On the other hand"; (2) "however"; (3) "then . . . . now"; and (4) "but rather." The Gentile Galatians' "not knowing God" before their conversion parallels Jewish Christians' being under the Law before *their* conversion. The Gentile Galatians' having "slaved for those who by nature [that is, inherently] aren't gods" parallels Jewish Christians' having slaved under the Law. These parallels should deter the Galatians from subjecting themselves to the Law, for such subjection would put them in a state essentially no different from paganism. "Not knowing God" and "having now come to know God" deal respectively with the inexperience and experience of a personal acquaintance with God as Abba, Father, through the reception of his Son's Spirit (4:6), not just an intellectual recognition of God's existence. By the same token, "having come to be known by God" means not only that he has taken the initiative to save the Galatians (compare Amos 3:2), but also that he experiences fatherhood to them by hearing the Spirit of his Son shout in their hearts, "Abba! Father!"—hence a reciprocity of acquaintance, of experiential knowledge.

Paul describes "the . . . elements" as "weak" in that they can't make anybody live eternally (see 3:21 and compare Romans 8:3), and describes them as "bankrupt" in that the Law holds its subjects under slavery rather than buying them out from under it (4:5). The question how it is that the Galatians "are turning back again" to such elements implies that subjecting themselves to the Law would put them back into the same condition of slavery they endured under pagan religion. As to enslavement, the monotheistic Law rates no better than polytheistic rules and regulations. For both that Law and those rules and regulations count as "the weak and bankrupt elements." "For which you *want* to slave" carries some irony and a tinge of sarcasm, while "all over again" heightens the irony and sarcasm and renews the parallel, if not equation, between enslavement to the Law and enslavement to polytheistic rules and regulations. "You're scrupulously observing days and months and seasons and years" indicates that the Galatians have started observing the calendrical features of the Law (for which see Leviticus 23:1–44; 25:1–55; Numbers 10:10; 28:11 and so on), though to further the parallel with polytheistic rules and regulations Paul uses terms that could apply also to pagan religious calendars. "*Scrupulously* observing" registers the care that ancients took to make sure they performed their religious duties at exactly the prescribed times. "Ineffectually" means that Paul fears lest the Galatians depend on works of the Law and thereby not be saved in the end (compare 5:2, 4; 1 Corinthians 15:1–2). "Lest *somehow* I've labored for you ineffectually" indicates that he's at a loss what he has or hasn't done that would have led to the Galatians' defecting. But "labored" appeals to the investment of himself in them.

4:12–14: I'm **begging you, brothers, become as I** [am], **because I also** [became] **as you** [were] [compare 1 Corinthians 9:19–23]. **You did me not even one injustice,** [13]**and you know that because of weakness of the flesh** [= a physical infirmity] **I evangelized you at first.** [14]**And you didn't make light of the testing of you in my flesh, nor did you spit. Instead, you welcomed me as** [you'd have welcomed] **an angel of God, as** [you'd have welcomed] **Christ Jesus!** Paul's fear that the Galatians might not be saved in the end (4:11) leads him to "beg" them and address them with an affectionate "brothers." "Become as I [am]" means that they should abandon works of the Law just as he has done. "Because I also [became] as you [were]" matches his Law-free faith with their Law-free faith before they started succumbing to influence from distorters of the gospel. In effect, Paul

is saying, "Please, get back on the same page with me, the one we used to occupy together." Continuing the theme of a return to their good old days, he reminds them that he evangelized them because a physical infirmity led him to visit Galatia, that despite the infirmity they didn't mistreat him, and that they welcomed him instead. By implication, they should again welcome him as represented by this letter just as they originally welcomed his very person. And, of course, to welcome him is to welcome his gospel of sheer grace. Ancient people often mistreated those who suffered a physical infirmity by making light of their infirmity and by spitting, which they thought would shield them from catching the infirmity themselves, as they feared they might, especially if the infirm person looked at them with what they considered "an evil eye." We don't know the nature of Paul's infirmity, nor do we have to know for an understanding of this passage; and he doesn't identify his infirmity to the Galatians, because they already knew what it was (compare 2 Corinthians 12:7–10). But he does call it "the testing of [the Galatians] in [his] flesh." They passed the test by welcoming him rather than mistreating him even a little bit—moreover, by welcoming him as they'd have welcomed "an angel [= a messenger] of God" and as they'd have welcomed "Christ Jesus" himself! Given their Christian profession, a better welcome is hard to imagine. Paul continues in this vein.

4:15–16: **So where** [is] **the pronouncing of yourselves fortunate?** When Paul first visited the Galatians, they pronounced themselves fortunate because he was proclaiming to them the gospel of God's grace apart from works of the Law (compare their having welcomed him [4:14]). Paul's present question implies that the distorters of this gospel have convinced the Galatians otherwise by telling them it was unfortunate that Paul omitted the necessity of their doing works of the Law. **For I'm testifying to you that if possible you'd have given me your eyes after digging** [them] **out of** [their sockets]. [16]**And so, have I become your enemy by telling you the truth?** "For" introduces the reason why Paul has just asked the whereabouts of the Galatians' former self-congratulation. Its absence is astonishing, given the extreme to which they would once have gone to help him. That if possible they'd have given him their eyes suggests an infirmity of his eyes in 4:12–14, though he may be using a gift of eyes only but emphatically as a figure of speech for the strongest possible desire to help him. "If possible" implies the impossibility of giving Paul their eyes with any benefit to him, but "after digging [them] out of [their sockets]" puts extra emphasis on how fortunate the Galatians once considered themselves for having Paul proclaim to them the Law-free gospel. And "I testify" suggests they're on trial. Paul hopes his complimentary testimony will help turn them back to belief in that gospel. But since the testimony will condemn them if they don't turn back, Paul asks plaintively whether in their well-socketed eyes he has become their enemy—and this for telling them the truth, which is "the truth of the gospel" (2:5, 14) as opposed to the distorters' Law-laden nongospel (1:6–7).

4:17–18: They [the distorters of the gospel (1:7)] **aren't courting you nobly; instead, they want to close you off** [from the Law-free gospel and/or me, its representative] **in order that you should court them.** [18]**But** [it's] **always noble to be courted in a noble** [cause], **and not only when I'm present with you.** Paul doesn't bother to identify "they," but the Galatians know right well that he's referring to those who've distorted the gospel of sheer grace by augmenting it with works of the Law. Those distorters are so much in the forefront of his mind that he probably doesn't even think of identifying "they." But he does go on to describe them as courters of the Galatians. "Courting" connotes zealous wooing. But though zealous, says Paul, this wooing isn't noble; for noble wooing wouldn't arise out of a desire to close the Galatians off from the Law-free gospel and/or its representative Paul, who'd evangelized them, and wouldn't arise out of the self-serving and hypocritical purpose of becoming the objects of the Galatians' wooing. The Law-free gospel of sheer grace is the kind of cause for which it's always noble to be courted. "And not only when I'm present with you" implies both that Paul has courted the Galatians nobly in the cause of this gospel and that in this letter he's doing so again despite his bodily absence from them.

4:19–20: **My children, in regard to whom I'm suffering birth pangs again until Christ is formed in you,** [20]**I would like to be present with you right now and to change my tone, because I'm at a loss in your case.** The affectionate address, "brothers" (4:12), shifts here to the even more affectionate address, "my children," to set up for Paul's comparing himself to a pregnant woman in labor. "Again" implies that his present pain matches the intensity of the pain he initially had out of concern for their conversion. For mixing grace with Law-keeping amounts to de-conversion and losing out on final justification. Strikingly, though, Paul doesn't speak of his giving birth to the Galatians a second time, as would be expected from the address, "my children," and from the reference to his suffering birth pangs again. Instead, he speaks of suffering birth pangs until Christ is formed in the Galatians, as though he wants *them* to play the role of an impregnated woman—and *expects* them to do so as a result of this letter: "*until* Christ is formed in you." Paul's birth pangs will cease only when Christ is formed in the Galatians; and Christ will be formed in them, like an embryo in the womb, only when they rest their faith again solely on "the grace of Christ" (1:6). "Right now" indicates that Paul would like to be with the Galatians at the time he's writing this letter so that he wouldn't have to write it but could speak to them face to face and modulate his tone to suit their evident reactions. His absence puts him at a loss, though, because he doesn't know how they'll react. But his loss is our gain, for otherwise we wouldn't have the letter.

4:21–27: **Tell me, you who're wanting to be under the Law, you hear the Law, don't you?** [22]**For it's written that Abraham had two sons, one by a slave girl and** one by a free [woman]. [23]**On the one hand, however, the** [son] **by the slave girl was born in accordance with flesh. On the other hand, the** [son] **by the free** [woman was born] **through the promise.** [24]**Which** [events] **are being allegorized** [in the following explanation]: **For these** [mothers] **are** [= symbolize] **two covenants: from Mount Sinai one** [covenant], **which as such is Hagar, birthing** [a son] **into slavery, on the one hand.** [25]**And the Hagar-Sinai mountain is in Arabia and stands with the current Jerusalem in the same column, for she is slaving** [under the Law] **along with her children.** [26]**The Jerusalem above, on the other hand, is free, which** [Jerusalem] **as such is our mother.** [27]**For it's written, "Celebrate, you barren** [woman] **who aren't bearing** [children]. **Burst out and cheer, you who aren't suffering birth pangs, because the children of the** [woman] **destitute** [of children are] **more than** [than the child of] **the** [woman] **who has a husband** [Isaiah 54:1]." For the Old Testament background see Genesis 16:1–16; 17:18–19; 21:1–2. Since Paul has just said he's at a loss concerning the Galatians, he now says in effect, "*You* tell *me!*" As in 4:9, his description of them as "*wanting* to be under the Law," which entails slavery to it, carries a good deal of irony and a tinge of sarcasm, both of which can arise paradoxically out of deep affection such as Paul has recently expressed. "You hear the Law, don't you?" furthers the irony and sarcasm and implies both the answer "Yes" and the Law's having been read to the Galatians by the gospel's distorters. So Paul cites the Law for *his* side of the argument, which sets out contrasts in parallel columns, so to speak: two contrasting sons, two contrasting mothers, two contrasting births, two contrasting covenants, and two contrasting cities. "For it's written" stresses the scriptural and therefore authoritative basis of these contrasts.

The two sons are Ishmael and Isaac. But to rivet attention on their respective conditions of slavery and freedom, Paul never does mention Ishmael's name, waits till 4:28 to mention Isaac's name, and mentions it then to highlight the Galatians' likeness to Isaac in respect to their and Paul's Isaac-like freedom from the Law. To rivet attention on Sarah's as well as Isaac's representation of this freedom, Paul similarly avoids mentioning by name Sarah, the mother of Isaac, delays mentioning Hagar, Ishmael's mother, to stress her as well as Ishmael's representation of enslavement to the Law, but does mention her name in 4:24–25 to highlight the likeness of the Law's slaves to a non-Jew who, as Paul will note in 4:30, was thrown out of Abraham's family. Hagar's birthing a son "in accordance with flesh" means that she bore Abraham a son apart from God's promise simply because she was of childbearing age and fertile. "The [son] by the free [woman was birthed] through the promise" in that the free woman was past childbearing age. Yet God had promised Abraham offspring through her. "On the one hand, however . . . . On the other hand" underlines the contrast.

"Which [events] are being allegorized" introduces a symbolic interpretation of the just-mentioned historical events. Paul equates the Law-covenant, decreed from Mount Sinai, symbolically with Hagar and says she birthed her son into slavery. "Which *as such*" accents the enslavement resulting from the Law-covenant. Then Paul mentions the location of the Hagar-Sinai mountain "in Arabia" to dissociate the Law-covenant from the land of Canaan, promised as an inheritance to Abraham and his seed and symbolizing for Paul the eternal life inherited by believers. He also puts the Hagar-Sinai mountain in the same column that "the current Jerusalem" occupies; and he does so even though, geographically speaking, the current Jerusalem is located not in Arabia, where Mount Sinai is located, but on Mount Zion in the promised land of Canaan. That is to say, theology trumps geography; for slavery to the Law that was decreed from Mount Sinai emanates now from Jerusalem. The "children" of this Jerusalem are those who now subject themselves voluntarily but wrongly to slavery under the Law.

Paul describes another Jerusalem as "free," by which he means free of enslavement to the Sinaitic law. We expect a Jerusalem *yet to come* for a contrast with "the *current* Jerusalem." But with "the Jerusalem *above*" Paul switches from chronology to location for an indication that it was from heaven that God issued his Law-free promise to Abraham and because believers in the unaugmented grace of Christ receive from heaven their inheritance, consisting in eternal life. "Which *as such*" accents the freedom of this Jerusalem from the Law, and "is our mother" indicates that believers in Jesus are born free of the Law. At this thought Paul quotes the celebratory text in Isaiah 54:1, for freedom from the Law calls for celebration. As applied by Paul and without naming her, "you barren [woman] who aren't bearing [children]," "you who aren't suffering birth pangs," and "the [woman] destitute [of children]" refer to Abraham's wife Sarah as she was during her long period of infertility. Again as applied by Paul, "the [woman] who has a husband" and a child by him refers to Hagar, who became Abraham's surrogate wife. The greater number of children that the barren woman finally had refers not to Sarah's biological children, for she birthed only one (Isaac)—rather, to the large number of Isaac-like believers in Jesus ("the seed of Abraham" as Paul called them in 3:29).

4:28–31: "But you, brothers, are children of the promise in accordance with Isaac [that is, in correspondence to him]. ²⁹As then, indeed, the [son] born in accordance with flesh was persecuting the [son born] in accordance with the Spirit, however, so too now. ³⁰Nevertheless, what is the Scripture saying? "Throw out the slave girl and her son, for by no means will the son of the slave girl inherit along with the son" of the free [woman] [Genesis 21:10]. ³¹Therefore, brothers, we aren't children of the slave girl—rather, of the free [woman]. In line with calling the Galatians "children of the promise in accordance with Isaac," Paul returns to his affectionate address, "brothers," and thus includes himself with them as such a child. And in line with the preceding contrast between promise and Law, "of the promise" describes him and them as free of slavery

under the Law (though the Galatians stand in danger of losing that freedom and thereby falling under the Law's curse). Paul interprets the playing of Hagar's son Ishmael (Genesis 21:9) as Ishmael's making sport of Sarah's son Isaac, and then compares that to the persecution of Christians, Law-free as they are, by unbelieving Jews, enslaved to the Law as they are (compare 6:12; 2 Corinthians 11:26; Philippians 3:6; 1 Thessalonians 2:14–16; 1 Timothy 1:13; Acts 8:3 and so on). "Indeed" accents the comparison. See the comments on 4:23 for "born in accordance with flesh." Here, though, Paul switches from "[born] through the promise" to "[born] in accordance with the Spirit" to describe Isaac's birth as made possible by the Spirit and to recall God's having "sent the Spirit of his Son out of [heaven] into our hearts" (4:6) and thus imply that as Abraham's seed (3:29) believers too are born in accordance with the Spirit.

"Nevertheless" introduces the following scriptural quotation as a command that the Galatians reject the distorters of the gospel by disciplining them out of the Galatians' churches. But since the slave girl herself stands for the Sinaitic covenant of Law (4:24), the command to throw out her as well as her son indicates that the Galatians should reject that covenant as well as its purveyors. "By no means" stresses that those who trust at all in their observance of the Law will be excluded from the inheritance of eternal life in God's kingdom, represented by the promised land.

"Therefore" introduces Paul's conclusion from the preceding argument as a whole, and another "brothers" adds endearment to the conclusion. "We aren't children of the slave girl—rather, of the free [woman]" declares the Galatians to be with Paul free of enslavement to the Law. If the Galatians will only recognize themselves as such, they'll not lose out on the inheritance (about which see the comments on 3:11, 17–18, and 5:21 with 6:8).

5:1: With the freedom [of "children . . . of the free woman" (4:31)] **Christ has set us free. Therefore** [= because of being set free] **stay standing and don't ever let yourselves get held in a yoke of slavery again.** The combination of "freedom" and "set . . . free" highlights the freedom of Christians from slavery under the Law of works (see 3:13 for the method of liberation). "Set *us* free" includes in this liberation Paul, a Jewish Christian, and thus all other Jewish Christians—and if them, certainly Gentile Christians such as the Galatians. "Stay standing," a positive command, and "don't ever let yourselves get held in a yoke of slavery again," a negative command, complement each other. Standing firm in freedom contrasts with being hunched under a yoke, whose purpose is to hold in control its bearer. "Of slavery" describes the yoke as a well-known figure of speech for the Law. "Again" harks back to the Galatians' enslavement to the weak and bankrupt elements of the world before the Galatians became Christians—elements that in principle don't differ from the Law, so that submitting to enslavement under the Law wouldn't differ essentially from prior enslavement to pagan rules and regulations (see the comments on 4:3, 8–9). "Don't ever let yourselves get held . . ." indicates that such enslavement is a matter of choice, not of compulsion as in the case of enslaving those defeated in war. So Paul's commanding the Galatians to stand comes close to a general's commanding his troops to stand firm in battle lest they get captured and enslaved.

5:2–4: Look! I, Paul, am telling you that if you're getting circumcised [as the first step in keeping the Law for your salvation], **Christ won't benefit** [Greek: *ōphēlesei*] **you at all.** [3]**And I'm testifying again to every man who's getting circumcised that he's a debtor** [Greek: *opheiletēs*] **to do the whole Law** [= obligated to keep all the Law's commandments, not just the commandment to get circumcised]. [4]**You've been abolished from Christ, you who as such are trying to be justified in** [the sphere of] **the Law. You've fallen out of the grace** [of Christ (compare 1:6)]. "Look!" calls special attention to what follows. "I . . . am telling you" intensifies the call. And the self-identification "Paul" intensifies it yet further with an allusion to Paul as "an apostle [sent] not from [mere] human beings or through [the agency of] a [mere] human being—rather, [sent] through [the direct action of] Jesus Christ and God the Father" (1:1), and therefore as one whose words had better be heeded. To get circumcised is to renounce the all-sufficiency of Christ's grace (see 1:6–10; 2:4, 16, 21; 3:13, 22). So Paul warns that getting circumcised deprives the Galatians of that benefit. They'll lose out on salvation; they'll miss out on justification. "And I'm *testifying* again" lends gravity to Paul's following statement that "every man who's getting circumcised" is "a debtor to do the whole Law." "Again" harks back to the immediately preceding statement that Christ won't at all benefit those who are getting circumcised, implies that in that statement as well as this one Paul was testifying, and may hark back also to 3:10: "For it's written, 'Accursed [is] everyone who isn't abiding in all the things written in the book of the Law so as to do them'" (compare James 2:10). The repetition adds further gravity to Paul's statement; and just as "to do the *whole* Law" allows none of its commandments to be excepted, "to *every* man" allows no man to be excepted who gets circumcised. The switch from "every man," "himself," and "he" back to "you" sharpens the point of Paul's declaration, "You've been abolished from Christ," which for emphasis repeats with different phraseology the earlier declaration, "Christ won't benefit you at all" (5:2). "Not . . . at all" rules out any mixture of faith and works of the Law in the attainment of justification. It's none of such works, or no justification whatever. To be "abolished from Christ" means not to be "in Christ" any more. "You who *as such*" underlines the condition of abolishment from Christ. "Are trying to be justified" implies an inevitably unsuccessful attempt, and "in [the sphere of] the Law" makes another contrast with being in Christ. "You've fallen out of grace" parallels "You've been abolished from Christ," because only in him is the grace of justification to be found, and also caps Paul's warning that the grace of Christ resists any addition of works of the Law, so that gravitating to the Law

makes his grace ineffective for justification. Moreover, the condition of having "fallen" out of grace makes for a sad contrast with "standing" in freedom from the Law (5:1; compare Romans 5:2).

5:5–6: For because of faith we're eagerly expecting by the Spirit the hope of justification. [6]**For in Christ Jesus neither circumcision nor uncircumcision has any strength** [for the gaining of justification]; **rather, faith takes effect through love.** Paul first tells the reason why the Galatians will have fallen out of Christ's grace if they get circumcised. Supplying the reason is the incompatibility of "trying to be justified in [the sphere of] the Law" (5:4) and "because of faith eagerly expecting by the Spirit the hope of justification." Eager expectation points forward to final justification at the Last Judgment. The felt gift of the Spirit anticipates that justification and thus makes the expectation eager. "The hope" of such justification makes the expectation confident, for confidence rather than uncertainty characterizes Paul's use of "hope." And in opposition to the Law as a sphere in which justification is attempted, faith is the mainspring of eager expectation. Next, Paul tells the reason why "we," including Gentile as well as Jewish believers, have this eager expectation. Supplying the reason are both the irrelevance in Christ Jesus of both circumcision and uncircumcision and the all-sufficiency of faith in him. Paul describes this faith as "tak[ing] effect through love," by which he means that the replacement of circumcision and uncircumcision with faith destroys this physically divisive difference between Jews and Gentiles and thus effects the prevalence of love in Christian churches. For the trio of faith, hope, and love see also 1 Corinthians 13:13; 1 Thessalonians 1:3; 5:8; Romans 5:1–5.

5:7–10: You were running beautifully. Who cut in so as to dissuade you of the truth? [8]**The dissuasion** [does] **not** [originate] **from the one who's calling you.** [9]**"A little leaven leavens the whole batch of dough."** [10]**In the Lord I'm persuaded regarding you that you'll think nothing other** [than what I've told you as the truth of the gospel]. **But the one who's stirring you up** [to defect (see 1:7)], **whoever he is, will bear judgment.** Paul compares the Galatians' Christian life to a race just as he compared his evangelization of them to a race (2:2). Till recently they've been running "beautifully." (The usual translation, "well," doesn't capture the element of admirability inherent in Paul's word.) "Who cut in . . . ?" implies that someone cut into the Galatians' path so as to block them from completing the race. We have no way of telling whether Paul had in mind someone in particular as the one who cut in (such as a leader of those who were distorting the gospel [1:7; 5:12] or Satan [1 Thessalonians 2:18]) or no one in particular. "The truth" of which an attempt was being made to dissuade the Galatians was, of course, "the truth of the gospel" (2:5, 14). "The one who's calling [the Galatians]" is God (compare 1:6, 15), and dissuasion from the truth certainly doesn't originate from him. The present tense in "who's calling" is due to the Galatians' tending toward apostasy. They still need God's effective call to save them from an eternally dreadful fate. See the comments on 1 Corinthians 5:6 for the saying on leaven, and Mark 8:15; Matthew 16:6 for leaven as a figure of speech for corruption. "A little leaven" may stand for the nongospel of those who are distorting the gospel of sheer grace. But since "the whole batch of dough" almost certainly stands for the Galatian Christians, "a little leaven" more likely stands for the one who's "cut[ting] in so as to dissuade [them] of the truth," later called "the one who's stirring [them] up [to defect]." Paul uses "in the Lord" instead of the more usual "in Christ" to stress the authority of Paul's persuasion that the Galatians "will think nothing other [than what he has told them is the gospel]." This high compliment ("*nothing* other . . .") has the purpose of encouraging them to get back on the racetrack, for people tend to rise to others' expectations of them. In view of the double anathema in 1:8–9, the judgment to be borne by the one who's stirring them up will consist in eternal damnation. Again, "the one" may or may not refer to someone in particular; but "whoever he is" makes his judgment regardless of power or prestige.

5:11–12: But I, brothers, if I'm still proclaiming circumcision, why am I still being persecuted? Then [= if in fact I'm still proclaiming circumcision] the snare [consisting] of the cross has been abolished. [12]O that those who are upsetting you would even get [their penises and testicles] **cut off!** "But I" stands in contrast with "the one who's stirring you up [to defect]" (5:10); and the address "brothers" furthers the contrast by putting Paul in the same family with the Galatians and thereby distancing from them that agitator. He's an outsider. "If I'm still proclaiming circumcision" at least suggests and probably implies that those who were trying to impose circumcision on Gentile Christians were portraying Paul as a proclaimer of circumcision either prior to his conversion or at the time of his writing this letter. The parallel between "*still* proclaiming circumcision" and "*still* being persecuted" favors the latter. In either case, "why am I still being persecuted?" implies ongoing persecution for *not* proclaiming circumcision. But Paul is more concerned about the theological consequence of a portrayal of him as proclaiming circumcision than he is of the falsity of such a portrayal. That consequence is an abolishment of "the snare of the cross," which is to say that a proclamation of circumcision by Paul would seem to make unnecessary the crucifixion of Jesus, including its offensiveness to human sensibilities (compare the comments on 1 Corinthians 1:23), and would seem to make it so by propounding Law-keeping as the way to achieve justification before God (compare 3:21). "The snare of the cross" refers in particular to the offensiveness of Christ's having become "a curse" according to the Law by "hang[ing] on a tree" (3:13). But since Christ became such "on our behalf" (3:13 again), Paul wants the snare of the cross to be abolished no more than he wants the Galatians to be "abolished from Christ" (5:4), though the two events would correlate. Paul doesn't want the agitators to succeed in abolishing the snare of the

cross by using a false portrayal of him as still proclaiming circumcision. So strong is his desire that they not succeed—after all, the Galatians' justification at the Last Judgment is at stake—that he breaks out in a wish that the agitators would even get their penises and testicles "cut off" (or "chopped off," as his verb could equally well be translated) just as they've already had their foreskins cut off (compare Philippians 3:2). Then they couldn't "enter the Lord's assembly" even according to the Law that they refuse to give up and try to impose on others (Deuteronomy 23:1; compare Leviticus 21:20; 22:24)! "Those who are upsetting you" doesn't connote emotional distress so much as incitement to rebel against the gospel of sheer grace. For "cut[ting] *in*" so as to dissuade the Galatians of the truth (5:7), these agitators deserve to have their privates "cut *off*." Lying in the background may be the self-castration practiced in Galatia by devotees of the goddess Cybele.

A WARNING AGAINST LICENSE
Galatians 5:13–6:10

5:13–15: For you were called on the ground of freedom, brothers. Only [don't turn] the freedom into a basis for the flesh; rather, through love slave for one another. [14]For the entire Law is fulfilled in a single statement—in the [statement], "You shall love your neighbor as [you love] yourself [Leviticus 19:18]." [15]But if you're biting and devouring one another, be watching out lest you be consumed by one another. "You were called on the ground of freedom" tells why Paul has just wished the agitators would have their privates cut off. Capitulation to the agitators' demand for circumcision would take away not only the Galatians' foreskins but also their freedom from the Law of works and thus consign them to an enslavement impossible to pull off successfully (Romans 7:7–8:3)—and therefore to eternal damnation. "Called on the ground of freedom" means that the call of God which effected their conversion goes hand in glove with freedom from the Law of works. The two are inextricably linked. The affectionate address, "brothers," signals an upcoming warning not to misconstrue this freedom as license to sin (compare Romans 6:1–2). As often elsewhere, "flesh" connotes moral weakness, so that "a basis for the flesh" means "a pretext to let the lusts of the flesh run amok." Over against such license Paul sets the command to "slave for one another." We expect the command to "love one another"; and indeed "through love" fulfills the function of that command. Moreover, Paul follows up with the command to love your neighbor as you love yourself. Nevertheless, putting the command first in the form of *slaving* for one another qualifies freedom from the Law shockingly; and the shock underscores that freedom doesn't equate with license. "Through love" echoes the statement in 5:6 that "faith takes effect through love" and thereby sets mutual love in the framework of faith rather than the Mosaic law. So slaving lovingly for one another's benefit replaces slaving for one's own benefit under the Law.

The statement that "the entire Law is fulfilled [in the command to love your neighbor]" tells why the Galatians should slave for one another through love. Moreover, slaving for one another defines loving your neighbor in terms of doing as well as feeling. But in what sense is the entire Law fulfilled in the single command to love your neighbor? Notably, it isn't *obedience* to this command that constitutes a fulfillment of the entire Law. It's the *statement* of the command that constitutes this fulfillment. So "is fulfilled" means "is summed up." In other words, loving your neighbor as you love yourself substitutes commanded kindnesses for prohibited injuries and shows love for God, who created in his own image your neighbor as well as you (see also the comments on Mark 12:31; Luke 10:36–37). "Slave *for one another*" applies the command to love your neighbor to relations between Christians in that by definition "your neighbor" means someone near you, and Christians are near each other both physically, in their assemblies, and theologically, in Christ. "But if you're biting and devouring one another" suggests that the agitators' nongospel has triggered conflicts among the Galatians, contrasts those conflicts with slaving for one another through love, and compares the conflicts to the fighting with each other of animals—say, street-roaming dogs—that bite one another and devour the flesh they bite off. Paul warns that fighting among Christians will likewise result in mutual destruction of a figuratively cannibalistic sort. The solution doesn't lie in compromise, though—rather, in the freedom of faith that takes effect through love.

5:16–18: And I'm saying, walk around by the Spirit and by no means will you bring to completion the lust of the flesh. [17]For the flesh lusts against the Spirit, and the Spirit [lusts] against the flesh. For these oppose each other, lest you be doing these things, whatever [they are], that you're wanting [to do]. [18]But if you're being led by the Spirit, you're not under the Law. "And I'm saying" puts an accent on the following command to "walk around by the Spirit." To walk around by the Spirit is to behave as the Spirit leads and enables you to behave. Negatively, this kind of behavior means not "bring[ing] to completion the lust of the flesh." "By no means" emphasizes the Spirit's superiority over the flesh in enabling you to frustrate its lust. Counting as lust is any overpowering desire—in the case of lust of the flesh, a desire so strong that by capitalizing on the moral weakness represented by "flesh" it leads to the transgressing of moral boundaries, both sexual and other (as in our expressions "the lust for power," "the lust for prestige," "the lust for wealth," and so forth). (The translation "desire" is too weak.) For the lust of the flesh to be brought to completion would be for the lust to prevail in your actual behavior.

The *command* to walk around by the Spirit, so that this completion doesn't take place, implies freedom of action and the personal responsibility accompanying it. Starting with "For," Paul tells why he has issued that command. The reason is twofold: (1) the flesh lusts against the Spirit in that your moral *weakness* paradoxically produces in you a *strong* desire to transgress the moral boundaries which the Spirit strongly desires you to honor, and (2) the Spirit lusts against the flesh in that the Spirit strongly desires you not to bring to completion the lust of the flesh. "For these oppose each other" explains that the respective lusts, those of the flesh and those of the Spirit, are dead set against each other. No compromise is possible, so that either the Spirit keeps you from doing the evil your flesh wants you to do or your flesh keeps you from doing the good the Spirit wants you to do. "But if you're being led by the Spirit" explains what it means to "walk around by the Spirit." It means to let the Spirit determine your behavior, indeed to empower you to behave in opposition to the lust of the flesh. And there may be some wordplay between "being *led* by the Spirit" and the contrastive condition of being under the Law as your childminder (3:24–25). For more literally translated, the word for "childminder" comes out as "child*leader*." We expect Paul to say that if you're being led by the Spirit you won't be led by your lustful flesh, or words to that effect (as in the earlier statement, "by no means will you bring to completion the lust of the flesh"). But he surprises us with the conclusion, "you're not under the Law," which brings out that Spirit-led behavior gives evidence of freedom from the Law. So you shouldn't submit to circumcision and the slavery it entails (compare 3:2–5).

5:19–21: And the works of the flesh are obvious, which as such [that is, as fleshly] are fornication, impurity, licentiousness, [20]idolatry, magic arts, hostilities, strife, jealousy, outbreaks of rage, rivalries, dissensions, factions, [21]envies, bouts of drunkenness, carousals, and things similar to these, about which I'm telling you beforehand [= before the Last Judgment] just as I told you before [when I was with you] that those who are practicing such things won't inherit God's kingdom. "The works of the flesh" parallel the frequently mentioned "works of the Law" (2:16; 3:2, 5, 10) to indicate that the flesh takes advantage of the Law because of the Law's powerlessness to resist the lust of the flesh. Paul declares the works of the flesh "obvious" to point out that you don't need the Law to recognize them as evil. The Law is needless as well as powerless. "Fornication" refers to sexual immorality of all kinds, but especially to having sex with a prostitute. Though "impurity" could refer to various vices as moral stains, Paul's sandwiching it between "fornication" and "licentiousness" makes it refer here to the impurity of illicit sex, perhaps with a hint at the stains of bodily fluid involved (for "impurity" means "uncleanness"). "Licentiousness" refers to sexual immorality of a flagrant sort—shameless and brazen. "Idolatry" means the worship of idols and occurs here because fornication, impurity, and licentiousness took place prominently at temples devoted to idolatry. Prostitutes did sex work there under the auspices of priests, and banquets in and near those temples often featured sexual dalliances. "Magic arts" follows "idolatry" because these arts called on the gods to do the bidding of those who practiced such arts.

With "hostilities, strife, jealousy, outbreaks of rage, rivalries, dissensions, factions, envies" Paul turns from what characterized plainly pagan behavior to what he described figuratively in 5:15 as "biting and devouring one another" in the Christian community, rent asunder by a nongospel. At the same time these behaviors also grew out of the "bouts of drunkenness" and "carousals" that characterized the symposiums (drinking sessions) following banquets and that characterized the worship of Bacchus, the Greek god of wine. By bookending the fleshly behaviors of some professing Christians with these two additional pagan behaviors, Paul categorizes the fleshly behavior of those supposed Christians with the behavior of outright pagans. "And things similar to these" leaves the list open-ended. Other vices could be added, but Paul has made his point well enough. His having told the Galatians twice now that "those who are practicing such things won't inherit God's kingdom" sharpens the point, interprets the inheritance promised to Abraham and his seed (3:16–18, 29; 4:7) as the inheritance of God's kingdom (in the form of eternal life according to 6:8), and implies that those who practice the works of the flesh show themselves not to have received the Spirit and therefore not to have been justified yet and not to be justified at the Last Judgment. So too the command in 5:16 to "walk around by the Spirit" means that through Spirit-led behavior you must prove your justification by faith. Not that such behavior earns your justification to any degree; only—but importantly—that it gives evidence thereof.

5:22–24: But the fruit of the Spirit is love, joy, peace, patience, magnanimity, goodness, faithfulness, ²³gentleness, self-control. There's no law against such things. ²⁴And those who belong to the Christ have crucified the flesh with its passions and lusts. Obviously, "the fruit of the Spirit" contrasts with the preceding "works of the flesh." Because "the works of the flesh" consist in the deeds that the flesh as moral weakness produces, we might have expected Paul to speak contrastively of "the works of the Spirit," that is, of deeds produced by the Spirit who indwells believers. But thus far in Galatians "works" has had unfavorable associations with "the Law" and "flesh." So Paul switches to "fruit," which has the advantage of being a standard figure of speech connoting evidence, as in Matthew 7:19, for example: "you shall recognize them by their fruits." Paul is talking about behavioral evidence of having the Spirit, then, and therefore about behavioral evidence of present and future justification. It's therefore a mistake to fix on "fruit" as used for the connotation of effortless outgrowth in opposition to "works" of obedient effort. Shortly, in fact, Paul will use "work" in a favorable sense (6:4); and elsewhere he uses "works" a number of times for Christian behavior (see 1 Corinthians 3:11–15, for example). "Works" has occurred in the plural for what the flesh produces (5:19). But despite listing nine virtues produced by the Spirit, Paul uses the singular in "fruit" because the first-listed fruit is "love," the doing of which entails the entire Law according to 5:14. So

love encompasses the following eight virtues. A unified, single fruit results (compare Colossians 3:12–14). And whereas the works of the flesh were made up mainly by activities, the fruit of the Spirit is made up mainly by traits of character. "Love" does translate, however, into activities of self-sacrificial helpfulness toward your neighbor, which in this context means your fellow Christian (see the comments on 5:14). Where love is, there too are joy, peace, patience, magnanimity, goodness, faithfulness, and self-control.

"Peace" has to do not so much with peace of mind as with peaceful relations with fellow Christians—that is, with the opposite of "biting and devouring one another," figuratively speaking (5:15)—so that communal relations might prosper rather than break down. "Patience" means having a long fuse, as opposed to "outbreaks of rage," one of the works of the flesh (5:20). "Kindness," the translation that usually stands where "magnanimity" stands here, captures a good deal of what Paul's underlying word means. But "magnanimity" rightly adds to kindness the connotation of rising above pettiness and mean-spiritedness. "Goodness" includes generosity. "Faithfulness" translates a word often translated "faith, belief," but in a list of virtuous traits of character more likely means faithfulness to one another in the Christian community. "Gentleness" is opposed to "hostilities" (5:20), and "self-control" is opposed to other "works of the flesh": "fornication, impurity, licentiousness . . . bouts of drunkenness, carousals" (5:19, 21).

By saying that there's no law against the foregoing virtues Paul is saying in effect that if you allow the Spirit to lead you along these lines, you needn't fear being shut out of God's kingdom for breaking any laws. At the Last Judgment you'll have in hand the evidence of having received the Spirit in connection with justification by faith. "Those who belong to the Christ" belong to him because of being in him, again by faith. "The Christ" thus refers to the corporate Christ, not to Christ as a lone individual. Those people "have crucified the flesh" by believing in him, so that when he was crucified, their moral weakness was crucified along with him (compare 2:19–20). Paul's statement personifies the flesh as a victim of crucifixion, makes those who belong to the Christ themselves the crucifiers of the flesh as moral weakness, and states their having crucified it as an event that has taken place in the past. Paul isn't commanding the Galatians to crucify their flesh, their moral weakness. He's stating this crucifixion as a fact accomplished in Christ's crucifixion and appropriated by the Galatians when they believed in the crucified Christ (see Romans 6:11 for an exhortation that applies this truth to daily conduct). In 5:16 Paul spoke of "the lust of the flesh." Here he adds "passions" and uses the plural in "lusts" to emphasize how different are the characteristics of the flesh from the fruit of the Spirit.

5:25–26: If we're living by the Spirit, let's also be keeping in line with the Spirit. ²⁶Let's not become vainglorious, challenging one another [to a fight], being envious of one another. "If we're living by the Spirit" assumes that we are and refers, not to behavior (in which case we might have expected "walk[ing] around by the Spirit," as in 5:16), but to believers' having eternal life by the Spirit, as will come out clearly in 6:8 (see also Romans 8:2, 6, 10; 1 Corinthians 15:45; 2 Corinthians 3:6 and the comments on Galatians 3:11). Because we have eternal life by the Spirit, we should be "keeping in line with the Spirit," behaviorally speaking, as he leads us (5:18). In Paul's original Greek "be keeping in line" is the verbal form of the world's "elements," which according to 4:3 enslaved the Galatians before they became Christians and which he described in 4:9 as "weak and bankrupt." So he puts keeping in line with the life-giving Spirit, the possession of whom spells freedom, in opposition to enslavement under those elements, which have no power or resources to give eternal life. Part of keeping in line with the Spirit is "not becom[ing] vainglorious." To become vainglorious would be to vie for an honor that's empty because you don't deserve it, perhaps also because it comes from human beings rather than from God. You become vainglorious by challenging another in your community (a local church in the Galatians' case) to some sort of combat or contest in which the winner gains honor at the expense of the other's honor. Challenges of this sort arise especially from envy of the other's honor. Paul will now spell out a better way.

6:1: Brothers, even if a person is caught [in the act of] **some transgression, you Spiritual ones rehabilitate such a person in the Spirit of gentleness, seeing to yourself lest you too be tempted** [to transgress]. The address "Brothers" lends seriousness to the following command and puts it in the framework of family obligations (compare "members of the household of the faith" in 6:10). "*Even* if a person is caught [in the act of] some transgression" implies that catching the person in it might incline the catcher to react with self-righteous repudiation. Against that possibility, Paul commands a rehabilitation of the transgressor (compare Matthew 18:15–17). "Some transgression" means one of "the works of the flesh" (5:19–21). To "rehabilitate" means to get the transgressor to mend his or her ways by ceasing to transgress. "You Spiritual ones" means "you who have the Spirit and are keeping in line with the Spirit" (hence the capitalization of "Spiritual" [see 5:25 with 3:3, 5; 5:16]). "In the Spirit of gentleness" contrasts with the possibility of repudiation, alludes to gentleness as part of "the fruit of the Spirit" (5:22–23), and therefore locates the activity of rehabilitation not in the human spirits of believers but in the Holy Spirit, who grows that fruit in believers. But gentleness as opposed to repudiation can expose the would-be rehabilitator to temptation, the temptation of joining the transgressor in his or her transgression. So Paul adds "seeing to yourself lest you too be tempted." In other words, keep a certain emotional distance; don't get too sympathetic. Though not at all to be neglected, rehabilitative love of your neighbor does have its moral risk (compare 1 Corinthians 10:12–13; Jude 22–23). The switch from the plural, "you Spiritual ones," to the singular, "yourself," and the awkwardness of this switch underscore the moral risk at an individual level.

6:2–5: Be bearing one another's burdens, and in this way you'll completely fulfill the law of the Christ [compare 1 Corinthians 9:19–23]. ³**For if someone supposes** [himself] **to be something, though being nothing, he's deluding himself.** ⁴**But each is to be testing his own work, and then he'll have a basis for boasting in regard to himself alone and not in regard to another** [person]. ⁵**For each will bear his own load.** "Burdens" represents hardships that weigh down a person economically, physically, emotionally, socially. To bear one another's burdens is to take such burdens on yourself through lovingly helpful deeds and thus obey the command to love your neighbor as you love yourself (5:14), which Paul now calls "the law of the Christ." Since Paul said that "the *entire* Law is fulfilled [that is, summed up]" in the statement of this command, here he says that obeying it "will *completely* fulfill the law of the Christ." He ascribes this law to the Christ because Jesus taught it in his capacity as the Christ, the Messiah (Mark 12:31; Matthew 19:19; 22:39; Luke 10:25–37) and because faith in Jesus as the Christ frames this law and thus extracts it from the Law of works (see the comments on 5:13–15). So the expression, "the law of the Christ," reinforces that freedom from the Mosaic law doesn't imply license to sin.

Supposing oneself "to be something" means supposing oneself to be above bearing others' burdens. The qualification, "though being nothing," notes the falsity of this supposition and means that nobody is above bearing others' burdens. "He's deluding himself," which literally refers to leading astray his own intellect, supplies a reason to bear one another's burdens. For nobody wants to be victimized by self-delusion. Testing one's own work, which Paul commands, contrasts with deluding oneself, against which he warns. "His own work" refers to the work of bearing one another's burdens, and testing often connotes approval as a consequence of the test (see, for example, Romans 2:18; 14:22; 1 Corinthians 11:28; 16:3; 2 Corinthians 8:22; 1 Thessalonians 2:4). So testing to the point of approving one's own work of bearing others' burdens gives one a basis for boasting. Justified boasting wasn't frowned on in first-century Mediterranean culture, just as in contemporary culture justified self-esteem isn't frowned on. In fact, the kind of boasting Paul is talking about comes closer to exultant self-esteem than to offensive braggadocio. "Each . . . his own" stresses individual responsibility as opposed to testing others' work, which is God's prerogative. "Boasting in regard to himself and not in regard to another [person]" reinforces the point and favors that "each will bear his own load" refers to what will happen at the Last Judgment (compare 1 Corinthians 4:3–5). We'll be judged individually on how we bore our own workload in behalf of others, not on their performances. Reason enough to test one's own work!

6:6: But the person being instructed as to the word [of the gospel] **is to be sharing in all good things with the person instructing** [him]. An instructed person's "sharing in all good things with the person instructing [him]" provides an instance of bearing another's burden. For the instructor's devoting time and energy in instruction lays on him an economic burden that the instructee needs to bear. "All good things" therefore refers to all kinds of material support needed by the instructor (compare the connotation of generosity in "goodness," part of "the fruit of the Spirit" in 5:22–23; also Matthew 10:10; Luke 1:53; 10:7; 12:18–19; 16:25; 1 Corinthians 9:1–14; 1 Timothy 5:18).

6:7–8: Don't ever deceive yourselves. God isn't snooted at. For whatever a human being sows—this he'll also reap, [8]because the one sowing into his own flesh will reap corruption out of [his own] flesh; but the one sowing into the Spirit will reap eternal life out of the Spirit. The alternative translation, "Don't ever *be* deceived," differs a little from "don't ever deceive *yourselves*"; but "he's deluding himself" in 6:3 favors the reflexive translation over the passive one. "God isn't snooted at" means that you don't turn up your nose at God and get away with doing so. Paul has just commanded the sharing of material goods; and in the only other passages where he uses the figure of sowing-and-reaping (1 Corinthians 9:10–11; 2 Corinthians 9:6), this figure has to do with material support. Here, then, snooting at God refers in particular to disobeying "the law of the Christ" that an instructee should bear his instructor's burden by providing him with material support. "God" and "a human being" stand over against each other as judge and judged stand over against each other. The human being's "sowing into his own flesh" compares his flesh to soil and stands for using his material resources to satisfy only his own physical needs and desires. Such sowing could therefore count as another one of "the works of the flesh" (5:19–21). The contrast with reaping eternal life shows that "reap[ing] corruption out of [his own] flesh" means consignment to eternal damnation (compare 1 Corinthians 15:50). (An allusion to circumcised flesh, which eventually decays, seems far-fetched here.) "Sowing into the Spirit" compares the Spirit to soil, stands for "sharing in all good things" with an instructor (6:6), and portrays such sharing as part of the fruit of the Spirit that's a necessary evidence of having the Spirit and therefore of being justified by faith (5:22–23; 6:1). "Reap[ing] eternal life out of the Spirit" means gaining eternal life at the resurrection and Last Judgment. For the Spirit as the source of eternal life, see the references in the comments on 5:25. The principle enunciated in 6:7–8 has many other applications, of course.

6:9–10: And let's not be giving up in doing the noble thing, for we'll reap at the opportune time, provided we don't get slack. [10]So then, as we have opportunity, let's be producing the good thing toward all, but especially toward members of the household of the faith. "Doing the noble thing" and "producing the good thing" describe "sharing in all good things" with instructors in the word of the gospel (6:6). "At the opportune time" refers to the season of harvest, which stands for the Last Judgment. "Not giving up" and "not get[ting] slack" have to do with perseverance in the sharing of material

resources, a perseverance that gives evidence of true faith. "*Let's* not be giving up" and "*let's* be producing" represent a shift from commands to exhortations, which soften Paul's tone and include him with the Galatians in the need for perseverance. "As we have *opportunity*" makes a wordplay with "we'll reap at the *opportune* time." The point of the wordplay is that at the opportune time for final judgment we'll be judged on whether we took advantage of opportunities to do the noble and good thing of sharing our material resources with those in need. "Toward all" broadens the scope of such sharing to include everyone in need, including non-Christians, not just instructors in the word. "But especially toward members of the household of the faith" concentrates on fellow Christians in that they're the Galatians' closest neighbors because of regular assemblies (the very meaning of "churches") and in that persecution made Christians economically needy. "The household of the faith" portrays them as a family formed by their common faith in Christ Jesus (compare "Abraham's seed" in 3:26–29). The expression may owe something to the prevalence of early Christians' meeting in private homes.

CONCLUSION
Galatians 6:11–18

6:11: Look at what big letters I've written to you with my hand! This exclamation signals the beginning of the end of the letter. "Look . . . !" calls attention to Paul's handwriting in big letters to assure the Galatians that he did indeed write this letter, an assurance designed in view of the letter's disputatious contents to reemphasize that it carries the authority of "an apostle [sent] not from [mere] human beings nor through [the agency of] a [mere] human being—rather, [sent] through [the direct action] of Jesus Christ and God the Father" (1:1). "What big letters" adds further emphasis on this assurance of authenticity, but it's hard to know whether the big letters have to do only with emphasis or also with poor eyesight on Paul's part or a lack of scribal expertise on his part (compare youngsters' writing with large letters when just learning penmanship; and note that the roughness of ancient papyrus made writing on the papyrus more difficult than writing on modern paper is). There are other possibilities. "I've written to you" almost certainly reflects the Galatians' standpoint when the letter is read to them. By that time Paul will have written in the past. Given this near certainty, Paul's own handwriting covers only 6:11–18. A scribal secretary will have written 1:1–6:10 at Paul's dictation. We know from Romans 16:22 with 15:15 that Paul used such a secretary in writing to the Romans, and from 1 Corinthians 16:21; Colossians 4:18; 2 Thessalonians 3:17–18; Philemon 19 that Paul often (if not always) used his own penmanship at the ends of his letters.

6:12–14: As many as want to put on a fine face in flesh—these are trying to force you to get circumcised. [They're doing so] only not to be persecuted for the cross of the Christ. [13]For not even those who them-

selves are trying to get [you] **circumcised are themselves keeping the Law; rather, they're wanting you to get circumcised in order that they may boast in your flesh.** [14]**As for me, may it not happen that I be boasting except in the cross of our Lord, Jesus Christ, through which the world has been crucified so far as I'm concerned, and** [through which] **I** [have been crucified] **so far as the world is concerned.** Distorters of the gospel of sheer grace are trying to force the Galatians to get circumcised by telling them that final justification requires present circumcision. (That circumcision was the crucial issue shows how male-dominated was the culture, for the Law didn't prescribe female circumcision.) "A fine face in flesh" was to be the *distorters'* face in the *Galatians'* flesh, specifically in the flesh of their circumcised penises. Two ironies: (1) though used figuratively for any sort of a fine show because the face is the most visible part of a person's body, "a fine *face*" hardly comports with a circumcised penis that's hidden behind clothing; (2) "a *fine* face" hardly comports with a penis disfigured by circumcision. Since only Jews would associate circumcision with a fine face/show, the ones trying to force circumcision on the Galatians must be Jews; and their doing so "not to be persecuted for the cross of the Christ" specifies them as Jewish Christians, for non-Christian Jews needn't fear persecution for that reason. "The Christ" portrays Jesus as the Messiah and implies persecution of Jewish Christians by non-Christian Jews because the Jewish Christians were proclaiming as the Messiah a man who'd been crucified, hung on a tree, and therefore accursed according to the Mosaic law (3:13). "*Only* not to be persecuted for the cross of the Christ" makes avoidance of persecution the sole purpose of the distorters' trying to force circumcision on the Galatians. If the distorters can boast that they persuaded the Galatians to get circumcised and thereby make them proselytes to Christianity as a branch of Judaism, non-Christian Jews might overlook the cross of Christ and not persecute Jewish Christians.

In and of itself the verb translated intensively, "themselves are trying to get [you] circumcised," is ambiguous. It could also be translated reflexively, "are getting themselves circumcised," or passively, "are being circumcised," or reciprocally, "are circumcising one another." But Jewish Christians would already have been circumcised, and the intensive translation adopted here agrees both with the Jewishness of the distorters and with Paul's emphasis on the forcefulness of their attempt to get the Galatians circumcised. But how can Paul say that "not even [the distorters] are themselves keeping the Law"? He can say so on the ground he has already established, namely, that since the Law requires obedience to itself as a whole, pronounces a curse on everyone who doesn't abide by *all* things written in it through doing them (3:10), and can't provide justification or life (2:16; 3:21), then nobody—not even the distorters of grace with Law—are keeping the Law in every respect. And this failure gives Paul his reason for saying they're trying to force circumcision on the Galatians only to avoid persecution. A true concern for Law-keeping would center on the distorters' own transgressions, not on Gentile Christians' uncircumcision.

Paul sets his wish not to boast except in the cross over against the distorters' purpose to boast in the Galatians' flesh. Any cross was considered the utmost of shame, though. It wasn't polite even to speak of a cross. To counteract the shamefulness of Jesus Christ's cross, then, Paul calls it "the cross *of our Lord*, Jesus Christ." Particularly in connection with this cross, "the world" means the world of unbelievers (1 Corinthians 1:18–23). So far as Paul is concerned, then, that world has been crucified through the cross—and stays crucified—because unlike the distorters, Paul doesn't care what unbelievers think of him. Through the cross, conversely, Paul has been crucified—and stays crucified—so far as the world is concerned in that unbelievers don't care what he thinks of them. He especially has in view unbelieving Jews who persecute him for proclaiming a cross that makes circumcision and uncircumcision irrelevant. They represent "the world." Paul values the cross, they despise it. So there's no compatibility. The cross forms a fence between them, and indeed the verb for "crucify" also means "make a fence."

6:15–16: For neither is circumcision anything [to boast about], **nor** [is] **uncircumcision** [anything to boast about]; **rather, a new creation** [is something to boast about].** [16]**And as many as will keep in line with this ground rule—peace** [will be] **on them and mercy** [will be] **also on the Israel of God.** The initial "For" makes the subsequently stated irrelevance of circumcision and uncircumcision an explanation of the previously stated wish not to boast except in the cross of the Lord, Jesus Christ. In other words, his cross makes circumcision nothing for a Jew to boast about, and uncircumcision nothing for a Gentile (with Greek repugnance against circumcision) to boast about. But "a new creation" *is* worth boasting about. Since circumcision and uncircumcision have to do with individuals, the new creation that contrasts with them has to do with individuals created anew in Christ, where neither circumcision nor uncircumcision counts (see 2 Corinthians 5:17 with comments). See the comments on 5:25 for the expression, "will keep in line with." "This ground rule" refers to the irrelevance of circumcision and uncircumcision in "a new creation." Paul predicts peace on those in general who in opposition to the distorters maintain the ground rule. "Peace" connotes all the benefits of salvation, which according to 1:8–9 those distorters won't receive—rather, an anathema. "Mercy" refers to God's taking pity in particular on "the Israel of God," by which he probably means "all Israel" that "will be saved" when "the deliverer will come out of Zion" and "remove ungodliness from Jacob" (Romans 11:25–27 [see the comments on that passage]).[2]

---

[2]Many commentators equate "the Israel of God" and "as many as will keep in line with this ground rule," and take Paul to be wishing rather than predicting both peace and mercy on them. Among other considerations, though, "also" and the repetition of "on" before "the Israel of God" seem to distinguish this Israel as a subset of the line-keepers.

6:17: From now on no one is to cause me beatings [a figure of speech for troubles], **for I'm bearing in my body the brand-marks of Jesus.** The word for "beatings" is usually translated "trouble(s)," but the literal translation links with "the brand-marks" on Paul's body, that is, with the scars he got from being beaten and struck by stones (Acts 14:19; 2 Corinthians 11:24–25). "From now on no one is to cause [Paul] beatings" means that this letter to the Galatians should put a stop to the agitators' causing him trouble by proclaiming to his converts a Law-laden nongospel. Bearing the brand-marks of Jesus complements bearing one another's burdens (6:1) in that Paul bears those brand-marks to unburden the Galatians of the works of the Law that the agitators are imposing on them. "Of Jesus" makes the brand-marks a sign that Paul is slaving for Jesus, as 1:10 has already indicated in prosaic language. Paul's bearing such a sign gives plenty of reason not to cause him trouble.

6:18: The grace of our Lord, Jesus Christ, [be] with your spirit, brothers. Amen. "Grace" always occurs in Paul's farewells, but here it carries extra freight because throughout this letter he has argued for the gospel of sheer grace over against a nongospel that demands works of the Law. "Your" distinguishes the Galatians' "spirit" (a collective singular) from the Holy Spirit, and Paul singles out their spirit rather than their flesh as the recipient of grace because "flesh" has connoted circumcision and moral weakness throughout the letter. The address "brothers" and "Amen" close the letter on a note of affection and an affirmation of the wish for grace.

EPHESIANS

This letter, written while Paul was in prison, contains a meditation on the high privileges of Christian believers, plus instruction on how in view of such privileges these believers should conduct themselves in the face of hostile spiritual forces.

GREETINGS
Ephesians 1:1–2

1:1–2: Paul, an apostle of Christ Jesus through God's will, to the saints who are . . . and [who are] **believers in Christ Jesus: ²Grace and peace to you from God, our Father, and the Lord, Jesus Christ.** Paul's self-designation matches his self-designation in 2 Corinthians 1:1; Colossians 1:1; 2 Timothy 1:1 exactly, but see the comments on 1 Corinthians 1:1 for the meanings of the terms used. As usual, "the saints" describes the addressees as consecrated by God to himself. The very earliest and best manuscripts lack the phrase "in Ephesus" after "we are"—hence the elliptical dots (". . .")—and this lack corresponds to Paul's having "heard" about the addressees' faith (1:15) and to their having "heard" about his ministry (3:2). By contrast, he'd evangelized the city of Ephesus for more than two years and therefore knew the Ephesian Christians intimately, as they also knew him (Acts 18:18–21; 19:1–20:1, 17–38). Probably, then, so-called Ephesians was a letter circulated from Ephesus to outlying churches, so that the geographical location of the saints was to be filled in by the reader in accordance with the city where they were living. Compare Colossians 4:16, where Paul refers to a letter (quote possibly our very "Ephesians") that's coming to Colossae from Laodicea, in which case the reader in Laodicea would have filled the blank with "to the saints who are *in Laodicea*," and the reader in Colossae would have filled the blank with "to the saints who are *in Colossae*." Paul balances his description of the addressees as consecrated by God with a description of them as "believers," which refers to their exercise of faith. "In Christ Jesus" locates their faith and thus the believers themselves (compare 1:13, 15 and see the comments on Romans 8:8–11 for the meaning and rationale of believers' location in Christ Jesus). The placement of "Christ" before "Jesus" gives "Christ" the connotation of a title: "Messiah Jesus." For the rest of the greeting, see the comments on Romans 1:7; 1 Peter 1:2; 2 John 3.

THE PRIVILEGES OF CHRISTIANS
Ephesians 1:3–3:21

Roughly the first half of Ephesians (after the greeting) deals with the privileges of Christians as a basis for exhortations in the second half.

BLESSING GOD FOR BLESSINGS
PLANNED BY GOD THE FATHER,
ACCOMPLISHED BY HIS BELOVED SON,
AND APPLIED BY THE HOLY SPIRIT
Ephesians 1:3–14

1:3–6: Blessed [be] **the God and Father of our Lord, Jesus Christ, who** [referring to God] **has blessed us in every Spiritual blessing in the heavenly** [realms] **in Christ, ⁴just as he** [God] **selected us in him** [Christ] **before the founding of the world that we might be sacred and blameless in his sight in love, ⁵by predestining us for adoption as** [his] **sons through Jesus Christ for himself** [that is, for God] **in accordance with the good pleasure of his will, ⁶for the praise of the glory of his grace, with which he graced us in** [his] **beloved** [Son] **. . . .** Here begins a sentence that extends all the way though 1:14. The very length of the sentence indicates how much God deserves to be blessed for the blessings he has bestowed on us, the saints, the believers, of 1:1. "Blessed [be] . . ." doesn't mean only that God *deserves* to be blessed, though. It means also that God *is* being blessed in what Paul writes throughout 1:3–14. To bless God is to favor him with praise (see the comments on 1 Peter 1:3 concerning the whole initial phrase). For him to bless "us" (referring to the addressees, Paul, and all other Christians) is for him to shower favors on us, so that those favors constitute the very environment in which we live—hence, "*in* every Spiritual blessing," the first of three successive "in"-phrases telling the location of us the saints. "*Every* Spiritual blessing" means every kind of favor bestowed by God through the agency of his Spirit, as specified in the rest of 1:3–14.

"In the heavenly [realms]," a fancy way of saying "in heaven," plays up our location as saints in heaven. Since Christ is in heaven and we are in him, we too are in heaven. So just as despite our still living on earth God looks on us as crucified, buried, and resurrected with Christ by virtue of our being in Christ (see, for example, Romans 6:4–6; Galatians 2:20), so too God looks on us as exalted in Christ to the heavenly realms despite our still living on earth (compare 2:6; Colossians 3:1–3). Paul traces our Spiritual blessings back to God's having selected us out of the mass of humanity, and having done so "before the founding of the world," so that the selection didn't depend on anything meritorious which we'd done (see Romans 9). "In him" indicates that even our location in Christ was planned by God before his "founding of the world." The selection's purpose was Godward: "that we might be sacred [that is, saints, holy, consecrated to him (1:1)] and blameless in his sight [as saints are and will in fact be at the Last Judgment (5:27), because God looks on us as in Christ, who is blameless]." If *God* sees nothing blameworthy, salvation is assured; and if our sacredness, our consecration, to God and blamelessness are due to his having "selected us in him [Christ]," "in love" is likely to reference God's loving us because of our sacredness and blamelessness in Christ. The selection of us entailed predestination "for [the purpose of] adoption as [God's] sons" (compare "our Father" in 1:2; also Romans 8:29).

"Through Jesus Christ" makes him the agent of adoption in that as believers we are in him and in that he is himself God's Son quite apart from adoption (4:13). "For himself" makes clear that "adoption as sons" means adoption as *God's* sons. "In accordance with the good pleasure of his will" personifies God's will, makes it take pleasure in the predestining of us for adoption, and attributes the predestinating to God's will as distinct from our will as human beings. "For the praise of the glory of his grace" adds to predestination another purpose besides that of adoption. Grace, God's ill-deserved favor as shown in the adoption, isn't the object of praise. "The *glory* of his grace" is the object, which way of putting it accents God's grace as glorious. The addition to "his grace" of the clause, "with which he graced us," doubles the accent on the glory of his grace. "In [his] beloved [Son]" locates us again in Christ, but calls him the one whom God loved to confirm that God loves us because of our sacredness and blamelessness in Christ (compare, for example, Mark 1:11; 9:7; 12:6; 2 Peter 1:17).

Paul's sentence continues in *1:7–10*: **in whom** [referring to Christ as God's beloved Son] **we have redemption through his blood, the forgiveness of trespasses in accordance with the wealth of his grace,** [8]**which** [grace] **he lavished on us in all wisdom and discernment** [9]**when making known to us the secret of his will in accordance with his good pleasure, which he** [God] **planned in him** [Christ] [10]**for the administration of the fullness of the seasons,** [that is,] **to head up all things for himself in the Christ—the things in the heavens and the things on the earth** . . . . "Redemption" means liberation from slavery. "Through his blood" marks Christ's blood as the cost of this liberation, and "blood" implies a violent death (compare the connotation of violence in our expression "bloodshed") and, given his blamelessness, a sacrificial death. As sacrificial, Christ's death also brings "the forgiveness of trespasses," which means their discharge, so that the trespasser doesn't have to suffer punishment for them. Christ suffered it for us.

"The forgiveness of trespasses" also suggests that the redemption consists in liberation from slavery to those trespasses (compare Romans 6:12–23). This redemption and forgiveness accord with God's grace—no, with "the *wealth* of his grace," more than enough to provide redemption and forgiveness, as further indicated by his having "lavished" that grace "on us" or, more literally, "into us," as though filling us to overflowing with a favor that's ill-deserved because of our trespasses. "In all wisdom and discernment" refers to all the wisdom and discernment required to understand "the secret of his [God's] will," a secret he has "made known to us." Such wisdom and discernment are the mental environment within which God lavished his grace on us. Without this environment we wouldn't have recognized and received his grace for what it is. The use of two synonyms, "wisdom" and "discernment," underlines their accompaniment of grace.

Paul mentions "the secret of his [God's] will" as a teaser that he'll explain in 2:11–3:13. Meanwhile, the making known "to us" of "the secret" which consists in "his will" enhances "the wealth of his grace." The accordance of his making the secret known with "his good pleasure" enhances further "the wealth of his grace" by putting a happy face on God in his lavishing the grace (see also the comments on 1:5 for this phrase). That God "planned" his good pleasure "in him [Christ]" dovetails with God's having "selected us in him [Christ] before the founding of the world" (1:4) and with his having "predestin[ed] us for adoption as [his] sons through Jesus Christ for himself in accordance with the good pleasure of his will" (1:5). The purpose of God's plan in Christ was "the administration of the fullness of the seasons," which means the imposition of his government when the epochs of human history have reached their full extent according to God's plan. He'll do this "for himself" (in the sense of carrying out his plan) by putting the entirety of creation ("the things in the heavens and the things on the earth") under the Christ's headship. "*The* Christ" adds the formality of a title to his headship.

Paul's sentence takes up again in *1:11–12*: **in him in whom we were also allotted** [to God] **by being predestined in accordance with the plan of him who is working all things in accordance with the intention of his will** [12]**that we who've hoped in the Christ beforehand might be for the praise of his glory** . . . . Paul correlated our being in Christ with God's having blessed us in every Spiritual blessing (1:3), having selected us for consecration and blamelessness (1:4), having graced us (1:6), and having redeemed and forgiven us (1:7). Now Paul correlates our being in Christ with our also having been allotted to God, which means that in his Son, Jesus Christ, God has acquired Christian believers as his own possession (see 1:14). This allotment occurred in conjunction with our being predestined ("for adoption as sons through Jesus Christ" according to 1:5), and this predestination triggered the carrying out of God's plan. To assure us that the execution of this plan hasn't been frustrated, Paul refers to God as "him who is working all things in accordance with the intention of his will." "*All* things" leaves nothing outside his plan. To stress God's will as determinative, Paul personifies God's "will" by ascribing to it an "intention." There follows a definition of God's will, namely, that "we . . . might be for the praise of his glory." Earlier, the glory of God's grace was to be the object of praise (1:6). Now it's the glory of God himself that's to be the object of praise. But why his *glory* rather than him *himself*? Because the praise of his glory has to do with the brilliance of his plan and of his working it out (compare Romans 11:33–36). Paul doesn't say that we are to praise God's glory. He says that God willed us *to be* for the praise of his glory. That is to say, our very existence as those "who've hoped in the Christ beforehand" is to be for the praise of God's glory. "Hope" carries the note of confidence in relation to Christ's return and attendant events, so that "hoped . . . beforehand" means to have put confidence in the Christ prior to his coming back as the one who *will* come back when "the fullness of the seasons" (1:10) has been reached.

1:13–14: in whom [referring to "the Christ"] **also you, when hearing the word of truth,** [that is,] **the gospel of your salvation, in whom also** [you], **when believing** [the gospel], **were sealed with the Spirit of promise, the Holy** [Spirit], [14]**who is the downpayment on our inheritance till the redemption of the acquisition,** [which redemption will be] **for the praise of his glory.** Here we have in Christ a sealing of Christians with the Holy Spirit—quite naturally, since the Spirit is Christ's Spirit (Romans 8:9). This sealing occurred when they heard "the word of truth" and believed it (in confirmation of the translation "believers" rather than "faithful" in 1:1). Paul identifies this word as the gospel and describes the word as a message containing truth. Then he describes the gospel, which means "good news," as "of salvation," which means "of deliverance." But deliverance from what? Paul reserves the answer to this question till 2:1–10, where salvation turns out to be deliverance from God's wrath, the just desert of our sins, trespasses, and fleshly lusts. "*Your* salvation" limits this deliverance to those who've heard and believed the gospel. "*Also . . . also*" doesn't mean "you as well as us"—rather, hearing and believing as well as hoping (1:12). The temporary shift from "we," "our," and "us" to "you" and "your" highlights for the addressees what happened to them at their conversion.

"Were sealed with the Spirit" means being stamped with the Spirit, so to speak, as a sign of being owned by God. "Of promise" is usually interpreted to be describing the Spirit as promised (as, for example, in Galatians 3:14; Luke 24:49; Acts 2:33; Ezekiel 36:26–27; 37:14). In view of the immediately following description of the Spirit as "the downpayment on our inheritance," however, it's better to interpret "the Spirit of promise" as the Spirit who, because he's the downpayment, is himself the promise of our inheritance that's yet to come in the form of resurrection to eternal life (compare 2 Corinthians 1:22; 5:5). Paul supplements "of promise" with "the Holy" to make

the sealing of believers with the Spirit the basis of calling them "saints," which means "holy ones, consecrated ones" (1:1, 4). "*Till* the redemption" supplements a past liberation from enslavement to trespasses (1:7) with a future liberation. Paul probably has in mind our liberation from mortality at the resurrection (Romans 8:23), but he avoids defining the liberation in terms of what it will mean for us and thus centers attention on what it will mean for God. It will mean his getting "the praise of his glory" (about which see the comments on 1:6, 12) from "the acquisition," that is, from the redeemed people he has acquired at the cost of Christ's blood (1:7; see also the comments on 1:11). This magnificent sentence that blesses God for his blessings has come to an end; but a final note should be taken of God the Father's prominence in 1:4–6, of Christ's prominence in 1:7–12, and of the Holy Spirit's prominence in 1:13–14.

A THANKSGIVING AND PRAYER
Ephesians 1:15–23

1:15–19: Because of this [your having heard the word of truth and believed in Christ (1:13)], **I too** [in addition to God's having sealed you with his Holy Spirit (1:14)], **having heard about your belief in the Lord, Jesus, and about** [your] **love for all the saints,** [16]**don't stop giving thanks for you when mentioning** [you] **on** [the occasion of] **my prayers** [17]**that the God of our Lord, Jesus Christ, the Father of glory, may give you the Spirit of wisdom and of revelation in the knowledge of him**—[18]**the eyes of** [your] **heart having been enlightened—so that you may know what is the hope of his calling, what** [is] **the wealth of the glory of his inheritance in the saints,** [19]**and what** [is] **the surpassing greatness of his power—for us who believe—in accordance with the working of the might of his strength . . . .** As in 1:12–13, Paul locates the addressees' faith in Christ, its object; only now he switches from "the Christ" to "the Lord," whom he identifies as "Jesus," to renew emphasis on Jesus' deity over against the "many lords" in paganism (1 Corinthians 8:5–6). This emphasis prepares for the detailing of Jesus' lordship later in the prayer. Paul has heard about his addressees' love as well as about their belief. "Love" includes loving deeds as well as loving sentiments. "For all the saints" makes fellow Christians, without exception, the beneficiaries of those deeds and sentiments. Hearing about his addressees' belief and love has spurred Paul to be giving thanks for the addressees. "When mentioning [you] on [the occasion of] my prayers" implies a giving of thanks to God. "I . . . don't stop giving thanks" doesn't mean that Paul is giving thanks continuously—rather, that when he prays for these Christians he always thanks God for them. The mention of his regular thanksgiving compliments them on their belief and love so as to win from them a favorable hearing of this letter when it's read to them in church meetings. The details of Paul's multiple prayers for them should likewise win a favorable hearing.

As to those details, "the God of our Lord, Jesus Christ" recalls "the God and Father of our Lord, Jesus Christ" in

1:3. But now "Father" is reserved for a followup in "the Father of glory." "The God of our Lord" doesn't imply worship of God by Jesus Christ, for that would contradict Jesus Christ's lordship. It implies, rather, that as "our Lord," Jesus Christ represents God to us. "The Father" refers to God, of course, not to Jesus Christ; and "of glory" describes the Father as both glorious and deserving of glorification through our praising "the glory of his grace" (1:6; see also 1:12, 14). Paul prays that this God may give to the letter's recipients "the Spirit of wisdom and of revelation in the knowledge of him [that is, of God]." According to 1:13–14 they've been sealed with the Holy Spirit. So they already have the Spirit as such. So what Paul prays for here is a giving in respect to the Spirit's function of providing wisdom and revelation in addition to the function of sealing (compare 3:3–5; Colossians 1:9–10; 1 Corinthians 2:6–16). God is the object of the knowledge gained through the Spirit of wisdom and of revelation. As in the often-used euphemism of a man's "knowing" a woman sexually (see Genesis 4:1 for the first biblical instance), the knowledge of God connotes an intimate relation with him (though not a sexual one, of course, for that sort of relation with a god characterizes pagan religion). Nevertheless, Paul's mention of wisdom, revelation, enlightenment, and (several times) "what" is to be known accents the informational component of knowledge. Without this component, knowledge as full intimacy turns into knowledge as mere flirtation.

The heart was considered an organ of knowing as well as of feeling. So that Paul portrays the heart as having eyes to see and by seeing to gain knowledge. "Having been enlightened" rests on the observation that you can't see in the dark and implies that the addressees used to live in mental darkness but that at conversion they were transferred into the realm of mental light, so that now they can see what the Spirit reveals to them (4:17–18; 5:8; Colossians 1:13). What then are they to know? *First*, "the hope of his calling." But what is that hope? Elsewhere Paul uses "hope" for confidence in Jesus' return and the eternal salvation it brings (see with comments Romans 5:2; 12:12; 15:4, 13; 1 Thessalonians 1:3; 5:8; 2 Thessalonians 2:16). This confidence comes as a result of God's having effectively called to himself those he selected for salvation (4:1, 4; Romans 8:29–30; 9:11; 1 Corinthians 1:26–29; 2 Timothy 1:9). But they need to have the Spirit inform them of the second coming as the ground of their confidence. *Second*, "what [is] the wealth of the glory of his [God's] inheritance in the saints." God's inheritance consists in the saints, those he has acquired (1:11, 14) and consecrated to himself (1:1). Usually a father *gives* or *leaves* an inheritance. This Father has *gained* an inheritance, one that is wealthy with glory. The glorious Father has a glorious inheritance. For Christians to know that they constitute the wealth of the glory of God's inheritance should fortify their hope, their confidence. Perhaps the wealth of the glory of God's inheritance in the saints reflects the growing mass of converts, especially among Gentiles (2:11–3:13; Romans 9–11). *Third*, "what [is] the surpassing greatness of his [God's] power."

Paul will tell what it is in 1:20–21. Meanwhile, to fortify his addressees' confidence even more, he interposes a description of God's power as "for us who believe" and heightens the power by talking about its "greatness" and describing its greatness as "surpassing." This greatness tallies with "the working" done by God's "might," which derives from "his strength." Paul has pretty well exhausted his thesaurus of synonyms for power. But where is this confidence-reinforcing work of power evident?

1:20–21: which as such [referring to God's working as mighty and strong] **he** [God] **worked in the Christ when he raised him from among the dead and seated** [him] **at his right** [hand] **in the heavenly** [realms] **²¹above every rulership and authority and power and lordship and every name being named not only in this age but also in the** [age] **that's going to come.** "Which [working] . . . he worked" emphasizes the activity of God's power. "As such" intensifies the emphasis by recalling attention to his working as mighty and strong. The evidence thereof consists in God's having raised the Christ from among the dead and seated him at God's right hand (compare Psalm 110:1). The seated position represents sovereignty, as when a ruler sits on a throne; and a position at the right hand of God represents his favor. Since believers are "in Christ," his sitting at God's right hand "in the heavenly [realms]" provides the basis for Paul's having located them "in the heavenly [realms]" (see the comments on 1:3), where in Christ they too enjoy God's favor and share Christ's sovereignty over hostile angelic powers (see 6:10–20). Likewise, the mention of God's having raised the Christ from among the dead provides the basis for believers' future redemption as one of liberation from mortality by way of resurrection (1:14). "Every rulership and authority and power and lordship" refers to hostile angelic powers (2:2; 3:10; 6:12). "Every name being named" picks up on the multiplicity of their preceding designations and widens the purview to include whatever other designations may apply to them at present and in the eternal future. In other words, the Christ outranks them all, and will forever outrank them. So take confidence, you who are in him (see 6:10–20 again for the circumstance that calls for confidence).

1:22–23: And he [God] **"has subjected all things under his** [the Christ's] **feet** [Psalm 8:6]" **and given him to the church as head over all things, ²³which** [church] **as such** [= as headed by the Christ] **is his body, the fullness of him who is being filled all in all** [= altogether, entirely]. God's subjection of all things under the Christ's feet complements God's having seated him above every hostile angelic power (1:20–21 [compare 1 Corinthians 15:24–28]). "And given him to the church as head over all things" recalls the heading up of all things in the Christ when "the fullness of the seasons" has arrived (see the comments on 1:10). So far as the church is concerned, though, he's already the head over all things. He's in charge. "*Given* him to the church [which here is the church universal, not just a local church]" anticipates the comparison in 5:22–33 of Christ's relationship to the church with the relationship of a husband to his wife. In 1 Corinthians 12:12–31a, especially 12:21, Paul called the church Christ's body but didn't make him the body's head, which could there represent a church member but certainly not Christ himself. Here, though, Paul attributes headship to Christ for an emphasis on Christ's sovereignty (compare 4:15–16; Colossians 1:18 as well as Ephesians 5:22–33). "The fullness" refers to the church as Christ's body in that he fills it (see 3:17 and especially 4:7–16 for what he fills the church with). "Of him who is being filled" refers to Christ as the one filled with deity (Colossians 1:19; 2:9). He's not *just* a human being. "Is being filled" makes God's filling the human Christ with deity ongoing, and "all in all" makes the filling entire. No part of the human Christ is lacking deity or ever will be lacking it.

THE SALVATION OF SINNERS BY GOD'S GRACE
Ephesians 2:1–10

2:1–3: And you, being dead in respect to your trespasses and sins, ²in which once upon a time you walked around [= behaved] in accordance with the age of this world, [that is,] in accordance with the ruler of the authority of the air, the spirit who is now working in the sons of disobedience, ³among whom also we all comported ourselves once upon a time in the lusts of our flesh, doing [time after time] the wishes of the flesh and of the reasonings [prompted by the flesh], and were by nature children of wrath as also the rest [are]—. Here Paul begins turning attention from what God has done for Christ (1:20–23) to what he has done for the addressees, who've believed in Christ. "Once upon a time" puts "being dead" in the past—specifically, prior to Christian conversion. "You walked around" refers to behavior and thus shows that being dead didn't mean the addressees used to be physically dead. "In respect to your trespasses and sins" defines their former state of death as one of moral death, such as Paul vividly describes in Romans 7:7–25, especially 7:9–13, 24, and 8:6 (see Romans 6:21–23 for this moral death as ending, apart from faith in Christ, in eternal death). Stressing the moral death is Paul's use of both "trespasses" and "sins." "In which . . . you walked around" makes them the very environment of behavior (so too "in the lusts of our flesh" with "comported ourselves" later on).

The occurrence of "in this age" in 1:21 might lead us to have expected here "in accordance with this age" or perhaps, in view of Galatians 1:4, "in accordance with this present evil age." But though "the age" refers to the present age, Paul delays "this" so as to attach it to "world" in the phrase, "of this world." As in 1 Corinthians 3:19; 5:10, "this world" refers to human society, in particular to the society of non-Christians, and anticipates the later-mentioned "sons of disobedience." So "the age of this world" means the current epoch as characterized by non-Christian society. This society set the standard for the addressees' pre-Christian behavior. So too did "the ruler," whom Paul will identify as "the Devil" in 4:27;

6:11 and as "the evil one" in 6:16. In parallel with "rulership" Paul has recently used "authority" to designate an angelic being hostile to God (1:21). So "the authority" here in 2:2 likely refers to the same sort of being, and "the ruler of the authority" means the ruler as himself the authority rather than the ruler over another authority. This use of synonymous designations underscores the Devil's dominance over "this world" of non-Christians (compare 2 Corinthians 4:4). To show this dominance as active and to confirm "the age" as present, Paul designates "the authority" who is the Devil as "the spirit who is now working in the sons of disobedience." Like father, like sons. So "the sons of disobedience" emphasizes the disobedience to God that characterizes "this world." The Devil's working "in" them, as he can because he's a "spirit," prompts their disobedience, whereas "of the air" portrays him as flying around to pursue his dirty work.

"Among whom also we all comported ourselves once upon a time" recalls "in which ['trespasses and sins'] once upon a time you walked around" but includes along with the addressees Paul and all other Christians in the pre-Christian behavior now termed as "the lusts of our flesh." Because flesh is physically weak (it decomposes at death and leaves only the bones to which it was attached), flesh came to stand for weakness, here for the moral weakness of susceptibility to sins of all kinds, not just to sins engaging the body (yet those are prominent). Though morally weak, the flesh as a moral category has strong desires just as bodily flesh has strong desires (for food and drink and sleep and sexual gratification, to take some obvious examples). Thus "the lusts of our flesh" refers to desires strong enough to prompt transgressions of moral boundaries. "*Doing* the wishes of the flesh" highlights the actuality of our repeated transgressions of those boundaries. Lusts as wishes turned into lusts as deeds. "And of the reasonings" adds that the flesh as moral weakness premeditates and rationalizes its transgressive desires. "We were children of wrath" describes us in our preconversion state as so helplessly destined to suffer God's wrath for our disobedience that it was as though the wrath of God had begotten us for the very purpose of such suffering. "By nature" points to such begetting and makes the destiny inherent to a state prior to conversion. "As also the rest" refers to those who haven't become Christians. Apart from conversion, they're destined for wrath.

Having left the preceding sentence incomplete, Paul starts a new one in **2:4–7: But God, being wealthy in mercy because of his much love with which he loved us ⁵even when we were dead in respect to [our] trespasses, made [us] alive together with the Christ—by grace you've been saved!—⁶and raised [us] together with [him] and seated [us] together with [him] in the heavenly [realms] in Christ Jesus ⁷in order that he [God] might exhibit in the ages that are coming upon [us] the surpassing wealth of his grace in magnanimity toward us in Christ Jesus.** As a contrast to "And you" in 2:1, "But God" shifts attention from our plight as sinners to God as him who has intervened in our behalf. "Being wealthy in mercy" means that he had a lot of pity for us (compare Romans 10:12–13; Titus 3:5–6). After all, we were destined for his wrath (2:3). Paul attributes God's "being *wealthy* in mercy to "*much* love"; and to underline how much God loved us Paul adds, "with which [love] he loved us *even* when we were dead in respect to [our] trespasses" (compare Romans 5:6–8). As in 2:1, this deadness was moral. By contrast, then, "God . . . made us alive" refers to a resurrection to morality, not to bodily resurrection, which obviously has yet to take place in the case of Paul and his addressees. But "together with the Christ [= 'the Anointed One']" follows from our being "in Christ" and from his past resurrection. God looks on us as having been made alive with Christ when he made Christ live again. And since Christ died for our sins, his renewed life had no more to do with sin. So far as God is concerned, then, Christians were made alive in Christ at their conversions so as to have no more relations with sin (see further Romans 6:8–14; 8:10–13; Colossians 3:1–11).

The remention of our trespasses, the first mention of which triggered a reference to God's retributive wrath (2:1–3), makes Paul interrupt his sentence with the exclamation, "by grace you've been saved!" By grace indeed, for our trespasses made our salvation illdeserved. And saved from the richly deserved wrath of God! "You've *been* saved" implies a saved condition at present as well as an event of salvation in the past. "And raised [us] together with [Christ]" reprises the earlier statement, "God . . . made [us] alive together with the Christ," but with wording that welds the resurrection to exaltation for our being "seated together with [him] in the heavenly realms" (compare 1:20), where as a result God has "blessed us in every Spiritual blessing" (1:3). Our location "*in* Christ Jesus" provides the basis of our being raised and seated "together *with* [him]." But our benefit doesn't constitute the ultimate goal of what God has done for us in Christ Jesus. Its ultimate goal consists in the eternal exhibition of the grace he has shown us. To jack up God's grace to the highest imaginable level Paul describes it as a "wealth" of grace, describes this wealth as even "surpassing" what was needed for our salvation, and attaches to it the phrase "in magnanimity" (compare 1:19). A repetition of the phrase "in Christ Jesus" locates us yet again in him, for it's in him where God exercises his grace. "In the ages that are coming upon [us]" portrays the eternal future as a succession of ages, one after another. The surpassing wealth of God's grace requires for its exhibition an endless succession of ages. For eternal life depends on eternal grace.

2:8–10: For by grace you've been saved through faith, and this [condition of having been saved] **[has]n't** [originated] **out of you. [It's] God's gift. 9[It has]n't** [originated] **out of [your good] works, lest anyone should boast. 10For we are *his* workmanship, having been created in Christ Jesus for good works, which God prepared beforehand in order that we might walk around in them** [= make them the sum and substance of our behavior]. See the comments on 2:5 for "by grace

you've been saved." Here Paul repeats the statement to make it an explanation, introduced by "For," of the justmentioned "surpassing wealth of his [God's] grace" (2:7). The addition, "through faith," indicates the means by which human beings appropriate salvation. Apart from believing the gospel concerning salvation in Christ, no saving occurs (compare Romans 10:13–17). In English translation "this" which "[has]n't [originated] out of you" but is "God's gift" and "[has]n't [originated] out of [your good] works"—this "this" might appear to refer back to "faith." Not so, however, because in Paul's Greek grammar a pronoun such as "this" needs to agree with its antecedent in gender and number. But the Greek for "faith" (and for "grace," incidentally) is feminine, whereas the Greek for "this" is neuter. The disagreement rules out "faith." So the neuter pronoun "this" refers in a regular grammatical fashion to the action in the verb, "have been saved." It's your "hav[ing] been saved" which hasn't originated out of you but is God's gift to you who've exercised faith and which hasn't originated out of your works, that is, any good deeds that you've done. "Lest anyone should boast" shows faith to be receptive, not meritorious, and makes the eternal exhibition of the wealth of God's grace (2:7) exclusive of any exhibition of your good works (among other passages, see Romans 3:27; 4:1–8; 11:6; 2 Timothy 1:9; Titus 3:5).

"For we are *his* [God's] workmanship" explains why salvation doesn't originate out of human works. (The mention of our trespasses and sins [see 2:1–3] has already explained why God's workmanship was necessary.) "Having been created in Christ Jesus for good works" makes our having been "made alive together with the Christ" (2:5) a work of new creation that's to replace those earlier trespasses and sins with good deeds (compare the contrast in 2:1–5 between moral death and moral resurrection, and see 4:24; 2 Corinthians 5:17; Galatians 6:14–16). Just as prior to their coming into existence those selected for salvation were prepared in the mind of God to receive his mercy (Romans 9:23), so the good works that had yet to be done were prepared in his mind for those saved by grace through faith to do (compare 1:4). So let's do them! Paul implies. And he'll detail them in chapters 4–6 (see his use of "walk around" as a figure of speech for behavior also in 4:1, 17; 5:2, 8, 15).

THE RECONCILIATION OF GENTILES
WITH GOD AND WITH JEWS
Ephesians 2:11–22

2:11–13: Therefore be remembering that once upon a time you, the Gentiles in flesh, the ones called "uncircumcision" by what's called "circumcision," handmade in flesh [as it is]**—12that you were at that time apart from Christ, alienated from the citizenship of Israel and strangers to the covenants of promise, having no hope and absent God in the world. 13But now in Christ Jesus you, who once upon a time were far away, have become near in the blood of the Christ.**

"Therefore" bases the following on the previously outlined salvation by grace through faith so as to produce a new creation in Christ (2:10). The command that the Gentiles be remembering their condition prior to Christian conversion has the purpose of making them in particular appreciate the surpassing wealth of grace that God has shown them (2:7). "In flesh" prepares for the Jews' derogatorily calling them "uncircumcision" because Gentile males didn't have their foreskins cut off, as the Mosaic law required be done to all Jewish males (Genesis 17:9–14). But Paul engages in a little dissing of his own by referring to the Jews, though he himself is one of them, as "what's called 'circumcision'" and then by describing the circumcision as "handmade in flesh," which means humanly performed on the penis as opposed to divinely performed in the heart (contrast also "his [God's] workmanship" in 2:10). This dissing has the purpose of making physical circumcision inconsequential so far as the new creation in Christ is concerned (compare with comments Romans 2:27–28).

"That you were at that time" reprises "Therefore be remembering that once upon a time you, the Gentiles" after the sidetrack into their uncircumcision. Paul then lists five preconversion disadvantages that they had as compared with the Jews: (1) being "apart from Christ," which means not having any expectation of a messianic savior; (2) being "alienated from the citizenship of Israel," which means not having membership in God's chosen nation; (3) being "strangers to the covenants of promise," which means exclusion from the covenants containing God's promises to Abraham, David, and Israel (see, for example, Genesis 12:1–3; 2 Samuel 7:1–17; Jeremiah 31:31–34); (4) "having no hope," which in view of 1 Corinthians 15:19 probably means devoid of confidence in a coming resurrection; and (5) being "absent God in the world," which means not that *he* was absent but that *they* were, because their enmeshment in polytheism made them ignorant of him as the one true God (contrast the Jews' advantages listed in Romans 9:4–5). "But now in Christ Jesus" contrasts with the Gentile believers' once being "apart from Christ" and "absent God in the world," which former conditions Paul escalates by describing them in terms of being a long distance from God ("far away"). Now they "have become near." *How* near? As near as "in Christ Jesus"! And *because of* being in him. How so? "In the blood of the Christ," which refers to his messianic role of loving self-sacrifice on a cross (compare Galatians 2:20). Most translations have "*by* the blood of the Christ," which is legitimate enough. But "*in* the blood of the Christ," an equally legitimate translation, suits better both the overarching theme of being "in Christ," only with a particular reference to reaping the benefits of his self-sacrifice, and also the upcoming parallels with "in his flesh" and "in it [referring to 'the cross']."

2:14–16: For he [the Christ] **is himself our peace, he who has made the both** [to be] **one and broken down the middle wall of partition, **[15]**the hostility, by having annulled in his flesh the Law** [consisting] **of command-ments** [couched] **in decrees, in order that he might create in himself one new human being by making peace **[16]**and** [in order that] **he might reconcile the both in one body to God through the cross by having killed in it the hostility.** This sentence explains what it meant to "have become near in the blood of the Christ" (2:13). "He himself" emphatically picks up "Christ Jesus" as "*the* Christ" (2:13 again). "Is . . . our peace" means that he embodies it, which turns out to be peace between Jews and Gentiles in the church and peace between them and God. Paul calls the former "hostility" between those Jews and Gentiles "the middle wall of partition" and traces the hostility to "the Law"—that is, the Mosaic law— "[consisting] of commandments [couched] in decrees." This law set up barriers, such as circumcision and dietary taboos for the Jews, which occasioned the hostility. But Christ "has made the both [that is, the formerly divided Jews and Gentiles who have now believed in him] [to be] one." He accomplished this unification by breaking down the middle wall of partition, which breaking down Paul explains as Christ's "having annulled . . . the Law." Though elsewhere Paul reiterates some of the Law, in particular its moral commandments, as binding on Christians (see, for example, Romans 13:8–10; but note there the omission of the ritual commandment to observe the Sabbath), he declares the Mosaic law as such to have been annulled. "In his [Christ's] flesh" complements "in the blood of the Christ" (2:13), thereby implies the violent separation of his flesh and blood (as represented in the Eucharist [see the comments on 1 Corinthians 11:23–26]), and indicates that his sacrificial death under the penalty which the Law exacted for our trespasses and sins rendered the Law henceforth inoperative. Paul's describing the Law as "[consisting] of commandments [couched] in decrees" exacerbates its former hold on us and thus heightens the good news of its annulment.

The purpose that Christ "might create in himself one new human being" brings back into view (as often) believers' being "in Christ," uses "one . . . human being" as a figure of speech for the oneness of Jewish and Gentile believers in him, and describes this corporate human being as "new" to emphasize elimination of the old hostility. "By making peace" accents this emphasis and justifies the opening statement that the Christ "is himself our peace." Paul finishes his sentence by identifying another purpose behind Christ's "having annulled in his flesh the Law." It's that Christ "might reconcile the both [believing Jews and believing Gentiles] in one body [the church as Christ's body, of which he's the head (1:23; 4:4, 12, 16; 5:23, 30)] to God [as well as to one another] through the cross [on which Christ's flesh and blood were sacrificially sundered from each other]." "By having killed the hostility in it" personifies the hostility to God that characterized the Jews and Gentiles before their conversion (see Romans 5:10; 8:7; Colossians 1:21) and indicates that "*in* it [the cross]" this hostility was killed, just as Gentile believers have become near "*in* the blood of the Christ" and just as he has broken down the hostility between believing Jews and Gentiles "*in* his flesh" (2:13).

2:17–18: And on coming, he [the Christ] **proclaimed peace as good news for you, the ones far away** [= you Gentiles according to 2:11–13], **and peace for the ones near** [= Jews, by contrast], [18]**in that through him we both have access in one Spirit to the Father.** The coming of Christ most naturally refers to his first advent, as in 1 Timothy 1:15: "Christ Jesus came into the world to save sinners." In general, "peace" refers to all the benefits of salvation (compare Luke 4:16–21). But Christ didn't proclaim such peace as good news to the Gentiles, for he limited his proclamation to Jews. So some interpreters say he proclaimed peace to the Gentiles through the agency of Paul and others (compare 3:1–10). But that interpretation doesn't sit well with Christ's "coming" to proclaim peace. It's better, then, to change the usual translation, "*to* you, the ones far away," into "*for* you, the ones far away," and understand Paul to be saying that Christ's proclamation of peace to Jews *applies* also to Gentiles—just as Peter said to a house full of Gentiles: "The word that he [God] sent to the sons of Israel by proclaiming as good news peace through Jesus Christ—this one is Lord *of all.* . . . To this [Jesus] all the prophets bear witness that *everyone* who believes in him receives forgiveness of sins through his name" (Acts 10:36, 43 [compare Acts 10:47; 11:18]). The particular benefit of salvific peace that Paul is expounding consists in the peace with God that allows those who by faith are *in* Christ, and therefore have been "adopt[ed]" by God as his "sons" (1:5)—this peace allows them access to him as their Father *through* Christ. "We *both* have access" brings peace between Gentile and Jewish believers alongside the peace that together they have with God. Access to the Father erases the distance of Gentiles from him, if they believe in Christ; but even Jews, near to God though they are because of their status as his chosen people (compare Romans 9:4–5), have had to get access to him through Christ, as in the case of a Jewish remnant (Romans 9:27; 11:5). "In one Spirit" parallels "in one body" (2:15–16) and supplements "through him [Christ]" in a way that stresses unity: "in *one* Spirit" (compare 4:4; Philippians 1:27; 1 Corinthians 12:9, 11–12, and especially 13–14; and see Romans 8:9 for the location of believers "in the Spirit").

2:19–22: Therefore then, you're no longer strangers and resident aliens; rather, you're citizens together with the saints and [you're] **members of God's household,** [20]**having been built on the foundation** [consisting] **of the apostles and prophets** [compare 4:11; 1 Corinthians 12:28], **Christ Jesus himself being the cornerstone,** [21]**in whom all the building, being fitted together, is growing into a sacred temple in the Lord,** [22]**in whom you too are being built together with** [Jewish believers] **into God's dwelling place in the Spirit.** The combination of "Therefore" and "then" refers emphatically back to Gentile as well as Jewish believers' having "access in one Spirit to the Father" (2:18). As from 2:11 onward, "you" means "you Gentile believers." "No longer strangers" means "no longer foreigners just passing through," and "citizens together with the saints"

reverses that former status, described in other terms back in 2:11–12. Paul doesn't identify "the saints"; but since he's addressing Gentile Christians, "the saints" probably has primary and perhaps exclusive reference to Jewish Christians. "No longer resident aliens" means "no longer foreigners who've settled among people not of your own ilk," and "members of God's household" reverses that former status. The thought of a "*house*hold" leads Paul to shift from the figures of citizens and family members to that of a building (compare the ancient practice of adding rooms onto a house to accommodate the growing family as sons married and had children of their own. Paul then distinguishes between the building's foundation, cornerstone, and superstructure, and classifies the building as a temple rather than an ordinary house (though a temple is the house of a god).

In view of 1 Corinthians 15:5–9 (to take one example), "the apostles" covers not only the original Twelve, but also others—such as Paul—to whom Jesus appeared after his resurrection and whom he commissioned. "The . . . prophets" refers not to Old Testament prophets but to Christian prophets as those who passed on direct revelations from God, as was needed in the new epoch of the church. Together the apostles and prophets form the building's foundation in that, chronologically and doctrinally speaking, the superstructure rests on what they said and did as spokespersons of Jesus and God, respectively. But "Christ Jesus *himself*" underscores that he's "the cornerstone," which was the first stone laid and therefore the one from which the foundation stones were lined out (compare 1 Peter 2:6). So what he said and did established the standard for what the apostles and prophets said and did. As "citizens *together with* the saints" and "members of God's *household*" stress the unity of Gentile believers with Jewish believers, so too do "*all* the building, being fitted *together*" and "you [Gentiles] *too* are being build *together with* [Jewish believers]." Ancient temples were built largely of stones without the use of mortar, so that "being fitted together" implies careful stonecutting, grinding, and smoothing so as to make the fits exact. The unity of Gentiles and Jews in Christ is to be no less exact. "In whom all the building . . . is growing" puts the building *in* Christ Jesus the cornerstone! Since being in him entails being members of his body (1:22–23; 2:16; 4:4, 12; 15–16; 5:23, 30) and since a body grows, Paul speaks of the building that's in Christ as "growing." Paul will explain the nature of this growth in 4:11–16. Meanwhile, "growing" and "being built" indicate progress toward a maturity and completion not yet attained.

"Into God's dwelling place" defines "into a . . . temple" as for God, not for one of the pagan gods whose temples dotted cityscapes in the Roman Empire. The addition of "sacred" to "temple" alludes to the saints as making up the temple, for the very word "saints" means "sacred people, consecrated people." Furthermore, it goes without saying that a temple is sacred, consecrated to the god who dwells in it. So Paul needn't have added "sacred" unless he wanted to highlight that saints make up the temple. That they do make it up leads him to describe it further as "in the Lord," for the saints are what they are—that is, sacred to God—because they're in Christ; and in Paul's vocabulary "the Lord" normally refers to Christ. Paul calls him "the Lord" to emphasize his deity, which suits the imagery of a temple. But so strong is Paul's doctrine of the saints' location in Christ that not only is all the building growing and being built up in Christ Jesus, but also the temple is "in the Lord" rather than the Lord's being in the temple! "God's dwelling place" corrects this architecturally ineffable oddity—but only momentarily, for "in the Spirit" parallels "in the Lord" and therefore puts the saints as God's dwelling place in the Spirit rather than the Spirit in God's dwelling place. See Romans 8:1, 9 for another passage according to which believers are both in Christ and in the Spirit. The use of "Spirit" has the purpose of avoiding the connotation of a temple as housing the graven image of a pagan god.

PAUL'S SENSE OF PRIVILEGE IN PROCLAIMING THE SECRET OF THE CHRIST
Ephesians 3:1–13

3:1–4: On account of this I, Paul, a prisoner of the Christ, Jesus, in behalf of you, the Gentiles—²if indeed you've heard about the administration of God's grace, which [grace] **was given to me for you** [Gentiles] **³in that by way of a revelation the secret was made known to me, just as I wrote earlier in brief, ⁴with reference to which** [secret] **you can, by reading** [this letter]**, understand my insight into the secret about the Christ . . . .** In Paul's Greek, "On account of" (*charin*) is a form of "grace" (*charis*). The resultant wordplay, which will be repeated in 3:14, highlights the theme of God's grace that runs throughout this letter (1:2, 6–7; 2:5, 7–8; 3:2, 7–8; 4:7, 29; 6:24). Here, "On account of this" refers to Gentile believers' being fitted and built together by the grace of God with Jewish believers (2:19–21). The addition of "Paul" to "I" highlights Paul's describing himself as "the prisoner of the Christ, Jesus." "Of *the* Christ" highlights Jesus' messianic office, which so overshadows the imperium of Caesar that Paul doesn't even mention his own awaiting a trial before the emperor (compare the prophet Elijah's saying to King Ahab, "As the Lord, the God of Israel, lives, before whom I stand," even though he was standing before the king [1 Kings 17:1]). Paul calls himself the Christ's prisoner because it's his proclamation of Jesus as the Christ that has led to the imprisonment (see Acts 21–28 for the full story). "In behalf of you, the Gentiles" aims for a favorable reception of this letter and specifies that Paul's proclamation carried out Christ's having sent him to evangelize Gentiles (Acts 9:15; 22:21; 26:17–18; Romans 1:5; Galatians 1:15–17; 2:9; 1 Timothy 2:7; 2 Timothy 4:17). The sending itself should also elicit a favorable reception of the letter on the part of Gentiles who'd believed in Christ.

As we can tell from 3:14–19, Paul has just now started to introduce a prayer for his addressees, but his sense of privilege in evangelizing the Gentiles overwhelms him

to such an extent that he interrupts himself to verbalize this sense. The dash in the translation right after "you, the Gentiles" represents the interruption. Paul will reintroduce his prayer and lay it out in 3:14–19. Doubtless the addressees have heard about Paul's evangelization of Gentiles. It's likely, in fact, that though he himself hadn't evangelized them, their evangelization had taken place as an indirect result of his having evangelized the nearby city of Ephesus (see the comments on 1:1). But "if indeed you've heard about the administration of God's grace, which [grace] was given to me for you [Gentiles]" is Paul's way of expressing his sense of privilege self-effacingly. "The administration of God's grace" refers to the proclamation of God's grace as the way of salvation (2:5, 8). "Which [grace] was given to me for you" means that Paul's own salvation by the grace of God had the larger purpose of salvation for Gentiles through Paul's proclamation to them of that grace (compare 2:17). "Was *given* to me" expresses again Paul's sense of privilege, and "for *you*" aims again for a favorable reception of this letter. "By way of a revelation" tells how he came to know "the secret" that God's grace was to be administered to Gentiles (see especially Galatians 1:15–17 for the revelation). "Just as I wrote earlier in brief" alludes back to 1:9–14; 2:1–22. "By reading [this letter]" means "by having it read to you in your church meetings" (as would have been the practice in Paul's day). "You can . . . understand my insight" provides a justification for Paul's writing a letter to churches he hasn't founded. He sends it as an instrument for the understanding that will give them strength of confidence in their struggle against hostile angelic powers (6:10–20). "Into the secret about the Christ" defines Paul's insight in terms of what used to be hidden but is now revealed, namely, that "the Christ" incorporates in himself Gentile as well as Jewish believers without distinction.

3:5–7: which [secret] **in other generations wasn't made known to the sons of men as it has now been revealed to his holy apostles and prophets in the Spirit, ⁶[the secret] that through the gospel Gentiles are coheirs and comembers of the body and copartakers of the promise in Christ Jesus** [compare 2:11–22]**, ⁷of which** [gospel] **I've become a server in accordance with the gift of God's grace that was given to me, in accordance with the working of his power . . . .** The contrast between "now" and "other generations" shows that "other generations" means past generations. "To his holy apostles and prophets" distinguishes them in particular from "the sons of men," which refers to human beings in general. In 2:20 Paul portrayed "the apostles and [Christian] prophets" as the foundation of the church, God's "holy temple." Here Paul shifts "holy" from the temple to the apostles and prophets, who make up its foundation (see the comments on 2:20 for the meanings of "apostles" and "prophets"). This shift reinforces the apostles' and prophets' importance as the foundation. Likewise reinforcing their importance are (1) the attachment to them of "his" (referring to God, in view of 1 Corinthians 12:28; Colossians 1:26–27); (2) the revelation to them as a group, not just to Paul as an individual (so 3:3); and (3) the shift of "in the Spirit" from "God's dwelling place" (so 2:22) to the apostles and prophets (which way of taking "in the Spirit" is supported also by the parallel with the location "in Christ Jesus" of the "copartakers of the promise" [see Romans 8:1, 9 for being in the Spirit as well as in Christ]).

With a revelation so broad-based, the secret "that through the gospel Gentiles [who believe it] are coheirs and comembers [with Jewish believers] of the body [of Christ] and copartakers [with them] of the promise [the Holy Spirit as the downpayment promising an inheritance of eternal salvation (see 1:13–14 with comments)] in Christ Jesus [where God views believers as located (about which location see the comments on Romans 8:8–11)]"—this now-revealed secret should give believers courageous strength in their struggle against hostile angelic powers (see 6:10–20 again). Paul has become a server of this gospel, this good news, in the sense that he serves it to people, especially to Gentiles, as a waiter at table would serve good food to diners. "In accordance with the gift of God's grace that was given to me" reprises a similar phrase in 3:2 ("the administration of God's grace, which [grace] was given to me for you [Gentiles])," but here Paul replaces "for you" with "in accordance with the working of his [God's] power" to give God the glory for the evangelistic success of Paul's serving the gospel to Gentiles (compare the self-effacement in 3:2, plus the power of gospel-preaching in Romans 1:16; 1 Corinthians 1:18, 23–24; 2:4–5 and especially 2 Corinthians 4:7). In view of 1 Corinthians 12:10 ("workings of miracles") and Galatians 3:5 ("who . . . works miracles"), "the working of his power" may also allude to the miracles that accompanied Paul's proclamation of the gospel; for in its plural form "power" means "miracles" (compare Romans 15:18–19; 2 Corinthians 12:12).

3:8–9: to me, the one less than the least of all the saints, this grace was given so that to the Gentiles I might proclaim as good news the incalculable wealth of the Christ ⁹and enlighten all as to what [is] the administration of the secret that for ages was hidden in God, who created all things . . . . "To me" picks up "to me" in the middle of 3:7. Paul doesn't call himself merely the least of the saints. He calls himself "*less* than the least of *all* the saints" to magnify the grace of God that was given him so that he might proclaim it as good news to the Gentiles. "The incalculable wealth of the Christ" describes this grace. In 1:7; 2:7 Paul referred to the wealth of God's grace. Here he ascribes wealth of grace to "the Christ," for it's in Christ as God's "anointed one" where those who believe him to be the Christ are saved by grace. In 2:7 Paul also described God's grace as "surpassing." Here he describes the Christ's grace as "incalculable" with special reference to the inclusion of Gentile believers together with Jewish believers. This is "the secret that for ages was hidden in God." "The administration of the secret" consists in proclaiming it to the Gentiles. The "enlighten[ing] of all" parallels the

proclamation to Gentiles and compares this proclamation to the enlightenment of the heart's eyes about which 1:18 spoke (see the comments there). The "what" of the secret's administration is that "all," including Gentiles, are to see that the Christ wants his grace administered to them. "The secret that for ages was hidden in God" means that he kept this secret to himself until its recent revelation to the apostles and prophets (3:2–6). The description of God as him "who created all things" prepares for the mention in 3:10 of hostile angelic powers. They are his creatures, not themselves gods. So fight them rather than fearing them (6:10–20).

3:10–12: in order that through the church God's multifaceted wisdom might now be made known to the rulerships and the authorities in the heavenly [realms] ¹¹in accordance with the eternal purpose that he carried out in the Christ, Jesus our Lord, ¹²in whom we have boldness and access with confidence through faith in him. Paul describes God's wisdom as "multifaceted" in that it has to do with the union of both Gentile and Jewish believers in the church, the body of Christ. Behind Paul's evangelizing and enlightening of Gentiles lies the purpose of God that this wisdom be made known "now," as opposed to the past ages of the secret's being hidden in him, and made known "to the rulerships and the authorities in the heavenly [realms]" as an indication that they've lost their dominance over those Gentiles who used to behave "in accordance with the ruler of the authority of the air" (2:2) but are now engaged in a struggle against that ruler and his minions (6:12: "against rulerships, against authorities, against the world rulers of this darkness, against the spiritual [forces] of evil in the heavenly [realms]"). Though these hostile angelic powers occupy "the heavenly [realms]," Christ is seated above them, which position indicates superiority and dominance (1:20–21); and since Christians are "seated together with [him] in the heavenly [realms] in Christ Jesus" (2:6), they too are seated above the hostile angelic powers and thus share his superiority and dominance over them. But it's "through the church" as visible on earth in its Jewish-Gentile diversity that God's multifaceted wisdom is now made known to them. The eternality of God's purpose that his wisdom be made known to them links up with his having "selected us . . . before the founding of the world" and "predestin[ed] us for adoption as [his] sons" (1:4–5 [see also 1:11]) and gives confidence to embattled Christians that God isn't improvising as he goes along. The carrying out of his purpose "in the Christ, Jesus our Lord" sets Christ over against the rulerships and the authorities. In him "we have boldness and access" to God as our Father (1:2) because Christ is his beloved Son, seated at his right hand, the side of favor (1:20). "Boldness" has to do with speech, and "access" with approach. "With confidence" heightens the boldness and eases access. "Through faith in him [Christ]" tells the means of our having attained such boldness and access in Christ (see the comments on Galatians 2:15–16 against the translation "through his [Christ's] faithfulness").

3:13: Therefore I'm asking [you] not to give up over my afflictions in your behalf, which as such are your glory. "My afflictions" refers especially to the present imprisonment of Paul (3:1). "In your behalf" attributes the afflictions to his evangelization of Gentiles, such as the addressees even though he hadn't evangelized them directly (see the comments on 3:1–4). "Which *as such*" stresses his afflictions as "in your behalf." "Are your glory" describes those afflictions as resulting in what he called "the wealth of the glory of his [God's] inheritance in the saints" (1:18). As God's inheritance *they* are wealthy with "the glory of his grace" (1:6). Consequently, they shouldn't give up when contemplating Paul's afflictions. They should understand those afflictions as for their benefit.

A PRAYER FOR STABILITY THROUGH INCREASED COMPREHENSION
Ephesians 3:14–19

3:14–19: On account of this I bow my knees before the Father, ¹⁵by whom[1] every family in heaven and on earth is being named, ¹⁶that in accordance with the wealth of his glory he may give you to be made mighty with power through his Spirit in the inner human being, ¹⁷so that the Christ may dwell in your hearts through faith, that you, having been rooted and founded in love, ¹⁸may be strong enough to comprehend with all the saints what [is] the breadth and length and height and depth—¹⁹and to know the Christ's love that surpasses knowledge, in order that you may be filled with all the fullness of God. Here we have the prayer that Paul started to introduce in 3:1 but that 3:2–13 interrupted. So see the comments on 3:1 for "On account of this." Since Jews such as Paul usually prayed standing (see Mark 11:25; Matthew 6:5; Luke 18:11, 13; 22:46), "I bow my knees" indicates that he prays for his addressees very earnestly. The earnestness with which he prays for them should make for their favorable reception of his letter. Because he hadn't evangelized them or ever visited them, he repeatedly writes in ways designed to ensure such a reception. Since fathers normally named their children as an acknowledgment of having fathered them, "before the Father" prepares for the clause, "by whom every family in heaven and on earth is being named" (compare 1:16–17).

Since God is the Father of believers in Jesus (1:2) and since Paul's Greek plays on the related words "Father" (*patera*) and "family" (*patria*), "by whom every family in heaven and on earth is being named" most likely has in view every company of deceased believers, now in heaven, and every company of believers living presently on earth. "Family" isn't to be understood in the sense of a modern nuclear family, then, or even in the sense of an extended biological family—rather, as a family

of faith. "*Every* family" relates all such families to each other through God's fatherhood despite their separate locations both on earth and between heaven and earth (compare the comments on 4:6). "Is being *named*" uses naming as a figure of speech for God's acknowledgment of these families as his own (compare their "adoption as [his] sons" in 1:5). "Is *being* named" has to do with God's acknowledging as his own each new company of believers that is coming into being through evangelism.

Paul prays first that God "may give you to be made mighty." By what standard? "In accordance with the wealth of his glory." In other words, the giving of might will never cease, because the wealth of God's might will never be depleted and because the glory of the wealth of God's grace (1:6–7; 2:7) will keep him giving on and on. Made mighty by what means and through whose agency? "With power through his [God's] Spirit" (see Isaiah 31:3; Zechariah 4:6 for the association of spirit with power). Made mighty where? "In the inner human being," and therefore not having to do with physical strength. The result of being made mighty? The Christ's "dwell[ing] in your hearts through faith," which indwelling will keep the addressees from losing faith as they struggle against hostile angelic forces (6:10–20). Made mighty for what purpose? "That you . . . may be strong enough to comprehend . . . and to know Christ's love," for it's this comprehension and knowledge that keeps believers from losing faith.

"With all the saints" favors that "having been rooted [an agricultural metaphor] and founded [an architectural metaphor] in love" refers to the love of believers for one another. The metaphors portray such love as a basis for comprehending Christ's love. Christians see the love of Christ reflected in their fellow believers' love for them. "To be able to stand against the schemes of the Devil" (6:11), believers need to be "strong enough" to comprehend. "What [is] the breadth and length and height and depth" provides the immediate object of this comprehension and points to the magnitude of Christ's love, which for emphasis on comprehension Paul reintroduces with "and to know." "That surpasses knowledge" describes Christ's love as of such magnitude that even those "strong enough" to comprehend its dimensions aren't capable of tracing out those dimensions to their full extent. His love is too broad, long, high, and deep (compare Romans 8:39). The purpose of comprehending it, so far as that is possible, is that the addressees "may be filled with all the fullness of God," which means being filled with Christ himself in that God fills him with deity (see the comments on 1:23 and Colossians 1:19; 2:9). "Filled with *all* the fullness of God" points to entire absorption with Christ as the purpose and result of knowing his love.

A DOXOLOGY
Ephesians 3:20–21

3:20–21: And to him [God the Father] **who in accordance with the power that's working in us has the power to do extravagantly above all the things we ask**

---

[1] Most standard translations have "from whom." But with a passive verb, as here in "is being named," "from" can mean "by," as for example in 2 Corinthians 2:2: "being made sorrowful from [= by] me."

or think, [21]to him [belongs] **the glory in the church and in Christ Jesus for all the generations of the age of the ages. Amen!** "The power that's working in us" echoes being "made mighty with power through his Spirit in the inner human being" (3:16), but there's a more distant echo of 1:19–21 too. This power sets the standard for God's having "the power to do extravagantly above all the things we ask or think," which way of describing it mirrors the description of Christ's love as "surpass[ing] knowledge" (3:19). "To him [belongs] the glory in the church and in Christ Jesus" states that the glory of God, which here is the magnificence of his power, is rightfully seen in the church and in Christ Jesus—and will be seen in them "for all the generations of the age of the ages," which for emphasis is an expanded way of saying "forever and ever," as though eternity consists in an age which, personified, has the offspring of multiple ages. "*All* the generations" leaves God's glory out of none of them. "Amen!" caps the doxology with an enthusiastic "Let it be so!"

THE RESPONSIBILITIES OF CHRISTIANS
Ephesians 4:1–6:20

Now that Paul has detailed the privileges of Christians (1:3–3:21), he details the responsibilities that come along with those privileges.

MAINTENANCE OF CHRISTIAN UNITY
Ephesians 4:1–16

4:1–3: **Therefore I, a prisoner in the Lord, exhort you to walk around** [= behave] **worthily of the calling with which you were called,** [2][that is,] **with all humility and meekness, with patience, putting up with one another in love,** [3]**being diligent to keep the unity of the Spirit in the bond of peace.** "Therefore" means "in view of the privileges that you, especially you Gentiles, have in Christ." The addition of "the prisoner" to "I" recalls 3:1. But there "of the Christ, Jesus" was added to "a prisoner" to tell whose prisoner Paul really was (not Caesar's). Here Paul adds "in the Lord" to tell the real whereabouts of his imprisonment (not Rome). Though "the Lord" refers to Christ, this designation calls attention to his authority, so that the following exhortations carry the force of his lordship over against Caesar's. Paul is speaking the exhortations from within the Lord! Paul's Greek contains a wordplay between three words that share the same root: "I . . . exhort [*parakalō*] . . . calling [*klēseōs*] . . . you were called [*eklēthēte*]." This wordplay underlines the exhortation. "The calling with which you were called" harks back to 1:18 ("that you may know what is the hope of his [God's] calling" and refers to the invitation with which God effected the addressees' salvation. Paul then explains "worthily" as meaning a behavior characterized by "all humility" (= an entirely lowly attitude in relations with fellow Christians), "all . . . meekness" (= no retaliation whatever when wronged), "patience" (= being long- rather than short-tempered), "putting up with one another in love" (= forbearance

seasoned with love), and "being diligent to keep the unity of the Spirit in the bond of peace" (= eager effort to preserve in practice the unity in principle of Christians, whether Jewish or Gentile, which unity they have because the Holy Spirit has baptized them all into the body of Christ [1 Corinthians 12:13], so that peaceful relations bind them together). Such behavior was countercultural in that pagans thought that to preserve and heighten your honor and avoid shame you should *not* be humble, meek, patient, forbearing, or noncombative. Paul sees, though, that pride, retaliation, impatience, forbearance, and competition for honor will destroy the behavioral unity that should mirror the Spiritual unity of Christians (compare 2:14–16). Another wordplay between Paul's self-description as "the prisoner" (literally, "the bound one" [*ho desmios*]) and "the bond [*tō syndesmō*] of peace" accents the exhortation to peaceful relations.

4:4–6: [There is] **one body and one Spirit, just as also you were called in one hope of your calling.** [5][There is] **one Lord, one faith, one baptism.** [6][There is] **one God and Father of all, who is over all and through all and in all.** The foregoing reference to "the unity of the Spirit" leads directly to the statement, "[There is] one body [representing the church as a unity] and one Spirit [whose oneness ensures the oneness of the church in that all Christians are 'in the Spirit' according to Romans 8:9]." "Just as also you were called" harks back to 4:1–3: "the calling with which you were called." But "in one hope of your calling" harks farther back to 1:18, "the hope of his [God the Father's] calling [you]," so that "just as *also* you were called" matches the one Spirit's having made one body out of Christians, on the one hand, with God the Father's having called them in one hope, on the other hand. The calling of them gave them hope, which means confidence of eternal salvation at Jesus' return, so that "*in* one hope" makes this confidence the element in which the call took place (compare the comments on 1:18). "In *one* hope" implies that since Christians have a common destiny, they should live in unity now just as they will eternally. The repeated use of "one" in 4:4–6 (seven occurrences in all) lays enormous stress on unity.

The "one Lord" is Jesus Christ. The "one faith" is belief in him. The "one baptism" is baptism "in one Spirit into one body," which is "the [corporate] Christ" (1 Corinthians 12:12–13), as represented by water baptism in Jesus' name (compare Acts 2:38; 8:12, 16; 10:48; 19:5; 22:16). The "one God" is "Father" to all believers in his Son, Jesus Christ (compare 1:2, 5 and [with comments] 3:14–15). God the Father is "over" them all in his sovereignty, "through" them all because of Jesus Christ's agency, and "in" them all by his Spirit's indwelling them. As does the sevenfold use of "one," the threefold use of "all" underscores unity. With the oneness of the Spirit, of the Lord, and of God, and with the persons of the Trinity in this order, compare 1 Corinthians 12:4–13 (see 8:6 too).

4:7–10: **But to each one of us grace was given in accordance with the measure of the Christ's gift.** [8]**Therefore** [because of this gift of grace] **it** [Scripture] **says,**

"When ascending into the height [of heaven] he captured a host of captives; he gave gifts to human beings [Psalm 68:18]." ⁹And as to "he ascended," what does it mean except that he also descended into the lower parts of the earth? ¹⁰He who descended is himself also the one who "ascended" above all the heavens in order that he might fill all things. It will turn out in 4:11–13 that apostles, prophets, evangelists, pastors and teachers constitute the grace given by the Christ "to each one of us." Through no merit of their own, in other words, the Christ has favored Christians with these people among them; and there's no Christian who doesn't benefit from their apostolic, prophetic, evangelistic, pastoral and didactic ministries. "In accordance with the measure of the Christ's gift" indicates differences in the giftedness of the apostles, prophets, evangelists, pastors and teachers. Paul makes this gift of grace the reason why Psalm 68:18 says what it says. In other words, what was to come determined what was said in the Old Testament. But what has now come to pass also leads Paul to update his Old Testament text by changing its reference from the Lord God to the Lord Christ (for Christ as Lord has acted on God's behalf) and by changing the Lord God's receiving of gifts from rebellious but defeated human beings (as in the Hebrew version of the psalm) to the Lord Christ's giving of gifts to submissive and favored human beings (that is, Christians). Therefore Christ's capturing a host of captives when he ascended into the height of heaven corresponds to God's having "raised him from among the dead and seated [him] at his right [hand] in the heavenly [realms] above every rulership and authority and power and lordship and every name being named not only in this age but also in the [age] that's going to come. And he [God] 'has subjected all things under his feet'" (1:20–22a). Though in relation to Christians those hostile angelic powers are still engaged in a struggle (6:10–20), in relation to Christ the powers are already his captives, his prisoners of war, so that Christians are assured of their own victory at his second coming.

The spoils of Christ's victory consist now in the gifts of grace given to Christians, seated as the Christians are (from God's standpoint) in the heavenly realms in Christ Jesus (2:6). Since Christ is the "one Lord" (4:5), Paul infers that Christ's ascent implies a descent. Otherwise, an ascent needn't imply a descent. (Take the case of Elijah, for example [2 Kings 2:1–14].) In referring back to Psalm 68:18 Paul changes "When ascending" to "he ascended" for a match with "he also descended." In Psalm 63:9 "go[ing] into the lower parts of the earth" has to do with burial, so that here in Ephesians "he also descended into the lower parts of the earth" means that Christ was buried after his crucifixion as well as that he ascended after his resurrection (already mentioned in connection with his heavenly exaltation [1:20–21]). The descent in burial makes a fine contrast with ascension "above all the heavens" despite their multiplicity (compare 2 Corinthians 12:2). "Is himself the one who 'ascended'" underscores the identity of the ascender with the descender to reinforce the descender's consequent supremacy. "In order

that he might fill all things" supplements this supremacy with an infusion of the whole universe with his presence and power (compare 1:10).

4:11–13: And he himself gave some [to be] apostles, and some [to be] prophets, and some [to be] evangelists, and some [to be] pastors and teachers [compare 1 Corinthians 12:28] **¹²with a view to the equipping of the saints for the work** [consisting] **of service for the building up of the body of the Christ ¹³till we all attain to the unity of the faith and of the knowledge of God's Son, to a mature male, to the measure of the stature of the Christ's fullness . . . .** "And he *himself* gave" underscores the identity of the giver with the ascender (compare the final comments on 4:7–10). The gifts with which the ascended Christ has graced the human beings who make up the church—these gifts are themselves human beings: (1) apostles and prophets (about whom see the comments on 2:20); (2) evangelists (Greek: *euangelistas*), those who travel around proclaiming the gospel (Greek: *euangelion*) with the aim of converting people though they (the evangelists) may not have the qualifications of an apostle or the gift of prophecy; and (3) pastors and teachers, that is, leaders in local churches who shepherd others, in part by teaching them, and teachers who don't otherwise lead. Since the apostles and prophets are foundational (2:20) and the evangelists missional, it may well be that "the equipping of the saints" spells out only, but importantly, the purpose for which the Christ has given pastors and teachers to local churches. "The saints" are the rest of the believers who make up local churches and whose equipping has the purpose of *their* doing "the work [consisting] of service [that is, of serving one another in accordance with their respective Spiritual gifts, for which see Romans 12:6–8 and 1 Corinthians 12:8–10 as well as 12:28]." This service has, in turn, the purpose of "the building up of the body of the Christ" (compare the earlier mixing of structural and physical metaphors in 2:21–22).

As implied by "till we all," "the body of the Christ" means the church as a whole, of which local churches are microcosms. "The unity of the faith" means the unity that's produced by a shared belief in Jesus. "The unity . . . of the knowledge of God's Son" means the unity that's produced by a shared knowledge of Jesus as God's Son, through whom believers have gained adoptive sonship to God (1:5). To know God's Son is to know about him and grow into a right and intimate relation with him (compare 2:21; Philippians 3:10). "Attain[ing] . . . to a mature male" builds on "attain[ing] to the unity of the faith and of the knowledge of God's Son." In Greek culture "a mature male" represented the acme of growth (and of beauty as well). Since the word translated "male" ordinarily refers to an adult male, Paul's addition of "mature" puts extra emphasis on maturity. "To the measure of the stature of the Christ's fullness" then builds on the phrase, "to a mature male." Since the Christ's fullness consists in his being filled with deity (see the final comments on 1:22–23), Paul sets out a tall measure indeed! He doesn't mean that Christians are to become, or will become, divine by nature. But he does mean that they are to become, and will become, divine in their character and conduct. When will such attainment be realized? In view of Colossians 1:28 ("in order that we may present every human being mature in Christ") and 1 Corinthians 13:10 ("But when the complete [= 'the mature'] comes, the piecemeal [= 'the partial, incomplete, immature'] will be discontinued," and this followed up immediately by a contrast between an infant and an adult male)—in view of these cross-references, the attainment of which Paul speaks will happen at the end, at Christ's second advent. Meanwhile the church is to grow toward such full maturity so as to minimize whatever further growth will occur on that occasion.

4:14–16: in order that we might no longer be infants, being wave-tossed and carried about by every wind of doctrine in the wiliness of human beings in trickery resulting in an artifice of error, ¹⁵but [in order that] by speaking the truth in love we might in all respects grow up to him who is the head, [namely] Christ, ¹⁶by whom all the body, being fitted together and compacted together through every supportive connection in accordance with the working in measure of each individual [body] part, causes the body's growth for the building up of itself in love. Most likely, this passage expands the purpose of Christ's giving some to be apostles, prophets, evangelists, pastors and teachers, which purpose is to keep other Christians from heretical doctrines. Paul compares such doctrines to the waves and wind of a stormy sea. "*Every* wind of doctrine" indicates a multiplicity of heresies over against "the *unity* of the faith" (4:13). "Tossed and carried about" stands for being swayed by the heresies in belief and behavior. "Infants" is the polar opposite of "a mature male" (4:13) and a figure of speech for someone theologically powerless to row against the winds and waves of false doctrines. "In order that we might *no longer* be infants" implies that such powerlessness would have characterized us prior to conversion, but no longer should, and that being swayed by false doctrines would keep us from "attain[ing] to the faith and of the knowledge of God's Son, to a mature male, to the measure of the stature of the Christ's fullness" (4:13).

"The wiliness *of human beings*" sets the false teachers over against *deity* in the Spirit, the Lord, and God the Father (4:4–6), and the false teachers' *wiliness* over against "the word *of truth*" (1:13) and "*truth . . . in Jesus*" (4:21). For emphasis on the danger of heresy, Paul describes the wiliness as encased "in trickery," which results "in an artifice [something cleverly designed]" characterized by "error." If we're not swayed by false doctrines we'll not take them on our lips to further the deception by repeating them. Instead, we'll be "speaking the truth [= the gospel uncorrupted by error]." "In love" describes speaking it as designed to benefit rather than deceive others. Such speaking will contribute to the positive purpose of Christ's gifting the church, which is that "we might in all respects grow up to him who is the head, [namely] Christ." This is another way of talking

about "attain[ment] . . . to the measure of the stature of the Christ's fullness" (see the comments on 4:13). "In all respects" covers the whole of Christian conduct.

"The head, [namely] Christ" recalls 1:22 ("And he [God] has given him [the Christ] to the church as head over all things") and thereby calls attention to the supremacy of Christ, as shown here by his fitting and compacting the body together (see the comments on 3:15 for the translation "by whom" instead of "from whom"). Against the fractiousness of heresies, Paul stresses again (as he did in 4:4–6) Christian unity: "*all* the body, being fitted *together* and compacted *together* through *every* supportive connection in accordance with the working of *each* individual [body] part." "Through every supportive connection" has to do with Christians' sticking together for the purpose of mutual support. "In accordance with the working . . . of each individual [body] part" puts every Christian to work in a mutually supportive role. "In measure" suits the work of each one to his or her Spiritual gift. Thus "all the body . . . causes the body's growth for the building up of itself." But the body can do so only by virtue of being fitted together and compacted together by Christ. The building up of itself "in love" recalls speaking the truth "in love" and indicates not only that love for one another should *imbue* "the working in measure of each individual [body] part" but also that love *consists in* such work.

MORAL CONDUCT
Ephesians 4:17–5:14

4:17–19: In the Lord, therefore, I'm saying and testifying this, that you no longer be walking around [= behaving] just as also the Gentiles [= pagans] are walking around in the inanity of their mind, ¹⁸being in a state of darkness as to [their] reasoning, alienated from the life of God because of the ignorance that's in them because of the callousing of their heart, ¹⁹who as such [referring to the Gentiles] being in a state of numbness have given themselves over to licentiousness for the working of every [kind of] impurity in prurience.² "Therefore" picks up "Therefore" in 4:1 and like it bases the following exhortation on the privileges of Christians, particularly those of Gentile origin, as spelled out in chapters 1–3. The addition of "testifying" to "saying" infuses the exhortation with solemnity; and echoing 4:1 again, "in the Lord" infuses Paul's speaking and testifying with the authority of the Lord himself. "Walking around" echoes 4:1 yet again, but "that you no longer be walking around as also the Gentiles are walking around" implies that at least to some extent Paul's addressees may still be behaving as unconverted Gentiles do. He identifies the behavior as licentiousness and spares no pains in tracing such behavior to moral stupidity, which in contrast to "the knowledge of God's Son" (4:13) he describes in terms of (1) mental inanity;

---

²The usual translation "greed" doesn't take account of the contextual discussion of sexual immorality—hence, "prurience."

(2) reasoning in the dark (compare 1:18); (3) alienation from the life of God; (4) inner ignorance; (5) a calloused heart (the heart being considered an organ of thinking as well as of feeling); and (6) numbness because of the callousing.

Paul doesn't say the unconverted Gentiles are alienated from *God* (though they are). He says they're alienated from God's *life*, which alienation fits "being dead in respect to . . . trespasses and sins" (2:1, 5). "Who *as such*" stresses "the callousing of their hearts" as the cause of "being in a state of numbness." "Licentiousness" means lack of moral restraint. "For the working of every [kind of] impurity" states the purpose—deliberate though stupid—of the unconverted Gentiles' having given themselves over to licentiousness. For the variety of impurity see especially Romans 1:24–27, though there it is God who gives them over, because they didn't glorify him as God or give thanks to him (Romans 1:21–23, where their stupidity is featured, as here). (Just as divine selection to salvation and salvation by human exercise of faith run along parallel tracks, so divine and human givings over to licentiousness run along parallel tracks.) "In prurience" describes "the working of every kind of impurity" as an effort to get more and more sexual satisfaction. But such working doesn't work; for satisfaction is found within moral boundaries, not outside them. Hence the "trickery" of false doctrines leading to licentious behavior.

4:20–24: But you—you did not learn the Christ in this way, [21]if indeed you heard about him and were taught in him, just as truth is in Jesus, [22]that in regard to [your] former conduct you have put off the old human being, who was being corrupted in accordance with deceitful lusts [23]and [you] are being renewed in the spirit of your mind [24]and have put on the new human being, who has been created in accordance with God in the righteousness and piety of the truth. "But you" draws an emphatic contrast with the unconverted Gentiles of 4:17. The addressees learned Christ in the sense that at conversion they not only learned about him. They also learned him himself as their model of behavior. "Not . . . in this way" draws another contrast, this time between learning Christ as a model of behavior and the moral stupidity outlined in 4:17–19. "If indeed you heard about him" is a gentle way of reminding the addressees that they have indeed heard about him, and refers to reports of him as a model of behavior. "You . . . were taught in him" makes him the locale of the learning. Only through being in him by faith can you learn him as your model of behavior (compare 1:15; 3:12, 17; 4:5). "Just as truth is in Jesus" contrasts with "deceitful lusts" in the present passage and with "the wiliness of human beings in trickery resulting in an artifice of error" back in 4:14.

"The old human being" is what you were, so far as your conduct was concerned, prior to conversion. By converting, you put it off the way you take off dirty clothes. And why not? It was being corrupted in accordance with deceitful lusts anyway! To the degree they

were being engaged in they were causing decay (the meaning of "corruption"); and the decay wasn't only moral, though it was that (see 1 Corinthians 15:33). It was also deadly, propelling you toward eternal death (compare 1 Corinthians 15:42, 50, 53–54 with Romans 6:21–23), not to mention corporeal death (Genesis 2:17; 3:3, 19; 5:5, 8, 11 and so on). Putting off the old human being required, and resulted in, your "being renewed in the spirit of your mind." "Of your mind" rules out the Holy Spirit as the spirit in view, so that the whole expression means "the disposition that governs your thinking" (compare the parallelism of "mind" and "heart" in 4:17–19 and contrast the inanity and callousing of the mind and heart in that passage with the renewal here). "The new human being" is what you are, so far as your conduct is concerned, as a Christian. You put it on at conversion the way you put on clean clothes. But keeping these behavioral clothes clean requires an ongoing renewal in the spirit of your mind (compare Romans 12:2). "In the righteousness and piety of the truth" defines what it means for the new human being to have been "created in accordance with God" (compare 2 Corinthians 5:17). Here, "righteousness" means doing the right thing. "Piety" connotes religious devotion that is scrupulous in practice. "Of the truth," which truth is "in Jesus," equates with "the gospel of your salvation" according to 1:13. This equation makes righteous and pious conduct part and parcel of the gospel, not by way of basing salvation on good deeds but by way of God's creating believers anew in sheer grace.

4:25–27: Therefore having put off falsehood [= lying], "be speaking truth, each of you, with his neighbor [Zechariah 8:16]," because we're one another's [body] parts. [26]"Be getting angry and don't be sinning [Psalm 4:4]." The sun isn't to be setting on the provocation of your anger, [27]and don't be giving a place for the Devil. The addressees "put off falsehood" when they "put off [their] old human being" (4:22). They are now to be "speaking truth" as an outgrowth of their having "put on the new human being, who has been created . . . in righteousness and piety *of the truth*" (4:24). "Each of you" stresses individual responsibility. "Because we're one another's [body] parts" alludes to membership in the church as the body of Christ and therefore interprets "with his neighbor" as a reference to fellow Christians. Lying to one another would destroy "the unity of the Spirit" that Paul exhorted his addressees "to keep . . . in the bond of peace" (4:3). Not that Christians are free to lie in their relations with non-Christians, of course; but those relations aren't Paul's present concern. In 4:31 he'll say, "All bitterness and anger . . . is to be removed from you." Although "Be getting angry" is a command, then, it needs to be understood as conditional, almost as satirical, so that the emphasis falls on "don't be sinning." How is anger to be removed from you so that you aren't sinning? By immediately making peace with the person who provoked you to anger. Then you won't be giving the Devil a divisive place in the church. By implication, where anger-caused division exists in the church, there the Devil is.

4:28–29: The person who's stealing is no longer to be stealing, but rather to be laboring, producing the good with his own hands in order that he may have [something] to be sharing with the person who has a need. There was no governmental welfare program and many, probably most, Christians were poor. So it's not hard to imagine that some of them may have practiced stealing just to survive. On the other hand, Paul's command to be laboring and his distinguishing between a needy person and the one who should be laboring suggest that some Christians were stealing out of an avoidance of labor. What labor produces is "good" because it can be used, and should be used, for "sharing with the person who has a need." Sharing will contribute to unity (see 4:1–3 again). "With his own hands" specifies manual labor, which higher classes despised (compare the exhortation to "all humility" in 4:2; see also 1 Thessalonians 4:11 and Paul's own example of manual labor according to Acts 20:34; 1 Corinthians 4:12). Were some Christians stealing to avoid the supposed shame of manual labor? In any case, Paul commands a shift from indolence and thievery to industry and charity. **²⁹No unwholesome word [statement] is to be coming out of your mouth; rather, if [there's] any good [word] having the effect of a needed building up,** [that word is to be coming out of your mouth] **in order that it may give grace to those hearing** [it]. The contrast with a word that's good because it has the effect of building people up makes an "unwholesome word" mean a word that has the effect of tearing people down. As indicated by the vocabulary of "building up," Paul is dealing with conversation between Christians. They need to build each other up in their conversation, and the building up has to do broadly with encouragement to live christianly, not only and narrowly with psychological encouragement. You're doing your fellow Christians a favor (the meaning of "grace") when speaking such a word in their hearing.

4:30–32: And don't be grieving God's Holy Spirit [compare Isaiah 63:10], **in whom you were sealed till the day of redemption. ³¹All bitterness and anger and wrath and clamor and slander, along with all malice, is to be removed from you. ³²And keep being magnanimous to one another, compassionate, graciously forgiving each other just as also God in Christ has forgiven you graciously.** Paul designates the Holy Spirit as "God's" to make clear a distinction from "the spirit of your mind" in 4:23. Disobedience to the preceding exhortation would grieve the Spirit, and grieving him implies his personhood over against an impersonal influence. "In whom you were sealed" recalls "you . . . were sealed with the Spirit" in 1:13, but "with the Spirit" is replaced by "in whom" to stress the closeness to the Spirit that makes Christians' disobedience grieve him (see also Romans 8:9 for the location of Christians "in the Spirit"). Concerning "till the day of redemption" see the comments on 1:14. For removal Paul mentions "bitterness" first. It arises out of the aforementioned provocation to anger (4:26) and therefore leads naturally to "anger," to which Paul adds "wrath" for emphasis. "Clamor" refers

to shouting matches. "Slander" means false accusations, which would contradict "speaking truth" (4:25). "All" eliminates from proper Christian attitude and behavior the entirety of these feelings and their outworkings. The addition, "with all malice," makes malice the accompaniment of bitterness, anger, wrath, clamor, and slander. Magnanimity "to one another" is to replace all those vices. Compassion and mutual forgiveness define the magnanimity. Graciousness describes the forgiveness as un- and even ill-deserved, and God's having forgiven ill-deserving believers in Christ sets the standard for gracious forgiveness (compare 2 Corinthians 2:7, 10; 12:13; Colossians 2:13; 3:13).

5:1–2: Therefore [because in Christ God has graciously forgiven you] **keep becoming imitators of God as** [his] **beloved children, ²and be walking around in love just as also the Christ loved us and gave himself over** [to death] **as an offering and sacrifice to God in our behalf with the result of a fragrant aroma** [pleasing to God]. Since children imitate their fathers, behaving lovingly toward one another, for which "walking around in love" is a figure of speech, should come naturally to Christians as God's children, loved by him. Imitating him in this respect has to be ongoing ("keep becoming imitators of God"), because new and changing circumstances call for repeated episodes of imitation. Christ's loving us literally to death sets the highest possible standard for Christians' loving one another and specifies self-sacrificial deeds for one another's benefit as the outcome of this love (compare Galatians 2:20). "As an offering and sacrifice to God in our behalf" describes the Christ's love in a twofold way: (1) as an offering *to God* and (2) as a sacrifice *in our behalf.* "With the result of a fragrant aroma" echoes Old Testament descriptions of burning animal sacrifices as giving off "a pleasing aroma to the Lord" (Leviticus 1:9, 13, 17 and so on) and implies that self-sacrificial love for one another on the part Christians will likewise please God.

5:3–5: But fornication and every [kind of] **impurity, or prurience, aren't even to be being named among you, just as it's proper for saints** [that these things *not* be named among them]; **⁴and shame and foolish talk, or coarse jesting, which in their nature aren't appropriate** [for the saints], [mustn't be named among you]. **But rather thanksgiving** [should be named among you]. **⁵For be cognizant by knowing this, that no fornicator or impure or prurient person, which sort of person is an idolater, has an inheritance in the kingdom of the Christ and of God.** Paul sets sexual immorality over against loving one another in imitation of God and in comparison with the Christ's loving us self-sacrificially. For sexual immorality has the purpose of self-gratification. "Fornication" refers to sexually immoral behavior in general; but because the term refers most prominently to having sex with a prostitute, Paul adds "every [kind of] impurity," which describes all illicit sex as morally dirty. "Or prurience" refers to the lust for more and more illicit sex as distinguished from the illicit acts themselves (see the comments on 4:19). Since fathers normally named their children as an acknowledgment of having fathered them, the command that sexual immorality isn't even "to be being named among you" means that making it a topic of conversation implies acknowledgment of its legitimacy, an acknowledgment improper for those who are consecrated to God ("saints" [compare the comments on 3:15]).

Paul goes on to identify the "nam[ing]" of sexual immorality with "shame and foolish talk," distinguishes "coarse jesting" about sexual immorality from ordinary conversation about it, describes both such conversation and such jesting as inappropriate, prohibits them, and commands that thanksgiving replace them. It goes without saying that the thanksgiving is to be directed to God, but the context may also imply that he should be thanked for the sexual satisfaction he provided in the institution of marriage, which in the Bible is only between a man and a woman (1 Corinthians 7:1–5). "But rather" makes for a strong contrast between thanksgiving and decadent talk. "For be *cognizant* by *knowing* this" emphasizes a contrast with "*foolish* talk" and introduces a reason for not taking sexual immorality so lightly as to make it a topic of acceptable or jocular conversation. For "no fornicator or impure or prurient person" see the foregoing comments. "Which sort of person is an idolater" equates the lust for more and more illicit sex ("prurience") with idolatry in that such lust replaces the worship of God with the worship of self through the pursuit of sexual gratification outside the divinely drawn boundary of marriage (compare Colossians 3:5). The inheritance refused to sexually immoral persons consists in the enjoyment of eternal life in the kingdom of the Christ and of God. Such enjoyment will outmatch the fleeting pleasures of illicit sex, and the pursuit of these pleasures marks a person as non-Christian (compare 1 Corinthians 6:9–10; Galatians 5:19–21). Since the Christ who "loved us and gave himself over . . . in our behalf" (5:2) has been "seated at his [God's] right hand" (1:20), Paul ascribes "the kingdom" to Christ as well as to God. The two of them share rulership. As often in Ephesians, "*the* Christ" calls attention to his messianic office.

5:6–12: Nobody is to be deceiving you with empty words. For [contrary to such words] **God's wrath is coming on the sons of disobedience because of these** [sexual misbehaviors]. [7]**Therefore don't be becoming partakers** [of such misbehaviors] **along with them** [the sons of disobedience]. [8]**For once upon a time you were darkness, but now** [you are] **light in the Lord. Be walking around as children of light** [9]**(for the fruit of the light** [consists] **in all goodness and righteousness and truth),** [10]**proving out** [in your sexually moral behavior] **what is pleasing to the Lord;** [11]**and don't be participating in the unfruitful deeds of the darkness, but instead be even censuring** [them]. [12]**For it's shameful even to talk about the** [deeds] **being brought to pass by them** [the sons of disobedience] **in secret.** Paul might have issued the direct command, "Don't be deceived." But his indirect command, "Nobody is to be deceiving you,"

only implies that the addressees shouldn't allow anybody to deceive them, and thus carries an implicit compliment that Paul doesn't expect them to be deceived. The compliment encourages their compliance, for people tend to rise to what's expected of them. "With empty words" refers to words empty of truth, here to the truth that "God's wrath is coming on the sons of disobedience." The word translated "disobedience" connotes that the disobedience arises out of a lack of persuasion concerning the coming of this wrath. In accordance with the adage "Like father, like son," "the sons of disobedience" personifies disobedience as a father, attributes offspring to him, and describes his offspring as taking after him. The coming of God's wrath on these offspring gives reason not to be deceived into emulating their sexual misbehaviors (compare 2:1–3). This wrath will arrive at the end (see Romans 2:5–8; 5:9; 9:22; 1 Thessalonians 1:10; 5:9), but the present tense of "is coming" makes it so sure to arrive then that it might as well be arriving already, as supported also by the present revelation of God's wrath in his giving the sons of disobedience over to their lusts (Romans 1:18, 24–32).

The coming of wrath supports not only the command, "Nobody is to be deceiving you with empty words," but also the command not to become partners with the sons of disobedience in their sexual adventures. Paul adds further support for this latter command. It's that "once upon a time [that is, before your conversion] you were darkness, but now [that is, since your conversion] [you are] light in the Lord." Illicit sex is portrayed as darkness because illicit sex usually occurs at night, in the dark, when others can't see what's happening (compare "in secret" at the end of this passage and Shakespeare, *The Rape of Lucrece* 674: "For light and lust are deadly enemies"). The equation of unconverted people with darkness implies that they *are* what they *do*. Their deeds define them. By the same token, "but now [you are] light" means that sexually moral behavior, represented by the light, defines Christians. "In the Lord" refers to Jesus, whose lordship governs the behavior of those genuinely in him by faith. "Be walking around as children of light" opposes becoming participants in sexual misbehaviors along with "the sons of disobedience," and "children" may connote a more intimate relation to light than "sons" did in relation to disobedience. So Christians are offspring of light in addition to being light personified.

The personification of light as Christians' parent shades then into an explanatory comparison of them to a tree that bears "fruit," a figure of speech for "all goodness and righteousness and truth," that is, conduct that's entirely good and right and true to the gospel. "Proving out what is pleasing to the Lord [in whom you are]" keeps goodness, righteousness, and truth from abstraction and translates them into the actualities of behavior (compare 2:10; Romans 12:1–2; Galatians 5:22; 2 Chronicles 31:20). The deeds of the darkness were unfruitful in that they lacked the aforementioned fruit of goodness, righteousness, and truth; and since Paul's addressees used *to be* darkness, those unfruitful deeds were *theirs*. The command not to be participating in such deeds provides a counterpoint to the command to be behaving as children of light and leads to the further command to substitute censure of those deeds in place of participation in them. The contrast between participation and censure shows the censure to be verbal. How then to explain Paul's earlier command that sexual immorality not even be named among Christians (5:3–5)? Well, naming had to do with accepting such immorality as a legitimate topic of conversation rather than as "shame and foolish talk, or coarse jesting," into which categories verbal censure doesn't fall. "For it's shameful even to talk about the [unfruitful deeds of darkness]" brings back the shame of such conversation as a reason to censure them instead. "*Even* to talk about [them]" implies that participation in them will follow from conversation about them. "Being brought to pass by them in secret" ascribes the darkness of the deeds to the shame of the unconverted, who *are* the darkness. They don't want their deeds exposed to censure in the light of day.

5:13–14: But all the [deeds of darkness], **being censured by the light, are being disclosed; for every** [such deed] **that's being disclosed is light.** [14]**Therefore** [because of this disclosure] **it says, "Get up, you who are sleeping; and rise from among the dead; and the Christ will shine on you."** Since Christians *are* the light according to 5:8, they are the ones censuring all the deeds of darkness if they (the Christians) obey the preceding command to be censuring them. This censuring discloses the dark and therefore shameful nature of the deeds. "*All* the [deeds of darkness]" and "*every* [such deed]" leave none of those deeds undisclosed by Christians' censuring them (again, if the Christians obey the preceding command). Paul then explains that by being disclosed, every deed of darkness is light, which is a strong way of saying that the censuring of such deeds exposes them to the light of day, so that they're no longer secret. So light now stands for verbal exposure, whereas it stood earlier for the Christians who are to do such exposing. Since in 4:8 "it says" clearly introduced a quotation of Scripture, the same introduction probably does so here as well, even though the following quotation corresponds in its wording to no single scriptural passage. Apparently Paul combines passages such as Isaiah 26:19; 51:17; 52:1; 60:1. (We find composite quotations of the Old Testament elsewhere in the New Testament, too—for example in Mark 1:2–3 and Matthew 27:9–10.) "Rise from among the dead" implies that "Get up, you who are sleeping" commands awaking and arising from the sleep of death, which harks back to "being dead" because of "your trespasses and sins" (2:1, 5) and therefore identifies the command as what Christians are to say to non-Christians by way of censuring the non-Christians' deeds of darkness. "And the Christ will shine on you" promises the light of messianic salvation if the censure is accepted, so that those who used to be darkness itself, and whose deeds because of censure became light itself, become themselves light because now they're Christians (as in 5:6–12).

WISE BEHAVIOR
Ephesians 5:15–21

5:15–17: **Therefore** [because of God's coming wrath] **be watching carefully how you're walking around** [= behaving]—[that is, take care] **not** [to be walking around] **as unwise people** [do]; **rather, as wise people** [do]— [16]**redeeming the time, because the days are evil.** [17]**On account of this** [the evil of these days] **don't be getting nitwitted; rather, be understanding what the Lord's will** [is]. If you don't watch carefully how you're walking around you'll stumble into the sin of apostasy and fall under God's coming wrath. Because of this wrath, "as unwise people [do]" describes non-Christians as unwise in their immoral behavior. "Rather, as wise people [do]" describes Christians, at least true ones, as contrastively wise in their moral behavior, given the coming of God's wrath. "Redeeming" means buying and liberating (as in the buying and liberating of slaves). "The days" that make up "the time" are "evil." So to redeem the time means to buy and liberate it from the evil that dominates its days. This redemption is to occur in the behavior of Christians. But the evil of these days, particularly the evil of the sexual immorality against which Paul has inveighed at length in 5:3–14, is seductive. So he warns against "getting nitwitted" by the seduction (compare Proverbs 5:1–23; 6:20–7:27; 9:13–18) and commands an understanding of the Lord's will. Since this command echoes the command in 5:5 to "be cognizant by knowing" that sexually immoral people don't have an inheritance in the kingdom of the Christ and of God, the theme of sexual morals has spilled over into the first part of this new section. The Lord has willed sexual morality.

5:18–21: **And don't be getting drunk with wine, in which there's dissipation. Rather, be getting filled in the Spirit** [19]**by speaking to each other in psalms and hymns and Spiritual songs, singing and psalming with your heart to the Lord,** [20]**always giving thanks to God—that is, the Father—for all things in the name of our Lord, Jesus Christ,** [21]**subordinating yourselves to one another in the fear of Christ.** The prohibition of getting nitwitted (5:17) makes Paul think of getting drunk with wine, which puts the drunk out of his wits and which Paul therefore prohibits. "In which there's dissipation" sounds like our describing a drunk as "in his cups" and identifies drunkenness as an excess that leads to ruin (compare Proverbs 20:1; 23:29–35). The usual translation, "be getting filled *with* the Spirit," is grammatically wrong. The correct translation, ". . . *in* the Spirit," parallels "*in* which [getting drunk with wine] there's dissipation" and corresponds to Romans 8:9, "rather, [you're] *in* the Spirit," and to 1 Corinthians 12:13, "we've all been baptized *in* one Spirit" (see also Ephesians 2:18, 22; 3:5; 6:18). Instead of telling *what* to get filled with, then, Paul tells *where* to get filled ("in the Spirit") and *how* to get filled ("by speaking to each other in psalms and hymns and Spiritual songs, singing and psalming . . . , always giving thanks to God . . . , subordinating yourselves to one another . . . ." "Speaking to each other" links up with the exhortation to mutual edification that dominates 4:1–5:2. So far as they can be distinguished, "psalms" come from the book of Psalms in the Old Testament, "hymns" refers to standard Christian songs, and "Spiritual songs" means Christian songs improvised on the spot under the Holy Spirit's influence. But we can't be sure of these distinctions. "Singing and psalming" (the latter of which may include instrumental accompaniment) defines "speaking" as melodious. "With your heart" requires the singing and psalming to be ardent as well as melodious. "To the Lord" directs the melodious and ardent speaking to Jesus Christ as well as "to each other."

"Always giving thanks to God" tells the content of the psalms, hymns, and Spiritual songs. "That is, the Father" distinguishes "God" from "the Lord," who is then identified as "our Lord, Jesus Christ," so that as often throughout Ephesians all three persons of what came to be called the Trinity make an appearance in conjunction with each other. "In the name of our Lord, Jesus Christ" requires that thanks to God the Father be channeled through Jesus Christ, whose name "Lord" indicates his right to relay the thanksgiving of those who confess his lordship on to God the Father. "Always . . . for all things" requires the thanksgiving to be constant and comprehensive. "Subordinating yourselves to one another" follows naturally from thanksgiving to God in the name of Jesus Christ as "our Lord," for his lordship rules out Christians' lording it over each other (compare 4:5: "one Lord") and should engender "the fear of Christ"—that is, of him as an object of fear (compare "the fear of the Lord" in Proverbs 9:10 and elsewhere). For he'll not take kindly to anyone's usurping his lordship. Moreover, "subordinating yourselves to one another" (1) makes for unity in a church (see again 4:1–5:2 and compare Romans 12:10; Philippians 2:3); (2) parallels "speaking to each other," "singing and psalming," and "giving thanks"; and (3) therefore along with them deals with interactions in meetings of a local church, not in the private homes of families. Paul will deal with home life next.

A CODE FOR CHRISTIAN HOUSEHOLDS
Ephesians 5:22–6:9

5:22–24: Wives, [be subordinating yourselves] to your own husbands as [you subordinate yourselves] to the Lord, [23]**because a husband is the head of** [his] **wife as also the Christ,** [is] **the church's head. He himself** [is] **the Savior of the body** [the church]. [24]**Nevertheless** [= despite his saviorhood, which could make members of the church think too highly of themselves as the objects of salvation], **as the church is subordinating herself to the Christ, in this way also you wives,** [be subordinating yourselves] **to** [your] **husbands in everything.** The commanded subordination to one another in meetings of a local church (5:21) carries over for a command that Christian wives subordinate themselves to their husbands. "To your *own* husbands" exempts the

wives from subordinating themselves to men not their husbands. "As to the Lord" makes the women's subordination as wives to their own husbands comparable to subordination as Christians to Jesus Christ, the Lord, so that insubordination to their own husbands compares with insubordination to the Lord.

Paul cites the headship of the husband in relation to his wife as the reason she should subordinate herself to him. The further comparison to the headship of Christ in relation to the church interprets headship as a figure of speech for supervisory authority. For "as the church is subordinating herself to the Christ" furthers the comparison in terms of subordination to a higher authority; and 1:20–23 has already associated his headship with his exaltation "above every rulership and authority and power and lordship and every name," has indicated the subjection of "all things under his feet," and has described him as "head over all things" in relation "to the church." As a title, "the Christ," which occurs twice in this passage, joins "the Lord" to underscore headship as authority. "He himself [is] the Savior of the body [the church]" switches the focus abruptly and emphatically, however, from authority to beneficence in preparation for the command that husbands love their wives "just as also the Christ loved the church and gave himself over [to death] in her behalf" (5:25), and also in preparation for the statement that "husbands too ought to be loving their own wives as [they love] their own bodies" (5:28). "In everything" makes the wife's subordination comprehensive, though Paul's commanding husbands next probably shows that he has in mind a Christian household in which the husband wouldn't try getting his wife to do anything antithetical to their shared faith (compare Colossians 3:18; also 1 Peter 3:1–6, where however the case of a Christian wife with a non-Christian husband is also addressed).

5:25–27: Husbands, be loving [your] **wives just as also the Christ loved the church and gave himself over** [to death] **in her behalf** [compare 5:2] [26]**in order that he might consecrate her** [the church] **by cleansing** [her] **by the washing with water in the word** [compare 1 Corinthians 6:11; Titus 2:14; 3:5; Ezekiel 16:8–14] [27]**in order that he himself might present to himself the church as glorious, not having a blemish or a wrinkle or anything of these sorts—rather, in order that** [the church] **might be sacred and blameless** [compare 1:4; Colossians 1:22; 3:19]. That Paul presumed to command wives how they should behave toward their husbands violated the husbands' prerogative to do so. But he was an apostle. So now he violates the prerogative of husbands to decide for themselves how they should behave toward their wives. "Just as also the Christ loved the church" sets a standard for the command that husbands love their wives. For "*just* as also" elevates "*as* also" from a *comparison* relevant to wives (so in reference to Christ's headship [5:23]) to a *standard*. "And gave himself over [to death] in her [the church's] behalf" defines the commanded love as self-sacrificial and beneficial to its object and also defines its extent as ultimate. "In her behalf" is then defined in terms of Christ's purpose to consecrate the church, which consecration has the purpose of cleansing her. This pair of purposes is then summarized in the purpose "that [the church] might be sacred and blameless." "In order that he himself might present [the church] to himself" makes the purpose of the consecration a segregating of the church to become, in distinction from the rest of humanity, Christ's own (compare 2 Corinthians 11:2). "He *himself . . . to himself*" accents this purpose and implies that the self-giving, self-sacrificial love of a husband for his wife will redound to his advantage. As is the church in relation to Christ, she will be her husband's alone ("sacred") and faithful to him ("blameless"), that is, "glorious" in her consecration to him and having no blemish or wrinkle of infidelity or any other moral failing in her marital relation. At least these are the probable results of a husband's Christ-like love. They are the certain results of Christ's love for the church.

Though for a special reason Paul will later refer to husbands' "*own*" wives, here he leaves out "your own" before "wives." This omission contrasts with "your own husbands" in 5:22. But here in 5:25, loving means self-sacrificial service within marriage. So it goes without saying that husbands should love only their own wives, whereas it didn't go without saying that wives had no need to subordinate themselves to men other than their husbands. Christ's "cleansing" the church "by the washing with water" may allude to the practice of a prenuptial bath. But the allusion shouldn't be pressed, because Paul is presently portraying the church more as Christ's body than as Christ's bride and wife. "In the word" identifies the cleansing water as the proclaimed gospel, belief in which washes away the filth of our trespasses and sins. So the cleansing occurs at conversion, but the presentation will occur once the church is complete, at the second coming. Then the church will have no moral blemish (similar to a blemish on the skin) and no moral wrinkle (similar to a wrinkle in the skin).

5:28–30: In this way [= as the Christ loved the church and gave himself over to death in her behalf] **husbands too ought to be loving their own wives as** [they love] **their own bodies. He who is loving his own wife is loving himself.** [29]**For no one has ever hated his own flesh; rather, he nourishes and bosoms it just as also the Christ** [nourishes and bosoms] **the church** [30]**because we're parts of his body.** The statement, "Husbands too ought to be loving their own wives," makes Christ-like love of wives a moral debt owed to them. Though omitting "their own" in 5:25, Paul now incorporates it for a parallel with "their own bodies." "As [they love] their own bodies" draws a comparison, but the standard for a husband's love of his wife remains Christ's having loved the church and given himself over to death in her behalf. The comparison to husbands' loving their own bodies evolves into a husband's "loving himself." His body is himself, at least in part. But why the equation of "loving his own wife" with "loving himself"? "For no one has ever hated his own flesh" supplies the answer. But

does it? "His own flesh" doesn't equate with "his own wife," does it? Wait and see. For the moment, though, Paul dwells on a husband's nourishing and bosoming his own flesh, which means making sure it gets enough food and warmth (as when a nursing mother hugs her suckling to her bosom [1 Thessalonians 2:7]), and states that such nourishing and bosoming rises to the standard of Christ's nourishing and bosoming the church. "Because we're parts of his body" identifies "the church" with "we [Christians]" and intimates that as parts of Christ's body we are, figuratively speaking, his flesh. Since "no one has ever hated his own flesh," no wonder Christ nourishes and bosoms us, the church. By implication, husbands are to nourish and bosom their wives, make sure they get enough food and warmth (which in large parts of the contemporary world is still as hard to do as it was in the first-century Roman Empire). Paul is now ready to explain how it is that a husband's loving his wife equates with loving himself, with loving his own flesh.

5:31–33: "**Because of this a man shall leave** [his] **father and mother and shall cleave to his wife, and the two shall be one flesh** [Genesis 2:24]." [32]**This secret is great, but I'm speaking in reference to Christ and in reference to the church.** [33]**Nevertheless, each one of you is also to be loving his own wife in this way,** [that is,] **as** [he loves] **himself; and the wife** [is to see] **that she fears** [her] **husband.** In Genesis 2:24, which Paul quotes, "Because of this" means "Because the woman (Eve) was taken out of the man (Adam)." Here in Ephesians, "Because of this" means "because of the parallel between the obligation of a husband to love his wife and the actuality of Christ's having loved the church." Grammatically, "shall leave," "shall cleave," and "shall be," which use the future tense for commands (as in "You shall have no other gods before me" [Exodus 20:3; Deuteronomy 5:7]), could be shifted to predictions: "will leave," "will cleave," and "will be." But the hortatory tenor of 5:25–33 favors commands. A man's leaving his parents and cleaving to his wife leads to their becoming one flesh in coitus, which explains how it is that a husband's loving his wife by serving her self-sacrificially, as he's commanded to do, equates with loving himself, with loving his own flesh. "But I'm speaking in reference to Christ and in reference to the church" defines "this secret" as the heretofore hidden parallel between a husband's loving his wife and Christ's having loved the church. The secret is "great"—that is, "large"—in that the love of Christ for the church, a large body, dwarfs the love of a husband for his wife. "Nevertheless" means that despite this difference in size, it's still incumbent on the individual husband ("each one of you") to be loving his own wife in the way he loves himself. "Also" draws a parallel between him and Christ. And since "the fear of Christ" is to characterize Christians (5:21) and since a husband as the head of his wife parallels Christ as the head of the church (5:23), the wife is to see "that she fears [her] husband," which means fearing to displease him by insubordination to him just as Christians should fear displeasing Christ by insubordination to him.

6:1–3: **Children, be obeying your parents in the Lord, for this is right.** [2]**"Be honoring your father and mother (which is in fact the first commandment with a promise)** [3]**in order that it may go well for you and** [in order that] **you may be long-lived on the earth** [Exodus 20:12; Deuteronomy 5:16 (compare Colossians 3:20)]." The children whom Paul addresses must be old enough to understand his exhortation. "Your parents" includes your mother as well as your father. Though she's to subordinate herself to him (5:22–24), she outranks you children. "In the Lord" doesn't restrict the obedience to Christian parents. It describes obedience to parents as the right thing for Christian children to do: "for this [obedience to parents] is right." Since Christian children are in the Lord by having believed in him, obedience to their parents takes place in him. He's the setting that determines behavior (see Colossians 2:6 with comments). As usual, "the Lord" refers to Jesus Christ. By quoting the Old Testament commandment to honor your father and mother, Paul reinforces his own command to obey them and equates obeying them with honoring them. His interruption of the quotation ("which is in fact the first commandment with a promise") interprets in advance the rest of the quotation. Interpreting the rest as a promise provides a motive for obedience. "In fact" highlights the promise of living well and long on the earth, given obedience to your parents. Naturally, this promise is a generalization that has exceptions. The Mosaic law prescribed death as a penalty for striking, cursing, or persistently disobeying parents (Exodus 21:15, 17; Deuteronomy 21:18–21), so that doing well and living long in the land of Canaan originally dealt with avoiding that penalty. For Paul, obedience to parents brings the Lord's blessings regardless of earthly locale. In view of 6:4, Paul may have in mind that in God's economy, parental commands are imbued with the wisdom of age (compare Proverbs 1:8–9 and similar passages scattered throughout Proverbs). The second of the Ten Commandments talks about God as showing kindness to those who love him and keep his commandments (Exodus 20:6; Deuteronomy 5:10). But there we have not so much a promise as a self-description. Strictly speaking, then, obedience to parents in this fifth of the Ten Commandments has a good purpose and a good result that together count validly as a promise, the first one.

6:4: **And, fathers, don't be provoking your children to anger; rather, be nourishing them in the discipline and admonition of the Lord** [compare Colossians 3:21]. The preceding command that children obey both their parents might lead us to expect mothers to be included here alongside fathers. So the present omission of mothers implies that their commands to children should echo the fathers' commands. Fathers had absolute authority over their children—even to the points of beating them, imprisoning them, selling them into slavery, and having them killed. So Paul's commands circumscribe Christian fatherhood. "Don't be provoking your children to anger" prohibits carping at them and placing on them unreasonable demands, both of which are sure to elicit anger.

"In the discipline and admonition of the Lord" interprets the commanded nourishing of children (which contrasts sharply with provoking them to anger) not as making sure they have enough food for their physical growth—rather, as training them how to live in a way that pleases the Lord and as advising them that it's intelligent to live that way. "Of the Lord" makes Jesus the ultimate source of such discipline and admonition.

6:5–8: **Slaves, be obeying** [your] **fleshly lords** [= masters/owners] **with fear and trembling in the integrity of your heart, as** [you obey] **the Christ,** [6]**not in accordance with eye-slavery, as pleasers of human beings** [do]—**rather, as Christ's slaves, doing God's will from** [your] **soul,** [7]**slaving with agreeability as** [slaving] **for the Lord and not for human beings,** [8]**knowing that each person, whether slave or free, whatever good** [deed] **he does—he will be requited this** [good deed] **by the Lord** [compare Colossians 3:22–25]. Slavery was widespread in the first-century Roman Empire. It wasn't color-based. Because the Romans hadn't conquered sub-Saharan Africa, in fact, fair-skinned slaves must have outnumbered dark-skinned ones. Prisoners of war were enslaved, but by the first century most slaves were probably so by birth. Households, especially those of the well-to-do, often included slaves who performed household duties. Other slaves were put to work in the fields, in mines, and elsewhere. Some attained positions of management, tutoring, and the like. Free persons occasionally sold themselves into slavery for the benefits of care and accommodation. But the conditions of slavery and the treatment of slaves varied widely. Slaves might buy their freedom with savings from their allowances; or their masters might free them, especially when the slaves became too old to work hard. The addressing of slaves here and elsewhere indicates that a number of slaves became Christians and—as in the case of wives and children in relation to their husbands and parents, respectively—treats the slaves as equal in Christ to their social superiors (compare Galatians 3:28; 1 Peter 2:18–25).

Where most translations have "masters" or "owners," the foregoing translation has "lords" to bring out the parallel between Jesus Christ as the Lord and the slave-masters/slaveowners as lords. (Paul uses the same Greek word for both.) "Fleshly lords" portrays the slaveowners as lords only in respect to their and their slaves' physical relationship to each other. As shown by the parallel in Colossians 3:22 ("fearing the Lord"), "be obeying . . . with fear" doesn't mean to fear your fleshly lords. It means to fear disobeying the Lord by disobeying your fleshly lords (compare the comments on 1 Peter 2:18). "And trembling" heightens this fear of the Lord to the point of bodily quivering (compare Philippians 2:12–13). "In the integrity of your heart" prohibits the inner duplicity of obeying halfheartedly. "As [you obey] the Christ" draws a comparison between obeying your fleshly lords and obeying your divine Lord, whom as Christians you obey wholeheartedly (for otherwise you're non-Christians). "Not in accordance with eye-slavery" means not with an eye to obey only when your fleshly lords are watching, which kind of obedience would betray a duplicitous heart. "As pleasers of human beings [do]" points up that your fleshly lords aren't your divine Lord (they're only human) and implies that though eye-slavery stands a chance of pleasing your unknowing, merely human lords, it certainly displeases your divine Lord. "Rather [in contrast to eye-slavery], as Christ's slaves [which you are], [be] doing God's will [that you obey your fleshly lords in the prescribed manner] from [your] soul [that is, 'in the integrity of your heart'], slaving with agreeability [as opposed to resistance and back talk] as [slaving] for the Lord [when you're obeying your fleshly lords from your soul] and not for human beings [so that from the Lord's standpoint obeying your fleshly lords doesn't even count as slaving for them—rather, as slaving only for him]." "Knowing that each person . . . will be requited this [good deed]" provides a reason for Christian slaves to follow Paul's command. The requital will come at the Last Judgment. "Each person" gives assurance of individual and exceptionless requital. "Whether slave or free" puts the slave on the same level as the free person "before the judgment platform of the Christ" (2 Corinthians 5:10), so that the slave will suffer no disadvantage. "Whatever good [deed] he does" shows that the requital in view is one of reward and ensures that no good deed, such as an act of wholehearted obedience to a fleshly lord, will go unrewarded. At the judgment the Lord will do good for the doer of good, including the slave as well as the free (compare 2:10; 4:28–29; 6:9). "By the Lord" implies that all Christians, including socially free ones, are the Lord's slaves.

6:9: And, lords [= masters], **be doing the same things to them** [your slaves], **forgoing the bullying** [of them], **knowing that both their Lord** [= Owner/Master] **and yours is in heaven; and there's no favoritism with him** [compare Colossians 4:1]. "The same things" are the "good" of 6:8; which in the case of masters means treating their slaves well and not bullying them with threats of beating, sexual harassment, the splitting of families through sale, and such like—much less the actual imposition of such mistreatment. Recognition that you as well as your slaves are a slave of the Lord should lead you to obey this command. His location "in heaven" puts him high above you in rank; and the fact that "there's no favoritism with him" gives you, so far as he's concerned, no advantage over your slaves.

EMPOWERMENT FOR BATTLE
Ephesians 6:10–20

6:10–13: As for the remainder [of my exhortation], **be getting empowered in the Lord and in the might of his strength** [compare 1:19]. [11]**Put on the full armor of God so that you may have power to stand against the Devil's artifices** [= strategies of battle], [12]**because we don't have** [on our hands] **a struggle against blood and flesh—rather, against the rulerships, against the authorities, against the cosmic mights of this dark-ness, against the spiritual** [beings] **of evil in the heav-enly** [realms]. [13]**Because of this** [our struggle against the spiritual beings of evil in the heavenly realms rather than against the blood and flesh of human beings], **take up the full armor of God in order that you may have power to withstand in the evil day and, on having implemented all things** [that is, having put on the full armor of God], **to stand.** "In the Lord [Jesus]" is the place to get empowered to do battle with the Devil and his minions of evil spirits. It's the might consisting in the Lord's strength that empowers you. Paul portrays this might in terms of God's full armor—that is, the armor that he supplies—*full* armor for *full* protection. Maybe being chained to a Roman soldier prompted Paul to use this portrayal (compare 3:1; 4:1; 6:20 with Acts 28:16, 20). "So that you may have power *to stand*" puts forward a sharp contrast with "being *wave-tossed* and *carried about* by every wind of doctrine" (4:14); hence, standing represents resistance. "Against the Devil's artifices" portrays the Devil as on the attack, and his mode of attack as a bag of tricks consisting in false doctrines peddled by false teachers and leading to bad behavior (see 4:14 again: "in trickery resulting in an artifice of error"). Armor will protect against such tricks; but it takes *God's* armor to do so, because we Christians aren't fighting against mere human beings, called "blood and flesh" against the background of physical warfare in which blood and flesh are sundered from each other through slaying with a sword, blood being put first in the pair to stress bloodshed. In view of his own imprisonment for proclaiming the gospel, Paul uses "we" to include himself in the struggle.

After mentioning the Devil, Paul broadens his purview to include the Devil's minions of evil spirits. For emphasis on the danger they pose to Christians, Paul lists them with four designations, uses designations that connote power, and prefixes each designation with "against." "Cosmic *mights*" means forces that control the world consisting of non-Christian society, over against "the *might* of [the Lord's] strength." In accordance with 5:8, 11, "of this darkness" refers to the moral darkness brought on by the influence of these cosmic mights on human beings. "Spiritual [beings] of evil" means evil spirits; and their location "in the heavenly [realms]" means that Christians, also located there (1:3; 2:6), aren't out of the evil spirits' reach so far as the doctrinal-behavioral influence of those spirits is concerned. "Take up the full armor of God in order that you may have power to withstand" recalls "Put on the full armor of God so that you may have power to stand," but "in the evil day" replaces "against the Devil's artifices" for correspondence with "the spiritual [beings] of evil" (compare 5:16: "the days are evil"). "The evil day" refers to any day when "the spiritual beings of evil" attack. "To stand against . . . . to withstand . . . to stand" puts a triple emphasis on not succumbing to the Devil's artifices.

6:14–17: Therefore [because of our struggle against evil spirits in the heavenly realms] **stand, having girded your waist with truth and having put on the breast-**

plate [consisting] **of righteousness** [15]**and having shod** [your] **feet with the preparation of the gospel of peace,** [16]**with all** [these pieces of armor] **taking up the shield of faith, with which you'll have power to extinguish all the flaming arrows of the evil one.** [17]**And grab the helmet of salvation and the sword of the Spirit, which is God's word . . .** [compare Isaiah 11:4–5; 59:17]. We read yet another "stand," but this time in a command predicated on having been empowered by the donning of God's full armor, which Paul now details piece by piece. Back of "having girded your waist" lies Roman soldiers' wearing a leather apron to protect the hips, groin, and thighs. Paul makes this apron stand for the truth of the gospel that protects against every wind of deceitful doctrine (4:14). The metal breastplate worn by Roman soldiers stands for righteousness, which here means behavior consistent with the gospel's truth and contrary to the bad behavior fostered by false doctrines. Roman soldiers wore thick-soled sandals whose hobnails, like modern cleats, enabled them to dig into the ground for withstanding an enemy's onslaught. Paul makes these sandals symbolize the gospel of peace, which prepares us to stand *against* the Devil's doctrinal-behavioral onslaught by standing *in* that gospel. Since the Christ "is himself our peace" by virtue of "making peace" and "proclaim[ing] peace as good news" (2:14–17), he has prepared us to stand firmly in the only gospel that brings peace with God and peace with one another. Notably and ironically, this already-secured peace prepares us to prevail in an ongoing war.

The kind of shield to which Paul refers was large enough to protect the whole torso of a Roman soldier. The shield's thick wood was covered with canvas and, over the canvas, with calfskin, and was tipped with metal and studded with metal in its center. Just before a battle the shields were immersed in water, so that the water-soaked calfskin, canvas, and wood extinguished any flaming arrows that lodged in the shields. For Paul, the Christian's shield consists in faith—that is, faith in the just-mentioned "gospel of peace." This faith will extinguish "all the flaming arrows" shot by the Devil, called "the evil one" to link him with "the spiritual [beings] of evil" and "the evil day" of his onslaught (6:12–13). Like the waves and wind of 4:14, the arrows represent false doctrines, which lead to bad behavior. "Flaming" describes them as specially dangerous. Professing Christians who succumb to them will lose out on salvation (compare Galatians 5:2–4). "The helmet of *salvation*" follows "the shield of *faith*," because we've "been *saved*" by grace "through *faith*" (2:8). The Roman soldier's metal helmet was designed to save him from a fatal blow to the head. He'd grab the helmet and his short, double-edged sword just before engaging in hand-to-hand combat. "Of the Spirit" describes the Christian's sword in a way that counters "the spiritual [beings] of evil in the heavenly [realms]" (6:12) and ascribes power to "God's word," which the sword represents. For "spirit" connotes power (Isaiah 31:3) and in the case of God's Spirit, as here, overwhelming

power (Zechariah 4:6). "God's word" doesn't mean the Old Testament, let alone the whole Bible. It means the recently mentioned and widely proclaimed "gospel of peace" (see also 5:26; Romans 10:8–10, 16–18), whose truth not only girds the Christian's waist but also fends off every "artifice of error" (4:14).

6:18–20: through every prayer and supplication praying in the Spirit in every season, and to this [end of prayer and supplication] **staying awake with all persistence and supplication for all the saints,** [19]**and in my behalf in order that a word** [= an utterance] **may be given me in the opening of my mouth so as to make known in boldness** [of speech] **the secret of the gospel,** [20]**for which** [secret] **I'm acting as an ambassador in a chain, in order that in it** [the chain] **I may speak boldly** [about the secret], **as it's necessary that I speak** [compare Colossians 4:3–4]. "Through every prayer" presents prayer as the means of grabbing the helmet of salvation and the sword of the Spirit and, by extension, as the means of putting on God's full armor. The addition of "supplication" defines the prayer as petitionary, so that we're to ask God for the helmet, sword, and pieces of armor. "Through *every* prayer . . . in *every* season" prescribes praying for every occasion of onslaught and prescribes supplication as the mode of every prayer. Since according to 2:18 "we have access in one Spirit to the Father," Paul locates our praying "in the Spirit," in whom from God's standpoint we are, just as we're in Christ (see also 2:21–22; 3:5; 5:18; Romans 8:1, 9; Jude 20). This location gives our prayers power and potency. But to pray "in every season" of onslaught, "staying awake" is required. In other words, lose sleep in order to pray more (compare Mark 14:38). "With all persistence" calls for being engrossed in prayer. "And supplication for all the saints" means praying that all Christians put on God's armor for protection against doctrinal-behavioral heresies.

Since "we" in 6:12 included Paul in all the saints' struggle against evil spiritual forces, he now asks that supplication be made for him in particular. Despite being "in a chain" he wants to make known the secret of the gospel "in boldness [of speech]," which suits an ambassador, who as such has diplomatic immunity (compare 2 Corinthians 5:20). He may be "in a chain" so far as the Roman government is concerned. But so far as he himself is concerned, he's a prisoner "in the Lord" (4:1) and "a prisoner of the Christ, Jesus" (3:1), not of the Caesar, and therefore is as free as an ambassador to speak boldly especially to the Caesar but also to the imperial guard (Philippians 1:12–13). "The secret of the gospel" is that Gentiles who believe the gospel will be saved without distinction alongside believing Jews (see 2:11–3:13). Naturally, this secret would have special relevance to the Caesar and his guard. Paul wants a chance to utter the secret boldly. Apparently he got it (see Philippians 1:12–13 again; also Acts 28:28, 30–31). Prayers answered! The necessity that he utter the secret boldly arises out of Christ's having commissioned him to proclaim it as good news "to the Gentiles" (3:8).

CONCLUSION
Ephesians 6:21–24

6:21–22: But in order that you also may know my circumstances, [that is,] **how I'm doing, Tychicus—my beloved brother and faithful servant in the Lord,** ²²**whom I've sent to you for this very purpose—will make known to you all** [my circumstances] **in order that you may know the circumstances concerning us and** [in order that] **he may encourage your hearts** [compare Colossians 4:7–8]. "But in order that you *also* may know my circumstances" and "to you *all*" probably allude to Tychicus's carrying this letter to various churches (see the comments on 1:1–2), so that "you also" means "you in this local church as well as all others in local churches elsewhere." The absence of a public postal service required someone such as Tychicus to carry the letter. But Tychicus will spell out Paul's circumstances ("how I'm doing") in addition to delivering the letter. "In order that . . . he may encourage your hearts" implies that Paul is doing well despite his imprisonment and that the addressees, though not having known him face to face (1:15; 3:2), are concerned about him. To assure them that Tychicus will report Paul's circumstances accurately and fully ("all [my circumstances]"), Paul describes him affectionately ("my beloved brother"), commendably ("my . . . faithful servant"), and christianly ("in the Lord [= Christ]"). Tychicus is serving Paul faithfully by carrying the letter and making known Paul's circumstances (but in addition to Colossians 4:7–8, see Acts 20:4; 2 Timothy 4:12; Titus 3:12). The shift from "*my* circumstances" to "the [circumstances] concerning *us*" implies that others are with Paul. He lists their names in Colossians 4:10–14, and they include two fellow prisoners (see also Colossians 1:1; Philemon 23).

6:23–24: Peace [be] **to the brothers, and love with faith** [be to them] **from God the Father and the Lord, Jesus Christ.** ²⁴**Grace** [be] **with all those who love our Lord, Jesus Christ, in imperishability.** The "peace" and "grace" of the greeting (1:2) appear now in reverse order for the farewell. See the comments on Romans 1:7; 1 Peter 1:2; 2 John 3 for the meaning of these terms, though 2:11–18 adds the element of peace between Gentiles and Jews who believe in "the gospel of peace" (6:15). This element and the preceding context of warfare with the Devil and his minions may have induced Paul to mention peace first. He also adds to peace "love from God the Father and the Lord, Jesus Christ," because their love accompanies their peace. "With faith" is added to "love," because love from God and Jesus Christ has to be appropriated by faith. But since the addressees have already been saved by grace "through faith" (2:8), the faith that Paul wishes to come from God and Jesus Christ must be faith that perseveres in the face of the Devil's doctrinal-behavioral onslaughts (6:10–20), just as "those who love our Lord, Jesus Christ, in imperishability" means those whose love of the Lord perseveres rather than perishing in the face of those onslaughts. Notably, love *for* the Lord balances love *from* God and the Lord. But love from them comes first, because love for the Lord comes by way of response (compare 1 John 4:19). The generality of "to the [Christian] brothers" and "with *all* those who love our Lord" suits the circularity of this letter and, even more broadly, the letter's emphasis on the oneness of the universal church (2:19–22; 4:4–6, 13, 16).

PHILIPPIANS

This letter, written while Paul was in prison, explains his circumstances, thanks Christians living in Philippi, Macedonia, for a recent financial gift, exhorts them to practice Christian virtues, and warns against heretics.

GREETINGS
Philippians 1:1–2

1:1–2: Paul and Timothy, slaves of Christ Jesus, to all the saints in Christ Jesus who are in Philippi, along with [= including] **the supervisors and assistants:** **²Grace and peace to you from God, our Father, and the Lord, Jesus Christ.** Though Paul's subsequent use of "I," "my/mine," and "me" shows him to be the author of this letter, the inclusion of Timothy alongside him adds weight to it in that what Paul says, Timothy says too. (On Timothy, see especially Acts 16:1–3; 2 Timothy 1:3–8.) "Slaves of Christ Jesus" implies that the writing and sending of this letter carries out a work-order of Christ Jesus, so that the Philippians should pay heed to the letter's contents. The placement of "Christ," a title equivalent to the Hebrew "Messiah," before "Jesus" suits the authority of Jesus in having Paul and Timothy as slaves and giving them this work to do for him. "The saints" describes the addressees as consecrated by God to himself and therefore as unlike non-Christians in this respect. "In Christ Jesus" describes the saints' Spiritual location. That is to say, God looks on them as being in Christ Jesus, and therefore consecrated to God, because they have within them the Spirit who himself indwells Christ, so that they too indwell him (Romans 8:1–11). The second placement of "Christ" before "Jesus" suits again Jesus' messianic authority, but this time over the saints, who are in him. "To *all* the saints" prepares for an upcoming, expansive compliment. "Who are in Philippi" indicates their geographical location, which is noticeably secondary to their Spiritual location in Christ Jesus (see the comments on Acts 16:11–40 for Paul and company's evangelization of this Macedonian city). Among all the saints in Philippi Paul makes special mention of "the supervisors [of the saints] and the assistants [of the supervisors, that is, those who help them in supervision]." (The traditional translation "bishops and deacons" doesn't adequately identify the activities of these people.) For the rest of the greeting, see the comments on Romans 1:7; 1 Peter 1:2; 2 John 3.

PAUL'S THANKSGIVING AND PRAYER FOR THE PHILIPPIANS
Philippians 1:3–11

1:3–6: I thank my God on the occasion of every remembrance of you, ⁴always in every supplication of mine for all you ⁵making the request with joy because of your sharing for the gospel from the first day until now, ⁶[I] being persuaded of this very thing, that he who began a good work in you [compare Galatians 3:3] **will be completing** [it] **until the day of Christ Jesus . . . .** "Remembrance of you" refers to Paul's remembering the Philippians, not to their remembering him. Thanking God for them when remembering them pays them a compliment, which is designed to make them receptive of what Paul will say throughout this letter. At the same time, though, God gets the credit for what it is about them that prompts Paul's thanksgiving. To his thanksgiving Paul adds supplications—that is, prayer-requests—in behalf of the Philippians. (For what he requests, see 1:9–11.) These supplications show concern for them, but "with joy" tempers the concern with an optimism borne of their "sharing for the gospel," which refers to their monetary contributions in support of his evangelistic work (see 4:14–15; Romans 12:13; 15:26; 2 Corinthians 8:4; 9:13; Galatians 6:6 for sharing in a monetary sense). "From the first day until now" means that the Philippians started this sharing right after their conversion and have continued it right up to the present (see also 4:14–18). Hence, the making of supplications in their behalf compensates them for this sharing. Enhancing Paul's compliment and concern is the emphasis to be seen in the following buildup: "on the occasion of *every* remembrance of you, *always* in *every* supplication of mine for *all* you." (The italicized words rest on forms of a single, repeated word in Paul's Greek.) And "*my* God" indicates that even in Paul's most intimate moments with God, thanksgiving and concern for the Philippians always play a part.

Paul's persuasion rests on their sharing as evidence that God has begun a good work in them and will continue to do so until it's complete at "the day of Christ Jesus," which is the day of his return, when salvation is finalized. Ordinarily "a good work" means a good deed done by a human being. Why then does Paul use the expression here for what God is doing? Answer: Because the sharing of financial resources for evangelism is a good deed that not only gives evidence of salvation but that also, like salvation itself, is engendered by God (compare Ephesians 2:10; 2 Corinthians 9:8; Genesis 1:31–2:3). Just as in Paul's thanking God, then, God gets the credit for the good work, the good deed. "Will be completing [it] until the day of Christ Jesus" suggests that God will continue his good work of inducing the Philippians to support evangelism financially till the second coming, when evangelism will cease, and that God will do so to generate further evidence of their salvation, which will then reach completion (compare the use of "complete" in connection with financial sharing in Romans 15:28; 2 Corinthians 8:6, 11). "This very thing" underlines the completion, of which Paul is persuaded.

1:7–8: just as it's right for me to have this attitude about all you, because I have you in my heart, all you being sharers together with me of grace both in my bonds and in the defense and confirmation of the gospel. [8]For God [is] my witness, how I'm longing for all you in the vitals of Christ Jesus. "Just as it's right for me to have this attitude about you" harks back to Paul's persuasion that God will be completing in the Philippians the good work he has begun in them (1:6). "Because I have you in my heart" adds affection to thought and makes the affection a trigger of the thought. "Grace" means "favor." The grace of salvation is ill-deserved favor. But "in my bonds and in the defense and confirmation of the gospel" alludes to the Philippians' "sharing [their financial resources] for the gospel from the first day [when Paul was still free to defend and confirm the gospel] till now [while he's bound in prison]" (1:5). Moreover, Paul uses "grace" for God's having favored him with an apostolic ministry (Romans 1:5; 12:3; 15:15; 1 Corinthians 3:10; Galatians 2:9), and also for God's favoring Christians with the ministry of sharing their financial resources (see with comments 2 Corinthians 8:1–2, 4, 6–7, 19; 9:8, 14). So "sharers together with [me] of my grace" means that by exercising the grace of sharing their financial resources with Paul they've shared with him in the grace of his apostolic ministry.

"In the defense and confirmation of the gospel" probably alludes to his battle against the so-called Judaizers (for which see especially Galatians) in preparation for his warning the Philippians against them (3:1–2). "For God is my witness" introduces with emphasis an explanation of Paul's having the Philippians in his heart. "How I'm longing for all you" explains it. He doesn't say he's longing *to see* them, though doubtless he does long to. He longs *for them themselves* (as though he wants to hug them, we might say [compare 2:24]). "The vitals" are internal organs, used here and elsewhere as a figure of speech for deep affection. Paul doesn't say "in *my* vitals," as he does in Philemon 12, 20. He says "in the vitals *of Christ Jesus*" to equate his longing for the Philippians with the affections for them of Christ Jesus himself. For if he's in Christ, as he certainly is, he participates in Christ's affections (compare Philemon 20, where Paul says "my vitals" but adds "in Christ"). No fewer than

three occurrences in these verses of "*all* you," added to "*all* the saints" and "*all* you" in 1:2, 4, enhance further Paul's complimenting the Philippians so as to gain from them a receptive hearing of the letter.

1:9–11: And I'm praying this: that your love may flourish still more and more in knowledge and total perception [10]so that you may be approving the things which are superlative in order that you may be sterling and irreproachable for the day of Christ, [11][you] filled with the fruit [consisting] of righteousness, the [fruit borne] through Jesus Christ for the glory and praise of God. Here Paul spells out the supplications he mentioned in 1:3. He has been referencing the Philippians' sharing of financial resources for evangelism, has expressed confidence that God will continue inducing them to do so, and elsewhere associates the sharing of financial resources with love (see 2 Corinthians 8:7–8, 24). So Paul's praying that the Philippians' "love may *flourish still more and more*" asks God for increased as well as continued such sharing for the gospel on the Philippians' part. But Paul sets such love in the framework of "knowledge and total perception," for knowledge of the gospel and perception of people's need to hear it will lead to the flourishing of this financial love "still more and more." "*Total perception*" accents the recognition of people's need to hear the gospel.

"So that you may be approving the things which are superlative" expands Paul's purview to include not only financial love but also moral excellence in general. "Approving" means putting behaviors to a moral test and then putting into practice those behaviors that pass the test (compare Romans 2:18; 12:2). Beyond the purpose of such approval lies the purpose of being "sterling and irreproachable for the day of Christ [= with a view to being found genuinely blameless when he returns to judge us (2 Corinthians 5:10)]" because of being "filled with the fruit [consisting] of righteousness." For "fruit" as a figure of speech for behavior and its outcome see 1:22; Romans 6:21–22; Galatians 5:22; Ephesians 5:9 (in addition to passages outside Paul's letters). For "fruit" as a figure of speech for sharing financial resources see 4:17; Romans 1:13 (with comments); 15:28. For "righteousness" as the sharing of financial resources see 2 Corinthians 9:9–10. For "righteousness" as right conduct in general see (among other passages) Romans 6:13–20; 2 Corinthians 6:7, 14; Ephesians 4:24; 5:9; 6:14; 1 Timothy 6:11; 2 Timothy 2:22; 3:16. "*Filled* with the fruit of righteousness" points to having an abundance of righteous conduct, including that of sharing financial resources for purposes of evangelism, to show at the Last Judgment. But "through Jesus Christ" makes him the generator within us of such fruit, so that no glory or praise accrues to us. Thus the ultimate purpose of love's flourishing consists in "the glory and praise of God," who by his Spirit has put Christ in us as well as us in Christ (see again Romans 8:1–11). The doubling in "glory and praise" accents this ultimate purpose.

PAUL'S PREACHING IN PRISON, PROSPECT OF RELEASE, AND READINESS TO DIE
Philippians 1:12–26

1:12–14: But I want you to know, brothers, that my circumstances have actually resulted in the advancement of the gospel; [13]**and so among the whole imperial guard and all the rest my bonds have become obvious** [as being] **in Christ,** [14]**and** [so] **the majority of the brothers, persuaded in the Lord by my bonds, are extraordinarily daring to speak the word of God fearlessly.** "I want you to know" emphasizes the following information over against what the Philippians might think because of Paul's being in bonds, that is, imprisoned (1:7). "Brothers" (meaning "fellow Christians," both male and female) adds affection to the emphasis and recalls the expressions of Paul's affection for the Philippians in 1:7–8. "My circumstances" refers to his imprisonment. They've "*actually* resulted in the advancement of the gospel" means they've done so *rather than* resulting in stalled evangelism. So the advancement has come not *despite* the imprisonment, but *because of* the imprisonment. "And so" introduces how the advancement has taken place. It has taken place by way of Paul's bonds becoming obvious as being in Christ. If Paul is in Christ, so too are the bonds with which he is chained (compare 3:10). Paul is saying that the gospel has become known through his imprisonment. Why is he in bonds? Because he has been proclaiming the gospel. What gospel? The gospel concerning Christ. Who is he and what has he done that has led Paul to proclaim good news about him? Paul has answered this last question by explaining the gospel "among the *whole* imperial guard and *all* the rest," which is to say that the gospel has been heard in quarters unlikely to have reverberated with it apart from Paul's imprisonment. He doesn't define "all the rest," but association with "the imperial guard" points to high governmental officials.

There's another way in which the gospel has advanced because of Paul's imprisonment. "The majority of the brothers" are speaking "the word of God," which phrase Paul uses to stress that the gospel is fail-safe (see especially Romans 9:6; 1 Thessalonians 2:13; 2 Timothy 2:9). They're not just *speaking* this word. They're *daring* to speak it. They're not just *daring* to speak it. They're *extraordinarily* daring to speak it. They're not just *extraordinarily* daring to speak it. They're extraordinarily daring to speak it *fearlessly*. Furthermore, it's the *majority* who are doing so. If Paul is proclaiming the gospel because of his imprisonment, why shouldn't they be proclaiming it because of their freedom? They are! But their persuasion is "in the Lord," not in Paul, so that Christ is the generator of their extraordinary daring just as he's the generator of "the fruit of righteousness" (1:11). What a two-pronged advancement of the gospel, then!

1:15–18c: On the one hand, some [are speaking God's word] **even because of envy and strife. On the other hand, some are also proclaiming the Christ because of goodwill.** [16]**The latter, on the one hand,** [are doing so] **out of love, knowing that I'm destined for the defense of the gospel.** [17]**The former, on the other hand, are announcing the Christ out of rivalry, not purely** [that is, not with the purity of goodwill and love], **fancying to raise pressure for my bonds.** [18a–c]**So what? Only that in every way, whether for a show or for the truth, Christ is being announced; and in this** [fact] **I'm rejoicing.** Envy of Paul led to rivalry with him. Striving against him took the form of trying to raise pressure for his bonds, that is, to worsen his affliction by increasing the tightness of his chains, so to speak. He provides no specifics; but here we have a striking instance ("*even because of envy and strife*") of a culture in which honor was highly valued but thought to be of limited supply, so that people competed for it at the cost of others' shame. Paul doesn't compete in this zero-sum game, but his self-conceived rivals do. In contrast with them, others "are proclaiming the Christ [an expression that defines what it means in 1:14 'to speak the word of God'] because of goodwill [toward Paul]" and "out of love [toward him]." This goodwill and love stem from the supporters' knowing that God destined Paul to defend the gospel (compare Galatians 1:15–16). They recognize the futility of competing for honor against God's appointee. By implication, Paul's rivals are stupid in their "fancying," as opposed to his supporters' "knowing." As for him, he cares only that "Christ is being announced." Indeed, he's rejoicing in this fact, whether it's "for a show" of the announcer to gain honor, or "for the truth" of the gospel to gain converts.

1:18d–20: I will rejoice, however. Paul is setting his future rejoicing in a temporal contrast with his present rejoicing (1:18c). [19]**For I know that "this for me will turn out to result in salvation** [Job 13:16]**" through your supplication and the supply of the Spirit of Jesus Christ** [20]**in accordance with my eager expectation and hope that in no respect I'll be ashamed—rather, that with all boldness even now, as always, Christ will be magnified in my body, whether through life or through death.** In the earlier part of 1:18, Paul said he presently rejoices that the Christ is being proclaimed. Now he explains the reason why he'll rejoice also in the future. The reason is that "this for me will turn out to result in salvation." What does "this" refer to? Well, the same word has just occurred in 1:18c. There it referred clearly to Christ's being proclaimed. We have no reason to see a change of reference here. So if this proclamation of Christ "will turn out to result in salvation," what salvation is in view? Eternal salvation in accordance with 1:28; 2:12. Whose salvation is in view? "For me" might seem to indicate that Paul's salvation is in view. He doesn't say "*my* salvation," though, as would be expected from expressions in 1:28; 2:12; 2 Corinthians 1:6; Ephesians 1:13 ("*your* [own] salvation") and Romans 13:11 ("*our* salvation"). The following reference to Paul's "boldness" therefore favors that "for me" has to do with Paul's proclamation of the gospel that will result in the salvation of those who respond in faith to that proclamation. "Through your supplication" makes the Philippians' praying a means of the proclamation's salvific success. "Through . . . the supply of the Spirit" makes empowerment by the Holy Spirit a coactive means of such success (compare the pairing of "the sword of the Spirit, which is God's word" with "prayer and supplication" in Ephesians 6:17–18; and for the Spirit as empowering successful evangelism see Romans 15:18–19; 1 Corinthians 2:4–5; 1 Thessalonians 1:5). God supplies his Spirit for this empowerment.

Paul adds "of Jesus Christ" to "the Spirit" because Christ is the subject of the proclamation empowered by the Spirit (compare Romans 8:9), and then elaborates his own evangelistic efforts (as in 1:12–14). He has "eager expectation and hope [which in his usage connotes confidence] that in no respect will [he] be ashamed [that is, ashamed to proclaim the gospel (compare Romans 1:18: 'For I'm not ashamed of the gospel'; also 2 Timothy 1:8, 12)]." The contrast with "boldness" favors the translation "*be* ashamed" rather than "be *put* to shame." Paul attaches "all" to "boldness" for emphasis on boldness in proclaiming the gospel "even now," when because of his imprisonment it might be thought by others that he would clam up. "As always" indicates the exercise of just as much boldness as he exercised prior to his imprisonment. He puts his bold proclamation of Christ in terms of Christ's being "magnified," that is, being made big through the announcement that he's no less a personage than the Christ, the Messiah. "In my body" implies that through his Spirit, Christ indwells Paul's body (Romans 8:1–11; 1 Corinthians 6:19); and Christ will be magnified in it both if Paul continues living as a proclaimer of Jesus as the Christ and if Paul dies as a proclaimer of Jesus as the Christ.

1:21–26: For to me, living [is] Christ [compare Galatians 2:20] and dying [is] gain. ²²And if living in flesh [is my lot], I [have] this [as] the fruit of [my] work. And I don't know what I'll prefer; ²³and I'm being hemmed in between the two [possibilities of living in flesh, which living is Christ, and dying] because of having a strong desire to depart [from you] and be with Christ. For [that would be] very much better [for me than living in flesh is]. ²⁴But on account of you, to stay in the flesh [is] more necessary. ²⁵And persuaded of this [greater necessity], I know that I'll stay [in the flesh] and stay with all you for the purpose of your advancement and joy of faith, ²⁶in order that in me, [that is,] through my coming again to you, your boast may be flourishing in Christ Jesus. Paul now explains why he spoke of Christ's being magnified in Paul's body, whether through life or through death. "To me" means "in my case/so far as I'm concerned." "Living [is] Christ" in that so long as Paul is living he's proclaiming Christ. But Paul allies his living to his proclamation of Christ so closely that he *equates* his living with Christ! "Dying [is] gain" in that Paul will then "be with Christ," which would be "very much better" than "living in flesh." Flesh is that part of the body which returns to dust upon death (Genesis 3:19). Given Paul's not yet attaching "my" to "flesh," then, the switch from "in my body," where "Christ will be magnified" (1:20), to "in flesh" denotes mortal life *as such*. Nevertheless,

"living in flesh" has a saving feature, namely, "this [as] the fruit of [Paul's] work." But what does "this" refer to here? In both 1:18 and 1:19 it referred to Christ's being proclaimed. So too here, for Paul's continuing to live in flesh would mean his continuing to proclaim Christ. This proclamation would result in successful evangelism.

The future tense in "what I'll prefer" looks forward to the time of Caesar's verdict. Meanwhile, "being hemmed in" describes figuratively "I don't know what I'll prefer." Paul can't make up his mind right now. "Having a strong desire to depart and be with Christ" stems from its being "very much better" than living in flesh. But Paul judges that staying with all the Philippians for their "advancement and joy of faith" is "more necessary" than the betterment of his situation even though departing and being with Christ would be "*very* much better" for Paul. Because of the greater necessity of "stay[ing] in the flesh," he says, "I *know* that I'll stay [in the flesh, which is to stay alive] and stay with all you [which implies a visit from Paul, as confirmed by 'my coming again to you' [see also 2:24]." See the final comments on 1:7–8 for "*all* you." "Your advancement and joy of faith" refers to the Philippians' increasing in the exercise of faith and to their joy in that exercise, both the increase and the joy coming as a result of Paul's visit. The Philippians' boast will flourish. What will they be boasting about when Paul visits them? They'll be boasting about the answer to their prayer that he be spared to visit them and continue proclaiming the gospel of salvation (see the comments on 1:19). But "in Christ Jesus" locates the flourishing of their boast where it brings no credit to them for praying. The credit goes to him, through whom God will have answered their prayer.

EXHORTATIONS
Philippians 1:27–2:18

1:27–30: Only be conducting yourselves as citizens worthily of the gospel about the Christ in order that whether coming and seeing you or being away from [you], I may be hearing things concerning you, [specifically,] that you're standing in one Spirit, with one soul contending together for the faith of the gospel ²⁸and not being scared in any respect by those who are set against you, which as such is in their case an indication of ruin but of your salvation—and this from God, ²⁹because to you it has been graciously given in Christ's behalf not only to be believing in him but also to be suffering in his behalf, ³⁰you having the same sort of struggle that you saw in my case and are now hearing [to be] in my case. "Only" introduces the following exhortations as what the Philippians should obey rather than succumbing to discouragement over Paul's imprisonment (compare 1:12–14). "Be conducting yourselves as citizens [of heaven according to 3:20]" alludes to and contrasts with the character of Philippi as a Roman colony populated originally by Roman citizens who were army veterans (compare Acts 16:35–40, where the issue of Roman citizenship comes up in Philippi). "Worthily of the gospel about the Christ" is defined by "standing in one Spirit, with one soul contending together for the faith of the gospel and not being scared in any respect by those who are set against you." Paul wants to hear of such heavenly citizen-worthy conduct whether he comes and sees the Philippians (in case he's released from prison) or stays absent from them (as now).

Because of the parallelism with "one soul," which refers to the Philippians' collective soul, many translations have "one spirit," a reference to the Philippians' collective spirit. (Since the earliest Greek manuscripts were written all in capital letters, capitalization versus noncapitalization in English becomes a question of interpretation rather than of simple translation.) On the other hand, Paul appears to have written Philippians and Ephesians around the same time and from the same imprisonment; and in Ephesians 4:4 "one Spirit" clearly refers to the Holy Spirit (see also 1 Corinthians 6:17). Even more impressively, in Ephesians 2:18 Paul uses the very same phrase that he uses here, "*in* one Spirit," again with clear reference to God's Spirit (so too in 1 Corinthians 12:13). And the difference between "*in* one Spirit" and "*with* one soul" weakens the parallelism between these phrases. Therefore it's better to take "standing in one Spirit" as a reference to the shared Holy Spirit, who gives the Philippians strength to stand firm as "with one soul"—that is, with a deeply felt unity—they're "contending together for the faith of the gospel" (an athletic metaphor, elaborated in 2:16; 3:12–14, for maintaining and propagating the belief whose object is the gospel).

To stand and contend requires "not being scared in any respect" by opponents who would persecute you. "Which *as such*" refers to the quality of not being scared. This quality will show that your opponents are headed for ruin in the hereafter but that you're headed for salvation in the hereafter, for otherwise you'd have reason to be scared of them. "And this" refers again to your "not being scared." "From God" gives him rather than you credit for not being scared. He gives you freedom from fear of your persecutors "because to you it has been graciously given in Christ's behalf not only to be believing in him but also to suffer in his behalf." In other words, the opportunity to believe in him is matched by the opportunity to suffer in his behalf, the opportunity to suffer in his behalf being as much a gracious gift as the opportunity to believe in him (compare 3:10). These gifts are given (by God, it's implied) in Christ's behalf—that is, to benefit him—and you suffer (persecution, it's implied from "those who are set against you") likewise in Christ's behalf—that is again, to benefit him. It's a benefit to him that you believe in him; and it's a benefit to him that you suffer persecution for propagating your belief, because believing in him and suffering to propagate this belief makes his sacrificial death worth the cost to him (compare 2 Corinthians 8:9). Then Paul draws a parallel between the Philippians' struggle against their opponents, their persecutors, and the same sort of struggle they saw in his case when he evangelized them and was thrown in jail (Acts 16:12–40; 1 Thessalonians 2:2) and

are now hearing in reference to his imprisonment. Mention of the parallel should ease their minds. They have good company in their struggle (compare Acts 14:22; 2 Thessalonians 1:4–10).

2:1–4: Therefore if in Christ [there's] **any encouragement, if any consolation of love, if any sharing of the Spirit, if any vitals** [= internal organs as a figure of speech for affections] **and compassions, ²fill my joy.** [I say this] **in order that you may be of the same attitude, having the same love, co-souled, being of one attitude, ³[doing] nothing in accordance with rivalry or in accordance with vainglory—rather, with lowliness of attitude** [= humility] **regarding each other as being superior to yourselves, ⁴each** [one of you] **not looking out for your own interests** [alone]**—rather, each** [of you all] [looking out for] **the interests of others as well** [compare 1 Corinthians 10:24; 13:5]. "Therefore" bases the following exhortation on the Philippians' knowing the sort of struggle Paul has undergone in the past and is now undergoing as a prisoner. Consequently, "encouragement," "consolation," "sharing of the Spirit," and "vitals and compassions" have to do with the Philippians' encouragement (and so on) of Paul. The quadrupled "if any" doesn't call in question the presence of these dispositions "in Christ." For since the Philippians are in him (1:1) and since such dispositions characterize Christ himself, a plentiful supply of them is available to the Philippians. So "if any" challenges the Philippians to draw on this supply for Paul's encouragement and consolation. "Of love" describes the consoling of him as stemming from love for him. All Christians have been baptized in one Spirit into one body (1 Corinthians 12:13). Hence they do share the Spirit in the sense of having him as common property (so to speak); and since love is the first-listed fruit of the Spirit (Galatians 5:22), "sharing of the Spirit" provides the basis for "consolation of love." Paul has already ascribed "vitals" to "Christ Jesus" (see 1:8 with comments). Here the pairing with "compassions" produces the meaning, deep feelings of compassion.

"Fill my joy" means, "Make me full of joy." Of course, Paul is already rejoicing in the Philippians' financial support of his evangelistic work (1:4–5) and in others' proclamation of the gospel (1:18). But his joy won't be full unless he learns that the Philippians have patched up differences which have disunited them (see, for example, 4:2–3). Therefore his exhortation to adopt "the same attitude" toward one another, which attitude he defines as "the same love" for each other. "Co-souled" then describes them, if they obey, as consequently harmonious with one another at their very core. "Being of *one* attitude" echoes the exhortation to be "of the *same* attitude," this time to be followed first, however, by what to avoid that would *destroy* oneness of attitude rather than by what to implement for *achieving* the sameness of attitude. Both "rivalry" and "vainglory" destroy oneness of attitude by pitting people against each other. In fact, an attitude of rivalry characterizes those near Paul who are "fancying" to make his imprisonment worse

(1:17). He prefixes "vain-" to "glory" to indicate that the glory which comes from fellow human beings is empty of the glory that comes from God. Paul adds vainglory to rivalry and for emphasis repeats "in accordance with." The connective "or" implies that rivalry leads to vainglory and that vainglory leads to rivalry, so that neither one should characterize Christians. "Nothing" rules out both of them entirely. "Lowliness of attitude" regarding yourself identifies "the same attitude/the one attitude" recently commanded; and "regarding each other as superior to yourselves" defines "lowliness of attitude." Moreover, looking out for others' interests as well as for your own tells what it entails activitywise to regard each other as superior to yourselves. Paul shifts from the singular in "each [one of you]" to the plural in "each [of you all]" to point up the responsibility of all members of the local Christian community to care for their fellow Christians' interests, and two instances of "rather" make for strong oppositions between what Paul prohibits and what he commands.

2:5–11: For have this attitude among you, which [is] **also** [the attitude proper to your being] **in Christ Jesus** [compare 4:2; Romans 15:5], **⁶who though existing in the form of God didn't regard being equal with God as something to take advantage of** [compare Romans 15:3]. **⁷Instead, he emptied himself by taking the form of a slave on coming to be in the likeness of human beings. ⁸And on being found in respect to fashion as a human being, he lowered himself by becoming obedient to the extent of death—but death on a cross! ⁹Therefore God also lifted him above** [everyone else] **and graced him with the name above every name ¹⁰in order that in the name of Jesus every knee might bow, of heavenly and earthly and subterranean** [beings], **¹¹and** [in order that] **every tongue might confess, "Jesus Christ** [is] **Lord," for the glory of God the Father.** "For" introduces this passage as a reason why the Philippians should obey the injunctions to lowliness of attitude (and so forth) in 2:1–4. Paul starts by noting that such an attitude is proper to being in Christ Jesus, as the Philippian Christians are according to 1:1, and then switches to him as an example of this attitude. His exemplifying it *makes* it proper for the interrelations of those in him by faith. "Who though existing in the form of God" ascribes preexistent deity to Christ, as confirmed by his "being equal with God." ("Form" refers to a way of being that makes someone who he is.) At the same time, this equality with God differentiates him from God, so that at the end of the passage we read of "God" as "the Father" and of "Jesus Christ" as "Lord." That Christ Jesus "didn't regard being equal with God as something to take advantage of" not only confirms his having equality with God because of existing in the form of God, but also models an absence of any "rivalry or vainglory" (2:3). "Instead, he emptied himself by taking the form of a slave" exhibits "lowliness of attitude" and "looking out for . . . the interests of others" (2:3–4).

"On coming to be in the likeness of human beings" portrays the divine Christ's incarnation as the precondition of his emptying himself by taking the form of a slave. "And on being found in respect to fashion [= mode of existence] as a human being" reiterates this precondition, and "lowered himself by becoming obedient to the extent of death" reiterates his emptying himself by taking the form of a slave. So death, not incarnation, defines his self-emptying. In other words, incarnation as a human being made possible his self-emptying in death, as confirmed by the correspondence between obedience and the form of a slave. For what is expected of a slave if not obedience? And since "to the extent of death" describes the obedience, self-emptying by taking the form of a slave equates with becoming obedient to the extent of death. Furthermore, "death on a cross" suits a slave, for crucifixion was regarded as the quintessential way to execute a slave, or somebody who was to be treated as a slave. "*But* death on a cross" sets crucifixion apart from other ways of execution and dying because of its suitability to slaves and those being treated as such. Hovering in the background is Isaiah 53:12, where the Slave of the Lord is said to have "poured out [= emptied] his soul to [the extent of] death."

Some linguistic notes: (1) "Soul" can mean both "life" and "himself," as when Jesus said the Son of Man came "to give *his soul/life* as a ransom" (Mark 10:45; Matthew 20:28) and Paul, quoting him, says "he gave *himself* as a ransom" (1 Timothy 2:6 [see also Titus 2:14]). (2) Hebrew, the language of Isaiah, had no reflexive pronoun such as "himself," so that "soul/life" served the function of a reflexive. (3) Isaiah 52:13–53:12 has words corresponding not only to "slave" but also to "form," "likeness," and "fashion" here in Philippians 2:5–11. And (4) these last-listed words of Paul should be taken as synonyms dealing with identity, not merely with similarity.

Crucifixion was considered the most shameful of deaths. (Its pain was secondary to its shame.) So in compensation for Christ's having "*lowered* himself," God "*lifted* him above [everyone else]." The gracing of Jesus with the name "*above* every name" and the listing of "heavenly and earthly and subterranean beings" as those whose every knee will "bow" in Jesus' name imply the addition of "everyone else" after "lifted him *above*." "Also" makes conspicuous the contrastive pairing of God's gracious uplift of Jesus with Jesus' obedient comedown. The universal bowing in Jesus' name and the universal confession, "Jesus Christ [is] Lord," bring together body language (the bowing of knees) and verbal language (the confession of tongues) in acknowledgment that the human Jesus is also the divine Lord (compare Isaiah 45:23). For "Lord" corresponds to LORD (Hebrew: Yahweh) as the most sacred of divine names in the Old Testament and therefore counts as "the name above every name." Furthermore, "Lord" connotes the ownership and mastery of slaves and therefore makes the lordship of Jesus compensate for his having taken the form of a slave. But why "for the glory of God the Father" rather than "for the glory of Jesus Christ"? Because God the Father is the one who lifted him and graced him with his own name and therefore merits glory for doing so.

And if even the universal acclamation of Jesus Christ as Lord has the purpose of glorifying God the Father, how much more should obeying the injunction to follow Jesus' example have that purpose.

2:12–13: And so [as a result of Christ's "becoming obedient to the extent of death" (2:8)], **my beloved, just as you've always obeyed, not only when in my presence but now much more in my absence be working at your own salvation with fear and trembling. ¹³For the one who is working in you both the wanting and the working for** [his] **good pleasure is God** [compare 1:6]. The address "my beloved" means "I love you" and implies both that you Philippians should reciprocate my love for you by obeying my following injunction and that this injunction flows out of a love which desires your salvation. "Just as you've always obeyed" provides a complimentary basis for obedience to the injunction. "Not only when in my presence" looks forward to Paul's visiting the Philippians, as he hopes to do (1:24–27; 2:24). But he doesn't want them to delay their obedience; so he adds "but now much more in my absence." Why "much more"? Because their not yet having Paul to exhort them in person might induce negligence.

The injunction, "be working at your own salvation," means to produce it, to implement it. For though salvation has already occurred by divine grace through human faith apart from good works (Ephesians 2:8–9; Romans 4:5–6), salvation has yet to be finalized at the Last Judgment; and this finalization will require good works to certify the past occurrence of salvation (Ephesians 2:10; 2 Corinthians 5:10; Romans 14:10). "With fear and trembling"—that is, with a fear so strong that it causes trembling—underscores the danger of lacking such certification, a danger which should drive you to be working at salvation. "Your *own* salvation" stresses the one self-interest allowable, indeed indispensable (compare the implication in 2:4 of "not looking out for your own interests [alone]—rather, . . . [for] the interests of others *as well*"). But why work at salvation if it's not by your working? Because if you don't, you'll betray that God isn't working in you. But if you do, you'll show that he is in fact working in you. Paul doesn't say, "For God is the one who is working in you . . . ." Rather, "For the one who is working in you . . . is God." This way of putting it lays emphasis on God (as the one who is working in you) rather than on the one who is working in you (as God). Thus, though you must work at your own salvation, you can't take any credit for your working. All credit goes to God. Moreover, his working in you includes your wanting to work as well as the actuality of your working, so that your working pleases you as well as God, though "[his] good pleasure" is what really counts. Since you work as a result of his working, it's no surprise that he takes pleasure in your working. All in all, then, God's working in you doesn't *relieve* you of working; it gives you *reason* to be working.

2:14–18: Be doing all things without grumblings and arguments, ¹⁵in order that you may become blameless and guileless, God's faultless children amid "a crooked and perverted generation [Deuteronomy 32:5],**" among whom you're shining as luminaries in the world, ¹⁶by holding fast the word of life, so that for the day of Christ I**['ll have] **a basis for boasting that I neither ran ineffectually nor labored ineffectually. ¹⁷Even if, however, I'm being poured out as a drink-offering on the sacrifice and ministry of your faith, I'm rejoicing—and I'm rejoicing together with all you. ¹⁸And in the same** [way] **you too, be rejoicing—and be rejoicing together with me.** The prohibition of "grumblings and arguments" shows that "all things" have to do particularly with the communal life of church members. The grumblings allude to the ancient Israelites' grumblings against Moses and Aaron despite their appointment by God to lead the Israelites (Exodus 15:24; 16:2, 7–9, 12 and so forth; compare 1 Corinthians 10:10). The Israelites also *argued* with Moses and Aaron (see Exodus 16:3; 17:1–3, for example). The special mention in 1:1 of "supervisors and [the supervisors'] assistants" and the upcoming command that the Philippians welcome back Epaphroditus, their "apostle and minister," and to hold such people as Epaphroditus "in esteem" (2:25–30) suggest grumblings against and arguments with leaders of the church in Philippi. Grumblings and arguments destroy being of one and the same attitude, having the same love, and being co-souled, all of which Paul commanded in 2:2, and would fit rivalry and vainglory, which he prohibited in 2:3 and countered with Christ's example in 2:5–11.

The emphatic twofoldness of "blameless and guileless" corresponds to the emphatic twofoldness of "grumblings and arguments." Grumblings are blameworthy, and arguments (at least the kind Paul has in mind) are guileful in that they are specious. As though "blameless and guileless" weren't enough, Paul adds "God's faultless children" for a contrast with the "crooked and perverted generation" amid whom the Philippians (and all Christians) are set. The twofoldness of "crooked and perverse" corresponds to that of "grumblings and arguments" and contrasts with that of "blameless and guileless." The obviousness of the contrast leads Paul to add "among whom you're shining as [moral] luminaries in the world." "By holding fast the word of life" tells how to become "blameless and guileless, God's faultless children." "The word of life" is the message about eternal life, to which message you must hold fast behaviorally as well as doctrinally if you're to attain that life (compare 1 Timothy 4:16). For Paul's hope of boasting on the day of Christ, the day of his return, see the comments on 2 Corinthians 1:14; 1 Thessalonians 2:19; and with the possibility of Paul's having run and labored "ineffectually [literally, 'with an empty result']" compare Galatians 2:2; 1 Thessalonians 3:5. Running and laboring portray Paul's evangelism in a twofold way: as a race to be won and as a job to be finished. Ineffectual running means losing the race, then, and ineffectual laboring means leaving the job unfinished. So far as the Philippians are concerned, Paul will lose his race and leave his job unfinished unless they prove their salvation "by holding fast the word of life"—in short, by perseverance.

"Even if . . . I'm being poured out as a drink-offering" harks back figuratively to the possibility that the trial of Paul will end in his martyrdom, a possibility first broached in 1:20–23 (compare 2 Timothy 4:6). For the pouring out of wine onto a sacrifice, see Exodus 29:40; Leviticus 23:13; Numbers 15:5, 7, 10; 28:14. Since Paul had Roman citizenship (Acts 16:37–38; 22:25–29; 23:27; 25:16) and the Romans used beheading to execute their condemned citizens, he may be comparing the resultant bloodshed to the pouring out of wine (as Jesus compared his shed blood to wine [Mark 14:24; Matthew 26:28; Luke 22:20]). "On the sacrifice and ministry of your faith" means the sacrifice consisting of the ministry prompted by the Philippians' faith and refers figuratively to the monetary gifts they've sent to support Paul in his evangelistic work (1:5–7; 2:30; 4:10–18). "Even if, however" stresses that not even the possibility of martyrdom is killing his joy over receiving their financial gift (1:4–5) and over the proclamation of Christ because of Paul's imprisonment (1:12–18), or is killing Paul's rejoicing with the Philippians over the brighter prospect of his being spared martyrdom at this juncture and then visiting them (1:25–26)—and also over the return of Epaphroditus to them, a return that will have taken place by the time they hear this letter read in their assembly (2:25–30). For "all you," see the final comments on 1:7–8. Then Paul turns from *assuming* that the Philippians are rejoicing to *commanding* them to rejoice, in particular to be rejoicing with him over what gives him joy. His imprisonment and possible martyrdom haven't made him a killjoy. To the contrary! The Philippians should follow suit ("And in the same [way] you too").

THE SENDING OF TIMOTHY AND EPAPHRODITUS TO PHILIPPI
Philippians 2:19–30

2:19–24: And I'm hoping in the Lord, Jesus, to send Timothy to you soon in order that I too may be well-souled [= heartened] by knowing the matters concerning you. [20]For I have no one of a soul equivalent [to mine] who as such will genuinely care about the matters concerning you. [21]For all [the others] are seeking their own interests, not the [interests] of Jesus Christ. [22]But you know his [Timothy's] mettle, that as a child [slaves] for [his] father he [Timothy] has slaved together with me for the gospel. [23]On the one hand, therefore, I'm hoping to send him at once when I get a bead on the matters concerning me. [24]On the other hand, I'm persuaded in the Lord that I myself too will come soon. As usual, Paul's "hoping" exudes confidence. "In the Lord, Jesus" undergirds the confidence, especially because *as* the Lord, Jesus has authority to fulfill Paul's hope. And since Timothy as well as Paul is Jesus' slave (1:1), the lordship of Jesus implies that Timothy will act on Jesus' orders when he arrives in Philippi. For "lord" refers to the owner and master of a slave. "Soon" indicates a sending of Timothy in the near future. So

the Philippians had better shape up now. "In order that I *too* may be well-souled" includes Paul as well as Timothy in the purpose of being heartened. The use of "well-souled" in the sense of "heartened" makes for a wordplay with "co-souled" (= harmonious) in 2:2. As a prisoner presently unable to visit Philippi himself, Paul wants to be heartened by hearing from Timothy good news regarding the state of affairs in the Philippian church ("by knowing the matters concerning you").

Why the hope to send Timothy rather than someone else? Because Paul has "no one of a soul equivalent" to his. This expression refers to having the same heartstrings for the Philippians that Paul has so as to "genuinely care" about the matters concerning the Philippians during his enforced absence from them; and the expression carries forward the wordplay with "co-souled" and "well-souled." This wordplay underscores these sentiments. So too does "who *as such*" in the case of Paul's having no one of an equivalent soul. Timothy and Epaphroditus, who is to be mentioned next, are the contextually obvious exceptions (the latter because he'll have returned to Philippi by the time the Philippians hear the letter read to them [see 2:25–30]). The reason that no one else will genuinely care is that they're all "seeking their own interests, not the [interests] of Jesus Christ." In 2:4 Paul told the Philippians to look out for "the interests *of others*" as well as for their own interests. Here he describes all who are with him as "seeking *their own* interests, not the [interests] *of Jesus Christ*," so that the interests of others, in this case of the Philippians, turn out to be the interests of Jesus Christ—naturally, because as Christians the others are in him, so that their interests are his too. How sadly un-Christian it is that his interests go unsought when the interests of others in him go unsought.

The tried-and-true character of Timothy constitutes his "mettle." The Philippians "know" it from the time he spent with them during Paul's second and third missionary journeys (Acts 16:1–40; 19:22; 20:3–4). This knowledge should join the possibility of Timothy's coming "soon" to make the Philippians shape up (concerning which see 4:2–3 and the allusions to disunity, grumblings, and arguments in 2:1–4, 14). "That as a child [slaves] for [his] father he has slaved together with me for the gospel" specifies what they know about his mettle. Paul says "together with me" rather than "for me" because he too is a slave of Christ Jesus in the work of advancing the gospel (1:1, 12). "Therefore" has Timothy's mettle as its basis. For "I'm hoping to send him," see the foregoing comments on "I'm hoping . . . to send Timothy." Here, though, instead of a vague "soon" Paul writes specifically, "at once when I get a bead on the matters concerning me," which means when he sees how his trial is going to turn out. Like his "hoping in the Lord, Jesus" in regard to sending Timothy, Paul's being "persuaded in the Lord" that he as well as Timothy "will come soon" exudes the confidence of one who is working as a slave for his Lord/Owner/Master (compare 1:25). Given his not yet having gotten a bead on the outcome of his trial,

Paul lapses back to a vague "soon" in regard to his coming. Nevertheless, it's soon enough; and the addition to "I" of "myself too" chimes in to help make it another reason for the Philippians to shape up forthwith.

2:25–30: But [though I'm not yet coming] **I've regarded it as necessary to send to you Epaphroditus, my brother and fellow worker and fellow soldier and your apostle and minister to my need,** [26]**since he was longing for all you and dismayed because you'd heard that he was sick.** [27]**For indeed he was sick, nearly to death. God had mercy on him, however, and not only on him but also on me lest I have sorrow upon sorrow.** [28]**Therefore I've sent him more urgently in order that on seeing him again you may rejoice and I may be more unsorrowful.** [29]**Therefore be welcoming him in the Lord with all joy, and be holding such people** [as him] **in esteem,** [30]**because on account of the work of Christ he came close to death by hazarding** [his] **life in order that he might make up for your deficit of ministry to me.** Given the lack of a public postal system, Paul is almost certainly sending Epaphroditus with this letter in hand. The past tense in "I've regarded it as necessary" reflects the Philippians' standpoint upon receiving the letter. The threefold description of Epaphroditus as Paul's "brother," "fellow worker," and "fellow soldier" uses figures of speech relating to family, labor, and battle to commend Epaphroditus so fulsomely that despite the possibility of the Philippians' having grumbled against him and argued with him and their other leaders (see the comments on 2:14), the Philippians shouldn't dare refuse him the joyful welcome that Paul commands they give him—especially since Timothy and Paul are likely to come soon themselves and check up on the reception given to Epaphroditus. Then despite the possibility of Epaphroditus's having been a butt of the Philippians' grumblings and arguments, Paul implies in what would then be a tour de force that the Philippians themselves commended Epaphroditus by sending him as their "apostle and minister" to Paul's financial need (compare 1:4–5; 4:10–18). Here, "apostle" has the sense of one whom they sent with authority to act on their behalf; and "minister" has the sense of one honored with the duty of priestly service, which like apostleship is representative service on the Philippians' behalf. Epaphroditus ministered like a priest by carrying a financial contribution to Paul, as though it were a sacrificial offering.

"Since he was longing for all you and dismayed" explains why Paul "regarded it as necessary" to send Epaphroditus. As regards longing for them *themselves* rather than longing *to see* them, see the comments on 1:8; and concerning "*all* you," see the final comments on 1:7–8. The longing and dismay of Epaphroditus is explained by the Philippians' having "heard that he was sick." Apparently he wanted to show them in person that he'd recovered. Paul explains with an emphatic "indeed" that Epaphroditus had been sick—and worse, "nearly to death." This explanation has the purpose of endearing Epaphroditus to the Philippians by implying that it was while acting on their behalf that he became sick. "God

had mercy on him, however" ascribes to God Epaphroditus's recovery and thus portrays him as getting from God a commendation of sorts. If God himself had mercy on Epaphroditus, the Philippians should do no less than give him a joyful welcome. "And [God had mercy] not only on him but also on me lest I have sorrow upon sorrow" portrays Paul as likewise commended in that God has spared him from having sorrow over a death of Epaphroditus laid on top of the sorrow over Epaphroditus's nearly fatal sickness. "Therefore" bases "I've sent him" on the recovery from sickness. "More urgently" describes the sending. This description compares the sending to one which, absent Epaphroditus's longing and dismay, wouldn't have been especially urgent. "In order that on seeing him again you may rejoice" assumes that the Philippians have enough sympathy for him that they'll be glad to see him back in good health, or at least identifies Paul's purpose in sending him back. "And [that] I may be more unsorrowful" adds another purpose. "*More* unsorrowful" means being spared sorrow over inability to send Epaphroditus back to the Philippians (had he died) in addition to being spared sorrow over his death itself (had it occurred).

"In the Lord" describes the commanded welcome of Epaphroditus as proper to his and his fellow Philippians' Spiritual location (compare the comments on 2:5). In favor of Paul's purpose that they may rejoice on seeing Epaphroditus again, "with all joy" rules out any and all grumblings and arguments such as 2:14 prohibits. So too does the command to "be holding such people [as him] in esteem," though this command broadens the objects of esteem to include other church leaders, such as the supervisors and their assistants of 1:1. Paul's threefold description of Epaphroditus at the start of this passage has already set an example of holding him and others like him in esteem. As a particular reason to hold Epaphroditus in esteem, Paul cites Epaphroditus's coming close to death on account of the work of Christ. Thus Paul identifies the Philippians' financial gift to him as the work of Christ, and Epaphroditus's coming close to death in the delivery of the gift as "hazarding [his] life in order that he might make up for [the Philippians'] deficit of ministry to [Paul]"—that is, for the deficit of the very ones who may have grumbled against him (Epaphroditus) and who may have argued with him. He certainly deserves from them a joyful welcome for having run a dangerous errand on their behalf. "Your deficit of ministry" is *not* to be understood as caused by negligence on their part—rather, as caused by their lack of opportunity, as Paul will state explicitly in 4:10.

A WARNING AGAINST JUDAIZERS
Philippians 3:1–4:1

3:1–4a: As for the rest [of this letter], **my brothers, be rejoicing in the Lord. To write the same things to you** [is]**n't onerous for me, on the one hand. For you, on the other hand,** [it's] **a safeguard.** [2]**Be watching out for the dogs. Be watching out for the wicked workers. Be watching out for the cutting** *down*. [3]**For**

we—we are the cutting *around*, the ones doing religious service by God's Spirit and boasting in Christ Jesus and not being confident in flesh, [4a]even though I [might be] having confidence even in flesh. The address "*my* brothers" introduces the rest of this letter on a particularly affectionate note designed to ensure that the Philippians take seriously the following exhortations, especially the warnings against false teachers. In 2:29 Paul told the Philippians to welcome Epaphroditus "in the Lord with all joy." Now he puts the rejoicing itself, which he commands, "in the Lord." As usual, "the Lord" refers to Christ Jesus; and rejoicing in him will keep the Philippians from thinking they need to keep the Mosaic law, starting with circumcision, as the false teachers whom Paul is about to excoriate were saying they had to do (see 3:7–11 for the sufficiency of Christ Jesus as Lord). "The same things" Paul is now going to write repeat what he has told the Philippians before, presumably when with them in person. He doesn't mind repeating himself; and because the false teachers (popularly called Judaizers) pose a serious threat to the gospel, he considers the repetition to be "a safeguard" against them.

How serious Paul considers the threat can be gauged from three successive, staccato-like commands, each one of which starts, "Be watching out." The first calls the false teachers "the dogs." The Mosaic law declared dogs to be ritually unclean (Leviticus 11:27); and since Gentiles didn't maintain ritual purity in accordance with the Law, Jews called Gentiles dogs (see Mark 7:26–28; Matthew 15:22, 26–27 for the epithet; and for an example of Jews' considering Gentiles ritually unclean see Acts 10:1–48, especially 10:28). So by calling the Judaizing teachers "dogs," Paul is turning against them the very epithet they use for Gentiles, including Gentile Christians, whom they tell to practice the Law so as not to be "dogs" any more! The Judaizing teachers stress doing the works of the Law so as to be righteous according to its terms. But Paul calls these teachers "*wicked* workers," that is, workers of wickedness because they teach it's necessary for salvation to keep the Mosaic law. Keeping the Law started with circumcision, which means "a cutting *around*," that is, a cutting around the penis to get rid of its foreskin. But Paul derides the Judaizers for their insistence on circumcision by calling them "the cutting *down*," as though they amputate the whole penis (and/or the testicles?), so that it dropped off. Then he justifies these warnings by identifying Christians, whether physically circumcised or not, as "the cutting around," and explains this identification as a Spiritual circumcision by adding that they're "the ones doing religious service by God's Spirit and boasting in Christ Jesus [the sole basis of salvation]" as opposed to "being confident in flesh [that has been cut off]" (compare Romans 2:25–29; 1 Corinthians 7:19; Ephesians 2:11; Colossians 2:11; Jeremiah 4:4; 9:25–26). The doing of religious service contrasts with the Judaizers as "wicked workers," and "even though I [might be] having confidence even in flesh" sets up for Paul's citing himself as an example of someone who *could* put confidence in flesh but *doesn't* despite having more apparent

reasons to do so than the Judaizers have. "*Even* in flesh" highlights the stupidity of putting confidence in it.

3:4b–6: If anyone else presumes to have confidence in flesh, I [presume] more [to do so, being] [5]an eight-dayer so far as circumcision is concerned; from the stock of Israel; of Benjamin's tribe; a Hebrew [born] of Hebrews; as to the Law, a Pharisee; [6]as to zeal, pursuing the church; as to the righteousness [stipulated] in the Law, being blameless. "If anyone else presumes to have confidence in flesh" implies that "the dogs," "the wicked workers," "the cutting down" of 3:2 presume to have confidence in flesh—particularly in their circumcised flesh, though it represents the entirety of their allegiance to the Mosaic law. With "I [presume] more [to have confidence in flesh]," Paul sets forth his presumption for the sake of argument, but as unjustified (it will turn out) even though the presumption has a stronger basis than the others' serious presumption. His circumcision was performed on the eighth day after his birth, exactly as stipulated by the Law for a Jewish baby boy (Genesis 17:12; Leviticus 12:3). "From the stock of Israel" gives Paul's biological pedigree. Nobody could scorn him as only a Gentile who had converted to Judaism. "Of Benjamin's tribe" gives his tribal pedigree (see also Romans 11:1), a pedigree he could be proud of because this tribe was the only one that stayed loyal to the tribe of Judah (1 Kings 12:21; Ezra 4:1; 10:9), which God had designated the tribe from which Israel's kings, including the Davidic Messiah, should come (see, for example, Genesis 49:8–12; Isaiah 9:6–7). As *Saul* of Tarsus, Paul appears to have been named after Israel's first king, a Benjamite (1 Samuel 9:1–2; Acts 13:9). "A Hebrew [born] of Hebrews" means that despite coming from Tarsus, a pagan city far from Jerusalem and the land of Israel, Paul had grown up in a Jewish home where the Greek language wasn't spoken and Jewish customs were strictly observed. But not only were his parents "Hebrews" in this sense. He himself had maintained his Hebraistic upbringing. So "a Hebrew [born] of Hebrews" marks a transition from Paul's heritage to Paul's choices. "As to the Law, a Pharisee" means that he practiced the Law in accordance with the oral traditions of a sect widely admired among the Jews for careful observance of it. "As to zeal, pursuing the church" goes beyond Law-keeping, means *persecuting* the church, and prepares for a wordplay in that 3:12 will speak quite differently of Paul's presently pursuing resurrection from among the dead, and of 3:14 of his pursuing "the prize of God's upward call in Christ Jesus" (compare Galatians 1:13). "As to the righteousness [stipulated] in the Law, blameless" means that as a matter of observation none of his fellow Jews found fault, or could have found fault, with his practice of Judaism (Galatians 1:14). (But see Romans 7:7–25 for his inner moral failure at the time.)

3:7–11: Whatever gains I had, however—*these* I came to regard as a loss because of the Christ. [8]On the contrary, however, I'm also regarding *all things* as a loss because of the superiority of knowing Christ

Jesus, my Lord, because of whom I've suffered the loss of all things and am regarding [them] as feces in order that I may gain Christ ⁹and be found in him, not having my righteousness, the [righteousness derived] from the Law—rather, the [righteousness derived] through faith in Christ, the righteousness [derived] from God on the basis of faith, ¹⁰in order to know him [Christ] and the power of his resurrection and the sharing of his sufferings, being conformed to his death, ¹¹if somehow I may make it to the resurrection from among the dead. "Whatever gains I had" refers to the items in 3:4b–6 that Paul cited as reasons he could put more confidence in flesh than the Judaizers do. But at his conversion he came to regard these gains as a loss. "Gains" and "loss" are financial figures of speech appropriate to Paul's writing this letter in part to thank the Philippians for their recent financial gift (1:5; 4:10–18). The shift from a plural in "gains" to the singular in "a loss" treats the gains as a collective loss, especially when introduced as here with "Whatever." "Because of the Christ" makes Jesus as the Messiah the reason why Paul changed his mind about his supposed gains. The change didn't simply neutralize the supposed gains; it turned them into a loss. Not that there was anything wrong with a Jewish heritage and Law-keeping. But such gains turn into a loss once they're compared with the Christ, whom Paul saw risen from among the dead (see 1 Corinthians 9:1; 15:8; Galatians 1:15–16). To put the point another way, self-righteousness turns into unrighteousness when set beside the Christ (compare Isaiah 64:6).

"On the contrary, however" strengthens the preceding, stand-alone "however" and draws another contrast, but this time not one that Paul arrived at in the past with respect only to his self-righteousness—rather, a contrast that for him is ongoing in the present and includes "all things." In comparison with the Christ, everything is a loss. Only he is a gain. The earlier phrase, "because of the Christ," expands into "because of the superiority of knowing Christ Jesus, my Lord." So Christ is gain only if you know him. To know him, as Paul goes on to say, is to experience him at work in your life as a result of believing in him. And such knowledge is so superior to all else that by comparison all else should be regarded as a loss. The addition of "Jesus" (a personal name) to "Christ" (a title) identifies who "the [aforementioned] Christ" is. The further addition of "my Lord" harks back to God's having given him "the name above every name" in order that "every tongue might confess, 'Jesus Christ [is] Lord'" (2:9–11) and reflects the intimacy ("my Lord") of Paul's knowing Christ in personal experience. "Because of whom I've suffered the loss of all things" doesn't refer to an objectively external loss (as, for example, of material wealth or physical well-being). This statement revives the figurative language of financial loss in regard to Paul's mental estimation of all things. But the revival has the purpose of shifting that language to the equally figurative but more astringent, indeed scatological language of "feces," which in view of the warning against "the dogs" in 3:2 may refer specifically to dog-doo.

"In order that I may gain Christ" states the purpose of regarding all things as feces in comparison with him, portrays him as the one true gain in contrast with the imaginary gains summarized as self-righteousness, and implies that you won't gain Christ unless you do regard all things as feces in comparison with him. When will you "gain Christ and be found in him"? On the Last Day (see 2 Corinthians 5:3; 2 Timothy 1:18 for being found or not found on that day). Not that believing in him hasn't already gained him for you and placed you in him from God's point of view. But as confirmed by the condition, "if somehow I may make it to the resurrection from among the dead" and by the next paragraph (3:12–16), this gain and this placement have yet to be finalized on the Last Day; and the finalization will require a certification of your having suffered the loss of all things by regarding them as feces (compare the comments on 2:12–13). "Not having my righteousness, the [righteousness derived] from the Law" encapsulates the list of imaginary gains in 3:5–6. "The righteousness [derived] from God" contrasts with the self-righteousness ("my righteousness") derived "from the Law" (that is, from Law-keeping) and consists in God's declaring righteous those sinners who have believed in Jesus, and declaring them so because in his death Jesus suffered the wrath of God against their sin (see the comments on Romans 3:21–26). But Paul wants so much to emphasize faith in Christ as the sole means of attaining righteousness at the Last Judgment that he delays the explicit reference to this righteousness till after the phrase, "through faith in Christ," and then adds "on the basis of faith" after "the righteousness [derived] from God" (compare Romans 9:30–10:10, and see the final comments on Galatians 2:15–16 against the translation, "through Christ's faithfulness").

"In order that I may gain Christ and be found in him" gets expanded in the rest of this paragraph ("in order to know him [and so on]"), and the expansion furthers the purpose of "regarding [all things] as feces" in comparison with Christ. So "the superiority of knowing Christ Jesus" becomes the reason "to know him." And to know him is to know "the power of his resurrection" (see Romans 1:4), that is, to experience it at the Last Day. (For that day has been in view since the reference to gaining Christ and being found in him.) This power contrasts with the weakness of flesh (Romans 6:19; 8:3–8; 1 Corinthians 15:50; Galatians 4:13) and guarantees believers' resurrection to eternal life (1 Corinthians 6:14; 15:43; 2 Corinthians 13:4). To know—that is, to experience—"the sharing of his sufferings" steps back to present time. Bearing in mind that Paul probably wrote Colossians and Philippians around the same time, see the comments on Colossians 1:24–26a for the sharing of Christ's sufferings. "Being conformed to his death" takes place in this sharing, for there you learn to consider yourself dead to sin because of having died with Christ so far as God is concerned. Thus conformity to Christ's death means considering yourself dead in him to sin (see Romans 6:1–11, and compare Romans 8:17; 2 Corinthians 1:9; 4:10–12; 2 Timothy 2:11).

"If somehow I may make it to the resurrection from among the dead" corresponds to "know[ing] the power of his resurrection" and thus confirms that knowing it has to do with the bodily resurrection of believers on the Last Day as guaranteed by Christ's resurrection in the past. So Paul has shifted from the future (knowing the power of Christ's resurrection) to the present (sharing Christ's sufferings), stayed in the present (being conformed to his death), and shifted back to the future (making it to the resurrection). Scholars would call this an A-B-B′-A′ arrangement. The "somehow" of making it to the resurrection is defined by the middle two terms B (sharing Christ's sufferings) and B′ (being conformed to his death), which relate back to regarding all things as a loss, and even as feces, in order to gain Christ and be found in him with God's righteousness. "The resurrection *from among* the dead" refers to the resurrection of Christians to eternal life. "The dead" are non-Christians, with whose resurrection to eternal doom Paul isn't concerned in writing to Christians (but see Acts 24:15).

3:12–16: Not that I've already obtained [resurrection from among the dead] **or have already been completed** [by God through that resurrection], **but I'm pursuing** [it] **if also** [as well as pursuing it] **I may grasp** [it], **because I was also grasped by Christ Jesus.** [13]**Brothers, I don't count myself to have grasped** [it]. **But** [I'm doing] **one thing: forgetting the things behind** [me] **on the one hand, stretching out for the things ahead** [of me] **on the other hand,** [14]**in accordance with the goal in view I'm pursuing to the prize of God's upward call in Christ Jesus** [compare 1 Corinthians 9:24–27]. [15]**Therefore let as many of us as** [are] **complete have this attitude. And if in regard to anything you have a different attitude, God will reveal even this to you.** [16]**Nevertheless, as to what we've attained** [thus far], **be keeping in line with the same.** Both negatively and positively Paul correlates his responsible human action with God's and Christ's sovereign divine action (compare 2:12–13). It's obvious that Paul hasn't already obtained resurrection or already been completed by God through it. For Paul hasn't even died yet. The two occurrences of a negated "already" point up this obviousness. But Paul states the obvious as a basis for pursuing the resurrection for which he was grasped by Christ Jesus. Pursuing it contrasts with pursuing the church by way of persecution (3:6) and means running a race whose goal is resurrection from among the dead. Except for resurrection, the language is figurative. "I was grasped by Christ Jesus" rules out self-righteousness in the case of Paul's ultimately grasping the resurrection. Christ Jesus grasped him at his conversion.

The address, "Brothers," lends a note of affectionate seriousness to the following denial of having grasped resurrection, as though it were guaranteed for Paul even if he stopped pursuing it. "But one thing" sets single-mindedness of pursuit against dividing attention between the race thus far run and what remains of it. Because of the paragraph-ending exhortation to be keeping in line with what has thus far been attained, "forgetting

the things behind [me]" means forgetting Paul's apostolic accomplishments to date rather than his Judaistic past. To keep your accomplishments in mind is to trust in them. "Stretching out" represents maximum effort, like that of a sprinter straining for the finish line. "For the things ahead" refers to what lies between Paul's present location on the race course and "the goal in view," that is, to what of Christ's sufferings is yet to be shared and what conformity to Christ's death is yet to be actualized before reaching the goal of resurrection from among the dead, which is "the prize of God's upward call in Christ Jesus"—an *upward* call in that the very word "resurrection" means in literal translation "a standing *up*" of formerly supine corpses. Paul adds "in Christ Jesus" because believers will be resurrected by virtue of incorporation into him, who has already been resurrected from among the dead.

"*In accordance with* the goal in view" means that the goal should determine how to run, that is, with forgetfulness of the things behind and with stretching out for the things ahead. "Therefore" bases the following exhortation on the necessity of forgetting and stretching out if one is to make it to the resurrection. The exhortation takes the form of encouragement rather than command, and Paul includes himself. But "let as many of us as [are] complete have this attitude" is ironic, because Paul has just denied that he has already been completed through resurrection; nor have any other Christians been completed through it. "As many of us as [are] complete" doesn't refer to some Christians as distinct from other Christians, then. It includes them all—but ironically, so that "this attitude" which Paul encourages is the attitude that in fact we have *not* yet been completed, and "a different attitude" is the mistaken one of having been completed already. "In regard to anything" means there's no past accomplishment whatever that will guarantee our resurrection to eternal life if we don't finish the race successfully; and "even this God will reveal to you" means that in fact he will reveal to you that you haven't yet been completed. But when will he reveal it? On the Last Day, at the Last Judgment. Then and there, though, the revelation will do you no good. The die will have been cast. Your certification will be lacking. "Nevertheless" means "despite the necessity of forgetting the things behind"— that is, "what we've attained [so far]." "Be keeping in line with the same" commands nondeviation, because thus far you've been heading in the right direction, "toward the prize of God's upward call in Christ Jesus."

3:17–19: Become fellow imitators of me, brothers, and be on the lookout for those who are walking around [= behaving] **in this way, just as you have us** [Paul and Timothy (1:1)] **as a role model.** [18]**For many are walking around, about whom I've told you often but am now telling you while even weeping—**[who are walking around] **as enemies of the cross of the Christ,** [19]**whose** [referring to the enemies] **end** [is] **ruination, whose god** [is their] **belly, and** [whose] **glory** [is] **in their shame** [compare Hosea 4:7], **those whose attitude** [is geared to] **earthly things** [compare Colossians 3:2].

The command that the Philippians become fellow imitators of Paul makes reference to the preceding autobiographical passage, in which he spoke of his forgetting the things behind and pursuing to the things ahead. *"Fellow imitators"* presses the point of unity among the Philippians in their imitation of Paul. In 3:2, three occurrences of "Watch out for" carried a note of warning: beware of. Here, "be on the lookout for" carries the note of a quest: be searching for those who are behaving the way Paul and Timothy behave. The Philippians need good role models in addition to Paul and Timothy, because *"many* are walking around . . . as enemies of the cross of Christ." Two good role models aren't enough to counterbalance, much less outweigh, those many bad role models, namely "the dogs," "the wicked workers," "the cutting down" of 3:2.

Paul has told the Philippians often about those Judaizers, and is telling them now, because of the constant threat the Judaizers pose. "While even weeping" describes him in a way that rules out all personal recrimination and expresses deep sorrow both over the eternal doom of the Judaizers and over their opposition to "the cross of the Christ" (compare Galatians 5:11; 6:12–14). For only his cross offers the way of salvation, so that by insisting on the self-righteousness derived from Law-keeping, the Judaizers are attacking the cross. They'll lose this battle, though; for their "end [is] ruination [= eternal punishment]." In this context, their *"walking around* . . . as enemies of the cross of the Christ" contrasts with Paul's *"pursuing* to the prize of God's upward call in Christ Jesus" (3:14). Though professedly monotheistic, the Judaizers' "god [is] the belly," Paul sarcastically says in a probable reference to their insistence on keeping the Mosaic food laws. See the use of "belly" with this association in Mark 7:19 and Matthew 15:17, which record a saying of Jesus that Paul may be alluding to. The Philippians would of course know that the Judaizers were teaching adherence to food laws and would therefore catch the association of "belly" with those laws. And though the Judaizers profess to give glory to God, their "glory [is] in their shame," Paul says with equal sarcasm in a probable back reference to their insistence on circumcision, what in 3:2 he sarcastically called "the cutting down" instead of "the cutting around" (compare 1 Corinthians 12:23–24, where Paul portrays the private parts of the body as unpresentable and therefore as needing to be covered with clothing to avoid shame). "Whose *god* . . . and [whose] *glory"* are both ironic, of course; and the gearing of the Judaizers' "attitude" to "earthly things" has to do with insistence on circumcision and kosher food, among other elements of the Mosaic law (compare 3:3–6). Now Paul will tell why to beware of the Judaizers and be fellow imitators of him instead.

3:20–21: For our citizenship exists in heaven, from where we're also [in addition to having our citizenship in heaven] **eagerly expecting a Savior—the Lord, Jesus Christ—**²¹**who will refashion our body of lowliness** [so as to be] **conformed to his body of glory in accordance with the working of his being powerful** [enough] **even**

to subject all things to himself. In 1:27 Paul exhorted the Philippians to be conducting themselves "as citizens worthily of the gospel about the Christ." The exhortation alluded to the character of Philippi as a Roman colony populated originally by Roman citizens who were army veterans. Here, Paul's statement that "our citizenship exists in heaven" makes for a contrast with Roman citizenship, based as it is on earth, to whose "things" the Judaizers' "attitude" is geared (3:19). Since Christians are located "in Christ Jesus" (1:1), his location determines the location of their citizenship. He's presently located in heaven. So their citizenship "exists in heaven." That's where they're living from God's point of view, which ought to translate into their point of view too. But Christ won't stay in heaven: *"from where* we're also eagerly expecting . . . Jesus Christ" (an obvious reference to the second coming). Before naming Jesus Christ, though, Paul says "a Savior" to indicate that Jesus Christ will save us citizens of heaven from the eternal "ruination" toward which the Judaizers are heading (3:19), and then adds "the Lord" to recall the universal acclamation, "Jesus Christ [is] Lord," at the end (2:11). His "refashion[ing] our body of lowliness" makes us expect him "eagerly." Since Christ *"lowered* himself by becoming obedient to the extent of *death"* (2:8), "our body of *lowliness"* means our *mortal* body (compare Romans 7:24; 8:10–11; 1 Corinthians 15:42–44, 50–54; 2 Corinthians 5:4). By way of contrast, "his body of glory" means his resurrected, immortal body, to which in this respect our body will be conformed (for the association of glory with resurrection to eternal life, see especially Romans 2:7, 10; 6:4; 1 Corinthians 15:42–43; Colossians 3:4; 2 Timothy 2:10–11). Christ will refashion our body "in accordance with the working of his being *power*ful [enough] even to subject all things to himself" (compare "the *power* of his resurrection" in 3:10). If he can *"even* subject *all things* to himself," he can surely refashion our bodies into conformity with his gloriously immortal body.

4:1: And so [in view of Christ's coming from heaven and of the Judaizing threat to your eternal salvation]**, my beloved and longed-for brothers, my joy and crown, be standing this way in the Lord, beloved.** "My beloved and longed-for brothers" means that Paul loves and longs for the Philippians as his fellow family members in Christ (compare 1:8; 2:12). "My joy and crown" means that they've brought him joy with their financial support of him (1:4–5) and that as his converts they've crowned him with victory in his evangelistic pursuit (see the comments on 1 Corinthians 9:24–25; 1 Thessalonians 2:19–20 for the crown as an imperishable wreath given to the victor in a race; also 2 Timothy 4:7–8 for receiving a crown at the second coming because of having finished one's race). "Be standing" contrasts with being "wave-tossed and carried about" (Ephesians 4:14) by the wind of the Judaizing heresy warned against in chapter 3 (compare 1:27). "This way" describes the standing as watching out for the Judaizers, imitating Paul, looking for other good role models too, and keeping in line with what has thus far been attained rather than deviating into the Judaizing heresy. "In the Lord" implies that deviating would betray a location outside the Lord, where no salvation is to be had. Because Paul loves the Philippians and longs for them as his brothers, he doesn't want them to lose out on salvation by falling prey to the Judaizers. Because they're his joy and crown, he doesn't want to be saddened and denied his crown by their apostatizing (compare 2:16). The repetition of "beloved" underscores that he issues this exhortation out of love for the Philippians.

EXHORTATIONS
Philippians 4:2–9

4:2–3: I exhort Euodia and I exhort Syntyche to be of the same attitude in the Lord [compare 2:2]. **³Yes, I ask you too, genuine yokemate: help them, who indeed for me struggled in the gospel along with both Clement and the rest of my coworkers, whose names** [are] **in the scroll of life.** The naming of the woman Euodia and Syntyche and the repetition of "I exhort" make for an exhortation that's both pointed and emphatic. For "be[ing] of the same attitude," see 2:2. Here, the addition of "in the Lord" makes being of the same attitude proper to these two women's location in him by virtue of having his Spirit (see the comments on 2:5–11 and Romans 8:1–11). "Yes" stresses the following request that Paul makes of someone in Philippi he calls a "genuine yokemate." "You *too*" indicates someone different from the women. More than that we can't tell, though some have suggested the capitalization, "Yokemate," to indicate another proper name. By way of a compliment, in any case, "genuine" describes "yokemate" as a true partner in the Lord's work, but whether of Paul or Euodia and Syntyche or all three of them isn't clear.

"Help them" means to help them "be of the same attitude in the Lord." "Who indeed . . . struggled in the gospel" describes Euodia and Syntyche as heavily engaged in evangelism. (The struggle portrays evangelism as an athletic contest with the forces of evil.) This description of the women gives "yokemate" a strong reason to help them. "For me" adds Paul's personal touch to the reason, so that helping them will amount to helping him as well. "Along with both Clement and the rest of my coworkers" sets out Euodia's and Syntyche's partnering with them in evangelism as a template for Euodia's and Syntyche's being of the same attitude in the Lord. For "in the gospel" parallels "in the Lord." "Whose names [are] in the scroll of life" suits the naming of at least the women and Clement (a man) and also underwrites the legitimacy, indeed the commendability, of their "struggl[ing] in the gospel," so that the "genuine yokemate" has even more reason to help Euodia and Syntyche. We know no more about Clement, nor what it was about him that led Paul to name him despite not naming the rest of Paul's coworkers. "The scroll of life" contains the names of professing Christians (see further the comments on Revelation 3:5).

4:4–7: Be rejoicing in the Lord always. Again I'll say, be rejoicing. ⁵Your mild-manneredness is to be known to all human beings [compare 2 Corinthians 10:1]. **The Lord** [is] **near. ⁶Don't be worrying about anything** [compare Matthew 6:25–34; Luke 12:22–32]. **Instead, your requests are to be made known to God in every** [circumstance] **by means of prayer and supplication with thanksgiving. ⁷And God's peace, which surpasses all thinking, will guard your hearts and your thoughts in Christ Jesus.** See the comments on 3:1 for the command, "Be rejoicing in the Lord." Here, the addition of "*always*" prepares for the prohibition, "Don't be worrying about *anything*." For constant joy drives out every worry. The repetition of "be rejoicing" and its emphatic introduction by "Again I'll say" reinforce this preparatory command. "Mild-manneredness" is a natural concomitant of joy. So Paul commands it too or, more particularly, that it "is to be *known* to all human beings," which way of putting the command prepares for the command that "your requests are to be made *known* to God." Thus the testimony of joyful mild-manneredness to all human beings is matched, and even made possible, by the directing of requests to God. The lynchpin of these exhortations is found in the statement, "The Lord [is] near." For if Jesus' return is near, Christians can afford to be mild-mannered even to their enemies; and they needn't worry about anything. "In *every* [circumstance]" corresponds to "about *anything*." "By means of prayer" tells how the requests are to be made known to God. "And supplication" defines the prayer as petitionary. "With thanksgiving" requires that thanks for what God has already supplied accompany the supplication. As a result, "God's peace"—that is, the blessings of salvation now and yet to come—"will guard your hearts and your thoughts"—that is, will keep you from heartbreak and neurosis. "Which surpasses all thinking" describes God's peace as so unimaginably good that it has this effect. And "in Christ Jesus" locates God's peace where believers themselves are located. So they enjoy it naturally.

4:8–9: As for the rest [of my exhortations], **brothers, as many things as** [are] **true, as many things as** [are] **respectable, as many things as** [are] **right, as many things as** [are] **pure, as many things as** [are] **charming, as many things as** [are] **laudable—if** [there's] **any virtue and if any praiseworthiness—be pondering these things. ⁹The things that you've both learned and received and heard and seen in me, be practicing these things; and the God of peace will be with you.** In 3:1, "As for the rest" seems to have referred to the rest of the letter. Now the phrase seems to refer to the rest of Paul's exhortations, which he introduces, as often, with the affectionate address "brothers." The sixfold repetition of "as many things as" underlines comprehensiveness in what Christians are to ponder. And they're to ponder them because thinking affects behavior. Paul ranges what is morally true against what is morally false, what is morally respectable against what is morally scandalous, what is morally right against what is morally wrong, what is morally pure against what is morally dirty, what is morally charming against what is morally loathsome, and what is morally laudable against what is morally reprehensible. Then he speaks of "virtue," which is moral excellence, and "praiseworthiness," which is moral commendability. The pairing of these terms with a twofold "if any" ensures the moral connotation of "as many things as [are] true [and so on down the preceding list]." "The things that you've both learned and received and heard and seen in me" are exactly those virtuous and praiseworthy things just listed. When Paul was with the Philippians, they "learned" these things by having "received" them as tradition passed on by him (the tradition probably originating in Jesus' moral teaching), by having "heard" them in Paul's own original teaching, and by having "seen" them in his behavior. Now it's up to the Philippians to "be practicing these things." For learning is useless unless it's put into practice. "The God of peace" turns around "the peace of God" in 4:7. Just as his peace will guard the hearts and thoughts of those who make their requests known to him with thanksgiving, so too the God of peace will himself be with those who practice virtuous, praiseworthy things as a result of pondering them. Moreover, he'll be with them till the Lord (Jesus), who is near, returns.

THANKS FOR FINANCIAL ASSISTANCE
Philippians 4:10-20

4:10-13: And I've rejoiced in the Lord greatly because now at last you've made your attitude [of concern] for me to blossom again. [I say so] on the basis that you were also of that attitude [earlier], but you weren't having an opportunity [to make it blossom again]. **¹¹Not that I'm speaking in accordance with lack. For I've learned to be content in my circumstances; ¹²I know even to be lowered; I know even to flourish. In every [circumstance] and in all [circumstances] I've been initiated both into being sated and into being hungry, both into flourishing and into lacking. ¹³In him who empowers me I'm strong enough for all** [those circumstances]. Paul sets an example of the rejoicing that he has told the Philippians to practice (3:1; 4:4). The addition of "greatly" highlights their financial gift to him that gave *him* reason to rejoice. But "in the Lord" gives credit to the Lord for what they've done. "Now at last" implies a period of noncontribution. "You've made your attitude [of concern]" correlates *their* action with the *Lord's* (compare 1:5-6; 2:12-13), and also correlates their attitude of concern for Paul with the attitude that he has exhorted them to have toward one another (2:1-11). "To blossom again" describes their financial concern for him as morally beautiful. "Again" refers to its *re*blossoming in a recent gift brought to Paul by Epaphroditus (2:25-30). Paul then makes clear that the Philippians aren't to be blamed for the hiatus in their giving, for they wanted to contribute all along but had no opportunity to do so. "Not that I'm speaking in accordance with lack" means that he isn't hinting that they haven't sent him enough money. "For I've learned to be content in my circumstances" means that he has no need to judge the adequacy of their gift. "I know even to be lowered" refers to experiences of financial distress. "I

know even to flourish" refers to experiences of financial surplus. "In *every* [circumstance] and in *all* [circumstances]" emphasizes the financial lows and highs into which Paul has been initiated by experience. "Both into being sated . . . and into flourishing" interprets the highs as having more than enough money to buy food for the satisfaction of his hunger; and "into being hungry . . . and into lacking" interprets the lows as not having enough money to do so. In view of 3:10, 21; Ephesians 6:10, "him who empowers me" refers to the Lord, Jesus Christ. By stating that it's in him that he's "strong enough for all [these circumstances]," Paul takes no credit for his ability to be content, but gives all credit to the Lord.

4:14-16: Nevertheless [despite my ability to be content in any and all circumstances]**, you did beautifully by sharing with me in respect to the pressure** [I'm under]. **¹⁵And also you yourselves know, Philippians, that in the beginning of the gospel** [that is, when you first heard and believed it]**, when I went out from Macedonia** [where Philippi is located]**, in the matter of giving and receiving no church shared with me except for you** [plural] **alone. ¹⁶[I say so] because even** [when I was] **in Thessalonica** [which is also in Macedonia] **you sent [a gift] for my need both once and twice.** "You did *beautifully* by sharing with me" alludes to the "*blossom*[ing] again" of the Philippians' financial support of Paul (4:10), and "in respect to the *pressure* [that I'm under]" alludes to the pressure of his "bonds," his chains, a pressure that others were "fancying to raise" (1:17). "And also you . . . know" means "you as well as I know." The additions to "you" of "yourselves" and "Philippians" underline the addressees' knowing in that the object of their knowledge consists in what they themselves did, which is that they supported Paul financially: they gave, he received. "No church shared with me except for you alone" highlights their giving by way of a contrast with other churches. "Even [when I was] in Thessalonica" highlights further their giving by noting that they started giving immediately upon their conversion. For Thessalonica was the next stop after Philippi during Paul's second missionary journey (Acts 16:40-17:1). "Both once and twice" means several times and highlights yet further their giving by calling attention to its plurality, and this despite Paul's having stayed in Thessalonica for no longer than several weeks so far as we can tell from Acts 17:1-10. And "for my need" attributes their giving to concern for Paul as the Lord's evangelist.

4:17-20: Not that I'm seeking for a gift; rather, I'm seeking for fruit that proliferates for your account. ¹⁸And I have all things and am flourishing. I've been filled by having received from Epaphroditus the [gifts] from you, [which are] an odor of fragrance [= a fragrant odor], an acceptable sacrifice well-pleasing to God. ¹⁹And my God will fill all your need in accordance with his wealth in glory in Christ Jesus. ²⁰And to our God and Father [belongs] glory forever and ever. Amen! The foregoing compliments might seem to be a backhanded way of seeking for a further financial gift from the Philippians. So "not that I'm seeking for a gift" denies such a motivation. "I'm seeking for fruit that proliferates for your account" does encourage the Philippians to continue giving—for their own sake, however, not for Paul's. Though salvation depends on God's righteousness, not the self-righteousness of human beings (3:9), for the evaluation of their faith the Philippians have an account with God. "Fruit" stands for credit in that account, and proliferation of the fruit stands for the buildup of credit through further deposits in the form of gifts for evangelism. But to reaffirm that he's not dissatisfied with the Philippians' most recent gift, Paul adds, "And I have all things," which connotes being paid in full. "And am flourishing" means that for the present he has more than enough money (especially for the purchase of food, since Roman prisoners depended largely on family or friends to bring them food). "I've been filled by having received from Epaphroditus the [gifts] from you" recalls 1:11: "that you may be . . . filled with the fruit [consisting] of righteousness," which includes the sharing of financial resources. But here it's Paul, not the Philippians, who has been filled with the fruit of their righteousness. For the description of their gifts as "an odor of fragrance, an acceptable sacrifice well-pleasing to God," see the comments on 2:17; Ephesians 5:2; Romans 12:1–2. The similar description in Ephesians 5:2 of Jesus' self-sacrifice makes it a high compliment that Paul would use such language for the Philippians' gifts to him. Notably, a sacrificial gift to Paul equates with a sacrificial gift to God, because Paul is doing God's work.

Since God is well-pleased with the Philippians' gifts, he'll "fill all [their] need," which means first and foremost (if not exclusively) that he'll supply all their financial need. "My God" reflects an intimacy with God that enables Paul to issue this promise (compare 1:3). "In accordance with his wealth" indicates an ever-sufficient supply. Paul locates God's wealth both "in glory," to indicate how dazzling it is in its volume, and "in Christ Jesus," to indicate its availability to those who themselves are in him by faith (compare Ephesians 3:16: "in accordance with the wealth of his [God the Father's] glory"). Because God will supply all the needs of the Philippians and, through them, of Paul, the apostle ascribes glory to God forever and ever and punctuates the ascription with "Amen!" Thus "glory" shifts from what is dazzling to what is honorific, and "forever and ever" makes God's glory limitless in time just as his wealth is limitless in volume. And "*our* God and Father" replaces the earlier "*my* God," because God will supply what the Philippians need just as he has supplied what Paul needed (compare 1:2).

CONCLUSION
Philippians 4:21–23

4:21–22: Greet every saint in Christ Jesus. The brothers [who are] with me greet you. ²²All the saints, and especially those of Caesar's household, greet you. The command, "Greet *every* saint in Christ Jesus," suits Paul's earlier exhortations to church unity at Philippi (see especially 2:1–11; 4:2–3). "In Christ Jesus" provides the framework of such a greeting, for the saints' location in him makes them neighbors to each other in distinction from the world of unbelievers. "The brothers" who are with Paul are Timothy and the noncompetitive preachers of 1:14–15. Paul calls them "the brothers" to portray the church as an extended family. "All the saints" includes all the believers where Paul is imprisoned (traditionally and most probably Rome). "And especially those of Caesar's household" recalls the success of the gospel in high places because of Paul's imprisonment (1:12–13). That "*all* the saints" send greetings through this letter sets for the Philippians an example of what Paul has just told them to do: "Greet *every* saint in Christ Jesus."

4:23: The grace of the Lord, Jesus Christ, [be] with your spirit. This benediction comes very close to the one in Galatians 6:18. See the comments on that verse.

COLOSSIANS

This letter, written while Paul was in prison, exalts the person and work of Christ over against false teaching that was devaluing him. Then Paul exhorts his addressees to behave in ways appropriate to Christ's person and work.

INTRODUCTION
Colossians 1:1–12

The introduction to Colossians consists in a greeting (1:1–2), a thanksgiving (1:3–8), and a prayer (1:9–12). The prayer will shade almost imperceptibly into a doctrinal discussion (1:13–2:23).

1:1–2: Paul, an apostle of Christ Jesus through God's will, and Timothy, the brother, ²to the saints in Colossae, even believing brothers in Christ: Grace and peace to you from God, our Father. Paul's self-designation matches his self-designation in 2 Corinthians 1:1; Ephesians 1:1; 2 Timothy 1:1 exactly, but see the comments on 1 Corinthians 1:1 for the meanings of the terms used. "The brother" describes Timothy as the Christian brother of Paul and the Colossians. The inclusion of Timothy alongside Paul adds weight to the letter in that what Paul says, Timothy says too, and also prepares for addressing the Colossians likewise as Christian "brothers." But Paul's "I," "my," and "me" (1:23–25, 29 and following) point to him as the letter's author. For Timothy, who in addition to those listed in 4:10–14 is with Paul at the time of writing, see especially Acts 16:1–3; 2 Timothy 1:3–8. "To the saints in Colossae" addresses the letter to Christians living in the city of that name and describes them not as outstandingly virtuous but as consecrated to God. They're his special possession as distinct from the non-Christians among whom they live. Colossae lay in the river valley of a mountainous region in southwest central Asia Minor. Many translations have "even *faithful* brothers" rather than "even *believing* brothers." The difference shouldn't be pressed, though, because faithfulness stems from belief; and belief engenders faithfulness. Here it seems that believing produces brotherhood; and "in Christ" doesn't indicate Christ as the object of belief so much as it indicates the union with Christ that believing in him effects. This union effects, in turn, the union of fellow believers with one another as brothers (compare 1:4; Ephesians 1:1 and the emphasis in Ephesians 2:8 on salvation "through faith [= belief]"). For the rest of this greeting ("Grace and peace . . .") see the comments on Romans 1:7; 1 Peter 1:2; 2 John 3.

1:3–8: We [Paul and Timothy] **are always thanking God, the Father of our Lord, Jesus Christ, when praying for you, ⁴having heard about your faith in Christ Jesus and** [about] **the love that you have for all the saints ⁵because of the hope reserved for you in heaven, which** [hope] **you heard about earlier in the word of the truth of the gospel ⁶that has come to you just as also in all the world it is bearing fruit and growing, just as also among you** [it has been bearing fruit and growing] **since the day you heard** [the gospel] **and came to know God's grace in truth, ⁷just as you learned** [the gospel] **from Epaphras, our beloved fellow slave, who is the Christ's faithful servant on our behalf, ⁸the one who has also indicated to us your love in the Spirit.** Paul's and Timothy's "thanking God" because of having heard about the Colossians' faith and love compliments the Colossians at the same time that it gives credit to God for their faith and love. "Always" enhances the compliment as well as the crediting, and the compliment aims for a favorable reception of the letter. The description of God as "the Father of our Lord, Jesus Christ" supplements the description of him in 1:2 as "our Father" but distinguishes Jesus Christ's sonship to God as divine. He's "our Lord," though he and we have the same Father. "When praying for you" adds concern to thankfulness for the Colossians. The mention of this concern should likewise make for their favorable reception of the letter. "Having heard" implies that neither Paul nor Timothy founded the church in Colossae (compare Ephesians 1:15). No wonder, then, the efforts of Paul to gain a favorable reception for his letter.

"About your faith in Christ Jesus" supports the translation "believing brothers in Christ" back in 1:2, for "faith" and "belief" go back to the same Greek word (see the comments on 1:2 for "in Christ Jesus"). Since love includes deeds done for the benefit of those who are loved (1 John 3:16–18) and since faith works through love (Galatians 5:6), Paul adds to the Colossians' faith in Christ Jesus "the love" that according to report they "have for all the saints." Since love includes beneficial deeds, as just noted, "for all the saints" probably means for all fellow Christians in Colossae, though hospitality to fellow Christians passing through Colossae may be included. See further the initial comments on Ephesians 1:15–19. "Because of the hope reserved for you in heaven" identifies the basis of the Colossians' faith and love. "Hope" completes the triad of cardinal Christian virtues (1 Thessalonians 1:3; 5:8 and, in a different order, 1 Corinthians 13:13; Galatians 5:5–6) and refers to the confidence of entering eternal life at Jesus' second coming. Such confidence undergirds faith and love. "Reserved for you in heaven" doesn't mean you'll go to heaven to enjoy eternal life there. For your bodies will be resurrected to enjoy eternal life on a renewed earth (Romans 8:18–25). "Hope" stands for the eternal life that's hoped for, and it's reserved in heaven in the sense that eternal life is being kept safe till as believers in Christ you start enjoying it at the second coming, resurrection, and renewal of the earth (see also 1 Peter 1:3–5; Revelation 21:1–4). The Colossians heard about this hope "earlier," that is, when "the word [= the message]" characterized by "the truth" that's contained in "the gospel" came to them, that is, into their hearing. "Just as also in all the world it is bearing fruit and growing" implies that the gospel is doing so in Colossae ("also"). But to keep the Colossians from falling prey to false doctrines which according to 2:4, 8, 16–23 are circulating among them, Paul emphasizes the gospel's bearing fruit and growing "in *all* the world." That is to say, "Don't trade the universal gospel for a local aberration."

In 1:10 Paul will explain fruit-bearing in terms of good deeds, and growing in terms of increase in the knowledge of God. "Just as also among you" makes explicit the implication of the earlier phrase, "just as *also* in all the world," and uses the gospel's fruit-bearing and growing among the Colossians up to this point as a deterrent against the possibility of falling prey to false doctrines that wouldn't bear the fruit of good deeds or advance the knowledge of God. "Since the day you heard it [the gospel]" underscores the gospel's effects as a deterrent by calling attention to their immediacy and continuance. "And came to know God's grace" refers to conversion as both an understanding and an experiencing of God's ill-deserved favor, the favor consisting in "the hope reserved . . . in heaven" and received by "faith in Christ Jesus." This grace makes for good news (the meaning of "gospel"). "In truth" probably tells how the Colossians came to know God's grace—that is, truly as opposed to falsely supposed knowledge in the acceptance of false doctrines—but knowing truly rests on believing "the word *of the truth* of the gospel."

"Just as you learned [the gospel] from Epaphras" parallels "just as also among you [the gospel has been bearing fruit and growing since the day you heard it]" and thereby indicates that Epaphras evangelized Colossae. Because he did, Paul calls him "our [referring to Paul and Timothy] beloved fellow slave"—a *"fellow* slave" because he as well as they are slaving for the Lord, Jesus Christ, in the work of evangelism (4:12–13) and because he (Epaphras) has joined Paul in prison (Philemon 23). The brotherly love Paul and Timothy feel for Epaphras, one of the Colossians' own number (4:12), establishes rapport with the Colossians through Epaphras. "The Christ" (Greek) means "the Messiah" (Hebrew) or, literally, "the Anointed One." So "who is the Christ's faithful servant" alludes to Jesus' messianic office, which makes having a servant appropriate, and describes Epaphras as faithful in having served the gospel of the Christ to

the Colossians. "On our behalf" indicates that Epaphras evangelized Colossae in place of Paul and Timothy, who had never gone to Colossae. The phrase may also imply that Paul and Timothy evangelized Colossae through the agency of Epaphras, who was very possibly their convert during the evangelization of Ephesus, 120 miles west of Colossae (Acts 19). "The one who has also [in addition to having evangelized you] indicated to us your love in the Spirit" (1) alludes to the Colossians' earlier-mentioned "love" that they "have for all the saints"; (2) states that Epaphras has delivered to Paul and Timothy a report of this love, which therefore they've "heard about"; and (3) locates the Colossians' love "in the Spirit" (for love is the first-mentioned "fruit of the Spirit" [Galatians 5:22], Paul has just talked about the gospel's bearing fruit among the Colossians, and they're in the Spirit, where the love is [Romans 8:9]).

1:9–12: **Because of this** [Epaphras's report] **we also, since the day we heard** [about your "love in the Spirit"], **don't stop praying for you and asking that you be filled with the knowledge of his** [God's] **will in all Spiritual wisdom and insight** [10]**so as to walk around** [= behave] **worthily of the Lord** [= Jesus Christ] **for the purpose and with the result of** [giving him] **all pleasure by** [your] **bearing fruit in all good work and by growing in the knowledge of God** [11]**while being empowered with all power in accordance with the might of his glory for the purpose and with the result of** [producing in you] **all perseverance and patience as with joy** [12]**you're giving thanks to the Father, who has qualified you for a portion of the allotment of the saints in the light . . . .** "We also . . . don't stop praying for you" picks up "when praying for you" in 1:3 and, yet again to ensure the letter's favorable reception, enhances the praying by describing it as constant ("don't stop") and petitionary ("asking") as well as thankful (so 1:3). "That you be filled with the knowledge of his will" refers to God's will (as later clarified by the phrase, "in the knowledge of God," but see already in 1:6 "you . . . came to know God's grace in truth"). The will of God is that his saints behave well (for the details of which see 3:1–4:6 and Ephesians 4:1–6:9, especially 5:17). To be "filled" with the knowledge of God's will is both to know about it fully and to carry it out fully, this in opposition to the intellectual and behavioral deficit of knowledge in false doctrines. "In all Spiritual wisdom and insight" escalates being filled to the nth degree and adds the practicality of wisdom and the discernment of insight to the informational and experiential components of knowledge. "Spiritual" describes the wisdom and insight as deriving, like the love in 1:8, from the Holy Spirit. No need, then, to listen to false teachers. "So as to walk around worthily of the Lord" identifies good behavior as the outcome, almost as the definition, of being filled with the knowledge of God's will. "Worthily of the Lord" implies that the Lord, Jesus Christ, is worthy of good behavior on the part of Christians, his slaves (compare Ephesians 4:1). For "the Lord" connotes the owner and master of slaves.

In addition to having "*all* Spiritual wisdom and insight," as the Lord's slaves Christians should give him "*all* pleasure by bearing fruit in *all* good work and by growing in the knowledge of God while being empowered with *all* power in accordance with the might of his glory for the purpose and result of *all* perseverance and patience." "All good work" means "every kind of good deed" and defines fruit-bearing. "Growing in the knowledge of God" counteracts decreasing in the knowledge of him through succumbing to false doctrines. The redundancy in "while being em*powered* with all *power*" accents the need of growth in the knowledge of God to enable resistance to those doctrines. "With the *might* of his glory" strengthens the accent, and the addition of "his glory" to "the might" (rather than a simple "his might") anticipates "the hope of glory" (1:27) at the Lord's second advent (3:4 [compare Ephesians 1:18–20]). This coming glory should make Christians mighty in their resistance to false doctrines. Paul puts this resistance in terms of perseverance and patience coupled with joyful thanksgiving for the coming glory, which Paul identifies as "a portion [your own individual share] of the allotment [compare the allotments in the land of Canaan to the tribes of Israel (Joshua 13–21)] of the saints [considered collectively as God's new people] in the light [a figure of speech for the kingdom of God's Son as opposed to 'the authority of the darkness' in 1:13–14, so that 'in the light' tells the whereabouts of 'a portion of the allotment' (compare 'the hope reserved for you in heaven' [1:5] and the comments on Ephesians 5:8–10 for 'the light')]." There's a wordplay in Paul's Greek between "joy" (*charas*) and "giving thanks" (*eucharistountes*). The wordplay underlines the God-given power to combine perseverance and patience with thanksgiving and joy. "To the Father, who has qualified you" implies that by qualifying you God has acted as a father to you, his children; and since "has qualified" connotes sufficiency, his qualifying you means that he has given you a sufficient amount of perseverance and patience to inherit "the allotment of the saints in the light," the promise of which allotment gives reason for perseverance and patience along with joyful thanksgiving.

THE PREEMINENCE OF CHRIST
IN CHRISTIAN DOCTRINE
Colossians 1:13–2:23

As does Ephesians, Colossians falls into two main sections, the first primarily doctrinal and the second primarily hortatory.

CHRIST'S CREATIVE AND REDEMPTIVE WORK
Colossians 1:13–23

That the start of the doctrinal section ("who . . .") is grammatically tied to Paul's and Timothy's preceding prayer for the Colossians (1:9–12) attests to what was noted in the introduction to Colossians, namely, that the prayer shades almost imperceptibly into the doctrinal section.

1:13–14: **who** [referring back to "the Father" in 1:12] **rescued us out from the authority of the darkness and transferred** [us] **into the kingdom of the Son of his love,** [14]**in whom we have redemption, the forgiveness of sins** . . . . "The darkness" represents immoral behavior, and its "authority" refers to the hold such behavior gets on people (see Ephesians 4:17–24). "Rescued us" implies deliverance from its authority, and also the authority's leading us to no good end—indeed, to the eventual suffering of "God's wrath" (3:6). So we've been rescued both from the present hold of darkness and from the future suffering of God's wrath. The rescue is supplemented by transferral "into the kingdom of the Son of his [God the Father's] love." The personification of love as a father underlines God's love for his Son and therefore underlines God's love for us as well, for as believers we are in Christ the Son ("*in whom* we have redemption"). Paul will later speak of "God's kingdom" (4:11), but here he speaks of the Son's kingdom; for God and his Son, seated at God's right hand (3:1), share rulership (Ephesians 5:5). And since the life of believers "has been hidden with the Christ in God" (3:3), transferral into the kingdom of God's Son doesn't imply *subjection* to his rule (however true that may be according to other passages)—rather, *participation* in his rule, which participation fits nicely with the immediately mentioned redemption. For "redemption" means liberation from slavery, and our having redemption in Christ means experiencing liberation from enslavement to the authority of the darkness so as to participate in the Son's kingly rule over the evil to which we used to be enslaved. Our redemption equates with our rescue, in other words. But Paul adds another equation, that of "the forgiveness of sins" with "redemption." By definition, "forgiveness" means "dismissal." So it's the dismissal of our sins from us, the severing of their connection with us, that constitutes the flip side of redemption. Their dismissal cancels our guilt *for* committing them as well as ending our enslavement *in* committing them.

1:15–16: **who** [referring to the Son] **is the image of the invisible God, the firstborn of all creation,** [16]**because in him were created all things in heaven and on earth, the visible things and the invisible things, whether thrones or lordships or rulerships or authorities. All things exist as created through him and for him.** By virtue of incarnation, the Son is the visible image of the otherwise invisible God. "The firstborn of all creation" doesn't mean that the Son was the first to be created, because this passage goes on to say that he created all things as opposed to being created himself. "Firstborn" sometimes lost both its temporal and its biological meanings so as to be used as a figure of speech for the highest possible status, as in Psalm 89:27: "I will also make him firstborn, the highest of the earth's kings" (see also Genesis 49:3). So some translations have "the firstborn *over* all creation." But there may be more. Just as firstborn sons enjoyed higher status than their brothers, so too they got the largest share of family inheritance (a double portion according to Deuteronomy 21:15–17;

compare the use of "firstborn" by Philo, a first-century Jewish philosopher, in his work, *Who Is the Heir?* 117–119). "The firstborn of all creation" may allude, then, to God the Father's giving his Son "all creation" as an inheritance (compare the later statement, "All things exist as created . . . for him"). "*All* creation" would then mark an enlargement of the usual double portion—naturally, since Christ's sonship to God is unique. Paul ascribes the Son's status as firstborn to the creation of all things "in him." It's tempting to translate with "*by* him" instead of "*in* him," but that would destroy the parallel with "all things cohere in him" in 1:17. So the creation of all things in him probably means that he's the source of their existence just as in 1:17 he'll be portrayed as the source of their sustenance.

The three occurrences in this paragraph of "all things," to be followed in succeeding paragraphs by several more occurrences, emphasize that nothing was created apart from the Son. Reinforcing this emphasis are the additions to "all things" of "in heaven and on earth," of "the visible things [on earth] and the invisible things [in heaven]," and of "whether thrones or lordships or rulerships or authorities [which in view of 'the authority of the darkness' in 1:13 as well as predominant usage elsewhere (see Romans 8:38; 1 Corinthians 15:24; and especially Ephesians 1:20–21; 3:10; 6:12) probably refer to angelic spirits, often deified and associated with the stars]." Could it be that false teachers in Colossae assigned parts of the universe to these spirits, so that Paul is counteracting such teachers by assigning the very existence of the spirits to the Son's creation of them? "Through him" makes the Son his Father's agent in creation, and "for him" makes him his Father's point in creation, the why and wherefore of creation, perhaps in the sense of making him the heir of all things. So the one who rescued us and in whom we have redemption (1:13–14) has enemies but no rivals, a blessed assurance of those who by faith are in him.

This assurance continues in *1:17–18a*: **And he himself** [the Son] **is prior to all things, and all things cohere in him.** [18a]**And he himself is the head of the body, the church . . . .** The temporal priority of the Son to all things, which have already been ascribed to his creation of them, confirms that "the firstborn of all creation" (1:15) didn't mean he was the first to be created. As explained earlier, the coherence of all things in him means he's the source of their sustenance, indeed continuance, as an ordered universe. As "the head of the body" he exercises supervisory authority over the church, just as physiologically speaking the head determines the activities of the body (compare the topmost position of the head, a position representing authority). Two occurrences of "he *himself* is" imply "he and no created thing is" and therefore stress that no rivals to him arise out of the created order.

1:18b–20: **who** [referring to the Son] **is the beginning, the firstborn** [resurgent] **from among the dead, so that in all things he might become the holder of first place,** [19]**because in him all the fullness** [of God] **was pleased to dwell** [20]**and through him to reconcile all things to him by making peace through the blood of his cross** [= the blood shed by the Son on his cross], **through him whether the things on earth or the things in heaven.** After the interlude of 1:17–18b, "who is the beginning" makes a new start reminiscent of "who is the image of the invisible God" (1:15). But the followup, "the firstborn [resurgent] from among the dead," differs from the first followup, "the firstborn of all creation," to shift attention from the Son's creatorship (as summarized in 1:17: "And he himself is prior to all things, and all things cohere in him") to the Son's headship (as introduced in 1:18a: "And he himself is the head of the body, the church"). Now "firstborn" returns to its original temporal meaning, though the biological meaning is still missing. The reference is to the Son's resurrection from among the dead as "the beginning" of the resurrection (compare 1 Corinthians 15:20: "Christ was raised from among the dead as the firstfruits of those who've fallen asleep"). The purpose behind his resurrection was that "in all things," which he'd created, "he might become the holder of first place." The wordplay between "the *first*born from among the dead" and "the holder of *first* place" emphasizes this purpose. Since the Son holds first place, those who make up the church needn't kowtow even to angels (see 2:18–19).

Providing the reason the Son's resurrection had the purpose of his holding first place is that "in him all the fullness was pleased to dwell." In other words, the entirety of God delighted to indwell him. Since by itself "fullness" indicates entirety, the addition of "all" to "the fullness" highlights God's entirety. Apart from this fullness, the Son wouldn't be "the head of the body, the church" (1:18a). All the fullness of God was also pleased to reconcile all things to the Son by making peace through the blood of his cross. Because "God's wrath is coming" (3:6), this reconciliation can't mean universal salvation. It must therefore mean, as Paul himself says, universal pacification ("making peace"), which includes salvation for believers, defeat for others (including hostile spirits according to 2:15), and the renewal of creation (if Romans 8:18–22 is brought into the picture). The Son's sacrificial death, represented by "the blood of his cross," made possible this pacification (compare 1:14; 2:14; Ephesians 1:7; 2:13, 16). For emphasis, "through him" reprises "through the blood of his cross"; and "whether the things on earth or the things in heaven" reemphasizes the pacificatory reconciliation of all things. The placement in 1:16 of the created things in heaven before the created things on earth corresponded to the order in Genesis 1:1. Because the Son shed his blood here on earth, though, the pacification of the things on earth is here placed before the pacification of the things in heaven.

1:21–23: **And you, once upon a time** [prior to your conversion] **being alienated** [from God (compare Ephesians 4:18)] **and hostile** [to him] **so far as** [your] **intellect was concerned,** [as evident] **in** [your] **evil deeds** [for what people do reflects what they think]—²²**but** [despite your hostility] **he has now reconciled** [you] [to himself] **in the body** [consisting] **of his** [the Son's] **flesh through death to present you** [to himself as] **sacred and blameless and unaccusable in his sight,** ²³**if indeed you stay founded and settled on the faith and not being shifted away from the hope** [consisting] **in the gospel that you heard,** [the gospel] **that has been proclaimed in all the creation under heaven, a server of which** [gospel] **I, Paul, have become.** "In the body [consisting] of his [the Son's] flesh" (1) distinguishes "the body" here from "the body, the church" in 1:18; (2) makes clear a literal rather than figurative meaning; (3) complements "through the blood of his [the Son's] cross"; and (4) thus implies the violent separation of Christ's blood and flesh (as represented in the Eucharist [see 1 Corinthians 11:23–27]). Consequently, "through death" means "through a *sacrificial* death." (All sacrificial deaths are violent, though not all violent deaths are sacrificial.) "To present you [as] sacred" means "to present you as consecrated to God." "Blameless" means not to be blamed by God, and "unaccusable" means not to be successfully accused by others or, in particular, by the Devil, whose very name means "accuser." But such a presentation is conditioned by "stay[ing] founded . . . on the faith," which in view of 1:4; 2:5, 7, 12 means "grounded in your belief," not in the faith as a body of doctrine. To stress the need of such stable faith Paul adds "indeed" to "if," adds "and settled" to "founded," and adds "not being shifted away" to "founded and settled." "From the hope" means "from your confidence." "In the gospel" tells the proper location of confidence. "That you heard" specifies the gospel by which you were converted, as opposed to new-fangled doctrines being peddled among you by false teachers (2:6–23). Also in opposition to those doctrines, "that has been proclaimed in all the creation under heaven" celebrates this gospel as universal rather than local (compare 1:6). The meaning isn't that every creature has heard the gospel. Paul has yet to proclaim it in Spain, for example (Romans 15:23–24). So he means that the proclamation of it knows no boundaries on earth. "A server of which [gospel] I, Paul, have become" puts on it the imprimatur of Paul as a church-wide apostle in contrast with false teachers local to Colossae. Both because of those teachers and because of Paul's not having evangelized Colossae, the Colossians needed to hear his imprimatur on what they'd originally heard from Epaphras and believed (1:7).

PAUL'S PROCLAMATION OF CHRIST
Colossians 1:24–2:5

1:24–26a: **I'm now rejoicing in** [my] **sufferings for you, and in** [Christ's] **stead I'm filling up in my flesh the insufficiencies of the afflictions of the Christ**—[I'm filling them up] **on behalf of his body, which is the church,** ²⁵**a servant of which I became in accordance with God's administration, given to me for you, to fulfill God's word,** ²⁶ᵃ**the secret that was hidden from the ages** [past] **and from the generations** [past]. The sufferings of Paul stem from his proclamation of the gospel. Since this proclamation has effected the conversion of many, he rejoices in his evangelistic sufferings; and since he's writing from prison, "now" accents the joy he feels in such sufferings. But in view of his not having evangelized Colossae, what should we make of "for you." Half the answer lies in 1:27, where Paul will speak of God's will that Gentiles be converted, and the other half in 1:7, where Paul spoke of the Colossians' having learned the gospel from Epaphras. Paul had an apostolic commission to evangelize Gentiles (see Ephesians 3:1–9; Galatians 1:15–16a among other passages), and the description in 3:5–11 of the Colossians' pre-Christian behavior points to a Gentile pedigree for at least most of them (compare Ephesians 2). So "for you" describes Paul's evangelistic sufferings as for the conversion of Gentiles such as the Colossians and in particular for the Colossian Gentiles because he grandfathered their church through Epaphras (compare the comments on 1:7). "I'm filling up *in my flesh* the insufficiencies of the afflictions of the Christ" draws a parallel with God's having reconciled the Colossians to himself "in the body [consisting] *of his* [Christ's] *flesh*" (1:22). "In [his] stead" reinforces the parallel, and "filling up . . . the insufficiencies" means making up for them.

But what are the Christ's "afflictions," and in what respect are they insufficient? They're the afflictions he feels in the persecution of Christians (Acts 9:1–5; 22:4–8; 26:9–15), and especially in the persecution of Paul and company (2 Corinthians 1:5–6; 4:10–12). The insufficiencies of these afflictions consist in the necessity of suffering further afflictions in the cause of Christian evangelism. For there's more evangelism to be done. "In behalf of his [the Christ's] body, which is the church" is explained by Paul's having become "a servant" of the church, which parallels his having become "a server" of the gospel (1:23). He serves the church by serving the gospel on the church's behalf. That is, he represents the church in his evangelistic labors. "In accordance with God's administration" alludes to a divine commission (see Galatians 1:15–16a again). "Given to me for you" portrays the commission as for the benefit of Gentiles, such as the Colossians. "To fulfill God's word" defines the administration given to Paul and means to proclaim the gospel. Apart from its proclamation it doesn't reach its potential. God's word isn't the Bible or any part thereof. It's "the secret" which Paul will identify in 1:26b–29 and whose past hiddenness he emphasizes with two phrases, "from the ages and from the generations." The emphasis plays up what he's about to call "the wealth of the glory of this secret."

1:26b–29: **But now it** [the secret] **has been disclosed to his saints,** ²⁷**to whom God willed to make known among the Gentiles what** [is] **the wealth of the glory of this secret, which** [secret] **is Christ in you,** [Christ] **the hope of glory,** ²⁸**whom we are proclaiming by admonishing every human being and teaching every human being in all wisdom in order that we may present every human being** [as] **mature in Christ,** ²⁹**to** which [end] **I'm also laboring, struggling in accordance with his working that is at work in me in power.** "But now" draws a contrast with the just-mentioned "ages" and "generations" past. The secret that has now been disclosed to God's saints—that is, to Christians as consecrated to him—is "Christ in you." God's willing to make known this secret "among the Gentiles" parallels the disclosure of it "to his saints." Combined with the secret's definition as "Christ in you," the parallel puts the primary focus on the location of Christ in Gentile saints such as those in Colossae, who make up at least the bulk of the church there. "The wealth" describes "the glory" of this secret as of great volume in that the secret includes Gentile as well as Jewish believers. "The glory" describes "the secret" as consisting in "the hope of glory," that is, in the confidence of what Paul in 3:4 will call the Colossians' being "manifested with [Christ] in glory" at the second coming (compare the glory of Christians' resurrected bodies on that occasion according to 1 Corinthians 15:43; 2 Corinthians 4:17; Philippians 3:21). As Christians are in Christ through the agency of his Spirit, so Christ is in them through his Spirit's agency. His Spirit indwells them both, so that they indwell each other (see especially Romans 8:1–11, but also 2 Corinthians 13:5; Galatians 2:20; 4:19; Ephesians 3:17).

Paul and Timothy's proclaiming "Christ in you" as "the hope of glory" specifies the way "God willed to make known [this secret] among the Gentiles." The proclamation consists in admonishment (putting it into the hearers' minds to believe in the now-disclosed secret) and teaching (explaining the secret so as to enable belief in it). The twofold use of "every human being" as the object of "admonishing" and "teaching" includes Jews as well as Gentiles, so that "every human being" may mean "every kind of human being." "In all wisdom" implies the entire foolishness of the false doctrines circulating in Colossae and describes Paul's and Timothy's admonition and teaching as leading along the right path. The purpose of such admonition and teaching is to present to God at the Last Judgment "every [kind of] human being [as] mature in Christ"—that is, as *in* Christ by faith and as *mature* in him by having stayed "founded and settled on [their] faith" rather than "being shifted away from the hope [consisting] in the gospel" (1:23). To impress on the Colossians the high level of his concern that they not succumb to false doctrines and fail to attain such maturity in Christ, Paul underlines his "laboring," which itself connotes hard toil, with the addition of "struggling," which escalates the labor to a fight against false doctrines and their perpetrators. "In accordance with his working" enlists Christ as Paul's commander in the fight. "That is at work in me in power" then assures the Colossians that Paul will win this fight, so that they should stick with him on the winning side (compare 1 Timothy 4:1–10).

2:1–3: For I want you to know how great a struggle I'm having in your behalf and [in behalf of] **the** [saints] **in Laodicea and as many** [saints] **as haven't seen my face in the flesh,** ²**in order that their hearts may be encouraged,** [they and you] **being compacted together**

in love [compare 3:14], **and for all the wealth of the full assurance of insight,** [that is,] **for the knowledge of God's secret,** [namely] **Christ,** ³**in whom are hidden all the treasures of wisdom and knowledge** [compare 1:9–10, 26–27; Proverbs 2:1–8]. This sentence elaborates Paul's struggling (1:29). "I want you to know" impresses on the Colossians the concern he has for them. Knowing his concern for them will make them take his letter seriously. "*How great* a struggle" accents Paul's high degree of concern to elevate the degree of their seriousness. "In your behalf" pinpoints the Colossians as objects of his concern (contrast the generalizing "every human being" in 1:28). An addition of "the [saints] in Laodicea" brings Christians in a nearby city (about 12 miles away) under the umbrella of Paul's beneficial "struggle" and anticipates the instruction in 4:16 that this letter to the Colossians be read also to the Laodiceans. The present statement will then inform the Laodiceans that Paul's great struggle is for them as well as for the Colossians. "And as many [saints] who haven't seen my face in the flesh [that is, who haven't seen me face to face]" includes at least the saints in Hieropolis (another city near Colossae), whom Paul will mention in 4:13, and perhaps also saints in yet other cities among which the letter called "Ephesians" was being circulated (see the introduction to Ephesians). He wants all of them to know how great is his struggle for them "in order that their hearts may be encouraged," the heart being considered a center of thought, will, and emotions. If Paul is struggling greatly for their benefit, they should take courage to maintain their faith in the gospel and not be diverted to false teachings. "Being compacted together in love" puts forward loving one another for a united front in resisting such teachings. "For all the wealth of the full assurance of insight" tells the purpose of being encouraged, which purpose is then rephrased: "for the knowledge of God's secret, [namely] Christ." In combination these phrases mean that Paul is struggling in this very letter to assure the saints who'll hear it read to them that in the gospel concerning Christ they already know everything needed for salvation and Christian life. Emphasizing the plenitude of this knowledge is the mention first of "*all* the *wealth*" consisting of "the *full* assurance" that comes from "*insight*"; and as if that emphasis weren't enough, Paul adds that in Christ as God's secret "are hidden *all* the *treasures* of *wisdom* and [again] *knowledge*." So pay no attention to false teaching concerning "thrones or lordships or rulerships or authorities" (1:16 [compare 2:8, 15, 18]). No treasures of wisdom and knowledge are hidden in them!

2:4–5: I'm saying this [that in Christ are hidden all the treasures of wisdom and knowledge] **in order that no one may be duping you with a specious argument** [to the opposite effect, namely, that there's further salvific wisdom and knowledge to be found outside the person and word of Christ]. ⁵**For even though I'm away** [from you] **so far as the flesh is concerned, I'm nevertheless with you so far as the Spirit is concerned, rejoicing and seeing** [as I do] **your orderliness and the stability of**

your faith in Christ. Paul's fleshly absence from the Colossians explains why he's saying what he says in a letter rather than in person. A contrast with the body would favor a reference to Paul's human spirit (as in 1 Corinthians 5:3). But the contrast with flesh favors a reference to God's Spirit (as in Galatians 5:16–25). It is through the eyes of the Spirit that Paul rejoices to see the Colossians' orderliness and stability (for the Spirit portrayed as eyes, see Zechariah 4:1–10). "Orderliness" means alignment with "God's secret, [namely] Christ" (2:2). "Stability" describes the Colossians' "faith in Christ" in a way just opposite of "being wave-tossed and carried about by every wind of doctrine in the wiliness of human beings in trickery resulting in an artifice of error" (Ephesians 4:4). Paul's rejoicing to see this orderliness and stability pays the Colossians a compliment that like other compliments in the letter is designed to gain for it a favorable reception (compare 1:3–8).

CHRIST'S SUFFICIENCY OVER AGAINST FALSE TEACHINGS IN COLOSSAE
Colossians 2:6–23

2:6–7: **Therefore** [given the possibility of someone's duping you and my presence with you so far as the Spirit is concerned], **as you received the Christ, Jesus the Lord, keep walking around in him,** 7**rooted and being built up in him and being established** [in him] **as to** [your] **faith (just as you were taught), flourishing in thanksgiving** [compare 1:10–12]. Here Paul tells the Colossians to add behavior in Christ to faith in Christ, and to make this addition as a natural followup to their original reception of Christ, whom Paul calls "*the* Christ" and identifies as "Jesus *the Lord*" to stress Jesus' messianic and divine authority to govern the behavior of believers in him. For the Colossians' original reception of Christ, Paul uses a verb that connotes the reception of a tradition that's being passed on—here, the Christ, Jesus the Lord, as an item of tradition contrasting with an upcoming tradition of human beings (2:8–10). As often, "walking around" stands for behavior, and "in him" makes Christ the setting that determines behavior as well as faith. "Rooted . . . in him" harks back to reception of Christ by faith in him as the basis of behavior in him. "Being built up in him" switches from a horticultural metaphor to one of construction, and from a past event that has a continuing result (rootedness) to an ongoing action. To keep from being duped, Christians need to be built up constantly. Likewise in regard to "being established," which means to be constantly confirmed as to faith in and conformity with original teaching as opposed to newfangled doctrines. So Paul has returned to orthodoxy (right doctrine) as the basis of orthopraxy (right behavior). "Thanksgiving" for all the treasures of wisdom and knowledge that you have in Christ will keep you from any dissatisfaction that would open your heart to false doctrines. "Flourishing" heightens the thanksgiving to a point where it excludes such dissatisfaction entirely.

2:8–10: **Be watching out lest anyone be your captor through philosophy and empty deceit in accordance with the tradition of human beings,** [that is,] **in accordance with the elements of the world and not in accordance with Christ,** 9**because in him dwells all the fullness of the Deity bodily;** 10**and you're filled in him, who is the head of every rulership and authority . . . .** The threat of a false teacher, whom Paul compares to a captor (somebody who takes you as a prisoner of war with his false teaching), requires constant vigilance. Paul calls the false teaching "philosophy" because this term means "love of wisdom" and he has recently said by contrast that in Christ are hidden "all the treasure of wisdom and knowledge" (2:3). True philosophy should love the wisdom that's in Christ, then. But the philosophy of the teachers Paul warns against carries "deceit," not wisdom. This deceit is "empty" of the wisdom that's in Christ, because the would-be captor is peddling "the tradition of human beings" rather than "the Christ, Jesus the Lord," whom you received as an item of divinely originated tradition (2:6–7). This tradition of human beings is their teaching that "the elements of the world"—earth, air, fire, and water—are divine, so that human beings are bound to live under the regulations of these deified elements (associated with but probably to be distinguished from the apparently heavenly though likewise deified "thrones," "lordships," "rulerships," and "authorities" of 1:16). "And not in accordance with Christ" indicates that there can be no blending of homage to the deified elements with adherence to Christ, "because in him dwells all the fullness of the Deity bodily." It's his body, not the elements of the world, where the Deity dwells, as in a temple—"all the fullness of the Deity," so that no supplement of deity is needed from earth, air, fire, or water (compare the comments on Galatians 4:3, 9). As in 1:19, the redundancy of "*all* the *fullness*" stresses that there's no lack of the Deity in Christ. He's no inferior deity to be compared with the world's elements. "And you're filled in him" means that since you're in Christ and the fullness of the Deity dwells in him, you too were filled with the Deity at your conversion and continue to live in a state of such fullness. Not that you have become divine yourself, of course—rather, in the person of the divine Christ you're filled with the Deity. And because all the fullness of the Deity indwells Christ bodily, he's "the head of every rulership and authority." Just as "he himself is the head of the body" means that he has authority over the church (1:18), so he has authority over every rulership and authority (see the comments on 1:16 for their identity as angelic spirits). All rule and authority belong to him. The so-called rulerships and authorities are no deities, not even of a subaltern sort. They're only creatures.

2:11–12: **in whom** [referring to Christ] **also** [in addition to being "filled in him" (2:10)] **you were circumcised with a circumcision not handmade in the divesting of the body of flesh in the circumcision of the Christ,** 12**when buried with him in baptism, in which you were also raised together with** [him] **through**

[your] **faith in the working of God, who raised him from among the dead.** "A circumcision not *hand*made" means a circumcision not *man*made—therefore *God*-made. Manmade circumcision consists in the divesting of foreskin, a small piece of flesh. The circumcision Paul is speaking about consists in "the divesting of the *body* of flesh." But whose body of flesh? Paul answers, "in the circumcision of the Christ," which corresponds to Christ's "body of flesh" (1:22) and to the dwelling in him of all the fullness of the Deity "bodily" (2:9). Since earlier on, "through death" immediately followed "in the body of his flesh" and since burial immediately follows divestiture in the present passage, it's easy to understand that here the divesting of Christ's body of flesh refers to his death on a cross, already mentioned in 1:20 and about to be mentioned again in 2:14. In other words, Paul compares the death of Christ to a circumcision of his whole body and, furthermore, includes Christians in such a circumcision of Christ because they're in Christ, so that God looks on them as having been crucified, "circumcised" whole-bodily, with Christ, as symbolically implied by burial in the waters of baptism (compare 2:20; Romans 6:3–11; Galatians 2:20). But since Christ didn't stay dead and since Christians don't stay under the waters of baptism but are raised up out of them, Paul adds that in baptism "you were also raised together with him [Christ]," so that despite the futurity of your body's resurrection, God looks on you and treats you not only as already dead and buried but also as already resurrected. "Through [your] faith" identifies the means by which you gained this status in Christ (compare Ephesians 2:8). Baptism portrayed the gaining of this status but didn't effect it. Faith did. "The working of God" identifies the object of your faith, and the description of him as the one "who raised him [Christ] from among the dead" identifies God's particular work that became the object of your faith (compare Romans 10:9: "and believe in your heart that God raised him from among the dead").

2:13–15: And you, being dead in trespasses and the uncircumcision of your flesh—he [God] made you alive together with him [Christ], when graciously forgiving all [our] trespasses for us, [14][that is,] when blotting out the certificate of indebtedness that was against us in respect to [God's] decrees [as to how we should behave], which [certificate] was opposed to us; and he has taken it out of the midst by nailing it to the cross. [15]By divesting the rulerships and the authorities he [God] disgraced [them] in public by triumphing over them in it [the cross]. In portraying our dying together with Christ as being "circumcised" in the circumcision of Christ (2:11–12), Paul was apparently saving the vocabulary of death for "being dead in trespasses." See the comments on Ephesians 2:1 for being dead in trespasses as a state of moral death prior to Christian conversion. Here Paul adds "and [in] the uncircumcision of your flesh" for an allusion to previous immorality as typical of Gentiles, such as at least a majority of the Colossians were (compare 1:27). See the initial comments on Ephesians 2:4–7 for God's having "made you

alive together with him [Christ]." Here Paul adds "when *graciously* forgiving *all* [our] trespasses for us," which defines what it means in Ephesians 2:5, 8 to be saved "by *grace*." The switch from "you" and "your" to "us" reflects the thankfulness of Paul for his own salvation by grace.

As in 1:14, "forgiveness" means "dismissal." So the dismissal of our trespasses from us, the severing of their connection with us, accompanied being made alive together with Christ. Paul portrays their dismissal as a "blotting out" of "the certificate of indebtedness," our IOU to God in which our trespasses counted as moral debts owed to him (compare Matthew 6:12, "And forgive our *debts* for us," with Luke 11:4, "And forgive our *sins* for us"). The certificate "was against us" in that our moral indebtedness was heading us toward the debtors' prison of God's coming wrath (3:6). "In respect to [God's] decrees" interprets the indebtedness in terms of trespassing against what God has decreed should characterize our behavior. "Which was opposed to us" repeats for emphasis that the moral indebtedness recorded on the certificate was heading us toward the debtors' prison of God's coming wrath. To the figure of blotting out that record Paul adds the figure of "tak[ing] it out of the midst [where it stood between God and us] by nailing it to the cross [so that it interpreted the crucifixion of Christ as his paying for us our debt of trespasses]." Then Paul turns attention back to the rulerships and authorities whose deification by pagans was adopted by the false teachers. Whereas crucifixion divested Christ of his body of flesh (2:11), God used that divestiture to divest the rulerships and authorities of their rule and authority. That is to say, Christ's crucifixion, which he suffered in the nude, was supposed to disgrace him in public; but God transformed it into a triumphal procession in which the rulerships and authorities were led, so to speak, as naked prisoners of war, their lack of deity exposed in the public proclamation of Christ as the only Lord and Savior.

2:16–17: Therefore no one is to be passing judgment on you in regard to food and in regard to drink or in the matter of a festival or of a new moon or of a Sabbath [day], **[17]which [matters] are a shadow of the things that were going to come; but the body [is] the Christ's.** "Therefore" uses God's having divested the rulerships and authorities as the basis of the command, "no one is to be passing judgment on you." Hence, the false teachers, whom Paul called the Colossians' would-be "captor[s]" (2:8), must have combined with their teaching concerning those pagan rulerships and authorities various Jewish practices concerning food, drink, festivals, new moons, and Sabbaths. Such practices were related to the Mosaic law, if not by way of wholesale prohibition (as regards food and drink) at least by way of implication (as regards ritual defilement [compare Daniel 1:8–16; Romans 14:1–13]). The false teachers' passing judgment on the Colossians probably means they're telling them that they'll go to hell if they don't follow these practices. Since Paul doesn't address the false teachers directly, his indirect command ("no one is to be passing judgment on you") aims at keeping the Colossians from taking seriously the false teachers' judgments. His description of the Jewish practices as "a shadow of the things that were going to come" means that those practices symbolized such things as abstinence from immorality and as the festivity and relief that have now come in the new era of Christ's gospel. "But the body [is] the Christ's" contrasts substance with shadow, reality with symbol, even fulfillment with promise. Because Paul has just mentioned food and drink and will shortly mention "unsparing [= ascetical] treatment of the body" (2:23), however, one wonders whether he means that since a Christian's body belongs to the Christ, it shouldn't be mistreated with asceticism (compare 1 Timothy 4:1–5).

2:18–19: No one is to be regulating you by indulging in humility and the homage of angels, spouting off about things that he has seen, being unwarrantedly puffed up by the mind of his flesh, ¹⁹and not holding fast the head [Christ], **by whom all the body, being supported and compacted together through** [its] **connections and ligaments, grows the growth of God.** A second indirect command ("No one is to be regulating you") aims at keeping the Colossians from taking seriously the false teachers' regulations. These teachers try to regulate the Colossians' practices by the influence of example. The mention of "humility" just before and in coordination with "homage of angels" probably interprets the homage as directed by the false teachers to angels rather than as directed by angels to God. For it would seem to go without saying that participation with angels in doing homage to God would entail humility. Since in Romans 8:38 Paul coordinates "angels" with "rulerships," says in 1 Corinthians 6:3 that Christians will judge angels, and in 2 Corinthians 11:14 calls Satan "an angel of light," in the present text "homage of angels" appears to mean homage to angelic rulerships and authorities; and the false teachers appear to be doing them homage in addition to obeying the supposed dictates of the world's elements. "*Indulging in* humility and the homage of angels" means going in for and getting religious pleasure out of such humility and homage.

"Spouting off about things that he has seen" refers to the contents of visions seen, or at least claimed to have been seen, during the course of doing homage to angels. "Spouting off" about those contents came from "being unwarrantedly puffed up [a figure of speech for getting stuck on oneself] by the mind of his flesh [his thoughts being weakly submissive to angels, since "flesh" connotes weakness]." So visions became the source of pride. Pride became the source of spouting off. And, ironically, the spouting off exposed feeblemindedness. "Unwarrantedly" describes the visions as worthless. "Not holding fast" implies both an initial or apparent holding and a letting go. "The head" refers to Christ as the authority in opposition to the false teachers' being puffed up by the mind of the flesh, and "all the body" stands for the church (1:18, 24; 3:15). A body grows as a result of ingesting food and drink through the mouth, located in the head. It's therefore by Christ as the church's head that

his body, the church, "grows the growth of God," which means producing for God the fruit of good deeds (1:6, 10; Ephesians 2:21; 4:15–16). "*All* the body" leaves no body part unsupported and uncompacted in the unity effected by Christ through the body's connections and ligaments. No help is needed from another source.

2:20–23: If you've died together with Christ [as you have, with the result of being freed] **from the world's elements** [whose regulations you used to obey], **why while living in the world are you submitting yourselves to decrees** [designed to placate those elements]—²¹**"You shouldn't handle** [this]; **you shouldn't taste** [that]; **you shouldn't touch** [such-and-such]," ²²**which things are all** [meant] **for dissolution by way of consumption** [because God provided them to be eaten, drunk, and otherwise used by human beings rather than avoided]—**in accordance with the** [ascetical] **commandments and teachings of human beings** [= not even of the world's supposedly authoritative elements, much less of God, and therefore certainly *un*authoritative (compare Mark 7:7; Matthew 15:9)], ²³**which** [commandments], **to be sure, have the reputation of wisdom** [as implied in "philosophy," meaning "the love of wisdom" (2:8), and as illustrated in "being *unwarrantedly* puffed up" (2:18)], **in indulgent homage** [to angels] **and humility** [before them] **having to do with unsparing** [ascetical] **treatment of the body** [by not handling, tasting, or touching what God has provided for food, drink, and other uses], **not with any value in relation to satedness of the flesh** [because God wants your body's flesh to be satisfied with food, drink, clothing, and other physical necessities (see 1 Timothy 4:3–5)]. "Died together with Christ" confirms that being circumcised "in the circumcision of the Christ" (2:11) had to do with his death as the cutting off of his whole body of flesh. The Colossians *are* living in the world, but they're to be living in it as *dead* in Christ to it, that is, as unresponsive to the decrees of its falsely deified elements. "Why . . . are you submitting yourselves to decrees [that require asceticism]?" implies that the false teachers have made inroads among the Colossians, so that Paul's earlier compliments of the Colossians represent their fundamental condition, whereas their submission to the decrees represents, thus far, an aberration. The commandments contained in the decrees "have the reputation of wisdom" in that many people think asceticism is a religiously wise lifestyle to practice whether or not they themselves practice it. "To be sure" underscores the wide extent of this reputation, but it's *only* a reputation. "Which things are *all* [meant] for dissolution by way of consumption" does away with the entirety of ascetical prohibitions.

THE PREEMINENCE OF CHRIST
IN CHRISTIAN CONDUCT
Colossians 3:1–4:6

Here begins the primarily hortatory main section of Colossians. Its exhortations are based on the doctrine spelled out in 1:13–2:23.

THE MENTAL APPLICATION OF UNION WITH CHRIST IN HIS DEATH, RESURRECTION, AND EXALTATION
Colossians 3:1–4

3:1–4: Therefore [given your having died together with Christ from the world's elements (2:20)] **if you've been raised together with the Christ, be seeking the things above, where the Christ is, sitting at God's right** [hand] [compare 2:12–13, 20; Ephesians 2:5–6; Romans 6:1–11; Galatians 2:20; Psalm 110:1]. **²Be thinking the things above, not the things on earth. ³For you've died, and your life is hidden together with the Christ in God. ⁴When the Christ, your life, is manifested, then you too will be manifested together with him in glory.** As in the case of having died together with Christ, "raised together with the Christ" has to do with the way God looks at you because of your being in Christ, who has already died and been raised. "*If* you've been raised" doesn't call in question your having been raised. It implies you should do something as a result of the fact you've been raised. Paul will list "the things above" in 3:12–4:6. They're "above" because they relate to Christ—and he's above, "sitting at God's right [hand]." So be seeking them because you've been raised together with the Christ. They're within reach. In Christ you are where they are, because "raised together with the Christ" includes exaltation to heaven as well as resurrection from among the dead. But finding the things above takes effort—hence the command to be seeking them. Seeking starts with thinking; for "as [a man] thinketh in his heart, so is he" (Proverbs 23:7 King James Version), and Paul's verb for thinking connotes an attitude favorable toward the objects of thought and therefore an attitude convertible into action. But you shouldn't be thinking favorably "the things on earth," which Paul will list in 3:5–9. Your death with Christ has put those things in your past. So they shouldn't even enter your thinking.

"Your life" alludes to your having been raised from death to life together with the Christ. "Is hidden" describes your life as yet to be manifested. "Together with the Christ" describes him too as yet to be manifested. "Hidden . . . in God" locates your life and the Christ for the time being—that is, till its and his manifestation—in "the invisible God" (1:15). Since it's together with the Christ that you've been raised from death to life, Paul designates "the Christ" as "your life"; and since this life is yours, Paul makes concurrent your manifestation and the Christ's manifestation. "In glory" identifies the circumstance of your and his manifestation in a way that dates the manifestation at the second coming and describes it as so resplendent as to provide plenty of motivation for seeking the things above, not the things below. For the association of glory with the second coming and attendant events, see 1:27 (where "hope" means confidence in the second coming); Romans 5:2; 8:18, 21; 1 Corinthians 15:43; 2 Corinthians 4:17; Titus 2:13.

THE APPLICATION OF DEATH WITH CHRIST TO SINFUL ACTIONS
Colossians 3:5–11

3:5–7: Therefore put to death [your body] **parts that are on earth: fornication, impurity, passion, bad lust, and prurience, which as such is idolatry, ⁶because of which things the wrath of God is coming, ⁷in which things even you walked around once upon a time,** [that is,] **when you were living in these things.** Your having died in God's point of view (3:3) means that in your conduct you should "put to death [your body] parts that are on the earth," which equate with "the things on the earth" that according to 3:2 you're not to "think." Paul is using "[your body] parts" as a figure of speech for the vices that he proceeds to list, because you use your body parts as instruments for the practice of those vices. "On earth" puts these figurative body parts in a location different from that of you yourself, for you've been raised together with the Christ to God's right hand in heaven above. Since your body parts stand for vices, the distance you should put between yourself and the vices is equivalent to the distance that separates heaven and earth.

More vices will be listed later, but those listed here all have to do with sexual immorality. They head the list and appear under no fewer than five designations because the strength of human libido makes illicit sex a matter of common occurrence. "Fornication" means sexual immorality in general, but refers especially to sexual intercourse in which one party is a prostitute. "Impurity" describes sexual immorality as moral defilement. "Passion" refers to out-of-control libido (compare Romans 1:26; 1 Thessalonians 4:5), and "lust" similarly to desire so strong that it leads to the trespassing of moral boundaries. Even by itself "lust" usually has this meaning, but here Paul adds "bad" to "lust" for emphasis on the harmful effects of sexual immorality. "Prurience" means greediness for more and more sexual gratification, a greediness that catapults a person into promiscuity. "Which as such is idolatry" compares such greediness to the worship of an idol, the idol of limitless sexual gratification. The comparison came easily to Paul, because lots of sexual immorality took place in and around pagan temples, which housed idols (compare the comments on Ephesians 4:19 [including the footnote]; 5:3–5; also 1 Corinthians 10:14, where in a discussion of sexual immorality Paul says to flee idolatry, and Galatians 5:20, where he lists idolatry right after three designations of sexual immorality). For the coming of God's wrath, see the comments on Ephesians 5:6; 1 Thessalonians 1:10. "In which things even you walked around once upon a time" parallels "when you were living in these things" and pictures the vices as the very habitat of the Colossians before their conversion—like living in a brothel, one might say. "*Even* you" underscores this reminder. "*Living* in these things" once upon a time makes it necessary to "put [them] *to death*" at the present time, and the earthly locale of living in them (compare 2:20) contrasts with the heavenly locale of "your life" that's "hidden together with the Christ in God" (3:3).

3:8–11: But now [as opposed to when you were living in these vices] **you, even you—put off all the** [following] **things: wrath, rage, malice, slander, shameful talk out of your mouth.** ⁹**Don't be lying to one another, since you've divested yourselves of the old human being together with his practices** ¹⁰**and have put on the new** [human being] **that's being renewed for the purpose and with the result of knowledge in accordance with the image of the one who created him,** ¹¹**where there's no Greek and** [no] **Jew,** [no] **circumcision and** [no] **uncircumcision,** [no] **barbarian,** [no] **Scythian,** [no] **slave,** [no] **free** [person]—**rather,** [where] **Christ** [is] **all things and in all.** "You, even you" pinpoints the Colossians as targets of Paul's subsequent exhortation. The figure of "put[ting] to death" (3:5–7) shifts to a figure of "put[ting] off," as when taking off dirty clothes, the following vices being compared to items of such clothing. "All" emphasizes that none of these vices should characterize Christian behavior. Their number as five implies that the five virtues to be listed in 3:12 ("affections of pity, magnanimity, humility, meekness, patience") should replace them. "Rage" arises out of "wrath," and "slander" out of "malice." For "shameful talk" see the comments on Ephesians 5:3–5. "Out of your mouth" seems almost to portray the tongue as clothed with slander and shameful talk. Paul turns from slander and shameful talk to untruthful talk in the command, "Don't be lying to one another" (compare Ephesians 4:25). As a rationale for the command, he says that "you've divested yourselves of the old human being together with his practices [such as lying] and have put on the new [human being]." Some commentators interpret "the old human being" as an allusion to Adam, because according to 1 Corinthians 15:22 "in the Adam all die," and "the new [human being]" as an allusion to Christ, because according to 1 Corinthians 15:22 "all will be made alive in the Christ" (compare Ephesians 2:15). But it's hard to think that as the new human being, Christ "is being renewed for the purpose and with the result of knowledge in accordance with the image of the one who created him." For in him "are hidden all the treasures of wisdom and of knowledge" (2:3), no renewal being necessary; and Christ, "in whom all things were created" (1:16), wasn't "created" as the new human being is said to have been created. So it's better to understand "the old human being" as the Colossians' preconversion self, together with its vices, and "the new [human being]" as their converted self, together with its virtues.

The Colossians stripped off their old self and put on their new self by faith, but it remains for them to work out in their behavior the effects of this metaphorical change of clothing. (A failure to work out those effects would invalidate their faith.) "That's being renewed" indicates progressive conformity in behavior to "the image of the one [Christ] who created him [the new human being]" by way of putting off old vices and putting on new virtues (see 1:15 for Christ as "the image

of the invisible God," and compare Romans 8:29; 12:2; 2 Corinthians 4:16; Titus 3:5 and especially Ephesians 4:20–24 for renewal). This renewal has the purpose and result of "knowledge," about which see the comments on 1:9–10. "*Where* there's no Greek and [no] Jew . . ." refers to Christ, who created the new human being/the new self, as the location in whom ethnic, cultural, physical, and social differences *make* no difference. See the comments on Galatians 3:28 for the use of "Greek" instead of "Gentile," and on 1 Corinthians 14:11 for the meaning of "barbarian." "Circumcision" stands for Jews because they practiced circumcision, and "uncircumcision" for Gentiles because they didn't practice it. Scythians lived on the steppes north of the Black Sea. Paul mentions them probably as an example of barbarians. Christ is not only the one in whom these differences disappear so far as God is concerned, and so far as Christians should be concerned. Christ is also "all things" to them in the sense of supplying them with all they need for salvation now and hereafter, so that they shouldn't stray into false doctrines. Moreover, he's "in all" who are in him by faith, so that he and they indwell each other.

THE APPLICATION OF HAVING BEEN RAISED WITH CHRIST TO RIGHTEOUS ACTIONS
Colossians 3:12–4:6

3:12–13: Therefore [because Christ is all things *to* you and is *in* all you (3:11)] **as God's selected ones, sacred** [to him] **and loved** [by him], **put on affections of pity, magnanimity, humility, meekness, patience,** ¹³**putting up with one another and graciously forgiving each other if someone has a grievance against someone** [else]. **Just as also the Lord has graciously forgiven you, in this way you too** [be graciously forgiving each other]. For obedience to the following commands, "as God's selected ones" appeals to the Colossians' sense of ill-deserved privilege. Selection by God (for which see, above all, Romans 9) results in being consecrated to him and loved by him just as in the case of the Jewish nation according to the Old Testament (see, for example, Deuteronomy 4:37; 10:15; 14:2), though Paul doesn't draw out the parallel here. The listed virtues are to be put on like items of clean clothing. "Magnanimity," which means kindness uncorrupted by pettiness and mean-spiritedness, arises out of "affections of pity." "Meekness," which means nonretaliatory gentleness, arises out of "humility," a lowly attitude in relations with fellow Christians. "Putting up with one another," with which compare Ephesians 4:2, arises out of "patience." And "graciously forgiving each other" arises out of all the immediately preceding virtues. The "grievance" that someone might have against someone else consists in something genuinely blameworthy, not in a mere annoyance. For failure to forgive graciously as you've been graciously forgiven, see Matthew 18:21–35; and with Christ the Lord's exercising gracious forgiveness, compare Mark 2:1–12; Matthew 9:1–8; Luke 5:17–26 (also Ephesians 4:32 for God's forgiveness "in Christ").

3:14–15: And over all these [virtues], [put on] love, which is the bond of maturity. ¹⁵And the Christ's peace is to be arbitrating in your hearts, to which [peace] you were also called in one body. And be thankful [compare 2:7]. The putting of love over all the just-mentioned virtues suggests an overgarment. On the other hand, the description of love as a "bond," something that binds together other items of clothing, suggests a waistband, a belt, a sash. In any case, love binds together the other virtues so as to produce maturity, full growth in virtue (compare 1:28; 4:12; 1 Corinthians 12:31b–13:13 [especially 13:9–11]). The bonding force of love leads naturally to thoughts of peace and arbitration. According to Ephesians 2:14–17 the Christ "is himself our peace" and "proclaimed peace as good news," thus "making peace" so as to "create in himself one new human being . . . in one body . . . by having killed . . . the hostility." Hence in Colossians, closely related as it is to Ephesians, "the Christ's peace" means the peace that he himself is, that he proclaimed as good news, and that he made so as to kill hostility between Christians as members of his body, the church, and to substitute arbitration for hostility. "In your hearts" makes the arbitration an outgrowth of love rather than an imposition forced from outside (like Pax Romana, the Roman peace dictated to subjugated peoples). "To which [peace] you were also called" (as well as its being commanded) might seem to contradict "in your hearts," for the calling is effective (as elsewhere in Paul). But it's still an invitation accepted with thankful hearts. "In one body" celebrates church unity resulting from arbitration by Christ's peace; and given peaceful unity of the church as the object of thanksgiving, the command to be thankful should be easy to obey. See further the comments on Ephesians 4:1–3, and for "*one body*" see Romans 12:4–5; 1 Corinthians 12:12–14; Ephesians 2:16; 4:4.

3:16–17: The word of the Christ is to be dwelling among you richly as you're teaching and admonishing each other in all wisdom, singing psalms, hymns, Spiritual songs with gratitude in your hearts to God. ¹⁷And in regard to everything whatever that you're doing in word [= speaking] or in deed [= working], [be doing] all things in the name of the Lord, Jesus, while giving thanks through him to God, the Father. "The word of the Christ" is the message about Jesus as the Messiah, which message is to eclipse any words about "thrones or lordships or rulerships or authorities" (1:16) or about "angels" (2:18). "Is to be dwelling among you" personifies this message as a fellow member of the churchly household, a message always being spoken at meetings of the church. "Richly" describes the dwelling of this message as valuable because it conveys "the wealth [= riches] of the glory of this secret, which [secret] is Christ in you, [Christ] the hope of glory" (1:27). It's this word, this message, that's to be used in "teaching [= instructing] and admonishing [= exhorting] each other [tasks that to one degree or another, depending on Spiritual gifts, all Christians are to engage in]." "In all wisdom" describes the teaching and admonishing in that their

subject matter features the Christ, "in whom are hidden all the treasures of wisdom and knowledge" (2:3), over against the false doctrines being peddled in Colossae. For "singing . . . with gratitude . . ." see the comments on Ephesians 5:18–20. Doing things "in the name of the Lord, Jesus" means doing them in acknowledgment that Jesus is what his designation "the Lord" indicates—in other words, doing them as his obedient slaves. "In regard to *everything whatever* that you're doing *in word or in deed* . . . *all* things" leaves absolutely no activity of Christians outside Jesus' domain (compare 1 Corinthians 10:31). "While giving thanks through him to God, the Father" makes Jesus the gateway to God, makes God fatherly in rescuing you "out from the authority of the darkness" and transferring you "into the kingdom" where Jesus exercises lordship with love (compare 1:13), and makes wholesale servitude to Jesus as Lord something for which to thank God (compare Ephesians 5:20).

3:18–21: Wives, be subordinating yourselves to [your] husbands, as it's appropriate [for you to do] in the Lord. ¹⁹Husbands, be loving [your] wives, and don't be getting embittered against them. ²⁰Children, be obeying [your] parents in all respects, for this is pleasing in the Lord. ²¹Fathers, don't be nagging your children, lest they get demoralized. This passage presents a reduced version of Ephesians 5:22–6:4. So see the comments on that passage for the present parallels. Concerning the few distinctive features here in Colossians, "as it's appropriate [for you to do] in the Lord" tells Christian wives that their position in Christ, designated "the Lord" to highlight his authority, calls for self-subordination to their husbands. "In the Lord" describes the wives' self-subordination rather than limiting it to Christian husbands. That husbands aren't to be "getting embittered against" their wives doesn't mean they're to avoid letting their wives embitter them—rather, to avoid treating their wives harshly out of anger and wrath (see Ephesians 4:31 for the association of "bitterness" with "anger and wrath"). Such treatment would run contrary to loving their wives. "In all respects" strengthens the command that children be obeying their parents; and the rationale, "for this [obedience] is pleasing in the Lord," replaces the rationale in Ephesians 6:1, "for this is right." But what's right always pleases him. As in the instruction to wives, "in the Lord" tells children that their position in Christ, again designated "the Lord" to highlight his authority, calls for obedience to their parents. "In the Lord" also describes the children's obedience rather than limiting it to Christian parents and presumes Christian faith on the part of the children being addressed. The command that fathers not be nagging their children substitutes for the similar command in Ephesians 6:4 that they not be provoking their children to anger, and here Paul adds a reason not to nag them: "lest they get demoralized." Demoralization by a Christian father would thwart his Christian influence on his and his wife's children.

3:22–25: Slaves, be obeying [your] fleshly lords [= human master/owners] in all respects, not with eye-

slavery as pleasers of human beings—rather, with integrity of heart, fearing the Lord. ²³Whatever you're doing, be working [at it] from [your] soul, as [working] for the Lord and not for human beings, ²⁴knowing that from the Lord you'll get back a restitution [consisting] of [your] inheritance. Be slaving for the Lord, [namely] Christ; ²⁵for the [lord/master] who injures [you] will be requited what he injured [in other words, your injurious master will suffer the Lord's injurious judgment on the Last Day], and there's no favoritism [with the Lord]. See the comments on Ephesians 6:5–8 for parallels in the present passage. As in the instruction to children, "in all respects" strengthens the command that slaves be obeying their "fleshly lords." "Fearing the Lord" shows that "with fear and trembling" in Ephesians 6:5 has to do with fearing to disobey the Lord, not with fearing the fleshly lords. "A restitution [consisting] of [your] inheritance" contrasts with slaves' having little or no hope of getting an inheritance in their present lifetimes and means participation "in the kingdom of the Christ and of God" (Ephesians 5:5), that is, in what Paul called in 1:12 "a portion of the allotment of the saints in the light" (compare Ephesians 1:14). "Fleshly lords," as Paul calls them, often punished their slaves with physical injuries. So to support his command to be slaving for the Lord who is Christ by obeying fleshly lords, Paul assures Christian slaves that injurious lords will in the end get their comeuppance from the Lord Christ.

4:1: You lords [= masters/owners of slaves], **be granting** [your] **slaves what** [is] **just and fair, knowing that you too have a Lord in heaven.** As in Ephesians 6:9, the foregoing translation uses "lords" for masters/owners of slaves to bring out the wordplay between those lords and the Lord, who is Christ Jesus. Another wordplay is harder to bring out in English. It's that the Greek for "what [is] just" (*to dikaion*) is related to the Greek in 3:25 for "injures/injured" (*adikōn/ēdikēsen*). Paul's point: granting slaves what is just contrasts with injuring them, which would instance what is *un*just. In simpler English, "treat your slaves justly and fairly." "Knowing that you too have a Lord in heaven" should motivate slaveowners to obey Paul's command. As Christians they're slaves to a master who ranks much higher than they do: "a Lord in heaven."

4:2–4: Be engrossed in prayer, staying awake in it with thanksgiving, ³praying at the same time also for us that God may open to us [Timothy and Paul according to 1:1] **a door for the word so that** [we] **may tell the secret of the Christ (because of which** [secret] **I'm even bound** [in chains as a prisoner]**), ⁴in order that I may disclose it as it's necessary for me to tell** [it]. To be engrossed in prayer requires "staying awake," that is, losing sleep so as to devote more time to praying (compare Mark 14:38). For "with thanksgiving," see the final comments on 1:9–12 and 3:16–17. "Praying *at the same time* also for us" stresses that the Colossians should always pray for Paul and Timothy as well as for themselves—in particular, that God may open to Paul and Timothy "a

door for the word," a figure of speech for an opportunity to tell "the secret of the Christ." Especially because of Paul's imprisonment, God will have to open the door. "The secret of the Christ" is "Christ in you [who believe in him]," the Christ who is "the hope of glory" and thus himself "God's secret" (see 1:26b–27 with 2:2). "Because of which [secret] I'm also bound" is Paul's compressed way of saying that at the time of writing he's chained as a prisoner because of having told the secret to Gentiles (see Acts 21:27–29; 22:21–23; 26:19–23 for the evangelizing of Gentiles as what led to his imprisonment). "I'm *even* bound" implies the incongruity of being chained as a prisoner for telling the Gentiles such good news. "That I may disclose it as it's necessary for me to tell [it]" shows that Paul wants to use even his imprisonment to continue telling the secret (see further the final comments on Ephesians 6:18–20).

4:5–6: Be walking around in wisdom [= behaving wisely] **toward outsiders, redeeming the time. ⁶Your word** [is to be] **always with grace,** [your word] **having been seasoned with salt, so that** [you] **may know how it's necessary for you to answer each individual** [outsider]. "Walking in wisdom" means behaving according to "[God's] will in all Spiritual wisdom and insight so as to walk around worthily of the Lord . . . bearing fruit in all good work" (1:9–10). "Toward outsiders" designs such behavior for conversion of the non-Christians with whom Christians interact. For "redeeming the time," see the comments on Ephesians 5:16, especially given the possibility that Ephesians will make its way as a circular letter to the church in Colossae (see the comments here on 4:16). Redeeming the time combines with wise behavior for the purpose of converting non-Christians. That is to say, be setting free (= redeeming) your time for the sake of evangelism. Since "the word" in 4:3 has just now referred to "the secret of the Christ" and has earlier meant both "the word of the truth of the gospel" (1:5), "God's word" (1:25), and "the word of the Christ" (3:16), "your word" probably means the message of the gospel that you speak to outsiders. In that case, "always with grace" requires this word always to contain the good news of salvation by "God's grace" (1:6 [compare Ephesians 2:5, 7–8]). "Having been seasoned with salt" has gotten a variety of interpretations. But in view of Jesus' comparing salt with the fire of divine judgment (Mark 9:49: "For everyone will be salted with fire"), the seasoning of your word with salt refers likely to warning outsiders that a refusal of God's grace will lead to the suffering of God's judgmental wrath (3:6). "So that [you] may know how it's necessary for you to answer each individual [outsider]" makes two points: (1) the combination of God's grace and God's judgment in answer to questions about your behavior as a Christian—this combination is what's "necessary" in your answer; (2) "to answer each individual [outsider]" calls for person-to-person evangelism (personal work, as it used to be called) in addition to public proclamation (1:28). In sum, Christian behavior ("walking around") and verbal witness ("your word") go together.

CONCLUSION
Colossians 4:7–18

The conclusion divides into the coming of Tychicus and Onesimus (4:7–9), greetings and final instructions (4:10–17), and a farewell and benediction (4:18).

4:7–9: Tychicus, [my] **beloved brother and faithful servant and fellow slave in the Lord, will make known to you all my circumstances,** [8]**whom I've sent to you for this very purpose, that you may know the circumstances concerning us** [Timothy and me] **and** [that] **he may encourage your hearts,** [9]**along with Onesimus,** [my] **faithful and beloved brother, who is** [one] **of you. They'll make known to you all the circumstances here.** The many close parallels with Ephesians 6:21–22, and also with Philemon as a whole, imply that Paul wrote Ephesians, Colossians, and Philemon during the same period and sent them together at the same time. His recommendation of Tychicus aims at ensuring that the Colossians welcome Tychicus hospitably and listen believingly to Tychicus's report of Paul's circumstances. "Whom I've sent to you" is spoken from the standpoint of the Colossians after Tychicus's arrival. See the comments on Ephesians 6:21–22 for Tychicus as a "beloved brother" and "faithful servant" and for other details. Here Paul adds both a description of Tychicus as a "fellow slave" (of the Lord, Jesus Christ) and a mention of Onesimus as a "faithful and beloved brother" (though according to Philemon 16 Onesimus was also Philemon's slave). The added description of Tychicus and the addition of Onesimus with a replacement of his status as a slave by his status as a faithful and beloved brother are designed to level out the statuses in Christ of Paul, Tychicus, and Onesimus, and to do so in order that the Colossian Christians, not just Philemon, may welcome Onesimus into their midst (see 3:11). "Who is one of you" describes Onesimus further as from Colossae and may also carry the overtone of his being the Colossians' fellow Christian now that he has been converted (Philemon 10–11, 15–16). Onesimus was converted only recently (during Paul's present imprisonment according to Philemon 10), so that he has had little chance to prove his faithfulness. "Faithful . . . brother" may therefore need to be understood as "believing . . . brother" (compare 1:2 with comments). In either case, "*They*'ll make known to you all the circumstances here" coordinates Onesimus with Tychicus as a fellow reporter. "Here" probably alludes to Rome in accordance with Acts 28. Knowing all Paul's circumstances will enable the Colossians to pray for Paul and Timothy intelligently (4:3).

4:10–11: Aristarchus, my fellow prisoner, greets you. Also [greeting you are] Mark, [who is] Barnabas's cousin (about whom you've received commands: if he comes to you, welcome him), [11]and Jesus, the one called Justus. As for those who are of the circumcision [that is, Jews], these [three] alone [are my] fellow workers for God's kingdom, who as such have become a comfort to me.** To greet in a letter means to send greet-

ings through it. We don't know how Aristarchus, who appears also in Philemon 24; Acts 19:29; 20:4; 27:2, came to be Paul's fellow prisoner. Perhaps he volunteered to join Paul in prison for the purpose of protecting him from abuse (compare Romans 16:7). Mark, also named John, appears often in Acts and Paul's letters. According to very early church tradition, Mark wrote the Gospel according to Mark. His presence with Paul, so that he sends greetings to the Colossians, indicates the healing of a rift between the two men, for which rift see Acts 15:36–40. If the commands that the Colossians received concerning Mark date from prior to Paul's writing this letter, we know nothing more about them. It's possible, though, that "you've received commandments" is spoken from the standpoint of the Colossians after the letter's arrival (as in "whom I've sent" [4:8]) and therefore refers to the following words: "if he comes to you, welcome him." Then the plural of "commands" implies the multiple aspects of welcoming, such as a cordial reception and the provision of room and board. "Barnabas's cousin" distinguishes this Mark from many others having the same name. "The one called Justus" likewise distinguishes "Jesus" from many others called Jesus as well as from Jesus the Lord. (Jesus, a Greek spelling of the Hebrew name Joshua, was still a popular boy's name among Jews living in the first century; for the heroic successor of Moses was named Joshua.)

Of the Jews where Paul is imprisoned, only Aristarchus, Mark, and Jesus Justus are Paul's "fellow workers for God's kingdom," that is, fellow evangelists. Their being an exception to the rule gives Paul, himself a Jew and one who is suffering imprisonment because of opposition from unbelieving Jews, special comfort. Working for God's kingdom hints at a contrast with the kingdom of the Caesar before whom Paul is going to stand trial. Since Paul identifies Aristarchus as his fellow prisoner, Mark as Barnabas's cousin, and Jesus as also called Justus and then identifies all three as Jews and fellow workers with him, they were probably otherwise unknown to the Colossians (who are likely to have known Barnabas at least by reputation because of his prominence in the early church). Despite their unacquaintance with Aristarchus, Mark, and Jesus Justus, then, Paul includes greetings from his three Jewish fellow workers to impress on the Colossians that the contents of his letter have considerable backing. His not having founded the church in Colossae combined with the threat of false teachings there to make the mention of such backing helpful to a favorable reception of the letter.

Paul continues to relay greetings, this time from Gentile Christians, in **4:12–14: Epaphras, who** [is one] **of you, a slave of Christ Jesus,** [greets you], **always struggling for you in** [his] **prayers that you may stand mature and fully assured in all God's will.** [13]**For I bear him witness that he has pain for you** [= emotional distress for you because of the threat posed by false teachers in Colossae] **and the** [saints] **in Laodicea and the** [saints] **in Hierapolis.** [14]**Luke, the beloved physician, greets you; and Demas** [greets you]. Though as a Colossian himself and therefore well-known to the Colossians, Epaphras gets the distinction of being called "a slave of Christ Jesus" to remind them that he founded their church in obedience to Christ Jesus (1:7) and that they should therefore stick to the gospel he taught them. "Always struggling for you in [his] prayers that you may stand mature and fully assured in God's will" highlights the intensity of Epaphras's concern that the Colossians not veer into newfangled false teachings (compare 1:28). God's will is opposed to those teachings and expressed in "the word of the truth of the gospel" that the Colossians "learned from Epaphras" (1:5–9). Further intensifying the intensity of this concern is the observability ("I bear him witness") of the emotional distress ("pain") evident in Epaphras's constant struggling in prayer for the saints in Colossae, and for the saints in nearby Laodicea and Hierapolis as well. They too might be threatened, or were threatened, by the false teachings. Paul describes Luke as "the beloved physician." But "the" often functions as a possessive pronoun, such as "my," so that Luke may have acted as Paul's personal physician. Demas gets no identification apart from his name (but see 2 Timothy 4:10).

4:15–17: Greet [for me] **the brothers in Laodicea, plus Nympha and the church** [that meets] **in her house.** [16]**And when the** [present] **letter has been read to you, make** [sure] **that it's read also in the church of the Laodiceans; and** [make sure] **that you too read the** [letter that's coming] **from Laodicea.** [17]**And tell Archippus, "See to the service which you've received in the Lord, that you be fulfilling it."** Because this letter is addressed to the Colossians, Paul asks them to relay his greetings to the Laodicean Christians, whom he calls "brothers" to underline his and their familial relation despite never having become acquainted face to face. But his mentioning Nympha by name suggests that he may have met her elsewhere—say, in Ephesus—as he had Epaphras (see the comments on 1:7). "The church [that meets] in her house" appears to differ from "the brothers in Laodicea" and from "the church of the Laodiceans." Perhaps, then, the church that met in Nympha's house was none other than the church in Hierapolis (compare 4:13: "the [saints] in Hierapolis").

Paul's command that his letter to the Colossians be read "also in the church of the Laodiceans" suggest that that church too was being threatened by false teachings. Would the Laodiceans then pass the letter on to the saints in Hierapolis? But what letter is it that the Colos-

sians are to read (that is, *have* read to them) when it comes from Laodicea? A letter that hasn't survived to our own day? Perhaps so, since we know of other Pauline letters that haven't survived (see the introduction to 2 Corinthians). On the other hand, Ephesians appears to have been a letter circulated in the region (see the comments on Ephesians 1:1–2). So Tychicus and Onesimus may have dropped off so-called Ephesians in Laodicea before traveling from the west a bit farther to Colossae to deliver Colossians there. In that case, Ephesians would arrive in Colossae somewhat later as "the letter [that's coming] from Laodicea."

Paul doesn't address Archippus, probably because he doesn't know him. Presumably Epaphras has told Paul about Archippus, though; and for Archippus to have the whole church address to him Paul's command puts great pressure on Archippus command to obey. "The service" which Archippus has "received" seems to imply that in Epaphras's absence, Archippus has been given the reins of leadership (compare Philemon 2). The reception of this service "in the Lord" makes the service one of service to the Lord, who is Jesus. The command that Archippus "be fulfilling it" is due to Epaphras's staying imprisoned with Paul (Philemon 23) rather than returning to Colossae with Tychicus and Onesimus. In view of Epaphras's continuing absence from Colossae, Archippus has more service to do, and therefore to fulfill. That it's the Colossians who are to tell him so has the purpose of making them the willing beneficiaries of his service and of giving him encouragement because of their willingness.

4:18: The greeting with my hand, Paul's [hand]. **Be remembering my bonds. Grace** [be] **with you.** The appearance of the final greeting in Paul's own handwriting implies that up to this point he has dictated the letter to a writing secretary. His handwriting, emphasized by the addition of "Paul's" to "my hand," had the purpose of guaranteeing the letter's authenticity. Because of the threat of false teachings and their actual presence in Colossae at this time, such a guarantee was needed. And because of the association of memory (Greek: *mnēmoneuete*) with the mention (Greek: *mneian*) of people in prayer (Romans 1:9–10; Ephesians 1:16; Philippians 1:3; 1 Thessalonians 1:2; Philemon 4), the command, "Be remembering my bonds," implies remembering to pray for Paul in view of his imprisonment. The grace that he wishes to be with the Colossians is the ill-deserved favor of God by which we're saved.

FIRST THESSALONIANS

In this letter Paul compliments Christian believers in the city of Thessalonica on their progress in faith and then exhorts them to live christianly in anticipation of Jesus' return on the Day of the Lord.

ADDRESS AND GREETING
1 Thessalonians 1:1

1:1: Paul and Silvanus and Timothy to the church of the Thessalonians [which is] **in God, the Father, and the Lord, Jesus Christ: Grace and peace to you.** Paul, Silvanus, and Timothy cofounded the Thessalonian church (see Acts 15:22, 32, 40–41; 16:1–3 with 17:1–9, "Silas" being the Aramaic form of the Latinized "Silvanus"). But the apostle Paul counts as leader of the other two and therefore as the author of this letter (see 2:18; 2 Thessalonians 3:17). By adding weight to the letter, his inclusion of Silvanus and Timothy with himself aims for a wholeheartedly favorable reception on the Thessalonians' part. "The *church* of the Thessalonians" means "the *assembly* of the Thessalonians." But since an assembly could consist of non-Christians, Paul adds "in God, the Father, and the Lord, Jesus Christ" and thus limits the address to Christians, whose assembly the word "church" connotes. The letter will be read to them when they assemble. They lived in Thessalonica, a major city in what is now northern Greece but was then Macedonia. Instead of saying "the church *in Thessalonica*," though, Paul says (as just noted) "the church of the Thessalonians *in God, the Father, and the Lord, Jesus Christ.*" Thus a theological address trumps a geographical address and thereby encourages the addressees. For dwelling physically in the city of Thessalonica, where they suffer persecution (2:14; 2 Thessalonians 1:4–7), doesn't determine their destiny. Dwelling through the Holy Spirit in God and Jesus Christ does (see 1:5–6; 4:8; 5:19 for the Thessalonians' having the Holy Spirit).

"The Father" designates God but leaves it unspecified whose Father he is. It will come out soon enough, however, that he's "our Father," the Father of Christians such as Paul and company (1:3; 3:11, 13), as well as of Jesus Christ (1:10). "The Lord" designates Jesus Christ. This term can refer to human beings—masters of slaves, owners of property, and rulers, for example—as well as to pagan deities. But the present conjunction with "God, the Father" in an indication of the Christians' sphere of existence points to Jesus' deity, especially in opposition to pagan deities and the emperor cult. "Jesus" is a personal name, "Christ" a title (meaning "Anointed One")

that has evolved into a second personal name. Putting a comma between "the Lord" and "Jesus Christ" underscores the true lordship of Jesus Christ over against the untrue lordship of pagan deities and deified emperors. For the meaning of "Grace and peace to you" see the comments on 1 Peter 1:2; 2 John 3.

A COMPLIMENTARY THANKS FOR THE THESSALONIAN BELIEVERS
1 Thessalonians 1:2–5

1:2–5: We're always thanking God for all of you, constantly making remembrance [of you] **in our prayers, [3]remembering your work of faith and labor of love and endurance in hope of our Lord, Jesus Christ, in the presence of God, even our Father, [4]knowing—brothers loved by God—**[his] **selection of you, [5]in that our gospel didn't get to you only with a** [spoken] **word—rather, also with power and with the Holy Spirit and with much full assurance, just as you know what kind of** [men] **we proved to be among you because of you.** As distinguished from "you" and "your," "we" and "our" refer to Paul and company. Which isn't to say, however, that "our Lord," "our Father," and "our gospel" exclude the addressees from the same relationships to Jesus, God, and the gospel. Thanks go to God for the Thessalonian Christians because of his seeing to their conversion, which made the evangelization of Thessalonica successful. "*Always* thanking God" stresses the extent of thanksgiving, and "for *all* of you" stresses the extent of his making the evangelization successful. "Prayers" provide the occasion for thanking God. "Making *remembrance*" means making *mention*. "Constantly" joins the plural of "prayers" to stress the regularity of mentioning the Thessalonian Christians thankfully in prayer.

"Remembering your work . . . and labor . . . and endurance" means mentioning in prayer these activities of the Thessalonian Christians as what in particular Paul and company thank God for. The "work" stems from "faith"—that is, from belief in Jesus—and means the doing of good deeds (see 2 Thessalonians 1:11; 2:17), especially for fellow Christians (4:9–12). The "labor" stems from "love" and connotes affectionate exertion for others' benefit (3:12 [compare the combination of work, labor, and love in 5:12–13]). The "endurance" stems from "hope," which means a confident expectation, not an uncertain wish. (An even more literal translation, "endurance *of* hope," would sound as though hope was *being* endured, whereas the less literal translation, "endurance *in* hope," allows hope to be the *source* of endurance.) "Of our Lord, Jesus Christ" defines the hope as a confident expectation of his second coming, and this expectation enables the endurance of persecution (2:14; 3:3–4; 2 Thessalonians 1:4–7; Acts 17:5–9). Hope comes last in this trio of Christian virtues because it looks forward to the second coming (so too in 5:8; Colossians 1:4–5), whereas in 1 Corinthians 13:13 love comes last as the highest virtue (compare Romans 5:1–5). "In the presence of God" goes with "remembering" and thus indicates that "prayers," in which the remembrance occurs, put us in his presence (3:9–10 [compare Hebrews 4:16; 7:19, 25; 10:1, 22]).

Knowledge that God selected the addressees for salvation leads Paul to address them with "brothers loved by God." They're Christian brothers in relation to Paul and company as well as to one another (Matthew 23:8). Calling attention to this relationship makes for a favorable reception of the letter, and calling attention to God's love for the addressees both encourages them in their hopeful endurance of persecution and contrasts sharply with pagan gods' usual lack of love for their devotees, who therefore needed to placate them. "Knowing . . . the selection" provides the basis for thanksgiving, and providing the basis of this knowledge is God's seeing to it that the gospel got to them not only verbally but also powerfully. Since by definition miracles are "powerful acts" or, more literally, "powers," the phrase "with power" indicates that the performance of miracles accompanied the spoken word. "With the Holy Spirit" indicates the source of this power. And "with . . . full assurance" indicates its effect on the Thessalonians. In conjunction with the spoken word the power converted them. "Much" raises their "full assurance" to the nth degree (compare Romans 15:18–19; 1 Corinthians 2:4–5; 2 Corinthians 6:7; 12:12; Galatians 3:5). Their knowledge of "what kind of [men]" Paul and company "proved to be" among them balances Paul's knowledge that God lovingly selected the Thessalonians, and also prepares for a description in 2:1–12 of the way Paul and company evangelized Thessalonica. This very appeal to the Thessalonians' knowledge of their behavior among them, plus the description of that behavior as "because of you," forecasts a favorable description in the upcoming passage and means that Paul and company behaved so as to benefit the Thessalonians with the gospel. All in all, the extended thanksgiving for the Thessalonians in 1:2–5 compliments them for the purposes of gaining their ready acceptance of the letter's further contents and of encouraging their further progress in faith-filled work, love-filled labor, and hope-filled endurance.

A COMPLIMENTARY DESCRIPTION OF THE THESSALONIAN BELIEVERS
1 Thessalonians 1:6–10

1:6–10: **And you proved to be imitators of us and of the Lord by having welcomed the word in much affliction with the joy of the Holy Spirit, 7so that you became a role model to all the believers in Macedo-** nia and in Achaia. **8For from you the word about the Lord reverberated forth not only in Macedonia and in Achaia; rather, your faith toward God has gone forth in every place, so that we have no need to say anything. 9For people themselves are reporting about us in reference to what kind of entrance to you we had, even how you turned to God from idols to slave for the living and true God 10and to await his Son from the heavens, whom he** [God] **raised from among the dead,** [namely] **Jesus, the one who rescues us from the coming wrath.**

As Paul and company proved to be good for the addressees (1:5), so the addressees have proved to be imitators of them and of the Lord, who has twice been identified as Jesus Christ (1:1, 3). Like the compliment in 1:2–5, this compliment has the purpose of gaining a ready acceptance of the letter and of encouraging its recipients. They became imitators of Paul and company and of the Lord by "having welcomed the word." The word of the gospel called on the Thessalonians "to slave for the living and true God" as Paul and company were doing and as the Lord, Jesus Christ, did. So welcoming this word meant "turn[ing] to God from idols" to slave for him, and welcoming it "in . . . affliction" adds an element to the imitation in that both Paul and company and the Lord suffered affliction—that is, persecution—in slaving for God. The Lord suffered it in his crucifixion, they in their evangelistic labors (Acts 16:16–17:15).

"Much" magnifies the like affliction suffered by the addressees. Likewise, "with the joy of the Holy Spirit" magnifies the compliment in that they welcomed the word joyfully *despite* the suffering of much affliction. Mention of the Holy Spirit as the source of this unnatural or, rather, supernatural joy balances the preceding mention of the Holy Spirit as the source of the power with which the word came to them (1:5) and implies by way of a further compliment that this joy gives evidence of their having received the Holy Spirit. Their joyful welcome of the word despite much affliction has made them "a role model" to be imitated just as they imitated Paul and company and the Lord. "To all the believers in Macedonia [roughly the northern part of modern Greece] and in Achaia [roughly the southern part]" enhances the compliment by displaying the extent to which the Thessalonian believers became a role model, and "For" introduces an explanation of the way they became such a model: the gospel, called "the word about the Lord," had "reverberated forth" from them as some of them traveled out of Thessalonica into Macedonia and Achaia and even elsewhere ("in every place," a deliberate exaggeration for emphasis on their far-flung evangelism [for some Thessalonian believers as Paul's traveling coevangelists see Acts 19:29; 20:4; 27:2; Colossians 4:10; Philemon 24]). "Not only . . . *rather,*" where we'd expect "not only . . . *but also,*" is a particularly emphatic way of stating the hyperbole; and "*your faith* toward God" restates "the word *about the Lord*" in terms of personal testimonies. These testimonies made them role models to be imitated.

We might have expected "your faith *in Jesus,*" but "your faith *toward God*" prepares for a description of the addressees' having "turned to God from idols." The addressees' own testimonies of faith toward God made it unnecessary for Paul and company to report their converts' faith. Because of those testimonies, in fact, people who heard them were reporting "what kind *of entrance*" Paul and company had to the addressees. "Even how you turned to God from idols" defines the entrance in terms of evangelism so successful as to be comparable to a triumphal entry such as victorious generals and celebrated orators, philosophers, and teachers enjoyed when entering a city. "From idols" also implies both that the Thessalonian believers didn't merely add God to the gods represented by idols, as pagans often multiplied their gods in a fashion similar to diversifying investments nowadays for the sake of economic safety (see Acts 17:1–4), and that most of the Thessalonian believers were Gentiles, for few Jews worshiped idols after their Assyrian and Babylonian exiles during the Old Testament period. "To slave" for God means to work for him—evangelistically in this context—and counts as an honor and privilege because he's "the *living* and *true* God" in contrast with "idols," dead and undivine as they are. God's having "raised ['his Son'] from among the dead" has made it possible for him (Jesus the Son) to come back "from the heavens" and rescue "us" (now including the addressees as well as Paul and company) "from the coming wrath" (that is, from the future cataclysm of God's final judgment on unbelievers). Since this wrath is coming and therefore not yet here, the present tense of "rescues" implies that the rescue is so certain that it might as well be happening already.

AN EXPLANATORY DESCRIPTION OF THE EVANGELIZATION OF THESSALONICA
1 Thessalonians 2:1–12

2:1–2: For you yourselves know, brothers, our entrance to you, that it hasn't proved empty [= void of success]. **²Rather, though having suffered earlier and been treated outrageously in Philippi, as you know, we made bold in our God to speak to you the gospel of God in** [the midst of] **an enormous struggle.** Here Paul and company start explaining the success of their entrance to the Thessalonians, first mentioned in 1:9. The explanation starts with an appeal to the Thessalonians' knowledge of that success. The addition of "yourselves" to "you" and the endearing address "brothers" strengthen the appeal, designed as it is to enlist agreement with the explanation. "Rather" shifts attention from the success as such to a reason for it. The reason consisted in evangelistic boldness. Boldness of speech was highly admired, and this boldness deserved more admiration than usual because Paul and company had recently suffered and been treated outrageously in Philippi (Acts 16:11–40). "In [the midst of] an enormous struggle" adds to the background of boldness the fierce opposition faced right in Thessalonica (Acts 17:1–9). Admirable as the boldness was, though, "in our God" gives God the credit for it. Just as the Spiritual location of the addressees "in God, the Father, and the Lord, Jesus

Christ" trumped their physical location in Thessalonica (1:1), so the Spiritual location of Paul and company in God trumped their circumstantial location in danger, so that they gained boldness of speech. "The gospel of God" means the good news of what God has done through his Son, Jesus (1:9–10).

2:3–4: For our urging [people to welcome the gospel] [does] **not** [stem] **from misguidance, and not from impurity, and not from flimflammery. ⁴Rather, just as we've been certified by God so as to be entrusted with the gospel, we speak in this way: not as pleasing human beings—rather,** [as pleasing] **God, the one who certifies our hearts.** This second explanation of the evangelistic success in Thessalonica consists in the bona fides of Paul and company. They speak and act not only boldly but also out of concern for truth (as opposed to "misguidance"), out of unselfish motives (as opposed to "impurity"), and out of sincerity (as opposed to "flimflammery"). Each of the two occurrences of "rather" introduces a contrast with "misguidance," "impurity," and "flimflammery," all three of which would be designed to please human beings without their recognition of the misguidance, impurity, and flimflammery. The first contrast consists in "not pleasing human beings," the second in "[pleasing] God." To these contrasts are added two certifications by God: (1) his certification of Paul and company as trustworthy proclaimers of the gospel and (2) his certification of their hearts as pleasing to him. Since then they proclaim the gospel to please him rather than human beings, he saw to it that their evangelization of Thessalonica proved successful.

2:5–8: For neither at any time did we appear on the scene with a word of flattery, just as you know [we didn't]**, nor with a ruse** [in the service] **of greed—God** [is our] **witness** [that we didn't]**—⁶nor** [did we ever appear on the scene] **seeking glory from human beings, either from you or from others, though able as Christ's apostles to be with weight** [that is, to throw our weight around]**. ⁷Rather, we appeared on the scene** [as] **infants among you. As if a nursing** [mother] **were bosoming her own children, ⁸in this way yearning for you** [= having a soft spot in our hearts for you] **we were delighted to deliver to you not only the gospel of God but also our own selves, because you've become beloved to us.** This third explanation of the evangelistic success in Thessalonica consists in the self-effacement of Paul and company. "Just as you know" enlists the Thessalonians' agreement that they hadn't flattered them to gain a personal following. Human beings can detect flattery, but only God can see greed in the heart. So Paul and company then enlist God as a witness to their using no ruse to satisfy any greed of theirs, the satisfaction of which greed would have come at the Thessalonians' expense.

In the Greco-Roman culture of honor and shame it was *expected* that people—especially itinerant orators, philosophers, and teachers of religion—seek "glory [= admiration] from [their fellow] human beings" by virtue of their oratorical, philosophical, and didactic skills. It was also thought *proper* that they should seek such glory. But Paul denies that he and his companions sought it and implies that it would have been un-Christian for them to do so. "Either from you or from others" extends the denial to their evangelization elsewhere too, and this despite having ability (in the sense of authorization) as Christ's apostles to throw their weight around. (Obviously, "apostles" is used here in a sense wider than the original Twelve [compare especially Acts 14:14].) Rather than presenting themselves as apostolic heavyweights and acting accordingly, they presented themselves as infants, lightweights lacking authority over their audience.[1] "Infants" is a figure of speech that highlights how innocent of greed were Paul and company among the Thessalonians. A shift to the figure of a nursing mother highlights how affectionately they acted toward them—so affectionately in fact that they weren't simply willing, they were even delighted to deliver to the Thessalonians their very own selves as well as the gospel of God. And they did deliver their own selves to the Thessalonians by serving them gratis. "Because you've become beloved to us" translates the figure of a nursing mother "bosoming her own children" into the actuality of a loving relationship. How different from the flimflam artists who preyed on their gullible audiences with self-glorifying, self-aggrandizing, crowd-pleasing preachments!

2:9–12: For you remember, brothers, our labor and hardship. While working night and day so as not to impose a burden on any of you, we proclaimed to you the gospel of God. [10]**You and God [are] witnesses to how devoutly and righteously and blamelessly we appeared on the scene for you who believe,** [11]**as indeed you know how** [we were treating] **each one of you as a father** [treats] **his own children by encouraging you and comforting** [you] **and testifying** [12]**that you should walk** [= conduct yourselves] **worthily of God, who is calling you into his own kingdom and glory.** This fourth explanation of the evangelistic success in Thessalonica consists in Paul and company's supporting themselves rather than taking money for their proclamation of the gospel (compare 1 Corinthians 9:18; 2 Corinthians 11:7–12; 12:13–14; Acts 18:3; 20:33–35). (Note: Each of the four explanations is introduced with the conjunction "For" [2:1, 3, 5, 9].) "You remember" both reminds the Thessalonians that Paul and company supported themselves and enlists the Thessalonians' agreement that they did. For the address "brothers" see the comments on 1:4. "Our labor and hardship" means "our hard labor." "While working *night* and day" details how hard their labor was, for working hours normally stretched from sunrise to sunset, but no further. Greek elites despised manual labor; and itinerant orators, philosophers, and religious teachers didn't deign to engage

in it. "*While* working night and day" indicates that Paul and company combined evangelism with manual labor: they used their workplaces to proclaim the gospel of God. "To you" puts the Thessalonians in the audience at those workplaces. "So as not to impose a burden on any of you" states the merciful purpose of self-support. In 2:5–8 Paul and company appealed to God as the witness to his and his companions' humanly invisible lack of greed. Now they appeal to the Thessalonians as well as to God, because working night and day was visible to the Thessalonians just as to God, though only he could attest to the inward purpose of not burdening the Thessalonians. They and God testify that the hard labor of Paul and company counted as religiously devout, morally righteous, ethically blameless, and meant for the benefit of the Thessalonian believers.

Here and earlier, "appeared on the scene" is a verbal equivalent of the noun "entrance" in 1:9; 2:1. "As indeed you know" appeals again to the Thessalonians' knowledge, underscored this time with "indeed" (compare 2:1–2, 9–10), and introduces Paul and company's treatment of them "as a father [treats] his own children." "Each one of you" individualizes the treatment for emphasis. The earlier comparison to a nursing mother's bosoming her own children featured motherly affection. The present comparison features fatherly encouragement, comfort, and deposition in regard to conduct worthy of God, that is, conduct which brings to him the glory he's worthy of. Since he is calling believers "into his own kingdom and glory," they owe him this kind of conduct. "His *own*" stresses the privilege of citizenship in that kingdom and of sharing there in God's glory. To share in that glory is to be compensated for not seeking glory from human beings any more than Paul and company did (2:6). God's call isn't just an invitation to be accepted or rejected. It's an effective tugging into his glorious kingdom.

A REPRISE OF PRAYERFUL THANKS FOR THE THESSALONIANS AND OF THE COMPLIMENTARY DESCRIPTION OF THEM
1 Thessalonians 2:13–16

2:13: And we're also thanking God constantly because of this, [namely,] **that on receiving from us the heard word of God** [= the gospel of God that you heard spoken by us]**, you welcomed** [it] **not** [as] **the word of human beings—rather, just as it truly is, the word of God, who is also working among you who believe.** Paul and company have just referred to their past fatherly treatment of the Thessalonians (2:9–12). Now they add a reprise of their thanking God for them (see 1:2–10 with comments). This time—in view of the intervening self-description (2:1–12)—they stress that the Thessalonians welcomed what they heard as God's true word, not as a merely human message. And to deflect credit from themselves for their hard labor Paul and company credit God with working among the Thessalonians (compare Philippians 1:6). Alternatively, as is grammatically possible, they credit God's word ("which" instead of "who")

---

[1]Some ancient manuscripts, followed by most English translations, have "gentle" instead of "infants." But "infants" has better manuscript support and, being more difficult to understand, the greater likelihood of having been changed by copyists.

with working among them (compare 1 Corinthians 1:18). In either case, Paul and company are living up to "not seeking glory from human beings" (2:6).

2:14–16: For you, brothers, became imitators of God's churches in Christ Jesus that are in Judea, in that you too have suffered the same things at the hands of your own countrymen just as also they themselves [did] **at the hands of the Jews,** [15]**who killed both the Lord,** [namely] **Jesus, and the** [Old Testament] **prophets, and** [who] **pursued us out** [of Thessalonica]**, and who don't please God, and** [who are] **hostile to all human beings,** [16][as evident in their] **trying to prevent us from speaking to the Gentiles that they might be saved, with the result that they** [the unbelieving Jews] **are always filling up their sins. And the wrath has arrived first upon them to the max.** The long sentence that starts this paragraph explains why Paul and company thank God constantly for the Thessalonians' welcoming God's word (2:13). As in 1:6, the reason lies in their welcoming it despite persecution; and complimenting them on their doing so has the purpose yet again of ensuring their ready acceptance of what is to follow in the letter. The affectionate address "brothers" enhances the compliment. According to 1:6 the addressees had become imitators of Paul and company and of the Lord in suffering persecution. Here they're said to have become "imitators of God's churches . . . that are in Judea." Since conversion to God entails "slaving for God" (1:9), those assemblies of his slaves belong to him—hence, "*God's* churches." But besides locating them geographically in Judea the text locates them Spiritually "in Christ Jesus" (see the comments on 1:1). The placement of "Christ" before "Jesus" retains something of the original titular meaning: "the Christ, [namely] Jesus" or "Messiah Jesus."

Another "you yourselves," plus "too" and "the same things," highlights the parallel between the addressees' suffering at the hands of their unbelieving fellow Thessalonians and the Judean churches' suffering at the hands of their unbelieving fellow Judeans (see especially Acts 8:1b–3). Adding to this parallel, the tradition of such persecution—a tradition which goes back through the killing of Jesus all the way to the killing of the Old Testament prophets—reinforces the point that the addressees aren't alone in their suffering of persecution. "[Who] pursued us out [of Thessalonica]" spotlights unbelieving Jews outside Judea, too, and alludes to what happened according to Acts 17:1–9, though the same sort of pursuit had happened elsewhere (Acts 9:26–30; 13:45–50; 14:5–6, 19–20; 17:13–14; 2 Corinthians 11:24–26). Since God sent the prophets and Jesus his Son and owns believers, it follows that their unbelieving persecutors aren't pleasing God. And the Jewish persecutors' "hostil[ity] to all human beings," not just to Christians, shows itself in the attempt to prevent the evangelization and consequent salvation of Gentiles. This attempt is "filling up their [the persecutors'] sins" in that they not only disbelieve but also try to keep the Gentiles, whom they hate, from believing. "Always" describes their attempt as ongoing. "The wrath" refers back to "the coming wrath" in 1:10,

so that the past tense of "has arrived" portrays this future cataclysm of divine wrath as so sure to come that it might as well have come already (compare the present tense in "Jesus, the one who rescues us from the coming wrath" [1:10], as though the rescue is so sure to happen that it might as well be happening already). "First" indicates that the Jewish persecutors will suffer God's wrath before unbelieving Gentiles do (compare Romans 2:9). "To the max" matches the magnitude of coming wrath to the magnitude of "always filling up their sins."

PAUL AND COMPANY'S CONCERN FOR AND JOY IN THE THESSALONIAN BELIEVERS
1 Thessalonians 2:17–3:10

2:17–18: But we, brothers, having been orphaned from you for an hour's time [= a short while]**—as to face, not as to heart** [= so far as a face-to-face but not a heart-to-heart relationship is concerned]**—in our immense yearning were all the more eager to see your face.** [18]**Therefore we wanted to come to you—indeed I, Paul, both once and twice** [= more than once]**—and Satan cut in on us** [so as to block our way and thus thwart us]. "But we" shifts attention from the persecutors to Paul and company. Another affectionate address, "brothers" (for which see the comments on 1:4), introduces their yearning for the addressees. "Immense" magnifies the yearning, and "orphaned from you" gives a reason for it and compares it to an orphaned child's hopeless and therefore all the greater yearning to see his or her parents. That Paul and company have been separated from the Thessalonian believers for only a short while makes their immense yearning even greater evidence of their love for those believers. "*Not* [orphaned] as to heart" is the reason for being "all the *more* eager to see your face." Because of this eagerness Paul and company, but especially Paul as their leader and the author of this letter ("I, Paul"), wanted to visit the Thessalonian believers. "Indeed" and "both once and twice" stress this desire of his. "And Satan cut in on us" absolves Paul and his companions from any blame for having failed to visit the persecuted Thessalonians.

2:19–20: For what [is] **our hope or joy or crown of boasting** [that is, a crown to boast about]**—for sure** [it's] **even you, isn't it?—in the presence of our Lord, Jesus, at his coming?** [20]**For you are our glory and joy!** "For" introduces another reason, this time forward-looking, for the immense yearning to visit the Thessalonian believers. The word translated "what . . . ?" could also be translated "who . . . ?" But "what . . . ?" does a better job of leaving the answer to the question in suspense. "Hope" means confident expectation and prepares for a reference to the second coming (see the comments on 1:3) but here refers to the Thessalonian believers at the second coming ("for sure [it's] even you, isn't it?") rather than to that coming itself. "Or joy *or* crown" sets out a range of further possibilities. But all of them complement each other. "Crown" means a wreath such as victorious athletes were given. To boast is to express pride.

But Paul and company are so bent on expressing pride in the Thessalonian believers rather than in themselves that they interrupt their question before finishing it. The interruption ("for sure [it's] even you, isn't it?") answers the initial question with another, self-answering question. "In the presence of our Lord, Jesus, at his coming" indicates that on that occasion Paul and company will express joyful pride in the Thessalonian believers because by staying true despite persecution these believers will have met the confident expectation of Paul and company. See the comments on 4:15 for the word "coming." "For you are our glory and joy" reiterates the interruptive answer to the foregoing question. "Our hope" drops out, "joy" stays, and "our glory" replaces "crown of boasting" to indicate that whatever honor Paul and company get at the second coming will derive from their converts in Thessalonica. See the comments on 1 Corinthians 9:24–25 on the crown as an imperishable wreath.

3:1–3a: Therefore [because Satan thwarted our coming to you] **when we could no longer bear** [wondering how you were doing], **we thought it good to be left alone in Athens ²and sent Timothy, our brother and God's coworker in the gospel about the Christ, to stabilize you and encourage** [you] **for the sake of your faith ³ªso that no one would be perturbed by these afflictions.** The sending of Timothy left Paul and Silvanus alone. "Our brother and God's coworker" commends Timothy so as to ratify his ministry among the Thessalonians during his past visit, and during another visit too if he's the carrier of this letter to them. (There was no public postal service.) See 2:13 (with comments) and Philippians 1:6 for God as a worker. What a high honor to be working with him! "In the gospel" makes the good news "about the Christ" a kind of workshop where God and Timothy cooperate in the task of evangelism, which goes beyond the converting of people to include their stabilization and encouragement. "The Christ" highlights Jesus' office of messiahship, so that "the gospel about the Christ" makes a kind of brand name over against the supposed gospel of a reigning Caesar. ("Gospel" was used for the good news of a Caesar's accomplishments.) Given the Thessalonian believers' afflictions, Timothy was to stabilize them lest their faith falter, and to encourage them lest even one of them be so much as perturbed by the afflictions.

3:3b–5: For you yourselves know that we're destined for this [the suffering of afflictions/persecution]. **⁴For in fact when we were with you, we were telling you ahead of time, "We're going to be afflicted," just as also it has happened and** [just as] **you know** [from your own experience of persecution]. **⁵Because of this** [the fulfillment of our prophecy], **when I too** [Paul in addition to Silvanus] **could no longer bear** [wondering how you were doing], **I sent** [Timothy] **to ascertain your faith, lest somehow the tempter had tempted you and our labor had drawn a blank.** Knowledge of predestination to persecution explains why you needn't be perturbed by the persecution. It holds no surprise. The addition of "yourselves" to "you" stresses the Thes-

salonians' knowledge and therefore not needing to be perturbed. Paul and company's prophesying the persecution explains the Thessalonians' knowledge that it was coming on them, as it now has. "*We're going to be afflicted*" includes Paul and company with their addressees in the past prophecy. Its very fulfillment helps steel them all against discouragement and loss of faith. A second mention of Timothy's sending serves to stress the concern of Paul, the leader, over the unknown state of the Thessalonians' faith. He calls Satan, who had thwarted him and his companions (2:18), "the tempter" who "had tempted" the Thessalonians by stirring up the persecution in Thessalonica so as to tempt the believers there into apostatizing (see the comments on James 1:2–4 on temptation as testing, and on testing as temptation). If they had yielded to the temptation, the labor that Paul and company had expended on them would have "drawn a blank," that is, proved empty of a lasting result in eternal life for the Thessalonians. But "somehow" implies that Paul doubted the tempter had succeeded, and that this doubt characterized Paul even at the time of his not yet knowing the state of their faith. Thus he compliments them with his confidence in them.

3:6–8: But now, since Timothy has come to us [Paul and Silvanus] **from you and told us good news about your faith and love and that you always have a good remembrance of us** [that is, you think kindly of us whenever we come to mind, as we often do], **longing to see us just as indeed we also** [long to see] **you, ⁷because of this** [your "good remembrance of us" and "longing to see us"] **we were encouraged over you, brothers, on** [the occasion of] **our every adversity and affliction,** [encouraged, that is,] **through your faith, ⁸because we now live if you're standing in the Lord** [as you are, in contrast with falling away from him to escape persecution]. "But now" signals a shift from previous concern to present relief. Given the earlier concern over stability and courage in faith, Timothy's good news was that the Thessalonians' faith had made them stable and courageous in persecution. But he had more good news: love and pleasant memories of Paul and company also characterized them (see 1:3; 5:8 for the correlation of faith and love, and 3:12 for love of fellow believers and all others as well). The Thessalonians' "good remembrance" rests on the good conduct of Paul and company as described in 2:1–12. Evidence of the good remembrance derives from the Thessalonians' longing to see them to the same degree they long to see the Thessalonians. "Indeed" underscores this equality of longing. And just as Timothy was sent to encourage the Thessalonians (3:2), his good news concerning their faith and love has encouraged Paul and company, whose concern over them has therefore changed to encouragement over them.

The address "brothers" adds a note of affection that tells why the good news encouraged Paul and company. "On [the occasion of] our every adversity and affliction" reflects back on their persecutions around the time of Timothy's bringing the good news (see in particular Acts 18:5, 12–17) and draws a parallel between the hard circumstances in which they received encouragement and the hard circumstance in which the Thessalonians received from them encouragement through Timothy. "Every" stresses the circumstantial adversity and affliction that made the good news brought by Timothy so encouraging. The faith of the Thessalonian believers was the object of his encouragement (3:2), but now their faith has become the means of encouragement to Paul and company. "Because we now live" implies that Paul and company had been (as we would say) "worried to death" over the possibility of the Thessalonians' having apostatized under the pressure of persecution (compare Mark 14:34; Matthew 26:38). "If you're standing" doesn't imply doubt that they're standing, for such doubt would contradict the encouragement derived from Timothy's good news. This news implies that as a matter of fact they *are* standing. "If" simply introduces standing as a condition, the fulfillment of which has given encouragement. Nevertheless, the very stating of this condition implies that the Thessalonians must continue standing if the encouragement of Paul and company is also to continue. "In the Lord" qualifies the standing as sticking true to belief in Jesus as the Lord rather than apostatizing to the worship of Caesar and pagan deities as though they were lords (compare the comments on 1:1 for "*in* the Lord"). The Lord supplies stability for standing.

3:9–10: For what thanks can we return to God concerning you on [the basis of] **all the joy with which because of you we rejoice in the presence of our God,** [10]**night and day begging extravagantly hard to see your face** [= to see you face to face] **and make up for the deficiencies in your faith?** This question explains the reason why Paul and company are living rather than dying (so to speak [3:8]) out of concern over the Thessalonians. The reason is that the Thessalonians' "standing in the Lord" makes it impossible to thank God *enough* for the joy they've brought to Paul and company. "*All* the joy" and the redundancy in "all the *joy* with which . . . we *rejoice*" heighten the degree of joy. "In the presence of our God" points to the expression of joy in thankful prayer, which puts Christians in his presence (1:3). "Night and day" and "extravagantly" stress how insistent is Paul's and Silvanus's "begging" God in prayer that they might see the Thessalonians, as Timothy has recently done. Timothy's report has increased the longing of Paul and Silvanus to see them. The implication of this longing in prayer should make the Thessalonians take seriously the instruction and exhortations to follow. But Paul and Silvanus are begging God extravagantly also that when seeing them they might "make up for the deficiencies in [the Thessalonians'] faith." Their faith is stable in that they're "standing in the Lord." But it's deficient in content, as will come out in chapters 4–5.

A BENEDICTION
1 Thessalonians 3:11–13

A benediction closes out chapters 1–3 and prepares for the instruction and exhortations in chapters 4–5.

3:11: And may God himself, even our Father, and our Lord, Jesus, straighten our way [figuratively speaking] **to you.** This first part of the benediction has to do with God's and Jesus' acting for the benefit of Paul and Silvanus (and Timothy unless he's carrying the letter to Thessalonica). They wish God and Jesus to straighten their way to the Thessalonian believers despite Satan's thwarting more than one prior attempt to visit them (2:18)—"straighten," because a straight road gets people from A to B faster than a crooked road would. "Himself" emphasizes God as one who has *power* to straighten the road in answer to the praying described in 3:10. "Even our Father" portrays him as one who has *sympathy* to do so in answer to that praying. "Our Lord" identifies Jesus as one who has *authority* to do so. That he would thus act in conjunction with God the Father and in answer to prayer implies his deity, and the singularity of the Greek verb underlying "straighten" despite its having a plural subject indicates that God and Jesus act in unison.

3:12–13: And may the Lord make you increase and flourish in love for one another and for all [people], **just as indeed we** [increase and flourish in love] **for you,** [13]**so as to stabilize your hearts as blameless in consecration in the presence of God, even our Father, at the coming of our Lord, Jesus, with all his consecrated ones** [compare 4:14; Zechariah 14:5]. This second part of the benediction has to do with Jesus' acting for the benefit of the Thessalonian believers. "The Lord" identifies him again as one who has authority to take such action. Love already characterizes the believers (1:3; 3:6). But because of continuing persecution, an increase in love is needed to maintain stability in Christian belief. Wishing them to "flourish" in love means wishing them to have *more* than enough love to maintain this stability. "For one another" points to a love that will bind them together in a unity so close-knit that it will enable them collectively to resist further temptations to apostatize. "For all [people]" points to a love that will also lead the believers to convert unbelievers, including persecutors, with charitable words and deeds. "Just as *indeed*" emphatically rementions the love of Paul and company for their addressees as a template for the addressees' love for one another and all people. An increase and flourishing of love will stabilize the addressees' "hearts." Since evil originates in the heart, one's inner being (Mark 7:21–23; Romans 1:24), "blameless" hearts produce blameless persons. "In consecration" means that such persons belong to God, as others do not. "In the presence of God . . . at the coming of our Lord, Jesus" means that stability in blamelessness of hearts—that is, perseverance in the face of persecution—ensures the enjoyment of God's presence "with all the consecrated ones" at the second coming. "Even our Father" describes God as one whose presence will be enjoyable because nobody will be able to cast blame on the addressees. They won't have apostatized. For Jesus' coming as "our *Lord*," see the comments on 4:13–5:3. But who are "all his consecrated ones"? "All the consecrated [= holy] ones" in Zechariah 14:5 refers to angels, and 2 Thessalonians 1:7 will say that at his revelation from heaven Jesus will be accompanied by "his powerful angels." But "the consecrated ones" at his coming in 2 Thessalonians 1:10 seem to equate with "those who believe," and 1 Thessalonians 4:14 says that God will bring deceased believers with Jesus. On the whole, then, "with all his consecrated ones" here in 3:13 probably means "with all deceased believers" and anticipates the discussion in 4:13–18. Comfortingly, "all" stresses that no deceased believer will be left out.

AN EXHORTATION TO SEXUAL MORALITY
1 Thessalonians 4:1–8

4:1–2: Therefore, brothers, as to the rest [of this letter] **we ask you and exhort** [you] **in the Lord, Jesus, that just as you received from us** [instructions on] **how it's necessary for you to walk around** [a figure of speech for conduct in everyday life] **and to please God, just as you** *are* **walking around** [that is, conducting yourselves], **that you be flourishing more** [by way of God-pleasing conduct]. ²**For you know what orders we gave you through the Lord, Jesus.** This exhortation to sexual morality starts a series of exhortations that fill out the rest of the letter, except for a conclusion in 5:23–28. The initial "Therefore" makes Paul's preceding wish that the Lord stabilize the Thessalonians' hearts as "blameless" (3:13) a basis for the following exhortation. The address "brothers" lends to the exhortation the weight of Paul and company's affection for the Thessalonian believers. The exhortation is driven by concern for their welfare. The use of "ask" as well as "exhort" adds further weight. To ask is to request. To exhort is to encourage strongly. "In the Lord, Jesus" locates Paul and company, the addressees, the asking, and the exhorting in Jesus as the Lord, whose lordship adds even further weight to the exhortation. He himself is the sphere in which these parties participate in the give-and-take of exhortation. "Just as you received from us" indicates that the exhortation shouldn't surprise the Thessalonians, as though Paul were going to spring on them something new and onerous. They heard the upcoming exhortation when Paul and company were with them in Thessalonica. "How it's necessary" justifies a repetition of the exhortation despite its being old hat. For of necessity "turn[ing] to God from idols to slave for the living and true God" (1:9) issues in conduct pleasing to him. "Just as you *are* walking around" provides a complimentary and therefore encouraging base on which to build the exhortation to "be flourishing more" by way of God-pleasing conduct. They're already flourishing; that is, their conduct is already more than good enough to please God. But they should build up an even greater excess of such conduct lest there be any doubt as to the genuineness of their faith, love, and hope (1:3). "For you know what orders we gave you" appeals to their already existing knowledge of what pleases God and, to ensure a ready acceptance of the exhortation, compliments them for that knowledge. "Through the Lord, Jesus" means that though Paul and company gave the orders, God had channeled those orders first through Jesus as the authoritative Lord. So obedience is necessary.

4:3–6: For this is God's will—[namely,] **your consecration—that you be keeping your distance from fornication;** ⁴**that each of you know to be acquiring his own vessel in consecration and honor,** ⁵**not in the passion of lust** [= lustful passion] **as indeed also the Gentiles** [fornicate] **who don't know God;** ⁶**that none** [of you] **infringe on and rip off his brother in the matter** [by committing adultery with his fellow Christian's wife], **because the Lord** [is] **an avenger in regard to all these** [matters], **just as also we told you before** [when we were with you] **and solemnly testified** [so that you'd be forewarned]. "Consecration" ("sanctification" in many translations) has to do with being set apart from profane use, here for the doing of God's will. The Thessalonian believers are to consecrate themselves by keeping their distance from fornication, a term used for all kinds of sexual immorality but referring especially to sexual intercourse with prostitutes. Because it often took place with prostitutes who plied their trade in pagan temples, fornication there would amount to consecration to the god or goddess of the temple rather than to "the living and true God" (1:9). Paul is writing in particular to Christian men. But God's will isn't only that these men keep away from fornication. Taking account of their sexual urge, he wills also that they marry a woman so as to help them keep their distance from fornication (1 Corinthians 7:1–9). A woman is a "vessel" for seminal fluid ejaculated by a man (compare the comments on 1 Peter 3:7, where a woman as "the *weaker* vessel" implies that the man is a container of seminal fluid just as she's a receptacle for it). "His *own* vessel" indicates a woman who becomes the man's wife. "Acquiring" describes marriage as a man's gaining sexual property (see more on this description below, and compare Exodus 20:17; Deuteronomy 5:21). "That *each* of you *know* to be acquiring his own vessel" means that God wants every Christian man to know his approval of such an acquisition. (The Greek text contains no word for "how," so that the translation "know *how* to be acquiring his own vessel," as though it were a question of manner or method, is misleading.) "In consecration" defines sexual intercourse in marriage as a kind of consecration that God wills. "In . . . honor" defines it as a behavior he honors as well as wills. "Not in the passion of lust" relates back to the practice of fornication, with which marital sexual intercourse contrasts. "As indeed the Gentiles [fornicate]" draws a distinct line of separation between sexual behavior proper to Christians and sexual misbehavior characteristic of non-Christians. "Who don't know God" describes non-Christians as ignorant of God's will in this regard because they don't know God himself (compare Romans 1:18–32).

Next, Paul and company shift from fornication, presumably with prostitutes, to adultery with fellow Christians' wives, calling it an infringement and rip-off because the wife of a brother is by acquisition his sexual property. This isn't all that Paul has to say about the status of married women, of course. See 1 Corinthians

7:2–5 for their having as much sexual authority over their husbands' bodies as husbands do over the bodies of their wives (compare Ephesians 5:22–33). For the moment, though, Paul is zeroing in on men's bad behavior. The defrauded husband won't have to take vengeance on the brother who committed adultery with his wife. The Lord himself will avenge the defrauded brother, and the fleeting pleasure of adultery isn't worth suffering vengeance at the Lord's hands. Though it's left unstated how and when he'll take vengeance, see 1 Corinthians 5:1–5. "But in *all* these [matters]" includes fornication as well as adultery. So the Lord (Jesus) will avenge not only a defrauded husband. He'll also avenge God for a Christian man's violating his consecration to God by having sex with a prostitute (which in the pagan world of that day was generally considered legitimate). "Just as we told you before" reminds the Thessalonians again that this exhortation should come as no imposition on them of a new and onerous moral burden. "And solemnly testified" adds that the past exhortation in their presence was given with the same seriousness that characterizes this written version of it. No excuses, then!

4:7–8: For God has not called us on the ground of uncleanness—rather, in consecration. Here Paul supports his exhortation with an appeal to the call of God, by which God effectively draws people into his kingdom. "Uncleannesss" refers to the moral contamination of illicit sex, as opposed to moral consecration to him. "Not . . . on the ground of uncleanness" means that his call shares no ground with the sexual immorality that formed part and parcel of much pagan religion. "In consecration" locates his call separate from such uncleanness. [8]**Therefore indeed** [because *God* has called us] **the one who disregards** [God's having called him in consecration] **isn't disregarding a human being; rather,** [he's disregarding] **God, who also gives his Holy Spirit to you.** "The one who disregards" suggests that Timothy had brought back a report that a man or a class of men in the Thessalonian church were disregarding the exhortation to sexual morality which Paul and company had issued when evangelizing Thessalonica. In any case, to disregard human authorities, such as them, is ill-advised. To disregard God is positively dangerous, as emphasized by "Therefore *indeed.*" But the description of him as the one "who also gives his Holy Spirit to you" explains both why it's necessary to keep your consecration to God inviolate (compare 1 Corinthians 6:18–20) and how it is that you're "in the Lord, Jesus" (4:1). Since the Holy Spirit indwells him, for you to have the Holy Spirit is for you also to indwell the Lord, Jesus.

AN EXHORTATION TO MUTUAL LOVE
1 Thessalonians 4:9–12

4:9–10a: But concerning brotherly love, you have no need [for us] **to write to you. For you yourselves are God-taught to be loving one another.** [10a]**For you're actually doing it,** [that is, showing love] **to all the brothers in the whole of Macedonia.** For two reasons

the Thessalonian believers don't need an exhortation to love one another: (1) They're already doing it so spontaneously that Paul credits it to God's direct teaching, which implies that Paul and company hadn't told them earlier to love one another (compare Isaiah 54:13; John 6:45). The addition of "yourselves" to "you" highlights their mutual love. (2) "*Actually*" and "to *all* the brothers [fellow Christians] in the *whole* of Macedonia" excitedly acknowledge an expansion of this love far beyond the city limits of Thessalonica, so that for this reason too no exhortation is needed. Since love entails "labor" for others' benefit (1:3), the Thessalonian Christians must have been helping Christians throughout other parts of Macedonia financially and in other practical ways.

4:10b–12: But we exhort you, brothers, to flourish more [in mutual love] [11]**and to aspire to being quiet and doing your own things and working with your own hands, just as we ordered you** [when we were with you] [12]**that you should walk around** [= conduct yourselves] **respectably toward outsiders and** [that] **you might have need of nothing.** Now it turns out that the lack of *need* for an exhortation to mutual love transmutes into a *reason* for such an exhortation—but with this difference, that the exhortation has to do with increase rather than making up for a deficiency. Another address with "brothers" stresses the exhortation. "To flourish more" implies that love is already flourishing. But there's never too much of love among Christians, especially when they're being persecuted as the Thessalonian believers were (1:6; 2:14; 3:3–5). So "more" urges an even greater excess of love for one another. Such love will enable them to retire from seeking favors from wealthy, powerful patrons in return for noisily broadcasting the supposed virtues of those patrons. "Working with your own hands" defines "doing your own things" and indicates that doing manual labor for self-support provides the means by which one can achieve the aspiration of "being quiet" because of independence from patrons. Despite the elites' disdain for manual labor, Christians' gaining economic independence ("need of nothing") by "working with [their] own hands" would gain the respect of most non-Christians ("outsiders" [compare the comments on 2 Thessalonians 3:6–13]).

AN EXHORTATION TO BE COMFORTED IN REGARD TO DECEASED FELLOW BELIEVERS
1 Thessalonians 4:13–18

4:13–14: And we don't want you to be ignorant, brothers, concerning those who are sleeping [the sleep of death], **lest you grieve just as** [do] **the rest** [unbelievers]**, who have no hope.** [14]**For if we believe** [as we do] **that Jesus died and resurrected—in this way too God will bring those who've fallen asleep through Jesus with him.** Yet another address with "brothers" introduces a new exhortation on an affectionate note. This exhortation includes an instruction designed to do away with ignorance. Some Thessalonian believers had died. The figure of sleeping refers to the supine posture of corpses lying in a tomb or a grave, not to the condition of disembodied souls (for which see 2 Corinthians 5:6–9; Philippians 1:21–23 so far as Paul is concerned). The Christians still living were grieving, apparently out of ignorance that their deceased fellow Christians would resurrect at the second coming. To resurrect is, literally, to have your corpse "stand up" out of its supine posture because of renewed life. Pagans lacked hope of a bodily resurrection for life on a renewed earth (compare the ancient epitaph: "I didn't exist. I did exist. I don't exist. I don't care"). "Lest you grieve just as [do] the rest, who have no hope" implies that the Thessalonian believers likewise lacked this hope, though they did believe that Jesus had resurrected. Paul and company explain that there's no reason to grieve out of lack of hope, because Jesus' resurrection ensures the resurrection of deceased Christians as God's way of bringing them with Jesus at the second coming. Paul is so eager to make this point that he breaks off the sentence that begins, "For if we believe," skips saying something like "we should also believe that," and jumps to the conclusion: "in this way too [= through a resurrection like that of Jesus] God will bring those who've fallen asleep through Jesus with him." "Will bring . . . with him" means that God will bring the disembodied souls of deceased believers with Jesus at the second coming to be united with their bodies in resurrection. "Those who've fallen asleep through Jesus" means that he's the agent whose death and resurrection ensures that the death of believers in him will issue in a resurrection like his. For, after all, they're "in . . . the Lord, Jesus Christ" (1:1) and thus are "the dead in Christ" (4:16; compare Romans 8:1–11; 1 Corinthians 15:22–23).

4:15–18: For this we say to you by the word of the Lord, that we who are living, who are being left behind [by those who've passed on] **till the Lord's coming, will by no means precede those who've fallen asleep, ¹⁶because the Lord himself will come down from heaven with a summons, with the archangel's voice, and with God's trumpet** [compare 1 Corinthians 15:52; Matthew 24:31]; **and the dead in Christ will resurrect first. ¹⁷Then we who are living and who are** [now] **being left behind will be snatched up together with them in clouds to meet the Lord in the air. And in this way we'll always be with the Lord. ¹⁸And so** [as a consequence], **be encouraging one another with these words.** "For" introduces the basis on which the preceding assurance rests. "The word of the Lord" constitutes that basis. It's tempting to think of some saying of Jesus that's recorded in one or more of the Gospels. But he's not recorded as having said anything like the key point here, which is that believers still living at the second coming won't precede deceased believers. So "the word of the Lord" likely refers to a prophetic revelation given by Jesus after his ascension to heaven (compare the use of this phrase for prophetic revelations in 1 Kings 13:2, 5, 9, 17, 18, 20, 26, 32; 20:35; Isaiah 1:10; Jeremiah 1:4 and other passages). "Lord" was increasingly used for the Roman emperor, and "coming" was often used for his (as well as other dignitaries') arrivals. So "the Lord's coming" pits

Jesus' arrival as the true, heavenly emperor against that of the earthly Caesar. "Will by no means" emphatically denies a precedence of living believers over deceased believers on that occasion. The Lord's coming will feature a descent from heaven. The addition of "himself" to "the Lord" underscores his heavenly lordship. "A summons" refers to a shout of command that "the dead in Christ" resurrect. "The archangel's voice" and a blast of "God's trumpet" add further decibels to the shout, which will awake and rally to renewed life "those who've fallen asleep." That the trumpet is *God's*, that the voice is the *arch*angel's, and that "the [Christian] dead" are "*in Christ*" and "will resurrect *first* [that is, before living believers are involved]" add such prestige to the deceased believers that nobody should grieve over their fate. They "will resurrect first" because they'll need bodies with which to meet the Lord appropriately. Living believers won't need a resurrection, of course. The meeting will occur "in the air" because of the Lord's descent from heaven, on the one hand, and because of the need, on the other hand, to honor him with a welcoming party outside the world-city and with an escort for the rest of his descent to the earth. For the arrivals of an emperor or other dignitary were regularly celebrated in this way, though horizontally rather than vertically. A meeting in the air requires not only that the Lord "come down from heaven" but also that resurrected and living believers "be snatched up." "Together with them" assures living believers that they won't be left out any more than they've feared that deceased believers would be left out. "In clouds" identifies the air where the meeting will take place as the earth's upper atmosphere. This meeting describes the way believers will come to be "always . . . with the Lord" (compare "presence" as another meaning of the Greek word behind "coming"). "Encouraging" connotes comfort in regard to deceased fellow believers, and possibly also in regard to living believers who face the prospect of dying before the Lord's coming.

AN EXHORTATION TO EXPECTANT READINESS FOR THE DAY OF THE LORD
1 Thessalonians 5:1–11

5:1–3: But concerning the times and the occasions, brothers, you have no need [for anything] **to be written to you. ²For you yourselves know correctly that the Day of the Lord is coming in this way: as a thief** [comes] **in the night. ³When people are saying, "Peace and security," then sudden destruction bears down on them, as indeed labor pain** [bears down on] **a pregnant woman; and by no means will they escape.** The address "brothers" introduces a new exhortation on an affectionate note. "The times and the occasions" have to do with the date of the Lord's coming as described in 4:13–18. The Thessalonians don't need a written instruction about that date, because prior oral instruction has already given them as much knowledge as is available. The addition of "yourselves" to "you" stresses their knowledge and adds to the compliment of their having it. As usual, the compliment aims for a good reception of what the authors have further to write. "Correctly" heightens the compliment and stresses the accuracy of knowing that "the Day of the Lord is coming in this way: as a thief [comes] in the night."

Old Testament prophets spoke often about "the Day of the Lord," by which they meant a day when the Lord would step into human affairs so as to judge the wicked and deliver the righteous (see, for example, Amos 5:18, 20). Since 4:13–18 spoke about "the coming of the Lord [Jesus]," Paul takes over the Old Testament phrase, "the Day of the Lord," and uses it for the day of Jesus' coming as the Lord to judge the wicked and deliver believers in him. Since the Day of the Lord is the day of the Lord's coming, "is coming" personifies the day: *it* is coming because *he* is coming. The present tense of "is coming" makes the coming so sure that the day might as well be already on its way. "As a thief [comes] in the night" points to unexpectedness. The contrast between the bearing down of "sudden destruction" and people's saying, "Peace and security," slightly favors that the people are expecting peace and security rather than, or more than, that they are describing a condition current at the time. In either case, there's a warning that the peace and security claimed and advertised by Roman rulers will prove illusory at worst, ephemeral at best. "Sudden destruction" refers to ruination, not annihilation, that will occur on the Day of the Lord. It's the Lord, Jesus, who at his coming on his day brings ruin on the people who are saying, "Peace and security." The contrast with "peace" implies a day of battle. The contrast with "security" stresses the destruction that will take place as a consequence of the battle. And the suddenness of this destruction contributes to its unexpectedness. The comparison to labor pain, emphasized with "indeed," highlights both the suddenness and the inevitability of destruction. Just as labor pain suddenly stabs the body of a pregnant woman who has come to term, so too will destruction suddenly strike the wicked when the Day of the Lord arrives. Furthermore, the unstoppability of giving birth once labor pain starts—this unstoppability leads the authors to add "and by no means will they [those who say, 'Peace and security'] escape."

5:4–5: But you, brothers, aren't in darkness so that the Day [of the Lord] **would catch you** [by surprise], **as a thief** [would]. **⁵For all you are sons of the light and sons of the day. We don't belong to the night, nor to the darkness.** "But you" distinguishes the audience of Christian believers from the preceding "they/them" on whom the Day of the Lord will bring ruin. As explained in 4:13–18, the coming of the Lord on his day will bring to believers, not ruin, but the very peace and security that unbelievers mistakenly expect for themselves. Another address with "brothers" underscores the distinction between believers and unbelievers in this regard. "You . . . aren't in darkness" is a figurative way of repeating the compliment that as informed believers the addressees are already in the know. But if there's nothing to be known about the date of the Day of the Lord, why won't that day catch believers as well as unbelievers by

surprise? Answer: 2 Thessalonians 2:1–12 will remind the addressees of events preceding the Day of the Lord, the observation of which events will keep them from being caught by surprise (though in 2 Thessalonians the present *non*observation of those events is meant to keep the addressees from thinking the day has already arrived), whereas unbelievers won't recognize the preceding events as signals that the Day of the Lord is about to arrive. In the meantime, though, Paul explains that along with other believers the Thessalonians are "sons of the light"—that is, people characterized by the light of knowledge—and therefore also "sons of the day"—that is, people whose knowledge makes the Day of the Lord welcome for them rather than threatening, as it is to unbelievers. "*All* you" heightens the compliment, which is also an encouragement. Since nighttime is at odds with daytime, "we don't belong to the night" means that we aren't at odds with the Day of the Lord. "Nor to the darkness" means that we're not characterized by ignorance concerning the Day of the Lord's coming. "We" includes Paul and company along with the addressees and implies their joyful anticipation of that day.

5:6–11: Therefore, then, let's not be sleeping, as the rest [of humankind are sleeping, because they belong to the night and to darkness]. **Rather, let's stay awake and sober. ⁷For those who sleep do their sleeping during the night, and those who get drunk do their getting drunk during the night. ⁸But because of belonging to the day, let's be staying sober as a result of having suited up with the breastplate** [consisting] **of faith and love, and with the hope of salvation as a helmet** [compare 1:3; Ephesians 6:14–17; Isaiah 59:17], **⁹because God hasn't set us for wrath—rather, for the obtaining of salvation through our Lord, Jesus Christ, ¹⁰who died for us in order that whether we're staying awake or sleeping we'll live together with him. ¹¹Therefore be encouraging one another and building up** [each other], **one on one, just as also you're doing** [compare 4:1, 10]. "Therefore" means "[for the reason that] we don't belong to the night, nor to the darkness" (5:5). The addition of "then" to "therefore" underlines this reason for not sleeping. Not as in 4:13–15, where sleeping represented death, now it represents failure to be looking out for the events that will signal the soon coming of the Day of the Lord. As noted earlier, 2 Thessalonians 2:1–12 will spell out those events by way of a reminder of what Paul had taught when in Thessalonica but what for the moment he takes for granted the Thessalonian believers remember. So "let's not be sleeping" urges looking for the signaling events. "As the rest" alludes to unbelievers' not looking out for these events because of ignorance concerning them. "Rather" underscores both staying awake, the counterpart to not sleeping, and the additional exhortation to stay sober.

We shouldn't interpret staying sober as only a figure of speech for maintaining self-control (see the comments on 1 Peter 1:13; 4:7; 5:8). Drunkenness leads to sleep. Drunken sleep characterizes unbelievers and stands for their ignorance of the events that will signal the near arrival of the Day of the Lord—and hence for the unbelievers' coming failure to recognize those signals. Neither drunkenness and drunken sleep nor what they symbolize should characterize Christians. Sobriety enables the exercise of "faith," which has earlier been said to issue in "work" (1:3), which in turn can't be done by those who are sleeping. Sobriety also enables the exericise of "love," which has earlier been said to issue in "labor" (1:3 again), which in turn and likewise can't be done by those who are sleeping. Faith and love are compared to a breastplate, protection for the vital organs in the chest. "The hope of salvation" means *confident* expectation of salvation at the Day of the Lord. This hope is compared to a helmet, protection for the head. These pieces of armor stand for believers' protection from the destruction that the Day of the Lord will bring on unbelievers. "Because God hasn't set us for wrath" means that there's no need to drown our troubles, such as persecution, in drunkenness. Our exemption from his coming wrath (compare 1:10) and our destiny to obtain salvation from it give more than enough reason to face the future awake and sober. "Through our Lord, Jesus Christ" reminds us that we'll obtain this salvation at his future coming because he "died for us" in the past.

"Our Lord, Jesus Christ" identifies Jesus rather than the Caesars or pagan deities as the Lord of Christians. "We'll live together with him" recalls "we'll always be with the Lord" (4:17), expresses the purpose of his dying for us, and alludes to his past resurrection, deceased believers' future resurrection, and the continued living of believers who survive till the coming of the Lord on his day. So "whether we're staying awake or sleeping" means whether we stay alive till his coming or we're sleeping the sleep of death by that time (compare 4:13–17). "Therefore be encouraging one another" recalls 4:18 for emphasis and helps identify "the Day of the Lord" as the time of "the coming of the Lord" in 4:13–18. "And building up [each other]" portrays encouragement in terms of building a structure that will withstand the pressures of persecution. "One on one" individualizes the encouragement that's to be done. "Just as also you're doing" draws a comparison whose complimentary character should elicit further activity of an encouraging sort.

MISCELLANEOUS EXHORTATIONS
1 Thessalonians 5:12–22

5:12–13: And we ask you, brothers, to acknowledge those who are laboring among you and presiding over you in the Lord and admonishing you; ¹³and [we ask you] to regard them extravagantly in love because of their work. Another address with "brother" introduces a further exhortation on an affectionate note designed to elicit a favorable response. "And we *ask* you" issues this exhortation on the cordial note of a request. "To acknowledge" is to show a deference that's deserved because of labor, authority, and admonition. For "laboring among you" is exhausting, "presiding over you" is "in the Lord" (that is, an execution of Jesus' lordship), and "admonishing you" is for your benefit. "Admonishing

you" refers to putting you on notice as to what Christian conduct requires. Acknowledgement is one thing, attitude another. So Paul asks the addressees to regard their local leaders "in love," and to do so "extravagantly." ("Presiding over" may refer not so much to governing as to hosting a house church, which hosting entailed a certain authority in arranging meetings of the church.) **Be at peace among yourselves.** This exhortation encapsulates the preceding one in that deferring to the leaders and loving them extravagantly will forestall rebellion and thus maintain peaceful relations between believers.

5:14–15: And we exhort you, brothers, be admonishing the disorderly. See the comments on 5:12 for "brothers." "Exhort" strikes a stronger note than that of "ask" in the preceding exhortation. This greater strength suits an admonition concerning the disorderly, whose misbehavior disrupts the just-commanded peaceful relations among believers. Given 4:11; 2 Thessalonians 3:6–16, "the disorderly" describes those who refuse to work for their living and sponge off wealthy patrons instead. Ordinary church members as well as the leaders are to put the disorderly on notice that they must stop this behaving out-of-line, which causes peace-disrupting resentments among believers. **Be reassuring the discouraged.** Persecution, which the addressees have been suffering according to 1:6; 2:14; 3:3–4; 2 Thessalonians 1:4–7, can cause discouragement, especially when some fellow Christians are taking economic refuge in the good graces of their patrons. The teaching on the Lord's coming in 4:13–5:11 can be put to good use in reassuring the discouraged. **Be helping the sick.** Why? Because their weakness keeps them from helping themselves—by working for their living as they could and should do if they were well, for example. **Be patient toward all**—that is, toward the disorderly, the discouraged, the sick, and (presumably) outsiders as well, including persecutors. For such people can try your patience innocently as well as culpably. ¹⁵**Be seeing that no one repays anyone harm in return for harm; rather, always be pursuing what's good for one another** [in the church] **and for all** [unbelievers too]. Believers as a community have a responsibility to see that none of their number plays tit for tat when it comes to harmful behavior. The opposition to each other of "harm" and "good" indicates that "what's good" refers to what is beneficial to others. "Always" and "be pursuing" stress the persistence and vigor which should characterize doing good for others rather than harming them.

5:16–22: Always be rejoicing. ¹⁷Be praying constantly. ¹⁸In every [circumstance] be giving thanks. Rejoicing, praying, and thanksgiving feed off each other. Thanksgiving validates praying, and praying gives rise to rejoicing in that God answers prayer. Joy, which isn't characteristic of pagan religion, produces more thanksgiving, so that the cycle repeats itself interminably, whereas failure to do one or another damages your doing of the others. So do all three in conjunction—regularly, as indicated by "always," "constantly," and "in every [circumstance]." **For this** [rejoicing, praying, and thanksgiving] [is] **God's will in Christ Jesus for you** [to do]. The will of God should drive believers to rejoice, pray, and give thanks; and his will is located "in Christ Jesus" in the sense that since believers are "in God the Father and the Lord, Jesus Christ" (1:1), they should do God's will that they find there. See the comments on 2:14 for "Christ Jesus." [19]**Don't be extinguishing the Spirit.** [20]**Don't be treating prophecies as of no account.** [21]**But be testing all things. Be holding tight the good.** [22]**Be keeping your distance from every sort of evil** [compare Isaiah 1:16–17]. Implied is a comparison of the Spirit to fire. Since the word of the Lord is like a burning fire in the heart of a prophet (Jeremiah 20:9), "Don't be treating prophecies as of no account" interprets "Don't be extinguishing the Spirit" (see the comments on 1 Corinthians 14:3 for Christian prophecy as inspired speech, whether or not predictive, that has the purposes of upbuilding, exhortation, and reassurance). On the other hand there's false prophecy as well as true. So Paul follows up with the instruction, "But be testing all things" (compare 1 Corinthians 12:10; 14:29). Some things will test out good. Other things will test out evil. Believers are to hold tight the good, but keep their distance from evil. Since they've already been told to keep their distance from fornication (4:3), Paul enlarges the exhortation to include "*every sort* of evil." The contrast with "keeping your distance" makes "holding tight" mean allying yourself as closely as possible with what's good.

A BENEDICTION AND FINAL INSTRUCTIONS
1 Thessalonians 5:23–28

5:23–24: And may the God of peace himself consecrate you entirely, and may your spirit and soul and body be kept blamelessly complete at the coming of our Lord, Jesus Christ. [24]**The one calling you** [is] **faithful, who also will do** [the consecrating and keeping]. "The God of peace" is the God who grants believers the peace that consists in all the blessings of salvation (see the comments on 1 Peter 1:2; 2 John 3), a peace to be reflected and symbolized in "peace among yourselves" (5:13). For God to consecrate you is for him to set you apart from unbelievers and thus treat you as sacred to himself. The addition of "himself" to "the God of peace" stresses Paul's wish that God act in this way (compare

4:3, though there the associated command to keep away from fornication favors *self*-consecration to him). "Entirely" indicates the insufficiency of any consecration less than 100 percent. A repetitive and expansive followup drives home the point: (1) "Your spirit and soul and body" expands the earlier "you" for emphasis on the entirety of the person, including the physical body, often denigrated in pagan thought. The expansion doesn't make fine distinctions between three parts of the human constitution any more than the command to love God with your whole heart and soul and mind and strength (Mark 12:30) makes fine distinctions between four parts of the human constitution. (2) "Be kept" corresponds to God's consecrating you in the earlier wish. (3) "Blamelessly complete" refers to the result of entire consecration, a result that will be achieved "at the coming of our Lord, Jesus Christ." "The one calling you" is God (see the comments on 2:12 for the call). His faithfulness will display itself in consecrating and keeping you in addition to calling you.

5:25–28: Brothers, be praying for us too. [26]**Greet all the brothers with a sacred kiss.** [27]**I put you under a solemn oath before the Lord** [as a witness] **to have the letter** [this one] **read to all the brothers.** [28]**The grace of our Lord, Jesus Christ,** [be] **with you.** As before, the address "Brothers" refers to the Thessalonian Christians in general and introduces the final lines of this letter affectionately. "Be praying for us *too*" implies that the immediately preceding benediction ("And may the God of peace himself . . .") reflected a prayer for the Thessalonian believers such as they should now pray for Paul and company. "Greet" literally means "embrace." Paul commands that "a sacred kiss" supplement the embrace. "Sacred" doesn't describe the kiss as chaste, though it should be, but as symbolic of accepting one another as consecrated to God, his sacred ones, his saints (see the comments on 1 Corinthians 1:1–3). Presumably, "you" (plural) whom Paul ("I") puts "under a solemn oath . . . to have the letter read to all the brothers" are the church leaders referenced in 5:12–13. "Before the Lord" strengthens the adjuration. For the church's united further progress, Paul insists that no believer be denied a hearing of the letter in an assembly. He used "grace," the ill-merited favor of God and Jesus Christ, as a hello (1:1) and now uses it as a goodbye. Both coming and going their grace is never to be forgotten.

SECOND THESSALONIANS

This letter assures Christians in Thessalonica, Macedonia, that they'll be delivered from persecution at Jesus' return on the Day of the Lord, explains that that day won't arrive till after a massive rebellion against God, and specifies ways to behave properly in the meantime.

ADDRESS AND GREETING
2 Thessalonians 1:1–2

1:1–2: Paul and Silvanus and Timothy to the church of the Thessalonians [which is] **in God, our Father, and the Lord, Jesus Christ:** [2]**Grace and peace to you from God the Father and the Lord, Jesus Christ.** See the comments on 1 Thessalonians 1:1. There, "our" is missing from the first instance of "Father" but present in 1:3, whereas the reverse is true here. Furthermore, "from God, the Father, and the Lord, Jesus Christ" now specifies the source of grace and peace, as wasn't done in 1 Thessalonians 1:1. Given the ongoing persecution of the Thessalonian believers and their apparent alarm, both of which are about to be mentioned, this specification has the purpose of encouraging them, so that a greeting from Paul and company escalates into a greeting from God and Jesus Christ as well, even at the expense of repetitiousness. See also the final comments on the greeting in 1 Corinthians 1:3

PERSECUTION
2 Thessalonians 1:3–12

Though it consists of one long sentence, this passage divides into a thanksgiving for the Thessalonian believers' progress in the midst of persecution (1:3–4), an assurance of deliverance from persecution and of divine judgment on the persecutors at the Lord's coming (1:5–10), and a prayer for the Thessalonian believers (1:11–12).

1:3–4: We ought to be thanking God always for you, brothers, just as it's fitting [that we do]**, because your faith is luxuriating and** [because] **the love of each one of you all for one another is increasing,** [4]**so that we ourselves are boasting in you among all the churches of God regarding your endurance and faith in all your persecutions and afflictions that you're putting up with . . . .** "We *ought* to be thanking God for you" doesn't imply that Paul and company haven't been praying for the addressees (see 1:11)—rather, that though they had evangelized Thessalonica, God deserves the credit for the luxuriating of the addressees' faith and for the increase in their love for one another.

"Always" underscores his deserving this credit, and "just as it's fitting" adds propriety to obligation in this giving of thanks to God. The endearing address "brothers" helps make the thanksgiving also a compliment on the Thessalonians' faith and mutual love. Though 1 Thessalonians was peppered with references to their faith and mutual love, a large number of features in the present passage heighten this thank-filled compliment, which should open the Thessalonians' hearts to the encouragement, instruction, and exhortations contained in the rest of the letter. Here are those features: (1) "because your faith is *luxuriating*" (whereas 1 Thessalonians 3:10 referred to a need to "make up for the *deficiencies* in your faith" despite earlier commendations of it); (2) "the love *of each one* of you *all* for one another *is increasing*" (in fulfillment of the prayer and exhortation in 1 Thessalonians 3:12; 4:9–10); (3) Paul and company's "*boasting*" in the addressees (whereas in 1 Thessalonians 1:8–10 they had "no need to say anything," because others were reporting the Thessalonians' faith); (4) their boasting in the Thessalonian believers "among *all* the churches of God" (except the church in Thessalonica, of course); (5) the addition of "*ourselves*" to "we" for emphasis on this boasting (as though they couldn't contain themselves even though the report of others left no need for boasting); (6) the prefixing of "your *endurance*" to "faith"; (7) the addition of "in *all* your *persecutions* and *afflictions*" to "faith" (which additions give "your endurance and faith" the sense of "persevering faith" and "faithful perseverance"); and (8) the notation that the addressees "are *putting up with*" their persecutions and afflictions. "Boasting *in* you" means that the boasting is centered on the Thessalonian believers, not on Paul and company's work of having evangelized them; and the Greek text mentions "in" twice for an untranslatable emphasis on them as the object of boasting. "Among all the churches" means "in all the assemblies," *not* in church buildings, of which there were none as yet. See the comments on 1 Thessalonians 2:14 for the additional phrase "of God." First Thessalonians 1:3 mentioned the addressees' faith, love, and hope. The present passage mentions faith and love—but not hope, because it has to do with the second coming, about which the addressees have become confused and therefore need correction (see chapter 2).

1:5–10: evidence of God's righteous judgment, so that you'll be considered worthy of God's kingdom, for which also you're suffering, [6]**if indeed** [it's] **right** [as it is!] **with God** [= in accordance with his justice] to repay with afflictions those who are afflicting you [7]and [to repay] with relief you who are being afflicted, along with us, at the revelation of the Lord, Jesus, from heaven with his powerful angels, by means of flaming fire [8]dealing vengeance [for believers] on those who don't know God and aren't obeying the gospel about our Lord, Jesus, [9]who [referring to the persecutors] as such [= as ignorant of God and disobedient to Jesus' gospel] will pay a penalty, [namely,] eternal destruction away from the Lord's face [= presence] and away from the glory of his strength, [10]when he comes to be glorified on that day among his consecrated ones [= Christians as consecrated to the Lord Jesus and through him to the one true God] and marveled at among all who believe, because our testimony to you was believed . . . . According to 1 Thessalonians 3:3b–4 Christians are destined to suffer afflictions that consist in persecution. Here, then, such afflictions are said to be "evidence of God's righteous judgment" in that they demonstrate that he will rightly consider persecuted Christians fit ("worthy") for entrance into his coming kingdom, because they've suffered for it, and will rightly repay their persecutors with affliction (compare Philippians 1:27–30). Not that Christians earn their way into God's kingdom by suffering for it; rather, that their endurance of persecution proves their faith genuine (compare 1 Peter 1:6–7). They suffer for God's kingdom because they profess it and proclaim it over against the kingdom of blasphemously deified Caesars and their successors. "Also" simply adds the thought of suffering to that of being considered worthy. "Along with us" adds the suffering of Paul and company to that of the addressees (see 1 Thessalonians 2:2, 15–16; 3:7 and numerous passages in Acts, including 17:1–13).

"If indeed [it's] right with God" echoes "God's righteous judgment" for emphasis on its rightness. "And [to repay] with relief [from persecution] you who are being afflicted" echoes "you'll be considered worthy of God's kingdom" for further emphasis on that rightness. "At the revelation of the Lord, Jesus, from heaven" echoes "the coming of the Lord . . . from heaven" on "the Day of the Lord" in 1 Thessalonians 4:13–5:2. But "the revelation" substitutes for "the coming" to indicate a public appearance for a balancing of the scales of justice. Since persecution has put the Christians to public shame, their vindication will require publicity. "With his powerful angels" portrays as irresistible their execution of justice at Jesus' command. "By means of flaming fire dealing vengeance" balances relief from affliction for Christians with God's fiery wrath for their persecutors (compare 1 Thessalonians 4:6, 13–5:10; Romans 12:19; 2 Samuel 22:48 = Psalm 18:47; Isaiah 66:15). The persecutors "don't know God" in the sense that they ignore him, don't acknowledge him, and therefore lack a personal acquaintance with him. They "aren't obeying the gospel of our Lord, Jesus" in that they're hearing it but not heeding it. Personified, the gospel commands people to repent of their sins and believe in Jesus as the Lord. "*Our* Lord" includes Paul and company with the addressees.

"Vengeance" works itself out as "a penalty" on unbelievers, and the penalty consists in "destruction," which means ruination, not annihilation (see the comments on Matthew 25:46). "Eternal" describes the ruination as everlasting. "Away from the Lord's face" means "distant from Jesus' presence" and makes a striking contrast with the assurance that believers "will always be with the Lord" (1 Thessalonians 4:17). "And away from the glory of his strength" contrastively anticipates his "be[ing] glorified among his consecrated ones" (compare Isaiah 2:10, 19, 21). For good measure, Paul adds "and marveled at among all who believe." "His strength" alludes to Jesus' wreaking vengeance on their persecutors and relieving believers of their persecutions. So "the glory of his strength" consists in believers' glorifying him for—and marveling at—the strength with which he turned the tables on their persecutors. To be away from that glory is ruinously not to participate in the glorifying and marveling. "On that day" refers to "the Day of the Lord," the day of his coming (2:1; 1 Thessalonians 4:13–5:2; compare Isaiah 2:11, 17). Though believers will do the glorifying and marveling, these activities are twice said to take place "among" them. This way of stating the matter points up Jesus' presence with them to receive their adulation, which presence of his is the correlate to their being "with the Lord" (1 Thessalonians 4:17). "*All* who believe" stresses that no believer will be left out (compare 1 Thessalonians 3:13; 5:5). "All who *believe*" contrasts with "not obeying the gospel." "Because our testimony to you was believed" assures the addressees that they're included among "all who believe" and therefore will enjoy the Lord's presence. This reference to a past testimony prepares for a reminder in 2:5 of past teaching.

1:11–12: to which [end] also we're always praying for you, that our God would consider you worthy of the calling [with which he will call you] and fulfill by [his] power every desire of goodness and [to fulfill] the work of faith, [12]so that the name of our Lord, Jesus, may be glorified in you, and you in him, in accordance with the grace of our God and the Lord, Jesus Christ [compare Isaiah 24:15; 66:5]. See the comments on 1 Thessalonians 1:2–3 for "always praying for you." "To which [end]" points forward to the addressees' being relieved of persecution because of God's considering them "worthy of the calling." Since they'll be relieved "at the revelation of the Lord, Jesus, from heaven," "the calling" refers to God's calling them into his eternal kingdom on the occasion of Jesus' revelation from heaven (see the comments on 1:5; 2:14; 1 Thessalonians 2:12; 5:24). God's considering them worthy of this calling depends on the exercise of his power to "fulfill . . . every desire of goodness and [to fulfill] the work of faith." But whose desire? God's? The addressees'? Paul and company's? That Paul and company "are always praying" to this end favors a reference to *their* desire that goodness characterize the addressees, and the Greek word underlying "desire" carries the connotation that Paul and company will "delight" in goodness on the addressees' part (compare 1 Thessalonians 5:15). "*Every* desire of goodness" then multiplies the desire in accordance with Paul and company's being three in number. Accompanying goodness will be "the work of faith," which doesn't mean that belief in Jesus is a work—rather, that good deeds grow out of belief in him (see the comments on 1 Thessalonians 1:3 and compare Galatians 5:6; Ephesians 2:8–10; James 2:14–26). Again, though, the fulfillment of this desire and of this work can come about only by God's exercise of power—hence the praying to this end (compare Philippians 1:6). The purpose and result of fulfillment will be twofold: (1) the glorification of Jesus' name (that is, of him as "Lord" when he comes "on that day" [1:10; compare Philippians 2:9–11]) and (2) the glorification of believers in him (so that because they're in him by virtue of having the Holy Spirit that indwells him as well as them, they'll share his glory [compare Romans 8:17; Colossians 3:4]). "In accordance with the grace of our God and the Lord, Jesus Christ" reminds that sharing in Jesus' glory isn't due to any merit on our part—rather, to the ill-merited favor that originates in God and that Jesus mediates. "*Our* God" and "*our* Lord, Jesus" joyously distinguish the God and the Lord of grace from those ungracious gods and lords from whose idols the addressees have turned away (1 Thessalonians 1:9).

THE DAY OF THE LORD
2 Thessalonians 2:1–17

This passage divides into a denial that the Day of the Lord has arrived (2:1–2), an affirmation of necessary precursors to that day (2:3–15), and a benediction (2:16–17).

2:1–2: And concerning the coming of our Lord, Jesus Christ, and the gathering of us to him, we ask you, brothers, ²to stop being quickly shaken from your rationality and to stop being alarmed—whether through a spirit or through a word or through a letter, as though through us—to the effect that the Day of the Lord has arrived. The address "brothers" introduces a soothing instruction on an affectionate note. "The coming of the Lord" echoes 1 Thessalonians 2:19; 4:15, and "the gathering of us to him" summarizes the catching up of Christians to meet the Lord in the air according to 1 Thessalonians 4:16–17. The Greek word that underlies "*concerning* the coming . . . and the gathering" suggests a rescue of those events from a misconception on the addressees' part. "Us" includes only Christians, of course, such as Paul and company and their addressees. "To stop being *quickly* shaken" implies that the misconception has already disturbed the addressees despite the recency of their conversion and of Paul and company's having taught them in person about the Lord's coming and the gathering of Christians to him on that occasion. "Shaken from your *rationality*" indicates a mental mistake. "And to stop being *alarmed*" indicates an accompanying and resultant emotional upheaval. "Whether through a spirit" points to the possibility of a prophetic revelation claimed to derive from the Holy Spirit but attributed here by Paul and company to some other spirit.

"Or through a word" points to the possibility of an oral report. "Or through a letter" points to the possibility of a written communication. "As though through us" probably refers to all three possibilities. That is, Paul, Silvanus, and Timothy don't know how the Thessalonian believers got mixed up concerning the Lord's coming and the gathering; so they conjecture that somebody has told those believers that Paul and company received a new prophetic revelation, or that somebody has brought an oral report of their supposedly new teaching, or that somebody has delivered to the Thessalonians a letter containing it and forged in the names of Paul and company. Regardless of the way the Thessalonians got a false impression that Paul and company had revised their teaching on the Lord's coming and the gathering, the Thessalonians' misconception of those events consisted in a belief that the Day of the Lord had already arrived (see the comments on 1 Thessalonians 5:2 for the Day of the Lord). The consequent emotional upheaval implies that the Thessalonians were disappointed that the Day of the Lord hadn't relieved them of their persecution by including the Lord's coming to bring them that relief.

2:3–4: No one should delude you in any way, because [the Day of the Lord can't arrive] **unless the rebellion comes first and the human being of lawlessness is revealed, the son of destruction, ⁴the one opposing and elevating himself over everyone called "god" or object of worship** [such as an idol], **so that he sits in God's temple, publicizing himself** [so that people will say,] **"He's God!"** Compare Daniel 11:36; Mark 13:14; Matthew 24:15; Acts 12:21–22; Revelation 13. "In any way" includes the three possible ways just mentioned ("a spirit . . . a word . . . a letter"). "Delude" stresses the falsity of the notion that "the Day of the Lord has arrived" (2:2). Two recognizable events have to take place first: (1) a climactic rebellion against God and (2) a revelation of its leader (compare "the Antichrist" in 1 John 2:18, 22; 4:3; 2 John 7 and "the beast" in Revelation 11:7; 13:1–4 and following). "The human being" stresses his humanity over against his false claim to deity and over against the Lord of the Day of the Lord. "Of lawlessness" means "characterized by the breaking of God's laws" (see Romans 4:7; 6:19; 2 Corinthians 6:14; Titus 2:14 for Paul's other uses of "lawlessness"). "Is revealed" sets the revelation of this rebel over against, and prior to, "the revelation of the Lord, Jesus, from heaven with his powerful angels" (1:7). "The son of destruction" describes the rebel as destined to be ruined, so that in the end his rebellion against God won't succeed. He won't just claim himself to be a god alongside other gods, as some Caesars and other rulers did. He'll claim to be the one and only God and so successfully publicize himself as such that people will proclaim him God. But what's meant by his sitting in God's temple? One immediately thinks of the Jewish temple in Jerusalem, which was still standing when 2 Thessalonians was written. But elsewhere Paul consistently speaks of God's temple as Christians, because the Spirit of God indwells them (see 1 Corinthians 3:16–17; 6:19; 2 Corinthians 6:16; Ephesians 2:21). So under the assumption that Paul and company had spoken of Christians as God's temple when they were in Thessalonica (compare 1 Thessalonians 1:5–6; 4:8; 5:19), it may be better to think of the present text as meaning that "the human being of lawlessness" will arise as an apostate within the church (see again 1 John 2:18, 22; 4:3; 2 John 7 and compare the use of the word "rebellion" for apostasy, that is, for a religious rebellion). His posture of sitting, as on a throne, suits a claim to deified rulership.

2:5–6: You remember, don't you, that when I was still with you I was telling you these things? [6]And now [because of my previous teaching] **you know what's holding down** [the lawless human being], **so that he'll be revealed in his own season** [that is, at the proper time for his revelation]. "I" is Paul (compare 1 Thessalonians 2:18). "Don't you . . . ?" implies that the addressees do remember, so that they shouldn't believe that the Day of the Lord has arrived, as though Paul had changed his tune. "And now you know what's holding [the lawless human being] down" compliments the Thessalonians on their present remembrance of Paul's past teaching, but also uses that remembrance for a soothing correction of their current misconception that the Day of the Lord has arrived without the Lord's coming to relieve them from persecution. They know not only that the lawless human being hasn't yet been revealed. They also know what's holding him down till the proper time for his revelation. But for lack of Paul's teaching when he was in Thessalonica, *we* don't know what's holding down the lawless human being. It's enough for us to know that he hasn't been revealed, that he must be revealed prior to the Lord's coming on the Day of the Lord, and that he'll be revealed at the right time according to God's eschatological calendar.

2:7: For the secret of lawlessness is already at work. Only the one who's presently holding down [the lawless human being will keep doing so] **till he gets out of the midst** [= out of the way]. Paul uses the term "secret" for information formerly unknown but now revealed to Christians, though it remains a mystery to non-Christians. Here the secret consists in the working of lawlessness (that is, the activity of breaking God's laws) already (that is, prior to the revelation of the lawless human being), so that the ground is presently being prepared for the future but short-lived success of his publicizing himself as God. It's only the counter activity of "the one who's presently holding [him] down" that keeps him from being revealed immediately. "*What's* holding [him] down" (2:6) has changed here to "*who's* . . . holding [him] down." This change has caused much interpretive speculation: that Paul shifts from Roman law ("what") as a deterrent over to the Roman emperor ("who") as the enforcer of that law, for example, or that Paul refers to the Holy Spirit as the deterrer and shifts from the neuter gender of the "Spirit" in the Greek language, grammatically speaking ("what"), to the personhood of the Holy Spirit, theologically speaking ("who"). A number of other identifications have been suggested. Again, though, we don't know the reason for the shift

because we lack knowledge of Paul's prior teaching in Thessalonica, so that we have to satisfy ourselves with knowing that the lawless human being has to be revealed before the Lord's coming on the Day of the Lord.

2:8–10: And then [after the one who's holding him down gets out of the way] **the lawless** [human being] **will be revealed, whom the Lord** [Jesus] **will do away with by the breath of his mouth** [compare Exodus 15:18; Psalm 33:6] **and deactivate by the epiphany that consists in his coming, [9]whose coming** [referring now to the lawless human being's coming *as opposed to* the Lord's coming] **is in accordance with Satan's working by means of every** [kind of] **miracle and signs and wonders in the service of a lie** [= the lie that the lawless human being is God] **[10]and by means of every** [kind of] **dishonest deception** [aimed] **at those who are perishing because they didn't welcome the love of the truth** [that Jesus is Lord rather than that the lawless human being is God] **so that they'd be saved** [from God's wrath (see 1 Thessalonians 5:9)]. Clearly, the revelation of the lawless human being will precede the revelation of the Lord. 1:5–10 portrayed the revelation of the Lord as the occasion for his bringing retribution on the persecutors of Christians and for his relieving the Christians from persecution. 2:1 portrayed his revelation as the occasion for his gathering Christians to himself. Now 2:8–10 portrays his revelation as the occasion for his doing away with the lawless human being. But because Paul has just used the vocabulary of revelation in reference to the coming of the lawless human being, for Jesus he shifts from "the revelation" to "the epiphany," which has the added advantage of connoting a powerful manifestation of deity, in contrast with the mere humanity of the lawless human being. The word that's translated "breath" because of the following phrase, "of his mouth," is elsewhere translated "Spirit" or "spirit" and therefore produces a wordplay: the Lord's breath is the Lord's Spirit, by whom he does away with the lawless human being and who is not the "spirit" that might have been mistakenly thought to inspire the notion of the Day of the Lord's having arrived already. "Deactivate" describes the Lord's epiphany as effecting the lawless human being's loss of power. The equation of the Lord's epiphany with his coming sets up for a contrast with the coming of the lawless human being, which Paul attributes to Satan's working and describes as including miracles, signs, wonders, and dishonest deception. By definition "deception" is "dishonest," but the redundancy is emphatic. "At those who are perishing" limits to non-Christians the effectiveness of the lawless human being's deception and describes their fate as an ongoing loss of salvation. This loss derives, in turn, from their failure to welcome, not just the truth (as we expect Paul to say), but "the *love* of the truth." You have to love the truth if you're to welcome it. For loving what 1 John 2:15–16 calls "everything [that's] in the world—[namely,] the lust of the flesh and the lust of the eyes and the braggadocio of livelihood" keeps you from loving the truth by way of welcoming it as your guide for belief and conduct.

2:11–12: And because of this [their nonwelcome of the love of the truth] **God is sending them a work of delusion, so that they'll believe the lie** [that the lawless human being is God], [12]**in order that all who haven't believed the truth—rather, have delighted in the dishonesty—may be judged.** The present tense of "is sending" for a future event connotes certainty. "A *work* of delusion" is a delusive *effect*. So God will judge nonwelcome of the love of the truth by making the nonwelcomers unable to avoid delusion and by making inevitable their believing the lie that the lawless human being is God. People's nonwelcome of the love of the truth, so that they "haven't believed the truth," actually leads God *to purpose* their judgment, their punishment (compare Jesus' telling parables in Mark 4:11–12 for the purpose of hiding the truth from people who hadn't accepted his plain speech). Their "hav[ing] delighted in the dishonesty" of satanic "deception" is the correlate of not believing the truth and of not welcoming the love of it.

2:13–14: But we ought to be thanking God always for you, brothers loved by the Lord [Jesus], **because God chose you for himself from the beginning for salvation by means of the Spirit's consecration and** [by means of your] **belief in the truth** [of the gospel], [14]**into which** [divine choosing for salvation] **he** [God] **also called you through our gospel for the purpose of** [your] **obtaining the glory of our Lord, Jesus Christ.** See the comments on 1:3 about the obligation to be always thanking God. The attachment of "loved by the Lord" to the address "brothers" adds Jesus' affection for the addressees to that of Paul and company for them and thus aims to encourage them in their endurance of continued persecution, which would have ceased if the Day of the Lord had arrived, as they mistakenly thought it had. "Loved" connotes an ongoing love. The basis for thanksgiving—namely, God's having chosen the addressees for salvation—amplifies the encouragement (compare 1 Thessalonians 1:4). "From the beginning" locates God's choice in the primordial past and therefore describes it as so long-standing as not to be withdrawn.[1] "By means of the Spirit's consecration" assures the addressees that they're sacred to God; and "[by means of your] belief in the truth," which contrasts with "all who haven't believed the truth" (2:12), balances the sovereign action of God's Spirit with the responsible exercise of faith on the part of human beings. God's primordial choice is likewise balanced by his temporal call through Paul and company's proclamation of the gospel. "For the purpose of [your] obtaining the glory of our Lord, Jesus Christ" looks forward to what will happen at Jesus' revelation from heaven (see 1:12 for Christians' sharing Jesus' glory in recompense for the shame of their persecution).

2:15–17: Therefore then, brothers, be standing [firm] **and holding on to the traditions that you were taught, whether through word** [of mouth when we were evangelizing Thessalonica] **or through our letter** [that is, 1 Thessalonians]. See the comments on 1 Thessalonians 5:6 for "Therefore then." As often, "brothers" introduces an exhortation affectionately. Persecution elicits the exhortation to be "standing [firm]." The addressees' misconception concerning the Lord's coming and the gathering elicits the exhortation to "be . . . holding on to the traditions" (see 2:1–5). [16]**And may our Lord himself, Jesus Christ, and God, our Father who loved us and by grace gave** [us] **eternal encouragement and good hope,** [17]**encourage your hearts and stabilize** [you] **in every** [kind of] **good deed and word** [compare 1 Thessalonians 3:11–13]. "Himself" stresses the identity of "Jesus Christ" as "our Lord" over against the supposed lordships of pagan deities and rulers. "Our Father" stresses the identity of "God" as the one "who loved us [as fathers love their children] and by grace [= ill-merited favor] gave [us] eternal encouragement [in the promise of eternal life] and good hope [in the sure and certain prospect of the Lord's coming to relieve us from our afflictions]." "And may [our Lord and God] . . . encourage your hearts [to withstand persecution in the meantime] and stabilize [you] in every [kind of] good deed and word." "*Every* [kind of]" stresses the variety of good deeds and words that characterize Christians. Stability in such outward deeds and words despite persecution will stem from hearts inwardly encouraged by good hope and will give evidence of genuine Christian faith. Thus this wish represents Paul and company's prayer for the addressees.

MISCELLANEA
2 Thessalonians 3:1–15

This passage divides into a plea for prayer (3:1–2), expressions of confidence (3:3–4), a wish for love and stability (3:5), and a command to exercise discipline (3:6–15).

3:1–2: As to the rest [of this letter], **brothers, be praying for us that the Lord's word may be running and glorified, just as** [it was] **also in your case,** [2]**and that we may be rescued from deviant and evil human beings** [who pose to us a constant threat]. **For faith** [in the gospel] **doesn't characterize all** [human beings]. The address "brothers" introduces this plea for prayer on a familial note. "The Lord's word" is the gospel concerning Jesus Christ. "May be running" personifies it (compare Psalm 147:15). The personification portrays it as a runner who wins a race and gets "glorified"—that is, honored—for his victory. Here the running stands for the speedy spread of the gospel through Paul and company's evangelistic itinerations, and the glorification stands for conversions. For converts glorify the gospel by believing it. "Just as also in your case" presents the evangelization and conversion of the Thessalonian believers as an interpretive example of this figure of speech. Prayer for rescue "from deviant and evil human beings" has the purpose of enabling Paul and company to continue their itinerant

---

[1]Some very good ancient manuscripts read "as first fruits" instead of "from the beginning"; but the city of Philippi, not Thessalonica, provided the first converts in Macedonia.

evangelism (compare 1 Thessalonians 5:25). "Deviant" means "out of place," that is, dislocated from the will of God; and "evil" means "causing pain." Together, these terms describe persecutors. Disbelief in the gospel underlies their attempts to thwart evangelism by means of persecution.

3:3–4: But the Lord is faithful, who will stabilize you and protect [you] **from the evil one.** [4]**And we're persuaded about you in the Lord, that you're doing, and will do, the things which we're commanding.** The faithfulness of the Lord (Jesus) contrasts with the just-noted faithlessness of deviant, evil human beings (3:2). They lack *trust* whereas he has trust*worthiness*. His trustworthiness will demonstrate itself in stabilizing the Thessalonian believers to endure their afflictions and in protecting them from the evil one—in other words, in keeping them from the apostasy that Satan wants to induce by means of the persecution he foments (compare 2:17; 1 Thessalonians 2:18; 3:2, 5, 13; 5:24). To the same end of such protection, the Lord will use Paul and company's persuasion that the addressees are doing, and will do, the things being commanded them in this letter. For expressions of confidence both in the Lord and in the addressees themselves will encourage them to match the Lord's faithfulness with their own.

3:5: And may the Lord direct your hearts into God's love and into the Christ's endurance. The preceding expressions of confidence have here morphed into a wish that reflects Paul and company's prayer for the addressees. As usual, "the Lord" refers to Jesus, to whom therefore the prayers are addressed. "God's love" could be the addressees' love for God or his love for them. But "the Christ's endurance" likely refers to Jesus' endurance of suffering and shame, particularly in his crucifixion. So the parallel between these phrases favors God's love for the addressees. The directing of their hearts into his love for them therefore means, more literally, the straightening of the road that their hearts, personified as travelers, should take into God's love. A straight road will get them there quicker than a crooked one would (compare the comments on 1 Thessalonians 3:11). "Hearts" suits "love," because the heart pounds rapidly when affected. Here, God's love for the addressees is to affect their hearts by way of keeping them loyal to him despite their afflictions. Similarly, a straight road into the Christ's endurance will affect their hearts by way of keeping them loyal to him, too, despite their afflictions. After all, he endured afflictions for their sakes—indeed, for their salvation—and in so doing provided them a role model of such endurance (compare Hebrews 12:1–3; 1 Peter 2:20b–21). "*The* Christ" points up the messianic character of his exemplary endurance.

3:6–9: But we command you, brothers, in the name of our Lord, Jesus Christ, that you shun every brother who walks around in a disorderly way, that is, not in accordance with the tradition which they received from us [compare 1 Thessalonians 4:11–12]. [7]**For you yourselves know how it's necessary for you to imitate us, because we didn't act disorderly among you;** [8]**that is, we didn't eat bread** [= food] **for free from anyone. Rather, in labor and hardship** [we were] **working night and day so as not to burden any of you** [compare 1 Thessalonians 2:9]. [9]**Not that we don't have authority** [to demand material support for our ministry]**—rather,** [we supported ourselves] **in order that we might give ourselves as a role model to you for** [you] **to imitate us.** The shift from a wish to a command triggers the address "brothers," which softens the command. But lest it therefore not be taken seriously, Paul and company state it "in the name [that is, with the authority] of our Lord, Jesus Christ" (compare 1 Corinthians 5:4). The addressees' likely hesitancy to "shun every brother [fellow Christian] who walks around in a disorderly way" prompted this appeal to Jesus' authority, expressed in full with "our Lord, Jesus Christ." In particular, the naming of Jesus Christ as "Lord" puts his authority front and center. "Shun *every* brother" disallows any favoritism and presumably has the purpose of making the fellow Christian who's guilty of disorderly behavior miss fellowship with other Christians so much that he'll correct his behavior. The disorderly behavior that is to draw shunning consists in defending and praising a patron in return for his material support rather than working for one's own living. Paul and company put themselves forward as role models of self-support, models well-known to the addressees because of Paul and company's past behavior in their midst, and also because of Paul and company's past teaching of self-support ("the tradition that you received from us"). The addition of "yourselves" to "you" stresses the addressees' "know[ing] how it's necessary for [them] to imitate [Paul and company's self-support]." The use of "know *how* it's necessary" rather than "know *that* it's necessary" highlights the self-supporting manner, not just the fact, of Paul and company's self-support. Also highlighting its manner are the statements "we didn't eat bread for free *from anyone*," "in labor *and hardship* [we were] working *night* and day so as not to burden *any* of you," "*not* that we don't have *authority* [to demand material support]," and "[we supported ourselves] in order that we might *give* ourselves as a role model to you."

3:10–13: For also when we were with you we were commanding you, "If anyone doesn't want to work, neither is he to eat." [11]**For we hear** [that] **some** [are] **walking around disorderly among you,** [that is,] **working not at all—rather, working around.** [12]**And we're commanding and exhorting such people in the Lord, Jesus Christ, that as a result of working in a quiet fashion they eat their own bread** [rather than somebody else's]. [13]**But you, brothers—you shouldn't give up in doing good.** Now it comes out clearly why refusal to work for a living has gotten the description, "disorderly." It violates the previous command. The command that the person isn't to eat who doesn't work because he doesn't *want* to work—this command means that his fellow Christians shouldn't feed him. Hunger may teach him to work for his own food. His fault lies in a lack of desire, not in the job market. Some Christians in the Thessalonian church are so loathe to work that they're "working not at all," which equates with "walking around disorderly." How then does "working not at all" contrast with "working around"? Both expressions posit working. The contrast lies between "not at all" and "around." Working not at all means not working quietly to make one's own living. Working around means working at the expense of a patron to defend and praise him nosily around town. Ironically, the contrast between these workings also carries an implicit equation between them in that working around counts as working not at all. A second use of "commanding," the addition of "exhorting," a reference to "such people," and the locating of the command and exhortation "in the Lord, Jesus Christ" (where ultimate authority lies) strengthen immeasurably the command that those unwilling to work shouldn't eat, which then turns into a command that they eat their own food as a result of working. "But you, brothers" shifts from "such people" as are "working not at all" to those who are "doing good"—in other words, who are acting nobly not only by working for their own living but also by providing material support to those who want to work but for one reason or another can't and therefore find themselves in dire straits. Despite the hardship of supporting the needy as well as themselves, doers of good "shouldn't give up."

3:14–15: But if anyone doesn't obey our word [of command that you support yourselves by working], **be taking note of that** [man] **so as not to affiliate yourselves with him, in order that he may feel ashamed.** [15]**And** [in your nonaffiliation] **don't be regarding him as an enemy; rather, be admonishing** [him] **as a brother** [compare 1 Thessalonians 5:14]. The earlier command that anyone who doesn't want to work shouldn't eat— that is, shouldn't be given a handout—escalates here into a command to shame him by shunning him. If hunger doesn't teach him to work, maybe shame will, especially since non-Christians have already rejected him (1 Thessalonians 2:14; compare 1 Corinthians 5:9–11, where nonaffiliation includes not eating together). On the other hand, he's not to be considered an enemy; for then your speaking to him would turn hostile. Brotherly admonition should characterize it instead. But nonaffiliation is

to confine the speaking to such admonition and rule out all other social intercourse.

CONCLUSION
2 Thessalonians 3:16–18

This conclusion is made up of a threefold wish (3:16, 18) wrapped around a greeting (3:17).

3:16: And may the Lord of peace give you peace through all [time] **in every way** [compare Numbers 6:26]. **The Lord** [be] **with you all.** As usual, "the Lord" is Jesus. "Peace" consists in all the blessings of salvation. So "of peace" describes Jesus the Lord as the source of those blessings. "Give you peace" wishes the addressees the blessings, which are to be reflected and symbolized by peaceful relations among Christians (1 Thessalonians 5:13, 23); and the wish represents Paul and company's prayer. "Through all [time] in every way" calls for blessings unlimited in time and kind. "The Lord [be] with you [now]" anticipates Christians' being always with the Lord from his future coming onward (1 Thessalonians 4:17), and the fulfillment of this prayerful wish will steel the addressees to stand firm in the midst of persecution. The addition of "all" to "you" implies the need for unity if Christians are to stand firm. They need one another along with the Lord's presence.

3:17: The greeting [is written] **by my hand,** [that is,] **Paul's, which** [referring to his penmanship as different from that of the scribe to whom he has dictated the letter up to this point] **is a sign** [of my authorship] **in every letter** [of mine]. **This is the way I write.** Paul, the main author, calls attention to his penmanship to guarantee the authenticity of this letter (compare especially Galatians 6:11, where he calls attention to the large size of the characters in his handwriting). Though he writes the final greeting himself in all his letters, his present mention of the practice arises out of the aforementioned possibility of a letter forged in his and his companions' names (2:2).

3:18: The grace of our Lord, Jesus Christ, [be] **with you all.** For this benediction see the comments on 1 Thessalonians 5:28, and for the present addition of "all" to "you" see the comments on 3:16 right here in 2 Thessalonians.

FIRST TIMOTHY

This letter contains instructions on how Timothy, a young associate of Paul, is to guard against heresy and both organize and administrate the church in Ephesus, a city in western Asia Minor.

INTRODUCTION
1 Timothy 1:1–2

1:1–2: Paul, an apostle of Christ Jesus in accordance with the command of God, our Savior, and of Christ Jesus, our hope, ²to Timothy, my genuine child in faith: Grace, mercy, peace from God, the Father, and Christ Jesus, our Lord. "Christ" is Greek for the Hebrew term, "Messiah," both meaning "Anointed One"; and "apostle" refers to someone sent with delegated authority. So "an apostle of Christ Jesus" designates Paul, the author, as someone sent by the Messiah, who is Jesus, to speak and act on his behalf. This letter will therefore carry the authority of the Messiah himself. "In accordance with the command of God . . . and of Christ Jesus" coordinates God and Christ Jesus in commanding Paul to perform his apostolic function. "Our Savior" identifies God as Paul's and Timothy's shared Savior from sin and its eternally disastrous consequences. Since "hope" connotes confidence, "our hope" identifies Christ Jesus as Paul's and Timothy's shared basis of confidence of eternal life, to be entered fully at Jesus' second coming. "My genuine child in faith" identifies Timothy, the recipient, affectionately and probably as Paul's convert (compare Acts 14:6–23; 16:1–3 with Philemon 10), who has turned out to be true to his belief in Paul's gospel. For "Grace" and "peace" see the comments on 1 Peter 1:2; 2 John 3. Paul inserts "mercy" in anticipation of 1:12–16 and again coordinates God and Christ Jesus, but now as the source of grace, mercy, peace. "The Father" replaces "our Savior" for a designation of God. This designation supersedes the fathering of Timothy by Paul as his child "in faith," makes Paul as well as Timothy a child of God, and implies Jesus' Sonship to God. "Our Lord" replaces "our hope" as a designation of Christ Jesus and thus ascribes deity to him in conjunction with God his Father.

A WARNING AGAINST HERESY, PLUS PERSONAL REMINISCENCES
1 Timothy 1:3–20

1:3–7: Just as when traveling on to Macedonia [north of Greece] **I exhorted you to stay in Ephesus** [near the west coast of Asia Minor] **that you might**

order some not to teach aberrantly ⁴**and not to be paying attention to myths and endless genealogies, which as such give rise to speculations rather than to God's house-law in faith—.** Paul leaves the foregoing sentence incomplete. ⁵**But the goal of the order** [you're to issue] **is love** [originating] **out of a pure heart and a good conscience and an unhypocritical faith, ⁶from which some, by going amiss, have veered out of** [faith] **into pointless talk, ⁷wanting to be teachers of the Law though not understanding either the things that they're saying or** [the things] **about which they're speaking confidently.** Apparently Timothy wanted to go with Paul when Paul was leaving Ephesus for Macedonia. So Paul had to exhort him to stay in Ephesus for the purpose of "order[ing] some not to teach aberrantly," that is, not to teach anything different from the apostolic tradition. Paul knew that some were in fact teaching aberrantly. He even knew that the aberrant teaching included "myths and endless genealogies," which in view of "some . . . wanting to be teachers of the Law" point to legendary tales spun out of Old Testament genealogies which themselves were being extended to no useful end (compare Titus 1:14). The exhortation that Timothy issue an order implies authority, probably authority to issue an order on Paul's behalf. Timothy is to issue an order not even to pay attention to the myths and genealogies, much less teach them. For their mythological character and interminability "give rise to speculations" about matters that can't be known. "Which *as such*" underscores the deleteriously speculative rather than beneficially practical effect of these speculations.

"God's house-law" contrasts with merely human speculations and refers to the practicalities of God's dealing with the members of his household. "In faith" alludes to the members as a household of faith, for faith in Christ Jesus provides the household's framework. That is to say, belief in God's self-revelation through Christ Jesus trumps the speculations of "some." The order Timothy is to issue has to do with faith/belief. But its goal has to do with conduct/behavior—in particular, with love, by which is probably meant love of one another in the Christian household (see, for example, Galatians 5:13–14). Speculations make the heart dirty by rationalizing sinful behavior, make the conscience bad by producing such behavior, and make faith hypocritical by subverting its genuineness. So love originates only "out of a *pure* heart and a *good* conscience and an *un*hypocritical faith." Some have gone amiss from these and veered out of faith into "pointless talk," which describes the speculations as aimless. They're a bridge to nowhere. "Wanting to be teachers of the Law" describes the speculators in relation to the Mosaic law and makes a contrastive wordplay with "God's house-law." Thus the law of Moses stands over against the law of faith (compare, for example, Romans 3:27; Galatians 2:16). Beyond "myths and endless genealogies" Paul doesn't identify what the speculators teach about the Law. Presumably Timothy knew what it was. Instead, then, Paul describes the speculators as "not understanding either the things that they're saying [when quoting the Law] or [the things] about which they're speaking confidently [when interpreting the Law]." As it often does, ignorance bred false confidence.

1:8–11: **But we** [Paul and Timothy] **know that the Law** [is] **good if someone uses it lawfully** [9]**by knowing this,** [namely,] **that the Law isn't meant for a righteous person, but for lawless and rebellious people, for ungodly and sinful people, for undevout and profane people, for killers of their own fathers and killers of their own mothers, for murderers** [in general], [10]**fornicators, sodomites, slave traders, liars, perjurers. And if anything else is opposed to healthful teaching** [11]**in accordance with the gospel of the glory of the blessed God, with which** [gospel] **I was entrusted,** [the Law was meant for those who engage in that "anything else"]. "But we know . . . by knowing" sets up a double contrast with the ignorance of the would-be teachers of the Law (1:7). "The Law isn't meant for a righteous person" implies that those teachers are misusing the Law for righteous people, that is, people who are righteous by faith in Christ (Philippians 3:9). It's by believing "the gospel of the glory of the blessed God," not by keeping "the Law," that people become righteous. "The Law [is] good" (compare Romans 7:12), but to teach it as the vehicle of righteousness is to use the Law unlawfully, in opposition to its own purpose and character (compare Romans 7:7–25). The lawful use of the Law, emphasized by a wordplay between "the Law" and "lawfully," has to do with an *un*righteous person. Paul doesn't define this use (but see Romans 3:19–20; 5:20–21; Galatians 3:23–24). Here his only point is that the would-be teachers of the Law are misusing it for people already righteous through believing the gospel.

The lengthy description of unrighteous people as "lawless," "rebellious," "ungodly," "sinful," "undevout," "profane," and so forth has the purpose of highlighting by contrast that those who are righteous through believing the gospel don't need the Law as a vehicle of righteousness. For they aren't "killers of their own fathers," "killers of their own mothers," "murderers," "fornicators," "sodomites," "slave traders," "liars," "perjurers," or any of the preceding. (The inclusion of "slave traders" implies a moral condemnation of slavery.) Since the speculators want to be teachers of the Law but don't understand what they're saying, Paul describes and lists unrighteous people in fluctuating degrees of contrast with the Ten Commandments. "Lawless," "rebellious," "ungodly," and "sinful" contrast very loosely with the commandments to have no other gods before the Lord God and not to

make idols or worship them. Less loosely, "undevout" and "profane" contrast with the commandments not to take the Lord's name in vain and to observe the Sabbath day. "Killers of their own fathers and killers of their own mothers" contrasts sharply with the commandment to honor your father and your mother. "Murderers" contrasts obviously with the commandment not to commit murder. "Fornicators" (a general term for sexually immoral people) and "sodomites" (males who play the masculine role in homosex [see Leviticus 18:22; 20:13]) contrast expansively with the commandment not to commit adultery (which means having sex with someone else's spouse). "Slave traders," referring to those who steal human beings, contrasts narrowly with the commandment not to steal anything at all. "Liars" and "perjurers" contrast in detail with the commandment not to bear false witness. "And if anything else is opposed to healthful teaching" would include disobedience to the commandment not to covet (though compare Jesus' stopping short of citing this commandment in Mark 10:19; Matthew 19:18–19; Luke 18:20) and recalls the catchall phrase, "and things similar to these," at the end of Paul's list of "the works of the flesh" in Galatians 5:21 (compare also the catchall but affirmatory clause in Romans 13:9, "and if [there's] any other commandment"; and see Exodus 20:3–17; Deuteronomy 5:7–21 for the Ten Commandments). "Healthful teaching" promotes moral health, and such teaching accords with the gospel in that the gospel pits the glory of God against human sinning (Romans 3:23). Paul calls God "blessed" in the sense that those who are righteous praise God for his gospel. "With which [gospel] I was entrusted" sets this gospel as a divine entrustment over against the worthless speculations of the would-be teachers of the Law.

1:12–14: **I have gratitude for him who empowered me—**[namely,] **for Christ Jesus, our Lord—because he considered me trustworthy** [compare 1 Corinthians 7:25] **by putting** [me] **into service** [13]**even though** [I] **was formerly a blasphemer and persecutor and aggressor. I was shown mercy, however, because being ignorant I acted in unbelief;** [14]**and the grace of our Lord increased lavishly along with the faith and love that** [are] **in Christ Jesus.** Here "our Lord" points to Christ Jesus' divine ability and authority in empowering Paul to speak and act (often miraculously, for "miracles" means "acts of power" [see Romans 15:18–19; 2 Corinthians 12:12; Galatians 3:5]) as his apostle (1:1). Christ Jesus considered Paul trustworthy by anticipation of the effect on him of being empowered, for at the time of Christ's "putting [him] into [apostolic] service" Paul hadn't yet proved himself trustworthy. On the contrary, he'd been "a blasphemer [that is, a slanderer of Christ] and persecutor [of believers in Christ (see 1 Corinthians 15:9; Galatians 1:13, 23; Philippians 3:6; Acts 7:58; 9:1–2, 13–14, 21; 22:4–5; 26:9–11)] and aggressor [so that violence characterized his persecution of them]." Hence his "gratitude." "However" contrasts the mercy shown to Paul with his former unmerciful activities. "Because I acted ignorantly in unbelief" explains why he was shown mercy and traces his acting ignorantly to unbelief. Not to believe the gospel leads to ignorant activity. Despite the ignorance of Paul as a blasphemer, persecutor, and aggressor, the Lord's grace (= ill-deserved favor) had to increase lavishly for the empowerment of Paul as an apostle. Along with that grace, faith in Christ Jesus had to increase lavishly on the part of Paul because of his former blasphemy of Christ. So too did Paul's love have to increase lavishly because of his former persecution of the church and aggression against it. He locates this faith and love "in Christ Jesus" because he himself is in Christ Jesus (see 2 Timothy 3:12, for example) and therefore is able to believe in him and love others who are in him by faith. The repetition of "our Lord" draws Timothy into the sphere in which Paul operates.

1:15–17: Trustworthy and deserving of total acceptance [is] the saying: "Christ Jesus came into the world to save sinners," of whom I am foremost. ¹⁶I was shown mercy, however, because of this: that in me [as] foremost [among sinners] Christ Jesus might exhibit total patience for an example of those who were going to believe on him for eternal life. ¹⁷And to the King of the ages, the imperishable, invisible, only God, [be-long] **honor and glory forever and ever. Amen!** Paul starts this paragraph with the quotation of a saying that he describes as "trustworthy and deserving of total acceptance" because of his own experience of mercy and lavish grace. "Trustworthy" means "worthy of belief," and "deserving of total acceptance" means deserving to be accepted as true without a shred of doubt that it's true. Just as Christ Jesus considered Paul trustworthy (1:12), Paul presents this saying as trustworthy. The occurrence of "trustworthy" (Greek: *pistos*) in these two instances gives occasion to point up a concentration of terms all based on a Greek stem, underlined above and below, that carries the meaning of faith, belief, trust. Besides the two statements just mentioned, see 1:2, 4 ("in faith" [*pistei*]), 5 ("an unhypocritical faith" [*pisteōs*]), 11 ("I was entrusted" [*episteuthēn*]), 13 ("in unbelief" [*apistia*]), 14 ("along with faith" [*pisteōs*]), 16 ("those who were going to believe" [*pisteuein*]), 19 ("while having faith" [*pistin*]), plus further occurrences in the following chapters, 2 Timothy, and Titus. The play on this stem highlights the efficacy of faith, belief, trust over against Law-keeping as taught by the speculators. "Christ Jesus came into the world" means that he entered human society and implies, though it doesn't emphasize, his preexistence outside this world (compare 2 Corinthians 8:9; Philippians 2:5–8 and the implication of Colossians 1:15–20). "To save sinners" means to save them from the wrath of God that's directed at them because of their sin (Romans 1:16–18). "Of whom I am foremost" cites Paul as proof that Christ Jesus' coming into the world to save sinners is trustworthy and deserving of total acceptance. Since Christ Jesus has saved Paul, the foremost of sinners, he'll save any sinner who believes the gospel.

"However" contrasts Paul's position as the foremost sinner with his having been shown mercy. In 1:13 he cited his acting ignorantly in unbelief as the reason for

being shown mercy. Here he supplements that reason with another one: Christ Jesus' purpose to exhibit in Paul as the foremost among sinners "total patience"—in other words, the patience required for Christ to tolerate Paul's blasphemy, persecution, and aggression prior to showing him mercy, putting him into apostolic service, and empowering him for it. The patience had to be "total" (we might say "maximal") because of Paul's foremost-ness among sinners. "For an example" doesn't refer to him as an example to be imitated by others—rather, as an example of Christ Jesus' patience that more than suffices for the lesser sinners "who were going to believe on him for eternal life." The early correlations of Christ Jesus with God (1:1–2) and the mention of eternal life lead Paul to break into a doxology to God, whom he first calls "the King of the ages [Greek: *tōn aiōnōn*]"—that is, the eternal King, who gives "eternal [Greek: *aiōnion*] life"—to whom honor and glory belong eternally—that is, "forever and ever [Greek: *tous aiōnas tōn aiōnōn*]." As eternal, he's "imperishable." As the "only God" (compare Deuteronomy 6:4), he's "invisible," unlike the many so-called gods whose images dotted the religious landscape of the first-century Roman Empire. "Amen!" underlines this ascription of honor and glory to him.

1:18–20: I'm entrusting this order to you, Timothy [my] child, in accordance with foregoing prophecies [spoken] about you, in order that by them [the prophecies] **you may be fighting the good fight ¹⁹while having faith and a good conscience, rejecting which** [good conscience] **some have suffered shipwreck in regard to the faith, ²⁰belonging to whom are Hymenaeus and Alexander, whom I've given over to Satan in order that they may be disciplined not to be blaspheming** [compare 2 Timothy 2:16–18; 1 Corinthians 5:3–5]. "This order" refers back to the order in 1:3–4 that Timothy tell "some not to teach aberrantly and not to be paying attention to myths and endless genealogies." Now Paul describes the order as an entrustment to Timothy in that Timothy will have to issue it in Paul's absence. The naming of Timothy in a direct address and the description of him as Paul's "child," both as in 1:2, appeal to Timothy's religious debt to Paul and to Paul's affection for him as reasons to issue the order. "In accordance with foregoing prophecies [spoken] about you" refers to prophecies delivered at Timothy's ordination (4:14) and cites those prophecies as the basis for Paul's entrusting the order to Timothy. "Foregoing" describes the prophecies as predictive; and predictive prophecies—at least those inspired by God's Spirit (as here goes without saying)—will reach fulfillment and thus established a solid basis for Paul's entrustment of the order to Timothy. Furthermore, such prophecies become the means by which Timothy "fight[s] the good fight," which is good because he's to fight for "the gospel of the glory of the blessed God" (1:11) and against "myths and endless genealogies" (1:4). Because this fight is good, Timothy has "a good conscience"; and because of the foregoing prophecies spoken about him, he has "faith" (compare 1:5). The "some" who are teaching "aberrantly" (1:3) and "wanting to be teachers of the Law" (1:7) are now said to have "rejected" the good conscience that Timothy has and to have "suffered shipwreck in regard to the faith" that he also has. The suffering of shipwreck is a figure of speech for the ruination which comes from "hav[ing] veered out of [faith] into pointless talk" (1:6 [compare Paul's own literal shipwrecks according to 2 Corinthians 11:25; Acts 27]). Paul knows by name two of the shipwrecked. This knowledge enabled him to give them "over to Satan" for whatever mayhem Satan might inflict on them that will teach them not to be blaspheming—that is, not to be slandering the gospel of faith in Christ, as Paul used to do (1:13). (Unlike God, Satan mistreats those under his charge.)

THE ORGANIZATION OF THE
CHURCH BY TIMOTHY
1 Timothy 2:1–3:13

This section of 1 Timothy divides into the topics of prayer (2:1–7), the churchly decorum of men and women (2:8–15), qualifications for supervisors (3:1–7), and qualifications for their assistants (3:8–13).

2:1–4: First of all, therefore, I exhort that supplications, prayers, invocations, thanks be made for all people, ²for kings and all those who are in [positions of governmental] **prominence so that we may lead a tranquil and quiet life in total piety and respectability. ³This** [making of supplications, prayers, invocations, thanks] **[is] good and acceptable in the sight of our Savior, God, ⁴who wants all human beings to be saved and come into a knowledge of the truth.** "Therefore" alludes to the need for practical piety as opposed to the impractical speculations decried in 1:3–11, 18–20. "First of all" refers to the first in a series of exhortations to such piety. The piling up of terms in "supplications, prayers, invocations, thanks" serves both to emphasize this exhortation and to identify the various elements that make up what, broadly speaking, is called prayer. In view of the would-be teachers of the Law, which was addressed to Jews (1:7), and in view of the upcoming reference to Paul as "a teacher of Gentiles" (2:7), he designs "all people" to include Gentiles as well as Jews. But also in view of the Roman government, he adds "for kings and all those who are in [positions of governmental] prominence."

Even private prayers were spoken aloud, and even in private homes meetings of a church were open to the non-Christian public (1 Corinthians 14:23–25). So if Christians became known by non-Christians to be praying for them and for governmental authorities, the general population and those authorities would be more likely to let Christians "lead a tranquil and quiet life," that is, pursue a tranquil and quiet livelihood apart from persecution, which could deprive them of their livelihood. They'd have a well-earned reputation for a piety that's "total" in that it includes praying for the totality of human society, and a well-earned reputation for a respectability that's "total" in that their respect for the totality of the human race breeds in return a respect for them. But not only will non-Christians, including kings and other governmental superiors, look kindly on the Christians for making supplications, prayers, invocations, and thanks in behalf of all. So too will God, for he looks on it as "good and acceptable." And he looks on it as such because he's not only "*our* Savior." He also "wants *all* human beings to be saved and come into a knowledge of the truth." This truth consists in the gospel, and knowledge of the truth includes an experience of its salvific effect when believing the gospel accompanies hearing it. So the Christians' reputation for total piety and respectability will aid a fulfilling of God's desire that all human beings be saved. Which is not to say that all of them *will* be saved, however; for not all will believe. Yet God's approval of prayers for all should motivate Christians to pray for all.

2:5–7: For [there is] **one God, one intermediary also between God and human beings,** [namely,] **the human being Christ Jesus, ⁶who gave himself as a ransom in substitution for all, a testimony** [to be borne] **in his** [God's] **own times, ⁷for the purpose of which** [testimony] **I was instated as a proclaimer and an apostle— I'm telling the truth; I'm not lying—as a teacher of Gentiles in faith and truth.** Here Paul explains what the truth is and why God wants all human beings to come into a saving knowledge of it. The truth is that there's one God, not many gods (1 Corinthians 8:5–6; Galatians 3:20; Ephesians 4:6; Deuteronomy 6:4). Since he's the one and only God of all, he's the source of salvation for all who'll believe (Romans 3:29–30). The truth is also that there's one intermediary between God and human beings. Since Christ Jesus is this one and only intermediary, he's the agent of salvation for all who'll believe. But Paul introduces him first as "the human being" to indicate his qualification to give himself as a ransom in substitution for all other human beings (compare Mark 10:45; Matthew 20:28). His *self*-giving parallels God's "*want*[ing] all human beings to be saved." "A ransom" alludes to redemption (liberation from enslavement to sin and death) by way of a self-sacrificial payment (compare 1 Peter 1:18–21). "A testimony" refers to the proclamation of Christ Jesus as the one intermediary between the one God and all human beings. "[To be borne] in his own times" refers to the present as appropriate, indeed as decreed by God, for this proclamation (compare Titus 1:3). Paul cites himself as an example of bearing this testimony "as a proclaimer and an apostle," and underlines his exemplary role by declaring, "I'm telling the truth; I'm not lying" (compare Romans 9:1), and by adding, "as a teacher of the Gentiles." The declaration prepares for a discussion of teaching in 2:11–15 and suggests that the would-be teachers of the Law were questioning or denying Paul's "instate[ment]" as a proclaimer and an apostle." The addition suggests that their misuse of the Law was driving away Gentiles or ruling them out genealogically (compare 1:4). Paul's inclusion of the Gentiles conforms to God's wanting all human beings to be saved. "In faith" distinguishes Paul's teaching as Law-free, and "in . . . truth" distinguishes it from the false teaching put forward by the would-be teachers of the Law.

2:8: Therefore I want the men in every location to pray, lifting up devout hands without wrath and disputation. This verse harks back to the exhortation in 2:1–4. So see the comments on that exhortation for the meaning of "Therefore." "The men" refers to adult Christian males, whom Paul wants to lead in prayer during church services. "In every location" means wherever in the world a church is located, but especially in Ephesus, where Paul has left Timothy (1:3; compare 1 Corinthians 1:2; 2 Corinthians 2:14; 1 Thessalonians 1:8; Malachi 1:11). "Lifting up devout hands" adds body language appropriate to the supplications, prayers, invocations, and thanks mentioned in 2:1 (compare Psalms 28:2; 141:2). "Without wrath and disputation" defines the meaning of "devout" and itself means the absence of angry arguments between the men who are leading a congregation in prayer. Such arguments would keep the antagonists from joining each other in a communal prayer led by one of them.

2:9–10: In the same way [I want] women to attire themselves in decorous apparel along with modesty and discretion, not in braids [= braided hair] and gold or pearls or expensive clothing—¹⁰rather (in relation to what's proper for women professing reverence for God), [to attire themselves] by means of good deeds. "In the same way" means, "Just as I want the men to do such-and-such, I want the women to do such-and-such." Though the such-and-suches differ, Paul's desire is the same. Positively, he wants the women to dress themselves modestly and discreetly. A play in the Greek text on the two related words *kosmein*, "to attire," and *kosmiō*, "decorous," adds emphasis to the instruction. Decorous apparel was understood to signal chastity and in Paul's day consisted of an unrevealing robe. Negatively, he prohibits braided hair, gold, pearls, and expensive clothing, all of which gave off an air of ostentation (the braids piled high on top of the head with gold-colored netting). Furthermore, making a show of pearls and expensive clothing signaled sexual availability, as in the case of well-paid prostitutes but also in the case of married women claiming the sexual independence enjoyed by their husbands (compare 5:6; 2 Timothy 3:6–7, and see especially Revelation 17:4–5; 18:12, 16). Paul wants Christian women both to *look* respectable and to *be* respectable. But respectability isn't enough. Women who profess reverence for God must also busy themselves with good deeds, which will constitute a kind of clothing that God respects.

2:11–14: In quietness a woman is to be learning in total subjection. ¹²And I don't permit a woman to teach and assume authority over a man—rather, to be in quietness. ¹³For [out of clay] Adam was molded as the first [human being], then Eve [Genesis 2:7, 18–22]; ¹⁴and Adam wasn't deceived, but the woman, having been completely deceived, fell into a transgression [of God's command not to eat from the tree of the knowledge of good and evil (Genesis 2:16–17; 3:1–7)]. "In total subjection" explains the reason for a woman's learning "in quietness." Since she's to learn in quietness, she's not to teach a man. Since she's to learn in total subjection, she's not to assume authority over a man *by* teaching him. "Rather, to be in quietness" reemphasizes learning in total subjection. Paul substantiates this instruction by citing God's having created Adam before creating Eve, and also by citing Adam's not being deceived whereas Eve, "having been completely deceived, fell into a transgression." Paul doesn't deny that Adam transgressed, nor does he blame Eve for persuading Adam to transgress (see Romans 5:12–21). But whereas Adam wasn't *deceived* into transgressing, Eve transgressed *because* she was deceived—completely (Genesis 3:13).

Several questions of interpretation need to be asked and answered. To whom is a woman to be totally subject? To God or to a man? Favoring subjection to a man are (1) the nonmention of God in 2:11–14; (2) the contrast in this same passage between a woman and a man; (3) the prohibition of a woman's teaching and assuming authority over a man; and (4) the explicit mention of a man as the one to whom a woman is to subject herself in Ephesians 5:22; Colossians 3:18; Titus 2:5; 1 Peter 3:1 (compare 1 Corinthians 14:33b–36 and note her *self*-subjection to the man rather than her subjection *by* the man, and also Paul's devoting in Ephesians 5:22–33 three and a half more lines to the responsibility of a man to his wife than to the woman's toward her husband [see also 1 Peter 3:7]).

If so favored by context, the Greek words for "man" and "woman" can equally well be translated "husband" and "wife," as in the passages just listed. So to what man is a woman to be totally subject here in 1 Timothy 2:11–14? To any man who is speaking in a meeting of the church, or only to her husband at home? In Ephesians 5:22–24; Titus 2:5; 1 Peter 3:1; 1 Corinthians 14:33b–36 "her/their *own* man/men" indicates the meaning "her/their own *husband/husbands*"; and in Colossians 3:18–21 the exhortations that men love their women, that children obey their parents, and that fathers not nag their children indicate again the meaning "husbands" and "wives" (so too Ephesians 5:25–6:4). But the present lack of such indications, the prohibition of a woman from teaching a man, and the clarity of church settings in the comparable passages 1 Corinthians 11:2–16; 14:33b–36 point to the woman's subjection here to any man who is speaking in a meeting of the church rather than to the subjection of a wife to her husband at home. (The switch from "a woman" in 2:11–14 to "they" in 2:15 shows that the singular of "woman" and "man" is generic rather than indicative of "husband" and "wife.")

Might Paul's instructions apply, then, only to a local condition in Ephesus, where Timothy was serving at the time? Hardly, because similar instructions occur in 1 Corinthians, Ephesians, Colossians, Titus, and 1 Peter, sent respectively to churches in Corinth, cities surrounding Ephesus, Colossae, Crete, and Roman provinces throughout Asia Minor. Furthermore, "as in *all* the churches of the saints" introduces the most similar instruction in 1 Corinthians 14:33b–36; and "*total* subjection" rules out that Paul is correcting only some Ephesian women's *abuse* of a freedom to teach men by teaching them heretically and/or authoritatively.

Might Paul's instructions apply, finally, only to a cultural condition prevalent throughout the first-century Roman Empire and to any like condition in other times and places? First to be noted is that such a condition may help explain why he issues his instructions, but they needn't limit the application of those instructions. To draw an analogy, the Judaizing heresy in Galatia prompted Paul to defend the doctrine of justification by faith apart from Law-keeping; but this doctrine doesn't suffer a limitation thereby. To judge between limited and unlimited application, attention must be paid to whatever reason or reasons Paul gives for his instructions as well as to a cultural condition. Concerning the latter and as intimated above, some women in the first-century Roman Empire, especially wealthy ones, may have mounted a kind of women's liberation movement by declaring independence from household duties. If so, criticism of this movement was coming from outside Christian circles, and Paul too would be responding critically to the movement insofar as it had appeared in churches. But is he responding to save the gospel from the disrepute being suffered by that movement? Perhaps so, but he doesn't say so. Instead, he appeals to the creation of Adam as the first human being, and of Eve only thereafter (compare 1 Corinthians 11:8–9); and in contrast with the nondeception of Adam he appeals also to the complete deception of Eve, whom he now calls "the woman" to underline her representation of "a woman" who in church "is to be learning in total subjection" and "in quietness" rather than "teach[ing] and assum[ing] authority over a man." The implication seems to be that Eve succumbed to deception because of failure to subject herself quietly to Adam. In any case these appeals, dealing as they do with the quintessential human beings Adam and Eve at creation and the fall, and therefore before human beings developed any culture, favor that Paul is thinking and speaking fundamentally as well as conditionally.[1] Notably, Paul doesn't base his instructions to slaves on any such appeals, but cites only the cultural condition that disobedience to masters will tarnish the gospel's reputation, whereas obedience will adorn it (6:1–2; Titus 2:9-10).

2:15: But she [the woman as represented by Eve] **will be saved** [from God's eternal wrath, as often throughout 1–2 Timothy and Titus] **through childbearing** [a proper function for the married woman (5:14)] **if they** [women as represented by Eve] **abide in faith** [= belief in Christ Jesus] **and love** [of fellow Christians] **and consecration** [= devotion to God] **along with discretion** [such as that described in 2:9–14]. These practices won't earn salvation, but they'll give evidence of "a pure heart and a good conscience and an unhypocritical faith," which guarantee salvation (1:5; compare Philippians 2:12–13). Reassuringly, then, homemaking is just as salvifically valuable for a woman as anything a man can do; and a man's teaching falsehood is just as salvifically dangerous as anything a woman can do (1:19–20).

3:1–7: Trustworthy [is] **the saying: "If someone is reaching out for supervision** [of a church], **he's desiring a good work."** [2]**Therefore** [because such supervision is a good work] **it's necessary that the supervisor be unimpeachable, a man of one woman, temperate** [in the use of wine], **discreet, decorous, hospitable, competent to teach,** [3]**not addicted to wine, not a brawler—rather, mild-mannered, uncombative, unloving of money,** [4]**presiding well over his own household, having** [his] **children in subjection along with total respectability** [5]**(but if someone doesn't know to preside over his own household, how will he take care of God's church?),** [6]**not a neophyte** [a new convert] **lest on becoming conceited he fall into the Devil's judgment.** [7]**And it's also necessary that** [he] **have a good testimony from the outsiders** [= non-Christians] **lest he fall into disgrace and the Devil's trap.** "Trustworthy [is] the saying" echoes 1:15. But the saying here differs from the one there. "Is reaching out for" stands for aspiring to, that is, "desiring"; and supervision, or oversight, stands for leadership, what Paul refers to as presiding over (5:17). "Good" describes the "work" of supervision in that Christians need church leaders to teach them the truth and counteract teachers of falsehood, such as the would-be teachers of the Law referenced in 1:3–7 (compare Acts 20:28–30; Titus 1:5–16). But this good work calls for a person known to be good. Alone, aspiration doesn't suffice and might even indicate a hunger for power and status. So Paul lays out qualifications that, if met, make the supervisor a role model for the Christians being supervised. Older English versions of the New Testament translated with "the bishop." Newer English versions have "the overseer." But "the supervisor" probably connotes the meaning of management a bit better.

Paul says first that a supervisor is to be "unimpeachable," which after listing the specifics of unimpeachability Paul restates positively as "hav[ing] a good testimony from the outsiders" (compare the concern for Christians' good reputation in chapter 2). Heading the list of specifics making for unimpeachability is that the supervisor should be "a man of one woman," which in line with

---

[1]Yet in church meetings women with a properly covered head may pray aloud, which doesn't count as teaching, and may prophesy, which counts as superior to teaching and consists in relaying a divine revelation rather than explaining it (1 Corinthians 11:2–16; 12:28). Priscilla's and Aquila's "expounding [literally, 'setting out']" to Apollos "the way of God more accurately" might not count as teaching either, but only as relaying to him Paul's teaching; but quite apart from that possibility it doesn't count as the kind of public teaching prohibited to women here, for they "took [Apollos] aside" (Acts 18:24–26). Neither does older women's teaching younger women domesticity (Titus 2:3–5) or Timothy's being taught since his infancy the sacred Scriptures by his grandmother and mother (2 Timothy 1:5; 3:14–15). For women as Paul's co-workers in the gospel, presumably under the guidelines laid down here, see Romans 16:3–6, 12; Philippians 4:2–3.

the later qualification, "competent to teach," and the earlier prohibition of a woman's teaching or exercising authority over a man (2:12–13) rules women out of supervision of a church. "A man of one woman" probably means a man who, if married, is known to have been sexually faithful to his wife (compare "a woman of one man" in 5:9).[2] "Discreet" and "decorous" follow "temperate" because intemperance in the use of wine leads to behavioral indiscretions and indecencies apparent to all. "Hospitable" follows next, because hospitality was considered a public virtue and travelers often needed hospitality in private homes; then "competent to teach," because persuasive teaching of the truth over against heresy constitutes part of the supervisory role. "Not addicted to wine" recalls "temperate" to introduce "not a brawler," because drunkenness breeds brawling; and brawling would tarnish the church's reputation. "Mild-mannered" and "uncombative" contrast with brawling. "Unloving of money" implies payment by the church to a supervisor for his "good work" (5:17–18; Galatians 6:6) but guards against a pecuniary aspiration (6:9–10).

"Presiding well [= admirably] over his own household [which in the case of men of means might include an extended family and slaves]" would augur a corresponding ability to preside well over a church. A particular evidence of such ability would be "having [his] children in subjection," for a supervisor will need to keep church members in subjection to the requirements of Christian belief and behavior (Hebrews 13:17). "Along with total respectability" calls for entirely respectable behavior on the part of a supervisor's children, for he's responsible to ensure total respectability on the part of those church members. "But if someone doesn't know to preside over his own household" implies that failure to do so portends an unwillingness to take care of the church if he were to be made a supervisor. Paul switches from "preside" to "take care of" to indicate that a supervisor's presiding over other Christians should be imbued with care for them—this because the church is "God's," not the supervisor's. A quick advancement to supervisorship could easily lead to conceit. So Paul prohibits

[2]Polygyny wasn't frequent enough in the first-century Roman Empire to have required a prohibition thereof, and such a prohibition would require the complementary phrase in 5:9 to prohibit polyandry. But polyandry wasn't practiced at all. Though marriage is presumed as usual (compare 1 Corinthians 7:2), Paul's endorsement of celibacy, given sexual self-control (1 Corinthians 7:25–40), and his own celibacy (1 Corinthians 7:7; 9:5) disfavor a requirement of marriage here; and the complementary phrase in 5:9 can't require the woman to be celibate. For there the woman is a widow, who *by definition* is celibate. Widows were praised for not remarrying. But widowers were not, and Paul urges younger widows to remarry (5:14; compare Romans 7:1–3; 1 Corinthians 7:8–9, 39). It remains possible that a supervisor shouldn't be someone who remarried after a divorce (see Luke 16:18, for example). But despite Jesus' and Paul's stricter-than-usual standards in this matter, such remarriage wasn't generally considered improper. So Paul's present concern for public reputation disfavors that he had in mind the question of divorce-and-remarriage.

such an advancement with a warning against conceit. "Judgment" usually refers to punishment by God (see, for example, Romans 2:2–3). So "the Devil's judgment" probably means punishment *suffered* by the Devil at God's hands (compare Revelation 20:10). To fall into the same judgment would be, then, a terrible fate (compare Revelation 20:15). On the other hand, to "fall into . . . the Devil's trap" means falling into the trap of conceit *set* by the Devil (compare 2 Timothy 2:26). And falling into this trap would include "fall[ing] into disgrace," for "the outsiders" would ridicule a church's supervisor who didn't "have a good testimony," that is, who lacked a good reputation.

3:8–10: **In the same way** [it's necessary that] **assistants** [to supervisors] [be] **respectable, not duplicitous** [= speaking out of both sides of their mouth], **not addicted to much wine, not mercenary, [9]holding the secret** [consisting] **of the faith in a clean conscience. [10]And these** [assistants] **are to be made sure of first. Then, if being unaccusable, they are to assist.** "In the same way" draws a parallel between the necessities that supervisors have a good reputation and that assistants do too. Traditional English translations read "deacons" instead of "assistants," but "deacons" obscures that these people are to serve the supervisors by assisting them. The qualifications of respectability and unaccusability frame the intervening specifics and match the qualification that supervisors have a good reputation, lest otherwise the gospel's progress be stalled. Duplicity in speech would make for a bad reputation, as would addiction to wine. As compared with "not addicted to wine" in 3:3, Paul prefixes "much" to "wine," probably in anticipation of telling Timothy in 5:23 to "be using a *little* wine" because of his "stomach and . . . illnesses." "Not mercenary" corresponds to "unloving of money" in 3:3 and implies, as there, payment for services or, if assistants had the task of distributing charitable funds, requires that assistants be above suspicion of any tendency toward embezzlement. "The secret [consisting] of the faith" anticipates "the secret of piety" in 3:16 and refers to the gospel for Gentiles as well as Jews (compare 2:7; 3:16), hidden as such in times past but now revealed, and featuring faith rather than Law-keeping (contrast 1:3–11). "*Holding* the secret . . . in a clean conscience" means adhering to it in conduct as well as belief, so that the conscience is clean. Since "holding" doesn't correspond to teaching, this requirement makes something of a contrast with the requirement that supervisors be "competent to teach" (3:2). The function of teaching seems reserved for supervisors, then. But "to be made sure of first" corresponds to supervisors' not being neophytes (3:6).

3:11: **In the same way** [it's necessary] **that women be respectable, not slanderous, temperate** [in the use of wine], **trustworthy in all** [respects]. Romans 16:1 designates a woman named Phoebe as an assistant; and since "assistant" had no grammatically feminine form in Greek but occurred for females as well as males, to make plain a reference to female assistants Paul uses "women" and inserts a snippet concerning them before reverting to male assistants in 3:12–13. That no similar snippet was inserted for female supervisors agrees with Paul's requiring women to learn "in total subjection" and "not to exercise authority over a man" (2:11–12), and that he doesn't require a female assistant to have an aptitude for teaching any more than he required male assistants to have that aptitude agrees with his not permitting a woman to teach a man (2:12). "Respectable" matches exactly the requirement that male assistants be "respectable" (3:8). "Not slanderous" has to do with speech just as "not duplicitous" did in connection with male assistants (3:8). "Temperate" parallels "not addicted to much wine" (3:8), and "trustworthy in all [respects]" expands on "not mercenary" (3:8).

Back to males in *3:12–13*: **Assistants are to be men of one woman, presiding well over** [their] **children and their own households.** ¹³**For those who've assisted well are acquiring for themselves a good standing and much boldness in the faith** [that is] **in Christ Jesus.** See the comments on 3:2, 4–5 for the requirements, "men of one woman" and "presiding well over [their] children and their households." Since 3:6–7 probably looks forward to the Last Judgment (see the comments on that passage), the acquiring of "a good standing and much boldness" on the part of "those who've assisted well" probably looks forward to a good standing and much boldness at the Last Judgment. Both the standing and the boldness contrast with a conceited supervisor's falling into judgment/punishment. They'll have acquired "a good *standing* . . . in the faith" because they will have been "*holding* the secret [consisting] of the faith with a clean conscience." The faith is "in Christ Jesus" because he's the location where believing the gospel puts a person. And in Christ Jesus a believer can afford to have much boldness at the Last Judgment. Reason enough for assistants to serve "well"!

<h3 style="text-align:center">THE ADMINISTRATION OF THE CHURCH BY TIMOTHY</h3>
1 Timothy 3:14–6:19

This section divides into the topics of preserving the church as a bastion of orthodoxy against heterodoxy (3:14–4:16) and pastoring members of the church (5:1–6:19).

<h3 style="text-align:center">PRESERVING THE CHURCH AS A BASTION OF ORTHODOXY AGAINST HETERODOXY</h3>
1 Timothy 3:14–4:16

3:14–16: **I'm writing these things to you while hoping to come to you with speed** [= soon]. ¹⁵**But if I delay,** [I'm writing] **in order that you may know how it's necessary to conduct yourself in God's household, which as such is the church of the living God,** [which is] **the pillar and base of the truth.** ¹⁶**And the secret of piety is confessedly great: Who** [referring to Christ] **was manifested in flesh, vindicated in** [the] **Spirit, seen by angels, proclaimed in** [= among] [the] **nations, believed on in** [the] **world, taken up in glory.** Here Paul switches from qualifications for supervisors and assistants, whom presumably Timothy is to appoint, to how Timothy should conduct himself "in God's household." The possibility of Paul's delay in coming to Timothy gives rise to the instruction, and the necessity of knowing how Timothy should conduct himself arises out of God's ownership of the household. "Which *as such* is the church of the living God" portrays the church emphatically as God's extended family. But the description of God as "living," unlike lifeless idols, calls to mind a house in which he lives, so that Paul then portrays the church as "the pillar and base of the truth." As a pillar holds up the roof of a house and as a base holds up the pillar, so the church holds up the truth, which is the aforementioned "secret [consisting] of the faith" (3:9; see also 2:4–7). Timothy has the task of seeing to it that the Ephesian church remains a "pillar and base of the truth."

Not content with the generality of the aforementioned secret, Paul now spells out some of its details and introduces it as "the secret of piety" that "is confessedly great." Piety, which is biblically admirable, grows out of the believed secret, because the secret contains the truth; and the secret is great in the sense that its truth is magnificent, encompassing salvation for believing Gentiles as well as believing Jews—"*confessedly* great" not in contrite admission but in confident declaration (contrast the declaration, "Great [is] Artemis of the Ephesians!" in Acts 19:27–28, 34–35). The Christian confession takes the form of six declarations concerning Christ: (1) "Manifested in flesh" refers to the result of incarnation and assumes his preexistence. (2) "Vindicated in [the] Spirit" refers to Christ's resurrection as vindicating him over against others' having crucified him as though he were a criminal. We might have expected "*by* [the] Spirit," but "*in* [the] Spirit" locates the resurrected Christ in the Holy Spirit just as believers "aren't in the flesh—rather, in the Spirit—if indeed the Spirit of God is residing in [them]" (Romans 8:9). (3) "Seen by angels" refers to the risen Jesus' appearance to the angelic world (compare angels' presence at the empty tomb of Jesus [Mark 16:5–7; Matthew 28:1–7; John 20:11–13] and his appearance to angels in heaven on arrival there [Revelation 5]). (4) "Proclaimed in [= among] [the] nations" refers to their evangelization, especially to the evangelization of Gentiles, and shows that "the secret" is now an *open* secret. (5) "Believed on in [the] world" refers to the widespread success of that evangelism. (6) "Taken up in glory" refers to Christ's ascension and, with the allusion to incarnation in the first declaration, frames the intervening declarations. Thus "was taken up" complements "was manifested," "was seen" complements "was vindicated," and "was believed on" complements "was proclaimed." Likewise, "in glory" complements "in flesh," "by angels" complements "in [the] Spirit," and "in the world" complements "in [= among] [the] nations."

4:1–5: **But the Spirit says expressly that in later times some will apostatize from the faith by paying** attention to deceitful spirits and teachings of demons **²in the hypocrisy of liars who've cauterized their own conscience, ³forbidding [people] to marry, [teaching them] to abstain from foods, which God created to be partaken with thanksgiving by believers—that is, those who've come to know the truth—⁴because every creation of God [is] good; and if being taken with thanksgiving, not one is to be thrown away. ⁵For it's being consecrated through God's word and an invocation.** "But the Spirit says" introduces a prophetic pronouncement inspired by the Holy Spirit. For emphasis the present tense of "says" vivifies the pronouncement regardless of when it was made. "Expressly" describes its meaning as unambiguous. And its prediction of apostasy from the faith makes a contrast with the immediately preceding, confessedly great secret of piety (3:16). "Some will apostatize" refers to the "some" who "by going amiss have [already] veered out of [faith]" (1:3–7); so "in later times" means present times as the period immediately preceding the end, when Christ returns (compare 2 Timothy 3:1–7). The lack of surprise in this apostasy should therefore keep Christians from following suit. "From the faith" draws an implicit contrast with Law-keeping as taught by those dismissively called "some" (see too 1:3, 6, 19). The designation "demons" identifies the "deceitful spirits" in opposition to "the Spirit," who speaks expressly and, as can be seen, truthfully about them. The deceitfulness of these demonic spirits falsifies their "teachings," so that "paying attention" to the spirits and their teachings leads to disaster and thus contrasts with the eternal benefit of confessing "the truth" contained in the great secret of piety (3:15–16) taught by Paul (2:7). The plural of these heretical "teachings" contrasts with the singularity of "the healthful teaching" (1:10; 4:6; 2 Timothy 4:3; Titus 1:9; 2:1), which unlike those teachings has an inner consistency.

Paul then shifts from the spirits as deceitful and demons as the source of heretical teachings to the "some" who peddle those teachings. He calls them "liars" and accuses them of "hypocrisy." They're liars in that they falsify the purpose of the Law (1:6–11). They're hypocritical in that they pretend to faith while actually resting themselves on speculations (contrast "unhypocritical faith" in 1:5). They've "cauterized their own consciences" and thus made them insensitive, so that they lie without compunction. Apparently their "forbidding [people] to marry" grew out of their teaching the Law "aberrantly" with reference to "myths and endless genealogies . . . though not understanding either the things that they're saying or [the things] about which they're speaking confidently" (1:3–7). More clearly, their teaching people "to abstain from foods" stems from a failure to recognize that Mosaic kosher laws are no longer in effect (see Romans 14; 1 Corinthians 8–10; Colossians 2:16–23; Mark 7:19c). Paul counters this teaching with an appeal to God's having created "foods . . . to be partaken [according to Genesis 9:3] with thanksgiving by believers [as opposed to Law-keepers]—that is, those who've come to know the truth [of the Law-free gospel

(compare Mark 7:18–19)]—because every creation of God [is] good [according to Genesis 1:31]; and if being taken with thanksgiving [to God for having created all foods to be eaten (compare Romans 14:6; 1 Corinthians 10:30)], not one [kind of food] is to be thrown away [as ritually unclean and therefore unfit to be eaten]. For it's being consecrated [= set aside for consumption] through God's word [the passages in Genesis alluded to above] and an invocation [which describes the aforementioned 'thanksgiving' in terms of a prayer said over the food (compare Romans 14:6; 1 Corinthians 10:16, 30)]."

4:6–10: By laying down these [directives] for the brothers [Christians as an extended family] **you'll be a good servant of Christ Jesus while being nourished with the words of the faith and of the good teaching that you've followed. ⁷But be avoiding the profane and old-womanly myths, and be exercising yourself for piety. ⁸For "bodily exercise is beneficial in a minor respect, but piety is beneficial in all respects because of its holding a promise of life that's now and that's going to come." ⁹Trustworthy and deserving of total acceptance [is] the [just-quoted] saying. ¹⁰For to this end we're laboring and competing, because we've set our hope on the living God, who is the Savior of all [kinds of] people, namely of believers.** In 3:13 Paul spoke of servants ("assistants") who've served well ("assisted well"; Greek: *kalōs diakonēsantes*). Here he speaks hopefully of Timothy as "a good servant" (Greek: *kalos . . . diakonos*). But those servants served supervisors as their assistants. Timothy is a servant "of Christ Jesus," not of supervisors in local churches. The preceding discussion of partaking foods in a literal sense gives rise to Timothy's "being nourished" in a figurative sense "with the words of the faith," which means the healthful words of the gospel that feature believing in Christ Jesus rather than Law-keeping as the way of salvation. Paul then describes these words as the content of "the good teaching" that Timothy has "followed" with the result that Paul left him in charge at Ephesus (1:3–4). By nourishing Timothy in mind and heart they'll enable him to continue "laying down these [directives] for the brothers," which activity creates a need for continual such nourishment.

Nourishment with "the good teaching" makes for "a good servant," and this good teaching contrasts with "the profane and old-womanly myths" that equate with the "teachings of demons" in 4:1, which equate in turn with the "myths and endless genealogies" of the would-be teachers of the Law in 1:4, 6–7. All these make a bad diet for the mind and heart, so that Paul commands Timothy to "be avoiding" them. The good diet of good doctrine will give Timothy the nourishment necessary for obedience to Paul's command that he "be exercising [himself] for piety." This command is necessary because orthodoxy (believing correctly) turns hypocritical apart from orthopraxy (behaving correctly). Paul describes the myths as "profane" in that they don't lead to piety, and as "old-womanly" in that they do lead to the religious senility that both characterizes a lack of exercise for piety and prevents such exercise. (Since only men engaged in athletic exercise, "old-womanly" connotes senility.)

Paul supports his exhortation by quoting a maxim that he describes as "trustworthy and deserving of total acceptance" (compare 1:15). According to this maxim bodily exercise benefits the body; but the benefit is minor in comparison with that of religious exercise for piety, because this kind of exercise benefits a person "in all respects." "Because of its holding a promise of life that's now and that's going to come" defines "in all respects" temporally as both present and future and grounds the superiority of the benefit in this both/and. That is to say, bodily exercise carries benefit only for "life that's now." Exercise for piety carries the benefit of "life . . . that's going to come," which is eternal life. But for believers eternal life, though entered fully not till Christ's return (hence "a *promise*" thereof), starts now by way of a foretaste. So it's present as well as future. Just as the maxim supported Paul's exhortation, so the reference to his and Timothy's laboring and competing supports the exhortation. "Competing" maintains the metaphor of athletic exercise, and "laboring" introduces the complementary metaphor of toiling hard (compare present-day athletes' saying, "No pain, no gain"). "To this end" refers to attaining the eternal life that's going to come (compare Philippians 3:10–14). "Our hope" is the confidence appropriate to the aforementioned "promise." As "living," God is the basis of hope for the eternal life of those for whom he's "the Savior," that is, for "believers." A Greek word that in Paul's letters outside 1–2 Timothy and Titus is translated "especially" seems to mean in these letters "namely," because (to take the present case as an example) God is the Savior only of believers, so that "all people" means all kinds of people, particularly Gentiles as well as Jews (compare the distinction in 2:3–4 between God as "*our* Savior" and his "*want*[ing] all people to be saved," and see the comments on 2:5–7; also 3:16). ("All" often means "all kinds of" rather than "every without exception.")

4:11–13: Be commanding and teaching these [things]. **¹²No one is to be despising your youthfulness. Rather, become for the believers a role model in speech, in behavior, in love, in faith, in chastity. ¹³Till I come, be paying attention to reading, to exhortation, to teaching.** The prefixing of commanding to teaching makes the teaching that Timothy is to do both authoritative and purposeful of obedience on the part of listeners. No one is to be despising his youthfulness, for despising it would forestall obedience to the commands embedded in his teaching. As implied by the plural "you" in 6:21, the Ephesian Christians will hear this letter read to them though it's addressed to Timothy. So the command, "No one is to be despising your youthfulness," is indirectly addressed to them. We don't know the age-bracket to which Timothy's youthfulness points; but the respect for older age that characterized both Jewish and Greco-Roman culture—a respect reflected in the upcoming designation of superintendents as "elders" (4:14; 5:17, 19; compare 5:1–2)—heightened

the possibility of people's despising Timothy's youthfulness. Becoming "a role model" despite, or even because of, youthfulness will lessen and perhaps eliminate that possibility. "A role model in speech" will teach others how to speak truthfully, as Christians ought to speak (2:7; Ephesians 4:25). "A role model . . . in behavior" will teach others to conduct themselves righteously (1:8–11). "A role model . . . in love" will teach others to love one another in deed as well as in word (1:5; 2:15; 6:11). "A role model . . . in faith" will teach others to believe the truth rather than myths and teachings of demons (1:4; 4:1, 7). And "a role model . . . in chastity" will teach others sexual morality; for if even as a young man Timothy can keep his libidinal urges under control, as by the Holy Spirit he can according to Galatians 5:22–23, so too can the others, whether young or old. "Till I come" indicates that Paul will come back to Ephesus but doesn't indicate how soon he will. To make up for his absence in the meanwhile, Timothy is told to be "paying attention to reading," which means to engage in reading Scripture (at that time the Old Testament) and apostolic documents to assembled Christians (see 2 Corinthians 7:8; Colossians 4:16; 1 Thessalonians 5:27; 2 Thessalonians 3:14 for the latter, 2 Timothy 3:16–17 for the former, and 2 Peter 3:16 for both). Exhortation is to grow out of such reading, and teaching is to be based on such reading.

4:14–16: Don't be careless about the gracious gift [that's] **in you, which was given to you through prophecy along with a laying on of the hands of the board of elders. ¹⁵Be taking care for these things, exist in them, in order that your progress may be manifest to all. ¹⁶Be paying attention to yourself and the teaching. Be staying in them** [these things]. **For by doing this you'll save both yourself and those who hear you.** Since Timothy could be careless about the gracious gift that's in him, this gift consists in ability for ministry, an ability given him by the Holy Spirit, not the Holy Spirit himself (compare especially 1 Corinthians 12:4–11). The carelessness would consist in not exercising the ability. This gift was given to Timothy "through prophecy" (compare 1:18), for Spirit-inspired prophecy not only ensures fulfillment but also causes it (see the comments on Revelation 10:2b–4). "With a laying on of the hands of the board of elders" adds the body language of prophecy to its verbal language (compare Numbers 27:18–23; Deuteronomy 34:9, and for Old Testament examples of prophetic body language see 2 Kings 13:14–19; Isaiah 20:1–6; Jeremiah 19:10–13; Ezekiel 4:1–5:17 among other passages). "Be taking care for these things" is the flip side of "Don't be careless about the gracious gift" and equates with "be paying attention to reading, to exhortation, to teaching" (4:13). To "exist in them" is to be absorbed in the doing of them. "In order that your progress may be manifest to all" alludes back to the need for Timothy to become "a role model in speech, in behavior, in love, in faith, in chastity" (4:12). In view of the statement that by paying attention to himself and the teaching he'll "save" himself, his "progress" refers to progress toward final salvation. "Be staying in them" equates with "exist[ing]" in "reading, exhortation, and teaching" and highlights perseverance in these activities as Timothy's working at his own salvation (see the comments on Philippians 2:12-13). Thus "to be paying attention to reading, to exhortation, to teaching" comes out to "be paying attention to yourself and the teaching" for the sake of Timothy's own salvation—and also for that of his hearers, because a resultant similar perseverance on their part will culminate in salvation for them too (compare Romans 11:14; 1 Corinthians 7:16; 9:22).

PASTORING MEMBERS OF THE CHURCH
1 Timothy 5:1-6:2d

5:1-2: You shouldn't tongue-lash an older [man]; **rather, be exhorting** [him] **as** [you would] **a father, younger** [men] **as** [you would] **brothers,** [2]**older** [women] **as** [you would] **mothers, younger** [women] **as** [you would] **sisters,** [that is,] **in total chastity.** In 4:12 Paul said that no one is to be despising Timothy's youthfulness. Lest Timothy abuse his authority as Paul's delegate, however, Paul now tells him to exhort those under his charge with the same loving respect owed to family members; for a church is a family of sorts, a household (3:15). Agewise in a church, men older than Timothy are like his father, male peers like his brothers, women older than he like mothers to him, and female peers like his sisters. Subjecting older men to a tongue-lashing would show disrespect. Likewise in regard to younger men, older women, and younger women. (The mention of younger men as well as older men before older as well as younger women reflects a male-dominated culture, and mention of the older before the younger reflects a culture in which age trumped youth.) "In total chastity" echoes 4:12, except that Paul has added "total" to underscore the need for Timothy to control his youthful libido (compare the "libidinal" younger widows of 5:11, who might welcome his sexual advances). Otherwise he'll show carnal as well as verbal disrespect for the younger women. Only respectful exhortations will prove effective.

5:3-8: Be honoring widows who really are widows. [4]**But if any widow has children or grandchildren, they are to learn first to be practicing piety in regard to their own household and to make repayments to** [their] **progenitors. For this is acceptable in God's sight.** [5]**But the real widow—that is, the one who has been left alone—has set her hope on God and is continuing in supplications and prayers night and day.** [6]**But the** [widow] **who lives voluptuously is dead while she lives.** [7]**And be commanding these things in order that they may be unimpeachable.** [8]**But if anyone isn't providing for his own—even, namely, the members of** [his] **household—he has denied the faith and is worse than an unbeliever.** Because men usually married women a number of years younger than they were, the numbers of widows in the first-century Roman Empire was disproportionately large. Also, a women's liberation movement may have encouraged young widows

not to remarry, lest they lose their newfound independence, and thus exacerbated the disproportion. In view of 5:16-18, "Be honoring widows" includes supporting them financially (compare Acts 6:1-6). But in view of the burgeoning number of widows, "who really are widows" has the purpose of relieving an increasing financial strain on the church. Paul defines real widowhood as including more than bereavement of a husband. A widow who has children or grandchildren old enough to support her doesn't qualify as a real widow, so that Paul says the children or grandchildren "are to learn first [before the church takes on her support and therefore as a matter of priority for the offspring] to be practicing piety [under the assumption they too are Christians] in regard to their own household [to which their widowed mother or grandmother belongs] and to make repayments [consisting of financial support in return for having nurtured them earlier in life] to [their] progenitors [here, in particular, to their widowed mothers or grandmothers]." This practice is "acceptable in God's sight" because of its justice as a *re*payment. Notably, learning issues in practicing; otherwise no learning has occurred. For Christians the acceptability of this practice in the sight of God, whose point of view counts for even more than that of human society (compare 2:3), provides reason enough to engage in it; and since by definition discipleship consists in learning, nonlearning means nondiscipleship.

"In regard to their *own* household" stresses a widow's membership in the household of her child or grandchild. But "the one who has been left alone" refers to a widow bereft of children and grandchildren as well as of her husband. To qualify as a real widow, though, she also has to have "set her hope on God" (that is, as a Christian convert to have put her confidence in God as the source of eternal life for her) and be "continuing in supplications and prayers night and day," so that the church's financial support becomes payment for her ministry of supplications and prayers. The twofoldness of "supplications and prayers" and of "night and day" accents this ministry as deserving of financial support. The placement of "night" before "day" not only reflects the Jewish view that a 24-hour day starts at sundown. It also highlights the ministry as occupying nighttime as well as daytime. The widow "who lives voluptuously" already has plenty of money and spends it in ways that leave no time for continuing in supplications and prayers night and day (compare 2:9; 5:11-15). The oxymoronic definition of voluptuous living as a living death portends eternal death instead of eternal life (contrast the reverse oxymoron in 2 Corinthians 6:9 of living though dying). Timothy is to be "commanding these things"—that is, commanding the churchly support of real widows and the children's or grandchildren's support of widows in their households—"in order that they [the church members, children, and grandchildren] may be unimpeachable [and therefore not a blot on the reputation of the church]." But to save the church an unnecessary financial strain, emphasis falls on the children's and grandchildren's responsibility in that failing this responsibility amounts to an economic if not verbal denial of Christian belief ("the faith") and therefore marks the professing Christian as "worse than an unbeliever"—that is, worse than someone who makes no profession of Christian belief—and therefore as sure to face impeachment at the Last Judgment whether or not ahead of time in human society. "His own—even, namely, the members of [his] household" intensifies the earlier stress on a widow's membership in the household of her child or grandchild.

5:9–10: A widow is to be listed if she is not less than sixty years [old], **a woman of one man** [prior to being widowed], **¹⁰being attested for good deeds—if she has reared children, if she has shown hospitality to strangers, if she has washed the saints' feet, if she has given aid to people being afflicted, if she has followed** [the practice of doing] **every** [kind of] **good deed.** Here Paul refers to listing real widows for the reception of financial support from the church. "Not less than sixty years [old]" adds to the qualifications laid out in 5:3–5 and restricts the list severely because of a much shorter life expectancy than typifies societies benefited by modern medicine. Further qualifications follow: "A woman of one man" means that a listed widow must be known to have been sexually faithful to her husband (compare 3:2). "Being attested for good deeds" means that others must testify to her performance of such deeds, which include the rearing of children (compare the bearing of children as a christianly proper function of married women according to 2:15), the showing of hospitality to strangers (see the comments on 3:2), the washing of the feet of saints (= fellow Christians, called "saints" because of their consecration to God), and the giving of aid "to people being afflicted" (that is, fellow Christians under the pressure of persecution). So the widow will have welcomed into her home fellow Christians previously unknown to her because in flight from persecution they had come from elsewhere; and her welcome of them started with washing their feet, soiled from walking dusty roads in open sandals (compare Genesis 18:4; Luke 7:44; John 13:1–11), and continued with aiding the refugees by providing them room and board (compare Matthew 10:23, 40–42; 25:35, 40). Along with the initial "being attested for good deeds," the closing qualification, "if she has followed [the practice of] every [kind of] good deed," frames the intervening examples but also stresses the doing of good deeds as a habit of life and adds "every" to "good deed" for the inclusion of good deeds other than those just specified.

5:11–12: But decline [putting] **younger widows** [on the list]. **For when they become libidinal against the Christ, they want to get married, ¹²incurring judgment because they've set aside** [their] **first faith.** Younger widows, those at least younger than sixty and—more particularly—premenopausal (see 5:14 for their ability to bear children), are liable to become "libidinal against the Christ," which is to say that their libido is liable to lead them into sexual promiscuity. This promiscuity will contradict their profession of Jesus as the

Messiah and make them want to get remarried even to an unbeliever, which kind of remarriage Paul prohibits in 1 Corinthians 7:39 and describes here as "incurring judgment," the suffering of eternal punishment (see the comments on 3:6), "because they've set aside [their] first faith [the belief in Jesus as the Messiah that they had at first]." For such a remarriage would almost certainly entail apostasy, its being the case that a wife was expected to adopt her husband's religion.

5:13: And at the same time [that they're living promiscuously and wanting to get married even to an unbeliever] **they also learn** [to be] **lazy** [if the church is supporting them financially], **going around from house to house, and not only lazy but also babbling and working around** [= meddling in others' business] **as they talk about things that shouldn't** [be talked about]. Learning to be lazy contrasts with learning to practice piety in the doing of every kind of good deed (5:4, 10). "Going around from house to house" contrasts with a woman's proper functions of childrearing and practicing hospitality in her own home (5:10). "Babbling" contrasts with "continuing in supplications and prayers night and day" (5:5). "Working around" through meddling in others' business contrasts with "follow[ing] [the practice of doing] every [kind of] good deed" in their behalf (5:10 again). And "talk[ing] about things that shouldn't [be talked about]" defines the gossip as verbal meddling.

5:14–16: Therefore [because they're liable to "become libidinal against the Christ" and lazy, gossipy meddlers] **I want younger** [widows] **to get married, to bear children, to manage a household, to give the opponent no occasion for ridicule. ¹⁵For some** [younger widows] **have already veered off behind Satan. ¹⁶If any believing** [woman] **has widows** [in her family or household], **she's to be giving them aid; and the church isn't to be burdened** [with caring for them], **in order that it** [the church] **may give aid to those who really are widows.** Since widows are still in view, "to get married" has to do with remarriage; and since Paul has just condemned remarriage to an unbeliever, in opposition to the heresy that forbids marriage (4:3) he now exhorts remarriage to a believer. "To bear children" recalls childbearing in 2:15 as a married woman's way of working at her salvation and implies here that at least some of the widows Paul has in mind haven't yet come close to sixty years of age. "To manage a household" includes not only the childrearing of 5:10 but also all sorts of other domestic duties, for which see Proverbs 31:10–31 (where the duties, though domestic, by no means confine the woman to her dwelling) and from which duties a first-century women's movement may have sought to liberate women. Because of a following reference to Satan, "the opponent" may refer to him. But elsewhere in the New Testament the words for opposition and ridicule are never used for him—rather, for human beings and what they do—and Paul has consistently expressed a concern that Christians maintain a good reputation for the sake of evangelism. So "the opponent" is likely any unbeliever who would fault with ridicule younger widows for not supporting the family as society's basic and vital unit by remarrying and taking up domestic duties again. Paul issues this exhortation because "some [younger widows] have already veered off behind Satan" by following him in their sexually promiscuous behavior (compare the "veer[ing] out of [faith] into pointless talk" by the would-be teachers of the Law [1:6–7]). And to ensure the church's ability to aid real widows, Paul adds to a younger Christian woman's domestic duties the duty of aiding widows such as her mother, mother-in-law, grandmother, grandmother-in-law, and any widowed slaves in her household.

5:17-18: The elders who preside well are to be considered worthy of a double honorarium, namely those who labor in speaking and teaching. ¹⁸For the Scripture says, "You shall not muzzle an ox when it's treading grain [Deuteronomy 25:4]"; and "the worker [is] worthy of his pay [Luke 10:7: compare Matthew 10:10; Numbers 18:31]." The command in 5:3–16 to "honor" real widows with financial support leads Paul to command now "a double honorarium" for "the elders who preside well." Presiding well is associated with a supervisor (overseer) in 3:4–5 (though in that passage the presiding over his own household morphs into "tak[ing] care of God's church"). So "the elders" here equate with supervisors; and the shift in terminology arises out of the immediately preceding discussion of widows "not less than sixty years [old]" (5:9) and, somewhat farther back, of elderly men and women in general (5:1–2) and of "the board of elders" (4:14). "Supervisor" designates an elder by his function. "Elder" designates a supervisor by his age-related status. "The board of elders" in 4:14, the plural of "elders" here, the plural of "supervisors and assistants [deacons]" in Philippians 1:1, and "the elders [plural] of the church [singular]" in Ephesus (Acts 20:17, 28), where Timothy is located, all combine to favor a plurality of elders/supervisors in a single local church, unless Paul and Luke lump together more than one house-church in a large city (against which possibility, however, see Romans 1:7; 16:5, 14–15). Such labor defines what it means to preside well; for speaking and teaching take time and effort away from a money-making occupation, so that these elders deserve an honorarium. There's no necessary implication that elders who don't speak and teach are presiding poorly. "A double honorarium" probably means an honorarium twice as large as one given to elders who, though competent to teach, expend time and effort in presiding over a church but not to the extent of speaking and teaching. "Are to be *considered* worthy" implies an ungrudging payment; and in view of the requirement that a supervisor be "competent to teach" (3:2), "speaking and teaching" probably means speaking by way of teaching. It remains possible that speaking refers to exhortation based on what is taught, though for that we might have expected the reverse order, teaching before speaking, and also "exhorting" instead of "speaking," as in 6:2e. To support the giving of a double honorarium, Paul first cites Scripture and then a saying of Jesus. In the scriptural citation the ox that's treading grain to separate kernels from chaff is made to stand for the elders who labor in speaking and teaching; and the nonmuzzling of the ox, so that it can munch on the grain it is treading out, is made to stand for these elders' getting a double honorarium (compare 1 Corinthians 9:9–14; Galatians 6:6). Paul uses the saying of Jesus to interpret the Scriptural citation.

5:19-20: Don't be accepting an accusation against an elder except "on [the evidence of] **two or three witnesses** [Numbers 35:30; Deuteronomy 17:6; 19:15]." ²⁰**Be censuring in the sight of all** [church members] **the** [elders] **who are sinning, in order that the rest may have a fear** [of sinning]. These two commands balance each other. On the one hand, an elder's presiding over nonelders might lead especially one of the nonelders to rebel by laying a false charge against the elder. So Paul commands Timothy not to be accepting the accusation except when it's supported by two or three witnesses. On the other hand, elders sometimes fall into sinning and thereby set a bad example for those under their supervision, and for the other elders too. So to counteract the bad example, Timothy is to censure the sinning elder openly. What a way for Timothy not to let anyone despise his youthfulness (4:12)! Obviously, he'll be acting as Paul the apostle's delegate.

5:21-22: In the sight of God and Christ Jesus and the selected angels I solemnly testify that you should observe [= carry out] **these** [directives] **without prior judgment, by doing nothing in accordance with prior inclination. ²²Don't be laying hands hastily on anyone** [by way of ordination into eldership]**, and don't be participating in others' sins. Be keeping yourself chaste.** "In the sight of God and Christ Jesus and the selected angels" portrays Paul's testimony as given before the heavenly court. That court calls for a testimony no less than solemn, and the angels are those "selected" in that the risen Christ appeared to them (3:16). "Without prior judgment" means "without prejudice," and "nothing in accordance with prior inclination" means "nothing in accordance with favoritism." "Don't be laying hands hastily on anyone" means not to ordain a neophyte into eldership just because the censuring of an elder has created a vacancy on the board of elders. Since an ordained neophyte is liable to "fall into the Devil's judgment" (3:6), the command that Timothy "not be participating in others' sins" includes a warning not to share in a neophyte's sins by having ordained him hastily (compare Romans 1:32; 2 John 11). In view of Timothy's youthful libido, "Be keeping yourself chaste" harks back to 4:12, "Rather, become for the believers a role model . . . in chastity," and to 5:2, "be exhorting . . . younger [women] as [you would] sisters, [that is,] in total chastity" (compare 2 Timothy 2:22). If Timothy were not to keep himself chaste and if he were to participate in others' sins, he'd lose the moral authority to censure sinning elders.

5:23: No longer be drinking [only] **water; rather, be using a little wine because of your stomach** [to help your digestion] **and your frequent illnesses.** This command implies that Timothy has been drinking only water and indicates outright that he has been having stomach trouble and suffering from it frequent bouts of illness. Paul's prescription of wine was typical; but the precaution "a *little* wine" keeps the prescription healthful and Timothy himself from falling into the trap of addiction to wine (3:3, 8; Titus 1:7). The precaution may also reflect the ancient practice of diluting wine rather heavily with water (see the comments on Revelation 14:10; 18:6). To drink undiluted wine was considered intemperate.

5:24–25: The sins of some people are very clear, preceding [them] **into judgment; but also in the case of some** [people] [their sins] **follow** [them into judgment]. **²⁵In the same way also the good deeds** [of some people are] **very clear, and the** [good deeds] **that are otherwise** [that is, not very clear at present] **can't be hidden** [forever]. Paul has recently commanded the open censure of elders who are sinning (5:20) and prohibited both prior judgment (5:21) and participation in others' sins (5:22). So after his digression into a prescription for Timothy's health (5:23), Paul reverts to the theme of sin and judgment. But now "judgment" refers to the Last Judgment, not to prior judgment. When sins are obvious ("very clear"), they precede to the Last Judgment those who commit them. So the punishment of such sins won't surprise anybody. When sins aren't obvious, they follow to that judgment those who commit them. So the punishment of such sins will surprise people, perhaps even the sinners themselves. The same is true of obvious and unobvious good deeds. So professing Christians should take both warning and encouragement, and Timothy shouldn't worry about inevitable failures to detect for censure the secret sins of some people (especially of some elders) and to detect for commendation the secret good deeds of others. At least eventually the truth will out and justice will prevail.

6:1–2d: As many as are under a yoke as slaves are to be regarding their own masters as deserving of total honor, lest God's name and [our] **teaching be slandered** [compare Romans 2:24; Isaiah 52:5]. "As many as" leaves no Christian slave exempt from obedience to Paul's command, no matter whether the slave has a Christian master or a non-Christian master. A yoke was placed over the necks of animals (for example, oxen) and connected to a vehicle or agricultural implement for the purpose of pulling it. So for slaves to be "under a yoke" stands for their being put to work for their masters (see Galatians 5:1 for a different application of this figure of speech). That Christian slaves are to be regarding their masters "as deserving of honor" doesn't depend on the masters' disposition, which might be cruel rather than kind, but on the masters' higher social status. As compared with the much lower social status of slaves, the masters' status calls for rendering them "*total* honor." Not a smidgen of honor is to be held back. But such

honor is reserved for "their *own* masters." For honoring a master consists in working for him, and a slave is bound to work only for *his* master. Paul doesn't want "God's name [= reputation]" and his and Timothy's "teaching [= the gospel]" to "be slandered [= defamed, maligned]" by a failure of Christian slaves to honor their masters totally (compare Titus 2:5, 10). In other words, evangelism takes precedence over social reform in the world at large (though social reform within the church, as per Galatians 3:28 and Philemon, may enhance evangelism and set an agenda for such reform outside the church [compare the comments on slave traders in 1:10]). Now Paul turns to a subcategory of slaves. ²ᵃ⁻ᵈ**And the** [slaves] **who have believing** [= Christian] **masters aren't to be despising** [them] **because they** [the masters] **are brothers** [in Christ to their slaves]**; rather, they** [the slaves] **are to be slaving the more** [for them] **because the** [masters] **who benefit from** [their slaves'] **well-doing are believers and beloved.** The reference to believing masters as Christian slaves' "brothers" erases in Christ the distinction between masters and slaves. Precisely because of this brotherly relation, however, the slaves should defer to that distinction not only by honoring their believing masters but also by loving them so much as to slave for them "more," that is, to do more for them than assigned tasks. Doing so will vault the slaves into the socially superior status of benefactors of their masters (whether or not others will recognize this reversal of roles).

ON TEACHING AND EXHORTING
1 Timothy 6:2e–10

6:2e–5: Be teaching and exhorting these things [compare 4:11]. **³If anyone is teaching different things and isn't agreeing with healthful words—those of our Lord, Jesus Christ—and the teaching that accords with piety, ⁴he's conceited, understanding nothing—rather, being diseased with debates and disputes over words, out of which** [debates and disputes] **develop envy, strife, slanders, evil suspicions, ⁵constant friction between people depraved in mind and defrauded of the truth, supposing** [as they do] **that piety is a means of** [monetary] **gain.** In the first part of this paragraph we read of teaching that issues in exhortation; then of different teaching that doesn't agree with healthful words, which because of antithetical parallelism refer to the aforementioned exhortation; and finally of teaching that accords with the piety effected by exhortation. Timothy is to teach so that others may learn, and to exhort so that the others may put their learning into the practice of piety. "Healthful words" and "the teaching that accords with piety" describe "these things" that Paul tells Timothy to be teaching and exhorting, and "these things" refers in general to the contents of 1 Timothy (compare the morally healthful teaching in 1:10; also 2 Timothy 1:13; 4:3; Titus 1:9, 13; 2:1–2, 8). To stress their binding force, Paul identifies the healthful words as "those of our Lord, Jesus Christ" (a reference to Jesus' moral teachings). The teaching of "different things" equates with the aberrant teaching mentioned in 1:3–4, doesn't agree with healthful words, and therefore produces the vices that Paul goes on to list. Disagreement with the healthful words and teaching that accord with piety betrays a morally diseased conceit that destroys insight ("understanding nothing") by prompting "debates and disputes over words." That is to say, conceit turns the very words that are meant to engender piety into objects of debates and disputes, which are nothing more than competitions for honor. The listed vices ("envy, strife, slanders . . .") constitute effects of the debates and disputes. Envy produces strife. Strife produces slanders. Slanders produce evil suspicions ("evil" in the sense of "villainous"). And evil suspicions produce constant friction "between people depraved in mind [because of disagreement with the healthful words] and defrauded of the truth [and thus 'understanding nothing' but 'supposing that piety is a means of (monetary) gain']." Notably, conceit corrupts thinking and robs its victims of truth, in this case the truth of Christian teaching; and the conceited mistake their debates and disputes for exercises in piety, and mistake such supposed piety for a means of money-making (because of listeners' financial contributions to those admired as winners in the debates and disputes).

6:6–10: But piety [combined] **with contentment is procurative of great gain** [apart from money]: [1] **⁷For we carried nothing into the world.** [2] **Because neither can we carry anything out of** [the world] [compare Job 1:21; Psalm 49:17; Ecclesiastes 5:15]. **⁸And if having meals and clothes, with these we'll be content. ⁹But those who want to be wealthy fall into a temptation and a trap and many mindless and harmful lusts which as such plunge people into destruction and ruin. ¹⁰For the love of money** [contrast 3:3, 8] **is the root of all the bad things, by reaching out for which** [money] **some have been led astray from the faith and have stabbed themselves with many pangs.** Contentment means being satisfied with bare necessities (compare 2 Corinthians 9:8; Philippians 4:11–12). True piety breeds a contentment that forestalls engagement in debates and disputes for the purpose of making money; and such piety is "procurative of great gain" in that it eventuates in eternal life, which has far greater value than money has. Paul substantiates this greater value by noting in two ways money's inferiority to the greater gain of eternal life: (1) At birth we brought nothing, such as money, into the world; (2) at death we're unable to take anything, not even the money we've made, out of the world.[3] In other words, money had no value for us prior to our mortal existence (naturally), and it will have no value for us following our mortal existence (just as naturally). Speaking for himself and Timothy, then, Paul says they'll be content with the bare necessities of "meals

[for nourishment] and clothes [for warmth]" in anticipation of the "great gain" of eternal life hereafter and in contrast with "want[ing] to be wealthy [that is, to have more money than what is presently required to buy food and clothing]" here and now.

Paul then describes "those who want to be wealthy" as "fall[ing]." To "fall into temptation" is to yield to it. To "fall into . . . a trap" is to be caught and confined by it. "Lusts" are what the temptation and the trap represent. So to "fall into . . . lusts" is to yield to them and be caught and confined by them. These lusts are "many" in that wanting to be wealthy looks forward to acquisitions far more numerous than meals and clothes. The lusts are "mindless" in that it makes no sense to aim for temporary wealth at the cost of the great gain consisting in eternal life. And the lusts are "harmful" in that they "plunge people into destruction and ruin." "Which *as such*" stresses the lusts as harmful. The destruction and ruin are eternal and therefore worse than falling for the moment into a temptation, a trap, and lusts. "Plung[ing] people" portrays their "destruction and ruin" as being shoved into the watery depths of the sea, from which there's no escape. And the pairing of "ruin" with "destruction" portrays the destruction as wreckage rather than annihilation (compare the pairings of "meals" and "clothes," "a temptation" and "a trap," "mindless" and "harmful"; also the comments on Matthew 25:44–46). And it's merely "want[ing] to be wealthy" that starts a chain reaction ending in eternal destruction and ruin. Why? Because "the love of money [= wanting to be wealthy] is the root [a figure of speech for the originating source] of all the bad things [the 'many mindless and harmful lusts which as such plunge people into destruction and ruin']." "Reaching out" for money comes from loving it. The "some" who "have been led astray from the faith" by reaching out for money are the same as those dismissively called "some" who "by going amiss have veered out of [faith] into pointless talk, wanting to be teachers of the Law" (1:3–7; see 1:19–20; 4:1–3 as well). They're also the same as those "supposing that piety is a means of [monetary] gain" (6:5). It's sadly ironic that by "reaching out for [money]" they've unknowingly grabbed a dagger and "stabbed themselves [a figure of speech for self-destruction and self-ruination] with many pangs [the many pains of hell that correspond to money-lovers' 'many mindless and harmful lusts']." See 6:17–19 for the benevolent use of wealth as a contrast with reaching out for money.

LEADING BY EXAMPLE
1 Timothy 6:11–16

6:11–12: But you, O man of God, be fleeing these things; and be pursuing righteousness, piety, faith, love, endurance, a meek disposition. ¹²Be competing the good competition for the faith. Take hold of eternal life, to which you were called and [for which] **you confessed the good confession in the sight of many witnesses.** The address to Timothy, "O man of God," sets him over against "those who want to be wealthy" (6:9).

---

[3]Since our inability to take anything out of the world hardly follows from our having brought nothing into it, it's better to treat "*For* we carried nothing . . ." and "*Because* neither can we carry anything . . ." as independent rationales of the foregoing rather than to make the second a consequence of the first.

They've been entrapped in their lusts, to which they therefore belong and which they therefore serve (Matthew 6:24; Luke 16:13). Timothy belongs to God and serves him. "O" is emphatic of Timothy as God's man; and the Greek word underlying the translation "man" doesn't refer to Timothy as a male in distinction from a female, but to him as a human being in distinction from God, his owner and master (compare this designation of Timothy with Deuteronomy 33:1; Joshua 14:6 [and so on]). "These things" that Timothy is to "be fleeing" are the "many mindless and harmful lusts" that derive from "want[ing] to be wealthy," from "the love of money," from "reaching out for [money]" (6:9–10). "Fleeing" them is to be complemented by "pursuing" the subsequently listed virtues (compare 2 Timothy 2:22). Temptation calls for flight, virtues for pursuit. As for the virtues, righteousness (= upright conduct) arises out of piety (the practice of true religion). Piety arises out of faith (ongoing belief in Jesus Christ). Faith operates through love (of fellow believers [Galatians 5:6]). And endurance (of hardship, especially of persecution, which often leaves nothing but food and clothing) is enabled by a meek disposition (nonretaliation). The command to "be pursuing" these virtues leads Paul to revive the metaphor of athletic competition in his command, "Be competing" (compare 4:10), which denotes strong effort marked by self-discipline. The parallel between pursuing and competing denotes the running of a race, the goal of which is to "take hold of eternal life" at what Paul is about to call "the epiphany [= appearance at the second coming] of our Lord, Jesus Christ" (6:14; 1 Corinthians 9:24–27; Philippians 3:11–14; 2 Timothy 4:7). This competition is "good" because it's "for the faith" and thereby entails "the good confession," which according to 6:13 Christ Jesus, too, confessed. The wordplay in and the parallel between competing the good competition and confessing the good confession call special attention to the competition and the confession. "For the faith" contrasts with "some" who "have been led astray from the faith" (6:10). "In the sight of many witnesses" indicates a public confession/declaration. Taking hold of eternal life contrasts with reaching out for money, which nobody can carry out of the world (6:6–10); and "to which you were called" refers to God's having effectively called Timothy to eternal life. Thus Paul correlates the divine and human elements in salvation.

6:13–16: I command [you] in the sight of God, who gives life to all things, and of Christ Jesus, who testified the good confession before Pontius Pilate, ¹⁴that as spotless, [that is] unimpeachable, you keep the command until the epiphany of our Lord, Jesus Christ, ¹⁵which [epiphany] he [God] will exhibit in his own times—[he being] the blessed and only Potentate, the King of those who exercise kingship and Lord of those who exercise lordship [compare Revelation 17:14; 19:16], **¹⁶the only one having immortality, inhabiting unapproachable light, whom no human being has seen or can see** [compare Exodus 33:20; John 1:18], **to whom** [belong] **honor and eternal might. Amen** [com-

pare 1:17]! Though Timothy "confessed the good confession in the sight of many [human] witnesses" (6:12), Paul doesn't have many human witnesses to observe him writing (or dictating) this letter to Timothy. So to lend weight to the present command, Paul echoes his solemn testimony to Timothy "in the sight of God and Christ Jesus and the selected angels" (5:21) but drops the angels in favor of adding the description of God as the one "who gives life to all things" and the description of Christ Jesus as the one "who testified the good confession before Pontius Pilate." These additions add to the weight of Paul's command. God is not only "living," unlike idols (3:15; 4:10). He's also life-giving, so that all living things derive their life from him. This description of him grows out of the "eternal life" that Timothy is to "lay hold of" according to 6:12. It will be the self-given life of God.

Since for Paul the good confession by Timothy before many witnesses was a confession of Jesus to be Lord (see Romans 10:9–10), Jesus' exemplary good confession before Pontius Pilate appears to have been a confession by Jesus of his own lordship. But we have no record of such a confession by him before Pontius Pilate (see Mark 15:1–15; Matthew 27:1–2, 11–26; Luke 23:1–7, 13–25; John 18:28–19:16). So Paul seems to be depending on a tradition unrecorded in the Gospels, or interpreting a tradition such as that in John 18:36–37, where Jesus tells Pilate that his (Jesus') kingdom isn't "from this world" and that he "came into the world," as equivalent to a confession of his lordship. In any case, Christ Jesus' good testimony even before Pontius Pilate, a Roman governor, should steel Timothy to maintain his own similarly good confession in obedience to Paul's command. For both God and Christ Jesus are bearing witness to the command, which has just preceded in 6:11–12. If Timothy keeps it, he'll be "spotless," which Paul explains as "unimpeachable."

"Until the epiphany of our Lord, Jesus Christ" extends the commanded obedience to the second coming, which Paul calls an "epiphany" to connote a glorious appearance that brings eternal salvation to believers in him, a salvation far grander than any temporal salvation brought by the so-called epiphany of a Roman emperor. God "will exhibit ['the epiphany of our Lord (which can also be translated "Emperor"), Jesus Christ'] in his [God's] own times"—that is, in the future as appropriately determined by God (compare 2:6; Titus 1:3). An epiphany is indeed an exhibition. Then to set God as well as the Lord, Jesus Christ, over against the Roman emperors of lesser epiphanies, Paul calls God "the blessed [= worthy of praise] and only Potentate [= the sole possessor of absolute power], the King of those who exercise kingship and Lord of those who exercise lordship [so that they are more subjects and slaves than kings and emperors], the only one having immortality [as opposed to those so-called kings and emperors, despite their supposed immortalization after death according to decrees of the Roman senate], inhabiting unapproachable light [in contrast with the approachability of kings and emperors, who dwell in dimly lit palaces], whom [apart from his incarnate Son] no human being has seen or can see [whereas kings and emperors are visible and seen both in person and in the form of images scattered throughout the Roman Empire], to whom [rather than to those kings and emperors] belong honor and eternal might [unlike the kings' and emperors' fading honor and short-lived might]." Paul caps this doxology with an enthusiastic "Amen!"

WARNING THE WEALTHY
1 Timothy 6:17–19

6:17–19: Be commanding those who are wealthy in the present age [as opposed to the coming age, called eternity] **not to be thinking high things** [about themselves because of their wealth] **and not to set** [their] **hope on the unclarity** [a figure of speech for the uncertainty] **of wealth—rather, on God** [compare 4:10; 5:5], **who wealthily** [= richly] **grants us all things for** [our] **enjoyment.** [18][Be commanding them] **to be doing benevolent work** [with their wealth], **to be wealthy in good works** [5:6], **to be generous, sharing,** [19]**treasuring up for themselves a good foundation for what's going to come** [hereafter], **in order that they may take hold of what is really life** [compare Matthew 6:19–20; Luke 12:21]. Now the command*ee*, Timothy (6:13), is commanded to be a command*er*—of "those [Christians] who are wealthy," no less, not just of "those who *want* to be wealthy" (6:9), and this despite the worldly power and prestige that wealth brings. But since we can't carry anything out of the world (6:7), to be wealthy only "in the present age" makes people of this description suitable targets for a command by Timothy. The temporariness of current wealth invalidates pride for having it, and the uncertainty of current wealth invalidates putting confidence in it even for the present age, much more for eternity, the age to come. Only the placing of hope on God is justified. To present him as the basis of hope for eternal life, Paul describes him as the one "who [already in the present age] wealthily grants us all things for [our] enjoyment." By "things" Paul means the "foods" which the would-be teachers of the Law put off-limits but all of which Paul says God created to be eaten with thanksgiving (4:3–5). As believers, in other words, our enjoyment of all foods, created by God in rich variety, anticipates the enjoyment hereafter of eternal life, which is "*really* life." But this life is guaranteed to the currently wealthy only if they show the reality of their professed faith in

Christ by using their money in "doing benevolent work," which makes them "wealthy in good works" and requires them "to be generous, sharing." And their generous sharing of present wealth will amount to "treasuring up a good foundation [= a confirmation of genuine faith] for what's to come [the real life of eternal life]." "In order that they may take hold of what is really life" echoes Timothy's own commanded "tak[ing] hold of eternal life" (6:12) and contrasts again with reaching out for money, which nobody can carry out of the world (6:6–10).

CONCLUSION
1 Timothy 6:20–21

6:20–21: O Timothy, guard what has been entrusted [to you] **while veering away from the profane, empty jabberings and inconsistencies of falsely named knowledge,** [21]**by professing which some have gone amiss in respect to the faith. Grace** [be] **with you** [plural]. Suitably for a conclusion, the descriptive address in 6:11, "O man of God," has shaded here into the personal address, "O Timothy." But "O" is still emphatic of Paul's concern that Timothy obey a final command. "What has been entrusted" to Timothy is the orthodox Christian faith. To "guard" it is to protect it from heterodoxy, such as the heresy first mentioned in 1:3–7 and now referenced as "profane, empty jabberings and inconsistencies of falsely named knowledge." As the would-be teachers of the Law "have veered out of [faith] into pointless talk," to guard the faith Timothy must be "veering" in a different direction, "away from" those jabberings, which match the earlier-mentioned pointless talk, and inconsistencies, which match in turn the earlier-mentioned teaching that's aberrant because it contradicts the faith. Paul describes the jabberings as "profane" (lacking in piety) and "empty" (lacking in truth), and the inconsistencies as producing "falsely named knowledge" (compare Paul's earlier description of the would-be teachers of the Law as "not understanding either the things that they're saying or [the things] about which they're speaking confidently"). "By professing which some have gone amiss in respect to the faith" harks back to those who "by going amiss have veered out of [faith]" (see also 1:18–20). The wishing of grace (God's favor) to be "with you" implies that the Ephesian Christians as well as Timothy will hear this letter read to them, for "you" is plural in Paul's Greek. So those Ephesians will know what Paul expects of them in response to Timothy's commands.

SECOND TIMOTHY

This letter contains an encouragement to Timothy that he exercise courage in Christian ministry, oppose false teaching, and come to Paul, the imprisoned author, who is facing martyrdom in the near future.

INTRODUCTION
2 Timothy 1:1–2

1:1–2: Paul, an apostle of Christ Jesus through God's will in accordance with the promise of the life that [is] in Christ Jesus, ²to Timothy, [my] beloved child: Grace, mercy, peace from God, the Father, and Christ Jesus, our Lord. After identifying himself by name, Paul cites his apostleship to undergird the contents of this letter with the very authority of Christ Jesus himself, who delegated Paul to represent him. See further the comments on 1 Corinthians 1:1. "In accordance with the promise of the life . . ." means that Christ Jesus authorized Paul to proclaim a message of life, which according to Titus 1:1–3 is eternal life and according to 1 Timothy 4:8 is both "now," by way of a foretaste, and "going to come," by way of full enjoyment. "The promise" of this life is contained in the message; and "that [is] in Christ Jesus" locates the life in him, so that to gain it those who hear the message must believe in him to take a position in him. For believers, he's the habitat of eternal life. "To Timothy, [my] . . . child" identifies the letter's recipient affectionately and probably as Paul's convert (compare Acts 14:6–23; 16:1–3 with Philemon 10). Perhaps because Paul is facing martyrdom (4:6–7), the tender description "beloved" replaces the authenticating description "genuine" that occurs in the similar address at 1 Timothy 1:2 (though see 1 Corinthians 4:17). For "grace" and "peace" see the comments on 1 Peter 1:2; 2 John 3. Here Paul inserts "mercy" in anticipation of 1:16, 18, where it has to do with finding the Lord's mercy on the Day of Judgment, and coordinates "God, the Father, and Christ Jesus, our Lord" as the source of "Grace, mercy, peace."

EXHORTATIONS TO DOCTRINAL AND BEHAVIORAL FIDELITY TO THE GOSPEL
2 Timothy 1:3–4:8

This main body of 2 Timothy, whose contents the foregoing subtitle summarizes, doesn't follow a progressive outline, but switches back and forth between Paul's citing good and bad doctrines, good and bad behaviors, and good and bad role models—all within the framework of exhorting Timothy in regard to his ministry.

1:3–5: I have [= give] **thanks to God, for whom I'm doing religious service with a pure conscience the way** [my] **progenitors** [did], **as I constantly have a remembrance concerning you in my supplications night and day, ⁴longing to see you** [compare 4:21a], **having called to memory your tears, that I might be filled with joy, ⁵having taken remembrance of the unhypocritical faith that** [is] **in you, which as such dwelled first in your grandmother Lois and your mother Eunice; and I'm persuaded that** [it dwells] **also in you . . . .** Paul interrupts his thanksgiving to God to say that he's doing religious service for God, as in Romans 1:9. But there the service consists in evangelism. Here it consists in his martyrdom, which in 4:6 he'll describe as a drink-offering already in process. The distinction is inconsequential, though, because he's being martyred on account of his service of evangelism. "With a pure [= clear] conscience" may imply that he doesn't deserve martyrdom but mainly, if not exclusively, reflects back on what 4:7 will call his good competition, finishing the race, and keeping the faith. "The way [my] progenitors [did]" refers to the religious service rendered to God by Israel's patriarchs (such as Abraham, Isaac, and Jacob), ascribes to Paul a venerable heritage of such service (compare Acts 24:14), and thus makes his own service a template for Timothy to follow. Since love fosters memory, "as I constantly have a remembrance concerning you in my supplications" grows out of Timothy's being a beloved child of Paul (1:2) and tells what happens when Paul is giving thanks to God. Invariably he remembers to pray for Timothy. "Night and day" not only reflects the Jewish view that a 24-hour day starts at sundown. By specifying "constantly," the phrase also highlights that Paul's supplications occur at night as well as during the day. "Longing to see you" tells what happens when Paul remembers Timothy in prayer, and "having called to memory your tears" explains why Paul longs to see Timothy and therefore alludes probably to Timothy's tears when he and Paul last parted from each other.

"That I might be filled with joy" contrasts with Timothy's tears and again tells why Paul longs to see Timothy. "Having taken remembrance of the unhypocritical faith that [is] in you" finally identifies what it is Paul thanks God for in his supplications. In particular, the lack of hypocrisy in Timothy's faith contrasts with the disappointment of Paul in others (see 1:15; 2:17–18; 4:10) and reinforces his thanksgiving. Moreover, interior faith ("faith that [is] in you") contrasts with faith limited to the exterior by way of pretense. The interplay of "have a remembrance," "having called to memory," and "having taken remembrance" underlines Paul's love for Timothy (almost in the sense that "absence makes the heart grow fonder") and thereby supplements the apostolic authority of Paul with his father-like affection for Timothy. The combination is designed to enhance this letter's effect on Timothy. "Which *as such*" stresses his faith as interior and therefore "unhypocritical" and goes on to ascribe this kind of faith to his grandmother Lois and his mother Eunice. "First" makes Lois the first convert in the family to Christian faith, and by implication makes Eunice the second convert. "And I'm persuaded that [it dwells] also in you" calls attention again to the interiority of Timothy's faith and gives him a venerable family heritage of faith similar to Paul's venerable ancestral heritage of religious service for God. Because Paul is (so to speak) passing the baton to Timothy, Paul's heritage will converge with Timothy's; and Timothy will entrust this heritage to his own successors (2:1–2). Paul's statement, "I'm persuaded," bespeaks a confidence that should motivate Timothy to rise to the occasion of the exhortations now directed to him.

Paul's long sentence continues in *1:6–7*: **for which reason I'm reminding you to be rekindling God's gracious gift, which is in you through the laying on of my hands. ⁷For God didn't give us a spirit of cowardice** [compare Romans 8:15]—**rather, [the Spirit] of power and love and sensibility.** Paul's reminder arises out of being persuaded of Timothy's unhypocritical faith, echoes the three remembrances in 1:3–5, and consists in an exhortation "to be rekindling God's gracious gift." A wordplay between "*re*minding" (Greek: *anamimnēskō*) and "*re*kindling" (Greek: *anazōpurein*) underlines the reminder to rekindle. Paul's imminent martyrdom and consequent passing of the baton to Timothy created a need for Timothy to stoke the fire of God's gracious gift to him. In other words, Timothy should make fresh use of the gift. This ill-deserved gift is the Holy Spirit, whom Paul describes as "of power and love and sensibility." The presence of this gift in Timothy (see also 1:14) correlates with the presence of unhypocritical faith in him (1:5). The laying of Paul's hands on Timothy provided the medium through which God gave his Spirit to Timothy (compare Acts 8:17–18; 9:12, 17; 19:6), probably occurred at Timothy's conversion, and seems to have differed from a gracious gift of ministry later given him "through prophecy along with a laying on of the hands of the board of elders" (1 Timothy 4:14). A danger of cowardice, which would keep Timothy from preaching the gospel, isn't likely to have originated in a personality trait of his. To the contrary, see the comments on 1 Corinthians 16:10. The danger is likely to have arisen from Paul's impending martyrdom. But God's Spirit isn't a spirit that breeds cowardice. Instead, the Spirit brings power for gospel-preaching (Romans 15:13, 18–19; 1 Corinthians 1:18; 2:1–5; 1 Thessalonians 1:5; Acts 1:8). He pours out love, again for gospel-preaching (Romans 5:5; 2 Corinthians 5:5, 14, 20). And he conveys sensibility, yet again for gospel-preaching (2 Corinthians 5:5, 13,

20). Hence Paul's martyrdom, which is about to occur, shouldn't make Timothy too cowardly to carry forward the heritage of gospel-preaching.

1:8–12a: **Therefore** [because God gave us the Spirit of power, love, and sensibility] **you shouldn't be ashamed of our Lord's testimony or of me, his prisoner. Instead, suffer mistreatment with** [me] **for the gospel in accordance with the power of God, ⁹the one who has saved us and called** [us] **with a holy calling, not in accordance with our works—rather, in accordance with his own purpose and grace, which was given to us in Christ Jesus before eternal times ¹⁰but has now been manifested through the epiphany of our Savior, Christ Jesus, who has incapacitated death, on the one hand, and on the other hand has brought life and imperishability to light through the gospel, ¹¹for which** [gospel] **I was instated a proclaimer and apostle and teacher** [compare 1 Timothy 1:12; 2:7], ¹²ᵃ**because of which reason I'm also suffering these things.** "Our Lord's testimony" means "the good confession" that "Christ Jesus . . . testified . . . before Pontius Pilate," a confession by Jesus of his own lordship (1 Timothy 6:13). Association with a crucified Christ and with Paul, imprisoned for preaching that such a Christ is Lord, might well make Timothy ashamed to carry forward Paul's extension of the Lord's testimony (compare 1 Corinthians 1:18). But because God has given Christians, such as Paul and Timothy, the Spirit of power, love, and sensibility, Timothy shouldn't be ashamed to carry it forward (compare Romans 1:16). Though Paul is a prisoner of Caesar, as in Ephesians 3:1; 4:1; Philemon 9 he calls himself the Lord's prisoner (see the comments on Ephesians 3:1). If Timothy comes to Paul, as Paul will tell him to do "before winter" (4:21), he's liable to "suffer mistreatment with [Paul] for the gospel [that is, for preaching the good news that Jesus, not Caesar, is Lord]" (compare 3:12). But along with Paul, Timothy is to suffer mistreatment for it to the extent God's power makes endurance possible, and there's no limit to that power (compare 2 Corinthians 1:3–11; 4:7–15; 12:10; 13:3–4; Philippians 3:10).

"The one who has saved us" describes God in a way that confirms his power. If he has saved us from our sins and eternal punishment, surely he's powerful enough to help us suffer mistreatment for the gospel. And no amount or degree of temporal mistreatment can cancel out our eternal salvation. "The one who has . . . called [us]" describes God as having effectively invited us to believe and be saved. The doubling in "*called* with a holy *calling*" emphasizes the effectiveness of this invitation. Our calling is "holy" in that it consecrates us to God at the same time it exposes us to mistreatment and exposes the treatment as *mis*treatment. "Not in accordance with our works" means that no good deeds which we might have done, or which God foresaw we would do, had anything to do with God's calling us with a holy calling (compare Romans 4:1–8; Ephesians 2:8–9; Titus 3:5). The calling had to do solely with God's "purpose [his plan] and grace [his ill-deserved favor]," the independence of which purpose and grace from "our works" is accented by "his own" (compare Romans 8:28; 9:10–13; Ephesians 1:11; 3:8–12). "Which was given to us in Christ Jesus" describes God's grace as a gift encapsulated in the person and work of Christ Jesus. But God gave us his grace in the past eternity ("before eternal times"), because that's when he purposed to call us with a holy calling (compare Titus 1:2).

"Through the epiphany of our Savior, Christ Jesus" this grace, "which was given to us in Christ Jesus" already in the concealment of eternity past, "has now been manifested" for all to see in its verbal portrayal through gospel-preaching. See the comments on 1 Timothy 6:14 for the connotation of "epiphany." Paul prefixes "our Savior" to "Christ Jesus" to identify Christ Jesus as God's agent in saving us through the incapacitation of death and the bringing of life and imperishability to light. He incapacitated death and brought life and imperishability to light by dying himself and rising from among the dead and thus becoming the Spirit who produces imperishable life for others (1 Corinthians 15:20–26, 45, 53–54; compare Romans 8:11). But to take effect in these ways, his death and resurrection must be proclaimed—hence "brought to light through the gospel." Finally Paul refers back to himself as a duly instated and therefore exemplary proclaimer of the gospel, an apostle sent to spread it abroad, and a teacher explaining it. This instatement and Paul's carrying out the responsibilities attached to it have additionally caused his suffering of "these things [his imprisonment and imminent martyrdom]."

1:12b–d: Nevertheless [despite my sufferings for the gospel] **I'm not ashamed, for I know him whom I have believed and am persuaded that he's able to guard till that day my deposit.** Here Paul cites himself as an example of the unashamedness he has told Timothy to show (1:8). In view of Titus 3:8b–c ("those who've believed God"), "him whom I [Paul] have believed" probably refers to God, not to Christ. Paul's knowing him to be God persuades Paul that God has the power ("he's able") to protect from heresy ("to guard") till the Day of Judgment ("that day") the gospel that Paul has entrusted to Timothy ("my deposit" [compare 1:14; 2:2; 1 Timothy 6:20]). In other words, God will see to it that the proclamation of the gospel will persist despite the incursions of heresy.

1:13–14: Be holding to the pattern of healthful words which you've heard from me. [Be holding to that pattern] **in the faith and love that** [are] **in Christ Jesus.** [14]**Guard through the Holy Spirit, who is dwelling in us, the good deposit.** "The pattern" to which Timothy is supposed to hold consists in "healthful words." These words are none other than the gospel that according to 1:12 Paul has deposited with Timothy. Because the words are theologically and morally healthful, Paul calls them "the *good* deposit." "Holding" to them as a pattern means to be guarding them from heresy. That Timothy is to guard them "through the Holy Spirit" indicates that God will guard Paul's deposit by using Timothy as its guardian just as he has used Paul as its guardian, and

do so by virtue of the Holy Spirit's indwelling Timothy (1:6–7). "Which you've heard from me" indicates that Paul has passed the healthful words on to Timothy for holding/guarding. "In the faith and love that [are] in Christ Jesus" locates the holding/guarding in the faith and love that are also located in him. Working backward, the faith and love are in him because Christians, such as Timothy, are in Christ Jesus and therefore able both to believe in him and to love others who are in him by faith (see 1 Timothy 1:14). In this faith and love, holding the pattern of healthful words—that is, guarding the good deposit—becomes necessary. Outside this faith and love, the guarding/holding makes no sense. For the healthful words have to do precisely and exclusively with the faith and love that are in Christ Jesus (compare 1 Timothy 1:18–19).

1:15–18: You know this, that all [who are] **in Asia, including Phygelus and Hermogenes, have turned away from me.** [16]**May the Lord give mercy to the household of Onesiphorus, because he often refreshed me and wasn't ashamed of my chain.** [17]**Instead, on coming to be in Rome he diligently searched for me and found** [me]. [18]**May the Lord give him to find mercy from the Lord in that day. And you know very well how many ways he served** [me] **in Ephesus.** Ephesus was the major city in Asia (a Roman province in western Asia Minor). While Timothy was there, Paul wrote to him that he should counter heretics active among the Christians in the city (see 1 Timothy 1:3–7, 18–20; 4:1–5; 5:15; 6:3–5, 20–21). Timothy may still be in Ephesus. Even if by now he has left, though, he knows that "all [who are] in Asia have turned away from [Paul]." Included are "Phygelus and Hermogenes," about whom we know no more. In 4:4 and Titus 1:14, "turned away" has the truth of the gospel as its object. So turning away from Paul probably means treating as false his claim to be proclaiming this truth. That "*all* [who are] in Asia have turned away" therefore points to a massive defection. It looks as though the heretics won the day against Timothy, and he as well as Paul knows that they have. Timothy shouldn't emulate them. Paul will ask Timothy to come to him (4:13, 21). So he cites Onesiphorus for emulation, because Onesiphorus, on arrival in Rome, diligently searched for Paul and found him despite Rome's large population and Onesiphorus's initial ignorance of Paul's address. On finding Paul, moreover, Onesiphorus "refreshed" Paul often (that is, time and again brought him provisions unavailable in prison) and "wasn't ashamed of [Paul's] chain" (though association with Paul exposed Onesiphorus himself to the danger of arrest and imprisonment) just as Timothy shouldn't be ashamed of Paul the prisoner (1:8). If Onesiphorus did thus, surely Timothy can follow his lead. For the sake of Onesiphorus, who by now may be dead, Paul wishes the Lord to give mercy to Onesiphorus's household. And even more for Onesiphorus's sake Paul wishes the Lord to grant him "to find mercy from the Lord in that day [the Day of Judgment]" just as Onesiphorus "found" Paul in Rome after searching for him diligently. A happy kind of poetic justice—though not by way of merit, for the two occurrences of "give" maintain the gracious character of a merciful judgment (see Titus 3:5). The redundancy in "May *the Lord* give him to find mercy *from the Lord* in that day" stresses the Lord as the giver of mercy. Mention of "how many ways [Onesiphorus] served [= assisted Paul] in Ephesus" adds further support to Paul's wish but mainly—because of Timothy's "know[ing] very well" those ways—underscores the need for Timothy to emulate Onesiphorus. Timothy "know[s]" the bad example of those who've turned away from Paul, but he knows the good example of Onesiphorus "very well"—that is, better—and therefore has more reason to emulate him than to emulate the others.

2:1-7: Therefore [because of the bad example of the Asians, who've turned away from me, and because of the good example of Onesiphorus, who served me well] **you, my child—be getting empowered in the grace that** [is] **in Christ Jesus.** [2]**And the things that you've heard from me in the presence of many witnesses—entrust these things to faithful people who as such will be competent to teach others also.** [3]**As a good soldier of Christ Jesus suffer mistreatment with** [me]. [4]**In order that he may please the one who recruited** [him], **no one serving as a soldier entangles himself in matters of livelihood.** [5]**And also if anyone competes as an athlete, he isn't crowned** [as the victor] **unless he has competed lawfully** [that is, according to the rules]. [6]**It's necessary that the hardworking farmer be partaking of the fruits** [of his labor] **first.** [7]**Understand what I'm saying, for the Lord will give you insight into all things** [compare Proverbs 2:6]. An emphatic "you," buttressed by "my child" (about which see the comments on 1:2), pinpoints Timothy as the target of Paul's subsequent commands. In 1:8 Paul commanded Timothy to suffer mistreatment with him "for the gospel in accordance with the power of God"; and in 1:13–14 Paul commanded Timothy to "guard through the Holy Spirit . . . the good deposit," which is "the pattern of healthful words." So the present command to "be getting empowered" looks to God as the source of power through his Spirit for guarding the gospel from misrepresentation by false teaching and bad behavior, which feed on each other. "In the grace that [is] in Christ Jesus" recalls 1:2, 6, 9 and, by identifying the location where empowerment by God's Spirit takes place, rules out any self-empowerment for which Timothy could take credit. "The things that you've heard" are none other than the aforementioned gospel/pattern of healthful words/good deposit. "From me" identifies Paul as their proclaimer, apostle, and teacher (1:11).

"In the presence of . . . witnesses" implies that they'll know whether what Timothy entrusts to others corresponds to the things he has heard from Paul. A description of the witnesses as "many" reinforces the point, which amounts to a warning that Timothy won't be able to get away with subverting Paul's gospel. Timothy is to entrust this gospel to others just as Paul has entrusted it to him (1:12–14; 1 Timothy 1:18; 6:20). These others must be "faithful [that is, trustworthy] people," so that the gospel may continue to be guarded/protected from misrepresen-

tation by false teaching and bad behavior. "Who *as such*" underlines the necessity of trustworthiness. Because the pure gospel needs to be passed on geographically and temporally, these faithful/trustworthy people must be "competent to teach others also" (compare 1 Timothy 3:2; 5:17; Titus 1:9). In 1 Timothy 1:18 Paul told Timothy to "be fighting the good fight [Greek: *strateuē . . . tēn kalēn strateian*]." Now he tells him to suffer mistreatment with Paul "as a good soldier [Greek: *kalos stratiōtēs*] of Christ Jesus" (compare 1:8; 4:5). It takes a good soldier to fight a good fight, and also to "guard the good deposit [Greek: *tēn kalēn parathēkēn* (1:14)]." The soldier is good in the sense of admirable, noble in his willingness to suffer mistreatment with Paul. Timothy is liable to suffer it with Paul if he visits Paul in prison (4:13, 21).

Carrying on his comparison of Timothy to a soldier and of Christ Jesus to the commander who enlisted him, Paul observes that "no one serving as a solider entangles himself in matters of livelihood" (that is, the affairs of everyday life, such as earning a living). To please the one who recruited him, the soldier forswears normal living in favor of soldiering. Paul is telling Timothy to engage in what used to be called "fulltime Christian service." For reinforcement the figure of speech shifts from soldiering to athletic competition, and from pleasing the recruiter to winning a victor's crown. Competing according to the rules represents again the forswearing of normal living, this time in favor of the regimen of physical training. See the comments on 1 Corinthians 9:24–25; Philippians 3:12–14, though in those passages the issue is the gaining of eternal life whereas here it's Timothy's engaging in fulltime Christian service so as to fulfill his commission and gain honor. For yet more emphasis Paul adds a third figure of speech, that of a farmer whose hard work, comparable to Timothy's fulltime Christian service, makes it "necessary" (divinely so, we might say) that he "be partaking of the fruits [of his labor] first [that is, most of all (compare this use of 'first' in 1 Timothy 1:15–16; 2:1)]." The figure of soldiering stresses the suffering of mistreatment so as to please the recruiter. The figure of athletic competition stresses self-discipline so as to win a victor's crown. The figure of farmwork stresses hard labor so as to get a reward. And the command, "Understand what I'm saying," stresses Timothy's need to please Christ Jesus, discipline himself, and work hard. Paul issues this command on the ground that the Lord (Jesus) will give Timothy "insight into all things," that is, into all that he must do to be a good soldier, a victorious athlete, and a well-rewarded farmer. Since the Lord *will* give him such insight, Timothy should obey with faith.

2:8-13: Keep remembering Jesus Christ, raised from among the dead, [descended] **from among David's seed, according to my gospel,** [9]**in which I'm suffering hardship to the extent of bonds** [= chains] **as an evildoer. God's word isn't bound** [= chained]**, however!** [10]**Because of this** [that God's word isn't bound] **I'm enduring all things because of the selected ones** [those chosen by God from among the human race] **in order that they too may attain the salvation** [that's] **in**

Christ Jesus along with eternal glory. ¹¹Trustworthy [is] the saying: "For if we died together with [him], we'll also live together with [him]. ¹²If we're enduring, we'll also reign together with [him]. If we'll disown [him], that one [Christ Jesus] will also disown us. ¹³If we're unfaithful, that one remains faithful; for he can't disown himself." In 1:3 Paul spoke of remembering Timothy, in 1:4 of remembering Timothy's tears, in 1:5 of remembering Timothy's unhypocritical faith. In 1:6 he "remind[ed]" Timothy to rekindle God's gracious gift. Now *Timothy* is to "keep remembering Jesus Christ" as him who now lives as "raised from among the dead." Why remember him as such? Because if he lives as a result of resurrection, so too will those who are in him by faith. There's no need to fear martyrdom, then, so that Timothy needn't hesitate to risk his life by visiting the about-to-be-martyred Paul. Parallel to "raised from among the dead" is "[descended] from among David's seed," which calls attention to "Jesus" as "Christ," the "Anointed One" who upon his return will reign as the messianic king. (To conform to the chronological order of Jesus' past resurrection and future messianic reign, alluded to by Davidic descent, Paul reverses the order found in Romans 1:3–4.) "According to my gospel" makes Paul's proclamation of Jesus as the resurrected and Davidic Christ/Messiah the standard by which Timothy's remembering is to be measured (see Romans 2:16; 16:25 for other instances of "my gospel").

"In which I'm suffering hardship" portrays the gospel as the arena in which, for proclaiming it, Paul is suffering hardship. The "hard-" in "hardship" connotes harm, injury. Accenting this connotation is a wordplay, *kakopathō . . . hōs kakourgos*, which when translated literally comes out as "suffering bad . . . as a doer of bad." "To the extent of bonds" stresses how badly Paul is suffering. "As an evildoer [a doer of what's bad]" means that he is being treated as a criminal though he isn't one. Here, "God's word" doesn't mean Scripture. It means the orally proclaimed gospel. This gospel isn't bound even though Paul, a proclaimer of it, is bound. Though he's in chains, God's word is being proclaimed (in Philippians 1:12–18 even *because of* Paul's imprisonment, though not necessarily this one). Paul cites two bases for his endurance: (1) the fact that God's word isn't bound and (2) the fact that God has selected whom he wants for salvation through hearing and believing his word. To these bases for endurance in the proclamation of God's word, Paul adds a purpose: "in order that they too [the selected ones in addition to you, Timothy, and me] may attain the salvation [that's] in Christ Jesus." "May attain" puts this salvation in the future. Since salvation is in Christ Jesus, to attain it you have to gain a position in him by believing in him. Negatively, the salvation consists in deliverance *from* eternal shame. Positively, salvation consists in deliverance *for* eternal glory.

In 1 Timothy 6:12; Titus 1:2; 3:7 Paul has spoken of eternal life. Here he shifts to eternal glory not only for a contrast with eternal shame but also for a contrast with the short-term shame of his imprisonment as a supposed criminal (compare Romans 3:23; 8:19–21). "The salva-

tion [that's] in Christ Jesus" leads to the trustworthy saying cited by Paul to support such a salvation. If as God sees them believers are in Christ, they "died together with [Christ]" when he died, and will "live together with [him]" when he comes back to bring them his own resurrected, eternal life (compare Romans 6:8). And since eternal glory characterizes this life, believers will also reign with him if they endure, if they demonstrate the genuineness of their faith by persevering in their suffering for the gospel (compare 3:12: "And also all who want to live piously in Christ Jesus will be persecuted"; also Matthew 19:28; Luke 22:30; Revelation 20:4). "If we'll disown [him in the balance of the present age], that one will also disown us [at the start of the age to come, when the Last Judgment occurs]." This statement recalls Matthew 10:33; Luke 12:9. "If we're unfaithful" equates with disowning him. So we expect Paul to say next that Christ will be unfaithful to those unfaithful to him, that is, disown them for their unfaithfulness. But Paul springs a surprise by saying "that one remains faithful." The two occurrences of "that one" underscore Christ as the disowner, on the one hand, and as the one who remains faithful, on the other hand. He remains faithful/trustworthy, so that others may still believe in him for eternal life, eternal glory, and co-kingship with him. Here is Paul's rationale for that one's remaining faithful: "For he can't disown himself." That is to say, Christ Jesus can't get away from his identity as the one in whom are eternal life, eternal glory, and kingship. His faithfulness is unswerving; ours is precarious.

2:14–15: Keep reminding [God's selected ones] of these things [located in the trustworthy saying of 2:11–13] by solemnly testifying [to them] in God's sight that they're not to be disputing over words, [which disputing is] useful for nothing, [which disputing leads] to catastrophe for those who hear [such disputing]. ¹⁵Be diligent to present yourself to God [as] attested, an unashameable worker, cutting straight [a figure of speech for teaching accurately] the word of truth. For the command, "Keep reminding," see the comments on 2:8–13. Now Timothy is to remind God's selected ones as Paul has told him to keep remembering Jesus Christ. "By solemnly testifying [to them]" highlights the seriousness of the reminder (compare 4:1; 1 Timothy 5:21). "In God's sight" adds to this seriousness; for with God as an eyewitness to the selected ones' hearing of Timothy's solemn testimony, they won't be able to plead ignorance if failing to heed the testimony. For the prohibition of "disputing over words," see the comments on 1 Timothy 6:4. Such disputing is "useful for nothing" in the sense that it doesn't promote the practice of piety; rather, it leads "to catastrophe," which probably means eternal punishment for lack of a practical piety that would confirm genuine, persevering faith. "Be diligent" calls for strong and careful effort on Timothy's part. By solemnly testifying to the selected ones "in God's sight," Timothy will be presenting himself to God (compare Romans 6:13); and he must do so, Paul says, as "attested" because of being "an unashameable worker" who in his solemn testimony is "cutting straight the word of truth [that is, 'God's word' (2:9) as conveying gospel-truth]" (compare "worker" with "farmer" [literally, "worker of soil"] in 2:6, and contrast "evildoer" [literally, "worker of bad"] in 2:9).

2:16–19: But be keeping clear of profane, empty jabberings. For they [those who engage in such jabberings] **will progress to more and more ungodliness** [compare 1 Timothy 4:7; 6:20–21; Titus 3:9]. [17]**And their word will spread like gangrene, by which** [word] **Hymenaeus and Philetus are characterized,** [18]**who as such have deviated from the truth by saying the resurrection has already happened, and are upsetting the faith of some** [compare Titus 1:11]. [19]**God's firm foundation stays standing, however, having this seal: "The Lord knows those who are his** [compare Numbers 16:5], **and everyone who names the Lord's name is to depart from unrighteousness** [compare Isaiah 26:13]." According to 2:14 God's selected ones "are not to be disputing over words." Now Timothy himself is told to be "keeping clear of profane, empty jabberings [= gobbledygook lacking any value for piety]." He's to be keeping clear because those who don't keep clear "will progress to more and more ungodliness," as though—ironically—an increase in ungodliness marks progress (compare 3:9, 13). In addition, "their word will spread like gangrene [that is, will infect those who listen to their jabberings]." Paul mentions by name two men characterized by these gangrenous jabberings: Hymenaeus, blacklisted also in 1 Timothy 1:20, and Philetus, unmentioned elsewhere. "Who *as such*" emphasizes this characteristic of theirs, because of which they "have deviated from the truth." The truth is to be found in "the word of truth," as opposed to "their word," which not only lacks truth but also conveys the falsehood that "the resurrection has already happened." We don't know for sure, but presumably Hymenaeus and Philetus denied all resurrections except Christ's, which happened in the past, whereas in 1 Corinthians 15:13 Paul risks Christ's resurrection in an argument for believers' future resurrection: "But if there's not a resurrection of dead people, neither was Christ raised." By "upsetting the faith of some" Hymenaeus and Philetus are leading others into apostasy. In contrast with the upsetting of some, "God's firm foundation stays standing." In view of this contrast, the subsequent statement that "the Lord knows those who are his" and the description in 1 Timothy 3:15 of "the church of the living God" as "the pillar and base of the truth," God's firm foundation is the church. But since the professing church is made up of true and false believers, Paul adds that "the Lord knows those who are his" and that "everyone who names the Lord's name is to depart from unrighteousness." Those who belong to the Lord and therefore depart from unrighteousness are what make the church God's firm foundation for the truth of the gospel and make him stamp the church with the seal of his ownership.

2:20–21: But in a big house there are not only gold and silver vessels, but also wood and clay [ones], **and some for honor, on the one hand, and some for dishonor, on the other hand.** [21]**Therefore if someone cleanses himself from these, he'll be a vessel for honor, consecrated, useful to the Master, prepared for every** [kind of] **good deed** [contrast "useful for nothing" in 2:14]. The "foundation" in 2:19 suggested the figure of "a . . . house." But this house is "big" in that it refers to the professing church, which includes false as well as true believers. Its "gold and silver vessels" symbolize the true; its wood and clay vessels symbolize the false (for example, Hymenaeus and Philetus). Gold and silver suit the vessels made out of them for honorable use (say, as a decorative vase). Wood and clay suit the vessels made out of them for dishonorable use (say, as a chamber pot, a vessel used as a toilet [compare Romans 9:21–23]). "For honor" is a figurative way of saying "for eternal glory" (2:10). "For dishonor" is a figurative way of saying "for the eternal shame of being disowned by Christ at the Last Judgment" (compare 2:12). "On the one hand . . . on the other hand" stresses these contrasts. "Therefore" means "in view of true and false believers in the church" and implies that Timothy shouldn't be surprised at this mixture (compare Matthew 13:24–30, 36–43, 47–50). "If someone cleanses himself from these" refers to purging away the gangrenous jabberings with which that "someone" has been infected. Such a purging takes the form of repentance (2:25) and will result in "be[ing] a vessel for honor, consecrated [to God], useful to the Master [Christ Jesus], prepared for [= equipped to perform] every [kind of] good deed [in contrast with the 'unrighteousness' mentioned in 2:19]." In other words, there's still hope for those infected with the "gangrene."

2:22–26: But keep fleeing from youthful lusts; and keep pursuing righteousness, faith, love, peace with those who call on the Lord out of a pure heart [compare 1 Timothy 1:5; Romans 10:13]. [23]**But keep avoiding foolish and uneducational debates, knowing that they breed battles.** [24]**And the Lord's slave mustn't be battling—rather,** [must] **be gentle toward all, competent to teach** [them], **tolerant of mistreatment,** [25]**with meekness educating those who resist. Perhaps God will give them repentance for a knowledge of the truth** [26]**and that they might get sober again** [so as to escape] **out of the Devil's trap** [compare 1 Timothy 3:7], [they] **having been caught by him for** [the doing of] **that one's will.** Here Paul shifts back to addressing Timothy directly. In 1 Timothy 4:12 he told Timothy to "become for believers a role model . . . in chastity" despite, or perhaps because of, his "youthfulness"; and in 1 Timothy 5:2 Paul told him to "be exhorting . . . younger [women] as [he would] sisters, [that is,] in chastity." So the present exhortation "to keep fleeing youthful lusts" has to do with maintaining sexual chastity. Since Timothy is to exhort young women (among others), Paul can't tell him to flee from the objects of youthful lusts. So he tells him to flee from the lusts themselves. It's not enough to "keep *fleeing*," though. Timothy must also "keep *pursuing*." Among his objects of pursuit, "righteousness" (in the sense of right conduct) grows out of "faith" (in the sense of right belief); "faith takes effect through love" (Galatians 5:6); and "love" produces "peace" (Romans 14:15, 19, Galatians 5:22; Ephesians 4:1–3; Colossians 3:14–15). But "along with those who call on the Lord out of a pure heart" limits to true Christians the pursuit of peace by Timothy. Instead of pursuing peace with Hymenaeus, Philetus, and their like, he's to educate them and, if they resist, compete against them (2:25; 1 Timothy 6:12).

For another contrast with pursuing, Paul tells Timothy to "keep avoiding foolish and uneducational debates," that is, debates that don't educate people in the knowledge of gospel-truth (compare 2:14, 16–17; 1 Timothy 6:4; Titus 3:9). The description of Timothy as "knowing that they [such debates] breed battles [rather than educating people]" shows him to be educated enough to avoid those debates. Whereas Paul compared Timothy to a soldier in 2:3–4, he now compares him to a slave of the Lord (Jesus). This comparison doesn't suit battling (hence Timothy "mustn't be battling"), but it does suit being "gentle toward all, competent to teach [for slaves were often teachers], tolerant of mistreatment [which slaves often suffered]," and also the "meekness" with which Timothy as a slave-like teacher should be "educating those who resist." Others' resistance shouldn't cause him to retaliate. Thus God may use Timothy's education of them to "give them repentance for a knowledge of the truth and that they might get sober again [as though their 'foolish and uneducational debates' could have arisen only out of drunkenness after an earlier, sober commitment to the truth] [so as to escape] out of the Devil's trap [into which they'd fallen in a kind of drunken stupor], [they] having been caught by him for [the doing of] that one's will [which contrasts with 'God's will' in 1:1 and equates engagement in the 'foolish and uneducational debates' with doing the Devil's will]." "That one" underscores that the Devil is sponsoring those debates; and apart from escape through repentance, his trap will plunge a person into eternal destruction and ruin (1 Timothy 3:6–7; 6:9).

3:1–5a: But knowing this, that in the last days difficult times will arrive [compare 1 Timothy 4:1–3]. **²For people will be lovers of themselves, lovers of money, boastful, arrogant, slanderers, unobedient to parents, ungrateful, undevout, ³unaffectionate, unappeasable, accusatory, undisciplined, untamed** [= savage, brutal]**, unloving of what's good, ⁴betrayers** [compare Matthew 24:10]**, impulsive, conceited, lovers of pleasure rather than lovers of God, ⁵ªhaving a form of piety but having denied its power.** Paul wants Timothy to know that though there's hope for the retrieval of opponents (2:24–26), "in the last days difficult times will arrive." Paul and Timothy are already living in the last days (see Acts 2:17; 1 Corinthians 10:11; Hebrews 1:2; 1 Peter 1:20; 2 Peter 3:3; 1 John 2:18; Jude 17–18). But because Paul is about to be martyred (4:6), he uses the future tense in regard to the difficult times that his successor Timothy will face. The descriptive list of people that follows tells why the times will be difficult. And as shown by the last item on the list ("holding a form of piety but having denied its power"), what will make the times difficult for Timothy is that such

people as are damningly described in the list will profess to be Christians, so that as a church leader he'll have to deal with them. As "lovers of themselves" they'll love money for what it can do for them and love pleasure for their selfish enjoyment rather than loving God for who he is and what he has done for them. Self-lovers and money-lovers fall naturally into boastfulness and arrogance; and they slander others so as to feed their boastfulness and arrogance at others' expense. There follows in the list a series of descriptors starting with "un-": "*un*obedient to parents, *un*grateful, *un*devout, *un*affectionate, *un*appeasable." "Accusatory" interrupts the series temporarily by showing that such people "hav[e] been caught" in "the Devil's trap" so as to do "that one's will" (2:26). For "the Devil" means "the Accuser." Then the series fills out with "*un*disciplined, *un*tamed, *un*loving of what's good." It's easy to imagine that disobedience to parents goes with ingratitude, lack of devotion, and lack of affection, that accusatoriness is the flip side of unappeasability, and that lack of self-control shows itself in the brutality of untamability. On the whole, though, we should look on the list as a grab bag of largely unassorted items. As to the last item, according to 1:7–8 the power of piety derives from God through his Spirit. So to deny the power of piety amounts to disowning God and his Spirit (compare the disowning of Christ Jesus in 2:13) and thus amounts to having only "a form [that is, an appearance] of piety" (compare Titus 1:16).

3:5b–9: And be turning away from these [men]. **⁶For [some] of these are those who slink into households and captivate little women heaped with sins,** [the women] **being led by various lusts, ⁷always learning and never able to come to a knowledge of the truth. ⁸And in the way Jannes and Jambres withstood Moses, in this way these** [men who captivate little women] **too are withstanding the truth,** [being] **men of a deeply corrupted mind, disqualified in regard to the faith. ⁹They'll not progress further, however. For their blankmindedness will be evident to all, as also the** [blankmindedness] **of those** [Jannes and Jambres] **became** [evident to all]. Timothy is to be turning away from those who refuse his attempt to educate them in a knowledge of the truth (2:24–26). To justify this turning away, Paul notes that some of them "slink into households and captivate little women [a derogatory term for adult women, like calling them giddy teenagers]." Because these women are giddy, the men who slink into their homes find the women easy to "captivate." This captivation results in the men's heaping sins on the women. But the women aren't blameless, for they're "being led by various lusts," which refer predominantly in Paul's writing to sexual lusts (compare 1 Timothy 5:6, 11; Titus 3:3). "Various" may refer to the changing of sexual partners, which would then link with the heaping up of sins. As a result the women, who should be learning from their husbands at home (1 Corinthians 14:35), are "always learning and never able to come to a knowledge of the truth." They're learning one falsehood after another from the apostates who've slinked in during the husbands' absence.

Paul then compares the slinkers' opposing the truth of the gospel with the opposition to Moses of Jannes and Jambres, names given in Jewish tradition to Pharaoh's magicians who opposed Moses (Exodus 7:8–8:19), and describes the slinkers as "men of a deeply corrupted mind" (for otherwise they'd teach and practice the truth) and as "disqualified in regard to the faith" (that is, destined as apostates for eternal punishment [compare 1 Timothy 1:19; 1 Corinthians 9:27; 2 Corinthians 13:5]). Just as the imitation of Moses' miracles by Pharaoh's magicians was cut short (Exodus 8:16–19), the so-called progress of the slinkers in their peddling of lust-satisfying heresy will be cut short (see the comments on 2:16 for the ironical use of "progress"). "For their blankmindedness will be evident to all." Thus their public shame will match that of Pharaoh's magicians. Paul equates a "*corrupted* mind" with "*blank*mindedness," for moral corruption empties the mind of truth. The exposé of this blankmindedness, to which exposé Timothy is to contribute by his ministry, will put a stop to the slinkers' progress so far as all true believers are concerned.

3:10–11: But you've followed my teaching, conduct, purpose, faith, patience, love, endurance, [11]persecutions—sufferings such as happened to me in Antioch, in Iconium, in Lystra [cities in central Asia Minor], **such persecutions as I bore. And out of them all the Lord rescued me** [compare Psalm 34:17, 19]! Over against the men of deeply corrupted mind and consequent blankmindedness in 3:5b–9 Paul cites himself as a good role model, whose ministry Timothy has followed and should continue to follow. This "follow[ing]" includes emulation as well as cognizance (compare 1 Timothy 4:6). Paul's "conduct" corresponds to his "teaching." His "faith," which probably carries here the meaning of faithfulness as well as belief, corresponds to his "purpose," that is, a determination to carry out his commission to proclaim the gospel, especially to Gentiles. His "patience" corresponds to his "love," which makes the patience possible. His "persecutions" correspond to his "endurance" in that they've required it. For an accent on his endurance of persecutions he adds "sufferings such as happened to me in Antioch, in Iconium, in Lystra, such persecutions as I bore" (for which see Acts 13:14–14:20, especially 13:45, 50; 14:2, 4–6, 19). This accent has the purpose of urging on Timothy the necessity that he too endure persecutions, especially those that might come upon him if at Paul's request he visits Paul, a prisoner condemned to die as though he were a criminal (1:8, 12; 2:3, 8–13; 4:5–18, 21a). But Paul balances the necessity of enduring persecutions with an encouragement: "And out of them all the Lord rescued me!" Which isn't to say that Paul won't be martyred soon (see 4:6). But he's still alive despite his close scrapes in the past. So Timothy shouldn't think that coming to visit Paul will necessarily cost him (Timothy) his life.

3:12–15: And also [= besides me] **all who want to live piously in Christ Jesus will be persecuted. [13]But evil people and charlatans will progress** [from bad to worse, deceiving [others] **and being deceived. [14]But you—keep abiding in the things you've learned and been convinced of, knowing from whom** [plural] **you've learned** [them] **[15]and** [knowing] **that since** [you were] **an infant you've known the sacred Scriptures, which have the power to make you wise for salvation through the faith** [that's] **in Christ Jesus.** "All who *want* to live piously in Christ Jesus" consist of true believers in distinction from those who in their self-satisfaction, and therefore outside Christ Jesus, have only "a form [an appearance] of piety" (3:5a). In Christ Jesus alone will truly pious living take place; and because such living contradicts the lifestyle of non-Christians, it generates persecution from them. The "evil people and charlatans" are still the slinking peddlers of lust-satisfying heresy in 3:5b–9. There Paul said they "will *not* progress further." But he was talking about progress in the deception of true believers, which he said will be cut short. Here he's talking about the heretics' progressing in the deception of untrue believers and in being deceived themselves, as though going in these respects from bad to worse marks "progress" (see the comments on 2:16 for this irony). "But you" sets Timothy in emphatic contrast to the heretics. "Keep abiding in the things you've learned and been convinced of" commands both doctrinal and behavioral perseverance in the truth of the gospel. To support this command Paul appeals to Timothy's knowing his grandmother Lois and his mother Eunice, from whom even as an infant he learned "the sacred Scriptures [the Old Testament] which [because they point forward to Christ] have the power to make you wise for [the purpose and result of] salvation through the faith [that's] in Christ Jesus." By implication, Timothy's grandmother and mother weren't giddy women "heaped with sins, led by various lusts, always learning and never able to come to a knowledge of the truth" (3:6–7). No, he learned from Lois and Eunice the gospel of truth as supported by the sacred Scriptures (1:5; Acts 16:1). (In that culture age and tradition counted for a lot whereas, generally speaking, novelty drew suspicion.) That the sacred Scriptures have the power to make a person wise for salvation corresponds (1) to their inspiration (3:16) by "the Spirit . . . of power" (1:7); (2) to "the gospel" as "in accordance with the power of God" (1:8); and (3) to the "power" of "piety" (3:5a). "Wise for salvation" contrasts with "being deceived." See the comments on 1 Timothy 3:13 for "the faith [that's] in Christ Jesus."

Now Paul tells why it is that "the sacred Scriptures . . . have the power to make you wise for salvation." **3:16–17: Every Scripture** [is] **God-breathed and beneficial for teaching, for censuring, for correction, for education in righteousness, [17]in order that God's person may be outfitted for every** [kind of] **good deed.** The books of what is now called the Old Testament hadn't yet been gathered together and published as a whole, nor was the term "Scripture" used for an individual book. "Every Scripture" therefore refers to every passage that goes to make up "the sacred Scriptures." Paul is saying, then, that every such passage is "God-breathed" in the figurative sense that it is an exhalation of God and in the literal sense that his Spirit guided its writing. For "-breathed" (Greek: -*pneustos*) is related to "Spirit" (Greek: *pneuma*), as though the Holy Spirit is the breath that God exhales in the form of the sacred Scriptures. The emphasis falls first on their authority, and then on their practical benefit "for teaching [explanation of the gospel], for censuring [rebuke of professing Christians sinning against it], for correction [of Christians deviating into heretical beliefs and behaviors], for education in righteousness [bringing apostates to repentance, if possible (2:24–26; 1 Timothy 1:20)]." All these benefits of Scripture have the purpose of outfitting "God's person" (one who belongs to him) "for every [kind of] good deed" (without which authentication of "the faith [that's] in Christ Jesus" [3:15] there's only "a form [appearance] of piety" [3:5a]).

4:1–2: I solemnly testify in the sight of God and Christ Jesus, who is going to judge the living and the dead [that is, those still living at the time of his return and those who've died by then (compare 1 Thessalonians 4:13–17)], **and** [I solemnly testify] **in view of his epiphany** [appearance] **and his reign** [that will follow the epiphany]: **²Proclaim the word. Be at the ready when the time seems appropriate, when the time seems inappropriate. Censure. Reprimand. Exhort with total patience and teaching.** For emphasis on his commissioning of Timothy, Paul supplies an elaborate introduction by (1) stating "I . . . testify"; (2) intensifying his testifying with "solemnly"; (3) setting his testimony "in the sight of God"; (4) adding "[in the sight of] Christ Jesus" (compare 1 Timothy 5:21), so that the legal requirement of two or three witnesses is met (1 Timothy 5:19; Numbers 35:30; Deuteronomy 17:6; 19:15); (5) describing Christ Jesus as him "who is going to judge the living and the dead," so that whether Timothy is still living when Christ returns or has died by then, along with everyone else he'll face judgment by Christ, only in his (Timothy's) case by the standard of Paul's solemn testimony; (6) stressing the certainty of this judgment with "*is going* to judge" rather than writing a simple "will judge"; (7) providing his testimony with the perspective of Christ's "epiphany," which should motivate Timothy to carry out Paul's commission and thereby share in the glory of that epiphany (about which see the comments on 1 Timothy 6:14); and (8) providing the testimony with the further perspective of Christ's "reign," which should likewise motivate a carrying out of the commission so as to share in that reign.

Five commands make up the commission itself: (1) "Proclaim the word," namely, "God's word," which according to 2:9 "isn't bound," "the saying [= word]" that Paul calls "trustworthy" and quotes in 2:11–13, and "the word of *truth*" in 2:15. (2) "Be at the ready [to proclaim the word] when the time [to do so] seems appropriate, when the time seems inappropriate [in other words, *all* the time]." (3) "Censure [professing Christians who keep sinning against the word]." (4) "Reprimand [those who refuse to reform as a result of censure]." (5) "Exhort [all others in the church] with total patience and teaching [that is, with totally patient teaching]."

Now Paul supplies the reason for his commissioning of Timothy. **4:3–4: For there'll be a time when people won't tolerate healthful teaching. Instead, itching as regards** [their] **hearing** [that is, wanting to have their ears scratched], **they'll heap up for themselves teachers in accordance with their own lusts ⁴and will turn** [their] **hearing away from the truth, on the one hand, and on the other hand will veer out of** [truth] **to myths.** "There'll be a time" echoes 3:1, and "healthful teaching" echoes 1:13 (see also 1 Timothy 1:10; 6:3; Titus 1:9, 13; 2:1–2, 8). Such teaching promotes good behavior on the basis of correct beliefs; but because some people want to behave badly, they won't tolerate healthful teaching. So they want teachers to tell them what will be in accord with their own lusts. Paul compares the lusts to itching in the ears, and false teaching to scratching the ears to gratify the itch. "Their own lusts" draws a sharp contrast with "want[ing] to live piously in Christ Jesus" (3:12), and also with scriptural "education in righteousness" (3:16). The "heap[ing] up" of "teachers in accordance with their own lusts" recalls the "little women heaped with sins, being led by various lusts, always learning and never able to come to a knowledge of the truth" (3:6–7). It's almost as though the heaping up of permissive teachers equates with being heaped with sins. At least a heap of sins will be the outcome of a heap of such teachers. There's also something sarcastically comical about a heap of teachers. "For themselves" means that the self-lovers of 3:2 falsely think the heap will benefit them. Listening to the heaped-up, toadying teachers will entail the listeners' "turn[ing] [their] hearing away from the truth," that is, turning their heads so as not to hear the truth of God's word. Then instead of saying that they'll turn their *hearing* to myths, Paul says "*they . . .* will veer out of [truth] to myths," so that the turning of their hearing from the truth will have a deleterious effect on their whole selves. "On the one hand . . . on the other hand" underscores this sequence. The myths will kill compunctions against bad behavior (compare 1 Timothy 1:4; 4:7; Titus 1:14).

4:5–8: But you—keep sober in all [situations]. **Suffer hardship. Do the work of an evangelist. Fill out your service. ⁶For I myself am already being poured out as a drink-offering, and the time of my departure has arrived. ⁷I've competed the good competition. I've finished the race. I've kept the faith. ⁸As for what remains, the crown of righteousness is reserved for me, which the Lord, the righteous judge, will repay me on that day, and not to me only—rather, to all who've loved his epiphany.** "But you" puts Timothy emphatically over against the people with itching ears and their ear-scratching teachers (compare 3:10, 14). "Keep sober" is usually taken figuratively, but Paul's command in 1 Timothy 5:23 that Timothy "be using a little wine" because of stomach trouble favors a warning against drunkenness. After all, "difficult times" (3:1) could drive him to drink more than a little wine. "In all [situations]" calls for sobriety whatever the difficulty of the times. And their difficulty likewise calls for Timothy to "suffer hardship," as Paul is doing according to 2:9 (see the comments there). For hardship is sure to come on Timothy in the carrying out of Paul's commission. "Do the work of an evangelist" means that Timothy should proclaim the gospel far and wide as Paul himself has done (Romans 15:19; Acts 13–28). "The work" makes evangelism Timothy's vocation, not merely an avocation (something done on the side). "Your service" refers to his work as an evangelist. To "fill [it] out" would be to leave nothing undone in his evangelistic service. Why? Because Paul is passing off the scene, as emphasized by his saying, "For I *myself* [over against "But *you*"] am already being poured out as a drink-offering" (about which see the final comments on Philippians 2:14–18). "And the time of my departure [in death] has arrived" explains the figure of a drink-offering. "Already," "has arrived," and the connotation of appropriateness or fixedness in the term "time" all point to Paul's conviction that his imprisonment and trial will end in martyrdom (contrast Philippians 1:13–14, 23–26; 2:24).

Since a drink-offering put the finishing touch on a sacrifice, it suits Paul to use the figure for the end of his self-sacrificial service as an apostle (compare 1 Timothy 1:12). He then shifts to another figure of speech, that of athletic competition, and calls the competition "good" because it's for "the good confession" of Christ Jesus as Lord (1 Timothy 6:12–13). "I've finished the race" defines the competition as a footrace (compare 1 Corinthians 9:24–26a; Philippians 2:16; 3:12–14; Acts 20:24). "I've kept the faith" means that in his teaching Paul has kept the gospel's "healthful words" from the gangrene-like infection of "profane, empty jabberings" (1:13; 2:16–17). Thus he stands as an example of what it would mean for Timothy to "fill out [his own] service." And as an encouragement to do so, Paul says that "the crown of righteousness" remains for him (Paul). It signifies victory in the competition, the race (see further the comments on 1 Corinthians 9:24–25). "Of righteousness" describes the crown as awarded for good behavior (2:22; 3:16; 1 Timothy 6:11), which in this context of athletic competition might compare with competing according to the rules. "Reserved for me" describes the crown further as guaranteed for future delivery. "On that day" denotes the Day of Judgment as the date of that delivery. "Repay[ment]" by "the Lord [Jesus], the righteous judge" makes the delivery well-deserved. "And not to me only—rather, to all who've loved his epiphany" gives further encouragement to Timothy along with other Christians, characterized as true by their having lovingly looked forward to the Lord Jesus' appearance at the second coming.

CONCLUSION
2 Timothy 4:9–22

The conclusion divides into a request for Timothy to come soon (4:9–15), news about Paul's trial (4:16–18), and greetings along with a further plea for Timothy to come and a benediction (4:19–22).

4:9–11: Be diligent to come to me soon. [10]**For because of having loved the present age Demas has abandoned me and traveled to Thessalonica. Crescens** [has traveled] **to Galatia, Titus to Dalmatia.** [11]**Luke alone is with me. On picking up Mark, bring** [him] **along with yourself; for he's useful to me for service.** Because only Luke is with Paul whereas others have left him, Timothy is to make every effort to join Paul in Rome and to bring Mark as well. The description of Mark as "useful" to Paul "for service" indicates a reversal of the breakup we read about in Acts 13:13; 15:37–40 (see also Colossians 4:10; Philemon 24) and probably refers to Paul's needing Mark to help bring him food, drink, and other necessities in prison, where such items were in short supply. According to early church tradition, Mark and Luke wrote the second and third Gospels (in canonical order), and Luke the book of Acts too. Along with Luke, Demas had been a traveling companion of Paul (Colossians 4:14; Philemon 24). But Paul puts Demas in a poor light by saying Demas "abandoned" him "because of having loved the present age." Apparently he hadn't "loved [the Lord's] epiphany" (4:8), at least not enough to "suffer mistreatment with [Paul] for the gospel in accordance with the power of God," as Paul has told Timothy to do (1:8). Paul is in Rome, Italy (1:17). Demas has gone to Thessalonica in Macedonia, Crescens (about whom we know nothing more) to Galatia in central Asia Minor, and Titus to Dalmatia (roughly modern Croatia on the east coast of the Adriatic Sea opposite the leg of Italy). Paul doesn't say why Crescens and Titus left, though Paul's "hav[ing] *sent* Tychicus to Ephesus" (4:12) suggests departures by Crescens and Titus not commissioned by Paul yet not blameworthy like that of Demas. Paul wrote a letter to Titus that we have, and Titus appears a number of times elsewhere in Paul's letters.

4:12–13: But I've sent Tychicus to Ephesus. [13]**When coming** [to me]**, bring the cloak that I left behind in Troas with Carpus—also the books, namely the parchments.** The sending of Tychicus contrasts with Demas's abandonment of Paul and with Crescens' and Titus's simply leaving him. Paul may be sending Tychicus *with* this letter, for he has previously used Tychicus to carry letters (see Ephesians 6:21; Colossians 4:7). If so, the past tense of "I've sent" takes the temporal standpoint of Timothy on receiving the letter. And if Tychicus is delivering the letter to Timothy in Ephesus, Timothy is still there, as he was when Paul wrote 1 Timothy to him (1 Timothy 1:3). Perhaps Tychicus is to replace Timothy in Ephesus. (In that case it seems likely that Paul sent Artemas rather than Tychicus to Crete [Titus 1:5; 3:12]). "When coming [to me]" presumes that Timothy will heed Paul's call to come to him (4:21; compare 1:4). "The cloak" was a heavy cape worn in cold weather and also used as a blanket. Paul tells Timothy to bring it because, as 4:21 will imply, winter is approaching; and prisoners weren't supplied with clothes or blankets. We don't know why Paul left his cloak behind in Troas with Carpus, nor do we know anything more about Carpus. But "with Carpus" gives Timothy something of an address "in Troas" where he can pick up the cloak. Troas lay on the coast of the Aegean Sea at the northwest corner of Asia Minor. If Timothy is in Ephesus, he'll travel north to Troas and probably take the Via Egnatia, a famous Roman road, toward the city of Rome. Paul wants Timothy to bring also "the books, namely the parchments" that he (Paul) had left with Carpus. The books might be scrolls or codices (like modern books). But codices were easier to travel with, parchments (skins processed for writing) were used for codices, and the Greek word often translated "especially" seems to mean "namely" in 1–2 Timothy and Titus (see the final comments on 1 Timothy 4:6–10). Hence "books" rather than "scrolls," and "namely" to equate the books with "the parchments." We don't know their contents.

4:14–15: Alexander the coppersmith showed me many harmful things [= did me much harm]. "The Lord will repay him in accordance with his deeds [Psalm 62:12; Proverbs 24:12]," [15]**against whom** [referring to Alexander] **you also be guarding yourself. For he withstood our words vigorously.** Alexander the coppersmith may have been Alexander the Jew whom Jews put forward during a riotous assembly in Ephesus (Acts 19:32–34) and/or Alexander the heretic whom Paul gave over to Satan (1 Timothy 1:20). But Alexander was a common name; and we don't know what sort of harm this Alexander did to Paul, only that it was "much," so that in addition to coming to Paul, Timothy should be on guard against Alexander. Paul takes satisfaction in the Lord's future repayment of Alexander "in accordance with his deeds." As the Lord will repay Paul in kind (that is, with a crown [4:8]), so he'll repay Alexander in kind (that is, with harm); for the Lord is "the righteous judge" (4:8). He'll set right the scales of justice. Not mainly for personal safety, though—rather, for the sake of Paul's and Timothy's "words," the words of the gospel previously described as "healthful." For Alexander opposed ("withstood") those words (compare 3:8). "Vigorously" highlights the danger Alexander poses to the words, just as "many" highlighted the harmful things he did to Paul.

4:16–18: At my first defense no one showed up alongside [me to support me]; rather, all abandoned me [compare Psalm 22:1]. May it [their abandoning me] **not be counted** [against them at the Last Judgment]. [17]**But the Lord stood alongside me and empowered me in order that through me the proclamation** [of the gospel] **might be filled out and all the Gentiles might hear** [it]. **And I was rescued out of the lion's mouth** [compare Psalm 22:21]. [18]**The Lord will rescue me from every evil deed** [compare Psalm 22:8] **and save** [me] **for his heavenly reign** [compare Psalm 22:27–28], **to whom** [belongs] **the glory forever and ever. Amen!** "My first defense" implies that Paul's trial isn't over, though according to 4:6 he's sure he'll be condemned to execution. The absence of somebody to support him—say, by a testimony in his behalf—cast a shadow over that defense. "Rather, all abandoned

me" recalls 1:15; 4:10. Paul's wish that the abandonment not be counted against the "all" shows he doesn't consider them apostates; and the sending of greetings from several named people and "all the brothers and sisters," apparently residents in Rome (4:21), suggests that the "all" who abandoned him had been his traveling companions. The Lord's presence and empowerment (compare 2:1) enabled him to proclaim the gospel in his first defense. This proclamation "filled out" Paul's apostolic commission as a herald of the gospel to "all the Gentiles," represented as a whole in Caesar's court. "The lion's mouth" stands for execution. Paul was rescued from it in that his first defense eventuated in a delay of execution, a delay that has made it possible for him to write this letter and, he hopes, to receive a visit from Timothy before winter sets in. At Paul's resurrection the Lord will have rescued him "*from* every evil deed" perpetrated against him, including his impending martyrdom, and will have "saved" him "*for* his [the Lord's] heavenly reign," in which Paul will share (2:12) and which will originate from heaven but come to earth (4:1; Philippians 3:20). At this thought Paul breaks into a glorious doxology capped by a triumphant "Amen!"

4:19–22: Greet Prisca and Aquila and the household of Onesiphorus. [20]**Erastus stayed in Corinth, and I left Trophimus ill in Miletus.** [21]**Be diligent to come before winter. Eubulus greets you; and Pudens and Linus and Claudia and all the brothers and sisters** [greet you]. [22]**The Lord** [be] **with your spirit. Grace** [be] **with you** [plural]. Prisca (known also by the diminutive form of her name, Priscilla) and Aquila are no longer in Rome (see Acts 18:1–3, 18, 24–26; Romans 16:3–5a; 1 Corinthians 16:19), but are probably again in Ephesus, where Timothy likely is. "The household of Onesiphorus" appeared in 1:16–18. Paul sends greetings to them as well as to Prisca and Aquila. No greetings are to be relayed by Timothy to Erastus and Trophimus. "Erastus stayed in Corinth" implies that Paul recently passed through Corinth, Greece (Acts 19:22; Romans 16:23). "I left Trophimus ill in Miletus," located on the Aegean coast of Asia Minor not far from Ephesus, likewise implies that Paul had passed through Miletus recently but also that illness prevented Trophimus from continuing with Paul (Acts 20:4; 21:29). As a specification of "soon" in 4:9, "Be diligent to come before winter" arises out of the halting of travel, particularly of travel by sea, during winter. Storms made it too dangerous (see Acts 27). Eubulus, Pudens, Linus, Claudia, and "all the brothers and sisters" appear to be Christian residents in Rome. Unlike Paul's erstwhile traveling companions, these people may have had no opportunity to testify in behalf of Paul during his first defense. He wishes that "the Lord [be] with [Timothy's] *spirit*," because it's there that Timothy needs courage to share mistreatment with Paul by coming to him. As usual, God's grace functions as a Christian goodbye as well as hello (1:2). The plural in "with you" implies that Timothy will share this letter with other Christians, such as Prisca, Aquila, and the household of Onesiphorus.

TITUS

In this letter Titus is told to appoint supervisors over Christians living in his area of ministry. Qualifications for supervisorship are spelled out, as are also the behavioral precepts that Titus himself is to teach.

INTRODUCTION
Titus 1:1-4

1:1-4: Paul, a slave of God and an apostle of Jesus Christ in accordance with the faith of God's selected ones and [in accordance with] **the knowledge of the truth that accords with piety** [2]**on the basis of hope for eternal life, which God, who doesn't lie, promised before eternal times.** [3]**But in his own seasons he manifested his word** [= message] **in the proclamation with which I've been entrusted in accordance with the command of our Savior,** [namely] **God,** [4]**to Titus,** [my] **genuine child in accordance with shared faith: Grace and peace from God, the Father, and Christ Jesus, our Savior.** On the one hand, God owns Paul, and therefore as his slave Paul works for him. On the other hand, Jesus Christ sent Paul to speak to people (especially to Gentiles) on his behalf. Thus working for God and speaking for Christ equate with each other. Paul's speaking has the purpose of eliciting faith in those whom God has selected out of the human race as a whole. Paul's speaking has the parallel purpose of eliciting in God's selected ones a knowledge of the truth. Thus faith consists in believing the truth, and a knowledge of the truth consists in believing it. (Faith and knowledge coalesce.) The truth elicits piety, the practice of faith and knowledge, so that they aren't purely mental. Piety has for its basis the hope for eternal life. (Otherwise, why practice faith and knowledge?) To those who have faith/knowledge of the truth, God promised eternal life.

Paul is sending his letter to the island of Crete (1:5). Unlike its inhabitants, who are "always liars" according to one of their own (1:12) and perhaps also unlike the god Zeus, who according to mythology lied to have sex with a human female and whose tomb the Cretans claimed to have on their island, God doesn't lie; and he promised eternal life for his selected ones in the past eternity. (For that's when he selected them for the purpose of giving them eternal life.) The primal character of this promise and the unlying character of God imbue this hope with confidence. The eternality of the promised life corresponds to the eternality of God's promise of it. In his own decreed and therefore appropriate seasons God manifested his word (the message of the promised

eternal life). Those seasons are recent, as can be seen from the fact that the manifestation has taken place in the proclamation which has now been entrusted to Paul as God's slave and Jesus Christ's apostle. This entrustment came by way of a command. Paul's and Titus's Savior issued the command to Paul (Galatians 1:15-16). That Savior is none other than God, whose authority infinitely outweighs the authority of a Roman emperor, often called "savior." As a whole, then, Paul's self-description authenticates the letter's following contents.

Paul addresses his letter to Titus and calls him his child, which probably designates him as Paul's convert, so that they share faith in Christ with each other (compare the comments on 1 Timothy 1:1-2 concerning Timothy). The perseverance of Titus in this sharing of faith marks him as Paul's "*genuine* child." For the greeting "Grace and peace" see the comments on 1 Peter 1:2; 2 John 3, and on 1 Timothy 1:1-2 for the replacement of "our Savior" with "the Father" as a designation of God. By shifting "our Savior" to "Christ Jesus" after calling God "our Savior," Paul presents God the Father and Christ Jesus as co-Saviors, or one Savior in two persons, at the level of deity.

THE APPOINTMENT AND QUALIFICATIONS OF SUPERVISORS
Titus 1:5-9

1:5-9: For this reason I left you behind in Crete, that you might set straight the remaining matters and appoint elders city by city, as I ordered you, [6]**if someone is unaccusable, a man of one woman,** [someone] **who has believing children not charged with dissipation or rebellious** [acts]. [7]**For it's necessary that as God's manager a supervisor be unaccusable, not headstrong, not hot-tempered, not addicted to wine, not a brawler, not mercenary—**[8]**rather, hospitable, loving what's good, sensible, righteous, devout, self-restrained,** [9]**devoting himself to the trustworthy word** [= message] **that's in accordance with the teaching** [he has received] **in order that he may be able both to be exhorting** [people] **in the teaching that's healthful and to be censuring those who are speaking against** [it]. "I left you behind in Crete" implies that Paul had been in Crete. "That you might set straight the remaining matters" implies that he had done some work there but left before finishing it, and that the work consisted in setting straight some matters that were threatening, or indeed were corrupting, the churches located there. Titus had the job of appointing elders so that they might help in setting straight those matters, for by virtue of their status and appointment they'll have authority to help. "City by city" implies the existence of a number of local churches on Crete. "As I ordered you" indicates that before Paul left he told Titus to appoint elders. So Paul is reminding Titus of that order, and this reminder of the order evolves into a reminder of qualifications for eldership.

Following are the qualifications that match those for supervisors in 1 Timothy 3:1–7 (but note that here in Titus 1:7 "a supervisor" shows that the elders under discussion are supervisors [see too the comments on 1 Timothy 5:17–18]): "a man of one woman" (compare also 1 Timothy 3:12), "not addicted to wine" (compare also 1 Timothy 3:8), "not a brawler," "hospitable," and "sensible" (see the comments on 1 Timothy 3:1–7 concerning these qualifications). "Who has believing children not charged with dissipation or rebellious [acts]" comes close to "having children in subjection along with total respectability" in 1 Timothy 3:4, 12, especially if such subjection includes Christian faith on the children's part. And "not hot-tempered" comes close to "mild-mannered, uncombative" in 1 Timothy 3:3. With regard to the elder, "unaccusable," which occurs twice here in Titus, comes close to "unimpeachable" in 1 Timothy 3:2 but matches the qualification of assistants/deacons in 1 Timothy 3:10, as also "not mercenary" matches the qualification of assistants/deacons in 1 Timothy 3:8. "As God's manager . . . unaccusable" implies that on behalf of God an elder has the duty and supervisory authority to manage a church, or to help manage a church if it has more than one elder (see again the comments on 1 Timothy 5:17–18). To suit management, Paul switches from "elders" to "a supervisor." "Devoting himself to the faithful word" has the purpose of enabling the elder/supervisor "to be exhorting [people] in [theologically-ethically] healthful teaching [compare the requirement in 1 Timothy 3:2 that a supervisor have an aptitude for teaching] and to be censuring those who are speaking against [that word (compare 1 Timothy 5:19–20)]." So in fact some in the church are speaking against it.

THE SUPPRESSION OF FALSE TEACHERS
Titus 1:10–16

1:10–14: For there are many rebels, blowhards, and deceivers of [people's] minds—namely those of the circumcision—¹¹whose mouths must be stopped, who as such are upsetting whole households by teaching for mercenary reasons things that mustn't [be taught]. ¹²A certain one of their own, a prophet of theirs, said, "Cretans are always liars, bad beasts, lazy bellies [Callimachus (3ʳᵈ century B.C.), *Hymn to Zeus*, line 8, or Epimenides (5ᵗʰ or 6ᵗʰ century B.C.)]." ¹³This testimony is true, for which reason be censuring them sharply in order that they may be healthy in the faith ¹⁴by not paying attention to Jewish myths and commandments of human beings who turn away from the truth. Here Paul tells the reason why Titus should appoint elders who meet the just-listed qualifications.

The reason is that rebels/blowhards/deceivers (and there are many of them) have arisen in the churches. They're rebelling against the apostolic tradition by teaching aberrantly (1 Timothy 1:3). As blowhards they're engaging in pointless talk (1 Timothy 1:6). And they're deceiving people's minds with their myths and endless genealogies (1 Timothy 1:4). (It appears that Titus has to deal with the same sort of heretics on Crete that Timothy has to deal with in Ephesus.) "Namely those of the circumcision" marks the heretics as Jewish (compare the would-be teachers of the Law in 1 Timothy 1:7). For the sake of the churches it's a divine necessity that the heretics' mouths be stopped, so that the verbal rebellion, pointless talk, and deception may cease. In their supervisory roles, elders—whose qualifications are to set them in stark contrast with the heretics—will have authority to do the stopping. "Who *as such*" stresses the heretics as rebels, blowhards, and deceivers who therefore "are upsetting whole households." "Whole" and the plural in "households" highlight the necessity of stoppage. "Upsetting" is a figure of speech for deception. "By teaching for mercenary reasons" attributes to the heretics a bad motive, the very motive which, like verbal rebellion against apostolic tradition, would disqualify anyone from eldership/supervisorship (1:6–7; compare 1 Timothy 6:5). Again in regard to divine necessity, "things that mustn't [be taught]" are coming out of "mouths" that "must be stopped."

The heretics are Jewish, but they're also Cretans. So Paul cites against them as Cretans "one *of their own*," which emphasizes this one's being himself a Cretan, and calls him "a prophet of theirs," which means he's their spokesman (compare Exodus 7:1) but also connotes authority in what he says. What he *has* said, then, amounts to an authoritative description of them which despite its vilification of Cretans warrants belief. "Cretans are *always* liars," so that Paul's description of the Cretan heretics as deceivers is to be believed. (If asked why then the Cretan prophet should be believed, Paul might say this prophet is the exception that proves the rule.) Cretans had the reputation for lacking the sophistication of Greco-Roman culture—hence the figurative description of them as "bad beasts," that is, as injurious because wild. (Ironically, the island of Crete lacked wild animals!) Paul uses this description as a tie-in to his calling the heretics "rebels" against the healthful apostolic tradition. And "lazy bellies" describes them as gluttonous and therefore lazy because they're always filling their bellies with food, bought with the money for which they're teaching heresy, rather than working to support themselves as Paul does (see 1 Corinthians 9:11–12, 18; 2 Corinthians 11:7; Acts 18:3; 20:33–35). After quoting the prophecy Paul calls it a "testimony" that's "true," as though it were delivered in a courtroom to expose the heretics' lies. Whereas he told Titus to appoint elders/supervisors able to censure the heretics (1:9), Paul is so exercised against them that he now tells Titus himself to "be censuring them," and to do so "sharply" because the faith is under serious threat. But they're not beyond hope; for if under Titus's censuring of them they shift their attention from "Jewish myths and commandments of human beings" (compare 1 Timothy 1:3–7; 4:3) back to "the teaching that's healthful" (1:9), the heretics themselves will be "healthy in the faith." "Of human beings" implies a contrast with commandments issued by God (compare Mark 7:7; Matthew 15:9; Isaiah 29:13); and the very term "commandments" contrasts with "the faith," which distinguishes healthy teaching from Law-keeping. "Human beings who turn away from the truth," which consists in "the faith," can't help but turn into liars those who issue commandments based on falsehood.

1:15–16: **All** [foods are] **pure to pure** [people]. **But to the polluted and unbelieving, not one** [food at all is] **pure. Instead, both their mind and** [their] **conscience** [are] **polluted.** [16]**They profess to know God; but with their deeds they're denying** [him], [they] **being abominable and disobedient and disqualified so far as any good deed is concerned.** The reference to "lazy bellies" in 1:12 helps turn Paul to the heretics' teaching of adherence to kosher law (compare 1 Timothy 4:1–5). But there's irony in his applying the saying about idle *gluttons* to those who teach *avoidance* of nonkosher foods. Pure people are those morally purified by Christ, their redeemer (2:14; 1 Timothy 1:5; 2 Timothy 2:22). For them, all foods are ritually pure because Christ declared them so (Mark 7:18–19; Luke 11:41; compare Romans 14:14, 20). For people morally polluted because of failure to have believed in Christ the purifier, not one food at all is pure, Paul says, because their moral pollution makes even the kosher food they eat ritually impure. "Instead" doesn't draw a contrast with Paul's judgment. It shifts the topic from foods to the heretics' "mind and conscience," which he describes as "polluted" by wrong thinking and wrong doing (compare the "cauterized . . . conscience" of kosher-teaching "liars" in 1 Timothy 4:2–3). Then Paul sets the heretics' behavioral denial of God over against their verbal profession of knowing God. The behavioral denial, which consists in the substitution of "foolish debates and genealogies and controversies and battles over the Law" (3:9) for "any good deed"—this behavioral denial of God makes the heretics "abominable [literally, 'stinky,' though in a moral sense] and disobedient [to God's commands as opposed to human beings' commands] and disqualified so far as any good deed is concerned [that is, for lack of any good deed]." See the comments on 1 Corinthians 9:27; 2 Corinthians 13:5–6 concerning "disqualified."

THE TEACHING OF GOOD CONDUCT
Titus 2:1–3:8c

2:1–2: **But you—keep articulating the things that are consistent with healthful teaching:** [2][that] **elderly men** [are] **to be temperate, respectable, sensible by being healthy in respect to the faith, love, endurance.** "But you" introduces a strong contrast between Titus, as Paul wants him to be, and the abominable, disobedient, disqualified heretics of 1:14–16, who teach Jewish

myths and the commandments of human beings rather than of God. The "elderly men" to whom Titus is to be articulating "the things that are consistent with healthful teaching"—these men aren't limited to the elders/supervisors of 1:5–9. They include nonelders/nonsupervisors too. "Temperate" has to do with the use of wine in particular, "respectable" with the elderly men's reputation for good behavior, "sensible" with their thinking, which affects behavior. These characteristics will arise out of healthy faith (correct belief), healthy love (doing good to fellow believers in particular), and healthy endurance (perseverance in the face of persecution [compare 2 Timothy 3:10–11]).

2:3–5: **In the same way** [that elderly men are to be as just described], **elderly women** [are to be] **reverent in demeanor, not slanderous, not enslaved to much wine, teachers of what is good** [4]**in order that they may be sensitizing the young** [wives] **to be lovers of** [their] **husbands, lovers of** [their] **children,** [5]**sensible, chaste, working at home, good, subjecting themselves to their own husbands in order that God's word may not be slandered** [compare Isaiah 52:5]. For "reverent in demeanor," see 1 Timothy 2:9–15. "Not slanderers" repeats for all elderly Christian women what is required of male assistants/deacons in 1 Timothy 3:11. "Not enslaved to much wine" echoes what is required of male assistants/deacons in 1 Timothy 3:8, though enslavement acts here as a metaphor for what there is called addiction. In 1 Timothy 2:12 Paul prohibited a woman from teaching a man. But here he wants elderly women to teach young wives what is good, which teaching he describes as sensitizing them (bringing them to their senses) and which good he specifies as the young wives' loving their husbands and their children, being sensible (compare 2:1–2), chaste by way of sexual fidelity to their husbands, working at home rather than gadding about (like those in 1 Timothy 5:13–15), good in the sense of kind (since the antonym "bad" can mean "injurious"), and subjecting themselves to their own husbands (compare 1 Timothy 2:11; Ephesians 5:22; Colossians 3:18; 1 Peter 3:1, 5). For the sake of evangelism, Paul doesn't want "God's word," which is the gospel (1:3), to be slandered (= defamed, maligned) by young wives' throwing off domesticity and chastity, perhaps under the influence of a first-century Roman women's liberation movement (about which see the comments on 1 Timothy 2:11–14). For outside Christian circles such liberation was coming under criticism.

2:6–8: **In the same way** [that elderly men and elderly women are to be as just described], **be exhorting younger men to be sensible** [7]**in all** [respects], **offering yourself** [to the younger men as] **a role model of good deeds,** [offering] **integrity in** [your] **teaching, respectability,** [8]**a healthful word** [= message], [offering yourself as] **irreproachable in order that** [your] **adversary may be embarrassed by having nothing disparaging to say about us.** Titus's verbal exhorting of younger men to be "sensible" in all respects is to be backed up by exemplary "good deeds" on his part. These good deeds will make him the opposite of the heretics, "disqualified" as they are for lack of "any good deed" (1:16). It will be sensible for younger men to follow Titus's example. To follow that of the heretics would betray bad thinking. The "integrity" that Titus is to offer in his teaching consists in not teaching out of a mercenary motive, which would corrupt what he teaches (1:11). Such integrity will breed both a "respectability" such as the younger Christian men should emulate and "a healthful word," that is, a message calling for morally healthy behavior. "[Offering yourself as] irreproachable" complements the role model of good deeds with the absence of anything blameworthy. "Your adversary" is probably a generic reference to the Jewish Christian heretics referenced in 1:10 (compare 1 Thessalonians 2:14–16). They oppose the "healthful word." But irreproachable behavior on Titus's part and on the part of younger men following his example will cause the heretics embarrassment, public shame in that they'll have nothing disparaging to say about Titus and Paul. The truth of a message has a way of showing itself in its effects. What a testimony to Paul, Titus, and their gospel if it produces irreproachable conduct even in frisky young men!

2:9–10: [Keep exhorting] **slaves to be subjecting themselves to their own masters in all** [respects]**, to be well-pleasing** [to them]**, not talking back** [at them], [10]**not pilfering** [from them]—**rather, exhibiting total trustworthiness,** [which is] **good, in order that they** [the slaves] **may adorn the teaching about our Savior, God, in all** [respects]. The slaves whom Titus is to exhort are Christians, but "their own masters" may or may not be Christian (compare 1 Timothy 6:1–2). In either case, these slaves are "to be subjecting themselves to their own masters in all [respects]." Such subjection will make them "well-pleasing" in that they'll do their master's bidding without talking back and won't engage in stealing what they can of their master's goods. (Slaves were reputed to do much pilfering, and the reputation was probably well-earned.) This well-pleasing behavior will not only produce a "total trustworthiness" that's "good." It will also put such trustworthiness on public display, which Paul calls "exhibiting," so that by "adorning the teaching about our Savior, God, in all [respects]" with their trustworthiness the slaves themselves (yes, even *as* slaves) will attract people, perhaps especially non-Christian masters, to that teaching. This adornment of the teaching stands over against the slandering of God's word in 2:5.

2:11–14: **For God's grace, salvific** [as it is] **for all human beings, has appeared,** [12]**training us that by rejecting ungodliness and worldly lusts we should live sensibly and righteously and piously in the present age** [13]**while waiting expectantly for the gladsome hope, that is, the epiphany of the glory of our great God and Savior, Jesus Christ,** [14]**who gave himself for us that he might redeem us from every** [kind of] **lawlessness** [compare Psalm 130:8] **and purify for himself**

a people specially his own, zealous for good deeds. In this passage Paul tells Titus the reason why he is to do the articulating and exhorting detailed in 2:1–10. Supplying the reason is the recent appearance of "God's grace," which, given our "ungodliness and worldly lusts," means his ill-deserved favor. The Greek behind "has appeared" is a verbal form of the noun translated "epiphany," which as noted in connection with 1 Timothy 6:14 had associations with the glorious appearance of an emperor bringing political salvation. In that earlier passage Paul used the term in reference to Jesus' second coming, as eventually he does in the present passage. First, though, he refers to Jesus' first coming or, more particularly, to his resultant self-sacrifice on a cross, but calls it an epiphany of God's grace in that as "our great God and Savior, Jesus Christ . . . gave himself for us that he might redeem us . . ." (compare 2 Timothy 1:10). Grace indeed! For redemption amounts to salvation from bondage to sin and corruption. "Salvific for all human beings" doesn't mean that all of them will be saved by grace. For not all have believed or will believe. But the phrase highlights God's *wanting* all human beings to be saved (see 1 Timothy 2:3–6; 2 Peter 3:9). His grace is educative as well as salvific, because through redemption "from every [kind of] lawlessness" and through purification "for good deeds" the redeemed and purified are being trained to reject ungodliness and worldly lusts and live sensibly (in their mental lives) and righteously (in their moral lives) and piously (in their religious lives). These aspects of living interpenetrate each other, of course. For it's sensible to live righteously and piously. It's right to live sensibly and piously. And it's pious to live sensibly and righteously. The "worldly lusts" associated with "ungodliness" aren't excessive desires for earthly things so much as they are transgressive desires characteristic of those who make up human society apart from God's people (compare 1 John 2:15–17).

"The gladsome hope" (traditionally, "the blessed hope") is confidence that just as God's grace appeared in the past, his glory will appear in the future. This hope is "gladsome" in that we can consider ourselves fortunate to have this prospect ahead of us. Waiting expectantly for the hope means waiting expectantly for its fulfillment, the hope being so sure of fulfillment that to wait for the hope *is* to wait for its fulfillment. Such waiting enables both a rejection of ungodliness and worldly lusts and a sensible, righteous, and pious lifestyle during "the present age." The fulfillment will come in "the epiphany of the glory of our great God and Savior, Jesus Christ." Paul speaks of an epiphany of glory at the second coming, not of Jesus Christ himself, just as he spoke of an epiphany of grace at Jesus Christ's first coming, not of him himself, so that the accents fall on grace and glory—attributes of Jesus Christ as therefore "our *great* God and Savior," infinitely more gracious and glorious than any emperor. He was gracious to "give himself for us" (about which see the comments on 1 Timothy 2:5–7). He'll be glorious in fulfilling "our gladsome hope." Our being redeemed "from every [kind of] lawlessness" (for which lawlessness see 1 Timothy 1:8–11) is reformulated as our being purified so as to become "a people specially his own," as was Israel in the Old Testament (compare Exodus 19:5; Deuteronomy 7:6; Ezekiel 36:25–33; 37:23) and as distinguished from the unbelieving peoples of the world. The redemption "*from* every [kind of] lawlessness" makes us "zealous *for* good deeds."

2:15: Keep articulating these things and exhorting and censuring [people in regard to them] **with total command. No one is to be disdaining you.** Paul's command echoes 2:1, 6 and, more distantly, 1:13. In obedience to Paul's command Titus is to engage in articulation, exhortation, and censure "with total command" on his own part. He's Paul's delegate, so that he mustn't hold back, as though giving only advice. "*Total* command" means commanding with Paul's own apostolic authority, which in turn is the authority of Jesus Christ himself, an authority delegated by him to Paul and now by Paul to Titus. No wonder no one should disdain Titus. To dare doing so would be dangerous, at the Last Judgment if not sooner. But if anyone does dare, Titus mustn't be dissuaded from carrying out orders.

3:1–2: Keep reminding them to be subjecting themselves to rulers, [that is,] **authorities, to be complying** [with the rulers' orders], **to be ready for every** [kind of] **good deed,** [2]**not to slander anyone, not to be brawlers,** [to be] **mild-mannered, exhibiting total meekness toward all people.** "Them" whom Titus is to "keep reminding" are the Cretan Christians. "Reminding" implies earlier similar instruction of them. Paul adds "authorities" to "rulers" to legitimize the rulers and thus justify his reminder. "To be complying [with their orders]" defines what it means for Cretans "to be subjecting themselves." For details see Romans 13:1–7. Compliant subjection doesn't suffice for Christians, though. They're also "to be ready for every [kind of] good deed" (for an example of which see the parable of the Good Samaritan [Luke 10:25–37]). Such readiness means preparedness to do good whenever ability and opportunity converge, and "*every* [kind of] good deed" combines with the exhibition of "*total* meekness toward *all* people" to show that here Paul has in mind the doing of good in society at large, not just among Christians. "Exhibiting" implies a public testimony to the philanthropic effect of the gospel, an effect designed to attract belief in Jesus. "Total meekness" calls for no retaliation, whatever the wrongs suffered; and "toward all people" includes even the Christians' persecutors. "Not to slander anyone" prohibits verbal abuse. "Not to be brawlers" prohibits physical violence. "[To be] mild-mannered" bridges both the nonbrawling and the exhibiting of total meekness.

3:3–8a: For once upon a time we ourselves, too, were mindless, disobedient, deceived, slaving for various lusts and pleasures, leading our lives in malice and envy, abhorrent, hating one another. [4]**"But when the magnanimity and love of our Savior, God, for humanity appeared,** [5]**he saved us not by deeds that we ourselves had done in righteousness—rather,** **in accordance with his mercy through the washing of regeneration and renewal of the Holy Spirit,** [6]**whom he richly poured out on us through Jesus Christ, our Savior,** [7]**in order that having been declared righteous by that one's grace we might become heirs in accordance with the hope of eternal life."** [8a]**The** [just-quoted] **saying** [is] **trustworthy.** This paragraph presents conversion as the reason Christians should obey the injunctions that Titus is to convey according to 3:1–2. "Once upon a time" refers to a time prior to conversion. "We" includes Paul and Titus along with the Cretan Christians whom Titus is to exhort. The addition of "ourselves" to "we" and the further addition of "too" stress that once upon a time Christians were morally no better than non-Christians and that therefore it was due solely to God's magnanimity, love, and mercy that they were converted. As to their preconversion selves, "mindless" describes them as stupid in their disobedience to God's laws (compare 1 Timothy 1:9–10). Because of this stupidity, they fell victim to moral deception; and because of this deception they mistook lusts as promising freedom, and pleasures (which are the outworkings of lusts) as granting freedom. But they found both lusts and pleasures to be enslaving instead. The variety of lusts and pleasures added to their deceptive attractiveness. Undermining those pleasures, however, were malice (animosity) and envy (jealousy) due to the notion that others' pleasures depleted their own pleasures. Malice and envy made the preconversion selves abhorrent *to* each other and thus hateful *of* each other.

"The magnanimity . . . of our Savior, God" contrasts with the preconversion selves' malice and envy, and his love contrasts with those selves' hating each other. Remarkably, he loved those who were abhorrent to one another. Just as the salvific grace of God appeared in an epiphany (2:11), so his salvific magnanimity and love for humanity appeared in an epiphany. They appeared in the first coming of Christ; but instead of saying that Christ appeared, Paul says that God's magnanimity and love appeared. Paul says so for an emphasis on what it took to convert us, that is, to save us from mindlessness, disobedience, deception, enslavement to various lusts and pleasures, malice, envy, mutual abhorrence, and mutual hate. Those vices ruled out self-salvation by "deeds that we ourselves had done in righteousness." The second addition of "ourselves" to "we" stresses our inability to perform deeds done in the orbit of righteousness, deeds that would erase the moral stain of deeds done in the orbit of unrighteousness. The contrast between "God" and "humanity" highlights our inability, on the one hand, and his power to save, on the other hand. "In accordance with his mercy" adds mercy to the aforementioned magnanimity and love of God for humanity and to his earlier- and later-mentioned grace (2:11; 3:7). The piling up of these terms puts enormous emphasis on his initiative in our salvation.

"Through the washing of regeneration and renewal of the Holy Spirit" stands over against the negated expression, "by deeds that we ourselves had done in righteousness." The washing *consists in* regeneration and therefore represents it as a cleansing from sins. "Renewal *of the Holy Spirit*" means renewal *by* the Holy Spirit and portrays the regenerated person as reborn to clean living, made possible by the Holy Spirit (compare Romans 8:1–17; 2 Corinthians 5:17; Galatians 5:16–25; Ezekiel 36:25–27). That God has poured out on us his Spirit "richly"—that is, generously—makes clean living both possible and actual for true Christians (compare Acts 2:17; Joel 2:29). "Through Jesus Christ" makes him the agent of God's pouring out the Holy Spirit (Acts 2:33). Application of the title "our Savior" to Jesus Christ portrays him again as the co-Savior with God (compare 1:3–4). Accompanying salvation, cleansing, regeneration, renewal, and an outpouring of the Holy Spirit was the forensic declaration of us as righteous (concerning which see above all Romans 3:21–4:25). Though it remains to be finalized at the Last Judgment, this declaration has already been made; and it was made by virtue of the ill-deserved favor ("grace") of Jesus Christ. "That one" identifies him emphatically as the source of justifying grace (1 Timothy 1:14; 2 Corinthians 8:9). So just as "our Savior" applies both to God and Jesus Christ, "grace" is ascribed to both of them (compare 2:11 with 3:7). Being declared righteous had the result of our becoming heirs. This heirship looks forward to the enjoyment of eternal life and in the meantime gives us "hope," which in Paul's vocabulary connotes confidence rather than wishful uncertainty. Hence the description of this just-quoted saying as "trustworthy."

3:8b–c: And concerning these things I want you to insist that those who've believed God be intent on engaging in good deeds. The presence of heresy in Cretan churches calls for Titus's insistence on engagement in good deeds. For heresy breeds bad behavior, which damages evangelism by giving the gospel a poor reputation, whereas good deeds promote evangelism by enhancing the gospel's reputation. To be "intent" on engaging in good deeds means to have the doing of them in the forefront of our minds. "Those who've believed God" have believed him to be the one who saves us because of his magnanimity and love of humanity, not *because of* the good deeds we're supposed to do but *for* the doing of them.

CONCLUSION
Titus 3:8d–15

The conclusion to Titus divides into a summary (3:8d–11), personal instructions to Titus (3:12–14), greetings and a benediction (3:15).

3:8d–11: These things are good and beneficial for human beings. [9]But be keeping clear of foolish debates and genealogies and controversies and battles over the Law. For they're unbeneficial and pointless. [10]After a first and second admonition be ousting [from the church] a factious person, [11]knowing that such a person is perverted and sinning, being self-condemned. "These things" refers to the preceding "good deeds."

The redundancy in saying that the good deeds "are good" emphasizes their moral beauty. "And beneficial for human beings" tells why they're good and portrays Christians, who do the good deeds, as benefactors of the human race in general—and this not simply by way of dispensing charity to all but also by way of bringing the unconverted to Christian faith through charity. (Benefaction was a highly admired activity in the culture of the first-century Roman Empire.) Because by contrast "they're unbeneficial and pointless [that is, serving no good purpose]," Titus is to "be keeping clear of foolish debates and genealogies and controversies and battles over the Law" (about which see 1 Timothy 1:3–7; Titus 1:15–16). Anyone who does engage in those debates, genealogies, controversies, and battles is "a factious person," one who causes divisions in the church. Such a person is to be given two admonitions, if necessary, to stop his engagement. But Paul's emphasis doesn't fall on the admonitions—rather, on Titus's subsequent need to oust the factious person, and to do so because of "knowing" at that point "that such a person is perverted and sinning, being self-condemned" for not having heeded the repeated admonition (compare 1 Timothy 6:3–5).

3:12–14: When I send Artemas or Tychicus to you, be diligent to come to me in Nicopolis; for I've decided to spend the winter there. [13]Diligently send forward Zenas the lawyer and Apollos so that nothing be lacking for them. [14]And our [people] are also to be learning to engage in good deeds for essential needs lest they be unfruitful. We know nothing more about Artemas; but for Tychicus as a traveling companion, helper of Paul, and letter-carrier for him see Acts 20:4; Ephesians 6:21–22; Colossians 4:7–8; 2 Timothy 4:12. Nicopolis lay on the northwest coast of Greece opposite the foot of Italy. "I've decided to spend the winter there [not 'here']" indicates that Paul hasn't yet arrived in Nicopolis. So we don't know where he was at the time of writing this letter (but see Romans 15:19 for his presence, perhaps at this time, in Illyricum, a region north of Nicopolis). He'll send Artemas or Tychicus to replace Titus in Crete. Then Titus is "to be diligent" to join Paul in Nicopolis. Paul's decision to spend the winter in Nicopolis favors that the commanded diligence includes Titus's coming before winter's onset. For sailing during winter, as Titus would have to do when leaving the island of Crete, was dangerous and usually avoided (see Acts 27 for Paul's recognition of the danger, involving Crete). So the commanded diligence in a sending of Zenas the lawyer and Apollos is also likely to include action taken before winter's onset (compare 2 Timothy 4:9, 21).

We know nothing more about Zenas. The relation of his name to that of the Greek god Zeus ("Zenas" meaning "a gift of Zeus") favors that he didn't come from Jewish stock and therefore had legal expertise outside Jewish law. Apollos appears in Acts 18:24–19:1 and repeatedly in 1 Corinthians, beginning at 1:12. He seems to have ministered cooperatively but independently from Paul. Since Paul addresses Titus alone, at the time of writing Zenas and Apollos have yet to arrive in Crete. They're probably carrying Paul's letter to Titus. But Paul wants them to rejoin him. Titus's sending forward Zenas and Apollos while he himself waits for the arrival of Artemas or Tychicus before going himself to Paul—this sending forward includes supplying Zenas and Apollos with whatever they need for their journey to Paul: food, money, and such like. And for a supply that will leave nothing lacking, Cretan Christians (whom Paul calls "our [people]") are "to be engaging in good deeds," which in this case means supplying Zenas's and Apollos's "essential needs." These Cretans will be learning by the actual doing (compare 1 Timothy 5:4, 13). "*Also* to be learning" seems to mean learning by doing *as well as* learning by listening to Titus's exhortations. "Lest they [the Cretan Christians] be unfruitful [a figure of speech for lacking in good deeds]" carries an implicit warning that failure to engage in good deeds indicates a failure to have received the saving grace of God (see 2:11–14).

3:15: **All who** [are] **with me greet you** [singular]. **Greet those who love us in the faith. Grace** [be] **with all you** [plural]. "All who [are] with me" refers to Paul's traveling companions, such as Artemas and Tychicus (3:12; Galatians 1:2; Philippians 4:21), though "all" suggests a larger number than those two and assures Titus ("you") of the friendship of everyone in Paul's company. Titus is to relay the greetings of Paul and his companions to "those who love [them] in the faith," that is, Cretan Christians who love them for their having brought these Cretans to Christian faith when with them on the island. "All you [plural]" for whom Paul wishes grace includes along with Titus both Zenas and Apollos and all those "who love [Paul and his companions] in the faith." Paul used "grace," the ill-deserved favor of God and Christ Jesus, as a hello (1:4) and now uses it as a goodbye. Both coming and going, their grace is never to be forgotten.

PHILEMON

In this letter Paul asks Philemon, a slaveowner, to receive kindly, perhaps even to release, his recently converted slave named Onesimus, who is now returning. The letter divides into an introductory greeting (verses 1–3); a thanksgiving for Philemon, the letter's main addressee (verses 4–7); a plea for Onesimus, Philemon's slave (verses 8–22); and concluding greetings, plus a benediction (verses 23–25).

1–3: Paul, a prisoner of Christ Jesus, and Timothy, the brother, to Philemon, our beloved [brother] **and fellow worker, ²and to Apphia, the sister, and to Archippus, our fellow soldier, and to the church in your** [singular for Philemon's] **house: ³Grace and peace to you** [plural for all the addressees] **from God, our Father, and the Lord, Jesus Christ.** Paul fills his greeting with numerous features designed to make Philemon amenable to granting some upcoming requests: (1) Paul designates himself "a prisoner of Christ Jesus" in the sense that his proclamation of Christ Jesus has led to imprisonment (see Acts 21–28 for the full story). This self-designation calls attention to the high price Paul has paid for the proclamation, so that when he presents his requests, Philemon should consider the granting of them a comparatively small price to pay. (2) To his own name Paul adds that of Timothy and designates him "the brother," that is, a fellow member of Paul's, Philemon's, and the other addressees' family of faith. This addition and designation add weight to the upcoming requests in that what Paul says, Timothy says too. For further information about Timothy, see the comments on 1 Timothy 1:1–2. (3) Paul designates Philemon as "our beloved [brother]." "Our" establishes a brotherly bond between Paul, Timothy, and Philemon; and "beloved" adds affection to the bond. Such a bond should make it easy for Philemon to grant the coming requests. (4) Paul also designates Philemon as his and Timothy's "fellow worker," which has to do with working for the cause of the gospel just as Paul and Timothy do. Hosting a church in his house examples such work on the part of Philemon. So he should consider the granting of Paul's requests an extension of this work. (Grammatically, "the church in your house" could refer to the church in Archippus's house. But pointing to Philemon's house are Paul's directing the following requests to Philemon and Philemon's owning a slave, which seems to indicate that he's a man of some means and therefore a man whose house would be large enough for church meetings.) (5) Paul names Apphia as an addressee alongside Philemon

and designates her "the sister" for another reference to the family of faith, in which family Paul's requests for the sake of the gospel are to be honored. Apphia might well be Philemon's wife, included here because a church meets in her and his house (though the "your" that modifies "house" is singular, referring to Philemon as the owner). Whether the wife of Philemon or an otherwise prominent Christian woman, Apphia is addressed by name and called a sister to garner her influence on him for the granting of Paul's requests. (6) To the same end Paul also names Archippus as an addressee and designates him as Paul's and Timothy's "fellow soldier." See the comment on Colossians 4:17 for the likelihood that Archippus took leadership of the Colossian church once Epaphras, its founder, left town. "Fellow soldier" then describes Archippus militarily as fighting for the gospel, perhaps against the false teachings in Colossae that Paul himself attacks in his letter to the Colossians—hence, "*our* fellow soldier," that letter having started, "Paul . . . and Timothy . . . to the saints in Colossae." In any case, since Colossians locates Archippus in Colossae, a city in central Asia Minor, his appearance here in Philemon 1–3 locates the man Philemon also in Colossae and favors that this letter and Colossians were sent together. (7) Paul addresses the church that meets in Philemon's house to put Christian communal pressure on Philemon to accede to Paul's upcoming requests. For the whole church, along with Apphia and Archippus, will join Philemon in hearing the letter read in their assembly. Concerning the rest of the greeting, see the comments on Romans 1:7; 1 Peter 1:2; 2 John 3. (Note: the church isn't a building; it's the Christians meeting in Philemon's house.)

4–5: I'm always thanking my God when mentioning you [singular for Philemon] **on** [the occasion of] **my prayers, ⁵because of hearing about your love for all the saints and** [about] **the faith that you have toward the Lord, Jesus.** It's a compliment to Philemon that he loves the saints who make up the church that meets in his house, and especially that he loves all of them. That he hosts their meetings expresses his love concretely. (As usual, "the saints" designates Christians as consecrated to God in distinction from other human beings, whom he hasn't consecrated to himself.) It's also a compliment to Philemon that he has directed his faith "toward the Lord," who is "Jesus," rather than toward the "thrones," "lordships," "rulerships," and "authorities" to whom false teachers in Colossae were trying to divert the faith of Christians there (Colossians 1:16, 23; 2:4–10,

15–23). And it enhances these compliments that Paul thanks God because of hearing about Philemon's love and faith. This thanksgiving accompanies Paul's prayers for him "always" and thus heightens the enhancement of the compliments. The prayers also show Paul's concern for Philemon. "*My* God" indicates that even in Paul's most intimate moments with God, thanksgiving and concern for Philemon always play a part. As do various elements in the greeting, these compliments have the purpose of making Philemon amenable to granting the upcoming requests.

6–7: [I pray] **that your faith's participation may become effective in the knowledge of every** [kind of] **good** [deed which is] **among you** [plural for all those mentioned in verses 1–2] **with a view to Christ.** [7]**For by reason of your** [singular for Philemon's] **love** [for all the saints, as previously indicated]**, I've had much joy and encouragement, because the vitals of the saints have been refreshed through you, brother.** "Your faith's participation" alludes to what Paul prays will be the participation of Philemon's faith in the granting of Paul's upcoming requests, for "faith takes effect through love" (Galatians 5:6). "May become effective" alludes to the granting itself. "In the knowledge of every [kind of] good [deed]" puts the granting in the category of good deeds, "knowledge" carrying the connotation of putting something into practice. "[Which is] among you" describes "every [kind of] good [deed]" as already characteristic of the addressees, so that the good deed of Philemon's granting Paul's requests should follow as a matter of course. "With a view to Christ" describes "every [kind of] good [deed]" that characterizes the addressees as directed toward the advancement of Christ in church life. As the basis of this prayer, Paul cites the joy and encouragement he has already gotten from reports of Philemon's love and faith, which he now describes as the refreshment of the saints' (his fellow Christians') "vitals," that is, their inner organs, standing for the emotions necessary to perseverance in Christian faith and life. Like the earlier compliments, this one too has the purpose of making Philemon amenable to granting Paul's upcoming requests. Enhancing the compliment are the twofoldness of "joy and encouragement," the addition to them of "much," and the addressing of Philemon with "brother." If Philemon has brought much joy and encouragement to Paul thus far, surely he might do so again, Paul implies.

8–12: Therefore [because of the joy and encouragement your actions have brought me]**, though having much boldness in Christ to command you in regard to what's proper,** [9]**because of love I'm exhorting you instead. Being such a one as this**—[that is,] **as Paul, an old** [man] **but now also a prisoner of Christ Jesus**—[10]**I'm exhorting you concerning my child, whom I've fathered in** [my] **bonds,** [namely] **Onesimus,** [11]**who once** [was] **useless to you but now** [is] **useful to you and to me,** [12]**whom I've sent back to you—himself, that is, my vitals** . . . . Paul has "much boldness in Christ

to command" Philemon because Christ made Paul an apostle, someone with the authority to speak and act on Christ's behalf (see 1 Corinthians 15:8–10, for example). "In regard to what's proper" alludes forward to what Paul will advise Philemon is proper for him to do in relation to Onesimus, a slave of Philemon. Because of Paul's love for Philemon (see also verse 1), Paul forgoes a bold command in favor of an exhortation. But his exhortations often include commands (see, for example, Romans 12:1–2; 1 Corinthians 4:16; 16:15), and he will shortly speak of Philemon's "obedience" (verse 21). So the present contrast between a command and an exhortation has to do with the boldness with which Paul could issue a command and the love with which he's going to issue an exhortation that needs to be obeyed. In agreement with the loving exhortation Paul appeals not to his apostolic authority, but to his old age and (for the second time) to his being "a prisoner of Christ Jesus" (for which see the comments on verse 1). Paul underscores these appeals by introducing them with the self-reference, "such a one as this," by repeating his name (compare verse 1), and by calling attention to his being a prisoner of Christ Jesus as an addition to his old age ("but now *also*") and as a hardship for an old man ("but *now* also").

A second "I'm exhorting you" introduces Onesimus as the subject of Paul's exhortation. Paul calls him "my child, whom I've fathered in [my] bonds," which means that Paul converted Onesimus during Paul's imprisonment. (Imprisonment should probably be understood as being chained to a Roman soldier in quarters rented by Paul [see Acts 28:16, 20, 30].) In view of verse 18 ("And if he [Onesimus] has wronged you [Philemon] somehow or owes [you money]"), Onesimus appears to have been detrimental to Philemon. But here Paul describes Onesimus only as "once useless" to Philemon to prepare Philemon for an exhortation to accept Onesimus back as more than his slave, that is, as a beloved brother just as Philemon is to Paul and Timothy (verse 1) and even as Philemon would accept Paul himself (verses 15–17). "Onesimus" means "useful." Masters often gave this name to boys born as slaves into their households, and did so in the hope that the boys would prove useful as slaves. So Paul is engaging in wordplay by saying that now as a Christian slave, Onesimus will live up to the meaning of his name whereas before conversion he didn't. Useful to Philemon, yes; but in preparation for Paul's mentioning that he (Paul) was planning to keep Onesimus to serve him on Philemon's behalf (verse 13) and hinting that Philemon free Onesimus to serve Paul (verse 21), Paul adds here, "[Onesimus] now [is] useful . . . *to me*." As an old man in prison he needs the use of Onesimus, as Philemon should agree. Then to stress his consideration of Philemon's ownership of Onesimus, Paul says he has sent Onesimus back to Philemon—but escalates Onesimus' usefulness to Paul by comparing Onesimus to his own "vitals"—that is, to Paul's inner organs, the seat of his affections (compare the comments on verse 7)—and accents the comparison with "himself," referring to Onesimus.

13–14: whom I was planning to hold tightly to myself in order that on your behalf he might be serving me in [my] gospel-bonds. ¹⁴But apart from your determination I didn't want to do anything, lest your good [deed] be as in accordance with compulsion—rather, [that your good deed might be] in accordance with willingness. Paul was planning to hold Onesimus tightly to himself. This planning makes more impressive the shift to Paul's allowing Philemon to make his own determination concerning Onesimus. "In order that *on your behalf* he might be serving me" appeals to Philemon's sense of opportunity to serve Paul's personal needs through the agency of Onesimus. (Prisoners needed family or friends to bring them adequate food, drink, and other necessities.) "In [my] gospel-bonds" is supposed to revive Philemon's sympathy for Paul, remind him that proclaiming the gospel landed Paul in prison, and foreclose any thought on Philemon's part that Paul had been planning to keep Onesimus for selfish reasons. That is to say, Onesimus would have been serving Paul in a way that would contribute to Paul's proclaiming the gospel even when chained up, as exemplified in the conversion of Onesimus himself. Then Paul submits his plan to Philemon's "determination," which submission suits a loving exhortation as opposed to a bold command (compare verses 8–9). "I didn't *want* to do anything [by way of holding Onesimus 'tightly to myself']" portrays Paul's wanting to defer to Philemon's determination as stronger than Paul's planning to hold tightly to Onesimus—and as stronger for Philemon's benefit, because a good deed performed by Philemon under "compulsion" from Paul wouldn't be so much of a credit to Philemon at the Last Judgment as a good deed done in accordance with Philemon's own "willingness." "*As* in accordance with compulsion" doesn't mean "as *if* in accordance with compulsion." It means "as *a matter of fact* in accordance with compulsion." But for Philemon's benefit Paul has steered clear of that matter of fact.

15–17: For maybe he [Onesimus] was parted [from you] for an hour because of this, that you might have him back eternally, ¹⁶no longer actually as a slave—rather, more than a slave, a beloved brother, especially to me but how much more to you both in the flesh and in the Lord. ¹⁷If therefore you hold me [to be] a partner, accept him as [you'd accept] me. "For" introduces a reason why Paul has deferred to Philemon's determination. "Maybe" gives the reason some delicacy, a possibility for Philemon to think about. If Onesimus was a runaway slave, as he seems to have been (see verse 18), "he *was parted* [from you]" not only softens his running away but also interprets it as very possibly divinely providential (compare Genesis 50:20). "For an hour" softens the running away further by calling attention to the shortness of Onesimus' absence (for which shortness "an hour" is a figure of speech, an hour being the shortest unit of time then in use). Those softenings should make Philemon sympathetic to Onesimus and to Paul's following requests concerning him. "That you might have him back eternally" points forward to an eternal life to be shared with Onesimus, as opposed to "an hour" of Onesimus' absence and as opposed to having him as a slave only for as long as mortal life lasts. "No longer actually as a slave" implies that in Christ, Onesimus isn't Philemon's slave any more, even now. Paul doesn't follow up by saying Onesimus is now "more than *as* a slave"—rather, "more *than* a slave." Paul has gone beyond a comparison and is dealing in an actuality.

"A beloved brother" defines the meaning of "more than a slave" and gives Onesimus a status in relation to Philemon which is on par with that of Philemon to Paul and Timothy (see verse 1)! "Especially *to me*" gives Onesimus a status also in relation to Paul which is on par with that of Philemon to Paul and Timothy. "*Especially* to me" alludes to Paul's having converted Onesimus and raises to the nth degree Onesimus' being incomparably more a beloved brother to Philemon ("how much more to you" than even "especially to me"). "[Beloved] *in the Lord*" is unsurprising, given Paul's emphasis elsewhere on equality in Christ (see for example, Galatians 3:28). But "[beloved] *in the flesh*"? And more so to Philemon than to Paul? In Ephesians 6:5; Colossians 3:22 Paul describes the masters of slaves as "fleshly" or, literally, "in accordance with flesh." That description concerns a hierarchical relation in human society at large, a relation in which masters wield authority over their slaves. Here Paul describes the relation between a master and his slave in the church. It's nonhierarchical—rather, lovingly brotherly. "If *therefore*" means "If in view of Philemon's and Onesimus' loving relation as brothers." Paul doesn't say, "If therefore you hold *yourself* [to be] a partner [with me]." He says, "If therefore you hold *me* [to be] a partner [with you]" and thus accents Philemon's attitude toward Paul rather than Paul's already delineated attitude toward Philemon. This accent makes Philemon's response to Paul's requests a test of his partnership with Paul for the gospel. Thus "accept him [Onesimus] as [you'd accept] me" means "accept him as your partner in the gospel."

18–20: And if he has wronged you somehow or owes [you money], be charging this to my account. ¹⁹I, Paul, have written [this] with my hand [= in my own handwriting]. I'll repay [you]—lest I tell you that you owe me even yourself in addition [to Onesimus' debt to you that I've just now assumed]. ²⁰Yes, brother, let me get a benefit from you in the Lord. Refresh my vitals in Christ. "Has *wronged* you" is vague. "Or *owes* [you money]" is specific and narrows down the wrongdoing to a theft—but only by implication; for to lighten Onesimus' load of guilt and make Philemon agreeable, Paul studiously avoids using the vocabulary of theft. "And if . . ." leaves it up to Philemon to judge whether Onesimus has wronged him or owes him money. "Somehow" highlights this contingency to impress on Philemon that the judgment is up to him, so that Paul's telling him to charge Paul's account stands out as an example of magnanimity that Philemon might well imitate. To accent his willingness to repay Philemon for any wrongdoing or unpaid debt on Onesimus' part, Paul identifies himself by name for the third time (see also verses 1, 9), promises to repay Philemon, and writes at least the self-identification and promise (if not the whole letter) with his own hand rather than dictating it to a secretary. ("I have written" is written from the later standpoint of those, like Philemon, hearing the self-identification and promise read to them.) Then Paul mentions—as if it were an afterthought, though it isn't—that Philemon owes him even Philemon's own self. In other words, Philemon owes his salvation to Paul's evangelism. (We don't know any other details of Philemon's conversion.)

"In addition" invites a comparison of Onesimus' possible monetary debt to Philemon with Philemon's certain salvific debt to Paul (see also Romans 15:27). The comparison makes Philemon's debt to Paul far bigger than Onesimus' to Philemon. The unexpectedness, indeed offhandedness, of this comparison ("lest I tell you" means "not to mention," though the mention is nevertheless made)—this offhandedness and "even yourself" spotlight the disparity between the debts, a disparity that works to Paul's advantage in saying, "Yes, brother, let me get a benefit from you in the Lord." "Yes" affirms this disparity. The address, "brother," appeals to Philemon's familial relation to Paul "in the Lord." "A benefit from you" would consist not just in Philemon's accepting Onesimus as he would accept Paul (verse 17), but also in carrying out Paul's plan to have Onesimus serving him on Philemon's behalf (verse 13), and "even more" (verse 21). The verb for getting a benefit (*onaimēn*) and Onesimus' name (*Onēsimon*) look and sound similar to each other. The resultant wordplay highlights how beneficial to Paul would be his having a useful Onesimus. Paul then escalates getting a benefit in the Lord to refreshment of his vitals "in Christ." There's a parallel with "in the Lord," but the switch from getting a benefit to the refreshing of Paul's vitals—that is, his internal organs—comes close to comparing the benefit to the saving of his emotional life. In verse 7 he addressed Philemon with "brother," as here, and complimented him on having refreshed the vitals of the saints. Now Paul wants him to refresh his (Paul's) vitals too. After all, Paul is a saint no less than are the saints who make up the church that meets in Philemon's house. In verse 12 Paul called Onesimus "my vitals." So the refreshing of Paul's vitals would have to do with Onesimus *as* Paul's vitals. "Let me get" expresses a wish, not even a loving exhortation, much less a bold command. Such delicacy should be hard for Philemon to resist. But the delicate wish modulates into an outright command, "Refresh my vitals in Christ," which prepares for a reference to Philemon's "obedience." The command should jerk Philemon out of whatever complacency Paul's delicacy may have lulled him into.

21–22: **Persuaded of your** [singular for Philemon's] **obedience, I've written to you knowing that you'll do even more than the things I'm telling** [you to do]. **22But at the same time** [as you do even more than I'm telling you to do], **also be preparing a guest room for me. For I'm hoping that through your** [plural] **prayers I'll be graciously given to you** [plural]. "Your obedience" relates back to the command, "Refresh my vitals in Christ"

(verse 20). Paul's persuasion of Philemon's obedience adds yet another compliment to him, and "knowing that you'll do even more than the things I'm telling [you to do]" heightens the compliment. Like the earlier compliments, this one has the purpose of motivating Philemon to justify the compliment in his response. Again, "I've written" is written from the later standpoint of those, like Philemon, hearing the letter read to them (compare verse 19). Paul has told Philemon to accept Onesimus as a beloved Christian brother and to refresh Paul's vitals by letting Paul get a benefit from Philemon, that is, the benefit of keeping Onesimus for himself (verse 20). But Onesimus is Philemon's slave. So "more than the things I'm telling [you to do]" alludes to Philemon's liberating, not just loaning, Onesimus to serve Paul in the cause of the gospel. "*Even* more" strengthens the allusion; and "*knowing* that you'll do even more" puts pressure on Philemon beyond that of Paul's being "persuaded" of his obedience, especially since Apphia, Archippus, and the whole church that meets in Philemon's house will be listening to the letter along with him. If he's to be preparing a guest room for Paul, Paul must expect to be released from prison soon (compare Philippians 1:7, 12–26; 2:24). So the followup of this letter with a visit by Paul to Philemon's house and a stay there puts extra pressure on Philemon to do even more than Paul is telling him to do in relation to Onesimus. "For I'm hoping . . ." explains why Philemon should prepare a guest room for Paul to stay in. As usual in Paul's letters, hoping connotes confidence, not uncertainty. He rests his confidence on the prayers of Philemon and the other addressees. "Through your prayers" assumes they're praying for Paul's release and a visit from him. "That . . . I'll be graciously given to you" interprets the expected release and visit as God's answering their prayers in accordance with his unmerited favor.

23–24: **Epaphras, my fellow prisoner in Christ Jesus, greets you** [singular]. **24Mark, Aristarchus, Demas, Luke—my fellow workers—**[greet you]. To greet in a letter is to send greetings through it. The singular of "you" pinpoints Philemon as the object of greetings from Epaphras and the others (contrast the plural of "you" in the greeting from Epaphras at Colossians 4:12–13). The pinpointing of Philemon despite an addressing of the letter to others as well (verse 2) ratchets up yet again the pressure on him to do what Paul wishes, exhorts, commands, expects, and even knows he'll do. Epaphras's having founded the church in Colossae (Colossians 1:7)—that is, the church which meets in Philemon's house—can't help but weigh on Philemon's mind as he contemplates what Paul has said. We don't know how Epaphras came to be Paul's "fellow prisoner," but this description explains why Epaphras isn't returning to Colossae and also adds weight to his greeting. Surely Philemon wouldn't want to disappoint Epaphras, who founded the church that meets in Philemon's house, any more than he'd want to disappoint Paul, to whose evangelism he owes his salvation. Though the physical location of Paul and Epaphras in a (house-)prison is due to the evangelistic outworking of their Spiritual location in Christ Jesus, the Spiritual location is more worth mentioning than is the physical location. The shift of "my fellow prisoner" from Aristarchus (Colossians 4:10) to Epaphras may indicate that these two took turns joining Paul in prison voluntarily so as to help him and defend him from abuse. The shift probably occurred between the writing of Colossians and Philemon (though not necessarily in that order). For Mark, Aristarchus, Demas, Luke, and the designation "my fellow workers," see the comments on Colossians 4:10–14. Adding greetings from these further fellow workers with Paul heightens for the last time the pressure on Philemon to respond favorably, obediently, lavishly. Jesus Justus, mentioned in Colossians 4:11, has apparently left Paul or joined him between the writing of Colossians and Philemon.

25: The grace of the Lord, Jesus Christ, [be] **with your** [plural] **spirit.** Notably, Paul attributes grace to Jesus Christ and designates him as "the Lord" to put him on the level of deity with God his Father. "*Your* spirit" distinguishes Philemon and company's spirit from the Holy Spirit, and the plural of "your" makes the singular of "spirit" collective. Usually Paul wishes grace to be "with you (all)." Here, though, he singles out "your spirit" because Philemon and company's praying for his release and a visit to them indicates a concern for him deep within them.

HEBREWS

Hebrews was written anonymously, and neither its contents and style nor early church tradition enables us to guess with confidence who may have written it. The address and greeting that usually introduce an ancient letter are missing from Hebrews, but it closes like an ancient letter (13:18–25). Apart from the traditional title, "To the Hebrews," several factors favor an original audience consisting at least for the most part of Jewish Christians: (1) warnings not to apostatize as an early generation of Jews did; (2) a presupposition of the recipients' knowledge of Jewish ritual; and (3) constant appeal to the Old Testament. Whatever his own identity, the author portrays Jesus Christ distinctively as a high priest who, having offered none other than himself as a completely sufficient sacrifice for sins, now ministers in the heavenly sanctuary. The purpose of this portrayal, which emphasizes his superiority to every aspect and hero of Old Testament religion, is to ensure that the letter's recipients stick true to their Christian faith.

THE SUPERIORITY OF GOD'S SON TO THE OLD TESTAMENT PROPHETS AND TO ANGELS, WITH A WARNING AGAINST APOSTASY
Hebrews 1:1–2:18

1:1–4: **After speaking in the prophets long ago to the [fore]fathers in many parts [= bit by bit] and in many ways, ²God has spoken to us at the last—[that is,] during these days—in a son, whom he positioned as the heir of all things, through whom also he made the ages, ³who being the radiance of [God's] glory and the exact imprint of his [God's] essence and carrying all things by the word of his power, on accomplishing the cleansing of sins, sat down at the right [hand] of the Greatness in the heights ⁴because of having become much superior to the angels inasmuch as he has inherited a more illustrious name in comparison with them.** "The [fore]fathers" means the ancestors of the Jewish Christians addressed in this letter. "Long ago" refers to Old Testament times, when God spoke to their ancestors. "In the prophets" has to do with God's using the prophets as his spokespersons (compare the use of "prophet" for Aaron as Moses' spokesman [Exodus 7:1 with 4:14–16; 16:9]). "In many parts [= bit by bit] and in many ways" points up the intermittence and variety of God's messages spoken through the prophets. There's little difference in meaning between these phrases, but the author uses the two of them to highlight a qualitative contrast with the singularity of God's having spo-

ken in a son. For a son can convey his father's speech more definitively than an unrelated spokesperson can. Adding to the qualitative contrast are both a contrast in addressees between "to us" and "to the [fore]fathers," so that God has spoken to us directly (we're not limited to figuring out how what he said to them applies to us), and a temporal contrast between "at the last—[that is,] during these days" and "long ago." "These days" *are* "the last" in that God's having spoken in a son constitutes his final word, so that we dare not neglect it.

Sonship entails heirship. Therefore the author supplements the son's communicative superiority to the prophets with the superiority of God's having put his son in the position of an heir, such as the prophets were not. "Of all things" grows out of God's having created and thereby owning all that exists, and thus maximizes the son's inheritance. The background of creation then leads the author to pronounce the son God's agent in creation: "through whom also [in addition to positioning him as heir] he made the ages." "All things" referred to the physical universe. "The ages" refers to the eras of time in which the universe exists; and to link up with the temporal contrast between "long ago" and "at the last—[that is,] during these days," the author refers to these eras rather than repeating "all things."[1]

To sonship, heirship, and agency in creation the author adds the son's being "the radiance of [God's] glory and the exact imprint [on human flesh (compare 2:14)] of his [God's] essence." In other words, the son is deity in human form, as the prophets were not, so that from now on we'll usually capitalize "Son." As deity, the Son is "carrying all things," that is, sustaining the universe of which he's the heir. "By the word of his power" means "by the Son's powerful word." Now he, the Son rather than God, is speaking; and the power with which he speaks is his own. As God has spoken communicatively, then, the Son is speaking sustainingly and therefore even

---

[1] It's commonly thought that "ages" came to mean the physical universe, like "all things," because 11:3 says "the ages . . . have been prepared by God's word, so that what is seen has come into existence out of things that aren't apparent [to the eye]." On the contrary it should be noted (1) that "what is seen"—the physical and therefore visible—has come into existence *as a result of* God's preparing the ages, so that the two aren't quite the same; (2) that 11:1–12:3 features an emphasis on faith as faithfulness that looks forward through time; and (3) that everywhere else in Hebrews "age" carries a temporal meaning (see especially 6:5; 9:26, but also numerous uses in phrases translated less literally with "forever").

more powerfully than God spoke in the prophets (but compare God's speaking the universe into existence in Genesis 1; also John 1:1–3).

More than anything the prophets did, the Son "accomplished the cleansing of sins" (in the sense of washing them away) and "sat down at the right [hand] of the Greatness in the heights" (compare Psalm 110:1). Sitting there links with the Son's heirship and codeity with God and connotes rulership, because rulers sit on a throne. The right hand represents favor (see, for example, Genesis 48:8–22; Matthew 25:31–46), such as suits God's having positioned the Son to be the heir of all things. The author calls heaven "the heights" to stress the height to which God has exalted the Son, and he calls God "the Greatness" to stress the Son's corresponding greatness in that he sits enthroned beside God. But the mention of enthronement in heaven's heights leads to the thought of angels, who also inhabit heaven. So the author shifts to the Son's superiority even to them as well as to the prophets. The Son became "much superior to the angels inasmuch as he has inherited a more illustrious name in comparison with them." Earlier he was said to have been made "the heir *of all things*." Now he's said to have "inherited a . . . *name*." A double inheritance, then! The inherited name is "Son," as the next verse will indicate; and that's "a *more illustrious* name" than "angels." Hence "name" denotes a species and has the sense of "designation" rather than referring to a personal name or even a title. The author doesn't say here who the Son is. Saving the identification till 2:9 will make for a climax.

Next, the author starts supporting with Scripture his assertion of the Son's superiority to angels. *1:5–6:* **For to which of the angels did he** [God] **ever say, "You're my Son; today I've fathered you** [Psalm 2:7]"? **And again** [to which of the angels did God ever say], **"He'll have me as** [his] **Father, and I'll have him as** [my] **Son** [2 Samuel 7:14; 1 Chronicles 17:13]"? **⁶And when he** [God] **brings** [his] **firstborn again into the inhabited** [earth], **he says, "And all God's angels are to worship him** [the firstborn] [Deuteronomy 32:43; Psalm 97:7 according to an earlier Greek translation of the standard Hebrew text translated in English versions]." Divine sonship outranks angelhood as well as prophethood. Finally, God's fatherhood, only implied till now, comes out explicitly. "Fathered" symbolizes that he has positioned the Son at his right hand, as is appropriate for a son and heir. The "today" of fathering probably refers to the time when the Son "sat down at the right [hand] of the Greatness in the heights." At this point, though, the author isn't concerned with the time of God's having fathered the Son so much as with God's having addressed the Son as quoted, and not having addressed any angel in that way (compare 12:16; Genesis 49:3; Deuteronomy 21:17). The quotations of Psalm 2:7; 2 Samuel 7:14; 1 Chronicles 17:13 have to do with David's royal line, of which the Son is the culmination (compare 7:14). "When he [God] brings [his] firstborn again into the inhabited [earth]" (1) implies the Son's heavenly origin; (2) refers to the second coming ("again" [compare

9:28]); (3) implies the Son's preexistence as deity; (4) anticipates God's having other sons and therefore the Son's having brothers (see 2:10–12); and (5) ranks the firstborn Son above them.

1:7–9: **And on the one hand he** [God] **says in reference to the angels, "The one who makes his angels winds and** [who makes] **his attendants a flame of fire** [Psalm 104:4, again according to an earlier Greek translation of the Hebrew]." **⁸On the other hand** [he says] **in reference to the Son, "Your throne, God, is forever and ever; and a scepter of rectitude** [is] **the scepter of your reign. ⁹You've loved righteousness and hated lawlessness. Because of this, God—your God—has anointed you more than your partners with the olive oil of gladness** [Psalm 45:6–7]." In Psalm 104:4 a psalmist refers to God as "the one who makes his angels winds [and so on]." But the author of Hebrews considers the psalmist to be a prophet, or at least like a prophet, and therefore a mouthpiece for what God says. The present tense of "says" gives the following quotation a contemporary relevance. The comparison of angels to winds arises out of the nature of angels as spirits, the Greek as well as Hebrew word for which also means "winds." The word underlying "attendants" has to do with religious service such as angels perform for God. The contrast with the eternality of the Son's throne, stressed by the addition of "and ever" to "forever," makes angels, by comparison, as evanescent as "winds" and "a flame of fire." To this contrast are added a number of items that demonstrate the superiority of the Son to angels: (1) his throne itself, in that angels have no throne; (2) the affirmation of the Son's deity by God himself when using "God" to address his Son; (3) God's attributing to him a reign of rectitude, symbolized by a scepter,² and describing him as a lover of righteousness and a hater of lawlessness; and (4) God's celebration of the Son's kingship because the Son has loved righteousness and hated lawlessness. "God—your God" highlights the close relation of the Son to his Father. Anointing with olive oil not only had to do with choosing a king. It also had to do with the festivity of a celebration. A host anointed with olive oil the heads of his guests to make their heads shine as a sign of gladness (compare the comments on Matthew 6:17; Luke 7:46). Playing the host, God has anointed his Son, so to speak, with more olive oil than he has used on his other guests and thus has treated his Son as the honored guest. Given the flow of argument, "more than your partners" probably means "more than the angels," though an anticipation of the Son's "brothers" (2:10–12) and "partners" (3:14) raises the possibility of another or additional identification with Christians (compare 12:22–23). Psalm 45, part of which the author quotes, dealt originally with a king's wedding. The author of Hebrews applies it to God's Son as the ultimate king and again has God speaking through the psalmist as his mouthpiece.

---

²A scepter is an ornamented rod or staff held by rulers on ceremonial occasions to symbolize their rulership.

1:10–12: Also [God says], "You at the beginning, Lord, founded the earth; and the heavens are the works of your hands. [11]They'll perish; but you'll last throughout [that is, forever]. And all [the heavens] will age as a garment [ages], [12]and you'll roll them up [for disposal] as if [they were] a cloak. As a garment [is changed] they too will be changed. But you are the same, and your years won't run out [Psalm 102:25–27]." Again God uses a psalmist as his mouthpiece and speaks relevantly to the present time. Now, though, he addresses his Son with "Lord," implies the Son's eternal preexistence by locating him "at the beginning," and attributes to him the founding of the earth and the creation of the heavens (compare 1:2; John 1:1–3; and Genesis 1:1: "In the beginning God created the heavens and the earth"). To complement the Son's eternal preexistence, God draws a contrast between the Son's eternal future and the perishing of all the heavens. Indeed, the Son himself will dispose of them. "All" means that not a single heavenly body will survive.

1:13–14: **But to which of the angels has he** [God] **ever said, "Sit at my right** [hand] **till I place your enemies as a footstool for your feet** [Psalm 110:1]**"?** Implied answer: To none of the angels. [14]**They're all attendant spirits, aren't they, being sent for the purpose of service because of those who are going to inherit salvation?** Implied answer: Yes. "Sitting" is the characteristic posture of a king on his throne, and God tells his Son to sit at his (God's) right hand, the hand of favor (see the comments on 1:3), and to sit there till God places his Son's enemies as a footstool for the Son's feet. To become a footstool is to suffer defeat and subjugation. By contrast, the angels serve as "attendant spirits," but they don't rise above that level. The word for "spirits" is the same as the word for "winds" in 1:7, but translated here in accordance with its other meaning, "spirits," because of the combination with "attendant" (for which see the comments on 1:7). As attendant spirits the angels are sent to serve "those who are going to inherit salvation," that is, Christians, who will inherit salvation when God places the enemies of his Son—those who persecute them—as a footstool for the Son's feet at the second coming. So the salvation will consist in the Christians' deliverance from persecution. Since the author's interest lies in demonstrating the Son's superiority to angels—here in a contrast between the Son's enthronement and the angels' servitude—the author doesn't tell how they serve Christians. But mentioning the Christians' future inheritance of salvation leads him next to inject a warning not to forfeit that inheritance by apostatizing.

2:1–4: **Because of this** [the Son's superiority to angels as well as to the ancient prophets] **it's necessary for us to be taking with utter seriousness the things that were heard, lest we drift away.** [2]**For if the word spoken through angels became firm and every transgression and disobedience got** [its] **just deserts** [as it did], [3]**how will we escape if we've become careless of such a great salvation, which as such, having gotten its start**

by being spoken through the Lord, was confirmed to us by those who heard [him] [4]while God joined in testifying by means of both signs and wonders and various miracles and distributions of the Holy Spirit according to his [God's] will? Implied answer: There's no way of escaping if we're careless, and we're careless if we lack utter seriousness. Not escaping looks ahead to punishment in hellfire (6:8; 10:26–31; 12:29). Therefore "necessary" means necessary for salvation from such a fate. By including himself with his audience in "for us" the author establishes rapport with them; and they'll think correctly that if utter seriousness is necessary for his salvation, it must be for theirs too. "The things that were heard" consist in what God spoke "in a son" (1:1–2) and was then proclaimed to the audience. To drift away would be not to take those things with utter seriousness and thus to apostatize and lose out on salvation.

The author supports his warning with an allusion to the history of the Mosaic law, and calls that law "the word spoken through angels." This appellation (1) rests on a Jewish tradition growing out of Deuteronomy 33:2 that God used angels to relay the Law to Moses (compare Acts 7:38, 53; Galatians 3:19); (2) establishes a contrast between God's having spoken through angels in ancient times and his having spoken "in a son" and "at the last—[that is,] during these days" (1:1–2 again); and (3) links up with the preceding description of the Son as superior to angels, so as to highlight that it's even more important to take very seriously the things God spoke in his Son than it was to take seriously what God had spoken through angels. As will come up in detail at 3:7–4:13, the history of Israel shows that violations of the good but inferior word spoken through angels incurred punishment. To stress his point the author uses two terms, "transgression" and "disobedience," modifies them with "every," and describes the punishment as well-deserved ("just deserts"). The word spoken through angels "became firm," then, in its rightly inflexible and consistent enforcement. Much more will a carelessness that leads to drifting away from the gospel incur a punishment that consists in failure to gain salvation; for the gospel promises a salvation greater than anything promised Israel, such as rest from the labors of Egyptian slavery in the land of Canaan (4:1–13).

The gospel promises rest in a heavenly country free from the wars of persecution (3:7–4:16; 11:16; 12:22–29; 13:14). The greatness of this salvation—that is, deliverance—gets emphasis from "*such* a great salvation" and from "which as such [= as great]." It would insult God and his Son to be careless about a salvation of this magnitude. "Having gotten its start by being spoken" describes the salvation in terms of an initial message (compare 4:2–3; 5:12; 6:1; Luke 4:16–19). "By being spoken through the Lord" alludes to God's having spoken "in a son" (1:1–2). So "the Lord" is the Son, as already in 1:10. God his Father spoke salvation through him when he'd brought him into the inhabited earth "at the last—[that is,] during these days" (1:1–2, 6). Earwitnesses (the original disciples) confirmed to the author and his audience what

God had said through the Lord. And God joined his own testimony to that of the earwitnesses by enabling them to perform "both signs and wonders and various miracles" and by individually distributing to them the Holy Spirit for such enablement (compare 6:4, also the law of two or three witnesses in Numbers 35:30; Deuteronomy 17:6; 19:15). The piling up of synonyms, the description of the miracles as "various," and the additional phrase, "according to his [God's] will," lay enormous emphasis on God's testifying in this way to what he'd spoken through the Lord, his Son, and earwitnesses had confirmed.

For reinforcement of his exhortation not to apostatize, the author returns now to the topic of the Son's superiority to angels. *2:5–8a:* **For he** [God] **didn't subject to angels the inhabited** [earth] **that's about to come, about which** [earth] **we're speaking.** **⁶But somewhere someone bore solemn testimony by saying, "What is a human being, seeing that you** [God] **remember him, or a son of a human being, seeing that you take notice of him? ⁷For a short while you've made him somewhat inferior to angels. You've crowned him with glory and honor. ⁸ªYou've subjected all things under his feet** [Psalm 8:5–7]**."** "The inhabited [earth] *that's about to come*" makes one think of "the *new* earth" of Revelation 21:1. "About which *we*'re speaking" brings the audience into the author's argument, as though they're echoing what he's saying, and distinguishes this coming earth from "the inhabited [earth]" into which God has already brought his "firstborn" (1:6), that is, "the earth" which God's Son, addressed with "Lord," "founded in the beginning" (1:10). "About to come" stresses the nearness and certainty of the present earth's replacement with another earth of restful deliverance from current woes.

Despite their high position as "God's angels" (1:6), he didn't subject to them the coming earth. The Son will still be superior. The combination of the past in "he didn't subject" and the future in "the inhabited [earth] that's about to come" alludes to a decision God has already made concerning a future state of affairs. "But somewhere someone bears solemn witness" introduces a contrast with what might have been the case (subjection of the coming earth to angels) but isn't. The twofold indefiniteness of "somewhere someone" lets attention rest solely on the solemnity of the following testimony rather than splitting attention between that testimony and its location or speaker, and this solemnity is supposed to keep the audience from taking the testimony less seriously than they were to take the warning in 2:1–4. Within the quoted testimony two occurrences of "seeing that" introduce the reasons for asking, "What is a human being . . . ?" Given that God remembers him though his inferiority as a human being makes him forgettable, in other words, and given that God takes notice of him though this inferiority makes him unnoteworthy, what is it about a human being that prompts God to remember and notice him? The question remains unanswered, and the absence of an answer makes the question an expression of astonishment at God's remembering and noticing a human being.

But who is this human being? In Psalm 8:5–7 (the passage being quoted) he's any and every human being. So too here in Hebrews, since the Son has been called "God" and "Lord" and not yet been identified clearly as also a human being. But three echoes of chapter 1 indicate that the author is starting to focus on God's Son as the representative human being: (1) "For he [God] didn't subject to angels the inhabited [earth] that's about to come" echoes 1:13: "But to which of the angels has he [God] ever said [as he said to his Son], 'Sit at my right [hand] till I place your enemies as a footstool for your feet'?" (2) "You've subjected all things under his feet" likewise echoes 1:13, in particular, "till I place your enemies as a footstool for your feet." And more particularly, (3) the "all things" that are so subjected echo the "all things" of which the Son is heir according to 1:2 and which he sustains according to 1:3. In the psalmist's view the "short while" of human life in general makes human beings "somewhat inferior to angels." The author of Hebrews transforms this observation of the psalmist into an observation on the Son as just such a human being. But the psalmist adds the observation, drawn from Genesis 1:26–30, that despite their inferiority because of short lives, God has crowned human beings with glory and honor and subjected to them all things. The author of Hebrews transforms this observation of the psalmist into scriptural support for God's subjecting to the Son all the things making up the inhabited earth that's about to come. The author will now support this transformation.

2:8b–9: **For in subjecting all things to him** [the human being, implied to be the Son by the echoes of chapter 1]**, he** [God] **left not one thing unsubjected to him. But now we don't yet see all things subjected to him. ⁹But we do see the one who was made somewhat inferior to angels for a little while—**[namely,] *Jesus*—**because of the suffering of death** [= so that he might suffer death]**,** [we see him] **crowned with glory and honor,** [his suffering of death having the purpose] **that by God's grace he should taste death on behalf of everyone.** "Left not one thing unsubjected to him" underlines the totality of God's "subjecting all things" to the Son. "But now we don't yet see all things as having been subjected to him" might seem to contradict the statement in 2:8a that God has subjected all things under the feet of his Son, the representative human being. But that statement had to do with the subjection to him of "the inhabited [earth] *that's about to come*" (2:5), not the present earth. And because it had to do with a future earth, "we don't *yet* see all things as having been subjected to him." But we *do* see Jesus—with the mind's eye (compare 3:19; 10:25), since he has ascended through and beyond the heavens into God's heaven (1:3; 4:14; 7:26; 8:1; 9:24). We see Jesus because of the Son's having become a human being with all that that entails, especially some inferiority to angels because of a short life as a result of suffering death. The author has finally identified God's Son explicitly as the human being called Jesus, and has done so at the climactic mention of the Son's incarnation, death, and crowning with glory and honor. But picking up again on Psalm 8:5–7, the author notes that we see Jesus already "crowned with glory and honor" even though the coming earth isn't yet subjected to him. This notation refers back to Jesus' having been positioned at God's right hand as the heir of all things, having inherited a more illustrious name than the angels, and having been anointed with the oil of gladness more than his companions have been (1:2–4, 9). Then to prepare for a spelling out of the saving effects of Jesus' death, the author backs up to add that suffering it had the purpose of "tast[ing] death on behalf of everyone," and that the grace of God—his ill-deserved favor—led God to count Jesus' death as beneficial for everyone (on condition of persevering faith, it's understood from 2:1–4 and confirmed in later passages). Tasting death portrays death as a poisonous food or drink the mere taking of which is lethal.

2:10–13: For it was fitting for him, because of whom all things [exist] and through whom all things [exist], that in bringing many sons to glory he [God] should complete through sufferings the founding leader of their salvation. **[11]For both he who consecrates [them] and they who are being consecrated [are] all from one** [that is, Jesus the Son and God's people, consisting of both Old Testament believers, such as those to be celebrated in chapter 11, and Christians, all have one Father, God]**, for which reason he [Jesus] isn't ashamed to call them brothers **[12]**when saying, "I'll proclaim your name to my brothers; in the midst of the assembly I'll sing your praise** [Psalm 22:22]**"; **[13]**and [when saying] again, "I'll base my trust on him** [Isaiah 8:17]**"; and** [when saying] **again, "Behold, I and the children that God has given me** [Isaiah 8:18]**!"** At first we might be inclined to see God as the one "because of whom all things [exist] and through whom all things [exist]." But "because of whom all things [exist]" corresponds to the Son's "carrying [= sustaining] all things" according to 1:3, and "through whom all things [exist]" corresponds to the Son's being the one "through whom" God "made the ages" according to 1:2. So it was fitting for Jesus the Son that God should "complete" him "through sufferings." This completion refers to a completion of Jesus' human experience through sufferings that reached their endpoint in his "tast[ing] death on behalf of everyone" (2:9 [compare 12:2–3]), and the completion was fitting in that it enabled God's "bringing many sons to glory." "Many sons" refers to God's people, distinguishes them from Jesus as God's "firstborn" Son (1:6), implies God to be their Father and Jesus to be their brother, counts them as numerous though they don't include "everyone" on behalf of whom Jesus tasted death (2:9), and thus encourages the audience to persevere because they're far from alone in their sufferings (compare 11:1–12:3). "To glory" pictures "their salvation" as a transition from the shame of suffering persecution (10:32–34; 12:2–3) to a glory like that of Jesus, which he wears as a crown (2:9).

The author calls Jesus "the founding leader of their salvation," its pioneer, in that he has already been crowned with glory whereas they haven't yet been crowned with it. Then the author supports his descrip-

tion of Jesus as "the founding leader of their salvation" by noting Jesus' and their common ancestry: they've all descended, theologically speaking, from God the Father, whose oneness Jewish Christians would have confessed in the words of Deuteronomy 6:4 since before their conversions. Strikingly, though, the author makes Jesus rather than God the Father the one who consecrates them, that is, sets them apart from the rest of humanity to be God's people. The common ancestry of Jesus and them makes him unashamed to call them "brothers." Unbelievers shame them through defamation and ostracism, but he honors them by designating them his brothers. The quotation of Psalm 22:22 indicates that Jesus designates them thus in speaking to God himself, whose opinion counts whereas that of unbelievers doesn't. Naturally, he'll accept the designation made by Jesus his Son. Originally, the psalmist spoke of his own proclaiming the name of the Lord to fellow Israelites and singing the Lord's praise in their assembly at the temple in Jerusalem. As will come out in 12:20–24, the author of Hebrews applies the text to Jesus' proclamation of God's name to God's ancient people now assembled in heaven because of their decease, and similarly relocates the singing of the Lord's praise. ("Assembly" and "church" translate one and the same Greek word, but in Hebrews it represents a heavenly congregation initially made up of Old Testament believers.)

In the combination of quotations from Isaiah 8:17 and 8:18 the representation of Jesus as a firstborn brother shifts to a representation of him as a father: "I and the children that God has given me." Or is it that God has given believers as his own children to Jesus as their firstborn brother? In either case, "Behold" makes the gift an object of exclamation such as should encourage the audience to persevere by basing their trust on God as Jesus based his trust on him when suffering (compare 2:13 with 12:2–3). Isaiah's "I" was Isaiah himself, and "the children" God had given him were Isaiah's disciples. But where *God* was said to speak through scriptural writers in chapter 1, here *Jesus* is said to do the same through Isaiah. No problem, though; for Jesus the Son shares deity with God his Father.

2:14–18: Since then the children have shared [and therefore do share] **in blood and flesh, he too has partaken of the same** [blood and flesh] **in order that through death he might neutralize the one who has the power of death—that is, the Devil—**[15]**and set free these** [people], [namely,] **as many as through the fear of death were held in slavery all** [their] **lifetime.** [16]**For doubtless he doesn't take hold of angels** [by way of helping them]**; rather, he takes hold of Abraham's seed** [by way helping Abraham's offspring]**.** [17]**Hence it was incumbent** [on him] **to be made like** [his] **brothers in all respects in order that he might become a merciful and faithful high priest in the things that relate to God,** [in other words,] **to be making an expiation for the people's sins.** [18]**For in that he himself has suffered by having been tested, he can come to the aid of those who are being tested.** So the neutralization of the

Devil as the one who has the power of death required Jesus' death as "an expiation [that is, an atonement] for the people's sins," Christians being portrayed as God's people along with believers of old and death being the penalty for sinning (9:27–28a; Genesis 3:1–24; 5:1–31). (Jesus' sacrificial death expiated sins and thereby propitiated [that is, appeased] God, wrathful as he was because of our sins; but only expiation is in view here.) The present tense in "to be making an expiation" puts the past death of Jesus front and center for contemporary emphasis on its expiatory value. A satisfactory expiation requires the sacrifice of like on behalf of like, in this case of a human being on behalf of human beings. The divine Son's incarnation in Jesus therefore made possible his death as such an expiation, and the children's shared "blood and flesh" therefore required Jesus to partake of the same. "Blood" comes first because it represents life (Genesis 9:4; Leviticus 17:11, 14; Deuteronomy 12:23) and because "without the pouring out of blood forgiveness [doesn't happen]" (9:22). "Flesh" represents mortality because it decomposes upon death.

The Devil's "power of death" consists in people's fear of death. It's the Devil's in that he brought this fear on them by enticing them into sinning, for which, as just mentioned, death is the penalty; and the fear of death enslaves them emotionally throughout their lifetime, so that they need to be set free in the anticipation of eternal life (compare 7:16). "As many as" underscores how universally human beings fear death (whatever their protestations to the contrary, we might add). Then the author explains further the purpose of the Son's incarnation: Despite the inferiority of human beings to angels, he "takes hold of Abraham's seed [by way of helping them]" rather than taking hold of angels by way of helping them. The angels didn't need help. Abraham's seed did. And the present tense in "takes hold of" indicates that his help is ongoing right now. But who are Abraham's seed? Not all human beings—rather, the earlier-mentioned "children," also called Jesus' "brothers." Here they're called Abraham's seed because ancient believers are included, perhaps also because the original audience of Hebrews consisted at least mainly of Jewish Christians, physically descended from Abraham and/or because of their having followed Abraham's example of faith (11:8–12 [compare Romans 4:1–25; Galatians 3:6–29, though there with special reference to Gentile Christians]). "Doubtless" stresses the Son's helping them, and this help consists in his having become a high priest to make himself an expiation for the sins of God's people, for which expiation he had to "be made like [his] brothers in all respects." Because their sins made them undeserving of his atonement for those sins, the author describes Jesus as "a *merciful* . . . high priest." In anticipation of pointing up Jesus' faithfulness to God's will (3:1–6; 10:5–9), the author also describes Jesus as "a . . . *faithful* high priest." And since suffering for his "brothers" tested his faithfulness to God's will, he can help those whose own faithfulness is now being tested. He knows what it's like to be tested (compare especially 4:14–16; 12:1–4).

THE SUPERIORITY OF JESUS TO MOSES, WITH A WARNING AGAINST APOSTASY
Hebrews 3:1–4:13

3:1–4: Hence, holy brothers, partakers of a heavenly calling, fix your mind on the apostle and high priest of our confession—[namely,] **Jesus**—²[he] **being faithful to the one who made him** [the apostle and high priest of our confession] **as Moses too** [was faithful] **in his house** [compare 1 Samuel 2:35; 1 Chronicles 17:14]. ³**For this** [Jesus] **was considered worthy of more glory than Moses inasmuch as the preparer** [= both the builder and the furnisher] **of a house has more honor than it** [does]. ⁴**For every house is prepared by someone, but God** [is] **the one who has prepared all things.** "Hence" introduces a conclusion drawn from the preceding portrayal of Jesus. For the first time the author addresses his audience directly, calling them "holy brothers," not in the sense that they're sinless but in the sense that they like him have been consecrated by Jesus so as to become sons of God and thus brothers of one another as well as of Jesus, God's firstborn Son (see 2:10–13). The author also calls them "partakers of a heavenly calling," which means they're participating together in a calling that came from heaven, God's invitation that effects an acceptance and that promises an eternal inheritance (9:15 [compare 5:4]). This twofold address establishes rapport with the audience and lends conviction to the following exhortation. They're to fix their mind on Jesus to keep from drifting away, from apostatizing (2:1; 12:1–2). Before mentioning Jesus by name, the author calls him "the apostle and high priest of our confession." "The apostle" designates Jesus as the one sent by God to speak for God with the very authority of God himself (1:1–2; 2:3 [compare 1:6, where God's bringing him into the inhabited earth corresponds to sending him in the present text]). "High priest" recalls Jesus as the helper of Christians being tested by persecution (2:16–18). The "confession" consists in a declaration of belief in him as such an apostle and high priest (see 11:13; 13:15 for confession as a declaration). "Our" describes this confession as shared between the author and his audience and therefore as providing a basis for the author's following discussion. The description of Jesus as "faithful to the one who made him [the apostle and high priest]"—that is, faithful to God—makes Jesus an example of faithfulness that Christians should emulate instead of apostatizing. Though inferior to him, Moses too provides such an example. The author doesn't spell out the details of Moses' faithfulness. So only faithfulness as such is in view.

Given the subsequent statement that "God [is] the one who has prepared all things [including houses, according to the context]" and given the reference in 10:21 to Jesus as "a great high priest over God's house," here the phrase "in his house" refers to God's house, not to Moses' or Jesus' house. The meaning of "house" blends the meanings of a building in which a family lives and the family itself, the "household." In other words, the household is comparable to the house. The household with which Moses had to do was God's ancient people, Israel. The household with which Jesus has had to do is the church, into which Israel has evolved. "For this [Jesus] was considered . . ." introduces a reason to fix the mind on Jesus rather than on Moses despite Moses' having also set a good example. Moses represents the Judaism back into which Jewish Christians would be tempted to apostatize for the avoidance of persecution. But if God considered Jesus worthy of more glory than Moses was worthy of, so that Jesus presently has the greater glory, then Jewish Christians should resist that temptation. The comparison with Moses may indicate that "the preparer of a house" who "has more honor [compare the 'more glory' of Jesus]" alludes to Jesus as well as stating a general rule. If so, he has prepared in God's behalf just as he has spoken in God's behalf (1:1–2; 2:3); but God remains "the one who [through his Son's agency] has prepared all things" (compare the Son's agency in "mak[ing] the ages" [1:2], an agency so intimate that God calls him "God" [1:8]). "For every house is prepared by someone" explains why more honor goes to the preparer of a house than to the house itself. The greater glory of Jesus consists in his having "sat down at the right [hand] of the Greatness in the heights" (1:3), as Moses has not.

3:5–6: And on the one hand "Moses [was] faithful in his whole house" as "a butler [Numbers 12:7]" for a testimony of the things that were going to be spoken. 6On the other hand Christ [is faithful] as a son over his house, whose house we are if in fact we hold tight [our] confidence and hopeful boast. "His . . . house" is still God's household, not that of Moses. He was only a butler, a chief servant, in it. But he was faithful, as Christians ought to be. "In his [God's] *whole* house" underlines that Moses remained faithful to his task despite the unfaithfulness of all his fellow Israelites (except for Joshua and Caleb), and Moses had the task of serving up "a testimony of the things that were going to be spoken." Those things consist in the message of "such a great salvation" that "got its start *by being spoken* through the Lord" (2:3). Scattered throughout Hebrews, numerous citations of the books of Moses (Genesis–Deuteronomy) give ample evidence of this Mosaic testimony. "On the one hand . . . . On the other hand" highlights a contrast with Christ's faithfulness, though. He is faithful as "a son" and "over" God's household, whereas Moses was faithful only as "a butler" and "in" God's household. Sonship outclasses butlership, and supremacy outstrips servitude, even servitude of a supervisory sort. For the first time our author uses "Christ" for Jesus, and does so to supplement the superiority of Jesus as God's Son with the superiority of Jesus as Messiah (the Hebrew equivalent of "Christ," which is Greek for "Anointed One"). In this twofold way, then, the statement about Moses which in the context of Numbers 12:7 exalted him above prophets becomes a footlight for Christ. Moses' service as a butler lies in the past. Jesus' rule as God's Son and messianic king is ongoing in the present, so that the author identifies us Christians as the household of God over which

Christ rules. But the author adds an emphatic qualification. The identification holds true only "if *in fact* we hold tight [our] confidence and hopeful boast." Hope is confident in the New Testament, especially here, and thus leads to boasting. But not to boasting in prideful self-confidence—rather, to boasting in the faithfulness of Christ as God's Son over us, who are God's household if we hold tight. The word for "confidence" connotes confidence to speak in public, "boast" connotes speaking in public, and "hopeful" describes the boast as looking forward with assurance to Christ's return. So holding tight our confidence and hopeful boast means not only to maintain Christian *belief.* It means also to maintain Christian *witness* in the world at large despite its antagonism.

3:7–11: Therefore [= because we're God's household only if we hold tight], **just as the Holy Spirit says, "Today, if you hear his voice, 8you shouldn't harden your hearts as** [they did] **in the embitterment during the day of testing in the wilderness, 9where your** [fore] **fathers tested** [me] **with scrutiny and saw my works for forty years. 10Therefore** [= because of their testing me and seeing my works] **I was vexed at this generation and said, 'They're always straying at heart, and they haven't known my paths. 11So I swore in my wrath, ". . . if they'll enter into my rest [Psalm 95:7–11]."'"** Israel's history as recorded and referred to in Exodus 17:1–7; Numbers 13:1–14:35; 20:1–13; Deuteronomy 1:19–46; 6:16 provides broad background for the quotation of Psalm 95:7–11 in this passage. But just as the author of Hebrews quoted God as speaking in Scripture (1:5–13) and quoted God's Son as speaking in Scripture (2:12–13), now he quotes the Holy Spirit as speaking in Scripture. Shades of the Trinity! In 4:7, moreover, the author of Hebrews will attribute the quoted psalm to David and say that God (4:4–5) is "speaking in David." So when the Holy Spirit says, "if you hear his voice," God's voice is being referred to. But the reference to God's *voice* quickly turns into the "I," "my," and implied "me" of God himself. The present tense in "the Holy Spirit *says*" joins "Today," the first-quoted word, to give the whole quotation relevance to the audience of Hebrews. They, and we, are the "you" to whom the Holy Spirit is speaking. "Today" also lends urgency to the command not to harden our hearts.

"If you hear his voice" doesn't call in question the hearing of God's voice, but in the context of Hebrews refers back to God's having spoken to us in a son, as confirmed by earwitnesses (1:1–2; 2:3). "You shouldn't harden your hearts," because hardened hearts represent stubborn resistance to what you hear. "As in the embitterment" refers to the ancient Israelites' bitterness over the spartan conditions of life in the wilderness after the exodus from Egypt. We therefore expect "during the day of testing in the wilderness" to refer to God's testing *them* under those conditions. But "where your [fore]fathers tested *me*" corrects our expectation by indicating that those Israelites tested *God* with their bitterness, that is, tested his patience. "With scrutiny" adds to their testing of God a close examination of the deeds they saw him perform over a period of forty years, an examination that had the purpose of justifying their own bitterness despite God's delivering them from slavery in Egypt and supplying them with the food and water they needed to survive in the wilderness. His patience ran out. He "was vexed at this generation" of Israelites in the wilderness and described them as "straying," as though they were sheep, and therefore as ignorant of his "paths" (a figure of speech for the conduct he requires of his people). "*Always* straying" describes them as consistently disobedient. "At heart" describes their disobedience as deep-rooted. Such disobedience, consistent and deep-rooted, characterizes the apostasy against which the author of Hebrews warns his audience. God's vexation with the Israelites who came out of Egypt issued in an angry oath, the first part of which lies unexpressed. If we were to fill in what's meant to be supplied, "I'll be damned" would capture the meaning except for its sounding flippant, whereas God was utterly serious in swearing the oath. So "if they'll enter into my rest" means that they most emphatically won't enter into it. Originally, "my rest" referred to rest in the land of Canaan from their slave labor in Egypt and from their trekking through the Sinai wilderness (Deuteronomy 12:9), a rest that God would have given them but for their disobedience. For a reason yet to become apparent, though, our author avoids mentioning Canaan.

3:12–15: Be watching out, brothers, lest there'll ever be in anyone of you an evil heart of unfaithfulness in apostatizing from the living God. [13]**Rather** [= instead of apostatizing from him], **be encouraging one another each day by each day, as long as it's called "Today,"** **in order that none of you be hardened by the deceitfulness of sin.** [14]**For we've become the Christ's partners if in fact we hold tight the beginning of** [our] **assurance firm till the end** [15]**while** [it's still] **to be said, "Today, if you hear his voice, you shouldn't harden your hearts as** [you did] **in the embitterment** [Psalm 95:7–8]**."** For the address "brothers" see the comments on 3:1. Here it lends weight to the warning. "Be watching out . . . lest there'll ever be" demands constant vigilance. "In anyone of you" arises out of concern not only that an individual Christian might apostatize but also that his apostasy might influence others to do the same (see 12:15). "Unfaithfulness" arises out of unbelief. Indeed "unbelief" could equally well translate the underlying Greek word. Unbelief and resultant unfaithfulness identify what makes the "heart" of a human being, out of which proceed his deeds, "evil" (compare the hardening of hearts warned against in 3:8). Such a heart betrays itself in "apostatizing from the living God." He's described as "living," unlike dead idols, to point up that he can and will punish apostates (10:31 [compare 4:12]).

"Each day by each day" is an especially emphatic way of telling the audience to be encouraging one another daily. Not a day is to pass without such encouragement, which includes the element of urging one another not to apostatize. "As long as it's called 'Today'" adds to constancy the element of perseverance. That is to say,

the perseverance of Christians in their faith/faithfulness requires that they persevere also in encouraging one another. "Today" will last until the second coming. "In order that none of you" corresponds to the earlier expression, "lest there'll ever be in anyone of you an evil heart"; but "be hardened by the deceitfulness of sin" replaces "an evil heart" in an echo of 3:8: "you shouldn't harden your hearts." If you've hardened your hearts, sin has deceived you into thinking that stubborn resistance to what God tells you won't bring his punishment. The punishment will consist in a loss of partnership with the Christ. As a title "the Christ," which means "the Anointed One," recalls that God "anointed" his Son "with the olive oil of gladness" more than he anointed his Son's "partners" with it (1:9). "If in fact we hold tight" stresses what's necessary for partnership with him, which partnership will eventuate in being brought "to glory" and "see[ing] the Lord" after suffering the shame of persecution (2:10; 12:1–2, 14). To "hold tight" is to keep from "drift[ing] away" (2:1). It's "the *beginning* of [our] assurance," not the assurance as a whole, that needs to be held tight. For if its beginning had the strength to convert us, it has the strength to keep us from apostatizing. "Firm" describes "the beginning" as strong enough to forestall apostatizing "till the end [= till the second coming]" (2:1–4; 3:6; 6:11, 19; 13:9). The author then quotes Psalm 95 again but this time stops short of "during the testing in the wilderness." Thus the command to take advantage of "today" by not "harden[ing] your hearts" gets all the emphasis. The danger of apostasy requires it.

3:16–19: For who were bitter after hearing [God's voice]**? Rather, all those who came out of Egypt through Moses' agency** [were bitter, weren't they]**?** Implied answer: Yes, all of them. [17]**And at whom was he vexed for forty years? At those who sinned, wasn't it, whose carcasses fell in the wilderness?** Implied answer: Yes. [18]**And to whom did he swear that** [they] **wouldn't enter into his rest, if not to those who were disobedient?** [19]**And we see that because of unfaithfulness they couldn't enter.** In 3:14 "For" introduced a reason to encourage one another. Another "For" now introduces a reason not to "harden your hearts," that is, not to apostatize. The author puts the reason in the form of three rhetorical questions and a concluding observation. The implied affirmative answer to the first two questions draws the audience into agreement with the author and thus strengthens his exhortation. Why not apostatize? Answer: because of what happened to the apostates who'd come out of Egypt. "After hearing [God's voice]" refers to their having heard it at Mount Sinai (12:18–20; Exodus 20:18–19; Deuteronomy 4:12; 5:22–27; 18:16) and thus excoriates their bitterness as inexcusable. "Rather" implies that we wouldn't have expected "all those who came out of Egypt" to have been bitter after hearing God's voice at Sinai. "Through Moses' agency" alludes back to the service he performed according to 3:5. God's vexation "at those who sinned" describes their unbelief, unfaithfulness, and hardening of hearts as sinful. According to 3:9 they saw God's works for forty years. Here he's said to have been vexed at them for forty years, so that their seeing his works and his vexation at them ran both long and concurrently. The shifting of forty years from their seeing his works to his vexation at them heightens to a red alert the warning not to apostatize. "Whose carcasses fell in the wilderness" describes dying there as falling, in contrast with entering into rest (compare 4:11). The word translated "carcasses" originally meant "limbs" and in connection with falling implies skeletal remains lying unburied (see Numbers 14:29, 32–33, also Leviticus 26:30; 1 Samuel 17:46; Isaiah 66:24), an appalling and therefore alarming fate. "Disobedient" may allude to the Israelites' refusal to invade Canaan because ten of their twelve spies had brought back a discouraging report. Their lack of faith made them unfaithful (Number 13–14).

4:1–2: Therefore [= because of what happened to the Israelites who came out of Egypt and apostatized] **let us fear lest at any time, while a promise to enter into his** [God's] **rest remains, anyone of you should seem to have come too late** [to enter it]. [2]**For we too have had good news proclaimed** [to us] **just as indeed they too** [those Israelites had good news proclaimed to them]. **But the word of hearing didn't benefit those** [Israelites] **because they didn't mix themselves by faith** [= they didn't associate themselves by faith] **with those who heard.** See 10:26–31 for an elaboration of why we should "fear." By including himself in "let us fear," the author enlists the audience to share his concern that some of them might apostatize and thus not only fail to enter into God's rest but also influence others not to. "At any time" makes these possibilities ever-present, and therefore the need for fear ever-necessary. "While a promise to enter . . . *remains*" implies that time will run out. The promise will be withdrawn. Entrance will become impossible. "A *promise* to enter" implies an entrance in the future for those who won't "have come too late." "To enter" portrays God's "rest" as a kind of place as well as a certain condition. "Come too late" not only warns of a lost opportunity. It also alludes to the Israelites who came out of Egypt. Because ten of their twelve spies brought from Canaan a discouraging report, those Israelites refused to enter Canaan. The Lord then declared they'd never enter, but wander in the wilderness for forty years and die there. Next morning they changed their mind and tried to enter. But it was too late. The Lord wasn't among them, and the Canaanites beat them back (Numbers 13:25–14:45). "Lest . . . anyone of you should *seem* to have come too late" reserves to God a final judgment as to apostasy but indicates that Christians should beware even the appearance of apostasy. "*For* we too" introduces a reason why we should fear lest anyone apostatize. "For we *too*" introduces a parallel between the recent proclamation of good news to the Christian audience of Hebrews and the much earlier proclamation of good news to the Israelite emigrants from Egypt. "Just as indeed" cements the parallel. The good news proclaimed to the present audience consisted in God's having spoken "to us [human beings] in a son" (1:1–2 [see also 2:9–18]). Beyond the implication of

God's swearing the emigrants from Egypt wouldn't enter into his [unspecified] rest, though, our author doesn't identify the good news proclaimed to them. From the Old Testament we'd judge it to be the promise of rest in the land of Canaan. But to help the present parallel the author leaves Canaan unmentioned. He calls the good news proclaimed to the wilderness generation "the word of hearing," which means the good news as heard when it was proclaimed to them. This word didn't benefit them, "because they didn't mix themselves by faith with those who heard." In 2:3 "those who heard" were the earwitnesses of God's Son during his time on earth. The echo of 2:3 indicates that "those who heard" here in 4:2 are those same earwitnesses, Jesus' original disciples. The Israelites who came out of Egypt didn't mix themselves by faith with those disciples in the sense that unlike the disciples, who believed and passed on the good news, those Israelites didn't likewise believe the good news spoken to them in their own time.

4:3–5: For we who've believed are entering into the rest, just as he [God] **has said, "As I swore in my wrath, '. . . if they'll enter into my rest** [Psalm 95:11],'" **even though the works** [of God] **came into existence from** [his] **founding of the world.** [4]**For somewhere he has spoken in this way about the seventh** [day], **"And God rested on the seventh day from all his works** [Genesis 2:2]." [5]**And in this** [passage] **again, ". . . if they'll enter into my rest** [Psalm 95:11]."** Two instances of the conjunction "For" (roughly equivalent to "because") introduce stages in an explanation why God's rest "remains." "We who've believed" sets up a contrast with those ancient Israelites who didn't exercise faith (4:2). "Are entering the rest" sounds as though the entrance is going on right now. And in a sense it is, so long as we are holding tight our confession and not drifting away (2:1–4; 3:12–14). But as noted above, "a promise to enter" implies a primarily future entrance. (Shall we say "a *grand* entrance"?) Confirming a primarily future entrance are the exhortations not to apostatize and come too late for entrance (compare 4:6, 9, 11). See the comments on 3:11 for God's swearing an oath. His "works" refers to what he did in the six days of creation according to Genesis 1 (compare Hebrews 1:10; 2:7). We expect the author to say those works came into existence *at* the founding of the world. But he says they did "*from* the founding of the world" for an allusion to the long timespan that separates them from now. The allusion will help make the point that God's rest has an origin that predates even the time of Israel's exodus from Egypt, and therefore that God swore those Israelites wouldn't enter into it *even though it had long been available* or, perhaps, even though he'd been waiting a very long time to have human beings share it with him. For "*somewhere* he has spoken in this way," see the comments on 2:6. "Has spoken in this way" alludes to the present record of his speaking in Scripture (compare 1:5–14). God's "works" in "his founding of the world" lead to a contrast with "rest[ing] on the seventh day from all his works," and the reference to rest leads back to his oath that the wilderness generation wouldn't enter his rest. This correlation implies that God is still resting from his works of creation. So "the seventh day" has lasted a long time and makes "my rest" not only the rest that God has promised to his faithful people, but also the rest that he himself enjoys. He wants others to share his enjoyment of it. So it can't be identified with the land of Canaan.

4:6–8: Therefore, since it remains for some to enter into it [God's rest]**, and those who formerly had good news proclaimed** [to them] **didn't enter** [into it] **because of disobedience,** [7]**he marks out a certain day**—[that is,] **"Today"**—**by saying in David after so long a time, just as it has been said before, "Today, if you hear his voice, you shouldn't harden your hearts** [Psalm 95:7–9]**."** [8]**For if Joshua had rested them** [= given the wilderness generation rest], **he** [God] **wouldn't have spoken about another** [day] **after these days** [of Joshua's time]. "Therefore" means "in view of God's swearing that the wilderness generation wouldn't enter his rest." "Since" introduces two observations as reasons to draw a conclusion: (1) God's rest remains for some others to enter into it; and (2) despite having had good news proclaimed to them, disobedience kept the wilderness generation from entering into God's rest. The word for disobedience connotes not being persuaded, which comes close to lack of faith (as in 4:2). The conclusion: God "marks out a certain day—[that is,] 'Today'—by saying in David after so long a time [a reference to the long interval between the wilderness generation and David] . . . ." David's "Today" postdates by centuries the exodus period, so that "it remains for some to enter into [God's rest]." Compare the comments on God's speaking "in a son" (1:1–2) for God's speaking "in David." "Just as it has been said before" refers back to previous quotations of Psalm 95:7–8 in Hebrews 3:7–8, 15. The author quotes it again for a reminder. Then he argues from Joshua's case. Joshua didn't lead the wilderness generation into rest. Of course not, for their carcasses had fallen in the wilderness (3:17). Joshua did lead the *next* generation of Israelites into Canaan. But to keep attention riveted on the wilderness generation as a frightful example of apostatizing, the author pays no attention to the next generation; and he avoids mentioning Canaan, as he has all along, because for him God's rest isn't located in Canaan. God isn't resting there. He's resting in heaven, as he has been since the founding of the world. To enter his rest, then, is to enter his heavenly rest at Jesus' second coming. So Canaan was only a pointer to God's already existent heavenly rest. It's another question whether to enter into God's rest Christians will go *to* heaven, or God will bring his rest *from* heaven to Christians on earth. Their awaiting Christ's second coming with salvation (9:28) and the reference in 2:5 to "the inhabited [earth] *that's about to come*" favor a heavenly origin for the rest rather than a heavenly destination for the Christians (compare Revelation 21:1–2).[3]

4:9–10: There remains, then, a Sabbath [rest] **for God's people.** [10]**For the person who has entered into his** [God's] **rest has also himself rested from his works as indeed God** [did] **from his own works.** Since David's "Today" shows that "rest" didn't come through Joshua on an earlier day, a rest remains for God's people. The author adds "Sabbath," which means "rest," for a link with God's resting on the seventh day, called the Sabbath, following the six days of creation (4:4). "God's people" covers both the ancient Israelites and contemporary Christians. According to 6:10; 10:24 Christians are still working. So entrance into God's rest and thereby resting from one's own works must lie in the future, and the past tense in "the person who has entered . . . has also himself rested" presents this future event in terms of a principle that's timelessly true. "*For* the person . . . has also himself rested" adds a reason for the use of "a Sabbath rest" in the preceding sentence. The switch from "God's people" in general to "the person who . . . also himself" brings the matter down to the level of individual responsibility. The parallel between God's good works of creation and the individual Christian's works favors the Christian's good works, performed after conversion (see 6:10; 10:24), rather than the "dead works," performed prior to conversion (6:1; 9:14). Entrance into God's rest in the hereafter will have the effect of resting from one's own (good) works, so that God's rest becomes the Christian's, too. "Also himself" (referring to the Christian) and "his own" (referring to God) tighten the parallel, and "as indeed" underlines it.

4:11–13: Therefore [since a Sabbath rest remains for God's people] **let's be diligent to enter into that rest lest anyone fall by way of the same example of disobedience.** [12]**For God's word** [is] **living and effective and sharper than every double-edged sword, and** [is] **piercing to the point of a division of the soul and of the spirit, and of joints and of marrow, and** [is] **judgmental of the heart's imaginations and thoughts.** [13]**And no creature is unapparent in his sight** [= out of sight to him]**, but all things** [are] **bare and exposed to the eyes of him with whom we have an account** [so that we'll have to give him an account of ourselves at the Last Judgment (compare 13:17)]. Entrance into God's rest requires diligence. Otherwise we'll "drift away" (2:1–4). "Lest anyone *fall* by way of the same example of disobedience" alludes back to the falling of the ancient Israelites' carcasses in the wilderness (3:17). See the comments on 4:6 for the connotation of "disobedience." "For" introduces a reason for diligence. "God's word" is what he has spoken in the prophets (1:1), in Jesus his Son (1:2), and in Scripture (1:5–14 [compare 4:2; 6:1; and especially 13:7]). The author says this

---

[3]Incidentally, the Greek text of Hebrews makes no distinction between the names of the Old Testament Joshua, who succeeded Moses, and Jesus of Nazareth. For "Jesus" is the Greek form of the Hebrew name "Joshua," and the author of Hebrews is writing in Greek. But he makes nothing of Jesus' and Joshua's having the same name. So to avoid confusing them with each other, English versions of the New Testament regularly use "Joshua" instead of "Jesus" for Moses' successor.

word is "living," as God is (3:12; 9:14; 10:31; 12:22), and thereby personifies it. The personification leads to the description "effective" since it's active with the very life of God. Earlier, his word appeared as good news (4:2, 6). But to stress the need for diligence, it appears now as judgmental, for which description the author uses a comparison to sharp, double-edged swords. But God's word is sharper in its judgments than any such sword, though like double-edged swords it has no dull edge, so that it cuts whether going or coming. The sharpness of God's word has to do with its laying bare, its exposing, the core of a human being, even his "heart's imaginations and thoughts" (the heart being conceived as the seat of intellect as well as emotion), so that we should recall the repeated admonitions not to harden our hearts (3:8, 15; 4:7). For no heart is so hard as to resist the cutting edges of God's judgmental word. And the straying, unbelieving heart of an apostate (3:10, 12) will surely feel those cutting edges. The author doesn't speak of the word's dividing *between* the soul and the spirit—rather, "*of the* soul and *of the* spirit." In other words, both the soul and the spirit represent the inmost core of a human being; and the author uses the two of them as synonyms to underscore the penetrating power of God's word. Similarly, the word doesn't divide *between* joints and marrow. It divides a joint, so to speak, as a sword divides a joint if it happens to strike at the juncture between two bones; and if it strikes elsewhere it cuts into the bone as far as the marrow. Like soul and spirit, but figuratively, joints and marrow stand for the core of a human being; and the piercing stands for exposure of inward reality as differentiated from outward appearances. The doubling of these expressions and others ("living and effective," "the heart's imaginations and thoughts," "no creature is unapparent . . . but all things [are] bare . . . ," "bare and exposed") puts enormous emphasis on God's word as judgmentally discerning. The word translated "account" is the same as the one translated "word." It carries different meanings in accordance with its contexts. But the author is playing on these two meanings, as though to say that at the Last Judgment we'll have to say a word (that is, give an account) about our obedience or disobedience to the word (that is, what God has said).

THE SUPERIORITY OF JESUS AS HIGH PRIEST TO AARON AND HIS DESCENDANTS AS HIGH PRIESTS, WITH WARNINGS NOT TO APOSTATIZE
Hebrews 4:14–10:39

This extensive section of Hebrews presents Jesus' human sympathy and divine appointment to high priesthood (4:14–5:14); an exhortation to maturity, with a warning against apostasy (6:1–20); an explanation of the patterning of Jesus as high priest after Melchizedek (7:1–10); the inferiority of the Levitical priesthood (7:11–28); the heavenly realities of Jesus' high priestly ministry (8:1–10:18); and a warning against apostasy (10:19–39).

JESUS' HUMAN SYMPATHY AND DIVINE APPOINTMENT TO HIGH PRIESTHOOD
Hebrews 4:14–5:14

4:14–16: Having therefore a great high priest who has gone through the heavens—[namely,] **Jesus the Son of God**—**let's be keeping a grip on** [our] **confession.** [15]**For we don't have a high priest who can't sympathize with our weaknesses, but one who has been tested in accordance with all things** [= in all respects] **in accordance with the likeness** [of our tests (= just as we're tested)]—**apart from sin** [in the sense that he didn't sin when tested]. [16]**Therefore let's be coming with confidence to the throne of grace in order that we may receive mercy and find grace for well-timed help** [= mercy and favor that will help us when we need help, that is, during our tests]. The first "therefore" bases the exhortation to "be keeping a grip on [our] confession" on the judgmental word of God, every creature's exposure to his sight, and our accountability to God (4:12–13). See 3:1; 11:13; 13:15 for confession as a declaration. Here, a confession of Jesus as the Son of God brings exposure to persecution and therefore the need for an exhortation to keep a grip on the confession. Having Jesus as our high priest picks up this portrayal of him in 2:17–3:1 for further support of the exhortation to be keeping a grip. Several additions enhance the earlier portrayal so as to reinforce this further support of the exhortation: (1) the addition of "great" to "high priest"; (2) the further addition of "who has gone through the heavens"; and (3) the addition of "the Son of God" to "Jesus." These additions also prepare for a discussion of Jesus as a high priest superior to Aaron, Moses' brother and the original Jewish high priest, and superior to Aaron's high priestly descendants. The greatness of Jesus as a high priest matches God as "the Greatness in the heights" (1:3). In other words, Jesus shares his Father's greatness because he shares his Father's deity (compare God's calling his Son "God" in 1:8). And by calling Jesus "a great high priest who has gone through the heavens" the author sets him over against Caesar, whose Latin title *Pontifex maximus* meant "the greatest high priest" (in the imperial religion). Caesar hadn't gone through the heavens! "Who has gone through the heavens" tells how Jesus came to sit down "at the right [hand] of the Greatness in the heights" (1:3 [compare 1:8, 13; 2:9]). "*Through the* heavens" implies a plurality of heavens between earth and the heaven of God's throne (compare our distinction between the sky near earth and "outer space"). "The Son of God" harks back to 1:2, 5, 8; 3:6. For "keeping a grip on [our] confession," see the comments on 3:1.

Out of the earlier description of Jesus as "a merciful and faithful high priest . . . . in that he himself has suffered by being tested" (2:17–18), the author infers that "we don't have a high priest that can't sympathize with our weaknesses." "But one who has been tested" confirms this inference from the earlier passage. Jesus' sympathy gives still more reason to be keeping a grip despite "our weaknesses," that is, despite the tendencies we have to loosen our grip because of the persecutions that test us. His sympathy will help us keep holding tight—if we keep in mind his sympathy (compare 12:1–4). He underwent a comprehensive test like ours that now enables him to sympathize. The juxtaposition of two synonymous phrases, each introduced by "in accordance with," spotlights this basis for his sympathy. "Apart from sin" preserves Jesus' sinlessness in that the test didn't lead him to fail through sinning. (Every test carries a temptation to sin.) Most translations insert "yet" before "apart from [or 'without'] sin." But the author adds the phrase without a connective, so that its abruptness is emphatic. Despite Jesus' being tested comprehensively, he didn't sin! "Apart from sin" also tells Christians that like Jesus they can pass their tests by not sinning. A second "therefore" bases the exhortation to "approach the throne of grace" on Jesus' ability to "sympathize with our weaknesses." "With confidence" connotes boldness of speech in asking for help (compare the comments on 3:6). Since a high priest represents God's people to God, "the throne of grace" refers to God's throne (1:3; 8:1; 12:2), so that our confidence lies in Jesus the great high priest's representing us successfully before God. "Of grace" describes the throne as a place where God's ill-deserved favor is to be found and his mercy received. The figure of a throne implies authority to dispense mercy and grace. With approaching God, compare 10:21–22; 11:6; 12:22–24 and possibly 13:13. Here, the approach contrasts with "stray[ing] at heart" and "apostatizing from the living God" (3:10, 12), has the purpose of praying to him through Christ for grace and mercy (compare 7:25; 13:15, 18 and, for Christ's setting an example of prayer, 5:7), and gives Christians marginalized on earth (13:12–13) assurance of heavenly hospitality.

5:1–3: For every high priest, when being taken from among human beings, is constituted [a high priest] **in behalf of human beings concerning things** [having to do] **with God,** [in other words,] **that he** [the high priest] **may offer** [to God] **both gifts and sacrifices for sins,** [the high priest] **being able to deal moderately with those who are ignorant and straying, since he himself too is encompassed in respect to weakness** [that is, since moral weakness limits him as it does his fellow human beings] [3]**and because of it he's obligated to make sin offerings, just as for the people, thus too for himself** [Leviticus 4:3–12; 9:7–14; 16:6–14]. The initial "For" makes the following an explanation of how it is we can receive helpful "mercy and grace" if we "approach with boldness the throne of grace" (4:16). Since a high priest has to represent human beings to God, the high priest must himself be a human being. The balance between "*from among* human beings" and "*in behalf of* human beings" highlights this representation of human beings by a fellow human being. "Is constituted [a high priest]" prepares for a later mention of divine appointment to high priesthood (5:4). "That he [the high priest] may offer [to God] both gifts and sacrifices for sins" not only explains what it means to act priestly "in behalf of human beings." It also recalls and explains how it was

that God's Son "accomplish[ed] the cleansing of sins" (1:3) and "mad[e] an expiation for the people's sins" (2:17). Our author will later develop this explanation in detail. "*Both* gifts *and* sacrifices" typifies the author's pairing of synonyms for emphasis.

A high priest's moral weakness, because of which he lapses into sinning as do the people he represents, enables him "to deal moderately" with them rather than angrily. The tacking of "himself too" onto "he" accents the high priest's sharing their moral weakness. But "apart from sin" in 4:15 has already differentiated Jesus as a high priest from the sinning high priests that the author is now talking about. And whereas they "deal moderately" with sinners because of their own sins, Jesus deals sympathetically with sinners out of sheer grace. "Those who are ignorant and straying," which refers to sinners, is often interpreted in terms of unintentional, unwitting sins (Leviticus 4:2, 13, 22, 27; 5:15, 18; 22:14; Numbers 15:24, 27–29; Ezekiel 45:20) as distinguished from intentional, willful sins, those committed "with a high hand" (Numbers 15:30–31). But "those who are ignorant and straying" echoes 3:9–10, where straying and ignorance occurred as synonyms for the sinning of Israelites *who had seen the Holy Spirit's works in the wilderness for forty years*, so that they sinned willfully and intentionally and paid the price of not entering God's rest. In 5:2, then, "ignorant" doesn't have the sense of "uninformed"—rather, of deliberately ignoring God's "paths" and thus willfully straying from them (see the comments on 3:10 for this figurative language). The "sin offerings" that a high priest was obligated to make for the people and for himself were a class of offerings sacrificed for the atonement of sins (Leviticus 6:24–30).

5:4–6: And no one takes the honor [of high priesthood] **on his own; rather,** [he takes it] **when being called by God, just as indeed even Aaron** [did]. [5]**Thus even the Christ didn't glorify himself so as to become a high priest; rather,** [the one who glorified him thus is] **the one who said to him, "You're my Son; today I've fathered you** [Psalm 2:7, quoted earlier in Hebrews 1:5]," [6]**just as also he says in a different** [passage], **"You** [are] **a priest forever in alignment with Mechizedek** [Psalm 110:4]" . . . . In pagan religion men often took the honor of priesthood by purchasing the office, and in the New Testament period Jewish high priests were political appointees. But the author of Hebrews is referring to the Mosaic law when writing that "no one takes the honor on his own" and then citing as an example Aaron, the first Jewish high priest (Exodus 28:1). "Indeed even Aaron" stresses that despite Aaron's being Moses' elder brother, he needed God's call to become a high priest. "Honor" and "glorify" suit "being called by God . . . . to become a *high* priest"; and use of the title, "the Christ," suits the office of a high priest in that high priests were anointed (Exodus 28:41; 29:7, 29; 30:22–33; 40:13, 15; Leviticus 8:12, 30) and "the Christ" means "the Anointed One." The use of "the one who said to him" where we might have expected "God said to him" keeps the focus on "the Christ" but in the following quotation adds divine sonship to high priesthood. Neither Aaron nor his successors had that relation to God (compare the superiority of Jesus as God's Son to angels [1:5] and to Moses [3:5–6]), but at this point the author is using the Christ's divine sonship as a setup for "learn[ing] obedience" as a son (5:8). The next quotation, that of Psalm 110:4, shows that God called the Christ to become a high priest just as he'd called Aaron and his successors. But "forever" suits the eternality of the Christ as God's Son (compare 1:8), and "in alignment with Melchizedek" differentiates the Christ's eternal priesthood from the priesthood of Aaron and his successors. Later again, the author will elaborate this difference.

5:7–8: who [referring to "the Christ" of 5:5] **in his days of flesh—when he'd offered both requests and entreaties, along with a loud cry and tears, to him who was able to save him out from death and** [when] **he'd been heeded because of his piety—**[8]**even though being a son, learned obedience from the things that he suffered.** "His days of flesh" refers to the Christ's earthly lifetime. Resurrection revived him bodily, of course; but "of flesh" connotes mortality (see 2:14 with comments). The pairing of "entreaties" with "requests," emphasized by "both . . . and," and the pairing of "tears" with "a loud cry" imply intensity in the sufferings by which the Christ "learned obedience." The plural of "requests" and "entreaties" points up even further the implied intensity by indicating multiple pleas. "Though being a son" implies that ordinarily a son doesn't have to suffer so intensely in the learning of obedience. The similarity in sound between the Greek words *emathen* ("he learned") and *epathen* ("he suffered") underscores the correlation between suffering and learning. "He learned obedience from the things he suffered" in the sense that suffering taught him experientially what it means, what it entails, to obey God's will as a human being (see 10:4–10). The pious learning and the pious obedience contrast, respectively, with the sinful ignorance and the sinful straying of those whom he represents as a priest (3:10; 5:2). But for what did he plead loudly and tearfully? We think naturally of the accounts of Jesus' praying in Gethsemane (Mark 14:32–42; Matthew 26:36–46; Luke 22:34–46). There he prayed that if possible his Father might exempt him from death. Here the description of his Father as "him who was able to save him *out from* death" combines with the "heed[ing]" of his pleas, which indicates a granting of them, to make a different point: The Christ pleaded that God would resurrect him, and because of the Christ's piety in suffering obediently to God's will, God did "save him out from death" by "bring[ing him] out from among the dead" (13:20 [compare 11:19, 35]).

5:9–11: And having been matured, he became for all who are obeying him the determinant of eternal salvation, [10]**having been designated by God a high priest in alignment with Melchizedek,** [11]**about whom** [referring to Melchizedek] **we** [have] **a considerable word to speak** [= much to say] **and hard to explain, since you've become sluggish so far as** [your] **ears are**

concerned. "Having been matured" prepares for a contrast between maturity and infancy in 5:13–14 and interprets Jesus' having "learned obedience from the things he suffered." Through that experience he grew up, so to speak. "Having been designated by God a high priest" balances "having been matured" by showing the immediate outcome of his maturation. But emphasis falls on the ultimate outcome: his becoming "the determinant of eternal salvation" for "all who are obeying him." "*Eternal* salvation" means deliverance out from death into eternal life as a result of God's heeding Jesus' pleas "to save him out from death." "The determinant" of such salvation makes Jesus its causative basis, whereas "obeying him" is the condition that has to be met for capitalizing on the consequent availability of eternal salvation. This obedience corresponds to Jesus' obedience to the extent of "tast[ing] death on behalf of everyone" (2:9) and contrasts with the disobedience of those Israelites who came out of Egypt but apostatized in the wilderness (3:7–4:3). The contrast defines obedience as persevering, not drifting away, holding tight the beginning of our assurance, being diligent, keeping a grip on our confession (2:1; 3:12, 14; 4:11, 14). "For *all* who are obeying him" gives assurance, however, that none who do persevere will come too late for entrance into God's rest of eternal salvation (contrast 4:1). See the comments on 5:6 for the phrase "in alignment with Melchizedek." The author warns that he has a lot to say about Melchizedek and that it's "hard to explain" because the audience have lazy ears, quickly tired to the point of boredom and nonlistening. Together, the warning and the description challenge the audience to prove the author wrong. Later, as a matter of fact, he'll go into a long and difficult explanation of Melchizedek (chapter 7). So in effect the author is saying, "As I shamed you in what I've just said, shame me in return by listening avidly and understandingly." "About whom *we* [have] a considerable word to speak" draws the audience into what the author has to say about Melchizedek and thus backhandedly invites them to prove the author wrong.

The invitation continues in *5:12–14:* **For even though you ought to be teachers because of the time** [that has elapsed since your conversions], **you have a need that someone be teaching you again the initial elements of God's oracles, not** [feeding you] **solid food.** [13]**For everyone who partakes of milk** [is] **untested by the word** [= message] **of righteousness, for he's an infant.** [14]**But solid food is for mature** [people], **ones who because of habit have organs of sense exercised for the discerning of both good and evil.** "For" introduces an explanation of the effect that the sluggishness of the audience's ears has had on the audience. By now they should have matured to the point of teaching others. Instead, they need to be taught—not advanced information, either; rather, the ABCs of the gospel, "the initial elements of God's oracles." Since "oracles" means *short* pronouncements of a deity, the author is building on his preceding description of the audience as incapable of tolerating and understanding a long discussion of Melchizedek. "A need that someone be teaching you *again*" implies they've forgotten those ABCs, which the author will remind them of in 6:1–2. He compares the ABCs to milk and therefore compares the audience now, not just to children in an elementary school, but to suckling infants incapable of eating solid food. Will they get mad enough at him to prove him wrong? Solid food would consist of "the word of righteousness," that is, advanced information about Melchizedek, whose very name—as will be noted in 7:2—means in Hebrew "king of righteousness." All Christians who are milk-drinking infants, so to speak, are "untested" by the solid food of advanced information because given their infancy, nobody has even dared to test their ability to feed on such advanced fare (compare 1 Corinthians 3:1–2). "But solid food is for mature [people]" sets out for the audience a possibility to which, in view of the author's shaming them, he hopes they'll aspire (compare 1 Corinthians 14:20). Then he describes mature Christians in terms of athletic exercise. They exercise their moral sensibilities the way athletes exercise their physical bodies (compare 1 Corinthians 9:24–27). Practice makes perfect, so that distinguishing between good and evil becomes a "habit." Given what the author has already said and will yet say, he has in mind particularly the good of perseverance and the evil of apostasy. To discern that *perseverance* is good is to *practice* it. To discern that *apostasy* is evil is to *avoid* it.

AN EXHORTATION TO MATURITY, WITH A WARNING AGAINST APOSTASY
Hebrews 6:1–20

6:1–3: Therefore [because you're like infants and need to mature] **leaving the Christ's initial word** [= the ABCs of the gospel, called in 5:12 "the initial elements of God's oracles" (compare God's having spoken "in a son" according to 1:1–2 and such a great salvation's "having gotten its start by being spoken through the Lord" according to 2:3)], **let us allow ourselves to be carried on to maturity, not laying again the foundation consisting in repentance from dead works and in faith toward God,** [2]**in teaching about baptisms and laying on of hands, and** [in teaching] **about the resurrection of dead** [people] **and eternal judgment.** [3]**And we'll do this, if in fact God permits.** "Leaving" doesn't mean "abandoning." It means "advancing beyond." See the comments on 3:14 and especially on 5:5 for "the Christ." Since the author has compared his audience to infants (5:11–14) and since infants need to be carried, he exhorts, "let us allow ourselves to be carried on to maturity." To soften the sarcasm he includes himself with "us" and "ourselves," as though he too were an infant (compare the comments on 5:11). Who is to do the carrying doesn't make an appearance. The author is concerned only with the need for maturity so that he can feed his audience with the solid food of extensive, hard-to-understand teaching about Melchizedek.

The figure then changes from infants to builders. "Not laying *again* the foundation" indicates that the au-

thor and his audience have already laid the foundation. They laid it at their conversions. But by listing its elements the author teaches the audience again what those elements are, just as 5:12 indicated the audience need to be retaught "the initial elements of God's oracles." So the foundation consists in the ABCs of the gospel in terms especially appropriate to Jewish Christians. "Repentance from dead works" means the renunciation of misdeeds that for our salvation required the death of Christ (see 9:14 in the context of 9:11–28). Complementing such repentance is "faith toward God," which means belief in and faithfulness to God as the one who has spoken to us in his Son (see especially 10:19–25, 36–39; 12:2; 13:7–8 with 1:1–2). "Teaching about baptisms" probably refers to teaching about baptism in Jesus' name as distinguished from John the Baptist's "baptism of repentance" (see Acts 18:24–19:5). "Laying on of hands" often accompanied Christian baptism for reception of the Holy Spirit (see Acts 8:17–19; 9:12, 17; 19:6). According to the gospel, "the resurrection of dead [people]" grows out of Christ's resurrection (compare 13:20) and issues in their "eternal judgment," that is, in a judgmental sentence that has an eternal consequence for good or for ill (9:27; 12:23 [compare "eternal salvation" in 5:9; "eternal redemption" in 9:12; "eternal inheritance" in 9:15; "eternal covenant" in 13:20; and condemnatory judging in 10:27, 30; 13:4)].

"And we'll do this" means "we'll allow ourselves to be carried on to maturity." Again the author includes himself to soften the sarcasm of his allusion to infants' having to be carried. Immediately, though, he waves a flag of warning: "if in fact God permits." God might not permit us to let ourselves be carried on to maturity. Our infancy could be a form of apostasy that makes it too late for us to enter into his rest (4:1). Time to get scared and hope for permission! "If *in fact*" stresses the danger of *non*permission.

6:4–6: For [it's] **impossible in the case of those who've once been enlightened and tasted the heavenly gift and become partakers of the Holy Spirit** [5]**and tasted God's word as good and the miracles of the age that's about to come** [6]**and have fallen by the wayside**—[it's impossible] **to renew** [them] **again with the result of repentance** [= so that they repent anew], **since they're recrucifying God's Son for themselves and making a spectacle** [of him as shamefully recrucified]. The author uses a series of phrases to underscore what it means for people to have been converted. "Enlightened" means "wised up to the truth of the gospel" (see 10:26). "The heavenly gift" is the "heavenly calling" put in terms of a gift that comes from heaven (see 3:1 with comments). To have "tasted" the gift means to have accepted it, as though it were a delicious morsel of food, just as when Jesus "tasted death" he accepted it, but as though it were bitter poison (2:9). (In neither case is there any thought of less than full ingestion.) The laying on of hands in 6:2 alluded to reception of the Holy Spirit. The heavenly gift equates with the heavenly calling of 3:1. And 3:1 spoke of "*partakers* of a heavenly calling."

So now the author speaks about having become "*partakers* of the Holy Spirit," as though the Holy Spirit is food or drink to be ingested (compare 1 Corinthians 12:13). Back to the figure of tasting, then. The tasting of "God's word" refers to the acceptance of what he has spoken in a son (1:1–2) as confirmed by earwitnesses (2:3). "As good" refers explicitly to the deliciousness of this word and emphasizes acceptance of it precisely because it's delicious in its promise of salvation. The author associated "word" and "power" in 1:3, and in 2:4 associated "miracles" (literally, "powers" [= powerful acts]) with "the Holy Spirit." So now he adds "miracles" as another object of taste, as though they too were food ingested by faith at conversion because they helped confirm the testimony of earwitnesses to what had "gotten its start by being spoken through the Lord" (2:3–4). "Of the age that's about to come [= the future eternity]" describes the miracles as a foretaste of final confirmation, when by God's power Christians who've persevered will enter God's rest at last and forever.

"Who've *once* been enlightened [and so on]" doesn't simply mean they were enlightened once upon a time. It means more fully that enlightenment was a one-time event, not to be repeated, as then comes out in the statement that "[it's] impossible . . . to renew [them] again with the result of repentance." The redundancy of "*re*new [them] *again*" stresses the impossibility of a second conversion for an apostate: a frightening reason not to apostatize but to allow ourselves to be carried on to maturity lest we do apostatize. "Have fallen by the wayside" describes apostates in a fashion that recalls those original apostates, the Israelites who came out of Egypt only to have their carcasses fall in the wilderness (3:17; 4:11). Just as those who rejected Jesus during "his days of flesh" (5:7) crucified him physically, apostates now recrucify him— but reputationally. "For themselves" draws an implicit parallel with the original crucifiers of Jesus, and "making a spectacle [of him]" defines the fashion in which apostates recrucify him and alludes both to crucifixion as the most shameful way to die and to the practice of locating crucifixions beside thoroughfares to maximize the shame. By apostatizing you're saying to the whole wide world that in your opinion Jesus deserved crucifixion as a pretender. To bring out this point the author uses "God's Son," plus a wordplay in saying that it's impossible to "*re*new" those who are "*re*crucifying" God's Son. And the lengthy description of what the apostates had experienced in conversion serves to heighten the horror of apostasy and thus the justice of nonrenewal.

6:7–8: For soil that has drunk the rain coming on it many times and [that] is bearing vegetation useful for those because of whom it [the soil] is also cultivated receives together with [them] favor from God. ⁸But if producing thorns and thistles, [it's] disapproved and close to a curse [compare Genesis 3:17–18], whose end [is] for burning [that is, the fate of such ground is to be burned]. The initial "For" introduces a metaphorical reason for the impossibility of renewing apostates again to repentance. A nonapostate is like soil. The rain

that comes many times throughout a season of growth is like the manifold blessings listed in 6:4–5 (enlightenment, the heavenly gift, and so on). The soil's drinking the rain is like accepting these blessings (compare the figure of drinking with the preceding figure of tasting). Bearing vegetation is like persevering rather than apostatizing. "Useful" describes vegetation as edible by "those because of whom it [the soil] is also cultivated." "Also" adds cultivation to rainfall. The soil receives favor from God together with the people because of whom the soil was cultivated. His favor comes on them in the form of edible vegetation. But how does his favor come on the soil? Not literally, for this soil receives no more rainfall than soil that produces thorns and thistles. The soil that bears edible vegetation receives favor from God only in its capacity of standing for Christians who persevere rather than apostatizing. His favor consists, then, in their eternal salvation. It follows obviously that soil which is producing thorns and thistles stands for apostates, that its being disapproved stands for God's not allowing a renewal of the apostates, that "close to a curse" stands for facing condemnation in the near future at the Last Judgment, and that "whose end [is] for burning" stands for the suffering of hellfire as a result of that condemnation.

Back in 6:4 the author shifted from "we" and "us" to "those who" in describing apostates. We see the reason for that shift in *6:9–12*: **But we're persuaded superior things about you, beloved, even things containing salvation, though we're also speaking in this way. ¹⁰For God [is] not unjust so as to forget your work, even the love that you've exhibited for his name by having served the saints and continuing to serve [them]. ¹¹But we long that each of you be exhibiting till the end the same diligence for the realization of [your] hope, ¹²lest you become sluggish, but [that you become] imitators of those who through faith and patience inherit the promises.** The author has been using "we" and "us" for himself and his audience. Now "you" stands for the audience over against "we." Who then are the "we"? It's usually thought that at least here, if not earlier too, the author is using an editorial "we" for himself alone. But more likely he's trying to rope the audience into thinking and feeling about themselves the way he does. For them to do so would forestall their apostasy and ensure their perseverance. The address "beloved" underlines his persuasion of "superior things" concerning them and also his longing that they persevere in those things. "Even things containing salvation" implies that the danger he has been warning against consists in damnation. "Though we're also speaking in this way" alludes to the necessity of warning them in addition to expressing his persuasion of "things containing to salvation." "For" then introduces a reason for the persuasion: it would be unjust of God to forget the evidence of their faith/faithfulness so long as they don't fall by the wayside. The evidence lies in their "work," which the author identifies as their love for God's "name," a love exhibited in their past and current service to fellow Christians. The author calls their fellow Christians "the saints" because

God has consecrated them for himself, so that they're associated with God's name—in other words, with who he is as "God." So serving the saints equates with loving God's name. It will come out in 10:32–34 that the audience have suffered persecution in the form of public ridicule, imprisonment, and loss of property. Serving the saints, then, consisted in exposing themselves to public ridicule by taking food to fellow Christians in prison (within which food wasn't provided) and giving board and room to fellow Christians who'd had their property taken from them. Such acts of service put their love for God's name on exhibit for all the world to see as well as for him to see (compare 13:1–3).

After citing this exhibit as evidence of the "superior things" that "contain salvation," the author returns to the need for perseverance, this time not in terms of a warning so much as in terms of his deep desire ("But we *long* . . ."). "That *each* of you . . ." leaves out no one. The author doesn't want to see a single apostate down the road. He wants the past and current exhibitions of the work of love to continue "till the end," when Christ returns (9:28). Such continuance will require "the same diligence" they've already exhibited and are still exhibiting (contrast the carelessness warned against in 2:1–4), and at the end such diligence will issue in "the realization of [their] hope." Their confidence of entering God's rest won't be disappointed. "Lest you become sluggish" injects a note of warning and seems at first to contradict the statement in 5:11, "you've become sluggish." But that statement was qualified by the added phrase, "so far as [your] ears are concerned," and therefore referred to their inability to be taught advanced doctrine (about Melchizedek) before being retaught the ABCs of the gospel. Here, on the other hand, sluggishness would mean slacking off from charitable service to persecuted fellow Christians, perhaps in part to avoid exposing *themselves* to persecution. The author doesn't identify in particular "those who through faith and patience inherit the promises." So the accent falls on imitating their faith and patience, whoever they are. The promises consist primarily in a repeated promise of entering God's rest, which will make for an eternal inheritance (see especially 4:1; 9:15). That entrance hasn't yet taken place. So "those who . . . inherit the promises" aren't inheriting them now. They're on their way to inheriting them by now exercising "faith and patience." The pairing of "patience" with "faith" gives faith the sense of faithfulness, belief that doesn't collapse when tested. "Patience" produces perseverance till the end, the second coming.

6:13–15: For when God made a promise to Abraham, since he had no one greater to swear by, he swore by himself [compare Genesis 22:16], [14]**saying, "Unequivocally, by favoring** [you] **I'll favor you; and by multiplying** [you] **I'll multiply you** [Genesis 22:17]." [15]**And by being patient, in this way he** [Abraham] **attained to the promise.** "For" introduces two reasons why the author has just exhorted his audience to diligence for the inheriting of God's promises: (1) the certainty of God's keeping the promises, as illustrated in Abraham's

life, and (2) the patience required for the attainment of God's promises, as illustrated again in Abraham's life. God promised to favor Abraham by multiplying him through many descendants; and God did, as was more than abundantly evident by New Testament times. But "by being patient" Abraham "attained to the promise" already in his own lifetime. His patience showed itself during the sixty years that intervened between the birth of his son Isaac, which merely *duplicated* Abraham (so to speak), and the birth of Abraham's grandsons Jacob and Esau, which started the *multiplication* of Abraham (Genesis 25:26). God's swearing by himself, than whom none is greater, emphasizes the certainty of his promise-keeping. Further emphasis accrues to this certainty from elements within the oath: (1) "Unequivocally"; (2) the doubling in "by *favoring* [you] I'll *favor* you"; and (3–4) the addition of and further doubling in "by *multiplying* [you] I'll *multiply* you." Emphasis accrues to Abraham's "being patient" by the addition of "in this way," which refers back to it. The promise to favor and multiply Abraham previews the promise of entering God's rest. Abraham's patience previews the patience required of Christians till Jesus returns. And Abraham's attaining to God's promise to him previews Christians' attaining to God's rest if they're patient.

6:16–20: For human beings swear by someone greater [literally, "against the greater one," so that the oath-taker is inviting the deity in whose name the oath is taken to make war on him if he doesn't make good on his oath]; **and for them an oath for the purpose of confirmation** [is] **the termination of every dispute,** [17]**by which** [oath of his] **God, wanting to exhibit all the more to the heirs of** [his] **promise the immutability of his will, intervened with an oath** [18]**in order that through two immutable acts, in which** [it's] **impossible for God to lie, we who've fled** [to him] **for refuge might have strong encouragement to seize the hope lying ahead** [of us], [19]**which** [hope] **we have as an anchor, both secure and firm, for the soul and** [as an anchor] **that enters farther in than the curtain,** [20]**where Jesus as a forerunner has entered in our behalf by having become a high priest forever in alignment with Melchizedek.** The author is using the illustration of Abraham as a segue into the discussion of Melchizedek that follows in chapter 7. For Melchizedek first appears in the story of Abraham (see 7:1–2 with Genesis 14:18–20). "For" introduces the present paragraph as an explanation of God's swearing a promise to Abraham. The explanation draws an analogy with the purpose and result of human beings' swearing an oath. The purpose is the confirmation of a promise. The result is "the termination of every dispute." God swore an oath to confirm his promise so that Abraham wouldn't dispute the certainty of God's keeping it. But the author discreetly drops his earlier reference to the promise God swore to Abraham, because he shifts now to God's promise of eternal salvation to people of persevering faith (7:25) and emphasizes the certainty that God will keep this promise just as he kept the one made to Abraham.

Several features of the text underline this certainty: (1) God's "wanting to exhibit *all the more* [than human beings do] . . . the immutability of his will [to keep the promise]"; (2) his "interven[ing] with an oath," so that the oath sworn to Abraham counts by extension for the promise of eternal salvation made to us; (3) the distinguishing of "two immutable acts," that is, the promising and the swearing of a supportive oath; (4) the observation that given these two immutable acts it's "impossible for God to lie"; (5) the resultant "encouragement to seize the hope lying ahead [of us]"; (6) the description of this encouragement as "strong"; (7) the comparison of the hope to an anchor; and (8) the description of the anchor as both "secure" and "firm" and as one that "enters . . . where Jesus . . . has entered," so that the hope is a well-founded expectation.

The description of us as "we who've fled [to God] for refuge" refers to conversion for the purpose of escaping eternal damnation, and "to seize the hope *lying ahead* [of us]" refers to the final attainment of eternal salvation. More particularly, "seize" points to the end result of holding tight to our confession. The anchor, representing hope, is "for the soul"—the self, but with emphasis on interiority, where confident hope resides—and the anchor is "firm" because God's oath "con*firm*[ed]" his promise. By saying that the anchor "enters farther in than the curtain," the author personifies the anchor so as to indicate that our hope follows Jesus, it's object, all the way into the heavenly Holy of Holies, where God himself dwells. In the earthly Jewish sanctuary a curtain divided the Holy of Holies from the outer room, called simply the Holy Place. The Jewish high priest entered the Holy of Holies with sacrificial blood in behalf of God's people once a year, on the Day of Atonement. As "a high priest forever in alignment with Melchizedek," Jesus "has entered for us [who are now God's people]." "As a forerunner" doesn't imply that we'll follow him there. It means that he has gone there "in our behalf" (compare the comments on 5:1). And so the author has prepared the ground for a full discussion of Christ's Mechizedek-like priesthood.

AN EXPLANATION OF THE ALIGNMENT OF JESUS AS HIGH PRIEST WITH MELCHIZEDEK
Hebrews 7:1–10

This section begins with a sentence in which the subject ("this Mechizedek") appears immediately, but the verb ("remains") appears only after a lengthy series of descriptions of the subject. **7:1–3: For this Mechizedek—king of Salem, priest of God Most High, who** [referring to Melchizedek] **met Abraham as he** [Abraham] **was returning from the slaughter of the kings and who blessed him,** **²to whom also Abraham apportioned a tenth of all** [the spoils of battle], **on the one hand** [his name] **first being translated "king of righteousness," then also on the other hand** [being] **king of Salem, which is** [= means] **"king of peace," ³fatherless, motherless, genealogyless, having neither a beginning of days nor an end of life but being like God's Son—re-**

mains a priest perpetually. "For this Melchizedek . . . remains a priest *perpetually*" brings out the parallel in Jesus' having become a high priest *forever* in alignment with Melchizedek" (6:20). "King of Salem" and "priest of God Most High" come from Genesis 14:18 as designations of Melchizedek. "The slaughter of the kings" refers to Abraham's defeating with his private army some kings who'd plundered Sodom and Gomorrah and taken captive Abraham's nephew Lot, a resident of Sodom (Genesis 14:1–16). Melchizedek blessed Abraham—that is, in view of his victory pronounced him favored by God—when Abraham was returning with the spoils of battle; and Abraham in turn gave Melchizedek a tenth of those spoils (Genesis 14:17–20). "Of *all* [the spoils of battle]" underscores Abraham's deference toward him.

The author then translates the Hebrew name "Melchizedek" as meaning "king of righteousness" (= "righteous king"). Since Jesus is a high priest in alignment with Melchizedek, "king" suits Jesus' enthronement and coronation according to 1:3, 8, 13; 2:9; and "of righteousness" suits Jesus' having "loved righteousness and hated lawlessness" (1:9). "Salem," a short form of "Jerusalem," relates to *shalōm*, Hebrew for "peace," so that "king of Salem" means "king of peace" (= "peaceful king"). Jesus' enthronement and coronation are recalled again, then; and "peace" associates him anticipatively with "the God of peace" in 13:20 and, because peace connotes all the benefits of salvation, makes Jesus "the founding leader of [our] salvation" and "the determinant of eternal salvation" (2:10; 5:9). "On the one hand first . . . then also on the other hand" highlights this twofold theological interpretation of Melchizedek's name and title. "Priest of God Most High" presents him in a capacity that makes Jesus' alignment with him a *priestly* alignment. "Fatherless" and "motherless" aren't to be understood biologically—rather, as indicating that the Old Testament *identifies* neither his father nor his mother; hence, "genealogyless." Similarly, "having neither a beginning of days nor an end of life" means that the Old Testament records neither his birth nor his death and therefore portrays him symbolically as a perpetual priest. He's like God's Son, so to speak, who "at the beginning . . . founded the earth," who "will last throughout," and whose "years won't run out" (1:10–12).

7:4–5: And be observing how great [is] **this** [Melchizedek], **to whom Abraham the patriarch gave a tithe** [= a tenth] **out of the battle spoils, the choicest ones** [literally, "the top spoils of the heap"]. **⁵And on the one hand those out of the sons of Levi** [= members of the Israelite tribe descended from Levi, one of Jacob's twelve sons] **who receive the priesthood have a commandment to collect from the people—that is, from their brothers** [= fellow Israelites]—**a tithe** [out of all the agricultural produce] **in accordance with the Law** [Numbers 18:21; 2 Chronicles 31:4–5], **even though they** ["their brothers"] **have come out of Abraham's loins** [the location of his reproductive organs]. The symbolism that the author finds in the Old Testament portrayal of Melchizedek is getting "hard to explain" (5:11). So the author commands his audience to "be observing how great [was] this Melchizedek." The command itself and "*how* great" heighten the greatness of Melchizedek in that it calls for observation. Illustrating his greatness is Abraham's giving him "a tithe out of the battle spoils" (compare Jesus' greatness according to 4:14; 10:21; 13:20). By describing Abraham as "the patriarch" and the battle spoils as "the choicest ones," the author enhances the illustration. "Those out of the sons of Levi who receive the priesthood" are Aaron and his male descendants within the tribe of Levi. Their having a commandment in the Law to collect tithes from their fellow Israelites indicates superiority to them despite those Israelites' sharing Abrahamic ancestry with the Levitical priests. Mention of this superiority sets the stage for a superior superiority, though. (Nonpriestly Levites collected tithes as did priests, but the author's interest in Jesus' priesthood leads him to deal only with the priests.)

7:6–10: On the other hand, the one who doesn't have a genealogy traced from them has collected a tithe from Abraham and blessed the one who had the promises [= Abraham (see Genesis 14:19)]. **⁷And without any contradiction the inferior entity is blessed by the superior entity. ⁸And here, on the one hand, dying human beings receive tithes** [not while they're dying, but despite their coming deaths]. **There, on the other hand, being testified that he lives,** [Melchizedek received a tithe]. **⁹And, so to speak, through Abraham even Levi** [representing the priests]**, the one who receives tithes** [from other Israelites]**, has paid a tithe** [to Melchizedek]**. ¹⁰For he** [Levi] **was still in the loins of** [his] [fore]**father** [Abraham] **when Melchizedek met him.** "On the other hand" in 7:6 sets Melchizedek over against the Levitical priests in 7:5. "Who doesn't have a genealogy traced from them" means that the Old Testament doesn't put him in the priestly line starting with Aaron and his sons. Obviously not, because Melchizedek was living as a contemporary of Abraham hundreds of years prior to the lifetimes of Aaron and his sons! Nevertheless, Melchizedek collected a tithe from Abraham just as Abraham's priestly descendants were commanded in the Law to collect tithes from Abraham's nonpriestly descendants through Isaac and Jacob. "*Has* collected . . . and blessed" is spoken from the standpoint of the extant scriptural record concerning Melchizedek. So he ranks superior in rank to tithe-paying Abraham even though Abraham forefathered the Levitical priests, who ranked superior to other Israelites, and even though Abraham "had the promises [about which see 6:13–15; 11:8–19]." To confirm this hierarchical superiority of Melchizedek to Abraham in blessing Abraham, the author states that "the inferior entity is blessed by the superior entity." To accent inferiority versus superiority, the author doesn't say that "the inferior *person* is blessed by the superior *person*." He speaks rather of entities to focus on the *qualities* of hierarchical inferiority (in the case of Abraham) and hierarchical superiority (in the case of Melchizedek). "Without any contradiction" makes the confirmation of Melchizedek's superiority absolute.

There's also a point of temporal superiority. Though receiving tithes shows the superiority of Levitical priests to their fellow Israelites, these priests die. The author calls them "human beings" for a contrast with the living God. Because the Scripture doesn't say that Melchizedek died, though, it testifies to his symbolically ongoing life. "Here, on the one hand . . . . There, on the other hand" highlights the contrast between dying and living forever. And yet another element in Melchizedek's superiority: the Levitical priests who receive tithes from their fellow Israelites paid a tithe to Melchizedek through the agency of their forefather Abraham. "So to speak" alerts us to the prospective nature of Abraham's acting as an ancestral proxy for the Levitical priests long before their lifetimes. "*Even* Levi" stresses the Levitical priests' acknowledgment through Abraham of Melchizedek's superiority to them.

THE INFERIORITY OF THE LEVITICAL PRIESTHOOD
Hebrews 7:11–28

7:11–14: So if in fact completion had been through the Levitical priesthood (for the people [of Israel] **have been legislated** [as recorded in Scripture] **on the basis of it** [the Levitical priesthood]**), what need** [would there] **still** [have been] **for another priest to stand up in alignment with Melchizedek and not be designated in alignment with Aaron? ¹²For when the priesthood is changed, out of necessity a change also of the Law takes place. ¹³For the one about whom these things are said has partaken of** [= belongs to] **a different tribe** [from that of Levi]**, from which** [different tribe] **no one has done duty at the altar. ¹⁴For** [it's] **very clear that our Lord has arisen out of Judah, in reference to which tribe Moses said nothing about priests** [compare Deuteronomy 33:7–11]. Most translations have "perfection" instead of "completion." "Perfection" isn't a bad translation, but it may not connote sufficiently well the process of being brought to a desired end or goal, as when other forms of the underlying Greek word deal with the completion of Jesus' education through the things he suffered (2:10; 5:8–9) and with the present audience's needing completion by growing up into Christian maturity (hence the translations "mature" and "maturity" in 5:14; 6:1). Here the author argues that the Lord's declaring long after the institution of the Levitical priesthood, "You are a priest forever in alignment with Melchizedek" (Psalm 110:4), indicated the inability of that priesthood, emphasized with "if in fact," to complete the work of salvation. Otherwise, there'd have been no need to announce a different kind of priesthood.

But the author doesn't speak only in the abstract about priesthood. He speaks also of "another priest," for he has in mind Jesus as that other priest. Since "to stand up" is a verbal form of the noun "resurrection" (literally, the "standing up" of what had been a supine corpse), one wonders whether the author implies that in "stand[ing] up" this other priest (Jesus) resurrected into his Melchizedek-aligned priesthood. "And not be designated in alignment with Aaron" underlines the difference of Melchizedekian priesthood from the Aaronic priesthood, which couldn't bring salvation to completion. "For the people [of Israel] have been legislated on the basis of it" tells why the Levitical priesthood's inability to bring salvation to completion was worrisome. The inability left God's people stranded so far as their salvation was concerned. The author will later explain in detail how the Levitical priesthood underlay the Law in that its priests offered sacrifices for transgressions—but inadequate sacrifices. Given the need for another priest in alignment with Melchizedek rather than with Aaron, the law that stipulated Levitical priests from Aaron onward had to be changed. In the next paragraph the author will cite Psalm 110:4 again as just such a divinely declared change. Meanwhile, he explains why Jesus didn't qualify to bring salvation to completion through the Levitical priesthood. Jesus had the wrong ancestry. He arose out of the nonpriestly tribe of Judah. But the author first calls him "the one about whom these things are said" to equate him with "You" whom the Lord declared to be "a priest forever in alignment with Melchizedek," and then calls him "our Lord" to highlight his exaltation to heavenly high priesthood and thus encourage the audience's perseverance with a recognition of their and his (the author's) shared privilege of having a lordly—that is, divine as well as human—high priest (compare 1:10; 13:20–21). With his having "partaken of a different tribe," compare his having "partaken of blood and flesh" (2:14). "Very clear" reinforces the argument that Jesus' ancestry requires a change in the law concerning priesthood, a change that conforms to Psalm 110:4. Further reinforcement comes from Moses' having "said nothing about priests" in reference to Jesus' tribe of Judah.

Even further reinforcement follows in *7:15–19*: **And it's still more abundantly clear if a different priest stands up in accordance with the likeness of Melchizedek,** [16]**who** [referring to "a different priest"] **has become** [such a priest] **not in accordance with the law of a fleshly commandment** [that is, the law requiring physical descent from Levi], **but in accordance with the power of an indestructible life.** [17]**For it's being testified** [to him], **"You** [are] **a priest** *forever* **in alignment with Melchizedek** [Psalm 110:4]." [18]**For on the one hand there takes place a removal of the foregoing commandment** [requiring Levitical priests] **because of its weakness and uselessness.** [19]**For the Law completed nothing. On the other hand** [there takes place] **the introduction of a superior hope, through which we're drawing near to God.** If a priest different from a Levitical one *actually* stands up and matches the aforementioned characteristics of the priest Melchizedek, as "our Lord" has done, then "it's still more abundantly clear" than it was from our Lord's non-Levitical ancestry that the Mosaic law had to be changed in regard to priesthood. See the comments on 7:11 for "stands up." "But in accordance with the power of an indestructible life" alludes to Jesus' resurrection and sets it over against "the law of a fleshly commandment." Resurrection to an in-

destructible life trumps physical descent. "The power" prepares for a contrast with the "weakness" of the Levitical commandment and its priests (7:18, 28), and "an indestructible life" prepares for a contrast with the mortality of Levitical priests (7:23).

That Jesus received his Melchizedek-like priesthood by a divine testimony addressed to him validates it beyond question. "It's being testified to him" makes the testimony current in that the Scripture contains it as an ongoing testimony. The removal of the Mosaic commandment concerning priesthood took place by virtue of this testimony and provided the reason for it. The present tense of "takes place" makes the removal, now past, stand out so vividly that it seems to be going on right now. The addition to "weakness" of "uselessness" and of the explanation, "For the Law completed nothing," puts a double accent on the reason for "a removal of the foregoing commandment." For "completed," see the comments on 7:11. "The introduction of a superior hope" contrasts with "a removal of the foregoing commandment." "On the one hand . . . on the other hand" plays up the contrast. "Hope" for the future replaces "the foregoing commandment," which required a backward, uncertain look. The hope is "superior" in that it gives us so much confidence that "we're drawing near to God" (compare 4:14–16 and contrast 12:20–21).

7:20–22: **And inasmuch as** [it was] **not without the swearing of an oath** [that our Lord has become a priest]— [21]**for on the one hand they** [the Levitical priests] **have become priests** *without* **the swearing of an oath; on the other hand he** [has become a priest] *with* **the swearing of an oath through the one saying to him, "The Lord swore and won't change his mind, 'You** [are] **a priest forever** [Psalm 110:4]'"—** [22]**by this much Jesus has become the guarantor of a superior covenant.** Here the author continues to play up the superiority of the hope we have in the different priesthood of our Lord. As in 7:1–3, the sentence starts, gets interrupted with a lengthy interlude, and then comes to an end. If we leave out the interlude, it reads, "And inasmuch as [it was] not without the swearing of an oath [that our Lord became a priest] . . . by this much Jesus has become the guarantor of a superior covenant." In other words, just as an oath-swearing guaranteed the eternal priesthood of Jesus, so by virtue of his priesthood he has become the guarantor of a superior covenant. A superior priesthood entails a superior covenant. The author will have a lot more to say about this covenant later on. For now he's content to note it as superior alongside the superior priesthood of Jesus; and this twofold superiority should keep the audience holding tight their Christian confession rather than apostatizing.

"*Not without* the swearing of an oath" poses a negative but emphatic way of saying, "Indeed it *was* with the swearing of an oath." Adding to this emphasis is the quotation of the first part of Psalm 110:4, omitted till now: "The Lord swore and won't change his mind." The oath-swearing that made Jesus a priest contrasts with the absence of oath-swearing at the installation of Levitical priests. The Lord didn't think their priesthood worth his swearing an oath. For theirs was temporary, Jesus' priesthood is eternal—hence too the shortening of the quotation of Psalm 110:4, so that it lacks "in alignment with Melchizedek" and ends with "forever." "For on the one hand . . . on the other hand" highlights the contrast between the swearing of an oath for Jesus' priesthood and the absence of oath-swearing for Levitical priesthood. "Through the one saying to him" refers to God as "the Lord" who swears the oath. But the author has recently referred to Jesus as "our Lord" (7:14). No matter, though. For if God can call his Son "God," as he did in 1:8, and call him "Lord," as he did in 1:10, then the author of Hebrews has warrant to use "Lord" for both Jesus and God the Father. Nevertheless, "the swearing of an oath *through* the one saying to him" centers attention on the oath-swearing, for which God the Lord is the mouthpiece. "And won't change his mind" secures the eternality of Jesus' priesthood.

7:23–25: And those who have become priests, on the one hand, are very numerous because of being prevented by death from continuing on. [24]**Because he** [Jesus] **continues forever, on the other hand, he holds** [his] **priesthood as unencroachable.** [25]**Hence he can also save to entire completion those who are coming to God through him, always living** [as he is] **to intercede in their behalf.** The high number of Levitical priests, due to their dying and therefore needing successors to step over into their vacant positions—this high number contrasts with the singularity of Jesus' priesthood, due to his "continu[ing] forever" and therefore not needing a successor. He'll never vacate his position. So it's "unencroachable." As usual, "on the one hand . . . on the other hand" highlights the contrast. The unencroachability of Jesus' priesthood issues not only in his "continu[ing] forever" but also in an ability to "save to entire completion." His staying on the job of priestly intercession for God's people will bring their salvation to full and final completion. As emphasized by "entire," no component will be missing. "*Always* living" corresponds to "continues *forever*." And "those who are coming to God through him [Jesus]" defines God's people as believers in Jesus. So don't renounce your confession of him, for if you do you'll never come to God.

7:26–28: For it was fitting that we [have] **such a high priest: devout, innocent, undefiled, having been separated** [by exaltation] **from the sinners** [among whom he lived on earth] **and become higher than the heavens,** [27]**who doesn't have day by day a necessity, as indeed the** [Levitical] **high priests** [did], **to offer sacrifices first for his own sins, then for the** [sins] **of the people.** [28]**For he did this once for all by offering himself** [for our sins, since he had none of his own]. **For the Law constitutes as high priests human beings who have weakness, but the word of the oath-swearing subsequent to the Law** [constitutes as the high priest] **a son who has been completed forever.** The initial "For" makes the following an explanation of why Jesus can "save to entire comple-

tion those who are coming to God through him." He can because he's the kind of priest who fits our need for an entirely complete salvation. The author details the kind of priest Jesus is, and the very piling up of details emphasizes his suitability: (1) "devout," and therefore in good stead with God; (2) "innocent," and therefore free of any evil of his own that would make him an unfit sacrifice on our behalf; (3) "undefiled," and therefore free of any moral contamination that would exclude him from God's presence, where his intercession for us has to take place; (4) "having been separated from the sinners and become higher than the heavens [the sun, moon, stars, and planets]," and therefore in God's presence where, as just stated, intercession for us has to take place; and (5) "who doesn't have day by day a necessity . . . to offer sacrifices first for his own sins, then for the [sins] of the people," and therefore able to intercede for us without the daily interruptions of having to offer sacrifices. "As indeed the [Levitical] priests [did]" brings out the superiority of Jesus' priesthood in this respect. Then the author explains why Jesus needn't offer daily sacrifices even for the people's sins. It's that he offered himself as a sacrifice. "Once for all" describes his self-sacrifice as eternally sufficient to atone for our sins. Finally the author tells why that self-sacrifice is eternally sufficient: unlike the merely human, morally, and mortally weak Levitical priests, Jesus is God's eternal and divine Son who underwent completion as also a human being (compare 5:8–9); and unlike the Law-constituted Levitical priests, Jesus is a priest constituted as such by a divine oath that postdated the Law and therefore outdated it.

THE HEAVENLY REALITIES OF
JESUS' HIGH PRIESTHOOD
Hebrews 8:1–10:18

8:1–2: And the head thing over and above the things being said [here]: **we have such a high priest** [as has just been described in 7:26–28], **who sat down at the right** [hand] **of the throne of the Greatness in the heavens** [compare 1:3 with comments], [2]**an attendant at the sanctuary, even the true tent** [traditionally, "the true tabernacle"], **which the Lord, not a human being, pitched.** "The head thing over and above the things being said [here]" means the main point up to which the preceding has been leading. What is that point? Not just Jesus' high priesthood, already mentioned. Rather, the location of Jesus' priestly attendance at a heavenly sanctuary. "Even the true tent" distinguishes this sanctuary. It's "true," not as opposed to false, but as real and substantial in contrast with what will be called "a blueprint and shadow" (8:5 [compare 9:24 and Revelation 15:5; 21:3 with comments]). Human beings pitch tents on earth. The example of Moses' doing so will come up in 8:5. But no human being could pitch a tent "in the heavens." The Lord did, though, in that he established a sanctuary there (compare 1:10, though in reference to the heavenly bodies, not a sanctuary). His pitching the heavenly tent makes it superior to any humanly pitched, earthly tent.

8:3–5: For every high priest is constituted [a high priest] **for the purpose of offering both gifts and sacrifices** [compare 5:1]. **Hence, [it's] necessary also for this** [high priest, Jesus] **to have something that he might offer.** [4]**Therefore if he indeed were on earth, he wouldn't be even a priest, because there are those** [on earth] **who are offering gifts in accordance with the Law,** [5]**who as such do religious service in a blueprint and shadow of the heavenly things** [= "of the true tent" in 8:2], **just as Moses stands warned** [in Scripture] **when he was about to complete the tent** [= the tabernacle]. **For he** [God] **says, "See, you** [Moses] **shall make all things according to the design that was shown you on the mountain** [Sinai] [Exodus 25:40]**."** The initial "For" introduces an argument why Jesus acts as a high priest in heaven rather than on earth. The argument starts with a notation that "every high priest is constituted [a high priest] for the purpose of offering both gifts and sacrifices." "Both . . . and" stresses this purpose. So if Jesus is to be a high priest, he has to have a gift or sacrifice to offer. What might that be? The answer has already been given in 7:26–27: "For he did this once for all by offering *himself* [for our sins]." Hence the author skips to a conclusion signaled by "therefore" and drawn from the high priestly necessity of having something to offer. The conclusion is that Jesus wouldn't be even an ordinary priest, much less a high priest, "if he indeed were on earth" instead of seated "at the right [hand] of the throne of the Greatness in the heavens" (8:1). He could offer nothing here, because the Mosaic law excluded him, a non-Levite, from offering gifts and sacrifices. He had the wrong ancestry (7:13–14). "Indeed" and "even" emphasize this exclusion from priestly service on earth. Supporting the exclusion further are those Levitical priests "who are offering gifts in accordance with the Law." Jesus' priestly service isn't *needed* on earth any more than it would be *lawful* here.

The Levitical priests "do religious service in a blueprint and shadow of the heavenly things." The Mosaic tent now comes explicitly into view. As a twofold description of it, "a blueprint and shadow" stresses its inferiority to "the heavenly things." And stressing the need for the Mosaic tent to be a fully accurate blueprint for and shadow of the heavenly sanctuary is the warning to "make all things according to the design that was shown to [Moses] on the mountain." As a blueprint, the Mosaic sanctuary looked *forward* to the heavenly sanctuary. As a shadow, it *fore*shadowed the heavenly sanctuary. "When he [Moses] was about to complete the [earthly] tent" doesn't mean he was on the verge of finishing it—rather, that he was about to bring the tent to completion by starting its construction in accordance with the God-given design.

8:6–12: **But now he** [Jesus] **has obtained a more excellent attendance** [of sacred things in the true tent (see 8:2)] **inasmuch as he's the intervener of a superior covenant, which as such has been legislated on the basis of superior promises** [compare 6:12]. [7]**For if that first** [covenant] **had been faultless, no place would have been sought for a second** [covenant]. [8]**For finding fault with them** [the nation of Israel], **he says, "Behold, the days are coming," says the Lord, "and** [= when] **I'll complete a new covenant with the household of Israel and with the household of Judah,** [9]**not in accordance with the covenant that I made with their** [fore]**fathers on the day when I took hold of their hand to lead them out of Egypt!** [I'll complete a new covenant with them,] **in that they didn't remain in my covenant and** [as a result] **I wasn't solicitous for them," says the Lord,** [10]**"in that this** [is] **the covenant which I'll covenant for the household of Israel after those days," says the Lord, "by giving my laws into their mind. And I'll inscribe them onto their hearts. And they'll have** [me] **as** [their] **God, and I'll have them as** [my] **people.** [11]**And by no means will each one teach his** [fellow] **citizen, even each one his brother, by saying, 'Know the Lord,' because they all, from the small to their great, will know me,** [12]**because I will be propitiated in regard to their unrighteousnesses** [= their unrighteous acts] **and by no means will I remember their sins any more** [Jeremiah 31:31–34]**."**

"But *now*" implies that prior to enthronement at God's right hand Jesus hadn't yet "obtained a more excellent attendance [of sacred things in the true tent]" and therefore, as indicated by the description of the Mosaic tent as a blueprint and (fore)shadow, that the heavenly tent hadn't yet been pitched. "Has obtained" alludes to God's having sworn an oath which effected Jesus' obtaining "a more excellent attendance." "*More* excellent" draws a comparison with the priestly service performed in the mere blueprint and (fore)shadow of the true tent and implies excellence in that service, but emphasizes greater excellence in the priestly service Jesus has performed in heaven. This greater excellence accrues from his intervention. "He's the intervener of a superior covenant" in the sense that he stepped in to establish a superior covenant in replacement of an inferior one, a second, new covenant in replacement of a first, old one. Many translations have it that Jesus is "the mediator." But that translation suggests a mediation between two parties in which there's give-and-take before agreement is reached. No, no, no. By intervention Jesus imposed a superior covenant unilaterally. Take it or leave it. Take it by faith, or leave it by unbelief and apostasy. As to its terms, you have no say-so. Hence the author says it "has been legislated" (compare 7:11 and "the intervention" of God's "will" in 6:17).

"A superior covenant" echoes 7:22 and has "superior promises" as the basis of its superiority. These promises are spelled out in the following quotation of Jeremiah 31:31–34 but recall also the promise of entering God's rest (4:1) as well as many other promised benefits of salvation that pepper the text of Hebrews—for example, future glory (2:10) and an eternal inheritance (9:15). The legislation of a superior covenant grew out of the faultiness of the first (Mosaic) covenant associated with the inferior tent. Otherwise, "no *place* would have been sought for a second [covenant]" in the sense that Jesus, "the intervener of a superior covenant," wouldn't have found a place in heaven to pitch the true tent of new covenantal activity (compare 12:17, where Esau is said to have found "no place" for a change in his father's mind). Then the author explains the faultiness of the first covenant in terms of the Lord's "finding fault" with the nation of Israel. So the first covenant was faulty in that it couldn't do away with the faults of God's people.

In the quotation of Jeremiah 31:31–34 "the Lord" (as the author of Hebrews calls him) refers to the covenant that he made with the "[fore]fathers," and according to 9:19–20 "God" commanded blood-sprinkling at the inauguration of that first covenant. So here, "he says" and "says the Lord" refer to God's speech, not to that of Jesus. "Behold" makes the Lord's announcement of a new covenant exclamatory. It's worth an exclamation! "The days are coming" makes the covenant new in time. But "not in accordance with the covenant that I made with their [fore]fathers" makes it new also in kind. For our author the time has now come, and the difference in kind has now been achieved, so that Jeremiah's time of fulfillment "after those days" is present time. "I'll *complete* a new covenant" means that the Lord will establish it. "*With* the household of Israel and *with* the household of Judah" means that they'll be the objects of his new covenantal legislation. Too awkwardly for an English translation, the Greek text adds "upon" to "with" ("I'll complete a new covenant with upon . . ."). The addition suggests divine imposition alongside divine benevolence. With the use of "household" compare the comments on 3:2–6. The distinction between "the household of Israel" and "the household of Judah" derives from the date of Jeremiah's prophecy after the united kingdom of Israel had split into a northern division ("Israel") and a southern division ("Judah"). But the prophecy looks forward to a reuniting, which for the author of Hebrews has taken place in the churchly household into which God's people have evolved (see again the comments on 3:2–6).

Why not a renewal of the old covenant rather than the establishing of a new kind of covenant? Because God's people "didn't remain" in the old one. Theirs was a history of apostasy, starting already with the generation that the Lord led out of Egypt (see chapters 3–4). As a result, he "wasn't solicitous for them." He stopped caring for them, as shown by their defeats and exiles. Thus the initial "in that" introduced the reason why a new covenant was needed. Another "in that" introduces the reason why the second covenant is described as new. It's described thus because the Lord will give his covenantal laws into the "mind" of the people and inscribe them "onto their hearts," which means that they'll obey out of thinking and feeling God's laws for themselves rather than obeying, and often disobeying, out of thinking and feeling God's laws as alien to them. "Inscribe" implies a permanent writing of those laws "onto their hearts." (The verb is stronger than "write" [compare Jeremiah 17:1].) The results, "they'll have [me] as [their] God, and I'll have them as [my] people," mean that no more will they reject God in favor of idols and that no more will he reject them by withdrawing his care. Hence the

happily emphatic expression, "the *covenant* that I'll *covenant* for [the benefit of] the household of Israel." Three occurrences of "says the Lord" add to the emphasis. So mindful will be his people of the laws and so heartfelt will be their obedience that neither the teaching of theology ("Know the Lord") nor the need to teach it will exist. Stressing these absences are several expressions: (1) "by *no* means"; (2) "*each* one" (occurring twice); (3) "*even* each one" (in the second occurrence); (4) the parallelism of "his [fellow] citizen" and "his brother"; (5) "they *all*"; (6) "from the small to their great"; and (7) the negation of "Know the Lord" by "they all . . . will know me." A second "because"-clause tells the reason why they'll all know the Lord. It's that the Lord "will be propitiated in regard to their unrighteousnesses."

As noted in the comments on 2:17, sins can be expiated (that is, atoned for); but persons are propitiated (that is, their anger is assuaged). "*I* will be . . ." shows that "propitiated" correctly fills out the present verbal phrase; and the previous statement, "I wasn't solicitous for them," establishes the requisite background of divine anger. Jesus' "making expiation for the people's sins" according to 2:17 has answered in advance *how* it is that the Lord has been propitiated. His not "remember[ing] their sins any more" issues from that propitiation. "Any more" implies that once he did remember them. But "by no means" underscores the permanence of his nonremembrance. To remember sins would be not merely to call them to mind. It would be to act judgmentally against them as a result of calling them to mind. So nonremembrance indicates exemption from eternal punishment. We Christians are the people thus exempted according to Hebrews. So let us hold tight our confession.

8:13: By saying "new" he has made the first [covenant] **old** [in the sense of "obsolete"]. **And what is being made old and is aging** [is] **close to disappearance.** The Mosaic covenant is obsolete so far as God is concerned. He "has made" it so. But "is being made old and aging" and "close to disappearance" both allude to the illegitimate continuance of that covenant so far as unbelieving Jews are concerned, and also predict its soon disappearance even for them.

9:1–2: On the one hand, therefore, the first [covenant], **too, had regulations for religious service; and** [its] **sanctuary** [was] **worldly** [that is, located in this world rather than in heaven]. ²**For a tent was prepared, the first one** [= the first to be entered], **in which** [were] **both the lampstand and the table and the presentation of loaves of bread, which** [tent] **as such** [that is, as just described] **is called the Holy Place.** "On the one hand" prepares for a comparison of the Holy Place with the Holy of Holies in 9:3–5. "Therefore" means that because the new covenant has a heavenly sanctuary with regulations for religious service (chapter 8), the first covenant, which foreshadowed the new, also had such regulations and a sanctuary, though a this-worldly one. "For" then introduces an explanation of the worldly sanctuary. To stress the preeminent sanctity of its Holy of Holies, the author treats the two rooms of the Mosaic tent as two tents. The preparation of the first one, the Holy Place, included its furnishings as well as its construction. The furnishings included (1) the lampstand in the shape of a tree with six upward turned branches, plus a central trunk, each of which held a lamp bowl fueled with olive oil and containing a wick that was kept burning; (2) a table; and (3) a presentation of loaves of bread by their being placed on the table week by week (see Exodus 25–31; 35–39; 40:17–33; Leviticus 24:1–9).

9:3–5: On the other hand, after the second curtain [which implies a first curtain at the entrance of the Holy Place] [was] **a tent called the Holy of Holies** [as though this second tent, being the most holy, was the sanctuary of the first tent], [4]**having a gold altar of incense** [= an altar on which incense was burned] **and the box of the covenant** [= the covenantal chest or, traditionally, the ark of the covenant], **entirely gold-plated all around, in which** [box were] **a gold jar containing the manna, and Aaron's staff that had budded and the tablets of the covenant** [= the covenantal tablets, on which were inscribed the Ten Commandments (Exodus 25:16; 37:1–9; 40:20; Deuteronomy 10:5)], [5]**and above it** [the box] [were] **cherubim** [winged angelic creatures] **of** [God's] **glory overshadowing the place of expiation and propitiation** [traditionally called the mercy seat (Exodus 25:10–22)], **about which things now isn't** [the time] **to speak item by item.** "On the other hand" introduces another tent, the inner sanctum called the Holy of Holies, meaning the very most sacred space. "The second curtain" separated it from the first tent, the Holy Place. According to the Old Testament the altar of incense stood the other side of this curtain from the Holy of Holies (Exodus 30:1–6; Leviticus 16:11–19). But once a year, on the Day of Atonement, the high priest had to take a firepan of burning coals from this altar, described as located "before the Lord," and then had to put incense on the coals and bring them inside the curtain so that the smoke of incense would cover the mercy seat (Leviticus 16:12–13). So to highlight the ceremonial association of the altar with the Lord's presence in the Holy of Holies, the author speaks of the altar as "after the second curtain." In the form of its coals and incense the high priest transferred it, so to speak, from the Holy Place into the Holy of Holies.

The redundancy of describing the covenantal box as "*entirely* gold-plated *all around*" joins the gold of both the altar of incense and the jar containing manna (about which see Exodus 16) to showcase the high value of these furnishings. If they were of such high value yet only a blueprint and shadow of the heavenly sanctuary (8:5), how much more valuable the heavenly one, where Jesus ministers. According to Exodus 16:33–34 the jar of manna was to be put before the covenantal box, and likewise—according to Numbers 17:1–11—Aaron's staff that budded. But just as the author brought the altar of incense into the Holy of Holies to associate the smoke of incense with the mercy seat, so too he brings the jar of manna and Aaron's rod into the covenantal box to

associate them with the tablets containing the Ten Commandments. Each item thus located in the box evoked memories of sin. In righteous rage Moses broke the first pair of tablets on seeing God's people worshiping the golden calf (Exodus 32:1–20), so that two replacements had to be inscribed (Exodus 34). God gave the manna to the Israelites because of their grumbling over not having a diet in the wilderness such as they'd had as slaves in Egypt. And Aaron's staff miraculously budded as a sign of God's ordination of Moses and Aaron, over against a jealous rebellion against their leadership (Number 16–17). By placing the jar of manna and Aaron's staff alongside the tablets as mementos of sin inside the covenantal box, then, the author implies the inability of the first covenant to do away with sin (7:11, 18–19; 8:6–13; 10:1–18).

For the association of cherubim with God's glory see Ezekiel 9:3; 10:1–22; 11:22–23 (compare Exodus 40:34–38), and for the meaning and combination of expiation and propitiation, see the comments on 2:17; 8:12. If "now isn't [the time] to speak item by item" about these things, why did the author list them? Answer: To underline his main point that the new covenant was foreshadowed in detail by the first covenant with its regulations and sanctuary.

9:6–10: And when these things have thus been prepared, the priests go continually into the first tent, on the one hand, completing [= fully performing] **the religious services.** [7]**Into the second** [tent], **on the other hand, only the high priest** [goes] **once during the year, not without blood that he offers for himself and the people's ignorances** [8]**as the Holy Spirit is making this clear,** [that] **the way of the Holy** [of Holies] **hasn't yet been manifested while the first tent still has standing** [= is still standing, still exists], [9]**which** [tent or standing] **as such** [that is, as a clarification by the Holy Spirit] [is] **a parable** [= a comparative symbol] **for the current time, in accordance with which** [parable] **both gifts and sacrifices are offered that can't complete the person doing religious service in accordance with** [his] **consciousness** [in other words, can't bring him to the goal of having a consciousness that he has accomplished the expiation of his sins and propitiation of God which his gifts and sacrifices need to have accomplished], [10][the gifts and sacrifices being] **only fleshly regulations on the basis of foods and drinks and different immersions,** [fleshly regulations] **imposed till the time of straightening.** "The priests" (plural) refers to ordinary priests as differentiated from "the high priest" (singular). The ordinary priests go into the Holy Place ("the first tent") repeatedly every day ("continually") in connection with the offering of sacrifices, incense-burning, fueling the lamps, trimming their wicks, and—once a week—changing the loaves of bread on the table ("the religious services").

The high priest alone goes into the Holy of Holies ("the second [tent]") on the Day of Atonement ("once during the year," meaning on only one day during the year) with sacrificial blood (Leviticus 16:17, 34). "Not without blood" is a negative way of emphasizing the importance of the high priest's taking with him sacrificial blood. Offering it "for himself" recalls the sinfulness of the succession of Levitical high priests (5:1–3; 7:27–28) as opposed to Jesus' sinlessness (4:15; 7:26–27). See the comments on 5:2 for "the people's ignorances" as instances of deliberately ignoring God's commandments, not as inadvertent sins (compare Leviticus 16:34). "As the Holy Spirit is making this clear" means that he uses the high priest's solo entrance into the Holy of Holies one day a year to show that entrance into the heavenly Holy of Holies "hasn't yet been manifested"—that is, hasn't yet been opened up to Christian believers by Jesus' blazing the trail for them—while the first tent, the Mosaic tabernacle, still stands (8:1–2; 9:12, 24–26; 10:20; compare the Holy Spirit's "making this clear" with "the Holy Spirit says" in 3:7 [see also 10:15]). The author calls this clarification "a parable" not in the sense of an illustrative story but in the sense of a comparative symbol pointing to Jesus' priestly activity in the heavenly Holy of Holies. "For the current time" refers to the time current with the existence of the Mosaic sanctuary, during which the Holy Spirit was using that sanctuary as a parable, so that verbs in the present tense ("the priests *go*," "the high priest . . . *offers*," "the Holy Spirit *is making* this clear," "while the first tent *has* standing," and "both gifts and sacrifices *are offered*") are spoken from the standpoint of someone living at the time of the Mosaic tabernacle, which perished later during the Old Testament period.

Since the consciousness of expiation and propitiation is at issue, "the person doing religious service" probably includes the bringer of gifts and sacrifices as well as the priest who offers them (compare 10:1). The author describes the gifts and sacrifices as "only fleshly regulations" because they're based on dietary laws concerning what foods are allowable to eat, what drinks are allowable to drink, and "different immersions" (dippings in water) required to get rid of ritual impurity (see, for example, Leviticus 8:6, 21; 9:14; 11:1–47; 13:6, 34, 54, 56, 58). Violation of these laws would invalidate the gifts and sacrifices. Jesus partook of blood and flesh (2:14) in order to inaugurate a new and living way into the heavenly Holy of Holies by the sacrifice of his blood and flesh (10:19–20). But his sacrifice wasn't "only [in the sense of 'merely'] fleshly"; for it was based on his sinlessness, not on ritual purity. "Till the time of straightening" means till Jesus' time, when God straightened things out by replacing the faulty first covenant with the faultless new covenant (8:6–13).

9:11–12: But Christ, having arrived as high priest of the good things that have taken place, entered through the greater and more goal-effective tent not made with [human] hands—that is, not of this creation— [12]**and [he entered] not through the blood of he-goats and calves but through his own blood once for all into the Holy [of Holies], having himself found eternal redemption** [for us]. The formality of "Christ" (properly a title meaning "Anointed One" as distinguished from the purely personal name "Jesus") suits the context of high

priestly activity (so too in 9:14, 24, 28). "Having arrived" refers to Christ's arrival in heaven upon his resurrection and ascension. "The good things" of which he's the high priest consist in the benefits of salvation, such as those listed in 6:4–5: enlightenment, a heavenly gift, and so on (see too 1:14 [inheritance of salvation]; 2:10 [future glory], 11 [sonship to God and brotherhood with his Son], 14–15 [deliverance from the fear of death], 17 [expiation of sins]; 4:1 [entrance into God's rest], and "eternal redemption" right here in 9:12). "That have taken place" describes these good things in terms of redemptive events, similar to those under which Israel experienced redemption from slavery in Egypt, but events that Christ brought to pass. He "entered through the greater and more goal-effective tent" when he ascended through heaven right into God's very presence. "Greater" implies that the Mosaic tent had a certain amount of greatness. But the heavenly tent has greater greatness. "More goal-effective" implies that religious service in the Mosaic tent had some foreshadowing effectiveness in bringing people toward the goal of a consciousness of having accomplished the expiation of sins and the propitiation of God (see 9:9). But Christ's religious service in the heavenly tent fully effects the reaching of this goal. "Not of this creation" defines "not made with [human] hands" and highlights the superiority of "the greater and more goal-effective tent" (compare 9:24 and "the true tent, which the Lord, not a human being, pitched" [8:2], in contrast with the "worldly" sanctuary of 9:1).

"*Through* the . . . tent" carries a spatial meaning. "Not *through* the blood of he-goats and calves but *through* his own blood" carries an instrumental meaning. In other words, it was his own sacrificial blood rather than that of sacrificed animals that enabled Christ to enter into the heavenly Holy of Holies, where God himself dwells. "Once for all" underscores the entire and eternal sufficiency of Christ's blood, which represents the taking of his very life (Genesis 9:4; Leviticus 17:11, 14; Deuteronomy 12:23), to expiate our sins and propitiate God (compare 7:27; 9:7, 21–22; 10:10). According to 4:16 we "find grace" at the throne of grace. Here Christ is said to have "found eternal redemption." Since 9:14 will say that "the blood of the Christ . . . will cleanse our consciousness from dead works," this redemption is for sinners, not for him. So "having *himself* found" (rather than "having found *for* himself") underscores that the finding of redemption for us is due to his activity, not ours. And "having himself *found*" implies a successful *search* for our redemption, as though God sent him into the world on a search-and-rescue mission (compare the designation of Jesus as "the apostle [= sent one] . . . of our confession [3:1]"). "Redemption" means liberation, purchased here at the cost of "his own blood." The description of redemption as "eternal" implies liberation from enslavement to sin and eternal death so as to enjoy forgiveness and eternal life.

9:13–14: For if the blood of he-goats and bulls and a heifer's ashes that sprinkle those who've been defiled consecrate [them] with the result of a purification of

[their] **flesh,** [14]**by how much more will the blood of the Christ, who through the eternal Spirit offered himself unblemished to God, cleanse our consciousness from dead works so that** [we] **do religious service for the living God!** "For" introduces an explanation of why Christ's blood enabled him himself to find eternal redemption for us. The explanation: If sacrificial animals' blood and ashes bring ritual purification to defiled people, much more will the Christ's blood bring moral purification to sinners. "By how much more" makes the explanation exclamatory; and "*the* Christ," a title, lends it extra weight. For variety of expression, "bulls" replaces the earlier-mentioned and yet-to-be-mentioned "calves" (9:12, 19); and in line with his reference to ritual purification, the author brings in "a heifer's ashes," which were mixed with water and sprinkled on ritually defiled people to consecrate them and thus get rid of their fleshly impurity. (A heifer is a young cow that hasn't birthed a calf.) Since Numbers 19, where the heifer's ashes are prescribed, speaks only of purification, we're surprised that our author brings in consecration as that which results in purification. But it's in view of the frequently mentioned consecration of Christians to God by Jesus' body and blood (2:11; 10:10, 14, 29; 13:12) that the author introduces consecration into his reference to ritual purification.

"Through the eternal Spirit" means that the Holy Spirit enabled the Christ to act as both priest and sacrifice, but the use of "eternal" rather than "Holy" or "of God" alludes to the eternality of the effected redemption (9:12 [compare 5:9; 6:2; 9:15]). As sacrificed animals had to be *ritually* unblemished, the Christ offered himself *morally* unblemished to God. So the cleansing of "our *consciousness*" replaces "the purification of *flesh*." Many English translations have "conscience" instead of "consciousness," but "consciousness" may better get across the thought of "dead works" playing on the mind so as to interdict the doing of religious service. The author calls sins "dead works" in that they are deeds which for our eternal redemption necessitated the Christ's self-sacrificial death. "For the *living* God" draws a contrast with "dead works" and suggests eternal life as an entailment of eternal redemption (9:12) and an eternal inheritance (9:15).

9:15: And because of this [the Christ's self-offering to God] **he's the intervener of a new covenant, so that those who've been called** [those effectively called by God into the membership of his people] **may receive the promise of an eternal inheritance, since a death has taken place with the purpose and result of a redemption from the transgressions based on the first covenant.** For "the intervener" see the comments on 8:6. "Of a new covenant" recalls 8:6–13. The Christ's self-offering made him this covenant's intervener. "The promise of an eternal inheritance" means the promise *consisting in* an eternal inheritance. To receive the promise, then, is to receive the inheritance; and by intervening a new covenant the Christ purposed a reception of the inheritance by "those who've been called." They'll

receive the promised inheritance when he'll "appear a second time with the purpose and result of salvation" (9:28 [see also 10:35–39]), just as they'll enter God's rest at that time (4:1, 11]). For God's rest *is* their inheritance (compare the land of Canaan as an inheritance promised to but not yet received by Abraham, Isaac, and Jacob [11:8–9]). The inheritance is "eternal" in that it entails "eternal salvation" (5:9), "eternal redemption" (9:12), and an "eternal covenant" (13:20), all of which are related to a "judgment" that's "eternal" in its consequences for good or ill (6:2). "Since a death has taken place" points back to the Christ's self-offering (9:14) as the new covenant's basis and as the price of redemption in that redemption means liberation from slavery at a cost. "From the transgressions based on the first covenant" personifies those transgressions as the transgressors' slavemasters. Since transgressions incur the penalty of death (Genesis 2:16–17; 3:1–7; 5:1–31), we should compare the "set[ting] free" of "as many as through the fear of death were held in slavery all [their] lifetime" (2:15). So transgressions enslave transgressors through the fear of death. "Based on the first covenant" means that the transgressions are defined as such by the Mosaic covenant. Take the Ten Commandments, for example.

In 9:15 the author stated that "a death has taken place" and mentioned "a new covenant" and "the first covenant." So now he relates a covenant-maker's death to a particular kind of covenant, a last will and testament, which as such doesn't take effect till the testator dies. **9:16–17: For where** [there's] **a testamentary covenant,** [there's] **a necessity that the death of the one who made the testamentary covenant be carried** [into the picture]. [17]**For a testamentary covenant** [is] **firm** [by taking effect] **on the basis of dead people** [that is, because makers of testamentary covenants have died], **since it never carries force when the one who made the testamentary covenant is living.** The initial "For" introduces a positive explanation why reception of the promise consisting in an eternal inheritance required a death. Since Jesus died to establish a new, testamentary covenant, he's "the Lord" who said he'd "complete a new covenant" (8:8). "That the death . . . be carried [into the picture]" is a picturesque way of saying that the testator's death has to be authenticated for the testamentary covenant to take effect. A second "For" introduces a restated positive explanation and then a corresponding negative explanation why reception of the promise required a death. It's that a testamentary covenant "never carries force when the one who made the testamentary covenant is living."

9:18–22: Hence [that is, because of the necessity of a death] **not even the first** [covenant] **stands inaugurated** [in Scripture] **without blood.** [19]**For when every commandment had been spoken by Moses to all the people in accordance with the Law, on taking the blood of calves and he-goats with water and scarlet wool and hyssop, he sprinkled both the book itself and all the people** [20]**while saying, "This** [is] **the blood of the covenant that God has commanded for**

you [Exodus 24:8]." ²¹**And he likewise sprinkled with the blood both the tent and all the utensils for religious service. ²²And almost all things are cleansed with blood in accordance with the Law, and without the pouring out of blood forgiveness doesn't happen.** "Not . . . without blood" is a negative but emphatic way of saying that blood was indeed used. In view of the immediately preceding references to death (9:15–17) the author might have said "not . . . without a death." But he uses "blood" to specify a death in which blood is shed violently and therefore sacrificially. The statement, "not *even* the first [covenant] stands inaugurated [in Scripture] without blood," stresses that every covenant starts with a bloody sacrifice. But the inauguration of the first covenant didn't involve the death of God, the covenant-maker. It involved bloody animal sacrifices instead, so that our author has now abandoned the analogy of a testator's having to die. Furthermore, the analogy of a *testamentary* covenant is abandoned in favor of a *legislative* covenant ("For when every *commandment* had been spoken . . . in accordance *with the Law*"). "By Moses to all the people" specifies the Mosaic covenant. The record of its inaugural ceremony in Exodus 24:1–8 lacks the element of water, used for cleansing. The addition here of "water" to "the blood of calves and he-goats" points up by association the cleansing power of sacrificial blood, whereas nonsacrificial blood stains rather than cleanses (see the comments on Revelation 7:14 for the oxymoron of blood that cleanses). The scarlet color of the wool corresponds to the color of blood, and the wool and the hyssop (a branchy plant) get mentioned as instruments for sprinkling "the blood of the covenant." Apparently the wool was twisted into thread and used as a string to tie together the branches of hyssop.

"All the people" occurs once in connection with Moses' speaking "every commandment," and again in connection with being sprinkled with the blood. The first occurrence points up the *obligation* of everyone counted among God's people to obey each commandment without exception. The second occurrence points up the *privilege* of everyone sprinkled to be counted among God's people. The sprinkling also of the book containing every commandment in the Law brings that book and all the people together under "the blood of the covenant that God has commanded for you" (as Moses puts it). "Has commanded" reprises the legislative character of the covenant. The similar blood-sprinkling of "both the tent and all the utensils for religious service" brings under the covenant subsequent sacrifices for transgressions of God's commandments, as indicated by the closing statement that "without the pouring out of blood forgiveness doesn't happen." Exodus 24:3–8 says that Moses sprinkled sacrificial blood on the altar and the people but doesn't say that he sprinkled it on the book of the Law, the tent, and "all the utensils for religious service" (though compare Leviticus 14:1–9). Our author, however, includes the altar among the utensils and adds the book and the tent for the aforementioned purpose of bringing as many things as he can of the first covenant

under sacrificial blood (compare Exodus 12:22; Leviticus 8:15–19; 14:4). "*Almost* all things are cleansed with blood" leaves room, however, for the "heifer's ashes" as a cleansing agent when mixed with water (9:13 [see also Leviticus 5:11–13; 15:10, 13; 16:26, 28; 22:6; Numbers 19:1–22; 31:21–24]). The blood of sacrificial animals effected the "forgiveness" of ritual impurity but couldn't effect the forgiveness of transgressions (see especially 10:3–4, 11). So "the pouring out of blood" in the case of those animals prefigured the shedding of Jesus' blood, which *has* effected forgiveness. "Pouring out" alludes to the draining of a sacrificial animal's blood after its throat has been slit (compare Leviticus 17), which practice prefigures the shedding of Jesus' blood.

9:23–24: Therefore [because of the necessity of cleansing by sacrificial blood] **a necessity** [existed] **on the one hand that the blueprints of the things in the heavens** [the blueprints consisting of the earthly sanctuary, which foreshadowed the heavenly sanctuary] **be cleansed with these** [sacrifices of calves and he-goats], **on the other hand that the heavenly things themselves** [be cleansed] **with sacrifices superior to these** [sacrifices of calves and he-goats]. ²⁴**For Christ didn't enter into a sanctuary made with** [human] **hands, a counterpart to the true** [sanctuary]—**rather, into heaven itself, now to appear before God's face in our behalf.** "Blueprints" (plural) alludes to the multiplicity of items making up the tabernacle and its furnishings (see especially 9:1–5). Similarly, "the things in the heavens" (a twofold plural) alludes to the multiplicity of items making up the heavenly sanctuary (God's throne and a curtain in particular). The cleansings of the earthly and heavenly sanctuaries shouldn't be regarded negatively as cleansings from ritual impurities that they had contracted, as though even the heavenly sanctuary could contract ritual impurity. Rather, the cleansings should be regarded positively as ensuring ritual purity at the inauguration of the sanctuaries. "Themselves" underscores this insurance so far as "the heavenly things" are concerned. Though Christ sacrificed himself "once for all" (7:27; 9:12; 10:10 [compare 9:26, 28]), the author uses the plural ("with sacrifices superior to these") to imply that Christ's sacrifice amounted in its worth to all the inferior sacrifices and more. For "Christ," see the comments on 9:11. The contrast between "a sanctuary made with [human] hands" and "the true [sanctuary]," to which the handmade sanctuary was a counterpart, recalls that "the Lord, not a human being, pitched the true tent" (8:2). The author switches back to the singular of "heaven" and adds "itself" to highlight Christ's entrance into the true sanctuary. This past entrance issues in his present appearance there ("now"). "In our behalf" makes this ongoing appearance high priestly (compare 7:25: "always living [as he is] to intercede in their behalf"). "Before God's face" indicates that God is looking right at him as he (God) listens to Christ's intercession in our behalf.

9:25–26: Nor [did Christ enter into the heavenly sanctuary] **to offer himself many times, as indeed the**

high priest enters into the [earthly] **Holy** [of Holies] **year by year with another's blood** [that is, with the blood of a sacrificed animal], **²⁶since it would have been necessary that he** [Christ] **suffer many times since the founding of the world. But now he has appeared once, at the consummation of the ages** [compare 1:6], **with the purpose and result of the removal of sin through his self-sacrifice.** Several contrasts characterize this pair of verses: (1) the heavenly sanctuary versus the earthly one; (2) Christ's self-sacrifice versus high priests' offering an animal sacrifice; (3) Christ's appearing "once" to remove sin versus high priests' entering the earthly sanctuary "year by year" with no permanent result; and (4) "now" versus "the founding of the world." "With *another's* blood" accents the contrast with Christ's *self*-sacrifice. "Year by year" refers to the annual Day of Atonement (about which see the comments on 9:7). "Since the founding of the world" broadens "many times"; for sacrifice on the Day of Atonement had to do only with sins committed during the past year, whereas people started sinning right from the founding of the world. So repeated self-sacrifices by Christ would need to have started then if pre-Mosaic sins were to be atoned for. Many times indeed! But not in fact; for "now," reinforced by "once, at the consummation of the ages," erases the hypothetical "many times since the founding of the world."

"The consummation of the ages" refers to their being brought together in a completion of what they were aimed toward (compare 8:8 with comments). So just as God "made the ages" through his *preincarnate* Son (1:3), he has brought them to completion through his *incarnate* Son. "Has appeared" indicates a past event with a continuing result. But since the Son's appearance on earth inaugurated the consummation of the ages, "now" covers both the time of that appearance on earth and all time till he appears a second time on earth (9:28). His first appearance here made possible his appearance as our high priest before God's face in the heavenly sanctuary (9:24). "The *removal* of sin" corresponds to a multiplicity of similar expressions having to do with cleansing, expiation, offering, sacrificing, taking up, and taking away (1:3; 2:17; 5:1, 3; 7:27; 9:28; 10:4, 11–12) except that here the author uses the singular, "sin," rather than the plural, "sins," used elsewhere. In this way he lumps sins into one package for their one-time removal. In 7:27 "once for all" described the self-sacrifice of Christ. Here, "once" describes his appearance on earth for the removal of sin through that self-sacrifice. "Appeared" thus sets the stage for his second appearance on earth (9:28).

9:27–28: And inasmuch as dying once is reserved for human beings [= is destined for them], **and after this a judgment** [is reserved/destined for them], **²⁸so too the Christ, having been offered once "to take up the sins of many** [Isaiah 53:12]," **will without sin appear a second time with the purpose and result of salvation for those who are eagerly awaiting him.** "Reserved" stresses that death and subsequent judgment are unavoidable for human beings. The judgment may be for good or ill, for eternal life or eternal damnation. "So too"

sets up a parallel between the Christ and other human beings. But the parallel is only partial. For though both they and he die "once," his death is an offering. Theirs is not. In fact, his is an offering "to take up the sins of many," whereas they die only for their own sins. "The Christ" (a title) underlines his official capacity as God's "Anointed One" to fulfill this function. "To *take up* the sins" is to assume them, so that he died as though they were his own and therefore demanded his death. "Of many" contrasts with him as a lone figure. But who are the "many"? All human beings regardless of their belief or unbelief in the gospel? Or only believers? "Salvation for those who are eagerly awaiting him" favors believers, but without any implication that a person can't believe unless the Christ took up that person's sins. If a person believes, the Christ took them up. As a result of having "taken up the sins of many," the Christ's appearance will be "without sin." He removed them when he took them up, and dying as an offering for them disposed of them so far as he was concerned too. As a result of their disposal Christian believers can, and should, await his second appearance on earth "eagerly." For the flip side of sin's disposal is "salvation," that is, deliverance from eternal damnation for having sinned.

10:1–2: For the Law—having a shadow of the good things that were going to come, not the image itself of the accomplishments [that is, the actualized good things]—**can never by means of the same sacrifices that they** [the Levitical high priests] **continually offer year by year complete those who come to** [the sanctuary with those sacrifices], **²since wouldn't they** [the sacrifices] **not have stopped being offered because the ones doing religious service** [by offering sacrifices], **having been cleansed once, wouldn't have even one consciousness of sins any more?** "The Law" refers to the Mosaic law, here with particular attention to its sacrificial system (as also in 8:4; 9:19, 22; 10:8). In 8:5 "a shadow" described the earthly sanctuary, where sacrifices were offered. Here "a shadow" describes the sacrifices themselves; and for a contrast the author adds "the image" that casts the shadow—backward in time, since the image consists in "the good things that *were going to come* [in the future]." Those good things equate with "the accomplishments," for which "the image" is a figure of speech just as "a shadow" represents the sacrifices figuratively. "Itself" intensifies "the image" as a figure of good things more substantial than the shadowy sacrifices. For a list of the accomplished good things, see the commentary on 9:11. They were going to come "at the consummation of the ages," that is, "now" (see 9:26). Stressing the ongoing inability of the sacrifices to complete those who offered them are "never," "the *same* sacrifices," "that they *continually* offer," and "year by year" (in particular reference to sacrifices on the annual Day of Atonement, about which see the comments on 9:7 [compare 9:25]). Noncompletion of those who come to the sanctuary with their sacrifices means the failure of offering them to give their offerers a consciousness that they've expiated their sins and propitiated God (see the comments on 9:9). If the offerers had thought a sacrifice all-sufficient to cleanse them from every sin and for all time, the author asks, wouldn't they have then and there stopped any further sacrificing?

10:3–4: On the contrary [as opposed to the possibility of "having not even one consciousness of sins any more"], **year by year** [there's] **a reminder of sins in these** [sacrifices]. ⁴**For** [it's] **impossible for the blood of bulls and of he-goats to take away sins.** Worse than the lingering consciousness of sins unexpiated and of God unpropitiated by the offering of animal sacrifices is the annual reminder of these failures by the repetition of sacrifices every Day of Atonement. In fact, the repetition produces a recognition of perpetual impossibility. The sins stay stuck to the sinner, "for [it's] impossible for the blood of bulls and of he-goats to take away sins." The Day of Atonement turns out to be a reminder of sins retained rather than, as hoped, an assurance of sins removed.

10:5–10: Therefore [because of the impossibility of sins' being taken away by the blood of bulls and of he-goats] **when entering into the world he** [Christ] **says, "You didn't want sacrifice and offering. But you furnished me a body. ⁶You didn't delight in whole burnt offerings and sin offerings. ⁷Then I said, 'Behold, I've come (it's written about me in the book-scroll) to do your will, God** [Psalm 40:6–8]!'" ⁸**When saying above, "you neither wanted nor delighted in sacrifices and offerings and whole burnt offerings and sin offerings," which as such are offered in accordance with the Law,** ⁹**then he has said** [as it now stands written in Scripture], **"Behold, I've come to do your will!" He takes up** [and away] **the first** [the offering of sacrifices] **in order that he might establish the second** [the doing of God's will], ¹⁰**by which will we've been consecrated through the offering of Jesus Christ's body once for all.** "When entering the world" refers to Christ's birth, when God furnished him a body, and implies Christ's preexistence (compare 1:1–2, 6; 2:14). The author interprets "You" in the quotation of Psalm 40:6–8 to be God, and "I" and "me" to be the Christ. As in 2:11–13, the Christ is portrayed as speaking in the Old Testament. Where Psalm 40:6 has "you've dug ears for me [to hear your will (as though God dug earholes in the head for this purpose)]," Hebrews has "you furnished me a body." This revision shifts the focus from hearing God's will to doing it through bodily self-sacrifice. In fact, being furnished a body has the purpose of enabling such a sacrifice in obedience to God's will (compare 5:7–8). "Sacrifice and offering" and "whole burnt offerings and sin offerings" run the gamut of various kinds of animal sacrifices prescribed in the Mosaic law (see especially Leviticus 1–7). In the psalm, God doesn't want them and takes no delight in them apart from conduct otherwise obedient to his will. In view of their inferiority and Christ's self-sacrifice, though, the author transmutes God's lack of desire and delight into a wholesale rejection. So "*then I said*" means that Christ spoke the following words when God furnished him a sacrificial human body because he (God) had rejected animal sacrifices.

"Behold" makes Christ's first coming an object of exclamation, as indeed it should be since it was to do God's will instead offering unwanted animal sacrifices. "When entering into the world" has preinterpreted "I've come" as a coming into the world. For the author of Hebrews "the book-scroll" where it's written about Christ could be any one of the Old Testament books quoted in Hebrews (see chapter 1, for example), but perhaps preeminently the Psalms-scroll in view of the heavy use of Psalm 110:1, 4 for Christ's enthronement and priesthood and the present topic of sacrifice. "To do your will, God" draws an implicit contrast between Christ's sacrificing himself in obedience to God and animals' being sacrificed through no obedience of their own. "Which as such" refers to those sacrifices as unwanted by God despite their being offered "in accordance with the Law." Just as the Law concerning priesthood has been changed (7:12), so too the Law concerning sacrifices.

"*Then* he has said" points up the transition from God's neither wanting nor delighting in sacrifices and offerings to the repeated exclamation by Christ that he has come to do God's will as opposed to the offering of animal sacrifices. Christ is a priest, but not one to offer such sacrifices as those. He takes them up and away *verbally* (by denying God's delight in various sacrifices) in order that he might establish God's will *deedfully* (through the sacrifice of his own body). "By which will we've been consecrated" means that the doing of God's will by Christ's self-sacrifice has resulted in the consecration of Christians as God's people (2:11; 10:29; 13:12). Emphasis falls on this consecration as an accomplished fact (but see the comments on 10:14). The author's use of "we" stems from the personal pleasure he takes in sharing the consecration with his audience. "Through the offering of Jesus Christ's body" defines the doing of God's will as the method of consecration. The combination of "Jesus" and "Christ" emphasizes the character of the offering as human ("Jesus") and messianic ("Christ"). In the quotation of Psalm 40:6–8, "body" meant a human body furnished Christ at his birth ("when entering into the world"). Here, "through the offering" gives "body" the connotation of a corpse (as elsewhere, though by no means exclusively, in ancient Greek literature). And "once for all" stresses the sufficiency of Christ's self-sacrifice in contrast with "the same sacrifices that they continually offer year by year" (10:1 [compare 7:27; 9:12]).

10:11–14: And on the one hand every priest stands day by day doing religious service and offering the same sacrifices many times, which [sacrifices] **as such** [= as repeated many times] **can never take away sins from around** [the offerers]. ¹²**On the other hand this** [priest, Jesus Christ], **having offered one sacrifice for sins in perpetuity, sat down at God's right** [hand] ¹³**while eagerly waiting out the remainder** [of time] **till his enemies are placed as a footstool for his feet.** ¹⁴**For by one offering he has in perpetuity completed those who are being consecrated.** This paragraph reemphasizes the insufficiency of animal sacrifices (compare 10:1–4) and the all-sufficiency of Christ's self-sacrifice (compare

10:5–10). "Every priest" refers to every Aaronic priest and therefore excludes Christ, the priest in alignment with Melchizedek rather than Aaron. "Doing religious service" is defined by the Aaronic priests' "offering . . . sacrifices." Stressing the insufficiency of those sacrifices are (1) "day by day"; (2) "the *same* sacrifices"; (3) "many times"; and (4) "which can never take away sins." "From around [the offerers]" adds further stress by picturing the offerers as clothed by sins, which those sacrifices can never strip off. Whereas the high priest offered sacrifices year by year on the Day of Atonement (9:7, 25; 10:1), ordinary priests offered sacrifices "day by day." But not even this multiplication suffices. "The same sacrifices" means one animal after another.

As a followup to "on the one hand," "on the other hand" underscores the contrast between Christ and the Aaronic priests. "Having offered one sacrifice for sins in perpetuity" contrasts with "offering the same sacrifices many times." "For sins" describes Christ's one sacrifice in a way that implies it takes away sins, whereas "the same [animal] sacrifices" offered by the Aaronic priests "can never take away sins." "In perpetuity" doesn't mean that Christ keeps on sacrificing himself for sins, which would contradict "one sacrifice" and "once for all" in 7:27; 9:12; 10:10. Just as "by one offering he has in perpetuity completed those who are being consecrated" means that their completion is forever done and over with, so his "having offered one sacrifice for sins in perpetuity" means that because of its all-sufficiency "the offering of his body" (10:10) is forever done and over with. Emphasizing this point is that after offering the one sacrifice, he "sat down." No need for further sacrifice, no need for further standing to offer one. He can sit down, whereas every Aaronic priest "stands" because his religious service of offering sacrifices doesn't cease (compare the contrast between sitting and standing in 2 Chronicles 6:10–12). And where does Christ sit down? "At God's right [hand]," the place of God's supreme favor and enthronement with him (see the comments on 1:3; 8:1). Christ sacrificed himself as a priest and sat down as a king. "While eagerly waiting out the remainder [of time] till his enemies are placed as a footstool for his feet" refers to the interim between Christ's enthronement and second coming (compare the comments on 1:13).

"One offering" equates with the previously mentioned "one sacrifice" and provides the means by which Christ "has in perpetuity completed those who are being consecrated." Their completion provides the reason why he has sat down and refers to giving them a consciousness of sins expiated and God propitiated (see the comments on 9:9; 10:1). But in view of their *having been* consecrated (10:10), how do we understand their "*being* consecrated"? Sometimes an expression like this puts the action front and center for emphasis, as though it were going on even though it's past or future in temporal fact. Either that kind of emphasis applies here, or the author is alluding to ongoing conversions that entail the consecration of one new believer after another.

10:15–18: **And also** [in addition to our being consecrated] **the Holy Spirit testifies to us. For after having said,** [16]**"'This** [is] **the covenant that I'll covenant'"** in reference to them **"'after those days,'" the Lord says: 'By giving my laws onto their hearts I'll also inscribe them onto their mind,'"** [17]**and, "'By no means will I remember their sins'" and their lawlessnesses "'any more** [Jeremiah 31:33–34]." [18]**And where** [there's] **forgiveness of these** [sins and lawlessnesses], [there's] **no longer an offering having to do with sin.** With the Holy Spirit's testifying in Scripture compare his speaking in Scripture at 3:7–11. Here in 10:15–18 what he testifies equates with what "the Lord says." The present tense of "testifies" and "says" gives the stated testimony contemporary relevance. For "to us," see the comments on "we" in 10:10. "*For* after having said" introduces an explanation of the Holy Spirit's testimony to us.

The following quotation of Jeremiah 31:33–34 repeats in part, and with some changes, the quotation in 8:8–12 (see the comments on that passage). This repetition adds emphasis to Jeremiah's prophecy. In line with "to us" and in comparison with the earlier quotation, several substitutions and omissions make the prophecy more applicable to Christians: (1) the omission of references in 8:8–9 to "a new covenant with the household of Israel and the household of Judah," to the covenant "made with their [fore]fathers," to their exodus from Egypt, to their failure to remain in that covenant, and to the consequent withdrawal from them of the Lord's care; (2) the substitution of a vague "in reference to them" where 8:10 had "for the household of Israel"; (3) the omission of "they'll have [me] as [their] God, and I'll have them as [my] people" (8:10); (4) the omission of no one's teaching a fellow citizen to know the Lord because all the people will know him (8:11); and (5) the substitution of forgiveness in place of propitiation (8:12). By reversing the order of "their mind" and "their hearts" (so 8:10), the author gets their mind as well as their hearts *inscribed* with the Lord's laws, and their hearts as well as their mind *given* the Lord's laws. The addition of "their *law*lessnesses" to "their sins" as another object of the Lord's nonremembering balances "giving my *laws* onto their hearts," and the substitution of "*onto* their hearts" for "*into* their mind" makes "giving" synonymous with "inscribe." "Also" adds the inscription to the covenant. "Where" refers to the location of forgiveness. The audience know the location from 6:19–20. It's the heavenly Holy of Holies: "farther in than the curtain, where Jesus as a forerunner has entered on our behalf." In that location there's "no longer an offering having to do with sin," because no further need exists for such an offering. Jesus "offered one sacrifice for sins in perpetuity" (10:12).

A WARNING AGAINST APOSTASY
Hebrews 10:19–39

10:19–22: **Therefore** [because there's forgiveness of sins and no more need for a sin offering], **brothers, having confidence for entrance into the Holy** [of Holies] by the blood of Jesus, [20]which [entrance] he inaugurated for us as a recently slain and living way through the curtain—that is, his flesh—[21]and [having] a great priest over God's household, [22]let us be coming to [God] with a true heart in the full assurance of faith because we've been sprinkled, so far as [our] hearts are concerned, [so as to be cleansed] from an evil consciousness and because we've been washed, so far as [our] body is concerned, with clean water [= cleansing water]. The address "brothers" refers to the audience and strikes a note of affectionate concern. As their fellow Christian (hence also "we" and "us" from here through 10:26), the author wants them to take seriously the following warning (compare the comments on 3:1 and especially 3:12). The warning starts with encouraging exhortations (10:19–25) but builds up to a frightening possibility (10:26–31) and then settles down to a promising conclusion (10:32–39).

The first exhortation is to approach God. The author bases this exhortation on the confidence he and his audience can have "for entrance into the Holy [of Holies]," the innermost part of the heavenly sanctuary, where God himself dwells. "Confidence" connotes freedom of speech as well as freedom of access. Only the Aaronic high priests could enter the earthly Holy of Holies, and then only once a year and only to burn incense and make an inferior, ineffective atonement (Leviticus 16:11–19). But because of Jesus' having made a superior, effective atonement in the heavenly Holy of Holies (9:12–18, 23–26), Christians can enter and speak their requests to God whenever they need "mercy and grace for well-timed help" (4:14–16). Some translations read, "since we have confidence." But nothing in the original Greek text corresponds to "since" or demands the supplying of "since." So it's better to understand that the exhortation to approach God includes an exhortation to have confidence for entrance into his presence.

The entrance consists in "a . . . way through the curtain" that divides the Holy of Holies, the inner sanctum, from the Holy Place, the outer sanctum. In other contexts the word for "way" is translated with "path" or "road." Jesus inaugurated the way so that we might travel it by prayer into God's presence, and Jesus did so by his blood (for which see again 9:12–14, 23–26). With reference to the bloody self-sacrifice of Jesus earlier in the first century, the author describes this way as "recently slain";[4] and with reference to Jesus' resurrection, the author describes the way also as "living" (compare 13:20). As self-sacrificed and resurrected, then, Jesus is himself our way into the Holy of Holies. And "living" means that he can now act further as our "great priest" by interceding in our behalf (7:25; 9:24).

The author calls the curtain Jesus' "flesh," which supplements Jesus' "blood" to indicate the violent separation of blood and flesh in a sacrifice (compare 2:14). Aaronic high priests passed through the inner curtain of the earthly sanctuary. In prayer, Christians pass through the inner curtain of the heavenly sanctuary. But since the curtain consists of Jesus' sacrificed flesh, "through the curtain" means entrance by means of his flesh in addition to going through it spatially as through a curtain.[5] And thus having him as "a great priest" joins "having confidence for entrance" to provide a second encouragement to approach God (compare 4:14–16; 13:20 and see 7:25 for God as the object of approach). "A great priest" substitutes for "a high priest," though from 2:17 onward Jesus has repeatedly been called a high priest and in 4:14 "a great high priest." Jesus is "great" in that he's enthroned at the right hand of God, who is "the Greatness in the heights/heavens" (1:3; 8:1 [see further the comments on 4:14]). Jesus' greatness puts him "over God's household" (compare 3:1–6).

"A true heart" is usually understood as a sincere and faithful one (compare Isaiah 38:3). But "after having received the knowledge of the truth" (10:26) suggests that a true heart is one that's filled with that knowledge. "Faith" means belief in and faithfulness to the gospel. Such belief and faithfulness stem from "the full assurance" of the gospel's truth (compare 4:2–3; 6:1, 11–12; 11:6 and contrast "an evil heart of unbelief/unfaithfulness in apostatizing from the living God" [3:12]). "A true heart in the full assurance of faith" thus underlies approaching God, fortifies against apostasy, and prepares for the exemplars of faithful faith throughout chapter 11, plus Jesus in 12:1–3.

In 9:13–14 there was an implication of being sprinkled with Christ's blood. Now the implication turns into an outright declaration: "because we've been sprinkled" (see also 12:24). Sprinkling stands for application. "So far as [our] hearts are concerned" excludes a literal sprinkling of blood on our bodies and points to a figurative sprinkling, that is, an application of Christ's atonement to our hearts (themselves a figure of speech for our inner being), where as just said we have "the full assurance of faith" and where, as said next, "an evil consciousness" (= a consciousness of our own evil) is cleansed away because of the application of Christ's atonement. There's no more consciousness of evil because atonement has removed the evil itself (compare 9:14). As in 9:13–14, 19–23, sprinkling effects cleansing—there, ritual cleansing; here, moral cleansing. "Because we've been washed"

---

[4]Most translations have "new" instead of "recently slain." It's true that the Greek word came to have the general meaning of "new." But elsewhere our author uses two other words for "new" (8:8, 13; 9:15; 12:24); and, more importantly in view of the possibility of another synonym, the present context of Jesus' sacrificial blood favors retention of the original meaning, "recently slain."

[5]Note: Jesus doesn't go through the curtain. We do. Furthermore, Hebrews doesn't say the curtain was split apart. So there's no allusion here to the splitting of the curtain at Jesus' death (Mark 15:38; Matthew 27:51; Luke 23:45). Besides, if the centurion and those with him at the cross saw the splitting of the curtain, as Matthew 27:54 indicates they did, it would have to have been the outer curtain at the entrance to the Holy Place on earth, not the inner curtain dividing the Holy of Holies from the Holy Place in heaven and spoken of here in Hebrews 10:19–20.

gives a second reason (after "because we've been sprinkled") to approach God "in the full assurance of faith." "With *clean* water" ensures that the washing cleanses. "So far as [our] body is concerned" points to water baptism as an outward counterpart to the inward cleansing of hearts (compare 6:2 with comments).

10:23: Let us be holding tight the confession of [our] **hope as unwavering** [referring to "the confession," not to "hope"], **for he who promised** [the hope] [is] **faithful.** Both 3:6 and 3:14 set forth a condition: "*if* in fact we hold tight." Here we have an exhortation: "*Let* us hold tight." The object of our holding tight—namely, "the confession of [our] hope"—recalls the exhortation in 4:14: "let's be keeping a grip on [our] confession." See the comments on that verse for confession as a declaration, here as the declaration of our hope, which declaration brings exposure to persecution, which exposure brings in turn a temptation to clam up, and which temptation creates, again in turn, the need for an exhortation to hold tight the confession rather than letting it go by clamming up. "As unwavering" describes the confession as undeterred by persecution or the threat of it. "[Our] hope" is our sure and certain expectation of final salvation (3:6; 6:11, 18; 7:19). The faithfulness of God, who promised what we hope for, makes the hope a sure and certain expectation and therefore a reason to hold tight our confession of it.

10:24–25: And let us be fixing our minds on one another for the purpose of incitement to love and good deeds, [25]**not abandoning the assembly of ourselves, as some** [have] **the habit** [of doing]—**rather, encouraging** [one another]**, and by so much the more as you see the day drawing near.** Love issues in doing good deeds for its objects (6:10). Fixing our minds on one another in the Christian community enables us to recognize each other's needs and thus incites us to love with good deeds. "Not abandoning the assembly of ourselves" keeps our minds fixed on one another, for out of sight means out of mind. ("Assembly" is related to "synagogue" and designates church meetings with a term resonant for Jewish Christians of their pre-Christian past.) In view of the upcoming mention of persecution (10:32–34), "the habit" of some to abandon the assembling of themselves with other Christians probably has the purpose of avoiding persecution. But to forestall a consequent apostasy, they should encourage one another in their assemblies. The drawing near of the day of Jesus' return, which will bring a judgment fatal to apostates, should intensify the mutual encouragement. To "see" the day drawing near is to recognize in persecutions an indication of its soon arrival.

And so 10:22 exhorts us to be approaching God with a true heart in the assurance of *faith*; 10:23 to be holding tight the confession of our *hope*; and 10:24–25 to be fixing our minds on one another for the purpose of incitement to *love* and good deeds (compare the Christian virtues of faith, hope, and love in 1 Corinthians 13:13).

10:26–27: For if we're sinning willfully after having received the knowledge of the truth, a sacrifice consisting in a sin offering is no longer left over. [27]**But** [there *is*] **something** [left over], **a fearsome expectation of judgment, even of "a fervor of fire that's going to eat the opponents** [Isaiah 26:11 (compare Psalm 79:5; Zephaniah 1:18; 3:8; Hebrews 12:29; Deuteronomy 4:24)]**."** "For" introduces a reason for the three exhortations ("let us . . .") in 10:19–25. "Having received the knowledge of the truth" means "having converted through accepting the gospel as true." "Sinning *willfully*" is reminiscent of "sinning with a high hand"—that is, rebelliously—in the Old Testament (see Numbers 15:30–31, for example). It will turn out in the rest of this chapter that the author is referring to apostasy, to a voluntary renunciation of Christ's self-sacrifice as a sin offering and therefore to a failure to hold tight the Christian confession. Under the Levitical system another sin offering could always be sacrificed. But those sacrifices, being of animals, were ineffective; and Christ's self-sacrifice was once-for-all effective (7:27; 9:12; 10:10). As emphasized by "no longer," therefore, a voluntary renunciation of it leaves no sin offering that could atone for the apostasy. Filling this vacuum is an "expectation of judgment." The apostate may not expect judgment, but he should; and our author is speaking from the standpoint of Christians like himself who know that judgment is coming (compare 9:27) and who in view of their expecting it need to warn each other not to apostatize. Judgment may be for good or ill. So our author describes the expectation of the judgment facing apostates as "fearsome." By describing the expectation rather than the judgment as fearsome he uses the expectation as an emotional tool to forestall apostasy. Underlining the expectation's fearsomeness is the equation of "judgment" with "a *fervor* of fire that's about to eat the opponents." This equation of judgment with fervor personifies the judgment. The fervor is fire-hot in its zeal to punish apostates. Then "fire" is also personified in that it's "about *to eat* the opponents" (compare James 5:3 among other passages that portray fire as eating). The opponents are none other than the apostates, who have turned against the truth they used to acknowledge. "*Going* to eat the opponents" denotes a judgment that's sure and soon.

10:28–31: On disregarding the law of Moses someone dies without pity [by execution] **"on the basis of two or three witnesses** [who testify to his flouting the Mosaic law] [Deuteronomy 17:6]**."** [29]**Of how much worse punishment do you suppose he'll be deemed deserving who has trampled God's Son and regarded as defiled the covenantal blood by which he was consecrated and** [who has] **insulted the Spirit of grace** [= the gracious Spirit]**?** [30]**For we know the one who said,** **"Retribution** [belongs] **to me, I'll give back in return** [Deuteronomy 32:35],**" and again, "The Lord will judge his people** [Deuteronomy 32:36; Psalm 135:14]**."** [31]**Falling into the hands of the living God** [is] **fearsome.** To disregard the law of Moses was to remove it from its position as the determinant of one's conduct. Supported by sufficient testimony, such disregard incurred execution "without pity." Apostasy from a Christian confession will incur "much worse punishment." But how can it be much worse than execution without pity? It can be so in that apostasy incurs eternal death whereas disregarding the Mosaic law incurred temporal death. By putting the much worse punishment of an apostate in the form of a question ("Of how much worse punishment do you suppose he'll be deemed deserving . . . ?"), the author asks his audience to think for themselves that the punishment will be much worse. Such reflection is likely to dissuade them from apostatizing.

To show how well deserved is this punishment that's worse than execution without pity, the author describes apostasy (1) as trampling God's Son, whereas God told the angels to worship him, addressed him with "God," proclaimed his eternal enthronement, and anointed him with the olive oil of gladness more than his partners (1:6, 8–9); (2) as debasing his covenantal blood to the function of a pollutant rather than the sole means of consecration in the cleansing away of sins (9:11–14, 28); and (3) as insulting the grace-giving Spirit, whereas it was through this Spirit that Christ "offered himself unblemished to God" for the cleansing of the apostate's consciousness from dead works (9:14). Knowledge of the one who claimed the right of retribution—that is, knowledge of God—justifies asking the question, "Of how much worse punishment do you suppose he [the apostate] will be deemed deserving . . . ?" Knowing God to be the final retributor, the terminal retaliator, and the Lord who'll judge even his people—knowing him to act in these capacities forces us to contemplate the worse than pitiless but just fate of an apostate. Quotations of Scripture undergird this portrayal of God. The trampler of God's Son will fall in his trampling. Hands represent operative power. Because God is "living" as idols are not, then, he has operative power to retribute, retaliate, and judge. A fearsome prospect, indeed a fearsome *certainty*, for apostates! Much more fearsome than falling into the hands of persecutors.

10:32–34: But remind yourselves of the former days, during which, after being enlightened, you endured a considerable struggle [consisting] of sufferings, ³³partly by being made a public spectacle through both vilifications and afflictions, partly by having become sharers with those being treated in this way. ³⁴For you showed sympathy even to the prisoners [compare 13:3] **and welcomed with joy the seizure of your possessions, knowing that you yourselves have a superior and lasting possession.** The switch from "we" and "us" in 10:19–31 to "you," "your," and "yourselves" marks a shift from exhortations to commands. "But rem to encouraging reminiscence. Reminding yourselves means ind yourselves" also marks a shift from dire warning more than calling the past to mind. It means also to recreate the past in your present conduct, here to recreate in your present persecution your past perseverance under persecution. This history of yours doesn't repeat itself automatically. Self-reminders are needed. "After being enlightened" means "after your conversions" (compare 6:4) and slides into the meaning, "because you were

converted." The resultant persecution is compared to "a considerable struggle [consisting] of sufferings," as in a strenuous athletic contest that entails physical injuries. (Ancient athletic contests often did entail such injuries.)

Verbal "vilifications" had brought shame, and "afflictions" appear to have gone further. Not only had some of the audience been made a public spectacle in these ways. Their fellow Christians had exposed themselves to like persecution by sharing their resources with them. For example, they showed sympathy with their imprisoned fellow Christians by taking them food and drink, which weren't provided in prisons except perhaps for a little bread and water, and also by staying in prison with them to prevent their abuse by jailers (see the comments on 13:3). "*Even* to the prisoners" stresses the risk entailed in such sharing, and this risk turned into the actuality of having their possessions seized. So we have vilifications, physical abuse, and economic deprivation as elements in the persecution. "Welcomed with joy the seizure of your possessions" strikes a sharp contrast with the possibility of apostatizing. The basis of this joyful welcome lay in the knowledge of a future possession, superior and lasting. It will consist of a heavenly country, a lasting city, and a lasting kingdom (11:14–16; 12:26–28; 13:14). "Knowing" connotes certitude, and "yourselves" stresses "you" as the possessors of these heavenly, eternal realities.

10:35–38: Therefore [because of having a superior and lasting possession] **don't throw away your confidence, which as such has a big payback.** As earlier, "confidence" means boldness in the declaration of Christian faith. Throwing away your confidence therefore results in apostatizing under persecution and carries the connotation of selling your confidence too cheap. After all, the confidence that results in perseverance has a big payback in eternity, namely, the superior possession of a heavenly country, of a lasting city, and of a lasting kingdom. Now we hear the first reason for the command not to throw away the confidence: ³⁶**For you have need of endurance in order that after doing God's will you may procure the promise.** Persecution creates the need for endurance, and endurance has the purpose and result of procuring the promise, that is, of getting the promised possession which is superior and lasting. But the procurement must follow the doing of God's will, which in this context means maintaining your Christian confession despite being persecuted for it. Now a second reason for the command not to throw away confidence: ³⁷**For yet "in a very, very little** [while] **he who is coming will arrive and won't delay** [Isaiah 26:20; Habbakkuk 2:3]**."** The one who's coming is Jesus (9:28). "In a very, very little [while]" and "won't delay" put a double accent on his coming soon. The addition of "will arrive" to "is coming" points up certainty. The soonness and certainty of Jesus' second coming provide reason not to throw away confidence. "Yet" refers to the meantime. ³⁸**"But my righteous person** [as distinguished from the one who is coming] **shall live by faith/faithfulness; and if he were to shrink back, my soul won't delight in him** [Habakkuk 2:4]**."** "My righteous person" refers to the Christian who doesn't throw away his confidence but does the right thing by enduring persecution (compare 11:4; 12:23). He endures through living by faith in the second coming, a faith that makes him faithful to his Christian confession. But if he were to shrink back from persecution by unfaith in the second coming and unfaithfulness to his Christian confession, God says, "My soul [a strong way of saying 'I myself, who am the final judge'] won't delight in him," so that he won't get the superior, lasting possession. "*Were* to shrink back" puts forward an unexpected possibility. "*Won't* delight in him" puts forward a sure consequence if the possibility nevertheless materializes.

Now the author expresses his conviction that the audience won't apostatize, as he did also in 6:9–10, though here he includes himself with them as he did not in the earlier passage. Since people tend to conform to what others say about them in direct communication with them, this expression of conviction that the audience won't apostatize, an expression buttressed by the author's tactful inclusion of himself, has the purpose of turning present expectation into future actuality. *10:39*: **But we—we aren't characterized by shrinking back into destruction; rather,** [we're characterized] **by a faith/ faithfulness that results in the preservation of life.** "But we—we" stresses the contrast with a person who shrinks back. Whereas the previous mention of shrinking back implied apostasy for the purpose of avoiding persecution, here the addition of "into destruction" indicates the result of apostasy. "Destruction" means lostness and eternal ruin (compare the comments on John 17:12). Opposite shrinking back stands a "faith" that perseveres in "faithfulness" and "results in the preservation [as opposed to 'destruction'] of life [in eternity]." So perseverance in life-threatening persecution effects preservation in eternal life and corresponds to "keeping a grip on [our] confession" (4:14 [compare 3:6, 14; 10:23]).

ENCOURAGEMENT FROM OLD TESTAMENT HEROES OF FAITH
Hebrews 11:1–40

The author has just described his audience and himself as those who "are characterized by a faith/faithfulness that results in the preservation of life" (10:39). So now he elaborates such faith/faithfulness (11:1–3) and illustrates it with examples drawn from the Old Testament (11:4–40). These examples have the purpose of encouraging the audience to persist in their own faith/ faithfulness. They'll know that they're not alone in doing so, and that it's possible to persist. Many others already have. The examples will start with Abel in the first book of the Old Testament and lead up to Jesus, the prime example of faith/faithfulness, in the next section (12:1–3).

11:1–3: **And faith is assurance concerning accomplishments hoped for** [that is, confidence that accomplishments of God's promises will in fact take place (see the comments on 6:18; 10:1, where "acts" and "accomplishments" represent the Greek word used here)], **conviction concerning things not seen** [that is, certitude that they exist even though they're presently invisible]. [2]**For by this** [= by faith] **the elders** [in the sense of God's ancient people] **were attested** [see the rest of chapter 11]. The statement that the elders were attested by faith personifies faith as God's agent in the attesting (compare 11:4, 39). He puts their faith on the witness stand as proof of their assurance and conviction. [3]**By faith we understand the ages to have been prepared by God's word, so that what is seen has come into existence out of things that aren't apparent** [to the eye]. See the footnote to 1:2 on the meaning of "ages" in relation to "what is seen." "Ages" establishes a temporal framework for a faith that looks forward to final salvation. The word of God provided the means of his temporal creation, and out of that invisible creation ("the ages" as "things that aren't apparent [to the eye]") there came into existence the physical creation ("what is seen"). "We understand" the invisible creation and its visible result "by faith" because we weren't there in the beginning, but faith consists in assurance and conviction that such a creation lies behind what we see. Assurance and conviction that God created the ages modulates faith as belief into faith as faithfulness in that the carrying out of his plan for the ages gives reason for faithfulness.

11:4: **By faith Abel offered to God more of a sacrifice than Cain** [did], **through which** [faith] **he was attested to be righteous in that on the basis of his** [Abel's] **gifts God was attesting** [him], **and through it** [Abel's faith] **he's still speaking despite having died** [Genesis 4:1–10 (compare Hebrews 12:24)]. The author interprets the plurals in Abel's bringing "[some] of the firstlings of his flock and of their fat portions" as "gifts" to mean that he offered to God "*more* of a sacrifice" than did Cain, whose offering is spoken of in the singular: "an offering of the fruit of the ground" (Genesis 4:3–4). Abel had confidence ("assurance") that God would fulfill Abel's hope to have his flock replenished, depleted as it was by the sacrifices, and Abel had certitude ("conviction") that replenishment was in the offing even though he didn't yet see it. This two-pronged faith prompted him to make multiple offerings. As in 11:2, his attestation through faith personifies faith as God's agent of attestation. "God was attesting [him]" interprets "the Lord had regard for Abel and his offering" (Genesis 4:4). According to Genesis 4:10 the Lord said to Cain, "The voice of your brother's blood is crying to me from the ground." Our author transmutes Abel's voice of *blood* into the speaking of Abel's *faith*. "Still speaking despite having died" underlines the exemplary relevance of Abel's faith to the audience of Hebrews.

11:5–6: **By faith Enoch was transferred** [from earth to heaven] **so as not to see death** [in the sense of experiencing it]; **and he wasn't being found, because God transferred him. For he has been attested to have pleased God prior to the transfer** [Genesis 5:18–24]. Hebrews interprets "God took him [Enoch]" in Genesis

5:24 as a transfer to heaven, and "he was not" in the same verse as an indication that Enoch didn't die. The addition of "he wasn't being found" (not in Genesis) implies that people were searching for him unsuccessfully. Their lack of success underlines the transfer that was due to his faith. Two further mentions of the transfer underline the faith that led to it; and the pleasing of God interprets "Enoch walked with God," which occurs twice in Genesis 5:22, 24. "He [Enoch] has been attested" is spoken from the standpoint of someone who has just heard a reading of the scriptural account. The author now draws a conclusion: [6]**And without faith** [it's] **impossible to please** [God]. **For the person who is coming to God must believe that he exists and** [that] **he becomes an awarder to those who are earnestly seeking him.** The logic is simple: It's impossible to please God without faith, because if you don't believe he exists, as unfaith would have it, you can't even approach God, much less please him, as Enoch did in walking with him. A God-pleaser must believe that God exists even though God is unseen, and must believe that God "becomes an awarder [of things 'hoped for,' we might add from 11:1] to those who are earnestly seeking him." (The Greek word for "are seeking" connotes intensity—hence the addition of "earnestly" [compare 12:17: "even though seeking it earnestly *with tears*"].) Enoch wasn't found by seekers who had seen him, but God is found by seekers who've never seen him.

11:7: **By faith Noah, having been warned about things not yet being seen, showing piety, prepared an ark** [literally, "a box," but a big floating one] **for the salvation of his household** [that is, for their deliverance from the flood], **through which** [faith] **he condemned the world and became an heir of the righteousness that's in accordance with faith** [Genesis 6–9]. "Having been warned about things not yet being seen" indicates that Noah's flood was the first flood. So the faith of Noah consisted in assurance and conviction that what hadn't been seen but had been warned about would indeed be accomplished. This faith led him to prepare an ark, and preparing it showed piety in that he prepared the ark in obedience to God's command. Given our author's interest in salvation (see also 1:14; 2:3, 10; 5:9; 6:9; 7:25; 9:28), the salvation of Noah's household from the flood adumbrates our eternal salvation. Noah condemned the world through his faith in that the contrast between it and the unfaith of his contemporaries ("the world") issued in their destruction by the flood. Over against the world's condemnation stands Noah's becoming "an heir of the righteousness that's in accordance with faith." But what is this righteousness? Not his own righteousness; for Genesis 6:9 describes him as already "a righteous man," whereas "an *heir* of righteousness" points to a righteousness yet to come. So this righteousness is God's righteousness in that he did the right thing by saving Noah and his household, and this was the right thing to do because it was "in accordance with [Noah's] faith" that God saved him and his household. Salvation and God's righteousness are often put in synonymous parallelism (for one of many examples, see Isaiah 61:10: "He

['God'] has clothed me with garments of salvation; he has wrapped me with a robe of righteousness"). Noah's becoming "an heir" of this salvific righteousness prepares for Abraham's "inheritance" in the next paragraph.

11:8–12: **By faith Abraham, when being called, obeyed by going out into a place that he was going to receive for an inheritance; and he went out despite not knowing where he's going.** [9]**By faith he resided as an alien in a land of promise—**[a land] **thus belonging to others—dwelling in tents with Isaac and Jacob, coheirs of the same promise.** [10]**For he was expectantly awaiting the city that has the foundations, whose framer and builder** [is] **God** [Genesis 12:1–9 and later passages]. [11]**By faith he** [Abraham] **received power for the throwing down of seed** [that is, for the ejaculation of sperm] **both in relation to sterile Sarah herself and** [though being himself] **past the time of maturity** [that is, beyond the age of virility], **since he considered him faithful who had promised** [them a son]. [12]**Therefore** [as many descendants] **as the stars of heaven in multitude and as the innumerable sand along the seashore have been fathered even by one** [man, Abraham], **who also in these respects** [= so far as virility for so many offspring was concerned] **had died** [Genesis 15:5; 17:19; 18:1–15; 21:1–7; 22:17]. Hebrews calls Canaan "a place" and "a land"; but it was only promised to Abraham, so that when he resided there it "belong[ed] to others" and he had the status of an "alien." "Dwelling [nomadically] in tents" as opposed to dwelling settledly in a city highlights that status. On the other hand, "he was going to receive ['a place'] for an inheritance." He never did receive it, though; and "dwelling in tents *with Isaac and Jacob*, coheirs of the same promise" extends the nonreception into the lifetimes of a son and a grandson of Abraham. So "a place," "a land of promise," turns out to be not Canaan, a geographical name that Hebrews avoids, but what will later be called a superior, heavenly fatherland (11:16), whose capital city, "a heavenly Jerusalem" according to 12:22, has "the foundations" that the "tents" of Abraham, Isaac, and Jacob didn't have. These foundations intimate eternal settledness for citizens in contrast with nomadic unsettledness for aliens. The fact that God will have framed and built this city suits its heavenly origin (compare Revelation 21:1–2) and connotes its permanence.[6] In 8:1–5 the earthly sanctuary was compared to a *blueprint* and shadow of the heavenly sanctuary. In the present passage, the earthly land in which Abraham, Isaac, and Jacob resided as aliens is rather like a *map* and shadow of the superior, heavenly fatherland, which features "the city that has the foundations." In both cases the earthly gives way to the heavenly.

"By faith Abraham . . . obeyed," "by faith he resided as an alien," and "by faith he received power." "When being

---

[6]Most English translations have "architect" instead of "framer." But "architect" is limited to the designer and supervisor of construction whereas the Greek word has to do also with the actual construction, so that "framer" and "builder" are synonymously emphatic.

called" indicates that his obedience was instantaneous. It coincided with the call. The present tense in "where he's going" vivifies the obedience by making it look as though it's occurring before our eyes. And "despite not knowing where he's going" conforms to the definition of faith as "assurance concerning accomplishments hoped for" and as "conviction concerning things not seen" (11:1). "For he was expectantly awaiting the city" confirms this correspondence to the definition of faith. And the statement that Abraham "considered him faithful who had promised" makes Abraham's faith meet the condition that "the person who's approaching God must believe that he exists and [that] he becomes an awarder to those who are earnestly seeking him" (11:6). "Him . . . who had promised" refers to God as a promise-keeper whose faithfulness gets elaborated in the references to the innumerability of Abraham's descendants and whose faithfulness also correlates to the faithfulness of his people, such as Abraham. "Fathered *even* by *one* [man]" stresses the innumerability by contrast. Sarah's sterility and Abraham's old age (emphasized by "*even* in relation to sterile Sarah *herself*") and Abraham's impotence (emphasized by mention both of his old age and of his death as to virility) highlight Abraham's faith as well as God's faithfulness. Abraham hoped for procreative power from God, but he couldn't see it. He had the assurance and conviction that constitute faith, though; and God honored it, so that the fulfillment of his promise of a son foreshadowed the yet future fulfillment of the promise of the superior, heavenly fatherland with its city that has the foundations. Abraham is said to have done one more thing "by faith," but first our author pauses for an interlude in which he picks up the just-mentioned topic of death ("who also in these respects had died") to summarize what he has said about Abraham, Isaac, and Jacob.

11:13–16: These all died in accordance with faith, not having received the promises—rather, having seen them from a distance and greeted [them] and confessed that they are foreigners and exiles on the earth. [14]For those who say such things make it quite clear that they're seeking a fatherland. [15]And if they were actually remembering that [fatherland] from which they had gone out, they'd have had time [and therefore opportunity] to return [compare Genesis 24:6–9]. [16]But now they're reaching out for a superior [fatherland], that is, a heavenly one. Therefore God isn't ashamed of them, [isn't ashamed] to be called their God [Genesis 26:24; 28:13; Exodus 3:6, 15; 4:5]. For he has prepared a city for them. The dying of "these all" who were "seeking a fatherland" different from the one out of which "they had gone" excludes Abel, Enoch, and Noah—none of whom emigrated—so that only Abraham, Isaac, and Jacob—the family whose earliest patriarch (Abraham) emigrated from Mesopotamia (modern Iraq)—are included. That these three patriarchs all died without having received the promises stresses their failure to have inherited an earthly land of promise, which failure points to a heavenly land of promise. "In accordance with faith" describes the manner of their dying: they

died still believing that God would keep his promise of a landed inheritance. The plural of "promises" points to repetitions of this promise. To have "received" the promises wouldn't have been merely to get a verbal pledge. The patriarchs already had that. It would have been to get *what* was promised.

Abraham, Isaac, and Jacob saw the land of Canaan at close range. They resided there as nomads. So "having seen them ['the promises,' that is, what had repeatedly been promised] *from a distance*" means that by faith they saw the promised *heavenly* fatherland, far from earth though it was. This farseeing faith doesn't contradict the definition of faith as "conviction concerning things not seen" (11:1), for in that definition "not seen" means "invisible because of not having materialized in one's *present* experience," whereas here in 11:13 "having seen . . . from a distance" means "visible as a materialization in one's *future* experience." "Greeted [them]" treats the promises as though they were persons to be greeted (compare the population of the heavenly Jerusalem with God, his people, angels, and Jesus in 12:22–24). Faith is friendly. But like the seeing, the greeting too was extended by faith "from a distance," the distance of space and time.

Seeing and greeting the promises as having to do with a heavenly and therefore distant fatherland led Abraham, Isaac, and Jacob to confess "that they are foreigners and exiles on the earth" (see Genesis 23:4). The present tense in their confession ("are") highlights their citizenship in the God-framed, God-built city that has its foundations laid in a heavenly fatherland superior to the fatherland from which they'd emigrated. The patriarchs' confession encourages Christians to maintain their confession, and to make it "quite clear," as was the patriarchs' confession, rather than blurring it to avoid persecution. "Seeking a fatherland" when residing in an earthly land of promise shows that they didn't find there the true land of promise. But not finding it there didn't prompt them to return to their original fatherland. They didn't even remember it as a fatherland to which they might return. "Actually" stresses their lacking a remembrance of that sort (compare Genesis 24:6, where Abraham forbids a return). So too Christians shouldn't even consider the possibility of apostatizing back into their preconversion state. "Reaching out for a superior [fatherland]" contrasts with the possibility of taking the opportunity to return. The distant, heavenly location of this superior fatherland required a reaching out, to which corresponds the need for Christians to persevere. "Now" and the present tense in "they're reaching out" contemporize this correspondence.

For God to have been ashamed of the patriarchs would have been for him to be ashamed of being called their God. But because "these all died in accordance with faith," a faith by which they reached out, he isn't ashamed. Which poses the question for Christians, Will God be ashamed of you and ashamed to be called your God, so that you'll lose out on salvation? Better stick true. Supporting the unashamedness of God in regard to the patriarchs is his having "prepared a city for them."

Citizenship had to do with a city, not a country. Paul was "a citizen of not an insignificant city [Tarsus]," for example (Acts 21:39). Better not give up your citizenship in the most significant city of all, the one that will later be called "the city of the living God, the heavenly Jerusalem" (12:22 [see already 11:10]).

11:17–19: By faith Abraham, when being tested, has offered Isaac; and he who'd taken up the promises was offering a one-and-only [son]—[18]**to whom** [Abraham] **it was said, "In Isaac will your seed be called"** [that is, "God will count Isaac as the continuation of your lineage" (Genesis 21:12)]—[19]**because of reasoning that God** [was] **able even to be raising** [Isaac] **from among the dead. Hence he** [Abraham] **got him back even in a comparable way** [that is, not by resurrection but by being spared when on the verge of being sacrificed—indeed, when lying bound on the altar with Abraham's knife at the ready (Genesis 22:1–19)]. Having finished the interlude of 11:13–16, the author returns in particular to Abraham with a fourth "by faith"-statement concerning him (see 11:8–9, 11 for the first three). His being tested adumbrates the testing of Hebrews' audience and, indeed, of Jesus (see 2:18 and compare 10:32–34). Will the audience pass their test as Abraham (and Jesus) did? Abraham's example encourages them to do so. "Abraham . . . has offered [but not sacrificed] Isaac" is spoken from the standpoint of someone who has just heard a reading of the scriptural account. For "the promises" as repetitions of a single promise see the comments on 11:13. "He who'd taken up the promises" describes Abraham as acting on them (compare his making a confession on the basis of them in 11:13). "A one-and-only [son]" designates Isaac as Abraham's sole offspring through Sarah and therefore as the one in whom according to God's promise Abraham's seed would be called (so too the implication of 11:11–12). The quotation of Genesis 21:12 stresses the strength of Abraham's faith in that the offering of Isaac seemed to contradict the promises that God would count Isaac and his descendants as the continuation of Abraham's lineage. Abraham didn't reason out a contradiction, though, because he did reason out God's ability to raise Isaac from among the dead and thus perpetuate Abraham's lineage. "Even" and "to be raising" (as though it could have been going on already) highlight this reasoning, and such reasoning comes from faith in an unseen, unrealized possibility. Hebrews interprets Abraham's statement in Genesis 22:5, "We [Isaac and I] will return to you [after 'worship[ing]' by means of the sacrifice of Isaac]," as based on Abraham's reasoning that God could raise Isaac from among the dead for a return with Abraham.

11:20–22: By faith Isaac blessed Jacob and Esau even concerning things that were going to happen [Genesis 27:27–29, 39–40]. "*Even* concerning things that *were going* to happen" underscores Isaac's faith as consisting in an assurance and conviction concerning things not seen at the time of the blessing (compare 11:1). [21]**By faith Jacob, when dying, blessed each of Joseph's sons** [Genesis 48] **and "bowed in worship on the top of his staff** [Genesis 47:31]." "When dying" indicates that despite "not having received the promises" (11:13) Jacob blessed Joseph's sons by a faith, like Isaac's, in realities as yet unseen. "*Each* of Joseph's sons" stresses that there was no shortfall of faith which would have left out one of the sons. Jacob's "bow[ing] in worship on the top of his staff" has the effect of describing faith as piety toward God, as in the case of Noah (11:7). [22]**By faith Joseph, when coming to his end** [= completing his lifetime], **remarked concerning the exodus of the sons of Israel and commanded concerning his bones** [that they be taken from Egypt to Canaan (Genesis 50:24–25; Exodus 13:19; compare Joshua 24:32)]. "When coming to his end" corresponds to "when dying" in the case of Jacob and, as there, indicates that despite "not having received the promises" (11:13) Joseph predicted the exodus and commanded concerning his bones by faith in a reality as yet unseen. "Commanded" exhibits how assured and convinced he was by faith in regard to the future event.

11:23–26: By faith Moses, when he'd been born, was hidden for three months by his parents, because they saw [he was] **a cute baby and** [because] **they didn't fear the king's edict** [that every male baby of the Israelites be thrown into the Nile River to drown (Exodus 1:15–2:2)]. By implication, Moses' parents had the assurance and conviction of faith that he'd be saved from death under the king's edict. This assurance and conviction kept them from fearing that edict. Their example tells the audience of Hebrews not to fear persecution, even martyrdom; for in the end God will save them eternally. Keep the faith! Hold tight your confession! Don't lose your grip! [24]**By faith Moses, when he'd become big** [= grown up], **refused to be called the son of Pharaoh's daughter** [who'd rescued and reared Moses (Exodus 2:3–10)] [25]**by choosing rather to endure ill-treatment with God's people than to have sin's temporary pleasure,** [26]**by considering vilification for the Christ** [to be] **greater wealth than Egypt's treasures. For he was looking away** [from Egypt's treasures] **to the payback** [Exodus 2:11–12]. Christians' endurance of persecution corresponds to Moses' endurance of ill-treatment with God's ancient people, Israel; for Christians are now God's people. "*With* God's people" indicates that faith entails sharing ill-treatment with one's fellows in the community of the faithful (compare 10:32–34). Moses' "choosing" to share in this way puts faith in the category of decision. Opting out would amount to apostasy, which brings the "pleasure" of enjoying the world's acceptance and approval but which Hebrews calls "sin" and describes as "temporary." Given that God's people will enjoy "eternal salvation" (5:9), "eternal redemption" (9:12), and "an eternal inheritance" (9:15) under "an eternal covenant" (13:20), it's not a bad choice to endure ill-treatment with God's people rather than to have sin's *temporary* pleasure. This choice equates with "considering vilification [a form of ill-treatment] for the Christ [to be] greater wealth than Egypt's treasures" which, judging from the cache in King Tut's tomb, must have been considerable indeed (compare Psalm 89:50–51). "For the Christ" describes Moses' faith as the assurance and conviction of an unseen but future reality. But how can vilification be considered wealth at all, much less as greater wealth? Answer: Its reward lasts forever whereas Egypt's wealth will soon perish (compare 1:10–12; 12:25–29 and see the comments on 10:35 for "the payback").

11:27: **By faith he [Moses] left Egypt, not having feared the king's anger; for he persisted as though seeing the unseeable one.** According to Exodus 2:13–22 Moses "fled from the presence of Pharaoh" because Pharaoh was trying to kill him upon hearing of Moses' killing an Egyptian who was beating one of Moses' fellow Israelites. Moses was afraid, but the text doesn't say he was afraid of Pharaoh's anger—rather, of a broadcast of Moses' having killed the Egyptian. Apparently our author noticed this distinction and then described Moses as not having feared the king's anger *when he killed the Egyptian before leaving Egypt.* "For he persisted" refers to his subsequent stay of forty years in the land of Midian (Acts 7:29–30). Like parents, like son. Moses' parents "didn't fear the king's edict" (11:23). Moses hadn't feared the king's anger. Nor should Christians fear their persecutors, even a Caesar. And their perseverance should match Moses' persistence. "The unseeable one" was "the Christ," for whom Moses considered vilification to be "greater wealth than Egypt's treasures" (11:26). The Christ was unseeable, however, because he hadn't yet appeared on the scene. But Moses "persisted *as though seeing the unseeable one,*" for faith consists in "assurance concerning accomplishments hoped for, conviction concerning things not seen" (11:1). Likewise Christians, if they're truly Christian, will persevere as though seeing the unseeable Christ till they do see him at his second coming (9:28).

11:28: **By faith he [Moses] has performed the Passover [that is, carried out the rite] and the pouring forth of the blood [of Passover lambs], lest the one who was decimating the [Egyptians'] firstborns touch them [the Israelites (Exodus 12:1–30)].** As before, "he has performed" is spoken from the standpoint of people who have just heard the scriptural account read to them. The performance grew out of an assurance and conviction concerning the future and therefore unseen decimation of firstborn sons except for those in households protected by the blood of Passover lambs. By the same token, a Christian has protection from furious judgment if he hasn't "regarded as defiled the covenantal blood by which he was consecrated" (10:26–31). Since Exodus 12:23 says the Lord will smite the Egyptians but also distinguishes "the decimater" from the Lord, presumably the decimater is the angel of the Lord, his alter ego.

11:29: **By faith they [the Israelites] passed through the Red Sea as though through dry land, which the Egyptians, on taking a test [at doing], were swallowed down [into the sea, so that they drowned (Exodus 14)].** The Israelites passed through the Red Sea by a faith that assured and convinced them that the Red Sea wouldn't

drown them, though it looked as though it would. They believed in a result as yet unseen. Stressing this happy result are the phrase "as though through dry land" and the Egyptians' drowning when they tested whether they could do the same. By faith Christians can pass through their sea, sometimes red with the blood of martyrs, without drowning in a divine judgment worse than drowning in the Red Sea.

11:30–31: **By faith the walls of Jericho fell after being encircled for seven days** [Joshua 6:1–21]. "After being encircled" shows that the walls didn't have faith; rather, the Israelites did who encircled them in the belief that the walls would fall even though the Israelites didn't see them falling in the meantime. "For seven days" showcases the Israelties' exemplary perseverance in this belief. [31]**By faith Rahab the prostitute, having welcomed the spies with peace, didn't perish along with those who were unpersuaded** [that the Lord would give Jericho into the Israelites' hands (Joshua 2:1–24; 6:22–25)]. Identifying Rahab as "the prostitute" points up that despite her prostitution, by faith she didn't perish along with her fellow townspeople, whom Hebrews describes as lacking the persuasion generated by faith. Her faith showed itself in welcoming the Israelite spies "with peace," that is, in greeting them with Middle Eastern hospitality. Likewise, the faith that saves Christians from perishing forever shows itself in their "pursu[ing] peace with all [people]" (12:14) and welcoming with hospitality their persecuted fellow Christians (10:33; 13:1–3).

11:32–34: **And what should I still say? For time will leave me behind [= get away from me] if I recount [the stories] about Gideon, Barak, Samson, Jephthah, and David and Samuel and the prophets,** [33]**who through faith prevailed against kings, administered justice, obtained promises, shut the mouths of lions,** [34]**put out the power of fire [= extinguished raging fire], escaped the mouths [= edges] of a sword, [coming] from a state of weakness were made mighty, became strong in battle, felled the regiments of foreigners** [see, for example, Judges 4–8, 11–12, 14–16; 1 Samuel 1:1–1 Kings 2:11; Daniel 3, 6 (especially 6:22)]. They prevailed against kings when they could only see defeat staring at them. They administered justice when the prevalence of injustice seemed insurmountable. They obtained promises when circumstances looked hopeless.[7] They shut the mouths of lions when they could only see the lions' mouths wide open to devour them. They put out the power of fire when they could only see its flames licking at them. They escaped a double-edged and therefore specially dangerous sword when they could only see its flashing blades ("edges," plural) headed toward them. They were made mighty when they could only see themselves as weak. They became strong in battle when they could only see their frailty (compare 2 Corinthians

---

[7]These heroes of faith did obtain what was promised for their earthly lifetimes, whereas according to 11:13, 39 the patriarchs and others did not obtain during their earthly lifetimes what was promised by way of an eternal inheritance.

12:9–10). They felled the regiments of foreigners when they could only see overwhelming odds arrayed against them. But what they could not see but believed in overcame what they did see. Faith overcame sight. Assurance overcame apprehension. Conviction overcame doubt.

11:35–38: Women received [back] their dead by resurrection; and others were tortured, not accepting release, in order that they might obtain a superior resurrection. ³⁶And different ones took a test consisting of mockings and floggings and, further, of fetters and prison. ³⁷They were stoned. They were sawn apart. They died by murder with a sword. They went around in sheepskins, in goatskins, being destitute, afflicted [literally, "pressured"], ill-treated—³⁸of whom the world wasn't worthy—wandering in deserts and mountains and caves and holes in the ground. This passage highlights faith as faithfulness. Though faith isn't mentioned explicitly, it carries over from 11:33. The passage also alludes to stories such as are found in Judges 14:5–6; 1 Samuel 17:34–36; 1 Kings 17:17–24; 18:4, 13; 19:1–18; 2 Kings 4:8–37; 2 Chronicles 24:20–21; Jeremiah 20:1–2; 26:20–23; 37:15–16; Daniel 3, 6; in some Jewish books outside the Old Testament; and particularly in a tradition that the prophet Isaiah was sawn apart. "Wandering in deserts" means wandering in regions largely or wholly devoid of human population, whether arid or not. Women's receiving back their dead by a preliminary resurrection augurs Christians' receiving back their dead, especially the martyred ones, by the final resurrection. Others didn't accept release from torture—that is, didn't recant so as to bring their torture to a halt. Thus they set an example of faithfulness for persecuted Christians to follow. The "superior resurrection" that such faithfulness gains will be what Daniel 12:2 calls an awakening "to everlasting life" as opposed to an awakening "to disgrace, to everlasting abhorrence." The faithless world is worthy of this shameful resurrection because they were unworthy of God's faithful people. The staccato-style in the second half of this paragraph suggests that a speaker is trying to fit as many examples of faith-in-action as possible into the time remaining. The more examples, the greater the encouragement for his audience to follow suit.

11:39–40: And all these, though attested through faith, didn't receive the promise, ⁴⁰since God had foreseen something superior for us in order that they might not be completed apart from us. See the comments on 11:2, 4 for personified faith as God's agent of attestation, and the comments on 11:13 for "didn't receive the promise." The Old Testament heroes of faith didn't receive—that is, didn't realize—the promise because it was based on Christ's high priestly work in the heavenly sanctuary, a work not yet initiated during their lifetimes. God had foreseen it as something yet to be provided "for us." So he foresaw what the Old Testament heroes of faith didn't see. "Something superior" summarizes the earlier-mentioned superior hope, superior covenant, superior sacrifices, superior possession, superior fatherland, and superior resurrection (7:19, 22; 8:6; 9:23; 10:34; 11:16, 35). "In order that they might not be completed apart from us" implies we Christians are God's people just as those Old Testament heroes were. So don't apostatize from Christianity back to Judaism as though you'd be rejoining God's people. You already belong, and to abandon faith in Christ would be to forfeit your status as one of God's people.

ENCOURAGEMENT FROM THE EXAMPLE OF JESUS
Hebrews 12:1–3

12:1–3: Therefore indeed, because of having so large a cloud of witnesses lying around us, on putting off every impediment—that is, the easily hampering sin—let us too [in addition to those witnesses] **be running with endurance the race lying ahead of us, ²while looking off to the founding leader and completer of the faith,** [namely] **Jesus, who in place of the joy lying ahead of him endured a cross by flouting** [its] **shame** [that is, the shame which crucifixion brings on its victim] **and has sat down at the right** [hand] **of God's throne** [compare Psalm 110:1]. **³For bring your reasoning up** [to the level of] **him who has endured such hostility as this** [that has been exercised] **by sinners against themselves** [referring to their crucifixion of him] **lest by getting tired out you exhaust yourselves.** The author includes himself in "us" to establish rapport with his audience and thus make them more receptive of his exhortation. The addition of "indeed" to "therefore" intensifies the exhortation. This intensification fits the comparison of the Christian life to a footrace, because here the word for "race" gets its particular meaning from the association with running. (Generally, it refers to any kind of struggle.) Because of the preceding and following context of persecution, "the race" stands for the Christian life as a struggle against persecution. "With endurance" fits both the figure of a footrace and the need of Christians to endure persecution rather than dropping out of the race by apostatizing in order to avoid persecution.

Encouragement to be running the race comes from "a cloud of witnesses," who are the past heroes of faith featured in chapter 11. They're "a cloud" in the figurative sense of a crowd engulfing us in the heavenly stands surrounding our earthly racecourse. They're "witnesses" in the double sense of watching us run our race and of cheering us on with the testimony of their own example of having run with the endurance that exhibits faith/faithfulness. In 11:2, 4–5, 39 they were *objects* of witness/testimony by being "attested." Here they are *subjects* who bear witness/testimony to us. "So large" underlines with high numerics their encouraging, cheering testimony. "*Lying* around us" implies their enjoyment of repose after running the race, contrasts with our present running, and thus encourages us to run with endurance right to the finish. "Lying *around* us" brings the past witnesses close at hand for this encouragement.

"The easily hampering sin" identifies what the "impediment" would be. At Greco-Roman athletic contests runners ran naked and barefoot so as not to be impeded by clothes and sandals. Sin hampers runners of the Christian race, and does so "easily." Therefore, and because sinning can eventuate in apostasy, they should strip themselves of "*every* [such] impediment." Notably, it's not persecution but sin that hampers the running (compare the comments on 10:11). "The race lying *ahead of us*" points to the remainder of our Christian lives on this earth and complements the cloud of witnesses "lying *around us*." "Looking off to . . . Jesus" complements "putting off every impediment" and implies fixing our gaze on Jesus rather than on our persecution, which to look at would slow or even stop our running, as when sprinters make the mistake of turning their heads to see how close their competitors might be. Hebrews calls Jesus "the founding leader and completer of the faith" in that he ran the same racecourse of persecution ahead of us, endured without "shrinking back" (to borrow a phrase from 10:39), and now awaits us at the finish line (compare the comments on 2:10). As usual, "the faith" means belief that endures, faithfulness that perseveres.

The race lies ahead of us, but joy lay ahead of Jesus. In place of the joy, meanwhile, was endurance of a cross; that is, he had to endure crucifixion before reaching the goal of joy ("the joy of victory" as opposed to "the agony of defeat"). Not "*the* cross" (as wrongly in most translations, which thus conjure up Christians' gilding it later on), but "*a* cross," just one of many ordinary pieces of wood used in the execution of criminals. In view of ultimate joy Jesus endured his cross by "flouting [its] shame." Crucifixion was considered the most shameful possible way to die, an execution fit for a slave, not so much for its pain as for its disgrace. In it Jesus was stripped naked, exposed to public view and mockery, and denied by death an opportunity to retrieve his honor. God had other ideas, of course, so that Jesus estimated such shame a small price to pay for the joy awaiting him "at the right [hand] of God's throne" (see the comments on 1:3). Sitting there constitutes his joy and implies that with our mind's eye we should be "looking off" to him as he sits there, no longer running, as we too will finish our running when we reach the throne he occupies with God.

"*For* bring your reasoning [up to the level of] him who has endured such hostility as this" explains how Christians are to go about obeying the exhortation to be "running with endurance." "Him who has endured such hostility as this" reemphasizes Jesus' exemplary endurance of crucifixion. The word for "hostility" includes the verbal accusations and mockery that accompanied crucifixion. "By *sinners*" defines Jesus' crucifixion as just such a sin as he sacrificed himself to expiate. Most translations have "by sinners against *himself* [Jesus]." But the best ancient manuscripts have "by sinners against *themselves*," so that those who crucified Jesus sinned against themselves—that is, to their own detriment— just as according to Numbers 16:38 rebels against the God-ordained leadership of Moses and Aaron are said

to have sinned "against themselves" (taking "their souls/ lives" as the Hebrew way of saying "themselves"). Running a race can tire us out to the point of an exhaustion that keeps us from finishing. Likewise, the suffering of persecution can tire us out to the point of apostatizing. But Jesus' example shows we needn't, and shouldn't, exhaust ourselves, that is, give up by apostatizing and thus failing to finish our race, failing to follow Jesus' example of bringing faith/faithfulness to completion.

ENCOURAGEMENT TO ACCEPT THE DISCIPLINE OF PERSECUTION
Hebrews 12:4–13

12:4–7: **You haven't yet resisted to the point of** [shedding your] **blood while struggling against sin,** **[5]and you've quite forgotten the encouragement which as such** [= in its function of encouragement] **is being addressed to you as to sons: "My son, don't be belittling the Lord's discipline** [of you], **and don't be getting tired out when being convicted by him** [of your sins]. **[6]For whom the Lord loves he disciplines, and he flogs every son whom he welcomes** [as his own] **[Proverbs 3:11–12]." [7]Endure** [persecution] **for the purpose of discipline. God is treating you as sons. For what son** [is there] **whom a father doesn't discipline?** Though already persecuted (10:32–34), the audience—unlike Jesus, who shed his blood (9:12, 14; 10:19, 29; 12:24; 13:12, 20)—"haven't yet resisted [their persecutors' attempts to make them apostatize] to the point of [shedding their own] blood." But they might have to in the future ("haven't *yet* . . ."). Since "struggling" is the verbal equivalent of the noun "race" in 12:1, "while struggling against sin" refers to running the Christian race with endurance so as not to commit the sin of apostasy—or other sins, which would hamper the running and tend toward apostasy. Except for "putting off . . . the easily hampering sin" in 12:1, we could say here that Christians are racing against sin. With the charge, "you've quite forgotten," compare especially the command in 10:32–34 to remember past persecution. The encouragement they've quite forgotten is found in Proverbs 3:11–12. According to this quoted passage, sonship and discipline go together.

Though not from the standpoint of its perpetrators, from the Lord's standpoint persecution is discipline; and discipline is a sign of sonship to him. So he uses others' persecution of Christians as his own means of "flog[ging] every son whom he welcomes [as his own]." "Some welcome!" we might be tempted to respond. But the father who's advising his son in Proverbs has forestalled such a response by commanding, "don't be belittling the Lord's discipline [of you], and don't be getting tired out when being convicted by him [of your sins]." As applied to the audience of Hebrews, to belittle the Lord's discipline would be to treat persecution as not a sign of sonship and therefore as something to avoid by apostatizing, for which "getting tired out" is a figure of speech. Compare 5:11–14 with being convicted, though here in 12:4–7 it's the Lord's use of persecution that exposes sin on the part of Christians. Since discipline has to do with punishment as a way of education, he uses persecution to flog the sin out of them. Such discipline exhibits his love. Such flogging signals his welcome. (Flogging stands for persecution; but just as a literal flogging consists in corporal punishment, so persecution often takes a corporal turn.) "He flogs *every* son whom he welcomes" states an exceptionless rule. So don't think the Lord is singling you out unfairly when he uses persecution to discipline you. Instead, "endure [persecution]," for "God is treating you as sons." Let this treatment spur you farther down the racecourse rather than making you drop out, "for what son [is there] whom a father doesn't discipline?"

12:8–10: But if you're without discipline [from God], **of which all** [his sons] **have become partakers, then you're bastards, that is, not** [God's legitimate] **sons. ⁹Furthermore, on the one hand we had fathers of our flesh as disciplinarians; and we were respecting them. On the other hand, shall we not subject ourselves much more to the Father of the spirits and live? ¹⁰For on the one hand they** [our earthly fathers] **were disciplining** [us] **for a few days in accordance with what to them was seeming** [to be] **good** [for us]. **On the other hand he** [God] **[disciplines us] for what is advantageous** [to us] **with the purpose and result of** [our] **sharing in his sanctity.** "Bastards" are those who to avoid the discipline of persecution have apostatized and thus proved they're not legitimate sons of God. "Of which [discipline] *all* [his sons] have become partakers" reiterates that you shouldn't think he's singling you out unfairly when he disciplines you through persecution. The author returns to "we" and "our" in his drawing a parallel between God's disciplining us as our Father and our biological fathers' having disciplined us in our minority (compare the comments on 12:1–3). Respecting our biological fathers as disciplinarians translates into subjecting ourselves to God by accepting the discipline of persecution. But since he ranks much higher than our biological fathers, we should subject ourselves to him "much more" than we did to them. The author's putting this point in the form of a question has the purpose of eliciting the audience's agreement and a corresponding followup in their conduct. Appropriately to the context of fathers and sons, he calls God "the Father." The addition, "of spirits," contrasts God the Father with the "fathers of our flesh." As human males fathered our flesh, God fathered our spirits (compare "the spirits of completed righteous [people]" in 12:23). "Shall we not . . . live?" holds out the assurance of eternal life for us who subject ourselves to the Father of spirits. Supporting such subjection are (1) the implicit parallel between the "few days" of our biological fathers' disciplining us and the short time (by comparison with eternal life) of our spiritual Father's disciplining us through persecution; and (2) the explicit parallel between "what to them [our biological fathers] was seeming [to be] good [for us]" and "what [in God's plan] is [definitely] advantageous [to us]" in that it has "the purpose and result of our

sharing in his sanctity." Most translations have "holiness" instead of "sanctity," but "sanctity" does a better job of getting across the basic meaning of detachment, whether moral or ritual, from impurity.

12:11–13: And all discipline seems for the present not to be joyful, on the one hand—rather, painful. Later, on the other hand, it yields the peaceful fruit of righteousness for those who've been exercised through it. ¹²Therefore straighten up [your] **slackened hands and enfeebled knees.** In other words, lift your hands, tighten their grip on your confession of Jesus as God's Son (compare 4:14), stand up, and put your knees to work in running the Christian race with endurance. **¹³And be making straight tracks with your feet** [compare Proverbs 4:26] **in order that what's lame may not be dislocated—rather, be healed** [compare Isaiah 35:3]. Just as Jesus had to endure a cross before enjoying a seat at God's right hand (12:2), Christians have to endure painful discipline "for the present" before enjoying "the peaceful fruit of righteousness" yielded by that discipline. "Painful" recalls the disciplinary flogging in 12:6. But what is "the peaceful fruit of righteousness"? Because the discipline consists in persecution, "righteousness" refers to God's vindication of those who endure the pain of persecution, not to their own upright character and conduct. To vindicate them for their endurance is the right thing for God to do. "Fruit" is a figure of speech for this righteousness as an outcome of endurance. But what does the description "peaceful" mean? Well, we know that "peace" (*shalōm* in Hebrew) represents all the benefits of salvation (see the comments on 7:2). So "the peaceful fruit of righteousness" means the benefits of salvation that make up God's vindication of "those who've been exercised through it [the discipline of persecution]." This discipline has exercised them in the sense of training them to run with endurance. The vindication will come "later"; for as elsewhere in Hebrews, salvation is put in terms of a final outcome at Jesus' return (see especially 1:14; 9:28). "Be making straight tracks with your feet" commands running straight for the goal without turning away through apostasy (compare 12:1–2). "What's lame" stands for a tendency toward apostasy. "May not be dislocated" stands for *not* apostatizing, and "rather, be healed" for a correction of that tendency.

A WARNING AGAINST APOSTASY
WITH THE EXAMPLE OF ESAU
Hebrews 12:14–29

12:14–17: Pursue peace with all [people (compare Psalm 34:14)], **and sanctification (without which no one will see the Lord) ¹⁵by seeing to it that** [there] **not** [be among you] **anyone coming too late for God's grace,** [that] **not any root of bitterness, by springing up, cause trouble and through it** [the root of bitterness] **many be defiled, ¹⁶**[that among you there] **not** [be] **any fornicator or profane person like Esau, who gave away his very own rights as a firstborn** [son] **in exchange for a single meal** [literally, "a single eating/repast"].

¹⁷**For you know that even afterwards, when wanting to inherit the blessing** [which would bestow on him his birthrights]**, he was rejected; for he didn't find a place of repentance even though having sought it earnestly with tears** [Genesis 27:1–38, especially 34–38]. Chapter 12 started with the figure of running a race. Now it continues with a double pursuit. Like "let us be running," "pursue" demands strenuous effort. The first object of Christians' pursuit is "peace with all [people]." "All" admits of no exceptions, not even of persecutors (who, incidentally, are pursuers, though the author of Hebrews never uses "pursue" for persecuting). The second object is "sanctification," for peaceful relations can suck a person into defiling relations (compare the comments on "sanctity" in 12:10). So Christians are to pursue peace horizontally in relation to all other human beings, and are to pursue sanctification vertically in relation to the Lord. That no one will see him without sanctification gives the strongest possible reason to pursue it. To see the Lord a person has to be ushered into his presence at the end. But since he's the very standard of sanctity, the unsanctified won't get ushered in. Their presence would pollute the atmosphere (for the sanctification of true believers see 2:11; 9:13–14; 10:10, 14, 29; 13:12).

"Coming too late for God's grace" recalls the danger of coming too late to enter God's rest (4:1), credits seeing the Lord to God's grace, and anticipates Esau's coming too late to inherit the blessing "afterwards," which like the present coming too late represents the hopeless fate of apostates. As the spartan conditions of the wilderness embittered the Israelites who came out of Egypt and caused them to apostatize (see 3:8, 15 with comments), so persecution can embitter Christians and cause them to apostatize. A *root* of bitterness stands for a *tendency* toward apostasy. Its springing up—that is, sending a shoot above ground—stands for *actual* apostasy (compare Deuteronomy 29:18). And as indicated by the defiling of many "through it," "cause trouble" refers to the apostate's leading others by example to apostatize with him. Because of this possibility Christians are to be "seeing to it" that no one among them apostatizes and in this respect become a bellwether for others. "*Many* be defiled" highlights the danger of numerous apostasies, reinforces the necessity of communal countermeasures, and by describing apostates as defiled denies them the sanctification without which no one will see the Lord.

Apostasy then broadens out to include non-Christian behavior in addition to the letting go of a Christian confession: "[that among you there] not [be] any fornicator or profane person." A profane person is one who disregards sanctity. Our author cites Esau as a deterrent specimen of such a person and, so far as fornication (having sex with prostitutes) is concerned, may be following a Jewish interpretation of Esau's marrying pagan women who were "a bitterness of spirit" to his parents, Isaac and Rebekah (Genesis 26:34–35; 36:2–3). The profanity of Esau came out in his disregarding the rights he had as a firstborn son, rights emphasized by "his very own," rights he should have considered sacrosanct but

that he gave away (to use the traditional expression) "for a mess of pottage" (Genesis 25:27–34). A firstborn son got the biggest and best share of an inheritance. In view of the designation of God's Son as "firstborn" (1:6) and of Christians as "firstborns" (12:23), Hebrews uses Esau's birthrights as a figure of speech for final salvation through Christ, uses the exchange of those birthrights for apostasy, and uses "a single meal" for "sin's temporary pleasure," that is, enjoyment of the world's acceptance and approval for having apostatized (11:25).

"For you know" appeals to the audience's knowledge of the scriptural story and by indirectly complimenting them for that knowledge seeks their taking to heart the dangerous example of Esau. "Even afterwards, when wanting to inherit the blessing" stresses the tragedy of his rejection because of the earlier exchange. The final "for" introduces the reason for his rejection: "he didn't find a place of repentance even though having sought it earnestly with tears." Repentance means a change of mind that issues in a change of conduct. But whose repentance is in view here? Not Esau's, because he did change his mind about the birthrights. Now he wanted them and went about to get them, whereas formerly he'd disregarded them and given them up. So Esau sought to change Isaac his father's mind. But he couldn't find there "a place" for change. Not even an earnest and tearful search turned up such a place. Similarly, an apostate won't find in God's mind a place for him to change "judgment" by "a fervor of fire" into "the peaceful fruit of righteousness" (see 6:4–8; 10:26–31 over against 12:11). According to 6:6 it's impossible for someone else to change an *apostate's* mind concerning the crucified Son of God. Here it's impossible for the apostate to change *God's* mind concerning the apostate's fearsome judgment. Poor, profane Esau! Unlike the heroes of faith in chapter 11, he exchanged what he couldn't yet see but should have believed in (his birthrights) for what he could see right before his eyes (a single meal). No delayed gratification for him, either in his mind or in his fate. Budding apostates, beware!

12:18–24: **For you haven't come to something tangible** [like Mount Sinai, it will turn out, where the Mosaic law was given] **and a kindled fire and pitch-blackness and a whirlwind** [as on Mount Sinai] ¹⁹**and the blast of a trumpet and the sound of words, a word of which** [sound] **those who heard begged not to be added to them.** That is, the Israelites didn't want to hear a single word more (Exodus 19:10–25; 20:18–21; Deuteronomy 4:10–12, 15, 24; 5:4, 22–27; Psalm 68:7–8). ²⁰**For they weren't bearing the brunt of what was being commanded: "If even a beast should touch the mountain, it shall be stoned** [Exodus 19:12–13]." ²¹**And what was being displayed** [on Mount Sinai] **was fearsome in this way: Moses said, "'I'm terrified' and tremulous** [that is, quivering with fear] [Deuteronomy 9:19]." ²²**Rather, you've come to Mount Zion and the city of the living God** [compare 11:10, 16]**, the heavenly Jerusalem; and to tens of thousands** [= myriads] **of angels,** ²³**an all-inclusive concourse** [of them]**; and to an assembly of** firstborns enrolled in heaven; and to God the judge of all; and to the spirits of completed righteous [people]; ²⁴and to Jesus the intervener of a new covenant; and to the blood of sprinkling [= his sprinkled blood] **that is speaking superiorly as compared with Abel's** [blood]. In 12:17 "For" introduced a reason to pursue peace and sanctification, with the use of Esau as a warning example. Now in 12:18 "For" introduces another reason to pursue peace and sanctification, this time with a contrast between unapproachable Mount Sinai, a threat to apostates, and Mount Zion, a welcoming site for persevering Christian pilgrims. "Tangible" describes Mount Sinai by way of a contrast with Mount Zion, which because of its being the locus of the heavenly Jerusalem is untouchable by earthlings. (The terrestrial Jerusalem rests on the terrestrial Mount Zion, of course.)

"A kindled fire and pitch-blackness and a whirlwind and the blast of a trumpet and the sound of words" all allude to the fearsome phenomena that accompanied God's giving the Mosaic law at Mount Sinai to the generation of Israelites that have appeared earlier, in Hebrews 3–4, as ancient apostates. Those phenomena portended their fate and, by extension, the fate of apostates from Christian faith. Several features of the text underline this symbolic warning: (1) the ancients' begging not to hear another threatening word; (2) the explanation of their begging as a failure to "bear the brunt of what was being commanded"; (3) the command that even a wild animal ("a beast") which happened to touch Mount Sinai should be stoned (with the implications that a domestic animal which did so should much more be stoned, and that a human being who did so should much, much more be stoned); (4) the description of "what was being displayed" as "fearsome"; and (5) its fearsomeness as prompting Moses to say he was trembling in terror.

Nevertheless, more emphasis falls on Christians' having "come to Mount Zion" and to "the city of the living God" located on it. He's described as "living" not just for a contrast with dead idols, but also for an indication that in contrast with the deadly dangerous Mount Sinai (merely touching it demanded death), coming to Mount Zion puts you in touch with the very life of God. The description of Jerusalem as "heavenly" recalls "the heavenly fatherland" in 11:16, "the heavenly things" of "the true tent" in 8:1–5; 9:23, "the heavenly gift" in 6:4, and the "heavenly calling" in 3:1. Given the portrayal in 1:13–14 of all angels as "attendant spirits . . . being sent out for the purpose of service because of those who are going to inherit salvation," the myriads of angels to whom Christians have come sounds a very favorable note, indeed a festive one when restated as "an all-inclusive concourse [of them]." For "assembly" see the comments on 2:12. "The firstborns" are believers such as those celebrated in chapter 11 (see especially 11:8–10, 16). They're called such not only because through brotherhood with God's firstborn Son they share the Son's high status (1:5–6; 2:10–18; contrast Esau, who gave up his rights as a firstborn), but also because they're now "enrolled in heaven" as God's earliest and now deceased

people, as then comes out in "the spirits of completed righteous [people]." They're called "spirits" because of disembodiment through death, and "completed" because of Jesus' having offered himself on their behalf, their having endured a full complement of suffering just as he did, and Christians' now having joined them in faith (2:10; 5:8–9; 7:28; 10:14; 11:40). Their assembly in the heavenly Jerusalem, metropolitan goal of pilgrimage, leaves out no ancient pilgrim who persevered. What encouragement for Christian pilgrims still on the road!

In the present context the designation of God as "the judge of all" connotes especially the vindication of his deceased righteous people. To this vindication is added "Jesus the intervener of a new covenant [see 8:6–13; 9:15, though here the word for 'new' connotes recency more than novelty, as in the earlier passages], and to the blood of sprinkling [see 10:22 and compare 9:11–22] that is speaking superiorly as compared with Abel's blood." The sprinkled blood of Jesus speaks forgiveness by removing sin (9:23–28) whereas the blood of Abel cried out for vengeance against his brother and murderer, Cain (Genesis 4:10). But just how is it that Hebrews' living audience and we as living Christians have "come to" a heavenly location and its heavenly population? The answer has already been given in 4:16 ("let's come to the throne of grace that we may receive mercy and find grace for well-timed help"); 10:19–22 (excerpt: "having confidence for entrance into the Holy [of Holies] by the blood of Jesus . . . let us be coming to [God] with a true heart in the full assurance of faith"); and 11:6 ("the person who's coming to God must believe that he exists and [that] he becomes an awarder to those who are earnestly seeking him"; compare 7:25: "he [Jesus] can also save to entire completion those who are coming to God through him, always living [as he is] to intercede in their behalf"). In short, then, living Christians "come to" a heavenly location and its heavenly population through prayer. As the hymn-writer said, it's the "sweet hour of prayer that calls me from a world of care and bids me *at my Father's throne* make all my wants and wishes known." Through prayer Christian pilgrims have arrived at their final destination before they've arrived at their final destination.

12:25–27: **Watch out lest you refuse the one who's speaking. For if those** [Israelites at Mount Sinai] **didn't escape after refusing the one who was warning them on earth, much more** [will] **we** [not escape] **who turn away from the one** [who's warning us] **from heaven,** ²⁶**whose voice shook the earth then** [when he gave the Law (Psalms 68:7–8; 77:18; 114:7)]**! But now he has promised by saying, "Once more I'll shake not only the earth, but also the heaven** [Haggai 2:6]**."** ²⁷**And the** [phrase] **"once more" indicates the removal of the things being shaken, as of things that have been made, in order that the things not being shaken might last.** Here the author shifts from Jesus' blood that speaks (12:24) over to God, who spoke warningly on Mount Sinai and is still speaking warningly, only now from heaven through our author's use of Scripture: "whose voice [referring to God's voice] shook the earth *then*!

But *now* he has promised by saying," plus a quotation of Haggai 2:6 (compare "the Holy Spirit says," plus a quotation in 3:7–11 of Psalm 95:7–11 and the author's using that quotation as a warning right through 4:13, to which passage the present one harks back). To disregard the warning is to refuse the one who's speaking it, and it's deadly to refuse God when he's speaking. A warning spoken from heaven outweighs a warning spoken on earth. Hence current apostates have less chance of escaping God's judgment than did the Israelites who came out of Egypt and apostatized, and they didn't escape (compare 2:3: "For if the word spoken through angels became firm and every transgression got [its] just deserts [as it did], how will we escape if we've become careless of such a great salvation . . . ?"). God's shaking the earth at Mount Sinai signified judgment, especially judgment against those early apostates bivouacked at the base of the mountain. "He has *promised*" to do some shaking once more, next time of heaven as well as earth, but only once more because the shaking will remove things that are shakeable. "As of things that have been made" identifies the shakeable things, which are to be shaken and thus removed, as those of human construction (compare the "sanctuary made with [human] hands" in 9:24 by way of contrast with the "tent not made with [human] hands" in 9:11). The removal of those things has the purpose of leaving "the things not being shaken" (because they're unshakeable) to last forever.

What these things are becomes clear in *12:28–29*: **Therefore because of receiving an unshakeable kingdom, let us have a thanks**[giving]**, through which we may do religious service pleasingly to God with piety and awe. **²⁹For "our God** [is] **also an incinerating fire** [Deuteronomy 4:24; 9:3]**."** The unshaken things that will last are those that make up the "unshakeable kingdom" of God's Son, whose "throne . . . is forever and ever" (1:8), who himself "will last throughout" (1:11), and whose "years won't run out" (1:12). Believers who persevere are receiving this kingdom as though the future shaking has already occurred, so sure are they to receive it; and receiving it means receiving corulership with God's Son in compensation for having endured persecution. This sure and certain prospect should lead us to hold a thanksgiving service. Holding it will please God with the piety and awe that it evinces. And we need to please him with our piety and awe because he's "an incinerating fire" as well as a shaker of earth and heaven.

PRACTICAL EXHORTATIONS
Hebrews 13:1–19

Growing out of Christians' reception of "an unshakeable kingdom" and God's being "an incinerating fire" (12:28–29) are practical exhortations designed to prevent apostasy.

13:1–3: Brotherly love is to continue. **²Don't be forgetting** [to show] **love to strangers, for through this some were unaware of having entertained angels** [when in fact they had]. **³Keep remembering those in fetters** [= prisoners] **as though fettered with** [them]— [that is,] **those being ill-treated—as also yourselves being in a body** [and therefore likewise vulnerable to the ill-treatment of imprisonment]. Love between biological brothers was considered a very strong and close relationship. Here the author uses "brotherly love" to stress how strong and close should be the relationship of love between fellow Christians. The statement in 10:33 that the addressees had "become sharers with those being treated in this way [= 'through vilifications and afflictions']" implies a brotherly love which had sustained them in an earlier persecution. The author therefore commands a continuance of such love, for persecution is unlikely to cease. "To show love to strangers" is often translated "to show hospitality." What we have here does remind us of the Middle Eastern law of hospitality, according to which room and board should be provided to traveling strangers. But the underlying Greek verb contains the same element of "love" that has just occurred in "brotherly love," and the context of persecution makes it probable that the author of Hebrews has particularly in mind the provision of room and board to fellow Christians who are fleeing persecution (compare Matthew 10:23, 40–42; 25:31–46). Because they've fled from elsewhere, they're strangers. But because they're fellow Christians, providing them room and board is comparable to entertaining angels unawares, for which Genesis 18:1–8 with 19:1–3 supplies the historical background (compare Judges 6:11–24). So the provision of such hospitality examples one way in which brotherly love is to continue.

"Don't be forgetting" corresponds to "is to continue" and suggests not only a tendency to forget this Christian duty, because a brother "out of sight" in a prison easily transmutes into a brother "out of mind," but also a temptation to forget the duty out of a desire to avoid persecution oneself. For to associate with the persecuted is to invite one's own persecution. According to 10:34 the addressees had "show[n] sympathy even to the prisoners." So "keep remembering those in fetters" commands a continuance of this form of brotherly love. For examples of imprisonment as persecution see especially Acts 12:1–11; 16:19–40; 2 Corinthians 11:23. Imprisonment wasn't used as a form of punishment—rather, as a way of securing the accused for an upcoming trial. Prisoners got at most, if at all, a little bread and water from the jailer, who might also abuse the prisoners physically. To remember prisoners therefore meant not simply to keep them in mind. It meant to keep them in mind by way of taking them adequate food and drink and even to stay with them for the prevention of abuse. "As though fettered with them" refers to staying with them though not being chained as they are. "Those being ill-treated" are the fettered, malnourished, and abused prisoners. Their treatment is "ill" also in that they don't deserve such treatment. Confessing Christ and living as a Christian shouldn't draw imprisonment. "As also yourselves being in a body" commands the addressees to risk physical ill-treatment themselves by staying with their imprisoned fellow Christians.

The topic of love within the Christian community now shifts into the topics of marriage and the love of money. *13:4:* **Marriage [is to be] valued in all respects and the bed** [where sexual intercourse takes place] **undefiled** [by illicit sex], **for God will judge fornicators and adulterers.** Marriage is to be valued in all respects, but in particular as the sole legitimate framework for a fulfillment of sexual desire. Outside that framework, sexual intercourse defiles the bed where it takes place and thus debases marriage. God's coming judgment of fornicators and adulterers proves the point. "Adulterers" refers to persons who have sexual intercourse with another person's spouse. "Fornicators" can refer to persons who engage in any form of illicit sex (premarital intercourse, incest, bestiality, and homosex as well as adultery) but because of being paired with "adultery" probably refers especially to men who have sex with prostitutes. For it was widely thought legitimate even for husbands to do so, if for no other reason than to spare the wife of constant pregnancy and birthing. Apart from repentance and consequent reformation of conduct, God's judgment will decree eternal damnation, no matter what the fornicators' and adulterers' profession of Christian faith.

13:5–6: [Your] **deportment [is to be] absent the love of money, because of being content with the things** [you have] **at hand. For he himself** [the Lord] **has said, "By no means will I ever let go of you, and by no means will I ever abandon you** [Deuteronomy 31:6, 8]," [6]**so that being confident we say, "The Lord** [is] **my helper, and I'll not be frightened. What will a human being do to me** [by way of damage, if the Lord helps me] [Psalms 56:11; 118:6]**?"** The love of money would destroy brotherly love, especially in a culture where economy was often thought to be a zero sum game in which one person's gain entails another person's loss. So contentment with present possessions should forestall love of money. Why be contented with them, though? Because of the Lord's faithfulness (expressed in the quotations of Deuteronomy 31:6, 8 and Psalms 56:11; 118:6). Emphasizing his faithfulness are (1) the addition of "himself" to "he"; (2) the tense of "has said," which indicates the permanence of his assurance of faithfulness; (3) "by no means"; (4) the doubling of the assurance, including a second "by no means"; (5) the changing of "he [the Lord God]" in Deuteronomy to "I" here in Hebrews so as to make the twofold assurance the Lord's own words to Christians; (6) a mention of their resultant confidence despite lack of money; and (7) the use of Psalms 56:11; 118:6 to express that confidence. "*We* say" draws the audience together with the author in this expression of confidence. The Lord's help does away with fright. "What will a human being do to me?" implies that persecution has caused the lack of money (see 10:34: "For you . . . welcomed with joy the seizure of your possessions, knowing that you yourselves have a superior and lasting possession"). The lack of money can engender a love of money. But can't human beings, persecutors in particular, do economic and other damage to a Christian despite the Lord's helping him?

Don't they? Yes, of course. So why not be frightened? Because divine vindication and final salvation await the faithful Christian at the Last Judgment. In comparison, what a human being does to me now shouldn't count, and doesn't.

13:7–8: **Keep in mind your leaders, who as such spoke God's word to you. By closely observing the outcome of their conduct, imitate** [their] **faith/faithfulness.** [8]**Yesterday and today Jesus Christ** [is] **the same—and forever!** "As such" means that by speaking God's word to the addressees of Hebrews their leaders had led them into Christian faith. Keeping the leaders in mind equates with "closely observing the outcome of their conduct"; and the outcome of their conduct consists in their faith, which as usual means belief that keeps the believer faithful as opposed to apostatizing. Such faith/faithfulness is to be imitated (compare 6:12). In recollection of 12:1–3 the author cites Jesus as the supreme example of faith/faithfulness. The addition of "Christ" to "Jesus" underscores his exemplifying it. He's "the same" in that his faith/faithfulness has remained constant from past ("yesterday") to present ("today"). The separate addition of "and forever!" extends his faith/faithfulness everlastingly (compare 5:6 and especially 7:24–25: "Because he [Jesus] continues forever, . . . he can also save to entire completion those who are coming to God through him, always living [as he is] to intercede in their behalf").

13:9: **Don't be letting yourselves be carried aside** [from the racecourse of 12:1–2?] **by various and strange teachings. For** [it's] **good to let** [your] **heart be firmed up by grace, not by foods, in which those who walk around have not been benefited.** To let ourselves be carried aside by various and strange teachings would count as unfaithfulness. "Various" describes the teachings as multiple in contrast with the singularity of God's having "spoken to us at the last, [that is,] during these days, in a son" (1:1–2); and "strange" describes the teachings as foreign to what God has spoken in a son. It's likely but not certain that such teachings were designed for the avoidance of persecution. The followup, which supports the exhortation, even suggests that these teachings urged Christians to make like non-Christian Jews by practicing the dietary regulations of the Mosaic law (compare the comments on 9:9–10). For Roman law exempted Jews from persecution even though they refused to worship the emperor. Since walking around is an often-used figure of speech for lifestyle, "those who walk around [in foods]" means "those who practice dietary regulations." Just as the author has described animal sacrifices under the Mosaic law as nonbeneficial, so now he describes the practice of Moses' dietary regulations as nonbeneficial, and ranges over against them God's "grace," which is to be found under the new covenant at "the throne of grace" in the heavenly Holy of Holies rather than in an earthly sanctuary (see, for example, 4:14–16). This grace will firm up the heart by way of strengthening it to persevere in the face of persecution.

13:10–14: We have an altar from which those who do religious service at the [Mosaic] **tent don't have authority to eat.** [11]**For the corpses of these living** [creatures (= animals)], **whose blood is carried by the high priest into the Holy** [of Holies on the Day of Atonement year by year] **as a sin offering—**[their corpses] **are burned outside the camp.** [12]**Therefore Jesus too, in order that he might consecrate the people through his own blood, suffered outside the gate.** [13]**Well, then, let us be going out to him, outside the camp, by carrying his vilification.** [14]**For we don't have a lasting city here; rather, we're earnestly seeking the** [city] **that's going to come.** Because of the contrast with Moses' earthly tent, the altar from which the Levitical high priests "don't have authority to eat" must be an altar in the heavenly sanctuary, which like the earthly sanctuary also has an altar, a curtain, a Holy of Holies, and a throne from which mercy and grace are dispensed in correspondence to the Old Testament mercy seat (4:16; 7:13; 8:1–2, 5; 9:1–14, 23–26; 10:19–22). The author supports the Levitical high priests' lack of authority by appealing to the burning of the corpses of animals sacrificed every Day of Atonement (Leviticus 16:27). A high priest carried their blood into the Holy of Holies as a sin offering; but without being salvaged for meat to be eaten (as in the case of some other sacrifices [Leviticus 6:24–7:38]), the animals' blood-drained corpses were burned outside the Israelites' campsites in the wilderness. Though the author is referring to Levitical high priests and their sacrifices of long ago, when the Mosaic tabernacle stood, he uses the present tense in "[they] don't have authority to eat [from the heavenly altar]," "is carried," and "are burned." The present tense dramatizes the inferiority of those high priests and their sacrifices by making them contemporary, so to speak, with the superior high priest, Jesus, and his self-sacrifice. The animals sacrificed by the Levitical high priests had been "living [creatures]"; but absent their blood, in which resided their life (Genesis 9:4; Leviticus 17:11, 14; Deuteronomy 12:23), they'd become "corpses." So Hebrews makes the Levitical high priests' lack of authority to eat meat from sacrifices made on the Day of Atonement symbolic of those priests' lack of authority to eat Christ's flesh from the heavenly altar. They lacked authority to eat literally the meat of those sacrificed animals. Because they weren't Christians they lacked authority to eat figuratively—that is, by faith—the sacrificed flesh of Christ.

Hebrews also makes the burning "outside the camp" symbolic of Jesus' suffering "outside the gate [of Jerusalem]" (for which see Mark 15:20; Matthew 27:31–33; and especially John 19:17, 20 [compare Mathew 21:39]). In fact, he's said to have suffered outside the gate for the very purpose of fulfilling this symbolism, and fulfilling it in this way had the purpose of consecrating "the people"—that is, past and present believers—"through his own blood." Consecrating them means making them God's people as distinct from unbelievers, including Christians-turned-apostate (2:11–12). "*His own* blood" stresses the superiority of Jesus' self-sacrifice over the Levitical priests' sacrifice of mere animals. Jesus' suffering outside the gate doesn't correspond to the animals' being sacrificed at the earthly sanctuary, though. The high priest carried their blood into the Holy of Holies *before* the burning of their corpses outside the camp, whereas Jesus carried his blood into the heavenly Holy of Holies *after* suffering outside the gate. To offset this lack of correspondence, the author makes Jesus' suffering "outside the camp" symbolic of the vilification that persecuted Christians have to endure just as Jesus did (compare the shame of his crucifixion in 12:2). The shift from his suffering "outside the *gate*" to Christians' going to him "outside the *camp*" reestablishes a correspondence in respect to the burning of sacrificed corpses outside the Israelites' camp in the wilderness and Christians' going to Jesus "outside the camp" of Judaism, and being vilified for doing so. "For we don't have a lasting city here" makes Jerusalem the present equivalent of the Israelites' camp in the wilderness and points up the obsolescence of this earthly Jerusalem now that Jesus has suffered its vilification of him. Christians' "*carrying* his vilification" calls to mind Simon of Cyrene's carrying the crossbar of Jesus' cross through jeering crowds on the way to Golgotha (see the comments on Mark 8:34) and means enduring vilification for belief in the shamefully crucified Jesus. Going out to him from the earthly camp/city constitutes an earnest search for the heavenly Zion/city that's coming (compare 11:10, 16; 12:22).

13:15–16: Through him, therefore [because "we don't have a lasting city here; rather, . . . a (city) that's going to come"], **let us be continually offering to God a sacrifice of praise, that is, the fruit of** [our] **lips as they confess his name.** [16]**And don't be forgetting the doing of good and sharing, for God is pleased with such sacrifices** [as opposed to animal sacrifices (compare Psalm 50:14)]. Christians are to offer sacrifices to God "through him [Jesus]" just as the Israelites were to bring their sacrifices to Levitical priests, who then presented the sacrifices to God. But "continually" distinguishes Christians' offerings both from the recently mentioned sin offerings sacrificed only once a year, on the Day of Atonement, and from Jesus' self-sacrifice "once for all" (7:27; 9:12; 10:10). "Of praise" distinguishes this sacrifice by Christians from animal sacrifices, and especially from the self-sacrifice of Jesus since it accomplished the expiation of sins and propitiation of God and thus made God deserving of praise for having brought his firstborn Son into the inhabited earth for the accomplishment of those feats (1:6; 2:17; 8:12). Since by definition "praise" means a public declaration—of what God has done in this case—the author picks up on the earlier allusion to soil that bears vegetation (6:7–8) to describe praise figuratively as "the fruit of [our] lips," as though our lips were fruit-bearing soil. To confess God's name is to declare him to be who his name says he is—namely, God—in praise for what he has done in the demonstration of his deity. But words of praise need supplementation by good deeds, a second kind of sacrifice that Christians must offer to God through Jesus. See the comments on 13:2

for the command, "don't be forgetting." "Sharing" defines "the doing of good" with particular reference to sharing resources with fellow Christians who are enduring economic losses through persecution (for which sharing see 10:32–34 [compare 13:1–3]). God's taking pleasure in such sacrifices provides motivation for making them, and the plural in "such sacrifices" calls for repeated good deeds of sharing.

13:17: Be obeying your leaders and submitting [to them]**, for they themselves are keeping watch over your souls as those who'll give back** [to God] **an account** [concerning your response to their leadership]. [Be obeying and submitting] **in order that they may do this with joy and not** [be] **sighing** [with grief over your lack of obedience and submission]. **For this** [would be] **disadvantageous to you.** As a hedge against the "various and strange teachings" warned against in 13:9, the author commands obedience and submission to the addressees' leaders. The verb for obedience has to do with letting yourself be persuaded—in other words, with taking advice—and the verb for submission has to do with yielding to the leaders' attempts at persuasion. "Themselves" highlights "they" for emphasis on the leaders' concern for the Christians they lead. "Are keeping watch over your souls" compares the leaders implicitly to shepherds (see 13:20, where Jesus as "the *great* shepherd of the sheep" distinguishes him from these leaders, their ordinary shepherds). Like shepherds of sheep, faithful Christian leaders have concern for those they lead; and apparently the author knows his addressees' leaders to be true in their concern, which in turn gives reason to obey them and submit to them. "Your souls" means "your very selves," with a focus on inner being and probably also on eternal destiny since "soul" often means "life" in reference to eternity as well as present time (see Mark 8:34–38, for example). "As those who'll give back [to God] an account" describes the leaders further as laboring under the recognition that at the Last Judgment they'll have to tell how well or badly their charges obeyed and submitted, so that their concern arises out of an unselfish motive. They want to avoid having to give God an account disadvantageous to their charges.

13:18–19: Be praying for us; for we're convinced that we, wanting to conduct ourselves well in all respects, have a good consciousness. [19]**But I'm exhorting you all the more to do this in order that I may very quickly be restored to you.** With "us," "we," and "ourselves" the author includes himself with his audience's leaders, so that the preceding command to obey and submit includes obedience and submission to what the author has written in this letter. But just as the audience need to obey their leaders and submit to them, the leaders need their audience to pray for them—in part, presumably, because persecution falls first and hardest on the leaders. Their having "a good consciousness"— that is, a consciousness of "wanting . . . to conduct themselves well"—gives the audience reason to pray for the author and his fellow leaders. "In all respects" en-

hances the reason. The author exhorts the audience "all the more" to pray specifically that he may "very quickly be restored" to them. So he's one of them though away from them at the time of writing and, by implication, believes they need his personal presence to help keep them from apostatizing, and need it desperately—hence, "very quickly." We don't know what circumstance required a "restor[ation]" of the author, as opposed to his merely coming to them.

CONCLUSION
Hebrews 13:20–25

Hebrews started without the usual features of an ancient letter: the author's name, an address, a greeting. But like a letter it now ends with greetings, personal news, and benedictions.

13:20–21: And may the God of peace, the one who in/by the blood of the eternal covenant brought up, out from among the dead, the great shepherd of the sheep—our Lord, [namely,] **Jesus—**[21]**equip you with every good thing so as to do his will by** [God's] **doing in us what** [is] **pleasing in his sight through Jesus Christ, who** [has] **the glory forever. Amen.** "May" goes with "equip" to produce the wish, "And may the God of peace . . . equip you . . ."; and "in/by the blood of the eternal covenant" goes with "brought up . . . the great shepherd of the sheep," not with "the God of peace." As elsewhere, "peace" connotes all the blessings of salvation," so that "the God of peace" credits God for the provision of those blessings. The further description of him as "the one who . . . brought up, out from among the dead, . . . our Lord, [namely,] Jesus" tells the means by which God ensured for believers the blessings of salvation. "Brought *up*" may suggest exaltation to God's right hand, as in 1:3, 13; 8:1; 10:12; 12:2 in addition to resurrection "out from among the dead." "Our *Lord*" favors this suggestion, and "*our* Lord" brings the author together with his audience under Jesus' lordship. To maintain rapport with them, in other words, the author is assuring them that he doesn't think himself exempt from that lordship. Not only does "the great shepherd of the sheep" portray Jesus as a shepherd, and indeed as the ruler of his people in that shepherding often stood for ruling (see, for example 2 Samuel 5:2; Matthew 2:2, 6). This figure of speech also implies a comparison of the author and his audience to sheep, who as such are bound to follow Jesus' lead, that is, submit to his lordship. "The *great* shepherd of the sheep" places him above the aforementioned leaders (13:17) just as "a *great* high priest" placed him above the Levitical high priests (4:14; 10:21).

But what does it mean that God brought Jesus up "in/by the blood of the eternal covenant"? Well, according to 9:11–12 Christ entered once for all into the heavenly Holy of Holies "through [the instrumentality of] his own blood." So "in/by the blood" means that God used Jesus' sacrificial blood as the sphere in which, and/or as the means by which, he brought Jesus up to the heavenly Holy of Holies for the presentation of his blood as an expiation (atonement) for our sins and a propitiation (appeasement) of God (2:17; 8:12). "Of the eternal covenant" describes the blood as having inaugurated the covenant, and "eternal" describes the covenant in that "those who've been called" have "receive[d] the promise of an eternal inheritance" (9:15 [compare 5:9; 9:12; Jeremiah 32:40; Zechariah 9:11]).

"Equip you with every good thing so as to do his will" recalls "the doing of good and sharing" (13:16) and wishes God's enablement for so doing (see 10:7 for the example of Jesus' doing God's will[8]). It takes "every good thing" by way of equipment to do the "good" of sharing. That it's "his will" we do this good provides reason enough for God's people to share (about which see the comments on 13:16). By equipping us with every good thing so as to do his will, God is "doing in us what's pleasing in his sight," so that we have no basis for self-righteous boasting. Naturally, he's "pleas[ed]" with "his will" that he's "doing in us." If he weren't pleased with it, he wouldn't be doing it. "In his sight" recalls that "all things [are] bare and exposed to the eyes of him with whom we have an account" (4:13). "Through Jesus Christ" makes him God's agent in doing in us what God wants us to do—that is, makes him God's agent in equipping us to do it, just as he was God's agent in "mak[ing] the ages" (1:2). Most translations have "to whom [be] the glory." But according to 1:3; 2:9; 3:3 he already has glory—hence the translation, "who [has] the glory." The full name "Jesus Christ" suits his possession of glory. "Forever" describes it as unending. And "Amen" caps it with the author's affirmation.

13:22–23: I exhort you, brothers: Be putting up with the word of exhortation [= this message that consists in my exhortations], **for—besides—I've written you a letter with few** [words]. [23]**Know that our brother Timothy** [is] **released, with whom, if he comes very quickly, I'll see you.** For the address "brothers," see the comments on 3:1, 12. Here it lends weight to the exhortation to put up with the overall exhortation that constitutes this letter. "Put up with" is intended to

---

[8]At 13:21 some excellent ancient manuscripts add "for him [God]" to "do his will," in which case we're to do the will of God for God's sake as well as for the sake of those whom we treat well.

quash any resistance that may have been building up against it during its reading to the audience. With an aside, the author then supports this exhortation to put up with the overall exhortation by citing its brevity ("a letter with few [words]"). Since the letter takes about an hour to read aloud, the author may be writing pen in cheek (or tongue in cheek if he's using a scribe to write at dictation, as most authors did). But the similar statement in 1 Peter 5:12 suggests a conventional statement that has the purpose of encouraging an audience not to dismiss the letter because of what they might think to be its excessive length. Given the stakes of eternal redemption because of perseverance versus eternal damnation because of apostasy, the letter has few enough words! The news of Timothy's release implies not only that he has been in prison (compare 10:34; 13:3) but also that the author and his audience know Timothy and know about his recent imprisonment. "With whom, if comes very quickly" implies that Timothy isn't present with the author at the time of writing, that he's expected to arrive at the author's location, and that in answer to the audience's prayers that the author be restored to them "very quickly" (13:19) he'll see them soon whether or not Timothy arrives in time to accompany him. "I'll see you" carries an implicit warning that he, perhaps with the backing of Timothy in person, will check up on the audience's response to this "word of urging." For more on Timothy see especially Acts 16:1–3; 2 Timothy 1:1–5.

13:24–25: Greet all your leaders and all the saints. The [saints] **from Italy greet you** [that is, send you greetings through this letter]. [25][May] **grace** [be] **with you all.** For "the saints" see the comments on 6:10. "The [saints] from Italy" probably refers to Christians who used to live in Italy but are now living wherever the author is located outside Italy. The phrase probably implies as well that the audience are living in Italy and therefore would welcome greetings from Italian expatriates. These voluntary greetings and the commanded ones have the purpose of strengthening Christian cohesion so as to guard against apostasy because of persecution. The author wishes that God's grace be with the audience to achieve this same purpose, for "grace" is needed "for well-timed help" in the test of persecution (4:16). "*All* your leaders," "*all* the saints," and "with you *all*" exhibit the goal of not losing even one soul to apostasy.

JAMES

This letter is a manual of Christian conduct that assumes a foundation of faith. The manual deals especially with Christians' conduct toward one another.

ADDRESS AND GREETING
James 1:1

1:1: James, a slave of God and of the Lord, Jesus Christ, to the twelve tribes in the Diaspora: [I wish you] **to rejoice** [= the Greek way of saying "Greetings" or "Hello"]. As was customary, the letter writer starts by identifying himself. The name "James" in the New Testament is equivalent to the name "Jacob" in the Old Testament. Though several Jameses appear in the New Testament, the present James is probably to be identified with a half brother of Jesus and full brother of the author of Jude. For more information, see the comments on Jude 1–2. "A slave of God and of the Lord, Jesus Christ" implies that James is carrying out orders by writing this letter. To be a slave of someone prominent and powerful, moreover, brought great honor on the slave. And who greater than God and the Lord, Jesus Christ? So James's audience had better listen up. He's carrying out orders from above. The designation of Jesus Christ as "the Lord" and the pairing of him with "God" point to Jesus' sharing deity with God the Father. "The Diaspora" means "the scattering" and refers to Jews living scattered outside the land of Israel. Though the term is used figuratively in 1 Peter 1:1–2 for Christians as the new Israel regardless of ethnicity, James's specification of "the twelve tribes," the Jewish tone of the rest of the letter, and James's base in Jerusalem favor a limitation of this address to Jews. The reference to Jesus Christ as "the Lord" and especially the reference in 2:1 to James's audience as "holding faith in our glorious Lord, Jesus Christ" show that James is writing even more limitedly to Jewish *Christians* living abroad. According to Acts 12:17; 15:13; 21:18; Galatians 1:19; 2:9, 12 this James rose to leadership in the church at Jerusalem. According to Acts 8:4; 11:19 Jewish Christians living there were scattered to outlying countries because of a persecution associated with the martyrdom of Stephen (Acts 6:8–8:3). And from time to time James will bring up the testing of faith by persecution. So as those Jewish Christians' former pastor in Jerusalem, James may be writing to them in particular. Let's assume so.

AN EXHORTATION TO REJOICE WHEN TEMPTED IN TRIALS
James 1:2–4

1:2–4: Whenever you fall into various temptations, my brothers, consider [it] **all joy** [3]**because of knowing that the authenticity of your faith produces perseverance.** [4]**And perseverance is to have a complete product, so that you're complete and whole, lacking in nothing.** "Brothers" means fellow Christians. The attachment of "my" brings James himself into the brotherhood and thus expresses affection for his audience and establishes rapport with them. "Temptations" translates a Greek word which also means "trials" and is often translated with that word here. In fact, though, every trial consists in a temptation to lose faith; and every temptation consists in a trial of faith. To maintain the element of trials as temptations, then, and to link up with the topic of temptation in 1:12–15, the translation "temptations" will serve well. "Various" describes the temptations in that they included displacement from homeland, social ostracism, economic boycott, and the loss of loved ones and friends through martyrdom—all because of persecution. (Later, James himself suffered martyrdom.) The audience are to consider falling into these temptations to lose faith not merely *with* joy but *to be* joy. Furthermore, to be *all* joy—in other words, entirely joyful. How so, especially in view of the variety of trying temptations? Answer: Because perseverance under various temptations lets you know that your faith is authentic, and such knowledge should bring you joy. James then personifies perseverance and issues an indirect command that it "have a complete product." A complete product is a finished one, so that to "have" it is to have finished it. The finished product consists in a Christian who has persevered by resisting temptations to give up faith under trial. To stress the completeness of such a Christian, James adds "and whole, lacking in nothing"—that is, lacking in nothing that would authenticate his faith. No wonder he tells them to "consider [it] all joy," a command that picks up on James's greeting, "[I wish you] to rejoice" (1:1).

AN EXHORTATION TO ASK GOD FOR WISDOM
James 1:5–8

1:5: But if anyone of you lacks wisdom, he's to be asking [for it] **from God, who generously gives to all and doesn't demean** [the asker for asking]. **And it**

[wisdom] **will be given to him.** "Lacking in nothing" (1:4) triggers in James the thought that some in his audience may not yet be "complete and whole." They may lack wisdom, particularly on how to cope with temptations brought on by the trials of persecution. Such a Christian is to be asking for wisdom as a gift from God. Not "*you* ask," but "*he's* to ask." The indirectness of this command softens it and thus makes it sympathetic. Then James cites God's generosity as an encouragement to ask. The word translated "generously" means, when translated more literally, "singly." Unlike the double-minded doubter whom James is about to mention, God gives single-mindedly. He gives without going back and forth on whether to give. Strengthening this encouragement to ask are his giving "to all" (he doesn't play favorites among Christians) and his not "demean[ing]" any Christian for asking (they won't lose his respect). There's a qualification, however.

1:6–8: But he's to be asking in faith, doubting not at all [compare Mark 11:24; Matthew 21:21–22]**. For the person who's doubting is like sea surf being blown and tossed about by the wind.** [7-8]**For that man—double-minded, unstable in all his ways—isn't to suppose that he'll receive anything from the Lord.** James repeats the indirect command, "he's to be asking" (see the comments on 1:5). To ask in faith is not to doubt at all that God will grant a request for wisdom. Even the slightest such doubt would dishonor him by calling in question his generosity. And doubting not only says something about God that's uncomplimentary and untrue. It also says something about the asker that's uncomplimentary—but true in his case. He has two minds (or, more literally, "two souls," indicating a kind of split personality). With one he believes. With the other he doesn't. He switches back and forth between believing and not believing. (Doubt isn't disbelief; it's switching, waffling.) Being of two minds, the doubter is unstable—not a good condition for a persecuted Christian to be in. James makes a comparison to wind-blown, wind-tossed sea surf as opposed to terra firma, solid ground. "In all his ways" indicates that doubting God's generosity to give wisdom represents an instability caused by doubt in all other aspects of the asker's Christian life. In other words, doubt is pervasive. It can't be isolated. It produces instability all the way around. So why ask God *believingly* for wisdom? First, because an asker who *doubts* is like unstable sea surf. Second, because he won't receive *anything*—whether wisdom or anything else—from the Lord. In 1:1 James called Jesus Christ "the Lord." But in 1:5 he wrote about asking "God" for wisdom. Therefore God and the Lord Jesus Christ are interchangeable so far as their deity is concerned. Yet again James uses an indirect command (not "don't *you* suppose," but "*that man . . .* isn't to suppose"), which here suggests he doesn't expect anyone in his audience to fall into the category of a doubter: "that man [over there, as distinct from you] . . . isn't to suppose that he'll receive anything from the Lord." So the doubter, who because of his doubt can't be sure the Lord will give him wisdom if he asks for it, *can*

be sure the Lord won't give him anything at all because of his doubt.

AN EXHORTATION NOT TO DESIRE WEALTH
James 1:9–11

1:9–11: And the low brother [= the Christian of low social status because of lacking wealth] **is to be boasting in his height** [= high status before God because of being a Christian]. [10]**But the rich** [man is to be boasting] **in his lowering, because he'll pass away as the flower of grass** [passes away (compare Isaiah 40:6–7)]. [11]**For the sun rose with scorching heat and dried up the grass, and its flower fell off and the beauty of its face** [= appearance] **was lost. In this way the rich** [man] **too will fade away in the midst of his journeys.** James continues to use indirect commands. The boasting of a low brother doesn't connote arrogance. He has no accomplishments that would elevate him to an honorable position in worldly society. So he's to boast in the sense of expressing pride in having been elevated to an honorable position before God, and this through no merit of his own—rather, by God's grace. In view especially of 2:5–7, where the rich are said to be suppressing James's "beloved brothers" and slandering "the good name" of Jesus that was invoked over them (at baptism), the rich man here in 1:10 is hardly a Christian. If he isn't, James is using sarcasm in saying that as a non-Christian the rich man should be "boasting in his lowering"—that is, in God's lowering him into hell—as though even that kind of divine attention provides a ground for boasting. God's elevating the poor and persecuted combines with his lowering the rich and oppressive to encourage perseverance on the part of Christians. See the comments on 1 Peter 1:24 for the comparison to field grass and its flowers. Like the lowering of the rich man, his passing away and fading away allude to his dying and going to hell. "In the midst of his journeys" suggests that death (or the second coming?) will catch the rich man unawares during his travels, whether for business or for pleasure.

AN EXHORTATION TO PERSEVERE
James 1:12–18

1:12: Fortunate is a man who perseveres under a temptation [by resisting it]**, because on becoming authenticated he'll receive the crown of life that he** [the Lord] **has promised to those who love him.** The word for "a man" usually refers to an adult male. James uses it here to portray Christians, whatever their age or sex, who are "complete and whole, lacking in nothing" (1:4). Such Christians *can* persevere, *do* persevere, and thereby become authenticated as true Christians. As a result, they'll get "the crown of life," that is, eternal life portrayed in terms of a victor's wreath. Good fortune indeed! They will have conquered the temptation to give in under trial. James cites the Lord's promise as an encouraging assurance. "To those who love him" implies that the true Christian perseveres out of love for the Lord, and that temptation tests that love.

1:13–15: No one being tempted is to say, "I'm being tempted by God [in the sense that the temptation comes from him]**." For God is untemptable by evil** [beings], **and he himself tempts no one.** Again James issues a command in the third person ("No one") rather than in the second person ("You"). The accent therefore falls on "No one." No exceptions are allowed, for even one exception would impugn the character of God. Since there's nothing in his character that would make him succumb to temptation, there's nothing in his character that would make him want anybody else to succumb to temptation. So no one should blame him for a temptation or excuse succumbing to temptation on the ground that God wanted him to succumb (contrast the Devil in this respect). [14]**But each** [man] **is tempted when being dragged away and baited by his own lusts.** Lusts are desires so strong that that they drag a person into transgressing divinely set boundaries. "Dragged away and baited" stresses the accountability of lust for temptations, and "his *own* lust" stresses the man's accountability for lust. Again, God isn't at fault. [15]**Then lust, having conceived, gives birth to a sin; and the sin, having been brought to completion** [as in full growth]**, births death.** James personifies lust as a female who conceives a sin within herself. Then he personifies the sin as a child. The child's birth symbolizes the committing of a sin. When the sin is full grown, like its mother (lust) it too becomes a mother by giving birth to death. This death occurs at the end of life and for non-Christians eventuates not only in physical death but also in eternal punishment, elsewhere called "the second death" (compare Genesis 2:16–17; 5:3–32; Romans 6:23; Revelation 2:11; 20:6, 14; 21:8). Meanwhile, the completion of sin stands in horrid contrast with the completion of Christians by virtue of their perseverance (1:4).

1:16–18: Don't you be letting yourselves be led astray, my beloved brothers. [17]**All good giving and every complete gift is from above, coming down from the Father of lights, with whom there's no variation or shadow of turning** [= shifting shadow]**.** [18]**Having willed** [to do so]**, he birthed us by the word of truth so that we might be, and are, a certain first fruits of his creatures.** In 1:2 James addressed his audience with "my brothers." Now he adds "beloved" to highlight his love for them, strengthen rapport with them, and show concern that they not let themselves be led astray. A shift from the earlier indirect commands to a direct command ("Don't *you* be letting *yourselves* . . .") intensifies the command. To be led astray means to be led into apostasy, the recanting of Christian faith to escape persecution. "All good giving" means the giving of all good gifts and alludes back to the example of God's giving wisdom to a person who believingly asks him for wisdom on how to persevere in the various temptations brought on by persecution (1:2–8). "Every complete gift" means every gift, like wisdom, that makes a Christian "complete and whole, lacking in nothing" (1:4). The combination of "giving" and "gifts" reinforces the stress on God's generosity. "Is from above" prepares for "coming down from the Father of lights."

We could take "the Father of lights" to portray God as creator of the sun, moon, stars, and planets. But the use of "Father" for God in relation to Christians at 1:27; 3:9 favors that here he's portrayed as their Father who dwells in the heavens, where those heavenly bodies are located and from where "all good giving and every complete gift" come. ("Heaven" covers the whole spectrum from the starry heavens to the heaven of God's abode.) James introduces the phrase "of lights" to prepare for a description of God as stable, in contrast with the heavenly bodies, which are in constant motion—hence the variation in their positions above and the consequent shifting of shadows here below—and which were widely thought to be personal beings whose movements determine events on earth (astrology). God's stability contrasts also with the instability of the doubter in 1:5–8. James cites the stability of God—Christians can count on his generosity—to encourage their own stability in temptations.

As stable, God carried out his will to birth believers "by the word [= the gospel]." "Of truth" describes this word in a way designed to keep the audience of Christians from instability, that is, from letting themselves be led astray. Birth by the word of truth provides an example in addition to wisdom of good and complete giving from above and contrasts both with lust's giving birth to sin and with sin's giving birth to death (a bad gift if there ever was one). "So that" introduces an achieved purpose ("so that we might be [purpose], and are [result]"). The figure shifts from a birth to a harvest: "The first fruits" of a harvest, its initial portion, were offered to God (Exodus 22:29; 23:19; 34:26) and were highly valued because they marked the start of a long-awaited new harvest. So comparing Christians to the first fruits of God's creatures calls attention to the special pleasure he takes in Christians. Reason again not to let themselves be led astray. ("A *certain* first fruits" means first fruits of a human rather than agricultural kind.)

AN EXHORTATION TO BE
DOERS OF THE WORD
James 1:19–27

1:19–21: Be knowledgeable, my beloved brothers; and every person is to be quick to listen, slow to speak, slow to anger. [20]**For a man's anger doesn't work God's righteousness.** [21]**So on putting off all filth and surplus of evil** [carried over from your lives before conversion]**, with meekness welcome the implanted word that can save your souls** [= your*selves*, not your souls as distinct from your bodies]**.** Another "my beloved brothers" underlines this exhortation (compare the comments on 1:16). The switch from "[You] be knowledgeable" to "every person is to be quick to listen [and so forth]" accents "every person." Again, no exceptions are allowed. "Quick to listen" and "slow to speak" complement each other, and slowness to anger comes as a result of quickness to listen and slowness to speak. These three characteristics define what it means here to be knowledgeable. In "a man's anger" there occurs again the word that usually connotes an adult male. It's appropriate here because by and large only adult males had the social status giving them freedom to vent their anger. James is laying down instructions for peaceful relations in Christian assemblies, much as the private clubs of pagans had rules designed to maintain such relations between members. But James bases his instructions on "God's righteousness," which means here the righteous behavior that God requires of Christians. Therefore they should put off filth from their behavior as they would take dirty clothes off their bodies. This expression implies that hot-tempered speech in Christian assemblies counts as moral filth; and the additional expression, "*surplus* of evil," implies that such speech counts as carried over from pre-Christian behavior and therefore as inappropriate to someone who has been "birthed by the word of truth" (1:18). But hot-tempered speech isn't the only misbehavior characteristic of life before conversion. Hence James refers to putting off "*all* filth and surplus of evil."

"The implanted word" equates with "the word of truth." Implantation interprets this word in terms both of human seed (semen) that led to a birth and of agricultural seed that led to a harvest of first fruits (see 1:18 again). Though already having been born by means of the word and thus become a kind of first fruits, Christians must welcome the word anew. For this word includes not only the good news of salvation through Christ, but also a demand to "work God's righteousness." Conversion includes sanctification as well as salvation, and "the implanted word *that can save your souls*" implies there can be no salvation without sanctification. Once born by the word of truth, a person needs meekness to welcome it anew for sanctification. For having become God's highly prized "first fruits" might easily lead the Christian to bristle at the need for any further work of the word on his life. On the contrary, he should positively "welcome" the word for such work.

1:22–25: But become doers of the word and not just listeners, miscalculating yourselves, ²³because if anyone is a listener of the word and not a doer [of it]—this person is like a man contemplating the face of his genesis [= the face with which he was born] in a mirror. ²⁴For he contemplated himself and has gone off, and immediately he forgot what sort of [man] he was [in the mirror]. ²⁵But the [man] who has bent down [to peer] into the complete law of liberty and has stayed alongside [it], not having become a forgetful listener—rather, a doer of work—this [man] will be fortunate in his doing [of the work]. Here it comes out clearly that to "welcome the implanted word" means to put it into practice after listening to it. James uses "listeners" because he's referring to the spoken word of the gospel. Even when the word was written, people ordinarily listened to it being read in an assembly of Christians; for prior to the invention of the printing press in the 1400s, private copies were few and far between. (Hence the use throughout this commentary of "audience" rather than "readers" or "readership.") "Miscalculating yourselves" turns out to mean forgetting your identity, and forgetting your identity means forgetting that you were reborn

a child of "the Father of lights" and therefore bound to obey him. Yet again "a man" goes back to a Greek word that usually connotes an adult male but here occurs figuratively for a mature Christian who forgets the face of his birth, that is, the new identity he got at conversion. Naturally, this forgetting will issue in misbehavior, in not doing the word. "*Has* gone off" (where we expect a simple "*went* off") and "immediately" (where we expect length of time as contributing to forgetfulness) dramatize the danger and seriousness of forgetting. Bad behavior follows fast. Bending down to peer indicates concentration and seriousness of purpose. "Into the complete law of liberty" represents a shift in terminology from "word" to "law." The law doesn't differ from the word, which as already mentioned contains the demand to "carry out God's righteousness" as well as the good news of salvation. But the shift in terminology lays emphasis on the obligation to meet this demand. Peering into the complete law of liberty also indicates a shift from self-contemplation (which is good if not lost from memory) to contemplation of the law that a Christian was reborn to keep. James calls this law "complete" because it contains all the commands and prohibitions necessary for Christian conduct, also because keeping it will complete the process of sanctification necessary to demonstrate the genuineness of faith. "Of liberty" describes the law as liberating its keeper from "being dragged away and baited by his own lusts" (1:14). "Has stayed alongside [the law]" contrasts with going off and immediately forgetting, and leads to doing the work of righteousness that God requires. James writes that such a man "will be fortunate," because doing the word demonstrates a genuineness of faith that will eventuate in eternal life.

1:26–27: If anyone not bridling his tongue but deceiving his heart thinks [he] is religious, this [man's] religion [is] inconsequential. ²⁷So far as God, even the Father, is concerned, pure and undefiled religion is this: to look after orphans and widows in their distress, to keep oneself unsullied by the world. James has just written about the word of truth as law, and about putting it into practice after listening to it. So now he writes about the listener's own spoken word. "Not bridling his tongue" stands for uncontrolled speech—for example, the hot-tempered speech that 1:19–20 warned against. Such speech renders religion—the rituals of prayer, praise, worship, and the like—vacuous despite a person's thinking he's commendably religious for performing them. James puts "pure and undefiled religion" over against "religion" that's "inconsequential." The contrast implies that an unbridled tongue dirties and defiles its owner's religion (see also 1:19–21 with comments). "Inconsequential" means not eventuating in eternal life. Vice versa for consequential religion. Widows and orphans—of whom there were many—had "distress" because apart from others' religious charity they usually fell below the poverty line and often suffered exploitation (see, for example, Zechariah 7:10; Mark 12:40; Luke 18:2–3; Acts 6:1; 9:36–43). God is concerned that the weakest members of society be cared for. Because of describing consequential religion as "pure and undefiled," James supplements the religious exercise of charity toward widows and orphans with "keep[ing] oneself unsullied by the world," that is, by the sinful ways of unbelievers. To keep oneself unsullied is to avoid being drawn into those ways. The attachment of "even the Father" to "God" recalls attention to his rebirthing believers to live in accordance with "the implanted word," "the complete law of liberty," rather than according to the ways of the world.

AN EXHORTATION TO SHOW LOVE RATHER THAN PARTIALITY
James 2:1–13

2:1–4: My brothers, don't be holding faith in our glorious Lord, Jesus Christ, with favoritism. ²For if a gold-ringed man in lustrous clothing were to enter into your assembly, and also a poor [person] in dirty clothing, ³and [if] you were to look at the one wearing the lustrous clothing and say, "You sit here well[-positioned]," and [if] you were to say to the poor [person], "You stand there or [if you want to sit rather than stand,] sit under my footstool [= on the floor at the base of my footstool, as opposed to sitting on a chair or a bench or even on the footstool], ⁴you've made discriminatory judgments among yourselves, haven't you, and become judges characterized by evil calculations [compare Leviticus 19:15]? For "my brothers" see the comments on 1:2. "*Our* glorious Lord, Jesus Christ" adds to the rapport already established by "my brothers" between James and his audience. The lordship and glory of Jesus Christ allude to his heavenly exaltation and so outshine the gold ring and lustrous clothing of a rich man that it would insult Jesus Christ to show the rich man favoritism, as though he were worthy to be compared with Jesus Christ. The favoritism would thus contradict faith in Jesus Christ as the glorious Lord. Contrasts between the rich man and the poor person and between their respective treatments are striking: a gold ring and lustrous clothing versus poverty and dirty clothing; a good seat "here" versus standing "there" or sitting on the floor. The switch from "*your* [plural] assembly" and "if *you* [plural] were to say" to "under *my* [singular] footstool" signals a favoritism toward the rich man that arises from a sense of individual self-importance: "I'll treat the rich man the way I'd like to be treated and am treated—or treat myself—as I sit here on my chair with my feet on a footstool." Though applied differently, "discriminatory judgments" recall the doubt warned against in 1:6–8, because that doubt consisted in making discriminatory judgments between the possibilities of God's answering and not answering a request for wisdom and switching back and forth between these possibilities, whereas here the discriminatory judgments consist in doubting whether God has selected the poor (for which see 2:5). ("Doubt" and "discriminatory judgments" translate the same Greek word.) "Discriminatory

judgments" also betray "evil calculations." They're evil because they take into account only external appearances and, as mentioned above, don't take account of the preclusive glory of the Lord, Jesus Christ.

2:5–7: Listen, my beloved brothers: God selected the poor so far as the world is concerned, didn't he— [the poor being] **rich by means of faith and** [being] **heirs of the kingdom that he promised to those who love him** [compare Luke 6:20]? ⁶**But you've disgraced the poor** [person]. **The rich are suppressing you, aren't they, and themselves dragging you into courts?** ⁷**They themselves slander the good name that was invoked over you, don't they?** For "my *beloved* brothers" see the comments on 1:16. The command, "Listen," puts the audience in a position of having to follow up with doing what they hear (see 1:22–25). God's selection of the poor has to do with salvation and contrasts with the audience's showing favoritism to the rich, who as ungodly oppressors of Christians are headed for destruction (1:10–11; 5:1–6). "So far as the world is concerned" limits the poverty of Christians to the opinion of non-Christians. "[Being] heirs of the kingdom" defines what it means to be "rich by means of faith." James has already said that "faith" is "in our Lord, Jesus Christ" (2:1). "*Heirs of the kingdom*" reflects believers' having God as their "Father" (1:27) and therefore points to his kingdom, his reign, which is yet to come (compare Matthew 6:10; Luke 11:2). The promise of the kingdom to those who love God recalls "the crown of life that he has promised to those who love him" (1:12). Eternal life and inheriting the kingdom coalesce. "But you" lays heavy emphasis on the audience's contradicting, or at least doubting, God's selection of the poor to inherit the kingdom. They've contradicted or doubted it by disgracing the poor person. By shifting from the plural, "the poor," to the singular, "the poor [person]," James says that the disgracing of even one poor person calls in question or denies God's having selected those who are poor by the world's standards. Nor does it make sense for Christians to treat the rich royally, for the rich are suppressing them and indeed dragging them to court to sue them out of what little they have, though as already rich those who drag them to court have more than they need. So bent on fleecing the Christians are the rich that they don't have their slaves drag the Christians to court. "They *themselves*" do so—personally. Worse yet, "they themselves" personally slander the good name of the Lord, Jesus Christ, that was invoked over the Christians, presumably at their baptism, to indicate his ownership of them (compare the frequent use of this expression in the Old Testament to indicate God's ownership of Israel, for example in 2 Chronicles 7:14; and see Isaiah 63:19 for a people's *not* being called by his name as describing "those over whom [the Lord] has *never* ruled"). Were the rich entering Christian assemblies to "case" them for purposes of economic persecution, being treated royally by Christians so as to deflect such persecution, yet slandering the name of Jesus Christ right within the Christians' assemblies?

2:8-11: If, however, you're completing the kingly law in accordance with the Scripture, "You shall love your neighbor as [you love] yourself [Leviticus 19:18]," you're doing well. ⁹But if you're playing favorites [by treating the rich better than you treat the poor, for example], you're working sin, being convicted by the Law as transgressors. ¹⁰For whoever keeps the whole Law but stumbles [a figure of speech for transgressing] in one [point] has become guilty of [transgressing] all [its points]. ¹¹For he [God] who said, "You shouldn't commit adultery," also said, "You shouldn't commit murder [Exodus 20:13-14; Deuteronomy 5:17-18]." And if you don't commit adultery but do commit murder, you've become a transgressor of the Law. "However" draws a contrast between showing favoritism to a rich man and loving your neighbor as you love yourself, the latter of which would be exemplified by treating royally a shabbily dressed poor person. James uses "law" for the source of this love commandment to highlight its scriptural authority, and he calls the Law "kingly" because it contains rules for life in "the kingdom that he [God] promised to those who love him" (2:5; compare the quotation of Leviticus 19:18 by Jesus, whose preaching centered on God's kingdom [Mark 12:31; Matthew 19:19; 22:39; Luke 10:27]). In other words, loving God entails loving your neighbor as you love yourself. You don't love God if you don't love your neighbor thus. But if you do love your neighbor thus, "you're doing *well*," which reverses saying to the rich man, "You sit here *well*" (2:3). That is, you're doing well to love your neighbor as yourself *instead of* seating the rich man well. Otherwise, "you're working sin," which is the flip side of "not work[ing] God's righteousness" (1:20). So in this instance sin is the work you do when you play favorites. The Law that convicts you as transgressors when you play favorites is the Law that contains the commandment to love your neighbor. To transgress it is to overstep a boundary. Hence, the command to love your neighbor as you love yourself sets a boundary against playing favorites, especially against favoring the rich. But how can James go so far as to say that "whoever keeps the whole Law but stumbles in one [point] has become guilty of [transgressing] all [its points]"? He can say so because the Law is an indivisible whole. You can't pick and choose within it what to keep and what to transgress. And it's an indivisible whole because the will of God, who gave it, and indeed God himself are indivisible. James illustrates this truth by citing the prohibitions of adultery and murder as spoken by one and the same God, who alone is God (Deuteronomy 6:4). To spell out the illustration James notes that committing murder makes you "a transgressor of the Law" even if you don't commit adultery.

2:12-13: Speak in this way and act in this way, [that is,] as those who are about to be judged by the Law of liberty. ¹³For the judgment [will be] merciless for the person who hasn't exercised mercy. Mercy vaunts itself over judgment. Here James personifies the Law as God's agent of judgment. The description of the Law as liberating when it's obeyed (see the comments on

1:25) exacerbates both the guilt of disobeying it and the consequent mercilessness of judgment for disobeying it. God meant it for your good! "Who hasn't exercised mercy" interprets favoring a rich man at the expense of a poor person, and thus also interprets not loving your neighbor as you love yourself as a failure to exercise the sort of mercy you'd like to receive, but won't, at the Last Judgment. "Who are *about* to be judged" underscores that judgment as soon and certain. Strong reason, then, to speak and act in a way that will ensure merciful rather than merciless judgment. The combination of speaking and acting—emphasized as it is by the twofold use of "in this way," once with "speak" and again with "act"—sets up for a discussion of deeds as demonstrative of verbal claims (2:14–26). "In this way" implies speaking differently from the way illustrated in connection with the rich man and the poor person in 2:2–3, and implies acting differently from the way illustrated in connection with adultery and murder (2:11). James has personified the Law. By saying, "Mercy vaunts itself over judgment," he also personifies mercy and judgment as opponents in a battle over the eternal fates of human beings. Though judgment will have prevailed in the case of those who've been merciless, mercy will boast in triumph over judgment in the case of those who've exercised mercy.

AN EXHORTATION TO DEMONSTRATE FAITH BY DOING GOOD WORKS
James 2:14-26

2:14-17: What benefit [would it be], my brothers, if someone were to say he has faith but were not to have works [= deeds consonant with faith]? The faith [that lacks works] can't save him, can it? ¹⁵If a brother or a sister [= fellow Christians] were to be subsisting naked and lacking food for the day ¹⁶and one of you were to say to them, "Go in peace, warm yourselves, and feed yourselves full," but you weren't to give them the body's necessities [food and clothing], what benefit [is it for the brother or the sister for you to have said that to them]? ¹⁷So too faith, if it doesn't have works, is dead [because of being] by itself. For "my brothers" see the comments on 1:2. In view of the immediately preceding reference to the Last Judgment, James denies the benefit of someone's claiming then to have faith if he doesn't have good works to authenticate his claim. Faith without that authentication can't save him at the Last Judgment. "Naked" doesn't mean "nude"—rather, clad only in a skimpy undergarment or in rags full of holes. In either case, lots of skin is exposed to the cold. "Go in peace" presents an ironic farewell in that "peace" connotes prosperity, whereas the fellow Christian, cold and hungry, lacks bare necessities for the body, much more the sort of prosperity that would enable the stoking of a furnace (so to say) or getting full on food and having leftovers for the next day too. As in 2:1–13, James continues to press the need for charity among Christians ("a brother or a sister"), so that "your neighbor" refers especially to fellow Christians (compare Galatians 6:10). By describing as "dead" the faith which is unaccompanied by works ("faith . . . *by itself*"), James personifies such faith as he has earlier personified the Law, judgment, and mercy. By implication, then, "works" are being portrayed as the spirit that animates a person's body but leaves it at death, so that the body represents faith. In 2:26 James will draw out this implication explicitly. We expect the reverse, a representation of works as the body and of faith as the spirit, so that James's violation of our expectation accentuates the point he's making. A dead body does nobody any good, least of all the person whose body it is. Likewise, a dead faith does nobody any good, least of all the person whose faith it is. For dead faith augurs the death that consists in eternal punishment.

2:18–19: **However, someone will say, "You have faith, and I have works. Show me your faith apart from works, and I'll show you** [my] **faith by my works.** [19]**You believe that God is one** [as in monotheism, rather than many, as in polytheism (see Deuteronomy 6:4)]. **You're doing well** [to believe so]. **Even the demons believe and quake."** "Faith" translates a noun whose corresponding verb is "believe," so that the translation "belief" would highlight the correspondence between the noun and the verb. But "faith" has become traditional in this passage as a contrast to "works." "You [singular] have faith" responds to "if someone were to say he has faith" (2:14a). The respondent doesn't have to repeat the qualification "but were not to have works" (also in 2:14a). That's understood. Instead, then, the respondent transforms the qualification into a declaration concerning himself: "and I have works." And it's understood from 2:17 ("So too faith, if it doesn't have works, is dead [because of being] by itself") that the respondent's works give evidence of faith. But to make these understandings explicit, he issues a challenge to the "someone" of 2:14a. The challenge reads, "Show me your faith apart from works, and I'll show you my faith by my works." Who then is this second "someone" of 2:18 who responds to the initial "someone" of 2:14a? He's none other than James, for he's elaborating in a direct address *to* the "someone" of 2:14a what James said *about* him and his view in 2:14b–17. This direct address extends to the end of chapter 2. In other words, James puts himself in the role of another "someone" who is debating the earlier "someone." Therefore, the "However" at the start of 2:18 doesn't set the following argument, or even "You have faith, and I have works," over against James' argument in 2:14b–17; for, as noted, the whole of 2:18–26 elaborates the argument in 2:14–17. Instead, "However" sets James as the second "someone" over against his imaginary opponent in debate, the first "someone."

To review, then, "You have faith" means "You claim to have faith though you don't have the works that would prove you have it." "And I have works" means "And I have the works that prove I do have faith." These declarations then turn into a challenge: "Show me your faith apart from works, and I'll show you my faith by my works." As the second "someone," James next commends the first "someone" for "believ[ing] that God

is one." "You're doing well" repeats the commendation in 2:8 of the person who loves his neighbor as he loves himself. But here the commendation has a tinge of sarcasm in that "even the demons" share this item of faith but like the first "someone" don't do the deeds that would demonstrate a lively faith, one that would eventuate in eternal life. The demons go one better than the first "someone," in fact. Not only do they believe in God's oneness, as that "someone" does. They also "quake" in dread of merciless judgment, as the "someone" of 2:14a doesn't—but should.

The second "someone" (James) continues addressing the first "someone" in *2:20–24:* **"But do you want to know, O empty**[-headed] **human being, that faith apart from works is workless?** [21]**Wasn't Abraham our** [fore]**father justified by works when he brought up Isaac his son onto the altar** [Genesis 22:2, 9–10]? [22]**You see that faith was working together with his works, and** [that] **the faith was completed by the works.** [23]**And the Scripture was fulfilled that says, 'And Abraham believed God, and it** [his having believed God] **was credited to him as righteousness** [Genesis 15:6]**,' and he was called God's 'friend'** [2 Chronicles 20:7; Isaiah 41:8]**.'** [24]**You see that a human being is justified by works and not only by faith."** The sarcasm in 2:19 has now turned into outright vituperation with the address, "O empty[-headed] human being." James uses "human being" rather than the word for an adult male to strike a contrast between the first "someone" being addressed and the one God whom the addressee believes in (2:19). The contrast demeans further the empty-headed addressee. "But do you want to know . . . ?" confirms his ignorance, justifies the vituperative description "empty[-headed]," and suggests that his ignorance stems from a lack of desire to know (contrast John 7:17). He may not know that "faith apart from works is workless" because such knowledge would frighten him into doing the charitable deeds he doesn't want to do. They would cramp his lifestyle, uncharitably comfortable as it is. "Faith apart from works is workless" advances a wordplay that means workless faith isn't just faith apart from works. It's also faith that doesn't work salvation in a person. With the example of Abraham, James puts salvation in terms of justification, which means to be declared righteous. Though Abraham's bringing up Isaac onto the altar constituted a single "work," James uses a plural in "by works" to make the offering an example of the works he has been talking about. "By works" indicates the source on the basis of which Abraham was justified. "When he brought up Isaac . . . onto the altar" leaves room for the angel of the Lord's staying Abraham's hand lest he plunge in the knife. The addition of "his son" to "Isaac" showcases the strength of Abraham's desire to obey God, in contrast with the questionability of the empty-headed human being's desiring to know that faith apart from works is workless. But "you see" may exhibit some optimism on James's part that he's filling an empty head, through its eyes, with some knowledge; and in another wordplay the followup, "that faith was working together with his

[Abraham's] works," pairs faith and works as coworkers toward justification. Then the statement that "the faith [of Abraham] was completed by the works" makes the works a demonstration of what would otherwise be dead faith. This completion of faith by works fulfilled Scripture, Genesis 15:6 in particular, in the sense that Abraham's works enabled Scripture to say his having believed God "was credited to him [compare 2:14] as righteousness." But note well! It wasn't his works that were credited as righteousness. It was his having believed God that was credited so. As proofs of faith, his works enabled such a crediting of faith even though faith as such isn't righteousness. James weds faith and works; but he maintains a distinction between them. So the crediting of Abraham's faith as righteousness doesn't rest on an equation of faith and righteousness, but represents a crediting of faith as a righteousness that intrinsically faith is not. As one of numerous possible comparisons see Romans 2:26, where Paul says a Gentile Law-keeper's uncircumcision will be credited as circumcision even though intrinsically it is not circumcision. Though working together, then, faith and works play different roles. Faith plays an underlying role, works an evidential role. "And he [Abraham] was called God's 'friend'" gives encouragement to show faith by doing works consonant with it, for to be *called* such-and-such in Scripture is to *be* such-and-such. Furthermore, "friend" goes back to a word that denotes the recipient of love and affection (compare John 15:12–15 with comments). Who wouldn't want to have that kind of friendship from God? "A human being" calls attention to the marvel that God actually befriends a human being by justifying him, declaring him righteous. "Is justified by works [as evidence of faith] and not only by faith [apart from the evidence of works]" hits back at the claim of the first "someone" that he has faith, though he doesn't have works to prove that he has it (2:14).

The second "someone" of 2:18 (James) is still speaking in **2:25–26: "And likewise Rahab the prostitute, too, was justified by works, wasn't she, when she welcomed the messengers** [sent by Joshua to spy out the city of Jericho] **and thrust them out by a different way** [from the one their pursuers thought they would take (Joshua 2:1–24; 6:17, 25; Hebrews 11:31)]? [26]**For just as the body apart from the spirit is dead, so too faith apart from works is dead."** In conformity with the law that two or three witnesses are required to establish a legal case (Numbers 35:30; Deuteronomy 17:6; 19:15), James cites Rahab as an example in addition to that of Abraham. "The prostitute" describes her in a way that makes her justification truly remarkable. You'd expect her sex work to have canceled out her neighborly treatment of the spies. But so important are works as evidence of faith that prostitution didn't cancel out the evidence of her faith, so that she was justified, declared righteous. Her works proved her faith to be alive, not dead, and in that sense became the means of her justification.

A WARNING AGAINST UNRESTRAINED SPEECH
James 3:1–12

3:1–3: Don't many of you become teachers, my brothers, knowing that we [teachers] **will get greater judgment** [compare Mark 12:40; Matthew 12:36; Luke 12:47–48; 20:47]. [2]**For in many respects we all stumble. If anyone doesn't stumble in word** [= in what he says]**, this person** [is] **a complete man, able to guide with bit and bridle his whole body too** [= in addition to restraining his speech]. [3]**And if we thrust bits into the mouths of horses so that they obey us, we guide their whole body about too.** For "my brothers" see the comments on 1:2. In 1:19 James told his audience to be "quick to listen" and "slow to speak," which according to 1:26 entails "bridl[ing] the tongue." It's natural, then, that he should now warn against unrestrained speech. But since teachers speak more than others do, particularly when Christians meet together, the teachers stand a greater chance of sinning with their tongue. Moreover, they're in a position of influence by virtue of teaching, as in the commands of James himself that his audience "listen" to what he has to say (2:5) and "become doers of the word and not just listeners" (1:22–25). As a segue into his warning against unrestrained speech, then, James warns that not many of them should become teachers; for teachers will get judged by stricter standards than nonteachers will be judged by and will consequently suffer severer punishment if they've spoken wrongly and thus misled others.

"Knowing" about the "greater judgment" of teachers should motivate the majority in James's audience not to become teachers, whereas out of ignorance of the judgment they might seek the higher status of a teacher in their churches (see 1 Corinthians 14:26 for the possibility of anyone's teaching in church meetings). James has earlier used "stumbl[ing]" as a figure for sinning (2:10). Now his statement that "in many respects we all stumble" not only denies the sinless perfection of any Christian this side of eternity. It also supports the exhortation that not many should become teachers. How so? Well, "we all stumble" by sinning and do so "in many respects." "We all" who stumble in this way includes teachers along with nonteachers. And as already noted, teachers among the "we all" will be judged more strictly for such stumbling.

In writing that a nonstumbler in his speech is "a complete man," James reverts to the word for an adult male. Here it accents an ability to keep all his behavior, represented by "his whole body," free from sin as well as to keep his speech, about to be represented by the tongue, free from sin. The guiding of horses' whole bodies with the use of bits thrust into their mouths also represents this comprehensive avoidance of sin, starting with speech. A man doesn't guide his whole body "with bit and bridle." So this phrase applies to the "complete man" only figuratively, but sets up for the literal sense in the case of horses. "Guiding" equates with "not stumbling" (= not sinning).

3:4–5a: Behold, the ships too, though being as big [as they are] **and driven by rough winds, are guided about by a tiny rudder where the impulse of the** [ship's] **pilot wants** [the ship to go]**!** ⁵ᵃ**So too the tongue is a small part** [of the body] **and talks big.** "Behold" makes the additional comparison to ships and their rudder exclamatory. The larger size of ships as compared to horses gives rise to the exclamation (see the comments on Acts 27:33–38 for the size of big ships). The tiny size of a rudder that guides big ships despite their being "driven by rough winds" makes the comparison striking. The application of this comparison matches the tongue as "a small part [of the body]" with the "tiny rudder," and the tongue's "talk[ing] big" with the rudder's guiding a big ship despite the driving of rough winds. The rudder defies those winds. But the tongue talks big because of the person whose tongue it is. So James draws out the comparison further, not by matching the person with the ship's pilot, but by matching the person with the pilot's "impulse." This match points up the impulsiveness of much speech, its lack of restraint, against which impulsiveness and lack James warns. In other words, he personifies the pilot's impulse, so that it rather than the pilot "wants" the ship to go here or there. The personification highlights impulsiveness as such.

3:5b–6: Behold, how small a fire kindles how large a forest! ⁶**And the tongue** [is] **a fire. The tongue constitutes itself a world of injury among our** [body] **parts, which** [referring to the tongue] **sullies the whole body and sets on fire the wheel of life and is set on fire by hell.** Here we have another comparison and another "Behold" that makes it exclamatory. A forest is larger than a big ship; and a small fire, such as a single flame, is smaller than a ship's rudder. All the more reason for an exclamation, then. How apt is the comparison of the tongue to a fire! "Tongue" is even used for a flame of fire (see Acts 2:3). But here the accent shifts from impulse to injury. As a small fire kindles the burning of a large forest, so the tongue, used impulsively, unrestrainedly, injures people far and wide. "A *world* of injury" underscores the breadth of injury. "Constitutes itself"—or, as the verb could also be translated, "appoints itself"—adds intention to lack of restraint in the injurious use of the tongue. "Among our [body] parts" recalls the small size of the tongue as compared with the body as a whole. "Sullies the whole body" interprets speech that injures others as a pollutant that befouls all your behavior, which, as earlier, the whole body represents. "The wheel of life" is a figure of speech for the cycle of your existence in its unbroken entirety. That the tongue "sets on fire the wheel of life" means, then, that an unrestrained tongue destroys its owner as well as injuring his surrounding "world." And just as the tongue sets fires of injury and destruction, it "is set on fire by hell," the place of ultimate injury and destruction. No wonder the disastrous effects of an unrestrained tongue.

3:7–10: For every species both of beasts and of birds and of reptiles and of sea creatures is being sub- dued, and has been subdued, by the human species [compare Genesis 1:24–28]. ⁸**But not a single one of human beings can subdue the tongue.** [It's] **an unstable, evil** [body part]. [It's] **full of death-dealing poison.** ⁹**With it we praise the Lord, that is, the Father; and with it we curse human beings, who've come into existence in accordance with God's likeness.** ¹⁰**Out of the same mouth issues praise and a curse** [compare Matthew 15:11, 17–19]. **My brothers, these things oughtn't to be happening thus.** This paragraph tells why James has just concluded that an unrestrained, impulse-driven tongue "is set on fire by hell." He pits the ability of human beings to subdue all other species, each one as a whole, against the inability of human beings to subdue their own tongue, only a small part of their whole body. "Not a single one of human beings" stresses this inability and shows that the "complete man" of 3:2, who "doesn't stumble in word" but is "able to guide with bit and bridle his whole body too," doesn't exist in real life. The tongue's being "an unstable, evil [body part]," like a wild animal, stems from being "set on fire by hell." Its being "full of death-dealing poison," like a serpent (which is a reptile), echoes its constitution "as a world of injury" (compare the biblical portrayal of Satan as a serpent; see also Psalm 140:3; Proverbs 11:9). Its mixing curses against human beings with praise of the Lord exemplifies its being "unstable " (compare the instability of the "double-minded" man in 1:8). And its cursing of human beings exemplifies its being "full of death-dealing poison." "That is, the Father" keeps us from thinking here of the Lord who is Jesus Christ (compare 1:17, 27) and thereby segues into a reference to God as the one in accordance with whose likeness human beings came into existence. That they bear his likeness exacerbates the evil of using our tongue to curse them. It comes close to cursing God himself. "Out of the same mouth issues praise and a curse," being repetitious of the earlier such statement, reinforces the evil, thus leads James to insert a solemn "my brothers" (on which see 1:2 again), and sets up for water's gushing "out of the orifice" of a spring (3:11). "These things" that "oughtn't to be happening thus" are the curses and the mixing of them with praise. Consistency in speech is missing, but *should* be on the side of praise.[1]

3:11–12: A spring doesn't gush out of its orifice sweet [water] **and bitter, does it?** ¹²**My brothers, a fig tree can't produce olives, can it, or a grapevine** [produce] **figs? Nor** [can] **salty** [water] **make water sweet,** [can it]**?** The element of inability ("can't . . . can it?")

---

[1]Not only does James stress the tongue's influence. He also stresses the need to subdue the tongue. And not only does he stress the greater judgment of teachers for how they use their tongue. He also stresses the use of the tongue in praising the Lord and cursing human beings, activities in which others in addition to teachers engage. Therefore it's unlikely that James means his audience to understand "the whole body" of human beings and of horses and a big ship as figures of speech for Christians in general as distinct from their teachers, represented by the tongue, the bit, and the rudder.

recollects that "not a single one of human beings can subdue the tongue" (3:8). But to dramatize the inconsistency of mixing curses against human beings and praise of the Lord (3:9–10), James cites the inability of a spring to gush out both sweet water and bitter, of a fig tree to produce olives, of a grapevine to produce figs, and of salty water to make water sweet. As we might say, the human tongue violates a law of nature. Another "my brothers" calls special attention to this violation.

AN EXHORTATION TO COOPERATIVE WISDOM
James 3:13–4:3

3:13–16: **Who [is] wise and understanding among you? With the meekness of wisdom he's to show his works [= deeds] by good behavior.** [14]**But if you have bitter jealousy and ambition in your heart, don't be boasting and lying against the truth.** [15]*This* **wisdom isn't coming down from above; rather, [it's] earthly** [in its origin]**, soulish** [arising out of the human soul rather than infused by the Holy Spirit]**, demonic** [even worse than "soulish" because of being characteristic of demons (at best) or infused by demons (at worst)]**.** [16]**For where jealousy and ambition [exist], there [exist] instability and every sort of vile deed.** The preceding rhetorical questions lead James to introduce this following exhortation with another such question. It harks back to the theme of wisdom in 1:5. But there wisdom was possibly absent. Here it's possibly present. And for emphasis James adds "understanding" to "wisdom." The wisdom he's looking for among his audience is characterized by "meekness," the toleration of mistreatment (like being cursed?) without striking back (compare "slow to anger" in 1:19–21). Though generally despised in non-Christian culture, meekness is wise in that striking back only generates further conflict. The deeds of a wise and understanding Christian, then, are to be done with meekness or, more accurately, are to be *shown* with meekness. For showing them proves his faith (2:18). And "good behavior" defines his deeds as such proof, especially since "good" connotes visible goodness, even beauty.

Over against meekness and good behavior James ranges "bitter jealousy and ambition," both of which forestall meekness and wreak havoc on good behavior. "*Bitter* jealousy" recalls the bitter water of 3:11 and adds animosity to the jealousy. "In your heart" traces the bitter jealousy and ambition to their inner source, so that James saves himself from advocating that you show your good deeds to elevate your status among other Christians. Bitter jealousy and ambition normally lead to boasting for the purpose of achieving one-upmanship and higher status. But James writes that bitter jealousy and ambition should *keep* you from boasting; for if you have *them*, you don't have anything worth boasting about. And to boast would be to lie against the truth that in fact you don't have anything to boast about, which truth is part and parcel of the gospel: "Nothing in my hands I bring. Only to thy cross I cling." With "this wisdom" that "isn't coming down from above" James

shifts dramatically from the wisdom that characterizes meekness to the "earthly" wisdom that advocates boasting as the way to get ahead. Then he returns to the origins of boasting in jealousy and ambition and says that because jealousy and ambition spawn "instability and every sort of vile deed" (James is referring to disorder and recriminations of Christians against each other in their assemblies), the so-called wisdom characterized by jealousy and ambition deserves the downward spiraling descriptions unheavenly, earthly, soulish, and even demonic (see explanations interspersed in the foregoing translation). "Demonic" recalls that an unrestrained, impulse-driven tongue "is set on fire by hell."

3:17–18: **But the wisdom from above, on the one hand, is first pure, then peaceable, considerate, persuadable, full of mercy and good fruits** [a figure of speech for good deeds, but emphasizing origin in a good heart]**, undiscriminatory, unhypocritical.** [18]**And the fruit of righteousness is sown in peace by those who make peace.** "The wisdom from above" contrasts sharply with "this wisdom" that "isn't coming down from above" (3:15–16) and picks up for elaboration the "wisdom" that characterizes "meekness" (3:13). The contrasts aren't always exact; but broadly speaking, the purity of the wisdom from above contrasts with the moral pollution spread by unrestrained, impulsive speech (3:6). "First" describes the purity as heading a list of further praiseworthy characteristics. "Peaceable" describes this heaven-originated wisdom in opposition to injuriousness and instability, "considerate" in opposition to destructiveness and cursing, "persuadable" in opposition to "boasting," "full of mercy and good fruits" in opposition to death-dealing poison, "undiscriminatory" in opposition to "ambition," and "unhypocritical" in opposition to "lying against the truth." "The fruit of righteousness" is "the good fruits" that consist in righteous deeds. "Is sown" turns this fruit into seed that produces a crop of "peace," specifically, peaceful relations among Christians in their assemblies. The fruit is sown "in peace" in that peaceful behavior on the part of some produces peaceful behavior on the part of others and thus turns into peacemakers those who sow peace (compare Matthew 5:9).

James has written in 3:17–18 about peaceable wisdom and about peacemakers. Now he elaborates on a deplorably opposite state of affairs among his audience, a state of cursing one another, jealousy, ambition, and disorder, as introduced earlier in 3:8–10, 14–16. **4:1–3:** **Where do fights and where do quarrels among you [come] from? From here, don't they: [that is,] from your hedonisms [= pleasure-seekings] that battle in your [body] parts?** [2]**You lust and don't have [what you lust for]. You murder, and you're jealous; and you can't attain [your goals]. You quarrel and fight. You don't have [what you want] because you don't ask [for it].** [3]**You ask [for it] and don't receive [it] because you ask badly, [that is,] in order that you may spend [it] on your hedonisms.** The doubling of "where . . . from?" and the addition of "quarrels" to "fights" underline the question of source and therefore also its answer: "your hedonisms." Underlying the fights and quarrels that stem from hedonisms is the audience's belief that the enjoyment of pleasures is a zero-sum game: there's only so much pleasure in the world, so that one person's enjoyment of it robs another person of such enjoyment. Under this belief, pleasure seeking breeds competition, and competition breeds fighting and quarreling—not only outside Christian circles, but also among Christians ("among *you*" and "from *your* hedonisms"). Later, James will undercut the notion of a zero-sum game by writing that God "gives very great grace." Meanwhile, "lust" defines the pleasure seekings as desires so strong that they lead to overstepping the boundary from peacekeeping into warlike competition.

"You murder" recalls the death-dealing poison of the tongue (3:8) and therefore isn't to be taken literally any more than the battling of hedonisms "in your [body] parts" is to be taken literally. James doesn't mean that the hedonisms battle against each other—rather, that the lust for physical pleasures produces fights and quarrels between competing Christians. The description of jealously poisonous speech in terms of murder dramatizes its evil character. Words can kill, so to speak. The placement of murder before jealousy highlights the murderous effect of evil speech and the origin of such speech in jealousy. "You fight and quarrel" alludes back to the question, "Where do fights and quarrels among you [come] from?" and explains why "you . . . don't have [what you lust for]." The fights and quarrels keep the lusts from attaining their goals of satisfaction in pleasures. If only the Christians would ask God for what they need, as James told them to do (1:5–8), instead of fighting and quarreling in competition to satisfy their physical appetites. Well, they do ask God, but not for what they need—rather, for what they can "spend on [their] hedonisms." Selfish pleasures cost a lot, financially as well as morally. So James describes their asking as bad and uses this description to explain God's refusal to grant their requests. He gives good gifts (1:16–17) and therefore doesn't grant bad requests. James's audience should be asking in unwavering faith for the wisdom that's "pure, then peaceable, considerate, persuadable, full of mercy and good fruits, undiscriminatory [between rich and poor (see 2:1–9)], unhypocritical" (3:17). Then God would grant their request. Then their fights and quarrels would cease. Then they'd enjoy the worthwhile pleasures of fellowship with one another.

A WARNING AGAINST WORLDLINESS
James 4:4–10

4:4–6: Adulteresses, you know, don't you, that friendliness toward the world equates with hostility toward God? So whoever prefers to be the world's friend constitutes himself an enemy of God. ⁵Or do you suppose that the Scripture speaks emptily [= meaninglessly, unseriously]? He [God] longs to the point of envy for the spirit that he caused to settle within us. Elsewhere James uses "spirit" only for the human spirit (2:26), he has recently alluded to human beings' "com[ing] into existence in accordance with God's likeness" (3:9), and according to Genesis 2:7 "the Lord God formed man of dust from the ground and breathed into his nostrils the breath of life," which in Genesis 7:22 is called "the breath of the *spirit* of life." So James means that God longs for the human spirit's fidelity to him. ⁶**But he [God] gives very great grace. Therefore it [the Scripture] says, "God opposes haughty people but gives grace to humble people** [Proverbs 3:34 (compare Psalm 18:27)]." James is so worked up over his audience's pleasure seekings in the non-Christian "world" that he exchanges the repeated, affectionate address, "my (beloved) brothers," for the damningly accusatory address, "Adulteresses." The Old Testament prophets often portrayed Israel's relation to God as that of a wife to a husband and accused Israel of adultery for her worship of other gods (Jeremiah 3:6–10, 20; 13:27; Ezekiel 23:45; Hosea 1–3 [see also Matthew 12:39; 16:4]). The analogy between Israel and the church, exemplified by James's having called his Jewish Christian audience "the twelve tribes in the Diaspora" (1:1), leads him to accuse the audience similarly, their hedonisms being like gods other than God. Moreover, "friendliness" includes an element of love and affection, so that friendliness toward the world amounts to an adulterous relationship with the world and, worse yet, to outright "hostility toward God" in contrast with Abraham's having been called "God's friend" (2:23). "You know, don't you . . . ?" implies that the audience do know that friendliness toward the world equates with hostility toward God. Not only does this implication compliment the audience in a way that should prompt them to heed James's warning. But also, because of such knowledge the befriender of the world has "constituted *himself* an enemy of God." To sin knowledgeably is to sin rebelliously. James's asking whether the audience suppose "that the Scripture speaks emptily" implies that judged by their behavior, they might just suppose so. (That the Scripture does *not* speak emptily, see Isaiah 55:11.) "He [God] longs to the point of envy [and so forth]" paraphrases what "the Scripture speaks." His longing in envy of the world for its having captured the friendship of Christians highlights the pathos of their committing adultery with the world (compare the jealousy of God over his people Israel in Exodus 20:5; 34:14; Deuteronomy 4:24; Zechariah 8:2). Although he "opposes haughty people," then, he "gives very great grace to humble people" in accord with the Scripture. His opposing the haughty implies the haughtiness of Christians who befriend the world and thus become enemies of God (compare Psalm 18:27). His opposition is irresistible. So it's foolish to constitute yourself his enemy. But he "gives very great grace to humble people," that is, treats them very favorably. They're people of low station or, better, people who lower themselves in relation to God instead of behaving in haughty disregard of his commands.

4:7–10: **Therefore submit yourselves to God; but stand against the Devil, and he'll flee from you.** **[8]Draw near to God, and he'll draw near to you. Cleanse** [your] **hands, you sinners; and purify** [your] **hearts, you double-minded people.** **[9]Get miserable and mourn and weep. Your laughter must be turned into mourning** [compare Luke 6:25]**, and** [your] **joy into dejection.** **[10]Lower yourselves** [= humble yourselves] **in the Lord's sight, and he'll lift you up** [= exalt you (compare 1:9–10; Matthew 23:12; Luke 14:11; 18:14)]. "Therefore" bases submission to God on his opposing haughty people and giving very great grace to humble people (4:6). Indeed, submission to him defines their humility. In a contrastive sort of way, standing against the Devil complements submitting to God or, more literally, putting yourselves *under* God. "Against the Devil" associates him with the world that James's audience have befriended (4:1–6). So standing against the Devil entails breaking off friendship with the world. "And he'll flee from you" extends an assurance that encourages standing against him. Drawing near to God also complements standing against the Devil, again in a contrastive sort of way. Furthermore, you can't draw near to God *without* standing against the Devil. And the assurance that God "will draw near to you" encourages your "draw[ing] near to God," reciprocates it, and contrasts with the Devil's "flee[ing] from you."

The audience's hands are dirty from friendly contact with the world, and the dirt on their hands represents sinful deeds—hence the command, "Cleanse [your] hands, you sinners." Because of their lusts (4:1–3) the hearts of the audience are impure—hence the additional command, "and purify [your] hearts, you double-minded people." You daren't draw near to God with dirty hands and an impure heart (see Psalm 24:3–4). "Double-minded" recalls 1:8. There the description had to do with doubt, switching back and forth between belief and unbelief. Here it has to do with worldliness, switching back and forth between God and the world. "Mourn and weep" defines "Get miserable" and enjoins deep sorrow for sin and for the filth of worldliness. "Your laughter . . . and joy" are the laughter and joy of a hedonist (4:1). They're to be turned into the "mourning" and "dejection" of a penitent. The word for dejection means a casting of the eyes downward, which makes for a nice transition into the command, "Lower yourselves." "In the Lord's sight" becomes possible by virtue of having drawn near to him. "And he'll lift you up" corresponds to his "giv[ing] grace [favor] to humble people" (4:6).

AN EXHORTATION AGAINST FAULTFINDING
James 4:11–12

4:11–12: **Don't be speaking against one another, brothers** [compare Leviticus 19:16a; Psalm 50:20]. **The person who speaks against a brother** [= a fellow Christian] **or judges his brother is speaking against the law and judging the law. But if you judge the law, you're not a doer of the law—rather, a judge** [of it]. **[12]The law-giver and judge is one,** [namely,] **he who can save and destroy** [compare Isaiah 33:22]. **But you who are judging** [your] **neighbor—who are you?** Certainly not the sole lawgiver and judge! In line with his exhortation not to speak against a brother, James reverts to his affectionate address, "brothers" (contrast "adulteresses," "sinners," and "double-minded people" in 4:4, 8), and the exhortation itself reverts to the topic of unrestrained speech (as in chapter 3). In view of Matthew 5:21–22; 7:1 (on which see the comments), to speak against a brother means to denounce a fellow professing Christian as not a true Christian; and to judge him means to arrogate to yourself the prerogative of condemning him to hell. To do so equates with speaking against the law—not the Mosaic law; rather, the kingly law of God's kingdom as taught by Jesus (2:8 [see also 1:25; 2:9–12])—because this law reserves to God, or Jesus as his representative, the prerogative of judging people's eternal fate. To judge a fellow professing Christian false also equates with judging the law in that you're effectively condemning the law for reserving that prerogative to God or Jesus. Judging the law makes you a nondoer of the law, moreover; and a nondoer of it lacks saving faith and faces merciless judgment (2:12–26 [see also 1:26 for the ineffectiveness of religion if its practitioner doesn't bridle his tongue]). The legitimate judge is one and the same as the lawgiver. For James's audience of Jewish Christians, familiar as they were with their oft-recited Golden Text, Deuteronomy 6:4: "Hear, O Israel, the Lord is our God; the Lord is *one*," there was no need to identify by name the "one" lawgiver and judge (see 2:19). "Who can save and destroy" puts the issue in terms of eternal destiny. "But you who are judging [your] neighbor" contrasts this behavior with the kingly law's commanding in accordance with Scripture, "You shall love your neighbor as [you love] yourself" (2:8), and interprets your "brothers" as your neighbors. A neighbor is anyone close to you, and you and your fellow Christians get close to each other—physically—every time you assemble for worship, praise, teaching, and the Lord's Supper.

AN EXHORTATION AGAINST OVERCONFIDENCE
James 4:13–17

4:13–17: **Go now, you who are saying, "Today or tomorrow we'll travel to such and such a city and do a year there and engage in business and make a profit,"** **[14]you who as such** [that is, as traveling businessmen] **aren't cognizant concerning the matter of tomorrow** [compare 1:10; Proverbs 27:1]. "You who are saying" echoes "you who are judging" in the preceding verse. But the topic has shifted from judging your neighbor to overconfident planning. "Go now" is an ironic, almost sarcastic command that a traveling businessman had better get going—at once. But being ironic, the command isn't really meant to be obeyed, as immediately hinted by the switch away from the singular in "Go now" to the plural in "you who are saying" (so the original

Greek). The businessmen may have less time to do their business and make a profit than they expect to have and plan on having. Tomorrow remains unknown to them. **Of what sort** [is] **your life?** Here is James's explanation of that sort: **For you're steam that appears for a short while, then disappears too.** **¹⁵Instead of your saying,** ["Today or tomorrow we'll travel to such and such a city . . ." (4:13), you should say,] **"If the Lord wills, we'll both live and do this or that."** **¹⁶But now you're boasting in your ostentations. All such boasting is evil.** **¹⁷So for the person who knows to do good and doesn't do** [it], **for him it's sin** [not to do what he knows is a good thing to do]. "The matter of tomorrow" turns into the sort of life the businessmen have. It's short, and could be shorter than they think. In any event, they're like a puff of steam. Now you see it, now you don't. The Lord's will determines the length of life, and also determines what you're able to do during your lifespan. Rather than boasting ostentatiously and therefore evilly of your coming business ventures, you should acknowledge the Lord's will verbally. That would be a good use of your tongue, as opposed to speaking against your brother (4:11). Knowing this to be a good use of your tongue but not using it thus is sin. If you didn't know before, you do now. So if you don't obey, you're sinning. But the principle of knowing to do good but sinning by not doing it applies broadly, as also the brevity of life applies to others than Christian businessmen.

AN EXHORTATION TO WAIT PATIENTLY FOR THE SECOND COMING
James 5:1–11

This passage divides into a description of wealthy persecutors of Christians (5:1–6) and the consequent need for Christians to exercise patience in awaiting the Lord's return (5:7–11).

5:1–4: Go now, you rich [men]. **Weep, howling over your miseries that are coming upon you** [compare Luke 6:24–25]. **²Your riches have rotted, and your garments have become moth-eaten. ³Your gold and silver have rusted, and their rust will turn into a testimony against you and eat your flesh as a fire** ["eats" combustible material]. **You've treasured up** [gold and silver] **during the last days** [compare Matthew 6:19–21; Luke 12:33–34]. **⁴Behold, the wages of the workers who mowed your fields,** [wages] **defrauded by you, are crying out** [in testimony against you]; **and the pleas of those who harvested** [your fields] **have entered "into the ears of Lord Sabaoth** [Isaiah 5:9]"**!** The topic of traveling businessmen in 4:13–17 now leads into a verbal attack on wealthy, oppressive non-Christians. James addresses them as though they're part of his audience ("you rich [men]"). They aren't, though; for he's writing to Christians often victimized by these rich men. But the make-believe address dramatizes James's pronouncement of judgment on them, and the dramatization strengthens the following exhortation that his real audience should wait patiently for the second coming, when

they'll be delivered and rewarded and their wealthy oppressors dispossessed and punished. (Generally speaking, the Old Testament too portrayed the wealthy as oppressive of the righteous.)

For "Go now," see the comments on 4:13. The conjunction of "howling" with the command, "Weep," highlights those coming "miseries" of dispossession and punishment (compare the phraseology in 4:9). Like the English word "howling," James's underlying Greek word sounds like what it means, except that instead of representing an extended outcry, like the howl of a wolf, it represents brief but fast-repeated ululations such as one still hears Middle Eastern women utter at funerals and on other mournful occasions. (The Greek is *ololuzontes*, which refers to a high-pitched repetition of "o-lo-lo-lo-lo-lo [and so on].") The miseries that are coming on rich oppressors should spoil with despair their present enjoyment of wealth, but they're not listening. They enjoy plentiful food consisting of grain harvested from their fields. They have wardrobes filled with garments of high quality. And they have hoards of gold and silver coins with which to purchase whatever they desire. Since according to 5:5 they've been living "luxuriously and voluptuously," the coins needed to bankroll such a lifestyle haven't yet rusted; nor have their garments yet become moth-eaten or their wealth of food yet rotted. So by putting the rotting, the eating by moths, and the rusting in the past, James portrays the coming miseries as so certain to take place that they might as well already have done so. In 1:10–11; 4:14 James warned the rich that life is short. Here he notes that riches have a short shelf life. The ancients knew as well as we do that gold and silver don't rust. So James is saying that even the riches which ordinarily don't rust will in fact do so under God's judgment. Or is it that James is referring to coins only plated with gold and silver that will wear off and expose the remainder to rust? In either event, earthly wealth will pass away. Next, James personifies the rust as a witness testifying against the oppressive rich at the Last Judgment and then, given the redness of both rust and fire, compares the rust to the fire of hell that will eat their flesh as the rust "ate" the gold and silver coins they should have paid their hired hands (compare 3:5b–6).

"The last days" reference the present church age in that it immediately precedes the end, that is, the second coming (compare Acts 2:17; 2 Timothy 3:1; Hebrews 1:2; 2 Peter 3:3; 1 John 2:18; Jude 18). Treasuring up gold and silver for self-gratification at the expense of others betrays foolish disregard of the judgment that will accompany the soon-coming end. Joining the personified rust of gold and silver coins in testimony against the oppressive rich are the personified wages that according to custom should have been paid their hired hands at the close of each workday (Leviticus 19:13; Deuteronomy 24:14–15; Malachi 3:5; Matthew 20:1–16; compare the law requiring at least two witnesses to establish a matter in court [Numbers 35:30; Deuteronomy 17:6; 19:15]). The "crying out" of the wages highlights the gravity of their charge. They fairly scream it. The present tense of "are crying out" makes it sound as though court is now in session, so sure and soon is it to be so. And "the pleas" for payment that the defrauded harvesters addressed ineffectually to the rich have already entered "into the ears of the Lord Sabaoth." He has overheard those pleas and noted them for the Last Judgment. "Sabaoth" is Hebrew (such as James's audience of Jewish Christians would understand) for "of hosts" and refers to the Lord's heavenly army of angels. This designation of God assures James's audience that despite their present powerlessness in relation to their rich oppressors, all the power of heaven stands ready to turn the tables. Indeed, the designation implies that at the Last Judgment God will enlist his angels in a war against the rich oppressors of his poor people. "Behold" makes these statements exclamatory for an assurative emphasis.

James continues to address wealthy, oppressive non-Christians as though they're part of his audience. **5:5–6: You've lived on the earth luxuriously and voluptuously. You've nourished your hearts "in a day of slaughter** [Isaiah 30:25; Jeremiah 12:3]." **⁶You've condemned, you've murdered the righteous person** [compare 2:6]. **He doesn't stand against** [= resist] **you.** The staccato-like effect of these short, unconnected statements sharpens the charges contained in them. "You've lived . . . luxuriously and voluptuously" provides the basis for a future "eat[ing]" of "your flesh" by the "rust" of "your gold and silver . . . as a fire ['eats' combustible material]" (5:3). "On the earth" implies a contrast with hell, where fire will burn (compare Luke 16:19–25; Ezekiel 16:49). The pairing of "luxuriously" and "voluptuously" puts a twofold emphasis on the contrast with the poverty of defrauded hired hands. By living thus, the rich oppressors have nourished their hearts—that is, fattened themselves (compare Isaiah 6:10: "Make the hearts of this people fat")—for slaughter (compare the slaughter of "the fattened calf" in Luke 15:23). "*In* [or '*during*'] a day of slaughter" portrays the Day of Judgment as so soon and certain as to be practically equivalent to the present age. By gratifying themselves at the expense particularly of poor Christians, in other words, the rich oppressors have unwittingly prepared themselves for the slaughter that consists in everlasting doom. But they've done worse than defrauding their hired hands. They've gone so far as to use the courts, which favor the rich, for condemning "the righteous person," that is, a Christian (see 5:16 for this designation of a Christian). The judicial condemnation has issued in an execution, but the injustice of condemning a righteous person to death has turned the execution into a murder. The righteous person's nonresistance heightens the injustice (compare Matthew 5:5, 38–42).

5:7–8: Therefore be patient, brothers, until the coming of the Lord. Behold, the farmer waits expectantly for the precious fruit of the earth, being patient over it [the fruit] **until it receives early** [rain] **and late** [rain]! **⁸You too be patient. Stabilize your hearts, because the Lord's coming has drawn near.** With affection and sympathy for his audience in their poverty-stricken, persecution-ridden plight, James addresses them with "brothers." "Therefore" makes his exhortation to patience grow out of that plight, described in the immediately preceding excoriation of their persecutors. "Until the coming of the Lord" defines how long the patience is required and points to the second coming as the occasion of release. The word for "coming" (*parousia* in Greek) often had to do with the visit of an emperor, and the word for "Lord" (*kyrios* in Greek) increasingly referred to the emperor. So "the coming of the Lord" portrays Jesus' return as an imperial visitation whose purpose will be to deliver his people from persecution and punish their persecutors.

James has recently written about mowing the fields and harvesting the crops of large-scale farmers (5:4). Now he uses a small-scale farmer to illustrate the kind of patience required of poor, persecuted Christians. "Behold . . . !" showcases the illustration, and the illustration itself pictures such a farmer as waiting patiently for the fruit his little plot of land will produce. His wait lasts from the early rain in late October–early November to the late rain in late April–early May. The heaviest rain fell in midwinter, but to suit his exhortation to patience James mentions only the first and last rains, the first being necessary for the germination of seed and the last being necessary for the ripening of fruit (compare Deuteronomy 11:14; Jeremiah 5:24; Joel 2:23). James describes the fruit as "precious" because a small-scale farmer, living on an economic precipice, needs the fruit for his and his family's bare subsistence. But James describes the fruit as "precious" also because it represents Christians' coming deliverance from poverty and persecution. The farmer has to wait. Impatience would do no good. Likewise, impatience for the Lord's coming would do no good. On the contrary, it would produce an instability born of frustration. So James follows up the command, "You too be patient," with the command, "Stabilize your hearts," which means to settle your thinking and feeling on the nearness of "the Lord's coming." Only such stability will keep you from succumbing to the pressures of poverty and persecution. In view of James's repeated call for patience, the nearness of the Lord's coming means not that he *will* come soon but that he's *ready* to come soon.

5:9: Don't be whining, brothers, against each other, lest you be judged [compare Matthew 7:1–2]. **Behold, the judge has taken his stand right in front of the gates** [compare Matthew 24:33]! The preceding exhortation to patience in the face of persecution by non-Christians (5:7–8) morphs here into an exhortation not to whine against fellow Christians, who may try your patience, especially when they sin against you (compare especially 3:13–4:12). Again James addresses his audience with "brothers," this time because it would be unbrotherly for brothers to whine against each other. (Remember: to a considerable extent this letter consists in rules for behavior within a local church, portrayed in terms of a family.) And whereas in 5:7–8 the prospect of deliverance from persecution at "the Lord's coming" provides a basis for patience, now the prospect of judgment at that coming provides a basis for not whining against each other—hence a shift from "the Lord" to "the judge." In view of the judge's ability to destroy as well as save (see 4:12), "lest you be judged" means "lest you suffer eternal destruction in hell." How serious, then, is the issue of whining against fellow Christians! It distinguishes between true and false ones. The judge's having "taken his stand right in front of the gates" echoes James's declaration that "the Lord's coming has drawn near" (5:8). But why "in front of the gates"? Because in ancient Middle Eastern cities judicial proceedings took place just inside the city gates (see, for example, Zechariah 8:16). The judge stands ready to enter the gates of the world-city, so to speak, for making judgments at the appropriate spot. To intensify his warning, James prefixes "Behold" to his declaration of the judge's readiness.

5:10–11: As an example of suffering hardship and of patience, brothers, take the prophets who spoke in the Lord's name. ¹¹Behold, we pronounce those who persevered fortunate [compare Matthew 5:10–12; 23:37; Acts 7:52]**! You've heard about Job's perseverance, and you've seen the Lord's completion in that the Lord is abundantly compassionate and merciful** [compare Exodus 34:6; Psalm 103:8]. After digressing to the topic of whining (5:9), James now reverts to the topic of patience under persecution (5:7–8). So he also repeats the affectionate, sympathetic address "brothers" which introduced that topic. The prophets' "example of suffering hardship and of patience" is an example to be followed. The background of 5:1–8 defines "hardship" as persecution; and the addition, "of patience," produces the meaning, "an example of suffering persecution patiently." By definition, "the prophets" were those "who spoke in the Lord's name," that is, who conveyed to others messages from him. But James adds this definition to point up the reason for the prophets' suffering. People didn't like those messages. By implication, the testimony of Christians likewise brings suffering on them. "Behold . . . !" underscores the good fortune of the prophets who persevered because of their patience in the face of persecution. Originally, *Jesus* pronounced them fortunate (see Matthew 5:10–12 again). But "*we* pronounce [them] fortunate" indicates that James and his audience have chimed in with Jesus' pronouncement and therefore should consider themselves similarly fortunate if like the ancient prophets they too persevere. Satan himself persecuted Job (Job 1–2). But Job persevered through faith in God and therefore provided an example to be followed in addition to that of the prophets. "You've *heard* about Job's perseverance" in that the books of Scripture were read aloud to audiences, copies for private reading being extremely rare. "The Lord's completion" refers to the restoration by him of Job's prosperity (Job 42:10–17). The Lord will likewise bring Christians' suffering of hardship to completion with "the crown of [eternal] life" (1:12). Such a completion arises out of his compassion and mercy (contrast the "merciless judgment" to

be brought on merciless people in 2:13). The use of two descriptions, "compassionate" and "merciful," and their magnification with "abundantly" fortify James's assurance of a fortunate outcome.

AN EXHORTATION AGAINST OATHS
James 5:12

5:12: And ahead of all things [in importance]**, my brothers, don't ever swear either by heaven or by the earth or by any other oath. But your "Yes" is to be yes, and** [your] **"No"** [is to be] **no, lest you fall under judgment.** For "my brothers," see the comments on 1:2. Here, this address joins "ahead of all things" to punctuate the importance of James's prohibiting the swearing of oaths. The prohibition stems from Jesus' prohibition of swearing them (see Matthew 5:33–37 with comments).[2] But why does James rate this prohibition more important than all his other instructions? His answer: Because if your "Yes," unadorned with an oath, doesn't really mean yes, and if your "No," likewise unadorned with an oath, doesn't really mean no, you'll "fall under judgment," that is, suffer eternal doom (compare the comments on 5:9). But this answer only pushes the question one step back. For why should a failure at simple truth-telling draw so severe a penalty? Well, as recently mentioned, James writes largely to lay down rules governing relations between Christians in local churches; and as his extensive discussion of the tongue in chapter 3 shows, speech occupies first place in determining those relations. And first among the kinds of speech which make for good relations is telling the truth so consistently that no oaths are necessary to convince others you're telling it, and so consistently that swearing that you're telling it would call in question whether you *are* telling it if you don't swear with an oath that you are.

AN EXHORTATION TO MUTUALITY
James 5:13–18

5:13–16a: Is anyone among you suffering hardship? He's to be praying. Is anyone in good spirits? He's to sing praises. ¹⁴Is anyone among you sick? He's to summon the elders of the church; and they're to pray over him, anointing him with olive oil [that is, pouring or smearing it on him] **in the Lord's name. ¹⁵And the prayer of faith will save** [from his illness] **the one who's ill, and the Lord will raise him up** [from his sickbed]**. And if perchance he has committed sins, it** [the committing of them] **will be forgiven for him. ¹⁶ᵃTherefore be confessing** [your] **sins to one another and praying for one another so that you may be healed.** As before, "suffering hardship" refers to the suffering of persecution (see the comments on 5:10). Therefore the first-mentioned praying is to be understood as praying for deliverance from persecution; and the contrast between

---

[2]Swearing an oath by this or that or someone (such as a deity) differs from cussing, though cussing isn't thereby allowed.

suffering hardship and being "in good spirits" indicates that deliverance from persecution, as when God answers the prayer for such deliverance, has produced the good spirits and therefore requires the praising of God for the deliverance. Praising him consists in the public recitation of his mighty and merciful acts. The plural in "praises" indicates multiple recitations. And the "sing[ing]" of them suits the good spirits.

The sick Christian is "to summon the elders of the [local] church," because he's too weak to attend a church meeting, because it would be too much to ask all the church members to come to his sickroom, and because as mature Christians the church elders bear special responsibility for others in the church. "They're to pray over him" implies that the elders have heeded his summons and that he's lying on a sickbed. They're to pray for his healing, naturally. Olive oil was used as a medicament in the Greco-Roman world (see Mark 6:13; Luke 10:34 for scriptural examples), but pronouncement of "the Lord's name" is to accompany the anointing and thereby ensure its curative effect (see Acts 3:6, 16; 4:7, 10 for the power of Jesus' pronounced name in a miraculous healing, though James references "the *Lord's* name" to underline Jesus' mastery over illness). The effectiveness of anointing in the Lord's name doesn't depend ultimately—or, we could say, mechanically—on olive oil as such or on the mere pronouncing of the Lord's name. It depends, rather, on the elders' praying with faith for a cure (compare 1:6–8 and see Acts 3:16 again).

"And if perchance he [the sick peson] has committed sins" opens up two possibilities, each one carrying an implication: (1) he has committed sins, so that his illness is a punishment for them; and (2) he hasn't committed sins, so that his illness isn't a punishment for sins. In the first instance, the Lord's raising him up from his sickbed will give evidence of forgiveness. "Therefore be confessing [your] sins to one another" means that Christians who are sick as a punishment for their sins should confess their sins to other Christians so that in their praying the others can take account of the sins that need forgiveness and thereby pray effectively for a healing of the sick. Only the elders need visit the sick for the purpose of anointing and praying, but all the church members are to join in the praying.

5:16b–18: A righteous person's entreaty, being effective, is abundantly strong. ¹⁷Elijah was a human being with sensitivities like ours, and he prayed with a prayer that it not rain, and it didn't rain on the land [of Israel] **for three years and six months. ¹⁸And he prayed again; and the sky gave rain, and the land sprouted its fruit.** "A righteous person" harks back to 5:6, where James said to the rich, "You've murdered the righteous person," and marks a distinction between the Christian whose sins have resulted in illness and the Christian who, not having sinned, prays for the sinful one's healing. A shift from the plural in "be praying for one another" (5:16a) to the singular of "a righteous person" prepares for the example of Elijah as one who prayed. To encourage praying, James adds another word

for prayer ("entreaty"), describes the prayer as "effective," for good measure adds the further description "strong," reinforces "strong" with "abundantly," appends the effectiveness of Elijah's praying both for a drought and for its end, and adds "with a prayer" to "he prayed." Then to make the example of Elijah even more convincing, James describes him not as the prophet that he was but as "a human being with sensitivities like ours," which he also was (see 1 Kings 19). In other words, if Elijah could pray effectively, as he did, so can you.

Yet 1 Kings 17–18 doesn't say directly that Elijah prayed for a drought and then for its end, and it puts the end of the drought in its third year (18:1) whereas James says the drought lasted "three years and six months." Since Elijah's prediction of a drought in 17:1 isn't said to stem from a divine revelation (note the contrast between "my [Elijah's] word" in 17:1 and "the word of the Lord" in 17:2, 8, 24; 18:1; compare 17:14), apparently James interprets the prediction as based on prayer for a drought because it was during the drought that the Lord raised the widow of Zarephath's son in answer to a prayer of Elijah and apart from any word from the Lord (17:8–23). The Lord did reveal to Elijah the coming end of drought (18:1), but to demonstrate that the Lord rather than Baal (a pagan god of rainstorms) would end the drought, Elijah prayed successfully for fire to fall from heaven and consume his offering (18:36–38). Apparently James interprets this prayer as effecting the end of the drought as well. And just as an infant was considered two years old immediately on entering his second year, whereas we'd consider him two years old not until he'd completed his second year (see the comments on Matthew 2:16), so James interprets "in the third year [of the drought]" (1 Kings 18:1) as referring to the middle of what we'd call the second year—hence "three years and six months" (as also in Luke 4:25). To cap the effectiveness of Elijah's praying, James adds to "the sky gave rain" that as a result "the land sprouted its fruit."

AN ENCOURAGEMENT TO KEEP FELLOW CHRISTIANS FROM APOSTATIZING
James 5:19–20

5:19–20: My brothers, if anyone among you wanders away from the truth and someone turns him back [to the truth], **²⁰he's to know that the person who turns back a sinner out of the wandering of his path** [= the path he took in wandering from the truth] **will save his** [the sinner's] **soul from death and "will cover a multitude of sins** [Proverbs 10:12]**."** The possibility that sins have resulted in illness and the assurance of forgiveness as an outcome of "the prayer of faith" (5:14–18) lead into an exhortation regarding "a sinner" in the church who needs to be saved "from death" by having the "multitude of [his] sins" forgiven. The address, "my brothers," lends a note of seriousness as well as affection to this, the last of James's exhortations (compare 5:12 and see the comments on 1:2). Since walking and traveling often stand for behaving in a certain way, "to wander away from the truth" means to deviate from the "good behavior" required by "the truth" in "the word of truth" (see 3:13–14 with 1:18). Unless short-circuited, this wandering will end in total apostasy and thus in a "death" which is eternal. The command that the "someone" who "turns back" the sinning wanderer "*is to know*" he's saving the wanderer from such a death—this command is designed to encourage the reclamation of wanderers. Putting the command indirectly and in the singular ("*he's* to know") rather than directly and in the plural ("*you're* to know") brings out the responsibility of an individual Christian to reclaim the wanderer. "Will save his soul" echoes 1:21 and, as there, refers to the whole self of the wanderer, not just to his soul as distinct from his body. But here, "from death" adds to "soul" the connotation of life in

that the word translated "soul" often means "life" (compare the expression "a living soul," as in Genesis 2:7, and passages such as Mark 8:35–37). Since James has called the wanderer "a sinner," it's the wanderer's "multitude of sins" that the reclaimer "will cover." And just as in 1 Peter 4:8 "love covers a multitude of sins" in the sense that Christians' love for each other makes them forgive the sins committed against them by fellow Christians, so the reclaimer will forgive the sins which the wanderer has committed against him. Again we should remember that James is largely concerned to establish good relations between Christians in local churches, so that the wanderer's sins are understood to be sins against fellow Christians. Thus the reclamation of the wanderer entails the reclaimer's forgiving the wanderer's sins against him.

FIRST PETER

This letter's addressees were suffering persecution. Emphasis falls therefore on proper Christian conduct in the face of anti-Christian hostility and on the gift of salvation that will reach completion in the future.

ADDRESS AND GREETING
1 Peter 1:1–2

1:1–2: Peter, an apostle of Jesus Christ, to exiles of the Diaspora of Pontus, Galatia, Cappadocia, Asia, and Bithynia, [exiles] **selected** [2]**in accordance with the foreknowledge of God the Father by the Spirit's consecration for obedience and** [for] **the sprinkling of Jesus Christ's blood: May grace and peace be multiplied for you.** In the Roman Empire of the first century authors customarily identified themselves at the start of their letters. Peter follows this custom, calls himself by the nickname that Jesus gave him, and uses its Greek form ("Peter," which means "a stone") because he's writing in Greek. (Jesus, who spoke Aramaic most of the time, used the Aramaic form ["Cephas"], Aramaic being a Semitic language closely related to Hebrew.) "An apostle of Jesus Christ" means "sent by Jesus Christ with authority to speak and act on his behalf." This self-designation lends authority—indeed, Jesus Christ's own authority—to the letter. "Jesus" is a personal name. Strictly and originally, "Christ" was a title that meant "Anointed One"; but constant usage led to its being used as another personal name alongside "Jesus" (compare the way the title "King," as in "King George," could turn into a personal name, as in "George King").

"Diaspora" means "dispersion" (literally, "a seeding throughout," as when seed is scattered throughout a field). The Jews' Diaspora consisting of those who lived as expatriates scattered in various regions outside their homeland of Israel (compare their forced exile in Babylonia during the Old Testament period). Peter portrays his Christian audience as similarly scattered, but not because they live as Jews outside the land of Israel. For their idolatry prior to conversion (4:3) marks them as Gentiles rather than Jews, whose Babylonian exile had by and large cured them of idolatry. It will turn out that Peter's audience are suffering persecution, and that the persecution has taken the form mainly of their being mistreated through social ostracism, maliciously false accusations, and economic boycott by the non-Christians among whom they're scattered. So Peter portrays the Christians as exiled from their homeland in heaven. They live on earth as noncitizens. Similar parallels with the Jews will pile up throughout this letter. Pontus, Galatia, Cappadocia, Asia, and Bithynia were Roman provinces in Asia Minor (the Asian side of modern Turkey).

After indicating his audience's exilic address, Peter describes them as "selected," that is, as chosen out from the rest of the human race, like God's chosen nation of Israel. The Christians' selection comfortingly counterbalances the non-Christians' rejection of them. "In accordance with the foreknowledge of God" doesn't mean that he selected the Christians because he knew ahead of time they were going to believe the gospel—rather, that he selected them in accordance with his predetermined plan, just as in Acts 2:23 Peter puts God's foreknowledge right after, and in parallel with, "God's ordained plan" (compare Genesis 18:19, where the Lord says he has "known" Abraham in the sense of having chosen him; Jeremiah 1:5, where we read that before Jeremiah's conception and birth the Lord knew, consecrated, and appointed him to be a prophet; and Amos 3:2, where the Lord says he has known—that is, chosen—only Israel from among all the earth's families [see also 1 Peter 1:20]). Addition of "the Father" to "God" prepares for "God, even the Father of our Lord, Jesus Christ" and for God's "father[ing] us anew" in 1:3. Consecration by the Spirit means his setting Christians apart from non-Christians to be sacred to God, as non-Christians are not. This consecration is the means by which the Spirit carries out God the Father's selection. The purpose and result of the consecration, and ultimately of the selection, are obedience to the call of the gospel and, in consequence of that obedience, "the sprinkling of Jesus Christ's blood," that is, the application of his blood so as to purchase the redemption of believers (1:18–19 [compare Exodus 24:3–8; Hebrews 9:13–14; 12:24]). Notably, those who later came to be called the Trinity cooperate in this selection for redemption: (1) God the Father's foreknowledge provides its basis. (2) The Spirit's consecration provides the means of its being carried out. (3) Jesus' shed blood provides the purchase price.

"Grace" transforms the usual subjective greeting in Greek, "Rejoice," into an objective *basis* for rejoicing, namely, the grace of God in selecting some people for redemption. (In Greek, "rejoice" and "grace" go back to the same root.) "Grace" means God's ill-deserved favor. "Peace," the usual Semitic greeting, connotes prosperity as well as absence of conflict and in conjunction with "grace" refers to all the blessings of redemption. For "peace" as a Semitic greeting see examples in Matthew 10:12–13; Judges 19:20; Ezra 4:17; 5:7. Peter adds "be multiplied" because as religious exiles, persecuted for their Christian beliefs and behavior, his audience need as much of God's grace and peace as they can get. "For you" alludes to the benefit that will accrue to them.

PRAISE FOR THE HEAVENLY INHERITANCE OF PERSECUTED CHRISTIANS
1 Peter 1:3–12

Those who later came to be called the Trinity make another appearance: (1) 1:3–5 features God the Father as an object of praise; (2) 1:6–9 features Jesus Christ as an object of hope; and (3) 1:10–12 features the Spirit as the inspirer of messianic prophecy in the past and of evangelism in the present.

1:3–5: Praised [be] **the God and Father of our Lord, Jesus Christ, who** [referring to God] **in accordance with his abundant mercy has fathered us anew with the result of a living hope through Jesus Christ's resurrection from among the dead,** [4][that is,] **with the result of an inheritance indestructible and unpolluted and unfading, having been secured in heaven for you,** [5]**who are being guarded by God's power through faith with the result of a salvation ready to be revealed in the last time . . . .** Praise of God grows out of gratitude for his having selected a new chosen people. Pride in such selection would overlook how ill-deserved is the grace that underlay the selection. "Our Lord" puts Jesus Christ on the level of deity alongside his Father, makes the Father his God in that he represents God, and designates Jesus the owner and master of believers and therefore the one to whom they owe obedience and worship. Putting a comma between "our Lord" and "Jesus Christ" highlights Christians' confessing his lordship over against the falsely supposed lordship of pagan deities and deified Caesars. (The use of commas and other punctuation marks is a matter of interpretation, since ancient Greek manuscripts contain punctuation hardly at all.)

"In accordance with his abundant mercy" parallels "in accordance with the foreknowledge of God the Father" in 1:1–2. As his foreknowledge formed the basis of selection, so his mercy forms the basis of his "father[ing] us anew." "Abundant" describes his mercy because—given our disgusting conduct (see especially 4:3–5)—it took a lot of mercy to father us anew. The translation "has *fathered* us anew" reflects that Peter is writing about a new kind of fertilization (by the seed of God's word according to 1:23) which results in a new kind of conception followed by a new kind of birth. Because the conduct that characterized us before conversion would have ended in God's judgment (4:17–18), he has to father anew those he has selected so that they may have "a living hope." "Hope" means a well-based confidence as opposed to wishful uncertainty. "Living" means "lively" in that the hope enables Christians to live christianly despite the antagonism of non-Christians. It also means that Christians have confidence they'll be resurrected to eternal life, as indicated by the following phrase, "through Jesus Christ's resurrection from

among the dead" (compare "God's living word" in 1:23, the Lord Jesus as a "living stone" in 2:4, and Christians as "living stones" in 2:5). "With the result of an inheritance" defines eternal life in terms of an inherited land, a land to be inherited by those fathered anew into God the Father's family as the land of Israel was inherited by the Jews, born into the family of Abraham through Isaac and then Jacob. But though the Jews' inherited land was repeatedly sacked by invaders, Christians' inheritance will never, *can* never, suffer such a fate. It has been "secured in heaven." The Jews polluted their land with idolatry and immorality. But since Christians have "purified" themselves (1:22), they won't pollute their inheritance. Drought made the Jews' land fade. Christians' inheritance will never fade. "Having been secured" means already secured. "In heaven" puts the inheritance at a safe distance from earthly sources of destruction, defilement, and drought.

"Who are being guarded" indicates protection of Christians as heirs in addition to the security of their inheritance, so that they and the inheritance may come together "in the last time," the time of Jesus' return. Though Christians are exposed to persecution, in other words, God keeps them safe in grace and peace just as he has secured their inheritance in heaven. "By God's power" makes their safety absolute. "Through faith" is usually understood in terms of Christians' faith. But "faith" can mean faithfulness as well as belief, Peter is stressing divine protection, and 4:19 will speak of suffering Christians' "commit[ting] their souls [= entrusting themselves] to a faithful Creator." So it's better to understand Peter to be writing that God guards Christians not only powerfully but also faithfully. He doesn't fall asleep on the watch. The resultant salvation has to do with deliverance from persecution so as to take possession of the inheritance presently secured in heaven. "Ready to be revealed in the last time" points forward to such deliverance at Jesus' return, when the inheritance will come out of its present hiddenness in heaven. This revelation, which will be apparent to non-Christians as well as Christians, will compensate for public dishonor that the Christians suffered at the non-Christians' hands. "Ready to be revealed" indicates that only the arrival of "the last time," the set date on God's calendar, keeps the revelation from happening right now. No work on the inheritance remains to be done. Jesus has already done it all. So God selected Christians before their conversion, fathered them anew at their conversion, and guards them afterwards till they come into their inheritance, at which time guarding will no longer be necessary.

Peter's long sentence continues in **1:6–7: in which** [referring back to the revealing of salvation in the last time] **you're cheering up despite having now been saddened a little, if necessary, by various trials** [7]**in order that the authenticity of your faith,** [which authenticity is] **much more valuable than gold that gets lost even though being authenticated** [by being put] **through fire, may be found to result in praise and glory and honor at the revelation of Jesus Christ . . . .** "Various trials" refers to different sorts of persecution that test the Christians' faith and tempt them to renounce it for the preservation and improvement of their present lives. "*If necessary*" implies that being saddened now by various trials is *sometimes* necessary in order that the authentication of Christians' faith may bring them praise, glory, and honor at the revelation of Jesus Christ, when he returns. The stacking of "praise," "glory," and "honor" one on top of another puts a huge emphasis on compensation for the Christians' present suffering of calumny, disgrace, and shame. "The revelation of Jesus Christ" parallels the revelation of the Christians' inheritance. The two revelations will coincide; and they *should* coincide, for Jesus readied the inheritance through his death and resurrection. "A little" indicates, on the other hand, that the sadness currently caused by various trials doesn't measure up to these future revelations, in contemplation of which the Christians are cheering up. The compliment of noting that they're cheering up is intended to win, and should rightly win, a favorable reception for this letter. Successfully enduring trials authenticates faith. This authentication compares with the authentication of gold by putting it through fire without its being burned up. Peter writes about authentication, not refinement, and uses gold as the ancients' most precious known metal to highlight by comparison the value God places on authentic Christian faith. Trials test the mettle of faith just as fire tests a metal such as gold. People can lose gold authenticated by the test of fire, as in the loss of gold coins; but a Christian's faith that has been authenticated by the endurance of persecution will never be lost. "May be found" implies a search at the Last Judgment for authenticity in professed Christian faith.

Peter's sentence continues the compliment and gets longer yet in *1:8–9*: **whom** [referring back to "Jesus Christ"] **you love, though not having seen** [him], **in whom believing, though not seeing him right now— yet you're cheering up with indescribable and glorified joy, ⁹obtaining the goal of your faith,** [namely,] **the salvation of** [your] **souls . . . .** The love of Christians for Jesus Christ explains why trials authenticate their faith rather than obliterating it. "Though not having seen [him]" showcases the intensity of their love for him just as the stacking up of "praise," "glory," and "honor" showcased the value of their faith's authenticity (1:7). "In whom believing" calls attention to this parallel. "Though not having seen [him]" also distinguishes Peter's audience from Peter himself, for he did see Jesus during Jesus' lifetime on earth. The audience, living far away from Israel in Asia Minor, didn't see Jesus. And because of his resurrection and ascension, they don't see him at the present time, so that not seeing him showcases yet again the intensity of their love for him. But "right now" implies they *will* see him at his revelation in the second coming. Believing in him despite the lack of past or present seeing of him cheers them up, however, with a joy that's dispelling their sadness. This joy surpasses the ability of human language to express it adequately ("indescribable"), and it's "glorified" in the

sense of ennobled by its having arisen out of believing in Jesus without seeing him (compare John 20:29). The joy is also accompanied by the obtaining of faith's goal. That goal, defined as "the salvation of your souls," doesn't mean the salvation of souls apart from bodies. Jews like Peter often used "soul" for the whole self, so that the phrase means "the salvation of your*selves*" (compare the reference in 1:3 to Jesus' resurrection, which by definition was bodily). Obtaining this salvation at the present time ensures a final and full possession of it "in the last time" (1:5). Salvation is a process that starts now and will reach completion in the future.

The sentence continues in *1:10–11*: **concerning which salvation prophets who prophesied about the grace** [destined] **for you researched avidly and investigated avidly ¹¹by making investigation into what person or what particular time the Spirit of Christ within them was indicating by testifying ahead of time the sufferings** [destined] **for Christ and the glories** [destined for him] **after these** [sufferings] **. . . .** "Grace" defines "salvation" in terms of ill-deserved favor (compare the comments on God's "abundant mercy" in 1:3). The "prophets who prophesied" about it are Old Testament prophets, not Christian prophets. Though they prophesied about this grace, they didn't know in whom it would be revealed or when it would be revealed. "Or" indicates they'd like to have discovered at least one of these items of information. The prophets remained ignorant despite their avid research and investigation, however; and this ignorance enhances Christians' privilege in having both the whom and the when of grace revealed to them. Peter's adding "investigation" to "research" and describing both of them as "avid" furthers the enhancement. "The Spirit of Christ within them [the Old Testament prophets]" implies the preexistence and deity of Christ and attributes the messianic prophecies to his Spirit. "Testifying ahead of time" gives these now-fulfilled prophecies evidential value. Specifically, Peter mentions "the sufferings [destined] for Christ" to make Christians feel better about their own suffering of various trials. The plural "sufferings" of Christ match the variety of the Christians' trials (1:6) and may include social persecution, like that of Christians, in addition to crucifixion. The mention of "the glories [destined for Christ] after these [sufferings]" encourages Christians likewise by implying their own such destiny yet to come. The plural of "glories" refers to Jesus' resurrection and exaltation (see 3:18–22) and answers to the plural of "sufferings." There has been no shortfall in compensation. As for the Old Testament prophets, they couldn't reconcile their prophecies of Christ's sufferings with their prophecies of his glories; for the distinction between his first and second comings hadn't yet become clear.

Peter's sentence finally reaches completion in *1:12*: **to whom it was revealed that they were serving, not to themselves but to you, things that have now been announced to you through those who proclaimed the gospel to you by the Holy Spirit sent from heaven,** into which things angels long to bend down for a glimpse. The twice-occurring "things" are Christ's sufferings and subsequent glories. It's as though the "things that have now been announced" were food—say, food for consumption by faith—being served up by the Old Testament prophets to people such as Peter's audience who've believed the good news of God's grace in Jesus Christ as proclaimed by Christian evangelists. The revelation to the Old Testament prophets that they were serving future Christians rather than themselves, plus the longing of angels to bend down from heaven to catch a glimpse of God's salvific activity on earth, enhances yet further the encouraging privilege of Christians in having the good news announced to them that those ancient prophecies have now been fulfilled. "By the Holy Spirit" describes the evangelists' announcement as divinely inspired. "Sent from heaven" recalls the day of Pentecost (Acts 2) and describes the Spirit as commissioned by God the Father to inspire the evangelists. Such inspiration gives the announcement the highest possible authority and reliability.

AN EXHORTATION TO PERSONAL HOLINESS
1 Peter 1:13–21

1:13: On account of this, having hitched up the hips of your mind, staying sober, base your hope completely on the grace being brought to you at the revelation of Jesus Christ. "On account of this" bases the following exhortation on the proclamation of the gospel that Peter has just mentioned. Good news requires good behavior. To prepare for work, people in Peter's world customarily hitched up their long outer robe by tucking its hem into a belt worn around the waist, so that the robe covered only the hips and allowed the legs freedom of movement (a modern American equivalent: rolling up your shirtsleeves). Peter uses the custom as a figure of speech for preparing to think—in particular, to think properly about Christian conduct. Such thinking requires sobriety, for drunkenness muddles the mind. Were Christians tempted to drown the sorrows of persecution (1:6) in alcohol? (There's no good reason to treat "staying sober" figuratively, though many do.) See the comments on 1:3 for hope as well-based confidence. Here it obviously has to do with the second coming, called "the revelation of Jesus Christ" to assure Christians who love him though they've never seen him that they will see him at his return. When he comes, Peter writes, he'll be bringing them "grace." But what grace? Not the grace of a salvation already received, but the grace of a salvation yet to be received, that is, deliverance from persecution. The command, "base your hope completely on [this] grace," implies that the deliverance will rest solely on God's ill-deserved favor, not in the least on Christians' achievements, not even on their faithful endurance of persecution, though such endurance is required for the authentication of faith. There may be a wordplay in "completely," for Peter's Greek original has as its root *tel-*, the same as for the Greek behind "end,"

which refers to the time of Christ's return, the very time when he'll bring the grace on which hope is to be based "completely."

1:14–16: As obedient children not conforming yourselves to the former lusts [that characterized you] **in your ignorance** [prior to conversion]—[15]**rather, in accordance with the Holy One who called you** [= God, who selected you for salvation and effected it (1:1–5)]— **you yourselves also, become holy in all** [your] **behavior** [more literally, "at every turn," that is, in whatever you turn to do], [16]**because it's written, "You shall be holy, because I am holy** [= the Lord's command in Leviticus 11:44–45; 19:2; 20:7, 26]**."** "As obedient children" harks back to "God the Father," who "has fathered us anew" (1:2–3). As children must obey their earthly fathers (Exodus 20:12; Deuteronomy 5:16; Ephesians 6:1–3; Colossians 3:20), Christians must obey their heavenly Father. Persecution tempts them contrariwise to conform themselves back to their unpersecuted behavior prior to conversion. "Lusts" defines the behavior as having stemmed from desires so strong that they led to the trespassing of moral boundaries. "In your ignorance" refers to earlier ignorance of those boundaries, set as they were in divinely inspired Scripture unknown to pagans, and implies that Christians now know better than to backslide into their former lusts. Instead of backsliding, they're to "become holy" as and because the God of Scripture is holy. His calling them to save them should motivate them to a holiness like his. "You yourselves also" accents the demand that they mirror God's holiness. "In all [your] behavior" allows no behavioral exceptions, and the contrast with "lusts" gives "holy" a moral meaning. In other words, ritual sanctity has morphed into moral sanctity. And since Peter has drawn parallels with God's chosen people of Israel (1:1–5), he cites for Christians what the Lord commanded the Israelites.

1:17–21: And if you're appealing to him as [your] **Father who judges impartially according to each person's work, behave yourselves with fear throughout the time of your residence as aliens,** [18]**taking cognizance** [of the fact] **that you were redeemed out of your pointless behavior, passed down from your forefathers, not with perishable things—silver or gold** [for instance (compare Isaiah 52:3)]—[19]**rather, with valuable blood like** [that] **of an unblemished and spotless lamb,** [the blood] **of Christ,** [20]**foreknown on the one hand before the founding of the world, manifested on the other hand at the last of the times because of you** [21]**who through him believe in God** [in the sense of trusting him and therefore staying faithful to him], **who raised him out of from among the dead and gave him glory, so that your faith** [= trust] **and hope are in God.** As a matter of fact, Peter's audience *are* appealing to God as their Father. Probably they're asking him to deliver them from their persecutors as a father would deliver his child from a bully (compare Genesis 21:8–14). The reference to God's judging supports this probability. Since judges in that world regularly showed partiality to wealthy and powerful oppressors of the poor and powerless, the further description of God as impartial suggests that the Christians thought he'd give them overdue justice against their persecutors. But with the command, "behave yourselves with fear," Peter turns the Christians' comforting view of God also into a warning based on God's coming judgment of them too. Fear of that judgment should keep them from backsliding into their former lusts.

"Work" is collective for deeds, and "according to each person's work" makes God's judgment individual as well as impartial. Grace doesn't cancel out the necessity of good deeds as evidence of having received God's grace. He's a demanding as well as gracious Father, and as demanding he's also judgmental. "Throughout the time of your residence as aliens" demands perseverance so long as you live or until the second coming and reminds Christians that as resident aliens whose landed inheritance awaits its revelation from heaven, they should sit loose to the present world. Supporting such sitting will be a taking cognizance of their redemption, which portrays their past behavior as not only leading to no worthwhile end ("pointless") and thoughtlessly adopted ("passed down from your forefathers") but also as enslaving. For "you were redeemed" means "you were bought as a slave and then set free." Since traditional standards of behavior were generally regarded as safe and sound for both society and individuals, Peter's associating those standards with pointlessness, thoughtlessness, and enslavement turns the usual view upside down.

Normally and commercially, payment to free a slave was made with silver and gold coins. But here and theologically, payment is said to have been made with Christ's blood, which represents his sacrificially offered life (Genesis 9:4; Leviticus 17:11, 14). Silver and gold coins are perishable in that they can be lost, and often are (compare 1:7). Despite their high value, then, the contrast with Christ's blood escalates its value above that even of silver and gold. As free people now ransomed from enslavement to their former lusts, Christians have an imperishable inheritance. The comparison of Christ's blood to that of "an unblemished and spotless lamb" alludes to the redemption of Israel from slavery in Egypt by virtue of the shed blood of Passover lambs (Exodus 12). The absence of any blemish and spot represents the sinless perfection of Christ that qualified him to bear our sins on the cross (2:24). "Foreknown . . . before the founding of the world" means he was eternally predetermined to redeem Christians by shedding his blood as their purchase price (see the comments on 1:2 concerning foreknowledge). "Manifested . . . because of you" makes their redemption the very reason for Christ's appearance—and therefore Christ's appearance a reason itself for Christians not to backslide for self-protection from persecution. "At the last of the times" makes Christ's past appearance the beginning of the end-time (compare 2 Peter 3:3; Jude 18). Believing in God through Christ means trusting that God has used Christ's blood to purchase your redemption and therefore staying faithful rather than backsliding. God's resurrecting and glori-

fying Christ undergirds believing in God through Christ both in regard to an already accomplished redemption from slavery to lusts and in regard to the hope of a future deliverance from persecution.

AN EXHORTATION TO MUTUAL LOVE
1 Peter 1:22–25

1:22–25: Having purified your souls [= yourselves (see the comments on 1:9)] **by obedience to the truth for the purpose of unhypocritical brotherly affection, out of a clean heart love one another strenuously,** [23]**having been fathered anew not out of perishable seed—rather,** [out of] **imperishable** [seed] **through the living and lasting word of God,** [24]**because "all flesh** [is] **as grass** [is]**, and all its glory** [is] **as the flower of grass** [is]**. The grass has dried up, and the flower has fallen off;** [25]**but the word of the Lord is lasting forever** [Isaiah 40:6–8]**." And this** [word of the Lord] **is the word that was proclaimed to you as good news.** "The truth" consists in the good news of redemption. Because of the immediately preceding reference to believing in God through Christ, obedience consists in heeding the command to believe this good news. Since redemption has to do with liberation from enslavement to "the former lusts," the obedience entailed self-purification through the exercise of faith. From God's standpoint the self-purification had the purpose of producing "unhypocritical brotherly affection," that is, genuine affection for fellow Christians. The command to "love one another" grows out of that purpose, so that failure to obey the command would frustrate the purpose of the purification. "Out of a *clean* heart" confirms that mutual love among Christians originates in purification and implies that an absence of such love would betray a morally dirty heart. "Out of a clean *heart*" calls for affection as well as thought, the heart being considered an organ of both feeling and thinking. "Strenuously" describes the commanded love as requiring great effort, like that of a sprinter straining to finish first. Such effort doesn't imply that others' faults make mutual love difficult—rather, that the love will require much expenditure of energy in the doing of helpful deeds. Loving one another in this way comes naturally because of shared ancestry: Christians have all "been fathered anew"—by God according to 1:3—so that they're brothers and sisters to one another. Not the "perishable seed" of human semen, but "the imperishable [seed]" consisting of "the living and lasting word of God" provided the means by which he fathered them (compare Mark 4:3–8, 13–20). This word was the *spoken* word of the gospel. Peter describes it as "living" in that it generates life when received by faith, and as "lasting" in that the life never ends. It's eternal.

Peter quotes Isaiah in support. "All flesh" means all human beings with reference to their perishability in that their flesh decomposes when they die. The perishability of their flesh matches the perishability of their seed (semen) and compares with the perishability of flowering fieldgrass. The glory—that is, the beauty—of human flesh falls away as wildflowers fall off their dried-up stems of grass in the sun and heat of summer. (Peter grew up in Israel, where grass is green only in springtime.) So certain is the perishing that the verbs "has dried up" and "has fallen off" put it in the past. To stress a contrast with this perishability, "the word of the Lord is lasting" repeats the thought of "the lasting word of God"; but an addition of "forever" extends the thought endlessly to match the eternality of life that comes about by "having been fathered anew." To clinch his point, Peter equates the Lord's word as described by Isaiah with the word of the gospel. In summary, we believe in the imperishable word of God. The imperishable blood of Christ pays for our liberation from sin. And an imperishable inheritance becomes ours.

AN EXHORTATION TO PROGRESS IN SALVATION
1 Peter 2:1–10

2:1–3: Therefore [= because the word of the Lord was preached to you as good news] **on putting off all malice and all deceit and hypocrisies** [= pretensions] **and jealousies and all malicious remarks** [all of which in this list would destroy the mutual love commanded in 1:22–25], **²long for the verbal, undeceitful milk as newborn infants** [long for milk], **in order that by it you may grow for the purpose and with the result of salvation, ³if you've tasted "that the Lord** [is] **kind** [Psalm 34:8]" **. . . .** "Putting off" was used for taking off clothes. So putting off the listed vices is like taking off dirty clothes. Three occurrences of "all" underscore the need for complete divestiture of the vices. "Hypocrisies" gives an example of "deceit." "Jealousies" lie at the root of "malice." And "malicious remarks" give expression to the malice.

Though he has spoken of his audience as "fathered anew" (1:3, 23), Peter doesn't compare *them* to infants, as though they were converted only recently. Rather, he compares the *longing* they should have for "the verbal, undeceitful milk" to infants' longing to suckle. Failure to put off the vices would keep Christians from longing as they should for the milk. But what is that milk? The word translated with "verbal" could also be translated with "rational" (in the sense of "reasonable") or "nonliteral" (as opposed to a mother's milk [compare Romans 12:1]). But such translations would leave uncertain what the milk consists of. On the other hand, the definite reference in 1:23–25 to the spoken word of God favors here the meaning "verbal," not in the sense of having to do with verbs in particular but in the sense of having to do with words in general. "Verbal" (or however else the Greek *logikon* is translated) is the adjectival form of a Greek noun (*logos*) meaning "word" (among other things). Why then didn't Peter write "the undeceitful milk *of the word*" instead of "the *verbal,* undeceitful milk"? Probably because he wanted to frontload the nonliteral verbal makeup of the milk he had in mind and range this makeup alongside its undeceitful character

for a parallelistic description. In 1:23 God's word was compared to imperishable seed. Here it's compared to unadulterated milk; but the shift of figures from seed to milk should cause no more of a problem than does the shift from Peter's portrayal of Christ as a lamb (1:19) to the forthcoming portrayal of him as a stone (2:4–8), to take but one example of many such shifts. As applied to milk, "undeceitful" means "unadulterated, pure"; but as applied to God's word "undeceitful" makes it an example that Christians should follow in their own speech ("putting off . . . all deceit"). God's word is as undeceitful as a mother's milk is unadulterated. The words of Christians should be just as undeceitful.

As infants grow by drinking their mother's milk out of a craving for it, Christians grow by drinking God's word, so to speak, out of a craving for it. The analogy breaks down, though, as all analogies do at one point or another. (Otherwise we'd have identity rather than analogy.) A craving for mother's milk doesn't need to be commanded in the case of infants. For Christians a similar craving comes by way of obedience to a command. Their growth has the purpose and result of salvation at the Last Day (see 1:5–13 for the salvation as future). Without growth now there'll be no salvation then. The growth consists in progress toward that salvation through a behavior which demonstrates authenticity of faith (1:7).

"If you've tasted 'that the Lord [is] kind'" doesn't call in *question* that Peter's audience have tasted the Lord as kind; rather, it *appeals* to their having tasted him as kind. His kindness tasted delicious (as mother's milk tastes delicious to an infant?) in that he redeemed them from slavery to their former lusts, secured in heaven an inheritance for them, and gave them a joyful hope (chapter 1). By growing, Christians will taste the Lord's kindness at the Last Judgment just as they've already tasted it in and since their conversions. There's a wordplay between the Greek words for "kind" (*chrēstos*) and "Christ" (*christos*). So "the Lord" who is kind is Christ. This identification will be confirmed in 2:4. To drink the milk of God's word is to taste the Lord's kindness.

2:4–6: while coming to whom [referring to the Lord]—**a living stone rejected on the one hand by human beings, on the other hand selected** [as] **very valuable alongside God** [= in his estimation]—**⁵you yourselves as also living stones** [like the Lord Jesus] **are being built as a Spiritual house into a consecrated body of priests so as to offer Spiritual sacrifices acceptable to God through Jesus Christ, ⁶because it's contained in Scripture** [as follows]: **"Behold, I'm laying in Zion a stone, a corner**[stone] **selected** [as] **very valuable; and the person who believes on him will by no means be shamed** [Isaiah 28:16; Psalm 34:4–5]!" The rejection of the stone by human beings and its selection by God confirm that in 2:3 Christ was "the Lord" who was "kind" and whom Peter now compares to a stone. The rejection and selection of this stone assure Peter's audience that their own like rejection by non-Christians and selection by God follow the pattern of Christ's experience.

In the end, not a bad outcome. "While coming to him" connotes duration and therefore doesn't refer to conversion alone, but refers to the entirety of Christian life as a coming to Jesus. To prepare for the result of this coming in the resurrection to eternal life, Peter compares Jesus to "a *living* stone." The comparison is oxymoronic, for stones are proverbial for being dead (compare Matthew 3:9; Luke 3:8). But precisely because it is oxymoronic, the comparison highlights Jesus as living because of his resurrection from among the dead (1:3).

God's selection of this stone contrasts with human beings' rejection of the stone, and a further contrast between deity and humanity underlines the contrast between selection and rejection. The selection and the rejection have to do with using and not using the stone in the construction of a building. God selected Jesus because he saw great value in him for building a temple that he (God) would inhabit. As emphasized by "Behold . . . !" Jesus the stone has such great value that God selected him for the temple's cornerstone. (Builders lay a cornerstone as the first stone of a foundation and use it as a corner from which to lay out the rest of the foundation.) Coming to Jesus associates Christians so closely with him that they too become "living stones." His resurrected life infuses their mortal lives with the promise of a future resurrection to eternal life. So God is adding them as living stones to Jesus, the living stone, in the construction of a temple: people as temple, temple as people.

Peter calls the temple "a Spiritual house" because God will reside there as Spirit (hence the capitalization of "Spiritual" [contrast pagan temples as housing images made of lifeless stone, metal, and wood]). The emphatic "you yourselves" underscores Christians' privilege in being used along with Jesus in the construction of this house. The privilege outweighs the shame and dishonor being heaped on Christians by non-Christians. Since the Christians "are being built," the house hasn't yet reached completion, and won't reach it till the second coming. A temple needs priests, whose very vocation is that of worshiping God. "Being built as a Spiritual house into a consecrated body of priests" indicates that Christians will forever act as priests in the completed temple that they are also coming to be. A house is built, but not a body of priests, so that the incongruity of being built as a house into a body of priests heightens the astonishment. "Consecrated" describes the Christians as a body of priests set apart from the rest of humanity and from their own former lusts (1:1, 14–16).

What do priests do by way of worshiping God at a temple? They offer sacrifices. As priests, Christians will eternally offer "Spiritual sacrifices." If the house is Spiritual because God as Spirit inhabits it, the sacrifices are appropriately and likewise Spiritual in that they're prompted by God as the Spirit who will indwell the priests because they *are* his house. For the moment, Peter doesn't identify what those sacrifices will be. So the accent stays on the honor and privilege of Christians' priesthood. (In the world of pagan religion, priesthoods were sought and bought for their prestige.) Peter does

describe the sacrifices, though, as "acceptable to God"—naturally, since God as Spirit will prompt them and since Christians will offer them "through Jesus Christ," whom God selected as "very valuable." Just as faith in God has to be channeled through Christ to count for salvation (1:21), so sacrifices will have to be channeled through him to count as valuable to God. After all, he counted Christ's sacrificial blood as "valuable" (1:18–19), so that those who've based their faith on him have invested in the ultimate value stock.

Peter can assure his audience thus because of Scripture, which he quotes. "I'm laying in Zion a stone" makes the building of God's temple on Mount Zion in Jerusalem a foregleam of God's building a new temple for himself out of Christ and Christians. "The person who believes *on* him" favors that Peter interprets Isaiah 28:16 as referring to the foundational cornerstone rather than to a key- or capstone (compare the comments on Mark 12:9–11). "Will by no means be shamed" means that though Christians suffer shame in a society by and large antagonistic to them, those who base their faith on Christ won't suffer shame at the Last Judgment. By implication, they'll be awarded eternal honor while their persecutors are consigned to eternal shame. "By no means" describes this reversal of fortunes as absolutely certain, so that Christians may endure with confidence—and should.

2:7–8: Therefore [because the person who believes on Jesus will by no means be shamed] **you who believe** [have] **the value.** Just as the resurrected life of Christ the cornerstone rubs off on believers built as living stones with him, then, so the value of Christ to God rubs off on believers. They too are valuable to him. **But for those who don't believe, "the stone that the builders rejected—this has turned into the head of an angle** [Psalm 118:22]" [8]**and** [into] **"a stone of stumbling** [= a stone that people stumble over] **and a rock of tripping** [= a rock that people trip over] [Isaiah 8:14]**," who stumble by disobeying the word** [of the gospel]**, to which** [stumbling] **they were also appointed.** Rejection by "the builders" replaces rejection by "human beings" and echoes what Peter said in Acts 4:11 as well as Jesus' quotation of Psalm 118:22 in Mark 12:10; Matthew 21:42; Luke 20:17. In the Gospels, Jesus speaks of "the builders" as the Jewish leaders who in rejecting him engineered his crucifixion. Since in Acts 4:5–11 Peter makes the same identification, presumably that identification holds true here as well. "The head of an angle" doesn't connote high elevation, but refers to Jesus as the aforementioned cornerstone from which the rest of the foundation is laid out angularly (at right angles, for example). This headship represents God's making Jesus eminent in answer to the builders' rejection of him. The figure changes from a cornerstone into a stone lying in a path, for example, and a rock jutting up into a path, to take another example, both of which cause walkers to stumble and trip over them. Stumbling and tripping over Jesus the stone and rock represent falling into judgment by way of "disobeying the word [of the gospel]."

Unbelievers were "appointed"—that is, predestined—to stumble. But "were *also* appointed" reserves room alongside such predestination for the personal responsibility they bear for "disobeying the word."

2:9-10: **But you** [are] **a select breed, a kingly body of priests, a consecrated nation, a people for** [God's] **acquisition, so that you may proclaim the virtues of him who called you out of darkness into his marvelous light,** [10][you] **who once** [were] **"not a people" but now** [are] **God's people, who "hadn't been treated mercifully" but now have been treated mercifully** [Hosea 1:6, 9; 2:23 (compare also Exodus 19:6; Isaiah 42:12, 16; 43:20-21; Malachi 3:17)]. "Select" harks back to Peter's addressing his audience as "selected" (1:1-2) and puts them in parallel with Jesus, the stone that God "selected." As selected out from the rest of humanity, they're a new breed of human beings. The translation "breed" does a better job than "race" does of recalling God's having fathered—that is, bred—Christians anew (1:3, 23). Their "being built . . . into a *consecrated* body of priests" in 2:5 turns now into being "a *kingly* body of priests" for a parallel with Israel as "a *kingdom* of priests" according to Exodus 19:6, where the Lord also calls Israel "a consecrated nation," as Peter here calls Christians. ("Nation" doesn't have the connotation of a modern nation state—rather, of people with a shared culture.) As a nation of saints, Christians have replaced Israel as the nation consecrated by God to himself; and it's this consecration that makes them a nation despite their ethnic diversity, which includes Jews like Peter who have *not* rejected Jesus. "A people for [God's] acquisition" alludes to God's having purchased them with Jesus' blood so as to free them from slavery to their former lusts and make them his own property (1:13-21). For money deposited in a slave's bank account at a pagan temple was often used to buy the slave in the name of the temple's god and to set the slave free, though as now the property of that god. In combination with God's purchasing Israel with the blood of Passover lambs so as to free them from slavery in Egypt and possess them as his own special people, the pagan practice provides background for Peter's statement.

The Christians' status-elevating selection as a new breed, their royalty as a body of priests, and their consecration as a nation, plus God's acquiring them as a people, provide them with a manifold basis for perseverance under persecution at the same time that the distinctiveness of their lifestyle draws accusations which generate persecution and accusations of unsociability, even of hating the human race as seemingly shown by nonattendance at gladiatorial games and theaters and by refusal to worship the gods, whose consequent anger supposedly brings floods, earthquakes, fires, plagues, and famines that affect the non-Christians as well as the nonconforming Christians. But what counts for the Christians' longterm benefit has the larger and ultimate purpose of counting for God's glory. As recipients of his beneficence Christians should proclaim his virtues. Finally Peter has told what the "Spiritual sacrifices" are that

as "a consecrated body of priests" Christians will offer to God. These sacrifices will consist in proclamations of God's virtues, what Hebrews 13:15-16 calls "a sacrifice of praise to God" offered through Jesus and thus "pleasing" to God. Peter's describing God as "him who called you out of darkness into his marvelous light" exemplifies such a proclamation—not a private thanksgiving, but a public recital of his saving acts. Darkness imprisons (Isaiah 42:7) and here represents sin and death, whereas God's light represents salvation and eternal life (compare Revelation 22:5). "Marvelous" describes this light inasmuch as those called out of darkness into it didn't use to be a people—they were Gentiles, pagans—but now are *God's* people, no less, and this not by any virtue of their own but by virtue of God's graciously effective call. In times past he didn't treat them mercifully, but now he has. The borrowing of phrases from Hosea 1-2 extends the parallel between Israel as the people of God and Christians as his new people. In Hosea, Israel's description as "not a people" represented God's disowning them, and his treating them mercifully meant a restoring of their status as his people. But much as Paul does in Romans 9:25-26, Peter applies these descriptions to non-Jewish Christians, who never have been God's people but whom he has made his people for the first time

AN EXHORTATION TO GOOD DEEDS
1 Peter 2:11-12

Here starts a series of exhortations on how Christians ought to behave in a society dominated by often antagonistic non-Christians. The series extends through 4:19.

2:11-12: **Beloved, I urge** [you] **as noncitizens and exiles** [for which designations see the comments on 1:1-2] **to stay away from fleshly lusts, which as such wage war against the soul,** [12]**keeping your behavior good among the Gentiles** [in the sense of non-Christians, who aren't God's new chosen people as Christians are], **in order that in what they malign you about, as** [though you were] **doing evil, by observing some of** [your] **good deeds they may glorify God on the Day of Inspection** [compare Isaiah 10:3]. "Beloved" sets an example of the mutual love commanded in 1:22 and introduces the following exhortations on a note of affection. "I urge," where Peter might have bluntly issued a command, softens the note further—appropriately, since in 1:22 he linked the command to love one another with "brotherly affection." For the moment, in other words, Peter steps out of his apostolic role as a commander and into the brotherly role of an urger. "As noncitizens and exiles" not only recalls 1:1-2. It also prepares for the exhortation to stay away from the lusts that characterize the behavior of the non-Christians among whom the Christians live "as noncitizens." See the comments on 1:14 for a definition of "lusts." Here the added description of the lusts as "fleshly" points to physical desires so strong that "as such"—that is, as physical—they "wage war against the soul." As before, "the soul" means the whole self (see the comments on 1:9). Warring against the self, which Christians have "purified" (1:22), implies that in themselves they want to do right but that fleshly lusts attack them in this respect. To stay away from these lusts means not to embrace them so as to enjoy their enticement (while intending to resist them in the end, of course)—rather, to retreat from them, indeed to flee out of earshot when they sing their siren songs. Only thus can Christians keep their behavior good among non-Christians.

"Good" means morally beautiful and therefore admirable. Non-Christians malign Christians even in regard to their good behavior. In early church history, for example, non-Christians maligned Christians' love for each other by misrepresenting it in terms of illicit sex. But because of observing now some of the Christians' good deeds ("some," because nobody but God will have observed them all), non-Christians will glorify God on the Last Day, the day when God inspects everybody's past behavior. But why will they glorify *God* for Christians' good deeds rather than glorifying the *Christians* who did them? Because it will be apparent that those deeds, including the very ones non-Christians had misrepresented, arose out of God's having fathered Christians with the seed of his living and lasting word, so that they lived godly, as a matter of fact, rather than lustfully, as the non-Christians had charged.

AN EXHORTATION TO SOCIAL PROPRIETY
1 Peter 2:13–17

2:13–16: **Subordinate yourselves to every human institution because of the Lord, whether to a king as being supreme** [over you] **¹⁴or to governors as being sent by him** [the king] **for the purpose of punishing evildoers but of praising doers of good, ¹⁵because God's will is thus:** [for you] **to mute the ignorance of nitwitted people by doing good, ¹⁶**[subordinating yourselves] **as free** [people] **and not holding** [your] **freedom as a cover for evil. Rather,** [subordinate yourselves] **as God's slaves.** "Every human institution" refers to entities created by human beings. "Whether to a king . . . or to governors" defines "every human institution" as governmental figures created as such by their fellow human beings. They make one of their number into a king—in Peter's setting, an emperor. And as a human being the king, or emperor, makes others into governors. "Every" indicates that Christians should subordinate themselves throughout the successions of kings and governors. "Because of the Lord" means for the sake of the Lord's public reputation, since Christians' behavior determines that reputation. "As being supreme" identifies the societal circumstance in which subordination is necessary for the protection and enhancement of the Lord's reputation. Likewise in regard to governors "as being sent by him [the king]."

"For the purpose of punishing evildoers but of praising doers of good" adds governmental execution of justice to the supremacy of kings and governors. By implication, then, Christians should not subordinate themselves to their governmental superiors in any practice of *in*justice. But Peter's main point is that Christians should behave so extraordinarily well that the king's governors will praise them for their good deeds rather than punishing them for evil deeds. For his own reputation, God wants Christians "to mute the ignorance of nitwitted people by doing good." "To mute" implies that such people's "ignorance" speaks in malignment of the Christians' good behavior and therefore by extension in malignment of God. We expect the nitwitted *people* to be muted, not their *ignorance*. As it is, though, the muting of ignorance personifies and thereby spotlights it for what it is. That it characterizes *nit*wits underlines the exposé. "As free" describes the Christians as not slaves of the king and his governors, so that subordination to them should arise out of obedience to the command of Christians' true master, God. And obedience to his command that they subordinate themselves to the king and governors will keep them from using their nonenslavement to them "as a cover"—that is, as a pretext—to rebel, which to do would constitute "evil."

Consciousness of their high status before God and of their freedom from enslavement to governmental authorities could lead Christians to treat non-Christians dishonorably. But doing so would bring disrepute on God, whom the Christians serve as his slaves. Therefore Peter writes in **2:17**: **Honor all** [people]. **Keep loving the brotherhood. Keep fearing God. Keep honoring the king** [compare Proverbs 24:21]. "Keep" plus "-ing" forms of verbs puts emphasis on the last three commands. The importance of Christian community, the enslavement of Christians to God, and the supremacy of the king as a human institution all call for this emphasis. The command to honor "*all* [people]" strikes at what the ancients thought was a zero-sum game: there's a limited amount of honor, so that honoring some people keeps other people from being honored. Not so, writes Peter. There's an inexhaustible supply of honor. So spread it indiscriminately. "Loving the brotherhood"—that is, fellow Christians—goes beyond honoring them to an emotional attachment that leads in turn to acts of helpfulness (compare 1:22). To fear God is to fear disobeying your master; for as a Christian you're his slave, and disobedience brings punishment. Fearing God includes honoring the king in obedience to God. Furthermore, honoring the king goes beyond subordinating yourself to him because of his supremacy and extends to praising him for his execution of justice.

AN EXHORTATION THAT CHRISTIAN SLAVES SUBORDINATE THEMSELVES TO THEIR MASTERS
1 Peter 2:18–25

People in the Roman Empire considered the household the basic unit of society, so that in large part Christianity was judged by its effect on family life. So Peter now starts telling his audience how to live as Christians in their households. He addresses household slaves first, because as a class they were the most vulnerable of all Christians to mistreatment on account of their faith. Thus the Christian behavior required of them becomes a paradigm for the behavior required of other Christians who like them suffer mistreatment because of their faith. It will turn out, though, that even the slaves have their own paradigm in the behavior of Christ. Meanwhile, it is revolutionary of Peter even to address slaves with behavioral instructions. That was the prerogative of the slaves' masters. Yet the masters might not be Christian. So Peter must address their slaves directly. And even those slaves who have Christian masters also have a standing before God that justifies Peter's instructing them directly rather than telling their masters what to instruct them.

2:18–19: **Household slaves,** [you should be] **subordinating yourselves with all fear to** [your] **masters, not only to the good and considerate ones, but also to the crooked** [= perverse] **ones.** [19]**For this** [is] **credit, if because of God-consciousness someone bears up when suffering sorrows unjustly.** Obviously, concern for the Lord's reputation in defense of the gospel trumps concern for social justice and equality. "All" stresses the fear that should characterize the subordination of Christian household slaves to their masters. But this fear is not to be a fear of those masters—rather, the fear of God, just mentioned in 2:17 (compare Christians' freedom even from the king and his governors [2:16]). So the subordination of slaves to their human masters is to arise out of fear to disobey their higher master, God, and is to be ongoing ("subordinating yourselves"). Moreover, the fear of God allows no differentiation to be made by a slave between a good human master and a bad one. In fact, to keep up self-subordination despite a bad master's mistreatment brings credit. That is to say, God finds such behavior creditable because it stems from a consciousness of him so vivid that it overrides the perversity of the slave's human master. "Bears up" contrasts with the possibility of running away or rebelling, and "suffering sorrows" refers to being beaten to the point of tears. "Unjustly" implies that slaves have human rights despite the popular opinion in Greco-Roman society that they have none.

2:20–25: **For what particular kudos** [do you deserve] **if when sinning and getting pummeled** [by your master] **you endure? But if when doing good and suffering you endure, this** [is] **credit alongside God** [that is, in his estimation]. [21]**For you were called into this** [suffering when doing good], **because Christ too suffered for you, leaving behind an example for you in order that you follow in the steps of him** [22]**who "didn't commit sin, nor was deceit found in his mouth** [Isaiah 53:9]," [23]**who when being ridiculed wasn't ridiculing in return, when suffering wasn't threatening** [his persecutors] **but was giving** [them] **over to him who judges rightly,** [24]**who himself** [referring back to Jesus] **in his body "carried our sins** [Isaiah 53:4, 12]" **up onto the tree** [= the cross (compare Deuteronomy 21:22–23; Galatians 3:13)] **in order that on passing away from**

sins [in the sense of dying to them] **we should live for righteousness, "by whose wound you were healed** [Isaiah 53:5]." [25]**For like sheep you were straying** [compare Isaiah 53:6], **but now you've returned to the shepherd and inspector of your souls.** "Sinning" describes insubordination to a master. Insubordinate slaves were regularly pummeled. "Doing good," on the other hand, brings credit in God's record-keeping. Why? Because it's the vocation of a Christian slave to do good though enduring mistreatment, and while enduring it. Why so? Because Christ did. So like him, like the Christian slave. The word translated "example" referred originally and particularly to a written alphabet that children traced when learning to write. But here, "follow in his steps" shows that Peter is using the word in the broader sense of an example.

"Suffered *for you*" provides both reason and motivation to follow the example of Jesus. "*Leaving behind* an example" means that as his original disciples, including Peter, followed "in his steps" quite literally while stringing out behind him during his earthly itinerations, so Christian slaves are to follow "in his steps" figuratively by behaving as he did. "Who didn't commit sin" set an example for Christian slaves not to sin through insubordination, which counts as sin because it besmirches God's reputation. "Nor was deceit found in his mouth" set an example for them not to practice the verbal deceit commonly used by slaves to claim compliance and conceal noncompliance. Ridicule was something like what is now called "trash-talk," which is especially abusive when spoken by a superior to a subordinate, as here. Masters often ridiculed their slaves; but Christian slaves shouldn't return the favor, writes Peter, not even behind their master's back. For as the Christ, Jesus was in a position to ridicule his judges; but he didn't. And though in a position to threaten them, he didn't but "was giving [them] over to him who judges rightly," namely God in contrast with Jesus' judges and the slaves' perverse masters, who judge wrongly. Peter may mean instead that Jesus gave *himself* rather than his persecutors over to God, or Peter may leave a blank for his audience to supply either Jesus himself or his persecutors, or both. But the immediately preceding references to Jesus' not ridiculing and not threatening can have only his persecutors in view and therefore favor the same in connection with "giving over."

By now Peter is so carried away with Jesus' behavior that he stops spelling out its applications to the behavior of Christian slaves and expounds instead the theological foundation of the behavior required of them. This foundation consists in Christ's disposing of our sins on the cross. They were nailed to it when he was nailed to it. With "*our* sins" Peter includes himself and other Christians along with Christian slaves. Now he's painting on a broad canvas. Because Christ "in his body 'carried our sins' up onto the cross," we might expect Peter to personify our sins and say that they died when Christ died, and that they died with him. But Peter doesn't say so. He doesn't even say that Christ died or that his death brought, or bought, the forgiveness of our sins—rather, that because Christ carried our sins up onto the cross "we should live for righteousness" after *our* dying. But for our dying Peter uses the euphemism "passing away" to facilitate the addition of "from sins," which combination lines up with his earlier exhortation to "stay away from fleshly lusts" (2:11 [with the euphemism of "passing away" for dying compare the euphemism of "the tree" for "the cross"]). To stay away from fleshly lusts is to work out in everyday life our having passed away from sins. Peter doesn't say we passed away from them by dying with Christ on the cross, as Paul does in Romans 6:1–11. So the emphasis stays on conduct: living for righteousness after passing away from sins, as though dying out from under the control of one master and coming to life under the control of a new master. "By whose wound [singular] you were healed" alludes to the slitting of the throat of a sacrificial lamb (compare 1:18–19) and presents an oxymoron in that strictly speaking a wound doesn't *cause* healing. It *needs* healing. But out of Jesus' wound flowed medicinal blood that healed our sin-sickness. And again, the healing doesn't have to do with forgiveness of sins (for which 3:18 is more suitable)—rather, with sinless behavior, the opposite of straying from the path of righteousness. "But now you've returned to the shepherd and inspector of your souls" (1) refers to the conversion of Peter's audience; (2) implies that predestination to salvation made their conversion a return; (3) portrays God, who selected them, as a shepherd and an inspector (compare 2:12); and (4) makes their souls—that is, their selves (see the comments on 1:9)—the object of his inspection. Masters can inspect their slaves' work, but not their slaves' very selves. Only God can do that, and he does. Not even a clever slave, schooled in the art of deceiving his master, can fool God. After using "we" and "our" for all Christians, Peter returns to "you" and "your" (plural) for his final address to Christian slaves.

AN EXHORTATION THAT CHRISTIAN WIVES SUBORDINATE THEMSELVES TO THEIR HUSBANDS
1 Peter 3:1–6

After slaves, wives in Greco-Roman culture of the first century were the most vulnerable to mistreatment in a household. Given his overarching discussion of persecution, then, Peter tells Christian wives how to behave at home, particularly in relation to their husbands, some of whom weren't Christian.

3:1–4: Likewise, wives, [you should be] subordinating yourselves to your own husbands in order that even if any [of them] are disobeying the word, they may be gained [for Christ] through [you] wives' behavior apart from a word ²by observing your pure behavior, [practiced] in fear, ³[you] whose adornment is not to be the exterior [adornment] of braiding of hair and gold[-colored] netting or donning of clothes—⁴rather, whose [adornment is to be] the hidden humanity of the heart, [that is,] in the imperishable [adornment consisting] **of a meek and quiet spirit, which in God's sight is very costly** [compare Proverbs 31:30]. "Likewise" draws a parallel between the subordination commanded of wives and that commanded of slaves; and just as Peter instructed slaves directly rather than through their masters because some of them had non-Christian masters, so he instructs wives directly rather than through their husbands because some of them had non-Christian husbands. Furthermore, just as slaves with Christian masters had their own standing before God, so too wives with Christian husbands had their own standing before him. So Peter addresses them directly rather than telling their husbands what to instruct them. "To *your own* husbands" stresses the limitation of a wife's subordination to her husband. "Even if any are disobeying the word" implies subordination to a Christian husband but emphasizes subordination to a non-Christian husband. "Disobeying the word" means refusing God's command to repent and believe the gospel and presumes that the non-Christian husband has heard the gospel—at least from his wife, one would think. So "gained [for Christ] through [you] wives' behavior apart from a word" refers to conversion, not in the absence of a spoken word (see 1:23), but through a husband's "observing your pure behavior" after he has disobeyed the spoken word of the gospel. "Gained" implies that a converted husband becomes Christ's property. "Pure" has to do with chastity, so that subordination to the husband includes sexual fidelity to him. Once again, "in fear" bases the subordination on fear of God, not on fear of the husband (see the comments on 2:18). A husband will observe his wife's pure behavior by noting that she doesn't adorn herself externally, for such adornment would attract other men.

Since a wife was expected to worship her husband's gods, a non-Christian husband whose Christian wife refused to worship his gods suffered public humiliation by her refusal. Furthermore, she wasn't supposed to have friends of her own. So if in addition to refusing to worship her husband's gods a Christian wife glamorized herself to go to church without him, he might well suspect she was trying to seduce her male Christian friends, especially since Christians talked a lot about love—and we all know what that means. Yet again, the non-Christian husband would suffer disgrace not only from what society at large considered his Christian wife's insubordinate behavior (in refusing to worship his gods) but also from her seductive public appearance (through glamorizing herself). And since the public good was thought to depend on pleasing the gods and maintaining orderly households, the behavior of a Christian wife pertained through her husband to the larger society. Short of compromising her faith, then, she must step very carefully, because the progress of the gospel trumps considerations of social and domestic equality.

Peter identifies the external adornment as "braiding of hair and gold[-colored] netting or donning of clothes." To prohibit clothes entirely would be to command nudity, and nudity would contribute to unchastity.

Therefore Peter is prohibiting clothing and, by extension, hairstyling that call special attention to the woman adorned thus. (Fashionable women braided their hair, stacked the braids on top of their heads, and held the tiers in place with gold-colored netting.) "A meek and quiet spirit" defines "the hidden humanity of the heart." This humanity is hidden in that such a spirit resides in the heart rather than in braided hair, gold-colored netting, and fancy clothing. Nevertheless, the behavioral effects of a meek and quiet spirit are observable. "Humanity" contrasts personhood with cosmetic externals. "Imperishable" describes the commanded adornment in a way that contrasts with the perishability of those cosmetic externals, and describes that adornment with a term that has previously described Christians' inheritance, secured in heaven for them (1:4), and God's word, by which they've been fathered anew (1:23). High praise indeed! "The heart" stands for the inner self, out of which stems a person's behavior; and "spirit" refers to the human spirit, which has characteristics such as meekness and quietness. "Meek" means tolerant of mistreatment, which tolerance requires—incidentally—a great deal of strength rather than showing weakness. "Quiet" makes special reference to the absence of backtalk. "Which in God's sight is very costly" means that if he were to put such a spirit up for sale, the husband would have to pay a high price to get it in his wife. And God's appraisal is what counts.

Now Peter justifies his command with an appeal to Old Testament examples. **3:5–6: For in this way once upon a time the holy women too, who were hoping in God, used to adorn themselves,** [that is,] **by subordinating themselves to their own husbands,** ⁶**as Sarah obeyed Abraham** [Genesis 12:10–20; 20:1–7]**, calling him "lord"** [Genesis 18:12]**, whose** [referring to Sarah] **children you've become when doing good and not fearing any intimidation** [compare Proverbs 3:25]. "In this way" means by way of the subordination of Christian wives to their husbands that Peter has just commanded. "Once upon a time" appeals to ancient tradition, which people valued highly. The tried and true deserves perpetuation. "Holy" describes the ancient women Peter has in mind as sacred to God because they adorned themselves with subordination to their husbands. By implication, God will regard as sacred to himself contemporary Christian wives who behave this way; and "too" implies the complimentary expectation of Peter that they will obey his command to do so. "Hoping in God" describes the holy women of old as confident that he would bless them for their self-subordinating behavior. For Christian wives, a similar hope includes confidence of God's approval at the Last Judgment, whether or not a non-Christian husband converts in the meantime. Again, and therefore emphatically, "to their own husbands" limits the subordination of ancient wives to their husbands (compare 3:1).

Peter introduces Sarah as a specific example. The obedience she showed to her husband Abraham defines the subordination required of Christian wives. In addition to obedience, "calling him 'lord'" displayed a verbal acknowledgment of Abraham's authority over her and exemplifies "a meek and quiet spirit" that contrasts with backtalk. "Whose children you've become" compares imitation of Sarah's behavior with physical descent. But physical descent pales in value before behavioral descent, and Sarah's prominence as the ancestress of all Jews (Isaiah 51:2) contributes further to Peter's drawing of parallels between ethnically diverse Christians as God's new chosen people and the Jews as God's ancient chosen people. Whereas "adorn[ed] themselves" described wifely subordination cosmetically, "doing good" describes it ethically. It's the right thing to do. "Not fearing any intimidation" means that a Christian wife shouldn't allow her husband, if he's a non-Christian, to bully her into giving up the Christian faith and practice, so that subordination to the husband is to arise not out of fear of him, just as the subordination of a slave isn't to arise out of fear of his master—rather, out of fear of God and out of God-consciousness (compare 2:18–19). The previously mentioned social expectation that wives worship their husband's gods made "not fearing any intimidation" a necessary qualification for Christian wives who had non-Christian husbands. Not that Christian women should feel free to marry non-Christian men. They shouldn't, and vice versa too (1 Corinthians 7:39). But Peter is addressing the circumstance of a woman who became a Christian after getting married whereas her husband hadn't become one.

AN EXHORTATION TO CHRISTIAN HUSBANDS THAT THEY CONFER HONOR ON THEIR WIVES
1 Peter 3:7

3:7: Husbands, likewise [be] **cohabiting** [with your wife] **in accordance with knowledge as with a weaker vessel, the female** [vessel]**, conferring honor** [on her] **as also a coheir with** [you] **of the grace of life so that your prayers not be hindered.** The dominance of husbands in first-century Greco-Roman culture made the problems of Christian husbands, even those who had non-Christian wives, less severe than the marital problems of Christian wives, especially those who had non-Christian husbands. Hence the brevity of Peter's instruction to Christian husbands. This brevity doesn't imply the husbands are under less obligation than their (Christian) wives are. "Likewise" indicates to the contrary that a Christian husband is under just as much obligation to obey the following command as a Christian slave and a Christian wife are to obey the preceding commands. Peter calls the wife "a weaker *vessel*" because her body is constructed in such a way as to be a receptacle for seminal fluid. His calling her "a *weaker* vessel" has a number of implications: (1) that the husband too is a vessel, because his body is constructed in such a way as to contain seminal fluid; (2) that "knowledge" is therefore a euphemism for sexual intercourse (see Genesis 4:1 for the first of many biblical examples); (3) that this euphemism brings out the sexual connotation of the traditional translation, "[be] dwelling together"; (4) that this traditional but sexually vacuous translation should be changed to the sexually charged translation, "[be] cohabiting"; (5) that the husband has more brute strength than his wife has; (6) that "*as* with a weaker vessel" prohibits the husband from using roughhouse tactics in copulation; (7) that "[be] cohabiting in accordance with knowledge" commands the husband to take sexual satisfaction from his wife, not from other women such as prostitutes, and to give his wife sexual satisfaction just as her subordination requires giving it to him; (8) that it's his treating her sexually in this exclusive, considerate, and gentle way that "confer[s] honor [on her]"; (9) that such treatment suits her status as "a coheir . . . of the grace of life" (the ill-deserved favor of eternal life that came as a result of being "fathered anew with the result of a living hope" [1:23]), so that despite her lower status in society at large, before God she has a status equal to her husband's (note the wordplay between "*co*habiting" and "*co*heir" and the assumption that the Christian husbands whom Peter is addressing have Christian wives, as usually happened because wives normally followed their husbands in religious matters); and (10) that given Peter's addressing Christian husbands and given their obedience to Peter's instruction, the prayers that won't be hindered are their prayers, not including those of their wives, who can hardly be held accountable for disobedience on their husband's part. By implication, God won't answer the prayers of husbands who disobey the instruction.

For the most part, masters didn't suffer at the hands of their slaves, nor children at the hands of their parents, nor parents at the hands of their children (living at home as youngsters). So Peter hasn't instructed Christian masters how to behave toward their slaves, or parents how to behave toward their children, or children how to behave toward their parents. His instructions have concerned mainly those household relations that carried a potential for persecution.

AN EXHORTATION TO UNITY
1 Peter 3:8–12

3:8–9: Finally, all of you, [be] like-minded, sympathetic, affectionate to the brotherhood, compassionate, lowly-minded, ⁹not returning a malicious [remark] in place of a malicious [remark], or ridicule in place of ridicule—but on the contrary, blessing [in return], because you were called for this purpose, that you should inherit a blessing. "Finally" introduces a conclusion to the preceding commands. The conclusion, made up of further commands, deals with traits that underlie obedience to the earlier commands. "All of you" enlarges the address to include not only household slaves, wives, and husbands, but also all other Christians. "Like-minded" is opposed to wrangling with one another, and the likemindedness is assumed to tally with Peter's other instructions. "Sympathetic" means entering into another's suffering so as to share it. "Affectionate to the brother-

hood" has to do with fellow Christians. "Compassionate" connotes a feeling of pity in your gut. "Lowly-minded" means thinking of yourself as less important than others, a trait like the others at odds with the self-congratulation and rivalry for honor that prevailed, and still prevails, in society at large. Shared among Christians, however, the traits commanded by Peter will help the Christians endure persecution. "A malicious [remark]" likely refers to a persecutor's false accusation, and "ridicule" to a persecutor's verbal abuse. The command not to retaliate with such speech in defense of your honor but to speak a good word in return tells Christians how to relate to their non-Christian persecutors. "To bless" means to "speak well of" and may refer more especially to praying for God's favor on your persecutors (compare Matthew 5:44; Luke 23:34a). Christians should speak blessingly because their very vocation is to do so. Otherwise they won't win others to the gospel. And to speak blessingly exhibits an authenticity of Christian faith that leads to inheriting God's blessing, which consists in eternal life.

3:10–12: For "the person who wants to love life and see good days is to stop [his] tongue from [uttering] a malicious [remark] and [to stop his] lips so as not to speak deceit [Psalm 34:12–13]." ¹¹But "he's to decline from [= avoid] a malicious [remark] and to do a good [deed]. He's to seek peace and pursue it, ¹²because the Lord's eyes [are trained] on righteous people, and his ears [attuned] to their supplication. But the Lord's face [is turned] against those who do malicious things [Psalm 34:14–16a]." Christians' identity as the new Israel makes appropriate Peter's applying to them this long quotation from the Old Testament. Given the present necessity of "various trials," (1:6), "want[ing] to love life and see good days" means desiring to enjoy eternal life and to experience the goodness of "a salvation ready to be revealed in the last time" (1:5–6). "To stop [his] tongue from [uttering] a malicious [remark]" is the flip side of returning a blessing for a malicious remark (3:9). "So as not to speak deceit" recollects 2:1 and the undeceitful milk of God's word in 2:2. "A good [deed]" is to substitute for a malicious remark, so that the good deed accompanies the verbal blessing. "Seek[ing] *peace*" relates to like-mindedness, sympathy, loving fellow Christians, compassion, and lowly-mindedness in 3:8. "*Seeking* peace" implies effort, and "*pursu*[ing] it" escalates this effort to the nth degree. Since pursuit is the literal meaning of persecution, pursuing peace represents the polar opposite of persecution. So it looks as though Christians are to pursue peace not only among themselves but also with the very non-Christians who persecute them. As usual, peace includes well-being in addition to absence of conflict. "Righteous people" describes the pursuers of such peace. The Lord takes note of them, watches out for them so that they don't have to watch out for themselves, and heeds their supplications. In other words, he'll deliver them from their persecutors. Meanwhile, they can assure themselves that his face is glowering at their malicious persecutors in anticipation of condemning them at the Last Judgment.

AN EXHORTATION TO SUFFERING
FOR THE RIGHT REASONS
1 Peter 3:13–4:6

3:13–16: And who [is] the one who'll harm you if you were to become zealots for the good? [14]**Nevertheless, even if you might suffer on account of righteousness, [you're] fortunate** [compare Matthew 5:10]. **"But you shouldn't fear the fear of them. Neither should you get upset** [Isaiah 8:12].**"** [15]**But "consecrate" the Christ as "Lord" in your hearts** [Isaiah 8:13]**, always [being] ready to offer a defense to everyone who asks you [to give] a reason for the hope within you.** [Give it] **with meekness and fear, however,** [16]**maintaining a good conscience, in order that in the matter for which you're being spoken against, those who are vilifying your good behavior in Christ may be shamed.** "And who . . . ?" introduces a question that hopes for no persecution of Christians if they zealously do good deeds. "Even if . . ." introduces a counterbalancing recognition that they might suffer "on account of righteousness," that is, because of doing the very good that ought to exempt them from persecution. "Nevertheless, . . . [you're] fortunate" alludes back to the Lord's approval of their doing good (3:11–12). At the Last Judgment that approval will more than compensate for the persecutors' having harmed them. This good fortune should make Christians unafraid of their persecutors and calm them in the face of persecution. "*The* Christ" calls attention to Jesus' status as anointed and therefore approved by God (compare Mark 1:9–11; Matthew 3:16–17; Luke 3:21–22). Because God anointed and approved him, he's "Lord" over against deified Caesars and supposed deities in the pagan pantheon.

For Christians to consecrate the Christ as Lord is for them to acknowledge his status as divine and therefore as their owner and master. Since the heart was considered the seat of thinking as well as feeling, "in your hearts" encompasses an intellectually as well as emotionally exclusive consecration of the Christ as Lord. Peter then describes this inward consecration as "the hope within you," for acknowledgement of Christ's lordship produces an inward confidence that he'll return to take control of the world gone awry and rectify the injustices inflicted on Christians. And out of such confidence is to come a constant readiness to defend it with a reason whenever a non-Christian asks for one, as if Peter is saying, "Don't clam up to avoid persecution." He doesn't tell *what* reason should be given, though, but does tell *how* it ought to be given. For the manner of its presentation may prove more convincing than its content. Meekness and fear make up the manner that Peter commands. Meekness refers to tolerance of the question and modesty in relation to the questioner. Fear doesn't refer to fear of the questioner—rather (and as usual), to a fear of displeasing the Lord—here by unreadiness to offer a reasoned defense of the inward hope. Moreover, a good conscience born of good behavior must accompany the defense. A bad conscience kills confidence, and bad behavior would

justify vilification by persecutors. But how can those who vilify good behavior be shamed by the very behavior they vilify? It's the meekness and fear commanded by Peter that will shame them—at the Last Judgment—and their shame will include the predicament of eternal punishment as well as public embarrassment. The good behavior that's being vilified at present takes place "in Christ," so that just as your hearts contain him as Lord, he contains your good behavior. He's the biosphere of your conduct just as your heart is his biosphere.

3:17–22: For [it's] **better to suffer while doing good, if the will of God may will** [that you suffer so]**, than while doing bad** [= evil]**,** [18]**because Christ too suffered for sins, once for all, a righteous person for unrighteous persons, in order that he might bring you to God by having been put to death as to flesh on the one hand, having been made alive as to Spirit on the other hand,** [19]**in which** [Spirit] **he had also made a proclamation to the spirits in prison on having gone** [there]**,** [20]**who once upon a time had been disobedient when God's patience was waiting in the days of Noah while an ark was being constructed, in which a few—that is, eight souls** [= persons]**—were saved through water,** [21]**which as a counterpart now saves you too.** [Which is to say,] **baptism** [saves you now]**—not as a removal of dirt from flesh; rather, as an appeal to God for a good conscience—through the resurrection of Jesus Christ,** [22]**who by having gone into heaven is at God's right** [hand]**, angels and authorities and powers having been subordinated to him** [that is, to Jesus Christ]. "For" introduces an explanation of why Christians should obey the preceding command to do good despite the ever-present possibility and frequent actuality of suffering for it because of people's vilification. Such suffering is "better" than suffering for "doing bad," because Christ too suffered unjustly. Implied is that if the "good behavior" of Christians takes place "in Christ," as 3:16 says, their suffering for such behavior also takes place in him: "because Christ *too* suffered." The addition of "for sins" shows that Christians' suffering "*while* doing good" includes suffering *for* or *because of* their "good behavior in Christ." If they suffer for doing good, as confirmed by "a good conscience" (3:16 again), they may take comfort in the recognition that their suffering fits God's plan, emphasized by the compound expression "if the *will* of God may *will* [that you suffer]." Another implication: Christ's suffering for sins carried out God's plan. But whereas Christians may have to suffer only *because of* non-Christians' persecuting them unjustly, Christ suffered also *for* others' sins—that is, to remove the sins of people, which barred their way to God, and then to bring the people to God.

In the Greek translation of the Hebrew Old Testament often used by authors of the New Testament, the prepositional phrase "for sins" is repeatedly used like a noun for sin offerings, a category of sacrifices designed to atone for sins. "Once for all" stresses the sufficiency of Christ's suffering to accomplish atonement. As "a righteous person" he could suffer on behalf of "unrighteous persons," for he had no unrighteousness of his own to suffer for. "In order that he might bring you [plural] to God" puts Christians in the category of unrighteous persons for whom, and for whose unrighteousness, Christ suffered. "By having been put to death as to flesh" specifies the nature of his suffering, starts defining the way he has brought unrighteous persons to God, and sets up for a contrast with "having been made alive as to Spirit," which continues the definition. This contrast makes the resurrection of Christ's corpse by the Spirit God's answer to the infliction of bodily death on Christ by his persecutors. The most ancient Greek manuscripts were written all in capital letters, so that the question of capitalization versus noncapitalization in English translation is a matter of interpretation. So it is conceivable that here we should understand a contrast between the flesh of Christ and his human spirit rather than the Holy Spirit. But since only his flesh was put to death, his spirit didn't need to be "made alive." Hence, "as to flesh" tells what needed to be made alive, and "as to Spirit" tells who made it alive. "In which [Spirit]" tells how the disembodied Christ was enabled to go to hell, called a "prison," prior to his resurrection and proclaim victory through his death over certain spirits imprisoned there (compare "in Spirit" as a vehicle of transport for the seeing of visions in Revelation 1:10; 4:2; 17:3).

Peter describes those spirits as "disobedient" and dates their disobedience to the time of Noah's constructing the ark. "Spirits" regularly refers to angelic or demonic spirits unless qualified in such a way as to make clear a reference to human spirits, as for example in Hebrews 12:23: "spirits of perfected righteous people." Here, then, the imprisoned spirits are to be understood as the fallen angels, called "the sons of God" in Genesis 6:1–4 (compare Job 1:6; 2:1; 38:7), that corrupted the human race just prior to Noah's flood (see 2 Peter 2:4–5; Jude 6–7 for the spirits' imprisonment in hell). Christ's dying as a righteous person for unrighteous persons to bring them to God constituted a victory over those spirits, who'd nearly succeeded in taking the whole human race down the drain. The exceptions: Noah and his family. Christians will enjoy a similar victory over their persecutors. The time it took Noah to construct the ark tried God's patience in that those spirits deserved immediate imprisonment in hell. But time for constructing the ark was required for the salvation of a few human beings. So too now, the persecutors of Christians deserve immediate punishment and therefore try God's patience; but time is required for filling the ark of salvation with those human beings, a minority though they are, who've been selected in accordance with God's foreknowledge (1:1–2).

The "eight souls" of Noah and his family (his wife and three sons and their wives) were saved "through water." But flood water as such didn't save Noah and his family. It saved them only inasmuch as they entered the ark in faith that God would save them from destruction (see especially Genesis 6:13–7:7), so that the water upheld the ark. Similarly, baptismal water as such doesn't save

people. It saves them only inasmuch as getting baptized acts out "an appeal to God for a good conscience." Faith that God will honor the appeal prompts submission to baptism, and God honors the appeal by removing sins from the baptizee's conscience. A good conscience is a clear one. "Through the resurrection of Jesus Christ" makes his resurrection parallel to the salvation of Noah and his family "through water." Fundamentally, then, neither baptismal water as such nor an appeal to God for a good conscience saves a person. Jesus Christ's resurrection does by making the baptismal appeal effective and certifying God's acceptance of Christ's death as the suffering of "a righteous person for unrighteous persons." After his resurrection Christ went into heaven, so that now he sits at God's right hand. Christians will likewise be resurrected and exalted; and the heavenly beings consisting of "angels and authorities and powers" will be subordinated to them just as they've already been subordinated to Jesus Christ, for the Christians' good behavior will have been "in Christ" (3:16). Hence, what has happened to him will happen to them. Forget the imprisoned spirits and the persecutors. Even *un*imprisoned angels and their like have been subordinated to Christ.

4:1–2: Therefore, since Christ suffered as to flesh [= physically], **you too arm yourselves with the same mindset, because the person who has suffered as to flesh has ceased from sin** [2]**with the result of no longer living** [his] **remaining time in flesh** [= no longer spending the rest of his physical lifetime] **for the lusts of human beings—rather, for God's will.** "Therefore" refers back to Christ's suffering in 3:18. But to underscore it as the basis for a following command, Peter redundantly adds, "since Christ suffered as to flesh." "You *too* arm yourselves with the *same* mindset" implies that Christ had a mindset that made him determined to do good (the good of bringing people to God [3:18 again]) despite having to suffer for it. Peter portrays this mindset as armor which enables Christians as imitators of Christ to withstand persecution, even persecution inflicted on their flesh in addition to verbal abuse and ostracism by non-Christians. "As to flesh" draws a parallel with Christ's having been put to death "as to flesh" (3:18 yet again). A Christian hasn't ceased from sin because he suffered physically. Just the reverse: he has suffered physically because he ceased from sin; and since cessation from sinning provokes non-Christians to persecute him, he needs to arm himself with Christ's mindset. Moreover, ceasing from sin at conversion results in living from that point on for God's will (that is, to do it) rather than for the lusts that human beings act on unless they're converted. The shift from sinning to carrying out God's will provides the reason why Christians need to arm themselves with Christ's mindset. But why does this shift create such a need? Read on.

4:3–6: For the time that has elapsed [= your lifetime prior to conversion] [was] **enough** [for you] **to have executed the Gentiles' plan by having traveled** [a figure of speech for behaving] **in debaucheries,**

lusts, winebibbings, carousals, drinking sprees, and unsanctioned idolatries, ⁴in which [plan of the Gentiles] they're surprised when you're not running with [them] into the same glut of dissipation, slandering [you because you don't], ⁵who [referring to "the Gentiles"] will give an account to him [God] who is ready to judge living people and dead people. ⁶For with this result was the gospel proclaimed also to dead people, [namely,] that on the one hand they were judged in accordance with human beings as to flesh; on the other hand they're living in accordance with God as to Spirit. Peter uses irony in writing that the lifetime of his audience prior to their conversion was "enough" for them "to have executed the Gentiles' plan." They shouldn't have executed it at all! For it stands opposed to "God's will" (4:2). But with the emphasis of irony this statement tells why Christians are now suffering for their presently changed behavior and therefore need to arm themselves. In view of Peter's repeated portrayals of Christians as the new Israel, "Gentiles" is figurative for non-Christians. The "plan" of the Gentiles is to spend their whole lifetime in the sinful behavior whose specifics Peter lists. Then as now, debauched and lustful behavior went along with excessive drinking of alcoholic beverages; and such drinking went along with idolatrous feasts (compare the drunkenness that nowadays goes along with the idolization of star athletes at sporting events and in the bars and homes where the events are broadcast). Peter describes the idolatries as "unsanctioned" in that they violate God's law, which prohibits idolatry (Exodus 20:1–6; Deuteronomy 5:6–10).

Given their plan to live licentiously, the Gentiles "are surprised" at what seems to them the Christians' antisocial behavior, which from the Gentiles' standpoint disrupts families, cities, and the empire. "You're not *running* with [them]" changes their "travel[ing]" into a footrace. After working hours they can't get to their debaucheries fast enough. "Dissipation" is a strong word that in the original Greek means "not saving anything back," that is, giving free rein to lusts. But for Peter the word isn't strong enough. So he introduces it with "glut." And accompanying this "glut of dissipation" is a "slandering" of Christians because they don't join the slanderers in running into the same glut. Misery isn't the only condition that loves company. Guilt does too. For the encouragement of Christians in their countercultural behavior, though, Peter assures them that the Gentiles "will give an account" to God concerning their evil behavior, including their slandering of the Christians. God's "read[iness] to judge" matches the "read[iness]" of Christians' "salvation to be revealed in the last time" (1:5). The two events will coincide. "Living people and dead people" leaves nobody outside the judgment, not even the dead, so that it will determine everybody's eternal fate for good or ill. Then Peter explains two results of gospel-preaching not only to people still living but also to people who died but heard and believed the gospel before dying. First, they suffered unjust judgment at the hands of their fellow (but non-Christian) human beings. "As to flesh" implies the suffering of martyrdom, just as in 3:18 "as to flesh" had to do with Christ's "having been put to death." Second, the Holy Spirit will resurrect them to eternal life in accordance with God's just judgment.

LOVING SERVICE FOR THE GLORY OF GOD
1 Peter 4:7–11

4:7–8: **But the end of all things has drawn near. Therefore be sensible and sober for prayers** [= for the purpose of praying], ⁸**before all** [other things] **having strenuous love for each other, because "love covers a multitude of sins [Proverbs 10:12]."** The mention of judgment leads Peter to assure his audience that "the end of all things," including their "various trials" (1:6), "has drawn near" and therefore could happen soon (compare 1:20). This nearness should motivate them to "be sensible and sober for prayers." After the broadside leveled against "winebibbings," "carousals," and "drinking sprees" (4:3), there's every reason to understand "be . . . sober" to mean "don't get drunk." A drunk person isn't "sensible" so as to pray effectively. Yet the proximity of the end calls for multiple prayers. Even more important than prayers and all other Christian duties in a situation of persecution, though, is the maintaining of mutual love among Christians. For such love makes them forgive (the meaning of "covers" [see Psalms 32:1; 85:2; Romans 4:7]) the sins committed against each other and thus maintain the communal cohesion needed for the endurance of persecution (compare Peter's questions, "Lord, how many times shall my brother sin against me and I forgive him? Up to seven times?" and Jesus' answer in Matthew 18:21–35). And love needs to be "strenuous" for the fulfilling of this need (see the comments on 1:22; 2:1; 3:9).

4:9–10: [Be] **hospitable to one another without complaint.** ¹⁰**Just as each person has received a gift, [be] serving it to each other as good managers of the diverse grace of God.** Strenuous love entails uncomplaining hospitality and serving one another. The hospitality may include both having each other over for a meal and conversation and the hosting of church meetings with the serving of food. But given both Peter's writing to a wide geographical area (1:1), the frequency of travel, and the flight of Christians under persecution from one city to another (Matthew 10:23), the hospitality probably includes as well the giving of board and room to such refugees. Hosting them and hosting church meetings exposed the hosts themselves to persecution, so that Peter commands the exercise of uncomplaining hospitality.

God has given each Christian a gift of one sort or another; but it's to be used for other Christians' benefit, as though it were food being served to a guest (the predominant meaning of "serving"). And the gift might just consist of the means to offer board and room to a refugee, or one's house or apartment to the church as a meeting place. "The *diverse* grace of God" highlights the variety of gifts he gives to Christians, for the Greek words for "gift" and "grace" go back to the same root.

"*Good* managers" employ their gifts in service to others, as God their master and employer intends them to do.

Now Peter writes about two diverse forms of God's grace. *4:11*: **If someone speaks, [he's to speak] as the oracles of God [speak]. If someone serves, [he's to serve] as [one who serves] with the strength that God supplies, in order that in all things God may be glorified through Jesus Christ, who has the glory and the might forever and ever. Amen!** To speak "as the oracles of God" is to glorify him by conveying a message from him rather than concocting one's own message. Similarly, to serve "with the strength that God supplies" has the purpose of bringing him glory "in all things . . . through Jesus Christ," through whom Christians "offer Spiritual sacrifices acceptable to God" (2:5) consisting in the proclamation of God's "virtues" (2:9). For these virtues he merits glorification. Because "Jesus Christ" immediately precedes, "who" may seem to reference him. But "*the* glory" harks back to the glorification of God through Jesus Christ, and a similar doxology in 5:10–11 references God clearly. Here, then, "who" more likely references him rather than Jesus Christ. God already has eternal glory and might, so that to glorify him is to *acknowledge* his eternal glory and might. Peter adds "the might" to "the glory" to encourage his persecuted audience that God has the might to deliver them from their persecutors. At this thought, and to drive it home, Peter adds the exclamatory affirmation "Amen!"

AN EXHORTATION TO SUFFER
JOYFULLY AS A CHRISTIAN
1 Peter 4:12–19

4:12–14: **Beloved, don't ever be surprised at the burning among you—which is happening to you for the purpose of a test—as though a surprise is meeting up with you. [13]Instead, be rejoicing insofar as you're sharing Christ's sufferings in order that also at the revelation of his glory** [in the second coming as well as now in the midst of fiery trials] **you may rejoice, being cheered up. [14]If you're being vilified in the name of Christ** [= because as a Christian you bear his name (see 4:16)], [you're] **fortunate, because the Spirit of glory and of God rests on you** [compare Isaiah 11:2; Matthew 5:11–12]. Appropriately following the doxology in 4:11, "beloved" marks a new start and on a note of affection introduces another exhortation. This note exemplifies on Peter's part the mutual love among Christians that he has commanded his audience to exercise strenuously (1:22; 4:8). The note also suits the seriousness of the plight in which they find themselves. Peter portrays this plight as a fire that threatens to burn them up (compare Daniel 3), and he tells them it has the purpose of a test—that is, according to 1:6–7, of testing their faith to prove its authenticity. They shouldn't be surprised at being tested by persecution; for Christ their role model suffered too, so that they're sharing his sufferings. He suffered in their place once for all ("a righteous person for unrighteous persons" [3:18]). They're now suffering in his place

("being vilified in the name of Christ"). His suffering was atoning (2:24; 3:18). Theirs is evidential (of authentic faith [see 1:6–7 again]). But both theirs and his have to do with salvation so as to form a community of suffering. To the degree that Christians share the sufferings of Christ, then, they should rejoice, but not *because* they'll rejoice also at the revelation of his glory—rather, "*in order that*" they may. By implication, they won't rejoice then at the sight of his glory if they don't rejoice now in the sharing of his sufferings. For rejoicing in this sharing characterizes authentic faith. To underline the future joy, Peter adds "being cheered up." According to 1:6 his audience are already cheering up. How much greater will be their cheer at the revelation of Christ's glory! But they're also already fortunate in that the Spirit rests on them. "Of glory" describes the Spirit as a promise of their own glorification at the revelation of Christ's glory. Peter adds "of God" in recollection of his having described them as "a Spiritual house" (see the comments on 2:5). And "*rests* on you" assures them of the Spirit's permanent presence. He'll stay on them through thick and thin right up to the revelation of Christ's glory.

4:15–18: **For none of you is to be suffering as a murderer or a thief or an evildoer** [= a criminal of any sort], **or as a troublemaker. [16]But if** [one of you suffers] **as a Christian, he's not to be ashamed; but he's to be glorifying God in this name** [in that "Christian" incorporates the name "Christ"], **[17]because** [it's] **time for the judgment to begin from the house of God** [that is, starting with Christians, whom Peter has compared to a house, a temple, for God as Spirit [2:5]]. **But if** [judgment begins] **first from us, what** [will be] **the end** [= destiny] **of those who are disobeying the gospel of God? [18]And "if the righteous person is scarcely being saved, where will the ungodly and sinful person appear** [Proverbs 11:31]**?"** That is, where will he show up? Certainly not in the circle of saved people. The reintroduction of "as" in "as a troublemaker" sets troublemaking apart from the preceding crimes. Troublemaking—for example, meddling in other people's business—may not fall into the category of a crime, but it would bring disrepute on the gospel. So Peter commands abstinence from it too. But he states these prohibitions indirectly ("*none* of you is to be suffering as a . . .") rather than directly ("don't *you* be suffering as a . . ."). This indirection implies that the addressees are already complying. "For" makes their compliance a basis for the Spirit's resting on them (4:14).

In pagan society suffering was considered shameful, and persecutors of Christians set out to shame them. So Peter tells his audience not to be ashamed to suffer "as a Christian." For "the Spirit of *glory*," which is the opposite of shame, rests on them; and Christ, after whom they're named as Christians, will have his glory revealed even to their persecutors. So Christians should glorify God instead of succumbing to shame. Furthermore, "time for the judgment to begin from the house of God" calls for the glorification of him by Christians. But 4:6 indicated that their judgment is executed by human beings—namely, their persecutors—and consists in persecution even to the point of martyrdom. So now is the time for that kind of judgment, and the glorification of God for persecution corresponds to rejoicing for it in 4:13. Naturally, then, the judgmental persecutors face a destiny worse than persecution, and face it at the hands of the God whose gospel they disobey, not least by persecuting its Christian representatives. To make the disobeyers' destiny unimaginably worse, Peter puts it in two unanswered rhetorical questions, "what . . . ?" and "where . . . ?" and writes that "the righteous person is saved with difficulty," that is, with the difficulty of having to suffer persecution. "The gospel of God" means the good news about his providing salvation through Christ. "The ungodly and sinful person" contrasts with "the righteous person," and "ungodly" means "not worshiping God." It's sinful not to worship him, and this sin leads to other sins in that the ungodly person cuts loose from God's moral demands.

4:19: And so too, those who are suffering in accordance with God's will are to commit their souls [= themselves (see the comments on 1:9)] **to a faithful creator in the doing of good.** Here Peter adds a conclusion, as indicated by "And so too." "Suffering in accordance with God's will" summarizes the preceding command to make sure the suffering doesn't come as a result of wrongdoing—rather, as a result of doing good. "Are to commit their souls to a faithful creator" commands trust that God will prove true to his promise of final salvation, including deliverance from persecution. Peter calls him "creator" in opposition to "every human institution [literally, 'creation']," such as "a king" or "governors" (2:13–14), unfaithful to their duty of executing justice as they often are. And "in the doing of good" defines "God's will" in opposition to criminal and troublemaking behavior. To do good though suffering for it displays a trustful commitment of oneself to God, the faithful creator.

AN EXHORTATION TO HUMILITY IN THE CHURCH AND RESISTANCE TO PERSECUTION
1 Peter 5:1–11

5:1–4: Therefore as the fellow elder and witness of the Christ's sufferings, the sharer [referring to Peter] **also of the glory that's about to be revealed, I exhort elders among you: ²Shepherd God's flock among you by supervising** [it], **not under coercion** [from other Christians]**—rather, willingly in accordance with God** [who has given you this responsibility]**; and not for shameful gain** [that is, not to profit dishonestly, for elders got paid (compare 1 Corinthians 9:6–18; Galatians 6:6; 1 Timothy 3:3 with 5:17–18; Titus 1:7, 11; 2 Peter 2:3; Jude 11)]**—rather, eagerly** [regardless of both pay and the persecution that comes first and foremost on church leaders]**; ³and not as wielding authority over the allotments** [of Christians whom you're supposed to shepherd]**—rather, becoming role models for the flock. ⁴And when the chief shepherd has appeared, you'll get the unfading crown of glory.** "Therefore" bases the following commands on the reference to "doing good"

in 4:19. So here are examples of doing good. With "fellow elder" Peter identifies himself as a colleague of elders in his audience. By doing so, he includes himself among those who need to act in accord with his coming commands. "*The* fellow elder" gives him prominence among them, though, a prominence that enhances his influence on them. To the same effect, "the . . . witness of the Christ's sufferings" lays claim to having seen the crucifixion (see Luke 23:49, which says that "all his [Jesus'] acquaintances" were watching it, and the correlation in 3:18 of "suffered" and "put to death"). Also giving Peter prominence and influence is his being "the sharer also of the glory that's about to be revealed." Unlike the elders among his addressees, in other words, Peter participated in Christ's coming glory when he saw the transfiguration, which previewed a revelation of that glory at the second coming (compare 2 Peter 1:16–18; Mark 9:1–8; Matthew 17:1–8; Luke 9:28–36).

As a title, "the Christ" adds a note of formality that fits Peter's calling him "the chief shepherd." "Elders" connotes maturity and leadership. "Not under coercion, but willingly" implies that Christians might try shoving others into eldership to avoid persecution themselves. Because of the contrast with "becoming role models for the flock," "wielding authority over" connotes heavy-handedness. "The allotments" indicates that elders were assigned—by Christ the chief shepherd, presumably—the Christians whom they were supposed to supervise. Peter calls Christ "the chief shepherd" to make him a role model for the role models (the elders) and promises compensation for them if they imitate Christ, a compensation called "the unfading crown of glory." For a crown, victorious athletes got a wreath of leaves that quickly faded. But Peter's word for "unfading" alludes to a particular blossom whose red color didn't fade. The unfading crown symbolizes the glory of everlasting life. This glory intimates a sharing of Christ's glory at the second coming and will more than compensate for the present shame (as non-Christians think it to be) of persecution. For the figures of shepherd and flock, see 2:25; Luke 12:32; John 10:1–30; 21:15–17; Acts 20:28–29; Ephesians 4:11; Hebrews 13:20 among other passages.

5:5–7: Likewise, you younger [men]**, subordinate yourselves to elders. And all of you, clothe yourselves with lowly-mindedness toward one another, because God "opposes haughty people but gives grace to humble people** [Proverbs 3:34]**."** "Likewise" makes the younger men just as responsible to subordinate themselves to the elders as the elders are responsible to shepherd them willingly, honestly, and exemplarily. Peter singles out the younger men because they stand at the opposite end of the spectrum in age and possibly because they also stand in danger of becoming "Young Turks," rebellious against the elders' leadership. "All of you" includes elders, young men, and everybody in between. For "lowly-mindedness" see the comments on 3:8. As a kind of clothing, this trait will be evident to others. "Haughty people" are self-elevated. Literally, "humble people" means "low people." God opposes the haughty because they've elevated themselves to compete with him. He gives favor ("grace") to humble people because they've lowered themselves in subjection to him. **6Therefore humble yourselves** [= "lower yourselves"] **under God's mighty hand in order that he may exalt you** [= "lift you up"] **at the set time** [of Christ's second coming], **7casting every concern of yours on him because he's concerned for you.** Lowly-mindedness toward one another stems from self-lowering under God's hand, for under it there's no space for self-elevation over each other. By itself the hand symbolizes strength, as it does dozens of times in the Old Testament (see Genesis 31:29, for example: "It is in the power of my hand to . . ."). The addition of "mighty" reinforces the symbolism (compare Exodus 13:9). Not only does this might assure Christians of God's ability to exalt them—in particular, to exalt them over their persecutors. He also has a concern for them that will *move* him to do so. They should get rid of their own concerns, then, by the vigorous action of throwing them, every one of them, on God. Riddance of anxiety-producing concerns will enable the Christians to endure persecution till their exaltation.

5:8–9: Be sober. Be awake. Your enemy the Devil is prowling around "as a roaring lion [does] [Psalm 22:13]," **hunting for someone to devour, 9whom** [referring to the Devil] **resist, firm in** [your] **faith, knowing that the same** [experiences] **of sufferings** [that you're having] **are being perpetrated on your brotherhood** [the Christian community] **in the world** [= in places other than your own]. We expect "and" between the commands to sobriety and wakefulness, and "because" to introduce the Devil's prowling as a reason for these commands. The lack of "and" and "because" produces a staccato-like effect that carries a note of urgency. Get drunk, and you'll go to sleep. Be sober, and you can stay awake. Again Peter warns against drunkenness (see the comments on 4:3), because a sleeping drunk is easy prey for the Devil in that getting drunk to alleviate the pressures of persecution betrays a lack of faith. This lack will incline the drunk to apostatize. But a Christian who's sober and awake because of firm faith in God's care and coming exaltation of him can successfully resist the pressures to apostatize represented by the Devil as a lion prowling around to devour Christians. And the knowledge that other Christians are likewise suffering persecution promotes a worldwide communal solidarity that helps keep this faith firm.

5:10–11: And after [you] **have suffered a little** [concerning which estimate see the comments on 1:6], **the God of all grace, who has called you in Christ into his eternal glory, will himself repair, stabilize, strengthen, establish** [you]. **11He** [has] **the might forever. Amen!** "The God of all grace" means "the all-gracious God." His grace—that is, his ill-deserved favor—has shown itself in his calling Christians. This calling refers to his having selected them for salvation and already effected the start of their salvation (1:1–13). Here the salvation is put in terms of a future entrance into the very glory that God

himself has, a glory that will reverse the shame of persecution (as non-Christians think and intend it to be). The eternality of God's glory translates into the eternality of the Christians' glory. The shift from persecution to glory, from shame to honor, will take place because of God's having placed Christians "in Christ" (compare 3:16; 5:14), on whom God has already conferred glory (1:11; 4:13; 5:1) and therefore in whom Christians too will get glory. "*All* grace" points not only to his past calling of them but also to his present and ceaseless repairing, stabilizing, strengthening, establishing of Christians. "Will *himself* repair . . ." stresses the direct involvement of his "mighty hand" and therefore gives them encouragement. God's hand will repair the damage done to them by their persecutors, stabilize them against efforts to shake them loose from their Christian profession, strengthen them to resist the Devil, establish them on a firm foundation of faith. We expect "and" before the last of these tasks. The lack of "and" leaves the list unfinished and thereby displays Peter's eagerness to write another doxology, as though he can't wait to affirm God's possession of eternal might, by which he can accomplish the tasks and in which Christians can take confidence. An exclamatory "Amen!" underscores this might (compare 4:11).

CONCLUSION
1 Peter 5:12–14

5:12: Through Silvanus, the faithful brother (as I count [him to be]), **I've written to you through** [the instrument of] **a few** [words], **urging and testifying that this is God's true grace, in which you should take your stand.** A Christian from Jerusalem named Silas appears in Acts from 15:22 onward. According to Acts 16:16–40 he had Roman citizenship. The name "Silvanus" that we have here in 1 Peter 5:12 is a Latin form of the Greek name "Silas." So it looks as though Silvanus and Silas refer to the same man. "Through Silvanus" means that in the absence of a public postal system he delivered this letter. Peter's describing him as "the faithful brother" is designed to gain a favorable reception for the letter as well as for Silvanus himself. "Through a few [words]" minimizes the letter's length, again to gain a favorable reception. "*Urging* that . . . this is God's true *grace*" connotes comfort and encouragement. "*Testifying* that this is God's *true* grace" connotes reliability. See the comments on 5:10 for the multiformity of this grace, which means favor. In it Christians should take their stand, because to curry the favor of non-Christians for the avoidance of persecution would be to forfeit the far better favor of God.

5:13–14: The [brotherhood of Christians] **in Babylon, selected along with** [you], **greets you. Also Mark my son** [greets you]. **14Greet one another with a loving kiss.** The Jews, God's people of old, had been exiled in Babylonia. Peter has repeatedly portrayed Christians as God's new chosen people. And Rome has replaced Babylon as the capital city of an empire in which the people of God live as a diaspora (see the comments on

1:1–2). So Peter uses "Babylon" as a symbolic name for Rome (compare Revelation 17–18), his location at the time of writing (as also according to early church tradition), and sends a greeting from the Christians there. The greeting is designed to encourage his audience. "Selected along with [you]" harks back to God's having selected Christians for salvation (1:1–2; 2:9) and thus adds to the encouragement. Mark, also called John (but not to be confused with John the baptizer or John the apostle [see Acts 12:12]), appeared as Paul's helper in Acts 12:25–13:5, suffered rejection by him in Acts 15:36–40, and came back into fellowship with him according to Colossians 4:10. Peter calls Mark his son, not in a biological sense, but in the sense of a young helper of his. As with the greetings from the Roman church and Mark, the audience's greeting one another will encourage them to endure persecution together. There's strength in numbers. And "with a loving kiss" adds a physical greeting, which neither the Roman church nor Mark can give, to the verbal greetings already given by them. Peter adds his own verbal greeting: [May] **all of you who** [are] **in Christ** [have] **peace.** "In Christ" locates Peter's audience where they have peace. See the comments on 1:2 for the meaning of "peace."

SECOND PETER

The statement in 3:1–2 that this is the second letter Peter is writing to his audience implies that they are the same as the audience to whom he wrote 1 Peter (about whom see the comments on 1 Peter 1:1–2). Teachers who peddled false doctrine and practiced immorality were beginning to make serious inroads into the church. So 2 Peter polemicizes against these teachers, particularly against their denial of Jesus' second coming, and affirms the true knowledge of Christian belief to counter their heresy.

ADDRESS AND GREETING
2 Peter 1:1–4

1:1–2: Simeon Peter, Jesus Christ's slave and apostle, to those who by the righteousness of our God and Savior, Jesus Christ, have obtained a faith equal in value to ours: [2]May grace and peace be multiplied for you in the knowledge of God and of Jesus, our Lord . . . . "Simeon" represents the Semitic spelling of "Simon," a Greek spelling, and reflects Peter's native, Semitic language: Aramaic (see also Acts 15:14). Jesus gave him the nickname "Peter," which in Greek means "a stone" (Mark 3:16; Matthew 10:2; Luke 6:14; John 1:42). The placement of "Christ," properly a descriptive title meaning "Anointed One," after "Jesus," a personal name, shows that "Christ" too has taken on the role of a personal name (compare the comments on 1 Peter 1:1–2). By calling himself "Jesus Christ's slave," Peter implies that he's writing in obedience to his master's orders. By also calling himself "Jesus Christ's . . . apostle," he indicates that what he's writing carries Jesus Christ's own authority. For by definition an apostle speaks, acts, and writes with the authority of his sender. "Who . . . have obtained a faith" represents Christian faith as gained by lot, that is, through no merit of the recipient. As in 1:5 "faith" means believing as such, not what is believed. "By the righteousness of our God and Savior, Jesus Christ" identifies Jesus with God, credits him with salvation, and portrays his righteousness as the means by which the audience have obtained an equally valuable faith. "Our *God and Savior*" distinguishes him from the supposed gods and saviors of pagans. "*Our* God and Savior" includes the Christian audience. But "equal in value to *ours*" differentiates them by anticipatively comparing their faith with the faith of Peter and his fellow "eyewitnesses of [Jesus'] greatness" (see 1:16–18). The comparison implies that the audience didn't see the greatness of Jesus. By describing their faith as equal in value to that of eye-witnesses, though, Peter pays a compliment to his audience's faith (compare John 20:29). At the same time, the description of their faith as equally valuable sets up for a contrast with the valueless faith (or is it *un*faith?) of heretics whom Peter is going to attack. This two-sided compliment has the purpose of winning a favorable hearing for the letter. But how is a faith valuable, and what kind of righteousness does Peter have in view? A faith is valuable insofar as it has truth—here, the truth of the gospel—as its object. And elsewhere in 2 Peter "righteousness" means right conduct (see 2:5, 21; 3:13). So here Jesus Christ is said to have done right by seeing to it that the audience obtained a faith equal in value to that of Peter and other eyewitnesses.

Concerning the multiplication of grace and peace for the audience, see the comments on 1 Peter 1:2; 2 John 3. There the multiplication is needed because of persecution. Here it's needed because of the threat of heresy. "In the knowledge of God and of Jesus" tells where grace and peace are to be found. Knowledge of God and of Jesus means knowing *them*, not just knowing *about* them, and implies that knowing God requires knowing Jesus and that knowing Jesus entails knowing God. This knowledge brings the ill-deserved favor ("grace") and prosperity ("peace") of salvation and contrasts with ill-favored and poisonous heresy. Peter has just now distinguished God and Jesus in addition to having earlier identified Jesus with God. So here he tacks "our Lord" onto "Jesus" to reiterate Jesus' deity. "Our Lord" also contrasts Jesus with the supposed lords worshiped by pagans and makes a match with Peter's having described himself as "Jesus Christ's slave," for "lord" was used for the owner and master of a slave.

Peter's wish that grace and peace may be multiplied for his audience continues in **1:3–4: since his divine power has granted us all things pertaining to life and godliness** [= piety] **through the knowledge of him who called us by his own glory and virtue, [4]through which** [glory and virtue] **he has granted us valuable and very big promises in order that on escaping from the corruption in the world** [consisting] **in lust, through these** [promises] **you may become sharers of divine nature.** For several reasons "his divine power" means Jesus' divine power: (1) he's the one last mentioned in 1:2; (2) in Peter's Greek, "divine" is the adjectival form of "God"; and 1:1 called Jesus "our God," so that naturally he has divine power; and (3) 1:16 will speak of "the power . . . of our Lord, Jesus Christ." His divine power has enabled him, then, to grant Christians "all things pertaining to life and godliness." This grant enabled Peter, in turn, to wish with confidence that grace and peace be multiplied for his audience (1:2)—hence the introduction of 1:3 with "since." "*All* things" leaves no deficiency whatsoever. "Pertaining to life and godliness" means "necessary to live a godly life that eventuates in eternal life" (compare 1 Peter 3:7, 10 and contrast the corrupt conduct of the heretics headed for eternal destruction here in chapter 2). But the granting of such things has taken place only "through the knowledge of him who called us" (see the comments on 1:1–2 for "knowledge"). Though 1:2 spoke of the knowledge of God as distinct from Jesus, 1:2 also spoke of the knowledge of Jesus; and 1:8; 2:20; 3:18 will speak exclusively of the knowledge of Jesus. So he's likely the one "who called us." At the same time, Peter's calling Jesus "our God" yet distinguishing him from God the Father in 1:1–2, 16–17 implies that Jesus called us on God's behalf and that God called us through Jesus (compare 1 Peter 1:15; 2:9).

"Called" refers to an invitation that effected an acceptance. "Who called us" is therefore designed to highlight the privilege of having been invited and thus drawn "out of darkness into his [God's] marvelous light" (1 Peter 2:9). "By his own glory and virtue" means that Jesus' glorious moral excellence is what made the call effective. "His own" stresses that the excellence belonged to Jesus as much as to his Father, whom he represented. Bedazzled by this excellence, the called ones couldn't resist their invitation. And prompted by his own excellence, Jesus on God's behalf has granted them "promises" in addition to "all things pertaining to life and godliness." The promises are "valuable" in that they're "very big," and they're "very big" in that they enable Christians to "become sharers of divine nature"—a quantum leap in moral transformation that entailed "escaping from the corruption in the world." "In lust" defines this corruption as moral and therefore defines "divine nature" as Jesus' (and God's) previously mentioned glorious virtue, that is, moral excellence. To share it is to participate in it, as evident in your behavior. And to have escaped the corruption in the world isn't for it to have bypassed you. It's for you to have fled from it when you were called, when you were converted. For to be called into God's marvelous light is at one and the same time to be called out of the darkness of this morally murky world (compare 1:19 and, again, 1 Peter 2:9).

THE MORAL UNDERGIRDING OF CHRISTIAN BELIEF WITH CORRECT CONDUCT
2 Peter 1:5–11

1:5–9: **And even for this very reason** [that God's divine power has granted us all things pertaining to life and godliness, and so forth, in 1:3–4] **by applying all due diligence, supplement your faith with virtue, and** [supplement your] **virtue with knowledge,** ⁶**and** [your] **knowledge with self-control, and** [your] **self-control with perseverance, and** [your] **perseverance**

with godliness, ⁷**and** [your] **godliness with brotherly affection, and** [your] **brotherly affection with love.** ⁸**For these things, if existing and increasing in you, render** [you] **not workless and not unfruitful in the knowledge of our Lord, Jesus Christ.** ⁹**For with whom these things are *not* present—he's blind, seeing dimly, having forgotten about the cleansing of his sins of old.** To the flight from moral corruption that took place at conversion Peter now adds a series of supplementary actions that require taking pains ("by applying all due diligence"). Moreover, the verb "supplement" connotes a lavish supply as opposed to a meager addition. In 1:1 "faith" means belief, not faithfulness (see too 1 Peter 1:7, 9, 21; 5:9). So here Peter puts faith as Christian belief first. Such faith is good; but it needs the supplement of virtue (moral excellence), for "faith apart from works is workless" (James 2:20). Virtue too is good; but it needs the supplement of knowledge, for ignorance of God and of Jesus leaves virtue groundless and therefore precarious. Knowledge is good too; but it needs the supplement of self-control, for knowledge can lead to license growing out of arrogance, as in the case of the heretics of chapter 2. Self-control is good; but it needs the supplement of perseverance, for it's hard to maintain self-control for long, especially in the face of heretical enticements such as those discussed in chapter 2. Perseverance is good; but it needs the supplement of godliness—that is, piety—for perseverance arises out of dependence on God and reverence for him (contrast 2:10–11). Godliness is good; but it needs the supplement of brotherly affection, for godliness can degenerate into cold isolation from fellow Christians. And brotherly affection is good; but it needs the supplement of love—that is, helpful deeds done for others—for otherwise the affection will rise no higher than the emotional level. These qualities need not only to exist in you, but also to increase in you (compare 3:18: "But *be growing* in grace and the knowledge of our Lord, Jesus Christ"). Without them, you're "workless" and therefore "unfruitful," a figure of speech for failing to do good deeds—and this despite knowing our Lord, Jesus Christ. But the existence and increase of the supplements make for an assiduous production of good deeds as fruit. Why? Because their absence betrays blindness in the sense of seeing too dimly to work at the production of good deeds. This purblindness symbolizes forgetfulness, the inability to see back to the cleansing of your sins at conversion, a cleansing represented by baptism on that occasion (compare 1 Peter 3:20–21; Acts 22:16). "Of old" describes the sins as having been committed prior to conversion. Forgetfulness of that cleansing produces moral indolence and unfruitfulness and insults the one who cleansed away your sins.

1:10–11: **To the contrary therefore, brothers, be diligent to make sure for yourselves your calling and selection. For while doing these things you'll by no means stumble.** ¹¹**For in this way the entrance into the eternal kingdom of our Lord and Savior, Jesus Christ, will be richly supplemented for you.** "Therefore" bases the following exhortation on the danger of going forgetfully and thus morally blind. The affectionate address, "brothers," derives from the seriousness of the danger of apostasy, that is, of losing "your calling and selection," which entails salvation itself (compare the comments on 1:3). "Be diligent" connotes strenuous effort, and "to make sure for yourselves your calling and selection" is to ensure your salvation by making the supplements listed in 1:5–7. Such effort doesn't merit salvation; but it will keep you from stumbling so as not to enter the kingdom. The eternality of the kingdom and its belonging to "our Lord and Savior, Jesus Christ" associates it with eternal life. "Will be . . . supplemented for you" caps your supplements with Jesus' supplement of that entrance. "Richly" describes his supplement as more than compensatory for your supplementary efforts.

THE HISTORICAL RELIABILITY OF CHRISTIAN BELIEF, SUPPORTED BY EYEWITNESS TESTIMONY AND FULFILLED PROPHECY
2 Peter 1:12–21

1:12–14: Therefore [because the audience need to make sure for themselves their calling and selection] **I'll always be going to remind you about these things even though you know** [them] **and are stabilized by the truth that's coming to** [you]. [13]**And I consider it right to be arousing you by way of reminder so long as I'm in this tent,** [14]**knowing that the divestiture of my tent is imminent, just as also our Lord, Jesus Christ, made clear to me.** "The truth" consists in what Peter has written up till now, and is "coming" to his audience in the form of this letter. They already know the truth, and it has already stabilized them. But knowledge doesn't translate into action automatically, stability can freeze into inaction, and heresy threatens. So Peter determines to be "arousing [his audience] by way of reminder," that is, by reminding them to make sure for themselves their calling and selection. He might have written simply, "I'm reminding you." But his use of the future tense ("I'll"), plus "always" and "be going to," heightens the expression of determination—and therefore the need for constant reminding. Perseverance requires it, and the requirement makes it right to do. So Peter will keep up the reminding as long as he lives. His audience will have this letter as a reminder even after he dies. So the qualification, "as long as I'm in this tent [a figure of speech for his body]," seems vacuous unless he intends further reminders. Did he die before he had opportunity to give them? In any case, his putting the exhortation in terms of a reminder pays the audience a compliment by implying they already know what they need to do. As earlier, the compliment has the purpose of winning a favorable and obedient hearing.

After using "this tent" to represent his body (compare John 1:14; 2 Corinthians 5:1, 4), Peter doubles his figurative language by comparing the tent to an article of clothing that can be taken off. So "the divestiture of my tent" represents the laying aside of his body at death. He must be old, because his death is "imminent"; and

according to John 21:18–19 Jesus prophesied that Peter would die in old age. "Just as also our Lord, Jesus Christ, made clear to me" recollects Jesus' prophecy in addition to Peter's old age; and "made clear" points up the prophecy's temporal specificity. Knowing that he'll die soon contributes to the determination of Peter to keep up his reminders. Not for long will he be able to do so. Meanwhile, he seems not to tire of identifying Jesus Christ as "our Lord" in opposition to pagan deities and Roman emperors (compare 1:2, 8, 11 and numerous later references). The approaching fulfillment of Jesus' prophecy that Peter would die in old age prepares for an argument from the fulfillment of Old Testament prophecy.

1:15–16: And I'll also be diligent for you to have perpetually after my departure a reminder of these things. [16]**For not by following cleverly contrived fables did we make known to you the power and coming of our Lord, Jesus Christ—rather, by having become eyewitnesses of that one's greatness** [we made his power and coming known to you]. "Also" adds perpetuity to the present reminder. By having survived the death of Peter, this very letter of his counts as an ongoing reminder even now. But much as in 1:12, the future tense in "I'll . . . be diligent" implies an effort on his part to communicate further reminders so long as he stays alive. For his "departure" he uses the Greek word *exodon*, from which we get the Latinized spelling "exodus," a going out. This word appeared in Luke 9:31 for Jesus' departure in death. Providing yet another reason for reminders is the nonmythological nature of Jesus' power and coming. The message that he'll come with power is based on eyewitness reports, writes Peter. He singles out his and others' (James' and John's) having seen Jesus' greatness on the mount of transfiguration. Six days earlier, according to Mark 9:1, Jesus had prophesied they would see "God's reign [as] having come with power"; and later he prophesied that he himself would come with power (Mark 13:26; Matthew 24:30; Luke 21:27). According to very early church tradition Mark got his information from Peter. Not surprisingly, then, Peter refers to the transfiguration as Jesus Christ's "power and coming"; and since Jesus shares God's reign (see 1:11), Peter refers to "that one's greatness" and to Jesus Christ as "our Lord." "Lord" could refer to an emperor, a king, a ruler. "*His* greatness" would have sufficed. But "*that one's* greatness" distances Jesus in a way that portrays his greatness as transcendent. Peter uses a word for Jesus' "coming" that connotes the second coming (*parousia* [see also 3:4, 12]), because he's using the transfiguration as a preview that guarantees the second coming, which certain heretics deny and apparently describe as a fable cleverly devised by Peter and his apostolic associates to impose unnecessary behavioral restrictions on their followers (chapter 3). In addition to belief in the second coming and the moral implications of the judgment connected with it, the honesty and honor of Peter and other apostles are at stake. There follows now a short narrative of what happened on the mount of transfiguration.

1:17–18: **For on receiving from God the Father honor and glory when a voice such as this was carried to him** [Jesus] **by the Suitably Great Glory, "This is my beloved Son, in whom I've taken delight** [compare Matthew 17:5 and see the comments on Matthew 3:17 for allusions to the Old Testament]**"—**[18]**we ourselves, being with him** [Jesus] **on the sacred mountain** [compare Psalm 2:6]**, also heard this voice when it was carried** [to him from heaven (compare Mark 9:7; Matthew 3:17; Luke 9:35)]. Peter interprets God's statement regarding Jesus as a reception of "honor and glory." "Honor" connotes *estimated* value of a high order. "Glory" connotes *evident* value of a high order. God put a high estimate on Jesus' value and made the estimate evident by what he said (perhaps also by brightening Jesus' appearance, but Peter doesn't otherwise mention the brightness). Specifically, "beloved" and "in whom I've taken delight" express the "honor and glory" Jesus received at his transfiguration. Peter adds "the Father" to "God" in preparation for "This is my beloved *Son*" and then calls God the Father "the Suitably Great Glory" to make him the appropriate source of the glory Jesus received, and also the appropriate source of "that one's [Jesus'] greatness" (1:16). "A voice *such as this*" refers forward to the Suitably Great Glory's statement about Jesus. To stress the historical reliability of this eyewitness report Peter breaks off the sentence he began. For after "on receiving from God the Father honor and glory . . ." good grammar requires a reference to Jesus, the recipient. But Peter leaves the sentence incomplete and jumps to "we" (the apostolic eyewitnesses). Also stressing historical reliability are (1) the tacking of "ourselves" onto "we"; (2) the reference to "being with him [Jesus]" at the transfiguration; (3) the localizing of the event ("on the sacred mountain"); and (4) the hearing of the Suitably Great Glory's voice in addition to eyewitnessing Jesus' greatness. "Sacred" describes the mountain as consecrated by what happened there. No other mountain has hosted such a display of Jesus' honor and glory. "When it was carried [to him]" reprises "a voice such as this was carried to him" and, more importantly, anticipates the statement that "men [prophets] being carried by the Holy Spirit spoke from God" (1:21). By implication, the Holy Spirit carried the Suitably Great Glory's voice to Jesus, so that Peter and some other apostles heard it.

1:19–21: **And we very surely have the prophetic word, by paying attention to which as to a lamp shining in a murky place until day dawns and the morning star rises in your hearts you're doing well,** [20]**knowing this foremost: that not a single prophecy of Scripture develops from a person's own interpretation** [of things]. [21]**For never was a prophecy brought by the will** [= impetus] **of a human being; rather, men being carried by the Holy Spirit spoke from God.** After stressing the reliability of his and other apostles' report of Jesus' transfiguration, Peter now stresses the reliability of his and their "very surely" having the prophetic word, which refers to Old Testament prophecy (as indicated by the reference to "Scripture," which did not yet include the

New Testament). This reliability backs up what they saw and heard and derives from earlier prophets' having "spoke[n] from God" as they were "being carried by the Holy Spirit."

A twofold denial supports the reliability: (1) "Not a single prophecy of Scripture develops from a person's own interpretation." Peter isn't referring to the interpretation *of* prophecy. He's referring to prophecy *as* interpretation, the interpretation of past, present, and future events. "Of Scripture" limits this statement to prophecies recorded in the Old Testament, and "not a *single* prophecy . . ." rules all false prophecy out of the Old Testament. (Not that the Old Testament doesn't record some prophecies for exposure as false, of course [see, for example, 1 Kings 22:1–40].) "Knowing this *foremost*" and the present tense of "develops" vividly underline the denial that the Old Testament advances false prophecy. (2) "For never was a prophecy carried by the will of a human being [and so on]" furthers the denial and strengthens it with "never." "The will of a human being" contrasts with "being carried by the Holy Spirit" and thus with "speak[ing] from God." As God's voice was carried to Jesus at the transfiguration, the prophets themselves were being carried by the Holy Spirit to their audiences when they spoke, so that their speech came from God. Since Scripture recorded their speech, "we very surely have the prophetic word." Given this reliable word, Christians do well to pay attention to it; for the second coming brings judgment. Peter compares the word to a lamp (see Psalm 119:105) and describes the world in which it shines as "murky," morally dark and dismal. The lamp of this scriptural word presages the morning star, which will introduce a bright new day. In view of Revelation 22:16, Peter probably refers with this figure of speech to Jesus at his return in fulfillment of the rest of Old Testament prophecy. For not all messianic prophecy there was fulfilled during Jesus' first coming. It's on this basis as well as on the transfiguration that the apostles preached the second coming. Outside our hearts the second coming will be Jesus' *descent* in the clouds (Mark 13:26; Matthew 24:30; Luke 21:27; 1 Thessalonians 4:16; Revelation 1:7). Inside our hearts it will be an *ascent* that introduces the dawn of a new day, the Day of the Lord, God's Day (3:10, 12; compare Numbers 24:17). In fulfillment of Scripture, that dawn will eliminate any further need for the lamp of scriptural prophecy.

FALSE TEACHERS
2 Peter 2:1–22

This section divides into false teachers' appearance in the church (2:1–3), their future judgment (2:4–10a), and their immoral ways (2:10b–22). Throughout, comparisons should be made to the letter of Jude.

2:1: **But false prophets also came on the scene among the people** [of Israel during the Old Testament period]**, as also there'll be false teachers among you,** [false teachers] **who as such will stealthily bring in destructive dogmas, even disowning the Master who**

bought them, bringing on themselves imminent destruction. Though the false teachers are already present among Peter's audience according to the rest of chapter 2 and also chapter 3, he uses the future tense to indicate that false teachers will continue to exist among the audience after his death, which he has just described as imminent (1:14). The first "also" points to the past presence of false as well as true prophets in Israelite history (see 1:20–21 for the true). The second "also" points to the future presence of false as well as true teachers among Christians (see 1:12–18 for the apostles as the true). Since history repeats itself, Christians should be on guard. Peter shifts from false prophets to false teachers because the false teachers were denying prophecy rather than engaging in it (see chapter 3). "Who *as such*" stresses that because they're false, they'll introduce their dogmas "stealthily." All the more reason to be on guard, then.

"Destructive" describes the "dogmas" in a way that justifies our term "heretics" and that indicates a loss of eternal life for those supposed Christians who embrace those dogmas. (The word translated "destructive" is related to the verb "perish, be lost" in John 3:16, for example.) "Even disowning the Master who bought them" signals just how heretical are the dogmas. According to chapter 3 the disowning takes the form of denying Jesus' return in judgment. So he's the Master who bought them. According to the rest of chapter 2 the disowning takes the form of disobeying his command to live a righteous life. Such disobedience follows from denying a judgmental return of Jesus. No need to fear getting punished for misbehavior: Just adjust your dogmas to accommodate your disobedience! Dogmas and disobedience affect each other. By introducing destructive disobedience the false teachers are "bringing imminent destruction on themselves." So their missing out on eternal life will be their own fault. Peter describes the destruction as "imminent" because it will happen ironically at the very return of Jesus in judgment that they deny, and his return could happen soon (3:10–13). Jesus bought them to be his slaves. So disowning him comes close to making them runaway slaves.

2:2–3: And many will follow their debaucheries, on account of whom [referring to the false teachers] **the path of truth will be slandered.** ³**And in** [their] **greed they'll exploit you with phony words, for whom the judgment** [pronounced against them] **since long ago isn't idle. And their destruction isn't snoozing.** "Their debaucheries" describes the false teachers' behavior as immoral. "Follow[ing] their debaucheries" portrays their immoral behavior as teaching by example. "*Many* will follow" sets out a predictive prophecy by Peter that rings the alarm bell louder yet. "The path of truth" means conduct appropriate to the gospel (compare Psalm 119:30). But Peter calls the gospel "truth" for a contrast with the false teachers' "phony words." He also predicts that the false teachers' debaucheries will bring disrepute on the truly Christian way of living, because these teachers will claim to be Christians despite

disowning the Master who bought them (though they wouldn't admit to doing so). "Greed" and "exploit" point to their money-grubbing. "Phony words" means words molded so as to gain the desired end of fleecing people rather than improving their behavior. Judgment was pronounced against the false teachers "long ago." (Peter doesn't say where.) "*Since* long ago" adds that the judgment, though delayed, "isn't idle" (literally, "isn't workless"). It's already at work, and has been for a long time (as Peter is about to explain). "Their destruction" defines "their judgment" and again refers to eternal lostness (see the comments on 2:1). "Isn't snoozing" parallels "isn't idle" for emphasis. Peter has personified the judgment and destruction, as though they are God's employees, and denies that because the false teachers will thrive the judgment and destruction have shirked their duty and fallen asleep on the job. On the contrary, judgment is working and destruction is awake.

2:4: For if God didn't spare angels that had sinned—rather, by tartarizing [them—that is, consigning them to Tartarus, a Greek name for deepest hell] **gave** [them] **over to chains of pitch-blackness,** [the angels] **being kept for judgment . . . .** Here begins a long sentence. "Angels that had sinned" refers to "the sons of god" who according to Genesis 6:1–4 corrupted the human race by marrying "the daughters of human beings" (perhaps through demonic possession of human males [compare 1 Peter 3:18–22; Jude 6; and, for angels as "the sons of God," Job 1:6; 2:1; 38:7]). God's not sparing these angels but chaining them in hell for future judgment shows that the false teachers' judgment and destruction, being of one piece with the angels' judgment, aren't idle or dormant. Still personified, judgment and destruction are guarding the sinful angels till they carry out on them, as well as on the false teachers, God's judgmentally destructive will. The "chains" consist of the "pitch-blackness" that characterizes Tartarus in Greek mythology, and these chains of pitch-blackness bind the sinful angels in that the angels can't see their way out of Tartarus. Thus the chains guarantee that these angels won't go missing on the Last Day, the day when God will judge and destroy all evil. Nor will the false teachers go missing. Other ancient manuscripts read "to *dungeons* of pitch-blackness," in which case depth combines with pitch-blackness to prevent escape.

2:5: and [if] **he didn't spare the ancient world—rather, when bringing a deluge** [literally, "a downpour, a drenching down"] **on the world of ungodly people safeguarded Noah as the eighth, a proclaimer of righteousness . . . .** See Genesis 6:5–8 for the ungodliness of people just prior to Noah's flood and in connection with the aforementioned sin of angels. "The world of ungodly people" centers attention on their destruction rather than on that of the earth. The flood shows again that God's judgment and destruction aren't idle and dormant. But Peter introduces an additional element, the safeguarding of Noah. "As the eighth" alludes to Noah's being the eighth after a counting of his wife, their three sons, and the sons' three wives (see 1 Peter 3:20). God safeguarded all of them, but Peter singles out Noah as "a proclaimer of righteousness" in opposition to current and coming false teachers who teach *un*righteousness. God's safeguarding Noah from the flood presages God's safeguarding from eternal damnation those Christians who resist false teaching.

2:6–8: and [if] by reducing the cities of Sodom and Gomorrah to ashes he condemned [them] to catastrophe [literally, "a downturn"], having placed [them] as an example of the things that are going to happen to ungodly people, ⁷and rescued righteous Lot, [who was] getting worn out by the behavior in debauchery of unprincipled [men] ⁸(for by what he saw and heard day in and day out while dwelling among them, the righteous [Lot] was tormenting [his] righteous soul [= himself as a righteous person] with [their] lawless deeds) . . . [see Genesis 18:1–19:29]. The "*down*turn" of a catastrophe consisted in being burned down to the ground, so that only ashes lay scattered about (compare the detention of sinful angels down in the underworld called Tartarus [2:4] and the "*down*pour" in Noah's time [2:5]). God's "having placed" Sodom and Gomorrah has to do with the visibility of their ashes in ancient times (compare Zephaniah 2:9). You could go there and see the evidence of God's active, wakeful judgment; and Peter uses that evidence "as an example of the things that are going to happen to ungodly people," by whom he means false teachers and those who "follow their debaucheries" (2:2). Whereas he called Noah "a *proclaimer* of righteousness," he calls Lot *himself* "righteous" to mate right behavior with right teaching. The righteousness of Lot was evident in his "getting worn out" (we might say "tired to death") by his fellow townspeople's behavior. "In debauchery" describes the behavior as so bad that debauchery was the very atmosphere in which the behavior took place. Peter assigns this behavior to men who have no principles bridling it. "Tormenting [his] righteous soul" ratchets up "getting worn out" and means not just that the behavior of his fellow townspeople pained him, but that he took pains to *make* it pain him. He didn't let himself get used to it. "With [their] lawless deeds" identifies "what he saw and heard day in and day out while dwelling among them." And the whole parenthetical statement, introduced by "for," explains in greater detail the reason for Lot's "getting worn out," which Peter's own distress over the false teachers' bad behavior mirrors. He wants his audience not to get used to such behavior in their midst, but to torment their souls with it too. If they do, God will rescue them from the coming conflagration (for which see 3:7, 10–12) just as he rescued Lot. Reason enough!

2:9–10a: [if he rescued righteous Lot and condemned the ungodly] the Lord knows to be rescuing godly people out of temptation and to be keeping unrighteous people for the Day of Judgment, [the unrighteous] being punished [on that day], ¹⁰ᵃand especially those who are going after flesh with lust for pollution

and who are despising lordship. Despite other translations to the contrary, Peter doesn't write that the Lord knows "how" to rescue godly people. There's no word in the Greek text which has that meaning. Peter isn't concerned with the Lord's *method* in rescuing godly people—rather, with the *fact* that he rescues them, which fact encourages them not to forsake the path of righteousness. "Out of temptation" implies that their godly behavior puts them to the test because of persecution, and this test tempts them to follow the false teachers' debaucheries as a way of avoiding persecution (compare the whole of 1 Peter). A climactic rescue will occur at the second coming, which the false teachers deny (3:3–4). By contrast, God "knows . . . [also] to keep unrighteous people for the Day of Judgment." The false teachers and their prey are particularly in view. Again it's a matter of fact, not a matter of method. The keeping of unrighteous people for judgment matches the keeping of sinful angels for judgment. Such people have no more chance of avoiding judgment than do the angels of 2:4. "Being punished" underlines the judgment's negativity. Peter's audience wouldn't want such a fate. They'd better not fall prey to the false teachers, then. "Especially those who are going after flesh with lust for pollution" describes the teachers and their prey as hellbent on satisfying their physical appetites through lustful pursuits that pollute them. But it's not just that their lusts pollute them morally. It's also that they lust *for* pollution, which in the first instance refers quite literally to stains resulting from the exchange of bodily fluids through illicit sex. "Going after flesh" portrays their pursuit with a term reminiscent of the ancient Jews' "going after" idols, as though human flesh itself has become an idol for the false teachers and their adherents (see Deuteronomy 28:14; 1 Kings 11:10, for example). "And who are despising lordship" adds arrogance to lust. Peter has just written that "the Lord knows to rescue godly people." So the false teachers are despising the Lord's lordship in that they're disobeying his command to live righteously. But their arrogance includes a slandering of lesser authorities too.

2:10b–11: Headstrong daredevils, they don't tremble when slandering luminaries [more literally, "glories"], ¹¹whereas angels, though being greater in strength and power, aren't bringing against them [the luminaries] a slanderous judgment alongside the Lord [= in his presence]. The false teachers are headstrong in that they dare to do what even angels don't do. The luminaries ("glories") whom they slander are probably the angels of heaven, holy angels, since God chained in "pitch-blackness" the angels that sinned (2:4) and since 1:3, 17; 3:18 associate glory with him and Jesus. The angels who don't bring against the luminaries a slanderous judgment, then, are the angels that sinned. As angels they're "greater in strength and power" than the false teachers. Even so, these sinful angels don't bring against holy angels, the luminaries, a slanderous judgment in the Lord's presence (as Satan did against Job, for instance [Job 1:9–11; 2:4–5]). Of course not, because God "consigned [the sinful angels] to Tartarus" till the day of their own judgment. If he has seen to it that the sinful angels can't bring before him a slanderous judgment against the holy ones, the false teachers must indeed be headstrong daredevils to speak ill of holy angels without trembling in fear of a fate like that of the sinful angels. Presumably the false teachers slander the holy angels in that their denial of the second coming entails a denial also of those angels' participation in it (see especially Jude 14–15, but also Mark 8:38; 13:27; Matthew 13:39, 41, 49; 16:27; 24:31; 25:31; Luke 9:26; 1 Thessalonians 3:13; 2 Thessalonians 1:7).

2:12–14: But these [false teachers], **having been sired as irrational living** [creatures] **of instinct** [are sired] **for capture and corruption, slandering in matters they're ignorant of, in their corruption will also** *be* **corrupted,** [13]**getting injured as a wage of** [their] **injuriousness, considering going on a binge in daytime** [to be] **a pleasure, blots and blemishes, binging in their deceitful pleasures as they feast together with you,** [14]**having eyes full of an adulteress and incessant of sin** [= eyes that sin ceaselessly], **baiting unstable souls, having a heart** [a figure of speech for both thinking and feeling] **trained in greed, children of a curse** [= destined to suffer the curse of God's judgment]. Because of their foolhardiness in slandering the luminaries, Peter says the false teachers have been sired as animals have been sired—and as *wild* animals at that: sired only to be captured and killed (for which "corruption" is a figure of speech) because they live by instinct rather than by reason. With this kind of siring, contrast being "fathered anew" in 1 Peter 1:3, 23. ("Fathered" and "sired" go back to the same Greek verb, "fathered" being an appropriate translation for human beings, "sired" an appropriate translation for animals and for human beings compared to animals.) "Irrational" corresponds to "headstrong daredevils" in 2:10b, and "of instinct" corresponds to "going after flesh with lust for pollution" in 2:10a. "Capture" symbolizes being kept for the Day of Judgment (2:9), and "corruption" refers to judgmental decay (eternal damnation) as the wage for moral decay (compare Romans 6:23). "Slandering in matters they're ignorant of" harks back to the slandering of luminaries (2:10b), and the ignorance follows naturally from "having been sired as *irrational* living [creatures] of instinct [are sired]." In their state of moral corruption the false teachers will suffer the fate of judgmental corruption. "*Also* be corrupted" compares their judgmental corruption to the fate of irrational wild animals that hunters capture and kill. The false teachers are going to get injured, so to speak, by God's righteous judgment against their injurious unrighteousness. The unrighteousness injures not only them, but also others by seducing them into unrighteous behavior, so that they too will suffer the injury of God's righteous judgment. A wordplay is at work here in that Peter uses a pair of related words (a verb [*adikoumenoi*] and a cognate noun [*adikias*]) both of which have the coordinate meanings of injury and unrighteousness. According to 2:3 greed characterizes the false teachers. So it's appropriate that they'll get paid a wage, but not one they want—rather,

the injury of God's righteous judgment in payback for their unrighteousness.

Binge-drinking usually takes place at night. Doing it in daytime, when workaday duties should be fulfilled, exhibits shamelessness (compare Ecclesiastes 10:16; Isaiah 5:11). Considering it a pleasure to binge during the day heightens the shamelessness. As brazen bingers, the false teachers are moral blots and blemishes on the reputation of "the path of truth" (2:2). Peter calls the "pleasures" of binging "deceitful" in that they lead to the unexpected "corruption" of eternal damnation. "As they feast together with you" puts his audience in a danger zone, or makes the false teachers' taking of meals—in particular church suppers, it would seem—a real and present danger of moral rot spreading among Peter's audience. "Having eyes full of an adulteress" means ogling another man's wife who'll commit adultery with the false teacher. Presumably the ogling takes place at the church suppers (during which the Lord's Supper was celebrated). "*Incessant* of sin" joins "*full* of an adulteress" to describe the false teachers' eyes as so lustful as to be incapable of seeing anyone except an adulteress and incapable of ceasing to ogle her. This ogling baits "unstable souls"—that is, entices Christian women susceptible to these Don Juans of the theological world. The false teachers have also exercised their heart in greed as though training it for an athletic contest. Which of them can outdo the others in money-grubbing? So the curse of God's judgment awaits them despite their denial of its coming.

2:15–16: On leaving behind the straight path they've strayed by following the path of Balaam, the [son] **of Bosor, who** [referring to Balaam] **loved a wage of injury.** Balak, king of Moab, had offered to pay Balaam a lot of money if he'd pronounce an injurious curse on Israel (Numbers 22:1–20). But as noted earlier, the word translated "injury" also means "unrighteousness," so that the wage was to be paid for the unrighteous pronouncement of an injurious curse. Like Balaam, writes Peter, the heretics teach easygoing morality to pad their paychecks. "The straight path" equates with "the path of truth" in 2:2 (compare Mark 1:3; Matthew 3:3; Luke 3:4–5; Acts 13:10—and Proverbs 2:13 among other Old Testament passages). What's straight contrasts with what's crooked and therefore perverted (compare the colloquial use of "crook" for a dishonest person). In other contexts, as a matter of fact, the word for "straight" is translated "upright" (in a moral sense). So a straight path has to do with living uprightly. The Old Testament ascribes the name "Beor" to Balaam's father. So "Bosor," which shares B, o, and r with "Beor," appears to be a sarcastic transmutation of "Beor" into a name that's built on the Hebrew word for "flesh," whose consonants are *b-s-r*, just as in "Bosor" (compare the false teachers' "going after flesh with lust for pollution" in 2:10). [16]**But he** [Balaam] **had** [= got] **a conviction for his own breach of law.** "His own" stresses Balaam's guilt in breaching a law. The law Balaam breached and got convicted for breaching consisted in God's command that he not go with King

Balak's messengers to curse Israel (Numbers 22:12). **A voiceless donkey** [that is, one that couldn't ordinarily speak], **expressing itself in a human's voice, restrained the prophet's lunacy** [which almost resulted in his death according to the account in Numbers 22:21–35].

2:17–19: These [false teachers] **are waterless fountains and mists being driven by a gale, for whom the pitch-blackness of darkness has been kept** [= reserved]. [18]**For by expressing themselves in empty pomposities they bait** [= entice] **with lusts for flesh,** [that is,] **by means of debaucheries, those who are barely escaping from those who are living in error** [= conducting their lives erroneously], [19]**promising them** [the ones who are barely escaping] **freedom though themselves subsisting as slaves of corruption** [which, as earlier, connotes both moral and judgmental decay]. **For by what anybody has been overcome, by this he has been enslaved.** The comparison to waterless fountains means that the false teachers have nothing good to offer. But if there's no water, there's no fountain. So "waterless fountains" is something of an oxymoron which by being such underscores Peter's point (contrast John 4:14; Revelation 7:17; 21:6; Proverbs 10:11; 13:14; 14:27; 18:4). Along a similar line, mists being driven by a gale drop no rain as they pass by and therefore, like waterless fountains, don't have anything good to offer, just as false teachers don't. The combining of "pitch-blackness" with "darkness" doubles the gravity of their fate. The reservation of "the pitch-blackness of darkness" sounds like what Peter wrote about the angels that sinned (2:4), except that those angels are being kept in chains of pitch-blackness right now, whereas it's the pitch-blackness of darkness itself that has been kept for the false teachers to suffer in the future. The false teachers' eyes may be full of an adulteress; but their words, swollen with pride, are empty of truth. Nevertheless, they're able to bait Christians—that is, entice them—with the lusts for flesh in which they themselves engage, as though saying, "Come join in the fun!" The ones most liable to take the bait are "those who are barely escaping from those who are living in error." The latter are non-Christians, from morally dangerous camaraderie with whom new Christians are just now escaping (compare 1:4). The false teachers promise these new Christians freedom to return to the debaucheries they enjoyed prior to conversion. But the false teachers' own enslavement to corruption belies the promise of freedom. As Peter explains with the personification of corruption as a conqueror, to be overcome by corruption is to be enslaved rather than freed by it. For human beings weren't created to live corruptly or to suffer the corruption of eternal damnation.

2:20–21: **For if after escaping the world's pollutions through knowledge of our Lord and Savior, Jesus Christ** [compare 1:3–4], **yet they're again being overcome by getting entangled in these** [pollutions], **the last circumstances have become worse for them than the first ones** [were (compare Matthew 12:45; Luke 11:26)]. [21]**For it would have been better for them not to have known the path of righteousness than, having known** [it], **to turn back from the sacred commandment that had been given over to them.** Here we have a twice-stated and therefore highlighted reason why corruption enslaves rather than liberates. It's that apostasy puts the apostate in a worse state ("the last circumstances") than someone who never converted, so that it would have been better not to have converted in the first place. Reentanglement in the world's pollutions draws the chains of slavery tighter than they were before, because there's no possibility of reconversion or, to use Peter's metaphor, of reliberation once a person has "turned back from the sacred commandment," which he doesn't quote but which must have to do with morally upright behavior (walking "the path of righteousness"). He calls it "sacred" because Jesus issued it (3:2).

2:22: **The circumstance of the true proverb has met up with them: "A dog having returned to his own vomit; and a sow, after washing herself, to wallowing in the mud."** Peter caps his argument by quoting a proverb. It's twofold. The part about a dog comes from Proverbs 26:11, the part about a sow from some source outside Scripture. "The circumstance" is the state of affairs described in the proverb. "True" underlines the proverb's accuracy as regards the behavior of dogs and sows, and their behavior "has met up with" the apostates in the sense that the proverb applies to the apostates' behavior as well as to that of dogs and sows. Since a sow's wallowing in the mud parallels a dog's *returning* to his own vomit, the sow's having washed herself means she washed herself in the mud. Thus her wallowing in the mud represents a return to the mud, like the dog's return to his vomit. "Washing herself" is to be understood as a sarcasm, then; for a mudbath doesn't count as a washing. The sarcasm implies, in turn, that the apostates never had a washing, a true conversion—only a mudbath. And as a figure of speech for their present behavior, vomit is even more off-putting than mud.

THE SECOND COMING, FINAL DISSOLUTION, AND NEW CREATION
2 Peter 3:1–18a

In 3:1–10 Peter affirms the second coming of Jesus, the final dissolution of the universe, and the new heavens and earth. In 3:11–18a he uses this complex of events to call for godly living.

3:1–2: **Beloved, I'm now writing you this second letter, in which** [letters (plural, to include 1 Peter as well)] **I'm trying to arouse your ingenuous mind by way of a reminder** [2]**to remember the words previously spoken by the holy prophets, plus the Lord and Savior's commandment** [previously spoken by] **your apostles.** "Beloved" expresses the love of Peter for his audience (see further the comments on 1 Peter 2:11, and note the emphasis on Christians' loving one another in 1 Peter 1:22; 2:17; 2 Peter 1:7). Except for the possibility of an otherwise unknown letter, "this second letter" implies

1 Peter, in which the exhortation at 1:12–13 compares remarkably well with the present statement in 2 Peter 3:1–2. Here, as there, the use of a noun with a related verb ("by way of a *reminder* [*hypomnēsei*] to *remember*" [*mnēsthēnai*]) accentuates Peter's effort to arouse the audience's mind (see the comments on 1:12–13 for reminding as a compliment as well as an exhortation). He describes their mind as "ingenuous," that is, free of speciousness—literally, "sun-tested," but used figuratively for what we might call free of hidden agendas. In other words, just as he compliments his audience's memory, he compliments their mind, their thinking, by saying it isn't harboring the false teachers' heresy. Such a harboring would incline them not to give his letter a favorable hearing.

In opposition to the novel and therefore untrustworthy heresy of the false teachers, Peter appeals first to words previously spoken by the prophets and recorded in the Old Testament (compare 1:19–21). He calls these prophets "holy"—that is, consecrated to God as evident in their godly behavior—to contrast them with the currently misbehaving false teachers and to highlight the authority of what they ("the holy prophets") said. Then Peter appeals to Jesus' commandment relayed to Peter's audience by apostles (compare 1:16–18). This commandment was spoken and relayed more recently than the words spoken by the prophets, but it still predates the heretics' novel teaching and therefore in alliance with the prophets' words has greater reliability. Peter calls Jesus "the Lord and Savior," terms used outside Christianity for the Roman emperors, to underline the commandment's authoritativeness. The foregoing and following references to the false teachers' lustful debaucheries imply that the prophets' words and Jesus' commandment had to do with clean living. "*Your* apostles" probably refers to the traveling missionaries who evangelized the audience, rather than to the twelve original apostles (see the comments on Acts 14:4 for the wider meaning of "apostles"). That Peter reminds his audience of Jesus' commandment as relayed by their apostles probably implies that these apostles have traveled on to evangelize elsewhere.

3:3–4: [You should be] **knowing this foremost, that on the last days scoffers will come with scoffing while traveling** [a figure of speech for behaving] **in accordance with their very own lusts** [4]**and saying, "Where is the promise of his** [Jesus'] **coming? For ever since the** [fore]**fathers fell asleep** [a euphemism for dying] **all things continue in this way** [= undisturbed, as at present] **since the beginning of creation** [compare the proverb, 'The more things change, the more they stay the same'; in other words, they *don't* change]." Knowing that the proponents of a heresy were prophesied to come makes their arrival a fulfillment of prophecy which protects against their blandishments and gives assurance of a like fulfillment of the prophecy that Jesus will come again with judgment. In view of the heretical threat, which puts people's eternal fate at risk, such protective knowledge is of first and foremost importance. "On

the last days" points to the current age of the church as the period immediately preceding "the day of eternity" (3:18; compare Acts 2:17; 1 Timothy 4:1; 2 Timothy 3:1; Hebrews 1:2; 1 Peter 1:5, 20; 1 John 2:18; Jude 18 and similar but not identical references in Jeremiah 30:24; Ezekiel 38:16; Daniel 2:28; Hosea 3:5; Micah 4:1). The addition of "with scoffing" to "scoffers will come" puts emphasis on the scoffing. "While traveling in their very own lusts" suggests the false teachers' itinerancy and pairs lustful behavior with the scoffing. Thus behavioral scoffing joins verbal scoffing. "Their *very own* lusts" underlines the scoffers' accountability for lustful behavior; and the verbal scoffing cites Jesus' not yet having returned as the scoffers' basis for denying his return altogether and, absent the judgment accompanying it, for breathing easy about bad behavior. "Where is the promise of his coming?" treats the second coming as though it wasn't even promised (compare Jeremiah 17:15). The dead forefathers are ancient ancestors, parallel to the Old Testament prophets in 3:2. The false teachers argue that ever since those forefathers died, all things continue as they have "since the beginning." The addition, "of creation," describes the beginning as absolute. This argument ignores what Peter has already noted—namely, God's not sparing the angels that sinned, Noah's flood, and the judgment of Sodom and Gomorrah (2:4–6). In other words, things have *not* continued unchanged since the very beginning.

3:5–7: For this eludes them, as they *want* [it to elude them], **that by God's word the heavens have existed since long ago and** [that by God's word] **earth was composed out of water and through water,** [6]**through which** [plural, referring to "God's word" and "water"] **the onetime world, deluged with water, was destroyed.** [7]**But by the same word the current heavens and earth, being kept until the day of judgment and destruction of ungodly human beings, have been stored up for fire.** The scoffers don't want to know what they should know. Their lusts make them unwilling to know it, for knowing it would rob them of taking pleasure in their debaucheries (2:13 [contrast John 7:17]). What they should know but eludes them is that though God created the heavens by his word and since time immemorial has maintained them by his word, and though by it he brought earth out of the original watery chaos with the result that it emerged through the water so as to become dry land (Genesis 1:1–13; Psalm 33:6; 148:1–6; Hebrews 11:3), by God's word and water the antediluvian world was also *destroyed* in a flood.

"World" leaves out "the heavens," undisturbed by the flood, but includes the earth's population (except for Noah and his family) along with the earth itself. Though God promised not to destroy it again with the waters of a flood (Genesis 9:8–17), by his same judgmental as well as creative word he has stored up—that is, put in a lockbox—the current heavens and earth for destruction by fire, and is keeping them until the day of judgment and destruction by fire (compare the keeping of the sinful angels for judgment in 2:4). Here we expect to hear about the destruction of the heavens and the earth, and we will hear about that in 3:10. But because Peter is taking aim at the false teachers he puts "judgment" before "destruction" and adds "of ungodly human beings" in reference to these false teachers. So they're the ones who should fear and whom his audience should shun. Polluted by the teachers' immoralities, the current heavens and earth will have to be burned up by fire. Their being "*stored up* for fire" stresses the certainty of being burned up. Similarly, "since long ago" stresses the reliability of God's word. The "*onetime* world" stresses the pastness of the world destroyed by the flood and therefore, in turn, the certainty of a future destruction by fire.

3:8–9: Beloved, this one thing isn't to elude you, [namely], that one day [is] like a thousand years with the Lord [= so far as he's concerned], and a thousand years like one day. ⁹The Lord isn't tardy in regard to [his] promise, as some people think of tardiness [compare Habakkuk 2:3]**; rather, he's being patient toward you, not wishing that any people be destroyed—rather, that all advance to repentance.** A repetition of the address, "Beloved," adds urgency as well as affection to the following exhortation (see the comments on 3:1 and 1 Peter 2:11). "This one thing" sets up for "one day." "Isn't to elude you" seeks to save the audience from a delusion like that of the false teachers (3:5). On the basis of Psalm 90:4 ("For a thousand years in your [the Lord's] sight are like yesterday when it passes by"), Peter argues that the Lord doesn't calculate days and years in a way that would support a human notion of tardiness in bringing "the day of judgment and destruction." The Lord's "promise" is "the promise of [Jesus'] coming" (3:4), which coming will occur on that day. The "some people" who "think of tardiness" on the Lord's part are the false teachers. They mistake his patience for tardiness. So their impatience, which ends in denial and debaucheries, contrasts with his patience, which derives from his desire that nobody be destroyed but that "all," not just "some people," repent (among other passages, compare Psalm 145:8–9; Joel 2:13; Romans 2:4). Ironically, the false teachers take their extended opportunity to repent for an indication that they need *not* repent and that they may apostatize into their debaucheries with impunity and pleasure. To repent, on the contrary, would be to advance, as Peter's audience have already done according to a possible implication in the Lord's "being patient *toward* you."

3:10: But the Day of the Lord will come as a thief, on which [day] the heavens will pass away with a crackling sound and elements, being burned up, will be dissolved; and the earth and the works in it will be found. "The Day of the Lord" occurs often in the Old Testament with respect to the Lord's bringing judgment and/or salvation on various occasions. Here the phrase refers to "the day of judgment and destruction of ungodly human beings" (3:7 [see also 2:9]), when Jesus comes back (see 3:4 with 1:16). "As a thief" describes the coming of the day as unexpected—but only for the ungodly, because Peter is about to say in 3:11–13 that Christians await

the day expectantly (compare especially 1 Thessalonians 5:1–4, but also Matthew 24:43–44; Luke 12:39–40; Revelation 3:3; 16:15, though in these latter passages it's Jesus rather than the day that comes as a thief). "With a crackling sound" describes the heavens' passing away in terms of the sound made when dry wood and brush are burning. Such will be the fate of the sun, moon, stars, and planets. "Elements" probably means earth, air, fire, and water—what many ancient people thought to be the building blocks of our world. As logs disintegrate, fall apart, when burning in a fireplace or bonfire, these building blocks "will be dissolved," that is, come apart when being burned up. Then "the earth and the works in it will be found" in a judgmental conflagration just as in 3:14 Peter will contrastively speak of Christians' being "found . . . in peace without blot and without blemish" (for similar uses of being found, see 1 Peter 1:7; 2:22; Philippians 2:8; 3:9 among other passages). "The works in it [the earth]" consist of the products of human art and craftsmanship.

3:11–12: Since all these things are to be dissolved in this way, what sort of people it's necessary for you to be in holy behaviors and acts of godliness, ¹²expectantly awaiting and hastening the coming of the Day of God, because of which [day] the heavens, being incinerated, will be dissolved and the elements, being burned, melt! The length of this sentence tends to disguise its character as an exclamation. But an exclamation it is: "what sort of people it's necessary for you to be . . . !" The dissolution of "all these things" mentioned in 3:10 provides the exclamation's basis. "What sort of people" points forward to the "holy behaviors and acts of godliness" required of them. "Holy" sets these behaviors apart from and in contrast with the bad behaviors of the false teachers, and "acts of godliness" contrast with the false teachers' acts of ungodliness. The plural of "behaviors" and of "acts of godliness" counters the variety in those teachers' debaucheries, greed, fleshly lusts, and arrogance, all spelled out in chapter 2. "The Day of God" equates with "the Day of the Lord" (compare Revelation 16:14). But Peter has switched from "the Lord" to "God" in recollection of "God's word," by which—along with water—"the onetime world . . . was destroyed" (3:5–6) much as the current universe will be destroyed in fire "by the same word" (3:7). "Expectantly awaiting" the arrival of God's day arises out of not mistaking his patience for tardiness (3:8–9). "Hastening the coming of the Day of God" contrasts with the false teachers' thinking of tardiness and using it to deny the day's arrival. The word for "coming" is the same as that for Jesus' "coming" in 1:16; 3:2–4, for God's day will come when Jesus comes. Christians' godly behavior hastens its coming (compare Acts 3:19–21), and hastening its coming in this way contrasts sharply with the false teachers' indulging their lusts in the meantime. The incineration of the heavens explains why they'll "pass away with a crackling sound" and makes their dissolution correspond to that of the "elements" (see 3:10 with comments). The melting of the elements as a result of burning gives another take on their dissolution (compare Micah 1:4). The present tense of "melt" portrays the action as so certain to take place that it might as well be taking place right now. So much for the false teachers' denial!

3:13: But in accordance with his promise we expectantly await "new heavens and a new earth [Isaiah 65:17; 66:22; Revelation 21:1]**," in which righteousness resides.** Expectant waiting rests on God's promise. Earlier, the promise had to do with Jesus' coming (3:4, 9). Here it has to do with "new heavens and a new earth," because Jesus' coming will usher in new heavens and a new earth. We expect Peter to write that godly, righteous people will reside there. Instead, he personifies "righteousness" and writes that it resides there. As a result, a heavy accent falls on exclusion of the behavior that characterizes the false teachers. They'll have an address elsewhere.

3:14–16: Because of which, beloved—[that is,] be**cause you're expectantly awaiting these things—be diligent to be found by him in peace without blot and without blemish;** [15]**and regard the patience of our Lord as salvation, just as also our beloved brother Paul wrote to you in accordance with the wisdom given to him,** [16]**as also in all** [his] **letters, speaking in them about these things, in which** [letters] **are some things hard to understand, which things the unlearned and unstable distort, as** [they distort] **the remaining Scriptures too, with the result of their very own destruction.** For the third time in chapter 3 Peter addresses his audience with "beloved" (see 3:1, 8 and the comments on 1 Peter 2:11). "Because of which" looks backward to 3:13, but for emphasis Peter repeats the thought with "because you're expectantly awaiting these things." The "new heavens and a new earth" of 3:13 constitute "these things." "Be diligent" harks back to the command in 1:10 that the audience "be diligent to make sure for [them]selves [their] calling and selection." Only this time Peter puts the matter in terms of "be[ing] found by him [the Lord] in peace [= the blessings of salvation (see the comments on 1:2)] without blot and without blemish [terms used in the Old Testament to describe animals fit for sacrifice, but used here for moral rectitude (compare 1 Peter 1:19; Hebrews 9:14; Jude 24 among other passages) in contrast with the false teachers, whom Peter described in 2:13 as 'blots and blemishes']." Being found in peace without moral defect will occur at Jesus' coming, just as the earth's and its works' being found in conflagration will occur then. Instead of mistaking the Lord's patience for tardiness and a license to indulge in debaucheries, as the false teachers do, Peter's audience are to "regard the patience of our Lord as salvation," that is, as an extended opportunity for others than themselves to be saved (3:9).

Since "our Lord" means the Lord of Peter and his audience, "our beloved brother Paul" probably means Paul as a beloved brother of Peter and his audience (rather than excluding his audience in favor of his associates or fellow apostles). Paul's having written to Peter's audience

qualifies Paul as beloved to them, and Peter's inclusion of himself adds to this reflection of mutual love among fellow Christians (compare 1:7; 1 Peter 1:22; 2:17; 4:8; 5:14). "Beloved" occurs here for the fourth time in chapter 3. "All his letters" refers to however many Paul had written at the time and to however many Peter was aware of. He cites Paul's letters and describes them as containing "wisdom given to him [by God, it's understood]" to support the contents of his own letter (2 Peter). Peter says that "the unlearned and unstable distort some things" in Paul's letters that "are . . . hard to understand." This statement suggests that the distortion consisted in using Paul's doctrine of freedom from the Old Testament law to support the false teachers' licentious lifestyle. On the other hand, this distortion neglects Paul's emphases on not behaving in accordance with the flesh—rather, in accordance with the Spirit (see Galatians 5:13–25, for example)—and on the coming judgment as a motivation for godly behavior (see Romans 13:11–14; 14:10–12; 2 Corinthians 5:9–10; Galatians 5:10, for example; also Romans 2:4 for God's patience as leading to repentance). By describing these things as "hard to understand," Peter enables himself to describe the false teachers as too "unlearned and unstable" to understand anything difficult (compare their "expressing themselves in empty pomposities" [2:18]). Their distortion of "the remaining Scriptures too" has to do with the Old Testament, to which Peter has repeatedly appealed (1:19–21; 2:4–9, 15–16, 22; 3:2, 5–6), and implies that Paul's letters carry similar authority. "Their *very own* destruction" stresses that the false teachers won't escape it.

3:17–18a: You therefore, beloved, since you know [these things] **beforehand, guard yourselves lest being led away by the error of the unprincipled** [false teachers] **you fall out of your own stability.** [18a]**But be growing in grace and the knowledge of our Lord, Jesus Christ.** For the fifth time in this chapter Peter uses "beloved" (see the comments on 3:1; 1 Peter 2:11). An emphatic "you" puts Peter's audience over against "the unlearned and unstable" false teachers (3:16). "Therefore" signals the contrast between the false teachers' ignorance and the audience's knowledge. As in 3:14, "these things" are the new heavens and new earth that will replace the incinerated current heavens and earth. Knowing these things beforehand gives reason to guard against the apostasy of embracing the false teachers' error. Peter calls this apostasy "fall[ing] out of your own stability." Falling implies an elevated status for stability and a low status for apostasy. Who would want a drop in status? According to 1:12 Peter's audience are presently stable in their knowledge of the truth. Here, "your own" underlines this stability and thereby pays them a compliment that implies Peter doesn't expect them to fall out of their stability. Since people tend to rise to the level of what's expected of them, addition of the compliment strengthens the exhortation. Growing in grace means increasing in God's favor because of good behavior (see 1 Peter 2:2, 18–20). Growing in "the knowledge of our Lord, Jesus Christ" means increasing in the truth about him and his command to live righteously, as opposed to the error of the false teachers (2:21; 3:2). "*Be* growing" implies that salvation requires ongoing growth as evidence of authentic faith (1:2–11).

A DOXOLOGY
2 Peter 3:18b

3:18b: To him [belongs] **the glory both now and for the day of eternity.** "He" is "our Lord and Savior, Jesus Christ," just mentioned. A doxology for him implies his deity, which 1:1 indicated outright: "our *God* and Savior, Jesus Christ." Peter ascribes to him glory "now" in the good behavior of Christians (contrast 2:2 but compare 1 Peter 2:11–12). And Peter ascribes to him glory, probably from God the Father, "for the day of eternity" (see 1:17; 1 Peter 1:21; 4:11, 13; 5:1). The description of eternity as a "day" means that for the Lord a day may stretch out even longer than a thousand years (compare 3:8).

FIRST JOHN

Early in church history there arose a heresy called Gnosticism. According to a basic premise of Gnosticism, physical matter is inherently evil. So to avoid tarnishing Jesus Christ with evil some Gnostics taught that he was a phantom. He only seemed to have a physical body (the doctrine of docetism, so called after the Greek verb *dokein*, "to seem"). Other Gnostics taught that Christ, a divine spirit, differed from Jesus, a human being with a physical body, and descended on Jesus immediately after Jesus' baptism but left him just before his death on a cross, so that the divine spirit Christ underwent neither a physical birth nor a physical resurrection, both of which would have entailed participation in the evil inherent in physicality (the doctrine of Cerinthianism, so called after a Gnostic teacher named Cerinthus). Since Gnostics didn't consider their bodies a part of their true selves, some of them gave their bodies free rein to engage in sinful conduct. The true selves, consisting of their spirits, would bear no guilt and thus remain sinless. Or so they thought. And since they prided themselves on secret knowledge about such matters ("Gnostic" means "knower"), they disdained orthodox Christians, whom they considered ignorant, and separated from them. Over against the foregoing features of Gnosticism, 1 John emphasizes righteous conduct, love for fellow believers, and belief in the incarnation of God's Son in the indivisible person Jesus Christ. These emphases have the purpose of encouraging the author's audience to resist the blandishments of Gnostic teachers.

First John has no introductory address, greeting from the author, or concluding salutations. Yet numerous references to writing rule out a merely recorded oral sermon. The repeated affectionate address, "my children," implies an audience well known to the Apostle John, to whose authorship early church tradition assigns the book; and according to this tradition he lived in Ephesus during his old age. So 1 John is probably a tract for circulation among Christians in the region surrounding Ephesus (compare Paul's circular letter called "Ephesians"). John states clearly his purposes of strengthening their knowledge, joy, and assurance in true Christian faith (1:3–4; 5:13) over against Gnostic falsehoods (2:1–29; 4:1–21).

THE EAR-, EYE-, AND HAND-WITNESSED INCARNATION OF GOD IN JESUS CHRIST AS THE BASIS FOR CHRISTIAN FELLOWSHIP
1 John 1:1–4

1:1–2: What was from [= since] **the beginning, what we've heard, what we've seen with our eyes,** **what we observed and our hands felt—**[we're writing] **about the Word of life,** [2]**and the life was manifested** [= made visible], **and we've seen** [the life] **and are testifying to** [the life] **and announcing to you the eternal life, who as such was with the Father and was manifested to us.** John writes about a "what" that was not only original and audible, but also visible, tangible, present with God the Father, and eternally alive. So the "what" is a who, none other than the Word who according to John 1:1–4 was in the beginning with God and had life in himself. But why "what" instead of "who"? Answer: Whereas "who" would have stressed the Word's personal identity, "what" stresses the Word's qualities of preexistence ("from the beginning . . . with the Father"), communicativeness ("the Word" as "heard"), visibility ("seen . . . observed . . . manifested . . . manifested"), tangibility ("felt"), vitality ("the life"), and eternality ("the *eternal* life"). "*In* the beginning" (John 1:1–3) stressed existence already at creation, that is, preexistence. Here, "*from* the beginning" stresses ongoing existence in addition to preexistence and thus prepares for an equation of the Word with "the *eternal* life." The Word was "heard" in that he "explained" God (John 1:18). The Word was "seen" in that he "became flesh and tented among us" (John 1:14). Over against Gnostic denials of the incarnation, the additions of "with our eyes" and "observed" stress physical sight of a physical object (compare, for example, John 6:40); and "our hands felt" stresses physicality likewise. "Of life" describes "the Word" as both living (compare John 5:26; 11:25; 14:6) and life-giving (compare especially John 5:21, but also 3:15–16, 36; 5:24; 6:63, 68 among other passages). "The life was manifested" recalls Jesus' manifesting himself as resurrected back to life in John 21:1, 14. For similar combinations of seeing and testifying to what was seen, note John 1:34; 3:11, 32; 19:35. Since "the eternal life . . . was with the Father" as "the Word" was "with the Father" in John 1:1, "who" fits better a reference to "the eternal life" than "which" would. And "as such" underlines the attributes of "the Word" as living, life-giving, and eternal. "With the Father" implies that "the eternal life" is none other than the Son of God, and confirms that "the eternal life" is a "who," not a "which." "We" and "us" refer to John and his fellow eyewitnesses, earwitnesses, and touch-witnesses of the Son of God's incarnate ministry. Though the other foundational witnesses have probably all died by the time John writes, his including them with himself enhances the reliability of his written testimony.

1:3–4: What we've seen and heard we're announcing even to you in order that you too may have fellowship with us; and also our fellowship [is] with the Father and with his Son, Jesus Christ. ⁴And we're writing these things in order that our joy may be filled up. "What we've seen and heard" redoubles John's emphasis on the eye- and earwitnessed qualities of the Word of life's historical visibility and audibility. "*Even* to you" and "you *too*" emphasize the privilege of John's audience in sharing—through the foundational witnesses' "announc[ment]"—the eternal life's manifestation to those witnesses. This manifestation, in turn, constituted the foundational witnesses' sharing the eternal life and, through him ("the eternal life"), sharing God his Father as well (compare John 14:8–11). Finally, "Jesus Christ" identifies God's Son with an historical figure (compare the delayed identification of "the Word" with Jesus Christ in John 1:1–17). The combination of "Jesus" with "Christ" also speaks against the aforementioned Cerinthian distinction between a physically human Jesus and a spiritually divine Christ. The "fellowship" that John talks about consists in a communicative sharing of the Word of life's incarnation. Involved in this sharing are John's audience, John himself, other foundational witnesses, God's Son Jesus Christ, and God the Father. The sharing brings joy, and writing about it has the purpose of filling John and his fellow foundational witnesses with the joy of sharing their testimony (compare John 3:29; 8:56; 15:11; 16:20–24; 17:13; 20:20; 2 John 12). "*We're* writing" includes those witnesses besides John, as though they're testifying along with him despite being dead. His testimony incorporates theirs too.

RIGHTEOUS CONDUCT
1 John 1:5–2:6

1:5: And this is the message that we've heard from him [Jesus Christ] and are announcing to you, that God is light and [that] in him there's no darkness at all. As "the *Word* of Life" (1:1) Jesus Christ conveys a "message." Appropriately to his being God's "Son" (1:2–3), his message concerns "God." "We've heard from him and are announcing to you" reinforces John's earlier appeal to his and his colleagues' having earwitnessed "the Word of life." Whereas "the *life* was the light of human beings" in John 1:4, here "*God* is light" (compare Revelation 21:23; 22:5). So light now stands for the character of God *in himself* rather than for the manifestation of God *through his Son* (as in John 1:4). "In him [God] there's no darkness at all" describes God's character by way of a denial. Since darkness is associated with "evil deeds/works" (John 3:19–20) and light with "good deeds/works" (see John 10:32 with John 9:3–5), light describes God's character as good; and the total absence of darkness in him describes his character as untainted by evil. These descriptions of his character prepare for moral descriptions of true Christians and false ones and for definitions of good and evil in terms of love and hate. But when did John and the other foundational witnesses

hear from Jesus Christ the message that "God is light and [that] in him there's no darkness at all"? In none of the Gospels is Jesus quoted as using these words. In John 8:46, however, he's quoted as saying, "Who of you convicts me of sin?" and in John 10:30–32 he refers to "many good deeds/works" that he has shown "from the Father." These statements amount to saying that God is light (in that Jesus' good deeds derived from the Father) and that in God there's no darkness at all (in that Jesus, who embodied God his Father, had no sin, no evil deeds, to be convicted of).

1:6–7: If we say, "We're having fellowship with him [God]," and are walking around in the darkness, we're lying and not doing the truth. To have fellowship with God is to share with him his Son Jesus Christ. Walking around stands for conduct. So "walking around in the darkness" means doing evil deeds. Since God is light, walking around in the darkness falsifies our saying that we're having fellowship with him. In other words, then, we don't have a share with him in his Son. "Not doing the truth" equates with "walking around in the darkness" and shows that the truth is to be performed in good deeds, not just believed in good words (compare John 3:21). And the truth has to do with God's character as manifest in Jesus the Word (John 1:14, 17; 14:6; 1 John 5:20). **⁷But if we're walking around in the light as he himself [God] is in the light, we're having fellowship with one another; and the blood of Jesus his Son is cleansing us from every sin.** Since "God is light" (1:5), to walk around in the light is to do good deeds *in him* (compare John 3:21: "But the one who is doing the truth comes to the light in order that his deeds may be manifested [to the effect] that they were done *in God*," which is to say that they come to the light for the express purpose of having their deeds shown to have had their genesis in God rather than in any natural human ability [see also numerous later references to having been "born out of God," plus John 1:13; 3:3–7]). But if "God *is* light," how can he be "*in* the light"? It's as though his good character is the aura which surrounds him and in which, therefore, we can walk around. Moreover, God is "*in* the light" because he's in his Son Jesus Christ, who *is* the light (John 1:4–5, 7–9; 8:12; 10:38; 14:10–11; 17:21, 23). "Fellowship with one another" means, then, sharing Jesus Christ in common with other true believers, because he's the light in whom they too walk around. But to keep us in this light, where God is, "the blood of Jesus his Son" has to "cleans[e] us from every sin." For sin is represented by darkness, which doesn't exist in God "at all" (1:5). "From *every* sin" underscores thoroughness of cleansing and corresponds to the "*at all*" of the non-existence of darkness in God. Ordinarily, blood stains. But because Jesus' blood, though disdained by Gnostics because of its physicality, is sacrificial for the taking away of sin (John 1:29; 19:34), it acts as a cleansing agent (Revelation 7:14), perhaps even as an interior cleansing agent since—figuratively speaking in regard to faith—it has to be drunk (John 6:53–56).

1:8–10: **If we say, "We don't have sin** [as Gnostics are prone to say, because they regard sinful deeds, done in their physical bodies, as detached from their true, spiritual selves]**," we're misleading ourselves and the truth isn't in us.** So truth is supposed to *reside* in us in order that we may *do* it (1:6 [compare statements in John 14:6; 15:4; 17:23 that *Jesus* is the truth and resides in believers; also the comments on 2:4]. And the claim to sinlessness, and therefore to having no need for Jesus' blood to cleanse us from every sin, amounts to self-deception. We *do* have sin from which we need to be cleansed. And such self-deception will keep us from doing what we need to do to gain the cleansing—will keep us, that is, from confessing our sins. ⁹**If we confess our sins, he** [God] **is faithful and righteous, with the result that he forgives** [our] **sins for us and cleanses us from every** [act of] **unrighteousness.** To confess our sins is to say the same thing God says about them: they're evil and therefore need to be forgiven and forsaken. God *always* forgives our confessed sins (hence "faithful") and forgives them *rightly* (hence "righteous"). Given Jesus' sacrificial blood, shed to take away sin, it would be unfaithful and wrong of God not to forgive them. To forgive them is to make them go away from us, and "*for* us" highlights the advantage to us of their departure. "Cleanses" equates with "forgives," and "unrighteousness" with "sins." "Cleanses us from *every* [act of] unrighteousness" recalls "cleanses us from *every* sin" in 1:7 and reemphasizes thoroughness of cleansing. As Jesus' blood is the agent of cleansing, God is the launderer in that he's the forgiver. (In Revelation 7:14 the *redeemed* "have washed their robes . . . in the blood of the lamb," so that there the accent shifts from divine forgiveness to human faith.) ¹⁰**If we say, "We haven't sinned," we make him a liar, and his Word isn't in us.** Again John attacks the Gnostic claim to sinlessness. Such a claim makes God a liar in the sense of treating him as though he's a liar in declaring us sinful by sending his Son to take away the world's sin (John 1:29 again). "*His* Word" makes "the Word of life" (1:1) God's own in the person of his Son, Jesus the Word (1:3). "In us" refers then to Jesus Christ as God's Word indwelling us—unless we treat God as a liar by claiming a sinlessness that eliminates the need for confession, cleansing, and forgiveness. And not to have Jesus Christ as God's Word in us is not to be true Christians.

2:1–2: **My children, I'm writing to you in order that you not sin. And if anyone** [of you] **sins, we have with the Father a righteous representative, Jesus Christ.** ²**And he himself is the expiation for our sins, and not only for ours but also for** [those] **of the whole world.** Most translations have "*little* children" instead of "children." But elsewhere John uses diminutive nouns without reference to small size (as when, for example, he interchanges diminutive and nondiminutive words for sheep in John 21:15–17). "My children" remains an endearing address, however. John writes to forestall our sinning. But in 1:8, 10 he contradicted the Gnostic claim to sinlessness and therefore adds here that in the case of our sinning (and confessing our sin, it's to be assumed

from 1:9), Jesus Christ stands as our representative (see the comments on John 14:16 for "representative"). "With the Father" makes Jesus Christ's representing us effective where it counts. As God the Father is righteous to forgive and cleanse us (1:9), Jesus Christ is righteous so as to present us as righteous *in himself* (compare our abiding in him according to 2:24, 28; 3:6; John 15:4–7). As righteous, furthermore, Jesus stands in the Father's presence as the expiation for our sins. For Jesus' blood, which *cleanses* away every sin so far as we're concerned, *atoned* for our sins so far as the righteous God is concerned.[1] "Also for [the sins] of the whole world" leaves the door of forgiveness and cleansing open for all who will believe and confess (compare John 1:29; 3:16). "World" means the mass of sinful humanity.

2:3–6: **And by this we know that we've come to know him** [God]: **if we keep his commandments.** So obeying God's commandments brings us the knowledge (in the sense of assurance) that we know him (in the sense of being intimately and favorably acquainted with him). John is putting this true knowledge, which arises out of good behavior, over against Gnostics' false knowledge, which flaunts bad behavior. Though for the moment "to know him" could refer to knowing Jesus Christ (mentioned just recently in 2:1–2), 3:22–24 will identify the commandments as God's and therefore him as the object of knowledge. ⁴**The person who says, "I've come to know him," and isn't keeping his commandments is a liar; and the truth isn't in this person.** So disobedience to God's commands exposes both ignorance of God himself and falsehood in the claim to know him. The claimant is "a liar" precisely because "the truth isn't in him." In this regard he's incapable of telling the truth. And since 5:20 will identify Jesus Christ as "the *true* one" and "the *true* God," we may have here in 2:4 an indication that Jesus Christ is himself the truth which isn't in the liar (compare the comments on 1:8 [see also John 14:6]). ⁵**But whoever is keeping his word—in this person God's love has truly been completed.** "Keeping his word" equates with "keeping his commandments" (2:4). But since 1:1 has called Jesus Christ "the Word of life" and 1:10 has denied that God's "Word" exists in anybody who claims to be sinless, it appears that Jesus the Word personifies the word of God that consists in commandments. The relating of God's love to his word anticipates the manifestation of that love in the sending of his Son into the world for our salvation (4:7–10). Similarly, the interrelating of obedience to his word and the completion of his love anticipates the command to love one another in the Christian community (2:7–11; 3:11–24;

---

[1]Sins are expiated (that is, paid for, made amends for), whereas an angry person is propitiated (that is, appeased). In Romans 1:18–3:26 God himself is said to have put forth Christ Jesus as "a propitiation" to appease his own (God's) anger against human sin. Here in 1 John 2:2 sins are mentioned but God's anger goes unmentioned, so that "expiation" becomes a better translation than "propitiation" for the same word that occurs in Romans 3:25.

4:7–12, 15–5:3). God's love for us reaches completion when—and only when, as implied by "truly"—Christians extend it by loving one another. **By this** [that is, by keeping his word (compare 2:3)] **we know** [again in the sense of having assurance] **that we're in him. ⁶The person who says** [he] **is abiding in him ought also himself to be walking around just as that one** [Jesus Christ] **walked around.** So *being* in God equates with *abiding* in him, and "abiding in" carries the double connotation of staying ("*abiding* in") and closeness ("abiding *in*"). This connotation strikes out against heretics such as the Gnostics, who by departing from orthodox faith and practice exit not only from the true Christian community but also from God himself. Anyone who claims to abide in God has therefore the obligation of behaving just as Jesus Christ behaved ("that one [over there]" distinguishing him from God, just mentioned).

MUTUAL CHRISTIAN LOVE
1 John 2:7–17

2:7: Beloved, I'm not writing to you a new commandment—rather, an old commandment, which you've had from the beginning. The old commandment is the word that you've heard. "Beloved" expresses the love of John for his audience of fellow believers. But in view of his reference in 2:5 to God's love for us and the statement to come in 4:19 that "we love, because he [God] first loved us," the address "Beloved" also means "You who are loved by God." His love sets a divine example of the love for one another that John is about to command. Without yet identifying the command, John describes it as an old rather than new commandment. People in biblical times valued the old much more than most moderns do. So John's description of the commandment as old lends it weight, the weight of tradition and reliability over against a newfangled, hate-filled heresy like Gnosticism (compare 2 John 9). The commandment is old in that it goes back to Jesus himself (John 13:34–35; 15:12–13, 17). The commandment is old also in that John's audience "have had [it] from the beginning," that is, since their conversions. For they certainly didn't *have* it or *hear* it prior to their entrance into the Christian community. But they've heard it as "the word" ever since that entrance. Because Jesus issued the commandment, it's "the word" of "the Word."

2:8: Again, I'm writing to you a new commandment, which is true in him and in you, because the darkness is passing away and the true light is already shining. "Again" picks up the topic of the commandment for consideration from a different standpoint. Though old in that it goes back to Jesus and has been had and heard by believers ever since their conversions, Jesus himself described it as new (see John 13:34–35 again). It's new in that it replaces "as [you love] yourself" (Leviticus 19:18) with "just as I [Jesus] have loved you" (John 13:34–35 yet again; see also John 13:1 ["he loved them to the end"]; 15:13–14 ["No one has greater love than this, that someone lay down his life for his loved ones (usu-

ally translated 'friends'). You're my loved ones if you do the things I command you"]). In John's Greek, "which" is neuter, whereas its referent, "a new commandment," is feminine. But the neuter gender of "which" emphasizes the quality of newness in the commandment. "Which is true in him" means that Jesus exemplified the commandment in the self-sacrifice he made for his loved ones. "Which is true . . . in you" means that John's audience have likewise exemplified the commandment in self-sacrifices for one another. They've *done* truth by keeping the commandment (compare 1:6). The passing away of the darkness and the shining already of the light hardly supply the reason for the commandment's *truthfulness*. So the passing away and the shining probably supply the reason for John's *writing* a new commandment. Because of Jesus' first and second comings, the old age of hate, represented by the disappearing darkness, is in the process of passing away, going into oblivion, becoming irrelevant. The new age of love, represented by the shining light, has already started. It can be seen in the love of true Christians for one another and in Jesus' love for them. This light is "true" in that it's the ultimate light that all other lights merely point to (John 1:6–9; 5:33–35) or, like the sun, represent (John 8:12; 9:4–5; 11:9–10). Better not secede from the light-filled community of love and enter the dark, heretical community of hate, then. For otherwise you'll pass away with the darkness into which you've entered.

2:9–11: The person who says he's in the light and hates his brother is in the darkness till now. ¹⁰The person who loves his brother abides in the light, and there's not a cause of stumbling in it [that is, in the light]. **¹¹The person who hates his brother is in the darkness and is walking around in the darkness and doesn't know where he's going, because the darkness has blinded his eyes.** As in chapter 1, "the light" is Jesus Christ, God's Son. Hating and loving will be defined in 3:10–18, 23; 4:7–11. Meanwhile John sets hating a brother against being in the light and equates such hate with being in the darkness. "His brother" means a fellow believer. John is warning his audience not to turn into heretical haters of believers in the community they once counted their own. "Is in the darkness *till now*" means that such an apostate is still in the darkness and despite former appearances has always been in it. He never was in the light (compare 2:19: "They went out from us, but they weren't *of* us. For if they'd been *of* us, they'd have stayed *with* us [and so on]"). By contrast, the brother-loving person "abides [= stays] in the light." There's no abiding in the light apart from brotherly love, and no brotherly love apart from abiding in the light. Furthermore, only in the light does Jesus' blood cleanse us from every sin (1:7). Walking around stands for behaving. So walking around in the darkness stands for behaving toward a brother hatefully. Hate isn't limited to attitude, for attitude affects behavior as well as vice versa. The walker in darkness "doesn't *know* where he's going." So much for the Gnostics' claim to superior knowledge! John is declaring that the heretics are going to hell without knowing they are. As represented by darkness and exemplified by hate, evil blinds people to their disastrous destiny.

2:12–14: I'm writing to you, children, because/ that [your] sins have been forgiven for you on account of his name. [13]**I'm writing to you, fathers, because/ that you've come to know him who [was] from the beginning. I'm writing to you, young men, because/ that you've conquered the evil one** [Satan (compare 3:12; 5:18–19; John 17:15; Matthew 6:13)]**. I've written to you, children, because/that you've come to know the Father.** [14]**I've written to you, fathers, because/ that you've come to know him who [was] from the beginning. I've written to you, young men, because/ that you're strong and God's Word abides in you and you've conquered the evil one.** With "children" John addresses all his audience affectionately again. (He's an old man, as indicated by his calling himself "the elder" in 2 John 1; 3 John 1.) In line with the dominance of males in first-century Mediterranean culture, "fathers" and "young men" then select out the male segments of John's audience and divide them agewise, fathers first out of respect for their seniority. Right after these addresses there occurs a Greek word that can be translated equally well with "because" or "that," depending on the context. Here, "because" suits the context by introducing complimentary *reasons* for John's writing. But the compliments embedded in these reasons make "that" suitable for introducing also the *content* of John's writing. Hence a splicing of "that" to "because." Together, the reasons and the compliments tell John's audience they *shouldn't* apostatize over to Gnostic heresy because they don't *need* to: (1) The children already have their sins forgiven. (2) The fathers have already come to know him who was from the beginning. (3) The young men have already conquered the evil one. (4) The children have already come to know the Father. (5) The fathers have already come to know him who was from the beginning. (6) The young men are strong, have God's Word abiding in them, and have already conquered the evil one. John's audience shouldn't apostatize, because they already have all they need, and apostatizing would make them lose what they have.

"On account of his name" grounds the forgiveness of sins in Jesus' cleansing blood (1:7), as opposed to the Gnostic notion of a sinless divine spark within Gnostics. "Him who [was] from the beginning" identifies the bearer of that name as "the Word of life," who became incarnate in Jesus Christ, and confirms that "*What* was from the beginning" (1:1) emphasized the eternality of "the life" embodied in the indivisible *person*, Jesus Christ. As to the name, it's the one he shares with his Father, that is, "God" (see John 17:11–12 with 1 John 5:20; also John 1:18; 20:28). This name encapsulates the incarnate God's saving of believers by cleansing them from their sins. Since fathers antedate children, it suits fathers to have come to know "him who [was] *from the beginning.*" There's no need for them to become Gnostic knowers, for they already have the knowledge requisite for salvation.

Since young men constitute a fighting force, it's suitable for John to write that they've already conquered Satan, the evil one (compare 4:4; 5:4; John 16:33 and numerous passages in the book of Revelation). So the young men needn't gravitate to a Gnostic doctrine of escaping at death from the inherently evil world of physical matter.

For emphasis on the foregoing round of assurances, John repeats the sequence and switches from "I'm writing" (present tense) to "I've written" (past tense, referring to the foregoing round). His fondness for synonyms shows up in the use of a different Greek word for "children." This address is still endearing, though. Forgiveness of sins (as in the foregoing round) gives way to "hav[ing] come to know the Father." Calling God "the Father" suits calling the audience "children," for they're God's children as well as John's. And knowing the Father already—this knowledge eliminates any need to seek out the falsely called knowledge offered by Gnostic heretics. The addressing of human fathers follows naturally after a reference to God the Father. As in the foregoing round, the object of the fathers' knowledge is "him who [was] from the beginning." This repetition reinforces John's anti-Gnostic thrust. The physical strength of the young men stands for their strength in orthodox Christian faith. They needn't capitulate to heresy. The abiding of God's Word (incarnate in Jesus Christ) does away with any need to go after a heretical word/message. And just as the young men are strong because of the abiding of God's Word in them, they've conquered the evil one because they're strong (see the earlier comments on this conquest). Mention of the evil one now leads into a discussion of "the world," dominated as it is by him (5:19).

2:15–17: Don't be loving the world or the things in the world. If anyone is loving the world, the love of the Father isn't in him, [16]**because everything in the world—**[namely,] **the lust of the flesh and the lust of the eyes and the braggadocio of livelihood—isn't from the Father; rather, it's from the world** [= has its origin in the world rather than in the Father]. [17]**And the world is passing away, also its lust** [is passing away]. **But the person who's doing God's will abides forever.** Since "the things in the world" consist in lusts and braggadocio—characteristics of human beings—"the world" consists of human beings. The distinction between "the *things* in the world" and the world itself confirms that the world consists of human beings. And according to 3:1, 6; John 1:10 the world hasn't known God or his Son Jesus. But Christians do know them (2:12–14; 4:6–7; John 17:3). So "the world" includes only non-Christians. Astonishingly, then, John commands Christians not to love non-Christians. In his writings (John, 1–3 John, Revelation) only God loved the world (John 3:16). Not even Jesus is said to have loved them. And God loved them by way of sending his one-and-only Son for the salvation of believers, whom God has given to him from out of the world, so that they're no longer worldlings (4:9–10; John 3:16–17; 17:6). And given their not being "from the world" just as Jesus wasn't "from the world," they never were worldlings (John 15:19; 17:14, 16).

Why not love the world consisting of worldlings? Because loving them will lead to catching by contagion their lusts and braggadocio. "Lusts" means desires so strong as to result in the transgression of boundaries that God has set around legitimate desires. Flesh and eyes do the lusting. "The lust of the flesh" consists in an excessive desire to enjoy things (avid pleasure-seeking). "The lust of the eyes" consists in an excessive desire to have things (avid acquisitiveness). And "the braggadocio of livelihood" consists in showing off one's material successes (conspicuous consumption), such boastfulness being common in the first-century Mediterranean culture of honor and shame. These lusts and this braggadocio don't derive from God the Father, because he isn't the Father of worldlings. They're born from the Devil and the flesh (3:8, 10; John 3:6; 8:44), not from above, God, and the Holy Spirit (2:29; 3:9; 4:7; 5:1, 4, 18; John 1:13; 3:3–8). These lusts and this braggadocio derive from the world, so that nonworldlings (that is, Christians) shouldn't love worldlings. Only God can love them without getting tainted with their lusts and braggadocio. Since Jesus sent his disciples into the world as the Father sent him into the world (John 17:18; 20:21), Christians are to follow Jesus' example of bearing witness to worldlings without loving either them or their sinful characteristics. We might be tempted to interpret John as meaning that Christians should love sinners but not their sins. But John writes that Christians should love neither, and even that loving the world excludes loving the Father. You can't love both. "The love of the Father" can mean love *for* the Father, love *from* the Father, or both. Since Jesus said he loves the Father (John 14:31), might the nonresidence of love for the Father "in" worldlings suggest that as the embodiment of that love Jesus himself doesn't reside in them? If so, we could treat "the love of the Father" as another designation of Jesus, like "the Word of life" and "the eternal life" (1:1–2).

The passing away of the world doesn't refer to the passing away of the physical universe (for which see Revelation 20:11; 21:1). It refers to the passing away of the worldlings who make up "the world." Not that they'll cease to exist; rather, they're going into oblivion and becoming irrelevant, just as the darkness in which they're walking around is thus passing away (2:8). The world's "lust" (a collective singular for the lust of the flesh, the lust of the eyes, and the braggadocio of livelihood) is passing away along with the world and darkness. None of the three will have a place in the new heaven and new earth (Revelation 21:1–22:5); and they're already on their way out, just as "the true light is *already* shining" (2:8). In contrast, the doer of "God's will," which is not to love the world or its lusty and boastful "things," "abides forever"—that is, stays throughout eternity in the aura of God's light.

INCARNATIONAL CHRISTOLOGY
1 John 2:18–27

2:18–19: Children, it's the last hour; and just as you heard Antichrist is coming, even now many antichrists have come on the scene, from which fact we know that it's the last hour. **¹⁹They went out from us, but they weren't of us.** They've shown their true colors. **For if they'd been of us** [that is, had their true origin among us], **they'd have stayed** [= abode] **with us. But** [they went out from us] **with the result that they've been manifested** [in a disclosure] **that they all aren't of us** [= that *none* of them really belonged in our community]. The endearing address, "Children," signals a new topic. In John 4:21, 23; 5:25, 28–29; 16:2, 4 Jesus spoke of "an hour" that "is coming and now is" (1) when true worshipers will worship the Father in Spirit and truth rather than on Mount Gerizim or in Jerusalem; (2) when the dead will hear the voice of God's Son and live; and (3) when believers in Jesus will suffer martyrdom. Such features characterize the hour as "the last" in that whatever its length, it immediately precedes "the Last Day" (John 6:39–40, 44, 54; 11:24; 12:48). John and his audience are living in that hour. Antichrist will come during it. But John uses him only as a springboard for introducing "many antichrists" who've already appeared on the scene. Since in their opposition to Christ (signified by "anti-") they prefigure Antichrist, whose appearance is well-known to herald the end, their appearance guarantees that "the last hour" has already arrived and is in process. These antichrists are none other than Gnostics, whose false teachings oppose the truth about Christ and therefore Christ *as* the truth (compare 2 John 7). Their secession from orthodox Christians evinced a lack of love for them, exemplified an attitude of superiority based on supposedly advanced knowledge, and provided a visible demonstration that the secessionists never belonged among orthodox Christians in the first place.

2:20–21: And you have an anointing from the Holy One, and you all know—²¹I haven't written to you because/that you don't know the truth—rather, because/that you do know it and because/that every lie isn't [= no lie is] **from the truth.** "Anointing" is related to "Christ," which means "Anointed One." He was anointed not with olive oil, as were the ancient kings of Israel, but with the Holy Spirit, who "descend[ed] like a dove out of heaven and . . . abode on him" (John 1:32). On the evening of the first Easter Sunday Jesus "breathed into [his original disciples] and tells them, 'Receive the Holy Spirit'" (John 20:22). And John 6:69 designates Jesus "the Holy One of God." Therefore, "you have an anointing from the Holy One" means that as God's Holy One, Jesus has anointed John's audience with the Holy Spirit just as God anointed him (Jesus) with the Holy Spirit (compare John 15:26: "whom I'll send to you from alongside the Father, the Spirit of the truth, who proceeds out from alongside the Father"; also 16:7). In anticipation of 2:27, where John will write that "his anointing [= the anointing which Jesus gives] teaches you about all things," John here writes "you all know" to stress that no true Christian needs the falsely called knowledge which Gnostics tout (compare Jeremiah 31:34). But before telling *what* all his audience know, John interrupts the sentence to assure them he hasn't written to them either because or that they don't know the truth. For if they were to infer that he has written *because* they don't know it or has written *that* they don't know it, they'd be tempted to think the Gnostics do have something they need to know (see the comments on 2:15–17 for "because/that"). On the contrary, he assures them further, they do know the truth. Moreover, they know that the truth doesn't engender lies. "Every lie" alludes to the false doctrines of Gnostics, and it finally comes out that "the truth" is what "you all know" (see the comments on 1:8; 2:4 for a possible allusion to Jesus as "the truth").

2:22–23: Who's the liar if not the person who denies [the truth by saying,] **"The Christ isn't Jesus"? This person is the antichrist, the person who denies the Father and the Son.** [23] **Everyone who denies the Son doesn't have the Father either. The person who confesses the Son has the Father too.** A lie implies a liar. So John singles out the liar who denies that the Christ is Jesus by distinguishing between Christ as a divine spirit and Jesus as a fleshly human being (see the comments on Cerinthianism in the introduction to 1 John; also the comments on John 20:30–31). The person who makes this false distinction opposes Christ rather than championing him, and therefore as a precursor to "Antichrist" deserves the opprobrium "the antichrist." Furthermore, that person denies the Father as well as the Son by dismissing the Father's revelation of himself in the indivisible person of Jesus Christ. Because the Father is in the Son, to deny the Son is to deny the Father, too, and hence not to have the Father or the Son. To confess the Son is to affirm him as God incarnate in the one person Jesus Christ and consequently to have the Father as well as the Son.

2:24–25: What you've heard from the beginning [which is that the Christ *is* Jesus] **is to abide in you.** In other words, this doctrine needs to remain in you rather than being jettisoned in favor of the Gnostic denial that the Christ is Jesus. **If what you've heard from the beginning abides in you, you too will abide in the Son and in the Father.** [25] **And this is the promise that he himself promised us: eternal life.** In both of its instances, "from the beginning" means since your conversions (compare 2:7). The abiding of the doctrine in you ensures your abiding in the Son and in the Father, where alone there's eternal life. The promise of such life should eliminate any hankering after the supposedly advanced knowledge taught by Gnostics. "He *himself* promised" makes the promise absolutely trustworthy. But is "he himself" the Son or the Father? Probably the Son, because he's the one who repeatedly promised eternal life during his earthly lifetime (from John 3:15 onward throughout the Fourth Gospel), and he's the truth (John 14:6).

2:26–27: I've written these things to you about those who are trying to mislead you [= lead you astray from the truth that the Christ is Jesus]. [27] **And you** [as opposed to those who are trying to mislead you]—**the anointing** [with the Holy Spirit] **that you received from him is abiding in you** [as indicated by Jesus himself in

John 14:17], **and you have no need that anyone** [such as a Gnostic] **teach you** [for there's no better teacher than the Holy Spirit]. **Rather, as his anointing** [the anointing with the Spirit that Jesus gives] **is teaching you about all things** [again as indicated by Jesus in John 14:26; 16:13–15] **and is true and isn't a lie, and just as it has taught you, you're abiding in him.** "All things" means all that's necessary for salvation, so that no new Gnostic revelations are needed. The anointing is true because it consists in the Holy Spirit, that is, "the Spirit of the truth," who Jesus said "will guide you in all the truth" (14:17; 15:26; 16:13)—thus John's statement here: "it [the anointing that consists in the Holy Spirit] *has* taught you" as well as "*is* teaching you." This past and ongoing teaching suffices. "Isn't a lie" keeps the anointing free from any admixture of falsehood with the truth. So the anointing is reliable as well as sufficient. In correspondence with the anointing's past and present teaching ("as . . . just as"), it's imperative to abide in the anointing. Stick true to the truth!

RIGHTEOUS CONDUCT
1 John 2:28–3:9

2:28–29: And now, children, abide in him [Jesus Christ] **so that if he should be manifested, we may/will have boldness and not be shamed away from him at his coming.** [29] **If you know that he is righteous** [as you do know, for 2:1 called him our "righteous representative"], **you know that also everyone who is practicing righteousness has been born from him.** In 2:18 John wrote that "it's the last hour [= the period immediately prior to 'the Last Day']," and he's about to mention the manifestation of Jesus at his second coming, which will take place on the Last Day. So "now" references "the last hour" in distinction from and preparation for that manifestation. The address "children" introduces a shift from abiding in "the anointing" (2:27) to abiding "in him [Jesus]." "So that . . . we may/will" indicates both the purpose and the result of abiding in him. They consist in having boldness and not being shamed. "At his coming" tells when. And since salvation is predicated on abiding "*in* him," "*away from* him" connotes a shameful dismissal to eternal damnation. Having made a false profession of belief in him would contribute to the shame of such a dismissal (compare being "thrown into the lake of fire" [Revelation 20:15; see also Revelation 21:8, 27; 22:15]). "Boldness," on the other hand, connotes confidence in meeting Jesus and speaking with him at his coming (compare 4:18: "complete love casts fear outside"). "*If* he should be manifested" doesn't call in question the manifestation as such, but it does stress uncertainty concerning the time of his coming. John puts the coming in terms of a manifestation—that is, of physical visibility—so as to counteract Gnostic notions of pure, nonphysical spirituality. And "you know . . . you know" unleashes a one-two punch against Gnostic pretensions to knowledge that non-Gnostics don't have. Since "[Jesus] is righteous," "everyone who is practicing righteousness" gives evidence of having been "born from him." For given worldlings' preoccupation with lusts and braggadocio (2:15–17) and, as will be mentioned shortly, given worldlings' origin in the Devil (3:8, 10, 12 [compare 5:19; John 8:44]), Jesus provides the only source for righteous living. So "everyone" excludes all unbelievers from the circle of those who are practicing righteousness at the same time that it includes all such practitioners within the circle of true believers. And the practice of righteousness opposes the practice of unrighteousness by Gnostics who give lust free rein under the supposition that their true selves, consisting only of their spirits, don't incur any guilt from bodily activities (see the introduction to 1 John). Since John has just referenced the manifestation of Jesus at the second coming, "born from him" appears to mean "born from Jesus." Soon, however, believers will be said to have been born "from God" (3:9–10 [compare John 1:13]). Yet they're also said to be born "from the Spirit" (John 3:5–6, 8), and Jesus the Word is identified with God (5:20; John 1:1, 18; 20:28). So along with these other references, "born from him [Jesus]" completes the Trinity's involvement in what Jesus called being born "from above" (John 3:3, 7).

3:1: Look at what sort of love the Father has given us, [namely,] that we should be called God's children. And we are! On account of this, the world doesn't know us, because it didn't know him. "Look at . . ." plus "And we are!" sounds a happy note of assurance that there's no need to defect into Gnosticism. In 2:5 John wrote that the love of God for us is completed in our keeping God's commandments, which quickly centered on the command that we love other Christians (2:7–11). Now John shifts to identifying the sort of love God has for Christians. This sort of love consists in the gift of our being called "God's children." But to suit our being called "children," John shifts from "God's love" (2:5) to the love of "the Father." That he "has *given* us" this sort of love highlights his "grace" in "giv[ing] his one-and-only Son" for our salvation through unmeritorious belief (1:17; 3:14–18). To be *called* God's children is to *be* God's children—naturally (or *super*naturally), since we've been "born from him." "On account of this" points forward to the world's not knowing him—that is, not recognizing God the Father in his incarnate Son, Jesus Christ (John 1:1–18, especially verses 10–11)—as the reason for the world's not knowing us believers either—that is, not recognizing us as to be God's children. The Gnostics, who think they have superior knowledge, represent the world in this lack of knowledge.

3:2–3: Beloved, we're God's children now, and it hasn't yet been manifested what we'll be [at Jesus' coming]. We know that if he should be manifested, we'll be like him, because we'll see him just as he is. ³And everyone who has this hope on the basis of him purifies himself just as that one [Jesus Christ] is pure. "Beloved" means "you who are loved by God" (see 3:1) as well as "you who are loved by me [John]" (see the comments on 2:7). The address introduces a reemphasis on

the status of being God's children, but with the addition of "now" to stress that there's no need to turn Gnostic for the gaining of this status. "Now" also underlines having the status at present even though it's not yet manifested to the world, including those pompous Gnostics, as it will be at Jesus' coming. In what respect will true believers be "like him"? Answer: Just as by virtue of his resurrection he'll be visibly manifested to the world as God's Son, by virtue of their resurrection true believers in him will similarly be manifested to the world as God's children. For "*if* he should be manifested," see the comments on 2:28. "We'll see him" because his manifestation will make him *physically* visible. "Just as he is" compares such future visibility to his present visibility, scars of crucifixion included, *in heaven* (see Revelation 5:6). That is to say, the Gnostically denied incarnation didn't leave off at Jesus' ascension. He's still incarnate. Why will seeing him manifest as he is make us manifest like him? Because we abide in him, so that his manifestation will entail ours too in a reversal of the world's present nonrecognition of us as God's children. "This hope" of future manifestation contains no element of uncertainty (as the English word "hope" tends to do). It means *confident* expectation. Its basis in Jesus supplies the confidence. Self-purification has to do with getting rid of "the lust of the flesh and the lust of the eyes and the braggadocio of livelihood" in correspondence with the absence of these "things in the world" from the person of Jesus Christ (2:15–17). Having the hope and purifying yourself go together. They depend on each other. Lack of self-purification kills the hope. Lack of the hope kills self-purification. "Everyone" allows no exceptions to this rule.

3:4–6: Everyone who is practicing sin is also practicing lawlessness, and sin is lawlessness. ⁵And you know that that one [Jesus Christ] was manifested [made visible through incarnation in his first coming] in order that he might take away sins [John 1:29]. And sin isn't in him. ⁶Everyone who is abiding in him isn't sinning. Everyone who is sinning has neither seen him nor known him. Lawlessness consists in breaking Jesus' commandments (2:3–8). John equates sin with lawlessness to portray sin as criminally shameful rather than as a behavior to be arrogantly flaunted, as some Gnostics flaunted their sinning as a sign of supposedly superior knowledge. Though Jesus was manifested to take away sins, sin isn't in him, as might mistakenly be thought because of his taking them away. In this context, taking them away has the purpose of eliminating them from the behavior of believers in addition to the purpose of providing forgiveness. Since sin isn't in Jesus, it follows that our abiding in him entails our not sinning. Otherwise sin *would* be in him. And it follows further that everyone who *is* sinning not only isn't in him but also hasn't even seen him or known him. "Nor known him" lashes out against Gnostic claims to superior knowledge. "Neither seen him" excludes Gnostic teachers from the circle of eyewitnesses to "the Word of life" (1:1–4), so that Gnostic teachers don't merit the trust owed to those foundational witnesses.

3:7–8: Children, no one is to mislead you. The person who is practicing righteousness is righteous, just as that one [Jesus Christ] **is righteous** [see 2:1 again]. **⁸The person who is practicing sin is from the Devil, because the Devil is sinning from the beginning. The Son of God was manifested in order that he might demolish the works of the Devil.** The endearing address, "Children," lends weight to the following statements. Most translations read "*let* no one mislead [or 'deceive'] you," as though John were issuing a command to his audience. He isn't, though. The grammar of his Greek has it that he's issuing a command, in the audience's hearing, *to a third party*, who are the Gnostic teachers in absentia. In other words, John is telling his audience what a Gnostic teacher shouldn't be doing to them. The misleading consists in saying it's okay to sin if you vault above the rules by turning Gnostic, because your spirit, your only true self, won't be sinning. Only your loosely attached body will. But the person who is practicing sin on this basis (or any other, for that matter) "is from the Devil," because "the Devil is sinning from the beginning" (compare John 8:44). His sinning started at the dawn of human history so far as the biblical record goes (see 3:12 for his involvement in Cain's murder of Abel [Genesis 3–4]). "*Is* sinning" stresses that the Devil is still sinning by working in and through false teachers such as the Gnostics. But "the Son of God was manifested to demolish the works of the Devil"—in other words, to demolish what the Devil is doing in and through those teachers. And he *will* demolish them. John calls Jesus "the Son of God" for a contrast with those who because they practice sin are "from the Devil" ("the Devil's children" according to 3:10). Like father, like child. So too the practitioner of righteousness takes after Jesus Christ the righteous one, from whom—along with God the Father and the Holy Spirit—this practitioner was born (compare 2:1, 29 with comments). To say that "the Son of God was manifested" is to point up again his physical visibility as a result of incarnation, contrary to Gnosticism.

3:9: Everyone who has been born from God isn't practicing sin [= no one born from God is practicing sin], **because his** [God's] **seed is abiding in him; and he's unable to be sinning, because he has been born from God.** John uses "seed" (Greek: *sperma*) as a figure of speech for engendering children, but doesn't identify the seed any further than to say it is God's. To say that the seed "is abiding" in the nonpractitioner of sin is to say that God's offspring will continue in their avoidance of sin. They won't apostatize to the sinful behavior of Gnostics. For since God is sinless, his offspring don't practice sinning and can't be sinning. But how can we harmonize the nonpractice of sin by God's children and their inability to be sinning, on the one hand, with the statements in 1:6–2:1, on the other hand, that claims to sinlessness are not only false but also indicative of not having God's word/Word in oneself, that Christians need to confess their sins for cleansing from every unrighteousness, and that Jesus Christ acts as their advocate when they sin? Given a Gnostic backdrop, we should answer this ques-

tion by understanding John to mean that true Christians don't, and can't, go on sinning both as a habit of life and as a way of flaunting the supposed superiority of their spirits, the divine sparks imprisoned in but fundamentally unaffiliated with their physical bodies. In effect, then, 1:8–2:1 affirms that the human spirit sins when its associated body sins; and 3:4–10 affirms that true Christians can't and won't deliberately and regularly let their bodies go on sinning without confession and cleansing. (Note also the *non*continuous Greek tense in the clause, "if anyone sins," at 2:1).

MUTUAL CHRISTIAN LOVE
1 John 3:10–24b

Now John narrows down the practice of righteousness in general to the topic of loving fellow believers in particular. As usual, "brother(s)" means fellow believer(s). **3:10–12: By this are manifest** [= made visible and therefore recognizable] **God's children and the Devil's children: everyone who isn't practicing righteousness isn't from God** [= no one who fails to practice righteousness is from God]**, and** [everyone] **who isn't loving his brother** [isn't from God], **¹¹because this is the message which you've heard from the beginning, that we should love one another, ¹²not as Cain was from the evil one and slew his brother. And for what reason did he slay him? Because his deeds were evil but the** [deeds] **of his brother** [were] **righteous.** Failure to practice righteousness entails the practice of sin. Behavior is either good or evil; and it manifests a person's moral parentage, whether it's divine or devilish. As before, "everyone" rules out exceptions to the rule. Not actively loving a fellow believer instances the nonpractice of righteousness and thus betrays birth from the Devil. Sins of omission count! The reason for saying so consists in "the message . . . that we should love one another" (John 13:34–35; 15:12, 17). The hearing of this message "from the beginning"—that is, ever since conversion to the gospel—cuts off any excuse not to love a brother actively. John then cites Cain as an example of origination from the Devil ("the evil one" [compare John 8:44]) rather than from God, also as an example of not loving a brother in that Cain "slew his brother." Evidence enough of not loving! John makes Cain's anonymous biological brother (whom we know from Genesis 4:1–8 as Abel) stand for an anonymous Christian brother, that is, *any* fellow believer. John identifies neither the righteous deeds of Cain's brother nor the evil deeds of Cain that lay behind the slaying. So the accent falls solely on the contrast and on Cain's evil deeds as representing those of Gnostic libertines, and his brother's righteous deeds as representing those of true Christians.

3:13–15: And don't marvel, brothers, if the world is hating you. ¹⁴We know that we have transferred out of death into life [compare John 5:24] **in that we love** [our] **brothers. The person who isn't loving** [his brother] **is abiding in death. ¹⁵Everyone who is hating**

his brother is a murderer, and you know that every murderer doesn't have [= no murderer has] eternal life abiding in him. With the address "brothers" John includes himself in the true Christian community of love and stresses that brotherly love characterizes this community in contrast with the world that hates them. As elsewhere, "the world" consists of non-Christian people. Behind John's "don't marvel" lies Jesus' having warned his disciples of the world's hating them because of having hated him first and because of their not belonging to the world (John 15:18–19; also 17:14). So the hatred shouldn't come as a surprise or as an enigma. "We know" counters the Gnostics' false claims to knowledge. Love of fellow believers gives evidence on which is based the true knowledge of having transferred out of death into life. "Out of . . . into" indicates different realms of existence, and "have transferred" indicates a done deal, so that there's no need to defect to Gnosticism for escape from death and entrance into life. John then describes the life as "eternal," so that "death" refers to eternal death, what Revelation 2:11; 20:6, 14; 21:8 calls "the second death." "Is *abiding* in death" makes for a stark contrast with a completed transference out of death into life. "Hating" defines "not loving." If you don't love your brother, you're hating him. John leaves no neutral ground between love and hate. Furthermore, hating amounts to murder; and no murderer—that is, no hater—has eternal life (Revelation 21:8). Thus the person who is "abiding in death" by not loving—that is, by murdering—his brother "doesn't have eternal life abiding in him." In other words, the hater-murderer is abiding in death and therefore doesn't have its corresponding opposite, eternal life, abiding in him. And this "eternal life" that isn't abiding in him is none other than God's Son, Jesus Christ, called in 1:2 "the eternal life who as such was with the Father and was manifested to us." Yet again, "everyone" and "every murderer" allow no exceptions.

3:16–18: We've come to know love by this, that that one [Jesus Christ] laid down his life for us. And we ought to lay down our lives for [our] brothers. [17]And whoever has the livelihood of the world and sees his brother having a need and closes off his bowels from him—how is God's love abiding in him? Implied answer: It is *not* abiding in him. **[18]Children, let us not be loving by word or by tongue [= by using our tongue merely to speak lovingly]—rather, in deed and truth.** Jesus' having "laid down his life for us" (compare John 10:17–18; 15:13–14) exhibited his love for us believers (compare John 13:1) and provided that love as the object of our knowledge. Knowing is experiencing in conjunction with understanding, over against Gnostic claims to purely intellectual knowledge of secret revelations that exclude the love of Jesus in laying down his life (physical) for us. "For us" means for the sake of our salvation. John cites such love on Jesus' part as an example that we should follow. But following it isn't limited to dying for one another as he died for us. For John goes on to cite as an example of *not* laying down our lives for one another the case of a believer who sees a fellow believer

in need but does nothing to fill that need. So there are plenty of loving deeds to be done that fall short of dying for a brother but that qualify in a limited way as laying down our life for him (compare Luke 10:30–37, though there without John's limitation to the Christian brotherhood). At the same time, failure to fill a brother's need counts as hating him, even as murdering him, so serious is the failure. In John 7:37–38 the copious passing of water out of the belly because of drinking the water of life stands for the superabundance of life that's eternal. Similarly here, the expression "closes off his bowels" uses anal-retentiveness as a figure of speech for uncompassionate failure to release one's resources to fill a brother's need. These comparisons may strike us as crude, but such a judgment bespeaks a certain prudishness on our part. (We have to admit the comparisons are vivid!) "Children" underlines the exhortation that immediately follows John's rhetorical question, "how is God's love abiding in him?" which implies that God's love for a needy brother would show itself through the agency of the brother who could help him—if that brother, possessing the wherewithal, did indeed have God's love abiding in him. To love "in deed" is to love actively and practically (with the resources at our disposal). To love "in . . . truth" is to love genuinely (because of knowing the truth as it is in Jesus).

3:19–20: And by this we'll know that we're from the truth and will convince our heart in his presence [20]that if our heart is condemning [us]—that God is larger than our heart and knows all things. "And by this we'll know" echoes "By this we've come to know" in 3:16 with reference to Jesus' setting an example of self-sacrificial love. Here we have a reference to our following his example by loving one another in deed and truth. Such loving will give us knowledge "that we're from the truth" (compare 3:14: "We know that we have transferred out of death into life in that we love [our] brothers"). And such loving will also convince our heart in God's presence, where truth prevails over falsehood, that if our heart is condemning us because we've sinned (compare 1:7–2:1), we're still "from the truth," and that since "God is larger than our heart" and therefore contains within himself all knowledge, whereas our heart's capacity for knowledge is constricted by sin, he knows "we're from the truth" despite our heart's condemning us. In the Bible, the heart is an organ of knowing, not just of feeling; and "we'll know" lashes out, as often, against Gnostic pretensions to superior knowledge. "That we're from the truth" may refer to origin in Jesus the truth (John 14:6) as well as to origin in true doctrine, for he's the subject matter of his teaching. Sin troubles the heart of a true believer (contrast Gnostics who delight in sinning to show their supposed advancement beyond morality). Given the preceding context, does John have in mind the sin of not lovingly helping a brother in need?

3:21–22: Beloved [by me and by God, who is larger than our heart and knows all things], **if [our] heart isn't condemning [us], we have boldness toward God; [22]and we're receiving from him whatever we're asking**

for, because we're keeping [= obeying] his commandments and doing the things that are pleasing in his sight [compare John 8:29]. In 2:28 John wrote of boldness in relation to Jesus at the second coming. Here he writes of boldness toward God in the making of prayer requests. "*Toward* God" indicates a close, face-to-face relationship with him in prayer (compare John 1:1 in regard to the preexistent Word and God, though there an equation of the Word and God immediately follows). Our boldness in prayer is predicated on having a heart that isn't condemning us. As we might say, a bad conscience because of some sin precludes praying with confidence that God will grant our requests. "Keeping his commandments" produces a heart that doesn't condemn us, equates with "doing the things that are pleasing in his sight," and provides the reason why "we're receiving from him whatever we're asking for." We might be disposed to explain *un*answered prayer on the ground of our failure to keep God's commandments and do the things pleasing in his sight. But John showcases what is happening by way of prayer that *is* answered for believers who because of their obedience have an uncondemning heart and a pleased God. Their receiving from God whatever they ask for (and with "we" John includes himself among them) shows that they have no need to switch over to Gnosticism (compare 5:14–16; John 14:13–14; 15:7, 16; 16:23–24, 26).

3:23–24b: **And this is his** [God's] **commandment, that we believe the name of his Son Jesus Christ and be loving one another just as he gave us the commandment.** 24a–b**And the person who is keeping his commandments is abiding in him, and he himself** [God] [is abiding] **in him** [in the keeper of God's commandments (compare 4:12–16)]. "Just as he gave us the commandment" means that God gave it to us through the words of Jesus, for Jesus spoke the words of God (see John 3:34; 14:10; 17:8 with John 13:34–35; 15:12, 17). "His commandments" (plural [3:22]) have narrowed down in the first instance to "his commandment" (singular [3:23]) because of its essentiality. So far as salvation is concerned, disobedience to this commandment would make obedience to all other commandments inconsequential. But though singular in its essentiality, the commandment turns out to be twofold. Its second part (to love one another as believers) has appeared already in 2:7–11; 3:10–20, where John presented obedience to it as evidence of true Christian faith, and disobedience to it as evidence of apostasy. But love for fellow Christians depends on, and grows out of, obeying the first part of the commandment, that is, to "believe the name of [God's] Son Jesus Christ." Believers' love for one another doesn't count apart from right belief concerning the Son of God. John 1:12 speaks of "believ[ing] *in* his name," which means to entrust our fate to him *because of* who his name indicates he is—an existential decision (see also 1 John 5:13). But "believ[ing] his *name*" means believing *that* he's who his name indicates he is—an intellectual decision (compare John 14:11: "Believe me, that I am in the Father and [that] the Father [is] in me").

"His Son Jesus Christ" identifies the bearer of the name to be believed. But what is that name? According to John 17:11–12 it's the name the Son shares with his Father, the name "God" (John 1:1, 18; 20:28 and 1 John 5:20: "This [Jesus Christ] is the true God" [see also the comments on John 1:12; 17:11–12]). So believing the name of God's Son Jesus Christ means believing he's God, as opposed to the Gnostic heresy that separated off a merely human Jesus from a purely divine Christ. And loving one another on the basis of this shared belief is opposed to the Gnostics' unlovingly distancing themselves from true believers. The duality of the single commandment to believe and love leads back to the plural in "keeping [God's] commandments." The reciprocity of abiding in God and God's abiding in the commandment-keeper points to an intimate relation with God that needs no Gnostic improvement (see also 4:13, 15–16), and abiding in God points to perseverance in right belief and in right conduct just as God's abiding in the commandment-keeper points to the faithfulness of God to preserve him in eternal life.

INCARNATIONAL CHRISTOLOGY
1 John 3:24c–4:6

3:24c–4:1: **By this we know that he** [God] **is abiding in us: from the Spirit that he gave us.** 1**Beloved, don't be believing every spirit. Rather, test the spirits** [to determine] **whether they're from God, because many false prophets have gone out into the world** [compare 2:18–19, 22–23; 2 John 7]. As usual, "*we* know" implies that the Gnostics really don't know what their name (which means "knowers") claims they know. The Spirit given to true believers gives them knowledge that God is abiding in them; for, after all, the Spirit is God's and is their teacher (2:20, 27 [for the Spirit as given, see John 14:17, 26; 15:26; 16:13; 19:30; 20:22]). After this assurance, John introduces a warning with "Beloved." The address not only expresses the love of John for his fellow believers. It also casts the gift of the Spirit as evidence of God's love for them just as the giving of his one-and-only Son evinced his love for the world (John 3:16 [compare the comments on 1 John 2:7]). The warning calls attention to the activity of multiple spirits. Some of them have inspired false prophets (Gnostics in this case) to go out (from the community of true believers) into the world (of unbelievers), where they really belong (2:19). That these false prophets are "many" heightens the danger posed by their heretical teachings. Hence the commands not to believe every spirit and to test them as to "whether they're from God." For to believe what a false prophet says is to believe the spirit that inspires him. In the next two verses John formulates a criterion by which to test the spirits.

4:2–3: **By this you know** [= recognize] **the Spirit of God: every Spirit that confesses** [= affirms] **Jesus** [as] **Christ having come in flesh is from God,** 3**and every spirit that doesn't confess Jesus** [as Christ having come in flesh] **isn't from God. And this** [spirit] **is the** [spirit] of the Antichrist, in reference to which [spirit] **you've heard that it's coming. And now it is already in the world.** As ever, "you know" sets true Christians' knowledge over against the so-called knowledge of Gnostics. "Every spirit that confesses . . . and every spirit that doesn't confess" ties true and false prophets so closely to the spirits within them that what the prophets confess or don't confess is what the spirits confess or don't confess. "*Every* Spirit . . . from God" distributes the Holy Spirit, severally among those who make a good confession (compare the comments on Revelation 1:4). Likewise, "*every* spirit . . . not from God" distributes the spirit of the Antichrist severally among those who don't make a good confession. As constantly, John's use of "every" disallows exceptions. The good confession affirms that the God-sent Christ equates with the human Jesus in a body of flesh and blood. Gnostic false prophets refused to affirm this equation; rather, they denied it by distinguishing a physically human Jesus and a spiritually divine Christ, so that when John comes to those prophets he has to say only that they don't confess Jesus. The spirit of the Antichrist would seem to be the Devil. We don't know for sure how it was that John's audience had heard that this spirit was coming, but see Revelation 13:15; 16:13–14; 18:2 for an association of spirits with the dragon (Satan) and the beast (the Antichrist). John's writing that the Antichrist's spirit is "now . . . already in the world" associates this spirit with the Gnostic false prophets who "have gone out [from the community of true believers] into the world [of unbelievers]" (4:1). "Now . . . already" puts a double emphasis on the spirit's activity as present even prior to the Antichrist's appearance, an activity that's counteracted, however, by the "shining" of "the true light . . . *already*" (2:8).

4:4–6: You're from God, children; and you've conquered them [the Gnostic false prophets]**, because greater is the one in you** [God according to 3:24] **than the one** [the Devil/evil one] **in the world.** [5]**They** [the Gnostic secessionists] **are from the world. On account of this** [their being from the world] **they're speaking from the world** [= from the standpoint of worldlings] **and the world hears them** [in the sense of heeding them because they're saying things which other worldlings like to hear]. The peddling of pure spirituality at the expense of bodily morality appeals to worldlings. [6]**We're from God. The person who knows God hears us. [The person] who isn't from God doesn't hear us. From this** [difference between hearing us and not hearing us] **we know** [= recognize] **the Spirit of the truth and the spirit of the misleading.** "You're from God" assures John's audience they needn't turn Gnostic for their salvation. Calling them "children" suits their being "from God" and reinforces the assurance. They've conquered the false prophets by beating back the attempts of those prophets to mislead them into heresy. The greatness of God, who abides in them, surpasses that of the Devil, who inhabits the world (that is, worldlings such as Gnostic false prophets). God's superior greatness has enabled John's audience to win this theological victory in their

lives. By way of contrast with origination "from God," the false prophets have originated "from the world." But do the "we" and "us" who "are from God" differ from the "you" who "are from God"? Yes, because in accordance with 1:1–4; 4:14 "we" and "us" then refer to John and his fellow eye- and earwitnesses to the earthly life, death, and resurrection of Jesus as the Christ who came in flesh. Moreover, "we're from God" then balances "you're from God." "The person who knows God" knows him because that person is "from God" and as a result "hears us" because "we" too are "from God." On the other hand, nonorigin from God produces a person who "doesn't hear us." Thus knowing God in the sense of having a personal acquaintance with him proceeds to knowing the Spirit of the truth and the spirit of the misleading in the sense of recognizing the difference between them by whether or not their adherents hear the original eye- and earwitnesses. "The Spirit of the truth" recalls the same phrase in John 15:26; 16:13 and means the Spirit who teaches the truth about Jesus, that is, Jesus *as* the truth (John 14:6). "The spirit of the misleading" means the spirit that misleads people into an erroneous denial that Jesus came as the Christ in flesh (compare 2:26; 3:7; 2 John 7).

MUTUAL CHRISTIAN LOVE
1 John 4:7–21

4:7–8: Beloved, let us be loving one another, because love is from God and everyone who is loving [others in the Christian community] **has been born from God and knows God.** [8]**The person who isn't loving** [others in the Christian community] **didn't come to know God** [when that person professed conversion]**, because God is love.** In his typically repetitious style, John circles back to the topic of mutual Christian love, which he has discussed twice before (2:7–17; 3:10–24a). The repetitions are designed for emphasis, but they also contain further elaborations of the topic (so too in repetitions of the topics of righteous conduct and incarnational Christology). "Beloved" suits a reintroduction of mutual Christian love but quickly devolves to God's love for believers as the basis for an exhortation that they love one another (compare the comments on 2:7). John includes himself among believers beloved by God and therefore writes, "let *us* be loving one another." Believers are to love one another because love is from God, and they're from God in that they've been born from him and consequently know him. For like recognizes like, as in the saying, "It takes one to know one." But the pairing of birth from God and knowing him also casts knowing him in an interpersonal as well as intellectual mold. As over and over again, "everyone" disallows exceptions. Loving other believers is a sure sign of birth from God and a consequent knowledge of him, so that lovers of other believers can assure themselves that they needn't turn to Gnosticism for birth from God and the knowledge of him. Gnostics count as nonlovers of believers (after all, they seceded from the community of believers) and therefore as nonknowers of God. That a nonlover didn't come to know God when he professed Christian belief not only gives the lie to his present pretension to a knowledge of God that orthodox Christians don't have. It also confirms that the ignorant nonlover "went out from us" because he wasn't "of us" (2:19). That "God is love" unmasks a nonlover of God's beloved ones as a nonknower of God himself, because to know him is to be infused with his active love for believers. Knowledge is transforming.

4:9–10: By this God's love was manifested among us, in that God has sent his one-and-only Son into the world in order that we might live through him [the Son]. **¹⁰In this is love, not that we've loved God— rather, that he loved us and sent his Son** [to make] **expiation for our sins** [compare John 3:16–17]. "By this" points forward to "God has sent . . . ." "God's love was manifested" alludes to the physically visible incarnation of God's one-and-only Son (1:1–2), an incarnation which Gnostic false prophets denied but which displayed that "God loved the world" (John 3:16). "Among us" refers particularly to John and his fellow eye- and earwitnesses (see 1:1–4; 4:4–6 with comments). "His *one-and-only* Son" stresses the extent of God's love: he went so far as to send his irreplaceable nearest and dearest. As to the clause, "that we might live through him," "we" refers generally to John's audience and whoever else will believe in Jesus (see, for example, 2:2; 4:14; John 3:16; 4:42), and "live through him" refers to Jesus as "the Word of life," "the life," and "the eternal life" (1:1–2; 5:11–12, 20 [see also John 3:15; 6:51, 54, 57–58; 11:25–26; 14:6, 19]). So living "through him" results in living eternally—forever. John goes on to write that our love for one another, which is the topic under discussion, doesn't derive from our love for God. On the contrary, our love for one another derives from God's love for us. And to the repeated reference to God's having sent his Son, John now adds another reference to the Son's making "expiation for our sins" (see 2:2 for the first such reference and comments there for an explanation of expiation).

4:11–12: Beloved, if God loved us in this way [as he did by way of sending his Son to make expiation for our sins], **we too ought to be loving one another** [compare 3:11, 23; John 13:34–35; 15:12, 17]. **¹²No one has ever seen God. If we're loving one another, God is abiding in us and his love has been completed among us.** "Beloved" calls renewed attention to God's love for us, as the immediately following reference to it confirms. The expiatory love of God for us makes our nonexpiatory love for one another look meager by comparison and therefore not at all too much to demand from us (see again the comments on 2:7). Concerning "no one has ever seen God," see the comments on John 1:18; 5:37; 6:46, where the statement has to do with not seeing God the Father in and of himself as distinct from seeing him in the person of his incarnate Son. Here the statement forms a backdrop against which we see him, so to speak, in the persons of our fellow believers, in whom he abides, so that to love one another is to love him as well. Such love

is both the condition and the evidence of his abiding in us and of the completion of his love "among us" (see the comments on 2:5 for the completion of God's love).

4:13–14: By this we know that we're abiding in him and he in us, in that he has given us some of his Spirit. ¹⁴And we've seen and are testifying that the Father has sent [his] **Son** [to become] **the world's Savior.** "By this" points forward to the Spirit as God's gift to assure believers that they abide in God, and he in them. So the Spirit joins their love for one another to double the assurance, which should keep them from thinking they have to convert to Gnosticism. The Spirit's teaching of the truth contributes to this assurance (see 2:20, 27 with comments). "Some of his Spirit" implies that there's plenty of the Spirit to spare for believers outside John's immediate audience. The "we" in "we've seen and are testifying" refers to John and his fellow eye- and earwitnesses to Jesus' earthly life, death, and resurrection (see 1:1–4). In 4:9 John referred to God's having sent his Son to give us eternal life, in 4:10 to expiate our sins, and now to become "the world's Savior" (compare John 3:17; 4:42)—that is, to take out of worldly society those who don't belong in it because they originate from God rather from the world, just as the heretics, who don't belong in the Christian community, have gone out of it into worldly society because they originate from the world rather than from God. But saved from what? From being "lost" (John 3:16), from "God's wrath" (John 3:36), from "the resurrection of judgment" (John 5:29), and from "the lake of fire," which is "the second death" (Revelation 2:11; 20:6, 14; 21:8).

4:15–16: Whoever confesses that God's Son is Jesus—God is abiding in him [the confessor] **and he in God. ¹⁶And we've come to know and believe the love that God has among us. God is love; and the person who's abiding in love is abiding in God, and God is abiding in him.** The identity of God's Son is at issue: Is he the human being called Jesus, identical with Christ? Or is God's Son a divine spirit called Christ, different from the simply human Jesus, as some Gnostics taught? John assures confessors of God's Son as Jesus that God is abiding in them and they in God. John uses the singular "him" and "he" to individualize these confessors. Each one enjoys such reciprocal indwelling. The "we" in "we've come to know and believe" reverts to an inclusion of John's audience (contrast 4:14). To know God's love is to understand and experience it, so that Gnosticism holds no attraction. To believe God's love is to accept it as true—and let us remember that it prompted God to send his Son to make "expiation for our sins" (4:10), so that believing God's love means, moreover, believing his Son's death to have made such an expiation. God has love "*among* us" through the completion of his love *in our love for one another*, so that our love is his too (2:5; 4:12).

4:17–18: Love has been completed with us by this [that is, by our abiding in love and therefore in God and by his abiding reciprocally in us] **so that we may/will**

have boldness in the Day of Judgment, because just as that one [Jesus] is, we also are in this world. [18]There's no fear in love; rather, complete love casts fear outside [the lover], because fear has punishment [in the sense of dreading the punishment to be meted out on the Day of Judgment]. And the person who is fearing [punishment] hasn't been completed in love. John has consistently used the Greek proposition behind "with" for the fellowship of sharing (1:3, 6, 7; 2:19). So the completion of love "with us" means that God shares with us the exchange of love between members of the Christian community (2:5; 4:12). His participation in this exchange has both the purpose and the result of our having boldness in the Day of Judgment ("may/will"). The boldness arises out of obedience to the command that we love one another. John has recently written, "If we're loving one another, God is abiding in us" and "we're abiding in him" (4:12, 13). In John 17:11, 20–23 Jesus notes in prayer that his disciples are "in the world" though he isn't there any more, and asks God the Father that believers in him (Jesus) may be one as he and the Father are one: "I in them and you in me, in order that they may be completed in oneness." Here in 4:17, then, "just as that one [Jesus] is, we also are in this world" means that as Jesus in heaven is one with the Father, believers on earth are one with the Father. His abiding in us and our abiding in him match the oneness of him and his Son so far as love is concerned. For the giving of boldness in the Day of Judgment, this match supplements our obedience to the commandment that we love one another. John equates this boldness with lack of fear. Loving one another drives out the fear of judgment. The description of this love as "complete" alludes to its completing God's love for us by expanding it to include mutual love among Christians. But the person who's fearing punishment on the Day of Judgment has punishment already in the form of fear itself and hasn't himself been completed in love—that is, hasn't loved believers. Otherwise, he'd not have fear. As it is, his fear, arising from a failure to love, is well grounded. So "let us love one another" (4:7).

4:19–21: We love, because he [God] first loved us [4:9–11]. [20]**If anyone says, "I love God," and is hating his brother, he's a liar** [compare 2:3–5]. **For the person who's not loving his brother, whom he has seen, can't be loving God, whom he hasn't seen.** John reasons not just that it's *easier* to love someone we've seen, such as a needy brother (3:17), than someone we haven't seen, such as God (4:12), but even that it's *impossible* to love the unseen God without loving a needy brother, because God and the brother abide in each other. They're inseparable. We can't love one without loving the other. [21]**And we have this commandment from him, that the person who's loving God be loving his brother too.** "We're loving" states a matter of fact that confirms our birth from God. (The context has to do with loving God and loving one another as fellow believers, not with loving the world/worldlings [see 2:15].) Yet though evidential of salvation, our loving doesn't merit salvation; for it has arisen out of God's loving us. Grammatically, "first"

doesn't tell when God loved us. Rather, "first" goes with "he" to describe God himself, not his loving. Because he loved us, he occupies first place. To hate a brother is to falsify your claim to love God; and hating a brother equates with not loving him, which earlier counted as murdering him and consisted in withholding resources that would have helped him (3:15–17). "He's a liar" implies origin from the Devil (compare John 8:44 and see the comments on 1 John 3:23 for having a commandment from God in the words of Jesus [John 13:34–35; 15:12, 17]).

AN INTEGRATION OF MUTUAL CHRISTIAN LOVE, INCARNATIONAL CHRISTOLOGY, AND RIGHTEOUS CONDUCT
1 John 5:1–21

5:1: Everyone who believes that the Christ is Jesus has been born from God, and everyone who loves the one who did the engendering [that is, God] **loves also the person who has been born** [from him]. Again John lashes out against Gnostics' distinguishing between a divine, spiritual Christ and a human, physical Jesus. In 4:2, 15; 2 John 7, John writes about *confessing* Jesus Christ as one incarnate person. Here he writes about *believing* the same. The belief that underlies the confession lends the confession authenticity. As indicated by "born from God" and "who did the engendering," God played the role of a father, figuratively speaking, in siring true believers (compare 3:9). "Everyone who believes . . ." gives assurance. "Everyone who loves . . ." states an axiom. The first "everyone" strengthens the assurance in its breadth. The second "everyone" strengthens the axiom in its tying love for God inextricably to love for one another in the Christian community.

5:2–4a: By this we know that we're loving God's children when we're loving God and doing his commandments. [3]For this is love for God, that we keep his commandments. And his commandments aren't burdensome, [4a]because everything that has been born from God conquers the world. "By this" points forward to keeping God's commandments. So interdependent are loving God and loving his children that just as we know we're loving God when we're loving his children (4:7–12), we also know we're loving his children when we're loving God. In particular, "doing his commandments" means keeping the commandment to love one another (compare 3:22–24 and "do[ing] the truth" in 1:6). John equates loving God with keeping his commandments and therefore with loving one another. So we have an equation as well as interdependence (compare John 14:15, 21, 31). God's commandments aren't burdensome, because to be born from God is to have a divine power that conquers the world by giving the strength to keep his commandments despite the world's allurements and hatred (compare 2:13–14; 4:4 with comments). "*Every*thing" leaves no one born from God without world-conquering power. "Every*thing*" refers to every person born from God, but with stress on the quality of such parentage (compare the use of "what" in 1:3 for a similar stress on personal quality).

5:4b-5: And this is the conquest that conquered the world: our belief. ⁵And who is the person that is conquering the world if not the person who believes that the Son of God is Jesus? The mention in 5:4a of conquering the world as a consequence of keeping God's commandments shades now into conquering the world by believing that the Son of God is Jesus. This believing occurred at conversion and equates with a conquest of the world in that worldlings are made up of antagonistic *un*belief that the Son of God is Jesus. The unbelief isn't just an attribute of theirs. It *constitutes* who they are. The rhetorical question, "And who is the person . . . ?" implies there's no person who conquers the world apart from believing that the Son of God is Jesus. Of course not, since an unbeliever is himself part of the world (contrast 2:22). And though Gnostics think they conquer the world by rising above others through special knowledge, they don't conquer it at all. For their denial that the Son of God is Jesus makes them worldlings along with the others.

5:6-8: This is the one who came through water and blood, [namely,] Jesus Christ—not only in the water; rather, in the water and in the blood. ⁷And the Spirit is the one who is testifying, because the Spirit is the truth ⁸in that there are three who testify, the Spirit and the water and the blood; and the three are one. "This" points back to "the Son of God," namely "Jesus," in 5:5 and anticipates "Jesus Christ" later in its own sentence. "Through water" hardly refers to Jesus' baptism, because in his Gospel John didn't mention the baptism of Jesus, and likewise hardly refers to Jesus' birth, because unlike Matthew and Luke the Gospel of John carries no account of Jesus' birth. But John 19:34-35 records, with emphasis on eyewitness testimony, that "blood and water" came out of Jesus' side when a soldier pierced it with a spear. The blood that came out is the blood that "cleanses us from every sin" (1:7); and the water that came out symbolizes the Holy Spirit, by whom a believer is born from above (John 3:3-8) and who gives life eternal (John 6:63; 7:37-39). Not as in John 19:34, here the mention of water advances to first position for emphasis on the testimonial role of the Spirit, whom the water symbolizes (compare also the association of the Spirit and water in John 3:3-8 before the mention of Jesus' blood in John 6:53-56). "Through" is to be taken in the sense of passing through rather than in the sense of means or agency (see too John 4:4; 10:1-2, 9; 14:6; 19:23), so that passing "*through* water and blood" entailed being "*in* the water and *in* the blood." So determined and defined was Jesus by his mission to give believers in him the water of the life-producing Spirit (John 6:63) and his blood as the elixir of eternal life (John 6:53-56 again) that the water and the blood constituted the very elements through and in which he came (compare Jesus Christ's having come "in flesh" [4:2; 2 John 7]). "Not only in the water" indicates that apart from the shedding of his blood as the

expiation for our sins (2:2; 4:10), there'd be no giving of the Spirit.

The Spirit's testimony consists in teaching (2:20, 27; 3:24; 4:13). The Spirit testifies by teaching that the indivisible Jesus Christ came through and in water and blood and that the water and the blood which came out of Jesus' side demonstrated that the Son of God died as the *incarnate* "Word of life" (1:1-4). So powerfully do the water and the blood testify to this anti-Gnostic fact that John lists them as witnesses (rather like Jesus' testimonial "works" in John 5:36; 10:25) distinguishable from the Spirit but united with each other and the Spirit in their threefold testimony. "The three" alludes to the legal sufficiency of two or three witnesses (John 8:17; Numbers 35:30; Deuteronomy 17:6; 19:15); and the use of the masculine "who" for a reference to the water, the blood, and the Spirit, all three of which are neuter in John's Greek, personifies the water and the blood as witnesses alongside the Spirit. In 4:6 John described the Spirit as "*of* the truth." Here he *equates* the Spirit and the truth. This equation recalls Jesus' equating himself with the truth (John 14:6) and gives the reason why the Spirit is testifying. If the Spirit who's testifying is the truth personified, the Spirit's testimony must be true. And if Jesus as well as the Spirit is the truth, he and the Spirit are one just as he and the Father are one (John 10:30; 17:11, 22).

5:9-10: If we accept the testimony of human beings, the testimony of God is greater, because this is God's testimony in that he has testified concerning his Son. ¹⁰The person who believes in God's Son has the testimony within himself. The person who doesn't believe God has made him a liar, because he hasn't believed in the testimony that God testified concerning his Son. For the testimony of human beings see 1:1-4; John 1:7, 19; 5:31-37. God's testimony is greater in the sense of being more reliable, utterly reliable in fact; and it consists in the Spirit's testifying within a believer in God's Son that this belief suffices for eternal life. Recourse to Gnosticism would prove fatal. To believe "in God's Son" is to entrust our eternal fate to him because of his expiation for our sins (2:2; 4:10). "Not [to] believe God" is to treat him as a liar in what he has testified concerning his Son. And not to believe "in the testimony" is to draw back from entrusting our eternal fate to the reliability of God's testimony.

5:11-13: And this is the testimony, that God gave us eternal life and [that] this life is in his Son. ¹²The person who has the Son has the life. The person who doesn't have God's Son doesn't have the life. ¹³I've written these things to you, the ones who believe in the name of God's Son, in order that you may know that you have eternal life. God's testimony concerning his Son, a testimony that believers have within themselves through the Holy Spirit, assures them that God did indeed give them eternal life when they believed. So they needn't turn to Gnosticism. The person who has the Son has "the life"—that is, "*eternal* life"—because God's Son *is* "the eternal life, who as such was [preexistently] with the Father" (1:2 [compare John 14:6; 11:25–26]). Since he's the only source of this life, the person who doesn't have him doesn't have the life that God's Son himself is and gives (John 6:27, 33; 10:28; 17:2). "In order that you may know that you have eternal life" puts John's writing together with God's testimony for a double assurance that—contrary to Gnostic doctrine—the audience know all they need to know for eternal life. See the comments on 3:23 for the meaning of "believe in the name of God's Son."

5:14–15: And this is the boldness which we have toward him [God], **that if we're requesting anything according to his will, he hears us.** [15]**And if we know that he hears us in regard to whatever we're requesting, we know that we have the requests which we've requested from him.** The assurance given in 5:11–13 leads to boldness, in particular to boldness in making prayer requests, as in 3:21–22 (see the comments on those verses). There, the boldness was conditioned by our having a heart that doesn't condemn us because we're keeping God's commandments and doing the things that please him. Here, the boldness is conditioned by our making requests that agree with his will. Given the meeting of this condition, John writes, we have twofold knowledge: (1) that God hears us in regard to whatever requests fall within the circle of his will and (2) that we have those requests in the sense that God grants the requests on hearing them. The present tense in "we *have*" stresses the certainty of God's granting them. They're as good as ours already in the asking. Better knowledge than anything Gnosticism, a potpourri of doctrines purporting to provide knowledge, has to offer!

5:16–17: If someone sees his brother sinning a sin not resulting in death, he shall request [God to forgive such a sin for the brother (see 3:21–22 for God as the addressee of prayer requests)]**; and he** [God] **will give life to him,** [that is,] **to the one who's sinning** [a sin] **not resulting in death. There is a sin resulting in death. I'm not saying that he** [the one who sees his brother sinning] **should ask concerning *that*** [sin]. [17]**All unrighteousness is sin, and there's sin not resulting in death.** "Whatever we're requesting" (5:15) narrows down to the case of praying for God's forgiveness of a brother who's not sinning a sin that results in death. Just as "the life" is "eternal life" (5:11–12), so "death" refers to eternal death (2:17; 3:14; John 5:24–29; 8:51–52), what John calls "the second death" in Revelation 2:11; 20:6, 14; 21:8. The sin resulting in this death consists in apostatizing from the true Christian faith into heresy—here, into Gnosticism, one of "the works of the Devil" that God's Son came to "demolish" (3:8). The seceding apostate "hates his brother" and therefore "is a murderer," and "no murderer has eternal life abiding in him" (3:15 [see also 5:12]). On the one hand, John doesn't outright forbid asking God to forgive the sin of apostasy. On the other hand, love of fellow believers might seem to entail praying for them. But apostates aren't fellow believers. Therefore John's explicit denial that he's saying to pray

that God forgive a heretic's sin of apostasy implies *not* praying for him to forgive it. The emphasis falls, however, on asking God to forgive a sin short of apostasy for a fellow believer who commits such a sin. "He *shall* request" issues a command to make such a request. So this prayer request combines with the fellow believer's confession of the sin (1:9) and the advocacy of Jesus, based on his expiation for our sins (2:2), to ensure God's giving the brother life rather than death, salvation rather than damnation. Lest anyone think lightly of a sin that falls short of apostasy, though, John adds that "*all* unrighteousness is sin." (Note: because the unforgivable sin in Matthew 12:24, 31–32; Luke 12:10 is committed by those who like the Pharisees of Jesus' day have never made a profession of belief in him, the sin of apostasy that results in death is to be distinguished from the unforgivable sin.)

5:18: We know that everyone who has been born from God isn't sinning [= no one who has been born from God is sinning]**; rather, the person who has been born from God—he** [God] **is keeping him** [in the sense of protecting him]**, and the evil one isn't grabbing hold of him.** John shifts from the topic of praying or not praying in regard to sin resulting and not resulting in death— he shifts from that topic to the topic of not sinning at all. This topic occupied the discussion in 3:6–9 (see again the comments on that passage), but now John adds God's protection of his child from the evil one (the Devil), so that the evil one isn't grabbing hold of the child so as to capture him for heresy, such as Gnosticism. God keeps his true children safe (see especially John 17:15, but also John 6:39; 10:28–29; 17:12; 18:9).

5:19–21: We know that we're from God [in the sense of having been born from him as his children] **and** [that] **the whole world** [= the rest of human society] **is situated within the evil one** [as believers are contrastively and repeatedly said to abide in God and Christ]. [20]**But we know that God's Son has come and given us insight so that we may know** [and] **do know the true one. And we are in the true one, in his Son Jesus Christ. This one** [Jesus Christ] **is the true God and eternal life.** [21]**Children, keep yourselves away from idols.** True Christians, then, have an intense awareness of the radical difference between themselves and all other human beings, over whom the evil one holds sway. In 5:13 our knowing constitutes John's *purpose* in writing. In 5:15, 18–19, 20 he affirms again and again the actuality of our knowing over against false claims to knowledge by Gnostics (so-called "knowers"). In view of John 17:3, which mentions "the only true God" as distinct from "Jesus Christ," whom he "sent," "the true one" whom we know is God. As true, he stands over against Gnostic falsehood. But since God the Father and Jesus are one (John 10:30; 17:11, 21–22), to be "in [God] the true one" is to be also "in his Son Jesus Christ" as opposed to the whole world's being "situated within the evil one." It also follows that this Jesus Christ "is the true God and eternal life" as opposed to certain Gnostics' false separation of a divine spirit called Christ from a physical human being called Jesus (see 1:1–4 for "the eternal life" as a title for "the Word of life," who became incarnate in God's Son Jesus Christ, and John 1:1, 18; 20:28 for Jesus Christ as God). "Children" reflects "born from God" (5:18) and lends weight to the command, "keep yourselves away from idols." Mention of "the *true* God" leads to this warning against *false* gods consisting of idols. The Greco-Roman culture in which John and his audience lived was riddled with idolatry. It may also be that the Gnostic secessionists against whom John writes went in for images and idolatrous practices, including sexual intercourse with prostitutes who plied their trade at the temples that housed idols. After all, Gnostics divided off their bodies, lusts and all, from their true spiritual selves just as they divided off Jesus, physical body and all, from a divine spiritual Christ.

SECOND JOHN

The theme of Christian truth as the basis of mutual Christian love dominates 2 John so as to warn Christians against showing hospitality to false teachers.

ADDRESS AND GREETING
2 John 1–3

1–2: The elder to a select lady and her children, whom I love in truth—and not I alone, but also all who've come to know the truth—²because of the truth that's abiding in us. And it will be with us forever! According to tradition the Apostle John wrote this letter along with the Fourth Gospel, 1 John, 3 John, and Revelation. Given this tradition, John calls himself "the elder" to underline his authority. For in first-century Greco-Roman culture, age brought respect. Since John was probably the last surviving apostle, "the elder" could well have had the connotation of "the elder statesman of the church." In that case, John didn't need to identify himself by name. "To a . . . lady and her children" means "to a local church and the individual members that make it up." For if the lady were an individual mother, it's strange that in verse 13 her sister's children but not the sister herself send greetings (compare John's personifications of the church at large as a woman, a bride, and a wife in Revelation 12:1–17; 19:7; 21:2, 9; 22:17). Besides, the business of loving one another (verse 5) applies elsewhere to church life (John 13:34–35; 15:12, 17 and several times in 1 John); and it's more likely that a church than that an individual Christian lady and her children would be loved by "all who know the truth" (verse 1). John describes this local church as "a *select* lady" in the sense that like the original disciples of Jesus, they've been selected out of worldly society (compare John 6:70; 13:18; 15:16, 19, but above all see Revelation 17:14). God has selected them for salvation (John 6:37, 39; 17:12). Mention of the selection assures them that they needn't, and indeed shouldn't, pay heed to false teachers who tell them they lack what's needed for salvation. John is going to warn against such teachers.

"Whom I love" endears John to his audience and makes him an example of obeying the command that Christians love one another, a command he's about to bring up. "In truth" means both that he loves his audience truly and that he loves them within the sphere of truth about Jesus Christ, who *is* the truth (John 14:6). "In truth" lacks a "the" before "truth." This lack leaves emphasis on truth as such, on the quality of truthfulness in John's love and in the correct teaching about Jesus

Christ. By enlarging the circle of loving support from those "who've come to know the truth," the addition, "and not I alone, but also all who've come to know the truth," encourages John's audience to stick true to this truth. As often in 1 John, the accent on knowing the truth lashes out against false claims to knowledge by Gnostics (= "knowers"). "Who've *come* to know" means that true Christians already have the truth in hand. They don't have to look elsewhere for it (compare John 8:32; 1 John 2:21). Whereas "*in* truth" identified truth as the doctrinal sphere in which true Christians love one another, "*because of* the truth" identifies truth about Jesus Christ as the mainspring of their love: they love one another because God was first in loving them by sending his Son Jesus Christ as the expiation for their sins (1 John 4:10, 19). The "abiding" of the truth "in us" indicates intimacy (so as to breed love) and permanence (so as to prevent apostasy). We might also think of John's equating the Spirit with the truth (1 John 5:6) and of Jesus' claim to be the truth (John 14:6) and his promise to abide in us (John 15:4). The exclamation, "And it [the truth—or is it the Spirit and Jesus *as* the truth?] will be with us forever!" gives further assurance to John's audience that they needn't turn into Gnostics. The truth's staying "*with* us" complements its abiding "*in* us."

3: Grace, mercy, peace from God the Father and from Jesus Christ, the Father's Son, will be with us in truth and love. "Grace" refers to God's favor. This word (*charis* in Greek) is related to the word used for an ordinary greeting (*chairein* in Greek: "Rejoice!"). So along with other early Christians, John turns a mere "Hello" into a glorious reminder of God's favor that "came on the scene through Jesus Christ" (John 1:14, 16–17). "Mercy" reminds us further that because of our sin, God's favor is ill-deserved. And "peace," a typically Semitic greeting (*shalōm* in Hebrew), connotes all the blessings of messianic salvation, not just the absence of warfare (compare John 14:27; 16:33; 20:19, 21, 26 and our political expression, "peacetime prosperity." For "peace" as a Semitic greeting see examples in Matthew 10:12–13; Judges 19:20; Ezra 4:17; 5:7. We expect to read "Grace, mercy, *and* peace," but John leaves out the expected "and" and puts the verb "will be" in the singular (so the Greek original) despite the plurality of three words of greeting. Thus the three are merged into a single unit: "Grace-mercy-peace." Each one implies the other. Together, they come from both God the Father and Jesus Christ (compare the double security of believers in John 10:28–29 and the double abode alongside them in John 14:23). The addition of "the Father's Son" to "Jesus Christ" prepares for a warning against heretics who separate Jesus from Christ and deny Jesus' divine sonship (see the introduction to 1 John). The two references to God as "the Father" underscore this sonship. In verse 2, John wrote that "the truth . . . will be with us forever." Now he writes that "grace-mercy-peace will be with us in truth [which means 'truly' because of right belief about Jesus Christ as the Father's Son] and love [which means 'lovingly' because of right conduct (loving one another) among believers]." "Will be" turns what would otherwise be a *wishful* greeting, such as "*May* grace-mercy-peace be yours," into a *confident* greeting that brings yet more assurance to believers who are being courted by heretics. (Note that in verses 1–3 no fewer than four occurrences of "truth" aim against the falsehoods of heresy.) A normal greeting contains the phrase "to *you*," as in all Paul's and Peter's letters. But to show solidarity with his readers "in truth and love," John writes "with *us*." He shares with them the Father's and the Son's grace-mercy-peace.

MUTUAL CHRISTIAN LOVE AS AN ANTIDOTE TO HERESY
2 John 4–7

4–5: I've rejoiced greatly because I found some of your children walking around in truth, just as we received a commandment from the Father [that we do so]. **⁵And now I'm asking you, lady (not as though writing to you a new commandment—rather,** [a commandment] **which we've had from the beginning), that we be loving one another.** Having replaced the normal Greek greeting that told *others* to rejoice, John writes now that *he* rejoiced. Giving rise to the joy was his finding some of the church members "walking around in truth." This statement contains a compliment designed (quite rightly and sincerely) to win his letter a favorable hearing when it's read to the church. The greatness of John's rejoicing strengthens the compliment. "*Some* of your children" doesn't imply that he found other members of the church not walking around in truth. It implies only that he and the "some" had had contact with each other during his and/or their travels outside the locality of their church. "*Walking around* in truth" means that he found them behaving in accordance with the truth which the Spirit is and which Jesus spoke and is (contrast 1 John 1:6 and compare John 3:21, both dealing with *doing* the truth). The said behavior quickly turns out to be loving one another, as God the Father commanded through his Son (see the comments on 1 John 3:23–24a). "Just as *we* received a commandment" alludes to John and his fellow earwitnesses to Jesus' commandment in John 13:34–35; 15:12, 17 (compare 1 John 1:1–4). "And *now*" distinguishes John's present writing from his having heard Jesus issue the commandment in the past. For John's description of the commandment as not new, see the comments on 1 John 2:7. "We've had [it] from the beginning [of the Christian era]" lends the commandment the weight of tradition in addition to the weight

of its origin "from the Father." "That we be loving one another" broadens "we" to include John's audience as well as John himself and other earwitnesses to the command. Though arising out of the commandment, "that we be loving one another" indicates what John is "now . . . asking" the church to do.

6–7: And this is love, that we walk around [= behave] **according to his commandments** [compare John 14:15, 21; 1 John 3:16; 4:10–11 and especially 5:3]. **This is the commandment, just as you have heard** [it] **from the beginning, that you walk around in it** [= behave in obedience to it], **⁷because many deceivers, who aren't confessing Jesus** [as] **Christ coming in flesh, have gone out** [from us, the true Christian community] **into the world** [consisting of unbelievers]. **This** [sort of nonconfessor] **is the deceiver and the antichrist** [because of whose secession we should love one another, as the Father commanded, for the sake of mutual encouragement to resist the blandishments of such a Gnostic false prophet (compare 1 John 2:19; 4:1–2)]. John equates love with obedience to the Father's commandments; for children who love their fathers obey their fathers, and in this case the Father has commanded his children to show their love for him by loving one another. In verse 4 John celebrated the *actuality* of walking around in truth. Now in verse 6 he lays down the *necessity* of walking around according to the Father's commandments. The two occurrences of "walk around" double the accent on obedient behavior. As in 1 John 2:3–8; 3:22–23, the plural "commandments" narrows down to the singular "commandment" to love one another (alluded to in verse 5). Whereas "*we* [John and Jesus' other original disciples] received a commandment from the Father . . . which we've had from the beginning [of the Christian era—in particular, since the time Jesus relayed it to us at the Last Supper (verses 4–5; John 13:34–35; 15:12, 17)]," "*you* [John's audience] have heard it from the beginning [of your Christian lives—that is, since your conversions, as in 1 John 2:7, 24; 3:11]." "*Many* deceivers" highlights how serious is the threat that in the absence of mutual Christian love they might succeed in luring away members of the church (so too in 1 John 2:18; 4:1). "Deceivers" means "misleaders," those who would lead others to stray instead of walking around in the truth (compare 1 John 2:26; 3:7). They would mislead others into thinking that a human Jesus differs from a divine Christ. First John 4:2 spoke of Jesus Christ as "*having* come in flesh" (compare 1 John 5:6: "the one who *came*"). Here John writes of Jesus as Christ "*coming* in flesh," much as he writes that "Antichrist is coming" (1 John 2:18 [see also 1 John 4:3]). In John 21:22–23, moreover, Jesus is quoted as saying twice, "till I come," and in Revelation 1:4, 8; 4:8 John associates Jesus with the Father, "he who is coming." So it looks as though John supplements his other references to Jesus' having previously come as Christ in flesh with a reference to Jesus' coming *again* as Christ in flesh (see the comment on 1 John 3:2). Certainly the Gnostics against whom John is warning denied a physical return of Jesus Christ just as they denied his past incarnation.

A WARNING TO RESIST HERESY
2 John 8–11

8–9: Be watching out for yourselves in order that you not lose the things which we've accomplished—rather, that you receive full remuneration. [9]**Everyone who goes ahead** [into heresy] **and doesn't abide** [= stay] **in the doctrine of the Christ** [that he's coming again in flesh as Jesus] **doesn't have God. The person who abides in the doctrine** [= sticks true to it]**—this person has both the Father and the Son.** "Be watching out for yourselves in order that you not lose . . ." appeals to legitimate self-interest. "The things which we've accomplished" refers to the conversions, and therefore the salvation, of John's audience. It's implied that he and his colleagues converted them; but it will be members of the church he's addressing, not John and his colleagues, who'll suffer loss if any of the addressees apostatize and lose out on the salvation they otherwise would have had. The "remuneration" consists in salvation. Its description as "full" alludes to the eternality of the life which salvation provides. But "remuneration" doesn't imply that John's audience will have earned eternal life by working for it. On the contrary, "we" (John and his colleagues) accomplished the conversions by evangelistic work. (The Greek verb behind "accomplished" is related to the Greek noun for "work," for which "remuneration" is a wage.) So if they don't apostatize, John's audience will get the benefit of *others'* work. "Who goes ahead [into heresy]" may connote what the Gnostics would call progress. If so, John uses the expression sarcastically: going ahead into heresy isn't *pro*gress; it's *re*gress. "Not [to] abide in the doctrine of the Christ" is "not [to] have God," because the Christ who has come and will come in flesh as Jesus *is* God (1 John 2:23; 5:20; John 1:1, 18; 20:28). For the same reason, abiding in the doctrine is to have "both the Father and the Son."

10–11: If anyone comes to you [plural] **and isn't bringing this doctrine** [of the Christ that he's coming in flesh as Jesus], **don't ever receive him into** [your] **house, and don't ever tell him to rejoice** [which would be a normal, courteous greeting like our "Hello!" or "Good day!"]. [11]**For the person who's telling him to rejoice is participating in his evil deeds.** "If anyone *comes* to you and isn't *bringing* this doctrine" implies a traveling false prophet. "Don't ever receive him into [your] house" prohibits giving such a false prophet board and room, which would enable him to peddle his heresy locally. The heresy is so evil that even the Middle Eastern law of hospitality no longer applies. "Don't ever tell him to rejoice" prohibits even a religiously neutral greeting, much more the Christian greeting, "Grace" (for which see the comments on verse 3). For the giving of a religiously neutral greeting would still be to encourage the false prophet and thus participate "in his evil deeds." Those deeds include not only his peddling of heresy but also his murderous hate of true believers (1 John 3:13–15), his lying (1 John 1:6, 10; 2:4, 22; 4:20; 5:10; Revelation 2:2), and lustful, boastful behavior (1 John 2:15–17). Nonhospitality to false teachers instances not loving the world (1 John 2:15–17 again).

PARTING REMARKS
2 John 12–13

12–13: Though having many things to write to you, I haven't wanted to [do so] **with papyrus** [the ancient version of paper] **and ink. Instead, I'm hoping to come to you and speak mouth to mouth** [in other words, carry on a conversation with you face to face] **in order that our joy may be filled up.** [13]**The children of your select sister are greeting you.** Does "our joy" refer to that of John *and his colleagues* who shared with him the evangelization of his addressees, as favored by verse 8 and 1 John 1:4? Or does "our joy" refer to that of John *and his addressees*, as favored by "hoping to come to you and speak mouth to mouth"? In either case joy is an outgrowth of mutual Christian love (see John 3:29; 15:11; 16:24; 17:13 for other references to *fulfilled* joy). "The children of your select sister" are members of the local church where John is at the time he's writing. For the meaning of "select" see the comments on verse 1. "Are greeting you [singular for the addressed local church]" means "they're sending you greetings through this letter"—an example of Christian love between local churches in addition to love within a local church.

THIRD JOHN

This letter focuses on an ecclesiastical dispute, commends Gaius, criticizes Diotrephes, and recommends Demetrius, all of whose roles become apparent as the letter progresses.

ADDRESS AND WELL-WISHING
3 John 1–4

1–4: The elder to the beloved Gaius, whom I love in truth. ²Beloved, concerning all things [pertaining to you] **I pray that you may prosper and be healthy just as your soul is prospering. ³For I rejoiced greatly when brothers were coming and testifying to your truth, just as you're walking around in truth.** Here we have a genuinely private letter addressed to a Christian named Gaius. For "the elder," see the comments on 2 John 1. In agreement with church tradition, this commentary will refer to him as John. By describing Gaius as "beloved," adding "whom I love in truth," and addressing Gaius with "Beloved" here and two more times in verses 5 and 11, John underlines his affection for Gaius, aims to win Gaius's obedience to a following exhortation, and exemplifies his own obedience to the command that Christians "love one another" (John 13:34–35; 15:12, 17; 1 John 2:7–11; 3:11–18; 4:7–21; 5:2–3). But Christians love one another because God was first in loving them (1 John 4:19), so that "beloved" denotes God's as well as John's love for Gaius. "In truth" means "truly" and therefore indicates that John's saying he loves Gaius is more than a rhetorical ploy for the purpose of winning from Gaius a favorable response. "Truth" refers also to the truth about Jesus as the Christ and incarnate Son of God, and indeed to Jesus *as* the truth (John 14:6). Therefore "in truth" locates John's loving Gaius in the sphere where God loved us by giving his one-and-only Son for our salvation and where believers correspondingly love one another in a completion of God's love for them (see 1 John 2:5; 4:12, 17–18 with comments). In other words, Christian love is doctrinally based and in that sense circumscribed (compare 1 John 2:15–17).

In ancient private letters, well-wishing commonly followed an opening address and used the language of prayer. John conforms to this convention by wishing prosperity and good health for Gaius in all aspects of his life outside the life of his soul. His soul was already prospering! The separating out of Gaius's soul implies that "all things" and "be[ing] healthy" have to do with material and physical prosperity. Such prosperity would enable Gaius to obey John's upcoming exhortation to help missionaries in their ministry and on their way. For the moment, though, John refers back to some brothers' coming to where he is and testifying to Gaius's "walking around in truth," that is, behaving in accord with true doctrine about Jesus Christ. So devoted to such doctrine has Gaius proved that in addressing him John calls this truth "*your* truth." In other words, the brothers have testified to the prosperity of Gaius's soul, and their testimony has brought John great joy because of John's own concern for the truth (as evident, for example, in his Gospel and 1 John). So great is his joy that he adds in broader terms: **⁴I don't have a greater joy than these things,** [namely,] **that I hear my children** [to be] **walking around in the truth.** "My children" implies Christians younger than "the elder," reexhibits his affection for them, and alludes to his authority over them. "These things" refers to details in the report John had heard from the brothers concerning Gaius. All in all, a father takes joy in his children who behave well. But who are "the brothers" who've testified to Gaius's "walking in the truth"?

A COMMENDATION OF GAIUS FOR HIS HOSPITALITY TO TRAVELING CHRISTIAN WORKERS
3 John 5–8

5–7: Beloved, you are acting faithfully as regards whatever you are accomplishing for the brothers, even [accomplishing] **this** [for] **strangers** [that is, for brothers you've never met before], **⁶who've testified in the sight of the church to your love, whom you'll do well to send forward in a manner worthy of God. ⁷For taking nothing from the Gentiles, they went out** [from their home church] **on behalf of the name.** This last phrase, "on behalf of the name," for which name the brothers "went out," indicates that they are traveling Christian missionaries. For "the name" is the name that Jesus Christ shares with the Father, that is, the name "God" (see the comments on John 1:12; 17:11–12; 1 John 2:12; 3:23; 5:13). (John assumes that Gaius knows this implication of "the name.") So these brothers didn't "[go] out from us" because "they weren't of us," as did Gnostic false prophets (1 John 2:19). No, they went out as ambassadors for the truth that the Christ, God's Son, came as Jesus in flesh. Because they teach this truth and because Gaius himself walks around in it, he exercised love for these brothers by giving them hospitality to enable their ministry in his locality—and did so despite never having met them before.

"Whatever you're accomplishing for the brothers" refers to this hospitality and implies that Gaius's hospitable work of love has proved effective through the brothers' ministry. So gracious has been Gaius's hospitality that the brothers have testified about it "in the sight of the church" where John is. On the basis of their testimony John adds that Gaius is "acting faithfully." "You *are* acting faithfully as regards what*ever* you *are* accomplishing" leaves room for future accomplishments in addition to those already done. "Whom you'll do well to send forward" implies that the brothers will pass through Gaius's locality on a further mission and will need his financial help for that mission as well as temporary hospitality on the way. Hence John's wishing Gaius "prosperity" in "all things" (verse 2), apart from which prosperity Gaius wouldn't have the means to send the brothers forward. "In a manner worthy of God" implies that since the brothers are going out as ambassadors of God, to support them financially is to worship God. "For they went out" probably refers, not to their past mission, but to the mission on which they've just started and for which John has written this letter recommending them. One of them (Demetrius according to verse 12) is carrying the letter to give to Gaius in the hope of winning his financial support. "Taking nothing from the Gentiles" means taking nothing from non-Christians. For the church is the true Israel, and Christians are the true Jews (see the comments on Revelation 2:9; 3:9; 7:1–17; 21:12–14), so that "Gentiles," which properly means non-Jews in an ethnic sense, came to be used for non-Christians in a religious sense. Pagan philosophers and other teachers took pay for their services. Christian missionaries proclaimed the gospel for free and therefore depended on fellow Christians for support.

8: Therefore we ought to be taking in as guests such [brothers] **in order that we may become workers with the truth.** It's as though the truth of the gospel is at work in the world. Indeed, Jesus and the Spirit are the truth that's at work in the world (John 14:6; 1 John 4:6; 5:6); and those who support missionaries as well as the missionaries themselves are working with this truth. "Therefore" makes the missionaries' "taking nothing from the Gentiles" when going out "on behalf of the name" (verse 7) the basis for "taking [them] in as guests." "We *ought* to be taking in as guests such [brothers]" contrasts with the order in 2 John 9–11 not to give heretics any hospitality, or even an ordinary greeting.

A CONDEMNATION OF DIOTREPHES
3 John 9–11

9–10: I've written something to the church [of which you're a member]. **But Diotrephes, loving to be first of them** [= dominant over others in the church], **isn't welcoming us.** [10]**Because of this** [his nonwelcome], **if I come I'll bring up his deeds, which he's doing while casting absurd aspersions on us with evil words. And not being satisfied on the basis of these** [evil words], **neither is he himself welcoming the brothers. He's**

even forbidding those who want [to welcome them from doing so] **and throwing** [them] **out of the church** [that is, out of the assembly, not out of a church building]. We don't know what writing John refers to in saying, "I've written something to the church." Probably not 1 John, because it appears to be a letter circulated among a number of churches. Possibly 2 John. But since John immediately says that "Diotrephes . . . isn't welcoming us," perhaps John refers to an otherwise unknown letter recommending the brothers, who represent him, and perhaps laying out the possibility of a visit by him (as in the present letter: "if I come"). In any case, Diotrephes appears to be a church dictator who doesn't want his preeminence compromised by John and the brothers and therefore is refusing them hospitality, is "casting absurd aspersions" on them "with evil words" so that others in the church won't provide them hospitality either, and is even forbidding others to show John and the brothers hospitality and throwing out of the church those that do. The words are "evil" because the aspersions are "absurd." But evil words alone didn't satisfy Diotrephes. He followed up with evil actions. Maybe the church meets in Diotrephes' house, and maybe John writes to Gaius in part because Diotephes has thrown Gaius out, so that Gaius needs encouragement. In any case again, John threatens to deal with Diotrephes' deeds if he (John) comes along with the brothers. Does old age make John's visit uncertain?

11: Beloved, don't be imitating what's bad—rather, what's good. The person who's doing what's good is from God. The person who's doing what's bad hasn't seen God. "What's bad" alludes to Diotrephes' dictatorial behavior. "What's good" refers to hospitable behavior, such as Gaius has already exhibited and needs to exhibit again. This latter behavior demonstrates origin from God. But what does it mean that the doer of what's bad "hasn't seen God"? According to 1 John 4:12 "no one has ever seen God" (see also John 1:18; 5:37; 6:46). True, no one has seen God the Father in and of himself. But since Jesus Christ is God in human flesh, his original disciples saw God the Father in and through the person of his incarnate Son (John 14:8–11; 1 John 1:1–4). "The person who's doing what's bad" refers then to the likes of Diotrephes, and he hasn't seen God because he didn't belong to the circle of Jesus' original disciples and therefore lacks the authority of John, who did belong to that circle.

A RECOMMENDATION OF DEMETRIUS
3 John 12

12: It has been testified by all as to Demetrius and by the truth itself [that he does what's good (compare verse 11)]. **And we're testifying** [to the same], **and you know that our testimony is true.** Demetrius appears to be the brother who's delivering this letter to Gaius. John's recommendation certifies Demetrius as a trustworthy brother. The recommendation consists of a threefold testimony: (1) "by all"; (2) "by the truth itself," as though Demetrius is so trustworthy that truth, personified again (as in verse 8), develops its own mouth to testify in his favor even apart from any human mouthpiece; and (3) by John's own "we." Gaius knows John well enough to know that the testimony of John and his colleagues in Demetrius's favor is credible. Furthermore, in the mouth of two or three witnesses every matter shall be established (1 John 5:7; John 8:17; Numbers 35:30; Deuteronomy 17:6; 19:15).

PARTING REMARKS
3 John 13–15

13–15: I have many things to write to you, but I don't want to be writing to you with ink and a reed-pen. ¹⁴And I'm hoping to see you right away, and will speak mouth to mouth [for which expression see the comments on 2 John 12]. "I'm hoping to see you" harks back to "if I come" (verse 10); but uncertainty in the earlier "if" gives way to expectation, which "hoping" connotes. "Right away" adds haste to expectation. Diotrephes will get his comeuppance without delay, and Gaius and others whom Diotrephes has thrown out of the church will get vindication. ¹⁵**Peace** [will be] **to you. The loved ones are greeting you** [= are sending their greetings through this letter]. **Greet the loved ones name by name.** John didn't include "grace, mercy, peace" in verse 1 as he did in 2 John 1–3. So "Peace to you" makes up now for that omission. For the meaning of "peace" see the comments on 2 John 1–3; and since there John issues a promise ("will be"), we should probably supply "will be" here too. "The loved ones" are Christians where John is writing. Most translations have "the friends." Though not incorrect, that translation obscures the connection with John's repeated citations of the command that Christians love one another (compare the comments on John 15:12–15). Finally, John tells Gaius to greet the loved ones where he (Gaius) is. "Name by name" individualizes the greetings and calls on Gaius to imitate Jesus, the good shepherd who "calls his own sheep name by name" (John 10:3; compare John 1:42; 11:43; 14:9; 20:16; 21:15, 16–17).

JUDE

The letter of Jude warns against false teachers (compare 2 Peter, especially chapter 2) and divides into an address and greeting (verses 1–2); a rationale for writing the letter (verses 3–4); a description of the false teachers' ungodliness and coming judgment (verses 5–16); an exhortation to resist them (verses 17–23); and a doxology (verses 24–25).

1–2: Jude, a slave of Jesus Christ and a brother of James, to [you] called ones, loved by God the Father and kept for Jesus Christ: ²May mercy and peace and love be multiplied for you. "Jude" is an English spelling of "Judas," which in turn is a Greek spelling of the Hebrew "Judah." The English spelling, Jude, distinguishes the author of this letter from other men who had the same name (for example, Judas Iscariot and Judah, one of Jacob's twelve sons). The author is probably a half brother of Jesus, for he calls himself "a brother of James." Though more than one James appears in the New Testament, Jesus had a half brother by that name who rose to leadership in the early church and wrote a letter of his own in our New Testament. So Jude's referring to himself as the (full) brother of this James lends weight to the present letter (see Mark 6:3; Matthew 13:55; Acts 12:17; 15:13; 21:18; Galatians 1:19; 2:9, 12; James 1:1). In view of their disbelief in Jesus during his public ministry (Mark 3:20–21, 31–35; Matthew 12:46–50; John 7:1–9), it looks as though James and Jude converted as a result of Jesus' resurrection (Acts 1:14; 1 Corinthians 9:5; 15:7). Jude identifies himself first as "a slave of Jesus Christ" to impress on his audience that the letter contains what Jesus Christ wants him to say. Jude is carrying out orders. So listen up. Furthermore, it was an honor to be the slave of a powerful, prominent figure such as Jesus.

Jude dubs his audience "called ones" in the sense that God's invitation to the banquet of salvation has effected their favorable response. As called, they're loved by God the Father and consequently kept for Jesus Christ. Emphasis falls on the steady state of being loved and kept. The love contrasts with God's anger at the bad behavior of heretics Jude is about to skewer. And the keeping contrasts with their apostasy. Moreover, the love and the keeping compliment the audience on their high privilege and thus aim again for a favorable hearing of the letter. "Kept for Jesus Christ" means that God the Father keeps his called ones from apostatizing. Their apostasy would mean a loss for Jesus Christ, their Lord and hence their owner (verses 4–5, 9, 14, 17, 21, 25). Jude wishes for them "mercy," because only by God's mercy can they es-

cape apostasy. Jude wishes them "peace," because it connotes the blessings of salvation as opposed to damnation for apostasy. And he wishes them "love," because only by God's love can they continue to be kept for Jesus Christ instead of apostatizing. "Be multiplied" reflects the seriousness of the threat that heretics might lead them into apostasy. In other words, Jude's audience need a lot of protective mercy, peace, and love.

3–4: Beloved, although doing all diligence [= being wholly eager] **to write to you concerning our mutual salvation, I had the necessity to write you by way of urging you to contend vigorously for the faith that was once for all given over to the saints** [= Christians as consecrated to God]. **⁴For certain men have infiltrated, [men] who long ago were prescribed for this condemnation, ungodly [men] who've transmuted the grace of our God into debauchery and are disowning our only Master and Lord, Jesus Christ.** "Beloved" recalls God's love for the audience (verses 1–2) but introduces Jude's love for them too and thus makes for their favorable reception of the letter and its message. Jude's calling attention to his great eagerness and to sharing salvation with the audience also makes for a favorable reception. But the threat of heretics among them forced him to shift from the preferred topic of their shared salvation to the compulsory topic of "contend[ing] vigorously for the faith." "The necessity" of this shift emphasizes the seriousness of the threat, as do also Jude's "urging" and the strength of the athletic-military metaphor, "contend[ing] vigorously." People's eternal fate is at stake. It's not just that Jude is engaged in a fight against the heretics. With might and main his audience are to join in the fight. "For the faith" portrays the fight as a defense of the gospel. Here, "faith" adds the content of belief to the activity of believing. "That was . . . given over to the saints" refers to the delivery of this belief to those who because of believing it became consecrated to God. From verses 17–18 it looks as though this delivery originated with the apostles. "Once for all given over" excludes from the faith anything disagreeable with the original.

"Certain men have infiltrated" indicates that disguising themselves as true Christians, heretics had come in among Jude's audience. "This condemnation" anticipates the judgments about to be described and quoted in verses 5–15, which go back to Old Testament times and even to Enoch, prior to Noah's flood (compare Proverbs 16:4). A like judgment awaits the heretics. The great age of their prescription to condemnation stresses the certainty of coming condemnation. For in the culture of Jude and his audience, the older, the more reliable. Novelty, such as the heretics represented, rightfully looked suspicious. The heretics' ungodliness dooms them to condemnation. Regardless of *believing* in God's existence, the ungodly *behave* as though God—at least the God of Scripture, who demands upright conduct—doesn't exist. The grace of God is his ill-deserved favor toward sinners. The heretics have treated it as a license to sin more rather than as an incentive *not* to sin any more. "Debauchery" refers especially to sexual sins, as will come out shortly and graphically. "Have transmuted . . . and are disowning" have to do with misbehavior growing out of misbelief—*mis*belief because it wasn't in tune with "the faith that was once for all given over to the saints." The pairing of "Master" and "Lord" puts emphasis both on Jesus Christ's ownership of Christians, whom God the Father has kept for him (verse 1), and on the heretics' misbelief and misbehavior as exposing their *not* belonging to Jesus Christ. "Our *only* Master and Lord" heightens the emphasis on his ownership of true Christians yet more. And "*our* God" and "*our* only Master and Lord" recalls Jude's sharing salvation with his audience and thus furthers a rapport with them that he hopes will make them take his letter to heart.

5–7: And I want to remind you, though you know all things once for all, that on saving the people [of Israel] **out of the land of Egypt, Jesus on a second occasion destroyed those who didn't believe;** ⁶**and the angels that didn't keep their own jurisdiction but quit their own habitat he has kept in everlasting bonds** [= chains] **under pitch-blackness for the judgment of the great day,** ⁷**as Sodom and Gomorrah and the cities around them, having fornicated and gone after another kind of flesh in a manner similar to these** [angels], **are on exhibit as an instance of undergoing the punishment of eternal fire.** Reminding would compliment the audience by implying they already know what Jude is about to tell them. But instead of saying "I remind you," he says "I *want* to remind you." This softening of the reminder makes for a higher compliment. And heightening the compliment yet further, the would-be reminder turns into an explicit statement that the audience already know what Jude wants to remind them of—indeed, "*all* [these] things." (Not all things in general, of course.) As though he hasn't already heightened the compliment enough, Jude adds that they've come to know all these things, and therefore know them now, "once for all." This triply heightened compliment tightens the previously mentioned rapport that he hopes will make the audience pay heed. The "once for all" knowing of "all things" recalls the "once for all" delivery to the saints of "the faith" (verse 3) and, like that delivery, excludes from their proper knowledge anything disagreeable with what they already know, such as the heresy under discussion.

The saving of the people of Israel from slavery in Egypt forecast the saving of Christian believers ("the called" of verse 1) from their sins. But Jude's accent falls on a second event, the destruction of unbelievers among

the Israelites as a forecast of the eternal punishment of heretics among Christian believers. He's alluding to the Israelites who exodused from Egypt under divine power but didn't believe in it to conquer the promised land of Canaan and so perished in the wilderness of Sinai (see Numbers 13–14, especially 14:11–12). "Those who didn't believe" implies that the heretics likewise don't believe and contrasts with believers' "contend[ing] vigorously for the faith" (verse 3), for "believe" and "faith" translate the same root in Jude's Greek. Some ancient manuscripts read that "the Lord . . . destroyed those who didn't believe." But the better ones read that "Jesus" destroyed them (so too in regard to the angels, mentioned next). Therefore Jude appears to imply the existence of Jesus (perhaps as the Old Testament angel of the Lord) prior to his birth in Bethlehem. Jude also interprets "the sons of God" in Genesis 6:1–4 as angels (compare Job 1:6; 2:1; 38:7) who left their heavenly habitat, and thus lost their jurisdiction there, to intermarry "the daughters of human beings on earth" (see also 1 Peter 3:19–20; 2 Peter 2:4 with comments). "The judgment of the great day" refers to the judgment that will yet take place on a day called "great" because of that event. Jesus' having successfully "kept" the fallen angels "in everlasting bonds under pitch-blackness for the judgment" guarantees their eternal punishment and portends the same for the heretics. The fallen angels' having been "kept" for judgment contrasts with God the Father's having "kept" true Christians ("called ones") for Jesus Christ (verse 1). Sodom and Gomorrah and cities surrounding them, destroyed by fire and sulfur (Genesis 18:1–19:29), exhibit punishment by eternal fire such as the heretics will suffer. Fornication covers all kinds of sexual immorality. The fallen angels committed fornication by engaging in sexual intercourse with females of the human species. Similarly though not equivalently, the men of Sodom, Gomorrah, and surrounding cities engaged in sexual intercourse with "another kind of flesh," that is, flesh other than that of the females God created for them to copulate with. Jude has correctly deduced from the Sodomites' demanding Lot deliver to them his guests, who they thought were human males, that the Sodomites and their neighbors practiced homosexuality (plus bestiality?).

8–10: Because of dreaming, nevertheless [that is, despite the destruction of the unbelieving Israelites, the impending judgment of the apostate angels, and the burning of Sodom and Gomorrah], **these** [heretics] **too are similarly polluting flesh, on the one hand. They're rejecting lordship, on the other hand, and slandering luminaries** [more literally, "glories"]. ⁹**But Michael the archangel (he was arguing about Moses' corpse when disputing with the Devil) didn't dare bring a judgment of slander against** [the Devil]; **rather, he said, "May the Lord reprimand you** [compare Zechariah 3:2]." ¹⁰**But these** [heretics], **on the one hand, slander as many things as they don't comprehend. On the other hand, as many things as they understand by instinct, as** [do] **irrational living** [creatures]—**by these they're being corrupted.** "Are similarly polluting flesh" favors homosexual practice on the part of the heretics, as in the case of the Sodomites and their neighbors, and describes the ejaculation of semen on or into a fellow male as polluting his flesh literally (though there's a strong overtone of moral pollution, of course). "Dreaming" refers to dreams the heretics have had, or at least claim to have had, which gave them new revelation contradicting old revelation on matters of sexual behavior. Hence Jude's earlier emphasis on the reliability of old revelation. On the basis of these dreams the heretics are rejecting Jesus' lordship in both their teaching and their behavior. Hence Jude's earlier emphasis on Jesus' lordship (see especially verse 4). On the same basis they're "slandering luminaries," probably the angels of heaven, God's angels, since he has kept the fallen angels "under pitch-blackness," where their glory can't shine luminously. The heretics slander the glorious angels of God by denying that these angels will come with the Lord in judgment on the ungodly (compare verses 14–15 and the comments on 2 Peter 2:10b–11).

Then Jude writes about a dispute between Michael and the Devil over Moses' corpse. According to a Jewish tradition, the Devil accused Moses of murder and therefore unworthy of the honorable burial that Michael had come from God to give him (compare Deuteronomy 34:1–6). But when Michael wished the Lord to reprimand the Devil, the Devil withdrew, knowing that the Lord would side with his archangel Michael so as to give Moses an honorable burial. "A judgment of slander" means a judgment that the Devil was slandering Moses by accusing him of murder (as opposed to justifiable homicide in defending a fellow Israelite [compare Exodus 2:11–12]). Jude's point: if even God's chief angel didn't dare bring such a judgment against the Devil, evil as he is, how stupidly arrogant must be the merely human heretics to slander God's gloriously good angels. "As many things as they don't comprehend" exacerbates the heretics' stupidity and puts it over against the knowledge possessed by Jude's audience (verse 5). Adding to the moral stupidity is the heretics' immoral knowledge: they know all about barnyard sex, for it characterizes their behavior. In this connection, a second occurrence of "as many things as," a reference to "instinct" as opposed to reason, and a comparison to mindless animals exacerbate the heretics' stupidity yet further. All the while, "they're being corrupted," which carries two senses: (1) their misbehavior is causing them moral ruin, and (2) their moral ruin presages their eternal ruin.

11: Alas for them, because they've traveled Cain's path and for pay have abandoned themselves to Balaam's error and have perished by way of Korah's disputatiousness! Jude uses traveling a path as a figure of speech for behavior. Cain murdered Abel his brother. So far as we know, the heretics haven't murdered anybody. But Cain murdered his brother "because his deeds were evil" whereas those "of his brother [were] righteous" (1 John 3:12). So traveling Cain's path stands for doing evil. "Balaam's error" consisted in acting out of greed for money (see the comments on 2 Peter 2:15–16). In a more literal translation, "for pay they've abandoned

themselves" to Balaam's error comes out as "for pay they've been poured out by Balaam's error," as though the personified error of greed has poured out the heretics as a libation, a drink offering, on the altar of Mammon (for a contrast, see Philippians 2:17). In view of Jude's having excoriated them for sexual immorality, it helped the comparison to Balaam that Balaam advised the Moabites to use their women for seducing the men of Israel (Numbers 25:1–3; 31:15–16). "Korah's disputatiousness" consisted in a verbal assault on the God-ordained leadership of Moses and Aaron (Numbers 16:1–35; 26:9–10). The heretics have likewise launched a verbal assault, resulting in a behavioral assault, on the apostolic tradition of morally pure living (verses 3, 17–18). And as Korah and his cohorts perished by the earth's swallowing them up, the heretics are so sure to perish forever that Jude uses the past tense, "have perished." The progressive intensification in the verbs—"have *traveled*," "have *abandoned* themselves," and "have *perished*"—makes things go from bad to worse for the heretics.

12–13: These are the reefs in your love[-feasts] **while feasting with** [you], **fearlessly shepherding themselves;** [they are] **waterless clouds being carried along by winds** [compare Proverbs 25:14], **autumn trees without fruit, having died twice because of being uprooted,** [13]**wild waves of the sea foaming up their own shames, roaming stars for whom the pitch-blackness of darkness has been kept forever.** Love-feasts were church suppers during which the Lord's Supper was celebrated (see the comments on 1 Corinthians 11:17–34 for the difference between these suppers and modern potlucks). The heretics were participating. But because they only pretended to be true Christians (verse 4), Jude compares them to reefs, rocky ridges lying just below the surface of the sea and therefore posing a hidden danger of shipwreck. In terms of a shipwreck, then, Jude is warning against the hidden danger of apostasy and eternal ruin. The figure of speech shifts from reefs to shepherds. As self-appointed leaders, the heretics should be shepherding the Christians by word and example in the path of righteousness rather than in Cain's path (verse 11). Instead, they're shepherding themselves—that is, indulging their own appetite for money and immoral pleasures at the true Christians' expense (compare Ezekiel 34:8)—and stupidly doing so without fear of the punishment that's sure to come on them. Like clouds being blown along without dropping needed rain and like trees that should be laden with ripe fruit in the autumn, but aren't, the heretics have nothing good to offer. "Carried along by winds" may allude to their itineration from one Christian community to another. They're like trees that have died twice, first as evident in their failure to bear fruit and second in their having been uprooted because of that failure (compare the second death of eternal torment in Revelation 2:11; 20:6, 14; 21:8). The yet further figure of "wild waves of the sea foaming up their own shames" pictures the heretics as wild and shameless in their slimy immoralities. The plural of "shames" calls attention to the multiplicity of their immoral acts, and "their *own* shames" stresses the heretics' accountability for them. We would refer to "roaming stars" as "planets," which means "wanderers, roamers." This figure of speech represents the heretics' wandering off the course of true Christian behavior and belief (compare the use of "error," which is the noun form of "roaming," for Balaam's greed [verse 11]). The combination of "pitch-blackness" with "darkness" intensifies the heretics' doom, a doom they'll share with the fallen angels who've been kept under the same pitch-blackness (see verse 6). That this pitch-blackness of darkness "has been kept forever" guarantees their eternal punishment. God wouldn't have reserved it for them so long ago only to leave it unoccupied by them in the end (contrast true Christians' having been "kept for Jesus Christ" [verse 1]).

14–15: **And in reference also to these** [heretics] **the seventh from Adam,** [namely,] **Enoch, prophesied, saying, "Behold, the Lord came with his holy ten thousands** [or, less specifically, 'myriads' (compare Deuteronomy 33:2; Zechariah 14:5)] **¹⁵to execute judgment against all** [of them] **and to convict every soul** [= every person among them] **of all their ungodly deeds that they ungodlied, and of all the harsh things that they as ungodly sinners spoke against him!"** Jude calls Enoch "the seventh from Adam" because Enoch comes seventh in the genealogy at Genesis 5:3–24. We find Enoch's prophecy outside the Bible in a book called *First Enoch*, though Jude may not have had this book as we do—perhaps only a fragment thereof or a tradition later incorporated into the book. In any case, he quotes Enoch's words as a prophecy concerning the heretics who've infiltrated among Christians. "Behold" makes the prophecy exclamatory of the heretics' judgment at the coming of "the Lord," that is, at the second coming of "Jesus Christ, our Lord" (verse 25). The past tense in "the Lord came" portrays that coming as so certain it might as well have already happened. "With his holy ten thousands" refers to accompaniment by a vast angelic army. The heretics won't stand a chance. "Holy" describes the angels as consecrated to God in contrast with the angels he has kept for judgment (verse 6). "To execute judgment against all [of them]" means "to convict every soul [= every person among them]"—in other words, to issue a verdict of guilty against the heretics and inflict punishment on them. "All" and "every soul" leave no room for exceptions. In quoting Enoch, Jude likewise uses "all" for their deeds, another "all" for their harsh words, "ungodly" for their deeds, "ungodlied" as a verb (coined for English) to describe their deeds as doubly ungodly, and another "ungodly" to describe the heretics as "sinners." As a result, enormous emphasis falls on the evil of their deeds and words. The harshness of their words, spoken against the Lord, has to do with denying him as Christians' "only Master and Lord" and thus rejecting his "lordship" (compare their slandering of "luminaries" and their Korah-like verbal rebellion [verses 4, 8, 11]).

16: **These** [heretics] **are grumblers, complainers, traveling** [once again a figure of speech for behaving] **in accordance with their own lusts. And their mouth is speaking pomposities, marveling at faces for the sake of advantage.** "Grumblers" recalls the Israelites who came out of slavery in Egypt only to grumble about spartan conditions in the wilderness on their way to the promised land of Canaan (so a number of references, starting with Exodus 15:24; 16:2, 7–9, 12 [see also 1 Corinthians 10:10]). Similarly and specifically, "complainers" has to do with complaining about one's circumstances. To get handouts, in other words, the heretics engaged in "poor talk." To take financial advantage of wealthy Christians, they showed them partiality (the meaning of "marveling at faces"). And the heretics mouthed "pomposities" to give the impression they deserved bountiful gratuities, if not outright bribes. After all, it cost a lot to satisfy their lusts (compare James 2:1–9). "Their *own* lusts" underscores accountability again.

17–19: **But you, beloved, remember the words that were spoken beforehand by the apostles of our Lord, Jesus Christ, ¹⁸in that they were telling you, "At the end of time there'll be scoffers traveling** [yet again a figure of speech for behaving] **in accordance with their own lusts of ungodlinesses. ¹⁹These** [scoffers] **are the ones causing divisions, soulish, not having the Spirit.** "But you, beloved" emphatically demarcates Jude's audience of true Christians from the heretics, whose professed Christianity amounts to nothing more than pretense. Remembering goes beyond a recollection of the past to include an application of that recollection in the present—here, a recognition of the current heretics for what they truly are, namely, the fulfillment of apostolic prophecies that licentious scoffers would appear on the scene "at the end of time" (the church age as the last period before the end of history as we know it). "Of our Lord, Jesus Christ" describes the apostles in a way that favors a reference to the original twelve (except Judas Iscariot), plus Paul. For their prophecies concerning heretics, see Matthew 7:15–23 (in quotation of Jesus); Acts 20:26–30; 1 Timothy 4:1–3 (though of ascetical rather than licentious heretics); 2 Timothy 3:1–9, besides unrecorded such prophecies. The designation "scoffers" suggests that the heretics were scofflaws in their behavior because they scoffed at the prospect of judgment at the Lord's coming, prophesied by Enoch (verses 14–15); and again "their *own* lusts" points up the Lord's calling them to account at the Last Judgment. "Lusts *of* ungodlinesses" means "lusts *for* ungodly behaviors." The heretics are participating in Christians' love-feasts (verse 12). So they cause divisions within churches (they and their followers versus true Christians) rather than leaving churches with their followers (as in 1 John 2:19). "Soulish" describes them as having only a physically enlivening soul, as all human beings do, and therefore as "not having the Spirit," whom only true Christians have (though the heretics may have claimed to have the Spirit [compare their reliance on dreams according to verse 8]).

20–23: **But you, beloved, by building yourselves on your most sacred faith, by praying in the Holy Spirit,**

²¹**keep yourselves in God's love while waiting expectantly for the mercy of our Lord, Jesus Christ, that results in eternal life.** ²²**And on the one hand treat mercifully some who are wavering.** ²³**On the other hand, save some by snatching them out of the fire** [compare Zechariah 3:2]. **But treat some mercifully with fear, hating even the tunic** [an undergarment] **blotted by the flesh.** "But you, beloved" demarcates Jude's truly Christian audience sharply from the heretics once again (see verse 17). For the faith as a body of belief, see the comments on verse 3. There Jude described it as "once for all given over to the saints [= believers as 'sacred' to God]." So here Jude describes it as "your[s]," shifts the description "sacred" from them to their faith, and jacks up this description to "*most* sacred" for a contrast with the heretics' *un*faith, which God considers profane. Building on this faith portrays behavior in terms of construction and portrays the most sacred body of belief as the foundation for truly Christian behavior. "Praying in the Holy Spirit" means praying under his direction. Such praying combines with the truly Christian behavior represented by "building yourselves" to provide the means for "keep[ing] yourselves in God's love." So "kept [by God] for Jesus Christ" (verse 1) doesn't absolve Christians from their own responsibility to keep themselves in the love of God "while waiting expectantly" for mercy instead of condemnation at the second coming and Last Judgment. The expectation enables the waiting; the waiting requires the keeping; the keeping ensures the mercy; and the mercy results in eternal life. In his exhortation Jude notably involves the Holy Spirit, God, and Jesus Christ—all three persons of what has come to be called the Trinity.

But Christians who are praying in the Holy Spirit and keeping themselves in God's love while expectantly awaiting the mercy of Jesus Christ should extend their own mercy—or, better, offer his mercy by anticipation—to those wavering on the brink of apostasy. Mercifully pull them back, Jude is saying. Don't push them over out of dismay over their attraction to the heretics. Others are already falling over the brink, though. They should be snatched out of the fire of eternal damnation before it's too late—and that fire is licking at their feet, so to speak (compare Revelation 20:15). Others have just now started the licentious life of apostasy, represented in an undergarment stained by the flesh next to which it's worn (compare verse 8). In dealing with them, mercy needs to be tempered with a fear of contamination by the licentiousness. It may tempt you to follow suit. So develop a healthy hatred of undergarments stained with the fluids of fleshly lusts. Nevertheless, try carefully to retrieve new apostates before they're hardened in apostasy.

24-25: **And he who can protect you as non-stumblers** [= so that you don't stumble] **and** [who can] **make you stand unblemished with gladness within sight of his glory,** ²⁵[namely,] **the only God, our Savior through Jesus Christ, our Lord,** [has] **glory, greatness, might, and authority before every age and now and till all the ages. Amen!** "Before every age" refers to eternity past, which is already set. Therefore Jude can't wish for anything then, as though the past could be changed. What we have, therefore, isn't a wish ("*may he* have")—rather, a declaration ("he *does* have"), punctuated with an exclamatory "Amen!" "He who can protect you" relates this declaration to the preceding exhortation on dealing with near and new apostates. Stumbling into apostasy, and ultimately into eternal ruin, contrasts with standing upright, morally unblemished, at the Last Judgment. "With gladness" will mark the fulfillment of expectant waiting and replace the present fear of contracting moral pollution. "Within sight of his glory" will turn present proximity to "the tunic blotted by the flesh" (verse 23) into proximity to the unblotted glory of God. "The *only* God, our Savior" denies the deity and saviorhood of all other supposed gods and saviors, including the Caesars. "Through Jesus Christ" declares him to be God's agent of salvation from sin and judgment. "Our Lord" puts him on par with "the only God, our Savior." God has had "glory, greatness, might, and authority" since eternity past (as emphasized in the phrase, "before *every* age"), has them currently, and will have them forever and ever (as emphasized in the phrase, "till *all* the ages"). Jude makes this declaration to solidify his audience in resistance to heresy, to encourage them in their "contend[ing] vigorously for the faith that was once for all given over to the saints" (verse 3).

REVELATION

This book is also called the Apocalypse (Greek for "uncovering"). It reveals, or uncovers, things otherwise hidden from human beings—namely, the true state of present affairs in the world and in certain churches that are addressed, and also what's going to happen to them and the world in the future. The predictive element has the purpose, not of satisfying idle curiosity, but of encouraging Christians to resist worldly allurements and antagonism, including persecution to the point of martyrdom. The extravagant figures of speech used throughout Revelation typify apocalyptic style and may sound strange to modern ears, but they convey the cosmic proportions of described events far more effectively than prosaic language could ever do (compare the exaggerated figures in current cartoons, which moderns readily accept and understand). Early church tradition identifies John, the author according to 1:4, with the apostle of that name. Though John records multiple visions that he had, his book is called Revelation (singular), not Revelations (plural).

INTRODUCTION
Revelation 1:1–8

The introduction to Revelation contains a superscription (1:1–2), a blessing on the public reader and his audience (1:3), a greeting (1:4–5a), a doxology (1:5b–6), and a statement of theme (1:7–8).

1:1–2: The revelation of Jesus Christ, which God gave him to show to his slaves the things that must happen with speed. Since Jesus will say in 22:16 that he sent his angel "to testify these things to you [plural, for the audience]," Jesus Christ passed on the revelation that God gave him (but see the comments on 22:16 for Jesus' angel as his alter ego, as the angel of Lord is to the Lord in the Old Testament). "To his slaves" describes the Christian audience as belonging to God and as bound to obey his messages conveyed through Jesus Christ. (The translation "servants" softens too much the sense of divine possession and mastery.) "Which God gave him to show . . ." is reminiscent of God's giving Jesus a variety of gifts throughout John's Gospel (with a special concentration in chapter 17). "The things which must happen" echoes Daniel 2:28 and indicates that God is in control of the future, however bleak it may presently look. In view of 1:3 ("For the time is near"), "with speed" means "soon." **And he** [God] **signified** [this revelation] **by sending** [it] **through his angel to his slave John, ²who testified the word of God and the testimony of Jesus Christ,** [that is,] **as many things as he saw** [in visions that John will recount throughout this book]. John uses "signified" because it's a verbal form of "sign," which appears repeatedly in his Gospel and fits the symbolic language that characterizes Revelation. "Through his angel" is usually taken as a heavenly intermediary between Jesus and John, so that the revelation originated from God and was transmitted by Jesus through an angel to John. But the word for "angel" means "messenger" and often refers to a human rather than angelic messenger. Especially in chapter 10 Jesus will be portrayed as an angel-like messenger (compare the comments on John 1:51). Moreover, it's Jesus, not some other kind of messenger, through whom God first sends a revelation to John (see 1:9–3:22; also the comments on 4:1); and no angel shows John anything till 17:1. It seems, then, that Jesus is God's messenger through whom God signified Revelation. As God's slave, John performed the duty of testifying God's word. But since Jesus is the Word of God (see 1:9; 19:13; John 1:1, 18; 10:35 with comments), John testified to Jesus' being that Word: the word *of* God is the Word who *is* God speaking. Similarly, "the testimony *of* Jesus Christ" is the testimony who *is* Jesus Christ testifying, "the testimony" being in synonymous parallelism with "the Word," and "of Jesus Christ" being in synonymous parallelism with "of God" (compare 1 John 5:20 for John's equating "Jesus Christ" with "God"). In this book, then, John testifies to the testimony *whom* he saw. "To *as many things as* he saw" gives assurance that he left nothing out.

1:3: Fortunate [is] **the person who reads** [this book aloud to a congregation of Christians] **and** [fortunate are] **those who hear the words of the prophecy and keep** [= heed] **the things written in it, for the time is near!** "The Word of God" (1:2) will speak "words"; and these words will constitute a "prophecy," which consists in preaching and predicting. The preaching will concentrate in chapters 2–3, the predicting in the remaining chapters. To read, hear, and keep the words is to be fortunate because the time of their fulfillment is near; and to be informed ahead of time gives opportunity and reason to prepare.

1:4–5a: John to the seven churches in Asia [a Roman province in western Asia Minor]. **Grace** [will be] **to you and peace from he who is and he who was and he who is coming, and from the seven Spirits that are within sight of his throne, ⁵ᵃand from Jesus Christ, the faithful witness** [= testifier], **the firstborn of the**

dead, and the ruler of the kings of the earth. The address makes Revelation a kind of long letter to churches in Asia. Though the churches are local, their being seven in number—seven being a number of completeness, as in the seven days of creation (Genesis 1:1–2:3)—makes these churches representative of churches everywhere. For the meanings of "grace" and "peace" and for supplying a confident "will be" rather than a wishful "be," see the comments on 2 John 3. John writes "from *he* who is" instead of a grammatically correct "from *him* who is." The bad grammar produces a divine title ("he who is") that alludes to the divine title "I AM" in Exodus 3:14 (compare John 8:58). Similarly, "from . . . he who was" produces a divine title referring to God's existence throughout eternity past. But instead of an expected "from . . . he who *will be*," John writes "from . . . he who *is coming*" for a reference to the second coming as an introduction to the eternal future. But the second coming, described at length in 19:11–16, will feature Jesus, whereas the present part of John's greeting features God. Jesus is the Word who is God, however (see the comments on 1:2), so that their oneness with each other (John 10:30; 17:11, 21–22) means that God comes when Jesus comes (compare John 14:23). "Is coming" portrays this future event as so sure to take place that it might as well be happening right now.

Ancient Greek manuscripts don't distinguish between capital and small letters of the alphabet. So the distinction in English translation is a matter of interpretation. Because the spirits are seven in number, other translations leave "spirits" uncapitalized. As a whole, though, the greeting in 1:4–5a looks Trinitarian, with "Jesus Christ" put third to allow for a number of additions relating to him. So we should capitalize "Spirits" and understand John to mean the Holy Spirit distributed in his wholeness to each of the seven churches in Asia and hence representatively to all churches. "Within sight of his throne" underlines the intimate association of "the seven Spirits" with God, who sits on the throne.

Completing the Trinity is "Jesus Christ." "The faithful witness" anticipates 3:14 and alludes to 1:2: "the testimony of Jesus Christ," which meant not only the testimony that he gave but also the testimony that he is, just as "the word of God" meant not only the word that God speaks but also the Word that God is (see the comments on 1:2). In speaking the words of God *as* God's Word, Jesus testified throughout John's Gospel (see John 8:14 for an example). And in his testimony he was faithful to the point of death (see John 18:37 in the context of his trial and crucifixion; compare Revelation 2:10 and especially 2:13). The faithfulness of Jesus' past testimony makes believable what he'll now testify according to the book of Revelation. "The firstborn of the dead" means that he was the first to resurrect from the dead never to die again (compare 1 John 5:20). But since firstborn sons traditionally got the lion's share of an inheritance, "firstborn of the dead" also means first in rank over those who have yet to be resurrected. "The ruler of the kings of the earth" assures Christians that despite past, current, and

coming persecution at the hands of those kings, Jesus Christ maintains sovereignty over them and will someday subdue them. (Nero's brutal persecution of Christians in Rome loomed in memory, for example.) Though Jesus' kingdom "isn't from this world" (John 18:36), he'll impose it on the earth (Revelation 19:11–22:5).

1:5b–6: **To him who loves us and released us from our sins by his blood—**⁶**and he made us** [into] **a kingdom,** [into] **priests for his God and Father—to him** [belong] **the glory and the might** [= sovereignty] **forever and ever** [literally, "unto the ages of the ages," that is, for an unending succession of ages]. **Amen!** "Us" refers to John and his audience of fellow Christian believers. For Jesus' loving believers in him, see especially 3:9; John 13:1, 34; 15:9, 12. But there Jesus refers to his loving believers by dying for their salvation. Here John refers to Jesus' ongoing love for believers, which will lead him to deliver them from their persecutions. "Released us from our sins" implies that our sins had hold of us, as though we were their slaves. "By his blood" tells the price of our release (compare 5:9; 7:14; 12:11; John 6:53–56; 19:34; 1 John 1:7; 5:6–8). Blood points up the sacrificial character of Jesus' death (see Hebrews 9:22 with comments). "And he made us [into] a kingdom" alludes to Exodus 19:6 but doesn't mean he rules over us (though that may be true in other contexts). It means, rather, that we share his rule with him, as will become apparent upon his return (1:9; 5:10; 20:4–6; 22:5). "And he made us . . . [into] priests for God" continues the allusion to Exodus 19:6 and adds to the privilege of ruling with Jesus the privilege of leading in the worship of God. There's a contrast with worldly kingdoms and priests who lead in the worship of divinized but earthly kings, such as the emperor, as well as of pagan gods. Priesthoods of this sort were eagerly sought and bought. Jesus' blood has bought our priesthood for us. "His God and Father" confirms the Trinitarian cast of 1:4–6 and implies Jesus' divine sonship over against the claim of Caesars to be divinized sons of God. (The coins of a Caesar were stamped with *divi filius*, Latin for "God's son.") But only to Jesus, "the ruler of the kings of the earth" (1:5a), belong the glory and the sovereignty claimed by Caesars and promoted by priests in charge of emperor worship. Unlike the Caesars' supposed glory and sovereignty, that of Jesus will last throughout eternity. "Amen" adds an exclamation point to this truth, assuring as it is to the people of God.

1:7: **Behold, he's coming with the clouds** [compare Daniel 7:13]**; and every eye will see him, even those who as such pierced him** [compare John 19:34, 37]**; and all the tribes of the earth will beat themselves** [on the chest] **over him** [compare Zechariah 12:10]**. Yes! Amen!** "Behold" calls special attention to the second coming, a climactic event. As the reference to piercing dictates, "he" who "is coming" is Jesus Christ, the dominant figure in 1:5–6. But "who is coming" described God the Father in 1:4. So because of their oneness, what is true of him is true also of Jesus (see the comments on 1:4). The present tense of "is coming" makes this future event as certain as a current event. Clouds accompany manifestations of deity (see the comments on Mark 13:26, for example), so that Jesus' coming "with the clouds" signals his deity in union with God the Father. Up in the sky with the clouds as he comes, he'll be visible to "every eye" (compare Matthew 24:23–30). "Even those . . . who pierced him" pluralizes the single soldier who pierced Jesus' side in John 19:34. But since that solider was acting on behalf of the Jewish authorities to whom Pilate gave Jesus over for crucifixion (John 19:12–16), "those . . . who pierced him" refers to these Jews. "Even" and "as such" underscore Jesus' victory over the ones most directly responsible for his death. "All the tribes of the earth" corresponds to "every eye" and includes many more than those who pierced Jesus. The tribes "will beat themselves [on the chest]" to lament his having been pierced (compare 18:9 for a similar lament over the fall of Babylon). John isn't concerned to say whether the tribes lament in repentance (probably not, since only certain Jews had him pierced) or in despair over their coming judgment. The focus rests on lament as such to emphasize the injustice done to Jesus. This injustice parallels the injustices perpetrated on his followers, but his coming with the clouds forecasts a vindication for them like his vindication. "Yes!" is Greek. "Amen!" is Hebrew. Together they provide a twofold affirmation of the truth that Jesus is indeed coming with the clouds.

1:8: **"I am the alpha and the omega," says the Lord God, "he who is and he who was and he who is coming, the Almighty."** Since alpha and omega are the first and last letters in the Greek alphabet, saying "I am the alpha and the omega" is like saying in English "I am the A and the Z." In other words, the Lord God spans the alphabet from beginning to end (compare 21:6; 22:13)—a figurative way of saying what follows in prosaic language: "he who is and he who was and he who is coming" (for which see the comments on 1:4). This language described God the Father in 1:4 and therefore identifies "the Lord God" with him here too (as clearly also in 4:8; 21:22). Addition of "the Almighty" gives John's audience assurance that despite their persecutions, the Lord God will prevail over the persecutors. He's not only eternally existent. He's also eternally powerful. So not to fear the Caesars or other worldly authorities—or Hekate, a goddess who was worshiped in Asia Minor (as well as elsewhere) and about whom remarkably similar things were said.

CHRIST THE ROYAL PRIEST TENDING SEVEN LAMPSTANDS AND HOLDING SEVEN STARS
Revelation 1:9–20

1:9: **I John, your brother and fellow sharer in the affliction and kingdom and perseverance in Jesus, came to be in the island called Patmos** [in the Aegean Sea thirty-seven miles southwest of Miletus, a port on the west coast of Asia Minor] **because of the Word of God and the Testimony of Jesus.** "Your brother" means "your fellow Christian." This self-designation and "your . . . fellow sharer" are designed to win from the audi-

ence a favorable hearing. At the same time, though, they reflect the close partnership Christians have with one another. (This use of "brother" appears often in John's writings.) Literally, "the affliction" means "the pressure" and refers here to the pressure of persecution, as exemplified in John's having come to be on the island called Patmos "because of the Word of God and the Testimony of Jesus," which means because of John's preaching about the Word who is God and testifying about the Testimony who is Jesus (see the comments on 1:2). The association with "the affliction . . . and perseverance" points to Patmos as a place of exile because of John's preaching. Furthermore, "the affliction" comes because Christians constitute a kingdom not of this world and opposed by the kingdom of the beast (1:6; 5:10; 11:15; 16:10; 17:12–18). But through sharing, true Christians persevere under the affliction because of the kingdom. "In Jesus" doesn't tell the location of "the affliction and kingdom and perseverance" so much as it tells the location of "John" as a "brother and fellow sharer." And this location "in Jesus" takes precedence over John's location "in the island called Patmos" (compare believers' abiding in Jesus though they're in the world [John 15:1–7; 17:11; also 14:1–3, 20]).

1:10–11: **I came to be in the Spirit on the Lord's Day and heard behind me a loud voice, as of a trumpet [11]saying, "Write in a scroll what you're seeing and send [the scroll] to the seven churches: to Ephesus and to Symrna and to Pergamum and to Thyatira and to Sardis and to Philadelphia and to Laodicea."** Whereas John had a continuous location in Jesus (1:9), he *"came to be* in the Spirit." That is to say, the Holy Spirit engulfed him so that he could see prophetic visions (compare being baptized "in the Holy Spirit" and worshiping God the Father "in the Spirit" [John 1:33; 4:23–24]). See also 19:10, which identifies "the Testimony of Jesus" with "the Spirit of prophecy" much as John 1:1 identifies "the Word" with "God," so that taken together, these statements spell the Trinity. "The Lord's Day" means Sunday, when Christians celebrated "the Lord's Supper" (1 Corinthians 11:20), and stands over against "the Emperor's Day," celebrated monthly in honor of the Caesar. ("Lord's" and "Emperor's" translate the same Greek word, but "Lord's" fits a reference to Jesus whereas "Emperor's" fits a reference to Caesar.) "A loud voice" connotes authority and calls for attention. "As of a trumpet" reinforces the loudness. "Saying" relates to the trumpet, as though it's speaking, rather than to the voice and therefore adds further reinforcement. The command to "write in a scroll" presses the point that Revelation comes from God through Jesus to John—and therefore *through* John, not just *from* John to the churches. So they'd better take heed. Their locations are listed, beginning with Ephesus (closest to Patmos) and then circling north and finally southeast.

1:12–13: **And I turned around to see the voice which as such was speaking with me. And on turning around, I saw seven gold lampstands [13]and in the**

midst of the lampstands [a figure] **like a son of man** [= having the appearance of a human being (compare Daniel 7:13)], **clothed down to the feet and belted around at his breasts with a gold belt.** To see a *voice* seems strange, but no more strange than seeing and even handling "the *Word* of life" in 1 John 1:1–3. To write about "*see*[ing] the voice" emphasizes that the voice comes from God's *incarnate* and therefore *visible* Word, Jesus Christ (1:1; John 1:14). "Which *as such*" adds further emphasis on the voice as visible through the Word's incarnation. "Speaking *with* me" doesn't imply John's speaking too. It implies, rather, the proximity of the voice to John, so that we mustn't think that distance obscured the vision. His having seen and heard at close range makes the account trustworthy. The seven gold lampstands recall the gold lampstand (the menorah) in the Old Testament tabernacle. It was single, but had six branches and a central stem (the trunk), each of which held a bowl-shaped lamp fitted with a wick and fueled with olive oil (Exodus 25:31–40; 27:20; 37:17–24; Zechariah 4:2). Here, though, the menorah's six branches and stem are separated into seven individual lampstands for the upcoming symbolism of seven churches geographically separated from each other. (It would spoil the symbolism if each lampstand were to have six branches and a stem.) The high value of gold will represent the high value God places on the churches. Jesus appears to John *like* a human being because he *is* a human being, but likeness to a human being keeps his already highlighted deity in the forefront. "In the midst of the lampstands" puts him in a sanctuary, where priests work, and in a position to evaluate the light-giving of the lamps, and therefore the testimony of the churches they stand for. The lowest possible hemline of his robe ("down to the feet") and the highest possible placement of his belt ("at his breasts") dignify him as the highest of high priests, over against Caesar (*pontifex maximus*, Latin for "highest priest"), just as John will call him "King of kings and Lord of lords" (17:14; 19:16; compare 1:5 and see 1:6 for believers in Jesus as a priesthood, so that abiding in their high priest makes them priests too). We might think of the belt as a horizontally placed sash of gold-colored cloth; but Daniel 10:5–6, to which John alludes more than once, speaks about a belt of "pure gold of Uphaz." So a belt of this precious metal matches the lampstands made of the same precious metal and thus heaps further dignity on Jesus.

1:14–15: And his head—that is, his hair—[was] white, as wool [is] white, as snow [is white]; and his eyes, as it were, a flame of fire; [15]and his feet [were] like bronze made glowingly red hot in a furnace, as it were; and his voice, as it were, the voice [= sound] of many waters [compare Ezekiel 1:24; 43:2]. The comparisons to wool and snow come from Daniel 7:9–14. There the whiteness of hair has to do with "the Ancient of Days" (God the Father in Christian terminology) as distinct from "one like a son of man" (Jesus Christ in Christian terminology). But because of the oneness of God the Father and Jesus his Son, John regularly interchanges

their descriptors. White hair stands for great age, here for eternal age, and for the veneration that such age deserves. The twofoldness of the comparisons to wool and snow underlines the great age. "Eyes as a flame of fire" denote anger that strikes the object of sight with judgmental fire (see 19:12 in context; compare Daniel 7:9–12; 10:6 and the ancient notion of an "evil eye" [not evil in the sense of sinful, but evil in the sense of causing misfortune]). Likewise, glowingly red hot feet of bronze denote a trampling down in judgment with heavy metal feet fired in the furnace of divine anger (compare Daniel 10:6 again and contrast the brittle feet of clay in Daniel 2:31–45). Because of the association with thunder in 14:2; 19:6, "the voice of many waters" refers to the sound of a heavy rainstorm. The addition of this comparison to the comparison with a trumpet blast (1:10) heightens the emphasis on loudness and therefore on authority and the need to pay attention.

1:16: And [he was] holding in his right hand seven stars; out of his mouth [was] issuing a sharp, double-edged sword; and his face [was] as the sun shines in its strength. The stars form a necklace that he holds. As seven they consist of the sun, the moon, and the five planets known to ancient people (Mercury, Venus, Mars, Jupiter, and Saturn). What they stand for in Revelation remains to be seen, but the ancients regarded these heavenly bodies as personal beings of a higher order than humans and therefore as heavenly beings whose movements in the sky control events on earth (hence astrology). So apart from the upcoming Christian symbolism, Jesus' holding the seven stars shows him rather than them in control. Since most people are right-handed, the right hand represents strength as well as favor, so that Jesus is *firmly* in control. The issuing of a sword out of Jesus' mouth stands for the pronouncement of judgments. As sharp and double-edged it lays bare the truth however and whenever it strikes (see Hebrews 4:12). The comparison of Jesus' face to the sun at high noon depicts his glory as blindingly bright (compare John 1:4–5, 7–9; 3:19–21 among other passages). It's a mistake to draw even a mental picture of a sword coming out of Jesus' mouth, of glowingly red hot feet, and so on. John is making comparisons to highlight Jesus' glory, anger, pronouncements of judgment, eternity, and so on.

1:17–19: And when I saw him, I fell at his feet as though [I were] dead [compare Daniel 10:9–11]; and he put his right [hand] on me, saying, "Don't be afraid. I am the first and the last [compare Isaiah 41:4; 44:6; 48:12], [18]and the living one. And I became dead; and behold, I am living forever and ever! And I have the keys of death and of hades. [19]Therefore write down the things that you've seen and the things that are and the things that are going to happen after these things." The vision of Jesus so overpowers John that he falls, not just on his knees, but flat on the ground ("as though dead") at Jesus' feet (the lowest possible position in relation to him). The audience of Revelation is meant to understand that the sight of Jesus at his second coming will similarly overpower his and their enemies. But to show that his power doesn't threaten believers, he puts his right hand (the hand of favor) on John and tells him not to fear. "I am the first and the last" interprets "I am the alpha and the omega" in 1:8. But there the Lord God (the Father) was speaking. Here Jesus is speaking. Yet again, then, what's true of the one is true of the other because of their oneness in deity (see the comments on 1:4, 7). "I am . . . the living one" strikes a contrast with John's having fallen at Jesus' feet "as though [John were] dead." This contrast suggests an allusion to the actual deaths of Christian martyrs, so that Jesus' identifying himself as "the living one" promises Christians life even though they die as martyrs (compare 20:4–6 and John 11:25–26 among other passages).

Jesus goes on to say that unlike John, he became actually dead, as martyrs for him do; but now he's alive forevermore, as they will be too. "Behold" punctuates the point. Moreover, Jesus' "hav[ing] the keys of death and of hades [the underworld of the dead]" indicates that by virtue of his own resurrection he'll unlock the gates of hades to bring believers in him, most notably his martyrs, out from death into life (compare John 5:24–29, where emphasis falls also on present anticipation of the transition from death to life, and on resurrection to judgment as well as on resurrection to life). "*Therefore* write" means that because the resurrected Jesus has the keys of death and of hades, John should write. But why should Jesus' having those keys require John to write? The answer is twofold: (1) the Christian audience need the encouragement that will come from hearing read to them what John writes; and (2) like the *speaking* of a true prophecy, the *writing* of one ensures and even sets in motion its fulfillment, for God doesn't go back on his word (contrast John's being told *not* to write down a prophecy of the seven thunders lest they be fulfilled [10:1–4]). Since "the things that you've seen" have to do with John's experience of seeing them, "the things that are and the things that are going to happen after these things" likewise have to do with John's experience of seeing the rest of the present vision and further visions to come. In other words, these phrases have to do with the visions themselves, not with their fulfillments, which won't be ensured till he writes down the visions (see further the comments on 4:1).

1:20: "**As for the secret of the seven stars that you saw on my right** [hand] **and as for the seven gold lampstands, the seven stars are** [= symbolize] **the messengers of the seven churches; and the seven lampstands are** [= symbolize] **the seven churches.**" "The secret" (often translated "the mystery") indicates that "the seven stars" are symbolic. Likewise for the seven gold lampstands. Jesus interprets the symbols. "*In* my right hand" (1:16) changes to "*on* my right hand," perhaps to highlight the stars' visibility to John. Because of the prominence of angels in apocalyptic literature, including elsewhere in Revelation, most translations read "angels" instead of "messengers" for the stars. But John's Greek word means "messengers" and often refers to human

rather than angelic messengers; and it's hard, perhaps impossible, to think that John could address the messages in chapters 2–3 to angels. Do angels have post office box numbers? But according to 1:4 John addresses Revelation to the churches, and the messages in chapters 2–3 are to be heard in those churches. So it's easier to think that John is sending Revelation to the churches by way of human messengers who are visiting him, one each from those churches, and who will return with the scroll in hand (compare the portrayal in chapter 10 of Jesus as angel-like though human). As stars and lamps give light, so the messengers and their churches give the light of Christian testimony in a world of darkness (compare the portrayal of John the baptizer as a burning and shining lamp because of his testifying about Jesus [John 1:6–8, 19–36; 3:22–36; 5:35]).

A MESSAGE TO THE CHURCH IN EPHESUS
Revelation 2:1–7

2:1–3: "For the messenger of the church in Ephesus write [as follows]: **These things says the one who's gripping the seven stars** [= the messengers of the seven churches] **in his right** [hand], **who's walking around in the midst of the seven gold lampstands: ²I know your deeds and toil and your perseverance, and that you can't bear** [= put up with] **bad people and** [that] **you've tested those who are alleging themselves** [to be] **apostles (and they aren't) and have found them false** [in their claim to be apostles], **³and** [that] **you have perseverance and have borne** [affliction (cf. 1:9)] **because of my name and haven't tired out.**" Here and throughout the rest of this message "you" and "your" are singular for the church as represented by its messenger, who is to convey the book of Revelation to his church. So it's probably better to translate with "*for* the messenger" rather than with "*to* the messenger." "These things says the one" strikes a formal, indeed solemn, note. But here the note is encouraging, for "who's gripping the seven stars in his right [hand]" means that Jesus the speaker holds the messengers securely in the hand of his strength and favor. For obvious reasons, persecutors go after church leaders first and foremost; and if the messengers fall into that category, as seems natural to assume, they stand in special danger. But though their present life lacks security, their eternal life has it. For Jesus will never relax his grip on them. He'll not throw them into the lake of fire (for which see 20:15), and no one will snatch them out of his hand (John 10:28). "Who's walking around in the midst of the seven gold lampstands" implies that Jesus is trimming the wicks and replenishing the oil of the lamps to keep their light shining. By means of these messages to the seven churches, in other words, Jesus is encouraging them and correcting their behavior so as to keep the light of their testimony shining (compare 1 John 2:8: "the true light is already shining").

Nothing escapes Jesus' notice: "I know your deeds." For the most part they turn out to be good (compare John 3:21). "Toil" connotes exertion. Commendably, the Ephesian Christians have been hard at work in their testimony. "Perseverance" indicates that they haven't stopped. And their testimony has included intolerance of bad people in the church who would damage its testimony. Jesus calls these people self-proclaimed "apostles," not in the sense of the original Twelve but in the sense of itinerant preachers (for "apostles" refers to somebody "sent" on a mission). Ephesus lay on a main highway between East and West and therefore got a lot of such preachers traveling through (compare Acts 20:28–31). In accord with 1 John 4:1–3, the Ephesian church has tested such preachers as to their doctrine and behavior (the two are intertwined) and found some of them to be false, whereas in all John's writings Jesus is nothing if not about "truth" (see a concordance). "And they aren't [apostles]" indicates Jesus' agreement with the church's verdict of falsity. "Perseverance" comes in for a second mention, this time in connection with the bearing of "affliction" instead of "deeds and toil." The church hasn't buckled under persecution (which could take the form of social ostracism, economic loss, and such like in addition to physical torture and martyrdom). "Because of my name" indicates that the persecution hasn't arisen out of misbehavior on their part, but out of their Christian testimony. For Jesus' name, see the comments on John 1:12; 17:11–12. It's the name "God," which he shares with his Father. God isn't Zeus or Apollo or any other supposed divinity in the pagan pantheon. Nor is a Caesar, past or present, divine. Jesus is God, and testifying to that truth over against polytheism brought persecution. Despite the persecution, though, the Ephesian church hasn't "tired out" in giving testimony to Jesus as God (compare 1 John 5:20).

2:4–5: "Nevertheless, I have against you that you've left your first love. ⁵Therefore be remembering from where you've fallen and repent and do the first deeds. Otherwise, I'm coming to you; and I'll move your lampstand out of its place if you don't repent." "Your first love" is the love the Ephesian Christians originally had for one another in obedience to Jesus' command (John 13:34–35; 15:12, 17 and various passages in 1 John). Not as in Matthew 24:10–12, where loss of communal love grows out of betraying each other to escape persecution oneself, here the loss of such love seems to have grown out of the very concern for truth that had led the Ephesian church to test self-proclaimed apostles, who turned out to be false. Apparently the church had become overly suspicious of its own membership. "Therefore" refers back to Jesus' having something "against" the church. No church should want his opposition. "Be remembering" means to recreate in your thinking. "From where you've fallen" compares the church to a lamp that has fallen from its lampstand with the result that the lamp doesn't give light any more. Loss of mutual love in a church spoils the church's testimony to the world. "Repent" means "change your attitude." "Do the first deeds" means "change your behavior" and implies that "your first love" consisted in doing helpful deeds for one another, not just in warm feelings and kind

words (compare 1 John 3:17–18). Good memory leads to good attitude, and good attitude leads to good deeds. "Otherwise" introduces a frightening warning: Jesus will come (whether at the end or preliminarily doesn't matter) and move the lampstand out of its place (within Jesus himself, the abiding place where alone there is salvation [see the comments on John 14:1–3]). "If you don't repent" underlines this warning.

2:6–7: "Nevertheless, you do have this, [namely,] that you hate the deeds of the Nikolaitans, which I too hate. ⁷The person who has an ear had better hear what the Spirit is saying to the churches. The person who conquers—I'll give him [the right] to eat from the tree of life, which [tree] is in God's paradise." A second "Nevertheless" introduces a happier outlook than the first one did in 2:4. Balancing out the hopefully temporary departure from first love is hatred of the Nikolaitans' deeds. Jesus and the Ephesian church agree with each other in this hatred just as they agreed with each other in pronouncing self-proclaimed apostles false (2:2). John doesn't yet describe the deeds of the Nikolaitans (but see the comments on 2:14–15). So the accent rests on the point that there's good hate as well as bad, just as there's bad love as well as good (see 1 John 2:15–17). All depends on the objects of love and hate. It's bad to love the bad, bad to hate the good, good to love the good, and good to hate the bad. Jesus offers himself as an example of good hating. "The person who has an ear" switches from the church to the individual Christian. However a church responds to Jesus' message, an individual Christian has his or her own responsibility to respond obediently. Everybody has an ear, and it takes only one to hear with. So the command is inclusive. Jesus doesn't address the individual Christian directly, though. Instead he tells the church what the individual Christian is commanded to do. This indirectness preserves the address to the church as a whole, conforms to Jesus' speaking also about but not to the person who conquers and other individuals in the churches, and sets up these individuals as examples (whether positive or negative) to the churches. "Is saying *to the churches* [plural]" indicates not only that the book of Revelation will go to all seven churches but also that every Christian is to heed what is said to all the churches, not just his or her own church. For what's said to other churches may apply to the individual even though it doesn't apply to his or her church as a whole. "What the *Spirit* is saying"—but *Jesus* is dictating these messages. So John's coming to be "in the Spirit" and hearing Jesus' "voice" (1:10) means that what Jesus says the Spirit too is saying (compare John 14:26; 15:26; and especially 16:12–14), just as what Jesus said during his earthly ministry is what God his Father said (John 8:28; 12:50; 15:15). The unity of the Trinity yet again!

"The person who conquers" refers to every true believer, not to specially good Christians (compare 1 John 5:5). There's a wordplay with the aforementioned "Nikolaitans" in that "Nik-" comes from the Greek verb behind "conquers" (*nikan*). The Nikolaitans may have thought of themselves as conquerors, but Jesus counts true Christians as the real conquerors. Conquering means resisting successfully the world's allurements and antagonism, sticking true and testifying no matter the cost (compare 1 John 2:13; 4:4; 5:4). The seven gold lampstands in John's vision have alluded to the seven-pronged gold menorah in the Old Testament tabernacle. That menorah, or lampstand, represented the tree of life and its branches in the garden of Eden. In addressing the Ephesian church, Jesus identified himself as the one "who's walking around in the midst of the seven gold lampstands" (2:1). So it's appropriate for him to allude now to "the tree of life" after which the original gold lampstand was modeled. Because of eating forbidden fruit from the tree of the knowledge of good and evil, humankind was expelled from "God's paradise," the garden of Eden, so that they couldn't eat fruit from the tree of life and thus gain eternal life in a state of sin. To have done so would have wreaked irreparable moral havoc on God's good creation (Genesis 1–3). "Paradise" means a walled *garden* or *park*. In a new creation paradise will be restored as a walled *city*, the New Jerusalem, described in 21:1–22:5 and featuring multiple specimens of the tree of life (22:2). True Christians, the conquerors, will have the right to eat its fruit. That is to say, they'll live forever with Jesus "the Living One" (1:18).

A MESSAGE TO THE CHURCH IN SMYRNA
Revelation 2:8–11

2:8–9: "And for the messenger of the church in Smyrna write [as follows]**: These things says the first and the last, who became dead and came alive: ⁹I know your affliction** [the pressure of persecution] **and poverty** [a result of persecution]**. Nevertheless you're rich! And** [I know] **the slander** [that comes] **from those who allege themselves to be Jews. And they're not** [Jews]**; rather,** [they're] **Satan's synagogue."** For the introduction see the comments on 2:1. "The first and the last" echoes 1:17. "The first" lived before he "became dead," and because he then "came alive" he's also "the last." In other words, he lived throughout the eternal past as "the alpha," died, and resurrected to live as "the omega" throughout the eternal future, so that those who face the possibility of martyrdom because of believing in him should take courage and comfort in sharing his eternal life through "the first resurrection" (20:4–6 [compare John 1:1–4; 11:25–26; 14:6; 1 John 1:1–2; 5:20; and note that "Smyrna," the name of a city, is also the Greek word for "myrrh," which according to John 19:38–40 was used to perfume Jesus' body when he "became dead"]). Though often suggested, an allusion to Smyrna's past demise and revival seems doubtful. "I know your affliction and poverty" replaces commendation (2:2–3) with sympathy. Tradesmen had guilds (something like modern labor unions, but not over against employers), and the guilds had patron deities to whom worship and sacrifice were made. Christian tradesmen therefore lost business when they dropped out of the guilds because of these pagan practices. That loss is one likely cause of the Smyrnan Christians' poverty. But present poverty for Christ's sake spells eternal wealth, which will be portrayed in John's vision of the New Jerusalem, adorned with gold and precious gems (Revelation 21:9–22:5). This wealth is in the Smyrnan Christians' divinely guaranteed savings account, so to speak ("you are rich"). Withdrawal for its enjoyment awaits the second coming and beyond.

Jesus doesn't specify "the slander [that comes] from those who call themselves Jews," so that his point consists not in the substance but in the falsity of what they're saying about the Christians. And this falsity is matched by the falsity of their calling themselves Jews. For if they were truly "Abraham's children," they'd be "doing the works of Abraham," that is, "lov[ing]" Jesus and therefore loving others who love him rather than slandering them (John 8:39, 42). As it is, they're "from [their] father the Devil" (John 8:44), so that "they're not [Jews]; rather, [they're] Satan's synagogue" (a reference to the synagogue in Smyrna [compare excommunication from a synagogue in John 9:22, 34; 12:42; 16:2 and the concentration of opposition to Jesus among the Jewish authorities in Jerusalem throughout John's Gospel]). Jesus calls the synagogue "Satan's" because its members slander the Christians with false accusations just as the Jewish authorities slandered Jesus with a false accusation (John 18:28–30); and "Satan" means "accuser" (compare 3:9; 12:10 and the comments on Revelation 7:1–17; 21:12 for Christians as the true Israel). Thus "the synagogue" stands over against "the church" (both to be understood in a local sense).

2:10: "In no respect be afraid of the things you're going to suffer. Behold, the Devil is about to throw some of you into prison so that you'll be tested and have affliction for ten days! Be faithful to the point of death, and I'll give you the crown of life." "The things you're *about* to suffer" connotes the imminence and certainty of suffering. This suffering will escalate the already experienced "affliction and poverty" (2:9) to an imprisonment that will test these Christians with ten days of affliction. The ten days may be figurative for an indefinitely limited period of time. But imprisonment had the purpose not of punishing a criminal—rather, of holding the accused for trial. There seems to be an allusion to Daniel 1:8–16, where the ten days of testing Daniel and his friends on a kosher diet are to be taken literally. Here, then, ten days of testing under the pressure (the literal meaning of "affliction") of a trial that might lead to a death sentence may need to be taken literally. As does "Satan" (a Semitic word), "Devil" (a Greek word) means "accuser," a meaning suitable to a trial for which there's imprisonment of the accused. The Devil's participation implies that it will be members of "Satan's synagogue" who'll get some of the Christians thrown in prison for trial and possible martyrdom. "Behold" highlights that the Devil will incite the unbelieving Jews to do so. Further highlighting this incitement is a wordplay between "Devil," *diabolos* in Greek, and "throw," *ballein* in Greek; for -*bolos* comes from *ballein*: the Devil will "throw" accusations against Christians to get them "thrown" into prison. "So that" indicates testing and affliction as his attained purpose. In no respect are the Christians to be afraid, though. Even if it means martyrdom, faithfulness is to swallow up fear. For there awaits the faithful a crown of life. To be faithful to the point of death is to be so full of faith that the prospect of a crown of life eliminates the fear of death. The crown will consist in resurrection to eternal life and represents this resurrection as a victory over death, especially death by martyrdom, in that laurel wreaths were awarded to victors at athletic contests such as the Olympics. (Note the reference to conquering—that is, winning a victory—in the next verse.)

2:11: **"The person who has an ear had better hear what the Spirit is saying to the churches."** See the comments on 2:7a. **"By no means will the person who conquers be injured by the second death."** The implied first death refers especially, though not exclusively, to martyrdom. The second death refers to being thrown into the lake of fire after a resurrection to judgment (see 20:14 with John 5:28–29). But the second death won't even injure, much less defeat, the person who conquers (for which conquering see the comments on 2:7b). "By no means" underscores this assurance.

A MESSAGE TO THE CHURCH IN PERGAMUM
Revelation 2:12–17

2:12–13: **"And for the messenger of the church in Pergamum write** [as follows]: **These things says the one who has the sharp, double-edged sword: ¹³I know where you dwell,** [that is,] **where Satan's throne** [is]. **And you're keeping a grip on my name and didn't deny faith in me even during the days of Antipas, my faithful witness, who was killed alongside you, where Satan dwells."** For the introduction see the comments on 2:1. By designating himself as "the one who has the sharp, double-edged sword," Jesus forewarns the church in Pergamum of strong criticism to come. The sword will lay bare serious faults (compare the comments on 1:16). So as not to antagonize his audience, though, Jesus first recognizes their difficult circumstance and commends their perseverance. The church dwells "where Satan's throne [is]," which in view of 13:2; 16:10 probably means where satanically inspired worship of the Roman emperor is prominent. For in those later passages Satan, represented by a dragon, gives the emperor, represented by the beast, "his throne." The acropolis of Pergamum, very steep and high, may have suggested the figure of a throne. Recognition of the circumstance that the church resided in a center of emperor worship heightens the commendation that they're "keeping a grip on [Jesus'] name" (for which name see the comments on 2:3). That is, the church has refused to worship the emperor and persisted in reserving the name "God" for Jesus Christ. The flip side of confessing Jesus Christ to be God is not denying such faith in him despite pressure to do so. Pressure of that sort reached a height of intensity "during the days of Antipas . . . who was killed alongside you [Jesus

says], where Satan dwells." Even then and even though "alongside you" underscores the proximity of like fate for other Christians, and even though Satan dwells there on his throne (note the second mention of Satan as the inspirer of emperor worship), the church hasn't buckled under the pressure to deny that Jesus Christ is God. As for Antipas, Jesus calls him "my faithful witness," which designation recalls John's designation of Jesus himself as "the faithful witness" (1:5). No higher compliment than that! *"My* faithful witness" means not only that Jesus claims him as his own (compare John 10:1–30; 17:1–26 among other passages), but also that Antipas testified regarding Jesus. This testimony led to Antipas's being killed.

2:14–15: **"Nevertheless, I have a few things against you in that you have there** [people in your church who are] **keeping a grip on the teaching of Balaam, who was teaching Balak to thrust a snare within eyesight of the sons of Israel** [so that they'd] **eat** [meat] **sacrificed to idols and fornicate. ¹⁵In this way you too have** [people in your church who are] **similarly keeping a grip on the teaching of the Nikolaitans."** The things Jesus has against the church in Pergamum may be "few," but they're serious. Counting them as few, however, keeps his criticism from becoming such a broadside as to forestall a repentant response. The story of Balaam the prophet, Balak king of Moab, and Israel is found in Numbers 22:1–25:9; 31:1–20. After failing to prophesy a curse on Israel for Balak, Balaam advised him to use his Moabite women for luring the men of Israel into sacrificing to pagan gods, eating the sacrificial meat, and fornicating with the women. Jesus calls these women "a snare," that is, a stumbling block which trips up people—morally in this case. "Within eyesight of the sons of Israel" pictures the women as appealing to "the lust of the [men's] eyes" (1 John 2:16). It makes no interpretive difference whether "the teaching of Balaam" refers to a teaching only *like* that of the ancient Balaam or also to a teaching by a prophet in Pergamum whom Jesus sarcastically *calls* Balaam because of a similarity with the ancient Balaam's teaching. Though fornication was often used as a figure of speech for idolatry, sexual immorality commonly accompanied idolatrous feasts in New as well as Old Testament times. So we have good reason to take the reference to fornication just as literally as we take the story of Balaam, Balak, and Israel and, more particularly, just as literally as we take the reference to eating meat from animals parts of which had been sacrificed to idols. Idolatrous feasts took place in temples. Since 1 John ends with a command that Christians keep themselves away from idols (5:21), and since 1 John aims against Gnostics of a libertine sort, chances are that those in Pergamum "who are keeping a grip on the teaching of Balaam" are just such Gnostics. They flaunt the supposed superiority of their spirits by indulging their fleshly lusts at idolatrous feasts (see the introduction to 1 John). "In this way" refers to such behavior. "You too" means "you as well as the church in Ephesus," which encountered "the deeds of the Nikolaitans" (2:6). "Keeping a grip on the teaching of the Nikolatians" contrasts with "keeping a grip on [Jesus'] name" (2:13) but runs parallel to "keeping a grip on the teaching of Balaam." "Similarly" makes the teaching of the Nikolaitans synonymous with the teaching of Balaam (see further the comments on 2:6–7). But whereas the church in Ephesus commendably "hate[s] the Nikolaitans' deeds," the church in Pergamum reprehensibly "ha[s]" Balaam-inspired Nikolaitans in the sense of tolerating them or, as we might say, accepting them as members in good standing.

2:16: "Therefore repent. Otherwise I'm coming to you quickly and will war with them by means of the sword of my mouth." If the church in Pergamum that's keeping its grip on Jesus' name doesn't repent by dealing disciplinarily with the people who are keeping their grip on the contrary teaching of Balaam (= the Nikolaitans' teaching), Jesus himself will come—"quickly," because he won't allow the present state of affairs to go on any longer. He'll deal with those people in terms like those used in 19:11–21 to describe the second coming, which will bring God's wrath on the beast, the kings of the earth, and their armies. The Balaamite Nikolaitans will share their fate. Balaam was killed with a sword in war with Israel (Numbers 31:8 [compare the drawn sword of the angel of the Lord standing in Balaam's way in Numbers 22:23, 31]). Likewise a sword will smite the Balaamites; but it will be the sword that comes out of Jesus' mouth—that is, a pronouncement of eternal doom at the Last Judgment.

2:17: "The person who has an ear had better hear what the Spirit is saying to the churches. The person who conquers—I'll give him [some] of the hidden manna; and I'll give him a white pebble, and written on the pebble a new name that no one knows except the person receiving [it]." See the comments on 2:7 for hearing and conquering. God gave manna as food for the Israelites as they traveled the wilderness on their way from Egypt to Canaan (Exodus 16). But as in John 6:22–59, the manna here symbolizes Jesus as the bread of life, *eternal* life. According to a Jewish tradition, some manna was hidden away along with other sacred objects when the Babylonians destroyed Solomon's temple, and this manna was to be brought out of hiding at the dawn of the messianic age. Jesus uses this tradition to portray eternal life in him as now hidden from view but destined to be manifested at his coming again (compare 1 John 3:1–2). "A white pebble" has attracted a number of interpretations; but given the immediately preceding reference to the food called manna, most likely the white pebble alludes to the custom of giving such a pebble to a victorious athlete—here, "the person who conquers"—as the ticket of admission to a celebratory feast—here, "the lamb's marriage banquet" (19:6–9) at which the featured dish will be the manna of eternal life. But what is the "new name" that's "written on the pebble" and that "no one knows except the person receiving it"? It can't be Jesus' new name (3:12); for the recipient of the white pebble knows the name written on it, whereas "no one

knows [Jesus' new name] except for him" (19:12). To know somebody's name was thought to possess a certain power over its owner. Under demonic impulse, for example, a demoniac tried to resist exorcism by shouting with a loud voice, "What do I and you have to do with each other, *Jesus, Son of the Most High God*? I adjure you by God not to torture me" (Mark 5:7; compare a demon's addressing Jesus by name and saying, "I know you, [that is,] who you are. [You're] God's Holy One" [Mark 1:24]). When Jesus asked, "What [is] your name?" and received the answer, "Legion [is] my name, because we're many" (Mark 5:9), he succeeded at the exorcism. (He'd previously thought the demoniac had only one demon.) Similarly, to pray "in [Jesus'] name" lends power to the prayer (John 14:13–14; 15:16; 16:23–24, 26). So for Jesus to say that no one except the recipient will know the name written on the pebble is a way of saying that no one will have power over the recipient (compare 19:12). Christians suffer now under the power of satanic forces. But not in the "*new* heaven" and "*new* earth" of Revelation 21:1–22:5, to which the "*new* name" corresponds (compare also the "*new* song" of 5:9; 14:3). And "a *white* pebble" corresponds especially to "the *white* garments" with which conquerors, who as such don't "stain their garments" with misbehavior, will be clothed (3:4–5 [see also 7:13–14 among other passages]).

A MESSAGE TO THE CHURCH IN THYATIRA
Revelation 2:18–29

2:18–19: "And for the messenger of the church in Thyatira write [as follows]: These things says the Son of God, the one who has his eyes as a flame of fire and his feet like glowingly [red hot] bronze: ¹⁹I know your deeds and love and faith and service and your perseverance. And your last deeds [are] more than [your] first [deeds]." For the introduction see the comments on 2:1. Over against the Caesars, who claimed the title *divi filius* (Latin for "God's son"), and in anticipation of "my Father" (2:28), Jesus identifies himself as "the Son of God" (see also the pervasiveness of this identification in John's Gospel and 1–2 John). This self-identification underlines the authority with which Jesus dictates the following message. "The one who has his eyes as a flame of fire" forecasts severe judgment and echoes 1:14, as do the glowingly red hot feet of bronze (see the comments on 1:14). But much as in 2:13, Jesus first compliments the church so as not to antagonize his audience with an immediate broadside. The list of their virtues is long, various, and well-balanced. "Deeds" spring from "love," and "love" necessarily expresses itself in "deeds" (1 John 3:16–18). "Faith" means both the right belief that undergirds deeds and love, and faithfulness in the doing of loving deeds. "Service" defines the deeds as done for fellow believers' benefit, and "perseverance" brings out the meaning of faithfulness in the word "faith." "Your last deeds" means "your recent deeds," and "[your] first [deeds]" means "your earlier deeds." That the last are "more than" the first means that the church is increasing in its practical expressions of love for one another (contrast the leaving of "first love" in the church at Ephesus [2:4]).

2:20–23: "Nevertheless, I have against you that you're leaving alone [compare John 12:7] **the woman Jezebel, who alleges herself** [to be] **a prophetess and is teaching and misleading my slaves to fornicate and eat** [meat] **sacrificed to idols.** ²¹**And I've given her time to repent, and she isn't willing to repent from her fornication.** ²²**Behold, I'm throwing her into a bed, and those who are committing adultery with her into great affliction if they don't repent from her deeds.** ²³**And I'll kill her children by means of death. And all the churches will know that I am the one who examines kidneys and hearts** [compare Jeremiah 11:20; 17:10], **and I'll give to each of you according to your deeds."** "Leaving alone the woman Jezebel" means tolerating her, being lenient toward her (compare the similar use of "have" in 2:15, for synonymous expressions occur often in John's writings). Whereas a concern for truth led to the loss of mutual love at Ephesus, a concern for love led to the loss of truth at Thyatira. As Jesus sarcastically called the falsely self-identified Jews in Smyrna "a synagogue of Satan" (2:9), he now sarcastically calls a falsely self-identified prophetess "Jezebel," the name of Israel's most notoriously wicked, pagan queen (see 1 Kings 16:29–33 and following, especially 2 Kings 9:22 for her whoredoms, and compare the false apostles here in 2:2). For "slaves" as a designation of Christians, see the comments on 1:1. Jezebel misleads Jesus' slaves in Thyatira with her teaching that it's okay, even superior, "to fornicate and eat [meat] sacrificed to idols" (see further the comments on 2:24; on 2:14 for such meat; and Deuteronomy 13:1–5 for false prophets as misleaders). In 2:14 eating such meat came first as a run-up to engaging in fornication at idolatrous banquets. Here, fornication comes first for stress on this immoral outcome of participating in such banquets. Jezebel has proved successful in misleading Christians thus. (Of course, sexual and alimentary pleasures oiled her success.) "I've given her time to repent" implies a past warning. "She isn't willing to repent" makes her unrepentance stubborn as well as flagrant. "*Her* fornication" indicates that she practices what she teaches. (Since idolatry and sexual immorality went together, there's no sufficient reason to reduce "fornication" to a mere figure of speech for idolatry.)

"Behold" calls special attention to Jezebel's imminent judgment. The present tense of "I'm throwing her" makes the judgment as good as going on right now. "Throwing" indicates forcible action, as in judgmental statements throughout Revelation (see, for example, 19:20; 20:3, 10, 14–15). "Into a bed" stands for a bed of illness and, because of the failure to take an opportunity for repentance, for a bed in hell (compare Psalm 139:8 for a bed in the underworld). Furthermore, "into a bed" suits judgment for fornication, committed in a bed. Jezebel has lost her chance to repent. Only "those who are committing adultery with her" have such a chance. "Committing adultery" implies fornication in which one

or both parties are married, but not to each other. "Great affliction" anticipates "the great affliction" out of which will come those who've washed their robes white "in the blood of the lamb" (7:14). To be thrown into it because of failure to repent contrasts with coming out of it and therefore means to share the fate of the wicked. For failure to repent is to *be* wicked. "If they don't repent from *her* deeds" indicates that Jezebel's partners in adultery still have a chance to repent because she has misled them with her supposedly prophetic teaching. "Her children" implies that she has given birth to bastards through her wanton liaisons. Killing her children "by means of death" means killing them by means of a plague and visits further punishment on her as a mother (6:8; Ezekiel 33:27). "And all the churches will know" implies the notoriety of this scandal among the other six churches addressed in Revelation and makes for them a warning example. But the example turns their attention to Jesus himself as "the one who [with blazing eyes (2:18)] examines kidneys [considered the seat of emotions, because you feel them in the pit of your stomach] and hearts [considered the seat of thoughts, because your heart races on the excitement of them]." In passing judgment, then, Jesus sees through our exteriors so as to coordinate interior conditions with outward deeds (compare John 7:24). With "I'll give *each of you* according to your deeds" Jesus switches from "her" and "her children" so as to call on his audience to watch out for themselves individually rather than merely looking at, and perhaps gloating over, others' judgment (compare the comments on 2:6–7).

2:24–25: "But I say to the rest of you in Thyatira, as many as don't hold this teaching, who as such [= in that you don't hold it] **haven't known 'the deep things of Satan'** (as they call [them])**: I'm not throwing on you another burden;** ²⁵**only, till I come keep a grip on what you do hold."** "But I say [and so forth]" introduces with a certain stress the considerate minimalism of the "burden" with which Jesus is about to saddle "the rest of you in Thyatira . . . who don't hold this [Jezebel's] teaching." "As many as" comfortingly includes them all. "Who . . . haven't known" means "who . . . haven't experienced." "The deep things of Satan" sarcastically references what Gnostic snobs called "the deep things of God" (a take-off on Paul's expression in 1 Corinthians 2:10; compare Daniel 2:22 and Jesus' sarcasm in calling the prophetess "Jezebel" [2:20] and especially in calling Smyrnan Jews "*Satan's* synagogue" [2:9] whereas they doubtless thought of themselves as God's synagogue [see also 3:9]). Jesus heightens the sarcasm by saying that "they," Jezebel and her fellow adulterers, call the deep things *Satan's* when they surely called them *God's*. "The *deep* things" connotes supposedly profound doctrine, superior to that which disallows fornication and eating at pagan temples meat that has been sacrificed to idols. It's better to have a burden thrown "*on* you" than to be yourself thrown "*into* a bed" or "*into* great affliction" (2:22). The minimal burden consists in keeping a grip on what the rest "*do* hold," as opposed to Jezebel's teaching, which they "*don't* hold." And what they "*do* hold" consists in their "deeds and love and faith and service and [their] perseverance." "Till I come" holds out the promise of an end to burden-bearing.

2:26–29: "And the person who conquers and who keeps my deeds till the end—I'll give him authority over the Gentiles [in the religious sense of non-Christians regardless of ethnicity]; [27]**and he'll shepherd them with an iron rod, as clay jars are shattered** [compare 12:5; 19:15; Psalm 2:8–9], **as I too have received** [authority] **from alongside my Father.** [28]**And I'll give him** [the person who conquers] **the morning star."** "The person who conquers" does so by "keeping [Jesus'] deeds till the end" (see also the comments on 2:7 for conquering). The deeds are those of Jesus in that he both commanded them and exemplified them in his own behavior on earth. To keep them is to obey his commands to do them and to imitate his doing of them. He says "*my* deeds" in opposition to "*her* [Jezebel's] deeds" (2:22). "Till the end" rephrases "till I come" (2:25). "Authority over the Gentiles" so as to "shepherd them [a figure of speech for ruling them]" looks forward to the saints' thousand years of ruling non-Christians following Christ's return (5:10; 20:1–10). "With an iron rod, as clay jars are shattered" portrays the saints' rule as rigorous and, when necessary, punitive—a reversal of their present condition of subjugation and oppression (compare the comments on 12:5). "As I too have received [authority]" indicates that they'll "reign as kings with the Christ" (20:4 [compare 12:10; 18:1; John 5:27; 17:2]). "From alongside my Father" typifies the Father's giving him various things according to John 8:26, 40; 10:18; 15:15; 17:7 (all with the phrase "from alongside"). "The morning star"—that is, Venus—symbolized victory, so that it's fitting that the victor ("the person who conquers") will receive the victory. But according to 22:16 Jesus is "the bright morning star" (compare Numbers 24:17). So he'll give himself *as* the victory to the victor just as he'll give himself *as* the manna, the bread of life, to the conqueror (2:17 [compare John 6:51–52]). And this self-giving will take place on the morning that eternal life dawns in the new heaven and the new earth. [29]**"The person who has an ear had better hear what the Spirit is saying to the churches."** See the comments on 2:7a. From here on the indirect command to hear comes last for final emphasis on the need to hear, whereas up till now the final emphasis has fallen on promises to the person who conquers.

A MESSAGE TO THE CHURCH IN SARDIS
Revelation 3:1–6

3:1: "And for the messenger of the church in Sardis write [as follows]: **These things says the one who has the seven Spirits of God and the seven stars: I know your deeds, that you have a name** [= a reputation] **that you're living. And you're dead."** For the introduction see the comments on 2:1, also on 1:4 for "the seven Spirits." "Of God" confirms the earlier estimate of the seven Spirits as God's Holy Spirit distributed in his wholeness to each of the seven churches. Jesus identifies himself as "the one who has the seven Spirits" because he'll describe the church as "dead" and because "Spirit" connotes life (11:11; 13:15; John 6:63), so that Jesus has a full complement of the seven Spirits, including one to bring a dead church to life. And "the seven stars" stand for "the seven messengers of the seven churches" (1:20), so that Jesus likewise has a full complement of the seven messengers to carry Revelation back to the churches from which they've come. "I know your deeds"—but Jesus doesn't list them. The less said, the better, as indicated also by his putting criticism before compliment (contrast 2:2–4, 13–15, 19–21). The deeds give way to a false reputation for living. The use of "a name" for the church's reputation makes a wordplay with the use in 3:4–5 of "a few names" and of "his name" for individual exceptions. The contrast between living and being dead makes the issue one of eternal life versus the second death, not merely one of thriving versus vegetating. As a whole, this church stands in danger of being thrown into the lake of fire, which is the second death (20:14). In other words, the church is reputedly Christian but in fact non-Christian. It doesn't have even the one of the seven life-producing Spirits assigned to it.

3:2–3: "Get awake and stabilize the remaining things that were about to die. For I haven't found your deeds fulfilled in the sight of my God. [3]**Therefore** [= because they're unfulfilled] **be remembering how it was that you received and heard** [God's word (1:2)]**, and be keeping** [it] **and repent. Therefore** [once more because your deeds are unfulfilled] **if you don't wake up, I'll come as a thief** [comes]**; and by no means will you know what particular hour I'll come against you** [compare Matthew 24:43–44; Luke 12:39–40; 1 Thessalonians 5:2–4; 2 Peter 3:10]**."** Since death is often compared to sleep (as in John 11:11, for example), "Get awake" means, "Wake up from the sleep of death," and prepares for the warning against being caught unprepared for Jesus' coming. He hasn't found the church's deeds "fulfilled." So "the remaining things" refers to deeds that remain but lack fulfillment because they haven't been supplemented with further deeds. What's meant is deeds that give evidence of the Spirit and of life, eternal life. More of them are needed to give such evidence (contrast the increasing number of such deeds in the Thyatiran church [2:19]). "In the sight of my God" indicates that God sees the state of the church in Sardis and that Jesus' appraisal of the deeds agrees with God's. "My God" echoes John 20:17 and stresses the closeness of Jesus' association with God. This closeness ensures the accuracy and authority of Jesus' appraisal. The remaining deeds need stabilization by being fulfilled, supplemented, added to. Otherwise they'll collapse and die. Jesus personalizes the deeds, as though they could die and be dead like the church, which consists of people. We expect "*are* about to die." Instead, we read "*were* about to die." Jesus projects a favorable response and therefore speaks as though the church has indeed stabilized the remaining things by fulfilling them. The fulfillment begins by remembering how it was that the people received and heard God's word (compare 2:5). Mental re-creation of the past then leads to keeping—that is, obeying—God's word in the present. Repentance constitutes the first act of obedience. The church is to repent for not having done enough deeds to demonstrate true faith. If the church doesn't wake up by obeying these commands, Jesus' coming will be like that of a thief (he'll take the church by surprise), whose intent is hostile ("I'll come against you"). Since an hour was the shortest unit of time used by these ancients, "by no means will you know what particular hour I'll come" stresses the surprise. (It's often noted that twice in earlier history Sardis, which had a seemingly impregnable acropolis, fell under surprise attack; but attack by an army on a city doesn't suit very well Jesus' coming as a thief who enters a private home.)

3:4–6: "Nevertheless, you have a few names in Sardis that haven't stained their garments; and they'll walk around with me in white [garments], **because they're worthy** [to do so]. **⁵The person who conquers will in this way be clothed in white garments, and by no means will I blot his name out of the scroll of life. And I'll confess his name in the sight of my Father and in the sight of his angels. ⁶The person who has an ear had better hear what the Spirit is saying to the churches."** For conquering and hearing see the comments on 2:7. "Nevertheless" introduces the happy exception of "a few names in Sardis." The use of "names" for these true Christians plays on "a name" in the sense of a reputation (3:1), echoes Jesus' statement that as the good shepherd "he calls his own sheep name by name" (John 10:3), and thus anticipates his "shepherd[ing] them and lead[ing] them to the springs of the waters of life" (Revelation 7:17). Behind "haven't stained their garments" lies the historical fact that the art of dyeing wool was first discovered in Sardis. Commendably, the few names haven't stained their moral garments the way garment-makers in Sardis dye the wool of the garments they make. Since the garments of the "few names" aren't morally stained, they'll walk around with Jesus in white garments (compare 19:8, where the "bright, clean fine linen" with which the saints are clothed stands for their "righteous acts"). Walking around with Jesus indicates close fellowship and will take place in the New Jerusalem (21:1–22:5). To be clothed in white garments "in this way" means to be clothed in them worthily ("because they're worthy"). "The scroll of life" contains the names of professing Christians and will appear repeatedly later in Revelation (for background see Exodus 32:32–33; Psalm 69:28; Daniel 12:1). Those whose behavior proves their profession false will have their names blotted out, so that they won't attain eternal life. But because a "few names in Sardis . . . haven't stained their garments"—that is, haven't falsified their profession with bad behavior—Jesus won't blot out the name of any of them, so that at the Last Judgment their names will appear in the register of the New Jerusalem's citizens. "By no means" adds force to this assurance. Since to confess Jesus means to declare he is in fact who he professes to be (the Son of God), for him to confess "the person who conquers" is for him to

declare (at the Last Judgment) the person is in fact who *he* professes to be (a Christian). Jesus' confession will include the Christian's name (see again John 10:3). "In the sight of my Father and in the sight of his angels" puts the confession in a judicial setting (20:11–15) and makes Jesus' confession of the true Christian just as public as was the true Christian's confession of Jesus.

A MESSAGE TO THE CHURCH
IN PHILADELPHIA
Revelation 3:7–13

3:7: "And for the messenger of the church in Philadelphia write [as follows]: **These things says the Holy One, the True One, the one who has the key of David, who opens and no one will shut, and closes and no one opens** [compare Isaiah 22:22]." For the introduction see the comments on 2:1. Jesus calls himself "the Holy One" to indicate his transcendence (compare John 6:69; 1 John 2:20) and "the True One" to indicate his truthfulness (compare 1 John 5:20; Revelation 3:14). Transcendence lends authority to his message. Truthfulness lends reliability to it. Since God the Father is "holy and true" (6:10) and the Spirit is "the Spirit of truth" as well as "Holy" (John 14:17, 26; 15:26; 16:13), Jesus' identifying himself as "the Holy One, the True One" undergirds Trinitarianism. "The key of David" stands for authority to admit and refuse admittance into David's royal household (compare entrance by the gates into a new city of David, the New Jerusalem [22:14]). "David" was a prototype of the Messiah, so that admittance into his household represents admittance into Jesus' household—and similarly for nonadmittance. "And no one will shut . . . and no one opens" denotes the finality of Jesus' letting in those who belong to him and turning away those who don't.

3:8: "I know your deeds. Behold, I've given in your sight an opened door, which no one can shut! [I know] **that you have little power and have kept my word and not denied my name."** So eager is Jesus to encourage the Philadelphian church that he interrupts a commendation of their deeds with an exclamatory assurance that he has given them an opened door into his household ("Behold . . . !"). In view of 3:7, he himself has opened it; and it's a gift from him (see also 2:7, 10, 17; 21:6; John 10:28; 1 John 5:11, 16 for eternal life as a gift). "In your sight" puts the opened door so close to the Philadelphian church that they can anticipate entering through it soon. "Which no one can shut" makes their entrance sure as well as soon. (Differently from here, the figure of an opened door in 1 Corinthians 16:9; 2 Corinthians 2:12; and Colossians 4:3 represents opportunities for Christian service, especially evangelism.) "You have little power" doesn't criticize the church; rather, it recognizes the small size of the church in Philadelphia. Few people lived there after a disastrous earthquake struck in A.D. 17. "You . . . have kept my word" means that the church has obeyed Jesus' commands (compare 22:7; 1 John 2:5; John 8:51–52; 15:20; 17:6) and preserved orthodox doctrine (Jesus *as* God's Word [see especially 1:2, 9; 6:9; 19:13; 20:4; John 1:1, 14; 10:35; 1 John 1:1, 10; 2:14 with comments]). "And not denied my name" implies pressure to deny it and refers to the name that Jesus shares with his Father, that is, "God" (see the comments on John 1:12; 17:11–12).

3:9: "**Behold, I'm giving that some from Satan's synagogue, who allege themselves to be Jews and they're not—rather, they're lying—behold, I'll make them come and kowtow in the sight of your feet and acknowledge that I've loved you!**" Two further instances of "Behold . . . !" underscore Jesus' assurances, designed to encourage the little church in Philadelphia. The first "Behold" introduces an assurance of their vindication. Like an opened door into Jesus' royal household (3:8), the vindication is coming as a gift from Jesus. For "Satan's synagogue" and Jewish non-Jews see the comments on 2:9. On the basis of Isaiah 45:14; 49:23; 60:14 Jews expected Gentiles to bow and scrape before them in the messianic kingdom. But here the self-proclaimed Jews who because of their unbelief in Jesus aren't true Jews—they'll do the bowing and scraping before the true Jews, that is, believers in Jesus regardless of their ethnicity. "In the sight of your feet" portrays the true Jews' feet as though they have eyes to see—at ground level—those kowtowing there. The kowtowers will have to acknowledge Jesus' love for the believers (compare 1:5; John 13:1, 34; 14:21; 15:9–10, 12–13).

3:10: "**Because you've kept my word of perseverance, I'll also keep you from the hour of the test,** [the hour] **that's about to come on the whole inhabited** [earth] **to test those who dwell on the earth.**" "My word of perseverance" means Jesus' command to persevere in Christian conduct and testimony (see 3:11: "Keep a grip . . ."). "You've kept" means "you've obeyed." "I'll also keep you" means "I'll also protect you." (There's a wordplay on two meanings of the verb *keep*.) "The hour of the test" refers to what is elsewhere called "the great affliction [more traditionally, 'the great tribulation']" (7:14 [compare 2:22; Daniel 12:1]). In Mark 13:19, 24; Matthew 24:21, 29 the phrase has to do with the vicious persecution of Christians in a run-up to the second coming. Here the phrase has to do with the dreadful horrors that will plague non-Christians during that same run-up (though elsewhere in Revelation the persecution of Christians also comes into view [see 5:9–11; 11:1–13; 12:13–17 and so on]). Since an hour was the shortest unit of time used by these ancients, "the hour" is a figure of speech for a short period of time, specified later as 1,260 days, or forty-two months calculated at 30 days each (11:2–3; 12:6; 13:5 [compare Daniel 7:25; 12:7]). "The test" will expose the failure of "those who dwell on the earth" to repent in response to the horrors characterizing that hour. Throughout the rest of Revelation "those who dwell on the earth" refers to non-Christians as distinguished from Christians, who are "not of the world" but are "born from above" (John 3:3, 7; 17:14). An accent falls on the earthwide extent of the test. It won't be lim-

ited to the province of Asia, where Philadelphia and the other six churches were located. "That's about to come" adds an accent on nearness and certainty of arrival. In John 17:15 Jesus prays to his Father, "I'm not asking that you take them [my disciples] out of the world—rather, that you keep them from the evil one." Since "keep them from" is there opposed to "take them out," here in Revelation 3:10 "keep you from" doesn't mean "take you out." It means "protect you from the hour of the test while you're in the world" just as John 17:15 means "keep them from the evil one while they're in the world." And just as keeping Jesus' disciples from the evil one means protecting them from apostasy under Satan's influence, so keeping the Christians in Philadelphia from the hour of the test means protecting them from apostasy under the pressure of the great affliction.

3:11–13: "**I'm coming quickly** [compare 1:1; 2:5, 16; 22:6–7, 12, 20]. **Keep a grip on what you have so that no one takes your crown.** [12]**The person who conquers— I'll make him** [into] **a pillar in the temple of my God, and by no means will he** [the conqueror] **go out** [of the temple] **any more. And I'll write on him** [1] **the name of my God and** [2] **the name of the city of my God,** [that is,] '**The New Jerusalem,' which is coming down out of heaven from my God, and** [3] **my new name.** [13]**The person who has an ear had better hear what the Spirit is saying to the churches.**" For conquering and hearing see the comments on 2:7. Jesus hasn't found fault with this church. So "I'm coming quickly" constitutes a promise, not a threat (contrast 2:5, 16). The present tense and "quickly" highlight the nearness and certainty of Jesus' coming as an encouragement to the little church that they "keep a grip on what [they] have." "What [they] have" consists in the items mentioned earlier: an opened door, a little power, the word of Jesus (and Jesus as the Word), nondenial of his name, and coming vindication. "So that no one takes your crown" alludes to an athlete's having to forfeit his prize (a laurel wreath) for breaking the rules, and warns against a professing Christian's having to forfeit eternal life for failure to "keep a grip . . . ," that is, to persevere (see 2:10 for a crown as symbolic of eternal life). The word for "temple" means the very sanctuary itself, exclusive of surrounding courts and cloisters. Jesus is about to mention the New Jerusalem; and 21:22 will say that there's no temple in it, "for the Lord God Almighty is her temple—also the lamb [is her temple]" (compare John 2:19–21). So to be made into a pillar in that temple is to dwell in eternal unity with God and the lamb. Lying in the background may be the practice of sculpting some pillars into the shape of human beings, as in the often-photographed porch of the maidens on the acropolis of Athens. "By no means will he [the conqueror] go out." Of course not, because pillars don't walk! The picture is one of stability and permanence (compare John 10:28: "by no means will they [Jesus' 'sheep'] be lost"). Also lying in the background may be a practice of inscribing on pillars the names of benefactors who paid the cost of construction and therefore, in a manner of speaking, owned the pillar (compare 5:9). So writing on the pillar-like conqueror God's name, "The New Jerusalem," and Jesus' new name means that God, his city (which will turn out *to be* the saints of God), and Jesus will together claim the conqueror as their own. The conqueror belongs to them. See the comments on 3:2 for "my God." "Which is coming down out of heaven" portrays his city as currently in its downward motion, so soon and sure is its future descent (21:2). Jesus' "*new*" name would appear to be his name "that no one knows except for him" (19:12), for his old names are widely known. As new, his name corresponds to the conqueror's "new name" in 2:17 and to "The New Jerusalem," in which the conqueror will dwell. All this newness will suit the coming "new heaven" and "new earth" (21:1).

A MESSAGE TO THE CHURCH IN LAODICEA
Revelation 3:14–22

3:14: "And for the messenger of the church in Ladoicea write [as follows]: **These things says the Amen, the faithful and true witness, the beginning of God's creation.**" For the introduction see the comments on 2:1. Isaiah 65:16 speaks of "the God of Amen." As "the Word of God" (19:13; John 10:35) who *is* God (John 1:1, 18; 20:28; 1 John 5:20), Jesus identifies himself as the "Amen"-God of Isaiah. Since "Amen" can mean both "faithful" and "true," Jesus adds to his self-identification "the faithful and true witness." He'll testify to the state of affairs in the church at Laodicea. His testimony will be faithful to his high priestly role of trimming the wicks and replenishing the fuel of the lamps among whose lampstands he walks around—that is, to his role of correcting and enhancing the light of their Christian testimony (see the comments on 2:1–3). His testimony will also be true to the actual state of affairs in the Laodicean church. As will be seen, this church has been neither faithful to its role as a witness for Jesus nor true in its opinion of itself. In view of its supposed self-sufficiency, moreover, Jesus also calls himself "the beginning of God's creation," not in the sense that God created him first (for he *is* the beginning [22:13] and as the Word already *was* in the beginning [John 1:1]), but in the sense that as God's agent in creation he began it (compare John 1:3: "All things came into existence through him"). The Laodicean church will have to get the things they need from him through whom these things came into existence.

3:15–16: "**I know your deeds, that you're neither cold nor hot. O that you were cold or hot!** [16]**In this way, because you're tepid and neither hot nor cold, I'm about to vomit you out of my mouth.**" Jesus compares the church's deeds to a drink. As nowadays, people then liked their drinks either hot or cold but not tepid; and it may be that water which came to Laodicea by aqueduct from hot springs in nearby Denizli had grown tepid along the way. If so, it nauseated the person who drank it. (Jesus' use of hyperbole, if hyperbole it is, accents the point.) What makes the church's deeds like a tepid drink

remains to be spelled out. In the meantime, Jesus says he's about to vomit the church out of his mouth—an alarmingly graphic figure of speech for pronouncing eternal doom at the Last Judgment. He doesn't want to have to do so: "O that you were cold or hot!" But "in this way" points forward to such a possibility, and "I'm about to" stresses its nearness and certainty should no change in temperature occur. For as it is, the Laodiceans turn his stomach.

3:17–19: "**Because you're saying, 'I'm wealthy, and I've become wealthy, and in respect to nothing do I have a need,' and** [because] **you don't know** [= don't recognize] **that you're hard-pressed and pitiable and poor and blind and naked,** [18]**I advise you to buy from me gold refined by fire in order that you may be wealthy, and white garments in order that you may clothe yourself and** [in order that] **the shame of your nakedness may not be manifested** [= that your nakedness not be exposed and thus bring shame on you at the Last Judgment]; **and** [I advise you to buy from me] **salve to anoint your eyes in order that you may see.** [19]**I scold and discipline as many people as I love. Therefore be serious and repent.**" The city of Laodicea had plenty of wealth. An earthquake destroyed Laodicea in A.D. 60, but the city rebuilt itself without imperial financial help such as Philadelphia received. The church too could truly say, "I'm wealthy." The addition of "I've become wealthy" pridefully showcases the wealth as something attained as well as possessed. "And in respect to nothing do I have a need" betrays the fallacy of thinking that material prosperity supplies everything needed. The resultant complacency defines the tepid water that nauseates Jesus.

Jesus tries to shatter this complacency by portraying the church in terms that describe a beggar rather than a tycoon: (1) "hard-pressed" to gain the barest necessities rather than needing nothing more; (2) "pitiable" while sitting streetside rather than lounging in a mansion; (3) "poor" so as to be reduced to begging rather than raking in profits from investments; (4) "blind" and therefore unable to work for a living rather than earning one; and (5) "naked" because of clothing so ragged as to expose lots of skin rather than being covered with finery (compare the blind beggar in John 9). All the foregoing come not only despite the city's wealth but also despite the ready availability of salve for curing eye diseases and despite the local manufacture of garments noted for their soft black wool. Of course Jesus is talking figuratively about a condition that physical prosperity can't correct but can in fact foster. "You don't know" points up the church's ignorance of their sorry religious condition. The church thinks it's Christian, but it isn't.

Jesus might have commanded the church. Instead he advises it kindly, or perhaps sardonically. In place of its present wealth the church needs to buy from Jesus gold refined by fire, the pure gold like transparent glass that will characterize the New Jerusalem (21:18). This purified gold represents the wealth of eternal life that's entirely devoid of avarice and other pecuniary evils. The church also needs to buy from Jesus white garments, representing righteous deeds, to cover the present shame of their not doing such deeds (see the comments on 3:4–5). The figurative white garments contrast with the actual black wool garments manufactured in the region. And the church needs to buy from Jesus a mental salve that will cure its introspective blindness. But what can a destitute beggar use to buy the required kind of gold, garments, and eye salve? He has no moral money! Ah, but there's one currency that Jesus will accept in payment: serious repentance. That, in fact, is the *only* currency he'll accept. And despite the nausea the church causes Jesus, he loves the people of the Laodicean church (compare 3:9) and therefore scolds and disciplines them to bring them round as does a father his child (compare Proverbs 3:12). Advising an adult has turned into scolding a child, a verbal form of discipline. True love is never cruel, but it sometimes needs to be severe. So is Jesus' love here.

3:20–22: "Behold, I've come to stand at the door [the Greek text implying motion to the door prior to standing there]**; and I'm knocking! If anyone hears my voice and opens the door, I'll also come in to him** [not '*into* him'] **and dine with him, and he with me.** ²¹**The person who conquers—I'll give** [= grant] **him to sit with me in my throne as I also conquered and sat with my Father in his throne** [compare 7:17; 12:5; 22:1, 3]. ²²**The person who has an ear had better hear what the Spirit is saying to the churches."** For conquering and hearing see the comments on 2:7. Suddenly, the figure switches from that of the whole church as a blind beggar and Jesus as a retail merchant to that of Jesus as a traveler and the individual church member as a homeowner. Jesus is looking for lodging and by knocking on the homeowner's door is appealing to the Middle Eastern law of hospitality. "Hears my voice" recalls Jesus' saying in John 10:3–4, 16, 27 that his sheep hear his voice with recognition. So here in Revelation 3:20 a verbal appeal for entrance is added to the knocking. "Behold" makes this double appeal exclamatory. Hearing Jesus' voice and opening the door for him represent true conversion. His coming in to the homeowner and their dining with each other, emphasized by the double expression "I'll . . . dine with him, and he with me" and by the contrast with vomiting, will represent at an individual level the messianic banquet, called "the lamb's wedding banquet" in 19:9. It will take place at the second coming. Not to participate is not to be saved. So Jesus is trying to convert church members who are ignorant of their unconverted state ("you don't know . . ." [3:17])!

The figure switches again, this time to the familiar picture of a conqueror, and the conqueror turns out to be a victorious king (compare 2:26–27; also 1:6; 5:10; 22:5). He sits because he has conquered. Just as sitting with the Father on his throne portrays Jesus as a victorious king coreigning with his Father (compare John 16:33: "I've conquered the world") and prepares for the vision of God as sitting on his throne (chapters 4–5), so sitting with Jesus on his throne portrays the true Christian as a victorious king coreigning with Jesus. The coreigning of Jesus with his Father has already started. The

true Christian's coreigning with Jesus will start when he comes back to reign for a thousand years (20:4–6) and will extend forever and ever (22:5).

THE HEAVENLY COURT
Revelation 4:1–5:14

This passage divides into the praise and worship of God by four living creatures and twenty-four elders (4:1–11) and the appearance of Jesus to receive a seven-sealed scroll, plus further praise and worship, this time of Jesus as well as of God the Father (5:1–14).

PRAISE AND WORSHIP OF GOD
Revelation 4:1–11

4:1: After these things [the vision of Jesus and his messages as described in 1:9–3:22] **I looked and—behold, an opened door in heaven! And the first voice, which I'd heard,** [a voice] **as of a trumpet speaking with me** [= Jesus' voice as described in 1:10–11] [was] **saying, "Come up here, and I'll show you things that must happen after these things."** "After these things I looked" introduces the second vision recorded in Revelation. "Behold" spotlights the "opened door in heaven" that John sees. The opened door recalls 3:7–8, where Jesus told the Philadelphian church that he'd give them an opened door into David's royal household, that is, into the kingdom of God and Christ on earth (compare 20:1–22:5). Here the opened door has the purpose of letting John see a heavenly vision. He seems surprised and transfixed. So Jesus tells him, "Come up here" (see the comments on 1:10–11 for the comparison of Jesus' voice to a talking trumpet). "I'll show you things that must happen" echoes God's having given Jesus a revelation for him "to show his slaves the things that must happen with speed" and along with 1:9–3:22 reconfirms that Jesus is acting as God's "messenger" through whom the revelation is being channeled to John (1:1 [see the comments there also for the thought of divine necessity]). But another "after these things" replaces "with speed" to echo 1:19, which has to do with a succession of visions, not with successive fulfillments of them (for chapters 2–3 include future events [2:10, 22–23; 3:9 plus references to Jesus' return and to conquerors' coming rewards] and chapters 6–22 include past events [as in 12:1–5]).

4:2–4: At once I came to be in the Spirit. And behold, a throne was located in heaven, and one sitting on the throne! ³**And the one sitting** [was] **like a jasper stone and a carnelian in appearance, and a rainbow like an emerald in appearance** [was] **all around the throne** [compare Ezekiel 1:28]. ⁴**And all around the throne** [were] **twenty-four thrones; and sitting on the thrones** [were] **twenty-four elders clothed in white garments and** [having] **gold crowns on their heads.** John had come to be in the Spirit for his first vision (see the comments on 1:10). The same thing happens for this second vision. He takes for granted that his audience understand the effectiveness of Jesus' command, "Come up here"; but "at once" emphasizes its effectiveness in terms of coming to be in the Spirit. Another "behold" showcases a heavenly throne and its occupant. John is more taken by the location of the throne in heaven and by the one sitting on the throne than he is by his own new location in heaven and presence before heavenly royalty. And no wonder, for it will turn out that the throne is that of Jesus' Father, just referenced in 3:21 (see also 12:5; 22:1). Sitting on a throne in heaven indicates sovereignty over events on earth, so that John and his audience should take courage despite their suffering affliction "because of the Word of God and the Testimony of Jesus" (see the comments on 1:9). To drive home this encouraging point, John will refer to God as a throne-sitter time and time again. But instead of describing him with human analogies, John describes his glory with analogies to gemstones (contrast Ezekiel 1:26–27 and human representations of pagan gods in the form of idols, not to mention statues of deified emperors). Since 21:11 describes a jasper stone as "sparkling like crystal," "like a jasper stone" here in 4:3 may mean that the one sitting on the throne was sparkling like a diamond. A carnelian is red; but John makes nothing of its color, nor of the green color of an emerald, to which gemstone he compares the rainbow circling over the throne. So these gemstones simply combine to highlight the glory of God and his throne. On the other hand, the rainbow recalls God's making rainbows a sign that he'll never again destroy the earth with a flood (Genesis 9:8–17). Christians, then, may transmute that symbolism into a sign that they're exempt from God's punitive judgment.

Circled around the throne are twenty-four other thrones with twenty-four elders sitting on them. The elders correspond in their number to the number of the twelve apostles, whose names are inscribed one each on the twelve foundations of the New Jerusalem, plus the number of the twelve tribes of Israel, whose names are inscribed one each on the twelve gates of the New Jerusalem (21:12–14). But why add the number of the twelve apostles to the number of the twelve tribes of Israel? Well, in 7:1–8 John will *hear* about 12,000 from each of the twelve tribes of Israel, but when in 7:9–17 he *sees* them they'll turn out to be an innumerable multitude of the redeemed from all nations, that is, the church (compare his *hearing* about a lion that he then *sees* to be a lamb in 5:1–7). Add the twelve apostolic names to the symbolically equivalent twelve tribal names and you get twenty-four. So the twenty-four elders represent (though they don't constitute) the universal church portrayed as both founded on the apostles and consisting in the true Israel. In accordance with the description of Christians in 1:6, moreover, the elders are kings in that they're sitting on thrones and wearing crowns, and also are priests in that their numbering twenty-four accords with Israel's twenty-four platoons of priests (1 Chronicles 24:1–19). All in all, then, the twenty-four elders are proxy for the church, robed in white garments representing righteous acts (19:8–14) and crowned with eternal life (compare similar statements throughout chapters 2–3.

4:5–6a: And out from the throne are issuing flashes of lightning and rumblings and thunderclaps. And [there are] **seven lamps of fire, burning within sight of the throne, which** [lamps] **are the seven Spirits of God** [compare Zechariah 4:1–6]. **⁶ᵃAnd within sight of the throne** [is], **as it were, a glassy sea, like crystal.** The flashes of lightning, rumblings, and thunderclaps recall the evidences of God's presence on Mount Sinai just after he delivered Israel from their oppression in Egypt (Exodus 19:16–25). The rest of Revelation will look back on that deliverance as a pattern for the coming deliverance of the church, the new Israel, from persecution. Since the lightning flashes, rumblings, and thunderclaps proceed "out from the throne," they represent the might and majesty of God just as the gemstones represent his glory. For the seven Spirits of God within sight of his throne, see the comments on 1:4; 3:1. The comparison to seven burning lamps recalls the seven lampstands that stood for the seven churches. It's these Spirits as lamps that can make the testimony of the churches upholding the lamps shine as light in a world of darkness. Because of its constant motion and violent storms, the sea stands for the evil powers of chaos (see, for example, 13:1). But a glassy, crystalline sea is a sea of ice in which the powers of chaos are frozen into immobility. In other words, these powers pose no threat to God in heaven; and in the new heaven and earth "the sea doesn't exist anymore" (21:1). There'll be no more chaos (compare God's creation of "a *firmament*" to separate the waters above, which periodically fall in the form of rain, from the waters below, which fill the seas [Genesis 1:6–8a]).

4:6b–7: And in the middle of the throne and around the throne [that is, between the primary throne and the twenty-four other thrones encircling it] [are] **four living** [creatures] **full of eyes before and behind** [= looking forward and backward]. **⁷And the first living** [creature is] **like a lion, and the second living** [creature] **like an ox, and the third living** [creature] **having** [= has] **a face, as it were, of a human being, and the fourth living** [creature is] **like a flying eagle** [compare Isaiah 6:1–3; Ezekiel 1:5–25; 10:1–22]. "Four" is a number of totality, as in "the four corners of the earth" and "the four winds of the earth" (7:1; 20:8). So the four creatures represent the totality of God's creatures. A lion is the top-ranking wild beast, an ox the top-ranking domestic animal, an eagle the top-ranking bird, and a human being the top-ranking creature of all. But the eagle is listed last and described as "flying" to highlight the heavenly location of the four creatures. John describes them as "living" to distinguish them from the inanimate throne. Their having "eyes" means that they sparkle with glints of light comparable to twinkling eyes. In other words, the flashes of lightning that proceed out from the throne reflect off the bodies of the four living creatures. So glorious is the one sitting on the throne that these reflections gleam from all over the creatures' bodies, so that they're "*full* of [twinkling] eyes *before and behind.*"

4:8–11: **And the four living** [creatures], **each one of them having six wings apiece, are full of eyes all around** [on the outside] **and inside** [between the wings and the body]; **and day and night they have no rest** [= they don't stop flying], **saying, "Holy, holy, holy** [is] **the Lord God Almighty, who was and who is and who is coming** [for which see the comments on 1:4, 8 and compare Isaiah 6:1–3 again]." **⁹And when the living** [creatures] **give glory and honor and thanks to the one sitting on the throne, who lives forever and ever, ¹⁰the twenty-four elders will fall within sight of the one sitting on the throne and worship** [= kiss the ground in front of] **the one who lives forever and ever and throw their crowns within sight of the throne, saying, ¹¹"You're worthy, our Lord and God, to receive glory and honor and power, because you created all things; and because of your will they existed and were created."** The four living creatures' wings enable them to fly around the throne ceaselessly ("they have no rest") as they declare the holiness of the Lord God Almighty. With a pair of their wings they fly forward and backward, with another pair sideways (right and left), and with another pair up and down. Ceaseless motion in all directions contributes to the sparkling reflections of God's glory. So John reiterates that each of the creatures is "full of eyes," but for added emphasis replaces "before and behind" with "all around *and inside*." When the creatures spread their wings in flight, eye-like glints of God's glory reflect even off the parts of the creatures' bodies otherwise covered by the wings. The present tense in "*are* full of eyes" and "*have* no rest" vivifies the whole scene for yet more emphasis on the glory of the one sitting on the throne.

The throne-sitter is "holy" in the sense that he's transcendent, wholly other from the created order and therefore not to be confused with it or with any part of it. The threefoldness of "holy" highlights this transcendence, which in turn leads to a threefold identification of him as "Lord," "the God," and "the Almighty" (in a more literal translation). His transcendence embraces mastery ("Lord"), deity ("God"), and omnipotence ("Almighty"), in all of which the true and persecuted worshipers of him, represented by the twenty-four elders, may take comfort and encouragement. To the threefold description of him as "holy" and the threefold identification of him as "the Lord God Almighty" is added the threefold designation of him as the one "who was and who is and who is coming," as in 1:4, 8 except that here "who was" comes first instead of second to trace his eternality consecutively from the past through the present into the future (otherwise see the comments on 1:4, 8).

Since the four living creatures represent the totality of God's creatures, their giving him "glory and honor and thanks"—another set of three—means that all his creatures should join in. To give him glory, honor, and thanks is to acknowledge his glory, honor, and beneficence. Two more occurrences of "the one sitting on the throne" reiterate his mastery, deity, and omnipotence; and two occurrences of "who lives forever and ever" re-

iterate his eternality. These reiterations enhance comfort and encouragement for believers enormously. History is under God's control, so that the representative twenty-four elders fall down in thankful worship (for which see the comments on 1:17). So vigorous is their worship that they "*throw* their crowns within sight of the throne" in bodily as well as verbal acknowledgement that their crowns, which symbolize eternal life (2:10), are gifts from him. Out of his eternality has come their eternal life. Sitting eternally on his throne in heaven, he—not some Caesar sitting only temporarily on a throne in Rome—is "worthy" as "our Lord and God" to have his "glory and honor and power" fully acknowledged. For after all, he "created all things." "[His] will" effected their existence and creation. Without it they wouldn't have continued existing and would never have started existing. Just as his will effected the first heaven and the first earth, it will effect the new heaven and the new earth, where there'll be no more tears, death, grief, crying, or pain (21:1–4). So take heart!

PRAISE AND WORSHIP OF JESUS AS
WELL AS OF GOD THE FATHER
Revelation 5:1–14

5:1: **And I saw on the right** [hand] **of the one sitting on the throne a scroll written on the inside and on the outside, securely sealed with seven seals.** Right-handedness is usual, and "*on* the right [hand]" differs from "having" and "gripping" "*in* his right [hand]" (1:16; 2:1). These factors suggest that the scroll is lying on the palm of the throne-sitter's right hand, with which hand he offers the scroll to its rightful claimant. Because it was difficult to write across the bumpy vertical strips of papyrus pith that were glued to horizontal strips to make the ancient equivalent of paper, writers normally wrote along the horizontal strips, which therefore made up the front side. The vertical strips then made up the back side and were written on only for lack of space on the front side or for a brief indication of contents in the case of rolling or folding the papyrus so as to make the front side invisible. So "on the inside" means "on the front side," and "on the outside" means "on the back side."

Since nothing will happen till the seals are broken open, starting in chapter 6, the present writing on the outside probably *characterizes* the contents of the document rather than *continuing* its contents from the inside. But what kind of document is it? It can't be read till all seven seals, which secure the exposed edge of the papyrus, are broken so as to unroll or unfold the papyrus. Yet with the breaking of each seal events take place despite this unreadability (until the last seal is broken, of course). Furthermore, it is sealing, not inability to read, that keeps things from happening (permanently in 10:4; for the time being in Daniel 8:26; 12:4, 9); and it is unsealing, not reading, that makes things happen (22:10). So the scroll is likely to contain descriptions of the events that take place when the seals are broken one by one. It will turn out that those events will constitute a gradual taking control of the earth away from those who persecute Christians living there, this in answer to the Christians' prayers. We should therefore think of the scroll as a title deed to the earth. "*Securely* sealed with *seven* seals," seven being a number of completeness, stresses that only the rightful owner can validly take the title deed from the throne-sitter's hand and break open the seals so as to wrest his property from usurpers (contrast the already opened scroll in Ezekiel 2:8–3:3). To whom, then, does the earth rightfully belong? To whom has God deeded it?

5:2–4: And I saw a strong angel proclaiming in a loud voice, "Who [is] worthy to open the scroll and loosen its seals?" [3]**And no one in heaven or on earth or under the earth was able to open the scroll or look into it.** [4]**And I started weeping profusely, because no one was found** [who was] **worthy to open the scroll or look into it.** A loud voice suits a proclamation, and the angel needs to be strong to make his voice heard throughout the reaches of heaven, earth, and the underworld (= the world of the dead). Most proclamations consist in announcements. This one consists in a question. The question asks for the identity of the earth's rightful owner. "Worthy" has to do with rightful ownership because of having been deeded the earth. "To open the scroll *and* loosen its seals" means to open it *by* loosening them (compare 5:9). To look into the scroll upon opening it is to see the opener's ownership validated in the title deed. Because at first no one was able—that is, was enabled by dint of having been deeded the earth—to open the scroll or look into it even though a search was made throughout the universe, John started weeping profusely. Why should a failure of the search cause such distress on his part? Answer: Because so long as usurpers control the earth, Christians will continue to suffer persecution, including martyrdom. No deliverance will come. Their prayers for it will go unanswered.

5:5–7: And one of the elders says to me, "Stop weeping. Behold, the lion from the tribe of Judah, David's sprout, has conquered so as to open the scroll and its seven seals" [compare the portrayal of Jesus as a conqueror in 3:21]. [6]**And I saw in the middle of the throne and the four living** [creatures] **and in the middle of the elders** [that is, between the throne and the four living creatures on the one hand and the elders on the other hand] **a lamb standing, as** [a lamb that] **had been slain** [compare Isaiah 53:7]**, having seven horns and seven eyes, which are the seven Spirits of God** [that] **had been sent into all the earth.** [7]**And he came and took** [the scroll] **out from the right** [hand] **of the one sitting on the throne.** The present tense of "says" introduces emphatically the elder's telling John to stop weeping and the subsequent announcement, an announcement designed to comfort the audience of Revelation as well as John himself. "Behold" adds further emphasis to the announcement. "The lion from the tribe of Judah, David's sprout," alludes to Genesis 49:9–10; Isaiah 11:1, 10; Jeremiah 23:5; 33:15; Zechariah 3:8; 6:12 and refers to the messianic king who sprouted,

so to speak, from the cut-off stump of David's dynasty within the Israelite tribe of Judah (compare 22:16; Romans 15:12) and who has conquered so as to open the scroll and its seven seals. Conquering suits a lion, and also suits a sprout of David in that as David was a conqueror (see, for example, 2 Samuel 5:1–10). But what has the lion and sprout conquered, and how? If the reference is to Jesus, he "has conquered the world" (John 16:33), that is, human society as dominated by Satan and therefore as hateful of Jesus and believers in him (John 15:18–19, 24–25; 17:14; 1 John 3:13; 5:19). The elder speaking to John mentions neither the object nor the method of the Davidic lion's conquest, however—only its purpose and result: the ability to open the scroll by opening its seven seals. The conquest has made him so worthily able that he'll break open all seven of them and thus impose on the earth his ownership of it completely (see the comments on 1:4–5a for seven as a number of completeness).

When John sees the lion he has been told about, strikingly it turns out to be a lamb. We're not to think that he saw the actual figure of a lamb—rather, the figure of a human being whom he compares to a lamb, and therefore calls a lamb, because the human figure bears on his body the scars of a sacrificial death, the very scars of crucifixion that Jesus showed to his disciples (John 20:19–29). This sacrificial lamb isn't lying limp and dead on an altar, though. He's standing because of his resurrection just as John 20:19, 26; 21:4 portrays the resurrected Jesus as standing on several occasions. Furthermore, the Greek word translated "resurrection" means "standing up," a sign of life, as opposed to a corpse's lying down. Here then we have the method of conquest: Jesus conquered by sacrificially laying down his life and taking it again so as to stand up (compare John 10:17–18 with John 16:33). As scarred, he's the Passover lamb that took away the sins of the world (John 1:29, 36; compare John's chronological correlation of Jesus' crucifixion with the slaying of Passover lambs [see the comments on John 13:27; 18:28, for example]).

Ordinarily, lambs don't have horns. But this lamb does. Throughout the Bible horns stand for active, aggressive power (see Daniel 8:5–10, for example). "Having *seven* horns" makes Jesus completely powerful in his conquest. As "the lion from the tribe of Judah, David's sprout," he has already conquered by means of his sacrificial death like that of a Passover lamb. As a risen lamb "having seven horns" he'll butt his and his people's enemies off the face of the earth, which rightfully belongs to him and his people, not to his and their enemies. And since spirit spells life (see the comments on 3:1), as the one who took up his life again he has the full complement of God's seven Spirits. The lamb's seven eyes represent these seven Spirits to indicate that through their agency the lamb takes note of his people wherever on earth they suffer for the lamplight of their Christian testimony. Such sufferers may take comfort in this feature, because it presages their coming deliverance and vindication. Since the lamb-like Jesus was standing inside the circle of the elders, it was but a short distance for him to come and take the scroll. That the one sitting on the throne handed the scroll to him confirms the one elder's assurance that "the lion from the tribe of Judah, David's sprout, has conquered so as to open the scroll and its seven seals." He's able because he's worthy, and he's worthy because the throne-sitter had deeded the earth to him.

5:8–10: And when he took the scroll, the four living [creatures] **and the twenty-four elders fell within sight of the lamb, each** [of the elders] **having a harp and gold bowls full of incense, which** [incense] **is the prayers of the saints** [in the sense of symbolizing their prayers]; [9]**and they** [the twenty-four elders] **are singing a new song, saying, "You're worthy to take the scroll and open its seals, because you were slain and with your blood purchased for God** [individuals] **out of every tribe and tongue** [= language] **and people and nation;** [10]**and you made them for our God** [into] **a kingdom and priests. And they'll reign as kings on the earth."** Falling within sight of the seven-eyed lamb matches falling within sight of the one sitting on the throne in 4:10 and prepares for the giving of divine honors to the lamb as well as to the throne-sitter (5:11–14). Now even the four living creatures stop flying around and fall down. (In 4:10 only the twenty-four elders fell down.) David played a harp (1 Samuel 16:14–23). So it's appropriate for the elders to accompany with harps their singing a song that praises "the sprout of David." And because the elders represent the saints (see the comments on 4:4), it's also appropriate that in addition to their harps they each have a gold bowl full of incense symbolizing the saints' prayers. (That they couldn't fall down, play their harps, and hold bowls all at the same time only goes to show that we're dealing with symbolic language.) The ascending, sweet-smelling smoke of incense is like prayer that goes up to God and, in a manner of speaking, pleases his nostrils (compare Psalm 141:2). That the incense is contained in gold bowls demonstrates the high value he places on the prayers of saints; and John calls those who pray "the saints" in the sense that they're consecrated to God. So it's sacrilegious for the world to treat them as rubbish. But since the world does treat them so by despising, hating, and persecuting them, they pray for deliverance and vindication. "*Full* of incense" points up the huge volume of such praying. Though these prayers go up to God, the elders are holding their bowls full of incense "within sight of the lamb"—a symbolic way of saying that the saints are praying to God in Jesus' name, as Jesus said to do (John 14:13–14; 15:16; 16:23–24, 26).

The elders' "new song" anticipates the "new song" to be sung by the redeemed in 14:3–4 and therefore suits the new name to be received by true Christians ("conquerors" [2:17; 3:12]), the New Jerusalem (3:12; 21:2), the new heaven and the new earth (21:1), and all things new (21:5). For there and then the prayers for deliverance and vindication will have been answered. Meanwhile, the elders declare in a song addressed to the

lamb that he's worthy to receive the scroll and open its seals, that is, to start the process which will culminate in all this blessed newness. The lamb's worthiness rests on his having submitted himself to slaughter, purchased with the coin of his blood some people for God from every tribe and tongue and nation, and made them into a kingdom and priests for God (see the comments on 1:6). The two occurrences of "for God" emphasize Jesus' acting on behalf of his Father and for his Father's glory (compare John 17:4, among other passages; and for believers as belonging to God as well as to Jesus, see John 10:29; 17:6, 9–10). "For *our* God" recollects "*my* God and *your* God" in a message that Jesus addressed to his disciples (called his "brothers" [John 20:17]) and in the context of Revelation means that Caesar isn't a god. Nor is Zeus or Apollo or Artemis or any other member of the pagan pantheon. The heaping up of terms in the phrase "tribe and tongue and people and nation" and the prefixing of "every" highlight God's loving "the world" by giving his one-and-only Son (compare 5:9; 7:9 with comments; also John 1:29; 3:16; 10:16; 1 John 2:2). Since there's encouragement in numbers, the persecuted saints may draw courage from their belonging to an international body of believers. They're not alone. As to their being purchased at the cost of Jesus' shed blood, this purchase amounts to being redeemed out of enslavement to the satanic forces that oppress them and into the freedom of reigning on earth as kings and of enjoying priestly privileges in the eternal worship of God (1:6; 20:4–6; 22:5). More encouragement to persevere! Whereas Jesus' blood appears elsewhere in John's writings as drink (John 6:53–56; 19:34; 1 John 5:6), as an agent of cleansing (1:5; 7:14; 1 John 1:7), and as a weapon of conquest (12:11), here the blood of Jesus, representing his very life (Genesis 9:4; Leviticus 17:11, 14; Deuteronomy 12:23), counts as the price of redemption and makes this redemption follow the pattern of Israel's redemption from slavery in Egypt by virtue of the blood of Passover lambs. Thus the elders sing about the redeemed while representing them as part of their number (see the comments on 4:4).

5:11–12: And I saw and heard the voice of many angels around the throne and of the living [creatures] **and of the elders—and their number was ten thousands of ten thousands** [= 10,000 x 10,000 or, more generally, an indefinitely large number: "myriads upon myriads"] **and thousands of thousands** [as though 10,000 x 10,000 doesn't suffice as a numerical estimate, so large is the throng]—[12]**saying with a loud voice, "Worthy is the lamb who was slain to receive power and wealth and wisdom and strength and honor and glory and favor."** Only the redeemed, represented by the elders, can sing a song of redemption (14:3). So now John sees and hears "the voice of many angels . . . and of the living [creatures] and of the elders . . . *saying* with a loud voice," that is, shouting rather than singing an acclamation (see the comments on 1:10–12 for seeing a voice as well as hearing it). The angels and the four living creatures won't let the elders monopolize the praising of Jesus the lamb.

For he's worthy to be praised by the spectators of redemption as well as by its recipients. Added to the high decibels of all their shouting is the high number of the angels, for which the adjective "many" doesn't suffice, so that John adds the numerical phrases explained above. The angels' location "around the throne" implies that the lamb is now seated with God on his throne (as confirmed in advance by 3:21 [see also 7:17; 12:5; 22:1, 3]). The humongous size of the throng suits the inestimably high worthiness of the lamb whom they acclaim. Instead of acclaiming him with a direct address as the elders, singing alone, did ("*You* are worthy" [5:9]), this throng acclaims him with a proclamation *about* him ("Worthy is the lamb"). This proclamation, heard throughout the universe because of the throng's "loud voice," will lead all God's creatures to join in a further acclamation which will include him as well as the lamb (5:13–14). Here, "who was slain" bases the lamb's worthiness (as in 5:9). But from whom is he worthy to receive the items listed? In 4:11 God was declared worthy to receive some of the same items from his creatures in the form of their acknowledging his glory and honor and power. So too here, but in reference to the lamb. Yet since the lamb has been declared worthy to receive the scroll from God's hand (5:9), it may be that he's also being declared worthy to receive *from God* the items listed. There are seven of them to highlight complete worthiness. (Did the three items in 4:11 suggest the Trinity in line with 1:4–6?) In both number and substance the seven items completely counteract the world's false estimate of Jesus' crucifixion as a shameful death.

5:13–14: And I heard every creature that [is] **in heaven and on earth and under the earth and on the sea—that is, all the** [creatures] **in them—saying, "The one sitting on the throne and the lamb** [will have] **favor and honor and glory and might** [= sovereignty] **forever and ever!"** [14]**And the four living** [creatures] **were saying, "Amen!" and the elders fell down and worshiped** [the one seated on the throne and the lamb]. Here the acclamation comes from all creatures, whatever and whoever and wherever they are. The unnecessary, parenthetical addition of "that is, all the [creatures] in them [heaven, earth, the underworld, and sea]" emphasizes this universality as strongly as possible. The acclamation also pairs together the throne-sitter and the lamb, who's sitting with him on the throne, because the lamb is no less God than the one sitting on the throne is. "Forever and ever" requires the supplying of a future tense: "will have." This list of items is shorter than the preceding list of seven. Perhaps their numbering four, the number of universality (as in "the four corners of the earth" and "the four winds" [7:1; 20:8]), suits both the universality of this acclamation and the number of the rementioned living creatures. In any case, the additions of "forever and ever," of the four living creatures' saying "Amen!" and of the elders' falling down and worshiping—these additions more than make up for any shortfall in the number of items listed.

PLAGUES
Revelation 6:1–16:21

This section of Revelation contains prophecies of three series of plagues. Interspersed are prophetic visions of other events. The plagues are to be understood in a broad sense that includes disasters and judgments of various sorts.

THE FIRST SIX SEALS
Revelation 6:1–17

The vision that started in 4:1 continues. *6:1–2:* **And I looked when the lamb opened one of the seven seals; and I heard one of the four living** [creatures] **speaking as the sound of a thunderclap** [speaks]**: "Come."** [2]**And I looked—and behold, a white horse and the one sitting on it having a bow! And a crown was given to him; and he went out conquering, that is, with the purpose and result of conquering.** Since "the lamb" is a figure of speech for Jesus as a human being who bears the scars of crucifixion but stands resurrected, he's capable of opening a seal (as a literal lamb would not be). "One of the seven seals" means the first of them, and "one of the four living [creatures]" means the first one (see the comments on 6:3–4). Opening the first seal doesn't reveal any contents of the scroll, and no reading occurs. Instead, the mere opening makes something happen. John hears a thunderously loud voice commanding someone else, not him, to come. The magnitude of loudness makes the command effective. The first of "The Four Horsemen of the Apocalypse" makes his appearance. It's punctuated by John's statement and exclamation, "And I looked—and behold . . . !" That there'll be *four* horsemen corresponds to Zechariah 1:7–11; 6:1–8 and to the coming of the thunderous voice from one of the four living creatures of chapters 4–5 (so also in the following three cases). All four horsemen are personifications of plagues, not themselves persons.

Notably, it isn't God who commands this horseman or the rest of them. The four living creatures act as intermediaries between God and the four horsemen to indicate that the plagues represented by them won't arise directly out of God's will. They'll derive indirectly from it by reason and way of human wickedness, which requires justice to be done. Other things being equal, God would much rather shower blessings on his creatures (contrast 4:1, where Jesus himself tells his witness John, "Come up here"). Since horses are used for transport, those that John now sees represent the transport of plagues across the earth. The white color of the first horse recalls the sacred white horses that Parthians brought into battle to ensure victory over the Romans, and the bow of the first horseman likewise recalls the Parthians. For they fought as skillful bowmen while riding their horses in battle, and they defeated the Romans at the eastern end of the Roman Empire in A.D. 62 (compare 9:13–19 with comments). (The Romans didn't fight with bows and arrows as the Parthians did.) Whiteness has been associated with conquest in 2:17; 3:5; and a crown, representing victory, is given to the first horseman in the present episode. The horseman "went out conquering." Addition of "the purpose and result of conquering" underlines the success of his conquest. He accomplished what he set out to do. All in all, then, the first horseman represents a successful invasion from without of what will later be called the kingdom of the beast (16:10 [compare especially chapter 13]). The overthrow of Babylon (a code name for Rome) will result (17:12–18).

6:3–4: And when he [the lamb] **opened the second seal, I heard the second living** [creature] **saying, "Come." ⁴And another horse, a red one, came out; and to the one sitting on it—to him was given** [license] **to take peace from the earth; in other words, that people should slaughter one another; and a big sword was given to him.** "The *second* seal" confirms that in 6:1 "*one* of the seven seals" meant the *first* one, and "the *second* living [creature]" confirms that in 6:1 "*one* of the four living [creatures]" meant the *first* one. As also confirmed by the following reference to a sword, the red color of this second horse stands for bloodshed. The description of the sword as "big" indicates wholesale bloodshed. And people's "slaughter[ing] one another" indicates civil war in reminiscence of the civil war that broke out in Rome right after Nero's death in A.D. 68. (John's visions use events in the recent past as points of take-off for events yet to come.) Thus civil war within supplements invasion from without to produce a complete collapse. "To take peace from the earth" marks the end of Pax Romana (Latin for "the Roman Peace," a golden age of peace established by Augustus Caesar, who reigned 27 B.C.–A.D. 14 [compare John 14:27]). "Was given" may imply that it was God who gave the second horseman license to take peace from the earth. But John doesn't identify the giver. So the accent rests on civil war as such. It's becoming apparent that the horsemen represent effects of human wickedness and don't derive from God's wrath, though he allows such effects to flourish. Nor does John say from where the red horse "came out." So the expression simply means that the horse came into view.

6:5–6: And when he [the lamb] **opened the third seal, I heard the third living** [creature] **saying, "Come." And I looked—and behold, a black horse and the one sitting on it holding a pair** [of scales] **in his hand! ⁶And I heard a voice, as it were, in the midst of the four living** [creatures], **saying, "A choenix of wheat for a denarius, and three choenixes of barley for a denarius; and you** [singular] **shouldn't do damage to the olive oil and the wine** [in other words, 'leave them alone']**."** The usual statement and exclamation, "And I looked—and behold . . . !" punctuate the appearance of a black horse. Several features project a picture of famine, possibly recalling one or another of several recent famines in parts of the Roman Empire: (1) The color black suits a famine in that during a famine caused by drought, plants such as the seedlings of wheat and barley shrivel up and turn black. (2) The pair of scales in this horseman's hand has

the purpose of rationing out by weight what little wheat and barley is available. (3) The price of the wheat and barley is so high as to indicate a famine-caused shortage. (The combination of *weighing* out the grain and *measuring* it out shows that we're dealing with mixed metaphors [compare Leviticus 26:26; 2 Kings 7:1; Ezekiel 4:10, 16]).

The choenix was a dry measure of almost one quart. A denarius was a day's wage for a manual laborer (Matthew 20:1–16). To pay a denarius for one choenix of wheat was to pay around ten times the normal price. Barley was cheaper, but to pay a denarius for three choenixes of barley was to pay about five or six times the normal price. In other words, a day's wage for just enough food to feed the laborer for one day. What's his family to eat? Yet a voice sets these prices as an upper limit which aren't to be exceeded, and also tells the horseman not to damage the olive oil and the wine, which constituted other dietary staples (Deuteronomy 7:13). In other words, the drought, though bad enough to damage shallow-rooted grains, isn't to become so severe as to damage deep-rooted trees and vines. But whose voice is it that limits the famine thus? John locates the voice "in the midst of the four living creatures." These creatures immediately surround God's throne (4:6), so that we might think the voice to be that of God. But the lamb has approached the throne and taken the scroll out of God's right hand (5:7), so that the voice could equally well be the lamb's. John doesn't quite call it a voice, though—rather, "a voice, *as it were*." This qualification favors that the lamb is speaking, for we don't ordinarily think of lambs as having a voice. In either case, the setting of limits on the famine displays mercy designed to give reason and opportunity for repentance (compare 9:13–21, especially 20–21; 14:6–7; 16:8–9).

6:7–8: And when he [the lamb] **opened the fourth seal, I heard the voice of the fourth living** [creature] **saying, "Come." ⁸And I looked—and behold, a pallid horse! And the one sitting on it—he** [had] **the name "Death," and Hades** [the underworld of the dead] **was following with him** [= close behind him]**. And to them was given authority over a fourth of the earth so as to kill** [its population] **by means of sword and by means of famine and by means of death and by the wild beasts of the earth.** "A pallid horse" has the sallow color of a corpse. Appropriately, then, this horseman is named "Death." "Hades" follows close behind (apparently on foot since he's not said to be sitting on a horse), because people go to hades as soon as they die. The personification of death and hades would have struck a familiar chord in John's audience, because Greek mythology featured Death and Hades as divinities of a sort (contrast 1:18). Death and hades mark inevitable outcomes of the invasion, the civil war, and the famine of the first three seals. "Authority over a *fourth* of the earth so as to kill [its] population" suits both this seal as the fourth one and the fourfold means of killing: (1) "sword"; (2) "famine"; (3) "death" (in the sense of a plague like the Black Death of the Middle Ages [compare the plague that ravaged Rome in A.D. 80]); and (4) "the wild beasts of the earth." In John's first-century setting, "a fourth of the earth" probably meant a fourth of the Roman Empire. Warfare aggravates a drought-caused famine, because invading armies comb the countryside for food from what few crops are available, and sieges keep people in a city from getting food and water at distances outside the city. Physical weakness caused by famine results in succumbing to disease. And society falls apart, so that there's little defense against the wild kingdom (compare Leviticus 26:14–33; Deuteronomy 32:23–26; Ezekiel 5:16–17; 14:21).

6:9–11: **And when he** [the lamb] **opened the fifth seal, I saw under the** [heavenly] **altar the souls of those who'd been slain because of the Word of God and because of the Testimony that they'd held.** [10]**And they cried out with a loud voice, saying, "Until when, holy and true Sovereign, aren't you judging and extracting vengeance for our blood from those who dwell on the earth?"** [11]**And to each of them was given a white gown; and it was told them that they should rest for yet a little while, till their fellow slaves too—that is, their brothers who were about to be killed as also they** [had been killed]**—were fulfilled.** The souls aren't the deceased in general. They're Christians who've been disembodied by martyrdom. The very word "souls" calls attention to their disembodiment and to their awaiting the first resurrection of 20:4–6, on which occasion they'll be reembodied. The souls of those martyred under Nero in A.D. 64 may be particularly in view. See the comments on 1:2, 9 for the phrases, "because of the Word of God and because of the Testimony that they'd held." To *hold* the Testimony means to *maintain* it—and him; for like "the Word," "the Testimony" is a title for Jesus—to the point of martyrdom (compare 12:17; 19:10). "Who'd been slain" draws a parallel between these martyrs and Jesus the lamb who'd been slain, though now he's "standing" by virtue of his already accomplished resurrection (5:6, 9, 12). The word for "soul" also means "life" in that a soul animates its body. According to Leviticus 17:11 "the life of the flesh is in the blood," and according to Leviticus 4:7, 18; 8:15 sacrificial blood is to be poured out at the base of the altar of burnt offering. So it's appropriately symbolic that the souls of Jesus' sacrificially slain martyrs should be seen "under the altar." Their life's blood has soaked into the ground, so to speak, underneath the altar in the heavenly sanctuary (compare the Lord's saying to Cain, "The voice of your brother's [Abel's] blood is crying out to me from the ground" (Genesis 4:10).

The martyrs had been condemned to death in human courts. Now they appeal their case to a higher court, the heavenly one. The loudness of the appeal indicates urgency. In addressing God they appeal to his sovereignty, which as "holy" is uniquely superior to that of any human sovereign, and as "true" is genuinely real, not just illusory like that of the Caesars and other earthly rulers (compare 3:7, but there in reference to Jesus). "Until when . . . aren't you judging and extracting vengeance for our blood from those who dwell on the earth?" means "How long will you leave off judging . . . ?" But the pres-

ent tense of "*aren't* you judging and extracting" where we expect the future ("*will* you")—this present tense stresses what at the moment God *isn't* doing that the souls of the martyrs wish he *were* doing at the moment. Judging is the proper task of a sovereign. So too is the extracting of vengeance, and plaintiffs plead their own case. Although Christian martyrs have no right to take on themselves the extraction of vengeance, then, for the sake of the justice that's inherent in God's character they have every right to ask him to extract vengeance for their blood that the earth-dwellers shed (see the comments on 3:10 for earth-dwellers as unbelievers, and compare Matthew 23:29–36; Luke 18:7).

In answer to the martyrs' question, they're first given white gowns. Since disembodied souls are composed of superfine substance, they can be clothed as well as seen (compare 1 Samuel 28:7–14). We shouldn't think here in terms of short nightgowns or hospital gowns—rather, in terms of long, formal gowns like those worn nowadays as academic regalia in recognition of an accomplishment. Because of their whiteness these gowns symbolize victory (see again 2:17; 3:4–5 for the association of whiteness with conquest, that is, victory). In other words, they represent a heavenly recognition of the martyrs' victory *through* martyrdom in addition to the purity of their prior Christian testimony. "To each of them" highlights individuality of recognition. No graduation by group here. The martyrs walk the stage and get robed one by one. Then they're told "to rest for yet a little while." Before martyrdom they toiled at testifying for Jesus (14:13). During the millennium following his return they'll reign as kings with him (20:4–6). They deserve and need to rest up. "For *yet* a little while" implies that they've been resting since their martyrdom. "For yet a *little* while" links up with Jesus' coming "quickly" (1:1, 3; 2:16; 3:11; 22:7, 10, 12, 20). In 3:2 he described the deeds of the church in Sardis as "not fulfilled," because more deeds needed to be added. So here in 6:11 the martyrs have yet to be fulfilled by the addition of more martyrs. These further martyrs are called the existing martyrs' "fellow slaves." There's fellowship in slaving for Jesus as his witnesses. "Brothers" adds a familial touch characteristic of John's writings (see especially 1:9; 12:10; 19:10; 22:9; John 20:17; 21:23 and numerous passages in 1 and 3 John). Fellowship and brotherhood make good fences for demarcating Christians from "the world" of "earth-dwellers." "Who were *going* to be killed" portrays the further martyrdoms as sure and soon. And "as also they [had been killed]" may make the further martyrdoms similar to the earlier ones not only in occurrence but also in occurring "because of the Word of God and because of the Testimony that they'd held."

6:12–14: **And I looked when he opened the sixth seal; and a big shaking occurred; and the sun became black, as sackcloth made of** [black goat's] **hair** [is black]; **and the whole** [= full] **moon became, as it were, blood** [in color]; [13]**and the stars of the sky fell to the earth as a fig tree casts off its summer figs when being shaken by a big** [= fierce] **wind;** [14]**and the sky was split apart**

like a scroll being rolled up; and every mountain and island were moved out of their places [we'd say, "*was moved out of its place*"] [compare Isaiah 13:10; 34:4; 50:3; Ezekiel 32:7–8; Joel 2:10, 31; 3:15; Haggai 2:6–7, 21–22]. The shaking isn't limited to an earthquake. It encompasses the sky as well as the earth. The heavenly bodies are mentioned first because pagans considered them to be personal beings more powerful than human beings. But not even they will escape the shaking. The blackening of the sun may allude, if not to an eclipse, to its blackening by the eruption of Mount Vesuvius in A.D. 79 or by an eruption closer to Patmos in A.D. 60. The disintegration of sky and earth is magnified in a number of ways: (1) by the addition of "big" to "shaking"; (2) by the comparisons to black goats' hair and to blood; (3) by the addition of "whole" to "moon"; (4–5) by the analogies of a fig tree's casting off its summer figs and of a scroll's being rolled up; (6) by the description of the wind that shakes the fig tree as "big"; and (7) by the addition of "every" to "mountain and island." The blackness of the sun suits the blackness of the third horse and the famine it represented, for crops don't grow without sunshine (6:5–6). The redness of the full moon suits the redness of the second horse and the bloodshed it represented (6:3–4). The meteorite shower represents the downfall of astral deities. We expect the figs to *fall* off. Instead, the fig tree *casts* them off, a more vigorous way of expressing those deities' downfall. According to Mark 13:24–26; Matthew 24:29–30; Luke 21:25–27, all these celestial phenomena will immediately precede the second coming. The splitting apart of the sky will let Jesus descend through the opening, though for suspense John will save a description of the descent till 19:11–16. "Split apart like a scroll being rolled up" means like an unrolled scroll that's split apart at its middle, so that its two halves automatically roll up to their curled positions and their contents, to which the heavenly bodies are here compared, disappear. There's no more stability on earth than in heaven. Ancient people commonly thought of mountains and islands as rooted deep down beneath the seas and therefore as genotypes, so to say, of stability. Not so now! They're tossed about like unanchored ships on a stormy sea.

6:15–17: **And the kings of the earth and the court officials and the military commanders and the wealthy and the strong** [such as athletes], **plus every slave and free** [person], **hid themselves in the caves and among the rocks of the mountains;** ¹⁶**and they say to the mountains and the rocks, "Fall on us and hide us from the face of the one sitting on the throne and from the wrath of the lamb,** ¹⁷**because the big day of their wrath has come. And who is able to stand** [in the face of it] [compare Hosea 10:8]**?"** The list of those who hide themselves starts with the high and mighty, because they might seem to be the most secure. But they're no more secure than their slaves and ordinary free men. The list consists of seven categories so as to connote completeness: none of the earth-dwellers, unbelievers since they are, will be any more able to maintain their positions

than the mountains and islands will be able to maintain theirs. As emphasized by "every," not even those in the lowest, least desirable, and most obscure positions ("slave and free man") will be able to do so. "Slave" is listed before "free man" because a slave might conceivably have the support of his master, but a free man has only himself to depend on. The present tense in "they say" highlights the plea to the mountains and rocks. Better to be crushed by a rock-slide or a cave-in than by the wrath of God and the lamb. Better to be hidden by the debris of the mountain-moving, cave-collapsing earthquake, the last and largest big one, than to look into the scowling face of the one sitting on the throne and be bowled over by the seven-horned lamb. "The wrath of the lamb" may seem oxymoronic; but because of his seven horns, this lamb has turned into a ram. "The . . . day of their wrath" is "big" because of the large amount of wrath to be visited on worldlings for their hatred of Christians. That day is the day of Jesus' return, and it "has come." But people are still pleading for suicidal shelter. The wrath hasn't quite struck, then. So "has come" stresses that though the day of wrath has *barely* begun, it *has* begun. In the minds of those who ask it, the question, "And who is able to stand [as opposed to falling under the onslaught of divine wrath]?" may call for the answer, "Nobody!" (compare Psalm 1:5–6). But chapter 7 will provide a very different answer.

THE ONE HUNDRED AND FORTY-FOUR THOUSAND AND INNUMERABLE MULTITUDE
Revelation 7:1–17

This passage divides into John's hearing about 144,000 "slaves of God," to be protected from harm (7:1–8), and John's seeing an innumerable multitude who've come "out of the great affliction" (7:9–17).

7:1: **After this** [the lamb's opening of the first six seals] **I saw four angels standing at the four corners of the earth, gripping the four winds of the earth lest a wind blow on the earth or on the sea or against any tree.** It takes four angels to occupy the four corners of the earth and grip the four winds of the earth. "On the earth or on the sea" joins the threefold "four" to indicate a geographically unlimited expanse. The four angels recall the four living creatures of chapters 4–5. The four winds recall the four horsemen of chapter 6 and like them represent disaster. But unlike the four horsemen, who represented disasters arising out of human wickedness, the four winds represent disaster arising out of the wrath of God and the lamb, just referenced in 6:16–17— only the figure has shifted from a great shaking of the sky and earth (6:12–15) to windstorms from east, west, north, and south. This shift suits the question with which chapter 6 ended: "And who is able to stand [in the face of 'the great day of their wrath']?" For winds can blow down standing objects such as trees. But since the question has to do with human beings ("And *who* . . . ?"), the trees represent human beings. The shift from "*on* the earth or *on* the sea" to "*against* any tree" portends wrath that will blow down human beings with whom God and the lamb are displeased. "*Gripping* the four winds" means holding them back so that for the time being they don't blow, and the description of them as "of the earth" rather than "of heaven" (as in some Old Testament texts) indicates that when finally let go, they'll blow down "the earth-dwellers," as Revelation regularly calls non-Christians, because the earth-dwellers won't be able to stand (see 6:17 again). The "standing" of the four angels contrasts with the earth-dwellers' inability to stand and anticipates the ability to stand of others, yet to be identified.

7:2–3: And I saw another angel ascending from the rising of the sun, having the seal of the living God. And to the four angels to whom [license] **had been given to damage the earth and the sea he** [the angel] **shouted in a loud voice, ³saying, "You shouldn't damage the earth or the sea or the trees until we've sealed the slaves of our God on their foreheads."** "The slaves of our God" are Christians (1:1; 2:20 and so on). Sealing them means marking them as his property so as to protect them from the winds of his and the lamb's wrath (see Ezekiel 9:1–11 for background, and John 6:37, 39; 10:4, 12, 14, 16, 26–30; 17:2, 6, 9–10, 24 for Christians as the property of Jesus and his Father). "On their foreheads" makes the mark a brand (figuratively speaking) so easily visible that there's no chance of the four angels' mistakenly allowing divine wrath to blow against a slave of God (see 14:1; 22:3–4 for the mark as the names of the lamb and of God his Father, and 13:16–18; 14:9; 16:2; 20:4 for the contrastive mark of the beast, consisting in either his name or his number [666]). So as slaves of God, Christians won't suffer his and the lamb's wrath, though in the form of persecution, including martyrdom, they'll suffer the wrath of the unbelieving nations and of the dragon Satan (11:7–10; 12:17). "You shouldn't damage the earth or the sea or the trees *until* we've sealed the slaves of our God" implies that the four angels should release the winds of wrath once the sealing has occurred. Inclusion of the sea along with the earth and its trees means that not even unbelievers on the high sea will escape the winds' destructive force. On the other hand, John's description of the seal as "of the living God" not only strikes a contrast with lifeless idols (for which see 9:20) but also implies that God imparts his own life to his sealed slaves, so that they'll not suffer the second death under his and the lamb's wrath (compare 2:11; 20:6, 14; 21:8).

Who is the angel that has the seal? He's "ascending from the rising of the sun," that is, in the east. The land of Israel is east of Patmos (strictly speaking, southeast; but the location of Patmos in the northern hemisphere makes sunrise look simply east of the island). Both 12:5 and John 20:17 feature Jesus' ascension from the land of Israel, and he has already been portrayed as an angel in the sense of a human messenger (1:1) and will yet be portrayed as such (see especially chapter 10). So the recent depiction of Jesus as a lamb has changed. He now appears as the "angel ascending from the rising of the sun" who "shouted in a loud voice" to be heard by the angels standing far away at the four corners of the earth. If so, however, to whom besides himself does he refer when saying "until *we've* sealed the slaves of *our* God"? The others can't be the four angels, because they're to hold back the winds while "we" do the sealing. But Jesus has earlier identified himself as "the one who has the seven Spirits of God" (3:1), referring to a full complement of the Holy Spirit (especially in relation to the seven churches addressed in chapters 2–3 [see the comments on 1:4]). So the "we" who brand believers with "the seal of the living God" are Jesus, the one ascending as a result of taking up his life again (John 10:17–18), and "the Spirit of life from God" (11:11; John 6:63).

7:4–8: And I heard the number of those who'd been sealed: 144,000. [They'd been] **sealed from every tribe of the sons of Israel: ⁵from the tribe of Judah, twelve thousand** [had been] **sealed; from the tribe of Reuben, twelve thousand; from the tribe of Gad, twelve thousand; ⁶from the tribe of Asher, twelve thousand; from the tribe of Naphtali, twelve thousand; from the tribe of Manasseh, twelve thousand; ⁷from the tribe of Simeon, twelve thousand; ⁸from the tribe of Levi, twelve thousand; from the tribe of Issachar, twelve thousand; from the tribe of Zebulun, twelve thousand; from the tribe of Joseph, twelve thousand. From the tribe of Benjamin, twelve thousand** [had been] **sealed** [compare Judges 21:10]. In the absence of a description of the sealing, "who'd been sealed" indicates its accomplishment. The number 144,000 is the square of twelve multiplied by a thousand. Since Israel numbered twelve tribes in all, twelve squared (144) underlines completeness. Multiplication by a thousand underlines multitudinousness. "From *every* tribe of the sons of Israel" and the listing tribe by tribe with the number 12,000 add further emphasis on completeness and multitudinousness, recall similar emphases in John 6:37, 39; 10:16, 27–30; 12:12–19 (with comments), and develop further the parallel in Revelation between the deliverance of Israel from slavery in Egypt and the coming deliverance of Christians from persecution (compare the typology of exodus also in John 1:14, 17, 29, 36; 3:14). In line with the portrayal of Jesus as "the lion from the tribe of Judah" (5:5), John lists first "the tribe of Judah" instead of "the tribe of Reuben," which otherwise should come first since Reuben was Israel's (Jacob's) firstborn son. Because the tribe of Dan went into idolatry first (Judges 18:30 [compare 1 Kings 12:28–30]) and because John and John's Jesus attack idolatry (2:14, 20; 13:15; 21:8; 22:15; 1 John 5:21), that tribe falls out. The tribe of Manasseh replaces that of Dan even though the later-listed tribe of Joseph included the tribe of Joseph's son Manasseh. Along with the tribe of Joseph's other son, Ephraim, the tribe of Manasseh inherited Joseph's double portion of land allotted to him in Canaan. But the tribe of Joseph is listed instead of that of Ephraim because Ephraim's tribe was the main rival of the first-listed, royal tribe of Judah, out of which, as mentioned above, Jesus arose as "the lion of the tribe of Judah" (5:5). Though sometimes omitted from Old Testament lists because it didn't receive an allotment of tribal territory in Canaan, the tribe of Levi, from which came Israel's priests, *is* listed here because Jesus has made Christians, represented by the 144,000, into "priests for God and his Father" (1:6; 5:10; 20:6). "[Were] sealed" is repeated at the end for the tribe of Benjamin to re-emphasize protection from the winds of God's and the lamb's wrath.

Do the 144,000 represent Christians, whatever their ethnicity, rather than ethnic Israelites? The aforementioned application of exodus typology to Christians and Jesus' saying earlier that members of Satan's synagogue who claim they're Jews really aren't Jews (2:9; 3:9) and calling Nathaniel "*truly* an Israelite" (John 1:47) favor an affirmative answer (compare 9:4, where a plague of demonic locusts affects only those who don't have God's seal on their foreheads, so that those who do have it would appear to be God's people, whatever their ethnicity). But there's more to consider in *7:9–10*: **After these things** [seeing the angels and hearing about the 144,000] **I looked—and behold, a big crowd, which no one could number, from every nation and** [from all] **tribes and peoples and tongues, standing within sight of the throne and within sight of the lamb, clothed** [referring to the crowd, not the lamb] **with white gowns! And palm fronds** [were] **in their hands,** ¹⁰**and they are shouting in a loud voice, saying, "Our God, who is sitting on the throne, and the lamb** [have] **salvation!"** In 5:5–6 John was told about a lion but then saw it to be a lamb (compare Jesus' being "the lamb of God that takes away the sin *of the world*," not just of ethnic Israelites [John 1:29]). Likewise here, John heard the number of the sealed Israelites, 144,000, but now sees them to be an innumerable crowd "from every nation and [from all] tribes and peoples and tongues" (compare 5:5–7 and the comments on 4:2–4). "Every" and the piling up of four terms ("nation," "tribes," "peoples," and "tongues," corresponding to "the four angels standing at the four corners of the earth, gripping the four winds of the earth" [7:1]), point to comprehensive ethnicity, so that "every tribe of the sons of Israel" back in 7:4 portrayed the universal church as the true Israel (compare John 4:42; Genesis 15:5; 16:10; 22:17; 26:4). "Behold" calls attention to this identification of the 144,000 as the universal church. "A *big* crowd" corresponds to the symbolism of twelve squared, and "which no one could number" corresponds to the symbolism of multiplication by one thousand (compare the use of twelve, its square, and multiplication by one thousand in a description of the New Jerusalem, identified as "the bride, the lamb's wife," that is, as the universal church [21:9–22:5]).

"Standing" supplies an answer to the question in 6:17: "And who is able to stand [in the face of God's and the lamb's wrath]?" The answer: Saved people from every nation, represented as the true Israel by the sealed 144,000. Their standing indicates both not being blown over by the winds of divine wrath and also resurrection; for many of them will have been martyred (20:4–6), and the scarred lamb's standing represented Jesus' resurrection in that "resurrection" means "standing up" (5:6). Since in the Old Testament only soldiers were numbered (see, for example, Numbers 1:1–3; 2 Samuel 24:1–9), the 144,000 portrayed the church militant on earth. Now they stand triumphantly resurrected in heaven. "Within sight of the throne and within sight of the lamb" puts the large crowd near God and the lamb just as are the twenty-four elders, who represent them, and indeed just as are the seven Spirits of God (1:4; 4:10; 5:8). See the comments on 6:11 for the crowd's white gowns. "Palm fronds in their hands" recalls another crowd's acclaiming Jesus with palm branches at his triumphal procession and, as there, links up with a portrayal of the present crowd in terms of the true Israel in that palm branches symbolized Israel (see the comments on John 12:13). Since the crowd doesn't shout a command (as did the ascending angel in 7:2), the loudness of their shout underscores numerical vastness rather than authority (compare 5:11–12). The present tense of "are shouting" reinforces this emphasis. "*Our* God" echoes "*your* God" in the message of Jesus to his disciples (John 20:17), and "who is sitting on the throne" celebrates God's having exercised his sovereignty to the crowd's benefit. He and the lamb have salvation. It's as though the crowd are saying, "We know that God and the lamb have salvation to give, because they've saved us not only from persecution but also from the ferocious winds of their wrath—and from death. Look, we're standing!"

7:11–12: **And all the angels were standing around the throne and** [around] **the elders and the four living** [creatures] **and fell on their faces within sight of the throne and worshiped God,** ¹²**saying, "Amen! Our God** [will have] **the favor and the glory and the wisdom and the thanks and the honor and the power and the strength forever and ever. Amen!"** The angels form the outermost circle surrounding the throne. The elders are closer in, and the four living creatures closest. In distinction from the living creatures, who are four in number, and the elders, who are twenty-four, "all" takes in the entirety of the indefinitely large angelic throng. Without exception they respond with a hearty "Amen!" to the crowd's attributing salvation to God and the lamb, and they punctuate their verbal agreement with body language. They "were standing," but now they fall on their faces and worship God. Falling on their faces conjures up the physical meaning of the Greek verb for worshiping, which is to kiss the ground at someone's feet. "Within sight of the throne" puts the angels, though forming the outermost circle, close enough for their kissing the ground to count as worshiping at the throne-sitter's feet. By saying "our God" the angels align themselves with saved human beings. With them they're equally dependent on God. But since the angels haven't needed or experienced salvation, instead of saying that God has salvation, as the large crowd did, they say that God will have (1) "the favor"; (2) "the glory"; (3) "the wisdom"; (4) "the thanks"; (5) "the honor"; (6) "the power"; and (7) "the strength" (compare the similar list of seven in 5:12). "Forever and ever" requires a supplying of the future tense, "will have"; and the sevenfoldness of the acclamation connotes completeness. God will eternally have all the acclaim that can possibly be had. The occurrence of "the" with each of the seven listed items marks them for individual attention. God will *have* them all in the form of his creatures' *acknowledgment* that he has them. A second "Amen!" punctuates the truth of the angels' acclamation (compare the doubling of "Amen," though without interruption, numerous times in John's Gospel, beginning at 1:51).

7:13–15b: And one of the elders answered [= responded to the preceding acclamation] **by saying to me, "These who are clothed with white gowns—who are they, and where did they come from?"** [14]**And I said to him, "My lord, you know** [who they are and where they came from] [compare Ezekiel 37:3]." **And he told me, "These are the ones coming out of the great affliction; and they washed their gowns and whitened them in the blood of the lamb.** [15a–b]**Because of this** [the washing white of their gowns] **they're within sight of God's throne; and they're serving him in his temple day and night."** The elder knows the answer to his own question, but it's John's response that prompts the elder to verbalize the answer by telling John the identity and origin of the big, white-gowned crowd. In John's response, "My lord" means something like "Kind sir" or "Good sir" and shows proper respect for an elder. Concerning "the great affliction" out of which the crowd come, see the comments on 3:10. Since the crowd are already standing within sight of the throne and the lamb (7:9), the present tense in "coming out of the great affliction" is emphatic rather than temporal. It emphasizes the fact of exit. Jesus has kept them from apostasy (3:10), so that now they're free and clear and within sight of the throne and the lamb. Normally you don't wash clothing in blood, and normally blood stains fabric rather than whitening it. But we're dealing with figurative language in which Jesus' blood, though literally shed in "expiation for our sins" (1 John 2:2; 4:10), figuratively washes and whitens believers' figurative gowns (compare 1 John 1:7: "the blood of Jesus . . . is cleansing us from every sin"; also Revelation 1:5). Being "within sight of God's throne" puts the white-gowned crowd in his temple, so that they can serve him by performing there the priestly duties of worship (compare 1:6; 5:10; 20:6 and the mercy seat in the temple's inner sanctum as God's throne, on which he sat in his invisible presence). These duties occupy the crowd incessantly ("day and night"), as in the case of the four living creatures (4:8). The mention of day before night shows that John isn't using the Jewish method of counting a twenty-four day from sunset to sunset (see the comments on John 1:39). According to 21:22; 22:3 the Lord God Almighty and the lamb will *be* the temple in which God's slaves will serve him.

7:15c–17: "And the one sitting on the throne will tent over them [in the sense of sheltering them]. [16]**And they'll not hunger any more; neither will they thirst any more. Nor will the sun fall on them** [in the sense of beating down on them], **nor any scorching heat** [compare Isaiah 49:10], [17]**because the lamb in the middle of the throne will shepherd them and lead them to the springs of the waters of life. And God will wipe every tear out of their eyes** [compare Isaiah 25:8]." The mixed metaphor of sitting on a throne and tenting over saved people indicates sovereign and therefore absolute protection. The figure of a temple (7:15) has shifted to that of the tabernacle, the tent that Israel transported with them during their trek from Egypt to Canaan (compare John 1:14). Not hungering any more recalls John 6:35 and God's giving Israel manna in the wilderness (Exodus 16). Not thirsting any more recalls John 4:13–15; 6:35; 7:37–39 (compare John 19:28) and God's giving Israel water in the wilderness (Exodus 15:22–26; Numbers 20:1–13). The sun's not falling on the saved recalls the cloud of God's presence that shaded the tabernacle by day during Israel's trek through the wilderness (Exodus 33:7–11; Numbers 9:15–17). Only now God is himself the tabernacle that shades the saved, who serve as priests within it/him. "Nor any scorching heat" may refer to winds heated by the sun. In any case, the cool of shade is of high value in the Middle East and represents here the comfort of eternal life. Acting as shepherd of the saved, the lamb leads them "to the springs of the waters of life" (compare again Exodus 15:22–26; Numbers 20:1–13 and the earlier-cited passages in John's Gospel). The figure has shifted again, this time from that of the tabernacle and priests serving under its shade to that of a shepherd leading his sheep out in the wilderness (compare John 10:1–6, 11–16, 27–30). In an astounding reversal of roles, the shepherd is the lamb, whereas a lamb is normally part of the flock that follows the shepherd. But this lamb is "in the middle of the throne." That is, he's enthroned with his Father (as also in 3:21; 12:5; 22:1, 3), so that as a royal shepherd he has the right to lead his sheep (rulers being often compared to shepherds of their subjects [see Matthew 2:6, for example]). Springs give an ever-fresh supply of water, and "of life" describes "the waters" as flowing. But "of life" alludes also to eternal life in an ever-fresh supply (compare 21:6; 22:1 and contrast the springs of death-dealing bitter waters in 8:10–11; also the turning of springs of water into springs of judgmental blood in 16:4–7). God's wiping "every tear out of their eyes" points to the eternal state of the saints, described more fully in 21:1–7. No more sorrow at all, not even over the deaths of martyrs (see the comments on 5:4 for John's sorrowing over their deaths). Delivered from persecution, free of guilt in God's presence, and serving him—eternal safety, comfort, and satisfaction. What an encouraging destiny!

THE SEVENTH SEAL
Revelation 8:1–5

Chapter 7 interrupted the sequence of seven seals for an answer to the question with which the sixth seal ended: "the great day of their [God's and the lamb's] wrath has come, and who is able to stand?" The sequence resumes now with the seventh seal. **8:1: And when he** [the lamb] **opened the seventh seal, there was silence in heaven for about half an hour.** So the heavenly acclamations and prayer in chapters 4–7 cease for about half an hour, that is, for a very short period of time, because an hour was the shortest named unit of time used by these ancients. Cut it in half and you make it very short indeed, the "little while" of 6:11. But why silence? And why very short? The silence can hardly give time to prepare for the trumpet blasts that will start in 8:6–7, because the sixth seal brought us to the beginning of the end (see the comments on 6:12–17), so that given their contents the trumpets will start with events farther back in something of an overlap with earlier seals. Nor can the silence very well prepare for the new creation after the pattern of primeval silence leading up to God's speaking order out of chaos (Genesis 1), for he won't create the new heaven and the new earth till a thousand years after what happens under the seventh seal (19:11–21:1). Nor is it likely that the silence enables God to hear the saints' prayers before answering them; for the silence in 8:1 appears to precede the offering up of those prayers in 8:3–4, and during the period of silence God appears to be occupied with giving trumpets to the seven angels standing before him (8:2). But the interlude in chapter 7 started with a portrayal of his and the lamb's wrath (6:16–17) in terms of judgmental winds that no one except the sealed for salvation can withstand. We all know about the short but eery calm that precedes a storm. It's best, then, to think of the half hour of silence as a calm before the fierce winds of tribulation-closing judgment start blowing. The silence occurs in heaven because the command to release those winds will issue from heaven. When the angels holding them back release them at the opening of the seventh seal, the winds will bring a judgmental storm of thunderclaps nearby, rumblings of distant thunder, and flashes of lightning, plus an earthquake (8:5).

8:2: And I saw the seven angels who stand within sight of God, and seven trumpets were given to them. For further suspense (in addition to the interlude of chapter 7), John introduces seven angels and their being given seven trumpets, which will constitute the next series of plagues. (Will we ever be told about the seventh seal?) Sitting on a throne is the proper posture for a sovereign. But in his presence, standing is the proper posture for others. So the seven angels stand. "*The* seven angels" distinguishes them as angels privileged with a specially close proximity to God. "Within sight of God" indicates as much, but also implies that he's the one who gives them their trumpets. Unlike the plagues under the seals, then, the plagues that take place when the trumpets are blown will derive directly from God's will (see the comments on 6:1–2). Why trumpets? Because the plagues will constitute calls on the earth-dwellers, non-Christians, to repent (9:20–21 [compare Ezekiel 33:1–6; Joel 2:15]).

8:3: And another angel, holding a gold censer [= a bowl in which to burn incense], **came and stood at the altar** [compare Amos 9:1]. **And much incense was given to him so that he'd give** [it] **along with the prayers of all the saints onto the gold altar within sight of the throne.** "The altar" alludes to the altar underneath which John saw the souls of martyrs. That was the altar of burnt offering, where sacrificial blood was poured out (see the comments on 6:9–11). But now this altar is associated with the offering of incense and thus described as "the *gold* altar," like the entirely different altar of incense in the Old Testament tabernacle (Exodus 30:1–10). So the nongolden altar of burnt offering and the gold altar of incense have been merged into a single altar so as to interpret the saints' prayers as prayers for deliverance from the persecution that shed the martyrs' blood. In 5:8 the twenty-four elders had gold bowls full of incense identified as the saints' prayers. Here the censer is likewise gold, along with the gold altar. All this gold shows the high value God places on the prayers—"of *all* the saints," not just of those already martyred, because all Christians want deliverance from such persecution as led to the martyrdom of the souls underneath the altar. "Much incense" is required to represent so many prayers as all the saints send up to heaven. There's a play on the *giving* of the incense to the angel and the angel's *giving* the incense in turn onto the gold altar. "*Along with* the prayers of all the saints" indicates that the incense represents those prayers (see 5:8 again); and "within sight of the throne" indicates proximity to God, to whom the prayers are addressed, and implies his giving of the incense to the angel. But who is the angel that relays them from the saints to God? "Another" distinguishes this angel from the just-mentioned seven angels. At 1:1; 4:1; 7:2 we noted portrayals of Jesus as an angel, that is, a messenger, and will note an even clearer such portrayal in chapter 10. In 1:12–20, moreover, Jesus appeared robed as a priest walking among the seven lampstands of a heavenly sanctuary. Here in 8:3 the altar and incense point to priestly function in that same sanctuary. So "another angel" refers to Jesus, acting as a priestly messenger who relays to God all the saints' prayers (compare praying in Jesus' name according to John 14:13–14; 15:16; 16:23–24, 26).

8:4–5: And the smoke from the incense, along with the saints' prayers, ascended within God's sight out of the angel's hand. [5]**And the angel took the censer and filled it with some of the fire from the altar and threw** [it] **onto the earth** [compare Ezekiel 10:2]; **and thunderclaps and rumblings and flashes of lightning and an** [earth]**quake occurred.** Naturally, the ascent of smoke from the burning incense pictures the ascent of prayers to God (compare Psalm 141:2). "Out of the angel's hand" underlines Jesus' angelically priestly role of relaying them to God and prepares for the subsequent actions of taking, filling, and throwing. The angel already has the censer (8:3); so his taking the censer at this point simply emphasizes those further actions. Filling the censer "with some of the fire from the altar" implies that the incense is now burned up and therefore that the saints' prayers are now completed. The coals of fire that replace the incense come from the fire that so to speak burned up the sacrificed martyrs, whose blood soaked into the ground beneath the altar. The very fire of their sacrifice is now used for judgment on the earth-dwellers, whose hands shed the martyrs' blood. (The symbolism of fire for judgment pervades Revelation and other literature, but see 20:9 for one example.) "*Filled it with fire*" indicates a judgment commensurate with the crimes. The martyrs will get all the vengeance they deserve (see 6:10). "Threw it [the censer filled with fire]" indicates a vigorous visitation of judgment in answer to the saints' prayers. "To the earth" aims the judgment at earth-dwellers (about whom see the comments on 3:10). Suddenly a storm replaces fire as a figure of this judgment. The judgmental winds of 7:1–3 blow in a storm of nearby thunderclaps, rumblings of distant thunder, and flashes of lightning, plus an earthquake, all reminiscent of God's descent onto Mount Sinai at the time of Israel's exodus from Egypt (Exodus 19:16–19; Psalm 77:17–18). Only this time it's God's descent *in Jesus*, or Jesus' descent *as God*, that causes these phenomena, though for suspense John will delay his description of the descent itself till 19:11–16. In 4:5 lightning was listed first as the precursor of thunderous rumblings in the distance and thunderclaps nearby. Because of a heavenly setting no earthquake occurred. Here the thunderclaps come first because of their proximity and loudness. Rumblings of distant thunder come next. And lightning follows, because it appears to strike the earth and therefore sets up for the addition of an earthquake.

THE FIRST SIX TRUMPETS
Revelation 8:6–9:21

Here begins a second series of plagues under the figure of trumpets. Since the seals came to a climax with the second coming under the seventh seal, the trumpets will mark a stepping back to sometime earlier in the great affliction. As in the seven seals, the first four trumpets will form a quartet; and again as in the seals, for suspense there'll be an interlude prior to the seventh trumpet. This suspense enhances the climactic character of each seventh.

8:6–7: And the seven angels who were holding the seven trumpets prepared themselves to blow their trumpets. Parenthetically introduced in 8:2, these angels now prepare themselves by hoisting the trumpets to their lips and taking a deep breath. **⁷And the first [angel] blew his trumpet, and there occurred hail and fire mixed with blood** [compare Exodus 9:22–26; Ezekiel 38:22; Joel 2:30]. **And they were thrown onto the earth, and a third of the earth [= land] was burned up; that is, a third of the trees was burned up; and all yellow green grass was burned up.** Now the thunderstorm, blown in by God's judgmental winds, produces hail along with fire that was ignited by the lightning strikes mentioned in 8:5 and that corresponds to the fire thrown onto the earth by "another angel" (also in 8:5). This plague recalls one of the plagues on Egypt that led up to the exodus (Exodus 9:13–35; Psalm 78:47; 105:32–33). "Mixed with

blood" doesn't feature in the Egyptian plague, probably refers to the fire as red-colored like blood (alternatively to morning redness of sky preceding a storm [Matthew 16:3] or to wind-blown red sand from the Sahara), and almost certainly alludes to shedding the earth-dwellers' blood in recompense for their having shed the martyrs' blood (see especially 14:17–20, but also 6:10; 16:6; 17:6; 18:24; 19:2). As before, "the earth" probably refers to the Roman Empire (see the comments on 6:8). Forest fires burn up one third of the trees occupying one third of its land mass. But all yellow green grass—that is, grass that has started to dry out and is therefore less resistant to fire than trees are—is burned up, not just one third of such grass. Notably, one third takes in more than the one fourth that characterized a plague under the fourth seal (6:7–8). The hail and fire spell an ecological disaster so far as the food chain is concerned (compare the famine in 6:5–6).

8:8–9: And the second angel blew his trumpet; and a big mountain burning with fire, as it were, was thrown into the sea. And a third of the sea became blood [as to its color, not its chemistry (compare Exodus 7:20, but there in reference to a river)]; **⁹and a third of the creatures in the sea—those** [in the sea] **that had souls** [= living creatures]**—died; and a third of the ships were obliterated** [compare Jeremiah 51:25, but there in reference to land-locked Babylon]. Here John sees a volcanic island that destroys itself in a massive eruption. "As it were" indicates that because of its self-destructive eruption the big mountain is fast becoming a nonmountain. It's disappearing. "Burning with fire" carries forward the theme of judgmental fire from 8:5, 7. In John's setting, "the sea" refers to the Mediterranean. Its turning blood-red in color refers to the red hot lava flowing into it and again corresponds to the martyrs' blood, for which vengeance is being taken. The explosion takes the lives of one third of the sea creatures. ("Souls" refers to the physical life that animates the bodies of creatures living in the sea.) The corresponding obliteration of one third of the ships at sea takes also the lives of their human occupants.

8:10–11: And the third angel blew his trumpet, and a big star burning as a lamp [burns] fell out of the sky [compare Isaiah 14:12]. **And it fell on a third of the rivers and on the springs of waters; ¹¹and the name of the star is called Wormwood** [a very bitter herb]**; and a third of the waters became wormwood** [that is, very bitter like the herb]. **And many of the human beings died from the waters, because they** [the waters] **had been made bitter** [= poisonous (compare Jeremiah 9:15; 23:15)]. In modern terms, John sees an asteroid burning because of friction as it enters the earth's atmosphere, striking the earth, and polluting a third of the sources of fresh water much as the exploding volcano adversely affected the salty waters of the sea and the creatures living in it. The similarly phrased Isaiah 14:12 has to do with the downfall of the king of Babylon, and Rome's downfall as a new Babylon will be described in chapters

17–18. But the present asteroid hardly symbolizes Rome, for the first four trumpets deal with ecological disasters: first to plant life, second to sea water, now to fresh water, and next to sources of light. The plagues of the final three trumpets will strike "those who ruin the earth" (11:18) rather than the earth itself. "Wormwood" refers to an herb whose dark green oil was used as a folk remedy to kill intestinal worms. Though not poisonous to human beings, its bitter taste seems poisonous, so that the asteroid is called "Wormwood" because the waters polluted by it bring death to "many" (contrast "the springs of the waters of life" in 7:17 and the sweetening of bitter waters in Exodus 15:22–25).

8:12: And the fourth angel blew his trumpet, and a third of the sun was struck—also a third of the moon and a third of the stars—so that a third of them was darkened and [so that] **the day didn't shine** [with sunlight] **for a third** [of the day], **and the night likewise** [didn't shine with moonlight and starlight for a third of it] [compare Exodus 10:21–23]. "Was struck" indicates a blow that blots out all sources of heavenly light for a third of the day and a third of the night. This plague mimics the plague of darkness on Egypt, except that the three whole days of darkness there have become one-thirds of darkness here for an indefinite number of days (indefinite because no one but God knows the day and hour of Jesus' return [see 3:3; 16:15 with Mark 13:32; Matthew 24:36]). Just as the plagues on Egypt were a countdown to the deliverance of Israel from slavery there, so the similar plagues in Revelation will be a countdown to the deliverance of Christians from persecution at the second coming. They can therefore take comfort during "the great affliction" in the nearness of their deliverance. On the other hand, since these celestial phenomena don't rise to the level of those described in 6:12–17, which mark the beginning of the end, this fourth trumpet has an earlier fulfillment.

8:13: And I looked and heard a single eagle flying in midsky [= directly overhead], **saying in a loud voice, "Woe! Woe! Woe to the ones who dwell on the earth—**[woe to them] **because of the remaining trumpet blasts of the three angels who are about to blow their trumpets."** Is this flying eagle the fourth living creature, whom John described in 4:7 as "like a flying eagle," but now as "single" (or "lone") because of separation from the other three living creatures? Probably not, because the fourth living creature was only *like* an eagle whereas we have here an eagle. In either case, though, this eagle heralds the last three trumpets in terms of three woes directed against the earth-dwellers, non-Christians. Alas for them! The word for woe means "alas for [plus an object]" and in the original Greek sounds like a screech such as an eagle emits: *ouai*, pronounced oo-EYE (compare 18:10, 16, 19). It suits an eagle, a bird of carrion (and vultures were classified among eagles), to pronounce woes. In Greek mythology an eagle acted as Zeus's messenger. The present eagle acts as a messenger of the one and only true God and screeches out woes as

a warning designed to call earth-dwellers to repentance and assure God's people that their vindication is coming soon. "Flying in midsky" makes the eagle visible to all. "Saying in a loud voice" makes the eagle audible to all. No earth-dweller will be able to plead ignorance as an excuse for not repenting. "Who are *about* to blow their trumpets" indicates that the remaining plagues under the trumpets are soon and certain to come. There's no room for doubt or delay. So repent now.

9:1: And the fifth angel blew his trumpet, and I saw a star that had fallen out of the sky to the earth. And the key of the shaft of the abyss [= the key to the shaft that connects the netherworld with the surface of the earth] **was given to him** [the one portrayed as the fallen star]. Plagues under the first four trumpets attacked sources for the sustenance of human life. Plagues under the final three trumpets, the three woes announced in 8:13, will attack human beings themselves. Stars were regarded as personal beings (see the comments on 1:16; also Judges 5:20; Job 38:6–7; Daniel 8:10). In view of 12:7–9, which relates the throwing of Satan from heaven to earth, the fallen star here represents Satan. His being given "the key to the shaft of the abyss" makes for a parody of Jesus' having the keys of death and of hades (1:18), for "the abyss" refers to the netherworld of the dead and of demons. The key stands for authority to open and shut. "Was *given* to him" indicates derived authority as opposed to inherent authority. Since in 20:1–3 an angel descending out of heaven will have the key to the abyss, bind Satan, and throw him into the abyss, Satan will have authority to open the shaft of the abyss only temporarily. And since death and hades are more or less synonymous with the abyss, Jesus, who has the keys to them, must be the one who gives Satan the key to the shaft (as he'll also be the angel who throws Satan into the abyss at 20:1–3). (Literally, "abyss" means "without a bottom" and is therefore often translated "bottomless pit.")

9:2–3: And he [Satan, the fallen star] **opened the shaft of the abyss; and smoke ascended out of the shaft, the smoke of a big furnace, as it were; and the sun and the atmosphere became dark because of the smoke from the shaft.** It's tempting to infer hellfire in the abyss as producing smoke. But John limits his description to the smoke as such, to its ascent out of the shaft (not explicitly out of the abyss), and to its great volume: "the smoke of a *big* furnace, as it were," so that "the sun and the atmosphere became dark" (contrast the smoke of incense ascending before God with the saints' prayers in 8:3–4; but compare Joel 2:10, 30–31; 3:15, especially in view of Joel's describing the effect of a cloud of locusts and John's following description of a plague of locusts). The darkening of the sun and atmosphere suits the association of darkness with evil in 16:10; John 1:5; 3:19; 8:12; 12:35, 46; 1 John 1:5; 2:8–11. Figuratively speaking, the hour of great affliction will be a time of specially intense darkness. [3]**And out of the smoke came locusts onto the earth; and authority was given to them, as the scorpions of the earth have authority** [compare Exodus 10:1–20; Joel 1:2–2:11]. Since these locusts come out of the smoke that has ascended out of the shaft of the abyss, they represent demons who ordinarily live in the abyss but whom Satan lets out to do his work on earth. A swarm of locusts in flight looks like a cloud of smoke. John compares the authority given these hellish locusts to the authority that earthly scorpions have. Scorpions can inflict on human beings an extremely painful sting, so that theirs is an authority based on people's fear of them. Likewise, the locust-like demons are given an authority based on people's fear of being painfully possessed by them (compare the accounts in Matthew, Mark, and Luke of demoniacs' physical travails). The demons impose a reign of terror that contrasts with God's love for the world (John 3:16). John doesn't say who gave the demons their authority, but Satan's having the key to the shaft of the abyss suggests him as the giver, though the authority derives ultimately from Jesus (see the comments on 9:1).

9:4–5: And it was told them that they shouldn't damage the grass of the earth or any green [plant] **or any tree, except that** [they should damage] **the human beings who as such** [that is, as human in distinction from vegetable matter] **don't have the seal of God on** [their] **foreheads.** "It was told them" by whoever gave them their authority (9:3). We might think of what they're told as a setting of limits, as in 6:6, 7–8; 8:7–9, 11–12. But except for the limitation to human beings who "don't have the seal of God on [their] foreheads" (compare 7:1–8), telling the locusts that they shouldn't damage any green vegetation simply confirms that the locusts represent demons. For the insects called locusts *would* damage green vegetation by devouring it but wouldn't damage human beings by devouring them. The locust-like demons will damage human beings by painfully possessing them—only non-Christians, though; for Christians will be exempt from this wave of widespread demonic possession. All who lack God's seal on their foreheads will be fair game. The text leaves it an open possibility that all the human beings who lack the seal may suffer possession. [5]**And it was given to them that they** [the demons] **shouldn't kill them—rather, that they** [the human beings] **should be tormented for five months. And their torment** [the torment inflicted by the demonic locusts] [was] **as torment by a scorpion** [is] **when it strikes a human being.** Two more limitations: (1) no killing, only torment; (2) five months, no longer. These limitations give non-Christians reason and opportunity to repent. If demonic possession were to go beyond torment to killing, there'd be no such opportunity. But the opportunity won't last forever. "Five months" represents the normal life span of locusts and coincides with the length of the summer season, during which locusts flourish. Whether literal or symbolic, the five months of widespread demonic possession will come to an unhappy end for those who refuse to repent.

9:6: And in those days human beings will seek Death and by no means will find him; and they'll crave to die, and Death flees away from them. As death was personified in 6:8, so too here in that death will flee away—hence the capitalization, "Death." So painful will be the demonic possession that its victims will try to commit suicide, but the demons that torment them will keep them alive to torment them further. "Will crave to die" doubles up on "will seek Death," and "by no means will find him" doubles up on "Death will flee away from them." These doublings lay enormous emphasis on the pain of the coming demonic possessions. Ironically, "will crave" is a verbal form of the noun "lusts" in 18:14; John 8:44; 1 John 2:16–17. Under this plague those who've lusted for enjoyable evils will lust for the ultimate evil, death, but won't get it. Not yet, as emphasized by the present tense of "flees away."

9:7–10: And the likenesses of the locusts [were] **like horses prepared** [= equipped] **for battle. And on their heads** [they had], **as it were, crowns like gold; and their faces** [were] **as faces of human beings** [are]. [8]**And they had hair—as it were, women's hair; and their teeth were as** [those] **of lions** [are]. [9]**And they had breastplates—iron breastplates, as it were; and the sound of their wings was, as it were, the sound of chariots of many horses running into battle** [= of many horse-drawn chariots rushing into battle]. The demons have been compared to locusts. Now the locusts are compared to horses and chariots (compare Joel 2:4–5). A locust looks like an armored warhorse, so that the plague of demonic possession resembles a fullscale military attack. In a parody of Jesus as "like a son of man" wearing "a gold crown" (14:14), the demonic locusts have "on their heads . . . crowns like gold." In other words, the locusts' antennae look like the projections of a radiate gold crown. The comparison to gold crowns, emphasized by the addition of "as it were" to "like," points to the demons' ruling people by possessing them. Looked at straight on, locusts' faces resemble the faces of human beings. This comparison marks the demons as intelligent beings. A locust's legs look hairy—hence the comparison to women's head-hair (understood to be noticeably long). This comparison calls to mind the long hair of Parthian cavalrymen (see the comments on 6:1–2) and the strength of Samson so long as he kept his long hair (Judges 13–16). The demons will overpower their victims. The ability of locusts to devour all vegetation in their path makes for a comparison with lions' teeth (also in Joel 1:6). The demons will likewise destroy human flourishing (contrast the salvation effected by the lion-like lamb of chapter 5). The scaly chest of a locust looks like a soldier's iron breastplate and represents the inability of human beings to destroy a swarm of locusts and therefore an equal inability to withstand a plague of demonic possession. (A swarm of locusts can number in the millions, spread over several miles in width, build up to several feet in depth, and destroy a whole territory's food supply in a few days.) The whirring wings of a swarm of locusts in flight sounds like the rumble of horses' hooves and chariot wheels as they're rushing into battle. Thus will be the swiftness of the coming demonic attack on human beings—a blitzkrieg. [10]**And they have tails like scorpions—that is, stingers—and in their tails [is] their authority to do damage to human beings for five months.** The upward-curving tails of locusts look like scorpions' tails. As insects, locusts don't have stingers in their tails. But these demonic locusts do. The pain of being possessed by them resembles the pain of a scorpion's sting. "Their authority to do damage to human beings" refers to capability plus authorization to exercise it (see also the comments on 9:3). "For five months" repeats the aforementioned chronological limit to stress the brevity of time left for repentance.

9:11–12: They have over them a king, the angel of the abyss. As to Hebrew, his name [is] Abaddon. And in Greek he has the name Apollyon. Because Satan will be cast into the abyss in 20:1–3, we may recognize Satan in "the angel of the abyss" who rules over the demons as their king (contrast God's reign, which appears repeatedly in Matthew as "the reign *of heaven*"). But John calls this angel "Abaddon," Hebrew for "destruction," and "Apollyon," Greek for "destroyer" (contrast John 3:16, where the verbal form of "destroyer" is used: "And so he [God] gave [his] one-and-only Son in order that everyone believing in him might not be destroyed [or 'lost,' an alternative translation], but might have eternal life"). These names point out Satan's desire to destroy human well-being, and indeed human beings as such, so that the limitation not to kill (9:5) must have been divinely set. That is to say, Satan doesn't protect his own, as God and Jesus do their own (John 10:28–30; 17:11–15). Satan doesn't love the world. God does (John 3:16 again). Satan hates his subjects just as he and his subjects hate God, Jesus, and Christians. The naming of Satan as a destroyer in both Hebrew and Greek stresses his destructiveness and parodies the inscription on Jesus' cross in Hebrew, Latin, and Greek (John 19:20). But here Latin is omitted to center attention on Apollyon as a wordplay on the god Apollo, with whom the emperor Nero, a destroyer of Christians in Rome, had identified himself. Not only does Apollyon call to mind Nero's patron deity, Apollo; but also Apollo had the locust as a symbol of himself. [12]**The one woe** [= the first woe, which is the fifth trumpet (compare the comments on 6:1–4)] **has gone away. Behold, two woes are yet coming after these things!** John's vision of demonic possession has ceased. Next he'll see and hear the second and third woes (the sixth and seventh trumpets). The interruptive announcement of them reemphasizes the need of non-Christians to repent. "Behold" makes this reemphasis exclamatory.

9:13–14: And the sixth angel blew his trumpet, and I heard a single voice from the horns of the gold altar within God's sight, [14]**saying to the sixth angel who had a trumpet, "Set loose the four angels who've been tied up at the big river Euphrates."** The best manuscripts read "the horns," not "the *four* horns." Horns on an altar projected upward from the corners of its top to keep the wood for burning a sacrifice and the sacrifice itself from rolling off the altar. But inanimate horns can't speak. So

whose voice emanated from the horns of the gold altar? "A *single* voice" eliminates the four living creatures as a group. And "within God's sight" eliminates him. Last seen at the gold altar was Jesus, offering up the incense of the saints' prayers and throwing a censer full of fire onto the earth (see 8:3–5 with comments). And he has appeared as a lamb with horns (5:6). So John hears the voice of Jesus the horned lamb coming not just from the altar—more specifically, from its horns. Since horns stand for active power, Jesus is portrayed here as answering *with power* the saints' prayers for deliverance from persecution by way of judgment on their persecutors, who live in the Roman Empire. The judgment will take the form of an invasion from the east side of the Euphrates River, which marked the empire's eastern border. Echoing Genesis 15:18; Deuteronomy 1:7; Joshua 1:4, John describes the river as "big": it's almost two thousand miles long. The four angels have been tied up there lest the invasion, which they're itching to launch, start sooner than planned by God (compare 16:12–16).

9:15–16: And the four angels who'd been prepared for the hour and day and month and year were set loose so as to kill a third of human beings. [16]**And the number of the forces of cavalry [was] twenty thousands of ten thousands** [20,000 x 10,000 = 200,000,000]. **I heard their number.** "For the hour and day and month and year" highlights the arrival of the exact time to begin operations in accordance with God's calendar. The angels are "set loose to kill a third of human beings"—probably within the Roman Empire, since this trumpet has to do with invading it—but the angels do their killing through the agency of 200,000,000 cavalry. "I heard their number" abruptly and repetitiously underlines the vastness of this army. As cavalry they're reminiscent of the Parthians (see the comments on 6:1–2). The number of them is overwhelming but limited, unlike the innumerable number of the redeemed in 7:9–10 and the indefinitely large number of the heavenly host of angels in 5:11–12.

9:17–19: And I saw the horses in this way—[that is,] **by way of a vision—also those sitting on them, having breastplates [that were] fiery red and violet and sulfurously yellow. And the heads of the horses [were] as the heads of lions [are], and out of their mouths are issuing fire and smoke and sulfur.** [18]**By these three plagues—by the fire and the smoke and the sulfur issuing out of their mouths—a third of human beings were killed.** [19]**For the authority of the horses is in their mouth and in their tails, for their tails [are] like serpents that have heads. And with them [the tails] they do damage.** This passage contains more reminiscences of the feared Parthians. They fought on horseback. Bright colors typified their breastplates. They didn't trim their horses' manes—therefore the comparison to the heads of lions. Parthian cavalry shot their arrows both when charging into battle—hence the comparison to the issuing of fire and smoke and sulfur out of the mouths of the snorting, wheezing warhorses—and when retreating from the frontline to refill their quivers before charging again. In retreat, the cavalry turned on their horses and shot over the horses' tails, which were bound up—hence the comparison to serpents that have heads spitting out venom in the form of deadly arrows. It doesn't hurt the comparison that Satan will be compared to a serpent (12:9, 14–15; 20:2). Sulfur is yellow and burns with a reddish blue—that is, violet—flame. These colors of the cavalry's breastplates (1) correspond to the figurative fire, smoke, and sulfur issuing out of the horses' mouths; (2) recall the destruction of Sodom and Gomorrah by fire and burning sulfur; and (3) anticipate the lake of fire and sulfur (19:20; 20:10, 14–15; 21:8; Genesis 19:1–29). The repetition of "fire and smoke and sulfur" and the addition of "the" to each of these three items underscore the effectiveness of this onslaught from the East, which results in the killing of one third of the Roman Empire's human population. "The authority of the horses" consists in their ability to carry the cavalry forward and rearward in battle as the cavalry shoot death-dealing arrows whichever way the horses are running. Contrast the demonic locusts' being prohibited from killing their victims (9:5–6). Things are getting worse.

9:20–21: And the rest of the human beings, who weren't killed by these plagues, didn't even repent of the products of their hands so as not to worship the demons and the gold and silver and bronze and stone and wooden idols that can neither see nor hear nor walk around. ²¹And they [the rest of the human beings] didn't repent of their murders or of their magic arts or of their fornications or of their thefts. Not even the first two woes, which gave reason and opportunity for repentance, induced the non-Christian survivors to repent. Not that they didn't have plenty to repent of: the worship of demons, as opposed to God and the lamb; the worship of idols that are blind, deaf, and immobile because they're dead, as opposed to the living God and resurrected lamb who see, hear, and move about (see Deuteronomy 32:16–17; 1 Corinthians 10:14–22 for worshiping idols as worshiping the gods, sarcastically called "demons," whom the idols represent); and murders, magic arts (the use of charms, potions, spellcasting, and such like), fornications (various kinds of sexual immorality), and thefts, all of which the non-Christians learned from their gods in the myths concerning them (among other passages, see Deuteronomy 4:28; Psalms 115:4–8; 135:15–18). John's listing in descending order of value the materials out of which idols are made—gold, silver, bronze, stone, and wood—degrades idolatry intellectually and symbolizes the moral degradation of idolaters (compare Daniel 5:4, 23; Acts 17:29). Whenever the one true God isn't worshiped, there's idolatry of one sort or another; and you become like what you worship.

AN INTERLUDE
Revelation 10:1–11:13

Just as chapter 7 interrupted the sequence of seven seals to build up suspense for the finale in the seventh seal, so too 10:1–11:13 interrupts the sequence of seven

trumpets to build up suspense for the finale in the seventh trumpet, which will be the third and final woe (8:13). These interruptions delay John's *accounts* of the seventh in each sequence, but not the *fulfillments* of each seventh. The present interruption divides into the canceling of seven thunderclaps (10:1–7), John's eating the opened scroll (10:8–11), and two witnesses (11:1–13).

The Canceling of Seven Thunderclaps to Avoid Further Waiting
Revelation 10:1–7

10:1–2a: And I saw another angel, a strong one, descending out of heaven, clothed with a cloud. And the rainbow [was] **over his head; and his face** [was shining] **as the sun** [shines]; **and his feet** [were burning] **as pillars of fire** [burn]; ²ᵃ**and** [he was] **holding in his hand an opened scroll.** The term "angel" can refer either to a human messenger or to an angelic one. We'll see plenty of reasons to identify this "angel" with Jesus (compare the comments on 1:1, 20; 4:1; 7:2; 8:3–5). "Another" distinguishes him from the six angels with trumpets (8:6–9:21), from "the angel of the abyss" (9:11), and from the four angels set loose at the Euphrates River (9:14–15 [compare "another angel" for Jesus in 8:3]). John describes him as "strong" to prepare for his taking control of the sea and earth (10:2b). "Descending out of heaven" points to Jesus' second coming for the taking of such control (compare the heaven as "opened" for his descent in 19:11; also 18:1; 20:1 and the frequent use of "descend" for his first coming in John's Gospel [3:13, for example]). "Clothed with a cloud" recalls Jesus' second coming "with the clouds" in 1:7. There the clouds presented a divine mode of transport. Here a cloud presents a divine article of clothing (compare 14:14–16, where "one like a son of man," a phrase referring to Jesus in 1:13, sits on a cloud as though it were a divine throne). "The rainbow over his head" harks back to 4:3, where "a rainbow" overarched the throne of God (compare Ezekiel 1:26–28); and according to 3:21; 7:17; 12:5; 22:1, 3 Jesus sits with God the Father on his throne (see also the comments on 5:11–12). Here the rainbow follows him in his descent to indicate his codeity with the Father (as elsewhere throughout Revelation, John's Gospel, and 1–2 John) and possibly to assure the saints that he's coming to deliver them, not to judge them (compare Genesis 9:8–17). The shining of the angel's face as the sun shines recalls the description of Jesus' face in 1:16 (compare 21:23). The comparison of the angel's feet to "pillars of fire" implies that his legs are included with the feet. Otherwise "pillars" would make nonsense. "Feet" is used as a part for the whole to recall the description of Jesus' feet in 1:15; 2:18 and thus identify this angel with him. But the earlier figure of "feet like bronze as made glowingly red hot in a furnace," which warned the ungodly of a trampling down in judgment, has now shifted to pillars of fire, which promise deliverance of the saints from their persecutors just as the Lord's pillar of fire stood between Israel and Pharaoh's pursuing army in Exodus

13–14. The single pillar of fire there has doubled here to accommodate the angel's two feet-and-legs. Since John describes the scroll held by the angel as already "opened," we should understand it as the seven-sealed scroll, the title deed to the earth that Jesus the lamb took and all of whose seals he opened in 5:1–8:5. Holding it open indicates that he's now ready to take control of the earth as his rightful possession. And so he will do. Many translations have "a *little* scroll," as though this diminutive scroll differs from "the scroll" in chapter 5. Though the underlying Greek words differ slightly in their endings, however, the word in chapter 5 is also diminutive; and that same Greek word will crop up here in 10:8. So for variety John is using variations of the same word just as he often uses synonyms for the same reason.

10:2b–4: And he placed his right foot on the sea and his left [foot] on the land ³and shouted in a loud voice just as a lion roars. And when he shouted, the seven thunderclaps spoke with their rumblings [compare Psalm 29]. **⁴And when the seven thunderclaps spoke, I was about to write** [what they said]**; and I heard a voice from heaven saying, "Seal up the things that the seven thunderclaps said, and you shouldn't write them down."** As in Deuteronomy 1:36; 11:25; Joshua 1:3–6, placing the feet on something stands for taking possession of it. Most people are right-handed, and right-handed people are normally right-footed; so the angel's right foot comes first. (From here on we'll call him Jesus.) The placement of his right foot on the *sea* is mentioned first to highlight his conquest of the chaotic forces of evil represented by the sea (compare the comments on 4:5–6a). The foot doesn't sink into the sea (compare Jesus' walking on the sea in John 6:16–21). The placement of his left foot on the land completes his taking over the earth. To emphasize this takeover, John will mention Jesus' *standing* triumphantly on the sea and on the land in 10:5, 8. The present placing of his feet issues in his later standing (compare the comments on 5:6 for standing as an indication of resurrection). He "shouted in a loud voice" so as to be heard and heeded by the seven thunderclaps up in the sky. "Just as a lion roars" not only reinforces this loudness. It also confirms the angel's identity as Jesus. For 5:5 called him "the lion of the tribe of Judah." "*Just* as" underlines the comparison. The thunderclaps responded noisily. The noise consisted in speech that John was going to write down. Obviously, the thunderclaps are being personified. But what does their speech represent? Given the parallel with seven seals, seven trumpets, and upcoming seven bowls, all of which represent plagues and judgments of various sorts, the seven thunderclaps must represent another such series. If John were to write them down, they'd have to happen; for a word of true prophecy is sure to be fulfilled. But a voice from heaven (God's, since Jesus is standing on the earth; compare especially 18:4) tells him not to write them down—rather, to seal them up. Since unsealing the seven-sealed scroll didn't just reveal coming events but actually triggered them in John's vision, sealing them up doesn't just hide them. It keeps them from happening.

In other words, the plagues of the seven thunderclaps are canceled (compare the cutting off, or shortening, of the days of the great affliction according to Mark 13:19–20; Matthew 24:20–22; and contrast the prohibition of sealing in Revelation 22:10, because leaving the book of Revelation *un*sealed will ensure the fulfillment of its contents). You don't seal up a piece of writing till you've written it. Telling John to "seal up the things that the seven thunderclaps have said" before telling him "you shouldn't write them down" therefore creates an incongruity. Moreover, if John hasn't yet written down what the thunderclaps said, there's nothing to seal up! This double incongruity, purposeful as it is, puts enormous stress on cancellation—for the sake of a speedy end, as we'll now see.

10:5–7: And the angel that I saw standing on the sea and on the land raised his right hand to heaven ⁶and swore by the one who lives forever and ever, who created heaven and the things in it and the earth and the things in it and the sea and the things in it, "There'll be no more time [that has to be waited out]**! ⁷Rather, during the days of the voice of the seventh angel, when he's about to blow his trumpet, also the secret of God was finished, as he** [God] **proclaimed** [it] **to his own slaves, the prophets, as good news."** The body language of raising the right hand to heaven corresponds to the verbal language of swearing by God, enthroned in heaven. But for several reasons John calls him "the one who lives forever and ever": (1) to make a contrast with the lifeless idols mentioned just recently in 9:20; (2) to encourage Christians who face the possibility of martyrdom with God's eternal life, which he has promised them; (3) to suit the announcement of no more waiting for the arrival of eternal life; and (4) to echo Daniel 12:7–9. But unlike the figure there, Jesus doesn't raise his left hand along with the right, because his left is holding the opened scroll (10:2). And John adds a reference to God as the creator of all that exists, again in opposition to the manmade idols of 9:20, and changes Daniel's waiting period from three and a half "times" to no waiting "time" at all. For after this interlude comes the seventh trumpet blast, which like the opening of the seventh seal brings us to the second coming, though for suspense John reserves a description of it as such till 19:11–16.

Since God is often said to swear by way of taking an oath (Exodus 6:8; Numbers 14:30; Luke 1:73; Acts 2:30; Hebrews 3:11, 18; 4:3; 7:21) and even to swear by himself (Deuteronomy 32:40; Hebrews 6:13), it should come as no surprise that Jesus swears by God, especially in view of his subordinating himself to God as a son to his father throughout John's Gospel. The present oath has the purpose of banishing all doubt that the end has finally arrived. The past tense in "the secret of God was finished" shows that even though the seventh trumpet hasn't been blown quite yet, it's to be blown so soon that the accompanying finish of God's secret might as well be historical already. The secret is the good news of salvation, that is, of deliverance from persecution and of resurrection from death by martyrdom to eternal life. Though proclaimed by God "to his own slaves, the prophets," this deliverance has remained a secret to their persecutors. The secret will be finished by the accomplishment of this salvation at the second coming. "*Also the secret*" means the finishing of the secret in addition to the blowing of the seventh trumpet at the same time. "His *own* slaves" stresses God's ownership of Christians. They don't belong to Caesar or to any of the pagan deities. Elsewhere in Revelation language is often borrowed from Old Testament prophetical books, but the Old Testament prophets themselves don't appear with any clarity. Christians do appear as prophets, however (see the comments on 11:3, 10, 18; 16:4–6; 18:20, 24; 22:6, 9). So "his own slaves, the prophets" are Christians, to whom God has revealed his secret as good news.

John's Eating the Opened Scroll
Revelation 10:8–11

10:8–9: And the voice that I heard from heaven [was] **speaking with me again and saying, "Go take the opened scroll in the hand of the angel who is standing on the sea and on the land." ⁹And I went away to the angel, telling him to give me the scroll. And he tells me, "Take** [it] **and eat it up. And it will make your stomach bitter. In your mouth, though, it'll be sweet as honey."** See the comments on 10:4 for the voice from heaven as God's. As in 1:12, "speaking *with* me" doesn't imply John's speaking too. It implies, rather, the proximity of the voice to John. At 4:1–2 he went up to heaven. From that vantage point he has been seeing events on earth, so that when God now tells him to "go take the opened scroll in the hand of the angel who is standing on the sea and on the land," he has to go "away" from heaven and proximity to God's voice. On orders from God, then, John tells the angelic Jesus to give him the scroll. As God the Father's obedient Son, Jesus is more than willing to give John the scroll, and indeed repeats God's command that John take the scroll (compare John 5:19, 30; 7:16; 8:26). The present tense in "he tells me" emphasizes the repetition. But Jesus adds a command to eat the scroll (compare Ezekiel 2:8–3:3). "Eat it *up*" stresses complete consumption, a devouring of the scroll in its entirety so as not to miss any of its prophetic effects. Since the scroll is a title deed to the earth and since Jesus has now opened it and thus taken possession of the earth, the resultant deliverance of Christians from their persecution is honey-sweet to the taste; and the resultant judgment on non-Christians is bitter to the stomach. As a prophet who has to deliver this two-pronged message, John will both taste the sweetness and feel the bitterness.

10:10–11: And I took the scroll out of the hand of the angel and ate it up; and in my mouth it was sweet as honey; and when I'd eaten it, my stomach was made bitter. ¹¹And they tell me, "It's necessary that you prophesy again concerning many peoples and nations and tongues [= languages] **and kings** [compare Jeremiah 1:10]**.**" What John was told about the effects of eating the scroll comes to pass. God has spoken to him twice (10:4, 8). Jesus has just spoken to him (10:9). So "they" who now speak to him are God and Jesus. They impress on John the necessity of his prophesying, because this activity is the very means of ensuring that divinely ordained events take place. No prophecy, no fulfillment. The present tense in "they tell me" underscores the necessity. "Again" looks forward to further prophecies in addition to those already made. "Peoples and nations and tongues" constitute the human population out of which come the redeemed (see 5:9; 7:9) and the remainder of which come in for judgment, so that John's further prophecies concerning them will include both the sweet and the bitter. "Kings" replaces the expected "tribes" in this foursome (compare also 11:9; 13:7; 14:6) to highlight both the victory of Christians as a kingdom of kings (see 1:6 with 21:24) and the judgment of those non-Christian kings who persecuted them (see especially chapters 17–18). The listing of four indicates earthwide scope (7:1; 20:8), and "many" adds numerousness to that scope.

Two Witnesses
Revelation 11:1–13

11:1–2: And a reed like a staff was given to me, saying [as though the reed was talking!]**, "Get up and measure the temple of God and the altar and the ones worshiping in it** [in the temple, that is (compare Ezekiel 40–42, especially 41:13)]**; ²and throw outside** [= leave out] **the courtyard outside the temple; and you shouldn't measure it, because it has been given to the Gentiles** [in the religious sense of non-Christians regardless of ethnicity] **and** [because] **they'll trample the holy city for forty-two months."** "A reed like a staff" amounts to a measuring rod. It will turn out in 11:3 that God is talking to John through the reed. The word for "temple" means the sanctuary proper, exclusive of any surrounding courtyard. "The altar" brings back into view the heavenly altar of 6:9; 8:3, 5 and therefore locates the temple, which houses it, likewise in heaven (as will be explicitly confirmed in 11:19). Later, "the holy city" will be identified as the New Jerusalem, which will be identified in turn as "the bride, the lamb's wife," that is, the redeemed, the saved, the saints (19:7–8; 21:2, 9–10; 22:17). The Lord God Almighty and the lamb are said to *be* the temple of this bridal city (21:22); and as priests, Christians are worshiping in the heavenly temple which is God and the lamb (compare 1:6; 5:10; 20:6 with 11:1; also 3:12 and the mutual indwelling of believers, Jesus, and God in John 14–17 [see especially the comments on John 14:16–23]). Since the *un*measured courtyard "has been given to the Gentiles" with the result that "they'll trample the holy city [that is, the saints]," the *measuring* of the temple proper and those worshiping in it symbolizes protection. The measuring of worshipers as well as the temple shows that we're dealing with symbolic language. So these two verses say that true worshipers of God have protection from his and the lamb's wrath by virtue of worshiping and abiding in God and the lamb, who are their heavenly temple. But these worshipers are exposed on earth, like the outer courtyard in John's vision, to the wrath of their persecutors, led by the dragon, Satan (12:17; compare Christian believers' being in the world but not of the world [John 17:11–18] and therefore located simultaneously on earth and in heaven [John 17:21]). The suffering of persecution will reach its peak in "the great affliction" of "forty-two months" just prior to the second coming (compare 7:14 with 11:2 and the combination of protection from divine wrath and the suffering of persecution in chapter 7 as a whole).

11:3–4: "And I'll give [prophecies] to my two witnesses and, clothed in sackcloth, they'll prophesy for 1,260 days. ⁴These are the two olive trees and the two lampstands that stand within sight of the Lord of the earth [compare Zechariah 4]." As noted above, God is speaking through the reed (yet another indication of symbolic language). The witnesses stand for Christians on earth during the great affliction of 1,260 days (= 42 months of 30 days each [11:2]). They are two in number, not because God will have only two prophets to testify for him during that period, but because the testimony of the innumerable multitude of Christians who'll come out of the great affliction (7:14) will satisfy the law that requires the united testimony of at least two witnesses to establish a matter in court (John 8:17; Numbers 35:30; Deuteronomy 17:6; 19:15). "Two" is symbolic, in other words. "They'll prophesy" means that they'll preach. "Clothed in sackcloth" symbolizes their preaching of repentance; for the wearing of sackcloth (made of rough goat's hair) symbolizes sorrow, such as the sorrow for sins that characterizes repentance (see Matthew 11:21, for example). They're called "the two olive trees" in that olive trees provide the olive oil that fuels lamps, and Zechariah 4:6 interprets this provision in terms of empowerment by the Holy Spirit. So the Holy Spirit will empower Christians, represented by the two witnesses, to prophesy. They're also called "the two lampstands" in that lampstands hold up lamps, which burn with the light of Christian testimony. The seven lampstands in 1:20 stood for seven local churches. The two here stand for all Christians in the legal sufficiency of their testimony. Unrepentant earth-dwellers will have no excuse. "Standing within sight of the Lord of the earth" alludes to the heavenly location of the earthly Christians as discussed in the foregoing paragraph (compare Elijah's saying to King Ahab, "As the Lord God of Israel lives, before whom I stand" [1 Kings 17:1]). "The Lord of the earth" refers to Jesus as the earth's owner, who in chapter 10 was portrayed as taking possession of it away from those who'd usurped control over it to the detriment of Christians. In succession, then, the Christians have been represented as "worship[ers]," as "the holy city," as "two witnesses," as "prophes[iers]," as "two olive trees," and as "two lampstands."

11:5–6: "And if anyone wants to harm them, fire issues out of their mouth and eats up their enemies. And if anyone wants to harm them, it's necessary that he be killed in this way. ⁶These have the authority to shut the sky so that rain doesn't precipitate for as long as the days of their prophesying. And they have authority over the waters so as to turn them into blood and to strike the earth** [= the land as distinct from 'the waters'] **with every kind of plague as often as they want."** For the time being, Christians—still represented by the two witnesses—will have the authority to defend themselves against their persecutors and thus complete their prophetic testimony, and authority also to impose plagues that will undergird their preaching of repentance. The authority comes from God or, more specifically, from the Holy Spirit of Zechariah 4:6 and consists in authorization and enablement to perform wonders such as Elijah and Moses once performed. See 2 Kings 1:9–12 for fire that "ate up" Elijah's enemies (so a literal translation; compare Jeremiah 5:14); 1 Kings 17:1; Luke 4:25; James 5:17 for Elijah's imposing a drought; Exodus 7:14–25 for Moses' turning water to blood; and Exodus 7:14–12:30 for Moses' striking the earth with every kind of plague (compare 1 Samuel 4:8). Elijah called down fire from heaven, whereas the two prophets issue fire from their mouths. But the difference isn't so great as it might seem, for issuance out of the mouth is a figurative representation of a verbal command that fire eat up the enemies. Presumably the fire consists in lightning that appears to come down from heaven and strike them dead. The fire's eating them up makes for a deadly contrast with John's eating up the lamb's title deed in 10:10–11.

11:7–8: "And when they've finished their testimony, the beast that's coming up out of the abyss will do battle with them and conquer them and kill them [compare Daniel 7:21]." "The beast" means "a *wild* beast" as opposed to a domestic animal. ⁸**"And their corpses** [will lie] **on the wide** [square] **of the big city which as such** [= as big] **is spiritually called Sodom and Egypt, where also their Lord was crucified."** The two witnesses, representing the last generation of Christians, will have finished their testimony at the end of the 1,260 days, that is, at the end of the great affliction. Though able to defend themselves during that period, afterward they'll suffer martyrdom at the hands of "the beast." More about the beast in chapters 13 and 17. His mention here is a teaser. For the moment we're told only that he originates from the abyss, out of which emanated the locust-like demons of 9:1–11 (not a good omen), and that he'll kill the Christians, their martyrdom being compared to a defeat in warfare. Furthermore, they'll suffer the disgrace of having their corpses lie unburied. "On the wide [square] of the big city" refers to a spacious city square. But what city is Jesus talking about? In 16:19; 17:18; 18:10, 16, 18, 19, 21 "the big city" is explicitly identified as "Babylon," a code name for Rome. But this city stands for its empire, and Jesus' description of the city as "big" recalls the popular Stoic philosophers' comparing the world to a city. Closer to home, we've already noted that the New Jerusalem will appear as a city *of people*, namely, "the bride, the lamb's wife" (= Christians [21:9]); and throughout John's Gospel and 1 John "the world" means non-Christians. So it makes sense to say that "the big city" symbolizes all non-Christians in the Roman Empire just as the New Jerusalem symbolizes all Christians. "Is Spiritually called" means "is called by 'the Spirit of prophecy' [19:10]"—hence the capitalization of "Spiritually." The Spirit calls the city "Sodom" because non-Christians, who make up this worldwide city, are headed for the lake of fire and sulfur, the very elements that destroyed Sodom (Genesis 19:24). The Spirit also calls the city "Egypt," because non-Christians will already be suffering during the great affliction the sorts of plagues that fell on Egypt in preparation for the exodus. "Where also their Lord was crucified" doesn't refer to Jerusalem, Israel, any more than Sodom refers to the long-destroyed city of that name or than Egypt refers to a country in Africa. The names are historically symbolic. In view is the world-city, the society of non-Christians throughout the Roman Empire, as the location of Jesus' crucifixion (compare John 1:10: "He was in the world and the world came into existence through him, and the world didn't know [= didn't recognize] him"). He's called "their [the martyred Christians'] Lord" to counterbalance his crucifixion with his lordship, which includes his ownership of Christians.

11:9–10: "And some of the peoples and tribes and tongues and nations gaze at their corpse for three and a half days; and they don't allow their corpses to be put in a tomb; [10]**and those who dwell on the earth rejoice over them** [the corpses of God's witnesses] **and celebrate; and they'll send gifts to one another, because these two prophets had tormented those who dwell on the earth."** The reference to "some of the peoples and tribes and tongues and nations" confirms that the preceding reference to "the big city . . . where also their Lord was crucified" had to do with the world-city consisting of the Roman Empire. The present tense of "gaze," "don't allow," "rejoice," and "celebrate" underlines the perverse pleasure non-Christians will take both in the martyrdom of Christians, here called "these two prophets" because of their Elijah-like self-defense in 11:5–6 (see also the last comments on 10:7), and in the disgraceful exposure of their corpse. Though quickly changed to a plural, the singular of "corpse" is collective to highlight unity in martyrdom. The three and a half days of exposure correspond to the three and a half years of the great affliction, as though the non-Christians now get their revenge against the Christians for the Christians' having zapped and plagued them—but a revenge only in miniature. To set up for a dramatic reversal, the rejoicing and celebrating and exchanging of gifts join gazing to add glee to the perversity of the non-Christians' vengeful pleasure.

11:11–13: And after three and a half days the Spirit of life from God entered into them [the prophets' corpses (compare Ezekiel 37:5)]**, and they stood on their feet. And great fear fell on those who were watching them,** [12]**and they** [the two prophets] **heard a loud voice from heaven, saying to them, "Come up here." And they went up into heaven in the cloud** [with which the angelic Jesus was clothed in 10:1 (compare 2 Kings 2:11)]**. And their enemies gazed at them** [going up]**.** [13]**And in that hour a big** [earth]**quake took place; and a tenth of the city fell; and seven thousand names of human beings were killed in the** [earth]**quake; and the rest became terrified and gave glory to the God of heaven.** The pleasure taken by non-Christians in the Christians' martyrdom and disgrace is short-lived, for what 20:4–6 will call "the first resurrection" now takes place. "They stood" recalls both the slain lamb's "standing" resurrected in 5:6 and the very meaning of "resurrection" as a "standing up" by formerly supine corpses (see John 6:63 for the Spirit as the life-maker). "On their feet" underscores the transition from lying dead in the city square to standing up alive again. The earth-dwellers' great glee turns into great fear as they see this transition taking place in front of their eyes. "Fell" indicates that the fear took them by surprise and all of a sudden. "Come up here" echoes 4:1, where Jesus told John the same, and therefore probably identifies the "loud voice from heaven" as Jesus' voice. It has to be loud to travel all the way from heaven to earth. The Christians go up into heaven, it will turn out in 19:7–8, 14, to join Jesus and accompany him in his second coming. "In the cloud" indicates that we should understand "heaven" initially as a reference to the sky. (The original Greek word varies in meaning between the heaven of the sky and the heaven of God's abode, if it makes any distinction at all.) "The cloud" also anticipates the cloud on which Jesus as "one like a son of man" will sit and then reap a harvest of the saints (see 14:14–16 with comments, and compare his coming "with the clouds" according to 1:7, John liking to switch back and forth between the singular and the plural, as in this passage between "their corpse" and "their corpses"). The earth-dwellers' gazing in glee has turned into gazing with fear, so that they see the Christians' resurrection and ascension just as they see Jesus' return (1:7 again). Being seen resurrected and ascending gives the Christians vindication before their enemies.

"A big [earth]quake" recalls both the big quake with which "the big day of [God's and the lamb's] wrath" started in 6:12–17 and the "[earth]quake" that coincided with other accompaniments of Jesus' return at the opening of the seventh seal (8:1, 3–5). Because an hour was the shortest unit of time recognized by the ancients, "in that hour" emphasizes here the coincidence of the earthquake with Christians' resurrection and ascension. The falling of "a tenth of the city" matches the falling of fear on the earth-dwellers, contrasts with the standing up and ascension of the Christians, and refers to the destruction of a tenth of the Roman Empire in that the city represents the empire. The earthquake's killing of seven thousand marks a large number that's complete (seven being a number of completeness) and contrasts with the Lord's preservation of seven thousand who didn't bow the knee to the false god Baal in Elijah's time (1 Kings 19:18 [see the comments on 11:5–6 for other allusions to the story of Elijah]). The killed are called "*names of human beings*" to stress their personal identities and thus the judgmental tragedy of their deaths. The survivors, already afraid, get even more afraid ("terrified," an intensified form of "afraid"). They even "gave glory to the God of heaven." But there's nothing about repentance, which 16:9 requires, just as the earth-dwellers' fear didn't have God as its object, as the gospel requires it to have according to 14:6–7. "Of heaven" describes God for a contrast with "those who dwell on the earth" (11:10). In a contest between him and them, he always wins.

THE SEVENTH TRUMPET
Revelation 11:14–19

11:14–15: The second woe [= the sixth trumpet] **has gone away. Behold, the third woe is coming quickly!** See the comments on 8:13; 9:12. "Behold" calls special attention to the coming quickly of this climactic woe. The quickness of its coming matches the quickness of Jesus' coming according to 2:16; 3:11; 22:7, 12, 20; for in fact Jesus comes in conjunction with the third woe's coming. [15]**And the seventh angel blew his trumpet, and there were loud voices in heaven, saying, "The kingdom of the world has become** [the kingdom] **of our Lord and of his Christ** [compare Psalm 2:2]**, and he will reign as king forever and ever."** So the third and last of the three woes equates with the seventh and last of the seven trumpets. "Of our Lord and his Christ" suggests that the loud voices who use this phrase belong to the Christians who, after being martyred and then resurrected right after the great affliction, went up to heaven (11:12 [compare 14:1–5]). If so, their voices are loud because they themselves are innumerable (7:9–10). In any case, the announcement is celebratory. "The kingdom of the world" doesn't mean the kingdom consisting of the world. For "the world" refers to human society in its hostility to God and his people, as it does very often in John's Gospel and 1–2 John; and "kingdom" has to do with reigning. Just as "[the kingdom] of our Lord and of his Christ" refers to their reigning over the earth, then, so "the kingdom of the world" refers to ungodly society's reigning over the earth even though the earth doesn't belong to them (see 5:1–5 with comments). The loud voices announce the end of this usurpation, evident especially in the persecution of Christians (nonworldlings), with the earth's takeover by the Lord and his Christ. "Has become" anticipates the takeover that is momentarily to occur at Christ's return, though John delays till 19:11–16 a description of the return as such. "Lord" referred to Jesus as recently as 11:8 but now shifts to God. The shift exemplifies their codeity. With "our Lord," the Christians gladly confess themselves to be God's slaves. Since "Christ" means "anointed one," "*his* Christ" alludes to God's having anointed Jesus with the Holy Spirit (see John 1:32–34). The "he" who "will reign as king" refers to "our Lord" as reigning through "his Christ," or to "his Christ" as reigning on behalf of "our Lord." Either way, the end result is the same (compare 22:5). "Forever and ever" contrasts with the world's temporary reign, which has now come to an end.

11:16–18: And the twenty-four elders, who were sitting on their thrones within God's sight, fell on their faces and worshiped God, [17]**saying, "We thank you, Lord God Almighty, who are and who were, because you've taken your great power and begun to reign as king.** [18]**And the Gentiles** [in the sense of all non-Christians as opposed to Christians, the true Israelites (chapter 7)] **were enraged** [at your doing so]**. And your wrath has come, also the time of the dead to be judged and** [the time] **to give a reward to your slaves the prophets, even the saints—that is, to those who fear your name, both the small and the great—and to be ruining those who are ruining the earth."** See the comments on 4:4 concerning the twenty-four elders and their sitting on thrones. "Within God's sight" puts the elders close enough to fall immediately before him. "On their faces" implies the literal—that is, physical— meaning of "worshiped": they "kissed [the ground] in front of God." For "Lord God Almighty" see the comments on 4:8. We might have expected "who are coming" after "you . . . who are and who were" (as in 1:4, 8). But the second coming has now occurred, so that "who are coming" drops out (so too in 16:5). The greatness of the Lord God Almighty's power—he's *all*-powerful—has enabled him to begin ruling the earth as its king. But to do so he has "*taken* [his] great power," as though it's a tool or a weapon that till now he hasn't used in this way. Rage is added to the non-Christians' fear and terror in 11:11–13 (compare Psalm 2, especially verse 1). The seizure from them of their illegitimate rule has enraged them. Their rage and the elders' thankfulness stand in stark contrast with each other. But their rage is no match for God's wrath.

In 6:17 the non-Christians bewailed that "the big *day* of [God's and the lamb's] wrath" had come. But the *wrath* hadn't come quite yet, for they were still fleeing for refuge (and it was still the sixth seal, not the seventh). Here in 11:16–18 under the seventh trumpet, though, the wrath itself has come, and therefore "also the time of the dead to be judged." The word for "time" connotes *opportune* time or, as we'd say, a *season*. But according to chapter 20 the dead won't be judged till after a thousand years following the second coming. So the season for judging the dead, who include both Christians and non-Christians, starts with the second coming, extends through the thousand years, and culminates in the subsequent judgment.

The designation of Christians as "slaves" suits the preceding designation of God as "Lord," which means "master" and "owner." The designation of Christians as "prophets" suits the same designation of the two witnesses, who represented all Christians earlier in the present chapter (11:10). As "saints" they are consecrated to God and therefore unlike "the world." Their fear of his name makes for another stark contrast with the non-Christians' raging against him. The elders speak about fearing God's "name" where we might have expected them to speak about fearing God. But their use of "name" alludes to the saints' refusal to apply "God," the name shared by the Father and Jesus his Son (John 17:11), to any other supposed deity, a refusal that incurred persecution. (Pagans blamed Christians for disasters such as fires, floods, famines, and earthquakes: the gods were venting their anger because of Christians' refusal to acknowledge their deity and worship them.) "The small" are unnoteworthy Christians, the socially and economically insignificant. "The great" are prominent Christians, the socially and economically successful. To stress that even the unnoteworthy will get the reward of eternal life, the elders mention them ahead of the prominent. The ruin of those who ruin the earth will consist in the second death, the opposite of eternal life (2:11; 20:6, 14; 21:8). And they ruin the earth by warring with each other, which has all sorts of pernicious effects, by attracting satanic and demonic activity up from the abyss to the earth's surface, and by drawing with their wickedness God's wrath in the form of earth-ravaging plagues (see chapters 6, 8–9 as well as later passages such as 12:12; 16:1–21). They're responsible, not God. Their behavior is ruining his property. This ruination will require the new earth of 21:1–5.

11:19: And God's temple, the one in heaven, was opened; and the ark of his covenant appeared [= became visible] in his temple; and bolts of lightning and rumblings [of thunder in the distance] **and thunderclaps** [nearby] **and an** [earth]**quake and big hail came about.** The ark of the covenant was a wooden box overlaid with gold and having a solid gold lid called "the mercy seat" because God sat on it in his invisible presence as Spirit (Exodus 25:10–22; 26:31–34; 37:1–9). As a whole, the ark represented God's having covenanted to dwell among his ancient people, Israel (hence, "*his* covenant"). But Christians, whatever their ethnicity, now constitute the true Israel (see the comments on chapter 7), so that here the ark represents God's having covenanted to dwell with *them* (see especially 21:3). The temple in heaven is called "God's" because he dwells there. The ark was hidden from public view in the innermost room of the earthly temple, a room called the Holy of Holies. But the heavenly temple is opened in John's vision to make the ark publicly visible. What's the significance of its visibility? Well, 1:7 highlighted the visibility of Jesus at his return; and 22:4 will highlight the visibility of God and the lamb in the eternal state of the saved. So the appearance of the ark because of the opening of the heavenly temple projects a renewed visibility of God incarnate in Christ, starting with the second advent and continuing throughout eternity for God's people—*renewed* visibility because divine incarnation at the first advent constituted an original visibility, as emphasized for example in John 1:14; 14:8–9; 20:14, 18, 20, 25, 29; 1 John 1:1–3, and because Jesus' going back to his Father in heaven has withdrawn that visibility for the time being (see, for example, John 16:28; 17:11). The occurrence of lightning bolts, rumblings, thunderclaps, and an earthquake matches what happened under the seventh seal and therefore confirms that that seal and the seventh trumpet (= the third woe) dealt with the

same occasion, that of the second coming. See the comments on 8:5 for the order of items there as compared with those in 4:5, except that 4:5 lacks an earthquake. The order here in 11:19 reverts to that in 4:5, adds an earthquake as in 8:5, and for good measure throws in "big hail" as well. The first trumpet included hail (8:7). But this hail has the description "big," which suits the climactic trumpet (see 16:21 for the weight of "big hail"). As for the present order, bolts of lightning are listed first as a natural followup to the visibility of the ark in the heavenly temple. It's as though the lightning illuminates the ark. Then rumblings of thunder reverberate from the distant heaven. Nearby, they become thunderclaps that shake the atmosphere just as a quake shakes the earth. The hail brings this storm to a natural conclusion. The end comes with a bang, not with a whimper.

A DRAGON, A WOMAN, AND HER MALE CHILD
Revelation 12:1–17

12:1–2: And a big sign appeared in heaven: a woman clothed with the sun. And the moon [was] **under her feet, and on her head** [was] **a crown of twelve stars.** ²**And having** [a child] **in** [her] **womb, she also screams, being racked with labor pains and suffering torment so as to give birth.** "Sign" indicates symbolism (compare the use of "sign" in John's Gospel for Jesus' miracles as symbolizing what happens when a person believes in him). "Big" describes this sign because it includes a sky-wide panorama of the sun, moon, and stars and thus will counterbalance "another sign" consisting of "the *big* red dragon" in 12:3. "In heaven" points to the location where the sun, moon, and stars can be associated with the woman. (At this point and throughout chapter 12 we should remember that the word translated "heaven" also means "sky" and that there's no necessary distinction between these meanings.) Collectively, Christians will be called "the bride, the lamb's wife" in 21:9 (see also 19:7–8; 21:2); and local churches are compared to a lady and her sister in 2 John 1, 5, 13. The Old Testament, moreover, compares Israel to a woman, including one who gives birth (see, for example, Isaiah 54:1–8; 66:7–9). Similarly, the woman in John's vision represents Christians as the true Israel, a representation already featured especially in chapter 7. In line with this representation the sun, moon, and twelve stars reflect the dream of Joseph in Genesis 37:9–10, where the sun and moon stand for Israel (Jacob) and his wife Rachel, respectively, and the stars for Israel's twelve sons, patriarchs of the twelve tribes listed in Revelation 7:5–8 and mentioned in 21:12 (compare the twelve constellations of the zodiac). The woman's garment of sunlight portrays Christians as radiant with the glory of God (compare 21:23–24; 22:5; 1 John 1:5–7). "The moon [was] under her feet" portrays her as ruling (compare the description of Christians in terms of rulership at 1:6; 5:10; 20:4–6; 22:5). Her crown stands for victory (compare the references in chapters 2–3 to true Christians as conquerors). Her screaming because of labor pains gets emphasized with the present tense of "screams," echoes

Isaiah 66:7; Micah 4:10, thereby confirms the woman's portraying Christians as the true Israel, and has nothing to do with the birth of Jesus. For John's Gospel doesn't contain a narrative of Mary's giving birth to Jesus, but it does contain something about a woman's suffering labor pains: in John 16:19–22 Jesus compares the sorrow his disciples will feel at and because of his departure to the pains of a woman giving birth.

12:3–4a: And another sign appeared in heaven: and behold, a big red dragon that had seven heads and ten horns and seven diadems on his heads! [4a]**And his tail takes in tow a third of the stars of heaven and threw them onto the earth.** "In heaven" suggests that a constellation such as Scorpio represents the large red dragon. In any case, "behold" highlights this sign. Its size as "big" matches that of the preceding sign. Its red color, like that of the red horse in 6:4, indicates bloodshed—but here the shedding of martyrs' blood rather than the blood of people in general as a result of civil war (6:10; 16:6; 17:6; 18:24; 19:2). The dragon is to be visualized as having a long, upright neck out of which jut seven crowned heads, one above the other. The ten horns don't project from the heads—rather, up from the long, horizontal body of the dragon. We have pictorial representations of such dragons in ancient near eastern iconography. "Diadems" connotes crowns of rulership as distinct from a crown of victory, such as the woman wears. The seven heads and ten horns will receive interpretation in 17:9–14. In Daniel 8:9–10 the throwing of stars from heaven to earth symbolizes the persecution of ethnic Israel by Antiochus Epiphanes, a Syrian ruler, in the second century B.C. The present allusion to that passage produces a symbol of the persecution of the church, the multiethnic true Israel (see chapter 7 again). The present tense of "takes in tow" highlights the persecution, and "a third" indicates the persecution of a very large proportion of the church (compare the corresponding one-thirds in the plagues of chapters 8–9).

12:4b–6: And the dragon stood within sight of the woman, who was about to give birth, in order that when she gave birth to her child he might eat up [the child]. [5]**And she gave birth to a son, a male** [child] **who was about to be shepherding all the Gentiles with an iron rod** [compare Psalm 2:9]**; and her child was snatched up to God and to his throne.** [6]**And the woman fled into the wilderness, where she has there a place prepared by God in order that they might nourish her for 1,260 days.** "Within sight of the woman" indicates the dragon's proximity to her. "That . . . he might eat up [her child]" indicates the dragon's purpose to destroy the child, who represents Jesus, by getting him killed, so that an implication is developing that the dragon represents Satan, who engineered the killing of Jesus according to John 6:70–71; 8:44; 13:2, 26–27 (see the comments on Revelation 12:1–2 for a reference to Jesus' death, not birth). Hovering in the background is Pharaoh's attempt to kill all the male babies of Israelite women before the exodus (Exodus 1:7–2:10). The addi-

tion of "a male [child]" to "a son" reinforces that background. The figure of "shepherding" represents ruling, as in 2 Samuel 5:2. "With an iron rod" indicates rigorous and, when necessary, punitive ruling by Jesus, as in 2:26–27 and especially 19:15 (contrast the usual wooden rod of a shepherd [see Numbers 17:8, for example]). "*Was about* to be shepherding" stresses the soonness and certainty of Jesus' rule. Because of the clear reference in 19:15 to "the Gentiles" as non-Christians subject to God's wrath, we should understand "the Gentiles" here to mean non-Christians, regardless of their ethnicity, as opposed to Christians, the true Israel (compare 2:9; 3:9). "*All* the Gentiles" underlines the universality of Jesus' soon-to-come rule.

The child's being "snatched up to God" represents God's transforming Jesus' otherwise shameful crucifixion into glorification—a "lifting up" on the cross as opposed to being knocked down by stoning—and God's combining this lifting up in exaltation with Jesus' resurrection and ascension to produce a threefold but continuous upward movement (see John 8:28, 59; 10:31–39; 11:8; 12:23, 32–34; 13:31–32; 17:1, 5, 24). "To his throne" not only includes Jesus' ascension, as in John 20:17. It also includes Jesus' enthronement with God on God's throne (3:21; 7:17; 22:1, 3). The woman's fleeing into the wilderness represents Christians' flight from persecution just as ancient Israel fled Pharaoh's mistreatment of them by going out from Egypt into the wilderness of Sinai. Here, then, the wilderness represents protection from persecution just as in 11:1–6 Christians, represented by the two witnesses, are given means of protection from their persecutors for the 1,260 days of the great affliction. "A place prepared by God" and the redundancy of "where . . . there" emphasize God's providing protection in the wilderness after the pattern of Israel at the time of their exodus (compare John 14:2–3). Nourishment adds sustenance to protection and recalls God's providing Israel with manna and quail in the wilderness (Exodus 16). Since the text has just said that Jesus was snatched up to God and his throne, "they" who are to nourish the woman for 1,260 days are God and Jesus. And since the woman is now on earth though John originally saw her to be in heaven, the dragon's throwing a third of the stars of heaven onto the earth must have entailed her being thrown down. For both she and the stars have represented Christians (12:1, 4a).

12:7–9: And a battle took place in heaven: Michael and his angels [sallying forth] **to fight with the dragon. And the dragon and his angels fought** [back]**;** [8]**and he wasn't strong enough** [to prevail]**; nor was their place found in heaven any more.** [9]**And the big dragon was thrown—the ancient serpent, the one called the Devil and Satan, who misleads the whole inhabited** [earth]**— he was thrown onto the earth** [compare Isaiah 14:12–15; Ezekiel 28:11–19]**; and his angels were thrown with him** [onto the earth]. The persecution of Christians on earth entails a simultaneous battle in heaven. For just as Daniel 10:13, 21; 12:1 portrays Michael as the archangelic protector of ethnic Israel, the present passage portrays him as the archangelic protector of Christians, the multiethnic true Israel. He has angels at his command, as does the dragon, now identified as Satan. (The dragon's heaven-based angels differ from the locust-like demons based in the abyss [9:1–11]). But the dragon and his angels suffer defeat, so that they lose "their place" in heaven (contrast the woman's having on earth "a place prepared by God"). This loss implies their having had access to God heretofore, as indicated in 12:10 ("who has been accusing them *in our God's sight*") and as illustrated in Job 1:6–12; 2:1–6. (Note: a prehistoric fall of the dragon and his angels isn't in view—rather, a fall that occurs at the start of the great affliction that precedes Jesus' second coming.) The repetition of "big" as a description of the dragon heightens his defeat. Not even his enormity saves him. "The ancient serpent . . . who misleads the whole inhabited [earth]" recollects the serpent's misleading Eve in Genesis 3:1–7, 13; and "the one called the Devil and Satan" anticipates his being called "the accuser of our brothers" in 12:10, for both "the Devil" (Greek) and "Satan" (Hebrew) mean "accuser" (compare 20:2 and see the comments on 2:10). The use of both terms emphasizes that he'll no longer be able to accuse Christians before God. The serpent's misleading "the whole inhabited [earth]" alludes to deception of the earth-dwellers, those who haven't recognized or accepted the truth of the gospel. He threw a third of the stars (Christians) onto the earth (12:4). Now in a comeuppance he and his angels suffer the same fate. The use of "thrown" no fewer than three times underscores this fate.

12:10–12: And I heard a loud voice in heaven, saying, "Right now have occurred our God's salvation and power and reign and his Christ's authority, because the accuser of our brothers has been thrown [onto the earth], **the one who has been accusing them in our God's sight day and night. **[11]**And they conquered him** [the dragon] **because of the blood of the lamb and because of the word of their testimony. And they didn't love their life even to the point of death. **[12]**Because of this celebrate, O heavens and you who dwell in them! Woe to** [= alas for] **the land and the sea, because the Devil has descended to you, having great rage, knowing that he has little time!"** The "loud voice" that speaks of "our brothers" recalls the "loud voice" of the early martyrs in 6:9–10, who were told to rest "for yet a little while" till "their brothers" were killed as they'd been. So the loud voice here belongs to those very same early martyrs (see also 5:11; 7:10; 19:1 for the singular of "voice" with many speakers). In 6:9–10 their voice was loud by way of appeal. Here it's loud by way of celebration. Their wait is over! Since the Devil has "little time" to vent his rage on earth, "Right now" indicates the start of "God's salvation and power and reign" and of "his Christ's authority" *in heaven* with the throwing down of Satan and his angels at the start of the 1,260 days of the great affliction, which equate with the "little time." From now on God will start exercising his power earthward to save his people from satanically inspired persecution and finally establish his reign on earth through his Christ's exercise of authority.

"*Our* God" implies the rejection of all other supposed gods, for which rejection the early martyrs, who are speaking here, were killed. "Accusing them . . . day and night" indicates constant accusation by Satan up till now (compare Jesus' having to act as believers' advocate in 1 John 2:1–2).

The early martyrs describe their fellow martyrs of late date as having conquered the dragon by braving martyrdom rather than defeatedly recanting their Christian testimony. "Because of the blood of the lamb" alludes to their sins having been washed away by the blood of Jesus as the Passover lamb, so that Satan's accusations were thrown out of court before he himself was thrown out (1:5; 7:14; 1 John 1:7). "Because of the *word* of their testimony" alludes to the maintaining of a testimony about Jesus as the *Word* despite the threat of martyrdom (see 1:2, 9; 6:9; 20:4 with comments). "They didn't love their life" enough to make them withdraw their testimony for the sake of escaping martyrdom. "Because of this" refers to their conquest of the dragon. The very heavens are personified and told to celebrate along with those who dwell there. This celebration counters the short-lived celebration of "earth-dwellers" over Christians' martyrdom right after the 1,260 days (11:7–10). These last martyrdoms are yet to come, so that the celebration is limited to heaven. Meanwhile, the conquest by martyrdom is so soon and sure to come that a heavenly celebration begins already. The word for "dwell" in regard to those in heaven differs from the word for "dwell" in regard to non-Christians on earth and alludes to Christians, the multiethnic Israel, as living in heavenly tents, so to speak, just as ethnic Israel lived in tents during the period of the exodus. The Devil's rage parallels the wrath of God and the lamb (6:16–17; 11:18) and marks his reaction to being thrown out of heaven. In the time he has left he'll take out his anger on the land and the sea. Not that he'll take it out *against* the land and the sea; rather, because of his polluting them with the blood of Christians (11:7), they'll be obliterated (20:11; 21:1b).

12:13–14: And when the dragon saw that he'd been thrown onto the earth, he pursued the woman who as such [that is, in her capacity as a woman] **had given birth to the male. **[14]**And the two wings of a big eagle were given to the woman in order that she might fly into the wilderness,** [that is,] **into her place, where— away from the face of the serpent—she's nourished there for a time and times and half of a time.** By definition, to be persecuted is to be pursued. So the dragon's pursuing the woman symbolizes the Devil's instigating the persecution of Christians. "Who as such had given birth to the male" harks back to the sorrow Jesus' disciples felt at and because of his return to the Father in heaven, a sorrow compared earlier to a woman's labor pains. Calling Jesus "the male" and dropping the earlier designation "child" suit a reference to his glorification (a maturation of sorts) through crucifixion, resurrection, and ascension (see the comments on 12:1–2). Giving the woman the two wings of an eagle for her aforementioned flight into the wilderness (12:6) recalls the same figure of speech in Exodus 19:4; Deuteronomy 32:9–14, where it had to do with the Israelites' flight from Egypt, and now represents the true Israelites', the Christians', initial protection from martyrdom, despite persecution, during the great affliction, which in accordance with Daniel 7:25; 12:7 is said to last "for a time [= one year] and times [= two years (a use of the plural for the obsolete dual number in Greek)] and half a time [= half a year]"—that is, the very forty-two months of thirty days each, or 1,260 days, during which the two witnesses, also symbolizing Christians, were said to avoid martyrdom despite being persecuted (11:1–6). It takes the wings of "a *big* eagle" to enable a woman to fly (compare the supernatural powers given the two witnesses to avoid martyrdom), and this big eagle corresponds to the big sign (12:1), the big dragon (12:3, 9), the big voice (meaning "a loud voice," as translated in 12:10), and the big rage (meaning "great rage," as translated in 12:12). See the comments on 12:6 for the woman's "place" and being "nourished" in the wilderness for 1,260 days. "Away from the face of the serpent" stresses avoidance of martyrdom during this period.

12:15–16: And the serpent spewed out of his mouth after the woman water—a river, as it were—in order that he might render her river-removed [= swept away by a river]. **¹⁶And the earth came to the woman's aid, and the earth opened its mouth and drank down the river that the dragon had spewed out of his mouth.** Still denoting Satan, John shifts briefly from "the dragon" to "the serpent" to suit *poisonous* water, the river rapids of venomous accusations spoken on earth "out of his mouth" against Christians just as "the ancient serpent" used to speak venomous accusations against them in heaven (contrast this deadly water with the water of life in 7:17; 21:6; 22:1, 17; John 4:10–11, 14; 7:37–38). But the serpentine dragon isn't the only one who has a big mouth. The personified earth has one too and "opened its mouth and drank down the river"; for like ethnic Israel at the time of the exodus, the woman has fled to her place in the Sinai wilderness, where water sinks into the desert sands. In other words, the satanically inspired accusations don't produce martyrdoms during the period of Christians' protection and preservation.

12:17: And the dragon was enraged at the woman and went off to do battle with the rest of her seed [= offspring], **those who keep God's commandments and hold the Testimony of Jesus** [compare Genesis 3:15–16 for background]. Just as "the serpent" shifted back to "the dragon" in 12:16, the figure of a river of accusations now shifts back to the figure of doing battle (12:7–9). This time, though, Michael and his angels don't appear on the scene to fight the dragon. So just as according to 11:1–10 "the beast . . . out of the abyss will do battle with [the two witnesses] and conquer them and kill them" after the 1,260 days of their protected prophesying, here the enraged dragon, whose agent the beast is (13:1–2), will succeed in making martyrs after that period of protection. "The rest of [the woman's] seed" refers to

individual Christians in addition to Jesus, her original offspring (but see again the comments on 12:1–2 that the woman, representing Christians, is Jesus' mother only in the sense that his departure brought them pain like that of a woman suffering birthpangs). For Christians as keepers of God's commandments see 14:12 and a host of passages in 1 John, starting at 2:3 (compare keeping Jesus' commandments in John 13–15); and for Christians as holding the Testimony of Jesus both in the sense of maintaining a testimony *about* him and in the sense of possessing the Testimony who *is* Jesus, see the comments on 1:2 with 1:9.

TWO BEASTS
Revelation 12:18–13:18

This passage divides into the description of a beast that comes up out of the sea (12:18–13:10) and the description of a beast that comes up out of the land (13:11–18). In both cases, the word for "beast" connotes a wild one.

12:18–13:1: And he [the dragon] **stood on the sand of the sea** [= on the seashore]. Thus the dragon, Satan, stands at the border of the sea, out of which the first beast will arise, and of the land, out of which the second beast will arise. For he will inspire and empower both beasts. **¹And I saw a beast coming up out of the sea,** [a beast] **having ten horns and seven heads and** [having] **on his horns ten diadems and on his heads names of blasphemy** [= names that slander God]. "A beast coming up out of the sea" recalls the beasts in Daniel 7, which come up out of the sea and stand for heathen empires. There are four of them; and since the third one has four heads, they have seven heads in toto. Moreover, the fourth beast has ten horns. The beast in John's vision comes by way of interbreeding the beasts in Daniel's vision. This interbreeding implies that the present beast represents an empire—the Roman Empire of the first century, during which John received the visions recorded in Revelation. Since the sea symbolizes the evil forces of chaos, "coming up out of the sea" joins the recollection of Daniel 7 to mark this imperial beast as heathen like those earlier ones. See the comments on 12:3 for a physical description of the dragon, whose heads and horns match those of the beast. Like father, like son? The dragon's heads were mentioned first, then his horns. But the beast's horns are mentioned first, then his heads. Putting the heads last prepares for a followup concerning a mortal blow suffered by one of them. The dragon's seven *heads* were said to have diadems on them. The beast's ten *horns* are said to have diadems on them. This oddity—and it is an oddity for horns to be wearing diadems—prepares for a portrayal of the horns as representing kings (17:12) just as the dragon's seven heads, wearing diadems in 12:3, will represent kings by way of their reappearance on the seven heads of the beast (17:9–10). As in 12:3, "diadems" symbolize rulership, not victory, which "crowns" symbolize. The horns symbolize active power and parody the horns of the slain but standing lamb in 5:6, though each of the ten kings is symbolized by only one horn whereas the one lamb has seven horns, representing complete power in action. The "names of blasphemy" will reappear in 17:3 and may refer to a single name written multiply on each head. John doesn't identify the names or name. But his description of them, or it, as blasphemous implies human rulers' acceptance and arrogation to themselves of one or more divine titles. We know that the Caesars did exactly that (compare Daniel 11:36–37; 2 Thessalonians 2:3–4).

13:2: And the beast that I saw was like a leopard; and his feet [were] as a bear's [feet are], and his mouth [was] as a lion's mouth [is]. And the dragon gave him his power and his throne and great authority. The comparison to a leopard that has bear-like feet and a lion-like mouth represents a composite of the first three beasts in Daniel 7. Leopards, bears, and lions are all carnivorous. The swiftness of a leopard enables it to catch prey. The clawed feet of a bear enable it to tear its victims in pieces. And a lion's mouth enables it to devour its victims. These characteristics portray the Roman Empire as carnivorous of its Christian subjects and strike a contrast with the lion of the tribe of Judah, who conquered by sacrificing himself as a Passover lamb for the eternal life of his subjects, those same Christians (5:5–6). The dragon's giving the beast "his power and his throne and great authority" represents Satan's giving the Roman Empire his own ability to rule, his own position of rulership, and his own right to rule (hijacked though that right is). In other words, Satan rules through the agency of the Roman Empire. The heaping up of the three terms "power," "throne," and "authority" and the attachment of "great" to "authority" stress the dominance granted this beastly empire by the dragon, Satan. Particularly in view is Roman persecution of Christians. Satan's giving his power, throne, and authority to the Roman Empire with its rulers parodies God the Father's giving his authority to Jesus his Son and enthroning him with himself (3:21; 7:17; 12:5; 22:1, 3; John 5:27; 17:2).

13:3a–b: And [I saw] one of his heads [to be], as it were, slain to death; and the wound of his death [= his mortal wound] was healed. "One of his heads . . . slain" symbolizes the violent death of a ruler who headed up the Roman Empire. The redundant additions of the phrases, "to death" and "the wound of his death," stress an occurrence of actual death. The healing of his mortal wound represents a coming back to life (see 13:14)—but not of the slain head, for the Greek possessive pronoun in "*his* death" disagrees with "head" but agrees with "beast." So the empire but not the head revives after the ruler represented by the head is slain (see too 13:12; 17:8, 11). But who was this ruler? Well, the emperor Nero slew himself in June of A.D. 68. After his death the civil war portrayed in 6:3–4 broke out; but the empire revived when Vespasian took the throne in July of A.D. 69. Thus the empire suffered a political death in the physical death of Nero and came back to political life with the accession of Vespasian. "As it were" alludes to the mixture

of political death and physical death. This episode in Roman history, symbolically represented here, parodies the death and resurrection of the lamb Jesus, "slain" like the beast's head and resurrected like the beast himself. In Jesus' case, though, he was physically slain and physically resurrected as one and the same person. Notably, as Nero slew himself, Jesus laid down his life on his own (John 10:17–18).

13:3c–4: And the whole earth [a personification of the earth to represent all earth-dwellers, that is, non-Christians] **was amazed,** [so that they followed] **behind the beast** [as disciples follow behind their teacher] [4]**and worshiped the dragon because he'd given authority to the beast. And they worshiped the beast, saying, "Who** [is] **like the beast, and who can do battle with him?"** For the phraseology of this question, though in reference to God, see Exodus 15:11; Psalm 89:6–7; Isaiah 40:25; Micah 7:18. Because the beast's kingdom is subject to invasion from without (see 6:1–2; 9:13–21; 16:12–14), "the whole earth" probably refers to the Roman Empire alone (compare our old expression, "the known world"). Nevertheless, the accent falls on discipleship to the beast and on worship of the dragon (Satan) and of the beast (that is, emperor worship) by all non-Christians within the empire (compare 2 Thessalonians 2:8–12). Following behind the beast and worshiping the dragon and the beast parody Christians' following Jesus and worshiping God his Father and Jesus. The parody even extends to the reason for worshiping the dragon. Non-Christians will worship him because he gave the beast authority just as Christians worship God because he gave Jesus authority (see again 3:21; 5:13; 22:1, 3; John 5:27; 17:2). The question, "Who [is] like the beast, and who can do battle with him?" implies the answer that no one can defeat him in battle but will get a resoundingly opposite answer in 19:11–21, which starts with Jesus' coming to "judge and do battle in righteousness" and ends with the beast's defeat and consignment to the lake of fire burning with sulfur (see also 17:12–14).

13:5–6: And there was given to him [the beast] **a mouth speaking big** [claims for himself], **that is, blasphemies; and there was given to him authority to act** [in these ways] **for forty-two months** [compare 11:2–3; 12:6, 14; Daniel 7:20, 25; 11:36]. "Was given . . . a mouth" means permission to speak. The limitation to forty-two months of the beast's authority to act probably rules out the dragon as the giver of this authority (contrast 13:2), for the dragon would hardly set such a limit on his own protégé—unless so ordered by God. Ultimately, in any case, the limitation derives from God's will and calendar; and the passive voice of "was given," which occurs twice, leaves the stress both on the beast's mouth that speaks claims for him so big that they belittle Jesus and God, and on the limitation to forty-two months of the beast's authority to act thus. [6]**And he opened his mouth with the purpose and result of blasphemies against God,** [that is,] **to blaspheme his name and his dwelling,** [in other words,] **those who dwell in heaven.** The Roman

Empire (the beast) blasphemes God's name by confiscating the term "God" (*deus* in Latin) for its rulers. Just as 13:3 personified the earth, so that it represented the earth-dwellers (non-Christians), 13:6 personifies God's tent-like dwelling, heaven, so that it represents those who dwell (literally, "tent") there (see the comments on 12:12 for the difference between the Greek words translated with "dwell"). To blaspheme heaven-dwellers is to slander them by denying them recognition as God's children (1 John 3:1). Do they include only those who've died and gone to heaven and are waiting there till they return at the second coming? Probably not, because living Christians are portrayed as located in heaven and on earth at the same time (see the comments on 11:1–2).

13:7–8: And it was given him to do battle with the saints and to conquer them; and authority was given him over every tribe and people and tongue and nation. ⁸And all those who dwell on the earth [= non-Christians]—[everyone] **whose name hasn't been written since the founding of the world in the scroll of life belonging to the slain lamb—will worship him** [the beast]. Doing battle with the saints and conquering them harks back to chapters 11–12 and the martyring of them after pursuing—that is, persecuting—them for 1,260 days. As in 13:5, "was given," which occurs twice here as it did there, probably implies divine permission. "Saints" means "those whom God has consecrated to himself" and therefore lends Christians assurance of his favor despite the beast's disfavor. The fourfoldness of "tribe and people and tongue and nation" combines with "every" and "all those who dwell on the earth" to emphasize the vast extent of the Roman Empire, represented by the beast (compare "four" in 7:1; 20:8). "Tongue" refers to human beings bound together by a shared native language. "Nation" doesn't carry the connotation of a modern nation state—rather, of human beings who have the same ethnicity (race and culture). "Whose name hasn't been written . . . in the scroll of life" describes an earth-dweller as destined not to have eternal life (see the comments on 3:5). "Belonging to the slain lamb" ties eternal life, represented by the scroll of life, to Jesus' death as a Passover sacrifice (as throughout John's Gospel, beginning at 1:29). "Since the founding of the world" adds the note of *pre*destination (compare John 6:39, 44; 15:16; 17:2, 24, and see Revelation 17:8 for linking "since the founding of the world" to the writing of the name rather than to the slaying of the lamb). In John's writing "the world" normally refers to human society, so that "since the founding of the world" may refer to the creation of human beings in particular rather than to the creation of the earth (or universe) in general. Such a reference would suit well the present topic of human destiny. Worship of the beast comes in for a second mention to underline the dragon's having given him "his power and his throne and great authority" (13:2, 4), and "*will* worship" makes the worship future to John's writing of Revelation.

13:9–10: If anyone has an ear, he'd better hear [what's being read to him (see 1:3)]. **¹⁰If anyone** [is des-

tined to go] **into captivity, he's going into captivity. If anyone** [is destined] **to be killed by a sword, his being killed by a sword** [is going to happen]. **Here's the perseverance and the faith of the saints.** These verses are often read in terms of Christians' destiny to be persecuted and martyred. But John has just referred to the earth-dwellers as having their names missing from the scroll of life; and the phraseology of 13:10 echoes that of Jeremiah 15:2, where the Lord pronounces doom on the ungodly. So it's better to read these verses in terms of the earth-dwellers' judgmental destiny. The indirect command to hear implies both the difficulty of accepting the predestinationism just mentioned and now to be elaborated, and also the necessity of accepting it despite that difficulty (for similar commands to hear see 2:7, 11, 17, 29; 3:6, 13, 22 and passages in the first three Gospels such as Mark 4:23). Here, and as often, capture leads to execution (see 6:4, 8; 13:14 for slaying/killing with a sword). John will describe Jesus as returning with a sword issuing out of his mouth so as to kill his and his followers' enemies (19:11–21). (To be sure, the Greek word for a sword there will differ from that for a sword here; but John likes to use synonyms without distinction, and killing with a sword characterizes both passages.) So "be[ing] killed by a sword" stands for being sentenced to "the second death" by the judgmental word that issues like an executioner's sword out of Jesus' mouth (for the second death see 2:11; 20:6, 14; 21:8). The certainty of this destiny for the persecutors provides saints with the encouragement needed to persevere and stay faithful. "The faith of the saints" means belief that keeps them faithful.

13:11–12: And I saw another beast, coming up out of the earth [= the land as opposed to the sea in 13:1; but see Daniel 7:17]; **and he had two horns like a lamb and was speaking as a dragon** [speaks]; **¹²and he exercises all the authority of the first beast in his** [the first beast's] **sight and causes the earth and those who dwell in it to worship the first beast, whose mortal wound was healed.** In 13:3 the earth was personified in reference to earth-dwellers. So a beast's "coming up out of the earth" means that he arose from among the earth-dwellers, non-Christians. His having "two horns like a lamb" parodies the horns of the lamb Jesus (5:6). But Jesus has a full complement of horns—seven. John pairs having two horns with the second beast's speaking, so that having two horns suggests conformity to the law requiring at least two witnesses, as in the case of "the two witnesses" in 11:1–13, whose duality is emphasized by the additional expressions "the two olive trees," "the two lampstands," and "these two prophets" (see also John 8:17 for an explicit citation of this law, and 1:35, 37, 40; 20:4, 12; 21:2 for twoness elsewhere in John's Gospel). As usual, horns symbolize active power, so that the pairing of the horns with speaking symbolizes persuasive speech. This second beast will powerfully persuade earth-dwellers to worship the first beast. "Speaking as a dragon [speaks]" means speaking deceitfully, for the dragon is "the ancient serpent [who deceived Eve according to Genesis 3:1–6; 1 Timothy 2:14], the one called the Devil and Satan, who misleads the whole inhabited [earth]" (12:9). The second beast "exercises all the authority of the first beast" in that he enforces the first beast's demand to be worshiped (13:4–8). The present tense of "exercises" and the addition of "all" to "the authority" underline the enforcement. "In his [the first beast's] sight" indicates proximity to the beast's image (to be mentioned shortly). "The earth and those who dwell in it" personifies the earth again to stand for the earth-dwellers. But this double-barreled way of referring to them emphasizes their being caused to worship the first beast. The emphasis makes Christian refuseniks stand out by contrast. "The first beast, whose mortal wound was healed," references the Roman Empire, which came back to life after the civil war that erupted upon Nero's suicide (see the comments on 13:3).

13:13–14: **And he** [the second beast] **performs big signs, so that he even causes fire to come down out of heaven onto the earth in the sight of people;** [14]**and he misleads those who dwell on the earth because of the signs that were given him to perform in the beast's sight, telling those who dwell on the earth to make an image for the beast who has the sword-wound and came alive.** The second beast's performing signs parodies Jesus' performing signs throughout John's Gospel, where John uses the same verb and noun. The present tense of "performs" and the addition of "big" to "signs" prepare for a particularly impressive sign: "he even causes fire to come down out of heaven onto the earth." "Even" and the present tense of "causes" heighten the impressiveness of this sign. Fire from heaven denotes lightning, which appears to originate in the sky and strike the earth. This sign parodies the fire that issues from the mouths of the two witnesses in 11:5 and devours their enemies. "In the sight of people" parodies Jesus' performing signs "in the sight of his disciples" (John 20:30) and results in deception of the earth-dwellers. Emphasized by the present tense of "misleads," the deception implies error in telling the earth-dwellers to make an image for the beast as though he were a deity to be worshiped. The statement that "the signs . . . were given him [the second beast] to perform" parodies God the Father's having given Jesus "works" to do (John 5:36; 17:4). (In John's Gospel "works" and "signs" alternate with each other.) But the passive voice of "were given" leaves the giver out of the picture and puts emphasis on the giving as such. "In the beast's sight" means in proximity to the first beast's image, which was replicated throughout the Roman Empire—including the province of Asia in western Asia Minor, where the seven churches addressed in Revelation were located—in temples dedicated to the worship of past and present emperors. So the second beast stands collectively for priests who officiated at those temples. The image is "*for* the beast" because it's *of* the beast, the empire represented by an image of its emperor, so as to benefit the empire through worship of the emperor. Such worship had the purpose of solidifying allegiance to the beastly empire. A reference

to living despite the sword-wound establishes a basis of amazement for the worship and again parodies Jesus the lamb's death and resurrection. The present tense in "who *has* the sword-wound" parodies even further Jesus' still having the scars of sacrificial death after his resurrection (5:6; John 20:19–29). The particular reference to a sword alludes to Nero's cutting his throat with a sword.

13:15–17: **And it was given to him** [the second beast] **to give a spirit to the image of the** [first] **beast so that the beast's image even speaks and causes as many people as didn't worship the beast's image to be killed** [in the sense of executed]; [16]**and he** [the second beast] **causes all—the small and the great, and the rich and the poor, and the free and the slaves—that they** [*not* those just listed] **give them** [those just listed] **a mark on their right hand or on their forehead** [17]**and that no one be able to buy or sell except a person who has the mark,** [which is] **the beast's name or the number of his name.** For "it was given" see the comments on 13:14. Yet again we have a parody of Jesus, to whom the first beast most closely (though evilly) corresponds. For just as Jesus was given the Spirit (John 1:32–33) and consequently has the Spirit (Revelation 3:1; 5:6; John 7:37–39; 20:22), so the first beast's image is given a spirit. And just as the Spirit makes alive (11:11; John 6:63), so the spirit makes the beast's image speak as though it were alive (compare the portrayal of Jesus as "the Word" who is constantly speaking "words" throughout John's Gospel; see also Revelation 19:13). The spirit speaking in the image commands the execution of all who don't worship the image (compare John 16:2, but there in a synagogal setting). "Causes *all*," plus the specification of various social classes, stresses as exceptionless the second beast's requiring everybody to bear of the first beast's mark and parodies the inclusion of "the small and the great" among the saints (11:18). The plural "they" who "give them a mark" brings out that the second beast symbolizes a whole bureaucracy of priests who direct worship of the first beast's image in temples dedicated to such worship. Throughout this passage the present tense of verbs dramatizes the events. The beast's mark goes "on the right hand" because the right-handedness of most people means they extend their right hand to pay for and take an item that they're buying, and to take payment and fork over an item that they're selling. Alternatively, the mark goes on the forehead. In either location, the mark is easily recognizable and therefore its requirement easily enforceable. Interpretations of the mark include branding, tattooing, and the handling of coins with Caesar's image and divine titles stamped on them. Three things are certain: (1) the mark consists in either a name or a number; (2) lack of the mark brings economic persecution; and (3) the mark contrasts with the seal of God, consisting of his and the lamb's name written on the foreheads of the 144,000, who represent true Christians (7:3; 14:1; 21:4)—not on their right hands, though, because God's seal has nothing to do with buying or selling. Now it's highly unlikely that John means Christians have, or will have, the name of God and the lamb physically inscribed on their foreheads. To have that inscription means, rather, to be protected from God's and the lamb's wrath because of worshiping them, refusing to worship the beast, and being known for such worship and nonworship. By the same token, to have the mark of the beast doesn't mean to have it physically inscribed on the right hand or forehead. It means to have worshiped the beast, to be known to have done so, and thus to be free from economic persecution.

13:18: Here's wisdom: the person who has a mind [or, as we might say, a brain] **had better calculate the beast's number; for it's the number of a human being, and his number is 666** [compare 17:9; Daniel 12:10]. The wisdom consists in calculating the beast's number, that is, in figuring out the meaning of 666. How does the number identify the beast personally and theologically? The indirect command to calculate the number implies a danger of deception in failing to do so. "The number of a human being" implies a human being who claims divinity and is worshiped as divine but isn't divine—hence, a Roman emperor. But which Roman emperor? Nero, for he's the head of the beast that got a mortal wound (see the comments on 13:3); and the numerical value of "Caesar Nero" when written in Hebrew characters (and see 9:11; 16:16; John 5:2; 19:13, 17, 20; 20:16 for John's interest in Hebrew) is 666, one short in each of its three digits of what would be the perfectly divine number of the Holy Trinity: 777. And the dragon (Satan), the first beast (the Roman Empire, embodied in its emperors), and the second beast (priestly enforcers of emperor worship) do form a contrastively *un*holy trinity. Note: Arabic numerals were unknown in the first century, so that letters of the alphabet were used for numbers: 1 = a, 2 = b, and so on up to 10, plus tens and hundreds covered by further letters of the alphabet (compare Roman numerals: I = 1; V = 5; X = 10; L = 50; C = 100; D = 500; and M = 1,000). Since a variety of numerically valued letters could add up to 666, it requires wisdom to figure out the reference to Nero.

THE 144,000 WITH THE LAMB ON MOUNT ZION
Revelation 14:1–5

14:1: And I looked—and behold, the lamb standing on Mount Zion, and with him 144,000, having his name and the name of his Father written on their foreheads [compare 22:4]! "Behold" showcases the lamb as a contrast to the dragon and the wild beasts of chapter 13, the second of which had "two horns like a lamb" (13:11). As in 5:6, "standing" portrays the lamb as resurrected. Because the present passage has to do with his final triumph, however, the earlier reference to the scars of his sacrificial death has dropped out. The Jewish temple stood on Mount Zion in Jerusalem. But a reference to heaven in 14:2 locates the present "Mount Zion" there. Just as heaven has a temple (see especially 11:19), it also has a Mount Zion; and just as John 12:15 brought Zion into association with the first coming of Jesus, Zion now gets associated with his second coming. Since Psalm 2:6

says that the Lord has installed his king on the "holy hill of Zion," the lamb's standing on Mount Zion represents his taking of kingship with a victory over his and his followers' foes (compare 11:15–18; 17:12–14; 19:11–21). The 144,000 seem to be standing along with the lamb. If so, they're resurrected too; and together they're celebrating in heaven the victory they've won with the lamb over the dragon and the two beasts, at whose instigation many of them had suffered martyrdom (compare the martyrdom, resurrection, and ascension to heaven of the two witnesses after the great affliction in 11:7–13, and also the census of the 144,000 in 7:4–8 as a military roll call similar to the same in Numbers 1:1–46). The inscription of the lamb's name and that of his Father on the foreheads of the 144,000 defines "the seal of our God" on the foreheads of the 144,000 in 7:3. This inscription contrasts with the mark of the beast, which consists in his name or its number (see 13:16–17 with comments). The lamb's name and that of his Father don't necessarily differ. According to John 17:11–12, in fact, Jesus and his Father share a name; and according to John 1:1 that name is "God" (compare John 20:28; 1 John 5:20), so that we might well translate here with "having his name, *even* his Father's name." John's calling God the lamb's "Father" cements their sharing deity with each other. And having "God" inscribed on the forehead, where all can see the name, symbolizes open, public confession of the Father and the lamb as God to the exclusion of all other supposed deities, especially the Roman emperors, the worship of whom the second beast in chapter 13 tried to enforce—unsuccessfully in the case of the 144,000, who stand for all true Christians (see the comments on chapter 7).

14:2–3: And I heard a voice [= sound] **from heaven—a voice of many waters, as it were** [compare 1:15], **and a voice of loud thunder, as it were; and the voice that I heard** [was], **as it were,** [the voice] **of harpists harping on their harps.** ³**And they're singing, as it were, a new song within sight of the throne and within sight of the four living** [creatures] **and the elders** [compare 5:9–10]. **And no one could learn the song except for the 144,000, those who'd been purchased from the earth** [compare the comments on 5:9; also Isaiah 35:10]. As noted above, "from heaven" points to a heavenly Zion. But it also implies that John hears a heaven-originated voice from a standpoint on earth (compare 4:1 with 10:8 for John's commuting between heaven and earth to see visions). The mention of "thunder" favors that "waters" refers to a rainstorm. "Many" describes the waters as overwhelming in number, just as chapter 7 described the 144,000 as innumerable when John actually saw them after hearing about them (so that the number was symbolic rather than literal [for "many waters" compare Ezekiel 1:24; 43:2]). "Loud" describes the thunder as overpowering in its volume because of the innumerability of the harpists who accompany their own singing. Four occurrences of "as it were" show John straining to describe adequately what he heard and saw. The sound was like that of a heavy rainstorm and loud thunder, but louder. The sound was like that of harpists playing their harps, but more melodious. The singing was like that of a chorale, but more harmonious. The present tense of "they're singing" brings the audience of John imaginatively into his experience of hearing the song. He describes the song as "new" in that it arises out of the resurrection of the 144,000 and out of their getting Jesus' new name (3:12). The description also anticipates the new heaven, the new earth, and the New Jerusalem (21:1–2, 5 [compare Psalm 33:1–3; 96:1–2; 149:1–9; Isaiah 42:10–13]). "Within sight of the throne and within sight of the four living [creatures] and the elders" confirms the heavenly setting of this scene and the ascension to heaven of the 144,000 after their resurrection (see the same in 11:11–12). They have to "learn" the song because it's "new." But to learn it you have to have "been purchased from the earth," that is, experienced the song's subject matter: redemption. So none but the 144,000 are singing the song. "Purchased" implies liberation from slavery (= redemption) at the cost of Jesus the lamb's blood, just as ethnic Israel was liberated from slavery in Egypt at the cost of the blood of Passover lambs. In 13:3, 11–12 John used "the earth" as a personification of non-Christians, the earth-dwellers; and "purchased from human beings" will follow now in 14:4. So "purchased from the earth" here in 14:3 means that the 144,000 have been segregated by redemption from the rest of the human race.

14:4–5: These [144,000] are the ones who've not been defiled with women, for they're virgins. These [are] the ones who follow the lamb wherever he goes. These have been purchased from human beings [as] first fruits for God and the lamb; ⁵and no lie was found in their mouth [compare Zephaniah 3:13]. They're blameless. Just as the 144,000 Israelites symbolize Christians as an innumerable army, so too does the present description of them as undefiled with women in that they're virgins. For in ancient Israel soldiers had to consecrate themselves and preserve their ritual purity before going into battle. Part of this preparation consisted in abstinence from sexual intercourse (Deuteronomy 23:9–14; 1 Samuel 21:4–5; compare the refusal of Uriah the Hittite, a soldier, to have sex with this wife so long as Israel was at war [2 Samuel 11:6–13]). John isn't interested in ritual purity as such. For him it symbolizes the moral and religious purity that characterizes true Christians (compare 19:7–8; 21:2 and Paul's portraying the Corinthian church to a "pure virgin" [2 Corinthians 11:2]). In particular, the ritual virginity of undefilement with women symbolizes the moral and religious purity of never having worshiped the beast and his image or engaged in the sexual immorality associated with idolatry. Instead of such worship the 144,000 "follow the lamb wherever he goes," even to a sacrificial death like his (though his was a sacrifice for others' sins, theirs a sacrifice in proclamation of the gospel) and now to heaven to return with him. They haven't apostatized.

Ordinarily a lamb does the following rather than being followed. But this lamb is a shepherd (7:17; John

10:1–30). "Purchased from human beings" parallels "purchased from the earth" in 14:3 and refers, as there, to segregation by redemption from the rest of the human race, the earth-dwellers. (The phrase does *not* imply that "human beings" sold them.) According to Moses' law the first fruits of a harvest (its initial portion) belonged to God (see Exodus 23:16, 19, for example). Hence, the description of the 144,000 as "first fruits for God and the lamb" marks them as belonging to God and the lamb (compare Jeremiah 2:2–3). That the lamb shares this ownership with God accords with the lamb's sharing deity with him. Contextually, the statement that "no lie was found in their mouth" has to do with the lie of confessing the beast to be a deity, implies searching for such a lie, and happily declares the search a failure so far as the 144,000 are concerned (compare John 8:44; 1 John 2:18–23). "They're blameless" pronounces crisply, and therefore emphatically, a verdict of innocence.

THREE ANGELIC MESSAGES
Revelation 14:6–12

The first of three angelic messages contains eternal good news (14:6–7). The second contains an announcement of the fall of Babylon (14:8). And the third contains a warning against worship of the beast (14:9–12). This passage well illustrates the basic meaning of "angel," which is "messenger."

14:6–7: And I saw another angel flying in midsky [= directly overhead], having eternal good news [= gospel] to proclaim as good news over those who sit on the earth—that is, over every nation and tribe and tongue and people—⁷saying in a loud voice, "Fear God and give him glory, because the hour of his judgment [= the hour for him to judge] has come; and worship him who made the heaven and the earth and sea and springs of waters." The phrase "another angel," which will also designate two more angels in the present trio, harks back to the trio of angels that blew the last three trumpets, called "woes," in 8:13. They were introduced by "a single eagle flying in midsky" and "speaking in a loud voice" just as here the angel is "flying in midsky" and "speaking in a loud voice." He flies in midsky so that everybody can see him. He speaks in a loud voice so that everybody can hear him. Therefore nobody will have an excuse for failure to believe the good news that he proclaims. (He'll proclaim it through the earthwide witness of Christians, as in 11:3–6.) The redundance of "good news . . . as good news" accents the goodness of the news. It's good in that it's "eternal," and it's eternal in that it offers eternal life to those who believe it (contrast the merely temporal prosperity proclaimed as good news by Roman Caesars). "Over," which occurs twice, means that the angel proclaims eternal good news from high in the sky. "Those who *sit* on the earth" equates with the more usual "those who *dwell* on the earth," but "sit" makes a better contrast with the angel's "flying" overhead. The elaboration of these earth-sitters with "every nation and tribe and tongue and people" emphasizes God's love for the world and desire that those who make up the world be saved rather than lost (John 3:16 [compare Revelation 5:9; 7:9 with comments]). Because of chapter 13, believing the good news so as to get eternal life takes the form of fearing, glorifying, and worshiping God as represented by Jesus the lamb rather than fearing, glorifying, and worshiping the dragon as represented by the beast (who like the dragon has seven heads and ten horns [12:3; 13:1; 17:3, 9–13]). The arrival of the hour of judgment urges a positive response on the ground that the earth-sitters have one last chance—a short one, since an hour was the shortest unit of time then in use. The judgment hasn't taken place yet, but its hour has arrived. Better hurry! Worshiping him who "made" the universe makes better sense than worshiping the beast's image that the worshipers themselves "made" (13:14). "The heaven and the earth" balance each other vertically. "Sea and springs of waters" balance each other in respect to salt water and fresh.

On the heels of the good news in 14:7–8 comes bad news. At least it's bad for those who've rejected the good news. **14:8: And another angel, a second one, followed, saying, "It fell, it fell—Babylon, the big** [city] **that caused all the Gentiles** [= all non-Christians, the earth-dwellers, regardless of their ethnicity, as opposed to Christians, the true Israelites] **to drink some of the wine of the rage of her whoredom** [= raging sexual immorality of all kinds] [compare 17:1–6; 18:2; Isaiah 21:9; Jeremiah 51:7–8]." "Followed" seems to imply that the second angel was also flying in midsky. As will become clear in chapters 17–18, "Babylon" is a code name for Rome. In Old Testament times, Mesopotamian Babylon stood for idolatry, immorality, and oppression of God's people (note the Jews' Babylonian exile). In these respects Rome has taken old Babylon's place. Roman Babylon hasn't fallen quite yet (see chapters 17–18 for that event), but its fall is so soon and sure to occur that the angel uses a past tense ("It fell") and doubles this announcement (compare 6:17). Though the fall of Roman Babylon spells bad news for non-Christians, who make up her religious citizenship, it spells good news for Christians, whom she has persecuted. "The rage of her whoredom" doesn't carry the sense of anger—rather, the sense of out-of-control passion (compare the intertwining of idolatry and sexual immorality in chapters 2–3). "Some of the wine" doesn't mean "just a little wine"— rather, enough to cause idolatrous and sexual passion to rage out of control (contrast 14:4 as interpreted above).

14:9–11: And another angel, a third one, followed them [the first two angels], **saying in a loud voice, "If anyone worships the beast and his image and receives a mark** [consisting of the beast's name or number (13:17)] **on his forehead or on his hand, ¹⁰he himself will also drink some of the wine of God's rage, [wine] that's mixed unmixed in the cup of his wrath. And he** [the beast-worshiper] **will be tormented with fire and sulfur within sight of holy angels and within sight of the lamb. ¹¹And the smoke of their** [the beast-worshipers']

torment goes up forever and ever, and those who worship the beast and his image don't have rest day and night. And if anyone receives the mark of his name [he doesn't have rest day and night]." "Followed" seems again to imply flying in midsky, as the first of these three angels did; and "speaking in a loud voice" adds high volume to wide visibility yet again, so that earth-dwellers are duly warned. With poetic justice and a wordplay on the two meanings of "rage," the third angel follows up the preceding reference to the raging passion of Babylon's sexual immorality with a reference to the judgmental rage of God's wrath on those who reject the eternal good news. Both references use the figure of wine, which in the one case leaves the inebriated helpless to resist the raging passion of sexual immorality and in the present case leaves them helpless to resist the raging wrath of divine judgment. Ordinarily wine was mixed with water. So "mixed unmixed" compares the raging wrath of God to wine mixed with more wine so as to produce an incapacitating belt of undiluted wine. In other words, his coming wrath will be undiluted with mercy and utterly overpowering. Worshipers of the beast will drunkenly stagger and fall under judgment. The redundant addition, "in the cup of his wrath," accents the severity of judgment all the more (compare Isaiah 51:17; Jeremiah 25:15–16). At one and the same time, "anyone" and "he himself" universalize and individualize this warning, which also promises persecuted Christians vindication and vengeance (compare 6:9–11).

"Tormented with fire and sulfur" means "tormented with burning sulfur," recalls the destruction of the wicked cities of Sodom and Gomorrah with burning sulfur (Genesis 19:24), and implies conscious suffering similar to the scorpion-like torment of demonic possession in 9:5–6, a temporary torment that prefigured the eternal torment here. Burning sulfur gives off a stiflingly acrid smell. "Within sight of holy angels and within sight of the lamb" indicates proximity, so that shame is added to pain and stench. The addition of "holy" to "angels" distinguishes these angels from the dragon's angels (12:7) and describes them as consecrated to God. The absence of a "the" before "holy angels" emphasizes the quality of their consecration to him. It's enough for the persecuted Christians to have gotten their vindication and vengeance. So the torment of their persecutors, the beast-worshipers, isn't said to be "within sight of the saints." The going up of the smoke of the beast-worshipers' torment "forever and ever" indicates burning without burning up. The present tense of "goes up" adds emphasis; and "don't have rest day and night" excludes any interruptive spells of relief, again with emphasis added by the present tense. It's as though the ceaseless torment is already going on (compare 19:3; 20:10; Isaiah 34:9–10).

14:12: "Here's the perseverance of the saints, those who keep God's commandments and faith in Jesus [compare 12:17]." "The saints" means "the holy [human beings]" who like the angels of 14:10 are holy in the sense of consecrated to God. Obedience to his commandments and a faith in Jesus that stays faithful to him define the saints' perseverance and characterize them even under the duress of persecution. "*Here's* the perseverance of the saints" refers back to the torturous fate of the beast-worshipers as an encouragement to endure momentary persecution for the sake of vindication and just vengeance (compare the comments on 13:10).

A BEATITUDE AND TWO HARVESTS
Revelation 14:13–20

This passage divides into a beatitude (14:13), a harvest of wheat (14:14–16), and a harvest of grapes issuing in a grapestomp (14:17–20).

14:13: **And I heard a voice from heaven, saying,** "Write [as follows]: **Fortunate** [are] **the dead**—[that is,] **the ones who die in the Lord—from right now on!**" "**Yes,**" **says the Spirit,** "[they die] **so that they rest from their toils; for their deeds follow along with them.**" To write prophetically is to ensure fulfillment as well as to encourage or warn, as the case may be—here to encourage Christians who face martyrdom by assuring them of relief and reward. Because the context has dealt with mass martyrdom at the close of the great affliction (6:11; 11:7–10; 12:7–17; 13:15–18), the encouragement is directed in particular to Christians facing martyrdom at that time. As martyrs, they'll die "in the Lord," who died for them (compare abiding in Jesus [John 15:1–10], coming to be "in the Spirit" [Revelation 1:10; 4:2; 17:3], and "the dead in Christ" [1 Thessalonians 4:16], plus Revelation 11:8 for a clear use of "the Lord" for Jesus). "From right now on" tells when these martyrs are fortunate, not when they die. They're fortunate because their martyrdom marks the end of the great affliction, so that they'll rise from the dead and ascend to heaven "after [only] three and a half days" (11:11). The Spirit's affirming the beatitude suggests, though it doesn't prove, that the voice which spoke from heaven was God's, so that the Spirit and he agree in the designation of Jesus as "the Lord." The good fortune of the martyrs consists in resting from their toils, and the Spirit affirms that this rest results from dying in the Lord. "From their toils" portrays Christian testimony as hard labor because of persecution. The plural of "toils" anticipates the plural of "deeds." "For their deeds follow along with them" gives the reason for resting from their toils: the deeds that led to their martyrdom justify the rest granted them afterward (compare 2:23; 6:11; 20:12; 22:12, plus 2:2 for a similar concurrence of "deeds" and "toil," and contrast the beast-worshipers' having *no* rest day and night forever and ever [14:11]).

14:14: **And I looked—and behold, a white cloud, and sitting on the cloud one like a son of man, having on his head a gold crown and in his hand a sharp sickle!** "Behold" calls special attention to the cloud and the one sitting on it. John mentions the cloud first and separately because it signals deity (see the comments on Mark 13:26, for example; and compare Revelation 4:2 for a mention of God's throne before the mention of the one

sitting on it). "A *white* cloud" contrasts with the smoke of the beast-worshipers' torment (14:11 [see 9:2 for smoke as an agent of darkness, and the comments on 6:1–2 for white as connoting victory as well as purity]). According to 1:7 Jesus "is coming with the clouds" (see also 10:1 with comments), and according to 1:13 he's "one like a son of man." In other words, he looks like a human being because he *is* one. John's present vision has to do with the second coming, then. But coming with clouds has shifted to sitting on a cloud for contrast with "those who sit on the earth" (14:6), that is, non-Christians as opposed to Christians, who at their resurrection will "go up into heaven in the cloud" (11:12). Since the cloud signals deity and enthronement entails sitting, the sitting of one like a son of man on a white cloud anticipates "the big white throne and the one sitting on it" in 20:11. A human being sits enthroned as God. His gold crown symbolizes victory, a victory shared by the twenty-four elders, who represent all true Christians and likewise wear gold crowns (4:4); and his holding a sharp sickle foreshadows a harvest.

14:15–16: **And another angel came out of the temple, shouting in a loud voice to the one sitting on the cloud, "Send your sickle** [onto the earth] **and harvest** [it], **because the hour to harvest** [it] **has come, because the earth's harvest has dried up.**" As long as the wheat is still green because of hydration, the time for harvest hasn't arrived (compare John 4:35: "the fields . . . they're already *white* for harvest"). [16]**And the one sitting on the cloud threw his sickle onto the earth, and the earth was harvested.** "Another angel" means another in addition to the three angels in 14:6–12 (see the comments on 14:6). As usual in Revelation, the heavenly temple is in view. By definition, angels are messengers. So this angel comes out of the temple bearing a message from God, who dwells there. The message consists in a command (compare Jesus' doing what his Father commands throughout John's Gospel, as in 4:34; 5:30; 8:28–29, for example). The angel shouts in a loud voice so as to be heard by Jesus the cloud-sitter. (Within the heavenly realm some distance is implied between the temple, where God dwells, and the clouds below.) The command, "*Send* your sickle," sounds strange but echoes Joel 3:13 according to a literalistic translation of the original Hebrew. Just as "*threw* his sickle onto the earth" doesn't have the sense of releasing the sickle—rather, the sense of a forceful thrust (compare our saying that a person "throws himself into his work")—so too sending the sickle has the sense of its forceful application to grain ready for harvest. Since an hour was the shortest named unit of time, the coming of "the hour of harvest" refers to the precise time for harvest on God's calendar as a first reason for the command to send the sickle. "Because the earth's harvest has dried up" provides a second reason, this time in reference to the earth's calendar, which is to say that on earth the full complement of Christian martyrs has been reached (6:11). In 14:7 "the hour" for God to judge was said to have come. Here, however, we have the hour for a salvific harvest of wheat, "first fruits for God and the lamb" as 14:4 calls the 144,000, who symbolize Christians as the true Israel (chapter 7). There's nothing about separating chaff from wheat and burning up the chaff in judgment, such as would correspond to the judgmental grapestomp coming up in 14:19–20 or to Matthew 3:12; Luke 3:17. This harvest symbolizes Christians' being resurrected and gathered up to heaven, where 14:1 placed them. So the present passage describes how they got there (compare again 11:11–12; also 1 Thessalonians 4:13–18).

14:17–18: And another angel, he also having a sharp sickle, came out of the temple in heaven. [18]**And another angel, the one who had authority over the fire, came out from the altar and called with a loud voice** [literally, "*voiced* with a loud voice"] **to the one who had the sharp sickle, saying, "Send your sharp sickle and pick the grape clusters of the vineyard of the earth, because its** [the vineyard's] **bunches** [of grapes] **have ripened."** For "another angel," which occurs twice here, see the comments on 14:6, 15. The angel who has authority over the fire "came out from the altar." Therefore the fire is the fire of the heavenly altar beneath which John saw the souls of martyrs, who prayed for vengeance (6:9–11), at which altar "another angel" offered up all the saints' prayers (symbolized by the smoke of burning incense in 8:3–4), and from which altar he threw fire onto the earth in answer to the saints' prayers (8:5). "Another angel" in 8:3–5 was Jesus (see the comments there). "Another angel . . . having authority over the fire" here in 14:17–18 is that same angelic Jesus (compare the comments on 1:1; 4:1; 7:2 and chapter 10 for past comments on Jesus as an angel). But the figure of judgmental fire now shifts to the figure of a judgmental harvest of grapes. A sickle doesn't suit grape-harvesting. John mentions the sharp sickle twice in connection with it, though, because the wildness of swinging a sharp sickle to pick grapes *does* suit God's rage, which comes out in 14:19–20. The loudness of Jesus' command to the angel with a sharp sickle emphasizes the need to wreak vengeance on the persecutors of Christians. "The vineyard of the earth" compares non-Christians, earth-dwellers represented as in 13:3, 11–12; 14:3 by the personified earth, to a vineyard (see the comments on John 15:1–4 for the translation "vineyard" instead of "vine," though here in Revelation "vine" would make equally good sense).

14:19–20: And the angel threw [= thrust] **his sickle onto the earth and picked the vineyard of the earth** [of its grape clusters] **and threw** [them] **into the big winepress of God's rage.** [20]**And the winepress was stomped outside the city, and blood came out of the winepress up to horses' bridles away to** [= for a distance of] **1,600 stades** [about 184 miles (compare Isaiah 63:1–6)]. Stomping grapes in a winepress had long since become the stock image for a bloodbath. This winepress has to be big to accommodate all the beast-worshipers and the magnitude of God's rage inflicted on them. Vineyards and their associated winepresses were located outside cities. Since beast-worshipers lived all over the Roman Empire, "outside the city" means throughout the empire of the new Babylon, namely, Rome (14:8). The red grape juice flowing out of the winepress represents the blood of those beast-worshipers for their having shed the blood of Christian martyrs (compare this grape juice, which comes out of "the big winepress of God's rage," with "the wine of God's rage" in 14:10). So profuse is the bloodflow that the white horses carrying a heavenly army at the second coming (19:14–15) will have to wade through it up to their bridles. Because of the numerical symbolism that pervades Revelation, the flowing of the beast-worshipers' blood for a distance of 1,600 stades probably represents the number four, symbolizing breadth (as in "the four corners of the earth" at 7:1; 20:8), but squared to symbolize fullness and multiplied by a hundred to symbolize great extent (compare the squaring of twelve and multiplying the result by a thousand in 7:4; 14:3 for the redeemed as the true and enlarged Israel). So God responds to the Roman Empire's trampling of Christians, whose suffering of persecution was symbolized by the trampled outer court in 11:2, with a trampling of the Roman Empire.

THE SEVEN BOWLS
Revelation 15:1–16:21

15:1: And I saw another big and astonishing sign in heaven: seven angels who had seven plagues—the last ones, because God's rage was finished in them. "Another *big* . . . sign in heaven" harks back to the "big sign . . . in heaven" at 12:1 (though see also "another sign . . . in heaven" at 12:3). Now John adds "and astonishing" to his description of the sign as "big." The reason for this double description will come out in 15:3. The description of the seven plagues as "the last ones" makes them the immediate precursors of Jesus' return. Before the opening of the seventh and last seal (8:1), which dealt with accompaniments to that return (8:3–5), there was a topical (though not chronological) interlude (7:1–17); and before the blowing of the seventh trumpet (11:15a), which likewise dealt with accompaniments to Jesus' return (11:15b–19), there was a topical interlude (10:1–11:14). Here, though, a topical interlude comes between John's seeing of seven angels with seven plagues (15:1) and the actual infliction of the plagues (16:1–21). So all seven of these plagues are "the last" in that they occur along with the events of the seventh seal and the seventh trumpet. In these last plagues God's rage against the beast-worshipers and persecutors of Christians will be poured out of bowls containing it till they're empty. But "*was* finished" treats this emptying as so soon and sure that it might as well be already done.

15:2–4: And I saw, as it were, a sea of glass mixed with fire; and [I saw] **standing on the sea of glass, having harps of God, the ones who'd been conquering** [and thus had come] **out from the beast** [victorious] **and from his image and from the number of his name.** [3]**And they're singing the song of Moses, God's slave, and the song of the lamb, saying, "Big** [in the sense of 'great'] **and astonishing** [are] **your deeds, Lord God Almighty. Right and true** [are] **your ways, king of the Gentiles** [in the religious sense of all non-Christians, regardless of ethnicity, as opposed to Christians, the true Jews (compare Daniel 4:37)]. ⁴**Who won't fear** [you], **Lord, and glorify your name? Because you alone** [are] **holy. Because all the Gentiles will come and worship in your sight. Because your righteous acts have been manifested** [compare Jeremiah 10:7]." For the meaning and theological significance of "as it were, a sea of glass," see the comments on 4:6. Here, though, John substitutes "mixed with fire" for "like crystal," which appeared there. Since fire is red in color, "mixed with fire" makes for an allusion to the Red Sea, through which ancient Israelites marched on their way out from slavery in Egypt. (More likely the Israelites marched through the Sea of Reeds, but that sea had already come to be called the Red Sea.) The heavenly Red Sea isn't opened up as the earthly Red Sea was, however. Instead, it's frozen solid so as to become like glass. As a result, the conquerors—true Christians (about whom see chapters 2–3 and 12:11; 21:7)—can and do stand right on the sea whereas the ancient Israelites stood on the far side of the sea. As in 5:6; 7:9, standing indicates resurrection; for as noted before, "resurrection" means the "standing up" of a formerly supine corpse. The conquerors have now risen from the dead and ascended to heaven in preparation for accompanying Jesus when he returns to earth. The chaotically churning sea on earth, out of which sea came the beast, threatens them no more. They've conquered (1) "the beast"; (2) "his image"; and (3) "the number of his name." This list puts a triple emphasis on the conquerors' having come out of "the great affliction" victorious over pressure to make them apostatize. "The beast" was represented by "his image" and by "the number of his name," for its number is a way of representing his name (see chapter 13 with comments). "Who'd been conquering" alludes to the duration of the great affliction: forty-two months, or 1,260 days (11:2; 12:6). The conquerors persevered throughout.

The conquerors are not only victorious. They're also joyful: "they're singing" and accompanying their singing by playing "harps of God," which may mean harps given them by God but more probably means harps used to accompany a song in praise of God (compare 5:8–10; 14:2; 1 Chronicles 16:42). Though the event lies in the future, John uses the present tense in "they're singing" to underline the nearness and certainty of the conquerors' joy. "The song of Moses" harks back to Exodus 15:1–18, which records a song sung to the Lord by Moses and the Israelites after their passage through the Red Sea, and confirms an allusion to the Red Sea in "a sea of glass *mixed with fire.*" Another confirmation comes in "the song of the lamb," in that the Israelites fled from Egypt through the Red Sea by virtue of sacrificed Passover lambs. Jesus is the ultimate Passover lamb (see the comments on 5:6), so that the song of the lamb is a new song of Moses (compare 14:3) that takes up words and themes from a song of Moses recorded in Deuteronomy 31:30–32:43 as well as from the one in Exodus 15:1–18.

Since Jesus stands in resurrection just as the conquerors do (see 5:6), "the song of the lamb" implies that Jesus is singing along with them as Moses sang along with his fellow Israelites. In an echo of Exodus 14:31 (immediately preceding the song of Moses), John calls Moses "God's slave" to make him a forerunner of Christians as God's slaves (1:1; 2:20; 7:3; 10:7; 11:18 and so on).

"Big and astonishing" describes the deeds of the Lord God Almighty just as "big and astonishing" described the sign that John saw in heaven (15:1). He described the sign that way because it includes this description of the Lord God Almighty's deeds. In the present context, prefixing "Lord" to "God" points to God's ownership of his slaves, Moses and Christians; and adding "Almighty" to "God" points to the power he has displayed in delivering his people from oppression. "Your ways" is a figure of speech for God's conduct (compare the similar use of "walk around," as in 16:15, for example). "Right" describes the conduct of God as doing justice for his persecuted people. "True" describes his conduct as reliable: he has been true to his word, the promises he made to them. "King of the Gentiles" alludes to the establishment of his rule over the non-Christians remaining on earth (compare 20:4, 7–10). "Who won't fear [you], Lord, and glorify your name?" implies the answer, "Nobody!" because God has established his rule irresistibly. The proximity of "king of the Gentiles" favors the connotation of emperorship in the address, "Lord"; for the word often translated "Lord" also means "Emperor." God, not any Caesar, is the true emperor. "And glorify your name" has to do with honoring the name "God" by withdrawing it from the Caesars (and from the entire pagan pantheon) and reserving it for the Lord alone. John cites three reasons for fearing the Lord and glorifying his name: (1) Only he is holy. Here John uses a word for "holy" that doesn't mean "differentiated from all others and therefore peerless in transcendence" (as the more usual word for "holy" does when applied to God [see 4:8, for example]) so much as "scrupulous in all his dealings" (though too much shouldn't be made of this difference, because John likes to use synonyms without distinction). (2) All non-Christians (even they!) will come and worship—that is, bow face down on the ground—in God's sight. Doing so gives evidence of their fearing the Lord and glorifying his name, but doesn't indicate conversion to the gospel, because according to 20:7–10 "the Gentiles in the four corners of the earth" will rebel against the rule of Christ and the saints. (3) God's righteous acts have become visible for all to see. These acts consist in delivering Christians and punishing their persecutors. All reasons enough to fear the Lord and glorify his name.

15:5–6: And after these things I looked, and the temple of the tent of the testimony in heaven was opened. ⁶And the seven angels who had the seven plagues came out of the temple, clothed with clean bright linen and belted around the breasts with gold belts. As in 11:19 at the blowing of the seventh trumpet, the opening of the heavenly temple marks an end to the 1,260 days of great affliction, so that Christ is now going to return. "The temple of the tent" means "the temple which *is* the tent." "The tent" alludes to the so-called tabernacle pitched for God as Spirit to dwell in during the period following Israel's exodus from Egypt (compare the many other allusions in this chapter to the events of that period). "Of the testimony" adds a reference to the Ten Commandments, which in the Old Testament are called "the testimony" in that they testified to God's covenant with Israel—hence, "the tablets of the covenant" and "the ark of the covenant" because of the placement of the tablets in the ark, which in turn was placed in the tabernacle (among many other passages see Exodus 25:16, 21–22; 31:18; 34:28; Deuteronomy 9:9, 11, 15). For all to see, God is now keeping his covenantal promises to the true Israel, consisting of Christians.

The temple was opened to let out seven angels. They come out to fulfill for God his covenant, represented by the testimony. They'll fulfill it by inflicting seven plagues (compare the curses for covenantal unfaithfulness in Deuteronomy 28:15–68). In 19:8 "clean, bright fine linen" will be said to represent "the righteous acts of the saints." So the angels' being "clothed with clean, bright linen" represents God's "righteous acts," just celebrated in 15:4 (see the comments on that verse). He's going to act righteously—that is, with justice in behalf of his people—through the agency of these angels. And their being "belted around the breasts with gold belts" symbolizes the angels' high rank for the carrying out of God's righteous acts (see further the comments on 1:13).

15:7–8: And one of the four living [creatures] gave the seven angels seven gold bowls full of the rage of the God who lives forever and ever [compare 14:9–11]. [8]And the temple was filled with smoke from God's glory and from his power, and no one could enter into the temple till the seven plagues of the seven angels were finished [compare Isaiah 6:1–4]. For the four living creatures, see the comments on 4:6–8. Since they're closest to the throne of God and the lamb, one of them gives the seven bowls of God's rage to the seven angels. Only gold, the most precious of metals, suits a container of God's rage. "Who lives forever and ever" describes God in opposition to the Caesars, who die and who—usually and ironically—are deified *after* they die! The filling of the temple with smoke recalls the smoke of incense that in 8:3–4 ascended to God from the gold altar in the heavenly temple (see also 5:8). There it symbolized all the saints' prayers. Here it symbolizes his answering those prayers with the exercise of his glorious power in the seven upcoming plagues. Since smoke darkens (9:2), nobody can enter the temple till the smoke has dissipated with the finish of the plagues. God's glorious power will have carried out the covenantal promises.

16:1–2: And I heard a loud voice from the temple saying to the seven angels [who'd come out of the heavenly temple according to 15:1, 5–6], **"Go and pour out onto the earth the seven bowls containing God's rage."** Since according to 15:8 no one could enter the temple, the voice emanating from within the temple must be

God's. He speaks loudly so as to be heard by the angels outside the temple. Previews of his rage have appeared in 14:10, 19; 15:1, 7. Chapter 16 will now detail it. The figure of pouring his rage out of bowls derives from its having been compared to wine that's "mixed unmixed" (see the comments on 14:10). **[2]And the first [angel] went off and poured out his bowl onto the earth, and a bad and pernicious sore proliferated on the people who had the mark of the beast and were worshiping his image.** Because of an upcoming reference to "the sea" (16:3), here "the earth" means the land mass, where people live. With poetic justice, the people who have the mark of the beast as a result of worshiping his image get "a bad and pernicious sore" (compare a similar plague on the Egyptians, who'd enslaved the ancient Israelites [Exodus 9:8–11]). It's as though the mark festers and turns into a boil ("as though," because the mark is symbolic without being physical [see the comments on 13:15–17]).

16:3: And the second [angel] poured out his bowl onto the sea; and it turned into blood—as it were, [the blood] of a dead [person]. And every soul of life—that is, the [creatures] in the sea—died. In the setting of John and his audience, "the sea" meant the Mediterranean Sea. At the blowing of the second trumpet, a third of this sea turned into blood and a third of the living creatures in the sea died as a result (8:8–9). Now the whole sea turns into blood. The broadening of this phenomenon suits the climactic character of "the seven last plagues" (15:1), connected as they are with the second coming (though as usual and for suspense John delays its description till 19:11–16). The addition of "as it were, [the blood] of a dead [person]" is often interpreted in terms of coagulated blood. More likely, the expression refers to blood flowing from a person mortally wounded and alludes to the previously shed blood of martyrs (6:10 and later). Poetic justice again: the punishment mirrors the crime. In biblical usage the "soul" provides physical life, and human beings aren't the only creatures who have such life. So "every soul of life" means the creatures living in the sea. Because of the pollution that's compared to blood, they all die (contrast the life-giving blood of Jesus [John 6:54]). The redundancy in adding "of life" to "every soul" underlines the catastrophe of dying.

16:4–6: And the third [angel] poured out his bowl onto the rivers and the springs of waters, and they turned into blood. [5]And I heard the angel of the waters, saying, "You—the one who are and who were, the holy one—are righteous [in the sense of doing justice]**, in that you've judged these things** [the waters of the rivers and springs] **[6]because they** [non-Christians] **poured out the blood of saints and prophets; and you've given them** [again the non-Christians] **blood to drink. They're worthy!"** As the second bowl of God's rage turned salty sea water into blood, the third bowl turns the fresh waters of rivers and springs into blood (so too in the first plague on Egypt [Exodus 7:17–21; Psalm 78:44; 105:29]; contrast the springs of living water, representing eternal life, offered by Jesus through his Spirit [7:17; 21:6; 22:17; John 4:14; 7:37–39; 19:34]). The two witnesses in 11:6 had authority to turn water into blood; and at the blowing of the third trumpet, a third of the rivers and springs turned poisonously bitter (8:10–11). But the present plague knows no such limitation (compare the comments on 16:3). "The angel of the waters" is the angel that pours out God's wrath on the waters of rivers and springs (compare the angels in charge of winds and fire at 7:1; 14:18). Because human beings depend so much and so directly on fresh water, especially for drinking, this angel breaks out in an exclamation that extols the justice of God in avenging the martyrs' blood by giving the persecutors blood to drink (compare the undiluted, blood-colored wine of God's rage in 14:10). At times, and always when God does the avenging, vengeance is justice, so that failure to avenge would be an injustice. As at the blowing of the seventh trumpet, which likewise has to do with the second coming (11:15–17), the angel's description of God as "You . . . who are and who were" lacks the followup, "who are coming," because God is coming in the person of Jesus on this very occasion (contrast 1:4, 8; 4:8). "The holy one" makes up for the lack. "Holy" indicates that God is distinctively scrupulous in doing justice (see the comments on 15:4). The pouring out of his rage corresponds to the persecutors' pouring out the blood of martyrs. "Saints and prophets" doesn't distinguish between different classes of martyrs (compare 18:20, 24). For the two witnesses in chapter 11 symbolized all true Christians, 11:10 called them "prophets," and from 5:8 onward Christians in general have been called "saints." So all true Christians are prophets as well as saints in the sense that by their witness they call people to repentance and belief in the gospel. We should therefore understand the martyred "saints and prophets" to mean "saints, *that is,* prophets." "They're worthy" could mean that these martyrs are worthy to be avenged of their martyrdom. But the closest parallel, which is found in 3:4, referred to the last-mentioned people, so that here in 16:6 "they're worthy" seems to mean that the last-mentioned people, killers of martyrs, deserve the judgment they're getting—a verdict of guilty comparable in its emphatic crispness to the contrary verdict, "They're blameless," pronounced concerning the 144,000 (14:5).

16:7: And I heard the altar saying, "Yes, Lord God Almighty, your judgments [are] **true and right** [compare Daniel 4:37]**!"** Just as according to 11:1, 3 God was speaking through a reed, we should understand that the martyrs whose souls cried out for vengeance from beneath the heavenly altar (6:9–11) are now speaking through this altar. "Yes" affirms the angel's preceding declaration. The martyrs acknowledge God's honoring their cry for vengeance and describe it as an example of his judgments which are "true" in the sense that he has proved himself true to his promises, and which are "right" in the sense that he has proved himself just.

16:8–9: And the fourth [angel] **poured out his bowl onto the sun, and** [ability] **was given it to scorch people with fire. ⁹And people were scorched with a big scorch** [= a severe sunburn]**; and they blasphemed the name of God, who has authority over these plagues, and they didn't repent so as to give him glory.** The plague on Egypt recorded in Exodus 9:23 included fire, but fire in the form of lightning. Here, a sunburn proves so severe as to be compared with the effect of fire (contrast 7:16; Isaiah 49:10). "Big" puts the sunburn on a grand scale. Indeed, from here on through the remaining plagues "big" will repeatedly describe them—and appropriately, because they happen in connection with the climactic event of Jesus' return. The people who suffer the big scorch don't repent "so as to give him glory." Quite oppositely—and like the beast, whom they worship and therefore imitate—they blaspheme God's name, which is to say that they refuse to stop applying it to the Caesars and the pantheon of their gods and use it exclusively for the one true God, the creator (compare 9:20–21; 13:5–6; 14:7).

16:10–11: And the fifth [angel] **poured out his bowl onto the throne of the beast, and his kingdom became dark, and people were gnawing their tongues because of pain, ¹¹and they blasphemed the God of heaven because of their pains and because of their sores** [= because of their painful sores]**, and they didn't repent of their deeds** [see Daniel 2:37, 44 for "the God of heaven"]**.** The beast's throne came by donation from the dragon Satan (13:2). Here it refers to Caesar's throne in Rome and to the thrones on which his image sits in temples dedicated to the worship of him throughout the empire (13:14–15). A plague of darkness in Egypt (Exodus 10:21–23) and the darkening by a third of the sun, moon, and stars at the blowing of the fourth trumpet (8:12) provide background for this bowl of darkness that covers the empire (the beast's "kingdom"). For the suitability of darkness to evil, see the comments on 9:2–3. The present darkness marks a dramatic and disconcerting shift from the blazing sun that has just preceded. And the sore that proliferated on the beast-worshipers in 16:2 has now become painful, so painful that they can only gnaw their tongues as the darkness engulfs them. But again as the beast did in 13:5–6, they blaspheme—this time God himself rather than his name. They slander him by blaming him for their sores rather than blaming themselves for their failure to repent. And they don't repent of their deeds even now (see 9:20–21 for a list of those deeds). This second reference to unrepentance supports the justice of God's judgment and demonstrates the depth of human depravity. The nonelect are self-determined in wrongdoing. Their perseverance in wickedness matches as a polar opposite the perseverance of the elect in godliness.

16:12–14: And the sixth [angel] **poured out his bowl onto the big river Euphrates; and its water was dried up, so that the way of the kings from the rising of the sun** [= from the east] **was prepared. ¹³And I saw three spirits—unclean, as frogs** [are unclean]**—**[issuing] **out of the mouth of the dragon** [Satan] **and out**

of the mouth of the beast [the Roman Empire] **and out of the mouth of the false prophet** [collective for the guild of priests enforcing worship of the emperors, who represent the empire; see the comments on chapter 13 and contrast the comparison of the Holy Spirit to a dove (John 1:32) and Jesus' breathing the Holy Spirit on the apostles (John 20:22)]. [14]**For they are spirits of demons** [= demonic spirits], **performing signs, who issue forth to the kings of the whole inhabited** [earth] **to gather them together for the battle on the big day of God Almighty.** A blowing of the sixth trumpet brought an invasion of the Roman Empire from the east. Despite similarities, though, the pouring out of this sixth bowl triggers the forming of a coalition between east and west. The description of the Euphrates River as "big" echoes 9:14; Genesis 15:18; Deuteronomy 1:7; Joshua 1:4 and refers to its length of almost 2,000 miles and to its never drying up—till now. The comparison of three unclean spirits to frogs, declared to be ritually unclean in Leviticus 11:9–12, 41–43, points here to religious and moral uncleanness (17:4; 18:2–3) and recalls a plague of actual frogs in Egypt (Exodus 8:1–15; Psalm 78:45). There's an unclean spirit for each of the unholy trinity: one for the dragon, another for the beast, and a third for the false prophet. "The false prophet" designates the second beast of chapter 13, because "he misleads those who dwell on the earth" (13:14 [compare 1 John 4:1–3]). The spirits' issuing out of the mouths of the unholy trinity symbolizes demonically inspired, persuasive speech, what somebody has called seductive propaganda. So the satanically sponsored, Caesar-ruled, false prophet-propagandized beast called the Roman Empire persuades kings of the east to cross the Euphrates River, the empire's eastern border, and ally themselves with the beast in a battle to obliterate God's people, the Christians (compare Ezekiel 38–39 and a second such attempt after the millennium [Revelation 20:7–10]). The threefold occurrence of "out of the mouth" underscores the persuasiveness of this seductive speech. The performance of signs enhances the seduction. In 3:10; 12:9; 13:3 "the whole inhabited [earth]" seems to have referred to the Roman Empire, what John and his contemporaries considered the civilized world. So "the kings of the whole inhabited [earth]" seem to be kings ruling parts of the empire under Roman auspices in addition to kings that come from outside the empire. This massive coalition will make for a "big day" on the part of God Almighty. And it will be God Almighty's big day; for the size of the coalition, massive though it is, will be no match for God's almightiness. The kings think they're going to obliterate Christians; but God will obliterate the kings, and the Christians will have just been taken to heaven for their return with Christ (see 15:1–4; 19:11–21).

16:15: **"Behold, I'm coming as a thief** [comes]! **Fortunate** [is] **the person who is staying awake and keeping his clothes on** [= staying dressed], **lest he walk around naked and people see his shame** [= the indecency of his exposed private parts]." The preceding reference to "God Almighty's big day" leads Jesus to break in with a declaration of his coming on God's behalf. Or is it God who breaks in with a declaration of Jesus' coming on his behalf? Either way, "behold" makes the declaration into an exclamation. At this point, the present tense in "I'm coming" indicates that Jesus' return is in process, or at least that the starting gun has just sounded. "As a thief [comes]" echoes 3:2–3 (compare Matthew 24:42–44; Luke 12:39–40; 1 Thessalonians 5:2; 2 Peter 3:10) and describes Jesus' return as unexpected on the part of the coalition of kings. Despite wide success in martyring Christians (see, for example, 11:7–10), the Lord will take the kings by surprise. "Staying awake" means watching for the second coming. "Keeping his clothes on" means persevering in Christian life and witness. To "walk around naked" would be to stop living and witnessing as a Christian—this to avoid persecution and martyrdom. It's at the Last Judgment that such apostasy will be exposed in a manner comparable to having your genitals exposed to public view. Shame will precede the pain of being thrown into the lake of burning sulfur (20:15 [compare the shame of having to pursue a thief without your clothes on]).

16:16: **And they** [the demonic spirits] **gathered them** [the kings] **to the place called Harmageddon in Hebrew.** For John's interest in Hebrew terms, see 9:11; John 5:2; 19:13, 17, 20; 20:16. "Har-" corresponds more closely to the original than does the more usual English "Ar-." It means "mountain," and "-mageddon" refers to the town of Megiddon in northern Israel. (As here, the Hebrew of Zechariah 12:11 tacks –n onto Megiddo-.) Thus "Harmageddon" means "the mountain of Megiddon." But Megiddon isn't located near a mountain, much less on a mountain. It's located on the edge of a plain. So "Harmageddon" doesn't make topographical sense. What does the term symbolize, then? Well, during the period of Israel's exodus from Egypt, to which exodus Revelation has been making numerous allusions, God descended onto a mountain (Sinai) to the accompaniment of lightning, thunder, and an earthquake (Exodus 19:16–18), which will also accompany his descent in the person of Jesus Christ at the second coming (see the very next verses here). Furthermore, famous battles took place on what Zechariah 12:11 calls "the *plain* of Megiddon," which unlike "the *mountain* of Megiddon" is topographically correct (see Judges 5:19; 2 Kings 23:29). Tack "-mageddon" onto "Har-" for a Hebrew term that means "the mountain of Megiddon" and you get a topographically incorrect but theologically powerful symbol of God's coming down in the person of Jesus to do battle with the combined forces of evil.

16:17–21: **And the seventh** [angel] **poured out his bowl onto the air, and a loud voice came out of the temple from the throne, saying, "It has come about!"** [18]**And flashes of lightning and rumblings and thunderclaps came about** [compare Isaiah 29:6]. **And a big** [earth]**quake came about such as hasn't come about since humankind came about on the earth, so great** [was] **the quake. That** [is] **how big!** [19]**And the big city**

came about in three parts [= was split into three parts], and the cities of the Gentiles [non-Christians, regardless of ethnicity, as distinguished from Christians as true Jews] fell. And Babylon, the big [city], was remembered in God's sight so as to give her the cup of the wine [consisting] of the rage of his wrath [= his raging wrath, or his wrathful rage]. ²⁰And every island fled, and no mountains were found. ²¹And big hail—as it were, talents [a talent = a unit of weight, so that each hailstone weighed almost ninety-four pounds]—came down out of the sky on people. And the people blasphemed God because of the plague of hail, because its plague is extremely big. Here we have accompaniments to the second coming without a description of the second coming itself, reserved as usual till 19:11–16. The exclamatory shout, "It has come about!" reverberates with several following instances of the verb "come about." And numerous instances of "big" magnify the significance of the event. The seventh bowl is poured "onto the air" so as to trigger flashes of lightning, rumblings of distant thunder, and nearby thunderclaps, all of which occur in the air (compare a following hailstorm). The coming of a voice "out of the temple from the throne" indicates God's voice (compare Isaiah 66:6). As in 16:1, the voice is "loud" so as to be heard outside the temple though originating inside it.

"It has come about!" announces an end to the great affliction, which end has come into view before (8:1, 3–5; 10:15–19; 15:1). With the description of the earthquake as unprecedented, compare Daniel 12:1. John spares no pains in describing it as unprecedented: (1) "big"; (2) "such as hasn't come about since humankind came about on the earth"; (3) "so great [was] the quake"; and (4) "That [is] how big!" As usual, "the big city" is Rome under the code name "Babylon" (see the comments on 11:7–8 for its representing the society of non-Christians in the Roman Empire). The big earthquake splits the big city into three parts, corresponding to the three unclean spirits that came out of the mouths of the unholy trinity (16:13). Each member of this trinity can have a fragment to chew on. The city is no longer big. "The cities of the Gentiles" consist of non-Christians who make up cities throughout the Roman Empire. Under the force of the big, unprecedented earthquake, these cities collapse in ruins. In other words, the people fall under God's judgment. "Babylon . . . was remembered in God's sight" means that God brought to his mind's eye Rome's persecution of his people, and that he did so to make her suffer his wrath in just retribution. The big earthquake accomplishes the dissolution of islands and mountains as well as the collapse of cities (compare 6:14). The "big hail" is defined by weight and recalls the plague of hail on Egypt (Exodus 9:13–35; Psalms 78:47; 105:32–33). The addition of "came down from the sky," which didn't occur in the reference to hail at 11:19, underscores that this plague originates from God in heaven ("sky" and "heaven" translating the same Greek word) and represents "the rage of his wrath." The redundancy of this last phrase lays heavy emphasis on his judging those who

persecuted his people. The people on whom the big hail falls don't include the people of God, for his people have ascended to heaven for the purpose of returning with Jesus (11:11–12; 14:14–16). Meanwhile the plague of hail, emphasized by the addition of "extremely" to "big" and by the present tense of "is," causes its depraved sufferers to blaspheme God (see the comments on 13:6; 16:9 and especially 16:11).

Here we may pause to compare the seventh bowl with the seventh seal (8:1–5) and the seventh trumpet (11:15–19) to show that each one has had to do with what happens at Jesus' return. The seventh seal featured the altar in the heavenly temple. The seventh trumpet featured the ark of the covenant in the heavenly temple. And the seventh bowl featured a voice coming out of the heavenly temple from the throne. Each seventh featured lightning, thunder, and an earthquake. The seventh trumpet and the seventh bowl added "big hail." And each seventh offered an indication that the end has arrived: (1) the seventh seal featured the throwing of fire on the earth in answer to the martyrs' plea for vengeance; (2) the seventh trumpet featured the coming of God's and Christ's kingdom and the time of judgment and reward (see also 10:7: "the secret of God was finished" at the blowing of the seventh trumpet); and (3) the seventh bowl featured both the exclamation, "It has come about!" and the fall of Babylon and of the cities of the Gentiles and the dissolution of the islands and mountains. Since each seventh referred to the end of the great affliction, there must have been at least some overlap in the preceding seals, trumpets, and bowls.

THE FALL OF BABYLON
Revelation 17:1–18:24

Chapters 17–18 elaborate the fall of Babylon, introduced in 14:8 and reintroduced at the pouring out of the seventh bowl of God's rage (16:17–21 [see the comments on 14:8 for Babylon as a code name for Rome]). Chapter 17 describes Babylon as a whore and relates her to the first beast of chapter 13. Chapter 18 describes God's judgment on her and quotes the laments of those who've pleasured themselves with her. Since at the pouring out of the seventh bowl Babylon was given "the cup [consisting] of the wine of the rage of his [God's] wrath" (16:19), it's appropriate for one of the angels that poured out the bowls to escort John in this next vision.

17:1–2: And one of the seven angels that had the seven bowls came and spoke with me, saying, "[Come] here! I'll show you the judgment [= punishment] of the big whore who's sitting on many waters, ²with whom the kings of the earth whored; and those who inhabit the earth got drunk with the wine [consisting] of her whoredom." This woman differs, of course, from the one who fled into the wilderness after birthing a male child (12:1–17). Since John says nothing, "spoke *with* me" indicates the angel's proximity to John in speaking to him about her. The angel calls her "the *big* whore" because she'll represent a *big* city; and as a whore, she'll portray the city as having seduced her clients, both rulers ("the kings of the earth") and their non-Christian subjects ("those who inhabit the earth"). The whoredom in which they engaged as her clients included idolatrous religion, the sexual immorality that accompanied it, and the pursuit of wealth at the cost of human lives. "Drunk with the wine of her whoredom" symbolizes as out of control the pursuits of wealth, sexual pleasure, and idolatry—in particular, the worship of Roman emperors and perhaps also of the goddess of the city of Rome, namely, Roma. The comparison of these pursuits to whoredom has numerous parallels in the Old Testament (see, for example, Ezekiel 16:1–63; 23:1–49). You can't literally sit on water, but the whore's "sitting on many waters" echoes a description of old, Mesopotamian Babylon in Jeremiah 51:13. Figuratively, the description suits both the location of old Babylon on the Euphrates River close to the Persian Gulf and the location of Rome, the new Babylon, on the Tiber River close to the Mediterranean Sea. These locations on waterways, especially that of Rome, contribute to the commercialism which will become prominent in chapter 18.

17:3–6: And he [the angel] **carried me away in the Spirit into a wilderness. And I saw a woman sitting on a crimson beast full of blasphemous names, having seven heads and ten horns. ⁴And the woman was clothed with purple and crimson** [= the colors of her clothing] **and gilded with gold** [jewelry] **and precious stone and pearls, having a gold cup in her hand,** [a cup] **full of abominations and of the unclean things** [consisting] **of her whoredom** [compare Jeremiah 51:7], **⁵and on her forehead a name written, a secret: "Big Babylon, the mother of the earth's whores and abominations." ⁶And I saw that the woman was drunk with the blood of the saints, that is, with the blood of Jesus' witnesses. And on seeing her, I marveled a big marvel** [= I was completely dumbfounded]. As in Ezekiel 3:12–15; 8:3; 11:1, 24; 37:1; 43:5, "the Spirit" becomes a divine mode of transport for the seeing of a prophetic vision (compare 1:10; 4:1–2; and especially 21:10). In 17:1–2 John *heard* about a whore "sitting on many *waters*." Now in a desert he *sees* her "sitting on a crimson *beast*." A reason for the shift to a desert will come out in 17:16. Since the description of the beast equates him with the beast of 13:1–10 that represented the Roman Empire, the shift from many waters that support the woman to the beast that supports her distinguishes her from the empire at large and identifies her as the city of Rome, supported religiously, politically, and commercially by that empire (religion, politics, and commerce being inseparably intertwined) and ruling over the empire (for sitting as the posture of rulership, compare 18:7: "I'm sitting as a queen"). The beast's crimson color (a deep red) stands for the Christian martyrs' blood, already shed and (from John's standpoint) yet to be shed throughout the empire (compare 13:7). "Full of blasphemous names" describes the beast in terms of emperor worship throughout the empire (compare 13:11–18). Specifically, the use of a divine name such as "God" for

emperors constituted blasphemy, that is, slander against the one true God.

The woman's purple clothing stands for Rome's rulership (compare Daniel 5:7; John 19:2, 5); and her crimson clothing, like the crimson color of the beast, stands for the shedding of martyrs' blood and recollects Nero's massacre of Christians right in Rome during A.D. 64. But just as purple represents royalty, crimson also represents luxury, for the pigment used to dye textiles crimson cost a lot (compare 18:12; Proverbs 31:21). Showcasing the luxury further are (1) "gilded with gold [jewelry]" with its twofold reference to gold; (2) "gilded with . . . a precious stone," in which "gilded" carries the broader meaning of "adorned" and "precious stone" is a collective singular for gemstones; (3) "gilded with . . . pearls," listed separately because, strictly speaking, they're not gemstones but abnormal growths within mollusks such as oysters; and (4) "having a gold cup in her hand." This description makes the woman out to have been a high class prostitute, a whore who got rich with the money her clients paid her and who was consequently able to deck herself out expensively for the purpose of attracting still more clients (with her lurid colors contrast the pure white clothing of the twenty-four elders and the true Christians they represent in 3:4–5, 18; 4:4 and so on till 19:14). Like a successful whore, in other words, the city of Rome has grown fabulously wealthy at the expense of her empire. In view of "the wine [consisting] of her whoredom" (17:2) we expect her cup to be full of wine. But John describes it as "full of abominations," which are sacrileges consisting of idols (here, especially images of deified emperors [compare Daniel 9:27; 11:31; 12:11]), and "full . . . of the unclean things [consisting] of her whoredom," which are the fornications that went along with idolatry (especially in connection with temple prostitutes). She advertised her business by wearing her name on her forehead (as whores may have done with the use of inscribed headbands; compare the mark of the beast on the foreheads of beast-worshipers [13:16] and contrast the name of God and the lamb as God's seal on the foreheads of Christians [7:3; 14:1; 22:4]).

This whore's name is "secret" in that it's symbolic: "Big Babylon" symbolizes Rome, biggest city in the Roman Empire, identifies "the big whore" of 17:1, and echoes "big Babylon" in Daniel 4:30. "The mother of the earth's whores and abominations" describes Rome further as a cesspool that has overflowed so as to permeate the empire with her sexual immorality and idolatry. According to 17:2 the earth-dwellers "got drunk with the wine [consisting] of her whoredom." Now we're told that she herself is drunk, as suits a whore in revelry—but "with the blood of the saints, that is, with the blood of Jesus' witnesses" (among other passages see Isaiah 49:26 for getting drunk on blood, and compare again Nero's massacre of Christians in Rome). "Jesus' witnesses" don't just belong to him. They also testified concerning him (compare 1:2, 9; 2:13; 6:9; 11:3, 7; 12:11, 17; 19:10; 20:4; 22:18, 20 and a host of passages in John's Gospel, 1 John, and 3 John). The connection of the whore's drunkenness with that of the earth-dwellers lies in Christians' refusal to join the earth-dwellers in the abomination of emperor worship and in the sexual immoralities which, as already noted, went along with idolatry, and the bloodletting of their martyrdom in Rome for that refusal (see 14:20 for a comparison of blood with red wine). The big whore, Rome, has gotten drunk in celebration over the killing of Christians; but this celebratory drunkenness will quickly turn into staggering and falling under God's judgment. John's dumbfoundment at what this vision might mean sets up for an explanation by the angel who's escorting him.

17:7–11: And the angel said to me, "Why have you marveled? I'll tell you the secret of the woman and of the beast that's carrying her, [the beast] that has seven heads and ten horns. ⁸The beast that you saw was and isn't and is about to come up out of the abyss [compare 11:7], and he's going into destruction. And those who dwell on the earth, whose names haven't been written in the scroll of life since the founding of the world, will be amazed when [they] see the beast, that it was and isn't and will arrive [compare 13:8]. ⁹Here [is] the mind that has wisdom [compare 13:18]: The seven heads are seven mountains, where the woman is sitting on them. ¹⁰They are also seven kings. Five have fallen. One [the sixth] is. The other [the seventh] hasn't yet come. And whenever he comes, it's necessary that he stay a little while. ¹¹And the beast that was and isn't is himself also an eighth [king] and is from the seven [= one of the seven] and is going into destruction." "The secret *of* the woman and *of* the beast" means the secret *concerning* them. It now comes out that the secret concerning the woman—that is, concerning the symbolism of her name, "Big Babylon" (17:5)—includes the beast that carries her. The beast's having seven heads and ten horns identifies it with the beast of 13:1–10, the Roman Empire. But in contrast with 13:1 the angel mentions the seven heads first, so that he'll explain them before explaining the ten horns. "Was and isn't and is about to come up" recalls the slaying of one of its *heads* and the healing of the *beast's* mortal wound in 13:3. But whereas the beast came up initially "out of the *sea*" (13:1), here the beast "is about to come up out of the *abyss*," from where the demonic locusts came in 9:1–3. The sea represented the evil forces of chaos as the beast's origin. The abyss represents the underworld of the dead and therefore suits the beast's reviving after suffering a mortal wound and thus makes the whole expression into a parody of Jesus' preexistence as the Word ("was" [see 19:13 with John 1:1]), death ("isn't"), and resurrection ("is about to come up out of the abyss" [compare 1:18; 2:8 and see the comments on 13:3–4 for the political death of the Roman Empire upon the emperor Nero's slaying himself, and for the empire's coming back to life with the accession of Vespasian after a year of civil war]).

Despite the beast's revival, it—that is, the Roman Empire—"is going into destruction." The present tense of "is going" underlines the certainty of future destruction. The beast sponsored by the destroyer Satan will it-

self be destroyed (see the comments on 9:11 for Satan as the destroyer, and compare Daniel 7:3–26). But as those "whose names haven't been written in the scroll of life" (for which see the comments on 3:5), the earth-dwellers don't know that the beast is headed for destruction. So they're amazed at the beast's revival. "Since the founding of the world" doesn't mean that their names weren't written in the book *between* the world's founding and now; rather, they weren't written there already *at* the world's founding. This phrase echoes 13:8 and stresses predestination, a common theme in John's writings (though not to the exclusion of human responsibility to believe and persevere). "That it [the beast] was and isn't and will arrive" parodies the preexistence of Jesus as the Word and his death (as earlier), but now of *his coming again* as the resurrected one. For the verb translated "will arrive" is related to the Greek noun *parousia* properly pronounced par-oo-SEE-ah, used for the second coming (as in 1 John 2:28, for example).

"Here's the mind that has wisdom" means, "The following explanation will clue you in to 'the secret,' that is, the symbolism." The seven heads stand for the seven hills on which Rome, represented by the woman, was built. But the hills are called "mountains" for an allusion to the supposed stability of Rome as a city (see the comments on 6:14 for mountains as symbols of stability). The woman's sitting on the mountains stands for the supposed stability of Rome's rule; for, as noted earlier, sitting is the posture of rulership. The ungrammatical redundancy in "*where* the woman is sitting *on them*" stresses the supposed stability of this rule. The seven heads of the beast also stand for seven kings, that is, for seven Roman emperors. The first five have fallen in that they've died. They run from Augustus through Tiberius, Gaius (Caligula), and Claudius to Nero. Galba, Otho, and Vitellius don't count during A.D. 69, because the civil war that raged then (and that was portrayed under the second seal in 6:3–4) marked the temporary death of the beastly empire. The sixth head, who "is," represents the emperor Vespasian. The seventh, who "hasn't yet come," represents Titus, who'll "stay a little while." His reign was short (A.D. 79–81), so that "a little while" has the sense of "*only* a little while." "It's necessary" attributes the brevity of Titus's reign to divine predetermination. God is controlling human events despite appearances to the contrary. Christians living under the next emperor, Domitian, and looking back on Titus's reign would likely have wished it had lasted a lot longer; for emperor worship became an increasing problem for them under Domitian. Because of this increase the eighth king, Domitian, escalates into the whole beast instead of remaining merely one of its heads. The description, "that was and isn't," harks back to Nero's suicide and the consequent political death of the empire during a year of civil war, and characterizes Domitian as "from the seven" in that he's another Nero—Nero revived, so to speak—who wanted to be addressed both orally and in writing as *dominus et deus* (Latin for "Lord and God"). For a second time and hence for emphasis (again with use of the present tense), "is going into destruction" predicts the demise of the Roman Empire. Though not under Domitian, it did fall. But seven symbolizes completeness, as in the seven seals, the seven trumpets, and the seven bowls; and the folding of Domitian, the eighth king, back into the seven kings maintains the symbolism of completeness. Therefore the beast with seven heads represents all worldly powers opposed to God's people, and especially a final such power, whichever that may be, just prior to the second coming.

That the beast "isn't" during the civil war after Nero but "is about to come up" suggests that John received this vision and wrote Revelation during that year (A.D. 69). But the present tense of "is" in connection with the sixth head, Vespasian, suggests a reception and writing during his reign (A.D. 69–79). Again, however, the present tense of "is" in connection with the eighth king, Domitian, suggests reception and writing during his reign (A.D. 81–96). From the use of the present tense, then, we can't tell when John received the vision and wrote Revelation. Apparently the angel speaking to him uses the present tense for vividness.

17:12–14: "And the ten horns that you saw are ten kings who as such haven't yet received kingship. Nevertheless, they're receiving authority as kings with the beast for one hour. [13]These have one purpose, and they give their power and authority to the beast. [14]These will battle with [= against] the lamb; and the lamb will conquer them, because he's the Lord of lords and the King of kings [compare 19:16; Deuteronomy 10:17; Psalm 136:2–3; Daniel 2:47]. And the called and selected and faithful ones with him [will conquer the beast and ten kings] [compare Daniel 7:7–28]." "Who as such" means "who as kings" and therefore stresses their kingship despite its futurity. Likewise, the present tense in "they're receiving authority as kings" stresses the certainty of their coming kingship. "With the beast" indicates alliance with the beast, as confirmed by their common purpose to "give their power and authority to the beast." Their portrayal as horns highlights this power and authority; for horns symbolize active power, and the present tense of "give" highlights their giving it to the beast in the sense of using it for his benefit. Since the dragon, Satan, gave his own authority to the beast (13:4), it's likely that these ten kings too get their power and authority from Satan. "For one hour" means that they'll possess and exercise power and authority with the beast only a short while, an hour being the shortest unit of time then named. This hour may equate with "the hour of the test, [the hour] that's about to come on the whole inhabited [earth]" (3:10). Since the "eighth [king]," who is "from the seven"—that is, Domitian as a new Nero—was called "the beast" (17:11), the ten horns represent kings who'll join forces with the beast (the Roman Empire in whatever new form it will take, just as the Babylonian Empire took a new form in the Roman Empire) to battle against the lamb by trying to obliterate the church through persecution and martyrdom (compare 16:16). The number of these kings, ten, symbolizes plenty of power and authority. At his second coming, though, the lamb will conquer the kings and the beast with whom they've allied themselves. He can, and will, because he's "the Lord of lords," which means "the Emperor of emperors" such as the Roman Caesars, and "the King of kings" such as these ten who "give their power and authority to the beast." The ones "with him [the lamb]" are counterposed to the kings "with the beast," are "called" in the sense of invited to the marriage banquet of the lamb (19:9), are "selected" in the sense of chosen out from the society of unbelievers (John 6:70; 13:18; 15:16, 19; 2 John 1, 13), and "faithful" in the sense of persevering because of genuine belief. Their sharing in the lamb's conquest of the beast reverses the beast's earlier conquest of them through persecuting and killing them (11:7; 13:7). In 13:4 the beast's admirers asked, "Who can do battle with him?" Their question is now answered. The lamb and his followers can.

17:15–18: And he [the angel] tells me, "The waters that you saw, where the whore is sitting, are peoples and crowds and nations and tongues. [16]And the ten horns that you saw and the beast—these will hate the whore and cause her to be deserted and naked, and they'll eat her flesh and burn her up with fire. [17]For into their hearts God has given the executing of his purpose and the giving of their kingship to the beast till the words of God will be finished [in the sense of realized, accomplished]. [18]And the woman whom you saw is the big city that has kingship over the kings of the earth." The interruption of the explanation with "And he tells me," plus the present tense of "tells," highlights the rest of the explanation, which springs a surprise. It's that peoples, crowds, nations, and tongues—all represented by the waters of the Mediterranean Sea around which their homelands are located—will turn against ("hate") Rome, the big whore that sits in rulership over them. With support from the ten kings, the beast that symbolizes those homelands and subjects will devastate the city. Now we know why John was taken into a wilderness to see the whore (17:3). Rome will be deserted as by definition a wilderness is deserted. Like an aged whore, she has no more clients and therefore no more income with which to maintain her luxurious lifestyle. Nakedness in bed suits a whore. But nakedness out in the open is shameful, yet suitable as punishment for a whore. Stripped away are the expensive purple and crimson garments, gold jewelry, gemstones, and pearls. And "the lust of the flesh" (1 John 2:16) takes on new meaning, cannibalism instead of sexual fondling and carnal intercourse: "they'll eat her flesh" as a carnivorous beast eats its victim. "And burn her up [her inedible parts] with fire," as a city is burned to the ground, carries overtones of the judgmental fire that appears repeatedly throughout Revelation (compare 2 Kings 9:21–37). This fate of Rome adumbrates the fate of the beast and ten kings whom God uses to judge Rome despite their own evil. He judges evil with evil. The past tense in "God has given the executing of his purpose" treats a future event as good as done, because he has spoken of it. "The words of God" that "will be finished" constitute the book of

Revelation (see especially 22:9, 18–19). Whatever the big city into which Rome is recast during the great affliction, its finish will finish God's frightful words concerning it.

18:1: After these things [referring to the sights of the preceding vision] **I saw another angel descending out of heaven, having great authority; and the earth was lit up by his glory.** "Another angel" distinguishes this angel from "one of the seven angels that had the seven bowls" (17:1), who was escorting John and speaking to him throughout chapter 17. "Descending out of heaven" (1) recalls "another angel . . . descending out of heaven" in 10:1, whom we found plenty of reasons to identify as Jesus; (2) anticipates the "angel descending out of heaven" in 20:1, whom again we'll find reason to identify as Jesus; and (3) links up with the portrayal of Jesus in John 3:13; 6:33, 41–42, 50–51, 58 as having descended out of heaven at his first coming. The present descent constitutes his second coming, so that he'll announce the fall of Babylon as an event that has just occurred (in the vision, of course, not in real time). "Having great authority" harks back to "Christ's authority" in 12:10 and to "another angel . . . having authority over the fire" in 14:18, whom also we found reasons to identify as Jesus (compare his authority according to John 5:27; 10:18; 17:2). The statement that "the earth was lit up by his glory" (1) recalls the earth's shining with God's glory in Ezekiel 43:2; (2) anticipates the lighting up of the New Jerusalem, which like the angel descends out of heaven, by the glory of God and Jesus the lamb (21:1–4, 23–25; 22:5); and (3) alludes to the divine glory of Jesus that's featured in 5:12–13; 21:23 and throughout John's Gospel (1:14; 2:11 and so on [compare also the portrayal of Jesus as the light of the world in John 1:4–9; 3:19–21; 8:12; 9:5; 12:46 with the lighting up of the earth here in Revelation 18:1]). Enough said to demonstrate that we have here Jesus, portrayed as a messenger (the meaning of "angel").

18:2–3: And he shouted in a strong voice, saying, "It fell, it fell—Babylon, the big [whore (compare Isaiah 21:9; Jeremiah 51:7–8)]**. And she has become a dwelling place of demons and an asylum of every kind of unclean spirit and an asylum of every kind of unclean bird** [that is, birds of carrion] **and an asylum of every kind of unclean and hated** [wild] **beast,** [3]**because all the Gentiles** [in the religious sense of pagans, non-Christians, whether Jewish or non-Jewish] **have fallen because of the wine** [consisting] **of the rage of her whoredom** [= Babylon's raging religious and sexual immorality] **and** [because] **the kings of the earth have whored with her** [compare Isaiah 23:17] **and** [because] **the merchants of the earth have gotten rich because of the** [economic] **power of her overindulgence."** Usually a voice is described as "loud," but here as "strong" to point up the efficacy of the announcement (the very speaking of a divine word effects as well as ensures its accomplishment) and to link the angel's voice with Jesus, the "strong" angel of 10:1, and with the description in 18:8 of the Lord God as "strong" (compare the comments on 18:21). In other words, John supplies a further

reason to identify this angel as Jesus. The announcement of Babylon's fall echoes 14:8 (see the comments there for the doubling of "It fell" and for the use of "Babylon" as a code word for Rome). The populating of Babylon with demons and ritually unclean and hated creatures of all sorts echoes passages such as Isaiah 13:19–22; 34:8–15; Jeremiah 50:39–40; 51:37 and implies that Babylon has been depopulated of human beings so as to become a wilderness, which by definition means an area devoid of them, or at least of very many of them (compare the comments on 17:16). The populating of Babylon with demons and unclean and hated creatures suits the moral and religious character of its former human population. "The Gentiles [non-Christians] have fallen" in that they *are* the fallen Babylon, just as the New Jerusalem will *consist* of Christians. These contrasting cities are the people who populate them, not just the places where people live (see the comments on 21:1–22:5). The Babylonians (if we may call the Romans such) have fallen under God's judgment as though in a drunken stupor. See the comments on 14:8; 17:1–2, 18 for "the wine [consisting] of the rage of her whoredom," for "the kings of the earth" as client kings under Roman auspices, and for the kings' whoring with Roman Babylon.

18:4–5: And I heard another voice from heaven, saying, "Come out of her, my people, lest you participate with [Babylon the whore] **in her sins and lest you receive some of her plagues,** [5]**because her sins have piled up to heaven and** [because] **God has remembered her injustices** [compare Isaiah 48:20; 52:11; Jeremiah 50:8; 51:6, 9, 44–45]**."** Since Jesus is the angel that descends out of heaven and shouts in 18:1, "my people" identifies "another voice from heaven" as God's. The reference to "God" in the quotation doesn't rule out God as the speaker; for he can refer to himself with "God," as he'll do in 21:5–8. Here he'll speak all the way through 18:20, though quote others in 18:16–17a, 18–19. His addressing Christians with "my people" portrays them as the true Israel (compare especially chapter 7). The command, "Come out of her [Babylon]," calls for a new exodus, just as the return of Jews from exile in Babylonia replicated their earlier exodus from Egypt (Jeremiah 31). But this new exodus isn't to be geographical as were those exoduses in Old Testament times; rather, it's to be moral and religious: nonparticipation in the big whore's sins of idolatry (especially emperor worship) and its accompanying sexual immorality (though the injustice of economic exploitation is about to come in for heavy emphasis). The messages to churches in the province of Asia contained a number of indications that some professing Christians were participating in such sins (2:6, 14–15, 20–24; 3:2–4, 15–17). To stay in Babylon morally and religiously is to "participate with [her] in her sins" and to "receive some of her plagues," that is, to be judged as a non-Christian despite your Christian profession (see 15:1; 16:1–21 for "the seven last plagues" in which "God's rage was finished"). If you don't come out of Babylon, you won't enter the New Jerusalem. "Lest you receive *some* of her plagues" implies that if you come out you won't receive *any* of them, much less all of them. "Piled up" means that Babylon's—that is, Rome's—sins have been bonded together, as were the bricks with mortar in the Tower of Babel, to build a new such tower that reaches to heaven and therefore provokes God, who dwells there, to put a stop to the building (Genesis 11:1–9). "Her injustices" adds to "her sins" crimes against humanity such as will shortly be detailed. "God has remembered her injustices" means that he has brought them to mind so as to balance the scales of justice (compare Psalm 109:14; Hosea 9:9).

18:6–8: "Pay her back as also she has paid [others], **and double the doubles in accordance with her deeds** [compare Jeremiah 50:15, 29]. **In the cup** [of wine] **that she has mixed** [for others] **mix a double for her** [compare Isaiah 40:2; Jeremiah 16:18]. ⁷**As much as she has glorified herself and overindulged, to this extent give her torment and grief, because in her heart she's saying, 'I'm sitting as a queen, and I'm not a widow, and by no means will I see** [= experience] **grief.'** ⁸**On this account her plagues will come in a single day: death** [in the sense of a deadly epidemic; compare 6:8] **and grief and famine** [compare Isaiah 47:7–11; Ezekiel 14:21]. **And she'll be burned down with fire, because the Lord God, who judges her,** [is] **strong."** To double is to duplicate, and a double is a duplicate. So "double the doubles in accordance with her deeds" means "make her punishments match her sins and injustices," and "mix a double for her in the cup that she has mixed [for others]" means "prepare a cup of wine that will make her fall down dead drunk as she has prepared a cup of wine that has made her paramours fall down dead drunk" (see 14:10 with comments for mixing wine with wine, rather than as usual with water, to produce a judgment undiluted with mercy). "As much as she has glorified herself and overindulged, to this extent give her torment and grief" joins "pay her back as also she has paid [others]" to frame the two commands that feature doubling and to confirm the need for balancing the scales of justice. The amassing of four synonymous commands—"pay her back," "double the doubles," "mix a double," and "give her torment and grief"—gives them enormous emphasis.

But whom is God commanding to execute this tit-for-tat justice? Well, there's no indication that he has stopped talking to Christians, whom he has just addressed with "my people." They'll accompany Jesus at his return as "the armies in heaven" to share in the judgment of the wicked (19:11–21). And though hidden in English translation, the "you" who are commanded to "pay her back," "double the doubles," "mix a double," and "give her torture and grief"—this "you" is plural like the "you" who are commanded as God's people to "come out of her." So he commands them, his people, to avenge themselves on Roman Babylon, the primary source of their persecution from Nero's reign onward.

Babylon's self-glorification contrasts with God's and the Holy Spirit's having glorified Jesus (see 18:1 with John 8:54, among other passages). She glorified herself by overindulging in the pleasures of wealth and sexual

immorality. But the torment of eternal punishment will replace those pleasures (14:10–11; 20:10), and the replacement will bring grief (contrast the absence of grief in Christians' eternal state [21:4]). Implied is Rome's having tormented and grieved the rest of the empire with her self-glorifying overindulgence, which robbed the rest of the empire of needed assets. Her false but prideful sense of security leads God to command the taking of vengeance on her. "In her heart she's saying" means "she says to herself." The present tense in "she's saying" highlights her false sense of security. She regards herself as royalty: "I'm sitting as a queen" (compare her sitting, the posture of royalty, on seven mountains in 17:9). She denies she's a widow. And she predicts she'll never suffer the grief that a widow suffers over the death of her husband (and because women were usually married to men older than they, widows were numerous as well as destitute). Despite having aged as a whore she foolishly expects a never-ending succession of clients.

"On this account" reemphasizes Babylon's self-glorification and overindulgence as reasons for her punishment. But the commands to punish her yield to a prediction of her punishment—with a new wrinkle, the rapidity with which "her plagues will come." "In a single day" tells how rapidly they'll come: in "the big day of their [God's and the lamb's] wrath" (6:17), "the big day of God Almighty" (16:14), when Jesus comes "as a thief [comes]" (16:15). Four plagues will come on her all on the same day, but will last forever: (1) an epidemic that will issue in the second death of eternal torment as opposed to eternal life; (2) everlasting grief worse than that of a widow and in contrast with the absence of grief in the Christians' eternal state (21:4); (3) unending famine as opposed to the fruits of the tree of life in the New Jerusalem (22:2); and (4) a fire that burns down Babylon—that is, burns down those who constitute the city without burning them up (see 14:10–11; 19:20; 20:14–15; 21:8 and compare the fire that burned much of Rome in A.D. 64 and sparked Nero's persecution of Christians living there). "Because the Lord God, who judges her, [is] strong" implies that only he can destroy Babylon, Rome, or whatever reproduction thereof may exist at Jesus' return. His strength associates him with Jesus, the strong angel with the strong voice (10:1; 18:2, 21 [compare Jesus' and God's sharing divine attributes throughout John's Gospel, 1–2 John, and Revelation]).

18:9–10: "And the kings of the earth, who'd whored with her and overindulged [with her], **will weep and beat themselves** [on the chest] **over her when they see the smoke of her burning** ¹⁰**as they stand at a distance on account of fear of her torment, saying, 'Woe, woe, O big city, O Babylon the strong city, because in a single hour your judgment has come** [compare 8:13, and for general background see Ezekiel 27]!'"** Here is the first of three laments over the fall of Babylon, each one beginning with "Woe, woe, O big city," this one by the "kings of the earth," the second by "the merchants" (18:15–17a), and the third by various classes of seamen (18:17b–20). "The kings of the earth" appear to be the client kings, represented by the beast's ten horns, who turned against Rome and burned her down in 17:16–18. Why then do they lament over her "when they see the smoke of her burning"? Because that smoke portends the smoke of their own eternal burning (see 14:10–11 again). "On account of fear of her torment" means "because of fear of being tormented as she is being tormented." After all, these kings have whored with Roman Babylon—that is, participated with her in emperor worship, idolatry in general, and the sexual immorality that accompanied it. Therefore the kings deserve a punishment like hers (compare the way God in the Old Testament used one wicked nation to punish another nation and then punished for its wickedness the one he'd used). "Standing at a distance" contrasts with formerly lying in bed with the big whore. For "beat[ing] themselves [on the chest]" in addition to weeping see the comments on 1:7. The future tense of "will weep and beat themselves" points to an event future to John. Since smoke darkens (9:2), "the smoke of her burning" contrasts with the angelic Jesus's "glory," by which "the earth was lit up" (18:1). "Woe" means "Alas" and in the original Greek sounds like what it means (oo-EYE). Repetition of the woe intensifies it. Babylon (Rome) is "strong" because she's "big," but not strong enough to resist successfully the Lord God her judge, who is "strong" (18:8), or the "strong angel" who has "a strong voice" (18:2, 21). "In a single hour" narrows down "in a single day" (18:8) and thus adds to the woe another intensification, this time of even greater rapidity than before. Otherwise see the comments on 18:8, and note that in 17:12 "one hour" indicates the *duration* of the ten kings' reign whereas here "one hour" indicates the unit of time *within* which an event takes place.

18:11–13: **"And the merchants of the earth are weeping and grieving over her, because no one is buying their cargo any more—**[12]**cargo** [consisting] **of gold and silver and precious stone** [a collective singular for gemstones] **and pearls and fine linen and purple** [cloth] **and silk and crimson** [cloth]—**and** [because no one is buying] **any kind of** [object made of] **sandarac wood** [a hard, aromatic wood from a North African tree of the pine family] **and any kind of ivory object and any kind of object** [made] **of invaluable wood** [because the wood is exotic] **and** [made] **of brass and of iron and of marble,** [13]**and** [because no one is buying] **cinnamon and amomum** [an Indian spice plant] **and incense and perfume and myrrh** [an aromatic resinous gum] **and wine and olive oil and fine flour and wheat and cattle and sheep and** [cargo] **of horses and carriages and bodies** [a reference to slaves considered as mere bodies to be bought as merchandise], **even souls of human beings** [a reference to slaves considered as human lives]." The present tense of "are weeping and grieving" and in "no one is buying their cargo any more" makes this future event so vivid that it seems to be occurring right now. And it might as well be, so certain is its occurrence. The list of imported goods, almost entirely upscale, includes jewelry and textiles (compare 17:4), furniture and utensils, spices and fragrances, foodstuffs and wine,

livestock and conveyances, and—last of all, as though of least inherent worth and therefore disposable when no longer useful—slaves. The merchants had brought to Rome these goods from all around the Mediterranean Sea and from as far away as Arabia, Armenia, India, and even China. But now the merchants' source of income has dried up or, more accurately, burned down. Note: slavery in the Roman Empire wasn't racially based, but was so extensive that historians think slaves may have constituted a third or even a half of the empire's human population.

Since the merchants aren't clearly quoted till 18:15–17a, it is God's voice, coming out of heaven in 18:4, that continues speaking by way of an address to Roman Babylon in **18:14**: **"And the late summer fruit of your soul's lust** [= the ripe fruit that your soul craved] **has gone away from you, and all the sumptuous and glitzy things have gone missing from you, and by no means will they** [the merchants] **find them** [for you] **any more."** Ripe fruit stands ready for plucking and eating, whets the appetite, and here stands for staples and especially luxuries imported to Rome from her empire and beyond. The Greek word translated "soul" means physical life. So "your soul's lust" refers to craving for the physical pleasures of a luxurious lifestyle. But "the late summer fruit" that makes possible such a lifestyle "has gone away from" Rome instead of being imported to Rome as before. "All the sumptuous and glitzy things" summarizes most of the imported goods listed in 18:11–13. "All" and the similar sounds of the Greek words underlying the rest of the phrase, *ta lipara* (TAH lee-pah-RAH) and *ta lampra* (TAH lahm-PRAH), stress that because of Rome's destruction, none of those goods are being imported any more. The collapse of trade is complete. For further emphasis, "have gone missing from you" echoes "has gone away from you." "And by no means will they [the merchants] find them ['all the sumptuous and glitzy things'] [for you] any more" reechoes the thought for yet further emphasis.

18:15–17a: **"The merchants of these things who got rich from her will stand at a distance on account of fear of her torment, weeping and grieving,** [16]**saying, 'Woe, woe, O big city clothed in fine linen and purple and crimson and gilded with gold** [jewelry] **and precious stone and pearl** [collective singulars], [17a]**because in a single hour such great wealth has been turned into a wilderness** [= voided (compare the use of this same verb in 17:16 for the whore's being deserted by her clients and the use of the corresponding noun, "wilderness," in 17:3 for the location where John was taken to see her)].'" Rome's paying for the merchants' goods, most of them high-priced, had made the merchants rich. But just as her former intimates the kings of the earth stood at a distance for fear of being tormented as the big whore is being tormented, so too do her former intimates the merchants. For just as those kings whored with her in terms of emperor worship, idolatry in general, and the sexual immorality that accompanied it, so the merchants have whored with her by pirating the assets of subject peoples to line their own pockets with the huge profits made from selling those assets to her. The merchants have good reason to fear. Rome's strength was important to the kings—hence their describing her as "the strong city" (18:10). But Rome's wealth was important to the merchants—hence their describing her as "clothed in fine linen and purple and crimson and gilded with gold [jewelry] and precious stone and pearl," none of which she can afford to buy from them any more. For the rest, see the comments on 18:10.

18:17b–19: **"And every helmsman and everyone sailing to a place** [= somewhere] **and sailors and as many as work the sea** [= make their living by it] **stood at a distance** [18]**and were shouting as they saw the smoke of her burning, saying, 'Who** [is] **like the big city?'** [19]**And they threw dust on their heads and were shouting, weeping and grieving, saying, 'Woe, woe, O big city by which all those who have ships at sea got rich from her preciousness** [that is, from the high prices Rome paid for the cargo imported to her], **because in a single hour she has been turned into a wilderness** [= voided of those imports].'" The kings of the earth were portrayed as lamenting in the future (18:9), the merchants as lamenting in the present (18:11). Seamen are now portrayed as lamenting in the past. This progression puts an increasing emphasis on the certainty of Babylon's downfall. In the end it's as good as done already, so that professing Christians who are compromising with her should take warning and true, faithful Christians should take heart. Travelers by sea are put together with helmsmen and sailors because there were no passenger ships. Such travelers had to sail on cargo ships. "As many as work the sea" brings in fishermen and pearl-divers as well. "Every," "everyone," and "as many as" leave no exceptions. They all stand at a distance, as did the kings and the merchants. Fear of being tormented as the big whore is being tormented has twice been cited as the reason for standing at a distance (18:10, 15) and therefore needn't be cited again. But for emphasis "the smoke of her burning" comes in for a second mention (compare 18:9 with comments). In 18:10, 15–17a, the kings and the merchants were "saying" their laments. Here, those listed "were shouting" so as to be heard across the waters by one another when asking, "Who [is] like the big city?" which echoes "Who [is] like the beast?" in 13:4. No other city compared in greatness with Rome, the new Babylon, or will compare with whatever newest Babylon will exist at Jesus' return. Nevertheless, the city is burning down, as evidenced by her smoke that these questioners see in the distance. They punctuate their question by throwing dust on their heads, a gesture of despair corresponding to the kings' and merchants' fear, in addition to weeping and grieving. We might wonder where these seamen got the dust. But Ezekiel 27:29–30, which is echoed here, has them disembarked onto land for lack of any more trade by sea. So they're shouting across the waters to one another from their bases on land. "Were shouting" occurs a second time to stress the following double "Woe," which occurs for a third time. And for a third

time it's the rapidity of Babylon's downfall that gives rise to the double "Woe" ("in a single day" [18:8], even "in a single hour" [as already in 18:10]). And for a second time we read that "she was turned into a wilderness" (see the explanation of 18:17a). The ungrammatical shift from a direct address, "O big city," to speaking about the city ("her" and "she") reflects the seamen's attempt to distance themselves from her. The laments have ended.

Just as in 18:14 the voice of God (18:4) addressed personified Babylon directly, so he speaks now in a direct address, but not to Babylon. *18:20*: **"Celebrate over her, O heaven and saints and apostles and prophets, because God has judged your judgment from her** [that is, has pronounced and executed the judgment on her that she had pronounced and executed on you when persecuting and killing you (compare Jeremiah 51:48–49)]**."** A similar call to celebrate, including a personification of heaven, appeared in 12:12. Here, "saints and apostles and prophets" define the personified heaven, which locates them in heaven as now ready to return with Jesus (compare 11:11–12; 14:1, 14–16). The twelve apostles will be mentioned in 21:14. But 2:2 and John 13:16 use "apostle(s)" in the wider sense of Christians sent to testify for Jesus. So just as all Christians are saints in that they're consecrated to God (5:8; 8:3–4 and so forth), so too all Christians are apostles in that they're sent to testify about Jesus (John 20:21). Likewise, all Christians are prophets in that they preach repentance (10:7; 11:10, 18; 16:6). The celebration is to acknowledge God's answer to the martyrs' cry for vengeance in 6:10. Compare Deuteronomy 19:16–21, where what a false witness had hoped would be done to the accused is to be done to the false witness instead.

18:21–24: **And a single strong angel picked up a stone—a big upper mill[stone], as it were—and threw [it] into the sea, saying, "In this way will Babylon, the big city, be thrown down with force** [compare Jeremiah 51:59–64]**; and by no means will she be found any more,** [22]**and by no means will the sound of harpists and musicians and flutists and trumpeters be heard in you any more, and by no means will any craftsman of any craft be found in you any more, and by no means will the sound of a mill be heard in you any more,** [23]**and by no means will the light of a lamp shine in you any more, and by no means will the voice of a bridegroom and** [the voice] **of a bride be heard in you any more** [compare Jeremiah 25:10, but contrast the bustling activity and glorious lamplight of the New Jerusalem according to 21:1–22:5]**, because your merchants were the earth's tycoons, because all the Gentiles** [again in the sense of non-Christians regardless of ethnicity] **were misled by your magic arts.** [24]**And in her was found the blood of prophets and of saints and of all who've been slain on the earth."** "A *single* strong angel" parallels the "single day" and "single hour" in which the downfall of Babylon occurred. "A single *strong* angel" identifies this angel with the angel in 18:1–2, who had "a strong voice" and whom we found reason to identify as Jesus in the role of a messenger (the meaning of "angel"). "Strong" has shifted from his voice, where it pointed up the efficacy of his announcement, to him himself, where it points up the strength he has to pick up a huge boulder and throw it forcefully. No lesser angel than Jesus has the strength to overthrow Babylon. For the comparison to "a big upper mill[stone]" see the comments on Mark 9:42. As a prophetic announcement effects an accomplishment of the announced event, so a prophetic action, such as the throwing of this stone, effects an accomplishment of the event symbolized by the action (as in the acted-out prophecies of Ezekiel [see Ezekiel 4–5, 12, for example] and perhaps most dramatically in 2 Kings 13:14–19, where King Joash's striking the ground with arrows at the prophet Elisha's command only three times effected three coming victories over Syria *but no more*). "Into the sea" references the Mediterranean Sea, across which merchant ships brought Rome her goods. Appropriately, she'll disappear into the very sea that provided waterways for the transportation of those goods. So Rome isn't only *burned* down (17:16; 18:8). She's also *thrown* down. (We have to think, then, of figurative language.)

"In this way . . . with force" adds a forceful throwing to the force of gravity. Babylon will sink like a stone to the sea bottom never to surface. "By no means will she be found any more" stresses the permanence of her disappearance. Five more occurrences of "by no means . . . any more" add up to a sixfold emphasis on this permanence. Babylon will be voided not only of her paramours and imported goods. She'll also be voided of her own human population and therefore of the wholesome activities that go along with urban life as it ought to be: making music for enjoyment and comfort, working at crafts by way of employment, grinding at a mill in preparation of food, lighting a lamp to illuminate a home, getting married. The list alternates between (1) the heard sound of harpists, musicians, and flutists; (2) the finding of craftsmen; (3) the heard sound of a mill; (4) the shining of a lamp; and (5) the heard voice of a bridegroom and a bride. No more of these audible and visible felicities, only dead silence and emptiness such as characterized the primeval chaos before God broke the silence by speaking the cosmos into existence and populating it (Genesis 1). Two reasons for the dead silence and emptiness: (1) the getting rich of Babylon's merchants at the expense of others' assets and (2) Rome's misleading of non-Christians with her magic arts, in particular with the "big signs" that deceived them into worshiping the emperors and thus the beastly empire represented by them (13:11–18).

The strong angel started out referring to Babylon in the third person ("she") but shifted to the second person ("you" and "your") to lend verbal force to the physical force of throwing. Now he shifts back to the third person ("her"). "In her was found the blood of prophets and saints" alludes especially to Nero's shedding of Christians in Rome. As in 18:20, "prophets and saints" designates all true Christians. But "the apostles" of 18:20 drop out here to make room for "the blood . . . of all who've been slain on the earth," which makes Babylon

symbolic of murderous injustice wherever, whenever, and whomever it has struck. "Was found" implies God's searching for such injustice so as to punish its perpetrators, but leaves the accent on the injustice as such.

HEAVENLY PRAISE OF GOD
Revelation 19:1–10

19:1–2: After these things I heard, as it were, the loud voice of a large crowd in heaven, saying, "Hallelujah! Salvation and glory and power belong to our God, ²because his judgments [are] **true and right, because he has judged** [= punished] **the big whore, who as such** [= in line with her whoredom] **was corrupting the earth with her whoredom, and has avenged his slaves' blood,** [which was shed] **by her hand** [compare Genesis 4:11; 2 Kings 9:7; Daniel 4:37]." "After these things" segues a shift of scenes from earth to heaven. John compares the voice that he heard to that of a large crowd. "A *large* crowd" produces a "*loud* voice" and harks back to the innumerably "large crowd" who were shouting an acclamation to God and the lamb "with a loud voice" in 7:9–10. That crowd consisted of saved people standing "within sight of the throne [God's] and within sight of the lamb." So too here. The saved have ascended to heaven to return with Jesus (11:11–12; 14:14–16; 19:11–14). Their using the Hebrew exclamation, "Hallelujah!" which means "Praise the Lord," marks them as true Israel just as in chapter 7 the 144,000 from Israel's twelve tribes turned out to be an innumerable crowd of saved people from every tribe and all tribes and peoples and tongues. The preceding and following contexts feature the beast and Babylon; so "salvation" refers particularly to God's deliverance of Christians from their persecutors, and to his having done so with his glorious power (compare 7:14, where the saved who in 7:10 attributed their salvation to God are said to have "come out of the great affliction" [also 12:10]). "Belong to our God" means that it is right and proper to give him credit (1) for having saved his people from the great affliction; (2) for having sent his angelic Son, whose glory lighted up the earth, to throw down Babylon, the source of their persecution (chapter 18); and (3) for thus exercising his power in their behalf (compare the pairing of his glory and power in the pouring out of the seven last plagues [15:7–8]). "*Our God*" puts him as the one true God over against the Caesars and other false gods. The judgments of God consist in his condemnations and consequent punishments. They're "true" in the sense that they show him to be true to his promise of deliverance for his people. They're "right" in the sense that they're just. It was only right that the big whore should be punished for corrupting the earth with her whoredom and for shedding the blood of Christians, called God's "slaves" (as from 1:1 onward), and that they get the vengeance which the martyrs expressed a longing for in 6:10. The truth and rightness of God's judgments in general and of the big whore's judgment in particular provide the bases for this acclamation (compare 5:12; 15:3; 16:7; Deuteronomy 32:43; 2 Kings 9:7).

19:3: And they've said "Hallelujah!" a second time. "And her smoke goes up forever and ever." One "Hallelujah!" wasn't enough. This second "Hallelujah!" praises the Lord for the everlasting burning of the big whore. Since the whore represents the city of Rome, her being burned suits Nero's having burned Christians in Rome as torches to illuminate his gardens at night (compare 14:10–11; 18:9, 18; Genesis 19:28; Isaiah 34:9–10). Thus "Eternal Rome," as the city was called, has become eternal in the smoke of her burning rather than eternal in the magnificence of her power and wealth.

19:4: And the twenty-four elders and the four living [creatures] fell down and worshiped God, who was sitting on the throne, saying, "Amen! Hallelujah [compare Psalm 106:47–48]!" For the twenty-four elders and the four living creatures see the comments on 4:4, 6b–8. These representations of the saved and these heavenly creatures closest to God render him obeisance and praise in response to the acclamation given him by the large crowd. "Fell down" suits worshiping him in that to worship means literally to kiss the ground in front of the object of worship. "Sitting on the throne" anticipates God's having begun to rule the earth from his throne in heaven (see 19:6 and compare 11:15–19). "Amen" is Hebrew for a strong "Yes!" which affirms the crowd's preceding acclamations (compare 1:7; 22:20). This affirmation picks up "Hallelujah!" from those acclamations and for a third time portrays that crowd, through their use of this Hebrew term, as true Israel (see the comments on 19:1–2).

19:5: And a voice came out from the throne, saying, "Praise our God, all you his slaves—that is, you the small and the great, who fear him." "Praise our God" rules out the voice as God's. But the voice emanates from the throne, Jesus occupies the throne with God (3:21; 7:17; 12:5; 22:1, 3), and in a message to his disciples he referred to "my God and your God" (John 20:17), which comports with "our God" in the present command. So the voice is that of Jesus. But he isn't God's slave—hence "*you* his slaves"; and believers are his "friends" (literally, "loved ones"), not his slaves (John 15:13–15)—hence "you *his* [God's] slaves." "Who fear him" describes God's slaves appropriately, for a slave fears to disobey his master (compare 11:18; 14:7; 15:4). It's healthy and wise to fear God. "The small [lacking prominence] and the great [possessing prominence]" adds emphasis to the already emphatic "all." None of the saved are to fail giving God praise.

The saved have already praised God (19:1–3). But even more praise is needed and deserved—hence **19:6–8: And I heard, as it were, the voice of a large crowd and, as it were, the sound of many waters and, as it were, the sound of strong thunderclaps, saying, "Hallelujah, because the Lord our God, the Almighty, has started reigning as king! [7] Let us rejoice and be glad and give him glory, because the wedding of the lamb has come, and his wife has prepared herself. [8] And it has been given to her that she be clothed with bright,** clean fine linen; for the fine linen is the righteous acts of the saints." The crowd of saved people who praised God in 19:1–3 praise him again in obedience to the command in 19:5. Again John compares their voice to that of a large crowd. But he turns the volume up, so to speak, by replacing the earlier description "loud" with further comparisons to "the sound of many waters" (a heavy rainstorm) and to "the sound of strong thunderclaps" (compare 14:2, though there the "loud thunderclap" is singular). For "Hallelujah!" see the comments on 19:1. But this fourth one gets an explicit justification: "because the Lord . . . has started reigning" (see 11:15 with comments). Since "lord" means an owner of slaves, God's slaves (as they were addressed in 19:5) acknowledge his ownership of them by calling him "the Lord." "Our God" echoes 19:1, 5 and sets him over against false lords and gods (compare 1 Corinthians 8:4–6). "The Almighty" highlights his omnipotence, which enables him to start reigning. The reign of the dragon, beast, and false prophet is over. And God's reign starts with a wedding. So joy and gladness are in order, as is giving him glory, that is, acknowledging his glory by praising him for scheduling this wedding. A wedding marks the coming together of a man and a woman for lifelong cohabitation. The lamb's wedding marks the coming together of Jesus the lamb and the church his wife for eternal cohabitation. No more will the distance between heaven and earth separate them from each other (compare 21:22–22:5 and contrast especially John 17:11–15). Lambs don't have weddings or wives. But this lamb is a shepherd (7:17), and shepherds do have weddings and wives. By anticipation the crowd refer to themselves as the lamb's "wife" (compare the comments on Matthew 1:18–19 regarding Joseph as Mary's "husband" though they were still only engaged). Old Testament passages that speak of Israel as the Lord's wife combine with the portrayal of Christians as the lamb's wife to further their identity as the true Israel (compare John 3:28–29 and see, for example, Hosea 2:19–20).

The wife has prepared herself for the wedding by donning "bright, clean fine linen," which symbolizes "the righteous acts of the saints." She *is* the saints, those who are consecrated to God; and to don such clothing she has to have acted righteously during her earthly lifetime as evidence of true faith. No wonder she's consecrated to God. The Greek word translated "bright" is the adjectival form of the Greek word for a lamp. So the brightness of the wife's linen represents the lamplight of her testimony (see the comparison of local churches to lampstands in 1:20 and of Christians to lamp-like witnesses in 11:1–10; 12:11, 17). The cleanness of her linen represents the purity of her religious, moral, and economic conduct (these three aspects being intertwined). She has come out of Babylon (18:4). And the fineness of her linen represents the high value that God puts on her good conduct and testimony (contrast the garish garb of the big whore in 17:4; 18:12, 16). That "it has been given" to the lamb's wife that she be clothed in this way indicates God's acknowledgment of her righteous acts, perhaps also that they're not self-generated but "done in God" (see the comments on John 3:21). Incidentally, the facts that the Lord "has started reigning," that the lamb's wedding "has come," that the lamb's wife "has prepared herself," and that "it has been given" her to wear bright, clean fine linen all show that the command to praise God in 19:5 wasn't addressed to Christians still on earth, and that such Christians didn't join in the present acclamation. No Christians are left on earth. At this point they're all in heaven.

19:9–10: And he [the angel of 17:1, 7, 15] **says to me, "Write** [as follows]**: Fortunate** [are] **those who've been invited to the lamb's wedding banquet." And he says to me, "These words of God are true."** [10]**And I fell down at his feet to worship him. And he says to me, "See** [that you] **not** [do this]**. I'm your and your brothers' fellow slave,** [your brothers] **who hold the Testimony of Jesus. Worship God, for the Testimony of Jesus is the Spirit of prophecy."** "And he says to me" features a verb in the present tense and occurs three times in these two verses. The first occurrence stresses the command to write a beatitude ("Fortunate [are] . . .") and the beatitude itself. The writing ensures that the beatitude will come to pass; for "these words of God [the words of his beatitude] are true." Invitees to the wedding banquet of the lamb are fortunate because it's a celebratory meal that starts an eternity of living with the lamb. Corporately, true Christians constitute the lamb's wife. Individually, they constitute wedding guests. This shift from one figure of speech to another differs no more than the portrayals of Jesus as a bridegroom on the one hand and as a lamb on the other hand. The persistence of "lamb"-terminology keeps pointing to his death as a Passover sacrifice that makes possible this banquet, a kind of Passover meal (see the portrayal of Jesus as a Passover lamb throughout John's Gospel, starting in 1:29, 36; and compare the eating of Jesus' flesh and the drinking of his blood for eternal life in John 6:48–58). The wedding banquet takes place at the return of Jesus, for it's then that "the wedding of the lamb has come" (19:7). But the banquet as such gets no description, probably because it represents an eternity of celebration. A second "and he says to me" comes between the beatitude and the assurance that "these words of God are true." This interruption and the present tense of "says" underscore the assurance (compare John 17:17).

With John's falling down at the angel's feet to worship him compare the comments on 19:4. Here, "at his feet" probably implies an intention to kiss the angel's feet. In any case, the angel prohibits John from carrying out his intention in falling down. Only God and Jesus the lamb are to be worshiped (see 4:10; 5:8, 13–14, for example). The third "and he says to me" stresses the angel's prohibition. He derogates himself to the level of John's and other Christians' fellow slave, belonging to God, and describes Christians as those "who hold the Testimony of Jesus," which means both that they maintain their testimony *about* him and that they possess the Testimony who *is* Jesus, just as Jesus is the Word (see the comments on 1:2

with 1:9). And just as "the Word [Jesus] was *God*" (John 1:1), so too "the Testimony of Jesus is the *Spirit*." Put these statements together, and you have the doctrine of the Trinity. "Of prophecy" describes the Spirit in terms of his generating John's visions (1:10; 2:7; 3:1; 4:2; 14:13; 17:3; 21:10; 22:6, 17). Since the Testimony who is Jesus is the Spirit of prophecy, when Jesus is testifying the Spirit is prophesying, and vice versa. The unity of Jesus as the Testimony with the Spirit of prophecy gives the reason for worshiping God. For only in Jesus and the Spirit can true worship of God take place (see John 4:24 with comments: "God is Spirit, and it's necessary that those who worship him worship [him] in Spirit and truth").

JESUS' SECOND COMING
Revelation 19:11–16

In 19:1–10 John *heard* about a lamb, a wife, a wedding, a wedding banquet, and invitees to it. Now he'll *see* about a warrior-ruler, armies, a battle, a grisly banquet, and invitees to it. The lamb turns into a warrior-ruler and the wife into his armies, so that a battle is added to the wedding and a grisly banquet for birds of carrion is added to the wedding banquet for followers of the lamb.

19:11–13: And I saw heaven opened [= in an opened state, not in the process of being opened]**. And behold, a white horse and sitting on it the one called faithful and true! And with righteousness** [in the sense of justice] **he's judging and making war** [compare Isaiah 11:3–4]**.** [12]**And his eyes** [are]**, as it were, a flame of fire. And on his head** [are] **many diadems,** [he] **having a name written that no one knows except for him;** [13]**and** [he] **was clothed with a garment that had been dipped in blood. And his name is called the Word of God** [that is, he's the Word of God; so that's the name by which he's called (compare 1:2, 9; 6:9; 20:4)]. The heaven was opened to let Jesus and his armies come down (compare 11:19; 15:5). "Behold" functions like an exclamation mark that showcases the white horse and its rider. As in 6:2 the whiteness of the horse symbolizes victory; and both passages feature a successful invasion from without (see the comments on 6:1–2). On the other hand, "faithful and true" distinguishes the present rider from the earlier one. For this description see the comments on 3:14; also 1:5; and compare 21:5; 22:6. As Jesus in 3:14 was faithful to his high priestly role and true in describing the deplorable state of affairs in the Laodicean church, he'll now be faithful to his role as judge and warrior and true in rectifying the unjust state of affairs in the non-Christian world. He judges—that is, punishes—*by* making war. The present tense of these verbs portrays the punishment of his and the saints' enemies as so sure that it might as well be happening right now. For the comparison of his eyes to "a flame of fire" see the comments on 1:14; 2:18. The diadems on his head represent rulership. They appear to be stacked on top of one another. The dragon had seven diadems, but only one per head (12:3). The beast out of the sea had ten diadems, but only one per horn (13:1). The indefinitely large number of diadems on Jesus' head ("many") symbolizes the universal reach of his rule. It knows no limit. Since to know someone's name, especially the name of a deity or a demon, was to possess a certain power over him, Jesus' "having a name written that no one knows except for him" means that he can't be overpowered (see the more extensive comments on 2:17 and the refusal of God to give his name to Jacob in Genesis 32:29 and the angel of the Lord's similar refusal in Judges 13:17–18). Is this name written on his many diadems as the names of the first beast were written on his heads (but not on his diadems)? John doesn't say so, perhaps because a visible inscription would make the name publicly known. Otherwise, the name is written on Jesus' head or diadems but remains undecipherable.

Isaiah 63:3 provides something of a background for Jesus' being "clothed with a garment that has been dipped in blood." But there the blood was of the Lord's enemies. Here Jesus' enemies aren't slain quite yet. Nor can his garment be stained with the blood of his martyrs, for their blood would make him responsible for their martyrdoms whereas the crimson color of the first beast and of the big whore's clothing (17:3–4; 18:16) made them responsible for those martyrdoms. So we're left with Jesus' blood. According to 7:14 the saints washed their robes white in the blood of the lamb. But the garment he wears is dyed with his blood just as his resurrected body still bears the scars of crucifixion (5:6; John 20:20, 24–27). In addition to his name that's unknown to all but himself, he's called "the Word of God"—not only the Word that God speaks and the Word who speaks about God, but also the Word who *is* God (see John 1:1, 18 and, with comments, John 10:35). John introduces this name here because Jesus represents and conveys "the true words of God" (19:9). As will be symbolized by a sharp sword issuing out of his mouth, however (19:15), here he'll speak a harsh word of judgment rather than the word "full of grace and truth" that he spoke in his first coming (John 1:14, 17).

19:14–16: And the armies in heaven, clothed in white, clean fine linen, were following him on white horses. [15]And out of his mouth is issuing a sharp sword in order that with it he should strike the Gentiles [in the sense of non-Christians, whether Jewish or non-Jewish, as opposed to Christians as true Jews (see especially chapter 7)]. And he'll shepherd them with an iron rod [that is, rule them rigorously and, when necessary, punitively (see the comments on 12:5)], and he's stomping the winepress of the wine [consisting] of the rage of the wrath of God Almighty. [16]And he has a name written on his garment, that is, on his thigh [= written on his garment midway between his knees and his hips]: "King of kings and Lord of lords." Since 19:8 described the lamb's wife—that is, Christians—as arrayed in "bright, clean fine linen," the description of Jesus' armies as arrayed similarly identifies them as Christians. Here, "white" replaces "bright" to match the whiteness of their horses, which matches in turn the whiteness of Jesus' horse and thus signifies their sharing in his victory, which the color white symbolizes. For "clean fine linen"

see the comments on 19:8, and for the "sharp sword" that's "issuing out of his mouth" see the comments on 1:16. To strike the Gentiles with this sword is to issue a sharp judicial sentence. Shepherding non-Christians with an iron rod contrasts dramatically with the lamb's shepherding Christians by leading them "to the springs of the water of life" (7:17). And the figure of shepherding with an iron rod shifts to stomping grapes in a winepress. "The big winepress of God's rage" was referenced in 14:19 (see the comments there). To heighten the fearsomeness of this judgment John uses the present tense ("is stomping") and piles one phrase on top of another ("the winepress of the wine [consisting] of the rage of the wrath of God") and then adds "Almighty" to point up the irresistibility of God's raging wrath. Warriors wore their swords on their thighs (see Exodus 32:27; Judges 3:16, 21; Psalm 45:3; Song of Solomon 3:8). But Jesus' sword issues out of his mouth. Replacing a sword on his thigh, then, is a name written on his garment: "King of kings and Lord of lords." The present tense in "he *has* a name" highlights the name's importance. See the comments on 17:14, where this name has already appeared. But not as there, "King of kings" precedes "Lord of lords" to prepare for a focus on the kings of the earth (19:18–19). The numerical value of this name adds up to 777 when written in Aramaic without "and," but John makes nothing of it as he does make something of 666 in 13:18. Better to leave that interpretation aside, then.

THE DEFEAT OF THE BEAST, FALSE PROPHET, KINGS OF THE EARTH, AND THEIR ARMIES
Revelation 19:17–21

19:17–18: And I saw a single angel standing in the sun; and he shouted in a loud voice, saying to all the birds that were flying in midsky, "[Come] here! Gather together for God's big banquet [18]in order to eat the flesh of kings and the flesh of commanders and the flesh of strong [men] and the flesh of horses and of those sitting on them and the flesh of all kinds of [people], both free and slave, both small [lacking prominence] and great [possessing prominence]." In 18:21 John described "a strong angel" as "single" to emphasize that the angel was strong enough to pick up a huge boulder by himself and throw it into the sea. Here he describes an angel as "single" to emphasize that by himself the angel outshines the sun and so can be seen despite "standing in the sun." Or is it that standing in the sun compares his glory to the sun's brightness? In either case, we're reminded of that very comparison in reference to Jesus' glory at 1:16; 10:1; 21:23; 22:5. So can this angel, like the ones already in 1:1; 7:2; 8:3–5; 10:1–11; 14:17–19; 18:1, 21, be Jesus? Why not? He has appeared earlier in chapter 19 as a lamb, as a bridegroom, as a royal warrior, and as a royal shepherd—now as a messenger. For "angel" means "messenger." He "shouted in a *loud* voice" so as to be heard by "*all* the birds that were flying in midsky." Flying there portrays them as birds of carrion—vultures, for example—circling directly over a battlefield and waiting to swoop down on prey, the corpses of slain troops. The angel's message gives them encouragement and calls the coming slaughter "God's big banquet" for the birds—"big," because the sword issuing out of Jesus' mouth will slay the whole of the armies mustered to make war with him and his armies. None of these armies will escape, no matter what their rank or station in life. Throw in horsemeat too. Adding to the grisliness of God's big banquet for the birds (and what a contrast with the joyous wedding banquet of the lamb!) is the plural of "flesh" in John's original Greek: literally, "the fleshes of kings and the fleshes of commanders [and so on]." You can picture the vultures tearing pieces of flesh out of a corpse and eating them (compare Ezekiel 39:17–20, and contrast the eating of Jesus' flesh [singular] in John 6:48–56 as a symbol of believing in him for eternal life).

19:19–21: And I saw the beast [see 13:1–10] **and the kings of the earth** [see especially chapters 17–18] **and their armies gathered together to make war with** [= against] **the one sitting on the horse and with his army. ²⁰And the beast was seized and along with him the false prophet who'd performed signs in his sight, by which** [signs] **he deceived those who'd taken the mark of the beast, that is, who'd been worshiping his image** [see 13:11–18 with comments]. **The two** [of them] **were thrown alive into the lake of fire burning with sulfur. ²¹And the rest were killed by the sword of the one sitting on the horse,** [by the sword] **that issued out of his mouth. And all the birds were sated with their flesh** [= the flesh of the rest of those gathered against the faithful and true Word of God and his army]. Ironically, the beast, the kings, and their armies "gathered together" to make war against Jesus and the saints without knowing that the birds had been told to "gather together" to feast on the carrion of these very kings and their armies. But since Christians have gone to heaven, it seems that the beast and his client kings muster their armies for war because they do know that Jesus has started to return with the Christians. What the beast and the king intended to be a battle turns out to be a capture of the beast, the final emperor of chapters 13 and 17 (or the Antichrist, as he's called in 1 John 4:3), and of the false prophet (as in 16:13, an identification of the second beast in chapter 13), plus a wholesale slaughter of their armies. The false prophet's past performance of signs in the beast's sight and resultant deception of the beast-worshipers contrast with Jesus' performance of signs throughout John's Gospel and with the description of Jesus here in 19:11 as "faithful and true." "Who worshiped the beast" defines "the mark of the beast" as symbolic of that worship rather than physical in character (compare the comments on 13:16–17).

The usual "and" fails to introduce the sentence, "The two [of them] were thrown alive into the lake of fire burning with sulfur." The consequent abruptness is jolting, as a statement of such judgment should be. "Alive" implies conscious torment such as 14:10–11 described in detail. "The lake of fire" produces a frightful contrast with the

heavenly sea of ice (4:6) on which the raptured saints stood before returning with Jesus (15:2). Better to stand on the ice of a frozen sea than to drown in the fire of a lake. "Burning with sulfur" adds stench to pain. Since the kings and their armies "were killed by the sword . . . that issued out of his [Jesus'] mouth," and since that sword symbolizes a judicial condemnation, the slaughter takes place through the utterance of a destructive word spoken by the one called "the Word of God," just as conversely "all things came into being" by the utterance of a creative word spoken by the Word who was God (see John 1:1–3 with Genesis 1:3–27). "The rest were killed" but will be raised for the Last Judgment following a thousand years (chapter 20). Meanwhile the throwing of the beast and the false prophet into the lake of fire burning with sulfur previews the ultimate fate of the rest who were killed and will be raised for that judgment, just as the death and resurrection of Jesus previewed the fate of his followers (concerning the lake of fire burning with sulfur, see the comments on 20:14–15).

THE MILLENNIUM
Revelation 20:1–10

This passage divides into the binding of Satan for a thousand years (20:1–3), the reign of Christ and the saints for that period (20:4–6), and the loosing of Satan, a rebellion, and its defeat at the end of the period (20:7–10).

20:1–3: And I saw an angel descending out of heaven, having the key to the abyss and a big chain on his hand. ²And he grabbed the dragon—the ancient serpent, who is the Devil and Satan—and bound him [with the chain] **for a thousand years ³and threw him into the abyss and locked and sealed** [it] **over him lest he mislead the Gentiles** [= non-Christians] **any more till the thousand years be finished. After these things it's necessary that he be released for a little while.** The angel's "descending out of heaven" recalls the very same in 10:1 and 18:1, in both of which passages we found ample reason to identify the angel as Jesus at his second coming. And the present angel's "having the key to the abyss" recalls 1:18, where Jesus said he has "the keys of death and of hades," both of which entities figure later here in chapter 20 (see also the comments on 9:1 and compare 3:7). Therefore John is seeing again a vision of Jesus' second coming, as he did in 19:11–21, but now in relation to what happens to Satan at that event whereas 19:11–21 had to do with what happens then to the beast, the false prophet, the kings of the earth, and their armies (contrast especially the throwing of the beast and the false prophet *into the lake of fire* [19:20] with the throwing of Satan *into the abyss* [on which see 9:2, 11 with comments]). Because Satan is "a *big* dragon" (12:3, 9), to chain him up Jesus has to have "a *big* chain." "*On his* hand" means that the chain is looped across his hand (and then hangs down, of course). In 12:9 the big dragon Satan was thrown onto the earth from heaven. Here he's thrown from the earth into the abyss. See the comments on 12:9 for the dragon as "the ancient serpent, who is the Devil and Satan." The locking and sealing of the abyss over him join his being chained to put a triple emphasis on his confinement (compare the abyss's having to be unlocked to let out the demonic locusts in 9:1–3). No one can loosen a chain Jesus has fastened, open a hatch he has locked, or break a seal he has pressed. "Lest he [Satan] mislead the Gentiles *any more* till the thousand years were finished" implies that the thousand years follow the second coming. For during the preceding church age Satan keeps busy, and his business includes misleading (2:9–10, 13, 24; 3:9; 12:1–17; 13:1–4; 16:12–16). So his millennium-long confinement can hardly symbolize the church age. Since other numbers in Revelation are symbolic (as in the case of the 144,000, for example [see the comments on chapter 7]), the one thousand years are probably to be taken as symbolizing a long time. The repetition of this number could imply a literal millennium, but could equally well emphasize the symbolism. The necessity of Satan's release after the thousand years arises out of God's plan. The reigning of the saints over the Gentiles during the millennium suggests he thinks it necessary that the saints get requited for having suffered at the Gentiles' (= non-Christians') hands. The "little while" of Satan's period of release contrasts with the preceding thousand years of his confinement and with the following eternity of his torture (20:10).

20:4–5a: And I saw thrones, and people sat on them, and judgment was given to them; and [I saw] **the souls of those who'd been beheaded because of the Testimony of Jesus and because of the Word of God. And whoever hadn't worshiped the beast or his image and hadn't taken the mark** [of the beast] **on** [their] **forehead and on their hand** [sat on thrones, and judgment was given to them]. **And they came alive and reigned as kings with the Christ for a thousand years.** ⁵ᵃ**The rest of the dead didn't come alive till the thousand years were finished** [compare 2:26–27; 3:21; Ezekiel 37; Daniel 7:9–27]. Sitting on thrones symbolizes rulership, of course. Since 1:6 and 5:10 portrayed Christians as a kingdom of kings who'll rule over the earth, the people who sit on these thrones are Christians; and their subjects are the non-Christians ("Gentiles") of 20:3 whom Satan can't mislead any more till the thousand years are finished. During this millennium Christians will make judicial decisions concerning them ("judgment [of non-Christians] was given to them") just as during the preceding age of the church non-Christians made judicial decisions concerning the Christians. Implied: not all non-Christians were slain at the second coming in 19:11–21—rather, only the armies of the kings of the earth—and the rest passed into the millennium. "The souls of those who'd been beheaded because of the Testimony of Jesus and because of the Word of God" recalls "the souls of those who'd been slain because of the Word of God and because of the Testimony that they'd held" in 6:9–11. See the comments on that passage, and on 1:2, 9 for testifying about the Testimony who is Jesus and preaching about the Word who is Jesus, "Testimony" and

"Word" being capitalized to indicate titles for him. Beheading was a typical Roman method of execution, especially for Roman citizens such as the Apostle Paul, who according to early church tradition suffered martyrdom by that method. The singling out of martyrs for special mention has the purpose of encouraging Christians who face martyrdom as a possibility and, in many cases, as an actuality (today as well as in John's day). But "whoever hadn't worshiped the beast [and so on]" broadens out the reference to Christians in general, as initially ("people sat on them [the thrones]"). "Souls" alluded to disembodiment by martyrdom (as in 6:9); but "they came alive" refers to bodily resurrection of Christians, both martyrs and nonmartyrs, as a prelude to "reign[ing] as kings . . . for a thousand years" (compare 2:8). The reigning draws out the implication of sitting on thrones and being given judgment. "With the Christ" alludes to his messianic reign (compare 11:15, 17) and makes Christians his client kings just as the beast had "the kings of the earth" as his clients. Since Christians came alive at the start of the thousand years, "the rest of the dead" who "didn't come alive till the thousand years were finished" are non-Christians (compare John 5:28–29).

20:5b–6: This [is] **the first resurrection.** ⁶**Fortunate and holy** [= consecrated to God] [is] **the person who has part in the first resurrection. Over these** [participants] **the second death has no authority. On the contrary, they'll be priests of God and of the Christ; and they'll reign as kings with him for a thousand years.** "The first resurrection" implies a second resurrection yet to come. Participants in the first one are fortunate because they won't suffer the second death of the fiery lake. "Over these the second death has no *authority*" personifies the second death. (Translations that have "power" instead of "authority" obscure the personification slightly.) "They'll be priests of God" echoes 1:6; 5:10, where their priesthood was paired with rulership, as here (see the comments on 1:6 for interpretation, and compare Isaiah 61:6). "And of the Christ" pairs Jesus with God as the object of priestly worship and thus comports with the deity of Jesus that John stresses throughout his writings. "*The* Christ" (= "the anointed one") points up the status of Jesus as the one whom God anointed with his Spirit to be the King of kings and Lord of lords. A second mention of reigning with the Christ for a thousand years reencourages Christians to endure martyrdom, if necessary, rather than apostatizing.

20:7–8: And when the thousand years are finished, Satan will be released from his prison ⁸**and go out to mislead the Gentiles in the four corners of the earth, Gog and Magog, to gather them together for the war, whose number** [will be] **as the sand of the sea.** In other words, "Gentiles" will be comparable in number to the grains of sand on the seashore (compare Joshua 11:4; 1 Samuel 13:5). "Prison" substitutes for "abyss" (20:1–3), because the abyss has been locked up like a prison. According to 12:9 Satan was misleading "the whole inhabited [earth]." Here he goes back to his business of misleading people, called "the Gentiles," non-Christians living "in the four corners of the earth," which means all over the earth (7:1). Therefore "Gog and Magog," which originally referred to a prince (Gog) and a far northern region (Magog) that he ruled (see Ezekiel 38–39, especially 38:1–3; 39:1–2), now stands for the enemies of God's people wherever they live. "To gather them together for the war" reenacts after the millennium a similar gathering prior to it (see 19:19; also 16:14, 16). "*The* war" hints that this war carries forward the earlier war, which was scarcely fought since the beast and the false prophet were immediately captured and the kings of the earth and their armies were slain without a fight by Jesus' utterance of a judgmental word. The number of the present Gentiles is like the grains of sand on the seashore because Gog and Magog are spread over the whole earth.

20:9–10: **And they went up on the breadth of the earth and encircled the saints' camp, that is, the beloved city. And fire came down out of heaven and devoured them. [10]And the Devil, who'd been misleading them, was thrown into the lake of fire and sulfur, where both the beast and the false prophet [are] and [where] they'll be tormented day and night forever and ever.** "The breadth of the earth" means the whole wide earth (compare its "four corners" in 7:1; 20:8). "Camp" ordinarily means a military camp, the present passage has a military cast, and the portrayal of Christians as the true Israel (see especially chapter 7) adds an allusion to ancient Israel's camping in a military arrangement of her tribes on their journey from Egypt to Canaan (Numbers 1:2–3; 2:1–34; see Revelation 7:4–8 for a military roll call of Christians and 14:4–5 for them as ritually pure soldiers [though their ritual purity symbolizes their moral and religious purity]). But just as "on the breadth of the earth" indicates that the Gentiles "went up" all over the wide earth, it also indicates that the saints are encamped all over the wide earth. We're not to think of a single location, then; and in anticipation of the New Jerusalem, "the beloved city" pictures the saints as a city (they *are* the city) beloved by God (compare 1 John 3:1–3; 4:19, for example) and thus consecrated ("holy") to him (compare the comments on 21:1–22:5 and the "going up" to old Jerusalem throughout the Old Testament, the Gospels, Acts, and Galatians 2:1–2). So wherever on earth Christians are living and ruling, the non-Christians muster under Satan's deceptive leadership to attack the Christians. Before they attack, though, fire comes down from heaven and devours the would-be attackers (compare 2 Kings 1:10, 12, 14; Ezekiel 38:22). "Fire . . . out of heaven" refers to lightning (compare the comments on 8:4–5, where lightning accompanied the second coming prior to the millennium). "Devoured them" compares the lightning's effect to the consumption of food (compare 11:5). The rebels are thus killed only to be quickly resurrected for the Last Judgment in 20:11–15. The Devil doesn't have a body to be killed, though. So incapable of resurrection, he's thrown immediately into the lake of fire and sulfur to join there his protégés, the beast and the false prophet (see the com-

ments on 19:20; 20:14–15 for the lake of fire and sulfur). "They" who'll "be tortured day and night forever and ever" refers to this unholy trinity.

THE LAST JUDGMENT
Revelation 20:11–15

20:11: **And I saw a big white throne and the one who was sitting on it, from whose face the earth and the heaven fled away. And no place was found for them.** The throne is big to represent the universality of the reign of God and his Christ (12:10 [compare "the big winepress of God's rage" in 14:19]). The throne's color, white, symbolizes the victory just won over the rebels (for this symbolism see, for example, 2:17 with comments). John doesn't say who was sitting on the throne. Usually God the Father is in view. But Jesus sits there with him (3:21; 7:17; 12:5; 22:1, 3), and according to John 5:22 "the Father . . . has given all judgment to the Son." The earth and the heaven flee away as though they were persons struck with fear of the throne-sitter. Their flight symbolizes the doing away of the old earth and old heaven in preparation for the "new heaven and new earth" (21:1). Here the earth gets mentioned before heaven because the scene of judgment is set on earth (another reason to regard the throne-sitter as Jesus, who has descended to the earth), whereas in 21:1 the new heaven gets mentioned before the new earth because according to 21:2 the New Jerusalem will "descend out of heaven from God." "And no place was found for them [the old earth and heaven]" continues the personification, indicates their disappearance, and might even imply a failed search for them (contrast 12:6, 14, but compare 12:8; 16:20). Since this judgment has to take place somewhere and since the sea, Death, and Hades (the underworld) have yet to give up their dead (20:13), John has apparently advanced for emphasis the disappearance of the old earth and heaven.

20:12: **And I saw the dead, the great** [possessing prominence] **and the small** [lacking prominence], **standing within sight of the throne.** "The great and the small" indicates a socially all-inclusive judgment. As forecast in 20:5 and evident in 5:6; 7:9; 15:2 (among other passages), "standing" indicates that "the dead" have been resurrected. "Within sight of the throne" indicates proximity to it. **And scrolls were opened** [compare Isaiah 65:6; Daniel 7:10]**; and another scroll was opened, which is** [the scroll] **of life** [compare Isaiah 4:3; Daniel 12:1]**; and the dead were judged according to their deeds by the things written in the scrolls.** The deeds recorded in the scrolls tell whether the doers of those deeds were Christians (see 2:23; 14:13; 22:12 among other passages). It takes more than one scroll to record the multiple deeds of everybody, but only one "scroll of life" to record the names of true Christians. "According to their deeds" underlines the justice of this judgment and thus warns the ungodly and encourages the righteous. The juxtaposition of the scrolls of deeds and the scroll of life strikes a balance between human moral responsibility and divine predestination (see the comments on 17:8 for the latter in connection with the scroll of life).

20:13: And the Sea gave up the dead [that were] **in it, and Death and Hades gave up the dead** [that were] **in them. And each** [of the resurrected dead] **was judged according to their deeds.** "Gave up the dead," which occurs twice, backs up to tell how it came about that John saw the dead—non-Christians, who as such didn't participate in the first resurrection (20:4–6)—standing, and therefore resurrected, close to the big white throne. "Gave up" also personifies "the Sea" along with "Death and Hades" (see the comments on 6:7–8 for Death and Hades as divinities of a sort in Greek mythology). First mention of the Sea stresses that those lost or drowned at sea and therefore never given a proper burial—even they won't escape judgment. For a second time "judged according to their deeds" affirms the justice of this judgment, this time with an added accent on its individuality and universality ("each [of the resurrected dead]").

20:14–15: And Death and Hades were thrown into the lake of fire. This is the second death, the lake of fire. In other words, being thrown into the lake of fire constitutes dying a second time. [15]**And if someone wasn't found written in the scroll of life, he was thrown into the lake of fire** [not to be confused with "the abyss" of 20:1, 3 and earlier]. The throwing of Death and Hades into the lake of fire completes their personification. They represent the *first* death and its aftermath (disembodied existence in the underworld). The first death dies in that everybody has died once; and there's no more need for hades in that all disembodied souls, who used to reside there, have received resurrected bodies. Only the possibility of eternal life or a second death remains. "If someone wasn't found written in the scroll of life" implies the presence of Christians as well as non-Christians at this last judgment, and also implies a search for names lest anyone be mistakenly thrown into the lake of fire. For the scroll of life see the comments on 3:5. Lakes consist of water, and water puts out a fire. So "the lake of fire" presents a contradiction in terms. But just as all deliberately created oxymorons make for an emphasis of one kind or another, the very contradiction in "the lake of fire" underlines the severity of punishment. Could it be, on the other hand, that the Dead Sea provides some background in real life? The Dead Sea is really a lake. At its southern end the Lord rained down sulfur and fire on Sodom and Gomorrah, so that smoke "ascended like the smoke of a furnace" (compare 14:10–11 with Genesis 19:24–25, 28); and Lot's wife turned into a pillar of salt during the episode (Genesis 19:26). The lake's location in the lowest spot on earth contrasts with Mount Zion, the eternal dwelling place of the redeemed (compare 14:1 with 21:10); and the extreme heat resulting in large part from low elevation sends up smoke-like haze. Furthermore, the saltiness of the lake can burn the skin, and the lake can smell sulfurous. Appropriately, the person who followed the beast, the false prophet, and the Devil will follow them into the lake of fire.

THE NEW HEAVEN, THE NEW EARTH, AND THE NEW JERUSALEM
Revelation 21:1–22:5

21:1–2: And I saw a new heaven and a new earth, for the first heaven and the first earth had gone away [compare 20:11: "the earth and the heaven fled away. And no place was found for them"]. **And the sea doesn't exist any more.** [2]**And I saw the holy city, the New Jerusalem, descending out of heaven from God, prepared as a bride adorned for her husband** [compare Isaiah 48:2; 49:18; 52:1–10; 61:10; 62:1–5; 65:17–19; 66:22; Ezekiel 16:6–14]. The first heaven had a sea of ice in which the forces of evil and chaos were frozen into immobility (see the comments on 4:6; 15:2); and the first earth had a sea out of whose chaotic waters came the first beast, the enemy of Christians (13:1). Since that beast has been thrown into the lake of fire along with his false prophet and their sponsor, the dragon Satan (19:20; 20:10), the sea, which represented the pernicious activity of that unholy trinity, doesn't exist any more either on the new earth or in the new heaven. That is to say, the forces of evil and chaos are no longer active on earth and don't even need to be immobilized in heaven. Stressing this point is the use of the present tense for a future state of affairs: "*doesn't* exist any more."

"Prepared as a bride adorned for her husband" echoes 19:7: "his [the lamb's wife] has prepared herself." The preparation had to do with her "be[ing] clothed with bright, clean fine linen; for the fine linen is the righteous acts of the saints" (19:8). There the saints made up the bride. Here, then, the preparing of the city "as a bride adorned for her husband" equates the city with the lamb's wife and therefore with the saints. In other words, the city *is* the saints, so that a description of the city tells what they themselves will be like in their eternal state, not what their living quarters will be like. (They'll be living all over the new earth in their resurrected bodies.) John describes the city as "holy" because the city is "the saints" of 19:8; and by definition "the saints" means "the holy ones," an expression that has been used for Christians as consecrated to God from 5:8 onward. "The holy city" also recalls "the holy city" in 11:1–2, where the phrase referred to Christians (see the comments there) and hence confirmed in advance that John is now describing Christians themselves in terms of a city (see also 20:9 with comments). "The New Jerusalem" identifies "the holy city" in a way that recalls the comparison of Christians to Israel, whose capital was Jerusalem, located on Mount Zion (7:1–17; 14:1–5). The identification also strikes up a contrast with the big whore, Rome as the new Babylon (chapters 17–18). In 11:11–12 Christians were said to have ascended into heaven at the end of the great affliction (compare 14:14–16) so as to follow Jesus at his return in 19:11–14. So how come John sees them "descending out of heaven" in the form of the New Jerusalem a thousand years later? Well, the first heaven, from which they returned with Jesus, and the first earth, to which they returned with him, have both "gone away."

With the appearance of the new heaven, then, Christians find themselves there rather than on the new earth, for they've been "born . . . out of God" and thus "born from above" (John 1:12–13; 3:3, 7 [compare John 17:6, 14, 16]), so that they now descend from their place of heavenly origin to their place of earthly destination (compare 3:12). "From God" underscores this origin. Another question: Why does John use "bride" here but "wife" in 19:7 though there the wedding and the wedding banquet hadn't taken place quite yet? Answer: The use of "bride" here indicates that the wedding banquet is ongoing. It symbolizes an eternity of celebration for the saints (compare Isaiah 62:5).

21:3–4: And I heard a loud voice from the throne, saying, "Behold, the tent of God [is] with human beings; and he'll tent with them [compare 7:15; 13:6; Ezekiel 37:27; Zechariah 2:10–11 among other passages]**! And they'll be his peoples, and God himself will be with them."** The theme of God's presence with his people appears often in the Old Testament, famously in Isaiah 7:14. **"And he'll wipe away every tear out of their eyes, and there won't be death any more. Neither will there be grief or crying or pain any more, because the first things have gone away** [compare 7:17; Isaiah 25:6–9; 35:10; 51:10–11]**."** The voice comes from the throne and refers to God in the third person ("God," "he," "himself," and "his") rather than in the first person ("I," "myself," and "my"). But see the comments on 18:4–5 that God can refer to himself in the third person. "The throne" refers back to "the big white throne" of 20:11, occupied both by Jesus, acting there as the judge (compare 3:21; 7:17; 12:5; 22:1, 3), and by God his Father, acting here and in 21:5–8 as the speaker. God speaks loudly so as to be heard throughout the new heaven and the new earth that John has just seen. "Behold" punctuates the exclamation that God is now dwelling with the saints. But their being called "human beings" highlights the marvel that the God of heaven is dwelling on earth with them. "Tent" describes his dwelling with them to draw a parallel with his dwelling in a tent, traditionally called the tabernacle, among Israelites in the Old Testament (compare Exodus 29:44–45 [see again Revelation 7 for Christians as the true Israel; and compare John 1:1, 14 for the tenting "among us" of Jesus the Word, who was God]). "And they'll be his peoples" joins the double use of "tent," once as a noun and once as a verb, to further this parallel with ancient Israel. But the plural in "his peoples" points up a difference: ancient Israel consisted of one people, whereas the true Israel consists now of many peoples, just as in chapter 7 the 144,000 Israelites about whom John heard turned out to be, when he saw them, "a large crowd, which no one could number, from every nation and [from all] tribes and peoples and tongues." With the addition of "himself," the marvel of God's tenting with human beings gets further emphasis in "God *himself* will be with them." "He'll wipe away every tear out of their eyes" indicates God's tender comfort and the total absence henceforth of the grief, crying, and pain caused by death. "There won't be death any

more" because "Death and Hades were thrown into the lake of fire" (20:14). "The first things" that characterized the first heaven and the first earth—namely, grief, crying, and pain—"have gone away." Death, grief, and crying accompanied the fall of Roman Babylon (18:8–9, 11, 19), and pain accompanied one of the last plagues poured out on beast-worshipers (16:10–11). But here the extermination of death, grief, crying, and pain makes a special though not exclusive allusion to past martyrdom and its effects (see 2:10, 13; 6:9; 11:7 and so on). No more!

21:5–8: And the one sitting on the throne said, "Behold, I'm making all things new!" And he says, "Write [what you've just heard]**, because these words are faithful and true** [see 22:6; also 3:14; 19:9, 11]**." 6And he said to me, "They have come into being! I am the alpha and the omega, the beginning and the end. To the person who's thirsting I'll give as a gift** [water] **from the spring of the water of life** [compare Psalm 36:8; Isaiah 49:10; 55:1–2; Jeremiah 2:13]**. 7The person who conquers will inherit these things, and I'll be God for him, and he'll be a son for me** [compare Exodus 29:45; Leviticus 26:11–12; Jeremiah 31:33; Ezekiel 37:27; 43:7; Zechariah 8:8]**. 8But the craven and unbelieving and abominable and murderers and fornicators and practicers of magic arts and idolaters and all the liars** [have] **their part** [of inheritance] **in the lake burning with fire and sulfur, which is the second death."** "The one sitting on the throne" and speaking refers to himself as "God": "I'll be God for him . . . ." So we have confirmation that God was speaking about himself in 21:3–4. "Behold," the use of the present tense for a future event in "I'm making all things new," and a repetition of the essential thought of 21:1–2 put a strong accent on the certainty of a new creation to encourage sufferers of persecution, who might be tempted to despair. "*All* things new" covers the new heaven, new earth, and New Jerusalem of 21:1–2.

"And he says," which interrupts the words of God, indicates a shift from the announcement aimed at a general audience to the addressing of a command to John, an individual. The present tense of "says" stresses the command to write. Prophetic writing ensures fulfillment. The new creation is sure to come, because "these words are faithful [in the sense of trustworthy]"; and they're trustworthy because they're "true." "They" that "have come into being" are the new heaven and the new earth (compare John 1:3 for the use of this verb in connection with creation, as opposed to translations such as "It has happened" and "It is done"). The use of a past tense for a future event in "have come into being" puts even more emphasis on certainty of fulfillment than the present tense did in "I'm making all things new." See the comments on 1:8 for "I am the alpha and the omega" (also 1:17; 2:8; 22:13; Isaiah 41:4; 44:6; 48:12). "The beginning and the end" provides an interpretation in terms of Genesis 1:1: "In the beginning God created the heavens and the earth," though here in Revelation God *is* the beginning in that he began the new heaven and the new earth just as he began the first heaven and the first earth (compare John 1:1–3). And he's the end in that he ended the first heaven and the first earth along with their death, tears, grief, crying, and pain. With his giving the thirsty person a drink, compare 7:17; 22:17; John 4:13–14; 7:37–39. "The spring" connotes an ever-new supply of fresh water appropriate to the "new earth" (contrast the undrinkable salt water of the chaotic sea). "Of life" describes the water as flowing and connotes life that is eternally ongoing. "Give as a gift" puts double emphasis on eternal life as free of charge and agrees with the constant portrayal in John's Gospel and 1 John of eternal life as a gift to believers (contrast buying and selling in the beast's kingdom [13:17]).

As throughout chapters 2–3, "the person who conquers" refers to true Christians, those who haven't apostatized despite the pressure of persecution to do so (see also 1 John 2:13–14; 4:4; 5:4–5, and compare Jesus himself as a conqueror in Revelation 5:5; 17:14; John 16:33). Inheriting "these things" means inheriting the new heaven and the new earth and leads to God's saying that the conqueror will be "a son" for him. Sons get an inheritance. That statement and "I'll be God for him" echo the adoptive language of 2 Samuel 7:14: "I'll be a father to him [David's royal offspring], and he'll be a son to me" (compare the portrayal of Christians as a kingdom of kings in 1:6 and later and, on the other hand, as a bride and wife in 19:7; 21:2, 9; 22:17). But the use of "God" instead of "Father" links up with "God" as the one from whom the New Jerusalem descends out of heaven and whose tent is with human beings (21:2–3 [see John 20:17 for the possibility that "Father" could otherwise have been used here despite some commentators' statements to the contrary]). "Craven" describes people, including professing Christians, afraid to refuse the false prophet's demand that they worship the beast (13:11–18). "Unbelieving" describes people who don't believe in Jesus, including those who lack the faith to keep them faithful to their Christian profession. "Abominable" describes people, again including professing Christians, who commit the abomination of worshiping the beast and his image. "Murderers" describes especially those who kill Christians and perhaps includes professing Christians who betray fellow Christians to save their own necks (compare Matthew 24:10). "Fornicators" describes people who practice sexual immorality, especially in temples dedicated to worship of the beast and other false gods. "Practicers of magic arts" is self-explanatory but may also describe people who because of practicing such arts fall prey to the false prophet's use of these arts to mislead them into worshiping the beast and his image (see 13:11–15). "Idolaters" describes such worshipers. And "all the liars" contrasts with the 144,000, in whose mouths no lie was found (14:1–5), and describes people who mouth the lie that a Caesar, represented by a head of the beast, is a god. None of these liars, not even those who have professed to be Christians, will escape the second death; and the categories of fornicators, practicers of magic arts, and idolaters may likewise include false professors of Christian faith. Lying earns condemnation throughout John's writings. "*Which*

is the second death" may refer either to "their *part* in the lake" or to the "*burning* with fire and sulfur."

21:9–14: And one of the seven angels who had the seven bowls that were full of the seven last plagues came and spoke with me, saying, "[Come] here! I'll show you the bride, the lamb's wife." ¹⁰And he took me away in the Spirit onto a big and high mountain and showed me the holy city, Jerusalem, descending out of heaven from God, ¹¹having God's glory [compare Ezekiel 40:1–2 and, among other passages, Exodus 40:34–35; Isaiah 60:1–2, 19]. **Her luster** [is] **comparable to a very precious stone, like a jasper stone that's sparkling like crystal** [compare Isaiah 54:11–12], **¹²having a big and high wall, having twelve gates and at the gates twelve angels and names inscribed** [on the gates], **which are the names of the twelve tribes of the sons of Israel. ¹³[As one comes] from the east, [there were] three gates, and from the north three gates, and from the south three gates, and from the west three gates, ¹⁴and the wall of the city having twelve foundations and on them the twelve names of the lamb's twelve apostles.** "And one of the seven angels who had the seven bowls" echoes 17:1, where such an angel—perhaps the same one—showed John God's judgment on the big whore. "That were full of the seven last plagues" combines echoes of 15:1 and 15:7. To sharpen a contrast between Babylon and the New Jerusalem the same angel as before, or the same sort of angel, now shows John the city called "the bride, the lamb's wife" as he earlier showed him the city called "the big whore." The twofold designation, "the bride, the lamb's wife," combines "the lamb's wife" in 19:7 with the comparison to "a bride" in 21:2. The angel's taking John away in the Spirit recalls the same in 17:3, where it had to do with the big whore, and thus sharpens the contrast further. "Onto a mountain" contrasts with "into a wilderness" in 17:3. Location in a wilderness symbolized desertion of the big whore (Roman Babylon) by her clients (see the comments on 17:16). Location on a mountain symbolizes the bridal, wifely New Jerusalem as the city up and into which pilgrims will flock, just as pilgrims went up and into the old Jerusalem, located on Mount Zion. John is taken onto the mountain to see the New Jerusalem because the city will land there on its descent out of heaven, just as he was taken into a wilderness to see Babylon because it was located there. "Big and high" describes the mountain. It has to be big to accommodate the enormous size of the city (yet to be delineated), and it's high to symbolize its security. For cities built on mountaintops were more easily defended than those built on a plain, as Mesopotamian Babylon found out to its sorrow (Daniel 5).

John hears about a bride-wife; but he sees "the holy city, Jerusalem, descending out of heaven from God." This phraseology repeats 21:2 for emphasis (see the comments on that verse), though John omits the earlier "New" before "Jerusalem." Yet he adds "having God's glory" to introduce the comparison of "her luster" to "a very precious stone" (in general) and to "a jasper stone" (in particular) that's "sparkling like crystal." Since the bridal, wifely city consists of Christians, these comparisons symbolize that eternal wealth will replace the temporary poverty that Christians suffered under persecution (2:9). "Sparkling like crystal" suggests what we'd call a diamond. The "big and high wall" is thick and tall and thus enhances the saints' eternal security, already symbolized by location on a big and high mountain (compare Isaiah 26:1). Properly, the word translated "gates" means "gateways." But 21:21 will equate each gateway with a pearl. The pearls suit a gate better than they do a gateway because pearls can be used as gates to close a gateway. Why then does John use here the word for a gateway in reference to the pearly gate fitted to it? Answer: to indicate that the openings will never be closed, as though they have no gates (21:25). The twelve gates that have inscribed on them the names of Israel's tribes, which took their names after those of Israel's (Jacob's) twelve sons, add to the portrayal of Christians as the true Israel (see chapter 7 again). As God stationed the cherubim at the east of the garden of Eden to keep sinful humanity from the tree of life (Genesis 3:22–24), so angels stationed at each gate of the New Jerusalem will keep the ungodly from entering the city to eat fruit from the tree of life within her but allow the saints free access to do so (21:8, 24–27; 22:14–15). Each of the wall's four sides has three gates. The list reflects Ezekiel 48:30–34 and starts with the east side because the Old Testament tabernacle, to which the New Jerusalem corresponds, was entered from the east (but compare also the angelic Jesus' ascending from the east in 7:2). North seems to come naturally before south (compare Luke 13:29); and west comes last to frame north and south between east and west, so that the order of east–north–south–west echoes Ezekiel 42:15–20 and may reflect that Israel's enemies generally came from the eastnorth and from the westsouth. (Oriented to the poles, we would say northeast and southwest, but people then were oriented to the rising and setting sun.) "*From* the east . . . and *from* the north [and so forth]" may allude to saints' coming from all directions to make up the city that represents them (compare 7:9: "from every nation and [from all] tribes and peoples and tongues"), though insofar as chapter 7 compared the multiethnic church to Israel's twelve tribes we might think each Christian "tribe" (so to speak, but not denominationally) has its own gate through which to enter. The wall's twelve foundations aren't stacked on top of one another; rather, one foundation supports each of the twelve segments of the wall that result from its being pierced by the twelve gates. The names of the twelve apostles, one each on these foundations, correspond to the names of Israel's twelve tribes, one each on the gates, and confirm that the church, founded on the apostles and symbolized by the city, is the true Israel (see the comments on 14:2–5). "Of the lamb" describes the apostles, recalls Jesus' choice of them according to John 15:16, and points as often to him as the Passover sacrifice that takes away sin (1:29).

21:15–18: And the [angel] speaking with me had a gold measuring reed in order that he might measure the city, that is, her gates and her wall. **¹⁶And the city is laid out four-cornered, and her length [is] as much as also [her] width [compare Ezekiel 45:2]. And he measured the city with the reed at 12,000 stades [almost 1,400 miles]. Her length and width and height are equal. ¹⁷And he measured her wall at 144 cubits [about 216 feet]—a human measurement, which is the angel's [measurement]. ¹⁸And the material of her wall [is] jasper, and the city [is] pure gold, comparable to pure [= clear] glass.** In 11:1–2 measuring symbolized protection (see the comments there). Here it highlights the city's huge dimensions, which represent the saints as the true and enlarged Israel. The measuring reed in 11:1–2 wasn't gold because it had to do with the saints' poverty-stricken circumstances at the present time. The gold of the reed used here suits the wealth of the saints, symbolized by the city, in their eternal state. Gates are included with the wall in the measuring because the gates contribute to the length and width. "Laid out four-cornered" means that the city is laid out as a square, and the four corners picture the saints as drawn from the four corners of the earth (7:1; 20:8). The number 12,000 symbolizes the saints as the true and enlarged Israel. As in 7:4–8, twelve alludes to the number of Israel's tribes, and multiplication by a thousand underlines multitudinousness. The addition of equal height to equal length and width makes the city a cube, which has twelve edges, so that 12 x 12,000 comes to 144,000, just as in 7:4–8; 14:1. The squaring of twelve underlines completeness. Furthermore, a cubic shape makes the city (the saints) the Holy of Holies of the tent (the tabernacle) that God will pitch "with human beings" (21:3). He'll be with them because he'll indwell them just as he indwelt the cube-shaped Holy of Holies, the inner sanctum of the Old Testament tabernacle (compare 1 Kings 6:20). There the tabernacle was pitched among the Israelites, only one of whom (the high priest) could enter the Holy of Holies, and that only once a year, on the Day of Atonement (Leviticus 16). As the true Israelites in the coming eternity, Christians will *be* the Holy of Holies (compare the present anticipation of this indwelling at John 14:23; 15:4–5). That is to say, Christians will be God's most sacred dwelling place, the innermost room of his new creation, the ultimate in-group of people who are presently outsiders because they've come out of Babylon so as not to participate in her sins (18:4). For the encouragement of these current outsiders their coming cubical shape turns things outside in. Thus the whole of the city embodies the glory of God because the whole of the city is the Holy of Holies, filled as in the Old Testament with the glory of his presence.

A cubit is the length of a human forearm from the point of the elbow to the tip of the little finger (about eighteen inches)—thus "a human measurement" in that it's based on a part of the human anatomy.[1] But it's "the angel's [measurement]" too in that the angel used it. The wall measured 144 cubits. Again the number symbolizes

---

[1]There was a longer cubit, measuring about twenty-one inches. It was used mainly in Egypt, however.

the saints as the true Israel, 144 being the square of 12 (see the foregoing comments). Since the city's height of 12,000 stades far exceeds 144 cubits, the angel appears to have measured the wall's thickness rather than its height (compare Ezekiel 40:5); and this thickness makes the wall unbreachable, which is to say that the saints will never again be exposed to persecution. See the comments on 21:11 for "jasper," which along with "gold" represents the eternal wealth of Christians in compensation for the poverty they suffered under persecution (2:9; compare the overlaying of the Holy of Holies with pure gold in Solomon's temple [1 Kings 6:20]). The purity of the city's gold, which makes it as transparent as glass, means that this wealth will have been untainted by the economic injustices that besmirched the big whore's opulence (chapters 17–18).

21:19–21: **The foundations of the city's wall** [were] **adorned with every kind of precious stone** [compare Isaiah 54:11–12]. **The first foundation** [was] **a jasper, the second a sapphire, the third an agate, the fourth an emerald,** [superscript]20[/superscript]**the fifth an onyx, the sixth a carnelian, the seventh a peridot, the eighth a beryl, the ninth a topaz, the tenth a chrysoprase, the eleventh a jacinth, the twelfth an amethyst.** [superscript]21[/superscript]**And the twelve gates** [were] **twelve pearls. Each one of the gates consisted of a single pearl. And the wide** [square] **of the city** [is] **pure gold, as glass** [is] **transparent** [so that "pure gold" means "clear gold," as in 21:18]. The foundations were "adorned with every kind of precious stone" just as the city was "prepared as a bride adorned for her husband" (21:2), because the city, including her foundations, *is* the bride. The adornment of the foundations looks at first as though they were faced with gemstones. It turns out, though, that just as each gate consisted of a single, gigantic pearl, each of the foundations consisted of a single, gigantic gemstone supporting a segment of the wall ("The first foundation [was] a jasper [and so on]"), as plotted below (looking from above and leaving open spaces for the gateways):

These gemstones recall the twelve gemstones adorning the chestpiece of the Jewish high priest (Exodus 28:17–20; 39:10–14 [compare Ezekiel 28:13]) and thereby recall as well the description of Christians as God's priests (1:6; 5:10; 20:6). The twelve pearls that make up the twelve gates add to the symbolism of wealth, as does the gold of the city square (often interpreted as a main street, but see 11:8). The gold's purity, which makes it transparent like glass, pictures again the saints' eternal wealth as untainted by economic injustice (compare 21:18).

21:22–27: **And I didn't see a temple in her** ["temple" in the sense of a sanctuary proper]. **For the Lord God Almighty is her temple—also the lamb** [is her temple]. [superscript]23[/superscript]**And the city has no need of the sun or of the moon to illumine her, for the glory of God lights her up, and her lamp** [is] **the lamb.** [superscript]24[/superscript]**And the nations will walk by her light, and the kings of the earth are bringing their glory into her.** [superscript]25[/superscript]**And by no means will her gates be closed during daytime, for night won't be there.** [superscript]26[/superscript]**And they** [the saints as new kings of the earth] **will bring into her the glory and the affluence of the nations.** [superscript]27[/superscript]**And by no means will anything defiling and** [any-one] **who's doing an abomination and a lie enter into her, but only those who've been written in the lamb's scroll of life** [compare Isaiah 60, especially verses 3, 5, 11–12, 19–20; and Ezekiel 43:5]. Ordinarily a city has a temple, and certainly John expected to see one in the New Jerusalem, since the old Jerusalem had one. But he didn't see one. And ordinarily a god dwells in a temple. But here the Lord God Almighty and the lamb *are* the temple, so that the city, since it is the cubically shaped Holy of Holies, is located in the temple—a striking reversal of temples' usual location in cities. This reversal means that the saints will dwell in God and the lamb just as God and the lamb will dwell in them (22:3). We can see the correctness of this deduction by glancing at 3:12, where in reference to "the New Jerusalem" Jesus promised to make "the person who conquers" into "a pillar in the temple of my [Jesus'] God," which in view of 21:22 we should read as "the temple which *is* my God." And since the temple replaced the tent/tabernacle in the Old Testament, we should likewise understand "the tent of God" back in 21:3 to mean "the tent which *is* God," because he'll dwell "with human beings" forever and ever (compare his statement in 21:6 that he *is* the beginning, not just that he was *in* the beginning).

Just as God's glory filled Solomon's temple when the ark of the Lord's covenant had been brought into the cubically shaped Holy of Holies (1 Kings 8:10–11), so the glory of God lights up the city, whose temple he is, so that the saints, who are the city, don't need the sun or the moon. The temple, and before it the tabernacle, had the menorah to give interior light for the priests ministering there. The menorah supported seven lamps. But this new temple, which is the lamb as well as the Lord God Almighty, needs no lamp other than the lamb himself to give Christians, the new priests, interior light (contrast the non-Christian, who doesn't have "the light . . . *in him*" [John 11:10]). The unbelieving nations and kings of the earth have met their doom in the lake of fire (20:11–15). So the saints, redeemed from those nations, have themselves become nations who "will walk by her [the New Jerusalem's] light." And because "they'll reign as kings forever and ever" (22:5), they've become the new "kings of the earth," whole nations of kings, who "are bringing their glory into her [the New Jerusalem]" (see John 17:22 for Jesus' having given his glory to believers). They'll bring their glory into the city so as to *become* the glorious city. For apart from them the city doesn't exist. Because of the ever-present light of God and the lamb, no night will be there; and because no night will be there, the gates will never be closed. "Be closed" doesn't refer to a state of closure—rather, to the act of closing. This act would occur before nightfall, as indicated by "during daytime." But "by no means" stresses nonoccurrence because of the absence of night. The repetition of bringing "glory" into the city and the addition of "affluence" to "glory" put a second, heightened accent on the saints' eternal wealth, which will compensate for their prior poverty due to persecution. The accent on "bringing . . . into her" gets counterbalancing, warning accents on the exclusion of "anything defiling and [anyone] who's doing [= committing] an abomination and a lie" (about which see the comments on 21:8 [compare 1 John 1:6]) and on the entrance of "only those who've been written in the lamb's scroll of life" (about which see the comments on 3:5). There's entering but no exiting, for 3:12 says that "by no means will he [the conqueror] go out [of the temple] any more." No one will want to leave!

22:1-2: And he [the angel] **showed me the river of the water of life, bright** [= sparkling] **like crystal, issuing out from the throne of God and the lamb** [2] **in the middle of her** [the city's] **wide** [square]. **And on this and that side of the river** [was] **the tree of life, producing twelve fruits, yielding its fruit each month by each month; and the leaves of the tree** [are] **for the healing of the nations** [compare Genesis 2:10; Psalm 46:4; Ezekiel 47:1-12; Zechariah 14:8]. The river of the water of life doesn't flow beside the city or even through it from outer source to outer destination as in ancient Babylon. Rather, it wells up within the city, coming from the throne of God and the lamb, who indwell the cubical city of superlative holiness—that is, who indwell the saints ("the holy ones"). And suitably to the size of the city—that is, to the innumerability of the saints (7:9)—"the *spring* of the water of life" in 21:6 has swollen into "the *river* of the water of life," just as "a *spring* of water leaping up into eternal life" in John 4:14 swelled into "*rivers* of living water" in John 7:38. The light of God's glory (21:23) makes the water sparkle like crystal (compare the sparklingly bright, clean fine linen of the lamb's wife in 19:8). Issuance of the river from the throne of God and the lamb symbolizes that they give their own eternal life to the saints. The throne sits in the middle of the city square to symbolize again God's and the lamb's indwelling the city, which symbolizes in turn the saints (compare the location of the tabernacle, which contained God's throne—known as "the mercy seat" on the ark of the covenant—in the middle of ancient Israel's encampments during the wilderness wanderings [Numbers 2:1-2]). Again suitably to the saints' innumerability, the river is lined with multiple specimens of the tree of life, not just one such tree as in the garden of Eden (Genesis 2:9; 3:22, 24). "Twelve fruits" is often interpreted as meaning twelve varieties of fruit. But "the tree of life" symbolizes eternal life, pure and simple. So it's better to interpret "twelve fruits" as twelve crops of the same fruit, which is eternal life—thus "yielding its fruit [singular] each month by each month," that is, all year long without seasonal interrup-

tion. One crop per month from each tree produces a never-ending and therefore sufficiently large and eternal supply of life. The leaves of the tree of life contrast with the fig leaves that Adam and Eve used in the garden of Eden to cover their private parts (Genesis 3:7). The gowns of bright, clean fine linen that the saints are wearing (19:8) leave no need for fig leaves. But the leaves of the tree of life will be used as a poultice for the healing of the nations of redeemed peoples who make up the New Jerusalem—a promise of eternal good health for their resurrected bodies. Not that the saints will get sick—rather, preventive medicine to the utmost.

22:3-5: And no more will there be any curse; and the throne of God and of the lamb will be in her [the city]; **and his slaves will serve him** [4] **and see his face; and his name** [will be] **on their foreheads;** [5] **and night will be no more; and they** [God's slaves] **have no need of the light of a lamp and of the light of the sun, because the Lord God will shed light on them; and they'll reign as kings forever and ever.** For the redeemed, the promise of no more curse negates God's curse on fallen, sinful humanity in Genesis 3:16-19 and therefore follows naturally after allusions to the garden of Eden in Revelation 22:1-2 (Zechariah 14:11). The throne of God and of the lamb will be in the New Jerusalem—that is, among the saints, who will have descended out of heaven—no longer far off in heaven (7:15; 21:2). Jesus called his disciples his friends rather than his slaves (John 15:15). Hence "his slaves" means God's slaves rather than the lamb's slaves, so that the face they'll see is God's. No longer will it be said: "No one has seen God at any time" (John 1:18). They'll "serve him" means that his slaves will do priestly service of worship in the temple, which God and the lamb are, and in the cubical Holy of Holies, which the slaves are (compare Isaiah 61:6). For God's "name on their foreheads," see 7:3; 9:4; and especially 14:1. It seals them as his property, eternally exempt from his wrath. It was said in 21:25 that "night won't be *there*" (a matter of location). Now it's said that "night will be *no more*" (a matter of time [see John 9:4 for the present evil age as nighttime]). But there'll be night along with day for those tormented forever and ever in the lake of fire (14:10-11; 20:10). The contrast with God's continuous light repeats 21:23-24 for emphasis, though here "Lord," which means "Master," is added to "God" for a complement to "his slaves." And their reigning as kings forever and ever contrasts with the defeat of the non-Christian kings of the earth in 19:19-21 (compare 20:7-10).

CONCLUSION
Revelation 22:6-21

Making up this conclusion are assurances (22:6-7); an episode that ends with a command to worship God (22:8-9); further assurances, combined with warnings (22:10-16); invitations (22:17); a further warning (22:18-19); a yet further assurance combined with another invitation (22:20); and a benediction (22:21).

22:6–7: And he said to me, "These words [are] faithful and true. And the Lord, the God of the Spirits of the prophets, has sent his angel to show his slaves the things that must happen with speed. ⁷And behold, I'm coming quickly! Fortunate [is] the person who keeps the words of the prophecy of this scroll." "He" naturally refers to the angel that spoke with John in 21:9. "These words" refers to the whole book of Revelation (compare 22:18–19). The words are "faithful" in that they're worthy of belief, and they're worthy of belief because they're "true" (21:5 [compare 19:11–12 for a description of Jesus, who showed John the contents of Revelation, as "the Word of God" who is "faithful and true"; also 3:14]). "And the Lord . . . sent his angel to show his slaves the things that must happen with speed [and so on]" appears, however, to be John's own comment as a followup echoing 1:1–3, which refers not to the angel that spoke to John in 21:9 but to Jesus as the messenger (= "angel") whom God had "show to his slaves the things that must happen with speed" (1:1 [see the comments on 1:1–2 and compare the constant use of "send" for Jesus in John's Gospel, starting in 3:17, and in 1 John 4:9–10, 14]). "The Lord," which means "the Master," anticipates the following reference to "his slaves." "The God of the Spirits of the prophets" describes God in terms appropriate to the predictive element in "show[ing] his slaves the things that must happen with speed." Just as "the seven Spirits of God" in 1:4; 3:1; 4:5; 5:6 were the Holy Spirit distributed in his wholeness to each of the seven churches addressed in Revelation, so "the Spirits of the prophets" are the Holy Spirit distributed in his wholeness to each Christian prophet (and see the comments on 11:10, 18 for every Christian as a prophet). As in 10:17; 11:18 and the Old Testament (Jeremiah 7:25, for example), God's prophets are his slaves; and all Christians belong to God as his slaves (so 1:1 and following). "Behold, I'm coming quickly!" adds an echo of 1:7; 2:16. ("Behold" comes from 1:7, the rest from 2:16.) The beatitude ("Fortunate [is] . . .") echoes 1:3 (see the comments there).

22:8–9: And I, John, [am] the one who was hearing and seeing these things [compare 1:9–11]. And when I heard and saw [them], I fell down to worship before the feet of the angel who was showing me these things. ⁹And he tells me, "See [that you] not [do this]. I am a fellow slave [of God] with you and your brothers the prophets, that is, those who keep the words of this scroll. Worship God." This passage returns to the angel, one of the seven that had seven bowls full of the seven last plagues, who showed John the New Jerusalem (21:9). Since in 19:10 John mistakenly fell down to worship this or a similar angel and was told not to, you wonder whether John mistakes the angel here for the angelic Jesus, whom he has just referenced in an echo of 1:1–3. See the comments on 19:4, 10 for falling down to worship before the angel's feet. Since 11:10 characterized all Christians as prophets, "those who keep the words of this scroll" equate with "your brothers the prophets"; and "your brothers" means your fellow Christians in the family of God (1:9; 6:11; 12:10; 19:10; John 20:17; 21:23 and

often in 1 and 3 John), "brothers" being gender-inclusive as are also "bride" and "wife" (19:7; 21:9; 22:17). "Worship God" produces a punch line that by implication prohibits worship of the beast—that is, of the Caesars—and of any other supposed deity.

22:10–11: And he tells me, "You shouldn't seal up the words of the prophecy of this scroll. For the time [of fulfillment] is near. ¹¹The person who is doing unrighteousness is to do unrighteousness still; and the dirty person is to be dirtied still; and the righteous person is to do righteousness still; and the holy person is to be made holy still [compare Daniel 12:10]." "And he tells me" occurred also in 22:9, so that the present repetition seems to indicate that the angel who has just refused worship continues speaking to John. On the other hand, 22:12–16 will continue with no indication of a shift in speakers, yet Jesus is speaking in those verses ("Behold, I'm coming quickly . . . . I, Jesus"); and what's said in 22:10–11 would fall appropriately from his lips. So either the angel of 21:9; 22:9 continues speaking here and John will break in with a quotation of Jesus at 22:12, or Jesus starts speaking right here in 22:10. The present tense of "tells" stresses the following prohibition and pronouncements. "Don't seal up the words of the prophecy of this scroll" reverses 10:3–4 (which had to do with words unrecorded in this scroll, however) and has the purpose not only of ensuring the reading of these words in the churches addressed in 1:4, 11 but also of ensuring the quick fulfillment of the prophecy. For sealing up the words would at most cancel them (as in 10:3–4) and at least delay their fulfillment till an unsealing (as in Jesus' breaking open the seals of the seven-sealed scroll at 6:1–17; 8:1–5 [see also Daniel 12:4, 9]). But "the time [of fulfillment] is near." "Doing unrighteousness" is compared to moral dirtiness, and "do[ing] righteousness" is compared to moral sanctity. (Apart from association with unrighteousness and righteousness, "dirty" and "holy" have to do with ritual rather than moral opposites.) To do unrighteousness is to be morally dirtied. To do righteousness is to be morally sanctified (compare 19:8). "Still" looks to the future, and "is to do" and "is to be" deliver judgmental commands to the effect at this point in the prophetic timeline that it's too late for anyone's moral character to change, or that the great affliction will harden the unrighteous in their unrighteousness and confirm the righteous in their righteousness (compare 9:20–21; 16:8–11). The end has come. The last opportunity has become the lost opportunity. The judgmental commands are indirect: not "*do* unrighteousness still"—rather, "the person . . . *is* to do unrighteousness still." This indirection makes the command an observation spoken to third parties, rather than an address to the person who is supposed to obey. In this way the commands turn into a warning to the third parties to make sure now, before it's too late, that they don't fall into the category of an unrighteous, morally dirty person, and into an encouragement to the third parties to make sure now, before it's too late, that they do fall into the category of a righteous, morally holy person.

22:12–13: "**Behold, I'm coming quickly; and my wage** [is] **with me to give back** [in the form of payment] **to each person as his work is** [compare 2:23; 20:12; Proverbs 24:12; Isaiah 40:10]!" In other words, he'll get what he deserves. [13]"**I** [am] **the alpha and the omega, the first and the last, the beginning and the end.**" Obviously, Jesus is speaking. In 22:7 the exclamation that he's coming quickly was followed by a beatitude. Here it's accompanied by a warning or an encouragement (as the case may be in accordance with the immediately preceding references to doing unrighteousness and doing righteousness). The warning or encouragement arises out of Jesus' coming to pay people whatever wage they've earned during their lifetimes of unrighteous or righteous work. "To *each* person" stresses individual responsibility. Others' work won't affect your wage. Your own work alone will determine it (compare the promises to individual conquerors, regardless of the churches to which they belong, in chapters 2–3). To establish his authority for determining people's eternal fate, Jesus identifies himself as the alpha and the omega, that is, as the first and last letters of the Greek alphabet, which then symbolize his beginning all things at creation and his ending all things at the Last Judgment so as to give everybody their due. In 1:8; 21:6 God said, "I am the alpha and the omega." In 21:6 he also said, "I am . . . the beginning and the end." In 1:17; 2:8 Jesus said, "I am the first and the last." By putting these phrases all together here in 22:13 and especially by applying to himself those phrases that earlier applied to God, Jesus highlights his eternal deity, which qualifies him to determine people's eternal fate.

22:14–15: "**Fortunate** [are] **those who are washing their gowns so that theirs may be the authority over the tree of life and** [so that] **they may enter into the city by** [her] **gates** [compare John 10:7–9]. [15]**Outside** [are] **the dogs and the practicers of magic arts and the fornicators and the murderers and the idolaters and everyone who loves and does a lie.**" So far as can be told, Jesus continues speaking here (compare 22:16: "I, Jesus"). See the comments on 6:11; 7:13–14 for "gowns" and the washing of them. "Authority over the tree of life" means authority to eat its fruit—that is, to enjoy eternal life—and contrasts with the Lord God's barring access to this tree in Genesis 3:22–24 lest mankind "take from the tree of life and eat and live forever" in a morally disastrous state of sin. "Enter[ing] into the city [the New Jerusalem] by [her] gates" joins that authority to define the fortune of "those who are washing their gowns." It's a good fortune. To be outside the city isn't to be outside it on earth. It means to be on earth not at all—rather, in the lake of fire. For the city is made up of the saints, the royalized nations of the redeemed who populate the whole of the new earth. There's no room for anyone else. The list of outsiders, who are the former insiders of the big whore Babylon, parallels to a considerable extent the list in 21:8. But the "craven" and the "unbelieving" who headed that list drop out here, and "dogs" replaces the "abominable," who came next in 21:8, and echoes Deuteronomy 23:17–18, where "a dog" parallels "a sodomite"

and where "the wages of a dog" complements "the hire of a whore" and is described along with the latter as "an abomination to the Lord your God" (see 1 Kings 14:24 for another pairing of sodomites with abominations). The use of "dogs" here and of "abomination" in 21:8 indicates, then, that Jesus is using "dogs" as an epithet for sodomites. The remainder on this list appear in an order different from that in 21:8, except for the last two (see the comments on 21:8).

22:16: "**I, Jesus, have sent my angel to testify to you** [plural] **these things concerning the churches** [= the seven churches addressed in chapters 1–3]. **I am the sprout and the scion of David, the bright morning star** [compare Numbers 24:17]." According to 1:1; 22:6 *God* sent Jesus as his angel (= messenger). Here *Jesus* has sent his angel "to testify . . . these things"; and in 22:18 the "I" who testifies will seem to be Jesus, "the one who is testifying these things" in 22:20 and saying, "Yes, I'm coming quickly!" Therefore we should understand Jesus' angel in the way we understand "the angel of the Lord" in the Old Testament, not as a messenger distinct from the Lord—rather, as the Lord in the form of a messenger (for the Lord's "sending" his angel see Genesis 24:7, 40; Exodus 23:20 with 23:23; Daniel 3:28; 6:22). Jesus' angel is Jesus in the form of a messenger, then; and for him as a witness who testifies see 1:5; 3:14; John 3:11, 31–33; 4:44 and so on. But who are "you" (plural) to whom he has testified "these things concerning the churches"? Since in chapters 2–3 Jesus dictated a message concerning each church to its "messenger" (see the comments on 1:20), he sent his angel, his alter ego, to testify these things to those messengers. And it's appropriate that he identify himself as "the bright morning star" to the messengers, because he identified them as "the seven stars" that John saw in Jesus' right hand (1:16, 20). "These things concerning the churches" include the whole of Revelation, not just chapters 2–3. For the rest, too, affects the churches. "The scion of David" describes Jesus as the descendent of a famous family—here, David's. See the comments on 5:5 for "the sprout . . . of David," and on 2:28 for Jesus as "the . . . morning star." Here he adds "bright" to suit the sparkling glory of the New Jerusalem. Though Venus is also the evening star, the city will have no night and therefore no evening star—only Jesus as the bright morning star signifying the eternal dawn of a new heaven and a new earth.

22:17: **And the Spirit and the bride are saying, "Come." And the person who hears is to say, "Come." And the person who is thirsting is to come. The person who wants to is to take the water of life as a gift** [= without cost (compare 21:6; Isaiah 55:1)]. "The Spirit" is God's. "The bride" is the saints. "The person who hears" is the individual Christian who hears Revelation read in a church meeting (1:3). "Is to say" is another indirect command and therefore an observation addressed to the churches' messengers, whom Jesus addressed in 22:16, regarding what individual Christians in the churches are supposed to do. But whom are the Spirit and the bride telling to come, and whom should individual Christians tell to come? In 22:7, 12 Jesus said he's coming, and in 22:20 he'll say so again. Furthermore, 22:20 will also feature the prayer, "Come, Lord Jesus"; and "Come" here in 22:17 is likewise singular. So the two present instances of "Come" are often understood as prayers for the second coming, as doubtlessly in 22:20. But it's a little odd that the Spirit should be asking Jesus to come; and it's a stretch to explain that the Spirit is inspiring the bride to pray for the second coming, for the text tells what the Spirit as well as the bride is saying. Moreover, the double invitation to come is immediately followed by an indirect command that "the person who is thirsting is to come," to which is added the further indirect command that "the person who wants to is to take the water of life as a gift," which not only echoes 21:6 (see the comments there) but also parallels John 7:37–38, where Jesus says, "If anyone thirsts, let him *come* to me and drink. . . . 'Out of his belly will flow rivers of living water.'" Note the singular for a thirsty person and the followup in John 7:39 concerning the Spirit. So we have here in 22:17 a triple invitation for such a person—that is, the person who wants eternal life—to come to Jesus for it.

22:18–19: **"I testify to everyone who hears the words of the prophecy of this scroll: If anyone adds to them, God will add to him the plagues that have been written in this scroll. ¹⁹And if anyone takes away from the words of the scroll of this prophecy, God will take his part away from the tree of life and out of the holy city, which have been written about in this scroll** [compare Deuteronomy 4:1–2; 12:32]**."** Here John may be breaking in with "I testify" (see 1:2 for him as a testifier), but Jesus' testifying undoubtedly in 22:20 favors that it's he who is testifying here. After all, he's the one who has revealed the contents of this scroll (1:1). The scroll contains the whole of Revelation (compare "the plagues that have been written in this scroll," plagues whose description has occupied the large majority of its text). "Who hears" refers to individuals listening to

the reading of Revelation in a church meeting (see 1:3 again). "Everyone" stresses individual responsibility. "Adds to" and "takes away" refer to corrupting the book of Revelation (the whole Bible is not in view) by adding contradictory teaching and subtracting unwelcome teaching. (Apocalyptic literature outside Revelation often underwent revisions.) "Which have been written about" refers to "the tree of life" and to "the holy city." To have one's part in them taken away is to suffer the second death.

22:20: **The one who is testifying these things says, "Yes, I'm coming quickly!" Amen! Come, Lord Jesus!** As "the one who is testifying these things" Jesus indicates that he is his own angel whom he sent to testify according to 22:16 (so too in 22:18–19). The present tense of "is testifying" and of "I'm coming" is emphatic. "Yes" strongly affirms Jesus' coming quickly. "Amen!" starts a Christian response with a corresponding Hebrew affirmation that reflects the identity of Christians as the true, enlarged Israel. "Come, Lord Jesus!" is their prayer for the second coming, especially to deliver them from persecution. For the most part, this prayer translates the Aramaic "Marana tha" of 1 Corinthians 16:22 ("Our Lord, come!"), Aramaic being a language closely related to Hebrew. But "Jesus" is added to identify the Lord. This prayer that Jesus come lends urgency to the command in 22:17 that "the person who is thirsting is to come . . . and take the water of life as a gift." Better do so before Jesus comes!

22:21: **The grace of the Lord Jesus** [will be] **with all.** See the comments on 1:4 and especially on 2 John 3 for "grace" as a Christian greeting and for supplying the confident "will be" rather than a wishful "be." The greeting offers a happy prediction. "The Lord Jesus" echoes 22:20, and both that verse and this one affirm Jesus' lordship over against that of the Caesars. "With all" refers to all true Christians (the "conquerors" of chapters 2–3 and elsewhere).